Cassell's Dictionary of Word Histories

CASSELL'S DICTIONARY OF
Word Histories

Adrian Room

CASSELL

Cassell
Wellington House
125 Strand
London
WC2R 0BB

First published 2000
by Cassell & Co.

This edition 2002

Distributed in the United States by Sterling Publishing Co. Inc.
387 Park Avenue South, New York, NY 10016–8810

British Library Cataloguing in Publication Data
A catalogue entry for this book is available from the British Library

ISBN 0–304–36383–9

Printed and bound in Finland by
W S Bookwell Ltd

Contents

Acknowledgements

Editor	Adrian Room
Publisher	Richard Milbank
Database Editors	Charles Buchan
	Rebecca Skipwith
	Alex Williams
Proof-readers	Alice Grandison
	Michael Janes
	Patricia Moore
Database Technology	Gentian I.T. Consultants
Typesetting	Gem Graphics

Introduction

This new dictionary gives the origins of some 20,000 words and word elements, ranging across the whole spectrum of the English language, from the everyday to the esoteric, the slang to the scientific.

The origins of English

English has been written only since the 8th century AD, when Roman missionaries introduced the Latin alphabet to Britain. The language of these early texts is now usually known as Old English. It is still sometimes known as Anglo-Saxon, since it was largely the Angles and Saxons who became the English people. Whatever we call it, it soon became quite distinct from the other Germanic dialects that evolved in Continental Europe, and in particular from the West Germanic language division of Germanic to which it originally belonged.

To modern English speakers, this early form of the language looks decidedly Germanic. As with Modern German, Old English had four cases (nominative, accusative, genitive, dative) in the singular and plural and a number of declensions. As also in German, each noun had a gender (masculine, feminine or neuter), and this determined the form of the accompanying articles and adjectives. Verbs were inflected for each person (first, second and third), and both nouns and verbs had strong and weak forms of their inflections. Traces of this formal structure remain today, so that not all nouns have a plural in *s* (*foot* has *feet*, *child* has *children*) and there are many verbs with a past form distinct from the present (*write* and *wrote*, *sing* and *sang*, *buy* and *bought*). But the old forms have now mostly disappeared.

It was in the 8th century that the Anglo-Saxons in Britain suffered an invasion from the Vikings, the Scandinavian marauders who were their former neighbours in northern Europe. The incomers eventually settled down with the natives in what became the Danelaw, chiefly in northern and eastern England. Though the English language survived, its vocabulary absorbed several words from the raiders' dialects, giving us such words as *awkward*, *birth*, *egg*, *sky* and *window*. Their contribution to the language is now generally distinguished by the name of Old Norse or, more generally, Scandinavian.

Following this disruption, the survival of English was not threatened until the Norman Conquest of 1066, when the use of the new arrivals' Old French dialect in government and literature brought the Old English period to a close.

The Conquest imposed a new political and cultural life on the Anglo-Saxons and radically altered the development of their language. The native English language was relegated to an inferior position, and for some three centuries remained only the spoken tongue of the common people. Norman French was the language of supremacy, of the courts and their administration. The Church provided a further foreign input in Latin, the language in which it conducted all its affairs. The imposition of French and Latin on the islanders was in the end beneficial, however, since native English borrowed and absorbed much of the vocabulary of the settlers. And although the two distinct tongues, Romance and Germanic, continued in parallel for some time, the Middle English that finally emerged in the 14th century was an infinitely richer language than its predecessor. It was split as before into dialects, but accents began to level out and the language itself began to consolidate into a single tongue under the influence of its written form, more conservative than its spoken form. Modern English was the result, the language that we speak and write today in all its variety.

The vocabulary of Modern English is now approximately half Germanic (Old English and Scandinavian) and half Romance (French and Latin), with various importations from Greek in science and technology and borrowings from Dutch, Italian, Spanish, German and Arabic and many other languages. The words for many basic concepts in English are often Old English in origin and exist in pairs. Examples are *heaven* and *earth*, *love* and *hate*, *beginning* and *end*, *life* and *death*, *day* and *night*, *month* and *year*, *hot* and *cold*, *way* and *path*. Cardinal numbers come from Old English, as do all ordinal numbers except *second*, which comes from Latin. Most personal pronouns are also of Old English origin, although *they*, *their* and *them* are Scandinavian. Many nouns would be identical whether they came from Old English or Scandinavian: *father*, *mother*, *brother* (but not *sister*), *man*, *wife*, *ground*, *land*, *tree*, *grass*, *summer* and *winter* are examples. Interesting comparisons exist between sense areas of English and French origin. Thus *president*, *representative*, *congress* and *parliament* are all French, as are *duke*, *marquis*, *viscount* and *baron*, but *king*, *queen*, *lord*, *lady*, *earl* and *knight* are English. *City*, *village*, *court*, *palace*, *manor*, *mansion* and *residence* are all French, but *town*, *hall*, *house*, *room* and *home* are all English. Words of similar or identical meaning are generally more human and concrete when of English origin and more intellectual and abstract when from French: *freedom* is English but *liberty* French, *truth* is English but *veracity* French. It is thus not perhaps too much of a surprise to find that *breakfast*, a mostly utilitarian meal, is of English origin, while *supper* and *dinner*, as social occasions, are from French. The English peasant's *cows*, *sheep* and *pigs* became *beef*, *mutton* and *pork* on his Norman master's table.

Modern scholarship has been able to trace the roots of English back to the time before its earliest written record. It has shown that English and most of the other languages of Europe, as well as several in Asia, are apparently descended from a common ancestor, known (rather clumsily) as Indo-European. It is not known exactly when or where this mother tongue was spoken, but it must be older than the earliest known written texts, which are Hittite and date as far back as 1700 BC. It goes without saying that Indo-European, lacking a written record, is a hypothetical language. But common words such as modern *father* and *mother* can be reconstructed in it, and a historical line can be confidently traced from Indo-European to Germanic to West Germanic to Old English to

Modern English. Put another way, it is possible in many cases to take a modern word and thread it back through variant related forms to its original form and thus account for most of the forms it takes in the languages of the Indo-European family today.

The dictionary entries

Where practicable, and where the origin is certain, *The Cassell Dictionary of Word Histories* aims to trace a particular word's history back to its ultimate language. This mainly holds true of well established English words. Thus **ecstasy** goes back through Old French and Late Latin to Greek, in that order. But where the word is still obviously foreign, or at any rate not yet fully assimilated into English, the history will often be restricted to the immediate language of origin. Thus **savonette** is taken back to French *savon*, 'soap' but not to the ultimate source of that word (which happens to be Germanic), while Japanese **sashimi** is explained only in terms of the word's literal meaning. On the other hand, if a foreign word has a particularly interesting origin or one relevant to English, a fuller history may be given. Thus Turkish **effendi** is traced back through Modern Greek to the Classical Greek word *authentēs*, which (although not explicitly stated as such here) is in fact related to the English word 'authentic'.

Each entry is presented in two parts and sometimes in three.

The first part is the <u>definition</u>, e.g. for **eccentric** as: 'peculiar or odd in manner or character'. The word's grammatical status is also given here, as *a.* (adjective) or *n.*(noun). (For a full list of abbreviations used, see pp.xi-xii.) Many standard dictionaries also include usage labels, such as 'informal', 'literary', 'poetical' or 'offensive'. The present dictionary, however, concerns itself with word origins, not word usage, and such labels do not feature. Indeed, the definition is given simply to identify the particular word. As such it is usually fuller than in other etymological dictionaries. (*Word Histories* thus defines **nomad** as 'a member of a people that wanders about seeking pasture for their flocks' while *The Oxford Dictionary of English Etymology* has simply 'one of a wandering race'.) To a certain degree, therefore, *Word Histories* doubles as a standard defining dictionary.

The second part is the <u>word history</u> proper. It begins with an indication of the period when the word was first recorded in English. These are conventionally abbreviated as follows: pre-1200 (before the 13th century), 11–12C (11th–12th century), 12–14C (12th–14th century), 14–15C (14th–15th century), then in individual centuries from 15C to the 20th century, which is divided into early 20C (1900–29), mid-20C (1930–69) and late 20C (1970–99). The immediate source language is then given, as e.g. Greek, Late Latin, French, Old Norse. In the case of Latin words, nominative and genitive forms are given for nouns in *-io* (as *collisio*, *collisionis*) and for present participles of verbs (as *sciens*, *scientis*). Following the word history, there may be one or more cross-references to related (and sometimes unrelated) words or elements. Thus **edifice** cross-refers to the related **edify**, and **satire** to the unrelated **satyr**.

The third part, where it exists, is a <u>note or comment</u> on the history. This is frequently in the form of a summary of the word's change or changes of meaning or usage over the years. Thus **proscribe** originally had the literal sense to write something in front of something else, while **randy** at first meant loudmouthed. Similarly **scandal** originally had a specific application to religion, while **eccentric** was part of the vocabulary of astronomy. Where a relatively modern word has been a deliberate invention, as for the names of a number of chemical elements and minerals, the name of the namer and year of naming, where known, is supplied. Thus the element **scandium** was discovered and named in 1879 by the Swedish physicist Lars F. Nilson. Other notes may perhaps mention a now discredited origin, as for **saunter**, which some formerly derived from French *Sainte-Terre*, 'Holy Land', alluding to the journeying of pilgrims, or repeat a popular but false etymology, such as the belief that the **earwig** is so called because it lives in an **ear** of corn. Again, an elucidation may be provided, such as (famously) why the **tank** as a military vehicle came to be named after the **tank** that is a waterholder.

In some cases, frustratingly and disappointingly, the origin remains unknown or at best uncertain, and one simply has to say so, as for **saunter** already mentioned above. But such cases are a clear minority.

Readers in search of convoluted or unexpected word histories will find some gems among the plainer stones, such as **assassin**, **Isabel**, **jade**, **jeopardy**, **jubilee**, **juggernaut**, **limousine**, **muscle**, **nice**, **noon**, **pamphlet**, **tawdry**, to name just a dozen.

Word Histories can thus serve not simply for reference but for enlightenment and even entertainment. Whatever the use to which it is put, from now on no reader need ever feel dazed and confused wordwise with the *Cassell Dictionary of Word Histories* to hand.

Adrian Room
August 1999

Chief Abbreviations

a.	adjective	exc.	except
aa.	adjectives	fem.	feminine
abbr.	abbreviation	fig,	figurative, figuratively
abl.	ablative	fl.	floruit, flourished
acc.	accusative, according	freq.	frequentative
adapt.	adaptation	fut.	future
adv.	adverb	fut.p.	future participle
alln.	allusion		
alt.	altered, alteration; alternative	gen.	genitive
appar.	apparently	ger.	gerund, gerundive
assim.	assimilated, assimilation		
at. no.	atomic number	imit.	imitative, imitatively
attrib.	attributive, attribute	imper.	imperative
augm.	augmentative	impers.	impersonal
aux.	auxiliary	incept.	inceptive
AV	Authorized Version of the Bible	ind.	indicative
		inf.	infinitive
b.	born	influ.	influenced
		int.	interjection
c.	circa, about	intens.	intensive
C	century	intr.	intransitive
cent.	century	iron.	ironical, ironically
cents.	centuries	irreg.	irregular, irregularly
cogn.	cognate		
coll.	colloquial; collateral	lit.	literally
collect.	collective		
comb.	combination	m.	masculine
comb. form	combining form	med.	medieval
comp.	comparative	mod.	modern
cond.	conditional		
conf.	confusion	N	North, northern
conj.	conjunction; conjugation	n.	noun
constr.	construction, constructed;	neg.	negative, negatively
	construed	neut.	neuter
contr.	contraction	nn.	nouns
corr.	corruption; corresponding	nom.	nominative
cp.	compare	NT	New Testament
d.	died	obs.	obsolete
dat.	dative	opp.	opposed, opposition
def.	definition	orig.	originally, origin
deriv.	derivation, derivative	OT	Old Testament
derog.	derogatory		
dial.	dialect, dialectal	part.	participle
dim.	diminutive	pass.	passive
		perf.	perfect
E	East, eastern	perh.	perhaps
esp.	especially	pers.	person; personal
etym.	etymology	phr.	phrase
euphem.	euphemism	pl.	plural

poet.	poetical, poetry		sl.	slang
pop.	popular, popularly		subj.	subjunctive
poss.	possessive; possibly		suf.	suffix
p.p.	past participle		superl.	superlative
pred.	predicative		syl.	syllable
pref.	prefix			
prep.	preposition		tr.	transitive
pres.	present		trans.	translation
pres.p.	present participle			
priv.	privative		ult.	ultimately
prob.	probably		usu.	usually
pron.	pronoun; pronounced			
pronun.	pronunciation		v.	verb
prop.	proper, properly		var.	variant
prov.	provincial		verb.a.	verbal adjective
			verb.n.	verbal noun
redupl.	reduplication, reduplicative		v.i.	verb intransitive
ref.	reference, referring		voc.	vocative
reflex.	reflexive		v.refl.	verb reflexive
rel.	related		v.t.	verb transitive
rel. pron.	relative pronoun		vv.	verbs
S	South, southern		W	West, western
sing.	singular			

Cross-references, Symbols and Proprietary Terms

Cross-references

The word cross-referred to appears as small capitals for usual lower case, e.g. Abbr. of FABULOUS[1].

Symbols

Obsolete and archaic words are preceded by a dagger sign †.
Uncertain or speculative word histories are preceded by a query ?, which may be interpreted as 'perhaps'.
Hypothetical word forms are preceded by an asterisk *.

Proprietary Terms

This book includes some words which are or are asserted to be propietary names. The presence or absence of such assertions should not be regarded as affecting the legal status of any proprietary name or trademark.

a *a.* a weakened form of *one*, sometimes called the indefinite article, used before singular nouns or noun phrases to denote an individual of a class. **WH:** pre-1200. Reduced form of *an*, from Old English *ān* ONE.

a-[1] *pref.* on, in, engaged in, as in *afoot*, *aboard*, *accursed*. **WH:** Reduced form of ON.

a-[2] *pref.* of, from, as in *akin*, *athirst*. **WH:** Reduced form of OF.

a-[3] *pref.* away, out, intensifying the action of verbs, as in *arise*, *awake*. **WH:** Old English *ā-*, corr. to Old High German *ar-*, *ir-*, Gothic *us-*, *ur-*.

a-[4] *pref.* from, as in *avert*. **WH:** Latin pref., from AB-[1].

a-[5] *pref.* at, to, as in *ascent*, *astringent*. **WH:** Latin pref., from AD-, used before *sc*, *sp*, *st*.

a-[6] *pref.* not, without, as in *achromatic*, *amoral*. **WH:** Greek *a-* not, without. Cp. AN-[3].

-a[1] *suf.* forming nouns, esp. ancient or Latinized names for plants and animals, as in *calendula*, *amoeba*; geographical names, as in *Asia*; names of oxides, as in *magnesia*; ancient or Latinized feminine forenames, as in *Gloria*, *Claudia*. **WH:** Latin or Greek *-a*, 1st declension fem. sing. n. ending.

-a[2] *suf.* forming plural nouns, as in *criteria*, *errata*, and names of zoological groups, as in *Carnivora*, *Lepidoptera*. **WH:** Latin or Greek *-a*, 2nd declension neut. pl. ending in nn. ending *-um* and *-on* respectively.

aardvark *n.* the African anteater, *Orycteropus afer*. **WH:** 18C. Afrikaans *aard* EARTH + *vark* pig. Rel. to FARROW.

aardwolf *n.* a hyena-like carnivorous mammal, *Proteles cristatus*, of southern Africa. **WH:** 19C. Afrikaans *aard* EARTH + *wolf* WOLF.

Aaronic *a.* of or relating to Aaron, his descendants, or the Jewish priesthood. **WH:** 17C. *Aaron*, the first Jewish high priest + -IC.

aasvogel *n.* a vulture. **WH:** 19C. Afrikaans *aas* carrion + *vogel* bird. Cp. FOWL.

ab-[1] *pref.* off, from, away, apart, as in *abrogate*, *abuse*. **WH:** Latin pref., from prep. *ab*, from, away, from Indo-European. In Latin and French derivatives *b* is often dropped or assimilated to a subsequent consonant. See A-[4]. Cp. Greek *apo*, English *of*, *off*, German *ab*.

ab-[2] *pref.* signifying motion towards, direction to, adherence etc., as in *abbreviate*. **WH:** Latin pref., from AD- with *d* assim. to *b*.

abaca *n.* Manila hemp. **WH:** 18C. Spanish *abacá*, from Tagalog *abaká*.

aback *adv.* with the sails pressed against the mast. **WH:** pre-1200. Old English *on bæc* at (the) back. See A-[1], BACK[1].

abactinal *a.* of or relating to that part of a radiate animal that is opposite the mouth. **WH:** 19C. Latin AB-[1] + *actinal*. See ACTINO-.

abacus *n.* a counting-frame; an apparatus of beads sliding on wires for facilitating arithmetical calculations. **WH:** 14–15C. Latin, from Greek *abax* counting table, ? from Hebrew *'ābāq* dust. It was originally a board sprinkled with fine sand for marking on.

Abaddon *n.* a destroyer, the angel of the Bottomless Pit, Apollyon (Rev. ix.11). **WH:** 12–14C. Hebrew *'ăḇaddon* (place of) destruction, from *'āḇad* to be lost.

abaft *adv.*, *prep.* in, on, or towards the rear of a ship. **WH:** 16C. A-[1] + Middle English *baft* behind, from Old English *bæftan*, from *bi* BY + *æftan* AFT.

abalone *n.* an edible gastropod mollusc of the genus *Haliotis*, that has an ear-shaped shell, perforated with breathing holes. **WH:** 19C. American English alt. of *avalone*, from Mexican Spanish *aulone*, from Costanoan *aūlun* red abalone.

abandon *v.t.* to give up completely. *Also n.* **WH:** 14–15C. Old French *abandoner* to leave to one's mercy, from *abandon* surrender, from *a bandon* at the power of, from *a* at (AD-) + *bandon* power, of Frankish origin. Cp. BAN.

à bas *int.* down with. **WH:** 18C. French, from *à* to + *bas* bottom, BASE[1].

abase *v.t.* to humble or degrade. **WH:** 16C. Alt., influ. by BASE[2], of Middle English *abaishen*, from Old French *abaissier* to bring low, from *a* (AD-) + *baissier* to make lower, from Popular Latin *bassiare*, ult. from Late Latin *bassus* short of stature.

abash *v.t.* to embarrass or put to shame by exciting a sense of guilt, mistake or inferiority. **WH:** 12–14C. Middle English *abaishen*, *abassen* to lose one's composure, from Old French *esbaïr*, *esbaïss-* to be astonished, from *es-* out (EX-) + *baïr* to open. Cp. BAY[2]. Rel. to ABEYANCE.

abask *adv.*, *a.* in the sunshine, basking. **WH:** 19C. A-[1] + BASK.

abate *v.t.* to lessen, esp. to make less violent or intense. *Also v.i.* **WH:** 12–14C. Old French *abatre* to beat down, from Popular Latin *abattere*, from AD- + *battere* to beat. Rel. to BAT[1], BAT[4].

abatis *n.* a defence work made of felled trees with their boughs directed outwards. **WH:** 18C. French, from *abatre* to beat down. See ABATE.

abatjour *n.* a skylight. **WH:** 19C. French *abat-jour*, from *abattre* to beat down + *jour* day, light. Cp. ABATE, JOURNAL.

abattoir *n.* a slaughterhouse. **WH:** 19C. French, from *abattre* to fell. See also -ORY[1].

abaxial *a.* facing away from the stem. **WH:** 19C. AB-[1] + *axial* (AXIS[1]).

abaya *n.* an outer garment without sleeves, as worn by Arabs. **WH:** 19C. Arabic *'abāya*.

abba *n.* father (in the invocation *Abba, father*). **WH:** 14–15C. Ecclesiastical Latin, from Ecclesiastical Greek, from Aramaic *'abbā* father. Cp. ABBOT. The word is ultimately of imitative origin. Cp. PAPA[1].

abbacy *n.* the office and jurisdiction of an abbot. **WH:** 16C. Ecclesiastical Latin *abbacia*, *abbatia*, from *abbas*, *abbatis* ABBOT. See also -ACY.

Abbasid *n.* a caliph or other member of the dynasty that ruled in Baghdad from 750 to 1258. *Also a.* **WH:** 18C. *'Abbās*, 566–652, uncle of Muhammad. See also -ID.

abbé *n.* a French abbot. **WH:** 16C. French, from Ecclesiastical Latin *abbas*, *abbatis* ABBOT.

abbess *n.* the lady superior of an abbey. **WH:** 12–14C. Old French *abbesse*, from Late Latin *abbatissa*, fem. of *abbas*, *abbatis* ABBOT.

Abbevillian *n.* the period or culture of the early Palaeolithic in Europe. *Also a.* **WH:** mid-20C. French *Abbevillien*, from *Abbeville*, a town in N France. See also -IAN.

abbey *n.* a monastic community governed by an abbot or abbess. **WH:** 12–14C. Old French *abaïe*, from Medieval Latin *abbatia*, from *abbas*, *abbatis* ABBOT. See also -Y[2].

abbot *n.* the superior of an abbey. **WH:** 11–12C. Late Latin *abbas*, *abbatis*, from Late Greek *abbas*, from Aramaic *'abbā* father. Cp. ABBA.

abbreviate[1] *v.t.* to shorten (esp. a word or phrase) by omitting certain parts of it. **WH:** 14–15C. Late Latin *abbreviatus*, p.p. of *abbreviare* to make brief, from Latin AB-[2] + *breviare* to shorten. See BRIEF, also -ATE[3].

abbreviate[2] *a.* shortened, cut short. **WH:** 15C. Late Latin *abbreviatus*, p.p. of *abbreviare*. See ABBREVIATE[1], also -ATE[2].

ABC *n.* the alphabet. **WH:** 11–12C. First three letters A, B, C.

abdicate *v.t.* to resign, to renounce formally. *Also v.i.* **WH:** 16C. Latin *abdicatus*, p.p. of *abdicare* to renounce, from AB-[1] + *dicare* to proclaim.

abdomen *n.* the part of the body which lies between the thorax and the pelvis and contains the stomach, bowels etc. **WH:** 17C. Latin, ? from *abdere* to conceal, from AB-[1] + comb. form *-dere* to put, place. See DO. The abdomen may have been seen as a concealing place for viscera.

abducent *a.* having the property of drawing back or away (applied to muscles, the function of which is to draw away or pull back the parts to which they belong. WH: 17C. Latin *abducens, abducentis,* pres.p. of *abducere,* from AB-¹ + *ducere* to lead. Cp. ABDUCT.

abduct *v.t.* to kidnap; to take away illegally (esp. a woman or child) by guile or force. WH: 19C. Latin *abductus,* p.p. of *abducere.* See ABDUCENT.

abeam *adv.* on a line at right angles to the keel of a ship or the length of an aircraft; opposite the middle (of a ship etc.). WH: 19C. A-¹ + BEAM.

abecedarian *n.* a person who teaches or is learning the alphabet. *Also a.* WH: 17C. Medieval Latin *abecedarium* alphabet, from letters A, B, C, D. See also -ARIAN.

†abed *adv.* in bed, gone to bed. WH: 14–15C. A-¹ + BED.

abele *n.* the white poplar, *Populus alba.* WH: 14–15C. Old French *aubel, abel,* from Medieval Latin *albellus,* dim. of *albus* white.

abelia *n.* a shrub of the genus *Abelia,* that is evergreen and has pink or white flowers. WH: 19C. Modern Latin, from Clarke *Abel,* 1780–1826, English botanist. See also -IA.

abelian *a.* (of a group) whose members are commutative in binary operations. WH: 19C. Niels Henrik *Abel,* 1802–29, Norwegian mathematician. See also -IAN.

Aberdeen *n.* a breed of rough-haired Scotch terrier. WH: 19C. *Aberdeen,* a city and former county in NE Scotland.

aberdevine *n.* the siskin. WH: 18C. Of unknown origin. It is said to be a birdcatcher's name.

aberrant *a.* deviating from the normal type. WH: 16C. Latin *aberrans, aberrantis,* pres.p. of *aberrare,* from AB-¹ + *errare* to wander. Cp. ERR.

aberration *n.* deviation from, or inconsistency with, the norm. WH: 16C. Latin *aberratio, aberrationis.* See ABERRANT, also -ATION.

abet *v.t.* to encourage or aid (a person) in crime or wrongdoing by word or deed. WH: 12–14C. Old French *abeter,* from *a* to + *beter* to hound on, from Germanic *bētan* to incite, or from Scandinavian *beita* to cause to bite. Cp. BAIT, BITE.

abeyance *n.* the state of being suspended or temporarily unused. WH: 16C. Anglo-French *abeiance* (legal) expectation, from Old French *abeance,* from *abeer* to aspire after, from *a* at, after + *beer* to open. Cp. ABASH. The original legal sense broadened to mean suspension (of credibility, honour etc.), then general disuse.

abhor *v.t.* to hate extremely, loathe. WH: 14–15C. Latin *abhorrere* to shrink away, from AB-¹ + *horrere* to bristle. See HORROR.

Abib *n.* the first month of the ancient Hebrew calendar, corresponding to Nisan. WH: 16C. Hebrew *'āḇīḇ* ear of corn.

abide *v.t.* to endure, tolerate. *Also v.i.* WH: pre-1200. Old English *ābīdan* to remain, from A-³ + *bīdan* to stay. See BIDE.

†abigail *n.* a waiting-maid. WH: 17C. *Abigail,* a 'waiting gentlewoman' in Beaumont and Fletcher's play *The Scornful Lady* (1616). The character was named after the wife of Nabal and subsequently of David in the Bible (I Sam. xxv).

ability *n.* the capacity or power (to do something). WH: 12–14C. Middle English *ablete,* from Old French *ablete,* from Latin *habilitas,* from *habilis* easy to manage. See ABLE, also -ITY.

ab initio *adv.* from the beginning. WH: Latin *ab* AB-¹ + *initio,* abl. sing. of *initium* beginning. Cp. INITIAL.

abiogenesis *n.* the theoretical process by which animate matter can be produced from something inanimate; the supposed spontaneous generation of animate matter. WH: 19C. Greek *abios,* from A-⁶ + *bios* life + GENESIS. The term was coined in 1870 by the English biologist T.H. Huxley.

abiotic *a.* not living, not produced by living organisms. WH: 19C. A-⁶ + BIOTIC.

abject *a.* miserable and wretched. *Also n.* WH: 14–15C. Latin *abiectus,* p.p. of *abiicere* to reject, from AB-¹ + *iacere* to throw. Cp. JET². The original sense was literal but became metaphorical in the 16C.

abjure *v.t.* to renounce or retract upon oath. *Also v.i.* WH: 14–15C. Latin *abiurare* to deny on oath, from AB-¹ + *iurare* to swear. See JURY.

Abkhazian *n.* a native or inhabitant of Abkhazia. *Also a.* WH: 19C. *Abkhazia,* a territory in the Caucasus. See also -IAN.

ablactate *v.t.* to wean from the breast. WH: 14–15C. Late Latin *ablactus,* p.p. of *ablactare* to wean, from AB-¹ + *lactare* to suckle, LACTATE¹. See also -ATE³.

ablation *n.* the surgical removal of any body tissue or part. WH: 14–15C. French, or from Late Latin *ablatio, ablationis,* from Latin *ablatus,* p.p. of *auferre* to take away. See also -ATION. Cp. ABLATIVE.

ablative *a.* taking away, separating, subtractive. *Also n.* WH: 14–15C. Old French *ablatif,* from Latin *ablatus,* p.p. of *auferre* to take away. See also -IVE. The term was coined (as *casus ablativus*) by Julius Caesar, as there was no corresponding Greek case from which the name could be adopted.

ablator *n.* the heat shield of a space vehicle that melts away during re-entry into the atmosphere. WH: mid-20C. Latin *ablatus,* p.p. of *auferre* (see ABLATIVE) + OR¹.

ablaut *n.* a vowel change in the middle of a word indicating modification in meaning, as *sit, set, rise, raise, ring, rang, rung.* WH: 19C. German, from *ab* off + *Laut* sound.

ablaze *adv., pred. a.* on fire, in a blaze. WH: 19C. A-¹ + BLAZE¹.

able *a.* having sufficient power or acquired skill, or sufficient financial and other resources to do something indicated. *Also v.t.* WH: 12–14C. Old French *hable, able,* from Latin *habilis* easily managed, from *habere* to hold. Rel. to HABIT.

-able *suf.* that may be, is fit or suitable for, as in *eatable, movable, saleable.* WH: French, from Latin *-abilis,* form of *-bilis* when added to vv. in *-are* (French *-er*).

ablegate *n.* a papal envoy sent with insignia to new cardinals etc. WH: 17C. Latin *ablegatus,* p.p. of *ablegare* to dismiss, from AB-¹ + *legare* to send on a message. See LEGATE.

abloom *a., adv.* blooming, in a state of bloom. WH: 19C. A-¹ + BLOOM¹.

ablush *a., adv.* blushing, ruddy. WH: 19C. A-¹ + BLUSH.

ablution *n.* the act of washing, cleansing or purifying by means of water or other liquids. WH: 12–14C. Old French, or from Late Latin *ablutio, ablutionis,* from AB-¹ + *luere* to wash. See also -ION.

abnegate *v.t.* to deny oneself, to renounce. WH: 17C. Latin *abnegatus,* p.p. of *abnegare,* from AB-¹ + *negare* to deny. See NEGATE, also -ATE³.

abnormal *a.* not normal or typical, departing from the ordinary type. WH: 19C. Alt. of *anormal,* from Latin *abnormis,* from AB-¹ + *norma* NORM. See also -AL¹.

Abo *n.* an Australian Aborigine. *Also a.* WH: early 20C. Abbr. of ABORIGINE.

aboard *adv., prep.* on board, on or in (a boat, ship, train, aircraft etc.). WH: 14–15C. A-¹ + BOARD.

abode *n.* place of residence; a habitation. WH: 12–14C. Verb.n. of ABIDE. The original meaning was delay, stay, but gave way to the present sense in the 16C.

aboil *a., adv.* boiling, on the boil. WH: 19C. A-¹ + BOIL¹.

abolish *v.t.* to do away with, put an end to. WH: 14–15C. Old French *abolir, aboliss-,* from Latin *abolere* to destroy, rel. to *abolescere* to die out. Cp. ADOLESCENT. See also -ISH².

abomasum *n.* the fourth stomach in a ruminating animal. WH: 17C. AB-¹ + OMASUM.

abominate *v.t.* to loathe, to hate exceedingly. WH: 16C. Latin *abominatus,* p.p. of *abominari* to deplore (as an evil omen), from AB-¹ + *ominari* to prophesy, from *omen, ominis* OMEN. The word is not from Latin *ab homine* inhuman (literally from the man).

aboral *a.* away from the mouth, opposite the mouth. WH: 19C. AB-¹ + ORAL.

aborigine *n.* an indigenous or original inhabitant of a continent, country or district. WH: 19C. Latin *aborigines,* prob. from *ab origine* from the beginning. See AB-¹, ORIGIN.

aborning *adv., a.* (while) being born or produced. WH: mid-20C. A-¹ + *borning,* verb.n. of *born,* irreg. from BORN. See also -ING¹.

abort *v.t.* to cause (a foetus) to be expelled from the womb before it is able to survive independently; to cause (a mother) to undergo an abortion. *Also v.i., n.* WH: 16C. Latin *abortus,* p.p. of *aboriri* to miscarry, from AB-¹ + *oriri* to come into being. Rel. to RISE.

abortion *n.* a procedure to induce the premature expulsion of a foetus. WH: 16C. Latin *abortio, abortionis.* See ABORT.

abortive *a.* fruitless, failing in its effect. *Also n.* WH: 14–15C. Old French *abortif,* from Latin *abortivus.* See ABORT.

ABO system *n.* a system for typing human blood according to the presence or absence of certain antigens. WH: mid-20C. Blood types A, B, AB and O.

aboulia *n.* loss of will-power, as a symptom of mental illness. WH: 19C. Greek, from A-⁶ + *boulē* will. See also -IA.

abound *v.i.* to be present in great quantities. WH: 12–14C. Old French *abunder*, *abonder*, from Latin *abundare*, from AB-¹ + *undare*, from *unda* wave.

about *prep.* concerning, in connection with. *Also adv.* WH: pre-1200. Old English *abūtan*, form of *onbūtan*, from *on* ON + *būtan* outside of, from *bī* BY + *ūtan* outside, from *ūt* OUT.

above *prep.* over, at or to a higher point than. *Also adv., n., a.* WH: pre-1200. Old English *abufan*, reduced form of *onbufan*, from *on* ON + *bufan* over, from *bī* BY + *ufan* over. Rel. to UP.

ab ovo *adv.* from the beginning. WH: 16C. Latin from the egg, from *ab* AB-¹ + abl. sing. of *ovum* egg. See OVUM.

abracadabra *int.* a word used as a magic word by conjurors when performing tricks. *Also n.* WH: 16C. Latin, cabbalistic word first found 2C, ult. from Greek, of unknown orig. ? Rel. to Greek ABRAXAS.

abrade *v.t.* to rub or wear away by friction. WH: 17C. Latin *abradere*, from AB-¹ + *radere* to scrape. Cp. ABRASION.

Abrahamic *a.* of or relating to Abraham or the dispensation under which he lived. WH: 19C. *Abraham*, the biblical patriarch. See also -IC.

abranchial *a.* without gills. *Also n.* WH: 19C. A-⁶ + BRANCHIA. See also -AL¹.

abrasion *n.* the act of rubbing away or wearing down. WH: 17C. Latin *abrasio*, *abrasionis*, from *abrasus*, p.p. of *abradere* to scrape off, from AB-¹ + *radere* to scrape. See RAZE.

abraxas *n.* a word used as a charm, denoting a power which presides over 365 others, and used by some Gnostics to denote their supreme god. WH: 18C. Late Greek, of unknown orig. Cp. ABRACADABRA. The word is said to have been coined in the 2C by the Egyptian Gnostic Basilides to express 365, each Greek letter having a numerical value.

abreaction *n.* the ridding oneself of a complex by reliving in feeling or action repressed fantasies or experiences. WH: early 20C. AB-¹ + REACTION.

abreast *adv.* side by side with the fronts in line. WH: 14–15C. A-¹ + BREAST.

abridge *v.t.* to reduce the length of (a book etc.), to shorten, curtail. WH: 12–14C. Old French *abreger*, *abregier*, from Latin *abbreviare*. See ABBREVIATE¹.

abroach *adv.* broached, pierced. *Also a.* WH: 14–15C. Anglo-French *abroche*, from Old French, from *a-* + *brochier* (Modern French *brocher*) BROACH.

abroad *adv.* in or to a foreign country. WH: 12–14C. A-¹ + BROAD. The original sense of widely, at large, became out of doors, then as now in the 16C.

abrogate *v.t.* to annul by an authoritative act; to repeal. WH: 16C. Latin *abrogatus*, p.p. stem of *abrogare*, from AB-¹ + *rogare* to propose a law. Rel. to RIGHT.

abrupt *a.* sudden, unexpected. WH: 16C. Latin *abruptus*, p.p. of *abrumpere* to break off, from AB-¹ + *rumpere* to break. Cp. RUPTURE.

abs- *pref.* away, off, from, as in *abstain*, *abscond*, *abstruse*. WH: Latin pref., from AB-¹, used before *c*, *qu*, *t*.

abscess *n.* a gathering of pus in any tissue or organ, accompanied by pain and inflammation. WH: 16C. Latin *abscessus*, from *abscedere* to withdraw, from ABS- + *cedere* to go. Cp. CEDE.

abscise *v.t.*, *v.i.* to separate from the stem of a plant by abscission. WH: 17C. Latin *abscisus*, p.p. of *abscidere*, from ABS- + *caedere* to cut. Cp. SCISSORS.

abscissa *n.* the x co-ordinate that shows the distance of a point from a vertical axis along a horizontal line. WH: 17C. Modern Latin *abscissa* (*linea*) cut (line), from fem. p.p. of *abscindere* to cut off, from AB-¹ + *scindere* to cut.

abscond *v.i.* to go away secretly or in a hurry. *Also v.t.* WH: 16C. Latin *abscondere* to conceal, from ABS- + *condere* to put together, from CON- + *-dere* to put.

abseil *v.i.* to descend a vertical or steeply sloping surface, such as a rock face, using a rope attached at the top and wound round the body. *Also n.* WH: mid-20C. German *abseilen*, from *ab* down + *Seil* rope.

absence *n.* the state of being absent from a place, event etc. WH: 14–15C. Old French, from Latin *absentia* (ABSENT¹).

absent¹ *a.* away from or not present in a place; not in attendance. WH: 14–15C. Old French, from Latin *absens*, *absentis*, pres.p. of *abesse*, from AB-¹ + *esse* to be. See also -ENT.

absent² *v.t.* to keep oneself away. WH: 14–15C. Old French *absenter*, or from Late Latin *absentare* to be away. See ABSENT¹.

absinthe *n.* wormwood. WH: 14–15C. French, from Latin *absinthium*, from Greek *absinthion* wormwood, ult. of non-Indo-European orig.

absit omen *int.* may the threatened evil not take place; God forbid. WH: 16C. Latin may this omen be absent, from *absit*, 3rd pers. pres. subj. of *abesse* to be absent + *omen* OMEN.

absolute *a.* complete, utter. *Also n.* WH: 14–15C. Latin *absolutus* freed, completed, p.p. of *absolvere* to set free. See ABSOLVE.

absolution *n.* acquittal, forgiveness. WH: 11–12C. Old French, from Latin *absolutio*, *absolutionis* completion, acquittal, from *absolvere* to set free. See ABSOLVE, also -TION.

absolve *v.t.* to pardon; acquit, pronounce not guilty. WH: 12–14C. Latin *absolvere* to set free, from AB-¹ + *solvere* to loosen. See SOLVE.

absonant *a.* discordant, inharmonious, unreasonable. WH: 16C. Latin AB-¹ + *sonans*, *sonantis*, pres.p. of *sonare* SOUND¹. The word is based on CONSONANT, DISSONANT, etc.

absorb *v.t.* to suck or soak up. WH: 14–15C. Old French *absorber*, or from Latin *absorbere*, from AB-¹ + *sorbere* to suck in, ult. from Indo-European.

absquatulate *v.i.* to run away, make off quickly, scram. WH: 19C. Facetious blend of ABSCOND + *squatule* (to depart) + PERAMBULATE.

abstain *v.i.* to keep oneself away, refrain (from). WH: 12–14C. Old French *abstenir*, from Latin *abstinere*, from ABS- + *tenere* to hold. Cp. TENANT.

abstemious *a.* sparing, not self-indulgent, esp. in the use of food and strong liquors. WH: 17C. Latin *abstemius*, from ABS- + *temus*, base of *temetum* intoxicating drink. See also -OUS.

abstention *n.* the act of abstaining or refraining, esp. from exercising one's right to vote. WH: 16C. French, or from Late Latin *abstentio*, *abstentionis*, from *abstinere* ABSTAIN. See also -ION.

abstinence *n.* the act or practice of refraining from some indulgence. WH: 12–14C. Old French, from Latin *abstinentia*, from *abstinens*, *abstinentis* pres.p. of *abstinere* ABSTAIN. See also -ENCE.

abstract¹ *v.t.* to draw or take away, remove. WH: 14–15C. Partly from ABSTRACT², partly from Latin *abstractus*, p.p. of *abstrahere* to draw off.

abstract² *a.* not related to tangible, concrete or particular instances. *Also n.* WH: 12–14C. Old French, or from Latin *abstractus*, p.p. of *abstrahere*, from ABS- + *trahere* to draw. Cp. TRACT¹. The original sense was derived, withdrawn (now *abstracted*). The present meaning arose in the 16C.

abstraction *n.* the act of abstracting or separating. WH: 12–14C. Old French, or from Late Latin *abstractio*, *abstractionis*. See ABSTRACT², also -ION.

abstractive *a.* possessing the power or quality of abstracting. WH: 14–15C. Medieval Latin *abstractivus*, from Latin *abstractus*. See ABSTRACT².

abstruse *a.* difficult to understand. WH: 16C. French *abstrus*, or from Latin *abstrusus*, p.p. of *abstrudere* to conceal, from ABS- + *trudere* to thrust. Rel. to THREAT.

absurd *a.* ridiculous, ludicrous. *Also n.* WH: 16C. French *absurde*, or from Latin *absurdus* out of tune, from AB-¹ + *surdus* deaf, mute. Cp. SURD.

abundance *n.* a more than sufficient quantity or number (of). WH: 12–14C. Old French (Modern French *abondance*), from Latin *abundantia*, from *abundans*, *abundantis*, pres.p. of *abundare* ABOUND.

abuse¹ *v.t.* to put to an improper use, misuse. WH: 14–15C. Old French *abuser*, and from Popular Latin *abusare*, from Latin *abusus*, p.p. of *abuti*, from AB-¹ + *uti* USE¹. The original sense of to misrepresent, to deceive, gradually became obsolete, but partly remains in its contrary, DISABUSE.

abuse[2] *n.* improper treatment or employment, misuse. WH: 14–15C. Old French *abus*, or from Latin *abusus*. See ABUSE[1].

abut *v.i.* to be contiguous. *Also v.t.* WH: 12–14C. Blend of Old French *abouter* to join end to end, from a- (AD-) + *bout* end, and Old French *abuter* to touch with an end, from a- (AD-) + *but* end, BUTT[3].

abuzz *a.*, *adv.* buzzing with activity, conversation etc. WH: 19C. A-[1] + BUZZ.

abysm *n.* an abyss. WH: 12–14C. Old French *abisme* (Modern French *abîme*), from Medieval Latin *abysmus*, alt. of *abyssus* ABYSS.

abyss *n.* a vast physical chasm or cavity. WH: 16C. Greek *abussos*, from A-[6] + *bussos* bottom. ? Rel. to Greek *bathos* depth. See BATHOS.

Abyssinian *a.* belonging to Abyssinia or its inhabitants. *Also n.* WH: 18C. *Abyssinia*, a country in NE Africa (now Ethiopia) + -AN.

ac- *pref.* signifying motion towards, direction to, adherence etc., as in *accommodate*, *accord*, *acquire*. WH: Latin pref., from AD- with *d* assim. to *c*, *k*, *qu*.

-ac *suf.* of or relating to, as in *cardiac*, *demoniac* (adjectives so formed are often used as nouns). WH: French *-aque*, or from Latin *-acus*, from Greek *-akos*, form of suf. *-kos* belonging to.

acacia *n.* a tree of the extensive genus *Acacia*, with pinnated leaves or else phyllodes, and small flowers in balls or spikes: some species yield catechu and others gum arabic. WH: 12–14C. Latin, from Greek *akakia* shittah tree. The word is probably related to Greek *akē* point, and so to EDGE.

academe *n.* academia. WH: 16C. Latin *academia*. See ACADEMY.

academic *a.* of or relating to an academy, college or university. *Also n.* WH: 16C. Old French *académique*, or from Latin *academicus*, from *academia*. See ACADEMY.

academy *n.* a society or institution for promoting literature, science or art. WH: 14–15C. Latin *academia*, from Greek *akadēmeia*, from *Akadēmos*, name of a hero of the Trojan war. Plato set up a school in a grove near Athens in the 4th century BC and named it in honour of Akademos.

Acadian *a.* belonging to Acadia. *Also n.* WH: 18C. *Acadia*, a former French colony on the N American Atlantic Coast which included the present Nova Scotia + -AN. Cp. CAJUN.

acajou *n.* the cashew-nut tree, *Anacardium occidentale*. WH: 16C. French CASHEW.

-acal *suf.* forming adjectives, as in *demoniacal*, *maniacal*. WH: -AC + -AL[1]. Adjectives ending in *-ac* often came to be used as nouns, so *-al* was added to distinguish the adjective.

acanthopterygian *a.* belonging to the Acanthopterygii, a large order of fishes, having the dorsal fin or fins entirely, and the other fins partially, supported by spinous rays. *Also n.* WH: 19C. Greek *akanthos* ACANTHUS + *pterugion* fin, dim. of *pterux* wing.

acanthus *n.* any plant or shrub of the genus *Acanthus*, which is native to the Mediterranean but widely grown for its large spiny leaves and white or purple flowers. WH: 16C. Greek *akanthos*, from *akantha* thorn, ? from *akē* point. Cp. ACACIA.

a cappella *a.*, *adv.* (of choral music) without instrumental accompaniment. WH: 19C. Italian in chapel style. See AD-, CHAPEL.

acarpous *a.* producing no fruit. WH: 18C. A-[6] + Greek *karpos* fruit. See also -OUS.

acarus *n.* a mite of the genus *Acarus*. WH: 17C. Modern Latin, from Greek *akari*.

acatalectic *a.* having the full number of metrical feet. *Also n.* WH: 16C. Greek *akatalēktos*, from A-[6] + *katalēktikos* (CATALECTIC).

acausal *a.* not causal. WH: mid-20C. A-[6] + *causal*. See CAUSE.

accablé *a.* crushed, overwhelmed. WH: 19C. French, p.p. of *accabler* to overwhelm, from Latin AC-, + French dial. *aachabler* to fell, from Popular Latin *catabola*, ult. from Greek *katabolē* throwing down. See CATABOLISM.

accede *v.i.* to agree (to), assent (to). WH: 12–14C. Latin *accedere*, from AC- + *cedere* to go. See CEDE.

accelerando *a.*, *adv.* with increasing speed. *Also n.* WH: 19C. Italian, pres.p. of *accelerare* ACCELERATE.

accelerate *v.t.* to increase the speed or rate of progress of. *Also v.i.* WH: 16C. Latin *acceleratus*, p.p. of *accelerare*, from AC- + *celer* swift. See also -ATE[3].

accent[1] *n.* a manner of speaking or pronunciation peculiar to an individual, a locality or a nation. WH: 12–14C. Old French, or from Latin *accentus*, from AC- + *cantus* song. Cp. CHANT.

accent[2] *v.t.* to lay stress upon (a syllable or word, or a note or passage of music). WH: 16C. Old French *accenter*. See ACCENT[1].

accentor *n.* a bird of the genus *Prunella* (formerly *Accentor*), as the hedge sparrow. WH: 19C. Late Latin, from AC- + *cantor* singer. Cp. ACCENT[1]. The literal sense is one who sings with another.

accept *v.t.* to consent to take (something offered). WH: 12–14C. Old French *accepter*, or from Latin *acceptare*, freq. of *accipere* to receive, from AC- + *capere* to take.

access *n.* admission to a place or person. *Also v.t.*, *a.* WH: 12–14C. Old French *acces*, or from Latin *accessus*, p.p. of *accedere* to approach. See ACCEDE. The early sense of an attack of disease became obsolete in the 16C.

accession *n.* coming to the throne; becoming the holder of an office, rank or dignity; entering upon a particular condition or status. *Also v.t.* WH: 16C. Old French, or from Latin *accessio*, *accessionis*, from *accessus*. See ACCESS, also -ION.

accessory *n.* a supplementary thing, esp. an additional part designed to improve the appearance, performance, comfort etc. of a vehicle, appliance etc. *Also a.* WH: 14–15C. Medieval Latin *accessorius*, from *accessus*. See ACCESS.

acciaccatura *n.* a short grace note played rapidly. WH: 19C. Italian, from *acciaccare* to crush, ? from Spanish *achacar* to accuse falsely.

accidence *n.* that part of grammar which deals with the inflection of words. WH: 16C. Late Latin *accidentia*, neut. pl. pres.p. of *accidere*. See ACCIDENT, also -ENCE.

accident *n.* an event proceeding from an unknown cause; the unforeseen effect of a known cause. WH: 12–14C. Old French, from Latin *accidens*, *accidentis*, pres.p. of *accidere* to happen, from AC- + *cadere* to fall. See also -ENT. The original sense was a happening of any kind. The present sense prevailed from the 19C.

accidie *n.* an abnormal mental condition characterized by extreme apathy and listlessness. WH: 19C. Old French *accide*, from Medieval Latin *accidia*, alt. of Late Latin *acedia*, from Greek *akēdia*, from A-[6] + *kēdos* care, concern.

accipiter *n.* a raptorial bird of the genus *Accipiter*, containing the hawks. WH: 19C. Latin hawk, bird of prey, from *accipere*, to receive, ACCEPT.

acclaim *v.t.* to greet or receive with great enthusiasm. *Also v.i.*, *n.* WH: 16C. Latin *acclamare*, from AC- + *clamare* to shout, with spelling assim. to CLAIM.

acclimatize *v.t.* to habituate to a new climate or environment. *Also v.i.* WH: 19C. French *acclimater*, from a- (AD-) + *climat* CLIMATE. See also -IZE.

acclivity *n.* an upward slope, as distinct from *declivity*. WH: 17C. Latin *acclivitas*, from *acclivus*, from AC- + *clivus* slope. See also -ITY.

accolade *n.* an award or honour, (an expression of) praise and approval. WH: 17C. French, from Provençal *acolada*, ult. from Latin AC- + *collum* neck. See also -ADE.

accommodate *v.t.* to provide lodging for. WH: 16C. Latin *accommodatus*, p.p. of *accommodare*, from AC- + *commodus* fitting. See COMMODE, also -ATE[3].

accompany *v.t.* to go with, attend as a companion. *Also v.i.* WH: 16C. Old French *accompagner*, from a- (AD-) + *compaignier*, from *compain* COMPANION[1].

accomplice *n.* a partner, esp. in crime. WH: 16C. Alt. of *complice*, from Late Latin *complex*, *complicis* partner, prob. by assoc. with ACCOMPANY or ACCOMPLISH.

accomplish *v.t.* to complete, to finish. WH: 12–14C. Old French *accomplir*, *accompliss*-, ult. from Latin AC- + *complere* to fill. See COMPLETE, also -ISH[2].

accord *v.t.* to grant, to bestow. *Also v.i.*, *n.* WH: pre-1200. Old French *acorder* (Modern French *accorder*), from Latin AC- + *cor*, *cordis* heart. Popular Latin *accordare* was based on Latin *discordare* to disagree and *concordare* to agree.

accordion *n.* a small portable keyed instrument in which the notes are produced by bellows acting on metallic reeds. WH: 19C. German *Akkordion*, from Italian *accordare* to tune. Cp. ACCORD.

accost *v.t.* to approach, to speak to. *Also v.i.*, *n.* WH: 16C. French *accoster*, from Italian *accostare*, ult. from Latin AC- + *costa* rib, side. Cp. COAST. The original sense was literal, to lie alongside. The current sense prevailed from the 17C.

accouchement *n.* confinement, lying-in, delivery. WH: 18C. French, from *accoucher*, from *a-* (AD-) + *coucher* to lie. See COUCH[1].

account *v.t.* to regard as, to consider. *Also v.i., n.* WH: 12–14C. Old French *acunter*, *aconter*, from *a-* (AD-) + *cunter*, *conter* COUNT[1].

accountant *n.* a person whose occupation is the keeping or preparation of business accounts. WH: 14–15C. Old French *acontant*, pres.p. of *aconter*, *aconter*. See ACCOUNT.

accoutre *v.t.* to dress, to equip. WH: 16C. Old French *accoutrer*, from *acostrer* to arrange, from Popular Latin *accosturare*, from *costura* a sewing. See COUTURE.

accredit *v.t.* to attribute (a saying, discovery etc.) (to a person). WH: 17C. French *accréditer*, from *a-* (AD-[1]) + *crédit* CREDIT.

accrescence *n.* continued growth, increase. WH: 17C. Late Latin *accrescentia*, from Latin *accrescere*, from AC- + *crescere* to grow. See also -ENCE.

accrete *v.i.* to grow together. *Also a.* WH: 18C. Latin *accretus*, p.p. of *accrescere*. See ACCRESCENCE.

accrue *v.i.* to grow, to increase. *Also v.t.* WH: 14–15C. Anglo-French *accru*, from Old French *accreu*, p.p. of *acreistre*, from Latin *accrescere*. See ACCRESCENCE.

acculturate *v.i.* to adopt the values and traits of another culture. *Also v.t.* WH: mid-20C. AC- + CULTURE. See also -ATE[3].

accumulate *v.t.* to heap up, pile one thing above another. *Also v.i.* WH: 15C. Latin *accumulatus*, p.p. of *accumulare*, from AC- + *cumulus* heap. See CUMULATE[1], also -ATE[3].

accurate *a.* in precise accordance with a rule or standard or with the truth. WH: 16C. Latin *accuratus*, p.p. of *accurare* to take care of, from AC- + *curare* to take care of. See CURE, also -ATE[2].

accursed *a.* lying under a curse. WH: 17C. P.p. of *accurse*, from A-[1] + CURSE.

accusative *a.* of or belonging to the formal case of direct objects in inflected languages. *Also n.* WH: 14–15C. Old French *accusatif*, or from Latin *accusativus casus* accusative case, from *accusatus*, p.p. of *accusare* ACCUSE. See also -IVE. Latin *accusativus casus* arose from a mistranslation of Greek *ptōsis aitiatikē* case of that which is caused, through association with Greek *aitiasthai* to accuse.

accuse *v.t.* to charge with a crime, offence or fault. WH: 12–14C. Old French *acuser*, from Latin *accusare* to call to account, from AC- + *causa* CAUSE.

accustom *v.t.* to habituate (oneself, someone) (to), to make familiar by use. *Also v.i.* WH: 14–15C. Anglo-French *acustumer*, from *a-* (AD-) + *costume* CUSTOM.

AC/DC *a.* bisexual. WH: mid-20C. Alternating current (*AC*) and direct current (*DC*) are the opposite varieties of electrical current.

ace *n.* the single point on cards or dice. *Also a., v.t.* WH: 12–14C. Old French *as*, from Latin *as* unity. The Roman *as* was a pound of 12 ounces, also a copper coin, originally a pound in weight. The spelling *ace* evolved only in the 15C. The original sense was a throw of one at dice, the lowest possible. The present sense as the highest throw or card prevailed from the 16C.

-acea *suf.* used to form names of classes or orders of animals, as in *Cetacea*, *Crustacea* etc. WH: Modern Latin, from Latin, neut. pl. of *aceus* -ACEOUS.

-aceae *suf.* used to form names of orders or families of plants, as in *Rosaceae*. WH: Modern Latin, from Latin, fem. pl. of *aceus* -ACEOUS.

-acean *suf.* used to form singular nouns or adjectives corresponding to collective nouns in *-acea*, as in *crustacean*, *cetacean*. WH: Modern Latin -ACEA + -AN.

acellular *a.* not having or consisting of cells. WH: mid-20C. A-[6] + CELLULAR.

acentric *a.* without centre. WH: 19C. A-[6] + *-centric* (CENTRE).

-aceous *suf.* of the nature of, belonging to, like: forming adjectives from nouns in natural science, as in *crustaceous*, *cretaceous*, *farinaceous*, *filaceous*. WH: Latin *-aceus* of the nature of. Cp. -EOUS, -OUS.

acephal- *comb. form* headless: used to form various scientific terms, chiefly botanical and zoological. WH: 18C. Greek *akephalos*, from A-[6] + *kephalē* head. See also -OUS.

acer *n.* a tree or shrub of the genus *Acer*, comprising over 100 species including the sycamore and maples. WH: 19C. Latin maple.

acerbic *a.* sour, astringent. WH: 19C. Latin *acerbus* sharp. See also -IC.

acerbity *n.* sourness, with roughness or astringency, as of unripe fruit. WH: 16C. French *acerbité*, or from Latin *acerbitas*, from *acerbus* ACERBIC. See also -ITY.

acerose *a.* shaped like a needle, needle-sharp. WH: 18C. Latin *acerosus*, from *acus*, *acus* needle, confused with *acer*, *acris* maple, or *acer*, *acris* sharp, acute. See also -OSE[1].

acet- *comb. form* of the nature of vinegar. WH: Latin *acetum* vinegar.

acetabulum *n.* an ancient Roman vessel for holding vinegar. WH: 14–15C. Latin *acetum* vinegar + *-abulum* vessel, container. Cp. ACETIC.

acetal *n.* any of a class of compounds formed by the reaction of an alcohol with an aldehyde. WH: 19C. ACETIC + -AL[2].

acetaldehyde *n.* a volatile liquid aldehyde used in the manufacture of organic compounds. WH: 19C. ACETIC + ALDEHYDE.

acetate *n.* a salt of acetic acid. WH: 18C. ACETIC + -ATE[1].

acetic *a.* of or relating to vinegar, akin to vinegar. WH: 18C. French *acétique*, from Latin *acetum* vinegar. See also -IC.

acetify *v.t.* to convert into vinegar. *Also v.i.* WH: 19C. Latin *acetum* vinegar + *-i-* + -FY.

acetone *n.* an inflammable liquid obtained by distilling acetated or organic substances and used in the manufacture of chloroform and as a solvent. WH: 19C. ACETIC + -ONE.

acetous *a.* having the character of vinegar, sour. WH: 14–15C. Late Latin *acetosus*, from *acetum* vinegar. See also -OUS.

acetyl *n.* the radical of acetic acid. WH: 19C. ACETIC + -YL.

acetylene *n.* a gas composed of carbon and hydrogen, which burns with an intensely brilliant flame; ethyne. WH: 19C. ACETYL + -ENE.

Achaean *a.* of or relating to Achaea in ancient Greece. *Also n.* WH: 16C. Latin *Achaeus*, from Greek *Akhaios*, from *Akhaia*, Achaea, a district of the Peloponnese + -AN.

Achaemenid *a.* of or relating to a dynasty of Persian kings from Cyrus I to Darius III (553–330 BC). *Also n.* WH: 18C. Greek *Akhaimenēs* Achaimenes, the legendary founder of the dynasty.

acharnement *n.* bloodthirsty fury, ferocity. WH: 18C. French, from *acharner* to give a taste of flesh (to dogs), from *a-* (AD-) + Old French *char* (Modern French *chair*), from Latin *caro*, *carnis* flesh, meat, + -MENT.

ache *v.i.* to suffer continuous dull pain; to be the source of an ache. *Also n.* WH: pre-1200. Old English *acan* (v.), *æce* (n.), ? rel. to Greek *agos* guilt. The noun was pronounced as AITCH to 17C. Cp. BAKE/BATCH, MAKE[1]/ MATCH[1], SPEAK/ SPEECH.

achene *n.* a small dry carpel, with a single seed, which does not open when ripe. WH: 19C. Modern Latin *achaenium*, from Greek A-[6] + *khainein* to gape.

Acheulian *a.* of or relating to the period of Lower Palaeolithic culture, typified by remains discovered in St-Acheul, and placed by archaeologists between the Chellean and the Mousterian epochs. *Also n.* WH: early 20C. French *Acheuléen*, from St-*Acheul*, a town in N France.

achieve *v.t.* to accomplish, finish. WH: 12–14C. Old French *achever* to come (bring) to a head, from *a chief* to (a) head. See AD-, CHIEF. The original French sense gave the English sense to kill to the 16C.

achillea *n.* any plant of the genus *Achillea*, such as the milfoil or yarrow, which are aromatic and have white, yellow or purple flowers. WH: 16C. Greek *Akhilleios*, a plant said to have been used medicinally by Achilles.

Achillean *a.* like Achilles. WH: 16C. Greek *Akhilleus* Achilles, the hero of Homer's *Iliad*. See also -AN.

achilous *a.* without lips. WH: 19C. A-[6] + Greek *kheilos* lip.

achiral *a.* (of a crystal or molecule) not chiral. WH: mid-20C. A-[6] + CHIRAL.

achlamydeous *a.* having neither calyx nor corolla, as the willows. WH: 19C. A-[6] + Greek *khlamus*, *khlamudos* cloak + -EOUS.

achondroplasia *n.* a hereditary bone disorder in which cartilage fails to ossify into long bones, resulting in very short limbs. WH: 19C. Greek *akhondros*, from A-[6] + *khondros* cartilage + -PLASIA.

achromatic *a.* colourless. WH: 18C. French *achromatique*, from Greek *akhrōmatos*, from A-[6] + *khrōma* colour. See CHROMATIC.

acicular *a.* resembling a needle in shape or sharpness. WH: 18C. Late Latin *acicula*, dim. of *acus* needle. See also -CULE, -AR[1].

acid *a.* sour, sharp to the taste. *Also n.* WH: 17C. French *acide*, or from Latin *acidus*, from *acere* to be sour.

acidosis *n.* a condition characterized by the appearance of excess acid in the urine and bloodstream. WH: early 20C. ACID + -OSIS.

acidulous *a.* a little sour or acid, moderately sharp to the taste, subacid. WH: 18C. Latin *acidulus*, from *acidus* sour. See ACID, also -ULOUS.

acierate *v.t.* to turn into steel. WH: 19C. French *aciérer*, from *acier* steel + -ATE[3].

acinus *n.* any of the drupels that make up a compound fruit, such as the raspberry. WH: 18C. Latin berry growing in a cluster.

-acious *suf.* abounding in, characterized by, inclined to. WH: French *-acieux*, or from Latin *-ax*, *-acis* + -OUS.

-acity *suf.* the quality of: forming nouns of quality from adjectives in -ACIOUS. WH: French *-acité*, from Latin *-acitas*, *-acitatis*. Cp. -ACIOUS.

ack-ack *a.* anti-aircraft. *Also n.* WH: early 20C. Phonetic names for the letters AA. *ack* was replaced by *able* in 1942.

ackee *n.* a tropical African tree, *Blighia sapida*, also cultivated in the W Indies. WH: 18C. Prob. from Kru *ā-kee*.

†ack-emma *n.* morning, a.m. WH: early 20C. Phonetic names for the letters AM. See ACK-ACK.

acknowledge *v.t.* to admit the truth of, accept. WH: 15C. Middle English *acknowlechen*, from blend of *acknow* to admit and *knowlechen* to admit, from *knowleche* KNOWLEDGE.

-acle *suf.* diminutive of nouns, as in *tabernacle*, *miracle*. WH: Latin *-aculum*.

aclinic *a.* not dipping, situated where the magnetic needle does not dip. WH: 19C. Greek *aklinēs*, from A-[6] + *klinein* to bend, to lean + -IC.

acme *n.* the top or highest point, perfection (of achievement, excellence etc.). WH: 16C. Greek *akmē* highest point, rel. to *akē* point. Cp. EDGE.

acne *n.* a skin condition characterized by pimples. WH: 19C. Modern Latin, from Late Greek *aknē*, misspelling of *akmē* highest point. See ACME. The original Greek was misspelled by Aetius in the 6C.

acolyte *n.* a person assisting a priest in a service or procession. WH: 12–14C. Old French *acolyt*, or from Ecclesiastical Latin *acolytus*, from Greek *akolouthos* following, follower.

aconite *n.* a plant of the genus *Aconitum*, esp. *A. napellus*, the common monkshood or wolfsbane. WH: 16C. French *aconit*, or from Latin *aconitum*, from Greek *akoniton*, of unknown orig.

acorn *n.* the fruit of the oak. WH: pre-1200. Old English *æcern*, rel. to ACRE. Not rel. to OAK, CORN[1].

acotyledon *n.* any plant of the class *Acotyledones*. WH: 18C. Modern Latin *acotyledones*, from Greek A-[6] + COTYLEDON.

acoustic *a.* of or relating to hearing, sound or acoustics. *Also n.* WH: 17C. Greek *akoustikos*, from *akouein* to hear. See also -IC. Rel. to HEAR.

acquaint *v.t.* to make (someone, oneself) aware of or familiar with (usu. followed by *with*). WH: pre-1200. Old French *acointier* to make known, from Late Latin *accognitare*, from Latin *accognitus*, p.p. of *accognoscere*, from AC- + *cognoscere* to know. See COGNITION.

acquiesce *v.i.* to submit or remain passive. WH: 17C. Latin *acquiescere*, from AC- + *quiescere* to rest. See QUIET. The original sense was to remain quiet. This gave way to the present sense from the 18C.

acquire *v.t.* to gain, or obtain possession of, by one's own exertions or abilities. WH: 15C. Old French *aquerre*, from Latin *acquirere* to gain in addition, from AC- + *quaerere* to seek.

acquisition *n.* the act of acquiring. WH: 14–15C. Latin *acquisitio*, *acquisitionis*, from *acquisitus*, p.p. of *acquirere*. See ACQUIRE.

acquit *v.t.* to declare not guilty. *Also v.refl.* WH: 11–12C. Old French *acquiter*, *aquiter*, from Medieval Latin *acquitare*, from AC- + *quitare* QUIT.

acre *n.* a measure of land containing 4840 sq. yd. (0.4 ha). WH: pre-1200. Old English *æcer* (tilled) field, rel. to Latin *ager*, Greek *agros* field. The original meaning was as much as an ox could plough in a day.

acrid *a.* pungent, biting to the taste. WH: 18C. Latin *acer*, *acris*, appar. assim. to ACID + -IC.

acridine *n.* a colourless, crystalline solid used in the making of dyes and drugs. WH: 19C. German *Acridin*. See ACRID.

acriflavine *n.* an aniline dye, solutions of which form a strong antiseptic. WH: early 20C. ACRIDINE + FLAVIN.

Acrilan® *n.* a type of acrylic fibre or fabric used for clothing, carpets etc. WH: mid-20C. ACRYLIC + *-i-* + Latin *lana* wool.

acrimony *n.* bitter, bad-tempered and accusatory feeling or speech. WH: 16C. French *acrimonie*, or from Latin *acrimonia*. See ACRID, -MONY.

acro- *comb. form* situated on the outside, beginning, termination, extremity, point or top, as in *acrobat*, *acrogenous*. WH: Greek *akro-*, from *akros* tip, peak. See also -O-.

acrobat *n.* a performer of daring gymnastic feats, such as a tumbler or a tightrope walker. WH: 19C. French *acrobate*, from Greek *akrobatēs*, from *akrobatos* walking on tiptoe, from *akro-* ACRO- + base of *bainein* to walk.

acrogen *n.* a cryptogam, a plant distinguished by growth from growing points at the extremity of the stem. WH: 19C. ACRO- + -GEN.

acrolith *n.* a statue having only the head and extremities of stone. WH: 19C. ACRO- + -LITH.

acromegaly *n.* a disease the chief feature of which is the enlargement of the face and of the extremities of the limbs. WH: 19C. ACRO- + Greek *megas*, *megalos* great. Cp. MEGA-, also -Y[2].

acronychal *a.* taking place in the evening or at sunset. WH: 16C. Greek *akronukhos* at nightfall, from *akro-* ACRO- + *nux* night + -AL[1].

acronym *n.* a word formed from initials, e.g. *NATO*, *laser*. WH: mid-20C. ACRO- + -ONYM.

acropetal *a.* in the direction of the apex. WH: 19C. ACRO- + Latin *petere* to seek + -AL[1].

acrophobia *n.* an abnormal dread of high places. WH: 19C. ACRO- + *-phobia* (-PHOBE).

acropolis *n.* the citadel or elevated part of a Greek town, esp. that of Athens. WH: 17C. Greek *akropolis*, from *akro-* ACRO- + *polis* city.

across *prep.* from one side to the other of. *Also adv.* WH: 12–14C. Old French *a croix* in a cross. See CROSS. The original sense was crosswise, in the form of a cross. The present prepositional sense emerged in the 16C.

acrostic *n.* a composition in which the lines are so disposed that their initial letters taken in order constitute a word or short sentence. *Also a.* WH: 16C. French *acrostiche*, from Greek *akrostikhis*, from *akro-* ACRO- + *stikhos* row, line of verse, with assim. to -IC. Cp. STICH.

acroter *n.* a pedestal on a pediment, for the reception of a figure. WH: 17C. Greek *akrōtērion* extremity. See ACRO-.

acrylic *a.* denoting or made from polymers of acrylic acid or its derivatives. *Also n.* WH: 19C. *acrolein* (from Latin *acer*, *acris* sharp + *oleum* oil + -IN[1]) + -YL + -IC.

act *n.* something that is done or being done, a deed. *Also v.t.*, *v.i.* WH: 12–14C. Latin *actus* a doing, from p.p. of *agere* to do. See AGENT.

actinia *n.* a sea anemone of the genus *Actinia*. WH: 18C. Modern Latin, from Greek *aktis*, *aktinos* ray + -IA.

actinic *a.* of or relating to rays, esp. the radiation from the sun. WH: 19C. Greek *aktis*, *aktinos* ray + -IC.

actinide *n.* any of a series of radioactive elements beginning with actinium and ending with lawrencium. WH: mid-20C. ACTINIUM + -IDE (after *lanthanide*, see LANTHANUM).

actinium *n.* a radioactive metallic element, at. no. 89, chem. symbol Ac, found in pitchblende. WH: early 20C. Greek *aktis*, *aktinos* ray + -IUM. The name was adopted from that of a supposed element, a metal discovered in 1881 in association with zinc, and so called because of the action of light on its salts.

actino- *comb. form* indicating a radial shape or structure. WH: Greek *aktis*, *aktinos* ray.

actinograph *n.* an instrument which registers the variations of chemical influence in solar rays. WH: 19C. ACTINO- + -GRAPH.

actinometer *n.* an instrument for measuring the intensity of radiation, esp. of the sun's rays. WH: 19C. ACTINO- + -METER.

actinomorphic *a.* having a radial shape or structure that is symmetrical about its axis, like the buttercup. WH: 19C. ACTINO- + *-morphic* (-MORPH).

actinomycete *n.* any of an order of filamentous bacteria, Actinomycetales, that includes both soil-inhabiting and disease-producing microorganisms. WH: early 20C. ACTINO- + Greek *mukētes*, pl. of *mukes* fungus.

actinotherapy *n.* the treatment of disease by exposure to actinic radiation. WH: early 20C. ACTINO- + *therapy* (THERAPEUTIC).

action *n.* the state, condition or fact of acting or doing. *Also int.*, *v.t.* WH: 12–14C. Old French, from Latin *actio, actionis*. See ACT, also -ION.

activate *v.t.* to make active, to set going. WH: 17C. ACTIVE + -ATE³.

active *a.* characterized by action, work or the performance of business; busy. WH: 12–14C. Latin *activus*. See ACT, also -IVE.

acton *n.* a vest or jacket of quilted cotton, worn under mail. WH: 12–14C. Old French *auqueton* (Modern French *hoqueton*), from Spanish *alcoton*, from Arabic *al-ḳuṭūn* the cotton.

actual *a.* existing in act or reality, real, genuine. WH: 12–14C. Old French *actuel*, from Late Latin *actualis* active, practical, from *actus* ACT. See also -AL¹.

actuary *n.* an officer of a mercantile or insurance company, skilled in statistics, esp. on the expectancy of life and the average proportion of losses by fire and other accidents. WH: 16C. Latin *actuarius* copyist, from *actus* ACT. See also -ARY¹.

actuate *v.t.* to put in action, to cause to operate. WH: 16C. Medieval Latin *actuatus*, p.p. of *actuare*, from *actus* ACT. See also -ATE³.

acuity *n.* sharpness, acuteness (of a point, an acid, disease or wit). WH: 14–15C. Old French *acuite*, or from Medieval Latin *acuitas*, from *acuere*. See ACUTE, also -ITY.

aculeus *n.* a sting. WH: 19C. Latin, dim. of *acus* needle. Cp. ACUTE.

acumen *n.* acuteness of mind, shrewdness. WH: 16C. Latin, from *acuere*. See ACUTE.

acuminate¹ *a.* tapering to a point. WH: 16C. Late Latin *acuminatus*, p.p. of *acuminare*. See ACUMEN, also -ATE².

acuminate² *v.t.* to sharpen, to point, to give keenness or poignancy to. WH: 16C. Late Latin *acuminatus*, p.p. of *acuminare*. See ACUMEN, also -ATE³.

acupressure *n.* massage using the fingertips applied to the points of the body used in acupuncture. WH: 19C. Latin *acu* with a needle + PRESSURE.

acupuncture *n.* a system of medical treatment in which the body surface is punctured by needles at specific points to relieve pain, cure disease or produce anaesthesia. WH: 17C. Latin *acu* with a needle + PUNCTURE.

acushla *n.* darling. WH: 19C. Irish, short for *a cuisle mo* O vein of my (heart) from *a* O + *chuisle*, voc. of *cuisle* vein + *mo* (of) my (*chroidhe* gen. of *croidhe* heart).

acute *a.* sharp, penetrating. *Also n.* WH: 12–14C. Latin *acutus*, p.p. of *acuere* to sharpen, from *acus* needle.

-acy *suf.* forming nouns of quality, state, condition etc., as in *fallacy*, *infancy*, *magistracy*, *piracy*. WH: Latin *-acia, -atia*, from Greek *-ateia*. Cp. -CY.

acyclovir *n.* an antiviral drug used in the treatment of Aids and herpes. WH: late 20C. *acyclic* (from A-⁶ + CYCLE + -IC) + -O- + *viral DNA*. See VIRAL.

acyl *n.* the monovalent radical of a carboxylic acid. WH: 19C. Greek, from Latin *acidum* ACID. See also -YL.

AD *abbr.* in the year of our Lord, Anno Domini. WH: Latin in the year of the lord, abl. sing. of *annus* year + gen. sing. of *dominus* lord. See ANNUAL, DOMINATE.

ad *n.* an advertisement. WH: 19C. Abbr. of *advertisement* (ADVERTISE).

ad- *pref.* signifying motion towards, direction to, adherence etc., as in *adduce*, *adhere*, *adjacent*, *admire*. WH: Latin pref., from prep. *ad* to. For reasons of pronunciation *d* is often assimilated to a subsequent consonant. See A-⁵, AB-², AC-, AF-, AG-, AL-, AN-¹, AP-, AR-, AS-, AT-.

-ad¹ *suf.* forming nouns denoting a group or ˙unit of a specific number, as in *monad*, *triad*. WH: Latin *-as, -adis*, from Greek *-as*, *-ados*.

-ad² *suf.* forming nouns, as in *salad*, *ballad*. WH: French *-ade*. See -ADE.

-ad³ *suf.* forming adverbs, esp. in anatomical descriptions, indicating direction towards a specified part, as in *caudad*. WH: See AD-.

Ada *n.* a computer programming language developed for real-time applications, esp. in military systems. WH: late 20C. Augusta *Ada* King, Countess of Lovelace, 1815–52, mathematician. Ada King, the daughter of Lord Byron, created a program for computer pioneer Charles Babbage's 'analytical engine' in 1843.

adage *n.* a proverb; a pithy maxim handed down from old time.

WH: 16C. French, from Latin *adagium*, from AD- + root *ag*-, rel. to *aio* I say.

adagio *adv.* slowly, gracefully. *Also a., n.* WH: 17C. Italian, from *ad agio* at ease. Rel. to AGIO.

Adam¹ *n.* the first man, in the Bible and in the Koran. WH: 11–12C. Hebrew *'āḏām* man, understood as a name.

Adam² *a.* of or relating to a decorative style of architecture and furniture of the 18th cent. WH: 19C. Robert *Adam*, 1728–92, James *Adam*, 1730–94, Scottish architects and designers.

adamant *a.* stubbornly determined. *Also n.* WH: 17C. Old French *adamaunt-*, from Latin *adamans, adamantis*, from Greek *adamas*, *adamantos* hardest metal, from A-⁶ + *daman* to tame. Cp. DIAMOND. The original meaning was magnet, lodestone, by association with Latin *adamare* to have a strong liking for. The present figurative sense prevailed only in the 20C.

Adamite *n.* a descendant of Adam. WH: 16C. ADAM¹ + -ITE¹.

adapt *v.t.* to adjust, to make suitable for a new purpose or conditions. *Also v.i.* WH: 14–15C. French *adapter*, from Latin *adaptare*, from AD- + *aptare*, from *aptus* APT.

Adar *n.* the sixth civil month, or twelfth ecclesiastical month of the Jewish year (corresponding to part of February and March). WH: 14–15C. Hebrew *'ăḏār*.

adaxial *a.* facing the stem. WH: early 20C. AD- + *axial* (AXIS¹).

add *v.t.* to put together with or join with. *Also v.i.* WH: 12–14C. Latin *addere*, from AD- + base of *dare* to give.

addax *n.* a species of antelope, *Addax nasomaculatus*. WH: 17C. Latin, from an African language.

addendum *n.* a thing to be added, an addition. WH: 17C. Latin, neut. ger. of *addere* ADD.

adder *n.* the common viper, *Vipera berus*. WH: pre-1200. Old English *nǣdre*. The initial *n* was lost in the 14–15C through a wrong division of *a naddre* as *an addre*. Cp. APRON, AUGER. The word originally meant serpent in general. The present restricted sense emerged in the 12C.

addict¹ *v.t.* to cause (someone, oneself) to become dependent on something, esp. a narcotic drug. WH: 16C. Latin *addictus*, p.p. of *addicere*, from AD- + *dicere* to appoint. The direct source of the word was the English p.p. *addicted*, replacing the earlier p.p. *addict*.

addict² *n.* a person who has become addicted to some habit, esp. the taking of drugs. WH: early 20C. ADDICT¹.

Addison's disease *n.* a disease characterized by undersecretion of steroid hormones from the adrenal cortex, causing weakness, weight loss and browning of the skin. WH: 19C. Thomas *Addison*, 1793–1860, English physician.

addle *a.* (of an egg) putrid, bad. *Also n., v.t., v.i.* WH: 12–14C. Old English ˙*adela* mud, mire, liquid filth, of unknown origin.

address *n.* the place where a person lives or a business, an organization etc. has its premises. *Also v.t., v.i.* WH: 12–14C. Old French *adresser*, from Popular Latin *addirectiare* to make straight, from Latin AD- + *directus* DIRECT. The noun dates from the 16C. The verb formerly had the additional senses to make straight, to dress, to direct the aim of, reflecting its Latin origin. This partly remains in *to address the ball*, i.e. to direct it.

adduce *v.t.* to bring forward as a proof or illustration, to cite, to quote. WH: 12–14C. Latin *adducere*, from AD- + *ducere* to lead, to bring.

-ade *suf.* forming nouns denoting action, as in *cannonade, ambuscade*; a person or body involved in action, as in *brigade, cavalcade*; product of action, as in *masquerade*; sweet drink, as in *lemonade*. WH: French, from Provençal, Spanish and Portuguese *-ada*, and from Italian *-ata*, all from Latin *-ata*, orig. fem. of p.p. ending *-atus*. See -ATE¹.

adenectomy *n.* the surgical removal of a gland. WH: 19C. ADENO- + -ECTOMY.

adenine *n.* one of the four purine bases in DNA and RNA. WH: 19C. Greek *adēn* ADENO- + -INE.

adenitis *n.* inflammation of the lymphatic glands. WH: 19C. Greek *adēn* ADENO- + -ITIS.

adeno- *comb. form* connected with a gland or glands, glandular; used in medical terms, e.g. *adenitis, adenopathy*. WH: Greek *adēn* gland. See also -O-.

adenoid *a.* having the form of a gland, glandular. *Also n.pl.* WH: 19C. Greek *adēn* ADENO- + -OID.

adenoma *n.* a benign tumour formed of glandular tissue. WH: 19C. Greek *adēn* ADENO- + -OMA.

adenopathy *n.* disease of a gland or glands. WH: 19C. Greek *adēn* ADENO- + -PATHY.

adenosine *n.* a compound of adenine and the sugar ribose, that forms part of RNA and various compounds that provide energy in cells. WH: early 20C. Blend of ADENINE + RIBOSE.

adept[1] *a.* thoroughly versed, highly skilled. WH: 17C. Latin *adeptus*, p.p. of *adipisci* to attain.

adept[2] *n.* a person who is completely versed in any science or art. WH: 17C. Latin *adeptus*. See ADEPT[1].

adequate *a.* equal to a requirement, sufficient. WH: 17C. Latin *adaequatus*, p.p. of *adaequare*, from AD- + *aequus* equal. Cp. EQUABLE, EQUAL.

à deux *a., adv.* of or between two (people). WH: 19C. French *à* to + *deux* two.

adhere *v.i.* to stick (to). WH: 15C. Old French *adherer*, or from Latin *adhaerere*, from AD- + *haerere* to stick.

adherence *n.* the state or quality of adhering. WH: 15C. Old French, from Late Latin *adhaerentia*. See ADHERE, also -ENCE.

adhesion *n.* the act or state of sticking, attaching oneself to, or joining. WH: 15C. French *adhésion*, or from Latin *adhaesio*, *adhaesionis*, from *adhaesus*, p.p. of *adhaerere* ADHERE. See also -ION.

adhibit *v.t.* to apply, to administer (a remedy). WH: 16C. Latin *adhibitus*, p.p. of *adhibere*, from AD- + *habere* to hold.

ad hoc *a., adv.* for a particular purpose only, specially. WH: 17C. Latin to this, from *ad* AD- + neut. acc. sing. of *hic* this.

ad hominem *a., adv.* directed to or against the person, not disinterested. WH: 16C. Latin to the person, from *ad* AD- + acc. sing. of *homo*, *hominis* person, man.

adiabatic *a.* impervious, esp. to heat. WH: 19C. Greek *adiabatos* impassable, from A-[6] + *dia* through + *batos* passable. See also -IC.

adiaphorism *n.* indifference with regard to non-essential matters, esp. those not specifically prescribed or forbidden by Scripture, in religion or ethics; latitudinarianism. WH: 17C. Greek *adiaphoros*, from A-[6] + *diaphoros* differing. See also -ISM.

adieu *int.* goodbye, farewell. *Also n.* WH: 14–15C. Anglo-French *adeu*, from Old French *adieu*, from *a* to + *Dieu* god. Cp. ADIOS. The full original phrase was *a Dieu (vous) commant* I commend (you) to God.

ad infinitum *adv.* to infinity, without end. WH: 17C. Latin to infinity, from *ad* AD- + acc. of *infinitus* boundless (space). Cp. INFINITE.

ad interim *a., adv.* for the meantime. WH: 18C. Latin, from *ad* AD- + *interim* meanwhile. See INTERIM.

adios *int.* goodbye. WH: 19C. Spanish *adiós*, from *a* to + *Dios* god. Cp. ADIEU. The full original phrase was *a Dios vos acomiendo* I commend you to God.

adipocere *n.* a greyish-white fatty or soapy substance, into which the flesh of dead bodies buried in moist places is converted. WH: 19C. French *adipocire*, from Latin *adeps*, *adipis* fat + French *cire* wax.

adipose *a.* of or relating to animal fat, fatty. *Also n.* WH: 18C. Modern Latin *adiposus*, from *adeps*, *adipis* fat + -OSE[1].

adit *n.* an approach, entrance, passage. WH: 17C. Latin *aditus* approach, from *aditus*, p.p. of *adire*, from AD- + *ire* to go.

Adivasi *n.* a member of any of the aboriginal tribes of India. WH: mid-20C. Modern Sanskrit *ādivāsī*, from *ādi* the beginning + *vāsin* inhabitant.

adjacent *a.* lying next (to); bordering. WH: 14–15C. Latin *adiacens*, *adiacentis*, pres.p. of *adiacere*, from AD- + *iacere* to lie down. See also -ENT. Cp. ADJECTIVE.

adjective *a.* added to. *Also n.* WH: 12–14C. Old French *adjectif*, from Late Latin *adiectivus*, from *adiectus* p.p. of *adicere*, from AD- + *iacere* to lay, to throw.

adjoin *v.t.* to be next to and contiguous with. *Also v.i.* WH: 12–14C. Old French *ajoindre*, *ajoign-* (Modern French *adjoindre*), from Latin *adiungere*. See ADJUNCT.

adjourn *v.t.* to put off or defer till a later period. *Also v.i.* WH: 12–14C. Old French *ajorner* (Modern French *ajourner*), from phr. *a jorn (nomé)* to (a) day (appointed). The original sense was to appoint a day for. The current sense prevailed from the 17C.

adjudge *v.t.* to pronounce officially or formally. WH: 12–14C. Old French *ajuger* (Modern French *adjuger*), from Latin *adiudicare*. See ADJUDICATE.

adjudicate *v.t.* to give a decision regarding, to judge. *Also v.i.* WH: 18C. Latin *adiudicatus*, p.p. of *adiudicare*, from AD- + *iudex*, *iudicis* a judge. See also -ATE[3]. Cp. JUDGE.

adjunct *n.* any thing joined to another without being an essential part of it. *Also a.* WH: 16C. Latin *adiunctus*, p.p. of *adiungere*, from AD- + *iungere* to join. Cp. JOIN.

adjure *v.t.* to charge upon oath, or on pain of divine displeasure. WH: 12–14C. Latin *adiurare*, from AD- + *iurare* to swear, from *ius*, *iuris* oath. Cp. JURY. The original sense was to hold a person to their oath. The current sense prevailed from the 17C.

adjust *v.t.* to regulate; to make slight alteration to, esp. to achieve greater accuracy. *Also v.i.* WH: 17C. Obs. French *adjuster* (Modern French *ajuster*), from Old French *ajoster* (Modern French *ajouter* to add), ult. from Latin AD- + *iuxta* close to.

adjutant *n.* an officer in each regiment who assists the commanding officer in matters of business, duty and discipline. WH: 17C. Latin *adiutans*, *adiutantis*, pres.p. of *adiutare*, freq. of *adiuvare*. See ADJUVANT. The original sense was an assistant generally. The military sense soon prevailed.

adjuvant *a.* helping. *Also n.* WH: 16C. French, or from Latin *adiuvans*, *adiuvantis*, pres.p. of *adiuvare*, from AD- + *iuvare* to help. See also -ANT.

ad lib *adv.* at pleasure, to any extent. WH: 17C. Latin according to pleasure, from *ad* AD- + acc. sing. of *libitum* pleasure. The abbreviation dates from the 19C.

ad litem *a.* (of a guardian) appointed for a lawsuit. WH: 18C. Latin according to the lawsuit, from *ad* AD- + acc. sing. of *lis*, *litis* lawsuit. Cp. LITIGATE.

adman *n.* a person who works in advertising. WH: early 20C. AD + MAN.

admass *n.* the mass viewers and listeners to whom television and radio advertising is directed. WH: mid-20C. AD + MASS. The term was coined by the English writer J.B. Priestley in 1955.

admeasure *v.t.* to ascertain the dimensions, weight etc. of (a vessel) for the purposes of official registration or rating. WH: 12–14C. Old French *amesurer*, from Medieval Latin *admensurare*, from AD- + *mensurare* MEASURE.

admin *n.* administration, administrative work. WH: mid-20C. Shortening of *administration* (ADMINISTER).

adminicle *n.* an aid, support. WH: 16C. Latin *adminiculum* prop, support, from AD- + dim. suf. -*culum* -CULE.

administer *v.t.* to manage or conduct as chief agent. *Also v.i.* WH: 12–14C. Old French *aminister*, from Latin *administrare*, from AD- + *ministrare* MINISTER.

admirable *a.* worthy of admiration. WH: 14–15C. Old French, from Latin *admirabilis*, from *admirari* ADMIRE.

admiral *n.* the commander of a fleet or a division of a fleet (a rank having four grades in the Royal Navy: Admiral of the Fleet, Admiral, Vice-Admiral and Rear-Admiral). WH: 12–14C. Old French *amiral*, ult. from Arabic *'amīr* commander (AMIR), + -*al* -AL[1]. The inserted *d* was added by association with ADMIRABLE. Traditionally the word was said to come from Arabic *'amīr al-* commander of the, from titles such as *'amīr al-bahr* commander of the sea. The early sense to the 15C was emir. The naval sense prevailed from the 16C.

admiralty *n.* the office of admiral. WH: 15C. Old French *admiralté* (Modern French *amirauté*) (ADMIRAL). See also -TY[1].

admire *v.t.* to have a high opinion of, to respect. *Also v.i.* WH: 15C. Old French *amirer* (Modern French *admirer*), from Latin *admirari*, from AD- + *mirari* to wonder. Cp. MIRAGE. The early sense was to wonder, to be surprised. The current sense prevailed from the 16C.

admissible *a.* fit to be considered as an opinion or as evidence. WH: 17C. French, or from Medieval Latin *admissibilis*, from Latin *admissus*, p.p. of *admittere*. See ADMIT.

admit *v.t.* to concede, to acknowledge. *Also v.i.* WH: 12–14C. Latin *admittere*, from AD- + *mittere* to send. Cp. MISSION.

admix *v.t.* to mix, to mingle. WH: 14–15C. Latin *admixtus*, p.p. of *admiscere*, from AD- + *miscere* MIX.

admonish *v.t.* to reprove gently. WH: 12–14C. Old French *amonester*, ult. from Latin *admonere*, from AD- + *monere* to advise. The ending was assimilated to -ISH².

adnate *a.* growing or grown closely attached to another part or organ along its whole surface. WH: 17C. Latin *adnatus*, var. of *agnatus* AGNATE, by assoc. with AD-.

ad nauseam *adv.* to the point of producing disgust or nausea. WH: 17C. Latin to sickness, from *ad* AD- + acc. sing. of *nausea* NAUSEA.

adnominal *a.* of or relating to an adnoun. WH: 19C. Latin *adnomen*, *adnominis*, var. of *agnomen* AGNOMEN + -AL¹.

adnoun *n.* an adjective used as a noun. WH: 19C. AD- + NOUN, based on ADVERB.

Adnyamathanha *n.* an Aboriginal language of S Australia. WH: Native name.

ado *n.* activity. WH: 12–14C. Scandinavian *at do* (shortened), from Old Norse *at* as sign of inf. + DO.

-ado *suf.* forming nouns, as in *desperado*, *renegado*, *tornado*. WH: Spanish, or from Portuguese, masc. p.p. ending of vv. in *-ar*, from Latin *-atus* -ATE¹. See -ADE. Some words in *-ado*, e.g. *bravado*, *gambado*, *strappado*, are alterations of French words in *-ade*.

adobe *n.* a sun-dried brick. WH: 18C. Spanish, from *adobar* to plaster, from Arabic *aṭ-ṭūb*, from *al* the + *ṭūb* bricks.

adolescent *a.* growing up; between puberty and maturity. *Also n.* WH: 15C. Old French, from Latin *adolescentia*, from *adolescens*, *adolescentis* pres.p. of *adolescere*, from AD- + *alescere* to grow up, from *alere* to nourish. See also -ENT.

Adonai *n.* the Lord; a name for God in the Old Testament. WH: 14–15C. Hebrew *'ăḏōnāy* my lord. The name was originally a substitute for JEHOVAH.

Adonis *n.* a handsome young man; a beau, a dandy. WH: 16C. Greek *Adōnis*, a youth loved by Aphrodite in Greek mythology, ult. from Phoenician *'adōnī* my lord. Cp. ADONAI.

adopt *v.t.* to take into any relationship, as child, heir, citizen, candidate etc. WH: 15C. Old French *adopter*, or from Latin *adoptare*, from AD- + *optare* to choose. Cp. OPT.

adore *v.t.* to regard with the utmost respect and affection. *Also v.i.* WH: 12–14C. Old French *adourer* (Modern French *adorer*), from Latin *adorare*, from AD- + *orare* to speak, to pray. Cp. ORATION.

adorn *v.t.* to decorate, ornament. *Also n.* WH: 12–14C. Old French *adorner*, from Latin *adornare*, from AD- + *ornare* to furnish. Cp. ORNATE.

ad personam *adv.* to the person. *Also a.* WH: mid-20C. Latin to the person, from *ad* AD- + acc. sing. of *persona* PERSON.

ad rem *a.*, *adv.* to the point, to the purpose. WH: 16C. Latin to the matter, from *ad* AD- + acc. sing. of *res* thing, matter.

adrenal *a.* near the kidneys. WH: 19C. AD- + RENAL.

adrenalin *n.* a hormone secreted by the adrenal glands that stimulates the heart muscle and increases blood pressure. WH: early 20C. ADRENAL + -IN¹.

adrenocorticotrophic *a.* stimulating the adrenal cortex. WH: mid-20C. *adreno-*, comb. form of ADRENAL + CORTICO- + -TROPHIC.

adrift *a.*, *adv.* drifting; unable to steer. WH: 16C. A-¹ + DRIFT.

adroit *a.* dexterous, mentally or physically resourceful. WH: 17C. Old French, from phr. *à droit* according to right, from AD- + *droit*, from Late Latin *drictum*, from Latin *directum* (DIRECT).

adscititious *a.* assumed, adopted, derived from without, supplemental. WH: 17C. Latin *adscitus*, p.p. of *adsciscere* to admit, to adopt + -ITIOUS², based on ADVENTITIOUS.

adscript *a.* written after (opposed to subscript). *Also n.* WH: 17C. Latin *adscriptus*, p.p. of *adscribere*, from AD- + *scribere* to write. Cp. SCRIPT.

adsorb *v.t.* to take up and cause to adhere in a thin film on the surface. *Also v.i.* WH: 19C. Back-formation from *adsorption*, blend of AD- and *absorption* (ABSORB).

adulate *v.t.* to fawn upon, to flatter servilely. WH: 18C. Latin *adulatus*, p.p. of *adulari* to fawn upon. See also -ATE³.

adult *a.* grown to maturity. *Also n.* WH: 16C. Latin *adultus*, p.p. of *adolescere* (ADOLESCENT).

adulterate *v.t.* to corrupt or debase (something) by mixing it with an inferior substance. *Also a.* WH: 16C. Latin *adulteratus*, p.p. of *adulterare* to debauch, from AD- + *alterare* ALTER. See also -ATE³. Cp. ADULTERY. The original sense was to commit adultery. The current less specific sense evolved soon after.

adultery *n.* voluntary sexual intercourse on the part of a married person with someone other than their spouse. WH: 14–15C. Middle English *adulterie*, from Old French *avouterie*, from Latin *adulterare* ADULTERATE.

adumbrate *v.t.* to outline, to sketch out. WH: 16C. Latin *adumbratus*, p.p. of *adumbrare*, from AD- + *umbrare*, from *umbra* shade, UMBRA. See also -ATE³.

ad valorem *a.*, *adv.* (of a tax) in proportion to the value of the goods. WH: 17C. Latin according to the value, from *ad* AD- + acc. sing. of Late Latin *valor*. See VALOUR.

advance *v.t.* to bring or move forward or upwards. *Also v.i.*, *n.*, *a.* WH: pre-1200. Old French *avancer*, ult. from Late Latin *abante*, from AB-¹ + *ante* before. The spelling with *d* arose in the 16C because the initial *a-* was thought to represent Latin AD-.

advantage *n.* a favourable condition or circumstance. *Also v.t.* WH: 12–14C. Old French *avantage*, from *avant* before. See also -AGE.

advection *n.* the transfer of heat by the horizontal movement of air. WH: early 20C. Latin *advectio*, *advectionis*, from *advehere*, from AD- + *vehere* to carry. See also -ION. Cp. VECTOR, VEHICLE.

advent *n.* the season of the Christian year including the four Sundays before Christmas. WH: pre-1200. Old French, from Latin *adventus* arrival, from p.p. of *advenire*, from AD- + *venire* to come. The word originally meant the Christian season only. This was extended to the coming of Christ (15C) and to the general sense of arrival in the 18C.

adventitious *a.* accidental, casual. WH: 17C. Medieval Latin *adventitius*, from Latin *adventicius*, from *adventus* arrival, ADVENT. See also -ITIOUS².

adventure *n.* an undertaking in which hazard or risk is incurred and for which enterprise and daring are required. *Also v.t.*, *v.i.* WH: pre-1200. Old French *aventure*, ult. from Latin *adventurus*, fut. part. of *advenire*. See ADVENT, also -URE. The early senses, now obsolete, were chance, luck, risk. The current sense prevailed from the 14C.

adverb *n.* a word or phrase qualifying a verb, an adjective or another adverb. WH: 14–15C. French *adverbe*, or from Latin *adverbium*, from AD- + *verbum* VERB.

adversary *n.* an opponent. *Also a.* WH: 12–14C. Old French *adversarie* (Modern French *adversaire*), from Latin *adversarius* opposed, from *adversus*. See ADVERSE, also -ARY¹.

adverse *a.* unpropitious, unfavourable. WH: 12–14C. Old French *advers*, from Latin *adversus* against, p.p of *advertere* (ADVERT).

advert *v.t.* to attend to, to turn attention to, refer to. *Also v.i.* WH: 14–15C. Old French *avertir*, ult. from Latin *advertere*, from AD- + *vertere* to turn. Cp. ANIMADVERT.

advertise *v.t.* to publicly describe (a product, service, vacancy etc.) in order to promote awareness, increase sales, invite applications etc. *Also v.i.* WH: 14–15C. Old French *avertir*, *avertiss-*. See ADVERT. The early sense was to notice, to draw attention to. *Advertisement* similarly meant warning, attention. The current meaning prevailed from the 19C.

advertorial *n.* a newspaper feature which is commissioned and often supplied by an advertiser, though appearing in the form of an editorial or impartial report. WH: mid-20C. Blend of *advertisement* (ADVERTISE) and *editorial* (EDIT).

advice *n.* counsel, opinion as to a course of action. WH: Old French *avis*, ult. from Latin AD- + *visum*, neut. p.p. of *videre* to see. The original sense was opinion. This finally became obsolete only in the 17C. Cp. ADVISE.

advise *v.t.* to counsel (a person). *Also v.i.* WH: 12–14C. Old French *aviser*, ult. from Latin AD- + *visere*, freq. of *videre* to see. The original sense was to observe, to take thought. The current meaning prevailed from the 17C. Cp. ADVICE.

advocaat *n.* a sweet thick liqueur containing raw egg and brandy. WH: mid-20C. Dutch ADVOCATE¹. The liqueur was used by advocates to clear the throat.

advocate[1] *n.* a person who defends or promotes a cause. WH: 12–14C. Old French *avocat*, from Latin *advocatus*, p.p. (used as n.) of *advocare*, from AD- + *vocare* to call.See also -ATE[1].

advocate[2] *v.t.* to plead in favour of, recommend. WH: 16C. See ADVOCATE[1], also -ATE[3].

advowson *n.* the right of presentation to a vacant benefice in the Church of England. WH: 12–14C. Anglo-French *avoweson*, or from Old French *avoeson*, from Latin *advocatio*, *advocationis* (ADVOCATE[1]).

adynamia *n.* lack of power, nervous debility, physical prostration. WH: 19C. Modern Latin, from Greek, from A-[6] + *dunamis* power. See also -IA.

adytum *n.* the innermost and most sacred part of a temple. WH: 17C. Latin, from Greek *aduton*, neut. sing. (used as n.) of *adutos* impenetrable.

adze *n.* a cutting tool with an arched blade at right angles to the handle. *Also v.t.* WH: pre-1200. Old English *adesa*, of unknown orig.

adzuki *n.* a plant, *Vigna angularis*, grown esp. in China and Japan. WH: 18C. Japanese *azuki*.

ae *a.* one, a. WH: Scots form of OE *ān* ONE used as a.

-ae *suf.* forming the plural of non-naturalized Latin words, as in *laminae*, *Rosaceae*, *Homeridae*. WH: Latin, pl. ending of 1st declension nn. in -a.

aedile *n.* a magistrate in ancient Rome who had charge of public works, games, roads and buildings. WH: 16C. Latin *aedilis*, from *aedes* building. See also -IL, -EAN.

aegis *n.* in Greek myth, a shield belonging to Zeus or Athene. WH: 17C. Latin, from Greek *aigis*. The shield is said to have been made of goatskin, and the word is popularly derived from Greek *aix*, *aigos* goat.

aegrotat *n.* a note certifying that a student is sick. WH: 18C. Latin he is sick, 3rd pers. sing. pres. ind. of *aegrotare* to be ill, from *aeger*, *aegris* sick, ill.

-aemia *comb. form* of, relating to or denoting blood, esp. a specified condition of the blood. WH: Greek *haima* blood + -IA.

Aeolian *a.* of or relating to Aeolus. WH: 16C. Latin *Aeolius*, a. from *Aeolus*, god of the winds in Greek mythology + -IAN.

Aeolic *a.* of or belonging to Aeolia. *Also n.* WH: 17C. Latin *Aeolicus*, from Greek *Aiolikos* of Aeolia. See also -IC.

aeolipile *n.* an apparatus for demonstrating the force of steam generated in a closed chamber and escaping through a small aperture. WH: 17C. French *éolipyle*, from Latin *Aeoli pylae* doorway of Aeolus (see AEOLIAN).

aeolotropy *n.* change of physical qualities consequent on change of position, as of the refracting properties of Iceland spar. WH: 19C. Greek *aiolos* changeful + *tropia* turning. Cp. TROPE.

aeon *n.* a period of immense duration. WH: 17C. Ecclesiastical Latin, from Greek *aiōn* age.

aepyornis *n.* any of a genus, *Aepyornis*, of gigantic fossil birds much larger than the ostrich, found in Madagascar. WH: 19C. Modern Latin, from Greek *aipus* high, tall + *ornis* bird. The term was coined in 1859 by the French zoologist Isidore Geoffroy Saint-Hilaire.

aerate *v.t.* to subject to the action of atmospheric air. WH: 18C. Latin *aer* air + -ATE[3].

aerial *a.* of or relating to the air. *Also n.* WH: 16C. Latin *aerius*, from Greek *aerios*, from *aēr* air. See also -AL[1]. The noun sense evolved only in the 20C, so that an aerial was originally an aerial wire, i.e. a wire in the air.

aeriform *a.* of the form or nature of air; gaseous. WH: 18C. Latin *aer* air + -*i*- + -FORM.

aero- *comb. form* of or relating to the air or atmosphere, e.g. *aerodynamics*. WH: Greek *aēr* air. See also -O-.

aerobatics *n.pl.* spectacular flying or stunts by an aircraft. WH: early 20C. AERO- + *acrobatics* (ACROBAT).

aerobe *n.* an organism that requires oxygen for life. WH: 19C. French *aérobie*, from Greek *aēr* air + *bios* life. The word was coined by the French chemist Louis Pasteur in 1863.

aerobiology *n.* the study of airborne microorganisms. WH: mid-20C. AERO- + BIOLOGY.

aerodrome *n.* an area, with any buildings attached, for the operation of esp. light aircraft. WH: 19C. AERO- + -DROME. The early sense was aeroplane, literally an 'air runner'. The current sense prevailed from the early 20C.

aerodynamics *n.* the science which deals with the forces exerted by gases in motion. WH: 19C. AERO- + *dynamics* (DYNAMIC).

aerodyne *n.* any heavier-than-air machine, such as an aircraft. WH: early 20C. Shortening of AERODYNAMICS.

aeroembolism *n.* the formation of nitrogen bubbles in the blood and tissues, caused by too rapid a reduction in atmospheric pressure. WH: mid-20C. AERO- + EMBOLISM.

aero-engine *n.* an engine used to power an aircraft. WH: early 20C. AERO- + ENGINE.

aerofoil *n.* a winglike structure constructed to obtain reaction on its surfaces from the air; one of the flying surfaces of an aeroplane. WH: early 20C. AERO- + FOIL[1].

aerogram *n.* a radiogram, a wireless message. WH: 19C. AERO- + -GRAM.

aerography *n.* the description of the properties etc. of the air. WH: 18C. AERO- + -GRAPHY.

aerolite *n.* a stone which falls through the air to the earth. WH: 19C. AERO- + -LITE.

aerology *n.* the department of science that deals with the atmosphere. WH: 18C. AERO- + -LOGY.

aerometer *n.* an instrument for measuring the weight and density of air and gases. WH: 18C. AERO- + -METER.

aeronaut *n.* a person who pilots, navigates or flies in a balloon or airship. WH: 18C. AERO- + Greek *nautēs* sailor. Cp. ASTRONAUTICS, COSMONAUT.

aeronomy *n.* the science of the upper atmosphere of the earth and other planets. WH: mid-20C. AERO- + -NOMY.

aerophyte *n.* a plant which grows entirely in the air, as distinguished from one growing on the ground. WH: 19C. AERO- + -PHYTE.

aeroplane *n.* a mechanically-driven heavier-than-air flying machine with fixed wings as lifting surfaces. WH: 19C. French *aéroplane*, from *aéro-* AERO- + PLANE[4], stem of *planer* to soar (see PLANE[1]).

aerosol *n.* a suspension of fine particles in air or gas, as in smoke or mist. WH: early 20C. AERO- + SOL.

aerospace *n.* the earth's atmosphere and the space beyond. *Also a.* WH: mid-20C. AERO- + SPACE.

aerostat *n.* an aircraft that is supported in the air statically, i.e. lighter-than-air. WH: 18C. French *aérostat*, from *aéro-* AERO- + -STAT.

aerostation *n.* the science of flying lighter-than-air craft. WH: 18C. French *aérostation*, from *aérostat* AEROSTAT + -ION.

aerotowing *n.* the towing of gliders by powered aircraft. WH: mid-20C. AERO- + *towing* (TOW[1]).

aerotrain *n.* a train that glides above its track supported on a cushion of air. WH: mid-20C. French *aérotrain*, from *aéro-* AERO- + *train* TRAIN.

aeruginous *a.* of the nature of or resembling verdigris. WH: 17C. Latin *aeruginosus*, from *aerugo* rust of copper, from *aes*, *aeris* bronze, copper. See also -OUS.

aery *a.* airy. WH: 16C. Latin *aerius*, from *aer* air + suf. based on -Y[1].

Aesculapian *a.* of or belonging to Aesculapius. WH: 17C. Latin *Aesculapius*, the Roman god of medicine + -AN.

aesthesia *n.* capacity to feel or sense, sensibility. WH: 18C. Greek *aisthēsis* a perceiving. See AESTHETE, also -IA.

aesthete *n.* a person who professes a special appreciation of the beautiful, esp. in the arts. WH: 19C. Greek *aisthētēs* a person who perceives, from *aisthētikos*, from *aisthēta* things perceived by the senses, from *aisthanesthai* to perceive.

aestival *a.* of or belonging to the summer. WH: 14–15C. Old French *estival*, from Latin *aestivalis*, from *aestus* heat. See also -AL[1].

aetatis *prep.* at the age of. WH: 19C. Latin of the age, gen. sing. of *aetas* life, age.

aetiology *n.* the study of causation. WH: 16C. Greek *aitiologia*, from *aitia* cause + -*logia* -LOGY.

af- *pref.* signifying motion towards, direction to, adherence etc., as in *affect*, *affix*. WH: Latin pref., from AD- with *d* assim. to *f*.

afar *adv.* at or to a (great) distance. WH: 12–14C. Middle English *a fer*, alt. of *on fer* and *of fer*. See A-[1], A-[2], FAR.

†afeard *a.* afraid, frightened. WH: pre-1200. A-[3] + p.p. of Old English *fǣran* to frighten. The word was superseded by AFRAID.

affable *a.* friendly, approachable. WH: 14–15C. Old French, and from Latin *affabilis*, from *affari*, from AF- + *fari* to speak. See also -ABLE.

affair *n.* a matter, something that is to be done. WH: 12–14C. Old French *afaire* (Modern French *affaire*), from *a faire* to do. Cp. ADO, AFFAIRE.

affaire *n.* a love affair. WH: 19C. French AFFAIR (of the heart).

affairé *a.* busy. WH: early 20C. French, p.p. of (*s'*)*affairer* to be busy, from *affaire* AFFAIR.

affect[1] *v.t.* to have an effect upon, exert an influence upon. WH: 14–15C. French *affecter*, or from Latin *affectus*, p.p. of *afficere*, from AF- + *facere* to do.

affect[2] *v.t.* to make a pretence of, to feign. WH: 14–15C. See AFFECT[1]. The original sense was to aim at, reflecting the Latin source verb. The sense to have a liking for, to display openly evolved in the 16C, the current sense predominating from the 17C.

affect[3] *n.* an emotion or emotional state that is associated with or causes an idea or an action. WH: 14–15C. Latin *affectus*, n. of completed action of *afficere*. See AFFECT[1]. The current sense arose in the 16C or 17C through German *Affekt*.

affection *n.* fondness, love. *Also v.t.* WH: 11–12C. Old French, from Latin *affectio*, *affectionis*, from *affectus*. See AFFECT[1], also -ION. The original sense of *affectionate* was affected, meaning prejudiced, partial. The current favourable sense emerged in the 16C.

affective *a.* of or relating to the affections, emotional. WH: 14–15C. French *affectif*, from Late Latin *affectivus*, from *affectus*. See AFFECT[1], also -IVE.

affenpinscher *n.* a European breed of dog, resembling the griffon, that has tufts of hair on the face. WH: early 20C. German, from *Affe* APE + *Pinscher* terrier.

afferent *a.* bringing or conducting inwards or towards, esp. conducting nerve impulses towards the brain or spinal cord. WH: 19C. Latin *afferens*, *afferentis*, pres.p. of *affere*, from AF- + *ferre* to bring. See also -ENT.

affettuoso *adv.* with feeling. WH: 18C. Italian, from Late Latin *affectuosus*. See AFFECT[1].

affiance *v.t.* to promise solemnly in marriage, to betroth. *Also n.* WH: 15C. Old French *afiancer*, from Medieval Latin *affidare*, from AF- + *fidare* to trust. Cp. FIANCÉ.

affiant *n.* a person who makes an affidavit. WH: 19C. Old French *afier*, from Medieval Latin *affidare*. See AFFIANCE, also -ANT.

affiche *n.* a poster, placard. WH: 19C. French, from *afficher*, from Old French *aficher*, from Late Latin *affigicare*, from Latin AF- + *figere* to fix.

affidavit *n.* a voluntary affirmation sworn before a person qualified to administer an oath. WH: 16C. Latin he declared on oath, 3rd pers. sing. perf. ind. of Medieval Latin *affidare*. See AFFIANCE.

affiliate[1] *v.t.* to connect with a larger organization. *Also v.i.* WH: 17C. Medieval Latin *affiliatus*, p.p. of *affiliare*, from AF- + *filius* son. See also -ATE[3].

affiliate[2] *n.* a person, company, branch etc. that is affiliated to an organization. *Also a.* WH: 19C. Latin *affiliatus*, p.p. of *affiliare* (AFFILIATE[1]). See also -ATE[1].

affined *a.* joined in affinity; related; closely connected. WH: 16C. Latin *affinis* related to + -ED. See AFFINITY.

affinity *n.* a natural attraction or inclination to, or liking for, something. WH: 12–14C. Old French *afinite* (Modern French *affinité*), from Latin *affinitas*, from *affinis*, from AF- + *finis* end, border. See also -ITY.

affirm *v.t.* to assert positively or solemnly. *Also v.i.* WH: 12–14C. Old French *afermer* (Modern French *affirmer*), from Latin *affirmare*, from AF- + *firmus* FIRM[1].

affix[1] *v.t.* to fasten, attach. WH: 16C. Old French *affixer*, or from Medieval Latin *affixare*, from AF- + *fixare* FIX.

affix[2] *n.* an addition. WH: 16C. Latin *affixus*, p.p. of *affigere*, from *ad*-AF- + *figere* to fasten. See FIX.

afflatus *n.* inspiration. WH: 17C. Latin, from *afflatus*, p.p. of *afflare*, from AF- + *flare* to blow. Cp. INFLATE.

afflict *v.t.* to inflict bodily or mental pain on; to trouble. WH: 12–14C. Latin *afflictare*, or from *afflictus*, p.p. of *affligere*, from AF- + *fligere* to strike. The word originally had the literal sense to throw down. The current sense emerged in the 16C.

affluent *a.* wealthy, prosperous. *Also n.* WH: 15C. Old French, from

Latin *affluens*, *affluentis*, pres.p. of *affluere*, from AF- + *fluere* to flow. Cp. FLUENT.

afflux *n.* a flowing towards or in. WH: 17C. Medieval Latin *affluxus*, from p.p. of *affluere* (AFFLUENT).

afford *v.t.* to be able to bear the expense of, to have the money, the means etc., to. WH: pre-1200. Old English *geforthian*, from *ge*- pref. denoting completion + *forthian* to further, from *forth* FORTH. The current spelling is an alteration of Middle English *aforthen*, with change of *th* for *d* as for BURDEN, MURDER. The original Old English sense was to set forward, to carry out. The current meanings evolved from the 15C.

afforest *v.t.* to plant trees on; to convert into forest. WH: 16C. Medieval Latin *afforestare*, from AF- + *foresta* FOREST.

affranchise *v.t.* to make free; to set at liberty physically or morally. WH: 15C. Old French *afranchir*, *afranchiss*- (Modern French *affranchir*), from *a*- (AD-) + *franc* free. Cp. FRANK.

affray *n.* a fight or disturbance involving two or more persons in a public place. *Also v.t.* WH: 14–15C. Anglo-French *affrai*, from Old French *effrei* (Modern French *effroi*), from Popular Latin *exfridare*, from Latin EX- + Germanic base related to German *Friede* peace. The original sense was attack, disturbance. The current narrower sense evolved in the 15C.

affreightment *n.* (a contract for) the hiring of a ship for conveyance of goods by sea. WH: 18C. French *affrètement*, from *affréter*, from *à* (AD-) + *fret* freight. The spelling has been assimilated to FREIGHT.

affricate *n.* a speech sound, such as *ch* in *church*, combining an initial plosive with a following fricative or spirant. WH: 19C. Latin *affricatus*, p.p. of *affricare*, from AF- + *fricare* to rub. See also -ATE[1].

†affright *v.t.* to frighten, to terrify. *Also a., n.* WH: 14–15C. Middle English p.p. *afright*, from Old English p.p. *āfyrhted*. See A-[3], FRIGHT, also -ED.

affront *v.t.* to insult openly. *Also n.* WH: 12–14C. Old French *afronter* (Modern French *affronter*), ult. from Latin *ad frontem* to the face. See AF-, FRONT. The verb originally had a much stronger sense, implying physical opposition. The current sense emerged in the 16C. Cp. INSULT[1], OFFEND.

affusion *n.* a pouring on of liquid. WH: 17C. French, or from Late Latin *affusio*, *affusionis*, from *affusus*, p.p. of *affundere*, from AF- + *fundere* to pour. See also -ION.

Afghan *a.* of or belonging to Afghanistan. *Also n.* WH: 18C. Pashto *afghāni*.

aficionado *n.* a keen follower or fan. WH: 19C. Spanish amateur, p.p. (used as n.) of *aficionar* to become fond of, from *afición*. See AFFECTION.

afield *adv.* away, at a distance, abroad. WH: 12–14C. A-[1] + FIELD.

afire *adv., pred.a.* on fire. WH: 12–14C. A-[1] + FIRE.

aflame *adv., pred.a.* flaming. WH: 16C. A-[1] + FLAME.

aflatoxin *n.* a carcinogenic toxin produced in badly stored peanuts, maize etc. by the mould *Aspergillus flavus*. WH: mid-20C. Modern Latin *A*(*spergillus*) *fla*(*vus*) + TOXIN.

afloat *a., adv.* floating. WH: pre-1200. A-[1] + FLOAT.

aflutter *a., adv.* in an excited or nervous state. WH: 19C. A-[1] + FLUTTER.

afoot *adv.* on foot. WH: 12–14C. A-[1] + FOOT.

afore *adv., prep.* before. WH: pre-1200. Old English *onforan*. See ON, FORE.

a fortiori *adv.* with still more reason, much more, still more conclusively. WH: 17C. Latin *a fortiori* (*argumento*) from stronger (evidence).

afoul *a., adv.* fouled, entangled, in collision. WH: 19C. A-[2] + FOUL.

afraid *a.* filled with fear, terrified. WH: 12–14C. P.p. of AFFRAY used as a.

afreet *n.* a demon or monster of Muslim mythology. WH: 18C. Arabic *'ifrīt*, prob. from Persian *āfrīda* created being.

afresh *adv.* again. WH: 15C. A-[3] + FRESH.

African *a.* of or relating to Africa. *Also n.* WH: pre-1200. Old English *Africanas* (pl.), from Latin *Africanus*, from *Africa terra* land of the *Afri*. See also -AN.

Afrikaans *n.* the language, descended from and similar to Dutch, spoken by Afrikaners and some people of mixed descent in S Africa (one of the official languages of the Republic of S Africa). WH: early 20C. Dutch AFRICAN. Cp. AFRIKANER.

Afrikander *n.* a breed of longhorn, humpbacked cattle originating from southern Africa; an animal of this breed. WH: 19C. Afrikaans, from *Afrikaan* AFRICAN + *-der*, based on *Hollander* Dutchman. The original meaning was AFRIKANER.

Afrikaner *n.* a person born in S Africa of white parents whose mother tongue is Afrikaans. WH: 19C. Afrikaans, from *Afrikaan* AFRICAN + *-er* pers. suf. See AFRIKANDER.

Afro *a.* (of a hairstyle) characterized by thick, bushy hair. *Also n.* WH: mid-20C. From AFRO- or AFRICAN + -O.

Afro- *comb. form* of or relating to Africa or Africans. WH: 19C. Latin, from *Afer, Afris* AFRICAN. See also -O-.

Afro-Caribbean *n.* a person of African descent from the Caribbean. *Also a.* WH: mid-20C. AFRO- + *Caribbean* (CARIB).

Afrocentric *a.* centred on African or Afro-American history and culture, esp. in order to promote a sense of cultural pride and identity in black Americans. WH: mid-20C. AFRO- + -CENTRIC.

afrormosia *n.* any tree of the African genus *Afrormosia*, with dark hard wood used for furniture. WH: mid-20C. Modern Latin, from AFRO- + *Ormosia*, a related genus, from Greek *hormos* necklace. See also -IA.

aft *a., adv.* towards or at the stern of a vessel. WH: 17C. Prob. from ABAFT.

after *prep.* at a later time than. *Also a., adv., conj.* WH: pre-1200. Old English *æfter* next, following, from Germanic, from Indo-European.

aftermath *n.* consequences or after-effects. WH: 15C. AFTER + dial. *math* a mowing, from Old English *mæth.* Rel. to MOW[1]. The original meaning was a second or later mowing after the first main one. The current figurative sense emerged in the 17C.

aftermost *a.* nearest the stern. WH: 18C. Prob. AFTER + -MOST as in FOREMOST etc., or Old English *æftemæst*, a double superl.

afternoon *n.* the latter part of the day between noon or lunchtime and evening. *Also a., int.* WH: 12–14C. AFTER + NOON. The word may have been formed after Latin *post meridiem* after noon. Cp. FORENOON.

Ag *chem. symbol* silver. WH: Latin *argentum*.

ag- *pref.* signifying motion towards, direction to, adherence etc., as in *aggravate, aggregate.* WH: Latin pref., from AD- with *d* assim. to *g.*

Aga® *n.* a type of stove with several ovens which is permanently lit. WH: mid-20C. Acronym of Swedish Svenska Aktiebolaget *Ga*sackumulator, Swedish Gas Accumulator Company, the orig. manufacturers.

aga *n.* a Turkish civil or military officer of high rank. WH: 16C. Turkish *aǧa* master, lord, from Mongolian *aqa.*

again *adv.* a second time, once more. WH: pre-1200. Old English *ongēan* toward, AGAINST. The earliest sense was back, in the opposite direction. The current meaning developed from the 14C.

against *prep.* in opposition to. WH: pre-1200. Old English *ongēan* AGAIN, + -S[2] + *t* as in *amidst* (AMID), *amongst* (AMONG), etc.

agal *n.* a band worn by Bedouin Arabs that keeps the keffiyeh in place. WH: 19C. Bedouin pronun. of Arabic *'iḳāl* bond, rope.

agama *n.* any land lizard of the Old World genus *Agama.* WH: 18C. ? Carib.

agamic *a.* characterized by absence of sexual action, asexual, parthenogenetic. WH: 19C. Greek *agamos*, from A-[6] + *gamos* marriage + -IC.

agamogenesis *n.* asexual reproduction. WH: 19C. Greek *agamo(s)* (AGAMIC) + GENESIS.

agamospermy *n.* the formation of seeds without fertilization by division of the ovule. WH: 19C. Greek *agamo(s)* (AGAMIC) + -SPERM + -Y[2].

agapanthus *n.* an ornamental plant with bright blue flowers, of the African genus *Agapanthus* and of the order Liliaceae. WH: 18C. Modern Latin, from Greek *agapē* love + *anthos* flower.

agape[1] *a., adv.* in an attitude or condition of wondering expectation. WH: 17C. A-[1] + GAPE.

agape[2] *n.* a 'love-feast', a kind of feast of fellowship held by the early Christians in connection with the Lord's Supper. WH: 17C. Greek *agapē* brotherly love.

agar-agar *n.* a gelatinous substance obtained from seaweeds and used for the artificial cultivation of bacteria. WH: 19C. Malay.

agaric *n.* any fungus of the family Agaricaceae, which have a cap and a stalk and include the edible mushroom. *Also a.* WH: 14–15C. Latin *agaricum*, from Greek *agarikon* tree fungus, from *Agaria*, a place in Sarmatia.

agate *n.* any semi-pellucid variety of chalcedony, marked with bands or clouds, or infiltrated by other minerals, and used for seals, brooches etc. WH: 15C. Old French, from Latin *achates*, from Greek *akhatēs*, of unknown orig. The word is popularly derived from *Achates*, the river in Sicily where the chalcedony is said to have been first found.

agave *n.* any of a genus of spiny-leaved plants, *Agave*, that includes the century plant. WH: 18C. Modern Latin, from Greek *Agauē*, pers. name in mythology, fem. of *agauos* noble.

agaze *adv.* gazing, in a gazing attitude. WH: 14–15C. A-[1] + GAZE.

age *n.* the length of time that a person or thing has existed. *Also v.i., v.t.* WH: 12–14C. Old French (Modern French *âge*), from Popular Latin *aetaticum*, from Latin *aetas, aetatis*, from *aevum* age of time. Cp. AEON.

-age *suf.* forming nouns, denoting actions, as in *breakage, passage*; a collection, group or set, as in *acreage, peerage*; a state or condition, as in *dotage, bondage*; a charge or fee payable, as in *postage*; the result of an action, as in *damage, wreckage*; a place or house, as in *anchorage, orphanage.* WH: Old French, from Late Latin *-aticum*, neut. of nn. in *-aticus* -ATIC.

agee *adv.* to one side. WH: 18C. A-[1] + GEE[1].

agenda *n.* a list of the business to be transacted. WH: 17C. Latin, pl. of *agendum*, neut. ger. of *agere* (AGENT).

agent *n.* a person who acts or transacts business on behalf of another. WH: 14–15C. Latin *agens, agentis*, pres.p. of *agere* to do. Rel. to ACT.

agent provocateur *n.* a person employed to detect suspected political offenders by leading them on to some overt action. WH: 19C. French provocative agent. Cp. AGENT, PROVOKE.

ageratum *n.* a plant of the tropical genus *Ageratum*, usu. having clusters of purple flowers. WH: 16C. Modern Latin, from Latin *ageraton*, from Greek, neut. of *agēratos*, from A-[6] + *gēras, gēratos* old age. Cp. GERIATRICS. The name was originally that of some 'everlasting' flower.

agger *n.* a mound. WH: 14–15C. Latin, from *aggere*, from AG- + *gerere* to carry.

agglomerate[1] *v.t.* to heap up or collect into a ball or mass. *Also v.i.* WH: 17C. Latin *agglomeratus*, p.p. of *agglomerare* to add to, from AG- + *glomerare*, from *glomus, glomeris* ball. See also -ATE[3].

agglomerate[2] *a.* collected into a mass; heaped up. *Also n.* WH: 19C. Latin p.p. *agglomeratus.* See AGGLOMERATE[1], also -ATE[2].

agglutinate[1] *v.t.* to cause to adhere; to glue together. *Also v.i.* WH: 16C. Latin *agglutinatus*, p.p. of *agglutinare*, from AG- + *glutinare*, from *gluten* glue. See also -ATE[3]. Cp. GLUTEN.

agglutinate[2] *a.* glued together. WH: 16C. Latin p.p. *agglutinatus.* See AGGLUTINATE[1], also -ATE[2].

aggrandize *v.t.* to make great in power, wealth, rank or reputation. WH: 17C. Old French *agrandir, agrandiss-*, from a- (AD-) + *grandir*, from Latin *grandis* GRAND.

aggravate *v.t.* to make worse or more severe. WH: 16C. Latin *aggravatus*, p.p. of *aggravare*, from AG- + *gravare*, from *gravis* heavy. See also -ATE[3]. Cp. GRAVE[2]. The early literal sense was to load, to burden. The current figurative sense gradually prevailed from the 17C.

aggregate[1] *v.t.* to collect together. *Also v.i.* WH: 14–15C. Latin *aggregatus*, p.p. of *aggregare*, from AG- + *grex, gregis* flock. See also -ATE[3].

aggregate[2] *a.* collected together; collected into a mass. *Also n.* WH: 14–15C. Latin p.p. *aggregatus.* See AGGREGATE[1], also -ATE[2].

aggress *v.i.* to begin an attack or quarrel. *Also v.t.* WH: 16C. Old French *agresser*, from Latin *aggressus*, p.p. of *aggredi* to attack, from AG- + *gradi* to proceed, to step.

aggrieve *v.t.* to cause grief, annoyance or pain to. WH: 12–14C. Old French *agrever* to make heavier, ult. from Latin *aggravare* (AGGRAVATE).

aggro *n.* aggressive, annoying behaviour; troublemaking. WH: mid-20C. Abbrev. of *aggravation* (AGGRAVATE) or *aggression* (AGGRESS). See also -O.

aghast *a.* appalled, horrified. WH: 12–14C. Var. of *agast* p.p., from A-³ + *gast*, from Old English *gǣstan*, from Germanic base of GHOST etc.

agile *a.* having the ability to move quickly and gracefully. WH: 14–15C. Old French, from Latin *agilis*, from *agere* to do. See also -IL.

agin *prep.* against. WH: 19C. Var. of obs. *again* AGAINST.

agio *n.* the difference in value between one kind of currency and another. WH: 17C. Italian *agio* ease, convenience. Rel. to EASE.

agist *v.t.* to provide pasture for (the cattle of others) at a certain rate. WH: 14–15C. Old French *agister*, from *a-* (AD-) + *gister*, from *giste* lodging. Cp. GÎTE.

agitate *v.t.* to shake or move briskly. Also *v.i.* WH: 14–15C. Latin *agitatus*, p.p. of *agitare*, freq. of *agere* to do, to drive. See also -ATE³.

agitato *adv.*, *a.* in an agitated manner. WH: 19C. Italian. Cp. AGITATE.

agitprop *n.* the dissemination, usu. through the arts, of political, esp. pro-Communist, propaganda. WH: early 20C. Russian *agit(atsiya)* agitation (AGITATE) + *prop(aganda)* PROPAGANDA.

aglet *n.* the metal tag of a lace. WH: 14–15C. Old French *aiguillette*, dim. of *aiguille* needle. See also -ETTE.

agley *adv.* astray, awry. WH: 18C. A-¹ + *gley* to squint, of unknown orig.

aglow *adv.*, *pred.a.* in a glow. WH: 19C. A-¹ + GLOW.

agma *n.* the symbol (ŋ) used to represent the speech sound ng as in *sing*. WH: mid-20C. Late Greek, from Greek fragment.

agnail *n.* a piece of torn skin or a sore at the root of a toe- or fingernail. WH: pre-1200. Old English *angnægl*, from Germanic base meaning compressed, tight + *nægl* NAIL.

agnate *n.* a descendant through the male line from the same male ancestor. Also *a.* WH: 16C. Latin *agnatus*, from AG- + *natus* born.

agnolotti *n.* small pieces of pasta stuffed with meat etc. WH: mid-20C. Italian, a dim. pl. of *agnolo* lamb.

agnomen *n.* a fourth name sometimes appended to the cognomen by the ancient Romans, usu. in honour of a great exploit. WH: 17C. Latin, from AG- + *nomen* NAME.

agnosia *n.* loss of the ability to recognize familiar things or people, esp. after brain damage. WH: early 20C. Greek *agnōsia* ignorance, from A-⁶ + *gnōsis* knowledge. See also -IA.

agnostic *n.* a person who believes that knowledge of the existence of God is impossible. Also *a.* WH: 19C. A-⁶ + GNOSTIC. The word was coined by the English biologist T.H. Huxley in 1869, but has been found earlier in a letter from Isabel Arundell of 1859.

Agnus Dei *n.* a figure of a lamb bearing a flag or cross. WH: 14–15C. Latin Lamb of God, from *agnus* lamb + gen. sing. of *deus* god.

ago *adv.* before this time. WH: 12–14C. A-³ + GO¹.

agog *a.*, *adv.* in a state of eager expectation. WH: 16C. Prob. French *en gogues*, from *en* IN + pl. of *gogue* merriment, of unknown orig.

agogic *a.* of or characterized by variations of stress in speech or musical rhythm produced by the lengthening of a syllable or note. WH: 19C. German *agogisch*, from Greek *agōgos* leading, from *agein* to lead. See also -IC.

à gogo *adv.* in abundance, galore. WH: mid-20C. French, from *à* + *gogo*, redupl. of base of *gogue*. See AGOG. Cp. GO-GO.

-agogue *comb. form* indicating a person or thing that leads, as in *demagogue*, *pedagogue*. WH: Greek *agōgos* leading, from *agein* to lead.

agoing *adv.* in a state of motion. WH: 17C. A-¹ + GO¹ + -ING¹.

agon *n.* (in ancient Greece) a festival or games at which prizes were competed for. WH: 17C. Greek *agōn* contest.

agonic *a.* having no dip, denoting an imaginary line on the earth's surface, drawn through the two magnetic poles. WH: 19C. Greek *agōnos*, from A-⁶ + *gōnia* angle + -IC.

agonist *n.* any muscle whose action is opposed by another muscle. WH: 17C. Greek *agōnistēs* contestant. See AGON, also -IST.

agonize *v.t.* to subject to extreme pain; to torture. Also *v.i.* WH: 16C. French *agoniser*, or from Late Latin *agonizare*, from Greek *agonizesthai*. See AGON, also -IZE.

agony *n.* anguish of mind. WH: 12–14C. Old French *agonie*, or from Late Latin *agonia*, from Greek *agōnia*. See AGON, also -Y².

agora¹ *n.* the public square, forum or market place of an ancient Greek town. WH: 16C. Greek.

agora² *n.* a monetary unit of Israel equal to one hundredth of a shekel. WH: mid-20C. Hebrew, *'ăḡōrāh* a small coin.

agoraphobia *n.* abnormal dread of open spaces. WH: 19C. Greek *agora* AGORA¹ + -*phobia* (-PHOBE).

agouti *n.* a small W Indian and S American rodent, *Dasyprocta agouti*. WH: 16C. French, or from Spanish *aguti*, from Tupi-Guarani *akutí*.

agraffe *n.* a sort of hook, formerly used as a clasp or fastening. WH: 17C. French *agrafe*, from *agrafer* to hook. Rel. to GRAB, GRAPPLE, GRASP.

agraphia *n.* loss of the cerebral power of expressing one's ideas in writing. WH: 19C. A-⁶ + Greek -*graphia* writing. See -GRAPH, also -IA.

agrarian *a.* of or relating to the land and cultivation. Also *n.* WH: 17C. Latin *agrarius*, from *ager*, *agri* land. See also -ARIAN.

agree *v.i.* to be of one mind, to hold the same opinion. Also *v.t.* WH: 12–14C. Old French *agréer*, ult. from Latin AG- + *gratus* pleasing. The earlier sense in the 14C was to please, to become favourable. The current sense prevailed from the 16C.

agreeable *a.* pleasing, pleasant. WH: 12–14C. Old French *agréable*. See AGREE, also -ABLE.

agreement *n.* the fact of being of one mind; concurrence in the same opinion. WH: 15C. Old French *agrément*. See AGREE, also -MENT.

agrestic *a.* rural, rustic. WH: 17C. Latin *agrestis*, from *ager*, *agri* field + -IC.

agribusiness *n.* agriculture conducted as a strictly commercial enterprise, esp. using advanced technology. WH: mid-20C. AGRI-CULTURE + BUSINESS.

agriculture *n.* the science and practice of cultivating the soil, growing crops and rearing livestock. WH: 14–15C. French, or from Latin *agricultura*, from *ager*, *agri* field + *cultura* CULTURE.

agrimony *n.* any plant of the genus *Agrimonia*, one species of which (*A. eupatoria*) was formerly valued as a tonic. WH: 14–15C. Late Latin *agrimonia*, misreading of *argemonia*, from Greek *argemōnē* poppy.

agro- *comb. form* of or relating to fields, soil or agriculture. WH: Greek *agros* land, field. See also -O-.

agrobiology *n.* the study of plant nutrition etc., in relation to soil management. WH: mid-20C. AGRO- + BIOLOGY.

agrochemical *n.* a chemical for use on the land or in farming. Also *a.* WH: mid-20C. AGRO- + CHEMICAL.

agroforestry *n.* farming that incorporates the cultivation of trees. WH: mid-20C. AGRO- + FOREST + -RY.

agronomy *n.* the science of land management, cultivation and crop production. WH: 19C. French *agronomie*, from *agronome* agriculturist, from Greek *agros* land + -*nomos* arranging. See AGRO-, -NOMY.

aground *a.*, *adv.* on the shallow bottom of any water. WH: 12–14C. A-¹ + GROUND¹. The earliest sense was on the ground generally. The current sense, with reference to ships etc., prevailed from the 16C.

ague *n.* a malarial fever, marked by successive hot and cold paroxysms, the latter attended with shivering. WH: 12–14C. Old French, from Medieval Latin *acuta*, a. used as n., from phr. *acuta febris* sharp fever. See ACUTE.

AH *abbr.* in the year of the Hegira (AD 622), from which is dated the Muslim era. WH: Latin *anno Hegirae* in the year of the Hegira, abl. sing. of *annus* year + gen. of HEGIRA.

ah *int.* used to express various emotions, according to the manner in which it is uttered, e.g. sorrow, regret, fatigue, relief, surprise, admiration, appeal, remonstrance, aversion, contempt, mockery. WH: 11–12C. Old French *a* (Modern French *ah*), from Latin *ah*.

aha *int.* an exclamation of surprise, triumph or mockery. WH: 11–12C. AH + HA.

ahead *adv.* in front, further on. WH: 16C. A-¹ + HEAD¹.

ahem *int.* an exclamation used to attract attention or merely to gain time. WH: 18C. Lengthened form of HEM².

ahimsa *n.* the Hindu and Buddhist doctrine of non-violence towards all living things. WH: 19C. Sanskrit, from *a-* A-⁶ + *hiṃsā* violence.

ahistorical *a.* not historical; taking no account of history. WH: mid-20C. A-⁶ + *historical* (HISTORIC).

-aholic *comb. form* (a person) having an addiction. WH: mid-20C. *(alc)oholic* (ALCOHOL).

ahoy *int.* used in hailing another ship or to attract attention. **WH:** 18C. AH + HOY[1].

à huis clos *adv.* behind closed doors, in private; in camera. **WH:** 19C. Obs. French *à* to, *huis* door, *clos* m. pl. p.p. of *clore* to close, from Latin *claudere*. Cp. *in camera* (CAMERA). The obsolete French *huis* has now been replaced by *porte*, and *clore* by *fermer*.

ai *n.* a three-toed sloth, *Bradypus tridactylus*, from S America. **WH:** 17C. Tupi, imit. of the animal's cry.

aid *v.t.* to assist, to help. *Also n.* **WH:** 14–15C. Old French *aïdier* (Modern French *aider*), from Latin *adiutare*, freq. of *adiuvare*, from AD- + *iuvare* to help.

aide *n.* an assistant, a help. **WH:** 18C. Abbr. of French *aide-de-camp* camp adjutant. See AID, CAMP[1].

Aids *n.* a condition in which the body's immune system is attacked by a virus, leaving the body defenceless against disease. **WH:** late 20C. Acronym of *a*cquired *i*mmune *d*eficiency *s*yndrome.

aigrette *n.* an ornamental feather or plume, esp. from the egret. **WH:** 18C. French. See EGRET.

aiguille *n.* a slender, needle-shaped peak of rock. **WH:** 18C. French needle.

aikido *n.* a Japanese martial art using throws, locks and twisting techniques to turn an opponent's own momentum against them. **WH:** mid-20C. Japanese *aikidō*, from *ai* together + *ki* spirit + *dō* way.

ail *v.i.* to be in pain, trouble or ill health. *Also v.t.* **WH:** pre-1200. Old English *eglan*, rel. to *egle* troublesome.

aileron *n.* the hinged portion on the rear edge of the wing-tip of an aeroplane that controls lateral balance. **WH:** early 20C. French, dim. of *aile* wing.

aim *v.t.* to point at a target with (a missile or weapon), to level (a gun) at a target. *Also v.i., n.* **WH:** 12–14C. Partly from Old French *amer*, dial. var. of *esmer*, from Latin *aestimare* (ESTIMATE[1]), partly from Old French *aemer*, ult. from Latin AD- + *aestimare*.

ain't *contr.* are not. **WH:** 18C. Contr. of *are not*.

Ainu *n.* an indigenous Japanese people living in N Japan, Sakhalin, the Kuriles and adjacent parts. **WH:** 19C. Ainu, lit. person, man.

aioli *n.* mayonnaise flavoured with garlic. **WH:** early 20C. French, from Provençal *ai* garlic + *oli* oil.

air *n.* the mixture of gases which envelops the earth, chiefly consisting of oxygen and nitrogen; the atmosphere. *Also v.t., v.i.* **WH:** pre-1200. Old French, from Latin *aer*, from Greek *aēr*. Rel. to AURA.

Airedale *n.* a large breed of terrier with a rough-haired, tan-coloured coat; a dog of this breed. **WH:** 19C. *Airedale*, from (River) *Aire* + DALE, a district in Yorkshire, where orig. bred.

airt *n.* a point of the compass, a direction. **WH:** 12–14C. Gaelic *àird*, from Old Irish *aird*.

airy *a.* well-ventilated. **WH:** 14–15C. AIR + -Y[1].

aisle *n.* a division of a church, esp. one parallel to, and separated by pillars from, the nave. **WH:** 12–14C. Old French *ele* (Modern French *aile*), from Latin *ala* wing. The spelling with *s* is due to confusion with ISLE.

ait *n.* a small island, esp. one in a river or lake. **WH:** pre-1200. Old English *iggath*, ult. from *īeg* island + dim. suf.

aitch *n.* the letter *h*. **WH:** 16C. Old French *ache*, prob. imit. of sound.

aitchbone *n.* the rump bone. **WH:** 15C. Old French *nache*, pl. *naches*, from Late Latin *naticas*, acc. pl. of *naticae*, from Latin *natis* buttock + BONE. See NATES. The initial *n* was lost as for ADDER, APRON, AUGER. The current form may owe something to the supposed resemblance of the bone to the letter *H*.

ajar[1] *a., adv.* (of a door) partly open. **WH:** 17C. A-[1] + *char*, from Old English *cerr* turn. See CHAR[3].

ajar[2] *adv.* in a jarring state, at discord. **WH:** 19C. A-[1] + JAR[1].

Akela *n.* the adult leader of a group of Cub Scouts. **WH:** early 20C. Name of leader of wolf pack in Rudyard Kipling's *Jungle Book* (1894) and *Second Jungle Book* (1895), from Hindi single, solitary.

akimbo *adv.* with the hands resting on the hips and the elbows turned outwards. **WH:** 14–15C. Middle English *in kenebowe* in a keen (sharp) bow, with assim. of *in* to A-[1].

akin *a.* allied by blood relationship. **WH:** 16C. A-[2] + KIN.

Akkadian *n.* a member of a Semitic people inhabiting Akkad (now central Mesopotamia) before 2000 BC. *Also a.* **WH:** 19C. *Akkad*, a city and district in ancient Babylonia + -IAN.

al- *pref.* signifying motion towards, direction to, adherence etc., as in *alliteration*, *allude*. **WH:** Latin pref., from AD- with *d* assim. to *l*.

-al[1] *suf.* forming adjectives, as in *annual*, *equal*, *mortal*. **WH:** Latin *-alis*, a. suf.

-al[2] *suf.* forming nouns, esp. denoting the enactment of the action of a verb, as in *arrival*, *acquittal*. **WH:** Latin *-alis*, a. suf. used as n.

ala *n.* a wing or winglike anatomical or plant part. **WH:** 18C. Latin wing.

à la *prep.* in the fashion of, after the manner of, after. **WH:** 16C. French, from À LA MODE.

alabaster *n.* a fine, soft, usu. white or semi-transparent form of gypsum, widely used for making ornaments. *Also a.* **WH:** 12–14C. Old French *alabastre* (Modern French *albâtre*), from Latin *alabaster*, from Greek *alabastos* vase (of alabaster), ? from Egyptian **a-la-baste* vessel of (the goddess) Bast.

à la carte *a., adv.* (of a menu) having each dish priced separately. **WH:** 19C. French. See À LA, CARTE.

†alack *int.* used to express sorrow. **WH:** 12–14C. AH + LACK, based on ALAS.

alacrity *n.* briskness, eagerness. **WH:** 14–15C. Latin *alacritas*, from *alacer*, *alacris* brisk. See also -ITY.

Aladdin's cave *n.* a place that contains fabulous treasures or great riches. **WH:** 19C. *Aladdin*, a character in the *Arabian Nights' Entertainment*, who found such a cave.

à la mode *adv., a.* fashionable. **WH:** 16C. French. See À LA, MODE.

alarm *n.* warning of approaching danger. *Also v.t.* **WH:** 12–14C. Old French *alarme*, from Italian *allarme*, from phr. *all' arme* to arms! An early sense, developing from the Old French original, was a surprise attack. The current meaning took over from the 17C.

alas *int.* used to express sorrow, grief, pity or concern. **WH:** pre-1200. Old French *a las* (Modern French *hélas*), from *a* AH + *las*, from Latin *lassus* weary.

alb *n.* a long white surplice with close sleeves worn by priests and servers at some church services. **WH:** pre-1200. Old English *albe*, from Ecclesiastical Latin *alba*, use as n. of fem. of Latin *albus* white.

albacore *n.* a large long-finned species of tuna, *Thunnus alalunga*. **WH:** 16C. Portuguese *albacor*, from Arabic *al-bakūra*, prob. from *al* the + *bakūr* premature.

Albanian *a.* of or relating to Albania or its inhabitants. *Also n.* **WH:** 16C. *Albania*, a country in W part of the Balkan peninsula + -AN.

albata *n.* an alloy like silver; a variety of German silver. **WH:** 19C. Latin, fem. of *albatus* clothed in white, from *albus* white.

albatross *n.* any long-winged large-bodied bird of the family Diomedeidae, esp. *Diomedea exulans*, the largest known seabird, the great albatross. **WH:** 17C. Alt. of *alcatras* (appar. by assoc. with Latin *albus* white), from Spanish *alcatraz* pelican, from Arabic *al-ġaṭṭās* the diver. The figurative sense, an inescapable burden or handicap, comes from Coleridge's *The Rime of the Ancient Mariner* (1798), in which the albatross shot by the ancient mariner is hung about his neck by his shipmates as a sign of guilt.

albedo *n.* the fraction of incident light reflected by a planet or other body or surface. **WH:** 19C. Ecclesiastical Latin whiteness, from *albus* white.

albeit *conj.* although, even though, notwithstanding. **WH:** 12–14C. ALL + BE + IT[1], in sense all though it be (that).

albert *n.* a short kind of watch-chain, fastened to a waistcoat buttonhole. **WH:** 19C. Prince *Albert*, 1819–61, consort of Queen Victoria, who sported one.

albescent *a.* becoming or passing into white; whitish. **WH:** 18C. Latin *albescens*, *albescentis*, pres.p. of *albescere* to become white, from *albus* white. See -escent (-ESCENCE).

Albigenses *n.pl.* a sect of Catharist reformers in Languedoc, who separated from the Church of Rome in the 12th cent. **WH:** 17C. Medieval Latin, from *Albiga*, Latin name of *Albi*, a city in SW France, where the sect arose.

albino *n.* a human being, or animal, having the colour pigment absent from the skin, the hair and the eyes, so as to be abnormally light in colour. **WH:** 18C. Spanish and Portuguese, from *albo* white + *-ino*. See also -INE. The term was originally applied by the Portuguese to albinos among African blacks.

Albion *n.* Britain or England. **WH:** pre-1200. Old English, from Latin, from Celtic, prob. rel. to Latin *albus* white, alluding to the white cliffs of Britain.

albite *n.* white feldspar, soda feldspar. **WH:** 19C. Latin *albus* white + -ITE[1].

album *n.* a blank book for the insertion of photographs, poetry, drawings or the like. **WH:** 17C. Latin blank tablet, use as n. of neut. of *albus* white. The word was first current in English from the German use of the Latin phrase *album amicorum* album of friends.

albumen *n.* the white of an egg. **WH:** 16C. Latin, from *albus* white.

albumin *n.* any of several water-soluble proteins existing in animals, in the white of egg, in blood serum and in plants. **WH:** 19C. French *albumine*. See ALBUMEN, also -IN[1].

alburnum *n.* the sapwood in exogenous stems, between the inner bark and heartwood. **WH:** 17C. Latin, from *albus* white.

alcaic *a.* of or relating to Alcaeus, or to a kind of verse he invented. *Also n.* **WH:** 17C. Late Latin *alcaicus*, from Greek *alkaikos*, from *Alkaios* Alcaeus, *c.*611–*c.*580 BC, Greek lyric poet. See also -IC.

alcalde *n.* the judge or mayor of a Spanish, Portuguese or Latin American town. **WH:** 16C. Spanish, from Arabic *al-ḳāḍī* the judge. Cp. CADI.

alcayde *n.* the governor of a fortress in Spain, Portugal etc. **WH:** 16C. Spanish, from Arabic *al-ḳā'id* the leader.

alchemy *n.* the chemistry of the Middle Ages, the search for an alkahest, the philosophers' stone, and the panacea. **WH:** 12–14C. Old French *alkemie* (Modern French *alchimie*), from Medieval Latin *alchimia*, from Arabic *al-kīmiyā'*, from *al* the + *kīmiyā'*, from Greek *khēmeia* art of transmuting metals.

alcheringa *n.* the golden age or dreamtime in the mythology of Australian Aboriginals. **WH:** 19C. Australian Aboriginal (Aranda) in the dreamtime, from *aljerre* dream + *-nge*, abl. suf., from.

alcid *n.* a bird of the auk family. **WH:** 19C. Modern Latin *Alcidae*, from *Alca* genus name. See AUK.

alcohol *n.* a colourless liquid produced by fermenting sugars and constituting the intoxicating agent in various drinks. **WH:** 16C. French (now *alcool*), from Arabic *al-kuḥl* the kohl (KOHL). The sense passed from KOHL (powder to darken the eyelids) to chemical powders and finally to liquid distillates and essences.

alcopop *n.* an alcoholic drink tasting and packaged like a soft drink. **WH:** late 20C. ALCOHOL + POP[1].

alcotot *n.* a small sachet of an alcoholic drink. **WH:** late 20C. ALCOHOL + TOT[1].

alcove *n.* a recess in a wall. **WH:** 16C. French *alcôve*, from Spanish *alcoba*, from Arabic *al-ḳubba* the vault. Not rel. to COVE[1].

aldehyde *n.* a volatile liquid that can be obtained from alcohol by oxidation; acetaldehyde, ethanal. **WH:** 19C. Abbr. of Modern Latin *alcohol dehydrogenatum* alcohol deprived of hydrogen.

al dente *a.* (esp. of cooked pasta) firm when bitten. **WH:** mid-20C. Italian to the tooth, from *al* to the + *dente* tooth. See DENT[2].

alder *n.* a tree, *Alnus glutinosa*, growing in moist places. **WH:** pre-1200. Old English *alor*, *aler*, rel. to Latin *alnus*. The spelling with *d* dates from the 14C.

alderman *n.* (in England and Wales) a civic dignitary, elected from among members of a council, ranking next below the mayor. **WH:** pre-1200. Old English *aldormann*, from *aldor* chief (cp. OLD) + MAN. Cp. EALDORMAN.

Alderney *n.* an animal of a breed of cattle originating on Alderney Island. **WH:** 18C. One of the Channel Islands, where it was bred.

Aldine *a.* of, belonging to or printed by Aldus Manutius or his family. **WH:** 19C. Modern Latin *Aldinus*, from *Aldus* Manutius, 1450–1515, Venetian printer. See also -INE.

Aldis lamp *n.* a hand-held lamp for sending signals in Morse code. **WH:** early 20C. Arthur C.W. Aldis, 1878–1953, its inventor.

aldosterone *n.* a steroid hormone produced by the adrenal glands that regulates salt levels. **WH:** mid-20C. *aldo-*, comb. form of ALDEHYDE + STEROL + -ONE.

aldrin *n.* an extremely poisonous chlorine containing insecticide. **WH:** mid-20C. Kurt *Alder*, 1902–58, German chemist, + -IN[1].

ale *n.* an intoxicating drink made from malt by fermentation, orig. distinguished from beer in not being flavoured with hops. **WH:** pre-1200. Old English *ealu*, from Germanic, from Indo-European **alu* bitter.

aleatory *a.* depending upon an uncertain event or chance. **WH:** 17C. Latin *aleatorius*, from *aleator* dice player, from *alea* a die. See also -Y[1].

alec *n.* a stupid person. **WH:** 19C. Shortening of *smart alec*. See SMART.

alee *a.*, *adv.* on the lee side. **WH:** 14–15C. A-[1] + LEE, influ. by Old Norse *á hlé* on (the) shelter.

alegar *n.* vinegar made from ale. **WH:** 14–15C. ALE, based on VINEGAR.

Alemannic *n.* the group of High German dialects of Alsace, Switzerland and SW Germany. **WH:** 18C. Late Latin *Alemannicus*, from *Alemanni*, pl. name of a Germanic tribe, prob. from same source as ALL + MAN. Cp. French *Allemagne* Germany. The name probably denoted a wide alliance of peoples.

alembic *n.* a vessel made of glass or copper formerly used for distilling. **WH:** 12–14C. Old French, from Medieval Latin *alembicus*, from Arabic *al-'anbīḳ* the still cap, from Greek *ambix*, *ambikos* cup. The word was originally the term for the cap of a still, the vessel itself being the CUCURBIT.

aleph *n.* the first letter of the Hebrew alphabet. **WH:** 12–14C. Hebrew *'ālep* ox. Cp. ALPHA. The Hebrew letter evolved from the hieroglyph of an ox's head.

alert *a.* watchful, vigilant. *Also n.*, *v.t.* **WH:** 16C. French *alerte*, from Italian *all'erta*, from *alla* at the + *erta* lookout (tower).

aleuron *n.* a protein found in the form of grains in ripening seeds. **WH:** 19C. Greek *aleuron* flour.

alevin *n.* a young fish, esp. a young salmon. **WH:** 19C. Old French, ult. from Latin *allevare* to raise. See ALLEVIATE.

alewife *n.* a N American fish, *Alosa pseudoharengus*, resembling the shad but smaller. **WH:** 17C. Orig. uncertain, alt. of (N) American Indian word, influ. by *alewife* (ALE).

alexanders *n.* a European plant, *Smyrnium olusatrum*, formerly used as a vegetable. **WH:** pre-1200. Old English *alexandre*, from Medieval Latin *alexandrum*, prob. from Latin *olus atrum*, from *holus*, *olus* pot herbs, vegetables + *atrum* neut. sing. of *ater* black.

Alexander technique *n.* a technique involving exercises, manipulation etc., designed to improve posture and movement by increasing awareness of them and thus avoid physical strain. **WH:** mid-20C. Frederick Matthias *Alexander*, 1869–1955, Australian-born physiotherapist.

Alexandrian *a.* of or relating to Alexandria. *Also n.* **WH:** 16C. *Alexandria*, a city in N Egypt + -AN. Alexandria was founded by *Alexander* the Great, 356–323 BC, King of Macedonia.

alexandrine *n.* a verse line containing twenty syllables in French, or six iambic feet in English prosody, usu. divided by a caesura. **WH:** 16C. French *alexandrin*, from *Alexandre* Alexander (the Great), the hero of the Old French romance in which the metre was used. See ALEXANDRIAN.

alexandrite *n.* a dark green chrysoberyl. **WH:** 19C. *Alexander* II, 1818–81, tsar of Russia + -ITE[1].

alexia *n.* (a brain defect resulting in) the inability to understand written or printed words, word-blindness. **WH:** 19C. A-[6] + Greek *lexis* speech, by confusion with Latin *legere* to read + -IA.

alexin *n.* a substance present in blood serum, which, combining with an antibody or antiserum, gives protection against disease. **WH:** 19C. Greek *alexein* to ward off + -IN[1].

alexipharmic *a.* preserving against poison. *Also n.* **WH:** 17C. French *alexipharmique*, from Modern Latin *alexipharmacum*, from Greek *alexipharmakon*, neut. sing. (used as n.) of *a.* from *alexein* to ward off + *pharmakon* poison. Cp. PHARMACO-.

alfalfa *n.* a plant, *Medicago sativa*, with flowers and leaves similar to those of clover, that is widely cultivated as forage, a salad vegetable and a commercial source of chlorophyll. **WH:** 19C. Spanish, from Arabic *al-faṣfaṣa* the best (kind of) fodder.

alfresco *a.*, *adv.* in the open air, open-air. **WH:** 18C. Italian *al fresco* in the fresh. See FRESCO.

alga *n.* a seaweed or other plant belonging to the Algae, a major group of simple aquatic or subaquatic plants, including the seaweeds, that lack differentiation into stems, roots and leaves. **WH:** 16C. Latin seaweed.

algebra *n.* the branch of mathematics in which letters are used as symbols for quantities, and signs represent arithmetical processes. WH: 12–14C. Italian, Spanish and Medieval Latin, from Arabic *al-jabr*, from *al* the + *jabar* reunion of (broken) parts, from *jabara* set of (broken) bones, to reunite. The word originally applied to the surgical treatment of fractures. The current sense came from the book title *'ilm al-jabr wa'l-muḳābala* (the) science of reintegration and reduction (9C). See ALGORISM.

-algia *comb. form* denoting pain (in a particular place), as in *neuralgia*. WH: Greek *algos* pain + -IA.

algid *a.* cold, esp. after feverishness. WH: 17C. Latin *algidus*, from *algere* to be cold. See also -ID.

Algol *n.* a computer language used chiefly for mathematical purposes. WH: mid-20C. *algo(rithmic)* (ALGORITHM) + LANGUAGE.

algolagnia *n.* sexual gratification derived from inflicting or suffering pain. WH: early 20C. Greek *algos* pain + *lagneia* lust.

algometer *n.* an instrument for estimating degrees of sensitiveness to pain. WH: 19C. Greek *algo(s)* pain + -METER.

Algonquian *n.* a family of N American Indian languages. *Also a.* WH: 19C. Var. of ALGONQUIN.

Algonquin *n.* a member of a N American Indian people formerly living in the valley of the Ottawa and around the northern tributaries of the St Lawrence. *Also a.* WH: 17C. French, ? from Micmac *algoomeaking* at the place of spearing fish and eels.

algorism *n.* the Arabic system of counting, the decimal system. WH: pre-1200. Old French *augorisme*, *algorisme*, from Medieval Latin *algorismus*, from Arabic *al-Ḵwārizmī* the man of *Ḵwārizm* (Khiva), surname of mathematician Abū Ja'far Muḥammad ibn Mūsā (*fl. c.*800–47), writer of works on arithmetic and algebra. al-Ḵwārizmī was the author of the book that gave the current sense of ALGEBRA.

algorithm *n.* a rule or set procedure for solving a mathematical problem, esp. using a computer. WH: 17C. Var. of ALGORISM, influ. by Greek *arithmos* number.

alguazil *n.* a mounted official at a bullfight. WH: 16C. Spanish, from Arabic *al-wazīr*, from *al* the + *wazīr* VIZIER.

Alhambra *n.* the Moorish palace and citadel at Granada in Spain. WH: 16C. Arabic *al-ḥamrā'* the red (house).

alias *adv.* otherwise (named or called). *Also n.* WH: 14–15C. Latin at another time, from *alius* other. Rel. to ELSE.

alibi *n.* the plea (of a person accused) of having been elsewhere when the offence was committed; the evidence to support such a plea. *Also v.t., v.i.* WH: 17C. Latin elsewhere, loc. adv. of *alius* other. The original sense was legal only.

alicyclic *a.* (of an organic compound) having aliphatic properties but containing a ring of carbon atoms. WH: 19C. ALIPHATIC + CYCLE + -IC.

alidad *n.* an arm or index showing degrees on a circle in an astrolabe, quadrant, theodolite etc. WH: 14–15C. French *alidade*, from Arabic *al-'iḍāda*, from *al* the + *'aḍud* upper arm.

alien *a.* unfamiliar; strange. *Also n., v.t.* WH: 12–14C. Old French, from Latin *alienus* belonging to another, from *alius* other.

alienate *v.t.* to cause to become unfriendly or hostile. WH: 16C. Latin *alienatus*, p.p. of *alienare*, from *alienus*. See ALIEN, also -ATE³.

aliform *a.* shaped like a wing. WH: 18C. Modern Latin *aliformis*, from Latin *ala* wing. See also -FORM.

alight¹ *v.i.* to get down, descend. WH: pre-1200. Old English *ālīhtan*, from *ā* A-³ + *līhtan* to get down (from a horse). See LIGHT³.

alight² *adv., pred.a.* on fire. WH: 12–14C. Middle English, from Old English *onlīhtan*, from *on* ON + *līhtan* to light (LIGHT¹). The current form was influenced by ABLAZE, AFIRE etc.

align *v.t.* to range or place in a line. *Also v.i.* WH: 14–15C. Old French *alignier* (Modern French *aligner*), from phr. *à ligne* into line, from *à* (AD-) + *ligne* LINE¹.

alike *a.* similar. *Also adv.* WH: 11–12C. Old English *gelīc*, from *gē-* together + *līc* LIKE¹.

aliment *n.* nutriment, food. *Also v.t.* WH: 15C. French *alimenter*, from Late Latin *alimentum*, from *alere* to nourish. See also -MENT.

alimony *n.* maintenance. WH: 17C. Latin *alimonia*, from *alere* to nourish. See also -MONY. Rel. to ALIMENT.

aliped *a.* having a winglike membrane connecting its digits. *Also n.* WH: 18C. Latin *ala* wing + *pes, pedis* foot.

aliphatic *a.* fatty. WH: 19C. Greek *aleiphar, aleiphatos* unguent + -IC.

aliquot *a.* of or relating to a number that is contained an integral number of times by a given number. *Also n.* WH: 16C. French *aliquote*, from Latin *aliquot* some, several, from *alius* one of two + *quot* how many.

alive *adv.* living, existent. WH: pre-1200. Old English *on līfe*, from *on* ON + *līfe*, dat. of *līf* LIFE.

alizarin *n.* the red colouring matter of madder. *Also a.* WH: 19C. French *alizarine*, from Arabic (coll.) *al-'iṣāra* the juice pressed out. See also -IN¹.

alkahest *n.* the universal solvent of the alchemists. WH: 17C. Imit. Arabic, prob. invented by Paracelsus.

alkali *n.* a compound of hydrogen and oxygen with sodium, potassium or other substances, which is soluble in water, and produces caustic and corrosive solutions capable of neutralizing acids and changing the colour of litmus to blue. WH: 12–14C. Medieval Latin, from Arabic *al-ḳalī* the calcined ashes of saltwort, etc.

alkane *n.* any of a series of aliphatic hydrocarbons including methane, ethane, butane and octane. WH: 19C. ALKYL + -ANE.

alkanet *n.* a red dye material obtained from *Alkanna tinctoria*. WH: 12–14C. Arabic (coll.) *al-ḥannat*, from *al-ḥinnā'*, from *al-* the + *ḥinnā'* HENNA.

alky *n.* an alcoholic. WH: 19C. Abbr. of *alcoholic* (ALCOHOL + -IC). See also -Y³.

alkyd *n.* any of a group of synthetic resins derived from alkyls and acids, used in paints, protective coatings and adhesives. WH: early 20C. ALKYL + ACID.

alkyl *n.* any monovalent hydrocarbon radical of the alkane series, e.g. methyl, ethyl, butyl. WH: 19C. German, from *Alkohol* ALCOHOL. See also -YL.

all *a.* the whole (quantity, duration, extent, amount, quality or degree) of. *Also pron., n., adv.* WH: pre-1200. Old English *eall, al,* ult. from Indo-European **alnos.*

alla breve *n.* a time signature including two or four minims to the bar. WH: 18C. Italian according to the breve, from *alla* to the + *breve* BREVE.

Allah *n.* the name of God among Muslims. WH: 16C. Arabic *'allāh*, contr. of *al-'ilāh* the god, from *al* the +*'ilāh* god.

allantois *n.* a foetal membrane acting as an organ of respiration and excretion in reptiles, birds and mammals. WH: 17C. Modern Latin, from Greek *allantoiedēs*, from *allas, allantos* sausage. The organ is so named from its shape in a calf.

allay *v.t.* to quiet, to calm (fear); to diminish (suspicion). *Also v.i.* WH: pre-1200. Old English *alecgan*, from A-³ + *lecgan* LAY¹. The current sense has been influenced by ALLEGE and ALLEVIATE.

allegation *n.* the act of alleging. WH: 14–15C. Old French *allégation*, or from Latin *allegatio, allegationis*, from *allegare*. See ALLEGE.

allege *v.t.* to affirm positively but without or before proof. WH: 12–14C. Anglo-French *alegier*, from Old French *esligier*, from Late Latin *exlitigare*, from EX- + *litigare* to contend at law (LITIGATE), but influ. by Latin *allegare* to charge.

allegiance *n.* the obligation of subjects to their sovereign or citizens to their country or government. WH: 14–15C. Old French *ligeance* (cp. LIEGE), influ. by Anglo-Latin *alligantia* ALLIANCE.

allegory *n.* a story, play etc. in which the characters and events depicted are meant to be understood as representing other, usu. abstract spiritual or psychological, entities. WH: 14–15C. Old French *allégorie*, from Latin *allegoria*, from Greek *allēgoria*, from *allos* other + *-agoria* speaking. The sense is speaking otherwise than one seems to speak.

allegro *a.* brisk, lively. *Also adv., n.* WH: 17C. Italian lively. Rel. to ALACRITY.

allele *n.* an allelomorph. WH: mid-20C. German *Allel*, abbr. of ALLELOMORPH.

allelomorph *n.* any of two or more contrasted characteristics, inherited as alternatives, and assumed to depend on genes in homologous chromosomes. WH: early 20C. Greek *allēl-* one another + -O- + -MORPH.

alleluia *int.* praise be to God. *Also n.* WH: pre-1200. Ecclesiastical Latin, from Greek *allēlouia*, from Hebrew *hallēlūyāh* praise Jah (God) (see JEHOVAH), from imper. pl. of *hallēl* to praise.

allemande *n.* any of various German dances of the 17th and 18th cents. WH: 17C. French, fem. of *allemand* German.

Allen screw *n.* a screw with a hexagonal socket in the head. WH: mid-20C. *Allen* Manufacturing Company, Hartford, Connecticut.

allergy *n.* an abnormal response or reaction to some food or substance innocuous to most people. WH: early 20C. German *Allergie*, from Greek *allos* other, different, based on *Energie* ENERGY.

alleviate *v.t.* to lighten, lessen. WH: 14–15C. Late Latin *alleviatus*, p.p. of *alleviare* to lighten, from Latin *alleviare*, from AL- + *levare* to raise, influ. by *levis* light. See also -ATE³.

alley *n.* a passage, esp. between or behind buildings. WH: 12–14C. Old French *alee* (Modern French *allée*), from *aler* (Modern French *aller*), to go, from Latin *ambulare* to walk.

alliaceous *a.* of or relating to the plant genus *Allium*, which contains the onion and garlic. WH: 18C. ALLIUM + -ACEOUS.

alliance *n.* the act of allying; the state of being allied. WH: 12–14C. Old French *aliance* (Modern French *alliance*). See ALLY¹.

alligator *n.* a large reptile, native to America and China, that resembles a crocodile but differs from it esp. by having a broader snout. WH: early 20C. Spanish *el lagarto* the lizard, ult. from Latin *lacerta* LIZARD.

alliterate *v.i.* to commence with the same letter or sound. WH: 18C. Back-formation from *alliteration*, from Late Latin *alliteratio*, *alliterationis*, from Latin AL- + *littera* letter + -ATION.

allium *n.* a plant of the genus *Allium*, containing garlic, leeks, onions etc. WH: 19C. Latin garlic.

allo- *comb. form* different, other, as in *allomorph*, *allopathy*. WH: Greek *allos* other, different. See also -O-.

allocate *v.t.* to assign, allot. WH: 16C. Late Latin *allocatus*, p.p. of *allocare*, from Latin AL- + *locare* LOCATE. See also -ATE³.

allochthonous *a.* (of rocks, deposits) formed elsewhere than where they are presently situated. WH: early 20C. German *allochthon*, from Greek *allos* other (ALLO-) + *khthōn* earth, soil. See also -OUS.

allocution *n.* a formal address, esp. one delivered by the Pope to the bishops and clergy, or to the Church generally. WH: 17C. Latin *allocutio*, *allocutionis*, p.p. of *alloqui* to address, from AL- + *loqui* to speak. See also -ION.

allodium *n.* landed property held in absolute ownership. WH: 17C. Medieval Latin, from Frankish *all* ALL + *ōd* estate, wealth.

allogamy *n.* cross-fertilization. WH: 19C. ALLO- + -GAMY.

allograft *n.* a tissue graft from a genetically unrelated donor. WH: mid-20C. ALLO- + GRAFT¹.

allograph *n.* a signature written by one person on behalf of another. WH: mid-20C. ALLO- + -GRAPH.

allomorph *n.* any of the two or more forms of a morpheme. WH: mid-20C. ALLO- + -MORPH.

allopathy *n.* the treatment of disease by including effects of a different kind from those produced by the disease; ordinary medical practice, as opposed to homoeopathy. WH: 19C. ALLO- + -PATHY.

allopatric *a.* occurring in geographically separated areas. WH: mid-20C. ALLO- + Greek *patra* fatherland. See also -IC.

allophone *n.* any of the two or more forms of a phoneme. WH: mid-20C. ALLO- + -PHONE.

allot *v.t.* to distribute, to assign as one's share. WH: 15C. Old French *aloter* (Modern French *allotir*), from *a*- (AD-) + *lot* LOT.

allotropy *n.* variation of physical properties without change of substance (e.g. diamond, graphite and charcoal are allotropic forms of carbon). WH: 19C. ALLO- + Greek *tropos* turn, from *trepein* to turn. Cp. TROPE.

allow *v.t.* to permit. WH: 12–14C. Old French *alouer*, partly from Latin *allaudere*, from AL- + *laudare* to praise (LAUD), partly from Medieval Latin *allocare* ALLOCATE.

alloy¹ *n.* an inferior metal mixed with one of greater value. WH: 16C. Old French *aloi*, from *aloier*, earlier *aleier* to mix with a baser metal, from Latin *alligare* to bind, from AL- + *ligare* to tie. Cp. ALLY¹.

alloy² *v.t.* to mix with a baser metal. WH: 17C. French *aloyer*. See ALLOY¹.

allseed *n.* any of various many-seeded plants, esp. *Radiola linoides* of the flax family. WH: 17C. ALL + SEED.

allspice *n.* (a spice prepared from) the berry of the pimento, said to combine the flavour of cinnamon, cloves and nutmeg. WH: 17C. ALL + SPICE.

allude *v.i.* to make indirect reference (to), to hint at. WH: 15C. Latin *alludere*, from AL- + *ludere* to play. An early sense was to pun, to make play with words. This became obsolete from the 17C.

allure *v.t.* to attract or tempt by the offer of some real or apparent good. *Also n.* WH: 15C. Anglo-French *alurer*, from Old French *aloirrier*, *aleurier*, from *a*- (AD-) + *loirre* LURE.

alluvion *n.* the wash of the sea against the land. WH: 16C. French, from Latin *alluvio*, *alluvionis*, from *alluvium* ALLUVIUM.

alluvium *n.* (a fine-grained fertile soil derived from) transported matter which has been washed away and later deposited by rivers, floods or similar causes. WH: 17C. Latin, neut. of *alluvius* washed against, from *alluere*, from AL- + -*luere*, comb. form of *lavare* to wash.

ally¹ *v.t.* to unite by treaty, confederation, marriage or friendship. WH: 12–14C. Old French *alier*, from Latin *alligare*, from AL- + *ligare* to bind. Cp. ALLAY, ALLOY¹.

ally² *n.* a person or group etc. who helps or supports another. WH: 12–14C. Partly from Old French *alié*, p.p. (used as n.) of *alier* ALLY¹, partly direct from ALLY¹. The original meaning was relative, kinsman. The current sense emerged in the 15C.

ally³ *n.* a superior kind of playing-marble or taw. WH: 18C. ? Dim. of ALABASTER.

alma *n.* an Egyptian dancing girl. WH: 18C. Arabic *'ālima* singer, orig. (as fem. a.) learned, from *'alima* to know.

almacantar *n.* an instrument for determining time and latitude. WH: 12–14C. Late Latin *almucantarath*, or from obs. French *almucantarat*, from Arabic *al-muḳanṭarāt* circles of celestial latitude, from *al* the + *ḳanṭara* arch.

alma mater *n.* the university, college or school that a person attended. WH: 17C. Latin bounteous mother. This was originally the title given to certain Roman goddesses, such as Ceres and Cybele.

almanac *n.* a register of the days of the year, with astronomical data and calculations, civil and ecclesiastical festivals etc. WH: 12–14C. Medieval Latin, from Late Greek *almenikhiaka*, of unknown orig. ? From Coptic.

almandine *n.* a precious deep red garnet. WH: 14–15C. Obs. French, alt. of *alabandine*, from Medieval Latin *alabandina*, from *Alabanda*, a city of Caria in Asia Minor.

almighty *a.* omnipotent. *Also adv.*, *n.* WH: pre-1200. Old English *ælmihtig*, from *æl*- ALL + *mihtig* MIGHT + -Y¹. The word is probably a translation of Latin *omnipotens* OMNIPOTENT.

almond *n.* a small widely cultivated tree of the rose family, *Prunus dulcis*. WH: 12–14C. Old French *alemande*, *almande*, from Medieval Latin *amandula*, from Greek *amugdalē*, of unknown orig. Cp. AMYGDALA.

almoner *n.* an official distributor of alms or bounty. WH: 12–14C. Old French *aumonier* (Modern French *aumônier*), from Popular Latin *almosinarius*, var. of Late Latin *elemosinarius*, from *eleemosyna* ALMS. Cp. ELEEMOSYNARY.

almost *adv.* nearly, very nearly. WH: pre-1200. Old English *ealmǣst*, from *eal*- ALL + *mǣst* MOST¹.

alms *n.pl.* anything given out of charity to the poor. WH: pre-1200. Old English *ælmyssa*, from Germanic, ult. from alt. of Late Latin *eleemosyna*, from Greek *eleēmosunē*. See ELEEMOSYNARY. Cp. ALMONER.

aloe *n.* a succulent plant of the genus *Aloe*, having fleshy, toothed leaves and bitter juice. WH: pre-1200. Old English *alwe*, from Latin *aloe*, from Greek *aloē*, of unknown orig.

aloft *adv.* high up, on high. WH: 11–12C. Old Norse *á lopt*, from *á* in + *lopt* air, sky. Cp. LOFT.

alogical *a.* not logical, not rational. WH: 17C. A-⁶ + *logical* (LOGIC).

alone *a.*, *adv.* with no other present. WH: 11–12C. Middle English *al* ALL + *one* ONE.

along *prep.* from one end to the other of. *Also adv.* WH: pre-1200. Old English *andlang*, from *and* against + *lang* LONG¹.

aloof *adv.* away, at a distance, apart. *Also a.* WH: 16C. A-¹ + Middle English *loof* LUFF. The word originally had a nautical sense, to windward! The current figurative sense emerged soon after.

alopecia *n.* baldness. WH: 14–15C. Latin, from Greek *alōpekia* fox mange, from *alōpēx*, *alōpekos* fox. See also -IA.

aloud *adv.* audibly. WH: 12–14C. A-[1] + LOUD.

alow *adv.* in or into the lower part of a ship, opposed to aloft. WH: 14–15C. A-[1] + LOW[1].

alp *n.* a high mountain. WH: 14–15C. French *Alpes*, from Latin, from Greek *Alpeis*, of unknown orig.

alpaca *n.* the domesticated llama of Peru. WH: 18C. Spanish, from Aymara *allpaca*.

alpargata *n.* a light, rope-soled canvas shoe, an espadrille. WH: 19C. Spanish.

alpha *n.* the first letter of the Greek alphabet (A, α). WH: 11–12C. Latin, from Greek, from Semitic. Cp. ALEPH.

alphabet *n.* the letters or characters used in writing a language, arranged in order. WH: 14–15C. Late Latin *alphabetum*, from Greek *alphabetos*, from ALPHA, BETA, the first two letters of the alphabet.

alphanumeric *a.* consisting of or using both letters and numbers. WH: mid-20C. Blend of *alpha(betic)* (ALPHABET) and *numeric* (NUMERAL).

already *adv.* beforehand, before some specified time. WH: 12–14C. ALL + READY.

Alsatian *a.* belonging to Alsace. *Also n.* WH: 17C. Medieval Latin *Alsatia* Alsace, a region of E France + -AN.

alsike *n.* a species of clover, *Trifolium hybridum*. WH: 19C. *Alsike*, a place near Uppsala, Sweden.

also *adv., conj.* in addition, as well. WH: pre-1200. Old English *alsurā*, from *all* ALL + *swā* SO.

alstroemeria *n.* a plant of the originally S American genus *Alstroemeria*, of the amaryllis family, cultivated for their brightly coloured orchid-like flowers. WH: 18C. Modern Latin, from Klas von Alstroemer, 1736–96, Swedish naturalist + -IA.

alt *n.* high tone; the higher register of sounds. WH: 16C. Provençal, from Italian *alto* ALTO.

Altaic *a.* of or relating to the peoples, and to the languages of the peoples (Turanian or Ural-Altaic), lying near the Altai mountains and the Arctic ocean. WH: 19C. *Altai*, mountains in central Asia + -IC.

altar *n.* a sacrificial block or table; a place of sacrifice, commemoration or devotion. WH: pre-1200. Old English, from Latin *altus* high. The word has been related by some to Latin *adolere*, to burn up, to consume. The usual Old English word for altar was *wēofod*, from *wīg* idol + *bēod* table.

altazimuth *n.* an instrument for measuring altitude and azimuth. WH: 19C. ALTITUDE + AZIMUTH.

alter *v.t.* to cause to vary or change in some degree. *Also v.i.* WH: 12–14C. Old French *altérer*, from Late Latin *alterare*, from Latin *alter* other.

altercate *v.i.* to dispute hotly. WH: 16C. Latin *altercatus*, p.p. of *altercari* to wrangle. See also -ATE[3].

alter ego *n.* a second self. WH: 16C. Latin other self. Cp. ALTER, EGO.

alternate[1] *v.t.* to arrange or perform by turns. *Also v.i.* WH: 16C. Latin *alternatus*, p.p. of *alternare* to do things in turn. Cp. ALTER. See also -ATE[3].

alternate[2] *a.* done or happening by turns, first one and then the other. WH: 16C. Latin *alternatus*, p.p. of *alternare*. See ALTERNATE[1], also -ATE[2].

alternative *a.* offering a choice of two things. *Also n.* WH: 16C. French *alternatif*, or from Medieval Latin *alternativus*. See ALTERNATE[1], also -ATIVE.

alternator *n.* a dynamo for generating an alternating electric current. WH: 19C. ALTERNATE[1] + -OR.

althorn *n.* an instrument of the saxhorn family, esp. the E flat alto or tenor saxhorn. WH: 19C. German, ALT + HORN.

although *conj.* though, notwithstanding. WH: 12–14C. ALL + THOUGH.

alti- *comb. form* high, highly, height. WH: Latin *altus* high, *alte* highly + -i-.

altimeter *n.* an instrument that indicates height above a given datum, usu. sea level. WH: 19C. ALTI- + -METER.

altissimo *adv.* in the second octave above the treble stave. WH: 18C. Italian, superl. of *alto* ALTO.

altitude *n.* vertical height. WH: 12–14C. Latin *altitudo, altitudinis*, from *altus* high. See also -TUDE.

alto *n.* the lowest female voice, contralto. *Also a.* WH: 16C. Italian, from Latin *altus* high.

altocumulus *n.* in meteorology, intermediate-altitude cloud in rounded masses with a level base. WH: 19C. Modern Latin *alto-*, from *altus* high + CUMULUS.

altogether *adv.* completely, entirely. WH: pre-1200. Old English *eall* ALL + *tōgædere* TOGETHER.

alto-relievo *n.* high relief, standing out from the background by more than half the true proportions of the figures carved. WH: 17C. Italian *alto-rilievo*, from *alto* high + *rilievo* RELIEVO.

altostratus *n.* in meteorology, intermediate-altitude cloud forming a continuous level layer. WH: 19C. Modern Latin *alto-*, from *altus* high + STRATUS.

altrices *n.pl.* birds whose young are very immature after hatching and depend entirely on the parents for food. WH: 19C. Modern Latin, pl. of *altrix*, fem. of *altor* nourisher, from *alere* to nourish. Cp. ALIMENT.

altruism *n.* devotion to the good of others (as opposed to *egoism*). WH: 19C. French *altruisme*, from Italian *altrui* somebody else. See also -ISM. The word was apparently coined in 1830 by the French philosopher Auguste Comte, based on *égoïsme* egoism (EGO).

alula *n.* the bastard wing. WH: 18C. Modern Latin, dim. of *ala* wing.

alum *n.* a double sulphate of aluminium and potassium. WH: 12–14C. Old French, from Latin *alumen*, rel. to *aluta* tawed leather.

alumina *n.* the oxide of aluminium occurring as corundum and a constituent of all clays. WH: 18C. Latin *alumen, aluminis* ALUM.

aluminium *n.* a white, ductile metallic element, at. no. 13, chem. symbol Al, with good resistance to corrosion, used as a basis for many light alloys. WH: 19C. ALUMINA + -IUM. The word is an altered form of *aluminum*, the original name given in 1812 by the element's discoverer, the British chemist Sir Humphry Davy.

aluminosilicate *n.* a silicate containing a proportion of aluminium, esp. a rock-forming silicate such as feldspar. WH: early 20C. *alumino-*, comb. form of ALUMINIUM + SILICA + -ATE[1].

aluminous *a.* composed of or relating to aluminium or alumina. WH: 14–15C. Latin *aluminosus*, from *alumen, aluminis* ALUM. See also -OUS.

alumnus *n.* a former pupil or student (of a particular place of education). WH: 17C. Latin nursling, vestigial pres. pass. part. of *alere* to nourish. Cp. ALMA MATER.

alveolus *n.* a little cavity. WH: 17C. Latin, dim. of *alveus* cavity.

always *adv.* on all occasions, in all cases. WH: 12–14C. ALL + WAY. The *s* comes from Middle English *wayes*, the adverbial genitive form of *way*.

alyssum *n.* a plant of the cruciferous genus *Alyssum*, that includes *A. saxatile*. WH: 16C. Modern Latin, from Latin *alysson*, from Greek *alusson*, from A-[6] + *lussa* rabies, for which believed to be a cure.

Alzheimer's disease *n.* a degenerative disease of the central nervous system characterized by a deterioration of mental faculties resembling premature mental senility or dementia. WH: early 20C. Alois *Alzheimer*, 1864–1915, German neurologist.

amabile *adv.* amiably, tenderly, sweetly. WH: 17C. Italian amiable.

amadou *n.* a tinder prepared from a dried fungus steeped in saltpetre, used as a match and a styptic. WH: 18C. French, of uncertain orig. The word is said to derive from Provençal *amadou* amorous, from its readiness to ignite.

amah *n.* (in the Far East and India) a maidservant or nanny. WH: 19C. Portuguese *ama* nurse.

amain *adv.* energetically, violently, in full force, at full speed, at once. WH: 16C. A-[1] + MAIN[1].

amalgam *n.* a compound of different things. WH: 15C. French *amalgame*, or from Medieval Latin *amalgama*, prob. ult. from Greek *malagma* emollient.

amanuensis *n.* a person employed to write what another dictates or to copy manuscripts. WH: 17C. Latin, from *a manu*, in phr. *servus a manu* slave at hand + -*ensis* belonging to. See also -ESE.

amaranth *n.* an imaginary flower supposed never to fade. WH: 16C. French *amarante*, or from Modern Latin *amaranthus*, from Latin *amarantus*, from Greek *amarantos* unfading, from A-[6] + *marainein* to wither. The spelling has been influenced by Greek *anthos* flower.

amaryllis *n.* an autumn-flowering bulbous plant. WH: 18C. Modern Latin, from name of *Amaryllis*, a country girl in the writings of Theocritus, Virgil and Ovid.

amass *v.t.* to make or gather into a heap. WH: 15C. Old French *amasser*, or from Medieval Latin *amassare*, from Latin AD- + *massa* MASS.

amateur *n.* a person who practises anything as a pastime, as distinguished from one who does so professionally. *Also a.* WH: 18C. French, from Italian *amatore*, from Latin *amator* lover. Cp. AMATORY.

amative *a.* amorous. WH: 17C. Medieval Latin *amativus*, from Latin *amatus*, p.p. of *amare* to love. See also -ORY[2].

amatol *n.* an explosive consisting of a mixture of ammonium nitrate and trinitrotoluene. WH: early 20C. AMMONIUM + *toluene* (see TOLU).

amatory *a.* of or relating to love or sexual desire. WH: 16C. Latin *amatorius*, from *amator* lover, from *amare* to love. See also -ORY[2].

amaurosis *n.* partial or total blindness from disease of the optic nerve, usu. without visible defect. WH: 17C. Greek *amaurōsis*, from *amauroun* to darken. See also -OSIS.

amaze *v.t.* to astound, to overwhelm with wonder. *Also n.* WH: pre-1200. Old English *āmasian*, from A-[3] + *masian* to confuse. Rel. to MAZE. The original meaning was to stun, then to terrify, to fill with panic. The current sense prevailed from the 17C.

Amazon *n.* any of a fabled race of Scythian female warriors. WH: 11–12C. Latin, from Greek *Amazōn*, explained by the Greeks as meaning breastless, as if from A-[6] + *mazos* breast, but prob. of foreign orig. The Amazons were said to cut off the right breast to draw the bow more freely.

ambassador *n.* a high-ranking diplomat sent by a state as its permanent representative in another country or on a particular mission abroad. WH: 12–14C. French *ambassadeur*, from Italian *ambasciatore*, from Medieval Latin *ambactia*, *ambaxia*, from Germanic *andbahts* servant, from Latin *ambactus* servant, vassal, from Gaulish. Cp. EMBASSY.

amber *n.* a yellowish translucent fossil resin, found chiefly on the southern shores of the Baltic, used for ornaments, mouthpieces of pipes, and in the manufacture of some varnishes. *Also a.* WH: 12–14C. Old French *ambre*, from Arabic *'anbar* AMBERGRIS.

ambergris *n.* a light, fatty, inflammable substance, ashy in colour, found floating in tropical seas (a secretion from the intestines of the cachalot or sperm whale, it is used in perfumery, and was formerly used in cookery and medicine). WH: 14–15C. Old French *ambre gris* grey amber, as distinct from *ambre jaune* yellow amber. Cp. AMBER.

ambidextrous *a.* using both hands with equal facility. WH: 17C. Late Latin *ambidexter*, from Latin *ambi-* both + *dexter* right-handed. See also -OUS. Cp. DEXTER[1].

ambient *a.* surrounding, encompassing on all sides; of or relating to the immediate surroundings. WH: 16C. French *ambiant*, or from Latin *ambiens*, *ambientis*, pres.p. of *ambire* to go round, from *ambi-* both + *ire* to go. Cp. AMBIGUOUS.

ambiguous *a.* susceptible of two or more interpretations. WH: 16C. Latin *ambiguus* doubtful, from *ambigere* to go round. See AMBIENT, also -OUS.

ambisonics *n.* a system of multi-channel high-fidelity sound reproduction which surrounds the listener with sound. WH: late 20C. Latin *ambi-* both + *sonics* (SONIC).

ambit *n.* scope, extent. WH: 12–14C. Latin *ambitus* circuit, compass, from p.p. *ambitus* (AMBITION).

ambition *n.* a desire for power, success etc. WH: 12–14C. Old French, from Latin *ambitio*, *ambitionis*, from *ambitus*, p.p. of *ambire*. See AMBIENT, also -ION. The word originally had an undesirable sense, inordinate striving after rank and wealth. The current favourable sense evolved from the 17C.

ambivalence *n.* the simultaneous existence in the mind of two incompatible feelings or wishes. WH: early 20C. German *Ambivalenz*, based on *Äquivalenz* equivalence (EQUIVALENT), from Latin *ambi-* both + *valens* being worth.

ambivert *n.* a person who fluctuates between introversion and extroversion. WH: early 20C. Latin *ambi-* both + *vertere* to turn. The word is based on INTROVERT[1] and EXTROVERT.

amble *v.i.* to walk at a leisurely relaxed pace. *Also n.* WH: 12–14C. Old French *ambler*, from Latin *ambulare* to walk. Cp. AMBULANCE.

amblyopia *n.* dimness of vision without any obvious defect in the eye. WH: 18C. Greek *ambluōpia* dimsightedness, from *ambluōpos*, from *amblus* blunt. See -OPIA.

ambo *n.* a pulpit or reading desk in early medieval churches. WH: 17C. Medieval Latin *ambo*, *ambonis*, from Greek *ambōn* rim of cup.

amboyna *n.* the finely variegated wood of *Pterocarpus indicus*. WH: 19C. *Amboina* (Ambon), an island in the Moluccas, Indonesia.

ambrosia *n.* the fabled food of the gods. WH: 16C. Latin, from Greek immortality, from *ambrotos* immortal, from A-[6] + *brotos*, from **mbrotos* mortal. Cp. MORTAL.

ambsace *n.* both aces, the lowest possible throw at dice. WH: 11–12C. Old French *ambes as*, from Latin *ambo* both + *as* ACE.

ambulance *n.* a vehicle for the transport of wounded, injured or sick people. WH: 19C. French, from *hôpital ambulant* mobile (horse-drawn) field hospital, from Latin *ambulans*, *ambulantis*, pres.p. of *ambulare* to walk. See also -ANCE.

ambulate *v.i.* to walk about. WH: 17C. Latin *ambulatus*, p.p. of *ambulare* to walk. See also -ATE[3].

ambulatory *a.* of or relating to walking. *Also n.* WH: 17C. Latin *ambulatorius*. See AMBULATE, also -ORY[2].

ambuscade *n.* an ambush, a lying in wait to attack an enemy. *Also v.i., v.t.* WH: 16C. French *embuscade*, from Italian *imboscata* or Spanish *emboscada*, Portuguese *emboscada*. See AMBUSH, also -ADE.

ambush *n.* a surprise attack by forces. *Also v.t., v.i.* WH: 15C. Old French *embusche*, from *embuschier*, from *en-* IN + *busche* wood, BUSH[1].

AMDG *abbr.* to the greater glory of God. WH: Latin *ad maiorem Dei gloriam*.

ameliorate *v.t.* to make better, to improve. *Also v.i.* WH: 18C. French *améliorer*, from Old French *ameillorer*, from *a-* (AD-) + *meillorer* to better, from Late Latin *meliorare* to improve. The direct source is in MELIORATE.

amen *int.* so be it, may it be as it has been asked, said or promised (said esp. at the end of a prayer or hymn). *Also n.* WH: pre-1200. Ecclesiastical Latin, from Greek *amēn*, from Hebrew *'āmēn* certain, from base *'mn* to be certain.

amenable *a.* willing to cooperate, readily persuaded. WH: 16C. Old French *amener* to bring to, from *a-* AD- + *mener* to bring, from Popular Latin *minare* to drive (animals), from Latin *minari* to threaten. Rel. to MENACE. See also -ABLE.

amend *v.t.* to alter (a person or thing) for the better, to improve. *Also v.i.* WH: pre-1200. Old French *amender*, from Latin *emendare*. See EMEND. The original sense was to mend literally, as of clothes and roads. This then passed to MEND itself from the 14C.

amende honorable *n.* an open or public apology, often accompanied by some form of amends. WH: 17C. French honourable reparation. Cp. AMEND, HONOUR.

amenity *n.* the quality of being pleasant or agreeable; attractions, charms. WH: 12–14C. Old French *aménité*, or from Latin *amoenitas*, from *amoenus* pleasant. See also -ITY.

amenorrhoea *n.* the abnormal cessation of menstruation. WH: 19C. A-[6] + MENO- + -RRHOEA.

ament *n.* a catkin. WH: 18C. Latin *amentum* thong, strap.

amentia *n.* severe congenital mental deficiency. WH: 14–15C. Latin madness, from *amens*, *amentis* mad, from A-[6] + *mens*, *mentis* mind. See also -IA. Cp. MENTAL[1].

Amerasian *a.* of mixed American and Asian parentage. *Also n.* WH: mid-20C. AMERICAN + ASIAN.

amerce *v.t.* to punish by fine. WH: 14–15C. Anglo-French *amercier*, in phr. *estre amercié* to be placed at the mercy of another, from *à merci* at (the) mercy. See MERCY.

American *a.* of or relating to the continent of America, esp. to the US. *Also n.* WH: 16C. Modern Latin *Americanus*, from *America*, the continent. See also -AN.

americium *n.* an artificially-created, metallic radioactive element, at. no. 95, chem. symbol Am. WH: mid-20C. *America* + -IUM. The element was produced in 1944 by four US scientists, Glenn T. Seaborg, Ralph A. James, Leon O. Morgan and Albert Ghiorso.

Amerind *n.* an American Indian. *Also a.* WH: 19C. Contr. of *American Indian*. See AMERICAN, INDIAN.

amethyst *n.* a violet-blue variety of crystalline quartz, supposed by the ancients to prevent intoxication. WH: 12–14C. Old French *ametiste*, from Latin *amethystus*, from Greek *amethustos lithos* intoxicated stone, from A-⁶ + *methuein* to be intoxicated + *lithos* stone. The quartz is so called because it was believed to prevent intoxication.

Amharic *n.* the official language of Ethiopia. *Also a.* WH: 18C. *Amhara*, a region of central Ethiopia + -IC.

amiable *a.* friendly, likeable. WH: 12–14C. Old French, from Late Latin *amicabilis* AMICABLE. The current sense was influenced from the 18C by Modern French *aimable* lovable, likeable.

amianthus *n.* a variety of asbestos, a fibrous kind of chrysolite of a greenish colour. WH: 17C. Latin *amiantus*, from Greek *amiantos*, from A-⁶ + *miainein* to defile. The mineral is so called because it is rendered stainless when thrown on a fire, being itself incombustible. The spelling with *h* was influenced by POLYANTHUS etc.

amicable *a.* friendly. WH: 14–15C. Late Latin *amicabilis*, from *amicus* friend. See also -ABLE.

amice¹ *n.* a piece of white linen worn on the neck and shoulders at Mass by Roman Catholic and some Anglican priests. WH: 12–14C. Medieval Latin *amicia*, *amisia*, of unknown orig. The earlier form was *amit*. Not rel. to AMICE².

amice² *n.* a hood, cap or cape worn by members of certain religious orders. WH: 12–14C. Old French *aumusse*, from Medieval Latin *almucia*, *almucium*, of unknown orig.

amicus curiae *n.* a disinterested adviser in a court of law. WH: 17C. Modern Latin friend of the court. Cp. AMICABLE, CURIA.

amid *prep.* in the midst or middle, among. WH: pre-1200. A-¹ + MID².

amide *n.* any of various organic compounds constituted as if obtained from ammonia by the substitution of one or more univalent organic acid radicals for one or more atoms of hydrogen. WH: 19C. AMMONIA + -IDE.

Amidol® *n.* a compound of phenol, chemical formula $C_6H_3(NH_2)_2(OH).2HCl$, used in the form of a soluble crystalline powder as a photographic developer. WH: 19C. AMIDE + -OL.

amigo *n.* a friend (also often used as a form of address). WH: 19C. Spanish, from Latin *amicus* friend.

amine *n.* any of various organic compounds derived from ammonia by the substitution of one or more univalent hydrocarbon radicals for one or more atoms of hydrogen. WH: 19C. AMMONIA + -INE.

amir *n.* the title of several Muslim rulers, esp. formerly in India and Afghanistan. WH: 16C. Persian and Urdu, from Arabic *'amīr* commander, from *amara* to command. Cp. ADMIRAL.

Amish *a.* of or belonging to a strict US Mennonite sect. *Also n.pl.* WH: 19C. Appar. from German *amisch*, from Jacob *Ammann*, 17C Swiss Mennonite elder.

amiss *a.* faulty, wrong. *Also adv.* WH: 12–14C. Old Norse *á mis* so as to miss, from *á* on + *mis* MISS¹.

amitosis *n.* cell division without mitosis. WH: 19C. A-⁶ + MITOSIS.

amitriptyline *n.* a tricyclic antidepressant drug with a mildly tranquillizing effect. WH: mid-20C. *ami(no)* (AMINE) + TRI- + *(he)ptyl* (from HEPTA- + -YL) + -INE.

amity *n.* friendship, mutual good feeling. WH: 14–15C. Old French *amitié*, from Popular Latin *amicitas*, *amicitatis*, from Latin *amicus* friend.

ammeter *n.* an instrument for measuring the strength of the electric current in a circuit. WH: 19C. AMPERE + METER.

ammonal *n.* an explosive compound containing aluminium mixed with ammonium nitrate. WH: early 20C. AMMONIUM + ALUMINIUM.

ammonia *n.* a pungent volatile gas, powerfully alkaline, a compound of nitrogen and hydrogen first obtained from sal ammoniac. WH: 18C. Modern Latin, from *sal ammoniacus* sal ammoniac (see SAL¹), from Greek *ammōniakos*, *ammōniakon* of Ammon. Sal ammoniac was said to be obtained from camel dung near the temple of Jupiter Ammon, Siwa, Egypt. Cp. AMMONITE.

ammonite *n.* the shell of a genus of fossil cephalopods, curved like the ram's horn on the statue of Jupiter Ammon. WH: 18C. Modern Latin *ammonites*, from Medieval Latin *cornu Ammonis* horn of Ammon. See also -ITE¹. The fossils were so named from their supposed resemblance to the involuted horn of Jupiter Ammon (see AMMONIA).

ammonium *n.* the ion or radical derived from ammonia by addition of a hydrogen ion or atom. WH: 19C. AMMONIA + -IUM.

ammunition *n.* any projectiles, e.g. bullets, shells, rockets, that can be discharged from a weapon. *Also a.* WH: 16C. French, from misdivision of *la munition* the MUNITION as *l'amunition*. The original sense was military supplies generally. The current narrower sense emerged in the 17C.

amnesia *n.* loss of memory. WH: 18C. Greek *amnēsia* forgetfulness, from A-⁶ + *mimnēskesthai* to recall. Cp. AMNESTY.

amnesty *n.* a general pardon. *Also v.t.* WH: 16C. Obs. French *amnestie* (Modern French *amnistie*), or from Latin *amnestia*, from Greek *amnēstia* forgetfulness. Cp. AMNESIA.

amniocentesis *n.* the removal of a sample of amniotic fluid from the womb, by insertion of a hollow needle, in order to test for chromosomal abnormalities in the foetus. WH: mid-20C. *amnio-*, comb. form of AMNION + Greek *kentēsis* pricking, from *kentein* to prick.

amnion *n.* the innermost membrane with which the foetus in the womb is surrounded. WH: 17C. Greek caul, dim. of *amnos* lamb.

amoeba *n.* a microscopic organism of the simplest structure, consisting of a single protoplasmic cell, which is extensile and contractile so that its shape is continually changing. WH: 19C. Modern Latin, from Greek *amoibē* change, alteration.

amok *adv.* in a frenzy, esp. as below. WH: 16C. Malay *amuk* fighting furiously, battling in a homicidal frenzy. Not rel. to MUCK.

among *prep.* in the midst of; surrounded by. WH: pre-1200. Old English *onmang*, from *on* ON + *(ge)mang* crowd. Rel. to MINGLE.

amontillado *n.* a kind of medium dry sherry. WH: 19C. Spanish, from *Montilla*, a town in S Spain + -ADO. The sherry-type wine *Montilla* takes its name from the same town.

amoral *a.* not concerned with morals; having no moral principles. WH: 19C. A-⁶ + MORAL.

amoretto *n.* a cupid. WH: 16C. Italian, dim. of *amore* love.

amorist *n.* a person who makes a study of or writes about love. WH: 16C. Latin *amor*, or from French *amour* love + -IST.

amoroso¹ *adv.*, *a.* to be performed lovingly. WH: 17C. Spanish and Italian, from Medieval Latin *amorosus* AMOROUS.

amoroso² *n.* a full rich type of sherry. WH: 17C. Spanish amorous. Cp. AMOROSO¹. The wine is so named from its sweetness.

amorous *a.* naturally inclined to love. WH: 12–14C. Old French (Modern French *amoureux*), from Medieval Latin *amorosus*, from Latin *amor* love. See also -OUS.

amorphous *a.* shapeless. WH: 18C. Modern Latin *amorphus*, from Greek *amorphos*, from A-⁶ + *morphē* shape. See also -OUS. Cp. MORPH.

amortize *v.t.* to liquidate (a debt) by instalments or by regular transfers to a sinking fund. WH: 12–14C. Old French *amortir*, *amortiss-* to deaden, from Popular Latin *admortire*, from AD- + *mors*, *mortis* death. Cp. MORTAL, MORTGAGE.

amount *v.i.* to run into an aggregate by the accumulation of particulars; to mount up (to), to add up (to). *Also n.* WH: 12–14C. Old French *amunter*, from *amont* upward, from Latin *ad montem* to the mount, from *ad* AD- + *mons*, *montis* MOUNT².

amour *n.* a love affair, esp. a secret one; an amorous intrigue. WH: 12–14C. Old French, from Latin *amor* love. The original meaning was love itself. The current sense prevailed from the 16C.

amour propre *n.* self-esteem. WH: 18C. French self-love, from *amour* love + *propre* own. See AMOUR, PROPER.

ampelopsis *n.* any climbing or creeping plant of the genus *Ampelopsis*, that includes the Virginia creeper. WH: 19C. Modern Latin, from Greek *ampelos* vine + *opsis* appearance.

ampere *n.* a unit by which an electric current is measured, the current sent by 1 volt through a resistance of 1 ohm. WH: 19C. André-Marie *Ampère*, 1775–1836, French physicist.

ampersand *n.* the sign '&'. WH: 19C. Alt. of *& per se and* '&' by itself, 'and'. See AND. The word comes from the former way of naming letters, especially those that made a word, e.g. *A per se A*, 'A' by itself, (the word) 'A', *O per se O*, 'O' by itself, (the word) 'O'. The character itself is probably a blend of *E* and *t*, from Latin *et* and.

amphetamine *n.* (a derivative of) a synthetic drug which has a stimulant action on the brain. WH: mid-20C. *alpha-methyl-phenethylamine*. See ALPHA, METHYL, PHENYL, ETHYL, AMINE.

amphi- *comb. form* both. **WH:** Greek *amphi-* both, of both kinds, on both sides, around.

amphibian *n.* any vertebrate animal of the class Amphibia, that have an aquatic gill-breathing larval stage followed by a terrestrial lung-breathing adult stage. *Also a.* **WH:** 17C. Modern Latin *amphibium*, from Greek *amphibion*, neut. (used as n.) of *amphibios*, from AMPHI- + *bios* life + -AN.

amphibiology *n.* the branch of zoology which deals with the Amphibia. **WH:** 19C. *amphibia* (AMPHIBIAN) + -LOGY.

amphibole *n.* any of a group of silicate and aluminosilicate minerals including hornblende and tremolite that usu. occur in the form of long slender dark-coloured crystals. **WH:** 17C. French, from Latin *amphibolus* ambiguous, from Greek *amphibolos*, from AMPHI- + *ballein* to throw. The original sense was ambiguity. The minerals are so named because of the variety in their structure. Cp. AMPHIBOLOGY.

amphibology *n.* an ambiguous expression, esp. a sentence composed of unambiguous words that is susceptible of a double meaning because of its construction. **WH:** 14–15C. Old French *amphibologie*, from Late Latin *amphibologia*, from Latin *amphibolia* AMPHIBOLE (in orig. sense). See -LOGY.

amphibrach *n.* a metrical foot of three syllables, the middle one long and the first and third short. **WH:** 16C. Latin *amphibrachys*, from Greek *amphibrakhus* short at both ends, from AMPHI- + *brakhus* short. Cp. AMPHIMACER.

amphictyon *n.* a delegate to the council of an amphictyony. **WH:** 16C. Greek *amphiktuones* dwellers around, from AMPHI- + *ktizein* to found.

amphimacer *n.* CRETIC. **WH:** 16C. Latin *amphimacrus*, from Greek *amphimakros* long at both ends, from AMPHI- + *makros* long. Cp. AMPHIBRACH.

amphimixis *n.* sexual reproduction. **WH:** 19C. AMPHI- + Greek *mixis* mingling.

amphioxus *n.* a lancelet. **WH:** 19C. Modern Latin, from AMPHI- + Greek *oxus* sharp.

amphipod *n.* any small sessile-eyed crustacean of the order Amphipoda, having two kinds of feet, one for walking and one for swimming. *Also a.* **WH:** 19C. Modern Latin *amphipoda*. See AMPHI-, -POD.

amphiprostyle *n.* a temple having a portico at each end. **WH:** 18C. Latin *amphiprostylus*, from Greek *amphiprostulos*, from AMPHI- + PROSTYLE.

amphisbaena *n.* a fabled snake said by the ancients to have a head at each end, and to be able to move in either direction. **WH:** 14–15C. Latin, from Greek *amphisbaina*, from *amphis* both ways (cp. AMPHI-) + *bainein* to go, to walk.

amphitheatre *n.* an oval or circular building with rows of seats rising one above another round an open space. **WH:** 16C. Latin *amphitheatrum*, from Greek *amphitheatron*, from AMPHI- + THEATRE.

amphora *n.* an ancient two-handled vessel for holding wine, oil etc. **WH:** 12–14C. Latin, from Greek *amphoreus*, from AMPHI- + *phoreus* bearer. Cp. AMPULLA.

amphoteric *a.* of two (opposite) kinds. **WH:** 19C. Greek *amphoteros*, comp. of *amphō* both (see AMPHI-) + -IC.

ampicillin *n.* a semisynthetic penicillin used to treat infections esp. of the urinary and respiratory tract. **WH:** mid-20C. *am(ino)* (AMINE) + PENICILLIN.

ample *a.* of large dimensions. **WH:** 18C. Old French, from Latin *amplus* large, abundant.

amplexicaul *a.* embracing or clasping the stem. **WH:** 18C. Modern Latin *amplexicaulis*, from Latin *amplexus* embrace + *caulis* stem.

amplify *v.t.* to increase, esp. the strength of (a signal) or the loudness of (sound). *Also v.i.* **WH:** 14–15C. French *amplifier*, from Latin *amplificare* to enlarge, from *amplus* AMPLE. See also -FY.

amplitude *n.* extent, size, bulk, greatness. **WH:** 16C. French, or from Latin *amplitudo*, from *amplus* AMPLE. See also -TUDE.

ampoule *n.* a sealed phial containing one dose of a drug. **WH:** 17C. French, from Latin AMPULLA.

ampulla *n.* a nearly globular flask with two handles, used by the ancient Romans. **WH:** 14–15C. Latin, dim. of *ampora* AMPHORA.

amputate *v.t.* to cut off (a limb or part of a limb) from an animal

body by surgical operation. **WH:** 16C. Latin *amputatus*, p.p. of *amputare*, from *am-* var. of *ampi-* around (cp. AMPHI-) + *putare* to prune, to lop. See also -ATE³.

amrita *n.* the ambrosia of the gods in Hindu mythology. **WH:** 18C. Sanskrit *amṛta* an immortal, nectar. Cp. AMBROSIA.

amtrac *n.* an amphibious tracked vehicle for landing assault troops. **WH:** mid-20C. *am(phibious)* (AMPHIBIAN) + TRACTOR. The spelling with *k* has been influ. by TRACK. Cp. *Amtrak*, the US passenger train operator.

amulet *n.* anything worn about the person as an imagined preservative against sickness, witchcraft etc. **WH:** 16C. Latin *amuletum*, of unknown orig. The word is not from Latin *amolitus*, p.p. of *amolire* to put away, to avert.

amuse *v.t.* to cause to laugh or smile. **WH:** 15C. Old French *amuser* to entertain, from *à* AD- + *muser* MUSE². The original English sense was to delude, to deceive, then to distract, to divert. The main modern sense dates from the 17C.

amygdala *n.* an almond-shaped body part, such as a tonsil or a lobe of the cerebellum. **WH:** 14–15C. Latin, from Greek *amugdalē* ALMOND.

amyl *n.* a monovalent group, C_5H_{11}, derived from pentane. **WH:** 19C. Latin *amylum* starch + -YL.

Amytal® *n.* a crystalline compound used as a sedative and hypnotic. **WH:** early 20C. AMYL + euphonic *t* + -AL².

†tan *conj.* if. **WH:** 12–14C. Weakened form of AND.

an. *abbr.* in the year. **WH:** Latin *anno*, abl. of *annus* year.

an-¹ *pref.* signifying motion towards, direction to, adherence etc., as in *annex*, *announce*. **WH:** Latin pref., from AD- with *d* assim to *n*.

an-² *pref.* up, as in *anode*. **WH:** Greek pref., from ANA-, used before vowels.

an-³ *pref.* not, without, as in *anaesthesia*, *anarchy*. **WH:** Greek pref., from A-⁶, used before vowels.

-an *suf.* of, belonging or relating to, as in *human*, *pagan*, *publican*, *Christian*, *European* etc. **WH:** Latin *-anus*. Cp. -IAN.

ana *n.* literary gossip or anecdotes, usu. of a personal or local kind. **WH:** 18C. See -ANA.

ana- *pref.* up, as in *anadromous*. **WH:** Greek pref., from prep. *ana* up, back, again.

-ana *suf.* objects relating to, as in *Africana*, *Americana*, *victoriana*. **WH:** Latin, neut. pl. of aa. in *-anus*. See -AN.

Anabaptism *n.* a second baptism. **WH:** 16C. Ecclesiastical Latin *anabaptismus*, from Greek *anabaptismos*, from ANA- + *baptismos* baptism (BAPTIZE). See also -ISM.

anabas *n.* a fish of the genus *Anabas* that includes the climbing perch, which can leave the water. **WH:** 19C. Modern Latin, from Greek *anabas*, part. of *anabainein* to walk up, from ANA- + *bainein* to walk. Cp. ANABASIS.

anabasis *n.* a military advance up-country. **WH:** 18C. Greek going up, from ANA- + *basis* going. Cp. KATABASIS.

anabatic *a.* (of wind or air currents) moving upwards. **WH:** 19C. Greek *anabatikos*, from *anabatēs* person who goes up, from *anabainein* to go up. See ANA-, also -IC.

anabiosis *n.* a state of suspended animation or greatly reduced metabolism. **WH:** 19C. Greek *anabiōsis* return to life, from *anabioein* to come to life again. See ANA-, also -OSIS.

anabolism *n.* the building up of complex substances by assimilation of nutriment, with storage of energy. **WH:** 19C. Greek *anabolē* a throwing up, from *anaballein*, from ANA- + *ballein* to throw. See also -ISM.

anabranch *n.* a tributary rejoining the main stream of a river and thus forming an island. **WH:** 19C. *ana(stomosing)*, pres.p. of ANASTOMOSE + BRANCH.

anachronism *n.* the assigning of an event, custom or circumstance to a wrong period or date. **WH:** 17C. French *anachronisme*, or from Greek *anakhronismos*, from *anakhronizesthai* to refer to a wrong time, from ANA- + *khronos* time. See also -ISM.

anacoluthon *n.* lack of grammatical sequence in a sentence. **WH:** 18C. Late Latin, from Greek *anakolouthon*, neut. sing. of a. *anakolouthos* lacking sequence, from AN-³ + *akolouthos* following.

anaconda *n. Eunectes murinus*, a very large semiaquatic S American boa. **WH:** 18C. Alt. of Latin *anacandaia* python, from Sinhalese *henakaṅdayā* whip snake, prob. from *heṅa* lightning + *kanda* stem.

anacreontic *a.* of or relating to Anacreon, or the metre used by him. *Also n.* WH: 17C. Late Latin *anacreontic*, from Greek *Anakreōn*, *Anakreontos* Anacreon, *c.*570–*c.*475 BC, Greek lyric poet. See also -IC.

anacrusis *n.* an upward beat at the beginning of a verse, consisting of an unstressed syllable or syllables. WH: 19C. Modern Latin, from Greek *anakrousis* prelude, from ANA- + *krouein* to strike.

anadem *n.* a garland or fillet. WH: 17C. Latin *anadema*, from Greek *anadema* headband, from ANA- + *deein* to bind. Cp. DIADEM.

anadromous *a.* (of fish) ascending rivers to deposit spawn. WH: 18C. Greek *anadromos* running up, from ANA- + *dromos* running (cp. -DROME). See also -OUS.

anaemia *n.* lack of haemoglobin or of red corpuscles in the blood, leading to pallor and lack of energy. WH: 19C. Modern Latin, from Greek *anaimia*, from AN-[3] + *haima* blood. See also -IA.

anaerobe *n.* an organism that thrives best, or only, in the absence of oxygen. WH: 19C. AN-[3] + AEROBE.

anaesthesia *n.* loss of bodily sensation due to nerve damage or other abnormality. WH: 18C. Modern Latin, from Greek *anaisthēsia*, from AN-[3] + *aisthēsis* sensation. See also -IA.

anaglyph *n.* a composite photograph in superimposed complementary colours which gives a stereoscopic image when viewed through special glasses. WH: 16C. Greek *anagluphē* work in low relief, from ANA- + *gluphein* to carve.

anagnorisis *n.* in Greek tragedy, a recognition that leads to the denouement. WH: 18C. Greek *anagnōrisis*, from ANA- + *gnōrizein* to recognise.

anagoge *n.* mystical, allegorical or spiritual interpretation. WH: 14–15C. Greek *anagōgē* (religious) elevation, from *anagein* to lift up, from ANA- + *agein* to lead.

anagram *n.* a word or sentence formed by transposing the letters of another word or sentence. WH: 16C. French *anagramme*, or from Modern Latin *anagramma*, from ANA- + Greek *gramma* letter.

anal *a.* of, relating to or situated near the anus. WH: 18C. Modern Latin *analis*. See ANUS, also -AL[1].

analects *n.pl.* crumbs which fall from the table. WH: 14–15C. Latin *analecta*, from Greek *analekta* things gathered up, from *analegein*, from ANA- + *legein* to gather.

analeptic *a.* restorative, increasing the strength. *Also n.* WH: 16C. Late Latin *analepticus*, from Greek *analēptikos* restorative, from ANA- + *lambanein* to take. See also -IC.

analgesia *n.* loss of sensibility to pain. WH: 18C. Greek *analgēsia* painlessness, from AN-[3] + *algeein* to feel pain.

analogous *a.* presenting some analogy or resemblance. WH: 17C. Latin *analogus*, from Greek *analogos*. See ANALOGY, also -OUS.

analogue *n.* an analogous word or thing, a parallel. *Also a.* WH: 19C. French, from Greek *analogon*, neut. sing. of *analogos*. See ANALOGY.

analogy *n.* similarity; a comparison used to demonstrate this. WH: 14–15C. French *analogie*, or from Latin *analogia*, from Greek equality (of ratios), proportion, from *analogos* proportionate, from ANA- + *logos* ratio, reason. Cp. LOGOS, -LOGY.

analyse *v.t.* to take to pieces, resolve into its constituent elements. WH: 16C. French *analyser*, v. from n. *analyse* ANALYSIS. The original meaning was literal, to dissect. The application to abstract objects emerged from the 18C.

analysis *n.* the process of analysing; a report or statement of the results of this process. WH: 16C. Medieval Latin, from Greek, from *analuein* to unloose, from ANA- + *luein* to loose.

analyst *n.* a person who analyses. WH: 17C. French *analyste*, from *analyser* to analyse (see ANALYSIS) based on nn. in -*iste* -IST.

analytic *a.* of or relating to analysis. WH: 16C. Late Latin *analyticus*, from Greek *analutikos*, from *analuein*. See ANALYSIS, also -IC.

anamnesis *n.* recollection. WH: 16C. Greek *anamnēsis* remembrance, from *anamimnēskein* to remember.

anamorphosis *n.* a distorted projection of any object so contrived that if looked at from one point of view, or reflected from a suitable mirror, it will appear properly proportioned. WH: 18C. Greek *anamorphōsis* transformation. See ANA-, MORPHOSIS.

ananas *n.* the pineapple plant or its fruit. WH: 16C. French and Spanish, from Portuguese *ananás*, from Guarani *naná*.

anandrous *a.* lacking stamens. WH: 19C. Greek *anandros* without males, from AN-[3] + *anēr*, *andros* man (here, stamen) + -OUS.

anapaest *n.* a metrical foot consisting of three syllables, the first two short and the third long, a reversed dactyl. WH: 16C. Latin *anapaestus*, from Greek *anapoistos* reversed, from ANA- + *paiein* to strike.

anaphora *n.* the commencement of successive sentences or clauses with the same word or words. WH: 16C. Latin, from Greek repetition, from ANA- + *pherein* to carry.

anaphrodisiac *a.* that suppresses or decreases sexual desire. *Also n.* WH: 19C. AN-[3] + APHRODISIAC.

anaphylaxis *n.* a condition of increased or extreme sensitivity to a foreign substance introduced into the body following previous contact. WH: early 20C. Modern Latin, from ANA- + Greek *phulaxis* watching.

anaplasty *n.* plastic surgery. WH: 19C. French *anaplastie*, from Greek *anaplastos*. See ANA-, -PLASTY.

anaptyxis *n.* the insertion of a short vowel between two consonants to facilitate pronunciation. WH: 19C. Modern Latin, from Greek *anaptuxis* unfolding, from ANA- + *ptuxis* folding.

anarch *n.* a promoter of anarchy or leader of revolt. WH: 17C. Greek *anarkhos* without a chief, from AN-[3] + *arkhos* chief. Cp. -ARCHY.

anarchy *n.* disorder, lawlessness. WH: 16C. Medieval Latin *anarchia*, from Greek *anarkhia*. See ANARCH, also -Y[2]. The original sense was absence of government. This then broadened to mean absence of order generally, and disorder, confusion, upheaval from the 19C.

anarthrous *a.* without the (Greek) article. WH: 19C. Greek AN-[3] + *arthron* joint, definite article + -OUS.

anasarca *n.* dropsy in the cellular tissue. WH: 14–15C. Medieval Latin, from Greek *anasarx*, from ANA- + *sarx* flesh.

anastigmat *n.* a lens free from astigmatism, which refers every point on the scene accurately to a corresponding point image. WH: 19C. ANA- + *stigmatic* (STIGMA).

anastomose *v.i.* to communicate by anastomosis. *Also v.t.* WH: 17C. Greek *anastomōsis*, from *anastomoun* to provide with a mouth, from ANA- + *stoma* mouth. See also -OSIS.

anastrophe *n.* inversion of the natural order of the words in a sentence or clause. WH: 16C. Greek *anastrophē* turning back, from ANA- + *strephein* to turn. Cp. STROPHE.

anathema *n.* an object of loathing. WH: 16C. Ecclesiastical Latin, from Greek var. of *anathēma* votive offering, from *anatithenai* to set up, from ANA- + *tithenai* to put, to place.

Anatolian *a.* of or relating to Anatolia. *Also n.* WH: 16C. *Anatolia*, now the E part of Turkey (cp. Greek *anatolē* east) + -AN.

anatomy *n.* the science of the structure of organized bodies. WH: 12–14C. Old French *anatomie*, from Late Latin *anatomia*, from Greek, from ANA- + *temnein* to cut. See also -TOMY. The word also originally meant skeleton. Cp. ATOMY[1].

anbury *n.* a soft wart on a horse's neck. WH: 16C. ? Old English *ang*- painful (cp. AGNAIL) + BERRY, in sense of berry-like mark or growth.

-ance *suf.* forming nouns denoting a state or action, as in *distance*, *fragrance*, *parlance*, *riddance*. WH: French, from Latin -*antia*, from pres.p. endings -*ans*, -*antis* -ANT, or -*entia*. See -ENCE.

ancestor *n.* any person from whom another person is descended; a progenitor. WH: 12–14C. Old French *ancestre* (Modern French *ancêtre*), from Latin *antecessor*, from ANTE- + *cessus*, p.p. of *cedere* to go.

anchor *n.* a heavy hooked iron instrument dropped from a ship to grapple the bottom and prevent drifting. *Also v.t., v.i.* WH: pre-1200. Old English *ancor*, from Latin *ancora*, from Greek *agkura*, rel. to *agkulos* crooked. See ANGLE[2]. The spelling with *h* is from erroneous Latin *anchora*.

anchorite *n.* a religious recluse, a hermit; an early Christian recluse. WH: 14–15C. Medieval Latin *ancorita*, *anchorita*, from Ecclesiastical Greek *anakhōrētēs*, from *anakhōrein* to retire, to retreat, from ANA- + *khōrein* to withdraw, from *khōros* place, space.

anchovy *n.* any of various small fish of the herring family, esp. *Engraulis encrasicolus*, caught in the Mediterranean, pickled for exportation, and used in sauces etc. WH: 16C. Spanish and Portuguese *anchova*, of unknown orig. The word is perhaps from Latin *apua* a type of small fish, from Greek *aphuē*.

anchusa *n.* any Eurasian plant of the genus *Anchusa*, similar to borage. WH: 16C. Latin, from Greek *agkhousa*.

ancien régime n. the political and social system of France before the French Revolution. WH: 18C. French former regime. Cp. ANCIENT[1], REGIME.

ancient[1] a. of or belonging to time long past. Also n.pl. WH: 12–14C. Anglo-French auncien, from Old French ancien, from Popular Latin anteanus, from ANTE- + -anus -AN. The spelling with t is by association with adjectives in -ANT, -ENT.

ancient[2] n. a flag, a standard. WH: 16C. Alt. of ENSIGN by assoc. with ANCIENT[1].

ancillary a. auxiliary, esp. providing support to a central service or industry. Also n. WH: 17C. Latin ancillaris, from ancilla, fem. dim. of anculus servant. See also -ARY[1].

ancipital a. flattened and having two sharp edges. WH: 18C. Latin anceps, ancipitis two-headed, from an- (from ambi- both) + caput, capitis head + -AL[1].

ancon n. a bracket or console supporting a cornice. WH: 18C. Latin, from Greek agkōn nook, bend.

-ancy suf. forming nouns expressing quality or state, as in constancy, elegancy, infancy, vacancy. WH: Latin -antia -ANCE. Cp. -ENCY.

and conj. the copulative which joins words and sentences: connecting words that are to be considered together or in relation to each other; implying consequence; implying a sequence in time; used to join identical words with an intensifying force; used to join identical words but implying a contrast. WH: pre-1200. Old English, rel. to Latin ante before, Greek anti against, Sanskrit atha thereupon. Cp. ANSWER.

-and suf. forming nouns meaning a person or thing that is about to undergo a specified process. WH: Latin -andus, ger. of vv. in -are.

Andalusian a. of or relating to Andalusia. Also n. WH: 17C. Andalusia, a region in S Spain + -AN.

andante a., adv. moderately slow. Also n. WH: 18C. Italian, pres.p. of andare to go.

Andean a. of or relating to the Andes mountains. WH: 19C. Andes, a mountain range in S America + -AN.

Anderson shelter n. an air-raid shelter formed of arched corrugated steel. WH: mid-20C. Sir John Anderson, 1882–1958, UK Home Secretary when the shelter was adopted, 1939.

andesite n. a fine-grained volcanic rock. WH: 19C. Andes (ANDEAN) + -ITE[1].

andiron n. a horizontal bar raised on short legs with an ornamental upright in front, placed on each side of the hearth to support logs in a wood fire; a firedog. WH: 12–14C. Old French andier, ? from Gaulish andero- bullock, referring to decorative forms of early andirons. The spelling has been assimilated to IRON.

andro- comb. form of or relating to the male sex, or to male flowers. WH: Greek anēr, andros man. See also -O-.

androecium n. the stamens of a flower collectively. WH: 19C. Modern Latin, from ANDRO- + Greek oikion house. See also -IUM.

androgen n. a male sex hormone. WH: mid-20C. ANDRO- + -GEN.

androgyne n. a hermaphrodite. WH: 16C. French, or from Latin androgynus, from Greek androgunos, from ANDRO- + gunē woman.

android n. a robot having human form. WH: 18C. Modern Latin androides, from ANDRO- + Greek -eidēs -OID.

andromeda n. a plant of a genus of heaths, Andromeda. WH: 18C. Latin, from Greek Andromedē Andromeda, the daughter of Cepheus and Cassiope in Greek mythology, who was rescued from the sea monster by Perseus.

androsterone n. a male sex hormone occurring in the testes and in urine. WH: mid-20C. ANDRO- + -sterone, from STEROL + KETONE.

-androus suf. having male organs or stamens, as in diandrous. WH: Modern Latin -andrus, from Greek -andros, from anēr, andros man. See ANDRO-.

-ane suf. forming adjectives, as in humane, mundane, urbane. WH: Var. of -AN. The suffix usually serves to differentiate, as HUMAN/HUMANE, URBAN/URBANE.

anecdote n. a brief account of an interesting or amusing fact or incident, esp. a biographical one. WH: 17C. French, or from Modern Latin anecdota, from Greek anekdota things unpublished, neut. pl. of anekdotos, from AN-[3] + ekdotos, from ekdidōnai to publish. The original English meaning was a secret history, e.g. of the doings of a prince. The current sense prevailed from the 18C.

anechoic a. free from echoes. WH: mid-20C. AN-[3] + ECHO + -IC.

†anele v.t. to anoint with oil. WH: 11–12C. Old English an- A-[1] + Middle English elien to oil, from Old English ele, from Latin oleum oil.

anemo- comb. form wind. WH: Greek anemos wind. See also -O-.

anemograph n. an instrument which automatically records the velocity and direction of the wind. WH: 19C. ANEMO- + -GRAPH.

anemometer n. an instrument for measuring the velocity of wind, a wind gauge. WH: 18C. ANEMO- + METER.

anemone n. any of a genus of plants, Anemone, with brilliantly-coloured flowers, esp. Anemone nemorosa, sometimes called the windflower, common in Britain. WH: 16C. Latin, from Greek anemōnē, from anemos wind + -ōnē daughter of. The flower is so called because it was believed to open only when the wind blows.

anemophilous a. wind-fertilized; having the pollen carried away by the wind. WH: 19C. ANEMO- + -philous (-PHILE).

anencephaly n. a congenital defect in which part or all of the brain is missing. WH: 19C. Greek AN-[3] + egkephalos ENCEPHALON + -Y[2].

†anent prep. concerning, touching, in respect of. WH: pre-1200. Old English on efen, from on ON + efen EVEN[2]. The earlier senses in company with, facing, became obsolete from the 19C.

-aneous suf. forming adjectives, as in extraneous. WH: Latin -aneus. Cp. -EOUS, -OUS.

aneroid a. operating without liquid. Also n. WH: 19C. French anéroïde, from Greek A-[6] + nēros wet, damp. See also -OID.

aneurin n. thiamine. WH: mid-20C. ANTI- + POLYNEURITIS + VITAMIN.

aneurysm n. an abnormal dilatation in an artery, particularly of the aorta. WH: 14–15C. Greek aneurusma dilatation, from aneurunein to widen out, from AN-[2] + eurunein, from euros wide.

anew adv. again; once again. WH: 11–12C. A-[2] + NEW.

anfractuose a. winding, sinuous, tortuous. WH: 16C. Late Latin anfractuosus, from Latin anfractus a bending. See also -OUS.

angary n. the confiscation or destruction by a belligerent of neutral property, esp. shipping, subject to claim for compensation. WH: 19C. French angarie, from Italian or Late Latin angaria forced service, from Greek aggareia, from aggaros courier, from Persian.

angel n. a messenger from God. WH: pre-1200. Old English engel, from Latin angelus, from Greek aggelos messenger. The soft g comes from Old French angele.

Angeleno n. a native or inhabitant of Los Angeles, California. WH: 19C. American Spanish.

angelica n. an umbelliferous plant, Angelica archangelica, used in medicine, and as a preserve or sweet. WH: 16C. Medieval Latin, from herba angelica angelic plant. The plant is so called from its reputed power against poison and plague, and also for its sweet scent.

angelus n. a short devotional exercise in the Roman Catholic Church in honour of the Incarnation. WH: 17C. Latin, from the opening words, Angelus domini nuntiavit Mariae An angel of the Lord announced to Mary. Cp. ANGEL.

anger n. rage, fierce displeasure. Also v.t., v.i. WH: 12–14C. Old Norse angr grief, from Germanic also of German eng narrow. Rel. to ANGUISH. The original meaning was trouble, affliction. The current sense emerged from the 14C.

Angevin n. a native or inhabitant of Anjou in N central France. Also a. WH: 17C. French, from Medieval Latin Andegavinus, from Andegavum Angers, the capital of Anjou.

angina n. any disease causing inflammation or constriction of the throat, esp. quinsy. WH: 16C. Latin quinsy, from Greek agkhonē strangling, assim. to Latin angere. See ANGUISH.

angina pectoris n. a heart condition marked by paroxysms of intense pain due to over-exertion when the heart is weak or diseased. WH: 18C. Latin quinsy of the chest, from ANGINA + gen. sing. of pectus breast, chest. Cp. PECTORAL.

angio- comb. form vascular; of or relating to the vessels of organisms. WH: Greek aggeio-, from aggeion vessel. See also -O-.

angiography n. X-ray photography of the blood vessels. WH: mid-20C. ANGIO- + -GRAPHY.

angioma n. a tumour composed of blood or lymph vessels. WH: 19C. Modern Latin, from Greek aggeion vessel + -OMA.

angioplasty n. an operation undertaken to repair or unblock a blood vessel, e.g. by laser or by the insertion and inflation of a balloon. WH: early 20C. ANGIO- + -PLASTY.

angiosperm n. a plant of the class Angiospermae, that has its seed enclosed in a vessel or ovary. WH: 19C. ANGIO- + Greek *sperma* seed. Cp. SPERM.

Angle n. a member of one of the Low German tribes that settled in Northumbria, Mercia and E Anglia. WH: pre-1200. Latin *Anglus*, pl. *Angli*, from Germanic, people of *Angul* (Angeln), a district in N Germany. The district was so named from its shape, like an ANGLE[1]. Cp. ENGLISH.

angle[1] n. the inclination of two lines towards each other. Also v.t., v.i. WH: 12–14C. Old French, or from Latin *angulus* corner.

angle[2] v.i. to fish with rod and line. Also v.t. WH: 14–15C. Middle English, from ANGLE[1]. A fish hook is bent at an ANGLE[1].

Anglican a. of or belonging to the Church of England or any Church in communion with it. Also n. WH: 17C. Medieval Latin *Anglicanus*, from *Anglicus*, from Latin *Angli*. See ANGLE.

anglice adv. in English. WH: 17C. Medieval Latin, from Latin *Anglus*. See ANGLE.

Anglicism n. an English idiom. WH: 17C. Medieval Latin *Anglicus*, from *Anglus* (ANGLE) + -ISM.

Anglo n. an Anglo-American. Also a. WH: 19C. Independent use of ANGLO-.

Anglo- comb. form English; of or belonging to England or the English. WH: Latin *Anglus* (ANGLE) + -O-.

Anglo-American n. an American of English parentage or descent. Also a. WH: 18C. ANGLO- + AMERICAN.

Anglo-Catholic a. Anglican, but of Catholic not Protestant tendencies. Also n. WH: 19C. ANGLO- + CATHOLIC.

Anglocentric a. considering England as the centre or English customs, practices etc. as the norm. WH: 19C. ANGLO- + -CENTRIC.

Anglo-French a. of, relating to or between England or Britain and France. Also n. WH: 19C. ANGLO- + FRENCH.

Anglo-Indian n. an English person born, or long resident, in the Indian subcontinent. Also a. WH: 19C. ANGLO- + INDIAN.

Anglo-Irish a. of or between Britain and Ireland, esp. the Republic of Ireland. Also n. WH: 18C. ANGLO- + IRISH.

Anglomania n. excessive fondness for English manners and customs. WH: 18C. ANGLO- + -MANIA.

Anglo-Norman a. of or relating to the Normans in England after the Norman Conquest. Also n. WH: 18C. ANGLO- + NORMAN.

Anglophile n. an admirer of England or of the English. Also a. WH: 19C. ANGLO- + -PHILE.

Anglophobe n. a hater of England or of the English. WH: 19C. ANGLO- + -PHOBE.

anglophone n. a person who speaks English. Also a. WH: early 20C. ANGLO- + -PHONE.

Anglo-Saxon a. of or relating to the English people before the Norman Conquest. Also n. WH: 17C. Modern Latin *Anglo-Saxones*, from Medieval Latin *Angli Saxones*, from Old English *Angulseaxan*. See ANGLE, SAXON.

angora n. a goat with long silky hair. WH: 19C. *Angora* (Ankara), a city in Turkey.

angostura n. a febrifugal bark, used also in the preparation of bitters. WH: 18C. *Angostura* (now Ciudad Bolívar), a town in Venezuela.

angst n. a nonspecific feeling of anxiety and guilt produced esp. by considering the imperfect human condition. WH: early 20C. German *Angst*, rel. to ANGER, ANGUISH, ANXIOUS.

ångström unit n. a unit of length used to express the wavelengths of different kinds of radiations, equivalent to 1/254,000,000 in. (10^{-10} m). WH: 19C. Anders Jonas Ångström, 1814–74, Swedish physicist.

anguine a. of, relating to or resembling a snake; snaky. WH: 17C. Latin *anguinus*, from *anguis* snake. See also -INE.

anguish n. excessive pain or distress of body or mind. Also v.t. WH: pre-1200. Old French *anguis* (Modern French *angoisse*), from Latin *angustia* straits, distress, from *angustus* tight, narrow. Rel. to ANGER, ANGINA.

angular a. having angles or sharp corners. WH: 12–14C. Latin *angularis*, from *angulus* ANGLE[1]. See also -AR[1].

angwantibo n. a rare small, gold-coloured primate, *Arctocebus calabarensis*, of W central Africa, similar to the loris. WH: 19C. Efik.

anharmonic a. not harmonic. WH: 19C. AN-[3] + HARMONIC.

anhedral n. the downward angle between the wing of an aircraft and the horizontal. Also a. WH: 19C. AN-[3] + -hedral. See -HEDRON.

anhinga n. a darter, esp. the American *Anhinga anhinga*. WH: 18C. Portuguese, from Tupi *áyinga*.

anhydride n. a chemical substance formed from another, esp. an acid, by removing the elements of water. WH: 19C. AN-[3] + HYDROUS + -IDE. Cp. ANHYDROUS.

anhydrite n. a colourless, orthorhombic mineral, calcium sulphate or anhydrous gypsum. WH: 19C. AN-[3] + HYDROUS + -ITE[1].. Cp. ANHYDROUS.

anhydrous a. having no water in the composition. WH: 19C. Greek *anudros* waterless, from AN-[3] + *hudōr*, *hudr*- water. See also -OUS.

ani n. any of various S and Central American birds of the genus *Crotophaga* of the cuckoo family, that have black plumage, a curved bill and a long tail. WH: 19C. Spanish *aní*, Portuguese *anum*, from Tupi *anū*.

aniconic a. that symbolizes but does not resemble. WH: 19C. AN-[3] + *iconic* (ICON).

anil n. the indigo plant. WH: 16C. French or Portuguese, from Arabic *an-nīl*, from *an*, form of *al* the + Arabic and Persian *nīl*, from Sanskrit *nīlī* indigo, from *nīla* dark blue.

anile a. of or resembling an old woman. WH: 17C. Latin *anilis*, from *anus* old woman. See also -IL.

aniline n. a chemical base used in the production of many beautiful dyes, and orig. obtained from indigo, now chiefly from nitrobenzene. WH: 19C. ANIL + -INE.

anima n. a person's true inner self, as opposed to the *persona*. WH: early 20C. Latin air, breath, mind.

animadvert v.i. to criticize or censure (with *on* or *upon*). WH: 14–15C. Latin *animadvertere*, from *animum* mind + *advertere* ADVERT. The earliest sense was to observe, to note. The current unfavourable sense may have developed by association with Latin *adversus* against, or with ADVERSE itself.

animal n. an organized being possessing life, sensation and the power of voluntary motion. Also a. WH: 12–14C. Old French, or from Latin *animalis* having breath, from ANIMA. The earliest sense was adjectival, contrasting with VITAL and NATURAL. *Animal* functions were thus those of the brain and nervous system, *vital* those of the heart, lungs and other vital organs, *natural* those of nutrition and assimilation.

animalcule n. an animal so small as to be invisible to the naked eye. WH: 16C. Modern Latin *animalculum*, dim. of *animal*. See ANIMAL, also -CULE.

animate[1] v.t. to give life or spirit to; to enliven, to vivify. WH: 15C. Latin *animatus*, p.p. of *animare* to give life to, from ANIMA. See also -ATE[3].

animate[2] a. living, endowed with life. WH: 14–15C. Latin *animatus*, p.p. of *animare* (ANIMATE[1]). See also -ATE[2].

animateur n. a person who is the animating force behind something; a promoter, a sponsor. WH: mid-20C. French animator. See ANIMATE[1].

animatronics n. the technique of making and using lifelike, esp. animal, robots. WH: late 20C. Blend of *animated* (ANIMATE[1]) and *electronics* (ELECTRONIC).

animé n. a W Indian resin, used for varnish. WH: 16C. French, from Tupi *wana'ni*.

animism n. the attribution of a living soul to inanimate objects and to natural phenomena. WH: 19C. Latin ANIMA + -ISM.

animosity n. hostility, extreme dislike. WH: 14–15C. Old French *animosité*, or from Late Latin *animositas*, from *animosus* spirited. See ANIMUS, also -OSITY. An early sense was high spirit, courage. The current meaning developed from the 17C.

animoso adv. with spirit. WH: 18C. Italian. See ANIMUS.

animus n. animosity. WH: 19C. Latin spirit, mind.

anion n. an ion that moves towards the anode, a negatively charged ion; cp. *cation*. WH: 19C. ANODE or ANA- + ION.

anise n. an umbelliferous plant, *Pimpinella anisum*, cultivated for its aromatic seeds, which are carminative, anciently confused with the dill. WH: 12–14C. Old French *anis*, from Latin *anisum*, from Greek *anison* dill, anise.

aniso- comb. form odd, unequal, unsymmetrical. WH: Greek *anisos* unequal. Cp. AN-[3], ISO-.

anisomeric *a.* not isomeric. WH: 19C. ANISO- + Greek *meros* part. Cp. *isomeric* (ISOMER).

anisometric *a.* having unsymmetrical parts or unequal measurements. WH: 19C. ANISO- + -METRIC.

anisotropy *n.* the fact of possessing different physical properties in different directions, as with wood along and across the grain. WH: 19C. ANISO- + Greek *tropos* turn (cp. TROPE) + -Y².

ankh *n.* a cross with a loop above the crosspiece, that was in ancient Egypt the emblem of life, or male symbol of generation. WH: 19C. Egyptian life, soul.

ankle *n.* the joint by which the foot is united to the leg. *Also v.i.* WH: 12–14C. Old English *ancleow*, ult. from Indo-European base rel. to ANGLE¹.

ankus *n.* an elephant goad. WH: 19C. Hindi *ǎkus*, from Sanskrit *aṅkuśa*.

ankylosaur *n.* a member of a suborder of dinosaurs, *Ankylosauria*, which were heavily armoured, short-legged, herbivorous quadrupeds. WH: late 20C. Modern Latin *Ankylosaurus*, from Greek *agkulōsis* (ANKYLOSE) + *sauros* lizard.

ankylose *v.t.* to stiffen (a joint) by the fusion of bones or fibrous tissue. *Also v.i.* WH: 18C. Greek *agkulōsis* crooking of joints, from *agkuloun* to crook, from *agkulos* crooked.

anna *n.* a former monetary unit and coin of India, Burma and Pakistan, equal to one-sixteenth of a rupee. WH: 17C. Hindi *ānā*.

annals *n.pl.* a narrative of events arranged in years. WH: 16C. French *annales*, or from Latin *annales*, m. pl. (used as n.) of *annalis* yearly, from *annus* year. See also -AL¹.

annates *n.pl.* the first year's revenue of Roman Catholic ecclesiastics on their appointment to a benefice, paid to the Pope. WH: 16C. French, from Medieval Latin *annata* a year's proceeds, from *annus* year.

annatto *n.* an orange-red dye used to colour food, fabric etc. WH: 17C. Carib.

anneal *v.t.* to temper (glass or metals) by subjecting them to intense heat, and then allowing them to cool slowly. *Also v.i., n.* WH: pre-1200. Old English *onǣlan*, from *on* A-¹ + *ǣlan* to kindle, to burn, from *āl* fire, burning.

annelid *n.* any of the Annelida, a class of invertebrate animals with elongated bodies composed of annular segments that includes the earthworm. WH: 19C. French *annélide*, or from Modern Latin *annelida*, from French *annelés* ringed ones, from Old French *anel* ring, from Latin *anellus*, dim. of *anulus*, itself dim. of *anus*. See ANUS, also -ID.

annex *v.t.* to add on to, esp. to something larger. WH: 12–14C. Old French *annexer*, from Latin *annexus*, p.p. of *annectere*, from AN- + *nectere* to tie, to fasten.

annihilate *v.t.* to reduce to nothing, to blot out of existence, to destroy completely. *Also v.i.* WH: 16C. Late Latin *annihilatus*, p.p. of *annihilare*, from AN-¹ + *nihil* nothing. The verb superseded the earlier *annihil*. See also -ATE³.

anniversary *n.* the annual return of any remarkable date. *Also a.* WH: pre-1200. Latin *anniversarius* returning yearly, from *annus* year + *versus* turning + -*arius* -ARY¹.

Anno Domini *adv.* in the year of Our Lord (indicating a date reckoned from the beginning of the Christian era). *Also n.* WH: 16C. Latin in the year of the Lord, from abl. of *annus* year + gen. of *dominus* lord.

annotate *v.t.* to make notes or comments upon. *Also v.i.* WH: 16C. Latin *annotatus*, p.p. of *annotare*, from AN-¹ + *nota* mark. See also -ATE³. Cp. NOTE.

announce *v.t.* to make known, to proclaim. WH: 15C. French *annoncer*, from Latin *annuntiare*, from AN-¹ + *nuntiare*, from *nuntius* messenger.

annoy *v.t.* to cause to feel irritated or angry. *Also v.i., n.* WH: 12–14C. Old French *anuier*, *anoier* (Modern French *ennuyer*), from Latin *in odio*, from phr. *mihi in odio est* it is hateful to me. The verb originally had a much stronger sense, even denoting physical hurt and destruction. The current weaker meaning evolved from the 16C.

annual *a.* returning or happening every year. *Also n.* WH: 12–14C. Old French *annuel*, from Late Latin *annualis*, from Latin *annalis*, from *annus* year. See also -AL¹.

annuity *n.* a sum of money payable annually. WH: 14–15C. French *annuité*, from Medieval Latin *annuitas*, from *annuus*, from Latin *annus* year. See also -ITY.

annul *v.t.* to render void, cancel. WH: 12–14C. Old French *adnuller* (Modern French *annuler*), from Late Latin *annullare*, from AN-¹ + *nullum* nothing, neut. sing. of *nullus* NULL.

annular *a.* ring-shaped. WH: 16C. French *annulaire*, or from Latin *annularis*, from *annulus*, dim. of *anus* ring. See ANUS, also -AR¹.

annunciate *v.t.* to announce, to proclaim the approach or arrival of. WH: 14–15C. Medieval Latin *annunciatus*, from Latin *annuntiatus*, p.p. of *annuntiare*. See ANNOUNCE, also -ATE³.

annus mirabilis *n.* a remarkable year (usu. applied in English history to 1666, year of the Great Fire of London etc.). WH: 17C. Modern Latin wonderful year. Cp. ANNUAL, ADMIRABLE.

anoa *n.* a small deerlike water buffalo native to Sulawesi. WH: 19C. Sulawesi.

anode *n.* the positive electrode or pole in an electrolytic cell. WH: 19C. Greek *anodos* way up, from AN-² + *hodos* way. Cp. CATHODE.

anodyne *a.* assuaging pain. *Also n.* WH: 16C. Latin *anodynus*, from Greek *anōdunos* free from pain, from AN-³ + *odunē* pain.

anoesis *n.* a state in which consciousness of sensation is not accompanied by thought. WH: early 20C. A-⁶ + Greek *noēsis* understanding.

anoestrus *n.* a state of sexual quiescence or inactivity. WH: early 20C. AN-³ + OESTRUS.

anoint *v.t.* to smear with oil or an ointment, esp. to pour oil on as a religious ceremony. WH: 12–14C. Anglo-French, from Old French *enoint*, p.p. of *enoindre*, from Latin *inungere*, from IN-¹ + *ungere* to smear. Cp. UNGUENT.

anole *n.* any small tropical American lizard of the genus *Anolis*, esp. *A. carolinensis*, the green anole. WH: 18C. Carib.

anomalure *n.* a squirrel-like rodent of the family Anomaluridae that have tails with rough scales on the underside. WH: 19C. Modern Latin *Anomalurus*, from Greek *anōmalos* anomalous (ANOMALY) + *oura* tail.

anomaly *n.* (an) irregularity. WH: 16C. Latin *anomalia*, from Greek *anōmalia*, from *anōmalos*, from AN-³ + *homalos* even + -OUS.

anomie *n.* the breakdown or absence of moral and social standards in an individual or society. WH: mid-20C. French, from Greek *anomia*, from *anomos* lawless, from A-⁶ + *nomos* law.

anon *adv.* immediately, thereupon. WH: pre-1200. Old English *on ān* into one, from *on* ON + *ān* ONE.

anonymous *a.* nameless. WH: 16C. Late Latin *anonymus*, from Greek *anōnumos*, from AN-³ + *onuma* name + -OUS.

anopheles *n.* any of a genus of mosquitoes, *Anopheles*, that includes the malarial mosquito *A. maculipennis*. WH: 19C. Modern Latin, from Greek *anōphelēs* useless, unprofitable.

anorak *n.* a warm waterproof jacket, usu. with a hood. WH: early 20C. Eskimo (Inuit) *ánorâq*.

anorexia *n.* loss of appetite. WH: 16C. Late Latin, from Greek, from AN-³ + *orexis* appetite. See also -IA.

anorthosite *n.* a coarse-grained rock that consists almost entirely of plagioclase feldspar. WH: 19C. French *anorthose* plagioclase, anorthoclase, from AN-³ + Greek *orthos* straight + -ITE².

anosmia *n.* absence or loss of the sense of smell. WH: 19C. AN-³ + Greek *osmē* smell + -IA.

another *a.* an additional, one more. *Also pron.* WH: 11–12C. *an* A + OTHER. The word was written as two words as late as the 16C.

ANOVA *n.* a statistical procedure to divide the variations in a set of observations into particular components. WH: late 20C. Acronym of *analysis of variance*.

anovulant *n., a.* (a drug) that inhibits ovulation. WH: mid-20C. AN-³ + *ovulation* (OVULATE) + -ANT.

anoxia *n.* deficiency of oxygen to the tissues. WH: mid-20C. AN-³ + OXY-² + -IA.

ansate *a.* having a handle. WH: 19C. Latin *ansatus*, from *ansa* handle.

Anschluss *n.* the forced union of Austria with Germany in 1938. WH: early 20C. German, from *anschliessen* to join, to annex.

anserine *a.* of or belonging to the goose. WH: 19C. Latin *anserinus*, from *anser* goose. See also -INE.

answer *n.* a reply to a question. *Also v.t., v.i.* WH: pre-1200. Old English *andswaru*, from *and-* against (cp. AND) + *-swaru* affirmation, from *swerian* SWEAR.

ant *n.* a small, social, hymenopterous insect of the family Formicidae. WH: pre-1200. Old English *ǣmette*, from *ǣ-* off, away + *mette* cutter, hewer. The literal meaning is one that cuts away (i.e. leaves).

-ant *suf.* forming adjectives, as in *distant, elegant, trenchant.* WH: French, or from Latin *-ans, -antis*, pres.p. ending of vv. in *-are*, or *-ens, -entis* (see -ENT).

antacid *a.* counteracting acidity. *Also n.* WH: 18C. ANTI- + ACID.

antagonist *n.* an opponent; a person who contends or strives with another. WH: 16C. French *antagoniste*, or from Late Latin *antagonista*, from Greek *antagōnistēs* adversary, from *antagōnizesthai*, from ANTI- + *agōnizesthai* to struggle.

antalkali *n.* something that neutralizes an alkali. WH: 19C. ANTI- + ALKALI.

Antarctic *a.* of or belonging to the S Pole or the region within the Antarctic Circle. *Also n.* WH: 14–15C. Old French *antartique* (Modern French *antarctique*), from Latin *antarcticus*, from Greek *antarktikos* opposite the north. See ANTI-, ARCTIC.

ante *n.* the stake which a poker player puts down after being dealt a hand, but before drawing. *Also v.t.* WH: 19C. Latin before. See ANTE-.

ante- *pref.* before in time or position. WH: Latin pref., from prep. *ante* before.

ante-bellum *a.* existing before the war, esp. the American Civil War. WH: 19C. Latin *ante bellum* before the war, from *ante* ANTE- + acc. sing. of *bellum* war.

antecede *v.t.* to precede. WH: 15C. Latin *antecedere*, from ANTE- + *cedere* to go.

antechamber *n.* an anteroom. WH: 17C. French *antichambre*, from Italian *anticamera*. See ANTE-, CAMERA. The original spelling was *antichamber.*

antechapel *n.* the part of a chapel between the western wall and the choir screen. WH: 18C. ANTE- + CHAPEL.

antedate *n.* a date preceding the actual date. *Also v.t.* WH: 16C. ANTE- + DATE[1].

antediluvian *a.* of or relating to the period before the biblical Flood. *Also n.* WH: 17C. ANTE- + Latin *diluvium* DELUGE + -AN.

antelope *n.* an animal of the genus *Antilope*, of the family Bovidae, containing ruminants akin to the deer and the goat. WH: 14–15C. Old French *antelop*, or from Medieval Latin *antalopus*, from Medieval Greek *antholops*, of unknown origin. It was originally the name of some mythical creature or heraldic animal. The current meaning dates from the 17C.

antenatal *a.* happening or existing before birth. WH: 19C. ANTE- + NATAL[1].

antenna *n.* a sensory organ occurring in pairs on the heads of insects and crustaceans; a palp, a feeler. WH: 17C. Latin, alt. of *antemna* sailyard.

antenuptial *a.* happening before marriage. WH: 19C. ANTE- + NUPTIAL.

antependium *n.* a covering for the front of an altar, a frontal. WH: 16C. Medieval Latin, from ANTE- + Latin *pendere* to hang.

antepenult *n.* the last syllable but two. WH: 16C. Abbr. of *antepenultimate*, from ANTE- + *penultimate* (PENULT).

ante-post *a.* (of betting) done in advance of the event concerned, esp. before the runners' numbers are posted. WH: early 20C. ANTE- + POST[1].

anterior *a.* at the front, more to the front. WH: 16C. French *antérieur*, or from Latin *anterior*, comp. of *ante* before. See ANTE-, also -IOR.

antero- *comb. form* front, in front, used in the formation of technical adjectives and adverbs. WH: Latin, comb. form of ANTERIOR. See also -O-.

anterograde amnesia *n.* loss of memory of events subsequent to a trauma causing brain damage, while the memory of previous events remains relatively unimpaired. WH: 19C. ANTERO- + -GRADE. See AMNESIA.

anteroom *n.* a room leading into or forming an entrance to another. WH: 18C. ANTE- + ROOM. The word is based on ANTECHAMBER.

anthelion *n.* a mock sun, a luminous ring projected on a cloud or fog bank opposite the sun. WH: 18C. Greek *anthēlion*, neut. of *anthēlios* opposite the sun, from *anth-*, var. of ANTE-, + *hēlios* sun.

anthelmintic *a.* destroying or remedial against parasitic, esp. intestinal, worms. *Also n.* WH: 17C. *anth-*, var. of ANTE-, + Greek *helmins, helminthos* worm + -IC.

anthem *n.* a portion of Scripture or of the Liturgy set to music, often in an elaborate choral setting. WH: pre-1200. Old English *antemn*, from Ecclesiastical Latin *antiphona* ANTIPHON. The spelling with *th* dates from the 15C. The anthem was originally a church chant alternating between priest and choir or between two choirs. The sense of religious song or hymn prevailed from the 16C.

anthemion *n.* a palmette, honeysuckle or conventional leaf or floral design. WH: 19C. Greek *flower*.

anther *n.* the pollen-bearing organ of flowering plants. WH: 16C. French *anthère*, or from Modern Latin *anthera*, from Greek *anthēra*, fem. of *antherōs*, a. from *anthos* flower.

antheridium *n.* the male spore-bearing organ, analogous to an anther, of cryptogams. WH: 19C. Modern Latin ANTHER + -*idium*, var. of -IUM.

antherozoid *n.* a motile male gamete produced in an antheridium. WH: 19C. ANTHER + -O- + -*zoid*. See ZOO-, also -ID.

anthocyanin *n.* any of a class of scarlet to blue plant pigments. WH: 19C. German *Anthocyan*, from Greek *antho-*, comb. form of *anthos* flower + *kuanos* blue. See also -IN[1].

anthology *n.* any collection of selected poems or other literary pieces. WH: 17C. French *anthologie*, or from Medieval Latin *anthologia*, from Greek *anthos* flower. See -LOGY. The original sense was a collection of flowers of verse, especially Greek selections of this type. The sense then passed to any literary collection or selection and even to other art forms.

Anthony *n.* the smallest in a litter of pigs. WH: 14–15C. *Anthony*, patron saint of swineherds, to whom one of a litter was dedicated. Cp. *tantony* in the same sense, from *Saint Anthony*.

anthozoan *n.* any of a class, Anthozoa or Actinozoa, of radiated animals containing the sea anemones and coral polyps. WH: 19C. Modern Latin *Anthozoa*, from Greek *anthos* flower + *zōia* animals (cp. ZOO-) + -AN.

anthracene *n.* a crystalline substance with blue fluorescence obtained from tar, used in the manufacture of chemicals. WH: 19C. Greek *anthrax, anthrakos* coal (cp. ANTHRACITE) + -ENE.

anthracite *n.* a non-bituminous coal, burning with intense heat, without smoke, and with little flame. WH: 16C. Greek *anthrakitēs*, from *anthrax, anthrakos* coal + -ITE[1].

anthracnose *n.* a fungal disease of plants that causes dark, sunken spots to appear. WH: 19C. French, from Greek *anthrax, anthrakos* coal + *nosos* disease.

anthracosis *n.* a lung disease caused by the inhalation of coal dust. WH: 19C. Greek *anthrax, anthrakos* coal + -OSIS.

anthrax *n.* an infectious, often fatal bacterial disease of sheep and cattle transmissible to humans. WH: 12–14C. Latin carbuncle, from Greek *anthrax, anthrakos* coal. The word was originally used of a boil that burnt like a coal.

anthropic *a.* of or relating to human beings. WH: 19C. Greek *anthrōpikos*. See ANTHROPO-, also -IC.

anthropo- *comb. form* human. WH: Greek *anthrōpos* human being. See also -O-.

anthropocentric *a.* centring on human beings. WH: 19C. ANTHROPO- + -CENTRIC.

anthropogeny *n.* the science or study of the origin of human beings. WH: 19C. ANTHROPO- + -GENY.

anthropogeography *n.* the geography of the distribution of the races of mankind. WH: 19C. ANTHROPO- + GEOGRAPHY.

anthropoid *a.* resembling human beings, of human form. *Also n.* WH: 19C. ANTHROPO- + -OID.

anthropology *n.* the study of human beings, esp. in regard to the customs, societies, rituals etc. they have evolved. WH: 16C. ANTHROPO- + -LOGY.

anthropometry *n.* the scientific measurement of the human body. WH: 19C. ANTHROPO- + -METRY.

anthropomorphic *a.* possessed of a form resembling that of a human being. WH: 19C. ANTHROPO- + -*morphic* (-MORPH).

anthropophagous *a.* feeding on human flesh, cannibal. WH: 19C. Latin *anthropophagus*, from Greek *anthrōpophagos*. See ANTHROPO-, -PHAGOUS.

anthropophyte *n.* a plant accidentally introduced into an area during cultivation of another species. WH: 19C. ANTHROPO- + -PHYTE.

anthroposophy *n.* a system of esoteric philosophy enunciated by Rudolf Steiner (1861–1925), who defined it as 'the knowledge of the spiritual human being ... and of everything which the spirit man can perceive in the spiritual world'. WH: early 20C. ANTHROPO- + Greek *sophia* wisdom. Its earlier sense in the 19C was 'knowledge of the nature of man'.

anti *prep.* opposed to. *Also n.* WH: 18C. Greek opposite. See ANTI-.

anti- *pref.* forming nouns and adjectives indicating opposition to something, as in *anti-apartheid*; the prevention of something, as in *antibody*; the opposite of something, as in *antithesis*; a rival, as in *Antichrist*; something that is unlike the conventional form, as in *anti-hero*. WH: Greek pref., from prep. *anti* opposite, against.

antiar *n.* the upas tree. WH: 19C. Javanese *antjar*.

antibody *n.* a substance produced in the blood in response to the presence of an antigen and capable of counteracting toxins. WH: early 20C. ANTI- + BODY, translating German *Antikörper*.

antic *n.* ridiculous or troublesome behaviour. *Also a., v.t., v.i.* WH: 16C. Italian *antico* ancient, from Latin *antiquus*, *anticus* ANTIQUE. Rel. to ANCIENT[1]. The word was originally used as an equivalent of Italian *grottesco* GROTESQUE, i.e. in the sense fantastic figure. The meaning then passed to a grotesque pageant or theatrical display. Its use in the singular was mainly obsolete by the 17C.

Antichrist *n.* a personal antagonist of Christ spoken of in the New Testament. WH: pre-1200. Old French *antecrist* (Modern French *antéchrist*), or from Ecclesiastical Latin *antichristus*, from Greek *antikhristos*. See ANTI-, CHRIST. The word's original occurrence was in the Greek New Testament (I John ii.18).

anticipate *v.t.* to foresee. *Also v.i.* WH: 16C. Latin *anticipatus*, p.p. of *anticipare*, from ANTE- + *cip-*, var. base of *capere* to take. See also -ATE[3].

anticlinal *a.* forming a ridge so that the strata lean against each other in opposite directions. *Also n.* WH: 19C. ANTI- + Greek *klinein* to lean, to slope + -AL[1].

antidote *n.* a medicine designed to counteract poison or disease. WH: 14–15C. French, or from Latin *antidotum*, from Greek *antidoton*, use as n. of neut. of *antidotos*, from ANTI- + *do-*, stem of *didonai* to give.

antidromic *a.* (of a nerve impulse) moving in the opposite direction to normal in the nerve fibre. WH: early 20C. ANTI- + Greek *dromos* running (cp. -DROME) + -IC.

antigen *n.* a substance introduced into the body which stimulates the production of antibodies. WH: early 20C. German, from French *antigène*. See ANTI-, -GEN.

antihelix *n.* the curved elevation within the helix of the ear. WH: 18C. Var. of *anthelix*. See ANTI-, HELIX.

antilogy *n.* contradiction in terms or in ideas. WH: 17C. French *antilogie*, from Greek *antilogia*, from ANTI- + -logia -LOGY.

antimony *n.* a bright bluish-white brittle metallic element, at. no. 51, chem. symbol Sb, occurring naturally and used esp. in the manufacture of alloys and semiconductors. WH: 14–15C. Medieval Latin *antimonium*, of unknown orig. The name is said to come from an Arabic word such as *'oṭmud*, itself perhaps from Greek *stimmis* eye powder. It is popularly derived from Greek *anti* ANTI- + French *moine* MONK, against the monks, i.e. 'monk's bane'.

antinomian *a.* opposed to the moral law. *Also n.* WH: 17C. Medieval Latin *Antinomi*, name of sect (see ANTINOMY) + -AN.

antinomy *n.* a contradiction between two laws. WH: 16C. Latin *antinomia*, from Greek, from ANTI- + *nomos* law. See also -Y[2].

antipasto *n.* an hors d'oeuvre. WH: 17C. Italian, from ANTE- + Latin *pasto* food. The word was not generally current until the mid-20C.

antipathic *a.* of contrary character or disposition. WH: 19C. ANTI-PATHY + -IC.

antipathy *n.* hostile feeling towards; aversion. WH: 16C. French *antipathie*, or from Latin *antipathia*, from Greek *antipatheia*, from *antipathēs* opposed in feeling. See ANTI-, -PATHY.

antiphon *n.* a sentence sung by one choir in response to another.

WH: 14–15C. Ecclesiastical Latin *antiphona*, fem. sing. from Greek neut. pl. of *antiphōnos* responsive, from ANTI- + *phōnē* sound. Cp. -PHONE.

antiphrasis *n.* the use of words in a sense contrary to their ordinary meaning. WH: 18C. Late Latin, from Greek, from *antiphrazein* to express by the opposite, from ANTI- + *phrazein* to declare, to tell. Cp. PHRASE.

antipodes *n.pl.* a place on the surface of the globe diametrically opposite to another. WH: 12–14C. French, or from Late Latin, from Greek, pl. of *antipous* with feet opposite, from ANTI- + *pous*, *podos* foot. The Antipodes are virtually opposite Britain geographically. The word originally applied to the inhabitants of the antipodes, rather than the place itself. The current sense prevailed from the 16C.

antiquary *n.* a student, investigator, collector or seller of antiquities or antiques. WH: 16C. Latin *antiquarius*, from *antiquus* ANTIQUE. See also -ARY[1].

antiquated *a.* old-fashioned, out of date. WH: 16C. Latin *antiquatus*, p.p. of *antiquare* to make old, from *antiquus* ANTIQUE + -ED.

antique *a.* ancient, that has been in existence for a long time. *Also n., v.t.* WH: 15C. French, or from Latin *antiquus*, *anticus*. See ANTE-. Cp. ANTIC.

antiquity *n.* the state of being ancient, great age. WH: 12–14C. Old French *antiquité*, from Latin *antiquitas*, from *antiquus* ANTIQUE. See also -ITY.

antirrhinum *n.* any plant of a genus, *Antirrhinum*, that includes the snapdragon. WH: 16C. Latin, from Greek *antirrhinos*, from *anti-* (ANTI-) counterfeiting + *rhis*, *rhinos* nose. The flowers resemble an animal's mouth.

antistrophe *n.* the return movement from left to right of a Greek chorus, answering the movement of a strophe. WH: 16C. Late Latin, from Greek *antistrophē*, from *antistrephein* to turn against. See ANTI-, STROPHE.

antithesis *n.* the direct opposite. WH: 14–15C. Late Latin, from Greek, from *antitithenai*, from ANTI- + *tithenai* to set, to place. Cp. THESIS.

antitype *n.* the thing or person that is represented by a type or symbol. WH: 17C. Late Latin *antitypus*, from Greek *antitupos*, from ANTI- + *tupos* TYPE.

antivenin *n.* serum obtained from animals immunized against snake venom, used as an antidote against snake-bite. WH: early 20C. ANTI- + VENIN.

antler *n.* a branch of the horns of a stag or other deer. WH: 12–14C. Anglo-French var. of Old French *antoillier* (Modern French *andouiller*), of uncertain orig. The word may derive from Late Latin *antocularis*, from ANTE- + *ocularis* of the eyes (cp. OCULAR), referring to the position of the horns on the head.

Antonine *a.* of or relating to the Roman emperors Antoninus Pius (reigned AD 138–161) and Marcus Aurelius Antoninus (reigned AD 160–80). *Also n.* WH: 16C. Latin *Antoninus*, from *Antonius* Anthony. See also -INE.

antonomasia *n.* the substitution of an epithet for a proper name, e.g. *the Corsican* for Napoleon. WH: 16C. Latin, from Greek, from *antonomazein*, to name instead, from ANTI- + *onoma* name. See also -IA.

antonym *n.* a term expressing the reverse of some other term, as 'good' to 'bad'. WH: 19C. French *antonyme*, from ANTI- + Greek *onuma* name. See -ONYM.

antre *n.* a cavern or cave. WH: 17C. Latin ANTRUM.

antrum *n.* a natural anatomical cavity, particularly one in bone. WH: 19C. Latin, from Greek *antron* cave.

anuran *n.* any tailless amphibian vertebrate of the order Anura which includes the frogs and toads. *Also a.* WH: 19C. Modern Latin *Anura*, from Greek AN-[3] + *oura* tail. See also -AN.

anuria *n.* inability to secrete urine, usu. due to kidney disorder. WH: 19C. Greek AN-[3] + -URIA.

anus *n.* the lower, excretory opening of the intestinal tube. WH: 14–15C. Latin ring.

anvil *n.* the iron block, usu. with a flat top, concave sides and a point at one end, on which smiths hammer and shape their work. *Also v.t., v.i.* WH: pre-1200. Old English *anfilte*, from *an-* ON + *-filte* something beaten. Rel. to FELT.

anxious *a.* troubled or fearful about some uncertain or future event. WH: 17C. Latin *anxius*, from *anxus*, p.p. of *angere* to choke, to oppress. See ANGUISH, also -IOUS.

any *a., pron.* one, unspecified, among several. *Also adv.* WH: pre-1200. Old English *ænig*, from *ān* ONE + -*ig* -Y[1].

Anzac *n.* a soldier in the Australian or New Zealand forces, in the war of 1914–18. WH: early 20C. Acronym of *Australian and New Zealand Army Corps*.

Anzus *n.* a pact for the security of the Pacific, formed in 1952 by Australia, New Zealand and the US. WH: mid-20C. Acronym of *Australia, New Zealand, United States*.

A-OK *a.* in good or perfect working order. WH: mid-20C. Abbr. of *all systems OK*. See OK.

aorist *n.* a Greek tense expressing indefinite past time. *Also a.* WH: 16C. Greek *aoristos* (*khronos*) indefinite (time), from A-[6] + *horistos* delimited, from *horizein* to define. Cp. HORIZON.

aorta *n.* the largest artery in the body. WH: 16C. Greek *aortē*, from base of *aeirein* to raise. Cp. ARTERY.

à outrance *adv.* to the end. WH: 17C. French, from *à* to + *outrance* going beyond bounds, from Old French *outrer* to pass beyond, from *outre*. See OUTRAGE, also -ANCE. Cp. OUTRÉ.

ap- *pref.* signifying motion towards, direction to, adherence etc., as in *appear, apply*. WH: Latin pref., from AD- with *d* assim. to *p*.

apace *adv.* at a quick pace, speedily, fast. WH: 14–15C. Old French *à pas* to the step. See AD-, PACE[1]. The original sense was step by step, at a walking pace.

Apache *n.* a member of a N American Indian people of the SW US and N Mexico. *Also a.* WH: 18C. Mexican Spanish, prob. from Zuñi *Ápachu* enemy.

apanage *n.* lands or an office assigned for the maintenance of a member of a royal house, esp. a younger son. WH: 17C. Old French *apanage*, from *apaner* to nourish, to dower (a daughter), from Medieval Latin *appanare* to provide with means of sustenance, from Latin AP- + *panis* bread. See also -AGE.

apart *adv.* parted, at a distance from one another. WH: 14–15C. Old French (Modern French *à part*), from Latin *a parte* at the side. See AD-, PART.

apartheid *n.* (a policy of) racial segregation. WH: mid-20C. Afrikaans separateness, from Dutch *apart* APART + -*heid* -HOOD.

apartment *n.* a suite of rooms, lodgings. WH: 17C. French *appartement*, from Italian *appartamento*, from *appartare* to separate, from *a parte* APART. See also -MENT.

apatetic *a.* (of an animal's coloration) closely resembling that of another species or of its surroundings. WH: 19C. Greek *apatētikos* fallacious, from *apatan* to cheat, to trick. See also -IC. Cp. APATITE.

apathy *n.* absence of feeling or passion. WH: 17C. French *apathie*, from Latin *apathia*, from Greek *apatheia*, from *apathēs* without feeling. See A-[6], -PATHY.

apatite *n.* a common mineral, consisting of calcium phosphate in combination with other elements, esp. fluorine, that is used in the making of fertilizers. WH: 19C. Greek *apatē* deceit + -ITE[1]. The mineral is so called from its resemblance to other minerals.

apatosaurus *n.* a very large herbivorous dinosaur of the genus *Apatosaurus*, formerly *Brontosaurus*, having a long neck and tail, a small head and trunklike legs. WH: 19C. Greek *apatē* deceit + *sauros* lizard. The dinosaur is so called from the deceptive similarity between some of its bones and those of certain other fossil reptiles.

ape *n.* a tailless primate, esp. one of the Pongidae (a gorilla, chimpanzee, orang-utan or gibbon). *Also v.t.* WH: pre-1200. Old English *apa*, from Germanic, of unknown orig.

apeak *adv., a., pred.* in a vertical or nearly vertical position; pointed upwards. WH: 16C. French *à pic* to the top. See AD-, PEAK[1].

aperçu *n.* a concise exposition, an outline, a brief summary. WH: 19C. French, p.p. of *apercevoir* to perceive.

aperient *a.* laxative, purgative, deobstruent. *Also n.* WH: 17C. Latin *aperiens, aperientis*, pres.p. of *aperire* to open. See also -ENT. Cp. APERITIF.

aperiodic *a.* not occurring regularly. *Also n.* WH: 19C. A-[6] + PERIOD + -IC.

aperitif *n.* a short drink, usu. alcoholic, taken as an appetizer. WH: 19C. French *apéritif*, from Medieval Latin *aperitivus*, var. of Late Latin *apertivus*, from *apertus*, p.p. of *aperire* to open. An aperitif is regarded as opening the digestive processes.

aperture *n.* an opening, a hole. WH: 14–15C. Latin *apertura*, from *apertus*, p.p. of *aperire* to open. See also -URE.

apetalous *a.* without petals. WH: 18C. Greek *apetalos* leafless. See A-[6], PETAL, also -OUS.

APEX[1] *abbr.* Association of Professional, Executive, Clerical and Computer Staff. WH: Acronym of *Association of Professional, Executive, Clerical and Computer Staff* or of *Association of Professional, Executive, Clerical and Computer Staff*.

APEX[2] *n.* a discounted fare on some air, sea and rail journeys paid for no later than a specified number of days before departure. WH: late 20C. Acronym of *advance-purchase excursion*.

apex *n.* the top or summit of anything. WH: 17C. Latin tip, top.

apfelstrudel *n.* a dessert of Austrian origin consisting of flaky pastry filled with a spiced apple mixture. WH: mid-20C. German, from *Apfel* apple + STRUDEL.

aphaeresis *n.* the taking away of a letter or syllable at the beginning of a word. WH: 16C. Late Latin, from Greek *aphairesis*, from *aphairein* to take away, from *aph*-, var. of APO-, + *hairein* to take.

aphagia *n.* inability or unwillingness to swallow. WH: 19C. Greek, from A-[6] + *phagein* to swallow. See also -IA.

aphasia *n.* (partial) loss of the power to express or understand anything in words. WH: 19C. Greek, from *aphatos* speechless, from A-[6] + *phanai* to speak. See also -IA.

aphelion *n.* the point most distant from the sun in the orbit of a planet or a comet. WH: 17C. Greek form of Modern Latin *aphelium*, from Greek *aph*-, var. of APO-, + *hēlios* sun. The word is based on Latin *apogaeum* APOGEE.

apheliotropic *a.* bending or turning away from the sun. WH: 19C. Greek *aph*-, var. of APO-, + *hēlios* sun + -*tropic* (-TROPE). Cp. HELIOTROPE.

aphesis *n.* a form of aphaeresis, in which an unaccented vowel at the beginning of a word is lost. WH: 19C. Greek letting go, from *aphienai*, from *aph*-, var. of APO-, + *hienai* to let go. The term was coined in 1880 by Sir James Murray, editor of the *Oxford English Dictionary*.

aphid *n.* any of a family of minute insects, Aphididae, which are very destructive to vegetation, comprising among others the greenfly, black fly, American blight etc. WH: 19C. Back-formation from *aphides*, pl. of APHIS.

aphis *n.* an aphid, esp. of the genus *Aphis*. WH: 18C. Modern Latin, from Greek, of uncertain orig. The term was coined or first applied by Linnaeus, perhaps based on Greek *koris* bug.

aphonia *n.* inability to speak or loss of voice caused by disease of the vocal tract. WH: 17C. Greek *aphōnia* speechlessness, from A-[6] + *phōnē* voice. Cp. -PHONE.

aphorism *n.* a pithy sentence, containing a maxim or wise precept. WH: 16C. French *aphorisme*, from Late Latin *aphorismus*, from Greek *aphorismos* definition, from *aphorizein* to define, from *aph*-, var. of APO-, + *horizein* to set bounds to. Cp. HORIZON.

aphrodisiac *a.* exciting sexual desire. *Also n.* WH: 18C. Greek *aphrodisiakos*, from *aphrodisios*, from *Aphroditē*, the Greek goddess of love, corresponding to the Roman Venus. See also -AC. Cp. VENEREAL.

aphthae *n.pl.* the minute specks seen in the mouth and tongue in thrush. WH: 17C. Latin, pl. of *aphtha*, from Greek, rel. to *haptein* to set on fire. The term was originally applied to ulcers associated with thrush.

aphyllous *a.* without leaves. WH: 19C. Greek *aphullos*, from A-[6] + *phullon* leaf. See also -OUS.

apian *a.* of or relating to bees. WH: 19C. Latin *apianus*, from *apis* bee. See also -AN.

apiarian *a.* relating to bees or bee-keeping. *Also n.* WH: 19C. Latin, from *apiarium* apiary, from *apis* bee. See also -AN.

apiculate *a.* terminating abruptly in a little sharp point. WH: 19C. Modern Latin *apiculus*, dim. of APEX + -ATE[2].

apiculture *n.* bee-keeping; bee-rearing. WH: 19C. Latin *apis* bee + CULTURE.

apiece *adv.* for or to each, severally. WH: 14–15C. A-[1] + PIECE.

APL *n.* a computer programming language designed for mathematical applications. WH: Abbr. of *a programming language*.

aplanatic *a.* (of a lens etc.) free from spherical aberration. WH: 18C. Greek *aplanētos* free from error, from A-⁶ + *planan* to wander + -IC.

aplasia *n.* defective or arrested development in a body tissue or organ. WH: 19C. A-⁶ + -PLASIA.

aplenty *adv.* in plenty, in abundance. WH: 19C. A-¹ + PLENTY.

aplomb *n.* self-possession, coolness. WH: 18C. French *à plomb* according to the plummet. Cp. PLUMB¹.

apnoea *n.* a breakdown or cessation of breathing. WH: 18C. Modern Latin, from Greek *apnoia*, from *apnous* breathless, from A-⁶ + *pnoia* breath. See also -IA.

apo- *pref.* away, detached, separate, as in *apology*, *apostrophe*. WH: Greek pref., from prep. *apo* off, from, away.

apocalypse *n.* any revelation or prophetic disclosure, esp. relating to the end of the world. WH: pre-1200. Old French, from Ecclesiastical Latin *apocalypsis*, from Greek *apokalupsis*, from *apokaluptein* to uncover, from APO- + *kaluptein* to cover.

apocarpous *a.* having the carpels wholly or partly distinct. WH: 19C. APO- + Greek *karpos* fruit + -OUS.

apochromat *n.* a lens that reduces chromatic aberrations. WH: early 20C. APO- + CHROMATIC.

apocope *n.* a cutting off or dropping of the last letter or syllable of a word. WH: 16C. Late Latin, from Greek *apokopē*, from *apokoptein* to cut off, from APO- + *koptein* to cut.

apocrine *a.* (of a gland) whose secretions include parts of the cells of the gland. WH: early 20C. APO- + Greek *krinein* to separate.

apocrypha *n.pl.* writings or statements of doubtful authority. WH: 14–15C. Ecclesiastical Latin, neut. pl. of *apocryphus*, from Greek *apokruphos* hidden, from *apokruptein* to hide. See APO-. The term was originally applied to any works of uncertain authorship. Its application to non-canonical Old Testament books dates from the 16C.

apod *n.* a footless creature, a bird, fish or reptile in which the feet or corresponding members are absent or undeveloped. WH: 19C. Greek *apous*, *apodos* without feet, from A-⁶ + *pous*, *podos* foot.

apodictic *a.* clearly demonstrative. WH: 17C. Latin *apodictus*, from Greek *apodeiktos*, from *apodeiknunai* to demonstrate, from APO- + *deiknunai* to show.

apodosis *n.* the consequent clause in a conditional sentence, answering to the protasis. WH: 17C. Late Latin, from Greek, from *apodidonai* to give back, from APO- + *didonai* to give.

apodyterium *n.* the apartment in ancient baths or palaestras where clothes were taken off. WH: 17C. Latin, from Greek *apoduterion*, from *apoduein* to strip, from APO- + -*duein* to put, to dress.

apogamy *n.* the absence of sexual reproductive power, the plant perpetuating itself from an unfertilized female cell. WH: 19C. APO- + -GAMY.

apogee *n.* the point in the orbit of the moon or any planet or satellite which is at the greatest distance from the earth. WH: 16C. French *apogée*, or from Modern Latin *apogeum*, from Greek *apogaion*, neut. (used as n.) of *apogaios* far from the earth, from APO- + *gaia*, *gē* earth.

apolitical *a.* uninterested in political affairs, politically neutral. WH: mid-20C. A-⁶ + POLITICAL.

Apollinaris *n.* an effervescent mineral water from a spring in the Ahr valley. WH: 19C. *Apollinarisburg*, a place near Bonn, W Germany. Cp. POLLY¹. The place itself is named for St *Apollinaris*.

Apollonian *a.* of or relating to Apollo. WH: 17C. Latin *Apollonius*, from Greek *Apollōnios* of Apollo, the Greek and Roman god of the sun, music and poetry. See also -IAN.

apologetic *a.* regretfully acknowledging or excusing an offence. WH: 14–15C. French *apologétique*, or from Late Latin *apologeticus*, from Greek *apologētikos* fit for defence, from *apologisthai*. See APOLOGY, also -IC.

apologia *n.* a vindication or formal defence of one's conduct, views etc. WH: 18C. Latin. See APOLOGY.

apologue *n.* a fable designed to impress some moral truth upon the mind, esp. a beast-fable or a fable of inanimate things. WH: 16C. French, or from Late Latin *apologus*, from Greek *apologos* story, from APO- + *logos* discourse. See also -LOGUE.

apology *n.* a regretful acknowledgement of offence. WH: 16C. French *apologie*, or from Late Latin *apologia*, from Greek speech in defence, from *apologeisthai* to speak in one's defence, from APO- + *legein* to speak.

apolune *n.* the point in a body's lunar orbit where it is furthest from the moon. WH: mid-20C. APO- + Latin *luna* moon.

apomixis *n.* reproduction without fertilization. WH: early 20C. APO- + Greek *mixis* mingling.

apophthegm *n.* a terse pointed saying, a maxim expressed in few but weighty words. WH: 16C. French *apophthegme*, or from Modern Latin *apophthegma*, from Greek, from *apophtheggesthai* to speak one's opinion, from APO- + *phtheggesthai* to speak.

apoplexy *n.* a sudden loss of sensation and of power of motion, generally caused by rupture or obstruction of a blood vessel in the brain, a stroke. WH: 14–15C. Old French *apoplexie*, from Late Latin *apoplexia*, from Greek *apoplēxia*, from *apoplēssein* to disable by a stroke, from APO- + *plēssein* to strike.

apoptosis *n.* the death of cells as part of the normal growth and development of an organism. WH: 19C. Greek *apoptōsis* falling away, from APO- + PTOSIS.

aporia *n.* in rhetoric, a real or affected doubt about what to do. WH: 16C. Late Latin, from Greek, from *aporos* impassable, from A-⁶ + *poros* passage. See also -IA.

aport *adv.* on or towards the port side of a ship. WH: 16C. A-¹ + PORT⁴.

aposematic *a.* (of the colouring of some animals) providing protection against predators. WH: 19C. APO- + SEMATIC.

aposiopesis *n.* a stopping short for rhetorical effect. WH: 16C. Latin, from Greek *aposiōpēsis*, from *aposiōpaein* to be silent, from APO- + *siōpaein* to be silent.

apositic *a.* causing aversion to food. WH: 19C. Greek *apositikos*, from *apositos* without appetite, from APO- + *sitos* food.

apostasy *n.* (a) renunciation of religious faith, moral allegiance or political principles. WH: 14–15C. Ecclesiastical Latin *apostasia*, from Late Greek alt. of *apostasis* defection, from APO- + *stasis* a standing. See also -Y².

apostate *n.* a person who commits apostasy. *Also a.* WH: 12–14C. Old French, from Ecclesiastical Latin *apostata*, from Late Greek *apostatēs* runaway slave, from APO- + *stat-*, rel. to *histanai* to cause to stand.

a posteriori *a.*, *adv.* reasoning from consequences, effects, things observed to causes; inductive, as opposed to *a priori* or *deductive*. WH: 17C. Latin from what comes after. Cp. POSTERIOR. The opposite is A PRIORI.

apostil *n.* a marginal note, gloss, annotation. WH: 16C. Old French, from *apostiller*, ? from Latin *post illa verba* after those words.

apostle *n.* any one of the twelve men appointed by Christ to preach the gospel. WH: pre-1200. Ecclesiastical Latin *apostolus*, from Greek *apostolos* messenger, from *apostellein* to send forth, from APO- + *stellein* to send.

apostrophe¹ *n.* the sign (') used to denote the omission of a letter or letters, and as the sign of the English possessive case. WH: 16C. French, or from Late Latin *apostrophus*, from Greek *apostrophos* mark of elision, use as n. of a., turned away. See APOSTROPHE².

apostrophe² *n.* a rhetorical figure in which the speaker addresses one person in particular, or turns away from those present to address the absent or dead. WH: 16C. Latin, from Greek *apostrophē*, from *apostrephein* to turn away, from APO- + *strephein* to turn.

apothecary *n.* a person who prepares and sells medicines, a druggist or pharmaceutical chemist. WH: 12–14C. Old French *apotecaire* (Modern French *apothicaire*), from Late Latin *apothecarius* storekeeper, from *apotheca*, from Greek *apothēkē* storehouse. See also -ARY¹. Cp. BOUTIQUE. The word was originally used of a seller of general merchandise. The narrower sense of medical practitioner dates from the 17C.

apothecium *n.* the spore-case in lichens. WH: 19C. Modern Latin, from Greek *apothēkē*. See APOTHECARY, also -IUM.

apotheosis *n.* deification, transformation into a god. WH: 16C. Ecclesiastical Latin, from Greek *apotheōsis*, from *apotheoun* to deify, from APO- + *theos* god.

apotropaic *a.* intended or supposed to avert evil influences. WH: 19C. Greek *apotropaios* averting evil, from *apotrepein* to turn away, from APO- + *trepein* to turn. See also -IC.

appal *v.i.* to grow pale, to grow faint or feeble. *Also v.t.* WH: 12–14C. Old French *appalir*, from *a-* (AD-) + *palir* (Modern French *pâlir*) PALE¹. The original sense was to grow pale, to make pale. The current sense prevailed from the 16C.

Appaloosa *n.* a N American breed of horse with a spotted coat. WH: early 20C. Prob. from *Palouse*, a river in Idaho, USA.

apparat *n.* the party organization of the Communist party in the former Soviet Union and similar states. WH: mid-20C. Russian, from German APPARATUS.

apparatus *n.* equipment generally. WH: 17C. Latin from *apparare* to make ready, from AP- + *parare* PREPARE.

apparel *n.* clothes. *Also v.t.* WH: 12–14C. Old French *apareil* (Modern French *appareil*), ult. from Latin AP- + dim. of *par* equal. Cp. PAR[1].

apparent *a.* to be seen, visible, in sight. WH: 12–14C. Old French *apparant* (Modern French *apparent*), from Latin *apparens, apparentis*, pres.p. of *apparere* APPEAR. See also -ENT.

apparition *n.* the fact of appearing or becoming visible, esp. suddenly or strangely. WH: 14–15C. Old French, from Latin *apparitio, apparitionis* attendance, from *apparitus*, p.p. of *apparere* APPEAR. See also -ITION.

apparitor *n.* an officer in a civil or ecclesiastical court who summons witnesses to appear. WH: 12–14C. Latin public servant, from *apparitus*. See APPARITION, also -OR.

appeal *v.i.* to make an earnest request (for). *Also v.t., n.* WH: 12–14C. Old French *apeler* to call (Modern French *appeler*), from Latin *appellare* to accuse, to impeach, from AP- + *pell-*, stem of *pellere* to drive.

appear *v.i.* to become or be visible. WH: 12–14C. Old French *apareir* (Modern French *apparoir*), from Latin *apparere*, from AP- + *parere* to come into view.

appease *v.t.* to pacify, to calm. WH: 12–14C. Anglo-French *apeser*, from Old French *apaisier* (Modern French *apaiser*), from *a-* (AD-) + *pais* PEACE.

appellant *a.* appealing, challenging. *Also n.* WH: 14–15C. Old French *apelant*, pres.p. of *apeler* APPEAL. See also -ANT.

appellation contrôlée *n.* a guarantee, in the labelling of some French wines and foodstuffs, that the product conforms to statutory regulations in respect of its origin, quality, strength etc. WH: mid-20C. French controlled appellation. See APPEAL, CONTROL.

append *v.t.* to add or subjoin. WH: 14–15C. Latin *appendere* to hang to, from AP- + *pendere* to hang.

appendectomy *n.* the excision of the vermiform appendix. WH: 19C. Latin *appendix, appendicis* APPENDIX + -ECTOMY.

appendicitis *n.* inflammation of the vermiform appendix. WH: 19C. Latin *appendix, appendicis* APPENDIX + -ITIS.

appendicle *n.* a small appendage. WH: 17C. Latin *appendicula*, dim. of *appendix, appendicis* APPENDIX. See also -CULE.

appendix *n.* a supplement to a book or document containing useful material. WH: 16C. Latin *appendix, appendicis*, from *appendere* APPEND.

apperceive *v.t.* to be conscious of perceiving. WH: 12–14C. Old French *aperceveir* (Modern French *apercevoir*), ult. from Latin AP- + *percipere* PERCEIVE.

appertain *v.i.* to relate (to). WH: 12–14C. Old French *apartenir* (Modern French *appartenir*), from Popular Latin *appartenere*, var. of Late Latin *appertinere*, from AP- + *pertinere* PERTAIN.

appetence *n.* instinctive desire, craving, appetite. WH: 17C. French *appétence*, or from Latin *appetentia* longing after, from *appetere*. See APPETITE, also -ENCE.

appetite *n.* desire for food. WH: 12–14C. Old French *apetit* (Modern French *appétit*), from Latin *appetitus* desire towards, from p.p of *appetere* to seek after, from AP- + *petere* to seek.

applaud *v.i.* to express approbation, esp. by clapping the hands. *Also v.t.* WH: 15C. Partly from Latin *applaudere*, from AP- + *plaudere* to clap, partly from French *applaudir*. Cp. PLAUDIT.

apple *n.* the round, firm, fleshy fruit of the apple tree. WH: pre-1200. Old English *æppel*, from Germanic, from Indo-European. Related words in other languages include German *Apfel*, Welsh *aval*, Irish *úll*, Russian *yabloko*.

Appleton layer *n.* an ionized layer in the upper atmosphere, above the Heaviside layer, which reflects radio waves. WH: mid-20C. Edward V. *Appleton*, 1892–1965, English physicist.

appliqué *n.* ornamental work laid on some other material. WH: 18C. French, use as n. of p.p.t of *appliquer* APPLY.

apply *v.t.* to put to (practical) use, to employ. *Also v.i.* WH: 12–14C. Old French *aplier*, from Latin *applicare*, from AP- + *plicare* to fold.

appoggiatura *n.* a grace note before a significant note. WH: 18C. Italian, from *appoggiare* to lean on, to rest.

appoint *v.t.* to nominate, designate (to a position, office). *Also v.i.* WH: 12–14C. Old French *apointer*, from *à point* to a point (see POINT).

apport *n.* in spiritualistic terminology, a material object made to appear without material agency. WH: 14–15C. Old French *aport* action of bringing, from *aporter* (Modern French *apporter*) to bring.

apportion *v.t.* to share out in just or suitable proportions. WH: 16C. Old French *apportionner*, or from Medieval Latin *apportionare*, from AP- + *portionare* (PORTION).

apposite *a.* appropriate. WH: 16C. Latin *appositus*, p.p. of *apponere* to apply, from AP- + *ponere* to place, to put.

appraise *v.t.* to estimate the worth, value or quality of. WH: 14–15C. Alt. of APPRIZE, by assim. to PRAISE.

appreciate *v.t.* to esteem highly. *Also v.i.* WH: 16C. Late Latin *appreciatus*, p.p. of *appretiare* to set a price on, from AP- + *pretium* PRICE. See also -ATE[3].

apprehend *v.t.* to grasp or lay hold of mentally. *Also v.i.* WH: 12–14C. French *appréhender*, or from Latin *apprehendere*, from AP- + *prehendere* to seize. The original meaning was to learn (cp. Modern French *apprendre*). The current meaning emerged in the 16C.

apprentice *n.* a person who is bound by a formal agreement or indentures to work for an employer in order to learn some trade or craft which the employer agrees to teach. *Also v.t., v.i.* WH: 12–14C. Old French *aprentis* (Modern French *apprentis*), from *aprendre* to learn, from Latin *apprendere*, contr. of *apprehendere* APPREHEND. See also -ICE.

apprise *v.t.* to inform, to bring to the notice of. WH: 17C. French *appris*, p.p. of *apprendre* to teach, to learn. See APPRENTICE.

†apprize *v.t.* to put a price on. WH: 14–15C. Old French *aprisier*, from *a-* (AD-) + *pris* PRICE, assim. to PRIZE[1].

approach *v.i.* to come or go near or nearer. *Also v.t., n.* WH: 12–14C. Old French *aprocher* (Modern French *approcher*), from Ecclesiastical Latin *appropiare*, from AP- + *propius* nearer, comp. of *prope* near.

approbate *v.t.* to express approval of. WH: 14–15C. Latin *approbatus*, p.p. of *approbare*. See APPROVE, also -ATE[3].

approbation *n.* the act of approving. WH: 14–15C. Old French, from Latin *approbatio, approbationis*, from *approbatus*. See APPROBATE, also -ATION.

appropriate[1] *v.t.* to take e.g. land as one's own, esp. unlawfully or without permission. WH: 14–15C. Latin *appropriatus*, p.p. of *appropriare* to make one's own, from AP- + *proprius* own, proper. See also -ATE[3].

appropriate[2] *a.* suitable, fit. WH: 14–15C. Late Latin *appropriatus*, p.p. of *appropriare*. See APPROPRIATE[1], also -ATE[2].

approve *v.t.* to sanction, confirm. *Also v.i.* WH: 12–14C. Old French *aprover* (Modern French *approuver*), from Latin *approbare* to make good, from AP- + *probus* good, just.

approximate[1] *v.t.* to cause to approach (esp. in number or quantity), to make almost the same as. *Also v.i.* WH: 17C. APPROXIMATE[2], or from Late Latin *approximatus*, p.p. of *approximare* to draw near to, from AP- + *proximus* very near. See also -ATE[3].

approximate[2] *a.* nearly approaching accuracy. *Also n.* WH: 14–15C. Late Latin *approximatus*, from *approximatus* (p.p.). See APPROXIMATE[1], also -ATE[2].

appui *n.* the stay (of a horse) upon the bridle-hand of its rider. WH: 16C. French, from *appuyer* to support, to rest on, from Late Latin *appodiare* to lean on, from AP- + *podium* support. Cp. PODIUM.

appulse *n.* the very close approach of two celestial bodies without the occurrence of occultation or eclipse. WH: 17C. Latin *appulsus* a driving towards, from *appulsus*, p.p. of *appellere*, from AP- + *pellere* to drive.

appurtenance *n.* an accessory, an appendage. WH: 12–14C. Anglo-French *apurtenaunce*, from Old French *apartenance*, ult. from Latin *appertinere* APPERTAIN. See also -ANCE.

apraxia *n.* (partial) loss of the ability to execute voluntary movements. WH: 19C. German *Apraxie*, from Greek *apraxia* inaction, from A-[6] + *praxis* action.

après-ski *n., a.* (of or intended for) the social time following a day's skiing. WH: mid-20C. French after skiing, from *après* after + SKI.

apricot *n.* a soft-fleshed, yellow to orange stone-fruit allied to the plum. WH: 16C. Portuguese *albricoque*, or from Spanish *albaricoque*, from Arabic *al-barḳūḳ*, from *al* the + *barḳūḳ*, from Late Greek *praikokion*, from Latin *praecoquum*, from neut. (used as n.) of var. of *praecox* early ripe. The word was assimilated to French *abricot* and perhaps also influenced by Latin *apricus* ripe.

April *n.* the fourth month of the year. WH: pre-1200. Latin *Aprilis*, ? from *aperire* to open. The name has also been derived from that of *Aphrodite* (Venus), the goddess to whom the month was dedicated in the Roman calendar.

a priori *adv.* from the cause to the effect; from abstract ideas to consequences; deductively. *Also a.* WH: 16C. Latin from what is before. Cp. PRIOR[1]. The opposite is A POSTERIORI.

apron *n.* a garment worn in front of the body to protect the clothes, or as part of a distinctive dress. WH: 12–14C. Old French *naperon* (Modern French *napperon* tablemat), from *nape* tablecloth, from Latin *mappa* napkin. The initial *n* of the original French was lost by misdivision (*an apron* for *a napron*), as for ADDER, AUGER etc. The current French word for apron is TABLIER.

apropos *adv.* opportunely, seasonably. *Also a.* WH: 17C. French *à propos*, from *à* to + *propos* purpose. Cp. PROPOSE.

apse *n.* a semicircular, or polygonal, and generally dome-roofed, recess in a building, esp. at the east end of a church. WH: 19C. Latin *apsis* APSIS. Cp. the pairs BASE[1]/ BASIS, AXE/ AXIS[1] etc.

apsis *n.* either one of two points at which a planet or satellite is at its greatest or least distance from the body around which it revolves. WH: 17C. Latin *apsis, apsidis*, from Greek *hapsis* arch, vault, ? from *haptein* to join.

apt *a.* suitable, relevant. WH: 12–14C. Latin *aptus*, p.p. of *apere* to fasten, to attach.

apteral *a.* without columns at the sides. WH: 19C. A-[6] + Greek *pteron* wing + -AL[1].

apterous *a.* (of insects) wingless, or having only rudimentary wings. WH: 18C. Greek *apteros* not winged, from A-[6] + *pteron* wing + -OUS.

apteryx *n.* the kiwi, a bird from New Zealand, about the size of a goose, with rudimentary wings. WH: 19C. Modern Latin, from Greek A-[6] + *pterux* wing.

aptitude *n.* a natural talent or ability. WH: 14–15C. Old French, from Late Latin *aptitudo*, from Latin *aptus*. See APT, also -TUDE. Cp. ATTITUDE.

apyretic *a.* without fever. WH: 19C. A-[6] + PYRETIC.

apyrexy *n.* the intermission or abatement of a fever. WH: 17C. Modern Latin *apyrexia*, from Greek *apurexia*, from A-[6] + *puressein* to be feverish + -Y[2].

aq. *abbr.* water. WH: Latin *aqua* water.

aqua *n.* water, liquid, solution. *Also a.* WH: mid-20C. Latin water.

aqua- *comb. form* of or relating to water. WH: Latin *aqua* water.

aquaculture *n.* the cultivation of aquatic organisms for human use. WH: 19C. AQUA- + CULTURE.

aqua fortis *n.* nitric acid. WH: 15C. Latin strong water. See AQUA. Cp. FORTE[2].

aqualeather *n.* tanned fishskin. WH: early 20C. AQUA- + LEATHER.

Aqua Libra® *n.* a drink made from mineral water and fruit juices. WH: late 20C. Latin *aqua* water + *libra* balance. The name perhaps puns on EQUILIBRIUM.

aqualung *n.* a portable diving apparatus, strapped on the back and feeding air to the diver as required. *Also v.i.* WH: mid-20C. AQUA- + LUNG.

aquamarine *n.* a bluish-green variety of beryl, named from its colour. *Also a.* WH: 18C. Latin *aqua marina* seawater. See AQUA, MARINE.

aquanaut *n.* a skin-diver. WH: 19C. AQUA- + Greek *nautēs* sailor.

aquaplane *n.* a board on which one is towed, standing, behind a motorboat. *Also v.i.* WH: early 20C. AQUA- + PLANE[1].

aqua regia *n.* a mixture of nitric and hydrochloric acids, capable of dissolving gold and platinum. WH: 17C. Latin royal water. The mixture is so called because it can dissolve the 'noble' metals (gold and platinum).

aquarelle *n.* a kind of painting in Chinese ink and very thin transparent watercolours. WH: 19C. French, from Italian *acquarella* watercolour, from *acqua*, from Latin AQUA.

aquarist *n.* the keeper of an aquarium. WH: 19C. AQUARIUM + -IST.

aquarium *n.* an artificial tank, pond or vessel in which aquatic animals and plants are kept alive. WH: 19C. Neut. sing. (used as n.) of Latin *aquarius* pertaining to water, from *aqua* water. The word is based on VIVARIUM. See also -ARIUM.

Aquarius *n.* a zodiacal constellation giving its name to the 11th sign, which the sun enters on 21 January. WH: pre-1200. Latin water carrier, use as n. of a. *aquarius*. See AQUARIUM.

aquarobics *n.* exercises performed in water to music. WH: late 20C. Blend of AQUA- and *aerobics*. See AEROBE.

aquatic *a.* living or growing in or near water. *Also n.* WH: 15C. Old French *aquatique*, or from Latin *aquaticus*, from *aqua* water. See also -ATIC. The original sense was simply watery. The current sense evolved in the 17C.

aquatint *n.* a method of etching on copper to produce tones similar to those of watercolour. WH: 18C. French *aquatinte*, or from Italian *acquatinta* coloured water. See AQUA-, TINT.

aquavit *n.* an alcoholic spirit flavoured with caraway seeds. WH: 19C. Norwegian, Swedish and Danish *akvavit* AQUA VITAE.

aqua vitae *n.* strong spirits, brandy etc. WH: 15C. Latin water of life. Cp. *eau de vie* (see EAU), USQUEBAUGH. The phrase was originally an alchemists' term for unrectified alcohol.

aqueduct *n.* an artificial channel, esp. an artificial channel raised on pillars or arches for the conveyance of (drinking) water from place to place. WH: 16C. Obs. French *aqueduct* (Modern French *aqueduc*), or from Latin *aquae ductus*, from gen. of *aqua* water + *ductus* conveying. Cp. AQUA, DUCT.

aqueous *a.* consisting of, containing, formed in or deposited from water. WH: 17C. Medieval Latin *aqueus*, from *aqua* water. See also -EOUS.

aquifer *n.* a water-bearing layer of rock, gravel etc. WH: early 20C. Latin *aqui-* AQUA- + *-fer* bearing, from *ferre* to carry, to bear.

aquiform *a.* in the form or state of water. WH: 19C. Latin *aqui-* AQUA- + -FORM.

aquilegia *n.* a plant of the genus *Aquilegia*, having backward-pointing spurs, commonly known as COLUMBINE. WH: 16C. Prob. from Latin *aquilegus* water-collecting, from *aqui-* AQUA- + *legere* to gather, to collect. The name is popularly derived from Latin *aquila* eagle, alluding to the form of the petals.

aquiline *a.* of or relating to an eagle; eagle-like. WH: 17C. Latin *aquilinus*, from *aquila* eagle. See also -INE.

aquosity *n.* wateriness. WH: 14–15C. Late Latin *aquositas*, from Latin *aquosus*, from *aqua* water. See also -ITY.

ar- *pref.* signifying motion towards, direction to, adherence etc., as in *arrest, arrive.* WH: Latin pref., from AD- with *d* assim. to *r*.

-ar[1] *suf.* forming adjectives, as in *angular, linear, lunar.* WH: Latin *-aris*, or from Old French *-aire, -ier*. Cp. -AL[1].

-ar[2] *suf.* forming nouns, as in *pillar.* WH: Latin *-ar*, from *-aris* (see -AR[1]), or from French *-er*.

-ar[3] *suf.* forming nouns, denoting the agent, as in *mortar, vicar.* WH: Latin *-arius*, or from French *-aire, -ier*.

-ar[4] *suf.* forming nouns, as in *liar.* WH: Alt. of -ER[1], -OR, assim. to -AR[3].

Arab *n.* a member of a Semitic people orig. inhabiting Arabia and now much of the Middle East. *Also a.* WH: 14–15C. French *Arabe*, from Latin *Arabs*, from Greek *Araps, Arabos*, from Arabic *'arab*.

araba *n.* an Oriental wheeled carriage. WH: 19C. Turkish, from Arabic *'arrāba* gun carriage.

arabesque *a.* Arabian in design. *Also n.* WH: 17C. French, from Italian *arabesco*, from *arabo* ARAB. See also -ESQUE. Moorish architecture uses intricate ornamentation as Islam forbids the representation of living creatures.

arabica *n.* coffee or coffee beans from the tree *Coffea arabica*, widely grown in S America. WH: early 20C. Latin, fem. of *arabicus*, from Greek *arabikos*. See ARAB, also -IC.

arabis *n.* a plant of the genus *Arabis* of cruciferous plants largely grown on rockwork, also called *rock cress*. WH: 17C. Latin, from Greek, from fem. (used as n.) of *Araps* ARAB.

arable *a.* (of land) ploughed or capable of being ploughed. WH: 14–15C. Old French, from Latin *arabilis*, from *arare* to plough. See also -ABLE.

Araby *a.* Arabic. *Also n.* WH: 12–14C. Old French *arabi*, prob. from Arabic *'arabī*, from *'arab* ARAB.

arachnid *n.* any individual of the class Arachnida, which contains the spiders, scorpions, ticks and mites. WH: 19C. French *arachnide*, or from Modern Latin *Arachnida*, from Greek *arakhnē* spider. See also -ID.

aragonite *n.* a grey or white mineral, composed of calcium carbonate, found in sedimentary rocks. WH: 19C. *Aragon*, a region in NE Spain + -ITE[1].

Araldite® *n.* an epoxy resin used as a strong adhesive. WH: mid-20C. Orig. uncertain. The adhesive was developed by Aero Research Ltd of Duxford, Cambridgeshire. The company was colloquially known as ARL, and this probably gave the main element of the name + -ITE[1].

Aramaean *a.* of or relating to ancient Aram, or Syria, or its language. *Also n.* WH: 19C. Greek *aramaios*, from Hebrew *'ārām* Aram + -AN.

Aran *a.* knitted in a style that originated in the Aran Islands, typically with a thick cream-coloured wool. WH: mid-20C. *Aran* Islands, off the W coast of Ireland.

Aranda *n.* a member of an aboriginal tribe of central Australia. *Also a.* WH: 19C. Australian Aboriginal.

araneidan *a.* of or belonging to the Araneida (or Araneae), the order comprising spiders. *Also n.* WH: 19C. Modern Latin *Araneida*, from *aranea* spider + -AN.

arapaima *n.* a very large primitive freshwater fish of S America. WH: 19C. Tupi.

arational *a.* not concerned with reason, non-rational. WH: mid-20C. A-[6] + RATIONAL.

araucaria *n.* a tree of the coniferous genus *Araucaria*, one species of which (*A. araucana*), the monkey-puzzle, is common in Britain as an ornamental tree. WH: 19C. Modern Latin, from Spanish *Arauco*, a province of Araucanía, Chile. See also -ARY[1].

arbalest *n.* a large, medieval crossbow for firing arrows and other missiles. WH: pre-1200. Old French *arbaleste*, from Late Latin *arcuballista*, from *arcus* bow. See ARC, BALLISTA.

arbiter *n.* a judge. WH: 14–15C. Latin judge, from AR- + *baetere* to go.

arbitrage *n.* traffic in bills of exchange or stocks so as to take advantage of rates of exchange in different markets. WH: 14–15C. Old French, from *arbitrer*, from Latin *arbitrari*. See ARBITRATE.

arbitrament *n.* decision by arbitrators. WH: 14–15C. Old French *arbitrement*, from Latin *arbitramentum*, from *arbitrari*. See ARBITRATE.

arbitrary *a.* (apparently) random, irrational. WH: 14–15C. Latin *arbitrarius*, or from French *arbitraire*, from Latin *arbiter* judge. See ARBITER, also -ARY[1].

arbitrate *v.t.* to hear and judge as an arbitrator. *Also v.i.* WH: 16C. Latin *arbitratus*, p.p. of *arbitrari* to examine, to give judgement. See ARBITER, also -ATE[3].

arbitress *n.* a female arbiter in a dispute etc. WH: 14–15C. Old French *arbitresse*, fem. of *arbitre* ARBITER.

arbor *n.* a main shaft or axle on which something, e.g. a cutting or milling tool, rotates in a machine. WH: 17C. French *arbre* tree, assim. in spelling to Latin *arbor*.

arboraceous *a.* resembling a tree. WH: 19C. Latin *arbor* tree + -ACEOUS.

Arbor Day *n.* a spring holiday in the US, Australia and other countries dedicated to tree-planting. WH: 19C. Latin *arbor* tree + DAY.

arboreal *a.* of or relating to trees. WH: 17C. Latin *arboreus*, from *arbor* tree + -AL[1].

arborescent *a.* having treelike characteristics. WH: 17C. Latin *arborescens*, *arborescentis*, pres.p. of *arborescere* to grow into a tree, from *arbor* tree. See -escent (-ESCENCE).

arboretum *n.* a botanical garden for the rearing and exhibition of rare trees. WH: 19C. Latin place with trees, from *arbor* tree.

arboriculture *n.* the systematic culture of trees and shrubs. WH: 19C. Latin *arbor* tree + CULTURE.

arborization *n.* treelike appearance. WH: 18C. Latin *arbor* tree + -ization. See also -IZE.

arbor vitae *n.* the tree of life. WH: 17C. Latin tree of life. See ARBOR, VITAL.

arbour *n.* a bower formed by trees or shrubs planted close together or trained on lattice-work; a shady retreat. WH: 12–14C. Anglo-French *erber*, from Old French *erbier* (Modern French *herbier*), from *erbe* herb + -ier (see -ARIUM). See also -OUR. The word is not related to Latin *arbor* tree, but the spelling has been influenced by it. The sense of shady retreat arose through association with HARBOUR as a place of shelter.

arbovirus *n.* any of a group of viruses transported by mosquitoes, ticks etc. that cause diseases such as yellow fever. WH: mid-20C. ARTHROPOD + BORNE + VIRUS.

arbutus *n.* an evergreen shrub or tree of the genus *Arbutus*, of which *A. unedo*, the strawberry tree, is cultivated as an ornamental tree in Britain. WH: 16C. Latin.

arc *n.* a portion of the circumference of a circle or other curve. *Also v.i.* WH: 12–14C. Old French, from Latin *arcus* bow, arch.

arcade *n.* a walk or passage with an arched roof. WH: 17C. French, from Provençal *arcada*, or from Italian *arcata*, ult. from Latin *arcus* ARC. See also -ADE.

Arcadian *a.* of or relating to Arcadia, the ideal region of rural happiness. *Also n.* WH: 16C. Latin *Arcadius*, from *Arcadia*, from Greek *Arkadia*, a mountainous district of the Peloponnese + -AN.

Arcady *n.* Arcadia, as the idealized rural paradise. WH: 14–15C. Latin *Arcadia*, from Greek *Arkadia*. See ARCADIAN.

arcana *n.* either of the two divisions, major or minor, of the Tarot pack. WH: 16C. Latin, pl. of ARCANUM.

arcane *a.* secret, esoteric. WH: 16C. Old French, or from Latin *arcanus*, from *arcere* to shut up, from *arca* chest. See also -ANE. Cp. ARK.

arcanum *n.* anything hidden. WH: 16C. Latin, neut. sing. (used as n.) of *arcanus*. See ARCANE.

arch[1] *n.* a curved structure, used as an opening or a support, e.g. for a bridge. *Also v.t., v.i.* WH: 12–14C. Old French *arche*, ult. from Latin *arcus* ARC.

arch[2] *a.* self-consciously teasing, roguish or mischievous. WH: 16C. Independent use of ARCH-.

arch- *pref.* chief, principal, as in *archbishop, archdeacon, archdiocese*. WH: Latin, from Greek *arkhi-*, from *arkhos* chief.

Archaean *a.* of, relating to or belonging to the earliest geological period or the rocks formed in this time. WH: 19C. Greek *arkhaios* ancient + -AN. Cp. ARCHAEO-.

archaeo- *pref.* of or relating to ancient times; primitive. WH: Greek *arkhaios* ancient. See also -O-.

archaeoastronomy *n.* the study of prehistoric sites with a view to establishing the astronomical beliefs and practices of ancient civilizations. WH: late 20C. ARCHAEO- + ASTRONOMY.

archaeobotany *n.* the study of plant remains that are found at archaeological sites. WH: late 20C. ARCHAEO- + BOTANY.

archaeology *n.* the science or special study of antiquities, esp. of prehistoric remains. WH: 17C. Modern Latin *archaeologia*, from Greek *arkhaiologia*. See ARCHAEO-, -LOGY. The word was originally used to mean ancient history, antiquities. The current sense evolved in the 19C.

archaeomagnetism *n.* the dating of prehistoric objects by reference to the direction and intensity of the earth's magnetic field in previous ages. WH: mid-20C. ARCHAEO- + *magnetism*. See MAGNET, also -ISM.

archaeopteryx *n.* a bird of the fossil genus *Archaeopteryx*, containing the oldest known bird. WH: 19C. ARCHAEO- + Greek *pterux* wing.

Archaeozoic *a.* of or relating to the earliest geological era, the dawn of life on the earth. *Also n.* WH: 19C. ARCHAEO- + -ZOIC.

archaic *a.* old-fashioned, antiquated. WH: 19C. French *archaïque*, from Greek *arkhaikos*, from *arkhaios* ancient. See also -IC.

archaize *v.i.* to imitate or affect ancient manners, language or style. *Also v.t.* WH: 19C. Greek *arkhaizein* to copy the ancients, from *arkhaios* ancient. See also -IZE.

archangel *n.* an angel of the highest rank. WH: pre-1200. Anglo-French *archangele*, from Ecclesiastical Latin *archangelus*, from Ecclesiastical Greek *arkhaggelos*, from Greek *arkhi-* ARCH- + *aggelos* ANGEL.

archbishop *n.* a chief bishop; a metropolitan; the spiritual head of an archiepiscopal province. WH: pre-1200. Late Latin *archiepiscopus*, from Greek *arkhiepiskopos*. See ARCH-, BISHOP. The original Old English word was *hēah-biscop*, from *hēah* high.

archdeacon *n.* a church dignitary next below a bishop in the care of the diocese. WH: pre-1200. Late Latin *archidiaconus*, from Late Greek *arkhidiakonos*. See ARCH-, DEACON.

archdiocese *n.* the see of an archbishop. WH: 19C. ARCH- + DIOCESE.

archduke *n.* a chief duke, esp. a son of an Emperor of Austria. WH: 16C. Old French *archeduc* (Modern French *archiduc*), from Latin *archidux, archiducis*. See ARCH-, DUKE.

archegonium *n.* the female sex organ in mosses, ferns and some conifers. WH: 19C. Modern Latin, from Greek *arkhegonos* progenitor, from *arkhe-* ARCH- + *gonos* race. See also -IUM.

arch-enemy *n.* a principal enemy. WH: 16C. ARCH- + ENEMY.

archer *n.* a person who uses the bow and arrow, a bowman. WH: 12–14C. Anglo-French, from Old French *archier* (Modern French *archer*), ult. from Latin *arcus* bow. See also -ER².

archetype *n.* the primitive or original type, model or pattern. WH: 16C. Latin *archetypum*, from Greek *arkhetupon*, neut. sing. (used as n.) of *arkhetupos*, from *arkhe-* ARCH- + *tupon* model. Cp. TYPE.

arch-fiend *n.* the chief fiend. WH: 17C. ARCH- + FIEND.

arch-foe *n.* a principal foe. WH: 17C. ARCH- + FOE.

arch-hypocrite *n.* a person notorious for extreme hypocrisy. WH: 17C. ARCH- + *hypocrite* (HYPOCRISY).

archidiaconal *a.* of, relating to or holding the office of an archdeacon. WH: 14–15C. Latin *archidiaconalis*. See ARCH-, DIACONAL.

archiepiscopal *a.* of or relating to an archbishop or an archbishopric. WH: 17C. Ecclesiastical Latin *archiepiscopus*, from Greek *arkhiepiskopos* archbishop. See ARCH-, BISHOP, also -AL¹.

Archilochian *a.* of or relating to Archilochus, or to the metre he reputedly introduced. *Also n.* WH: 18C. Latin *Archilochius*, from Greek *Arkhilokhos* Archilochus, *fl.*714–676 BC, Greek satiric poet + -AN.

archimage *n.* a chief magician. WH: 16C. Greek *arkhimagos*. See ARCH-, MAGUS.

archimandrite *n.* the superior of a monastery or convent in the Greek Church, corresponding to an abbot in the Roman Catholic Church. WH: French, or from Ecclesiastical Latin *archimandrita*, from Ecclesiastical Greek *arkhimandritēs*, from *arkhi-* ARCH- + *mandra* enclosure, monastery. See also -ITE¹.

Archimedean *a.* of, relating to or invented by Archimedes. WH: 19C. Late Latin *Archimedus*, from Greek *Arkhimēdēs* Archimedes, *c.*287–212 BC, Greek mathematician + -AN.

archipelago *n.* any area of sea or water studded with islands. WH: 16C. Italian *arcipelago*, from Greek *arkhi-* ARCH- + *pelagos* sea. Cp. PELAGIAN.

architect *n.* a person who plans and draws the designs of buildings, and superintends their erection. WH: 16C. French *architecte*, from Italian *architetto*, from Latin *architectus*, from Greek *arkhitektōn*, from *arkhi-* ARCH- + *tektōn* builder. Cp. TECTONIC.

architectonic *a.* of or relating to architecture or architects. WH: 17C. Latin *architectonicus*, from Greek *arkhitektonikos*, from *arkhitektōn*. See ARCHITECT, also -IC.

architrave *n.* the lowest portion of the entablature of a column, immediately resting on the column itself. WH: 16C. French, from Italian, from *archi-* ARCH- + *trave*, from Latin *trabs, trabis* beam.

archive *n.* a place in which (historical) records are kept. *Also v.t.* WH: 17C. French *archives* (pl.), from Latin *archiva*, from Greek *arkheia* public records, from neut. pl. (used as n.) of *arkheios* governmental, from *arkhē* government. Rel. to ARCH-.

archivolt *n.* the inner contour of an arch. WH: 17C. Italian *archivolto*, or from French *archivolte*, ult. from Latin *arcus* ARC + *volta* VAULT¹.

archlute *n.* a large bass lute with a double neck. WH: 17C. French *archiluth*, or from Italian *arciliuto*. See ARCH-, LUTE¹.

archon *n.* any one of the nine chief magistrates of ancient Athens after the time of Solon. WH: 16C. Greek *arkhōn* ruler, from *arkhein* to rule.

arch-priest *n.* a senior priest among the secular clergy of the Orthodox Church. WH: 14–15C. Old French *archeprestre* (Modern

French *archiprêtre*), from Late Latin *archipresbyter*, from Greek *arkhipresbuteros*. See ARCH-, PRESBYTER, PRIEST.

-archy *comb. form* denoting government or rule of a particular type or by a particular group, as in *oligarchy, monarchy*. WH: Greek *arkheia* government, from *arkhēs* ruling. Rel. to ARCH-. See also -Y².

arcology *n.* an ideal city where architecture and ecology are harmoniously combined. WH: mid-20C. *architectural* (ARCHITECT) + ECOLOGY. The word was coined in 1969 by the US architect Paolo Soleri.

Arctic *a.* of or relating to the North, the N Pole, or the region within the Arctic Circle. *Also n.* WH: 14–15C. Old French *artique* (Modern French *arctique*), from Latin *arcticus*, from Greek *arktikos*, from *arktos* bear. See also -IC. Cp. ANTARCTIC. The region is so named as it lies beneath the Great Bear (Ursa Major) constellation.

arctophile *n.* a person who loves or collects teddy bears. WH: mid-20C. Greek *arktos* bear + -PHILE.

arcuate *a.* curved like a bow. WH: 14–15C. Latin *arcuatus*, p.p. of *arcuare* to curve, from *arcus* ARC. See also -ATE².

arcus senilis *n.* a bow- or ring-shaped opaque area around the cornea of the eye, often seen in elderly people. WH: 18C. Latin *senile* bow. See ARC, SENILE.

-ard *suf.* denoting disposition to do something to excess, as in *drunkard, sluggard*. WH: Old French -*ard*, from German -*hart*, -*hard* hardy. Cp. HARD.

ardent *a.* glowing, intense, zealous. WH: 14–15C. Old French *ardant* (Modern French *ardent*), from Latin *ardens, ardentis*, pres.p. of *ardere* to burn. See also -ANT, -ENT.

ardente *a.* ardent, fiery. WH: 18C. Italian, from Latin *ardens, ardentis*. See ARDENT.

ardour *n.* intensity of emotion, fervour. WH: 14–15C. Old French (Modern French *ardeur*), from Latin *ardor*, from *ardere* to burn.

arduous *a.* laborious, difficult, involving a lot of effort. WH: 16C. Latin *arduus* steep, difficult + -OUS.

are *n.* a metric unit of area equal to 100 square metres (1076.44 sq. ft.). WH: 18C. French, from Latin AREA.

area *n.* a particular extent of surface, a region. WH: 16C. Latin vacant piece of level ground (in a town).

areca *n.* a tree of a genus of palms, *Areca*, esp. *A. catechu*, which yields the betel-nut. WH: 16C. Portuguese, from Malayalam *aḍekka*, form of Tamil *aḍaikāy*, from *aḍai* close cluster + *kāy* nut, fruit.

arena *n.* an area enclosed by seating in which sports events or entertainments take place. WH: 17C. Latin sand, place strewn with sand.

aren't *contr.* are not. WH: 18C. Contr. of *are not*.

areography *n.* the description of the physical features of the planet Mars. WH: 19C. Greek *areos*, from *Arēs* Mars + -GRAPHY.

areola *n.* a dark circle round the human nipple. WH: 17C. Latin, dim. of AREA.

arête *n.* a sharp ascending ridge of a mountain. WH: 19C. French, from Latin *arista* ear of corn, fishbone. Cp. ARRIS.

argali *n.* the wild sheep of Asia, *Ovis ammon*. WH: 18C. Mongolian.

argent *n.* the white colour representing silver. *Also a.* WH: 16C. French, from Latin *argentum* silver.

Argentine *a.* of or relating to Argentina. *Also n.* WH: 19C. Spanish *Argentina*, lit. silvery. The country is named after the Río de la Plata, from Spanish *plata* silver.

argentine *a.* of or containing silver. *Also n.* WH: 15C. Old French *argentin*, from Latin *argentum* (ARGENT) + -INE.

argil *n.* white clay, potter's earth. WH: 14–15C. Old French *argille*, from Latin *argilla*, from Greek *argillos* clay.

arginine *n.* one of the essential amino acids found in plant and animal proteins. WH: 19C. German *Arginin*, ? from Greek *arginoeis* shining bright. See also -INE.

Argive *a.* of or relating to Argos. *Also n.* WH: 16C. Latin *Argivus*, from Greek *Argeios*, from *Argos* Argos, a city-state in ancient Greece.

argol *n.* an impure acid potassium tartrate deposited from wines. WH: 12–14C. Anglo-French *argoile*, of unknown orig.

argon *n.* an inert gas, at. no. 18, chem. symbol Ar, one of the gaseous constituents of the atmosphere, discovered in 1894. WH: 19C. Greek, neut. of *argos* idle, inactive, from A-⁶ + *ergon* work. The gas was so named in 1894 for its inertness by its discoverers, Lord Rayleigh and Sir William Ramsay.

Argonaut n. any of the legendary heroes who accompanied Jason in the ship *Argo* to seek the Golden Fleece. WH: 16C. Latin *argonauta*, from Greek *argonautēs*, from *Argo* Argo + *nautēs* sailor. The ship itself was named from Greek *argos* swift, earlier shining.

argosy n. a large vessel for carrying merchandise. WH: 16C. Appar. from Italian *Ragusea* of Ragusa (now Dubrovnik), but pop. assoc. with *Argo* (ARGONAUT).

argot n. the phraseology or jargon of a class or group. WH: 19C. French, of unknown orig. The word is perhaps related to Old French *hargoter* to quarrel, a variant of *harigoter* to tear. It is not related to JARGON[1].

argue v.t. to (try to) exhibit or prove by reasoning. Also v.i. WH: 12–14C. Old French *arguer*, from Latin *argutari*, freq. of *arguere* to make clear.

argument n. an exchange of views, esp. an angry or passionate one. WH: 12–14C. Old French, from Latin *argumentum*, from *arguere*. See ARGUE, also -MENT.

Argus n. a vigilant watcher or guardian. WH: 14–15C. Latin, from Greek *Argos* Argos, the hundred-eyed guardian of Io in Greek mythology.

argute a. shrill, sharp. WH: 14–15C. Latin *argutus*, p.p. of *arguere* to make clear. See ARGUE.

argy-bargy n. (a) dispute, argument. Also v.i. WH: 19C. Redupl. of ARGUE.

argyle a. knitted or woven with a diamond-shaped pattern in two or more colours. Also n. WH: 18C. *Argyll*, a former county of Scotland. The Argyll branch of the Campbell clan has a tartan of this pattern.

aria n. a song, esp. in an opera or oratorio, for one voice supported by instruments. WH: 18C. Italian, from Latin *aera*, acc. of *aer* AIR.

Arian a. of or relating to Arius or his doctrine. Also n. WH: 14–15C. Ecclesiastical Latin *Arianus*, from *Arius*, from Greek *Arios* Arius, c.250–336, Libyan theologian.

-arian suf. forming adjectives meaning belonging to, believing in, or nouns meaning a person who belongs to, believes in, or is associated with, as in *humanitarian*, *Sabbatarian*, *sexagenarian*. WH: Latin *-arius* -ARY[1] + -AN.

arid a. dry, parched, without moisture. WH: 17C. French *aride*, or from Latin *aridus*, from *arere* to be dry. See also -ID.

ariel n. a Middle Eastern and African gazelle. WH: 19C. Arabic *'aryal*.

Aries n. the Ram, the first of the zodiacal constellations, which the sun enters in the month of March. WH: pre-1200. Latin *aries* ram.

arietta n. a short lively air, tune or song. WH: 18C. Italian, dim. of ARIA.

ariette n. an arietta. WH: 19C. French, from Italian ARIETTA.

aright adv. right, rightly, properly, becomingly. WH: pre-1200. Old English *on riht*, *ariht*, from A-[1] + *riht* RIGHT.

aril n. an accessory seed-covering, more or less incomplete but often brightly coloured and fleshy, formed by a growth near the hilum. WH: 18C. Modern Latin *arillus*, of unknown orig.

arioso a., adv. in a songlike style, melodious(ly). Also n. WH: 18C. Italian, from ARIA.

-arious suf. forming adjectives meaning connected with, belonging to, as in *gregarious*, *vicarious*. WH: Latin *-arius* -ARY[1] + -OUS.

arise v.i. to appear, to come into being. WH: pre-1200. Old English *ārīsan*, from A-[3] + *rīsan* RISE.

arista n. an awn. WH: 17C. Latin awn, ear of grain. Cp. ARÊTE.

aristo n. an aristocrat. WH: 19C. French, abbr. of *aristocrate* aristocrat. See ARISTOCRACY.

aristocracy n. the nobility. WH: 15C. Old French *aristocratie*, from Greek *aristokratia*, from *aristos* best. See also -CRACY.

Aristophanic a. of or relating to Aristophanes. WH: 19C. Latin *Aristophanicus*, from Greek *Aristophanikos*, from *Aristophanēs* Aristophanes, c.448–c.385 BC, Greek comic dramatist. See also -IC.

Aristotelian a. of or relating to Aristotle, or to his philosophy. Also n. WH: 16C. Latin *Aristotelius*, from Greek *Aristoteleios*, from *Aristotelēs* Aristotle, 384–322 BC, Greek philosopher and scientist. See also -AN.

Arita n. a type of Japanese porcelain with asymmetrical decoration. WH: 19C. Arita, a town in S Japan.

arithmetic[1] n. the science of numbers. WH: 12–14C. Old French *arismetique*, ult. from Latin *arithmetica*, from Greek *arithmētikē tekhnē* counting art, from *arithmein* to reckon, from *arithmos* number. The Old French *arismetique* came to be associated with Latin *ars metrica* art of measure.

arithmetic[2] a. of or relating to arithmetic. WH: 17C. French *arithmétique* ARITHMETIC[1].

-arium suf. forming nouns meaning place for or connected with, as in *aquarium*, *sacrarium*. WH: Latin, neut. of aa. in *-arius*. See -ARY[1].

ark n. a ship, a boat, esp. Noah's ark. WH: pre-1200. Old English *ærc*, from Latin *arca* box, coffer. The English word translates two unrelated Hebrew nouns in the Bible: (1) Noah's ark (Gen. vi–ix) and the 'ark of bulrushes' in which the baby Moses was found (Exod. ii.3); (2) the Ark of the Covenant (Deut. x.2,5).

arm[1] n. the upper limb of the human body on either side, from the shoulder to the hand. Also v.t. WH: pre-1200. Old English, from Germanic.

arm[2] n. a weapon. Also v.t., v.i. WH: 12–14C. Old French *armes*, from Latin *arma* weapons.

armada n. an armed fleet, esp. the fleet sent by Philip II of Spain against England in 1588. WH: 16C. Spanish, fem. of *armado* armed, p.p. of *armar*, from Latin *armare*, from *arma* weapons. Cp. ARM[2].

armadillo n. any of several small burrowing edentate animals of the family Dasypodidae, native to S America, encased in bony armour, and capable of rolling themselves into a ball. WH: 16C. Spanish, dim. of *armado* armed (man), from Latin *armatus*, p.p. of *armare* to arm. See ARM[2].

Armageddon n. the final battle between good and evil at the end of the world. WH: 19C. Greek *Armageddōn*, prob. from Hebrew *harmegiddōn* mount of Megiddo, a city in Palestine, which was the site of important battles in the history of the Israelites. The name is used in the Bible (Rev. xvi.16) for the site of the last battle at the Day of Judgement.

Armagnac n. a dry brandy from SW France. WH: 19C. French, former name of a region of SW France.

Armalite® n. a lightweight automatic high-velocity rifle. WH: mid-20C. ARM[2] + -a- + *lite*, alt. of LIGHT[2].

armament n. the arms and munitions of war, esp. the weapons with which a warship, aircraft etc. is equipped. WH: 17C. Latin *armamentum*, from *armare* to arm. See ARM[2], also -MENT.

armamentarium n. the equipment, medicines etc. collectively, that are available to a doctor or other medical practitioner. WH: 19C. Latin arsenal, armoury, from *armamentum*. See ARMAMENT, also -ARIUM.

armature n. the revolving part, wound with coils, of an electric motor or dynamo. WH: 14–15C. French, from Latin *armatura*, from *armatus*, p.p. of *armare* to arm. See ARM[2], also -URE. The original sense was arms, armour. The current specialized sense dates from the 18C.

Armenian a. of or relating to Armenia. Also n. WH: 16C. Latin *Armenia*, a country of SW Asia, from Greek, from Old Persian *Armina* + -IAN.

armes parlantes n.pl. coats of arms which show devices that directly illustrate the name of the bearer, e.g. that represent the name Churchill by a church and a hill. WH: 18C. French speaking arms. See ARM[2], PARLEY.

armet n. a kind of helmet consisting of a rounded iron cap, a spreading protection for the back of the neck, and visor, beaver and gorget in front, which superseded the basinet in the 15th cent. WH: 16C. French, influ. by *armes* (ARM[2]), from Spanish *almete*, or from Italian *elmetto* HELMET.

armiger n. an esquire. WH: 16C. Latin bearing arms, from *arma* arms (ARM[2]) + *gerere* to bear. See also -GEROUS.

armillary a. of or relating to bracelets. WH: 17C. Modern Latin *armillaris*, from *armilla*, dim. of *armus* shoulder. See also -ARY[2].

Arminian a. of or relating to Arminius, who maintained the doctrine of free will against Calvin. Also n. WH: 17C. Latin *Jacobus Arminius* Jacob Harmensen, 1560–1609, Dutch theologian + -AN.

armipotent *a.* powerful or mighty in arms (an epithet of Mars). WH: 14–15C. Latin *armipotens, armipotentis*, from *arma* arms (ARM²) + *potens* powerful, POTENT.

armistice *n.* a cessation of fighting for a stipulated time during war. WH: 18C. French, or from Modern Latin *armistitium*, from *arma* arms (ARM²) + *-stitium*, from *sistere* to stop. The word is based on Latin *solstitium* SOLSTICE.

armlet *n.* a small ornamental band worn on the arm. WH: 16C. ARM¹ + -LET.

armoire *n.* a chest, a cupboard. WH: 16C. French cupboard. See AUMBRY.

Armoric *a.* of or relating to Brittany. *Also n.* WH: 15C. Latin *Armoricae* Armorica, modern Brittany, from Gaulish *are* in front of + *mor* sea + -AN.

armory *n.* the science of heraldry. WH: 14–15C. Old French *armoirie* (Modern French *armoiries*), from *armoier* to blazon, from *arme* arm. See ARM², also -Y².

armour *n.* a defensive covering worn by a person in combat, esp. by a medieval warrior. *Also v.t.* WH: 12–14C. Old French *armure*, from Latin *armatura* ARMATURE. See also -OUR.

army *n.* a body of people organized for land warfare. WH: 14–15C. Old French *armée*, fem. p.p. of *armer*, from Latin *armare*. See ARM², also -Y².

arnica *n.* a tincture prepared from *Arnica montana*, mountain tobacco, and used as an application for bruises, sprains etc. WH: 18C. Modern Latin, of unknown orig. The word is said by some to derive from Greek *arnakis* lambskin, with reference to the texture of the leaves.

aroid *a.* belonging to the family Araceae, which includes the *Arum* genus of plants. WH: 19C. ARUM + -OID.

†aroint *int.* avaunt! begone! WH: 17C. Orig. unknown. The word is perhaps from English dialect *rointree* rowan tree, said to be efficacious against witches.

aroma *n.* the fragrance in a plant, spice, fruit, wine etc. WH: 12–14C. Latin, from Greek *arōma* spice.

aromatic *a.* of or relating to an aroma. *Also n.* WH: 14–15C. Old French *aromatique*, from Late Latin *aromaticus*, from Greek *arōmatikos*, from *arōma* (AROMA).

around *prep.* surrounding, round about. *Also adv.* WH: 12–14C. Prob. from A-¹ + ROUND.

arouse *v.t.* to stir up, awaken. WH: 16C. A-³ + ROUSE. The verb is based on such pairs as RISE/ ARISE, WAKE¹/ AWAKE.

arpeggio *n.* a chord played on a keyed instrument by striking the notes in rapid succession instead of simultaneously. WH: 18C. Italian, from *arpeggiare* to play on the harp, from *arpa* HARP.

arrack *n.* a distilled spirit from the East, esp. one distilled from coconut or rice. WH: 17C. Arabic *'araḳ* sweat, sweet juice, from *'araḳ al-tamr* juice of dates.

arraign *v.t.* to cite before a tribunal to answer a criminal charge. WH: 14–15C. Old French *araisnier, areisnier*, from Late Latin *arrationare*, from Latin AR- + *ratio, rationis* account, REASON.

arrange *v.t.* to adjust, to put in proper order. *Also v.i.* WH: 12–14C. Old French *arangier, arengier* (Modern French *arranger*), from a- (AD-) + *rangier* RANGE. The original sense was military, to draw up in battle array. The current general sense took over from the 18C.

arrant *a.* notorious, downright, unmitigated. WH: 14–15C. Var. of ERRANT.

arras *n.* a rich tapestry. WH: 14–15C. *Arras*, a town in NE France, where the fabric was manufactured.

array *n.* an impressive display or collection. *Also v.t.* WH: 12–14C. Old French *arei* (Modern French *arroi*), ult. from Latin AR- + Germanic base meaning to prepare, rel. to READY.

arrears *n.pl.* that which remains unpaid or undone. WH: 12–14C. Old French *arere*, *ariere* (Modern French *arrière*), from Latin *adretro*, from AR- + *retro* backward, behind.

arrest *v.t.* to apprehend and take into legal custody. *Also n.* WH: 12–14C. Old French *arester* (Modern French *arrêter*), from Late Latin *adrestare* from AR- + *restare* to stay, to stop, REST¹.

arrhythmia *n.* an irregularity or alteration in the rhythm of the heartbeat. WH: 19C. Greek, from A-⁶ + *rhuthmos* RHYTHM.

arrière-ban *n.* in French history, a summons to the king's vassals to do military service. WH: 16C. French, from Old French *ariereban*, alt. of *arban*, from Germanic *hari* army + *ban* proclamation, BAN. The term has been influenced by Old French *arere* (Modern French *arrière*) behind. See ARREARS.

arrière-pensée *n.* a mental reservation. WH: 19C. French, lit. behind-thought. Cp. ARREARS, PENSÉE.

arris *n.* the line in which two straight or curved surfaces forming an exterior angle meet each other. WH: 17C. Alt. of early Modern French *areste* sharp ridge, ARÊTE.

arrive *v.i.* to come to a place, position, during a journey or movement; to reach a destination. *Also v.t.* WH: pre-1200. Old French *ariver* (Modern French *arriver*), from Late Latin *arribare, arripare*, from Latin AR- + *ripa* shore. Cp. RIVER. The verb originally denoted an arriving by water only. The current wider sense dates from the 16C.

arrivederci *int.* goodbye, to our next meeting. WH: 19C. Italian until we see each other again, from *a* until + *rivedere* to see again + *ci* us. Cp. AUF WIEDERSEHEN, AU REVOIR.

arriviste *n.* a social climber, a parvenu. WH: early 20C. French, from *arriver* ARRIVE. See also -IST.

arroba *n.* a unit of weight used in some Spanish-speaking countries equivalent to 25 lbs (11.35 kg). WH: 16C. Spanish, from Arabic *ar-rub'*, from *ar*, form of *al* the + *rub'* quarter. The weight was originally a quarter of a quintal.

arrogance *n.* the act or quality of being arrogant. WH: 12–14C. Old French *arrogance*, from Latin *arrogantia*, from *arrogans, arrogantis*. See ARROGANT, also -ANCE.

arrogant *a.* overbearing, haughty. WH: 12–14C. Old French, from Latin *arrogans, arrogantis*, pres.p. of *arrogare* to claim for oneself. See ARROGATE.

arrogate *v.t.* to make unduly exalted claims or baseless pretensions to (a thing) for oneself or for someone else. WH: 16C. Latin *arrogatus*, p.p. of *arrogare* to claim for oneself, from AR- + *rogare* to ask. See also -ATE³.

arrondissement *n.* a territorial division of a French department. WH: 19C. French from *arrondir, arrondiss-* to make round. See also -MENT.

arrow *n.* a slender, straight, sharp-pointed missile shot from a bow. *Also v.t., v.i.* WH: pre-1200. Old English *arwe, arewe*, from Old Norse, from Germanic base. Rel. to ARC.

arroyo *n.* a dried-up watercourse, a rocky ravine. WH: 19C. Spanish.

arse *n.* the buttocks, the rump, the hind parts. WH: pre-1200. Old English *ærs*, from Germanic, from Indo-European.

arsenal *n.* a place for the storage, or manufacture and storage, of naval and military weapons and ammunition. WH: 16C. French, from obs. Italian *arzanale* (now *arsenale*), ult. from Arabic *dār-aṣ-ṣinā'a* workshop, from *dār* house + *as*, form of *al* the + *ṣinā'a* art, manufacture. The word originally meant a naval dock, especially that at Venice. The current wider sense developed early in English, although Spanish *arsenal* still means dockyard.

arsenic¹ *n.* a brittle, semi-metallic steel-grey element, at. no. 33, chem. symbol As. WH: 12–14C. Old French, from Greek *arsenikon* yellow orpiment, from Arabic *az-zarnīḳ*, from *az*, form of *al* the + *zarnīḳ*, orpiment, from Persian, from *zar* gold. The Greek source has been misidentified with *arsenikos* male, supposedly referring to the element's powerful qualities.

arsenic² *a.* of or containing arsenic, esp. applied to compounds in which arsenic combines as a pentavalent element. WH: 19C. ARSENIC¹, with ending taken to be -IC.

arsis *n.* the stressed syllable in metre, esp. in Greek or Latin verse. WH: 14–15C. Late Latin, from Greek lifting, raising, from *airein* to raise.

arson *n.* the wilful setting on fire of another's house or other property, or of one's own with intent to defraud the insurers. WH: 17C. Old French, from Late Latin *arsio, arsionis*, from *arsus*, p.p. of *ardere* to burn. Cp. ARDENT.

arsy-versy *adv.* backwards; in reverse order. WH: 16C. ARSE + Latin *versus* turned. See VERSUS. The final -y in both parts is simply to make a jingle.

art *n.* creative activity concerned with the production of aesthetic objects or of beauty in general. *Also a.* WH: 12–14C. Old French, from Latin *ars, artis*, from base stem *ar-* to fill.

artefact *n.* a product of human skill or workmanship. WH: 19C. Latin *arte* by art, abl. of *ars* ART + *factum*, neut. p.p. of *facere* to make.

artel *n.* a cooperative organization of peasants, craftsmen etc. in the former Soviet Union or pre-revolutionary Russia. WH: 19C. Russian *artel'*, from Italian *artiere* artisan, craftsman.

artemisia *n.* any herbaceous, perennial plant of the genus *Artemisia*, that includes wormwood, mugwort and sagebrush. WH: 12–14C. Latin, from Greek wormwood, from *Artemis*, Diana, the goddess to whom it was sacred.

artery *n.* any of the membranous pulsating vessels conveying blood from the heart to all parts of the body. WH: 12–14C. Latin *arteria*, or from Greek *artēria*, prob. from *airein* to raise. See also -Y[2].

artesian well *n.* a well in which water is obtained by boring through an upper retentive stratum to a subjacent water-bearing stratum, the water being forced to the surface by natural pressure. WH: 19C. French *artésien* of *Artois* (Old French *Arteis*), a region of NE France, where such wells were first made. See also -IAN.

Artex® *n.* a textured paint covering for ceilings and walls. *Also v.t.* WH: mid-20C. Blend of ART and TEXTURE.

arthralgia *n.* pain in a joint. WH: 19C. Greek *arthron* joint + -ALGIA.

arthritic *a.* of or suffering from arthritis. *Also n.* WH: 12–14C. Old French *artetique*, from Late Latin *arteticus*, from Latin *arthriticus*, from Greek *arthritikos*, from *arthron* joint. See also -ITIC.

arthro- *comb. form* of or relating to joints. WH: Greek *arthron* joint. See also -O-.

arthromere *n.* a body segment of an arthropod. WH: 19C. ARTHRO- + Greek *meros* part.

arthroplasty *n.* surgical repair of a joint. WH: 19C. ARTHRO- + -PLASTY.

arthropod *n.* a member of the Arthropoda, a phylum of invertebrate animals with segmented bodies and jointed limbs, including the insects, arachnids and crustaceans. WH: 19C. Modern Latin *Arthropoda*, from Greek *arthron* joint + -POD.

Arthurian *a.* of or relating to King Arthur or his knights. WH: 17C. *Arthur*, *fl.*6C, semilegendary king of the Britons + -IAN.

artichoke *n.* a composite plant, *Cynara scolymus*, somewhat like a large thistle: the receptacle and fleshy bases of the scales are eaten as a vegetable. WH: 16C. Italian *articiocco*, *arciciocco*, alt. of Old Spanish *alcarchofa*, from Arabic *al-ḵaršūf*. Not rel. to CHOKE.

article *n.* an item, a piece, a distinct element. *Also v.t.* WH: pre-1200. Old French, from Latin *articulus*, dim. of *artus* joint. See also -CLE. Rel. to ART. The earliest English sense of the word was a clause of the Apostles' Creed (cp. the modern Thirty-Nine Articles in the Book of Common Prayer). The sense of moment, nick of time, followed (14C), then a piece of business, a matter (15C). The sense journalistic piece dates from the 18C.

articular *a.* of or relating to the joints. WH: 14–15C. Latin *articularis*, from *articulus*. See ARTICLE, also -AR[1].

articulate[1] *v.t.* to utter (words) distinctly. *Also v.i.* WH: 16C. Latin *articulatus*, p.p. of *articulare*, from *articulus*. See ARTICLE, also -ATE[3]. The original sense was to formulate in articles. This then gave way to the current sense.

articulate[2] *a.* able to express oneself clearly and coherently. WH: 16C. Latin *articulatus*, p.p. of *articulare*, from *articulus*. See ARTICLE, also -ATE[2]. The original sense was having meaningful sounds in speech. The current sense developed from the 18C.

artifice *n.* a clever expedient, a contrivance. WH: 14–15C. Old French, from Latin *artificium*, from *ars*, *artis* ART + *fic-*, var. of *fac-*, stem of *facere* to make. The original sense was favourable, as workmanship, work of art. The current unfavourable sense began to emerge from the 16C.

artificial *a.* made or produced by human agency, not natural. WH: 12–14C. Old French *artificiel*, or from Latin *artificialis*, from *artificium*. See ARTIFICE, also -AL[1].

artillery *n.* large-calibre guns, cannons, mortars etc., with their equipment for use in land warfare. WH: 12–14C. Old French *artillerie*, from *artiller*, alt. of *atillier* to equip, to arm, from *a-* (AD-) + *tire* order. See TIER, also -ERY. The original sense was munitions generally. The current narrower sense dates from the 18C.

artiodactyl *a.* having an even number of toes. *Also n.* WH: 19C. Modern Latin *Artiodactyla*, from Greek *artios* even + *daktulos* finger, toe.

artisan *n.* a skilled manual worker. WH: 16C. French, from Italian *artigiano*, from Latin *artitus*, p.p. of *artire* to instruct in the arts, from *ars*, *artis* ART. See also -AN.

artist *n.* a person who practises any of the fine arts, esp. that of painting. WH: 16C. Old French *artiste*, from Italian *artista*, from *arte* ART. See also -IST.

artiste *n.* a public performer, an actor, dancer, musician, acrobat etc. WH: 19C. French ARTIST.

arugula *n.* rocket, a Mediterranean plant used in salads. WH: mid-20C. Italian dial., ult. from Latin *eruca* ROCKET[2].

arum *n.* a plant of the European genus *Arum*, usu. with a white spathe and arrow-shaped leaves, e.g. the cuckoo pint. WH: 14–15C. Latin, from Greek *aron*.

arundinaceous *a.* resembling a reed. WH: 17C. Latin *arundinaceus*, from *arundo* reed. See also -ACEOUS.

arvo *n.* afternoon. WH: mid-20C. AFTERNOON + -O. The spelling reflects the pronunciation of the first syllable.

-ary[1] *suf.* forming adjectives meaning of or relating to, connected with, belonging to, engaged in, as in *elementary*, *necessary*, *voluntary*. WH: Latin *-arius*. See also -Y[1].

-ary[2] *suf.* equivalent to -AR[1] and sometimes to -ARY[1], as in *exemplary*, *military*, *contrary*. WH: Latin *-aris*, or from French *-aire*. See also -Y[1].

Aryan *n.* a member of any of the peoples speaking a language of the Indo-European family, esp. the Indo-Iranian branch. *Also a.* WH: 15C. Sanskrit *ārya* noble + -AN.

aryl *n.* any monovalent aromatic hydrocarbon radical, e.g. phenyl. WH: early 20C. AROMATIC + -YL.

as[1] *adv.* in or to the same degree (followed by *conj.* governing pronoun, n. phr. or relative clause). *Also conj.*, *pron.* WH: pre-1200. Reduced form of Old English *alswā* ALSO.

as[2] *n.* a Roman copper coin, orig. of 12 oz (340 g) but frequently reduced. WH: 16C. Latin. Cp. ACE.

as- *pref.* signifying motion towards, direction to, adherence etc., as in *assail*, *assimilate*. WH: Latin pref., from AD- with *d* assim. to *s*.

asafoetida *n.* a gum resin, with a strong unpleasant smell of garlic, obtained from some plants of the genus *Ferula*, formerly used in medicine and currently as a herbal remedy and in cookery. WH: 14–15C. Late Latin, from *asa* (from Persian *āzā* mastic) + *foetida*, fem. of *foetidus* FETID.

asana *n.* any of the positions taught in yoga. WH: mid-20C. Sanskrit *āsana*, from *āste* he sits.

asbestos *n.* a fibrous form of certain minerals that is practically incombustible and resistant to chemicals, formerly widely used as a heat-resistant or insulating material. *Also a.* WH: pre-1200. Old French *abeston*, from Latin, from Greek *asbeston*, acc. of *asbestos* unquenchable, from A-[6] + *sbestos* quenched. The term was originally applied to a fabulous 'unquenchable' stone. The current meaning dates from the 17C.

ascarid *n.* any of the genus *Ascaris* of intestinal nematode worms. WH: 14–15C. Modern Latin, from Greek *askaris* intestinal worm.

ascend *v.i.* to go or come from a lower to a higher place, position or degree. *Also v.t.* WH: 14–15C. Latin *ascendere*, from A-[5] + *scandere* to climb.

ascension *n.* the act of ascending. WH: 12–14C. Old French, from Latin *ascensio*, *ascensionis*, from *ascensus*, p.p. of *ascendere* ASCEND. See also -ION.

ascent *n.* the act or process of ascending, upward motion. WH: 16C. ASCEND, based on pair DESCEND/ DESCENT.

ascertain *v.t.* to discover or verify by investigation, examination or experiment. WH: 14–15C. Old French *acertener*, from *a-* (AD-) + CERTAIN. The earlier sense was to make certain. The current meaning became established in the 18C.

ascesis *n.* the practice of self-discipline. WH: 19C. Greek *askēsis* exercise, from *askein* to exercise.

ascetic *a.* practising rigorous self-discipline, esp. for spiritual or religious ends. *Also n.* WH: 17C. Late Latin *asceticus*, or from Greek *askētikos*, from *askētēs* monk, hermit, from *askein* to exercise. See also -IC.

ascidian *n.* a tunicate of the order Ascidiacea, the adults of which are sedentary, e.g. the sea squirt. WH: 19C. Greek *askidion*, dim. of *askos* wineskin. See also -AN.

ascidium *n.* a pitcher- or flask-shaped plant part, such as the leaf of the pitcher plant. WH: 19C. Modern Latin, from Greek *askidion*. See ASCIDIAN.

ASCII *n.* a standard system for representing alphanumeric symbols as binary numbers, used in data processing. WH: mid-20C. Acronym of *American Standard Code for Information Interchange*.

ascites *n.* dropsy causing swelling of the abdomen. WH: 14–15C. Late Latin, from Greek *askitēs* dropsy, from *askos* wineskin.

Asclepiad *n.* a line of verse consisting of a spondee, two (or three) choriambs and an iambus. WH: 17C. Late Latin *asclepiadeus*, from Greek *asklēpiadeios*, from *Asklēpiadēs*, Greek poet of 3C BC, who invented it.

asclepias *n.* a plant of the genus *Asclepias*, or order Asclepiadaceae, containing the milkweeds etc., principally from N America. WH: 16C. Latin, from Greek *asklēpias*, from *Asklēpios* Aesculapius, the Roman god of medicine.

asco- *comb. form* indicating an ascus or bladder. WH: Greek *askos* bladder. See also -O-.

ascomycete *n.* a fungus of the Ascomycetes, a large class of fungi, including penicillium and yeasts, having spores formed in asci. WH: 19C. Modern Latin *Ascomycetes*, from ASCO- + Greek *mukētes*, pl. of *mukēs* fungus.

ascorbic acid *n.* vitamin C, occurring in vegetables, fruits etc. WH: mid-20C. A-⁶ + SCORBUTIC.

ascot *n.* a cravat with wide square ends. WH: early 20C. *Ascot*, a village in Berkshire, from its being sported at race meetings there.

ascribe *v.t.* to attribute, to assign (to). WH: 12–14C. Latin *ascribere*, from A-⁵ + *scribere* to write.

ascription *n.* the act of ascribing; a thing which is ascribed. WH: 16C. Latin *ascriptio, ascriptionis*, from *ascriptus*, p.p. of *ascribere* ASCRIBE. See also -ION.

ascus *n.* a cell in which spores are formed in an ascomycete. WH: 19C. Modern Latin, from Greek *askos* bag, sac.

asdic *n.* an early form of apparatus for detecting the presence and position of submarines. WH: early 20C. Acronym of *Anti-Submarine Detection Investigation Committee*.

-ase *suf.* forming nouns denoting enzymes, as in *DNase*. WH: See DIASTASE.

aseismic *a.* free of, or virtually free of, earthquakes. WH: 19C. A-⁶ + SEISMIC.

aseity *n.* the fact of being self-derived, having no other source. WH: 17C. Late Latin *aseitas*, from Latin A-⁴ from + *se* oneself. See also -ITY.

asepsis *n.* the condition of being aseptic. WH: 19C. A-⁶ + SEPSIS.

asexual *a.* without sex, sexual organs or sexual functions. WH: 19C. A-⁶ + SEXUAL.

ASH *abbr.* Action on Smoking and Health. WH: The name also puns on (cigarette) ASH¹.

ash¹ *n.* the residuum left after the burning of anything combustible. WH: pre-1200. Old English *æsce, æxe*. Rel. to Latin *arere* to be dry. See ARID.

ash² *n.* a forest tree, *Fraxinus excelsior*, with grey bark, pinnate leaves and tough, close-grained wood. *Also a.* WH: pre-1200. Old English *æsc*, from Germanic.

ashamed *a.* feeling shame, either abashed by consciousness of one's own error or guilt or on account of some other person or thing. WH: pre-1200. Old English *āsceamod*, p.p. of *āsceamian* to feel shame, from A-³ + *sceamu* SHAME.

ashen¹ *a.* ash-coloured, between brown and grey. WH: 14–15C. ASH¹ + -EN³.

ashen² *a.* of or relating to the ash tree. WH: 12–14C. ASH² + -EN³.

ashet *n.* a large flat plate or dish. WH: 16C. French *assiette* plate.

Ashkenazi *n.* an E European or German Jew. WH: 19C. Modern Hebrew, from *Ashkenaz*, a descendant of Japheth (Gen. x.3).

ashlar *n.* a square-hewn stone used in a building. WH: 12–14C. Old French *aisselier*, from Latin *axilla*, dim. of AXIS¹ board, plank. The sense has transferred from woodwork to stonework.

ashore *adv.* to the shore. WH: 16C. A-¹ + SHORE¹.

ashram *n.* (in India) a hermitage for a holy man or place of retreat for a religious community. WH: early 20C. Sanskrit *āśrama* hermitage.

Asian *a.* of, relating to or belonging to Asia or its people. *Also n.* WH: 14–15C. Latin *Asianus*, from Greek *Asianos*, from *Asia*, the continent. See also -AN.

Asiatic *a.* Asian. *Also n.* WH: 17C. Latin *Asiaticus*, from Greek *Asiatikos*, from *Asia*, the continent. See also -IC.

aside *adv.* at, to or towards one side. *Also n.* WH: 12–14C. A-¹ + SIDE.

asinine *a.* stupid, ridiculous. WH: 15C. Latin *asininus*, from *asinus* ASS. See also -INE.

ask *v.t.* to put a question to, to inquire of; to put (a question) to. *Also v.i.* WH: pre-1200. Old English *āscian*, from Germanic.

askance *adv.* obliquely, sideways, askew, squintingly. *Also v.t.* WH: 15C. Orig. unknown. According to some, it is from an early form of AS¹ + Latin *quasi* as if.

askari *n.* an indigenous E African soldier. WH: 19C. Arabic *'askarī* soldier.

askew *adv.* in an oblique direction. *Also a.* WH: 16C. A-¹ + SKEW.

aslant *adv., a.* in a slanting or oblique direction. *Also prep.* WH: 12–14C. A-¹ + SLANT.

asleep *adv., pred.a.* in or into a state of sleep. WH: 12–14C. A-¹ + SLEEP.

aslope *a.* sloping, oblique. *Also adv.* WH: 14–15C. Of uncertain orig. Predates SLOPE.

asmoulder *a., adv.* smouldering. WH: 19C. A-¹ + SMOULDER.

asocial *a.* not social. WH: 19C. A-⁶ + SOCIAL.

asp *n.* a small venomous hooded serpent, *Naja haje*, the Egyptian cobra. WH: 12–14C. Old French *aspe*, from Latin *aspis*, from Greek.

asparagine *n.* an amino acid occurring in proteins, found in asparagus and other vegetables. WH: 19C. ASPARAGUS + -INE.

asparagus *n.* any plant of the genus *Asparagus*, esp. *A. officinalis*, a culinary plant, the tender shoots of which are eaten. WH: 12–14C. Latin, from Greek *asparagos*. A well-known popular variant is *sparrow-grass* (see SPARROW, GRASS).

aspartame *n.* an artificial sweetener derived from aspartic acid. WH: late 20C. ASPARTIC ACID + phenylaline (see PHENYL) + METHYL + ESTER, its chemical constituents.

aspartic acid *n.* a nonessential amino acid present in many proteins, that acts as a neurotransmitter. WH: 19C. French *aspartique*, from ASPARAGUS. See also -IC.

aspect *n.* a particular element or feature of something. WH: 14–15C. Latin *aspectus*, from p.p. of *aspicere* to look at, from A-⁵ + *specere* to look.

aspen *n.* a poplar, *Populus tremula*, remarkable for its quivering leaves; also called *trembling poplar*. *Also a.* WH: 14–15C. ASP + -EN³. The word was originally an adjective, but is now a noun. An earlier form was *asp*, from Old English *æspe*.

asper *n.* a small Turkish silver coin, later only a monetary unit. WH: 14–15C. French *aspre*, from Late Greek *aspron*, from Latin *asper nummus* newly minted coin.

asperate *a.* with a rough surface from being covered with short stiff hairs. *Also v.t.* WH: 15C. Latin *asperatus*, p.p. of *asperare*, from *asper* rough. See also -ATE².

asperge *v.t.* to besprinkle, esp. with holy water. *Also n.* WH: 16C. French *asperger*, or from Latin *aspergere*, from A-⁵ + *spargere* to sprinkle.

asperity *n.* harshness of manner. WH: 14–15C. Old French *asperité*, or from Latin *asperitas*, from *asper* rough. See also -ITY.

aspermia *n.* total absence of semen. WH: 19C. A-⁶ + Greek *sperma* seed + -IA. Cp. SPERM.

asperse *v.t.* to spread disparaging reports about, to defame. WH: 15C. Latin *aspersus*, p.p. of *aspergere* ASPERGE.

asphalt *n.* a bituminous pitch that occurs naturally or as a residue from petroleum distillation. *Also v.t.* WH: 12–14C. French *asphalte*, from Late Latin *asphalton*, from Greek, of non-Greek orig.

asphodel *n.* a mythical undying flower, said to bloom in the Elysian fields. WH: 14–15C. Latin *asphodilus, asphodelus*, from Greek *asphodelos*, of unknown orig. Cp. DAFFODIL.

asphyxia *n.* a lack of oxygen in the blood, leading to unconsciousness or death. WH: 18C. Modern Latin, from Greek, from A-⁶ + *sphuxis* pulsation. See also -IA. The original meaning was stoppage of the pulse. The current sense evolved soon after.

aspic *n.* a savoury jelly used as a garnish or in which game, hard-boiled eggs, fish etc., may be embedded. WH: 18C. French ASP. The jelly is probably so called because its colours are like those of the snake.

aspidistra *n.* a plant of the liliaceous genus *Aspidistra*, formerly often grown as a house plant. WH: 19C. Modern Latin, from Greek *aspis, aspidos* shield, from shape of stigma + *-istra*, from *Tupistra*, a related genus.

aspirate¹ *v.t.* to pronounce with an exhalation of breath. WH: 17C. Latin *aspiratus*, p.p. of *aspirare* ASPIRE. See also -ATE³.

aspirate² *a.* pronounced with an exhalation of breath. *Also n.* WH: 16C. Latin *aspiratus*, p.p. of *aspirare* ASPIRE. See also -ATE².

aspire *v.i.* to long, desire eagerly. *Also v.t.* WH: 12–14C. Old French *aspirer*, from Latin *aspirare*, from A-⁵ + *spirare* to breathe. The sense in the 16C was literal, to rise up, to mount, perhaps influenced by SPIRE¹. This soon became obsolete, except in poetry.

aspirin *n.* (a tablet containing) acetylsalicylic acid, used as a painkiller. WH: 19C. German *a(cetylierte) Spir(säure)* acetylated salicylic acid + -IN¹. See ACETYL, SPIRAEA, also -IN¹.

asplenium *n.* any fern of the genus *Asplenium* that is found worldwide and includes several species, e.g. the bird's nest fern, that are grown as house plants (cp. *spleenwort*). WH: 19C. Greek A-⁶ + *splēn* SPLEEN. The plant is said to cure spleen disorders. Cp. *spleenwort* (SPLEEN).

asquint *adv.* out of the corner of the eye, obliquely. WH: 12–14C. Appar. A-¹ + a Low German or Dutch word now found in Dutch *schuinte* obliquity, slant, from *schuin* oblique. Cp. SQUINT.

ass *n.* either of two wild quadrupeds, *Equus africanus* (of Africa) and *E. hemionus* (of Asia), allied to the horse, but of smaller size, with long ears and a tufted tail. WH: pre-1200. Old English *assa, asa*, from Celtic, from Latin *asinus*.

assai *adv.* very, as *largo assai*, very slow. WH: 18C. Italian enough, from Popular Latin *adsatis*, from *satis*. Cp. ASSETS.

assail *v.t.* to attack violently by physical means. WH: pre-1200. Old French *asalir* (Modern French *assaillir*), from Late Latin *assalire*, from Latin AS- + *salire* to leap. The verb has been influenced by ASSAY.

Assamese *a.* of or relating to Assam, its people or its language. *Also n.* WH: 19C. *Assam*, a state in NE India + -ESE.

assassin *n.* a person who kills someone, esp. for money or for fanatical, political etc. motives. WH: 16C. French, or from Late Latin *assassinus*, from Arabic *ḥašīšī* HASHISH-eater. The word was originally used of religious fanatics in the mountains of Lebanon who drugged themselves with hashish when about to murder a king or public figure.

assault *n.* a violent physical or verbal attack. *Also v.t., a.* WH: 12–14C. Old French *assaut* (Modern French *assaut*), ult. from Late Latin *assalire*. See ASSAIL.

assay *n.* the scientific determination of the quantity of metal in an ore, alloy, bullion or coin. *Also v.t., v.i.* WH: 12–14C. Old French *assai, assay*, var. of *essai* ESSAY¹.

assegai *n.* a slender lance of hard wood, esp. that of the southern African tribes. *Also v.t.* WH: 17C. Obs. French *azagaie* (Modern French *zagaie, sagaie*), or from Portuguese *azagaia*, or from Spanish *azagaya*, from Arabic (coll.) *az-zaġāya*, from *az*, form of *al* the + Berber *zaġāya* spear.

assemble *v.t.* to call together. *Also v.i., n.* WH: 12–14C. Old French *asembler* (Modern French *assembler*), ult. from Latin AS- + *simul* together.

assent *v.i.* to express agreement. *Also n.* WH: 12–14C. Old French *assenter*, ult. from Latin *assentire*, from AS- + *sentire* to feel, to think.

assert *v.t.* to affirm, to declare positively. WH: 17C. Latin *assertus*, p.p. of *asserere* to claim, to affirm, from AS- + *serere* to join.

assess *v.t.* to judge the quality or worth of; to value. WH: 14–15C. Old French *assesser*, from Latin *assessus*, p.p. of *assidere* to sit by, from AS- + *sedere* to sit. Cp. ASSIZE.

assets *n.pl.* all the property of a person or company which may be liable for outstanding debts. WH: 16C. Old French *asez* (Modern French *assez* enough), ult. from Latin AS- + *satis* enough. The word was originally a collective singular, but is now regarded as plural.

asseverate *v.t.* to affirm with solemnity. WH: 18C. Latin *asseveratus*, p.p. of *asseverare*, from AS- + *severus* grave, SEVERE. See also -ATE³.

assibilate *v.t.* to pronounce (a sound) with or as a sibilant. *Also v.i.* WH: 19C. Latin *assibilatus*, p.p. of *assibilare*, from AS- + *sibilare* to hiss. See also -ATE³.

assiduous *a.* hard-working, conscientious. WH: 16C. Latin *assiduus*, from *assidere* (ASSESS) + -OUS.

assign *v.t.* to allot, to apportion. *Also n.* WH: 12–14C. Old French *asigner* (Modern French *assigner*), from Latin *assignare*, from AS- + *signare* SIGN.

assignat *n.* paper money issued by the Revolutionary Government of France (1790–96) on the security of state lands. WH: 18C. French, from Latin *assignatum*, neut. p.p. of *assignare*. See ASSIGN.

assimilate *v.t.* to take as nutriment and convert into living tissue, to incorporate in the substance of an organism. *Also v.i.* WH: 14–15C. Latin *assimilatus*, p.p. of *assimilare*, from AS- + *similis* SIMILAR. See also -ATE³.

assist *v.t.* to help, to give support to. *Also v.i., n.* WH: 14–15C. Old French *assister*, from Latin *assistere*, from AS- + *sistere* to take one's stand. The meaning to stand near, to attend, developed from the 16C (cp. Modern French *assister à*), and became closer to Old French in the sense to be present at in the 17C. Both senses became obsolete from the 19C.

assize *n.* from 1815 to 1971, the sessions held periodically by the judges of the Supreme Court in each county in England and Wales for the administration of civil and criminal justice. *Also v.t.* WH: 12–14C. Old French *asise, assise*, fem. (used as n.) of *assis*, p.p. of *asseeir* (Modern French *asseoir*) to sit, to assess, from Latin *assidere*. See ASSESS.

associate¹ *v.t.* to connect in the mind or imagination. *Also v.i.* WH: 14–15C. Latin *associatus*, p.p. of *associare*, from AS- + *socius* sharing. See also -ATE³.

associate² *a.* connected or joined in a common enterprise. *Also n.* WH: 14–15C. Latin *associatus*, p.p. of *associare*. See ASSOCIATE¹, also -ATE².

assonant *a.* corresponding in sound. *Also n.* WH: 18C. French, from Latin *assonans, assonantis*, pres.p. of *assonare* to respond to, from AS- + *sonare*, from *sonus* sound. See also -ANT.

assort *v.t.* to arrange or dispose in groups of the same type, to classify. *Also v.i.* WH: 15C. Old French *assorter* (Modern French *assortir*), from *a-* (AD-) + *sorte* SORT. The spelling has assimilated to Latin verbs in *ass-*, from AS-.

assuage *v.t.* to soothe, to lessen the violence or pain of. *Also v.i.* WH: 12–14C. Old French *asouagier*, from Latin AS- + *suavis* sweet. Cp. SUAVE.

assume *v.t.* to take for granted, to accept without proof or as a hypothesis. *Also v.i.* WH: 14–15C. Latin *assumere*, from AS- + *sumere* to take.

assumpsit *n.* an oral or unsealed contract, founded on a consideration. WH: 16C. Latin he has taken upon himself, 3rd pers. sing. perf. ind. sing. of *assumere* ASSUME.

assumption *n.* the act of assuming or undertaking a task etc. WH: 12–14C. Old French *asompsion* (Modern French *assomption*), or from Latin *assumptio, assumptionis*, from *assumptus*, p.p. of *assumere* ASSUME. See also -ION.

assure *v.t.* to give confidence to, to convince. WH: 14–15C. Old French *assurer*, from Latin AS- + *securus* SECURE.

assurgent *a.* pointing upwards; rising upwards in a curve. WH: 16C. Latin *assurgens, assurgentis*, pres.p. of *assurgere*, from AS- + *surgere* to rise. See also -ENT.

Assyrian *a.* of or relating to the ancient kingdom of Assyria. *Also n.* WH: 14–15C. Latin *Assyrius*, from Greek *Assurios*, from *Assuria* Assyria, an ancient empire in Mesopotamia + -AN.

astable *a.* not stable. WH: mid-20C. A-⁶ + STABLE¹.

astarboard *adv.* on or towards the starboard side of a ship. WH: 15C. A-¹ + STARBOARD.

astatic *a.* not remaining fixed; unstable, unsteady. WH: 19C. Greek *astatos* unstable + -IC.

astatine *n.* a radioactive element, at. no. 85, chem. symbol At, formed in minute amounts by radioactive decay or made artificially. WH: mid-20C. Greek *astatos* unstable + -INE.

aster *n.* any of a genus, *Aster*, of composite plants with showy, daisy-like heads. WH: 17C. Latin, from Greek *astēr* star.

-aster *suf.* forming nouns meaning an inferior practitioner of an art, as in *criticaster, poetaster*. WH: Latin.

asteriated *a.* (of a crystal or gemstone) exhibiting asterism. WH: 19C. Greek *asterios* starry + -ATE² + -ED.

asterisk *n.* a mark (*) used in printing to call attention to a note, to mark omission etc. *Also v.t.* WH: 14–15C. Late Latin *asteriscus*, from Greek *asteriskos*, dim. of *astēr* star.

asterism *n.* a small cluster of stars. WH: 16C. Greek *asterismos*, from *astēr* star. See also -ISM.

astern *adv., a.* in, at or towards the stern of a ship. WH: 14–15C. A-¹ + STERN².

asteroid *n.* any of the small celestial bodies that orbit the sun, esp. between the orbits of Mars and Jupiter, a planetoid, a minor planet. *Also a.* WH: 19C. Greek *asteroeidēs* starlike, from *astēr* star. See also -OID.

asthenia *n.* absence of strength; debility, diminution or loss of vital power. WH: 18C. Modern Latin, from Greek *astheneia* weakness, from *asthenēs* weak, from A-⁶ + *sthenos* strength. See also -IA.

asthma *n.* a respiratory disorder, usu. allergic in origin, characterized by wheezing, constriction of the chest, and usu. coughing. WH: 14–15C. Greek, from *azein* to breathe hard.

Asti *n.* an Italian white wine. WH: 19C. *Asti*, a province in NW Italy.

astigmatism *n.* a defect of the eye or of a lens as a result of which a point source of light tends to be focused as a line. WH: 19C. A-⁶ + Greek *stigma, stigmatos* point + -ISM. Cp. STIGMA.

astilbe *n.* any plant of the perennial saxifragaceous genus *Astilbe*, having spikes or plumes of tiny red or white flowers. WH: 19C. Modern Latin, from Greek A-⁶ + *stilbē*, fem. of *stilbos* glittering. The plant is so called because its individual flowers are very small.

astir *a., adv.* in motion. WH: 18C. A-¹ + STIR¹.

astomatous *a.* mouthless. WH: 19C. Greek *astomatos*, from A-⁶ + *stoma, stomatos* mouth. See also -OUS.

astonish *v.t.* to strike with sudden surprise or wonder, to amaze. WH: 16C. *astony* or *astone*, from Old French *estoner* (Modern French *étonner*), from EX- + Latin *tonare* to thunder + -ISH². The original meaning was to shock, to dumbfound, also literally to stun, to stupefy. The more general sense evolved from the 17C. Cp. ASTOUND.

astound *v.t.* to strike with amazement, to shock with surprise. WH: 14–15C. *astounded*, from *astound*, form of *astoned*, p.p. of *astone* (ASTONISH) + -ED. The original sense was to shock, to stun. The current sense evolved from the 16C.

astraddle *adv.* in a straddling position. WH: 17C. A-¹ + STRADDLE.

astragal *n.* a small semicircular moulding or bead, round the top or the bottom of a column. WH: 17C. Latin *astragalus*, from Greek *astragalos*.

astrakhan *n.* the tightly curled, usu. black or grey fleece obtained from lambs orig. from Astrakhan. WH: 18C. *Astrakhan*, a city in central Asia (now in SW Russia).

astral *a.* of or relating to the stars. *Also n.* WH: 17C. Late Latin *astralis*, from *astrum* star. See also -AL¹.

astraphobia *n.* a morbid fear of thunder and lightning. WH: 19C. ASTRO- + -*phobia* (-PHOBE). The original sense was fear of the stars. The current sense has been influenced by Greek *astrapē* lightning.

astray *a., adv.* in or into sin, crime or error. WH: 12–14C. Anglo-French var. of Old French *estraié*, p.p. of *estraier* to stray, ult. from Latin *extra*- out of bounds + *vagari* to wander. Cp. STRAY.

astride *a., adv.* with a leg on either side. *Also prep.* WH: 17C. A-¹ + STRIDE.

astringent *a.* causing contraction of body tissues. *Also n.* WH: 16C. French, from Latin *astringens, astringentis*, pres.p. of *astringere*, from A-⁵ + *stringere* to bind. See also -ENT.

astro- *comb. form* of or relating to the heavenly bodies, planets or stars, as in *astrology, astronomy*. WH: Greek *astron* star. See also -O-.

astrobiology *n.* a branch of biology concerned with the search for life beyond the earth. WH: mid-20C. ASTRO- + BIOLOGY.

astrochemistry *n.* the study of the chemistry of celestial bodies and particles in interstellar space. WH: mid-20C. ASTRO- + CHEMISTRY.

astrodome *n.* a dome window in an aircraft to enable astronomical observations to be made. WH: mid-20C. ASTRO- + DOME¹.

astrodynamics *n.* the study of the motion of bodies in outer space and of the forces acting on them. WH: mid-20C. ASTRO- + *dynamics* (DYNAMIC).

astrogeology *n.* the study of the geology of the moon, etc. WH: mid-20C. ASTRO- + GEOLOGY.

astrohatch *n.* an astrodome in an aircraft. WH: mid-20C. ASTRO- + HATCH¹.

astroid *n.* a hypocycloid with four cusps (resembling a square with concave sides). WH: 19C. ASTRO- + -OID.

astrolabe *n.* an instrument, usu. consisting of a graduated disc with a sighting device, formerly used to measure the altitude of celestial bodies and as an aid to navigation. WH: 14–15C. Old French *astrelabe*, from Late Latin *astrolabium*, from Greek *astrolabos* star-taking.

astrology *n.* the study of a supposed connection between the changing aspects of the heavenly bodies and the changing course of human life, with predictions of events and advice on conduct. WH: 14–15C. Old French *astrologie*, from Latin *astrologia*, from Greek. See ASTRO-, -LOGY. The original sense was that of ASTRONOMY. The current sense evolved from the 16C.

astrometry *n.* the branch of astronomy concerned with measuring the position and motion of heavenly bodies. WH: 19C. ASTRO- + -METRY.

astronautics *n.* the science of travel through space. WH: early 20C. ASTRO- + -*nautics*, based on *aeronautics* (AERONAUT).

astronavigation *n.* navigation of a ship, aircraft or spaceship by observation of the stars. WH: mid-20C. ASTRO- + *navigation* (NAVIGATE).

astronomy *n.* the science which studies all phenomena of the heavenly bodies, space and the physical universe. WH: 12–14C. Old French *astronomie*, from Latin *astronomia*, from Greek. See ASTRO-, -NOMY. The word shared the sense of ASTROLOGY to the 18C, when the two senses were distinguished.

astrophotometer *n.* an instrument for measuring the intensity of sidereal light. WH: 19C. ASTRO- + PHOTOMETER.

astrophysics *n.* the branch of astronomy concerned with the physics and chemistry of celestial objects and their origin and evolution. WH: 19C. ASTRO- + PHYSICS.

Astroturf® *n.* an artificial grass surface, esp. for sports fields. WH: mid-20C. *Astro*(*dome*), an indoor baseball ground in Houston, Texas, where it was first used + TURF.

astute *a.* acute, discerning. WH: 17C. Obs. French *astut*, or from Latin *astutus*, from *astus* cunning.

astylar *a.* without columns or pilasters. WH: 19C. Greek *astulos* without columns, from A-⁶ + *stulos* column + -AR¹.

asunder *adv.* apart, in different pieces or places. WH: pre-1200. Old English *on sundran*. See A-¹, SUNDER.

asylum *n.* protection from extradition given by one country to a person, esp. a political refugee, from another. WH: 14–15C. Latin, from Greek *asulon* refuge, neut. (used as n.) of *asulos* inviolable, from A-⁶ + *sulē* right of seizure.

asymmetry *n.* lack of symmetry, or of proportion; an instance of this. WH: 17C. Greek *asummetria*. See A-⁶, SYMMETRY.

asymptomatic *a.* (of a disease) not exhibiting symptoms. WH: mid-20C. A-⁶ + *symptomatic* (SYMPTOM).

asymptote *n.* a straight mathematical line continually approaching some curve but never meeting it within a finite distance. WH: 17C. Greek *asumptōtos*, from A-⁶ + SYM- + *ptōtos* liable to fall.

asynchronous *a.* not coincident in point of time. WH: 18C. A-⁶ + SYNCHRONOUS.

asyndeton *n.* a rhetorical figure by which the conjunction is omitted, as 'I came, I saw, I conquered'. WH: 16C. Modern Latin, from Greek neut. (used as n.) of *asundetos* unconnected, from A-⁶ + *sundetos* bound together.

asynergia *n.* lack of coordination between muscles or parts, e.g. as a result of brain disease or damage. WH: 19C. Modern Latin, from A-⁶ + SYNERGY. See also -IA.

asyntactic *a.* loosely organized with regard to syntax; irregular, ungrammatical. WH: 19C. A-⁶ + *syntactic* (SYNTAX). See also -IC.

asystole *n.* the absence of heartbeat. WH: 19C. A-⁶ + SYSTOLE.

at *prep.* denoting nearness or precise position in time or space or on a scale. WH: pre-1200. Old English *æt*, from Germanic, rel. to Latin *ad* AD-.

at- *pref.* signifying motion towards, direction to, adherence etc., as in *attempt*, *attribute*. WH: Latin pref., from AD- with *d* assim. to *t*.

ataman *n.* an elected leader or general of the Cossacks. WH: 19C. Russian HETMAN.

ataraxia *n.* impassiveness, calmness, indifference, stoicism. WH: 17C. French *ataraxie*, from Greek *ataraxia* impassiveness, from A-[6] + *tarassein* to disturb. See also -IA.

atavism *n.* recurrence of some characteristic of a more or less remote ancestor. WH: 19C. French *atavisme*, from Latin *atavus* forefather, from *at-* beyond + *avus* grandfather. See also -ISM.

ataxia *n.* loss of the power of coordination of the muscles, resulting in irregular, jerky movements. WH: 19C. Modern Latin, from Greek, from A-[6] + *-taxia*, from *taxis* order. See also -IA, -Y[2].

-ate[1] *suf.* forming nouns of office or function, as in *curate*. WH: Latin *-atus*, n. suf. See -ATE[2].

-ate[2] *suf.* forming participial adjectives, as in *desolate*, *separate*, *situate*. WH: Latin *-atus*, p.p. suf. of vv. in *-are*.

-ate[3] *suf.* forming verbs, as in *desolate*, *separate*, corresponding to adjectives in the same form, or others produced on the same model, as in *fascinate*, *isolate*. WH: Latin -ATE[2], or influ. by French vv. in *-er*. Many verbs in *-ate* are formed from the past participle stem of Latin verbs in *-are*.

Atebrin® *n.* quinacrine. WH: mid-20C. Orig. unknown.

atelectasis *n.* failure of the lung to inflate at birth. WH: 19C. Greek *atelēs* imperfect + *ektasis* extension.

atelier *n.* a workshop, an artist's studio. WH: 17C. French, from Old French *astelier*, from *astelle* splinter of wood.

a tempo *adv., a.* in the original tempo or time. WH: 18C. Italian in time. Cp. TEMPO.

Athanasian *a.* of or relating to Athanasius, or the creed attributed to him. *Also n.* WH: 16C. Latin *Athanasius*, 293–373, bishop of Alexandria + -AN.

atheism *n.* disbelief in the existence of a God or gods. WH: 16C. French *athéisme*, from Greek *atheos* without God, from A-[6] + *theos* god. See also -ISM.

atheling *n.* a member of an Anglo-Saxon noble family, often restricted to a prince of the royal blood or to the heir apparent. WH: pre-1200. Old English *ætheling*, from Germanic, from base meaning race, family. See also -ING[3].

athematic *a.* not based on themes. WH: 19C. A-[6] + *thematic* (THEME).

athenaeum *n.* a literary or scientific club or institution. WH: 18C. Latin *Athenaeum*, from Greek *Athēnaion* temple of Athene in ancient Athens, where teachers taught and speakers and writers declaimed.

Athenian *n., a.* (a native or inhabitant) of Athens. WH: 16C. Latin *Atheniensis*, from *Athenae*, from Greek *Athēnai* Athens, the leading city of ancient Greece and its modern capital.

athermancy *n.* the power of stopping radiant heat or infrared radiation. WH: 19C. Greek *athermantos* not heated, from A-[6] + *thermainein* to heat (cp. THERM). See also -CY. Not rel. to -MANCY.

atheroma *n.* the deposition of fatty material on the inner coat of the arteries. WH: 16C. Latin, from Greek *athērōma*, from *athērē* groats. See also -OMA.

atherosclerosis *n.* thickening of the artery walls characterized by deposits of fatty material in the arteries. WH: early 20C. Greek *athērōma* (ATHEROMA) + SCLEROSIS.

athetosis *n.* a condition, caused by a cerebral lesion, that is characterized by involuntary writhing movements of the fingers and toes. WH: 19C. Greek *athetos* without position + -OSIS.

athirst *a.* thirsty, oppressed with thirst. WH: pre-1200. Old English *ofthyrst*, shortening of *ofthyrsted*, p.p. of *ofthyrstan* to suffer thirst. Cp. OFF, THIRST.

athlete *n.* a person trained to compete in events, such as running, weight-throwing and jumping, requiring strength, agility, speed or stamina. WH: 14–15C. Latin *athleta*, from Greek *athlētēs*, from *athlein* to contend for a prize, from *athlon* prize.

Atholl brose *n.* a mixture of whisky and honey, often with oatmeal. WH: 18C. *Atholl* (*Athole*), a district of central Scotland + BROSE.

-athon *suf.* denoting an event or contest that continues for a long time, as in *talkathon*, *danceathon*. WH: From MARATHON.

athwart *prep.* from side to side of, across. *Also adv.* WH: 14–15C. A-[1] + THWART.

-atic *suf.* forming adjectives, as in *aquatic*, *fanatic*, *lunatic*. WH: French *-atique*, or from Latin *-aticus*, combining -IC with v. or n. stems in *-at-*.

-atile *suf.* forming adjectives chiefly denoting possibility or quality, as in *volatile*. WH: French *-atile*, or from Latin *-atilis*, combining -ilis -IL with v. or n. stems in *-at-*.

atilt *a., adv.* tilted up. WH: 16C. A-[1] + TILT.

-ation *suf.* forming abstract nouns from verbs, as in *approbation*, *conservation*, *ovation*. WH: Old French *-acion* (Modern French *-ation*), from Latin *-atio*, *-ationis*. Cp. -TION, -ION.

-ative *suf.* forming adjectives, as in *demonstrative*, *representative*, *talkative*. WH: French *-atif*, or from Latin *-ativus*, combining *-ivus* -IVE with v. stems in *-at-*.

Atlantean *a.* of or like the Titan Atlas; very strong. WH: 17C. Latin *Atlanteus*, from *Atlas*, *Atlantis* (ATLAS). See also -EAN.

Atlantic *a.* of or occurring in or near the Atlantic Ocean. *Also n.* WH: 14–15C. Greek *Atlantikos*, from *Atlas*, *Atlantis*. See ATLAS, also -IC.

atlas *n.* a book containing a collection of maps. WH: 16C. Latin, from Greek *Atlas*, the Titan said to hold up the pillars of the universe. It was a practice to place a picture of Atlas supporting the heavens on the front page of collections of maps.

atman *n.* in Hinduism, the innermost self, the soul or the Universal Soul, the supreme spiritual principle. WH: 18C. Sanskrit *ātman* breath, soul.

atmo- *comb. form* of or relating to vapour or to the atmosphere. WH: Greek *atmos* vapour.

atmolysis *n.* the separation of gases in combination based on their different rates of diffusion through a porous substance. WH: 19C. ATMO- + LYSIS.

atmometer *n.* an instrument for measuring the moisture exhaled in a given time from any humid surface. WH: 19C. ATMO- + -METER.

atmosphere *n.* the gaseous envelope surrounding any of the celestial bodies, esp. that surrounding the earth. WH: 17C. Modern Latin *atmosphaera*, from Greek *atmos* vapour + *sphaira* SPHERE.

atoll *n.* a coral island, consisting of an annular reef surrounding a lagoon. WH: 17C. Maldivian *atoḷu*, ? from Malayalam *aḍal* uniting, closing.

atom *n.* the smallest particle taking part in chemical action, the smallest particle of matter possessing the properties of an element. WH: 14–15C. Old French *atome*, from Latin *atomus*, from Greek *atomos*, use as n. of a., indivisible, from A-[6] + *tomos* a cutting, from *temnein* to cut. Cp. TOME. The word was originally used as a hypothetical particle of matter that could not be further divided. The current sense dates from the 19C.

†atomy[1] *n.* a minute particle, an atom. WH: 16C. Prob. Latin *atomi*, pl. of *atomus* ATOM, but assoc. with ATOMY[2].

†atomy[2] *n.* a skeleton, an anatomical preparation. WH: 16C. ANATOMY, as if *an atomy*.

atonal *a.* without a fixed key. WH: early 20C. A-[6] + TONAL.

atone *v.i.* to make expiation or satisfaction for some crime, sin or fault. *Also v.t.* WH: 12–14C. AT + ONE. The original sense was to reconcile, then to appease, then as now to expiate from the 17C.

at-oneness *n.* the condition of being at one, reconcilement, harmony. WH: 19C. *at one* + -NESS. Cp. ATONE.

atonic *a.* without an accent, unaccented. *Also n.* WH: 18C. A-[6] + TONIC.

atop *adv.* on or at the top. *Also prep.* WH: 17C. A-[1] + TOP[1].

atopy *n.* a hereditary tendency to acute allergic reactions. WH: early 20C. Greek *atopia* unusualness, from *atopos* unusual, from A-[6] + *topos* place. See also -Y[2].

-ator *suf.* forming nouns denoting a person or thing performing an action as in *equator*, *agitator*, *commentator*. WH: French *-ateur*, or from Latin *-ator*. Cp. -OR.

-atory *suf.* forming adjectives meaning related to or involving a verbal action, as in *commendatory*. WH: Latin *-atorius*. Cp. -ORY[2].

atrabilious *a.* melancholic. WH: 17C. Latin *atra bilis* black bile. See also -IOUS. The Latin phrase translates Greek *melankholia* MELANCHOLY.

atrazine *n.* a white crystalline compound widely used as a weed-killer. WH: mid-20C. *a(mino)* (AMINE) + *tr(i)azine*.

atrium *n.* the central court in an ancient Roman house. WH: 16C. Latin, of unknown orig.

atrocious *a.* very bad, execrable. WH: 17C. Latin *atrox, atrocis* fierce, cruel. See also -IOUS.

atrophy *n.* a wasting of the body, or (one of) its organs, through lack of nourishment or disease. *Also v.t., v.i.* WH: 17C. French *atrophie*, or from Late Latin *atrophia*, from Greek lack of food. See A-[6], -TROPHY.

atropine *n.* a poisonous alkaloid obtained from deadly nightshade, *Atropa belladonna*, used in the treatment of intestinal spasm and to counteract the slowing of the heart. WH: 19C. Modern Latin *Atropa*, from Greek *Atropos* inflexible, one of the Fates in mythology + -INE. Atropos was the Fate who cut the thread of life. The plant was named from its toxic nature.

attaboy *int.* used to express encouragement. WH: early 20C. Prob. from *that's the boy!*. The word is mostly used to encourage a male. Cp. *attagirl* for a female.

attach *v.t.* to connect, affix. *Also v.i.* WH: 12–14C. Old French *atachier* (Modern French *attacher*), ult. from Germanic. Rel. to STAKE[1].

attaché *n.* a junior member of an ambassador's staff. WH: 19C. French, p.p. of *attacher* ATTACH.

attack *v.t.* to launch a physical or armed assault on. *Also v.i., n.* WH: 17C. French *attaquer*, from Italian *attaccare* to join battle, ATTACH.

attain *v.i.* to arrive at some object. *Also v.t.* WH: 12–14C. Old French *ataindre* (Modern French *atteindre*), from Latin *attingere* to touch on, from AT- + *tangere* to touch.

attainder *n.* the forfeiture of civil rights as the legal consequence of a sentence of death or outlawry for treason or felony. WH: 14–15C. Anglo-French *attainder*, use as n. of inf. *atteinder*, from Old French *ataindre* ATTAIN. See also -ER[4].

attaint *v.t.* to condemn or subject to attainder. *Also a., n.* WH: 12–14C. Old French *ataint*, p.p. of *ataindre* ATTAIN.

attar *n.* a fragrant essence, or essential oil, esp. of roses. WH: 17C. Persian *'itr*, or from Arabic *'iṭr*, coll. Arabic *'aṭar* perfume, essence.

attempt *v.t.* to try, endeavour (to do, achieve etc.). *Also n.* WH: 12–14C. Old French *attempter* (Modern French *attenter*), from Latin *attemptare*, from AT- + *temptare* TEMPT.

attend *v.t.* to be present at. *Also v.i.* WH: 12–14C. Old French *atendre* (Modern French *attendre* to wait for), from Latin *attendere*, from AT- + *tendere* to stretch. Cp. TEND[1].

attention *n.* the act or state of concentrating the mind on some object. *Also int.* WH: 14–15C. Latin *attentio, attentionis*, from *attentus*, p.p. of *attendere* ATTEND. See also -ION.

attentive *a.* paying attention; listening carefully. WH: 12–14C. French *attentif*, from *attente*, from Old French *atente*, fem. p.p. (used as n.) of *atendre* ATTEND + -IVE.

attenuate[1] *v.t.* to make thin or slender. *Also v.i.* WH: 16C. Latin *attenuatus*, p.p. of *attenuare*, from AT- + *tenuare* to make thin, from *tenuis* thin. See also -ATE[3]. Cp. TENUITY.

attenuate[2] *a.* slender. WH: 14–15C. Latin *attenuatus*, p.p. of *attenuare*. See ATTENUATE[1], also -ATE[2].

attest *v.t.* to vouch for, to certify. *Also v.i., n.* WH: 16C. French *attester*, from Latin *attestari*, from AT- + *testari* to witness, from *testis* witness. Cp. TESTIFY.

Attic *a.* of or belonging to Attica, its capital, Athens, or the Greek dialect spoken there. *Also n.* WH: 16C. Latin *Atticus*, from Greek *Attikos* of Attica, a district of ancient Greece. See also -IC.

attic *n.* the top storey of a house. WH: 17C. French *attique* ATTIC. The storey is so called from its situation at the top of the house, corresponding to the site of the Attic order above the main façade. The sense of top storey evolved as a noun from the adjective in the 19C.

attire *v.t.* to dress, esp. in fine or formal clothing. *Also n.* WH: 12–14C. Old French *atirier* to arrange, to equip, from *a tire*, Provençal *a tieira* in order. Cp. TIER. The original sense was to put in order, to equip, as of a horse for war or a knight with armour. The more general sense evolved from the 15C.

attitude *n.* a mental position or way of thinking with respect to someone or something. WH: 17C. French, from Italian *attitudine*, or

from Spanish *attitud* fitness, disposition, from Late Latin *aptitudo, aptitudinis* APTITUDE.

atto- *comb. form* denoting a factor of 10^{-18}. WH: Danish or Norwegian *atten* eighteen. See also -O-.

attorn *v.t.* to acknowledge (a new owner) as one's landlord. *Also v.i.* WH: 12–14C. Old French *atorner* to assign, to appoint, from *a-* (AD-) + *torner* TURN.

attorney *n.* a legally authorized agent or deputy. WH: 12–14C. Old French *atorné*, p.p. (used as n.) of *atorner*. See ATTORN.

attract *v.t.* to draw to oneself or itself or cause to approach. *Also v.i.* WH: 12–14C. Latin *attractus*, p.p. of *attrahere*, from AT- + *trahere* to draw.

attribute[1] *n.* a quality ascribed or imputed to any person or thing. WH: 14–15C. Old French *attribut*, or from Latin *attributum*, neut. p.p. (used as n.) of *attribuere* ATTRIBUTE[2].

attribute[2] *v.t.* to regard as caused by. WH: 15C. Latin *attributus*, p.p. of *attribuere*, from AT- + *tribuere* to allot. Cp. TRIBUTE.

attrit *v.t.* to wear down (an enemy, opponent) by constant (small-scale) action. WH: mid-20C. From ATTRITION.

attrition *n.* the act or process of wearing away, esp. by friction. WH: 14–15C. Late Latin *attritio, attritionis*, from *attritus*, p.p. of *atterere*, from AT- + *terere* to rub.

attune *v.t.* to accustom, acclimatize. *Also n.* WH: 16C. AT- + TUNE.

atypical *a.* not typical, not conforming to type. WH: 19C. A-[6] + TYPICAL.

Au *chem. symbol* gold. WH: Latin *aurum* gold.

aubade *n.* a poem or musical piece announcing or greeting dawn. WH: 17C. French, from Spanish *albada*, from *alba* dawn.

auberge *n.* an inn in France. WH: 16C. French, from Provençal *alberga* lodgings, rel. to German *Herberge* inn, from Old High German *heriberga* army shelter. Cp. HARBOUR.

aubergine *n.* the eggplant, *Solanum melongena*. WH: 18C. French, from Catalan *alberginia*, from Arabic *al-bāḏinjān*, from *al* the + Persian *bāḏingān*, from Sanskrit *vātiṃgana*.

aubrietia *n.* a plant of a genus, *Aubretia*, of dwarf, perennial, spring-flowering rock plants of the family Cruciferae. WH: 19C. Modern Latin *Aubrieta*, from Claude *Aubriet*, 1668–1743, French botanist. See also -IA.

auburn *a.* reddish-brown. *Also n.* WH: 14–15C. Old French *alborne, auborne*, from Medieval Latin *alburnus* whitish, from Latin *albus* white. The word was originally used of a yellowish or brownish white colour. The current sense, reddish brown, arose through a false association with BROWN.

AUC *abbr.* (in Roman dates) from the foundation of the city. WH: Latin *ab urbe condita*, lit. from the founded city, with ref. to Rome. The dates were calculated from 753 BC, a year arbitrarily fixed by Varro.

au courant *a.* fully informed, up to date with the situation. WH: 18C. French in the current. See CURRENT.

auction *n.* a public sale of goods, usu. one in which each bidder offers a higher price than the preceding. *Also v.t.* WH: 16C. Latin *auctio, auctionis* increase, from *auctus*, p.p. of *augere* to increase. See also -ION.

auctorial *a.* of or relating to an author or the occupation of an author. WH: 19C. Latin *auctor* AUTHOR + -IAL.

audacious *a.* bold, daring. WH: 16C. Latin *audax, audacis* bold, from *audere* to dare. See also -ACIOUS.

audible *a.* capable of being heard. WH: 15C. Late Latin *audibilis*, from *audire* to hear.

audience *n.* an assembly of hearers or spectators at a meeting, play, concert etc. WH: 14–15C. Old French, from Latin *audientia*, from *audiens, audientis*, pres.p. of *audire* to hear. See also -ENCE.

audile *a.* of or relating to sound or hearing. *Also n.* WH: 19C. Latin *audire* to hear + -IL.

audio *a.* of or relating to sound or its reproduction, transmission or broadcasting. *Also n.* WH: early 20C. Independent use of AUDIO-.

audio- *comb. form* of or relating to hearing. WH: Latin *audire* to hear. See also -O-.

audiology *n.* the science of hearing. WH: mid-20C. AUDIO- + -LOGY.

audiometer *n.* an application of the telephone for testing the sense of hearing. WH: 19C. AUDIO- + -METER.

audiophile *n.* a person with an enthusiastic interest in high-fidelity sound reproduction. WH: mid-20C. AUDIO- + -PHILE.

audiovisual *a.* (esp. of teaching methods or aids) directed at or involving hearing and sight. WH: mid-20C. AUDIO- + VISUAL.

audiphone *n.* an instrument which, when pressed against the teeth, enables people with some types of deafness to hear by conveying sound waves to the auditory nerves. WH: 19C. Latin *audire* to hear + Greek *phōnē* sound. The word is based on TELEPHONE.

audit *n.* an official examination of accounts. *Also v.t.* WH: 14–15C. Latin *auditus* hearing, p.p. (used as n.) of *audire* to hear.

audition *n.* a trial performance by a singer, musician, actor etc. applying for a position or role. *Also v.t., v.i.* WH: 16C. Latin *auditio, auditionis*, from *auditus*, p.p. of *audire* to hear. See also -ION.

auditor *n.* a person appointed to audit accounts. WH: 14–15C. Old French *auditeur*, from Latin *auditor*, from *auditus*. See AUDIT, also -OR.

auditorium *n.* the part of a building occupied by the audience. WH: 17C. Latin, neut. (used as n.) of *auditorius* concerning hearing. See AUDITORY, also -ORIUM.

auditory *a.* of or relating to the organs or sense of hearing, perceived by the ear. *Also n.* WH: 16C. Late Latin *auditorius*, from Latin AUDITOR. See also -ORY².

au fait *a.* having up-to-date knowledge, fully informed. WH: 18C. French to the fact. Cp. FACT.

au fond *adv.* basically. WH: 18C. French at the bottom. Cp. FUND.

auf Wiedersehen *int.* farewell, goodbye. WH: 19C. German to the seeing again, from *auf* to + *wieder* again + *sehen* to see. Cp. ARRIVEDERCI, AU REVOIR.

Augean *a.* of or relating to Augeas. WH: 16C. Latin *Augeas*, from Greek *Augeias* Augeas, a mythical king of Elis, whose stables had not been cleaned for 30 years until Hercules turned the River Alpheus through them + -AN.

auger *n.* a carpenter's tool, somewhat resembling a very large gimlet, worked with both hands, for boring holes in wood. WH: pre-1200. Old English *nafogār*, from *nafu* NAVE² + *gār* spear, piercer. The initial *n* was lost through misdivision of *a nauger* as *an auger*. Cp. ADDER, APRON.

†aught *n.* anything whatever. *Also adv.* WH: pre-1200. Old English *āwiht*, from Germanic. Cp. AYE², WIGHT.

augite *n.* a greenish, brownish-black or black variety of aluminous pyroxene found in igneous rocks. WH: 19C. Greek *augitēs*, from *augē* lustre. See also -ITE¹.

augment¹ *v.t.* to increase, to make larger or greater in number, degree, intensity etc. *Also v.i.* WH: 14–15C. Old French *augmenter*, or from Late Latin *augmentare*, from *augmentum*, from *augere* to increase.

augment² *n.* a grammatical prefix in the form of a vowel used in the older Indo-European languages to denote past time. WH: 14–15C. Old French, or from Late Latin *augmentum*. See AUGMENT¹, also -MENT. The original sense was an increase.

au gratin *a.* (of a dish) with a light crust, usu. made by browning breadcrumbs and cheese. WH: 19C. French with the GRATIN.

augur *v.t.* to foretell from signs or omens. *Also v.i., n.* WH: 16C. Latin soothsayer, ? from *avis* bird and root of *garrire* to chatter. Cp. GARRULOUS.

August *n.* the eighth month of the year, named in honour of Augustus Caesar. WH: pre-1200. Latin *augustus*, after *Augustus* Caesar. See AUGUSTAN.

august *a.* inspiring reverence and admiration. WH: 17C. Old French *auguste*, or from Latin *augustus* consecrated, venerable.

Augustan *a.* of or belonging to Augustus Caesar or his age, in which Latin literature reached its highest development. *Also n.* WH: 16C. Latin *Augustus*. See -AN. Augustus Caesar (reigned 27 BC–AD 14), born Gaius Octavius, was granted the title *Augustus* in 23 BC in recognition of his services and status.

auguste *n.* a type of circus clown who plays the role of the clumsy bungler. WH: early 20C. French, from German *August* the forename (Augustus). The German forename came to mean fool, clown, presumably as an ironic use of the 'noble' original. See AUGUST, AUGUSTAN.

Augustine *n.* an Augustinian friar. WH: 14–15C. Old French *augustin*, from Latin *Augustinus* St Augustine of Hippo, 354–430, a Father of the Church.

auk *n.* a northern seabird of the family Alcidae, with black and white plumage, heavy body and short wings, esp. the great auk (now extinct), the little auk and the razorbill. WH: 17C. Old Norse *álka* razorbill.

auld *a.* old. WH: 14–15C. Var. of OLD, representing pronun. of Old English (Anglian) *ald*.

aulic *a.* of or relating to a royal court. *Also n.* WH: 18C. French *aulique*, or from Latin *aulicus*, from Greek *aulikos*, from *aulē* court. See also -IC.

aumbry *n.* a niche or cupboard in a church for books and sacred vessels. WH: 12–14C. Old French *almarie*, var. of *armarie* (Modern French *armoire* cupboard), from Latin *armarium* closet, from *arma* utensils.

au naturel *a., adv.* in the natural state. WH: 19C. French. Cp. NATURAL.

aunt *n.* the sister of one's father or mother. WH: 12–14C. Old French *ante* (Modern French *tante*), from Latin *amita*. The initial *t* of French *tante* comes from *antante*, a childish reduplication. Cp. French *tata* auntie.

au pair *n.* a person, esp. a girl, from a foreign country who performs domestic tasks in exchange for board and lodging. *Also v.i.* WH: 19C. French on equal terms. Cp. PAIR, PAR¹.

aura *n.* a distinctive atmosphere or quality. WH: 14–15C. Latin, from Greek breath, breeze.

aural *a.* of or relating to the ear. WH: 19C. Latin *auris* ear + -AL¹.

aureate *a.* golden, gold-coloured. WH: 14–15C. Late Latin *aureatus*, from *aureus* golden, from *aurum* gold. See also -ATE².

aureole *n.* the gold disc surrounding the head in early pictures of religious figures, and denoting glory, a nimbus. WH: 15C. French *auréole*, from Latin *aureola*, fem. of *aureolus*, dim. of *aureus* golden, from *aurum* gold.

au revoir *int.* farewell, goodbye. WH: 17C. French to the seeing again, from *au* to the + *revoir* to see again. Cp. ARRIVEDERCI, AUF WIEDERSEHEN, Spanish *hasta la vista*, Russian *do svidaniya*, English *see you (later)*.

auric *a.* of or relating to gold, applied to compounds in which gold is trivalent. WH: 19C. Latin *aurum* gold + -IC.

auricle *n.* an atrium of the heart. WH: 14–15C. Latin *auricula*. See AURICULA, also -CLE.

auricula *n.* a garden flower, *Primula auricula*, sometimes called bear's ear, from the shape of its leaves. WH: 17C. Latin, dim. of *auris* ear. See also -CULE.

auricular *a.* of, relating to, using or known by the sense of hearing. *Also n.* WH: 14–15C. Late Latin *auricularius*, from *auricula*. See AURICULA, also -AR¹.

auriferous *a.* yielding or producing gold. WH: 17C. Latin *aurifer* gold-bearing, from *aurum* gold. See also -FEROUS.

Aurignacian *a.* of or relating to the period of Upper Palaeolithic culture typified by human remains and implements etc. of stone, horn and bone found in the cave of Aurignac, Haute-Garonne. WH: early 20C. French *Aurignacien*, from *Aurignac*, a place in SW France, where remains of it were found.

aurochs *n.* the extinct wild ox, *Bos primigenius*. WH: 18C. German, var. of *Auerochs*, from Old High German *ūrohso*, from *ūro* aurochs + *ohso* OX.

aurora *n.* a peculiar illumination of the night sky common within the polar circles, consisting of streams of light ascending towards the zenith. WH: 14–15C. Latin *Aurora*, a goddess of the dawn in Roman mythology, from an Indo-European source that also gave EAST.

auscultation *n.* listening with the ear or stethoscope to the sounds made by the internal organs, to judge their condition. WH: 17C. Latin *auscultatio, auscultationis*, from *auscultatus*, p.p. of *auscultare* to hear attentively. See also -ATION.

Auslese *n.* a usu. sweetish white wine from Germany or Austria made from selected ripe grapes. WH: 19C. German, from *aus* out + *Lese* picking, vintage.

auspex *n.* in ancient Rome, a person who took the auspices; an augur. WH: 16C. Latin, from *avispex*, from *avis* bird + *-spex* observer, from *specere* to look.

†auspicate *v.t.* to inaugurate, initiate. *Also v.i.* WH: 17C. Latin *auspicatus*, p.p. of *auspicari*, from *auspicium*. See AUSPICE, also -ATE³.

auspice n. patronage, protection. WH: 16C. French, or from Latin *auspicium* taking omens from birds. See AUSPEX.

Aussie n. an Australian. *Also a.* WH: early 20C. Abbr. of AUSTRALIAN. A variant spelling *Ozzie* represents a pronunciation of *Aussie*.

austenite n. a solid solution of carbon or another element with one of the phases of iron. WH: early 20C. Sir William Roberts-*Austen*, 1843–1902, English metallurgist + -ITE[1].

Auster n. the south wind. WH: 14–15C. Latin, rel. to EAST.

austere a. severely simple, unadorned. WH: 12–14C. Old French *austère*, from Latin *austerus*, from Greek *austēros* severe.

Austin a., n. (an) Augustinian. WH: 12–14C. Contr. of Old French *augustin*. See AUGUSTINE.

austral a. southern. WH: 15C. Latin *australis* southern, from AUSTER. See also -AL[1].

Australasian a. of or relating to Australasia, a general name for Australia, New Zealand, Tasmania and the surrounding islands. *Also n.* WH: 19C. *Australasia* (from *Australia* + *Asia*) + -AN.

Australian a. of or belonging to Australia. *Also n.* WH: 17C. French *australien*, from Latin *australis*, in name *Terra Australis* southern land, supposed continent and islands in southern hemisphere. The named region now includes Australasia, Polynesia and parts of southern S America. Australia was originally *Terra Australis Incognita*, unknown southern land.

Australopithecus n. a fossil primate of the extinct genus *Australopithecus* whose remains have been found in southern Africa. WH: early 20C. Modern Latin, from Latin *australis* southern + -O- + Greek *pithēkos* ape.

Australorp n. an Australian utility-type of black Orpington fowl. WH: early 20C. AUSTRALIAN + ORPINGTON.

Austrian n. a native or inhabitant of Austria. *Also a.* WH: 17C. *Austria*, a country in central Europe + -AN. The German name of Austria is *Österreich* eastern kingdom.

Austro-[1] comb. form German. WH: AUSTRAL. See also -O-.

Austro-[2] comb. form Austrian. WH: AUSTRIAN. See also -O-.

autacoid n. an internal secretion, a hormone or chalone. WH: early 20C. Greek *autos* self (AUTO-) + *akos* remedy + -OID.

autarch n. an absolute sovereign, an autocrat. WH: 19C. Greek *autos* self (AUTO-) + *arkhos* ruler.

autarky n. self-sufficiency, esp. national economic self-sufficiency. WH: 17C. Greek *autarkia*, from *autarkēs* self-sufficient, from AUTO- + *arkein* to suffice.

autecology n. (the study of) the ecology of an individual organism or species. WH: early 20C. AUTO- + ECOLOGY.

auteur n. a film director who is thought of as having a more than usually dominant role in the creation of their films and a unique personal style. WH: mid-20C. French AUTHOR.

authentic a. of undisputed origin, genuine. WH: 14–15C. Old French *autentique* (Modern French *authentique*), from Late Latin *authenticus*, from Greek *authentikos* principal, genuine, from *authentēs* one acting on own authority. The original sense was authoritative. The current sense gradually took over from the 15C.

author n. the composer of a literary work. *Also v.t.* WH: 12–14C. Old French *autor* (Modern French *auteur*), from Latin *auctor*, from *augere* to increase, to promote.

authority n. legitimate power to command or act. WH: 12–14C. Old French *autorité*, from Latin *auctoritas*, from *auctor*. See AUTHOR, also -ITY.

authorize v.t. to give authority to, to empower. WH: 14–15C. Old French *autoriser*, from Medieval Latin *auctorizare*, from *auctor*. See AUTHOR, also -IZE.

autism n. a disorder of mental development, usu. evident from childhood, marked by complete self-absorption, lack of social communication and inability to form relationships. WH: early 20C. Greek *autos* self + -ISM.

auto- comb. form self. WH: Greek, from *autos* self.

autoantibody n. an antibody produced in reaction to an antigen contained within the organism itself. WH: early 20C. AUTO- + ANTIBODY.

autobahn n. a motorway in Germany, Austria or Switzerland. WH: mid-20C. German, from *Auto* automobile + *Bahn* road.

autobiography n. a memoir of one's life, written by oneself. WH: 18C. AUTO- + BIOGRAPHY.

autocar n. a vehicle driven by its own mechanical power, a motor vehicle. WH: 18C. AUTOMOBILE + CAR.

autocephalous a. (of an eastern Church) having the power to appoint its own synod, bishop etc. WH: 19C. AUTO- + -*cephalous* (-CEPHALIC).

autochanger n. a device that allows records to be dropped one by one from a stack on to a turntable. WH: mid-20C. AUTO- + *changer* (CHANGE).

autochthon n. any one of the original or earliest known inhabitants. WH: 16C. Greek *autokhthōn* indigenous, from AUTO- + *khthōn* earth, soil.

autoclave n. a sealed vessel used for chemical reactions at high temperature and pressure. *Also v.t.* WH: 19C. French, from AUTO- + Latin *clavus* nail or *clavis* key. The vessel is so called because it is self-fastening.

autocracy n. absolute government by a single person. WH: 17C. Greek *autokrateia*, from *autokratēs* AUTOCRAT. See also -CRACY.

autocrat n. a sovereign with uncontrolled authority. WH: 19C. French *autocrate*, from Greek *autokratēs*, from AUTO- + *kratos* power, authority.

autocross n. the sport of motor racing across country or on unmade roads. WH: mid-20C. AUTOMOBILE + *cross*(-*country*) (see CROSS).

Autocue® n. a device that displays the text to be spoken by a person on television. WH: mid-20C. AUTO- + CUE[1].

autocycle n. a pedal cycle with motor attachment. WH: early 20C. AUTOMOBILE + BICYCLE.

auto-da-fé n. a sentence pronounced by the Inquisition. WH: 18C. Portuguese act of faith, from *auto* act + *da* of + *fé* faith.

autodestruct a. having the power to destroy itself or to initiate self-destruction. *Also v.i.* WH: late 20C. AUTO- + *destruct* (DESTRUCTION).

autodidact n. a self-taught person. WH: 18C. Greek *autodidaktos* self-taught. See AUTO-, DIDACTIC.

autodyne a. (of an electrical circuit) in which the same elements and valves are used both as oscillator and detector. WH: early 20C. AUTO- + HETERODYNE.

auto-erotism n. self-produced sexual pleasure or emotion, e.g. masturbation. WH: early 20C. AUTO- + *erotism* (EROTIC).

autofocus n. a facility in some cameras for automatically focusing the lens. WH: mid-20C. AUTO- + FOCUS.

autogamy n. self-fertilization. WH: 19C. AUTO- + -GAMY.

autogenous a. self-engendered, self-produced, independent. WH: 19C. Greek *autogenēs*. See AUTO-, -GENOUS.

autogiro n. an aircraft in which the lifting surfaces are the freely-rotating blades of a large horizontal airscrew. WH: early 20C. Spanish, from AUTO- + *giro* gyration.

autograft n. a surgical graft that moves tissue from one point to another in the same individual's body. WH: early 20C. AUTO- + GRAFT[1].

autograph n. a signature written esp. by a celebrity for an admirer. *Also a., v.t.* WH: 17C. French *autographe*, or from Late Latin *autographum*, from Greek *autographon*, from neut. (used as n.) of *autographos* written with one's own hand. See AUTO-, -GRAPH. The current popular sense dates from the 19C.

Autoharp® n. a zither-like instrument having dampers which stop selected strings from sounding and allow chords to be played. WH: 19C. AUTO- + HARP.

autohypnosis n. the process of putting oneself into a hypnotic trance. WH: early 20C. AUTO- + HYPNOSIS.

autoimmune a. of or caused by antibodies that attack the molecules, cells etc. normally present in the organism producing them. WH: mid-20C. AUTO- + IMMUNE.

autointoxication n. reabsorption of toxic matter produced by the body. WH: 19C. AUTO- + *intoxication* (INTOXICATE).

autolysis n. the breakdown of cells by the action of enzymes produced in the cells themselves. WH: early 20C. AUTO- + LYSIS.

automat n. a vending machine. WH: 17C. German, from French *automate*, from Latin AUTOMATON.

automatic a. operating without direct or continuous human intervention. *Also n.* WH: 18C. Greek *automatos* + -IC. See AUTOMATON.

automation n. the use of self-regulating or automatically programmed machines in the manufacture of goods. WH: mid-20C.

AUTOMATIC + -ATION. The term was coined by Delmar S. Harder, a manufacturing executive of the Ford Motor Company, who in 1947 organized a group of specialists he called 'automation engineers'.

automatism n. the quality of being automatic. WH: 19C. French *automatisme*, from *automate*. See AUTOMATON.

automaton n. a machine that is activated by a concealed mechanism and power source within itself, a robot. WH: 17C. Latin, from Greek, from neut. (used as n.) of *automatos* acting of itself, from AUTO- + -*matos* thinking, animated.

automobile n. a motor car. Also a. WH: 19C. French, from AUTO- + MOBILE. The original automobiles were self-propelling, as distinct from horse-drawn vehicles.

automotive a. self-propelling. WH: 19C. AUTO- + MOTIVE.

autonomy n. the right of self-government. WH: 17C. Greek *autonomia*, from *autonomos* having its own laws, from AUTO- + *nomos* law. See also -NOMY.

autopilot n. automatic pilot. WH: mid-20C. AUTO- + PILOT.

autopista n. a motorway in Spain. WH: mid-20C. Spanish, from *auto* automobile + *pista* track, PISTE.

autoplasty n. repair of a lesion by healthy tissue from the same body. WH: 19C. AUTO- + -PLASTY.

autopsy n. a post-mortem examination. Also v.t. WH: 17C. French *autopsie*, or from Modern Latin *autopsia*, from Greek, from *autoptēs* eyewitness. See AUTO-, OPTIC.

autoradiograph n. a photograph produced by radiation from, and showing the distribution of, radioactive particles in a body. WH: early 20C. AUTO- + RADIOGRAPH.

autorotation n. rotation resulting from the shape or structure of an object in an airflow, not from a power source. WH: early 20C. AUTO- + *rotation* (ROTATE[1]).

autoroute n. a motorway in France. WH: mid-20C. French, from *auto* automobile + *route* road, ROUTE.

autoschediasm n. something hastily improvised. WH: 19C. Greek *autoskhediasma*, from *autoskhediazein* to act or speak offhand, from *autoskhedios* offhand.

autosome n. a chromosome other than a sex chromosome. WH: early 20C. AUTO- + -SOME[2].

autostrada n. a motorway in Italy. WH: early 20C. Italian, from *auto* automobile + *strada* road. Cp. STRATUM.

autosuggestion n. suggestion arising from oneself, esp. the unconscious influencing of one's own beliefs, physical condition etc. WH: 19C. AUTO- + *suggestion* (SUGGEST).

autotelic a. that is an end in itself. WH: 19C. AUTO- + Greek *telos* end.

autotimer n. a device that can be set to turn an appliance, e.g. a cooker, on or off at a predetermined time. WH: mid-20C. AUTO- + *timer* (TIME).

autotomy n. voluntary separation of a part of the body, e.g. the tail, as in certain lizards. WH: 19C. AUTO- + -TOMY.

autotoxic a. self-poisoning. WH: early 20C. AUTO- + TOXIC.

autotrophic a. (of or relating to organisms) capable of manufacturing organic foods from inorganic sources, as by photosynthesis. WH: 19C. AUTO- + -TROPHIC.

autotype n. a facsimile. Also v.t. WH: 19C. AUTO- + -*type* (TYPE).

autowinder n. an electrically powered device that automatically winds on the film in a camera after a photograph has been taken. WH: mid-20C. AUTO- + *winder* (WIND[2]).

autoxidation n. oxidation that occurs spontaneously on exposure to atmospheric oxygen. WH: 19C. AUTO- + *oxidation* (OXIDE).

autumn n. the season of the year between summer and winter. Astronomically, it extends from the autumnal equinox to the winter solstice; popularly, it comprises the months from September to November in the northern hemisphere and from March to May in the southern. WH: 14–15C. Old French *autompne* (Modern French *automne*), from Latin *autumnus*, of unknown orig.

autumnal a. relating to, characteristic of or produced in autumn. Also n. WH: 16C. Latin *autumnalis*, from *autumnus* AUTUMN. See also -AL[1].

autunite n. a mineral consisting of a hydrous phosphate of uranium and calcium. WH: 19C. *Autun*, a town in E France, + -ITE[1].

auxiliary a. helping, aiding. Also n. WH: 14–15C. Latin *auxiliarius*, from *auxilium* help. See also -ARY[1].

auxin n. any of a group of growth-promoting plant hormones. WH: mid-20C. Greek *auxein* to increase + -IN[1].

Av n. the fifth ecclesiastical month, or 11th civil month of the Jewish year (corresponding roughly with August). WH: 18C. Hebrew *'āḇ*.

avadavat n. an Indian and SE Asian waxbill of the genus *Amandava*. WH: 17C. *Ahmadabad*, a city in W India, where the birds were sold.

avail v.i. to be of value, use, profit or advantage. Also v.t., n. WH: 12–14C. VAIL[2]. The word was apparently formed on an analogy with pairs such as AMOUNT/ MOUNT[1].

available a. capable of being employed; at one's disposal. WH: 14–15C. AVAIL + -ABLE.

avalanche n. a mass of snow, ice and debris falling or sliding from the upper parts of a mountain. Also v.i., v.t. WH: 18C. French, from Romansh, alt. of dial. *lavanche* (of unknown orig.) blended with *avaler* to descend.

avant adv., a. before, in front. WH: French before, ult. from Latin *ab* from + *ante* before. Cp. AVAUNT.

avant-garde a. in advance of contemporary artistic tastes or trends; experimental, progressive. Also n. WH: 14–15C. French AVANT + *garde* GUARD. Cp. VANGUARD.

Avar n. a member of a people of the NE Caucasus. WH: 18C. Avar.

avarice n. excessive desire for wealth; greed. WH: 12–14C. Old French, from Latin *avaritia*, from *avarus* greedy. See also -ICE.

avascular a. without blood vessels. WH: early 20C. A-[6] + VASCULAR.

avast int. stay! stop! desist! WH: 17C. Dutch *hou'vast*, *houd vast* hold fast. The first syllable has been assimilated to A-[1].

avatar n. in Hinduism, the descent of a god or released soul to earth. WH: 18C. Sanskrit *avatāra* descent, from *ava* down, away + *tār-* to pass over.

†**avaunt** int. be off! away with you! begone! WH: 14–15C. Old French *avant* to the front. Cp. AVANT.

ave int. hail! welcome! farewell! (in allusion to the classical custom of greeting the dead). Also n. WH: 12–14C. Latin, 2nd pers. sing. imper. of *avere* to be well, to fare well.

avenaceous a. of, relating to or resembling oats. WH: 18C. Latin *avenaceus*, from *avena* oats. See also -ACEOUS.

avenge v.t. to execute vengeance on account of or on behalf of. Also v.i. WH: 14–15C. Old French *avengier*, from A-[1] + *vengier*, from Latin *vindicare* VINDICATE.

avens n. a rosaceous plant of the genus *Geum*, esp. the wood avens or herb bennet, *G. urbanum*, and the water avens, *G. rivale*. WH: 12–14C. Old French *avence*, from Medieval Latin *avencia*, of unknown orig.

aventail n. the movable part of a helmet in front, which may be lifted to admit fresh air. WH: 12–14C. Old French *esventail* airhole, from *esventer* (Modern French *éventer*), ult. from Latin EX- + *ventus* wind. See also -AL[2].

aventurine n. a gold-spangled Venetian glass (made by a process which was discovered accidentally, hence the name). WH: 18C. French, from Italian *avventurino*, from *avventura* chance. See ADVENTURE, also -INE.

avenue n. a way or means of approaching an objective or gaining an end. WH: 17C. French, fem. p.p. (used as n.) of *avenir* to arrive, from Latin *advenire*, from AD- + *venire* to come. Cp. ADVENT. The association with trees is apparently due to Evelyn, who defined an avenue as 'the principal walk to the front of the house, or seat' (1664).

aver v.t. to assert or declare positively. WH: 14–15C. Old French *avérer*, from *a-* (AD-) + *veir*, *voir*, from Latin *verus* true.

average n. the typical or prevailing number, quantity, proportion, level or degree; the general standard. Also v.t., v.i., a. WH: 15C. French *avarie*, from Italian *avaria*, from Arabic *'awār* damage to goods + -AGE. The original sense was a duty or tax on goods, and specifically expense or loss arising from damage to goods at sea. The current sense evolved from the special sense of an equal distribution of expense or loss among all interested parties, hence any distribution based on a median estimate. The -age element was influenced by words such as DAMAGE.

Averroist n. a follower of Averroës, who taught a kind of pantheism blending Aristotelian and Islamic ideas. WH: 18C. *Averroës*, 1126–98, Islamic philosopher and physician + -IST.

averse *a.* unwilling, reluctant (to). WH: 16C. Latin *aversus*, p.p. of *avertere* AVERT.

avert *v.t.* to turn away. WH: 14–15C. Partly from Old French *avertir*, partly from Latin *avertere*, from A-[4] + *vertere* to turn.

Avesta *n.* the sacred scriptures of Zoroastrianism. WH: 19C. Persian, from Pahlavi *âvistâk* lore. Cp. ZEND.

avgolemono *n.* Greek chicken soup made with egg yolks and lemon. WH: mid-20C. Modern Greek *augo* egg + *lemono* lemon.

avian *a.* of or relating to birds. WH: 19C. Latin *avis* bird + -AN.

aviation *n.* the subject of aircraft; the practice of operating aircraft. WH: 19C. Latin *avis* bird + -ATION.

aviculture *n.* the breeding and rearing of birds. WH: 19C. Latin *avis* bird + CULTURE.

avid *a.* very keen, enthusiastic. WH: 18C. French *avide*, or from Latin *avidus*, from *avere* to long for. See also -ID.

avidin *n.* a protein found in egg white that prevents the absorption of biotin. WH: mid-20C. AVID + -IN[1].

avifauna *n.* the birds in any district taken collectively. WH: 19C. Latin *avis* bird + FAUNA.

avionics *n.* (the science concerned with) the development and use of electronic and electric equipment in aircraft and spacecraft. WH: mid-20C. AVIATION + *electronics* (ELECTRONIC).

avirulent *a.* not virulent. WH: early 20C. A-[6] + VIRULENT.

avitaminosis *n.* (a) disease resulting from vitamin deficiency. WH: early 20C. A-[6] + VITAMIN + -OSIS.

avizandum *n.* private consideration by a judge or court before passing judgement. WH: 17C. Medieval Latin, neut. ger. of *avizare* to consider, ADVISE.

avocado *n.* the pear-shaped fruit of a Central American tree, *Persea americana*. Also *a.* WH: 17C. Spanish, alt. (influ. by *avocado* lawyer, ADVOCATE[1]) of *aguacate*, from Nahuatl *ahuacatl*.

avocation *n.* a minor employment or occupation. WH: 16C. Latin *avocatio*, *avocationis*, from *avocatus*, p.p. of *avocare*, from A-[4] + *vocare* to call. Cp. ADVOCATE[1].

avocet *n.* a wading bird of the genus *Recurvirostra*, having a long slender bill curved upwards. WH: 17C. French *avocette*, from Italian *avosetta*, of unknown orig.

Avogadro's constant *n.* the number of molecules or atoms in one mole of substance. WH: 19C. Count Amadeo *Avogadro*, 1776–1856, Italian scientist.

avoid *v.t.* to keep at a distance from, to shun. Also *v.i.* WH: 14–15C. Anglo-French *avoider*, from Old French *esvuidier*, *evuider*, from *es-* EX- + *vuide* empty, VOID. The original sense was to empty, to make void. This gave the further meaning to withdraw, to retire. Both senses are now obsolete, and the current meaning evolved from the 16C.

avoirdupois *n.* a system of weights based on the unit of a pound of 16 ounces, equal to 7000 grains (0.4536 kg). WH: 12–14C. Old French *aveir de peis* goods of weight, from *aveir* (Modern French *avoir*), use as *n.* of *avoir* to have (from Latin *habere* to have) + *de* of + *peis*, *pois* (Modern French *poids*) weight. Cp. POISE[1].

†avouch *v.t.* to affirm, vouch for, guarantee as certain. Also *v.i.*, *n.* WH: 15C. Old French *avochier*, from Latin *advocare* ADVOCATE[1].

avow *v.t.* to own, to acknowledge, to admit (of one's free will). Also *n.* WH: 12–14C. Old French *avouer* to acknowledge as valid, from Latin *advocare* ADVOCATE[1]. Cp. AVOUCH.

avulsion *n.* the act of tearing away or violently separating. WH: 17C. French, or from Latin *avulsio*, *avulsionis*, from *avulsus*, p.p. of *avellere*, from A-[4] + *vellere* to pluck.

avuncular *a.* of or relating to an uncle. WH: 19C. Latin *avunculus* maternal uncle, dim. of *avus* grandfather + -AR[1].

aw *int.* used to express sympathy, disapproval, appeal etc. WH: 19C. Imit. Cp. O.

awa' *adv.* away, gone. WH: See AWAY.

await *v.t.* to wait for, look out for, expect. Also *v.i.* WH: 12–14C. Anglo-French *awaitier*, from Old French *aguaitier*. See AD-, WAIT.

awake *v.i.* to wake from sleep, cease sleeping. Also *v.t.*, *a.* WH: pre-1200. Old English *āwæcnan*, *āwacian*. See A-[3], WAKE[1].

award *v.t.* to grant or confer, esp. as a prize for merit or as something needed. Also *n.* WH: 14–15C. Anglo-French *awarder*, var. of Old French *esguarder* to consider, to ordain. See EX-, WARD.

aware *a.* conscious, cognizant. WH: pre-1200. Old English *gewær*, from *ge-*, intens. pref. + *wær* WARE[2].

awash *adv.* on a level with the water. Also *a.* WH: 19C. A-[1] + WASH.

away *adv.* from a place, person, cause or condition. Also *a.*, *n.*, *int.* WH: pre-1200. Old English *on weg*. See ON, WAY.

awe *n.* dread mingled with veneration. Also *v.t.* WH: pre-1200. Old English *ege*, from Germanic. Rel. to AIL.

aweary *a.* tired, weary. WH: 16C. A-[1] + WEARY.

a-weather *adv.* to the weather side, as opposed to the lee side. WH: 16C. A-[1] + WEATHER.

aweel *int.* well; well then. WH: 19C. *ah well!*. See AH, WELL[1].

aweigh *adv.* (of an anchor) raised vertically just off the bottom. WH: 17C. A-[1] + WEIGH. Not rel. to AWAY.

awful *a.* extremely disagreeable; very bad of its kind. WH: pre-1200. Old English *agheful*. See AWE, also -FUL. The original sense was full of awe, a sense now chiefly assumed by *awesome*.

awheto *n.* a caterpillar affected with a parasitic fungus, from the dried body of which a tattoo dye is obtained. WH: 19C. Maori.

awhile *adv.* for some time; for a little. WH: pre-1200. Old English *āne hwīle*, from *āne* A, ONE + *hwīle* WHILE. It was originally two words.

a-wing *adv.*, *a.* on the wing, flying. WH: 17C. A-[1] + WING.

awkward *a.* lacking dexterity, bungling, clumsy. WH: 14–15C. Obs. *awk* untoward, backhand, from Old Norse *afugr* + -WARD. The original literal meaning of turned the wrong way gave the sense perverse, cantankerous in the 16C, then finally the current sense from about the same time.

awl *n.* a hand tool with a cylindrical tapering blade, sharpened at the end, for making holes for stitches in leather. WH: pre-1200. Old English *æl*, from Germanic, of unknown orig. Cp. German *Ahle*.

awn *n.* any one of the bristles springing from a bract in the inflorescence of some cereals and grasses. WH: pre-1200. Old Norse *agn-*, stem of *ǫgn*, from Germanic, of unknown orig. Cp. German *Ahne*.

awning *n.* a covering of tarpaulin, canvas or other material used as a protection from sun or rain, as above the deck of a ship. WH: 17C. Orig. unknown. According to some, the word is from French *auvent* awning.

AWOL *a.*, *adv.* absent without authorization from one's post or position of duty. Also *n.* WH: Acronym of *absent without official leave*, or *absent without leave*.

awry *adv.* obliquely, crookedly. Also *a.* WH: 14–15C. A-[1] + WRY.

axe *n.* a hand tool for cutting or chopping, consisting of an iron or steel blade with a sharp edge fitted to a handle or helve. Also *v.t.* WH: pre-1200. Old English *æx*, *eax*, from Germanic. Cp. German *Axt*.

axel *n.* a jump in ice-skating incorporating one and a half turns. WH: mid-20C. *Axel* Rudolph Paulsen, 1855–1938, Norwegian skater.

axenic *a.* uncontaminated by undesirable micro-organisms. WH: mid-20C. A-[6] + Greek *xenikos* alien, strange + -IC. Cp. XENO-.

axil *n.* the hollow where the base of a leaf joins the stem or where a branch leaves the trunk. WH: 18C. Latin *axilla*, dim. of *ala* wing.

axiology *n.* the philosophy of values. WH: early 20C. French *axiologie*, from Greek *axia* value + -O- + -LOGY.

axiom *n.* a self-evident or generally accepted truth. WH: 15C. French *axiome*, or from Latin *axioma*, from Greek, from *axioun* to think worthy, from *axios* worthy.

axis[1] *n.* a real or imaginary straight line round which a body revolves, or round which its parts are arranged, or to which they have a symmetrical relation. WH: 12–14C. Latin AXLE.

axis[2] *n.* a S Asian deer with a white-spotted coat, *Cervus axis*. WH: 17C. Latin an Indian animal.

axle *n.* the pin or bar on which a wheel revolves or wheels revolve, or which revolves with a wheel or wheels. WH: 12–14C. Old Norse *oxull*, from *oxultré* axle TREE. Rel. to AXIS[1].

Axminster *n.* a variously coloured and patterned woven carpet with a tufted pile. WH: 19C. *Axminster*, a town in Devon, where a carpet of this type was woven.

axolotl *n.* a salamander of the genus *Ambystoma* that retains the larval form when fully grown, esp. a small Mexican salamander, *A. mexicanum*. WH: 18C. Nahuatl, from *atl* water + *xolotl* servant.

axon *n.* the projection from a nerve cell that typically conducts impulses away from the cell. **WH:** 19C. Greek *axōn* axis.

axonometric *a.* (of a drawing etc.) showing vertical and horizontal lines projected to scale but inclined to the principal axes of the object represented. **WH:** early 20C. Greek *axōn* axis + -O- + -METRIC.

ayah *n.* a nurse for European children or a maidservant in a European household in the Indian subcontinent or in other former British territories. **WH:** 18C. Portuguese *aia*, fem. of *aio* tutor.

ayatollah *n.* a leader of the Shiite Muslims in Iran. **WH:** mid-20C. Persian, from Arabic *'āyatu-llāh* sign of God, from *āya* sign, model + ALLAH.

aye¹ *adv., int.* yes. *Also n.* **WH:** 16C. Appar. I, influ. by YEA. Cp. YES.

†aye² *adv.* always, ever. **WH:** 12–14C. Old Norse *ei, ey*, from Germanic. Rel. to AEON and ult. to AGE.

aye-aye *n.* a small lemur found in Madagascar, *Daubentonia madagascariensis*. **WH:** 18C. French, from Malagasy *aiay*, from the animal's cry.

Aylesbury *n.* a breed of large domestic duck. **WH:** 19C. *Aylesbury*, a town in Buckinghamshire.

Aymara *n.* a member of an Indian people of Bolivia and Peru. *Also a.* **WH:** 19C. Bolivian Spanish.

ayond *prep.* beyond. **WH:** 18C. A-¹ + BEYOND, based on AFORE, BEFORE.

Ayrshire *n.* a breed of cattle highly prized for dairy purposes. **WH:** 19C. *Ayrshire*, a former county in SW Scotland.

ayurveda *n.* an ancient Hindu system of medicine, health and healing. **WH:** early 20C. Sanskrit *āyur-veda* science of life. See VEDA.

azalea *n.* any of various shrubby plants of the genus *Rhododendron*, with showy and occasionally fragrant flowers. **WH:** 18C. Modern Latin, from Greek, fem. (used as n.) of *azaleos* dry. The plant flourishes in dry soil.

azeotrope *n.* a mixture of liquids in which the boiling point remains constant during distillation at a given pressure. **WH:** early 20C. A-⁶ + Greek *zeo-, zein* to boil + -TROPE.

Azerbaijani *n.* a native or inhabitant of Azerbaijan. *Also a.* **WH:** 19C. *Azerbaijan*, a country in SW Asia + -I³. Cp. AZERI.

Azeri *n.* a member of a people living in Azerbaijan, Armenia, and adjacent regions. *Also a.* **WH:** 19C. Turkish *azeri*, from Persian fire. The people are said to have been fire-worshippers.

azide *n.* a salt or ester of hydrazoic acid, containing the monovalent group or ion N_3. **WH:** early 20C. AZO- + -IDE.

Azilian *a.* of or relating to the period of culture typified by the remains found in the cavern of Mas-d'Azil. *Also n.* **WH:** 19C. Mas-d'*Azil*, a location in the French Pyrenees + -IAN.

azimuth *n.* an angular distance from a point of the horizon to the intersection with the horizon of a vertical circle passing through a celestial body. **WH:** 14–15C. Old French *azimut*, from Arabic *as-samt*, from *as*, form of *al* the + *samt* way, direction. Cp. ZENITH.

azine *n.* an organic compound with more than one nitrogen atom in a six-atom ring. **WH:** 19C. AZO- + -INE.

azo- *comb. form* having two adjacent nitrogen atoms. **WH:** French *azote* nitrogen, from A-⁶ + Greek *zōē* life.

azoic *a.* having no trace of life. **WH:** 19C. A-⁶ + ZOIC.

AZT *n.* an antiviral drug derived from thymine, used in the treatment of HIV. **WH:** late 20C. Abbr. of azidothymidine. See AZIDE.

Aztec *a.* denoting, of or relating to the leading Mexican Indian people at the time of the Spanish invasion (1519). *Also n.* **WH:** 18C. French *Aztèque*, or from Spanish *Azteca*, from Nahuatl *aztecatl* person from *Aztlan*, the people's legendary place of origin. The name is also said to be from Nahuatl *aztatl* heron + *tlan* near to, or Nahuatl *aztecatl* men of the north.

azure *n.* the deep blue of the sky. *Also a., v.t.* **WH:** 12–14C. Old French *asur, azur*, from Medieval Latin *azzurum*, from Arabic *al-lāzaward*, from *al* the + Persian *lāžward* lapis lazuli. Cp. LAPIS LAZULI.

azygous *a.* unpaired, occurring singly, not as one of a pair. *Also n.* **WH:** 17C. A-⁶ + Greek *zugon* yoke. See also -OUS.

baa *n.* the cry or bleat of a sheep. *Also v.i.* WH: 16C. Imit. Cp. French *bê*, German *mäh* etc.

Baagandji *n.* an extinct SE Australian Aboriginal language. WH: Native name.

Baal *n.* the chief male divinity among the Phoenicians. WH: 14–15C. Hebrew *ba'al*, from Canaanite lord. Cp. BEELZEBUB.

baas *n.* boss, overseer. WH: 17C. Dutch. Cp. BOSS[2].

baba *n.* a small cake soaked in rum. WH: 19C. French, from Popular Latin (married) peasant woman.

babacoote *n.* the indri, a short-tailed woolly lemur, *Indri indri*, from Madagascar. WH: 19C. Malagasy father-child, from *baba* father + *koto* child.

babassu *n.* a Brazilian palm tree, *Orbignya martiana* or *O. speciosa*. WH: early 20C. Brazilian Portuguese *babaçú*, from Tupi *ybá* fruit + *guasu* large.

Babbitt *n.* a dull, complacent businessman (or other person) with orthodox views and little interest in cultural values. WH: early 20C. George F. *Babbitt*, the main character in Sinclair Lewis's 1922 novel *Babbitt*.

babbitt *n.* an alloy of tin, antimony and copper, used in bearings to diminish friction. *Also v.t.* WH: 19C. Isaac *Babbitt*, 1799–1862, US inventor.

babble *v.i.* to talk incoherently. *Also v.t., n.* WH: 14–15C. Imit., from base *bab-*. Cp. French *babiller*, Dutch *babbelen*, German *pappelen* etc.

babe *n.* a young child, a baby. WH: 14–15C. Imit. form of childish utterance. Cp. MAMMA[1], NANA[2], PAPA[1] etc. See BABY.

babel *n.* noisy confusion. WH: 16C. *Babel*, city and tower where confusion of tongues is said to have taken place (Gen. xi), from Hebrew *bābel* BABYLON. The word is popularly associated with BABBLE.

Babi *n.* a follower of the Bab (1819–50), who forbade polygamy, begging and alcohol (and was executed for heresy). WH: 19C. Persian, from Arabic *bāb* intermediary, lit. gate.

babiche *n.* laces or thongs made of rawhide. WH: 19C. Canadian French, from Micmac *a:papi:č*.

babirusa *n.* the wild hog of eastern Asia, *Babyrousa babyrussa*, in the male of which the upper canines grow through the lip and turn backwards like horns. WH: 17C. Malay, from *babi* hog + *rusa* deer.

baboon *n.* a monkey of the genera *Papio* and *Mandrillus*, with long doglike snout, great canine teeth, hardened skin on the buttocks, and capacious cheek-pouches. WH: 14–15C. Old French *babuin* manikin, baboon, ? from Old French *babone* muzzle, grimace. The word is probably ultimately imitative of the animal's grimace and chatter. Cp. BABBLE.

babouche *n.* a Turkish heel-less slipper. WH: 17C. French, from Arabic *bābūj*, from Persian *pāpūš*, from *pa* foot + *pūš* covering. Cp. PUMP[2].

babu *n.* in the Indian subcontinent, Hindu gentleman, a respectful title corresponding to English Mr. WH: 18C. Hindi *bābū* father, ult. of imit. orig. Cp. ABBA, PAPA[1].

babul *n.* any of several trees of the genus *Acacia*, bearing small yellow flowers and yielding gum arabic and tannin. WH: 19C. Hindi *babūl* and Bengali *bābul*, from Sanskrit *babbūla*.

babushka *n.* a grandmother, an old woman. WH: mid-20C. Russian grandmother, dim. of *baba* old woman. Cp. BABA.

baby *n.* an infant; a child in arms. *Also a., v.t.* WH: 14–15C. Dim. of BABE. See -Y[3].

Babylon *n.* Rome, the papacy (regarded as corrupt by some Protestants). WH: 17C. Latin, from Greek *Babulōn*, from Akkadian *Bāb-ilān* gate of the gods, from *bābu* gate + *ilān* gods, name of the ancient Chaldean capital and of the mystical city of the Apocalypse. Cp. BABEL.

Bacardi® *n.* a Caribbean rum. WH: early 20C. Facundo *Bacardi*, the orig. manufacturer, 1862.

bacca *n.* tobacco. WH: 19C. Abbr. of TOBACCO. See -Y[3].

baccalaureate *n.* an examination qualifying successful candidates for higher education in more than one country. WH: 17C. French *baccalauréat*, or from Medieval Latin *baccalaureatus*, from *baccalaureus*. See BACHELOR, also -ATE[1].

baccarat *n.* a gambling card game between banker and punters. WH: 19C. French *baccara*, of unknown orig.

baccate *a.* bearing berries. WH: 19C. Latin *baccatus*, from *bacca* berry. See also -ATE[2].

bacchanal *a.* of or relating to Bacchus, the god of wine, or his festivities. *Also n.* WH: 16C. Latin *bacchanalis*, from *Bacchus*, from Greek *Bakkhos* Bacchus, the god of wine. See -AL[1].

bacchius *n.* a metrical foot of three syllables, two long and one short. WH: 16C. Latin, from Greek *bakkheios pous* Bacchic foot. See BACCHANAL.

bacci- *comb. form* of or relating to a berry or berries. WH: Latin *bacca* berry + *-i-*.

bacciferous *a.* bearing berries. WH: 17C. BACCI- + -FEROUS.

bacciform *a.* berry-shaped. WH: 19C. BACCI- + -FORM.

baccivorous *a.* berry-eating. WH: 17C. BACCI- + *-vorous* (-VORE).

bach *n.* a small cottage or habitable hut. WH: 19C. Abbr. of BACHELOR.

bachelor *n.* an unmarried man. WH: 12–14C. Old French *bacheler* young aspirant knight, from Medieval Latin **baccalaris*, prob. var. of *baccalarius*, ult. of unknown orig. The Medieval Latin form was later altered to *baccalaureus*, as if from *bacca lauri* laurel berry. Cp. BACCALAUREATE.

bacillus *n.* a microscopic, rodlike (disease-causing) bacterium. WH: 19C. Late Latin little rod, dim. of *baculus* rod, stick. Cp. BACTERIUM.

bacitracin *n.* an antibiotic used esp. in treating skin infections. WH: mid-20C. BACILLUS + *Trac(y)* + -IN[1]. Margaret Tracy b. *c*.1936 was the American child in whom the substance was first found in a wound, 1945.

back[1] *n.* the hinder part of the human body, from the neck to the lower extremity of the spine. *Also a., adv., v.t., v.i.* WH: pre-1200. Old English *bæc*, from Germanic. Rel. to BACON.

back[2] *n.* a large tub used in brewing, distilling, dyeing etc. WH: 16C. Dutch *bak*, and from Low German *back* large dish.

backgammon *n.* a game played by two persons on a table with pieces moved according to the throw of dice. *Also v.t.* WH: 17C. BACK[1] + early form of GAME[1]. Cp. GAMMON[2].

backwards *adv.* with the back foremost. WH: 12–14C. Orig. *abackward*, from ABACK + -WARD, -wards. The word was later associated with BACK[1].

bacon *n.* the cured back and sides of a pig. WH: 12–14C. Old French, from Old High German *bahho*, from Germanic, rel. to BACK[1]. The Modern French word for bacon is *lard*. See LARD.

Baconian *a.* of or relating to Bacon or his inductive philosophy. *Also n.* WH: 19C. Francis *Bacon*, 1561–1626, English philosopher + -IAN.

bactericide *n.* an agent that destroys bacteria. WH: 19C. BACTERIO- + -CIDE.

bacterio- *comb. form* of or relating to bacteria. WH: Latin BACTERIUM. See also -O-.

bacteriology *n.* the scientific study of bacteria. WH: 19C. BACTERIO- + -LOGY.

bacteriolysis *n.* the destruction of bacteria. WH: 19C. BACTERIO- + LYSIS.

bacteriophage *n.* a virus which destroys bacteria. WH: early 20C. French *bactériophage*. See BACTERIO-, -PHAGE.

bacteriostasis *n.* inhibition of the growth of bacterial cells. WH: early 20C. BACTERIO- + Greek *stasis* stopping.

bacterium *n.* a member of a large group of microscopic unicellular organisms found in soil, water and as saprophytes or parasites in organic bodies. WH: 19C. Modern Latin, from Greek *baktēria*, dim. of *baktēria* staff, cane. Cp. BACILLUS.

bacteroid *a.* of the nature of or resembling a bacterium. WH: 19C. BACTERIUM + -OID.

Bactrian *a.* of or relating to Bactria. WH: 14–15C. Greek *Baktrianos*, or from Latin *Bactrianus*, from *Bactria*, an ancient country of central Asia. See -IAN.

baculine *a.* characterized by the stick, cane or flogging. WH: 18C. Latin *baculum* rod, stick + -INE. Cp. BACILLUS.

bad *a.* not good, unpleasant. *Also n.* WH: 12–14C. ? Old English *bædling* effeminate man, pederast, from Germanic root rel. to Latin *foedus* foul, filthy.

badge *n.* a distinctive mark, sign or token. *Also v.t.* WH: 14–15C. Orig. unknown.

badger *n.* a nocturnal plantigrade mammal of the weasel family, with thick body and short legs and a head with two stripes, *Meles meles*, found in Britain, Europe and Asia. *Also v.t.* WH: 16C. ? From BADGE + -ARD, with ref. to its distinctive head markings. The Celtic name of the badger is BROCK.

badigeon *n.* a mixture of plaster and freestone used by sculptors to repair defects in stone, and by builders to present the appearance of stone. WH: 18C. French, of unknown orig.

badminton *n.* a game resembling tennis, but played, usu. indoors, with shuttlecocks instead of balls. WH: 19C. *Badminton* estate in Gloucestershire, seat of Duke of Beaufort, where first played, c.1870.

Baedeker *n.* any of the series of guide-books published by Baedeker. WH: 19C. Karl *Baedeker*, 1801–59, German publisher.

baffle *v.t.* to perplex, confound. *Also v.i.* WH: 16C. ? French *bafouer* to ridicule, or from French (obs.) *beffler* to mock, both prob. ult. from exclamation *baf!*, imit. of mockery. Cp. BAH, PAH, POOH.

baft *n.* a cheap coarse fabric. WH: 16C. Urdu, from Persian *bāft* a textile, *bāfta* woven.

bag *n.* a pouch, small sack or other flexible receptacle. *Also v.t., v.i.* WH: pre-1200. ? Old Norse *baggi* bag, bundle, of unknown orig. ? Rel. to PACK.

bagasse *n.* the refuse products in sugar-making. WH: 19C. French, from Spanish *bagazo* residue.

bagatelle *n.* a game played on a nine-holed board with pins obstructing the holes, with nine balls to be struck into them. WH: 17C. French, from Italian *bagatella*, prob. dim. of Latin *bacca* berry, or Italian *baga* baggage.

bagel *n.* a ring-shaped bread roll. WH: early 20C. Yiddish *beggel*, from Germanic. Rel. to BAIL⁴ and so ult. to BOW¹.

baggage *n.* luggage; belongings packed for travelling. *Also a.* WH: 14–15C. Old French *bagage*, from *baguer* to tie up or *bagues* bundles. Rel. to BAG.

bagnio *n.* a brothel. WH: 16C. Italian, from Latin *balneum* bath. Cp. STEW¹. A secondary sense, an oriental prison for slaves, is said to derive from a former Roman bath at Constantinople, converted into a prison.

bagpipe *n.* a musical instrument of great antiquity, now chiefly used in the Scottish Highlands, consisting of a windbag and several reed-pipes into which the air is pressed by the player. WH: 12–14C. BAG + PIPE.

baguette *n.* a narrow stick of French bread. WH: 18C. Latin, from Italian *bacchetto*, dim. of *bacchio*, from Latin *baculum* staff.

bah *int.* expressing contempt. WH: 19C. ? French, imit. Cp. PAH, POOH.

bahadur *n.* a ceremonious title formerly given in India to officers and distinguished officials. WH: 18C. Urdu and Persian *bahādur*, from Mongolian *baatar* brave, hero. The English soldier Lord Roberts, 1832–1914, was nicknamed Bobs Bahadur.

Baha'i *n.* a follower of a religious movement originating in Iran in the 19th cent., which stresses the validity of all world religions and the spiritual unity of all humanity. WH: 19C. Persian, from Arabic *bahā'* splendour. The name is directly from *Bahā'* Allāh, 1817–92, and his son 'Abd al-*Baha'*, c.1844–1921, who developed the movement from Babism (BABI).

Bahamian *n.* a native or inhabitant of the Bahamas. *Also a.* WH: 18C. *Bahama*, islands in W Atlantic + -IAN.

Bahasa Indonesia *n.* the official language of Indonesia. WH: mid-20C. Malay, from Sanskrit *bhāṣā* speech, language.

baht *n.* the standard unit of currency in Thailand. WH: 18C. Thai *bāt*.

baignoire *n.* a box at the theatre on the lowest tier. WH: 19C. French bath tub. Cp. BAGNIO. The French *baignoire* was orig. a dressing room at a public bath.

bail¹ *n.* the temporary release of a prisoner from custody on security given for their due surrender when required. *Also v.t.* WH: 12–14C. Old French power, custody, from *bailler* to take charge of, to hand over, from Latin *baiulare* to bear a burden, from *baiulus* carrier. Cp. BAIL³, BAILIFF.

bail² *n.* in cricket, either of the crosspieces laid on top of the wicket. *Also v.i., v.t.* WH: 12–14C. Old French *baile* palisade, enclosure, ? from Latin *baculum* rod. Cp. BAILEY.

bail³ *v.t.* to throw (water) out of a boat with a shallow vessel. WH: 17C. French *baille* bucket, from Latin *baiulus* carrier. Cp. BAIL¹.

bail⁴ *n.* a hoop or ring. WH: 14–15C. Prob. Old Norse *beygla* hoop. Cp. BAGEL.

bailee *n.* a person to whom goods are entrusted for a specific purpose. WH: 16C. BAIL¹ + -EE. Cp. BAILOR.

bailey *n.* the wall enclosing the outer court of a feudal castle. WH: 12–14C. Prob. Old French *bail* BAIL².

Bailey bridge *n.* a bridge of lattice steel construction made of standard parts for rapid erection and transport. WH: mid-20C. Sir Donald Coleman *Bailey*, 1901–85, English engineer, its designer.

bailie *n.* a Scottish municipal magistrate corresponding to an English alderman. WH: 12–14C. Old French, from *baillir* to have under one's care. Cp. BAIL¹, BAILIFF.

bailiff *n.* a sheriff's officer who executes writs and distrains. WH: 12–14C. Old French *baillif*, nom. *baillis*, from Medieval Latin *baiulivus*, a. from *baiulus* carrier, manager. See BAIL¹.

bailiwick *n.* the district within which a bailie or bailiff possesses jurisdiction. WH: 14–15C. BAILIE + Old English *wīce* function of an official. Cp. WICK².

bailor *n.* a person who entrusts another with goods for a specific purpose. WH: 16C. BAIL¹ + -OR. Cp. BAILEE.

Baily's beads *n.pl.* the brilliant points of sunlight that appear to be strung round the moon just at the beginning and end of a solar eclipse. WH: 19C. Francis *Baily*, 1774–1844, English astronomer.

bain-marie *n.* a vessel of boiling water into which saucepans are put for slow heating; a double saucepan. WH: 18C. French, translating Medieval Latin *balneum Mariae*, translating Medieval Greek *kaminos Marias* Maria's furnace, from Maria the Jewess, legendary alchemist.

Bairam *n.* either of two Muslim festivals following the Ramadan, the *Lesser* lasting three days, the *Greater*, which falls seventy days later, lasting four days. WH: 16C. Obs. Turkish *baïrām* (now *bayram*), ult. from Persian *baẕrām*.

bairn *n.* a child. WH: pre-1200. Old English *bearn*, from Germanic. Rel. to BEAR².

bait *v.t.* to furnish (a hook, gin, snare etc.) with real or sham food to entice prey. *Also v.i., n.* WH: 12–14C. Old Norse *beita* to hunt with dogs or hawks. Rel. to BITE. Cp. ABET.

baize *n.* a coarse woollen material something like felt. WH: 16C. French *baies*, fem. pl. (used as n.) of *bai* reddish-brown, BAY⁵. The material is presumably so called from its original colour.

bajra *n.* a type of Indian millet. WH: 19C. Hindi *bājrā*.

bake *v.t.* to cook by dry conducted (as opposed to radiated) heat, to cook in an oven or on a heated surface. *Also v.i.* WH: pre-1200. Old English *baecan*, from Germanic. Cp. BATCH.

Bakelite® *n.* a synthetic resin made from formaldehyde and phenol, used for insulating purposes and in the manufacture of plastics, paints and varnishes. WH: early 20C. Leo H. *Baekeland*, 1863–1944, Belgian-born US chemist + -ITE¹.

Baker day *n.* any one of the days during the British school year set aside for the training of teachers. WH: late 20C. Kenneth *Baker*, b.1934, British politician who introduced it in 1987.

Bakewell tart *n.* an open tart with a pastry base, containing jam and almond paste. WH: 19C. *Bakewell*, a town in Derbyshire.

baklava *n.* a cake made from layered pastry strips with nuts and honey. WH: 17C. Turkish.

baksheesh *n.* a gratuity, a tip (used without the article). WH: 18C. Persian *bakšīš*, from *bakšīdan* to give. Cp. BUCKSHEE.

balaclava *n.* a tight woollen covering for the head, ears, chin and neck. WH: 19C. *Balaklava*, a village in the Crimea, site of battle, 1854.

balalaika *n.* a three-stringed triangular-shaped musical instrument resembling a guitar. WH: 18C. Russian, prob. imit. of sound.

balance *n.* a pair of scales. *Also v.t., v.i.* WH: 12–14C. Old French, from Late Latin *bilanx, bilancis*, from BI- + *lanx* scales.

balas *n.* a rose-red variety of the spinel ruby. WH: 14–15C. Old French *balais*, from Medieval Latin *balascus*, from Arabic *balakš*, from Persian *Badakšān* Badakhshan, a district in N Afghanistan, where it is found.

balata *n.* any of various Central American trees which yield latex, esp. *Mankara bidentata.* WH: 17C. Carib *balatá.*

balboa *n.* the unit of currency in Panama. WH: early 20C. Vasco Núñez de *Balboa, c.*1475–1519, Spanish explorer and discoverer of the Pacific Ocean.

Balbriggan *n.* a knitted cotton fabric used for hose and other goods. WH: 19C. *Balbriggan*, a town near Dublin, Ireland, where first made.

balcony *n.* a gallery or platform projecting from a house or other building. WH: 17C. Italian *balcone*, prob. from Germanic and rel. to BAULK.

bald *a.* without hair upon the crown of the head. WH: 12–14C. Prob. from Celtic *bal* white spot + -ED. The Middle English form was *balled*, as if related to BALL[1] in the sense of something round and smooth.

baldachin *n.* a canopy over an altar, throne or doorway, generally supported by pillars, but sometimes suspended from above, formerly of a rich brocade of silk and gold. WH: 16C. Italian *baldacchino*, from *Baldacco* Baghdad, where it originated + -INE.

balderdash *n.* rubbish, nonsense. WH: 16C. Orig. unknown. ? Ult. of imit. orig., influ. by DASH. Earlier senses, now obsolete, were froth, mixture of drinks.

baldric *n.* a richly ornamented girdle or belt, passing over one shoulder and under the opposite, to support dagger, sword, bugle etc. WH: 12–14C. Germanic, ? from Latin *balteus* belt.

bale[1] *n.* a package. *Also v.t.* WH: 12–14C. Prob. Middle Dutch *bale*, from Old French *bale*, ult. rel. to BALL[1].

†bale[2] *n.* evil, mischief, calamity. WH: pre-1200. Old English *balu*, from Germanic.

bale[3] *v.i.* to abandon an aeroplane in the air and descend by parachute. *Also v.t.* WH: 17C. See BAIL[3].

baleen *n.* whalebone. *Also a.* WH: 12–14C. Old French *baleine* whale, from Latin *balaena.*

Balinese *n.* a native or inhabitant of Bali. *Also a.* WH: 19C. *Bali*, an island in Indonesia + -ESE, influ. by Dutch *Balinees.*

Balkan *a.* of or relating to the region of SE Europe which includes the Balkan Peninsula. *Also n.* WH: 19C. Turkish *balkan* chain of wooded mountains, assim. to words in -AN. The name is that of a chain of wooded mountains in Bulgaria.

ball[1] *n.* a spherical body of any dimensions. *Also v.t., v.i.* WH: 12–14C. Old Norse *bollr*, from Germanic, ult. rel. to BULL[1].

ball[2] *n.* a social assembly for dancing. WH: 17C. Old French *bal* dance, from Late Latin *ballare*, rel. to Greek *ballein* to throw. Cp. BALLAD, BALLET.

ballad *n.* a light simple song, esp. a slow sentimental one. *Also v.i., v.t.* WH: 15C. Old French *ballade*, from Provençal *balada* dance, song to dance to, from *balar* to dance. Cp. BALL[2], also -AD[2].

ballade *n.* a poem consisting of three eight-lined stanzas rhyming *a b a b b c b c*, each having the same line as a refrain, and with an envoy of four lines, an old form revived in the 19th cent. WH: 12–14C. See BALLAD.

ballast *n.* stones, iron or other heavy substances placed in the bottom of a ship or boat to lower the centre of gravity and make her steady. *Also v.t.* WH: 16C. Low German, ? from Scandinavian, ? comb. of *bar* bare and *last* load, in the sense of a load for the sake of weight only.

ballerina *n.* a female ballet dancer; a female dancer taking a leading part in a ballet. WH: 18C. Italian, fem. of *ballerino* dancing master, from *ballare* to dance. See BALL[2].

ballet *n.* a form of dramatic representation consisting of dancing and mime to set steps. WH: 17C. French, from Italian *balletto*, dim. of *ballo* BALL[2].

ballista *n.* a military engine used in ancient times for hurling stones, darts and other missiles. WH: 16C. Latin, ult. from Greek *ballein* to throw.

ballistic *a.* of or relating to the hurling and flight of projectiles. WH: 18C. See BALLISTA + -IC.

ballon d'essai *n.* a trial balloon. WH: 19C. French trial balloon. Cp. BALLOON, ESSAY[1]. The original sense was a small balloon sent up to determine the direction of the wind before a passenger balloon ascended.

balloon *n.* a spherical or pear-shaped bag of light material, which when filled with heated air or gas rises and floats in the air (to the larger kinds a car is attached, capable of containing several persons, and these balloons are used for scientific observations, reconnoitring etc.). *Also v.i., v.t.* WH: 16C. French *ballon*, or from Italian *ballone*, augm. of *balla* BALL[1]. See also -OON. A balloon was originally a large inflated ball for batting to and fro, then a type of airborne firework. The main sense dates from Montgolfier's balloon ascent, 1783, while the child's balloon dates from 19C.

ballot *n.* the method or system of secret voting. *Also v.t., v.i.* WH: 16C. Italian *ballotta*, dim. of *balla* BALL[1]. Cp. blackball (BLACK).

bally *a.* bloody. WH: 19C. Euphem. alt. of *bloody*, from Old English *blōdig*, from Germanic. See BLOOD, also -Y[1]. The form of the word may have been suggested by the euphemistic abbreviation *bl—y.*

ballyhoo *n.* noisy and unprincipled propaganda. WH: 19C. Orig. unknown.

ballyrag *v.t.* to revile, abuse, assail with violent language. *Also v.i.* WH: 18C. Orig. unknown. Cp. RAG[2].

balm *n.* the fragrant juice, sap or gum of certain trees or plants. *Also v.t.* WH: 12–14C. Old French *basme* (Modern French *baume*), from Latin *balsamum* BALSAM.

Balmoral *n.* a kind of Scottish cap. WH: 19C. *Balmoral* Castle, a royal residence in Scotland.

balneology *n.* the science of treating diseases by bathing and medicinal springs. WH: 19C. Latin *balneum* bath + -O- + -LOGY.

baloney *n.* idiotic talk, nonsense. WH: early 20C. Said to be from BOLOGNA sausage.

balsa *n.* an American tropical tree, *Ochroma lagopus.* WH: 17C. Spanish raft.

balsam *n.* a vegetable resin with a strong fragrant odour, balm. *Also v.t.* WH: pre-1200. Latin *balsamum*, from Greek *balsamon*, ? of Semitic orig. See BALM.

Balti *n.* a type of curry composed of meat and vegetables cooked in an iron pot. WH: late 20C. Hindi bucket, scoop, from shape of dish in which cooked.

Baltic *a.* denoting, of or relating to a sea in N Europe or its bordering countries. *Also n.* WH: 16C. Medieval Latin *Balticus*, from Late Latin *Balthae* Balts. See also -IC.

Baltimore *n.* a N American oriole, *Icterus galbula*, the male of which has a black head and orange plumage. WH: 17C. Charles Calvert, 3rd Baron *Baltimore*, 1637–1715, British proprietor of Maryland, after the colours of his coat of arms.

baluster *n.* a small column, usu. circular, swelling towards the bottom, and forming part of a series called a balustrade. WH: 17C. French *balustre*, from Italian *balaustro*, from *balausta* blossom of wild pomegranate, which a baluster resembles in shape. Cp. BANISTER.

bam *v.t.* to cheat, hoax, bamboozle. *Also v.i., n.* WH: 18C. Prob. from BAMBOOZLE.

bambino *n.* a child, a baby. WH: 18C. Italian, dim. of *bambo* silly. Cp. BIMBO.

bamboo *n.* any giant tropical grass of the subfamily Bambusidae. *Also v.t.* WH: 16C. Dutch *bamboes*, ult. from Malay *mambu*, ? from Kanarese.

bamboozle *v.t.* to mystify for purposes of fraud; to cheat. *Also v.i., n.* WH: 18C. Orig. uncertain. ? Rel. to BOMBAST[1]. Cp. BAM.

ban *v.t.* to forbid, to proscribe. *Also v.i., n.* WH: pre-1200. Old English *bannan*, from Germanic, base found also in Greek *phanai*, Latin *fari* to speak. Cp. BANNS.

banal *a.* commonplace, trite. WH: 18C. Old French, from *ban* BAN + -AL¹. The original sense was legal, belonging to compulsory feudal service. This eventually evolved to the current sense in the 19C.

banana¹ *n.* a tropical and subtropical treelike plant, *Musa sapientum*, closely allied to the plantain. WH: 16C. Spanish and Portuguese, from Mande.

banana² *n.* an opponent of all further construction on and development of land. WH: late 20C. Acronym of *build absolutely nothing anywhere near anyone*, punning on BANANA¹.

banausic *a.* mechanical, considered merely fit for a mechanic; uncultured. WH: 19C. Greek *banaustikos*, from *bainos* forge. See also -IC.

Banbury cake *n.* a kind of pastry cake filled with mincemeat, supposed to be made at Banbury. WH: 16C. *Banbury*, a town in Oxfordshire.

banc *n.* the judicial bench. WH: 18C. Latin *in banco* on the bench. Cp. BANK².

band¹ *n.* a flat slip of cloth (BAND²), used to bind together, encircle or as part of a garment. WH: 14–15C. Old French *bande*, orig. *bende*, from Germanic, from base of BIND. Cp. BEND, BAND².

†band² *n.* that which binds, confines or restrains. WH: pre-1200. Old Norse *band*, from Germanic, from base of BIND. Cp. BAND¹, BEND, BOND¹.

band³ *n.* a company of musicians playing together. WH: 15C. Old French *bande*, from Medieval Latin *banda*, prob. of Germanic orig. The word perhaps originates from the use of a band of cloth to identify members of a group of soldiers. Cp. BAND¹.

band⁴ *v.t.* to bind or fasten with a band. *Also v.i.* WH: 15C. Old French *bander*. See BAND¹.

bandage *n.* a strip of flexible material used to bind up wounds, fractures etc. *Also v.t.* WH: 16C. French, from Old French *bande* BAND¹ + -AGE.

bandanna *n.* a silk handkerchief of a type orig. of Indian manufacture, having white or yellow spots on a coloured ground. WH: 18C. Prob. from Portuguese, from Hindi. Cp. Hindi *bā̆dhnū* method of tie-dyeing, spotted cloth, from *bā̆dhnā* to tie.

bandeau *n.* a narrow band or fillet for the head. WH: 18C. French, from Old French *bandel*, dim. of *bande* BAND¹.

banderilla *n.* a little dart ornamented with ribbons, which bullfighters stick in the neck of the bull. WH: 18C. Spanish, dim. of *bandera* banner.

banderole *n.* a long narrow flag with a cleft end flying at a masthead. WH: 16C. French *banerole*, later *banderole*, from Italian *banderuola*, dim. of *bandiera* BANNER.

bandicoot *n.* a large Asian rat of the genus *Bandicota*. WH: 18C. Alt. of Telugu *pandi-kokku* pig-rat.

banding *n.* the action of binding or marking with a band. WH: 16C. BAND⁴ + -ING¹.

bandit *n.* a person who is proscribed, an outlaw. WH: 16C. Italian *bandito*, p.p. (used as n.) of *bandire* BAN.

bandog *n.* an aggressive cross-breed fighting dog. WH: 12–14C. BAND² + DOG.

bandolier *n.* a belt worn over the right shoulder and across the breast, with little leather loops to receive cartridges. WH: 16C. French *bandoulière*, ? from Spanish *bandolera*, from *banda* sash. Cp. BAND¹.

bandoline *n.* a gummy substance applied to the hair to keep it smooth and flat. WH: 19C. French BANDEAU + Latin *linere* to anoint, to bedaub.

bandore *n.* an old musical instrument somewhat resembling a lute. WH: 16C. Orig. uncertain. Prob. rel. to PANDORE.

bandy¹ *v.t.* to beat or throw to and fro as at the game of tennis or bandy. *Also v.i., n.* WH: 16C. ? French *bander* to take sides at tennis. Cp. BANDY³.

bandy² *a.* crooked, bent outwards. WH: 17C. Orig. uncertain. ? From *bandy*, curved stick used in a form of hockey, itself somehow rel. to BANDY¹. Cp. HOCKEY¹.

bane *n.* a cause of ruin or mischief. *Also v.t.* WH: pre-1200. Old English *bana* slayer, of Germanic orig. Ult. source unknown, but

prob. rel. to Greek *phonos* murder. The original sense was murderer. This evolved to poison from the 14C (hence plant names such as *fleabane*, *henbane*) and eventually gave the current weaker meaning in the 16C.

bang *v.t.* to slam (a door), fire (a gun), beat (a musical instrument) with a loud noise. *Also v.i., n., adv.* WH: 16C. Imit., ? of Scandinavian orig.

bangalay *n.* a variety of eucalyptus tree. WH: 19C. Australian Aboriginal.

Bangladeshi *n.* a native or inhabitant of Bangladesh. *Also a.* WH: late 20C. *Bangladesh*, a republic in the NE of the Indian subcontinent + -I³. Cp. BENGALI, BUNGALOW. The name of Bangladesh means Bengali country, from Hindi *banglā* Bengali + *desh* country.

bangle *n.* a ring-bracelet or anklet. WH: 18C. Hindi *banglī* coloured glass bracelet.

banish *v.t.* to condemn to exile. WH: 14–15C. Old French *banir*, *baniss-* (Modern French *bannir*), from Germanic, from base of BAN. See also -ISH².

banister *n.* a shaft or upright supporting a handrail at the side of a staircase. WH: 17C. Alt. of BALUSTER, partly through assoc. with BAR¹.

banjo *n.* a stringed musical instrument, having a head and neck like a guitar and a body like a tambourine, and played with the fingers. WH: 18C. Alt. of BANDORE, representing pronun. by American blacks.

bank¹ *n.* a raised area of ground. *Also v.t., v.i.* WH: 12–14C. Old Norse *bakki* ridge, from Germanic. Rel. to BENCH.

bank² *n.* an establishment which deals in money, receiving it on deposit from customers and investing it. *Also v.i., v.t.* WH: 15C. French *banque*, or from Italian *banca* (also *banco*), from Medieval Latin *bancus*, from Germanic. Cp. BANK¹. The word was originally used of a moneychanger's counter or shop. The sense stock of money evolved in the 16C and the current sense emerged in the 17C. The Bank of England was founded in 1694.

bank³ *n.* a platform or stage. WH: 12–14C. Old French *banc*, from Germanic. Cp. BANK¹, BENCH.

banker *n.* a sculptor's revolving table. WH: 17C. ? Alt. of Italian *banco* bench. See BANK³.

banket *n.* a gold-bearing conglomerate. WH: 19C. Afrikaans almond toffee. The rock is so named from its colour.

bankrupt *n.* a person who, becoming insolvent, is judicially required to surrender their estates to be administered for the benefit of their creditors. *Also a., v.t.* WH: 16C. Italian *banca rotta*, lit. bench broken, influ. by French *banqueroute* and assim. to Latin *ruptus* broken. The original sense was the breaking up of a trader's business because of his failure to pay creditors.

banksia *n.* an Australian flowering shrub or tree of the genus *Banksia* of the family Proteaceae. WH: 19C. Modern Latin, from Sir Joseph Banks, 1743–1820, English naturalist. See also -IA. The banksia rose is named for his wife Dorothea.

banlieue *n.* the territory outside the walls but within the jurisdiction of a town or city. WH: 19C. French, from Latin *banleuca*, from *bannus* BAN + *leuca* LEAGUE².

banner *n.* an ensign or flag painted with some device or emblem. *Also a.* WH: 12–14C. Old French *baniere* (Modern French *bannière*) and Medieval Latin *bandum* BAND³. The original Old French sense was the flag under which a particular group of troops formed.

banneret *n.* a knight entitled to lead a company of vassals under his banner, ranking above other knights and next below a baron. WH: 12–14C. Old French *baneres*, later *baneret*. See BANNER.

bannerette *n.* a small banner. WH: 12–14C. Old French *banerete*, dim. of *baniere*. See BANNER, -ETTE.

bannerol *n.* a banner about a yard or metre square, borne at the funeral of eminent personages and placed over the tomb. WH: 16C. See BANDEROLE.

bannock *n.* a flat round cake made of pease- or barley-meal or flour, usu. unleavened. WH: pre-1200. Old English *bannuc*, from Celtic, ? rel. to Latin *panis* bread.

banns *n.pl.* proclamation in church of an intended marriage, so that any impediment may be made known and inquired into. WH: 12–14C. Pl. of BAN, from Medieval Latin (pl.) *banna*.

banquet *n.* a sumptuous feast, usu. of a ceremonial character and followed by speeches. *Also v.t., v.i.* WH: 15C. Old French, dim. of *banc* bench, BANK³. The original Old French sense refers to benches placed at a table around which people are eating. An early English sense was a slight repast, a snack, as the exact opposite of the current meaning, but this was obsolete by the 17C.

banquette *n.* a built-in cushioned seat along a wall. WH: 17C. French, from Italian *banchetta*, dim. of *banca* bench, shelf. See also -ETTE.

banshee *n.* a supernatural being, supposed in Ireland and the Scottish Highlands to wail round a house when one of the inmates is about to die. WH: 17C. Irish *bean sídhe*, from Old Irish *ben síde*, from *ben* woman + *síde* of the fairies.

bantam *n.* a small domestic fowl, of which the cocks are very aggressive. WH: 18C. *Bantam*, a district of NW Java, where they are supposed to have been native.

banter *v.t.* to ridicule good-humouredly; to rally, to chaff. *Also v.i.*, *n.* WH: 17C. Orig. unknown.

banting *n.* the reduction of obesity by abstinence from fat, starch and sugar. WH: 19C. William *Banting*, 1797–1878, English cabinet-maker and dietician.

bantling *n.* a little child, a brat. WH: 16C. ? German *Bänkling* bastard, from *Bank* bench, BANK³. See -LING¹. Cp. BASTARD.

Bantu *n.* a group of languages of southern and central Africa. *Also a.* WH: 19C. Bantu, pl. of *-ntu* person.

banxring *n.* a Javanese squirrel-like tree-shrew, *Tupaia javanica*. WH: 19C. Javanese *bangsring*.

banyan *n.* a Hindu merchant or shop-keeper, a Bengali broker or hawker. WH: 16C. Portuguese, from Gujarati *vāṇiyo* man of the trading caste, from Sanskrit *vāṇija* merchant. The banyan tree came to be so called by Europeans from a particular tree under which traders had built a pagoda.

banzai *int.* a Japanese battle-cry, patriotic salute or cheer. *Also a.* WH: 19C. Japanese ten thousand years (of life to you). Cp. Chinese *wàn* ten thousand, *suì* year.

baobab *n.* an African tree, *Adansonia digitata*, bearing large pulpy fruit. WH: 17C. Prob. from an African language.

bap *n.* a large soft bread roll. WH: 16C. Orig. unknown.

baptize *v.t.* to sprinkle with or immerse in water as a sign of purification and consecration, esp. into the Christian Church. *Also v.i.* WH: 12–14C. Old French *baptiser*, from Ecclesiastical Latin *baptizare*, from Greek *baptizein* to dip, to immerse.

bar¹ *n.* a piece of wood, iron or other solid material, long in proportion to breadth; a pole. *Also v.t.* WH: 12–14C. Old French *barre*, of unknown orig.

bar² *n.* a unit of atmospheric pressure which is equivalent to 10^6 dynes per square centimetre (10^5 newton per square metre). WH: early 20C. Greek *baros* weight.

bar³ *prep.* except, apart from. WH: 18C. Imp. of BAR¹, from French *barrer*. Prob. based on EXCEPT, SAVE, etc. Cp. BARRING.

barathea *n.* a fabric made from wool mixed with silk or cotton, used esp. for coats and suits. WH: 19C. Orig. unknown.

barb¹ *n.* the appendages on the mouth of the barbel and other fishes. *Also v.t.* WH: 12–14C. Old French *barbe*, from Latin *barba* beard. Cp. BARBEL.

barb² *n.* a fine breed of horse. WH: 17C. French *barbe*, from Italian *barbero* of Barbary. See BARBARY.

Barbadian *n.* a native or inhabitant of Barbados. *Also a.* WH: 18C. *Barbados*, an island in the W Indies + -IAN.

barbarian *n.* a savage, a person belonging to some uncivilized people. *Also a.* WH: 12–14C. Obs. French *barbarien*, from Old French *barbare*, from Latin *barbarus*, from Greek *barbaros* non-Greek, foreign. Cp. BRAVE. The word is ultimately probably imitative of unintelligible speech. Cp. BARBARY, BABBLE.

Barbary *a.* of or relating to Barbary, an extensive region in the north of Africa. WH: 12–14C. Arabic *barbar* BERBER, whose speech was unintelligible to others. Cp. BARBARIAN.

barbastelle *n.* a bat of the genus *Barbastella* which roosts in trees or caves. WH: 18C. French, from Italian *barbastello*.

barbate *a.* bearded. WH: 18C. Latin *barbatus* bearded, from *barba* beard. See also -ATE².

barbecue *n.* an outdoor meal at which food is prepared over a charcoal fire. *Also v.t.* WH: 17C. Spanish *barbacoa*, ? from Arawak *barbacoa* raised framework of sticks. A barbecue was originally a

wooden framework for storage, sleeping on, etc., then an animal roasted on such a framework, then the meal itself from the 19C.

barbel *n.* a European freshwater fish, *Barbus vulgaris*, allied to the carp, named from the fleshy filaments which hang below the mouth. WH: 14–15C. Old French, from Late Latin *barbellus*, dim. of *barbus*, from *barba* beard. Cp. BARB¹.

barber *n.* a person who shaves and cuts beards and hair; a men's hairdresser. *Also v.t.* WH: 12–14C. Old French *barbier*, from *barbe* beard. See BARB¹, also -ER¹.

barberry *n.* a shrub of the genus *Berberis*, esp. *B. vulgaris*. WH: 14–15C. Old French BERBERIS, assim. to BERRY.

barbet *n.* a tropical bird of the family Capitonidae, allied to the toucans, having tufts of hair at the base of its bill. WH: 16C. French, from *barbe* beard. See also -ET¹.

barbette *n.* a mound of earth in a fortification on which guns are mounted to be fired over the parapet. WH: 18C. French, from *barbe* beard. See BARBET, also -ETTE.

barbican *n.* an outer fortification to a city or castle, designed as a cover to the inner works, esp. over a gate or bridge and serving as a watchtower. WH: 12–14C. Old French *barbacane*, from Medieval Latin *barbacana*, prob. ult. from Arabic.

barbie *n.* a barbecue. WH: late 20C. Abbr. of BARBECUE. See also -Y³.

barbituric *a.* denoting an acid obtained from malonic and uric acids. WH: 19C. French *barbiturique*, from German *Barbitur(säure)*, said to be from *Barbara*, woman's name (+ *Säure* acid). See URIC. However, malonic acid is extracted from beet, Italian *barbabietola*, and this seems a more likely origin.

barbola *n.* the attachment of small flowers etc. in paste to embellish vases etc. WH: early 20C. Alt. of *barbotine*, from French *barbotine*, from *barboter* to work noisily with the bill in water (as a duck), prob. ult. imit. Cp. BARBARIAN, BABBLE.

Barbour® *n.* a type of green waxed jacket. WH: mid-20C. John *Barbour*, 1874–1918, its orig. manufacturer.

barbule *n.* a hooked or serrated filament given off from the barb of a feather. WH: 19C. Latin *barbula*, dim. of *barba* beard. See also -ULE.

barcarole *n.* a song sung by Venetian gondoliers. WH: 18C. French *barcarolle*, from Italian (Venetian) *barcarola* gondolier, from *barca* BARK³.

barchan *n.* a shifting sand dune in the shape of a crescent. WH: 19C. Turkic *barkhan*.

bard¹ *n.* a Celtic minstrel. WH: 12–14C. Celtic. The word was originally used in Scotland and as a term of contempt, but was romanticized by Sir Walter Scott in e.g. *The Lay of the Last Minstrel* (1805) ('The last of all the bards was he,/ Who sung of Border chivalry').

bard² *n.* a slice of bacon put on meat or game before roasting. *Also v.t.* WH: 15C. Old French *barde*, ult. from Arabic *barda'a* saddle-cloth, stuffed saddle.

bardy *n.* an edible wood-boring grub. WH: 19C. Australian Aboriginal.

bare *a.* unclothed, naked, nude. *Also v.t.* WH: pre-1200. Old English *bær*, from Germanic, from Indo-European.

barège *n.* a light gauzy dress fabric. WH: 19C. *Barèges*, a village in SW France where orig. made.

barf *v.i.* to vomit, to retch. *Also n.* WH: mid-20C. Prob. imit.

bargain *n.* an agreement between parties, generally concerning a sale. *Also v.i., v.t.* WH: 12–14C. Old French *bargaine*, *bargane*, *barguine*, from *bargaignier* to trade, to dispute (Modern French *barguigner* to hesitate), from Italian *bargagnare*, from Medieval Latin *barcaniare*, prob. from Germanic. Ult. rel. to BORROW.

bargan *n.* a boomerang. WH: 19C. Australian Aboriginal.

barge *n.* a flat-bottomed freight-boat used principally on canals or rivers. *Also v.i., v.t.* WH: 12–14C. Old French, from Medieval Latin *bargia*, ? ult. from Greek *baris* Egyptian boat. Cp. BARK³.

barge- *comb. form* used as below. WH: Medieval Latin *bargus* kind of gallows.

barghest *n.* a doglike goblin whose apparition is said to portend calamity or death. WH: 18C. Orig. unknown. The word is said to be from German *Berggeist* mountain demon, but has also been related to German *Bahre* bier or *Bär* bear, the latter with reference to its supposed form.

barilla *n.* an impure alkali obtained from the ash of *Salsola soda* and allied species. WH: 17C. Spanish *barrilla*, dim. of *barra* bar.

baritone *n.* a male voice intermediate between a bass and a tenor. *Also a.* WH: 17C. Italian *baritono*, from Greek *barutonos* deep-sounding, from *barus* deep + *tonos* pitch.

barium *n.* a metallic divalent element, at. no. 56, chem. symbol Ba, the metallic base of baryta. WH: 19C. BARYTA + -IUM. The word was coined in 1808 by the English chemist Sir Humphry Davy. Cp. CALCIUM, STRONTIUM.

bark[1] *v.i.* to utter a sharp, explosive cry, like that of a dog. *Also v.t., n.* WH: pre-1200. Old English *beorcan*, from Germanic, ? ult. alt. of BREAK.

bark[2] *n.* the rind or exterior covering of a tree, formed of tissues parallel to the wood. *Also v.t.* WH: 12–14C. Old Norse *borkr*, ? rel. to BIRCH. The Old English word for bark was RIND.

bark[3] *n.* a ship or boat, esp. a small sailing vessel. WH: 14–15C. Old French, prob. from Provençal *barca*, from Late Latin. Cp. BARGE.

Barking bloke *n.* the stereotypical floating male voter. WH: late 20C. *Barking*, a district of E London, originally a town in Essex. Cp. ESSEX MAN.

barley *n.* a plant of the genus *Hordeum*, a hardy, awned cereal. WH: pre-1200. Old English *bærlic*, a. from root form of *bere* barley + *-lic* -LY[1].

barm *n.* the frothy scum which rises to the surface of malt liquor in fermentation, used as a leaven. WH: pre-1200. Old English *beorma*, prob. from Low German. Ult. rel. to FERMENT[2].

barmbrack *n.* sweet, spicy bread containing currants, dried peel etc. WH: 19C. Irish *bairín breac* speckled cake.

Barmecide *n.* a person who gives illusory benefits. *Also a.* WH: 18C. Arabic *barmakī* a name of a family in the *Arabian Nights' Entertainment*, one of whom invited a beggar to feast from empty dishes to test his humour.

bar mitzvah *n.* a Jewish boy who has reached the age of religious responsibility, usu. on his 13th birthday. WH: 19C. Hebrew *bar miṣwāh* son of commandment. Cp. BAT MITZVAH.

barn *n.* a covered building for the storage of grain and other agricultural produce. WH: pre-1200. Old English *beren*, *bern*, earlier *berern*, from *bere* BARLEY + *ærn*, *ern* house. Cp. BARTON.

barnacle *n.* the barnacle goose. WH: 12–14C. Medieval Latin *bernaca*, of unknown orig. According to some, the word is from Latin *Hibernicae*, *Hiberniculae* Irish goose. Cp. HIBERNIAN.

barnacles *n.pl.* a kind of twitch put on the nostrils of a restive horse while being shod. WH: 14–15C. Pl. of *barnacle*, alt. of Anglo-French *bernac*, of unknown orig.

barney *n.* a noisy argument or fight. WH: 19C. Orig. unknown. Perhaps *Barney* was a nickname for a typical noisy Irishman.

baro- *comb. form* weight, pressure. WH: Greek *baros* weight, usu. with sense of pressure. See also -O-.

barograph *n.* an aneroid barometer recording the variations of atmospheric pressure. WH: 19C. BARO- + -GRAPH.

barogyroscope *n.* a gyrostat used for demonstrating the rotation of the earth. WH: early 20C. BARO- + GYROSCOPE.

barology *n.* the science of weight. WH: 19C. BARO- + -LOGY.

barometer *n.* an instrument used for measuring the atmospheric pressure, thus indicating probable weather change, and also for measuring altitudes reached. WH: 17C. BARO- + -METER.

baron *n.* a member of the lowest rank of nobility. WH: 12–14C. Old French *baron*, acc. of *ber*, from Medieval Latin *baro*, *baronis* man, male, warrior, prob. of Frankish orig.

baronet *n.* a hereditary titled order of commoners ranking next below barons, instituted by James I in 1611. *Also v.t.* WH: 14–15C. Anglo-French *baronettus*. See BARON, also -ET[1]. The term (title) originally meant a lesser baron. The current title was officially instituted in 1611.

baroque *n.* a style of artistic or architectural expression prevalent esp. in 17th-cent. Europe, characterized by extravagant ornamentation. *Also a.* WH: 18C. French, from Portuguese *barroco*, Spanish *barrueco*, Italian *barocco*, ult. of unknown orig. The French word was originally a derogatory term used of rough or imperfect pearls.

baroreceptor *n.* a collection of nerve endings in the body that are sensitive to changes in pressure. WH: mid-20C. BARO- + *receptor*. See RECEPTION.

baroscope *n.* a weather glass. WH: 17C. BARO- + -SCOPE.

barothermograph *n.* an instrument combining a barometer and a thermometer. WH: 19C. BARO- + *thermograph*. See THERMOGRAPHY.

barouche *n.* a double-seated four-wheeled horse-drawn carriage, with a movable top, and a seat outside for the driver. WH: 19C. German (dial.) *Barutsche*, from Italian *baroccio* two-wheeled, ult. from Latin *birotus*, from BI- + *rota* wheel. Cp. French *brouette* wheelbarrow.

barquentine *n.* a three-masted vessel, with the foremast square-rigged, and the main and mizen fore-and-aft rigged. WH: 17C. From *barque* BARK[3] based on BRIGANTINE.

barracan *n.* a coarse cloth resembling camlet. WH: 17C. French *barracan*, *bouracan*, from Arabic *burrukān*, from Persian *barak* cloak made of camel's hair.

barrack[1] *n.* a temporary hut. *Also v.t., v.i.* WH: 17C. French *baraque*, from Italian *baracca* or Spanish *barraca* soldier's tent, ult. of unknown orig.

barrack[2] *v.i.* to jeer. *Also v.t.* WH: 19C. ? Irish (dial.) to brag, to boast. Pop. assoc. with BORAK.

barracoon *n.* a fortified African slave house. WH: 19C. Spanish *barracón*, augm. of *barraca*. See BARRACK[1], also -OON.

barracouta *n.* a large edible fish of the Pacific, *Thyrsites atun*. WH: 17C. Alt. of BARRACUDA.

barracuda *n.* a predatory tropical fish of the family Sphyraenidae. WH: 17C. Orig. unknown. ? From Carib.

barrad *n.* an Irish conical cap. WH: 19C. Irish *barreud*, *bairread*, from French *barrette* BARRET.

barrage *n.* an artificial bar or dam formed to raise the water in a river. WH: 19C. French, from *barre* BAR[1] + -AGE.

barramundi *n.* any of various percoid fishes found in Australian rivers, esp. *Lates calcarifer*. WH: 19C. Australian Aboriginal.

barranca *n.* a deep gorge, with steep sides. WH: 17C. Spanish.

barrator *n.* a person who out of malice or for their own purposes stirs up litigation or discord. WH: 14–15C. Old French *barateor* cheat, trickster, from *barater*, from Greek *prattein* to do, to perform. ? Influ. by Old Norse *barátta* contest. Cp. BARTER.

barre *n.* a wall-mounted horizontal rail used for ballet exercises. WH: early 20C. French BAR[1].

barré *n.* the laying of a finger across a particular fret of a guitar etc., to raise the pitch for the chord being played. WH: 19C. French, p.p. of *barrer* BAR[1].

barrel *n.* a cylindrical wooden vessel formed of staves held together by hoops. *Also v.t., v.i.* WH: 12–14C. Old French *baril*, from Medieval Latin *barriclus* small cask, ult. of unknown orig.

barren *a.* incapable of producing offspring. *Also n.* WH: 12–14C. Old French *barahaine*, *baraine*, *brehaine* (Modern French *bréhaigne*), of unknown orig.

barret *n.* a little flat cap. WH: 19C. French *barette*, from obs. Italian *baretta*. See BIRETTA.

barrette *n.* a hair-clasp. WH: early 20C. French, dim. of *barre* BAR[1].

barretter *n.* an appliance for keeping electric current in a circuit at constant strength. WH: early 20C. Orig. uncertain. ? From BARRATOR with the sense of exchange.

barricade *n.* a hastily formed rampart erected across a street or passage to obstruct an enemy or an attacking party. *Also v.t.* WH: 16C. French, from *barrique*, from Spanish *barrica* cask, from stem of *barril* BARREL. See also -ADE, -ADO. Barricades were originally built of barrels.

barrico *n.* a small cask, a keg. WH: 16C. Spanish *barrica* cask. See BARRICADE.

barrier *n.* an obstacle which hinders approach or attack. *Also v.t., a.* WH: 14–15C. Old French *barriere*. See BAR[1], also -IER.

barring *prep.* except, omitting. WH: 15C. Pres.p. of BAR[1]. See also -ING[1].

barrio *n.* a Spanish speaking community or district, usu. sited in the poorer areas of cities in SW US. WH: 19C. Spanish, ? from Arabic.

barrister *n.* a member of the legal profession who has been admitted to practise as an advocate at the bar; a counsellor-at-law. WH: 14–15C. See BAR[1]. The rest of the word is probably based on MINISTER.

barrow[1] *n.* a hill. WH: pre-1200. Old English *beorg*, from Germanic. Cp. BERG[2].

barrow[2] *n.* a shallow cart with two wheels pushed by hand. WH: pre-1200. Old English *bearwe*, from Germanic, from base of BEAR[2]. Cp. BIER. The cart was originally simply a frame on which a load was carried, including a stretcher and a bier. The current sense began to emerge in the 14C.

barter *v.t.* to give (anything except money) in exchange for some other commodity. *Also v.i., n.* WH: 14–15C. Prob. from Old French *barater*. See BARRATOR.

bartizan *n.* a battlement on top of a house or castle. WH: 16C. Scottish form of *bratticing*. See BRATTICE. The word was popularized in the 19C by Sir Walter Scott.

barton *n.* the part of an estate which the lord of the manor kept in his own hand. WH: pre-1200. Old English *bere-tūn*. See BARLEY, TOWN. Cp. BARN.

baryon *n.* any member of the heavier class of subatomic particles that have a mass equal to or greater than that of the proton. WH: mid-20C. Greek *barus* heavy + -ON from ELECTRON, PROTON.

barysphere *n.* the solid, heavy core of the earth, probably consisting of iron and other metals. WH: early 20C. Greek *barus* + SPHERE.

baryta *n.* barium oxide or barium hydroxide. WH: 19C. Based on *barytes*, from Greek *barutēs* weight + -*a* as in SODA, etc.

basalt *n.* a dark igneous rock of a black, bluish or leaden grey colour, of a uniform and compact texture, consisting of augite, feldspar and iron intimately blended, olivine also being often present. WH: 17C. Latin *basaltes*, var. of *basanites*, from Greek *basanitēs*, from *basanos* touchstone.

basan *n.* a sheepskin for bookbinding, tanned in oak or larch bark, as distinct from roan which is tanned in sumach. WH: 15C. Old French *basane*, from Provençal *bazana*, from Spanish *badana*, from Arabic *biṭāna* dressed sheepskin.

basanite *n.* a black variety of quartz. WH: 18C. Latin *basanites*. See BASALT, also -ITE[1].

bascule *n.* an apparatus on the principle of the lever, in which the depression of one end raises the other. WH: 17C. French see-saw, from stem of *battre* to beat + *cul* buttocks.

base[1] *n.* the lowest part on which anything rests. *Also v.t.* WH: 12–14C. Old French, or from Latin BASIS.

base[2] *a.* low in the moral scale; despicable. WH: 14–15C. Old French *bas*, from Medieval Latin *bassus* short, stout. Classical Latin had *Bassus* as a cognomen.

base jump *n.* a parachute jump from a fixed point such as a high building. WH: late 20C. Acronym of *b*uilding, *a*ntenna-tower, *s*pan, *e*arth, denoting the type of structure used.

basenji *n.* a small central African hunting dog which cannot bark. WH: mid-20C. Bantu, pl. of *mosenji, musengi* native.

bash[1] *v.t.* to strike, so as to smash or hurt. *Also v.i., adv., n.* WH: 17C. Ult. imit. ? Orig. blend of BANG and DASH or SMASH.

†bash[2] *v.t.* to dismay, abash. *Also v.i.* WH: 14–15C. Shortening of ABASH.

bashful *a.* shamefaced, easily embarrassed, excessively modest. WH: 15C. BASH[2] + -FUL.

bashibazouk *n.* a Turkish irregular soldier, noted for lawlessness and atrocious brutality. WH: 19C. Turkic *başı bozuk* wrong-headed, from *baş* head + *bozuk* out of order.

basho *n.* a tournament in sumo wrestling. WH: late 20C. Japanese place.

basi- *comb. form* of, relating to or forming the base; or at the base of. WH: BASE[1], BASIS + -*i*-.

BASIC *n.* a computer programming language using simple English terms. WH: mid-20C. Acronym of *B*eginners' *A*ll-purpose *S*ymbolic *I*nstruction *C*ode, based on *basic* (BASE[1]).

basicranial *a.* of or at the base of the cranium. WH: 19C. BASI- + *cranial*. See CRANIUM.

basidium *n.* a mother cell carried on a stalk and bearing spores characteristic of various fungi. WH: 19C. Modern Latin, from Greek BASIS, + -*idium*, Modern Latin dim. of -IUM.

basifugal *a.* growing away from the base. WH: 19C. BASI- + *fugal*. See FUGUE.

basil *n.* any herb of the genus *Ocimum*, species of which are used as culinary herbs, e.g. the sweet basil, *O. basilicum*. WH: 14–15C. Old French *basile*, from Medieval Latin *basilicum*, from Greek *basilikon* royal. See BASILICA. The herb was perhaps so called as it formed the basis of some 'royal' unguent or medicine.

basilateral *a.* at the side of a base. WH: 19C. BASI- + LATERAL.

Basilian *a.* of or relating to the monastic order instituted by St Basil in the Greek Church. *Also n.* WH: 18C. Latin *Basilius* Basil (St Basil the Great), *c.*330–379, Bishop of Caesarea + -AN.

basilica *n.* a large oblong building with double colonnades and an apse, used as a court of justice and an exchange. WH: 16C. Latin royal palace, from Greek *basilikē*, fem. (used as n.) of *basilikos* royal, from *basileus* king.

basilisk *n.* a fabulous reptile, said to be hatched by a serpent from a cock's egg, whose look and breath were reputedly fatal. WH: 14–15C. Latin *basiliscus*, from Greek *basiliskos*, dim. of *basileus* king. According to Pliny, the reptile was so called from a spot like a crown on its head.

basin *n.* a hollow (usu. circular) vessel for holding food being prepared or water, esp. for washing. WH: 12–14C. Old French *bacin* (Modern French *bassin*), from Medieval Latin *bascinus*, from *bacca* water container, ? from Gaulish.

basinet *n.* a light helmet, almost round, and generally without a visor. WH: 12–14C. Old French *bacinet*, dim. of *bacin* BASIN. See also -ET[1].

basipetal *a.* proceeding in the direction of the base. WH: 19C. BASI- + -*petal*, from Latin *petere* to seek.

basis *n.* the base or foundation. WH: 16C. Latin, from Greek stepping. Cp. BASE[1].

bask *v.i.* to expose oneself to the influence of warmth. *Also v.t.* WH: 14–15C. ? Scandinavian. Cp. Old Irish *badhask* to bathe oneself, from *badha* bathe. The earlier sense was to bathe in blood. The current sense dates from the 16C.

basket *n.* a wickerwork vessel of plaited twigs or similar material. *Also v.t.* WH: 12–14C. Anglo-French *baskettum*, of unknown orig. The word is said by some to derive from Latin *bascauda* a type of basin.

basmati rice *n.* a type of rice with a slender grain, delicate fragrance and nutty flavour. WH: 19C. Hindi *bāsmatī* fragrant.

basophil *n.* a white blood cell with basophilic contents. WH: 19C. Greek BASIS + -O- + -*phil* (-PHILE).

Basque *n.* a member of a people occupying both slopes of the western Pyrenees. *Also a.* WH: 19C. French, from Latin *Vasco* dweller in Vasconia, a region of the W Pyrenees. Cp. GASCON.

bas-relief *n.* low relief, a kind of sculpture in which the figures project less than one-half of their true proportions above the plane forming the background. WH: 17C. French, from Italian BASSO-RILIEVO.

bass[1] *n.* the lowest part in harmonized musical compositions; the deepest male voice. *Also a., v.t.* WH: 14–15C. BASE[2], with spelling assim. to Italian BASSO.

bass[2] *n.* the common European perch, *Perca fluviatilis*. WH: 14–15C. Alt. of *barse*, from Old English *baers, bears*, from Germanic.

bass[3] *n.* the inner bark of the lime tree or any similar vegetable fibre. WH: 17C. Alt. of BAST.

basset[1] *n.* a short-legged breed of dog, orig. used to drive foxes and badgers from their earths. WH: 17C. French, from *bas* low. See also -ET[1].

basset[2] *n.* the outcrop of strata at the surface of the ground. *Also a., v.i.* WH: 16C. Orig. unknown.

basset-horn *n.* a tenor clarinet with a recurved mouth. WH: 19C. German *Bassetthorn*, partial translation of French *cor de basset*, from Italian *corno di bassetto*, from *corno* horn, *di* of, *bassetto*, dim. of *basso* BASS[1].

bassinet *n.* an oblong wicker basket with a hood at the end, used as a cradle. WH: 16C. French, dim. of *bassin* BASIN. See also -ET[1].

basso *n.* a bass singer. WH: 18C. Italian low, from Latin *bassus*. Cp. BASS[1], BASE[2].

bassoon *n.* a wooden double-reed instrument, the bass to the clarinet and oboe. WH: 18C. French *bassoon*, from Italian *bassone*, augm. of *basso* low. See also -OON.

basso-rilievo *n.* low relief, bas-relief. WH: 17C. Italian, from *basso* low (see BASSO) + *rilievo* RELIEF[2].

bast *n.* the inner bark of the lime or linden tree. WH: pre-1200. Old English *bæst*, from Germanic, of unknown orig. Cp. BASS³.

bastard *n.* an illegitimate child or person. *Also a.* WH: 12–14C. Old French *bastart* (Modern French *bâtard*), from Medieval Latin *bastardus*, prob. from *bastum* packsaddle. See BAT³, also -ARD. The Old French word was used for a child of a nobleman and a woman other than his wife, born as a 'child of the packsaddle' (used as a bed while travelling). Cp. BANTLING.

baste¹ *v.t.* to moisten (a roasting joint etc.) with liquid fat, gravy etc. WH: 15C. Orig. unknown.

baste² *v.t.* to beat with a stick, to thrash, cudgel. WH: 16C. ? Fig. sense of BASTE¹. Appar. not rel. to BASH¹, which it predates.

baste³ *v.t.* to sew slightly, to tack, to fasten together with long stitches. WH: 14–15C. Old French *bastir* to tack, from Frankish, from Germanic. Rel. to BASTE.

bastille *n.* a fortified tower. WH: 14–15C. Old French, from *bastide*, from Provençal *bastida*, fem. p.p. (used as n.) of *bastir* to build. Cp. BASTION.

bastinado *n.* a method of corporal punishment or torture inflicted with a stick on the soles of the feet. *Also v.t.* WH: 16C. Spanish *bastinada*, from *bastón* stick, cudgel. See BATON, also -ADO.

bastion *n.* a projecting work at the angle or in the line of a fortification, having two faces and two flanks. WH: 16C. French, from Italian *bastione*, from *bastire* to build.

basuco *n.* an impure form of cocaine which is highly addictive. WH: late 20C. Columbian Spanish, ? rel. to Spanish *bazucar* to shake vigorously.

bat¹ *n.* a wooden instrument with a cylindrical handle and broad blade used to strike the ball at cricket or similar games. *Also v.t., v.i.* WH: pre-1200. ? Old French *batte*, from *batre*. See BATTER¹.

bat² *n.* a small nocturnal mouselike mammal of the order Chiroptera, having the digits extended to support a wing-membrane stretching from the neck to the tail, by means of which it flies. WH: 16C. Alt. of Middle English *bakke*, from Scandinavian. Cp. Old Swedish *natt-backa* night bat. The current spelling is perhaps from an association with Latin *blatta* moth. The Old English word for bat was *hrēremus* (modern English *rearmouse*), from *hrēran* to shake. Cp. German *Fledermaus* and English dial. *flitter-mouse*. (See FLITTER).

bat³ *n.* a packsaddle. WH: 14–15C. Old French, earlier *bast* (Modern French *bât*), from Provençal *bast*, from Medieval Latin *bastum* packsaddle. ? Rel. to Greek *bastazein* to bear.

bat⁴ *v.t.* to blink. WH: 17C. Var. of BATE³.

batata *n.* the sweet potato. WH: 16C. Spanish, from Taino. See POTATO.

Batavian *a.* of or relating to Batavia, an ancient district of the Netherlands. *Also n.* WH: 16C. Latin *Batavia*, from *Batavi* people of Betawe, an island between the Rhine and the Waal (in the modern Netherlands) + -AN.

batch *n.* any quantity produced at one operation or treated together. *Also v.t.* WH: 15C. Earlier *bach*, from Old English *gebæc* baking, something baked, from *bacan* BAKE. For the relationship between verb and noun, cp. WAKE¹/ WATCH, MAKE¹/ MATCH¹, SPEAK/ SPEECH.

bate¹ *n.* a rage. WH: 19C. See BAIT.

bate² *n.* alkaline lye used in tanning. *Also v.t.* WH: 19C. Of Germanic origin, rel. to BAIT and so to BITE.

†bate³ *v.t.* to beat the wings, flutter impatiently. *Also n.* WH: 12–14C. Old French *batre* to strike, beat (Modern French *battre*). See BATTER¹.

bateau *n.* a long, light, flat-bottomed river-boat, tapering at both ends, used in Canada. WH: 18C. French boat, from Old English, or from Scandinavian. See BOAT.

bateleur *n.* an African eagle, *Terathopius ecaudatus*, having a short tail and a crest. WH: 19C. French juggler, mountebank. The bird is so named for its distinctive aerobatics.

Batesian mimicry *n.* mimicry in which a species is protected by its resemblance to one that is harmful or inedible. WH: 19C. H.W. Bates, 1825–92, English naturalist + -IAN.

bath¹ *n.* the act of washing or immersing the body in water or other fluid. *Also v.t.* WH: pre-1200. Old English *bæth*, from Germanic. Rel. to BAKE.

bath² *n.* a liquid measure among the ancient Hebrews, containing about 6½ gallons. WH: 14–15C. Hebrew *baṭ*.

bathe *v.i.* to swim in a body of water for pleasure. *Also v.t., n.* WH: pre-1200. Old English *bathian*, from base of BATH¹.

batho- *comb. form* used in compound words employed in oceanography etc. WH: Greek *bathos* depth. See also -O-.

batholith *n.* a great mass of intrusive igneous rock, esp. granite. WH: early 20C. BATHO- + -LITH.

bathometer *n.* an instrument used to ascertain the depths reached in soundings. WH: 19C. BATHO- + METER.

bathos *n.* ridiculous descent from the sublime to the commonplace in writing or speech. WH: 17C. Greek depth. The main current sense was introduced by Pope in the treatise *Peri Bathous, or the Art of Sinking in Poetry* (1727), the title being a parody on Longinus' *Peri Huphous* ('On the Sublime') (1C AD).

bathy- *comb. form* used in compound words employed in oceanography, etc. WH: Greek *bathus* deep.

bathymetry *n.* the art or method of taking deep soundings. WH: 19C. BATHY- + -METRY.

bathyscaphe *n.* a submersible vessel for deep-sea observation and exploration. WH: mid-20C. French, from BATHY- + Greek *skaphos* ship.

bathysphere *n.* a strong steel deep-sea observation chamber. WH: mid-20C. BATHY- + SPHERE.

batik *n.* a method of printing designs on fabric by masking areas to be left undyed with wax. WH: 19C. Javanese painted.

batiste *n.* a fine cotton or linen fabric. *Also a.* WH: 19C. French, earlier *batiche*, ? from base of *battre*. See BATTER¹. According to some, the word is from *Baptiste* of Cambray, the original maker (13C).

bat mitzvah *n.* a Jewish girl who has reached the age (usu. 12 years) of religious responsibility. WH: mid-20C. Hebrew *baṭ miṣwāh* daughter of commandment, based on BAR MITZVAH.

baton *n.* the wand used by a conductor of an orchestra etc. in beating time. *Also v.t.* WH: 16C. French *bâton*, earlier *baston*, from Late Latin *bastum* stick.

batrachian *a.* of or relating to the order Anura (formerly Batrachia), which includes frogs and toads. *Also n.* WH: 19C. Modern Latin *Batrachia*, from Greek *batrakheia*, neut. pl. of *a.* from *batrakhos* frog. See also -AN.

battalion *n.* a main division of an army. *Also v.t.* WH: 16C. French *bataillon*, from Italian *battaglione*, augm. of *battaglia* BATTLE. See also -OON.

battels *n.pl.* provisions from the buttery at an Oxford college. WH: 16C. ? From dial. *battle*, to nourish, and rel. to BATTEN².

batten¹ *n.* a strip of sawn wood used for flooring. *Also v.t.* WH: 15C. Old French *batant*, pres.p. (used as n.) of *batre*. See BATTER¹, also -ANT.

batten² *v.i.* to thrive, to prosper (on). *Also v.t.* WH: 16C. Old Norse *batna* to improve. See also -EN⁵.

batten³ *n.* the movable bar of a loom which strikes the weft in. WH: 19C. French *battant*, pres.p. of *battre* to beat.

Battenberg *n.* a kind of oblong cake made with sponge of two colours. WH: early 20C. *Battenberg*, a town in W Germany. The cake is said to have been named for the marriage of Princess Victoria of Hesse-Darmstadt to Prince Louis of Battenberg in 1884. (The Prince took British nationality and changed his title to Mountbatten, 1917.)

batter¹ *v.t.* to strike with successive blows so as to shake or demolish. *Also v.i., n.* WH: 12–14C. Old French *batre* to strike, to beat (Modern French *battre*), from Latin *battuere*. Cp. BATTLE.

batter² *v.i.* to incline (as walls, parapets, embankments etc.) from the perpendicular with a receding slope. *Also n.* WH: 16C. Orig. unknown.

batter³ *n.* a batsman; a player who is batting. WH: 18C. See BAT¹ + -ER¹.

battery *n.* a connected series of electric cells, dynamos or Leyden jars, forming a source of electrical energy. WH: 12–14C. Old French *baterie* (Modern French *batterie*), from *batre*. See BATTER¹, also -ERY. The original sense was beating (as it is still in 'assault and battery'). Two senses then developed: first, battering by guns, then the guns themselves. The guns discharged shells, hence the modern batteries that discharge electricity. The current sense dates from the 18C.

batting *n.* using a bat, hitting with a bat. WH: 17C. See BAT¹ + -ING¹.

battle *n.* a fight or hostile engagement between opposing armies etc. *Also v.i., v.t.* WH: 12–14C. Old French *bataille*, from Late Latin *battualia* military exercises, from *battuere* to beat. Cp. BATTER¹.

battled *a.* drawn up in line of battle. WH: 12–14C. P.p. of obs. *battle* to provide with battlements + -ED. The word has been largely superseded by *embattled* EMBATTLE[1].

battledore *n.* the light racket used to strike a shuttlecock in an old racket game. WH: 14–15C. ? Provençal *batedor* beater, from *batre* to beat. See BATTER[1].

battlement *n.* a parapet with openings on the top of a building, orig. for defensive purposes. WH: 14–15C. Old French *bataillier* (see BATTLE) + -MENT.

battue *n.* driving game from cover by beating the bushes. WH: 18C. French, fem. p.p. (used as n.) of *battre* to beat. See BATTER[1].

battuta *n.* a bar. WH: 18C. Italian, from *battuere* to beat.

bauble *n.* a gewgaw, a showy trinket. WH: 12–14C. Old French *baubel, babel* child's toy, ? ult. from redupl. of *bel* beautiful. Cp. BIBELOT. For a similar reduplication, cp. BON-BON.

baud *n.* a unit which measures the rate of telegraphic or electronic transmission, equal to one information unit or (loosely) one bit of data per second. WH: mid-20C. Jean *Baudot*, 1845–1903, French engineer, inventor of the telegraph printing system.

Bauhaus *n.* (the principles of) a radical German school of architecture and the arts founded in 1919 and dedicated to achieving a functional synthesis of art design and technology. WH: early 20C. German house of building, from *Bau* building + *Haus* house, inversion of *Hausbau* building of a house.

baulk *n.* an obstacle, a hindrance, a check; a disappointment. *Also v.i., v.t.* WH: pre-1200. Old Norse *bálkr* partition, from Germanic, rel. to Old English *balca* beam. The word was originally used for a ridge, so that the verb meant to plough up in ridges from the 14C. The current sense evolved in the 17C from the idea of a ridge in one's way that had to be negotiated.

bauxite *n.* a clay which is the principal source of aluminium. WH: 19C. French, orig. *beauxite*, from Les *Baux* near Arles, S France. See also -ITE[1].

Bavarian *n.* a native or inhabitant of Bavaria. *Also a.* WH: 17C. *Bavaria* (German *Bayern*), formerly a kingdom in the German Empire, now a state in Germany + -AN.

bawbee *n.* an old Scots copper coin equivalent to about a halfpenny. WH: 16C. Alexander Orrock, laird of Sille*bawby*, mintmaster under James V, 16C.

bawd *n.* a procuress, a brothel-keeper. *Also v.i.* WH: 14–15C. Shortening of obs. *bawdstrot*, from Old French *baudetrot, baudestroy*, from *baut, baude* lively, shameless (cp. BOLD) + base of Anglo-French *trote* trot (old woman, hag). (Cp. Dame *Trot*, a character in children's chapbook literature.)

bawl *v.i.* to cry loudly, howl. *Also v.t., n.* WH: 14–15C. Imit. Cp. Medieval Latin *baulare* to bark, Icelandic *baula* to low (as an ox). The original sense was to bark, to howl. This soon passed from a dog to a human.

bawley *n.* a small fishing smack. WH: 19C. Orig. unknown.

bay[1] *n.* an inlet of the sea extending into the land, with a wide mouth. WH: 14–15C. Old French *baie*, from Old Spanish *bahia*, ? of Iberian orig.

bay[2] *n.* an opening or recess in a wall. WH: 14–15C. Old French *baie*, from *bayer* to stand open, to gape, from Medieval Latin *batare*, of unknown orig.

bay[3] *n.* barking. *Also v.i., v.t.* WH: 12–14C. Old French *bai*, from *abai* (Modern French *aboi*), from *abaillier* (Modern French *aboyer*) to bark, ult. of imit. orig.

bay[4] *n.* the bay tree or bay laurel, *Laurus nobilis*. WH: 14–15C. Old French *baie*, from Latin *baca* berry.

bay[5] *a.* reddish-brown in colour, approaching chestnut. *Also n.* WH: 12–14C. Old French *bai*, from Latin *badius* chestnut-coloured (of horses). Cp. Irish *buide* yellow.

bay[6] *n.* the second branch of a stag's horn, the next to the brow antler. WH: 19C. Abbr. of *bez-antler*, from Old French *besantoillier*, from *bes-* twice + *antoillier* ANTLER.

bay[7] *n.* a dam or embankment retaining water. *Also v.t.* WH: 14–15C. Orig. unknown.

bayadère *n.* a Hindu dancing girl. WH: 16C. French, from Portuguese *bailadeira*, from *bailar* to dance. Cp. BALL[2], BALLET.

bayonet *n.* a weapon for stabbing or thrusting, attached by a band to the muzzle of a rifle, so as to convert that into a kind of pike.

Also v.t. WH: 17C. French *baïonnette*, prob. from *Bayonne*, a city in S France, where first manufactured. See also -ET[1]. The term was originally used of a short dagger. The current sense dates from the 18C.

bayou *n.* the outlet of a lake or river. WH: 18C. American French, from Choctaw *bayuk*.

bazaar *n.* an Eastern market place, where goods of all descriptions are offered for sale. WH: 16C. Italian *bazarro*, from Turkish, from Persian *bāzār* market.

bazooka *n.* an anti-tank or rocket-firing gun. WH: mid-20C. Appar. from *bazoo* kazoo, from its resemblance to this instrument.

BBQ *abbr.* barbecue. WH: Abbr. of *barbecue* with *Q* representing pronun. of *-cue*.

BCG *abbr.* Bacillus Calmette-Guérin, used in anti-tuberculosis vaccine. WH: Albert *Calmette*, 1863–1933, and Camille *Guérin*, 1872–1961, French scientists who developed the vaccine, 1906.

bdellium *n.* a tree of any of several species of *Balsamodendron*, which produces gum resin. WH: 14–15C. Latin, from Greek *bdellion*, of Semitic orig.

be *v.*, *often aux.* to exist, to live, to have a real state of existence, physical or mental. WH: pre-1200. Inf. from Old English *bēon* to become, rel. to Latin *fui* I have been, Greek *phuein* to bring forth, Sanskrit *bhavati* exists; *am* from Old English *eom*, prob. based on *bēon*; *is* from Germanic stem *es-*, rel. to Latin *est*, Greek *esti* is; *are* from Germanic stem **ar-*, rel. to Latin *oriri* to arise, to come to be; *were* from Old English *wesan* to be.

be- *pref.* about, by, as in *besmear*, to smear all over, *bedaub*, to daub about, *before*, about the front of, *below*, on the low side of, *besiege*, to sit around. WH: pre-1200. Old English *be-*, weak form of *bī-* BY.

beach *n.* a sandy or pebbly seashore. *Also v.t.* WH: 16C. Orig. uncertain. ? From Old English *bæce, bece* brook. (Cp. BECK[2]). The sense would have developed from a river with pebbles to a river valley with pebbles, and then to a seashore with pebbles. It is not certain when the transference of sense occurred.

Beach-la-mar *n.* a Creole spoken in the W Pacific. WH: 19C. Alt. of Portuguese *bicho do mar*. See BÊCHE-DE-MER.

beacon *n.* a burning cresset fixed on a pole or on a building. *Also v.t., v.i.* WH: pre-1200. Old English *bēacn*, from Germanic, of unknown orig. Rel. to BECKON. The original sense was sign, standard. The association with fire dates from the 14C. Hence came the names Brecon Beacons, Dunkery Beacon etc., denoting hills where signal fires were lit.

bead *n.* a small globular perforated body of glass or other material. *Also v.t., v.i.* WH: pre-1200. Old English *bed-* (only in comb.) prayer. Cp. BID. Beads in the current sense were originally those on a rosary for keeping a count of prayers said. Beads on necklaces etc. date from the 16C.

beadle *n.* a messenger, crier or usher of a court. WH: pre-1200. Old English *bydel*, from Germanic, base of Old English *bēodan* BID.

beagle *n.* a small dog orig. bred for hunting hares by members of the hunt on foot. WH: 15C. ? Old French *beegueule* with open mouth, from *beer* to open wide (cp. BAY[2]) + *gueule* throat.

beak *n.* the pointed bill of a bird. *Also v.t.* WH: 12–14C. Old French *bec*, from Late Latin *beccus*, of Celtic orig.

beaker *n.* a large wide-mouthed drinking vessel. WH: 12–14C. Old Norse *bikarr*, from Popular Latin, ? from Greek *bikos* drinking bowl. Cp. PITCHER[1].

beam *n.* a large, long piece of timber squared on its sides, esp. one supporting rafters in a building. *Also v.t., v.i.* WH: pre-1200. Old English *bēam*, of Germanic orig. Cp. BOOM[2], German *Baum*. The original basic sense was tree, as still in *hornbeam, whitebeam* etc. The current sense also dates from the earliest times.

bean *n.* the kidney-shaped seed in long pods of *Faba vulgaris* and allied plants. *Also v.t.* WH: pre-1200. Old English *bēan*, from Germanic. Cp. German *Bohne*.

bear[1] *n.* a plantigrade mammal of the family Ursidae, with a large head, long shaggy hair, hooked claws and a stumpy tail. *Also v.i., v.t.* WH: pre-1200. Old English *bera*, from Germanic, ult. from Indo-European **bher-* light brown, rel. to source of BROWN. Cp. BEAVER[1].

bear[2] *v.t.* to carry, to show (e.g. armorial bearings). *Also v.i.* WH: pre-1200. Old English *beran*, from Germanic, from Indo-European base of Greek *pherein*, Latin *ferre* to carry, Sanskrit *bharati* carries. Cp. BORN.

beard *n.* the hair on the lower part of a man's face, esp. on the chin. *Also v.t.* WH: pre-1200. Old English *beard*, from Germanic, rel. to Latin *barba*, Russian *boroda* beard. Cp. German *Bart*.

Béarnaise sauce *n.* a rich sauce made with egg yolks, lemon juice or wine vinegar, herbs and shallots. WH: 19C. French, fem. of *Béarnais* of Béarn, a region of SW France.

beast *n.* any of the animals other than human beings. WH: 12–14C. Old French *beste* (Modern French *bête*), from Popular Latin *besta*, from Latin *bestia*. The Middle English *beste* was used to translate Latin *animal* and replaced Old English *dēor* in this sense. The sense of a human being like an animal dates from the 15C.

beat *v.t.* to strike with repeated blows. *Also v.i., n., a.* WH: pre-1200. Old English *bēatan*, from Germanic.

beatify *v.t.* in the Roman Catholic Church, to declare (a deceased person) blessed in heaven. WH: 16C. Old French *béatifier*, or from Ecclesiastical Latin *beatificare*, from *beatus* blessed. See also -FY.

beau *n.* a woman's lover. *Also v.t.* WH: 17C. French, a. used as n., ult. from Latin *bellus* fine, beautiful. Cp. BELLE.

Beaufort scale *n.* a scale of wind velocity ranging from 0 = calm to 12 = hurricane. WH: 19C. Sir Francis *Beaufort*, 1774–1857, English admiral and hydrographer.

beau idéal *n.* a person or thing seen as representing the highest standard of beauty or excellence. WH: 19C. French ideal beauty, now often misunderstood as 'beautiful ideal'. See BEAU, IDEAL.

Beaujolais *n.* a usu. red, light Burgundy wine from Beaujolais. WH: 19C. *Beaujolais*, a district of SE France.

Beaune *n.* a usu. red Burgundy wine. WH: 19C. *Beaune*, a town in E France.

beauty *n.* that quality which gives the eye or the other senses intense pleasure. WH: 12–14C. Old French *belte*, *beaute* (Modern French *beauté*), from Latin *bellus*. See BEAU, also -TY.

beaux arts *n.pl.* fine arts. WH: 19C. French *beaux-arts* fine arts, beautiful arts. The current sense was promoted by Charles Batteux' *Les Beaux-Arts réduits à un même principe* (1746), in which he divided the arts into the useful, the beautiful (sculpture, painting, music, poetry) and those which combined the useful and the beautiful (architecture, eloquence).

beaver[1] *n.* an amphibious rodent mammal, of the genus *Castor*, with broad tail, soft fur and habits of building huts and dams. WH: pre-1200. Old English *beofor*, *befor*, from Germanic, ult. from Indo-European, base rel. to BROWN. Cp. BEAR[1].

beaver[2] *n.* the lower part of a visor. WH: 15C. Old French *baviere* (child's) bib, from *baver* to slaver.

bebop *n.* a variety of jazz music which developed in the 1940s, distinguished from the earlier jazz tradition by its more complex melodies and harmonies and faster tempos (see BOP[1]). WH: mid-20C. Imit. of musical phrase. Cp. BOP[1].

becalm *v.t.* to deprive (a ship) of wind. WH: 16C. BE- + CALM.

because *conj.* by reason of, on account of. WH: 12–14C. Orig. two words (see BY, CAUSE) based on Old French *par cause de* by reason of.

beccafico *n.* a small migratory songbird, of the genus *Sylvia*, eaten as a delicacy in continental Europe. WH: 17C. Italian, from *beccare* to peck + *fico* FIG[1]. The bird is regarded as a delicacy when fattened on figs and grapes.

béchamel *n.* a white sauce made with cream or milk and flavoured with onions and herbs. WH: 18C. Louis, Marquis de *Béchamel*, 1630–1703, general of Louis XIV of France, its inventor.

†bechance *v.i.* to chance, to happen. *Also v.t., adv.* WH: 16C. BE- + CHANCE.

becharm *v.t.* to charm, to fascinate. WH: 12–14C. BE- + CHARM[1].

bêche-de-mer *n.* the sea-slug or trepang, *Holothuria edulis*, an echinoderm eaten by the Chinese. WH: 18C. Pseudo-French, from Portuguese *bicho do mar* worm of the sea. Trade in trepang with the Chinese was conducted in BEACH-LA-MAR.

beck[1] *n.* a nod, a gesture of the finger or hand. *Also v.i., v.t.* WH: 12–14C. Shortening of BECKON.

beck[2] *n.* a brook, a rivulet. WH: 12–14C. Old Norse *bekkr*, from Germanic. Cp. German *Bach* stream.

becket *n.* anything used to confine loose ropes, tackle or spars, such as a large hook, a rope with an eye at one end; a bracket, pocket, loop etc. WH: 18C. Orig. unknown.

beckon *v.i.* to make a signal by a gesture of the hand or a finger or by a nod. *Also v.t.* WH: pre-1200. Old English *bēcnan*, from Germanic. Rel. to BEACON.

becloud *v.t.* to cover with or as with a cloud. WH: 16C. BE- + CLOUD.

become *v.i.* to pass from one state or condition into another. *Also v.t.* WH: pre-1200. Old English *becuman*, from Germanic. See BE-, COME. Cp. German *bekommen* to obtain. The original sense was to come, to arrive. This became obsolete by the 18C.

becquerel *n.* a unit which measures the activity of a radioactive source. WH: 19C. Antoine Henri *Becquerel*, 1852–1908, French physicist.

becurl *v.t.* to curl. WH: 17C. BE- + CURL.

bed *n.* an article of domestic furniture to sleep on. *Also v.t., v.i.* WH: pre-1200. Old English *bed*, *bedd*, from Germanic. Rel. to Latin *fodere* to dig, Greek *bothros* pit, Welsh *bedd* grave. Cp. German *Bett*. A bed was originally a hole or pit to sleep in.

bedabble *v.t.* to sprinkle, to wet; to splash, to stain. WH: 16C. BE- + DABBLE.

bedad *int.* by God. WH: 18C. Alt. of *by God!* Cp. BEGAD, BEGORRA.

bedaub *v.t.* to daub over, to besmear. WH: 16C. BE- + DAUB.

bedazzle *v.t.* to confuse by dazzling. WH: 16C. BE- + DAZZLE.

bedeck *v.t.* to deck out, to adorn. WH: 16C. BE- + DECK.

bedeguar *n.* a mossy growth on rose briers. WH: 14–15C. French *bédégar*, from Persian *bād-āwar* wind-brought.

bedel *n.* an officer at an English university, esp. Oxford or Cambridge, who performs ceremonial functions. WH: 12–14C. See BEADLE.

bedevil *v.t.* to torment. WH: 16C. BE- + DEVIL.

bedew *v.t.* to moisten or sprinkle with dewlike drops. WH: 12–14C. BE- + DEW.

Bedford cord *n.* a tough woven fabric similar to corduroy. WH: 19C. *Bedford*, a town in Bedfordshire + CORD.

†bedight *a.* adorned, decked out. WH: 14–15C. p.p. of *bedight*, from BE- + *dight* to dress. See DIGHT.

bedim *v.t.* to render dim. WH: 16C. BE- + DIM.

bedizen *v.t.* to deck out in gaudy vestments or with tinsel finery. WH: 17C. BE- + *dizen* to dress, from base found in DISTAFF + -EN[5].

bedlam *n.* a scene of wild uproar. *Also a.* WH: 14–15C. Alt. of *Bethlehem*, from the Hospital of the Priory of St Mary of Bethlehem, London, incorporated as lunatic asylum, 1547, subsequently Bethlehem (Bethlem) Royal Hospital, now in Beckenham, SE London. The name came to apply to any madhouse in the 17C, and hence to a noisy disorder in such a madhouse.

Bedlington terrier *n.* a breed of grey, crisp-haired terrier. WH: 19C. *Bedlington*, a town in Northumberland.

Bedouin *n.* a nomadic Arab, as distinguished from one living in a town. *Also a.* WH: 14–15C. Old French *beduin* (Modern French *bédouin*), from Arabic *badawī*, pl. *badawīn*, from *badw* desert. See also -INE.

bedowrie shower *n.* a red dust storm. WH: mid-20C. *Bedourie*, a town in Queensland, Australia.

bedraggle *v.t.* to soil by trailing in the wet or mire. WH: 18C. BE- + DRAGGLE.

bee *n.* a four-winged insect of the genus *Apis*, which collects nectar and pollen and is often kept in hives for the honey and wax it produces. WH: pre-1200. Old English *bēo*, from Germanic.

Beeb *n.* the BBC. WH: mid-20C. Abbr. of pronun. of name.

beech *n.* a forest tree of the genus *Fagus*, esp. *F. sylvatica*, the common beech, with smooth bark and yielding nuts or mast. WH: pre-1200. Old English *bēce*, from Germanic base rel. to Latin *fagus* beech, Greek *phagos* edible oak. Cp. BUCKWHEAT, BOOK.

beef *n.* the flesh of the ox, cow or bull, used as food. *Also v.i.* WH: 12–14C. Old French *boef*, *buef* (Modern French *bœuf*), from Latin *bos*, *bovis* ox. Rel. to COW[1]. *Beefeater* means what it says, and is not from BUFFET[2].

Beelzebub *n.* the prince of evil spirits, Satan. WH: pre-1200. Late Latin *Beëlzebub*, from Hebrew *ba'al zĕbūb* lord of the flies, a Philistine god (II Kgs i.2). Greek *Beelzeboul* represents the same name for the 'prince of the devils' (Matt. xii.24).

beep *n.* a short sound as made by a car horn or an electronic device, usu. as a warning. *Also v.i., v.t.* WH: early 20C. Imit. Cp. BLIP, BLEEP.

beer *n.* an alcoholic drink brewed from fermented malt, hops, water and sugar. WH: pre-1200. Old English *bēor*, from Germanic, from Latin (monastic) *biber* drink, from *bibere* to drink. Cp. BEVERAGE, BIB.

beest *n.* the first milk drawn from a cow after calving. WH: pre-1200. Old English *bēost*, from Germanic, ult. of unknown orig. Not rel. to BEAST.

beet *n.* any plant of the genus *Beta*, whose root is used as a salad and in sugar-making. WH: pre-1200. Old English *bēte*, from Germanic, from Latin *beta*, ? of Celtic orig.

beetle[1] *n.* an insect of the order Coleoptera, the upper wings of which have been converted into hard wing-cases, the under ones being used for flight, if it is able to fly, the name being popularly confined to those of black colour and large size. WH: pre-1200. Old English *bitula*, *bitela*, from shortened base of *bītan* BITE. See also -LE[1].

beetle[2] *n.* a maul; a heavy wooden mallet for driving stones, stakes or tent-pegs into the ground, hammering down paving-stones and other ramming and crushing operations. *Also v.t.* WH: pre-1200. Old English *bētel*, from Germanic, from base of BEAT. See also -LE[1].

beetle[3] *v.i.* to jut out, hang over. *Also a.* WH: 14–15C. Orig. unknown. ? Rel. to BITE. The expression *beetle-browed* came to be associated with BEETLE[1], as bushy eyebrows resemble the tufted antennae of some species.

befall *v.t.* to happen to. *Also v.i.* WH: pre-1200. Old English *befeallan*. See BE-, FALL.

befit *v.t.* to be suitable to or for. WH: 16C. BE- + FIT[1].

befog *v.t.* to obscure, to confuse. WH: 17C. BE- + FOG[1].

befool *v.t.* to make a fool of. WH: 14–15C. BE- + FOOL[1].

before *prep.* in front of, in time, space, rank or degree. *Also adv., conj., a.* WH: pre-1200. Old English *beforan*, from Germanic. See BY, FORE.

befoul *v.t.* to make dirty, to soil. WH: 12–14C. BE- + FOUL.

befriend *v.t.* to become a friend of, to help. WH: 16C. BE- + FRIEND.

befuddle *v.t.* to confuse, baffle. WH: 19C. BE- + FUDDLE.

beg *v.i.* to ask for alms. *Also v.t.* WH: 12–14C. Prob. Old English *bedecian*, from Germanic base of BID.

†begad *int.* by God. WH: 16C. Alt. of *by God!* Cp. EGAD, BEDAD.

beget *v.t.* to generate, to procreate. *Also v.i.* WH: pre-1200. Old English *begetian*. See BE-, GET[1]. Cp. GET[2].

Beghard *n.* a lay brother belonging to a 13th-cent. Flemish religious order like the Beguines. WH: 16C. Medieval Latin *Beghardus*, from Old French *Bégard*, from stem of BEGUINE + -ARD.

begin *v.i.* to come into existence, to start. *Also v.t.* WH: pre-1200. Old English *beginnan*, from Germanic, from BE- + Germanic base of unknown orig., found in various compounds meaning to begin. The base may have had the sense to open, related to Latin *hiare* to gape. Old English *beginnan* was rare; the usual verb was *onginnan*, from ON + -*ginnan*.

begird *v.t.* to encircle with or as with a girdle. WH: pre-1200. Old English *begyrdan*. See BE-, GIRD[1].

begone *int.* get you gone, go away, depart. WH: 14–15C. Orig. *be gone*. See BE, GO[1].

begonia *n.* a plant of the genus *Begonia*, cultivated chiefly for their ornamental foliage. WH: 18C. Modern Latin, from Michel *Bégon*, 1638–1710, French patron of science. See also -IA.

begorra *int.* by God! WH: 19C. Alt. of *by God!* Cp. BEDAD, BEGAD, EGAD.

begrime *v.t.* to blacken or soil with grime. WH: 16C. BE- + GRIME.

begrudge *v.t.* to grudge. WH: 14–15C. BE- + GRUDGE.

beguile *v.t.* to deceive, to lead into by fraud. WH: 12–14C. BE- + GUILE.

Beguine *n.* a member of certain sisterhoods which arose in the Netherlands in the 12th cent. (some of which still exist), whose members are not bound by perpetual vows, and may leave the community when they please. WH: 14–15C. Old French *béguine*, from Medieval Latin *Beguina*, ? ult. from Middle Dutch v. meaning to mutter (prayers). See also -INE. According to some, the word is from Lambert (le) *Bègue* (Lambert the Stammerer), priest of Liège, founder of the order in the 12C.

beguine *n.* music or dance in bolero rhythm, of S American or W Indian origin. WH: early 20C. American French, from French *béguin* flirtation, fancy, from Old French *beguine* BEGUINE. The original sense of French *béguin* was Beguine headdress.

begum *n.* a queen, princess or lady of high rank in the Indian sub-continent. WH: 17C. Urdu *begam*, from Turkic *begim*, from source of BEY + 1st pers. sing. poss. suf. -*im*.

behalf *n.* interest, lieu, stead. WH: 12–14C. Comb. of earlier phrs. *on his halve* and *bihalve him*, both meaning on his side. See BY, HALF.

behave *v.refl.* to conduct oneself. *Also v.i., v.t.* WH: 14–15C. BE- + HAVE.

behead *v.t.* to cut the head off. WH: pre-1200. Old English *behēafdian*. See BE-, HEAD[1].

behemoth *n.* a huge person or thing. WH: 14–15C. Hebrew *běhēmōt*, intensive pl. of *běhēmāh* beast. According to some, the word is from Egyptian *p-ehe-mau* water ox, perhaps referring to the hippopotamus.

behest *n.* a command, an injunction. WH: pre-1200. Old English *behǣs*, from Germanic base meaning to bid, to call. See BE-, HEST, HIGHT.

behind *prep.* at the back of. *Also adv., n.* WH: pre-1200. Old English *behindan*, from *bi-* BY + *hindan* from behind. Cp. HIND[1].

behold *v.t.* to see. *Also v.i., int.* WH: pre-1200. Old English *bihaldan*, from Germanic. See BE-, HOLD[1].

behoof *n.* advantage, use, profit, benefit. WH: pre-1200. Old English *behōf*, from Germanic, from BE- + var. of base of HEAVE.

behove *v.t.* to befit, to suit. WH: pre-1200. Old English *behōfian*. See BEHOOF.

beige *n.* a light brownish yellow colour. *Also a.* WH: 19C. Orig. unknown. The original French sense was the colour of natural wool. The word is unlikely to be related to Italian *bambagia* cotton wool.

being *n.* existence. *Also conj., a.* WH: 12–14C. BE- + -ING[1].

bejabers *int.* used to express surprise. WH: 19C. Alt. of *by Jesus!*

bejewelled *a.* decorated with jewels. WH: 19C. p.p. of *bejewel*, from BE- + JEWEL.

bekah *n.* a Hebrew weight of ¼ ounce (Exod. xxxviii.26). WH: 17C. Hebrew *beqa'*.

bel *n.* a measure for comparing the intensity of noises, currents etc., the logarithm to the base 10 of the ratio of one to the other being the number of bels. WH: early 20C. Alexander Graham Bell, 1847–1922, Scottish-born US inventor of the telephone.

belabour *v.t.* to beat, to thrash. WH: 14–15C. BE- + LABOUR.

belar *n.* a variety of casuarina tree, *Casuarina glauca*. WH: 19C. Australian Aboriginal (Wiradhuri) *bilaarr*.

belated *a.* very late; behind time. WH: 17C. P.p. of *belate*, from BE- + LATE.

belay *v.t.* to fasten (a running rope) by winding it round a cleat or belaying-pin. *Also n., int.* WH: pre-1200. Old English *belecgan*. See BE-, LAY[1].

bel canto *n.* a style of operatic singing characterized by purity of tone and exact phrasing. WH: 19C. Italian fine song. Cp. BELLE, CANTO.

belch *v.i.* to eject wind noisily by the mouth from the stomach. *Also v.t., n.* WH: pre-1200. Old English *bælcan*, *belcettan*, prob. imit. ? Rel. to BELLOW.

†beldam *n.* an old woman. WH: 14–15C. Old French *bele*, fem. of *bel*, from Latin *bellus* beautiful. + DAM[2]. *Bel-* expresses a relationship. Cp. French *belle-mère* mother-in-law.

beleaguer *v.t.* to besiege. WH: 16C. Dutch *belegeren* to besiege. See BE-, LEAGUER.

belemnite *n.* a conical, sharply pointed fossil shell of a cephalopod of the order Belemnoidea, allied to the cuttlefish. WH: 17C. Modern Latin *belemnites*, from Greek *belemnon* dart. See also -ITE[1].

bel esprit *n.* a person of genius. WH: 17C. French fine mind. Cp. BELLE, ESPRIT.

belfry *n.* a bell tower attached to or separate from a church or other building. WH: 12–14C. Old French *berfrei*, later *belfrei* (Modern French *beffroi*), from Middle High German *bercfrit*, prob. from v. meaning to protect, from *berc-* protection, shelter + -*frit* peace. A belfry was originally a wooden tower used as a siege-engine. A similar tower was built beside churches to house bells, and this gave the later association with BELL[1] in the 15C.

belga *n.* a former Belgian unit of exchange, equivalent to 5 francs. WH: mid-20C. Latin *Belga* a Belgian.

Belgian *a.* of or relating to Belgium or to the Belgians. *Also n.* WH: 17C. *Belgium*, a country in W Europe + -AN.

Belial *n.* the Devil, Satan. WH: 12–14C. Hebrew *bĕliyya'al* worthlessness.

belie *v.t.* to tell lies about, to slander. WH: pre-1200. Old English *belēogan*. See BE- + LIE[1].

belief *n.* religion, religious faith. WH: 12–14C. Alt. of Old English *gelēafa*, from *gelēfan* earlier form of *belēfan* BELIEVE. Cp. German *glauben* to believe.

believe *v.t.* to accept as true. *Also v.i.* WH: pre-1200. Old English *belȳfan, belēfan,* earlier *gelēfan,* from Germanic.

†**belike** *adv.* likely, possibly, perhaps. WH: 16C. See BY, LIKE[1].

Belisha beacon *n.* a flashing orange globe on a post to indicate a street crossing for pedestrians. WH: mid-20C. Leslie Hore-*Belisha,* 1893–1957, British politician who was Minister of Transport when the beacon was introduced in the early 1930s.

belittle *v.t.* to depreciate or undermine verbally. WH: 18C. BE-+ LITTLE.

bell[1] *n.* a hollow body of cast metal, usu. in the shape of an inverted cup with recurved edge, so formed as to emit a clear musical sound when struck by a hammer. *Also v.i., v.t.* WH: pre-1200. Old English *belle,* prob. rel. to BELL[2].

bell[2] *n.* the cry of a stag at rutting time. *Also v.i.* WH: 16C. Old English *bellan* to bark, BELLOW.

belladonna *n.* deadly nightshade or dwale, *Atropa belladonna.* WH: 18C. Modern Latin, from Latin *bella donna* fair lady. The sap of the plant was formerly used as a cosmetic to dilate the pupils of the eyes.

belle *n.* a beautiful woman. WH: 17C. French, fem. of *bel* BEAU, from Latin *bella,* fem. of *bellus* beautiful, pretty, orig. dim. of *bonus* good.

belles-lettres *n.pl.* polite literature, the humanities, pure literature. WH: 17C. French fine letters. Cp. BEAUX ARTS.

bellicose *a.* inclined to war or fighting. WH: 14–15C. Latin *bellicosus,* from *bellicus* warlike, from *bellum* war. See also -IC, -OSE[1].

belligerent *a.* carrying on war. *Also n.* WH: 16C. Latin *belligerans, belligerantis,* pres.p. of *belligerare* to wage war, from *belliger* waging war, from *bellum* war. The Latin source was later assimilated to *gerens, gerentis,* present participle of *gerere* to bear, to carry. See -GEROUS, also -ENT.

bellow *v.i.* to emit a loud hollow sound. *Also v.t., n.* WH: 12–14C. ? Late Old English *bylgan,* rel. to BELL[2].

bellows *n.pl.* an instrument or machine for supplying a strong blast of air to a fire or a wind instrument. WH: 12–14C. Prob. Old English *belga, belgum,* pl. of *belg, bælg* BELLY. The Old English word for bellows was *blǣstbelg* blowing bag. Cp. BLAST.

Bell's palsy *n.* a paralysis of the face, usu. temporary. WH: 19C. Sir Charles *Bell,* 1774–1842, Scottish anatomist.

belly *n.* that part of the human body in front which extends from the breast to the insertion of the lower limbs. *Also v.t., v.i.* WH: pre-1200. Old English *belig,* var. of *bælig, bælg,* from Germanic bag, from base meaning to swell, to be inflated. Rel. to BELLOWS, BILLOW. The original meaning was bag, bellows. The current sense dates from the 14C.

belomancy *n.* divination by means of arrows. WH: 17C. Greek *belos* dart + -MANCY.

belong *v.i.* to be the property, attribute, appendage, member, right, duty, concern or business (of). WH: 12–14C. Prob. intens. of obs. *long* to be appropriate, to pertain, from ALONG. See BE-.

Belorussian *a.* of Belarus in E Europe. *Also n.* WH: mid-20C. *Belorussia,* from Russian *Belorossiya,* from *belyĭ* white + *Rossiya* Russia, a country (now Belarus) west of Russia and north of Ukraine + -AN.

beloved *a.* loved greatly. *Also n.* WH: 14–15C. P.p. of *belove,* from BE-+ LOVE.

below *prep.* under in place. *Also adv.* WH: 14–15C. Middle English *be-* BY + LOW[1].

Bel Paese® *n.* a mild Italian cream cheese. WH: early 20C. Italian beautiful country. Cp. BELLE, PAYSAGE.

belt *n.* a broad, flat strip of leather or other material worn around the waist or over the shoulder, esp. to hold clothes in place, to hold a weapon, as a safety restraint, or as a badge of rank or distinction. *Also v.t., v.i.* WH: pre-1200. Old English *belt,* from Germanic, from Latin *balteus* girdle, of Etruscan orig.

Beltane *n.* May Day (Old Style), one of the old Scottish quarter days. WH: 14–15C. Gaelic *bealltainn* said to mean bright fire, from words

rel. to Old English *bǣl,* rel. to Greek *phalos* shining, bright (as in *balefire*) and Irish *tine,* Welsh *tân* fire. Not rel. to BAAL.

beluga *n.* a large sturgeon, *Huso huso,* from the Black and Caspian Seas. WH: 16C. Russian, from *belyĭ* white + formative suf. -*uga.*

belvedere *n.* a turret, lantern or cupola, raised above the roof of a building to command a view. WH: 16C. Italian fair sight, from *bel, bello* beautiful + *vedere* to see. Cp. GAZEBO.

bema *n.* the sanctuary, presbytery or chancel of a church. WH: 17C. Greek *bēma* step, raised place.

bemean *v.t.* to render mean, to lower or debase. WH: 17C. BE-+ MEAN[3], prob. based on DEMEAN[1].

bemire *v.t.* to cover or soil with mire. WH: 16C. BE- + MIRE.

bemoan *v.t.* to moan over, to deplore. *Also v.i.* WH: pre-1200. Old English *bemǣnan,* from *be-* BE- + *mǣnan* to mean (to complain), later influ. by MOAN.

bemuse *v.t.* to make utterly confused or dazed. WH: 18C. BE- + MUSE[2].

ben[1] *n.* a mountain peak in Scotland etc. WH: 18C. Gaelic and Irish *beann* prominence, peak, height.

ben[2] *prep.* in or into the inner apartment of. *Also adv., n.* WH: 14–15C. Old English *binnan.* See BY, IN.

bench *n.* a long seat. *Also v.t., v.i.* WH: pre-1200. Old English *benc,* from Germanic, rel. to BANK[1], BANK[3].

bend *v.t.* to bring into a curved shape. *Also v.i., n.* WH: pre-1200. Old English *bendan,* from Germanic, from base of BAND[2].

beneath *prep.* below, under in place or position. *Also adv.* WH: pre-1200. Old English *binithan, bineothan,* from *bi-* BY + *nithan, neothan* below, down, from Germanic base of NETHER.

benedicite *int.* bless you, good gracious. *Also n.* WH: 14–15C. Latin, 2nd pers. pl. imper. of *benedicere* to wish well to, to bless, from *bene* well + *dicere* to say. The earliest sense was blessing, deliverance.

benedick *n.* a newly married man. WH: 19C. *Benedick,* character in Shakespeare's *Much Ado About Nothing* (1599), a confirmed bachelor who marries. Both Benedick's name and that of his bride, Beatrice, mean blessed (Latin *benedictus, beata*).

Benedictine *a.* of or relating to St Benedict, 480–543, or to the order of monks founded by him. *Also n.* WH: 17C. French *bénédictin* or Modern Latin *benedictinus,* from *Benedictus* Benedict.

benediction *n.* a blessing pronounced officially. WH: 14–15C. Old French *bénédiction,* from Latin *benedictio, benedictionis,* from *benedictus,* p.p. of *benedicere.* See BENEDICITE, also -ION.

benefaction *n.* a gift or endowment for charitable purposes. WH: 17C. Late Latin *benefactio, benefactionis,* from *bene facere* to do good to. See -FACTION.

benefice *n.* an ecclesiastical living. WH: 12–14C. Old French *bénéfice,* from Latin *beneficium* favour, support, from *bene* well + *fic-,* var. of *fac-,* root of *facere* to do, to make.

beneficent *a.* kind, generous, doing good. WH: 17C. Prob. from *beneficence* based on earlier BENEVOLENT, MAGNIFICENT. See also -ENT.

beneficial *a.* advantageous, helpful. WH: 14–15C. Old French *bénéficial,* or from Late Latin *beneficialis,* from *beneficium.* See BENEFICE, also -AL[1].

beneficiary *n.* a person who receives a favour. *Also a.* WH: 17C. Latin *beneficiarius,* from *beneficium.* See BENEFICE, also -ARY[1].

benefit *n.* advantage, gain. *Also v.t., v.i.* WH: 14–15C. Old French *bienfet, bienfait,* from Latin *benefactum* good deed, from *bene facere.* See BENEFACTION. The original meaning was good deed. The sense of advantage arose in the 15C, and financial sense in the 19C.

Benelux *n.* Belgium, the Netherlands and Luxembourg, with ref. to the customs union formed between the countries in 1947. WH: mid-20C. Acronym of *Be*lgium, *Ne*therlands, *Lux*embourg. The name was perhaps intended to suggest Latin *bene* well and *lux* light.

benevolent *a.* disposed to do good, generous. WH: 14–15C. Old French *benivolent,* from Latin *benevolens, benevolentis,* pres.p. of *bene velle* to wish well. See also -ENT.

Bengali *a.* of or relating to Bengal, a region coinciding with Bangladesh and the Indian state of W Bengal, formerly an Indian province, its people or language. *Also n.* WH: 18C. Hindi *baṅgālī.* Cp. BANGLADESHI, BUNGALOW.

benighted *a.* involved in moral or intellectual darkness; ignorant; uncivilized. WH: 17C. p.p. of *benight,* from BE- + NIGHT.

benign *a.* kind-hearted, gracious. WH: 12–14C. Old French *bénigne*, from Latin *benignus*, prob. from *bene* well + *-genus* born. Cp. MALIGN.

†**benison** *n.* a blessing. WH: 12–14C. Old French *beneiçon*, later *benisson*, from Latin *benedictio, benedictionis* BENEDICTION.

†**Benjamin** *n.* the youngest son. WH: 19C. *Benjamin*, youngest son of the patriarch Jacob (Gen. xliii).

benjamin *n.* benzoin. WH: 16C. Alt. of *benjoin*, var. of BENZOIN, by assoc. with male forename *Benjamin*.

bennet[1] *n.* herb bennet, *Geum urbanum*. WH: 14–15C. Old French *herbe benëite*, from Medieval Latin *herba benedicta* blessed plant. The plant was said to put the devil to flight.

bennet[2] *n.* a dry grass stalk. WH: 12–14C. Dial. form of BENT[2].

bent[1] *n.* an inclination, a bias. *Also a.* WH: 14–15C. Prob. from BEND. Cp. pairs DESCEND/ DESCENT, EXTEND/ EXTENT.

bent[2] *n.* stiff, rushlike grass, esp. of the genus *Agrostis*. WH: 12–14C. Old English *beonet*, from Germanic, of unknown orig.

Benthamism *n.* the utilitarian philosophy based on the principle of the greatest happiness of the greatest number. WH: 18C. Jeremy *Bentham*, 1748–1832, English jurist and writer.

benthos *n.* the sedentary animal and plant life on the ocean bed or at the bottom of a lake. WH: 19C. Greek depth of the sea.

bentonite *n.* an absorbent clay used in various industries as a filler, bonding agent etc. WH: 19C. Fort *Benton*, Montana, USA + -ITE[1].

ben trovato *a.* characteristic or appropriate, if not true. WH: 19C. Italian well found.

benumb *v.t.* to render torpid or numb. WH: 16C. P.p. of Old English *beniman* to deprive. See BE-, NIM. Cp. NUMB.

Benzedrine® *n.* amphetamine. WH: mid-20C. *benz(oic)* (BENZOIN) + *(eph)edrine* (EPHEDRA).

benzene *n.* an aromatic hydrocarbon obtained from coal tar and some petroleum fractions, used in industry in the synthesis of organic chemical compounds, as a solvent and insecticide. WH: 19C. *benz(oic)* (BENZOIN) + -ENE.

benzoin *n.* a resin obtained from trees of the genus *Styrax*, used in medicine and in perfumery, also called *(gum) benjamin*. WH: 16C. French *benjoin*, or from Arabic *lubānjāwī* incense from Java (*lu-* being taken for definite article, as Italian *lo*, and dropped).

bequeath *v.t.* to leave by will or testament. WH: pre-1200. Old English *becwethan*, from *be-* + *cwethan* to say. Cp. QUOTH.

berate *v.t.* to rebuke or scold vehemently. WH: 16C. BE- + RATE[2].

Berber *n.* a member of the Hamitic peoples of N Africa. *Also a.* WH: 18C. Arabic *barbar*. See BARBARY.

berberis *n.* any shrub of the genus *Berberis*. WH: 16C. Modern Latin or Old French, from Medieval Latin *barbaris*. See BARBERRY.

berceuse *n.* a lullaby, a cradle song. WH: 19C. French, from *bercer* to rock + fem. suf. *-euse*.

bereave *v.t.* to deprive or rob of anything. WH: pre-1200. Old English *berēafian*, from Germanic. See BE-, REAVE. The specific association with death dates from the 17C.

Berenice's hair *n.* a small northern constellation, near the tail of Leo. WH: 16C. Trans. of Latin *Coma Berenices*, from *coma* hair (cp. COMA[2]) + *Berenice, c.*273–221 BC, wife of Ptolemy III of Egypt. Berenice's hair was said to have been stolen from the temple of Venus and placed in the heavens.

beret *n.* a round, brimless flat cap fitting the head fairly closely. WH: 19C. French *béret*, from dial. and Old Provençal *berret*. See BIRETTA.

berg[1] *n.* an iceberg. WH: 19C. Abbr. of ICEBERG.

berg[2] *n.* a mountain or hill (often used in place names). WH: 19C. Afrikaans, from Dutch mountain. Cp. BARROW[1].

bergamot[1] *n.* a citrus tree, *Citrus bergamia*, which yields a fragrant essential oil used in perfumery. WH: 17C. *Bergamo*, a city and province in N Italy.

bergamot[2] *n.* a juicy kind of pear. WH: 17C. French *bergamotte*, from Italian *bergamotta*, from Turkish *begarmudu*, from *beg* prince (cp. BEY) + *armud* pear + poss. suf. *-u*.

bergschrund *n.* a crevasse or fissure between the base of a steep slope and a glacier or névé. WH: 19C. German, from *Berg* mountain (cp. BARROW[1]) + *Schrund* cleft, crevice.

Bergsonian *a.* of or relating to Henry Bergson, or his theory of creative evolution and the life force. *Also n.* WH: early 20C. Henri *Bergson*, 1859–1941, French philosopher.

beribboned *a.* decorated with ribbons. WH: 19C. BE- + p.p. of *ribbon*. See RIBBON.

beriberi *n.* a degenerative disease due to a deficiency of vitamin B₁. WH: 18C. Sinhalese.

berk *n.* an idiot. WH: mid-20C. Abbr. of *Berkeley hunt* (a hunt in Gloucestershire), rhyming sl. for CUNT. According to some, the word is from the (Royal) *Berkshire hunt*, as being more prestigious.

Berkeleian *a.* of or relating to Bishop George Berkeley or his philosophy, which denied that the mind, being entirely subjective, could know the external world objectively. *Also n.* WH: 19C. Bishop George *Berkeley*, 1685–1753, Irish philosopher + -AN.

berkelium *n.* an artificially produced radioactive element, at. no. 97, chem. symbol Bk. WH: mid-20C. *Berkeley*, California, USA + -IUM. Cp. CALIFORNIUM. The element is so named as it was produced at the University of California at Berkeley in 1949.

Berliner *n.* a native or inhabitant of Berlin. WH: 19C. German *Berlin*, a city in N Germany, the German capital + -ER[1].

berm *n.* a narrow ledge at the foot of the exterior slope of a parapet. WH: 18C. French *berme*, from Dutch *berm*, prob. rel. to BRIM.

Bermuda shorts *n.pl.* tight-fitting knee-length shorts. WH: mid-20C. *Bermuda*, a group of islands in the W Atlantic. The reference was originally to shorts worn by Americans holidaying or yachting in Bermuda.

Bernardine *a.* of or relating to St Bernard of Clairvaux or the Cistercian order. *Also n.* WH: 16C. Modern Latin *Bernardinus*, from St *Bernard*, 1091–1153, French abbot of Clairvaux, pioneer of the Cistercian order.

berry *n.* any smallish, round, fleshy fruit. *Also v.i.* WH: pre-1200. Old English *berige, berie*, from Germanic. Cp. German *Beere*.

bersagliere *n.* a skilled marksman. WH: 19C. Italian, from *bersaglio*.

berserk *n.* a Norse warrior possessed of preternatural strength and fighting with desperate fury and courage. *Also a., adv.* WH: 19C. Old Norse *berserkr*, acc. *berserk*, prob. from *bjorn* bear + *serkr* coat (cp. SARK), but poss. from *berr* BARE.

berth *n.* a sleeping place on board ship or in a railway carriage. *Also v.t., v.i.* WH: 17C. BEAR[2] + -TH[2]. The original sense was sea room. Cp. *to give a wide berth to*. The sense of sleeping place dates from the 18C.

bertha *n.* a wide, deep collar, often of lace. WH: 19C. French *Berthe*, *Bertha*, female forename.

Bertillon system *n.* a method of recording personal measurements and other characteristics, esp. for the purpose of identifying criminals. WH: 19C. Alphonse *Bertillon*, 1853–1914, French criminologist.

beryl *n.* a gem nearly identical with the emerald, but varying in colour from pale green to yellow or white. WH: 12–14C. Old French *beril* (Modern French *béryl*), from Latin *beryllus*, from Greek *bērullos*, prob. of foreign orig. Cp. French *besicles*, German *Brille* spectacles, the lenses for which were made from beryl in medieval times.

beryllium *n.* a light metallic element, at. no. 4, chem. symbol Be, used as a component in nuclear reactors and to harden alloys etc. WH: 19C. Modern Latin, from BERYL + -IUM. The element is so named as it was originally discovered as an oxide in beryl and in emeralds in 1798.

beseech *v.t.* to ask earnestly, implore. WH: 12–14C. Middle English *be-* BE- + *sechan* SEEK.

beseem *v.t., v.i.* to be fit, suitable, or proper (for), to be becoming (to) (*usu. impersonal*). WH: 12–14C. BE- + SEEM.

beseen *a.* seen, looking, appearing. WH: 14–15C. P.p. of obs. *besee*, from Old English *besēon*, from *be-* BE- + *sēon* SEE[1].

beset *v.t.* to set upon, to assail. *Also a.* WH: pre-1200. Old English *besettan*, from *be-* BE- + *settan* SET[1].

beside *prep.* by the side of, side by side with. *Also adv.* WH: pre-1200. Old English *be sīdan*, from *be* BY + *sīde* SIDE.

besiege *v.t.* to surround (a place) with intent to capture it by military force. WH: 12–14C. Obs. *assiege*, from Old French *asegier* (Modern French *assiéger*), from AS- + SIEGE, with BE- substituted for *as-*.

besmear *v.t.* to cover or daub with something unctuous or viscous. WH: pre-1200. Old English *besmierwan*, from *be-* BE- + *smerian* SMEAR.

besmirch v.t. to soil, discolour. WH: 16C. BE- + SMIRCH.

besom n. a broom made of twigs or heath bound round a handle. Also v.i., v.t. WH: pre-1200. Old English besema, besma, from Germanic. Cp. German Besen.

besot v.t. to infatuate. WH: 16C. BE- + SOT.

bespangle v.t. to cover over with or as with spangles. WH: 16C. BE- + SPANGLE.

bespatter v.t. to spatter over or about. WH: 17C. BE- + SPATTER.

bespeak v.t. to speak for, to arrange for, to order beforehand. Also v.i., n. WH: pre-1200. Old English bisprecan, from bi- BE- + sprecan SPEAK.

bespectacled a. wearing spectacles. WH: 18C. BE- + SPECTACLE + -ED.

bespread v.t. to spread over. WH: 12–14C. BE- + SPREAD.

besprinkle v.t. to sprinkle or scatter over. WH: 16C. BE- + SPRINKLE.

Bessemer process n. a process invented in 1856 for the elimination of carbon and silicon etc. by forcing air into melted pig-iron. WH: 19C. Sir Henry Bessemer, 1813–98, English engineer.

best a. of the highest quality. Also adv., n., v.t. WH: pre-1200. Old English betest, from Germanic superl. Cp. BETTER. See also -EST[1].

†bestead v.t. to help. Also v.i. WH: 16C. BE- + stead to help, to avail, v. from n. STEAD.

bested a. situated, circumstanced (usu. with ill, hard, hardly, sore etc.). WH: 12–14C. BE- + Old Norse staddr, p.p. of stethja to place, assim. to stead. See STEAD.

bestial a. brutish, inhuman. Also n. WH: 14–15C. Old French, from Late Latin bestialis, from Latin bestia BEAST. See also -IAL.

bestiary n. a person who fought with beasts in the Roman amphitheatre. WH: 19C. Medieval Latin bestiarum, from Latin bestia BEAST. See also -ARY[1].

bestir v.t. to rouse into activity. WH: 12–14C. BE- + STIR[1].

bestow v.t. to give as a present. WH: 12–14C. BE- + STOW.

bestrew v.t. to strew over. WH: pre-1200. Old English bestrēowian, from be- BE- + strēowian STREW.

bestride v.t. to sit upon with the legs astride. WH: pre-1200. Old English bestrīdan, from be- BE- + strīdan STRIDE.

bet n. an act of betting, a wager. Also v.t., v.i. WH: 16C. ? Shortening of ABET.

beta n. the second letter of the Greek alphabet (B, β). WH: 12–14C. Latin, from Greek.

betake v.refl. to take oneself (to). WH: 12–14C. BE- + TAKE[1].

betel n. a shrubby Asian plant with evergreen leaves, Piper betle. WH: 16C. Portuguese, from Malayalam verrila.

bête noire n. a pet aversion. WH: 19C. French black beast. Cp. BEAST, NEGRO.

beth n. the second letter of the Hebrew alphabet. WH: 12–14C. Hebrew bēṯ house, from orig. shape of letter.

bethel n. a Nonconformist chapel. WH: 17C. Hebrew bēṯ-'el, from bēṯ house (of) + 'el god. The Hebrew word is translated 'house of God' in Gen. xii.11–19.

bethesda n. a Nonconformist chapel. WH: 19C. Bethesda, name of pool in John v.2–4, from Aramaic bēṯ house (of) + hesdā grace, favour.

†bethink †v.t. to think of, to recollect. Also v.refl. WH: pre-1200. Old English bethencan, from be- BE- + thencan THINK.

betide v.t. to happen to. Also v.i. WH: 12–14C. BE- + obs. time to happen. See TIDE.

†betimes adv. at an early hour; in good time. WH: 12–14C. BE- + TIME + -S[2].

bêtise n. a foolish act or remark. WH: 19C. French stupidity, from bête foolish, from Old French beste BEAST.

betoken v.t. to foreshow, to be an omen of. WH: pre-1200. Old English betācnian, from be- BE- + tācnian TOKEN.

betony n. a labiate plant, Stachys officinalis, with purple flowers. WH: 12–14C. Old French bétoine, from Popular Latin var. of Latin betonica, from Vettonica, said to be from name of an Iberian tribe.

betray v.t. to deliver up a person or thing treacherously. WH: 12–14C. BE- + obs. tray, from Old French traïr (Modern French trahir), alt. of Latin tradere to deliver, from TRANS- + -dare to give.

betroth v.t. to contract (two persons) in an engagement to marry, to engage, to affiance. WH: 12–14C. Middle English bi- BE- + treuthen, from treuth pledge, TROTH. Cp. TRUTH.

better a. superior, more excellent. Also adv., n.pl., v.t., v.i. WH: pre-1200. Old English betera, from Germanic comp. Cp. BEST. See -ER[3].

bettong n. a small prehensile-tailed kangaroo. WH: 19C. Australian Aboriginal (Dharuk) bidung.

between prep. in, on, into, along or across the place, space or interval of any kind separating (two points, lines, places or objects). Also adv., n. WH: pre-1200. Old English betwēonum, from be- BE- + twēonum two each. Cp. TWO.

†betwixt prep., adv. between. WH: pre-1200. Old English betwēohs, betwēox, from be- BE- + twēox for two. Cp. TWO.

beurre manié n. a mixture of butter and flour added to a sauce to thicken it. WH: mid-20C. French handled butter. Cp. BUTTER, MANAGE.

bevatron n. an electrical apparatus for accelerating protons to high energies. WH: mid-20C. BeV, acronym of billion electronvolts + SYNCHROTRON, with -a- ? influ. by betatron (see BETA).

bevel n. a tool consisting of a flat rule with a movable tongue or arm for setting off angles. Also v.t., v.i., a. WH: 17C. Old French, dim. of baïf open-mouthed (Modern French biveau), from baer to gape. See BAY[2].

beverage n. any drink other than water. WH: 12–14C. Old French bevrage, beuvrage (Modern French breuvage), from beivre to drink, from Latin bibere. See also -AGE.

bevy n. a flock of larks or quails. WH: 14–15C. Orig. unknown.

bewail v.t. to wail over, to lament for. Also v.i. WH: 12–14C. BE- + WAIL.

beware v.i. to be wary, to be on one's guard. Also v.t. WH: 12–14C. Orig. be ware regarded as one word. Cp. BEGONE. See BE, WARE[2].

bewhiskered a. having whiskers. WH: 19C. P.p. of bewhisker, from BE- + WHISKER.

Bewick's swan n. a small white swan, native to E Asia and NE Europe, a race of Cygnus columbianus. WH: 19C. Thomas Bewick, 1753–1828, English engraver and naturalist.

bewig v.t. to adorn with a wig. WH: 18C. BE- + WIG[1].

bewilder v.t. to perplex, confuse. WH: 17C. BE- + WILDER.

bewitch v.t. to charm, to fascinate. WH: 12–14C. BE- + WITCH.

bey n. a governor of a Turkish town, province or district. WH: 16C. Turkish bēg. Cp. BEGUM.

beyond prep. on, to, or towards the farther side of. Also adv., n. WH: pre-1200. Old English begeondan, begondan, from be BY + geondan, gondan, from Germanic base of yond (see YON).

bezant n. a gold coin struck at Constantinople by the Byzantine emperors, varying greatly in value. WH: 12–14C. Old French besant, nom. besanz, from Latin Byzantius of Byzantium.

bezel n. a sloping edge like that of a cutting tool. WH: 16C. Old French (Modern French biseau, béseau), of unknown orig. ? From Latin bis twice.

bezique n. a game of cards for two players, using a double pack. WH: 19C. French bésigue, ? from Persian bāzīgar acrobat, from bāzī game.

bezoar n. a stony growth found in the stomach of certain animals and supposed to be an antidote to poisons. WH: 15C. French bézoar, ult. from Arabic bādizahr, bāzahr, from Persian pādzahr antidote, from pād protecting (from) + zahr poison.

bhaji n. an Indian vegetable dish. WH: mid-20C. Hindi bhājī fried vegetables.

bhang n. the dried leaves of hemp, Cannabis sativa. WH: 16C. Portuguese bangue, from Persian and Urdu bang, assim. to Hindi bhāṅg, from Sanskrit bhaṅga.

bhangra n. music based on a fusion of Asian and contemporary pop music. WH: mid-20C. Punjabi bhāṅgrā, name of a traditional harvest dance.

bharal n. a wild blue-coated sheep, Pseudois nayaur, of the Himalayas. WH: 19C. Hindi.

bheesti n. in the Indian subcontinent, a servant who supplies water to a house. WH: 18C. Urdu bhīstī, from Persian bihištī person of paradise, prob. of facet. orig.

bi a. bisexual. Also n. WH: mid-20C. Abbr. of BISEXUAL.

bi- pref. double, twice. WH: Latin, rel. to Greek DI-[2], twice, doubly.

biacuminate a. having two tapering points. WH: 19C. BI- + ACUMINATE[1].

biangular a. having two angles. WH: 19C. BI- + ANGULAR.

biannual a. half-yearly, twice a year. WH: 19C. BI- + ANNUAL. Cp. BIENNIAL.

biarticulate *a.* two-jointed. WH: 19C. BI- + ARTICULATE².

bias *n.* a leaning of the mind, inclination. *Also v.t., a., adv.* WH: 16C. Old French *biais*, from Provençal, ? from Greek *epikarsios* oblique.

biathlon *n.* an athletic event combining either cross-country skiing and rifle shooting or cycling and running. WH: mid-20C. BI- + Greek *athlon* contest, based on PENTATHLON.

biaxial *a.* having two (optical) axes. WH: 19C. BI- + *axial*. See AXIS¹.

bib *n.* a cloth or piece of shaped plastic put under a child's chin to keep the front of the clothes clean. *Also v.i.* WH: 16C. Prob. from Latin *bibere* to drink.

bibelot *n.* a small article of virtu, a knick-knack. WH: 19C. French, from redupl. of *bel* beautiful. Cp. BAUBLE, BON-BON.

Bible *n.* the sacred writings of the Christian religion, comprising the Old and New Testaments. WH: 12–14C. Old French *bible*, from Ecclesiastical Latin *biblia*, neut. pl. (taken as fem. sing.), from Greek *ta biblia* the books, from *biblion* book. The Greek *biblion* was originally a diminutive of *biblos* papyrus, scroll (of Semitic origin), but had already lost its diminutive sense to become the ordinary word for book before being applied to sacred writings.

biblio- *comb. form* of or relating to books. WH: Greek *biblion* book. See also -O-.

bibliography *n.* the methodical study of books, authorship, printing, editions, forms etc. WH: 17C. French *bibliographie*, or from Modern Latin *bibliographia*, from Greek. See BIBLIO-, -GRAPHY.

bibliolatry *n.* excessive admiration of a book or books. WH: 17C. BIBLIO- + -LATRY.

bibliology *n.* scientific study of books, bibliography. WH: 19C. BIBLIO- + -LOGY.

bibliomancy *n.* divination by books or verses of the Bible. WH: 18C. BIBLIO- + -MANCY.

bibliomania *n.* a mania for collecting and possessing books. WH: 18C. BIBLIO- + -MANIA.

bibliopegy *n.* the art of binding books. WH: 19C. BIBLIO- + Greek *-pēgia*, from *pēgnunai* to fix.

bibliophile *n.* a lover or collector of books. WH: 19C. French. See BIBLIO-, -PHILE.

bibliophobia *n.* a dread or hatred of books. WH: 19C. BIBLIO- + -phobia (-PHOBE).

bibliopole *n.* a bookseller, esp. one dealing in rare books. WH: 18C. Latin *bibliopola*, from Greek *bibliopōlēs*, from *biblion* book + *pōlēs* seller.

bibliotheca *n.* a library. WH: 19C. Latin, from Greek *bibliothēkē* library, from *biblion* book + *thēkē* repository. Cp. DISCOTHEQUE. Old English *bibliothēce* was the original name of the Bible in English.

bibulous *a.* addicted to alcohol. WH: 17C. Latin *bibulus* drinking freely, from *bibere* to drink. See also -ULOUS.

bicameral *a.* having two legislative chambers or assemblies. WH: 19C. BI- + Latin CAMERA chamber + -AL¹.

bicarbonate *n.* a salt of carbonic acid. WH: 19C. BI- + CARBON + -ATE¹.

bice *n.* any of various pigments made from blue or green basic copper carbonate. WH: 12–14C. Old French *bis* dark grey, of unknown orig. The sense evolved specifically from the French colours *azur bis* dark blue and *vert bis* dark green.

bicentenary *n.* a 200th anniversary. *Also a.* WH: 19C. BI- + *centenary* (CENTENARIAN).

bicephalous *a.* having two heads. WH: 19C. BI- + -*cephalous* (-CEPHALIC).

biceps *n.* the large muscle in front of the upper arm. *Also a.* WH: 17C. Latin from BI- + -*ceps*, from *caput* head. Cp. TRICEPS, QUADRICEPS.

bicker *v.i.* to quarrel or squabble over petty issues. *Also n.* WH: 12–14C. ? Middle Dutch *bicken* to slash, to attack + -ER⁵. The original sense was to fight, to skirmish. The meaning was then transferred to verbal skirmishing in the 15C.

bicky *n.* a biscuit. WH: early 20C. Dim. of BISCUIT. See also -Y³.

bicolour *a.* having two colours. *Also n.* WH: 19C. Latin *bicolor*, or from French *bicolore*. See BI-, COLOUR.

biconcave *a.* concave on both sides. WH: 19C. BI- + CONCAVE.

biconvex *a.* convex on both sides. WH: 19C. BI- + CONVEX.

bicultural *a.* having or consisting of two cultures. WH: mid-20C. BI- + *cultural* (CULTURE).

bicuspid *a.* having two points or cusps. *Also n.* WH: 19C. BI- Latin *cuspis, cuspidis* CUSP. See also -ID.

bicycle *n.* a two-wheeled pedal-driven vehicle, with the wheels one behind the other and usu. with a saddle for the rider mounted on a metal frame. *Also v.i.* WH: 19C. BI- + Greek *kuklos* circle, wheel, CYCLE. Cp. TRICYCLE.

bicyclic *a.* having two rings of atoms in the molecular structure. WH: 19C. BI- + Greek *kuklos* circle + -IC.

bid *v.t.* to offer, to make a tender of (a price), esp. at an auction or for work to be undertaken. *Also v.i., n.* WH: pre-1200. Old English *biddan* to ask, to entreat, from Germanic base of Old English *gebed* prayer (see BEAD), or from Old English *bēodan* to offer, to command, from Indo-European.

biddy *n.* an old woman. WH: 17C. Orig. unknown. ? From female forename *Bridget*. Cp. *chickabiddy* (CHICK¹), from CHICK¹ + -*a*- + BIDDY.

biddy-biddy *n.* a New Zealand grassland plant, *Acaena viridior*, related to the rose. WH: 19C. Alt. of PIRIPIRI.

bide *v.t.* to abide, await. WH: pre-1200. Old English *bīdan*, from Germanic. Cp. ABIDE.

bident *n.* a two-pronged fork. WH: 17C. Latin *bidens, bidentis* having two teeth. See BI-, DENT².

bidet *n.* a low basin for bathing the genital and anal area. WH: 17C. French pony, ass, from *bider* to trot, of unknown orig. The basin is so called from the position of the user.

bidirectional *a.* functioning in two directions. WH: mid-20C. BI- + *directional* (DIRECTION).

Biedermeier *a.* (of a style of furniture) common in Germany in the first half of the 19th cent. WH: early 20C. Gottlieb *Biedermeier*, a fictitious German poet created by Ludwig Eichrodt in 1855. Biedermeier was presented as a naive and unintentionally comic poet and his name came to be associated, at first contemptuously, with the art styles of the period, 1815–48.

biennial *a.* happening every two years. *Also n.* WH: 17C. Latin *biennis* of two years. See BI-, also -AL¹. Cp. BIANNUAL.

bier *n.* a stand or litter on which a corpse is placed, or on which the coffin is borne to the grave. WH: pre-1200. Old English *bēr*, from Germanic base of BEAR².

bifacial *a.* having two faces. WH: 19C. BI- + FACIAL.

bifarious *a.* double. WH: 17C. Latin *bifarius* twofold. See BI-, also -OUS.

biff *v.t.* to strike, to cuff. *Also n.* WH: 19C. Imit. Cp. BOP².

biffin *n.* a variety of deep red cooking apple. WH: 18C. Dial. pronun. of *beefing*, from BEEF (ref. to the colour) + -ING³.

bifid *a.* split into two lobes by a central cleft. WH: 17C. Latin *bifidus*, from BI- + base of *findere* to split. Cp. TRIFID.

bifocal *a.* with two foci. *Also n.pl.* WH: 19C. BI- + *focal*. See FOCUS.

bifold *a.* twofold, double. WH: 19C. BI- + -FOLD.

bifoliate *a.* having two leaves. WH: 19C. BI- + FOLIATE².

biform *a.* having or partaking of two forms. WH: 19C. Latin *biformis*, from BI- + *forma* shape, FORM.

bifurcate¹ *v.i.* to divide into two branches, forks or peaks. WH: 17C. Medieval Latin *bifurcatus*, p.p. of *bifurcare*, from *bifurcus* two-forked, from BI- + *furca* FORK. See also -ATE³.

bifurcate² *a.* divided into two forks or branches. WH: 19C. Medieval Latin *bifurcatus*. See BIFURCATE¹, also -ATE².

big *a.* large or great in size or intensity. *Also adv.* WH: 12–14C. Orig. unknown. ? Indirectly assoc. with BUG². The original sense was strong, stout, the idea of which survives today in certain contexts, e.g. *big boy, big with child*.

biga *n.* a two-horse chariot. WH: 17C. Latin.

bigamy *n.* marriage with another person while a legal spouse is living. WH: 12–14C. Old French *bigamie*, from *bigame*, from Late Latin *bigamus*, from BI- + -GAMY. Cp. MONOGAMY.

bight *n.* a bending, a bend. WH: pre-1200. Old English *byht*, from Germanic, rel. to BOW². Cp. BUXOM.

bignonia *n.* a shrub of the genus *Bignonia*, containing the trumpet flower. WH: 18C. Modern Latin. From Abbé Jean-Paul *Bignon*, 1662–1743, librarian to Louis XIV. See also -IA.

bigot *n.* a person intolerantly devoted to a particular creed or party. WH: 16C. Orig. unknown. The word is popularly said to represent the phrase *by God!* (of Germanic origin) as a term of disparagement or disagreement. It was first used of a hypocritical professor of religion, then applied more generally from the 17C.

bijou n. a jewel, a trinket. *Also a.* WH: 17C. French, from Breton *bizou* finger ring, from *biz* finger.

bike[1] n. a bicycle. *Also v.i.* WH: 19C. Abbr. of BICYCLE. Cp. TRIKE.

bike[2] n. a wasps', bees' or hornets' nest. WH: 12–14C. Orig. unknown.

bikini n. a brief, two-piece swimming costume. WH: mid-20C. *Bikini*, an atoll in the Marshall Islands, N Pacific, where the atom bomb was tested, 1946. The costume was apparently named from its 'explosive' effect when first seen. It is not related to BI-. Cp. MONOKINI.

bilabial a. of or denoting a consonant produced with both lips, e.g. b, p, w. *Also n.* WH: 19C. BI- + LABIAL.

bilateral a. having, arranged on, of, or relating to two sides. WH: 18C. BI- + LATERAL.

bilberry n. the fruit of a dwarf moorland shrub, *Vaccinium myrtillus*, also called *whortleberry* and *blaeberry*. WH: 16C. Prob. from Scandinavian. Cp. Danish *böllebær*, from *bölle* bilberry + *bær* BERRY.

†bilbo n. a rapier, a sword. WH: 16C. *Bilbao*, a city in N Spain, famous for its weapon manufacture.

Bildungsroman n. a novel dealing with the emotional and spiritual education of its central figure. WH: early 20C. German, from *Bildung* education + *Roman* novel.

bile n. a bitter yellowish fluid which is secreted by the liver and aids digestion. WH: 16C. French, from Latin *bilis* bile, anger.

bi-level a. having or operating on two levels. *Also n.* WH: mid-20C. BI- + LEVEL.

bilge n. that part on which a ship rests when aground, where the vertical sides curve in. *Also v.i., v.t.* WH: 15C. Prob. var. of BULGE. The sense of nonsense evolved in the 19C from *bilge-water*.

bilharzia n. a disease caused by blood flukes, characterized by blood loss and tissue damage, which is endemic to Asia, Africa and S America (also known as *schistosomiasis*). WH: 19C. Modern Latin, from Theodor *Bilharz*, 1825–62, German parasitologist. See also -IA.

bilingual a. knowing or speaking two languages. *Also n.* WH: 19C. Latin *bilinguis*, from BI- + *lingua* tongue + -AL[1].

bilirubin n. the chief pigment of bile, a derivative of haemoglobin. WH: 19C. Latin *bilis* BILE + *ruber* red + -IN[1].

bilk v.t. to cheat, to defraud. *Also n.* WH: 17C. Orig. uncertain. ? Alt. of BAULK.

bill[1] n. a statement of particulars of goods delivered or services rendered. *Also v.t.* WH: 12–14C. Anglo-French *bille*, or from Anglo-Latin *billa*, prob. from Old French *bulle*, from Medieval Latin *bulla* BULL[2]. The original sense was simply a written document. The sense statement of charges, poster dates from the 15C.

bill[2] n. the horny beak of birds or of the platypus. *Also v.i.* WH: pre-1200. Old English *bile*, of unknown orig. Poss. rel. to BILL[3].

bill[3] n. an obsolete weapon resembling a halberd. WH: pre-1200. Old English *bil*, from Germanic, of unknown orig. Cp. BILL[2].

billabong n. a stream flowing from a river to a dead end. WH: 19C. Australian Aboriginal (Wiradjuri) *bila* river + *bang* watercourse running only after rain. The word is popularly associated with the name of the *Bell* River, New South Wales.

billet[1] n. quarters assigned to a soldier or others, esp. in a civilian household. *Also v.t.* WH: 14–15C. Anglo-French *billette*, or from Anglo-Latin *billetta*, dim. of *billa* BILL[1]. See also -ET[1].

billet[2] n. a small log or faggot for firing. WH: 14–15C. Old French *billette*, *billot*, dims. of *bille* tree trunk, log of wood, from Medieval Latin *billa*, *billus* branch, trunk, prob. of Celtic orig. Cp. Irish *bile* sacred tree, large tree. See also -ET[1].

billet-doux n. a love letter. WH: 17C. French sweet note. See BILLET[1], DULCET.

billiards n. a game with three balls, which are driven about on a cloth-lined table with a cue. WH: 16C. French *billard* billiards, billiard cue, from *bille*. See BILLET[2], also -ARD.

billingsgate n. scurrilous abuse, foul language. WH: 17C. *Billingsgate*, a former London fish market, whose traders were noted for their foul language.

billion n. one thousand million, i.e. 1,000,000,000 or 10^9. *Also a.* WH: 17C. French from MILLION, with substitution of BI- for *mi-*.

billon n. base metal, esp. silver alloyed with copper. WH: 19C. Old French ingot, from *bille*. See BILLET[2], also -OON.

billow n. a great swelling wave of the sea. *Also v.i.* WH: 16C. Old Norse *bylgja*, from Germanic base rel. to that of BELLY.

billy n. a metal can or pot for boiling water etc. over a campfire. WH: 19C. Scottish dial. *billy-pot*, cp. *bally* milk pail. The word has probably been influenced by Australian Aboriginal *billa* river. See BILLABONG. The Scottish origin is due to Scots settlers in Australia.

billy-o n. used only in the phrase *like billy-o*. WH: 19C. Orig. unknown. There are many fanciful etymologies, e.g. from a Nonconformist minister *Biglio*, from an Italian army officer *Biglio*, from George Stephenson's locomotive Puffing *Billy*, as a euphemistic form of (*like*) *hell I will*, etc.

bilobed a. having or divided into two lobes. WH: 18C. BI- + *lobed*, *lobate*. See LOBE.

bilocular a. having two cells or compartments. WH: 18C. BI- + *locular*. See LOCULUS.

biltong n. strips of lean meat dried in the sun. WH: 19C. Afrikaans, from Dutch *bil* buttock + *tong* tongue.

bimanal a. two-handed; of or belonging to the group of animals with two hands, as in the higher primates and man. WH: 19C. Modern Latin *bimana* (neut. pl.) two-handed animals, from BI- + *manus* hand + -AL[1].

bimbo n. an attractive person, esp. a woman, who is naive or of limited intelligence. WH: early 20C. Italian little child, baby. Cp. BAMBINO.

bi-media a. using or relating to two media, such as radio and television. WH: mid-20C. BI- + MEDIA[1].

bimensal a. continuing for two months. WH: 19C. BI- + Latin *mensis* month + -AL[1].

bimeridian a. of, relating to or recurring at midday and midnight. WH: 19C. BI- + MERIDIAN.

bimetallism n. the employment of two metals (gold and silver) in the currency of a country, at a fixed ratio to each other, as standard coin and legal tender. WH: 19C. French *bimétallique*, from BI- + *métallique* METAL + -IC + -ISM.

bimillenary n. a period of 2000 years. *Also a.* WH: 19C. BI- + *millenary*. See MILLENNIUM.

bimodal a. having two modes. WH: early 20C. BI- + MODAL.

bimonthly a. occurring once in two months. *Also adv., n.* WH: 19C. BI- + *monthly*. See MONTH.

bin n. a receptacle for storing things. *Also v.t.* WH: pre-1200. Old English *bin*, *binn*, from Celtic. Cp. Welsh *ben* cart. Prob. rel. to BIND.

binary a. consisting of a pair or pairs. *Also n.* WH: 14–15C. Late Latin *binarius*, from *bini* two together. See also -ARY[1].

binaural a. relating to, having or using two ears. WH: 19C. *bin-* BI- + AURAL.

bind v.t. to tie together, to or on something. *Also v.i., n.* WH: pre-1200. Old English *bindan*, from Indo-European base rel. to that of BAND[1], BAND[2].

bindi-eye n. a small Australian herbaceous plant, *Calotis cuneifolia*, with burlike fruits. WH: early 20C. Australian Aboriginal (Kamilaroi and Yuwaalaraay) *bindayaa*, influ. by EYE[1].

bine n. a flexible shoot or stem, esp. of the hop. WH: 19C. Var. of BIND.

binervate a. having two nerves or leaf ribs. WH: 19C. BI- + NERVE + -ATE[2].

Binet–Simon scale n. an intelligence test employing graded tasks for subjects (usu. children) according to age. WH: early 20C. Alfred *Binet*, 1873–1911, and Théodore *Simon*, 1873–1961, French psychologists.

bing n. a heap, a pile. WH: 12–14C. Old Norse *bingr* heap.

binge n. a drinking spree. *Also v.i.* WH: 19C. Dial. *binge* to soak, of unknown orig.

bingo n. a game in which random numbers are called out and then marked off by players on a card with numbered squares, the winner being the first to mark off all or a predetermined sequence of numbers. WH: mid-20C. ? From exclamation of winner, from *bing*, imit. Cp. PING.

binnacle n. the case in which the ship's compass is kept. WH: 15C. Spanish *bitácula*, from Portuguese *bitacola*, from Latin *habitaculum* habitacle (dwelling-place), from *habitare*. See HABIT, also -CULE.

binocular a. having two eyes. *Also n.* WH: 18C. Latin *bini* two together + *oculus* eye + -AR[1].

binomial a. having two names, the first denoting the genus, the second the species. *Also n.* WH: 16C. French *binôme* or Modern Latin *binomium*, from BI- + Greek *nomos* part, portion + -AL[1].

binovular *a.* of, relating to or developed from two ova. WH: early 20C. bin- BI- + *ovular*. See OVULE.

bint *n.* a girl or woman. WH: 19C. Arabic daughter, girl. The word gained popular currency in English from its use by servicemen in Egypt in the 1st and 2nd World Wars, 1914–18, 1939–45.

binturong *n.* a SE Asian arboreal mammal, *Arctictis binturong*, with a shaggy black coat and a prehensile tail. WH: 19C. Malay.

bio- *comb. form* of or relating to life or living things. WH: Greek *bios* life. See also -O-.

bioassay *n.* the measuring of the strength and effect of a substance such as a drug by testing it on living cells or tissues. WH: early 20C. BIO- + ASSAY.

bioastronautics *n.* the study of the effects of space travel on living organisms. WH: mid-20C. BIO- + ASTRONAUTICS.

biochemistry *n.* the chemistry of physiological processes occurring in living organisms. WH: 19C. BIO- + CHEMISTRY.

biocide *n.* a chemical which kills living organisms. WH: mid-20C. BIO- + -CIDE.

biocoenosis *n.* the relationship between plants and animals that are ecologically interdependent. WH: 19C. Modern Latin, from BIO- + Greek *koinōsis* sharing, from *koinos* common.

biodegradable *a.* capable of being broken down by bacteria. WH: mid-20C. BIO- + DEGRADE + -ABLE.

biodiversity *n.* the existence of a wide variety of plant and animal species. WH: mid-20C. BIO- + DIVERSE + -ITY.

bioenergetics *n.* the study of energy relationships in living organisms. WH: mid-20C. BIO- + *energetics* (ENERGY).

bioengineering *n.* the provision of aids such as artificial limbs, hearts etc. to restore body functions. WH: mid-20C. BIO- + *engineering* (ENGINEER).

bioethics *n.* the study of ethical issues arising from advances in medicine and science. WH: late 20C. BIO- + *ethics* (ETHIC).

biofeedback *n.* a method of regulating involuntary body functions, e.g. heartbeat, by conscious mental control. WH: late 20C. BIO- + FEEDBACK.

bioflavonoid *n.* a group of substances found in citrus fruits and blackcurrants, also called *citrin* and *vitamin P*. WH: mid-20C. BIO- + *flavonoid*, from *flavone* (FLAVIN) + -OID.

biogas *n.* gas, such as methane, that is produced by the action of bacteria on organic waste matter. WH: late 20C. BIO- + GAS.

biogenesis *n.* the doctrine that living matter originates only from living matter. WH: 19C. BIO- + GENESIS.

biogeography *n.* the study of the distribution of plant and animal life over the globe. WH: 19C. BIO- + GEOGRAPHY.

biography *n.* the history of the life of a person. WH: 17C. French *biographie*, or from Modern Latin *biographia*. See BIO-, -GRAPHY.

biohazard *n.* a risk to human health or the environment from biological research. WH: mid-20C. BIO- + HAZARD.

biology *n.* the science of physical life or living matter in all its phases. WH: 19C. French *biologie*, from German. See BIO-, -LOGY.

bioluminescence *n.* the production of light by living organisms such as insects, marine animals and fungi. WH: early 20C. BIO- + *luminescence* (LUMINESCE).

biomass *n.* the total weight of living organisms in a unit of area. WH: mid-20C. BIO- + MASS.

biomathematics *n.* the study of the application of mathematics to biology. WH: early 20C. BIO- + MATHEMATICS.

biome *n.* a large ecological community, having flora and fauna which have adapted to the particular conditions in which they live. WH: early 20C. Greek *bios* life + -OME.

biomechanics *n.* the study of the mechanics of movement in living creatures. WH: early 20C. BIO- + *mechanics* (MECHANIC).

biomedicine *n.* the study of the medical and biological effects of stressful environments, esp. space travel. WH: mid-20C. BIO- + MEDICINE.

biometry *n.* the statistical measurement of biological data. WH: 19C. BIO- + -METRY.

biomorph *n.* a decoration representing a living thing. WH: 19C. BIO- + -MORPH.

bionics *n.* the science of applying knowledge of biological systems to the development of electronic equipment. WH: mid-20C. *bionic* (from BIO- + ELECTRONIC). See also -ICS.

bionomics *n.* ecology. WH: 19C. BIO- + (*eco*)*nomics* (ECONOMIC).

biont *n.* a living organism. WH: mid-20C. Greek *biont*-, pres.p. stem of *bioun* to live, from *bios* life. Cp. SYMBIONT.

biophysics *n.* the application of physics to living things. WH: 19C. BIO- + PHYSICS.

biopic *n.* a film, often giving a glamorized and uncritical account of the life of a celebrity. WH: mid-20C. *bio*(*graphical*) (BIOGRAPHY) + PIC.

bioplasm *n.* protoplasm. WH: 19C. BIO- + Greek *plasma* moulded thing. See PLASMA.

biopsy *n.* the removal and diagnostic examination of tissue or fluids from a living body. WH: 19C. Greek BIO- + *opsis* sight, based on NECROPSY.

biorhythm *n.* a supposed biological cycle governing physical, emotional and intellectual moods and performance. WH: mid-20C. BIO- + RHYTHM.

bioscope *n.* a cinematograph. WH: 19C. BIO- + SCOPE[1].

biosensor *n.* an electronic chip covered with a layer of e.g. an enzyme which can sense the presence of a particular substance, used in diagnosing illness, detecting the presence of drugs etc. WH: late 20C. BIO- + SENSOR.

-biosis *comb. form* forming nouns referring to a specific mode of life. WH: Greek *biōsis* way of life.

biosphere *n.* the portion of the earth's surface and atmosphere which is inhabited by living things. WH: 19C. German *Biosphäre*. See BIO-, SPHERE.

biosynthesis *n.* the production of chemical compounds by living organisms. WH: mid-20C. BIO- + SYNTHESIS.

biota *n.* the flora and fauna of a region. WH: early 20C. Modern Latin, from Greek *biotē* life.

biotechnology *n.* the use of micro-organisms and biological processes in industry. WH: mid-20C. BIO- + TECHNOLOGY.

biotic *a.* relating to life or living things. WH: 17C. Late Latin *bioticus*, from Greek *biōtikos*, from *bios* life. See also -IC.

biotin *n.* a vitamin of the B complex (also known as vitamin H) found esp. in liver and egg yolk. WH: mid-20C. Greek *biotos* life + -IN[1].

biotite *n.* a black or dark-coloured micaceous mineral. WH: 19C. Jean-Baptiste *Biot*, 1774–1862, French mineralogist + -ITE[1].

bioturbation *n.* the disturbance of layers of soil by the action of living creatures. WH: mid-20C. BIO- + Latin *turbatio, turbationis* disturbance. See also -ION.

biparous *a.* bringing forth two at a birth. WH: 18C. BI- + -PAROUS.

bipartisan *a.* involving or supported by two or more (political) parties. WH: early 20C. BI- + PARTISAN[1].

bipartite *a.* comprising or having two parts. WH: 14–15C. Latin *bipartitus*, p.p. of *bipartire*. See BI-, PARTITE.

biped *a.* having two feet. *Also n.* WH: 17C. Latin *bipes, bipedis*, from BI- + *pes, pedis* foot. Cp. TRIPOD.

bipetalous *a.* having two petals in a flower. WH: 19C. BI- + *petalous* (PETAL).

biphenyl *n.* an organic compound which contains two phenyl groups. WH: 19C. BI- + PHENYL.

bipinnaria *n.* a starfish larva with two bands of cilia. WH: 19C. BI- + Latin *pinna* feather, + Modern Latin -*aria*, neut. pl. of -*arius* -ARY[1].

bipinnate *a.* (of a pinnate leaf) having pinnated leaflets. WH: 18C. BI- + PINNATE.

biplane *n.* an aircraft with two sets of wings one above the other. WH: 19C. BI- + PLANE[4]. Cp. MONOPLANE.

bipolar *a.* having two poles or opposite extremities. WH: 19C. BI- + POLAR.

biquadratic *a.* raised to the fourth power. *Also n.* WH: 17C. BI- + QUADRATE[1] + -IC.

birch *n.* any tree of the genus *Betula*, with slender limbs and thin, tough bark. *Also a., v.t.* WH: pre-1200. Old English *birce, bierce*, from Germanic.

bird *n.* any feathered vertebrate animal of the class Aves. WH: pre-1200. Old English *brid*, of unknown orig. and with no corr. form in any Germanic language. Not rel. to BREED or BROOD, as formerly supposed. The standard Old English word for bird was *fugol* FOWL, so that *bird* was restricted to a young bird. The current general sense of the word evolved in the 12–14C.

birefringence n. the formation of two unequally refracted rays of light from a single unpolarized ray. WH: 19C. BI- + REFRINGENT + -ENCE.

bireme n. a Roman galley with two banks of oars. Also a. WH: 16C. Latin biremis, from BI- + remus oar. Cp. TRIREME.

biretta n. a square cap worn by clerics of the Roman Catholic and Anglican Churches. WH: 16C. Italian berretta and Spanish birreta, fem. dims. corr. to Old Provençal berret BERET, based on Late Latin birrus hooded cape, ? of Celtic orig. According to some, the word is from Greek purros flame-coloured, red.

birl v.i. to spin round, to rotate noisily. Also v.t., n. WH: 18C. Prob. imit. Cp. BURL[1].

Biro® n. a type of ballpoint pen. WH: mid-20C. László József Biró, 1899–1985, Hungarian inventor.

birostrate a. having two beaks or beaklike processes. WH: 19C. BI- + rostrate (ROSTRUM).

birth n. the act of bringing forth. WH: 12–14C. Old Norse byrth, corr. to Old English gebyrd, from Germanic, from base of BEAR[2]. See also -TH[2].

biscuit n. a thin flour-cake baked until it is highly dried. Also a. WH: 12–14C. Old French bescuit, besquit (Modern French biscuit), from Latin bis twice + coctus, p.p. of coquere. The cake was originally baked twice, being returned to the oven after initial cooking to make it long-lasting. The spelling was regularly bisket in the 16–18C, when the French form was readopted.

bise n. a keen, dry, northerly wind prevalent in Switzerland and adjacent countries. WH: 12–14C. French, of unknown orig. The word is not likely to derive from Popular Latin aura bisia grey wind, as sometimes proposed.

bisect v.t. to divide into two (equal) parts. Also v.i. WH: 17C. BI- + Latin sectus, p.p. of secare to cut.

biserial a. arranged in two rows. WH: 19C. BI- + SERIAL, seriate.

bisexual a. sexually attracted to both sexes. Also n. WH: 19C. BI- + SEXUAL.

bish n. a mistake. WH: mid-20C. Orig. unknown. ? Alt. of BOSH.

bishop n. a dignitary presiding over a diocese, ranking beneath an archbishop, and above the priests and deacons. WH: pre-1200. Old English biscop, from (pop. var. of) Ecclesiastical Latin episcopus, from Greek episkopos overseer, from EPI- + -skopos looking over. See -SCOPE.

bismillah int. in the name of Allah. WH: 18C. Arabic bi-smi-llāh in the name of God, the first word of the Koran. See ALLAH.

bismuth n. a reddish white crystalline metallic element, at. no. 83, chem. symbol Bi, used in alloys and in medicine. WH: 17C. Modern Latin bisemutum, from German Wismut, of unknown orig.

bison n. either of two large bovine mammals of the genus Bison, with a shaggy coat and a large hump, the European bison, B. bonasus, now very rare, and the American bison, B. bison, commonly called buffalo, once found in great numbers in the mid-Western prairies. WH: 14–15C. Latin, from Germanic base of WISENT.

bisque[1] n. a rich soup made by boiling down fish, birds or the like. WH: 17C. French crayfish soup. ? From Biscaye (Vizcaya), a province of N Spain (on the Bay of Biscay).

bisque[2] n. in tennis, golf etc., a stroke allowed at any time to the weaker party to equalize the players. WH: 17C. French, of unknown orig. The word is said on tenuous grounds to come from the province of Biscay (BISQUE[1]), whose inhabitants are experts at pelota, a game resembling tennis.

bisque[3] n. a kind of unglazed white porcelain used for statuettes. WH: 17C. See BISCUIT.

bissextile a. of or relating to a leap year. Also n. WH: 16C. Late Latin bissextilis annus year containing the bis sextus dies the doubled sixth day. The sixth day before the calends of March, i.e. 24th February, was reckoned twice every fourth year in the Roman calendar.

bistable a. (of a valve or electrical circuit) having two stable states. WH: mid-20C. BI- + STABLE[1].

bistort n. a plant with a twisted root and spike of flesh-coloured flowers, Polygonum bistorta. WH: 16C. French bistorte, or from Medieval Latin bistorta, from bis twice + torta, fem. p.p. of torquere to twist.

bistoury n. a small instrument used for making incisions. WH: 18C. French bistouri, earlier bistorie dagger, of unknown orig. The first element may be Latin bis twice. The word is popularly derived from

Pistoia, a town in Tuscany, S Italy, famous for its weapon manufacture. Cp. PISTOL.

bistre n. a transparent brownish yellow pigment prepared from soot. Also a. WH: 18C. French, of unknown orig.

bistro n. a small bar or restaurant. WH: early 20C. French, of uncertain orig. The word is perhaps from earlier bistingo, apparently a variant of colloquial bistouille drink of coffee mixed with brandy. It is probably not from Russian bystro! quick!, a supposed call of Russian soldiers for service in a bar.

bisulcate a. having cloven hoofs. WH: 19C. Latin bisulcus two-cleft, from BI- + sulcus furrow.

bisulphate n. a salt or ester of sulphuric acid. WH: 19C. BI- + SULPHATE.

bit[1] n. a small portion. WH: pre-1200. Old English bita, from Germanic, from base of BITE. Cp. BIT[2].

bit[2] n. the iron part of the bridle inserted in the mouth of a horse. Also v.t. WH: pre-1200. Old English bite, from Germanic, from base of BITE.

bit[3] n. in binary notation, either of the two digits, 0 or 1, a unit of information in computers and information theory representing either of two states, such as on and off. WH: mid-20C. Abbr. of bi(nary) (digi)t (see BINARY, DIGIT) based on BIT[1]. Cp. BYTE.

bitch n. the female of the dog. Also v.i., v.t. WH: pre-1200. Old English bicce, ? from Scandinavian.

bite v.t. to cut or crush with the teeth. Also v.i., n. WH: pre-1200. Old English bītan, from Germanic, rel. to Latin findere to split.

bitt n. a strong post fixed in pairs on the deck of a ship for fastening cables, belaying ropes etc. Also v.t. WH: 12–14C. Prob. from a Low German nautical term of unknown orig.

bitter a. sharp or biting to the taste. Also n., v.t. WH: pre-1200. Old English biter, prob. from Germanic base of BITE. The original sense was biting, cutting, then cruel, harsh, then finally sharp to the taste, with all three senses continuing concurrently from the 12C.

bitterling n. a small brightly coloured freshwater fish, Rhodeus amarus. WH: 19C. German, from source of BITTER (translating Latin amarus) + -LING[1].

bittern[1] n. any of the wading birds of the heron family, esp. of the genus Botaurus. WH: 14–15C. Old French butor, from Latin butio bittern (+ taurus bull). The spelling with -n is perhaps from an association with HERON.

bittern[2] n. the liquid obtained when sea water is evaporated to extract the salt. WH: 17C. Appar. from BITTER.

bitumen n. any of various solid or sticky mixtures of hydrocarbons that occur naturally or as a residue from petroleum distillation, e.g. tar, asphalt. WH: 14–15C. Latin. The Latin word also gave French béton concrete.

bivalent a. having a valency of two. Also n. WH: 19C. BI- + -valent (VALENCE).

bivalve a. having two shells or valves which open and shut. Also n. WH: 17C. BI- + VALVE.

bivious a. leading two different ways. WH: 17C. Latin bivius, from BI- + via way + -OUS. Cp. TRIVIAL.

bivouac n. a temporary encampment in the field without tents etc. Also v.i. WH: 18C. French, prob. from Swiss German Biwacht extra watch. See BY, WATCH. The word is said to have come from the 'citizen patrol' used in Aargau and Zürich to assist the ordinary town watch.

biweekly a., adv. occurring once a fortnight. Also n. WH: 19C. BI- + weekly. See WEEK.

biyearly a., adv. occurring every two years. WH: 19C. BI- + yearly. See YEAR.

biz n. business, work, employment. WH: 19C. Abbrev. of pronun. BUSINESS. Cp. showbiz (SHOW).

bizarre a. odd, strange. WH: 17C. French, from Italian bizzarro angry, of unknown orig. The word is related to Spanish and Portuguese bizarro handsome, brave, from Basque bizar beard (a symbol of strength).

blab v.t. to reveal indiscretely. Also v.i., n. WH: 14–15C. Prob. ult. imit., from Germanic base. Cp. BABBLE, BLUBBER, BLAH.

black a. intensely dark in colour (the opposite of white). Also n., v.t. WH: pre-1200. Old English blæc, from Germanic, ult. of unknown orig. ? Rel. to Greek phlox, phlogos flame.

blad *v.t.* to hit a thumping blow. *Also v.i., n.* WH: 16C. Prob. imit.

bladder *n.* a membranous bag in the animal body which receives the urine. WH: pre-1200. Old English *blædre*, from Germanic, from base of BLOW[1], with suf. corr. to Latin *-trum*, Greek *-tra, -tron*, Sanskrit *-tram*.

blade *n.* the thin cutting part of a knife, sword etc. *Also v.i.* WH: pre-1200. Old English *blæd*, from Germanic, ? rel. to BLOW[2].

blaeberry *n.* the bilberry or whortleberry. WH: 14–15C. Scottish *blae* BLUE, from Old Norse *blár*+ BERRY. Not rel. to BILBERRY despite sense.

blag *n.* robbery, esp. violent robbery. *Also v.t., v.i.* WH: 19C. Orig. unknown. ? Rel. to BLAGUE.

blague *n.* pretentiousness, humbug. WH: 19C. French, ? from Dutch *blagen* to swell.

blah *n.* foolish talk, chatter, exaggeration. WH: early 20C. Imit. Cp. BLETHER.

blain *n.* a pustule, a blister or sore. *Also v.t.* WH: pre-1200. Old English *blegen*, from Germanic. Cp. CHILBLAIN.

blakey *n.* a metal toe or heel cap on a shoe or boot. WH: 19C. John *Blakey*, the original manufacturer.

blame *v.t.* to censure, to find fault with. *Also n.* WH: 12–14C. Old French *blamer* (Modern French *blâmer*), from Popular Latin *blastemare*, from Ecclesiastical Latin *blasphemare* to revile, to reproach, from Greek *blasphēmein* BLASPHEME.

blanch *v.t.* to whiten by taking out the colour. *Also v.i., a.* WH: 12–14C. Old French *blanchir*, from *blanche*, fem. of *blanc* white. See BLANK.

blancmange *n.* milk (usu. sweetened) thickened with cornflour or gelatine to form a jelly-like dessert. WH: 14–15C. Old French *blanc mangier* (Modern French *blancmanger*), from *blanc* white + *mangier* food. Blancmange was originally a dish of white meat or fish. The current sense emerged in the 16C.

blanco *n.* a substance used by the armed forces to whiten or colour uniform belts, webbing etc. *Also v.t.* WH: 19C. French *blanc* white (see BLANK) + -O.

bland *a.* having very little taste. WH: 14–15C. Latin *blandus* soft, gentle.

blandiloquence *n.* smooth, ingratiating talk. WH: 17C. Latin *blandiloquentia*, from *blandiloquentus* smooth-talking, from *blandus* mild, gentle (see BLAND) + *loqui* to talk (cp. LOQUACIOUS). See also -ENCE.

blandish *v.t.* to flatter gently. WH: 12–14C. Old French *blandir*, *blandiss-*, from Latin *blandiri*. See BLAND, also -ISH[2].

blank *a.* empty, vacant. *Also n., v.t., int.* WH: 12–14C. Old French *blanc* white, from Germanic base of Old High German *blanc* white, shining. The original sense was white. The current meaning superseded this gradually from the 16C.

blanket *n.* a piece of woollen or other warm material, used as bedcovering. *Also a., v.t.* WH: 12–14C. Old French *blanchet*, from *blanc*, fem. *blanche* white. See BLANK, BLANCH, also -ET[1]. A blanket was originally a type of undyed woollen cloth for clothing.

blanquette *n.* a stew of white meat, esp. veal, in a white sauce. WH: 18C. French, from Provençal *blanqueto*, dim. of *blanc* white. Cp. BLANKET.

blare *v.i.* to roar, bellow. *Also v.t., n.* WH: 14–15C. Middle Dutch *bleren*, of imit. orig.

blarney *n.* smooth, flattering speech. *Also v.t., v.i.* WH: 18C. *Blarney*, a village and castle near Cork, S Ireland, where a stone is supposed to give a cajoling tongue to those who kiss it. The stone is said to commemorate the smooth-talking Cormac MacDermot MacCarthy, Lord of Blarney in the 16C.

blasé *a.* dulled in sense or emotion. WH: 19C. French, p.p. of *blaser* to cloy, from Dutch *blasen* to blow. Cp. BLADDER.

blaspheme *v.t.* to utter profane language against (God or anything sacred). *Also v.i.* WH: 12–14C. Old French *blasfemer* (Modern French *blasphémer*), from Ecclesiastical Latin *blasphemare* to revile, to reproach, from Greek *blasphēmein*, from *blasphēmos* evil-speaking, prob. from *blas-* false + *phēmē* speech. Cp. BLAME.

blast *n.* a violent gust of wind. *Also v.t., v.i., int.* WH: pre-1200. Old English *blæst*, from Germanic, from base of BLAZE[3].

-blast *comb. form* used in biological terms to indicate an embryonic cell or cell layer, as in *mesoblast*, *statoblast*. WH: Greek *blastos* sprout, stem.

blastema *n.* protoplasm. WH: 19C. Greek *blastēma* sprout.

blasto- *comb. form* of or relating to germs or buds, germinal. WH: Greek *blastos* sprout, germ. See also -O-.

blastocyst *n.* the modified blastula in mammals. WH: 19C. BLASTO- + CYST.

blastoderm *n.* the germinal membrane enclosing the yolk of an impregnated ovum which divides into layers that develop into embryonic organs. WH: 19C. BLASTO- + -DERM.

blastomere *n.* any one of the cells formed during the primary divisions of an egg. WH: 19C. BLASTO- + -MERE.

blastula *n.* a hollow sphere composed of a single layer of cells, produced by the cleavage of an ovum. WH: 19C. Modern Latin, from Greek *blastos*. See BLASTO-, also -ULE.

blatant *a.* very obvious, palpable. WH: 16C. ? Alt. of Scottish *blatand* bleating, assoc. with *blatter* to prate volubly. The original sense, as first used by Spenser, was clamorous, noticeably loud. The current sense emerged only in the 19C.

blawort *n.* the harebell, *Campanula rotundifolia*. WH: 18C. Scottish *blae* (see BLAEBERRY) + WORT.

blaze[1] *n.* a bright glowing flame. *Also v.i., v.t.* WH: pre-1200. Old English *blæse*, *blase*, from Germanic, rel. to BLAZE[2] through the sense shining.

blaze[2] *n.* a white mark on the face of a horse or other animal. *Also v.t.* WH: 17C. Orig. uncertain. ? Rel. to BALD or BLAZE[1].

blaze[3] *v.t.* to proclaim. WH: 14–15C. Middle Low German and Middle Dutch *blāzen* BLOW[1]. Cp. BLAST.

blazon *n.* the art of describing and explaining coats of arms. *Also v.t.* WH: 12–14C. Old French *blason* shield, of unknown orig. Not rel. to BLAZE[3].

-ble *suf.* tending to, able to, fit to (forming verbal adjectives), as in *durable*, *flexible*, *visible*. WH: Old French, from Latin *-bilis*, *-bilis*, in act. or pass. verbal aa. or p.p. stems. Cp. -ABLE, -IBLE, -UBLE.

bleach *v.t.* to make white by exposure to the sun or by chemical agents. *Also v.i., n.* WH: pre-1200. Old English *blæcan*, from Germanic, from base meaning shining, white, pale. Cp. BLEAK[1].

bleak[1] *a.* bare of vegetation. WH: pre-1200. Old English *blāc* shining, white, from Germanic, from base of BLEACH, with form influ. by Old Norse *bleikr* shining.

bleak[2] *n.* any of various small river fishes, esp. *Alburnus alburnus*. WH: 15C. Prob. from Old Norse *bleikja*, from Germanic. Cp. BLEAK[1].

†blear *a.* dim, indistinct, misty. *Also v.t.* WH: 12–14C. Orig. unknown. Cp. BLUR.

bleat *v.i.* to cry like a sheep, goat or calf. *Also v.t., n.* WH: pre-1200. Old English *blǣtan*, of imit. orig. Cp. BAA.

bleb *n.* a small blister or bladder. WH: 17C. Var. of BLOB.

bleed *v.i.* to emit or discharge blood. *Also v.t., n.* WH: pre-1200. Old English *blēdan*, from Germanic, from base of BLOOD.

bleep *n.* an intermittent, high-pitched sound from an electronic device. *Also v.i., v.t.* WH: mid-20C. Imit. Cp. BLIP, BEEP.

blemish *v.t.* to spoil the appearance of. *Also n.* WH: 14–15C. Old French *blemir*, *blemiss-* to render pale, to injure, prob. of Germanic orig. See also -ISH[1]. The verb has perhaps been influenced by French *blesser* to wound.

blench *v.t.* to flinch from. *Also v.i., n.* WH: pre-1200. Old English *blencan*, from Germanic, influ. by BLINK.

blend[1] *v.t.* to mix, to mingle (esp. teas, wines, spirits, tobacco etc. so as to produce a certain quality). *Also v.i., n.* WH: 12–14C. Prob. from Scandinavian, from *blend-*, pres. stem of Old Norse *blanda* to mix. Cp. *bland*, a drink of buttermilk mixed with water in N Scotland (Orkney and Shetland).

†blend[2] *v.t.* to blind, to make blind. WH: pre-1200. Old English *blendan*, from Germanic source of BLIND.

blende *n.* a native sulphide of zinc. WH: 17C. German, from *blenden* to deceive (cp. BLEND[2]), so called because it resembles galena but yields no lead. Cp. HORNBLENDE, *pitchblende* (PITCH[2]).

Blenheim *n.* a breed of spaniels. WH: 19C. *Blenheim* Palace, the Duke of Marlborough's seat at Woodstock, Oxfordshire. The palace was itself named after the duke's victory at Blenheim (now Blindheim) in Bavaria, 1704.

blennorrhoea *n.* excessive discharge of mucus, esp. from the genital and urinary organs. WH: 19C. Greek *blennos* mucus + -RRHOEA.

blenny *n.* any of a family of small, spiny-finned sea fishes, esp. of the genus *Blennius*. WH: 18C. Latin *blennius*, from Greek *blennos* slime. The name refers to the mucous coating of the fish's scales.

blent *a.* mingled. WH: 19C. P.p. of BLEND[1].

blepharitis *n.* inflammation of the eyelids. WH: 19C. Greek *blepharon* eyelid + -ITIS.

blepharo- *comb. form* of or relating to the eyelids. WH: Greek *blepharon* eyelid. See also -O-.

blesbok *n.* a subspecies of bontebok, a southern African antelope, having a white blaze on its forehead. WH: 19C. Afrikaans, from Dutch *bles* BLAZE[2] + *bok* BUCK[1].

bless *v.t.* to consecrate, to hallow. WH: pre-1200. Old English *blēt-sian*, *blēdsian*, from same base as that of BLOOD. The original Old English sense was to mark with blood (in a sacrificial rite). The current sense evolved from the use of this verb to translate Latin *benedicere* (see BENEDICITE). The sense to wish happiness is probably influenced by BLISS.

blet *v.i.* (of fruit) to become internally rotten, as a pear which ripens after being picked. WH: 19C. French *blettir*, from *blet*, fem. *blette*, from same base as that of *blesser* to wound.

blether *v.i.* to talk nonsense volubly. *Also n.* WH: 14–15C. Old Norse *blathra*, from *blathr* nonsense. Cp. BLITHERING.

blewits *n.* any fungus of the genus *Tricholoma*, with edible purplish tops. WH: 19C. Prob. from BLUE.

blight *n.* a disease caused in plants by fungoid parasites and various insects, mildew, smut, rust, aphids etc. *Also v.t.* WH: 16C. Orig. unknown. ? Ult. rel. to BLEACH.

Blighty *n.* (used by soldiers) Britain, home. WH: early 20C. Urdu *b'lāytī*, coll. form of *bilāyatī*, *wilāyatī* foreign, European, from Arabic *wilāyat* district. Cp. VILAYET. The spelling has been influenced by BLIGHT, BRIGHT etc.

blimey *int.* an exclamation of astonishment. WH: 19C. Alt. of *blind me!* or *blame me!* (see BLIND, BLAME). Cp. GORBLIMEY.

blimp *n.* a small airship used for observation. WH: early 20C. Appar. from (Type) *B-limp* (see LIMP[2]), code name of such a balloon in 1st World War, 1914–18. After the war the name was adopted for the cartoon character Colonel Blimp, created by David Low, 1891–1963.

blind *a.* unseeing. *Also n., v.t., v.i.* WH: pre-1200. Old English, from Germanic. ? Rel. to BLEND[1].

blink *v.i.* to move the eyelids. *Also v.t., a., n.* WH: 12–14C. Partly from obs. *blenk*, var. of BLENCH, partly from Dutch *blinken* to shine, to glitter. The sense of the word in the 16C was to glance, to peep, as if opening the eyes momentarily rather than closing them, as now.

blintz *n.* a thin, stuffed pancake. WH: early 20C. Yiddish *blintse*, from Russian *blinets*, dim. of *blin* pancake.

blip *n.* an irregularity in the linear trace on a radar screen indicating the presence of an aircraft, vessel etc. *Also v.i., v.t.* WH: 19C. Imit. Cp. BLEEP, BEEP.

bliss *n.* happiness of the highest kind. WH: pre-1200. Old English, from Germanic, from base of BLITHE. The sense has been influenced by BLESS.

blister *n.* a swelling raised on the skin caused by some injury, burn etc. and containing a watery fluid. *Also v.i., v.t.* WH: 12–14C. ? Old French *blestre*, *bloustre* swelling, pimple, itself from base of BLAST.

blithe *a.* cheerful, joyous. WH: pre-1200. Old English *blīthe*, from Germanic. Cp. BLISS.

blithering *a.* nonsensical, contemptible. WH: 19C. *blither*, var. of BLETHER + -ING[2].

B. Litt. *abbr.* Bachelor of Letters. WH: Latin *Baccalaureus Litterarum*. See BACCALAUREATE, BACHELOR. Cp. LITERAL.

blitz *n.* intense enemy onslaught, esp. an air raid. *Also v.t.* WH: mid-20C. Abbr. of German *Blitzkrieg*, from *Blitz* lightning + *Krieg* war.

blizzard *n.* a furious storm of snow and wind. WH: 19C. Orig. uncertain. ? Ult. imit. Cp.BLOW[1], BLAST. The original meaning of sharp blow, knock, soon became obsolete.

bloat *v.t.* to cause to swell. *Also v.i., a., n.* WH: 12–14C. Old Norse *blautr* soft. The verb dates from the 17C.

bloater *n.* a herring partially cured by steeping in dry salt and smoking. WH: 19C. BLOAT + -ER[1].

blob *n.* a globular drop of liquid. *Also v.i., v.t.* WH: 14–15C. Imit. Cp. BLUBBER, BUBBLE, PLOP.

bloc *n.* a combination of parties, or of nations. WH: early 20C. French BLOCK.

block *n.* a solid mass of wood or stone; a log, a tree stump. *Also v.t.* WH: 12–14C. Old French *bloc*, from Germanic, of unknown orig. ? Rel. to BLOW[2].

blockade *n.* the besieging of a place, so as to compel surrender by starvation or prevent communication with the outside. *Also v.t.* WH: 17C. BLOCK + -ADE, prob. based on AMBUSCADE.

bloke *n.* a man, a fellow. WH: 19C. Shelta, of unknown orig.

blond *a.* fair or light in colour. *Also n.* WH: 15C. Old French, from Medieval Latin *blundus*, *blondus* yellow, ? from Germanic.

blood *n.* the red fluid circulating by means of veins and arteries, through the bodies of man and other vertebrates. *Also v.t.* WH: pre-1200. Old English *blōd*, from Germanic, of unknown orig. ? Rel. to source of BLOOM[1].

bloom[1] *n.* a flower. *Also v.i., v.t.* WH: 12–14C. Old Norse *blóm* flower, blossom, from Germanic, from base of BLOW[3] also seen in FLOWER.

bloom[2] *n.* a mass of iron that has undergone the first hammering. *Also v.t.* WH: pre-1200. Old English *blōma*, from Germanic. The Germanic forms are identical to those for BLOOM[1] but the word is probably different in origin.

bloomer[1] *n.* a style of dress for ladies, consisting of a shorter skirt, and loose trousers gathered round the ankles. WH: 19C. Amelia Jenks *Bloomer*, 1818–94, US champion of women's rights and dress reform, who promoted (but did not invent) the style.

bloomer[2] *n.* a plant that blooms (*esp. in comb.*, as *early-bloomer*). WH: 18C. BLOOM[1] + -ER[1].

bloomer[3] *n.* an oblong crusty loaf with rounded ends and notches on the top. WH: mid-20C. Orig. unknown. The loaf is perhaps so called because it expands in baking or has a sheen (see BLOOM[1]) or because its shape suggests an ingot of metal (see BLOOM[2]).

Bloomsbury *n.* a group of writers, artists etc. associated with Bloomsbury in the early 20th cent. *Also a.* WH: early 20C. *Bloomsbury*, a district in W central London.

blooper *n.* a blunder; a silly mistake. WH: early 20C. *bloop*, imit. + -ER[1]. Cp. *whoops* (WHOOP).

blore *n.* a violent gust or blast. WH: 14–15C. Prob. imit. Cp. BLOW[1], BLAST.

blossom *n.* the flower of a plant, esp. considered as giving promise of fruit. *Also v.i.* WH: pre-1200. Old English *blōstm*, *blōstma*, from Germanic, prob. from same base as that of BLOOM[1].

blot[1] *n.* a stain of ink or other discolouring matter. *Also v.t., v.i.* WH: 14–15C. Prob. from Scandinavian. Cp. Old Norse *blettr* blot, stain. ? Rel. to BLISTER.

blot[2] *n.* an exposed piece at backgammon. WH: 16C. Prob. Dutch *bloot* naked, exposed.

blotch *n.* a mark on the skin. *Also v.t.* WH: 17C. Prob. blend of BLOT[1] and BOTCH[2].

blotto *a.* unconscious with drink. WH: early 20C. BLOT[1] + -O.

blouse *n.* a light, loose, upper garment. *Also v.t., v.i.* WH: 19C. French, of uncertain orig., ? from Germanic. The word was originally used of a man's garment, as a shirt or 'smock-frock'. It was applied to the woman's equivalent by the end of the 19C.

blouson *n.* a short, loose jacket fitted or belted in at the waist. WH: early 20C. French, from BLOUSE.

blow[1] *v.i.* to move as a current of air. *Also v.t., n.* WH: pre-1200. Old English *blāwan*, of Germanic orig., from Indo-European base that also gave Latin *flare* to blow.

blow[2] *n.* a stroke with the fist or any weapon. WH: 14–15C. Orig. unknown, but prob. influ. by BLOW[1].

†blow[3] *v.i.* to blossom. *Also n.* WH: pre-1200. Old English *blōwan*, from Germanic base of BLOOM[1], BLOSSOM and ? BLADE.

blowze *n.* a red-faced, bloated woman. WH: 16C. Orig. unknown. ? Rel. to BLUSH.

blub *v.i.* to weep noisily, shed tears. WH: 19C. Abbr. of BLUBBER.

blubber *n.* the fat underlying the skin in whales and other cetaceans, from which train-oil is prepared. *Also a., v.i., v.t.* WH: 15C. Prob. imit. Cp. BLEB, BLOB, BUBBLE. The original sense was foam, bubble. The current sense developed only in the 17C, when whaling had become established.

blucher *n.* a strong leather half-boot. WH: 19C. Gebhard von *Blücher*, 1742–1819, Prussian general, who wore them in battle.

bludge *v.i.* to evade work. *Also v.t.*, *n.* WH: early 20C. Back-formation from *bludger*, abbr. of *bludgeoner*, from BLUDGEON.

bludgeon *n.* a short, thick stick. *Also v.t.* WH: 18C. Orig. unknown.

blue *a.* of the colour of the cloudless sky or deep sea. *Also n.*, *v.t.* WH: 12–14C. Old French *bleu*, from Germanic, from base also of Latin *flavus* yellow.

bluff[1] *a.* (of a cliff, or a ship's bows) having a broad, flattened front. *Also n.* WH: 17C. Prob. of Low Dutch orig., taken up in nautical usage. The word has been applied to a person in the sense blunt from the 18C.

bluff[2] *n.* a blinker for a horse. *Also v.t.*, *v.i.* WH: 17C. Dutch *bluffen* to brag, to boast.

blunder *v.i.* to err grossly. *Also v.t.*, *n.* WH: 12–14C. Prob. from Scandinavian, and rel. to BLIND.

blunderbuss *n.* a short gun, of large bore, widening at the muzzle. WH: 17C. Alt. (by assoc. with BLUNDER) of Dutch *donderbus*, from *donder* thunder + *bus* gun (orig. box, tube), rel. to German *Büchse* BOX[1], gun. Cp. *thunderbox* (THUNDER).

blunge *v.t.* to mix (clay, powdered flint etc. with water) in a pugmill. WH: 19C. Blend of PLUNGE and words in *bl-* such as BLEND[1].

blunt *a.* dull, stupid, obtuse. *Also n.*, *v.t.*, *v.i.* WH: 12–14C. ? Scandinavian, from base of Old Norse *blundr* dozing, sleep. Cp. BLUNDER. The sense of abrupt dates from 16C.

blur *n.* a smear, a stain. *Also v.t.*, *v.i.* WH: 16C. Orig. uncertain. ? Var. of BLEAR.

blurb *n.* a description of a book, usu. printed on the dust jacket, intended to advertise and promote it. WH: early 20C. Fanciful word invented by US humorist Gelett Burgess, 1866–1951. Cp. BLAH, BLURT.

blurt *v.t.* to utter abruptly (*usu. with out*). *Also v.i.*, *n.* WH: 16C. Prob. imit.

blush *v.i.* to become red in the face from shame or other emotion. *Also v.t.*, *n.* WH: pre-1200. Old English *blyscan*, from Germanic. Cp. Swedish *bloss*, Danish *blus* torch.

bluster *v.i.* to blow boisterously. *Also v.t.*, *n.* WH: 14–15C. Prob. imit. Cp. BLAST.

BMX *abbr.* bicycle motocross, bicycle stunt riding over an obstacle course. WH: late 20C. Initials of *bicycle* + *motocross* + *X* representing *cross*.

bo *int.* an exclamation intended to surprise or frighten. WH: 14–15C. Imit. Cp. BOO.

boa *n.* a genus of large S American snakes of the family Boidae, which kill their prey by crushing. WH: 14–15C. Latin, of unknown orig. The word is perhaps imitative of an exclamation of terror. Cp. BO.

boanerges *n.* a loud, vociferous preacher or orator. WH: 17C. Greek, from Hebrew *b'nē regesh* sons of tumult, name given by Jesus to two sons of Zebedee (Mark iii.17). The Authorized Version has 'sons of thunder'. The brothers were so named because they offered to call down fire on the Samaritans.

boar *n.* the uncastrated male of the domesticated swine. WH: pre-1200. Old English *bār*, of Germanic orig. Appar. not rel. to BEAR[1].

board *n.* a piece of timber of considerable length. *Also v.t.*, *v.i.* WH: pre-1200. Old English *bord*, as comb. of two Germanic words meaning board, plank and border, ship's side. (Cp. French *bord* edge, border.)

boast *n.* excessively proud assertion. *Also v.i.*, *v.t.* WH: 14–15C. Orig. unknown. ? From a Germanic base that gave German *böse* bad, wicked. An earlier sense of threat was current to the 18C.

boat *n.* a small vessel, propelled by oars or sails. *Also v.t.*, *v.i.* WH: pre-1200. Old English *bāt*, from Germanic. Dutch *boot*, German *Boot* and French BATEAU have all come from English or Scandinavian.

boatel *n.* a floating hotel, a moored ship functioning as a hotel. WH: mid-20C. Blend of BOAT and HOTEL, based on MOTEL.

boatswain *n.* the foreman of the crew (in the RN a warrant officer) who looks after the ship's boats, rigging, flags, cables etc. WH: pre-1200. Old English *bātswegen*. See BOAT, SWAIN.

bob[1] *n.* a short jerking action, a curtsy. *Also v.t.*, *v.i.* WH: 14–15C. Orig. unknown. ? Partly imit.

bob[2] *n.* a person, a fellow. WH: 18C. Pet form of male forename *Robert*.

Bobadil *n.* a braggart. WH: 18C. Captain *Bobadill*, a boastful, cowardly soldier in Ben Jonson's comedy *Every Man in His Humour* (1598). The character's name is an alteration of *Boabdil*, otherwise Muhammad X (d.1527), sultan of Granada. This itself is a corruption of *Abū Abd'illāh* father of the servant of Allah.

bobbery *n.* a row. WH: 19C. Alt. of Hindi *Bāp re* O father!, exclamation of surprise or grief.

bobbie pin *n.* a hairgrip. WH: mid-20C. Prob. from BOB[1] + -Y[1], in sense of small, short. Cp. BOBBY[2], BOBBY SOX.

bobbin *n.* a spool or pin with a head on which thread for making lace, cotton, yarn, wire etc., is wound and drawn off as required. WH: 16C. French *bobine*, of unknown orig. The word is perhaps from the imitative *bob* that may lie behind BOB[1].

bobbitt *v.t.* to sever the penis of (one's husband or lover). WH: late 20C. Lorena *Bobbitt*, American who severed her husband's penis, 1993. The word happens to suggest *bob it* as if BOB[1] (in sense of cutting a horse's tail short).

bobby[1] *n.* a policeman, a police officer. WH: 19C. Pet form of male forename *Robert*, from Sir Robert Peel, 1788–1850, who introduced a new Police Act, 1828. Cp. PEELER.

bobby[2] *n.* a calf slaughtered for veal because it has been weaned. WH: early 20C. Prob. from BOB[1] + -Y[1]. See BOBBIE PIN.

bobby-dazzler *n.* an excellent striking person or thing, esp. an attractive girl. WH: 19C. Obscure 1st element + *dazzler*. See DAZZLE.

bobby sox *n.* ankle socks usu. worn by young girls. WH: mid-20C. Prob. from BOB[1] + -Y[1]. See BOBBIE PIN. *Sox* is a commercial spelling of *socks* (SOCK[1]).

bobolink *n.* a N American songbird, *Dolichonyx oryzivorus*. WH: 18C. Appar. imit. of bird's call.

bobstay *n.* a chain or rope for drawing a ship's bowsprit downward and keeping it steady. WH: 18C. *bob* (in some sense) + STAY[3].

bocage *n.* woodland scenery represented in ceramics. WH: 16C. French. See BOSCAGE.

Boche *n.* a German, esp. a soldier. *Also a.* WH: early 20C. French sl., from *Alboche*, var. of *Allemoche*, argot form of *Allemand* German. The inserted *b* is apparently by association with slang *caboche* head, or *tête de boche* wooden head.

bock *n.* a strong German beer. WH: 19C. French, from German abbr. of *Eimbockbier*, from *Einbecker Bier* Einbeck beer, from *Einbeck*, a town in central Germany.

bod *n.* a person. WH: 18C. Abbr. of BODY.

bodacious *a.* excellent, wonderful. WH: 19C. ? Var. of *boldacious*, blend of BOLD and AUDACIOUS.

bode *v.t.* to foretell. *Also v.i.* WH: pre-1200. Old English *bodian*, from Germanic, rel. to BID.

bodega *n.* a shop selling wine, esp. in a Spanish-speaking country. WH: 19C. Spanish, from Latin *apotheca*. See BOUTIQUE.

Bode's law *n.* a formula for measuring the distances of the planets from the sun. WH: 19C. Johann Elert *Bode*, 1747–1826, German astronomer.

Bodhisattva *n.* in Mahayana Buddhism, a person who postpones entry into nirvana in order to help suffering beings. WH: 19C. Sanskrit one whose essence is enlightenment, from *bodhi* perfect knowledge (see BUDDHA) + *sattva* essence, being. Cp. BO TREE.

bodice *n.* a tight-fitting outer vest for women. WH: 16C. pl. of BODY, with -*ce* representing earlier unvoiced sound of -S[1]. Cp. DICE. Cp. *body* in sense woman's close-fitting top.

bodkin *n.* a large-eyed and blunt-pointed needle for leading a tape or cord through a hem, loop etc. WH: 12–14C. Orig. uncertain. ? Dim. from Celtic. Cp. Irish *bod*, Welsh *bidog* dagger. The word was originally used of a type of dagger. The current sense dates from the 18C.

Bodleian *a.* of or relating to Sir T. Bodley, who in 1597 restored the Library at Oxford University which now bears his name. *Also n.* WH: 17C. Sir Thomas *Bodley*, 1545–1613, English diplomat.

body *n.* the material frame of a person or animal. *Also v.t.* WH: pre-1200. Old English *bodig*, from Germanic, of unknown orig. Old High German *botah* corpse was superseded by German *Leib*, rel. to LIVE[1].

Boer *n.* a S African of Dutch birth or extraction. *Also a.* WH: 19C. Dutch *boer* farmer. Cp. BOOR.

boffin *n.* a scientist, esp. one employed by the armed services or the government. WH: mid-20C. Orig. unknown. The word may have been suggested by Noddy *Boffin*, a character in Charles Dickens' *Our Mutual Friend* (1864).

Bofors gun *n.* an automatic anti-aircraft gun. WH: mid-20C. *Bofors*, name of the munition works in Sweden where first made.

bog *n.* a marsh, a morass. *Also v.t.* WH: 12–14C. Gaelic and Irish *bogach*, from *bog* soft.

bogey[1] *n.* in golf, one stroke over par on a hole. *Also v.t.* WH: 19C. Prob. from BOGEY[2], seen as an imaginary opponent.

bogey[2] *n.* a spectre. WH: 19C. Prob. rel. to BOGLE, BUG[2].

bogey[3] *v.i.* to bathe, to swim. *Also n.* WH: 19C. Australian Aboriginal (Dharuk) *bu-gi*.

boggard *n.* a hobgoblin. WH: 16C. Rel. to BOGGLE, BOGLE, BUG[2] etc.

boggle *v.i.* to shrink back from, start with fright (at). *Also v.t.* WH: 16C. Prob. of dial. orig. and rel. to BOGGARD, BOGLE etc.

bogie *n.* a revolving undercarriage. WH: 19C. Orig. unknown.

bogle *n.* a hobgoblin, a spectre, an imaginary object of terror. WH: 16C. Prob. rel. to BOGEY[2].

bogus *a.* sham, counterfeit. WH: 18C. Orig. unknown. ? Rel. to BOGEY[2].

bohea *n.* an inferior quality of black China tea. WH: 18C. Dial. Chinese *Bu-yi*, var. of *Wu-yi*, name of the hills in SE China where it was grown.

Bohemian *a.* of or relating to Bohemia, its people or their language. *Also n.* WH: 14–15C. *Bohemia*, a former kingdom in central Europe (now W part of Czech Republic) + -AN.

bohemian *n.* a gypsy. *Also a.* WH: 18C. French *bohémien* BOHEMIAN, since gypsies were said to come from Bohemia. The secondary sense of one leading a free, unconventional life owes much to Henri Murger's novel *Scènes de la vie de Bohème* (1847–9).

boho *n.* a bohemian. *Also a.* WH: early 20C. Abbr. of BOHEMIAN + -O.

bohrium *n.* an artificially manufactured radioactive chemical element, at. no. 107, chem. symbol Bh. WH: late 20C. Niels *Bohr*, 1885–1962, Danish physicist + -IUM.

boil[1] *v.i.* to be agitated by the action of heat, as water. *Also v.t., n.* WH: 12–14C. Old French *boillir* (Modern French *bouillir*), from Latin *bullire* to bubble, to boil, from *bulla* bubble.

boil[2] *n.* a hard, inflamed, suppurating tumour. WH: pre-1200. Old English *bȳl*, *bȳle*, from Germanic, influ. by (but not rel. to) BOIL[1].

boisterous *a.* wild, unruly. WH: 14–15C. Alt. of obs. *boistous* rough, of unknown orig., through its var. *boisteous*. The early meaning was stout, stiff, bulky, as of ship's cables or heavy clothing. This sense was obsolete by the end of the 17C.

bolas *n.* a missile, used by S American Indians, formed of balls or stones strung together and flung round the legs of the animal aimed at. WH: 19C. Spanish and Portuguese, pl. of *bola* ball.

bold *a.* courageous, daring. WH: pre-1200. Old English *bald*, rel. to German *bald* soon, Old Norse *ballr* dangerous, fatal, from Germanic.

bole[1] *n.* the stem or trunk of a tree. WH: 12–14C. Old Norse *bolr*, ? rel. to BAULK.

bole[2] *n.* a brownish, yellowish or reddish, soft unctuous clay, containing more or less iron oxide. WH: 12–14C. Late Latin BOLUS.

bolection *n.* a projecting moulding. WH: 17C. Orig. unknown.

bolero *n.* a lively Spanish dance. WH: 18C. Spanish, from *bola* ball.

boletus *n.* a mushroom or toadstool of the genus *Boletus*, having the undersurface of the pileus full of pores instead of gills. WH: 16C. Latin, or from Greek *bōlitēs*, ? from *bōlos* lump.

bolide *n.* a large meteor, usu. one that explodes and falls in the form of aerolites. WH: 19C. French, from Latin *bolis*, *bolidis*, from Greek *bolis* missile.

bolivar *n.* the standard unit of currency in Venezuela. WH: 19C. Simón *Bolívar*, 1783–1830, S American soldier and statesman.

boliviano *n.* the standard unit of currency in Bolivia, equal to 100 centavos. WH: 19C. Spanish. From Simón *Bolívar*. See BOLIVAR.

boll *n.* a rounded seed vessel or pod. WH: 12–14C. Middle Dutch *bolle*, or from Dutch *bol* round object, rel. to BOWL[1].

bollard *n.* a large post or bitt on a wharf, dock or on board ship for securing ropes or cables. WH: 12–14C. ? Old Norse *bolr* BOLE[1] + -ARD.

bollocks *n.pl.* testicles. *Also v.i.* WH: 18C. Pl. of *bollock*, var. of *ballock*, from Old English *bealluc*, dim. of Germanic base of BALL[1].

bologna *n.* a large smoked sausage of mixed meats, also called a *polony*. WH: 19C. *Bologna*, a city in N Italy. Cp. POLONY.

Bolognese *a.* of or relating to Bologna. *Also n.* WH: 18C. Italian of Bologna. See BOLOGNA, also -ESE.

bolometer *n.* an extremely sensitive instrument for measuring radiant heat. WH: 19C. Greek *bolē* ray of light + -O- + -METER.

Bolshevik *n.* a member of the Russian majority Socialist party which came to power under Lenin in 1917. *Also a.* WH: early 20C. Russian *bol'shevik* majority member, from *bol'she* greater, comp. of *bol'shoǐ* big. Cp. MENSHEVIK.

bolster *n.* a long underpillow, used to support the pillows in a bed. *Also v.t., v.i.* WH: pre-1200. Old English cushion, from Germanic, ? with base meaning to swell. Cp. German *Polster*.

bolt[1] *n.* a short thick arrow with a blunt head. *Also v.t., v.i.* WH: pre-1200. Old English, from Germanic, of unknown orig. The common sense of a sliding piece of iron for fastening a door dates from the 15C, that of a metal pin from the 17C. The latter emerged with the growth of ship-building.

bolt[2] *n.* a sieve for separating bran from flour. *Also v.t.* WH: 12–14C. Old French *bulter* (Modern French *bluter*), of unknown orig. The current spelling evolved by association with BOLT[1].

bolus *n.* medicine in a round mass larger than a pill. WH: 16C. Late Latin, from Greek *bōlos* clod, lump of earth.

bomb *n.* an explosive device triggered by impact or a timer usu. dropped from the air, thrown or placed by hand. *Also v.t., v.i.* WH: 16C. French *bombe*, from Italian *bomba*, prob. from Latin *bombus*, from Greek *bombos* booming, humming, of imit. orig. The word was originally used of an explosive shell fired from a mortar. The current sense effectively dates from the 1st World War, 1914–18, when bombs were dropped (originally thrown) from aircraft.

bombard[1] *v.t.* to attack with shot and shell. WH: 16C. French *bombarder*, from Old French *bombarde* BOMBARD[2].

bombard[2] *n.* the earliest form of cannon. WH: 14–15C. Old French *bombarde*, from Medieval Latin *bombarda*, prob. from Latin *bombus*. See BOMB.

bombarde *n.* a medieval alto-pitched shawm. WH: 14–15C. Old French *bombarde*. See BOMBARD[2]. The instrument is so called from its appearance.

bombardon *n.* a brass instrument related to the tuba. WH: 19C. Italian *bombardone*, augm. of *bombardo* BOMBARD[2].

bombasine *n.* a twilled dress fabric of silk and worsted, cotton and worsted, or of worsted alone. WH: 16C. Old French *bombasin*, from Medieval Latin *bombacinum*, from *bombacynus* silken, from BOMBYX. See also -INE.

bombast[1] *n.* high-sounding words. *Also a.* WH: 16C. P.p. of obs. *bombase* to stuff with wool, from Old French *bombace* raw cotton, from Medieval Latin *bombax*, *bombacis*, alt. of BOMBYX. Cp. BOMBASINE. The original sense was cotton wool, especially as used for padding for clothes. The current figurative sense evolved soon after.

bombast[2] *v.t.* to stuff out, to inflate. WH: 16C. See BOMBAST[1].

Bombay bowler *n.* a small, light pith helmet. WH: early 20C. Orig. uncertain. The word may be related in some way to *Bombay* (Mumbai), a city in India.

Bombay duck *n.* a small S Asian fish, *Harpodon nehereus*, when salted and dried eaten as a relish; also called *bummalo*. WH: 19C. Alt. of Marathi *bombīl*, source of *bummalo*, influ. by *Bombay* (Mumbai), a city in India.

bombe *n.* an ice cream dessert moulded into a rounded, bomb shape. WH: 19C. French BOMB.

bombé *a.* protruding or round-fronted, as of furniture. WH: early 20C. French, p.p. of *bomber* to swell out, from *bombe* BOMB.

bombora *n.* dangerous broken water, usu. at the base of a cliff. WH: mid-20C. Australian Aboriginal.

bombyx *n.* any moth of the genus *Bombyx*, containing the silkworm, *B. mori*. WH: 14–15C. Latin, from Greek *bombux*. Cp. BOMBASINE.

bona fide *adv.* in good faith. *Also a.* WH: 16C. Latin with good faith, abl. of *bona fides*, from *bonus* good + *fides* faith. Cp. BONUS, FIDELITY.

bonanza *n.* a rich mine. *Also a.* WH: 19C. Spanish fair weather, prosperity, from Latin *bonus* good.

Bonapartism *n.* attachment to the dynasty founded in France by Napoleon Bonaparte. WH: 19C. Napoleon *Bonaparte*, 1769–1821, emperor of France. See also -ISM.

bona vacantia *n.pl.* unclaimed goods. WH: 18C. Latin ownerless goods, from *bona* goods (from *bonus* good) + n. from *vacare* to be empty, to be ownerless. Cp. VACANT.

bon-bon *n.* a sweet, esp. of fondant. WH: 18C. French, redupl. of *bon* good.

bonce *n.* the head. WH: 19C. Orig. unknown. The original sense was a large playing-marble.

bond¹ *n.* a thing which binds or confines, as a cord or band. *Also v.t., v.i.* WH: 12–14C. Alt. of BAND¹, rel. to BIND, BOUND³.

bond² *a.* in serfdom or slavery. WH: pre-1200. Old Norse *bóndi* occupier and tiller of the soil (cp. HUSBAND), from *bóandi*, pres.p. (used as n.) of *bóa*, var. of *búa* to dwell, from Germanic base also of BOOTH.

bond³ *n.* a league of confederation. WH: 19C. Afrikaans, from Dutch, from *binden* to bind. Cp. German *Bund* confederation.

bondage *n.* slavery, captivity. WH: 12–14C. Anglo-Latin *bondagium*, from BOND². See also -AGE. The word has been influenced in sense by BOND¹.

bone *n.* the hard material of the skeleton of mammals, birds, reptiles and some fishes. *Also a., v.t.* WH: pre-1200. Old English *bān*, from Germanic. The word is not related to any word for bone outside Germanic. German *Bein* means leg but bone in compounds with *-bein*, as *Hüftbein* hip bone.

bonfire *n.* a large fire lit in the open air on an occasion of public rejoicing. WH: 14–15C. BONE + FIRE. A bonfire was originally a large outdoor fire for burning bones, also a fire for burning heretics, proscribed books, etc. Hence the 'celebratory' sense of the modern bonfire.

bong *n.* a low-pitched reverberating sound. *Also v.i.* WH: early 20C. Imit.

bongo¹ *n.* a small hand drum of a type often played in pairs. WH: early 20C. American Spanish *bongó*, from W African.

bongo² *n.* a rare antelope, *Tragelaphus euryceros*, which has spiralled horns and a red-brown coat with narrow cream stripes. WH: 19C. Kikongo.

bonhomie *n.* good nature, geniality. WH: 18C. French, from *bon homme* good man + *-ie* -Y².

bonito *n.* any of various striped tuna. WH: 16C. Spanish pretty, nice.

bonjour *int.* good day. WH: 16C. French good day, from *bon* good + *jour* day.

bonk *v.t.* to hit. *Also v.i., n.* WH: mid-20C. Imit.

bonkers *a.* crazy, mad. WH: mid-20C. Orig. unknown. ? Rel. to BONCE or BONK. See -ER⁶. The original meaning was slightly tipsy.

bon mot *n.* a witticism. WH: 18C. French good word, from *bon* good + *mot* word.

bonne *n.* a nursemaid. WH: 18C. French, fem. of *bon* good, implying woman. French children formerly addressed domestics as *ma bonne* my good (woman) or *ma chère bonne* my dear good (woman).

bonne bouche *n.* a tasty titbit. WH: 16C. French good mouth, meaning good taste in the mouth.

bonnet *n.* a hat tied beneath the chin, of various shapes and materials, formerly worn by women out of doors and now usu. by babies. *Also v.t., v.i.* WH: 14–15C. Old French *bonet*, from Medieval Latin *abonnis* headgear.

bonny *a.* beautiful, pretty. WH: 15C. ? Old French *bone*, fem. of *bon* good, of uncertain orig.

bonsai *n.* a potted tree or shrub cultivated into a dwarf variety by skilful pruning of its roots. WH: early 20C. Japanese, from *bon* tray + *sai* planting.

bonsella *n.* a tip, a present. WH: late 20C. Zulu *ibhanselo* gift and Xhosa *ukubasele* to give a present. Cp. BAKSHEESH.

bonspiel *n.* a curling match. WH: 16C. Prob. from Low German. Cp. German *Spiel* game.

bontebok *n.* a large antelope, *Damaliscus dorcas*, which has a deep reddish-brown coat, a white tail and white patches on its head and rump. WH: 18C. Afrikaans, from Dutch *bont* pied + *bok* BUCK¹.

bon ton *n.* fashion, good style. WH: 18C. French good tone, from *bon* good + *ton* tone.

bonus *n.* something over and above what is due. *Also v.t.* WH: 18C. Latin *bonus* good. The word is probably a misuse of masculine *bonus* for neuter *bonum* good thing. It was originally Stock Exchange slang.

bon vivant *n.* a person fond of good living. WH: 17C. French good living (person). Cp. BON VIVEUR.

bon viveur *n.* a bon vivant. WH: 19C. Pseudo-French good liver. Cp. BON VIVANT.

bon voyage *n., int.* a pleasant journey, farewell. WH: 17C. French good journey, from *bon* good + *voyage* journey, VOYAGE. English lacks a corresponding two-word wish. Cp. Italian *buon viaggio*, Spanish *buen viajo*, German *gute Reise*, Russian *schastlivogo puti*, Finnish *hyvä matkaa* etc.

bonza *a.* excellent. WH: early 20C. ? Alt. of BONANZA.

bonze *n.* a Buddhist religious teacher in Japan, China and adjacent regions. WH: 16C. French *bonze* and Portuguese *bonzo*, ? from Japanese *bonzō* priest.

boo *int., n.* a sound used to express contempt, displeasure, aversion etc. (imitating the lowing of oxen). *Also v.i., v.t.* WH: 19C. Imit. Cp. BO.

boob¹ *n.* an error, a blunder. *Also v.i.* WH: mid-20C. Abbr. of BOOBY.

boob² *n.* a woman's breast. WH: mid-20C. Either var. of *bub*, abbr. of *bubby* (cp. German dial. *Bübbi* teat) or abbr. of *booby*, alt. of *bubby*.

booboo *n.* a mistake. WH: early 20C. Redupl. of BOOB¹.

boobook *n.* a brown spotted owl, *Ninox novaeseelandiae*, native to Australia and New Zealand. WH: 19C. Australian Aboriginal (Dharuk) *bug bug*, imit. of bird's call.

booby *n.* a dull, stupid person; a dunce. WH: 17C. Prob. Spanish *bobo*, from Latin *balbus* stammering, stuttering. See also -Y³.

boodle *n.* money, capital, stock in trade. WH: 17C. Dutch *boedel*, *boel* possessions, disorderly mass. Cp. CABOODLE.

boogie *v.i.* to dance to pop music. *Also n.* WH: early 20C. Orig. unknown. ? Of W African orig. and rel. to BONGO¹.

book *n.* a collection of sheets printed, written on or blank, bound in a volume. *Also v.t., v.i.* WH: pre-1200. Old English *bōc*, from Germanic base prob. rel. to BEECH, as wood used for tablets on which runes were written.

Boolean *a.* being or relating to a logical system using symbols to represent relationships between entities. WH: 19C. George *Boole*, 1815–64, English mathematician + -AN.

boom¹ *n.* a loud, deep sound. *Also v.i., v.t.* WH: 14–15C. Imit. Cp. BOMB.

boom² *n.* a long spar to extend the foot of a particular sail. WH: 16C. Dutch tree, BEAM.

boomer *n.* a large kangaroo. WH: 19C. Prob. from BOOM¹ + -ER¹.

boomerang *n.* an Aboriginal Australian missile weapon, consisting of a curved flat stick so constructed that it returns to the thrower. *Also v.i.* WH: 19C. Australian Aboriginal (Dharuk) *bumarin*.

boon¹ *n.* a benefit, a blessing. WH: 12–14C. Old Norse *bón*, from Germanic, ? rel. to Latin *fari* to speak. The original sense was prayer, request. This then evolved to mean the thing prayed for, favour.

boon² *a.* close, intimate. WH: 14–15C. Old French *bon*, from Latin *bonus* good.

boondocks *n.pl.* remote or uncultivated country. WH: mid-20C. Tagalog *bundok* mountain.

boondoggle *n.* work of little practical value. *Also v.i.* WH: mid-20C. Orig. unknown. It was originally a braided lanyard worn by Scouts, so is perhaps a Scout coinage. Cp. WOGGLE.

boong *n.* an Aborigine. WH: mid-20C. Indonesian. ? Jakarata dial. var. of *bung* elder brother.

boongarry *n.* the N Queensland tree kangaroo, *Dendrolagus lumholtzi*. WH: 19C. Australian Aboriginal (Warrgamay) *bulnggari*.

boonies *n.pl.* the boondocks. WH: mid-20C. Abbr. of BOONDOCKS. See also -Y³.

boor *n.* a rude, awkward or insensitive person. WH: 16C. Low German *būr* or Dutch *boer*. Cp. BOER, NEIGHBOUR. The original sense was husbandman, peasant, especially when Dutch or German. The current general sense developed soon after.

boost *v.t.* to push upwards. *Also v.i., n.* WH: 19C. Orig. unknown.

boot¹ *n.* a kind of shoe that covers the whole foot and the lower part of the leg. *Also v.t.* WH: 12–14C. Old Norse *bóti*, or from Old French *bote* (Modern French *botte*), prob. rel. to *bot* blunt, stumpy, and ult. to BUTT¹.

boot² *n.* advantage, profit (used only in the expression *to boot*). WH: pre-1200. Old English *bōt*, from Germanic, from base also of BETTER, BEST.

booth n. a stall or tent at a fair, polling station etc. WH: 12–14C. Old Norse (var. of) *buth*, from *bóa*. See BOND[2].

booty n. spoil taken in war. WH: 14–15C. Middle Low German *būte*, *buite* exchange, distribution (cp. German *Beute*), rel. to Old Norse *býta* to deal out, of unknown orig. Influ. by BOOT[2].

booze n. an alcoholic drink. Also v.i. WH: 12–14C. Middle Dutch *būsen* to drink too much (Dutch *buizen*). The spelling *booze* dates only from the 18C. The earlier form was *bouse*.

bop[1] n. an innovative style of jazz music dating from the 1940s. Also v.i. WH: mid-20C. Imit. Cp. BEBOP.

bop[2] v.t. to hit, to strike. Also n. WH: 19C. Imit. Cp. BIFF.

bora[1] n. a keen dry, NE wind in the upper Adriatic. WH: 19C. Italian (dial. var of) *borea*, from Latin, from Greek *boreas* north wind.

bora[2] n. a ritual initiation rite. WH: 19C. Australian Aboriginal (Kamilaroi) *buurr-a*.

boracite n. native borate of magnesia. WH: 18C. Medieval Latin BORAX *boracis* + -ITE[1].

borage n. a hairy, blue-flowered plant of the genus *Borago*, esp. *B. officinalis*, formerly esteemed as a cordial, and used to flavour claret cup etc. WH: 12–14C. Old French *bourrache*, from Medieval Latin *borrago*, *borraginis*, ? from Arabic *'abū ḥurāš* father of roughness, ref. to leaves.

borak n. chaff, banter. WH: 19C. Australian Aboriginal (Wathawurung) *burag*.

borax n. the mineral salt sodium borate. WH: 14–15C. Medieval Latin, from Arabic (coll.) *būrāk*, from Pahlavi *būrak*.

borborygmus n. rumbling of the stomach. WH: 18C. Greek *borborugmos*, from *borboros* slime, mud.

bordar n. a villein of the lowest rank, doing manual service for a cottage which he held at his lord's will. WH: 12–14C. Anglo-Latin *bordarius*, from *borda*, from Old French *borde* small farm, from Frankish. Cp. BOARD.

Bordeaux n. a red, white or rosé wine from Bordeaux. WH: 16C. *Bordeaux*, a city in SW France.

bordello n. a brothel. WH: 16C. Italian, from Old French *bordel*, dim. of *borde*. See BORDAR.

border n. an edge, margin. Also v.t., v.i. WH: 14–15C. Old French *bordeüre* (Modern French *bordure*), from Germanic base of BOARD. See also -ER[2].

bordure n. the border of an escutcheon, occupying one-fifth of the shield. WH: 15C. Earlier form of BORDER.

bore[1] v.t. to make a hole through. Also v.i., n. WH: pre-1200. Old English *borian*, or from Germanic base rel. to Latin *forare* to bore, Greek *pharos* plough.

bore[2] n. a tidal wave of great height and velocity, caused by the meeting of two tides or the rush of the tide up a narrowing estuary. WH: 12–14C. ? Old Norse *bára* wave.

bore[3] n. a tiresome person. Also v.t. WH: 18C. ? French. The word is apparently not related to BORE[1] despite the suggestion of 'drilling'. It was originally used of a tiresome thing, not a person. The latter sense evolved in the 19C.

boreal a. of or relating to the north or the north wind. WH: 14–15C. Old French *boréal*, or from Late Latin *borealis*, from Latin *boreas*, from Greek north wind. See also -AL[1].

borecole n. a curled variety of winter cabbage, kale. WH: 18C. Dutch *boerenkool* peasant's cabbage, from *boer* BOOR + *kool* COLE.

boree n. any of several species of *Acacia* affording firewood. WH: 19C. Australian Aboriginal (Wiradhuri and Kamilaroi) *burrii*.

boreen n. a lane, a bridle path. WH: 19C. Irish *boíthrín*, dim. of *bóthar* road. See also -EEN.

born a. brought into the world. WH: pre-1200. Old English *boren*, p.p. of *beran* BEAR[2]. The word was distinguished early from BORNE.

borne a. carried by. WH: 17C. P.p. of Old English *beran* BEAR[2]. Cp. BORN.

borné a. narrow-minded, limited. WH: 18C. French, p.p. of *borner* to limit, from Popular Latin *bodina* limit, ? from Gaulish. Cp. BOUND[2].

Bornholm disease n. a rare viral disease, epidemic pleurodynia. WH: mid-20C. *Bornholm*, a Danish island in the Baltic Sea, where first described.

bornite n. a valuable copper ore found in Cornwall and elsewhere. WH: 19C. Ignatius von *Born*, 1742–91, Austrian mineralogist + -ITE[1].

boro- comb. form indicating salts containing boron. WH: BORON. See -O-.

boron n. the element, at. no. 5, chem. symbol B, present in borax and boracic acid. WH: 19C. BORAX, with ending taken from that of CARBON, which in some ways it resembles.

boronia n. any shrub of the genus *Boronia*. WH: 18C. Modern Latin, from Francesco *Borone*, 1769–94, Italian botanist.

borough n. a town possessing a municipal corporation. WH: pre-1200. Old English *burg*, *burh*, from Germanic, rel. to Old English *beorgan*. See BORROW. Cp. BURGH, BURROW. The original sense was a fortress or fortified town. The current official sense dates from the 16C.

borrow v.t. to obtain and make temporary use of. Also v.i. WH: pre-1200. Old English *borgian*, from Germanic, rel. to Old English *beorgan*, from Germanic base meaning to protect, to shelter, itself also rel. to BURY.

borsch n. Russian beetroot soup. WH: 19C. Russian *borshch*. The original sense was hogweed (Russian *borshchevik*), *Heracleum sphondylium*, from which the soup was at one time made. The name was retained when beetroot was substituted for hogweed.

Borstal n. a place of detention and corrective training for juvenile offenders, now called *youth custody centre*. WH: early 20C. *Borstal*, a village near (now district of) Rochester, Medway, where the first such institution opened, 1901. It is purely a coincidence that the place name Borstal means security place, from Old English *borg* security (cp. BORROW) + *steall* place (cp. STALL[1]). Cp. BORSTALL.

borstall n. a steep track on a hillside. WH: pre-1200. Old English *borg* security, refuge or *beorg* hill + *steall* place. The word is chiefly current in Kent and Sussex. Cp. BORSTAL.

bort n. small fragments split from diamonds in roughly reducing them to shape, used to make diamond powder. WH: 17C. Dutch *boort*.

borzoi n. a Russian wolfhound of a breed with a long silky coat. WH: 19C. Russian *borzoĭ*, from *borzyĭ* swift.

boscage n. wood, woodland. WH: 14–15C. Old French (Modern French BOCAGE), from Late Latin *boscum* BUSH[1]. See also -AGE.

bosh n. empty talk, nonsense, folly. Also int., v.t. WH: 19C. Turkish *boş* empty, worthless.

bosk n. a bush, a thicket, a small forest. WH: 12–14C. Var. of BUSH[1].

bosket n. a grove. WH: 18C. French *bosquet*, from Italian *boschetto*, dim. of *bosco* wood. Cp. BOUQUET, BUSH[1].

Bosnian a. of or relating to Bosnia. Also n. WH: 18C. *Bosnia*, a region in the Balkans, now part of Bosnia-Herzegovina + -IAN.

bosom n. the breast of a human being, esp. of a woman. Also v.t. WH: pre-1200. Old English *bōsm*, from Germanic, ? ult. from base of BOUGH.

boson n. a particle, or member of a class of particles, with an integral or zero spin, which behaves in accordance with the statistical relations laid down by Bose and Einstein. WH: mid-20C. Satyendra Nath *Bose*, 1894–1974, Indian physicist. See also -ON.

boss[1] n. a protuberant part. Also v.t. WH: 12–14C. Old French *boce* (Modern French *bosse*), of unknown orig. The word is perhaps from Frankish *botja* blow, hence a swelling caused by a blow, from *batan* to hit.

boss[2] n. a supervisor, manager. Also a., v.t. WH: 19C. Dutch *baas* master, of unknown orig..

boss[3] n. a miss, a bad shot, a bungle. Also v.t., v.i. WH: 19C. Orig. unknown.

bossa nova n. a Brazilian dance resembling the samba. WH: mid-20C. Portuguese new tendency, from *bossa* tendency + *nova*, fem. sing. of *novo* new.

boston n. a game of cards somewhat resembling whist. WH: 19C. *Boston*, a city in Massachusetts, USA. The gaming reference is to the siege of Boston (1775–6). The technical terms of the game are siege terms.

Boswell n. a biographer. WH: 19C. James *Boswell*, 1740–95, companion and biographer of Samuel Johnson.

bot n. a parasitic worm, the larva of the genus *Oestrus*. WH: 16C. Prob. from Low Dutch, cp. Dutch *bot*, of unknown orig. Prob. not rel. to BITE.

botany n. the science which treats of plants and plant life. WH: 17C. From *botanic* (from French *botanique* or Latin *botanicus*, from Greek *botanikos*, from *botanē* plant) + -Y[2].

botargo *n.* a relish made of the roes of the mullet and tuna. WH: 16C. Italian, from Medieval Greek *arghotarakho*, ? from Coptic *outarakhon*, from *ou* the + Greek *tarikhion* pickle.

botch¹ *n.* a clumsy patch. *Also v.t.* WH: 14–15C. Orig. unknown. ? From BOTCH².

botch² *n.* an ulcerous swelling. WH: 14–15C. Old French *boche*, var. of *boce* BOSS¹.

botcher *n.* a young salmon, a grilse. WH: 17C. Orig. unknown.

both *a., pron.* the one and also the other, the two. *Also adv.* WH: 12–14C. Old Norse *báthir*, representing *bá-thir* both they, from base also of Latin *ambo*, Russian *oba* both.

bother *v.t.* to tease, to vex. *Also v.i., int., n.* WH: 17C. Prob. from (or rel. to) Irish *bodhaire* deafness, noise, from *bodhraim* to deafen, to annoy.

bothy *n.* a rough kind of cottage. WH: 18C. Prob. rel. to Irish and Gaelic *both, bothán*, in turn rel. to BOOTH.

bo tree *n.* the peepul tree, a fig tree, *Ficus religiosa*, held sacred by the Buddhists and planted beside their temples. WH: 19C. Sinhalese *bōgaha*, from *bō*, from Pali and Sanskrit *bodhi* perfect knowledge (see BUDDHA) + *gaha* tree.

botryoid *a.* resembling a bunch of grapes in form. WH: 18C. Greek *botruoeidēs*, from *botrus* cluster of grapes. See also -OID.

bottine *n.* a buskin. WH: 16C. French, dim. of *botte* BOOT¹. See also -INE.

bottle¹ *n.* a vessel with a narrow neck for holding liquids. *Also v.t.* WH: 14–15C. Old French *boteille* (Modern French *bouteille*), from Medieval Latin *butticula*, dim. of Late Latin *buttis* BUTT².

bottle² *n.* a bundle of hay or straw. WH: 14–15C. Old French *botel*, dim. of *botte* bundle, from Middle Low German and Middle Dutch *bote* bundle of flax, prob. from Germanic base of BUTT⁴.

bottom *n.* the lowest part of anything, the part on which anything rests. *Also v.t., v.i., a.* WH: pre-1200. Old English *botm*, from Germanic, rel. to Latin *fundus*. Cp. FUND.

botulism *n.* a form of food poisoning caused by eating preserved food infected by *Clostridium botulinum*. WH: 19C. German *Botulismus*, from Latin *botulus* sausage. See also -ISM. Cp. BOWEL. The poisoning was originally caused (in Germany) by eating sausages.

bouclé *n.* a looped yarn. *Also a.* WH: 19C. French, p.p. of *boucler* to buckle, to curl. Cp. BUCKLE.

boudoir *n.* a small, elegantly furnished room, used as a lady's private apartment. WH: 18C. French *bouder* to sulk, to pout, based on *dortoir* dormitory, *parloir* parlour etc. French *bouder* is itself of imitative origin. Cp. POUT¹.

bouffant *a.* full, puffed out, as a hairstyle. WH: 19C. French, pres.p. of *bouffer* to swell, prob. ult. of imit. orig. Cp. PUFF.

bougainvillaea *n.* any tropical plant of the genus *Bougainvillaea*, the red or purple bracts of which almost conceal the flowers. WH: 19C. Modern Latin, from Louis-Antoine de *Bougainville*, 1729–1811, French navigator. See also -A¹.

bough *n.* a large branch of a tree. WH: pre-1200. Old English *bōg, bōgh*, from Germanic, rel. to Greek *pēkhus* forearm, cubit. Cp. BOW³. Related words are Icelandic *bogr*, Danish *boug*, German *Bog*, Dutch *boeg*, all meaning shoulder.

boughten *a.* bought. WH: 18C. Dial. p.p. of BUY.

bougie *n.* a wax candle. WH: 18C. French, from *Bougie* (Arabic *Bijāya*), a town in N Algeria with a former trade in wax candles. French *bougie* replaced *chandelle* CANDLE in the 19C.

bouillabaisse *n.* a rich fish stew or chowder, popular in the south of France. WH: 19C. French, from Provençal *bouiabaisso*, from imper. *bous* boil + *abaisse* lower, i.e. bring quickly to the boil then let simmer down.

bouilli *n.* meat gently simmered. WH: 17C. French, p.p. (used as n.) of *bouillir* BOIL¹. Cp. BULLY².

bouillon *n.* broth, soup. WH: 17C. French, from *bouillir* BOIL¹. Cp. COURT BOUILLON.

boulder *n.* a water-worn, rounded stone. WH: 14–15C. Shortening of *bouldersten*, of Scandinavian orig. Cp. Swedish dial. *bullersten*, ? rel. to Swedish *bullra* to rumble.

boule¹ *n.pl.* a French game resembling bowls, played with metal balls. WH: early 20C. French BOWL².

boule² *n.* a Greek legislative body. WH: 19C. Greek *boulē* senate, council.

boulevard *n.* a public walk on the rampart of a demolished fortification. WH: 18C. French, from Germanic. See BULWARK.

boulter *n.* a fishing line with a number of hooks attached. WH: 16C. Orig. unknown.

bounce *v.i.* to rebound. *Also v.t., n.* WH: 12–14C. ? Low Dutch (cp. Dutch *bons* thump), or of imit. orig. The original meaning was to beat, to thump. The current sense developed in the 16C.

bound¹ *n.* a leap, a spring. *Also v.i., v.t.* WH: 16C. Old French *bondir* to resound, (later) to rebound, from (var. of) Late Latin *bombitare*, var. of *bombilare* to buzz, from Latin *bombus*. Cp. BOMB.

bound² *n.* a limit, a boundary. *Also v.t.* WH: 12–14C. Anglo-French *bounde*, from Old French *bodne*, from Medieval Latin *bodina* border. Cp. BORNÉ, BOURNE.

bound³ *a.* under obligation, compelled, obliged. WH: 14–15C. P.p. of BIND.

bound⁴ *a.* prepared, ready. WH: 12–14C. Old Norse *búinn*, p.p. of *búa* to prepare, with *-d* from BOUND³.

bounty *n.* gracious liberality. WH: 12–14C. Old French *bonté*, from Latin *bonitas*, from *bonus* good. See also -TY¹. The sense of gratuitous payment arose in the 18C.

bouquet *n.* a bunch of flowers. WH: 18C. French, orig. clump of trees (cp. BOSK), from dial. var. of Old French *bos, bois* wood. Cp. BUSH¹. See also -ET¹.

bouquetin *n.* the Alpine ibex. WH: 18C. French, from Old French *boc estaign*, from STEINBOCK.

Bourbon *n.* a member of the royal family that formerly ruled France. WH: 18C. French *Bourbon*(-l'Archambault), a town in central France.

bourbon *n.* an American whisky made of wheat or Indian corn. WH: 19C. *Bourbon* County, Kentucky, USA. The county itself is named for the House of BOURBON.

bourdon *n.* a bass stop on an organ. WH: 12–14C. Old French drone, of imit. orig.

bourg *n.* a town built under the shadow of a castle. WH: 14–15C. Old French, from Medieval Latin *burgus* BOROUGH.

bourgeois¹ *n.* a person of the mercantile, shopkeeping or middle class. *Also a.* WH: 16C. French. See BURGESS.

bourgeois² *n.* a size of type around 9 point. WH: 19C. The word is said to be from name of printer, but ? so called for its intermediate size.

bourguignon *a.* (of meat dishes) stewed with (Burgundy) wine. WH: early 20C. French Burgundian. See BURGUNDY.

bourn *n.* a small stream, esp. a stream that runs periodically from springs in chalk. WH: 12–14C. S English var. of BURN². The word is common in place names, e.g. Bournemouth, Eastbourne, Burnham.

†bourne *n.* a bound, a limit, a goal. WH: 16C. French *borne*. See BOUND².

bourree *n.* a folk dance from the Auvergne and Basque provinces. WH: 17C. French *bourrée*, fem. p.p. (used as n.) of *bourrer* to hit, to knock. French *bourrée* originally meant a bundle of sticks, firewood. The current sense came from a dance around a fire of such sticks.

bourse *n.* a (French) foreign exchange for the transaction of commercial business. WH: 16C. French, from Medieval Latin *bursa* purse. See BURSA, PURSE.

boustrophedon *a., adv.* written alternately from left to right and from right to left. WH: 17C. Greek as the ox turns in ploughing, from *bous* ox + *-strophos* STROPHE + *-don* adverbial suf.

bout *n.* a turn, a round. WH: 16C. Var. of obs. *bought*, prob. from Low German *bucht*. See BIGHT.

boutique *n.* a fashionable clothes shop. WH: 18C. French, from Old Provençal *botica*, from Latin *apotheca*, from Greek *apothēkē* storehouse. Cp. APOTHECARY, BODEGA.

bouton *n.* a pimple, pustule, boil. WH: 19C. French BUTTON.

boutonnière *n.* a flower or flowers worn in the buttonhole. WH: 19C. French buttonhole. Cp. BOUTON.

bouts rimés *n.pl.* a game in which a list of rhymed endings is handed to each player to fill in and complete the verse. WH: 18C. French rhymed endings. Cp. BUTT³, RHYME.

bouzouki *n.* a Greek stringed instrument similar to the mandolin. WH: mid-20C. Modern Greek *mpouzouki*. Cp. Turkish *bozuk* spoilt, referring to roughly made instruments.

bovate *n.* the amount of land that an ox could plough in a season, approx. 13 acres. WH: 17C. Medieval Latin *bovata*, from Latin *bos*, *bovis* ox. See also -ATE[1].

bovine *a.* of or resembling oxen. WH: 19C. Late Latin *bovinus*, from Latin *bos*, *bovis* ox. See also -INE.

Bovril® *n.* a concentrated beef extract used for flavouring stews etc. WH: 19C. Latin *bos*, *bovis* ox + *vril*, imaginary form of energy described in Edward Bulwer-Lytton's novel *The Coming Race* (1871), from Latin *virilis* (VIRILE).

bovver *n.* a boisterous or violent commotion, a street fight. WH: mid-20C. Cockney pronun. of BOTHER.

bow[1] *n.* the doubling of a string in a slip-knot. *Also v.t.* WH: pre-1200. Old English *boga*, from Germanic. Cp. BOW[2].

bow[2] *v.i.* to bend forward as a sign of submission or salutation. *Also v.t.*, *n.* WH: pre-1200. Old English *būgan*, from Germanic. Cp. BOW[1].

bow[3] *n.* the rounded fore-end of a ship or boat. WH: 14–15C. Low German *boog* and Dutch *boeg*. See BOUGH. The pronunciation has been influenced by association with BOW[2].

bowdlerize *v.t.* to expurgate (a book). WH: 19C. Thomas *Bowdler*, 1754–1825, English editor who published an expurgated edition of Shakespeare, 1818.

bowel *n.* each of the intestines, a gut. *Also v.t.* WH: 12–14C. Old French *boël* (Modern French *boyau*), from Latin *botellus* pudding, sausage, small intestine, dim. of *botulus* sausage. Cp. BOTULISM.

bower[1] *n.* an arbour, a shady retreat, a summer house. WH: pre-1200. Old English *būr*, from Germanic, from base meaning to dwell. Cp. BUILD. The spelling has been influenced by FLOWER, TOWER etc. The original sense was simply dwelling. The meaning arbour arose in the 16C.

bower[2] *n.* either of the two knaves in euchre. WH: 19C. German *Bauer* husbandman, peasant. See BOOR.

bower[3] *n.* either of the two anchors carried in the bows. WH: 15C. BOW[3] + -ER[1].

bowie knife *n.* a long knife with the blade double-edged towards the point, used as a weapon in the south and south-west of US. WH: 19C. James *Bowie*, 1799–1836, US soldier.

bowl[1] *n.* a hollow (usu. hemispherical) vessel for holding liquids. WH: pre-1200. Old English *bolla*, from Germanic base meaning to swell. Cp. BOLL.

bowl[2] *n.* a solid ball, generally made of wood, slightly biased or one-sided, used to play various games with. *Also v.i.*, *v.t.* WH: 14–15C. Old French *boule*, from Latin *bulla* bubble. Cp. BULLA.

bowler *n.* an almost-hemispherical stiff felt hat. WH: 19C. William *Bowler*, the London hatter who designed it, 1850.

bowser *n.* a tanker used for refuelling aircraft on an airfield, or for supplying water. WH: early 20C. Name of company of oil storage engineers.

Bow Street officer *n.* a police officer. WH: 19C. *Bow Street*, London, the former location of the main magistrate's court.

bow-wow *int.* used to represent the bark of a dog. *Also n.* WH: 16C. Imit. Cp. WOOF[1].

bowyang *n.* a strap or string below the knee to prevent trousers from dragging. WH: 19C. Orig. unknown. The word is said to be from English dial. *booyangs*.

box[1] *n.* a case or receptacle usu. with a lid and rectangular, for holding solids. *Also v.t.* WH: pre-1200. Prob. from Late Latin *buxis*, *buxidis*, var. of Latin *pyxis* (PYX), box of boxwood. See BOX[2].

box[2] *n.* a genus of small evergreen shrubs, *Buxus*, esp. the common box tree, *Buxus sempervirens*. WH: pre-1200. Latin *buxus*, from Greek *puxos*.

box[3] *n.* a blow with the open hand on the ear or side of the head. *Also v.t.*, *v.i.* WH: 14–15C. Orig. unknown. ? Imit.

Box and Cox *n.* two people who share a job or a room but never meet. *Also a.*, *adv.*, *v.i.* WH: 19C. Title of play (1847) by J.M. Morton, in which two people unwittingly become tenants of the same room, one by night, the other by day.

boy *n.* a male child. *Also int.* WH: 12–14C. Orig. uncertain. ? Rel. to Old English male pers. names *Bōia*, *Bōja*. Cp. German *Bube* knave. ? Rel. to BABE. The original sense was a male servant. See KNAVE.

boyar *n.* a member of the old Russian nobility. WH: 16C. Russian *boyarin*, pl. *boyare*. ? Rel. to BEY.

boycott *v.t.* to combine to ostracize (a person) on account of their political opinions. *Also n.* WH: 19C. Captain Charles C. *Boycott*, 1832–97, land agent in Ireland, who was so treated by the Land League, 1880.

boyla *n.* a sorcerer. WH: 19C. Australian Aboriginal.

Boyle's law *n.* the principle that the pressure of a gas varies inversely with its volume at constant temperature. WH: 19C. Robert *Boyle*, 1627–91, English scientist.

boysenberry *n.* an edible hybrid fruit related to the loganberry and the raspberry. WH: mid-20C. Rudolph *Boysen*, 1895–1950, US horticulturist + BERRY.

bra *n.* a women's undergarment that supports the breasts. WH: mid-20C. Abbr. of BRASSIÈRE.

brace *n.* that which tightens or supports. *Also v.t.* WH: 14–15C. Old French the two arms, the distance between the fingertips with the arms outstretched (Modern French *brasse* fathom), from Latin *brachia*, pl. of *brachium* arm, from Greek *brakhiōn*. Cp. BRACHIO-, EMBRACE[1].

bracelet *n.* an ornamental band for the wrist. WH: 14–15C. Old French, from *bras* arm, from Latin *brachium* (BRACE). See also -EL, -ET[1].

brach *n.* a bitch hound. WH: 14–15C. Old French *brachez*, pl. of *brachet*, dim. of Provençal *brac*, from Frankish.

brachial *a.* of or belonging to the arm. WH: 14–15C. Latin *brachialis*, from *brachium* arm. See also -AL[1].

brachio- *comb. form* having arms or armlike processes. WH: Greek *brakhiōn* arm. See also -O-.

brachiopod *n.* a bivalve mollusc of the phylum Brachiopoda, with tentacles on each side of the mouth. WH: 19C. BRACHIO- + -POD.

brachiosaurus *n.* a herbivorous dinosaur of the genus *Brachiosaurus*, characterized by the length of its front legs and its huge size. WH: early 20C. BRACHIO- + Greek *sauros* lizard.

brachistochrone *n.* the curve between two points through which a body moves in a shorter time than any other curve. WH: 18C. Greek *brakhistos*, superl. of *brakhus* short + *khronos* time.

brachy- *comb. form* short. WH: Greek *brakhus* short.

brachycephalic *a.* short-headed. WH: 19C. BRACHY- + -CEPHALIC.

brachylogy *n.* concision of speech. WH: 16C. BRACHY- + -LOGY.

brack[1] *n.* a flaw or tear in a cloth or dress. WH: 12–14C. Old Norse *brak*, from Germanic base of BREAK. The original sense was noise, outcry. The given sense comes from BREAK.

brack[2] *n.* cake or bread containing dried fruit. WH: 19C. Shortening of BARMBRACK.

bracken *n.* a fern, esp. *Pteridium aquilinum*. WH: 12–14C. Old Norse. Cp. Swedish *bräken*, Danish *bregne*.

bracket *n.* a projection with a horizontal top fixed to a wall. *Also v.t.* WH: 16C. Breton *braguette* codpiece or Spanish *bragueta* codpiece, bracket, dim. of French *brague* mortise (in pl.) breeches, from Provençal *braga* breeches, from Latin *braca*, pl. *bracae* breeches. The sense has been influenced by Latin *brachium* arm.

brackish *a.* partly fresh, partly salt. WH: 16C. From obs. *brack* salt, from Germanic, of unknown orig. + -ISH[1].

bract *n.* a small modified leaf or scale on the flower stalk. WH: 18C. Latin *bractea*, var. of *brattea* thin metal plate, gold leaf.

brad *n.* a thin, flattish nail, with a small lip or projection on one side instead of a head. WH: 14–15C. Var. of obs. *brod* shoot, appar. from Old Norse *broddr* (cp. PROD).

bradawl *n.* a small boring-tool. WH: 19C. BRAD + AWL.

brady- *comb. form* slow. WH: 19C. Greek *bradus* slow.

bradycardia *n.* a slow heartbeat. WH: 19C. BRADY- + Greek *kardia* heart.

bradypeptic *a.* of slow digestion. WH: 19C. BRADY- + *peptic* (PEPSIN).

bradypod *n.* one of the sloth family. WH: 19C. BRADY- + -POD.

brae *n.* a slope bounding a river valley. WH: 12–14C. Old Norse *brá* eyelash (cp. German *Braue* eyebrow). See BROW for sense development.

brag *v.i.* to boast. *Also v.t.*, *n.*, *adv.* WH: 14–15C. Orig. unknown. ? Rel. to BRAY[1].

braggadocio *n.* an empty boaster. WH: 16C. Pseudo-Italian pers. name *Braggadochio*, boastful character in Spenser's *Faerie Queene* (1590, 1596). The name itself is based on BRAG or BRAGGART + -*occio* Italian augm. suf.

braggart n. a boastful person. Also a. WH: 16C. Obs. French bragard, from obs. braguer to boast, from bragues breeches + -art, var. of -ARD. Not rel. to BRAG.

Brahma n. the chief Hindu divinity, the Creator God. WH: 17C. Sanskrit brahman prayer.

brahma n. any bird of an Asian breed of domestic fowl. WH: 19C. Brahmaputra, a river in India.

Brahmin n. a member of the highest Hindu caste, the priestly order. WH: 12–14C. Sanskrit brāhmaṇa one of Brahmin caste, from brahman prayer.

braid[1] n. anything plaited or interwoven (esp. hair). Also v.t. WH: pre-1200. Old English bregdan to move quickly, to twist in and out, from Germanic, of unknown orig. Cp. UPBRAID. The word was originally used of a sudden jerky movement, such as brandishing a spear, drawing a sword etc. This sense was obsolete by the 15C.

braid[2] a. broad. WH: pre-1200. See BROAD.

braidism n. hypnotism, mesmerism. WH: 19C. Dr James Braid, 1795–1860, who first applied the system in 1842. Braid's own name for his system was HYPNOTISM.

brail n. a piece of leather with which to bind up a hawk's wing. Also v.t. WH: 14–15C. Old French braiel, braël, from Medieval Latin bracale waistbelt, from braca. See BRACKET.

Braille n. a system of writing or printing for the blind, by means of combinations of points standing in relief. Also v.t. WH: 19C. Louis Braille, 1809–52, French teacher of the blind, who invented it.

brain n. the soft, whitish, convoluted mass of nervous substance contained in the skull of vertebrates. Also v.t. WH: pre-1200. Old English brægen, from Germanic, ? rel. to Greek brekhmos front part of the head. Cp. BREGMA.

braird n. the first shoots of corn or grain. Also v.i. WH: 15C. Alt. of Old English brerd. Cf. Old High German brort, brord prow, margin.

braise v.t. to cook slowly in little liquid in a tightly closed pan. WH: 18C. French braiser, from braise live coals. Cp. BRAZIER.

brake[1] n. an appliance to a wheel to check or stop motion. Also v.t., v.i. WH: 18C. Prob. from brake winch of crossbow or brake bridle, curb.

brake[2] n. an instrument for breaking flax or hemp. Also v.t. WH: 14–15C. Middle Low German brake, or from Old Dutch braeke, rel. to BREAK.

brake[3] n. a mass of brushwood, a thicket. WH: pre-1200. ? Old English bracu, ? from Middle Low German brake branch, tree stump.

brake[4] n. bracken. WH: 12–14C. Prob. shortening of BRACKEN, taken as pl.

bramble n. the blackberry bush, Rubus fructicosus, or any allied thorny shrub. WH: pre-1200. Old English bræmbel, earlier brǣmel, from Germanic base also of BROOM. See also -LE[1].

Bramley n. a large green variety of cooking apple which has firm flesh. WH: early 20C. Matthew Bramley, a Nottinghamshire butcher, who first grew it in his garden, c.1850.

bran n. the husks of ground corn separated from the flour by bolting. WH: 12–14C. Old French bran bran (Modern French dial. excrement, filth), from Popular Latin brennus, from Gaulish.

branch n. a limb of a tree. Also v.i., v.t. WH: 12–14C. Old French branche, from Late Latin branca animal's paw, of unknown orig. The Late Latin word is found in the phrase branca ursina bear's foot. See BRANK-URSINE.

branchia n.pl. the gills of fishes and some amphibians. WH: 17C. Latin branchia, pl. branchiae, from Greek bragkhia gills.

branchio- comb. form of or relating to gills. WH: Greek bragkhia gills.

branchiopod n. an individual of a group of molluscoid animals with gills on the feet. WH: 19C. BRANCHIO- + -POD.

brand n. a particular kind of manufactured article. Also v.t. WH: pre-1200. Old High German brant and Old Norse brandr, from Germanic, from base also of BURN[1]. The word was originally used of a piece of burning wood. The transition of the sense to a trade mark arose through a marking by burning (as in branding cattle or criminals).

brandish v.t. to wave or flourish about (a weapon etc.). Also n.

WH: 12–14C. Old French brandir, brandiss-, from Germanic base of BRAND. See also -ISH[2].

brandling n. a small red worm with vivid rings, used as bait in angling. WH: 17C. BRAND + -LING[1].

brandreth n. a wooden stand for a barrel, a rick etc. WH: 14–15C. Old Norse brandreith grate, from brandr BRAND + reith carriage, vehicle.

brandy n. a spirit distilled from wine. Also v.t. WH: 17C. Dutch brandewijn, from branden to burn, to distil + wijn WINE.

brank n. buckwheat, Fagopyrum esculentum. WH: 16C. Orig. unknown.

brank-ursine n. the acanthus or bear's breech. WH: 14–15C. French branche ursine or Medieval Latin branca ursina bear's claw. See BRANCH, URSINE.

brash[1] a. vulgarly assertive or pushy. WH: 19C. ? From RASH[1].

brash[2] n. loose, disintegrated rock or rubble. Also a. WH: 18C. Orig. unknown.

brash[3] n. a slight indisposition arising from disorder of the alimentary canal. WH: 14–15C. ? Imit. The original sense was crash, blow, then attack, bout.

brass n. a yellow alloy of copper and zinc. Also a. WH: pre-1200. Old English bræs, of unknown orig.

brassard n. a badge worn on the arm. WH: 16C. French, from bras arm. See also -ARD.

brasserie n. a (usu. small) restaurant, orig. one serving beer as well as wine etc. with the food. WH: 19C. French, orig. brewery, from brasser to brew, from Latin braces spelt.

brassica n. any plant belonging to the genus Brassica of the Cruciferae family (turnip, cabbage etc.). WH: 19C. Latin cabbage.

brassière n. a women's undergarment for supporting the breasts. WH: early 20C. French child's reins, camisole, from bras arm.

brat n. a child, an infant, usu. one who is badly behaved. WH: 16C. ? Old English bratt, from Old Irish bratt cloak. Cp. English dial. brat, orig. cloak, then pinafore, scrap of clothing.

brattice n. a partition for ventilation in a mine. WH: 12–14C. Old French bretesche (Modern French bretèche), from Medieval Latin brittisca, from Old English brittisc BRITISH, i.e. BRETON. A brattice was originally breastwork erected on a fortress for use in a siege.

bratwurst n. a kind of German sausage. WH: early 20C. German, from Brat spit + Wurst sausage. Cp. WURST.

bravado n. ostentatious defiance. WH: 16C. Spanish bravada, from bravo BRAVO[2]. See also -ADO.

brave a. daring, courageous. Also n., v.t., v.i. WH: 15C. French, from Italian bravo bold or Spanish bravo courageous, from Latin barbarus barbarous (BARBARIAN).

bravo[1] int. capital! well done! Also n. WH: 18C. French, from Italian. See BRAVE.

bravo[2] n. a hired assassin. WH: 16C. Italian. See BRAVE.

bravura n. brilliance of execution. Also a. WH: 18C. Italian, from bravo BRAVE. See also -URE.

braw a. fine. WH: 16C. Var. of BRAVE.

brawl[1] v.i. to quarrel noisily. Also v.t., n. WH: 14–15C. Prob. ult. imit. Cp. Dutch brallen to brag. Rel. to BRAY[1].

brawl[2] n. a French dance like a cotillion. WH: 16C. French branle, from branler to shake, from Old French brandeler BRANDISH.

brawn n. muscle, flesh. WH: 12–14C. Old French braon fleshy part of hind leg, from Germanic. Cp. German Braten roast flesh, Old English brǣdan to roast.

braxy n. splenic apoplexy in sheep. Also a. WH: 18C. Orig. uncertain. ? From brack noise, outcry.

bray[1] v.i. to make a harsh, discordant noise, like an ass. Also v.t., n. WH: 12–14C. Old French braire to cry, from Popular Latin bragere, ult. of imit. orig.

†bray[2] v.t. to pound or grind small, esp. with pestle and mortar. WH: 14–15C. Old French breier (Modern French broyer), from Germanic base of BREAK.

braze v.t. to solder with an alloy of brass and zinc. Also n. WH: pre-1200. Old English brasian, from BRASS.

brazen a. made of brass. Also v.t. WH: pre-1200. Old English bræsen, from BRASS. See also -EN[3].

brazier n. a large pan to hold lighted charcoal. WH: 17C. French brasier, from braise live coals. Cp. BRAISE, BREEZE[2].

brazil *n.* a red dyewood produced by the genus *Caesalpinia*, which gave its name to the country in S America. WH: 12–14C. Medieval Latin *brasilium*, of unknown orig. The *Brazil nut* is named from *Brazil*.

breach *n.* the act of breaking. Also *v.t.*, *v.i.* WH: 12–14C. French *brèche*, from Frankish, from Germanic base of BREAK. The word superseded Old English *bryce*, to which it is ultimately related.

bread *n.* a food, made of flour or other meal kneaded into dough, generally with yeast, made into loaves and baked. Also *v.t.* WH: pre-1200. Old English *brēad*, from Germanic, of unknown orig. The regular Old English word for bread was *hlāf* LOAF[1], so that *brēad* meant simply piece, morsel. The current sense dates from the 13C.

breadth *n.* measure from side to side. WH: 16C. English dial. *brede*, from Old English *brǣdu*, from Germanic base of BROAD + -TH[2], based on LENGTH.

break *v.t.* to separate into pieces by violence. Also *v.i.*, *n.* WH: pre-1200. Old English *brecan*, from Germanic, from Indo-European base also of Latin *frangere* to break. Cp. FRACTION.

breaker *n.* a keg, a water-cask. WH: 19C. Spanish *bareca*, *barrica*. See BARRICO.

breakfast *n.* the first meal of the day. Also *v.i.*, *v.t.* WH: 14–15C. BREAK + FAST[2]. Cp. DÉJEUNER. The first meal of the day breaks the abstinence from food during the night.

bream[1] *n.* a freshwater fish of the genus *Abramis*, esp. *A. brama*. WH: 14–15C. Old French *bresme* (Modern French *brème*), from Frankish *brahsima*.

bream[2] *v.t.* to clear (a ship's bottom) of ooze, seaweed, shellfish etc. by burning. WH: 15C. Prob. from Low German, and rel. to BROOM. Cp. Dutch *brem* broom, furze.

breast *n.* either of the organs for the secretion of milk in women. Also *v.t.* WH: pre-1200. Old English *brēost*, from Germanic. Cp. German *Brust*.

breath *n.* the air drawn in and expelled by the lungs in respiration. WH: pre-1200. Old English *brǣth*, from Germanic, from Indo-European, from base meaning to burn, to heat. The original meaning was smell, scent. The current sense replaced Old English *æthm*, *anda*, related to ATMOSPHERE. Cp. German *atmen* to breathe.

breathe *v.i.* to inhale or exhale air. Also *v.t.* WH: 12–14C. See BREATH.

breccia *n.* a rock composed of angular, as distinguished from rounded, fragments cemented together in a matrix. WH: 18C. Italian gravel, rubble, rel. to French *brèche* BREACH.

breech *n.* the portion of a gun behind the bore. Also *v.t.* WH: pre-1200. Old English *brōc*, pl. *brēc*, from Germanic. The original sense (to the 17C) was a garment for the legs and trunk, giving current *breeches* in the 12–14C. The sense back part of a rifle or gun barrel dates from the 16C.

breed *v.t.* to bring forth. Also *v.i.*, *n.* WH: pre-1200. Old English *brēdan*, from Germanic, from base of BROOD.

breeks *n.pl.* breeches. WH: 12–14C. Var. of (pl. of) BREECH.

breeze[1] *n.* a light wind. Also *v.i.* WH: 16C. Prob. from Old Spanish and Portuguese *briza* (Spanish *brisa*) north-east wind. The word was originally used of a trade wind in the tropics, then of a cool wind blowing from the sea on tropical coasts. The general sense of light wind evolved in the 17C.

breeze[2] *n.* a gadfly. WH: pre-1200. Old English *briosa*, of unknown orig.

breeze[3] *n.* small cinders and cinder dust. WH: 16C. French *braise*, earlier *brese*, burning charcoal, hot embers. Cp. BRAZIER.

bregma *n.* the point on the skull where the coronal and sagittal sutures meet. WH: 16C. Greek front of the head.

brehon *n.* an ancient hereditary Irish judge. WH: 16C. Irish *breitheamhan*, gen. pl. of *breitheamh*, from *breith* judgement.

breloque *n.* an ornament attached to a watch-chain. WH: 19C. French drumbeat, prob. of imit. orig.

bremsstrahlung *n.* the electromagnetic radiation caused by an electron colliding with or slowed down by the electric field of a positively charged nucleus. WH: mid-20C. German, from *bremsen* to brake + *Strahlung* radiation.

Bren *n.* a type of light machine-gun. WH: mid-20C. *Br*no, a town in Moravia (now Czech Republic) where originally made + *En*field, a town in Middlesex (now a district of N London), where later made. Cp. *Lee-Enfield*, a rifle formerly used by the British Army,

from J.P. *Lee*, 1831–1904, US designer of the bolt action + *Enfield*, where made.

brent[1] *n.* the smallest of the wild geese, *Branta bernicla*, which visits Britain in the winter. WH: 14–15C. Orig. unknown.

brent[2] *a.* steep, precipitous, lofty. WH: pre-1200. Var. of Old English *brant*, rel. to Old Norse *brattr* steep, lofty.

brer *n.* brother. WH: 19C. Black or S US pronun. of BROTHER.

Breton *n.* a native of Brittany. Also *a.* WH: 14–15C. Old French, see BRITON. Brittany is so named for the Britons who crossed the English Channel to settle there when the Angles, Saxons and Jutes invaded Britain in the 5C.

breve *n.* a sign (˘) used in printing to mark a short vowel. WH: 12–14C. Var. of BRIEF.

brevet *n.* an official document conferring certain privileges. Also *a.*, *v.t.* WH: 14–15C. Old French, from Late Latin *breve* dispatch, note. See BRIEF, also -ET[1].

breveté *a.* patented. WH: 19C. French, p.p. of *breveter* to patent. See BREVET.

brevi- *comb. form* short. WH: Latin *brevis* BRIEF.

breviary *n.* in the Roman Catholic Church, a book containing the divine office. WH: 14–15C. Latin *breviarium* summary, from *breviare*. See ABBREVIATE[1], also -ARY[1].

breviate *a.* abbreviated, short. Also *n.*, *v.t.* WH: 14–15C. Latin *breviatus*, p.p. of *breviare*. See ABBREVIATE[1], also -ATE[2].

brevier *n.* a size of type around 7 point between bourgeois and minion, in which breviaries were formerly printed. WH: 16C. Dutch or German, from Medieval Latin use of *breviarum* BREVIARY, ? because used in printing of breviaries.

breviped *a.* short-footed, short-legged. WH: 19C. BREVI- + -*ped* (-PEDE).

brevipennate *a.* having short wings. WH: 19C. BREVI- + PENNATE.

brevirostrate *a.* having a short bill or beak. WH: 19C. BREVI- + *rostrate* (ROSTRUM).

brevity *n.* briefness, shortness. WH: 15C. Old French *breveté*, earlier *brieté*, from Latin *brevitas*, *brevitatis*, from *brevis* BRIEF. See also -ITY.

brew *v.t.* to make (beer, ale etc.) by steeping and fermenting. Also *v.i.*, *n.* WH: pre-1200. Old English *brēowan*, from Germanic, ? rel. to Latin *fervere* to boil, Greek *phrear* spring, well.

brewis *n.* broth. WH: 12–14C. Old French *broez*, *broets*, sing. *broet* (Modern French *brouet*), from *breu*, from Germanic base also of BROTH.

Briareus *n.* a many-handed person. WH: 17C. Greek *Briareōs* mythological giant with a hundred hands who aided Zeus against the Titans.

bribe *n.* a gift of money etc. offered to anyone to influence their conduct. Also *v.t.*, *v.i.* WH: 14–15C. Old French *briber*, *brimber* to beg, of unknown orig. The original sense of the verb was to steal. This was obsolete by the 16C and the current sense prevailed.

bric-a-brac *n.* fancy ware, curiosities. WH: 19C. French, from obs. *à bric et à brac* at random, prob. of imit. orig.

brick *n.* a block of clay and sand, usu. oblong, moulded and baked, used in building. Also *a.*, *v.t.* WH: 14–15C. Middle Low German and Middle Dutch *bricke*, *brike*, ult. of unknown orig. French *brique* comes from the same source.

brickle *a.* fragile, frail. WH: pre-1200. Var. of BRUCKLE. Cp. MICKLE, var. of *muckle*.

bricole *n.* in billiards, the rebound of a ball from a wall or cushion. WH: 16C. Old French, or from Provençal *bricola* or Italian *briccola*, of unknown orig.

bride *n.* a woman newly married or on the point of being married. Also *v.i.*, *v.t.* WH: pre-1200. Old English *brȳd*, from Germanic, of unknown orig. Not rel. to BIRD.

bridewell *n.* a house of correction, a prison. WH: 16C. St *Bride's Well*, in the City of London, where such a prison stood to the 19C.

bridge[1] *n.* a structure over a river, road etc. to carry a road or path across. Also *v.t.* WH: pre-1200. Old English *brycg*, from Germanic. Cp. German *Brücke*.

bridge[2] *n.* a card game descended from whist, played by partners one of whose hand is exposed at a particular point in the game. WH: 19C. Orig. uncertain. Prob. of E Mediterranean orig. ? Rel. to Russian *birich*, *birjuch* crier, herald.

bridle *n.* a headstall, bit and bearing or riding rein, forming the headgear of a horse or other beast of burden. *Also v.t., v.i.* WH: pre-1200. Old English *brīdel*, from Germanic base of BRAID[1].

Brie *n.* a soft white cheese orig. produced in France. WH: 19C. *Brie*, an agricultural region in NE France.

brief *a.* short in duration. *Also n., v.t.* WH: 12–14C. Old French *brief* (Modern French *bref*), from Latin *brevis* short.

brier[1] *n.* a thorny or prickly shrub, esp. a wild rose. WH: pre-1200. Old English *brēr, brǣr*, of unknown orig.

brier[2] *n.* the white or tree heath, *Erica arborea*. WH: 19C. French *bruyère* heath, from Gaulish, with spelling assim. to BRIER[1].

brig *n.* a square-rigged vessel with two masts. WH: 18C. Shortened form of BRIGANTINE.

brigade *n.* a subdivision of an army, varying in composition in different countries and at different dates. *Also v.t.* WH: 17C. French, from Italian *brigata* troop, company, from *brigare* to contend, to be occupied with, from *briga* strife, contention. See also -ADE.

brigalow *n.* any acacia tree, esp. *Acacia harpophylla*. WH: 19C. Australian Aboriginal, ? from Kamilaroi *burriigal*.

brigand *n.* a robber, a bandit. WH: 14–15C. French, from Italian *brigante*, orig. foot soldier, pres.p. (used as n.) of *brigare*. See BRIGADE.

brigantine *n.* a two-masted vessel square-rigged on both masts but with a fore-and-aft mainsail, and mainmast much longer than the foremast. WH: 16C. Old French *brigandine* (Modern French *brigantin*), from Italian *brigantino*, from *brigante*. See BRIGAND, also -INE.

bright *a.* lighted up, full of light. *Also adv., n.* WH: pre-1200. Old English *beorht, berht, breht*, from Germanic, ult. rel. to FLAGRANT and FLAME.

Bright's disease *n.* inflammation of the kidneys, nephritis. WH: 19C. Richard *Bright*, 1789–1858, English physician.

brigue *n.* strife, intrigue. *Also v.t., v.i.* WH: 14–15C. Old French, from Italian *briga*. See BRIGADE.

brill[1] *n.* a flat sea fish, *Scophthalmus rhombus*, allied to the turbot. WH: 15C. Orig. unknown.

brill[2] *a.* excellent, very pleasing. WH: late 20C. Abbr. of BRILLIANT.

brilliant *a.* shining, sparkling. *Also n.* WH: 17C. French *brillant*, pres.p. of *briller* to shine, from Italian *brillare*, prob. from Latin *berryllus* BERYL.

brim *n.* the upper edge of a vessel. *Also v.t., v.i.* WH: 12–14C. Orig. unknown. Cp. German *Bräme*, Old Norse *barmr* edge.

brimstone *n.* sulphur, esp. in the biblical context of the lake of brimstone. WH: pre-1200. Old English *brynstān*, prob. from *bryne* burning (see BURN[1]) + *stān* STONE.

brindle *a.* tawny, with bars of darker hue. WH: 17C. Alt. of obs. *brinded*, prob. of Scandinavian orig., rel. to *branded*. See BRAND. The *-l-* was probably added under the influence of *grizzled* (GRIZZLE[2]), *speckled* (SPECK) etc.

brine *n.* water strongly impregnated with salt. *Also v.t.* WH: pre-1200. Old English *brīne*, of unknown orig. Cp. Dutch *brijn* brine.

bring *v.t.* to cause to come along with oneself. WH: pre-1200. Old English *bringan*, from Germanic. Cp. German *bringen*.

brinjal *n.* esp. in the Indian subcontinent, an aubergine. WH: 17C. Portuguese *berinjela* AUBERGINE.

brink *n.* the edge or border of a precipice, pit etc. WH: 12–14C. Old Norse *brekka* slope, of unknown orig. Cp. German dial. *Brink* hill, Dutch *brink* grassland.

brio *n.* spirit, liveliness. WH: 18C. Italian liveliness, of Gaulish orig.

brioche *n.* a kind of light sweet bread. WH: 19C. French, from *brier*, alt. of *broyer*. See BRAY[2].

briolet *n.* a pear- or drop-shaped diamond cut with long triangular facets. WH: 19C. French *briolette*, prob. from *brillant*. See BRILLIANT.

briquette *n.* a block of compressed coal dust. *Also v.t.* WH: 19C. French, dim. of *brique* BRICK. See also -ETTE.

brisk *a.* lively, active. *Also v.t., v.i.* WH: 16C. Prob. from French BRUSQUE.

brisket *n.* that part of the breast of an animal which lies next to the ribs. WH: 12–14C. ? Old Norse *brjósk* cartilage, gristle + -ET[1].

brisling *n.* a small herring, a sprat. WH: early 20C. Norwegian and Danish sprat.

bristle *n.* a short, stiff, coarse hair, esp. on the back and sides of swine, in a beard or on a plant. *Also v.t., v.i.* WH: 12–14C. Old English *byrst* bristle + -LE[2].

Bristol board *n.* a thick smooth white cardboard. WH: 16C. *Bristol*, a city and port in W England.

bristols *n.pl.* a woman's breasts. WH: mid-20C. Rhyming slang, *Bristol Cities* = *titties*. See TIT[2]. The specific reference is to the football team *Bristol City*, probably influenced by BREAST and *Bristol milk*, a type of sherry.

Brit *n.* a Briton, a British subject. WH: early 20C. Abbr. of BRITON, BRITISH or *Britisher* (BRITISH).

brit *n.* the spawn and young of the herring and the sprat. WH: 17C. Orig. unknown.

Britannia *n.* Britain personified, esp. as a female figure in a helmet with a shield and trident. WH: pre-1200. Latin *Britannus, Brittanus* Britain. See BRITON.

British *a.* of or relating to Great Britain or the United Kingdom or its inhabitants. *Also n.* WH: pre-1200. Old English *Brettisc, Brittisc*, from *Brit* BRITON + -ISH[1].

Briton *n.* a member of the people inhabiting S Britain at the Roman invasion. WH: 12–14C. Old French *Breton*, from Latin *Britto, Brittonis*, or its Celtic equivalent. See BRYTHON. Cp. BRETON.

Britpop *n.* a type of pop music giving prominence to melody and often imitating 1960s British songs. WH: late 20C. BRITISH + POP[2].

brittle *a.* liable to break or be broken. *Also n.* WH: 14–15C. Old English *gebrythan* to break in pieces, from Germanic base of Old English *brēotan* to break up. See also -LE[3]. A sense transitory, impermanent, was current 16–18C.

britzka *n.* an open carriage with a calash top. WH: 19C. Polish *bryczka*, dim. of *bryka* wagon.

broach *v.t.* to mention, to make public. *Also v.i., n.* WH: 12–14C. Old French *brochier* (Modern French *brocher*), from *broche* spit, from Latin *brocchus*, in phr. *brocci dentes* projecting teeth, prob. from Gaulish. The original sense was to spur, to prick with spurs.

broad *a.* wide, extended across. *Also n., adv.* WH: pre-1200. Old English *brād*, from Germanic.

Brobdingnagian *a.* gigantic, huge. *Also n.* WH: 18C. *Brobdingnag*, land of giants in Swift's *Gulliver's Travels* (1726). See also -IAN.

brocade *n.* silken material with raised figures. *Also v.t.* WH: 16C. Spanish and Portuguese *brocado*, with blend of French *brocart* BROCKET[1], from Italian *broccato* embossed fabric, from *brocco* twisted thread. See also -ADE.

brocard *n.* an elementary principle of law. WH: 16C. French, or from Medieval Latin *brocardus*, from *Brocard* or *Burchard*, *c.*965–1025, bishop of Worms, complier of *Decretum*, a collection of canon law.

broccoli *n.* a variety of cabbage which has greenish flower heads. WH: 17C. Italian, pl. of *broccolo* cabbage sprout, dim. of *brocco* shoot, BROACH.

broch *n.* a prehistoric circular tower, common in Scotland. WH: 17C. Alt. of BURGH. Cp. Old Norse *borg* enclosure, castle.

broché *a.* brocaded, woven with a raised design. WH: 19C. French, p.p. of *brocher* to stitch, brocade. See BROACH.

brochette *n.* a skewer. WH: 15C. French, dim. of *broche* BROACH.

brochure *n.* a small pamphlet. WH: 18C. French stitched work, from *brocher* to stitch. See BROACH, also -URE.

brock *n.* a badger. WH: pre-1200. Old English *broc, brocc*, from Celtic base of Welsh *broch*, Irish, Gaelic *broc*.

Brocken spectre *n.* the shadow of an observer, often enlarged and surrounded by coloured lights, thrown on to a bank of cloud in a high mountain area. WH: 19C. *Brocken*, the highest of the Harz Mountains, N central Germany, where it is particularly observed.

brocket[1] *n.* a stag in its second year with its first horns, which are straight and unbranched. WH: 14–15C. Anglo-French *broquet*, dim. of *broque*, dial. var. of *broche* BROACH. Cp. French *brocard* young doe, brocket. See also -ET[1]. The stag is so called from its pointed horns.

brocket[2] *n.* any small deer of the genus *Mazama*, of Central and S America, which have short, straight antlers. WH: 14–15C. See BROCKET[1].

broderie anglaise *n.* open embroidery on cambric or linen. WH: 19C. French English embroidery. Cp. EMBROIDER, ANGLE.

brogue *n.* a sturdy shoe. *Also v.t.* WH: 16C. Irish and Gaelic *bróg*, from Old Norse *brók*. See BREECH. The sense dialectical accent dates from the 18C, apparently as a form of speech used by those who wore brogues and who referred to them as such.

broil[1] *n.* a tumult, disturbance, contention. WH: 14–15C. Old French *bröoillier* (Modern French *brouiller*), from base of Old French *breu*. See BREWIS.

broil[2] *v.t.* to cook on a gridiron; to grill. *Also v.i., n.* WH: 14–15C. Old French *bruler*, *bruller* to burn (Modern French *brûler*), ? from Germanic base of BURN[1] + Latin *ustulare* to burn up.

broke *a.* ruined, penniless. WH: 12–14C. Former p.p. of BREAK. Cp. BROKEN.

broken *a.* in pieces. WH: 12–14C. P.p. of BREAK.

broker *n.* an agent, a factor. WH: 12–14C. Anglo-French *brocour*, *brogour*, rel. to Provençal *abrocador*, of unknown orig. ? Rel. to BROACH. The original sense of trader, pedlar merged with the current sense in the 16C.

brolga *n.* a large Australian crane, *Grus rubicunda*, which has a red-and-green head and a trumpeting call. WH: 19C. Australian Aboriginal (Kamilaroi) *burralga*.

brolly *n.* an umbrella. WH: 19C. Alt. of UMBRELLA. See also -Y[3].

brome grass *n.* any grass of the genus *Bromus*, esp. *B. inermis*, a cultivated fodder-grass. WH: 18C. Modern Latin *Bromus*, from Latin *bromos*, from Greek *bromos*, *brōmos* oats.

bromelia *n.* any plant of the family Bromeliaceae, esp. of the genus *Bromelia*, which have short stems and stiff spiny leaves, such as the pineapple. WH: 19C. Modern Latin, from Olaf *Bromel*, 1639–1705, Swedish botanist. See also -IA.

bromine *n.* a non-metallic, dark red, liquid element, at. no. 35, chem. symbol Br, with a strong, irritating odour. WH: 19C. French *brome*, from Greek *brōmos* stink. See also -INE.

bromo- *comb. form* of or relating to bromine. WH: Comb. form of BROMINE. See also -O-.

bronc *n.* a bronco. WH: 19C. Abbr. of BRONCO.

bronchiectasis *n.* abnormal dilation of the bronchial tubes. WH: 19C. Greek *brogkhia*, pl. of *brogkhos* BRONCHUS + *ektasis* dilation.

bronchiole *n.* any of the tiny branches of the bronchi. WH: 19C. Modern Latin *bronchiolus*, dim. of Late Latin *bronchia*, from Greek *brogkhia* (BRONCHUS) + dim. suf. *-olus.* ·

bronchitis *n.* inflammation of the bronchial tubes. WH: 19C. BRONCHUS + -ITIS.

bronchocele *n.* abnormal swelling of the thyroid gland, goitre. WH: 17C. Greek *brogkhos* BRONCHUS + -O- + -CELE.

bronchodilator *n.* a substance which causes widening of the bronchi, used by people with asthma. WH: early 20C. Greek *brogkhos* BRONCHUS + -O- + *dilator* (DILATE).

bronchopneumonia *n.* pneumonia originating in the bronchial tubes. WH: 19C. Greek *brogkhos* BRONCHUS + -O- + PNEUMONIA.

bronchoscope *n.* an instrument which is inserted in the bronchial tubes for the purpose of examination or extraction. WH: 19C. Greek *brogkhos* BRONCHUS + -O- + -SCOPE.

bronchotomy *n.* the operation of opening the windpipe, tracheotomy. WH: 18C. Greek *brogkhos* BRONCHUS + -O- + -TOMY.

bronchus *n.* any of the main divisions of the windpipe. WH: 17C. Late Latin, from Greek *brogkhos* windpipe, pl. *brogkhia* ramifications of windpipe.

bronco *n.* a wild or half-tamed horse of California or New Mexico. WH: 19C. Spanish rough, rude.

brontosaurus *n.* an apatosaurus. WH: 19C. Modern Latin, from Greek *brontē* thunder + *sauros* lizard. The name alludes to the animal's great size.

bronze *n.* a brown alloy of copper and tin, sometimes with a little zinc or lead. *Also a., v.t., v.i.* WH: 17C. French, from Italian *bronzo*, prob. from Persian *birinj* brass.

brooch *n.* an ornamental clasp with a pin, worn on clothing. *Also v.t.* WH: 12–14C. Var. of BROACH.

brood *n.* a family of birds hatched at once. *Also v.i., v.t.* WH: pre-1200. Old English *brōd*, from Germanic, from Indo-European base meaning to warm, to heat. Cp. German *Brut*.

brook[1] *n.* a small stream. WH: pre-1200. Old English *brōc*, from Germanic, of unknown orig. Cp. German *Bruch* marsh, bog.

brook[2] *v.t.* to endure, to put up with. WH: pre-1200. Old English *brūcan*, from Germanic base meaning to use. Cp. German *brauchen* to use. Rel. to Latin *frui* to enjoy, and so to FRUIT. The sense to use was current to the 16C, and the current sense dates from then.

broom *n.* a shrub with yellow flowers belonging to the genus *Sarothamnus* or *Cytisus*, esp. *Cytisus scoparius*. *Also v.t.* WH: pre-1200. Old English *brōm*, from Germanic base also of BRAMBLE.

brose *n.* a kind of porridge made by pouring water on oatmeal or oatcake, with seasoning. WH: 17C. Var. of BREWIS.

broth *n.* the liquor in which anything, esp. meat, has been boiled. WH: pre-1200. Old English, from Germanic, from base of BREW.

brothel *n.* premises where prostitutes sell their services. WH: 14–15C. Ult. from Old English *brēothan* to deteriorate, to degenerate, of unknown orig. The original sense was worthless fellow, then prostitute, and the current sense is from *brothel-house*, house of prostitution.

brother *n.* a son of the same parents or parent. WH: pre-1200. Old English *brōther*, *brōder*, from Germanic, from Indo-European source that also gave Latin *frater*, Greek *phratēr*, Sanskrit *bhrātr*.

brougham *n.* a close, four-wheeled carriage drawn by one horse. WH: 19C. Henry Peter, Lord *Brougham*, 1778–1868, who designed it, c.1838.

brouhaha *n.* a tumult, a row. WH: 19C. French, of imit. orig.

brow *n.* the ridge over the eye. *Also v.t.* WH: pre-1200. Old English *brū*, from Germanic, from Indo-European. The original Old English (pl.) sense was eyelashes. The sense then passed to eyelids, to eyebrows, to the prominent part of the forehead, and finally to the forehead as a whole. Cp. BRAE.

brown *a.* of the colour of dark wood, scorched paper or dark soil; of the compound colour produced by a mixture of red, black and yellow. *Also n., v.t., v.i.* WH: pre-1200. Old English *brūn*, from Germanic. Ult. rel. to BEAR[1], BEAVER[1]. The original Old English sense was dark, dusky, and the current colour sense emerged in the 13C.

Brownian movement *n.* random agitation of particles suspended in a fluid caused by bombardment of the particles by molecules of the fluid. WH: 19C. Robert *Brown*, 1773–1858, English botanist + -IAN.

Brownism *n.* the Congregationalist scheme of Church government adopted in a modified form by the Independents. WH: 17C. Robert *Browne*, c.1550–c.1633, Puritan separatist + -ISM.

browse *v.t.* to nibble and eat off (twigs, young shoots etc.). *Also v.i., n.* WH: 14–15C. Old French *broster* to crop (Modern French *brouter*), from *brost* (Modern French *brout*) bud, young shoot, prob. from Germanic.

brucellosis *n.* an infectious bacterial disease in animals, caused by bacteria of the genus *Brucella*, which is also contagious to humans (also called *contagious abortion*, *Malta* or *undulant fever*). WH: mid-20C. Modern Latin, from Sir David *Bruce*, 1855–1931, Scottish physician + -*ella* + -OSIS.

brucine *n.* a poisonous alkaloid found in the seed and bark of *Nux vomica* and other species of *Strychnos*. WH: 19C. Modern Latin *Brucea*, from James *Bruce*, 1730–94, Scottish traveller. See also -INE.

brucite *n.* a mineral form of magnesium hydroxide. WH: 19C. Archibald *Bruce*, 1777–1818, US mineralogist + -ITE[1].

bruckle *a.* fragile, brittle, precarious, ticklish. WH: pre-1200. Old English -*brucol*, -*brycel*, ult. from Germanic base of BREAK.

Bruin *n.* (a personal name for) the brown bear. WH: 15C. Dutch brown, name of the bear in *Reynard the Fox* (12–13C). See BROWN.

bruise *v.t.* to crush, indent or discolour, by a blow from something blunt and heavy. *Also v.i., n.* WH: pre-1200. Old English *brȳsan*, influ. in Middle English by Old French *bruisier* (Modern French *briser*) to break, to smash, of unknown orig. The original sense was stronger, to crush, to mangle. The current weaker sense dates from the 16C. The former sense is still implicit in *bruiser*, meaning strong man.

bruit *v.t.* to rumour, to noise abroad. *Also n.* WH: 15C. Old French, p.p. (used as n.) of *bruire* to roar, from alt. of Latin *rugire* to roar, by assoc. with source of BRAY[1].

brûlé *a.* cooked with caramelized brown sugar. WH: early 20C. French burnt, p.p. of *brûler* to burn. Cp. BROIL[2].

Brum *n.* Birmingham, England. WH: 19C. Shortening of *Birmingham*. Cp. BRUMMAGEM.

brumby *n.* a wild horse. WH: 19C. Orig. unknown.

brume *n.* mist, fog, vapour. WH: 18C. French fog, from Latin *bruma* winter.

Brummagem *a.* cheap and ostentatious. *Also n.* WH: 17C. Dial. form of *Birmingham*. Cp. BRUM.

brunch *n.* a meal which combines a late breakfast with an early lunch. *Also v.i.* WH: 19C. Blend of BREAKFAST and LUNCH.

brunette *n.* a girl or woman with dark hair and a dark complexion. *Also a.* WH: 16C. French *brunet* (m.), *brunette* (fem.), dim. of *brun* BROWN. See also -ETTE.

brunt *n.* the shock or force of an attack. WH: 14–15C. Latin. Orig. unknown. ? From Scandinavian. Cp. Old Norse *bruna* to advance in battle with the speed of fire. To the 17C, the sense was blow, attack. Hence *to bear the brunt* to receive the blow, to face the assault.

bruscamente *adv.* strongly accented. WH: 19C. Italian roughly, abruptly, from *brusco* rough, abrupt. Cp. BRUSQUE.

bruschetta *n.* a type of Italian open toasted sandwich, eaten as an appetizer or snack. WH: late 20C. Italian, from *brusco* sour. Cp. BRUSQUE.

brush¹ *n.* an instrument for cleaning, generally made of bristles or feathers. *Also v.t., v.i.* WH: 12–14C. Old French *broisse*, *brosse* and (in the sense brushwood) *broce* (Modern French *brousse*), both prob. ult. from Latin *bruscum* excrescence on a maple.

brush² *n.* a young woman, a girl. WH: mid-20C. Prob. from BRUSH¹ (in sense of fox's tail). Cp. TAIL¹ (in slang sense of a woman, especially regarded sexually).

brusque *a.* rough or blunt in manner. WH: 17C. French lively, fierce, harsh, from Italian *brusco* sour, tart. Cp. BRISK.

Brussels *a.* made at or derived from Brussels. *Also n.* WH: 18C. *Brussels*, a city in the Low Countries, now the capital of Belgium.

brut *a.* (of wine) dry, unsweetened. WH: 19C. French rough, raw, from Latin *brutus*. See BRUTE.

brute *n.* an animal as opposed to a human being; a beast. *Also a.* WH: 14–15C. French *brut*, *brute*, from Latin *brutus* heavy, stupid.

bruxism *n.* the unconscious habit of grinding the teeth. WH: mid-20C. Greek *brukhein* to gnash the teeth + -ISM.

Brylcreem® *n.* a cream smoothed into the hair to make it shiny. WH: early 20C. Respelling of *brill(iantine)* (BRILLIANT) + CREAM.

bryology *n.* the science of mosses. WH: 19C. Greek *bruon* moss + -O- + -LOGY.

bryony *n.* a climbing plant of the genus *Bryonia*, esp. *B. dioica*, with whitish flowers. WH: pre-1200. Latin *bryonia*, from Greek *bruōnia*, from *bruein* to swell, to burgeon.

bryophyte *n.* a cryptogamous plant of the division Bryophyta, consisting of the liverworts and mosses. WH: 19C. Modern Latin *Bryophyta*, from Greek *bruon* moss + -PHYTE.

bryozoan *n.* any one of the lowest class of the mollusca, of the phylum Bryozoa, also called *polyzoan*. WH: 19C. Modern Latin *Bryozoa*, from Greek *bruon* moss + -ZOA.

Brython *n.* a member of the Celtic people occupying S Britain at the time of the Roman invasion, as distinguished from the Goidels. WH: 19C. Welsh BRITON.

BSE *n.* a disease of the central nervous system in cattle, usu. fatal, also called *mad cow disease*. WH: late 20C. Abbr. of bovine spongiform encephalopathy.

bub *n.* (as a form of address) boy. WH: 19C. Abbr. of *bubby*, childish form of BROTHER, or from German *Bube* boy.

bubal *n.* the hartebeest. WH: 18C. French *bubale*, from Latin *bubalus* BUFFALO.

bubble *n.* a sphere of water or other liquid filled with air or other gas. *Also a., v.i., v.t.* WH: 12–14C. Partly imit., partly alt. of BURBLE.

bubo *n.* an inflamed swelling of the lymphatic glands, esp. in the groin or armpit. WH: 14–15C. Latin, from Greek *boubōn* groin, swelling in the groin.

buccal *a.* of or relating to the cheek or the mouth. WH: 19C. Latin *bucca* cheek + -AL¹.

buccaneer *n.* a piratical rover, orig. on the Spanish Main. *Also v.i.* WH: 17C. French *boucanier*, from Tupi *mukem*, *mocaém* wooden frame for cooking. Cp. BARBECUE. See also -EER. A buccaneer was originally a hunter who cooked meat on such a frame.

buccinator *n.* the flat, thin muscle forming the wall of the cheek, used in blowing. WH: 17C. Latin, from *buccinare* to blow the trumpet, from *buccina* kind of trumpet, from *bucca* cheek. See also -ATOR.

Buchmanism *n.* a non-denominational evangelical religious movement of American origin, also known as the Oxford Group, now more usually Moral Rearmament. WH: early 20C. Frank *Buchman*, 1878–1961, US evangelist + -ISM.

buck¹ *n.* the male of the fallow deer, reindeer, goat, hare and rabbit. *Also a., v.i., v.t.* WH: pre-1200. Old English *buc* male deer, *bucca* he-goat, from Germanic.

buck² *n.* the body of a wagon or cart. WH: 17C. Prob. var. of *bouk* belly, body, from Old English *būc*, from Germanic.

buck³ *n.* a sawhorse. WH: 19C. Dutch *zaagbok*. See SAW¹, BUCK¹.

buckbean *n.* a water plant having pinkish-white flowers, of the genus *Menyanthes*, esp. *M. trifoliata*, also called the *bogbean*. WH: 16C. Flemish *bocks boonen* goat's beans. See BUCK¹, BEAN.

bucket *n.* a vessel with a handle, for carrying water. *Also v.t., v.i.* WH: 12–14C. Anglo-French *buket*, *buquet* tub, pail, ? from Old English *būc* belly, pitcher. See also -ET¹.

buckie *n.* a spiral shell, e.g. the whelk. WH: 16C. ? Latin *buccinum* whelk, from *buccina*. See BUCCINATOR.

buckle *n.* a link of metal etc., for fastening straps etc. *Also v.t., v.i.* WH: 12–14C. Old French *bocle* (Modern French *boucle*), from Latin *buccula* cheek strap of a helmet, dim. of *bucca* cheek.

Buckley's *n.* no chance at all. WH: 19C. Orig. uncertain. ? From William *Buckley*, 1780–1856, an escaped convict who lived for 32 years with Aborigines in Victoria, Australia. The word is also said to be from the firm *Buckley* and Nunn, so that one had two chances: *Buckley's* or NONE¹.

buckling *n.* a smoked herring. WH: early 20C. German *Bückling* bloater, from Middle Dutch *buckinc*, from *bok* BUCK¹. The herring is so named because of its goatlike odour.

buckminsterfullerene *n.* a form of carbon with 60 atoms arranged at the vertices of a polyhedron with hexagonal and pentagonal faces, also called a *Bucky ball*. WH: late 20C. Richard *Buckminster Fuller*, 1895–1983, US engineer and architect who invented the geodesic dome + -ENE.

bucko *n.* a swaggering or bullying person. *Also a.* WH: 19C. BUCK¹ + -O.

buckram *n.* a strong coarse kind of linen cloth, stiffened with gum. *Also a., v.i.* WH: 12–14C. Old French *boquerant* (Modern French *bougran*), ? from *Bukhara*, a town in central Asia (now in Uzbekistan). The change of *-n* to *-m* is as for GROGRAM, VELLUM. The original sense was fine linen. The current sense dates from the 15C.

Buck's Fizz *n.* a cocktail of champagne or sparkling wine mixed with orange juice. WH: mid-20C. *Buck's* Club, London + FIZZ. The cocktail is said to have been invented by the club's first barman, but it was known in Paris before the club was founded by Captain Herbert *Buckmaster* and others, 1919.

buckshee *n.* something for nothing, a windfall. *Also a.* WH: early 20C. Alt. of BAKSHEESH.

buckwheat *n.* a cereal plant of the genus *Fagopyrum*, esp. *F. esculentum*, the three-cornered seeds of which are given to horses and poultry, and in the US are used for cakes. WH: 16C. Middle Dutch *boecweite* or Middle Low German *bōkwēte* beech wheat. The plant is so called because its grains resemble beechmast.

bucolic *a.* pastoral, rustic. *Also n.* WH: 16C. Latin *bucolicus*, from Greek *boukolikos*, from *boukolos* herdsman, from *bous* ox. See also -IC.

bud¹ *n.* the germ of a branch, cluster of leaves or flower, usu. arising from the axil of a leaf. *Also v.i., v.t.* WH: 14–15C. Orig. unknown. ? Ult. rel. to source of BOIL¹.

bud² *n.* buddy, pal. WH: 19C. Abbr. of BUDDY.

Buddha *n.* the title given to Gautama, the founder of Buddhism, by his disciples. WH: 17C. Sanskrit enlightened, p.p. of *budh-* to awake, to know.

buddle *n.* an oblong inclined vat in which ore is washed. *Also v.t.* WH: 16C. Orig. unknown.

buddleia *n.* any shrub of the genus *Buddleia*, which have fragrant lilac, orange or white flowers. WH: 18C. Modern Latin, from Rev. Adam *Buddle*, 1660–1715, English amateur botanist. See also -IA.

buddy *n.* a close friend, pal. *Also a., v.i.* WH: 19C. Alt. of BROTHER or var. of BUTTY¹.

budge[1] *v.i.* to move from one's place. *Also v.t.* WH: 16C. French *bouger*, from (freq. form of) Latin *bullire*, from *bulla* bubble. Cp. Italian *bulicare* to bubble up.

budge[2] *n.* a kind of fur made of lambskin with the wool outwards. *Also a.* WH: 14–15C. Orig. unknown.

budgeree *a.* good, excellent. WH: 18C. Australian Aboriginal (Dharuk) *bujiri*.

budgerigar *n.* an Australian green parakeet, *Melopsittacus undulatus*. WH: 19C. Australian Aboriginal, ? mispronun. of Kamilaroi *gijirrigaa*. According to some, the word is from Dharuk *bujiri* good (see BUDGEREE) + *gar* cockatoo.

budget *n.* an estimate of receipts and expenditure, esp. the annual financial statement of the Chancellor of the Exchequer in the House of Commons. *Also v.i., v.t., a.* WH: 14–15C. Old French *bougette*, dim. of *bouge* leather bag, from Latin *bulga*. See BULGE, also -ET[1]. The original sense was pouch, wallet. This then evolved to bundle, stock, referring to the contents of a bag. The current parliamentary sense arose from the fact that the Chancellor 'opens his budget' when presenting his statement. It dates from the 18C.

budgie *n.* a budgerigar. WH: early 20C. Abbr. of BUDGERIGAR. See also -Y[3].

buff[1] *n.* the colour of buff leather, light yellow. *Also a., v.t.* WH: 16C. Shortened form of Old French *buffle*, from Italian *bufalo*. See BUFFALO.

buff[2] *n.* a blow, a buffet. WH: 14–15C. Old French *bufe* BUFFET[1]. Cp. BUFFER.

buffalo *n.* an Asiatic ox of the genus *Bubalus*, esp. *B. arnee*, the water buffalo. *Also v.t.* WH: 16C. Portuguese *bufalo* (now *bufaro*), from Late Latin *bufalus*, from Latin *bubalus*, from Greek *boubalos* wild ox, antelope. Cp. BUFF[1].

buffer *n.* a mechanical apparatus for deadening or sustaining the force of a concussion. *Also v.t.* WH: 14–15C. Prob. from BUFF[1], imit. of sound made by soft inflated object when struck + -ER[1]. Cp. BUFF[2].

buffet[1] *n.* a blow with the hand or fist, a cuff. *Also v.t., v.i.* WH: 12–14C. Old French *bufet*, dim. of *bufe* BUFF[2]. See also -ET[2].

buffet[2] *n.* a cupboard or sideboard for the display of plate, china etc. WH: 18C. French, from Old French *bufet*, *buffet*, of unknown orig.

bufflehead *n.* a black and white duck, *Bucephala albeola*, also called *butterball*. WH: 16C. From *buffle*, from Old French, from Italian *bufalo* (see BUFFALO) + HEAD[1].

buffo *n.* a singer in a comic opera. *Also a.* WH: 18C. Italian puff of wind, buffoon, from *buffare*. See BUFFOON.

buffoon *n.* a person who indulges in jests. WH: 16C. French *bouffon*, from Italian *buffone*, from Medieval Latin *buffo* clown, from v. of imit. orig. meaning to puff. See also -OON.

bug[1] *n.* any insect of the order Hemiptera, esp. the blood-sucking, evil-smelling insect, *Cimex lectularius*, found in bedsteads etc. *Also v.t.* WH: 17C. ? Old English *-budda* as in *scearnbudda* dung beetle, or rel. to BUG[2].

bug[2] *n.* a hobgoblin, a bugbear. WH: 14–15C. Rel. to BOGGARD, BOGLE etc. The connection with Welsh *bwg* ghost, hobgoblin is not clear.

bugger *n.* a sodomite. *Also int., v.t.* WH: 12–14C. Middle Dutch, from Old French *bougre*, orig. heretic, then sodomite, from Medieval Latin *Bulgarus* BULGARIAN. The word was originally used of a sect of Bulgarian heretics to whom homosexual practices were attributed in the 11C.

buggy *n.* a light, four-wheeled or two-wheeled vehicle, having a single seat. WH: 18C. Orig. unknown.

bugle[1] *n.* a hunting-horn, orig. made from the horn of a wild ox. *Also v.t., v.i.* WH: 12–14C. Old French, from Latin *buculus*, dim. of *bos* ox.

bugle[2] *n.* a long, slender glass bead, usu. black, for trimming dresses. WH: 16C. Orig. unknown.

bugle[3] *n.* a creeping plant of the genus *Ajuga*, esp. *A. reptans*. WH: 12–14C. Late Latin *bugula*.

bugloss *n.* any of various plants of the borage family, esp. the genus *Anchusa*, with rough, hairy leaves. WH: 14–15C. Old French *buglosse*, from Latin *buglossus*, from Greek *bouglōssus* ox-tongued, from *bous* ox + *glōssa* tongue. The name refers to the plant's rough, hairy leaves.

buhl *n.* brass, tortoiseshell etc. cut into ornamental patterns for inlaying. *Also a.* WH: 19C. German *Buhl* and French *boule*, from André Charles *Boule*, 1642–1732, French cabinetmaker.

build *v.t.* to make by putting together parts and materials. *Also v.i., n.* WH: pre-1200. Old English *byldan*, from *bold*, *botl* dwelling, house, from Germanic, from base meaning to dwell found also in BOWER[1].

bulb *n.* a subterranean stem or bud sending off roots below and leaves above, as in the onion or lily. *Also v.i.* WH: 14–15C. Latin *bulbus*, from Greek *bolbos* onion, bulbous root. The original sense was invariably onion. The present wider sense dates from the 17C. It was transferred to a light bulb in the 19C.

bulbul *n.* an Eastern bird of the family Pycnonotidae. WH: 17C. Persian, of imit. orig.

bulgar *n.* wheat that has been boiled and then dried. WH: early 20C. Turkish, from Persian *bulgūr* bruised grain.

Bulgarian *n.* a native or inhabitant of Bulgaria. *Also a.* WH: 16C. Medieval Latin *Bulgaria*, a country in the E Balkans + -IAN.

bulge *n.* a swelling on a surface. *Also v.i., v.t.* WH: 12–14C. Old French *boulge*, from Latin *bulga* leather sack, bag, of Gaulish orig. Cp. BUDGET. The original meaning was wallet, pouch. This sense was applied to a ship's hull in the 17C, but has now been superseded by BILGE. The general sense of swelling dates from the 18C.

bulimia *n.* a medical condition characterized by overeating. WH: 14–15C. Medieval Latin *bolismus*, or from Modern Latin *bulimia*, from Greek *boulimia* ravenous hunger, from *bou-* huge (from *bous* ox) + *limos* hunger. See also -IA.

bulk[1] *n.* magnitude of three dimensions. *Also v.i., v.t.* WH: 12–14C. Old Norse *búlki* cargo, influ. by *bouk* belly, bulk, from Old English *būc* belly.

bulk[2] *n.* a framework projecting in front of a shop for displaying goods. WH: 16C. Prob. from BAULK.

bulkhead *n.* an upright partition dividing a ship, aircraft etc. into compartments. WH: 15C. See BULK[2] + HEAD[1].

bull[1] *n.* the uncastrated male of any bovine mammal, esp. of the domestic species, *Bos taurus*. *Also a., v.i., v.t.* WH: pre-1200. Old English *bula*, from Old Norse *boli*, rel. to source of BULGE.

bull[2] *n.* a papal edict. WH: 12–14C. Old French *bulle*, from Latin BULLA seal, sealed document.

bull[3] *n.* a ludicrous contradiction in terms, supposed to be characteristic of the Irish, an Irish bull. WH: 17C. Orig. unknown, but usu. assoc. with *bullshit* (BULL[1]).

bull[4] *n.* drink made by putting water into an empty spirit cask to acquire the flavour of the liquor. WH: 19C. Orig. unknown.

bulla *n.* a round pendant worn by Roman children. WH: 19C. Latin bubble.

bullace *n.* a wild plum, *Prunus insititia*, having two varieties, one with white, the other with dark fruit. WH: 12–14C. Old French *buloce*, *beloce* sloe, ? of Gaulish orig.

bulldoze *v.t.* to level or cone used in firearms of small calibre. WH: 19C. ? From BULL[1] + alt. of DOSE. The colloquial sense would thus be to bully, to coerce with a dose fit for a bull. The word is not an alteration of *bull-nose* as sometimes explained.

bullet *n.* a metal ball or cone used in firearms of small calibre. WH: 16C. French *boulet*, *boulette*, dim. of *boule* BALL[1]. See also -ET[1]. The word was originally used in the sense cannonball. The current sense soon followed, but at first was usually defined by a distinguishing word such as little or musket.

bulletin *n.* an official report of some matter of public interest, e.g. of the condition of an invalid. *Also v.t.* WH: 17C. French, from Italian *bulletino*, *bolletino*, from *bulletta* passport, dim. of *bulla* BULL[2]. The original sense was note, warrant. The current sense evolved in the 18C, initially for a report on a sick person's health, then for a war or battle report.

bullion *n.* uncoined gold and silver in the mass. *Also a.* WH: 12–14C. Anglo-French, appar. mint, from var. of Old French *bouillon*, from Latin *bullire* to boil. See also -ION.

bully[1] *n.* a blustering, overbearing person. *Also a., v.t., v.i.* WH: 16C. Prob. from Middle Dutch *boole* lover. The original sense was sweetheart, darling, then good (male) friend, mate, then as now from the 17C.

bully[2] *n.* tinned beef. WH: 18C. Alt. of BOUILLI.

bully[3] *n.* in hockey, the starting of a game by striking sticks on the ground and then above the ball three times and then attempting to hit the ball. *Also v.i.* WH: 19C. Prob. from *bully*, a scrum in Eton football, of unknown orig.

bulrush n. either of two tall rushes growing in water, *Scirpus lacustris* and *Typha latifolia*, the reed mace or cat's-tail. WH: 14–15C. Prob. from BULL¹ in sense large, coarse (cp. *bullfrog*, *bullfinch*) + RUSH².

bulwark n. a rampart or fortification. *Also v.t.* WH: 14–15C. Middle Low German and Middle Dutch *bolwerk*, ult. from source of BOLE¹ + WORK.

bum¹ n. the buttocks. WH: 14–15C. Orig. unknown. The word is recorded earlier than BUMP¹.

bum² n. a tramp. *Also a., v.i., v.t.* WH: 19C. Prob. from German *bummeln* to stroll, to loaf. Cp. German *Bummel* stroll, journey.

bum³ v.i. to make a humming noise. WH: 14–15C. Var. of BOOM¹.

bumalo n. Bombay duck; a small Asian fish, dried and used as a relish. WH: 17C. ? Marathi *bombīl*.

Bumble n. a beadle. WH: 19C. *Bumble*, parish beadle in Charles Dickens' *Oliver Twist* (1838–41). The word already existed in the sense blunderer, idler.

bumble v.i. to buzz, to boom. *Also n.* WH: 14–15C. Partly from BOOM¹, BUM³ + -LE⁴, partly from *bumble* confusion, jumble, of imit. orig. Cp. BUMBLE.

bumboat n. a boat used to carry provisions to vessels. WH: 17C. Appar. from BUM¹ + BOAT. The original sense was a scavenger's boat appointed to remove 'filth' from the Thames.

bumf n. toilet paper. WH: 19C. Abbr. of *bum-fodder*. See BUM¹, FODDER.

bumiputra n. a Malaysian of indigenous Malay origin. *Also a.* WH: mid-20C. Malay, from Sanskrit son of the soil.

bumkin n. a small boom projecting from each bow to extend the foresail. WH: 17C. Dutch *boomken*, from *boom* tree, BOOM² + -ken -KIN.

bump¹ n. a thump, a dull, heavy blow. *Also v.t., v.i., adv.* WH: 16C. Imit., ? from Scandinavian. Cp. Middle Danish *bumpe* to strike with the fist.

bump² n. the cry of the bittern. *Also v.i.* WH: 16C. Imit.

bumpkin n. a country lout. WH: 16C. ? Dutch *boomken* little tree (see BOOM² + -KIN), or from Middle Dutch *bommekijn* little barrel, in sense squat figure.

bumptious a. disagreeably self-opinionated. WH: 19C. Prob. from BUMP¹, based on FRACTIOUS.

bun¹ n. a small sweet roll or cake. WH: 14–15C. Orig. unknown. ? Alt. of Old French *buignet* fritter.

bun² n. a squirrel. WH: 16C. Orig. unknown. Cp. BUNNY.

Buna® n. a type of artificial rubber. WH: mid-20C. German, from BUTADIENE + *Na*(*trium*) sodium.

bunce n. extra profit. WH: 18C. Orig. unknown.

bunch n. a cluster of several things of the same kind tied together. *Also v.t., v.i.* WH: 14–15C. Orig. unknown. The original sense was lump, swelling. The current sense arose in the 16C.

bund n. an embankment, a dam or causeway. WH: 19C. Urdu *band*, from Persian.

Bundesrat n. the Upper House of Parliament in Germany or Austria. WH: 19C. German, from gen. of *Bund* confederation + *Rat* council.

Bundestag n. the Lower House of Parliament in Germany. WH: 19C. German, from gen. of *Bund* confederation + *tagen* to confer.

bundle n. a number of things or a quantity of anything bound together loosely. *Also v.t., v.i.* WH: 14–15C. ? Old English *byndelle* binding, but later influ. by Low German, Dutch *bundel* bundle.

bundook n. a musket or rifle, a gun. WH: 19C. Urdu *bandūk*, from Persian *bundūk* firearm.

bundu n. the back of beyond, the far interior. WH: mid-20C. Shona *bundo* grasslands.

bung¹ n. a large cork stopper for a bung-hole. *Also v.t.* WH: 14–15C. Middle Dutch *bonghe*, of unknown orig.

bung² a. dead. WH: 19C. Australian Aboriginal (Jagara) *bang*.

bungalow n. a one-storeyed house. WH: 17C. Hindi *banglā* BENGALI. Cp. BANGLADESHI. The word was originally used of a single-storey house in India. The current sense, used of any one-storeyed dwelling, dates from the 19C.

bungee n. an elasticated cord. WH: early 20C. Orig. unknown.

bungle v.t. to botch. *Also v.i., n.* WH: 16C. Imit. Prob. from Scandinavian. Cp. Swedish *bangla* to work ineffectually, rel. to Old Swedish *banga* to strike. Cp. BANG.

bunion n. a swelling on the foot, esp. of the joint of the big toe. WH: 18C. ? Extension of *bunny* swelling, from Old French *buigne* bump on the head, from Old French *buignon*, from *buigne*. See also -OON.

bunk¹ n. a box or recess serving for a bed. *Also v.i.* WH: 18C. Orig. unknown. ? Rel. to BANK³ and so to BENCH.

bunk² v.i. to make off, to bolt. *Also n.* WH: 19C. Orig. unknown. ? Rel. in some way to BUNK¹. (A boy running away to sea would have his berth in a bunk.)

bunko n. a swindling game or confidence trick. *Also v.t.* WH: 19C. ? Spanish *banca* a card game.

bunkum n. insincere political talk. WH: 19C. *Buncombe* County, N Carolina, USA, whose representative, Felix Walker, made a long and pointless speech in Congress simply to please his constituents.

bunny n. a rabbit (used by or to children). WH: 17C. BUN² + -Y³.

Bunsen burner n. a burner or lamp in which air is mingled with gas to produce an intense flame. WH: 19C. Robert W. *Bunsen*, 1811–99, German chemist.

bunt¹ n. the middle part of a sail, formed into a cavity to hold the wind. WH: 16C. Orig. unknown.

bunt² n. a fungus, *Tilletia caries*, which attacks wheat. WH: 17C. Orig. unknown.

bunt³ v.t. (of an animal) to butt. *Also v.i., n.* WH: 18C. Prob. from BUTT⁴.

buntal n. straw obtained from the leaves of the talipot palm. WH: early 20C. Tagalog.

bunter n. new red sandstone. WH: 19C. German *bunter* (*Sandstein*), from *bunt* variegated.

bunting¹ n. a bird of the family Emberizidae, related to the finches. WH: 12–14C. Orig. unknown. ? Rel. to German *bunt* speckled. Cp. BUNTER.

bunting² n. a thin woollen material of which flags are made. WH: 18C. Orig. unknown.

bunya bunya n. a large conifer, *Araucaria bidwillii*, with edible seeds. WH: 19C. Australian Aboriginal (Jagara).

bunyip n. the fabulous rainbow serpent that lives in pools. WH: 19C. Australian Aboriginal (Wemba-Wemba) *banib*.

buoy n. an anchored float indicating a fairway, reef, shoal etc. *Also v.t.* WH: 12–14C. Prob. from Middle Dutch *boeye*, *boeie* (Dutch *boei*), from Germanic base meaning signal, and so rel. to BEACON, BECKON.

bur n. any prickly or spinous fruit, calyx or involucre. WH: 12–14C. Scandinavian (cp. Danish *burre* bur, burdock), or from French (cp. *bourre* vine bud). Cp. BURL¹.

burb n. a suburb. WH: mid-20C. Abbr. of SUBURB.

Burberry® n. a type of weatherproof cloth or clothing. WH: early 20C. Thomas *Burberry*, 1835–1926, English cloth manufacturer.

burble v.i. to talk inconsequentially or excitedly. *Also n.* WH: 12–14C. Imit. Cp. BABBLE, BARBARIAN.

burbot n. an eel-like flat-headed freshwater fish, *Lota lota*. WH: 12–14C. Old French *barbete* (Modern French *bourbotte*), prob. from Old French *borbe* mud, slime.

burden n. a load. *Also v.t.* WH: pre-1200. Old English *byrthen*, from Germanic, from base of BIRTH.

bureau n. a writing table with drawers for papers. WH: 17C. French (Old French *burel*), orig. woollen stuff, baize (used for covering writing desks), prob. from *bure*, var. of *buire* dark brown, from Latin *burrus* fiery red, from Greek *purros* red. The sense of office evolved in the 19C.

bureaucracy n. government by departments of state. WH: 19C. French *bureaucratie*. See BUREAU, -CRACY.

burette n. a graduated glass tube for measuring small quantities of liquid. WH: 19C. French, from *buire* ewer, from Frankish *būk* belly. Cp. BUCKET. See also -ETTE.

burg n. a fortress. WH: 18C. See BOROUGH, BURGESS.

burgage n. a tenure by which lands or tenements in towns or cities were held for a small yearly rent. WH: 14–15C. Medieval Latin *burgagium*, from *burgus*. See BURGESS, also -AGE.

burganet n. a light helmet for foot soldiers. WH: 16C. French *bourguignotte*, ? fem. of *bourguignot* Burgundian, with ending assim. to -ET¹.

burgee n. a kind of small coal suitable for furnaces. WH: 18C. Orig. uncertain. The sense triangular flag may come from French *bourgeois* (see BURGESS) master.

burgeon *v.i.* to sprout, to bud. *Also n.* WH: 12–14C. Old French *bourgeonner*, from *bourgeon* young shoot, bud, from Old French *borjon*, from Late Latin *burra* wool.

burger *n.* a flat round cake of minced meat or vegetables which is grilled or fried, e.g. *hamburger, beefburger.* WH: mid-20C. Abbr. of HAMBURGER.

burgess *n.* an inhabitant of a borough possessing full municipal rights, a citizen. WH: 12–14C. Old French *borjois* (Modern French *bourgeois*), from Late Latin *burgus* castle, fort (cp. BOROUGH) + *-ensis* -ESE.

burgh *n.* a Scottish town holding a charter. WH: 14–15C. Var. of BOROUGH.

burglar *n.* a person who breaks into premises with intent to commit a theft. WH: 16C. Obs. French *burgler*, from Anglo-Latin *burgulator*, appar. from base meaning pillage. Cp. Latin *latro* thief, which gave French *larron* thief, burglar.

burgomaster *n.* the chief magistrate of a municipal town in Austria, Germany, the Netherlands or Belgium. WH: 16C. Dutch *burgemeester*, from *burg* (see BOROUGH) + *meester*, from English MASTER.

burgoo *n.* a kind of oatmeal porridge or thick gruel eaten by sailors. WH: 17C. Arabic *burġul*. See BULGAR.

burgrave *n.* the commandant of a castle or fortified town. WH: 16C. German *Burggraf*, from *Burg* BOROUGH + *Graf* count.

burgundy *n.* red or white wine made in Burgundy. *Also a.* WH: 17C. *Burgundy*, French *Bourgogne* (cp. BOURGUIGNON), a region of E France, from Medieval Latin *Burgundia*, from Late Latin *Burgundii*.

burial *n.* the act of burying a dead body in the earth. WH: pre-1200. Old English *byrgels*, from Germanic. See BURY, also -LE². The original sense was place of burial. The current sense of an act of burying dates from the 15C.

burin *n.* the cutting tool of an engraver on copper. WH: 17C. French, from Italian *burino* (now *bulino*), from Germanic base of BORE¹.

burka *n.* the long veil or veiled, loose overgarment worn by Muslim women. WH: 19C. Urdu *burḳa'*, from Arabic *burḳu'*.

burke *v.t.* to kill secretly by suffocation. WH: 19C. William *Burke*, 1792–1829, Irish murderer, who suffocated or strangled his victims to sell their bodies for dissection.

Burkitt's lymphoma *n.* a malignant tumour of the white blood cells, associated with infection by the Epstein–Barr virus. WH: mid-20C. Denis P. *Burkitt*, 1911–93, British surgeon.

burl¹ *n.* a knot or lump in wool or cloth. *Also v.t.* WH: 14–15C. Old French *bourle* tuft of wool, dim. of *bourre*, from Late Latin *burra* wool. Cp. BUR.

burl² *n.* a spin (in a motor vehicle). WH: 19C. Var. of BIRL.

burlap *n.* a coarse kind of canvas used for sacking, upholstering etc. WH: 17C. Orig. unknown.

burlesque *a.* drolly or absurdly imitative. *Also n., v.t.* WH: 17C. French, from Italian *burlesco*, from *burla* ridicule, joke, fun, of unknown orig. See also -ESQUE.

burletta *n.* a comic opera. WH: 18C. Italian, dim. of *burla*. See BURLESQUE, also -ETTE.

burly *a.* stout, corpulent. WH: 12–14C. Prob. from same source as BOWER¹, from Old English *būr* + -LY¹. Cp. Old High German *burlīh* exalted, stately. The word was originally a term of approval, in the sense handsome, stately. This then modified to noble, and evolved to the current sense from the 14C.

Burmese *n.* a native or inhabitant of Burma. *Also a.* WH: 19C. *Burma* (now Myanmar), a country in SE Asia + -ESE.

burn¹ *v.t.* to destroy or scorch by fire. *Also v.i., n.* WH: pre-1200. Old English *bærnan* (trans.), *birnan* (intrans.), both from same Germanic base. Cp. German *brennen*.

burn² *n.* a small stream, a brook. WH: pre-1200. Old English *burna*, from Germanic base also of Dutch *bron*, German *Brunnen*. Cp. BOURN.

burnet *n.* a plant of the genus *Sanguisorba*, with pinkish flower heads. WH: 12–14C. Old French *brunet* (see BRUNETTE), *brunete* brown cloth, brown-flowered plant, dims. of *brun* BROWN. See also -ET¹.

burnish *v.t.* to polish, esp. by rubbing. *Also v.i., n.* WH: 12–14C. Old French *burnir*, *burniss-*, var. of *brunir* to make brown, from *brun* BROWN. See also -ISH².

burnous *n.* a mantle or cloak with a hood, worn by Arabs. WH: 16C. French, from Arabic *burnus*.

burp *n.* a belch. *Also v.i., v.t.* WH: mid-20C. Imit.

burpee *n.* an exercise that consists of a squat thrust from standing position, and back to this position. WH: mid-20C. Royal H. *Burpee*, 1897– , US psychologist.

burr *n.* a whirring noise. *Also v.t., v.i.* WH: 18C. Prob. imit., but ? assoc. with BUR, alluding to its roughness.

burrawang *n.* any of several palmlike trees of the genus *Macrozamia*. WH: 19C. Australian Aboriginal (Dharuk) *buruwan*.

burro *n.* a donkey. WH: 19C. Spanish donkey.

burrow *n.* a hole in the ground made by rabbits, foxes etc., for a dwelling-place. *Also v.i., v.t.* WH: 12–14C. Var. of BOROUGH.

burry *a.* characterized by burrs. WH: 14–15C. BUR + -Y¹.

bursa *n.* a synovial sac found among tendons in the body and serving to reduce friction. WH: 18C. Medieval Latin bag, PURSE.

burst *v.t.* to break with suddenness and violence. *Also v.i., n.* WH: pre-1200. Old English *berstan*, from Germanic.

Burton *n.* a beer from a brewery in Burton-upon-Trent. WH: mid-20C. *Burton*-upon-Trent, a town in Staffordshire.

burton *n.* a small tackle consisting of two or three pulleys. WH: 18C. Alt. of BRETON.

bury *v.t.* to place (a corpse) under ground, to inter, to consign to the grave (whether earth or sea). WH: pre-1200. Old English *byrgan*, from Germanic, from base also of BORROW.

bus *n.* a large passenger vehicle for transporting members of the public, hotel guests, employees etc., usu. on a set route. *Also v.i., v.t.* WH: 19C. Abbr. of OMNIBUS.

busby *n.* the tall fur cap worn by hussars. WH: 18C. Orig. unknown. ? From surname *Busby*. The busby was originally a type of wig.

bush¹ *n.* a thick shrub. *Also v.t., v.i.* WH: 12–14C. Partly from Old French *bos*, *bosc*, var. of *bois* wood, partly from Old Norse *buski*, from Germanic. Cp. German *Busch*.

bush² *n.* the metal lining of an axle-hole or similar orifice. *Also v.t.* WH: 15C. Middle Dutch *busse* BOX¹ (Dutch *bus*).

bushel¹ *n.* a dry measure of 8 gal. (36.37 litres). WH: 12–14C. Old French *boisell* (Modern French *boisseau*), prob. of Gaulish orig.

bushel² *v.t.* to mend or alter. *Also v.i.* WH: 19C. ? German *bosseln* to do odd jobs.

bushido *n.* the code of honour of the Japanese samurai. WH: 19C. Japanese military knight's way, from *bushi* samurai + *dō* way.

business *n.* employment, profession. WH: pre-1200. Old English *bisignis*, from *bisig* BUSY + *-nis* -NESS. The original sense was care, concern. This progressed to diligence, industriousness in the 13C, to occupation in the 14C, and finally to affair in the 16C.

busk¹ *v.i.* to perform in the street or in a public place, esp. beside a queue in order to collect money. WH: 17C. Obs. French *busquer* to seek, to hunt for, from Italian *buscare* or Spanish *buscar*, from Germanic.

busk² *n.* a stiffening bone or plate in a corset. WH: 16C. French *busc*, from Italian *busco* splinter, rel. to Old French *busche* (Modern French *bûche*) log, from Germanic.

†busk³ *v.t.* to prepare, to dress. *Also v.i.* WH: 12–14C. Old Norse *búask*, reflex. of *búa* to prepare. Cp. BOUND⁴.

buskin *n.* a kind of high boot reaching to the calf or knee. WH: 16C. Prob. from Old French *bousequin*, var. of *brousequin* (Modern French *brodequin*), prob. from Middle Dutch *broseken*, of unknown orig.

buss¹ *n.* a loud kiss. *Also v.t.* WH: 16C. Prob. alt. of *bass*, from Old French *baiser*, from Latin *basiare* to kiss.

buss² *n.* a herring boat with two or three masts. WH: 12–14C. Old French *buce*, later *busse*, influ. by Middle Dutch *buisse* (Dutch *buis*), ult. of unknown orig.

bust¹ *n.* a sculptured representation of the head, shoulders and breast of a person. WH: 17C. French *buste*, from Italian *busto*, from Latin *bustum* funeral pyre, tomb.

bust² *v.i.* to break or burst. *Also v.t., n., a.* WH: 18C. Var. of BURST.

bustard *n.* any large bird of the family Otididae, allied to the plovers and the cranes. WH: 15C. Appar. Anglo-French blend of Old French *bistarde*, *oustarde*, both from Latin *avis tarda* slow bird. The inappropriate adjective (the bird is a swift runner) is unexplained.

bustee *n.* in the Indian subcontinent, a settlement or a collection of huts. WH: 19C. Hindi *bastī* dwelling, settlement.

bustier *n.* a strapless bodice. WH: late 20C. French, from *buste* BUST[1].

bustle[1] *n.* activity with noise and excitement. *Also v.i., v.t.* WH: 14–15C. ? Var. of *buskle* BUSK[3].

bustle[2] *n.* a pad, cushion or framework, worn under a woman's dress to expand the skirts behind. WH: 18C. Orig. unknown.

busy *a.* fully occupied. *Also v.i., v.t., n.* WH: pre-1200. Old English *bisig* careful, anxious, of unknown orig.

but *prep.* except, barring. *Also conj., n., adv., v.t.* WH: pre-1200. Old English *būtan*, from BY, OUT.

butadiene *n.* the gas used in making synthetic rubber. WH: early 20C. BUTANE + DI-[2] + -ENE.

butane *n.* an inflammable gaseous compound; a hydrocarbon of the paraffin series found in petroleum. WH: 19C. BUTYL + -ANE.

butch *a.* masculine in manner or appearance. *Also n.* WH: mid-20C. Orig. uncertain. ? From BUTCHER.

butcher *n.* a person whose trade it is to slaughter domestic animals for food. *Also v.t.* WH: 12–14C. Anglo-French var. of Old French *boucher*, from *boc* he-goat (Modern French *bouc*), prob. from Celtic. See BUCK[1], -ER[2].

butler *n.* a servant in charge of the wine, plate etc. WH: 12–14C. Old French *bouteillier* cup bearer, from *bouteille* BOTTLE[1]. See also -ER[2].

butt[1] *n.* the thick end of anything, esp. of a tool or weapon. *Also v.i.* WH: 14–15C. Appar. rel. to Dutch *bot* stumpy (cp. BUTT[5]) and to base of BUTTOCK.

butt[2] *n.* a large cask. WH: 14–15C. Old French *bot* (Modern French *botte*), from Late Latin *buttis*.

butt[3] *n.* a goal. WH: 12–14C. Old French *but*, of unknown orig., ? influ. by *butte* rising ground. Cp. BUTTE.

butt[4] *v.i.* to strike, thrust or push with the head or as with the head. *Also v.t., n.* WH: 12–14C. Old French *bouter*, from Germanic.

butt[5] *n.* a flatfish of various kinds. WH: 12–14C. Middle Low German *but* and Middle Dutch *but, butte*, prob. rel. to Low German *but*, Middle Dutch *bot* stumpy. Cp. BUTT[1].

butte *n.* an abrupt, isolated hill or peak. WH: 19C. French. See BUTT[3].

butter *n.* the fatty portion of milk or cream solidified by churning. *Also v.t.* WH: pre-1200. Old English *butere*, from Germanic, from Latin *butyrum*, from Greek *bouturon*, from *bous* ox, cow + *turos* cheese.

buttery *n.* a room in which liquor and provisions are kept. WH: 12–14C. Anglo-French *boterie*, ? from *but* BUTT[2] or rel. to Old French *botelerie* butlery (see BUTLER). The word was originally used of a liquor and wine store. The sense then altered to a provisions store, perhaps influenced by BUTTER.

buttock *n.* either of the protuberant parts of the rump, the posterior. *Also v.t.* WH: pre-1200. Old English *buttuc*. See BUTT[1], also -OCK.

button *n.* a knob or disc used for fastening or ornamenting garments. *Also a., v.t., v.i.* WH: 12–14C. Old French *bouton*, from Germanic base also of BUTT[4].

buttress *n.* a structure built against a wall to strengthen it. *Also v.t.* WH: 12–14C. Old French (*ars*) *bouterez* thrusting (arch), from *bouter* BUTT[4].

butty[1] *n.* a partner, companion, a mate. WH: 18C. Prob. from *to play booty*. See BOOTY.

butty[2] *n.* a sandwich, a snack. WH: 19C. See BUTTER, also -Y[3].

butyl *n.* any of four isomeric forms of the chemical group C_4H_9. WH: 19C. *but*(*yric*) (BUTYRACEOUS) + -YL.

butyraceous *a.* having the nature or consistency of butter. WH: 17C. Latin *butyrum* BUTTER + -ACEOUS.

buxom *a.* (of women) plump and comely. WH: 12–14C. Stem of Old English *būgan* to bend, BOW[2] + -SOME[1]. The original meaning was obedient, compliant. The current sense dates from the 16C. The reasoning is that plump people are generally more good-natured and amenable than those who are thin and lean.

buy *v.t.* to obtain by means of money. *Also n.* WH: pre-1200. Old English *bycgan*, from Germanic. Cp. Old Norse *buggja* to let out, to lend.

buzz *n.* a sibilant hum, like that of a bee. *Also v.i., v.t.* WH: 14–15C. Imit.

buzzard[1] *n.* a bird of prey, esp. of the genus *Buteo*. *Also a.* WH: 14–15C. Old French *busard, buson*, from Latin *buteo, buteonis* falcon. See also -ARD.

buzzard[2] *n.* any large nocturnal insect. WH: 17C. BUZZ + -ARD.

bwana *n.* (in Africa) sir, master. WH: 19C. Kiswahili.

by *prep.* near, at, in the neighbourhood of, beside, along, through, via. *Also adv., a., n.* WH: pre-1200. Old English *bī, bi, be*, from Germanic, prob. rel. to 2nd syl. of Greek *amphi-*, Latin *ambi-* around.

bye[1] *n.* a subsidiary object. WH: 16C. Ellipt. use of BY.

bye[2] *int.* goodbye. WH: 18C. Child's version of GOODBYE.

bye-byes *n.* sleep, bedtime, bed (used by or to children). WH: 19C. Phr. or refrain used in lullabies, imit. of soothing sound or child's babble.

by-law *n.* a private statute made by the members of a local authority. WH: 12–14C. Prob. from (obs.) *byrlaw*, from Old Norse *býjar*, gen. sing. of *býr* dwelling, village (as in place names such as *Grimsby*) + *lagu* LAW[1], but assoc. with BY, LAW[1].

byre *n.* a cowshed. WH: pre-1200. Old English *bȳre*, ? rel. to BOWER[1].

Byronic *a.* like Lord Byron or his poetry. WH: 19C. George Gordon, Lord *Byron*, 1788–1824, English poet + -IC.

byssus *n.* a textile fabric of various substances. WH: 14–15C. Latin, from Greek *bussos*, of Semitic orig.

byte *n.* a series of usu. eight binary digits treated as a unit. WH: mid-20C. Arbitrary, based on BIT[3] and BITE.

Byzantine *a.* of or relating to Byzantium or Istanbul (formerly Constantinople). *Also n.* WH: 16C. French *byzantin* or Latin *Byzantinus*, from *Byzantium*, from Greek *Buzantron* Byzantium, the city later called Constantinople, now Istanbul. See also -INE.

C

c. *abbr.* about. WH: Latin CIRCA.

cab¹ *n.* a taxi. WH: 19C. Abbr. of CABRIOLET.

cab² *n.* an ancient Jewish measure of capacity equal to 4 pints (2.3l). WH: 16C. Hebrew *qab* hollow or concave vessel. 'The fourth part of a cab of camel's dung' (II Kgs. vi.25).

cabal *n.* a small body of persons closely united for some secret purpose; a junta, a clique. *Also v.i.* WH: 16C. French *cabale*, from Medieval Latin *cabbala*, from Hebrew (rabbinical) *qabbālāh* tradition, from *qibbēl* to receive, to accept. In the 17C the word was associated with a committee of five ministers under Charles II whose surnames happened to begin with C, A, B, A, L: Clifford, Arlington, Buckingham, Ashley and Lauderdale.

caballero *n.* a Spanish gentleman. WH: 19C. Spanish CAVALIER. Cp. CHEVALIER.

cabana *n.* a small hut, cabin or tent on the beach or at a swimming-pool, used for changing by bathers. WH: 19C. Spanish *cabaña*, from Late Latin *capanna, cavanna* CABIN.

cabaret *n.* an entertainment or floor show consisting of singing, dancing etc. WH: 17C. Old French, from var. of Middle Dutch *camaret, cambret*, from Old Picard *camberet* little room. Cp. CAMERA, CHAMBER. The word is not from Latin *caput arietis* ram's head, as sometimes proposed, in supposed allusion to a tavern sign.

cabbage *n.* any of the plain-leaved, hearted varieties of *Brassica oleracea*. WH: 14–15C. Old French *caboche* head, var. of Old French *caboce*, of unknown orig. Cp. BOCHE.

cabbala *n.* a traditional exposition of the Pentateuch attributed to Moses. WH: 16C. Medieval Latin *cabbala*, from Hebrew (rabbinical) *qabbālāh* tradition, from *qibbēl* to receive, to accept. Cp. CABAL.

caber *n.* a pole, the roughly-trimmed stem of a young tree, used in the Highland sport of tossing the caber. WH: 16C. Gaelic and Irish *cabar*.

Cabernet *n.* a variety of black grape used to make a dry red wine. WH: 19C. French, name of grape variety from Médoc, France.

cabin *n.* a small hut. *Also v.i., v.t.* WH: 12–14C. Old French *cabane*, from Provençal *cabana*, from Late Latin *capanna*, of unknown orig.

cabinet *n.* a piece of furniture with drawers, shelves etc., in which to keep or display curiosities or articles of value. WH: 16C. CABIN + -ET¹, influ. by French *cabinet*, from Italian *gabinetto* closet, chest of drawers.

cable *n.* a strong, thick rope of hemp or wire. *Also v.t.* WH: 12–14C. Anglo-French var. of Old French *chable* (Modern French *câble*, from Provençal *cable*), from Late Latin *capulum* halter, assoc. with Latin *capere* to hold. Cp. CAPTIVE.

caboched *a.* (in Heraldry) borne full-faced and showing no other feature, as the heads of some animals. WH: 16C. French *caboché*, p.p. of *cabocher*. See CABBAGE, also -ED.

cabochon *n.* a precious stone polished, and having the rough parts removed, but without facets. WH: 16C. Old French dim. of *caboche*. See CABBAGE, also -OON.

caboodle *n.* crowd, lot. WH: 19C. ? From *kit and boodle*. See KIT¹, BOODLE.

caboose *n.* the cook's house or galley on a ship. WH: 18C. Dutch *cabuse, combuse* (now *kabuis, kombuis*), from Low German *kabūse*, of unknown orig. ? Ult. rel. to CABIN, HOUSE¹.

cabotage *n.* coastal navigation or shipping. WH: 19C. French, from *caboter* to coast along, ? ult. from Spanish *cabo* CAPE². See also -AGE.

cabretta *n.* a type of soft leather made from the skin of a S American sheep. WH: 19C. Spanish *cabra* nanny goat + *-etta* -ETTE.

cabriole *a.* (of table and chair legs) shaped in a reflex curve. *Also n.* WH: 18C. French, from *cabrioler*, earlier *caprioler*, from Italian *capriolare*. See CAPRIOLE.

cabriolet *n.* a covered, horse-drawn carriage with two wheels. WH: 18C. French, dim. of *cabriole* leap. See CAPRIOLE, also -ET¹. The carriage is so named for its springy, bouncing motion.

ca'canny *n.* proceeding with caution or wariness. WH: 19C. Scottish *ca'*, var. of CALL + CANNY.

cacao *n.* a tropical American tree, *Theobroma cacao*, from the seeds of which chocolate and cocoa are prepared. WH: 16C. Spanish, from Nahuatl *cacauatl*, from *uatl* tree. Cp. COCOA.

cacciatore *a.* (of meat dishes, esp. chicken) cooked with tomatoes, onions, mushrooms, herbs etc. WH: mid-20C. Italian hunter.

cachalot *n.* a member of a genus of whales having teeth in the lower jaw, esp. the sperm whale. WH: 18C. French, from Spanish and Portuguese *cachalote*, from *cachola* big head.

cache *n.* a place in which provisions, arms etc. are hidden. *Also v.t.* WH: 18C. French, from *cacher* to hide.

cachet *n.* a seal. WH: 17C. French, from *cachet* to hide, to press, from alt. of Latin *coactare* to constrain. Rel. to COGENT.

cachexia *n.* a loss of weight from and weakness of the body resulting from chronic disease. WH: 16C. French *cachexie*, or from Late Latin *cachexia*, from Greek *kakhexia*, from *kakos* bad + *hexis* habit. See also -IA.

cachinnate *v.i.* to laugh immoderately. WH: 19C. Latin *cachinnatus*, p.p. of *cachinnare*, of imit. orig. See also -ATE³.

cacholong *n.* a white or opaque variety of opal or quartz. WH: 18C. French, from Mongolian *kas chilagun* precious stone.

cachou *n.* a small pill-like sweet for perfuming the breath. WH: 16C. French, from Portuguese *cachu*, from Malay *kacu*. Cp. CATECHU.

cachucha *n.* a lively Spanish dance in triple time. WH: 19C. Spanish small boat, cup, prob. from *cacho* shard, piece, prob. from Popular Latin *cacculus* pot, from alt. of Latin *caccabus* from Greek *kakkabos*, of Semitic orig.

cacique *n.* a chief of the indigenous inhabitants of the W Indies or the neighbouring parts of America. WH: 16C. Spanish or French, from Taino lord, chief.

cack *n.* excrement. WH: pre-1200. Old English *cac-*, as in *cachūs* dung house, from Latin *cacare* to excrete.

cackle *n.* the cackling of a hen. *Also v.i.* WH: 12–14C. Prob. from Low German and Middle Dutch *kākelen*, partly of imit. orig., partly from *kāke* jaw, cheek.

caco- *comb. form* bad, incorrect, unpleasant. WH: Greek *kakos* bad. See also -O-.

cacodemon *n.* an evil spirit. WH: 16C. Greek *kakodaimōn* evil genius. See CACO-, DEMON.

cacodyl *n.* a toxic organic compound of arsenic and methyl with an unpleasant smell. WH: 19C. Greek *kakōdēs* stinking + -YL.

cacoepy *n.* incorrect pronunciation of words. WH: 19C. Greek *kakoepia*, from *kakos* bad (see CACO-) + *epos* word (cp. EPOS). See also -Y².

cacoethes *n.* a bad habit. WH: 16C. Latin, from Greek *kakoēthes*, use as n. of a. *kakoēthes* ill-disposed. See CACO-, ETHOS.

cacography *n.* bad spelling. WH: 16C. CACO- + -GRAPHY, based on ORTHOGRAPHY.

cacology *n.* bad choice of words. WH: 17C. Greek *kakologia* vituperation. See CACO-, -LOGY.

cacomistle *n.* a ring-tailed American mammal, *Bassariscus astutus*, related to the raccoon. WH: 19C. American Spanish *cacomixtle*, from Nahuatl *tlacomiztli*, from *tlaco* half + *miztli* mountain lion.

cacomorphia *n.* malformation, deformity. WH: 19C. CACO- + -morphia, from Greek *morphē* shape, form. See also -IA.

cacophony *n.* a rough, discordant sound or mixture of sounds. WH: 17C. French *cacophonie*, from Greek *kakophōnia*, from *kakos* bad (see CACO-) + *phōnē* sound. Cp. EUPHONY.

cactus *n.* any succulent spiny plant of the family Cactaceae. WH: 17C. Latin, from Greek *kaktos* cardoon.

cacuminal *a.* (of a vowel or consonant) retroflected. *Also n.* WH: 19C. Latin *cacuminare* to make pointed, from *cacumen, cacuminis* top, summit + -AL[1].

cad *n.* an ill-mannered person, a person guilty of ungentlemanly conduct. WH: 18C. Abbr. of CADDIE or CADET.

cadastre *n.* an official register of the ownership of land as a basis of taxation. WH: 18C. French, from Provençal *cadastro*, from Italian *catastro*, earlier *catastico*, from Late Greek *katastikhon* list, register, from *kata stikhon* line by line.

cadaver *n.* a corpse, a dead body. WH: 14–15C. Latin, from *cadere* to fall.

caddie *n.* a person who assists a golfer, esp. by carrying clubs. *Also v.i.* WH: 17C. Scottish use of French *cadet* young gentleman who enters the military without a commission. See CADET. The original Scottish sense in the 18C was messenger, errand boy, giving the current sense from the 19C.

caddis[1] *n.* the larva of the caddis fly, which lives in water in a protective case of sand, stones, sticks, leaves etc. WH: 17C. Orig. unknown.

caddis[2] *n.* a type of worsted yarn. WH: 12–14C. Old French *cadas, cadaz*, from Provençal, of unknown orig.

caddy *n.* a small box in which tea is kept. WH: 18C. Alt. of CATTY.

cade *n.* (of a young animal) brought up by hand; domesticated. *Also n.* WH: 14–15C. Orig. unknown.

-cade *comb. form* a procession, as in *motorcade*. WH: See CAVALCADE.

cadelle *n.* a small beetle, *Tenebroides mauritanicus*, that feeds on stored grain, etc. WH: 19C. French, from Portuguese *cadello*, from Latin *catella*, fem. of *catellus* little dog.

cadence *n.* the sinking of the voice, esp. at the end of a sentence. *Also v.t.* WH: 14–15C. Old French, from Italian *cadenza*, from Popular Latin, from Latin *cadens, cadentis*, pres.p. of *cadere* to fall. See also -ENCE. Cp. CADENZA, CHANCE.

cadenza *n.* a vocal or instrumental flourish of indefinite form at the close of a movement. WH: 18C. Italian CADENCE.

cadet *n.* a young trainee in the army, navy, air force or police. WH: 17C. French, earlier *capdet*, from Gascon dial., from dim. of Latin *caput, capitis* head. See also -ET[1]. Cp. CADDIE. The original meaning, younger son or brother, arose because Gascon officers in the French army were usually younger sons or lesser heads of noble families.

cadge *v.t.* to get by begging. *Also v.i.* WH: 14–15C. Orig. unknown. ? Rel. to CATCH.

cadi *n.* the judge of a Muslim town or village. WH: 16C. Arabic *ḳāḍī* judge. Cp. ALCALDE.

Cadmean *a.* of or belonging to Cadmus. WH: 17C. Latin *Cadmeus*, from Greek *Kadmeios*, from *Kadmos* Cadmus, the legendary founder of Thebes + -AN.

cadmium *n.* a bluish-white metallic element, at. no. 51, chem. symbol Cd. WH: 19C. Latin *cadmia* (see CALAMINE) + -IUM as in SODIUM etc. The element was named in 1817 by Friedrich Stromeyer, the German chemist who discovered it.

cadre *n.* the permanent establishment or nucleus of a regiment; the skeleton of a regiment. WH: 19C. French, from Italian *quadro*, from Latin *quadrus* square.

caduceus *n.* the winged staff of Mercury, borne by him as messenger of the gods. WH: 16C. Latin, from Greek (Doric) *karukeion*, rel. to Attic Greek *kērukeion*, neut. a. (used as n.) from *kērux, kērukos* herald.

caducous *a.* falling off quickly or prematurely. WH: 17C. Latin *caducus* liable to fall, from *cadere* to fall + -OUS.

caecilian *n.* any wormlike legless amphibian of the order Apoda (or Gymnophiona) which burrows in moist soil. WH: 19C. Modern Latin *caecilia* genus name, from Latin *caecilia* slow-worm. See also -AN.

caecum *n.* the first part of the large intestine, which is prolonged into a blind pouch. WH: 14–15C. Latin *intestinum caecum* blind gut, translating Greek *tuphlon enteron*.

caenogenesis *n.* the development in an embryo, larva etc., of adaptations that disappear at the adult stage, when they are no longer needed. WH: 19C. Greek *kainos* new, recent + GENESIS.

Caen stone *n.* a soft, yellowish, oolitic building-stone from Caen. WH: 14–15C. *Caen*, a town in Normandy.

Caerphilly *n.* a mild-flavoured white cheese. WH: early 20C. *Caerphilly* (Welsh *Caerffili*), a town in S Wales.

caesalpiniaceous *a.* of, relating to or belonging to the Caesalpiniaceae, a family of chiefly tropical plants that includes brazil, carob, cassia and senna. WH: 19C. Modern Latin *Caesalpinia* genus name, from Andrea *Cesalpina* (Andreas Caesalpinus), 1519–1603, Italian botanist + -IA. See also -ACEOUS.

Caesar *n.* the title of the Roman emperors down to Hadrian, and of the heirs presumptive of later emperors. WH: pre-1200. Old English *cāsere*, from Germanic, from Latin family name of Gaius Julius *Caesar*, *c.*102–44 BC, Roman statesman. Cp. KAISER, TSAR.

caesious *a.* bluish or greenish grey. WH: 19C. Latin *caesius* + -OUS.

caesium *n.* a highly-reactive, silvery-white metallic element, at. no. 55, chem. symbol Cs, similar to sodium in many properties. WH: 19C. Latin *caesius* greyish-blue + -IUM. The element was so named in 1860 by Robert Wilhelm Bunsen (see BUNSEN BURNER) and Gustav Robert Kirchhoff from the two blue lines in its spectrum.

caespitose *a.* growing in tufts. WH: 18C. Latin *caespes, caespitis* sod, turf + -OSE[1].

caesura *n.* in classical prosody, the division of a metrical foot between two words, esp. in the middle of a line. WH: 16C. Latin, from *caesus*, p.p. of *caedere* to cut. See also -URE.

cafard *n.* depression, low spirits. WH: 16C. French cockroach, hypocrite, ? from Late Latin *caphardum* university gown. According to some, the word is from Arabic *kāfir* unbeliever. Cp. KAFFIR.

café *n.* a small restaurant serving coffee, tea etc. and light inexpensive meals or snacks. WH: 19C. French coffee, coffee house. Cp. COFFEE.

cafeteria *n.* a restaurant in which customers fetch their own food and drinks from the counter. WH: 19C. American Spanish, from *café* coffee. See CAFÉ.

cafetière *n.* a type of coffee-pot fitted with a plunger that forces the grounds to the bottom and holds them there while the coffee is poured. WH: 19C. French, from *café* coffee. See CAFÉ.

caff *n.* a café or cafeteria. WH: mid-20C. Abbr. of CAFÉ or CAFETERIA.

caffeic *a.* derived from coffee. WH: 19C. French *caféique*, from *café* coffee. See also -IC.

caffeine *n.* a vegetable alkaloid derived from the coffee and tea plants. WH: 19C. French *caféine*, from *café* coffee + -INE.

cage *n.* an enclosure of wire or iron bars, in which animals or birds are kept. *Also v.t.* WH: 12–14C. Old French, from Latin *cavea* stall, cage, coop.

cagey *a.* uncommunicative, secretive. WH: early 20C. Orig. unknown. The word is said to come from CAGE, alluding to wary animals in cages.

cagoule *n.* a lightweight weatherproof jacket, usu. hooded. WH: mid-20C. French cowl, from Latin *cucullus* hooded cape.

cahier *n.* a notebook. WH: 19C. French. See QUIRE.

cahoots *n.pl.* partnership, collusion. WH: 19C. Orig. unknown. The word is perhaps from French *cahute* cabin, with reference to an enclosed company.

Cain *n.* a murderer, a fratricide. WH: 12–14C. *Cain*, the eldest son of Adam, who murdered his brother Abel (Gen. iv).

†cain *n.* rent paid in kind, esp. farm produce. WH: 12–14C. Irish and Gaelic *cáin*.

caïque *n.* a light rowing boat used on the Bosporus. WH: 17C. French, from Italian *caicco*, from Turkish *kayık*.

cairn *n.* a pyramidal heap of stones, esp. one raised over a grave or to mark a summit, track or boundary. WH: 14–15C. Gaelic *carn*. Cp. Welsh *carn*.

cairngorm *n.* a yellow or brown variety of rock crystal (found in the Cairngorm mountains in NE Scotland). WH: 18C. *Cairngorm*, a mountain in central Scotland, from Gaelic *carn gorm* blue CAIRN.

caisson *n.* a large, watertight case or chamber used in laying foundations under water. WH: 17C. French large chest, from Italian *cassone*, assim. to French *caisse* CASE[2]. See also -OON.

†caitiff *n.* a despicable wretch or cowardly person. *Also a.* WH: 12–14C. Old French *caitif* captive, var. of *chaitif* (Modern French *chétif* wretched) from alt. of Latin *captivus* CAPTIVE.

cajole *v.t.* to persuade by flattery. *Also v.i.* WH: 17C. French *cajoler*, from Old French *gaioler* to cry, to cackle, from *geai* JAY[1], influ. by *cage* CAGE.

Cajun *n.* a descendant of the French-speaking Acadians deported to Louisiana in the 18th cent. *Also a.* WH: 19C. Alt. of ACADIAN.

cajuput *n.* a small tree, *Melaleuca leucadendron*, which yields a volatile oil. WH: 18C. Malay *kayuputih*, from *kayu* tree + *puteh* white.

cake *n.* a mixture of flour, butter, eggs, sugar and other ingredients, baked usu. in a tin. *Also v.t., v.i.* WH: 12–14C. Scandinavian, rel. to German *Kuchen*. Not rel. to COOK.

Calabar bean *n.* the highly poisonous seed of the climbing plant *Physostigma venenosum* of W Africa. WH: 19C. *Calabar*, a town and province in Nigeria + BEAN.

calabash *n.* a kind of gourd, esp. the fruit of the calabash tree. WH: 17C. French *calebasse*, from Spanish *calabaza*, ? ult. from Persian *karbuz* melon.

calaboose *n.* a prison. WH: 18C. S US blacks' French *calabouse*, from Spanish *calabozo* dungeon, prob. from Popular Latin *calafodium*, from *cala* protected place + Latin *fodere* to dig.

calabrese *n.* a type of green broccoli. WH: mid-20C. Italian Calabrian, from *Calabria*, a region of S Italy.

caladium *n.* any of a genus of plants belonging to the arum family, with starchy tuberous roots used in the tropics for food. WH: 19C. Modern Latin, from Malay *keladi*. See also -IUM.

calamanco *n.* a Flemish woollen cloth with a fine gloss, and chequered on one side, much in use in the 18th cent. WH: 16C. Orig. unknown. Cp. Dutch *kalmink*, German *Kalmank*, French *calmande*.

calamander *n.* a hard wood, marked with black and brown stripes, from India and Sri Lanka. WH: 19C. Sinhalese *kaḷumädiriya*, ? from English *Coromandel* (ebony), assim. to Sinhalese *kaḷu* black.

calamari *n.pl.* squid, esp. in Mediterranean cookery. WH: early 20C. Italian, pl. of *calamaro* squid. See CALAMARY.

†calamary *n.* a squid, esp. of the genus *Loligo*. WH: 16C. Medieval Latin *calmarium* pen case, neut. (used as n.) of Latin *calamarius*, from *calamus*, from Greek *kalamos* pen. See also -ARY[1]. The squid are so called from their shape and perhaps also from the ink that they squirt out.

calamine *n.* a pinkish powder of zinc carbonate and ferric oxide used in a lotion to soothe the skin. WH: 14–15C. Old French, from Medieval Latin *calamina*, from alt. of Latin *cadmia*, from Greek *kadmeia gē* Cadmean earth, from *kadmos*. See CADMEAN. Cp. CADMIUM.

calamint *n.* an aromatic herb of the genus *Clinopodium* (formerly *Calamintha*) of the mint family. WH: 12–14C. Old French *calament*, from Medieval Latin *calamentum*, from Late Latin *calaminthe*, from Greek *kalaminthē*, influ. by MINT[2].

calamite *n.* a fossil plant of the Carboniferous period, related to the horsetails. WH: 19C. Modern Latin *Calamites* genus name, from Latin *calamus*. See CALAMUS.

calamity *n.* extreme misfortune or adversity. WH: 14–15C. Old French *calamité*, from Latin *calamitas*. See also -ITY. The sense of disaster, misfortune developed in the 16C.

calamus *n.* the sweet flag, *Acorus calamus*. WH: 14–15C. Latin, from Greek *kalamos* reed.

calando *a., adv.* gradually becoming softer and slower. WH: 19C. Italian slackening, from *calare* to lower, to drop.

calandria *n.* a sealed cylindrical vessel with tubes passing through it, used as a heat exchanger, e.g. in nuclear reactors. WH: early 20C. Spanish, from Greek *kulindros* CYLINDER.

calash *n.* a light horse-drawn carriage, with low wheels and removable top. WH: 17C. French *calèche*, from German *Kalesche*, from Czech *kolesa* wheels, carriage.

calathea *n.* any plant of the genus *Calathea* of S America, many of which are grown as house plants, such as the zebra plant. WH: 19C. Modern Latin, from Latin *calathus*, from Greek *kalathos* basket. Cp. CALATHUS.

calathus *n.* in classical art, a wide-topped fruit basket used as a symbol of fruitfulness. WH: 18C. Latin, from Greek *kalathos* basket. Cp. CALATHEA.

calc- *comb. form* lime, calcium. WH: German *Kalk* lime, from Latin *calx, calcis* CALX. Cp. CALCI-.

calcaneum *n.* the bone of the heel. WH: 18C. Latin, from *calcar* spur. See CALCAR[2].

calcar[1] *n.* the reverberatory furnace in which the first calcination is made in glass-making. WH: 17C. Italian *calcara*, from Late Latin *calcaria* limekiln.

calcar[2] *n.* a spurlike process on a petal or on a bird's leg. WH: 18C. Latin spur, from *calx, calcis* heel. See CALX.

calcareous *a.* of or containing calcium carbonate; chalky or limy. WH: 17C. Latin *calcarius* of lime (see CALX, also -ARY[1]) + -OUS. Cp. CHALK.

calceolaria *n.* any plant of the genus *Calceolaria*, with slipper-like flowers; slipperwort. WH: 18C. Modern Latin, from Latin *calceolus*, dim. of *calceus* shoe + -aria. See also -ARY[1].

calceolate *a.* shaped like a slipper. WH: 19C. Latin *calceolus* (CALCEOLARIA) + -ATE[2].

calci- *comb. form* lime, calcium. WH: Latin *calx, calcis* lime + -i-. See CALX. The form usually has the sense calcium carbonate.

calcic *a.* of, relating to or containing calcium or lime. WH: 19C. CALCIUM + -IC.

calcicole *a.* (of a plant) thriving in chalk or limy soil. *Also n.* WH: 19C. CALCI- + Latin *colere* to inhabit.

calciferol *n.* a compound found in dairy products, vitamin D[2]. WH: mid-20C. CALCIFEROUS + -OL. The compound is so called because it promotes bone calcification.

calciferous *a.* (*Chem.*) yielding or containing calcium salts. WH: 18C. CALCI- + -FEROUS.

calcifuge *a.* (of a plant) not suited to chalky or limy soil. *Also n.* WH: 19C. CALCI- + -FUGE.

calcify *v.t.* to convert into lime. *Also v.i.* WH: 19C. CALCI- + -FY.

calcine *v.t.* to reduce to calcium oxide by heat. *Also v.i.* WH: 14–15C. Old French *calciner*, or from Medieval Latin *calcinare*, from Late Latin *calcina* lime, from Latin *calx, calcis* CALX.

calcite *n.* natural crystallized calcium carbonate. WH: 19C. Latin *calx, calcis* (see CALX) + -ITE[1].

calcitonin *n.* a hormone produced and secreted by the thyroid gland, which inhibits the loss of calcium from the skeleton and controls the amount of calcium in the blood. WH: mid-20C. CALCIUM + TONE + -IN[1].

calcium *n.* a silver-white metallic element, at. no. 20, chem. symbol Ca. WH: 19C. Latin *calx, calcis* (see CALX) + -IUM. The element was so named in 1808 by the English chemist Sir Humphry Davy. Cp. BARIUM, MAGNESIUM, STRONTIUM.

calcrete *n.* a rock made up of particles of sand and gravel held together with calcium carbonate. WH: early 20C. CALCI- + CONCRETE[1].

calculate *v.t.* to determine by mathematical process. *Also v.i.* WH: 14–15C. Late Latin *calculatus*, p.p. of *calculare*. See CALCULUS, also -ATE[3].

calculus *n.* a stony growth formed in various organs of the body, such as the kidney. WH: 17C. Latin small stone. The Romans used small pebbles for reckoning (calculating) on an abacus.

caldarium *n.* a Roman hot bath or room where such baths were taken. WH: 18C. Latin, from *calidus* hot.

caldera *n.* a large, deep volcanic crater. WH: 19C. Spanish, from Late Latin *caldaria* pot for boiling. Cp. CAULDRON.

Caledonian *a.* of or relating to Scotland; Scottish. *Also n.* WH: 17C. Latin *Caledonia*, Roman name of part of N Britain, later applied to Scotland + -AN.

calefacient *a.* causing heat or warmth. *Also n.* WH: 17C. Latin *calefaciens, calefacientis*, pres.p. of *calefacere*, from *calere* to be warm. See -FACIENT.

calendar *n.* a list of the months, weeks and days of the year, with the civil and ecclesiastical holidays, festivals and other dates. *Also v.t.* WH: 12–14C. Old French *calendier* (Modern French *calendrier*), from Latin *calendarium* account book, from *calendare* CALENDS (day on which accounts were due). See also -AR[3].

calender[1] *n.* a press or machine in which cloth or paper is passed between rollers to make it glossy. *Also v.t.* WH: 15C. Old French *calandrer*, of uncertain orig. The word is perhaps from Latin *calendra*, from Greek *kulindros* CYLINDER.

calender[2] *n.* a member of an order of mendicant dervishes. WH: 16C. Persian *ḳalandar* uncouth (man), ? from *ḳaland* pickaxe, shovel.

calends *n.pl.* the first day of any month in the ancient Roman calendar. WH: pre-1200. Old French *calendes*, from Latin *calendae*, *kalendae* first day of the month (when the order of days was proclaimed), from base of Latin *calare*, Greek *kalein* to call, to proclaim.

calendula *n.* a marigold, or any other plant of the genus *Calendula*. WH: 16C. Modern Latin, dim. of *calendae* CALENDS. The plant is so named because its flowers are reputed to last for a month.

calenture *n.* a fever or delirium caused by heat, esp. suffered by sailors in the tropics. WH: 16C. French, from Spanish *calentura*, from *calentar* to be hot, from Latin *calere* to be warm.

calescence *n.* increasing warmth or heat. WH: 19C. Latin *calescens*, *calescentis*, pres.p. of *calescere* to grow warm, from *calere* to be warm. See also -ESCENCE.

calf¹ *n.* the young of any bovine animal, esp. of the domestic cow. WH: pre-1200. Old English *cælf*, *cealf*, from Germanic. Cp. German *Kalb*.

calf² *n.* the thick fleshy part of the back of the leg below the knee. WH: 12–14C. Old Norse *kálfi*, of unknown orig. ? Rel. to CALF¹.

Caliban *n.* a brutish man; a savage, a boor. WH: 17C. *Caliban*, the partly human monster in Shakespeare's *The Tempest* (1611).

calibre *n.* the internal diameter of the bore of a gun or any tube. WH: 16C. Old French, from Italian *calibro*, or from Spanish *calibre*, ? from Arabic *ḳālib* mould, ult. from Greek *kalapous* shoemaker's last.

caliche *n.* a deposit of sand, gravel or clay containing minerals (esp. Chile saltpetre), found in very dry regions. WH: 19C. American Spanish, from Spanish pebble in a brick, from *cal* lime. See CALX.

calico *n.* cotton cloth formerly imported from the East. *Also a.* WH: 16C. Alt. of *Calicut* (now Kozhikode), a city and port in SW India, from which it was exported.

calid *a.* warm, tepid, hot. WH: 14–15C. Latin *calidus* warm.

Californian *a.* of or relating to California. *Also n.* WH: 18C. *California*, a state in W USA + -AN.

californium *n.* an artificially-produced radioactive element, at. no. 98, chem. symbol Cf. WH: mid-20C. *California* University, Berkeley, California, USA, where it was discovered, 1950 + -IUM. Cp. BERKELIUM.

†caliginous *a.* misty, murky. WH: 16C. Latin *caliginosus*, from *caligo*, *caliginis* mistiness. See also -OUS.

calipash *n.* that part of a turtle next to the upper shell, containing a dull green gelatinous substance. WH: 17C. ? W Indian, or alt. of Spanish *carapacho* CARAPACE. Cp. CALIPEE.

calipee *n.* that part of a turtle next to the lower shell, containing a light yellow substance. WH: 17C. ? W Indian. Cp. CALIPASH.

caliph *n.* the chief ruler in certain Muslim countries, who is regarded as the successor of Muhammad. WH: 14–15C. Old French *caliphe*, from Arabic *ḳalīfa* deputy (of God), from title *ḳalīfat Allāh*, or successor (of Muhammad), from title *ḳalīfat rasūl Allāh* successor of the Messenger of God, from *ḳalafa* to succeed.

calisaya *n.* bark from a tree of the genus *Cinchona*, esp. *Cinchona calisaya*; a type of Peruvian bark. WH: 19C. Spanish. ? From *Calisaya*, 17C Indian who revealed properties of quinine to the Spanish.

calix *n.* a cup or chalice. WH: 18C. Latin *calix*, *calicis* cup. Cp. CALYX.

calk¹ *v.t.* to copy (a drawing etc.) by rubbing the back with colouring matter and tracing the lines with a pointed instrument onto paper beneath. WH: 17C. French *calquer* to trace, from Italian *calcare*, from Latin *calcare* to tread. Cp. CALQUE.

calk² *n.* a calkin. *Also v.t.* WH: 16C. See CALKIN.

calkin *n.* a sharp projection on a horseshoe to prevent slipping. WH: 14–15C. Middle Dutch *kalkoen*, from Old French *calcain*, from Latin *calcaneum* heel, from *calx*, *calcis* heel.

call *v.t.* to name, to designate. *Also v.i., n.* WH: pre-1200. Old Norse *kalla* to cry, to summon loudly, from Germanic.

calla *n.* the arum lily, *Zantedeschia aethiopica*. WH: 19C. Modern Latin, from Greek *kallaia* cock's wattles, ? or from Greek *kallos* beauty.

caller *a.* cool, refreshing. WH: 14–15C. Alt. of *calver*. See CALVERED. Cp. SILLER.

calligraphy *n.* the art of beautiful handwriting. WH: 17C. Greek *kalligraphia*, from *kalligraphos* beautiful writer, from *kallos*, *kalli*- beauty. See -GRAPHY.

calliope *n.* a series of steam-whistles that produce musical notes when played by a keyboard. WH: 19C. Greek *Kalliopē* Calliope, the Muse of epic poetry, whose name means beautiful-voiced, from *kallos*, *kalli*- beauty + *ōps*, *opos* voice.

calliper *n.* compasses with bow legs for measuring convex bodies, or with points turned out for measuring calibres. *Also v.t.* WH: 16C. Appar. alt. of CALIBRE.

callipygous *a.* having beautiful buttocks. WH: 18C. Greek *kalli-pūgos*, epithet of a statue of Aphrodite (Venus), from *kallos*, *kalli*- beauty + *pūgē* buttocks. See also -OUS.

callisthenics *n.pl.* gymnastics promoting fitness and grace. WH: 19C. Greek *kallos*, *kalli*- beauty + *sthenos* strength + -ICS.

callop *n.* an Australian freshwater fish, *Plectroplites ambiguus*, used as food. WH: early 20C. Australian Aboriginal.

callous *a.* unfeeling, insensitive. WH: 14–15C. French *calleux*, from Latin *callosus*, from *callus* hardened skin. See also -OUS. Cp. CALLUS.

callow *a.* youthful, immature, inexperienced. *Also n.* WH: pre-1200. Old English *calu*, from Germanic, prob. from Latin *calvus* bald.

calluna *n.* the heather, *Calluna vulgaris*. WH: 19C. Modern Latin, from Greek *kallunein* to beautify, to sweep clean, from *kallos* beauty.

callus *n.* an area of hard or thick skin caused by friction, pressure etc. *Also v.i., v.t.* WH: 16C. Latin *callus*, more commonly *callum* hardened skin. Cp. CALLOUS.

calm *a.* still, quiet. *Also n., v.t., v.i.* WH: 14–15C. ? Popular Latin alt. of Late Latin *cauma*, from Greek *kauma* heat (of the day, of the sun), by assoc. with Latin *calere* to be warm.

calmodulin *n.* a protein found in most plant and animal cells, where it controls various processes involving calcium. WH: late 20C. CALCIUM + MODULATE + -IN¹.

calomel *n.* mercurous chloride, an active purgative. WH: 17C. Modern Latin, ? from Greek *kalos* beautiful + *melas* black. Calomel is a white powder but the powder is black at the initial stage of preparation.

Calor gas® *n.* a type of bottled gas used for cooking etc. WH: mid-20C. Latin *calor* heat + GAS.

caloric *a.* of or relating to heat or calories. *Also n.* WH: 18C. French *calorique*, from Latin *calor* heat. See also -IC.

calorie *n.* a unit of heat, equalling 4.1868 joules; the quantity of heat required to raise the temperature of 1 gram of water by 1°C, a small calorie. WH: 19C. French, from Latin *calor* heat, + French *-ie* -Y².

calotte *n.* a small skullcap worn by Roman Catholic ecclesiastics. WH: 17C. French, ? rel. to *cale* CAUL.

calotype *n.* an early photographic process invented by W.H. Fox Talbot; a talbotype. WH: 19C. Greek *kalos* beautiful + -*type*. See TYPE.

caloyer *n.* a Greek Orthodox monk, esp. of the order of St Basil. WH: 16C. French, from Italian *caloiero*, from Ecclesiastical Greek *kalogēros*, from *kalos* beautiful + *gērōs* old age.

calpac *n.* a high, triangular felt cap worn in the East. WH: 16C. Turkish *kalpak*.

calque *n.* a loan translation, a literal translation of a foreign expression. WH: mid-20C. French copy, tracing. See CALK¹.

caltrop *n.* an instrument formed of four iron spikes joined at the bases, thrown on the ground to impede the advance of cavalry. WH: pre-1200. Old English *calcatrippe*, from Medieval Latin *calcatrippa*, *calcatrappa*, from Latin *calx*, *calcis* heel + Medieval Latin *trappa* TRAP¹.

calumet *n.* the tobacco-pipe of the N American Indians, used as a symbol of peace and friendship; the peace pipe. WH: 17C. French, dial. var. of *chalumeau*, from Late Latin *calamellus*, dim. of *calamus* reed. See CALAMUS.

calumny *n.* a malicious misrepresentation of the words or actions of another. *Also v.t.* WH: 16C. Latin *calumnia* trickery, ult. from *calvi* to trick, to deceive. See also -ATE³. Rel. to CHALLENGE.

calutron *n.* a mass spectrometer that is used in the separation of isotopes. WH: mid-20C. *Cal(ifornia) U(niversity)* + CYCLOTRON.

calvados *n.* apple brandy made in Normandy. WH: early 20C. *Calvados*, a department in Normandy, France.

calvaria n. the upper part of the skull of a vertebrate animal. WH: 14–15C. Latin skull. See CALVARY.

Calvary n. the place where Christ was crucified. WH: 17C. Latin *calvaria* skull (from *calva* scalp, *calvus* bald), translating Greek GOLGOTHA.

calve v.i. to give birth to a calf. Also v.t. WH: pre-1200. Old English *calfian*, *cealfian*, from *cælf*, *cealf* CALF[1].

calvered a. (of salmon etc.) prepared in a particular way when fresh. WH: 12–14C. P.p. of *calver*, ? rel. to Middle Low German *keller*, from Germanic base meaning to be cold. Cp. CALLER.

Calvinism n. the tenets of Calvin, esp. his doctrine of predestination and election. WH: 16C. French *calvinisme* or Modern Latin *calvinismus*, from Jean *Calvin*, 1509–64, French Protestant reformer. See also -ISM.

calvity n. baldness. WH: 17C. Latin *calvitium*, from *calvus* bald.

calx n. ashes or fine powder remaining from metals, minerals etc. after they have undergone calcination. WH: 14–15C. Latin *calx*, *calcis* lime, prob. from Greek *khalix* pebble, limestone.

calycanthus n. a N American shrub of the genus *Calycanthus*. WH: 18C. Modern Latin, from *calyx*, *calycis* (see CALYX) + Greek *anthos* flower.

calyci- comb. form calyx. WH: Latin *calyx*, *calycis* CALYX.

calyciform a. having the form of a calyx. WH: 19C. CALYCI- + -FORM.

calycine a. of, belonging to, or in the form of a calyx. WH: 18C. Latin *calyx*, *calycis* CALYX + -INE.

calycle n. a small calyx. WH: 18C. Latin *calyculus*, dim. of *calyx*, *calycis* CALYX. See also -CLE.

calypso n. a W Indian narrative song, usu. performed to a syncopated accompaniment and made up as the singer goes along. WH: early 20C. Orig. uncertain. The word is apparently not from *Calypso*, an island nymph in Greek mythology.

calyptra n. a hood or cover, such as a root-cap. WH: 18C. Modern Latin, from Greek *kaluptra* covering, veil.

calyx n. the whorl of leaves or sepals (usu. green) forming the outer integument of a flower. WH: 17C. Latin *calyx*, *calycis* or Greek *kalux* shell, husk, from base of *kaluptein* to hide.

calzone n. a folded pizza containing a filling. WH: mid-20C. Italian trouser leg. The pizza is so called from its shape.

cam n. an eccentric projection attached to a revolving shaft for the purpose of giving linear motion to another part. WH: 18C. Dutch *kam* comb, as in *kamrad* cogwheel.

camaraderie n. comradeship. WH: 19C. French, from *camarade* COMRADE. See also -ERY.

camarilla n. a cabal. WH: 19C. Spanish, dim. of *camara* CHAMBER.

camass n. any liliaceous plant, of the genus *Camassia*, esp. *Camassia quamash* or *Camassia esculenta*, the bulb of which is eaten by various N American peoples. WH: 19C. Chinook Jargon *kamass*, ? from Nootka *chamas* sweet.

camber n. the curvature given to a road surface to make water run off it. Also v.t., v.i. WH: 14–15C. Old French *cambre*, from dial. var. of *chambre* arched, from Latin *camurus* curved inwards. Rel. to CAMERA, CHAMBER.

Camberwell beauty n. a butterfly, *Nymphalis antiopa*, having deep purple wings with yellow or cream borders. WH: 19C. *Camberwell*, a village near (now a district of) SE London, where it was seen.

cambist n. an expert in the science of financial exchange. WH: 19C. French *cambiste*, from Italian *cambista*, from *cambio* exchange. See CAMBIUM, also -IST.

cambium n. the cellular tissue which annually increases the girth of exogenous trees and other plants. WH: 16C. Medieval Latin change, exchange, from Latin *cambiare* to exchange. The original reference was to sap that becomes or exchanges form with vegetative cambium.

Cambodian a. of or relating to Cambodia. Also n. WH: 18C. *Cambodia*, a country in SE Asia + -AN.

cambrel n. a bent piece of wood used by butchers for hanging up carcasses. WH: 14–15C. Either Anglo-French var. of Old French *chambril* lath or rel. to Welsh *cambren* crooked tree, from *cam* crooked + *pren* wood, stick. Cp. GAMBREL.

Cambrian a. of or belonging to Wales. Also n. WH: 17C. Medieval Latin *Cambria* Wales, var. of *Cumbria* (see CUMBRIAN) + -AN.

cambric n. a type of very fine white linen or cotton. WH: 14–15C. Flemish *Kamerijk* Cambrai, a town in N France, where originally made.

Cambridge blue n., a. pale blue. WH: 19C. *Cambridge* University, England. University sports teams wear light blue as part of their clothing, as distinct from the dark blue of Oxford.

camcorder n. a video camera and recorder combined in one unit. WH: late 20C. CAMERA + RECORDER.

came n. a strip of lead used in framing glass in lattice windows. WH: 16C. Orig. unknown.

camel n. a large, hornless, humpbacked ruminant with long neck and padded feet, used in Africa and the East as a beast of burden. There are two species, the Arabian camel, *Camelus dromedarius*, with one hump, and the Bactrian camel, *C. bactrianus*, with two humps. Also a. WH: pre-1200. Latin *camelus*, from Greek *kamēlos*, from Semitic. Cp. Hebrew *gāmāl*.

camellia n. an evergreen shrub, of the genus *Camellia*, with beautiful flowers. WH: 18C. Modern Latin. From Georg Joseph *Kamel* (Camellus), 1661–1706, Moravian Jesuit missionary and botanist. See also -IA.

†camelopard n. the giraffe. WH: 14–15C. Latin *camelopardus*, from Greek *kamēlopardalis*, from *kamēlos* (see CAMEL) + *pardalis* (see PARD[2]).

Camembert n. a soft rich cheese from Normandy. WH: 19C. *Camembert*, a village in Normandy, France.

cameo n. a precious stone with two layers of colours, the upper being carved in relief, the lower serving as background. Also a. WH: 14–15C. Old French *camehu*, *camahieu* (Modern French *camaieu*), rel. to Medieval Latin *cammaeus*, of unknown orig.

camera n. an apparatus for taking photographs, which records an image (or a series of images in a cinecamera) on a light-sensitive surface. WH: 17C. Latin vault, arched chamber, from Greek *kamara* object with arched cover. Cp. CHAMBER. The photographic apparatus is from Latin *camera obscura* dark chamber, invented in the 18C.

camerlengo n. a papal treasurer. WH: 17C. Italian, from Frankish. See CHAMBERLAIN.

camion n. a heavy lorry. WH: 19C. French, of unknown orig.

camisade n. a night assault or surprise attack, in which the soldiers wore their shirts over their armour as a means of recognition. WH: 16C. Spanish *camisada*, from *camisa*, from Late Latin *camisia*. See CHEMISE.

camisole n. an underbodice. WH: 19C. French, from Italian *camiciola* or Spanish *camisola*, dim. of (respectively) *camicia*, *camisa*, from Late Latin *camisia*. See CHEMISE.

camlet n. a fabric, orig. of camel's hair, now a mixture of silk, wool and hair. WH: 14–15C. Old French *chamelot*, *camelot*, ult. from Arabic *ḳamla* nap, pile of velvet. The word has become popularly associated with CAMEL.

camomile n. an aromatic creeping plant belonging to the genera *Anthemis* or *Matricaria*, esp. *A. nobilis* or *M. chamomilla*. WH: 12–14C. Old French *camomille*, from Late Latin *camomilla*, alt. of *chamaemelon*, from Greek *khamaimēlon* earth apple, from *khamai* on the ground + *mēlon* apple. The plant is so called from the apple-like scent of its flowers.

Camorra n. a lawless secret society in S Italy, dating from the old kingdom of Naples. WH: 19C. Italian, ? from Spanish *camorra* dispute, quarrel.

camouflage n. disguise, esp. the concealment of guns, vehicles etc., from the enemy by means of deceptive painting and covering. Also v.t. WH: early 20C. French, from thieves' slang *camoufler*, from Italian *camuflare* to disguise, to deceive, ? assoc. with French *camouflet* snub, whiff of smoke in the face. See also -AGE.

camp[1] n. the place where an army is lodged in tents or other temporary structures. Also v.t., v.i. WH: 16C. Old French, from Italian *campo*, from Latin *campus* level field, place for games or military exercises. Cp. CAMPAIGN, CAMPUS.

camp[2] a. affectedly homosexual. Also v.i., n. WH: early 20C. Orig. unknown. Appar. not rel. to CAMP[1].

campaign n. a series of military operations aimed at a single objective. Also v.i. WH: 17C. French *campagne*, from Late Latin *campania*, fem. sing. and neut. pl. (used as n.) of *campanius*, from

Latin *campus*. See CAMP[1]. Cp. CHAMPAIGN. Military forces were out in the field in summer but in quarters in winter.

campanile *n.* a bell-tower, esp. a detached one. WH: 17C. Italian, from *campana* bell + *-ile* -IL.

campanology *n.* the art of bell-ringing. WH: 19C. Modern Latin *campanologia*, from Late Latin *campana* bell + -O- + -LOGY. Late Latin *campana* is derived from *Campania*, the region around Naples, Italy, whose bronze ware was used for making bells.

campanula *n.* any plant of the genus *Campanula* with bell-shaped flowers, such as the bluebell of Scotland, the Canterbury bell etc. WH: 17C. Modern Latin, from Late Latin *campana* bell. See also -ULE.

Campeachy wood *n.* logwood. WH: 17C. *Campeche*, a port and state of Mexico.

campestral *a.* of, relating to or growing in the fields or open country. WH: 18C. Latin *campester, campestris*, from *campus*. See CAMP[1], also -AL[1].

camphene *n.* a terpene found in many essential oils. WH: 19C. CAMPHOR + -ENE.

camphor *n.* a whitish, translucent, volatile, crystalline substance with a pungent odour, obtained from *Camphora officinarum, Dryobalanops aromatica* and other trees, used as an insect repellent, in liniment and in the manufacture of celluloid. WH: 12–14C. Old French *camphore* or Medieval Latin *camphora*, from Arabic *kāfūr*, from Malay *kapur*, ult. from Sanskrit *karpūra*.

camphorate *v.t.* to wash or impregnate with camphor. WH: 17C. CAMPHOR + -ATE[3].

campion *n.* any flowering plant of the genera *Lychnis* or *Silene*. WH: 16C. ? Rel. to CHAMPION. The name was originally used for Latin *lychnis coronaria*, Greek *lukhnis stephanōmatikē* rose campion used for garlands.

campo *n.* an area of level or undulating grassland, esp. in Brazil. WH: 19C. American Spanish or Portuguese *field, open country*, from Latin *campus*. See CAMP[1].

campshed *v.t.* to line (a river bank) with piles and planks to prevent it from being worn away. WH: 15C. Prob. CANT[2] + *shide* plank, beam (rel. to SHEATH, SHED[1], SKI).

campus *n.* the buildings and grounds of a university or college. WH: 18C. Latin. See CAMP[1]. The word was first used at Princeton University, New Jersey, USA.

campylobacter *n.* a bacterium that can cause gastroenteritis and other disorders. WH: late 20C. Modern Latin, from Greek *kampulos* bent. + BACTERIUM.

camwood *n.* barwood; a hard red wood from a W African tree, *Baphia nitida*. WH: 17C. Prob. from Temne *k'am* + WOOD.

can[1] *v.aux.* to be able to. WH: pre-1200. Old English *cunnan*, ult. from Indo-European base seen also in Latin *gnoscere*, Greek *gignōskein*. Cp. German *können*. Rel. to UNCOUTH.

can[2] *n.* a metal vessel for holding liquid. *Also v.t.* WH: pre-1200. Old English *canne*, ult. from Germanic, or from Late Latin *canna*. Cp. CANE.

Canaan *n.* a land of promise. WH: 17C. Ecclesiastical Latin *Chanaan*, from Ecclesiastical Greek *Khanaan*, from Hebrew *kěna'an* ancient name of W Palestine, a land promised to the children of Israel (Exod. iii.17 etc.).

Canadian *a.* of or relating to Canada. *Also n.* WH: 16C. *Canada*, a federal state in N America + -IAN.

canaigre *n.* a dock plant, *Rumex hymenosepalus* of the southern states of America (esp. Texas), the root of which is used in tanning. WH: 19C. Mexican Spanish.

canaille *n.* the rabble, the mob. WH: 16C. French, from Italian *canaglia* pack of dogs, from *cane* dog.

canal *n.* an artificial watercourse, esp. one used for navigation. *Also v.t.* WH: 14–15C. Old French, var. of *chanel* CHANNEL[1], from Latin *canalis*, or from Italian *canale*. Cp. KENNEL[2].

canaliculus *n.* a small channel or groove. WH: 16C. Latin dim. of *canalis*. See CANAL, also -CULE.

canapé *n.* a small thin piece of bread or toast topped with cheese, fish etc. WH: 19C. French bed curtain, from Latin *conopeum*. See CANOPY. The topping 'sits' on bread or toast as if on a sofa (now a secondary meaning).

canard *n.* an absurd story, a hoax, a false report. WH: 19C. French duck. The sense comes from the French phrase *vendre un canard*

à moitié to half-sell a duck, i.e. not to sell it at all, so to deceive, to make a fool of.

canary *n.* a small yellow cagebird, *Serinus canaria*, from the Canary Islands. *Also a.* WH: 16C. From *Canary* Islands, off the W coast of Africa. The islands were known in Roman times for large dogs. Hence their name, from Latin *canis* dog.

canasta *n.* a card game similar to rummy, played by two to six players, using two packs of playing cards. WH: mid-20C. Spanish basket, from Latin *canistrum* CANISTER. Cp. CANASTER.

canaster *n.* a coarse kind of tobacco. WH: 19C. Spanish *canastro* basket, from Medieval Latin. The tobacco is so named from the rush baskets in which it was originally brought from America. See CANISTER.

cancan *n.* a stage dance of French origin performed by female dancers, involving high kicking of the legs. WH: 19C. French, said to be redupl. of *canard* duck. Cp. CANARD. According to some, the word is from French *cancan* gossip, scandal, from Latin *quamquam* although, and yet, a word typical of scholarly discussion in medieval times.

cancel *v.t.* to annul, revoke. *Also n.* WH: 14–15C. Old French *canceller*, from Latin *cancellare* to make in the form of a lattice, to cross out, from *cancellus*, pl.*cancelli* crossbars. Cp. CHANCEL.

Cancer *n.* the fourth of the 12 signs of the zodiac, the Crab. WH: pre-1200. Latin crab. See CANCER.

cancer *n.* a malignant spreading growth affecting parts of the body. WH: pre-1200. Latin crab, creeping ulcer, from Greek *karkinos* crab. Cp. CANKER, CHANCRE.

candela *n.* a unit of luminous intensity. WH: mid-20C. Latin CANDLE.

candelabrum *n.* a high, ornamental candlestick or lampstand, usually branched. WH: 19C. Latin, from *candela* CANDLE.

candescent *a.* glowing with or as with white heat. WH: 19C. Latin *candere* to be white, to glow. See also -escent (-ESCENCE).

candid *a.* frank, sincere. WH: 17C. French *candide* or Latin *candidus*, from *candere* to be white, to glisten. See also -ID. Cp. CANDLE.

candida *n.* a yeastlike fungus of the genus *Candida*, esp. *C. albicans*, which causes thrush. WH: mid-20C. Modern Latin, fem. of Latin *candidus*. See CANDID. Cp. CANDLE.

candidate *n.* a person who seeks or is proposed for some office or appointment. *Also v.i.* WH: 17C. Old French *candidat* or Latin *candidatus* clothed in white. See CANDID, also -ATE[1].

candle *n.* a cylindrical body of tallow, wax etc. with a wick in the middle, used for lighting or ornament. *Also v.t.* WH: pre-1200. Latin *candela*, earlier *candela*, from *candere* to be white, to glisten. The word came into English with the adoption of Christianity.

candour *n.* frankness, sincerity. WH: 14–15C. Latin *candor*, from base of *candidus, candere*. See CANDID, also -OUR.

candy *n.* sugar crystallized by boiling and evaporation. *Also v.t., v.i.* WH: 16C. Orig. *sugar-candy* (see SUGAR), from Anglo-French *candi*, from Old French, from Arabic *kandī* candied, from *kand* candy, from Persian, from Sanskrit *khaṇḍa* piece, fragment, from *khaṇḍ-* to break.

candytuft *n.* a herbaceous plant, *Iberis umbellata*. WH: 17C. *Candy*, obs. form of *Candia*, the island of Crete + TUFT.

cane *n.* a slender, hollow, jointed stem of the bamboo, sugar cane or other reeds or grasses. *Also v.t.* WH: 14–15C. Old French *canne*, from Latin *canna* reed, cane, tube, from Greek *kanna*, from Semitic. Cp. Hebrew *qāneh* reed.

canella *n.* a W Indian tree of the genus *Canella* with aromatic bark, esp. *C. winterana*. WH: 17C. Medieval Latin, from Latin *canna* cane, tube. See CANE.

canephorus *n.* a sculptured figure of a young woman or young man carrying a basket on their head. WH: 17C. Latin, from Greek *kanēphoros*, from *kaneon* basket + *-phoros* carrying (see -PHORE).

canescent *a.* hoary, greyish-white. WH: 19C. Latin *canescens, canescentis*, pres.p. of *canescere* to grow hoary, from *canus* hoary. See also -escent (-ESCENCE).

canfield *n.* a gambling card game similar to patience. WH: early 20C. Richard A. *Canfield*, 1855–1914, US gambling-house proprietor.

cangue *n.* a heavy wooden collar or yoke, formerly fixed round the neck of criminals in China. WH: 17C. French, from Portuguese *canga* yoke, from Annamese *gong*.

canicular *a.* of or relating to Sirius, the dog-star. WH: 12–14C. Late Latin *canicularis*, from *canicula* dog-star, dim. of *canis* dog.

canine *a.* of or relating to dogs or the family Canidae. *Also n.* WH: 14–15C. French *canin* or Latin *caninus*, from *canis* dog. See also -INE. Rel. to HOUND.

canister *n.* a metal case or box for holding tea, coffee etc. WH: 15C. Latin *canistrum*, from Greek *kanastron* wicker basket, from *kanna* reed. See CANE. Ult. rel. to CAN².

canker *n.* an ulceration in the human mouth. *Also v.t., v.i.* WH: 12–14C. Old French *chancre* (see CHANCRE), from Latin *cancer, cancris* CANCER.

canna *n.* any of a genus of ornamental plants with brightly coloured flowers. WH: 18C. Modern Latin *Canna*, from Latin *canna* CANE.

cannabis *n.* any plant of the genus *Cannabis*, esp. the Indian hemp. WH: 18C. Latin, from Greek *kannabis*, ? ult. rel. to HEMP. Cp. CANVAS.

cannel *n.* a hard, bituminous coal, burning with a bright flame. WH: 12–14C. Old French *chanel*. See CHANNEL¹. Cp. CANAL, KENNEL².

cannelloni *n.pl.* rolls of sheet pasta filled with meat etc. and baked. WH: mid-20C. Italian, augm. pl. of *cannello* stalk. See also -OON.

cannelure *n.* a flute, a channel. WH: 18C. French, from *canneler* to groove, to flute, from *canne* reed. See CANE, also -URE.

cannibal *n.* a human being who feeds on human flesh. *Also a.* WH: 16C. Spanish *Canibales*, form (recorded by Columbus) of name *Caribes*, people of W Indies. See CARIB. The named people were believed to eat human flesh. The sense may have been reinforced by Spanish *can* dog.

cannikin *n.* a small can or cup. WH: 16C. Dutch *kanneken*. See CAN², also -KIN.

cannon¹ *n.* a heavy mounted gun. WH: 14–15C. Old French *canon*, from Italian *cannone*, augm. of *canna* tube. See CANE, also -OON.

cannon² *n.* a billiards stroke by which two balls are hit successively. *Also v.i.* WH: 19C. Alt. of CAROM.

cannula *n.* a small tube introduced into a body cavity to withdraw a fluid. WH: 17C. Latin, dim. of *canna* CANE.

canny *a.* knowing, shrewd, wise. WH: 16C. CAN¹ + -Y¹.

canoe *n.* a light narrow boat (orig. made from a hollowed-out tree trunk) propelled by paddles. *Also v.i.* WH: 16C. Spanish *canoa*, from Arawak, from Carib *canaoua*. The current spelling is due to French *canoë*.

canon *n.* a rule, a regulation, a general law or principle. WH: pre-1200. Latin, from Greek *kanōn* rule, rel. to CANE.

canoodle *v.i.* to kiss and cuddle amorously. WH: 19C. Orig. unknown. The word is perhaps from NOODLE², influenced by CUDDLE.

Canopus *n.* the bright star in the constellation Argo. WH: 16C. Latin, from Greek *Kanōpus* name of an ancient Egyptian city.

canopy *n.* a rich covering suspended over an altar, throne, bed, person etc. *Also v.t.* WH: 12–14C. Medieval Latin *canopeum* baldachin, alt. of Latin *conopeum* net over a bed, from Greek *kōnōpeion* Egyptian bed with mosquito curtains, from *kōnōps* mosquito, of unknown orig.

canorous *a.* tuneful, melodious, resonant. WH: 17C. Latin *canorus*, from *canere* to sing. See also -OUS.

cant¹ *n.* hypocritical talk; hypocritical sanctimoniousness. *Also a., v.i.* WH: 16C. Prob. from Latin *cantare* to sing. Cp. CHANT.

cant² *n.* a slope, a slant, an inclination. *Also v.t., v.i.* WH: 12–14C. Middle Low German *kant* point, creek, border, from var. of Latin *canthus* iron tyre.

cant³ *a.* strong, lusty. WH: 12–14C. ? From CANT². Cp. Dutch *kant* neat, clever.

Cantab. *a.* of Cambridge (University). WH: 18C. Abbr. of CANTA-BRIGIAN or Modern Latin *Cantabrigiensis*.

cantabile *a., adv.* in an easy, flowing style. *Also n.* WH: 18C. Italian that can be sung, from *cantare* to sing.

Cantabrigian *a.* of or relating to the town or University of Cambridge, England or of Massachusetts. *Also n.* WH: 16C. Latin *Cantabrigia* Cambridge (England) + -AN.

Cantal *n.* a hard strong-flavoured French cheese. WH: 19C. *Cantal*, a department of the Auvergne, France.

cantala *n.* a tropical American plant, *Agave cantala*, from which a coarse tough fibre is obtained. WH: 19C. Orig. unknown.

cantaloupe *n.* a small, round, ribbed musk-melon. WH: 18C. French. From *Cantaluppi*, a papal estate near Rome, where it was first grown on being introduced from Armenia.

cantankerous *a.* bad-tempered; quarrelsome. WH: 18C. ? Blend of *rancorous* (RANCOUR) and some other word of uncertain orig. The word is derived by some from Old French *contechier* to touch, to feel, from *con-* CON- and *teche*, related to *atachier* ATTACH.

cantata *n.* a poem, a short lyrical drama or (usu.) a biblical text, set to music, with solos and choruses. WH: 18C. Italian *aria cantata* sung air, with fem. p.p. of *cantare* to sing.

cantatore *n.* a male professional singer. WH: 19C. Italian singer, from Latin *cantator*, from *cantare* to sing. See also -OR.

canteen *n.* a restaurant or cafeteria in a factory or office where meals and light refreshments are sold at low prices to the employees. WH: 18C. French *cantine*, from Italian *cantina* cellar, ? from *canto* corner. See CANT².

canter *n.* an easy gallop. *Also v.t., v.i.* WH: 18C. Shortening of *Canterbury gallop*, easy pace of pilgrims riding to shrine of St Thomas à Becket at Canterbury.

canterbury *n.* a light stand with divisions for music portfolios etc. WH: 19C. *Canterbury*, a city in Kent, also a province in South Island, New Zealand.

cantharis *n.* Spanish fly, a coleopterous insect having vesicatory properties. WH: 14–15C. Latin, from Greek *kantharis*.

canthus *n.* the angle made at the corner of the eye where the eyelids meet. WH: 17C. Latin, from Greek *kanthos* corner of the eye. Cp. CANT².

canticle *n.* a brief song, a chant, esp. one of certain portions of Scripture said or sung in churches. WH: 12–14C. Latin *canticulum*, dim. of *canticum* song.

cantilena *n.* a ballad. WH: 18C. Italian, from Latin *cantilena* song, from *cantillare*. See CANTILLATE.

cantilever *n.* a projecting beam, girder or bracket for supporting a balcony or other structure. *Also v.i., v.t.* WH: 17C. Orig. uncertain. ? From CANT² + -i- + LEVER.

cantillate *v.t.* to chant or intone as in synagogues. WH: 19C. Latin *cantillatus*, p.p. of *cantillare* to sing low, to hum, from *cantare* to sing. See CHANT, also -ATE³.

cantina *n.* a bar or wine shop, esp. in Spanish-speaking countries. WH: 19C. Spanish and Italian. See CANTEEN.

cantle *n.* a fragment, a piece. *Also v.t.* WH: 12–14C. Old French *chantel* (Modern French *chanteau*), from Medieval Latin *cantellus*, dim. of *canthus*. See CANT², also -LE².

canto *n.* any one of the principal divisions of a poem. WH: 16C. Italian song, from Latin *cantus*. Cp. CHANT.

canton¹ *n.* a division of a country, a small district. WH: 16C. Old French, from Provençal, oblique case of var. of Latin *canthus*. See CANT².

canton² *v.t.* to divide into troops or cantons. WH: 16C. Partly from CANTON¹, partly from French *cantonner* to quarter, Italian *cantonnare* to canton, to quarter.

Cantonese *a.* of the city of Canton in S China, or its inhabitants. *Also n.* WH: 18C. *Canton*, English name of Guangzhou + -ESE.

cantor *n.* a precentor; a person who leads the singing in church. WH: 16C. Latin singer, from *canere* to sing.

cantrip *n.* a spell, an incantation, a charm. WH: 16C. Orig. unknown.

Cantuarian *a.* of or relating to Canterbury or its archiepiscopal see. WH: 16C. Latin *Cantuaria* Canterbury + -AN.

cantus *n.* a chant or style of singing used in the medieval church. WH: 16C. Latin song. Cp. CANTO, CHANT.

Canuck *n.* a Canadian. *Also a.* WH: 19C. Appar. from *Canada*. ? Influ. by CHINOOK.

canvas *n.* a coarse unbleached cloth, made of hemp or flax, used for sails, tents, paintings, embroidery etc. *Also a., v.t.* WH: 14–15C. Old French *chanevaz* (Modern French *canevas*), from Popular Latin *cannapaceus* made of hemp, from *cannapus*, from var. of Latin *cannabis* hemp, from Greek *kannabis*. Cp. CANNABIS.

canvass *v.t.* to solicit votes, interest, support, orders etc. from. *Also v.i., n.* WH: 16C. CANVAS, with unexplained alteration of sense. The word was perhaps adopted in the sense to sift (votes etc.) through canvas. The original meaning was to toss someone in a canvas sheet as a sport or punishment.

canyon *n.* a deep gorge or ravine with precipitous sides, esp. of the type formed by erosion in the western plateaus of the US. WH: 19C. Spanish *cañón* tube, pipe, augm. of *caña*, from Latin *canna*. See CANE, also -OON.

canzone *n.* a Provençal or Italian song. WH: 16C. Italian song. Cp. CHANSON.

caoutchouc *n.* raw rubber, the coagulated juice of certain tropical trees, which is elastic and waterproof. WH: 18C. French, from obs. Spanish *cauchuc*, from Quechua *kauchuk*.

cap *n.* a covering for the head, usu. soft and close-fitting, with or without a peak at the front. *Also v.t., v.i.* WH: pre-1200. Late Latin *cappa*, ? from Latin *caput* head. Cp. CAPE[1].

capable *a.* competent, able. WH: 16C. French, from Late Latin *capabilis*, from *capere* to take. See also -ABLE. Cp. CAPTIVE.

capacious *a.* able to hold or contain much. WH: 17C. Latin *capax, capacis*, from *capere* to take. See also -ACIOUS.

capacitate *v.t.* to make capable . WH: 17C. CAPACITY + -ATE[3].

capacity *n.* the power of containing, receiving, absorbing, producing etc. *Also a.* WH: 14–15C. French *capacité*, from Latin *capacitas*, from *capax, capacis*. See CAPACIOUS, also -ITY.

cap-à-pie *adv.* from head to foot (armed or dressed). WH: 16C. Old French *cap a pie* (Modern French *de pied en cap*) head to foot, from Latin *caput* head + *ad* to + *pes, pedis* foot.

caparison *n.* ornamental coverings or trappings for a horse or other beast of burden. *Also v.t.* WH: 16C. Obs. French *caparasson* (now *caparaçon*), from Spanish *caparazón* saddle cloth, ? from *capa* cape, cloak. Cp. CAPE[1].

cape[1] *n.* a sleeveless cloak. WH: 16C. French, from Provençal *capa*, from Late Latin *cappa*. See CAP.

cape[2] *n.* a headland projecting into the sea. WH: 14–15C. Old French *cap*, from Provençal, from Latin *caput* head. Several languages use the word for head to mean cape, e.g. Arabic *rā's*, Danish *hoved*, Welsh *pen*.

capelin *n.* a small Newfoundland fish, *Mallotus villosus*, of the smelt family, used as food or as bait for cod. WH: 17C. French, from Provençal *capelan* CHAPLAIN.

caper[1] *n.* a frolicsome leap. *Also v.i.* WH: 16C. Abbr. of CAPRIOLE.

caper[2] *n.* a prickly shrub, *Capparis spinosa*, of S Europe. WH: 14–15C. French *câpres*, or from Latin *capparis*, from Greek *kapparis*.

capercaillie *n.* the woodgrouse, *Tetrao urogallus*, also called the *cock of the wood*. WH: 16C. Gaelic *capull coille* horse of the wood. The variant spelling *capercailzie* with -*lz*- represents Middle English -*lz*-, the latter letter being YOGH. The bird is popularly said to be so named because the male's mating call resembles the whinnying of a horse, but the sense of horse is probably figurative, meaning large bird.

capias *n.* a judicial writ ordering an officer to arrest the person named. WH: 14–15C. Latin you are to seize, 2nd pers. sing. pres. subj. of *capere* to take.

capillaceous *a.* resembling a hair, hairlike. WH: 18C. Latin *capillaceus*, from *capillus* hair. See also -ACEOUS.

capillary *a.* resembling a hair, esp. in fineness. *Also n.* WH: 17C. Latin *capillaris*, from *capillus* hair. See also -ARY[2].

capital[1] *a.* chief, most important. *Also n., int.* WH: 12–14C. Old French, from Latin *capitalis*, from *caput, capitis* head. See also -AL[1].

capital[2] *n.* the head of a pillar. WH: 12–14C. Old French *capitel* (Modern French *chapiteau*), from Late Latin *capitellum*, dim. of *caput, capitis* head. The spelling with -*al* is by assoc. with CAPITAL[1].

capitate *a.* having a head. WH: 17C. Latin *capitatus*, from *caput, capitis* head. See also -ATE[2].

capitation *n.* a tax, fee or grant per person. WH: 17C. French or Late Latin *capitatio, capitationis*, from *caput, capitis* head. See also -ATION.

Capitol *n.* the national temple of ancient Rome, situated on the Capitoline Hill, dedicated to Jupiter. WH: 14–15C. Old French *capitolie*, later assim. to Latin *Capitolium*, from *caput, capitis* head. The earliest US senate house to be so named was that at Williamsburg, Virginia in 1699.

capitular *a.* of or relating to a cathedral chapter. *Also n.* WH: 16C. Late Latin *capitularis*, from Latin *capitulum*. See CHAPTER, also -AR[1].

capitulary *n.* a collection of ordinances, esp. those of the Frankish kings. WH: 17C. Late Latin *capitularius*, from Latin *capitulum*. See CHAPTER, also -ARY[1].

capitulate *v.i.* to surrender, esp. on stipulated terms. WH: 16C. Medieval Latin *capitulatus*, p.p. of *capitulare* to draw up under distinct heads, from Late Latin *capitulum*. See CHAPTER, also -ATE[3]. The original sense was to treat, to parley. The sense to surrender developed in the 17C.

capitulum *n.* a small head. WH: 18C. Latin, dim. of *caput, capitis* head. See also -ULE.

capiz *n.* a bivalve mollusc, *Placuna placenta*, found in the Philippines. WH: 19C. Tagalog.

cap'n *n.* captain. WH: 19C. Abbr. of CAPTAIN.

capo *n.* the head of a branch of the Mafia. WH: mid-20C. Italian, from Latin *caput* head.

capon *n.* a castrated cock, esp. fattened for cooking. *Also v.t.* WH: pre-1200. Old French *capon*, from Latin *capo, caponis*, rel. to Greek *koptein* to strike, to cut off.

caponier *n.* a covered passage across the ditch of a fortified place. WH: 17C. Spanish *caponera* capon pen. A caponier was originally a place for keeping capons. See CAPON.

caporal *n.* a coarse kind of French tobacco. WH: 19C. French CORPORAL[1]. The tobacco is so called from its superiority to the *tabac du soldat* soldier's tobacco.

capot *n.* the winning of all the tricks at piquet by one player. *Also v.t.* WH: 17C. French, ? from *capoter*, dial. var. of *chapoter* to castrate.

capo tasto *n.* a bar fitted across the fingerboard of a guitar or similar instrument, to alter the pitch of all the strings simultaneously. WH: 19C. Italian head stop.

capote *n.* a long cloak or overcoat, usu. with a hood. WH: 19C. French, dim. of *cape* CAPE[1].

capparidaceous *a.* of or relating to the Capparidaceae, a plant family that includes the caper. WH: 19C. Latin *capparis* CAPER[2]. See also -ACEOUS.

cappuccino *n.* white coffee, esp. from an espresso machine, often topped with whipped cream or powdered chocolate. WH: mid-20C. Italian. See CAPUCHIN. The coffee is so called from its colour, that of the habit worn by certain Capuchin monks.

capreolate *a.* having or resembling tendrils. WH: 18C. Latin *capreolatus*, from *capreolus* tendril. See CAPRIOLE, also -ATE[2].

capric *a.* of or relating to a goat. WH: 19C. Latin *caper, capri* goat + -IC.

capriccio *n.* a frisky movement, a prank, a caper. WH: 17C. Italian CAPRICE.

caprice *n.* a sudden impulsive change of opinion, mood or behaviour. WH: 17C. French, from Italian *capriccio* head with hair standing on end, horror, from *capo* head + *riccio* hedgehog (cp. URCHIN). The current sense evolved by association with Italian *capra* goat.

Capricorn *n.* the zodiacal constellation of the Goat. WH: pre-1200. Latin *capricornus*, from *caper, capri* goat + *cornu* horn, rendering Greek *aigokērōs* goat-horned.

caprification *n.* the practice of suspending branches of the caprifig on the cultivated fig, so that the (female) flowers of the latter may be pollinated by wasps parasitic on the flowers of the former. WH: 17C. Latin *caprificatio, caprificationis*, from *caprificatus*, p.p. of *caprificare*, from *caprificus* wild fig tree. See also -ATION.

caprifig *n.* the wild fig of S Europe and SW Asia Minor, *Ficus carica*, used in caprification. WH: 15C. Latin *caprificus* wild fig.

capriform *a.* having the form of a goat. WH: 19C. Latin *caper, capri* goat + -FORM.

caprine *a.* like a goat. WH: 14–15C. Latin *caprinus*, from *caper, capri* goat. See also -INE.

capriole *n.* a leap made by a horse without advancing. *Also v.i.* WH: 16C. French (now *cabriole*), from Italian *capriola*, from *capriolare* to leap, from *capriolo* roebuck, from Latin *capreolus*, dim. of *caper, capri* goat. See also -OLE[1].

Capri pants *n.pl.* women's tight-fitting trousers, tapering towards and ending above the ankle. WH: mid-20C. *Capri*, an island in the Bay of Naples. The trousers are so called as they are worn by tourists and holidaymakers on Capri. Cp. BERMUDA SHORTS.

caproic *a.* of or relating to a goat. WH: 19C. Latin *caper, capri* goat. + -*oic*. See also -O-, -IC.

Capsian *n.* a culture of the late palaeolithic period in N Africa and S Europe. *Also a.* WH: early 20C. French *capsien*, from Latin *Capsa* Gafsa, central Tunisia. See also -IAN.

capsicum *n.* a plant of the genus *Capsicum*, with mild or pungent fruit and seeds. WH: 16C. Modern Latin, ? from Latin *capsa* CASE².

capsid[1] *n.* any bug of the family Miridae, feeding on plants. WH: 19C. Modern Latin *Capsidae*, from *Capsus* genus name. See also -ID.

capsid[2] *n.* the outer casing of some viruses, made of protein. WH: mid-20C. Latin *capsa* CASE² + -ID.

capsize *v.t.* to upset, to overturn. *Also v.i., n.* WH: 18C. ? Spanish *capuzar* to sink (a ship) by the head, from *cabo* head + *chapuzar* to dive, to duck. The earlier English word was *overset*.

capstan *n.* a revolving pulley or drum, either power- or lever-driven, used to wind in a rope or cable. WH: 14–15C. Provençal *cabestan*, from *cabestre* halter, from Latin *capistrum*, from *capere* to seize. The Spanish equivalent word is *cabrestante*, formerly said to derive from *cabra* goat + *estante* standing, on the grounds that the word for goat in different languages is used for various mechanical devices. Cp. French *chèvre* sawhorse. But this is folk etymology.

capsule *n.* a small envelope of gelatin containing medicine. WH: 14–15C. French or Latin *capsula*, dim. of *capsa* CASE². See also -ULE.

captain *n.* a leader, a commander. *Also v.t.* WH: 14–15C. Old French *capitain* (Modern French *capitaine*), superseding earlier *chevetaigne* CHIEFTAIN and *chataigne*, from Late Latin *capitaneus* chief, from *caput, capitis* head.

caption *n.* the wording under an illustration, cartoon etc. *Also v.t.* WH: 14–15C. Latin *captio, captionis*, from *captus*, p.p. of *capere* to seize. See also -ION.

captious *a.* fault-finding, carping, cavilling. WH: 14–15C. Old French *captieux* or Latin *captiosus*, from *captio*. See CAPTION, also -OUS.

captivate *v.t.* to fascinate, to charm. WH: 16C. Late Latin *captivatus*, p.p. of *captivare*. See CAPTIVE, also -ATE³.

captive *n.* a person or animal taken prisoner or held in confinement. *Also a., v.t.* WH: 14–15C. Latin *captivus*, from *captus*, p.p. of *capere* to seize. See also -IVE.

capture *v.t.* to take as a captive. *Also n.* WH: 16C. French, from Latin *captura*, from *captus*. See CAPTIVE, also -URE.

capuche *n.* a hood, esp. the long pointed hood of the Capuchins. WH: 16C. French (now *capuce*), from Italian *cappuccio*. See CAPUCHIN.

capuchin *n.* a Franciscan friar of the reform of the 1520s. WH: 16C. French (now *capuchin*), from Italian *cappuccino*, from *cappuccio* hood, cowl, augm. of *cappa* CAPE¹. The friars are so named for their sharp-pointed hood. See CAPUCHE.

caput *n.* the head, the top part. WH: 18C. Latin head.

capybara *n.* a S American mammal, *Hydrochaerus hydrochaeris*, the largest living rodent, allied to the guinea pig. WH: 17C. Spanish *capibara* or Portuguese *capivara*, from Tupi *capiuára*, from *capĩ* grass + *uára* eater.

car *n.* a small road vehicle propelled by an internal-combustion engine, usu. having four wheels and seats for two to five passengers; a motor-car. WH: 14–15C. Old French *carre*, from var. of Latin *carrum, carrus*, from Celtic base seen in Irish *carr*, Welsh *car* wagon. Rel. to CARRY, CART and ult. to CURRENT. The sense development is: chariot (16C), passenger compartment of balloon etc. (18C), railway carriage (19C), motor vehicle (19C).

carabao *n.* the water buffalo. WH: 19C. Philippine Spanish, from Visayan *karabáw*.

carabid *n.* any beetle of the family Carabidae, the ground beetles. *Also a.* WH: 19C. Modern Latin *Carabidae*, from Latin *carabus* a kind of crab. See also -ID.

carabiniere *n.* a member of the national police force in Italy. WH: 19C. Italian carabineer. See CARBINE.

caracal *n.* a lynx, *Felis caracal*, of N Africa and S Asia, having black-tufted ears. WH: 18C. French or Spanish, from Turkish *karakulak*, from *kara* black + *kulak* ear.

caracara *n.* any of various American birds of prey that feed on carrion. WH: 19C. Spanish or Portuguese *caracará*, from Tupi-Guarani, of imit. orig.

caracol *n.* a half turn or wheel made by a horse or its rider. *Also v.i., v.t.* WH: 17C. French snail's shell, spiral. Rel. to ESCARGOT.

carafe *n.* a wide-mouthed glass container for wine or water at table. WH: 18C. French, from Italian *caraffa*, of unknown orig. The word is perhaps from Arabic *gharafa* to draw water.

carambola *n.* the star fruit. WH: 16C. Portuguese, prob. from Marathi *karambal*.

carambole *n.* in billiards, a cannon. *Also v.i.* WH: 18C. French red ball in billiards, from Spanish *carambola*, appar. from *bola* ball. Cp. CAROM. Appar. not rel. to CARAMBOLA.

caramel *n.* burnt sugar used for flavouring and colouring food and drink. WH: 18C. French, from Spanish *caramelo*, prob. from Medieval Latin *cannamella* sugar cane, appar. by folk etymology from Latin *canna* CANE + *mel, mellis* honey.

carangid *n.* any fish of the family Carangidae, including the scads, pilot fishes etc. *Also a.* WH: 19C. Modern Latin *Carangidae*, from *Caranx* genus name. See also -ID.

carapace *n.* the upper shell of an animal of the tortoise family. WH: 19C. French, from Spanish *carapacho*, of unknown orig.

carat *n.* a weight (standardized as the International Carat of 0.200 g) used for precious stones, esp. diamonds. WH: 14–15C. French, from Italian, from Arabic *ḳīrāṭ* weight equal to 1/24 of a miskal, from Greek *keration* fruit of the carob, dim. of *keras* horn.

caravan *n.* a mobile home, a vehicle for living in that can be towed by a car or (esp. formerly) by a horse. *Also v.i.* WH: 15C. French *caravane*, from Persian *kārwān*. Cp. VAN¹. Not rel. to CAR. The original sense was a company of merchants travelling together. The sense of mobile home emerged in the 17C and owed much to the wandering of gypsies.

caravanserai *n.* an Oriental inn with a large courtyard for the accommodation of caravans of merchants or pilgrims. WH: 16C. Persian *kārwānsarāy*, from *kārwān* (see CARAVAN) + *sarāy* palace (cp. SERAGLIO).

caravel *n.* any of various small light ships, such as a swift Spanish or Portuguese merchant vessel of the 15th–17th cents. WH: 16C. French *caravelle*, from Portuguese *caravela*, dim. of *caravo*, from Late Latin *carabus*, from Greek *karabos* horned beetle. The allusion is probably to the shape of the ship.

caraway *n.* a European umbelliferous plant, *Carum carvi*. WH: 12–14C. Medieval Latin *carui*, or some similar Romance form, from Arabic *karawiyā*, prob. ult. from Greek *karon* cumin.

carb *n.* a carburettor. WH: mid-20C. Abbr. of CARBURETTOR.

carbamate *n.* a salt or ester of carbamic acid, esp. carbaryl. WH: 19C. *carbam(ic)* + -ATE². See CARBO-, AMIDE.

carbanion *n.* a negatively charged ion at the carbon position. WH: mid-20C. CARBO- + ANION.

carbazole *n.* a substance obtained from coal tar, used to make dyes. WH: 19C. CARBO- + *azole* (see AZO-, -OLE¹).

carbide *n.* a compound of carbon with a metal, esp. calcium carbide. WH: 19C. CARBON + -IDE.

carbine *n.* a short rifle used by cavalry. WH: 17C. French *carabine*, from *carabin* mounted musketeer, of uncertain orig. The word is perhaps an alteration of *escarrabin* burier of plague victims (cp. SCARAB).

carbo- *comb. form* of, with, containing, or relating to carbon. WH: See CARBON, also -O-.

carbocyclic *a.* denoting a compound which includes a closed ring of carbon atoms. WH: 19C. CARBO- + *cyclic* (CYCLE).

carbohydrate *n.* an organic compound of carbon, hydrogen and oxygen, usu. having two atoms of hydrogen to every one of oxygen, as in starch, glucose etc. WH: 19C. CARBO- + HYDRATE.

carbolic *a.* derived from coal or coal tar. *Also n.* WH: 19C. CARBO- + -OL + -IC.

carbon *n.* a non-metallic element, at. no. 6, chem. symbol C, found in nearly all organic substances, in carbon dioxide and the carbonates, and occurring naturally as diamond, graphite and charcoal. WH: 18C. French *carbone*, from Latin *carbo, carbonis* coal.

carbonado *n.* a black, opaque diamond of poor quality, used industrially in drills etc. WH: 16C. Portuguese carbonated. See CARBON.

Carbonari *n.pl.* members of a secret republican society in Italy and France in the early part of the 19th cent. WH: 19C. Italian, pl. of *carbonaro* collier, charcoal burner, from *carbone* coal, ult. from

Latin *carbo, carbonis* CARBON. The Carbonari were reputed to evolve from a secret medieval society whose members were originally charcoal burners.

Carborundum® *n.* an abrasive material, esp. a silicon carbide used for grinding-wheels etc. WH: 19C. Blend of CARBON and CORUNDUM. The material was so named in 1891 by Edward G. Acheson, the US inventor who discovered silicon carbide, because the natural mineral form of fused alumina is called corundum.

carboxyl *a.* of or containing the monovalent radical -COOH. WH: 19C. CARBO- + OXY-[1] + -YL.

carboy *n.* a large globular bottle of green or blue glass, protected with wickerwork, used for holding corrosive liquids. WH: 18C. Persian *karāba* large glass flagon.

carbuncle *n.* a hard, painful boil without a core, caused by bacterial infection. WH: 12–14C. Old French *charbuncle*, from Latin *carbunculus* small coal. See CARBON, also -UNCLE.

carburation *n.* the process of mixing the correct proportions of hydrocarbon fuel and air in an internal-combustion engine etc. WH: 19C. From *carburet* (CARBURETTOR) + -ATION.

carburettor *n.* an apparatus designed to atomize a liquid, esp. petrol in an internal-combustion engine, and to mix it with air in the correct proportions to ensure ready ignition and complete combustion. WH: 19C. From *carburet* to charge with carbons (from CARBO- + -*uret*, from Medieval Latin -*uretum*) + -OR.

carby *n.* a carburettor. WH: mid-20C. Abbr. of CARBURETTOR + -Y[3].

carcajou *n.* the glutton or wolverine. WH: 18C. Canadian French, from Montagnais *kwa:hkwa:če:w*.

carcass *n.* the dead body of an animal. WH: 12–14C. Old French *charcois* (Modern French *carcasse*), of unknown orig. According to some, the word is from Latin *carchesium* a type of Greek beaker, from Greek *karkhision*.

carcinogen *n.* a substance that can give rise to cancer. WH: 19C. CARCINOMA + -GEN.

carcinology *n.* the branch of zoology which deals with the Crustacea. WH: 19C. Greek *karkinos* crab + -O- + -LOGY.

carcinoma *n.* a malignant tumour. WH: 18C. Latin, from Greek *karkinōma*, from *karkinos* crab + -OMA.

card[1] *n.* stiff paper or thin cardboard. WH: 14–15C. Old French *carte*, from Latin *charta* papyrus leaf, paper, from Greek *khartēs* papyrus leaf. Cp. CHART.

card[2] *n.* a toothed instrument for combing wool, flax etc. or raising a nap. *Also v.t.* WH: 14–15C. Old French *carde*, from Provençal *carda*, from *cardar* to tease, to comb, from Medieval Latin *cardo* teasel, from Latin *carere* to card.

cardamine *n.* any of a genus of cruciferous plants comprising the cuckoo-flower or lady's-smock. WH: 18C. Modern Latin, from Greek *kardaminē* some cresslike plant, from *kardamon* cress. Cp. CARDAMOM.

cardamom *n.* an aromatic plant of SE Asia, *Elettaria cardamomum*. WH: 14–15C. Old French *cardamome*, from Latin *cardamomum*, from Greek *kardamōmon*, from *kardamon* cress + *amōmon* amomum, an aromatic plant of the ginger family.

cardan joint *n.* in engineering, a type of universal joint which can rotate when out of alignment. WH: 18C. Gerolamo *Cardano*, 1501–76, Italian mathematician.

cardiac *a.* of or relating to the heart. *Also n.* WH: 14–15C. French *cardiaque*, from Latin *cardiacus*, from Greek *kardiakos*, from *kardia* heart. See also -AC.

cardie *n.* a cardigan. WH: mid-20C. Abbr. of CARDIGAN + -*ie* -Y[3].

cardigan *n.* a knitted jacket buttoned up the front. WH: 19C. James Thomas Brudenell, 7th Earl of *Cardigan*, 1797–1868, leader of the charge of the Light Brigade (1854) in the Crimean War, who wore such a jacket.

cardinal *a.* fundamental, chief. *Also n.* WH: pre-1200. Old French, from Medieval Latin *cardinalis*, from *cardo, cardinis* hinge. See also -AL[1].

cardio- *comb. form* of or relating to the heart. WH: Greek *kardia* heart. See also -O-.

cardiogram *n.* a reading from a cardiograph. WH: 19C. CARDIO- + -GRAM.

cardiograph *n.* an instrument for registering the activity of the heart. WH: 19C. CARDIO- + -GRAPH.

cardioid *n.* a heart-shaped curve. *Also a.* WH: 18C. Greek *kardioeidēs* heart-shaped, from *kardia* heart. See also -OID.

cardiology *n.* the branch of medicine concerned with the heart. WH: 19C. CARDIO- + -LOGY.

cardiomyopathy *n.* a disease of the heart muscle. WH: mid-20C. CARDIO- + MYO- + -PATHY.

cardiopulmonary *a.* of or relating to the heart and lungs. WH: early 20C. CARDIO- + PULMONARY.

cardiovascular *a.* of or relating to the heart and blood vessels. WH: 19C. CARDIO- + VASCULAR.

carditis *n.* inflammation of the heart. WH: 18C. Greek *kardia* heart. + -ITIS.

cardoon *n.* a thistle-like plant, *Cynara cardunculus*, allied to the artichoke, the leaf stalks of which are eaten as a vegetable. WH: 17C. French *cardon*, from *carde* edible part of artichoke, from Provençal *cardo*, from Latin *cardus* thistle, artichoke. See also -OON.

CARE *abbr.* Cooperative for American Relief Everywhere. WH: The acronym puns also on CARE.

care *n.* anxiety, concern. *Also v.i.* WH: pre-1200. Old English *caru*, from Germanic. Not rel. to Latin *cura* care.

careen *v.t.* to turn (a ship) on one side in order to clean, caulk or repair it . *Also v.i.* WH: 16C. French *carène*, from Italian (dial.) *carena*, from Latin *carina* keel. Cp. CARINA.

career *n.* a course or progress through life, esp. a person's working life. *Also a., v.i.* WH: 16C. French *carrière*, from Italian *carriera*, from Provençal *carreira*, from Latin *carrus* CAR.

caress *n.* a gentle touch. *Also v.t.* WH: 17C. French *caresse*, from Italian *carezza*, from Latin *carus* dear. See also -ESS[2]. Cp. CHARITY.

caret *n.* in writing or printing, a mark (^) used to show that something, which may be read above or in the margin, is to be inserted. WH: 17C. Latin it lacks, 3rd pers. sing. pres. ind. of *carere* to be without, to lack. Cp. CASTRATE.

cargo *n.* freight carried by ship or aircraft. WH: 17C. Spanish *cargo* a loading, or *carga* load, from *cargar* to load. See CHARGE.

Carib *n.* a member of the aboriginal people of the southern islands of the W Indies. *Also a.* WH: 16C. Spanish *caribe*, from Haitian creole. Cp. CANNIBAL.

Caribbee bark *n.* the bark of any of several W Indian trees of the genus *Exostema*, used for medicinal purposes. WH: 18C. Spanish *caribe* CARIB. Cp. *Caribbees*, old name of the W Indies, and specifically the Lesser Antilles.

caribou *n.* the N American reindeer. WH: 17C. Canadian French, from Micmac *xalibu* lit. snow shoveller. The native name refers to the animal's habit of pawing snow to find grass.

caricature *n.* a representation of a person exaggerating characteristic traits in a ludicrous way. *Also v.t.* WH: 18C. French, from Italian *caricatura*, from *caricare* to load, to exaggerate, from Late Latin *carricare*. See CHARGE, also -URE.

caries *n.* decay of the bones or teeth. WH: 16C. Latin decay.

carillon *n.* a set of bells played by the hand or by machinery. *Also v.i.* WH: 18C. French, from alt. of Old French *carignon, quarregnon*, from Popular Latin *quatrinio, quatrinionis*, from Latin *quaternio* group of four bells. Not rel. to CAROL.

carina *n.* a ridgelike or keel-shaped structure. WH: 18C. Latin keel. Cp. CAREEN.

carioca *n.* a S American dance like the samba. WH: 19C. Portuguese, from Tupi *cari* white + *oca* house.

†cark[1] *v.t.* to burden, to harass, to worry. *Also v.i., n.* WH: 12–14C. Old French *carche*, from *carchier*, from Late Latin *carricare*. See CHARGE.

cark[2] *v.i.* to break down. WH: mid-20C. Prob. from *cark* to caw (of imit. orig.), from assoc. of the crow with carrion.

carl *n.* a countryman. WH: pre-1200. Old Norse *karl* man, male, from Germanic. Rel. to CHURL.

carline *n.* any plant of the genus *Carlina*, allied to the thistle, esp. *C. vulgaris*. WH: 16C. French, from Medieval Latin *carlina*, ? from *cardina* (from Latin *cardo* thistle). The word has been influenced by the name of *Carolus* Magnus (Charlemagne), to whom its medicinal properties are said to have been revealed.

carling *n.* a strong fore-and-aft beam that supports the deck of a vessel. WH: 14–15C. Old Norse *karling* old woman, witch, fem. of *karl* CARL. The association of meaning is not clear.

Carlism n. adherence to Don Carlos and his heirs as the legitimate sovereigns of Spain. WH: 19C. French *carlisme*, from Spanish *carlismo*, from Don *Carlos*, 1788–1855, brother of King Fernando VII of Spain. See also -ISM.

carmagnole n. a lively song and dance popular during the French Revolution. WH: 18C. French style of jacket popular in French Revolution, from *Carmagnola*, a town in Piedmont, NW Italy.

Carmelite n. a member of an order of mendicant friars, founded in the 12th cent. on Mount Carmel; a White Friar. *Also a.* WH: 14–15C. French *carmélite*, from Medieval Latin *Carmelita*, from Mount *Carmel*, Palestine. See also -ITE¹.

carminative a. relieving flatulence. *Also n.* WH: 14–15C. Old French *carminatif* or Medieval Latin *carminatus*, p.p. of *carminare* to heal by incantation, from Latin *carmen, carminis* song. See CHARM¹, also -ATIVE.

carmine n. a vivid red or crimson pigment obtained from cochineal. *Also a.* WH: 18C. Old French *carmin*, ult. from Arabic *ḳirmiz*. See CRIMSON.

carnage n. slaughter, esp. of a large number of human beings. WH: 17C. French, from Italian *carnaggio*, from Medieval Latin *carnaticum*, from Latin *caro, carnis* flesh. See also -AGE.

carnal a. bodily, sexual. WH: 14–15C. Ecclesiastical Latin *carnalis*, from Latin *caro, carnis* flesh. See also -AL¹.

carnallite n. a white or reddish hydrous chloride of magnesium and potassium found in German and Iranian salt-mines. WH: 19C. Rudolph von *Carnall*, 1804–74, German mining engineer + -ITE¹.

carnassial n. in carnivores, a large tooth adapted for tearing flesh, the first lower molar or the last upper premolar. *Also a.* WH: 19C. French *carnassier* carnivorous + -AL¹.

carnation¹ n. the cultivated clove pink, *Dianthus caryophyllus*, with sweet-scented double flowers of various colours. WH: 16C. ? Ult. from misreading of Arabic *ḳaranful* clove, clove pink, from Greek *karuophullon*. See GILLYFLOWER.

carnation² n. a light rose-pink colour. *Also a.* WH: 16C. French, from Italian *carnagione*, from Late Latin *carnatio, carnationis*, from Latin *caro, carnis* flesh. See also -ATION.

carnauba n. a Brazilian palm, *Copernicia cerifera*. WH: 19C. Portuguese, from Tupi.

carnet n. a document allowing the transport of vehicles or goods across a frontier. WH: 19C. French notebook, from Old French *quaer* (Modern French *cahier* exercise book), from Popular Latin *quaternus*, from Latin *quaterni* set of four, from *quattuor* four. The original sense was a page folded into four. Cp. QUARTO.

carnify v.t. to convert to flesh. *Also v.i.* WH: 17C. Latin *caro, carnis* flesh. + -FY.

carnival n. a festival, esp. annual, usu. marked by processions and revelry. WH: 16C. Italian *carnevale*, from Medieval Latin *carnelevamen* Shrovetide, from Latin *caro, carnis* flesh + *levare* to put away. The word is not from Italian *carne* meat + Latin *vale* farewell.

carnivore n. any animal of the order Carnivora, a large order of mammals subsisting on flesh. WH: 19C. French, from Latin *carnivorus*, from *caro, carnis* flesh + -VORE.

Carnot cycle n. an ideal heat-engine cycle that gives maximum thermal efficiency and is reversible. WH: 19C. Sadi *Carnot*, 1796–1832, French scientist.

carnotite n. a yellow mineral, a vanadate of uranium and potassium, noted as an important source of radium. WH: 19C. M.A. *Carnot*, 1839–1920, French inspector general of mines + -ITE¹.

carny¹ v.i. to act in a wheedling manner. *Also v.t.* WH: 19C. Orig. unknown.

carny² n. a carnival . WH: mid-20C. Abbr. of CARNIVAL + -Y³.

carob n. the Mediterranean locust tree, *Ceratonia siliqua*. WH: 14–15C. Obs. French *carrobe* (Modern French *caroube*), from Medieval Latin *carrubia*, from Arabic *ḳarrūba*.

carol n. a joyous song or hymn, esp. sung at Christmas. *Also v.i., v.t.* WH: 12–14C. Old French *carole*, ? from Latin *chorus* CHOIR, influ. by Greek *khoraulēs* flute player, from *aulos* flute. The sense hymn of joy (especially Christmas carol) dates from the 14–15C. The original sense was a ring dance accompanied by a song.

Carolina duck n. a duck, *Aix sponsa*, found in the woodlands of N America. WH: 19C. *Carolina*, former British colony (now two states, N and S Carolina) of USA.

Caroline a. of or relating to the reigns of Charles I and II of Britain. WH: 17C. Medieval Latin or Modern Latin *Carolinus*, from Medieval Latin *Carolus* Charles.

Carolingian a. of or belonging to the dynasty of French kings founded by Charlemagne. *Also n.* WH: 19C. Var. of *Carlovingian*, from French *carlovingien*, from *Karl* Charles, based on *mérovingien* MEROVINGIAN.

Carolinian a. of or relating to either of the US states of N Carolina and S Carolina. *Also n.* WH: 18C. *Carolina* (see CAROLINA DUCK) + -IAN.

carolus n. any of various coins of the reigns of kings called Charles, esp. a gold coin of the time of Charles I of Britain. WH: 16C. Medieval Latin *Charles*.

carom n. in billiards, a cannon. *Also v.i.* WH: 18C. Abbr. of CARAMBOLE.

carotene n. an orange-red pigment found in plants, e.g. carrots, a source of vitamin A. WH: 19C. Latin *carota* carrot + -ene (alt. of -INE).

carotid a. of or related to either of the arteries (one on each side of the neck) supplying blood to the head. *Also n.* WH: 17C. French *carotide* or Modern Latin *carotides*, from Greek *karōtides*, pl. of *karōtis* drowsiness, from *karoun* to stupefy. The arteries are so called because compression of them was believed to cause stupor.

carouse n. a carousal. *Also v.i., v.t.* WH: 16C. German *gar aus* (*trinken*) (to drink) right out, completely.

carousel n. a merry-go-round. WH: 17C. French *carrousel*, from Italian *carosello* tourney, either from Italian dial. *carusello* ball of clay (which the contestants threw at each other), or from Arabic *kurraj* child's toy of model harnessed horses.

carp¹ n. any freshwater fish of the genus *Cyprinus*, esp. *C. cyprio*, the common carp. WH: 14–15C. Old French *carpe*, from Provençal *carpa*, or from Late Latin *carpa*.

carp² v.i. to talk querulously, to complain. WH: 12–14C. Old Norse *karpa* to brag, influ. by (or from) Latin *carpere* to pluck, to slander.

-carp comb. form a fruit, or a structure that develops into part of a fruit, as in *pericarp*. WH: Greek *karpos* fruit.

carpaccio n. an Italian hors d'œuvre comprising thin slices of raw meat or fish, sometimes served with a dressing. WH: early 20C. Italian, augm. of *carpa* CARP¹.

carpel n. the female reproductive organ of a flower, comprising ovary, style and stigma. WH: 19C. French *carpelle* or Modern Latin *carpellum*, from Greek *karpos* fruit. See also -EL.

carpenter n. a person who prepares and fixes the woodwork of houses, ships etc.; a skilled woodworker. *Also v.i., v.t.* WH: 12–14C. Old French *carpentier* (Modern French *charpentier*), from Late Latin *carpentarius artifex* carriage maker, from *carpentum* two-wheeled carriage, from Gaulish. Rel. to CAR. See also -ER².

carpet n. a woollen or other thick fabric, usu. with a pile, for covering floors and stairs. *Also v.t.* WH: 12–14C. Old French *carpite* or Medieval Latin *carpita*, from obs. Italian *carpita* woollen counterpane, from Latin *carpere* to pluck, to pull to pieces. Rel. to HARVEST.

carpo-¹ comb. form of or relating to the wrist. WH: Greek *karpos* wrist. See also -O-.

carpo-² comb. form of or relating to fruit. WH: Greek *karpos* fruit. See also -O-.

carpogonium n. the female reproductive organ of red algae. WH: 19C. CARPO-¹ + Greek *gonos* race + -IUM.

carpology n. the branch of botany which deals with fruits and seeds. WH: 19C. CARPO-² + -LOGY.

carpometacarpus n. in birds, a wing bone formed by fusion of the metacarpal bones with some of the carpal bones. WH: 19C. CARPO-¹ + METACARPUS.

carpophagous a. fruit-eating. WH: 19C. CARPO-² + -PHAGOUS.

carpophore n. in some flowers, an elongated part bearing the carpels and stamens. WH: 19C. CARPO-² + -PHORE.

carpospore n. a spore produced after fertilization of the carpogonium in red algae. WH: 19C. CARPO-² + SPORE.

carpus n. the wrist, the part of the human skeleton joining the hand to the forearm, comprising eight small bones. WH: 14–15C. Latin, from Greek *karpos* wrist.

carr *n.* an area of marshy ground or fen where willow, alder or similar trees or shrubs are found. WH: 12–14C. Old Norse *kjarr* brushwood.

carrack *n.* a large merchant ship; a galleon. WH: 14–15C. Old French *caraque*, ? from Spanish *carraca*, from Arabic, ? from *karākir*, pl. of *kurkūra* a type of merchant vessel.

carrageen *n.* an edible seaweed, *Chondrus crispus*, found on N Atlantic shores; Irish moss. WH: 19C. Irish *carraigín*, dim. of *carraig* rock. Cp. CRAG¹.

carrel *n.* a cubicle for private study in a library. WH: 16C. Appar. var. of CAROL in the sense ring.

carriage *n.* a passenger vehicle, esp. part of a train. WH: 14–15C. Old French *cariage*, from *carier* CARRY. See also -AGE.

carrick bend *n.* a knot for joining two ropes together. WH: 19C. ? Alt. of CARRACK + BEND.

carrier *n.* a person, thing or organization conveying goods or passengers for payment. WH: 14–15C. CARRY + -ER¹.

carriole *n.* a small open carriage. WH: 18C. French, from Italian *carriuola*, dim. of *carro* CAR. See also -OLE¹.

carrion *n.* dead, putrefying flesh. *Also a.* WH: 12–14C. Old French *charoigne* (Modern French *charogne*), from Latin *caro, carnis* flesh. Cp. CARNAL.

carronade *n.* a short naval cannon of large bore. WH: 18C. *Carron*, near Falkirk, Scotland, where orig. made + -ADE. Cp. CARRON OIL.

carron oil *n.* a mixture of linseed oil and lime water, formerly used for scalds and burns. WH: 19C. *Carron*, ironworks near Falkirk, Scotland, where much used + OIL.

carrot *n.* a plant, *Daucus carota*, with an orange-coloured tapering root, used as a vegetable. WH: 15C. Old French *carotte*, from Latin *carota*, from Greek *karōton*.

carry *v.t.* to transport or convey from one place to another by supporting and moving with the thing conveyed. *Also v.i., n.* WH: 14–15C. Anglo-French *carier*, var. of Old French *charier* (Modern French *charrier* to cart, to drag), from Late Latin *carricare*, from *carrus* CAR.

carse *n.* low fertile land, usu. near a river. WH: 12–14C. ? from pl. of CARR.

cart *n.* a strong two-wheeled vehicle for heavy goods etc., usu. drawn by a horse. *Also v.t., v.i.* WH: 12–14C. Old Norse *kartr*, prob. influ. by Anglo-French *carete* (Modern French *charrette*), dim. of *carre* CAR.

carte *n.* a card. WH: 14–15C. French, from Latin *charta*. See CARD¹, CHART.

cartel *n.* an agreement (often international) among manufacturers to keep prices high, to control production etc. WH: 16C. French, from Italian *cartello* placard, challenge, dim. of *carta*, from Latin *charta*. See CARD¹, CHART.

Cartesian *a.* of or relating to Descartes, or his philosophy or mathematical methods. *Also n.* WH: 17C. Modern Latin *Cartesianus*, from *Cartesius*, Latinized form of name of René *Descartes*, 1596–1650, French philosopher and scientist.

Carthusian *a.* of or belonging to an order of monks founded by St Bruno in 1084. *Also n.* WH: 16C. Medieval Latin *Carthusianus*, from *Carthusia* La Grande Chartreuse, a monastery near Grenoble, France. See also -IAN.

cartilage *n.* an elastic, pearly-white animal tissue; gristle. WH: 14–15C. French, from Latin *cartilago, cartilaginis*, ? rel. to Latin *cratis* wickerwork, CRATE.

cartogram *n.* a map showing statistical information in diagrammatic form. WH: 19C. French *cartogramme*, from *carte* map. See CARD¹, CHART, -GRAM.

cartography *n.* the art or practice of making maps and charts. WH: 19C. French *cartographie*, from *carte* map. See CARD¹, CHART, -GRAPHY.

cartomancy *n.* fortune-telling from a selection of playing cards. WH: 19C. French *cartomancie*, from *carte* CARD¹. See -MANCY.

carton *n.* a cardboard box. *Also v.t.* WH: 19C. French, from Italian *cartone*. See CARTOON.

cartoon *n.* an illustration, esp. comic, usu. dealing with a topical or political subject. WH: 16C. Italian *cartone*, augm. of *carta* CARD¹. See also -OON. The sense of comic drawing is first recorded in 1843 in *Punch*.

cartophily *n.* the hobby of collecting cigarette cards. WH: mid-20C. French *carte* card or Italian *carta* CARD¹ + -O- + -PHILY.

cartouche *n.* a scroll on the cornice of a column. WH: 17C. French, from Italian *cartoccio*, from *carta* CARD¹. Cp. CARTRIDGE.

cartridge *n.* a case, esp. of metal, holding the explosive charge of a gun etc., with or without a bullet. WH: 16C. Alt. of CARTOUCHE.

cartulary *n.* the register or collection of documents relating to a monastery or church. WH: 14–15C. Medieval Latin *cartularium*, from *cartula*, dim. of *carta*. See CARD¹, CHART, also -ULE, -ARY¹.

caruncle *n.* a small, fleshy excrescence. WH: 16C. Obs. French, from Latin *caruncula*, dim. of *caro, carnis* flesh. See also -UNCLE.

carve *v.t.* to cut (solid material) into the shape of a person, thing etc. *Also v.i.* WH: pre-1200. Old English *ceorfan*, from Germanic, prob. ult. rel. to Greek *graphein* to write.

Carver *n.* a chair with a rush seat and vertical and horizontal spindles in the back. WH: early 20C. John *Carver*, 1576–1621, first governor of Plymouth Colony.

caryatid *n.* a figure of a woman in long robes, serving to support an entablature. WH: 16C. French *caryatide*, from Italian *cariatide*, from Latin *caryatides*, from Greek *karuatides* (pl.) priestesses of Artemis (Diana) at *Karuai* (Caryae), Laconia.

caryophyllaceous *a.* belonging to, relating to or characteristic of the Caryophyllaceae, a family of plants that includes the pink and the carnation. WH: 19C. Modern Latin *Caryophyllaceae*, from *caryophyllus* clove pink, from Greek *karuophullon*. See GILLYFLOWER, also -ACEOUS.

caryopsis *n.* a fruit with a single seed, to which the pericarp adheres throughout, as in grasses. WH: 19C. Modern Latin, from Greek *karuon* nut + *opsis* appearance.

carzey *n.* a lavatory. WH: mid-20C. Italian *casa* house.

Casanova *n.* a man notorious for his amorous or sexual adventures. WH: early 20C. Giovanni Jacopo *Casanova* de Seingalt, 1725–98, Italian adventurer, famous for escapades and love affairs.

cascabel *n.* the rear part of a type of cannon. WH: 17C. Spanish, from Catalan *cascavel*, from Medieval Latin *cascabellus* little bell.

cascade *n.* a small waterfall, esp. one of a series of waterfalls. *Also v.i.* WH: 17C. French, from Italian *cascata*, from *cascare* to fall, from Latin *casus* fall. See CASE¹, also -ADE.

cascara *n.* the bark of a N American buckthorn, *Rhamnus purshiana*, used as a laxative. WH: 19C. Spanish *cáscara (sagrada)* (sacred) bark.

†cascarilla *n.* the aromatic bark of the W Indian shrub *Croton eluteria*. WH: 17C. Spanish, dim. of *cáscara* bark.

case¹ *n.* an instance, an occurrence. WH: 12–14C. Old French *cas*, from Latin *casus*, from base of *cadere* to fall. Cp. CADENCE. In the grammatical sense of a form of a declinable word, Latin *casus* translates Greek *ptōsis* fall.

case² *n.* a box or other container. *Also v.t.* WH: 14–15C. Old French *casse*, dial. var. of *chasse* (Modern French *châsse* frame), from Latin *capsa* box, bookcase, from base of *capere* to hold.

caseation *n.* the formation of cheese from casein when milk coagulates. WH: 14–15C. Medieval Latin *caseatio, caseationis*, from Latin *caseus* cheese. See also -ATION.

casein *n.* the protein in milk, forming the basis of cheese. WH: 19C. Latin *caseus* cheese + -IN¹.

casemate *n.* an armoured vault or chamber in a fortress or ship, containing an embrasure. WH: 16C. French, from Italian *casamatta*, earlier *casamata*, ? from Greek *khasma*, pl. *khasmata* CHASM. The word was formerly popularly derived from Italian *casa* house + Spanish *matar* to kill, as if meaning slaughterhouse.

casement *n.* a window or part of a window opening on hinges. WH: 14–15C. Anglo-Latin *cassimentum*, from *cassa* (Latin *capsa* CASE²). See also -MENT.

casern *n.* any of a series of temporary buildings for soldiers between the ramparts and the houses of a fortified town; a barrack. WH: 17C. French *caserne*, from Provençal *cazerna*, from Latin *quaterna* (hut) for four.

cash¹ *n.* coins and bank notes, as opposed to cheques etc. *Also a., v.t.* WH: 16C. French *casse* or Italian *cassa*, from Latin *capsa* CASE².

cash² *n.* any of various Eastern (esp. Chinese) coins of low value. WH: 16C. Obs. Portuguese *caxa*, from Tamil *kāsu*, influ. by CASH¹.

cashew *n.* the kidney-shaped nut of a tropical tree, *Anacardium occidentale*. **WH:** 16C. French *cachou*, from Portuguese *cachù*, from Tupi *acajú*.

cashier[1] *n.* a person who has charge of the cash or of financial transactions in a bank, shop etc. **WH:** 16C. Dutch *cassier* or French *caissier*, from *caisse* CASH[1]. See also -IER.

cashier[2] *v.t.* to dismiss from service, esp. from the armed forces, in disgrace. **WH:** 16C. Early Flemish *kasseren* to disband, to revoke, from French *casser* to break, to dismiss, from Latin *quassare* QUASH. The sense is said to have passed from Flemish into English through the contact of British soldiers with the Dutch in the Netherlands campaign of 1585.

cashmere *n.* a fine soft wool from the hair of the Himalayan goat. **WH:** 17C. *Kashmir*, a state in N of Indian subcontinent. Cp. CASSIMERE, KERSEYMERE.

casino *n.* a public establishment, or part of one, used for gambling. **WH:** 18C. Italian, dim. of *casa* house, from Latin *casa* cottage.

cask *n.* a barrel. **WH:** 16C. French *casque* or Spanish *casco* helmet. CASQUE.

casket *n.* a small case for jewels etc. *Also v.t.* **WH:** 14–15C. ? Anglo-French, alt. of Old French CASSETTE.

casque *n.* a helmet. **WH:** 17C. French, from Spanish *casco*. Cp. CASK.

Cassandra *n.* a person who prophesies evil or takes a gloomy view of the future, esp. one who is not listened to. **WH:** 17C. Latin, from Greek *Kassandra*, daughter of Priam, King of Troy, given power of prophecy by Apollo but condemned by him never to be believed.

cassareep *n.* the boiled-down juice of the bitter cassava root, used as a condiment. **WH:** 19C. Carib.

cassata *n.* a type of ice cream containing nuts and candied fruit. **WH:** early 20C. Italian little case.

cassation[1] *n.* annulment, abrogation. **WH:** 12–14C. Latin *cassatus*, p.p. of *cassare* to annul. See also -ATION.

cassation[2] *n.* an 18th-cent. instrumental composition similar to a divertimento. **WH:** 19C. German *Kassation* serenade, from Italian *cassazione*.

cassava *n.* a W Indian plant, the manioc, of the genus *Manihot*, esp. *M. esculenta*, the bitter cassava, or *M. dulcis*, the sweet cassava. **WH:** 16C. Taino *casávi*, *cazábbi*, influ. by French *cassave*, Spanish *cassava*.

Cassegrain telescope *n.* a type of reflecting telescope. **WH:** 19C. Giovanni *Cassegrain*, 1625–1712, French astronomer.

casserole *n.* an earthenware, glass etc. cooking pot with a lid. *Also v.t.* **WH:** 18C. French, from *cassole*, dim. of *casse*, from Provençal *casa*, from Late Latin *cattia* ladle, pan, from Greek *kuathion*, dim. of *kuathos* cup. See also -OLE[2].

cassette *n.* a small plastic case containing a length of audiotape, to be inserted into a cassette deck or cassette recorder; an audio cassette. **WH:** 18C. French, dim. of *casse*, *caisse* CASE[2]. See also -ETTE.

cassia *n.* any plant of the genus *Cassia*, including the senna. **WH:** pre-1200. Latin *cassia*, *casia*, from Greek *kasia*, from Hebrew *qĕṣī'āh*. The same source gave the name of Kezia, the second of Job's three beautiful daughters (Job xlii.14).

cassimere *n.* a fine twilled woollen cloth used esp. for suits. **WH:** 18C. Var. of CASHMERE.

cassingle *n.* a prerecorded audio cassette containing a single item of music, esp. pop or rock music, on each side. **WH:** late 20C. Abbr. of CASSETTE + SINGLE.

cassino *n.* a card game for two to four players. **WH:** 18C. Var. of CASINO.

cassis *n.* a usu. alcoholic cordial made from blackcurrants. **WH:** 19C. French blackcurrant, from Latin CASSIA.

cassiterite *n.* a black or brown mineral, stannic dioxide, a source of tin. **WH:** 19C. Greek *kassiteros* tin + -ITE[1].

cassock *n.* a long, close-fitting garment worn by clerics, choristers, vergers etc. **WH:** 16C. French *casaque* long coat, from Italian *casacca* riding coat, prob. from Turkic *kazak*. See COSSACK. According to some, the word is from Arabic *kazāgand* padded coat, from Persian *kazhāgand* from *kazh* raw silk + *āgand* stuffed.

cassoulet *n.* a dish consisting of haricot beans stewed with bacon, pork etc. **WH:** mid-20C. French, dim. of dial. *cassolo* stewpan, tureen.

cassowary *n.* a large flightless bird of the Australasian genus *Casuarius*. **WH:** 17C. Malay *kesuari*.

cast *v.t.* to throw, to hurl. *Also v.i., a., n.* **WH:** 12–14C. Old Norse *kasta* to throw.

castanet *n.* a small spoon-shaped concave instrument of ivory or hard wood, a pair of which is fastened to each thumb and rattled or clicked as an accompaniment to music. **WH:** 17C. Spanish *castañeta*, dim. of *castaña*, from Latin *castanea* chestnut. See CHESTNUT, also -ET[1]. The instruments are so called not from the wood from which they are made but from their chestnut-like shape.

caste *n.* any one of the hereditary classes of society in India. **WH:** 16C. Spanish and Portuguese *casta*, fem. (used as n.) of *casto* pure, unmixed, from Latin *castus*. See CHASTE.

castellan *n.* the governor of a castle. **WH:** 14–15C. Old French *castelain* (Modern French *châtelain*), from Medieval Latin *castellanus*, use as n. of Latin a., from *castellum* fortified place. See CASTLE, also -AN. Cp. CHATELAIN.

castellated *a.* having turrets and battlements. **WH:** 17C. Medieval Latin *castellatus*, from *castellum*. See CASTLE, also -ATE[2], -ED.

castigate *v.t.* to chastise, to punish. **WH:** 17C. Latin *castigatus*, p.p. of *castigare*, from *castus* pure. See also -ATE[3]. Cp. CHASTEN.

Castile soap *n.* a fine, hard soap, whose main constituents are olive oil and soda. **WH:** 14–15C. *Castile*, a province (formerly a kingdom) in Spain, where orig. made.

Castilian *n.* a native or inhabitant of Castile in Spain. *Also a.* **WH:** 15C. Spanish *Castellano*, from *Castella* Castile. See also -IAN.

castle *n.* a fortified building, a fortress. *Also v.i., v.t.* **WH:** pre-1200. Anglo-French *castel*, var. of *chastel* (Modern French *château*), from Latin *castellum*, dim. of *castrum* fortified place. See also -LE[1].

castor[1] *n.* a small swivelled wheel attached to the leg of a table, sofa, chair etc. **WH:** 14–15C. CAST + -OR.

castor[2] *n.* an oily compound secreted by the beaver, used in medicine and perfumery. **WH:** 14–15C. Old French or Latin, from Greek *kastōr* beaver.

castor[3] *a.* good, excellent. **WH:** mid-20C. ? Shortening of *castor sugar* (see CASTOR[1]), denoting something sweet.

castor oil *n.* an oil, used as a cathartic and lubricant, obtained from the seeds of the plant *Ricinus communis*. **WH:** 18C. CASTOR[2] + OIL. The oil, although not obtained from the beaver, became popularly associated with the compound that was from that source. The two substances in fact have quite different applications.

castrate *v.t.* to remove the testicles of, to geld. **WH:** 16C. Latin *castratus*, p.p. of *castrare*. See also -ATE[3].

castrato *n.* a male soprano castrated before puberty to retain the pitch of his voice. **WH:** 18C. Italian, p.p. (used as n.) of *castrare* CASTRATE.

casual *a.* happening by chance; accidental. *Also n.* **WH:** 14–15C. Old French *casuel*, from Latin *casualis*, from Latin *casus* CASE[1]. See also -AL[1].

casualty *n.* a person who is killed or injured in a war or in an accident. **WH:** 14–15C. Alt. of Medieval Latin *casualitas*, from *casualis* (see CASUAL), based on PENALTY, *royalty* (ROYAL) etc. See also -TY[1].

casuarina *n.* any tree of the genus *Casuarina*, of Australia and SE Asia, with jointed leafless branches. **WH:** 18C. Modern Latin, from *casuarius* cassowary. The tree's branches resemble the cassowary's feathers.

casuist *n.* a person who studies or resolves moral problems, esp. one who uses plausible but false reasoning. **WH:** 17C. French *casuiste*, from Spanish *casuista*, from Latin *casus* CASE[1]. See also -IST.

casus belli *n.* an act that provokes or justifies war. **WH:** 19C. Latin, from *casus* CASE[1] + *belli*, gen. of *bellum* war.

cat[1] *n.* any mammal of the genus *Felis*, comprising the lion, tiger, leopard etc., esp. *F. catus*, the domestic cat. *Also v.t., v.i.* **WH:** pre-1200. Old English *catt*, from Late Latin *cattus*, prob. ult. from an Afro-Asiatic source.

cat[2] *n.* a coal and timber vessel formerly used on the NE coast of England. **WH:** 17C. ? From CAT[1]. Cp. Old French *chat* merchant ship.

cat[3] *n.* a catalytic converter. **WH:** mid-20C. Abbr. of *catalytic* (CATALYSIS).

cata- *pref.* down; downwards. **WH:** Greek, from *kata* down, against, wrongly, completely.

catabasis n. a downward movement. WH: 19C. Greek *katabasis*, from *kata-* down + *basis* going.

catabolism n. the process of change by which complex organic compounds break down into simpler compounds, destructive metabolism. WH: 19C. Greek *katabolē*, from *kata-* down + *ballein* to throw. See also -ISM.

catacaustic a. formed by reflected rays. Also n. WH: 18C. CATA- + CAUSTIC.

catachresis n. the wrong use of one word for another. WH: 16C. Latin, from Greek *katakhrēsis*, from *katakhrēsthai* to misuse.

cataclasis n. the crushing of rocks by pressure. WH: mid-20C. CATA- + Greek *klasis* breaking.

cataclasm n. a violent break or disruption. WH: 19C. Greek *kataklasma*, from *kataklan* to break down, from *kata* down + *klan* to break.

cataclysm n. a violent upheaval or disaster. WH: 17C. French *cataclysme*, from Latin *catclysmos*, from Greek *kataklusmos* deluge, from *kata* down + *kluzein* to wash.

catacomb n. a subterranean burial place, with niches for the dead, esp. the subterranean galleries at Rome. WH: pre-1200. French *catacombes*, from Late Latin *catacumbas*, of uncertain orig. The word is perhaps from Greek *kata* down + *tumbos* TOMB.

catadromous a. (of fish) descending periodically to spawn (in the sea or the lower waters of a river). WH: 19C. CATA- + -*dromous*, based on ANADROMOUS.

catafalque n. a temporary stage or tomblike structure for the coffin during a state funeral service. WH: 17C. French, from Italian *catafalco*, of unknown orig. Cp. SCAFFOLD.

Catalan a. of or relating to Catalonia, its people or their language. Also n. WH: 14–15C. French, from Provençal and Spanish, from Spanish *Cataluña*, Catalan *Catalunya* Catalonia. See also -AN.

catalase n. an enzyme involved in the decomposition of hydrogen peroxide. WH: early 20C. CATALYSIS + -ASE.

catalectic a. having an incomplete metrical foot at the end of a line. Also n. WH: 16C. Late Latin *catalecticus*, from Greek *katalēktikos*, from *katalēgein* to leave off, from *kata* down + *lēgein* to cease. See also -IC.

catalepsy n. a state of trance or suspension of voluntary sensation. WH: 14–15C. French *catalepsie*, from Late Latin *catalepsia*, from Greek *katalēpsis*, from *katalambanein* to seize upon. See CATA-, also -Y[2].

catalogue n. a methodical list, arranged alphabetically or under class headings, e.g. of items for sale, books in a library etc. Also v.t. WH: 14–15C. Old French, from Late Latin *catalogus*, from Greek *katalogos*, from *katalegein* to pick out, from *kata* completely + *legein* to choose.

catalpa n. any tree of the chiefly N American genus *Catalpa*, with long, thin pods. WH: 18C. Creek.

catalysis n. the acceleration of a chemical reaction by a catalyst. WH: 17C. Modern Latin, from Greek *katalusis*, from *kataluein* to dissolve, from *kata* down + *luein* to set free.

catamaran n. a double-hulled boat. WH: 17C. Tamil *kaṭṭu-maram*, lit. tied wood. Cp. TRIMARAN.

catamenia n.pl. the menses. WH: 18C. Greek, neut. pl. of *katamēnios* monthly, from *kata* down + *mēn* month.

catamite n. a boy kept for homosexual purposes. WH: 16C. Latin *catamitus*, from Greek *Ganumēdēs* Ganymede, Zeus's cupbearer and presumed lover. Ganymede's name has been derived from Greek *ganos* sheen (as of wine) + *mēdea* genitals.

catamountain n. the leopard, panther, puma, lynx etc. WH: 14–15C. *cat of* (*the*) *mountain*. The word is not a translation of some other name.

catananche n. any plant of the genus *Catananche*, of the daisy family. WH: 19C. Modern Latin, from Latin *catanance* plant used in love potions, from Greek *katanagkē*, from *kata* down + *anagkē* compulsion.

cataphoresis n. the movement of charged particles under the influence of an electric field. WH: 19C. CATA- + Greek *phorēsis* being carried.

cataphyll n. a simplified or rudimentary leaf. WH: 19C. Greek *kata* down + *phullon* leaf.

cataplasm n. a poultice, a plaster. WH: 14–15C. Old French *cataplasme*, from Late Latin *cataplasma*, from Greek *kataplasma*, from *kataplassein* to plaster over, from *kata* down + *plassein* to plaster.

cataplexy n. temporary paralysis brought on suddenly by shock. WH: 19C. Greek *kataplēxis* stupefaction, from *kataplēssein*, from *kata* down + *plēssein* to strike.

catapult n. a device for propelling small stones, made from a forked stick with elastic between the prongs. Also v.t., v.i. WH: 16C. Old French *catapulte* or Latin *catapulta*, from Greek *katapeltēs*, from *kata* against + var. of base of *pallein* to hurl.

cataract n. a large, rushing waterfall. WH: 14–15C. Latin *cataracta* waterfall, from Greek *kataraktēs*, *katarrhaktēs*, from *kata* down + *rhattein* to dash, to break.

catarrh n. inflammation of a mucous membrane, esp. of the nose, causing a watery discharge. WH: 16C. French *catarrhe*, from Late Latin *catarrhus*, from Greek *katarrhous*, from *katarrhein* to run down, from *kata* down + *rhein* to flow.

catarrhine a. (of Old World monkeys) having the nostrils in a close, oblique position. Also n. WH: 19C. CATA- + Greek *rhis, rhinos* nose.

catastrophe n. a great misfortune or disaster. WH: 16C. Latin *catastropha*, from Greek *katastrophē* overturning, from *katastrephein*, from *kata* down + *strephein* to turn.

catatonia n. a syndrome often associated with schizophrenia, marked by periods of catalepsy. WH: 19C. CATA- + Greek *tonos* TONE + -IA.

catawba n. a N American variety of grape, *Vitis abrusca*. WH: 19C. *Catawba*, river in the Carolinas, USA.

catch v.t. to grasp, to take hold of. Also v.i., n. WH: 12–14C. Old French *cachier*, var. of *chacier* (Modern French *chasser*). See CHASE[1]. The original meaning was to chase. The sense to seize, to grasp has been influenced by LATCH.

catchpole n. a constable. WH: 14–15C. Var. of Old French *chacepol*, from var. of Latin *captare* (see CHASE[1]) + *pullus* fowl (cp. PULLET). The original meaning was tax-gatherer, literally chicken-chaser.

catechetic a. consisting of questions and answers; of or relating to catechism. WH: 17C. Ecclesiastical Greek *katēkhētikos*, from *katēkhētēs* catechist, from *katēkhein*. See CATECHIZE, also -IC.

catechism n. a form of instruction by means of question and answer, esp. the authorized manuals of doctrine of a Christian Church. WH: 16C. Ecclesiastical Latin *catechismus*, from Ecclesiastical Greek, from *katēkhizein*. See CATECHIZE, also -ISM.

catechize v.t. to instruct by means of questions and answers. WH: 14–15C. Ecclesiastical Latin *catechizare*, from Ecclesiastical Greek *katēkhizein*, *katēkhein* to sound through, to instruct orally, from *kata* down + *ēkhein* to sound, from *ēkhē*. See ECHO, also -IZE.

catechol n. a crystalline phenol found in catechu and other resins. WH: 19C. CATECHU + -OL.

catechu n. a brown astringent gum, obtained chiefly from the Asian tree *Acacia catechu*, used in tanning. WH: 17C. Modern Latin, from Malay *kacu*. Cp. CACHOU.

catechumen n. a person who is under Christian instruction preparatory to receiving baptism. WH: 14–15C. Old French *catéchumène*, or from Ecclesiastical Latin *catechumenus*, from Greek *katēkhoumenos* being instructed, pres.p. pass. of *katēkhein*. See CATECHIZE.

category n. an order, a class. WH: 14–15C. French *catégorie*, from Late Latin *categoria*, from Greek *katēgoria* statement, from *katēgorein* to speak against, from *kata* against + *agoreuein* to speak in the assembly. Cp. AGORA[1]. The word was originally a philosophical term. The sense of class, division evolved in the 17C.

catena n. a chain. WH: 17C. Latin, as in Ecclesiastical Latin *catena patrum* chain of the Fathers (of the Church).

catenane n. a chemical compound in which the molecules are linked together like a chain. WH: mid-20C. Latin *catena* chain + -ANE.

catenary n. a curve formed by a chain or rope of uniform density hanging from two points of suspension not in the same vertical line. Also a. WH: 18C. Modern Latin *catenaria*, fem. (used as n.) of Latin *catenarius*, from *catena* chain. See also -ARY[1].

cater[1] v.i. to supply food, entertainment etc. (for). Also v.t. WH: 16C. Middle English *acatour* caterer, purveyor, from Old French *achatour*, from *achater* to buy (Modern French *acheter*), ult. from Latin *captare* to take, to seize.

cater² †*n.* the number four on cards or dice. *Also adv.* WH: 14–15C. Old French *quatre* four. The original sense was four on a dice, the figures on which are placed diagonally.

cateran *n.* a Highland freebooter or irregular soldier. WH: 12–14C. Medieval Latin *cateranus*, from Gaelic *ceathairne* peasantry. Cp. KERN².

caterpillar *n.* the larva of a butterfly or other lepidopterous insect. WH: 14–15C. Prob. var. of Old French *chatepelose* lit. hairy cat, from Late Latin *catta* CAT¹ + *pelose* hairy, from Latin *pilosus*, from *pilus* hair (cp. PILE³), influ. by PILLAR. Cp. CHENILLE.

caterwaul *v.i.* to make the loud howling noise of a cat on heat. *Also n.* WH: 14–15C. CAT¹ + *-er-* + WAUL.

†cates *n.pl.* provisions. WH: 15C. Pl. of *cate*, from *acate* purchasing, from Old French *acat* (Modern French *achat*). See CATER¹.

Cathar *n.* a member of a medieval Manichaean sect in S France. WH: 17C. Medieval Latin *Cathari*, from Greek *katharoi* the pure (pl.). Cp. CATHARSIS.

catharsis *n.* the purging of the emotions by tragedy; emotional release achieved through dramatic art. WH: 19C. Modern Latin, from Greek *katharsis*, from *katharein* to cleanse, from *katharos* pure.

Cathay *n.* China. WH: 16C. Medieval Latin *Cataya, Cathaya*, from Turkic *Khitāy*. Cp. Russian *Kitaĭ* China.

cathedra *n.* the bishop's throne in a cathedral. WH: 14–15C. Latin, from Greek *kathedra* choir.

cathedral *n.* the principal church in a diocese, containing the bishop's throne. WH: 12–14C. Old French *cathédral*, from Late Latin *cathedralis*, from Latin CATHEDRA. See also -AL¹. As a noun the word is short for *cathedral church*.

Catherine wheel *n.* a firework that rotates like a wheel. WH: 16C. *Catherine*, legendary saint of Alexandria, martyred on a spiked wheel.

catheter *n.* a tube used to introduce fluids to, or withdraw them from, the body, esp. to withdraw urine from the bladder. WH: 17C. Late Latin, from Greek *kathetēr*, from *kathienai* to send down, to let down, from *kata* down + *hienai* to send.

cathetometer *n.* an instrument consisting of a telescope mounted on a vertical graduated support, used for measuring small vertical distances. WH: 19C. Latin *cathetus*, from Greek *kathetos grammē* perpendicular line (see CATHETER) + -O- + -METER.

cathexis *n.* concentration of mental or emotional energy on a single object. WH: early 20C. Greek *kathexis* holding, retention, rendering German (*Libido*)*besetzung* (libido)-filling.

cathode *n.* the negative electrode in an electrolytic cell. WH: 19C. Greek *kathodos* way down, from *kata* down + *hodos* way. Cp. ANODE.

catholic *a.* general, comprehensive. *Also n.* WH: 14–15C. Old French *catholique* or Latin *catholicus*, from Greek *katholikos* general, universal, from *kathalou* (*kath' holou*) in general, from *kata* in respect of + gen. of *holos* whole.

catholicon *n.* a universal medicine; a panacea. WH: 14–15C. French, from Modern Latin *catholicum* (*remedium*) universal (remedy). See CATHOLIC.

cation *n.* the positive ion which in electrolysis is attracted towards the cathode. WH: 19C. CATHODE or CATA- + ION.

catkin *n.* the pendulous flower head of the willow, birch, poplar etc. WH: 16C. Obs. Dutch *katteken* kitten. See CAT¹, also -KIN. The catkin is apparently so called from its soft downy appearance, suggesting a kitten's fur. There was no word for it in English until the botanist Henry Lyte adopted it from the Dutch in 1578. An earlier general word for the pendent part of a flower was AGLET.

catling *n.* a double-edged knife used in surgical amputations. WH: 17C. CAT¹ + -LING¹.

catoptric *a.* of or relating to a mirror or reflector, or to reflection. WH: 16C. Greek *katoptrikos*, from *katoptron* mirror. See also -IC.

cattalo *n.* a hardy cross between domestic cattle and American bison. WH: 19C. Blend of CATTLE and BUFFALO.

cattle *n.pl.* domesticated animals, esp. bovine mammals such as cows, bulls, oxen and bison. WH: 12–14C. Old French, var. of *chatel* CHATTEL. The original sense was personal property, which would have included the owner's livestock. The current, more specific sense emerged in the 16C. Cp. FEE, PECULIAR.

cattleya *n.* any epiphytic orchid of the genus *Cattleya*, with brightly coloured flowers. WH: 19C. Modern Latin, from William *Cattley*, d.1832, English horticultural patron. See also -A¹.

catty *n.* a unit of weight used in SE Asia, equal to about 1½ lb. (0.68 kg). WH: 16C. Malay and Javanese *kati*. Cp. CADDY.

Caucasian *a.* of or belonging to one of the main ethnological divisions of humankind, native to Europe, W Asia, and N Africa, with pale skin. *Also n.* WH: 17C. *Caucasus, Caucasia* the Caucasus, a mountainous region between the Black and Caspian Seas. See also -IAN.

caucus *n.* a preparatory meeting of representatives of a political party to decide upon a course of action, party policy etc. *Also v.i., v.t.* WH: 18C. ? Algonquian *cau'-cau'-as'u* adviser.

caudal *a.* of or relating to the tail or the posterior part of the body. WH: 17C. Modern Latin *caudalis*, from Latin *cauda* tail. See also -AL¹.

caudex *n.* the thickened stem and root of a plant, esp. of a palm or tree fern . WH: 18C. Latin, earlier form of CODEX.

caudillo *n.* in Spanish-speaking countries, a military leader or head of state. WH: 19C. Spanish, from Late Latin *capitellum*, dim. of *caput, capitis* head.

caudle *n.* a warm drink of wine and eggs formerly given to invalids. *Also v.t.* WH: 12–14C. Old French *chaudel* (Modern French *chaudeau*), from Medieval Latin dim. of Latin *caldum* hot drink, from *calidus* warm.

caul *n.* a part of the amnion, sometimes enclosing the head of a child when born. WH: 12–14C. ? Old French *cale* head covering.

cauld *a., n.* cold. WH: 12–14C. See COLD.

cauldron *n.* a large, deep, bowl-shaped vessel with handles, for boiling. WH: 12–14C. Anglo-French *caudron* (Modern French *chaudron*), augm. of var. of Latin *calidarium* cooking pot, from Latin *calidus* hot.

caulescent *a.* having a stem or stalk visible above the ground. WH: 18C. Latin CAULIS + *-escent* -ESCENCE.

cauliflower *n.* a variety of cabbage with an edible white flowering head. WH: 16C. Alt. (by assim. to COLE, FLOWER) of obs. French *chou fleuri*, prob. from Italian *cavolfiore*, pl. *cavoli fiori*, or from Modern Latin *cauliflora* flowered cabbage.

caulis *n.* the main stem or stalk of a plant. WH: 16C. Latin stem, stalk.

caulk *v.t.* to fill or seal with waterproof material. *Also n.* WH: 14–15C. Old French *cauquer, caukier*, var. of *cauchier* to tread, to press forcibly (Modern French *côcher*), from Latin *calcare* to tread, to press, from *calx, calcis* heel.

cause *n.* that which produces or contributes to an effect. *Also v.t.* WH: 12–14C. Old French, from Latin *causa* reason, motive. Cp. BECAUSE.

'cause *conj.* because. WH: 14–15C. Abbr. of BECAUSE. Cp. 'COS.

causerie *n.* an essay or article in a conversational style. WH: 19C. French, from *causer* to talk, from Latin *causari* to bring a lawsuit. See CAUSE.

causeway *n.* a raised road across marshy ground or shallow water. *Also v.t.* WH: 14–15C. From *causey* (from Old Northern French *cauciée* (Modern French *chaussée*), from Popular Latin *calciata via* paved way, from Latin *calx, calcis* lime (cp. CHALK)) + WAY. The original sense was a river embankment with a chalk base, and a similar raised way, path or road over marshy ground.

caustic *a.* burning, corrosive. *Also n.* WH: 12–14C. Latin *causticus*, from Greek *kaustikos*, from *kaustos* combustible, from *kaiein* to burn. See also -IC. The figurative sense first appeared in the 17C.

cauterize *v.t.* to burn or sear (a wound etc.) with a hot iron or a caustic substance. WH: 12–14C. Old French *cautériser*, from Late Latin *cauterizare*, from Greek *kautēriazein*, from *kautērion* branding iron, from *kaiein* to burn.

caution *n.* care to avoid injury or misfortune. *Also v.t.* WH: 12–14C. Old French, from Latin *cautio, cautionis*, from *cautus*, p.p. of *cavere* to take heed. See also -ION. Cp. CAVE², CAVEAT.

cavalcade *n.* a company or procession of riders on horseback. WH: 16C. French, from Italian *cavalcata*, from *cavalcare* to ride, from Latin *caballus* horse. Cp. CAVALRY.

cavalier *n.* a supporter of Charles I during the Civil War; a Royalist. *Also a., v.i.* WH: 16C. French, or Italian *cavaliere*, from Latin *caballus* horse. See also -IER. Cp. CHEVALIER.

cavalla n. any of various tropical fish, such as the *Gnathanodon speciosus*. WH: 17C. Spanish *caballo* horse, ? influ. by Italian *cavalli*, pl. of *cavallo* mackerel.

cavalry n. a body of soldiers on horseback, part of an army. WH: 16C. French *cavallerie*, from Italian *cavalleria*, from *cavallo* horse, from Latin *caballus*. See also -ERY, -RY.

cavatina n. a short, simple song. WH: 19C. Italian, from *cavata* production of sound, from *cavare* to extract, to dig out. Cp. CAVE¹.

cave¹ n. a hollow place in a rock or underground. *Also v.t., v.i.* WH: 12–14C. Old French, from Latin *cava*, fem. sing. (used as n.) of *cavus* hollow. The phrase *to cave in* is perhaps of Low German origin (cp. Dutch *afkalven* to fall away, *uitkalven* to fall out), influenced by CAVE¹.

cave² int. look out! WH: 14–15C. Latin beware!, imper. sing. of *cavere* to beware. Cp. CAVEAT.

caveat n. a warning, a caution. WH: 16C. Latin let him beware, 3rd pers. sing. pres. subj. of *cavere* to beware. Cp. CAUTION.

cavendish n. a kind of tobacco softened and pressed into cakes. WH: 19C. ? *Cavendish*, maker's or exporter's name.

cavern n. a large cave or underground chamber. *Also v.t.* WH: 12–14C. Old French *caverne*, from Latin *caverna*, from *cavus* hollow. Cp. CAVE¹.

caviar n. the salted roes of various fish, esp. the sturgeon, eaten as a delicacy. WH: 16C. Italian *caviale*, earlier *caviaro*, prob. from Medieval Greek *khaviari* (Modern Greek *khabiari*). Cp. Turkish *havyar*. Although associated with Russia, the Russian word for caviar is quite different: *ikra*.

cavicorn a. having hollow horns. *Also n.* WH: 19C. Latin *cavus* hollow + *cornu* horn.

cavil n. a petty or frivolous objection. *Also v.i., v.t.* WH: 16C. Old French *caviller*, from Latin *cavillari*, from *cavilla* mockery. Rel. to CALUMNY.

cavitation n. the formation of a cavity or cavities. WH: 19C. French, from *cavité* CAVITY. See also -ION.

cavity n. a hollow space or part. WH: 16C. Old French *cavité*, from Late Latin *cavitas*, from *cavus* hollow. See also -ITY.

cavo-rilievo n. a sculpture made by hollowing out a flat surface and leaving the figures standing out to the original level. WH: 19C. Italian hollow relief, from *cavo* hollow (cp. CAVE¹). + *rilievo* RELIEVO.

cavort v.i. to prance about; to caper or frolic. WH: 18C. ? Alt. of CURVET.

cavy n. a S American rodent of the family Cavidae, esp. any of the genus *Cavia*, including *C. cobaya*, the guinea pig. WH: 18C. Modern Latin *cavia*, from Galibi *cabiai*.

caw v.i. to cry like a rook, crow or raven. *Also n.* WH: 16C. Imit. Cp. CROW¹, ROOK¹.

Caxton n. a book printed by William Caxton. WH: 19C. William *Caxton*, c.1422–c.1491, English printer.

cay n. a reef or bank of sand, coral etc. WH: 17C. Spanish *cayo*, from French *quai* QUAY. Cp. KEY².

cayenne n. the powdered fruit of various species of capsicum, a very hot, red condiment. WH: 18C. Tupi *kyynha*, *quiynha*, assim. to *Cayenne*, a city and port in French Guiana.

cayman n. a tropical American reptile similar to an alligator, esp. any of the genus *Caiman*. WH: 16C. Spanish *caimán* or Portuguese *caimão*, from Carib *acayuman*.

cayuse n. a small American Indian horse. WH: 19C. Penutian, from name of people who bred it.

CD-ROM n. a compact disc used with a computer system. WH: late 20C. *CD* + *ROM*.

ceanothus n. any N American shrub of the genus *Ceanothus*, with small ornamental flowers. WH: 18C. Modern Latin, from Greek *keanōthos* a kind of thistle.

cease v.i. to come to an end, to stop. *Also v.t., n.* WH: 12–14C. Old French *cesser*, from Latin *cessare* to stop, from *cessus*, p.p. of *cedere* CEDE.

cecity n. blindness (physical or mental). WH: 15C. Latin *caecitas*, from *caecus* blind. See also -ITY.

cecropia moth n. a large N American moth, *Hyalophora* (or *Samia*) *cecropia*, with brightly coloured wings. WH: 19C. Modern Latin. From *Cecrops*, mythical first king of Athens.

cedar n. any evergreen coniferous tree of the genus *Cedrus*, with durable and fragrant wood, including the cedar of Lebanon. WH: pre-1200. Old French *cedre*, from Latin *cedrus*, from Greek *kedros*, ? from Semitic. Cp. Hebrew *qātar* it smoked.

cede v.t. to give up, to surrender. WH: 16C. French *céder* or Latin *cedere* to give way, to yield.

cedi n. the standard unit of currency in Ghana. WH: mid-20C. Ghanaian, ? alt. of SHILLING.

cedilla n. a mark (¸) placed under a *c* in French, Portuguese etc., to show that it has the sound of *s*. WH: 16C. Spanish (now *zedilla*), dim. of *zeda* (letter) Z. Cp. ZETA. The mark was formerly used in Spanish.

cee n. the third letter of the alphabet, C, c. WH: 16C. Representation of pronun. of letter name. Cp. DEE etc.

Ceefax® n. a teletext service operated by the BBC. WH: late 20C. Representation of init. elements of *seeing* + *facsimile*. Cp. FAX. The word also puns on *see facts*.

ceil v.t. to line (a ceiling), esp. with plaster. WH: 14–15C. Orig. uncertain. ? Rel. to Latin *celare*, French *céler* to hide, to conceal.

ceilidh n. an informal gathering, esp. in Scotland or Ireland, for music, dancing etc. WH: 19C. Irish *céilidhe* (now *céili*), from Old Irish *céilide* visit, from *céile* companion.

ceiling n. the inner, upper surface of a room. WH: 12–14C. CEIL + -ING¹. Not rel. to French *ciel* sky, heaven.

cel n. a celluloid for an animated film. WH: mid-20C. Abbr. of CELLULOID.

celadon n. a pale grey-green colour. *Also a.* WH: 18C. French *céladon*, from *Céladon*, sentimental lover who wore a green ribbon in Honoré d'Urfé's novel *L'Astrée* (1607–27). Cp. ISABEL.

celandine n. a yellow-flowered plant related to the poppy, *Chelidonium majus*, the greater celandine. WH: pre-1200. Old French *célidoine*, from Medieval Latin *celidonia*, ult. from Greek *khelidōn* swallow. For the inserted *-n-* cp. PASSENGER. The plant is so named because it flowers at the time of the arrival of swallows.

-cele comb. form a tumour or hernia. WH: Greek *kēlē* tumour.

celeb n. a celebrity. WH: early 20C. Abbr. of *celebrity*. See CELEBRATE.

celebrate v.t. to observe (a special occasion etc.) with festivities. *Also v.i.* WH: 14–15C. Latin *celebratus*, p.p. of *celebrare*, from *celeber*, *celebris* frequented, renowned. See also -ATE³.

celeriac n. a variety of celery with a turnip-like root eaten as a vegetable. WH: 18C. CELERY + arbitrary -AC.

celerity n. speed, swiftness, promptness. WH: 15C. French *célérité*, from Latin *celeritas*, from *celer* swift. See also -ITY.

celery n. a plant, *Apium graveolens*, the blanched leaf-stalks of which are eaten cooked or raw. WH: 17C. French *céleri*, from Italian (dial.) *selleri*, ult. from Greek *selinon* parsley.

celesta n. a keyboard instrument in which steel plates are struck by hammers. WH: 19C. Appar. pseudo-Latin form of French *céleste*. See CELESTIAL.

celestial a. of or relating to heaven; spiritual, angelic, divine. *Also n.* WH: 14–15C. Old French *celestial*, from Medieval Latin *caelestialis*, from Latin *caelestis*, from *caelum* heaven. See also -IAL.

celestine n. a blue, red or white mineral, strontium sulphate. WH: 19C. Latin *caelestis* CELESTIAL + -INE. The mineral is so named because of its occurrence as sky-blue crystals.

celibate a. unmarried. *Also n.* WH: 17C. Latin *caelibatus*, from *caelebs*, *caelibis* unmarried, bachelor. See also -ATE².

cell n. a small room, esp. one in a prison or monastery. WH: pre-1200. Old French *celle* or Latin *cella* storeroom, chamber, rel. to *celare* to hide and ult. to HALL.

cella n. the central chamber in a temple. WH: 17C. Latin. See CELL.

cellar n. an underground room or vault beneath a house used for storage. *Also v.t.* WH: 12–14C. Old French *celier* (Modern French *cellier*), from Late Latin *cellarium* set of cells, storehouse, from *cella* CELL. See also -AR¹.

cello n. a four-stringed bass instrument of the violin family rested on the ground between the legs. WH: 19C. Abbr. of VIOLONCELLO.

cellobiose n. a disaccharide obtained from cellulose. WH: early 20C. CELLULOSE + -O- + BI- + -OSE².

Cellophane® n. a transparent paper-like material made of viscose, chiefly used for wrapping. WH: early 20C. CELLULOSE + -O- + *-phane* based on *diaphane* (DIAPHANOUS).

cellular *a.* of, relating to or resembling a cell or cells. *Also n.* WH: 18C. French *cellulaire*, from Modern Latin *cellularis*, from Latin *cellula*, dim. of *cella* CELL. See also -ULE, -AR[1].

celluloid *n.* a transparent flammable thermoplastic made from cellulose nitrate, camphor and alcohol, used e.g. in cinema film. WH: 19C. CELLULOSE + -OID.

cellulose *n.* a carbohydrate of a starchy nature that forms the cell walls of all plants. *Also a.* WH: 19C. French, from *cellule*, from Latin *cellula* (see CELLULAR) + -OSE[2].

Celsius *a.* of or denoting a temperature scale in which the freezing point of water is designated 0° and the boiling point 100°. WH: 19C. Anders *Celsius*, 1701–44, Swedish astronomer, inventor of the centigrade temperature scale.

Celt *n.* a member or descendant of an ancient people comprising the Welsh, Cornish, Manx, Irish, Gaels and Bretons, inhabiting parts of England, Scotland, Ireland, Wales and northern France. WH: 16C. Latin *Celtae* (pl.), from Greek *Keltoi*, later *Keltai*.

celt *n.* a prehistoric cutting or cleaving implement of stone or bronze. WH: 18C. Medieval Latin *celtis* chisel.

cembalo *n.* a harpsichord. WH: 19C. Abbr. of CLAVICEMBALO.

cement *n.* a powdery substance, esp. used to make mortar or concrete and hardening like stone. *Also v.t., v.i.* WH: 12–14C. Old French *ciment*, from Latin *caementum* quarry stone, from *caedere* to hew. See also -MENT.

cemetery *n.* a public burial ground, esp. one that is not a churchyard. WH: 14–15C. Late Latin *coemeterium*, from Greek *koimētērion* dormitory, from *koiman* to put to sleep.

cenacle *n.* the room, or a representation of it, in which the Last Supper took place. WH: 14–15C. Old French *cénacle*, from Latin *cenaculum*, from *cena* dinner. See also -CULE.

-cene *comb. form* denoting a recent period of geological time, as in *Miocene, Eocene*. WH: Greek *kainos* new.

CENELEC *n.* the electrical standards organization of the EU. WH: Abbr. of French *Comité européen normalisation électrotechnique*, European Electrotechnical Standardization Committee.

cenospecies *n.* a species whose members are related to those of another species by the ability to interbreed. WH: early 20C. COENO- + SPECIES.

cenotaph *n.* a sepulchral monument raised to a person buried elsewhere. WH: 17C. French *cénotaphe*, from Late Latin *cenotaphium*, from Greek *kenotaphion*, from *kenos* empty + *taphos* tomb.

Cenozoic *a.* of or relating to the third and most recent geological era. *Also n.* WH: 19C. Greek *kainos* new, recent + -ZOIC.

cense *v.t.* to burn incense near or in front of. WH: 14–15C. Shortened form from Old French *encenser* INCENSE[1].

censor *n.* a public officer appointed to examine books, films etc., before they are published or released, to see that they contain nothing obscene, seditious etc. *Also v.t.* WH: 16C. Latin, from *censere* to pronounce as an opinion, to assess. See also -OR.

censure *n.* blame, reproach. *Also v.t., v.i.* WH: 14–15C. Old French, from Latin *censura* CENSUS. See also -URE.

census *n.* an official enumeration of the inhabitants of a country. WH: 17C. Latin, from *censere* to assess. Cp. CENSOR.

cent *n.* a hundredth part of the basic unit of many currencies, e.g. of the US dollar. WH: 14–15C. French, or from Italian *cento*, from Latin *centum* hundred. The name was adopted in 1786 in the USA for a coin value 1/100 dollar.

centaur *n.* a Greek mythological figure, half man, half horse. WH: 14–15C. Latin *centaurus*, from Greek *kentauros*, of unknown orig.

centaurea *n.* any plant of the genus *Centaurea*, including the cornflower, knapweed etc. WH: 19C. Modern Latin, from Late Latin *centauria*. See CENTAURY.

centaury *n.* any of various plants once used medicinally, esp. those of the genus *Centaurium*, such as *C. erythraea*. WH: 14–15C. Late Latin *centauria*, from Greek *kentauros* CENTAUR. The medicinal properties of the plant were said to have been discovered by the centaur Chiron.

centavo *n.* a hundredth part of the basic unit of currency of Portugal and some Latin American countries. WH: 19C. Spanish and Portuguese, from Latin *centum* hundred.

centenarian *n.* a person who has reached the age of 100 years. *Also*

a. WH: 19C. Latin *centenarius* containing a hundred, from *centum* hundred. See also -ARIAN.

centesimal *a.* hundredth. *Also n.* WH: 17C. Latin *centesimus* hundredth, from *centum* hundred. See also -AL[1].

centesimo *n.* a hundredth part of the basic unit of currency of Italy, Panama, Uruguay etc. WH: 19C. Italian *centesimo* and Spanish *centésimo*, from Latin *centesimus*. See CENTESIMAL.

centi- *comb. form* a hundred. WH: Latin *centum* hundred + -*i*-.

centiare *n.* a metric unit of area equal to one square metre (10.76 sq. ft.), a hundredth part of an are. WH: 19C. French, from Latin *centum* hundred + ARE.

centigrade *a.* Celsius. WH: 19C. French. See CENTI-, -GRADE.

centigram *n.* a metric unit of weight, a hundredth part of a gram. WH: 19C. French *centigramme*. See CENTI-, -GRAM.

centilitre *n.* a metric unit of capacity, a hundredth part of a litre. WH: 19C. French. See CENTI-, LITRE.

centillion *n.* in Britain and Germany, one million raised to the 100th power, 10^{600}. WH: 19C. CENTI- + second element based on MILLION, BILLION etc.

centime *n.* a hundredth part of the basic unit of many currencies, e.g. the French franc. WH: 19C. French, from Old French *centiesme*, *centisme* (Modern French *centième*), from Latin *centesimus*. See CENTESIMAL.

centimetre *n.* a metric unit of length, a hundredth part of a metre. WH: 18C. French *centimètre*. See CENTI-, METRE[1].

centimo *n.* a hundredth part of the basic unit of currency in Spain, Paraguay, Venezuela etc. WH: 19C. Spanish *céntimo*, from Latin *centesimus*. See CENTESIMAL.

centipede *n.* an arthropod of the class Chilopoda with many segments, each bearing a pair of legs. WH: 17C. French *centipède*, from Latin *centipeda*. See CENTI-, -PEDE.

centner *n.* a unit of weight equal to 100 lb. (45.4 kg). WH: 16C. German (now *Zentner*), from Latin *centenarius*. See CENTENARIAN.

cento *n.* a composition of verses from different authors. WH: 17C. Latin patchwork garment.

central *a.* proceeding from or situated in the centre. WH: 17C. French, or from Latin *centralis*, from *centrum* CENTRE. See also -AL[1].

centre *n.* the middle point or part. *Also v.t., v.i., a.* WH: 14–15C. Old French, from Latin *centrum*, from Greek *kentron* goad, peg, point of a pair of compasses, from base of *kentein* to prick.

-centric *comb. form* having a specified centre, as in *heliocentric*. WH: Greek *kentrikos*, from *kentron* CENTRE. See also -IC.

centrifugal *a.* tending to move away from the centre. WH: 18C. Modern Latin *centrifugus*, from *centrum* CENTRE + -*fugus* fleeing, from *fugere* to flee. See also -AL[1]. The word was coined by Sir Isaac Newton in 1687. Cp. CENTRIPETAL.

centriole *n.* a small rodlike part of an animal cell, which forms one of the poles of the spindle during cell division. WH: 19C. Modern Latin *centriolum*, dim. of *centrum* CENTRE. See -OLE[2].

centripetal *a.* tending to move towards the centre. WH: 18C. Modern Latin *centripetus*, from *centrum* CENTRE + -*petus* seeking, from *petere* to seek. See -AL[1]. The word was coined by Sir Isaac Newton in 1687. Cp. CENTRIFUGAL.

centro- *comb. form* central, centrally. WH: Latin *centrum* CENTRE. See also -O-.

centrobaric *a.* of or relating to the centre of gravity. WH: 18C. CENTRO- + Greek *baros* weight + -IC.

centroclinal *a.* (of a rock formation) with strata sloping downwards and inwards to a central point. WH: 19C. CENTRO- + Greek *klinein* to lean, to slope + -AL[1].

centroid *n.* the centre of mass, esp. of a geometrical figure. WH: 19C. CENTRE + -OID.

centromere *n.* the part of a chromosome by which it is attached to the spindle during cell division. WH: early 20C. CENTRO- + -MERE.

centrosome *n.* a small body of protoplasm near a cell nucleus, containing the centriole. WH: 19C. CENTRO- + -SOME[2].

centrosphere *n.* the part of the earth below the crust. WH: 19C. CENTRO- + SPHERE.

centrum *n.* the main part of a vertebra. WH: 19C. Latin CENTRE.

centum *a.* denoting the group of Indo-European languages in which the original velar stops were not palatalized, as distinct from *satem*. WH: early 20C. Latin *centum*. Latin *centum* is an example of a word (with 'hard' *c*) in which the velar stop was retained, as distinct from 'soft' *s* in Avestan *satem* hundred, in which it was not.

centuple *n.* a hundredfold. *Also a., v.t.* WH: 17C. French, or from Ecclesiastical Latin *centuplus*, var. of *centuplex*, from *centum* hundred.

centurion *n.* a Roman military officer commanding a company of a hundred men. WH: 12–14C. Latin *centurio, centurionis* CENTURY. See also -ION.

century *n.* a period of a hundred years. WH: 14–15C. Latin *centuria* hundred, from *centum* hundred. See also -Y². The original sense was a measure of land, then, in the 15C, a division of the Roman army of about a hundred men. The specific application to years evolved in the 17C.

ceorl *n.* in feudal times, an English freeman, below the thane and above the serf. WH: pre-1200. Old English, orig. form of CHURL.

cep *n.* a type of edible mushroom, *Boletus edulis*, with a brown shiny cap. WH: 19C. French *cèpe*, from Gascon *cep* tree trunk, mushroom, from Latin *cippus* stake.

cepaceous *a.* smelling or tasting of onion. WH: 17C. Latin *caepa* onion. See also -ACEOUS.

cephalalgia *n.* headache. WH: 16C. Latin, from Greek *kephalalgia*, from *kephalē* head. See -ALGIA, also -Y².

cephalic *a.* of or relating to the head. *Also n.* WH: 14–15C. Old French *céphalique*, from Latin *cephalicus*, from Greek *kephalikos*, from *kephalē* head. See also -IC.

-cephalic *comb. form* -headed, as in *brachycephalic*. WH: Greek *kephalē* head + -IC.

cephalin *n.* a compound of phosphorus occurring in the brain and in nerve tissue. WH: 19C. CEPHALO- + -IN¹.

cephalitis *n.* inflammation of the brain. WH: 19C. Greek *kephalē* head + -ITIS.

cephalization *n.* in animal evolution, the development of a head at the anterior end of the body. WH: 19C. CEPHALO- + -*ization* (-IZE).

cephalo- *comb. form* of or relating to the head. WH: Greek *kephalē* head. See also -O-.

cephalochordate *n.* any fishlike animal of the subphylum Cephalochordata, including the lancelet. WH: mid-20C. CEPHALO- + CHORDATE.

cephalometry *n.* the measurement of the human head by radiography, esp. in orthodontics. WH: 19C. CEPHALO- + -METRY.

cephalopod *n.* a mollusc of the class Cephalopoda, having a distinct head with prehensile and locomotive organs attached. WH: 19C. Modern Latin *Cephalopoda*. See CEPHALO-, -POD.

cephalosporin *n.* any of a group of antibiotics derived from fungi of the genus *Cephalosporium*. WH: mid-20C. Modern Latin *Cephalosporium* (see CEPHALO-, SPORE) + -IN¹.

cephalothorax *n.* the anterior division of the body, consisting of the coalescence of head and thorax in spiders, crabs and other arthropods. WH: 19C. CEPHALO- + THORAX.

cephalotomy *n.* the dissection of the head. WH: 19C. CEPHALO- + -TOMY.

cephalous *a.* having a head. WH: 19C. Greek *kephalē* head + -OUS.

cepheid *n.* a variable star with a regular cycle of variations in brightness, which allows its distance to be estimated. WH: early 20C. Latin *Cepheus*, from Greek *Kepheus*, father of Andromeda in Greek mythology + -ID.

ceraceous *a.* waxlike; waxy. WH: 18C. Latin *cera* wax + -ACEOUS.

ceramal *n.* a cermet. WH: mid-20C. CERAMIC + ALLOY¹. Cp. CERMET.

ceramic *a.* of or relating to pottery. *Also n.* WH: 19C. Greek *keramikos*, from *keramos* potter's earth, pottery. See also -IC.

cerargyrite *n.* a soft mineral that is a source of silver, consisting of silver chloride in crystalline form; horn silver. WH: 19C. Greek *keras* horn + *arguros* silver + -ITE¹.

cerasin *n.* the insoluble part of the gum of the cherry and plum trees. WH: 19C. Latin *cerasus* cherry tree + -IN¹.

cerastes *n.* any snake of the genus *Cerastes*, esp. the horned viper. WH: 14–15C. Latin, from Greek *kerastēs*, from *keras* horn.

cerastium *n.* any plant of the genus *Cerastium*, with horn-shaped capsules. WH: 18C. Modern Latin, from Greek *kerastēs* horned. See also -IUM.

cerate *n.* a hard ointment or stiff medicated paste containing wax. WH: 14–15C. Latin *ceratum*, from Greek *kerōton*, neut. of *kerōtos* covered with wax.

cerated *a.* waxed; covered with wax. WH: 18C. Latin *ceratus* covered in wax (see CERATE) + -ED.

cerato- *comb. form* horned. WH: Greek *keras, keratos* horn. See also -O-.

ceratodus *n.* any extinct lungfish of the genus *Ceratodus*, of the Mesozoic era. WH: 19C. Modern Latin, from Greek *keras, keratos* horn + *odous* tooth.

ceratoid *a.* horny; hornlike. WH: 19C. CERATO- + -OID.

Cerberus *n.* a three-headed dog, fabled to guard the entrance of Hades. WH: 17C. Latin, from Greek *Kerberos*.

cercaria *n.* a trematode worm or fluke in its second larval stage. WH: 19C. Modern Latin, from Greek *kerkos* tail. See also -ARY¹.

cercopithecoid *n.* any primate of the superfamily Cercopithecoidea, an Old World monkey. *Also a.* WH: 19C. Latin *cercopithecus*, from Greek *kerkopithēkos* long-tailed monkey, from *kerkos* tail + *pithēkos* ape. See also -OID.

cercus *n.* either of a pair of tail-like sensory appendages at the tip of the abdomen in some arthropods. WH: 19C. Modern Latin, from Greek *kerkos* tail.

cere *n.* the patch of waxlike skin at the base of the upper beak in many birds. *Also v.t.* WH: 15C. Latin *cera* wax.

cereal *a.* of or relating to wheat or other grain. *Also n.* WH: 19C. Latin *cerealis* pertaining to the cultivation of grain, from *Ceres* Roman goddess of agriculture. See also -AL¹. The sense of breakfast food dates from the 19C.

cerebellum *n.* a portion of the brain situated beneath the posterior lobes of the cerebrum, responsible for balance and muscular co-ordination. WH: 16C. Latin, dim. of CEREBRUM.

cerebro- *comb. form* of or relating to the brain. WH: Latin *cerebrum* brain. See also -O-.

cerebroside *n.* a lipid occurring in the myelin sheaths of nerves. WH: 19C. CEREBRO- + -OSE² + -IDE.

cerebrospinal *a.* of or relating to the brain and to the spinal cord. WH: 19C. CEREBRO- + SPINE + -AL¹.

cerebrovascular *a.* of or relating to the brain and its blood vessels. WH: mid-20C. CEREBRO- + VASCULAR.

cerebrum *n.* the main part of the brain, filling the upper cavity of the skull. WH: 17C. Latin brain.

ceremonial *a.* of or performed with ceremonies. *Also n.* WH: 14–15C. Late Latin *caerimonialis*, from *caerimonia* CEREMONY. See also -AL¹.

ceremony *n.* a prescribed rite, esp. in accordance with religion or tradition. WH: 14–15C. Latin *caerimonia* religious worship, of uncertain orig. See also -MONY. According to ancient scholars, the word is from *Caere* (now Cerveteri, Italy), the former capital of Etruria.

Cerenkov radiation *n.* the electromagnetic radiation produced by particles moving faster than the speed of light in the same medium. WH: mid-20C. Pavel A. *Cherenkov*, 1904–90, Russian physicist.

cereus *n.* any cactus of the genus *Cereus*, esp. *C. jamacaru* of Brazil, which can grow to a height of 40 ft. (13 m). WH: 17C. Latin waxen, from *cera* wax.

cerise *n.* a red colour, cherry red. *Also a.* WH: 19C. French cherry.

cerium *n.* a malleable grey metallic element of the rare earth group, at. no. 58, chem. symbol Ce. WH: 19C. *Ceres* (an asteroid discovered 1801, shortly before the element) + -IUM (as in POTASSIUM and names of other metals). The name was coined in 1803 by the Swedish scientists Jöns Berzelius and Wilhelm Hisinger.

cermet *n.* an alloy of a heat-resistant ceramic and a metal. WH: mid-20C. CERAMIC + METAL. Cp. CERAMAL.

CERN *n.* the European Laboratory for Particle Physics, a European organization for nuclear research. WH: Acronym of French *Conseil européen pour la recherche nucléaire*, European Organization for Nuclear Research, its former title (1952–54).

cero- *comb. form* of, relating to or composed of wax. WH: Latin *cera* or Greek *kēros* wax. See also -O-.

ceroc *n.* a jive dance for two people, originating in France. WH: mid-20C. French *c'est le roc* it's rock (and roll), on which it is based.

cerography *n.* the art or technique of writing, engraving etc. on or with wax. WH: 16C. CERO- + -GRAPHY.

ceroplastic *a.* modelled in wax. WH: 19C. CERO- + PLASTIC.

cerotype *n.* an engraving on a wax-coated copper plate, used to prepare an electrotype printing plate. WH: 19C. CERO- + -*type* (TYPE).

cert *n.* a certainty. WH: 19C. Abbr. of CERTAIN or *certainty*.

certain *a.* sure; confident. *Also pron.* WH: 12–14C. Old French, from extended form of Latin *certus* settled, sure.

certificate[1] *n.* a written testimony or document, esp. of status or ability. WH: 14–15C. French *certificat* or Medieval Latin *certificatum*, neut. p.p. (used as n.) of *certificare*. See CERTIFY, also -ATE[1].

certificate[2] *v.t.* to give a certificate to. WH: 18C. See CERTIFICATE[1].

certify *v.t.* to attest to, esp. in writing. WH: 12–14C. Old French *certifier*, from Late Latin *certificare*, from *certus*. See CERTAIN, also -FY.

certitude *n.* the state of being certain; certainty, conviction. WH: 14–15C. Late Latin *certitudo*, from *certus*. See CERTAIN, also -TUDE.

cerulean *n.* a deep blue colour. *Also a.* WH: 17C. Latin *caeruleus* sky-blue, from *caelum* sky, heaven. See also -EAN.

cerumen *n.* the waxlike secretion of the ear. WH: 17C. Modern Latin, from Latin *cera* wax.

ceruse *n.* white lead. *Also v.t.* WH: 14–15C. Old French *céruse*, from Latin *cerusa*, ? ult. from Greek *kēros* wax.

cervelat *n.* a kind of smoked sausage made from pork or beef. WH: 17C. French (now *cervelas*), from Italian *cervellata* Milanese sausage made of meat and pig's brain (Italian *cervello* brain).

cervical *a.* of or relating to the neck. WH: 17C. French, or from Modern Latin *cervicalis*, from Latin *cervix*, *cervicis*. See CERVIX, also -AL[1].

cervid *n.* any mammal of the family Cervidae, including the deer. *Also a.* WH: 19C. Modern Latin *Cervidae*, from Latin *cervus* deer. See also -ID.

cervine *a.* of or relating to the deer family. WH: 19C. Latin *cervinus*, from *cervus* deer. See also -INE.

cervix *n.* a necklike part of the body, esp. the passage between the uterus and the vagina. WH: 18C. Latin neck, of unknown orig. ? Rel. to Latin CEREBRUM + *vincire* to bind, to tie.

cess[1] *n.* a tax. *Also v.t.* WH: 15C. Shortening of ASSESS.

cess[2] *n.* luck. WH: 19C. Prob. from CESS[1].

cessation *n.* the act of ceasing. WH: 14–15C. Latin *cessatio*, *cessationis*, from *cessatus*, p.p. of *cessare*. See CEASE, also -ATION.

cesser *n.* cessation, coming to an end. WH: 16C. Use as n. of Old French *cesser* CEASE. See also -ER[4].

cession *n.* a yielding, a surrender; a ceding of territory, rights or property. WH: 14–15C. Old French, or from Latin *cessio*, *cessionis*, from *cessus*, p.p. of *cedere* CEDE. See also -ION.

cesspit *n.* a cesspool. WH: 19C. From imagined base of CESSPOOL + PIT[1].

cesspool *n.* an underground container or a hole in the ground for sewage to drain into. WH: 17C. Prob. alt. of *suspiral* (pipe, passage), from Old French *souspirail* (Modern French *soupirail*), from Medieval Latin *suspiraculum*, from *suspirare* to suspire + instr. suf. -*culum* (see also -CLE), assim. to POOL[1].

cestode *a.* ribbon-like. *Also n.* WH: 19C. Modern Latin *Cestoda*, from Latin *cestus* belt, girdle, from Greek *kestos* stitched. See also -ODE[1].

cetacean *a.* of, relating to or belonging to the Cetacea, an order of marine mammals including whales, dolphins etc. *Also n.* WH: 19C. Modern Latin *Cetacea*, from Latin *cetus*, from Greek *kētos* whale. See also -ACEAN.

cetane *n.* an oily, colourless hydrocarbon found in petroleum. WH: 19C. From *cetyl*, a related compound found in SPERMACETI (from Latin *cetus* + -YL) + -ANE.

ceteris paribus *adv.* other things being equal. WH: 17C. Latin, abl. pl. of *ceterus* remaining over + *par* equal.

cetology *n.* the study of whales. WH: 19C. Latin *cetus* whale + -O- + -LOGY.

Ceylon moss *n.* a red seaweed, *Gracilaria lichenoides*, of the E Indian Ocean, from which agar is obtained. WH: 19C. *Ceylon*, former name of Sri Lanka + MOSS.

cf. *abbr.* compare. WH: Latin *confer*, 2nd pers. sing. imper. of *conferre* to compare. See CONFER. Cp. CP..

cha *n.* tea. WH: 18C. Chinese *chá* tea.

chabazite *n.* a white or colourless mineral, a hydrated silicate of calcium, sodium, potassium and aluminium. WH: 19C. French

chabazie, from Greek *khabazie*, misreading of *khalazie*, voc. of *khalazios* hailstone, from *khalaza* hail. See also -ITE[1].

Chablis *n.* a dry white wine made at Chablis. WH: 17C. *Chablis*, central France.

cha-cha *n.* a ballroom dance of Latin American origin. *Also v.i.* WH: mid-20C. American Spanish, of imit. orig. Cp. CHACONNE.

chacma *n.* a southern African baboon, *Papio ursinus*. WH: 19C. Nama.

chaconne *n.* a set of variations over a continuously repeated ground bass. WH: 17C. French, from Spanish *chacona*, prob. of imit. orig., from sound of castanets used in dance. Cp. CHA-CHA.

chad *n.* the small pieces of paper removed when holes are punched in a computer card, paper tape etc. WH: mid-20C. Orig. unknown.

chador *n.* a large veil, worn over the head and body by Muslim women. WH: 17C. Urdu *chādar*, from Persian *čādar* sheet, veil.

chaeta *n.* a bristle on the body of the earthworm and other annelids, used in locomotion. WH: 19C. Modern Latin, from Greek *khaitē* long hair.

chaeto- *comb. form* characterized by bristles or a mane. WH: Greek *khaitē* long hair. See also -O-.

chaetodon *n.* any fish of the genus *Chaetodon*, with bristly teeth and brilliant colouring. WH: 18C. CHAETO- + Greek *odous*, *odontos* tooth.

chaetognath *n.* any marine worm of the phylum Chaetognatha, such as the arrow worm, with a ring of bristles around the mouth. WH: 19C. CHAETO- + Greek *gnathos* jaw.

chaetopod *n.* an oligochaete or polychaete. WH: 19C. CHAETO- + -POD.

chafe *v.t.* to rub so as to make sore or worn. *Also v.i., n.* WH: 14–15C. Old French *chauffer*, from var. of Latin *catefacere* to make warm, from *calere* to be warm + *facere* to make.

chafer *n.* a beetle of the family Scarabaeidae, such as the cockchafer. WH: pre-1200. Old English *ceafor*, *cefer*, from Germanic. Cp. German *Käfer* beetle. Rel. to CHAFF[1], JOWL.

chaff[1] *n.* the husks of grain. WH: pre-1200. Old English *cæf*, *ceaf*, ? from Germanic base meaning to gnaw, to chew. Rel. to CHAFER.

chaff[2] *n.* banter. *Also v.t., v.i.* WH: 19C. ? Var. of CHAFE.

chaffer *v.i.* to dispute about price, to haggle, to bargain. *Also v.t., n.* WH: 12–14C. Old Norse *kaupfor* trading journey. Cp. CHEAP, FARE.

chaffinch *n.* a common European bird, *Fringilla coelebs*. WH: pre-1200. Old English *ceaffinc*, from *ceaf* CHAFF[1] + *finc* FINCH. The bird feeds on chaff or grain.

Chagas' disease *n.* a tropical disease caused by the protozoan *Trypanosoma cruzi*, characterized by high fever and inflammation of the heart muscles. WH: early 20C. Carlos *Chagas*, 1879–1934, Brazilian physician.

chagrin *n.* vexation, disappointment, mortification. *Also v.t.* WH: 17C. French rough skin, from Turkish *çāgri*, influ. by French GRAIN. Cp. SHAGREEN.

chain *n.* a series of links or rings fitted into or connected with each other, for binding, joining, holding, hauling etc. or for decoration, esp. as jewellery. *Also v.t.* WH: 12–14C. Old French *chaine* (Modern French *chaîne*), from Latin *catena* chain, fetter. Cp. CATENA.

chair *n.* a movable seat with a back and usu. four legs for one person. *Also v.t.* WH: 12–14C. Old French *chaiere* (Modern French *chaise*), from Latin *cathedra* throne (see CATHEDRAL). The earlier Old English word for chair was *stōl* STOOL.

chaise *n.* a light horse-drawn carriage for travelling or pleasure. WH: 17C. French, var. of *chaire* CHAIR.

chakra *n.* in yoga, a centre of spiritual power in the human body. WH: 18C. Sanskrit *cakra* circle, rel. to WHEEL. Cp. CHARKA.

chalaza *n.* either of the two twisted albuminous threads holding the yolk in position in an egg. WH: 18C. Modern Latin, from Greek *khalaza* small knot.

chalazion *n.* a small cyst on the eyelid. WH: 18C. Greek *khalazion*, dim. of *khalaza*. See CHALAZA.

chalcanthite *n.* a blue mineral, a crystalline form of hydrated copper sulphate. WH: 19C. Latin *chalcanthum*, from Greek *khalkanthon*, from *khalkos* copper + *anthos* flower. See also -ITE[1].

chalcedony *n.* a cryptocrystalline variety of quartz. WH: 14–15C. Latin *calcedonius*, from Greek *khalkēdōn*, of unknown orig. The word is probably not related to *Chalcedon*, a city of ancient Bithynia, as if the quartz were originally found there.

chalcid *n.* any tiny parasitic insect of the family Chalcididae, which lays its eggs inside another insect. WH: 19C. Modern Latin *Chalcis* genus name, from Greek *khalkos* copper, brass. The name relates to the metallic sheen that many of the insects have.

chalco- *comb. form* of or relating to copper or brass. WH: Greek *khalkos* copper, brass. See also -O-.

chalcocite *n.* a grey or black mineral, copper sulphide. WH: 19C. CHALCO- + alt. of second element of orig. name, *chalcosine* (CHALCO- + -INE).

chalcography *n.* the act or process of engraving on brass or copper. WH: 17C. CHALCO- + -GRAPHY.

chalcolithic *a.* of or relating to a prehistoric period when both stone and copper or bronze implements were in use. WH: early 20C. CHALCO- + LITHIC.

chalcopyrite *n.* a yellow mineral, a sulphide of copper and iron; copper pyrites, a copper ore. WH: 19C. CHALCO- + *pyrite* (PYRITES).

Chaldean *a.* of or belonging to ancient Chaldea or its language. *Also n.* WH: 16C. Latin *Chaldaeus*, from Greek *Khaldaios* (m.), from *Khaldaia* (f.) Chaldea. See also -AN.

chalet *n.* a small house or hut on a mountainside, esp. in Switzerland. WH: 19C. Swiss French, dim. of Old French *chasel* farmstead, from deriv. of Latin *casa* hut, cottage.

chalice *n.* a cup, goblet or other drinking vessel. WH: pre-1200. Old French, or from Latin *calix, calicis* cup. Cp. CALIX, CALYX.

chalicothere *n.* any of a group of large extinct mammals of the Tertiary period. WH: early 20C. Modern Latin *Chalicotherium* genus name, from Greek *khalix, khalikos* gravel + *thērion* wild animal.

chalk *n.* soft white limestone or calcium carbonate, chiefly composed of the remains of marine organisms. *Also v.t.* WH: pre-1200. Old English *cealc*, from Germanic, from Latin *calx, calcis* lime. See CALX.

challah *n.* a loaf of white bread, usu. plaited, eaten by Jews on the Sabbath. WH: 19C. Hebrew *ḥallāh*, prob. from *ḥll* to hollow, to pierce.

challenge *n.* a summons or invitation to fight a duel. *Also v.t.* WH: 12–14C. Old French *chalenge*, from Latin *calumnia* CALUMNY. The original sense to the 17C was to accuse, to bring a charge against. The current sense dates from the 14–15C.

challis *n.* a light fabric of wool or cotton, used for clothing. WH: 19C. ? From surname *Challis*.

chalutz *n.* a member of a group of immigrants to Israel who established the first agricultural settlements (kibbutzim). WH: early 20C. Hebrew *ḥālūş* pioneer.

chalybeate *a.* impregnated with iron. *Also n.* WH: 17C. Modern Latin *chalybeatus*, from Latin *chalybs*, from Greek *khalups, khalubos* steel. See also -ATE².

chamade *n.* the beat of a drum or sound of a trumpet demanding or announcing a surrender or parley. WH: 17C. French, from Portuguese *chamada*, from *chamar*, from Latin *clamare*. See CLAIM, also -ADE.

chamaephyte *n.* a plant with buds close to the ground. WH: early 20C. Greek *khamai* low, on the ground + -PHYTE.

chamber *n.* the place where a legislative assembly meets. WH: 12–14C. Old French *chambre*, from Latin CAMERA.

chamberlain *n.* an officer in charge of the household of a sovereign or nobleman. WH: 12–14C. Old French (Modern French *chambellan*), from Frankish, from Old Saxon *kamera*, from Latin CAMERA. See also -LING¹. Cp. CAMERLENGO.

Chambertin *n.* a dry red Burgundy wine. WH: 18C. *Chambertin*, the vineyard of origin, in the Côte de Nuits, E France.

chambray *n.* a light cotton or linen fabric with a white weft and coloured warp. WH: 19C. *Cambrai*, a town in N France. Cp. CAMBRIC.

chambré *a.* (of wine) warmed to room temperature. WH: mid-20C. French, p.p of *chambrer* to keep in a room. Cp. CHAMBER.

chameleon *n.* a small African lizard having the power of changing colour. WH: 12–14C. Latin *chamaeleon*, from Greek *khamaileōn*, from *khamai* on the ground + *leōn* lion.

chamfer *n.* in carpentry, an angle slightly pared off. *Also v.t.* WH: 16C. Back-formation from *chamfering*, from French *chamfrain*, from *chant* edge (cp. CANT²) + *fraint*, p.p. of *fraindre*, from Latin *frangere* to break.

chamois *n.* a goatlike European antelope, *Rupicapra rupicapra*.

WH: 16C. Old French, prob. from a pre-Roman Alpine word rel. to German *Gemse* chamois.

champ¹ *v.t., v.i.* to bite with a crunching or grinding noise; to chew or munch noisily. *Also n.* WH: 12–14C. Prob. imit.

champ² *n.* a champion. WH: 19C. Abbr. of CHAMPION.

champac *n.* a kind of magnolia, *Michelia champaca*, much venerated in India. WH: 18C. Sanskrit *campaka* or Malay *cempaka*.

champagne *n.* a white sparkling wine made in the province of Champagne. WH: 17C. *Champagne*, a region of NE France, from Late Latin *campania* plain. See CHAMPAIGN.

champaign *n.* flat, open country. *Also a.* WH: 14–15C. Old French *champagne*, from Late Latin *campania* plain, from fem. sing. (used as n.) of *campanius*, from Latin *campus*. See CAMP¹. Cp. CAMPAIGN, CHAMPAGNE.

champers *n.* champagne. WH: mid-20C. CHAMPAGNE + -ers, form of -ER⁶.

champerty *n.* an illegal agreement to finance a party in a suit on condition of sharing the property at issue if recovered. WH: 14–15C. Anglo-French *champartie*, from Old French *champart* the feudal lord's share, from Latin *campus* (see CAMP¹) + *pars* PART.

champignon *n.* an edible mushroom, esp. the fairy-ring champignon, *Marasmius oreades*. WH: 16C. French, dim. of *champagne*. See CHAMPAIGN.

champion *n.* a person who defeats all competitors. *Also v.t., a., adv.* WH: 12–14C. Old French, from Medieval Latin *campio, campionis* combatant in the (athletic) field, from Latin *campus* field. See CAMP¹.

champlevé *n.* enamelling by the process of inlaying vitreous powders into channels cut in the metal base. *Also a.* WH: 19C. French, from *champ* field + *levé* raised. Cp. CAMP¹, LEVEE².

chance *n.* a risk, a possibility. *Also v.t., v.i., a.* WH: 12–14C. Old French *chëance* (Modern French *chance*), from *chëoir* to fall, to befall, var. of Latin *cadere* to fall.

chancel *n.* the eastern part of a church, usu. separated from the nave by a screen or by steps. WH: 12–14C. Old French (Modern French *cancel*), from Latin *cancelli* (pl.), dim. of *cancer* lattice, ? alt. of *carcer* barrier, prison.

chancellery *n.* a chancellor's court or council and official establishment. WH: 12–14C. Old French *chancellerie*, from *chancelier*. See CHANCELLOR, also -ERY.

chancellor *n.* the president of a court, public department, or university. WH: pre-1200. Old French *chancelier*, from Late Latin *cancellarius* porter, secretary, from *cancelli* (see CHANCEL) + -arius -ER². The word was originally the term for the officer stationed at the bar or latticework separating the judges from the public in a court of law.

chance-medley *n.* homicide by misadventure, as in repelling an unprovoked attack. WH: 15C. Anglo-French *chance medlee*, from *chance* CHANCE + *medlee*, fem. p.p. of *medler* to mix. See MEDDLE.

chancery *n.* the court of the Lord Chancellor, the highest English court of justice next to the House of Lords, comprising a court of common law and a court of equity, now a division of the High Court of Justice. WH: 14–15C. Contr. of CHANCELLERY.

chancre *n.* a hard syphilitic lesion. WH: 16C. French, from Latin CANCER. Cp. CANKER.

chandelier *n.* a hanging branched frame for a number of lights. WH: 17C. French, from *chandelle*. See CHANDLER, also -IER.

chandelle *n.* an abrupt upward turn of an aircraft, using its momentum to increase the rate of climb. *Also v.i.* WH: early 20C. French candle.

chandler *n.* a person who makes or sells candles. WH: 12–14C. Old French *chandelier*, from *candelle* (Modern French *chandelle*), from Latin *candela*. See CANDLE, also -ER².

change *v.t.* to make different, to alter. *Also v.i., n.* WH: 12–14C. Old French *changer*, from Late Latin *cambiare*, from Latin *cambire* to exchange, to barter, prob. of Celtic orig.

channel¹ *n.* the bed of a stream or an artificial watercourse. *Also v.t.* WH: 12–14C. Old French *chanel*, from Latin *canalis* pipe, groove, from *canna* CANE. See also -EL. Cp. CANAL.

channel² *n.* a plank fastened horizontally to the side of a ship to spread the lower rigging. WH: 18C. Alt. of *chain-wale* (see CHAIN, WALE). Cp. GUNNEL / GUNWALE.

chanson *n.* a song. WH: 15C. French, from Latin *cantio, cantionis*. See CANZONE.

chant *v.t.* to speak or sing rhythmically or repetitively. *Also v.i., n.* WH: 14–15C. French *chanter*, from Latin *cantare*, freq. of *canere* to sing. Cp. SHANTY².

chanterelle *n.* an edible fungus, *Cantharellus cibarius*. WH: 18C. French, from Modern Latin *cantharellus*, dim. of *cantharus*, from Greek *kantharos* drinking vessel. The fungus is so called because of its funnel shape.

chanteuse *n.* a female nightclub singer. WH: 19C. French, fem. of *chanteur* singer. See CHANT, also -OR.

chanticleer *n.* a name for a cock, esp. as the herald of day. WH: 12–14C. Old French *chantecler* (Modern French *chanteclair*), name of the cock in *Reynard the Fox* and Chaucer's *Nun's Priest's Tale*. Cp. CHANT, CLEAR. The name of the hen in these works is *Partlet*, from Old French *Pertelote*, a personal name of unknown origin.

Chantilly *n.* a delicate type of lace. WH: 18C. *Chantilly*, a town near Paris, France.

chantry *n.* an endowment for a priest or priests to say mass daily for some person or persons deceased. WH: 14–15C. Old French *chanterie*, from *chanter* to sing. See CHANT, also -ERY, -RY.

chaos *n.* confusion, disorder. WH: 15C. French or Latin, from Greek *khaos* vast chasm, void. Cp. GAS.

chap¹ *v.t.* to cause to crack or open in long slits. *Also v.i., n.* WH: 14–15C. Orig. unknown. Cp. CHOP¹.

chap² *n.* a man, a fellow. WH: 16C. Abbr. of CHAPMAN. Cp. CUSTOMER.

chap³ *n.* the jaws (usu. of animals), the mouth and cheeks; the chops. WH: 16C. Orig. unknown. Cp. CHOP³.

chaparajos *n.pl.* leather leggings worn by cowboys. WH: 19C. Mexican Spanish *chaparreras*, from *chaparra, chaparro*. See CHAPARRAL. The spelling with -*ajo*, -*ejo* has perhaps been influenced by Spanish *aparejo* equipment. The leggings were worn by cowboys to protect their trousers against the thorns of the chaparral.

chaparral *n.* a thicket of low evergreen oaks, or of thick undergrowth and thorny shrubs. WH: 19C. Spanish, from *chaparra, chaparro* dwarf evergreen oak.

chapati *n.* in Indian cookery, a round, thin loaf of unleavened bread. WH: 19C. Hindi *capātī*, from *capānā* to flatten, to roll out, ult. from Dravidian.

chapbook *n.* a small book, usually of tales, ballads or the like, formerly hawked by chapmen. WH: 19C. CHAPMAN + BOOK.

chape *n.* the catch or piece by which an object is attached, such as the tongue of a buckle. *Also v.t.* WH: 12–14C. Old French *cape*, hood. See CAPE¹.

chapeau *n.* a hat. WH: 15C. French, from Old French *chapel*, from Latin *capellum*, dim. of *cappa* CAP. Cp. CHAPLET.

chapel *n.* a place of worship connected with and subsidiary to a church. *Also a.* WH: 12–14C. Old French *chapele* (Modern French *chapelle*), from Medieval Latin *cappella*, dim. of *cappa* cape, cloak. See CAP. The chapel is so named from the cloak of St Martin, preserved by the Frankish kings in a sanctuary (chapel) as a sacred relic. Cp. CHAPLAIN.

chaperone *n.* a married or elderly woman who accompanies a young unmarried woman on social occasions or in public places. *Also v.t.* WH: 14–15C. Old French headdress, from *chape*. See CHAPE. A chaperone was originally a hood or cap. The current sense arose in the 18C to denote an older woman who 'sheltered' a younger woman as a hood shelters the face.

chapiter *n.* the upper part of the capital of a column. WH: 12–14C. Old French *chapitre*. See CHAPTER.

chaplain *n.* a clergyman who officiates in a private chapel, in the armed forces, or in some other establishment or institution. WH: 12–14C. Old French *chapelain*, from Medieval Latin *cappellanus*, orig. custodian of the cloak of St Martin, from *cappella*. See CHAPEL, also -AN.

chaplet *n.* a wreath or garland for the head. WH: 14–15C. Old French *chapelet*, dim. of *chapel* (Modern French *chapeau* hat). See CHAPEAU, also -LET.

†chapman *n.* a person who buys and sells. WH: pre-1200. Old English *cēapman*, from *cēap* (see CHEAP) + *man* MAN.

chappal *n.* a leather sandal worn in India. WH: 19C. Hindi *cappal*.

chaptalize *v.t.* to add sugar to (wine) during fermentation in order to increase the alcohol content. WH: 19C. J.A. *Chaptal*, 1756–1832, French chemist who invented the process + -IZE.

chapter *n.* a division of a book. *Also v.t.* WH: 12–14C. Old French *chapitre*, earlier *chapitle*, from Latin *capitulum*, dim. of *caput* head.

char¹ *v.t.* to burn slightly, to blacken with fire. *Also v.i.* WH: 17C. Appar. back-formation from CHARCOAL.

char² *n.* any small fish of the genus *Salvelinus*, of the salmon family, esp. *S. alpinus*. WH: 17C. Orig. unknown. ? From Celtic.

char³ *n.* a charwoman. *Also v.i.* WH: pre-1200. Old English *cerr* turn. Cp. CHORE. As a noun the word is an abbreviation of *charwoman*.

charabanc *n.* a coach for day trippers. WH: 19C. French *char-à-bancs* carriage with seats. Cp. CAR, BENCH. The charabanc was originally a horse-drawn vehicle, and was superseded by the motor coach.

characin *n.* any freshwater fish of the family Characidae, including the piranha. WH: 19C. Modern Latin *Characinus* genus name, from Greek *kharax* a kind of fish, lit. pointed stake. Cp. PIKE¹.

character *n.* the distinctive qualities peculiar to a person or thing. *Also v.t.* WH: 12–14C. Old French *caractère*, from Latin *character*, from Greek *kharaktēr* instrument for marking, from *kharassein* to engrave. The original sense (in the spelling *caracter*) was a symbol marked on the body or an imprint on the soul. The meaning person in a play or book evolved in the 17C.

charade *n.* a game in which a word is guessed from actions or utterances representing each syllable and the whole word. WH: 18C. French, from Provençal *charrado* conversation, from *charra* chatter, prob. of imit. orig.

charas *n.* hashish, cannabis resin. WH: 19C. Hindi *caras*.

charbroil *v.t.* to grill (meat etc.) over charcoal. WH: mid-20C. CHARCOAL + BROIL¹.

charcoal *n.* an impure form of carbon prepared from vegetable or animal substances, esp. wood partially burnt under turf. *Also a.* WH: 14–15C. From *char-* of uncertain orig. + COAL (in sense charcoal). The first element may relate to Old English *cerr* turn, in the sense of wood that has been turned (converted) into coal.

charcuterie *n.* a shop selling cold cooked meats and similar products. WH: 19C. French, from obs. *char* (Modern French *chair*) *cuite* cooked flesh. See also -ERY.

chard *n.* a variety of beet, *Beta vulgaris*, with stalks and leaves eaten as a vegetable, also called *Swiss chard*. WH: 17C. French *carde*, ? alt. by assoc. with *chardon* thistle. See CARDOON.

Chardonnay *n.* a white grape grown in the Burgundy region of France and elsewhere, used to make wine. WH: early 20C. *Chardonnay*, in E central France.

charge *v.t.* to ask as a price. *Also v.i., n.* WH: 12–14C. Old French *charger*, from Late Latin *carricare* to load, from Latin *carrus* CAR. Cp. CARRY.

chargé d'affaires *n.* a diplomatic agent acting as deputy to an ambassador. WH: 18C. French (one) charged with affairs. See CHARGE, AFFAIR.

chariot *n.* a carriage used in war, public triumphs and racing. *Also v.t., v.i.* WH: 14–15C. Old French, augm. of *char*, ult. from Latin *carrus* CAR.

charisma *n.* personal magnetism or charm enabling one to inspire or influence other people. WH: 17C. Ecclesiastical Latin, from Greek *kharisma*, from *kharis* favour, grace.

charity *n.* generosity to those in need, alms-giving. WH: pre-1200. Old French *charité*, from Latin *caritas*, from *carus* dear. See also -ITY. Cp. CARESS.

charivari *n.* a mock serenade of discordant music. WH: 17C. French, ? from Popular Latin *caribaria*, from Greek *karebaria* headache, or ult. of imit. orig.

charka *n.* an Indian spinning wheel, used esp. for spinning cotton. WH: 19C. Urdu *charḳa* spinning wheel, from Persian *čarḳa*, rel. to Sanskrit *cakra* wheel. Cp. CHAKRA, CHUKKA.

charlatan *n.* a person who pretends to have skill or knowledge; a quack; an impostor. WH: 17C. French, from Italian *ciarlitano*, from *ciarlare* to babble, to patter, of imit. orig. The word is said by some to derive from Italian *cerretano* inhabitant of *Cerreto*, a town in central Italy.

Charles' law *n.* the principle that all gases at constant pressure have the same coefficient of expansion. WH: 19C. Jacques-Alexandre-César *Charles*, 1746–1823, French physicist.

Charles's wain *n.* seven stars in the constellation the Great Bear; the Plough. WH: pre-1200. Old English *Carles wægn* Carl's wain. Carl is Charlemagne. The group may have been so named through association of the star Arcturus with King Arthur, who was himself associated with Charlemagne.

charleston *n.* a strenuous dance in 4/4 time with characteristic kicking outwards of the lower part of the legs. WH: early 20C. *Charleston*, a city in S Carolina, USA, where it became fashionable in the 1920s.

charley horse *n.* muscle stiffness or cramp, esp. in the arm or leg after exercise. WH: 19C. Orig. unknown.

charlie *n.* an utterly foolish person. WH: 19C. Dim. of male forename *Charles*. See also -Y³.

charlock *n.* a type of wild mustard, *Sinapis arvensis*; the field mustard. WH: pre-1200. Old English *cerlic*, *cyrlic*, of unknown orig.

charlotte *n.* a kind of pudding made with fruit and thin slices of bread or layers of breadcrumbs etc. WH: 18C. ? From female forename *Charlotte*. The pudding is popularly said to be named for Queen *Charlotte*, 1744–1818, wife of George III, who patronized apple growers.

charm¹ *n.* a power of alluring, fascinating etc. *Also v.t., v.i.* WH: 12–14C. Old French *charme*, from Latin *carmen* song, incantation.

charm² *n.* a blended noise or confusion of voices, as of birds or children. WH: pre-1200. Old English *cearm*, *cierm*, of Germanic orig. Cp. Dutch *kermen* to mourn, to lament.

Charmeuse® *n.* a soft silky fabric with a smooth finish. WH: early 20C. French, fem. of *charmeur* charmer. See CHARM¹.

charnel *a.* deathlike; sepulchral. WH: 14–15C. Old French, from Medieval Latin *carnale*, neut. (used as n.) of *carnalis* CARNAL.

Charolais *n.* a breed of large white beef cattle. WH: 19C. Monts du *Charollais*, E France, where orig. bred.

charpoy *n.* a light Indian bedstead. WH: 17C. Urdu *chārpāī*, from Persian four-footed, from *chār* four + *pāī* foot. Cp. QUADRUPED, to which it is ult. rel.

charqui *n.* beef cut into strips and dried in the sun, jerked beef. WH: 17C. American Spanish, from Quechua *cc'arkii*. Cp. JERK².

chart *n.* a map of some part of the sea, with coasts, islands, rocks, shoals etc., for the use of sailors. *Also v.t.* WH: 16C. Old French *charte*, from Latin *charta*. See CARD¹.

charter *n.* an instrument in writing granted by the sovereign or parliament, incorporating a borough, company or institution, or conferring certain rights and privileges. *Also a., v.t.* WH: 12–14C. Old French *chartre*, from Latin *chartula*, dim. of *charta*. See CARD¹.

Charterhouse *n.* a Carthusian monastery. WH: 14–15C. Old French *Chartreuse*, alt. of *Charteuse*, from Medieval Latin *Carthusius*, from *Carthusia* (see CARTHUSIAN), assim. to HOUSE¹. Cp. CHARTREUSE. Charterhouse School, now in Godalming, Surrey, was founded in 1611 on the site of a Carthusian monastery in London.

charter party *n.* an agreement in writing concerning the hire and freight of a vessel. WH: 14–15C. French *charte partie*, from Medieval Latin *charta partita* divided charter, indenture.

Chartism *n.* the principles of an English reform movement of 1838–48, including universal suffrage, vote by ballot, annual parliaments, payment of members, equal electoral districts and the abolition of property qualifications for members. WH: 19C. Medieval Latin *charta* legal writing, charter + -ISM. The movement was so named from the *People's Charter* that it published in 1838.

chartreuse *n.* a pale green or yellow liqueur made with aromatic herbs. *Also a.* WH: 19C. French, fem. of *Chartreux*. See CARTHUSIAN, CHARTERHOUSE. The liqueur was originally made by the Carthusian monks of La Grande Chartreuse, near Grenoble, France. The place name probably derives from the *Caturiges*, the Alpine people who settled in the region in pre-Roman times. Their own name in turn apparently derives from Gaulish *catu* battle + *riges*, pl. of *rix* king. They were thus the 'kings of battle'.

chary *a.* wary, prudent, cautious. WH: pre-1200. Old English *cearig*, from Germanic, from base of CARE. The original sense of the word was anxious, grievous, then dear, cherished. The current sense evolved in the 16C.

Charybdis *n.* one of a pair of alternative risks. WH: 14–15C. Latin, from Greek *kharubdis* a dangerous whirlpool in Greek mythology. Charybdis lay off the coast of Sicily opposite SCYLLA, a rock on the Italian shore. Boats passing between the two risked foundering in the former or running aground on the latter.

chase¹ *v.t.* to pursue, esp. at speed. *Also v.i., n.* WH: 12–14C. Old French *chacier* (Modern French *chasser*), from var. of Latin *captare*, freq. of *capere* to take. Cp. CATCH.

chase² *v.t.* to engrave, to emboss. WH: 14–15C. Appar. shortening of ENCHASE.

chase³ *n.* a rectangular iron frame in which type is locked for printing. WH: 16C. French *châsse*. See CASE².

chase⁴ *n.* a wide groove. WH: 17C. French *chas* enclosed space, from Provençal *caus*, from Medieval Latin *capsum* thorax.

chasm *n.* a deep cleft in the ground. WH: 16C. Latin *chasma*, from Greek *khasma* gaping hollow. Ult. rel. to YAWN.

chasmogamic *a.* having flowers that open to allow cross-pollination. WH: early 20C. CHASM + -O- + GAMIC.

chasse *n.* a liqueur drunk after coffee. WH: 18C. French, abbr. of *chasse-café*, lit. chase-coffee. See CHASE¹, CAFÉ.

chassé *n.* a gliding step in dancing. *Also v.i., v.t.* WH: 19C. French, p.p. of *chasser* to chase. See CHASE¹. The step is so called because one foot displaces the other as if chasing it.

chassepot *n.* a breech-loading rifle used in France, 1866–74. WH: 19C. Antoine A. *Chassepot*, 1833–1905, its French designer.

chasseur *n.* a huntsman. *Also a.* WH: 18C. French, from *chasser* (see CHASE¹) + -eur -OR.

chassis *n.* the framework of a motor vehicle, aeroplane etc. WH: 17C. French *châssis*, from Latin *capsa* CASE².

chaste *a.* abstaining from all sexual intercourse, or from sex outside marriage. WH: 12–14C. Old French, from Latin *castus*, rel. to *castrare* CASTRATE.

chasten *v.t.* to punish with a view to reformation; to correct; to discipline. WH: 16C. CHASTE + -EN⁵.

chastise *v.t.* to punish, esp. physically. WH: 12–14C. Appar. from obs. v. *chaste*, from Old French *chastier* (Modern French *châtier*), from Latin *castigare* CASTIGATE. Cp. CHASTEN.

chasuble *n.* a sleeveless vestment worn by a priest over the alb while celebrating Mass. WH: 12–14C. Old French *chesible*, later *chasuble*, from Late Latin *casubla*, alt. of Latin *casula* little cottage, hooded cloak, dim. of *casa* house.

chat¹ *v.i.* to talk easily and familiarly. *Also v.t., n.* WH: 14–15C. Abbr. of CHATTER.

chat² *n.* any of various birds, mostly songbirds or warblers, such as the stonechat or the whinchat. WH: 17C. Prob. imit.

chateau *n.* a castle or country house in French-speaking countries. WH: 18C. French CASTLE.

chateaubriand *n.* a thick steak of beef cut from the fillet. WH: 19C. François René, Vicomte de *Chateaubriand*, 1768–1848, French writer and statesman. The steak is said to be so called because it was specially prepared (grilled and served with Béarnaise sauce) for Chateaubriand by his chef, Montmirel, when he was French ambassador in London in 1822.

chatelain *n.* the lord of a castle. WH: 14–15C. Old French *chastelain* CASTELLAN (Modern French *châtelain*). A chatelaine was originally a female castellan who wore a special belt for carrying keys etc.

chatoyant *a.* having a changeable lustre or colour, like that of a cat's eye in the dark. *Also n.* WH: 18C. French, pres.p. of *chatoyer* to glisten, to shimmer, from *chat* CAT¹.

chattel *n.* moveable property. WH: 12–14C. Old French *chatel*, from Provençal *captal*, or from Medieval Latin *capitale*, neut. (used as n.) of Latin *capitalis*. See CAPITAL¹. Cp. CATTLE.

chatter *v.i.* to talk idly and thoughtlessly. *Also n.* WH: 12–14C. Imit., of freq. formation. Cp. CHITTER.

chatty *n.* an Indian earthen pitcher or water-pot. WH: 18C. Hindi *cātī*, from Tamil *caṭṭi*.

Chaucerian *a.* of or relating to Chaucer. *Also n.* WH: 17C. Geoffrey *Chaucer*, c.1343–1400, English poet + -IAN.

chaud-froid *n.* a dish of cold meat in an aspic sauce. WH: 19C. French, lit. hot-cold. Cp. CALID, FRIGID. The dish is so called because the hot cooked meat is allowed to grow cold before being eaten.

chauffeur *n.* a person employed to drive a motor car. *Also v.t., v.i.* WH: 19C. French stoker, fireman, from *chauffer* to heat. See CHAFE, also -OR.

chaulmoogra *n.* any of various trees of the family Flacourtiaceae, of tropical Asia, esp. *Hydnocarpus kurzii.* WH: 19C. Bengali *cāulmugrā*, from *cāul* rice + *mugrā* bowstring hemp.

chautauqua *n.* an institution providing adult education, entertainment etc., esp. at outdoor meetings in the summer. WH: 19C. *Chautauqua*, a county and lake in New York State, USA.

chauvinism *n.* exaggerated patriotism of an aggressive kind; jingoism. WH: 19C. Nicolas *Chauvin*, a Napoleonic veteran featuring as a character in the French vaudeville *La Cocarde tricolore* (1831) by Hippolyte Cogniard. See also -ISM. The historical Chauvin, although wounded, expressed a blind loyalty to Napoleon and the Empire that was at first admired but later ridiculed as a typical attitude of old soldiers.

chaw *v.t.* to chew (esp. tobacco). *Also n.* WH: 14–15C. Var. of CHEW. Cp. CHOW.

chay *n.* a chaise. WH: 19C. Back-formation from CHAISE taken as a pl.

chayote *n.* a tropical American climbing plant, *Sechium edule.* WH: 19C. Spanish, from Nahuatl *chayotli.*

chay root *n.* the root of an Indian plant, *Oldenlandia umbellata,* which yields a red dye. WH: 16C. Tamil *caya* + ROOT[1].

ChB *abbr.* Bachelor of Surgery. WH: Abbr. of Latin *Chirurgiae Baccalaureus.* Cp. CHM.

cheap *a.* low in price. *Also adv.* WH: pre-1200. Old English *cēap* price, bargain, from Germanic, from Latin *caupo* small tradesman, innkeeper. Cp. CHAPMAN. The current sense is elliptical for *good cheap* and arose in the 15C. Old English *cēap* market survives in such place names as Eastcheap and Cheapside (London), Chepstow and Chipping Norton.

cheat *v.t.* to defraud, to deprive. *Also v.i., n.* WH: 14–15C. Shortening of ESCHEAT.

Chechen *n.* a member of a people inhabiting the autonomous republic of Chechnya in SE Russia. *Also a.* WH: 19C. Obs. Russian *chechen* (now *chechenets*).

check[1] *n.* a test for accuracy, quality etc. *Also v.t., v.i., int.* WH: 12–14C. Shortening of Old French *eschec* (Modern French *échec*), from Medieval Latin *scaccus,* from Arabic, from Persian *šāh* king, SHAH. Cp. CHEQUE. The original reference was to the king in a game of chess when exposed to a direct attack and thus halted (checked) in its moves.

check[2] *n.* a chequered pattern, a cross-lined pattern. *Also a.* WH: 14–15C. Prob. abbr. of *checker* CHEQUER.

checkerberry *n.* a N American shrub, *Gaultheria procumbens,* with white flowers and edible red fruit. WH: 18C. From *checker,* var. of CHEQUER + BERRY. The shrub is so called from the chequered appearance of the fruit.

checkmate *n.* in chess, the winning move or situation when one king is in check and cannot escape from that position. *Also int., v.t.* WH: 12–14C. Shortening of Old French *eschec mat,* from Arabic *šāh māt,* representing Persian *šāh mat* the king is astonished, from *šāh* (see CHECK[1]) + *mat* astonished. Arabic *šāh māt* actually means the king is dead, but that is because Persian *mat* to be astonished was taken as *māta* to die.

Cheddar *n.* a hard, strong-flavoured yellow cheese. WH: 17C. *Cheddar,* a village in Somerset, where originally made.

cheddite *n.* an explosive made from a chlorate or perchlorate mixed with castor oil. WH: early 20C. *Chedde* in Haute-Savoie, E France, where originally made + -ITE[1].

cheek *n.* the side of the face below the eye. *Also v.t., v.i.* WH: pre-1200. Old English *cēoce,* from Germanic. Rel. to CHEW. The sense impudence, insolence dates from the 19C and comes from the expression *to give cheek* to speak impudently.

cheep *v.i.* to chirp feebly. *Also n.* WH: 16C. Imit. Cp. CHIRP, PEEP[2].

cheer *n.* a shout of joy, encouragement or applause. *Also v.t., v.i.* WH: 12–14C. Old French *chiere* face, from Late Latin *cara,* from Greek *kara* head. The original sense was face, then expression of face, then frame of mind, then cheerfulness. The sense shout of joy evolved in the 17C.

cheese[1] *n.* the curd of milk pressed into a solid mass and ripened by keeping. WH: pre-1200. Old English *cēse, cȳse,* from Germanic, from Latin *caseus,* of unknown orig. Cp. German *Käse.*

cheese[2] *n.* an important person. WH: 19C. Prob. from Urdu, from Persian *čīz* thing.

cheese[3] *v.t.* to stop. WH: 19C. Orig. unknown. ? From CEASE.

cheetah *n.* a leopard-like mammal, *Acinonyx jubatus,* the swiftest land animal. WH: 18C. Hindi *cītā,* from Sanskrit *citraka* leopard, lit. spotted.

chef *n.* a professional cook, esp. the head cook of a restaurant etc. WH: 19C. French head, CHIEF.

chef-d'œuvre *n.* a masterpiece. WH: 17C. French chief (piece) of work. Cp. CHEF, ŒUVRE.

Cheka *n.* the secret police in Russia (1917–22). WH: early 20C. Russian *che, ka,* pronunciation of initials of *Chrezvychaĭnaya komissiya* Extraordinary Commission. The full Russian title was *Chrezvychaĭnaya komissiya po bor'be s kontrrevolyutsieĭ i sabotazhem* Extraordinary Commission for Combating Counter-revolution and Sabotage.

Chekhovian *a.* of, resembling or relating to the style or works of the dramatist Chekhov. WH: early 20C. Anton Pavlovich *Chekhov,* 1860–1904, Russian writer + -IAN.

chela[1] *n.* a claw (as of a lobster or crab), a modified thoracic limb. WH: 17C. Modern Latin, from Latin *chele,* from Greek *khēlē* claw.

chela[2] *n.* a student or novice in esoteric Buddhism. WH: 19C. Hindi *celā.*

cheli- *comb. form* of or relating to a claw or claws. WH: Greek *khēlē* claw.

chelicera *n.* either of the clawlike appendages on the head of scorpions and spiders. WH: 19C. Modern Latin *chelicera,* from CHELA[1] + Greek *keras* horn.

cheliferous *a.* having a chela or chelae. WH: 18C. CHELI- + -FEROUS.

cheliform *a.* like a claw in form or shape. WH: 18C. CHELI- + -FORM.

cheliped *n.* either of the pair of legs carrying chelae. WH: 19C. CHELI- + -*ped* (-PEDE).

Chellean *a.* of or relating to the period of Lower Palaeolithic culture typified by the remains found at Chelles in the valley of the Marne; Abbevillian. WH: 19C. French *Chelléen,* from *Chelles* near Paris. See also -AN.

chelone *n.* any plant of the genus *Chelone,* cultivated for its white, pink or purple flowers. WH: 19C. Greek *khelōnē* tortoise. The flowers are said to resemble a tortoise's head.

chelonian *n.* any reptile of the order Chelonia, containing the turtles and tortoises. *Also a.* WH: 19C. Modern Latin *Chelonia,* from Greek *khelōnē* tortoise. See also -IA, -AN.

Chelsea bun *n.* a bun made of a roll of sweet dough with raisins. WH: 18C. *Chelsea,* a district in central London, where originally made + BUN[1].

chemical *a.* of or relating to chemistry, its laws or phenomena. *Also n.* WH: 16C. French *chimique* or Modern Latin *chimicus,* from Medieval Latin *alchimicus,* from *alchimia* ALCHEMY + -AL[1]. The earlier spelling was *chymical.* The original sense was alchemical.

chemico- *comb. form* chemical. WH: Comb. form of CHEMICAL. See also -O-. Cp. CHEMO-.

chemiluminescence *n.* luminescence occurring as a result of a chemical reaction, without production of heat. WH: 19C. *chemi-* (CHEMO-) + *luminescence* (LUMINESCE).

chemin de fer *n.* a variety of baccarat. WH: 19C. French railway (lit. road of iron). The game is said to be so named because of the speed at which it is played. French *chemin de fer* is a direct translation of English *railway.*

chemise *n.* an undergarment of linen or cotton worn by women. WH: 12–14C. Old French, from Late Latin *camisia* shirt, nightgown. Cp. CAMISOLE, SHIMMY.

chemisorption *n.* a process of adsorption involving chemical bonds. WH: mid-20C. *chemi-* (CHEMO-) + *adsorption* (ADSORB).

chemist *n.* a scientist specializing in chemistry. WH: 14–15C. French *chimiste,* from Modern Latin *chimysta,* from *alchimista* alchemist (ALCHEMY). The original sense was alchemist. The current sense evolved in the 17C.

chemistry *n.* the science which investigates the elements of which bodies are composed, the combination of these elements, and the reaction of these chemical compounds on each other . WH: 16C. CHEMIST + -RY.

chemmy *n.* chemin de fer. WH: early 20C. Abbr. of CHEMIN DE FER.

chemo- *comb. form* chemical . WH: Comb. form of CHEMICAL. See -O-. Cp. CHEMICO-.

chemoreceptor *n.* a sensory nerve ending which responds to a chemical stimulus. WH: early 20C. CHEMO- + *receptor* (RECEPTION).

chemosynthesis *n.* the production of organic material by some bacteria, using chemical reactions. WH: early 20C. CHEMO- + SYN-THESIS.

chemotaxis *n.* the property possessed by some cells or micro-organisms of being drawn towards or repelled by certain chemical substances. WH: 19C. CHEMO- + TAXIS.

chemotherapy *n.* the treatment of disease, esp. cancer, by drugs. WH: early 20C. German *Chemotherapie*, from CHEMO- + *Therapie* therapy (THERAPEUTIC). The term was coined in 1907 by the German biochemist Paul Ehrlich.

chemurgy *n.* the branch of chemistry which is devoted to the industrial utilization of organic raw material, esp. farm products. WH: mid-20C. CHEMO- + -*urgy*, based on METALLURGY.

chenille *n.* a round tufted or fluffy cord of silk or worsted. WH: 18C. French hairy caterpillar, from Latin *canicula*, dim. of *canis* dog. The material is so named from its furry appearance.

cheongsam *n.* a Chinese woman's long, tight-fitting dress with slit sides. WH: mid-20C. Chinese (Mandarin) *chángshān*, from *cháng* long + *shan* unlined upper garment.

cheque *n.* a draft on a bank for money payable to the bearer. WH: 18C. Var. of CHECK[1]. Not French *chèque*, which was borrowed from English. A cheque was originally so called as it was used to check forgery or the alteration of an agreed sum.

chequer *n.* a pattern made of squares in alternating colours, like a chessboard. *Also v.t.* WH: 12–14C. Shortening of EXCHEQUER. A chequer was originally a chessboard (cp. CHECK[1]). Hence *checkers* as the US equivalent of draughts.

cherish *v.t.* to treat with affection, to protect lovingly. WH: 12–14C. Old French *chérir*, *chériss-*, from *cher* dear, from Latin *carus*. See also -ISH[2].

chernozem *n.* a dark-coloured, very fertile soil found in temperate climates. WH: 19C. Russian, from *chërnyï* black + *zemlya* earth.

Cherokee *n.* a member of a N American Indian people now chiefly living in Oklahoma. *Also a.* WH: 17C. Obs. Cherokee *tsaraki* (now *tsaliki*).

cheroot *n.* a cigar with both ends cut square off. WH: 17C. French *cheroute*, from Tamil *curuṭṭu* roll of tobacco.

cherry *n.* a small stonefruit of the plum family. *Also a.* WH: 12–14C. Old French *cherise* (Modern French *cerise*), from Medieval Latin *ceresia*, ? from neut. pl. of *ceraseus*, from Latin *cerasus*, from Greek *kerasos* cherry tree.

chersonese *n.* a peninsula, esp. the Thracian peninsula. WH: 17C. Latin *chersonesus*, from Greek *khersonēsos*, from *khersos* dry + *nēsos* island. In ancient geography, the name applied to several peninsulas in Europe and Asia. It survives today in the city and port of *Kherson*, Ukraine, by the Tauric Chersonese (modern Crimea).

chert *n.* a flinty type of quartz; hornstone. WH: 17C. Orig. unknown.

cherub *n.* a celestial spirit next in order to the seraphim. WH: pre-1200. ult. from Hebrew *kĕrūḇ*, pl. *kĕrūḇîm* (English *cherubim*). The sense beautiful child derives from a rabbinic folk etymology that explains Hebrew *kĕrūḇ* as representing Aramaic *kĕ-rabyā* like a child.

chervil *n.* a garden herb, *Anthriscus cerefolium*, used in soups, salads etc. WH: pre-1200. Latin *chaerephylla*, from Greek *khaire-phullon*, from *khairein* to take pleasure in + *phullon* leaf.

Cheshire *n.* a mild-flavoured white or red cheese with a firm but crumbly texture. WH: 16C. *Cheshire*, a county in NW England where originally made.

chess[1] *n.* a game played by two persons with 16 pieces each on a board divided into 64 squares. WH: 12–14C. Shortening of Old French *esches* (Modern French *échecs*), pl. of *eschec* CHECK[1].

chess[2] *n.* any of the parallel baulks of timber used in laying a pontoon bridge. WH: 14–15C. Orig. unknown. ? Rel. to CHASE[1].

chessel *n.* a cheese mould. WH: 17C. Appar. from CHEESE[1] + WELL[2].

chest *n.* a large strong box. *Also v.t.* WH: pre-1200. Old English *cest*,

cyst, from Germanic, from Latin *cista*, from Greek *kistē* box. Cp. CIST[1].

chesterfield *n.* a deeply upholstered sofa with curved arms and back of the same height. WH: 19C. From an Earl of *Chesterfield*. A secondary sense, a kind of overcoat, is probably from Philip Dormer Stanhope, 4th Earl of Chesterfield, 1694–1773, English statesman and man of letters.

chestnut *n.* any tree of the genus *Castanea*, esp. the Spanish or sweet chestnut, *C. sativa*. *Also a.* WH: 16C. Old French *chastaine* (Modern French *châtaigne*), from Latin *castanea*, from Greek *kastanea*, short for *kastaneion karuon* nut of Castanaea + NUT. The original Greek town from which the tree was named may have been either Castanaea, Pontus, or Castana, Thessaly.

chetnik *n.* a member of a Serbian nationalist guerrilla force active before and during the two World Wars. WH: early 20C. Serbo-Croat *četnik*, from *četa* band, troop. See also -NIK.

cheval-de-frise *n.* a portable fence, consisting of a bar armed with two rows of long spikes, for checking attacks by cavalry etc. WH: 17C. French horse of Friesland. Cp. CHEVALIER, FRISIAN. The fences were named ironically from their use by the Friesians, who had no cavalry.

cheval glass *n.* a large swinging mirror mounted on a frame. WH: 19C. French *cheval* horse + GLASS. The mirror is so named because it is mounted on its frame, like a rider in the saddle.

chevalier *n.* a member of some foreign orders of knighthood or of the French Legion of Honour. WH: 14–15C. Old French, from Medieval Latin *caballarius*, from Latin *caballus* horse. See also -IER. Cp. CAVALIER.

chevet *n.* an apse. WH: 19C. French pillow, from Latin *capitellum* top opening in a tunic, from *caput*, *capitis* head. The eastern extremity of a French Gothic church, considered externally, resembles the top of a bed, where one rests one's head.

cheviot *n.* a breed of sheep with short thick wool. WH: 18C. *Cheviot* Hills, on the border between England and Scotland.

chèvre *n.* a type of cheese made from goats' milk. WH: mid-20C. French goat.

chevrette *n.* a thin goatskin leather used for gloves. WH: 19C. French, dim. of CHÈVRE. See also -ETTE.

chevron *n.* a V-shaped badge on the sleeve of a uniform, esp. of a non-commissioned officer in the armed forces. WH: 14–15C. Old French, from Latin *caper* goat. The badge is perhaps so called from the angular shape of a goat's hind legs.

chevrotain *n.* a small animal of the family Tragulidae, resembling a deer. WH: 18C. French, dim. of Old French *chevrot*, dim. of *chèvre* goat.

chew *v.t.* to grind with the teeth. *Also v.i., n.* WH: pre-1200. Old English *cēowan*, from Germanic. Cp. German *kauen*.

Cheyenne *n.* a member of a N American Indian people now chiefly living in Montana and Oklahoma. *Also a.* WH: 18C. Canadian French, from Dakota *šahíyena*.

Cheyne–Stokes *a.* of or denoting a cycle of respiration, esp. in comatose patients, in which breathing gradually becomes shallower, stops, then gradually increases again. WH: 19C. John *Cheyne*, 1777–1836, Scottish physician, and William *Stokes*, 1804–78, Irish physician.

chez *prep.* at the house of. WH: 18C. French, from Old French *chiese*, from Latin *casa* cottage.

chi *n.* the 22nd letter of the Greek alphabet (Χ, χ). WH: 14–15C. Greek *khi*.

chiack *v.t.* to tease, to poke fun at. *Also n.* WH: 19C. Orig. unknown. The word was apparently originally a costermonger's cry of commendation.

Chian *a.* of or relating to Chios. *Also n.* WH: 16C. Latin *Chius*, from Greek *Khios* (a.), from *Khios* Chios. See also -AN.

Chianti *n.* a dry red wine from Tuscany. WH: 19C. *Chianti* Mountains, Tuscany.

chiaroscuro *n.* the treatment or effects of light and shade in drawing, painting etc. *Also a.* WH: 17C. Italian *chiaro* clear, bright + *oscuro* dark, OBSCURE.

chiasma *n.* the connection or point of contact between paired chromosomes after crossing over during meiosis. WH: 19C. Modern Latin, from Greek *khiasma* crosspiece, from *khiazein*. See CHIASMUS.

chiasmus *n.* the inversion of order in parallel phrases, as in *you came late, to go early would be unreasonable*. WH: 17C. Modern Latin, from Greek *khiasmos*, from *khiazein* to mark with a chi, from *khi* CHI.

chibouk *n.* a long Turkish pipe for smoking. WH: 19C. French *chibouque*, from Turkish *çubuk*, earlier *çıbık*, tube, pipe.

chic *n.* smartness, style. *Also a.* WH: 19C. French, ? from German *Schick* skill, rather than Spanish *chico* little.

chicane *n.* an artificial obstacle on a motor-racing track. *Also v.i., v.t.* WH: 17C. French *chicaner* to pursue at law, to quibble, of unknown orig. The original sense was an instance of chicanery. The sense a hand without trumps at cards evolved in the 19C, and the current motor-racing sense in the mid-20C.

Chicano *n.* a person of Mexican origin living in the US. WH: mid-20C. Alt. of Spanish *mejicano* Mexican, from *Méjico* Mexico.

chichi *a.* showy, affectedly pretty or fashionable. *Also n.* WH: early 20C. French, prob. imit., but suggestive of CHIC. The word is not related to *chi-chi* half-caste girl, Eurasian woman, which is imitative of the speech of some Eurasians in India.

chick[1] *n.* a young bird about to be hatched or newly hatched. WH: 12–14C. Abbr. of CHICKEN.

chick[2] *n.* a door screen or blind made from strips of bamboo fastened together with twine. WH: 17C. Urdu *chik*, from Persian *čigh*.

chickadee *n.* any of various N American songbirds of the tit family, such as *Parus atricapillus*. WH: 19C. Imit. of the bird's call.

chicken *n.* the young of the domestic fowl. *Also a.* WH: pre-1200. Old English *cīcen*, prob. ult. rel. to COCK[1], and like it of imit. orig.

chickling *n.* the cultivated vetch. WH: 16C. French *chiche*, from Old French *cice*, from Latin *cicer* chickpea + -LING[1].

chickpea *n.* a dwarf species of pea, *Cicer arietinum*. WH: 18C. Alt. of *chiche-pease*, from French *chiche* (see CHICKLING) + PEA.

chicle *n.* the juice of the sapodilla, used in the making of chewing gum. WH: 19C. American Spanish, from Nahuatl *tzictli*.

chicory *n.* a blue-flowered plant, *Cichorium intybus*, the succory. WH: 14–15C. Obs. French *cicorée* endive (Modern French *chicorée*), from Medieval Latin *cicorea*, ult. from Greek *kikhorion*. Cp. SUCCORY.

chide *v.t.* to find fault with, to reprove. *Also v.i., n.* WH: pre-1200. Old English *cīdan*, of unknown orig. An earlier sense (to the 19C) was to wrangle, to brawl. The current sense dates from the 12–14C.

chief *a.* principal, first. *Also n.* WH: 12–14C. Old French *chef*, var. of Latin *caput* head.

chieftain *n.* a general, a leader. WH: 12–14C. Old French *chevetaine*, from Late Latin *capitaneus* (see CAPTAIN), assim. to CHIEF.

chiffchaff *n.* a European warbler, *Phylloscopus collybita*. WH: 18C. Imit.

chiffon *n.* a gauzy semi-transparent fabric. *Also a.* WH: 18C. French, from *chiffe* rag, from Germanic. Rel. to CHIP.

chigger *n.* a small W Indian and S American flea, *Tunga penetrans*. WH: 18C. Alt. of CHIGOE.

chignon *n.* a coil or knot of long hair at the back of the head. WH: 18C. French nape of the neck, from var. of Latin *catena* CHAIN. See also -OON.

chigoe *n.* the flea *Tunga penetrans*, a chigger. WH: 17C. French *chique*, from a W African language.

chihuahua *n.* a very small dog with big eyes and pointed ears. WH: 19C. *Chihuahua*, a city and state in Mexico.

chilblain *n.* an inflamed swelling of the hands or feet caused by bad circulation and cold. WH: 16C. CHILL + BLAIN.

child *n.* a young person. *Also v.t., v.i.* WH: pre-1200. Old English *cild*, rel. to Gothic *kilthei* womb, *inkiltho* pregnant. The sense is thus effectively fruit of the womb. German *Kind* child is not related.

†**Childermas** *n.* the festival of Holy Innocents (28 December). WH: pre-1200. Old English *cildramæsse*, from *cildra*, gen. pl. of *cild* CHILD + *mæsse* MASS.

Chilean *n.* a native or inhabitant of Chile. *Also a.* WH: 18C. *Chile*, a S American republic + -AN.

Chile pine *n.* the monkey-puzzle tree. WH: 19C. *Chile* (see CHILEAN) + PINE[1].

chiliad *n.* a thousand. WH: 14–15C. Late Latin *chilias, chiliadis*, from Greek *khilias, khiliados*, from *khilioi* one thousand. See also -AD[1].

chiliasm *n.* the doctrine of the millennium. WH: 17C. Greek *khiliasmos*, from *khilias* CHILIAD.

chill *n.* coldness. *Also v.t., v.i., a.* WH: pre-1200. Old English *cele, ciele*, of Germanic orig. Rel. to COLD.

chilli *n.* the hot-tasting ripe pod of a species of capsicum, esp. *Capsicum annuum*, used to flavour, sauces, pickles etc. WH: 17C. Spanish *chile*, from Nahuatl *chilli*.

chilo- *comb. form* lip-shaped, labiate. WH: Greek *kheilos* lip. See also -O-.

chilopod *n.* any arthropod of the class Chilopoda, including the centipedes. WH: 19C. Modern Latin *Chilopoda*. See CHILO-, -POD.

Chiltern Hundreds *n.pl.* certain Crown lands in Buckinghamshire and Oxfordshire, the nominal stewardship of which is granted to a Member of Parliament who wishes to vacate their seat. WH: 12–14C. *Chiltern Hills*, S England + HUNDRED + -S[1].

chime[1] *n.* the harmonic or consonant sounds of musical instruments or bells. *Also v.i., v.t.* WH: 12–14C. Prob. from Old English *cimbal* CYMBAL, interpreted as *chime bell*.

chime[2] *n.* the edge of a cask or tub formed by the ends of the staves. WH: 14–15C. Prob. from Old English *cim-*, in *cimstān* base, pedestal, *cimīren* clamp-iron, of Germanic orig.

chimer *n.* a bishop's outer robe. WH: 14–15C. Appar. rel. to Spanish *zamarra* sheepskin cloak, and to Italian *zimarra, cimarra* long robe. Cp. CYMAR.

chimera *n.* a fabulous fire-eating monster, with a lion's head, a serpent's tail, and the body of a goat. WH: 14–15C. Latin *chimaera*, from Greek *khimaira* she-goat, monster, from *khimaros* he-goat. The original chimera was said to be a monster personifying snow or winter (Greek *khiōn* snow, *kheimōn* winter).

chimichanga *n.* a deep-fried rolled tortilla with a savoury filling. WH: mid-20C. Mexican Spanish trinket.

chimney *n.* the flue, vent or passage through which smoke etc. escapes from a fire into the open air. WH: 12–14C. Old French *cheminée* chimney, fireplace, from Late Latin *caminata*, ? orig. from *camera caminata* room with a fireplace, from Latin *caminus* forge, furnace, from Greek *kaminos* oven.

chimp *n.* a chimpanzee. WH: 19C. Abbr. of CHIMPANZEE.

chimpanzee *n.* a large intelligent African anthropoid ape, *Pan troglodytes*. WH: 18C. French *chimpanzé*, from Kikongo.

chin *n.* the front part of the lower jaw. WH: pre-1200. Old English *cin*, from Germanic. Rel. to Latin *gena* cheek, Greek *genus* jaw. Cp. German *Kinn*.

china *n.* fine porcelain, first brought from China. *Also a.* WH: 16C. *China*, a country in E Asia.

China aster *n.* a Chinese garden plant, *Callistephus chinensis*, with showy aster-like flowers. WH: 18C. CHINA + ASTER.

chinch *n.* a N American insect, *Blissus leucopterus*, destructive to cereal crops. WH: 17C. Spanish *chinche*, from Latin *cimex, cimicis* bedbug.

chincherinchee *n.* a southern African plant of the lily family, *Ornithogalum thyrsoides*, with white flowers. WH: early 20C. Imit. of squeaky sound made by rubbing the plant's stalks together.

chinchilla *n.* any S American rodent of the genus *Chinchilla*. WH: 17C. Spanish, prob. from Aymara or Quechua, influ. by *chinche* CHINCH.

chin-chin *int.* a familiar form of salutation or drinking toast. WH: 18C. Chinese *qĭng-qĭng* please-please. The word is popularly associated with CHINK[2] as it is often said when clinking glasses in a toast.

Chindit *n.* a member of the Allied commando force in Burma (now Myanmar) during World War II. WH: mid-20C. Burmese *chinthé* griffin. The mythological creature, represented on Burmese pagodas, was adopted as a device of the troops under Major-General Orde Wingate (1903–44).

chine[1] *n.* the backbone or spine of any animal. *Also v.t.* WH: 12–14C. Shortening of Old French *eschine* (Modern French *échine*), from blend of Germanic source of SHIN and Latin *spina* SPINE.

chine[2] *n.* a deep and narrow ravine. WH: pre-1200. Old English *cinu*, from Germanic base of CHINK[1].

chine[3] *n.* the join between the side and bottom of a ship or boat. WH: 14–15C. Alt. of CHIME[2].

chiné *a.* (of fabric) having a mottled pattern. WH: 19C. French, p.p. of *chiner* to dye the warp of, from *Chine* China. The warp or weft threads of the fabric were dyed to give it a mottled pattern in a supposed Chinese style.

Chinese *n.* a native or inhabitant of China, or a person of Chinese descent. *Also a.* WH: 16C. China + -ESE.

Chink *a.*, *n.* (a) Chinese. WH: 19C. China, ? influ. by CHINK[1] with reference to the narrow eyes of the Chinese.

chink[1] *n.* a narrow cleft or crevice. *Also v.t., v.i.* WH: 16C. Orig. uncertain. ? From CHINE[2].

chink[2] *n.* a jingling sound as of coins or glasses. *Also v.t., v.i.* WH: 14–15C. Imit.

Chinky *n.* a Chinese person. *Also a.* WH: 19C. CHINK + -Y[3].

Chino- *comb. form* Chinese; of or relating to China. WH: China + -O-.

chino *n.* a tough, twilled cotton fabric. WH: mid-20C. American Spanish toasted. The original sense was a Spanish American of mixed blood, with skin of a light brown ('toasted') colour. The word was hence applied to military trousers of this colour.

chinoiserie *n.* a style of Western art and architecture using Chinese motifs. WH: 19C. French, from *chinois* CHINESE + -*erie* -ERY.

Chinook *n.* a member of a N American Indian people who formerly lived along the Columbia river. WH: 19C. Salish *tsinúk.*

chinook *n.* a warm dry wind blowing east of the Rocky Mountains. WH: 19C. CHINOOK. The Chinook formerly lived along the Columbia river, west of the Rocky Mountains, where the wet wind blows. The name was then extended to the dry wind blowing east of the Rockies.

chintz *n.* a printed cotton cloth with floral devices etc., usu. glazed. WH: 17C. Hindi *chīt* spattering, stain, from Sanskrit *citra-s* distinctive. Rel. to CHEETAH. The current form of the word is a fanciful spelling of *chints*, the plural of the original form, *chint.*

chip *n.* a small piece of wood, stone etc. detached. *Also v.t., v.i.* WH: pre-1200. Old English *cipp, cyp,* from Germanic, from Latin *cippus* stake, post, pillar. Cp. German *kippen* to clip.

chipmunk *n.* a N American rodent of the genus *Tamias lysteri,* resembling a squirrel. WH: 19C. Ojibwa *ačitamon* squirrel, lit. one that descends trees headlong.

chipolata *n.* a small sausage. WH: 19C. French, from Italian *cipollata* dish of onions, from *cipolla* onion. The sausage was originally flavoured with onion. The word is unrelated to CHIP.

Chippendale *a.* (of furniture) designed or made by Chippendale about the middle of the 18th cent., or in a similarly ornately elegant style. WH: 19C. Thomas *Chippendale,* 1718–79, English cabinetmaker.

chipper *a.* energetic and cheerful. WH: 19C. Orig. unknown. ? Influ. by form of CHIRRUP. Cp. *chirpy* (CHIRP).

chiral *a.* (of an optically active chemical compound) asymmetric, having a left-handed or right-handed structure. WH: 19C. Greek *kheir* hand + -AL[1].

chiro- *comb. form* manual. WH: Greek *kheir* hand. See also -O-.

chirograph *n.* a written or signed document. WH: 12–14C. French *chirographe,* from Latin *chirographum,* from Greek *kheirographon.* See CHIRO-, -GRAPH.

chiromancy *n.* divination by means of the hand; palmistry. WH: 14–15C. French *chiromancie,* from Latin *chiromantia,* from Greek *kheiromanteia.* See CHIRO-, -MANCY.

chiropodist *n.* a person skilled in the care of the feet, esp. in the removal of corns etc. WH: 18C. CHIRO- + -POD + -IST.

chiropractic *n.* spinal manipulation as a method of curing disease, disorders of the joints etc. WH: 19C. CHIRO- + Greek *praktikos.* See PRACTISE. The word is said to have been coined by a patient of Daniel Palmer, US founder of the Chiropractic School and Cure in 1895.

chiropteran *n.* any mammal of the order Chiroptera, with membranes connecting their fingers and used as wings, consisting of the bats. WH: 19C. Modern Latin *Chiroptera,* from CHIRO- + Greek *pteron* wing. See also -AN.

chirp *v.i.* (of a bird, insect etc.) to make a quick, sharp sound. *Also v.t., n.* WH: 14–15C. Imit. Cp. CHEEP, CHIRRUP.

chirr *v.i.* to make a trilling monotonous sound like that of the grasshopper. *Also n.* WH: 17C. Imit.

chirrup *v.i.* to chirp, to make a twittering sound. WH: 16C. Alt. of CHIRP made by trilling the *r.*

chisel *n.* an edged tool for cutting wood, iron or stone, operated by pressure or striking. *Also v.t., v.i.* WH: 14–15C. Old French (Modern French *ciseau,* pl. *ciseaux* scissors), or from Latin *cis-,* var. of *caes-,* stem of *caedere* to cut. See also -EL.

chi-square test *n.* a test used in statistics to compare data, esp. observed and theoretical values. WH: early 20C. CHI + SQUARE + TEST[1]. The test is so called because the letter chi is conventionally used to represent the square root of the sum of the squares of the differences between the two types of values.

chit[1] *n.* a child. WH: 14–15C. Orig. unknown. ? Var. of KIT[3]. Not rel. to CHILD or KID[1].

chit[2] *n.* a voucher for money owed. WH: 17C. Abbr. of *chitty,* from Hindi *ciṭṭhī,* from Sanskrit *citra* spot, mark. Rel. to CHEETAH, CHITAL.

chital *n.* the axis deer. WH: 19C. Hindi *cītal,* from Sanskrit *citrala* spotted. Cp. CHEETAH.

chit-chat *n.* chat, gossip, trifling talk. *Also v.i.* WH: 17C. Redupl. of CHAT[1].

chitin *n.* the horny substance that gives firmness to the exoskeleton of arthropods and to the cell wall of fungi. WH: 19C. French *chitine,* from Greek *khitōn.* See CHITON, also -IN[1].

chiton *n.* an ancient Greek tunic. WH: 19C. Greek *khitōn* tunic.

chitter *v.i.* to shiver, to tremble. WH: 12–14C. Imit. Cp. CHATTER.

chitterlings *n.pl.* the smaller intestines of animals, esp. as prepared for food. WH: 12–14C. Orig. uncertain. ? Rel. to Middle High German *kutel* (German *Kutteln*), in same sense.

chivalry *n.* the knightly system of the Middle Ages. WH: 12–14C. Old French *chevalerie,* from Medieval Latin *caballerius,* var. of *caballarius.* See CHEVALIER, also -ERY.

chive *n.* a small onion-like herb, *Allium schoenoprasum.* WH: 14–15C. Dial. var. of Old French *cive,* from Latin *cepa* onion.

chivvy *v.t.* to hurry; to pester or nag. *Also v.i., n.* WH: 18C. Said to be from *Chevy Chase,* scene of a skirmish in a Border ballad. The ballad was inspired by the battle of Otterburn (1388), in which there was a fierce encounter between Scottish and English troops.

chlamydia *n.* any disease-causing micro-organism of the genus *Chlamydia,* resembling both bacteria and viruses. WH: mid-20C. Modern Latin, from Greek *khlamus, khlamudos* CHLAMYS + -IA.

chlamys *n.* a Greek cloak or mantle. WH: 17C. Greek *khlamus* mantle.

chloasma *n.* a condition in which dark patches appear in a person's skin, usu. at a time of hormonal change. WH: 19C. Greek *khloazein* to become green.

chloracne *n.* a skin disease that results from exposure to chlorinated chemicals. WH: early 20C. CHLORO- + ACNE.

chloral *n.* a liquid made from chlorine and alcohol. WH: 19C. CHLORINE + ALCOHOL. The term was coined in 1831 by the German chemist Justus Liebig, based on earlier *ethal* (ETHER + -AL[1]).

chloramphenicol *n.* an antibiotic used to treat typhoid etc. WH: mid-20C. CHLORO- + AMIDE + PHENO- + NITRO- + GLYCOL.

chlorate *n.* a salt of chloric acid. WH: 19C. CHLORIC + -ATE[1].

chlorella *n.* any green freshwater alga of the genus *Chlorella.* WH: early 20C. Modern Latin, dim. of Greek *khlōros* green.

chloric *a.* of, relating to or containing pentavalent chlorine. WH: 19C. CHLORINE + -IC. Cp. CHLOROUS.

chloride *n.* a compound of chlorine with another element. WH: 19C. CHLORINE + -IDE.

chlorine *n.* a yellow-green, poisonous, gaseous element, at. no. 17, chem. symbol Cl, obtained from common salt, used as a disinfectant and for bleaching. WH: 19C. Greek *khlōros* green + -INE. The name was coined in 1810 by the English chemist Sir Humphry Davy with reference to the colour, but the element itself was discovered in 1774 by the Swedish chemist Carl Scheele.

chlorite[1] *n.* a green silicate mineral. WH: 18C. Latin *chloritis,* from Greek *khlōritis* a green precious stone. See CHLORO-, also -ITE[1].

chlorite[2] *n.* a salt of chlorous acid. WH: 19C. CHLORINE + -ITE[1].

chloro- *comb. form* of a green colour. WH: 19C. Greek *khlōros* green. See also -O-.

chlorofluorocarbon *n.* any of various compounds of carbon, hydrogen, chlorine and fluorine, used in refrigerators, aerosols etc., some of which are harmful to the ozone layer; a CFC. WH: mid-20C. CHLORO- + FLUORO- + CARBON, based on HYDROCARBON.

chloroform *n.* a volatile fluid formerly used as an anaesthetic. *Also v.t.* WH: 19C. CHLORO- + FORMIC. The fluid was named in 1834 by the French chemist Jean-Baptiste-André Dumas.

Chloromycetin® *n.* a brand of chloramphenicol. WH: mid-20C. CHLORO- + MYCETO- + -IN¹.

chlorophyll *n.* the green colouring matter of plants which absorbs the energy from sunlight, used in producing carbohydrates from water and carbon dioxide. WH: 19C. French *chlorophylle*. See CHLORO-, -PHYLL.

chloroplast *n.* a plastid containing chlorophyll. WH: 19C. CHLORO- + -PLAST.

chloroquine *n.* a drug used in the treatment of malaria. WH: mid-20C. CHLORO- + *quinoline* (QUINOL).

chlorosis *n.* a disease affecting young people due to deficiency of iron in the blood. WH: 17C. CHLORO- + -OSIS.

chlorous *a.* of, relating to or containing trivalent chlorine. WH: 19C. CHLORINE + -OUS. Cp. CHLORIC.

chlorpromazine *n.* a tranquillizing drug. WH: mid-20C. CHLORO- + PROMETHAZINE.

ChM *abbr.* Master of Surgery. WH: Abbr. of Latin *Chirurgiae Magister.* Cp. CHB.

choc *n.* a chocolate. WH: 19C. Abbr. of CHOCOLATE.

chocho *n.* a choko. WH: 18C. Spanish, of American Indian orig.

chock *n.* a wood block, esp. a wedge-shaped block used to prevent a cask, wheel, boat etc. from shifting. *Also v.t., adv.* WH: 12–14C. Prob. from Old French *choque* log, block of wood, var. of *çouche* (Modern French *souche*), of unknown orig. Some derivative senses, such as *chock-a-block* and *chock-full*, were probably influenced by CHOKE.

chocoholic *n.* a person who is very fond of or addicted to chocolate. *Also a.* WH: late 20C. Blend of CHOCOLATE and *alcoholic* (ALCOHOL).

chocolate *n.* a usu. sweet food made from the roasted and ground seeds of the cacao tree. *Also a.* WH: 17C. French *chocolat*, or from Spanish *chocolate*, from Nahuatl *chocolatl* (now written *xocoatl*) type of food made from cacao seeds, lit. bitter water, influ. by unrelated *cacauatl* drink made from cacao.

Choctaw *n.* a member of a N American Indian people of Alabama. *Also a.* WH: 18C. Choctaw *čahta*.

choice *n.* the power or act of choosing. *Also a.* WH: 12–14C. Old French *chois* (Modern French *choix*), from *choisir* to choose, from Germanic base of CHOOSE.

choir *n.* an organized body of singers. *Also v.i., v.t.* WH: 12–14C. Old French *quer* (Modern French *chœur*), from Latin *chorus*. See CHORUS. The original spelling was *quire*. The current spelling, based on the French and Latin words, was introduced in the 17C.

choke *v.t.* to block the windpipe (of), so as to prevent breathing. *Also v.i., n.* WH: 12–14C. Shortening of Old English *ācēocian*, from a- A-¹ + *cēoce* CHEEK.

choko *n.* a succulent vegetable like a cucumber. WH: 18C. Spanish, of Amer. Ind. orig.

choky *n.* a prison. WH: 17C. Hindi *caukī*, influ. by CHOKE.

cholagogue *n.* a medicine which promotes the flow of bile. WH: 17C. Greek *kholagōgos*, from *kholē* bile, gall + *agōgos* leading, eliciting.

cholangiography *n.* X-ray photography of the bile ducts. WH: mid-20C. CHOLE- + ANGIOGRAPHY.

chole- *comb. form* of or relating to bile. WH: Greek *kholē* bile, gall.

cholecalciferol *n.* a compound that occurs in fish-liver oils; vitamin D₃. WH: mid-20C. CHOLE- + CALCIFEROL.

cholecyst *n.* the gall bladder. WH: 19C. Modern Latin *cholecystis* gall bladder, from Greek *kholē* bile, gall + *kustis* bladder.

choler *n.* yellow bile, the humour supposed to cause irascibility. WH: 14–15C. Old French *colère*, from Latin CHOLERA.

cholera *n.* an acute, often fatal, bacterial infection, spread by contaminated water supplies, in which severe vomiting and diarrhoea cause dehydration. WH: 14–15C. Latin, from Greek *kholera*, from *kholē* bile, gall.

cholesterol *n.* a steroid alcohol occurring in body tissues, including blood and bile (high levels of cholestrol in the blood are thought to be a cause of arteriosclerosis and heart disease). WH: 19C. CHOLE- + Greek *stereos* stiff + -OL.

choli *n.* an Indian woman's garment, a short tight-fitting bodice worn under a sari. WH: early 20C. Hindi *colī*.

choliamb *n.* a scazon. WH: 19C. Late Latin *choliambus*, from Greek *khōliambos*, from *khōlos* lame. See IAMBUS.

cholic *a.* of, relating to or obtained from bile. WH: 19C. Greek *kholikos*. See CHOLE-, also -IC.

choline *n.* a substance occurring naturally in the body, important for the synthesis of lecithin etc. WH: 19C. CHOLE- + -INE.

cholla *n.* any of various cacti of the genus *Opuntia*, of Mexico and the south-west US. WH: 19C. Mexican Spanish, use of Spanish skull, head, of unknown orig.

Chomskian *a.* of or relating to Chomsky or his work. WH: mid-20C. Noam Avram *Chomsky*, 1928– , US linguistic scholar + -AN.

chondrify *v.i.* to be converted into cartilage. *Also v.t.* WH: 19C. Greek *khondros* cartilage + -FY.

chondrin *n.* gelatin from the cartilage of the ribs, joints etc. WH: 19C. Greek *khondros* cartilage + -IN¹.

chondrite *n.* a meteorite containing stony granules. WH: 19C. Greek *khondros* granule + -ITE¹.

chondritis *n.* inflammation of cartilage. WH: 19C. Greek *khondros* cartilage + -ITIS.

chondro- *comb. form* composed of or relating to cartilage. WH: Greek *khondros* cartilage. See also -O-.

chondrocranium *n.* a skull composed of cartilage, esp. that of the human embryo. WH: 19C. CHONDRO- + CRANIUM.

chondroid *a.* like cartilage. WH: 19C. Greek *khondros* cartilage + -OID.

chondrule *n.* any of the stony granules found in a chondrite. WH: 19C. CHONDRITE + -ULE.

choo-choo *n.* a railway train or steam engine (used by or to children). WH: early 20C. Imit. Cp. *chuff-chuff*, *puff-puff*.

chook *n.* a chicken or other domestic fowl. WH: mid-20C. Var. of CHUCK⁴. Cp. CHICK¹.

choose *v.t.* to select from a number. *Also v.i.* WH: pre-1200. Old English *cēosan*, from Germanic. Rel. to Latin *gustare* to taste. Cp. GUSTO.

chop¹ *v.t.* to cut with a sharp blow. *Also v.i., n.* WH: 14–15C. Var. of CHAP¹.

chop² *v.i.* (of the wind etc.) to change direction suddenly. *Also v.t., n.* WH: 14–15C. Orig. uncertain. ? Var. of CHAP¹ or from a form of CHEAP.

chop³ *n.* the jaw of an animal. WH: 14–15C. Var. of CHAP³.

chop⁴ *n.* in the Indian subcontinent and China, a seal or official stamp. WH: 17C. Hindi *chāp* stamp, brand.

chop-chop *adv., int.* at once, quickly. WH: 19C. Pidgin English var. of Chinese *kuài-kuài* quick-quick.

chopstick *n.* either of two small sticks of wood or ivory used by the Chinese to eat with. WH: 17C. Pidgin English *chop* (cp. CHOP-CHOP) + STICK¹. The Chinese word for chopsticks is *kuàizi*, from *kuài* fast, quick + *zǐ* son, small thing.

chop suey *n.* a Chinese dish of shredded meat and vegetables served with rice. WH: 19C. Chinese (Cantonese dial.) *zá suì* mixed bits.

choragus *n.* the leader or director of the chorus in the ancient Greek theatrical performances. WH: 17C. Latin, from Greek *khoragos*, from *khoros* CHORUS + *agein* to lead.

choral *a.* of, for or sung by a choir or chorus. WH: 16C. Medieval Latin *choralis*, from Latin CHORUS. See also -AL¹.

chorale *n.* a simple choral hymn or song, usually of slow rhythm. WH: 19C. German *Choralgesang*, translating Medieval Latin *cantus choralis* choral song.

chord¹ *n.* the simultaneous and harmonious sounding of notes of different pitch. *Also v.i.* WH: 12–14C. Shortening of ACCORD, influ. by CHORD².

chord² *n.* a straight line joining the extremities of an arc or two points in a curve. WH: 16C. Var. of CORD, based on Latin *chorda* string.

chordate *n.* any member of the Chordata, a phylum of animals with a backbone or notochord. *Also a.* WH: 19C. Modern Latin *Chordata*, from Latin *chorda* chord. See also -ATE¹.

chore *n.* a small regular task, esp. a household job. WH: 18C. Alt. of CHAR³.

chorea *n.* a nervous disorder characterized by irregular convulsive movements of an involuntary kind. WH: 17C. Latin, from Greek *khoreia* dance.

choreography n. the arrangement of steps (of a stage dance or ballet). WH: 18C. Greek *khoreia* dance + -O- + -GRAPHY.

choreology n. the study of the movements of dancing. WH: mid-20C. Greek *khoreia* dance + -O- + -LOGY.

choriamb n. a metrical foot of four syllables, of which the first and fourth are long, and the second and third short. WH: 18C. Late Latin *choriambus*, from Greek *khoriambos*, from *khoreios* of a chorus + *iambos* IAMBUS.

chorine n. a chorus girl. WH: early 20C. CHORUS + -INE.

chorion n. the outer membrane which envelops the embryo of a reptile, bird or mammal. WH: 16C. Greek *khorion* outer membrane of foetus.

chorister n. a person who sings in a choir, esp. a choirboy or choirgirl. WH: 14–15C. Anglo-French *cueristre*, *cueriste*, from Medieval Latin *chorista*, from Latin CHORUS + -IST. The current form gradually replaced earlier *chorist* from the 16C.

chorizo n. a highly seasoned pork sausage made in Spain or Mexico. WH: 19C. Spanish.

chorography n. the art or practice of describing and making maps of particular regions or districts. WH: 16C. French *chorographie*, or from Latin *chorographia*, from Greek *khōrographia*, from *khōra* country, district. See -GRAPHY.

chorology n. the science of the geographical distribution of plants and animals. WH: 19C. Greek *khōra* region + -O- + -LOGY.

chortle v.i. to make a loud chuckle. Also v.t., n. WH: 19C. Invented by Lewis Carroll in *Through the Looking-Glass* (1871). Appar. blend of CHUCKLE and SNORT.

chorus n. a large choir. Also v.t., v.i. WH: 16C. Latin, from Greek *khoros* dance, band of dancers, chorus.

chough n. a large black bird of the crow family, *Pyrrhocorax pyrrhocorax*, with red legs and bill. WH: 12–14C. Prob. imit. of cry.

choux pastry n. a rich light pastry made with eggs. WH: 18C. French pl. of *chou* cabbage, from Latin *caulis* + PASTRY. The pastry is so called because it is used for making cabbage-shaped buns.

chow n. food. WH: 19C. Abbr. of CHOW-CHOW.

chow-chow n. a dog of an orig. Chinese breed with thick coat and curled tail. WH: 18C. Pidgin English, ult. orig. unknown. The word is perhaps a reduplication of Chinese *zá* mixed, miscellaneous.

chowder n. a thick soup or stew made of fish, bacon etc. Also v.t. WH: 18C. ? French *faire la chaudière* to supply a pot for cooking a stew, from *chaudière* pot, cauldron.

chowkidar n. a watchman. WH: 17C. Urdu *chaukīdār*, from Hindi *caukī* CHOKY + Urdu and Persian *-dār* keeper.

chow mein n. a Chinese dish of meat and vegetables served with fried noodles. WH: 19C. Chinese *chăo miàn* fried noodles.

chowry n. a flapper for driving away flies. WH: 18C. Hindi *caūrī*, from Sanskrit *camara* (tail of a) yak.

chrematistic a. concerning moneymaking. WH: 18C. Greek *khrēmatistikos*, from *khrēmatizein* to make money, from *khrēma*, *khrēmatos* money. See also -IC.

chrestomathy n. a selection of passages with notes etc., to be used in learning a language. WH: 19C. French *chrestomathie* or Greek *khrēstomathia*, from *khrēstos* useful + *matheia* learning.

chrism n. consecrated oil, used in the Roman Catholic and Greek Orthodox Churches in administering baptism, confirmation, ordination and extreme unction. WH: pre-1200. Medieval Latin *crisma* and Ecclesiastical Latin *chrisma*, from Greek *khrisma*, from *khriein* to anoint.

Christ n. a title given to Jesus of Nazareth, and synonymous with the Hebrew Messiah. Also int. WH: pre-1200. Old English *Crīst*, from Latin *Christus*, from Greek *Khristos*, use as n. of a. meaning anointed, from *khriein* to anoint. The Greek name translates Hebrew *māshīāh* MESSIAH.

Christadelphian n. a member of a millenarian Christian sect claiming apostolic origin. Also a. WH: 19C. Late Greek *Khristadelphos* in brotherhood with Christ, from *Khristos* CHRIST + *adelphos* brother. See also -IAN.

christen v.t. to receive into the Christian Church by baptism; to baptize. Also v.i. WH: pre-1200. Old English *crīstnian*, from Latin *christianus* CHRISTIAN.

Christendom n. Christians collectively. WH: pre-1200. Old English *cristendōm*. See CHRISTEN, also -DOM.

Christian n. a person who believes in or professes the religion of Christ. Also a. WH: 14–15C. Latin *christianus*, from *Christus* CHRIST. See also -IAN.

Christie n. in skiing, a turn in which the skis are kept parallel, used esp. for stopping or turning sharply. WH: early 20C. Abbr. of *Christiania*, former name of Oslo, the capital of Norway. Oslo, refounded 1624, was named Christiania (for Christian IV of Denmark-Norway) to 1877 and then Kristiania to 1925.

Christingle n. a lighted candle held by children at Advent services etc., representing Christ as the light of the world. WH: mid-20C. Prob. alt. of German *Christkindl* Christ-child, Christmas present, influ. by INGLE.

Christmas n. the festival of the nativity of Jesus Christ celebrated on 25 December. Also a., int., v.i., v.t. WH: pre-1200. Old English *Crīstes mæsse*. See CHRIST, MASS.

Christo- comb. form of or relating to Christ. WH: Latin *Christus* or Greek *Khristos* CHRIST. See also -O-.

Christolatry n. the worship of Christ regarded as a form of idolatry. WH: 19C. CHRISTO- + -LATRY.

Christology n. the branch of theology concerned with Christ. WH: 17C. CHRISTO- + -LOGY.

Christophany n. an appearance of Christ to mankind. WH: 19C. CHRISTO- + Greek *-phaneia* appearance, from *phainein* to show.

chroma n. purity or intensity of colour. WH: 19C. Greek *khrōma* colour.

chromate n. a salt of chromic acid. WH: 19C. CHROMIC + -ATE[1].

chromatic a. of or relating to colour. WH: 14–15C. French *chromatique* or Latin *chromaticus*, from Greek *khrōmatikos*, from *khrōma*, *khrōmatos* colour. See also -IC. The word as used of a musical scale originally applied to one of three kinds of tetrachord in ancient Greek music, the others being DIATONIC and ENHARMONIC. The scale was so named since the intervals were 'coloured' by non-diatonic subdivision.

chromatid n. either of the two strands into which a chromosome divides during cell division. WH: early 20C. Greek *khrōma*, *khrōmatos* colour + -ID.

chromatin n. the portion of the nucleus of a cell, consisting of nucleic acids and protein, which readily takes up a basic stain. WH: 19C. Greek *khrōma*, *khrōmatos* colour + -IN[1].

chromato- comb. form of or relating to colour. WH: Greek *khrōma*, *khrōmatos* colour. See also -O-.

chromatography n. a technique for separating or analysing the components of a mixture which relies on the differing capacity for adsorption of the components in a column of powder, strip of paper etc. WH: 18C. CHROMATO- + -GRAPHY.

chromatophore n. a cell in some animals that can concentrate or disperse pigment, causing the animal to change colour. WH: 19C. CHROMATO- + -PHORE.

chromatopsia n. abnormal coloured vision. WH: 19C. CHROMATO- + Greek *-opsia* seeing. See OPTIC.

chrome n. chromium, esp. chromium-plating. Also v.t. WH: 19C. French, from Greek *khrōma* colour. The element was so named in 1797 by the French chemist Louis-Nicolas Vauquelin from the brilliant colours of its compounds. Cp. CHROMIUM.

chromic a. of, relating to or containing trivalent chromium. WH: 19C. CHROME + -IC.

chrominance n. the colour quality of light. WH: mid-20C. CHROMO- + *-inance* from *luminance* (LUMEN).

chromite n. a mineral consisting of chromium and iron oxide. WH: 19C. CHROME or CHROMIUM + -ITE[1].

chromium n. a bright grey metallic element, at. no. 24, chem. symbol Cr, remarkable for the brilliance of colour of its compounds, used as a protective or decorative plating. WH: 19C. CHROME + -IUM. The element was discovered in 1797 by the French chemist Louis-Nicolas Vauquelin, who originally named it CHROME.

chromo n. a chromolithograph. WH: 19C. Abbr. of CHROMOLITHOGRAPH.

chromo- comb. form of or relating to colour. WH: Greek *khrōma* colour, or (less commonly) CHROMIUM. See also -O-.

chromogen n. an organic colouring matter. WH: 19C. CHROMO- + -GEN.

chromolithograph n. a picture printed in colours by lithography. Also v.t. WH: 19C. CHROMO- + LITHOGRAPH.

chromophore *n.* a group of atoms that are responsible for the colour of a chemical compound. WH: 19C. CHROMO- + -PHORE.

chromosome *n.* any of the rod-shaped structures in a cell nucleus that carry the genes which transmit hereditary characteristics. WH: 19C. German *Chromosom*. See CHROMO-, -SOME². The term was coined in 1888 by the German histologist Wilhelm Waldeyer-Hartz. Cp. NEURONE.

chromosphere *n.* the gaseous envelope of the sun through which light passes from the photosphere. WH: 19C. CHROMO- + SPHERE.

chromotypography *n.* colour printing. WH: 19C. CHROMO- + TYPO-GRAPHY.

chronic *a.* (of a disease, social problem etc.) of long duration, or apt to recur. *Also n.* WH: 14–15C. French *chronique*, from Latin *chronicus*, from Greek *khronikos* of time, from *khronos* time. See also -IC.

chronicle *n.* a register or history of events in order of time. *Also v.t.* WH: 12–14C. Anglo-French *cronicle*, from var. of Old French *cronique* (Modern French *chronique*), from Latin *chronica*, from Greek *khronika* annals.

chrono- *comb. form* of or relating to time or dates. WH: Greek *khronos* time. See also -O-.

chronogram *n.* a date given by taking the letters of an inscription which coincide with Roman numerals and printing them larger than the rest. WH: 17C. CHRONO- + -GRAM.

chronograph *n.* an instrument for measuring and registering very small intervals of time with great precision. WH: 17C. CHRONO- + -GRAPH.

chronology *n.* the study of historical records etc. in order to determine the sequence of past events. WH: 16C. Modern Latin *chronologia*. See CHRONO-, -LOGY.

chronometer *n.* an instrument that measures time with great precision, esp. one used in navigation at sea. WH: 18C. CHRONO- + -METER.

chronoscope *n.* an instrument registering small intervals of time, used esp. for measuring the velocity of projectiles. WH: 18C. CHRONO- + -SCOPE.

chrysalis *n.* the last stage through which a lepidopterous insect passes before becoming a perfect insect. WH: 17C. Latin *chrysalis*, *chrysalidis*, from Greek *khrūsallis*, from *khrūsos* gold. The pupae of some butterflies have a golden sheen.

chrysanth *n.* a cultivated chrysanthemum. WH: early 20C. Abbr. of CHRYSANTHEMUM.

chrysanthemum *n.* any cultivated plant of the genera *Chrysanthemum* or *Dendranthema*, with brightly coloured flowers. WH: 16C. Latin, from Greek *khrūsanthemon*, from *khrūsos* gold + *anthemon* flower. The name originally applied specifically to the corn marigold with its golden flowers.

chryselephantine *a.* made partly of gold and partly of ivory. WH: 19C. Greek *khrūselephantinos*, from *khrūsos* gold + *elephas*, *elephantos* elephant, ivory. See also -INE.

chryso- *comb. form* of gold. WH: Greek *khrūsos* gold. See also -O-.

chrysoberyl *n.* a gem of a yellowish-green colour, composed of beryllium aluminate. WH: 17C. Latin *chrysoberyllus*. See CHRYSO-, BERYL.

chrysolite *n.* a yellowish-green or brown translucent orthorhombic mineral, a variety of olivine. WH: 14–15C. Old French *crisolite*, from Medieval Latin *crisolitus*, from Greek *khrūsolithos*. See CHRYSO-, -LITE.

chrysoprase *n.* an apple-green variety of chalcedony. WH: 12–14C. Old French *crisopace*, from Latin *chrysopassus*, from Greek *khrūsoprasos*, from *khrūsos* gold + *prason* leek.

chrysotile *n.* a fibrous mineral, a source of asbestos. WH: 19C. Greek *khrūsos* gold + *tilos* fibre.

chthonian *a.* of or relating to the underworld. WH: 19C. Greek *khthonios*, from *khthōn* earth + -AN.

chub *n.* a coarse river fish, *Leuciscus cephalus*. WH: 14–15C. Orig. unknown.

Chubb® *n.* a type of lock that cannot be picked. WH: 19C. Charles *Chubb*, 1773–1845, London locksmith.

chubby *a.* plump, rounded. WH: 17C. CHUB + -Y¹.

chuck¹ *v.t.* to fling, to throw. *Also n.* WH: 16C. ? Old French *chuquer*, earlier form of *choquer* to knock, of unknown orig. Cp. SHOCK¹.

chuck² *n.* a device for holding the work to be turned on a lathe, or for holding the bit in a drill. *Also v.t.* WH: 17C. Var. of CHOCK.

chuck³ *n.* the call of a hen to her chickens. *Also v.i.*, *v.t.* WH: 14–15C. Imit. Cp. CLUCK.

chuck⁴ *n.* darling, dear. WH: 16C. Alt. of CHICK¹, influ. by CHUCK³. Cp. CHOOK.

chuckle *v.i.* to laugh quietly to oneself. *Also n.* WH: 16C. CHUCK³ + -LE⁴.

chucklehead *n.* a stupid person. WH: 18C. Prob. var. of CHUCK² + HEAD¹.

chuddy *n.* chewing gum. WH: mid-20C. Orig. unknown. ? Var. of *chewie* (CHEW).

chuff *v.i.* (of a steam locomotive etc.) to make a short puffing sound. *Also n.* WH: early 20C. Imit. Cp. CHOO-CHOO.

chuffed *a.* pleased, happy. WH: mid-20C. Dial. *chuff*, of unknown orig. + -ED.

chug *n.* a short dull explosive sound, as of an engine. *Also v.i.* WH: 19C. Imit.

chukar *n.* an Indian partridge, *Alectoris chukar*, with red legs and bill. WH: 19C. Sanskrit *cakor*.

chukka *n.* any of the periods into which a polo game is divided. WH: 19C. Hindi *cakar*, from Sanskrit *cakra* circle, wheel. Not rel. to CHUCK¹.

chum¹ *n.* a close friend. *Also v.i.* WH: 17C. Prob. shortening of *chamber-fellow*. See CHAMBER, FELLOW. Cp. COMRADE. The word was originally Oxford University slang, corresponding to Cambridge University CRONY.

chum² *n.* chopped fish used by anglers as bait. WH: 19C. Orig. unknown.

chump *n.* a silly person. WH: 18C. ? Blend of CHUNK and LUMP¹ or STUMP.

chunder *v.i.* to vomit. *Also n.* WH: mid-20C. Orig. uncertain. The word is said to come from rhyming slang *Chunder Loo* SPEW, from a cartoon character, Chunder Loo of Akim Foo, originally drawn by Norman Lindsay and appearing in advertisements for Cobra boot polish, 1909–20.

chunk *n.* a short, thick lump of anything. WH: 17C. Appar. alt. of CHUCK².

Chunnel *n.* a tunnel connecting England and France under the English Channel. WH: early 20C. Contr. of *Channel Tunnel*. See CHANNEL¹, TUNNEL.

chunter *v.i.* to talk at length and meaninglessly. WH: 17C. Prob. imit., influ. by CHATTER.

church *n.* a building set apart and consecrated for public worship, esp. Christian worship. *Also v.t.*, *a.* WH: pre-1200. Old English *circe*, *cirice*, from Germanic, from Medieval Greek *kurikon*, from Greek *kuriakon*, short for *kuriakon dōma* house of the Lord, from *kurios* master, lord. Cp. KIRK.

churidars *n.pl.* tight-fitting trousers worn by Indian men and women. WH: 19C. Hindi *churi* + *dar* tight-fitting + -S¹.

churinga *n.* a sacred amulet. WH: 19C. Australian Aboriginal (Aranda) *tywerrenge*.

churl *n.* a surly, rude or ill-bred person. WH: pre-1200. Old English *ceorl*, from Germanic. Cp. CEORL. The original sense was man, as distinct from WIFE. In the Old English institution, a churl was a member of the lowest rank of freemen. After the Norman Conquest (1066) he was a serf or bondman.

churn *n.* a large can for carrying milk long distances. *Also v.t.*, *v.i.* WH: pre-1200. Old English *cyrin*, from Germanic.

churrasco *n.* a meat dish of S America, consisting of steak barbecued over wood or charcoal. WH: early 20C. American Spanish, prob. from dial. *churrascar* to burn.

chute¹ *n.* an inclined trough for conveying water, timber, grain etc. to a lower level. WH: 19C. French *fall* (of water etc.), from Old French *cheoite*, fem. p.p. (used as n.) of *cheoir* to fall, from Latin *cadere*, influ. by SHOOT.

chute² *n.* a parachute. WH: early 20C. Abbr. of PARACHUTE.

chutney *n.* a hot seasoned condiment or pickle. WH: 19C. Hindi *catnī*.

chutzpah *n.* barefaced audacity. WH: 19C. Yiddish, from Aramaic *huṣpā*.

chyle *n.* the milky fluid separated from the chyme by the action of the pancreatic juice and the bile, absorbed by the lacteal vessels, and assimilated with the blood. WH: 14–15C. Late Latin *chylus*, from Greek *khūlos* animal or plant juice. Cp. CHYME.

chyme *n.* the pulpy mass of digested food before the chyle is separated from it. WH: 14–15C. Late Latin *chymus*, from Greek *khūmos* animal or plant juice. Cp. CHYLE.

chypre *n.* a strong sandalwood perfume. WH: 19C. French Cyprus, where prob. orig. made.

ciabatta *n.* a moist type of Italian bread made with olive oil. WH: late 20C. Italian slipper (SLIP[1]), ref. to shape of loaf.

ciao *int.* used to express greeting or leave-taking. WH: early 20C. Italian dial. alt. of *schiavo* (I am your) slave, from Medieval Latin *sclavus* slave.

ciborium *n.* a vessel with an arched cover for the Eucharist. WH: 16C. Medieval Latin, from Greek *kibōrion* cup-shaped seed vessel of the Egyptian water-lily. In the sense eucharistic vessel the word has probably been influenced by Latin *cibus* food.

cicada *n.* any homopterous insect of the family Cicadidae, with stridulating organs. WH: 14–15C. Latin tree cricket, prob. from a Mediterranean language, and ult. of imit. orig. Cp. CRICKET[2].

cicatrice *n.* the mark or scar left after a wound or ulcer has healed. WH: 14–15C. Old French, or from Latin *cicatrix*, *cicatricis* scar.

cicatricle *n.* the germinating point in the yolk of an egg, or the vesicle of a seed. WH: 17C. Latin *cicatricula*, dim. of *cicatrix*. See CICATRICE, also -CULE.

cicely *n.* any of several umbelliferous plants, esp. sweet cicely. WH: 16C. Appar. from Latin *seselis*, from Greek, with assim. to female forename *Cicely*.

cicerone *n.* a guide who explains the curiosities and interesting features of a place to strangers. *Also v.t.* WH: 18C. Italian, from Latin *Cicero*, *Ciceronis*. See CICERONIAN. Cicero was a noted orator and the word was originally applied to the guides in Rome, famous for their verbosity.

Ciceronian *a.* resembling the style of Cicero; easy, flowing. *Also n.* WH: 16C. Latin *Ciceronianus*, from *Cicero*, *Ciceronis*, cognomen of Marcus Tullius *Cicero*, 106–43 BC, Roman politician and orator.

cichlid *n.* any tropical freshwater fish of the family Cichlidae, often kept in aquaria. *Also a.* WH: 19C. Modern Latin *Cichlidae*, from Greek *kikhlē* a kind of fish. See also -ID.

cicisbeo *n.* the recognized lover of a married woman. WH: 18C. Italian, of unknown orig. The word is said by some to be an inversion of Italian *bel cece* beautiful chickpea.

cicuta *n.* any umbelliferous plant of the genus *Cicuta*, including the water hemlock. WH: 14–15C. Latin.

-cide *comb. form* a person or substance that kills, as in *fratricide*. WH: French, from Latin *-cida* or *-cidum* cutting, killing, from *caedere* to cut, to kill.

cider *n.* an alcoholic drink made from the fermented juice of apples. WH: 12–14C. Old French *sidre*, earlier *cisdre* (Modern French *cidre*), from Ecclesiastical Latin *sicera*, from Ecclesiastical Greek *sikera*, from Hebrew *šēḵār* strong drink.

ci-devant *a.* former, of a past time. *Also adv., n.* WH: 18C. French formerly, from phr. *ci-devant noble* formerly a noble (formula used of an aristocrat who lost his title in the Revolution), from *ci* here + *devant* before.

Cie. *abbr.* Company. WH: French *compagnie* company.

cig *n.* a cigarette. WH: 19C. Abbr. of CIGARETTE.

cigar *n.* a roll of tobacco leaves for smoking. WH: 18C. French *cigare* or Spanish *cigarro*, from Mayan *sik'ar* smoking. According to some, the word is from Spanish *cigarra* grasshopper, alluding to its dark cylindrical shape. Cp. CIGARETTE.

cigarette *n.* a cylinder of cut tobacco or aromatic herbs rolled in paper for smoking. WH: 19C. French, from *cigare* (see CIGAR) + -ETTE.

ci-gît here lies (inscribed on gravestones). WH: early 20C. French here lies, from *ci* here + 3rd pers. sing. pres. ind. of *gésir* to lie, from Latin *iacere* to lie.

cilice *n.* cloth made from hair. WH: 16C. French, from Latin *cilicium*, from Greek *kilikion*, from *Kilikia* Cilicia, an ancient district of S Anatolia, now in S Turkey. The word was originally descriptive of cloth made of Cilician goat's hair.

cilium *n.* an eyelash. WH: 18C. Latin.

cimbalom *n.* a Hungarian type of dulcimer. WH: 19C. Hungarian, from Italian *cembalo*, *cimbalo* CYMBALO.

cimetidine *n.* a drug used in the treatment of gastric and duodenal ulcers. WH: late 20C. From *ci-*, alt. of CYANO- + METHYL + -*idine* (from -IDE + -INE).

cimex *n.* any insect of the genus *Cimex*, containing the bedbug. WH: 16C. Latin.

Cimmerian *a.* profoundly dark. WH: 16C. Latin *Cimmerius*, from Greek *Kimmerios* + -AN. The Cimmerians were a people fabled to live in perpetual darkness.

cinch *n.* a certainty. *Also v.t.* WH: 19C. Spanish *cincha* girth. The popular sense alludes to the firm hold that a saddle-girth gives a rider (originally a cowboy).

cinchona *n.* any S American tree of the genus *Cinchona*, whose bark yields quinine. WH: 18C. Modern Latin. From the Countess of *Chinchón*, 1576–1639, vicereine of Peru, who introduced the drug to Spain after being cured of a fever by powdered cinchona bark.

cincture *n.* a belt, a girdle. *Also v.t.* WH: 16C. Latin *cinctura*, from *cinctus*, p.p. of *cingere* to gird.

cinder *n.* a piece of coal that has ceased to burn but retains heat. WH: pre-1200. Old English *sinder*, of Germanic orig. From the 16C the word was assimilated to the unrelated French *cendre*, from Latin *cinis*, *cineris* ashes.

Cinderella *n.* a person whose merits are unrecognized. WH: 19C. *Cinderella*, the heroine of a fairy tale, a pretty girl forced to stay at home and do the chores. Cinderella was French *Cendrillon*, from *cendre* cinders, ashes + dim. ending *-illon*.

cine- *comb. form* cinema. WH: Abbr. of cinema.

cineaste *n.* a cinema enthusiast. WH: early 20C. French *cinéaste*, from *ciné* CINE- + *-aste* from *enthousiaste* enthusiast (ENTHUSIASM).

cinema *n.* a theatre where cinematographic films are shown. WH: early 20C. French *cinéma*, abbr. of *cinématographe* CINEMATOGRAPH.

cinematograph *n.* an apparatus for projecting very rapidly onto a screen a series of photographs, so as to create the illusion of continuous motion. WH: 19C. French *cinématographe*, from Greek *kinēma*, *kinēmatos* movement. See -GRAPH. The term was adopted in 1895 by the Lumière brothers, its inventors, but is recorded earlier in 1892.

cinéma-vérité *n.* cinema which approaches a documentary style by using realistic settings, characters etc. WH: mid-20C. French, lit. cinema verity. Cp. CINEMA, VERITY.

cinephile *n.* a person who likes the cinema. WH: mid-20C. CINEMA + -PHILE.

Cinerama® *n.* a method of film projection on a wide screen to give a three-dimensional effect. WH: mid-20C. CINEMA + -*rama* from PANORAMA.

cineraria *n.* a garden or hothouse plant, *Pericallis cruenta*, cultivated for its brightly coloured daisy-like flowers. WH: 16C. Modern Latin, fem. of Latin *cinerarius*. The name was originally that of the silver ragwort, *Senecio cineraria*, so called from its ash-coloured leaves.

cinerary *a.* of or relating to ashes. WH: 18C. Latin *cinerarius*, from *cinis*, *cineris* ashes. See also -ARY[1].

cingulum *n.* a girdle-like part or structure, such as the ridge that surrounds the base of a tooth. WH: 19C. Latin girdle.

cinnabar *n.* a bright red form of mercuric sulphide. *Also a.* WH: 12–14C. Latin *cinnabaris*, from Greek *kinnabari*, of unknown orig.

cinnamon *n.* a spice obtained from the aromatic inner bark of a SE Asian tree, *Cinnamomum zeylanicum*. *Also a.* WH: 14–15C. Old French *cinnamome*, from Latin *cinnamomum*, from Greek *kinnamōmon*, from Semitic, ? ult. from Malay.

cinque *n.* five, esp. the five at cards or dice. WH: 14–15C. Old French *cinc*, *cink* (Modern French *cinq*), from Latin *quinque* five.

cinquecento *n.* the revived classical style of art and literature that characterized the 16th cent., esp. in Italy. WH: 18C. Italian five hundred. Cp. QUATTROCENTO. Italian regards the 16C as the 1500s.

cinquefoil *n.* a plant of the genus *Potentilla*, with five-lobed leaves. WH: 12–14C. Latin *quinquefolium*. See CINQUE, FOIL[1]. The Latin name translated Greek *pentaphullon*, from *pente* five + *phullon* leaf.

Cinzano® *n.* an Italian vermouth. WH: early 20C. Francesco *Cinzano*, 1783–1859, Italian distiller.

cipher *n.* a code or alphabet used to carry on secret correspondence, designed to be intelligible only to the persons concerned. *Also v.i., v.t.* WH: 14–15C. Old French *ciffre* (Modern French *chiffre*), from Medieval Latin *cifra*, from Arabic *ṣifr* empty. Cp. ZERO. The sense secret writing dates from the 16C.

cipolin *n.* a green Italian marble with white zones. WH: 18C. French, from Italian *cipollino*, from *cipolla* onion, from Latin *cepa*. The marble is so called because its foliated structure resembles the coats of an onion.

circa *prep.* about, around (often used with dates). *Also adv.* WH: 19C. Latin about, around.

circadian *a.* (of biological cycles etc.) recurring or repeated (approximately) every 24 hours. WH: mid-20C. Latin *circa* about, around + *dies* day + -AN.

Circassian *a.* of or relating to Circassia, its inhabitants or their language. *Also n.* WH: 16C. *Circassia*, Latinized form of Russian *Cherkes*. See also -IA, -AN.

Circe *n.* an enchantress. WH: 14–15C. Latin, from Greek *Kirkē*, an enchantress in Greek mythology.

circinate *a.* rolled up (like the leaves of ferns). WH: 19C. Latin *circinatus*, p.p. of *circinare* to make round, from *circinus* pair of compasses. See also -ATE[2].

circle *n.* a plane figure bounded by a curved line, every point on which is equidistant from the centre. *Also v.t., v.i.* WH: pre-1200. Old French *cercle*, from Latin *circulus*, dim. of CIRCUS. See also -ULE. The spelling with -*i*- is based on the Latin original and dates from the 16C.

circlip *n.* a split metal ring fitted into a slot or groove on a bar, shaft etc. to hold something in place. WH: early 20C. Blend of CIRCULAR and CLIP[1].

circs *n.pl.* circumstances. WH: 19C. Abbr. of *circumstances* (CIRCUMSTANCE).

circuit *n.* the line enclosing a space, the distance round about. WH: 14–15C. Old French, from Latin *circuitus*, from p.p. of *circuire*, var. of *circumire*, from *circum* around + *ire* to go.

circular *a.* in the shape of a circle, round. *Also n.* WH: 14–15C. Old French *circulier* (Modern French *circulaire*), alt. of *cerclier*, from Late Latin *circularis*, from Latin *circulus* CIRCLE. See also -AR[1].

circulate *v.i.* to pass from place to place or person to person. *Also v.t.* WH: 15C. Latin *circulatus*, p.p. of *circulare*, from *circulus* CIRCLE. See also -ATE[3].

circum- *pref.* round, about. WH: Latin pref., from prep. *circum* around, about.

circumambient *a.* going round. WH: 17C. CIRCUM- + AMBIENT.

circumambulate *v.t.* to walk or go round. *Also v.i.* WH: 17C. CIRCUM- + AMBULATE.

circumbendibus *n.* a roundabout or indirect way. WH: 17C. CIRCUM- + BEND + Latin -*ibus*, abl. pl. ending.

circumcircle *n.* a circle that surrounds a triangle or other polygon, touching all the vertices. WH: 19C. CIRCUM- + CIRCLE.

circumcise *v.t.* to remove surgically or by ritual the prepuce or foreskin of (a male), or the clitoris of (a female). WH: 12–14C. Old French *circonciser*, from Latin *circumcidere*, from CIRCUM- + *caedere* to cut.

circumference *n.* the line that bounds a circle. WH: 14–15C. Old French *circonférence*, from Latin *circumferentia*, from *circumferre*, from CIRCUM- + *ferre* to carry, to bear. See also -ENCE.

circumflex *n.* a mark (ˆ, or ˆ in Greek) placed above a vowel to indicate accent, quality, length or contraction. *Also a., v.t.* WH: 16C. Latin *circumflexus*, p.p. of *circumflectere*, from CIRCUM- + *flectere* to bend, translating Greek *perispōmenos* drawn around.

circumfluent *a.* flowing round on all sides. WH: 16C. Latin *circumfluens, circumfluentis*, pres.p. of *circumfluere*, from CIRCUM- + *fluere* to flow. See also -ENT.

circumfuse *v.t.* to pour (a fluid etc.) round. WH: 16C. Latin *circumfusus*, p.p. of *circumfundere*, from CIRCUM- + *fundere* to pour.

circumjacent *a.* lying round. WH: 15C. Latin *circumiacens, circumiacentis*, pres.p. of *circumiacere*, from CIRCUM- + *iacere* to lie down. See also -ENT.

circumlocution *n.* a roundabout phrase or expression. WH: 14–15C. French, or from Latin *circumlocutio, circumlocutionis*, from CIRCUM- + *locutio, locutionis* LOCUTION, translating Greek PERIPHRASIS.

circumlunar *a.* situated or moving around the moon. WH: early 20C. CIRCUM- + LUNAR.

circumnavigate *v.t.* to sail or fly completely round. WH: 17C. CIRCUM- + NAVIGATE.

circumnutate *v.i.* (of the tips of growing plants etc.) to nod or turn successively to all points of the compass. WH: 19C. CIRCUM- + NUTATE.

circumpolar *a.* situated round or near one of the earth's poles. WH: 17C. CIRCUM- + POLAR.

circumscribe *v.t.* to draw a line around. WH: 14–15C. Latin *circumscribere*, from CIRCUM- + *scribere* to draw lines, to write.

circumsolar *a.* revolving round or situated near the sun. WH: 19C. CIRCUM- + SOLAR.

circumspect *a.* cautious, wary. WH: 14–15C. Latin *circumspectus*, p.p. of *circumspicere*, from CIRCUM- + *specere* to look.

circumstance *n.* an incident, an occurrence. *Also v.t.* WH: 12–14C. Old French *circonstance*, from Latin *circumstantia*, from *circumstans, circumstantis*, pres.p. of *circumstare*, from CIRCUM- + *stare* to stand. See also -ANCE.

circumstantial *a.* depending on circumstances. *Also n.* WH: 16C. Latin *circumstantia* CIRCUMSTANCE + -AL[1].

circumterrestrial *a.* situated or moving around the earth. WH: 19C. CIRCUM- + TERRESTRIAL.

circumvallate *v.t.* to surround or enclose with a rampart. WH: 19C. Latin *circumvallatus*, p.p. of *circumvallare*, from CIRCUM- + *vallare*, from *vallare* rampart. See also -ATE[3].

circumvent *v.t.* to go round, to avoid or evade. WH: 14–15C. Latin *circumventus*, p.p. of *circumvenire*, from CIRCUM- + *venire* to come.

circumvolution *n.* the act of rolling round. WH: 14–15C. Latin *circumvolutio, circumvolutionis*, from *circumvolutus*, p.p. of *circumvolutare*, freq. of *circumvolvere*, from CIRCUM- + *volvere* to turn + -ION.

circus *n.* a travelling company of clowns, acrobats, trained animals etc. WH: 14–15C. Latin circle, circus.

ciré *n.* satin or other fabric with a waxed surface. *Also a.* WH: early 20C. French, p.p. of *cirer* to wax.

cire perdue *n.* a method of casting bronze, using wax which is subsequently melted and replaced by the metal. WH: 19C. French lost wax, from *cire* wax + fem. p.p. of *perdre* to lose.

cirque *n.* a semicircular basin in a hillside or valley, caused by erosion. WH: 17C. French, from Latin CIRCUS.

cirrhosis *n.* a disease of the liver in which it becomes yellowish and nodular because of the death of liver cells and the growth of fibrous tissue. WH: 19C. Modern Latin, from Greek *kirrhos* orange-tawny (ref. to colour of liver in many cases). See also -OSIS. The term was coined in 1805 by the French physician René-Théophile-Hyacinthe Laënnec.

cirri- *comb. form* having fringelike appendages. WH: Latin *cirrus* curl, fringe.

cirriped *n.* any member of the Cirripedia, a class of marine animals related to the Crustacea, having cirriform feet and including the barnacles. WH: 19C. Modern Latin *Cirripeda*, from Latin CIRRUS + *pes, pedis* foot. The crustacean is so named from the appearance of the legs when they protrude from the valved shell.

cirro- *comb. form* denoting cloud formed at high altitudes. WH: Latin *cirrus* curl, fringe. See also -O-.

cirrocumulus *n.* a cloud at high altitude broken up into small fleecy masses. WH: 19C. CIRRO- + CUMULUS.

cirrostratus *n.* a horizontal or slightly inclined sheet of cloud more or less broken into fleecy masses. WH: 19C. CIRRO- + STRATUS.

cirrus *n.* a lofty feathery cloud. WH: 18C. Latin curl, fringe.

cis- *pref.* on this side of. WH: Latin pref., from prep. *cis* on this side of.

cisalpine *a.* on the Roman side of the Alps. WH: 16C. Latin *cisalpinus*. See CIS-, Alpine (ALP).

cisatlantic *a.* on the speaker's side of the Atlantic, as distinct from transatlantic. WH: 18C. CIS- + ATLANTIC.

cisco *n.* any of several freshwater whitefish of the genus *Coregonus* of N America. WH: 19C. Orig. unknown.

cislunar *a.* between the moon and the earth. WH: 19C. CIS- + LUNAR.

cismontane *a.* on the speaker's side of the mountains, esp. on the south side of the Alps. WH: 19C. Latin *cismontanus*. See CIS-, MONTANE.

cispadane *a.* on this side of the river Po, esp. south of the Po. WH: 18C. Latin *cispadanus*, from CIS- + *Padus* Po. See also -ANE.

†**cispontine** *a.* on the north side of the Thames in London. WH: 19C. Latin *cispontinus*, from CIS- + *pons, pontis* bridge. See also -INE. The north side of the Thames in London was originally better known than the south, and the City of London developed there.

cissoid *a.* contained within two intersecting curves. *Also n.* WH: 17C. Greek *kissoeidēs*, from *kissos* ivy. See also -OID. The cusp of the cissoid resembles the indentations of an ivy leaf.

cissus *n.* any plant of the genus *Cissus*, such as *C. antarcticus*, the kangaroo vine. WH: 19C. Greek *kissos* ivy.

cist[1] *n.* a tomb consisting of a kind of stone chest or a hollowed tree trunk. WH: 19C. Welsh chest.

cist[2] *n.* a casket or chest, esp. one used for carrying the sacred utensils in Greek antiquity. WH: 19C. Latin *cista*. See CHEST.

Cistercian *n.* a member of a monastic order founded in 1098. *Also a.* WH: 14–15C. French *cistercien*, from Latin *Cistercium* Cîteaux, near Dijon, France, where the order was founded. See also -IAN.

cistern *n.* a tank for storing water, esp. a water tank for a lavatory. WH: 12–14C. Old French *cisterne* (Modern French *citerne*), from Latin *cisterna*, from *cista* chest. Cp. CIST[2].

cisterna *n.* a sac or space containing fluid, such as cerebrospinal fluid. WH: 19C. Modern Latin, from Latin *cisterna* CISTERN.

cistron *n.* a functional gene, a section of a chromosome controlling a single function. WH: mid-20C. CIS- + TRANS- + -ON. The element *trans-* refers to the possibility that two genes could be in the same or different chromosomes.

cistus *n.* any plant of the genus *Cistus*, a rock rose. WH: 16C. Modern Latin, from Greek *kistos*.

citadel *n.* a castle or fortified place in a city. WH: 16C. French *citadelle* or Italian *citadella*, dim. of obs. *cittade* (var. of *città*), from Latin *civitas* CITY.

cite *v.t.* to quote, to allege as an authority. WH: 14–15C. Old French *citer*, from Latin *citare*, freq. of *ciere* to set in motion, to call.

cithara *n.* an instrument resembling a lyre. WH: 18C. Latin, from Greek *kithara*. Cp. GUITAR, ZITHER.

citizen *n.* a member of a state having political rights. *Also a.* WH: 12–14C. Anglo-French *citesein, citezein*, from alt. (influ. by DENIZEN) of Old French *citeain* (Modern French *citoyen*), from Latin *civitas* CITY.

citole *n.* a stringed musical instrument. WH: 14–15C. Old French, from Latin CITHARA. See also -OLE[2].

citrate *n.* a salt of citric acid. WH: 18C. *citric* (CITRUS) + -ATE[1].

citric acid *n.* the acid found in lemons, citrons, limes, oranges etc. WH: 18C. Latin CITRUS + -IC + ACID.

citrin *n.* bioflavonoid, vitamin P. WH: mid-20C. CITRUS + -IN[1].

citrine *a.* like a citron. *Also n.* WH: 14–15C. Old French *citrin* lemon-coloured, from Medieval Latin *citrinus*, from Latin CITRUS. See also -INE.

citro- *comb. form* citric. WH: Latin CITRUS. See also -O-.

citron *n.* a tree, *Citrus medica*, bearing large lemon-like fruit. WH: 16C. Old French, from Latin CITRUS, based on *limon* lemon. Rel. to CEDAR.

citronella *n.* any S Asian grass of the genus *Cymbopogon*. WH: 19C. Modern Latin, dim. of CITRON. The grass is so named from its citron-like smell.

citrus *n.* any tree of the genus *Citrus*, including the orange, lemon, citron etc. WH: 19C. Latin citron tree, thuja.

cittern *n.* a medieval instrument resembling a lute, with wire strings. WH: 16C. Var. of CITHARA, based on GITTERN. Cp. GUITAR, ZITHER.

city *n.* a town incorporated by a charter. *Also a.* WH: 12–14C. Old French *cité*, from Latin *civitas*, from *civis* citizen. See also -TY[1].

civet *n.* a civet cat. *Also v.t.* WH: 16C. French *civette*, from Italian *zibetto*, from Medieval Latin *zibethum*, from Arabic *zabād* musk.

civic *a.* of or relating to a city or citizens. WH: 16C. French *civique* or Latin *civicus*, from *civis* citizen. See also -IC.

civil *a.* of or relating to citizens. WH: 14–15C. Old French, from Latin *civilis*, from *civis* citizen. See also -IL.

civilize *v.t.* to bring out of barbarism. WH: 17C. French *civiliser*, from *civil*. See CIVIL, also -IZE.

civvy *n.* civilian clothes, as opposed to uniform. *Also a.* WH: 19C. Abbr. of *civilian* (CIVIL).

clachan *n.* a small village or hamlet in the Highlands of Scotland. WH: 14–15C. Gaelic and Irish *clachán*.

clack *v.i.* to make a sharp, sudden noise like a clap or crack. *Also v.t., n.* WH: 14–15C. Imit. Cp. CLUCK.

clad *v.t.* to provide with cladding. WH: 16C. Appar. from *clad*, p.p. of CLOTHE.

clade *n.* a group of organisms sharing a unique characteristic because of evolution from a common ancestor. WH: mid-20C. Greek *klados* branch.

clado- *comb. form* branching. WH: Greek *klados* branch, shoot. See also -O-.

cladode *n.* a flattened stem that resembles a leaf. WH: 19C. Late Greek *kladōdēs* with many shoots, from Greek *klados* shoot.

cladogram *n.* a diagram illustrating the cladistic relationship between species. WH: mid-20C. CLADO- + -GRAM.

claim *v.t.* to demand as a right. *Also v.i., n.* WH: 12–14C. Old French *clamer* to cry, to call, from Latin *clamare*. Cp. CLAMOUR.

clairaudience *n.* the (supposed) faculty of hearing voices and other sounds not perceptible to the senses. WH: 19C. French *clair* clear + AUDIENCE, based on CLAIRVOYANCE.

clairvoyance *n.* the (supposed) power of perceiving future events or objects not present to the senses. WH: 19C. French, from *clair* clear + *voyant*, pres.p. of *voir* to see. See also -ANCE.

clam *n.* any of several edible bivalve molluscs, esp. *Venus mercenaria*, the hard clam, and *Mya arenaria*, the soft clam. *Also v.i.* WH: 16C. Appar. from Old English *clām* mud, clay, rel. to CLAMP[1].

clamant *a.* crying or begging earnestly. WH: 17C. Latin *clamans, clamantis*, pres.p. of *clamare* to cry out. See also -ANT. Cp. CLAIM.

clamber *v.i.* to climb with hands and feet, to climb with difficulty. *Also v.t., n.* WH: 12–14C. Prob. freq. form of *clamb*, obs. past tense of CLIMB.

clammy *a.* moist, damp. WH: 14–15C. Old English *clām* mud, clay + -Y[1]. See CLAM.

clamour *n.* a loud and continuous shouting or calling out. *Also v.t., v.i.* WH: 14–15C. Old French *clamour*, from Latin *clamor*, rel. to *clamare* to cry out. See also -OUR. Cp. CLAIM.

clamp[1] *n.* a frame with two tightening screws to hold pieces of wood etc. together. *Also v.t.* WH: 12–14C. Prob. Low German in orig., from Germanic. Cp. CLAM.

clamp[2] *n.* a heap, mound or stack of turf, rubbish, potatoes etc. *Also v.t.* WH: 16C. Prob. from Dutch *klomp* heap, rel. to CLUMP.

clamp[3] *n.* a heavy footstep or tread. *Also v.i.* WH: 18C. Imit. Cp. CLOMP, CLUMP.

clan *n.* a tribe or number of families bearing the same name, descended from a common ancestor. WH: 14–15C. Gaelic *clann* offspring, family, stock, from Old Irish *cland* (modern Irish *clann*), from Latin *planta* sprout, scion, PLANT.

clandestine *a.* secret, underhand. WH: 16C. French *clandestin* or Latin *clandestinus*, from *clam* secretly. See also -INE.

clang *v.t.* to strike together, so as to cause a sharp, ringing sound. *Also v.i., n.* WH: 16C. Imit., but influ. by Latin *clangor*, from *clangere* to resound. Cp. CLANK, CLINK[1].

clank *n.* a sound as of solid metallic bodies struck together (usu. a deeper sound than *clink*, and a less resounding one than *clang*). *Also v.t., v.i.* WH: 14–15C. Imit. Cp. CLANG, CLINK[1], CLONK, CLUNK.

clap[1] *v.t.* to strike together noisily. *Also v.i., n.* WH: pre-1200. Old English *clappan*, from Germanic. Of imit. orig.

clap[2] *n.* gonorrhoea. WH: 16C. Old French *clapoir* venereal bubo.

clapboard *n.* a feather-edged board used to cover the roofs and sides of houses. *Also v.t.* WH: 16C. Partial trans. of obs. *clapholt*, from Low German *klappholt*, from *klappen* to crack + *holt* wood.

claque *n.* a body of hired applauders. WH: 19C. French, from *claquer* to clap. Of imit. orig. Cp. CLACK, CLAP[1].

clarabella *n.* an organ stop giving a powerful fluty tone. WH: 19C. Latin *clarus* (fem. *clara*) clear + *bellus* (fem. *bella*) beautiful.

clarence *n.* a closed four-wheeled carriage for four passengers, with a seat for the driver. WH: 19C. The Duke of *Clarence*, later William IV, 1765–1837.

Clarenceux *n.* the second King of Arms. WH: 14–15C. Anglo-French, from *Clarence*, English dukedom named from *Clare*, Suffolk.

clarendon *n.* a condensed type with heavy face. *Also a.* WH: 19C. Prob. from *Clarendon* Press, Oxford.

claret *n.* a light red Bordeaux wine. *Also a.* WH: 14–15C. Old French (*vin*) *claret* light-coloured (wine) (Modern French *clairet*), dim. of Old French *cler* CLEAR. Claret was originally so named in contrast to white or red wine.

clarify *v.t.* to make easier to understand. *Also v.i.* WH: 12–14C. Old French *clarifier*, from Late Latin *clarificare*, from Latin *clarus* clear + *-ficere* -FY.

clarinet *n.* a keyed woodwind instrument with a single reed. WH: 18C. French *clarinette*, dim. of *clarine*, var. of *claron* CLARION. See also -ETTE.

clarion *n.* a kind of trumpet, with a narrow tube, producing a loud and clear note. *Also a., v.t.* WH: 12–14C. Medieval Latin *clario*, *clarionis*, from Latin *clarus* clear.

clarity *n.* clearness. WH: 12–14C. Latin *claritas*, from *clarus* clear. See also -ITY.

clarkia *n.* any plant of the genus *Clarkia* of herbaceous annuals with showy purple, pink or white flowers. WH: 19C. Modern Latin, from William *Clark*, 1770–1838, US explorer. See also -IA.

clary *n.* any of several labiate plants of the genus *Salvia*, esp. *S. sclarea*, an aromatic herb. WH: 14–15C. Obs. French *clarie*, from Medieval Latin *sclarea*. The loss of the initial *s* is unexplained.

clash *v.i.* to make a loud noise by striking together. *Also v.t., n.* WH: 16C. Imit. Cp. CRASH[1].

clasp *n.* a catch, hook or interlocking device for fastening. *Also v.t., v.i.* WH: 12–14C. Orig. unknown. The final *-sp* suggests an association with GRASP, HASP etc.

class *n.* a number of persons or things ranked together. *Also v.t., a.* WH: 16C. Latin *classis* assembly, division of the Roman people. The Romans themselves related *classis* to *calare* to call out, to proclaim.

classic *n.* an author, artist etc. of the first rank. *Also a.* WH: 17C. French *classique* or Latin *classicus*, from *classis* CLASS. See also -IC.

classical *a.* belonging to or characteristic of the ancient Greeks and Romans or their civilization or literature. WH: 16C. Latin *classicus* CLASSIC + -AL[1].

classify *v.t.* to distribute into classes or divisions. WH: 18C. Back-formation from *classification*, from French, from *classe* CLASS. See also -FICATION.

clastic *a.* fragmentary; composed of materials derived from the waste of various rocks. WH: 19C. French *clastique*, from Greek *klastos* broken in pieces. See also -IC.

clathrate *n.* a solid compound in which the molecules of one component are trapped within the structure of another. WH: 19C. Latin *clathratus*, p.p. of *clathrare*, from *clathri* (pl.) lattice, from Greek *klēthra* bars. See also -ATE[2].

clatter *v.i.* to make a sharp rattling noise. *Also v.t., n.* WH: pre-1200. Old English *clatr-* in *clatrung* clattering, of imit. orig.

claudication *n.* limping. WH: 14–15C. Latin *claudicatio*, *claudicationis*, from *claudicatus*, p.p. of *claudicare* to limp, from *claudus* lame. See also -ATION.

clause *n.* a complete grammatical unit, usu. including a subject and predicate. WH: 12–14C. Old French, from Latin *clausula* close (of a rhetorical period), conclusion of a legal formula, fem. dim. of *clausus*, p.p. of *claudere* CLOSE[2].

claustral *a.* of or relating to a cloister or monastic foundation. WH: 14–15C. Late Latin *claustralis*, from *claustrum* CLOISTER. See also -AL[1].

claustrophobia *n.* an abnormal fear of being in a confined space. WH: 19C. Modern Latin, from Latin *claustrum* (see CLOISTER) + -O- + -*phobia* (-PHOBE).

clavate *a.* club-shaped. WH: 17C. Latin *clavatus*, from *clava* club. See also -ATE[2].

clave *n.* either of a pair of hardwood sticks that make a hollow sound when struck together. WH: early 20C. American Spanish, from Spanish *clave* keystone, from Latin *clavis* key.

clavicembalo *n.* a harpsichord. WH: 18C. Italian, from Medieval Latin *clavicymbalum*, from *clavis* key + *cymbalum* CYMBAL.

clavichord *n.* a soft-toned musical instrument, one of the first stringed instruments with a keyboard, a predecessor of the pianoforte. WH: 14–15C. Medieval Latin *clavichordium*, from Latin *clavis* key + *chorda* string. See CORD.

clavicle *n.* the collarbone. WH: 17C. Latin *clavicula*, dim. of *clavis* key. See also -CULE. The bone is so named because of its shape.

clavicorn *n.* any of a group of beetles, the Clavicornia, with club-shaped antennae. *Also a.* WH: 19C. Modern Latin *clavicornis*, from *clava* club + *cornu* horn.

clavier *n.* the keyboard of an organ, pianoforte etc. WH: 18C. German *Klavier* or French *clavier*, from Medieval Latin *claviarius* keybearer, from *clavis* key. See also -ER[2].

claw *n.* the sharp hooked nail of a bird or animal. *Also v.t., v.i.* WH: pre-1200. Old English *clawu*, oblique case of *clēa*, from Germanic. Cp. German *Klaue*.

clay *n.* heavy, sticky earth. *Also v.t.* WH: pre-1200. Old English *clǣg*, from Germanic base also of CLEAVE[2], CLIMB. Cp. German *Kleie*.

claymore *n.* a two-edged sword used by the Scottish Highlanders. WH: 18C. Gaelic *claidheamh* sword + *mór* great.

Clayton's *a.* sham; ersatz. WH: late 20C. Proprietary name of soft drink marketed as a substitute for alcohol. The drink was advertised with the slogan 'It's the drink I have when I'm not having a drink'.

-cle *suf.* diminutive, as in *cubicle*, *particle*. WH: French *-cle*, from Latin *-culus* -CULE.

clean *a.* free from dirt, contamination etc. *Also v.t., v.i., adv., n.* WH: pre-1200. Old English *clǣne*, from Germanic. Rel. to Dutch *kleen*, German *klein* small.

cleanly *a.* clean in person and habits. WH: pre-1200. Old English *clǣnlīce*, also -LY[1].

cleanse *v.t.* to make clean. WH: pre-1200. Old English *clǣnsian*, from *clǣne* CLEAN.

clear *a.* free from darkness or dullness. *Also adv., v.t., v.i.* WH: 12–14C. Old French *cler* (Modern French *clair*), from Latin *clarus* clear, bright.

clearance *n.* the act of clearing. WH: 16C. CLEAR + -ANCE.

clearcole *n.* a preparation of size and whiting, used as a primer. *Also v.t.* WH: 19C. French *claire colle* clear glue, from *clair* CLEAR + *colle* glue. Cp. COLLAGE.

clearing *n.* the act of making clear, free from obstruction etc. WH: 14–15C. CLEAR + -ING[1].

cleat *n.* a strip of wood secured to another one to strengthen it. *Also v.t.* WH: 12–14C. Of Germanic orig. Cp. Dutch *kloot* ball, sphere, German *Kloss* clod, dumpling. Rel. to CLOT, CLOUT.

cleave[1] *v.t.* to split apart, esp. with violence, to cut through, to divide forcibly. *Also v.i.* WH: pre-1200. Old English *clēofan*, from Germanic. Cp. German *klieben*.

cleave[2] *v.i.* to stick, to adhere. WH: pre-1200. Old English *cleofian*, from Germanic base also of CLAY, CLIMB. Cp. German *kleben*.

cleavers *n.* a loose-growing plant, *Galium aparine*, with hooked prickles that catch in clothes. WH: pre-1200. Old English *clīfe*, from base of CLEAVE[2].

clef *n.* a symbol at the beginning of a stave denoting the pitch and determining the names of the notes according to their position on the stave. WH: 16C. French, from Latin *clavis* key.

cleft[1] *a.* divided, split. WH: 14–15C. P.p. of CLEAVE[1]. Cp. CLOVEN.

cleft[2] *n.* a split, a crack, a fissure. WH: 12–14C. Of Germanic orig. Rel. to CLEAVE[1] and assim. to CLEFT[1]. Cp. German *Kluft*.

cleg *n.* a gadfly, a horsefly. WH: 14–15C. Old Norse *kleggi*, from Scandinavian.

cleisto- *comb. form* closed. WH: Greek *kleistos* closed. See also -O-.

cleistogamic *a.* having flowers that never open and are self-fertilized. WH: 19C. CLEISTO- + -*gamic* (-GAMY).

clematis *n.* any ranunculaceous plant of the genus *Clematis* including the traveller's joy, *C. vitalba*. WH: 16C. Latin, from Greek *klēmatis*, from *klēma* vine branch.

clement *a.* (of weather) mild. WH: 14–15C. Latin *clemens*, *clementis*, of unknown orig. See also -ENT.

clementine *n.* a small, bright orange citrus fruit with a sweet flavour. WH: early 20C. French *clémentine*, from Père *Clément*, French priest who first cultivated it near Oran, Algeria. See also -INE.

clench *v.t.* to close (the hands, teeth etc.) firmly. *Also n.* WH: pre-1200. Old English *-clencan*, from Germanic base also of CLING. Rel. to CLINCH.

clepsydra *n.* an ancient instrument used to measure time by the dropping of water from a graduated vessel through a small opening. WH: 14–15C. Latin, from Greek *klepsudra*, from *kleps-*, comb. form of *kleptein* to steal + *hudōr* water.

clerestory *n.* the upper part of the nave, choir or transept of a large church containing windows above the roofs of the aisles. WH: 14–15C. CLEAR + STOREY.

clergy *n.* the body of people set apart by ordination for the service of the Christian Church. WH: 12–14C. Partly from Old French *clergé*, from Ecclesiastical Latin *clericatus*, from *clericus* (see CLERK, also -ATE¹), partly from Old French *clergie*, from *clerc* CLERK + -*ie* -Y², influ. by *clergé*.

cleric *a.* clerical. *Also n.* WH: 17C. Ecclesiastical Latin *clericus*, from Ecclesiastical Greek *klērikos* belonging to the Christian ministry, from *klēros* lot, hostage. Cp. CLERK. Cp. Acts i.17: 'For he was numbered with us, and had obtained part of this ministry' (Greek *ton klēron tēs diakonias tautēs*).

clerical *a.* of or relating to the clergy. WH: 15C. Ecclesiastical Latin *clericalis*. See CLERIC, also -AL¹.

clerihew *n.* a satirical or humorous poem, usu. biographical, consisting of four rhymed lines of uneven length. WH: early 20C. Edmund *Clerihew* Bentley, 1875–1956, English writer, its inventor.

clerk *n.* a person employed in an office, bank, shop etc. to assist in correspondence, bookkeeping etc. *Also v.i.* WH: pre-1200. Old English *clēric* CLERIC, reinforced by Old French *clerc* from same source. The sense of scribe, secretary came about because medieval clergy performed writing and secretarial work. An earlier spelling was *clark*, reflected in the pronunciation and the surname Clark.

clever *a.* intelligent. WH: 12–14C. Germanic in orig., ? rel. to CLEAVE². Cp. Middle Dutch *klever* sprightly, smart.

clevis *n.* a forked iron at the end of a shaft or beam, or an iron loop, for fastening tackle to. WH: 16C. Prob. from CLEAVE¹.

clew *n.* the lower corner of a square sail. *Also v.t.* WH: pre-1200. Old English *cliwan, cleowen*, from Germanic, prob. from base also of CLAW. Cp. CLUE.

clianthus *n.* any plant of the Australian genus *Clianthus*, with clusters of red flowers. WH: 19C. Modern Latin, appar. from Greek *kleos, klei-* glory + *anthos* flower.

cliché *n.* a hackneyed phrase. WH: 19C. French, p.p. (used as n.) of *clicher* to stereotype, prob. of imit. orig. French *clicher* is said to represent the sound of a die striking molten metal. Cp. CLICK. The figurative sense of worn-out expression dates from the late 19C.

click *v.i.* to make a slight, sharp noise, as of small hard objects knocking together. *Also v.t., n.* WH: 16C. Imit. Cp. French *clique* tick (of a clock).

client *n.* a person who entrusts any business to a lawyer, accountant, architect etc. WH: 14–15C. Latin *cliens, clientis*, earlier *cluens*, pres.p. (used as n.) of *cluere* to hear, to obey. See also -ENT. The sense of one obtaining professional service, customer, dates from the 17C.

clientele *n.* clients collectively. WH: 16C. French *clientèle*, from Latin *clientela*. See CLIENT. The original sense, group of dependants, was taken from Latin. The current sense, clients of a professional person, dates from the 19C and was borrowed from French.

cliff *n.* a high, steep rock face, esp. on the coast. WH: pre-1200. Old English *clif*, from Germanic. Rel. to CLEAVE². The word is related by some to CLEAVE¹, since in many Indo-European languages the words for rock or cliff are from forms meaning to split, to cut, e.g. Russian *skala* rock, cliff from Indo-European base also of SCALE¹, SHELL.

climacteric *n.* a critical period in human life. *Also a.* WH: 16C. French *climactérique* or Latin *climactericus*, from Greek *klimaktērikos*, from *klimaktēr* critical period, from *klimax, klimakos*. See CLIMAX, also -IC.

climate *n.* the temperature of a place, and its meteorological conditions generally, with regard to their influence on animal and plant life. *Also v.i.* WH: 14–15C. Old French *climat* or Late Latin *clima, climatis*, from Greek *klima, klimatos* slope of ground, zone, region, from *klinein* to lean, to slope. Cp. CLIME. The original sense was a region of the earth between two parallels of latitude. The current meteorological sense dates from the 17C.

climax *n.* the highest point, culmination. *Also v.i., v.t.* WH: 16C. Late Latin, from Greek *klimax* ladder, climax. The original sense was the learned one for a series of rhetorical expressions in ascending order. The current sense of highest point dates from the 18C.

climb *v.t.* to ascend, esp. by means of the hands and feet. *Also v.i., n.* WH: pre-1200. Old English *climban*, from Germanic nasalized var. of base of CLEAVE².

clime *n.* a region, a country. WH: 14–15C. Late Latin *clima*. See CLIMATE.

clinch *v.t.* to drive home or settle (an argument, deal etc.). *Also v.i., n.* WH: 16C. Var. of CLENCH.

cline *n.* a gradation of forms seen in a single species over a given area. WH: mid-20C. Greek *klinein* to lean, to slope.

cling *v.i.* to adhere closely, esp. by grasping or embracing. *Also v.t., n.* WH: pre-1200. Old English *clingan*, from Germanic, from base also of CLENCH.

clinic *n.* a private hospital, or one specializing in one type of ailment or treatment. WH: 17C. French *clinique*, from Greek *klinikē* the clinical art, from *klinē* bed. Cp. *bedside* (BED). The original sense was a person confined to bed by sickness. The current sense, first the teaching of medicine at a sick person's bedside, then a private hospital, dates from the 19C.

clink¹ *n.* a sharp, ringing sound, as when glasses or metallic bodies are struck lightly together. *Also v.i., v.t.* WH: 12–14C. Prob. from Middle Dutch *klinken* to sound, to ring, of imit. orig. Cp. CLANG, CLANK.

clink² *n.* a prison. WH: 16C. Orig. unknown. The word was originally the name or nickname of a prison in Southwark, London. It is apparently unrelated to CLINK¹.

clinker¹ *n.* vitrified slag. WH: 17C. Dutch (early) *klinckaerd* (now *klinker*), from *klinken* to ring. See CLINK¹.

clinker² *n.* a clinch nail. WH: 12–14C. Dial. *clink*, var. of CLENCH + -ER¹.

clino- *comb. form* sloping, oblique. WH: Greek *klinein* to lean, to slope. See also -O-.

clinometer *n.* an instrument for measuring angles of inclination. WH: 19C. CLINO- + -METER.

clint *n.* any of the blocks that make up a limestone pavement. WH: 12–14C. Danish and Swedish *klint*, from Old Swedish *klinter* rock.

cliometrics *n.* the use of statistics and statistical methods in historical research, esp. in the study of economic history. WH: mid-20C. *Clio*, the Muse of history + -*metrics* as in ECONOMETRICS, etc. See also -ICS.

clip¹ *v.t.* to cut with shears or scissors. *Also v.i., n.* WH: 12–14C. Old Norse *klippa*, prob. imit.

clip² *n.* an appliance for gripping, holding or attaching. *Also v.t.* WH: 15C. CLIP¹.

clique *n.* an exclusive set. WH: 18C. Old French, from *cliquer* to make a noise, from Middle Dutch *klikken* CLICK.

clitellum *n.* the thick central part of the body of an earthworm. WH: 19C. Modern Latin, from Latin *clitellae* (pl.) pack saddle.

clitic *n.* an enclitic or a proclitic. *Also a.* WH: mid-20C. Base and ending of ENCLITIC and PROCLITIC.

clitoris *n.* a small erectile body situated at the apex of the vulva and corresponding to the penis in the male. WH: 17C. Modern Latin, from Greek *kleitoris*, dim. of *kleitōr* hill, rel. to *klinein* to lean, to slant.

cloaca *n.* the excretory cavity in certain animals, birds, insects etc. WH: 16C. Latin, rel. to *cluere* to cleanse.

cloak *n.* a loose, wide, outer garment, usu. sleeveless. *Also v.t., v.i.* WH: 12–14C. Old French *cloke, cloque*, dial. var. of *cloche* bell, cloak, from Medieval Latin *clocca*. Cp. CLOCK¹. The garment was originally so called from its bell-like shape.

clobber *n.* clothes. *Also v.t.* WH: 19C. ? Yiddish.

clock¹ *n.* an instrument for measuring and indicating time. *Also v.t.* WH: 14–15C. Middle Low German *klocke*, from Germanic, from Medieval Latin *clocca* bell, prob. from Celtic, ult. of imit. orig. Cp. CLOAK, French *cloche*, German *Glocke* bell. Clocks originally indicated time by sounding the hours on a bell, not by displaying hands on a dial.

clock² *n.* an ornamental pattern on the side of the leg of a stocking. WH: 16C. Orig. unknown. According to some, the original pattern was bell-shaped. See CLOCK¹.

clocking *n.* brooding, hatching. *Also a.* WH: 14–15C. Dial. *clock*, rel. to CLUCK + -ING¹.

clod *n.* a lump of earth or clay. *Also v.t., v.i.* WH: 14–15C. Var. of CLOT.

clog *n.* a kind of shoe with a wooden sole. *Also v.t., v.i.* WH: 12–14C. Orig. unknown. ? Rel. to LOG¹.

cloisonné *a.* partitioned, divided into compartments. *Also n.* WH: 19C. French, p.p. of *cloisonner*, from *cloison* partition, from Popular Latin *clausio*, *clausionis*, from *clausus*. See CLOSE[1].

cloister *n.* a series of covered passages usu. arranged along the sides of a quadrangle in monastic, cathedral or collegiate buildings. *Also v.t.* WH: 12–14C. Old French *cloistre* (Modern French *cloître*), from Latin *claustrum* lock, bar, from *clausus*, p.p. of *claudere* CLOSE[2] + *-trum* instr. suf.

clomp *v.i.* to walk or tread in a heavy and clumsy fashion. WH: 19C. Imit. Cp. CLAMP[3], CLUMP.

clone *n.* a number of organisms produced asexually from a single progenitor. *Also v.t.* WH: early 20C. Greek *klōn* twig, slip.

clonk *v.i.* to make a short dull sound, as of two solid objects striking each other. *Also v.t., n.* WH: 19C. Imit. Cp. CLANK, CLINK[1], CLUNK.

clonus *n.* a muscular spasm with alternate contraction and relaxation, as opposed to *tonic spasm*. WH: 19C. Latin, from Greek *klonos* turmoil.

clop *n.* the sound of a horse's hoof striking the ground. *Also v.i.* WH: 19C. Imit.

cloqué *n.* a type of fabric with an embossed surface. WH: early 20C. French blistered, from *cloque* blister, rel. to *cloche* bell.

close[1] *a.* near in time or space. *Also adv., n.* WH: 14–15C. Old French *clos*, from Latin *clausus*, p.p. of *claudere* CLOSE[2].

close[2] *v.t.* to shut. *Also v.i., n.* WH: 12–14C. Old French *clos-*, p.p. stem of *clore*, from Latin *claudere* to shut, to close.

closet *n.* a small room for privacy and retirement. *Also a., v.t.* WH: 14–15C. Old French, dim. of *clos*. See CLOSE[1], also *-ET*[1].

clostridial *a.* of or relating to a rod-shaped bacterium of the genus *Clostridium*, esp. one that causes disease. WH: mid-20C. Modern Latin *clostridium*, from Greek *klōstēr* spindle. See also *-IUM*, *-AL*[1].

closure *n.* the act of closing. *Also v.t.* WH: 14–15C. Old French, from Late Latin *clausura*, from *clausus*, p.p. of *claudere* CLOSE[2]. See also *-URE*.

clot *n.* a small coagulated mass of soft or fluid matter, esp. of blood. *Also v.t., v.i.* WH: pre-1200. Old English *clott*, from Germanic. Cp. CLEAT, CLOUT.

cloth *n.* a woven fabric of wool, cotton, silk etc. used for garments or other coverings. WH: pre-1200. Old English *clāth*, from Germanic, of unknown orig. Cp. German *Kleid* dress. The original sense was both woven material and garment. The plural was originally *clothes*, but after the sense garment became obsolete in the 14–15C, the plural *cloths* was formed to distinguish the two meanings.

clothe *v.t.* to provide or cover with or as with clothes. *Also v.i.* WH: pre-1200. Old English *geclathed*, part.a., from *clāth* CLOTH.

clothier *n.* a manufacturer of cloth. WH: 12–14C. CLOTH + *-ER*[1]. The original form was *clother*. The ending was assimilated to words denoting an occupation or profession ending in *-IER*.

cloture *n.* closure of debate in a legislative body. *Also v.t.* WH: 19C. French *clôture*, from Old French CLOSURE.

clou *n.* the centre of interest or attraction. WH: 19C. French nail, stud.

cloud *n.* a mass of visible vapour condensed into minute drops and floating in the upper regions of the atmosphere. *Also v.t., v.i.* WH: pre-1200. Old English *clūd*, prob. rel. to CLOT. The original sense was hill, preserved in such place names as Temple Cloud, Somerset, and The Cloud, a hill commanding wide views on the Cheshire-Staffordshire border. Cumulus clouds resemble a rocky hill. This means that there was a different Old English word for cloud, which was *wolcen*. See WELKIN.

clough *n.* a ravine. WH: pre-1200. Old English *clōh*, from Germanic, rel. to German dial. *Klinge* ravine.

clout *n.* a blow, esp. on the head. *Also v.t.* WH: pre-1200. Old English *clūt*, of Germanic orig. Rel. to CLEAT, CLOT. Cp. German *Kloss* lump, clod.

clove[1] *n.* a dried, unexpanded flower bud of the tree *Eugenia aromatica*, used as a spice. WH: 12–14C. Old French *clou de girofle* nail of gillyflower. See GILLYFLOWER.

clove[2] *n.* a small bulb forming one part of a compound bulb, as in garlic, the shallot etc. WH: pre-1200. Old English *clufu*, from Germanic base also of CLEAVE[1]. Cp. German *Knoblauch* garlic, in which the first element corresponds to that of Old Saxon *cluflōc* clove-leek.

clove hitch *n.* a knot used to fasten a rope round a spar or another rope. WH: 18C. From *clove*, p.p. of CLEAVE[1] + HITCH. The knot has a single loop at the front and is 'cloven' into two parallel lines at the back.

cloven *a.* divided into two parts. WH: 12–14C. P.p. of CLEAVE[1].

clover *n.* any plant of the genus *Trifolium*, with dense flower heads and usu. trifoliate leaves, used for fodder. WH: pre-1200. Old English *clāfre*, from Germanic, with 1st syl. corr. to Old High German *klēo*. Cp. German *Klee* clover.

clown *n.* a comic entertainer, usu. with traditional make-up and costume, in a circus or pantomime. *Also v.i., v.t.* WH: 16C. Prob. Low German in orig., from Scandinavian. Cp. Swedish dial. *kluns* clumsy fellow, Swedish *klump* lump. The word is not from Latin *colonus* husbandman, farmer, as suggested by Ben Jonson in 1633.

cloy *v.t.* to satiate, to glut. WH: 14–15C. Shortening of *accloy*, orig. with sense to prick a horse with a nail in shoeing, hence to stop up an aperture, to clog, from Old French *encloer*, from Medieval Latin *inclavare*, from *clavus* nail.

cloze test *n.* a test of readability or comprehension in which words omitted from the text must be supplied by the reader. WH: mid-20C. Phonetic representation of abbr. of CLOSURE + TEST[1].

club[1] *n.* a piece of wood with one end thicker and heavier than the other, used as a weapon. *Also v.t.* WH: 12–14C. Old Norse *clubba*, assim. form of *klumba*, rel. to CLUMP. The suit of cards is so named from a translation of Spanish *basto* club, the picture on Spanish cards. The picture has been replaced on English cards by that of a trefoil. Hence French *trèfle* trefoil, club (on cards).

club[2] *n.* an association of persons combined for some common object, such as politics, sport etc. *Also v.t., v.i.* WH: 17C. CLUB[1] in verbal sense to gather in a clublike mass.

cluck *n.* the guttural call of a hen. *Also v.i., v.t.* WH: 15C. Imit. Cp. CLOCKING.

clue *n.* anything that serves as a guide, direction or hint for the solution of a problem or crime. *Also v.t.* WH: 14–15C. Var. of CLEW. A clue serves as a guide, just as a clew was a ball of yarn used to trace a path through a maze (as for Theseus in the Labyrinth).

clumber *n.* a variety of spaniel with a broad head. WH: 19C. *Clumber Park*, near Worksop, Nottinghamshire, where originally bred.

clump *n.* a thick cluster of shrubs or flowers. *Also v.i., v.t.* WH: 12–14C. Partly from Middle Low German *klumpe*, rel. to Dutch *klomp* lump, mass (cp. CLAMP[2], CLUB[1]), partly imit.

clumsy *a.* awkward, ungainly. WH: 16C. Dial. *clumse*, prob. of Scandinavian orig. + *-Y*[1]. Cp. Swedish *klumsig* numb, clumsy.

Cluniac *n.* a member of a religious order, a reformed branch of the Benedictines, founded at Cluny in the 10th cent. *Also a.* WH: 16C. Medieval Latin *Cluniacus*, from *Clunaeum* Cluny (or Clugny), near Mâcon, France.

clunk *v.i.* to make a short, dull sound, as of metal striking a hard surface. *Also n.* WH: 18C. Imit. Cp. CLANK, CLINK[1], CLONK.

clupeid *n.* any fish belonging to the family Clupeidae, the herring family. *Also a.* WH: 19C. Modern Latin *Clupea* genus name, from Latin *clupea* a river fish + *-ID*.

cluster *n.* a number of things of the same kind growing or joined together. *Also v.i., v.t.* WH: pre-1200. Old English *clyster*, prob. from Germanic base also of CLOT.

clutch[1] *n.* a grip, a grasp. *Also v.t.* WH: 12–14C. Var. of dial. *clitch*, from Old French *clyccan*, from Germanic.

clutch[2] *n.* a set of eggs to be hatched. WH: 18C. Prob. S var. of dial. *cletch*, from *cleck* to hatch, from Old Norse *klekja*, ? rel. to CLUCK. Not rel. to CLUTCH[1].

clutter *v.i.* to make a confused noise. *Also v.t., n.* WH: 14–15C. Var. of dial. *clotter*, from CLOT + *-ER*[5], assoc. with CLATTER, CLUSTER.

Clydesdale *n.* a heavy, powerful breed of horse. WH: 18C. *Clydesdale*, the region around the River Clyde, Scotland, where originally bred.

clypeus *n.* the shieldlike part of an insect's head, which joins the labrum. WH: 19C. Latin *clipeus* round shield.

†clyster *n.* an enema. *Also v.t.* WH: 14–15C. Old French *clystère*, or from Latin *clyster*, from Greek *klustēr* syringe, from *kluzein* to rinse out.

cnida *n.* the stinging-cell of the jellyfish and other coelenterates. WH: 19C. Modern Latin, from Greek *knidē* nettle.

co. *n.* the others, similar or related people or things; only in *and co.* WH: Abbr. of COMPANY.

co- *pref.* with, together, jointly, mutually, as in *coalesce*, *cooperate.* WH: Latin pref., from COM-, used esp. before vowels, *h* and *gn-.*

coach *n.* a long-distance bus. *Also v.t., v.i.* WH: 16C. French *coche*, from Hungarian *kocsi szekér* cart from *Kocs*, a town in N Hungary, where such carts (carriages) were first made. The sense of private tutor, sports instructor dates from the 19C, probably with reference to the 'carrying' of pupils or trainees.

coact *v.i.* to act together or in concert. *Also v.t.* WH: 14–15C. Latin *coactus*, p.p. of *cogere* to compel (see COGENT).

coadjutor *n.* an assistant, a helper, esp. to a bishop. WH: 14–15C. Old French *coadjuteur*, from Late Latin *coadjutor*, from CO- + Latin *adiutor*, from *adiutus*, p.p. of *adiuvare*, from AD- + *iuvare* to help.

co-agent *n.* a person or thing that acts with another. *Also a.* WH: 16C. CO- + AGENT.

coagulate *v.t., v.i.* to curdle, to clot. WH: 14–15C. Latin *coagulatus*, p.p. of *coagulare*, from *coagulum* rennet, from CO- + Latin *agere* to drive.

coal *n.* a black, solid, opaque carbonaceous substance of vegetable origin, obtained from the strata usu. underground, and used for fuel. *Also v.t., v.i.* WH: pre-1200. Old English *col*, from Germanic. Cp. German *Kohle*. An earlier sense to the 19C was charcoal. See CHARCOAL.

coalesce *v.i.* to fuse into one. WH: 16C. Latin *coalescere*, from CO- + *alescere* to grow up, from *alere* to nourish. See also -ESCE.

coalition *n.* a combination of persons, parties or states, having different interests. WH: 17C. Medieval Latin *coalitio*, *coalitionis*, from *coalitus*, p.p. of *coalescere* COALESCE. See also -ION.

coalmouse *n.* a small dark bird, *Parus ater*, also called *coal tit* or *cole tit.* WH: pre-1200. Old English *colmāse*. See COAL, TITMOUSE.

coaming *n.* a raised border round a hatch etc. for keeping water out of the hold. WH: 17C. Orig. unknown.

coarctate *a.* pressed together. WH: 14–15C. Latin *coarctatus*, p.p. of *coarctare*, from CO- + *artare*, from *artus* confined.

coarse *a.* large in size or rough in texture. WH: 14–15C. Orig. unknown. The word is said by some to derive from COURSE in the sense of something ordinary, 'run of the mill'.

coast *n.* that part of the border of a country where the land meets the sea. *Also v.t., v.i.* WH: pre-1200. Old French *coste* (Modern French *côte*), or from Latin *costa* rib, flank, side. The verbal sense to freewheel downhill dates from the 19C, after earlier to slide downhill on a toboggan (18C). These both represent Modern French *côte* slope, hillside.

coat *n.* an outer garment with sleeves. *Also v.t.* WH: 12–14C. Old French *cote* (Modern French *cotte* petticoat), from Frankish, of unknown orig.

coati *n.* a racoon-like carnivorous mammal of the genera *Nasua* or *Nasuella*, with a long flexible snout, from Central or S America. WH: 17C. Spanish and Portuguese, from Tupi *cuati*, appar. from *cua* belt + *tim* nose. The variant *coatimundi* is from Portuguese *cuatimundi*, from Tupi *cuatimune*, from *cuati* + *mune* snare, trick.

co-author *n.* a person who writes a book together with someone else. *Also v.t.* WH: 19C. CO- + AUTHOR.

coax¹ *v.t.* to persuade by flattery. *Also v.i.* WH: 16C. Var. of *cokes* simpleton, of unknown orig. The original meanings (in spelling *cokes*) were to make a trial of, then to pet, to fondle, to caress. The current meaning and spelling evolved from the 17C.

coax² *n.* coaxial cable. WH: mid-20C. Abbr. of COAXIAL.

coaxial *a.* having a common axis. WH: 19C. CO- + *axial* (AXIS¹).

cob *n.* a lump or ball of anything, esp. coal. *Also v.t.* WH: 14–15C. Latin, from Greek, ult. from Indo-European, base giving COTTON. Orig. unknown.

cobalt *n.* a greyish-white, brittle, hard metallic element, at. no. 27, chem. symbol Co. *Also a.* WH: 17C. German *Kobalt* KOBOLD. The element is so called from the miner's belief that it was a worthless substance put in silver ore by mountain demons. Cp. NICKEL, WOLFRAM.

cobber *n.* a friend, a mate. WH: 19C. Prob. from dial. *cob* to take a liking to + -ER¹.

cobble¹ *n.* a rounded stone or pebble used for paving. *Also v.t.* WH: 14–15C. COB + -LE⁴.

cobble² *v.t.* to mend or patch (esp. shoes). WH: 15C. Back-formation from *cobbler*, of unknown orig.

co-belligerent *a.* waging war jointly with another. *Also n.* WH: 19C. CO- + BELLIGERENT.

coble *n.* a flat, square-sterned fishing boat with a lugsail and six oars. WH: pre-1200. ? Celtic. Cp. Welsh *ceubal* skiff, wherry.

COBOL *n.* a high-level computer language for commercial use. WH: mid-20C. Acronym of *common business-oriented language.*

cobra *n.* any venomous snake of the genus *Naja*, from tropical Africa and Asia, which distends the skin of the neck into a kind of hood when excited. WH: 17C. Portuguese *cobra de capella* snake with hood, ult. from Latin *colubra* snake.

coburg *n.* a loaf of bread with one or more cuts on top that spread out during baking. WH: 19C. Prince Albert of Saxe-*Coburg*, 1816–61, consort of Queen Victoria. Cp. ALBERT. The name arose soon after the marriage of Prince Albert and Queen Victoria in 1840.

cobweb *n.* the web or net spun by a spider for its prey. *Also a.* WH: 12–14C. Dial. *cop* spider + WEB. Dialect *cop* is itself an abbreviation of *attercop*, from Old English *āttorcoppe*, from *āttor* poison + (perhaps) *cop²*.

coca *n.* the dried leaves of a S American plant, *Erythroxylum coca* chewed as a narcotic stimulant. WH: 16C. Spanish, from Aymara *kuka* or Quechua *koka.*

Coca-Cola® *n.* a brown-coloured soft drink flavoured with coca leaves, cola nuts etc. WH: 19C. COCA + COLA.

cocaine *n.* a drug prepared from coca leaves or synthetically, used as a narcotic stimulant and medicinally as a local anaesthetic. WH: 19C. COCA + -INE.

coccidiosis *n.* a parasitic disease of the intestines, liver etc., found in domestic birds and mammals. WH: 19C. Modern Latin *coccidium*, from Greek *kokkis, kokkidos*, dim. of *kokkos* COCCUS + -OSIS.

coccolith *n.* a small round body found in chalk formations, prob. extinct plankton. WH: 19C. Greek *kokkos* COCCUS + -LITH.

coccus *n.* a spherical bacterium. WH: 18C. Modern Latin, from Greek *kokkos* grain, berry, seed.

coccyx *n.* the lower solid portion of the vertebral column, the homologue in human of the tail of the lower vertebrates. WH: 16C. Latin, from Greek *kokkux* cuckoo. The bone is so called from its resemblance (in humans) to a cuckoo's beak.

Cochin *n.* a breed of domestic fowl with feathered legs. WH: 19C. *Cochin* (-China), a former part of French Indo-China, now of Vietnam.

cochineal *n.* a red substance obtained from the dried bodies of the female cochineal insect, used in dyeing, as a food colouring and in the manufacture of scarlet and carmine pigments. WH: 16C. French *cochenille* or Spanish *cochinilla*, from Latin *coccinus* scarlet, from Greek *kokkos* COCCUS.

cochlea *n.* the anterior spiral division of the internal ear. WH: 16C. Latin snail shell, screw, from Greek *kokhlias*, prob. rel. to *kogkhē* CONCH.

cock¹ *n.* the male of birds, particularly of the domestic fowl. *Also v.t.* WH: pre-1200. Old English *cocc*, prob. from Medieval Latin *coccus*, of imit. orig. The sense of tap dates from the 15C, of the hammer of a gun from the 16C. The reason for these sense developments is not entirely clear, although there may be a link with COCK².

cock² *n.* the act of turning or sticking anything upward, such as a hat, the ears etc. *Also v.t., v.i.* WH: 12–14C. Appar. from COCK¹, with ref. to fighting cocks.

cock³ *n.* a small conical pile of hay. *Also v.t.* WH: 14–15C. ? Scandinavian. Cp. Norwegian *kok* heap, pile.

cockabully *n.* a small freshwater fish of New Zealand, esp. one of the genus *Gobiomorphus*. WH: 19C. Maori *kokopu.*

cockade *n.* a knot of ribbons worn in the hat as a badge. WH: 17C. French *cocarde*, from *bonnet à la coquarde*, from fem. of obs. *coquard* proud, saucy, from *coq* COCK¹. See also -ARD.

cock-a-leekie *n.* soup made from a fowl boiled with leeks. WH: 18C. COCK¹ + LEEK. See -Y³.

cockalorum *n.* a self-important little man. WH: 18C. Prob. alt. of obs. Flemish *kockeloeren* to crow, of imit. orig., influ. by Latin gen. pl. ending *-orum.*

cockatiel *n.* a small crested parrot, *Nymphicus hollandicus*, of Australia. WH: 19C. Dutch *kakatielje*, prob. dim. of *kakatoe* COCKATOO.

cockatoo *n.* a large crested parrot of the Cacatuidae, usu. white, from Australasia. WH: 17C. Dutch *kakatoe*, from Malay *kakatua*, influ. by COCK[1].

cockatrice *n.* the basilisk, a deadly mythical reptile. WH: 14–15C. Old French *cocatris*, from Medieval Latin *calcatrix*, from *calcare* to tread, to track, from *calx* heel, translating Greek *ikhneumōn* tracker. See ICHNEUMON.

cockboat *n.* a small ship's boat. WH: 14–15C. Obs. *cock*, from Old French *coque*, dial. var. of *coche*, from Medieval Latin *caudica*, from Latin *caudex* block of wood + BOAT.

cockchafer *n.* a large brown beetle, *Melolontha melolontha*, whose larvae feed on the roots of crops. WH: 18C. COCK[1] + CHAFER.

Cocker *n.* used only in the phrase *according to Cocker*, meaning properly, correctly. WH: 19C. Edward *Cocker*, 1631–75, English mathematician, author of a widely used text.

cockerel *n.* a young cock. WH: 12–14C. Dim. of COCK[1]. The dim. suf. *-rel*, from Old French *-erel* (Modern French *-ereau*), is also found in DOGGEREL, MONGREL, SCOUNDREL, where it has a pejorative sense.

cocker spaniel *n.* a small spaniel of a breed used in shooting snipe etc. WH: 19C. COCK[1] + -ER[1]. The dog is so called because it is trained to flush up woodcock.

cockle[1] *n.* a bivalve mollusc of the genus *Cardium*, esp. *C. edule*. WH: 12–14C. Old French *coquille* shell, from Medieval Latin, from Medieval Greek *kokhulia*, pl. of *kokhulion*, var. of *kogkhulion*, from *kogkhē* CONCH.

cockle[2] *n.* the corncockle. WH: pre-1200. Old English *coccul*, ? from Medieval Latin, dim. of Latin *coccum* berry. See also -LE[2].

cockle[3] *v.i.* to pucker up. *Also v.t.*, *n.* WH: 16C. French *coquiller* to blister in cooking, from *coquille* shell. See COCKLE[1].

cockle[4] *n.* a heating-stove with a kind of radiator. WH: 17C. ? Dutch *kākel*, from German *Kachel* stovetile, *Kachelofen* stove made of such tiles.

cockney *n.* a native of London (traditionally, a person born within sound of the bells of St-Mary-le-Bow, Cheapside). *Also a.* WH: 14–15C. Prob. from COCK[1] + -n- of gen. pl. + obs. *-ey* EGG[1]. Originally, cock's egg was a term for a small misshapen egg, as if one laid by a cock. The sense then passed in the 16C to an effeminate or weak person, esp. a 'soft' town dweller, as distinct from a full-blooded countryman. The nickname, at first derogatory, finally passed to a Londoner in the 17C.

cockroach *n.* an orthopterous insect, *Blatta orientalis* or *Periplaneta americana*, resembling a beetle, and a pest in kitchens. WH: 17C. Spanish *cucaracha*, from *cuca* caterpillar, assim. by 19C to COCK[1] + ROACH[2].

cocktail *n.* a drink taken esp. before a meal, usu. spirit mixed with fruit juice, bitters, other alcoholic liquor etc. *Also a.* WH: 17C. COCK[1] + TAIL[1]. The word was originally an adjective used of a cock-tailed horse. From the 19C it was a noun for such a horse and for an alcoholic drink that 'cocked the tail' of the drinker.

cocky[1] *a.* self-important, conceited. WH: 16C. COCK[1] + -Y[1]. The original meaning was lecherous. The current meaning evolved in the 18C.

cocky[2] *n.* a small farmer. WH: 19C. COCKATOO + -Y[3]. Cockatoo was originally a nickname of a convict serving a sentence on Cockatoo Island in Sydney Harbour, Australia. The name then passed to tenant farmers who were brought from Sydney to settle in the Port Fairy district, west of Melbourne.

coco *n.* a tropical palm tree, *Cocos nucifera*, the coconut palm. WH: 16C. Portuguese and Spanish, orig. grinning face, alluding to the three hollows in the base of the shell, which suggest the eyes and mouth of a grimacing face. The form *coco* arose, apparently by accident, from Dr. Johnson's Dictionary (1755), where he combines the entry for *coco* with that of *cocoa*. The spelling *coker* was formerly used in the commercial sense to avoid confusion with *cocoa*.

cocoa *n.* a preparation from the seeds of the cacao tree, *Theobroma cacao*. WH: 18C. Alt. of CACAO.

coco-de-mer *n.* a palm tree of the Seychelles, *Lodoicea maldivica*. WH: 19C. French coco from the sea. The tree is so called as it was first known from its nuts, which were found floating in the sea.

cocoon *n.* a silky covering spun by the larvae of certain insects in the chrysalis state. *Also v.t.*, *v.i.* WH: 17C. French *cocon*, from Medieval Provençal *coucoun* eggshell, cocoon, dim. of *coca* shell.

cocopan *n.* a small wagon used in mines, running on a narrow-gauge railway track. WH: early 20C. Zulu *i-ngqukumbana* stumpy wagon.

cocotte *n.* a small dish in which food is cooked and served. WH: 19C. French. The (dated) sense of prostitute is from the child's nickname for a hen (cp. French *poule* hen, promiscuous young woman). The sense cooking dish arose in the early 20C from French *cocasse*, from Latin *cucuma* cooking vessel.

co-counselling *n.* a form of amateur counselling in which people feeling the need for help listen to and advise each other. WH: late 20C. CO- + *counselling* (COUNSEL).

cod[1] *n.* any large deep-sea food fish, of the family Gadidae, esp. *Gadus morrhua*. WH: 12–14C. Orig. unknown.

cod[2] *n.* a husk or pod. WH: pre-1200. Old English *codd*, from Germanic. Cp. Swedish *kudde* cushion, Norwegian *kodd* scrotum.

cod[3] *n.* a parody. *Also a.*, *v.t.*, *v.i.* WH: 17C. Orig. unknown. The word is not from CODGER, which appeared later.

cod[4] *n.* nonsense. WH: mid-20C. Abbr. of CODSWALLOP.

coda *n.* an adjunct to the close of a composition to enforce the final character of the movement. WH: 18C. Italian, from Latin *cauda* tail.

coddle *v.t.* to treat as an invalid or baby, to pamper. *Also n.* WH: 19C. Prob. dial. var. of CAUDLE. Cp. *mollycoddle* (MOLLY[1]).

code *n.* a series of symbols, letters etc. used for the sake of secrecy. *Also v.t.*, *v.i.* WH: 12–14C. Old French, from Latin *codex*. See CODEX.

codeclination *n.* the polar distance of anything, the complement of its declination. WH: 19C. CO- + DECLINATION.

codeine *n.* an alkaloid obtained from morphine and used as a narcotic and analgesic. WH: 19C. Greek *kōdeia* head, poppy-head + -INE. The alkaloid was discovered and named in 1832 by the French chemist Pierre-Jean Robiquet.

codependency *n.* mutual dependency for the fulfilment of emotional needs within a relationship. WH: late 20C. CO- + *dependency* (DEPEND).

co-determination *n.* cooperation between management and employees, or their trade union representatives, in decision-making. WH: early 20C. CO- + DETERMINATION.

codex *n.* a manuscript volume, esp. of the Bible or of texts of classics. WH: 16C. Latin *codex*, *codicis* block of wood, block split into leaves, book.

codger *n.* an odd old person. WH: 18C. ? Var. of *cadger* (CADGE).

codicil *n.* an appendix to a will, treaty etc. WH: 14–15C. Latin *codicillus*, dim. of *codex*. See CODEX.

codicology *n.* the study of manuscripts. WH: mid-20C. French *codicologie*, from Latin *codex*, *codicis*. See CODEX, -O- + -LOGY.

codling *n.* a long, tapering kind of apple, used for cooking. WH: 14–15C. Anglo-French *Quer de lion* lion-heart (French *Cœur de lion*). The apple is so named from its hard centre, making it unsuitable as an eating apple.

codomain *n.* the set of values that a function can take in all possible expressions. WH: early 20C. CO- + DOMAIN.

codon *n.* a set of three nucleotides in DNA or RNA that specifies a particular amino acid. WH: mid-20C. CODE + -ON.

co-driver *n.* a person who shares the driving of a motor vehicle, esp. a rally car, with another. WH: mid-20C. CO- + *driver* (DRIVE).

codswallop *n.* nonsense. WH: mid-20C. Orig. unknown. According to some, the word is from COD[2] + *wallop*, an alteration of *ballock* (see BOLLOCKS). Cp. *balls* (BALL[1]).

coed *n.* a co-educational school. *Also a.* WH: 19C. Abbr. of *co-educational* (CO-EDUCATION).

co-education *n.* education of the two sexes together. WH: 19C. CO- + *education* (EDUCATE).

coefficient *n.* the numerical or constant factor of an algebraical number, as 4 in 4*ab*. WH: 17C. Modern Latin *coefficiens*, *coefficientis*. See CO-, EFFICIENT.

coelacanth *n.* a large bony sea fish, *Latimeria chalumnae*, the only known living representative of the primitive subclass Crossopterygii thought to be extinct until 1938. WH: 19C. Modern Latin *Coelacanthus* genus name, from Greek *koilos* hollow + *akantha* spine. The fish is so named from its hollow-spined fins.

coelenterate *n.* any invertebrate of the phylum Coelenterata, containing the jellyfish, corals, sea anemones etc. *Also a.* WH: 19C.

Modern Latin *Coelenterata*, from Greek *koilos* hollow + *enteron* intestine. See also -ATE².

coeliac *a.* of or relating to the abdomen. WH: 17C. Latin *coeliacus*, from Greek *koiliakos*, from *koilia* belly. See also -AC.

coelo- *comb. form* denoting a hollow part or cavity. WH: Greek *koilos* hollow. See also -O-.

coelom *n.* a body cavity, esp. the space between the body wall and the intestines. WH: 19C. Greek *koilōma*, *koilōmatos* hollow, cavity.

coelostat *n.* an astronomical instrument with a mirror that rotates to continuously reflect the light from a celestial object. WH: 19C. Greek *caelum* sky + -O- + -STAT.

coemption *n.* concerted action among buyers for forestalling the market by purchasing the whole quantity of any commodity. WH: 14–15C. Latin *coemptio*, *coemptionis*, from *coemptus*, p.p. of *coemere* to buy up. See also -ION.

coenaesthesis *n.* the collective consciousness of the body, as distinguished from the impressions of the separate senses. WH: 19C. Greek *koinos* common + *aisthēsis* sensation, perception.

coeno- *comb. form* common. WH: Greek *koinos* common. See also -o-.

coenobite *n.* a monk living in a monastic community. WH: 14–15C. Old French *cénobite* or Ecclesiastical Latin *coenobita*, from *coenobium*, from Greek *koinobion* community life, from *koinos* common + *bios* life. See also -ITE¹.

coenocyte *n.* a mass of protoplasm that contains many nuclei within a cell wall, occurring in fungi and algae. WH: early 20C. COENO- + -CYTE.

coenosteum *n.* the calcareous skeleton of a coral colony. WH: 19C. Greek *koinos* common + *osteon* bone.

coenzyme *n.* in biochemistry, a non-protein organic molecule that is necessary for the activity of certain enzymes. WH: early 20C. CO- + ENZYME.

co-equal *a.* equal with another. *Also n.* WH: 14–15C. Latin *coaequalis* of the same age. See CO-, EQUAL.

coerce *v.t.* to restrain by force. *Also v.i.* WH: 14–15C. Latin *coercere*, from CO- + *arcere* to restrain.

coessential *a.* of the same essence. WH: 15C. Ecclesiastical Latin *coessentialis*, translating Greek *homoousis* (see HOMOOUSIAN). See CO-, ESSENTIAL.

coetaneous *a.* of the same age or period. WH: 17C. Latin *coaetaneus* contemporaneous, from CO- + *aeternus*, from *aetas* age. See also -OUS.

coeternal *a.* equally or jointly eternal with another. WH: 14–15C. Ecclesiastical Latin *coaeternus* + -AL¹. See CO-, ETERNAL.

coeval *a.* of the same age. *Also n.* WH: 17C. Late Latin *coaevus*, from CO- + *aevum* age. See also -AL¹.

coexist *v.i.* to exist together at the same time or in the same place. WH: 17C. Late Latin *coexistere*. See CO-, EXIST.

coextend *v.i.* to extend equally in time or space. WH: 17C. CO- + EXTEND.

coffee *n.* a beverage made from the ground roasted seeds of a tropical Asiatic and African shrub, of the genus *Coffea*, esp. *C. arabica*. *Also a.* WH: 16C. Turkish *kahve*, ult. from Arabic *kahwa*, prob. through Dutch *koffie*. Cp. CAFÉ.

coffer *n.* a chest or box for holding valuables. *Also v.t.* WH: 12–14C. Old French *coffre*, from Latin *cophinus*. See COFFIN.

coffin *n.* the box in which a corpse is enclosed for burial or cremation. *Also v.t.* WH: 12–14C. Old French *cofin* little basket, case, from Latin *cophinus*, from Greek *kophinos* basket. Cp. COFFER.

coffle *n.* a travelling gang, esp. of slaves fastened together in a line. WH: 18C. Arabic *kāfila*.

cog *n.* a tooth or projection in the rim of a wheel or other gear for transmitting motion to another part. *Also v.t.* WH: 12–14C. Prob. from Scandinavian. Cp. Swedish *kugge* cogwheel.

cogent *a.* powerful, constraining, convincing. WH: 17C. Latin *cogens*, *cogentis*, pres.p. of *cogere* to drive together, to compel, from CO- + *agere* to drive. See also -ENT.

cogitate *v.i.* to think, to reflect, to meditate. *Also v.t.* WH: 16C. Latin *cogitatus*, p.p. of *cogitare* to think, from CO- + *agitare*. See AGITATE, also -ATE³.

cogito *n.* the principle that a being exists because it thinks or has awareness. WH: 19C. Latin I think, 1st pers. sing. pres. ind.

of *cogitare* COGITATE. The word comes from the formula *cogito, ergo sum* I think therefore I am by the French philosopher René Descartes, 1596–1650.

cognac *n.* French brandy of fine quality, esp. that distilled in the neighbourhood of Cognac. WH: 16C. *Cognac*, a town and region in W France.

cognate *a.* akin, related. *Also n.* WH: 17C. Latin *cognatus*, from CO- + *gnatus* born.

cognition *n.* the act of apprehending. WH: 14–15C. Latin *cognitio*, *cognitionis*, from *cognitus*, p.p. of *cognoscere* to get to know, from CO- + *gnoscere* to know. See also -ION.

cognizance *n.* knowledge, notice, recognition. WH: 12–14C. Old French *conissaunce*, var. of *conoissance* (Modern French *connaissance*), from Latin *cognoscens*, *cognoscentis*, pres.p. of *cognoscere*. See COGNITION, also -ANCE.

cognize *v.t.* to have knowledge or perception of. WH: 17C. From COGNIZANCE, based on RECOGNIZE etc.

cognomen *n.* a surname. WH: 17C. Latin, from CO- + *gnomen* name.

cognoscente *n.* a connoisseur. WH: 18C. Italian one who knows (now *conoscente*), Latinized form of *conoscente*, from Latin *cognoscens*, *cognoscentis*, pres.p. of *cognoscere*. See COGNITION, also -ENT.

cohabit *v.i.* to live together, esp. as husband and wife without being legally married. WH: 16C. Late Latin *cohabitare*, from CO- + *habitare* HABIT.

co-heir *n.* a joint heir. WH: 14–15C. CO- + HEIR.

cohere *v.i.* to stick together. WH: 16C. Latin *cohaerere*, from CO- + *haerere* to stick.

coheritor *n.* a co-heir. WH: 16C. CO- + *heritor* (HERITAGE).

cohesion *n.* coherence. WH: 17C. Latin *cohaesus*, p.p. of *cohaerere*. See COHERE, also -ION.

coho *n.* a Pacific salmon, *Oncorhynchus kisutch*. WH: 19C. Orig. unknown.

cohort *n.* a tenth part of a Roman legion, containing many maniples or six centuries. WH: 14–15C. Old French *cohorte* or Latin *cohors*, *cohortis* enclosure, company, from CO- + *hort-* as in *hortus* garden.

coif *n.* a close-fitting cap, esp. worn by nuns under a veil. *Also v.t.* WH: 12–14C. Old French *coife* headdress (Modern French *coiffe*), from Late Latin *cofia* helmet.

coiffeur *n.* a hairdresser. WH: 19C. French, from *coiffer* to dress the hair, from *coiffe* (COIF) + -*eur* -OR.

coign *n.* a quoin. WH: 14–15C. Var. of COIN. Cp. QUOIN.

coil¹ *v.t.* to wind (a rope etc.) into rings. *Also v.i., n.* WH: 16C. Old French *coillir* (Modern French *cueillir* to gather), from Latin *colligere*. See COLLECT¹.

†coil² *n.* noise, turmoil, confusion, bustle. WH: 16C. Orig. unknown.

coin *n.* a piece of metal stamped and current as money. *Also v.t., v.i.* WH: 12–14C. Old French *coin*, (obs.) *coing* wedge, corner, stamping die, from Latin *cuneus* wedge. The die originally used for stamping coin was wedge-shaped.

coinage *n.* the act of coining. WH: 14–15C. Old French *coigniage*, from *coignier* to mint, from *coin*. See COIN.

coincide *v.i.* to correspond in time, place etc. WH: 18C. Medieval Latin *coincidere*, from CO- + *incidere* to fall upon, to fall into.

coinheritance *n.* a joint inheritance. WH: 16C. CO- + *inheritance* (INHERIT).

coinsurance *n.* joint insurance, esp. when part of the risk is borne by the owner of the insured property. WH: 19C. CO- + *insurance* (INSURE).

Cointreau® *n.* a colourless orange-flavoured liqueur. WH: early 20C. Adolphe and Édouard *Cointreau*, orig. manufacturers in Angers, France in 1849.

coir *n.* coconut fibre. WH: 16C. Malayalam *kayaṟu* cord, coir.

coit *n.* the buttocks. WH: mid-20C. Var. of QUOIT.

coition *n.* copulation. WH: 16C. Latin *coitio*, *coitionis*, from *coitus*, p.p. of *coire*, from CO- + *ire* to go. See also -ION.

Coke® *n.* Coca-Cola. WH: early 20C. Abbr. of COCA-COLA®.

coke¹ *n.* coal from which gas has been extracted. *Also v.t.* WH: 14–15C. ? Var. of dial. *colk* core of apple, heart of wood etc., of unknown orig.

coke² *n.* cocaine. WH: early 20C. Abbr. of COCAINE.

col *n.* a depression in a mountain ridge; a saddle or elevated pass. WH: 19C. French, from Latin *collum* neck.

col- *pref.* with, as in *collect, collide.* WH: Latin pref., from COM- with *m* assim. to *l.*

cola *n.* a tropical African tree of the genus *Cola*, bearing a nut which contains caffeine. WH: 17C. Temne *k'ola* cola nut.

colander *n.* a culinary strainer having the bottom perforated with small holes. WH: 12–14C. ? Provençal *colador*, from Latin *colatus*, p.p. of *colare* to strain. See also -OR. The inserted *n* is as in MESSENGER, PASSENGER etc.

co-latitude *n.* the complement of the latitude; the difference between the latitude and 90°. WH: 18C. CO- + LATITUDE.

colcannon *n.* an Irish dish consisting of potatoes and green vegetables stewed together and mashed. WH: 18C. Irish *cál ceannann* white-headed cabbage. Cp. COLE.

colchicum *n.* any plant of the genus *Colchicum*, esp. the meadow saffron, the corm and seeds of which are used in medicine. WH: 16C. Latin, from Greek *kolkhikon*, use as n. of neut. of *Kolkhikos*, from *Kolkhis* Colchis, a region east of the Black Sea. The name alludes to the poisonous arts of Medea, the enchantress of Greek legend who helped Jason win the Golden Fleece in Colchis, her place of birth.

colcothar *n.* a red form of ferric peroxide used as a pigment and as a polishing powder. WH: 17C. Arabic *ḳalḳuṭār*, ? from Greek *khalkanthon* CHALCANTHITE.

cold *a.* low in temperature, esp. in relation to normal temperature. *Also adv., n.* WH: pre-1200. Old English *cald*, from Germanic, rel. to *gelu* frost. Cp. JELLY.

cold-short *a.* (of a metal) brittle when cold. WH: 17C. Swedish *kallskör*, neut. *kallskört*, from *kallr* cold + *skör* brittle, assoc. with SHORT (in sense brittle).

cole *n.* the cabbage. WH: pre-1200. Old English *cāwel, caul*, from Latin *caulis* stem, stalk, cabbage. Cp. KALE.

colectomy *n.* surgical removal of the colon or part of it. WH: 19C. COLON[2] + -ECTOMY.

coleopteran *n.* any insect of the order Coleoptera, including the beetles and weevils, having the forewings converted into sheaths for the hind wings. WH: 19C. Modern Latin *Coleoptera*, from Greek *koleopteros*, from *koleos* sheath + *pteron* wing. See also -AN.

coleoptile *n.* a protective sheath around the shoot tip in grasses. WH: 19C. Greek *koleos* sheath + *ptilon* feather.

coleorhiza *n.* the root sheath in the embryo of grasses. WH: 19C. Greek *koleos* sheath + *rhiza* root.

coleus *n.* any plant of the genus *Solenostemon*, cultivated for their variegated coloured leaves. WH: 19C. Modern Latin, from Greek *koleos* sheath. The name refers to the plant's united filaments.

coley *n.* an edible fish, *Pollachius virens*, resembling the cod. WH: mid-20C. Prob. abbr. of *coalfish.* See COAL, also -Y[1].

colibri *n.* a hummingbird of the genus *Colibri*. WH: 17C. French and Spanish, from Carib.

colic *n.* acute spasmodic pain in the intestines. WH: 14–15C. Old French *colique*, from Late Latin *colicus*, from COLON[2]. See also -IC. The pain is so called because it is associated with the lower intestine.

colitis *n.* inflammation of the colon. WH: 19C. COLON[2] + -ITIS.

collaborate *v.i.* to work jointly with another, esp. in literary, artistic or scientific work. WH: 19C. Late Latin *collaboratus*, p.p. of *collaborare*, from COL- + *laborare* LABOUR. See also -ATE[3].

collage *n.* a picture made of pieces of paper, fabric etc., glued on to a surface. WH: early 20C. French gluing, from *colle* glue, from Greek *kolla*. See also -AGE.

collagen *n.* a fibrous protein that yields gelatin when boiled. WH: 19C. French *collagène*, from Greek *kolla* glue. See -GEN.

collapsar *n.* hypothetical celestial region formed from a collapsed star, a black hole. WH: late 20C. COLLAPSE + -ar, based on PULSAR, QUASAR.

collapse *v.i.* to fall in, to give way. *Also v.t., n.* WH: 18C. Backformation from *collapsed*, from Latin *collapsus*, p.p. of *collabi*, from COL- + *labi* to fall (see LAPSE) + -ED.

collar *n.* something worn round the neck, esp. the part of a garment that goes round the neck. *Also v.t.* WH: 12–14C. Old French *colier* (Modern French *collier*), from Latin *collare*, from *collum* neck. See also -AR[1].

collard *n.* a kind of cabbage that does not grow into a head. WH: 18C. Reduced form of *colewort.* See COLE.

collarette *n.* a small collar worn by women. WH: 17C. French *collerette*, dim. of *collier* COLLAR. See also -ETTE.

collate *v.t.* to bring together in order to compare. WH: 16C. Latin *collatus*, p.p. of *conferre.* See CONFER, also -ATE[3].

collateral *a.* having the same common ancestor but not lineally related . *Also n.* WH: 14–15C. Medieval Latin *collateralis.* See COL-, LATERAL.

colleague *n.* a person associated with another in any office or employment; a fellow worker. WH: 16C. French *collègue*, from Latin *collega* partner in office, from COL- + *leg-*, stem of *lex* law, *legare* to dispute.

collect[1] *v.t.* to gather together into one mass or place. *Also v.i., a., adv.* WH: 14–15C. Old French *collecter*, or from Medieval Latin *collectare*, from Latin *collectus*, p.p. of *colligere*, from COL- + *legere* to collect, to assemble, to read.

collect[2] *n.* a brief comprehensive form of prayer, adapted for a particular day or occasion. WH: 12–14C. Old French *collecte*, from Latin *collecta* gathering, assembly, fem. p.p. (used as n.) of *colligere.* See COLLECT[1]. The sense does not relate to the assembly ('collection') of worshippers but to the 'collecting' of the petitions of members of the congregation into a single prayer.

collectanea *n.pl.* a collection of passages from various authors, a miscellany or anthology. WH: 17C. Latin, neut. pl. of *collectaneus*, from *collectus* (see COLLECT[1]). The word is used as an adjective in Caesar's *Dicta collectanea* (1C BC) and as a noun in Solinus' *Collectanea rerum memorabilium* (3C AD).

collection *n.* the act of collecting. WH: 14–15C. Old French, from Latin *collectio, collectionis*, from *collectus.* See COLLECT[1], also -ION.

collective *a.* tending to collect, forming a collection. *Also n.* WH: 14–15C. Old French *collectif* or Latin *collectivus*, from *collectus.* See COLLECT[1], also -IVE.

colleen *n.* a girl, a lass. WH: 19C. Irish *cailín*, dim. of *caile* countrywoman, girl. See also -EEN.

college *n.* an institution for further or higher education. WH: 14–15C. Old French *collège* or Latin *collegium* association, corporation, from *collega* COLLEAGUE. The sense of institution for further or higher education evolved in the 16C.

collegiate *a.* of or relating to a college. WH: 14–15C. Late Latin *collegiatus* member of a college, from *collegium* COLLEGE. See also -ATE[1].

collegium *n.* a college of cardinals. WH: 19C. Latin, see COLLEGE.

collenchyma *n.* plant tissue composed of elongated cells with thickened walls, occurring immediately under the epidermis in leaf-stalks, stems etc. WH: 19C. Greek *kolla* glue + *egkhuma* infusion.

Colles' fracture *n.* a fracture of the radius close to the wrist, with backward displacement of the hand. WH: 19C. Abraham *Colles*, 1773–1843, Irish surgeon.

collet *n.* a band or ring. WH: 14–15C. Old French, dim. of *col*, from Latin *collum* neck. See also -ET[1].

collide *v.i.* to come into collision or conflict. *Also v.t.* WH: 17C. Latin *collidere* to clash together, from COL- + *laedere* to hurt by striking.

collie *n.* a sheepdog with long silky hair and a pointed nose. WH: 17C. Prob. from COAL (from its orig. colour) + -ie (-Y[3]). According to some, the word is from the dog's pet name, a form of *Colin. Colle* occurs as the name of a dog in Chaucer.

collier *n.* a person who works in a coal mine. WH: 12–14C. COAL + -IER. The word originally meant a charcoal burner or seller. The current sense dates from the 16C.

colligate *v.t.* to bind together. WH: 16C. Latin *colligatus*, p.p. of *colligare*, from COL- + *ligare* to bind. See also -ATE[3].

collimate *v.t.* to adjust the line of sight of (a telescope). WH: 17C. Latin *collimare*, misreading in some editions of Cicero for *collineare* to aim, from COL- + *lineare* to bring into a straight line, from *linea* LINE[1]. See also -ATE[3].

collinear *a.* in the same straight line. WH: 18C. COL- + LINEAR.

Collins *n.* a drink of spirits mixed with soda water, fruit juice etc. WH: 19C. Prob. from name *Collins.* The cocktail is also known as *John Collins* or *Tom Collins*, the alleged name of its originator.

collision *n.* the act of striking violently together. WH: 14–15C. Late

Latin *collisio, collisionis*, from *collisus*, p.p. of *collidere* COLLIDE. See also -ION.

collocate *v.t.* to place together. WH: 16C. Latin *collocatus*, p.p. of *collocare*, from COL- + *locare* to place, LOCATE. See also -ATE³.

collocutor *n.* a person who takes part in a conversation or conference. WH: 16C. Late Latin, from *collocutus*, p.p. of *colloqui*, from COL- + *loqui* to talk. See also -OR.

collodion *n.* a syrupy solution of pyroxylin in ether and spirit, used in photography and medicine. WH: 19C. Greek *kollōdēs* gluelike, from *kolla* glue. See also -ODE¹.

collogue *v.i.* to talk confidentially or plot together. *Also v.t.* WH: 17C. Prob. alt. of COLLEAGUE, by assoc. with Latin *colloqui*. See COLLOCUTOR.

colloid *n.* an uncrystallizable, semi-solid substance, capable of only very slow diffusion or penetration. *Also a.* WH: 19C. Greek *kolla* glue + -OID.

collop *n.* a slice of meat. WH: 14–15C. Scandinavian, from a word represented by Old Swedish *kolhuppadher* roasted on coals, from *kol* COAL + *huppa* leap (cp. SAUTÉ). Cp. Swedish dial. *kollops* dish of stewed meat.

colloquial *a.* of, relating to or used in common or familiar conversation, not used in formal writing or in literature. WH: 18C. Latin *colloquium* conference, from *colloqui* + -AL¹. See COLLOCUTOR.

colloquy *n.* a conference, conversation or dialogue between two or more persons. WH: 14–15C. Latin *colloquium*. See COLLOQUIAL, also -Y².

collotype *n.* a method of lithographic printing in which the film of gelatin that constitutes the negative is used to produce prints. WH: 19C. Greek *kolla* glue + -O- + -*type* (TYPE).

collude *v.i.* to act in concert, to conspire. WH: 16C. Latin *colludere* to have a secret agreement, from COL- + *ludere* to play.

collusion *n.* secret agreement for a fraudulent or deceitful purpose. WH: 14–15C. Old French, or from Latin *collusio, collusionis*, from *collusus*, p.p. of *colludere* COLLUDE. See also -ION.

collyrium *n.* an eye-salve, a medicated eyewash. WH: 14–15C. Latin, from Greek *kollurion* poultice, eye ointment, from *kolluris* cake, dim. of *kollura* roll of bread.

collywobbles *n.pl.* a stomach-ache, an upset stomach. WH: 19C. COLIC + WOBBLE.

colo- *comb. form* colon. WH: Greek *kolon* COLON¹.

colobus *n.* a leaf-eating African monkey of the genus *Colobus*, with short or absent thumbs. WH: 19C. Modern Latin, from Greek *kolobos* curtailed, docked. The monkey is so named from its shortened thumbs.

colocynth *n.* the climbing plant, *Citrullus colocynthis*, the bitterapple, or its fruit. WH: 16C. Latin *colocynthis*, from Greek *kolokunthis, kolokunthidos*.

cologarithm *n.* the logarithm of the reciprocal of a number. WH: 19C. CO- + LOGARITHM.

cologne *n.* eau-de-Cologne. WH: 19C. Abbr. of French *eau-de-Cologne*, lit. water of Cologne. See EAU.

colon¹ *n.* a punctuation mark (:) used to mark the start of a list, a long quotation etc.; also used in expressing an arithmetical ratio. WH: 16C. Latin, from Greek *kōlon* limb, clause. The mark is so called because it was originally used to separate clauses.

colon² *n.* the largest division of the intestinal canal, extending from the caecum to the rectum. WH: 14–15C. Latin, from Greek *kolon* colon, food, meat. Not rel. to COLON¹.

colonel *n.* the commander of a regiment; an army officer ranking below a brigadier and above a lieutenant colonel. WH: 16C. Obs. French *coronel*, later *colonnel* (now *colonel*), from Italian *colonnello*, from *colonna* COLUMN. A colonel was originally the commander of a column of soldiers.

colonial *a.* of or relating to a colony, esp. to those of the British Empire or to those in America that became the United States in 1776. *Also n.* WH: 18C. COLONY + -AL¹, ? based on French *colonial*.

colonist *n.* a settler in or inhabitant of a colony. WH: 18C. COLONIZE + -IST.

colonize *v.t.* to found a colony in. *Also v.i.* WH: 17C. COLONY + -IZE.

colonnade *n.* a series or range of columns at regular intervals. WH: 18C. French, earlier *colonnade*, from *colonne* COLUMN, based on Italian *colonnato*. See also -ADE.

colony *n.* a settlement founded by emigrants in a foreign country, and remaining subject to the jurisdiction of the parent state. WH: 14–15C. Latin *colonia* farm, settlement, from *colonus* tiller, settler, from *colere* to cultivate. See also -Y².

colophon *n.* a publisher's identifying symbol. WH: 17C. Late Latin, from Greek *kolophōn* summit, finishing touch, prob. rel. to Latin *collis* hill. The current sense of publisher's imprint evolved in the mid-20C.

colophony *n.* a dark-coloured resin obtained from turpentine, rosin. WH: 12–14C. Latin *colophonia*, from *Colophonia resina* resin of *Colophon*, a town in Lydia. The origin of the town name is presumably as for COLOPHON.

Colorado beetle *n.* a small yellow and black striped beetle, *Leptinotarsa decemlineata*, very destructive to the potato plant. WH: 19C. *Colorado*, a state in W central USA + BEETLE¹.

colorant *n.* a substance used to impart colour, a pigment etc. WH: 19C. COLOUR + -ANT.

coloration *n.* colouring, marking, arrangement of colours. WH: 17C. French, or from Late Latin *coloratio, colorationis*, from *coloratus*, p.p. of *colorare* COLOUR. See also -ATION.

coloratura *n.* the ornamental use of variation, trills etc. in vocal music. WH: 18C. Italian, from Late Latin *coloratus*. See COLORATION.

colorific *a.* producing colour, having the power of imparting colour to other bodies. WH: 17C. French *colorifique* or Modern Latin *colorificus*, from Latin *color* COLOUR. See also -FIC.

colorimeter *n.* an instrument for measuring the hue, brightness, and purity of colours. WH: 19C. Latin *color* COLOUR + -*i*- + -METER.

colosseum *n.* the amphitheatre in ancient Rome. WH: 16C. Medieval Latin *coliseum*, use as n. of Latin *colosseus* colossal. See COLOSSUS.

colossus *n.* a statue of gigantic size. WH: 14–15C. Latin, from Greek *kolossos*, name given by Herodotus to statues of ancient Egyptian temples, appar. from an Aegean language. The name became widely familiar from the Colossus of Rhodes, a gigantic statue said to have stood astride the entrance to the harbour of Rhodes in ancient Greece in the 3C BC.

colostomy *n.* the surgical formation of an artificial anus by an incision made into the colon. WH: 19C. COLON² + Greek *stoma* mouth + -Y².

colostrum *n.* the first secretion from the mammary glands after parturition. WH: 16C. Latin beestings.

colotomy *n.* surgical incision into the colon. WH: 19C. COLON² + -TOMY.

colour *n.* the sensation produced by waves of resolved light upon the optic nerve. *Also v.t., v.i.* WH: 12–14C. Old French *colur, colour* (Modern French *couleur*), from Latin *color*. See also -OUR.

-colous *comb. form* inhabiting (a certain environment). WH: Latin -*colus*, from *colere* to inhabit. See also -OUS.

colporteur *n.* a person who travels about selling religious books, tracts etc. WH: 18C. French, from *colporter*, prob. alt. of *comporter*, from Latin *comportare* COMPORT. Cp. PORTER¹.

colposcope *n.* an instrument for examining the cervix and upper vagina. WH: mid-20C. Greek *kolpos* womb + -O- + -SCOPE.

Colt® *n.* an early type of American revolver. WH: 19C. Samuel *Colt*, 1814–62, US inventor.

colt *n.* a young horse, esp. a young male from its weaning until the age of four. *Also v.i., v.t.* WH: pre-1200. Orig. uncertain. Cp. Swedish *kult* half-grown animal, boy. ? Rel. to CHILD.

colubrid *n.* any snake of the family Colubridae, most of which are harmless. *Also a.* WH: 19C. Modern Latin *Colubridae*, from Latin *coluber, colubris* snake.

colugo *n.* a flying lemur. WH: 18C. Orig. unknown.

columbarium *n.* a pigeon house; a dovecote. WH: 18C. Latin, from *columba* dove. See also -ARIUM.

Columbian *a.* of or relating to the United States of America. WH: 18C. Modern Latin *Columbia*, poetic name of America, from Christopher *Columbus*, 1451–1506, Genoese explorer, who discovered it in 1492. See also -AN.

Columbine *n.* the female dancer in a pantomime, the sweetheart of Harlequin. WH: 18C. French, from Italian *Columbina*, use as n. of fem. of *colombino* dovelike in gentleness. Italian *Columbina* was originally the name of a servant girl in the *commedia dell'arte*.

columbine *a.* of, relating to or resembling a dove or pigeon. *Also n.* WH: 12–14C. Old French *colombine*, from Medieval Latin *columbina* dovelike, from *columba* pigeon. The flower of the columbine is said to resemble five clustered pigeons.

columbite *n.* an ore of niobium and tantalum, containing manganese and iron. WH: 19C. COLUMBIUM + -ITE[1]. The ore was so named in 1805 by the Scottish mineralogist Robert Jameson.

columbium *n.* niobium. WH: 19C. Modern Latin *Columbia*, poetic name of America (see COLUMBIAN) + -IUM. The element was named by the English chemist Charles Hatchett, who discovered it in a specimen of ore brought to England from Massachusetts in 1801. It was rediscovered in 1844 and renamed NIOBIUM.

columella *n.* the central pillar of a univalve shell, or of corals. WH: 16C. Latin, dim. of *columna* COLUMN.

column *n.* a pillar or solid body of wood or stone, of considerably greater length than thickness, usu. consisting of a base, a shaft and a capital, used to support or adorn a building, or as a solitary monument. WH: 14–15C. Partly from Old French *columpne* (Modern French *colonne*, from Italian *colonna*), partly from Latin *columna* pillar.

colure *n.* either of two great circles passing through the equinoctial points, and cutting each other at right angles at the poles. WH: 14–15C. Late Latin *coluri* (pl.), from Greek *kolourai*, pl. of *kolouros* truncated, from *kolos* docked + *oura* tail. The circles are so called because their lower part is permanently below the horizon in temperate latitudes.

colza *n.* the rape plant. WH: 18C. French (Walloon), earlier *colzat*, from Low German *kōlsāt* coleseed (see COLE).

com- *pref.* with, as in *component*, *competition*, *commend*, *combine*. WH: Latin pref., from prep. *cum* with, used before *b*, *p*, *m* and a few words beginning with vowels or *f*. For reasons of pronunciation *m* is often dropped or assimilated to a subsequent consonant. See CO-, COL-, CON-, COR-.

coma[1] *n.* a state of absolute unconsciousness, characterized by the absence of any response to external stimuli or inner need. WH: 17C. Modern Latin, from Greek *kōma*, *kōmatos*, rel. to *koitē* bed, *keisthai* to lie down.

coma[2] *n.* the nebulous covering of the nucleus of a comet. WH: 17C. Latin, from Greek *komē* hair of the head.

comate *a.* bearing a tuft of hair at the end. WH: 18C. Latin COMA[2] + -ATE[2].

comb *n.* a toothed instrument for separating, tidying and arranging the hair. *Also v.t., v.i.* WH: pre-1200. Old English *camb*, *comb*, from Germanic. Cp. German *Kamm*.

combat *v.i.* to fight, to struggle. *Also v.t., n.* WH: 16C. French *combattre*, from Late Latin *combattere*, from COM- + var. of *battuere* to fight, to beat. Cp. BATTER[1], BATTLE.

combe *n.* a valley on the side of a hill or mountain. WH: pre-1200. Old English *cum*, *cumb*, from Celtic. Cp. CWM.

comber *n.* a British fish, *Serranus cabrilla*, of the perch family. WH: 18C. Orig. unknown.

combi *n.* a machine or device that has a combined function. *Also a.* WH: mid-20C. Abbr. of COMBINATION.

combination *n.* the act or process of combining. WH: 14–15C. Old French (Modern French *combinaison*) or Latin *combinatio*, *combinationis*, from *combinatus*, p.p. of *combinare* COMBINE[1]. See also -ATION.

combine[1] *v.t.* to cause to unite or coalesce. *Also v.i.* WH: 14–15C. Old French *combiner*, or from Late Latin, from COM- + *bini* two at a time.

combine[2] *n.* a combination, esp. of persons or companies to further their own commercial interests. WH: 17C. COMBINE[1].

combo *n.* a small band in jazz and popular music. WH: 19C. Abbr. of COMBINATION + -O.

combs *n.pl.* combinations (the undergarment). WH: mid-20C. Abbr. of COMBINATION + -S[1].

combust *v.t.* to burn, to consume with fire. *Also a.* WH: 15C. Latin *combustus*, p.p. of *comburere* to burn up.

come *v.i.* to move from a distance to a place nearer to the speaker or hearer. *Also v.t., n., int.* WH: pre-1200. Old English *cuman*, from Germanic, from Indo-European base also of Latin *venire* to come.

come-at-able *a.* easy to reach, accessible. WH: 17C. From *come at* (see COME, AT) + ABLE.

Comecon *n.* an economic organization of E European states, 1949–91. WH: mid-20C. Abbr. of Council for Mutual Economic Assistance, translating Russian *Sovet ekonomicheskogo vzaimopomoshchi*.

comedian *n.* an entertainer who tells jokes, humorous anecdotes etc. WH: 16C. French *comédien*, from *comédie* COMEDY. See also -IAN.

comedienne *n.* a female comedian. WH: 19C. French, fem. of *comédien* COMEDIAN.

comedo *n.* a blackhead. WH: 19C. Latin glutton, from *comedere* to eat up. See COMESTIBLE. The word was originally applied to worms which devour the body. The matter from a comedo can be expressed in a wormlike mass.

comedy *n.* a dramatic composition of an entertaining character depicting and often satirizing the incidents of ordinary life, and having a happy ending. WH: 14–15C. Old French *comédie*, from Latin *comoedia*, from Greek *kōmōidia*, from *kōmōidos* comic actor, comic poet, from *kōmos* revel + *aoidos* singer.

comely *a.* pleasing in appearance or behaviour. WH: 12–14C. Prob. shortening of *becomely*. See BECOME.

comer *n.* a person who comes or arrives. WH: 14–15C. COME + -ER[1].

comestible *n.* food. WH: 15C. Old French, from Medieval Latin *comestibilis*, from Latin *comestus*, p.p. of *comedere* to eat up, from COM- + *edere* to eat. See also -IBLE.

comet *n.* a luminous heavenly body, consisting of a nucleus or head, a coma, and a train or tail, revolving round the sun in a very eccentric orbit. WH: pre-1200. Old French *comète*, from Latin *cometa*, from Greek *komētēs* long-haired, from *komaein* to wear the hair long, from *komē* hair. The Greeks saw a comet as having a 'head' with a 'tail' of long hair.

come-uppance *n.* retribution for past misdeeds. WH: 19C. COME + UP + -ANCE.

†**comfit** *n.* a sweet, esp. a nut or seed coated with sugar. WH: 12–14C. Old French *confit*, from Latin *confectum*, neut. (used as n.) of *confectus*, p.p. of *conficere* to prepare. See CONFECT.

comfort *v.t.* to console. *Also n.* WH: 12–14C. Old French *conforter*, from Late Latin *confortare* to strengthen, from CON- + *fortis* strong.

comfrey *n.* a tall wild plant of the genus *Symphytum*, esp. *S. officinale*, with rough leaves and white or purplish flowers, formerly used for healing wounds. WH: 12–14C. Old French *confire*, from Medieval Latin *cumfiria*, from Latin *conferva*, from *confervere* to heal, to boil together, from CON- + *fervere* to boil.

comfy *a.* comfortable. WH: 19C. Abbr. of *comfortable* (COMFORT) + -Y[1].

comic *a.* of or relating to comedy. *Also n.* WH: 16C. Latin *comicus*, from Greek *kōmikos*, from *kōmos* revel. See also -IC.

Cominform *n.* the Information Bureau of the Communist Parties, 1947–56, orig. including Yugoslavia. WH: mid-20C. Abbr. of Communist Information Bureau.

coming *a.* approaching. *Also n.* WH: 12–14C. COME + -ING[1].

Comintern *n.* the Third Communist International, founded in Moscow in 1919, dissolved in June 1943. WH: early 20C. Russian *komintern*, abbr. of *Kommunisticheskiĭ Internatsional* Communist International. See *communist* (COMMUNISM), INTERNATIONAL.

comitadji *n.* a member of a band of Balkan guerrillas. WH: early 20C. Turkish *komitacī* member of a (revolutionary) committee, from *komite* COMMITTEE[1].

comity *n.* affability, friendliness, courtesy, civility. WH: 16C. Latin *comitas*, from *comis* courteous. See also -ITY.

comma *n.* a punctuation mark (,), denoting the shortest pause in reading. WH: 16C. Latin, from Greek *komma* piece cut off, rel. to *koptein* to strike.

command *v.t.* to order, to call for. *Also v.i., n.* WH: 12–14C. Old French *comander* (Modern French *commander*), from Late Latin *commandare*, from COM- + *mandare* to commit, to enjoin. Cp. COMMEND.

commandeer *v.t.* to seize or make use of for military purposes. *Also v.i.* WH: 19C. Afrikaans *kommandeer*, from Dutch *commanderen*, from French *commander* COMMAND.

commander *n.* a person who commands or is in authority. WH: 12–14C. Old French *comander* (Modern French *commandeur*), from Late Latin *commandare*. See COMMAND, also -ER[2].

commandment *n.* an order, a command, esp. a divine command. WH: 12–14C. Old French *comandement* (Modern French *commandement*), from *comander* COMMAND. See also -MENT.

commando *n.* a body of men called out for military service; a body of troops. *Also a.* WH: 18C. Portuguese (now *comando*), from *commandar* COMMAND. The current sense of a soldier making daring raids dates from the Second World War (1939–45).

commeasure *v.t.* to be equal in extent, degree etc. to, to coincide with. WH: 17C. COM- + MEASURE.

comme ci comme ça *a.* middling, indifferent, so-so. *Also adv.* WH: mid-20C. French like this like that, from *comme* like, as + *ci* this, *ça* that.

commedia dell'arte *n.* Italian comedy of the 16th–18th cents., using improvisation and stock characters. WH: 19C. Italian comedy of art. See COMEDY, ART.

comme il faut *a.* as it should be, correct, genteel. WH: 18C. French as it is necessary, from *comme* like, as + *il* it + *faut*, 3rd pers. sing. pres. of *falloir* to be necessary.

commemorate *v.t.* to keep in remembrance by some solemn act. WH: 16C. Latin *commemoratus*, p.p. of *commemorare*, from COM- + *memorare* to relate, from *memor*. See MEMORY, also -ATE³.

commence *v.i.* to start, to begin. *Also v.t.* WH: 12–14C. Old French *comencier* (Modern French *commencer*), from Latin COM- + *initiare* INITIATE¹.

commend *v.t.* to commit to the charge of, to entrust. *Also n.* WH: 12–14C. Latin *commendare*, from COM- + *mandare* to commit, to entrust. Cp. COMMAND.

commendam *n.* the holding of a vacant ecclesiastical benefice in trust until an incumbent was appointed. WH: 16C. Ecclesiastical Latin, acc. sing of *commenda*, from phr. *dare in commendam* to give (a benefice) in charge, from *commendare* COMMEND.

commensal *a.* (of an organism) living in intimate association with, on the surface of or in the substance of another, without being parasitic. *Also n.* WH: 14–15C. French, from Medieval Latin *commensalis*, from COM- + *mensa* table. See also -AL¹.

commensurable *a.* measurable by a common unit. WH: 16C. Late Latin *commensurabilis*, from COM- + *mensurabilis* MENSURABLE. See also -ABLE.

commensurate *a.* having the same measure or extent. WH: 17C. Late Latin *commensuratus*, from COM- + *mensuratus*, p.p. of *mensurare*. See MEASURE, also -ATE².

comment *n.* a remark, an opinion. *Also v.i., v.t.* WH: 14–15C. Latin *commentum* invention, interpretation, from *commentus*, p.p. of *comminisci* to devise, to contrive.

commerce *n.* trade, financial transactions. *Also v.i.* WH: 16C. French, or from Latin *commercium* trade, trafficking, from COM- + *merx, mercis* merchandise.

commercial *a.* of or relating to commerce. *Also n.* WH: 16C. COMMERCE + -IAL.

commère *n.* a female compère. WH: early 20C. French, fem. of COMPÈRE.

commie *n., a.* (a) communist. WH: mid-20C. Abbr. of *communist* (COMMUNISM). See also -Y³.

comminate *v.t.* to threaten, to denounce. WH: 17C. Latin *comminatus*, p.p. of *comminari*, from COM- + *minari* to threaten. See also -ATE³.

commingle *v.t., v.i.* to mingle or mix together, to blend. WH: 17C. COM- + MINGLE.

comminute *v.t.* to make smaller. WH: 17C. Latin *comminutus*, p.p. of *comminere*, from COM- + *minuere* to lessen.

commis *n.* an agent. WH: 16C. French, p.p. (used as n.) of *commettre* to entrust. See COMMIT.

commiserate *v.i.* to feel or express sympathy (with). *Also v.t.* WH: 16C. Latin *commiseratus*, from COM- + *miserari*, p.p. of *commiserari* to lament, to pity, from *miser* wretched. See also -ATE³.

commissar *n.* the head of a department of government in the former USSR. WH: early 20C. Russian *komissar*, from French *commissaire*, from Medieval Latin *commisarius* COMMISSARY.

commissariat *n.* the department of the army charged with supplying provisions and stores. WH: 16C. Partly from Medieval Latin *commissariatus*, from *commisarius* COMMISSARY, partly from French *commisariat*. See also -ATE¹.

commissary *n.* a commissioner. WH: 14–15C. Medieval Latin *commissarius* officer in charge, from *commissus*. See COMMISSION, also -ARY¹.

commission *n.* the entrusting of a task or duty to another. *Also v.t.* WH: 12–14C. Old French, from Latin *commissio, commissionis*, from *commissus*, p.p. of *committere* COMMIT. See also -ION.

commissure *n.* a joint, a seam. WH: 14–15C. Latin *commissura*, from *commissus*. See COMMISSION, also -URE.

commit *v.t.* to entrust, to deposit. WH: 14–15C. Latin *committere* to join, to entrust, from COM- + *-mittere* to put, to send. See MISSION.

committee¹ *n.* a board elected or deputed to examine, consider, and report on any business referred to them. WH: 15C. COMMIT + -EE. The word was originally used of a single person to whom some function was committed. The current sense dates from the 16C. Cp. COMMITTEE².

committee² *n.* a person to whom the care of another person or their property is committed. WH: 15C. COMMIT + -EE.

commix *v.t., v.i.* to mix together, to blend. WH: 14–15C. Orig. p.p., from Latin *commixtus*, from COM- + *-mixtus*. See MIX.

commode *n.* a night commode. WH: 17C. French, from Latin *commodus*. See COMMODIOUS. The sense developed as follows: tall headdress worn by women (17C), chest of drawers (18C), covered chamber pot (19C). For this last, cp. *convenience* (CONVENIENT).

commodify *v.t.* to turn into or treat as a commodity. WH: late 20C. COMMODITY + -FY.

commodious *a.* roomy. WH: 14–15C. French *commodieux* or Medieval Latin *commodiosus*, from Latin *commodus* convenient, from COM- + *modus* measure. See also -OUS.

commodity *n.* an article of commerce, a product or raw material that can be bought and sold. WH: 14–15C. Old French *commodité* or Latin *commoditas*, from *commodus*. See COMMODIOUS, also -ITY.

commodore *n.* an officer ranking above captain and below rearadmiral. WH: 17C. Prob. from Dutch *komandeur*, from French *commandeur* COMMANDER.

common *a.* belonging equally to more than one. *Also n., v.i.* WH: 12–14C. Old French *comun*, from Latin *communis*, from COM- + *munia* duties.

commonality *n.* commonness; being shared by a number of individuals. WH: 14–15C. Var. of COMMONALTY.

commonalty *n.* the common people. WH: 12–14C. Old French *comunalté*, from Medieval Latin *communalitas*, from Latin *communis*. See COMMON, also -AL¹, -ITY.

commonplace *a.* common, trivial, trite, unoriginal. *Also n., v.t., v.i.* WH: 16C. Orig. *common place*, translating Latin *locus communis*, translating Greek *koinos topos* general theme.

commons *n.pl.* the common people, esp. as part of a political system. WH: 12–14C. Pl. of COMMON.

commonwealth *n.* the whole body of citizens, the body politic. WH: 14–15C. Orig. *common wealth*, from COMMON + WEALTH.

commotion *n.* violent motion. WH: 14–15C. Old French, or from Latin *commotio, commotionis*, from COM- + *motio, motionis* MOTION.

commove *v.t.* to disturb, to agitate, to excite. WH: 14–15C. Old French *commovoir*, from Latin *commovere*, from COM- + *movere* MOVE.

commune¹ *n.* a group of people, not related, living together and sharing property and responsibilities. WH: 17C. French, from Medieval Latin *communia*, neut. pl. of Latin *communis* COMMON, taken as fem. sing. in sense of group of people leading common life.

commune² *v.i.* to converse together familiarly or intimately. WH: 12–14C. Old French *comuner* to share, from *comun* COMMON.

commune³ *n.* intimate conversation. WH: 19C. COMMUNE².

communicate *v.t.* to pass on, to transmit. *Also v.i.* WH: 16C. Latin *communicatus*, p.p. of *communicare* to impart, to share, from *communis* COMMON. See also -ATE³.

communion *n.* the act of communicating or communing. *Also a.* WH: 14–15C. Old French, or from Latin *communio, communionis*, from *communis* common. See also -ION.

communiqué *n.* an official announcement. WH: 19C. French, p.p. (used as n.) of *communiquer* COMMUNICATE.

communism *n.* a theory of government based on common ownership of all property and means of production. WH: 19C. French *communisme*, from *commun* COMMON. See also -ISM.

communitarian *n.* a member of a community, esp. a communist community. *Also a.* WH: 19C. COMMUNITY + -ARIAN, based on *unitarian* (see UNIT) etc.

community *n.* a body of people living in a particular place. WH: 14–15C. Old French *comuneté* (Modern French *communauté*), assim. to Latin *communitas*, from *communis* COMMON. See also -ITY.

commute *v.t.* to exchange or interchange. *Also v.i.* WH: 14–15C. Latin *commutare* to change entirely, to exchange, from COM- + *mutare* to change. The sense to travel regularly to work and back by public transport arose in the 19C and developed from the American commutation ticket (season ticket) bought by such travellers at a reduced rate instead of the full-rate ticket.

comp *n.* a competition. *Also v.i., v.t.* WH: early 20C. Abbr. of COMPETITION.

comp. *abbr.* company. WH: 17C. Abbr. of COMPANY.

compact[1] *a.* closely packed or fitted together. *Also v.t.* WH: 14–15C. Latin *compactus*, p.p. of *compingere*, from COM- + *pangere* to fasten.

compact[2] *n.* a small flat case containing face powder, puff and mirror. WH: 16C. COMPACT[1].

compact[3] *n.* an agreement, a bargain, a covenant. WH: 16C. Latin *compactum*, neut. p.p. (used as n.) of *compacisci* to make an agreement. See COM-, PACT.

compadre *n.* a friend. WH: 19C. Spanish godfather, benefactor. Cp. GOSSIP.

compages *n.* a structure or system of many parts united. WH: 16C. Latin, from COM- + *pag-*, base of *pangere* to fasten, to fix, assim. to nn. in -AGE.

companion[1] *n.* a person who associates with or accompanies another. *Also a., v.t., v.i.* WH: 12–14C. Old French *compaignon* (Modern French *compagnon*), from Latin COM- + *panis* bread. Cp. COMPANY, French *copain* chum, crony, from same source.

companion[2] *n.* the raised window frame on the quarterdeck through which light passes to the cabins and decks below. WH: 18C. Alt., by assoc. with COMPANION[1], of obs. Dutch *kompanje* quarterdeck (now *campanje*), from Old French *compagne*, from Italian (*camera della*) *compagna* (room for) provisions.

company *n.* society, companionship. *Also v.t., v.i.* WH: 12–14C. Old French *compaignie*, from Latin COM- + *panis* bread. Cp. COMPANION[1]. See also -Y[2].

comparative *a.* of or involving comparison. *Also n.* WH: 14–15C. Latin *comparativus*, from *comparatus*, p.p. of *comparare*. See COMPARE, also -ATIVE.

compare *v.t.* to liken (one thing to another). *Also v.i., n.* WH: 14–15C. Old French *comparer*, from Latin *comparare* to pair, to match, from *compar* like, equal, from COM- + *par* equal.

comparison *n.* the act of comparing. *Also v.t.* WH: 12–14C. Old French *comparesoun* (Modern French *comparaison*), from Latin *comparatio, comparationis*, from *comparatus*, p.p. of *comparare*. See COMPARE, also -ISON.

compartment *n.* a division. WH: 16C. French *compartiment*, from Italian *compartimento*, from *compartire*, from Late Latin *compartiri* to share with another, from COM- + *partiri* to share.

compass *n.* an instrument indicating magnetic north, used to ascertain direction, to determine the course of a ship or aeroplane etc. *Also v.t.* WH: 12–14C. Old French *compas*, from *compasser*, from Popular Latin *compassare*, from Latin COM- + *passus* step, PACE[1].

compassion *n.* sympathy for the sufferings and sorrows of others. *Also v.t.* WH: 12–14C. Old French, from Ecclesiastical Latin *compassio, compassionis*, from *compassus*, p.p. of *compati* to suffer with. See COM-, PASSION.

compatible *a.* well-matched or well-suited. *Also n.* WH: 14–15C. French, from Medieval Latin *compatibilis*, from Late Latin *compati* to suffer with. See COMPASSION, -IBLE.

compatriot *n.* a fellow countryman. WH: 16C. Old French *compatriote*, from Late Latin *compatriota*, translating Greek *sumpatriōtēs*. See COM-, PATRIOT.

compeer *n.* an equal, a peer. *Also v.t.* WH: 14–15C. Old French *comper*. See COM-, PEER[2].

compel *v.t.* to force, to oblige. WH: 14–15C. Latin *compellere*, from COM- + *pellere* to drive.

compendium *n.* a handbook or reference book. WH: 16C. Latin profit, saving, from COM- + *pendere* to weigh. Cp. COMPENSATE.

compensate *v.t.* to recompense. *Also v.i.* WH: 17C. Latin *compensatus*, p.p. of *compensare* to weigh against another, from COM- + *pensare*, freq. of *pendere* to weigh. See also -ATE[3].

compère *n.* a person who introduces the items in a stage or broadcast entertainment. *Also v.t., v.i.* WH: 18C. French godfather, from Medieval Latin *compater*, from COM- + *pater* father. The current sense dates from the early 20C.

compete *v.i.* to contend as a rival (with). WH: 17C. Latin *competere* to strive together, from COM- + *petere* to aim at.

competent *a.* qualified, capable. WH: 14–15C. Old French *competent* or Latin *competens, competentis*, pres.p. of *competere* to coincide (cp. COMPETE). See also -ENT. The original sense (to the 18C) was suitable, appropriate. The current sense dates from the 17C.

competition *n.* the act of competing. WH: 17C. Late Latin *competitio, competitionis*, from *competitus*, p.p. of *competere*. See COMPETE, also -ITION.

compile *v.t.* to compose using material from various authors or sources. WH: 12–14C. Old French *compiler* to put together, prob. from Latin *compilare* to plunder, to plagiarize.

complacent *a.* smug, self-satisfied. WH: 17C. Latin *complacens, complacentis*, pres.p. of *complacere*, from COM- + *placere* to please. See also -ENT.

complain *v.i.* to express dissatisfaction or objection. *Also v.t.* WH: 14–15C. Old French *complaindre, complaign-*, from Medieval Latin *complangere*, from Latin COM- + *plangere* to lament. Cp. PLAIN[2].

complaisant *a.* courteous, deferential. WH: 17C. French obliging, pres.p. of *complaire* to acquiesce in order to please, from Latin *complacere*. See COMPLACENT, also -ANT.

compleat *a.* complete. WH: 14–15C. Var. of COMPLETE. The current use of this spelling derives from Izaak Walton's *The Compleat Angler* (1653).

complement[1] *n.* that which is necessary to make something complete. WH: 14–15C. Latin *complementum*, from *complere*. See COMPLETE, also -ENT. Cp. COMPLIMENT[1].

complement[2] *v.t.* to be a complement to. WH: 17C. COMPLEMENT[1].

complete *a.* finished. *Also v.t.* WH: 14–15C. Old French *complet*, or from Latin *completus*, p.p. of *complere* to fill up, to fulfil, from COM- + base of *plenus* full.

complex *a.* composed of several parts, composite. *Also n.* WH: 17C. French *complexe* or Latin *complexus*, p.p. of *complecti* to encompass, to embrace, from COM- + *plectere* to braid, to twine.

complexion *n.* the colour and appearance of the skin, esp. of the face. WH: 12–14C. Old French, from Latin *complexio, complexionis* combination, from *complexus*. See COMPLEX, also -ION. The current sense emerged in the 16C.

compliance *n.* the act of complying. WH: 17C. COMPLY + -ANCE. The sense has been influenced by PLY[1], so that *compliant* implies *pliant* (PLIABLE).

complicate *v.t.* to make complex or intricate. WH: 17C. Latin *complicatus*, p.p. of *complicare*, from COM- + *plicare* to fold. See also -ATE[3].

complicity *n.* participation, partnership, esp. in wrongdoing. WH: 17C. French *complicité*, from Old French *complice*, from Late Latin *complex, complicis* confederate, from COM- + base of *plicare* to fold. Cp. ACCOMPLICE.

compliment[1] *n.* an expression or act of praise, courtesy, respect or regard. WH: 17C. French, from Italian *complimento*, from Latin *complementum* COMPLEMENT[1].

compliment[2] *v.t.* to pay compliments to. WH: 17C. French *complimenter*, from *compliment*. See COMPLIMENT[1]. Cp. COMPLEMENT[1].

compline *n.* in the Roman Catholic Church, the last part of the divine office of the breviary, sung after vespers. WH: 12–14C. Alt., prob. based on *matines* (MATINS), of Old French *complie* (Modern French *complies*), fem. p.p. (used as n.) of obs. *complir*, from var. of Latin *complere*. See COMPLETE.

comply *v.i.* to act or be in accordance (with rules, wishes etc.). WH: 16C. Italian *complire*, from Catalan *complir* or Spanish *cumplir*, from Latin *complere*. See COMPLETE.

compo[1] *n.* any of various compounds, such as a kind of stucco. WH: 19C. Abbr. of COMPOSITION.

compo[2] *n.* compensation for injury etc. WH: 19C. Abbr. of *compensation* (COMPENSATE).

component *a.* serving to make up a compound or a larger whole. *Also n.* WH: 16C. Latin *componens, componentis*, pres.p. of *componere*. See COMPOUND[2], also -ENT.

comport v.t. to conduct (oneself), to behave. Also n. WH: 14–15C. Latin comportare, from COM- + portare to carry, bear. The original sense (to the 19C) was to endure, to tolerate. The current sense to behave arose in the 17C.

compose v.t. to make, esp. by putting together several parts to form one whole. Also v.i. WH: 14–15C. Old French composer, based on Latin componere (see COMPOUND²), but re-formed after Latin p.p. compositus (see COMPOSITE¹) and Old French poser. See POSE¹.

composite¹ a. made up of distinct parts or elements. Also n. WH: 14–15C. French, or from Latin compositus, p.p. of componere. See COMPOUND², also -ITE².

composite² v.t. to merge (related motions from different branches of a trade union, political party etc.) for presentation to a national conference. Also n. WH: mid-20C. COMPOSITE¹.

composition n. the act of composing or putting together to form a whole. WH: 14–15C. Old French, from Latin compositio, compositionis, from compositus, p.p. of componere. See COMPOUND², also -ION.

compositor n. a person who sets type. WH: 14–15C. Anglo-French compositour, from Latin compositor, from compositus. See COMPOSITION, also -OR.

compos mentis a. in one's right mind. WH: 17C. Latin, lit. master of the mind, from compos (COM- + potis powerful) + gen. sing. of mens, mentis mind. Cp. MENTAL¹, NON COMPOS MENTIS.

compossible a. capable of coexisting. WH: 17C. Old French, from Medieval Latin compossibilis. See COM-, POSSIBLE.

compost n. a fertilizing mixture of vegetable matter etc. Also v.t. WH: 14–15C. Old French composte (Modern French COMPOTE), from Latin composta, fem. p.p. (used as n.) of componere COMPOUND². Cp. COMPOSITE¹. Compost also had the sense of COMPOTE to the 18C.

composure n. tranquillity, esp. of the mind. WH: 16C. COMPOSE + -URE.

compote n. fruit stewed or preserved in syrup. WH: 17C. French, see COMPOST.

compound¹ a. composed of two or more ingredients or elements. Also n. WH: 14–15C. From compouned, p.p. of compoune, earlier spelling of COMPOUND². See also -ED.

compound² v.t. to make into a whole by the combination of several constituent parts. Also v.i. WH: 14–15C. Old French compondre, compoun-, from Latin componere, from COM- + ponere to place. The original spelling was compoune (see COMPOUND¹). The current form dates from the 16C and is based on EXPOUND.

compound³ n. an open enclosure where workers are housed, esp. in S African mines. WH: 17C. Portuguese campon or Dutch kampoeng, from Malay kampung enclosure, small village, with spelling influ. by COMPOUND¹.

comprador n. in China and Japan, a Chinese or Japanese person employed by a European business house as an agent or intermediary. WH: 17C. Portuguese buyer, from Latin comparator, from comparare to purchase, from COM- + parare to furnish.

comprehend v.t. to grasp mentally, to understand. WH: 12–14C. Old French comprehender (Modern French comprendre) or Latin comprehendere, from COM- + prehendere to seize.

comprehension n. the act or power of comprehending or understanding. WH: 14–15C. French compréhension, from Latin comprehensio, comprehensionis, from comprehensus, p.p. of comprehendere. See COMPREHEND, also -ION.

compress¹ v.t. to squeeze or press together. WH: 14–15C. Old French compresser, from Late Latin compressare, freq. of Latin comprimere, or from Latin compressus, p.p. of comprimere. See COM-, PRESS¹.

compress² n. a soft pad used to maintain pressure on an artery to stop bleeding. WH: 16C. French compresse, or from Old French compresser. See COMPRESS¹.

comprise v.t. to contain, to include, to consist of. WH: 14–15C. French compris, p.p. of comprendre COMPREHEND. Cp. APPRISE.

compromise n. a settlement by mutual concession. Also v.t., v.i. WH: 14–15C. Old French compromis, from Latin compromissum, neut. p.p. (used as n.) of compromittere to consent to arbitration, from COM- + promittere PROMISE. The original sense (to the 19C) was agreement, with no suggestion of concession.

compte rendu n. a statement, report or review. WH: 19C. French account rendered, from compte account, from Latin computare (see COMPUTE), + p.p. of rendre RENDER.

Comptometer® n. a type of calculating machine. WH: 19C. Appar. from French compte COUNT¹ + -O- + -METER.

comptroller n. a controller, a financial officer or executive. WH: 15C. Var. of controller (CONTROL), by wrong assoc. with source of COUNT¹.

compulsion n. the act of compelling by moral or physical force. WH: 14–15C. Old French, from Late Latin compulsio, compulsionis, from Latin compulsus, p.p. of compellere COMPEL. See also -ION.

compunction n. pricking or reproach of conscience. WH: 12–14C. Old French componction, from Ecclesiastical Latin compunctio, compunctionis, from Latin compunctus, p.p. of compungere to prick severely, to sting, from COM- + pungere to prick. See also -ION.

compurgation n. a trial in which a number of persons declared the accused's innocence on oath. WH: 17C. Medieval Latin compurgatio, compurgationis, from Latin compurgatus, p.p. of compurgare to purge completely. See COM-, PURGATION.

compute v.t. to determine by calculation. Also v.i. WH: 17C. French computer, or from Latin computare, from COM- + putare to settle, to reckon.

computer n. an electronic device which does complex calculations or processes data according to the instructions contained in a program. WH: 17C. COMPUTE + -ER¹. The original sense was a person who makes calculations. The current sense dates from the 19C.

comrade n. a friend, a companion. WH: 16C. French camerade, camarade, from Spanish camarada chamber-fellow, from camara chamber, from Latin CAMERA. See also -ADE.

Comsat® n. a communications satellite. WH: mid-20C. Abbr. of communications satellite.

comstockery n. excessive censorship of literary or artistic material on the grounds of immorality. WH: early 20C. Anthony Comstock, 1844–1915, member of the New York Society for the Suppression of Vice + -ERY.

con¹ n. a fraud, a swindle. Also v.t. WH: 19C. Abbr. of confidence (CONFIDE).

con² n. a reason against. Also prep., adv. WH: 16C. Abbr. of Latin contra CONTRA-.

con³ n. a convict. WH: 19C. Abbr. of CONVICT².

con⁴ v.t. to direct the steering of (a ship). WH: 17C. Appar. form of obs. cond, from Old French conduire, from Latin conducere CONDUCT².

†con⁵ v.t. to peruse carefully. WH: pre-1200. Var. of CAN¹.

con- pref. with, as in connect, conjunction. WH: Latin pref., from COM- with m assim. to c, d, f, g, j, n, q, s, t, v and occasionally vowels.

conacre n. the practice of subletting land already prepared for cropping. WH: 19C. CORN¹ + ACRE.

con amore adv. with devotion. WH: 18C. Italian with love, from con with, from Latin cum with + amore love, from Latin amor.

conation n. the faculty of desiring or willing. WH: 17C. Latin conatio, conationis, from conatus, p.p. of conari to endeavour. See also -ATION.

con brio adv. with vigour or spirit. WH: 19C. Italian with vigour, from con with, from Latin cum + BRIO.

concatenate v.t. to join or link together in a successive series. Also a. WH: 16C. Late Latin concatenatus, p.p. of concatenare, from CON- + catena CHAIN. See also -ATE³.

concave a. having a curve or surface hollow like the inner side of a circle or sphere, as distinct from convex. Also n., v.t. WH: 16C. Old French, or from Latin concavus, from CON- + cavus hollow. Cp. CAVE¹.

concavo- comb. form concave. WH: CONCAVE + -O-.

conceal v.t. to hide or cover from sight or observation. WH: 12–14C. Old French conceler, from Latin concelare, from CON- + celare to hide.

concede v.t. to give up, to surrender. Also v.i. WH: 15C. French concéder, from Latin concedere to withdraw, from CON- + cedere CEDE.

conceit n. a vain opinion of oneself. Also v.t., v.i. WH: 14–15C. From CONCEIVE, based on DECEIT etc. The current sense of vanity dates from the 16C.

conceive v.t. to become pregnant with. Also v.i. WH: 12–14C. Old French conceiv-, base of concevoir, from Latin concipere, from CON- + capere to take.

concelebrate *v.t.* to celebrate (Mass or the Eucharist) along with another priest. *Also v.i.* WH: 16C. Latin *concelebratus*, p.p. of *concelebrare*, from CON- + *celebrare* CELEBRATE. See also -ATE³.

concentrate *v.t.* to bring to a common focus, centre or point. *Also v.i., a., n.* WH: 17C. Latinized form of CONCENTRE. See also -ATE³.

concentre *v.t.* to draw or direct to a common centre. *Also v.i.* WH: 16C. French *concentrer*. See CON-, CENTRE. Cp. CONCENTRATE.

concentric *a.* having a common centre. WH: 14–15C. Old French *concentrique* or Medieval Latin *concentricus*. See CON-, CENTRE, also -IC.

concept *n.* a general notion, an abstract idea. WH: 16C. Late Latin *conceptus*, p.p. of *concipere*. See CONCEIVE.

conceptacle *n.* that in which anything is contained. WH: 17C. French, or from Latin *conceptaculum*. See CON-, RECEPTACLE.

conceptual *a.* of or relating to mental concepts or conception. WH: 17C. Medieval Latin *conceptualis*. See CONCEPT, also -AL¹.

conceptus *n.* the fertilized ovum or developing embryo and surrounding tissue in the womb. WH: 18C. Latin conception, embryo, from *conceptus*, p.p. (used as n.) of *concipere*. See CONCEIVE.

concern *v.t.* to relate or belong to. *Also v.i., n.* WH: 14–15C. Old French *concerner* or Late Latin *concernere* to distinguish, from Latin CON- + *cernere* to sift.

concert¹ *n.* a public musical entertainment. WH: 17C. French, from Italian *concerto*, from *concertare*. See CONCERT². Cp. CONSORT³.

concert² *v.t.* to plan, to arrange mutually. WH: 16C. French *concerter*, from Italian *concertare* to bring into harmony, of unknown orig.

concertante *n.* a piece of music containing a number of solo passages. WH: 18C. Italian, part. n. of *concertare*. See CONCERT².

concertina *n.* a portable instrument having a keyboard at each end with bellows between. *Also v.i.* WH: 19C. CONCERT¹ + -INA¹.

concertino *n.* a short concerto. WH: 18C. Italian, dim. of CONCERTO.

concerto *n.* a composition for a solo instrument with orchestral accompaniment. WH: 18C. Italian, from *concertare*. See CONCERT².

concession *n.* the act of conceding. WH: 14–15C. Old French, from Latin *concessio, concessionis*, from *concessus*, p.p. of *concedere*. See CONCEDE, also -ION.

conch *n.* a shellfish of the family Strombidae. WH: 14–15C. Latin *concha*, from Greek *kogkhē* mussel, cockle, shell-like cavity.

conchie *n.* a conscientious objector. WH: early 20C. Abbr. of pronun. of CONSCIENTIOUS. See also -Y³.

concho- *comb. form* shell. WH: Greek *kogkhē* shell. See also -O-.

conchoid *n.* a shell-like curve. WH: 18C. CONCH + -OID.

conchology *n.* the branch of zoology that deals with shells and the animals inhabiting them. WH: 18C. CONCHO- + -LOGY.

concierge *n.* a doorkeeper, a porter, a janitor. WH: 16C. French, from Old French *cumcerges*, ? from Popular Latin *conservius*, from Latin CON- + *servus* slave.

conciliar *a.* of or relating to a council, esp. an ecclesiastical council. WH: 17C. Medieval Latin *conciliarius* counsellor. See also -AR³.

conciliate *v.t.* to win the regard or goodwill of, to win over. WH: 16C. Latin *conciliatus*, p.p. of *conciliare* to combine, to procure, from *concilium* COUNCIL. See also -ATE³.

concinnous *a.* harmonious. WH: 17C. Latin *concinnus* skilfully put together. See also -OUS.

concise *a.* condensed, brief. WH: 16C. French *concis* or Latin *concisus* divided, broken up, p.p. of *concidere*, from CON- + *caedere* to cut.

conclave *n.* a secret assembly or private meeting. WH: 14–15C. French, from Latin, from CON- + *clavis* key. The sense of private meeting or assembly dates from the 16C.

conclude *v.t.* to bring to an end, to finish. *Also v.i.* WH: 12–14C. Latin *concludere*, from CON- + *claudere* to close, to shut.

concoct *v.t.* to prepare by mixing together. WH: 16C. Latin *concoctus*, p.p. of *concoquere* to cook together, from CON- + *coquere* to cook.

concomitant *a.* accompanying. *Also n.* WH: 17C. Late Latin *concomitans, concomitantis*, pres.p. of *concomitari* to accompany. See also -ANT.

concord *n.* agreement. WH: 12–14C. Old French *concorde*, from Latin *concordia*, from *concors, concordis* of one mind, from CON- + *cor, cordis* heart.

concordat *n.* a convention or treaty, esp. between a pope and a secular government. WH: 17C. French, or from Latin *concordatum*,

neut. p.p. (used as n.) of *concordare* to agree upon (see CONCORD) + -*at* (-ATE¹).

concours *n.* a competition. WH: mid-20C. French contest. See CONCOURSE.

concourse *n.* a confluence, a gathering together. WH: 14–15C. Old French *concours*, from Latin *concursus*, p.p. (used as n.) of *concurrere* CONCUR.

concrescence *n.* a growing together, coalescence. WH: 17C. CON- + -*crescence*, based on EXCRESCENCE etc.

concrete¹ *a.* existing, real. *Also n., v.t., v.i.* WH: 14–15C. French *concret*, or from Latin *concretus*, p.p. of *concrescere* to grow together, from CON- + *crescere* to grow. The sense of building material dates from the 19C.

concrete² *v.i.* to coalesce. *Also v.t.* WH: 16C. CONCRETE¹.

concretion *n.* the act of coalescing into a solid mass. WH: 16C. French *concrétion* or Latin *concretio, concretionis*, from *concretus*, p.p. of *concrescere*. See CONCRETE¹.

concubine *n.* a woman who cohabits with a man without being married to him. WH: 12–14C. Old French, from Latin *concubina*, from CON- + *cubare* to lie. Cp. CUBICLE.

concupiscence *n.* unlawful or excessive sexual desire. WH: 12–14C. Old French, from Late Latin *concupiscentia*, from *concupiscens, concupiscentis*, pres.p. of *concupiscere*, var. of *concupere*, from CON- + *cupere* to desire. Cp. CUPIDITY.

concur *v.i.* to coincide. WH: 14–15C. Latin *concurrere*, from CON- + *currere* to run. The sense was literal (to run together, to collide) to the 17C as well as figurative.

concuss *v.t.* to cause concussion in. WH: 16C. Latin *concussus*, p.p. of *concutere*, from CON- + *quatere* to shake.

condemn *v.t.* to censure, to blame. WH: 12–14C. Old French *condemner* (Modern French *condamner*), from Latin *condemnare*, from CON- + *damnare* to damage. See DAMN.

condense *v.t.* to make more dense or compact. *Also v.i., a.* WH: 14–15C. Old French *condenser*, from Latin *condensare*, from *condensus* very dense. See CON-, DENSE.

condescend *v.i.* to stoop, to yield. WH: 12–14C. Old French *condescendre*, from Ecclesiastical Latin *condescendere* to stoop, to accede, from CON- + *descendere* DESCEND. The original sense had no implication of assumed superiority. The current sense dates from the 14–15C.

condign *a.* worthy, adequate. WH: 14–15C. Old French *condigne*, from Latin *condignus* entirely worthy, from CON- + *dignus* worthy. Cp. DIGNITY.

condiment *n.* a seasoning or sauce. WH: 14–15C. Latin *condimentum*, from *condire* to preserve, to pickle, from *condere* to preserve. See also -MENT.

condition *n.* a stipulation, a requirement. *Also v.t.* WH: 12–14C. Old French *condicion* (Modern French *condition*), from Latin *conditio, conditionis* agreement, situation, rel. to *condicere* to agree upon, from CON- + *dicere* to declare, to say. See also -ION.

condo *n.* a group of dwellings (e.g. a block of flats) of which each unit is separately owned. WH: mid-20C. Abbr. of CONDOMINIUM.

condole *v.i.* to sorrow, to mourn, to lament. WH: 16C. Ecclesiastical Latin *condolere*, from Latin CON- + *dolere* to suffer pain, to grieve.

condom *n.* a contraceptive device, a rubber sheath worn over the penis during sexual intercourse. WH: 18C. Orig. unknown. ? From the name of its inventor.

condominium *n.* joint sovereignty over a state. WH: 18C. Modern Latin, from Latin CON- + *dominium* DOMINION.

condone *v.t.* to forgive or overlook (an offence etc.). WH: 19C. Latin *condonare* to deliver up, to surrender, from CON- + *donare* to give.

condor *n.* either of two vultures, *Vultur gryphus*, the Andean condor, and *Gynogyps californianus*, the California condor. WH: 17C. Spanish *cóndor*, from Quechua *kuntur*.

condottiere *n.* a leader of a troop of mercenaries, esp. in Italy. WH: 18C. Italian, from *condotta* contract, from fem. p.p. of *condurre* to conduct. See CONDUCE.

conduce *v.i.* to contribute (to a result). WH: 14–15C. Latin *conducere* to bring together, to contribute, from CON- + *ducere* to lead.

conduct¹ *n.* the way in which anyone acts or lives. WH: 12–14C. Old French *conduit*, from Latin *conductus*, p.p. (used as n.) of *conducere*. See CONDUCE, CONDUIT.

conduct[2] *v.t.* to lead, to guide. *Also v.i.* WH: 12–14C. Old French *conduit*, p.p. of *conduire*, from Latin *conducere* CONDUCE, assim. to Latin *conductus*. See CONDUCT[1].

conductus *n.* a Latin vocal composition of the 12th and 13th cents. WH: 19C. Medieval Latin. See CONDUCT[1].

conduit *n.* a channel, canal, or pipe, usu. underground, to convey water. WH: 12–14C. Orig. form of CONDUCT[1].

conduplicate *a.* having the sides folded in face to face. WH: 18C. Latin *conduplicatus*, p.p. of *conduplicare*. See CON-, DUPLICATE[2].

condyle *n.* an eminence with a flattened articular surface on a bone. WH: 17C. French, from Latin *condylus*, from Greek *kondulos* knuckle.

cone *n.* a solid figure described by the revolution of a right-angled triangle about the side containing the right angle. *Also v.i., v.t.* WH: 14–15C. French *cône*, from Latin *conus*, from Greek *kōnos* pine cone.

conf. *abbr.* compare. WH: Latin *confer*, 2nd pers. sing. imper. of *conferre* to compare.

confab *n.* a chat, a conversation. *Also v.i.* WH: 18C. Abbr. of *confabulation* (CONFABULATE).

confabulate *v.i.* to talk familiarly, to chat, to gossip. WH: 17C. Latin *confabulatus*, p.p. of *confabulari* to converse. See CON-, FABLE, also -ATE[3].

confect *v.t.* to make by combining ingredients. WH: 14–15C. Latin *confectus*, p.p. of *conficere* to put together, from CON- + *facere* to make.

confederate[1] *a.* united in a league. *Also n.* WH: 14–15C. Late Latin *confoederatus*, from CON- + *foederatus* federate (FEDERAL).

confederate[2] *v.t., v.i.* to unite in a league or alliance. WH: 16C. CON-FEDERATE[1]. See also -ATE[3].

confer *v.t.* to bestow, to grant. *Also v.i.* WH: 14–15C. Latin *conferre*, from CON- + *ferre* to bring.

confess *v.t.* to acknowledge, to admit. *Also v.i.* WH: 14–15C. Old French *confesser*, from Latin *confessus*, p.p. of *confiteri* to acknowledge, from CON- + *fateri* to declare, to avow.

confetti *n.* bits of coloured paper thrown at weddings etc. WH: 19C. Italian, pl. of *confetto* COMFIT. The word was originally used for small sweets thrown during carnivals in Italy, then for coloured paper imitating such sweets.

confidant *n.* a person entrusted with secrets, esp. with love affairs. WH: 17C. Alt. of *confident* (CONFIDE), prob. to reproduce pronun. of French *confidente*. See also -ANT.

confide *v.i.* to have trust or confidence (in). *Also v.t.* WH: 14–15C. Latin *confidere*, from CON- + *fidere* to trust.

configure *v.t.* to give shape or form to. WH: 14–15C. Latin *configurare* to fashion after a pattern, from CON- + *figurare* FIGURE.

confine[1] *v.i.* to have a common boundary (with or on). *Also v.t.* WH: 16C. French *confiner*, from Latin *confinia*. See CONFINE[2].

confine[2] *n.* a boundary, a limit. WH: 14–15C. French *confins*, from Latin *confinia*, pl. of *confine* and *confinium*, from *confinis* bordering, from CON- + *finis* end, limit.

confirm *v.t.* to establish the truth or correctness of. WH: 12–14C. Old French *confermer* (later *confirmer*), from Latin *confirmare*, from CON- + *firmare* to strengthen, from *firmus* FIRM[1].

confiscate[1] *v.t.* to take or seize, esp. as a penalty. WH: 16C. Latin *confiscatus*, p.p. of *confiscare*, from CON- + *fiscus* chest, treasury. See also -ATE[3].

confiscate[2] *a.* confiscated. WH: 16C. Part. a. of CONFISCATE[1]. See also -ATE[2].

confiteor *n.* a Roman Catholic formula of confession. WH: 12–14C. Latin I confess, first word of the formula *Confiteor Deo Omnipotenti* I confess to Almighty God, etc.

conflagration *n.* a large and destructive fire. WH: 15C. Latin *conflagratio, conflagrationis*, from *conflagratus*, p.p. of *conflagrare* to burn up, from CON- + *flagrare* to blaze. See also -ATION.

conflate *v.t.* to fuse together. WH: 14–15C. Latin *conflatus*, p.p. of *conflare* to kindle, to achieve, from CON- + *flare* to blow. See also -ATE[3].

conflict[1] *n.* a fight, a struggle. WH: 14–15C. Latin *conflictus*, p.p. (used as n.) of *confligere* to strike together, to clash, from CON- + *fligere* to strike.

conflict[2] *v.i.* to come into collision, to clash. WH: 14–15C. Latin *conflictus*. See CONFLICT[1].

confluent *a.* flowing or running together. *Also n.* WH: 15C. Latin *confluens, confluentis*, pres.p. of *confluere*, from CON- + *fluere* to flow. See also -ENT.

conflux *n.* confluence. WH: 17C. Late Latin *confluxus*, from CON- + *fluxus* FLUX.

confocal *a.* having common focus or foci. WH: 19C. CON- + *focal* (FOCUS).

conform *v.t.* to make like in form, to make similar (to). *Also v.i.* WH: 12–14C. Old French *conformer*, from Latin *conformare*, from CON- + *formare* FORM.

confound *v.t.* to throw into confusion. *Also int.* WH: 12–14C. Old French *confondre*, from Latin *confundere* to pour together, to mix up, from CON- + *fundere* to pour.

confraternity *n.* a brotherhood esp. for religious or charitable purposes. WH: 14–15C. Old French *confraternité* or Medieval Latin *confraternitas*, from *confrater*. See CONFRÈRE, CON-, FRIAR.

confrère *n.* a fellow-member of a profession, religion, association etc. WH: 14–15C. Old French, from Medieval Latin *confrater*. See CON-, FRIAR.

confront *v.t.* to face. WH: 16C. French *confronter*, from Medieval Latin *confrontare*, from Latin CON- + *frons, frontis* forehead, face, FRONT.

Confucian *a.* of or relating to Confucius or his philosophical system. *Also n.* WH: 19C. *Confucius*, 551–479 BC, Chinese philosopher + -AN.

confuse *v.t.* to confound, to perplex. WH: 12–14C. Back-formation from p.p. *confused*, from Old French *confus*, from Latin *confusus*, p.p. of *confundere* CONFOUND + -ED.

confute *v.t.* to overcome in argument. WH: 16C. Latin *confutare* to check, to restrain, from CON- + base of *refutare* REFUTE.

conga *n.* a Latin American dance performed by several people in single file. *Also v.i.* WH: mid-20C. American Spanish, from Spanish, fem. of *congo* of the Congo.

congé *n.* leave-taking, departure, farewell. *Also v.i.* WH: 14–15C. Old French *congié* (Modern French *congé*), from Latin *commeatus* passage, leave to pass, from *commeare* to go and come, from COM- + *meare* to go.

congeal *v.t.* to convert from the liquid to the solid state by cold, to freeze. *Also v.i.* WH: 14–15C. Old French *congeler*, from Latin *congelare*, from CON- + *gelare* to freeze. Cp. JELLY.

congelation *n.* the act or process of congealing. WH: 14–15C. Old French, or Latin *congelatio, congelationis*, from *congelatus*, p.p. of *congelare* CONGEAL.

congener *n.* a person or thing of the same kind or class. *Also a.* WH: 18C. Latin, from CON- + *genus, generis* race, stock.

congenial *a.* pleasant, agreeable. WH: 17C. CON- + GENIAL[1].

congenital *a.* existing from birth. WH: 18C. Latin *congenitus*, from CON- + *genitus*, p.p. of *gignere* to beget. See also -AL[1].

conger *n.* any marine eel of the family Congridae, esp. *Conger conger*. WH: 12–14C. Old French *congre*, from Latin *congrus, conger*, from Greek *goggros*.

congeries *n.* a collection or heap of particles, things, ideas etc. WH: 16C. Latin heap, pile, from *congerere*. See CONGEST.

congest *v.t.* to crowd, to obstruct, to block. *Also v.i.* WH: 14–15C. Latin *congestus*, p.p. of *congerere* to collect, to amass, from CON- + *gerere* to bear, to carry.

conglobate *v.t.* to form into a ball. *Also v.i., a.* WH: 17C. Latin *conglobatus*, p.p. of *conglobare*, from CON- + *globare* to make into a ball, from *globus* ball, GLOBE. See also -ATE[3].

conglomerate[1] *a.* gathered into a round body. *Also n.* WH: 14–15C. Latin *conglomeratus*, p.p. of *conglomerare*, from CON- + *glomus, glomeris* ball. See also -ATE[3].

conglomerate[2] *v.t., v.i.* to gather into a ball. WH: 16C. Latin *conglomeratus*, p.p. of *conglomerare*. See CONGLOMERATE[1], also -ATE[3].

conglutinate *v.t.* to glue together. *Also v.i.* WH: 14–15C. Latin *conglutinatus*, p.p. of *conglutinare*, from CON- + *glutinare* to glue, from *gluten, glutinis* glue. See also -ATE[3].

Congolese *a.* of or relating to the Congo or Zaire. *Also n.* WH: early 20C. French *Congolais*, from *Congo*, a region and country in W central Africa. See also -ESE.

congou *n.* a kind of Chinese black tea. WH: 18C. Abbr. of Chinese *gōngfu chá* tea for the discerning, from *gōngfu* effort + *chá* TEA.

congrats *n.pl.*, *int.* congratulations. WH: 19C. Abbr. of *congratulations* (CONGRATULATE).

congratulate *v.t.* to express pleasure or praise to, on account of some event or achievement. *Also v.i.* WH: 16C. Latin *congratulatus*, p.p. of *congratulari*, from CON- + *gratulari* to express one's joy, from *gratus* pleasing. See also -ATE[3].

congregate *v.t.* to gather or collect together into a crowd. *Also v.i.* WH: 14–15C. Latin *congregatus*, p.p. of *congregare* to collect together, from CON- + *grex*, *gregis* flock. See also -ATE[3].

congress *n.* a discussion, a conference. WH: 14–15C. Latin *congressus*, p.p. (used as n.) of *congredi* to go together, to meet, from CON- + *gradi* to proceed, to step.

congruent *a.* agreeing, suitable, correspondent. WH: 14–15C. Latin *congruens*, *congruentis*, pres.p. of *congruere* to meet together, to agree, from CON- + *ruere* to fall, to rush. See also -ENT.

conic *a.* of, relating to or having the form of a cone. *Also n.* WH: 16C. Modern Latin *conicus*, from Greek *kōnikos*, from *kōnos* CONE. See also -IC.

conidium *n.* an asexual reproductive cell or spore in certain fungi. WH: 19C. Modern Latin, from Greek *konis* dust + *-id-*. See also -IUM.

conifer *n.* any tree or shrub of the Coniferae, an order of resinous trees, such as the fir, pine and cedar, bearing a cone-shaped fruit. WH: 19C. Latin cone-bearing, from *conus* CONE + *-fer*, from *ferre* to carry, to bear.

coniine *n.* an alkaloid constituting the poisonous principle in hemlock. WH: 19C. Latin *conium*, from Greek *kōneion* hemlock + -INE.

conjecture *n.* guess, surmise. *Also v.t.*, *v.i.* WH: 14–15C. Old French, or from Latin *coniectura* conclusion, inference, from *coniectus*, p.p. of *coniicere* to throw together, from CON- + *iacere* to throw.

conjoin *v.t.* to cause to unite, to join. *Also v.i.* WH: 14–15C. Old French *conjoindre*, *conjoign-*, from Latin *coniungere*, from CON- + *iungere* JOIN.

conjugal *a.* of or relating to matrimony or to married life. WH: 16C. Latin *coniugalis*, from *coniunx*, *coniugis* consort, spouse, from CON- + stem of *iugum* yoke. See also -AL[1].

conjugate[1] *v.t.* to inflect (a verb) by going through the voices, moods, tenses etc. *Also v.i.* WH: 16C. Latin *coniugatus*, p.p. of *coniugare*, from CON- + *iugare* to join, to yoke, from *iugum* yoke. See also -ATE[3].

conjugate[2] *a.* joined in pairs, coupled. *Also n.* WH: 15C. Latin *coniugatus*, p.p. of *coniugare*. See CONJUGATE[1], also -ATE[2].

conjunct *a.* joined. *Also n.* WH: 14–15C. Latin *coniunctus*, p.p. of *coniungere*, from CON- + *iungere* to join. Cp. CONJOIN.

conjunctiva *n.* the mucous membrane lining the inner surface of the eyelids and the front of the eyeball. WH: 14–15C. Medieval Latin *(tunica) coniunctiva* conjunctive (membrane), from Late Latin *coniunctivus*, from *coniunctus*, p.p. of *coniungere*. See CONJUNCT.

conjure[1] *v.t.* to effect by or as if by magical influence. *Also v.i.* WH: 12–14C. CONJURE[2].

conjure[2] *v.t.* to appeal to by a sacred name, or in a solemn manner. *Also v.i.* WH: 12–14C. Old French *conjurer* to plot, to exorcise, from Latin *coniurare* to band together by an oath, from CON- + *iurare* to swear. Cp. JURY.

conk *n.* the head. *Also v.t.* WH: 19C. ? Alt. of CONCH.

conker *n.* the fruit of a horse chestnut. WH: 19C. ? From CONCH, assoc. with CONQUER. The children's game of conkers was originally played with snail shells.

con moto *adv.* briskly, with movement. WH: 19C. Italian with movement, from *con* with, from Latin *cum* + *moto* movement (see MOTION).

connate *a.* innate, inborn, congenital. WH: 17C. Late Latin *connatus*, p.p. of *connasci*, from CON- + *nasci* to be born. See also -ATE[2].

connatural *a.* inborn. WH: 16C. Late Latin *connaturalis*, from CON- + *naturalis* NATURAL.

connect *v.t.* to join or fasten together. *Also v.i.* WH: 14–15C. Latin *connectare*, from CON- + *nectere* to bind.

connection *n.* the act of connecting. WH: 14–15C. Latin *connexio*, *connexionis*, from *connexus*, p.p. of *connectere*. See CONNECT, also -ION.

conniption *n.* a fit of rage or hysteria. WH: 19C. Appar. invented word. ? Based on *corruption* (CORRUPT).

connive *v.i.* to conspire (with). *Also v.t.* WH: 17C. French *conniver*, from Latin *connivere*, from CON- + stem rel. to *nictare* (NICTITATE).

connoisseur *n.* a person skilled in judging, esp. in the fine arts. WH: 18C. Old French (Modern French *connaisseur*), from *conoistre*, *conoiss-* (Modern French *connaître*) to know + *-eur* -OR.

connote *v.t.* to imply, to betoken indirectly. WH: 17C. Medieval Latin *connotare*, from CON- + *notare* NOTE.

connubial *a.* of or relating to marriage. WH: 17C. Latin *connubialis*, from *connubium* wedlock, from CON- + *nubere* to marry. See also -AL[1].

conquer *v.t.* to win or gain, esp. by military force. *Also v.i.* WH: 12–14C. Old French *conquerre*, from Latin *conquirere* to seek for, to gain, from CON- + *querere* to seek.

conquest *n.* the act of conquering. WH: 12–14C. Old French (Modern French *conquête*), from Latin *conquista*, fem. p.p. (used as n.) of *conquirere*. See CONQUER.

conquistador *n.* any of the Spanish conquerors of America in the 16th cent. WH: 19C. Spanish, from *conquistar* to conquer, from *conquista* CONQUEST.

con-rod *n.* a connecting rod. WH: mid-20C. Abbr. of *connecting rod* (CONNECT).

consanguine *a.* of the same blood. WH: 17C. Latin *consanguineus* of the same blood, from CON- + *sanguis*, *sanguinis* blood. See also -OUS.

conscience *n.* moral sense. WH: 12–14C. Old French, from Latin *conscientia* privity of knowledge, from *conscire* to be privy to, from CON- + *scire* to know. See also -ENCE. The earlier English word was *inwit*, from IN + WIT[1].

conscientious *a.* scrupulous, diligent. WH: 17C. French *conscien-cieux*, from Medieval Latin *conscientiosus*, from Latin *conscientia*. See CONSCIENCE, also -OUS.

†**conscionable** *a.* regulated by conscience. WH: 16C. CONSCIENCE (with *-ce* wrongly taken to be *-S*[1]) + -ABLE. The word is still current in the negative form *unconscionable*.

conscious *a.* aware of one's own existence. *Also n.* WH: 16C. Latin *conscius* knowing something with others or in oneself, from *conscire*. See CONSCIENCE, also -OUS.

conscribe *v.t.* to conscript. WH: 15C. Latin *conscribere*. See CONSCRIPT[1].

conscript[1] *a.* enrolled, registered, enlisted compulsorily in the armed forces. *Also n.* WH: 16C. Latin *conscriptus*, p.p. of *conscribere* to write down, to enrol, from CON- + *scribere* to write. The original sense related to enrolled Roman senators. The current military sense dates from the 19C.

conscript[2] *v.t.* to enlist compulsorily. WH: 19C. Back-formation from *conscription*, from Late Latin *conscriptio*, *conscriptionis* levying of troops. See CONSCRIPT[1], also -ION.

consecrate *v.t.* to make sacred, to hallow. *Also a.* WH: 14–15C. Latin *consecratus*, p.p. of *consecrare*, from CON- + *sacrare* to dedicate, from *sacer* SACRED. See also -ATE[3].

consecution *n.* the state of being consecutive. WH: 14–15C. Latin *consecutio*, *consecutionis*, from *consecutus*, p.p. of *consequi* to follow closely, from CON- + *sequi* to pursue. See also -ION.

consecutive *a.* following without interval or break. WH: 17C. French *consécutif*, from Medieval Latin *consecutivus*, from *consecutus*. See CONSECUTION, also -IVE.

consensus *n.* general agreement, unanimity. WH: 17C. Latin agreement, from *consensus*, p.p. of *consentire*. See CONSENT.

consent *v.i.* to agree, to give permission. *Also v.t.*, *n.* WH: 12–14C. Old French *consentir*, from Latin *consentire*, from CON- + *sentire* to feel.

consentaneous *a.* mutually consenting, unanimous. WH: 16C. Latin *consentaneus*, from *consentire*. See CONSENT, also -ANEOUS.

consentient *a.* of one mind, unanimous. WH: 17C. Latin *consentiens*, *consentientis*, pres.p. of *consentire*. See CONSENT, also -ENT.

consequent *a.* following as a natural or logical result. *Also n.* WH: 14–15C. Old French *conséquent*, from Latin *consequens*, *consequentis*, pres.p. of *consequi* to follow closely. See CONSECUTION, also -ENT.

conservancy *n.* the official preservation of forests and other natural resources. WH: 18C. Alt. of *conservacy*, from Anglo-French *conservacie*, from Anglo-Latin *conservatia*, or from Latin *conservatio*, *conservationis* CONSERVATION. See also -ACY.

conservation *n*. the act of conserving. WH: 14–15C. Old French, or from Latin *conservatio*, *conservationis*, from *conservatus*, p.p. of *conservare*. See CONSERVE, also -ATION.

conservative *a*. tending or inclined to conserve what is established. *Also n*. WH: 14–15C. Late Latin *conservativus*, from Latin *conservatus*. See CONSERVATION, also -ATIVE. The name of the political party arose in the 19C, when the word was extended to apply to conservative attitudes in politics, religion etc. generally.

conservatoire *n*. a public school of music or other fine art. WH: 18C. French, from Italian *conservatorio* CONSERVATORY. Italian *conservatorio* was originally the term for a hospital or school for orphans and foundlings where a musical education was given.

conservator *n*. a person who preserves something from damage or injury. WH: 14–15C. Old French *conservateur*, from Latin *conservator* keeper, preserver, from *conservatus*. See CONSERVATION, also -OR.

conservatorium *n*. a conservatoire. WH: 19C. German, and from Modern Latin CONSERVATORY. See also -ORIUM.

conservatory *n*. a greenhouse for exotic plants. WH: 16C. Late Latin *conservatorium*, neut. (used as n.) of *conservatorius*, from *conservatus*. See CONSERVATION, also -ORY[1].

conserve *v.t*. to preserve from decay or loss. *Also n*. WH: 14–15C. Old French *conserver*, from Latin *conservare*, from CON- + *servare* to keep.

consider *v.t*. to think about, to contemplate. *Also v.i*. WH: 14–15C. Old French *considérer*, from Latin *considerare* to examine, prob. from CON- + *sidus*, *sideris* constellation, star. The original sense was probably to examine the stars, with reference to either augury or navigation.

consign *v.t*. to commit to the care, keeping or trust of another. *Also v.i*. WH: 14–15C. French *consigner*, from Latin *consignare* to attest with a seal, from CON- + *signare* SIGN.

consist *v.i*. to be composed (of). WH: 14–15C. Latin *consistere* to stand still, from CON- + *sistere* to place, to stand firm. The earliest sense (to the 19C) was to exist, to reside in. The current sense arose in the 16C.

consistory *n*. the court of a bishop for dealing with ecclesiastical causes arising in his diocese. WH: 12–14C. Old French *consistoire*, from Late Latin *consistorium*. See CONSIST, also -ORY[1].

consociate[1] *a*. associated together. *Also n*. WH: 14–15C. Latin *consociatus*. See CONSOCIATE[2], also -ATE[2].

consociate[2] *v.t*. to unite. *Also v.i*. WH: 16C. Latin *consociatus*, p.p. of *consociare*, from CON- + *sociare* to associate, from *socius* fellow. See also -ATE[3].

consocies *n*. a natural community with one dominant species. WH: early 20C. From *consociation* (CONSOCIATE[1]), based on SPECIES.

console[1] *v.t*. to comfort or cheer in trouble. WH: 17C. French *consoler*, from Latin *consolari*, from CON- + *solari* to soothe.

console[2] *n*. the control panel of an electric or electronic system. WH: 17C. French, ? from *consolider* CONSOLIDATE, influ. by *sole* SOLE[1] (in obs. sense foundation, supporting beam).

consolidate *v.t*. to form into a solid and compact mass. *Also v.i*. WH: 16C. Latin *consolidatus*, p.p. of *consolidare*, from CON- + *solidare* to make firm, from *solidus* SOLID. See also -ATE[3].

consols *n.pl*. consolidated annuities. WH: 18C. Abbr. of *consolidated annuities* (CONSOLIDATE) + -S[1].

consommé *n*. a clear soup made by boiling meat and vegetables to form a concentrated stock. WH: 19C. French, p.p. (used as n.) of *consommer*, from Latin *consummare*. See CONSUMMATE[2]. Not rel. to CONSUME. The soup is so called because the meat and vegetables have been concentrated by being boiled down.

consonant *a*. agreeing or according, esp. in sound. *Also n*. WH: 12–14C. Old French, from Latin *consonans*, *consonantis*, pres.p. of *consonare* to sound together, from CON- + *sonare* SOUND[1].

con sordino *adv*. with a mute. WH: 19C. Italian with *con* with, from Latin *cum* + SORDINO.

consort[1] *n*. a companion, an associate. WH: 14–15C. French, from Latin *consors*, *consortis* sharing in common, from CON- + *sors* portion, lot. The sense of husband or wife arose in the 17C.

consort[2] *v.i*. to associate, to keep company (with). *Also v.t*. WH: 16C. From CONSORT[1], influ. by SORT, CONSORT[3].

consort[3] *n*. a group of musical instruments of the same type playing together. WH: 16C. Partly from CONSORT[2], influ. by Latin CONSORTIUM, partly from early form of CONCERT[1].

consortium *n*. an association of companies, financial interests etc. WH: 19C. Latin, from *consors* CONSORT[1].

conspecific *a*. of or relating to the same species. WH: 19C. CON- + *specific* (SPECIFY).

conspectus *n*. a general sketch or survey. WH: 19C. Latin, p.p. (used as n.) of *conspicere*. See CONSPICUOUS.

conspicuous *a*. obvious, clearly visible. WH: 16C. Latin *conspicuus*, from *conspicere* to look at carefully, from CON- + *specere* to look at. See also -OUS.

conspire *v.i*. to combine secretly to do any unlawful act, esp. to commit treason, sedition, murder, or fraud. *Also v.t*. WH: 14–15C. Old French *conspirer*, from Latin *conspirare* to agree, to combine, from CON- + *spirare* to breathe.

con spirito *adv*. in a lively manner, with spirit. WH: 18C. Italian with spirit, from *con* with, from Latin *cum* + *spirito* SPIRIT.

constable *n*. a police officer of the lowest rank. WH: 12–14C. Old French *cunestable*, *conestable* (Modern French *connétable*), from Late Latin *comes stabuli* count of the stable. See COUNT[2], STABLE[2]. Cp. MARSHAL. The Latin title was first that of a head groom, then of the chief officer of the household of Frankish kings. The equivalent high rankings in English usage are now mainly historic.

constant *a*. continuous, unceasing. *Also n*. WH: 14–15C. Old French, from Latin *constans*, *constantis*, pres.p. of *constare* to stand firm, from CON- + *stare* to stand. See also -ANT.

constantan *n*. an alloy of copper and nickel used for electrical components because of its high electrical resistance at any temperature. WH: early 20C. CONSTANT + arbitrary -an.

Constantia *n*. a S African wine from Constantia. WH: 18C. *Constantia*, an estate near Cape Town, S Africa.

constellation *n*. a number of fixed stars grouped within the outlines of an imaginary figure in the sky. WH: 12–14C. Old French, from Late Latin *constellatio*, *constellationis*, from CON- + *stella* star.

consternate *v.t*. to frighten, to dismay. WH: 17C. Latin *consternatus*, p.p. of *consternare* to lay prostrate, from CON- + *sternare* to lay low. See also -ATE[3].

constipate *v.t*. to affect with constipation. WH: 16C. Latin *constipatus*, p.p. of *constipare*, from CON- + *stipare* to press, to cram. See also -ATE[3].

constituent *a*. constituting, composing. *Also n*. WH: 15C. French *constituant*, from Latin *constituens*, *constituentis*, pres.p. of *constituere* CONSTITUTE. See also -ENT.

constitute *v.t*. to make up or compose. WH: 14–15C. Latin *constitutus*, p.p. of *constituere* to establish, from CON- + *statuere* to set up.

constitution *n*. the act of constituting. WH: 12–14C. Old French, or from Latin *constitutio*, *constitutionis*. See CONSTITUTE, also -ION.

constitutive *a*. that constitutes or composes; component, essential. WH: 16C. Late Latin *constitutivus* confirmatory. See CONSTITUTE, also -IVE.

constrain *v.t*. to compel, to oblige (to do or not to do). WH: 12–14C. Old French *constraindre*, *constraign-* (Modern French *contraindre*), from Latin *constringere* to bind tightly together, from CON- + *stringere* (see STRAIN[1]).

constrict *v.t*. to make smaller, narrower or tighter. WH: 18C. Latin *constrictus*, p.p. of *constringere*. See CONSTRAIN.

construct[1] *v.t*. to make by putting parts together. WH: 14–15C. Latin *constructus*, p.p. of *construere* to lay, to build, from CON- + *struere* to lay, to build.

construct[2] *n*. something constructed. WH: 19C. CONSTRUCT[1].

construction *n*. the act or process of constructing. WH: 14–15C. Old French, from Latin *constructio*, *constructionis*. See CONSTRUCT[1], also -ION.

construe *v.t*. to explain, to interpret. *Also v.i*. WH: 14–15C. Latin *construere* CONSTRUCT[1].

consubstantial *a*. (esp. of the three persons of the Trinity) having the same substance or essence. WH: 14–15C. Ecclesiastical Latin *consubstantialis*, translating Greek *homoousios* HOMOOUSIAN. See CON-, SUBSTANTIAL.

consubstantiate *v.t., v.i.* to unite in one substance. WH: 16C. Late Latin *consubstantiatus* part. a. See CON-, SUBSTANTIATE.

consuetude *n.* custom, usage, habit. WH: 14–15C. Old French, from Latin *consuetudo*, from *consuetus*, p.p. of *consuescere* to accustom, to use, from CON- + *suescere* to become accustomed. See also -TUDE. Cp. CUSTOM.

consul *n.* an official appointed by a state to reside in a foreign country to protect its mercantile interests and citizens there. WH: 14–15C. Latin, rel. to *consulere* to take counsel. See CONSULT. The original sense was a magistrate in ancient Rome. The title then passed to that of a magistrate or similar official, with the current sense emerging in the 16C.

consult *v.i.* to take counsel together, to confer (with). Also *v.t., n.* WH: 16C. Old French *consulter*, from Latin *consultare*, freq. of *consultus*, p.p. of *consulere* to take counsel.

consume *v.t.* to eat or drink. Also *v.i.* WH: 14–15C. French *consumer*, from Latin *consumere*, from CON- + *sumere* to take.

consummate[1] *a.* complete, perfect. WH: 14–15C. Latin *consummatus*, p.p. of *consummare*. See CONSUMMATE[2].

consummate[2] *v.t.* to bring to completion, to perfect, to finish. WH: 16C. Latin *consummatus*, p.p. of *consummare*, from CON- + *summa* SUM or *summus* highest, supreme. See also -ATE[3].

consumption *n.* the act of consuming. WH: 14–15C. Old French *consomption*, from Latin *consumptio, consumptionis*, from *consumptus*, p.p. of *consumere* CONSUME. The original specific sense was the wasting of the body by disease.

contact *n.* touch, the state of touching. Also *v.t.* WH: 17C. Latin *contactus*, p.p. (used as n.) of *contingere* to touch closely, from CON- + *tangere* to touch.

contagion *n.* communication of disease by contact with a person suffering from it. WH: 14–15C. Latin *contagio, contagionis*, from CON- + base of *tangere* to touch. See also -ION.

contain *v.t.* to hold within fixed limits. WH: 12–14C. Old French *contenir*, from Latin *continere*, from CON- + *tenere* to hold.

contaminate *v.t.* to pollute, esp. with radioactivity. WH: 14–15C. Latin *contaminatus*, p.p. of *contaminare*, from *contamen, contaminis* contact, pollution, from base of *tangere* to touch. See also -ATE[3]. Cp. CONTAGION.

contango *n.* the postponement of a transaction on the Stock Exchange. WH: 19C. Appar. arbitrary, based on Latin v. with 1st pers. sing. in *-o*. The word is perhaps intended either to be understood as 'I make CONTINGENT' or to suggest CONTINUE.

Conté *a.* denoting a type of hard crayon or pencil used by artists etc. WH: 19C. Nicolas Jacques *Conté*, 1755–1805, French inventor.

conte *n.* a tale, esp. a short story in prose. WH: 19C. French tale, COUNT[1].

contemn *v.t.* to despise, to scorn. WH: 14–15C. Old French *contemner* or Latin *contemnere*, from CON- + *temnere* to despise.

contemplate *v.t.* to look at, to study. Also *v.i.* WH: 16C. Latin *contemplatus*, p.p. of *contemplari*, from CON- + *templum* open space for observation, TEMPLE[1]. See also -ATE[3].

contemporaneous *a.* existing, living or happening at the same time. WH: 17C. Latin *contemporaneus*, from CON- + *tempus, temporis* time. See also -OUS.

contemporary *a.* living at the same time. Also *n.* WH: 17C. Medieval Latin *contemporarius*, from CON- + *tempus, temporis* time, based on Latin *contemporaneus* (see CONTEMPORANEOUS) and Late Latin *contemporalis*. See CON-, TEMPORAL[1], also -ARY[1].

contempt *n.* scorn, disdain. WH: 14–15C. Latin *contemptus*, p.p. (used as n.) of *contemnere* CONTEMN.

contend *v.i.* to strive in opposition. Also *v.t.* WH: 14–15C. Old French *contendre* or Latin *contendere*, from CON- + *tendere* to stretch, to strive.

content[1] *a.* satisfied, pleased. Also *int., v.t., n.* WH: 14–15C. Old French, from Latin *contentus* that is satisfied, p.p. of *continere* to repress, to restrain. Cp. CONTAIN.

content[2] *n.* capacity or power of containing; volume. WH: 14–15C. Medieval Latin *contentum*, use as n. of *contentus*, p.p. of *continere* CONTAIN.

contention *n.* the act of contending. WH: 14–15C. Old French, or from Latin *contentio, contentionis*, from *contentus*, p.p. of *contendere*. See CONTEND, also -ION.

conterminous *a.* having a common boundary (with). WH: 17C. Latin *conterminus*, from CON- + TERMINUS. See also -OUS.

contessa *n.* an Italian countess. WH: 19C. Italian, from Medieval Latin *comitissa*. See COUNT[2], -ESS[1].

contest[1] *v.t.* to contend, to strive earnestly for. Also *v.i.* WH: 16C. Latin *contestari* to call to witness, from CON- + *testari* to bear witness.

contest[2] *n.* a struggle for victory or superiority. WH: 17C. CONTEST[1], or from French *conteste*, from *contester* CONTEST[1].

context *n.* the parts of a piece of speech or writing immediately connected with a sentence or passage quoted. WH: 14–15C. Latin *contextus*, p.p. (used as n.) of *contexere* to weave together, from CON- + *texere* to weave.

contexture *n.* the act or manner of weaving together. Also *v.t.* WH: 17C. French, prob. from Medieval Latin, from Latin CON- + *textura* TEXTURE.

contiguous *a.* touching, in contact. WH: 16C. Latin *contiguus* touching together, from *contingere*. See CONTINGENT, also -OUS.

continent[1] *n.* a large continuous tract of land. WH: 15C. French, from Latin *terra continens* continuous land, from TERRA + part. a. of *continere* to restrain. See CONTAIN, also -ENT. The sense of mainland dates from the 16C, and of one of the main land masses (Europe, Asia etc.) from the 17C.

continent[2] *a.* able to control one's bladder and bowel movements. WH: 14–15C. Latin *continens, continentis*, pres.p. of *continere* to restrain. See CONTAIN, also -ENT. The current specific sense emerged only in the mid-20C, as the opposite of earlier INCONTINENT[1].

contingent *a.* dependent on an uncertain issue, conditional. Also *n.* WH: 14–15C. Latin *contingens, contingentis*, pres.p. of *contingere* to be continuous, from CON- + *tangere* to touch. Cp. CONTIGUOUS.

continual *a.* frequently recurring. WH: 12–14C. Old French *continuel*. See CONTINUE, also -AL[1].

continuance *n.* the act or state of continuing. WH: 14–15C. Old French. See CONTINUE, also -ANCE.

continuation *n.* the act or an instance of continuing. WH: 14–15C. Old French, from Latin *continuatio, continuationis*, from *continuatus*, p.p. of *continuare*. See CONTINUE, also -ATION.

continue *v.t.* to carry on without interruption. Also *v.i.* WH: 12–14C. Old French *continuer*, from Latin *continuare* to make continuous, from *continuus* CONTINUOUS.

continuity *n.* the state of being continuous. WH: 14–15C. Old French *continuite*, from Latin *continuitas*, from *continuare*. See CONTINUE, also -ITY.

continuo *n.* a bass part with harmony indicated by shorthand marks; thorough bass. WH: 18C. Italian continuous, from Latin *continuus*. See CONTINUOUS.

continuous *a.* connected without a break in space or time. WH: 17C. Latin *continuus* uninterrupted, from *continere* to hang together, from CON- + *tenere* to hold. See also -OUS.

continuum *n.* an unbroken mass, series or course of events. WH: 17C. Neut. sing. (used as n.) of Latin *continuus*. See CONTINUOUS.

conto *n.* a Portuguese or Brazilian monetary unit, equal to 1000 escudos or cruzeiros. WH: 17C. Portuguese, from Latin *comptus* COUNT[1].

contort *v.t.* to twist with violence, to wrench. WH: 14–15C. Latin *contortus*, p.p. of *contorquere*, from CON- + *torquere* to twist.

contour *n.* the defining line of any figure or body, an outline. Also *v.t.* WH: 17C. French, from Italian *contorno*, from *contornare* to draw in outline, from CON- + *tornare* to turn.

contra[1] *n.* the opposite (usu. the credit) side of an account. Also *prep., adv.* WH: 17C. Latin *contra* (CONTRA-).

contra[2] *n.* a counter-revolutionary guerrilla fighter in Nicaragua. WH: late 20C. Abbr. of Spanish *contrarrevolucionario* counter-revolutionary (COUNTER-REVOLUTION).

contra- *pref.* against, opposite, contrary. WH: Latin, from *contra* against.

contraband *a.* prohibited, unlawful. Also *v.t., v.i., n.* WH: 16C. Spanish *contrabanda*, from Italian *contrabando* (now *contrabbando*), from *contra-* CONTRA- + *bando*. See BAN.

contrabass *n.* a double bass. WH: 19C. Italian *contrabbasso* (now *contrabbasso*), or from French *contrebasse*. See CONTRA-, BASS[1].

contrabassoon *n.* a double-reeded woodwind instrument with a range an octave lower than a bassoon. WH: 19C. CONTRA- + BASSOON.

contraception *n.* birth control, the taking of measures to prevent conception. WH: 19C. CONTRA- + *conception* (CONCEPTUS).

contract[1] *v.t.* to draw together. *Also v.i.* WH: 14–15C. Orig. p.p., from var. of Old French *contrait*, from Latin *contractus*, p.p. of *contrahere*. See CONTRACT[2].

contract[2] *n.* a formal agreement, esp. one recognized as a legal obligation. WH: 12–14C. Old French (Modern French *contrat*), from Latin *contractus*, p.p. (used as n.) of *contrahere*, from CON- + *trahere* to draw.

contractor *n.* a person who undertakes a contract, esp. to do or supply something for a specified sum. WH: 16C. Late Latin, from Latin *contractus* (see CONTRACT[2]), or direct from CONTRACT[1]. See also -OR.

contradict *v.t.* to deny the truth of (a statement etc.). *Also v.i.* WH: 16C. Latin *contradictus*, p.p. of *contradicere*, orig. *contra dicere* to speak against.

contradictory *a.* affirming the contrary. *Also n.* WH: 14–15C. Late Latin *contradictorius*. See CONTRADICT, also -ORY[2].

contradistinguish *v.t.* to distinguish by contrasting opposite qualities. WH: 17C. CONTRA- + DISTINGUISH.

contraflow *n.* a form of motorway traffic regulation, two-way traffic being instituted on one carriageway so that the other may be closed. WH: mid-20C. CONTRA- + FLOW.

contrail *n.* a condensation trail. WH: mid-20C. Contr. of *condensation trail*. See CONDENSE, TRAIL.

contraindicate *v.t.* to indicate the unsuitability of (a particular treatment or drug). WH: 17C. CONTRA- + INDICATE.

contralto *n.* the lowest of the three principal varieties of the female voice, the part next above the alto in choral music. *Also a.* WH: 18C. Italian. See CONTRA-, ALTO. Cp. COUNTERTENOR.

contraposition *n.* the act of placing opposite or in contrast to. WH: 16C. Late Latin *contrapositio, contrapositionis*, from *contrapositus*, p.p. of *contraponere*, from CONTRA- + *ponere* to place. See also -ITION.

contraption *n.* a strange or improvised device. WH: 19C. Prob. from CONTRIVE on pattern of pair such as *conceive/ conception*, assoc. with TRAP[1].

contrapuntal *a.* of, relating to or in counterpoint. WH: 19C. Italian *contrapunto* (now *contrappunto*), from Medieval Latin *contrapunctum*. See COUNTERPOINT, also -AL[1].

contrary[1] *a.* opposite. *Also n., adv., v.t.* WH: 12–14C. Old French *contraire*, from Latin *contrarius*, from *contra* against. See also -ARY[1].

contrary[2] *a.* wayward, perverse. WH: 12–14C. CONTRARY[1].

contrast[1] *v.t.* to set in opposition, so as to show the difference between. *Also v.i.* WH: 15C. French *contraster*, from Italian *contrastare*, from Medieval Latin, from Latin CONTRA- + *stare* to stand.

contrast[2] *n.* unlikeness of things or qualities. WH: 16C. French *contraste*, from Italian *contrasto* strife, opposition, from *contrastare* to withstand, from Medieval Latin. See CONTRAST[1].

contra-suggestible *a.* reacting to a suggestion by doing the opposite. WH: early 20C. CONTRA- + *suggestible* (SUGGEST).

contrate *a.* (of a wheel) having teeth or cogs at right angles to the plane of the wheel. WH: 15C. Medieval Latin *contrata*. See COUNTRY.

contravallation *n.* a chain of fortifications constructed by besiegers around the besieged place. WH: 17C. French *contravallation* or Italian *contravallazione*, from Latin CONTRA- + *vallatio, vallationis*, from Late Latin *vallare* to entrench, from VALLUM. See WALL, also -ATION.

contravene *v.t.* to violate, to infringe. WH: 16C. Late Latin *contravenire*, from CONTRA- + *venire* to come.

contredanse *n.* a French version of the English country dance. WH: 19C. French, alt. of *country dance* (COUNTRY) by assoc. with *contre* against, opposite.

contretemps *n.* an unexpected event which throws everything into confusion. WH: 17C. French, orig. motion out of time, from *contre* against + *temps* time.

contribute *v.t.* to give for a common purpose. *Also v.i.* WH: 16C. Latin *contributus*, p.p. of *contribuere*, from CON- + *tribuere* to grant.

contrite *a.* deeply sorry for wrongdoing, full of remorse. WH: 12–14C. Old French, from Latin *contritus*, p.p. of *conterere*, from CON- + *terere* to rub, to grind. Cp. TRITE.

contrive *v.t.* to devise, to invent. *Also v.i.* WH: 12–14C. Old French *controver* (Modern French *controuver* to invent), from Medieval Latin *contropare* to compare, prob. from CON- + *tropus* TROPE.

control *n.* check, restraint. *Also v.t.* WH: 16C. French *contrôle*, from *contrôler*, from obs. *contreroller*, from Medieval Latin *contrarotulare*, from *contrarotulus* copy of a roll, from Latin *contra* against + *rotulus* ROLL.

controversy *n.* a dispute or debate, esp. one carried on in public over a long period of time. WH: 14–15C. Latin *controversia*, from *controversus* disputed, from *contro-*, var. of CONTRA- + *versus*, p.p. of *vertere* to turn. See also -Y[2].

controvert *v.t.* to dispute. WH: 16C. Latin *contro-*, var. of CONTRA- + *vertere*. See CONTROVERSY.

contumacious *a.* perverse, obstinate, stubborn. WH: 16C. Latin *contumacia*, from *contumax, contumacis*, ? from CON- + *tumere* to swell. See also -ACIOUS.

contumely *n.* rude, scornful abuse or reproach. WH: 14–15C. Old French *contumelie*, from Latin *contumelia*, prob. from CON- + *tumere* to swell.

contuse *v.t.* to bruise without breaking the skin. WH: 14–15C. Latin *contusus*, p.p. of *contundere*, from CON- + *tundere* to beat, to thump.

conundrum *n.* a riddle. WH: 16C. Orig. unknown. The word is perhaps a parody of some learned Latin term. Cp. PANJANDRUM. The original sense was crank, pedant.

conurbation *n.* a cluster of towns and urban districts that merge to form a densely populated area. WH: early 20C. CON- + Latin *urbs, urbis* city + -ATION. The term was proposed in 1915 by the Scottish sociologist Sir Patrick Geddes, a pioneer of town planning.

conure *n.* any parrot of the genus *Pyrrhura*, with a long tail. WH: 19C. Modern Latin *Conurus* former genus name, from Greek *kōnos* CONE + *oura* tail.

convalesce *v.i.* to recover health after illness, surgery etc. WH: 15C. Latin *convalescere*, from CON- + *valescere* to grow strong, from *valere* to be strong, to be well.

convection *n.* the propagation of heat or electricity through liquids and gases by the movement of the heated particles. WH: 17C. Latin *convectio, convectionis*, from *convectus*, p.p. of *convehere*, from CON- + *vehere* to carry. See also -ION. Not rel. to CONVEY.

convenance *n.* conventional usage or propriety. WH: 15C. French, from *convenir*, from Latin *convenire*. See CONVENE, also -ANCE.

convene *v.t.* to call together. *Also v.i.* WH: 14–15C. Latin *convenire* to assemble, to agree, from CON- + *venire* to come.

convenient *a.* suitable, opportune. WH: 14–15C. Latin *conveniens, convenientis*, pres.p. of *convenire*. See CONVENE, also -ENT.

convent *n.* a community of religious persons, now usu. nuns. WH: 12–14C. Old French (Modern French *couvent*), from Latin *conventus* assembly, company, p.p. (used as n.) of *convenire* CONVENE. Cp. COVIN.

conventicle *n.* a clandestine gathering, esp. for worship. WH: 14–15C. Latin *conventiculum* place of assembly, dim. of *conventus* meeting. See CONVENT.

convention *n.* an agreement, a treaty. WH: 14–15C. Old French, from Latin *conventio, conventionis* meeting, covenant, from *conventus*. See CONVENT, also -ION.

converge *v.i.* to tend towards one point. *Also v.t.* WH: 17C. Late Latin *convergere* to incline together, from CON- + *vergere* to bend, to turn.

conversant *a.* having knowledge acquired by study, use or familiarity. WH: 12–14C. Old French, pres.p. of *converser*. See CONVERSE[1], also -ANT.

conversation *n.* the act of conversing. WH: 12–14C. Old French, from Latin *conservatio, conservationis*, from *conversari* CONVERSE[1]. The original sense was living together, way of behaving. The current sense emerged in the 16C.

conversazione *n.* a social meeting devoted to literary, artistic or scientific subjects. WH: 18C. Italian CONVERSATION.

converse[1] *v.i.* to talk easily and informally (with) etc. WH: 14–15C. Old French *converser*, from Latin *conversari*, from CON- + *versare*, freq. of *vertere* to turn. The original sense was to live with. The current sense (relating to CONVERSATION) arose in the 17C.

converse[2] n. something opposite or contrary. *Also a.* WH: 14–15C. Old French *convers*, from Latin *conversus*, p.p. (used as n.) of *convertere* CONVERT[1].

conversion n. the act or an instance of converting. WH: 12–14C. Old French, from Latin *conversio, conversionis*, from *conversus*, p.p. of *convertere* CONVERT[1].

convert[1] v.t. to change from one physical state to another. *Also v.i.* WH: 12–14C. Old French *convertir*, from var. of Latin *convertere* to turn, from CON- + *vertere* to turn.

convert[2] n. a person who is converted from one religion, party, belief or opinion to another, esp. one who is converted to Christianity. WH: 16C. CONVERT[1].

convex a. having a curve or surface rounded like the outer side of a circle or sphere, as distinct from concave. *Also n.* WH: 16C. Latin *convexus* vaulted, arched.

convey v.t. to carry, to transport. *Also v.i.* WH: 12–14C. Old French *conveier* (Modern French *convoyer*), from Medieval Latin *conviare*, from CON- + *via* way. Cp. CONVOY.

convict[1] v.t. to prove guilty. *Also a.* WH: 12–14C. Latin *convictus*, p.p. of *convincere* CONVINCE.

convict[2] n. a criminal sentenced to a term in prison. WH: 15C. Orig. p.p. of CONVICT[1].

convince v.t. to satisfy the mind of. WH: 16C. Latin *convincere* to convict of error, from CON- + *vincere* to overcome, to conquer.

convivial a. festive, social, jovial. WH: 17C. Latin *convivialis*, from *convivium* feast, from CON- + *vivere* to live. See also -IAL.

convocation n. the act of calling together. WH: 14–15C. Latin *convocatio, convocationis*, from *convocatus*, p.p. of *convocare*. See CONVOKE, also -ATION.

convoke v.t. to call or summon together. WH: 16C. Latin *convocare* to call together, from CON- + *vocare* to call.

convolute a. rolled or coiled together. WH: 17C. Latin *convolutus*, p.p. of *convolvere*, from CON- + *volvere* to roll.

convoy v.t. to accompany in transit by land or sea, for the sake of protection, esp. with a warship. *Also n.* WH: 14–15C. Old French *convoyer*, var. of *conveier* CONVEY.

convulse v.t. to agitate violently. WH: 17C. Latin *convulsus*, p.p. of *convellere* to pull violently, from CON- + *vellere* to pluck, to pull.

cony n. a rabbit. WH: 12–14C. Old French *conin*, from Latin *cuniculus* rabbit, ? of Iberian orig. Cp. Basque *untxi* rabbit.

coo v.i. to make a soft low sound, like a dove or pigeon. *Also v.t., n., int.* WH: 17C. Imit.

co-occur v.i. to occur at the same time or in the same place. WH: mid-20C. CO- + OCCUR.

cooee n. a call used to attract attention. *Also int., v.i.* WH: 18C. Imit. of call used by Aborigines and adopted by settlers in Australia, from Australian Aboriginal (Dharuk) *guuu-wi*.

cook n. a person who prepares food for the table with the use of heat. *Also v.t., v.i.* WH: pre-1200. Old English *cōc*, from Popular Latin *cocus*, from Latin *coquus*.

cookie n. a sweet biscuit. WH: 18C. Dutch *koekje*, dim. of *koek* cake.

Cook's tour n. an extensive but very rapid tour. WH: early 20C. Thomas *Cook*, 1808–92, English travel agent.

cool a. slightly or moderately cold. *Also n., v.t., v.i.* WH: pre-1200. Old English *cōl*, from Germanic, from base also of COLD. Cp. German *kühl*.

coolabah n. any of several species of eucalyptus trees, esp. *Eucalyptus microtheca*. WH: 19C. Australian Aboriginal (Kamilaroi) *gulabaa*.

coolie n. an unskilled hired labourer in or from the East, esp. India and China. WH: 16C. Hindi and Telugu *kūlī* day labourer, prob. from Tamil *kūli* to hire, assoc. with Urdu *ḵulī* slave, from Turkish.

coom n. refuse matter, such as soot, coal-dust or mould. WH: 16C. Appar. var. of CULM[2].

coon n. a raccoon. WH: 18C. Abbr. of RACCOON.

coon-can n. a card game like rummy. WH: 19C. ? Spanish *¿con quién?* with whom?

coop n. a cage or small enclosure for poultry or small animals. *Also v.t.* WH: 12–14C. Middle Low German *kūpe*, from Latin *cupa* tun, barrel.

co-op n. a cooperative society, business venture, or shop. *Also a.* WH: 19C. Abbr. of *cooperative*. See COOPERATE.

cooper n. a person whose trade is to make barrels, tubs etc. *Also v.t., v.i.* WH: 12–14C. Middle Low German *kūper*. See COOP, also -ER[1].

cooperate v.i. to work or act with another or others for a common end. WH: 16C. Ecclesiastical Latin *cooperatus*, p.p. of *cooperari*, from CO- + *operari* OPERATE. See also -ATE[3].

co-opt v.t. to elect onto a committee etc. by the votes of the members of that committee etc., as opposed to by the votes of a larger body of voters. WH: 17C. Latin *cooptare*, from CO- + *optare* to choose.

coordinate[1] a. of the same order, importance etc. *Also n.* WH: 17C. CO- + Latin *ordinatus* (ORDINATE), based on SUBORDINATE[1].

coordinate[2] v.t. to make coordinate. *Also v.i.* WH: 17C. CO- + Latin *ordinare* (ORDINATE), based on SUBORDINATE[2].

coot n. a small black British aquatic bird, *Fulica atra*, or any other bird of the same genus. WH: 12–14C. Prob. Low German in orig. Cp. Dutch *koet*.

cootie n. a body louse. WH: early 20C. ? Malay *kutu* a biting insect.

co-own v.t. to own jointly. WH: early 20C. Back-formation from *co-owner*, from CO- + *owner* (OWN[2]).

cop[1] v.t. to seize. *Also n.* WH: 18C. Prob. var. of CAP.

cop[2] n. a conical roll or thread on the spindle of a spinning-machine. WH: pre-1200. Orig. unknown.

copacetic a. excellent, very satisfactory. WH: early 20C. Orig. unknown. According to some, the word is from the Hebrew phrase *kōl b'sēder* all in order, or *kōl b'sēdeḵ* all with justice.

copaiba n. the balsam or gum-resin obtained from the plant *Copaifera officinalis* or allied species. WH: 17C. Portuguese *copáiba*, from Tupi *copaíba*.

copal n. a resin obtained from any of a number of tropical trees. WH: 16C. Spanish, from Nahuatl *copalli* incense.

coparcener n. a coheir or coheiress. WH: 14–15C. CO- + *parcener* (PARCENARY).

copartner n. a partner, an associate. WH: 14–15C. CO- + PARTNER.

cope[1] v.i. to encounter, to contend successfully (with). WH: 12–14C. Old French *colper* to strike, to cut (Modern French *couper*), from *colp* blow, from Medieval Latin *colpus*. See COUP[1]. Cp. COUP[2]. The original sense was literal. The current figurative sense dates from the 17C.

cope[2] n. an ecclesiastical sleeveless vestment worn in processions and at solemn ceremonies. *Also v.t., v.i.* WH: 12–14C. Medieval Latin *cupa*, from Late Latin var. of *cappa* CAP.

cope[3] v.t. to buy. *Also v.i.* WH: 14–15C. Low German *kōpen*. See CHEAP.

copeck n. a Russian monetary unit and coin, the hundredth part of a rouble. WH: 17C. Russian *kopeĭka*, dim. of *kop'ë* lance. The coin originally bore the figure of a tsar (Ivan IV) bearing a lance.

copepod n. any of the many, usu. tiny, salt-water and freshwater crustaceans of the subclass Copepoda, some parasitic, others found in plankton. WH: 19C. Modern Latin *Copepoda* (pl.), from Greek *kōpē* handle, oar + -POD.

Copernican a. of or relating to the astronomical system of Copernicus, which has the sun as its centre. WH: 17C. Nicolaus *Copernicus*, 1473–1543, Polish astronomer + -AN.

co-pilot n. a second or assistant pilot of an aircraft. WH: early 20C. CO- + PILOT.

coping saw n. a saw consisting of a blade in a U-shaped frame, used for cutting curves in wood etc. too large for a fretsaw. WH: 16C. COPE[1] + -ING[1] + SAW[1].

copious a. plentiful, abundant. WH: 14–15C. Old French *copieux* or Latin *copiosus*, from *copia*. See COPY, also -IOUS.

copita n. a tulip-shaped sherry glass. WH: 19C. Spanish, dim. of *copa*, from Popular Latin *cuppa* CUP.

coplanar a. lying on the same plane. WH: 19C. CO- + *planar* (PLANE[1]).

copolymer n. a polymer consisting of random or repeated sequences of more than one type of molecule. WH: mid-20C. CO- + POLYMER.

copper[1] n. a reddish-brown malleable, ductile metallic element, at. no. 29, chem. symbol Cu. *Also a., v.t.* WH: pre-1200. Old English *copor, coper*, from Germanic, from Late Latin *cuprum*, from Latin *cyprium* (*aes*) (metal) of Cyprus. Cp. German *Kupfer*. The metal is so named from its earliest known source.

copperas n. a green sulphate of iron, green vitriol. WH: 14–15C. Old French *couperose*, from Medieval Latin *cuprosa* flower of copper, ult. from Late Latin *cupri-*, comb. form of Latin *cuprum* copper + *rosa* ROSE, translating Greek *khalkanthon*.

coppice *n.* a small wood of small trees and undergrowth, cut periodically for firewood. *Also v.t., v.i.* WH: 14–15C. Old French *copeïz*, from Medieval Latin *colpus*. See COUP[1]. Cp. COPSE.

copra *n.* the dried kernel of the coconut, yielding coconut oil. WH: 16C. Portuguese and Spanish, from Malayalam *koppara*.

co-precipitation *n.* precipitation of more than one compound from a solution at the same time. WH: mid-20C. CO- + *precipitation* (PRECIPITATE[1]).

copresent *a.* present at the same time. WH: 19C. CO- + PRESENT[1].

copro- *comb. form* of or relating to or living on or among dung. WH: Greek *kopros* dung. See also -O-.

coprocessor *n.* a microprocessor which operates in conjunction with another processor in a computer by providing supplementary functions or performing specialized operations. WH: late 20C. CO- + *processor* (PROCESS[1]).

co-produce *v.t.* to produce (a film, play etc.) jointly with one or more other people. WH: mid-20C. CO- + PRODUCE[1].

coprolalia *n.* the obsessive repeated use of obscene language. WH: 19C. COPRO- + Greek *lalia* talk, prattle.

coprolite *n.* the fossil dung of various extinct animals, chiefly saurians, largely used as fertilizer. WH: 19C. COPRO- + -LITE.

coprology *n.* lewdness. WH: 19C. COPRO- + -LOGY.

coprophagan *n.* any insect belonging to the Coprophagi, lamellicorn beetles feeding on or living in dung. WH: 19C. Modern Latin *Coprophagi*, from COPRO- + Greek *phagein* to eat. See also -AN.

coprophilia *n.* morbid, esp. sexual, interest in excrement. WH: mid-20C. COPRO- + -PHILIA.

coprosma *n.* any of various evergreen Australasian shrubs or small trees of the genus *Coprosma*, which bear colourful berries. WH: 19C. Modern Latin *Coprosma*, from COPRO- + Greek *osmē* smell.

copse *n.* a coppice. *Also v.t.* WH: 16C. Contr. of COPPICE.

Copt *n.* an Egyptian at the time of the ancient Greek and Roman empires. WH: 17C. French *Copte* or Modern Latin *coptus*, from Arabic *al-ḳibṭ, al-ḳubṭ*, from Coptic *Gyptios*, from Greek *Aiguptios* Egyptian.

copula *n.* the word in a sentence or proposition which links the subject and predicate together. WH: 17C. Latin connection, linking of words, from CO- + *apere* to fasten. See also -ULE.

copulate[1] *v.i.* to have sexual intercourse. *Also v.t.* WH: 14–15C. Latin *copulatus*, p.p. of *copulare* to fasten together. See COPULA, also -ATE[3]. The original sense was to link together generally (to the 19C). The current specific sense dates from the 17C.

copulate[2] *a.* joined, connected. WH: 15C. Latin *copulatus*, p.p. of *copulare*. See COPULATE[1], also -ATE[2].

copy *n.* a transcript or imitation of an original. *Also v.t., v.i.* WH: 12–14C. Old French *copie*, from Latin *copia* abundance, plenty. The sense of transcript arose from Medieval Latin phrases such as *copiam describendi facere* to give the power of transcription, or *dare vel habere copiam legendi* to give or have the power of reading.

coq au vin *n.* a stew of chicken in red wine. WH: mid-20C. French cock in wine. See COCK[1], WINE.

coquelicot *n.* a name for any of the species of red-flowered field poppies. WH: 18C. French red poppy, var. of *coquerico* cock-a-doodle-do. The colour of the poppy flowers is compared with that of a cock's comb.

coquet *v.i.* to flirt (with). *Also a., n.* WH: 17C. French *coqueter*, dim. of COCK[1]. The noun was originally both masculine and feminine. The feminine subsequently became *coquette*. The allusion is to the cock's strutting gait and to its blatant courtship. Cp. COCKY[1].

coquilla *n.* the nut of *Attalea funifera*, a Brazilian palm, used in carving. WH: 19C. Appar. Spanish or Portuguese dim. of *coca* shell, from Old Spanish. See COQUINA.

coquina *n.* a type of soft, whitish limestone formed from broken shells and coral. WH: 19C. Spanish shellfish, cockle, or from Old Spanish *coca*, from Medieval Latin, from Latin *concha* shell.

coquito *n.* a Chilean nut-bearing palm tree, *Jubaea chilensis*. WH: 19C. Spanish, dim. of *coco* coconut.

cor[1] *int.* expressing surprise, amazement etc. WH: mid-20C. Alt. of *God*. Cp. GORBLIMEY.

cor[2] *n.* a horn. WH: 19C. French horn, from Latin *cornu*. French *cor anglais* is literally English horn, although said by some to derive from French *cor anglé* angled horn, with reference to the instrument's shape.

cor[3] *n.* a Hebrew measure, a homer. WH: 14–15C. Hebrew *kŏr*.

cor- *pref.* with, as in *correct, corrode*. WH: Latin pref., from COM- with *m* assim. to *r*.

coracle *n.* a light boat used in Wales and Ireland, made of wickerwork covered with leather or oiled cloth. WH: 16C. Welsh *corwgl, cwrwgl*. Cp. CURRACH.

coracoid *n.* a hooklike process of the scapula in mammals. *Also a.* WH: 18C. Modern Latin *coracoides*, from Greek *korakoeidēs* raven-like, from *korax* raven, crow. See also -OID. The projection resembles a crow's beak.

coradicate *a.* derived from the same root. WH: 19C. CO- + Latin *radicatus* rooted, from *radix, radicis* root.

coral *n.* the calcareous skeletal structure secreted by certain marine polyps or zoophytes of the class Anthozoa, deposited in masses on the bottom of the sea. *Also a.* WH: 12–14C. Old French (Modern French *corail*), from Latin *corallum, coralium*, from Greek *korallion*, ? of Semitic orig.

coram populo *adv.* in public. WH: 16C. Latin before the public, from *coram* in the presence of + abl. sing. of *populus* people.

coranto *n.* a rapid kind of dance. WH: 16C. Alt., by addition of Italian ending -*o*-, of COURANT.

corban *n.* among the ancient Jews, a thing consecrated to God. WH: 12–14C. Popular Latin, from Greek (New Testament) *korban*, from Hebrew *qorbān* offering, from *qāraḇ* to approach, to draw near.

corbeil *n.* a sculptured basket, esp. such as forms the ornamental summit of a pillar etc. WH: 18C. Old French *corbeille* basket, from Late Latin *corbicula*, dim. of *corbis* basket.

corbel *n.* a bracket or projection of stone, wood or iron projecting from a wall to support some superincumbent weight. *Also v.t.* WH: 14–15C. Old French crow, raven, corbel (Modern French *corbeau*), dim. of *corp*, from Latin *corvus*. The projection is so called because it suggests a raven's beak.

corbie *n.* a raven, a crow or a rook. WH: 14–15C. Old French *corb*, var. of *corp* (see CORBEL) + -*ie*-Y[3].

cord *n.* thick string or thin rope composed of several strands, or a piece of this. *Also v.t.* WH: 12–14C. Old French *corde*, from Latin *chorda*, from Greek *khordē* gut, string (of musical instrument). Cp. CHORD[2].

cordate *a.* heart-shaped. WH: 17C. Latin *cordatus*, from *cor, cordis* heart. See also -ATE[2].

Cordelier *n.* a Franciscan friar of the strictest rule (from the knotted rope worn round the waist). WH: 14–15C. Old French, from *cordelle*, dim. of *corde* CORD. The order is so called from the knotted cord worn round the waist.

cordial *a.* hearty, warm-hearted. *Also n.* WH: 12–14C. Medieval Latin *cordialis*, from Latin *cor, cordis* heart. See also -IAL.

cordiform *a.* heart-shaped. WH: 19C. Latin *cor, cordis* heart + -*i*- + -FORM.

cordillera *n.* a ridge or chain of mountains, esp. used (*in pl.*) of the Andes, and the continuation of these in Central America and Mexico. WH: 18C. Spanish, from *cordilla*, dim. of *cuerda*, from Latin *chorda* CORD.

cordite *n.* a smokeless explosive, prepared in stringlike grains. WH: 19C. CORD + -ITE[1]. The substance is so named from its stringlike appearance.

cordoba *n.* the basic monetary unit of Nicaragua, equal to 100 centavos. WH: early 20C. Fernando Fernández de *Córdoba, c.*1475–*c.*1525, Spanish governor of Nicaragua.

cordon *n.* a line or series of persons, posts or ships placed so as to guard or blockade a place. *Also v.t.* WH: 14–15C. Italian *cordone*, augm. of *corda* CORD and Old French *cordon*, dim. of *corde* CORD. See also -OON.

cordon bleu *a.* (of food or cookery) of the highest standard. *Also n.* WH: 18C. French blue ribbon, from *cordon* (see CORDON) + *bleu* BLUE. The original *cordon bleu* was the sky-blue ribbon worn by the Knights Grand Cross of the French order of the Holy Ghost, the highest order of chivalry under the Bourbon kings. The term then extended to other orders of excellence.

cordon sanitaire *n.* a line of guards surrounding a disease-infected area, to cut off communication and so prevent the spread of the disease. **WH:** 19C. French sanitary cordon, from *cordon* (see CORDON) + *sanitaire* SANITARY.

cordovan *n.* fine leather, esp. horsehide, orig. made at Cordova. **WH:** 16C. Spanish *cordován* (now *cordobán*), from *Córdova* (now *Córdoba*), a city in S Spain. Cp. CORDWAIN.

corduroy *n.* a stout-ribbed cotton cloth made with a pile. *Also a.* **WH:** 18C. Prob. from CORD + *duroy* name of a lightweight worsted material, of unknown orig. The word is popularly derived from French *corde du roi* king's cord or *couleur du roi* royal colour.

cordwain *n.* a kind of leather, finished as a black morocco, orig. from Córdoba in Spain. **WH:** 14–15C. Old French *cordewan, cordoan,* from *Cordoue,* Spanish *Córdova.* See CORDOVAN.

core *n.* the heart or inner part of anything. *Also v.t.* **WH:** 12–14C. Orig. uncertain. The word is perhaps from French *cœur,* Latin *cor* heart, or Old French *cor* horn.

coregent *n.* a joint ruler or governor. **WH:** 18C. CO- + REGENT.

coreligionist *n.* a person of the same religion. **WH:** 19C. CO- + RELIGION + -IST.

corella *n.* any of various small Australian cockatoos of the genus *Cacatua.* **WH:** 19C. Appar. Latinized form of Australian Aboriginal (Wiradhuri) *garila.*

coreopsis *n.* any of the many annual or perennial garden plants of the genus *Coreopsis,* with bright, mostly yellow flowers. **WH:** 18C. Modern Latin, from Greek *koris* bug + *opsis* appearance. The plant is so called from the shape of the seeds.

co-respondent *n.* a joint respondent in a lawsuit, esp. a divorce suit. **WH:** 19C. CO- + *respondent* (RESPOND).

corf *n.* formerly a basket, now usu. a wagon, for carrying ore or coal in mines. **WH:** 14–15C. Low German or Dutch *korf,* from Latin *corbis* basket.

corgi *n.* a small, smooth-haired, short-legged dog, orig. from Wales. **WH:** early 20C. Welsh, from *cor* dwarf + *ci* dog.

coriaceous *a.* made of or resembling leather. **WH:** 17C. Late Latin *coriaceus,* from CORIUM. See also -ACEOUS.

coriander *n.* an umbellifer, *Coriandrum sativum,* with aromatic and carminative seeds used as a spice in cooking. **WH:** 12–14C. Old French *coriandre,* from Latin *coriandrum,* from Greek *koriannon,* of unknown orig.

Corinthian *a.* of or relating to Corinth. *Also n.* **WH:** 16C. Latin *Corinthius,* from Greek *Korinthios,* from *Korinthos* Corinth, city of ancient and modern Greece.

Coriolis effect *n.* the apparent deflection, caused by the rotation of the earth, of a body moving relative to the earth, the deflection being to the right in the northern hemisphere and to the left in the southern hemisphere. **WH:** early 20C. Gustave-Gaspard *Coriolis,* 1792–1843, French engineer.

corium *n.* the innermost layer of the skin in mammals. **WH:** 19C. Latin skin, hide, leather.

cork *n.* a stopper for a bottle or cask. *Also a., v.t.* **WH:** 12–14C. Dutch and Low German *kork,* from Spanish *alcorque* cork-soled sandal, from Arabic *al-ḳurḳ,* from Latin *quercus* oak, cork-oak.

corm *n.* a bulblike, fleshy underground stem, sometimes called a solid bulb. **WH:** 19C. Modern Latin *cormus,* from Greek *kormos* trunk of a tree whose branches have been cut off.

cormorant *n.* any of the somewhat ducklike waterbirds of the genus *Phalacrocorax,* in Britain esp. *P. carbo,* a voracious seabird. **WH:** 12–14C. Old French *cormaran* (Modern French *cormoran*), from Medieval Latin *corvus marinus* sea raven. The final -*t* was added as with PEASANT, TYRANT etc.

corn¹ *n.* grain. *Also v.t.* **WH:** pre-1200. Old English, from Germanic, rel. to Latin *granum* GRAIN. Cp. German *Korn.*

corn² *n.* a horny excrescence on the foot or hand, produced by pressure over a bone. **WH:** 14–15C. Old French *cor,* from Latin *cornu* horn.

cornea *n.* the transparent forepart of the external coat of the eye, through which the rays of light pass. **WH:** 14–15C. Shortening of Medieval Latin *cornea tela* horny web, from Latin *corneus* CORNEOUS.

cornel *n.* a tree or shrub of the genus *Cornus,* which includes the cornelian cherry, *C. mas,* and the dogwood, *C. sanguinea.*

WH: 14–15C. Old French *corneille* (Modern French *cornouille*), from Latin *cornus.*

cornelian *n.* a variety of semi-transparent chalcedony. **WH:** 14–15C. Old French *corneline* (Modern French *cornaline*), ? rel. to Old French *corneille* CORNEL.

corneous *a.* horny. **WH:** 17C. Latin *corneus,* from *cornu* horn. See also -EOUS.

corner *n.* the place where two converging lines or surfaces meet. *Also v.t., v.i.* **WH:** 12–14C. Old French *cornier,* from Latin *cornu* horn, tip, corner. See also -ER².

cornet¹ *n.* a three-valved brass musical instrument shaped like a small trumpet. **WH:** 14–15C. Old French dim. of var. of Latin *cornu* horn. See also -ET¹.

cornet² *n.* the lowest commissioned officer in a cavalry regiment. **WH:** 16C. Old French *cornette,* dim. of *corne* horn, from alt. of Latin *cornua,* pl. of *cornu* horn. See also -ET¹. The officer is so named as he bore the colours, originally a standard tapering to a point.

cornetto *n.* an old woodwind instrument with finger holes and a cup-shaped mouthpiece. **WH:** 19C. Italian, dim. of CORNO.

cornice *n.* a moulded horizontal projection crowning a wall, entablature, pillar or other part of a building. **WH:** 16C. French *corniche,* from Italian *cornice,* prob. from Latin *cornix, cornicis* crow (cp. CORBEL), but blending with a deriv. of Greek *korōnis* coping-stone.

corniche *n.* a coast road, esp. one along the face of a cliff. **WH:** 19C. French. See CORNICE.

Cornish *a.* of or relating to Cornwall. *Also n.* **WH:** 14–15C. *Corn-,* from *Cornwall,* a county in SW England + -ISH¹.

corno *n.* a horn. **WH:** 19C. Italian, from Latin *cornu* horn.

cornu *n.* a hornlike process. **WH:** 17C. Latin horn.

cornucopia *n.* an abundant stock. **WH:** 16C. Late Latin, from Latin *cornu copiae* horn of plenty. The original cornucopia was a mythical horn that could provide whatever was desired. In Greek mythology, it was the horn of the goat Amalthaea, who suckled the infant Zeus.

cornuted *a.* horned or having hornlike projections. **WH:** 17C. Latin *cornutus* horned, from *cornu* horn + -ED.

corolla *n.* the inner whorl of two series of floral envelopes occurring in the more highly developed plants, the petals. **WH:** 17C. Latin, dim. of *corona* CROWN.

corollary *n.* an additional inference from a proposition. *Also a.* **WH:** 14–15C. Latin *corollarium* money paid for a garland, present, deduction, from COROLLA. See also -ARY¹.

corona¹ *n.* a disc or halo round the sun or the moon. **WH:** pre-1200. Latin CROWN.

corona² *n.* a kind of long cigar with straight sides. **WH:** 19C. Spanish *La Corona* the crown, orig. a proprietary name.

coronach *n.* in the Scottish Highlands and in Ireland, a dirge, a funeral lamentation. **WH:** 16C. Gaelic *corranach,* from *comhtogether* + *rànach* outcry.

coronagraph *n.* an optical instrument used to observe the sun's corona. **WH:** 19C. CORONA¹ + -GRAPH.

coronal¹ *a.* of or relating to a crown or the crown of the head. **WH:** 14–15C. French, or from Latin *coronalis,* from *corona* CROWN. See also -AL¹.

coronal² *n.* a circlet or coronet. **WH:** 14–15C. Appar. from Anglo-French *coroune* crown.

coronary *n.* a coronary thrombosis. *Also a.* **WH:** 17C. Latin *coronarius,* from *coronis.* See CORONAL¹, also -ARY¹.

coronation *n.* the act or ceremony of solemnly crowning a sovereign. **WH:** 14–15C. Old French, from Medieval Latin *coronatio, coronationis,* from *coronatus,* p.p. of *coronare* CROWN. See also -ATION.

coroner *n.* an officer of the Crown whose duty it is to inquire into cases of sudden or suspicious death, and to determine the ownership of treasure-trove. **WH:** 12–14C. Anglo-French *corouner,* from *coroune* CROWN (see -ER¹), from Latin title *custos placitorum coronae* guardian of the pleas of the crown. The coroner was originally an officer of the royal household responsible for safeguarding the private property of the Crown. The current sense emerged in the 17C.

coronet *n.* a little crown. **WH:** 14–15C. Old French *coronete,* dim. of *corone* CROWN. See also -ET¹.

co-routine *n.* part of a computer program functioning like a subroutine but which can be left and entered at any point. WH: late 20C. CO- + ROUTINE.

corozo *n.* a S American ivory-nut tree, *Phytelephas macrocarpa*, the source of vegetable ivory. WH: 18C. Spanish, var. of dial. *carozo* stone or core of fruit.

corporal[1] *n.* an army non-commissioned officer of the lowest grade. WH: 16C. Obs. var. of French *caporal*, or from Italian *caporale*, prob. from *corpo*, from Latin *corpus*, *corporis* body (of troops); assim. to Italian *capo* head. Cp. CORPORAL[2].

corporal[2] *a.* relating to the body. *Also n.* WH: 14–15C. Old French (Modern French *corporel*), from Latin *corporalis*, from *corpus*, *corporis* body. See also -AL[1].

corporate *a.* united in a body and acting as an individual. *Also n.* WH: 15C. Latin *corporatus*, p.p. of *corporare*, from *corpus*, *corporis* body. See also -ATE[2].

corporation *n.* a united body. WH: 14–15C. Late Latin *corporatio*, *corporationis*, from Latin *corporatus*. See CORPORATE, also -ATION. The sense prominent abdomen arose in the 18C under the influence of CORPULENT.

corporeal *a.* having a body. WH: 14–15C. Late Latin *corporealis*, from Latin *corporeus*, from *corpus*, *corporis* body. See also -AL[1].

corporeity *n.* material existence. WH: 17C. French *corporéité* or Medieval Latin *corporeitas*, from Latin *corporeus*. See CORPOREAL, also -ITY.

corposant *n.* a luminous electric body often seen on the masts and rigging on dark stormy nights; St Elmo's fire. WH: 16C. Old Spanish, Portuguese and Italian *corpo santo* holy body.

corps *n.* a body of troops having a specific function. WH: 16C. French, from Latin CORPUS.

corpse *n.* a dead body, esp. of a human being. WH: 12–14C. Alt. of CORSE based on Latin *corpus*, French *corps* body. The added *p* was at first mute, as in French, but began to be sounded from the 16C. The final *-e* was rare before the 19C, but was then added to differentiate from CORPS. The earliest sense was living body to the 18C, but the sense dead body was also current from the 14–15C.

corpulent *a.* excessively fat or fleshy. WH: 14–15C. Latin *corpulentus*, from *corpus* body. See also -ULENT.

corpus *n.* a body. WH: 14–15C. Latin body. The original sense was literal. The sense collection of writings dates from the 18C, and body of spoken or written material for linguistic analysis from the mid-20C.

corpuscle *n.* a cell, esp. a *white* or *red corpuscle*, suspended in the blood. WH: 17C. Latin *corpusculum*, dim. of *corpus*. See also -CULE.

corrade *v.t.* to wear down (rocks etc.), e.g. as a river does by mechanical force and solution. WH: 17C. Latin *corradere*, from COR- + *radere* to scrape.

corral *n.* an enclosure (orig. of emigrants' wagons in American Indian territory) for cattle, horses etc. or for defence. *Also v.t.* WH: 16C. Spanish and Portuguese *curral*. Cp. CRAWL[2], KRAAL.

correct *v.t.* to set right. *Also a.* WH: 12–14C. Latin *correctus*, p.p. of *corrigere*, from COR- + *regere* to lead straight, to direct.

corregidor *n.* the chief magistrate of a Spanish town. WH: 16C. Spanish, from *corregir*, from Latin *corrigere* CORRECT.

correlate *v.i.* to be reciprocally related. *Also v.t., a., n.* WH: 18C. Back-formation from *correlation* (16C), from Medieval Latin *correlatio*, *correlationis*, from Latin COR- + *relatio*, *relationis* RELATION.

correspond *v.i.* to be comparable or equivalent (to). WH: 14–15C. Old French *correspondre*, from Medieval Latin *correspondere*, from Latin COR- + *respondere* RESPOND.

corrida *n.* a bullfight. WH: 19C. Spanish course (of bulls). The full form is *corrida de toros* course of bulls. See COURSE, TOREADOR.

corridor *n.* a gallery or passage communicating with the apartments of a building. WH: 16C. French, from Italian *corridore*, alt. (by assim. to *corridore* runner) of *corridoio* running place, from *correre* to run, from Latin *currere*. The original sense was a covered way in a fortification. The sense then passed from outdoor covered way in the 17C to passage in a building in the 19C.

corrie *n.* a semicircular hollow or cirque in a mountainside, usu. surrounded in part by crags. WH: 16C. Gaelic and Old Irish *coire* cauldron, hollow.

corrigendum *n.* an error needing correction, esp. in a book. WH: 19C. Latin, neut. ger. of *corrigere* CORRECT.

corrigible *a.* capable of being corrected. WH: 14–15C. French, from Medieval Latin *corrigibilis*, from Latin *corrigere* CORRECT. See also -IBLE.

corroborate *v.t.* to confirm, to establish. WH: 16C. Latin *corroboratus*, p.p. of *corroborare*, from COR- + *roborare* to strengthen, from *robus*, *roboris* strength. See also -ATE[3].

corroboree *n.* a festive or warlike dance of the Australian Aborigines. WH: 18C. Australian Aboriginal (Dharuk) *garabari*. Not rel. to CORROBORATE.

corrode *v.t.* to consume gradually, esp. chemically. *Also v.i.* WH: 14–15C. Latin *corrodere*, from COR- + *rodere* to gnaw. Cp. RODENT.

corrugate[1] *v.t.* to contract or bend into wrinkles or folds. *Also v.i.* WH: 14–15C. Latin *corrugatus*, p.p. of *corrugare*, from COR- + *rugare*, from *ruga* wrinkle. See also -ATE[3].

corrugate[2] *a.* wrinkled. WH: 18C. Latin *corrugatus*. See CORRUGATE[1].

corrupt *a.* perverted by bribery or willing to be. *Also v.t., v.i.* WH: 12–14C. Old French, or from Latin *corruptus*, p.p. of *corrumpere* to destroy, to bribe, from COR- + *rumpere* to break.

corsac *n.* a small yellowish Asian fox, *Vulpes corsac*. WH: 19C. Russian *korsak*, from Turkic *karsak*.

corsage *n.* a flower or small bouquet or spray of flowers, usu. worn by a woman on the bodice or lapel of her dress. WH: 14–15C. Old French, from *cors* (Modern French CORPS) body. See also -AGE. The original sense was body in general, or size and shape of body. The sense of bodice dates from the 19C, and of posy from the early 20C.

corsair *n.* a pirate or a privateer, esp. formerly on the Barbary coast. WH: 16C. French *corsaire*, from Medieval Latin *cursarius*, from *cursa*, *cursus* hostile inroad, from Latin *cursus* COURSE.

corse *n.* a corpse. WH: 12–14C. Old French *cors* (Modern French CORPS). Cp. CORPSE. Two earlier senses, now both obsolete, were ribbon for ornamented girdle or garter to the 16C, and type of slender pillar to the 19C.

corset *n.* a close-fitting stiffened or elasticated undergarment worn by women to give a desired shape to the body. *Also v.t.* WH: 12–14C. Old French, dim. of *cors* body (Modern French CORPS). See also -ET[1]. Cp. BODICE.

Corsican *a.* of or relating to Corsica. *Also n.* WH: 18C. *Corsica*, an island in the Mediterrean + -AN.

corslet *n.* body armour. WH: 15C. Old French, dim. of *cors* body (Modern French CORPS). See also -LET.

cortege *n.* a procession, esp. at a funeral. WH: 17C. French *cortège*, from Italian *corteggio*, from *corteggiare* to attend court, from *corte* COURT.

Cortes *n.* the legislative assemblies of Spain and (formerly) Portugal. WH: 17C. Spanish and Portuguese, pl. of *corte* COURT.

cortex *n.* the layer of plant tissue between the vascular bundles and the epidermis. WH: 14–15C. Latin bark.

corticin *n.* an alkaloid obtained from the bark of the aspen. WH: 19C. Latin CORTEX, *corticis* bark + -IN[1].

cortico- *comb. form* of or relating to the cortex. WH: Latin CORTEX, *corticis* bark. See also -O-.

corticosteroid *n.* a steroid (e.g. cortisone) produced by the adrenal cortex, or a synthetic drug with the same actions. WH: mid-20C. CORTICO- + STEROID.

cortisone *n.* a corticosteroid, natural or synthetic, used to treat rheumatoid arthritis, allergies and skin diseases. WH: mid-20C. 17-hydroxy-11-dehydroxy*corticosterone*, chemical name. Cp. CORTICOSTEROID. It was originally named *Compound E* in 1936, but was renamed in 1949 by its discoverer, the US biochemist Edward C. Kendall.

corundum *n.* a rhombohedral mineral of great hardness, allied to the ruby and sapphire. WH: 18C. Tamil *kuruntam* or Telugu *kuruvindam*. Cp. CARBORUNDUM.

coruscate *v.i.* to sparkle, to glitter in flashes. WH: 18C. Latin *coruscatus*, p.p. of *coruscare* to vibrate, to glitter. See also -ATE[3].

corvee *n.* an obligation to perform a day's unpaid labour for a feudal lord, as the repair of roads etc. WH: 12–14C. Old French *corvée*, from Provençal *corroada*, from Latin *corrogata* (*opera*) requisitioned (work), from neut. pl. p.p. of *corrogare* to summon, from COR- + *rogare* to ask.

corvette *n.* a small, fast escort vessel armed with anti-submarine devices. WH: 17C. French, ult. dim. of Middle Dutch *korf* basket, type. See CORF, also -ETTE. The current sense dates from the mid-20C (World War II).

corvid *a.* corvine. Also *n.* WH: mid-20C. Modern Latin *Corvidae*, from Latin *corvus* raven. See also -ID.

corvine *a.* of or relating to the crows. WH: 17C. Latin *corvinus*, from *corvus* raven. See also -INE.

corybant *n.* a priest of Cybele, whose rites were accompanied with wild music and dancing. WH: 14–15C. Latin *Corybas, Corybantis*, from Greek *Korubas*, of unknown orig.

corylus *n.* any shrub of the genus *Corylus*, including the hazel. WH: 18C. Latin hazel.

corymb *n.* a raceme or panicle in which the stalks of the lower flowers are longer than those of the upper, so creating a flat-topped cluster. WH: 18C. French *corymbe* or Latin *corymbus*, from Greek *korumbos* summit, cluster of flowers.

coryphaeus *n.* the leader of a chorus in a classical play. WH: 17C. Latin, from Greek *koruphaios* chief, chorus leader, from *koruphē* head, top.

coryphée *n.* a chief dancer in a corps de ballet. WH: 19C. French CORYPHAEUS.

coryza *n.* nasal catarrh. WH: 16C. Latin, from Greek *koruza* nasal mucus, catarrh.

cos[1] *n.* a curly variety of lettuce introduced from the island of Cos in the Aegean. WH: 17C. *Cos*, one of the Dodecanese islands, in the Aegean Sea.

cos[2] *abbr.* cosine. WH: 18C. Abbr. of COSINE.

'cos *conj.* because. WH: 19C. Alt. of 'CAUSE.

Cosa Nostra *n.* the branch of the Mafia operating in the US. WH: mid-20C. Italian our thing, from *cosa* thing + *nostra*, fem. of *nostro* our.

cosec *abbr.* cosecant. WH: 18C. Abbr. of COSECANT.

cosecant *n.* the secant of the complement of an arc or angle. WH: 18C. Modern Latin *consecans, cosecantis*. See CO- + SECANT.

cosech *abbr.* hyperbolic cosecant. WH: 19C. COSECANT + *h* (for *hyperbolic* (HYPERBOLE)). Cp. COSH[2], COTH, SINH, TANH.

coseismal *a.* relating to the points simultaneously affected by an earthquake. Also *n.* WH: 19C. CO- + *seismal* (SEISMIC).

coset *n.* a set which forms a given larger set when added to another one. WH: early 20C. CO- + SET[2].

cosh[1] *n.* a heavy blunt weapon for hitting people with, e.g. a length of metal or hard rubber. Also *v.t.* WH: 19C. Orig. unknown.

cosh[2] *abbr.* hyperbolic cosine. WH: 19C. COS[2] + *h* (for *hyperbolic* (HYPERBOLE)).

coshering *n.* an Irish custom whereby the lord was entitled to exact from his tenant food and lodging for himself and his followers. WH: 16C. Irish *cóisir* feast + -ING[1].

co-signatory *n.* a person who signs jointly with others. WH: 19C. CO- + *signatory* (SIGNATURE).

cosine *n.* the sine of the complement of an arc or angle. WH: 17C. CO- + SINE[1].

cosmetic *a.* beautifying. Also *n.* WH: 17C. French *cosmétique*, from Greek *kosmētikos*, from *kosmein* to arrange, to adorn, from *kosmos* COSMOS[1]. See also -IC.

cosmic *a.* of or relating to the universe, esp. as distinguished from the earth. WH: 17C. COSMOS[1] + -IC.

cosmo- *comb. form* of or relating to the universe. WH: Greek *kosmos* COSMOS[1]. See also -O-.

cosmogony *n.* a theory, investigation or dissertation respecting the origin of the world. WH: 17C. Greek *kosmogonia* creation of the world, from *kosmos* COSMOS[1] + -*gonia* generation, production + -Y[2].

cosmography *n.* a description or delineation of the features of the universe, or of the earth as part of the universe. WH: 14–15C. French *cosmographie* or Late Latin *cosmographia*, from Greek *kosmographia*. See COSMO-, -GRAPHY.

cosmology *n.* the science which investigates the evolution and structure of the universe as an ordered whole. WH: 17C. French *cosmologie* or Modern Latin *cosmologia*. See COSMO-, -LOGY.

cosmonaut *n.* an astronaut, esp. in the former Soviet Union. WH: mid-20C. Russian *kosmonavt*, from *kosmo-* COSMO- + -*navt*, -*naut* as in AERONAUT. Cp. *astronaut* (ASTRONAUTICS).

cosmopolis *n.* a city inhabited by people from many different countries. WH: 19C. COSMO- + POLIS.

cosmopolitan *a.* at home in any part of the world. Also *n.* WH: 17C. Greek *kosmopolitēs*, from *kosmo-* COSMO- + *politēs* citizen + -AN. Cp. METROPOLITAN.

cosmos[1] *n.* the universe regarded as an ordered system. WH: 12–14C. Greek *kosmos* order, ornament, world.

cosmos[2] *n.* any plant of the tropical American genus *Cosmos*, grown in gardens for their showy flowers. WH: 19C. Modern Latin, from Greek *kosmos* ornament. See COSMOS[1].

cosmotron *n.* an electrical apparatus for accelerating protons to high energies. WH: mid-20C. COSMO- + -TRON.

co-sponsor *n.* a joint sponsor. Also *v.t.* WH: early 20C. CO- + SPONSOR.

Cossack *n.* a member of a people, probably of mixed Turkish origin, living on the southern steppes of Russia, and formerly furnishing light cavalry to the Russian army. WH: 16C. Russian *kazak*, from Turkic nomad, adventurer. Cp. KAZAKH.

cosset *v.t.* to pet, to pamper. Also *n.* WH: 16C. ? Anglo-French *coscet, cozet* cottager. If this is the origin, the reference would be to a lamb kept in a cottage and raised by the cottager's family. Cp. II Sam. xii.3.

cossie *n.* a swimming costume. WH: early 20C. Abbr. of COSTUME + -*ie* -Y[3].

cost *v.t.* to require as the price of possession or enjoyment. Also *v.i., n.* WH: 14–15C. Old French *coster, couster* (Modern French *coûter*), from var. of Latin *constare* to stand firm, to be fixed, from CON- + *stare* to stand. Cp. CONSTANT.

costa *n.* a rib. WH: 19C. Latin rib.

co-star *n.* a star appearing (in a film) with another star. Also *v.i., v.t.* WH: early 20C. CO- + STAR.

costard *n.* a large, round apple. WH: 12–14C. Anglo-French, from *coste* rib, from Latin COSTA. See also -ARD. The reference is to the apple's ribs. The word was a slang term for head from the 16C. Hence the children's taunt *cowardy custard* in the 19C.

Costa Rican *n.* a native or inhabitant of Costa Rica. Also *a.* WH: 19C. *Costa Rica*, a country of Central America + -AN.

cost-efficient *a.* giving a satisfactory return on the initial outlay. WH: mid-20C. COST + EFFICIENT.

coster *n.* a seller of fruit, vegetables etc., esp. from a street barrow. Also *a.* WH: 16C. COSTARD + MONGER. The word was originally used of an apple-seller. The abbreviation *coster* dates from the 19C.

costive *a.* having the motion of the bowels too slow, constipated. WH: 14–15C. Old French *costivé*, from Latin *constipatus*. See CONSTIPATE.

costmary *n.* an aromatic plant of the aster family, *Chrysanthemum balsamita*, cultivated for use in flavouring. WH: 14–15C. From the original name *cost* (from Latin *costum* or Greek *kostos*, from Arabic *ḳusṭ*, from Sanskrit *kuṣṭha*) + (St) Mary. Cp. ROSEMARY.

costume *n.* dress. Also *v.t.* WH: 18C. French, from Italian custom, fashion, habit, from Latin *consuetudo, consuetudinis*. See CUSTOM. The original sense was the custom and fashion proper for a historical or literary scene. The current sense dates from the 19C. Cp. HABIT.

cosy *a.* comfortable, snug. Also *n., v.t.* WH: 18C. Orig. unknown. ? from Scandinavian. Cp. Norwegian *koselig* cosy.

cot[1] *n.* a small bed with high barred sides for a young child. WH: 17C. Hindi *khāṭ* bedstead, couch, hammock.

cot[2] *n.* a cottage or hut. Also *v.t.* WH: pre-1200. Old English, from Germanic base rel. to that of COTE. Cp. COTTAGE.

cot[3] *abbr.* cotangent. WH: 18C. Abbr. of COTANGENT.

cotangent *n.* the tangent of the complement of an arc or angle. WH: 17C. CO- + TANGENT.

cote *n.* a sheepfold, or any small house or shelter for birds or animals. WH: pre-1200. Old English, from Germanic base rel. to that of COT[2]. Cp. COTTAGE.

cotenant *n.* a joint tenant. WH: 19C. CO- + TENANT.

coterie *n.* a set of people associated together for friendly conversation. WH: 18C. Old French, ult. from Middle Low German *kote* COTE. See also -ERY. The original Old French sense was a group of tenants holding land together.

coth *abbr.* hyperbolic cotangent. WH: 19C. COT[3] + *h* (for *hyperbolic* (HYPERBOLE)).

cothurnus *n.* the buskin worn by actors in ancient Greek and Roman tragedy. WH: 18C. Latin, from Greek *kothornos*.

co-tidal *a.* having the tides at the same time. WH: 19C. CO- + *tidal* (TIDE).

cotillion *n.* an 18th-cent. French ballroom dance for four or eight people. WH: 18C. French *cotillon* petticoat, dance, dim. of *cotte* COAT. Cp. COTTA. The dance is presumably so named from the costumes worn by women in the original peasant dance on which it is said to be based.

cotinga *n.* any bird of the tropical Central and S American family Cotingidae, the males of many species of which have bright plumage, naked patches of bright skin, peculiar wattles etc. WH: 18C. French, from Tupi *cutinga*, from *tinga* white.

cotoneaster *n.* an ornamental shrub of the genus *Cotoneaster*, belonging to the order Rosaceae. WH: 18C. Modern Latin, from Latin *cotoneum* QUINCE + -ASTER.

Cotswold *n.* a breed of sheep, formerly peculiar to the counties of Gloucester, Worcester and Hereford. WH: 16C. *Cotswold* Hills, mainly in Gloucestershire.

cotta *n.* a short surplice. WH: 19C. Italian, from Medieval Latin, from base also of COAT.

cottage *n.* a small country or suburban residence. *Also v.i.* WH: 14–15C. Anglo-French *cotage* or Anglo-Latin *cotagium*, from COT², COTE. See also -AGE. A cottage was originally a small dwelling for poor country people. The current sense, not implying poverty, dates from the 18C.

cottar *n.* a Scottish farm labourer living in a cottage belonging to a farm and paying rent in the form of labour. WH: pre-1200. COT² + -ER¹ (Scottish -*ar*). Cp. COTTIER.

cotter *n.* a key, wedge or bolt for holding part of a machine in place. WH: 12–14C. Orig. unknown. ? A shortening of *cotterel* hook or bar from which a pot is hung.

cottier *n.* a peasant living in a cottage. WH: 12–14C. Old French *cotier*, ult. from Germanic base also of COT². See also -IER.

cotton *n.* a downy substance resembling wool, growing in the fruit of the cotton plant, used for making thread, cloth etc. *Also a., v.t., v.i.* WH: 14–15C. Old French *coton*, from Arabic *kuṭn*.

cotyledon *n.* the rudimentary leaf of an embryo in the higher plants, the seed-leaf. WH: 16C. Latin navelwort, from Greek *kotulēdōn* cup-shaped cavity, from *kotulē* cup, socket.

couch¹ *n.* a long upholstered seat with a back, for more than one person. *Also v.t., v.i.* WH: 12–14C. Old French *couche*, from Latin *collocare*. See COLLOCATE. The original sense of the verb (to the 18C) was to lay down flat, to set in place, esp. horizontally.

couch² *n.* couch grass. *Also v.t.* WH: 16C. Var. of QUITCH.

couchant *a.* (of an animal) lying down with the head raised. WH: 14–15C. Old French, pres.p. of *coucher* COUCH¹. See also -ANT.

couchette *n.* a seat in a continental train which converts into a sleeping berth. WH: early 20C. French little bed. See COUCH¹, also -ETTE.

coudé *a.* (of a reflecting telescope) in which light rays are bent by mirrors to a point of focus, e.g. on a photographic plate, off the axis of the telescope. *Also n.* WH: 19C. French, p.p. of *couder* to bend at right angles, from *coude* elbow, from Latin *cubitum* CUBIT.

Couéism *n.* a therapeutic system based on auto-suggestion. WH: early 20C. Émile *Coué*, 1857–1926, French psychologist + -ISM.

cougar *n.* the puma. WH: 18C. French *couguar*, abbr. of Modern Latin *cuguacarana*, from alt. of Tupi *çuçuarana*, lit. false deer, from *suasú* deer + *rana* false. The cougar is so called because it resembles a deer but has a coat of a different colour.

cough *n.* a convulsive effort, accompanied by noise, to expel foreign or irritating matter from the lungs. *Also v.t., v.i.* WH: 12–14C. From imit. base represented by Old English *cohhetan* to shout. Cp. German *keuchen* to pant.

coulee *n.* a molten or solidified lava flow. WH: 19C. French *coulée* flow, from *couler* to flow, from Latin *colare* to filter, to strain, from *colum* strainer.

coulis *n.* a thin purée. WH: 19C. French, from Old French *coleiz*, from Latin *colare* to strain, to flow. The word was formerly current in English as *cullis* (14–15C), but was then used for a type of broth or gravy made from meat or fish, not a sieved sauce made of vegetables or fruit, as now.

coulisse *n.* a grooved timber in which a sluice-gate or a partition slides. WH: 19C. French, use as n. of fem. of *coulis* sliding. See CULLIS. Cp. PORTCULLIS.

couloir *n.* a steep gully or long, narrow gorge on a precipitous mountainside. WH: 19C. French channel, from *couler* to pour, from Latin *colare* to filter + -*oir* -ORY¹.

coulomb *n.* a unit of electrical charge, equal to the quantity of electricity transferred by one ampere in one second. WH: 19C. Charles-Augustin de *Coulomb*, 1736–1806, French physicist.

coulometry *n.* a method of quantitative chemical analysis involving the measurement of the number of coulombs used in electrolysis. WH: early 20C. COULOMB + -METRY.

coulter *n.* the iron blade fixed in front of the share in a plough. WH: pre-1200. Latin *culter* knife, ploughshare.

coumarin *n.* an aromatic crystalline substance extracted from the tonka bean and other plants, used in flavourings and as an anticoagulant. WH: 19C. French *coumarine*, from *coumarou*, from Portuguese and Spanish *cumarú*, from Tupi tonka bean. See also -IN¹.

coumarone *n.* a colourless aromatic liquid obtained from coal tar, used in the production of synthetic resins for use in paints and varnishes, adhesives etc. WH: 19C. COUMARIN + -ONE.

council *n.* a number of people met together for deliberation or some administrative purpose. *Also a.* WH: pre-1200. Anglo-French *cuncile*, *concilie*, from Latin *concilium* assembly, meeting, from CON- + *calare* to call, to summon. Not rel. to COUNSEL.

counsel *n.* advice. *Also v.t.* WH: 12–14C. Old French *cunseil* (Modern French *conseil*), from Latin *consilium* consultation, deliberating body. See CONSULT.

count¹ *v.t.* to reckon up in numbers, to total. *Also v.i., n.* WH: 14–15C. Old French *cunter* to reckon, to relate (Modern French *compter* to reckon, *conter* to relate), from Latin *computare* COMPUTE.

count² *n.* a foreign title of rank corresponding to a British earl. WH: 14–15C. Old French *conte* (Modern French *comte*), from Latin *comes*, *comitis* companion, overseer, from COM- + *itus*, p.p. of *ire* to go. Old French *conte* was used to render English EARL.

countenance *n.* the face. *Also v.t.* WH: 12–14C. Old French *contenance* bearing, behaviour, contents, from *contenir*. See CONTAIN, also -ANCE. The original sense to the 18C was bearing, demeanour, and to the 19C appearance, aspect. The current sense of face dates from the 14–15C.

counter¹ *n.* a table or desk over which business is conducted (in a shop, bank, library, cafe etc.). WH: 12–14C. Old French *conteoir* (Modern French *comptoir*), from Medieval Latin *computatorium*, from Latin *computare* COMPUTE. See also -ER². A counter was originally (to the 16C) a table or desk for counting money. The current sense dates from the 17C.

counter² *n.* the opposite, the contrary. *Also a., adv., v.t., v.i.* WH: 14–15C. COUNTER-.

counter- *comb. form* in return, duplicating. WH: Anglo-French *countre-* or Old French *contre-*, from Latin CONTRA¹.

counteract *v.t.* to act in opposition to. WH: 17C. COUNTER- + ACT.

counter-attack *v.t., v.i.* to make an attack after an attack by an enemy or opponent. *Also n.* WH: 19C. COUNTER- + ATTACK.

counter-attraction *n.* attraction in an opposite direction. WH: 18C. COUNTER- + *attraction* (ATTRACT).

counterbalance¹ *v.t.* to weigh against or oppose with an equal weight or effect. WH: 16C. COUNTER- + BALANCE. The original sense was to weigh or balance one thing against another. The current sense dates from the 17C.

counterbalance² *n.* an equal weight or force acting in opposition. WH: 16C. COUNTER- + BALANCE. The original sense was the opposite side of a balance. The current sense dates from the 17C.

counterblast *n.* an argument or statement in opposition. WH: 16C. COUNTER- + BLAST. The original sense was probably a blast blown on a trumpet in answer to a challenge.

counterchange *n.* exchange, reciprocation. *Also v.t., v.i.* WH: 16C. French *contrechange*. See COUNTER-, CHANGE.

countercharge *n.* a charge in opposition to another. *Also v.t.* WH: 18C. COUNTER- + CHARGE.

countercheck *n.* a check brought against another. *Also v.t.* WH: 16C. COUNTER- + CHECK¹.

counter-claim *n.* a claim made against another claim, esp. a claim brought forward by a defendant against a plaintiff. *Also v.t., v.i.* WH: 18C. COUNTER- + CLAIM.

counter-clockwise *adv.* anticlockwise. WH: 19C. COUNTER- + *clockwise* (CLOCK[1]).

counter-culture *n.* a way of life deliberately contrary to accepted social usages. WH: late 20C. COUNTER- + CULTURE.

counter-espionage *n.* work of an intelligence service directed against the agents of another country. WH: 19C. COUNTER- + ESPIONAGE.

counterexample *n.* an example or fact that does not fit a proposed theory, and which is used as an argument against it. WH: 18C. COUNTER- + EXAMPLE.

counterfeit *a.* made in imitation with intent to be passed off as genuine. *Also n., v.t., v.i.* WH: 14–15C. Old French *contrefait*, p.p. of *contrefaire*, from Medieval Latin *contrafacere*, from CONTRA- + *facere* to make.

counterfoil *n.* the counterpart of a cheque, receipt or other document, retained by the giver. WH: 18C. COUNTER- + FOIL[1].

counterfort *n.* a buttress, arch or oblique wall built against a wall or terrace to retain, support or strengthen it. WH: 16C. French *contrefort*, from Old French *contreforcier* prop, buttress.

counter-insurgency *n.* actions taken by a government, police force, army etc. to counter rebellion etc. WH: mid-20C. COUNTER- + *insurgency* (INSURGENT).

counterintelligence *n.* work of an intelligence service designed to prevent or damage intelligence gathering by an enemy intelligence service. WH: mid-20C. COUNTER- + INTELLIGENCE.

counter-intuitive *a.* going against what one intuitively feels to be right. WH: mid-20C. COUNTER- + *intuitive* (INTUITION).

counterirritant *n.* an irritant applied to the body to remove or lessen some other irritation. *Also a.* WH: 19C. COUNTER- + *irritant* (IRRITATE).

countermand *v.t.* to revoke, to annul. *Also n.* WH: 14–15C. Old French *contremander*, from Medieval Latin *contramandare*, from Latin CONTRA- + *mandare* to command.

countermarch *v.i.* to march in an opposite direction. *Also v.t., n.* WH: 16C. COUNTER- + MARCH[1].

countermeasure *n.* an action taken to counter a danger, thwart an enemy etc. WH: early 20C. COUNTER- + MEASURE.

countermine *n.* a gallery or mine to intercept or frustrate a mine made by the enemy. *Also v.t., v.i.* WH: 14–15C. COUNTER- + MINE[2].

countermove *n.* a movement in an opposite or contrary direction, or in opposition or retaliation. *Also v.i.* WH: 19C. COUNTER- + MOVE.

counter-offensive *n.* a counter-attack. WH: mid-20C. COUNTER- + *offensive* (OFFEND).

counteroffer *n.* a second, usu. lower, offer by a seller attempting to close a deal. WH: 18C. COUNTER- + OFFER.

counterpane *n.* a bedcover. WH: 17C. Alt. of obs. *counterpoint*, from Old French *contrepoint*, from alt. of Medieval Latin *culcita puncta*, from *culcita* cushion, mattress + *puncta*, fem. of *punctus*, p.p. of Latin *pungere* to prick, with -*point* assim. to PANE.

counterpart *n.* a person who is exactly like another in character, role etc. WH: 14–15C. COUNTER- + PART, based on Old French *contrepartie*.

counterplot *n.* a plot to defeat another plot. *Also v.t., v.i.* WH: 16C. COUNTER- + PLOT.

counterpoint *n.* a melodious part or combination of parts written to accompany a melody. *Also v.t.* WH: 14–15C. Old French *contrepoint*, from Medieval Latin *contrapunctum*, *cantus contrapunctus* song pricked opposite (i.e. to the original melody), from CONTRA- + Medieval Latin *punctus*, p.p. (used as n.) of Latin *pungere* to prick. 'Prick' means mark, write down, as distinct from music that was extemporized or traditional, as plainchant was.

counterpoise *n.* a weight in opposition and equal to another. *Also v.t.* WH: 14–15C. Old French *contrepeis*, *contrepois* (Modern French *contrepoids*). See COUNTER-, POISE[1].

counter-productive *a.* producing an opposite, or undesired, result. WH: mid-20C. COUNTER- + *productive* (PRODUCT).

counterproof *n.* in printing, a reversed impression taken from another just printed. WH: 17C. COUNTER- + PROOF.

counterproposal *n.* a proposal made as an alternative to a previous proposal. WH: 19C. COUNTER- + *proposal* (PROPOSE).

counterpunch *n.* a punch given in return. *Also v.i.* WH: 17C. COUNTER- + PUNCH[1].

counter-reformation *n.* a reformation of an opposite nature to or as a reaction to another. WH: 19C. COUNTER- + *reformation* (REFORM).

counter-revolution *n.* a revolution opposed to a former one, and designed to restore a former state of things. WH: 18C. COUNTER- + REVOLUTION.

counterscarp *n.* the exterior wall or slope of the ditch in a fortification, opposite the *scarp*. WH: 16C. French *contrescarpe*, from Italian *controscarpa*. See CONTRA-, SCARP[1].

countershaft *n.* an intermediate shaft driven by the main shaft and transmitting motion. WH: 19C. COUNTER- + SHAFT.

countersign *v.t.* to attest the correctness of by an additional signature. *Also n.* WH: 17C. French *contresigner*. See COUNTER-, SIGN.

countersink *v.t.* to chamfer (a hole) for a screw or bolt head. *Also n.* WH: 18C. COUNTER- + SINK.

counterstroke *n.* a stroke made in return. WH: 16C. COUNTER- + STROKE[1].

countertenor *n.* (a singer with) a voice higher than tenor, a male alto voice. WH: 14–15C. Old French *contretenor*, from obs. *contratenore*. See COUNTER-, TENOR. A countertenor was originally a part written against that for a tenor in the same range. Cp. CONTRALTO.

counterterrorism *n.* terrorism carried out to prevent or in retaliation for acts of terrorism by others. WH: mid-20C. COUNTER- + *terrorism* (TERROR).

countervail *v.t.* to act against with equal effect or power. *Also v.i.* WH: 14–15C. Anglo-French *countrevaloir*, from Latin *contra valere* to be of worth against. See CONTRA-, VAIL[2].

countervalue *n.* an equivalent value. WH: 17C. COUNTER- + VALUE.

counterweigh *v.t.* to counterbalance. WH: 14–15C. COUNTER- + WEIGH. Cp. COUNTERPOISE.

counterwork *v.t.* to work against. *Also n.* WH: 16C. COUNTER- + WORK.

country *n.* a territory or state. WH: 12–14C. Old French *cuntrée* (Modern French *contrée*), from Medieval Latin *contrata* (*terra*) (land) lying opposite (i.e. spread out before one), from Latin *contra* opposite. See also -Y[2].

county *n.* a division of land for administrative, judicial and political purposes. *Also a.* WH: 12–14C. Anglo-French *counté*, from Old French *conté* (Modern French *comté*), from Latin *comitatus*, from *comes*, *comitis*. See COUNT[2], also -Y[2]. The original sense was the territory of a count. Anglo-French *counté* was used by Normans in Britain as the equivalent of English SHIRE.

coup[1] *n.* a stroke, a telling or decisive blow. WH: 14–15C. Old French, from Medieval Latin *colpus*, from Latin *colaphus*, from Greek *kolaphos* blow with the fist. The original sense (to the 16C) was a blow in combat. The current sense dates from the 18C.

coup[2] *v.t.* to upset, to overturn. *Also v.i.* WH: 14–15C. Prob. var. of COPE[1].

coup de foudre *n.* a sudden and overwhelming event. WH: 18C. French stroke of lightning, from *coup* (see COUP[1]) + *de* of + *foudre* lightning, thunderbolt, from Latin *fulgur*, from *fulgere* to shine (cp. FULGENT).

coup de grâce *n.* a finishing stroke, an action that puts an end to something. WH: 17C. French stroke of grace, from *coup* (see COUP[1]) + *de* of + *grâce* GRACE. Cp. modern *mercy killing* (MERCY).

coup de main *n.* a sudden and energetic attack. WH: 18C. French stroke of the hand, from *coup* (see COUP[1]) + *de* of + *main* hand, from Latin *manus* (cp. MANUAL).

coup de soleil *n.* sunburn. WH: 18C. French stroke of the sun, from *coup* (see COUP[1]) + *de* of + *soleil* sun, from Latin *sol* (cp. SOLAR). Cp. *sunstroke* (SUN).

coup d'état *n.* a sudden and violent change of government, esp. of an illegal and revolutionary nature. WH: 17C. French stroke of state, from *coup* (see COUP[1]) + *d'* of + *état* STATE.

coup de théâtre *n.* a dramatic turn of events in a play. WH: 18C. French stroke of theatre, from *coup* (see COUP[1]) + *de* of + *théâtre* THEATRE.

coup d'œil *n.* a quick comprehensive glance. WH: 18C. French stroke of eye, from *coup* (see COUP[1]) + *d'* of + *œil* eye, from Latin *oculus* (cp. OCULAR).

coupe *n.* a dessert made of fruit or ice cream. WH: 19C. French goblet, from Medieval Latin *cuppa*. See CUP.

coupé *n.* a two-doored car with an enclosed body. WH: 18C. French, p.p. of *couper* to cut. See COUP[1]. In the sense of (car and) carriage, the word is short for *carrosse coupé* cut carriage, meaning one that has been shortened.

couple *n.* two. *Also v.t., v.i.* WH: 12–14C. Old French *cople* (Modern French *couple*), from Latin *copula* COPULA.

coupon *n.* a form that may be detached or cut out e.g. from an advertisement, and used as an order form, entry form for a competition etc. WH: 19C. French piece cut off, from *couper* to cut. See COPE[1], also -OON.

coupure *n.* in fortifications, a passage, esp. one cut through the glacis to facilitate sallies by the besieged. WH: 18C. French, from *couper* to cut. See COPE[1], also -URE.

courage *n.* bravery, boldness. WH: 12–14C. Old French *corage* (Modern French *courage*), from Latin *cor* heart. See also -AGE. The sense to the 17C was heart as the seat of feeling, so disposition, nature. A second earlier sense to the 17C was anger, pride. The current sense dates from the 14–15C.

courant *a.* in a running attitude. *Also n.* WH: 17C. French, pres.p. of *courir* to run, from Latin *currere*. See also -ANT.

courgette *n.* a small kind of vegetable marrow. WH: mid-20C. French, dim. of *courge* GOURD. See also -ETTE.

courier *n.* an employee of a private postal company offering a fast collection and delivery service usu. within a city or internationally. WH: 14–15C. Obs. French (now *courrier*), from Italian *corriere*, from *correre* to run, from Latin *currere*. See also -IER.

course *n.* continued movement along a path. *Also v.t., v.i.* WH: 12–14C. Old French *cours*, from Latin *cursus*, p.p. (used as n.) of *currere* to run. Some senses of the word relate more directly to French *course*.

court *n.* an enclosed piece of ground used for games. *Also v.t., v.i.* WH: 12–14C. Old French *cort* (Modern French *cour*), from Latin *cohors*, *cohortis*. See COHORT.

court bouillon *n.* a stock made with vegetables, water and wine or vinegar, used especially for cooking fish in. WH: 17C. French, from *court* short (see CURT) + BOUILLON.

Courtelle® *n.* a synthetic acrylic fibre. WH: early 20C. *Court*aulds, name of manufacturers + -*elle* -EL or French fem. suf. as in *éternelle* (from m. *éternel* ETERNAL).

courteous *a.* polite, considerate. WH: 12–14C. Old French *corteis* (Modern French *courtois*), from *cort* COURT + -*eis*. See also -EOUS. The literal sense is having manners that befit the court of a prince.

courtesan *n.* a prostitute or mistress. WH: 16C. French *courtisane*, from obs. Italian *cortigiana*, fem. of *cortigiano* courtier, from *corte* COURT. The literal sense is a court mistress, a prostitute attached to the court.

courtesy *n.* politeness, graciousness. WH: 12–14C. Old French *cortesie* (Modern French *courtoisie*), from *corteis*. See COURTEOUS, also -Y[2]. Cp. CURTSY.

courtier *n.* a person who is in attendance or a frequenter at a royal etc. court. WH: 12–14C. Old French *courtoyer* (see COURT), with ending assim. to -IER.

courtly *a.* polished, elegant, polite. *Also adv.* WH: 12–14C. COURT + -LY[1].

couscous *n.* a N African dish of pounded wheat steamed over meat or broth. WH: 17C. French, from Arabic *kuskus*, prob. of Berber orig.

cousin *n.* the son or daughter of an uncle or aunt. *Also a.* WH: 12–14C. Old French *cosin*, *cusin* (Modern French *cousin*), from Latin *consobrinus* mother's sister's child, from CON- + *sobrinus* second cousin, from *soror* sister.

couth *a.* well-mannered, sophisticated. WH: mid-20C. Backformation from UNCOUTH. The word existed earlier in English from pre-1200 in the sense known, familiar, famous. This sense was obsolete from the 18C.

couthie *a.* friendly, kindly, genial. *Also adv.* WH: 18C. COUTH + -*ie* -Y[3].

couture *n.* dressmaking. WH: early 20C. French, from Old French *cousture*, from Late Latin *consutura*, from Latin *consutus*, p.p. of *consuere* to sew together, from CON- + *suere* to sew.

couvade *n.* a custom among certain peoples, by which a father during the birth of his child performs certain acts and abstains from certain foods etc. WH: 19C. French, from *couver* to hatch, from Latin *cubare* to lie. See also -ADE. Cp. COVEY.

couvert *n.* a place setting in a restaurant. WH: 18C. French covering. See COVERT[1].

couverture *n.* chocolate for coating cakes, sweets etc. WH: mid-20C. French covering. See COVERT[1], -URE.

covalent *a.* having atoms linked by a shared pair of electrons. WH: early 20C. CO- + -*valent*, from Latin *valens*, *valentis*, pres.p. of *valere* to be strong. See also -ENT.

covariant *n.* a function standing in the same relation to another from which it is derived as any of its linear transforms do to a transform similarly derived from the latter function. WH: 19C. CO- + *variant* (VARIANCE).

cove[1] *n.* a small creek, inlet or bay. *Also v.t.* WH: pre-1200. Old English *cofa* chamber, from Germanic. Cp. German *Koben* pen, stall.

cove[2] *n.* a man, a fellow, a chap. WH: 16C. ? Romany *kova* thing, person, or rel. to Scottish *cofe* hawker, itself rel. (via CHEAP and CHAPMAN) to CHAP[2].

coven *n.* an assembly of witches. WH: 14–15C. Var. of COVIN.

covenant *n.* an agreement on certain terms, a compact. *Also v.t., v.i.* WH: 12–14C. Old French (Modern French *convenant*), use as n. of pres.p. of *covenir* to agree, from Latin *convenire* CONVENE. See also -ANT.

Coventry *n.* used only in the phrase *to send to Coventry*, meaning to ostracize. WH: 16C. *Coventry*, a city in Warwickshire (now a unitary authority) in central England. The phrase arose in the 18C, when Royalist prisoners captured in Birmingham in the English Civil War were sent to Coventry, a Parliamentary stronghold.

cover *v.t.* to overlay. *Also v.i., n.* WH: 12–14C. Old French *cuvrir*, *covrir* (Modern French *couvrir*), from Latin *cooperire*, from CO- + *operire* to cover.

coverlet *n.* an outer covering for a bed, a counterpane or bedspread. WH: 12–14C. Anglo-French *covrelet*, *covrelit*, from *covre*-, pres. stem of *covrir* COVER + *lit* bed. Not rel. to -LET.

covert[1] *a.* disguised, secret, private. WH: 12–14C. Old French (Modern French *couvert*), p.p. of *cuvrir*, *covrir* COVER.

covert[2] *n.* a place which covers and shelters. WH: 12–14C. Old French (Modern French *couvert*), p.p. (used as n.) of *cuvrir*, *covrir* COVER.

covertical *a.* having common vertices. WH: 19C. CO- + *vertical* (VERTEX).

covet *v.t.* to desire (something unlawful) inordinately. *Also v.i.* WH: 12–14C. Old French *coveitier* (Modern French *convoiter*), from Latin *cupiditas* CUPIDITY. A sense to the 16C was also specifically to desire sexually.

covey *n.* a brood or small flock of birds (prop. of partridges). WH: 12–14C. Old French *covée* (Modern French *couvée*), fem. p.p. (used as n.) of *cover*, from Latin *cubare* to lie.

covin *n.* an agreement between two or more persons to injure or defraud another. WH: 12–14C. Old French, from Medieval Latin *convenium*, from Latin *convenire* CONVENE. Cp. CONVENT.

cow[1] *n.* the female of any bovine species, esp. of the domesticated species *Bos taurus*. WH: pre-1200. Old English *cū*, from Germanic, from Indo-European base also of Latin *bos*, Greek *bous* ox. Cp. German *Kuh*.

cow[2] *v.t.* to intimidate, to deprive of spirit or courage, to terrify, to daunt. WH: 16C. Prob. from Old Norse *kúga* to oppress, to tyrannize. Not rel. to COWARD, COWER.

cowabunga *int.* used to express pleasure or satisfaction. WH: mid-20C. Prob. fanciful. The word originated as an exclamation of anger by a US cartoon character.

cowage *n.* a tropical climbing plant, *Mucuna pruriens*. WH: 17C. Hindi *kawāc*.

coward *n.* a person without courage. *Also a.* WH: 12–14C. Old French *cuard*, later *couard*, from var. of Latin *cauda* tail (in sense having tail between legs). See also -ARD. Not rel. to COW[2], COWER.

cower *v.i.* to stoop, to crouch. WH: 12–14C. Middle Low German *kūren* to lie in wait, of unknown orig. Not rel. to COW[2], COWARD.

cowl *n.* a hooded garment, esp. one worn by a monk. *Also v.t.* WH: pre-1200. Old English *cugele*, *cūle*, from Ecclesiastical Latin *cuculla*, from Latin *cucullus* hood of cloak.

co-worker *n.* a fellow worker. WH: 17C. CO- + *worker* (WORK).

cowrie *n.* a gastropod of the family Cypraeidae, esp. *Cypraea moneta*, with a small shell formerly used as money in many parts of southern Asia and Africa. WH: 17C. Hindi *kaurī*.

co-write *v.t.* to write something together with one or more other people. WH: 19C. CO- + WRITE.

cowslip *n.* a wild plant with fragrant flowers, *Primula veris*, growing in pastures. WH: pre-1200. Old English *cūslyppe*, *cūsloppe*. See COW[1], SLIP[2]. Cp. SLOP[1]. The plant is so named as it grows in pastures naturally fertilized by cow dung. Not rel. to LIP.

cox *n.* in rowing, the person who steers for a crew in a race. Also *v.t.*, *v.i.* WH: 19C. Abbr. of COXSWAIN.

coxa *n.* the hip. WH: 14–15C. Latin hip.

coxcomb *n.* a conceited person, a fop, a dandy. WH: 16C. Var. of *cockscomb* (COCK[1]). Cp. COCKY[1]. The original sense was fool, jester, from the cap that he wore, resembling a cock's comb.

Cox's orange pippin *n.* a sweet-tasting variety of eating apple with a green skin tinged with reddish orange. WH: 19C. R. *Cox*, d.1845, English horticulturist. See ORANGE, PIPPIN.

coxswain *n.* a person who steers a boat, esp. in a race, a cox. Also *v.t.*, *v.i.* WH: 12–14C. cock (COCKBOAT) + SWAIN. Cp. BOATSWAIN.

coy *a.* coquettish. Also *v.t.*, *v.i.* WH: 12–14C. Old French *coi*, earlier *quei*, from var. of Latin *quietus* QUIET. The original sense to the 17C was quiet, especially in phrases such as *to hold oneself coy*. The current sense dates from the 14–15C.

coyote *n.* the N American prairie wolf. WH: 18C. Mexican Spanish, from Nahuatl *coyotl*.

coypu *n.* a S American aquatic rodent, *Myocastor coypus*, naturalized in Europe. WH: 18C. Araucanian.

coz *n.* a cousin. WH: 16C. Abbr. of COUSIN.

cozen *v.t.* to deceive, to cheat. Also *v.i.* WH: 16C. ? Obs. Italian *cozzonare* to act as a horse-breaker, to cheat, from *cozzone* middleman, from Latin *cocio*, *cocionis* dealer. Not rel. to COUSIN.

cp. *abbr.* compare. WH: Latin *compara*, 2nd pers. sing. imper. of *comparare* COMPARE. Cp. CF.

crab[1] *n.* a decapod crustacean of the group Brachyura, esp. the common crab, *Cancer pagurus*, and other edible species. WH: pre-1200. Old English *krabba*, from Germanic. Cp. CRAB[2].

crab[2] *v.t.* to criticize savagely, to pull to pieces. Also *v.i.* WH: 16C. Low German *krabben*, rel. to CRAB[1]. The earliest sense is to scratch and fight (of hawks). The current sense dates from the 19C.

crab[3] *n.* a crab apple. Also *a.*, *v.i.* WH: 14–15C. Orig. uncertain. ? Alt. of Scots dial. *scrab*.

crabbed *a.* peevish, morose, sour-tempered. WH: 12–14C. Orig. from CRAB[1], but later assoc. with CRAB[3]. The gait and habits of the crab suggest a cross-grained nature.

crack *v.t.* to break without entire separation of the parts. Also *v.i.*, *n.*, *a.* WH: pre-1200. Old English *cracian*, ult. of imit. orig. Cp. CREAK.

crackle *v.i.* to make short, sharp crackling noises. Also *v.t.*, *n.* WH: 14–15C. From CRACK. See also -LE[4].

cracknel *n.* a hard, brittle biscuit. WH: 14–15C. Alt. of Old French *craquelin*, from Middle Dutch *krākeline*, from *krāken* CRACK. Cp. *cracker* (CRACK).

-cracy *comb. form* government or rule of, or influence of or dominance by, as in *aristocracy*, *democracy*, *plutocracy*, *theocracy*. WH: French *-cracie*, from Medieval Latin *-cratia*, from Greek *-kratia* power, rule (*kratos* strength).

cradle *n.* a baby's bed or cot, usu. rocking or swinging. Also *v.t.*, *v.i.* WH: pre-1200. Old English *cradol*, prob. from same base as that of German *Kratte* basket.

craft *n.* dexterity, skill. Also *v.t.* WH: pre-1200. Old English *cræft*, from Germanic. Cp. German *Kraft* skill, power. The original sense to the 16C was strength, power. The current sense of skill, cunning dates from the 12–14C, while the sense of boat arose in the 14–15C.

crafty *a.* sly, cunning. WH: pre-1200. Old English *cræftig*. See CRAFT, also -Y[1].

crag[1] *n.* a rugged or precipitous rock. WH: 12–14C. Celtic in orig. Cp. Irish *carraig*, Welsh *craig* rock, stone.

crag[2] *n.* shelly deposits, esp. in Norfolk, Suffolk and Essex, of the Pliocene age. WH: 18C. ? From CRAG[1].

crake *n.* the corncrake. Also *v.i.* WH: 12–14C. Old Norse *kráka*, of imit. orig. Cp. CROAK.

cram *v.t.* to push or press in so as to fill to overflowing. Also *v.i.*, *n.* WH: pre-1200. Old English *crammian*, from Germanic. Rel. to Dutch *krammen* to cramp, to clamp.

crambo *n.* a game in which one person says a word or line of verse to which the other person must find a rhyme. WH: 17C. Alt. of obs. *crambe*, from Latin, with ref. to Juvenal's *crambe repetita* cabbage dished up again, or *crambe bis cocta* cabbage twice cooked.

cramp[1] *n.* a spasmodic contraction of some limb or muscle, accompanied by pain and numbness. Also *v.t.* WH: 14–15C. Old French *crampe*, from Germanic, with basic sense bent. Cp. CRAMP[2], CRIMP[1].

cramp[2] *n.* a cramp-iron. Also *v.t.* WH: 14–15C. Middle Dutch *krampe*, of same orig. as CRAMP[1].

crampon *n.* a plate with iron spikes worn on climbing boots to assist in climbing ice-slopes etc. WH: 12–14C. Old French, from Frankish. Cp. CRAMP[2]. The current sense arose in the 18C.

cran *n.* a measure of 37½ gallons (170 l.) by which herrings are sold. WH: 18C. Gaelic *crann*, ? same as *crann* lot, share of fish given to each packer.

cranberry *n.* any shrub of the genus *Vaccinium*, esp. the American *V. macrocarpon* and the British *V. oxycoccos*, both with a small, red, acid fruit used in sauces etc. WH: 17C. German *Kranbeere*, from Low German *kranebeere*, lit. crane berry, of unknown orig. The name was adopted by early N American colonists from some Germanic source, then brought to England when cranberries were exported there.

crane[1] *n.* a long-necked bird of the family Gruidae, esp. the common crane of Europe, *Grus grus*, a migratory wading bird. Also *v.t.*, *v.i.* WH: pre-1200. Old English *cran*, of Germanic orig., rel. to Latin *grus*, Greek *geranos* crane. Cp. German *Kranich*.

crane[2] *n.* a machine for hoisting and lowering heavy weights. Also *v.t.* WH: 12–14C. From CRANE[1]. The machine's long arm suggests the bird's long neck.

cranio- *comb. form* of or relating to the skull. WH: Greek *kranion* skull. See also -O-.

cranium *n.* the skull, esp. the part enclosing the brain. WH: 12–14C. Medieval Latin, from Greek *kranion* skull.

crank[1] *n.* an arm at right angles to an axis for converting rotary into reciprocating motion, or the converse. Also *v.t.* WH: pre-1200. Old English *cranc-* in *crancstæf* weaver's implement, rel. to *crincan* to bend. Cp. German *krank* sick, with reference to the idea of being bent or crooked.

crank[2] *n.* an eccentric, esp. someone who is obsessed with a theory or fad. WH: 16C. Prob. ult. from CRANK[1]. The sense of eccentric person arose in the 19C as a back-formation from CRANKY.

crank[3] *a.* liable to capsize. WH: 18C. Either from CRANK[1] or a back-formation from CRANKY.

cranky *a.* eccentric, esp. obsessed with a theory or fad. WH: 18C. ? Orig. from obs. *crank* sick person (cp. German *krank*), but influ. by CRANK[2]. See also -Y[1].

crannog *n.* an ancient lake-dwelling, common in Scotland and Ireland, built up from the lake bottom on brushwood and piles, and often surrounded by palisades. WH: 17C. Irish *crannóg* or Gaelic *crannag* timber structure, from *crann* tree, beam.

cranny *n.* a crevice, a chink. WH: 14–15C. Old French *crané*, p.p. of a *v.* based on Old French *cran*, from Popular Latin *crena* incision. Cp. CRENATE.

crap[1] *n.* rubbish. Also *v.i.*, *v.t.*, *a.* WH: 14–15C. Old French *crappe*, from Medieval Latin *crappa* chaff, ? from Old Dutch *krappen* to cut off.

crap[2] *n.* a losing throw in the game of craps. WH: 19C. From CRAPS.

crape *n.* a gauzy fabric of silk or other material, with a crisped, frizzly surface, formerly usu. dyed black, used for mourning. Also *v.t.*, *a.* WH: 16C. French CRÊPE.

craps *n.* a gambling game played with two dice, with fixed winning and losing numbers. WH: 19C. Appar. alt. of *crabs*. Cp. CRAB[1].

crapulent *a.* given to intemperance. WH: 17C. Late Latin *crapulentus* very drunk, from Latin *crapula* inebriation, from Greek *kraipalē* hangover. See also -ULENT.

crash[1] *v.t.* to cause (a vehicle etc.) to hit something with great force. Also *v.i.*, *n.*, *a.*, *adv.* WH: 14–15C. Imit., ? partly suggested by CRAZE and DASH or by CRUSH.

crash[2] *n.* a coarse linen cloth, sometimes with cotton or jute in it, used for towelling. WH: 19C. Russian *krashenina* dyed coarse linen, from *krasit'* to dye, to colour.

crasis *n.* the contracting of the vowels of two syllables into one long vowel or diphthong. WH: 16C. Greek *krasis* mixture, combination.

crass *a.* loutish, boorish. WH: 15C. Latin *crassus* solid, thick, fat.

-crat *comb. form* a partisan or supporter of something denoted by a word ending in *-cracy*, as in *democrat*. WH: French *-crate*, from aa. ending in *-cratique*. See -CRACY.

cratch *n.* a manger, a hay-rack, esp. for feeding animals out of doors. WH: 12–14C. Old French *creche* (Modern French CRÈCHE), from Germanic base also of CRIB.

crate *n.* a large wicker case for packing crockery. *Also v.t.* WH: 14–15C. ? Dutch *krat* tailboard (of a wagon), of unknown orig.

crater *n.* the mouth of a volcano. *Also v.t.* WH: 17C. Latin, from Greek *kratēr* bowl.

craton *n.* any of the large, relatively stable and immobile parts of the earth's crust, forming the main part of a continent and continental shelf. WH: mid-20C. Alt. of *kratogen*, from Greek *kratos* strength + -GEN.

cravat *n.* a tielike scarf worn in an open-necked shirt, esp. by men. WH: 17C. French *cravate*, from *Cravate*, from German *Krabate*, from Serbo-Croat *Hrvat* CROAT. A scarf of this type was originally worn by Croatian mercenaries, and the French adopted the fashion.

crave *v.t.* to long for. *Also v.i.* WH: pre-1200. Old English *crafian*, from Germanic, rel. to Old Norse *krof* request.

craven *a.* cowardly, faint-hearted. *Also n., v.t.* WH: 12–14C. ? Anglo-French abbr. of Old French *cravanté* overcome, p.p. of *cravanter* to crush, to overwhelm, from Latin *crepans, crepantis,* pres.p. of *crepare* to rattle, later assim. to English p.p.s in -EN[6].

craw *n.* the crop or first stomach of birds or insects. WH: 14–15C. From or rel. to Middle Low German *krage* neck, throat, of unknown orig. Cp. German *Kragen* collar, neck.

crawl[1] *v.i.* to move slowly on one's hands and knees or with one's body close to the ground. *Also n.* WH: 12–14C. Orig. unknown. ? From Scandinavian and rel. to CRAB[1].

crawl[2] *n.* an enclosure in shallow water for keeping fish, turtles etc. alive. WH: 17C. Portuguese *curral.* Cp. CORRAL, KRAAL.

crayfish *n.* any of the many, mostly freshwater, species of lobster-like crustaceans of the families Astacidae and Parastacidae. WH: 12–14C. Old French *crevice, crevis* (Modern French *écrevisse*), from Frankish, from Germanic, from same base as for CRAB[1]. The second syllable has been assimilated to FISH[1].

crayon *n.* a stick or pencil of coloured chalk or similar material. *Also v.t.* WH: 17C. French, from *craie*, from Latin *creta* chalk, clay. See also -OON.

craze *v.t.* to make insane. *Also v.i., n.* WH: 14–15C. ? Old Norse. Cp. Swedish *krasa* to crack, to crunch.

creak *v.t.* to make a continued sharp grating or squeaking noise. *Also v.i., n.* WH: 12–14C. Imit. Cp. CROAK.

cream *n.* the fatty part of milk which rises and collects on the surface, often separated off and used in cakes, desserts etc. *Also v.t., v.i., a.* WH: 12–14C. Old French *creme, cresme* (Modern French *crème*), from blend of Late Latin *cramum* (? from Gaulish) with Ecclesiastical Latin *chrisma* CHRISM.

crease *n.* a line or mark made by folding or doubling. *Also v.t., v.i.* WH: 16C. Prob. var. of CREST. Cp. Old French *cresté* wrinkled, furrowed.

create *v.t.* to cause to exist. *Also v.i., a.* WH: 14–15C. Latin *creatus*, p.p. of *creare* to bring forth, to produce. See also -ATE[3].

creatine *n.* an organic compound found in muscular fibre. WH: 19C. Greek *kreas* flesh + -INE. The derivative was discovered and named in 1835 by the French chemist Michel-Eugène Chevreul.

creation *n.* the act of creating. WH: 14–15C. Old French *création*, from Latin *creatio, creationis.* See CREATE, also -ION.

creature *n.* a living being. *Also a.* WH: 14–15C. Old French *créature*, from Late Latin *creatura.* See CREATE, also -URE. An original early sense to the 17C was the created universe, otherwise creation.

crèche *n.* a day nursery in which young children are taken care of. WH: 18C. French. See CRATCH.

cred *n.* credibility, as in *street cred.* WH: late 20C. Abbr. of *credibility* (CREDIBLE).

credence *n.* belief, credit. WH: 12–14C. Old French *crédence*, from Medieval Latin *credentia*, from Latin *credens, credentis*, pres.p. of *credere* to believe. See also -ENCE. An additional sense from the 14–15C to the 18C was a document furnishing credentials.

credenza *n.* a credence table. WH: 19C. Italian, from Medieval Latin *credentia.* See CREDENCE.

credible *a.* deserving of or entitled to belief. WH: 14–15C. Latin *credibilis*, from *credere* to believe. See also -IBLE.

credit *n.* belief, trust. *Also v.t.* WH: 16C. French *crédit*, from Italian *credito*, or from Latin *creditum*, neut. p.p. (used as n.) of *credere* to believe, to put one's trust in.

credo *n.* the Apostles' Creed or the Nicene Creed. WH: 12–14C. Latin I believe, 1st pers. sing. pres. ind. of *credere* to believe. The word is from the opening phrase of the Apostles' Creed and Nicene Creed, *Credo in unum Deum* I believe in one God.

credulous *a.* disposed to believe, esp. without sufficient evidence. WH: 16C. Latin *credulus*, from *credere* to believe. See also -ULOUS.

Cree *n.* a member of a N American Indian people living in central Canada. *Also a.* WH: 18C. Canadian French *Cris*, abbr. of *Cristinaux*, from Algonquian (now *kinistino:*).

creed *n.* a brief summary of the articles of religious belief. *Also v.t.* WH: pre-1200. Old English *crēda*, from Latin *credo* I believe. See CREDO.

Creek *n.* a member of a N American people now living mostly in Oklahoma, or of a confederacy of which the Creeks were the dominant members. *Also a.* WH: 18C. CREEK. The people are so named from the creeks (streams) of the flatlands of Georgia and Alabama, their original territory.

creek *n.* a small inlet, bay or harbour, on the coast. WH: 12–14C. Old Norse *kriki* chink, nook or Old French *crique*, from Old Norse. Cp. Dutch *kreek* creek, bay.

creel *n.* an osier basket. WH: 12–14C. Orig. unknown.

creep *v.i.* to crawl along the ground. *Also n.* WH: pre-1200. Old English *crēopan*, from Germanic.

†creesh *n.* grease, fat. *Also v.t.* WH: 14–15C. Old French *craisse* (Modern French *graisse*), from Latin *crassa* thick, fat. Cp. GREASE[1].

cremate *v.t.* to dispose of a corpse by burning. WH: 19C. Latin *crematus*, p.p. of *cremare* to burn, or back-formation from *cremation* (17C), from Latin *crematio, cremationis.* See also -ATE[3].

crème *n.* cream. WH: 19C. French CREAM.

crème brûlée *n.* a dessert consisting of cream or custard covered with caramelized sugar. WH: 19C. French burnt cream, from CRÈME + fem. p.p. of *brûler* to burn. Cp. BRÛLÉ. The dessert was earlier known (from 18C) by its English name, *burnt cream.* Cp. CRÈME CARAMEL.

crème caramel *n.* a dessert consisting of a set custard coated with liquid caramel. WH: 19C. French, from earlier *crème au caramel* caramel cream. See CREAM, CARAMEL. It is the caramel that is 'burnt' in this dish and in CRÈME BRÛLÉE. *Crème au caramel* is now a different dessert, with caramel-flavoured cream, not a coating of caramel.

crème de cacao *n.* a chocolate-flavoured liqueur. WH: mid-20C. French chocolate cream, from CRÈME + *de* of + CACAO. French *crème* in the name of liqueurs denotes a creamlike smoothness. Cp. CRÈME DE CASSIS, CRÈME DE MENTHE.

crème de cassis *n.* a blackcurrant-flavoured liqueur. WH: mid-20C. French blackcurrant cream, from CRÈME + *de* of + CASSIS.

crème de la crème *n.* the pick, best, most select, elite. WH: 19C. French cream of the cream, from CRÈME + *de la* of the. English CREAM in the sense the best dates from the 16C.

crème de menthe *n.* a peppermint-flavoured liqueur. WH: early 20C. French (pepper)mint cream, from CRÈME + *de* of + *menthe* MINT[2].

crème fraîche *n.* a type of thick, slightly soured cream. WH: mid-20C. French fresh cream, from CRÈME + fem. of *frais* FRESH. Cp. FROMAGE FRAIS.

crenate *a.* notched. WH: 17C. Modern Latin *crenatus*, from Popular Latin *crena* incision, notch, of unknown orig. See also -ATE[2], -ED. Cp. CRANNY.

crenel *n.* a loophole through which to discharge musketry. WH: 15C. Old French (Modern French *créneau*), from dim. of Popular Latin *crena* (see CRENATE).

crenulate *a.* (of the edges of leaves, shells etc.) finely notched or scalloped. WH: 18C. Modern Latin *crenulatus*, from *crenula*, dim. of *crena*. See CRENATE, also -ATE[2].

Creole *n.* a person of European parentage in the W Indies or Spanish America. *Also a.* WH: 17C. French *créole*, earlier *criole*, from Spanish *criollo*, prob. from Portuguese *crioulo* black person born in Brazil, home-born slave, from *criar* to nurse, to breed, from Latin *creare* CREATE.

creophagous *a.* carnivorous, flesh-eating. WH: 19C. Greek *kreophagos*, from *kreas* flesh + -PHAGOUS.

creosote *n.* a liquid distilled from coal tar, used for preserving wood etc. *Also v.t.* WH: 19C. German *Kreosote*, from Greek *kreo-*, comb. form of *kreas* flesh + *sōtēr* saviour. The name was devised in 1832 to mean flesh-saving, referring to the liquid's antiseptic properties.

crêpe *n.* crape. WH: 18C. French, earlier *crespe*, use as n. of Old French *crespe* curled, frizzled, from Latin *crispus* curled. Cp. CRISP.

crepitate *v.i.* to crackle. WH: 17C. Latin *crepitatus*, p.p. of *crepitare* to crackle, from *crepare* to rattle. See also -ATE[3]. The original sense (to the 18C) was to break wind. The current sense dates from the 19C.

crepuscle *n.* morning or evening twilight. WH: 14–15C. Latin *crepusculum*, rel. to *creper* dusky, dark.

crescendo *n.* (a musical passage performed with) a gradual increase in the force of sound. *Also adv., a., v.i.* WH: 18C. Italian, pres.p. of *crescere* to increase, from Latin *crescere* to grow.

crescent *a.* shaped like a new moon. *Also n.* WH: 14–15C. Old French *creissant* (Modern French *croissant*), from Latin *crescens*, *crescentis*, pres.p. of *crescere* to grow. See also -ENT.

cresol *n.* a compound, occurring in three isomers, which is found in coal tar and creosote and is used in antiseptics and as a raw material for plastics. WH: 19C. Abbr. of *creosote* (see CREOSOTE) + -OL.

cress *n.* any of various cruciferous plants with a pungent taste, e.g. watercress, garden cress. WH: pre-1200. Old English *cressa*, *cresse*, from Germanic, ? from base of Latin *gramen* grass. Cp. German *Kresse*.

cresset *n.* a metal cup or vessel, usu. on a pole, for holding oil for a light. WH: 14–15C. Old French, from *craisse*, var. of *graisse* oil, GREASE[1]. See also -ET[1].

crest *n.* a plume on the head of a bird. *Also v.t., v.i.* WH: 12–14C. Old French *creste* (Modern French *crête*), from Latin *crista* tuft, plume.

cresyl *n.* each of three isomeric radicals derived from a cresol. WH: 19C. CRESOL + -YL.

cretaceous *a.* of the nature of or abounding in chalk. WH: 17C. Latin *cretaceus*, from *creta* chalk. See also -ACEOUS.

Cretan *n.* a native or inhabitant of Crete. *Also a.* WH: 16C. Latin *Cretanus*, from *Creta*, from Greek *Krētē* Crete, an island of the E Mediterranean. See also -AN.

cretic *n.* a metrical foot consisting of a short syllable preceded and followed by a long syllable. WH: 16C. Latin *creticus*, from Greek *krētikos*, from *Krētē*. See CRETAN, also -IC. The foot is so named as it is said to have originated with the Cretan poet Thaletas in the 7C BC.

cretin *n.* a person mentally and physically disabled because of a (congenital) thyroid malfunction. WH: 18C. French *crétin*, from Swiss French *creitin*, *crestin*, from Latin *Christianus* CHRISTIAN. The Swiss French name was originally applied to dwarfed or deformed persons in Alpine valleys. They were 'Christian' because, although disabled, they were obviously human beings, not animals.

cretonne *n.* a cotton fabric with pictorial patterns, used for upholstering, frocks etc. WH: 19C. French, of uncertain orig. According to some, the word is from *Creton*, a village in N France, where the fabric is said to have been originally made.

Creutzfeldt–Jakob disease *n.* a disease of human beings, related to BSE and scrapie, which causes brain degeneration, leading to death. WH: late 20C. Hans G. *Creutzfeldt*, 1885–1964, + Alfons M. *Jakob*, 1884–1931, German neurologists.

crevasse *n.* a deep fissure in a glacier. WH: 19C. French, from Old French *crevace*. See CREVICE.

crevice *n.* a crack, a cleft, a fissure. WH: 12–14C. Old French *crevace* (Modern French *crevasse*), from *crever* to burst, to split, from Latin *crepare* to rattle, to crack, to break with a crash.

crew *n.* the sailors on a ship or boat, esp. as distinct from the officers

or the captain. *Also v.t., v.i.* WH: 14–15C. Old French *creüe* increase (Modern French *crue*), fem. p.p. (used as n.) of *croistre* (Modern French *croître*), from Latin *crescere* to grow, to increase. The original sense (to the 16C) was an increase or reinforcement of a military force. The current sense dates from the 17C.

crewel *n.* fine two-threaded worsted. WH: 15C. Orig. unknown. ? Rel. to French *écru* raw, unbleached.

crib *n.* a child's cot. *Also v.t., v.i.* WH: pre-1200. Old English, of Germanic orig. The sense of text used for cheating evolved in the 19C from an earlier (now obsolete) use of crib to mean basket. A basket conceals what is inside, just as a crib (in the modern sense) is a secret or hidden translation.

cribbage *n.* a card game for two, three or four players. WH: 17C. Orig. unknown. ? Rel. to CRIB. If this is the origin, the reference would presumably be to the crib (store) of cards held by the dealer.

cribriform *a.* resembling a sieve; perforated like a sieve. WH: 18C. Latin *cribrum* sieve + -i- -FORM.

crick *n.* a spasmodic painful stiffness, esp. of the neck or back. *Also v.t.* WH: 14–15C. Orig. unknown. Cp. CRACK. The word is perhaps imitative of a sudden check or spasm.

cricket[1] *n.* an open-air game played by two sides of 11 players, consisting of an attempt to strike, with a ball, wickets defended by the opponents with bats. *Also v.i.* WH: 12–14C. Orig. uncertain. The word is generally said to derive from Old French *criquet* goalpost in game of bowls, stick, perhaps from Middle Dutch *cricke* stick, staff, rel. to CROOK, CRUTCH. Any connection with CROQUET is unlikely.

cricket[2] *n.* any grasshopper-like insect of the family Gryllidae, the males being noted for their chirping. WH: 12–14C. Old French *criquet*, from *criquer* to crackle, of imit. orig. The word alludes to the insect's chirping.

cricket[3] *n.* a low, wooden stool. WH: 17C. Orig. unknown.

cricoid *a.* ringlike. WH: 18C. Modern Latin *cricoides* ring-shaped, from Greek *krikoeidēs*, from *krikos* ring. See also -OID.

cri de cœur *n.* a heartfelt appeal or protest. WH: early 20C. French cry of the heart, from *cri* CRY + *de* of + *cœur* heart, from Latin *cor*.

crier *n.* a person who cries or proclaims. WH: 14–15C. Old French *criere*, from *crier* CRY. See also -ER[2].

crikey *int.* used to express astonishment. WH: 19C. Alt. of CHRIST. Cp. CRIPES, CRUMBS.

crim *n., a.* (a) criminal. WH: early 20C. Abbr. of CRIMINAL.

†crim. con. *n.* criminal conversation. WH: Abbr. of *criminal conversation*.

crime *n.* an act contrary to human or divine law. *Also v.t.* WH: 12–14C. Old French, from Latin *crimen* judgement, offence, from base of *cernere* to decide, to pass judgement.

crime passionel *n.* a crime, esp. murder, committed because of, usu. sexual, passion and jealousy. WH: early 20C. French crime of passion, from CRIME + *passionel*, a. from PASSION.

criminal *a.* of the nature of a crime, relating to (a) crime. *Also n.* WH: 14–15C. Late Latin *criminalis*, from Latin *crimen*, *criminis* CRIME. See also -AL[1].

criminate *v.t.* to accuse of a crime. WH: 17C. Latin *criminatus*, p.p. of *criminare*, from *crimen*, *criminis* CRIME. See also -ATE[3].

criminology *n.* the scientific study of crime and criminals. WH: 19C. Latin *crimen*, *criminis* CRIME + -O- + -LOGY.

criminous *a.* guilty of a crime, criminal. WH: 14–15C. Old French *crimineux*, from Latin *criminosus*, from *crimen*, *criminis* CRIME. See also -OUS.

crimp[1] *v.t.* to curl or put waves into (hair). *Also n.* WH: pre-1200. Old English *gecrympan*, from Germanic.

crimp[2] *n.* a person who decoyed men for military or naval service. *Also v.t.* WH: 17C. Orig. unknown.

Crimplene® *n.* a kind of crease-resistant synthetic fibre, or a fabric made from it. WH: mid-20C. Prob. from CRIMP[1] + TERYLENE. The name was perhaps partly suggested by *Crimple* Beck, a stream near the original maker's factory at Harrogate, N Yorkshire.

crimson *n.* a deep red colour. *Also a., v.t., v.i.* WH: 14–15C. Old Spanish *cremesín* or obs. French *cramoisin* (Modern French *cramoisi*), ult. from Arabic *ḳirmizī*, from *ḳirmiz* KERMES.

cringe *v.i.* to shrink back in fear. *Also v.t., n.* WH: 12–14C. Of Germanic orig. Rel. to Old English *cringan* to yield, Dutch *krengen* to keel over, German *krank* ill (cp. CRANK[2]).

cringle *n.* an iron ring on the bolt-rope of a sail for a rope to pass through. WH: 17C. Low German *kringel*, dim. of *kring* circle. Cp. CRANK[1], CRINKLE.

crinite *a.* hairy. WH: 16C. Latin *crinitus*, p.p. of *crinire* to cover with hair, from *crinis* hair. See also -ITE[2].

crinkle *n.* a wrinkle, a crease. *Also v.i., v.t.* WH: 14–15C. Freq. base of Old English *crincan*. See CRINGLE, also -LE[4].

crinoid *a.* lily-shaped. *Also n.* WH: 19C. Greek *krinoidēs* lily-like, from *krinon* lily. See also -OID.

crinoline *n.* a stiff fabric of horsehair formerly used for petticoats, etc. WH: 19C. French, from Latin *crinis* hair + *linum* thread.

criosphinx *n.* a sphinx with a ram's head. WH: 19C. From *crio-*, comb. form of Greek *krios* ram (see -O-) + SPHINX.

cripes *int.* used to express surprise. WH: early 20C. Alt. of CHRIST.

cripple *n.* a lame or disabled person. *Also v.t., v.i.* WH: pre-1200. Old English *crypel, cropel*, from Germanic, from same base as that of CREEP.

crisis *n.* a momentous point in politics, domestic affairs etc. WH: 14–15C. Medical Latin, from Greek *krisis* decision, judgement, from *krinein* to decide. The original specific sense was the turning point of a disease. The current general sense dates from the 17C.

crisp *a.* hard, dry and brittle. *Also v.t., v.i., n.* WH: pre-1200. Latin *crispus* curled, ? ult. of imit. orig.

crispate *a.* having curled, wrinkled or wavy edges. WH: 19C. Latin *crispatus*, p.p. of *crispare* to curl. See CRISP, also -ATE[2].

criss-cross *a., n.* (a network of lines) crossing one another. *Also v.t., v.i., adv.* WH: 17C. Alt. of *Christ-cross* Christ's cross (see CHRIST, CROSS), regarded as redupl. of CROSS.

crista *n.* a ridge or crest. WH: 19C. Latin. See CREST.

cristobalite *n.* one of the main forms of silica, occurring e.g. as opal. WH: 19C. Cerro San *Cristobál* in Mexico, where first found. See also -ITE[1].

crit *n.* a critical study or examination. WH: 18C. Abbr. of *criticism*. See CRITIC.

criterion *n.* a principle or standard by which anything is or can be judged. WH: 17C. Greek *kritērion* means of judging, from *kritēs* judge.

critic *n.* a judge, an examiner. WH: 16C. Latin *criticus*, from Greek *kritikos*, use as n. of a. from *kritēs* judge. See also -IC.

critique *n.* a critical essay or judgement. *Also v.t.* WH: 17C. French, from Greek *kritikē (tekhnē)*, the critical (art), criticism. See CRITIC.

critter *n.* a creature (an animal or, as a term of pity, a person). WH: 19C. Var. of CREATURE.

croak *v.i.* (of e.g. a frog or a raven) to make a hoarse low sound in the throat. *Also v.t., n.* WH: 12–14C. Imit.

Croat *n.* a native or inhabitant of Croatia in SE Europe. *Also a.* WH: 17C. Modern Latin *Croatae* (pl.), from Serbo-Croat *Hrvat*.

croc *n.* a crocodile. WH: 19C. Abbr. of CROCODILE.

croceate *a.* of or like saffron. WH: 19C. Latin *croceus*, from CROCUS. See also -ATE[2].

crochet *n.* a kind of knitting done with a hooked needle. *Also v.t., v.i.* WH: 19C. French, dim. of *croc* hook, dim. of *croc* hook, with *-ch-* from *crochié* hooked. Cp. CROOK.

crocidolite *n.* a silky fibrous silicate of iron and sodium, also called blue asbestos. WH: 19C. Greek *krokis, krokidos* nap of woollen cloth + -O- + -LITE.

crock[1] *n.* an earthenware vessel; a pot, a pitcher, a jar. *Also v.t.* WH: pre-1200. Old English *croc*, prob. rel. to *crōg* small vessel, from Germanic. Cp. German *Krug* tankard.

crock[2] *n.* a sick, decrepit or old person. *Also v.i., v.t.* WH: 14–15C. ? Flemish in orig. Prob. rel. to CRACK.

crocket *n.* a carved foliated ornament on a pinnacle, the side of a canopy etc. WH: 12–14C. Old French, var. of *crochet* CROTCHET.

crocodile *n.* a large amphibian reptile of the family Crocodylidae, with the back and tail covered with large, square scales. WH: 12–14C. Old French *cocodrille* (Modern French *crocodile*), from Medieval Latin *cocodrillus*, from Latin *crocodilus*, from Greek *krokodilos*, of unknown orig. Greek *krokodilos* has been interpreted through folk etymology as pebble worm, from *krokē* pebble + *drilos* earthworm.

crocus *n.* a small bulbous plant of the genus *Crocus*, belonging to the Iridaceae, with yellow, white or purple flowers, extensively cultivated in gardens. WH: 14–15C. Latin, from Greek *krokos*, of Semitic orig.

Croesus *n.* a very wealthy man. WH: 17C. Latin, from Greek *Kroisos*, King of Lydia, 6C BC, famous for his wealth.

croft *n.* a piece of enclosed ground, esp. adjoining a house. *Also v.i.* WH: pre-1200. Orig. unknown.

Crohn's disease *n.* chronic inflammation of the intestines, esp. of the small intestine, usually causing pain and diarrhoea. WH: mid-20C. Burrill B. *Crohn*, 1884–1983, US pathologist.

croissant *n.* a crescent-shaped roll of rich flaky pastry. WH: 16C. French. See CRESCENT. The word was originally a variant of CRESCENT. The current sense dates from the 19C.

Cro-Magnon *a.* denoting an early type of modern man, living in late Palaeolithic times. WH: 19C. *Cro-Magnon*, a hill near Les Eyzies in the Dordogne, France, containing a cave where the remains were found in 1868.

crombie *n.* an overcoat made from a type of woollen cloth. WH: mid-20C. J. & J. *Crombie* Ltd., Scottish clothmakers.

cromlech *n.* a circle of standing stones. WH: 17C. Welsh, from *crom*, fem. of *crwm* bowed, arched + *llech* flat stone.

crone *n.* an old woman. WH: 14–15C. Prob. from Middle Dutch *croonje* carcass, old ewe, rel. to CARRION.

cronk *a.* ill. WH: 19C. Prob. var. of CRANK[2].

crony *n.* an intimate friend. WH: 17C. Greek *khronios* long-lasting, from *khronos* time. The word was originally Cambridge University slang. Cp. CHUM[1].

crook *n.* a shepherd's or bishop's hooked staff. *Also a., v.t., v.i.* WH: 12–14C. Old Norse *krókr* hook, peg, bend, corner.

croon *v.i.* to sing in a low voice. *Also v.t., n.* WH: 15C. Middle Low German or Middle Dutch *krōnen* to lament, to groan, of imit. orig.

crop *n.* plants grown for food. *Also v.t., v.i.* WH: pre-1200. Old English, from Germanic, ult. of unknown orig. The original sense was craw, with the sense plants grown for food developing from it in the 12–14C. A bird's craw stores food just as cultivated fields 'store' the harvest.

croquet *n.* an open-air game played on a lawn with balls and mallets. *Also v.t., v.i.* WH: 19C. Orig. uncertain. ? French dial. var. of CROCHET.

croquette *n.* a savoury ball made with meat, potato etc. fried in breadcrumbs. WH: 18C. French, from *croquer* to crunch. See -ETTE.

crore *n.* in the Indian subcontinent, ten millions, a hundred lakhs (of rupees, people etc.). WH: 17C. Hindi *kror*, from Sanskrit *koṭi*.

crosier *n.* the hooked pastoral staff of a bishop or abbot. WH: 12–14C. Partly from Old French *croissier* cross-bearer, from *crois* (Modern French *croix*) CROSS, partly from Old French *crocier* bearer of a bishop's crook, from *croce* (Modern French *crosse*), from Germanic base also of CRUTCH.

cross *n.* an ancient instrument of execution made of two pieces of timber set transversely. *Also a., v.t., v.i.* WH: pre-1200. Old Norse *kross*, from Old Irish *cros*, from Late Latin var. of Latin CRUX, *crucis*.

crosse *n.* the long, hooked, racket-like stick used in the game of lacrosse. WH: 19C. French, from Old French *cruce* bishop's crook. See CROSIER.

crostini *n.pl.* small pieces of toasted or fried bread covered with a topping. WH: mid-20C. Italian, pl. of *crostino* little crust. Cp. CROUTON.

crotch *n.* a forking. WH: 16C. Prob. ult. rel. to Old French *croche* crosier, CROOK, but partly var. of CRUTCH.

crotchet *n.* a note, equal in length to one beat of a bar of 4/4 time. WH: 12–14C. Old French *crochet*, dim. of *croc* hook. See also -ET[1].

croton *n.* a plant of the genus *Croton*, euphorbiaceous medicinal trees and shrubs from the warmer parts of both hemispheres. WH: 18C. Greek *krotōn* sheep-tick. The plant is so called because its seeds resemble ticks.

crottle *n.* any of several species of lichens used for dyeing. WH: 18C. Gaelic and Irish *crotal* lichen.

crouch *v.i.* to stoop, to bend low. *Also n.* WH: 14–15C. Prob. Old French *crochir* to be bent, from *croche*. See CROTCH.

croup[1] *n.* the rump, the buttocks (esp. of a horse). WH: 12–14C. Old French *croupe*, from Germanic base rel. to that of CROP.

croup² *n.* inflammation of the larynx and trachea, characterized by hoarse coughing and difficulty in breathing. WH: 16C. Imit. Cp. COUGH.

croupier *n.* a person who superintends a gaming table and collects the money won by the bank. WH: 18C. French. See CROUP¹, -IER. A French *croupier* was originally a person who rode behind the croup of a horse. From this the sense passed to a person who stood behind a gambler to give advice, and finally to the current sense.

crouton *n.* a small cube of fried or toasted bread, served with soup or salads. WH: 19C. French, from *croûte* CRUST.

Crow *n.* a member of an American Indian people living mostly in Montana. WH: 19C. From CROW¹, trans. of their native name, *Absaroka*.

crow¹ *n.* a large black bird of the genus *Corvus*, esp. the hooded crow, and the carrion crow *C. corione*. WH: pre-1200. Old English *crāwe*, from Germanic base of CROW².

crow² *v.i.* to make a loud cry like a cock. *Also v.t., n.* WH: pre-1200. Old English *crāwan*, from Germanic, of imit. orig. Cp. CAW.

crowd¹ *n.* a number of persons or things collected closely together. *Also v.t., v.i.* WH: pre-1200. Old English *crūdan* to push, to crowd, from Germanic.

crowd² *n.* an old instrument somewhat like a violin, but with six strings (in early times three), four played with a bow and two with the thumb. *Also v.i.* WH: 12–14C. Welsh *crwth*. Cp. Gaelic *cruit* harp, violin, Old Irish *crot* harp.

crowdy *n.* meal and water (or milk) stirred together cold to form a thick gruel. WH: 16C. Orig. unknown.

crown *n.* the ornamental headdress worn on the head by monarchs as a badge of sovereignty. *Also a., v.t.* WH: 12–14C. Old French *corone* (Modern French *couronne*), from Latin *corona* wreath, chaplet, from Greek *korōnē* bent thing. Cp. CORONA¹.

croze *n.* the groove in barrel staves near the end to receive the head. *Also v.t.* WH: 17C. ? French *creux*, fem. *creuse*, from Old French *crues* hollow.

cru *n.* a French vineyard or group of vineyards producing wine of a particular quality. WH: 19C. French, from *crû*, p.p. of *croître* to grow.

crucial *a.* decisive. WH: 18C. French, from Latin *crux, crucis* cross. See also -IAL. The current sense derives from Latin *crux* cross in the sense of a finger-post at a crossroads, where a decision has to be made which way to go. This sense is reinforced by CRUX, so that the decision is a vital one.

crucian *n.* a small colourful fish, *Carassius carassius*, without barbels. WH: 18C. Alt. of Low German *karuse, karutze* (German *Karausche*), from Latin *coracinus*, from Greek *korax* raven. The fish is so named for its dark-coloured back, contrasting with its lighter sides.

cruciate *a.* cruciform. WH: 17C. Medieval Latin *cruciatus*, from Latin *crux, crucis* cross. See also -ATE².

crucible *n.* a melting pot of earthenware, porcelain or refractory metal, adapted to withstand high temperatures without softening, and sudden and great alterations of temperature without cracking. WH: 14–15C. Medieval Latin *crucibulum* night lamp, crucible, from Latin *crux, crucis* cross. The night lamp is said to be so called because it had crossed wicks.

crucifer *n.* a cross-bearer. WH: 16C. Ecclesiastical Latin, from Latin *crux, crucis* cross + -*i*- + *fer*, from *ferre* to carry, to bear.

crucifix *n.* a cross bearing a figure of Christ. WH: 12–14C. Old French, from Ecclesiastical Latin *crucifixus*, from Latin *cruci fixus* fixed to a cross. Cp. CRUCIFY.

cruciform *a.* cross-shaped. WH: 17C. Latin *crux, crucis* + -*i*- + FORM.

crucify *v.t.* to inflict capital punishment on by affixing to a cross. WH: 12–14C. Old French *crucifier*, from alt. of Ecclesiastical Latin *crucifigere*, from Latin *cruci figere* to fix to a cross. See CROSS, FIX.

cruck *n.* in old buildings, either of a pair of curved timbers which support the roof and extend to the ground. WH: 16C. Prob. var. of CROOK.

crud *n.* any dirty, sticky or slimy substance. WH: 14–15C. Earlier form of CURD.

crude *a.* raw, in a natural state. *Also n.* WH: 14–15C. Latin *crudus* raw, rough, cruel.

crudités *n.pl.* raw vegetables served as an hors d'œuvre, often with a dip or sauce. WH: mid-20C. French, pl. of *crudité* crudity. See CRUDE, -ITY. The vegetables are so called as they are raw.

cruel *a.* disposed to give pain to others. *Also v.t.* WH: 12–14C. Old French, from Latin *crudelis*, rel. to *crudus*. See CRUDE.

cruet *n.* a small container for pepper, salt etc. at table. WH: 12–14C. Anglo-French dim. of Old French *crue*, from Old Saxon *krūka*, from Germanic base also of CROCK¹.

cruise *v.i.* to sail to and fro, for pleasure or in search of plunder or an enemy. *Also v.t., n.* WH: 17C. Prob. from Dutch *kruisen* to cross, from *kruis* CROSS.

cruller *n.* a light, sweet, often ring-shaped cake, deep-fried in fat. WH: 19C. Dutch *kruller*, from *krullen* to curl.

crumb *n.* a small piece, esp. of bread. *Also v.t., v.i.* WH: pre-1200. Old English *cruma*, from Germanic. Cp. German *Krume*. The final *b* appeared in the 16C on an analogy with DUMB, THUMB etc.

crumble *v.t.* to break into small particles. *Also v.i., n.* WH: 14–15C. From an Old English v. that is ult. from the same Germanic base as CRUMB. See also -LE⁴.

crumbs *int.* used to express surprise or dismay. WH: 19C. Alt. of CHRIST.

crummy *a.* unpleasant, worthless. WH: 16C. CRUMB + -Y¹. The original sense was crumbly or crumblike. The current sense arose in the 19C on the basis that something strewn with crumbs is dirty or untidy.

crump *n.* the sound of the explosion of a heavy shell or bomb. *Also v.i.* WH: 17C. Imit. The original sense was verbal, to eat with a muffled crunch, as a horse or pig. The current sense evolved through army slang in the early 20C.

crumpet *n.* a thin, light, spongy teacake, often eaten toasted. WH: 17C. Orig. uncertain. ? Rel. to CRAMP¹, CRIMP¹ or CRUMPLE. A crumpet was originally a thin griddle cake.

crumple *v.t.* to crush. *Also v.i., n.* WH: 12–14C. CRUMP + -LE⁴.

crunch *v.t.* to crush noisily with the teeth. *Also v.i., n.* WH: 19C. Var. of *cranch*, of identical meaning and imit. orig., with assim. to MUNCH and CRUSH.

cruor *n.* coagulated blood. WH: 17C. Latin.

crupper *n.* a strap with a loop which passes under a horse's tail to keep the saddle from slipping forward. *Also v.t.* WH: 12–14C. Old French *cropiere* (Modern French *croupière*), from base of CROUP¹. See also -ER².

crural *a.* belonging to the leg. WH: 16C. French, or from Latin *cruralis*, from *crus, cruris* leg. See also -AL¹.

crusade *n.* any of several expeditions undertaken by Christians in the Middle Ages to recover possession of the Holy Land, then in Muslim hands. *Also v.i.* WH: 14–15C. Orig. from Medieval Latin *cruciata*, from Latin *crux, crucis* cross, but later (16C) partly from Old French *croisade*, alt. of *croisée* (from *crois* CROSS) by assim. to Spanish, partly from Spanish *cruzada* (from *cruz* CROSS). See also -ADE, -ADO.

†cruse *n.* a small pot, cup or bottle. WH: pre-1200. Old English *crūse*, of Germanic orig.

crush *v.t.* to press or squeeze together between two harder bodies so as to break, bruise or reduce to powder. *Also v.i., n.* WH: 12–14C. Old French *croissir* to gnash the teeth, to crack, ult. of unknown orig.

crust *n.* the hard outer part of bread. *Also v.t., v.i.* WH: 12–14C. Old French *crouste* (Modern French *croûte*), from Latin *crusta* rind, shell.

crustacean *n.* any animal of the class or subphylum Crustacea, including lobsters, crabs, shrimps, woodlice etc., named from their hard shells. *Also a.* WH: 19C. Modern Latin *Crustacea*, from neut. pl. (used as n.) of *crustaceus*, from Latin *crusta* CRUST. See also -AN.

crutch *n.* a staff, with a crosspiece to fit under the armpit, to support a lame or injured person. *Also v.t., v.i.* WH: pre-1200. Old English *crycc*, from Germanic base also of CROOK. Cp. CROTCH.

crutched *a.* wearing a cross as a badge. WH: 16C. Obs. *crouch* cross, from Latin CRUX, *crucis* + -ED.

crux *n.* the decisive or most important point. WH: 17C. Latin CROSS.

cruzado *n.* a former coin and monetary unit of Brazil, replaced by the cruzeiro. WH: 16C. Portuguese bearing a cross.

cruzeiro *n.* a coin and monetary unit of Brazil, equal to 100 centavos. WH: early 20C. Portuguese large cross.

cry *v.i.* to weep. *Also v.t., n.* WH: 12–14C. Old French *crier*, from Latin *quiritare* to raise a public outcry (lit. to call on the *Quirites* or Roman citizens for help). See QUIRITES.

cryo- *comb. form* very cold. WH: Greek *kruos* frost, icy cold. See also -O-.

cryobiology *n.* the study of the effects of cold on organisms. WH: 20C. CRYO- + BIOLOGY.

cryogen *n.* a freezing-mixture, a mixture of substances used to freeze liquids. WH: 20C. CRYO- + -GEN.

cryolite *n.* a brittle fluoride of sodium and aluminium from Greenland. WH: 19C. CRYO- + -LITE.

cryometer *n.* a thermometer for measuring low temperatures. WH: mid-20C. CRYO- + -METER.

cryonics *n.* the practice of preserving a dead body by deep-freezing it, in order to keep it until the discovery of a cure for the condition which caused the death. WH: mid-20C. Contr. of *cryogenics* (CRYOGEN).

cryophilic *a.* able to live or grow at low temperatures. WH: mid-20C. CRYO- + -*philic* (-PHILE).

cryophysics *n.* low-temperature physics. WH: mid-20C. CRYO- + PHYSICS.

cryoprecipitate *n.* a precipitate obtained from a substance which has been frozen and then thawed under controlled conditions. WH: late 20C. CRYO- + PRECIPITATE[2].

cryopreservation *n.* preservation of human sperm etc. by freezing. WH: late 20C. CRYO- + *preservation* (PRESERVE).

cryoprotectant *n.* a substance that stops tissues freezing or prevents damage by freezing. WH: late 20C. CRYO- + *protectant* (PROTECT).

cryopump *n.* a vacuum pump which uses liquefied gases. WH: mid-20C. CRYO- + PUMP[1].

cryostat *n.* an apparatus for maintaining, or for keeping something at, a low temperature. WH: early 20C. CRYO- + -STAT.

cryosurgery *n.* surgery involving the application of very low temperatures to specific tissues in order to cut or remove them. WH: mid-20C. CRYO- + SURGERY.

cryotherapy *n.* medical treatment involving the use of extreme cold. WH: mid-20C. CRYO- + *therapy* (THERAPEUTIC).

crypt *n.* a vault, esp. one beneath a church, used for religious services or for burial. WH: 14–15C. Latin *crypta*, from Greek *kruptē* vault, from *kruptos* hidden.

cryptanalysis *n.* the art of deciphering codes and coded texts. WH: early 20C. *crypt-* (CRYPTO-) + ANALYSIS.

cryptic *a.* hidden, secret. WH: 17C. Late Latin *crypticus*, from Greek *kruptikos*, from *kruptē*. See CRYPT, also -IC.

crypto *n.* a secret member or supporter of some organization etc. WH: mid-20C. CRYPTO- as independent word.

crypto- *comb. form* secret. WH: Greek *kruptos* hidden. See also -O-.

cryptocrystalline *a.* having a crystalline structure which is visible only under the microscope. WH: 19C. CRYPTO- + *crystalline* (CRYSTAL).

cryptogam *n.* a plant without pistils and stamens; any seedless plant such as a fern, lichen, moss, seaweed or fungus. WH: 19C. French *cryptogame*, from Modern Latin *cryptogamus*, from CRYPTO- + Greek *gamos* marriage. The plant is so called because its means of reproduction were not originally apparent.

cryptogram *n.* a text in code. WH: 19C. CRYPTO- + -GRAM.

cryptology *n.* the study of codes. WH: 17C. CRYPTO- + -LOGY.

cryptomeria *n.* a coniferous evergreen tree, *Cryptomeria japonica*, from the Far East, with many cultivated varieties. WH: 19C. Modern Latin, from CRYPTO- + Greek *meros* part. The tree is so called because the seeds are concealed by scales.

cryptonym *n.* a secret name. WH: 19C. CRYPTO- + -ONYM.

crystal *n.* a clear transparent mineral, transparent quartz, also called *rock crystal*. *Also a.* WH: pre-1200. Old French *cristal*, from Latin *crystallum*, from Greek *krustallos* ice. Rel. to CRUST.

crystallo- *comb. form* forming, formed of, of or relating to crystal, crystalline structure or the science of crystals. WH: Greek *krustallos* CRYSTAL. See also -O-.

crystallogeny *n.* the branch of science which studies the formation of crystals. WH: 19C. CRYSTALLO- + -GENY.

crystallographer *n.* a person who describes or investigates crystals and their formation. WH: 19C. CRYSTALLO- + -*grapher* (-GRAPH).

crystalloid *a.* like a crystal in appearance or structure. *Also n.* WH: 14–15C. CRYSTAL + -OID.

crystallomancy *n.* divination by means of a crystal or other transparent body. WH: 17C. CRYSTALLO- + -MANCY.

crystallometry *n.* the art or process of measuring the forms of crystals. WH: 19C. CRYSTALLO- + -METRY.

csardas *n.* a Hungarian national dance, moving from a slow to a quick tempo. WH: 19C. Hungarian *csárdás*, from *csárda* inn.

CS gas *n.* an irritant gas, causing tears, painful breathing etc., used in riot control. WH: mid-20C. Abbr. of *Carson Staughton*, from Ben B. *Carson*, 1896– , + Roger W. *Staughton*, 1906–57, US chemists who discovered its properties, 1928.

ctenoid *a.* comb-shaped. *Also n.* WH: 19C. Greek *kteis, ktenos* comb + -OID.

ctenophore *n.* a member of the Ctenophora, coelenterates with fringed or comblike locomotive organs. WH: 19C. Modern Latin *ctenophorus*, from Greek *kteis, ktenos* comb + -PHORE.

CT scanner *n.* a machine which produces X-ray photographs of sections of the body with the assistance of a computer. WH: late 20C. Abbr. of *computerized tomography* (see COMPUTER, TOMOGRAPHY) + *scanner* (SCAN).

Cu *chem. symbol* copper. WH: Abbr. of Latin *cuprum* copper.

cub *n.* the young of certain animals, e.g. the lion, bear or fox. *Also v.i., v.t.* WH: 16C. Orig. unknown. ? Rel. to COB. The equivalent Old English word was *hwelp* WHELP.

cubage *n.* the process of finding the solid contents of any body. WH: 19C. CUBE + -AGE.

Cuban *a.* of or relating to Cuba, or its people. *Also n.* WH: 16C. *Cuba*, an island in the W Indies + -AN.

cubby *n.* a cubby hole. WH: 17C. Rel. to dial. *cub* stall, pen, prob. from Low German. Rel. to COVE[1].

cube *n.* a solid figure contained by six equal squares, a regular hexahedron. *Also v.t.* WH: 16C. Old French, or from Latin *cubus*, from Greek *kubos*. Rel. to HIP[1].

cubeb *n.* the small spicy berry of *Piper cubeba*, a Javanese shrub used in medicine, cookery and medicated cigarettes. WH: 12–14C. Old French *cubèbe*, from Medieval Latin *cubeba*, from Spanish Arabic *kubēba*, from Arabic *kubāba*.

cubicle *n.* a portion of a bedroom partitioned off as a separate sleeping apartment. WH: 14–15C. Latin *cubiculum*, from *cubare* to lie. See also -CULE.

cubit *n.* an old measure of length, from the elbow to the tip of the middle finger, but varying in practice at different times from 18 to 22 in. (0.46 to 0.5 m). WH: 12–14C. Latin *cubitum* elbow, forearm, cubit.

cucking-stool *n.* a kind of chair, formerly used for ducking disorderly women, dishonest tradesmen etc. WH: 14–15C. Obs. *cuck* to defecate, of Scandinavian origin. + -ING[2] + STOOL. The chair was originally in the form of a close stool or commode.

cuckold *n.* a man whose wife is sexually unfaithful. *Also v.t.* WH: pre-1200. Var. of Old French *cucuault*, from *cucu* CUCKOO + pejorative suf. -*ald*, -*aud*. The reference is to the cuckoo's habit of laying its eggs in another bird's nest.

cuckoo *n.* a migratory bird of the family Cuculidae, esp. *Cuculus canorus*, which visits Britain in the spring and summer and lays its eggs in the nests of other birds. *Also a.* WH: 12–14C. Old French *cucu* (Modern French *coucou*), of imit. orig. Cp. Latin *cuculus*, Greek *kokkux*. The Old English name for the cuckoo was *gēac* GOWK.

cucullate *a.* hooded, resembling a hood. WH: 18C. Late Latin *cucullatus*, from *cucullus* hood. See also -ATE[2].

cucumber *n.* the elongated fruit *Cucumis sativus*, extensively used as a salad and pickle. WH: 14–15C. Latin *cucumis, cucumeris*. Rel. to GOURD. Cp. CUCURBIT. The English word was assimilated to Old French *cocombre* (Modern French *concombre*).

cucurbit *n.* a gourd. WH: 14–15C. Old French *cucurbite*, from Latin *cucurbita*. Rel. to GOURD. Cp. CUCUMBER.

cud *n.* food deposited by ruminating animals in the first stomach, from which it is drawn and chewed over again. WH: pre-1200. Old English *cudu*, earlier *cwudu*, of Germanic orig. Cp. German *Kitt* cement, putty.

cudbear *n.* a crimson dye obtained from *Roccella tinctoria* and other lichens. WH: 18C. Alt. of *Cuthbert* by Dr. Cuthbert Gordon, 18C Scottish chemist, who patented it. Cp. CUDDY¹.

cuddle *v.i.* to lie close or snug together. *Also v.t.*, *n.* WH: 16C. ? From COUTH (in sense snug) + -LE⁴.

cuddy¹ *n.* a donkey, an ass. WH: 18C. Prob. from *Cuddy*, pet form of male forename *Cuthbert*. Cp. NEDDY.

cuddy² *n.* a cabin in a ship where officers and passengers take their meals. WH: 17C. Prob. from early Dutch *kajute* (now *kajuit*), from Old French *cahute* shanty, of unknown orig.

cudgel *n.* a short club or thick stick, a bludgeon. *Also v.t.* WH: pre-1200. Old English *cycgel*, of unknown orig.

cudweed *n.* any plant of the genus *Gnaphalium*, esp. *G. sylvaticum*, a plant formerly administered to cattle that had lost their cud. WH: 16C. CUD + WEED.

cue¹ *n.* the last words of a speech, a signal to another actor that they should begin. *Also v.t.* WH: 16C. Orig. unknown. The word is said to represent letter *q*, from Latin *quando* when, marked at the point in an actor's script where he was to enter or begin his speech.

cue² *n.* a long straight rod used by players of snooker, pool etc. *Also v.t.*, *v.i.* WH: 18C. Var. of QUEUE.

cuesta *n.* a hill ridge with a gentle slope ending in a steep scarp slope. WH: 19C. Spanish slope, from Latin *costa*. See COAST.

cuff¹ *n.* the fold or band at the end of a sleeve. WH: 14–15C. Orig. unknown. Prob. not rel. to COIF.

cuff² *v.t.* to strike with the open hand. *Also n.* WH: 16C. Prob. imit. Cp. German slang *kuffen* to thrash, Swedish *kuffa* to thrust.

cui bono? *adv.*, *int.* for whose benefit?, who stands to gain? WH: 17C. Latin to whom (is it) a benefit?, from *cui*, dat. sing. of *qui* who, which + abl. sing. of *bonum* good thing (cp. BONUS). The full form of the phrase is *cui bono est?* to whom is it a benefit?, attributed by Cicero to one Lucius Cassius.

cuirass *n.* armour for the body, consisting of a breastplate and a backplate strapped or buckled together. WH: 14–15C. Old French *cuirace*, later *curas* (Modern French *cuirasse*), from alt. (based on Old French *cuir* leather) of fem. (used as n.) of Latin *coriaceus*, a. from *corium* leather. See also -ACEOUS.

cuisine *n.* a style of cooking. WH: 18C. French kitchen, from Latin *coquina*, *cocina*, from *coquere* to cook. Cp. KITCHEN.

cuisse *n.* a piece of thigh armour. WH: 12–14C. Old French *cuisseus*, pl. of *cuissel*, from Late Latin *coxale*, from *coxa* hip. The English word was originally plural.

culchie *n.* a country labourer, a yokel. *Also a.* WH: mid-20C. ? Alt. of first part of *Kilti*magh, a country town in County Mayo, Ireland.

cul-de-sac *n.* a street or lane open only at one end. WH: 18C. French bottom of the sack, from *cul* bottom + *de* of + *sac* SACK¹. The phrase was originally used in an anatomical sense of a sac (tube) closed at one end.

-cule *comb. form* used to form nouns, esp. indicating smallness, as in *molecule*. WH: French, from Latin *-culus*, dim. suf. Cp. -CLE, -UNCLE.

culex *n.* a dipterous insect of the genus *Culex*, containing the gnat and the mosquito. WH: 15C. Latin gnat.

culinary *a.* relating to the kitchen or cooking. WH: 17C. Latin *culinarius*, from *culina* kitchen. See also -ARY¹.

cull *v.t.* to select, to choose as the best. *Also n.* WH: 12–14C. Old French *coillier* (Modern French *cueillir*), from Latin *colligere* COLLECT¹.

cullet *n.* broken glass for recycling. WH: 19C. Var. of COLLET.

cullis *n.* a roof gutter. WH: 19C. French *coulisse*, use as n. of fem. of *coulis* sliding.

cully *n.* a pal, a mate. WH: 17C. Orig. unknown.

culm¹ *n.* a stem, esp. of grass or sedge. WH: 17C. Latin *culmus*.

culm² *n.* anthracite coal, esp. if in small pieces. WH: 12–14C. Prob. rel. to COAL.

culmen *n.* the ridge on the top of a bird's bill. WH: 17C. Latin, contr. of *columen* top, summit. Cp. CULMINATE.

culminate *v.i.* to reach the highest point. WH: 17C. Late Latin *culminatus*, p.p. of *culminare* to exalt, from *culmen*, *culminis* summit. See also -ATE³.

culottes *n.pl.* women's flared trousers cut to resemble a skirt. WH: 19C. French, pl. of *culotte* knee breeches, from *cul* bottom, backside.

culpable *a.* blamable, blameworthy. WH: 12–14C. Old French *coupable*, from Latin *culpabilis*, from *culpare* to blame, from *culpa* fault, blame. See also -ABLE.

culprit *n.* a person who is at fault. WH: 17C. ? From misinterpretation of written abbr. *cul.prist.*, from Anglo-French *Culpable: prest d'averrer notre bille* (You are) guilty: (we are) ready to aver our indictment, form of address to accused in trial. The original legal usage was in the formula *Culprit, how will you be tried?* said by the clerk to a prisoner who had pleaded not guilty.

cult *n.* a system of religious belief. *Also a.* WH: 17C. French *culte* or Latin *cultus* worship, from *colere* to inhabit, to protect, to honour with worship.

cultivar *n.* a variety of a naturally-occurring species, produced and maintained by cultivation. WH: early 20C. Blend of CULTIVATE and VARIETY. The term was devised in 1923 by the US horticulturist and botanist Liberty H. Bailey.

cultivate *v.t.* to till, to prepare for crops. WH: 17C. Medieval Latin *cultivatus*, p.p. of *cultivare*, from *cultivus* in *cultiva terra* arable land, from Latin *cultus*, p.p. of *colere*. See CULT, also -IVE, -ATE³.

cultrate *a.* shaped like a knife. WH: 19C. Latin *cultratus*, from *culter* knife. See also -ATE². Cp. COULTER.

culture *n.* a state of intellectual and artistic development. *Also v.t.* WH: 12–14C. French, or from Latin *cultura*, from *cultus*. See CULTIVATE, also -URE.

†culver *n.* a wood pigeon. WH: pre-1200. Old English *culfre*, *culfer*, from Latin *columbula*, dim. of *columba* dove, pigeon.

culverin *n.* a long cannon or handgun. WH: 15C. Old French *coulevrine*, from *couleuvre* snake, from Latin *colubra*, *coluber* snake. See also -INE. The names of reptiles were often applied to early types of cannon.

culvert *n.* a drain or covered channel for water beneath a road, railway etc. WH: 18C. Orig. uncertain. Prob. not from French *couvert* covered (see COVERT¹).

cum¹ *prep.* combined with, together with. WH: 14–15C. Latin with.

cum² *n.* ejaculated semen. WH: late 20C. Var. of COME.

cumber *v.t.* to hamper, to clog, to hinder, to impede. *Also n.* WH: 12–14C. Prob. shortening of *accumber* or ENCUMBER.

Cumberland sausage *n.* a coarse-grained savoury sausage, of a type orig. made in Cumberland. WH: mid-20C. *Cumberland*, a former county in NW England (now part of Cumbria) + SAUSAGE.

cumbia *n.* a type of dance music similar to salsa, orig. from Colombia. WH: mid-20C. Columbian Spanish, ? from Spanish *cumbé*.

Cumbrian *a.* belonging to the county of Cumbria in NW England, to the former county Cumberland, or the ancient British kingdom of Cumbria. *Also n.* WH: 18C. Medieval Latin *Cumbria*, from Welsh *Cymry* Welshmen, or a Brittonic word meaning compatriots. See also -AN. Cp. CAMBRIAN.

cum grano salis *adv.* with a pinch of salt, not too seriously. WH: 17C. Latin with a grain of salt, from CUM¹ with + abl. sing. of *granum* GRAIN + gen. sing. of SAL¹ salt.

cumin *n.* an umbelliferous plant of the parsley family, *Cuminum cyminum*, with aromatic and carminative seeds. WH: pre-1200. Old English *cymen*, from Latin *cuminum*, from Greek *kuminon*, of Semitic orig. Cp. German *Kümmel* a liqueur flavoured with caraway seeds.

cummerbund *n.* a waistband or sash, worn esp. by men with evening dress. WH: 17C. Urdu *kamar-band* loin band, waist band, from Persian, from *kamar* waist, loins + Persian and Urdu *-bandī* tie, band.

cumshaw *n.* in China etc., a present, a tip. *Also v.t.* WH: 19C. Chinese (dial.) *gǎmsiâ*, (Mandarin) *gǎnxiè*, from *gǎn* to be grateful + *xiè* to thank. The word was originally a phrase used by Chinese beggars.

cumulate¹ *v.t.*, *v.i.* to accumulate. WH: 16C. Latin *cumulatus*, p.p. of *cumulare*, from *cumulus* heap. See also -ATE³.

cumulate² *a.* heaped up, accumulated. WH: 16C. Latin *cumulatus*. See CUMULATE¹, also -ATE².

cumulo- *comb. form* (of cloud) cumulus. WH: CUMULUS. See also -O-.

cumulonimbus *n.* a very thick, dark cumulus cloud, usu. a sign of thunder or hail. WH: 19C. CUMULO- + NIMBUS.

cumulostratus *n.* a mass of cumulus cloud with a horizontal base. WH: 19C. CUMULO- + STRATUS.

cumulus *n.* a round billowing mass of cloud, with a flattish base. WH: 17C. Latin heap. The meteorological sense dates from the 19C.

cunctation *n.* cautious delaying. WH: 16C. Latin *cunctatio*, *cunctationis*, from *cunctatus*, p.p. of *cunctari* to delay. See also -ATION.

cuneate *a.* wedge-shaped. WH: 19C. Latin *cuneus* wedge + -ATE².

cunjevoi *n.* an Australian plant of the arum family, *Alocasia macrorrhiza*, grown for its edible rhizome. WH: 19C. Australian Aboriginal.

cunnilingus *n.* stimulation of the female genitals by the lips and tongue. WH: 19C. Latin one who licks the vulva, from *cunnus* female (external) genitals + *lingere* to lick.

cunning *a.* artful, crafty. Also *n.* WH: 12–14C. Old Norse *kunnandi* knowing, pres.p. of *kunna* to know (see CAN¹).

cunt *n.* the female genitalia. WH: 12–14C. Rel. to Old Norse *kunta*, Middle Dutch *kunte*, from Germanic, ult. of unknown orig. According to some, rel. to COT².

cup *n.* a vessel to drink from, usu. small and with one handle. Also *v.t.*, *v.i.* WH: pre-1200. Popular Latin *cuppa*, prob. from Latin *cupa* tub.

cupboard *n.* an enclosed case or recess with shelves to receive plates, dishes, food etc. Also *v.t.* WH: 14–15C. CUP + BOARD. A cupboard was originally a table on which to display cups, plates etc. Cp. *sideboard* (SIDE). The current sense dates from the 16C.

cupel *n.* a small shallow vessel used in assaying precious metals. Also *v.t.* WH: 17C. French *coupelle*, dim. of *coupe* CUP.

Cupid *n.* the Roman god of love. WH: 14–15C. Latin *Cupido*, personification of *cupido* desire, love, from *cupere* to desire.

cupidity *n.* an inordinate desire to possess, covetousness, avarice. WH: 14–15C. French *cupidité* or Latin *cupiditas*, from *cupidus* desirous, from *cupere* to desire. See also -ID, -ITY.

cupola *n.* a little dome. WH: 16C. Italian, from Late Latin *cupula* little cask, small vault, dim. of *cupa* cask.

cuppa *n.* a cup of tea. WH: mid-20C. Representation of spoken form of *cup of.*

cupreous *a.* of, like or composed of copper. WH: 17C. Late Latin *cupreus*, from *cuprum* COPPER. See also -OUS.

cupressus *n.* any conifer of the genus *Cupressus*, which includes the cypress. WH: 19C. Late Latin *Cupressus* genus name. See CYPRESS¹.

cupule *n.* an inflorescence consisting of a cup, as in the oak or hazel. WH: 14–15C. Late Latin *cupula*. See CUPOLA.

cur *n.* a mongrel, an aggressive dog. WH: 12–14C. Prob. from orig. form *cur-dog*, from Old Norse *kurr* grumbling or *kurra* murmur, of imit. orig. Cp. GROWL and *grr*, imit. of dog's growling.

curaçao *n.* a liqueur flavoured with bitter orange peel, sugar and cinnamon, orig. from Curaçao. WH: 19C. *Curaçao*, a Caribbean island of the lesser Antilles, producing oranges used in the liqueur's flavouring.

curare *n.* the dried extract of plants from the genera *Strychnos* and *Chondodendron*, used by the Indians of S America for poisoning arrows, and formerly employed in physiological investigations as a muscle relaxant. WH: 18C. Spanish and Portuguese, from Carib *kurari*.

curassow *n.* any turkey-like game bird of the family Cracidae, found in S and Central America. WH: 17C. Alt. of *Curaçao*. See CURAÇAO.

curate *n.* a member of the Church of England clergy who assists the incumbent of a parish. WH: 12–14C. Medieval Latin *curatus* person having cure (charge) of a parish, from *cura*. See CURE, also -ATE¹. A curate was originally so called because he had the care of (souls in) the parish. The current sense evolved in the 16C for an assistant to the incumbent, or for a clergyman who deputized for him in his absence. Cp. CURÉ.

curative *a.* tending to cure. Also *n.* WH: 14–15C. French *curatif*, from Medieval Latin *curativus*, from Latin *curatus*. See CURATOR, also -IVE.

curator *n.* a person who has charge of a library, museum or similar establishment. WH: 14–15C. Partly from Old French *curateur*, partly from Latin *curator*, from *curatus*, p.p. of *curare*. See CURE, also -OR.

curb *n.* a check, a restraint. Also *v.t.* WH: 15C. Prob. var. of obs. *courb* to bend, to bow, from Old French *courber*, from Latin *curvare* CURVE. Cp. KERB.

curch *n.* a piece of linen formerly worn by women, a kerchief. WH: 14–15C. Erron. sing. representing Old French *cuevrechés*, pl. of *couvrechef*. See KERCHIEF.

curculio *n.* a weevil of the family Curculionidae, esp. *Conotrachelus nenuphar*, which attacks fruit trees. WH: 18C. Latin corn weevil.

curcuma *n.* any plant of the genus *Curcuma*, tuberous plants of the ginger family. WH: 14–15C. Medieval Latin, from Arabic *kurkum*, from Sanskrit *kuṅkuma* saffron.

curd *n.* the coagulated part of milk, used to make cheese. Also *v.t.*, *v.i.* WH: 14–15C. Orig. unknown. ? Rel. to CROWD¹. Cp. CRUD.

curdle *v.t.* to break into curds. Also *v.i.* WH: 16C. Freq. of CURD. See also -LE⁴.

cure *n.* the act of healing or curing disease. Also *v.t.*, *v.i.* WH: 12–14C. Old French, from Latin *cura* care. Not rel. to CARE. The original sense was care, heed, concern (to the 17C). The medical sense evolved in the 14–15C.

curé *n.* a parish priest in France etc., a French rector or vicar. WH: 17C. French, from Medieval Latin *curatus*. See CURATE. The French *curé* corresponds in sense to the English vicar, while the English curate corresponds to the French *vicaire*. See VICAR.

curette *n.* a surgeon's instrument used for scraping a body cavity. Also *v.t.*, *v.i.* WH: 18C. French, from *curer* to take care of, to clean, from Latin *curare* to care for. See CURE, also -ETTE.

curfew *n.* a military or civil regulation to be off the streets or indoors between stated hours. WH: 12–14C. Old French *cuevrefeu* (Modern French *couvrefeu*), from *cuvrir* COVER + *feu* fire. A curfew was originally a regulation stipulating a time by which fires had to be covered or extinguished.

Curia *n.* the papal court. WH: 17C. Latin, ? from Old Latin **co-viria* coalition of men. See CO-, VIRILE.

curie *n.* the standard unit of radioactivity, 3.7×10^{10} disintegrations per second. WH: early 20C. Pierre and Marie *Curie*, 1859–1906 and 1867–1934, co-discoverers of radium, 1898. Cp. CURIUM.

curio *n.* a curiosity, esp. a curious piece of art; a bit of bric-a-brac. WH: 19C. Abbr. of *curiosity* (CURIOUS).

curiosa *n.pl.* unusual (collectable) objects. WH: 19C. Latin, neut. pl. of *curiosus*. See CURIOUS.

curious *a.* inquisitive, desirous to know. WH: 12–14C. Old French *curius* (Modern French *curieux*), from Latin *curiosus* careful, inquisitive, from *cura* care. See CURE, also -OUS.

curium *n.* an artificially-produced transuranic metallic element, at. no. 96, chem. symbol Cm. WH: mid-20C. Pierre and Marie *Curie* (see CURIE) + -IUM. The element was named by the US nuclear chemist Glenn T. Seaborg, who with co-workers discovered it in 1944.

curl *n.* a ringlet or twisted lock of hair. Also *v.t.*, *v.i.* WH: 14–15C. Appar. from an unrecorded Old English word rel. to Middle Dutch *crulle*, Middle High German *krol*, Norwegian *krull* all meaning curl.

curlew *n.* a migratory wading bird of the genus *Numenius*, esp. the European *N. arquatus*. WH: 12–14C. Old French *courlieu*, var. of *courlis*, orig. imit. of bird's cry but assim. to Old French *courliu* courier, messenger, from *courre* to run + *lieu* place. The curlew is a good runner.

curlicue *n.* a decorative curl or twist, esp. in handwriting. WH: 19C. *curly* (CURL) + CUE¹.

curmudgeon *n.* a miserly or churlish person. WH: 16C. Orig. unknown. The word is not from French *cœur méchant* malicious heart, as Dr. Johnson suggested.

currach *n.* a skiff made of wickerwork and hides, a coracle. WH: 14–15C. Irish and Gaelic *curach* small boat. Cp. CORACLE.

currant *n.* the dried fruit of a dwarf seedless grape orig. from the E Mediterranean. WH: 16C. Abbr. of *raisins of Corauntz*, from Old French *raisins de Corinthe*, lit. grapes of Corinth. See RAISIN. The fruit was originally exported from Corinth, Greece. It was not the present currant, however, but a type of raisin. The name was subsequently transferred to the black, red or white fruit of the genus *Ribes*, which its clusters resembled.

currawong *n.* an Australian crowlike songbird of the genus *Strepera*. WH: early 20C. Australian Aboriginal (Yagara) *garrawang*.

currency *n.* the circulating monetary medium of a country, whether in coin or paper. WH: 17C. CURRENT. See also -ENCY.

current *a.* belonging to the present week, month, year. *Also n.* WH: 12–14C. Old French *corant* (Modern French *courant*), pres.p. of *courre* (Modern French *courir*), from Latin *currere* to run. See also -ENT, -ANT.

curricle *n.* a two-wheeled chaise for a pair of horses. *Also v.i.* WH: 14–15C. Latin CURRICULUM. The original sense (to the 18C) was the running or course of one thing or several consecutive things. The carriage name dates from the 18C.

curriculum *n.* a fixed course of study at a school etc. WH: 19C. Latin running, course, race chariot, from *currere* to run.

currier *n.* a person who curries, dresses and colours leather after it has been tanned. WH: 14–15C. Old French *corier*, from Latin *coriarius*, from *corium* leather. See also -ER². Not rel. to CURRY².

curry¹ *n.* a highly-spiced orig. Indian dish of stewed meat, fish etc. in a sauce, usu. served with rice. *Also v.t.* WH: 16C. Tamil *kaṟi* sauce, relish for rice.

curry² *v.t.* to groom (a horse) with a curry-comb. WH: 12–14C. Old French *correier* (Modern French *courroyer*) to arrange, to equip, to curry (a horse), from Latin CON- + Germanic base of READY.

curse *v.t.* to invoke harm or evil upon. *Also v.i., n.* WH: pre-1200. Orig. unknown. Not rel. to CROSS.

cursillo *n.* an informal spiritual retreat of members of the Roman Catholic Church, esp. in Latin America. WH: mid-20C. Spanish little course.

cursive *a.* handwritten with joined characters, esp. with looped characters. *Also n.* WH: 18C. Medieval Latin *cursivus*, from Latin *cursus*, p.p. of *currere* to run. See also -IVE.

cursor *n.* on a VDU screen, a movable point of light or other indicator showing the position of the next action, e.g. the beginning of an addition or correction. WH: 12–14C. Latin runner, from *cursus*. See CURSIVE, also -OR. The original sense (to the 17C) was runner, running messenger. The mathematical meaning arose in the 16C and the computing application in the mid-20C.

cursorial *a.* adapted for running. WH: 19C. Latin *cursorius*. See CURSORY, also -AL¹.

cursory *a.* hasty, careless. WH: 17C. Latin *cursorius*, from CURSOR. See also -ORY².

curt *a.* abrupt, esp. rudely terse. WH: 14–15C. Latin *curtus* cut short, abridged. Rel. to SHORT.

curtail *v.t.* to shorten, lessen or reduce. WH: 15C. From CURTAL, but from 16C assoc. with TAIL¹ and later prob. with French *tailler* to cut (see TAILOR).

curtail step *n.* the bottom step of a flight of stairs, finished at its outer extremity in a scroll. WH: 18C. Orig. of first element unknown. The second is STEP.

curtain *n.* a length of material hanging beside a window or door, or round a bed, which can be drawn across. *Also v.t.* WH: 12–14C. Old French *cortine* (Modern French *courtine*), from Late Latin *cortina*, translating Greek *aulaia*, from *aulē* court.

†curtal *n.* a horse with a cropped tail. *Also a.* WH: 15C. French *courtault*, *courtauld* (now *courtaud*), from *court* short (cp. CURT) + pejorative suf. *-ault*.

†curtal axe *n.* a heavy sort of cutting sword, a cutlass. WH: 16C. Alt. of CUTLASS by assim. to CURTAL and AXE.

curtana *n.* the unpointed sword carried in front of the English sovereigns at their coronation as a symbol of mercy. WH: 12–14C. Anglo-Latin *curtana*, from Anglo-French *curtain*, from Old French *cortain*, from *cort* short (cp. CURT). Old French *Cortain* was the name of Roland's sword, so called because it had broken at the point when driven into a block of steel.

curtilage *n.* a piece of ground lying near and belonging to a dwelling and included within the same fence. WH: 12–14C. Old French *courtillage*, from *courtil* small court, kitchen garden, from *cort* COURT. See also -AGE.

curtsy *n.* an act of respect or salutation, performed by women by slightly bending the body and knees at the same time. *Also v.i.* WH: 16C. Contr. of COURTESY.

curule *a.* of high civic dignity. WH: 16C. Latin *curulis*, from *currus* chariot, from *currere* to run.

curvaceous *a.* (of a woman's body) generously curved. WH: mid-20C. CURVE + -ACEOUS.

curvature *n.* deflection from a straight line. WH: 14–15C. Old French, from Latin *curvatura*, from *curvatus*, p.p. of *curvare* CURVE. See also -URE.

curve *n.* a line of which no three consecutive points are in a straight line. *Also v.t., v.i.* WH: 14–15C. Latin *curvus* bent, curved. Cp. CURB.

curvet *n.* a particular leap of a horse raising the forelegs at once, and, as the forelegs are falling, raising the hindlegs, so that all four are off the ground at once. *Also v.i.* WH: 16C. Italian *corvetta*, dim. of *corva*, early form of *curva* CURVE, from Latin *curva*, fem. of *curvus* bent, curved.

curvi- *comb. form* curved. WH: Latin *curvus* bent, curved + -i-.

curvifoliate *a.* having revolute leaves. WH: 19C. CURVI- + FOLIATE¹.

curvilinear *a.* bounded by curved lines. WH: 18C. CURVI- + LINEAR, based on RECTILINEAR.

cuscus *n.* any of several nocturnal tree-dwelling marsupials of the genus *Phalanger* of N Australia, New Guinea etc. WH: 17C. French *couscous*, from Dutch *koeskoes*, from native Moluccas name.

cusec *n.* a unit of rate of flow of water, 1 cu. ft. (0.0283 m³) per second. WH: early 20C. Abbr. of *cubic foot per second*.

cush *n.* in snooker, pool etc., the cushion. WH: 19C. Abbr. of CUSHION.

cushat *n.* the wood pigeon or ring-dove. WH: pre-1200. Orig. unknown.

cush-cush *n.* a variety of yam, *Dioscorea trifida* of S America. WH: 19C. ? Ult. of African orig.

Cushing's syndrome *n.* a metabolic disorder in which the adrenal cortex produces excessive corticosteroid hormones, usu. resulting in obesity, hypertension and fatigue. WH: mid-20C. Harvey W. Cushing, 1869–1939, US surgeon.

cushion *n.* a kind of pillow or pad for sitting, kneeling or leaning on, stuffed with feathers, wool, hair or other soft material. *Also v.t.* WH: 12–14C. Old French *coissin* (Modern French *coussin*), from var. of Popular Latin *coxinum*, from Latin *coxa* hip, thigh.

Cushitic *n.* a group of Hamitic languages of E Africa. *Also a.* WH: early 20C. *Cushite* (from *Cush*, an ancient country in the Nile valley + -ITE¹) + -IC.

cushy *a.* (of a job etc.) well paid and with little to do. WH: early 20C. Urdu *kuśī* pleasure, from Persian *kuš*. Not rel. to CUSHION.

cusp *n.* a point, an apex, a summit. WH: 16C. Latin *cuspis*, *cuspidis* point, apex.

cuspidor *n.* a spittoon. WH: 18C. Portuguese spitter, from *cuspir* to spit, from Latin *conspuere*. See also -OR.

cuss *n.* a curse. *Also v.t.* WH: 18C. Var. of CURSE. The sense person, creature was later popularly taken to be abbr. of CUSTOMER.

custard *n.* a composition of milk and eggs, sweetened and flavoured. WH: 14–15C. Old French *crouste* CRUST. See also -ABLE. An earlier spelling was *crustade*. A custard was originally an open pie containing meat or fruit covered with broth or milk, thickened with eggs, sweetened and spiced. The current sense dates from the 17C.

custody *n.* guardianship, security. WH: 14–15C. Latin *custodia*, from *custos*, *custodis* guardian. See also -Y².

custom *n.* a habitual use or practice. *Also a., v.t., v.i.* WH: 12–14C. Old French *costume* (Modern French *coutume*), from alt. of Latin *consuetudo*, *consuetudinis*, from *consuescere* to become accustomed, from CON- + *suescere* to become accustomed. Cp. CONSUETUDE.

customary *a.* habitual, usual. *Also n.* WH: 16C. Medieval Latin *custumarius*, from *custuma*, from Anglo-French *custome*. See CUSTOM, also -ARY¹.

customer *n.* a purchaser. WH: 14–15C. Anglo-French *custumer* or Medieval Latin *custumarius*. See also -ER¹. An earlier sense (to the 19C) was a customs officer. The sense person of a particular character that one has to deal with dates from the 16C.

custos *n.* a keeper, a custodian. WH: 14–15C. Latin.

cut¹ *v.t.* to penetrate or wound with a sharp instrument. *Also v.i., int.* WH: 12–14C. Orig. uncertain. Prob. rel. to Norwegian *kutte*, Icelandic *kuta* to cut with a little knife. The word was probably already in Old English, although it has not been recorded.

cut² *n.* the action of cutting. *Also a.* WH: 14–15C. CUT¹.

cutaneous *a.* belonging to or affecting the skin. WH: 16C. Modern Latin *cutaneus*, from Latin *cutis* skin. See also -ANEOUS.

cutch *n.* catechu. WH: 18C. Malay *kachu*. Cp. CATECHU, CACHOU.

cute *a.* attractive, pretty. WH: 18C. Shortening of ACUTE.

cuticle *n.* the dead skin at the edge of fingernails and toenails. WH: 15C. Latin *cuticula*, dim. of *cutis* skin. See also -CULE.

cutis *n.* the true skin beneath the epidermis. WH: 17C. Latin skin.

cutlass *n.* a broad curved sword, esp. that formerly used by sailors. WH: 16C. French *coutelas*, from Latin *cultellus* (see CUTLER) + augm. suf. *-aceum*.

cutler *n.* a person who makes or deals in cutting instruments. WH: 12–14C. Old French *coutelier*, from Old French *coutel* (Modern French *couteau*) knife, from Latin *cultellus*, dim. of *culter* COULTER. See also -ER².

cutlet *n.* a small slice of meat, usu. from the loin or neck, for cooking. WH: 18C. French *côtelette*, earlier *costelette*, dim. of *coste* rib (now *côte*), from Latin *costa*. See also -EL, -ETTE. Not rel. to CUT¹ but assim. to it, + -LET.

cuttle *n.* a cuttlefish. WH: pre-1200. Old English *cudele*, from base of COD², alluding to its ink bag.

cutty *a.* short, cut short. *Also n.* WH: 17C. From *cut*, p.p. of CUT¹ + -Y³.

cuvée *n.* a batch or blend of wine. WH: 19C. French vatful, from *cuve*, from Latin *cupa* cask, vat. Cp. CUP.

cuvette *n.* a shallow dish for holding liquids in a laboratory. WH: 17C. French dim. of *cuve*. See CUVÉE, -ETTE.

cwm *n.* a valley in Wales. WH: 19C. Welsh valley. Cp. COMBE.

cwt. *abbr.* hundredweight. WH: Abbr. of Latin *centum* hundred. + WEIGHT.

-cy *suf.* forming nouns of quality from adjectives, and nouns of office (cp. -SHIP) from nouns, as in *fallacy, lunacy, tenancy, residency*. WH: Latin *-cia, -tia*, Greek *-keia, -teia*. See also -Y².

cyan *n.* a bluish-green colour. *Also a.* WH: 19C. Greek *kuanos* dark blue.

cyanamide *n.* a colourless crystalline weak acid, an amide of cyanogen. WH: 19C. *cyan-* (CYANO-) + AMIDE.

cyanate *n.* a salt of cyanic acid. WH: 19C. CYANIC + -ATE¹.

cyanic *a.* derived from cyanogen. WH: 19C. *cyan-* (CYANO-) + -IC.

cyanide *n.* any (very poisonous) compound of cyanogen with a metallic element. WH: 19C. *cyan-* (CYANO-) + -IDE.

cyanine *n.* a blue dye used in photographic emulsions. WH: 19C. *cyan-* (CYANO-) + -INE.

cyano- *comb. form* of a blue colour. WH: Greek *kuanos* dark blue. See also -O-.

cyanobacterium *n.* any prokaryotic organism of the division *Cyanobacteria*, containing a blue photosynthetic pigment, blue-green alga. WH: late 20C. CYANO- + BACTERIUM.

cyanocobalamin *n.* a vitamin of the B complex occurring in the liver, the lack of which can lead to pernicious anaemia, Vitamin B_{12}. WH: mid-20C. CYANO- + *cobalamin*, from COBALT + VITAMIN.

cyanogen *n.* a colourless, poisonous gas composed of carbon and nitrogen, burning with a peach-blossom flame, and smelling like almond. WH: 19C. French *cyanogène*. See CYANO-, -GEN. The gas was so named in 1815 by the French chemist Joseph Louis Gay-Lussac, as it is chemically related to Prussian blue.

cyanosis *n.* a condition in which the skin becomes blue or leaden-coloured owing to the circulation of oxygen-deficient blood. WH: 19C. Modern Latin, from Greek *kuanōsis* blueness. See CYANO-, also -OSIS.

cyanotype *n.* a photographic process in which a cyanide is employed, producing a blueprint. WH: 19C. CYANO- + -type (see TYPE).

cyber- *comb. form* denoting computer control systems, electronic communication networks and virtual reality. WH: Abbr. of CYBERNETICS.

cybernetics *n.* the comparative study of control and communication mechanisms in machines and living creatures. WH: mid-20C. Greek *kubernētēs* steersman, from *kubernan* to steer. See also -ICS. The study was so named by the US mathematician Norbert Wiener, who introduced it in his book *Cybernetics: or, Control and Communication in the Animal and the Machine* (1948).

cyberpunk *n.* a style of science fiction writing that features rebellious computer hackers in a bleak future world controlled by computer networks. WH: late 20C. CYBER- + PUNK.

cyberspace *n.* virtual reality, the notional environment created by computer in which people can physically interact. WH: late 20C. CYBER- + SPACE.

cyborg *n.* a form of robot of superhuman capabilities made from biological and mechanical parts. WH: mid-20C. Abbr. of *cybernetic organism*. See CYBERNETICS, ORGANISM.

cycad *n.* a tropical or subtropical palmlike plant of the order Cycadeles, an order of gymnosperms, allied to the conifers. WH: 19C. Modern Latin *Cycar* genus name, from erron. Greek *kukas*, mistranscription of *koikas*, acc. pl. of *koix* doum.

Cycladic *a.* of or relating to the Cyclades, a group of islands in the S Aegean Sea, esp. to the Bronze Age civilization that existed there. WH: early 20C. Latin *Cyclades*, from Greek *Kuklades*, from *kuklos* circle. See also -IC.

cyclamate *n.* any of several compounds derived from petrochemicals, formerly used as sweetening agents. WH: mid-20C. Contr. of *cyclohexylsulphamate*.

cyclamen *n.* any S European tuberous plant of the genus *Cyclamen*, having red, pink or white flowers. WH: 16C. Medieval Latin, from Latin *cyclaminos*, from Greek *kuklaminos*, prob. from *kuklos* circle. The name apparently refers to the plant's round root.

cycle *n.* a series of events or phenomena recurring in the same order. *Also v.i.* WH: 14–15C. French, or from Late Latin *cyclus*, from Greek *kuklos* circle.

cyclo- *comb. form* circular. WH: Greek *kuklos* circle. See also -O-.

cycloalkane *n.* a saturated hydrocarbon having a cyclic molecular structure, cycloparaffin. WH: mid-20C. CYCLO- + ALKANE.

cyclo-cross *n.* the sport of cross-country racing on a bicycle. WH: mid-20C. CYCLE (from BICYCLE) + *cross-country* (CROSS). Cp. BMX.

cyclograph *n.* an instrument for describing the arcs of large circles. WH: 19C. CYCLO- + -GRAPH.

cyclohexane *n.* a colourless liquid cycloalkane used as a paint remover and solvent. WH: 19C. CYCLO- + HEXANE.

cycloid *n.* the figure described by a point in the plane of a circle as it rolls along a straight line till it has completed a revolution. WH: 17C. Greek *kukloeidēs* circular. See CYCLE, also -OID.

cyclometer *n.* an instrument for recording the revolutions of a wheel, esp. that of a bicycle, and hence the distance travelled. WH: 17C. CYCLO- + -METER. The current arose in the 19C, influ. by CYCLE (in the sense BICYCLE).

cyclone *n.* a tropical cyclone. WH: 19C. Prob. from Greek *kuklōma* wheel, coil of a snake. The word was coined in 1848 by the English meteorologist Henry Piddington as a general term for any storm or atmospheric disturbance in which the wind has a circular course.

cycloparaffin *n.* a cycloalkane. WH: early 20C. CYCLO- + PARAFFIN.

cyclopedia *n.* an encyclopedia. WH: 17C. Abbr. of ENCYCLOPEDIA.

cyclopropane *n.* a colourless hydrocarbon gas used as an anaesthetic. WH: mid-20C. CYCLO- + PROPANE.

Cyclops *n.* a member of a race of mythical one-eyed giants supposed to have lived in Sicily. WH: 14–15C. Latin, from Greek *kuklōps* round-eyed, from *kuklos* circle + *ōps* eye.

cyclorama *n.* a curved wall or cloth at the rear of a stage, film set etc. WH: 19C. CYCLO- + -*rama* based on PANORAMA.

cyclosis *n.* circulation, as of blood, the latex in plants, or protoplasm in certain cells. WH: 19C. Greek *kuklōsis* encirclement.

cyclosporin *n.* an immunosuppressant drug used after transplant surgery to prevent rejection of grafts and transplants. WH: late 20C. CYCLO- + Modern Latin *polysporum* (from fungus *Trichoderma polysporum*) + -IN¹.

cyclostome *n.* any fish of the subclass Cyclostomata, with a circular sucking mouth, e.g. the lamprey and hag. WH: 19C. CYCLO- + Greek *stoma* mouth.

cyclostyle *n.* a machine for printing copies of handwriting or typewriting by means of a sheet perforated like a stencil. *Also v.t.* WH: 19C. CYCLO- + STYLE.

cyclothymia *n.* a psychological condition characterized by swings between elation and depression. WH: early 20C. CYCLO- + Greek *thumos* temper, mind + -IA.

cyclotron *n.* a particle accelerator designed to accelerate protons to high energies. WH: mid-20C. CYCLO- + -TRON. The accelerator is so called as the particles revolve in a magnetic field.

cygnet *n.* a young swan. WH: 14–15C. Old French *cigne* (Modern French *cygne*), or from Latin *cycnus, cygnus* swan, from Greek *kuknos*. See also -ET¹.

cylinder *n.* a straight roller-shaped body, solid or hollow, and of uniform circumference. WH: 16C. Latin *cylindrus*, from Greek *kulindros* roller, from *kulindein* to roll.

cyma *n.* a convex and a concave curve forming the topmost member of a cornice. WH: 16C. Modern Latin, from Greek *kuma* billow, wave, from *kuein* to become pregnant.

cymar *n.* a woman's light loose robe or undergarment of the 17th and 18th cents. WH: 17C. French *simarre*, from Italian *cimarra*, *zimarra*. Cp. CHIMER.

cymatium *n.* a cyma. WH: 16C. Latin ogee, Ionic volute, from Greek *kumation*, dim. of *kuma* CYMA.

cymbal *n.* a disc of brass or bronze more or less basin-shaped, clashed together in pairs or hit with a stick etc. to produce a sharp, clashing sound. WH: pre-1200. Latin *cymbalum*, from Greek *kumbalon*, from *kumbē* cup, hollow vessel.

cymbalo *n.* the dulcimer, a stringed instrument played by means of small hammers held in the hands. WH: 19C. Italian *cembalo*, *cimbalo*, from Latin *cymbalum* CYMBAL. Cp. CIMBALOM.

cymbidium *n.* any orchid of the genus *Cymbidium* having colourful, long-lasting flowers and a recess in the flower-lip. WH: 19C. Modern Latin, from Greek *kumbē* cup. The plant is so called from the hollow recess in the lip of the flower.

cymbiform *a.* (of certain bones and grasses) boat-shaped. WH: 19C. Latin *cymba* boat + -*i*- + -FORM.

cyme *n.* an inflorescence in which the central terminal flower comes to perfection first, as in the guelder rose. WH: 18C. French *cyme*, *cime* summit, top, from Latin CYMA.

cymophane *n.* a variety of opalescent chrysoberyl. WH: 19C. Greek *kumo*-, comb. form of *kuma* CYMA + *phanēs* showing.

Cymric *a.* of or relating to the Welsh. *Also n.* WH: 19C. Welsh *Cymru* Wales or *Cymry* the Welsh + -IC.

cynic *n.* a person who is pessimistic about human nature. *Also a.* WH: 16C. Latin *cynicus*, from Greek *kunikos* doglike, churlish, prob. from *Kunosarges* gymnasium where Antisthenes taught, but assoc. with *kuōn*, *kunos* dog. See also -IC.

cynocephalus *n.* a dog-headed man in ancient mythology. WH: 12–14C. Latin, from Greek *kunokephalos* dog-headed, from *kuōn*, *kunos* dog + *kephalē* head.

cynophobia *n.* a morbid fear of dogs. WH: 19C. Greek *kuōn*, *kunos* dog + -*phobia* (-PHOBE).

cynosure *n.* a centre of interest or attraction. WH: 16C. French, or from Latin *Cynosura*, from Greek *kunosoura*, from *kunos* gen. sing. of *kuōn* dog + *oura* tail. Latin *Cynosura* is the name of the constellation Ursa Minor (Little Bear). This contains the North Star (Pole Star), formerly used as a guide by sailors.

cy près *a.*, *adv.* as near as practicable (referring to the principle of applying a bequest as nearly as possible to the testator's aim when that aim is impracticable). *Also n.* WH: 19C. Anglo-French as near as (French *ci-près*).

cypress[1] *n.* a tree of the coniferous genera *Cupressus* or *Chamaecyparis*, esp. *Cupressus sempervirens*, valued for the durability of its wood. WH: 12–14C. Old French *cipres* (Modern French *cyprès*), from Late Latin *cypressus*, from Greek *kuparissos*, of non-Greek orig.

†cypress[2] *n.* a kind of satin that was highly valued. WH: 14–15C. Anglo-French *cipres*, *cypres*, from Old French *Cipre*, *Cypre* (Modern French *Chypre*) Cyprus, an island in the Mediterranean, from which the fabric was originally brought.

cyprine *n.* of or belonging to the fish suborder Cyprinoidea, containing the carp. WH: 19C. Latin *cyprinus* carp, from Greek *kuprinos*.

Cypriot *n.* a native or inhabitant of Cyprus. *Also a.* WH: 16C. Greek *Kupriōtēs*, from *Kupros* Cyprus.

cypripedium *n.* any orchid of the genus *Cypripedium*, esp. the lady's slipper, possessing two fertile stamens, the central stamen (fertile in other orchids) being represented by a shieldlike plate.

WH: 18C. Modern Latin, from Greek *Kupris* Aphrodite + *pedilon* slipper.

cypsela *n.* the dry single-seeded fruit of the daisy and related plants. WH: 19C. Modern Latin, from Greek *kupsēlē* hollow vessel.

Cyrenaic *a.* of or relating to Cyrene, an ancient Greek colony in the north of Africa, or to the hedonistic philosophy founded at that place by Aristippus. *Also n.* WH: 16C. Latin *Cyrenaicus*, from Greek *Kurēnaikos*, from *Kurēnē* Cyrene.

Cyrillic *a.* denoting the alphabet of the Slavonic nations who belong to the Orthodox Church, now esp. Russia and Bulgaria. *Also n.* WH: 19C. St *Cyril*, 826–69, apostle of the Slavs, deviser of the Glagolitic alphabet (from which Cyrillic was derived). See also -IC.

cyst *n.* a bladder, vesicle or hollow organ. WH: 18C. Late Latin *cystis*, from Greek *kustis* bladder.

cysteine *n.* a sulphur-containing amino acid, present in proteins and essential in the human diet. WH: 19C. From *cystine* (from Greek *kustos* bladder + -INE) + -*eine*, var. of -INE. Cystine, an oxidized dimer of cysteine, is so called because it was originally isolated from urinary calculi.

cysti- *comb. form* of or relating to the bladder. WH: Greek *kustis* bladder. See also -O-.

cystitis *n.* inflammation of the urinary bladder. WH: 18C. *cyst*- (CYSTI-) + -ITIS.

cystocele *n.* hernia caused by protrusion of the bladder. WH: 19C. *cysto*- (CYSTI-) + -CELE.

cystoscope *n.* an instrument or apparatus for the exploration of the bladder. WH: 19C. *cysto*- (CYSTI-) + -SCOPE.

cystotomy *n.* the surgical operation of cutting into the urinary bladder. WH: early 20C. *cysto*- (CYSTI-) + -TOMY.

-cyte *comb. form* a mature cell, as in *leucocyte*. WH: Greek *kutos* receptacle.

Cytherean *a.* of or relating to Venus, the goddess of love, who was connected with Cythera. WH: 18C. Latin *Cytherea*, a name of Venus, from *Cythera* Kithira, an Ionian island. See also -AN.

cytidine *n.* a nucleoside obtained from RNA by the condensation of ribose and cytosine. WH: early 20C. CYTO- + -*idine* (from -IDE + -IN[1]).

cyto- *comb. form* cellular. WH: Greek *kutos* receptacle. See also -O-.

cytoblast *n.* a cell nucleus. WH: 19C. CYTO- + -BLAST. The nucleus is so called because it was originally believed to be the germ from which the cell sprang.

cytochrome *n.* any of a group of naturally-occurring compounds consisting of a protein linked to a haem, of great importance in cell oxidization. WH: early 20C. CYTO- + Greek *khrōma* colour. See CHROME.

cytogenetics *n.* the branch of genetics concerned with inheritance where related to the structure and function of cells. WH: mid-20C. CYTO- + *genetics* (GENETIC).

cytology *n.* the study of cells. WH: 19C. CYTO- + -LOGY.

cytomegalovirus *n.* a variety of herpes virus that may cause serious nerve damage in those whose immune systems are weakened, esp. babies. WH: mid-20C. *cytomegalic* (see CYTO-, MEGA-) + VIRUS.

cytoplasm *n.* the protoplasm of a cell apart from the nucleus. WH: 19C. CYTO- + *plasm* (see PLASMA).

cytosine *n.* a pyrimidine occurring in all living tissues, being a component base of RNA and DNA. WH: 19C. CYTO- + -OSE[2] + -INE.

cytoskeleton *n.* a network of fibrous proteins that govern the shape and movement of a living cell. WH: mid-20C. CYTO- + SKELETON.

cytotoxin *n.* a substance which is poisonous to cells. WH: early 20C. CYTO- + TOXIN.

Czech *n.* a native or inhabitant of the Czech Republic. *Also a.* WH: 19C. Polish spelling of Czech *Čech*.

dab[1] *v.t.* to strike gently with some moist or soft substance. *Also n.* WH: 12–14C. Imit. Cp. DABBLE, DIB[1].

dab[2] *n.* a small flatfish, *Limanda limanda.* WH: 14–15C. Orig. uncertain. ? From DAB[1] in sense of something flattened. Cp. PAT (of butter) made flat by patting.

dabble *v.t.* to wet by little dips. *Also v.i.* WH: 16C. Obs. Dutch *dabbelen*, or DAB[1] + -LE[4].

dabchick *n.* the little grebe, *Tachybaptus ruficollis.* WH: 16C. ? Var. of DIP or DIVE + CHICK[1].

dabster *n.* a person who is expert at anything. WH: 18C. DAB[1] + -STER.

da capo *adv.* (repeat) from the beginning. WH: 18C. Italian from the beginning, from *da* from + CAPO.

dace *n.* a small river fish, *Leuciscus leuciscus.* WH: 14–15C. Old French *dars*, pl. of *dart* DANCE. The loss of *r* is similar to that in BASS[2].

dacha *n.* a country house or cottage in Russia. WH: 19C. Russian grant of land, from *dat'* to give.

dachshund *n.* a short-legged long-bodied breed of dog. WH: 19C. German badger dog, from *Dachs* badger + *Hund* dog, HOUND. The dog is so named not because it resembles a badger but because it was originally used to hunt them.

dacite *n.* a type of volcanic rock. WH: 19C. *Dacia*, an ancient Roman province in central Europe + -ITE[1]. The rock was so named in 1863.

dacoit *n.* in the Indian subcontinent or Burma (Myanmar), a member of a band of armed robbers. WH: 18C. Hindi *ḍakait*, from *ḍākā* gang robbery.

dactyl *n.* a metrical foot consisting of one long followed by two short syllables, or of one stressed followed by two unstressed syllables. WH: 14–15C. Latin *dactylus*, from Greek *daktulos* finger, date. The foot is so named from its three 'joints', like those of a finger.

dactylo- *comb. form* having fingers or digits. WH: Greek *daktulos* finger. See also -O-.

dactylogram *n.* a fingerprint. WH: 20C. DACTYLO- + -GRAM.

dactylology *n.* the art of conversing with the deaf by means of the fingers. WH: 17C. DACTYLO- + -LOGY.

dad *n.* father. WH: 16C. ? Imit. of infant's first speech. Cp. Welsh *tad*, Latin *tata* father.

Dada *n.* an early 20th-cent. school of art and literature that aimed at suppressing any correlation between thought and expression. WH: early 20C. French, lit. hobby-horse, from title of review first published in Zürich, 1916. French *dada* itself probably came from redupl. of *da*, var. of *dia*, cry to urge on a horse. Cp. *gee-up* (GEE[1]).

dado *n.* an arrangement of wainscoting or decoration round the lower part of the walls of a room. WH: 17C. Italian die, cube, from Latin *datum*. See DIE[2]. A dado was originally the cube of a pedestal, to which the lower part of a room wall corresponds.

daedal *a.* curiously formed. WH: 16C. Latin *daedalus*, from Greek *daidalos* skilful, variegated.

daff[1] *n.* a daffodil. WH: early 20C. Abbr. of DAFFODIL.

daff[2] *v.i.* to play the fool. WH: 16C. Orig. unknown. Cp. DAFT.

daffodil *n.* the yellow narcissus, *Narcissus pseudonarcissus.* WH: 16C. Alt. of *affodil*, from Medieval Latin *affodilus*, from var. of Latin *asphodilus*. The addition of the initial *d* is unexplained, but cp. *dapple-grey/apple-grey* (DAPPLE).

daffy *a.* crazy, daft. WH: 19C. DAFF[2] + -Y[1].

daft *a.* weak-minded, imbecile. WH: pre-1200. Old English *gedæfte*, from Germanic, from stem also of Gothic *gadaban* to become, to be fitting. The original sense was mild, meek, humble. The current sense arose in the 14–15C. Cp. DEFT.

dag *n.* a daglock. *Also v.t.* WH: 14–15C. Orig. unknown. Cp. TAG. The word formerly (to the 17C) had the sense of the hanging pointed portion of something, as in the lower edge of a garment.

dagga *n.* a type of hemp used as a narcotic. WH: 17C. Afrikaans, from Nama.

dagger *n.* a short two-edged weapon adapted for stabbing. WH: 14–15C. ? From obs. *dag*, influ. by French *dague* dagger, from Provençal.

daglock *n.* the dirt-covered clumps of wool around the hindquarters of a sheep. WH: 17C. DAG + LOCK[2].

dago *n.* a Spaniard, Italian or Portuguese. WH: 19C. Alt. of Spanish male forename *Diego* James. *Diego* is one of the most common Spanish male forenames, and that of the patron saint of Spain.

dagoba *n.* a dome-shaped Buddhist shrine containing relics. WH: 19C. Sinhalese *dāgaba*, from Pali *dhātu-gabbha* receptacle for relics.

daguerreotype *n.* the process of photographing on copper plates coated with silver iodide, developed by exposure to mercury vapour. *Also v.t.* WH: 19C. Louis-Jacques-Mandé *Daguerre*, 1789–1851, French inventor of this process. See also -O-, TYPE.

dahabeeyah *n.* a type of sailing-boat on the Nile. WH: 19C. Arabic *ḍahabīya* golden. The word was originally used for the gilded state barge of the Muslim rulers of Egypt.

dahlia *n.* a composite plant of the genus *Dahlia* from Mexico, cultivated for their flowers. WH: 19C. Andreas *Dahl*, 1751–89, Swedish botanist + -IA.

daily *a.* happening or recurring every day. *Also adv., n.* WH: 14–15C. DAY + -LY[1].

daimio *n.* the official title of a former class of feudal lords in Japan. WH: 18C. Japanese, from *dai* great + *myō* name.

daimon *n.* a genius or attendant spirit. WH: 19C. Greek *daimōn.* See DEMON.

dainty *a.* pretty, delicate. *Also n.* WH: 12–14C. Old French *daintié*, from Latin *dignitas* worthiness, beauty, from *dignus* worthy. See also -TY[1].

daiquiri *n.* a cocktail made of rum and lime-juice. WH: early 20C. *Daiquiri*, a rum-producing district of SE Cuba.

dairy *n.* the place or building or department of a farm where milk is kept and converted into butter or cheese. *Also a.* WH: 12–14C. Obs. *dey*, from Old English *dæge* female servant, from base meaning kneader (cp. LADY) + -RY.

dais *n.* a platform. WH: 12–14C. Old French *deis* (Modern French *dais*), from Medieval Latin DISCUS table. The original sense was a high table in a hall.

daisy *n.* a small composite flower, *Bellis perennis*, with white petals and a yellow centre. WH: pre-1200. Old English *dæges ēage* day's eye. The flower is so named because the yellow centre of the flower is revealed in the morning.

dak *n.* the Indian post or transport by relays of runners, horses etc. WH: 18C. Hindi *ḍāk.*

Dalai Lama *n.* the spiritual leader of Tibetan Buddhism, previously also the temporal ruler of Tibet. WH: 17C. Mongolian *dalai* ocean + LAMA. The sense of ocean is presumably meant to suggest breadth and depth of wisdom or range of power.

dalasi *n.* the standard monetary unit of the Gambia. WH: late 20C. Name of former local coin.

dale *n.* a valley, esp. from the English Midlands to the Scottish lowlands. WH: pre-1200. Old English *dæl*, from Germanic. Cp. German *Tal.*

dally *v.i.* to trifle (with), to treat frivolously. *Also v.t.* WH: 12–14C. Old French *dalier* to converse, to chat, of unknown orig. The original sense was to converse idly, to chat. The current sense evolved in the 14–15C.

Dalmatian *n.* a variety of hound, white with numerous black or brown spots, formerly kept chiefly as a carriage dog. *Also a.* WH: 16C. *Dalmatia*, a region on the Adriatic coast of Croatia + -AN.

dalmatic *n.* an ecclesiastical vestment worn by bishops and deacons in the Roman and Greek Churches at High Mass. WH: 14–15C. Old French *dalmatique* or Latin *dalmatica*, from *Dalmaticus* of Dalmatia. Cp. DALMATIAN. See also -IC. The vestment was originally made of Dalmatian wool.

dal segno *adv.* (repeat) from point indicated. WH: 19C. Italian from the sign, from *dal* from the + *segno* SIGN.

dalton *n.* an atomic mass unit. WH: mid-20C. John *Dalton*, 1766–1844, English chemist. Cp. DALTONISM.

daltonism *n.* colour-blindness, esp. inability to distinguish between red and green. WH: 19C. John *Dalton*, 1766–1844, English chemist, who suffered from colour blindness + -ISM.

dam[1] *n.* a bank or mound raised to keep back water (by humans to form a reservoir etc. or by a beaver). *Also v.t.* WH: 12–14C. From Germanic, ult. of unknown orig. Cp. German *Damm*.

dam[2] *n.* a female parent (chiefly of quadrupeds); used of a human mother in contempt. WH: 12–14C. Alt. of DAME.

damage *n.* injury or detriment to any person or thing. *Also v.t., v.i.* WH: 12–14C. Old French (Modern French *dommage*), from *dam* loss, damage, prejudice, from Latin *damnum* loss. See DAMN, also -AGE.

Damascene *a.* of or relating to Damascus. *Also n.* WH: 14–15C. Latin *Damascenus*, from Greek *Damaskēnos*, from *Damaskos* Damascus, an ancient city and the capital of Syria. Cp. DAMASK, DAMSON.

damascene *v.t.* to ornament by inlaying or incrustation, or (as a steel blade) with a wavy pattern in welding. *Also a., n.* WH: 18C. DAMASCENE.

damask *n.* a rich silk stuff with raised figures woven in the pattern, orig. made at Damascus. *Also a., v.t.* WH: 14–15C. Latin *Damascus* Damascus, where orig. produced. Cp. DAMASCENE.

dame *n.* a lady; a title of honour (now applied to the wives of knights and baronets). WH: 12–14C. Old French, from Latin *domina*, fem. equivalent of *dominus* lord. Cp. DAM[2], MADAM.

dammar *n.* any of various Asian and Australasian trees yielding resin. WH: 17C. Malay *damar* resin.

damn *int.* used to express annoyance. *Also v.t., v.i., n., a., adv.* WH: 12–14C. Old French *dampner* (Modern French *damner*), from Latin *damnare* to inflict loss upon, from *damnum* loss, damage.

Damoclean *a.* of or resembling Damocles; perilous, anxious. WH: 19C. Latin *Damocles*, from Greek *Damoklēs*, a flatterer whom Dionysius of Syracuse (4C BC) feasted while a sword hung by a hair above him demonstrating the dangerous nature of such exalted positions + -AN.

damp *a.* slightly wet; clammy. *Also n., v.t.* WH: 12–14C. Low German vapour, steam, smoke, from Germanic. Cp. German *Dampf* steam.

damsel *n.* a young unmarried woman. WH: 12–14C. Old French *dameisele* (Modern French *demoiselle*), alt. (influ. by *dame*) of *danzele*, *donsele*, from dim. of Latin *domina* lady. See DAME. Cp. DEMOISELLE.

damson *n.* a small dark purple plum. *Also a.* WH: 14–15C. Latin *damascenum prunum* Damascus plum. Cp. DAMASCENE.

dan[1] *n.* in martial arts, any of the black-belt grades of proficiency. WH: mid-20C. Japanese step, grade.

dan[2] *n.* a type of small deep-sea buoy. WH: 17C. Orig. unknown. ? From the male forename *Daniel*.

†dan[3] *n.* a title of respect placed before personal names (and before mythological names in the archaic poets). WH: 12–14C. Old French, from Latin *dominus* lord, master. Cp. DOM, DON.

dance *v.i.* to move, usu. to music, with rhythmical steps. *Also v.t., n.* WH: 12–14C. Old French *dancer* (Modern French *danser*), from Frankish *dintjan*, of unknown orig. The Old English equivalent verb was *sealtian*, related to Latin *saltare*. See SALTANT.

dancette *n.* the chevron or zigzag moulding in Norman work. WH: 19C. French *dancetté*, from *danché*, earlier obs. *dansié*, from Latin *dens*, *dentis* tooth.

dandelion *n.* a well-known composite plant, *Taraxacum officinale*, with a yellow rayed flower and toothed leaves. WH: 14–15C. French *dent-de-lion*, from Medieval Latin *dens leonis* lion's tooth. The name refers to the plant's strongly toothed leaves.

dander[1] *n.* temper, anger. WH: 19C. Orig. unknown. ? Alt. of DANDRUFF.

dander[2] *v.i.* to wander about idly. WH: 16C. Freq. of some v. with stem such as *dad-* or *dand-*. See -ER[5]. Cp. DAWDLE.

Dandie Dinmont *n.* a breed of short-legged, rough-coated terrier. WH: 19C. Name of a character in Sir Walter Scott's novel *Guy Mannering* (1815) who had a pair of terriers called Mustard and Pepper.

dandify *v.t.* to make smart, or like a dandy. WH: 19C. DANDY + -FY.

dandle *v.t.* to bounce (a child) up and down on one's knees or toss (it) in one's arms . *Also v.i.* WH: 16C. Orig. unknown. Cp. Italian *dandolare*, var. of *dondolare* to rock, to swing, to dandle.

dandruff *n.* scaly scurf on the head. WH: 16C. 1st element of unknown orig., 2nd ? same as dial. *rove* scab.

dandy *n.* a man extravagantly concerned with his appearance. *Also a.* WH: 18C. ? Shortening of *jack-a-dandy* (JACK[1]), where last element may be *Dandy*, pet form of male forename *Andrew*.

Dane *n.* a native or inhabitant of Denmark. WH: pre-1200. Old English *Dene*, as in *Denmark*.

danegeld *n.* an annual tax formerly levied on every hide of land in England to maintain forces against or furnish tribute to the Danes (finally abolished by Stephen). WH: pre-1200. Old Norse gen. of *Danir* Danes + *gjald* payment, tribute (cp. GELD[2]).

Danelaw *n.* the portion of England allotted to the Danes by the treaty of Wedmore (ad 878), extending north-east from Watling Street. WH: pre-1200. Old English *Dena lagu* Danes' law. See DANE, LAW[1].

danewort *n.* the dwarf elder, *Sambucus ebulus*, the flowers, bark and berries of which are used medicinally. WH: 14–15C. DANE + WORT. The plant is so named from the belief that it sprang up wherever the Danes had slaughtered the English, or had been slaughtered by them.

danger *n.* risk, hazard; exposure to injury or loss. WH: 12–14C. Old French *dangier* (Modern French *danger*), from Latin *domnus*, *dominus* lord, master. The original sense was the power of a lord or master, hence the power to harm or injure. Early senses to the 16C were liability to loss, difficulty, damage.

dangle *v.i.* to hang loosely. *Also v.t.* WH: 16C. Imit. Cp. Norwegian and Danish *dingle*, Swedish and Icelandic *dingla* to dangle.

Daniel *n.* an upright judge. WH: 16C. Prophet *Daniel*, a shrewd judge introduced in the apocryphal History of Susanna. The current usage owes much to Shakespeare's *Merchant of Venice* (IV.i) ('a Daniel come to judgement').

Daniell cell *n.* a type of primary voltaic cell having a copper anode and zinc cathode. WH: 19C. John F. *Daniell*, 1790–1845, English physicist.

Danish *a.* of or relating to Denmark. *Also n.* WH: pre-1200. Old English *Denis*, from Germanic, superseded by forms from Old French *daneis* (Modern French *danois*), from Medieval Latin *Danensis*, from Late Latin *Dani* Danes, subsequently assim. to aa. in -ISH[1].

dank *a.* damp, moist. *Also n.* WH: 12–14C. Prob. from Scandinavian. Cp. Swedish *dank* marshy spot.

danseur *n.* a male ballet dancer. WH: 19C. French dancer (DANCE) + -eur -OR.

Dantean *a.* of or relating to Dante. *Also n.* WH: 18C. *Dante* Alighieri, 1265–1321, Italian poet + -AN.

danthonia *n.* a pasture grass of the genus *Danthonia*. WH: early 20C. Modern Latin, from Étienne *Danthoine*, 19C French botanist. See -IA.

dap *v.i.* to fish by letting the bait fall gently into the water. *Also v.t., n.* WH: 17C. Var. of DAB[1], with *p* expressing lighter touch.

daphne *n.* any shrub of the genus *Daphne*. WH: 14–15C. Greek *daphnē* laurel, bay, from *Daphnē*, a nymph of Greek mythology who escaped Apollo's advances by being changed into a laurel.

dapper *a.* spruce, smart. WH: 14–15C. Middle Low German or Middle Dutch heavy, powerful, strong, from Germanic. Cp. German *tapfer* brave.

dapple *n.* a spot on an animal's coat. *Also a., v.t., v.i.* WH: 14–15C. From *dappled*, of uncertain orig. ? From Old Norse *depill* spot. Cp. Norwegian *dape* puddle. According to some, *dapple-grey* originated in (unrecorded) *apple-grey*, from APPLE + GREY, the markings on the animal's coat being compared to the dashes of colour on an apple.

darbies *n.pl.* handcuffs. WH: 17C. From *Father Darby's bands*, some form of rigid band for debtors. The identity of Father Darby is unknown.

Darby and Joan *n.* an elderly married couple living in domestic bliss. WH: 18C. Appar. from characters in a poem published in the *Gentleman's Magazine*, 1735.

dare *v.i.* to have the courage or impudence (to). *Also v.t., n.* WH: pre-1200. Old English *durran*, from Germanic, from Indo-European base also of Greek *tharsein* to be bold.

darg *n.* the quantity of work done in a day. WH: 14–15C. Contr. of *daywork*. See DAY.

daric *n.* a gold coin of Darius I of Persia. WH: 16C. Greek *Dareikos* of Darius. See also -IC.

dariole *n.* a dish cooked in a usu. flowerpot-shaped mould. WH: 14–15C. Old French, var. of *doriole* gilded. The Old French word was originally used for a type of bun with a golden brown exterior.

Darjeeling *n.* tea from Darjeeling. WH: 19C. *Darjeeling* (now Darjiling), a town and district in NE India.

dark *a.* without light. *Also n., v.i., v.t.* WH: pre-1200. Old English *deorc*, prob. from Germanic base. Cp. German *tarnen* to conceal, rel. to TARNISH.

darkie *n.* a dark-skinned person, esp. of African origin. WH: 18C. DARK + -*ie* -Y[3].

†darkle *v.i.* to grow dark. WH: 19C. Back-formation from *darkling*, from DARK + -LING[2].

darling *n.* a person who is dearly loved. *Also a.* WH: pre-1200. DEAR + -LING[1].

darn[1] *v.t.* to mend with stitches that cross or interweave. *Also n.* WH: 17C. ? From obs. *dern* to hide, to conceal, from Old English *diernan*, from Germanic.

darn[2] *int., v.t.* damn. WH: 18C. Alt. of DAMN.

darnel *n.* a kind of grass, *Lolium temulentum*, formerly believed to be poisonous, which grows among corn. WH: 12–14C. Orig. unknown.

dart *n.* a small pointed missile used in the game of darts. *Also v.t., v.i.* WH: 12–14C. Old French (Modern French *dard*), acc. of *darz, dars*, from Frankish spear, lance.

Dartmoor pony *n.* a breed of small hardy English pony. WH: 19C. *Dartmoor*, a moorland plateau in Devon + PONY.

Darwinian *a.* of or relating to Darwin or Darwinism. *Also n.* WH: 19C. Charler *Darwin*, 1809–82, English naturalist + -IAN.

dash *v.i.* to rush; to fall or throw oneself violently. *Also v.t., int., n.* WH: 14–15C. Prob. imit. Cp. Swedish *daska*, Danish *daske* to beat.

dashiki *n.* a type of loose shirt worn esp. by blacks in America. WH: mid-20C. Prob. from Yoruba, from Hausa.

dassie *n.* a hyrax, *Procavia capensis*. WH: 18C. Afrikaans, from Dutch *dasje*, dim. of *das*. Cp. German *Dachs* badger.

dastardly *a.* cowardly and nasty. WH: 16C. *dastard* (prob. from *dazed*, p.p. of DAZE + -ARD) + -LY[1].

dasypod *n.* any S American armadillo of the genus *Dasypodidae*. WH: 19C. Modern Latin *dasypus*, from Greek *dasupous, dasupodos*, from *dasus* rough, hairy + *pous, podos* foot.

dasyure *n.* any member of the genus *Dasyurus* of small marsupials, found in Australia, Tasmania and New Guinea. WH: 19C. French, from Modern Latin *dasyurus*, from Greek *dasus* rough, hairy + *oura* tail.

data *n.pl.* facts or information from which other things may be deduced. WH: 17C. Latin, pl. of DATUM. See also DATE[1].

dataria *n.* the papal chancery at Rome from which all bulls are issued. WH: 16C. Medieval Latin, from *datum* DATE[1]. See also -ARY[1].

date[1] *n.* a fixed point of time. *Also v.t., v.i.* WH: 12–14C. Old French, from Medieval Latin *data*, fem. (used as n.) of *datus*, p.p. of *dare* to give. The precise origin is from the Latin formula used in dating letters, e.g. *Dabam Romae prid. kal. Apr.* I gave (this) at Rome on 31st March. The later formula was simply *Data Romae* given at Rome. Hence *data*, the first word of this, as a term for the time and place stated.

date[2] *n.* the fruit of the date palm, an oblong fruit with a hard seed or stone. WH: 12–14C. Old French (Modern French *datte*), from Latin *dactylus*, from Greek *daktulos* finger, toe, date. The fruit is so called from the finger-like shape of the tree's leaves. Cp. DACTYL.

dative *a.* denoting the grammatical case used to represent the indirect object, or the person or thing interested in the action of the verb. *Also n.* WH: 14–15C. Latin *dativus* of giving, from *datus*, p.p. of *dare* to give. See also -IVE. In the grammatical sense, Latin *casus dativus* dative case translated Greek *ptōsis dotikē*.

datum *n.* a quantity, condition, fact or other premise, given or admitted, from which other things or results may be found. WH: 18C. Latin, neut p.p. of *dare* to give. Cp. DATA.

datura *n.* any solanaceous plant of the genus *Datura*, as the thorn apple, *D. stramonium*, which yields a powerful narcotic. WH: 16C. Modern Latin, from Hindi *dhatūrā*.

daub *v.t.* to smear or coat with a soft adhesive substance. *Also v.i., n.* WH: 14–15C. Old French *dauber*, from Latin *dealbare* to whiten, to whitewash, from DE- + *albus* white.

daube *n.* a stew of meat braised with wine etc. WH: 18C. French, from Italian *addobbo* adornment, influ. by French *adouber* to dub (a knight). Cp. DUB[1].

daughter *n.* a female child in relation to a parent or parents. WH: pre-1200. Old English *dohtor*, from Germanic, from Indo-European, which also gave Sanskrit *duhitṛ*, Greek *thugatēr*.

daunt *v.t.* to intimidate, to dishearten. WH: 12–14C. Old French *danter*, var. of *donter* (Modern French *dompter*), from Latin *domitare*, freq. of *domare* to tame.

dauphin *n.* the heir apparent to the French throne. WH: 14–15C. French, from Old French *daulphin* DOLPHIN. *Dauphin* was the family name of the lords of Viennois or *Dauphiné*.

davenport *n.* a small writing desk with drawers on both sides. WH: 19C. Appar. from one Captain *Davenport*, for whom early examples were made in the 18C.

davit *n.* a spar used as a crane for hoisting an anchor. WH: 15C. Old French *daviot* (Modern French *davier*), dim. of *Davi* David. The word is apparently from the biblical story of David being let down through a window (I Sam. xix.12).

Davy *n.* a miner's wire-gauze safety lamp. WH: 19C. Sir Humphry *Davy*, 1778–1828, English chemist.

Davy Jones *n.* an imaginary malign spirit with power over the sea. WH: 18C. Orig. unknown. ? From JONAH.

daw *n.* a jackdaw. WH: 14–15C. Of Germanic orig. Cp. German *Dohle* jackdaw.

dawdle *v.i.* to be slow, to linger. *Also n.* WH: 17C. Prob. from dial. orig. Cp. DODDER[1], TODDLE.

dawn *n.* the break of day. *Also v.i.* WH: 15C. Back-formation from *dawning*, alt. of *dawing*, from obs. *daw* to dawn, from Germanic base of DAY.

day *n.* the time the sun is above the horizon. WH: pre-1200. Old English *dæg*, from Germanic. Cp. German *Tag*.

Day-glo® *n.* a type of fluorescent paint. *Also a.* WH: mid-20C. DAY + GLOW.

daylight *n.* the light of day, as opposed to that of the moon or artificial light. WH: 12–14C. DAY + LIGHT[1].

daze *v.t.* to stupefy, to confuse. *Also n.* WH: 12–14C. From Scandinavian. Cp. Middle Dutch *dasen* to act foolishly.

dazzle *v.t.* to overpower with a glare of light. *Also v.i., n.* WH: 15C. DAZE + -LE[4].

DDR *abbr.* German Democratic Republic (the former E Germany). WH: Abbr. of German *Deutsche Demokratische Republik* German Democratic Republic.

de- *pref.* from. WH: Latin, from *de* off, from. In the privative sense it is partly through French *dé-*, from Old French *des-*, from Latin *dis-*, regarded as identical with Latin *de-*. Cp. DIS-.

deaccession *v.t.* (of a library, museum etc.) to dispose of and remove from the catalogue of holdings. WH: late 20C. DE- + ACCESSION.

deacon *n.* a cleric in orders next below a priest. *Also v.t.* WH: pre-1200. Ecclesiastical Latin *diaconus*, from Greek *diakonos* servant, Christian minister.

deactivate *v.t.* to render harmless or less radioactive. WH: mid-20C. DE- + ACTIVATE.

dead *a.* having ceased to live. *Also adv., n., v.i., v.t.* WH: pre-1200. Old English *dēad*, from Germanic, from p.p. of ult. base of DIE[1]. Cp. German *tot*.

deaden *v.t.* to diminish the vitality or force of. *Also v.i.* WH: 17C. DEAD + -EN[5]. *Deaden* replaced the earlier verb *dead* in the 17C.

deadly *a.* causing death; fatal. *Also adv.* WH: pre-1200. DEAD + -LY[1].

deaf *a.* incapable or dull of hearing. *Also n., v.t.* WH: pre-1200. Old English *dēaf*, from Germanic, from Indo-European base also of Greek *tuphlos* blind. Cp. German *taub*.

deal[1] *n.* a bargain, a business transaction. *Also v.t., v.i.* WH: pre-1200. Old English *dǣl*, from Germanic base also of DOLE[1]. Cp. German *Teil* part.

deal[2] *n.* a plank of fir or pine of a standard size, not more than 3 in. (7.6 cm) thick, 7 in. (17.8 cm) wide, and 6 ft. (1.8 m) long. WH: 12–14C. Middle Low German or Middle Dutch *dele* plank, floor, from Germanic. Cp. German *Diele* floorboard.

deambulatory *n.* a place for walking about in. WH: 14–15C. Medieval Latin *deambulatorium*, from *deambulatus*, p.p. of *deambulare* to walk about, from DE- + *ambulare* to walk. Cp. AMBULATE.

dean *n.* an ecclesiastical dignitary presiding over the chapter of a cathedral or collegiate church. WH: 12–14C. Old French *dien* (Modern French *doyen*), from Late Latin *decanus* chief of a group of ten, from Latin *decem* ten.

dear *a.* beloved, cherished; (a conventional form of address used in letter-writing). *Also n., adv., v.t., int.* WH: pre-1200. Old English *dēore*, from Germanic. Cp. German *teuer* dear, expensive.

dearth *n.* a scarcity, lack. WH: 12–14C. DEAR + -TH[2]. If a thing is scarce, it will be expensive.

deasil *n.* motion towards the right, in the direction of the hands of a clock or of the apparent motion of the sun. WH: 18C. Gaelic *deiseil*. Rel. to Latin DEXTER[1].

deaspirate *v.t.* to remove the aspirate from. WH: 19C. DE- + ASPIRATE[1].

death *n.* extinction of life; the act of dying. WH: pre-1200. Old English *dēath*, from Germanic base also of DIE[1]. See also -TH[2]. Cp. German *Tod*.

deattribute *v.t.* to end the attribution of (a work) to a particular artist etc. WH: late 20C. DE- + ATTRIBUTE[2].

deave *v.t.* to deafen. WH: pre-1200. Old English -*dēafian*. See DEAF.

deb[1] *n.* a debutante. WH: early 20C. Abbr. of *débutante* (DEBUT).

deb[2] *n.* a debenture. WH: early 20C. Abbr. of DEBENTURE.

debacle *n.* a complete failure. WH: 19C. French *débâcle*, from *débâcler* to unbar, from *dé* DE- + *bâcler* to bar.

debag *v.t.* to remove the trousers of (someone) by force. WH: early 20C. DE- + BAG.

debar *v.i.* to exclude from approach or action. WH: 14–15C. French *débarrer*, from Old French *desbarrer*, from *des*- DE- + *barrer* to bar.

debark[1] *v.t., v.i.* to disembark. WH: 17C. French *débarquer*, from *dé* DE- + *barque* BARK[3].

debark[2] *v.t.* to remove the bark from. WH: 18C. DE- + BARK[2].

debarrass *v.t.* to disembarrass. WH: 18C. French *débarrasser*, from *dé*- DE- + *embarrasser* EMBARRASS.

debase *v.t.* to lower in quality or value. WH: 16C. DE- + BASE[1]. Cp. ABASE.

debate *v.t.* to contend about by words or arguments, esp. publicly. *Also v.i., n.* WH: 14–15C. Old French *debatre* (Modern French *debattre*), from Latin *dis*- DE- + *battere* to fight.

debauch *v.t.* to corrupt in morals, to pervert. *Also v.i., n.* WH: 16C. French *débaucher*, from Old French *desbaucher*, from *des*- DE- + element of unknown orig.

debenture *n.* a written acknowledgement of a debt. WH: 14–15C. Latin *debentur* they are owing, 3rd pers. pl. pres. ind. pass. of *debere* to owe. The Latin word was apparently the first word of a certificate of indebtedness, although no examples of such a document are known. The ending was assimilated to -URE.

debilitate *v.t.* to weaken, to enfeeble; to enervate, to impair. WH: 16C. Latin *debilitatus*, p.p. of *debilitare* to weaken, from *debilis* weak. See also -ATE[3].

debit *n.* an amount set down as a debt. *Also v.t.* WH: 14–15C. Latin *debitum* DEBT.

debonair *a.* having self-assurance, carefree. WH: 12–14C. Old French *debonaire* (Modern French *débonnaire*), from *de bon aire* of good disposition.

debouch *v.i.* to march out from a confined place into open ground. WH: 18C. French *déboucher*, from *dé*- DE- + *bouche* mouth. Cp. DISEMBOGUE.

debrief *v.t.* to gather information from (someone, such as a soldier, diplomat or spy) after a mission. WH: mid-20C. DE- + BRIEF.

debris *n.* broken rubbish, fragments. WH: 18C. French *débris*, from obs. *débriser* to break down, to break up, from *dé*- DE- + *briser* to break.

debruised *a.* crossed or folded so as to be partly covered. WH: 16C. P.p. of *debruise*, from Old French *debruisier*, from *dé*- DE- + *bruiser* (Modern French *briser*) to break.

debt *n.* something which is owing from one person to another, esp. a sum of money. WH: 12–14C. Old French *dette*, from pl. (used as fem. n.) of Latin *debitum*, neut. p.p. of *debere* to owe. The -*b*- was introduced in the 16C after obsolete French *debte*.

debug *v.t.* to find and remove hidden microphones from. WH: mid-20C. DE- + BUG[1].

debunk *v.t.* to dispel false sentiment about, to destroy pleasing legends or illusions about. WH: early 20C. DE- + *bunk* (BUNKUM).

debus *v.t., v.i.* to (cause to) alight from a motor vehicle. WH: early 20C. DE- + BUS, based on DEBARK[1]. Cp. DETRAIN.

debut *n.* a first appearance before the public, esp. of a performer. *Also v.i.* WH: 18C. French *début*, from *débuter* to lead off.

deca- *comb. form* ten. WH: Greek *deka* ten.

decade *n.* a period of ten years. WH: 14–15C. Old French *décade*, from Late Latin *decas, decadis*, from Greek *dekas*, from *deka* ten. See also -AD[1].

decadence *n.* moral or cultural decay, deterioration; a falling-off from a high standard of excellence. WH: 16C. French *décadence*, from Medieval Latin *decadentia*, from *decadens, decadentis*, pres.p. of *decadere*, var. of *decidere* DECAY.

decaf *n.* decaffeinated coffee. *Also a., v.t.* WH: late 20C. Abbr. of *decaffeinated* (DECAFFEINATE).

decaffeinate *v.t.* to remove the caffeine from (coffee, tea etc.). WH: mid-20C. DE- + CAFFEINE + -ATE[3].

decagon *n.* a plane figure with ten sides and ten angles. WH: 17C. Medieval Latin *decagonum*, from Greek *dekagōnon*, from *deka* DECA- + -*gōnos* -GON.

decagram *n.* a weight of 10 grams (0.353 oz). WH: 19C. French *décagramme*, from *déca*- DECA- + *gramme* -GRAM.

decagynous *a.* having ten pistils. WH: 19C. DECA- + -GYNOUS.

decahedron *n.* a solid figure with ten sides. WH: 19C. DECA- + -HEDRON.

decal *n.* a transfer, a decalcomania. *Also v.t.* WH: mid-20C. Abbr. of DECALCOMANIA.

decalcify *v.t.* to clear (bone etc.) of calcareous matter. WH: 19C. DE- + CALCIFY.

decalcomania *n.* the process of transferring a design. WH: 19C. French *décalcomanie*, from *décalquer* to transfer a tracing + -*manie* -MANIA. Cp. CALQUE.

decalitre *n.* a liquid measure of capacity containing 10 litres (nearly 2½ gallons). WH: 19C. French *décalitre*, from *déca*- DECA- + LITRE.

Decalogue *n.* the Ten Commandments. WH: 12–14C. French *décalogue* or Ecclesiastical Latin *decalogus*, from Greek *dekalogos*, from *deka*- DECA- + *logos* saying, speech. See -LOGUE.

decametre *n.* a measure of length, containing 10 metres (393.7 in). WH: 19C. French *décamètre*, from *déca*- DECA- + *mètre* METRE[1].

decamp *v.i.* to break camp. WH: 17C. French *décamper*, from *dé*- DE- + *camp* CAMP[1].

decanal *a.* of or relating to a dean or a deanery. WH: 18C. Medieval Latin *decanalis*, from Late Latin *decanus*. See DEAN.

decant *v.t.* to pour off by gently inclining, so as not to disturb the sediment. WH: 17C. Medieval Latin *decanthare*, from Latin DE- + *canthus* angular lip of a jug, from Greek *kanthos* corner of the eye.

decapitate *v.t.* to behead. WH: 17C. Late Latin *decapitatus*, p.p. of *decapitare*, from DE- + *caput, capitis* head. See also -ATE[3].

decapod *n.* any cephalopod of the order Decapoda, having two tentacles and four pairs of arms. *Also a.* WH: 19C. French *décapode*, from Modern Latin *Decapoda*. See DECA-, -POD.

decarbonate *v.t.* to remove carbon from. WH: 19C. DE- + CARBON + -ATE[3].

decastyle *a.* having ten columns. *Also n.* WH: 18C. Greek *dekastulos* having ten columns, from *deka* ten + *stulos* column.

decasyllable *n.* a word or line of ten syllables. WH: 19C. DECA- + SYLLABLE.

decathlon *n.* an athletic contest consisting of ten events. WH: early 20C. DECA- + Greek *athlon* contest.

decay *v.i.* to rot. *Also v.t.*, *n.* WH: 15C. Old French *decair*, var. of *decheoir* (Modern French *déchoir*), from var. of Latin *decidere*, from DE- + *cadere* to fall. Cp. DECADENCE.

decease *n.* death, departure from this life. *Also v.i.* WH: 12–14C. Old French *décès*, from Latin *decessus* departure, death, from p.p. of *decedere* to go away, to depart, from DE- + *cedere* to go.

deceit *n.* the act of deceiving. WH: 12–14C. Old French, use as n. of p.p. of *deceveir* DECEIVE.

deceive *v.t.* to mislead deliberately or knowingly. *Also v.i.* WH: 12–14C. Old French *deceivre*, from Latin *decipere*, from DE- + *capere* to take.

decelerate *v.i.* to reduce speed, to slow down. *Also v.t.* WH: 19C. DE- + ACCELERATE.

December *n.* the twelfth and last month of the year. WH: 12–14C. Old French *décembre*, from Latin *December*, from *decem* ten. December was originally the 10th month of the Roman year. The meaning of *-ber* is unknown. Cp. SEPTEMBER etc.

decemvir *n.* any one of the various bodies of ten magistrates appointed by the Romans to legislate or rule, esp. the body appointed in 451 bc to codify the laws. WH: 14–15C. Latin, sing. of *decemviri*, orig. *decem viri* ten men. Cp. DUUMVIR.

decennary *n.* a period of ten years. *Also a.* WH: 17C. Medieval Latin *decenarius*, from *decena* tithing. See also -ARY[1].

decent *a.* becoming, seemly. WH: 16C. French *décent* or Latin *decens*, *decentis*, pres.p. of *decere* to be fitting. See also -ENT.

decentralize *v.t.* to break up (a centralized administration etc.), transfer from central control. WH: 19C. DE- + *centralize* (CENTRAL).

deception *n.* the act of deceiving. WH: 14–15C. Old French *déception* or Late Latin *deceptio*, *deceptionis*, from Latin *deceptus*, p.p. of *decipere*. See DECEIVE, also -ION.

decerebrate *a.* having undergone the removal of the cerebrum. WH: 19C. DE- + CEREBRUM + -ATE[2].

decern *v.t.* to decree. WH: 14–15C. Old French *décerner*, from Latin *decernere* to decide, to pronounce a decision, from DE- + *cernere* to separate, to sift.

dechristianize *v.t.* to pervert from Christianity; to divest of Christian sentiments and principles. WH: 19C. DE- + *Christianize* (CHRISTIAN).

deci- *pref.* a tenth part of. WH: Abbr. of Latin *decimus* tenth.

decibel *n.* a unit to compare levels of intensity, esp. of sound, one-tenth of a bel. WH: early 20C. DECI- + BEL.

decide *v.t.* to come to a decision about, to determine. *Also v.i.* WH: 14–15C. French *décider* or Latin *decidere* to cut off, to determine, from DE- + *caedere* to cut.

deciduous *a.* (of leaves etc. which fall in autumn and trees which lose their leaves annually) falling, not perennial. WH: 17C. Latin *deciduus*, from *decidere* to fall down, to fall off, from DE- + *cadere* to fall. See also -OUS.

decigram *n.* a weight equal to one-tenth of a gram (1.54 grain). WH: 19C. French *décigramme*, from *déci-* DECI- + *gramme* GRAM[1].

decile *n.* in statistics, any one of nine values of a random variable dividing a frequency distribution into ten equal groups. WH: 17C. French *décile*, prob. from Medieval Latin deriv. of Latin *decem* ten.

decilitre *n.* a fluid measure of capacity of one-tenth of a litre (0.176 pint). WH: 19C. French *décilitre*, from *déci-* DECI- + LITRE.

decillion *n.* a million raised to the tenth power, represented by 1 followed by 60 ciphers. WH: 18C. DECI- + *-llion* based on MILLION, BILLION etc.

decimal *a.* of or relating to ten or tenths. *Also n.* WH: 17C. Modern Latin *decimalis*, from Latin *decimus* tenth, from *decem* ten. See also -AL[1].

decimate *v.t.* to destroy a tenth or a large proportion of. WH: 16C. Latin *decimatus*, p.p. of *decimare*, from *decimus*. See DECIMAL, also -ATE[3]. The sense was originally to select and execute one man in ten. The current general sense probably arose from a misunderstanding of 'one in ten' as 'nine out of ten'.

decimetre *n.* the tenth part of a metre (3.937 in). WH: 18C. French *décimètre*, from *déci-* DECI- + *mètre* METRE[1].

decipher *v.t.* to turn from cipher into ordinary language. *Also n.* WH: 16C. DE- + CIPHER, based on French *déchiffrer*.

decision *n.* the act or result of deciding. WH: 14–15C. Old French *décision*, from Latin *decisio*, *decisionis*, from *decisus*, p.p. of *decidere* DECIDE. See also -ION.

decivilize *v.t.* to render less civilized. WH: 19C. DE- + CIVILIZE.

deck *n.* the plank or iron flooring of a ship, a platform forming a floor in a ship. *Also v.t.* WH: 14–15C. Middle Dutch *dec* roof, covering, cloak, from Germanic base of THATCH. The nautical deck was originally regarded as a roof rather than a floor. Cp. PLAFOND.

deckle *n.* a frame used in paper-making to keep the pulp within the desired limits. WH: 18C. German *Deckel*, dim. of *Decke* covering. See also -LE[1].

declaim *v.t.* to utter rhetorically or passionately. *Also v.i.* WH: 14–15C. French *déclamer* or Latin *declamare*, from DE- + *clamare* claim.

declaration *n.* the act of declaring or proclaiming. WH: 14–15C. Latin *declaratio*, *declarationis*, from *declaratus*, p.p. of *declarare* DECLARE. See also -ATION.

declare *v.t.* to assert or affirm positively. *Also v.i.* WH: 12–14C. Latin *declarare* to make clear, from DE- + *clarare*, from *clarus* CLEAR.

declass *v.t.* to remove from a social class. WH: 19C. French *déclasser*, from *dé-* DE- + *classer* CLASS. Cp. DÉCLASSÉ.

déclassé *a.* having lost social position or estimation. WH: 19C. French, p.p. of *déclasser*. See DECLASS.

declassify *v.t.* to remove (information) from the security list. WH: 19C. DE- + CLASSIFY.

declension *n.* the variation of inflection of nouns, adjectives and pronouns. WH: 14–15C. Old French *déclinaison*, from *décliner* DECLINE, alt. after Latin *declinatio*, *declinationis* DECLINATION.

declinate *a.* bending or bent downwards in a curve. WH: 19C. Latin *declinatus*, p.p. of *declinare* DECLINE. See also -ATE[2].

declination *n.* the act of bending or moving downwards. WH: 14–15C. Latin *declinatio*, *declinationis*, from *declinatus*, p.p. of *declinare* DECLINE. See also -ATION.

decline *v.i.* to deteriorate, to decay. *Also v.t.*, *n.* WH: 14–15C. Old French *décliner*, from Latin *declinare*, from DE- + *clinare* to bend.

declinometer *n.* an apparatus for measuring the declination of the needle of the compass. WH: 19C. DECLINATION + -O- + -METER.

declivity *n.* an inclination, a slope or gradual descent of the surface of the ground, as distinct from *acclivity*. WH: 17C. Latin *declivitas*, from *declivis* sloping down, from DE- + *clivus* slope.

declutch *v.i.* to release the clutch of a vehicle. WH: early 20C. DE- + CLUTCH[1].

deco *n.* art deco. WH: mid-20C. Abbr. of *Art Deco*. See ART.

decoct *v.t.* to boil down in hot water. WH: 14–15C. Latin *decoctus*, p.p. of *decoquere* to boil down, from DE- + *coquere* COOK.

decode *v.t.* to translate from code symbols into ordinary language. WH: 19C. DE- + CODE.

decoke *v.t.* to remove carbon from, to decarbonize. *Also n.* WH: early 20C. DE- + COKE[1].

†**decollate** *v.t.* to behead. WH: 14–15C. Orig. p.p., from Latin *decollatus*, p.p. of *decollare* to behead, from DE- + *collum* neck. See also -ATE[3].

décolleté *a.* (of a dress) low-necked. *Also n.* WH: 19C. French, p.p. of *décolleter* to expose the neck, from *dé-* DE- + *collet* collar of a dress.

decolonize *v.t.* to grant independence to (a colonial state). WH: mid-20C. DE- + COLONIZE.

decolour *v.t.* to deprive of colour, bleach. WH: 14–15C. French *décolorer* or Latin *decolorare*, from DE- + *colorare* to colour.

decommission *v.t.* to close or dismantle (a nuclear reactor etc.) which is no longer to be used. WH: early 20C. DE- + COMMISSION.

decompose *v.t.* to resolve into constituent elements. *Also v.i.* WH: 18C. French *décomposer*, from *dé-* DE- + *composer* COMPOSE.

decompound *a.* compounded of compounds. WH: 17C. DE- + COMPOUND[1].

decompress *v.t.* gradually to relieve pressure on. WH: early 20C. DE- + COMPRESS[1].

decongestant *a.* relieving congestion. *Also n.* WH: mid-20C. DE- + CONGEST + -ANT.

deconsecrate *v.t.* to withdraw consecrated status from; to secularize. WH: 19C. DE- + CONSECRATE.

deconstruction *n.* a method of literary and philosophical analysis by breaking down the structure of the language on the assumption that words have no fixed meaning outside of their relation to other words. WH: 19C. DE- + CONSTRUCTION.

decontaminate v.t. to clear of a poisonous substance or radio-activity. WH: mid-20C. DE- + CONTAMINATE.

decontrol v.t. to terminate government control of (a trade etc.). Also n. WH: early 20C. DE- + CONTROL.

decor n. the setting, arrangement and decoration of a room or of a scene on the stage. WH: 19C. French décor, from décorer DECORATE.

decorate v.t. to make more attractive by ornamentation. WH: 16C. Latin decoratus, p.p. of decorare to beautify, from decus, decoris embellishment. See also -ATE³.

decorous a. behaving in a polite and decent manner. WH: 17C. Latin decorus + -OUS.

decorticate v.t. to strip the bark, skin, husk or outside layer from. WH: 17C. Latin decorticatus, p.p. of decorticare, from DE- + cortex, corticis bark. See also -ATE³.

découpage n. the art of decorating furniture etc. with cut-out patterns. WH: mid-20C. French, from découper to cut up, to cut out, from dé- DE- + couper to cut.

decouple v.t. to separate, to end the connection between. WH: 17C. French découpler, from dé- DE- + coupler COUPLE.

decoy n. a bait, an attraction. Also v.t. WH: 17C. ? Dutch de kooi the decoy. See COY.

decrease¹ v.i. to become less. Also v.t. WH: 14–15C. Old French descreistre, descreiss- (Modern French décroître), from var. of Latin decrescere, from DE- + crescere to grow.

decrease² n. lessening, a diminution. WH: 14–15C. Old French decreis, from stem of descreistre. See DECREASE¹.

decree n. a law or ordinance made by superior authority. Also v.t., v.i. WH: 12–14C. Old French decré, var. of decret, from Latin decretum, use as n. of neut. of decretus, p.p. of decernere DECERN.

decrement n. decrease, diminution. WH: 16C. Latin decrementum, from decre-, stem of decrescere DECREASE¹. See also -MENT.

decrepit a. weak from age and infirmities. WH: 14–15C. Latin decrepitus, from DE- + crepitus, p.p. of crepare to rattle, to creak.

decrepitate v.t. to calcine in a strong heat, so as to cause a continual crackling of the substance. Also v.i. WH: 17C. DE- + Latin crepitatus, p.p. of crepitare to crackle. See also -ATE³.

decrescendo adv., a. diminuendo. Also n. WH: 19C. Italian, pres.p. of decrescere DECREASE¹. Cp. DIMINUENDO.

decrescent a. (of the moon) waning. WH: 17C. Latin decrescens, decrescentis, pres.p. of decrescere DECREASE¹. See also -ENT.

decretal a. of or relating to a decree. Also n. WH: 12–14C. Late Latin decretale, neut. sing. (used as n.) of decretalis, from decretus, p.p. of decernere DECERN. See also -AL¹.

decriminalize v.t. to make (an action) no longer illegal. WH: mid-20C. DE- + CRIMINAL + -IZE.

decry v.t. to cry down; to clamour against. WH: 17C. DE- + CRY, based on French décrier to cry down. Cp. DESCRY.

decrypt v.t. to decipher. WH: mid-20C. DE- + crypt-, from CRYPTOGRAM.

decumbent a. lying down, reclining; prostrate. WH: 17C. Latin decumbens, decumbentis, pres.p. of decumbere to lie down, from DE- + nasalized var. of cubare to lie. See also -ENT.

decuple a. tenfold. Also n., v.t., v.i. WH: 14–15C. Late Latin decuplus, from decem ten.

decurion n. a Roman officer commanding ten men. WH: 14–15C. Latin decurio, decurionis, from decuria, from decem ten, based on centurio, centurionis CENTURION.

decurrent a. attached along the side of a stem below the point of insertion (as the leaves of the thistle). WH: 14–15C. Latin decurrens, decurrentis, pres.p. of decurrere to run down, from DE- + currere to run. See also -ENT.

decurve v.t., v.i. to curve downward. WH: 19C. DE- + CURVE.

decussate¹ v.t., v.i. to intersect at acute angles, i.e. in the form of an X. WH: 17C. Latin decussatus, p.p. of decussare to divide crosswise, from decussis the numeral 10, intersection of lines crosswise (X), from decem ten. See also -ATE³.

decussate² a. intersecting at acute angles, in the form of an X. WH: 19C. Latin decussatus, p.p. of decussare. See DECUSSATE¹, also -ATE².

dedans n. an open gallery at the end of a real-tennis court. WH: 18C. French inside, interior.

dedicate v.t. to apply wholly to some purpose, person or thing. WH: 14–15C. Latin dedicatus, p.p. of dedicare to proclaim, to devote, from DE- + dicare, var. of dicere to say. See also -ATE³.

deduce v.t. to draw as a conclusion by reasoning, to infer. WH: 14–15C. Latin deducere, from DE- + ducere to lead.

deduct v.t. to take away, to subtract. WH: 14–15C. Latin deductus, p.p. of deducere DEDUCE.

deduction n. the act of deducting. WH: 14–15C. Old French déduction or Latin deductio, deductionis, from deductus. See DEDUCT, also -ION.

dee n. the fourth letter of the alphabet, D, d. WH: 18C. Representation of pronun. of D as letter's name.

deed n. a thing done with intention. Also v.t. WH: pre-1200. Old English dēd, from Germanic, from Indo-European base of DO. Cp. German Tat.

deejay n. a disc jockey. WH: mid-20C. Representation of pronun. of abbr. DJ. Cp. DEE, JAY².

deem v.t. to judge, to consider. Also v.i., n. WH: pre-1200. Old English dēman, from Germanic base of DOOM.

de-emphasize v.t. to remove the emphasis from. WH: mid-20C. DE- + emphasize (EMPHASIS).

deep a. extending far down. Also adv., n. WH: pre-1200. Old English dēop, from Germanic, from base also of DIP. Cp. German tief.

deer n. any ruminant quadruped of the family Cervidae, the males having antlers, except in the one domesticated species, the reindeer. WH: pre-1200. Old English dēor, from Germanic, from Indo-European source word with meaning breathing creature. The original sense was animal, beast (in general). Cp. German Tier animal, beast.

de-escalate v.t. to reduce the intensity of. WH: mid-20C. DE- + ESCALATE.

def a. very good, brilliant. WH: late 20C. Abbr. of definitive (DEFINITE). The word is popularly associated with DEATH.

deface v.t. to spoil the appearance or beauty of. WH: 12–14C. Obs. French défacer, earlier deffacer, var. of Old French desfacier, from des- DE- + FACE.

defalcate v.i. to commit embezzlement. Also v.t. WH: 16C. Medieval Latin defalcatus, p.p. of defalcare, from DE- + Latin falx, falcis sickle, scythe. See also -ATE³.

defame v.t. to speak maliciously about; to slander, to libel. Also n. WH: 12–14C. Old French diffamer, from Latin diffamare to spread about as an evil report, from DIS-, DE- + fama FAME. A sense to accuse was current to the 19C.

defat v.t. to remove fat(s) from. WH: early 20C. DE- + FAT.

default n. failure to do something, esp. to appear in court on the day assigned or to meet financial liabilities. Also v.i., v.t. WH: 12–14C. Partly from Old French défaute, from defaillir to fail, partly from Old French défaut, back-formation from défaute.

defeasance n. the act of annulling a contract. WH: 14–15C. Old French defesance, from defesant, pres.p. of defaire (Modern French défaire) to undo, from dé- DE- + faire to do. See also -ANCE.

defeat v.t. to overthrow, to conquer. Also n. WH: 14–15C. Old French deffait, desfait, p.p. of desfaire (Modern French défaire), from Medieval Latin disfacere to undo, from Latin dis- DE- + facere to make. The original sense (to the 17C) was to undo, to destroy. The current sense dates from the 16C (but was too late for Shakespeare).

defecate v.i. to eject faeces from the body. Also v.t. WH: 15C. Latin defaecatus, p.p. of defaecare, from DE- + faex, pl. faeces dregs. See FAECES, also -ATE³. The original sense was to purify, to clarify. The current sense dates from the 19C.

defect¹ n. absence of something essential to perfection or completeness. WH: 14–15C. Latin defectus, p.p. of deficere to leave, to desert, from DE- + facere to make, to do.

defect² v.i. to desert one's country or cause for the other side. WH: 16C. Latin defectus. See DEFECT¹.

defence n. the state or act of defending. Also v.t. WH: 12–14C. Old French defens (Modern French défense), from Late Latin, use as nn. of defensum, defensa neut. and fem. p.ps. of defendere. See DEFEND.

defend v.t. to shield from harm. Also v.i. WH: 12–14C. Old French défendre, from Latin defendere to ward off, to protect, from DE- + -fendere as in offendere OFFEND.

defenestration n. the action of throwing someone (or occasionally something) out of a window. WH: 17C. Modern Latin *defenestratio, defenestrationis*, from DE- + *fenestra* window. See also -ATION.

defer[1] *v.t.* to put off, to postpone. *Also v.i.* WH: 14–15C. Old French *différer* to defer, to differ. See DIFFER.

defer[2] *v.i.* to yield to the opinion of another. *Also v.t.* WH: 14–15C. Old French *déférer*, from Latin *deferre* to carry away, to refer (a matter), from DE- + *ferre* to bear, to carry.

deferent *n.* something which carries or conveys. *Also a.* WH: 14–15C. French *déférent* or Medieval Latin *deferens, deferentis*, pres.p. of *deferre*. See DEFER[2], also -ENT.

defervescence *n.* a cooling down; an abatement of symptoms of fever. WH: 18C. Latin *defervescens, defervescentis*, pres.p. of *defervescere* to cease boiling, from DE- + *fervescere* to begin to boil, from *fervere* to be hot. See also -ENCE.

defeudalize *v.t.* to deprive of feudal character or form. WH: 19C. DE- + *feudalize* (FEUD[2]).

defibrillator *n.* a machine used to apply an electric current to the chest and heart area to stop fibrillation of the heart. WH: mid-20C. DE- + FIBRILLATE[1] + -OR.

deficient *a.* defective; falling short. WH: 16C. Latin *deficiens, deficientis*, pres.p. of *deficere* to undo, to leave, from DE- + *facere* to make, to do. See also -ENT.

deficit *n.* a falling short of revenue as compared with expenditure. WH: 18C. French *déficit*, from Latin *deficit* it is wanting, 3rd pers. sing. pres. ind. of *deficere*. See DEFICIENT.

defilade *v.t.* to arrange the defences so as to shelter the interior works from an enfilade. *Also n.* WH: 19C. French *défiler* + -ADE. Cp. ENFILADE.

defile[1] *v.t.* to make foul or dirty; to soil, to stain. WH: 14–15C. Alt. of obs. *defoul* to trample down (from Old French *defouler*, from de- DE- + *fouler* to tread), based on obs. *befile* to befoul, to defile (from BE- + obs. *file* to defile). Influ. by FOUL.

defile[2] *n.* a long, narrow pass or passage, as between hills, along which people can march only in file. *Also v.i.* WH: 17C. French *défilé*, p.p. (used as n.) of *défiler* to defile, from dé- DE- + *file* FILE[1].

define *v.t.* to state the meaning of (a word etc.), to describe (a thing) by its qualities and circumstances. *Also v.i.* WH: 14–15C. Old French *definer*, from var. of Latin *definire*, from DE- + *finire*.

definite *a.* limited, fixed precisely. *Also n.* WH: 16C. Latin *definitus*, p.p. of *definire*. See DEFINE, also -ITE[2].

deflagrate *v.t.* to consume by means of rapid combustion. *Also v.i.* WH: 18C. Latin *deflagratus*, p.p. of *deflagrare* to burn up, from DE- + *flagrare* to burn. See also -ATE[3].

deflate *v.t.* to let down (a pneumatic tyre, balloon etc.) by allowing the gas to escape. *Also v.i.* WH: 19C. DE- + *-flate* from INFLATE.

deflect *v.i.* to turn or move to one side. *Also v.t.* WH: 16C. Latin *deflectere* to bend aside, from DE- + *flectere* to bend.

deflorate *a.* having shed its pollen. *Also v.t.* WH: 19C. Latin *defloratus*, p.p. of *deflorare*. See DEFLOWER, also -ATE[2].

deflower *v.t.* to deprive of virginity, to ravish. WH: 14–15C. Old French *defflourer* (Modern French *déflorer*), from var. of Late Latin *deflorare*, from DE- + *flos, floris* FLOWER. A second sense to the 18C was to select the finest parts (the 'flower') from a book. Cp. ANTHOLOGY.

defocus *v.t.* to put out of focus. *Also v.i.* WH: mid-20C. DE- + FOCUS.

defoliate *v.t.* to deprive of leaves, esp. in warfare. WH: 18C. Late Latin *defoliatus*, p.p. of *defoliare*, from DE- + *folium* leaf. See also -ATE[3].

deforce *v.t.* to withhold with violence. WH: 14–15C. Old French *deforcier*, from des- DE- + *forcier* FORCE[1]. Cp. ENFORCE.

deforest *v.t.* to clear of trees. WH: 16C. DE- + FOREST. Cp. DISAFFOREST, DISFOREST.

deform *v.t.* to render ugly or unshapely. *Also v.i., a.* WH: 14–15C. Old French *difformer* (Modern French *déformer*), from Medieval Latin *difformare*, from Latin *deformare*. See DIS-, DE-, FORM.

defraud *v.t.* to deprive of what is right by deception; to cheat. WH: 14–15C. Old French *defrauder* or Latin *defraudare*, from DE- + *fraudere* to cheat, from *fraus, fraudis* FRAUD.

defray *v.t.* to pay; to bear the charge of; to settle. WH: 14–15C. French *défrayer*, from dé- DE- + obs. *frai, frait* (pl. *frais*) expenses, cost, from Medieval Latin *fredum* fine for breach of the peace.

defrock *v.t.* to deprive (a priest etc.) of ecclesiastical status. WH: 17C. French *défroquer*, from dé- DE- + *froc* FROCK.

defrost *v.t.* to remove frost or ice from. *Also v.i.* WH: 19C. DE- + FROST.

deft *a.* neat in handling; dextrous, clever. *Also adv.* WH: 12–14C. Var. of DAFT. The original meaning was mild, meek, humble (the earliest sense of *daft*). The current sense arose in the 14–15C.

defunct *a.* dead, deceased. *Also n.* WH: 16C. Latin *defunctus*, p.p. of *defungi* to discharge, to perform, from DE- + *fungi* to perform.

defuse *v.t.* to render (a bomb) harmless by removing the fuse. WH: mid-20C. DE- + FUSE[2].

defy *v.t.* to disregard openly. *Also n.* WH: 12–14C. Old French *défier*, earlier *desfier*, from Latin *dis-* DE- + *fidus* faithful.

dégagé *a.* relaxed, casual, detached. WH: 17C. French, p.p. of *dégager* to set free, from dé- DE- + *-gager*, from *engager* ENGAGE.

degas *v.t.* to remove gas from. WH: early 20C. DE- + GAS.

degauss *v.t.* to neutralize the magnetization of (a ship etc.), by the installation of a current-carrying conductor. WH: mid-20C. DE- + GAUSS.

degenerate[1] *a.* having fallen from a better to worse state. *Also n.* WH: 16C. Latin *degeneratus*, p.p. of *degenerare*. See DEGENERATE[2], also -ATE[2].

degenerate[2] *v.i.* to fall off in quality from a better to a worse physical or moral state. WH: 16C. Latin *degeneratus*, p.p. of *degenerare* to depart from its race, from *degener* debased, from DE- + *genus, generis* kind. See also -ATE[3].

deglutition *n.* the act or power of swallowing. WH: 17C. French *déglutition* or Modern Latin *deglutitio, deglutitionis*, from *deglutitus*, p.p. of *deglutire* to swallow down, from DE- +*glutire* to swallow. Cp. GLUT.

degradation *n.* the act of degrading. WH: 16C. Old French *dégradation* or Ecclesiastical Latin *degradatio, degradationis*, from *degradatus*, p.p. of *degradare*. See DEGRADE, also -ATION.

degrade *v.t.* to reduce in rank or dignity. *Also v.i.* WH: 14–15C. Old French *dégrader*, from Ecclesiastical Latin *degradare*, from DE- + *gradus* rank, GRADE.

degrease *v.t.* to remove grease from. WH: 19C. DE- + GREASE[1].

degree *n.* a step in progression or rank. WH: 12–14C. Old French *degré*, from Latin DE- + *gradus* step, GRADE.

degressive *a.* reducing in quantity. WH: early 20C. Latin *degressus*, p.p. of *degredi* to descend + -IVE.

degust *v.t.* to taste so as to relish. WH: 17C. Latin *degustare*, from DE- + *gustare* to taste.

de haut en bas *adv.* condescendingly, in a manner assuming superiority. WH: 17C. French from above to below, from *de* from + *haut* high (cp. HAUTEUR) + *en* in, to + *bas* low (cp. BASE[2]).

dehisce *v.i.* (of the capsules or anthers of plants) to gape, to burst open. WH: 17C. Latin *dehiscere*, from DE- + *hiscere* to begin to open, from *hiare* to gape.

dehorn *v.t.* to remove the horns from. WH: 19C. DE- + HORN.

dehumanize *v.t.* to divest of human character, of feeling or tenderness; to brutalize. WH: 19C. DE- + *humanize* (HUMAN).

dehumidify *v.t.* to remove humidity from. WH: mid-20C. DE- + *humidify* (HUMID).

dehydrate *v.t.* to release or remove water or its elements from (the body, tissues etc.). WH: 19C. DE- + Greek *hudōr, hudr-* water + -ATE[3].

dehydrogenate *v.t.* to remove hydrogen from. WH: 19C. DE- + HYDROGEN + -ATE[3].

dehypnotize *v.t.* to awaken from a hypnotic condition. WH: 19C. DE- + *hypnotize* (HYPNOTISM).

de-ice *v.t.* to disperse or remove ice (from the wings and control surfaces of an aircraft, the windows of a car). WH: mid-20C. DE- + ICE.

deicide *n.* the killing of a god. WH: 17C. Ecclesiastical Latin *deicida* killer of a god, or from Latin *deus, dei* god. See also -CIDE.

deictic *a.* proving or pointing directly; demonstrative as distinct from *indirect* or *refutative*. *Also n.* WH: 19C. Greek *deiktikos*, from *deiktos*, verb.a. of *deiknunai* to show.

deid *a.* dead. WH: 12–14C. Var. of DEAD.

deify *v.t.* to make a god of. WH: 12–14C. Old French *déifier*, from Ecclesiastical Latin *deificare*, from Latin *deus* god. See also -FY.

deign *v.i.* to condescend. *Also v.t.* WH: 12–14C. Old French *degnier* (Modern French *daigner*), from Latin *dignare* to deem worthy, from *dignus* worthy.

deil *n*. the Devil. WH: 14–15C. Var. of DEVIL.

deindustrialize *v.t.* to make (a country etc.) less industrial. WH: 19C. DE- + *industrialize* (INDUSTRY).

deinothere *n*. an extinct mammal resembling an elephant, with tusks that curve downwards. WH: 19C. Modern Latin *Deinotherium*, from Greek *deinos* terrible + *thērion* wild animal.

deinstitutionalize *v.t.* to remove from an institution, esp. from a mental hospital. WH: mid-20C. DE- + *institutionalize* (INSTITUTE).

deionize *v.t.* to remove ions from (water or air). WH: early 20C. DE- + *ionize* (ION).

deipnosophist *n*. a person who discourses learnedly at meals, an excellent dinner table conversationalist (after the title of a work by Athenaeus). WH: 17C. Greek *deipnosophistēs*, used in pl. as title of a work by Athenaeus (3C BC) describing long discussions at a banquet, from *deipnon* dinner + *sophistēs* wise man.

deism *n*. the belief in the being of a god as the governor of the universe, on purely rational grounds, without accepting divine revelation. WH: 17C. Latin *deus* god + -ISM, based on French *déiste* deist, from Latin *deus* + -iste -IST.

deity *n*. a god; divine nature. WH: 12–14C. Old French *déité*, from Ecclesiastical Latin *deitas*, translating Greek *theotēs*, from *theos* god. See also -TY[1]. Ecclesiastical Latin *deitas* was coined by St Augustine, *c*.400.

déjà vu *n*. an illusion of already having experienced something one is experiencing for the first time. WH: early 20C. French already seen, from *déjà* already + p.p. of *voir* to see.

deject *v.t.* to depress in spirit; to dishearten. *Also a.* WH: 14–15C. Latin *deiectus*, p.p. of *deiicere* to throw down, from DE- + *iacere* to throw.

déjeuner *n*. breakfast, luncheon. WH: 18C. French, use as n. of *déjeuner* to break one's fast, from Old French *desjeüner*, from *des-* DE- + *jeün* fasting, from Latin *ieiunus*. Cp. DINE.

de jure *adv.* by right, legally. *Also a.* WH: 16C. Latin of law, from *de* of, from + abl. sing. of *ius, iuris* law.

dekko *n*. a quick look. *Also v.i.* WH: 19C. Hindi *dekho*, polite imper. of *dekhnā* to look.

delaine *n*. a kind of untwilled wool muslin. WH: 19C. Shortening of *mousseline de laine*. See MOUSSELINE.

†delate *v.t.* to accuse, to inform against. WH: 15C. Latin *delatus*, p.p. of *deferre*. See DEFER[2], also -ATE[3].

delay *v.t.* to postpone, to put off. *Also v.i., n.* WH: 12–14C. Old French *delayer*, var. of *deslaier*, prob. from *des-* DE- + *laier* to leave.

delayering *n*. the restructuring of a company or other organization by reducing the number of hierarchical layers. WH: late 20C. DE- + LAYER + -ING[1].

dele *v.t.* to take out, omit, expunge; to mark for deletion. *Also n.* WH: 18C. Latin, 2nd pers. sing. pres. imper. of *delere* DELETE.

delectable *a*. delightful, highly pleasing. WH: 14–15C. Old French *délectable*, from Latin *delectabilis*, from *delectare* to delight. See also -ABLE.

delegate[1] *n*. a person authorized to transact business. WH: 14–15C. Latin *delegatus*, use as n. of p.p. of *delegare*. See DELEGATE[2], also -ATE[1].

delegate[2] *v.t.* to depute as an agent or representative, with authority to transact business. WH: 14–15C. Latin *delegatus*, p.p. of *delegare*, from DE- + *legare* to send on a commission. See also -ATE[3].

delete *v.t.* to erase. WH: 14–15C. Latin *deletus*, p.p. of *delere* to blot out, to efface.

deleterious *a*. harmful; injurious to health or mind. WH: 17C. Medieval Latin *deleterius*, from Greek *dēlētērios* noxious. See also -OUS.

delft *n*. glazed earthenware of a type orig. made at Delft. WH: 17C. *Delft*, earlier *Delf*, a town in the Netherlands.

deli *n*. delicatessen. WH: mid-20C. Abbr. of DELICATESSEN.

Delian *a*. of or relating to Delos. WH: 16C. Latin *Delius*, from Greek *Dēlios* of Delos, a Greek island in the Cyclades + -AN.

deliberate[1] *a*. done or carried out intentionally. WH: 14–15C. Latin *deliberatus*, p.p. of *deliberare*. See DELIBERATE[2], also -ATE[2].

deliberate[2] *v.i.* to weigh matters in the mind, to ponder. *Also v.t.* WH: 16C. Latin *deliberatus*, p.p. of *deliberare*, from DE- + *librare* to weigh, from *libra* scales. See also -ATE[3].

delicacy *n*. the quality of being delicate. WH: 14–15C. DELICATE + -ACY.

delicate *a*. exquisite in form or texture. *Also n.* WH: 14–15C. Old French *délicat* or Latin *delicatus*, of unknown orig. See also -ATE[2]. The word is associated by folk etymology with Latin *deliciae* pet indulgences or *delicere* to allure, DELIGHT.

delicatessen *n*. a shop or part of a shop selling cold meats and cheeses and specialist prepared foods. WH: 19C. German *Delikatessen* (pl.) or Dutch *delicatessen* (pl.), from French *délicatesse*, from *délicat* DELICATE.

delicious *a*. giving great pleasure to the sense of taste. WH: 12–14C. Old French *delicieus* (Modern French *délicieux*), from Late Latin *deliciosus*, from Latin *delicia*, pl. *deliciae* DELIGHT.

†delict *n*. an offence, a delinquency. WH: 14–15C. Latin *delictum*, use as n. of *delictus*, p.p. of *delinquere*. See DELINQUENT.

delight *v.t.* to please greatly, to charm. *Also v.i., n.* WH: 12–14C. Old French *delitier*, from Latin *delectare* to allure, to charm, freq. of *delicere*, from DE- + *lacere* to entice. The spelling with *-gh-* dates from the 16C and arose on an analogy with English words such as LIGHT[1].

Delilah *n*. a temptress. WH: 16C. *Delilah*, a woman who betrayed Samson to the Philistines (Judg. xvi).

delimit *v.t.* to fix the boundaries or limits of. WH: 19C. French *délimiter*, from Latin *delimitare*, from DE- + *limitare*. See LIMIT.

delineate *v.t.* to draw in outline; to sketch out. WH: 16C. Latin *delineatus*, p.p. of *delineare* to outline, from DE- + *lineare* to draw lines, from *linea* LINE[1]. See also -ATE[3].

delinquent *n*. an offender, a culprit. *Also a.* WH: 15C. Latin *delinquens, delinquentis*, pres.p. of *delinquere* to be at fault, to offend, from DE- + *linquere* to leave. See also -ENT.

deliquesce *v.i.* to liquefy, to melt away gradually by absorbing moisture from the atmosphere. WH: 18C. Latin *deliquescere* to melt away, to dissolve, from DE- + *liquescere* to begin to melt, from *liquere* to be liquid. See also -ESCE.

delirious *a*. suffering from wandering in the mind, as a result of fever etc. WH: 16C. DELIRIUM + -OUS.

delirium *n*. a wandering of the mind, perversion of the mental processes, the results of cerebral activity bearing no true relation to reality, characterized by delusions, illusions or hallucinations, caused by fever etc. WH: 16C. Latin, from *delirare* to deviate, to be deranged, from DE-+ *lira* ridge between furrows, i.e. lit. to leave the furrow.

delitescent *a*. concealed, latent. WH: 17C. Latin *delitescens, delitescentis*, pres.p. of *delitescere* to hide away, to lurk, from DE- + *latescere* to begin to hide, from *latere* to lie hidden. See also -escent (-ESCENCE).

deliver *v.t.* to distribute, to present. *Also v.i.* WH: 12–14C. Old French *délivrer*, from Late Latin *deliberare*, from Latin DE- + *liberare* LIBERATE.

dell *n*. a hollow or small valley, usually wooded. WH: pre-1200. Old English, from Germanic, from base also of DALE. Cp. German *Tal* valley.

Della Cruscan *a*. of or relating to the Accademia della Crusca. *Also n.* WH: 19C. Italian (*Accademia*) *della Crusca* (Academy) of the bran. The Accademia della Crusca was established at Florence in 1582 to purify ('sift') the Italian language and subsequently published an authoritative dictionary.

delocalize *v.t.* to remove from its proper or usual place. WH: 19C. DE- + *localize* (LOCAL).

delouse *v.t.* to rid (a person or place) of vermin, esp. lice. WH: early 20C. DE- + LOUSE.

Delphic *a*. of or belonging to Delphi, where there was a celebrated oracle of Apollo. WH: 16C. *Delphi*, a town of Phocis in ancient Greece + -IC.

delphinium *n*. any plant of the genus *Delphinium*, having tall blue flowers. WH: 17C. Modern Latin, from Greek *delphinion* larkspur, from *delphis* DOLPHIN. The name alludes to the shape of the spur.

delphinoid *a*. of or relating to the division Delphinoidea, including dolphins, porpoises etc. *Also n.* WH: 19C. Greek *delphinoeidēs*, from *delphis* DOLPHIN. See also -OID.

delta *n*. the fourth letter of the Greek alphabet (Δ, δ). WH: 12–14C. Latin, from Greek.

deltiology *n*. the study and collecting of postcards. WH: mid-20C. Greek *deltion*, dim. of *deltos* writing tablet. See also -O- + -LOGY.

delude *v.t.* to deceive, to convince (someone) that something untrue is true. WH: 14–15C. Latin *deludere* to play false, to mock, from DE- + *ludere* to play, from *ludus* play, game.

deluge *n.* a general flood or inundation, esp. the biblical flood in the days of Noah. *Also v.t.* WH: 14–15C. Old French *déluge*, alt. (after other words in -*uge*) of *diluve*, from Latin *diluvium* (DILUVIAL).

delusion *n.* the act of deluding. WH: 14–15C. Late Latin *delusio*, *delusionis*, from *delusus*, p.p. of *deludere*. See DELUDE, also -ION.

delustre *v.t.* to remove the lustre from. WH: early 20C. DE- + LUSTRE[1].

de luxe *a.* luxurious, of superior quality. WH: 19C. French of luxury, from *de* of + LUXE.

delve *v.i.* to dip, to descend suddenly (into). *Also v.t., n.* WH: pre-1200. Old English *delfan* to dig, from Germanic.

demagnetize *v.t.* to remove magnetism from. WH: 19C. DE- + *magnetize* (MAGNET).

demagogue *n.* an agitator who appeals to the passions and prejudices of the people. WH: 17C. Greek *dēmagōgos*, from *dēmos* people + *agōgos* leading, from *agein* to lead.

demand *n.* an authoritative claim or request. *Also v.t., v.i.* WH: 12–14C. Old French *demander*, from Latin *demandare* to hand over, to entrust, from DE- + *mandare* to commission, to order.

demantoid *n.* a type of green garnet. WH: 19C. German, from *Demant* diamond.

demarcation *n.* the fixing of a boundary or dividing line. WH: 18C. Spanish *demarcación*, from *demarcar* to mark out the bounds of, from *de*- DE- + *marcar* MARK[1]. See also -ATION.

démarche *n.* a diplomatic approach. WH: 17C. French, from *démarcher* to take steps, from *dé*- DE- + *marcher* MARCH[1].

dematerialize *v.t.* to deprive of material qualities or characteristics; to spiritualize. *Also v.i.* WH: 19C. DE- + *materialize* (MATERIAL).

deme *n.* a subdivision or township in Greece (ancient and modern). WH: 19C. Greek *dēmos* DEMOS.

demean[1] *v.t.* to debase (oneself), to lower (oneself). WH: 17C. DE- + MEAN[3], based on DEBASE.

demean[2] *v.t.* to conduct (oneself), to behave. *Also n.* WH: 12–14C. Old French *démener* to lead, to exercise (*se démener* to behave), from Latin DE- + *minare* to drive (animals), from *minari* to threaten.

dement *v.t.* to madden; to deprive of reason. *Also n.* WH: 16C. Old French *dementer* or Late Latin *dementare*, from *demens*, *dementis* insane, from DE- + *mens*, *mentis* mind.

démenti *n.* an official contradiction of a rumour etc. WH: 16C. French, from *démentir* to contradict, from *dé*- DE- + *mentir* to lie.

dementia *n.* serious deterioration of the mental faculties, with memory loss, mood swings etc. WH: 18C. Latin, from *demens*. See DEMENT, also -IA.

demerara *n.* a type of brown sugar. WH: 19C. *Demerara*, a river and region of Guyana.

demerge *v.t., v.i.* to split into separate companies again. WH: late 20C. DE- + MERGE.

demerit *n.* something which merits punishment. WH: 14–15C. Old French *desmerite* or Latin *demeritum*, from *demeritus*, p.p. of *demereri* to merit, to deserve, from DE- + *mereri* MERIT. The original sense was something that deserves reward. The current sense evolved because *de*- was taken as negative.

demersal *a.* found in deep water or on the ocean bed. WH: 19C. Latin *demersus*, p.p. of *demergere* to submerge, to sink, from DE- + *mergere* to plunge, to dip. See also -AL[1].

demesne *n.* an estate in land. WH: 12–14C. Old French *demeine*, later Anglo-French *demesne*, use as n. of a., of a lord, from Latin *dominicus* of a lord, from *dominus* lord. Cp. DOMAIN.

demi- *pref.* half, semi-, partial, partially. WH: French *demi*, from Medieval Latin *dimedius* half, from Latin *dimidius*. Cp. DEMY.

demi-bastion *n.* in fortification, a single face and flank, resembling half of a bastion. WH: 17C. DEMI- + BASTION.

demigod *n.* a being who is half a god. WH: 16C. DEMI- + GOD.

demijohn *n.* a glass bottle with a large body and small neck, enclosed in wickerwork. WH: 18C. Prob. alt. of French *dame-jeanne*, lit. Lady Jane, assim. to DEMI- and JOHN. The French word is a corruption of Provençal *damajano*, perhaps from *demeg* half.

demilitarize *v.t.* to end military involvement in and control of. WH: 19C. DE- + *militarize* (MILITARY).

demi-mondaine *n.* a prostitute. WH: 19C. French, from *demi-monde*, lit. half world. The French word implies a world half in and half out of society.

demineralize *v.t.* to remove salts or other minerals from. WH: mid-20C. DE- + *mineralize* (MINERAL).

demi-pension *n.* (French) hotel accommodation with half board. WH: mid-20C. French half board, from DEMI- + PENSION[2].

†**demi-rep** *n.* a woman of doubtful chastity. WH: 18C. DEMI- + abbr. of REPUTABLE. Cp. REP[1].

demise *n.* death; the end of something. *Also v.t.* WH: 14–15C. Anglo-French, fem. p.p. (used as n.) of Old French *desmettre* (Modern French *démettre*) to dismiss.

demist *v.t.* to make clear of condensation. WH: mid-20C. DE- + MIST.

demit *v.t., v.i.* to resign, abdicate. WH: 16C. French *démettre*, from Old French *desmettre*, from *des*- DE- + *mettre*, replacing Latin *dimittere*. See DISMISS.

demitasse *n.* a small coffee cup. WH: 19C. French half-cup, from DEMI- + *tasse* cup (cp. TASS).

demiurge *n.* in Platonic philosophy, the creator of the universe. WH: 17C. Ecclesiastical Latin *demiurgus*, from Greek *dēmiourgos* craftsman, artisan, from *dēmios* public (see DEMOS) + -*ergos* working.

demi-veg *a.* not completely vegetarian, but including white meat and fish in the diet. *Also n.* WH: mid-20C. DEMI- + abbr. of *vegetarian* (VEGETABLE).

demivolte *n.* an artificial motion of a horse in which it raises its legs in a particular manner. WH: 17C. DEMI- + *volte* (VOLT[2]).

demo *n.* a demonstration . *Also a.* WH: mid-20C. Abbr. of *demonstration* (DEMONSTRATE).

demob *v.t.* to demobilize. *Also n.* WH: early 20C. Abbr. of DEMOBILIZE.

demobilize *v.t.* to disband, to dismiss (troops) from a war footing. WH: 19C. French *démobiliser*. See DE-, *mobilize* (MOBILE).

democracy *n.* the form of government in which the sovereign power is in the hands of the people, and exercised by them directly or indirectly. WH: 16C. Old French *démocratie*, from Late Latin *democratia*, from Greek *dēmokratia*. See DEMOS, -CRACY.

démodé *a.* out of fashion. WH: 19C. French, p.p. of *démoder* to go out of fashion, from *dé*- DE- + *mode* fashion, MODE.

demodulate *v.t.* to extract the original audio signal from (the modulated carrier wave by which it is transmitted). WH: mid-20C. DE- + MODULATE.

Demogorgon *n.* a mysterious divinity, first mentioned by a scholiast on the *Thebaid* of Statius as one of the infernal gods. WH: 16C. Late Latin, of uncertain orig. Cp. DEMOS, GORGON.

demography *n.* the study of population statistics dealing with size, density and distribution. WH: 19C. Greek *dēmos* people + -O- + -GRAPHY.

demoiselle *n.* the demoiselle crane, *Anthropoides virgo*. WH: 16C. French. See DAMSEL. The bird is so called from its elegance of form, like that of a young lady.

demolish *v.t.* to pull down, to raze. WH: 16C. Old French *démolir*, *démoliss*-, from Latin *demoliri*, from DE- + *moliri* to construct, from *moles* mass. See MOLE[3], also -ISH[2].

demon *n.* an evil spirit supposed to have the power of taking possession of human beings. WH: 12–14C. Medieval Latin, from Latin *daemon*, from Greek *daimōn* divinity, genius.

demonetize *v.t.* to deprive of its character as money. WH: 19C. French *démonétiser*, from *dé*- DE- + Latin *moneta* MONEY. See also -IZE.

demono- *comb. form* demon(s). WH: Greek *daimono-*, comb. form of *daimon* DEMON. See also -O-.

demonolatry *n.* the worship of demons or evil spirits. WH: 17C. DEMONO- + -LATRY.

demonology *n.* the study of demons or of evil spirits. WH: 16C. DEMONO- + -LOGY.

demonopolize *v.t.* to end the monopoly of. WH: 19C. DE- + *monopolize* (MONOPOLY).

demonstrate *v.t.* to show by logical reasoning or beyond the possibility of doubt. *Also v.i.* WH: 16C. Latin *demonstratus*, p.p. of *demonstrare*, from *de*- DE- + *monstrare* to show. See also -ATE[3].

demoralize *v.t.* to lower the morale of, to discourage. WH: 18C. French *démoraliser*, from *dé*- DE- + *moral* MORAL.

demos *n.* the people, as distinguished from the upper classes; the mob. WH: 18C. Greek *dēmos* people.

demote *v.t.* to reduce in status or rank. WH: 19C. DE- + PROMOTE.

demotic *a.* of or relating to the people. *Also n.* WH: 19C. Greek *dēmotikos* popular, from *dēmotēs* one of the people. See DEMOS, also -OT², -IC.

demotivate *v.t.* to cause to feel lack of motivation, to discourage. WH: late 20C. DE- *motivate* (MOTIVE).

demount *v.t.* to remove from a mounting. WH: 16C. French *démonter* DISMOUNT. The original sense was to dismount. The current sense derives from DE- + MOUNT¹.

demulcent *a.* softening, mollifying, soothing. *Also n.* WH: 18C. Latin *demulcens, demulcentis,* pres.p. of *demulcere* to stroke caressingly, from DE- + *mulcere* to stroke, to appease. See also -ENT.

demur *v.i.* to have or express scruples, objections or reluctance. *Also v.t., n.* WH: 12–14C. Old French *demourer* to delay, to linger (Modern French *demeurer*), from var. of Latin *demorari*, from DE- + *morari* to tarry, to delay.

demure *a.* reserved and modest. WH: 14–15C. Prob. from Old French *demouré*, p.p. of *demourer* (see DEMUR), influ. by Old French *mur* grave (Modern French *mûr*), from Latin *maturus* ripe, MATURE. The original sense was calm, settled, used of the sea. A later sense was grave, sober.

demurrage *n.* an allowance by the freighter of a vessel to the owners for delay in loading or unloading beyond the time named in the charter-party. WH: 17C. Old French *demourrage*. See DEMUR, also -AGE.

demutualize *v.t.* to end the mutual status of (a building society etc.). WH: late 20C. DE- + *mutualize* (MUTUAL).

demy *n.* a particular size of paper, 22½ × 17½ in. (444.5 × 571.5 mm) for printing, 20 × 15½ in. (508 × 393.7 mm) for drawing or writing (*N Am.* 21 × 16 in.). WH: 14–15C. DEMI-, or French *demi* half. The original sense was half, half-sized. The current sense dates from the 16C.

demystify *v.t.* to remove the mystery from, to clarify. WH: mid-20C. DE- + MYSTIFY.

demythologize *v.t.* to remove the mythological elements from (something, e.g. the Bible) to highlight the basic meaning. WH: mid-20C. DE- + *mythologize* (MYTHOLOGY).

den *n.* the lair of a wild beast. *Also v.i.* WH: pre-1200. Old English *denn*, from Germanic. Rel. to DENE¹.

denarius *n.* a Roman silver coin, worth 10 asses; a penny. WH: 14–15C. Latin *denarius nummus* coin containing ten (asses), from *deni* by tens. Cp. DENIER.

denary *a.* containing ten. WH: 19C. Latin *denarius* containing ten. See DENARIUS.

denationalize *v.t.* to transfer from public to private ownership. WH: 19C. French *dénationaliser*, from *dé-* DE- + *nationaliser* nationalize (NATIONAL).

denaturalize *v.t.* to render unnatural; to alter the nature of. WH: 19C. DE- + *naturalize* (NATURAL).

denature *v.t.* to change the essential nature or character of (something) by adulteration etc. WH: 17C. French *dénaturer*, from *dé-* DE- + NATURE.

denazify *v.t.* to purge of Nazism and its evil influence on the mind. WH: mid-20C. DE- + NAZI + -FY.

dendrite *n.* a stone or mineral with treelike markings. WH: 18C. French, from Greek *dendritēs* pertaining to a tree, from *dendron* tree. See also -ITE¹.

dendro- *comb. form* resembling a tree. WH: Greek *dendron* tree. See also -O-.

dendrochronology *n.* the study of the annual growth rings in trees. WH: early 20C. DENDRO- + CHRONOLOGY.

dendrogram *n.* a type of tree diagram showing relationships between kinds of organism. WH: mid-20C. DENDRO- + -GRAM.

dendroid *a.* treelike, branching, tree-shaped. WH: 19C. DENDRO- + -OID.

dendrology *n.* the natural history of trees. WH: 18C. DENDRO- + -LOGY.

dendrometer *n.* an instrument for measuring the height and diameter of trees. WH: 19C. DENDRO- + -METER.

dene¹ *n.* a valley. WH: pre-1200. Old English *denu*, from Germanic. Rel. to DEN.

dene² *n.* a sandy down or low hill, a tract of sand by the sea. WH: 12–14C. ? Rel. to Low German *düne* and Dutch *duin* DUNE.

denegation *n.* contradiction, denial. WH: 15C. French *dénégation*, from Late Latin *denegatio, denegationis,* from DE- + *negare*. See also -ATION. The original sense was refusal of what is asked. The current sense dates from the 19C.

dene-hole *n.* an excavation consisting of a shaft, from 2 ft. 6 in. to 3 ft. (about 75 cm to 1 m) in diameter and 20 ft. to 90 ft. (about 6 to 27 m) in depth, ending below in a cavern in the chalk, made originally to obtain chalk. WH: 18C. Orig. uncertain. ? From DANE + HOLE, but assoc. by later archaeologists with DENE¹ and DEN. The excavations are traditionally said to have been made by the Danes.

de-net *v.t.* to reduce the price of (a book) below that specified by the publisher (and protected by the Net Book Agreement). WH: late 20C. DE- + NET².

dengue *n.* an acute fever common in the tropics, characterized by severe pains, a rash and swellings. WH: 19C. West Indian Spanish, from Kiswahili *denga, dinga,* in turn from Spanish *dengue* affectation. The reference is to the stiffness of the neck and shoulders that the disease causes, giving the sufferer an affected or fastidious air.

denier *n.* a unit for weighing and grading silk, nylon and rayon yarn, used for women's tights and stockings. WH: 14–15C. Old French, from Latin DENARIUS. The application to silk etc. dates from the 19C.

denigrate *v.t.* to defame. WH: 14–15C. Latin *denigratus*, from DE- + *nigrare* to blacken, from *niger* black. See also -ATE³.

denim *n.* a coarse, twilled cotton fabric used for jeans, overalls etc. WH: 17C. Orig. *serge denim*, from French *serge de Nîmes* serge of Nîmes (a city in SW France). See SERGE.

denitrate *v.t.* to remove nitric or nitrous acid or nitrate from. WH: 19C. DE- + NITRATE¹.

denizen *n.* a citizen, an inhabitant, a dweller, a resident. *Also v.t.* WH: 14–15C. Anglo-French *deinzein*, from Old French *deinz* within (from Late Latin *de intus* from within) + *-ein*, from Latin *-aneus*, assim. to CITIZEN. A denizen is a person who lives within a country, as distinct from a foreigner, who lives outside its borders.

denominate *v.t.* to call, to designate. WH: 14–15C. Latin *denominatus,* p.p. of *denominare,* from DE- + *nominare* to name. See also -ATE³.

de nos jours *a.* of this period, of our time. WH: early 20C. French of our days, from *de* of + *nos,* pl. of *notre* our + *jours,* pl. of *jour* day.

denote *v.t.* to mark, to indicate, to signify. WH: 16C. Old French *dénoter* or Latin *denotare,* from DE- + *notare* NOTE.

denouement *n.* the unravelling of a plot or story. WH: 18C. French *dénouement,* from *dénouer* to untie, from *dé-* DE- + *nouer* to knot.

denounce *v.t.* to accuse or condemn publicly. WH: 12–14C. Old French *dénoncier* (Modern French *dénoncer*), from Latin *denuntiare* to give official information, from DE- + *nuntiare* to make known.

de novo *adv.* anew. WH: 17C. Latin from new, from *de* from + *novo,* abl. sing. of *novus* new.

dense *a.* compact; having its particles closely united. WH: 14–15C. French, or from Latin *densus* thick, crowded.

dent¹ *n.* a depression such as is caused by a blow with a blunt instrument. *Also v.t.* WH: 12–14C. Orig. var. of DINT, but later assoc. with INDENT¹. An early sense to the 16C was a dealing of blows, the vigorous wielding of a weapon.

dent² *n.* a tooth of a wheel, a cog. WH: 16C. French tooth.

dental *a.* of or relating to or formed by the teeth. *Also n.* WH: 16C. Late Latin *dentalis,* from Latin *dens, dentis* tooth. See also -AL¹.

dentalium *n.* a tusk shell (the mollusc or its shell). WH: 19C. Modern Latin, from Late Latin *dentalis.* See DENTAL.

dentate *a.* toothed. WH: 14–15C. Latin *dentatus,* from *dens, dentis* tooth. See also -ATE².

denti- *comb. form* of or relating to the teeth. WH: Latin *dens, dentis* tooth + -i-.

denticle *n.* a small tooth. WH: 14–15C. Latin *denticulus,* dim. of *dens, dentis* tooth. See also -CLE.

dentiform *a.* shaped like a tooth or teeth. WH: 18C. DENTI- + -FORM.

dentifrice *n.* powder, paste or other material for cleansing the teeth. WH: 14–15C. French, from Latin *dentifricium,* from *dens, dentis* tooth + *fricare* to rub.

dentil *n.* any one of the small square blocks or projections under the moulding of a cornice. WH: 16C. Italian *dentello* or obs. French *dentille* (now *dentelle*), fem. dim. of *dent* tooth, from Latin *dens, dentis*.

dentilingual *a.* formed by the teeth and the tongue. *Also n.* WH: 19C. DENTI- + LINGUAL.

dentine *n.* the ivory tissue forming the body of a tooth. WH: 19C. Latin *dens, dentis* tooth + -INE.

dentist *n.* a person skilled in and qualified in treating and preventing disorders of the teeth and jaws. WH: 18C. French *dentiste*, from *dent* tooth. See also -IST.

denuclearize *v.t.* to deprive of nuclear arms. WH: mid-20C. DE- + NUCLEAR + -IZE.

denude *v.t.* to make bare or naked. WH: 14–15C. Latin *denudare*, from DE- + *nudare* to bare, from *nudus* nude.

denumerable *a.* able to be put into a one-to-one correspondence with the positive integers; countable. WH: early 20C. Late Latin *denumerare*, from DE- + *numerare* to count out, to enumerate. See also -ABLE.

denunciate *v.t.* to denounce. WH: 16C. Medieval Latin *denunciatus*, from Latin *denuntiatus*, p.p. of *denuntiare*. See DENOUNCE, also -ATE³.

deny *v.t.* to assert to be untrue or non-existent. *Also v.i.* WH: 12–14C. Old French *deneier* (Modern French *dénier*), from Latin *denegare*, from DE- + *negare* to refuse, to say no.

deoch an doris *n.* a drink taken just before leaving. WH: 17C. Gaelic *deoch an doruis*, Irish *deoch an dorais* drink at the door, from *deoch* drink + *an* the + *dorus* door, gen. sing. *doruis* (Gaelic) or *doras*, gen. sing. *dorais* (Irish).

deodand *n.* a personal chattel which had been the immediate cause of the death of any person, and on that account was forfeited to be sold for some pious use. WH: 16C. Law French *deodande*, from Anglo-Latin *deodanda, deodandum*, from Latin *Deo dandum* thing to be given to God, from *Deus* God + *dare* to give.

deodar *n.* a large Himalayan cedar, *Cedrus deodara*. WH: 19C. Hindi *deodār*, from Sanskrit *devadāru* timber of the gods, from *deva* god + *dāru* wood.

deodorize *v.t.* to deprive of odour. WH: 19C. DE- + Latin *odor* ODOUR + -IZE.

Deo gratias *int.* thanks be to God. WH: 16C. Latin (we give) thanks to God, from *Deo*, dat. of *Deus* God + *gratias*, acc. pl. of *gratia*.

deontic *a.* of or relating to duty. WH: 19C. Greek *deōn, deontos*, neut. pres.p. of *dei* it is right + -IC.

Deo volente *int.* God willing; all being well. WH: 18C. Latin God willing, from *Deo*, abl. of *Deus* God + *volente*, abl. of *volens*, pres.p. of *velle* to wish, to be willing.

deoxidize *v.t.* to deprive of oxygen; to extract oxygen from. WH: 18C. DE- + *oxidize* (OXIDE).

deoxycorticosterone *n.* a hormone which maintains the sodium and water balance in the body. WH: mid-20C. DE- + OXY-¹ + CORTICO- + -*sterone* (from STEROL + KETONE).

deoxygenate *v.t.* to deoxidize. WH: 19C. DE- + *oxygenate* (OXYGEN).

deoxyribonucleic acid *n.* the full name for DNA. WH: mid-20C. DE- + OXY-¹ + RIBOSE + *nucleic* (from NUCLEUS + -IC) + ACID.

depart *v.i.* to go away, to leave. *Also v.t.* WH: 12–14C. Old French *départir*, from var. of Latin *dispertire* to divide. See DE-, PART.

department *n.* a separate part or branch of business or administration. WH: 14–15C. Old French *département*. See DEPART, also -MENT.

departure *n.* the act of departing; leaving. WH: 14–15C. Old French *departeüre*. See DEPART, also -URE.

depasture *v.t.* to graze upon. *Also v.i.* WH: 16C. DE- + PASTURE.

dépaysé *a.* that is away from home or familiar surroundings. WH: early 20C. French removed from one's country. See DE-, PAYSAGE.

dépêche *n.* a message; a dispatch. WH: 19C. French, from *dépêcher* to send, to dispatch, from *dé-* DE- + -*pêcher*, from Late Latin *pedicare*, from *pedica* FETTER. Cp. IMPEACH. Not rel. to DISPATCH.

depend *v.i.* to be contingent, as to the result, on something else. WH: 14–15C. Old French *dépendre*, from var. of Latin *dependere*, from DE- + *pendere* to hang, to be suspended.

depersonalize *v.t.* to divest of personality. WH: 19C. DE- + *personalize* (PERSON).

depict *v.t.* to paint, to portray. WH: 14–15C. Latin *depictus*, p.p. of *depingere* to portray, from DE- + *pingere* to paint.

depilate *v.t.* to remove hair from. WH: 16C. Latin *depilatus*, p.p. of *depilare*, from DE- + *pilare* to deprive of hair, from *pilus* hair. See also -ATE³.

deplane *v.i.* to disembark from an aeroplane. *Also v.t.* WH: early 20C. DE- + PLANE⁴.

deplete *v.t.* to reduce. WH: 19C. Latin *depletus*, p.p. of *deplere* to empty out, from DE- + base of *plenus* full.

deplore *v.t.* to express disapproval of, to censure. WH: 16C. Old French *déplorer* or Italian *deplorare*, from Latin *deplorare*, from DE- + *plorare* to wail, to bewail.

deploy *v.t.* to open out. *Also v.i.* WH: 15C. French *déployer*, from Latin *displicare* to unfold, from *dis-* DE- + *plicare* to fold. Cp. DISPLAY.

deplume *v.t.* to strip of feathers. WH: 14–15C. French *déplumer*, from Medieval Latin *deplumare*, from Latin DE- + *plumare* PLUME.

depolarize *v.t.* to free (the gas-filmed plates of a voltaic battery etc.) from polarization. WH: 19C. DE- + POLARIZE.

depoliticize *v.t.* to make non-political. WH: mid-20C. DE- + POLITICIZE.

depolymerize *v.t.* to break a polymer down into monomers. *Also v.i.* WH: 19C. DE- + *polymerize* (POLYMER).

depone *v.t.* to declare under oath; to testify. *Also v.i.* WH: 14–15C. Latin *deponere* to lay aside, to put down, from DE- + *ponere* to place.

depopulate *v.t.* to clear of inhabitants. *Also v.i.* WH: 16C. Latin *depopulatus*, p.p. of *depopulare* to ravage, from DE- + *populare* (from *populus* people) to lay waste. See also -ATE³. Latin *depopulare* was later understood as to deprive of people, although *de-* is properly an intensive.

deport *v.t.* to expel from one country to another. *Also n.* WH: 17C. French *déporter*, from Latin *deportare*, from DE- + *portare* to carry. The word is popularly associated with PORT¹, as if meaning from the port. Cp. IMPORT¹, EXPORT¹.

depose *v.t.* to remove from a throne or other high office. *Also v.i.* WH: 12–14C. Old French *déposer*, based on Latin *deponere* (see DEPONE), but re-formed after Latin *depositus* and Old French *poser*. See POSE¹.

deposit *v.t.* to lay down, to place. *Also n.* WH: 17C. Obs. French *dépositer* or Medieval Latin *depositare*, from Latin *depositum*, neut. p.p. (used as n.) of *deponere*. See DEPONE.

depot *n.* a place of deposit, a storehouse. WH: 18C. French *dépôt*, from Old French *depost*, from Latin *depositum*. See DEPOSIT.

deprave *v.t.* to make bad or corrupt. *Also v.i.* WH: 14–15C. Old French *dépraver* or Latin *depravare*, from DE- + *pravus* crooked, perverse.

deprecate *v.t.* to express disapproval of or regret for. WH: 17C. Latin *deprecatus*, p.p. of *deprecari*, from DE- + *precari* to pray. See also -ATE³.

depreciate *v.t.* to lower the value of. *Also v.i.* WH: 14–15C. Late Latin *depreciatus*, p.p., from Latin *depretiare*, from DE- + *pretium* price. See also -ATE³.

depredation *n.* plundering, spoliation. WH: 15C. French *déprédation*, from Late Latin *depraedatio, depraedationis*, from *depraedatus*, p.p. of *depraedari*, from DE- + *praedari* to plunder. See also -ATION.

depress *v.t.* to press down. WH: 14–15C. Old French *depresser*, from Late Latin *depressare*, freq. of Latin *depressus*, p.p. of *deprimere* to press down, from DE- + *premere* to press.

depressurize *v.t.* to reduce the atmospheric pressure in (a pressure-controlled area, such as an aircraft cabin). WH: mid-20C. DE- + *pressurize* (PRESSURE).

deprive *v.t.* to take from, to dispossess (of). WH: 12–14C. Old French *depriver*, from Medieval Latin *deprivare*, from DE- + *privare* to deprive.

de profundis *adv.* from the depths of penitence or affliction. *Also n.* WH: 14–15C. Latin from the depths, from *de* from + *profundis*, abl. pl. of *profundus* deep, PROFOUND. The phrase represents the opening Latin words of Ps. cxxx: *De profundis clamavi ad te, Domine* Out of the depths have I cried unto thee, O Lord.

deprogram *v.t.* to remove a program from (a computer). WH: late 20C. DE- + *program* (PROGRAMME).

deprogramme *v.t.* to persuade (someone) to reject obsessive beliefs, ideas and fears. WH: late 20C. DE- + PROGRAMME.

depth *n.* deepness. WH: 14–15C. DEEP + -TH², based on LONG¹/ LENGTH and similar pairs. The early equivalent was *deepness* pre-1200, from Old English *dēopnes*.

depurate *v.t.* to purify. *Also v.i.* WH: 17C. Medieval Latin *depuratus*, p.p. of *depurare*, from DE- + *purare* to purify, from *purus* pure. See also -ATE³.

depute¹ *v.t.* to appoint or send as a substitute or agent. WH: 14–15C. Partly from Old French *députer*, from Latin *deputare* to destine, to assign, from DE- + *putare* to consider, partly based on DEPUTE².

depute² *n.* a deputy. WH: 14–15C. Old French *député*, p.p. of *députer* DEPUTE¹. Cp. DEPUTY.

deputy *n.* a person who is appointed or sent to act for another or others. WH: 14–15C. Var. of DEPUTE², retaining final syl. of French.

deracinate *v.t.* to tear up by the roots. WH: 16C. French *déraciner*, from *dé-* DE- + *racine* root. See also -ATE³.

derail *v.t.* to cause to leave the rails. *Also v.i.* WH: 19C. French *dérailler*, from *dé-* DE- + *rail* RAIL¹.

derailleur *n.* a bicycle gear in which the chain is moved between different sprockets. WH: mid-20C. French *dérailleur*, from *dérailler* (see DERAIL) + *-eur* -OR.

derange *v.t.* to put out of line or order. WH: 18C. French *déranger*, from *dé-* DE- + *rang* RANK¹.

derate *v.t.* remove the liability for rates from. *Also v.i.* WH: early 20C. DE- + RATE¹.

deration *v.t.* to remove from the rationed category. WH: early 20C. DE- + RATION.

Derby *n.* a race for three-year-old horses, held at Epsom in May or June. WH: 17C. *Derby*, a city and county in the N Midlands of England, and an earldom named after the county. The Derby horse race was founded in 1780 by the 12th Earl of Derby.

derby *n.* any important sporting event. WH: 19C. DERBY, after the horse race.

derecognize *v.t.* to cease to recognize the rights of (a trade union). WH: mid-20C. DE- + RECOGNIZE.

de règle *a.* customary, correct. WH: 19C. French from the rule, from *de* from + *règle* rule.

deregulate *v.t.* to remove legal or other regulations from (transport services etc.), often so as to open up general competition. WH: mid-20C. DE- + REGULATE.

derelict *a.* forsaken, abandoned. *Also n.* WH: 17C. Latin *derelictus*, p.p. of *delinquere* to forsake entirely, to abandon, from DE- + *relinquere* to leave, to forsake.

derequisition *v.t.* to free (requisitioned property). WH: mid-20C. DE- + REQUISITION.

derestrict *v.t.* to free from restriction, e.g. to free a road from speed limits. WH: mid-20C. DE- + RESTRICT.

deride *v.t.* to laugh at, to mock. *Also v.i.* WH: 16C. Latin *deridere*, from DE- + *ridere* to laugh at.

de-rig *v.t.* to dismantle the rigging of. *Also v.i.* WH: 19C. DE- + RIG¹.

de rigueur *a.* required by fashion. WH: 19C. French from strictness, from *de* of, from + *rigueur* strictness, RIGOUR.

derive *v.t.* to obtain, to get. *Also v.i.* WH: 14–15C. Old French *dériver* or Latin *derivare*, from DE- + *rivus* brook, stream. The original sense (to the 19C) was to conduct water from a source into a channel. The current sense dates from the 16C.

derm *n.* skin. WH: 19C. Modern Latin *derma*, from Greek skin.

-derm *comb. form* skin, as in *pachyderm*. WH: Greek *derma* skin.

dermatic *a.* of or relating to the skin. WH: 19C. Greek *dermatikos*, from *derma* skin. See also -IC.

dermatitis *n.* inflammation of the skin. WH: 19C. DERMATO- + -ITIS.

dermato- *comb. form* of or relating to the skin. WH: Greek *derma*, *dermatos* skin, leather. See also -O-.

dermatoglyphics *n.* the science of skin markings of the hands and feet. WH: early 20C. DERMATO- + Greek *gluphikos* glyphic (see GLYPH) + -S¹.

dermatoid *a.* skinlike. WH: 19C. DERMATO- + -OID.

dermatology *n.* the science of the skin and its diseases. WH: 19C. DERMATO- + -LOGY.

dermatosis *n.* any disease of the skin. WH: 19C. DERMATO- + -OSIS.

dernier *a.* last. WH: 17C. French last, from Old French *derrenier*, from *derrein*, from Popular Latin *deretranus*, from *de-retro*, from *retro* behind. Cp. DERRIÈRE.

derogate¹ *v.i.* to detract, to withdraw a part (from). *Also v.t.* WH: 14–15C. Latin *derogatus*, p.p. of *derogare*, from DE- + *rogare* to ask, to question. See also -ATE³.

derogate² *a.* debased, degenerated. WH: 14–15C. Latin *derogatus*, p.p. of *derogare*. See DEROGATE¹, also -ATE².

derrick *n.* a hoisting machine with a boom stayed from a central post, wall, floor, deck etc., for raising heavy weights. WH: 17C. *Derrick*, surname of a noted London hangman, *c.*1600.

derrière *n.* the buttocks, the behind. WH: 18C. French behind, from Popular Latin *de-retro*. See DERNIER.

derring-do *n.* courageous deeds. WH: 16C. Misconstruction by Spenser (and others) of *dorryng do* daring to do, orig. in Chaucer, misprinted in 16C editions as *derrynge do*. The expression was later popularized by Sir Walter Scott.

derringer *n.* a short-barrelled large-bore pistol. WH: 19C. Henry Derringer, 1786–1868, US gunsmith.

derris *n.* an extract of the root of tropical trees of the genus *Derris*, which forms an effective insecticide. WH: 19C. Modern Latin, from Greek leather covering. The reference is to the leather covering of the pod.

derry *n.* dislike, antipathy. WH: 19C. Prob. shortening of (meaningless) refrain *derry down*, punning on DOWN¹.

derv *n.* diesel engine fuel oil. WH: mid-20C. Acronym of diesel-engined road vehicle.

dervish *n.* a member of one of the various Muslim ascetic orders, whose devotional exercises include meditation and often frenzied physical exercises. WH: 16C. Turkish *derviş*, from Persian *darvīš* poor, religious mendicant. Cp. FAKIR.

desalinate *v.t.* to remove salt from (sea water). WH: mid-20C. DE- + SALINE + -ATE³.

descale *v.t.* to remove scale or scales from. WH: mid-20C. DE- + SCALE¹.

descant¹ *n.* a song, a melody. WH: 14–15C. Old French *deschant* (Modern French *déchant*), from Medieval Latin *discantus* part-song, refrain, from DIS- + *cantus* song.

descant² *v.i.* to comment or discourse at length (on). WH: 14–15C. Old French *deschanter* (Modern French *déchanter*). See DESCANT¹.

descend *v.i.* to come or go down. *Also v.t.* WH: 14–15C. Old French *descendre*, from Latin *descendere*, from DE- + *scandere* to climb.

descent *n.* the act of descending. WH: 12–14C. Old French *descente*, from *descendre* DESCEND, based on pairs such as *attente/ attendre* (see ATTEND), *vente/ vendre* (see VEND).

descramble *v.t.* to convert (a scrambled signal) to intelligible form. WH: mid-20C. DE- + SCRAMBLE.

describe *v.t.* to set forth the qualities or properties of in words. *Also v.i.* WH: 14–15C. Latin *describere* to write down, to copy, from DE- + *scribere* to write.

descry *v.t.* to make out, to espy. WH: 12–14C. Old French *descrier* to cry down, to publish (Modern French *décrier*). The original sense was to disclose, to reveal. The current sense has come to be associated with DECRY.

desecrate *v.t.* to divert from any sacred purpose; to profane. *Also a.* WH: 17C. DE- + *-secrate* from CONSECRATE. Latin *desecrare* or *desacrare* properly meant to consecrate.

deseed *v.t.* to remove the seeds from. WH: mid-20C. DE- + SEED.

desegregate *v.t.* to end racial segregation in (an institution, e.g. a school). WH: mid-20C. DE- + SEGREGATE¹.

deselect *v.t.* to refuse to readopt as a candidate, esp. as a prospective parliamentary candidate. WH: mid-20C. DE- + SELECT.

desensitize *v.t.* to make insensitive to (a chemical agent etc.). WH: early 20C. DE- + *sensitize* (SENSITIVE).

desert¹ *n.* a waste, uninhabited, uncultivated place, esp. a waterless and treeless region. *Also a.* WH: 12–14C. Old French *désert*, from Late Latin *desertum*, use as n. of neut. of *desertus* left waste, p.p of *deserere* to leave, to forsake.

desert² *v.t.* to forsake, to abandon. *Also v.i.* WH: 14–15C. French *déserter*, from Late Latin *desertare*, from Latin *desertus*. See DESERT¹.

desert³ *n.* what one deserves, either as reward or punishment. WH: 12–14C. Old French, from *deservir* DESERVE.

deserve *v.t.* to be worthy of, to merit by conduct or qualities, good or bad, esp. to merit by excellence, good conduct or useful deeds. *Also v.i.* WH: 12–14C. Old French *deservir* (Modern French *desservir*), from Latin *deservire* to serve well, from DE- + *servire* SERVE.

desexualize *v.t.* to castrate or spay. WH: 19C. DE- + SEXUAL + -IZE.

deshabille *n.* state of undress, state of being partly or carelessly attired. WH: 17C. French *déshabillé*, use as n. of p.p. of *déshabiller* to undress, from *des-* DIS- + *habiller* to dress.

desiccate *v.t.* to dry, to remove moisture from. WH: 16C. Latin *desiccatus*, p.p. of *desiccare*, from DE- + *siccare* to make dry, from *siccus* dry. See also -ATE³.

†desiderate *v.t.* to feel the loss of. WH: 17C. Latin *desideratus*, p.p. of *desiderare* to desire, prob. from DE- + *sidus*, *sideris* star. See also -ATE³. Cp. CONSIDER.

desideratum *n.* anything desired, esp. anything to fill a gap. WH: 17C. Latin, neut. sing. (used as n.) of p.p. of *desiderare* DESIDERATE.

design *v.t.* to formulate, to project. *Also v.i.*, *n.* WH: 14–15C. Partly from Latin *designare* DESIGNATE¹, partly from French *désigner*.

designate¹ *v.t.* to indicate, to mark. WH: 18C. Latin *designatus*, p.p. of *designare*, from DE- + *signare* SIGN. See also -ATE³.

designate² *a.* nominated to but not yet holding an office. WH: 14–15C. Latin *designatus*, p.p. of *designare*. See DESIGNATE¹, also -ATE².

desire *v.t.* to wish (to do). *Also v.i.*, *n.* WH: 12–14C. Old French *désirer*, from Latin *desiderare* DESIDERATE.

desist *v.i.* to cease, to forbear; to leave off. WH: 14–15C. Old French *désister*, from Latin *desistere*, from DE- + *sistere*, redupl. of *stare* to stand.

desk *n.* a table for a writer or reader, often with a sloping top. WH: 14–15C. Medieval Latin *desca*, prob. from Provençal *desc* basket or Italian *desco* table, from Latin DISCUS, dish, disc. Cp. DISH.

deskill *v.t.* to reduce the level of skill required for (a job), esp. by automation. WH: mid-20C. DE- + SKILL.

desman *n.* either of two molelike aquatic mammals, *Desmana moschata* of Russia and *Galemys pyrenaicus* of the Pyrenees. WH: 18C. French, used from German, from Swedish *desman-råtta* muskrat, from *desman* musk.

desmid *n.* a member of a group of microscopic freshwater algae, differing from the diatoms in their green colour, and in having no siliceous covering. WH: 19C. Modern Latin *Desmidium* genus name, as if dim. of Greek *desmos* band, chain.

desolate¹ *a.* forsaken, lonely. WH: 14–15C. Latin *desolatus*, p.p. of *desolare*. See DESOLATE², also -ATE².

desolate² *v.t.* to deprive of inhabitants. WH: 14–15C. Latin *desolatus*, p.p. of *desolare* to abandon, from DE- + *solus* alone. See also -ATE³.

desorb *v.t.* to release (an absorbed substance) from a surface. *Also v.i.* WH: early 20C. Back-formation from *desorption*, from DE- + *adsorption* (ADSORB).

despair *v.i.* to be without hope. *Also v.t.*, *n.* WH: 12–14C. Old French *desperer*, from Latin *desperare*, from DE- + *sperare* to hope, from *speres*, old pl. of *spes* hope.

desperado *n.* a desperate or reckless ruffian. WH: 17C. Var. of DESPERATE (as n.), based on Spanish words in -ADO.

desperate *a.* reckless, regardless of danger. *Also adv.*, *n.* WH: 14–15C. Latin *desperatus*, p.p. of *desperare*. See DESPAIR.

despicable *a.* meriting contempt; vile. WH: 16C. Late Latin *despicabilis*, from *despicari* to look down on, from DE- + base rel. to *specere* to look. See also -ABLE.

despise *v.t.* to regard with contempt. WH: 12–14C. Old French *despire*, *despiss-*, from Latin *despicere*, from DE- + *specere* to look. Cp. DESPICABLE.

despite *prep.* in spite of. *Also n.*, *v.t.* WH: 14–15C. Abbr. of *in despite of*, from *despite*, from Old French *despit* (Modern French *dépit*), from Latin *despectus* looking down on, from p.p. of *despicere*. See DESPISE.

despoil *v.t.* to strip or take away from by force; to plunder. *Also n.* WH: 12–14C. Old French *despoiller* (Modern French *dépouiller*), from Latin *despoliare*, from DE- + *spolia* (see SPOIL).

despond *v.i.* to be low in spirits, to lose hope. *Also n.* WH: 17C. Latin *despondere* to give up, to resign, from DE- + *spondere* to promise.

despot *n.* an absolute ruler or sovereign. WH: 16C. French *despote*, from Medieval Latin *despota*, from Greek *despotēs* lord, master.

desquamate *v.i.* to scale or peel off, to exfoliate. *Also v.t.* WH: 18C. Latin *desquamatus*, p.p. of *desquamare* to scale off, from DE- + *squama* scale. See also -ATE³.

des res *n.* a desirable residence (used by estate agents). WH: late 20C. Abbr. of *desirable residence*.

dessert *n.* the last course of a meal, consisting of fruit or sweetmeats; the sweet course. WH: 16C. French, use as n. of p.p. of *desservir* to clear the table, from *des-* DIS- + *servir* SERVE.

destabilize *v.t.* to make unstable. WH: early 20C. DE- + *stabilize* (STABLE¹).

destination *n.* the place to which a person is going or to which a thing is sent. WH: 14–15C. Old French, from Latin *destinatio*, *destinationis*, from *destinatus*, p.p. of *destinare*. See DESTINE, also -ATION.

destine *v.t.* to appoint, fix or determine to a use, purpose, duty or position. WH: 12–14C. Old French *destiner*, from Latin *destinare* to make firm, from DE- + deriv. of *stare* STAND.

destiny *n.* the purpose or end to which any person or thing is appointed. WH: 12–14C. Old French *destinee*, from Latin *destinata*, fem. p.p. (used as n.) of *destinare*. See DESTINE, also -Y².

destitute *a.* deprived of money and the necessities of life. *Also v.t.*, *n.* WH: 14–15C. Latin *destitutus* forsaken, p.p. of *destituere*, from DE- + *statuere* to set up, to place.

destock *v.i.* to reduce one's stock. WH: mid-20C. DE- + STOCK.

†destrier *n.* a warhorse, a charger. WH: 12–14C. Old French, from Latin *dextera* right hand (see DEXTER¹). The horse was so called as it was led by the right hand of a squire.

destroy *v.t.* to demolish; to pull to pieces. WH: 12–14C. Old French *destruire* (Modern French *détruire*), from alt. of Latin *destruere*, from DE- + *struere* to pile up.

destruction *n.* the act of destroying. WH: 12–14C. Old French, from Latin *destructio*, *destructionis*, from *destructus*, p.p. of *destruere*. See DESTROY, also -ION.

desuetude *n.* disuse; cessation of practice or habit. WH: 17C. French *désuétude* or Latin *desuetudo*, from *desuetus*, p.p. of *desuescere* to become unaccustomed, from DE- + *suescere* to be accustomed. See also -TUDE.

desulphurize *v.t.* to free (an ore) from sulphur. WH: 19C. DE- + *sulphurize* (SULPHUR).

desultory *a.* passing quickly from one subject to another. WH: 16C. Latin *desultorius* pertaining to a vaulter, from *desultor*, from *desultus*, p.p. of *desilire* to leap down, from DE- + *salire* to leap. See also -ORY². The original sense was skipping about.

detach *v.t.* to disconnect, to separate. *Also v.i.* WH: 16C. French *détacher*, earlier *destacher*, from *des-* DIS- + stem of *attacher* ATTACH.

detail *n.* an item. *Also v.t.* WH: 17C. French *détail*, from *détailler*, from *dé-* DE- + *tailler* to cut in pieces. Cp. TAILOR.

detain *v.t.* to restrain; to keep in custody. *Also n.* WH: 14–15C. Old French *détenir*, from var. of Latin *detinere*, from DE- + *tenere* to hold.

detect *v.t.* to discover or find out. *Also a.* WH: 14–15C. Latin *detectus*, p.p. of *detegere*, from DE- + *tegere* to cover.

detent *n.* a pin, catch or lever forming a check to the mechanism in a watch, clock, lock etc. WH: 17C. French *détente*, from Old French *destente*, from *destendre* (Modern French *détendre*) to slacken, from *des-* DIS- + *tendre* to stretch.

détente *n.* relaxation of tension between nations or other warring forces. WH: early 20C. French slackening, relaxation. See DETENT.

detention *n.* the act of detaining. WH: 14–15C. French *détention* or Late Latin *detentio*, *detentionis*, from *detentus*, p.p. of *detinere* DETAIN. See also -ION.

détenu *n.* a person kept in custody, a prisoner. WH: 19C. French, use as n. of p.p. of *détenir* DETAIN.

deter *v.t.* to discourage or frighten (from). WH: 16C. Latin *deterrere*, from DE- + *terrere* to frighten.

detergent *n.* a chemical cleansing agent for washing clothes etc. *Also a.* WH: 17C. Latin *detergens*, *detergentis*, pres.p. of *detergere*, from DE- + *tergere* to wipe.

deteriorate *v.t.* to make inferior. *Also v.i.* WH: 16C. Late Latin *deterioratus*, p.p. of *deteriorare*, from *deterior* worse. See also -ATE³.

determinant *a.* determinative, decisive. *Also n.* WH: 17C. Latin *determinans*, *determinantis*, pres.p. of *determinare* DETERMINE. See also -ANT.

determinate *a.* limited, definite. WH: 14–15C. Latin *determinatus*, p.p. of *determinare* DETERMINE. See also -ATE².

determination *n.* resolution, strength of mind. WH: 14–15C. Old French *détermination*, from Latin *determinatio, determinationis*, from *determinatus*. See DETERMINATE, also -ATION.

determine *v.t.* to ascertain exactly. *Also v.i.* WH: 14–15C. Old French *déterminer*, from Latin *determinare* to bound, to limit, to fix, from DE- + *terminare* TERMINATE. The original sense was to bring to an end, as still in legal usage. The current sense arose in the 17C.

detest *v.t.* to hate exceedingly, to abhor. WH: 15C. Latin *detestari* to denounce, to renounce, from DE- + *testari* to bear witness, from *testis* witness. An earlier sense (to the 18C) was to curse, calling God to witness.

dethrone *v.t.* to remove or depose from a throne. WH: 17C. DE- + THRONE.

detinue *n.* unlawful detention. WH: 14–15C. Old French *detenue*, fem. p.p. (used as n.) of *detenir* DETAIN, assim. to Latin *detinere*.

detonate *v.t.* to cause to explode with a loud bang. *Also v.i.* WH: 18C. Latin *detonatus*, p.p. of *detonare*, from DE- + *tonare* to thunder. See also -ATE³.

detour *n.* a roundabout way. *Also v.t., v.i.* WH: 18C. French *détour* change of direction, from *détourner* to turn away.

detox¹ *n.* detoxification. WH: late 20C. Abbr. of *detoxification* (DE-TOXIFY).

detox² *v.t.* to detoxify. *Also v.i.* WH: late 20C. Abbr. of DETOXIFY.

detoxicate *v.t.* to detoxify. WH: 19C. DE- + Latin *toxicum* poison, based on INTOXICATE.

detoxify *v.t.* to remove poison or toxin from, esp. as a treatment for drug or alcohol addiction. WH: early 20C. DE- + Latin *toxicum* poison + -FY.

detract *v.t.* to diminish, to reduce. *Also v.t.* WH: 14–15C. Latin *detractus*, p.p. of *detrahere*, from DE- + *trahere* to draw.

detrain *v.t.* to cause to alight from a train. *Also v.i.* WH: 19C. DE- + TRAIN. Cp. DEBUS.

detribalize *v.t.* to make (a person) no longer a tribe member. WH: early 20C. DE- + TRIBAL + -IZE.

detriment *n.* harm, injury, damage; loss. *Also v.t.* WH: 14–15C. Old French *détriment* or Latin *detrimentum*, from *detri-*, stem of *deterere* to wear away, from DE- + *terere* to rub. See also -MENT.

detritus *n.* accumulated matter produced by the disintegration of rock. WH: 18C. Latin rubbing away, from *detri-*. See DETRIMENT.

de trop *a.* superfluous, in the way. WH: 18C. French excessive, from *de* of + *trop* too much.

detrude *v.t.* to thrust or force down. WH: 14–15C. Latin *detrudere*, from DE- + *trudere* to thrust.

detruncate *v.t.* to lop or cut off. WH: 17C. Latin *detruncatus*, p.p. of *detruncare*, from DE- + *truncare* TRUNCATE¹.

Dettol® *n.* a type of disinfectant. WH: mid-20C. Contr. of orig. name *Disinfectol*, from DISINFECT + -OL.

detumescence *n.* the diminution of swelling. WH: 17C. Latin *detumescere* to subside from swelling, from DE- + *tumescere* to swell. See also -ENCE.

detune *v.t.* to adjust (a musical instrument, car engine etc.) so that it is not tuned. WH: early 20C. DE- + TUNE.

deuce¹ *n.* a card or die with two spots. WH: 15C. Old French *deus* (Modern French *deux*), from Latin *duos* two.

deuce² *n.* the Devil, invoked as a mild oath. WH: 17C. Low German *duus*, prob. ult. from Latin *duos* two. A throw of two at dice was regarded as the worst possible.

deus *n.* god. WH: 12–14C. Latin god.

deuteragonist *n.* the second actor in a classical Greek play; the next actor in importance to the protagonist. WH: 19C. Greek *deuteragōnistēs*. See DEUTERO-, AGONIST. Cp. PROTAGONIST.

deuterate *v.t.* to replace hydrogen in (a substance) by deuterium. WH: mid-20C. DEUTERIUM + -ATE³.

deuterium *n.* heavy hydrogen, an isotope of hydrogen with double mass. WH: mid-20C. Greek *deuteros* second + -IUM. The isotope is so called because its atomic weight is approximately 2, whereas that of hydrogen is approximately 1.

deutero- *comb. form* second, secondary. WH: Greek *deuteros* second. See also -O-.

Deutero-Isaiah *n.* the supposed writer of Isa. xl–lv. WH: 19C. DEUTERO- + *Isaiah*.

deuteron *n.* a heavy hydrogen nucleus. WH: mid-20C. Greek *deuteros* second + -ON, based on PROTON.

Deuteronomy *n.* the fifth book of the Pentateuch, containing a recapitulation of the Mosaic law. WH: 14–15C. Ecclesiastical Latin *Deuteronomium*, from Greek *Deuteronomion*, from *deuteros* second + *nomos* law. The book is so named from a misunderstanding in the Septuagint (the Greek version of the Old Testament) of the original Hebrew, meaning a copy of the law (Deut. xvii.18).

deuteroscopy *n.* second sight. WH: 17C. DEUTERO- + -*scopy* (-SCOPE).

deutoplasm *n.* the portion of the yolk that nourishes the embryo, the food yolk of an ovum or egg-cell. WH: 19C. *deuto-* (form of DEUTERO-) + *plasm* (PLASMA), based on PROTOPLASM.

Deutschmark *n.* the standard unit of currency of Germany. WH: mid-20C. German German mark, from *Deutsch* German + MARK².

deutzia *n.* a Chinese or Japanese shrub of the genus *Deutzia*, with clusters of pink or white flowers. WH: 19C. Modern Latin, from Johann van der *Deutz*, 1743–88, Dutch patron of botany. See also -IA.

devalue *v.t.* to reduce the value of. WH: early 20C. DE- + VALUE.

Devanagari *n.* the formal alphabet in which Sanskrit and certain vernaculars are usually written. WH: 18C. Sanskrit, from *deva* god + *nāgarī* NAGARI, an earlier form of the script.

devastate *v.t.* to lay waste, to ravage. WH: 17C. Latin *devastatus*, p.p. of *devastare*, from DE- + *vastare* to lay waste. See also -ATE³.

devein *v.t.* to remove the main vein from. WH: mid-20C. DE- + VEIN.

develop *v.t.* to unfold, to bring to light gradually. *Also v.i.* WH: 17C. Old French *développer*, from Latin DIS- + base represented by Old French *voloper* to envelop, of unknown orig. Cp. ENVELOP.

devest *v.t.* to undress. WH: 16C. Old French *desvester*, from *des-* DIS- + Latin *vestire* to clothe, from *vestis* garment.

deviate¹ *v.i.* to turn aside. *Also v.t.* WH: 17C. Late Latin *deviatus*, p.p. of *deviare*, from Latin DE- + *via* way. See also -ATE³.

deviate² *n.* a person who deviates from the norm. *Also a.* WH: 16C. Late Latin *deviatus*, p.p. of *deviare*. See DEVIATE¹, also -ATE². The current sense is direct from the verb.

device *n.* a contrivance, an invention. WH: 12–14C. Old French *devis*, from Latin *divisus*, p.p. of *dividere* DIVIDE.

devil *n.* Satan, the chief spirit of evil. *Also v.t., v.i.* WH: pre-1200. Old English *dēofol*, from Ecclesiastical Latin *diabolus*, from Greek *diabolos* accuser, slanderer, from *diaballein*, from *dia-* across + *ballein* to throw. Greek *diabolos* translates Hebrew *Sātān* SATAN in the Septuagint (the Greek version of the Old Testament).

devious *a.* insincere and deceitful. WH: 16C. Latin *devius*, from DE- + *via* way. See also -OUS.

devise *v.t.* to invent, to form in the mind. *Also v.i., n.* WH: 12–14C. Old French *deviser*, from Latin *divisus*, p.p. of *dividere* DIVIDE. The original sense (to the 15C) was to divide, to distribute.

devitalize *v.t.* to deprive of vitality or of vital power. WH: 19C. DE- + *vitalize* (VITAL).

devitrify *v.t.* to deprive of vitreous qualities. WH: 19C. DE- + *vitrify* (VITREOUS).

devocalize *v.t.* to make (a sound) voiceless or nonsonant. WH: 19C. DE- + *vocalize* (VOCAL).

devoice *v.t.* to pronounce without vibrating the vocal cords. WH: mid-20C. DE- + VOICE.

devoid *a.* empty (of), lacking. *Also v.t.* WH: 14–15C. P.p. of obs. *devoid* to cast out, to vacate, from Old French *devoidier* (Modern French *dévider*), from *de-* DE- + *voider* VOID.

†devoir *n.* a duty. WH: 12–14C. Old French *deveir* (Modern French *devoir*), from Latin *debere* to owe. Cp. ENDEAVOUR.

devolution *n.* transference or delegation of authority, esp. from central to regional government. WH: 15C. Late Latin *devolutio, devolutionis*, from *devolutus*, p.p. of *devolvere* DEVOLVE.

devolve *v.t.* to pass, transfer (duties or power) to another. *Also v.i.* WH: 14–15C. Latin *devolvere*, from DE- + *volvere* to roll. The original sense was to roll down, to unroll. The current sense arose in the 17C.

Devonian *a.* of or relating to Devon. *Also n.* WH: 17C. Medieval Latin *Devonia*, from *Devon*, a county in SW England. See also -AN, -IAN.

devore *a.* (of a fabric, esp. velvet) having a design etched with acid. WH: early 20C. French *dévoré*, p.p. of *dévorer* to eat up, DEVOUR.

dévot *n.* a devotee. WH: 18C. French, use as n. of a., DEVOUT.

devote *v.t.* to dedicate; to give wholly up (to). **WH:** 16C. Latin *devotus*, p.p. of *devovere*, from DE- + *vovere* to vow.

devour *v.t.* to eat up quickly and greedily. **WH:** 12–14C. Old French *devorer*, from Latin *devorare*, from DE- + *vorare* to swallow.

devout *a.* deeply religious. **WH:** 12–14C. Old French *dévot*, from Latin *devotus*, p.p. of *devovere* DEVOTE.

dew *n.* moisture condensed from the atmosphere upon surface at evening and during the night. *Also v.t.*, *v.i.* **WH:** pre-1200. Old English *dēaw*, from Germanic. Cp. German *Tau*.

dewan *n.* chief financial minister of an Indian state. **WH:** 17C. Urdu, from Persian *dīwān* DIVAN (in sense fiscal register). Cp. DOUANE.

dewar *n.* a type of vacuum flask, used to keep liquids or gases warm in scientific experiments. **WH:** 19C. Sir James *Dewar*, 1842–1923, British physicist and chemist.

dewater *v.t.* to remove water from. **WH:** early 20C. DE- + WATER.

Dewey Decimal System *n.* a system of library classification using ten main subject classes. **WH:** 19C. Melvil *Dewey*, 1851–1931, US librarian + DECIMAL + SYSTEM.

dewlap *n.* the flesh that hangs loosely from the throat of cattle and some dogs. **WH:** 12–14C. DEW + LAP[1]. The fold of skin is said to be so called as it brushes the dew from the grass.

DEW line *n.* the radar network in the Arctic regions of N America. **WH:** mid-20C. Abbr. of *distant early warning* + LINE[1].

deworm *v.t.* to rid (an animal) of worms. **WH:** mid-20C. DE- + WORM.

Dexedrine® *n.* a dextrorotatory isomer of amphetamine. **WH:** mid-20C. Prob. from DEXTRO- + BENZEDRINE.

dexter[1] *a.* situated on the right of a shield (to the spectator's left) etc. **WH:** 16C. Latin right, from base represented also by Greek *dexios*.

dexter[2] *n.* a breed of small cattle originally from Ireland. **WH:** 19C. Appar. from a Mr *Dexter*, who established the breed.

dexterity *n.* manual skill. **WH:** 16C. French *dextérité*, from Latin *dexteritas*. See DEXTER[1], also -ITY.

dextral *a.* right-handed. *Also n.* **WH:** 17C. Medieval Latin *dextralis*, from Latin *dextra* right hand. See also -AL[1].

dextran *n.* a carbohydrate produced by the action of bacteria in sugar solutions, used as a substitute for blood plasma in transfusions. **WH:** 19C. DEXTRO- + -AN.

dextrin *n.* a gummy substance obtained from starch, so called from its dextrorotatory action on polarized light. **WH:** 19C. DEXTRO- + -IN[1]. The word was coined in 1833 by the French physicists Jean-Baptiste Biot and Jean-François Persoz.

dextro- *comb. form* turning the plane of a ray of polarized light to the right, or in a clockwise direction (as seen looking against the oncoming light). **WH:** Latin *dexter*, *dextra* right. See also -O-.

dextrocardia *n.* a condition in which the heart lies on the right side of the chest instead of the left. **WH:** 19C. DEXTRO- + Greek *kardia* heart + -IA.

dextroglucose *n.* dextrose. **WH:** 19C. DEXTRO- + GLUCOSE.

dextrogyrate *a.* causing to turn towards the right hand. **WH:** 19C. DEXTRO- + GYRATE.

dextrorotatory *a.* turning the plane of polarization to the right. **WH:** 19C. DEXTRO- + *rotatory* (ROTATE[1]).

dextrorse *a.* rising from left to right in a spiral line. **WH:** 19C. Latin *dextrorsum* toward the right side, from DEXTER[1] + *versus*, p.p. of *vertere* to turn.

dextrose *n.* a form of glucose which rotates polarized light clockwise; grape sugar. **WH:** 19C. DEXTRO- + -OSE[2].

dey *n.* the title of the old sovereigns of Algiers, Tripoli and Tunis. **WH:** 17C. French, from Turkish *dayı* maternal uncle (used as a courtesy title).

DF *abbr.* Defender of the Faith. **WH:** Cp. FID. DEF..

dhal *n.* a split grain, pulse. **WH:** 17C. Hindi *dāl*.

dharma *n.* in Hinduism and Buddhism, the fundamental concept of both natural and moral law, by which everything in the universe acts according to its essential nature or proper station. **WH:** 18C. Sanskrit established thing, decree, custom.

dhobi *n.* in the Indian subcontinent, a washerman. **WH:** 19C. Hindi *dhobī*, from *dhob* washing.

dhole *n.* an Asian wild dog, *Cuon alpinus*. **WH:** 19C. Orig. unknown.

dhoti *n.* a loincloth worn by male Hindus. **WH:** 17C. Hindi *dhotī*.

dhow *n.* a ship with one mast, a very long yard, and a lateen sail,

used on the Arabian Sea. **WH:** 18C. Arabic *dāwa*, prob. rel. to Marathi *ḍāw*.

di-[1] *pref.* asunder, apart, away, as in *digest*, *diminish*, *direct*. **WH:** Latin pref., from DIS- with *s* assim. to *b*, *d*, *g*, *l*, *m*, *n*, *r*, *s*, *v*, *j*.

di-[2] *pref.* twice, two, double, as in *dilemma*, *dimity*. **WH:** Greek pref., from *dis* twice.

di-[3] *pref.* through, as in *diocese*. **WH:** Greek pref., from DIA-, used before vowels.

dia- *pref.* through, as in *dialect*, *diatribe*. **WH:** Greek pref., from prep. *dia* through.

diabase *n.* an igneous rock which is an altered form of basalt. **WH:** 19C. French, from *dia-*, representing DI-[2] + *base* base. The implied sense is (rock with) two bases. The word may later have been associated with Greek *diabasis* transition.

diabetes *n.* a disease characterized by excessive discharge of urine containing glucose, insatiable thirst and emaciation. **WH:** 16C. Latin, from Greek, lit. syphon, from *diabainein* to go through. Cp. DIARRHOEA. The reference is to the excessive discharge of urine.

diablerie *n.* dealings with the devil. **WH:** 18C. French devilry, from *diable* DEVIL. See also -ERY.

diabolic *a.* of, relating to, proceeding from or like the devil. **WH:** 14–15C. Old French *diabolique*, from Ecclesiastical Latin *diabolicus*, from *diabolus* DEVIL. See also -IC.

diabolo *n.* a game with a double cone spun in the air by a cord on two sticks, an adaptation of the old game of the devil on two sticks. **WH:** early 20C. Italian, from Ecclesiastical Latin *diabolus* DEVIL.

diacaustic *a.* formed by refracted rays. **WH:** 18C. DIA- + Greek *kaustikos* burning. See CAUSTIC.

diachronic *a.* of or relating to the study of the historical development of a subject, e.g. a language. **WH:** 19C. DIA- + Greek *khronos* time + -IC.

diacid *a.* having two replaceable hydrogen atoms. **WH:** 19C. DI-[2] + ACID.

diaconal *a.* of or relating to a deacon. **WH:** 17C. Ecclesiastical Latin *diaconalis*, from *diaconus* DEACON. See also -AL[1].

diacoustic *a.* of or relating to the science of refracted sounds. **WH:** 18C. DIA- + ACOUSTIC.

diacritic *a.* distinguishing, distinctive. *Also n.* **WH:** 17C. Greek *diakritikos*, from *diakrinein* to distinguish, from *krinein* to separate. See DIA-.

diactinic *a.* transparent to or capable of transmitting actinic rays. **WH:** 19C. DIA- + ACTINIC.

diadem *n.* a fillet or band for the head, worn as an emblem of sovereignty. *Also v.t.* **WH:** 12–14C. Old French *diadème*, from Latin *diadema*, from Greek regal headband of Persian kings, from *diadein* to bind round.

diaeresis *n.* a mark placed over the second of two vowels to show that it must be pronounced separately, as in *naïve*. **WH:** 16C. Latin, from Greek *diairesis*, from *diairein* to take apart, from DIA- + *hairein* to take.

diagenesis *n.* the changes which occur in sediments before they consolidate into rock. **WH:** 19C. DIA- + GENESIS.

diagnosis *n.* determination of diseases by their symptoms. **WH:** 17C. Modern Latin, from Greek, from *diagignōskein* to distinguish, to discern, from DIA- + *gignōskein* KNOW.

diagometer *n.* an instrument for measuring the relative conductivity of substances, orig. used to detect adulteration in olive oil. **WH:** 19C. French *diagomètre*, from Greek *diagein* to carry across + *metron* measure. See -METER.

diagonal *a.* extending from one angle of a quadrilateral or multilateral figure to a nonadjacent angle, or from one edge of a solid to a nonadjacent edge. *Also n.* **WH:** 16C. Latin *diagonalis*, from Greek *diagōnios* from angle to angle, from DIA- + *gōnia* angle. See also -AL[1].

diagram *n.* a drawing made to demonstrate or illustrate some statement or definition. *Also v.t.* **WH:** 17C. Latin *diagramma*, from Greek *diagraphein* to mark out by lines, from DIA- + *graphein* to write. See -GRAM.

diagraph *n.* an instrument used for mechanically drawing outline sketches, enlargements of maps etc. **WH:** 19C. French *diagraphe*, from Greek *diagraphein*. See DIAGRAM.

diagrid *n.* a structure of diagonally intercepting beams or ribs. **WH:** mid-20C. DIAGONAL + GRID.

diaheliotropic *a.* growing or turning transversely to the light. WH: 19C. DIA- + *heliotropic* (HELIOTROPE).

diakinesis *n.* the last stage of the prophase of meiosis, when homologous chromosomes cross over and separate. WH: early 20C. DIA- + Greek *kinēsis* motion.

dial *n.* the graduated and numbered face of a timepiece. *Also v.t., v.i.* WH: 12–14C. Medieval Latin *diale* dial of a clock, from *dialiter* daily, from Latin *dies* day. See also -AL¹. The word was originally used of a sundial.

dialect *n.* a form of language peculiar to a particular district or people. WH: 16C. French *dialecte*, or from Latin *dialectus*, from Greek *dialektos* speaking, way of speaking, from *dialegesthai* to converse with, from DIA- + *legein* to speak.

dialectic *n.* dialectics. *Also a.* WH: 14–15C. Old French *dialectique* or Latin *dialectica*, from Greek *dialektikē* (*tekhnē*) dialectic (art), from *dialektikos* of discourse, from *dialektos*. See DIALECT.

diallage *n.* a dark-to-bright-green nonaluminous variety of pyroxene, common in serpentine rock. WH: 18C. Greek *diallagē* interchange, from *diallassein* to interchange, from DIA- + *allassein* to change, from *allos* other. The original sense was a rhetorical figure by means of which arguments are brought to bear on one point. The geological sense dates from the 19C. The mineral was so named for its dissimilar cleavages.

dialogue *n.* a discourse between two or more persons. *Also v.i., v.t.* WH: 12–14C. Old French *dialoge* (Modern French *dialogue*), from Latin *dialogus*, from Greek *dialogos* conversation, discourse, from *dialegesthai*. See DIALECT. The word is not from DI-², as if referring to a conversation between two speakers. Cp. DUOLOGUE.

dialysis *n.* the process of separating crystalloid from colloid ingredients in soluble substances by passing through moist membranes. WH: 16C. Latin, from Greek *dualusis*, from *dialuein* to part asunder, from DIA- + *luein* to set free.

diamagnetic *a.* tending, when magnetized, to assume a position at right angles to the magnetic field. *Also n.* WH: 19C. DIA- + *magnetic* (MAGNET).

diamanté *n.* material covered with glittering particles, such as sequins. *Also a.* WH: early 20C. French, p.p. of *diamanter* to set with diamonds, from *diamant* DIAMOND.

diameter *n.* a straight line passing through the centre of any object from one side to the other. WH: 14–15C. Old French *diamètre*, from Latin *diametrus*, from Greek *diametros* (*grammē*) diagonal (line), from DIA- + *metron* measure. See -METER.

diamond *n.* the hardest, most brilliant and most valuable of the precious stones, a transparent crystal of pure carbon, colourless or tinted. *Also a., v.t.* WH: 12–14C. Old French *diamant*, from Medieval Latin *diamas*, *diamantis*, from alt. of Latin *adamas* ADAMANT.

Diana *n.* a woman who hunts. WH: 14–15C. Latin *Diana*, Roman moon goddess and patron of virginity and hunting.

diandrous *a.* having only two stamens. WH: 18C. DI-² + Greek *anēr*, *andros* man + -OUS. The stamen is the flower's male reproductive organ. The female organ is the pistil.

dianoetic *a.* of or relating to the rational or discursive faculty. *Also n.* WH: 17C. Greek *dianoētikos*, from *dianoeisthai* to think, from DIA- + *noein* to think, to suppose. Cp. NOETIC.

dianthus *n.* any plant of the genus *Dianthus* including the pinks and carnations. WH: 18C. Greek *Dios* of Zeus + *anthos* flower.

diapason *n.* a harmonious combination of notes. WH: 14–15C. Latin, from Greek *diapasōn*, from *dia pasōn* (*khordōn*) through all (notes).

diapause *n.* a period of suspended growth in insects. WH: 19C. DIA- + PAUSE.

diaper *n.* a baby's nappy. *Also v.t.* WH: 12–14C. Old French *diaspre*, from Medieval Latin *diasprum*, from Medieval Greek *diaspros*, from DIA- + *aspros* white. The original sense was a silk or linen woven cloth, then a towel, napkin etc. made of such material, then (from the 16C) a baby's nappy, which was also originally made of it.

diaphanometer *n.* an instrument for measuring the transparency of the atmosphere. WH: 18C. Greek *diaphanēs* transparent (see DIAPHANOUS) + METER.

diaphanous *a.* (of a fabric) fine and almost transparent. WH: 17C. Medieval Latin *diaphanus*, from Greek *diaphanēs*, from DIA- + *phainein* to show. See also -OUS.

diaphoresis *n.* sweating. WH: 17C. Late Latin, from Greek, from *diaphorein* to carry away, to dissipate by sweating, from DIA- + *phorein* to carry.

diaphragm *n.* the large muscular partition separating the thorax from the abdomen. WH: 14–15C. Late Latin *diaphragma*, from Greek, from DIA- + *phragma* fence. The equivalent Old English derivative is MIDRIFF.

diaphysis *n.* the shaft of a bone as distinct from the ends. WH: 19C. Greek *diaphusis* growing through, from DIA- + *phusis* growth.

diapir *n.* an anticlinal fold in which the overlying rock has been pierced by material from below. WH: early 20C. Greek *diapeirainein* to pierce through, from DIA- + *peirainein*, from *peran* to pierce.

diapositive *n.* a positive photographic transparency; a slide. WH: 19C. DIA- + POSITIVE.

diarchy *n.* government by two rulers. WH: 19C. DI-² + -*archy* based on *monarchy* (MONARCH).

diarrhoea *n.* the excessive discharge of faecal matter from the intestines. WH: 14–15C. Late Latin, from Greek *diarrhoia*, from *dairrhein* to flow through. See DIA-, -RRHOEA.

diarthrosis *n.* an articulation of the bones permitting them to act upon each other; free arthrosis. WH: 16C. Greek *diarthrosis*, from DIA- + *arthrōsis* (see ARTHRO-, -OSIS).

diary *n.* an account of the occurrences of each day. WH: 16C. Latin *diarium* journal, daily allowance, from *dies* day. See also -ARY¹. Cp. JOURNAL.

diascope *n.* an optical projector for showing transparencies. WH: mid-20C. DIA- + -SCOPE.

Diaspora *n.* the dispersion of the Jews after the Babylonian captivity. WH: 19C. Greek, from *diaspeirein* to disperse, from DIA- + *speirein* to sow, to scatter. The term itself originated in the Septuagint (Greek version of the Old Testament): *hesē diaspora hen pasais basileiais tēs gēs* shalt be a dispersion in all kingdoms of the earth (AV. shalt be removed into all the kingdoms of the earth) (Deut. xxviii.25).

diastaltic *a.* of or relating to reflex action and the nerves governing this. WH: 17C. Greek *diastaltikos* serving to distinguish, from *diastellein*. See DIASTOLE.

diastase *n.* a nitrogenous substance produced during the germination of all seeds, and having the power of converting starch into dextrine, and then into sugar. WH: 19C. Greek *diastasis*. See DIASTASIS, also -ASE.

diastasis *n.* separation of bones without fracture, or of the pieces of a fractured bone. WH: 18C. Modern Latin, from Greek separation, from DIA- + *stasis* placing.

diastema *n.* a space between two adjacent teeth, as in most mammals. WH: 14–15C. Late Latin, from Greek *diastēma* space between.

diastole *n.* dilatation of the heart and arteries alternating with systole. WH: 16C. Late Latin, from Greek *diastolē* separation, expansion, from *diastellein*, from DIA- + *stellein* to place, to put.

diastrophism *n.* deformation of the earth's crust, giving rise to mountains etc. WH: 19C. Greek *diastrophē* distortion, dislocation, from DIA- + *strephein* to turn. See also -ISM.

diastyle *n.* an arrangement of columns in which the space between them is equal to three or four diameters of the shaft. *Also a.* WH: 16C. Partly from Latin *diastylos*, from Greek *diastulos* having space between the columns, partly from Greek *diastulion* space between the columns, both from DIA- + *stulos* column.

diatessaron *n.* a harmony of the four Gospels. WH: 14–15C. Late Latin, from Greek *dia tessarōn* composed of four. See DIA-. The term comes from the title given by Tatian (2C BC) to his *Evaggelion dia tessarōn* Gospel made of four, an account of the Gospels in a single narrative.

diathermancy *n.* the property of being freely pervious to heat. WH: 19C. French *diathermansie*, from Greek DIA- + *thermansis* heating, assim. to -ANCY.

diathermy *n.* the employment of high-frequency currents for the production of localized heat in the tissues. WH: early 20C. DIA- + Greek *thermos* heat + -Y².

diathesis *n.* a constitution of body predisposing to certain diseases. WH: 17C. Modern Latin, from Greek disposition, from *diatithenai* to arrange.

diatom *n.* a member of the class of algae *Bacillariophyceae*, which have siliceous coverings and which exist in immense numbers at the bottom of the sea, multiplying by division or conjugation, and occurring as fossils in such abundance as to form strata of vast area and considerable thickness. WH: 19C. Modern Latin *Diatoma* genus name, from Greek *diatomos* cut in two, from *diatemnein* to cut through.

diatonic *a.* of the regular scale without chromatic alteration. WH: 17C. Old French *diatonique* or Late Latin *diatonicus*, from Greek *diatonikos* at intervals of a tone, from DIA- + *tonos* TONE. See also -IC.

diatribe *n.* an angry speech; a piece of harsh criticism or denunciation. WH: 16C. French, from Latin *diatriba* learned discussion, from Greek *diatribē* spending of time, discourse, from DIA- + *tribein* to rub. Not rel. to TRIBE.

diazepam *n.* a type of tranquillizer and muscle relaxant. WH: mid-20C. Abbr. of *benzodiazepine* (see BENZENE) + AMIDE.

diazo *a.* (of a compound) having two nitrogen atoms and a hydrocarbon radical. *Also n.* WH: mid-20C. Abbr. of *diazotype*, from DI-[2] + AZO- + *-type* (TYPE).

dib[1] *v.i.* to dap. WH: 17C. Alt. of DAB[1].

dib[2] *n.* a sheep's knuckle-bone. WH: 18C. Prob. from DIB[1].

dibasic *a.* containing two bases or two replaceable atoms. WH: 19C. DI-[2] + BASE[1] + -IC.

dibble *n.* a pointed instrument used to make a hole in the ground for seed. *Also v.t., v.i.* WH: 14–15C. Appar. from DIB[1]. See also -LE[1].

dibranchiate *a.* of or relating to an order of cephalopods, *Dibranchiata*, having only two gills, the shell rarely external and never chambered. WH: 19C. Modern Latin *dibranchiata*, from DI-[2] + Greek *bragkhia* gills. See also -ATE[2].

dicast *n.* in Greek history, one of 6000 Athenians chosen each year to act as judges. WH: 19C. Greek *dikastēs* judge, from *dikazein* to judge, from *dikē* judgement.

dice *n.* a small cube marked with figures on the sides, used in gambling, being thrown from a box or cup. *Also v.i., v.t.* WH: 19C. Old French *dés*. See DIE[2].

dicephalous *a.* having two heads on one body. WH: 19C. Greek *dikephalos*, from DI-[2] + *kephalē* head. See also -OUS.

dicey *a.* risky, difficult. WH: mid-20C. DICE + -Y[1].

dichlamydeous *a.* having both corolla and calyx. WH: 19C. DI-[2] + Greek *khlamus, khlamudos* cloak + -EOUS.

dichloride *n.* a compound having two atoms of chlorine with another atom. WH: 19C. DI-[2] + CHLORIDE.

dichlorodiphenyltrichloroethane *n.* the full name for the insecticide DDT. WH: mid-20C. DI-[2] + CHLORO- + DI-[2] + PHENYL + TRICHLOROETHANE.

dichogamous *a.* having stamens and pistils maturing at different times, so that self-fertilization is prevented. WH: 19C. Greek *dikha* in two, apart + *gamos* marriage. See also -OUS.

dichotomy *n.* a separation into two. WH: 16C. Modern Latin *dichotomia*, from Greek *dikhotomia*, from *dikha* in two, apart + *tomos* section. See -TOMY.

dichroic *a.* assuming two or more colours, according to the direction in which light is transmitted. WH: 19C. Greek *dikhroos* two-coloured, from DI-[2] + *khrōs* colour. See also -IC.

dichromate *n.* a double chromate. WH: 19C. DI-[2] + CHROMATE.

dichromatic *a.* characterized by or producing two colours, esp. of animals. WH: 19C. DI-[2] + CHROMATIC.

dichromic *a.* having or perceiving only two colours. WH: 19C. Greek *dikhrōmos*, from DI-[2] + *khrōma* colour. See also -IC.

dick[1] *n.* a fellow or person. WH: 16C. *Dick*, male forename, alt. of *Ric-*, 1st element of Latin *Ricardus* Richard.

dick[2] *n.* a declaration. WH: 19C. Abbr. of DECLARATION.

dicken *int.* used to express disbelief or disgust. WH: 19C. Alt. of DICKENS.

dickens *n.* the devil, the deuce. WH: 16C. Prob. from surname *Dickens*, as euphem. form of DEUCE[2].

Dickensian *a.* of, relating to or in the style of Dickens. *Also n.* WH: 19C. Charles *Dickens*, 1812–70, English novelist + -IAN.

dicker *v.i.* to barter, to haggle; to carry on a petty trade. *Also v.t., n.* WH: 19C. Prob. from obs. *dicker* a quantity, a lot, from Germanic, from Latin *decuria* group of ten, from *decem* ten + *vir* man. Cp.

DECEMVIR. The original reference was to a quantity of ten hides, used by the Romans as a unit of barter on the frontier.

dicky[1] *n.* a false shirt front. WH: 18C. Appar. from male forename *Dicky*. See DICK[1], also -Y[3].

dicky[2] *a.* unsound, weak. WH: 18C. Orig. uncertain. Prob. from DICK[1] in proverbial expression *as queer as Dick's hatband*.

diclinous *a.* having the stamens and the pistils on separate flowers, on the same or different plants, as distinct from *monoclinous*. WH: 19C. Modern Latin *Diclines*, from DI-[2] + Greek *klinē* bed. See also -OUS.

dicotyledon *n.* any plant of the class *Dicotyledones* of flowering plants including all of those with two cotyledons. WH: 18C. Modern Latin *dicotyledones*. See DI-[2] + COTYLEDON.

dicrotic *a.* (of a pulse in an abnormal state) double-beating. WH: 19C. Greek *dikrotos* double-beating + -IC.

Dictaphone® *n.* an apparatus for recording sounds, used for taking down correspondence etc., to be transcribed afterwards. WH: early 20C. DICTATE[1] + -PHONE.

dictate[1] *v.t.* to read or recite to another (words to be written). *Also v.i.* WH: 16C. Latin *dictatus*, p.p. of *dictare*, freq. of *dicere* to say. See also -ATE[3].

dictate[2] *n.* an order, an injunction; a direction; a precept. WH: 16C. Latin *dictatum*, neut. p.p. (used as n.) of *dictare* DICTATE[1].

diction *n.* the use of words. WH: 16C. Old French, or from Latin *dictio, dictionis* saying, mode of expression, from *dictus*, p.p. of *dicere* to say.

dictionary *n.* a book containing the words of any language in alphabetical order, with their definitions, pronunciations, parts of speech, etymologies and uses, or with their equivalents in another language. WH: 16C. Medieval Latin *dictionarium* (*manuale*) (MANUAL) of words, or *dictionarius* (*liber*) (book) of words, from Latin *dictio, dictionis*. See DICTION, also -ARY[1].

dictum *n.* a positive or dogmatic assertion. WH: 16C. Latin, neut. p.p. (used as n.) of *dicere* to say.

dicynodont *n.* a large fossil reptile of a lizard-like form with turtle jaws. WH: 19C. Modern Latin *Dicynodontia*, from DI-[2] + Greek *kuōn, kunos* dog + -ODONT. The name refers to the reptile's two long canine teeth in the upper jaw.

didactic *a.* adapted or tending to teach, esp. morally. WH: 17C. Greek *didaktikos*, from *didak-*, stem of *didaskein* to teach. See also -IC.

diddle *v.t.* to cheat; to swindle. *Also v.i.* WH: 19C. Orig. uncertain. ? Alt. of FIDDLE, influ. by *fiddle-de-dee*. According to some accounts, the word is a back-formation from the name of Jeremy *Diddler*, a swindling character in James Kenney's farce *Raising the Wind* (1803).

diddly-squat *n.* anything at all. WH: late 20C. Orig. uncertain. ? From *doodle* excrement + *squat* to defecate. Cp. var. forms *diddly-poop*, *doodle-shit*.

diddums *int.* used to express commiseration to a baby. WH: 19C. Var. of *did 'em* did they (i.e. tease you, etc.).

didelphian *a.* of or relating to the Didelphidae, a family of marsupials, including the opossums. WH: 19C. Modern Latin *Didelphidae*, from DI-[2] + Greek *delphus* womb. See also -AN. The Didelphidae have a double uterus and vagina.

didgeridoo *n.* an Australian musical instrument, a long, hollow wooden tube that gives a deep booming sound when blown. WH: early 20C. Appar. of imit. orig. Not from an Australian Aboriginal language.

didicoi *n.* an itinerant traveller or tinker, who is not a true Romany. WH: 19C. Appar. alt. of Romany *dik akei* look here.

dido *n.* an antic, a caper. WH: 19C. Orig. unknown. The word is popularly associated with the name of the British corvette *Dido*, whose officers and crew were renowned for their smart appearance, as if dressed for a formal social occasion.

†didymium *n.* a mixture of the two elements neodymium and praseodymium, orig. thought to be a single element. WH: 19C. Greek *didumos* twin + -IUM. The mixture was so named by the Swedish chemist Carl G. Mosander, who discovered it in 1841, from its close association ('twin brotherhood') with lanthanum.

didymous *a.* twin, growing in pairs. WH: 18C. French *didyme*, from Greek *didumos* twin + -OUS.

didynamous *a.* having four stamens. WH: 18C. DI-[2] + Greek *dunamis* power + -OUS.

die[1] *v.i.* to lose life, to depart this life. *Also v.t.* WH: 12–14C. Old Norse *deyja*, from Germanic base of DEAD. There must have been a corresponding verb in Old English, but it is not recorded.

die[2] *n.* a dice. WH: 12–14C. Old French *dé*, pl. *dés*, from Latin DATUM. Latin *datum* means given, here applying to what is given or decreed by lot or fortune.

dieffenbachia *n.* any plant of the tropical American evergreen genus *Dieffenbachia*. WH: 19C. Ernst Dieffenbach, 1811–55, German horticulturist. See also -IA.

dieldrin *n.* an insecticide containing chlorine. WH: mid-20C. Otto *Diels*, 1876–1954, German chemist + ALDRIN.

dielectric *a.* nonconductive, insulating. *Also n.* WH: 19C. DI-[3] + ELEC-TRIC.

diene *n.* an organic compound which has two double bonds between carbon atoms. WH: early 20C. DI-[2] + -ENE.

dies *n.* a day. WH: 17C. Latin day.

diesel *n.* any vehicle driven by a diesel engine. WH: 19C. Rudolph *Diesel*, 1858–1913, German engineer.

diesis *n.* the double dagger (‡); a reference mark. WH: 14–15C. Latin, from Greek quarter-tone, from *diienai* to send through, from DI-[3] + *ienai* to send.

diet[1] *n.* a prescribed course of food followed for health reasons, or to reduce weight. *Also a., v.i., v.t.* WH: 12–14C. Old French *diète*, from Latin *diaeta*, from Greek *diaita* course of life.

diet[2] *n.* a legislative assembly or federal parliament holding its meetings from day to day (esp. as an English name for Continental parliaments). WH: 14–15C. Medieval Latin *dieta* day's journey, allowance, wages, assoc. with Latin *dies* day. The association with day (German *Tag*) is also present in German BUNDESTAG, LANDTAG, *Reichstag* (see REICH), all forms of legislative assembly.

diethyl ether *n.* ether. WH: 19C. DI-[2] + ETHYL + ETHER.

dif- asunder, apart, away, as in *different*, *diffract*. WH: Latin pref., from DIS- with *s* assim. to *f*.

differ *v.i.* to be dissimilar. *Also v.t., n.* WH: 14–15C. Old French *différer* to differ, to defer, from Latin *differre*, from DIF- + *ferre* to carry.

difference *n.* the state of being unlike or distinct. *Also v.t., v.i.* WH: 12–14C. Old French *différence*, from Latin *differentia*, from *different-*. See DIFFERENT, also -ENCE.

different *a.* unlike, dissimilar. WH: 14–15C. Old French *différent*, from Latin *differens*, *differentis*, pres.p. of *differre*. See DIFFER, also -ENT.

differentia *n.* something which distinguishes one species from another of the same genus. WH: 17C. Latin. See DIFFERENCE.

differential *a.* differing; consisting of a difference. *Also n.* WH: 17C. Medieval Latin *differentialis*, from Latin DIFFERENTIA. See also -AL[1].

differentiate *v.t.* to make different. *Also v.i.* WH: 19C. Medieval Latin *differentiatus*, p.p. of *differentiare*, from Latin DIFFERENTIA. See also -ATE[3].

difficult *a.* hard to do or carry out. WH: 14–15C. Back-formation from *difficulty*, from Latin *difficultas*, from DIF- + *facultas* (see FACULTY).

diffident *a.* lacking confidence in oneself or one's powers. WH: 14–15C. Latin *diffidens*, *diffidentis*, pres.p. of *diffidere*, from DIF- + *fidere* to trust. See also -ENT. The original sense was lacking confidence in others. The sense lacking confidence in oneself evolved in the 18C.

diffract *v.t.* to break into parts. WH: 19C. Latin *diffractus*, p.p. of *diffrangere* to break in pieces, from DIF- + *frangere* to break.

diffuse[1] *v.t.* to pour forth. *Also v.i.* WH: 14–15C. Latin *diffusus*, p.p. of *diffundere*. See DIFFUSE[2].

diffuse[2] *a.* scattered, spread out. WH: 14–15C. French *diffus*, or from Latin *diffusus*, p.p. of *diffundere* to pour out, from DIF- + *fundere* to pour.

dig *v.t.* to excavate or turn up with a spade or similar instrument, or with hands, claws etc. *Also v.i., n.* WH: 12–14C. ? Old English *dīc* DITCH. The word replaced earlier DELVE and GRAVE[1].

digamma *n.* (Ϝ) a letter in the oldest Greek alphabet, which had the sound of *w*. WH: 17C. Latin, from Greek, from DI-[2] + GAMMA. The letter is so named from its resemblance to two gammas placed one above the other.

digamy *n.* marrying a second time. WH: 17C. Late Latin *digamia*, from Greek, from *digamos* married to two people, from DI-[2] + -GAMY. Cp. BIGAMY.

digastric *a.* having a double belly or protuberance. *Also n.* WH: 17C. Modern Latin *digastricus*, from Greek DI-[2] + *gastēr* belly. See also -IC.

digest[1] *v.t.* to break (food) down in the stomach into forms which can be easily assimilated by the body. *Also v.i.* WH: 14–15C. Latin *digestus*, p.p. of *digerere*. See DIGEST[2].

digest[2] *n.* a compendium or summary. WH: 14–15C. Latin *digesta* matters methodically arranged, neut. pl. of *digestus*, p.p. of *digerere* to divide, to distribute, to digest, from DI-[1] + *gerere* to carry, to bear.

†dight *v.t.* to dress, to array, to adorn. *Also a.* WH: pre-1200. Orig. p.p., from Old English *dihtan*, from Latin *dictare* to appoint, to dictate. Cp. German *dichten* to write, to compose verse. Early meanings of the original verb included to direct, to appoint, to arrange, to compose. All these were obsolete by the 16C.

digit *n.* a finger or toe. WH: 14–15C. Latin *digitus* finger, toe.

digitalin *n.* an alkaloid obtained from the foxglove. WH: 19C. Modern Latin DIGITALIS + -IN[1].

digitalis *n.* the dried leaves of the foxglove, which act as a cardiac sedative. WH: 17C. Modern Latin, use as n. of Latin *digitalis* pertaining to the finger, based on German *Fingerhut* thimble, foxglove.

digitate *a.* having finger-like processes. WH: 17C. Latin *digitatus*. See DIGIT, also -ATE[2].

digitiform *a.* finger-shaped. WH: 19C. Latin *digitus* DIGIT + -*i*- + -FORM.

digitigrade *a.* (of an animal, as a cat, dog, hyena and weasel) having the heel raised above the ground and walking on their toes. *Also n.* WH: 19C. Latin *digitus* DIGIT + -*i*- + -*gradus* walking. Cp. PLANTIGRADE.

diglot *a.* bilingual. *Also n.* WH: 19C. Greek *diglōttos*, from DI-[2] + *glōtta* tongue.

diglyph *n.* a projection like a triglyph, but with two channels instead of three. WH: 18C. Greek *digluphos* doubly indented, from DI-[2] + *gluphein* to carve.

dignify *v.t.* to invest with dignity. WH: 14–15C. Old French *dignefier*, from Late Latin *dignificare*, from Latin *dignus* worthy. See also -FY.

dignity *n.* a serious and respectable manner. WH: 12–14C. Old French *digneté* (Modern French *dignité*), from Latin *dignitas*, from *dignus* worthy. See also -ITY.

digraph *n.* a combination of two letters to represent one simple sound, such as *ea* in *mead* or *th* in *thin*. WH: 18C. DI-[2] + -GRAPH.

digress *v.i.* to deviate, to wander from the main topic. WH: 16C. Latin *digressus*, p.p. of *digredi*, from DI-[1] + *gradi* to proceed, to step, from *gradus* step.

dihedral *a.* having two sides or surfaces. *Also n.* WH: 18C. DI-[2] + -*hedral* (-HEDRON).

dihybrid *n.* the offspring of parents that differ in two pairs of genes. WH: early 20C. DI-[2] + HYBRID.

dihydric *a.* containing two hydroxyl groups. WH: 19C. DI-[2] + HYDRIC.

dik-dik *n.* any of several small E African antelopes of the genus *Madoqua*. WH: 19C. E African name, of imit. orig.

diktat *n.* a settlement imposed, after a war, on the defeated. WH: mid-20C. German DICTATE[2].

dilacerate *v.t.* to tear into pieces. WH: 14–15C. Orig. p.p., from Latin *dilaceratus*, p.p. of *dilacerare*, from DI-[1] + *lacerare* to tear, to lacerate. See also -ATE[3].

dilapidate *v.t.* to damage, to bring into decay or ruin. *Also v.i.* WH: 16C. Latin *dilapidatus*, p.p. of *dilapidare*, from DI-[1] + *lapis*, *lapidis* stone. See also -ATE[3].

dilate *v.t.* to expand, to widen, to enlarge in all directions. *Also v.i., a.* WH: 14–15C. Old French *dilater*, from Latin *dilatare* to spread out, from DI-[1] + *latus* wide.

dilatory *a.* causing or tending to cause delay. WH: 14–15C. Late Latin *dilatorius* delaying, from Latin *dilator* delayer, from *dilatus*, p.p. of *differre* DEFER[1]. See also -ORY[2].

dildo *n.* an object serving as an erect penis, used as a sex aid. WH: 16C. Orig. unknown. The word originally occurred in the refrains of ballads, and has been derived either from Italian *diletto* delight, pleasure, or from English DALLY (in sense to toy, to sport).

dilemma *n.* an argument in which a choice of alternatives is presented, each of which is unfavourable. WH: 16C. Latin, from Greek *dilēmma*, from DI-[2] + *lēmma* assumption, premiss.

dilettante n. a lover or admirer of the fine arts. Also a. WH: 18C. Italian, use as verbal. a. of dilettare, from Latin delectare DELIGHT. Cp. AMATEUR.

diligence[1] n. steady application or assiduity in business of any kind. WH: 12–14C. Old French, from Latin diligentia, from diligent-. See DILIGENT.

diligence[2] n. a public stagecoach, formerly used in France and adjoining countries. WH: 17C. French, abbr. of carosse de diligence coach of speed.

diligent a. assiduous in any business or task. WH: 12–14C. Old French, from Latin diligens, diligentis, pres.p. of diligere to esteem highly, to choose, from DI-[1] + legere to choose. See also -ENT.

dill n. an annual umbellifer, Anethum graveolens, cultivated for its aromatic seeds, and for its flavour. WH: pre-1200. Old English dile, dyle, from Germanic, ult. of unknown orig. The word is translated anise in AV New Testament: 'mint and anise and cummin' (Matt. xxiii.23). See ANISE.

dilly n. a remarkable person or thing. Also a. WH: mid-20C. From 1st syl. of delightful (DELIGHT) or DELICIOUS + -Y[3].

dillybag n. an Australian Aboriginal basket or bag made of rushes or bark. WH: 19C. Australian Aboriginal (Yagara) dili coarse grass, bag woven from such grass + BAG.

dilly-dally v.i. to loiter about; to waste time. WH: 17C. Redupl. of DALLY.

dilute v.t. to make (a liquid) thin or weaken by adding water. Also a. WH: 16C. Latin dilutus, p.p. of diluere to wash away, to dissolve, from DI-[1] + -luere comb. form of lavare to wash.

diluvial a. of or relating to Noah's flood. WH: 17C. Late Latin diluvialis, from diluvian, from diluere. See DILUTE, also -AL[1].

dim a. lacking in light or brightness. Also v.t., v.i. WH: pre-1200. Old English, from Germanic. Rel. to DAMP, DANK.

dime n. a silver coin of the US, worth 10 cents, or one-tenth of a dollar. WH: 14–15C. Old French, from Latin decima, use as n. of fem. of decimus tenth.

dimension n. measurable extent or magnitude, length, breadth, height, thickness, depth, area, volume etc. WH: 14–15C. French, from Latin dimensio, from dimensionis, from dimensus, p.p. of dimetiri to measure out, from DI-[1] + metiri to measure.

dimer n. a chemical composed of two identical molecules. WH: early 20C. DI-[2] + -MER.

dimerous a. having two parts, joints, divisions etc., arranged in pairs. WH: 19C. Modern Latin dimerus, from Greek dimerēs bipartite. See also -OUS.

dimeter n. a verse of two metrical feet. WH: 16C. Late Latin, from Greek dimetros of two measures, from DI-[2] + metron measure.

dimethyl n. ethane, an organic compound in which two equivalents of methyl take the place of two of hydrogen. WH: 19C. DI-[2] + METHYL.

dimetrodon n. a large carnivorous reptile of the genus Dimetrodon, of the Permian period. WH: 19C. Modern Latin, from DI-[2] + Greek metron measure + -odon, from odous, odontos tooth.

dimidiate a. divided into two halves. WH: 18C. Latin dimidiatus, p.p. of dimidiare to halve, from dimidium half, from DI-[1] + MEDIUM. See also -ATE[2].

diminish v.t. to make smaller or less. Also v.i. WH: 14–15C. Blend of obs. diminue to diminish, from Old French diminuer, from Medieval Latin diminuere, from Latin deminuere to lessen, from DE- + minuere (see MINUTE[2]) and minish to diminish, from Old French menuisier, ult. from Latin MINUTIA (cp. MINCE).

diminuendo a., adv. gradually decreasing in loudness. Also n., v.i. WH: 18C. Italian diminishing, pres.p. of diminuire, from Latin deminuere. See DIMINISH.

diminutive a. small, tiny. Also n. WH: 14–15C. Old French diminutif, from Late Latin diminutivus, from diminutus, p.p. of diminuere. See DIMINISH.

dimissory a. dismissing, discharging; giving permission to depart. WH: 14–15C. Late Latin dimissorius, from Latin dimissus. See DISMISS, also -ORY[2].

dimity n. a strong cotton fabric with stripes or patterns, chiefly used for bed-hangings. WH: 14–15C. Italian dimito or Medieval Latin dimitum, from Greek dimitos, from DI-[2] + mitos thread of the warp. The origin of the final -y is unknown.

dimorphic a. having or occurring in two distinct forms. WH: 19C. Greek dimorphos, from DI-[2] + morphē form. See also -IC.

dimple n. a small natural depression on the cheek or chin. Also v.t., v.i. WH: 14–15C. Of Germanic orig., ? from nasalized form of DEEP. Rel. to DIP. The word is likely to have existed in Old English, but is not recorded.

dim sum n. a Chinese dish of small steamed dumplings with various fillings. WH: mid-20C. Chinese tím sam, from tím dot + sam heart. The name refers to the small centre filling.

dimwit n. a stupid person. WH: mid-20C. DIM + WIT[1].

DIN n. a method of classifying the speed of photographic film by sensitivity to light (the greater the light sensitivity the higher the speed). WH: Abbr. of German Deutsche Industrie-Norm German Industrial Standard.

din n. a loud and continued noise. Also v.t., v.i. WH: pre-1200. Old English dyne, from Germanic.

dinar n. the standard unit of currency in the countries which formerly made up Yugoslavia. WH: 17C. Arabic and Persian dīnār or Turkish and Serbo-Croat dinar, from Late Greek dēnarion, from Latin DENARIUS.

din-din n. dinner (used by or to children). WH: 19C. Childish redupl. of DINNER.

dine v.i. to take dinner. Also v.t. WH: 12–14C. Old French disner (Modern French dîner), prob. from desjeuner to break one's fast. Cp. DÉJEUNER.

dinero n. money. WH: 17C. Spanish coin, money, from Latin DENARIUS.

ding[1] v.t. to strike; to beat violently. Also v.i., n. WH: 12–14C. Prob. from Scandinavian. Cp. Old Norse dengja to hammer, Danish dænge to beat, to bang.

ding[2] n. a lively party. WH: mid-20C. Prob. shortening of DING-DONG or WINGDING.

Ding an sich n. a thing in itself. WH: 19C. German thing in itself, from Ding THING[1] + an in + sich self.

dingbat n. a stupid person. WH: 19C. Orig. uncertain. ? DING[1] (sound of bell) + batty (BAT[2]). According to some, ding- may represent German Ding thing.

ding-dong n. the sound of a bell. Also a., adv., v.i. WH: 16C. Imit. Cp. DING[1], DONG[1].

dinge n. a dent. Also v.t. WH: 17C. Orig. unknown.

dinges n. a name for any person or thing whose name is forgotten or unknown; a thingummy. WH: 19C. Dutch ding THING[1].

dinghy n. a small ship's boat. WH: 19C. Hindi ḍīgī, ḍĕgī. The English spelling with -gh- indicates the hard g.

dingle n. a dell, a wooded valley between hills. WH: 12–14C. Orig. unknown.

dingo n. the Australian wild dog, Canis dingo. WH: 18C. Australian Aboriginal (Dharuk) din-gu.

dingy a. soiled, grimy. WH: 18C. ? Old English dynge DUNG. See also -Y[1].

dinkum a. good, genuine, satisfactory. WH: 19C. Orig. uncertain. ? British dialect dinkum work, due share of work.

dinky[1] a. charming, dainty. WH: 18C. Prob. dial. dink finely dressed, spruce + -Y[1].

dinky[2] n. either partner of a socially upwardly mobile couple with two incomes and no children. WH: late 20C. Acronym of double income, no kids + -Y[1], based on DINKY[1].

dinner n. the main meal of the day. WH: 12–14C. Old French disner (Modern French dîner), use as n. of inf. See DINE.

dinoceras n. any member of an extinct genus of gigantic mammals of N America, apparently with three pairs of horns. WH: 19C. Modern Latin, from Greek deinos fearful, terrible + keras horn. Cp. DINOSAUR.

dinoflagellate n. any of a group of unicellular aquatic organisms with two flagella. WH: 19C. Modern Latin Dinoflagellata, from Greek dinos a whirling + Latin flagellum (see FLAGELLATE[2]).

dinosaur n. a gigantic Mesozoic reptile. WH: 19C. Modern Latin dinosauros, from Greek deinos fearful, terrible + sauros lizard. The name was coined in 1841 by the British palaeontologist Sir Richard Owen.

dint n. the mark or dent caused by a blow. Also v.t., v.i. WH: pre-1200. Old English dynt, from Germanic. Cp. DENT[1].

diocese n. the district under the jurisdiction of a bishop. WH: 12–14C. Old French *diocise* (Modern French *diocèse*), from Late Latin *diocesis*, from Latin *dioecesis* governor's jurisdiction, from Greek *dioikēsis* administration, from *dioikein* to keep house, from DI-³ + *oikos* house. Cp. PARISH.

diode n. a simple electron tube in which the current flows in one direction only between two electrodes. WH: 19C. DI-² + Greek *hodos* way. Cp. ANODE, CATHODE. The term was coined in 1886 by the Welsh electrical engineer Sir William Henry Preece.

dioecious a. having the stamens on one individual and the pistils on another. WH: 18C. Modern Latin *Dioecia*, from DI-² + Greek *oikos* house + -OUS. The *Dioecia* were a class in Linnaeus' sexual system.

dioestrus n. a period between periods of oestrus. WH: early 20C. DI-² + OESTRUS.

diol n. any alcohol with two hydroxyl groups in each molecule. WH: early 20C. DI-² + -OL.

Dionysiac a. of or relating to Dionysus (the Greek god of wine). WH: 19C. Late Latin *Dionysiacus*, from Greek *Dionūsiakos*, from *Dionūsos* Dionysus, the Greek god of wine. See also -AC. The cult of Dionysus was marked by ecstatic rites.

Diophantine equation n. an indeterminate equation which needs an integral or rational solution. WH: 18C. *Diophantus*, *fl*.3C AD, Greek mathematician + -INE.

diopside n. pyroxene, esp. the transparent variety. WH: 19C. French, from DI-² + Greek *opsis* aspect, later interpreted as from Greek *diopsis* view through. Cp. DIOPTASE.

dioptase n. an emerald-green ore of copper. WH: 19C. French, from Greek *dioptus* transparent, from DI-³ + *optos* visible. Both *dioptase* and DIOPSIDE were coined in 1801 by the French mineralogist René-Just Haüy.

dioptre n. a unit of refractive power, being the power of a lens with a focal distance of one metre. WH: 16C. French, from Latin *dioptra*, from Greek, from DI-³ + *optra*, from stem *op*- to see + instr. suf. *-tra*. The name was originally that of an ancient optical instrument for measuring angles. The current sense dates from the 19C.

diorama n. a painting in which natural phenomena are depicted by means of change of colour and light. WH: 19C. French, from DIA- + base of PANORAMA.

diorite n. a granite-like rock, consisting principally of hornblende and feldspar. WH: 19C. French, from Greek *diorizein* to distinguish, from DI-³ + *orizein* to limit. See also -ITE¹. The name was coined by the French mineralogist René-Just Haüy.

Dioscuri n.pl. the twins Castor and Pollux. WH: 16C. Greek *Dioskouroi*, from *Dios*, gen. of *Zeus* + *kouros* boy, son.

dioxan n. a colourless, insoluble, toxic liquid. WH: early 20C. DI-² + *ox*- (OXY-¹) + -AN.

dioxide n. one atom of a metal combined with two of oxygen. WH: 19C. DI-² + OXIDE.

dioxin n. a highly toxic substance found in some weedkillers which causes birth defects, cancers and various other diseases. WH: early 20C. DI-² + *ox*- (OXY-¹) + -IN¹.

DIP n. a kind of integrated circuit consisting of two rows of pins in a small piece of plastic or ceramic. WH: late 20C. Acronym of *dual in-line package*.

dip v.t. to plunge into a liquid for a short time. *Also v.i.*, n. WH: pre-1200. Old English *dyppan*, from Germanic base also of DEEP. Cp. German *taufen* to baptize.

dipeptide n. a peptide with two amino acid molecules in its structure. WH: early 20C. DI-² + PEPTONE + -IDE.

dipetalous a. bipetalous. WH: 18C. Modern Latin *dipetalus*. See DI-², PETAL, also -OUS.

diphase a. having two phases. WH: 19C. DI-² + PHASE.

diphosphate n. a compound containing two phosphate groups in the molecule. WH: 19C. DI-² + PHOSPHATE.

diphtheria n. an infectious disease characterized by acute inflammation and the formation of a false membrane, chiefly on the pharynx, nostrils, tonsils and palate, causing breathing difficulties. WH: 19C. Modern Latin, from French *diphthérie*, from Greek *diphthera* skin, hide. See also -IA. French *diphthérie* was substituted in 1855 by the French epidemiologist Pierre-Fidèle Bretonneau for

his original term of 1821, *diphthérite*, probably because medical terms in *-ite* (-ITIS) usually relate to the part of the body affected (cp. BRONCHITIS, LARYNGITIS etc.).

diphthong n. the union of two vowels in one syllable. WH: 14–15C. French *diphtongue*, from Latin *diphthongus*, from Greek *diphthoggos*, from DI-² + *phthoggos* voice, sound.

diphyllous a. having two leaves or sepals. WH: 18C. Modern Latin *diphyllus* (from DI-² + *phullon* leaf) + -OUS.

diphyodont a. of or relating to mammals which have two sets of teeth, one deciduous, the other permanent. WH: 19C. Greek *diphu-*, from *diphuēs* (from DI-² + *phuein* to generate) + -ODONT.

diplo- comb. form double. WH: Greek *diplos*, *diplous* double. See also -O-.

diploblastic a. having two germ layers. WH: 19C. DIPLO- + -BLAST + -IC.

diplocardiac a. having the heart double or the two sides separated. WH: 19C. DIPLO- + CARDIAC.

diplococcus n. any coccus occurring usually in pairs. WH: 19C. DIPLO- + COCCUS.

diplodocus n. a very large dinosaur of the genus *Diplodocus*, characterized by a large tail and a small head. WH: 19C. Modern Latin, from Greek DIPLO- + *dokos* beam, bar. The dinosaur was so named in 1878 by the US palaeontologist Othniel Charles Marsh for its 'double beam' (its long neck and long tail).

diploë n. the spongy tissue between the plates of the skull. WH: 16C. Greek *diploē* doubling, from *diploos* double.

diploid a. having the full number of paired homologous chromosomes. *Also n.* WH: 19C. DIPLO- + -OID. In the biological sense the 2nd element represents -ID.

diploma n. a certificate of a degree, licence etc. WH: 18C. Latin, from Greek folded paper, from *diploun* to make double, to fold, from *diploos* double. The original sense was that of a folded document conveying a privilege.

diplomacy n. the art of conducting negotiations between nations. WH: 18C. French *diplomatie*, from *diplomatique*, based on *aristocratie* ARISTOCRACY.

diplont n. an animal or plant with a diploid number of chromosomes in its cells. WH: early 20C. DIPLO- + -ONT.

diplopia n. a disorder of the eyes in which the patient sees objects double. WH: 19C. DIPLO- + -OPIA.

diplotene n. a stage of the prophase of the meiosis during which paired chromosomes separate. WH: early 20C. French *diplotène*, from DIPLO- + *-tène*, from Greek *tainia* band, ribbon.

dipnoous a. of or relating to an order of fishes, the Dipnoi, breathing both by gills and true lungs. WH: 19C. Modern Latin *Dipnoi*, from Greek *dipnoos* with two breathing apertures, from DI-² + *pnoē* breathing. See also -OUS.

dipody n. in prosody, a double foot. WH: 19C. Late Latin *dipodia*, from Greek, from DI-² + *pous*, *podos* foot. See also -Y².

dipole n. two equal and opposite electric charges or magnetic poles a small distance apart. WH: early 20C. DI-² + POLE².

dippy a. slightly mad. WH: early 20C. Orig. unknown. ? Rel. to DOPE.

dipsas n. a snake whose bite was said to produce unquenchable thirst. WH: 14–15C. Latin, from Greek causing thirst, from *dipsa* thirst.

dipso n. a dipsomaniac, an alcoholic. WH: 19C. Abbr. of *dipsomaniac* (DIPSOMANIA).

dipsomania n. alcoholism; an irresistible craving for stimulants. WH: 19C. Greek *dipso-*, comb. form of *dipsa* thirst (see also -O-) + -MANIA.

dipteral a. (of a temple) having a double row of columns all round. WH: 19C. Latin *dipteros*, from Greek two-winged, from DI-² + *pteron* wing. See also -AL¹.

dipterous a. of or relating to the Diptera, an order of insects which have two wings and two small knobbed organs called poisers. WH: 18C. Modern Latin *Diptera*, from Greek, from *dipteros* (see DIPTERAL). + -OUS.

diptych n. an altarpiece or other painting with hinged sides closing like a book. WH: 17C. Late Latin *diptycha*, from Late Greek *diptukha* pair of writing tablets, from *diptukhos* folded in two, from DI-² + *ptukhē* fold.

dire *a.* dreadful, fearful. WH: 16C. Latin *dirus* fearful, threatening, rel. to Greek *deinos* (see DINOSAUR).

direct *a.* straight. *Also adv., v.t., v.i.* WH: 14–15C. Latin *directus*, p.p. of *dirigere* to straighten, to guide, from DI-[1] + *regere* to make straight, to rule.

direction *n.* the act of directing. WH: 14–15C. French, or from Latin *directio, directionis*, from *directus*. See DIRECT, also -ION.

Directoire *a.* of or relating to the costume and furniture of the Directory period in France, 1795–99. WH: 18C. French DIRECTORY. The French revolutionary government known as the *Directoire* was so named for its five *directeurs* (directors) or ministers.

director *n.* a person who directs or manages. WH: 14–15C. Anglo-French *directour*, from Late Latin *director*, from Latin *directus*. See DIRECT, also -OR.

directory *n.* a book containing the names, addresses and telephone numbers of the inhabitants etc. of a district. *Also a.* WH: 14–15C. Late Latin *directorium*, neut. sing. (used as n.) of *directorius*, from *director* DIRECTOR. See also -ORY[1].

directrix *n.* a line determining the motion of a point or another line so that the latter describes a certain curve or surface. WH: 16C. Medieval Latin, fem. of Late Latin DIRECTOR. See also -TRIX. The geometrical sense dates from the 18C.

dirge *n.* a funeral song or hymn. WH: 12–14C. Latin *dirige*, 2nd pers. sing. imper. of *dirigere* DIRECT. The Latin word comes from the antiphon beginning *Dirige, Domine, Deus meus, in conspectu tuo viam meam* Direct, O Lord, my God, my way in thy sight (AV. Lead me, O Lord, in thy righteousness) (Ps. v.8), formerly in the Office of the Dead. Cp. PLACEBO, REQUIEM.

dirham *n.* the standard unit of currency of several N African and Middle Eastern countries. WH: 18C. Arabic, from Greek *drakhmē*. See DRACHM.

dirigible *a.* able to be directed or steered. *Also n.* WH: 16C. Latin *dirigere* DIRECT + -IBLE.

dirigisme *n.* state control of economic and social affairs. WH: mid-20C. French, from *diriger*, from Latin *dirigere* DIRECT. See also -ISM.

diriment *a.* nullifying, rendering a marriage null and void. WH: 19C. Latin *dirimens, dirimentis*, pres.p. of *dirimere*, from *dir-* DIS- + *emere* to take.

dirk *n.* a dagger, esp. one worn by a Highlander. *Also v.t.* WH: 16C. Orig. unknown. According to some, the word is from the male forename *Dirk*. Cp. German *Dietrich* picklock, skeleton key.

dirndl *n.* an Alpine peasant woman's dress with tight-fitting bodice and full gathered skirt. WH: mid-20C. German dial. dim. of *Dirne* girl.

dirt *n.* foul or unclean matter, matter that soils. *Also v.t.* WH: 12–14C. Old Norse *drit* excrement, rel. to Old English *gedrītan* to defecate.

dis *v.t.* to treat disrespectfully, to put down. WH: late 20C. Abbr. of DISRESPECT.

dis- *pref.* asunder, apart, away, as in *disaster, distant, disturb.* WH: Old French *des-, dis-* (Modern French *dés-, dé-, dis-*) or Latin *dis-* two ways, in two, from *duo* two. For reasons of pronunciation, s is often dropped or assimilated to a subsequent consonant. See DI-[1], DIF-.

disability *n.* weakness, handicap. WH: 16C. DIS- + ABILITY.

disable *v.t.* to render unable. WH: 14–15C. DIS- + ABLE.

disabuse *v.t.* to free from error or misapprehension, to undeceive. WH: 17C. DIS- + ABUSE[1].

disaccharide *n.* a sugar with two linked monosaccharides per molecule. WH: 19C. DI-[2] + *saccharide* (SACCHAR-).

disaccord *n.* disagreement; lack of harmony, incongruity. *Also v.i.* WH: 16C. DIS- + ACCORD.

disaccustom *v.t.* to do away with (a habit); to free from the force of custom. WH: 15C. Old French *desacoustumer* (Modern French *désaccoutumer*). See DIS-, ACCUSTOM.

disacknowledge *v.t.* to disown, to deny acquaintance with. WH: 16C. DIS- + ACKNOWLEDGE.

disadvantage *n.* an unfavourable position or condition. *Also v.t.* WH: 14–15C. Old French *désavantage*. See DIS-, ADVANTAGE.

disaffect *v.t.* to estrange, alienate the affection or loyalty of. WH: 17C. DIS- + AFFECT[1].

disaffiliate *v.t.* to end an affiliation to. *Also v.i.* WH: 19C. DIS- + AFFILIATE[1].

disaffirm *v.t.* to deny what has been affirmed. WH: 16C. DIS- + AFFIRM.

disafforest *v.t.* to strip of forest. WH: 14–15C. Anglo-Latin *disafforestare*. See DIS-, AFFOREST.

disaggregate *v.t.* to separate into components, parts or particles. WH: 19C. DIS- + AGGREGATE[1].

disagree *v.i.* to differ in opinion. WH: 15C. Old French *désagréer*. See DIS-, AGREE.

disallow *v.t.* to refuse to sanction or permit; to refuse assent to; to disavow, to reject; to prohibit. *Also v.i.* WH: 14–15C. Old French *desalouer*. See DIS-, ALLOW.

disambiguate *v.t.* to make unambiguous. WH: mid-20C. DIS- + AMBIGUOUS + -ATE[3].

disamenity *n.* a disadvantage, a drawback. WH: early 20C. DIS- + AMENITY.

disanchor *v.t.* to weigh the anchor of. *Also v.i.* WH: 14–15C. Old French *desancrer*. See DIS-, ANCHOR.

disannul *v.t.* to annul, to abrogate. WH: 15C. DIS- + ANNUL.

disanoint *v.t.* to annul the consecration of. WH: 17C. DIS- + ANOINT.

disappear *v.i.* to go out of sight; to become invisible. WH: 14–15C. DIS- + APPEAR, based on French *disparaître*.

disappoint *v.t.* to defeat the expectations, hopes or desires of. WH: 14–15C. Old French *désappointer*. See DIS-, APPOINT. The original sense was to reverse the appointment of, to deprive of an office. The current sense dates from the 15C.

disapprobation *n.* disapproval, condemnation. WH: 17C. DIS- + APPROBATION.

disappropriate *v.t.* to remove from individual possession. WH: 17C. Medieval Latin *disappropriatus*, p.p. of *disappropriare*, from DIS- + Latin *appropriare* APPROPRIATE[1].

disapprove *v.t.* to condemn, as not approved of. *Also v.i.* WH: 15C. DIS- + APPROVE. The original sense (to the 18C) was to disprove. The current sense dates from the 17C.

disarm *v.t.* to take the weapons away from. *Also v.i.* WH: 14–15C. Old French *désarmer*. See DIS-, ARM[2].

disarrange *v.t.* to put out of order. WH: 18C. DIS- + ARRANGE.

disarray *n.* disorder, confusion. *Also v.t.* WH: 14–15C. Old French *desaroi* (Modern French *désarroi*). See DIS-, ARRAY.

disarticulate *v.t.* to separate the joints of, to disjoint. *Also v.i.* WH: 19C. DIS- + ARTICULATE[1].

disassemble *v.t.* to take apart. WH: 17C. DIS- + ASSEMBLE.

disassimilation *n.* the conversion of assimilated substances into such as are less complex or waste substances; catabolism. WH: 19C. DIS- + *assimilation* (ASSIMILATE).

disaster *n.* a sudden misfortune. *Also v.t.* WH: 16C. French *désastre*, or from Italian *disastro*, from *dis-* DIS- + *astro* star, from Latin *astrum*. An early sense (to the 17C) was an unfavourable aspect of a star or planet.

disavow *v.t.* to deny the truth of, to disown; to disapprove; to disclaim. WH: 14–15C. Old French *désavouer*. See DIS-, AVOW.

disband *v.i.* to separate, to disperse. *Also v.t.* WH: 16C. Obs. French *desbander* (now *débander*). See DIS-, BAND[3].

disbar *v.t.* to deprive of status as a barrister; to expel from membership of the bar. WH: 17C. DIS- + BAR[1].

disbelieve *v.t.* to refuse credit to, to refuse to believe in. *Also v.i.* WH: 17C. DIS- + BELIEVE. *Disbelieve* superseded earlier *misbelieve* (MISBELIEF).

disbench *v.t.* to deprive of status as a bencher, to dismiss from senior membership of the Inns of Court. WH: 17C. DIS- + BENCH.

disbenefit *n.* a disadvantage, a drawback. WH: mid-20C. DIS- + BENEFIT.

disbound *a.* separated from a bound volume. WH: mid-20C. DIS- + BOUND[3].

disbowel *v.t.* to disembowel. WH: 14–15C. DIS- + BOWEL.

disbranch *v.t.* to strip of branches. WH: 16C. DIS- + BRANCH.

disbud *v.t.* to cut away (esp. superfluous) buds from. WH: 18C. DIS- + BUD[1].

disburden *v.t.* to remove a burden or encumbrance from. *Also v.i.* WH: 16C. DIS- + BURDEN.

disburse *v.t.* to pay out, to expend. *Also v.i.* WH: 16C. Old French *desbourser* (Modern French *débourser*). See DIS-, BURSA.

disc n. a flat circular plate or surface. WH: 17C. French *disque* or Latin DISCUS.

discalced a. (of a friar or a nun etc.) unshod, barefoot, wearing sandals . *Also n.* WH: 17C. Contr. of *discalceated*, p.p. of *discalceate*, from Latin *discalceatus*, from DIS- + *calceatus*, p.p. of *calceare* to shoe. See also -ATE³. The contraction was based on French *déchaux*.

discard¹ v.t. to get rid of, to reject. *Also v.i.* WH: 16C. DIS- + CARD¹. The earliest sense was to throw out a card from a hand.

discard² n. the playing of useless cards. WH: 18C. DISCARD¹.

discarnate a. having no flesh, disembodied. WH: 14–15C. DIS- + Latin *caro, carnis* flesh, or from Late Latin *carnatus* fleshy. See also -ATE².

discern v.t. to perceive distinctly with the senses, to make out. *Also v.i.* WH: 14–15C. Old French *discerner*, from Latin *discernere*, from DIS- + *cernere* to separate. The word became confused with DECERN.

†discerptible a. separable, capable of being torn apart. WH: 18C. Latin *discerptus*, p.p. of *discerpere*, from DIS- + *carpere* to pick, to pluck + -IBLE.

discharge¹ v.t. to unload from a ship, vehicle etc. *Also v.i.* WH: 12–14C. Old French *descharger* (Modern French *décharger*), from Late Latin *discaricare* to unload, from DIS- + *caricare*. See CHARGE.

discharge² n. the act of discharging. WH: 14–15C. DISCHARGE¹.

disciple n. a pupil of a leader etc. *Also v.t.* WH: pre-1200. Latin *discipulus* learner, from *discere* to learn.

discipline n. training of the mental, moral and physical powers to promote order and obedience. *Also v.t.* WH: 12–14C. Old French, from Latin *disciplina*, from *discipulus* DISCIPLE.

disclaim v.t. to deny, to repudiate. *Also v.i.* WH: 14–15C. Anglo-French *desclamer*. See DIS-, CLAIM.

disclose v.t. to make known, to reveal. *Also n.* WH: 14–15C. Old French *desclos-*, pres. stem of *desclore*, from Latin DIS- + *claudere* CLOSE².

disco n. a discotheque. *Also a.* WH: mid-20C. Abbr. of DISCOTHEQUE.

discobolus n. in ancient Greece, a discus-thrower. WH: 18C. Latin, from Greek *diskobolos*, from *diskos* DISCUS + *bolos* throwing, from *ballein* to throw.

discography n. a catalogue or list of gramophone records or compact discs, esp. by a particular artist or band. WH: mid-20C. DISC + -O- + -GRAPHY.

discoid a. having the shape of a disc. WH: 18C. Greek *diskoeidēs*, from *diskos*. See DISCUS, also -OID.

discolour v.t. to alter the colour of. *Also v.i.* WH: 14–15C. Old French *descolorer*, or from Medieval Latin *discolorare*, from Latin DIS- + *colorare* COLOUR.

discombobulate v.t. to confuse, to disconcert. WH: 19C. Prob. alt. of DISCOMPOSE or DISCOMFIT.

discomfit v.t. to embarrass and confuse. *Also n.* WH: 12–14C. Old French *desconfit*, p.p. of *desconfire* (Modern French *déconfire*), from Latin DIS- + *conficere* to put together, to destroy, from CON- + *facere* to do.

discomfort n. lack of ease or comfort. *Also v.t.* WH: 14–15C. Old French *desconfort* (Modern French *déconfort*). See DIS-, COMFORT.

discommend v.t. to blame, to censure; to disapprove of; to disparage. WH: 14–15C. DIS- + COMMEND.

discommode v.t. to cause inconvenience to. WH: 18C. Obs. French *discommoder*, var. of *incommoder* INCOMMODE.

discommon v.t. to prevent from being common land. WH: 14–15C. DIS- + COMMON.

discompose v.t. to destroy the composure of. WH: 15C. DIS- + COMPOSE.

disconcert v.t. to discompose, to disquiet. WH: 17C. Obs. French *desconcerter* (now *déconcerter*). See DIS-, CONCERT².

disconfirm v.t. to show or suggest the falseness of. WH: mid-20C. DIS- + CONFIRM.

disconformity n. a lack of conformity or agreement; inconsistency. WH: 16C. DIS- + *conformity* (CONFORM).

disconnect v.t. to remove (an electrical device) from its source of power, esp. by unplugging it. WH: 18C. DIS- + CONNECT.

disconsolate a. unable to be consoled or comforted. WH: 14–15C. Medieval Latin *disconsolatus*, from Latin DIS- + *consolatus*, p.p. of *consolari* CONSOLE¹.

discontent n. lack of content; dissatisfaction. *Also a., v.t.* WH: 16C. DIS- + CONTENT¹.

discontiguous a. not contiguous; having the parts not in contact. WH: 18C. DIS- + CONTIGUOUS.

discontinue v.t. to stop producing. *Also v.i.* WH: 14–15C. Old French *discontinuer*, from Medieval Latin *discontinuare*, from Latin DIS- + *continuare* CONTINUE.

discophile n. a person who collects gramophone records or compact discs. WH: mid-20C. DISC + -O- + -PHILE.

discord¹ n. lack of agreement; contention. WH: 12–14C. Old French *descord* (Modern French *discorde*). See DISCORD².

discord² v.i. to be out of harmony (with). WH: 12–14C. Old French *descorder* (Modern French *discorder*), from Latin *discordare* to be at variance, from *discors, discordis* discordant, from DIS- + *cor, cordis* heart.

discotheque n. a club or public place where people dance to recorded pop music. WH: mid-20C. French *discothèque* (orig.) record library, based on *bibliothèque* library. See DISC, BIBLIOTHECA.

discount¹ n. a deduction from the amount of a price. WH: 17C. Obs. French *descompte* (now *décompte*), from *descompter*. See DISCOUNT².

discount² v.t. to deduct a certain sum from (a price). *Also v.i.* WH: 17C. Obs. French *descompter* (now *décompter*), from Italian *discontare*, from Medieval Latin *discomputare*, from Latin DIS- + *computare* COMPUTE.

discountenance v.t. to disconcert, to abash. *Also n.* WH: 16C. DIS- + COUNTENANCE.

discourage v.t. to deprive of courage; to dishearten. WH: 14–15C. Old French *descouragier* (Modern French *décourager*). See DIS-, COURAGE.

discourse¹ n. talk, conversation, exchange of ideas. WH: 14–15C. Latin *discursus* running back and forth, argument, use as n. of p.p. of *discurrere*, from DIS- + *currere* to run. Cp. DISCURSIVE. The form of the word has been assimilated to COURSE.

discourse² v.i. to talk, to speak, to converse. *Also v.t.* WH: 16C. DISCOURSE¹.

discourteous a. impolite, rude. WH: 16C. DIS- + COURTEOUS.

discover v.t. to gain the first sight of. WH: 12–14C. Old French *descouvrir* (Modern French *découvrir*), from Late Latin *discooperire*, from Latin DIS- + *cooperire* COVER. The original sense was to make known, to divulge. The current sense dates from the 16C, the start of the geographical 'Age of Discovery' proper following Columbus's discovery of America in 1492.

discovert a. not having a husband, unmarried, widowed or divorced. WH: 14–15C. Old French *descovert* (Modern French *découvert*), p.p. of *descouvrir*. See DISCOVER.

discovery n. the act of discovering. WH: 16C. DISCOVER + -Y², based on the pair RECOVER/ *recovery* (RECOVER).

discredit n. lack or loss of credit. *Also v.t.* WH: 16C. DIS- + CREDIT, based on Italian *discreditare* or French *discréditer*.

discreet a. prudent, wary. WH: 12–14C. Old French *discret*, from Latin *discretus*, p.p. of *discernere* DISCERN, with sense influ. by *discretio, discretionis* DISCRETION. Cp. DISCRETE.

discrepancy n. a difference; an inconsistency, esp. between two figures or claims. WH: 17C. Latin *discrepantia*, from *discrepans, discrepantis*, pres.p. of *discrepare* to be discordant, from DIS- + *crepare* to creak. See also -ANCY.

discrete a. distinct, discontinuous, detached, separate. WH: 14–15C. Latin *discretus*. See DISCREET.

discretion n. the power or faculty of distinguishing things that differ, or discriminating correctly between what is right and wrong, useful and injurious. WH: 12–14C. Old French *discrétion*, from Latin *discretio, discretionis* separation, from *discretus*, p.p. of *discernere* DISCERN. See also -ION.

discriminate¹ v.i. to make a distinction or difference. *Also v.t.* WH: 17C. Latin *discriminatus*, p.p. of *discriminare*, from *discrimen, discriminis* division, distinction, from *discernere* DISCERN. See also -ATE³.

discriminate² a. distinctive; having the difference clearly marked. WH: 17C. Latin *discriminatus*, p.p. of *discriminare*. See DISCRIMINATE¹, -ATE². Cp. earlier INDISCRIMINATE.

discrown *v.t.* to divest or deprive of a crown; to depose. WH: 16C. DIS- + CROWN.

disculpate *v.t.* to free from blame. WH: 17C. Medieval Latin *disculpatus*, p.p. of *disculpare*, from Latin DIS- + *culpare* to blame, from *culpa* fault. See also -ATE³. Cp. EXCULPATE.

discursive *a.* passing from one subject to another; rambling. WH: 16C. Medieval Latin *discursivus*, from *discursus*. See DISCOURSE¹, also -IVE.

discus *n.* in ancient Greece, a metal disc thrown in athletic sports, a quoit. WH: 17C. Latin, from Greek *diskos*.

discuss *v.t.* to debate. WH: 14–15C. Latin *discussus*, p.p. of *discutere* to dash to pieces, to disperse, from DIS- + *quatere* to shake.

discutient *a.* having power to disperse tumours etc. Also *n.* WH: 17C. Latin *discutiens, discutientis*, pres.p. of *discutere*. See DISCUSS, also -ENT.

disdain *n.* scorn, a feeling of contempt combined with haughtiness and indignation. Also *v.t., v.i.* WH: 12–14C. Old French *desdeign* (Modern French *dédain*), alt. of Late Latin *dedignare*, from Latin DE- + *dignare, dignari* DEIGN.

disease *n.* any alteration of the normal vital processes of humans, the lower animals or plants, under the influence of some unnatural or hurtful condition. WH: 12–14C. Old French *desaise*, from *des-* DIS- + *aise* EASE. The original sense was absence of ease, trouble. The current sense dates from the 14–15C.

diseconomy *n.* the state of being uneconomic or unprofitable. WH: mid-20C. DIS- + ECONOMY.

disembark *v.i.* to leave a ship, aircraft, train etc. at the end of a journey. Also *v.t.* WH: 16C. French *désembarquer*, Spanish *desembarcar* or Italian *disimbarcare*, from DIS- + French *embarquer* EMBARK.

disembarrass *v.t.* to free from embarrassment or perplexity. WH: 18C. DIS- + EMBARRASS, prob. based on obs. French *désembarrasser* (now *débarrasser*).

disembellish *v.t.* to divest of ornament. WH: 17C. DIS- + EMBELLISH.

disembody *v.t.* to divest of body or the flesh; to free from a concrete form. WH: 18C. DIS- + EMBODY.

disembogue *v.t.* (of a stream) to pour out or discharge (water) at the mouth; to pour forth or empty itself. Also *v.i.* WH: 16C. Spanish *desembocar*, from *des-* DIS- + *embocar* to run into a creek or strait, from *em-* IN-¹ + *boca* mouth. Cp. DEBOUCH.

disembowel *v.t.* to lacerate so as to let the bowels protrude. WH: 17C. DIS- + EMBOWEL.

disembroil *v.t.* to free from confusion or perplexity. WH: 17C. DIS- + EMBROIL.

disemploy *v.t.* to cease to employ, to remove from employment. WH: 17C. DIS- + EMPLOY.

disempower *v.t.* to deprive of the power to act. WH: 16C. DIS- + EMPOWER.

disenable *v.t.* to disable, to incapacitate . WH: 17C. DIS- + ENABLE.

disenchant *v.t.* to free from enchantment or glamour, to free from a spell. WH: 16C. Old French *désenchanter*. See DIS-, ENCHANT.

disencumber *v.t.* to free from burden or hindrance. WH: 16C. DIS- + ENCUMBER, prob. based on Old French *désencombrer*.

disendow *v.t.* to strip of endowments. WH: 19C. DIS- + ENDOW.

disenfranchise *v.t.* to deprive of electoral privilege. WH: 17C. DIS- + ENFRANCHISE.

disengage *v.t.* to separate; to loosen, to detach. Also *n.* WH: 17C. DIS- + ENGAGE, prob. based on French *désengager*.

disentail *v.t.* to free from or break the entail of. WH: 17C. DIS- + ENTAIL.

disentangle *v.t.* to free from entanglement. Also *v.i.* WH: 16C. DIS- + ENTANGLE.

†disenthral *v.t.* to set free from slavery, to emancipate. WH: 17C. DIS- + ENTHRAL.

disentitle *v.t.* to deprive of a right. WH: 17C. DIS- + ENTITLE.

†disentomb *v.t.* to remove from a tomb. WH: 17C. DIS- + ENTOMB.

disequilibrium *n.* a lack of balance or equilibrium, esp. in economic affairs. WH: 19C. DIS- + EQUILIBRIUM.

disestablish *v.t.* to annul the establishment of, esp. to deprive (a Church) of its connection with the state. WH: 16C. DIS- + ESTABLISH.

disesteem *n.* a lack of esteem or regard. Also *v.t.* WH: 17C. DIS- + ESTEEM.

diseur *n.* a reciter. WH: 19C. French talker, from *dire* to say.

disfame *n.* disrepute, dishonour. WH: 14–15C. Orig. from Old French *desfame*, from *desfamer* DEFAME, later from DIS- + FAME.

disfavour *n.* a feeling of dislike or disapprobation. Also *v.t.* WH: 16C. DIS- + FAVOUR.

disfeature *v.t.* to deface, disfigure. WH: 17C. DIS- + FEATURE.

disfellowship *n.* lack of fellowship. Also *v.t.* WH: 17C. DIS- + *fellowship* (FELLOW).

disfigure *v.t.* to spoil the beauty or appearance of. WH: 14–15C. Old French *desfigurer* (Modern French *défigurer*), from Latin DIS- + *figura* FIGURE.

disforest *v.t.* to disafforest, to clear of forest. WH: 16C. Old French *desforester*. See DIS-, FOREST. Cp. DEFOREST.

disform *v.t.* to alter in form. WH: 14–15C. DIS- + FORM. Cp. DEFORM.

disfranchise *v.t.* to disenfranchise. WH: 14–15C. DIS- + FRANCHISE.

disfrock *v.t.* to strip of clerical attire. WH: 19C. DIS- + FROCK. Cp. DEFROCK.

disgarnish *v.t.* to strip of equipment etc., to despoil. WH: 14–15C. Old French *desgarnir* (Modern French *dégarnir*), from *des-* DIS- + *garnir*. See GARNISH.

disgorge *v.t.* to eject from the mouth or stomach; to vomit. Also *v.i.* WH: 15C. Old French *desgorger* (Modern French *dégorger*). See DIS-, GORGE.

disgrace *n.* the state of being out of favour. Also *v.t.* WH: 16C. French *disgrâce*, from Italian *disgrazia*, from *dis-* DIS- + *grazia*, from Latin *gratia* GRACE.

disgruntle *v.t.* to annoy, to disappoint. WH: 17C. DIS- + dial. *gruntle* to grunt, to grumble, from GRUNT + -LE⁴.

disguise *v.t.* to conceal or alter the appearance of, with unusual dress. Also *n.* WH: 12–14C. Old French *desguiser* (Modern French *déguiser*), from DIS-, GUISE. The original sense (to the 16C) was to alter the usual style or fashion of dress, without any idea of concealment.

disgust *v.t.* to cause loathing or aversion in. Also *n.* WH: 17C. Old French *desgouster* (Modern French *dégoûter*) or Italian *disgustare*, from DIS- + Latin *gustus* taste.

dish *n.* a broad, shallow, open vessel for serving up food at table. Also *v.t., v.i.* WH: pre-1200. Old English *disc*, from Germanic, from Latin DISCUS. Cp. German *Tisch* table. Rel. to DESK.

dishallow *v.t.* to make unholy; to profane. WH: 16C. DIS- + HALLOW.

disharmony *n.* lack of harmony; discord, incongruity. WH: 17C. DIS- + HARMONY, prob. based on DISCORD¹.

dishearten *v.t.* to discourage, to disappoint. WH: 16C. DIS- + HEARTEN, or from obs. *disheart* + -EN⁵, based on HEARTEN.

†disherit *v.t.* to disinherit; to dispossess. WH: 12–14C. Old French *desheriter* (Modern French *déshériter*), from Latin DIS- + *hereditare* to inherit. The now obsolete verb has been superseded by DISINHERIT.

dishevel *v.t.* to disorder (the hair). Also *v.i.* WH: 16C. Back-formation from *dishevelled*, from Old French *deschevelé*, p.p of *descheveler*, from *des-* DIS-+ *chevel* hair. + -ED.

dishonest *a.* destitute of honesty, probity or good faith. WH: 14–15C. Old French *deshoneste* (Modern French *déshonnête*), from alt. of Latin *dehonestus*, from *honestus* HONEST. See DE-, DIS-.

dishonour *n.* lack of honour. Also *v.t.* WH: 12–14C. Old French *deshoner* (Modern French *déshonneur*), from Latin DIS- + *honor* HONOUR.

dishorn *v.t.* to deprive of horns. WH: 16C. DIS- + HORN.

dishorse *v.t.* to unhorse. WH: 19C. DIS- + HORSE.

disillusion *v.t.* to free or deliver from an illusion; to undeceive. Also *n.* WH: 16C. DIS- + ILLUSION.

disimpassioned *a.* dispassionate; tranquillized. WH: 19C. DIS- + *impassioned* (IMPASSION).

disimprison *v.t.* to release from captivity; to liberate. WH: 17C. DIS- + IMPRISON.

disimprove *v.t.* to make worse. Also *v.i.* WH: 17C. DIS- + IMPROVE.

disincentive *n.* something which discourages. Also *a.* WH: mid-20C. DIS- + INCENTIVE.

disincline *v.t.* to make averse or indisposed (to). WH: 17C. DIS- + INCLINE¹.

disincorporate *v.t.* to deprive of the rights, powers or privileges of a corporate body. WH: 17C. DIS- + INCORPORATE¹.

disindividualize *v.t.* to take away the individuality of. WH: 19C. DIS- + *individualize* (INDIVIDUAL).

disinfect *v.t.* to free or cleanse from infection, often by chemical means. **WH:** 16C. French *désinfecter*, from *dés-* DIS- + *infecter* INFECT.

disinfest *v.t.* to rid of vermin, e.g. rats or lice. **WH:** early 20C. DIS- + INFEST.

disinflation *n.* a return to normal economic conditions after inflation, without a reduction in production. **WH:** 19C. DIS- + *inflation* (INFLATE).

disinformation *n.* the deliberate propagation or leaking of misleading information. **WH:** mid-20C. DIS- + *information* (INFORM[1]), based on Russian *dezinformatsiya*.

disingenuous *a.* not ingenuous. **WH:** 17C. DIS- + INGENUOUS.

disinherit *v.i.* to cut off from a hereditary right. **WH:** 14–15C. DIS- + INHERIT. The verb has superseded earlier DISHERIT.

disintegrate *v.t.* to reduce to fragments or powder. *Also v.i.* **WH:** 18C. DIS- + INTEGRATE[1].

disinter *v.t.* to dig up, esp. from a grave. **WH:** 17C. French *désenterrer*, from *dés-* DIS- + *enterrer* INTER.

disinterest *n.* impartiality, disinterestedness. *Also v.t.* **WH:** 17C. DIS- + INTEREST[1].

disinvest *v.i.* to reduce or withdraw one's investment (in). **WH:** 17C. DIS- + INVEST.

disinvolve *v.t.* to disentangle. **WH:** 17C. DIS- + INVOLVE.

disjecta membra *n.pl.* scattered fragments of a written work. **WH:** 18C. Alt. of Latin *disiecti membra poetae* limbs of a dismembered poet. The Latin phrase is from Horace.

disjoin *v.t., v.i.* to separate, to part. **WH:** 14–15C. Old French *desjoindre, desjoign-* (Modern French *déjoindre*), from Latin *disiungere*, from DIS- + *iungere* JOIN.

disjoint *v.t.* to put out of joint, to dislocate. *Also v.i., a.* **WH:** 14–15C. Old French *desjoint*, p.p. of *desjoindre*. See DISJOIN.

disjunction *n.* the act of disjoining; separation. **WH:** 14–15C. Old French (Modern French *disjonction*), or from Latin *disiunctio, disiunctionis*, from *disiunctus*, p.p. of *disiungere*. See DISJOIN, also -ION.

dislike *v.t.* to regard with repugnance or aversion. *Also n.* **WH:** 16C. DIS- + LIKE[2]. The verb has superseded earlier MISLIKE.

disload *v.t.* to unload. **WH:** 16C. DIS- + LOAD.

dislocate *v.t.* to put out of joint. **WH:** 16C. Prob. back-formation from *dislocation*, from Old French, or from Medieval Latin *dislocatio, dislocationis*, from *dislocatus*, p.p. of *dislocare*, from Latin DIS- + *locare* to place. See also -ION.

dislodge *v.t.* to eject from a place of rest, retirement or defence. *Also v.i.* **WH:** 14–15C. Old French *deslogier*, from *des-* DIS- + *logier* LODGE.

disloyal *a.* not true to allegiance. **WH:** 15C. Old French *desloial* (Modern French *déloyal*), from *des-* DIS- + *loial* LOYAL.

dismal *a.* dark, depressing. *Also n.pl.* **WH:** 12–14C. Anglo-French *dis mal*, from Medieval Latin *dies mali* evil days. The word was originally (as a noun) the term for the 24 evil or unlucky days (two in each month) in the medieval calendar. In the 14–15C this then became the adjective applied to such days. The current general sense emerged in the 16C.

disman *v.t.* to deprive of maleness; to divest of men. **WH:** 17C. DIS- + MAN.

dismantle *v.t.* to strip of covering, equipment or means of defence. **WH:** 16C. Old French *desmanteler* (Modern French *démanteler*), from *des-* DIS- + *manteler* to fortify.

dismask *v.t.* to unmask. **WH:** 16C. Obs. French *desmarquer* (now *démarquer*), from *des-* DIS- + *masquer* MASK.

dismast *v.t.* to deprive (a ship) of masts. **WH:** 18C. DIS- + MAST[1].

dismay *v.t.* to deprive of courage; to dispirit. *Also v.i., n.* **WH:** 12–14C. Old French **desmaier*, from Latin DIS- + Germanic base of MAY[1].

dismember *v.t.* to separate limb from limb. **WH:** 12–14C. Old French *desmembrer* (Modern French *démembrer*), from Latin DIS- + *membrum* MEMBER.

dismiss *v.t.* to send away; to disband. *Also v.i.* **WH:** 14–15C. Medieval Latin *dismissus*, var. of Latin *dimissus*, p.p. of *dimittere*, from DI-[1] + *mittere* to send.

dismount *v.i.* to alight from a horse or bicycle. *Also v.t., n.* **WH:** 16C. DIS- + MOUNT[1], prob. based on Old French *desmonter*.

disnature *v.t.* to render unnatural. **WH:** 14–15C. Old French *des-*

naturer (Modern French *dénaturer*), from *des-* DIS- + *naturer* to form, to shape, from Medieval Latin *naturare*, from *natura* NATURE.

Disneyesque *a.* of or relating to the type of cartoon film or character created by Disney. **WH:** mid-20C. Walt *Disney*, 1901–66, US cartoonist + -ESQUE.

disobedient *a.* refusing or neglecting to obey. **WH:** 14–15C. Old French *desobedient*, from alt. of Ecclesiastical Latin *inoboediens, inoboedientis*, from Latin *oboediens, oboedientis* obedient (OBEDIENCE). See DIS-.

disobey *v.t.* to neglect or refuse to obey. *Also v.i.* **WH:** 14–15C. Old French *désobéir*, from alt. of Ecclesiastical Latin *inoboedire*, from Latin *oboedire* OBEY. See DIS-.

disoblige *v.t.* to act in a way contrary to the wishes or convenience of. **WH:** 16C. Old French *désobliger*, from Latin DIS- + *obligare* OBLIGE.

disorder *n.* lack of order; confusion. *Also v.t.* **WH:** 15C. Appar. assim. to ORDER of earlier *v. disordain*, from Old French *desordener* (Modern French *désordonner*), from Latin DIS- + *ordinare* ORDAIN.

disorganize *v.t.* to destroy the arrangement of. **WH:** 18C. French *désorganiser*, from *dés-* DIS- + *organiser* ORGANIZE. This and related words in English date from the French Revolution, 1789–92.

disorient *v.t.* to disorientate. **WH:** 17C. French *désorienter*, from *dés-* DIS- + *orienter* ORIENT. Cp. DISORIENTATE.

disorientate *v.t.* to cause to lose one's sense of direction. **WH:** 18C. DIS- + *orientate* (ORIENT). Cp. DISORIENT. The original and literal sense was to turn from the east (and so cause to lose one's bearings).

disown *v.t.* to disclaim, to renounce, to repudiate. **WH:** 17C. DIS- + OWN[2].

disparage *v.t.* to treat or speak of slightingly. **WH:** 14–15C. Old French *desparagier*, from *desparage* unsuitable for marriage, from *des-* DIS- + *parage* equality of rank, from Latin *par* equal. See also -AGE. The original sense was to marry unequally (to the 18C). Cp. MÉSALLIANCE. The current sense dates from the 16C.

disparate *a.* dissimilar, discordant. *Also n.* **WH:** 14–15C. Latin *disparatus*, p.p. of *disparare* to separate, from DIS- + *parare* to prepare.

disparity *n.* (an) inequality. **WH:** 16C. French *disparité*, from Late Latin *disparitas*, from *paritas* PARITY[1]. See DIS-.

dispart *n.* the difference between the external semidiameter of a gun at the muzzle and at the breech. **WH:** 16C. ? From obs. *v. dispart* to split in two, from Italian *dispartire* to divide, to part, or from Latin *dispartire* to distribute, from DIS- + *partire* PART.

dispassionate *a.* calm, impartial. **WH:** 16C. DIS- + *passionate* (PASSION).

dispatch *v.t.* to send off to some destination, esp. with haste. *Also v.i., n.* **WH:** 16C. Italian *dispacciare*, from Spanish *despachar* to expedite, from DIS- + base (of unknown orig.) of Italian *impacciare* to hinder and Spanish *empachar* to impede.

dispel *v.t.* to dissipate, to disperse; to drive away, to banish. **WH:** 14–15C. Latin *dispellere*, from DIS- + *pellere* to drive.

dispensable *a.* able to be dispensed with, inessential. **WH:** 16C. Medieval Latin *dispensabilis*, from Latin *dispensare* DISPENSE. See also -ABLE.

dispensary *n.* a place where medicines are dispensed. **WH:** 17C. Medieval Latin *dispensarium*, use as n. of neut. of *dispensarius*, from Latin *dispensare*. See DISPENSE, -ARY[1]. A dispensary was originally a place where medicines were weighed out.

dispensation *n.* the act of dispensing; distribution. **WH:** 14–15C. Old French, from Latin *dispensatio, dispensationis*, from *dispensatus*, p.p. of *dispensare*. See DISPENSE, also -ATION. The theological sense translates Greek *oikonomia*. Cp. ECONOMY.

dispense *v.t.* to deal out, to distribute. *Also v.i., n.* **WH:** 14–15C. Old French *despenser*, from Latin *dispensare* to weigh out, to disburse, freq. of *dispendere*, from DIS- + *pendere* to weigh.

dispermous *a.* having only two seeds. **WH:** 18C. DI-[2] + Greek *sperma* seed + -OUS.

disperse *v.t.* to drive or throw in different directions. *Also v.i.* **WH:** 14–15C. Latin *dispersus*, p.p. of *dispergere* to scatter, from DIS- + *spargere* to strew.

dispersion *n.* the act of dispersing. **WH:** 14–15C. Late Latin *dispersio, dispersionis* scattering, from *dispersus*. See DISPERSE, also -ION.

dispirit *v.t.* to deprive of spirit or courage. **WH:** 17C. DIS- + SPIRIT.

displace v.t. to remove from the usual or proper place. WH: pre-1200. Partly from DIS- + PLACE, partly based on obs. French *desplacer* (now *déplacer*), from *des-* DIS- + *placer* PLACE.

display v.t. to exhibit, to show. *Also v.i., n.* WH: 12–14C. Old French *despleier* (Modern French *déployer* DEPLOY), from Latin *displicare* to scatter, to disperse, from DIS- + *plicare* to fold. Not rel. to PLAY.

displease v.t. to dissatisfy, to offend; to vex, to annoy; to be disagreeable to. *Also v.i.* WH: 14–15C. Old French *desplaisir, desplaire* (Modern French *déplaire*), from *des-* DIS- + *plaisir* PLEASE.

displeasure n. a feeling of annoyance or anger. *Also v.t.* WH: 14–15C. Old French *desplaisir*, use as n. of inf. (see DISPLEASE), later assim. to PLEASURE.

displume v.t. to strip of plumes, feathers or decorations. WH: 15C. DIS- + PLUME.

dispone v.t. to dispose, dispose of. WH: 14–15C. Latin *disponere* to arrange, to dispose, from DIS- + *ponere* to place. Cp. DISPOSE.

disport v.t. to amuse (oneself), to divert (oneself); to enjoy (oneself). *Also v.i., n.* WH: 14–15C. Old French *desporter* (Modern French *déporter* DEPORT), from *des-* DIS- + *porter* to carry, PORT[5]. Cp. SPORT.

disposal n. the act of disposing. WH: 17C. DISPOSE + -AL[2].

dispose v.t. to arrange, to set in order. *Also v.i., n.* WH: 14–15C. Old French *disposer*, based on Latin *disponere* (see DISPONE) but reformed from Latin p.p. *dispositus* and Old French *poser*. See POSE[1].

disposition n. the act of arranging or bestowing. WH: 14–15C. Old French, from Latin *dispositio, dispositionis*, from *dispositus*, p.p. of *disponere* DISPONE. See also -ITION.

dispossess v.t. to oust from possession, esp. of real estate. WH: 15C. Old French *despossesser*. See DIS-, POSSESS.

dispraise v.t. to censure, to express disapprobation of. *Also n.* WH: 14–15C. DIS- + PRAISE.

†dispread v.t. to spread in different directions. *Also v.i.* WH: 16C. DIS- + SPREAD.

disproof n. refutation. WH: 14–15C. DIS- + PROOF.

disproportion n. lack of proportion between things or parts. *Also v.t.* WH: 16C. DIS- + PROPORTION.

disprove v.t. to prove to be erroneous or unfounded. WH: 14–15C. Old French *desprover*. See DIS-, PROVE.

dispute v.i. to quarrel in opposition to another. *Also v.t., n.* WH: 12–14C. Old French *desputer* (Modern French *disputer*), from Latin *disputare* to estimate, from DIS- + *putare* to reckon.

disqualify v.t. to render unfit, to debar. WH: 18C. DIS- + QUALIFY.

disquiet v.t. to disturb, to make uneasy, to harass, to vex. *Also n., a.* WH: 16C. DIS- + QUIET.

disquisition n. a formal discourse or treatise. WH: 15C. Old French, from Latin *disquisitio, disquisitionis*, from *disquisitus*, p.p. of *disquirere*, from DIS- + *quaerere* to seek. See also -ITION.

disrate v.t. to degrade or reduce in rating or rank. WH: 19C. DIS- + RATE[1].

disregard v.t. to take no notice of; to neglect. *Also n.* WH: 17C. DIS- + REGARD.

disrelish n. a distaste or dislike; aversion, antipathy. *Also v.t.* WH: 16C. DIS- + RELISH.

disremember v.t. to be unable to remember; to forget. WH: 17C. DIS- + REMEMBER.

disrepair n. a state of being out of repair. WH: 18C. DIS- + REPAIR[1].

disreputable a. of bad repute, not respectable. WH: 18C. DIS- + REPUTABLE, based on *disrepute*.

disrespect n. lack of respect or reverence; rudeness, incivility. *Also v.t.* WH: 17C. DIS- + RESPECT.

disrobe v.t. to strip of a robe or dress; to undress (oneself). *Also v.i.* WH: 14–15C. DIS- + ROBE.

disrupt v.t. to interrupt, to prevent from continuing. *Also a.* WH: 14–15C. Latin *disruptus*, p.p. of *disrumpere*, from DIS- + *rumpere* to break.

dissatisfy v.t. to make discontented, to displease. WH: 17C. DIS- + SATISFY.

dissect v.t. to cut in pieces. WH: 16C. Latin *dissectus*, p.p. of *dissecare*, from DIS- + *secare* to cut. Not from DI-[2]. Cp. BISECT.

disseise v.t. to deprive of possession of estates etc.; to dispossess wrongfully. WH: 12–14C. Old French *dessaisir* to dispossess. See DIS-, SEIZE.

dissemble v.i. to hide one's feelings, opinions or intentions; to play

the hypocrite. *Also v.t.* WH: 14–15C. Alt. of obs. *dissimule*, from Old French *dissimuler*, from Latin *dissimulare* (see DISSIMULATE), assoc. with SEMBLANCE.

disseminate v.t. to spread (information) about. *Also v.i.* WH: 14–15C. Latin *disseminatus*, p.p. of *disseminare*, from DIS- + *semen, seminis* seed. See also -ATE[3].

dissension n. disagreement of opinion; strife. WH: 12–14C. Old French, from Latin *dissensio, dissensionis*, from *dissensus*, p.p. of *dissentire*. See DISSENT, also -ION.

dissent v.i. to differ or disagree in opinion. *Also n.* WH: 14–15C. Latin *dissentire* to differ in sentiment, from DIS- + *sentire* to feel.

dissentient a. disagreeing or differing in opinion; holding or expressing contrary views. *Also n.* WH: 17C. Latin *dissentiens, dissentientis*, pres.p. of *dissentire*. See DISSENT, also -ENT.

dissepiment n. a division or partition in an organ or part. WH: 18C. Latin *dissaepimentum*, from *dissaepire* to make separate, from DIS- + *saepire* to divide off by a hedge, from *saepes* hedge. See also -MENT.

dissertation n. a formal discourse on any subject; a disquisition, treaty or exile. WH: 17C. Latin *dissertatio, dissertationis*, from *dissertus*, p.p. of *dissertare* to argue, to debate, freq. of *disserere*. See also -ATION.

disservice n. a harmful act, a bad turn. WH: 16C. DIS- + SERVICE[1].

dissever v.t. to sever, to separate. WH: 12–14C. Old French *dessevrer*, from Late Latin *disseparare*, from Latin DIS- + *separare* SEPARATE[1].

dissident a. not in agreement; disagreeing. *Also n.* WH: 16C. French, or from Latin *dissidens, dissidentis*, pres.p. of *dissidere* to sit apart, to disagree, from DIS- + *sedere* to sit. See also -ENT.

dissimilar a. unlike in nature or appearances. WH: 16C. DIS- + SIMILAR, based on Latin *dissimilis* or French *dissimilaire*.

dissimilate v.t. to make (sounds) unlike. *Also v.i.* WH: 19C. DIS- + Latin *similis* similar, based on ASSIMILATE.

dissimilitude n. unlikeness, dissimilarity. WH: 14–15C. Latin *dissimilitudo*, from *dissimilis* unlike, from DIS- + *similis* alike. See also -TUDE.

dissimulate v.t., v.i. to dissemble, to conceal, to disguise. WH: 14–15C. Latin *dissimulatus*, p.p. of *dissimulare*. See DIS-, SIMULATE.

dissipate v.t. to scatter; to drive in different directions. *Also v.i.* WH: 14–15C. Latin *dissipatus*, p.p. of *dissipare*, from DIS- + *supare* to throw. See also -ATE[3].

dissociate v.t. to separate, to disconnect. *Also v.i.* WH: 16C. Latin *dissociatus*, p.p. of *dissociare*, from DIS- + *sociare* to join together, from *socius* companion. See also -ATE[3].

dissoluble a. able to be dissolved, decomposed or disconnected. WH: 16C. Old French, or from Latin *dissolubilis*, from *dissolvere*. See DIS-, SOLVE, also -BLE. Cp. earlier INDISSOLUBLE.

dissolute a. loose in morals; debauched. *Also n.* WH: 14–15C. Latin *dissolutus* loose, disconnected, p.p. of *dissolvere* DISSOLVE.

dissolution n. the act or process of dissolving, separating etc. WH: 14–15C. Old French, or from Latin *dissolutio, dissolutionis*, from *dissolutus*, p.p. of *dissolvere* DISSOLVE. See also -ION.

dissolve v.t. to diffuse the particles of (a substance) in a liquid. *Also v.i., n.* WH: 14–15C. Latin *dissolvere*, from DIS- + *solvere* to loosen, SOLVE.

dissonant a. discordant, inharmonious. WH: 14–15C. Old French, or from Latin *dissonans, dissonantis*, pres.p. of *dissonare* to disagree in sound, from DIS- + *sonare* SOUND[1].

dissuade v.t. to try to persuade not to do some act. WH: 15C. Latin *dissuadere*, from DIS- + *suadere* to advise, to persuade.

dissymmetry n. lack of symmetry between objects or parts. WH: 19C. DIS- + SYMMETRY.

distaff n. a cleft stick about 3 ft. (0.91 m) long, on which wool or carded cotton is wound for spinning. WH: pre-1200. Old English *distæf*, appar. from base of Middle Low German *dise, disene* distaff, bunch of flax. Cp. BEDIZEN. Rel. to STAFF[1].

distal a. applied to the extremity of a bone or organ farthest from the point of attachment or insertion. WH: 19C. DISTANT + -AL[1], based on DORSAL, *ventral* (VENTER) etc. Cp. PROXIMAL.

distance n. the space between two objects measured along the shortest line. *Also v.t.* WH: 12–14C. Old French *destance* (Modern French *distance*), or from Latin *distantia*, from *distant-*. See DISTANT, also -ANCE.

distant *a.* separated by intervening space. WH: 14–15C. Old French, or from Latin *distans, distantis*, pres.p. of *distare* to stand apart, from DIS- + *stare* to stand.

distaste *n.* disrelish, aversion of the taste. *Also v.t., v.i.* WH: 16C. DIS- + TASTE, based on Old French *desgoust* (Modern French *dégoût*) or Italian *disgusto* DISGUST.

distemper¹ *n.* a method of painting with colours soluble in water, mixed with chalk or clay, and diluted with size instead of oil. *Also v.t.* WH: 17C. Old French *destremper*, or from Late Latin *distemperare* to soak, to macerate. See DIS-, TEMPER.

distemper² *n.* a catarrhal disorder affecting dogs, foxes etc. *Also v.t.* WH: 16C. Partly from obs. *distemper* to temper incorrectly, to disturb, from Late Latin *distemperare* to soak, to mix (cp. DISTEMPER¹), partly from DIS- + TEMPER.

distend *v.t.* to spread or swell out; to inflate. *Also v.i.* WH: 14–15C. Latin *distendere*, from DIS- + *tendere* to stretch.

disthrone *v.t.* to dethrone. WH: 16C. DIS- + THRONE.

distich *n.* a couplet; two lines of poetry making complete sense. WH: 16C. Latin *distichon*, from Greek *distikhon*, use as n. of neut. of *distikhos* of two rows, from DI-² + *stikhos* row, line of verse.

distichous *a.* having two rows (of leaves etc.). WH: 18C. Latin *distichus*, from Greek *distikhos* (see DISTICH) + -OUS.

distil *v.t.* to extract by means of vaporization and condensation. *Also v.i.* WH: 14–15C. Latin *distillare*, alt. of *destillare*, from DE- + *stillare*, from *stilla* drop.

distinct *a.* clearly distinguished or distinguishable. *Also n.* WH: 14–15C. Latin *distinctus*, p.p. of *distinguere* DISTINGUISH.

distingué *a.* having an air of nobility or dignity. WH: 19C. French, p.p. of *distinguer* DISTINGUISH.

distinguish *v.t.* to discriminate, to differentiate. *Also v.i.* WH: 16C. French *distinguer* or Latin *distinguere* + -ISH². Cp. EXTINGUISH.

distort *v.t.* to alter the natural shape of. *Also a.* WH: 15C. Latin *distortus*, p.p. of *distorquere*, from DIS- + *torquere* to twist.

distract *v.t.* to draw or turn aside, to divert the mind or attention of. *Also a.* WH: 14–15C. Latin *distractus*, p.p. of *distrahere*, from DIS- + *trahere* to draw, to drag. Cp. DISTRAUGHT.

distrain *v.t.* to seize for debt; to take the personal property of, in order to satisfy a demand or enforce the performance of an act. *Also v.i.* WH: 12–14C. Old French *destreindre, destreign-*, from Latin *distringere* to draw asunder, from DIS- + *stringere* to draw tight.

distrait *a.* absent-minded, abstracted, inattentive. WH: 14–15C. French, from Old French *destrait*, p.p. of *destraire*, from Latin *distrahere* DISTRACT. Cp. DISTRAUGHT.

distraught *a.* bewildered, agitated. WH: 14–15C. Alt. of *distract*, obs. p.p. of DISTRACT, by assim. to *straught*, obs. p.p. of STRETCH.

distress *n.* extreme anguish or pain of mind or body. *Also v.t.* WH: 12–14C. Old French *destrese, destresse* (Modern French *détresse*), from Latin *districtus*, p.p. of *distringere*. See DISTRAIN.

distribute *v.t.* to divide or deal out amongst a number. WH: 14–15C. Latin *distributus*, p.p. of *distribuere*, from DIS- + *tribuere* to grant, to assign.

district *n.* a portion of territory specially defined for administrative etc. purposes. *Also v.t.* WH: 17C. French, from Medieval Latin *districtus* (territory of) jurisdiction, from Latin *districtus*, p.p. of *distringere*. See DISTRAIN. Cp. STRICT. The original sense was the territory under the jurisdiction of a feudal lord.

distrust *v.t.* to have no confidence in. *Also n.* WH: 14–15C. DIS- + TRUST, based on French *défier* DEFY or Latin *diffidare*.

disturb *v.t.* to agitate, to disquiet. *Also v.t.* WH: 12–14C. Old French *destorber*, from Latin *disturbare*, from DIS- + *turbare* to disturb, from *turba* tumult, crowd.

distyle *n.* a portico having two columns. WH: 19C. DI-² + Greek *stulos* column.

disulphide *n.* a compound in which two atoms of sulphur are united to another element or radical. WH: 19C. DI-² + SULPHIDE.

disunion *n.* the state of being disunited; disagreement, discord. WH: 15C. DIS- + UNION.

disunite *v.t.* to disjoin, to divide. *Also v.i.* WH: 16C. DIS- + UNITE.

disuse¹ *n.* a cessation of use, practice or exercise; the state of being disused; desuetude. WH: 14–15C. DIS- + USE¹.

disuse² *v.t.* to cease to use. WH: 14–15C. Old French *desuser*, from *des-* DIS- + *user* USE².

disutility *n.* harmfulness. WH: 19C. DIS- + UTILITY.

disyllable *n.* a word or metrical foot of two syllables. *Also a.* WH: 16C. Alt. (based on SYLLABLE) of French *disyllabe*, from Latin *disyllabus*, from Greek *disullabos* of two syllables, from DI-² + *sullabē* SYLLABLE.

dit¹ *n.* a word representing the dot in Morse code when this is spoken. WH: mid-20C. Imit.

dit² *a.* named. WH: 19C. French, p.p. of *dire* to say.

dital *n.* a thumb stop on a guitar or lute for raising the pitch of a string by a semitone. WH: 19C. Italian *dito* finger, based on PEDAL¹.

ditch *n.* a trench made by digging to form a boundary or for drainage. *Also v.t., v.i.* WH: pre-1200. Old English *dīc*, from Germanic, from base also of DYKE. Cp. DIG.

ditheism *n.* the theory of two co-equal gods or opposing powers of good and evil, the basic principle of Zoroastrianism and Manichaeism. WH: 17C. DI-² + THEISM.

dither *v.i.* to be distracted or uncertain; to hesitate, to be indecisive. *Also n.* WH: 17C. Var. of obs. *didder* to tremble, to shake, rel. to DODDER¹.

dithyramb *n.* in ancient Greece, a choric hymn in honour of Bacchus, full of frantic enthusiasm. WH: 17C. Latin *dithyrambus*, from Greek *dithurambos*, prob. of non-Indo-European orig.

ditriglyph *n.* the interval between two triglyphs. WH: 18C. French *ditriglyphe*, from DI-² + *triglyphe* TRIGLYPH.

ditrochee *n.* a metrical foot of two trochees. WH: 18C. Late Latin *ditrochaeus*, from Greek *ditrokhaios*, from DI-² + *trokhaios* TROCHEE.

dittany *n.* a herb, *Origanum dictamnus*, which was prized by the ancients for its medicinal properties. WH: 14–15C. Old French *ditain*, from Medieval Latin *ditaneum*, from Latin *dictamnus*, from Greek *diktamnon*. ? from *Diktē*, a mountain in Crete, where it grows.

ditto *n.* what has been said before. *Also a., v.t.* WH: 17C. Italian, dial. var. of *detto* said, from Latin *dictus*, p.p. of *dire* to say.

ditty *n.* a little poem, a song. *Also v.t.* WH: 12–14C. Old French *dité* composition, treaty, from Latin *dictatum*, neut. p.p. (used as n.) of *dictare* DICTATE¹. See also -Y². Cp. DICTATE¹.

ditty bag *n.* a sailor's bag for needles, thread and odds and ends. WH: 19C. First word of unknown orig. + BAG. The term may be a sailor's corruption of DILLYBAG.

ditzy *a.* scatterbrained. WH: late 20C. Orig. unknown. ? Blend of DIZZY and DOTTY.

diuresis *n.* an excess of urine secretion. WH: 17C. Modern Latin, from DI-³ + Greek *ourēsis* urination.

diurnal *a.* of or relating to a day or the day-time. *Also n.* WH: 14–15C. Late Latin *diurnalis*, from Latin *diurnus* daily, from *dies* day. See also -AL¹. Cp. JOURNAL.

diva *n.* a famous female singer, a prima donna. WH: 19C. Italian, from Latin goddess.

divagate *v.t.* to ramble, to diverge, to digress. WH: 16C. Latin *divagatus*, p.p. of *divagari* to wander about, from DI-¹ + *vagari* to wander. See also -ATE³.

divalent *a.* with a valency of two. WH: 19C. DI-² + -*valent*, from Latin *valens, valentis*, pres.p. of *valere* to be strong. See also -ENT.

divan *n.* in oriental countries, a court of justice, the highest council of state. WH: 16C. French, or from Italian *divano*, from Turkish *dīvān*, from Persian brochure, anthology, register, court, bench. Cp. DEWAN, DOUANE. A divan was originally an oriental council of state, held in a room with a cushioned seat. The current sense evolved from the seat in the 18C.

divaricate¹ *v.i.* to diverge into branches or forks. *Also v.t.* WH: 17C. Latin *divaricatus*, p.p. of *divaricare*, from DI-¹ + *varicare* to stretch (the legs) apart, from *varicus* straddling. See also -ATE³.

divaricate² *a.* spreading irregularly and wide apart. WH: 18C. Latin *divaricatus*. See DIVARICATE¹, also -ATE².

dive *v.i.* to plunge, esp. head first, under water. *Also v.t., n.* WH: pre-1200. Old English *dūfan*, from Germanic, from same base as for DEEP, DIP.

diverge *v.i.* to go in different directions from a common point. *Also v.t.* WH: 17C. Medieval Latin *divergere*, from DI-¹ + Latin *vergere* to bend, to turn.

†divers *a.* several, sundry. WH: 12–14C. Old French, from Latin *diversus*, p.p. of *divertere* DIVERT. Cp. DIVERSE.

diverse *a.* different, unlike. *Also v.t., v.i.* WH: 12–14C. Var. of DIVERS, influ. by ADVERSE, PERVERSE etc.

diversion *n.* the act of diverting or turning aside. WH: 14–15C. Late Latin *diversio, diversionis* turning away, from Latin *diversus*, p.p. of *divertere* DIVERT. See also -ION.

divert *v.t.* to turn from any course or direction. *Also v.i.* WH: 14–15C. French *divertir*, from Latin *divertere*, from DIS- + *vertere* to turn.

diverticulum *n.* an abnormal sac or pouch on the wall of a tubular organ, esp. the intestine. WH: 17C. Medieval Latin byway, var. of Latin *deverticulum*, from *devertere* to turn aside, from DE- + *vertere* to turn. See also -CULE.

Dives *n.* a wealthy man. WH: 14–15C. Late Latin rich man, use as n. of Latin *dives* rich (after the parable of Lazarus and the rich man, Luke xvi.19–31). The word is not a personal name, despite the capital initial.

divest *v.t.* to strip of clothing. WH: 17C. Alt. of DEVEST, based on Latin vv. in DI-¹.

divide *v.t.* to cut or part in two. *Also v.i., n.* WH: 12–14C. Latin *dividere* to force apart, to separate. Cp. DEVISE.

dividend *n.* the share of the interest or profit which belongs to each shareholder in a company, bearing the same proportion to the whole profit that the shareholder's capital bears to the whole capital. WH: 15C. Anglo-French *dividende*, from Latin *dividendum*, neut. ger. (used as n.) of *dividere* DIVIDE. See also -END.

divi-divi *n.* a tropical American tree, *Caesalpinia coriaria*. WH: 19C. American Spanish, from Carib.

divine¹ *a.* of or relating to God or gods. *Also n.* WH: 12–14C. Old French *devin*, later *divin*, from Latin *divinus*, from *divus* godlike, rel. to *deus* god.

divine² *v.t.* to find out by inspiration or intuition. *Also v.i.* WH: 14–15C. Old French *deviner*, from Latin *divinare* to foretell, to predict. Cp. DIVINE¹. The original sense was to determine by supernatural means.

divinity *n.* the quality of being divine. WH: 12–14C. Old French *divinité*, from Latin *divinitas, divinitatis*, from *divinus* DIVINE¹. See also -ITY.

divisible *a.* capable of division. WH: 14–15C. Old French, or from Late Latin *divisibilis*, from Latin *divisus*. See DIVISION, also -IBLE.

division *n.* the act of dividing. WH: 14–15C. Old French *devisiun* (Modern French *division*), from Latin *divisio, divisionis*, from *divisus*, p.p. of *dividere* DIVIDE. See also -ION.

divisive *a.* forming or noting separation or division, analytical. WH: 16C. Late Latin *divisivus*, from Latin *divisus*. See DIVISION, also -IVE.

divorce *n.* the dissolution of a marriage. *Also v.t., v.i.* WH: 14–15C. Old French, from Latin *divortium* separation, from *divortere*, *divertere* DIVERT.

divot *n.* a piece of turf torn up by the head of a golf club when driving. WH: 16C. Orig. unknown. The word originally occurred in the phrase *fail and divot*. See FAIL².

divulge *v.t.* to make known; to reveal. *Also v.i.* WH: 14–15C. Latin *divulgare*, from DI-¹ + *vulgare* to publish, to propagate, from *vulgus* common people. The original sense (to the 18C) was to make known publicly, to publish. The current sense dates from the 17C.

divvy¹ *n.* a dividend; a share. *Also v.t.* WH: 19C. Abbr. of DIVIDEND.

divvy² *n.* a stupid person; an idiot. *Also a.* WH: late 20C. Orig. unknown.

Diwali *n.* a Hindu festival honouring Lakshmi, the goddess of wealth, celebrated from October to November and marked by the lighting of lamps. WH: 17C. Hindi *diwālī*, from Sanskrit *dīpāvalī*, *dīpalī* row of lights, from *dīpa* light, lamp.

Dixie *n.* the US southern states. WH: 19C. Orig. unknown. According to some, the region is so named because it is south of the MASON-DIXON LINE¹. According to others, it is from *Dixie*, a nickname of New Orleans, so called from the ten-dollar bills printed there, from French *dix* ten.

dixie *n.* a pot for cooking over an outdoor fire. WH: early 20C. Hindi *degcī* cooking pot, from Persian *degča*, dim. of *deg* iron pot.

dizzy *a.* giddy, dazed. *Also v.t.* WH: pre-1200. Old English *dysig*, from Germanic. See also -Y¹. The Old English word is translated as foolish in the AV New Testament (in the parable of the wise and foolish virgins, Matt. xxv).

djellaba *n.* a cloak with wide sleeves and a hood, worn by men in N Africa and the Middle East. WH: 19C. Moroccan Arabic *jellāb*.

D.Litt. *abbr.* Doctor of Literature, Doctor of Letters. WH: Abbr. of Latin *Doctor Litterarum* Doctor of Letters.

DNA *n.* the main constituent of chromosomes, in the form of a double helix, which is self-replicating and transmits hereditary characteristics. WH: mid-20C. Abbr. of DEOXYRIBONUCLEIC ACID.

DNase *n.* an enzyme which hydrolyses DNA. WH: mid-20C. DNA + -ASE.

do *v.t.* to perform or carry out (a work, service etc.). *Also v.i., v.aux.*, *n.* WH: pre-1200. Old English *dōn*, from Germanic, from Indo-European base also of Sanskrit *dadhāmi* to put, Greek *tithēmi* I place, Latin *facere* to make, to do. Cp. DEED, DOOM.

dob *v.t.* to betray. WH: mid-20C. Var. of DAB¹.

dobbin *n.* a draught horse. WH: 16C. Male personal name *Dobbin* (dim. of *Dob*), alt. of *Robin* (*Rob*). Cp. ROBIN.

dobby *n.* an attachment to a loom for weaving small figures. WH: 17C. ? From pers. name *Dobbie*, from *Dob* (see DOBBIN) + -Y³.

dobe *n.* an adobe. WH: 19C. Shortening of ADOBE.

Dobermann *n.* a large breed of dog with a smooth black and tan coat, used as a guard dog. WH: early 20C. Ludwig *Dobermann*, 19C German dog breeder + *Pinscher* a type of terrier, ? orig. from *Pinzgau* valley, Austria.

dobra *n.* the standard monetary unit of Sao Tomé e Principe. WH: late 20C. Portuguese fold, from Latin *dupla*, fem. of *duplus* double, DUPLE.

dobsonfly *n.* a large N American neuropterous insect of the family Corydalidae, esp. *Corydalis cornutus*, whose larvae are used as fishing bait. WH: 19C. 1st element of unknown orig. + FLY¹.

doc *n.* a doctor. WH: 19C. Abbr. of DOCTOR.

Docetae *n.pl.* a sect in the early Church who maintained that Christ had not a natural but only a phantasmal or celestial body. WH: 18C. Medieval Latin, from Patristic Greek *Dokētai*, from Greek *dokein* to seem, to appear. Cp. DOXOLOGY.

docile *a.* tractable; easily managed. WH: 15C. Latin *docilis*, from *docere* to teach.

dock¹ *n.* an artificial basin in which ships are built or repaired. *Also v.t., v.i.* WH: 14–15C. From Germanic, of unknown orig.

dock² *n.* the enclosure for prisoners in a criminal court. WH: 16C. Prob. orig. cant word rel. to Flemish *dok* hen coop, rabbit hutch.

dock³ *n.* a common name for various species of the genus *Rumex*, perennial herbs, esp. the common dock, *R. obtusifolius*. WH: pre-1200. Old English *docce*, of Germanic orig.

dock⁴ *v.t.* to cut the tail off. *Also n.* WH: 14–15C. ? Identical to 2nd element of Old English *fingerdoccan* finger muscles, rel. to Frisian *dok* bunch, ball, Low German *dokke* bundle of straw, Old High German *tocka* doll.

docket *n.* a summary or digest. *Also v.t.* WH: 15C. Orig. uncertain. ? From DOCK⁴ + -ET¹.

doctor *n.* a qualified practitioner of medicine or surgery. *Also v.t., v.i.* WH: 12–14C. Old French *doctour*, from Latin *doctor* teacher, from *doctus*, p.p. of *docere* to teach. See also -OR. The current sense evolved from the teacher of medicine, or qualified doctor of medicine.

doctrinaire *a.* visionary, theoretical, impractical. *Also n.* WH: 19C. French, from DOCTRINE + -aire -ARY¹. The word was originally used by French political extremists of those who supported a 'doctrine' of compromise.

doctrine *n.* what is taught. WH: 14–15C. Old French, from Latin *doctrina* teaching, learning, from DOCTOR. See also -INE.

docudrama *n.* a television film of a dramatized version of a true story. WH: mid-20C. *documentary* (DOCUMENT¹) + DRAMA.

document¹ *n.* a written or printed paper containing information for the establishment of facts. WH: 14–15C. Old French, from Latin *documentum* lesson, proof, from *docere* to teach. See also -MENT.

document² *v.t.* to furnish with the documents necessary to establish any fact. WH: 17C. DOCUMENT¹.

dodder¹ *v.i.* to shake, to tremble, to totter. WH: 17C. Alt. of obs. *dadder* to quake, to tremble, of uncertain orig. Cp. DITHER.

dodder² *n.* a plant of the genus *Cuscuta*, which consists of slender, twining, leafless parasites, enveloping and destroying the plants on which they grow. WH: 12–14C. Of Germanic orig. Cp. German *Dotter*.

doddered *a.* (of an aged oak etc.) having lost its top or its branches. WH: 17C. Appar. from obs. *dod* to make the top of something blunt, rounded or bare, of unknown orig., later assoc. with DODDER² + -ED.

doddle *n.* something very easily accomplished. WH: mid-20C. Orig. uncertain. ? From var. of TODDLE or DAWDLE. Cp. DODDER¹.

dodeca- *pref.* twelve. WH: Greek *dōdeka* twelve.

dodecagon *n.* a plane figure of 12 equal angles and sides. WH: 17C. Greek *dōdekagōnon*, from *dōdeka* twelve + *-gōnos* -GON.

dodecagynian *a.* of or relating to the Dodecagynia, a Linnaean order of plants, containing those having from 12–19 free styles. WH: 18C. Modern Latin *Dodecagynia*, from Greek *dōdeka* twelve + *gunē* woman, female, (here) pistil. Cp. DODECANDROUS.

dodecahedron *n.* a solid figure of 12 equal sides, each of which is a regular pentagon. WH: 16C. Greek *dōdekaedron*, from *dōdeka* twelve + *hedron* seat, face.

dodecandrous *a.* of or relating to the Dodecandria, a Linnaean class of plants, comprising those having 12–19 free stamens. WH: 19C. Modern Latin *Dodecandria*, from Greek *dōdeka* twelve + *anēr, andros* man, male, (here) stamen + -OUS. Cp. DODECAGYNIAN.

dodecaphonic *a.* twelve-note. WH: mid-20C. DODECA- + *-phonic*, from Greek *phōnē* sound, voice + -IC.

dodecasyllable *n.* a metrical line of 12 syllables. WH: 18C. DODECA- + SYLLABLE.

dodge *v.i.* to move aside suddenly. *Also v.t., n.* WH: 16C. Orig. unknown. ? Rel. to Scottish dial. *dodd* to jog. Cp. SLED/ SLEDGE¹.

Dodgem® *n.* a bumper car in an amusement ground. WH: early 20C. DODGE + '*em* (THEM).

dodo *n.* a large extinct bird, *Raphus cucullatus*, formerly found in Mauritius. WH: 17C. Portuguese *doudo* simpleton, fool. Cp. DOTTEREL. The bird was so named from its awkward appearance.

Dodonaean *a.* of or relating to Jupiter, worshipped in the temple of Dodona, in Epirus, where there was a famous oracle. WH: 16C. Latin *Dodonaeus*, from Greek *Dōdōnaios*, from *Dōdōne* Dodona. See also -EAN.

doe *n.* the female of the fallow deer. WH: pre-1200. Old English *dā*, of unknown orig.

doek *n.* a head-cloth, worn by married women. WH: 18C. Afrikaans cloth. Cp. DUCK³.

doff *v.t.* to take off (clothing, esp. one's hat). *Also v.i.* WH: 14–15C. Contr. of *do off*. See DO, OFF. Cp. DON².

dog *n.* a domesticated mammal of numerous breeds classed together as *Canis familiaris. Also v.t.* WH: pre-1200. Old English *docga*, of unknown orig. The word was originally the name of a specific powerful breed of dog. The general Old English word was *hund* HOUND.

Dogberry *n.* an officious constable or policeman. WH: 19C. Name of a foolish constable in Shakespeare's *Much Ado About Nothing* (1599).

dogberry *n.* the fruit of the dogwood. WH: 16C. DOG + BERRY. Cp. DOGWOOD. The fruit is perhaps so named because it is regarded as inferior in size or quality. Cp. *dog Latin, dog-violet* (DOG).

doge *n.* the title of the chief magistrate of the republics of Venice and Genoa. WH: 16C. French, from Italian, from Venetian Italian *doze*, ult. from Latin *dux, ducis* leader. Cp. DUKE.

dogged *a.* stubborn, persistent. WH: 12–14C. DOG + -ED. The original sense was having the bad qualities of a dog, so mean, vicious, spiteful. The current sense evolved in the 14–15C.

dogger¹ *n.* a Dutch fishing boat with bluff bows like a ketch, employed in the North Sea in the cod and herring fishery. WH: 12–14C. Middle Dutch trawler, fishing boat. ? Rel. to DOG. Cp. CAT².

dogger² *n.* a large concretion occurring in some sedimentary rocks. WH: 17C. ? From DOG.

doggerel *n.* verses written with little regard to rhythm or rhyme. *Also a.* WH: 14–15C. Appar. from DOG + *-rel*, from Old French *-erel* (Modern French *-eau*), suf. denoting contemptuous or dim. sense, as in COCKEREL, DOTTEREL, MONGREL, SCOUNDREL. Cp. *dog Latin* (DOG).

doggone *a., adv.* damned. *Also int.* WH: 19C. Prob. alt. of *God damn* by kind of inversion.

dogie *n.* a motherless calf. WH: 19C. Orig. unknown.

dogma *n.* an established principle, tenet or system of doctrines put forward to be received on authority, esp. that of a Church, as opposed to one deduced from experience or reasoning. WH: 16C. Late Latin, from Greek *dogma, dogmatos* opinion, decree, from *dokein* to seem good, to think.

dogwood *n.* any shrub of the genus *Cornus*, esp. *C. sanguinea*, the wild cornel, with white flowers and purple berries. WH: 16C. DOG + WOOD. The shrub is apparently so named from the DOGBERRY that it bears. According to some, it is so called because its odour suggests that of a wet dog.

doh *n.* the first note of a major scale in the tonic sol-fa system of notation. WH: 18C. Arbitrary, replacing earlier UT.

doily *n.* a small ornamental mat or napkin on which to place cakes, sandwiches, bottles, glasses etc. WH: 17C. *Doiley (Doyley)*, name of a 17C London haberdasher.

doing *n.* something done or performed; an event, transaction, proceeding, affair. WH: 12–14C. DO + -ING¹.

†doit *n.* a small Dutch copper coin worth about half a farthing. WH: 16C. Middle Dutch *duit*.

doited *a.* crazed; mentally affected, esp. by old age. WH: 14–15C. Orig. uncertain. ? Alt. of *doted*, p.p. of DOTE.

dojo *n.* a room where martial arts are practised. WH: mid-20C. Japanese, from *dō* way, pursuit + *-jō* place.

dolabriform *a.* having the form of an axe; hatchet-shaped. WH: 18C. Latin *dolabra* pickaxe + *-i-* + -FORM.

Dolby® *n.* a system used to cut down interference on broadcast or recorded sound. WH: mid-20C. Ray M. *Dolby*, 1933– , US engineer, its inventor.

dolce *adv.* sweetly, softly. *Also a.* WH: 19C. Italian sweet, from Latin *dulcis*. Cp. DULCET.

Dolcelatte *n.* a kind of soft, blue-veined, Italian cheese. WH: mid-20C. Italian *dolce latte* sweet milk, from DOLCE + *latte* milk, from Latin *lac, lactis*.

doldrums *n.pl.* low spirits, the dumps. WH: 18C. *doldrum*, ? from DULL, based on TANTRUM + -S¹.

dole¹ *n.* unemployment benefit. *Also v.t.* WH: pre-1200. Old English *dāl*, from Germanic base also of DEAL¹. The sense to the 16C was part or division of a whole. The sense gift of food or money arose in the 14–15C and in turn gave the current colloquial sense early in the 20C.

dole² *n.* sorrow, lamentation. WH: 12–14C. Old French *dol, duel* mourning (Modern French *deuil*), from Popular Latin *dolus*, from Latin *dolere* to grieve.

dolerite *n.* a variety of trap-rock consisting of feldspar and pyroxene. WH: 19C. French *dolérite*, from Greek *doleros* deceptive. See also -ITE¹. The rock is so named because it is difficult to distinguish from diorite.

dolichocephalic *a.* long-headed (applied to skulls in which the width from side to side bears a less proportion to the width from front to back than 80%). WH: 19C. Greek *dolikhos* narrow + -CEPHALIC.

dolichos *n.* any plant of the genus *Dolichos*, having long pods allied to the kidney bean. WH: 18C. Modern Latin, from Greek *dolikhos* long, ref. to length of pods.

dolichosaurus *n.* a small snakelike reptile from the Cretaceous era. WH: 19C. Modern Latin, from Greek *dolikhos* long + *sauros* lizard.

dolina *n.* a funnel-shaped depression in the earth. WH: 19C. Slovene valley.

doll *n.* a child's toy representing a human figure. WH: 16C. Pet form of female forename *Dorothy*. Cp. MARIONETTE. A similar substitution of *l* for *r* in personal names occurs in the pairs *Hal/ Harry, Sal/ Sarah, Moll/ Mary*.

dollar *n.* the chief unit of currency of the US, Canada, Australia, New Zealand etc. WH: 16C. Early Flemish and Low German *daler*, from German *Taler* (formerly *thaler*), abbr. of *Joachimsthaler* coin from the silver mine of *Joachimstal* St Joachim's valley, now Jáchymov, Czech Republic. The name was originally that of a German coin, then (as *dollar*) of the Spanish *peso* (piece of eight) circulating in N America at the time of the American War of Independence, 1775–83. The dollar was officially established as US currency in 1785.

dollop *n.* a shapeless lump. *Also v.t.* WH: 16C. ? Scandinavian. Cp. Norwegian (dial.) *dolp* lump.

dolly *n.* a doll (used by or to children). *Also v.t., v.i., a.* WH: 17C. DOLL + -Y³.

Dolly Varden *n.* a large-patterned print dress. WH: 19C. *Dolly Varden*, a vain young woman in Charles Dickens's *Barnaby Rudge* (1841).

dolma *n.* a vine leaf stuffed with rice and meat. WH: 17C. Modern Greek *ntolmas*, from Turkish *dolma*, from *dolmak* to fill, to be filled.

dolman *n.* a long Turkish robe, open in front, and with narrow sleeves. WH: 16C. French *doliman*, from Turkish *dolama*, lit. act of winding, from *dolamak* to wind.

dolmen *n.* a cromlech; the megalithic framework of a chambered cairn, consisting usually of three or more upright stones supporting a roof-stone. WH: 19C. French, ? from Cornish *tolmen* hole stone. Cp. MENHIR.

dolomite *n.* a brittle, translucent mineral consisting of the carbonates of lime and magnesia. WH: 18C. French, from Déodat de *Dolomieu*, 1750–1801, French geologist. See also -ITE¹. Dolomieu also gave the name of the *Dolomite* mountains in the Italian Alps, where rocks contain the mineral.

doloroso *a., adv.* (to be performed) in a soft, dolorous manner. WH: 19C. Italian doloroso, from Latin *dolorosus*.

dolorous *a.* full of pain or grief. WH: 14–15C. Old French *doleros* (Modern French *douloureux*), from Late Latin *dolorosus*, from Latin *dolor*. See DOLOUR, also -OUS.

dolour *n.* pain, suffering, distress; grief, sorrow, lamentation. WH: 12–14C. Old French *dolor* (Modern French *douleur*), from Latin *dolor* pain, grief. See also -OUR.

dolphin *n.* any sea mammal of the family Delphinidae, having a beaklike snout. WH: 14–15C. Old French *daulphin*, from Provençal *dalfin*, from Medieval Latin *dalphinus*, from Latin *delphinus*, from Greek *delphin* (earlier *delphis*). Cp. DAUPHIN.

dolt *n.* a stupid person; a numskull. WH: 16C. ? Var. of *dulled*, p.p. of DULL.

DOM *abbr.* to God the best and greatest . WH: Abbr. of Latin *Deo Optimo Maximo* to God, the best, the greatest, from dat. of *Deus Optimus Maximus*.

Dom *n.* in the Roman Catholic Church, a title given to members of the Benedictine and Carthusian orders. WH: 17C. Abbr. of Latin *dominus* lord, master, or from Portuguese *dom*, from Latin *dominus*.

-dom *suf.* denoting power, jurisdiction, office or condition, a group of people, as in *kingdom, freedom*. WH: Old English *-dōm*, use as suf. of *dōm* DOOM. Cp. German *-tum*.

domain *n.* territory over which authority or control is exercised. WH: 14–15C. French *domaine*, alt. (by assoc. with Latin *dominus* lord, master) of Old French *demaine* DEMESNE.

domaine *n.* a vineyard. WH: mid-20C. French DOMAIN.

dome¹ *n.* a roof, usually central, the base of which is a circle, an ellipse or a polygon, and its vertical section a curved line, concave towards the interior; a cupola. *Also v.t., v.i.* WH: 16C. French *dôme*, from Italian *duomo* house, house of God, cathedral, cupola, from Latin *domus*. The poetic sense house, building comes direct from Latin *domus*.

†dome² *n.* doom. WH: 12–14C. Early form of DOOM.

Domesday *n.* a register of the lands of England compiled (1086) by order of William the Conqueror. WH: pre-1200. Old English *dōmes dæg*, from gen. of *dōm* DOOM + *dæg* DAY + BOOK. The *Domesday Book* is so called because its judgement was final, like that of Doomsday.

domestic *a.* employed or kept at home. *Also n.* WH: 14–15C. Old French *domestique*, from Latin *domesticus*, from *domus* house, based on *rusticus* RUSTIC etc.

domesticity *n.* the state of being domestic. WH: 18C. DOMESTIC + -ITY.

domicile *n.* a house, a home. *Also v.t., v.i.* WH: 14–15C. Old French, from Latin *domicilium*, from *domus* house.

dominant *a.* ruling, governing. *Also n.* WH: 14–15C. Old French, from Latin *dominans, dominantis*, pres.p. of *dominari* DOMINATE. See also -ANT.

dominate *v.t.* to predominate over. *Also v.i.* WH: 17C. Latin *dominatus*, p.p. of *dominari* to rule, to govern, from *dominus* lord, master. See also -ATE³.

dominee *n.* a minister in any of the Afrikaner Churches in S Africa. WH: mid-20C. Afrikaans and Dutch, from Latin *domine*, voc. of *dominus* lord, master. Cp. DOMINIE.

domineer *v.i.* to exercise authority arrogantly and tyrannically; to assume superiority over others. *Also v.t.* WH: 16C. Dutch *domineren*, from Old French *dominer*, from Latin *dominari* DOMINATE. See also -EER. Cp. COMMANDEER.

dominical *a.* among Christians, of or relating to the Lord or the Lord's Day. *Also n.* WH: 12–14C. Old French, or from Late Latin *dominicalis*, from Latin *dominicus*, from *dominus* lord, master. See also -IC, -AL¹.

Dominican *n.* a member of an order of preaching friars; a Black Friar. *Also a.* WH: 16C. Medieval Latin *Dominicanus*, from *Dominicus*, from St Dominic (Spanish *Domingo de Guzmán*), *c.*1170–1221, founder in 1215 of order named for him. See also -AN.

dominie *n.* a teacher, a schoolmaster. WH: 17C. Latin *domine*, voc. of *dominus* lord, master. Cp. DOMINEE.

dominion *n.* sovereign authority; control. WH: 12–14C. Old French, from Medieval Latin *dominio, dominionis*, from *dominium* property, from *dominus* lord, master.

domino *n.* any of 28 oblong dotted pieces, orig. of bone or ivory, used in playing dominoes. WH: 17C. French hood worn by priests in winter, ? ult. from Latin *dominus* lord, master. The original sense was a type of cloak with a mask worn at masquerades. The use of the word for dominos (the game) is said to derive from the black colour of the backs of the pieces, like that of the masquerade garment.

Don *n.* a title formerly restricted to Spanish noblemen and gentlemen, now common to all men in Spain, Sir, Mr. WH: 16C. Spanish, from Latin *dominus* lord, master.

don¹ *n.* a fellow or tutor of a college, esp. at Oxford or Cambridge. WH: 17C. DON.

don² *v.t.* to put on (clothing). WH: 14–15C. Contr. of *do on*. See DO, ON. Cp. DOFF.

dona *n.* a woman. WH: 17C. Portuguese or Spanish *doña*, from Latin *domina*, fem. of *dominus*. See DON. Cp. DONNA.

donate *v.t.* to bestow as a gift, esp. on a considerable scale for public or religious purposes. WH: 18C. Back-formation from DONATION.

donation *n.* the act of giving. WH: 14–15C. Old French, from Latin *donatio, donationis*, from *donatus*, p.p. of *donare* to give, from *donum* gift. See also -ATION.

Donatism *n.* the doctrine of an Arian sect, founded in ad 311 by *Donatus*, who denied the infallibility of the Church and insisted on individual holiness as a condition of membership. WH: 16C. Medieval Latin *Donationus*, from *Donatus*, 4C AD bishop of Carthage. See also -ISM.

donative *n.* a gift, a present, a gratuity, esp. an official donation. *Also a.* WH: 14–15C. Latin *donativum* largesse, from *donatus*. See DONATION, also -IVE.

done *a.* performed, executed. *Also int.* WH: 12–14C. P.p. of DO.

donee *n.* the person to whom anything is given. WH: 16C. DONOR. See also -EE.

doner kebab *n.* spit-roasted lamb served in pitta bread, usually with salad. WH: mid-20C. Turkish *döner kebap*, from *döner* rotating + *kebap* KEBAB.

dong¹ *v.i.* to make the sound of a large bell. *Also v.t., n.* WH: 16C. Imit. Cp. BONG, DING-DONG.

dong² *n.* the standard unit of currency of Vietnam. WH: 19C. Vietnamese coin, piastre.

donga *n.* a gully, a watercourse with steep sides. WH: 19C. Nguni.

dongle *n.* an electronic device used to protect software from unauthorized use. WH: late 20C. Arbitrary.

donjon *n.* the grand central tower or keep of a castle, esp. a medieval Norman one, the lower storey generally used as a prison. WH: 12–14C. Old French DUNGEON.

donkey *n.* a long-eared member of the horse family, an ass. WH: 18C. Orig. uncertain. The word originally rhymed with MONKEY, suggesting a derivation either in DUN¹ or in the male personal name *Duncan*. Cp. CUDDY¹, DICKY¹, NEDDY.

donna *n.* an Italian lady. WH: 17C. Italian lady, from Latin *domina*. See DONA.

donnée *n.* a subject, a theme. WH: 19C. French, fem. p.p. of *donner* to give.

donnybrook *n.* a rowdy brawl. WH: 19C. *Donnybrook*, a suburb of Dublin, Ireland, formerly famous for its annual fair.

donor *n.* a giver. WH: 14–15C. Old French *doneur*, from Latin *donator*, from *donatus*. See DONATION, also -OR.

doodah *n.* any small decorative article or gadget. WH: early 20C. Refrain *doo-dah* of Stephen Foster's plantation song 'Camptown Races' (1850).

doodle *v.i.* to draw pictures or designs absent-mindedly while thinking or listening. *Also n.* WH: 19C. ? From *doodle* foolish person, from Low German *dudel-* in *dudeltopf* simple fellow, influ. by DAWDLE.

doodlebug *n.* the earliest type of flying bomb used by the Germans in the war of 1939–45, the V-1. WH: 19C. DOODLE + BUG[1]. The sense of flying bomb dates from the mid-20C and may have been reinforced by BUG[2] since all other earlier senses lack the idea of worry or terror.

doohickey *n.* any small mechanical device. WH: early 20C. DOODAH + HICKEY.

doolally *a.* insane, eccentric. WH: early 20C. *Deolali*, a town near Bombay (Mumbai), India, location of a military sanatorium.

doolie *n.* a covered litter of bamboo. WH: 17C. Hindi *ḍolī*, dim. of *ḍolā* cradle, swing, litter, from Sanskrit *ḍolā* to swing.

doom *n.* fate (usu. in an evil sense). *Also v.t.* WH: pre-1200. Old English *dōm*, from Germanic, from base meaning to place, to set, represented also by DO.

Doona® *n.* a duvet. WH: late 20C. ? Based on DOWN[2].

door *n.* a frame of wood or metal, usually on hinges, closing the entrance to a building, room etc. WH: pre-1200. Old English *duru*, from Germanic, from Indo-European base also of Latin *foris* (see FOREIGN), Greek *thura*, Sanskrit *dur*.

doozy *n.* something wonderful or excellent. WH: early 20C. Said to be from *Deusenberg*, name of expensive and fashionable car.

dop *n.* a kind of cheap brandy. WH: 19C. Afrikaans, of uncertain orig. The word is perhaps from *doppe* husks of grapes or *dop* cup.

dopa *n.* an amino acid, a precursor of dopamine. WH: early 20C. German, from letters of Dihydroxyphenyl*a*lanine.

dopamine *n.* a chemical found in the brain, acting as a neurotransmitter, a precursor of adrenalin. WH: mid-20C. DOPA + AMINE.

dopant *n.* a substance used to dope a semiconductor. WH: mid-20C. DOPE + -ANT.

dope *n.* a varnish used for waterproofing, protecting and strengthening the fabric parts of an aircraft. *Also v.t., v.i., a.* WH: 19C. Dutch *doop* sauce, from *doopen* to dip, to mix.

doppelgänger *n.* the apparition of a living person; a wraith. WH: 19C. German, lit. double-goer, from *Doppel* double + *Gänger* goer.

Dopper *n.* a member of the Reformed Church of S Africa, characterized by extreme simplicity of manners and dress. WH: 19C. Orig. uncertain. ? Afrikaans *doper* baptist. Afrikaans *dompen* to suppress and *dorper* townsman have also been suggested.

dopplerite *n.* a black substance found in peat beds. WH: 19C. Christian *Doppler* (see DOPPLER'S PRINCIPLE) + -ITE[1].

Doppler's principle *n.* the principle that when the source of any wave motion is approached, the frequency appears greater than it would to an observer moving away. WH: 19C. Christian *Doppler*, 1803–53, Austrian physicist.

dor *n.* any of several insects that make a loud humming noise in flying, esp. the black dung-beetle, *Geotrupes stercorarius*. WH: pre-1200. Prob. imit.

dorado *n.* a fish, *Coryphaena hippurus*, of brilliant colouring. WH: 17C. Spanish gilded, from Late Latin *deauratus*, p.p. of *deaurare* to gild over. See DORY[1].

Dorcas Society *n.* a charitable association for providing clothes for the poor. WH: 19C. *Dorcas*, a woman in the New Testament who made coats and garments and who 'was full of good works and alms deeds' (Acts ix.36). The name Dorcas is a translation of Aramaic *Tabitha*, from Greek *dorkas* deer, gazelle.

Dorian *n.* an inhabitant of Doris. *Also a.* WH: 16C. Latin *Dorius*, from Greek *Dōrios* of Doris, a division of ancient Greece + -IAN.

dork *n.* a stupid or socially awkward person. WH: late 20C. Alt. of DICK[1] in sense penis.

Dorking *n.* a breed of domestic fowl, orig. from Dorking. WH: 18C. *Dorking*, a town in Surrey.

dormant *a.* in a state resembling sleep, inactive. WH: 14–15C. Old French, pres.p. of *dormir*, from Latin *dormire* to sleep. See also -ANT.

dormer *n.* a window set in a sloping roof with a vertical frame and a gable. WH: 16C. Old French *dormëor*, from *dormir* (see DORMANT). A dormer was originally the window of a dormitory.

dormitive *a.* promoting sleep; narcotic, soporific. *Also n.* WH: 16C. French *dormitif*, from Latin *dormitus*, p.p. of *dormire* to sleep. See also -IVE.

dormitory *n.* a sleeping room, esp. in a school or public institution, containing a number of beds. WH: 14–15C. Latin *dormitorium*, use as n. of neut. of *dormitorius*, from *dormitus*. See DORMITIVE, also -ORY[1].

Dormobile® *n.* a van equipped for living in while travelling. WH: mid-20C. DORMITORY + AUTOMOBILE (or MOBILE).

dormouse *n.* a small British hibernating rodent, *Muscardinus avellanarius*. *Also a.* WH: 14–15C. Orig. unknown. The word has become associated with French *dormir* or Latin *dormire* to sleep and MOUSE[1].

dormy *a.* in golf, of or relating to a player who is as many holes ahead of their opponent as there remain holes to play. WH: 19C. Orig. unknown. The word is popularly associated with French *dormir* to sleep (or the related past participle *endormi* asleep) as if the player can relax or take a nap.

dornick *n.* a stout damask linen cloth, orig. made at Tournai. WH: 14–15C. *Doornik*, Flemish name of Tournai, a town in SW Belgium.

doronicum *n.* leopard's bane. WH: 16C. Modern Latin, from Modern Greek *dōronikon*, from Persian *darūnak*.

dorp *n.* a small town. WH: 15C. Dutch village. Cp. THORP.

dorsal *a.* of or relating to the back. WH: 14–15C. Old French, or from Late Latin *dorsalis*, from Latin *dorsualis*, from DORSUM. See also -AL[1]. Cp. DOSSAL.

dorsiferous *a.* (of ferns) having seeds at the back of the frond. WH: 18C. *dorsi-* (DORSO-) + -FEROUS.

dorsiflexion *n.* a bending backwards. WH: 19C. *dorsi-* (DORSO-) + *flexion* (FLEXIBLE).

dorsigrade *a.* walking on the back of the toes. WH: 19C. *dorsi-* (DORSO-) + -GRADE, based on DIGITIGRADE or PLANTIGRADE.

dorso- *comb. form* of, relating to or situated on the back. WH: Latin DORSUM. See also -O-.

dorsum *n.* the back. WH: 18C. Latin back.

dory[1] *n.* a golden-yellow sea fish of the family Zeidae, esp. the John Dory. WH: 12–14C. French *dorée*, fem. p.p. (used as n.) of *dorer* to gild, from Late Latin *deaurare*, from Latin DE- + *aurare* to gild, from *aurum* gold.

dory[2] *n.* a small, flat-bottomed boat. WH: 18C. ? Miskito *dóri* dugout.

doryphore *n.* a self-righteous critic. WH: mid-20C. French Colorado beetle, from Greek *doruphoros* spear carrier. The word was coined by the English writer and critic Sir Harold Nicholson, 1886–1968. The Colorado beetle is a pest.

DOS® *n.* a particular computer operating system. WH: mid-20C. Acronym of *d*isk *o*perating *s*ystem.

dos-à-dos *a.* (of two books) bound together but facing in opposite directions. *Also n.* WH: 19C. French back to back, from *dos* back, from Popular Latin *dossum*, from Latin DORSUM + *à* to.

dose *n.* the amount of any medicine which is taken or prescribed to be taken at one time. *Also v.t.* WH: 14–15C. French, from Late Latin *dosis*, from Greek giving, gift, portion of medicine, from *didonai* to give.

do-se-do *n.* a square dance in which dancers pass each other back to back. WH: early 20C. Alt. of DOS-À-DOS.

dosh *n.* money. WH: mid-20C. Orig. uncertain. ? From DOSS implying money needed for a lodging house. The word is popularly said to be a blend of DOLLAR and CASH[1].

doss *v.i.* to sleep. *Also n.* WH: 18C. Orig. unknown. ? Rel. to Latin DORSUM.

dossal *n.* an ornamental hanging at the back of an altar or a stall, or round the sides of a chancel. WH: 17C. Medieval Latin *dossale*, neut. of *dossalis*, from Late Latin *dorsalis* DORSAL.

dossier *n.* a collection of papers and other documents relating to a person, a thing or an event. WH: 19C. French bundle of papers in a wrapper with a label on the back, from *dos* back, from Popular Latin *dossum*, from Latin DORSUM + *-ier* -ARY[1].

dot[1] *n.* a little mark made with a pointed instrument. *Also v.t., v.i.* WH: pre-1200. Old English *dott*. The Old English word has been recorded only once, with the sense head of a boil.

dot[2] *n.* a dowry. *Also v.i.* WH: 19C. French, from Latin *dos, dotis*. See DOWER.

dotage *n.* impairment of the intellect by age. WH: 14–15C. DOTE + -AGE.

dote *v.i.* to be silly or deranged, infatuated or feeble-minded. WH: 12–14C. From Germanic. Cp. Middle Dutch *doten* to be silly.

dotterel *n.* a small migratory plover, *Eudromias morinellus* (said to be so foolishly fond of imitation that it mimics the actions of the fowler, and so allows itself to be captured). WH: 14–15C. DOTE + *-rel*, from Old French *-erel* (Modern French *-ereau*), suf. denoting dim. or derog. sense (cp. COCKEREL, DOGGEREL, MONGREL, SCOUNDREL). Cp. DODO.

dottle *n.* a plug of tobacco left unsmoked in a pipe. WH: 14–15C. DOT[1] + -LE[2].

dotty *a.* unsteady of gait, shaky. WH: 19C. DOTE + -Y[1].

douane *n.* a Continental custom house. WH: 17C. French, from Italian *duana*, from Arabic *dīwān* office, from Old Persian *dīwān* DIVAN. Cp. DEWAN.

Douay Bible *n.* an English version of the Vulgate, made by the students of the Roman Catholic college at Douai and published 1582–1609. WH: 19C. *Douai*, a town in N France.

double[1] *a.* composed of two, in a pair or in pairs. *Also adv.* WH: 12–14C. Old French *doble* (Modern French *double*), from Latin *duplus* DUPLE.

double[2] *n.* twice as much or as many, a double quantity. *Also v.t., v.i.* WH: 12–14C. DOUBLE[1].

double entendre *n.* a word or phrase with two interpretations, one of which is usually indelicate. WH: 17C. Obs. French double understanding (now *double entente*), from *double* DOUBLE[1] + *entente* ENTENTE.

doublet *n.* either of a pair. WH: 12–14C. Old French, from *double*. See DOUBLE[1], also -ET[1]. The original sense was close-fitting garment, so called because it had a double layer of material (outer and lining). Cp. *singlet* (SINGLE).

doubletree *n.* the horizontal bar on a vehicle to which the swingletree for harnessing horses is attached. WH: 19C. DOUBLE[1] + TREE, based on *single-tree* (SINGLE), var. of *swingletree* (see SWINGLE). The bar is so called because it has a swingletree at each end.

doubloon *n.* a Spanish and S American gold coin (orig. the double of a pistole). WH: 17C. French *doublon* or Spanish *doblón*, from *doble* DOUBLE[1]. See also -OON.

doublure *n.* an ornamental lining for a book cover. WH: 19C. French lining, from *doubler* to line. See also -URE.

doubt *v.t.* to hold or think questionable. *Also v.i., n.* WH: 12–14C. Old French *doter* (Modern French *douter*), from Latin *dubitare* to waver, to hesitate, from *dubius* DUBIOUS. The current spelling arose in the 15C, based on the Latin original via obsolete French *doubter*.

douce *a.* sober, sedate, peaceable, sweet, pleasant. WH: 12–14C. Old French *dous* (Modern French *doux*), from Latin *dulcis* sweet.

douceur *n.* a small present; a gift, a bribe. WH: 14–15C. French, from var. of Latin *dulcor* sweetness.

douche *n.* a jet of water or vapour directed upon some part of the body. *Also v.t., v.i.* WH: 18C. French, from Italian *doccia* conduit pipe, from *docciare* to pour by drops, from Latin *ductus* DUCT.

dough *n.* the paste of bread etc. before baking; a mass of flour or meal moistened and kneaded. WH: pre-1200. Old English *dāg*, from Germanic, from Indo-European base meaning to smear, to knead. Cp. DUFF[1].

†doughty *a.* brave, valiant. WH: pre-1200. Old English *dohtig*, earlier *dyhtig*, from Germanic. Cp. German *tüchtig* capable, efficient, brave.

Douglas fir *n.* any tall American conifer of the genus *Pseudotsuga*, grown for ornament and timber. WH: 19C. David *Douglas*, 1798–1834, Scottish botanical explorer. See FIR.

doum *n.* an Egyptian palm, *Hyphaene thebaica*, remarkable for the dichotomous division of the trunk and branches. WH: 18C. Arabic *dawm*.

dour *a.* sullen; stern. WH: 14–15C. Prob. from Gaelic *dúr* dull, stupid, ? from Latin *durus* hard.

douroucouli *n.* a nocturnal ape of the genus *Aotus*, of Central and S America. WH: 19C. Native name in S America.

douse *v.t.* to plunge into water, to dip. *Also v.i.* WH: 16C. ? Imit. (cp. SOUSE). Cp. Dutch *doesen* to beat, to strike.

dove *n.* any bird of the family Columbidae, resembling a pigeon, but smaller and paler. WH: 12–14C. Old Norse *dúfa*, from Germanic base that is prob. imit. of bird's cry. Cp. German *Taube* dove. According to some, the word is related to DIVE, referring to the bird's dipping flight. Doves are usually thought of as 'coming down' from above.

Dover's powder *n.* a sweat-inducing compound, with opium, potassium sulphate and ipecacuanha. WH: 19C. Thomas *Dover*, 1660–1742, English physician.

dovetail *n.* a mode of fastening boards together by fitting tenons, shaped like a dove's tail spread out, into corresponding cavities. *Also v.t., v.i.* WH: 16C. DOVE + TAIL[1].

dowager *n.* a widow in possession of a dower or jointure. WH: 16C. Old French *douagiere*, from *douage* dower, from *douer* to portion out, from Latin *dotare*. See DOWER, also -ER[2].

dowdy *a.* dull, unfashionable. *Also n.* WH: 16C. From *dowd* shabby person, of unknown orig. + -Y[3].

dowel *n.* a pin or peg for connecting two stones or pieces of wood, being sunk into the side of each. *Also v.t.* WH: 12–14C. ? Middle High German *dovel*, from Germanic, from Indo-European base also of Greek *tuphos* wedge.

dower *n.* the part of a husband's property which his widow enjoys during her life. *Also v.t.* WH: 14–15C. Old French *douaire*, from Medieval Latin *dotarium*, from Latin *dotare* to endow, from *dos, dotis* dowry, DOT[2], rel. to *dare* to give. See also -ARY[1].

dowie *a.* dull, low-spirited, dreary. WH: 16C. Orig. uncertain. ? Ult. from DULL + -Y[1].

dowitcher *n.* a wading bird of the genus *Limnodromus*, found on the shores of arctic and subarctic N America. WH: 19C. Iroquoian, rel. to Mohawk and Cayuga *tawis*, Onondaga *tawish*.

Dow–Jones index *n.* an index of the prices of stocks and shares on the New York Stock Exchange. WH: early 20C. *Dow Jones & Co.*, US financial news agency, from Charles H. *Dow*, 1851–1902, and Edward D. *Jones*, *c.*1855–1920, US economists.

down[1] *adv.* towards the ground. *Also prep., a., v.t., v.i., n.* WH: pre-1200. Shortening of *adown*, from Old English *adūne*, from a- A-[1] + *dūn* DOWN[3].

down[2] *n.* the fine soft plumage of young birds or the plumage found under the feathers. WH: 12–14C. Old Norse *dúnn*, from Germanic. Cp. German *Daune*.

down[3] *n.* a tract of upland, esp. the chalk uplands of southern England, used for pasturing sheep. WH: pre-1200. Old English *dūn* hill, ? ult. from Celtic. Cp. DUN[3]. Rel. to DUNE, TOWN.

Down's syndrome *n.* a genetic disorder characterized by lower than average intelligence, short stature, sloping eyes and flattened facial features. WH: mid-20C. John Langdon-*Down*, 1828–96, English physician.

dowry *n.* the property which a wife brings to her husband. WH: 12–14C. Old French *douaire* DOWER.

dowse *v.i.* to use a dowsing rod for the discovery of subterranean waters or minerals. WH: 17C. Orig. unknown. Not rel. to DOUSE.

doxology *n.* a brief formula or hymn of praise to God. WH: 17C. Medieval Latin *doxologia*, from Greek, from *doxa* expectation, opinion, glory, from *dokein* to seem. See also -O- + -LOGY.

†doxy[1] *n.* a female lover. WH: 16C. Orig. unknown. ? Rel. to DOCK[4] with ref. to rump. Cp. TAIL[1] in sense woman regarded in sexual terms.

doxy[2] *n.* opinion, esp. in religious matters. WH: 18C. From last element of *orthodoxy* (ORTHODOX), *heterodoxy* (HETERODOX) etc.

doyen *n.* the senior member of a body of people. WH: 14–15C. French DEAN.

doze *v.i.* to sleep lightly. *Also v.t., n.* WH: 17C. Orig. uncertain. ? A dial. word. Cp. Danish *døse* to make drowsy.

dozen n. an aggregate of twelve things or people. Also a. WH: 12–14C. Old French dozeine (Modern French douzaine), ult. from Latin duodecim twelve.

Dr abbr. debit. WH: Abbr. of debtor (DEBT).

drab[1] a. of a dull brown or dun colour. Also n. WH: 16C. Prob. alt. of Old French drap cloth. See DRAPE. Cp. TRAP[3].

drab[2] n. a prostitute, a slut. Also v.i. WH: 16C. ? Dutch or Low German. Cp. Dutch drab dregs. Cp. DRABBLE.

drabble v.t. to draggle; to make wet and dirty, as by dragging through filth. Also v.i. WH: 14–15C. Low German drabbelen to walk or paddle in muddy water. See also -LE[4]. Cp. DRAB[2].

dracaena n. any shrub or tree of the genera Dracaena or Cordyline. WH: 19C. Modern Latin, from Greek drakaina, fem. of drakōn DRAGON. The bark of some species is a source of the resin used as a colouring for varnishes known as dragon's blood (DRAGON).

drachm n. an apothecaries' weight of 60 grains (1/8 oz, 3.542 g). WH: 14–15C. Old French dragme or Late Latin dragma, var. of Latin drachma, from Greek drakhme an Attic weight and coin. Cp. DRAM.

drack a. unattractive. WH: mid-20C. Orig. uncertain. Cp. dreck rubbish, trash. The word is popularly associated with Dracula, or more specifically with the film Dracula's Daughter (1936).

dracone n. a large, flexible container for liquids, towed by a ship. WH: mid-20C. Greek drakōn DRAGON.

draconian a. inflexible, severe, cruel. WH: 19C. Greek Drakōn Draco, 7C BC Athenian legislator, noted for his severe penal code + -IAN.

draff n. refuse, lees, esp. of malt after brewing or distilling. WH: 12–14C. ? Old English, from Germanic source prob. also of DRIVEL. Cp. German Träber husks, grains.

draft n. the first outline of any document. Also v.t. WH: 16C. Representation of mod. pronun. of DRAUGHT.

drag v.t. to pull along the ground by main force. Also v.i., n. WH: 12–14C. Old Norse draga, or from Old English dragan DRAW.

dragée n. a sweetmeat consisting of a nut, fruit etc. with a hard sugar coating. WH: 17C. See DREDGE[2].

draggle v.t. to make wet and dirty by dragging on the ground. Also v.i. WH: 16C. Dim. and freq. of DRAG. See also -LE[4].

dragoman n. a person who acts as guide, interpreter and agent for travellers in the Middle East. WH: 14–15C. Obs. French (now drogman), from Italian dragomanno, from Medieval Greek dragoumanos, from Arabic tarjumān, from tarjama to interpret, with last element assim. to MAN. Cp. TARGUM.

dragon n. a fabulous monster found in the mythology of nearly all nations, generally as an enormous winged lizard with formidable claws etc. WH: 12–14C. Old French, from Latin draco, draconis, from Greek drakōn serpent.

dragonnade n. the persecutions of Protestants in France during the reign of Louis XIV by means of dragoons who were quartered upon them. Also v.t. WH: 18C. See DRAGOON, also -ADE.

dragoon n. a cavalry soldier, orig. a mounted infantryman armed with a short musket or carbine called a dragon. Also v.t. WH: 17C. French DRAGON. See also -OON. The original sense was a type of carbine or musket, called dragon because it belched fire.

drail n. a piece of lead on the shank of the hook of a fishing rod. Also v.i. WH: 16C. Appar. alt. of TRAIL.

drain v.t. to draw off gradually. Also v.i., n. WH: pre-1200. Old English drēahnian, prob. from Germanic base also of DRY.

drake[1] n. the male of the duck. WH: 12–14C. Low German drake, drache, from Germanic base also of second element of German Enterich drake.

drake[2] n. the mayfly. WH: pre-1200. Old English draca, from Germanic, from Latin draco DRAGON. The original sense was dragon. The current sense emerged in the 17C.

Dralon® n. an acrylic fibre, or a fabric made from it, usu. used in upholstery. WH: mid-20C. Based on NYLON. The fabric is of German origin, so the first element may represent German Draht wire, referring to some part of the manufacturing process or the fibre itself.

dram n. a drachm in apothecaries' weight. Also v.i., v.t. WH: 14–15C. Old French drame or Medieval Latin drama, vars. of Old French dragme, from Late Latin dragma. See DRACHM.

drama n. a play, usually intended for performance by living actors on the stage. WH: 16C. Late Latin, from Greek drama, dramatos, from dran to do, to act, to perform.

dramatis personae n.pl. the set of characters in a play. WH: 18C. Latin persons of the drama, from Late Latin dramatis, gen. sing. of drama DRAMA + nom. pl. of persona PERSON.

dramatist n. a writer of plays. WH: 17C. Greek DRAMA + -IST.

dramatize v.t. to set forth in the form of a drama. Also v.i. WH: 18C. Greek DRAMA, dramatos + -IZE.

dramaturge n. a dramatist, a playwright. WH: 19C. French, from German Dramaturg, from Greek dramatourgos, from DRAMA, dramatos + -ergos worker.

Drambuie® n. a liqueur with a Scotch whisky base. WH: 19C. Gaelic dram buidheach satisfying drink or dram buidhe yellow drink (or both).

drape v.t. to cover, clothe or decorate with cloth etc. Also n. WH: 14–15C. Old French draper, from drap cloth, from Late Latin drappus, ? of Celtic orig. Cp. DRAB[1].

drastic a. acting vigorously; effective. WH: 17C. Greek drastikos active, effective, from dran to do. See also -IC.

drat int. damn. WH: 19C. Shortening of od-rat, from OD[1] + rat, alt. of ROT.

draught n. a current of air. Also v.t. WH: 12–14C. Old Norse dráttr, from Germanic base also of DRAW.

draughtsman n. a person who draws, designs or plans. WH: 18C. DRAUGHT + -'S + MAN.

draughty a. full of draughts or currents of air. WH: 19C. DRAUGHT + -Y[1].

Dravidian n. a member of the people of S India and Sri Lanka speaking Tamil, Telugu, Canarese and Malayalam. Also a. WH: 19C. Sanskrit drāvida pertaining to the Tamils, from Dravida Tamil. See TAMIL, also -IAN.

draw v.t. to draft, to picture. Also v.i., n. WH: pre-1200. Old English dragan, from Germanic. Cp. German tragen to draw, to pull. The earliest senses were to pull, to come towards. The remaining chief senses (to extract, to pull out to a greater length, to make a picture) all evolved in the 12–14C.

drawee n. the person on whom a bill of exchange or order for payment in money is drawn. WH: 18C. DRAW + -EE.

drawer[1] n. a sliding boxlike receptacle in a table etc. WH: 16C. DRAW + -ER[1], based on Old French tiroir, from tirer to draw, to pull.

drawer[2] n. a person who draws. WH: 12–14C. DRAW + -ER[1].

drawing n. the act of drawing. WH: 12–14C. DRAW + -ING[1]. In drawing room, the word is from withdrawing room (WITHDRAW).

drawl v.t. to utter in a slow, lengthened tone. Also v.i., n. WH: 16C. Of Germanic orig. Cp. Dutch dralen to delay, to linger. Rel. to DRAW.

drawn a. haggard. WH: 12–14C. P.p. of DRAW. The sense of haggard evolved in the 19C.

dray n. a low cart, generally of strong and heavy construction, used by brewers etc. WH: 14–15C. From base of Old English dragan DRAW.

dread v.t. to fear greatly. Also v.i., n., a. WH: pre-1200. Old English ādrǣdan, earlier ondrǣdan, from ond- (as in ANSWER) and Germanic base of unknown orig.

dream n. a vision. Also v.i., v.t. WH: 12–14C. Prob. from Old English drēam joy, gladness, music, of Germanic orig. Cp. German Traum.

dreary a. dismal, cheerless. Also n. WH: pre-1200. Old English drēorig, from drēor gore, from Germanic, from base of Old English drēosan to drop, to fall. See also -Y[1]. Cp. German traurig sad.

dredge[1] n. an apparatus for dragging under water to bring up objects from the bottom for scientific purposes. Also v.t., v.i. WH: 15C. ? Middle Dutch dregghe grappling hook. ? Rel. to DRAG.

dredge[2] v.t. to sprinkle (flour etc.). WH: 12–14C. Old French dragie (Modern French DRAGÉE), from Medieval Latin drageia, ? from Latin tragemata spices, from Greek. Cp. DRUG.

dree v.t. to suffer, to endure. WH: pre-1200. Old English drēogan, from Germanic base also of Gothic driugan to do military service, Old Norse drýgja to perpetrate.

dreg n. the sediment or lees of liquor. WH: 12–14C. Prob. from Scandinavian. Cp. Old Norse (pl.) dreggjar, Swedish (pl.) drägg.

dreich a. tedious, wearisome, long. WH: 12–14C. From Germanic base of DREE. Cp. Old Norse drjúgr enduring, lasting.

drench *v.t.* to wet thoroughly. *Also v.i.*, *n.* WH: pre-1200. Old English *drencan*, from Germanic. Rel. to DRINK, DROWN.

Dresden china *n.* fine, delicately decorated china. *Also a.* WH: 18C. *Dresden*, a city in E Germany, near which it is made. Cp. MEISSEN.

dress *v.t.* to clothe, to attire. *Also v.i.*, *n.* WH: 12–14C. Old French *dresser*, from Latin *directus* DIRECT. The original sense (to the 17C) was to set in order, to put straight. The current sense (earlier to attire in fine clothing) evolved in the 14–15C.

dressage *n.* the training of a horse in deportment, obedience and response to signals given by the rider's body. WH: mid-20C. French, lit. training, from *dresser* to train, to drill. See DRESS.

dresser[1] *n.* a kitchen sideboard with a set of shelves for displaying plates etc. WH: 14–15C. Old French *dresseur* (Modern French *dressoir*), from *dresser* to prepare. See also -ER[2]. Cp. DRESS. The sideboard is so called as food was 'dressed' (prepared) on it.

dresser[2] *n.* a person who dresses another, esp. an actor for the stage. WH: 12–14C. DRESS + -ER[1].

dressing *n.* the act of dressing. WH: 14–15C. DRESS + -ING[1].

drey *n.* a squirrel's nest. WH: 17C. Orig. unknown.

drib †*v.t.* to entice by degrees. *Also v.i.*, *n.* WH: 17C. Alt. of DRIP.

dribble *v.i.* to fall in a quick succession of small drops. *Also v.t.*, *n.* WH: 16C. Freq. of DRIB. See also -LE[1]. The sense to slaver is probably influenced by DRIVEL. The sense to manoeuvre a football is perhaps from a different source. Cp. Dutch *dribbelen* to toddle.

drice *n.* frozen carbon dioxide in granular form. WH: mid-20C. Contr. of *dry ice*.

drift *n.* something which is driven along by a wind or current. *Also v.i.*, *v.t.* WH: 12–14C. Orig. from Old Norse *drift* snowdrift, later from Middle Dutch *drift* drove, course, from Germanic base of DRIVE.

drill[1] *n.* a metal tool for boring holes in hard material. *Also v.t.*, *v.i.* WH: 17C. Middle Dutch *drillen* to bore, of Germanic orig., from Indo-European base ult. of THROW. To drill soldiers is to turn them round, as a drill does when boring a hole.

drill[2] *n.* a small trench or furrow, or a ridge with a trench along the top, for seeds or small plants. *Also v.t.*, *v.i.* WH: 18C. Prob. from DRILL[1].

drill[3] *n.* a baboon from W Africa, *Mandrillus leucophaeus*. WH: 17C. Of African orig. Cp. MANDRILL.

drill[4] *n.* a heavy cotton twilled cloth used for trousers etc. WH: 18C. Shortening of *drilling*, alt. of German *Drillich*, from Latin *trilix*, *trilicis* triple-twilled, from *tri-* three + *licium* thread. Cp. TWILL.

drily *adv.* amusingly and cleverly. WH: 14–15C. DRY + -LY[2].

drink *v.t.* to swallow (a liquid). *Also v.i.*, *n.* WH: pre-1200. Old English *drincan*, from Germanic. Cp. German *trinken*.

drip *v.i.* to fall in drops. *Also v.t.*, *n.* WH: pre-1200. Old English *dryppan*, from Germanic base also of DROP.

drive *v.t.* to push or urge by force. *Also v.i.*, *n.* WH: pre-1200. Old English *drīfan*, from Germanic. Cp. German *treiben*.

drivel *n.* slaver; spittle flowing from the mouth. *Also v.i.*, *v.t.* WH: pre-1200. Old English *dreflian*, prob. rel. to DRAFF. Cp. also -LE[4].

drizzle *n.* fine, small rain. *Also v.i.*, *v.t.* WH: 16C. Prob. from Old English *drēosan* to fall. See DREARY, also -LE[4].

Dr Martens® *n.pl.* heavy lace-up boots with thick, cushioned soles. WH: mid-20C. *Dr* Klaus *Maertens*, German inventor of the sole, 1945.

drogue *n.* a bag drawn behind a boat to prevent her broaching to. WH: 18C. Orig. unknown. ? Rel. to DRAG.

droguet *n.* a ribbed woollen fabric, a kind of rep. WH: 19C. French DRUGGET.

droit *n.* a right, a due. WH: 14–15C. Old French, from use as n. of var. of Latin *directum*, neut. of *directus* DIRECT.

droll *a.* ludicrous, laughable. *Also n.*, *v.i.* WH: 17C. French *drôle*, earlier *drolle*, ? from Middle Dutch *drolle* imp, goblin. Cp. TROLL[2].

drome *n.* an aerodrome. WH: early 20C. Abbr. of AERODROME.

-drome *comb. form* a large area specially prepared for some specific purpose, as in *aerodrome*, *hippodrome*. WH: Greek *dromos* course, running, rel. to *dramein* to run.

dromedary *n.* an Arabian camel. WH: 12–14C. Old French *dromedaire* (Modern French *dromedaire*) or Late Latin *dromedarius*, from Latin *dromas*, *dromadis* dromedary, from Greek *dromas kamēlos* running camel + -ARY[1].

dromond *n.* a large medieval ship. WH: 12–14C. Old French *dromont*, from Late Latin *dromo*, *dromontis*, from Late Greek *dromōn*, from Greek *dromos*. See -DROME.

-dromous *comb. form* running, as in *anadromous*. WH: Greek *dromos* (see -DROME) + -OUS.

drone *n.* the male of the bee, larger than the worker, which makes the honey. *Also v.i.*, *v.t.* WH: pre-1200. Old English *drān*, of Germanic orig., prob. from word meaning to boom.

drongo *n.* any glossy, black, insect-eating bird of the family Dicruridae. WH: 19C. Madagascan name.

droob *n.* an ineffectual person. WH: mid-20C. Orig. uncertain. ? Alt. of DROOP. Cp. DRIP.

drool *v.i.* to drivel, to slaver. *Also n.* WH: 19C. Contr. of DRIVEL.

droop *v.i.* to lean or bend down. *Also v.t.*, *n.* WH: 12–14C. Old Norse *drúpa* to hover, to hang the head in sorrow.

drop *n.* a globule or small portion of liquid in a spherical form. *Also a.*, *v.t.*, *v.i.* WH: pre-1200. Old English *dropa*, from Germanic base also of DROOP and DRIP. Cp. German *Tropfen*.

dropsy *n.* oedema. WH: 12–14C. Shortening of obs. *hydropsy*, from Old French *idropsie*, from Medieval Latin *hydropsia*, from Latin *hydropisis*, from Greek *hudrōpiasis*, from *hudrōps*, from *hudōr*, *hudr-* water. See -IASIS. Not rel. to DROP.

droshky *n.* a Russian open four-wheeled vehicle in which the passengers ride astride a bench, their feet resting on bars near the ground. WH: 19C. Russian *drozhki* (pl.), dim. of *drogi* wagon, hearse, pl. of *droga* centre pole of a carriage.

drosometer *n.* an instrument for measuring the quantity of dew collected on a surface during the night. WH: 19C. Greek *drosos* dew + -O- + -METER.

drosophila *n.* any of the small fruit flies of the genus *Drosophila*, used in laboratory genetic experiments. WH: 19C. Modern Latin, from Greek *drosos* dew + *philos* loving.

dross *n.* the scum or useless matter left from the melting of metals. WH: pre-1200. Old English *drōs* dregs, from Germanic, from Indo-European base also of DREG.

drought *n.* dryness, dry weather; long-continued rainless weather. WH: pre-1200. Old English *drūgath*, from Germanic base of DRY.

drouk *v.t.* to drench; to duck. WH: 16C. Orig. unknown. Cp. Old Norse *drukkna* to be drowned. See DROWN.

drove *n.* a collection of animals driven in a body. *Also v.t.*, *v.i.* WH: pre-1200. Old English *drāf*, from base of DRIVE. The original sense was an act of driving.

drown *v.i.* to be suffocated in water or other liquid. *Also v.t.* WH: 12–14C. Prob. from word of Old English orig., rel. to Old Norse *drukkna* to be drowned, from Germanic base of DRINK. Rel. to DRENCH.

drowse *v.i.* to be sleepy or half asleep. *Also v.t.*, *n.* WH: pre-1200. Old English *drūsian*, from Germanic base also of *drēosan* to fall. See DREARY. The original sense was to sink, to drop. The current sense dates from the 16C, the word arising as a back-formation from *drowsy*.

drub *v.t.* to beat with a stick; to cudgel. WH: 17C. Prob. ult. from Arabic *daraba* to beat.

drudge *n.* a person employed in menial work. *Also v.i.*, *v.t.* WH: 12–14C. Appar. from stem of Old English *drēogan* DREE, or var. of obs. *drug* to pull, to drag.

drug *n.* any substance used as an ingredient in medical preparations. *Also v.t.*, *v.i.* WH: 14–15C. Old French *drogue*, of unknown orig. According to some, the word is from Latin *drogia*, an altered form of *tragemata* spices (see DREDGE[2]).

drugget *n.* a coarse woollen fabric, felted or woven, used as a covering or as a substitute for carpet. WH: 16C. French *droguet*, of unknown orig. Cp. DROGUET.

Druid *n.* one of the priests or teachers of the early Gauls and Britons or perh. of pre-Celtic peoples, who taught the transmigrating of souls, frequently celebrated their rites in oak groves, and are alleged to have offered human sacrifices. WH: 16C. French *druide* or Latin *druidae* (pl.), from Greek *druidai*, from Gaulish *druides*, rel. to Irish *draoidh* magician, sorcerer. According to some, the Gaulish word is related to Irish *dair* and Welsh *derwen* oak, and so also to Old English *trēow* TREE.

drum[1] *n.* a musical instrument made by stretching parchment over the head of a hollow cylinder or hemisphere. *Also v.i., v.t.* WH: 14–15C. Prob. from Middle Dutch and Low German *tromme*, of imit. orig. Cp. RUB-A-DUB.

drum[2] *n.* a long, narrow ridge of drift or alluvial formation. WH: 18C. Gaelic and Irish *druim* back, ridge.

Drummond light *n.* limelight or oxyhydrogen light. WH: 19C. Thomas *Drummond*, 1797–1840, Scottish engineer.

drunk *a.* intoxicated, overcome with alcoholic liquors. *Also n.* WH: 12–14C. P.p. of DRINK, shortened from *drunken*.

drupe *n.* a fleshy fruit containing a stone with a kernel, such as the peach or plum. WH: 18C. Latin *drupa* overripe olive, from Greek *druppa* olive.

Druse *n.* a member of a politico-religious sect of Islamic origin, inhabiting the region of Mt Lebanon in Syria. WH: 18C. French, from Arabic *Durūz*, pl. of *Darzī*, from name of Muḥammad ibn *Ismāʾīl ad-Darazī*, d.1019, one of the founders. Darazī's own name means tailor. Hence the name of *Darzee*, the tailor bird in Rudyard Kipling's *Jungle Book* (1894).

druse *n.* a cavity in a rock lined or studded with crystals. WH: 19C. French, from German, from Old High German *druos* gland, bump.

dry *a.* devoid of moisture. *Also n., v.t., v.i.* WH: pre-1200. Old English *drȳge*, from Germanic. Cp. German *trocken*.

dryad *n.* in mythology, a nymph of the woods. WH: 14–15C. Old French *dryade*, from Latin *Dryades*, pl. of *Dryas*, from Greek *Druas*, from *drus* tree. See also -AD[1].

dryopithecine *n.* any member of the genus *Dryopithecus* of extinct apes, thought to be the ancestors of modern apes. WH: mid-20C. Modern Latin *Dryopithecus*, from Greek *drus* tree + *pithēkos* ape. See also -INE.

dual *a.* consisting of two. *Also n., v.t.* WH: 14–15C. Latin *dualis*, from *duo* two. See also -AL[1].

duan *n.* a canto. WH: 18C. Gaelic and Irish.

dub[1] *v.t.* to confer knighthood upon by a tap with a sword on the shoulder. WH: pre-1200. Anglo-French *duber*, shortening of *aduber*, from Old French *adober* to equip with armour, to repair (Modern French *adouber*), of unknown orig.

dub[2] *v.t.* to give a new soundtrack, esp. in a different language, to (a film). WH: early 20C. Abbr. of DOUBLE[1].

dub[3] *n.* a clumsy or unskilful person. *Also v.t.* WH: 19C. ? From DUB[1].

dub[4] *v.i.* to pay (up). WH: 19C. Orig. unknown.

dub[5] *n.* a deep pool in a stream; a puddle. WH: 14–15C. Orig. unknown.

dubbin *n.* a preparation of grease for preserving and softening leather. *Also v.t.* WH: 19C. Alt. of *dubbing*, from DUB[1] + -ING[1].

dubious *a.* doubtful; wavering in mind. WH: 16C. Latin *dubiosus*, from *dubium* doubt. See also -OUS.

dubitation *n.* doubt, hesitation, uncertainty. WH: 14–15C. Old French, from Latin *dubitatio*, *dubitationis*, from *dubitatus*, p.p. of *dubitare* to doubt. See also -ATION.

Dublin Bay prawn *n.* a small European lobster, *Nephrops norvegicus*. WH: mid-20C. *Dublin Bay*, Ireland. See PRAWN.

dubnium *n.* an artificially produced radioactive element, at. no. 105, chem. symbol Db. WH: late 20C. *Dubna*, Russia, location of the Joint Institute for Nuclear Research, where orig. produced + -IUM.

Dubonnet® *n.* a sweet, red, French aperitif. WH: early 20C. Joseph *Dubonnet*, 19C French chemist and wine merchant.

ducal *a.* of or relating to a duke or duchy. WH: 15C. French, from *duc* DUKE. See also -AL[1].

ducat *n.* a coin, of gold or silver, formerly current in several European countries. WH: 14–15C. Italian *ducato* or Medieval Latin *ducatus* duchy, territory of a duke, from Latin *dux*, *ducis*. See DUKE. A ducat was originally a silver coin minted in 1140 by Robert II of Sicily as Duke of Apulia.

Duce *n.* the official title of Benito Mussolini, 1883–1945, when head of the Fascist state in Italy. WH: early 20C. Italian leader. Cp. FÜHRER.

Duchenne muscular dystrophy *n.* a severe form of muscular dystrophy, which affects mainly boys. WH: 19C. Guillaume Benjamin Amand *Duchenne*, 1806–75, French neurologist.

duchess *n.* the wife or widow of a duke. WH: 14–15C. Old French *duchesse*, from Medieval Latin *ducissa*, from Latin *dux*, *ducis*. See DUKE, also -ESS[1].

duck[1] *n.* a web-footed waterbird of the family Anatidae, esp. the domestic duck. WH: pre-1200. Old English *duce*, from Germanic base of DUCK[2].

duck[2] *v.i.* to plunge under water. *Also v.t., n.* WH: 12–14C. From (unrecorded) Old English word of Germanic orig. Cp. German *tauchen* to dive, to plunge.

duck[3] *n.* a kind of untwilled linen or cotton fabric, lighter and finer than canvas, used for jackets, aprons etc. WH: 17C. Middle Dutch *doek* linen, from Germanic source of unknown orig. Cp. German *Tuch* cloth.

duct *n.* a tube, canal or passage by which a fluid is conveyed. *Also v.t.* WH: 17C. Latin *ductus* leading, from *ductus*, p.p. of *ducere* to lead. The original sense was the action of leading.

ductile *a.* able to be drawn out into threads or wire; malleable, not brittle. WH: 12–14C. Old French, or from Latin *ductilis*. See DUCT, also -IL.

dud *n.* a useless person or thing. *Also a.* WH: 14–15C. Orig. unknown. ? Ult. rel. to DEAD. A dud was originally an article of clothing, then (in pl.) ragged clothes (16C), then useless person (19C).

dude *n.* a fop, an affected person; an aesthete. WH: 19C. Prob. from dial. German fool. Cp. Low German *dudenkop*, lit. stupid head.

dudeen *n.* a short clay tobacco pipe. WH: 19C. Irish *duídín*, dim. of *dúd* pipe. See also -EEN.

dudgeon[1] *n.* anger, sullen resentment, indignation. WH: 16C. Orig. unknown.

†**dudgeon**[2] *n.* the root of the box tree. WH: 14–15C. Orig. uncertain. Cp. Anglo-French *digeon*.

due *a.* owed, that ought to be paid. *Also adv., n.* WH: 12–14C. Old French *dëu* (Modern French *dû*), from var. of Latin *debitus* (cp. DEBIT), p.p. of *debere* to owe.

duel *n.* a combat between two persons with deadly weapons to decide a private quarrel, usu. an affair of honour. *Also v.i.* WH: 15C. Italian *duello* or Latin *duellum*, var. of *bellum* war. The word is popularly associated with Latin *duo* two.

duello *n.* a duel. WH: 16C. Italian DUEL.

duende *n.* a demon, an evil spirit. WH: early 20C. Spanish.

duenna *n.* an elderly woman employed as companion and governess to young women, a chaperone. WH: 17C. Spanish *duenna* (now *dueña*), from Latin *domina* lady, mistress. Cp. DONA, DONNA.

duet *n.* a composition for two performers, vocal or instrumental. *Also v.i.* WH: 18C. German *Duett* or Italian *duetto*, from *duo* two. See DUO, also -ET[1].

duff[1] *n.* a stiff, flour pudding boiled in a bag. WH: 19C. Var. of DOUGH. Cp. pronun. of *enough*.

duff[2] *v.t.* in golf, to bungle (a shot). *Also a.* WH: 19C. Back-formation from DUFFER.

duffel *n.* a thick, coarse kind of woollen cloth, with a thick nap. WH: 17C. *Duffel*, a town in Belgium, where originally made.

duffer *n.* a stupid, awkward or useless person. WH: 18C. Orig. unknown. Cp. DUFF[2].

dug[1] *a.* that has been dug. WH: P.p of DIG.

dug[2] *n.* a teat, a nipple of an animal. WH: 16C. Orig. unknown.

dugong *n.* a large herbivorous aquatic mammal, *Dugong dugon*, with two forelimbs only, belonging to the Sirenia, and inhabiting the Indian seas. WH: 19C. Malay *duyung*.

dugout *n.* a canoe made of a single log hollowed out, or of parts of two logs thus hollowed out and afterwards joined together. WH: 18C. DUG[1] + OUT.

duiker *n.* any of several small African antelopes of the genus *Cephalophus*. WH: 18C. Dutch diver, from Middle Dutch *dūker*, from *dūken* to dive, DUCK[2]. The antelope is so called from its habit of plunging through bushes when alarmed.

duke *n.* a noble holding the highest hereditary rank outside the royal family. WH: pre-1200. Old French *duc*, from Latin *dux*, *ducis* leader, rel. to *ducere* to lead.

Dukhobor *n.* a member of a Russian mystical sect who were oppressed for their passive resistance to militarism, and migrated in large numbers from their homes in the Caucasus to Canada. WH: 19C. Russian, from *dukh* spirit + *borets* wrestler.

dulcet *a.* sweet-sounding. WH: 14–15C. Old French *doucet*, dim. of *doux*, fem. *douce*, refashioned after Latin *dulcis* sweet. See also -ET[1].

†dulcify *v.t.* to make sweet or gentle. WH: 16C. Latin *dulcificare*, from *dulcis* sweet. See also -FY.

dulcimer *n.* a musical instrument with strings of wire, which are struck with rods. WH: 15C. Old French *doulcemer*, said to der. from Latin *dulcis* sweet + *melos* song.

dulcitone *n.* a keyboard instrument with graduated tuning forks which are struck with hammers. WH: 19C. Latin *dulcis* sweet + TONE.

dulia *n.* the lowest of the three degrees of adoration recognized in the Roman Catholic Church, the reverence paid to angels, saints etc. WH: 14–15C. Medieval Latin, from Greek *douleia* servitude, from *doulos* slave.

dull *a.* slow of understanding; not quick in perception. *Also v.t., v.i.* WH: pre-1200. Old English *dol*, from Germanic. Cp. German *toll*.

dulse *n.* an edible kind of seaweed, *Rhodymenia palmata*. WH: 17C. Irish and Gaelic *duileasg*, rel. to Welsh *delysg* dulse.

duly *adv.* in a suitable manner; properly. WH: 14–15C. DUE + -LY[2].

Duma *n.* a legislative body in Russia and some other republics formerly in the USSR. WH: 19C. Russian, from base of *dumat'* to think, ult. rel. to DOOM.

dumb *a.* unable to utter articulate sounds. *Also v.t.* WH: pre-1200. Old English, from Germanic, ult. of unknown orig. Cp. German *dumm* stupid.

dumbfound *v.t.* to confuse, to astound. WH: 17C. Appar. from DUMB + CONFOUND.

dumdum *n.* a soft-nosed expanding bullet that lacerates the flesh. WH: early 20C. *Dum Dum*, a town and arsenal near Calcutta, India, where first produced. The town's name comes from Hindi *damdamā* mound.

dummy *n.* a ventriloquist's doll. *Also a., v.t., v.i.* WH: 16C. DUMB + -Y[3].

dump[1] *n.* a pile of refuse. *Also v.t., v.i.* WH: 12–14C. ? From Old Norse. Cp. Danish *dumpe* to fall suddenly, to fall plump. The current use is partly imitative.

dump[2] *n.* a leaden counter used in chuck-farthing, a game in which a farthing or other coin was pitched into a hole. WH: 18C. Appar. from 1st element of DUMPLING. Cp. DUMPY.

dumpling *n.* a mass of dough or pudding, boiled or baked, often enclosing fruit etc. WH: 17C. Orig. uncertain. Cp. DUMP[2], -LING[1].

dumps *n.pl.* sadness, depression, melancholy. WH: 16C. Prob. from Low German or Dutch. Cp. Middle Dutch *domp* exhalation, mist, rel. to DAMP.

dumpy *a.* short and thick; plump. *Also n.* WH: 18C. From 1st element of DUMPLING + -Y[1]. Cp. DUMP[2].

dun[1] *a.* of a dull brown or brownish-grey colour. *Also n., v.t.* WH: pre-1200. Old English, from Germanic. Prob. rel. to Old Saxon *dosan*. Cp. DUSK.

dun[2] *v.t.* to demand payment from with persistence. *Also n.* WH: 17C. Abbr. of *Dunkirk*, a town and port in N France, with ref. to a privateer from there.

dun[3] *n.* a hill, a mound, an earthwork (largely used in place names). WH: 18C. Irish *dún*, from Gaelic *dùn* hill, hill fort, rel. to obs. Welsh *din*. Cp. DOWN[3].

dunce *n.* a stupid person, a person who is slow in learning. WH: 16C. John *Duns* Scotus, *c.*1266–1308, scholastic theologian. The followers of Duns Scotus were discredited by humanists and reformers in the 16C, and this ultimately led to the current sense.

dunch *v.t.* to nudge. *Also n.* WH: 12–14C. Orig. unknown.

Dundee cake *n.* a fruit cake decorated with almonds. WH: 19C. *Dundee*, a city on the Firth of Tay, SE Scotland.

dunderhead *n.* a stupid person. WH: 17C. ? From *dunder* (var. of *dunner* resounding noise, ? imit. or freq. of DIN) + HEAD[1]. Cp. BLUNDERBUSS.

dune *n.* a hill, mound or ridge of sand on the seashore. WH: 18C. Old French, from Middle Dutch *dūne* (Dutch *duin*), rel. to Old English *dūn* DOWN[3].

dung *n.* the excrement of animals; manure. *Also v.t., v.i.* WH: pre-1200. Old English, from Germanic, ult. of unknown orig. Cp. Danish *dynge* heap.

dungaree *n.* a coarse kind of calico used for overalls. WH: 17C. Hindi *duṅgrī*.

dungeon *n.* a prison or place of confinement, esp. one that is dark and underground. *Also v.t.* WH: 12–14C. Old French *donjon*, from Popular Latin *dominio*, *dominionis* lord's tower, from Latin *dominus* lord, master. Cp. DONJON.

dunite *n.* a rock consisting essentially of olivine, frequently accompanied by chromite. WH: 19C. *Dun* Mountain, New Zealand + -ITE[1].

duniwassal *n.* a Highland gentleman of inferior rank, a yeoman. WH: 16C. Gaelic *duine* man + *uasal* noble, of gentle birth.

dunk *v.t.* to dip (a cake or biscuit) in what one is drinking, e.g. tea or coffee. WH: early 20C. Pennsylvanian German *dunke* to dip, from German *tunken*. Cp. DUNKER.

Dunker *n.* a member of a sect of German-American Baptists. WH: 18C. Pennsylvanian German dipper. See DUNK, -ER[1].

dunlin *n.* a small sandpiper, *Calidris alpina*, a common shorebird. WH: 16C. Prob. from DUN[1] + -LING[1]. The bird has greyish-brown upper parts in winter.

dunnage *n.* loose wood, faggots, boughs etc., laid in the hold to raise the cargo above the bilge-water, or wedged between the cargo to keep it from rolling when stowed. WH: 12–14C. Orig. unknown.

dunno *contr.* (I) don't know. WH: 19C. Representation of informal pronun. of (I) *don't know*.

dunnock *n.* the hedge sparrow, *Prunella modularis* (from its colour). WH: 15C. Appar. from DUN[1] + -OCK.

dunny[1] *n.* an outside lavatory. WH: 19C. ? From DUNG, or dial. *dunniken* lavatory.

dunny[2] *a.* hard of hearing. WH: 18C. Orig. uncertain. ? From dial. *dunch* deaf, blind.

dunt *n.* a blow or stroke. *Also v.t., v.i.* WH: 14–15C. ? Var. of DINT. Cp. DENT[1].

duo *n.* a pair of performers who work together. WH: 16C. Italian, from Latin two.

duodecennial *a.* occurring once every 12 years. WH: 17C. Latin *duodecennium* period of twelve years, from *duodecim* twelve + *annus* year. See also -AL[1].

duodecimal *a.* proceeding in computation by twelves (applied to a scale of notation in which the local value of the digits increases twelvefold as they proceed from right to left). *Also n.* WH: 17C. Latin *duodecimus* twelfth + -AL[1]. Cp. DECIMAL.

duodenary *a.* of or relating to the number 12. WH: 19C. Latin *duodenarius* containing twelve, from *duodeni* twelve each. See also -ARY[1].

duodenum *n.* the first portion of the small intestine. WH: 14–15C. Medieval Latin, from Latin *duodeni* twelve each. See DUODENARY. The duodenum is so called from its length of twelve fingers' breadth.

duologue *n.* a dialogue for two persons. WH: 18C. Latin *duo* two + *-logue*, based on MONOLOGUE. Cp. DIALOGUE.

duomo *n.* an Italian cathedral. WH: 16C. Italian. See DOME[1].

duopoly *n.* an exclusive trading right enjoyed by two companies. WH: early 20C. Latin *duo* two + *-poly*, based on MONOPOLY.

duotone *n.* an illustration in two tones or colours. *Also a.* WH: early 20C. Latin *duo* two + TONE.

dupe *n.* a person who is easily deceived; a credulous person. *Also v.t.* WH: 17C. Dial. *dupe* hoopoe, from bird's supposed stupid appearance.

dupion *n.* a double cocoon formed by two or more silkworms. WH: 19C. French *doupion*, rel. to Italian *doppione*, from *doppio* double.

duple *a.* double, twofold. WH: 16C. Latin *duplus*, from *duo* two.

duplex *n.* a duplex apartment or house. *Also a., v.t.* WH: 16C. Latin, from *duo* two + *plic-*, base of *plicare* to fold. The sense of duplex apartment or house arose in the early 20C.

duplicate[1] *a.* existing in two parts exactly corresponding. *Also v.t.* WH: 14–15C. Latin *duplicatus*, p.p. of *duplicare*. See DUPLICATE[2], also -ATE[2].

duplicate[2] *v.t.* to make or be a reproduction of. WH: 15C. Latin *duplicatus*, p.p. of *duplicare* to double. See DUPLE, also -ATE[3].

duplicity *n.* double-dealing, dissimulation. WH: 14–15C. Old French *duplicité* or Late Latin *duplicitas*. See DUPLEX, also -ITY.

dupondius *n.* a coin in ancient Rome, worth two asses. WH: 17C. Latin, from *duo* two + *-pondius*, from *pondus* weight (see POUND[1]).

duppy *n.* a malevolent ghost in W Indian folklore. **WH:** 18C. Orig. unknown. ? W African.

durable *a.* having the quality of endurance or continuance. **WH:** 12–14C. Old French, from Latin *durabilis*, from *durare* to harden, to endure, from *durus* hard. See also -ABLE.

Duralumin® *n.* an alloy of aluminium, copper and other metals, having great strength and lightness. **WH:** early 20C. ? From *Düren*, a town in Germany, where manufactured, or from Latin *durus* hard. See ALUMINIUM.

dura mater *n.* the first of three lining membranes of the brain and spinal cord. **WH:** 14–15C. Medieval Latin, lit. hard mother, rendering of Arabic *al-'umm al-jāfiya* coarse mother. Arabic *al-'umm* mother indicates a relationship between the parts. Cp. PIA MATER.

duramen *n.* the heartwood or central wood in the trunk of exogenous trees. **WH:** 19C. Latin hardness, from *durare*. See DURABLE.

†durance *n.* imprisonment. **WH:** 14–15C. Old French, from Latin *durare*. See DURABLE, also -ANCE.

duration *n.* continuance. **WH:** 14–15C. Old French, from Medieval Latin *duratio, durationis*, from Latin *duratus*, p.p. of *durare*. See DURABLE, also -ATION.

durbar *n.* an Indian ruler's court. **WH:** 17C. Urdu, from Persian *darbār* court.

durchkomponiert *a.* having different music for each stanza. **WH:** 19C. German, from *durch* through + *komponiert* composed.

duress *n.* constraint, compulsion, restraint of liberty, imprisonment. **WH:** 12–14C. Old French *duresse*, from Latin *duritia*, from *durus* hard. See also -ESS².

Durex® *n.* a condom. **WH:** mid-20C. Prob. from DURABLE + commercial suf. -ex.

durian *n.* a large tree, *Durio zibethinus*, grown in the Malay archipelago. **WH:** 16C. Malay, from *duri* thorn, prickle.

duricrust *n.* a hard, mineral crust found near the surface of soil in semi-arid regions. **WH:** early 20C. Latin *durus* hard + -*i*- + CRUST.

during *prep.* in or within the time of. **WH:** 14–15C. Pres.p. of *dure* to last, to continue (from Old French *durer*, from Latin *durare* to harden, to endure, from *durus* hard) + -ING², based on Old French *durant* and Latin abl. absolute (as in *durante vita* while life continues).

durmast *n.* a Eurasian oak, *Quercus petraea*. **WH:** 18C. ? Error for *dunmast*, from DUN¹ + MAST².

durra *n.* a kind of sorghum, *Sorghum bicolor*, cultivated for grain and fodder. **WH:** 18C. Arabic *ḍura*.

durrie *n.* a coarse cotton fabric, made in squares, and used in the Indian subcontinent for carpets, curtains, coverings for furniture etc. **WH:** 19C. Hindi *darī*.

durum *n.* a variety of spring wheat, *Triticum durum*, with a high gluten content, used mainly for the manufacture of pasta. **WH:** early 20C. Latin *durum*, neut. of *durus* hard.

durzi *n.* an Indian tailor. **WH:** 19C. Urdu, from Persian *darzī*.

dusk *n.* shade, gloom. Also *a., v.t., v.i.* **WH:** pre-1200. Old English *dox*, from Germanic, from Indo-European base also of Latin *fuscus* dark, murky (cp. FUSCOUS).

dust *n.* earth or other matter reduced to such small particles as to be easily raised and carried about by the air. Also *v.t., v.i.* **WH:** pre-1200. Old English *dūst*, from Germanic. Cp. German *Dunst* mist, vapour.

Dutch *a.* of or relating to the Netherlands. Also *n.* **WH:** 12–14C. Middle Dutch *dutsch* Dutch, German, rel. to Old English *thēodisc* Gentile, from *thēod* people. See also -ISH¹. Cp. German *Deutsch* German. The *thēod* reference is to a common Germanic people. The specific application to the Netherlands evolved in the 17C.

dutch *n.* a wife. **WH:** 19C. Abbr. of DUCHESS.

duty *n.* something which is bound or ought to be paid or done. **WH:** 14–15C. Anglo-French *deweté*, from *du*, var. of Old French *dēu*. See DUE, also -TY¹.

duumvir *n.* either of two officers or magistrates in ancient Rome appointed to carry out jointly the duties of any public office. **WH:** 17C. Latin sing. of *duum virum*, gen. of *duo viri* two men.

duvet *n.* a quilt stuffed with down or man-made fibres, used as a bed covering instead of blankets and a sheet. **WH:** 18C. French DOWN².

dux *n.* the top pupil of a school. **WH:** 18C. Latin leader.

dwaal *n.* a state of bewilderment. **WH:** mid-20C. Afrikaans to wander, to roam.

dwale *n.* the deadly nightshade, *Atropa belladonna*. **WH:** 12–14C. Prob. from Scandinavian. Cp. Danish *dvale* dead sleep, stupor.

dwam *n.* a daydream, absent-mindedness. Also *v.i.* **WH:** 16C. From Germanic base of DWELL. Cp. Middle Dutch *dwelm* stupefaction.

dwarf *n.* a human being, animal or plant much below the natural or ordinary size. Also *a., v.t., v.i.* **WH:** pre-1200. Old English *dweorg*, from Germanic. Cp. German *Zwerg*.

dweeb *n.* a stupid or contemptibly weak man or boy. **WH:** late 20C. Orig. unknown. ? Influ. by DWARF and WEED.

dwell *v.i.* to reside, to abide (in a place); to live, to spend one's time. Also *v.t., n.* **WH:** pre-1200. Old English *dwellan*, from Germanic. Cp. Old Norse *dvelja* to delay, to stay.

DWEM *n.* a dead white European male, esp. one who has been regarded as being of undue historical or literary importance because of belonging to a dominant section of society. **WH:** mid-20C. Acronym of *dead white European male*.

dwindle *v.i.* to become smaller. **WH:** 16C. Freq. of dial. *dwine* to fade, to pine away, from Old English *dwīnan*. See also -LE⁴.

dwt. *abbr.* pennyweight. **WH:** Abbr. of Latin *denarius* penny and *weight*. Cp. CWT.

DX *n.* long-range radio transmissions. **WH:** Abbr. of *distance* and *extension*.

dyad *n.* an operator which is two vectors combined. **WH:** 17C. Late Latin *dyas, dyadis*, from Greek *duas, duados*, from *duo* two. See also -AD¹.

Dyak *n.* a person belonging to the aboriginal race inhabiting Borneo, probably related to the Malays. **WH:** 19C. Malay up-country.

dybbuk *n.* in Jewish folklore, the soul of a dead sinner which enters the body of a living person and takes control of their actions. **WH:** early 20C. Yiddish *dibek*, from Hebrew *dibbūq*, from *dābaq* to cling, to cleave.

dye *v.t.* to stain, to colour. Also *v.i., n.* **WH:** pre-1200. Old English *dēagian*, presumably of Germanic orig. The spelling with *y* arose to distinguish from DIE¹.

dying *a.* about to die. Also *n.* **WH:** 14–15C. DIE¹ + -ING².

dyke *n.* a wall built to protect low-lying lands from being flooded. Also *v.t.* **WH:** 12–14C. Old Norse *dík*, from Germanic. See DITCH. Cp. German *Teich* pond.

dynameter *n.* an instrument for measuring the magnifying powers of a telescope. **WH:** 19C. Greek *dunamis* force + -METER.

dynamic *a.* of or relating to forces not in equilibrium, as distinct from *static*. Also *n.* **WH:** 19C. French *dynamique*, from Greek *dunamikos*, from *dunamis* force, power. See also -IC.

dynamism *n.* the restless energy of a forceful personality. **WH:** 19C. Greek *dunamis* force, power + -ISM.

dynamite *n.* a powerful explosive compound, extremely local in its action, consisting of nitroglycerine mixed with an absorbent material. Also *v.t.* **WH:** 19C. Greek *dunamis* force, power + -ITE¹. The explosive was so named in 1867 by its inventor, Alfred Nobel (see NOBEL PRIZE).

dynamo *n.* a machine for converting mechanical energy into electricity by means of electromagnetic induction. **WH:** 19C. Abbr. of *dynamoelectric machine*. See DYNAMOELECTRIC. The shortened form was recommended in 1882 by the English physicist Professor S.P. Thompson.

dynamo- *comb. form* of or relating to force or power. **WH:** Greek *dunamis* force, power. See also -O-.

dynamoelectric *a.* of or relating to the conversion of mechanical into electric energy or the reverse. **WH:** 19C. DYNAMO- + ELECTRIC. The term *dynamo-electric machine* was devised in 1867 by the German electrical engineer Werner von Siemens to distinguish it from the earlier *magneto-electric machine*. See MAGNETO.

dynamograph *n.* a dynamometer used for recording speed, power, adhesion etc. on electric railways. **WH:** 19C. DYNAMO- + -GRAPH.

dynamometer *n.* an instrument for the measurement of power, force or electricity. **WH:** 19C. French *dynamomètre*. See DYNAMO-, -METER.

dynamotor *n.* an electrical machine capable of acting as a motor and a generator which converts direct current into alternating current. **WH:** early 20C. Greek *dunamis* force, power + MOTOR.

dynast *n.* a ruler, a monarch. **WH:** 17C. Latin *dynastes*, from Greek *dunastēs*, from *dunasthai* to be able, to be powerful.

dynatron *n.* a four-electrode thermionic valve which generates continuous oscillation. **WH:** early 20C. Greek *dunamis* force, power + -TRON.

dyne *n.* a unit for measuring force, the amount that, acting upon a gram for a second, generates a velocity of one centimetre per second. **WH:** 19C. French, from Greek *dunamis* force, power.

dys- *comb. form* diseased, difficult or bad. **WH:** Greek *dus-*, rel. to Sanskrit *dus-*, Old High German *zūr-* (German *zer-*), Old Norse *tor-*.

dysaesthesia *n.* insensibility. **WH:** 18C. Modern Latin, from Greek *dusaisthēsia*, from *dus-* DYS- + *anaisthēsia* ANAESTHESIA.

dysentery *n.* an infectious tropical febrile disease, causing inflammation in the large intestines, and accompanied by mucous and bloody faeces. **WH:** 14–15C. Old French *dissenterie* or Latin *dysenteria*, from Greek *dusenteria*, from *dusenteros* afflicted in the bowels, from *dus-* DYS- + *entera* bowels. See also -Y².

dysfunction *n.* impaired or abnormal functioning, esp. of any organ or part of the body. **WH:** early 20C. DYS- + FUNCTION.

dysgenic *a.* unfavourable to the hereditary qualities of any stock or people. **WH:** early 20C. DYS- + -GENIC.

dysgraphia *n.* inability to write. **WH:** mid-20C. DYS- + Greek *graphia* writing.

dyslexia *n.* an impaired ability in reading and spelling caused by a neurological disorder. **WH:** 19C. DYS- + Greek *lexis* speech. Greek *legein* to speak has apparently been confused with Latin *legere* to read.

dyslogistic *a.* disparaging, disapproving, censuring. **WH:** 19C. DYS- + *eulogistic* (EULOGY).

dysmenorrhoea *n.* difficult or painful menstruation. **WH:** 19C. DYS- + MENORRHOEA.

dyspepsia *n.* indigestion. **WH:** 18C. Latin, from Greek *duspepsia*, from *duspeptos* difficult of digestion, from *dus-* DYS- + *peptos* cooked, digested. See also -IA.

dysphagia *n.* difficulty of swallowing. **WH:** 18C. Modern Latin, from Greek *dus-* DYS- + *phagia* (-PHAGE).

dysphasia *n.* difficulty in speaking or understanding speech, caused by injury to or disease of the brain. **WH:** 19C. DYS- + -PHASIA.

dysphemism *n.* the use of an offensive word or phrase in place of an inoffensive or mild one. **WH:** 19C. DYS- + EUPHEMISM.

dysphonia *n.* a difficulty in speaking arising from disease or malformation of the organs. **WH:** 18C. Greek *dusphonia*, from *dus-* DYS- + *phōnē* sound, voice. See also -IA.

dysphoria *n.* a morbid uneasiness; feeling unwell. **WH:** 19C. Greek *dusphoria* malaise, discomfort, from *dusphoros* hard to bear, from *dus-* DYS- + *pherein* to bear. See also -IA.

dysplasia *n.* abnormal growth of tissues. **WH:** early 20C. DYS- + -PLASIA.

dyspnoea *n.* difficulty of breathing. **WH:** 17C. Latin, from Greek *duspnoia*, from *dus-* DYS- + *pnoē* breathing. See also -A¹.

dysprosium *n.* a rare silvery-white metallic element, at. no. 66, chem. symbol Dy, of the rare earth group, used in laser materials etc. **WH:** 19C. Greek *dusprositos* hard to get at + -IUM. The name was coined in 1866 by the French chemist Paul-Émile Lecoq de Boisbaudran, with reference to the element's rarity. Cp. GALLIUM, SAMARIUM.

dysthymia *n.* anxiety and depression. **WH:** 19C. Greek *dusthumia* despondency, from *dus-* DYS- + *thumos* spirit. See also -IA.

dystocia *n.* difficult childbirth. **WH:** 18C. Greek *dustokia*, from *dus-* DYS- + *tokos* childbirth. See also -IA.

dystopia *n.* an imaginary wretched place, the opposite of a utopia. **WH:** 18C. DYS- + UTOPIA.

dystrophy *n.* any of various disorders characterized by the wasting away of muscle tissue. **WH:** 19C. DYS- + -TROPHY.

dysuria *n.* difficulty and pain in passing urine. **WH:** 14–15C. Late Latin, from Greek *dusouria*, from *dus-* DYS- + *ouron* urine. See also -IA.

DZ *abbr.* Algeria (International Vehicle Registration). **WH:** Abbr. of country's Arabic name, *al-Djazā'ir*.

dziggetai *n.* a variety of wild ass, *Equus hemionus*, somewhat resembling the mule, native to central Asia. **WH:** 18C. Mongolian *chiketei* having ears, eared, from *chiki* ear.

dzo *n.* a hybrid breed of Himalayan cattle developed from crossing the yak with common horned cattle. **WH:** 19C. Tibetan *mdso*.

E

e- *pref.* out of, from, as in *evade*, *emasculate*. WH: Latin pref., from EX-. For reasons of pronunciation, *x* is dropped before all consonants except *c, f, h, p, q, s, t*.

each *a., pron.* every one (of a limited number) considered separately. WH: pre-1200. Old English *ælc*, from Germanic phr. meaning ever alike (see AYE², ALIKE). Cp. German *jeglicher* any. The current spelling (without *l*) began to appear in the 16C.

eager *a.* excited by an ardent desire to attain, obtain or succeed. WH: 12–14C. Old French *aigre*, from Latin *acer, acris*. Cp. ACRID.

eagle *n.* any of various large birds of prey of the family Accipitridae, esp. of the genus *Aquila*, such as the golden eagle. *Also v.t.* WH: 12–14C. Old French *aigle*, from Latin *aquila*, ? from AQUA. Latin *aquila* named the black eagle, perhaps so called as it was the colour of a storm cloud. This word replaced Old English *earn* (ERNE).

eagre *n.* a bore in an estuary. WH: 17C. Orig. unknown.

ealdorman *n.* the highest royal official of a shire in Anglo-Saxon times, responsible for law and order and for levying and leading the local fyrd. WH: pre-1200. Historic form of Old English *aldormann* ALDERMAN.

-ean *suf.* belonging to, as in *European*. WH: Latin or Greek ending + -AN. The English suffix represents Latin *-aeus, -eus* or Greek *-aios, -eios* + -AN. In some cases the root of the word itself provides *-e*.

ear¹ *n.* the organ of hearing and balance, consisting of the external ear, middle ear and internal ear. WH: pre-1200. Old English *ēare*, from Germanic, from Indo-European base also of Latin *auris* (cp. AURAL) and of Greek *ous, ōtos* (cp. OTIC). Cp. German *Ohr*.

ear² *n.* a seed-bearing head of corn. *Also v.i.* WH: pre-1200. Old English *ēar*, from Germanic base rel. to Latin *acus, aceris* husk, chaff. Cp. German *Ähre*. Not rel. to EAR¹.

earing *n.* a small line for fastening the corner of a sail to a yard in reefing. WH: 17C. EAR¹ + -ING¹ or RING¹.

earl *n.* a British nobleman ranking next below a marquess and next above a viscount, equivalent to a COUNT². WH: pre-1200. Old English *eorl*, of unknown orig. Cp. JARL. Old English *eorl* may have been contrasted with *ceorl* CHURL.

early *adv.* before the proper, expected or usual time. *Also a., n.* WH: pre-1200. Old English *ǣrlīce*, based on Old Norse *arliga*. See ERE, also -LY².

earn *v.t.* to gain (money etc.) as the reward of labour. WH: pre-1200. Old English *earnian*, from Germanic, from base rel. to Old English *esne* labourer, man. Cp. German *Ernste* harvest.

earnest¹ *a.* serious, grave. *Also n.* WH: pre-1200. Old English *eornost*, from Germanic base represented also by Old Norse *ern* brisk, vigorous, of unknown orig. Cp. German *Ernst* seriousness.

earnest² *n.* an instalment paid to seal a contract or agreement. WH: 12–14C. Prob. ult. from Old French *erres* (Scottish dial. *arles*), appar. from Medieval Latin, dim. of Latin *arrha*, from Greek *arrabōn* earnest-money, assim. first to -NESS, then to EARNEST¹.

earth *n.* the globe, the planet on which we live, the third planet from the sun. *Also v.t., v.i.* WH: pre-1200. Old English *eorthe*, from Germanic. Cp. German *Erde*.

earwig *n.* any of various insects of the order Dermaptera, esp. *Forficula auricularia*, with curved forceps at its tail. *Also v.i., v.t.* WH: pre-1200. Old English *ēarwicga*, from *ēare* EAR¹ + *wicga* earwig, prob. rel. to WIGGLE. The insect was formerly believed to crawl into the human ear. The word is not from EAR², despite the presence of earwigs in cornstalks and chaff.

ease *n.* a state of freedom from labour, trouble or pain. *Also v.t., v.i.* WH: 12–14C. Old French *aise*, alt. of Latin *adiacens*, use as n. of pres.p. of *adiacere*. See ADJACENT.

easel *n.* a wooden frame used to support a picture, open book etc. WH: 16C. Dutch *ezel* ass. Cp. HORSE.

east *a.* situated towards the point where the sun rises during the equinox. *Also n., adv., v.i.* WH: pre-1200. Old English *ēast*, from Germanic, from Indo-European base also of Latin AURORA, Greek *auōs* dawn. Cp. German *Osten*.

Easter *n.* the festival in commemoration of the resurrection of Christ, taking place on the Sunday after the full moon that falls on or next after 21 March. WH: pre-1200. Old English *ēastre*, appar. from *Eostre*, Northumbrian var. of *Eastre*, the name of a goddess whose feast was celebrated at the vernal equinox, from Germanic. Cp. EAST.

eastern *a.* situated in the east. *Also n.* WH: pre-1200. Old English *ēasterne*, from Germanic, from base of EAST.

easy *a.* not difficult, not requiring great labour, exertion or effort. *Also adv., n., int.* WH: 12–14C. Old French *aisié* (Modern French *aisé*), p.p. of *aisier* to put to ease. See EASE, also -Y¹.

eat *v.t.* to chew and swallow as food. *Also v.i.* WH: pre-1200. Old English *etan*, from Germanic, from Indo-European base also of Latin *edere* (cp. EDIBLE), Greek *edein*. Cp. German *essen*.

eau *n.* water (used in compounds to designate various spirituous waters and perfumes). WH: 18C. French water, from Latin AQUA.

eaves *n.pl.* the lower edge of the roof which projects beyond the wall, and serves to throw off the water which falls on the roof. WH: pre-1200. Old English *efes*, from Germanic, prob. from base of OVER.

ebb *n.* the flowing back or going out of the tide. *Also v.i.* WH: pre-1200. Old English *ebba*, from Germanic, from base of OF and its var. OFF. The original sense was as if 'a running off'.

EBCDIC *n.* a code for alphanumeric characters. WH: Abbr. of extended binary-coded decimal-interchange code.

Ebola *n.* a virus occurring in parts of Africa, infection with which causes a serious illness. WH: late 20C. River *Ebola*, N Zaire (now Congo).

ebonics *n.* American black street slang. WH: late 20C. EBONY + *phonics* (PHONIC).

ebony *n.* the wood of various species of *Diospyros*, noted for its solidity and black colour, capable of a high polish, and largely used for mosaic work and inlaying. *Also a.* WH: 14–15C. Old French *eban* (Modern French *ébène*), from Latin *ebanus*, from Greek *ebanos* ebony tree, ? based on IVORY.

ebracteate *a.* without bracts. WH: 19C. Modern Latin *ebracteatus*, from Latin *e-* E- + *brachea* BRACT. See also -ATE².

ebriety *n.* drunkenness, intoxication. WH: 14–15C. French *ébriété* or Latin *ebrietas*, from *ebrius* drunk. See also -ITY.

ebullient *a.* overflowing with high spirits or enthusiasm, exuberant. WH: 16C. Latin *ebulliens, ebullientis*, pres.p. of *ebullire* to boil up, from *e-* E- + *bullire* BOIL¹. See also -ENT. The original sense was boiling, agitated as if boiling. The current sense evolved in the 17C.

eburnation *n.* an excessive deposition of bony matter, sometimes found in a diseased state of the joints. WH: 19C. Latin *eburnus* made of ivory, from *ebur*. See IVORY, also -ATION.

ecad *n.* in ecology, an organism which has been modified by the environment. WH: early 20C. Greek *oikos* house + -AD¹.

écarté *n.* a game of cards played by two people with 32 cards. WH: 19C. French, p.p. of *écarter* to discard from *é-* (EX-) + *carte* CARD¹. The game is so called because each player can discard certain cards.

ecbolic *n.* a drug that stimulates contractions and promotes the expulsion of the foetus. *Also a.* WH: 18C. Greek *ekbolē* expulsion + -IC.

Ecce Homo *n.* a painting or sculpture representing Christ crowned with thorns, as before Pilate. WH: 14–15C. Latin behold the Man, from *ecce* lo! + *homo* man. The phrase comes from the words of Pilate in the Vulgate (the Latin version of the Bible), AV 'Behold the man!' (John xix.5).

eccentric *a.* peculiar or odd in manner or character. *Also n.* WH: 14–15C. Late Latin *eccentricus*, from Greek *ekkentros*, from *ek-* EX- + *kentron*. See CENTRE, also -IC. The original sense was astronomical, of a circle or orbit not having the earth exactly in its centre. The current sense dates from the 17C.

ecchymosis *n.* a bruise, a discoloration of the skin due to the effusion of blood from blood vessels ruptured by a blow. WH: 16C. Modern Latin, from Greek *ekkhumōsis*, from *ekkhumonathai* to extravasate blood. See also -OSIS.

Eccles cake *n.* a small cake made of pastry and filled with dried fruit. WH: 19C. *Eccles*, a town in Lancashire (now Salford).

ecclesiastic *n.* a person in holy orders, a member of the clergy. *Also a.* WH: 14–15C. French *écclesiastique* or Ecclesiastical Latin *ecclesiasticus*, from Greek *ekklēsiastikos*, from *ekklēsiastēs* member of an assembly, from *ekklēsia* assembly, church, from *ek-* EX- + *kalein* to call, to summon.

ecclesiolatry *n.* excessive reverence for ecclesiastical forms and traditions. WH: 19C. Ecclesiastical Latin *ecclesia*, from Greek *ekklēsia* (see ECCLESIASTIC) + -O- + -LATRY.

ecclesiology *n.* the study of all matters connected with churches, esp. church architecture, decoration and antiquities. WH: 19C. Ecclesiastical Latin *ecclesia*, from Greek *ekklēsia* (see ECCLESIASTIC) + -O- + -LOGY.

eccrine *a.* denoting a gland that secretes externally, esp. the sweat glands. WH: mid-20C. Greek *ekkrinein* to secrete, from *ek-* EX- + *krinein* to separate. See also -INE.

ecdysis *n.* the casting of the skin, as by snakes, insects and crustaceans. WH: 19C. Greek *ekdusis*, from *ekduein* to put off, to shed, from *ek-* EX- + *duein* to put.

echelon *n.* (a group of persons in) a level, stage or grade of an organization etc. *Also v.t.* WH: 18C. French *échelon*, from *échelle* ladder, from Latin *scala*. See SCALE³, also -OON.

echeveria *n.* a succulent plant of the genus *Echeveria*, found in Central and S America. WH: 19C. Modern Latin, from Anastasio *Echeverría* or *Echeveri*, 19C Mexican botanical illustrator. See also -IA.

echidna *n.* a mammal of the genus *Tachyglossus* or *Zaglossus*, popularly known as the spiny anteater, which lays eggs instead of giving birth to live young like other mammals. WH: 19C. Modern Latin former genus name, from Greek *ekhidna* viper.

echinoderm *a.* of or relating to the Echinodermata. *Also n.* WH: 19C. Greek *ekhinos* hedgehog + -O- + -DERM.

echinus *n.* a sea urchin of the genus *Echinus*. WH: 14–15C. Latin, from Greek *ekhinos* hedgehog, sea urchin.

echo *n.* the repetition of a sound caused by its being reflected from some obstacle. *Also v.i., v.t.* WH: 12–14C. Old French *écho* or Latin *echo*, from Greek *ēkhō*, rel. to *ēkhē* sound. In Greek mythology, Echo was a mountain nymph who entertained Hera while Zeus dallied with other nymphs. Hera punished Echo for this ruse with a speech impediment, so that she could never begin a conversation but only repeat the words of others.

echovirus *n.* any of a group of viruses which can cause meningitis or intestinal or respiratory illnesses. WH: mid-20C. Acronym of enteric *cytopathogenic human orphan* + VIRUS.

echt *a.* genuine, authentic. WH: early 20C. German genuine, from Middle Dutch.

eclair *n.* an iced, finger-shaped cream-filled pastry. WH: 19C. French *éclair* lightning, from *é-* EX- + *clair*, or from Latin *clarus* bright, CLEAR. The word is popularly said to refer either to the pastry's gleaming coating of fondant icing or to the 'streak' of cream through its centre.

†éclaircissement *n.* an explanation or clearing up of a subject of dispute or misunderstanding. WH: 17C. French, from *éclaircir*, *éclairciss-* to clear up. See ECLAIR, also -MENT.

eclampsia *n.* convulsions or fits, particularly of the type that occur with acute toxaemia in pregnancy. WH: 19C. Modern Latin, from French *éclampsie*, from Greek *eklampsis* sudden development, from *eklampein* to shine out.

éclat *n.* brilliant success. WH: 17C. French, from *éclater* to burst out, from Popular Latin *exclapitare*, from EX- + v. of imit. orig. (cp. CLAP¹).

eclectic *a.* broad, not exclusive. *Also n.* WH: 17C. Greek *eklektikos*, from *eklegein* to select, from *ek-* EX- + *legein* to choose.

eclipse *n.* the total or partial obscuration of the light from a heavenly body by the passage of another body between it and the eye or between it and the source of its light. *Also v.t., v.i.* WH: 12–14C. Old French (Modern French *éclipse*), from Latin *eclipsis*, from Greek *ekleipsis*, from *ekleipein* to leave its place, to fail to appear, from *ek-* EX- + *leipein* to leave.

eclogue *n.* an idyll or pastoral poem, esp. one containing dialogue. WH: 14–15C. Latin *ecloga*, from Greek *eklogē* selection (of poems), from *eklegein*. See ECLECTIC.

eclosion *n.* emergence, esp. of a larva from an egg or of an insect from a pupa-case. WH: 19C. French *éclosion*, from *éclore* to hatch, ult. from EX- + Latin *claudere* to close.

eco- *comb. form* concerned with ecology, habitat or the environment. WH: First element of ECOLOGY.

ecocide *n.* the destruction of an environment, or of aspects of an environment. WH: mid-20C. ECO- + -CIDE.

ecoclimate *n.* the climate of an area, perceived as of ecological importance. WH: mid-20C. ECO- + CLIMATE.

ecofreak *n.* a person who attaches (too much) importance to the well-being of the environment. WH: late 20C. ECO- + FREAK.

eco-friendly *a.* not damaging to the environment. WH: late 20C. ECO- + *friendly* (FRIEND).

ecolabel *n.* a label on a food or household product asserting that the product contains nothing damaging to the environment. WH: late 20C. ECO- + LABEL.

E. coli *abbr.* Escherichia coli, a bacterium causing food poisoning. WH: mid-20C. Abbr. of *Escherichia coli*, from Modern Latin *Escherichia*, from Theodor *Escherich*, 1857–1911, German paediatrician + -IA + gen. of Latin COLON².

ecology *n.* the branch of biology dealing with the relations between organisms and their environment. WH: 19C. Greek *oikos* house + -O- + -LOGY.

econometrics *n.* statistical and mathematical analysis of economic theories. WH: mid-20C. ECONOMY + -METRIC. See also -ICS.

economic *a.* relating to the science of economics. WH: 14–15C. Old French *économique*, from Latin *oeconomicus*, from Greek *oikonomikos*, from *oikonomos*. See ECONOMY, also -IC.

economy *n.* the totality of goods and services produced and consumed by a community or state; the wealth or financial resources of a community etc. WH: 15C. Old French *économie* or Latin *oeconomia*, from Greek *oikonomia*, from *oikonomos* manager of a household, steward, from *oikos* house. See also -NOMY.

écorché *n.* an anatomical figure with the muscular system exposed for the purpose of study. WH: 19C. French, p.p. of *écorcher* to flay, from Popular Latin *excorticare*, from EX- + Latin CORTEX.

ecospecies *n.* a taxonomic species regarded as an ecological unit. WH: early 20C. ECO- + SPECIES.

ecosphere *n.* the parts of the universe, esp. the earth, where life can exist. WH: mid-20C. ECO- + SPHERE.

écossaise *n.* a Scottish dance in duple time. WH: 19C. French, fem. of *écossais* Scottish. Cp. SCHOTTISCHE.

ecosystem *n.* a system consisting of a community of organisms and its environment. WH: mid-20C. ECO- + SYSTEM. The term was coined in 1935 by the English botanist Arthur George Tansley.

ecoterrorism *n.* terrorist acts threatened or carried out in order to help environmentalist causes. WH: late 20C. ECO- + *terrorism* (TERROR).

ecotourism *n.* tourism managed on a small scale and in environmentally friendly ways. WH: late 20C. ECO- + *tourism* (TOUR).

ecotype *n.* a distinctive group within a species which has adapted to its particular environment. WH: early 20C. ECO- + *-type* (TYPE).

écraseur *n.* an instrument for removing tumours etc. without effusion of blood. WH: 19C. French crusher, from *écraser* to crush, from *é-* EX- + *-craser*, rel. to CRAZE.

ecru *a.* of the colour of unbleached linen. *Also n.* WH: 19C. French *écru* raw, unbleached, from *é-* EX- + *cru*, from Latin *crudus* (see CRUDE).

ecstasy *n.* a state of mental exaltation. WH: 14–15C. Old French *extasie*, from Late Latin *extasis*, from Greek *ekstasis*, from *eksta-*, stem of *existanai* to put out of place, from EX- + *histanai* to place. See also -Y². The literal sense of the word is being put out of place. Cp. *beside oneself* (BESIDE).

ecthyma *n.* a skin disease characterized by an eruption of pimples. WH: 19C. Modern Latin, from Greek *ekthuma*, from *ekthuein* to break out as heat.

ecto- *comb. form* of or relating to the outside of something. WH: Greek *ekto-*, stem of *ektos* outside. See also -O-.

ectoblast *n.* the membrane composing the walls of a cell. WH: 19C. ECTO- + -BLAST.

ectoderm *n.* the outer layer of the ectoblast. WH: 19C. ECTO- + -DERM.

ectogenesis *n.* the growth of an organism or part outside the body instead of inside. WH: early 20C. ECTO- + GENESIS.

ectomorph *n.* a person of slight or thin build. WH: mid-20C. ECTO- + -MORPH. The term was coined in 1940, together with ENDOMORPH and *mesomorph* (MESOMORPHIC), by the English paediatrician William Sheldon.

-ectomy *suf.* denoting the surgical removal of a part of the body, as *tonsillectomy*. WH: Greek *ektomē* excision, from *ek-* EX- + *temnein* to cut. Cp. -TOMY.

ectoparasite *n.* an organism parasitic on the outside of the host. WH: 19C. ECTO- + PARASITE.

ectopia *n.* congenital displacement of an organ or part. WH: 19C. Modern Latin, from Greek *ektopos* out of place, from *ek-* EX- + *topos* place. See also -IA.

ectoplasm *n.* the outer layer of protoplasm or sarcode of a cell. WH: 19C. ECTO- + -*plasm* (PLASMA).

ectosarc *n.* the outer transparent sarcode-layer of certain protozoa, as the amoeba. WH: 19C. ECTO- + Greek *sarx*, *sarkos* flesh.

ectozoon *n.* an animal parasitic on the outside of other animals. WH: 19C. ECTO- + Greek *zōion* animal.

ectype *n.* a copy, as distinguished from an original. WH: 17C. Greek *ektupon*, neut. of *ektupos* worked in relief, from *ek-* EX- + *tupos* figure. See TYPE.

ecu *n.* a currency unit used as a unit of account in the European Union, its value based on the value of several different European currencies. WH: late 20C. Abbr. of *E*uropean *C*urrency *U*nit, punning on ÉCU.

écu *n.* a French silver coin of varying value, usu. considered as equivalent to the English crown. WH: 16C. French, from Latin *scutum* shield.

ecumenical *a.* belonging to the Christian Church or Christian world as a whole. WH: 16C. Late Latin *oecumenicus*, from Greek *oikoumenikos* belonging to *hē oikoumenē* the inhabited world, the whole earth. See also -AL[1].

eczema *n.* an inflammatory disease of the skin, characterized by blisters and itching. WH: 18C. Modern Latin, from Greek *ekzema*, *ekzematos*, from *ekzein* to boil over, to break out, from *ek-* EX- + *zein* to boil.

-ed *suf.* forming the past tense and participle of regular verbs (used also as participial adjectives). WH: Old English *-ed*, *-ad*, *-od*, representing Germanic p.p. suf., from Indo-European.

edacious *a.* greedy, voracious, ravenous. WH: 19C. Latin *edax*, *edacis*, from *edere* to eat + -OUS. See also -ACIOUS.

Edam *n.* a kind of pressed, yellow cheese with a red outer skin of wax. WH: 19C. *Edam*, a town near Amsterdam, the Netherlands.

edaphic *a.* of or relating to the soil. WH: 19C. Greek *edaphos* floor + -IC.

Edda *n.* the title of either of two Icelandic books, the Elder or Poetic Edda and the Younger or Prose Edda (see ELDER[1], YOUNG). WH: 17C. Either from the name of the great-grandmother in the Old Norse poem *Rigsthul* or from Old Norse *ōthr* poetry.

eddo *n.* taro. WH: 17C. Of W African orig. Cp. Fante *edwó* yam, *ndwo* root.

eddy *n.* a small whirlpool. *Also v.i.*, *v.t.* WH: 14–15C. Prob. from base of Old English *ed-* again, back. Cp. Old Norse *itha* eddy.

edelweiss *n.* a small white composite plant, *Gnaphalium alpinum*, growing in rocky places in the Alps. WH: 19C. German, from *edel* noble + *weiss* white. The word is popularly said to have been coined to attract 19C visitors to the Alps, but it is more likely to be a folk name referring to the white starlike bracts.

Eden *n.* the region in which Adam and Eve were placed at their creation, according to the Bible. WH: 12–14C. Late Latin, from Greek *Edēn*, or from Hebrew *'ēḏen*, ? from Akkadian *edinu* from Sumerian *eden* plain, but assoc. with Hebrew *'ēḏen* delight.

edentate *a.* having no incisor teeth. *Also n.* WH: 19C. Latin *edentatus*, p.p. of *edentare* to render toothless, from *e-* E- + *dens*, *dentis* tooth. See also -ATE[2].

edge *n.* the sharp or cutting part of an instrument, such as a sword. *Also v.t.*, *v.i.* WH: pre-1200. Old English *ecg*, from Germanic, from Indo-European base meaning to be sharp, to be pointed, seen also in Latin *acies* edge (cp. ACUTE) and Greek *akis* point (cp. ACME). Cp. EGG[2], German *Ecke* corner.

edible *a.* fit for food, eatable. *Also n.* WH: 16C. Late Latin *edibilis*, from *edere* to eat. See also -IBLE.

edict *n.* a proclamation or decree issued by authority. WH: 12–14C. Latin *edictum*, neut. p.p. (used as n.) of *edicere* to proclaim, from E- + *dicere* to say, to tell.

edifice *n.* a building, esp. one of some size and pretension. WH: 14–15C. Old French *édifice* or Latin *aedificium*, from *aedis* (see EDIFY) + -*fic*-, var. of *fac*-, stem of *facere* to make.

edify *v.t.* to instruct; to improve; to build up esp. morally and spiritually. WH: 12–14C. Old French *édifier*, from Latin *aedificare*, from *aedis* dwelling, temple (orig. hearth) + -*ficare*. See also -FY. The original sense was to construct a building. The current sense dates from the 14–15C.

edit *v.t.* to prepare for publication or processing by compiling, selecting, revising etc. *Also n.* WH: 18C. Partly from French *éditer* to publish (from Latin *editus*, p.p. of *edere* to put forth, from E- + *dare* to put), partly a back-formation from *editor* (from Latin producer, exhibitor, from *editus*).

-edly *suf.* forming adverbs from the p.p. of verbs, as in *markedly*, *guardedly*. WH: -ED + -LY[2].

educate *v.t.* to train and develop the intellectual and moral powers of. WH: 14–15C. Latin *educatus*, p.p. of *educare*, rel. to *educere* EDUCE. See also -ATE[3].

educe *v.t.* to bring out, evolve, develop. WH: 14–15C. Latin *educere*, from E- + *ducere* to lead. Cp. EDUCATE.

edulcorate *v.t.* to sweeten. WH: 17C. Medieval Latin *edulcoratus*, p.p. of *edulcorare*, from E- + Late Latin *dulcor* sweetness, from Latin *dulcis* sweet. See also -ATE[3].

edutainment *n.* infotainment. WH: late 20C. Abbr. of *education* (EDUCATE) + *entertainment* (ENTERTAIN).

Edwardian *a.* of or relating to the periods of any of the kings of England named Edward, esp. that of Edward VII (1901–10). *Also n.* WH: 19C. *Edward*, male forename + -IAN.

-ee *suf.* denoting the recipient, as in *grantee*, *legatee*, *payee*, *vendee*. WH: From or based on Anglo-French *-é*, p.p. suf., from Latin *-atus* -ATE[2].

eel *n.* a snakelike fish of the genus *Anguilla*, esp. the common European species, *A. anguilla*. WH: pre-1200. Old English *ǣl*, from Germanic, of unknown orig. Cp. German *Aal*.

-een *suf.* forming feminine diminutive nouns, as in *colleen*. WH: Irish dim. suf. *-ín*.

-eer *suf.* denoting an agent or a person concerned with or dealing in, as in *charioteer*, *musketeer*, *pamphleteer*, *sonneteer*. WH: Representing French *-ier*, from Latin *-arius*. Cp. -IER, -ARY[1].

eerie *a.* strange and frightening. WH: 12–14C. Prob. from Old English *earg* cowardly. Cp. German *arg* evil, bad. The original sense was fearful (superstitiously). The current sense dates from the 18C.

ef- *pref.* out of, from, as in *efface*, *effuse*. WH: Latin pref., from EX-, with *x* assim. to *f*.

eff *v.i.*, *v.t.* a euphemism for FUCK. WH: mid-20C. Name of letter *F*, as euphem. abbr. of FUCK.

efface *v.t.* to destroy or remove (something), so that it cannot be seen. WH: 15C. Old French *effacer*, from *ef-* EF- + *face* FACE.

effect *n.* the result or product of a cause or operation, the consequence. *Also v.t.* WH: 14–15C. Old French (Modern French *effet*), or from Latin *effectus*, from p.p. of *efficere* to accomplish, from EF- + *facere* to make, to do.

effeminate *a.* (of a man) womanish; unmanly, weak. WH: 14–15C. Latin *effeminatus*, p.p. of *effeminare* to make feminine, from EF- + *femina* woman. See also -ATE[2].

effendi *n.* a learned man or a man of social standing in the eastern Mediterranean. WH: 17C. Turkish *efendı*, from Modern Greek *aphentē*, voc. of *aphentēs*, from Greek *authentēs* lord, master.

efferent *a.* conveying outwards. *Also n.* WH: 19C. Latin *efferens, efferentis,* pres.p. of *efferre,* from EF- + *ferre* to bring, to carry. See also -ENT.

effervesce *v.i.* to bubble up, from the escape of gas, as fermenting liquors. WH: 18C. Latin *effervescere,* from EF- + *fervescere* to begin to boil, from *fervere* to be hot, to boil. See also -ESCE.

effete *a.* feeble, effeminate. WH: 17C. Latin *effetus* exhausted through child-bearing, from EF- + *fetus* breeding. See FOETUS. The original sense (to the 19C) was no longer fertile, past bearing offspring. The current sense has probably been influenced by association with unrelated EFFEMINATE.

efficacious *a.* producing or having power to produce the effect intended. WH: 16C. Latin *efficax, efficacis,* from *efficere.* See EFFECT, also -ACIOUS.

efficient *a.* causing or producing effects or results. *Also n.* WH: 14–15C. Latin *efficiens, efficientis,* pres.p. of *efficere.* See EFFECT, also -ENT.

effigy *n.* a representation or likeness of a person, as on coins, medals etc. WH: 16C. Latin *effigies,* from *effig-,* stem of *effingere,* from EF- + *fingere* to fashion, to shape.

effleurage *n.* in massage, a stroking movement of the hand. *Also v.i., v.t.* WH: 19C. French, from *effleurer* to stroke lightly, lit. to remove the flower, from EF- + *fleur* flower.

effloresce *v.i.* to burst into flower, to blossom. WH: 18C. Latin *efflorescere,* from EF- + *florescere* to come into bloom, from *florere* to blossom, from *flos, floris* flower. See also -ESCE.

effluent *a.* flowing or issuing out; emanating. *Also n.* WH: 14–15C. Latin *effluens, effluentis,* pres.p. of *effluere.* See EFFLUVIUM, also -ENT.

effluvium *n.* an emanation affecting the sense of smell, esp. a disagreeable smell and vapour as from putrefying substances etc. WH: 17C. Latin, from *effluere,* from EF- + *fluere* to flow. See also -IUM.

efflux *n.* the act of flowing out or issuing. WH: 16C. Medieval Latin *effluxus,* from p.p. of *effluere.* See EFFLUVIUM.

effort *n.* an exertion of physical or mental power, a strenuous attempt, an endeavour. WH: 15C. Old French, earlier *esforz,* from *esforcier* (Modern French *efforcer*), from Latin EF- + *fortis* strong.

effrontery *n.* bold, shameless and rude behaviour. WH: 17C. French *effronterie,* from *effronté,* from Late Latin *effrons* barefaced, from EF- + *frons, frontis* forehead. See also -ERY.

effulgent *a.* shining brightly. WH: 18C. Latin *effulgens, effulgentis,* pres.p. of *effulgere* to shine brightly, from EF- + *fulgere* to shine. See also -ENT.

effuse[1] *v.t.* to pour out, to emit. WH: 14–15C. Latin *effusus,* p.p. of *effundere,* from EF- + *fundere* to pour.

effuse[2] *a.* (of an inflorescence) spreading loosely. *Also n.* WH: 16C. Latin *effusus,* p.p. of *effundere.* See EFFUSE[1].

E-fit *n.* a computerized form of photofit with a wide range of possible facial features, usu. used in helping police and witnesses build up a picture of suspects. WH: late 20C. Acronym of *electronic facial identification technique,* punning on FIT[1].

eft *n.* the common newt. WH: pre-1200. Old English *efeta,* of unknown orig. Cp. NEWT.

†eftsoon *adv.* soon after, speedily, forthwith. WH: pre-1200. Old English *eftsōna,* from *eft* again, from Germanic base of AFTER + *sōna* SOON.

e.g. *abbr.* for example. WH: Abbr. of Latin *exempli gratia* for the sake of an example, from gen. sing. of EXEMPLUM + abl. sing. of *gratia* goodwill, GRACE.

egad *int.* by God (a minced oath). WH: 17C. AH + GOD.

egalitarian *a.* believing in the principle of human equality. *Also n.* WH: 19C. French *égalitaire,* from *égalité,* from *égal,* from Latin *aequalis* equal. See also -ARIAN.

egence *n.* the state of being needy. WH: 19C. Latin *egens, egentis,* pres.p. of *egere* to be in need.

egest *v.t.* to eject. WH: 15C. Latin *egestus,* p.p. of *egerere,* from E- + *gerere* to bear, to carry.

egg[1] *n.* the ovum of birds, reptiles, fishes and many of the invertebrates, usu. enclosed in a spheroidal shell and containing the embryo of a new individual. *Also v.t., v.i.* WH: 12–14C. Old Norse, superseding Old English *æg,* from Germanic, prob. ult. rel. to Latin

OVUM and Greek *ōion* egg. The word is unlikely to be related to Latin *avis* bird, as some claim.

egg[2] *v.t.* to incite, to urge (on). WH: 12–14C. Old Norse *eggja* EDGE.

eglandulose *a.* without glands. WH: 19C. E- + *glandulose.* See GLAND, also -ULOUS.

eglantine *n.* the sweet-brier. WH: 14–15C. French *églantine,* from Old French *aiglent,* from Latin *acuteus* prickle. See also -INE.

ego *n.* individuality, personality. WH: 19C. Latin I.

egregious *a.* conspicuously bad, flagrant. WH: 16C. Latin *egregius* surpassing, from *e-* E- + *grex, gregis* flock. See also -IOUS. The sense was originally remarkably good but soon after became remarkably bad, as now.

egress *n.* departure. WH: 16C. Latin *egressus,* from p.p. of *egredi* to go out, from *e-* E- + *gradi* to proceed, to step.

egret *n.* a heron of those species that have long and loose plumage over the back, of the genus *Egretta* or *Bulbulcus.* WH: 14–15C. Old French *aigrette,* from Provençal *aigreta,* from stem of *aigron,* rel. to Old French HERON. See also -ET[1]. Cp. AIGRETTE.

Egyptian *a.* of or relating to Egypt or the Egyptians. *Also n.* WH: 12–14C. *Egypt,* a country in NE Africa + -IAN.

eh *int.* used to express doubt, inquiry, surprise etc. WH: 16C. Natural exclamation. Cp. AYE[1].

-eian *suf.* forming adjectives and nouns from nouns ending in *-ey,* as in *Bodleian.* WH: *-ey* + -AN.

Eid *n.* a Muslim festival. WH: 17C. Arabic 'īd festival, from Aramaic.

eider *n.* a large Arctic duck, *Somateria mollissima.* WH: 17C. Icelandic *æthur,* gen. *æthar,* in *ætharfugl* eider duck, from Old Norse *æthr.*

eidetic *a.* able to reproduce a vivid image of something previously seen or imagined. *Also n.* WH: early 20C. Greek *eidētikos,* from *eidos* form. See also -ETIC. The term was introduced in *c.* 1920 by the German psychologist Erich Jaensch.

eidograph *n.* an instrument for copying plans or drawings on an enlarged or reduced scale. WH: 19C. Greek *eidos* form + -GRAPH.

eidolon *n.* an image, likeness or representation. WH: 17C. Greek *eidōlon.* See IDOL.

eigen- *comb. form* characteristic, own. WH: German *eigen-* OWN[1].

eigenfrequency *n.* any of the natural frequencies of vibration of a system. WH: mid-20C. EIGEN- + FREQUENCY.

eigenfunction *n.* the function that satisfies a particular differential equation, esp. in wave mechanics. WH: early 20C. EIGEN- + FUNCTION.

eigenvalue *n.* a value for which a particular differential equation has an eigenfunction, esp. in wave mechanics. WH: early 20C. EIGEN- + VALUE.

eight *n.* the number or figure 8 or viii. *Also a.* WH: pre-1200. Old English *ehta,* from Germanic, from Indo-European base also of Latin *octo,* Greek *okto,* Sanskrit *aṣṭā.*

eighteen *n.* the number or figure 18 or xviii. *Also a.* WH: pre-1200. Old English *ehtatēne,* from Germanic base of EIGHT, -TEEN.

eighty *n.* the number or figure 80 or lxxx. *Also a.* WH: pre-1200. Old English *hundehtatig,* from *hund,* of unknown orig., + *ehta* EIGHT + *-tig* -TY[2]. The first element was lost early in Middle English. Cp. SEVENTY.

einkorn *n.* a variety of wheat, *Triticum monococcum,* used for feeding animals. WH: early 20C. German, from *ein* one + *Korn* CORN[1], seed.

einsteinium *n.* a radioactive element, at. no. 99, chem. symbol Es, artificially produced from plutonium. WH: mid-20C. Albert Einstein, 1879–1955, German-born US physicist + -IUM. The name was coined commemoratively in 1955, simultaneously with *fermium* (FERMI).

eirenicon *n.* a measure or proposal intended to make or restore peace. WH: 17C. Greek *eirēnikon,* neut. sing. of *eirēnikos* IRENIC.

eisteddfod *n.* a competitive congress of Welsh bards and musicians held annually to encourage native poetry and music. WH: 19C. Welsh session, from *eistedd* to sit.

either *a., pron.* one or the other of two. *Also adv., conj.* WH: pre-1200. Old English *ægther,* contr. of *æghwæther,* from Germanic phr. from bases of AYE[2] + WHETHER.

eiusdem generis *a.* of the same kind. WH: 17C. Latin of the same kind, from gen. sing. of IDEM + GENUS.

ejaculate[1] *v.t.* to utter suddenly and briefly; to exclaim. *Also v.i.* WH: 16C. Latin *eiaculatus*, p.p. of *eiaculari*, from E- + *iaculari* to dart, from *iaculum* dart, javelin, from *iacere* to throw. See also -ATE[3]. The original sense was the physiological one (to emit semen). The sense to utter arose in the 17C.

ejaculate[2] *n.* semen which has been ejaculated. WH: early 20C. EJACULATE[1]. See also -ATE[2].

eject[1] *v.t.* to cause to come out of e.g. a machine. WH: 14–15C. Latin *eiectus*, p.p. of *eicere*, from E- + *iacere* to throw.

eject[2] *n.* something that is not an object of our own consciousness but inferred to have actual existence. WH: 19C. Latin *eiectum*, neut. p.p. of *eicere* (see EJECT[1]), based on SUBJECT[1], OBJECT[2]. The word was coined in 1878 by the English mathematician William K. Clifford to express ideas and sensations that could not be classed as either subjects or objects.

eke *v.t.* to produce, support or maintain with difficulty. WH: pre-1200. Old English *ēacan*, from Germanic, from Indo-European base also of Latin *augere* to increase (cp. AUGMENT[1]) and Greek *aukhein*.

ekka *n.* a small one-horse carriage. WH: 19C. Hindi *ikkā*, lit. single, from Sanskrit *eka* one.

el[1] *n.* the 12th letter of the alphabet, L, l. WH: 19C. Representation of pronun. of *L* as letter's name.

el[2] *n.* an elevated railway. WH: early 20C. Abbr. of *elevated* (ELEVATE).

-el -LE[2]. WH: suf. representing Old French *-el*, from Latin dim. suf. *ellus*.

elaborate[1] *a.* carefully or highly wrought. WH: 16C. Latin *elaboratus*, p.p. of *elaborare*. See ELABORATE[2], also -ATE[2].

elaborate[2] *v.t.* to develop in detail. *Also v.i.* WH: 16C. Latin *elaboratus*, p.p. of *elaborare*, from E- + *labor* LABOUR. See also -ATE[3].

élan *n.* energy and confidence. WH: 19C. French, from *élancer*, from *é-* (EX-) + *lancer* LANCE.

eland *n.* a large oxlike antelope, *Tragelaphus derbianus*, from southern Africa. WH: 18C. Afrikaans, from Dutch elk, from obs. German *Elend* (now *Elen*), from Lithuanian *élnis*. Rel. to ELK.

elapse *v.i.* (esp. of time) to glide or pass away. WH: 16C. Latin *elapsus*, p.p. of *elabi* to slip away, from E- + *labi*. See LAPSE.

elasmobranch *n.* a fish of the subclass Elasmobranchii, having platelike gills, containing the sharks, rays and chimeras. WH: 19C. Modern Latin *Elasmobranchii* (pl.), from Greek *elasmos* beaten metal + *bragkhia* gills.

elasmosaurus *n.* an extinct marine reptile with platelike gills and a tough skin. WH: 19C. Modern Latin, from Greek *elasmos* beaten metal + *sauros* lizard. The name was coined in 1868 by the US palaeontologist Edward D. Cope.

elastane *n.* a polyurethane with elastic properties, used in the manufacture of close-fitting clothing. WH: mid-20C. ELASTIC + -ANE.

elastic *a.* having the quality of returning to that form or volume from which it has been compressed, expanded or distorted; springy, rebounding. *Also n.* WH: 17C. Modern Latin *elasticus*, from Greek *elastikos*, from *ela-*, stem of *elaunein* to drive.

elastomer *n.* a synthetic rubber-like substance. WH: mid-20C. ELASTIC + -O- + -MER.

Elastoplast® *n.* a gauze surgical dressing on a backing of adhesive tape, suitable for small wounds, cuts and abrasions. WH: early 20C. ELASTIC + -O- + PLASTER.

elate *v.t.* to raise the spirits of, to stimulate. *Also a.* WH: 16C. Latin *elatus*, p.p. of *efferre*, from EF- + *ferre* to bear. See also -ATE[3].

elater *n.* a coleopterous insect of the genus *Elater*, called click beetles or skipjacks, from their ability to spring up and alight on their feet. WH: 17C. Greek *elatēr* driver, from *ela-* stem of *elaunein* to drive. Cp. ELASTIC.

elaterite *n.* a soft elastic mineral, elastic bitumen. WH: 19C. Greek *elatēr* driver (see ELATER) + -ITE[1]. Cp. ELASTIC.

elaterium *n.* a powerful purgative obtained from the fruit of the squirting cucumber. WH: 16C. Latin, from Greek *elatērion*, from *ela-*. See ELATER, also -IUM. The purgative is so called as it 'drives out' the impurities of the body.

elbow *n.* the joint uniting the forearm with the upper arm. *Also v.t., v.i.* WH: pre-1200. Old English *elnboga*, from Germanic, from bases of ELL and BOW[1]. Cp. German *Ellenbogen*.

†eld *n.* old age. *Also a., v.t.* WH: pre-1200. Old English *eldu*, from Germanic. Cp. OLD.

elder[1] *a.* older. *Also n.* WH: pre-1200. Old English *eldra*, from Germanic. See also -ER[3]. Rel. to ELD, OLD.

elder[2] *n.* a tree of the genus *Sambucus*, esp. *S. nigra*, a small tree bearing white flowers and dark purple berries. WH: pre-1200. Old English *ellærn*, prob. orig. an a., of unknown orig. Not rel. to ALDER. See also -ER[3].

El Dorado *n.* any place where money or profit is easily obtained. WH: 19C. Spanish the gilded, from *el* the + DORADO. The name was originally that of a non-existent country or city where there was much gold, believed to exist on the Amazon in S America.

eldritch *a.* strange, weird, ghastly, frightful. WH: 16C. Orig. uncertain. ? Rel. to ELF.

Eleatic *a.* of or relating to Elea, a town of Magna Graecia. *Also n.* WH: 17C. Latin *Eleaticus*, from *Elea*, an ancient Greek city in SW Italy. See also -ATIC.

elecampane *n.* a composite plant, *Inula helenium*, used in cooking and medicinally. WH: 14–15C. Ult. from Medieval Latin *enula campana* (*enula* from Latin *inula*, from Greek *helenion* elecampane, *campana* prob. meaning of the fields, from Latin *campus* (CAMP[1])).

elect *v.t.* to choose for any office or employment. *Also a., n.* WH: 14–15C. Latin *electus*, p.p. of *eligere*, from E- + *legere* to choose. The original sense (to the 19C) was to select for a particular purpose.

Electra complex *n.* attraction of a daughter to her father accompanied by hostility to her mother. WH: early 20C. *Electra*, the daughter of Agamemnon and Clytemnestra in Greek mythology, who caused her mother's death in revenge for the murder of her father. See COMPLEX. Cp. OEDIPUS COMPLEX.

electret *n.* a permanently polarized piece of dielectric material. WH: 19C. *electricity* (ELECTRIC) + MAGNET.

electric *a.* containing, generating or operated by electricity. *Also n.* WH: 17C. Modern Latin *electricus*, from Latin *electrum* amber, from Greek *ēlektron* + -IC. The word was adopted with reference to the fact that amber produces an electrostatic charge when rubbed.

electricity *n.* a form of energy which makes its existence manifest by attractions and repulsions, by producing light and heat, chemical decomposition and other phenomena. WH: 17C. ELECTRIC + -ITY.

electro *n.* an electrotype. *Also v.t.* WH: 19C. Use of ELECTRO- as independent word.

electro- *comb. form* having electricity for its motive power. WH: ELECTRIC or ELECTRICITY. See also -O-.

electrobath *n.* a solution of a metallic salt used in electrotyping and electroplating. WH: 19C. ELECTRO- + BATH[1].

electrobiology *n.* electrophysiology, the science of the electric phenomena of living organisms. WH: 19C. ELECTRO- + BIOLOGY.

electrocardiograph *n.* an instrument which indicates and records the manner in which the heart muscle is contracting. WH: early 20C. ELECTRO- + CARDIOGRAPH.

electrochemistry *n.* the science of the chemical effects produced by electricity. WH: 19C. ELECTRO- + CHEMISTRY.

electroconvulsive *a.* (of a therapy for mental or nervous disorders) using electric shocks to the brain. WH: mid-20C. ELECTRO- + *convulsive* (CONVULSE).

electrocopper *v.t.* to give a copper coating to by electrolysis. WH: 19C. ELECTRO- + COPPER.

electroculture *n.* the application of electricity to horticulture. WH: early 20C. ELECTRO- + CULTURE.

electrocute *v.t.* to kill by an electric shock. WH: 19C. ELECTRO- + EXECUTE.

electrode *n.* any one of the poles of a galvanic battery or of an electrical device. WH: 19C. ELECTRIC + Greek *hodos* way, based on ANODE, CATHODE. The term was coined in 1834 by the English chemist and physicist Michael Faraday.

electrodialysis *n.* dialysis in which an electric field is applied across a semi-permeable membrane. WH: early 20C. ELECTRO- + DIALYSIS.

electrodynamics *n.* the branch of mechanics concerned with electricity in motion. WH: 19C. ELECTRO- + *dynamics* (DYNAMIC).

electroencephalograph *n.* an instrument recording small electrical impulses produced by the brain. WH: mid-20C. ELECTRO- + *encephalograph* (ENCEPHALOGRAPHY).

electroengraving *n.* engraving by means of electricity. WH: 19C. ELECTRO- + *engraving* (ENGRAVE).

electrograph *n.* a recording electrometer. WH: 19C. ELECTRO- + -GRAPH.

electroluminescence *n.* luminescence produced by the application of an electric current. WH: 19C. ELECTRO- + *luminescence* (LUMINESCE).

electrolyse *v.t.* to decompose by direct action of electricity. WH: 19C. From *electrolysis*, from ELECTRO- + -*lysis* (LYSIS), based on ANALYSE.

electromagnet *n.* a bar of soft iron rendered magnetic by the passage of a current of electricity through a coil of wire surrounding it. WH: 19C. ELECTRO- + MAGNET.

electromechanical *a.* of or relating to the use of electricity in mechanical processes etc. WH: 19C. ELECTRO- + MECHANICAL.

electrometallurgy *n.* the separation of metals from their alloys by means of electrolysis. WH: 19C. ELECTRO- + METALLURGY.

electrometer *n.* an instrument for measuring the amount of electrical force, or for indicating the presence of electricity. WH: 18C. ELECTRO- + -METER.

electromotion *n.* the passage of an electric current in a circuit. WH: 19C. ELECTRO- + MOTION.

electromuscular *a.* of or relating to the action of the muscles under electric influence. WH: 19C. ELECTRO- + MUSCULAR.

electron *n.* a particle bearing a negative electric charge, the most numerous constituent of matter and probably the cause of all electrical phenomena. WH: 19C. ELECTRIC + -ON. The term was coined in 1891 by the Irish physicist George J. Stoney.

electronegative *a.* passing to the positive pole in electrolysis. *Also n.* WH: 19C. ELECTRO- + *negative* (NEGATE).

electronic *a.* of or relating to electronics. WH: early 20C. ELECTRON + -IC.

electrophilic *a.* having an affinity for electrons. WH: mid-20C. ELECTRO- + -*philic* (-PHILE).

electrophorus *n.* an instrument for generating static electricity by induction. WH: 18C. ELECTRO- + -*phorus* (-PHORE).

electrophysiology *n.* the study of electric phenomena in living organisms. WH: 19C. ELECTRO- + PHYSIOLOGY.

electroplate *v.t.* to cover with a coating of silver or other metal by exposure in a solution of a metallic salt, which is decomposed by electrolysis. *Also n.* WH: 19C. ELECTRO- + PLATE.

electroplexy *n.* electroconvulsive therapy. WH: mid-20C. ELECTRO- + APOPLEXY.

electropolar *a.* denoting a conductor positively electrified at one end and negatively at the other. WH: 19C. ELECTRO- + POLAR.

electroporation *n.* the introduction of DNA etc. into bacteria by opening the pores of the cell membranes with an electric pulse. WH: late 20C. ELECTRO- + PORE[1] + -ATION.

electropositive *a.* having a tendency to pass to the negative pole in electricity. *Also n.* WH: 19C. ELECTRO- + POSITIVE.

electroscope *n.* an instrument for detecting the presence and the quality of electricity. WH: 19C. ELECTRO- + -SCOPE.

electroshock *a.* (of medical treatment) using electric shocks. WH: 19C. ELECTRO- + SHOCK[1].

electrostatic *a.* of or relating to the science of static electricity. WH: 19C. ELECTRO- + STATIC, based on *hydrostatic* (HYDROSTATICS).

electrotechnology *n.* the use of electricity in technology. WH: 19C. ELECTRO- + TECHNOLOGY.

electrotherapeutics *n.* the use of electricity to treat paralysis etc. WH: 19C. ELECTRO- + *therapeutics* (THERAPEUTIC).

electrothermancy *n.* the science of the relations of electric currents and the temperature of bodies. WH: 19C. ELECTRO- + Greek *thermansis* heating, assim. to -ANCY.

electrotonus *n.* the alteration in the activity of a nerve or muscle under the action of a galvanic current. WH: 19C. ELECTRO- + TONUS.

electrotype *n.* the process of producing copies of medals, woodcuts, type etc., by the electric deposition of copper upon a mould. *Also v.t.* WH: 19C. ELECTRO- + -*type* (TYPE).

electrovalent *a.* of or relating to bonding caused by electrostatic attraction between ions. WH: early 20C. ELECTRO- + -*valent* (VALENCE).

electroweak *a.* of or relating to a combination of electromagnetic and weak interactions. WH: late 20C. ELECTRO- + WEAK.

electrum *n.* an alloy of gold and silver in use among the ancients. WH: 14–15C. Latin, from Greek *ēlektron*.

electuary *n.* a purgative medicine mixed with some sweet confection. WH: 14–15C. Late Latin *electuarium*, prob. from Greek *ekleikton*, from *ekleikhein* to lick up.

eleemosynary *a.* given or done by way of alms. *Also n.* WH: 16C. Medieval Latin *eleemosynary*, from Ecclesiastical Latin *eleemosyna* alms, from Greek *eleēmosunē* compassionateness, from *eleēmōn* compassionate, from *eleos* mercy. See also -ARY[1]. Cp. ALMS.

elegant *a.* pleasing to good taste. WH: 15C. Old French *élégant* or Latin *elegans, elegantis*, rel. to *eligere* to select. See ELECT, also -ANT. The earliest sense was dressing tastefully.

elegy *n.* a lyrical poem or a song of lamentation. WH: 16C. Ecclesiastical Latin *élégie* or Latin *elegia*, from Greek *elegeia*, from *elegos* mournful poem. See also -Y[2]. Not rel. to ELEGANT.

element *n.* any one of the fundamental parts of which anything is composed. WH: 12–14C. Old French *élément*, from Latin *elementum* principle, rudiment, translating Greek *stoikheion* step, component, part. The source of Latin *elementum* is uncertain. Some hold that it was originally a grammar term representing a Latin-learning schoolboy's formation from the letters *l, m, n*. Cp. ABC.

elemi *n.* a gum resin obtained from the Philippine tree, *Canarium luzanicum*, used in pharmacy. WH: 16C. Modern Latin, from Arabic *al-lāmī*.

elenchus *n.* a refutation. WH: 17C. Latin, from Greek *elegkhos* argument of refutation.

elephant *n.* a large pachyderm, four-footed, with flexible proboscis and long curved tusks, of which two species now exist, *Elephas maximus* and *Loxodonta africana*, the former partially domesticated and used as a beast of draught and burden. WH: 12–14C. Old French *olifant, elefant* (Modern French *éléphant*), from alt. of Latin *elephans, elephantis*, from Greek *elephas, elephantos* ivory, elephant, prob. of non-Indo-European orig. There is no proven connection between Greek *elephas* and Latin *ebur* ivory.

Eleusinian *a.* relating to Eleusis, in ancient Attica, or to the mysteries in honour of Demeter celebrated there annually. WH: 17C. Latin *Eleusinius*, from Greek *Eleusinios* pertaining to Eleusis, a village near Athens + -AN.

elevate *v.t.* to lift up; to raise higher. WH: 14–15C. Latin *elevatus*, p.p. of *elevare*, from E- + *levare* to lighten, to raise. See also -ATE[3].

eleven *n.* the number or figure 11 or xi. *Also a.* WH: pre-1200. Old English *endleofon*, from Germanic, from base of ONE + base represented also by TWELVE. Old English regarded eleven as 'one left' (over ten).

elevon *n.* a wing-flap on a delta wing aircraft. WH: mid-20C. *elevator* (ELEVATE) + AILERON.

elf *n.* a tiny supernatural being supposed to inhabit groves and wild and desolate places and to exercise a mysterious power over human beings. *Also v.t.* WH: pre-1200. Var. of Old English *ylf*, from Germanic. Cp. German *Alp* nightmare.

elicit *v.t.* to draw out, evoke. WH: 17C. Latin *elicitus*, p.p. of *elicere* to draw forth by magic, from E- + *lacere* to deceive.

elide *v.t.* to strike out, omit, delete. WH: 16C. Latin *elidere* to crush out, from E- + *laedere* to dash.

eligible *a.* fit or deserving to be chosen. WH: 14–15C. French *éligible*, from Late Latin *eligibilis*, from *eligere* to choose. See also -IBLE.

eliminate *v.t.* to cast out, expel. WH: 16C. Latin *eliminatus*, p.p. of *eliminare* to thrust out of doors, to expel, from E- + *limen, liminis* threshold. See also -ATE[3]. The original sense was to drive out, to expel. The sense to remove, to get rid of arose in the 18C.

ELINT *n.* gathering intelligence by electronic means. WH: mid-20C. Abbr. of *electronic intelligence.

eliquation *n.* conversion from a solid (or gaseous) to a liquid form. WH: 17C. Late Latin *eliquatio, eliquationis*, from *eliquatus*, p.p. of *eliquare* to liquefy, from E- + *liquare* to melt, to dissolve. See also -ATION.

elite *n.* the best part, the most powerful. WH: 18C. French *élite*, fem. of obs. p.p. (used as n.) of *élire* from var. of Latin *eligere* ELECT.

elixir *n.* the alchemists' liquor for transmuting metal into gold. WH: 14–15C. Medieval Latin, from Arabic *al-'iksīr*, from *al-* the + Greek *xērion* drying powder for wounds, from *xēros* dry.

Elizabethan *a.* of or relating to Queen Elizabeth I or Queen Elizabeth II or the time of either of these. *Also n.* WH: 19C. *Elizabeth*, female forename + -AN. The name is that of two English queens: Elizabeth I (reigned 1558–1603) of England and Elizabeth II (reigned from 1952) of the United Kingdom.

elk *n.* the largest animal of the deer family, *Alces alces*, a native of northern Europe and of N America, where it is called the moose. WH: 15C. Prob. from Old English *elh*, with *k* for *h*. Cp. German *Elch*, Greek *elaphos* deer.

ell *n.* a measure of length, varying in different countries, for measuring cloth: the English ell is 45 in. (114.3 cm). WH: pre-1200. Old English *eln*, from Germanic, with orig. meaning arm, forearm, rel. to Latin ULNA and Greek *ōlēnē* elbow. Cp. ELBOW. The final -*n* of the Old English has disappeared as in MILL[1].

ellagic *a.* of or relating to gall-nuts or to gallic acid. WH: 19C. French *ellagique*, from a reversal of *galle* gall-nut + -*ique* -IC. French *galle* could not itself be used because *gallique* GALLIC already existed.

ellipse *n.* a regular oval; a plane curve of such a form that the sum of two straight lines, drawn from any point in it to two given fixed points called the foci, will always be the same. WH: 17C. French, from Latin *ellipsis*, from Greek *elleipsis* defect, from *elleipein* to leave out, to fall short, from *en* in + *leipein* to leave. In a conic section, the cutting plane makes a smaller angle with the base than the side of the cone does. It thus 'falls short' of the side of the cone.

elm *n.* any tree of the genus *Ulmus*. WH: pre-1200. Old French, from Germanic, from Indo-European base also of Latin *ulmus*. Cp. German *Ulme*.

El Niño *n.* a warm ocean current in the southern Pacific, arising every few years, which affects the S American coast directly and climatic disturbance over a much larger area. WH: 19C. Spanish *El Niño (de Navidad)* the (Christmas) Child, Baby Jesus. The name refers to the time when the current occurs, between Christmas and March.

elocution *n.* the art, style or manner of speaking or reading. WH: 14–15C. Latin *elocutio*, *elocutionis*, from *elocutus*, p.p. of *eloqui*. See ELOQUENCE, also -ION. The original sense (to the 19C) was oratorical expression, literary style. The current sense dates from the 17C.

eloge *n.* an encomium, a panegyric, esp. a discourse in honour of a deceased person. WH: 16C. French *éloge*, from Latin *elogium* short epitaph, from alt. of Greek *elegeia* ELEGY. The Latin altered form probably arose by confusion with *eulogium* (see EULOGY).

Elohim *n.* the ordinary name of God in the Hebrew Scriptures. WH: 16C. Hebrew *'ĕlōhīm* lit. gods. The Hebrew plural word to describe the one God is usually explained as a 'plural of majesty' although it may actually relate to a polytheistic culture.

†eloin *v.t.* to remove. WH: 15C. Old French *esloignier* (Modern French *éloigner*), from Late Latin *elongare*. See ELONGATE.

elongate *v.t.* to extend. *Also v.i., a.* WH: 14–15C. Late Latin *elongatus*, p.p. of *elongare*, from Latin E- + *longe* far off, from *longus* long. See also -ATE[3].

elope *v.i.* to run away with a lover, with a view to a secret marriage, in defiance of social or moral restraint. WH: 16C. Anglo-French *aloper*, prob. from a word rel. to LEAP. The original sense was to run away, to abscond. The current narrower sense evolved in the 17C.

eloquence *n.* fluent, powerful and appropriate verbal expression, esp. of emotional ideas. WH: 14–15C. Old French *éloquence*, from Latin *eloquentia*, from *eloquens*, *eloquentis*, pres.p. of *eloqui* to speak out, from E- + *loqui* to speak. See also -ENCE.

Elsan® *n.* a type of chemical lavatory. WH: mid-20C. Appar. from *E. L. Jackson*, its orig. manufacturer + *sanitation* (SANITARY).

else *adv.* besides, in addition, other. WH: pre-1200. Old English *elles*, gen. sing. of a Germanic word rel. to Latin *alius* other (cp. ALIEN) and Greek *allos* (cp. ALLO-).

elucidate *v.t.* to make clear and easy to understand. WH: 16C. Late Latin *elucidatus*, p.p. of *elucidare*, from E- + *lucidus* LUCID. See also -ATE[3].

elude *v.t.* to escape from by artifice or dexterity. WH: 16C. Latin *eludere*, from E- + *ludere* to play. The original sense (to the 18C) was to delude, to baffle. The current sense dates from the 17C.

Elul *n.* the sixth month of the Jewish ecclesiastical, and the 12th of the civil year, beginning with the new moon of September. WH: 16C. Hebrew *'ĕlūl*.

elute *v.t.* to wash out by the action of a solvent. WH: 18C. Latin *elutus*, p.p. of *eluere* to wash out, from E- + *luere* to wash.

elutriate *v.t.* to purify by straining or washing so as to separate the lighter and the heavier particles. WH: 18C. Latin *elutriatus*, p.p. of *elutriare* to wash out, from E- + *lutriare* to wash.

elvan *n.* intrusive igneous rock penetrating sedimentary strata in Cornwall, Devon and Ireland. WH: 18C. ? Cornish, from Welsh *elfen* element.

elver *n.* a young eel, esp. a young conger. WH: 17C. Alt. of dial. form of *eel-fare* (EEL).

Elysium *n.* in Greek mythology, the abode of the souls of heroes after death. WH: 16C. Latin, from Greek *Elusion (pedion)* (plain of the) blessed. The Greek name is of non-Greek origin.

elytron *n.* each of the horny sheaths which constitute the anterior wings of beetles. WH: 18C. Greek *elutron* sheath.

Elzevir *n.* a book printed by the Elzevirs. *Also a.* WH: 18C. Dutch *Elsevier*, name of a family who were printers in the Netherlands, 1583–1712.

em *n.* the 13th letter of the alphabet, M, m. WH: 12–14C. Representation of pronun. of *M* as letter's name.

em- *pref.* in, on, into, upon, as in *embank*, *empanel*. WH: Old French *pref.*, from EN- with n assim. to *b*, *m*, *p*.

emaciate *v.t.* to cause to lose flesh or become lean. *Also v.i.* WH: 17C. Latin *emaciatus*, p.p. of *emaciare*, from E- + *macies* leanness. See also -ATE[3].

emanate *v.i.* to issue or flow as from a source, to originate. *Also v.t.* WH: 18C. Latin *emanatus*, p.p. of *emanare*, from E- + *manare* to flow.

emancipate *v.t.* to release from bondage, slavery, oppression or legal, social or moral restraint. WH: 17C. Latin *emancipatus*, p.p. of *emancipare*, from E- + *mancipium* slave. See also -ATE[3].

emarginate[1] *v.t.* to take away the edge or margin of. WH: 17C. Latin *emarginatus*, p.p. of *emarginare* to remove the edge of, from E- + *margo*, *marginis* edge. See also -ATE[3].

emarginate[2] *a.* with the margin notched. WH: 18C. Latin *emarginatus*, p.p. of *emarginare*. See EMARGINATE[1], also -ATE[2].

emasculate[1] *v.t.* to castrate. WH: 17C. Latin *emasculatus*, p.p. of *emasculare* to castrate, from E- + *masculus* male. See also -ATE[3].

emasculate[2] *a.* castrated. WH: 17C. Latin *emasculatus*, p.p. of *emasculare*. See EMASCULATE[1], also -ATE[2].

embalm *v.t.* to preserve (e.g. a body) from putrefaction by means of spices and aromatic drugs. WH: 12–14C. Old French *embaumer*, from EM- + *baume* BALM.

embank *v.t.* to confine or defend with a bank or banks, dykes, masonry etc. WH: 16C. EM- + BANK[1].

embargo *n.* a prohibition by authority upon the departure of vessels from ports under its jurisdiction. *Also v.t.* WH: 17C. Spanish, from *embargar* to arrest, to impede, from Latin IM-[1] + *barra* BAR[1].

embark *v.t.* to put on board ship. *Also v.i.* WH: 16C. French *embarquer*, from EM- + *barque* BARK[3].

embarras de choix *n.* a perplexing number of things to choose from. WH: 17C. French embarrassment of choice, from *embarras* embarassment (see EMBARRASS) + *de* of + *choix* CHOICE.

embarrass *v.t.* to make (someone) feel ashamed or uncomfortable. *Also n.* WH: 17C. French *embarrasser*, from Spanish *embarazar*, prob. from Portuguese *embaraçar*, from *baraço* halter. The original sense was to hamper, to impede. The current sense arose in the 19C.

embassy *n.* the official residence or offices of an ambassador. WH: 16C. Old French *ambassé*, from Medieval Latin *ambascatia*. See AMBASSADOR, also -Y[2].

embattle[1] *v.t.* to array in order of battle. *Also v.i.* WH: 12–14C. Old French *embataillier*. See EM-, BATTLE.

embattle[2] *v.t.* to furnish with battlements. WH: 14–15C. EM- + Old French *bataillier*. See BATTLE. Cp. BATTLEMENT.

embay *v.t.* to enclose (a vessel) in a bay, to landlock. WH: 16C. EM- + BAY[1].

embed *v.t.* to lay as in a bed. WH: 18C. EM- + BED.

embellish *v.t.* to decorate in order to make more attractive. WH: 14–15C. Old French *embellir*, *embelliss*-, from EM- + *bel* beautiful. See also -ISH[2].

ember[1] *n.* a smouldering piece of coal or wood. **WH:** pre-1200. Old English *ǽmyrge*, from Germanic. Cp. Danish *emmer*, Swedish *mörja*. The *b* entered as for SLUMBER.

ember[2] *n.* an anniversary, a recurring time or season. **WH:** pre-1200. Old English *ymbren*, prob. alt. of *ymbryne* period, revolution of time, from *ymb* about, round + *ryne* course. The Old English word may have been partly based on the Ecclesiastical Latin *quatuor tempora* four seasons. Cp. German *Quatember* Ember day.

ember-goose *n.* the northern diver or loon, *Gavia immer*. **WH:** 17C. Norwegian *immer, imbre* + GOOSE.

embezzle *v.t.* to take fraudulently (what is committed to one's care). *Also v.i.* **WH:** 14–15C. Anglo-French *embesiler*, from EM- + *besiler* to embezzle, of unknown orig. The original sense (to the 18C) was to make off with, to steal.

embitter *v.t.* to cause (a person) to be bitterly resentful or hostile. **WH:** 15C. EM- + BITTER.

†**emblaze** *v.t.* to set in a blaze, to kindle. **WH:** 15C. EM- + BLAZE[1].

emblazon *v.t.* to blazon; to adorn with heraldic figures or armorial designs. **WH:** 16C. EM- + BLAZON.

emblem *n.* a symbolic figure; a picture, object or representation of an object symbolizing some other thing, class, action or quality, as a crown for royalty or a balance for justice. *Also v.t.* **WH:** 17C. Latin *emblema* inlaid work, from Greek *emblēma* insertion, from *emballein* to throw in, to insert, from EM- + *ballein* to throw.

emblements *n.pl.* growing crops annually produced by the cultivator's labour, which belong to the tenant, though the lease may terminate before harvest. **WH:** 15C. Old French *emblaement*, from *emblaer* to sow with corn (Modern French *emblaver*), from *blé* corn.

embody *v.t.* to incarnate or invest with a material body. *Also v.i.* **WH:** 16C. EM- + BODY, based on Latin *incorporare* (see INCORPORATE[1]).

embog *v.t.* to plunge into a bog. **WH:** 17C. EM- + BOG.

embogue *v.i.* to disembogue, to discharge (as a river into the sea). **WH:** 17C. Spanish *embocar*, from EM- + *boca* mouth. Cp. DISEMBOGUE.

embolden *v.t.* to give boldness to. **WH:** 16C. EM- + *bolden*, from BOLD + -EN[5].

embolism *n.* partial or total blocking-up of a blood vessel by a clot of blood, bubble of air etc. **WH:** 14–15C. Late Latin *embolismus*, from Greek *embolismos*, from *emballein* to throw in, from EM- + *ballein* to throw. See also -ISM. The original sense was the intercalation of days in a calendar (to correct an accumulating discrepancy). The medical sense dates from the 19C.

embonpoint *n.* plumpness of person or figure. *Also a.* **WH:** 17C. French phr. *en bon point* in good condition, from *en* IN + *bon* good + *point* POINT.

embosom *v.t.* to place or hold in or as in the bosom of anything. **WH:** 16C. EM- + BOSOM.

emboss *v.t.* to engrave or mould in relief. **WH:** 14–15C. Old French *embocer* (Modern French *embosser*), from EM-, BOSS[1].

embouchure *n.* the shaping of the lips to the mouthpiece of a brass or wind instrument. **WH:** 18C. French, from *s'emboucher* to discharge itself by a mouth, from *emboucher* to put in the mouth, from EM- + *bouche* mouth. See also -URE.

embow *v.t.* to arch, to vault. **WH:** 14–15C. EM- + BOW[1].

embowel *v.t.* to disembowel. **WH:** 16C. Old French *emboweler*, alt. of *esboueler*, from *es-* EX- + *bouel* BOWEL.

embower *v.t.* to enclose in or as in a bower. **WH:** 16C. EM- + BOWER[1].

embox *v.t.* to set or shut in or as in a box. **WH:** 17C. EM- + BOX[1].

embrace[1] *v.t.* to enfold in the arms. *Also v.i., n.* **WH:** 12–14C. Old French *embracer* (Modern French *embrasser*), from Latin IM-[1] + *bracchium* arm (cp. BRACE).

†**embrace**[2] *v.t.* to fasten or fix with a brace. **WH:** 15C. EM- + BRACE.

embracer *n.* a person who endeavours to corrupt a jury by threats, bribery etc. **WH:** 14–15C. Old French *embraseor* instigator, from *embraser* to set on fire, from EM- + *braise* live coals. Cp. ENTICE.

embranchment *n.* a branching out, as of the arm of a river. **WH:** 19C. French *embranchement*. See EM-, BRANCH, also -MENT.

embrangle *v.t.* to entangle, to complicate. **WH:** 17C. EM- + obs. *brangle* to shake, to make totter, from Old French *branler* to shake, influ. by WRANGLE.

embrasure *n.* the inward enlargement, bevelling or splaying of the sides of a window or door. **WH:** 18C. French, from obs. *embraser* (now *ébraser*) to widen (a door or window opening), of unknown orig. See also -URE.

embrave *v.t.* to inspire with courage, to embolden. **WH:** 16C. EM- + BRAVE.

embreathe *v.t.* to breathe into, inspire. **WH:** 14–15C. EM- + BREATHE.

embrittle *v.t.* to make brittle. **WH:** early 20C. EM- + BRITTLE.

embrocate *v.t.* to moisten, bathe or foment (as a diseased part of the body). **WH:** 17C. Medieval Latin *embrocatus*, p.p. of *embrocare*, from Late Latin *embroca*, from Greek *embrokhē* lotion. See also -ATE[3].

embroider *v.t.* to ornament with figures or designs in needlework. *Also v.i.* **WH:** 14–15C. Anglo-French *enbrouder*, from EM- + Old French *brouder* (Modern French *broder*), from Germanic.

embroil *v.t.* to throw into confusion. **WH:** 17C. French *embrouiller*. See EM-, BROIL[1].

embryectomy *n.* the surgical operation of removing the foetus through an incision in the abdomen. **WH:** 19C. EMBRYO- + -ECTOMY.

embryo *n.* an unborn offspring. *Also a.* **WH:** 14–15C. Late Latin, mistaken adoption of Greek *embruon* (from EM- + *bruein* to swell, to grow) as a n. in *-ōn, -ōnis*.

embryo- *comb. form* of or relating to the embryo or embryos. **WH:** EMBRYO. See also -O-.

embryoctony *n.* the destruction of the foetus in the womb. **WH:** early 20C. EMBRYO- + Greek *-ktonos*, from *ktenein* to kill.

embryogenesis *n.* the formation of an embryo. **WH:** 19C. EMBRYO- + GENESIS.

embryogony *n.* the formation of an embryo. **WH:** 19C. EMBRYO- + Greek *-gonia* production.

embryology *n.* the science of the embryo and the formation and development of organisms. **WH:** 19C. EMBRYO- + -O- + -LOGY.

embryotomy *n.* the cutting up of an embryo or foetus in the uterus to aid removal. **WH:** 18C. EMBRYO- + -TOMY.

embus *v.t.* to put troops into buses or lorries for transport. *Also v.i.* **WH:** early 20C. EM- + BUS, based on EMBARK. Cp. ENTRAIN[2].

emcee *n.* a master of ceremonies. *Also v.t., v.i.* **WH:** mid-20C. Representation of pronun. of letters *MC*.

-eme *suf.* in linguistics, forming nouns, meaning a smallest possible, indivisible unit, as in *morpheme, phoneme*. **WH:** Extracted from PHONEME.

emend *v.t.* to correct, to remove faults from. **WH:** 14–15C. Latin *emendare*, from E- + *menda* fault. Cp. AMEND.

emerald *n.* a variety of beryl, distinguished by its beautiful green colour. *Also a.* **WH:** 12–14C. Old French *esmeraude* (Modern French *émeraude*), from alt. of Latin *smaragdus*, from Greek *smaragdos*, var. of *maragdos*, from Hebrew *bāreqet* emerald, from *bāraq* to flash, to sparkle.

emerge *v.i.* to rise up out of anything in which a thing has been immersed or sunk. **WH:** 16C. Latin *emergere*, from E- + *mergere* to dip, to plunge.

emergency *n.* a sudden occurrence or situation demanding immediate action, a crisis. **WH:** 17C. Medieval Latin *emergentia*, from Latin *emergens, emergentis*, pres.p. of *emergere*. See EMERGE, also -ENCY.

emeritus *a.* having served one's term of office and retired with an honorary title. *Also n.* **WH:** 18C. Latin, p.p. of *emereri* to earn (one's discharge) by service, from E- + *mereri* to deserve. See MERIT.

emerods *n.pl.* haemorrhoids. **WH:** 14–15C. Alt. of HAEMORRHOIDS. Cp. I Sam. v.6.

emersion *n.* the action of emerging, esp. from water. **WH:** 17C. Late Latin *emersio, emersionis*, from Latin *emersus*, p.p. of *emergere*. See EMERGE. See also -ION.

emery *n.* a coarse variety of corundum, of extreme hardness, and black or greyish-black colour, used for polishing hard substances. **WH:** 15C. French *émeri*, from Old French *esmeril*, from Italian *smeriglio*, from Medieval Greek *smēri*, from Greek *smiris* polishing powder. Cp. SMEAR.

emetic *a.* inducing vomiting. *Also n.* **WH:** 17C. Greek *emetikos*, from *emetos* vomiting, from *emein* to vomit. See also -IC.

émeute *n.* a seditious or revolutionary outbreak. **WH:** 18C. French, from Old French *esmote*, from *esmeu* (Modern French *ému*), p.p. of *esmovoir* (Modern French *émouvoir*), based on *meute* crowd, uprising. Cp. EMOTION.

emiction *n.* the discharge of urine. WH: 17C. Medieval Latin *emictus*, p.p. of *emingere*, from E- + *mingere* to urinate. See also -ION.

emigrate *v.i.* to leave one's country in order to settle in another. *Also v.t.* WH: 18C. Latin *emigratus*, p.p. of *emigrare*, from E- + *migrare* to migrate. See also -ATE[3].

émigré *n.* an emigrant, esp. one of the royalists who left France at the time of the French Revolution. WH: 18C. French, p.p. of *émigrer*, from Latin *emigrare*. See EMIGRATE.

éminence grise *n.* a man in the background exercising power unofficially. WH: mid-20C. French, lit. grey eminence. The term was originally a nickname applied to Cardinal Richelieu's private secretary, the Capuchin Père Joseph (originally François Joseph le Clerc du Tremblay), 1577–1638. He was so called by contrast with Richelieu himself, the *Éminence rouge* Red Eminence (from the colour of his cardinal's robes).

eminent *a.* famous and respected. WH: 14–15C. Latin *eminens*, *eminentis*, pres.p. of *eminere* to project. See also -ENT.

emir *n.* in the Middle East and N Africa, a prince, chieftain, governor or commander. WH: 16C. French *émir*, from Arabic *'amīr*. See AMIR.

emissary *n.* a messenger or agent, esp. one sent on a secret, dangerous or unpleasant mission. *Also a.* WH: 17C. Latin *emissarius*, from *emissus*, p.p. of *emittere* EMIT. See also -ARY[1].

emission *n.* the act or process of emitting or being emitted. WH: 14–15C. Latin *emissio*, *emissionis*, from *emissus*. See EMISSARY, also -ION.

emit *v.t.* to give out, to give vent to, to issue, to discharge, to utter. WH: 17C. Latin *emittere*, from E- + *mittere* to send.

emmenagogue *n.* a medicine that induces or restores the menses. WH: 18C. Greek *emmēna* menses (from EM- + *mēn*, *menos* month) + *agōgos* leading, from *agein* to lead.

Emmental *n.* a type of Swiss cheese with holes in it. WH: early 20C. *Emmental*, a region in Switzerland.

emmer *n.* a variety of wheat, *Triticum dicoccum*, grown in Europe largely as livestock fodder. WH: early 20C. German, from Old High German *amer*.

emmet *n.* an ant. WH: pre-1200. Old English *æmete*, weak form of *æmete*. See ANT.

Emmy *n.* the television equivalent of an Oscar, awarded by the American Academy of Television Arts and Sciences. WH: mid-20C. Orig. uncertain. Prob. alt. of *Immy*, from *image* (*orthicon tube*) + -Y[3]. The name may have been assimilated to *Emmy* (pet form of the female forename *Emma*) to match the existing OSCAR.

emollient *a.* softening, relaxing. *Also n.* WH: 17C. Latin *emolliens*, *emollientis*, pres.p. of *emollire* to make soft, from E- + *mollis* soft. See also -ENT.

emolument *n.* the profit arising from any office or employment. WH: 14–15C. Old French *émolument* or Latin *emolumentum* gain, prob. orig. payment to a miller for the grinding of corn, from *emolere* to grind up, from E- + *molere* to grind. See also -ENT.

emotion *n.* agitation of the mind. WH: 16C. French *émotion*, from *émouvoir* to excite, to move the feelings of, ult. from Latin *emovere*, from E- + *movere* to move.

empanel *v.t.* to enter on the list of jurors. WH: 14–15C. Anglo-French *empaneller*. See EM-, PANEL.

empathy *n.* the capacity for identifying with the experience of others, or appreciating things or emotions outside ourselves. WH: early 20C. Greek *empathein*, from EM- + *pathos* feeling. See also -Y[2]. The word was created as a translation of German *Einfühlung* (from *ein* in + *Fühlung* feeling), itself coined in 1903 by the German philosopher and psychologist Theodor Lipps.

empennage *n.* the stabilizing parts at the rear of an aeroplane, including the rudder, the fin and the elevator. WH: early 20C. French feathering (of an arrow), from *empenner* to feather (an arrow), from EM- + *penne* feather, from Latin *penna*. See also -AGE.

emperor *n.* the sovereign of an empire. WH: 12–14C. Old French *emperere* (Modern French *empereur*), from Latin *imperator*, from *imperare* to command, from IM-[1] + *parare* to prepare. See also -OR.

emphasis *n.* a special prominence or significance put on an idea, policy etc. WH: 16C. Latin, from Greek appearance, from *emphainein* to exhibit, from EM- + *phainein* to show.

emphractic *a.* having the quality of closing the pores of the skin. *Also n.* WH: 18C. Greek *emphraktikos*, from *emphrattein* to obstruct, from EM- + *phrattein* to block. See also -IC.

emphysema *n.* distension in the tissue of the lung, causing breathing difficulties. WH: 17C. Late Latin, from Greek *emphusēma*, from *emphusan* to puff up.

empire *n.* the group of states or nations over which an emperor rules. *Also a.* WH: 12–14C. Old French, from Latin *imperium*, rel. to *imperator* EMPEROR.

empirical *a.* founded on experience or observation, not theory. *Also n.* WH: 16C. Latin *empiricus*, from Greek *empeirikos*, from *empeiria* experience, from *empeiros* skilled, from EM- + *peira* trial, experiment. See also -IC, -AL[1].

emplacement *n.* a setting in position. WH: 19C. French. See EM-, PLACE, also -MENT.

emplane *v.i.* to go on board an aeroplane. *Also v.t.* WH: early 20C. EM- + PLANE[4]. Cp. EMBUS, ENTRAIN[2].

employ *v.t.* to use, to exercise. *Also n.* WH: 14–15C. Old French *employer*, from Latin *implicare* to enfold, to involve. See IMPLICATE. Cp. IMPLY.

emplume *v.t.* to adorn with or as with plumes. WH: 17C. Old French *emplumer*. See EM-, PLUME.

empoison *v.t.* to mix poison with. WH: 14–15C. Old French *empoisoner* (Modern French *empoisonner*). See EM-, POISON.

emporium *n.* a large shop where many kinds of goods are sold. WH: 16C. Latin, from Greek *emporion*, from *emporos* merchant, from EM- + verbal stem *por-*, *per-* to journey.

empower *v.t.* to authorize. WH: 17C. EM- + POWER.

empress *n.* the wife or widow of an emperor. WH: 12–14C. Old French *emperesse*, from *emperere* EMPEROR. See also -ESS[1].

empressement *n.* cordiality, goodwill, eagerness. WH: 18C. French, from *empresser* to urge. See also -MENT.

†emprise *n.* an adventurous or chivalrous undertaking. *Also v.t.* WH: 12–14C. Old French, fem. p.p. (used as n.) of *emprendre*, from Latin EM- + *prehendere*, *prendere* to take. Cp. ENTERPRISE.

empty *a.* void, containing nothing. *Also n., v.t., v.i.* WH: pre-1200. Old English *æmtig*, from *æmta* leisure, prob. from neg. *ā* + *mōt* meeting (see MOOT). The original Old English sense was at leisure, unoccupied, unmarried.

empurple *v.t.* to tinge or colour with purple. WH: 16C. EM- + PURPLE.

empyema *n.* a collection of pus in a body cavity, esp. in the pleura. WH: 14–15C. Late Latin, from Greek *empuēma*, from *empuein* to suppurate, from EM- + *puon* pus.

empyrean *n.* the highest and purest region of heaven, where the element of fire was supposed by the ancients to exist without any admixture of grosser matter. *Also a.* WH: 14–15C. Medieval Latin *empyreus*, from Greek *empurios*, from EM- + *pur* fire. See also -EAN.

empyreuma *n.* the disagreeable smell and taste produced when animal and vegetable substances are burned. WH: 17C. Greek *empureuma* live coal covered with ashes, from *empureuein* to set on fire, from EM- + *pur* fire.

emu *n.* a large Australian cursorial bird of the genus *Dromaius*, esp. *D. Novaehollandiae*, resembling the cassowary but different in having no casque. WH: 17C. Portuguese *ema*, prob. from a Moluccan language. The name was originally used (to the 18C) for the cassowary, a related bird, and was applied to the present bird only in the 19C.

emulate *v.t.* to try to equal or excel. *Also a.* WH: 16C. Latin *aemulatus*, p.p. of *aemulari*, from *aemulus* rival. See also -ATE[3].

emulgent *a.* milking or draining out. WH: 16C. Latin *emulgens*, *emulgentis*, pres.p. of *emulgere*. See EMULSION, also -ENT.

emulous *a.* desirous of equalling or excelling others. WH: 14–15C. Latin *aemulus*. See EMULATE, also -ULOUS.

emulsion *n.* a colloidal suspension of one liquid in another. *Also v.t.* WH: 17C. French *émulsion* or Modern Latin *emulsio*, *emulsionis*, from Latin *emulsus*, p.p. of *emulgere* to milk out, from E- + *mulgere* to milk. See also -ION. Cp. MILK.

emunctory *a.* serving to wipe the nose. *Also n.* WH: 14–15C. Medieval Latin *emunctorius*, from Latin *emunctus*, p.p. of *emungere* to wipe the nose. See also -ORY[2].

emys *n.* the freshwater tortoise. WH: 19C. Modern Latin, from Greek *emus*.

en *n.* the 14th letter of the alphabet, N, n. **WH:** 18C. Representation of pronun. of *N* as letter's name. Cp. EM.

en- *pref.* in, on, into, upon, as in *encamp, encourage, engulf, enslave, enlighten, encomium, energy, enthusiasm.* **WH:** Greek pref., from prep. *en* in, inside. In Old French derivatives, *n* is often assimilated to a subsequent consonant. See EM-.

-en¹ *suf.* forming diminutives of nouns, as in *chicken, maiden.* **WH:** Old English, from Germanic, neut. base of -EN³.

-en² *suf.* forming feminine nouns, as in *vixen.* **WH:** Old English, from Germanic.

-en³ *suf.* forming adjectives from nouns, meaning pertaining to, made of, of the nature of, as in *golden, woollen.* **WH:** Old English, from Germanic. Cp. Greek *-inos*, Latin *-inus*. See -INE.

-en⁴ *suf.* forming the pl. of nouns, as in *oxen.* **WH:** Old English *-an*, orig. part of stem of weak nn.

-en⁵ *suf.* forming verbs from adjectives or nouns, meaning to become or cause to become, as in *enlighten.* **WH:** Old English *-nian*, from Germanic.

-en⁶ *suf.* forming the p.p. of strong verbs, as in *broken, fallen, spoken.* **WH:** Old English *-en*, from Germanic.

enable *v.t.* to make able. **WH:** 14–15C. EN- + ABLE.

enact *v.t.* to decree. *Also n.* **WH:** 14–15C. EN- + ACT, based on Medieval Latin *inactare*.

enallage *n.* a change of words, or a substitution of one mood, tense, number, case or gender of the same word for another. **WH:** Late Latin, from Greek *enallagē*, from base of *enallassein* to exchange, from EN- + *allassein* to change, from *allos* other.

enamel *n.* a vitreous, opaque or semitransparent material with which metal, porcelain and other vessels, ornaments etc. are coated by fusion, for decorative or preservative purposes. *Also v.t., v.i.* **WH:** 14–15C. Anglo-French *enameler*, from EN- + *amail* (Old French *esmail*), from Germanic. Rel. to SMELT¹.

enamour *v.t.* to captivate, to charm. **WH:** 12–14C. Old French *enamourer*, from EN- + AMOUR. Cp. INAMORATO.

enanthema *n.* an ulcer or other eruption on a mucus-secreting surface. **WH:** 19C. EN- + EXANTHEMA.

enantio- *comb. form* opposite, mirror image. **WH:** Greek *enantios* opposite. See also -O-.

enantiomer *n.* a molecule which is the mirror image of another. **WH:** mid-20C. ENANTIO- + -MER.

enantiomorph *n.* a crystal structure which is the mirror image of another. **WH:** 19C. ENANTIO- + -MORPH.

enantiosis *n.* a figure of speech by which one says (usually ironically) the reverse of what one means. **WH:** 17C. Greek, from *enantios* opposite.

enarch *v.t.* to arch over. **WH:** 14–15C. EN- + ARCH¹.

†enarration *n.* a narration or description. **WH:** 16C. Latin *enarratio, enarrationis*, from E- + *narratio, narrationis*. See NARRATE, also -ION.

enarthrosis *n.* a ball-and-socket joint. **WH:** 16C. Greek *enarthrōsis*, from *enarthros* jointed. See also -OSIS. Cp. EN-, ARTHRO-.

enation *n.* the production of outgrowths upon the surface of an organ. **WH:** 19C. Latin *enatio, enationis*, from *enari* to issue forth, to be born, from E- + *nasci* to be born. See also -ATION.

en avant *int.* forward! **WH:** 19C. French forward, from *en* into + AVANT.

en barbette *a.* (of guns) so mounted as to allow of their being fired over a parapet without embrasures or port-holes. **WH:** 18C. French, from *en* in + BARBETTE.

en bloc *adv.* as one unit, all together. **WH:** 19C. French in a block, from *en* in + BLOC.

en brosse *a.* (of hair) cut very short so that it stands on end. **WH:** early 20C. French in a brush, from *en* in + *brosse* BRUSH¹.

en cabochon *a.* (of a precious stone) polished, but without facets. **WH:** 19C. French in a cabochon, from *en* in + CABOCHON.

encaenia *n.pl.* a festival to commemorate the dedication of a church, the founding of a city etc. **WH:** 14–15C. Latin, from Greek *egkainia* dedication festival, from EN- + *kainos* new, recent.

encage *v.t.* to shut in or as in a cage. **WH:** 16C. EN- + CAGE¹.

encamp *v.i.* to form a camp. *Also v.t.* **WH:** 16C. EN- + CAMP¹.

encapsulate *v.t.* to enclose in a capsule. **WH:** 19C. EN- + CAPSULE + -ATE³.

encarnalize *v.t.* to make carnal. **WH:** 19C. EN- + CARNAL + -IZE.

encase *v.t.* to put into a case. **WH:** 17C. EN- + CASE².

encash *v.t.* to cash, to convert (bills etc.) into cash. **WH:** 19C. EN- + CASH¹.

encaustic *n.* a mode of painting in which the colours are fixed by heat (now chiefly of painting on vitreous or ceramic ware in which the colours are burnt in). *Also a.* **WH:** 16C. Latin *encausticus*, from Greek *egkaustikos*, from *egkaiein* to burn in, from EN- + *kaiein* to burn.

encave *v.t.* to hide in a cellar. **WH:** 17C. EN- + CAVE¹.

-ence *suf.* forming abstract nouns meaning a state or quality, as *absence, science.* **WH:** French, from Latin *-entia*, from pres.p. stems in *-ent-* -ENT, or *-antia* (see -ANCE).

enceinte *a.* pregnant. *Also n.* **WH:** 18C. French, from Latin *incincta*, fem. p.p. of *incingere* to gird in, from IN-¹ + *cingere* to gird.

encephalitis *n.* inflammation of the brain. **WH:** 19C. ENCEPHALO- + -ITIS.

encephalo- *comb. form* brain. **WH:** Greek *egkephalos* brain, from EN- + *kephalē* head. See also -O-.

encephalocele *n.* hernia of the brain. **WH:** 19C. ENCEPHALO- + -CELE.

encephalography *n.* radiography of the brain. **WH:** early 20C. ENCEPHALO- + -GRAPHY.

encephalomyelitis *n.* acute inflammation of the brain and spinal cord. **WH:** early 20C. ENCEPHALO- + MYELITIS.

encephalon *n.* the brain. **WH:** 18C. Greek *egkephalon* that which is in the head, from EN- + *kephalē* head.

encephalopathy *n.* any degenerative disease referable to a disorder of the brain. **WH:** 19C. ENCEPHALO- + -PATHY.

encephalotomy *n.* the operation of cutting into the brain. **WH:** 19C. ENCEPHALO- + -TOMY.

enchain *v.t.* to bind with chains. **WH:** 14–15C. Old French *enchaîner*, from EN- + Latin *catena* chain.

enchant *v.t.* to influence by magic, to bewitch. **WH:** 14–15C. Old French *enchanter*, from Latin *incantare*, from IN-¹ + *cantare* to sing. See CHANT.

enchase *v.t.* to set or encase within any other material, such as a gem in precious metal. **WH:** 14–15C. Old French *enchaser* to enshrine, to set (gems), from EN- + *chasse*. See CASE².

enchilada *n.* a Mexican dish of a meat-filled tortilla served with chilli sauce. **WH:** 19C. American Spanish, fem. of *enchilado*, p.p. of *enchilar* to season with chilli. See EN-, CHILLI.

enchiridion *n.* a handbook or manual, a small guide or book of reference. **WH:** 14–15C. Late Latin, from Greek *egkheiridion*, from EN- + *kheir* hand + dim. suf. *-ion*.

enchorial *a.* belonging to or used in a country. **WH:** 19C. Greek *egkhōrios* in the country, from EN- + *khōra* country. See also -AL¹.

encipher *v.t.* to put (a message etc.) into cipher, to encode. **WH:** 16C. EN- + CIPHER.

encircle *v.t.* to enclose or surround (with). **WH:** 16C. EN- + CIRCLE.

en clair *a., adv.* (of telegrams etc.) not in code or cipher. **WH:** 19C. French in clear, from *en* in + *clair* CLEAR.

enclasp *v.t.* to enfold in a clasp, to embrace. **WH:** 16C. EN- + CLASP.

enclave *n.* a territory completely surrounded by that of another state; an enclosure, as viewed from outside it. *Also a.* **WH:** 19C. French, from Old French *enclaver* to enclose, to dovetail, from Popular Latin, from Latin *inclavare*, IN-¹ + *clavis* key.

enclitic *a.* of or relating to a word which cannot, as it were, stand by itself, but is pronounced as part of the preceding word, on which it throws its accent, e.g. *thee* in *prithee.* *Also n.* **WH:** 17C. Late Latin *encliticus*, from Greek *egklitikos*, from *egklinein* to lean on, from EN- + *klinein* to lean, to slope. See also -IC.

enclose *v.t.* to shut in. **WH:** 12–14C. Old French *enclos*, p.p. of *enclôre*, from Popular Latin, from Latin *includere* INCLUDE.

encode *v.t.* to translate a message into code. **WH:** early 20C. EN- + CODE.

encomiast *n.* a person who composes an encomium, a panegyrist. **WH:** 17C. Greek *egkōmiastēs*, from *egkōmiazein* to praise, from *egkōmion* ENCOMIUM.

encomium *n.* a formal eulogy or panegyric. **WH:** 16C. Latin, from Greek *egkōmion* eulogy, neut. (used as n.) of *egkōmios*, from EN- + *kōmos* revel. Cp. COMIC.

encompass *v.t.* to surround, to invest. **WH:** 12–14C. EN- + COMPASS.

encore *int.* used as a call for a repetition at a concert, theatre etc. *Also n.*, *v.t.*, *v.i.* WH: 18C. French still, again, ? from Popular Latin *hinc-ad-horam* from then to this hour. The French equivalent word is *bis*, from Latin twice.

encounter *v.t.* to meet face to face. *Also n.* WH: 12–14C. Old French *encontrer* (Modern French *rencontrer*), from Latin IN-¹ + *contra* against.

encourage *v.t.* to give courage or confidence to. WH: 14–15C. Old French *encourager*, from EN- + *corage* COURAGE.

encrinite *n.* a fossil crinoid. WH: 19C. Modern Latin *encrinus*, from Greek EN- + *krinon* lily + -ITE¹.

encroach *v.i.* to intrude (upon) what belongs to another. WH: 14–15C. Old French *encrochier* to seize, to fasten on, from EN- + *crochier* to hook, from *croc* hook (cp. CROOK).

encrust *v.t.* to cover with a crust or hard coating. *Also v.i.* WH: 17C. French *incruster*, from Latin *incrustare*, from IN-¹ + *crusta* CRUST.

encrypt *v.t.* to put (information or a message) into code. WH: mid-20C. EN- + *crypt* in CRYPTOGRAM etc.

encumber *v.t.* to hamper, impede or embarrass by a weight, burden or difficulty; to burden. WH: 12–14C. Old French *encombrer* to block up, from EN- + *combre* river barrage, of Gaulish orig.

-ency *suf.* forming abstract nouns meaning state or quality, as in *emergency*. WH: Latin *-entia* -ENCE. Cp. -ANCY.

encyclical *n.* a circular letter, esp. a letter from the Pope to the bishops or to the Church at large. *Also a.* WH: 17C. Late Latin *encyclicus*, from Greek *egkuklios* circular, general, from EN- + *kuklos* circle. See also -IC, -AL¹.

encyclopedia *n.* a book containing information on all branches of knowledge, or on a particular branch, usu. arranged alphabetically. WH: 16C. Modern Latin, from pseudo-Greek *egkuklopaideia*, representing *egkuklios paideia* all-round education. Cp. ENCYCLICAL. The word was originally a term for the 'circle of learning', i.e. a general education. The current sense arose in the 17C.

encyst *v.t.* to enclose in a cyst, bladder or vesicle. *Also v.i.* WH: 18C. EN- + CYST.

end *n.* the extreme point or boundary of a line or of anything that has length. *Also a.*, *v.i.*, *v.t.* WH: pre-1200. Old English *ende*, from Germanic, from Indo-European. Cp. Sanskrit *anta* end, boundary, death.

-end *suf.* forming nouns meaning somebody or something to be perceived or treated in a particular way, as in *prebend*. WH: Latin *-endus*, ger. ending of vv. in *-ere*. Cp. -AND.

endamage *v.t.* to damage. WH: 14–15C. EN- + DAMAGE.

endanger *v.t.* to expose to danger. WH: 14–15C. EN- + DANGER.

endear *v.t.* to make dear (to). WH: 16C. EN- + DEAR, based on French *enchérir* (from EN- + *cher* dear).

endeavour *v.i.* to strive (after) a certain end. *Also v.t.*, *n.* WH: 14–15C. From phr. *to put oneself in devoir*, based on French *se mettre en devoir* to do one's utmost, lit. to put oneself in duty. See EN-, DEVOIR.

endeictic *a.* showing, exhibiting. WH: 17C. Greek *endeiktikos* probative, indicative, from *endeiknunai* to point out. See also -IC. Cp. APODICTIC, DEICTIC.

endemic *a.* peculiar to a particular locality or people. *Also n.* WH: 17C. French *endémique* or Latin *endemicus*, from Greek *endēmos* pertaining to people, native, from EN- + *dēmos* people. See also -IC.

endermic *a.* acting upon or through the skin, as an unguent applied after blistering. WH: 17C. EN- + Greek *derma* skin + -IC.

enderon *n.* the inner derm or true skin. WH: 19C. EN- + Greek *deros*, *derma* skin. The term was coined in 1859 by the English biologist T.H. Huxley.

endive *n.* a kind of chicory, *Cichorium endivia*, much cultivated for use in salads, or *C. intybus*, the wild endive. WH: 14–15C. Old French, from Medieval Latin *endivia*, from Medieval Greek *indibi*, from Latin *intibum*, from Greek *entubon*.

endo- *comb. form* of or relating to the inside of anything. WH: Greek, from *endon* within. See also -O-.

endocardium *n.* a membrane lining the interior of the human heart. WH: 19C. Modern Latin, from ENDO- + Greek *kardia* heart + -IUM.

endocarp *n.* the inner layer of a pericarp. WH: 19C. ENDO- + -CARP.

endocranium *n.* the thick membrane lining the cranial cavity. WH: 19C. ENDO- + CRANIUM.

endocrine *a.* (of a gland) having no duct and secreting directly into the bloodstream. *Also n.* WH: early 20C. ENDO- + Greek *krinein* to separate.

endoderm *n.* the inner layer of the blastoderm. WH: 19C. ENDO- + -DERM.

endogamous *a.* necessarily marrying within the tribe. WH: 19C. ENDO- + Greek *gamos* marriage. See also -OUS.

endogen *n.* a plant growing from within. WH: 19C. French *endogène*. See ENDO-, -GEN.

endolymph *n.* the serous fluid in the membranous labyrinth of the ear. WH: 19C. ENDO- + LYMPH.

endometrium *n.* the membrane lining the cavity of the womb. WH: 19C. Modern Latin, from ENDO- + Greek *mētra* womb + -IUM.

endomorph *n.* a person of plump, thick-set build. WH: 19C. ENDO- + -MORPH.

endoparasite *n.* a parasite living in the interior of its host. WH: 19C. ENDO- + PARASITE.

endophyllous *a.* denoting leaves evolved from a sheath. WH: 19C. ENDO- + Greek *phullon* leaf + -OUS.

endoplasm *n.* the partially fluid inner layer of protoplasm. WH: 19C. ENDO- + *plasm* (PLASMA).

endorphin *n.* any of a group of chemicals occurring naturally in the brain which have a similar effect to morphine. WH: late 20C. *endogenous* (ENDOGEN) + MORPHINE.

endorse *v.t.* to write (one's name) on the back of (a cheque) to specify oneself as the payee. WH: 15C. Medieval Latin *indorsare*, from Latin IN-¹ + *dorsum* back.

endoscope *n.* an instrument for inspecting internal parts of the body. WH: 19C. ENDO- + -SCOPE.

endoskeleton *n.* the internal bony and cartilaginous framework of the vertebrates. WH: 19C. ENDO- + SKELETON.

endosmosis *n.* the passage of a fluid from outside inwards through a porous diaphragm. WH: 19C. French *endosmose*, from ENDO- + Greek *ōsmos* pushing. See also -OSIS.

endosperm *n.* the albumen of a seed. WH: 19C. ENDO- + -SPERM.

endospore *n.* the inner layer of the wall of a spore. WH: 19C. ENDO- + SPORE.

endothelium *n.* a membrane lining blood vessels, tubes, cavities etc. WH: 19C. Modern Latin, from ENDO- + Greek *thēlē* nipple + -IUM.

endothermic *a.* occurring, or formed, with the absorption of heat. WH: 19C. ENDO- + *thermic* (THERMAL).

endotoxin *n.* a toxin present within a bacterium and only released at death. WH: early 20C. ENDO- + TOXIN.

endow *v.t.* to bestow a permanent income upon. WH: 14–15C. Anglo-French *endouer*, from EN- + Old French *douer*, from Latin *dotare*, from *dos*, *dotis* dowry, rel. to *dare* to give. The earliest sense was to give a dowry to a woman, or to provide a dower for a widow.

endozoic *a.* living inside an animal. WH: 19C. ENDO- + -ZOIC.

endue *v.t.* to endow, to furnish. WH: 14–15C. Old French *enduire*, partly from Latin *inducere* to lead in (see INDUCE), partly from EN- + *duire*, from Latin *ducere* to lead. The word has become associated in sense with Latin *induere* to put on (clothes).

endure *v.t.* to undergo, to suffer. *Also v.i.* WH: 12–14C. Old French *endurer*, from Latin *indurare* to harden, from IN-¹ + *durus* hard.

-ene *suf.* denoting a hydrocarbon, as in *benzene*, *naphthalene*. WH: Alt. of -INE.

enema *n.* a fluid injected into the rectum. WH: 14–15C. Late Latin, from Greek, from *enienai* to send in, to put in, to inject, from EN- + *hienai* to send.

enemy *n.* someone hostile to another person, or to a cause etc. WH: 12–14C. Old French *enemi* (Modern French *ennemi*), from Latin *inimicus*, from IN-² + *amicus* friend, friendly. This word replaced native Old English FOE.

energumen *n.* an enthusiast, a fanatic. WH: 18C. Late Latin *energumenus*, from Greek *energoumenos*, p.p. of *energein* to work upon, from EN- + *ergon* work.

energy *n.* internal or inherent power. WH: 16C. French *énergie* or Late Latin *energia*, from Greek *energeia*, from EN- + *ergon* work. See also -Y².

enervate *v.t.* to deprive of force or strength; to weaken. *Also a.* WH: 17C. Latin *enervatus*, p.p. of *enervare* to extract the sinews of, from E- + *nervus* sinew. See also -ATE³.

enface *v.t.* to write, print or stamp the face of (a document). WH: 19C. EN- + FACE, based on ENDORSE.

en face *adv.* opposite, facing. WH: 18C. French facing, from *en* in + *face* FACE.

en famille *adv.* at home with one's family. WH: 18C. French in the family, from *en* in + *famille* FAMILY.

enfant gâté *n.* someone whose character has been spoiled by over-indulgence. WH: 19C. French spoilt child, from *enfant* child (see INFANT) + *gâté*, p.p. of *gâter* to spoil, from Latin *vastare*, from *vastus* (see WASTE).

enfant terrible *n.* a person who embarrasses people by behaving indiscreetly, unconventionally etc. WH: 19C. French terrible child, from *enfant* child (see INFANT) + *terrible* TERRIBLE.

enfeeble *v.t.* to make feeble or weak. WH: 12–14C. Old French *enfeblir*, from EN- + *feble* FEEBLE.

enfeoff *v.t.* to invest with a fief. WH: 14–15C. Old French *enfeffer*, from EN- + *fief* FIEF.

en fête *adv.* dressed for a holiday, celebrating a holiday. WH: 19C. French in a festival, from *en* in + FÊTE.

enfetter *v.t.* to fetter. WH: 16C. EN- + FETTER.

enfilade *n.* a fire that may rake a position, line of works or body of troops, from end to end. *Also v.t.* WH: 18C. French, from *enfiler* to thread on a string, from EN- + *fil* thread. See FILE¹, also -ADE.

enfold *v.t.* to wrap, cover or surround. WH: 14–15C. EN- + FOLD².

enforce *v.t.* to compel obedience to (a law etc.). *Also v.i., n.* WH: 12–14C. Old French *enforcier*, from Latin IN-¹ + *fortis* strong.

enfranchise *v.t.* to give (someone) the right to vote. WH: 14–15C. Old French *enfranchir*, *enfranchiss*-, from EN- + *franc*, *franche* free. See FRANK.

engage *v.t.* to bind by a promise or contract, esp. by promise of marriage. *Also v.i., n.* WH: 14–15C. Old French *engager*, from EN- + base of WAGE.

engagé *a.* (of a writer, artist etc.) committed to a moral or political cause. WH: 19C. French, p.p. of *engager* ENGAGE.

en garde *int.* in fencing, used as a warning to be ready to receive attack. *Also a.* WH: 19C. French on guard, from *en* on + *garde* GUARD.

engender *v.t.* to cause to happen. *Also v.i.* WH: 12–14C. Old French *engendrer*, from Latin *ingenerare*, from IN-¹ + *generare* GENERATE.

engine *n.* an apparatus consisting of a number of parts for applying mechanical power, esp. one that converts energy into motion. *Also v.t.* WH: 12–14C. Old French *engin*, from Latin *ingenium* natural quality, device, from IN-¹ + *gen*-, base of *gignere* to beget. Cp. INGENIOUS, INGENUOUS. The earliest sense was natural talent, wit.

engineer *n.* a person who is trained or qualified in a branch of engineering. *Also v.t., v.i.* WH: 12–14C. Old French *engigneor* (Modern French *ingénieur*), from Medieval Latin *ingeniator*, from *ingeniare*. See ENGINE. The current form of the word comes direct from French *ingénieur* or Italian *ingegnere*, with the suffix assimilated to -EER. An engineer was originally a builder of engines of war.

engird *v.t.* to encircle, to encompass with or as if with a girdle. WH: 16C. EN- + GIRD¹.

engirdle *v.t.* to surround with or as with a girdle. WH: 16C. EN- + GIRDLE¹.

English *a.* of or relating to England or its inhabitants. *Also n., v.t.* WH: pre-1200. Old English *englisc*. See ANGLE, also -ISH¹. In its earliest recorded occurrence in Old English, the word had already lost its etymological sense relating to the Angles (as opposed to the Saxons).

englut *v.t.* to swallow. WH: 15C. Old French *englotir* (Modern French *engloutir*), from Late Latin *inglutire*, from IN-¹ + *gluttire* to swallow.

engorge *v.t.* to congest (with blood). WH: 15C. Old French *engorgier* to feed to excess (Modern French *engorger* to congest). See EN-, GORGE.

engraft *v.t.* to graft upon, to insert (a scion of one tree) upon or into another. WH: 16C. EN- + GRAFT¹.

engrail *v.t.* to indent in curved lines, to make ragged at the edges as if broken with hail. WH: 14–15C. Old French *engresler* to make thin (Modern French *engrêler*), from EN- + *gresle* (Modern French *grêle*) thin, from Latin *gracilis*.

engram *n.* the physical trace of a memory in the brain. WH: early 20C. German *Engramm*, from EN- + Greek *gramma* letter. The term was coined in 1904 by the German zoologist R. Semon.

en grande tenue *adv.* in full evening dress. WH: 19C. French in grand dress, from *en* in + fem. of *grand* great, GRAND + *tenue*, from *tenir* to hold, to keep, from Latin *tenere*.

en grand seigneur *adv.* like a lord, using or having a grand or arrogant manner. WH: 19C. French in (the manner of a) grand lord, from *en* in + *grand* great, GRAND + SEIGNEUR.

engrave *v.t.* to cut figures, letters etc. (on), with a chisel or graver. *Also v.i.* WH: 15C. EN- + GRAVE¹.

engross *v.t.* to monopolize, to occupy the attention entirely, to absorb. WH: 14–15C. French *engrosser*, from Medieval Latin *ingrossare*. See EN-, GROSS. The sense to monopolize comes from French *en gros*, from Medieval Latin *in grosso* in bulk, wholesale, from Late Latin *grossus* GROSS.

engulf *v.t.* to cast, as into a gulf. WH: 16C. EN- + GULF.

enhance *v.t.* to raise in importance, degree etc. *Also v.i.* WH: 12–14C. Anglo-French *enhauncer*, prob. alt. of Old French *enhaucier*, from Latin IN-¹ + *altus* high. The original sense (to the 16C) was to lift, to raise. The current sense evolved in the 16C.

enharmonic *a.* having intervals less than a semitone, as between G sharp and A flat. *Also n.* WH: 17C. Late Latin *enharmonicus*, from Greek *enarmonikos*, from EN- + *harmonia* HARMONY. See also -IC.

enhearten *v.t.* to encourage, cheer, strengthen. WH: 17C. EN- + HEARTEN.

enigma *n.* an inexplicable or mysterious proceeding, person or thing. WH: 16C. Latin *aenigma*, from Greek *ainigma*, from base of *ainissesthai* to speak allusively, from *ainos* fable. The earliest sense was riddle, allusive speech. The current sense dates from the 17C.

enjambment *n.* the continuation of a sentence or clause, without a pause in sense, from one line of verse or couplet into the next. WH: 19C. French *enjambement*, from *enjamber* to stride over, to go beyond, from EN- + *jambe*. See JAMB.

enjoin *v.t.* to direct, prescribe, impose (an act or conduct). WH: 12–14C. Old French *enjoindre*, *enjoign*-, from Latin *iniungere* to join, to attach, from IN-¹ + *iungere* JOIN.

enjoy *v.t.* to take pleasure or delight in. WH: 14–15C. Old French *enjoier* to give joy to, from EN- + *joie* JOY, or from Old French *enjoïr* to enjoy, from EN- + *joïr*, from Latin *gaudere*. The original sense (to the 16C) was to rejoice. A sense to make happy was also current (to the 17C).

enkephalin *n.* a chemical found in the brain, having a pain-killing effect similar to that of morphine. WH: mid-20C. Greek *egkephalos* brain. See ENCEPHALO-, also -IN¹.

enkindle *v.t.* to kindle, to set on fire. WH: 16C. EN- + KINDLE.

enlace *v.t.* to encircle tightly, to surround. WH: 14–15C. Old French *enlacier* (Modern French *enlacer*), from Latin IN-¹ + alt. of *laqueus* noose, but later taken as from EN- + LACE.

enlarge *v.t.* to make greater; to extend in dimensions, quantity or number. *Also v.i.* WH: 12–14C. Old French *enlarger*, from EN- + *large* LARGE.

enlighten *v.t.* to give mental or spiritual light to, to instruct. WH: 12–14C. Old English *inlīhtan* to shine, from IN-¹ + *līhtan* (see LIGHT²), later as from EN- + LIGHTEN¹ (or LIGHT¹ + -EN⁵). The original sense (to the 19C) was literally to make luminous, to put light into. The current sense evolved in the 14–15C.

enlist *v.t.* to enrol, esp. to engage for military service. *Also v.i.* WH: 16C. EN- + LIST¹, prob. based on Dutch *inlijsten* to inscribe on a list.

enliven *v.t.* to give spirit or animation to. WH: 17C. From obs. *enlive* (from EN- + LIVE¹) + -EN⁵.

en masse *adv.* in a group, all together. WH: 18C. French in a mass, from *en* in + *masse* MASS.

enmesh *v.t.* to entangle or catch in or as if in a net. WH: 17C. EN- + MESH.

enmity *n.* the state or quality of being an enemy. WH: 12–14C. Old French *enemitié* (Modern French *inimitié*), from Latin *inimicus*. See ENEMY, also -ITY.

ennea- *comb. form* nine. WH: Greek *ennea* nine.

ennead *n.* a set of nine things, esp. of nine books or discourses. WH: 16C. Greek *enneas*, *enneados*, from *ennea* nine. See also -AD¹.

enneagynous *a.* having nine pistils. **WH**: 19C. ENNEA- + -GYNOUS.

enneahedron *n.* a solid figure with nine sides. **WH**: 18C. ENNEA- + -HEDRON.

enneandrian *a.* having nine stamens. **WH**: 19C. ENNEA- + Greek *anēr, andros* man. + -IAN.

enneapetalous *a.* having nine petals. **WH**: 19C. ENNEA- + Greek *petalon* PETAL + -OUS.

enneaphyllous *a.* having nine leaflets composing a compound leaf. **WH**: 19C. ENNEA- + Greek *phullon* leaf + -OUS.

ennoble *v.t.* to make a noble of. **WH**: 15C. Old French *ennoblir*. See EN-, NOBLE.

ennui *n.* lack of interest in things, boredom. **WH**: 18C. French, from Latin *in odio* in hatred. See ANNOY.

enormous *a.* huge, immense. **WH**: 16C. Latin *enormis* (from E- + *norma* pattern) + -OUS. Something enormous is out of the normal.

enosis *n.* the proposal for the political union of Cyprus with Greece. **WH**: mid-20C. Modern Greek *henōsis*, from *hena* one. See also -OSIS.

enough *a.* sufficient or adequate for need or demand. *Also pron., int., adv.* **WH**: pre-1200. Old English *genōg*, from Germanic. Cp. German *genug*.

enounce *v.t.* to enunciate, state definitely. **WH**: 19C. French *énoncer*, from Latin *enuntiare* ENUNCIATE, based on ANNOUNCE, PRONOUNCE.

en papillote *adv.* baked in an envelope of foil or greased paper. **WH**: late 20C. French in a curlpaper, from *en* in + PAPILLOTE.

en passant *adv.* by the way. **WH**: 17C. French in passing, from *en-* in + *pres.p.* of *passer* PASS.

en pension *adv.* as a lodger, with meals provided. **WH**: 19C. French in a lodging house, from *en* in + PENSION².

enprint *n.* an enlarged photographic print. **WH**: mid-20C. Abbr. of *enlarged print*.

en prise *a.* in chess, of or relating to a piece which is exposed to capture. **WH**: 19C. In (a position to be) taken, from *en* in + fem. p.p. (used as n.) of *prendre* to take.

enrage *v.t.* to put in a rage. **WH**: 15C. Old French *enrager* to become enraged. See EN-, RAGE.

en rapport *adv.* in sympathy (with). **WH**: 19C. French in rapport, from *en* in + RAPPORT.

enrapture *v.t.* to fill with rapture, to delight. **WH**: 18C. EN- + RAPTURE.

enrich *v.t.* to make rich or richer. **WH**: 14–15C. Old French *enrichir*, from EN- + *riche* RICH.

enrobe *v.t.* to put a robe upon, to attire. **WH**: 16C. EN- + ROBE.

enrol *v.t.* to write down on or enter in a roll. *Also v.i.* **WH**: 14–15C. Old French *enroller* (Modern French *enrôler*), from EN- + *rolle* ROLL.

enroot *v.t.* to fix by the root. **WH**: 14–15C. EN- + ROOT¹.

en route *adv.* on the way; on the road. **WH**: 18C. French on the road, from *en* in + *route* road, way, ROUTE.

ens *n.* entity, being, existence. **WH**: 16C. Late Latin, pres.p. (used as n.), formed from *esse* to be, on a supposed analogy of *absens* from *abesse* (see ABSENT¹). Latin *esse* in fact has no pres.p., but some compounds do, such as *absens* from *abesse*, *praesens* from *praeesse* (see PRESENT¹).

Ensa *n.* an official organization for entertaining men and women in the armed services during World War II. **WH**: mid-20C. Acronym of *Entertainments National Service Association*.

†**ensample** *n.* an example, a pattern, a model. *Also v.t.* **WH**: 12–14C. Anglo-French *ensample*, alt. of Old French *essample* EXAMPLE.

ensanguine *v.t.* to smear or cover with blood. **WH**: 17C. EN- + Latin *sanguis, sanguinis* blood.

ensate *a.* shaped like a sword with a straight blade. **WH**: 19C. Modern Latin *ensatus*, from *ensis* sword. See also -ATE².

ensconce *v.t.* to settle (oneself) comfortably or securely. **WH**: 16C. EN- + SCONCE².

ensemble *n.* all the parts of anything taken together. *Also adv.* **WH**: 14–15C. Old French, from Latin *insimul*, from IN-¹ + *simul* at the same time.

enshrine *v.t.* to place in or as if in a shrine. **WH**: 14–15C. EN- + SHRINE.

enshroud *v.t.* to cover with or as if with a shroud. **WH**: 16C. EN- + SHROUD.

ensiform *a.* sword-shaped, as the leaf of an iris. **WH**: 16C. Latin *ensis* sword + -FORM.

ensign *n.* a national banner, a standard, a regimental flag, the flag with distinguishing colours carried by ships. *Also v.t.* **WH**: 14–15C. Old French *enseigne*, from Latin INSIGNIA. The earliest sense was signal, watchword, slogan.

ensilage *n.* a method of preserving forage crops whilst moist and succulent, without previously drying, by storing them en masse in pits or trenches. *Also v.t.* **WH**: 19C. French, from *ensiler*, from Spanish *ensilar*, from *en-* (see IN-¹) + SILO. See also -AGE.

enslave *v.t.* to make a slave of, to reduce to bondage. **WH**: 17C. EN- + SLAVE.

ensnare *v.t.* to entrap. **WH**: 16C. EN- + SNARE.

ensphere *v.t.* to place in or as if in a sphere. **WH**: 17C. EN- + SPHERE.

enstatite *n.* a rock-forming mineral, magnesium silicate. **WH**: 19C. Greek *enstatēs* adversary + -ITE¹. The rock is so named because of its refractory nature.

ensue *v.i.* to follow in course of time, to succeed. *Also v.t.* **WH**: 14–15C. Old French *ensiw-, ensu-*, stem of *ensivre* (Modern French *ensuivre*), from Latin *insequi*, from IN-¹ + *sequi* to follow.

en suite *adv.* in succession, as part of a set. *Also a.* **WH**: 18C. French in a suite, from *en* in + SUITE.

ensure *v.t.* to make certain (that). **WH**: 14–15C. Anglo-French *enseürer*, alt. of Old French *asseürer* ASSURE. Cp. INSURE. The original sense to the 17C was to promise to (someone). The current sense dates from the 18C.

enswathe *v.t.* to enwrap, to bandage. **WH**: 16C. EN- + SWATHE.

-ent *suf.* forming adjectives meaning causing or performing some action, or being in a condition, as in *apparent, astringent*. **WH**: French, or from Latin *-ent-*, pres.p. stem of 2nd, 3rd and 4th conj. vv., or *-ant-* (see -ANT).

entablature *n.* the upper part of a classical building supported upon the columns, consisting in upward succession of the architrave, frieze and cornice. **WH**: 17C. Italian *intavolatura* boarding, from *intavolare* to board up, from IN-¹ + *tavola* table. See also -URE.

entablement *n.* the platform or series of platforms supporting a statue, above the dado and base. **WH**: 17C. French, from *entabler*, from EN- + *table*. See TABLE, also -MENT.

entail *v.t.* to involve, to necessitate. *Also n.* **WH**: 14–15C. EN- + Anglo-French *taile* TAIL². The original sense was the (still current) legal one, to settle the succession of land or property. The general sense to involve, to necessitate, arose only in the 19C.

entamoeba *n.* any amoeba of the *Entamoeba* genus, which causes amoebic dysentery in humans. **WH**: early 20C. Modern Latin, from ENTO- + AMOEBA.

entangle *v.t.* to ensnare, as in a net. **WH**: 14–15C. EN- + TANGLE¹.

entasis *n.* the almost imperceptible convex curvature given to a shaft or a column. **WH**: 17C. Modern Latin, from Greek, from *enteinein* to strain.

entelechy *n.* (in Aristotle's philosophy) the complete realization or full expression of a function or potentiality. **WH**: 14–15C. Late Latin *entelechia*, from Greek *entelekheia*, from EN- + *telei*, dat. of *telos* end, perfection + *ekhein* to be in a (particular) state. See also -Y².

entellus *n.* an Indian monkey, the hanuman. **WH**: 19C. *Entellus*, an old man in Virgil's *Aeneid* (1C BC). The reason for the choice of name is uncertain, but the monkey does rather resemble an old man.

entente *n.* a friendly understanding. **WH**: 19C. French, obs. fem. p.p. (used as n.) of *entendre* to understand. See INTEND.

enter *v.t.* to go or come into. *Also v.i.* **WH**: 12–14C. Old French *entrer*, from Latin *intrare*, from *intra* within.

enteral *a.* of or relating to the intestines. **WH**: early 20C. Partly from Greek *enterikos* (see ENTERIC) + -AL¹, partly a back-formation from PARENTERAL.

enterectomy *n.* surgical removal of part of the small intestine. **WH**: 19C. *enter-* (ENTERO-) + -ECTOMY.

enteric *a.* of or relating to the intestines. *Also n.* **WH**: 19C. Greek *enterikos*, from *enteros* intestine. See ENTERO-.

enteritis *n.* inflammation of the small intestine, usu. causing diarrhoea. **WH**: 19C. Greek *enteron* intestine + -ITIS.

entero- *comb. form* of or relating to the intestines. **WH**: Greek *enteron* intestine. See also -O-.

enterocele *n.* a hernia containing part of the intestines. **WH**: 17C. ENTERO- + -CELE.

enterolite *n.* a stony calculus. **WH**: 19C. ENTERO- + -LITE.

enterology *n.* a treatise or discourse on the intestines, often extended to all the internal parts of the human body. WH: 18C. ENTERO- + -LOGY.

enteropathy *n.* disease of the small intestine. WH: 19C. ENTERO- + -PATHY.

enterostomy *n.* the surgical formation of an opening to the small intestine through the abdominal wall. WH: 19C. ENTERO- + Greek *stoma* mouth + -Y².

enterotomy *n.* the surgical opening up of the intestines. WH: 19C. ENTERO- + -TOMY.

enterovirus *n.* a virus which enters the body through the intestinal tract. WH: mid-20C. ENTERO- + VIRUS.

enterprise *n.* an undertaking, esp. a bold or difficult one. *Also v.t., v.i.* WH: 14–15C. Old French *entreprise*, fem. p.p. (used as n.) of *entreprendre*, later var. of *emprendre*. See EMPRISE.

entertain *v.t.* to receive and treat as a guest. *Also v.i.* WH: 14–15C. Old French *entretenir*, from Latin *inter-* among + *tenere* to hold. The sense to have as a guest evolved in the 15C, and the general sense to amuse in the 17C.

enthalpy *n.* the heat content of a substance per unit mass. WH: early 20C. Greek *enthalpein* to warm in, from EN- + *thalpein* to heat. See also -Y².

enthral *v.t.* to enslave, to captivate. WH: 14–15C. EN- + THRALL.

enthrone *v.t.* to place on a throne or place of dignity. WH: 16C. EN- + THRONE. This verb replaced ENTHRONIZE.

enthronize *v.t.* to enthrone, to induct. WH: 14–15C. Old French *introniser*, from Late Latin *intronizare*, from Greek *enthronizein*, from EN- + *thronos* THRONE. See also -IZE.

enthusiasm *n.* intense and passionate zeal. WH: 17C. French *enthousiasme* or Late Latin *enthusiasmus*, from Greek *enthousiasmos*, from *enthousiazein* to be inspired, to be possessed by a god, from *enthous* inspired, from EN- + *theos* god. Cp. GIDDY.

enthymeme *n.* a syllogism of which one premise is suppressed, and only an antecedent and a consequent expressed in words. WH: 16C. Latin *enthymema*, from Greek *enthumēma*, from *enthumeisthai* to consider, to infer, from EN- + *thumos* mind.

entice *v.t.* to attract. WH: 12–14C. Old French *enticier*, from Popular Latin *intitiare* to set on fire, from Latin IN-¹ + *titio* firebrand. The original sense (to the 17C) was to incite, to provoke. The current sense then prevailed.

entire *a.* whole, complete, perfect. *Also n.* WH: 14–15C. Old French *entier*, from Latin *integrum*, neut. of INTEGER.

entitle *v.t.* to give a right, title or claim to anything. WH: 14–15C. Old French *entiteler* (Modern French *intituler*), from Late Latin *intitulare*, from IN-¹ + *titulus* TITLE.

entity *n.* anything that has real existence, a being. WH: 15C. French *entité*, or from Medieval Latin *entitas*, from Late Latin ENS, *entis*. See also -TY¹.

ento- *comb. form* of or relating to the inside of anything. WH: Greek *entos* within. See also -O-.

entoblast *n.* the nucleus of a cell. WH: 19C. ENTO- + BLAST.

entomb *v.t.* to place in a tomb, to bury. WH: 14–15C. Old French *entomber*, from EN- + *tombe* TOMB.

entomic *a.* relating to insects. WH: early 20C. Greek *entoma* insects (see ENTOMO-) +-IC.

entomo- *comb. form* of or relating to insects. WH: Greek *entomon* insect, neut. of *entomos* cut up, from EN- + *temnein* to cut. Cp. INSECT. See also -O-.

entomoid *a.* resembling an insect. *Also n.* WH: 19C. ENTOMO- + -OID.

entomology *n.* the scientific study of insects. WH: 18C. French *entomologie* or Modern Latin *entomologia*. See ENTOMO-, -LOGY.

entomophagous *a.* feeding on insects. WH: 19C. ENTOMO- + -PHAGOUS.

entomophilous *a.* attractive to insects. WH: 19C. ENTOMO- + -philous (-PHILE).

entomostracous *a.* belonging to the Entomostraca, a division of crustaceans which are small in size, with the body segments usu. distinct, and gills attached to the feet or organs of the mouth. WH: 19C. Modern Latin *Entomostraca*, from ENTOMO- + Greek *strakon* shell + -OUS.

entophyte *n.* any parasitic plant growing in the interior of animal or vegetable structures. WH: 19C. ENTO- + -PHYTE.

entourage *n.* retinue, people following or attending on an important person. WH: 19C. French, from *entourer* to surround. Cp. French *entours* surroundings, *à l'entour* around. See also -AGE.

entozoon *n.* an animal living within the body of another animal. WH: 19C. ENTO- + -ZOON.

entr'acte *n.* the interval between the acts of a play. WH: 19C. Obs. French, (now *entracte*), from *entre* between + *acte* act.

entrails *n.pl.* the internal parts of animals; the intestines. WH: 12–14C. Old French *entrailles*, from Medieval Latin *intralia*, alt. of Latin *interanea*, neut. pl. (used as n.) of *interaneus* internal, from *inter*. See INTERIOR. Not rel. to TRAIL.

entrain¹ *v.t.* to draw after, to bring as a consequence. WH: 16C. Old French *entraîner*, from EN- + *traîner* to drag. See TRAIN.

entrain² *v.t.* to put into a railway train. *Also v.i.* WH: 19C. EN- + TRAIN.

entrain³ *n.* enthusiasm, high spirits. WH: 19C. French, from ENTRAIN¹.

entrammel *v.t.* to entangle, hamper, fetter. WH: 16C. EN- + TRAMMEL.

entrance¹ *n.* the act of entering, or an instance of entering. WH: 15C. Old French, from *entrer* ENTER. See also -ANCE.

entrance² *v.t.* to throw into a state of ecstasy. WH: 16C. EN- + TRANCE.

entrap *v.t.* to catch in or as in a trap. WH: 16C. Old French *entrapper*, from EN- + *trappe* TRAP¹.

entreat *v.t.* to beseech, to ask earnestly. *Also v.i.* WH: 14–15C. Old French *entraitier*, from EN- + *traitier* TREAT.

entrechat *n.* a leap in dancing, esp. one including a striking of the heels together several times. WH: 18C. French, from Italian (*capriola*) *intrecciata* complicated (capriole). Cp. INTRICATE.

entrecôte *n.* a beefsteak cut from between two ribs. WH: 19C. French, lit. between rib, from *entre* between + *côte* rib.

entrée *n.* freedom or right of entrance. WH: 18C. French. See ENTRY.

entremets *n.* a light dish served between courses. WH: 15C. French, from *entre* between + *mets* MESS.

entrench *v.t.* to put (oneself) in a defensible position, as if with trenches. *Also v.i.* WH: 16C. EN- + TRENCH.

entre nous *adv.* between ourselves, in private. WH: 17C. French between us, from *entre* between + *nous* us.

entrepôt *n.* a warehouse for the temporary deposit of goods. WH: 18C. French (earlier *entrepost*), from *entreposer* to store, from *entre* among + *poser* to place.

entrepreneur *n.* a person who undertakes a (financial) enterprise, esp. one with an element of risk. WH: 19C. French, from *entreprendre* to undertake + *-eur* -OR. Cp. IMPRESARIO.

entresol *n.* a low storey between two higher ones, usu. between the first and the ground floor, a mezzanine. WH: 18C. French, from Spanish *entresuelo*, from *entre* between + *suelo* storey.

entropion *n.* introversion of the eyelids. WH: 19C. Medieval Latin, from Greek *entropē*, from EN- + *trepein* to turn. Cp. ENTROPY.

entropy *n.* the property of a substance, expressed quantitatively, which remains constant when the substance changes its volume or does work with no heat passing into or from it, thus forming an index of the availability of the thermal energy of a system for mechanical work. WH: 19C. Greek EN- + *tropē* turning, transformation. See also -Y². The term was coined in 1865 by the German mathematical physicist Rudolf Clausius. He based it on ENERGY, which he (wrongly) understood to mean 'work contents'. *Entropy* was thus intended to mean 'transformation contents'.

entrust *v.t.* to commit or confide (something or someone) to a person's care. WH: 17C. EN- + TRUST.

entry *n.* the act of entering. WH: 12–14C. Old French *entrée*, from Latin *intrata*, fem. p.p. (used as n.) of *intrare* ENTER. See also -Y².

Entryphone® *n.* a telephonic device at the entrance to a block of flats etc., which allows visitors to communicate with the flat occupier. WH: mid-20C. ENTRY + PHONE¹.

entwine *v.t.* to twine or twist together. *Also v.i.* WH: 16C. EN- + TWINE.

enucleate *v.t.* to bring to light, elucidate, solve. WH: 16C. Latin *enucleatus*, p.p. of *enucleare* to extract the kernel from, to clarify, from E- + NUCLEUS. See also -ATE³.

enumerate *v.t.* to reckon up one by one, to count. WH: 17C. Latin *enumeratus*, p.p. of *enumerare*, from E- + *numerus* number. See also -ATE³.

enunciate *v.t.* to pronounce distinctly, articulate clearly. *Also v.i.* WH: 17C. Latin *enuntiatus*, p.p. of *enuntiare*, from E- + *nuntiare* ANNOUNCE. See also -ATE³.

enuresis *n.* involuntary urinating, incontinence of urine. WH: 19C. Modern Latin, from Greek *enourein* to urinate in.

envelop *v.t.* to enwrap, to enclose, to surround so as to hide, to enshroud. WH: 14–15C. Old French *envoluper* (Modern French *envelopper*), from EN- + *voloper* to wrap up. Cp. DEVELOP.

envelope *n.* a folded paper wrapper to contain a letter. WH: 16C. French *enveloppe*, from *envelopper*. See ENVELOP. The original sense was a wrapper or covering generally. The current sense of wrapper for a letter arose in the 18C.

envenom *v.t.* to make poisonous, to impregnate with poison. WH: 12–14C. Old French *envenimer*, from EN- + *venim* VENOM.

environ *v.t.* to surround, to be or extend round, to encircle. WH: 12–14C. Old French *environer* (Modern French *environner*), from *environ* surroundings, around, from EN- + *viron* circuit, from *virer* VEER[1].

environment *n.* surroundings. WH: 17C. ENVIRON + -MENT.

envisage *v.t.* to conceive of as a possibility. WH: 19C. French *envisager*. See EN-, VISAGE.

envision *v.t.* to visualize, to envisage. WH: early 20C. EN- + VISION.

envoi *n.* a postscript to a collection of poems, or a concluding stanza to a poem. WH: 14–15C. Old French, from *envoyer* to send, from phr. *en voie* on the way.

envoy *n.* a diplomatic agent, next in rank below an ambassador, sent by one government to another on some special occasion. WH: 17C. French *envoyé*, p.p. (used as n.) of *envoyer* to send, from phr. *en voie* on the way. Cp. ENVOI.

envy *n.* ill will at the superiority, success or good fortune of others, a grudging sense of another's superiority to oneself. *Also v.t., v.i.* WH: 14–15C. Old French *envie*, from Latin *invidia*, from *invidere* to look maliciously on, from IN-[1] + *videre* to see. Cp. INVIDIOUS.

enwind *v.t.* to wind or coil around. WH: 16C. EN- + WIND[2].

enwrap *v.t.* to wrap or enfold. WH: 14–15C. EN- + WRAP.

enwreathe *v.t.* to encircle with or as with a wreath. WH: 15C. EN- + WREATHE.

Enzed *n.* New Zealand. WH: early 20C. Representation of pronun. of *NZ* as abbr. of *New Zealand*. Cp. EN, ZED.

enzootic *a.* of or relating to a disease which affects animals in a certain district either constantly or periodically; endemic among animals. *Also n.* WH: 19C. EN- + Greek *zōion* animal + -IC.

enzyme *n.* a protein produced by living cells which acts as a catalyst, esp. in the digestive system. WH: 19C. German *Enzym*, from Modern Greek *enzumos* leavened. The term was coined in the scientific sense in 1877 by the German physiologist Wilhelm Kühne but was in use before this in English as a term for the leavened bread in the Eucharist.

Eocene *a.* of or relating to the lowest division of the Tertiary strata. *Also n.* WH: 19C. Greek *ēōs* dawn + -CENE. The term was coined in 1831 by the English scholar William Whewell for the geologist Charles Lyell. Cp. MIOCENE, PLIOCENE.

eohippus *n.* an extinct forerunner of the horse, the earliest known form of horselike mammal. WH: 19C. Greek *ēōs* dawn + *hippos* horse. The genus is also known by the English name *dawn horse*.

eolith *n.* a roughly-chipped flint dating from the very early palaeolithic age, found abundantly in parts of the North Downs, and originally thought to be artificial. WH: 19C. Greek *ēōs* dawn + -LITH, based on *neolith* (see NEOLITHIC).

eosin *n.* a red fluorescent dye, sometimes used in biology. WH: 19C. Greek *ēōs* dawn. + -IN[1]. The name alludes to the dye's red colour, like that of the morning sky.

-eous *suf.* forming adjectives meaning of the nature of, as in *igneous*, *ligneous*. Latin *-eus* + -OUS. Cp. -ACEOUS, -ANEOUS.

eozoon *n.* a member of a hypothetical genus of Protozoa found in the Laurentian strata in Canada, the supposed remains of which are now believed to be inorganic. WH: 19C. Greek *ēōs* dawn + *zōion* animal.

ep- *pref.* upon, at, to, besides, in addition, as in *epact*, *epoch*. WH: Greek *pref.*, from EPI-, used before vowels.

epact *n.* the moon's age at the beginning of the year. WH: 16C. Old French *épacte*, from Late Latin *epactae* (pl.), from Greek *epaktai* (*hēmerai*) intercalated (days), from *epaktos* brought in, from *epagein* to bring in, from EP- + *agein* to lead. The original sense was the number of days 'brought in' (intercalated) to determine the excess of the solar year over the lunar year of twelve months.

epagoge *n.* the bringing forward of particular examples to prove a universal conclusion. WH: 19C. Greek *epagōgē*, from *epagein* to bring in. See EPACT.

epana- *comb. form* denoting repetition, doubling. WH: EP- + ANA-.

epanadiplosis *n.* a rhetorical figure by which a sentence ends with the same word with which it begins. WH: 17C. EPANA- + DIPLO- + -OSIS.

epanalepsis *n.* a figure of speech by which the same word or clause is repeated after other words intervening. WH: 16C. EPANA- + Greek *lēpsis* a taking.

epanodos *n.* a rhetorical figure in which the second member of a sentence is an inversion of the first. WH: 16C. EPANA- + Greek *hodos* way.

epanorthosis *n.* a rhetorical figure by which a person retracts what they have said for the purpose of putting it more forcibly. WH: 16C. EPANA- + Greek *orthōsis* a setting straight, from *orthoein*, from *orthos* straight.

eparch *n.* the chief bishop of a diocese in the Russian Church. WH: 17C. Greek *eparkhos*, from EP- + *arkhos* chief.

epaulette *n.* an ornamental badge worn on the shoulder in military, naval and certain civil full dress uniforms. WH: 18C. French *épaulette*, dim. of *épaule* shoulder, from Latin SPATULA shoulder blade. See also -ETTE.

épée *n.* a duelling sword. WH: 19C. French sword, from Old French *espee*. See SPAY.

epeirogenesis *n.* the making of a continent by the pushing up of parts of the earth's crust. WH: 19C. Greek *ēpeiros* mainland, continent. + GENESIS.

epencephalon *n.* the hindmost division of the brain. WH: 19C. EP- + ENCEPHALON.

epenthesis *n.* the addition of a letter or letters in the middle of a word, as in *alitium* for *alitum*. WH: 19C. Late Latin, from Greek, from *epenthe-*, stem of *epentithenai* to insert, from EP- + EN- + *tithenai* to place.

epergne *n.* an ornamental stand, usu. branched, for the centre of a table etc. WH: 18C. ? French *épargne* a saving, economy.

epexegesis *n.* words added to elucidate something which has gone before. WH: 16C. Greek *epexēgēsis*. See EP-, EXEGESIS.

ephebe *n.* in ancient Greece, a freeborn youth between the ages of 18 and 20, qualified for citizenship. WH: 19C. Latin *ephebus*, from Greek *ephēbos*, from EP- + *hēbē* early manhood.

ephedra *n.* any evergreen shrub of the genus *Ephedra*, growing in America and Eurasia. WH: early 20C. Modern Latin, from Latin *equisetum*, from Greek.

ephemera *n.* an insect of the genus *Ephemoptera*, containing the mayfly. WH: 14–15C. Medieval Latin, use as n. of fem. of Late Latin *ephemerus* lasting only a day, from Greek *ephēmeros*, from EP- + *hēmera* day.

Ephesian *a.* of or relating to Ephesus. *Also n.* WH: 14–15C. Latin *ephesius*, from Greek *ephesios*, from *Ephesos* Ephesus, an ancient Greek city on the W coast of Asia Minor. See also -AN.

ephod *n.* an emblematic short coat covering the shoulders and breast of the Jewish High Priest. WH: 14–15C. Hebrew *'ēpōd*.

ephor *n.* any one of the five magistrates chosen at Sparta and invested with the highest power, controlling even the kings. WH: 16C. Latin *ephorus*, or from Greek *ephoros* overseer, from EP- + base of *horan* to seen.

epi *n.* a tuft of hair, esp. on a horse's forehead. WH: 19C. French *épi* tuft, SPIKE[2].

epi- *pref.* upon, at, to, besides, in addition, as in *epigram*, *episode*. WH: Greek pref., from prep. *epi* on, near to, above, in addition.

epiblast *n.* the outermost of the layers in the blastoderm. WH: 19C. EPI- + -BLAST.

epic *a.* narrating some heroic event in a lofty style. *Also n.* WH: 16C. Latin *epicus*, from Greek *epikos*, from *epos*. See EPOS, also -IC.

epicalyx *n.* a whorl of leaves forming an additional calyx outside the true calyx. WH: 19C. EPI- + CALYX.

epicanthus *n.* a fold of skin over the inner angle of the eye, characteristic of Chinese and other eastern Asian peoples. WH: 19C. EPI- + CANTHUS.

epicarp *n.* the outermost layer of fruits. WH: 19C. EPI- + -CARP.

epicedium *n.* a dirge. WH: 16C. Latin, from Greek *epikēdeion*, neut. (used as n.) of *epikēdeios* funeral (a.), from EPI- + *kēdos* care, grief.

epicene *a.* of common gender, having only one form for both sexes. *Also n.* WH: 14–15C. Late Latin *epicoenus*, from Greek *epikoinos*, from EPI- + *koinos* common.

epicentre *n.* the point on the earth's surface over the focus of an earthquake. WH: 19C. Greek *epikentron*, neut. of *epikentron* situated in a centre, from EPI- + *kentros* CENTRE.

epicontinental *a.* (esp. of a sea) situated over a continental shelf. WH: early 20C. EPI- + *continental* (CONTINENT¹).

epicotyl *n.* the part of the stem of an embryonic plant above the cotyledons. WH: 19C. EPI- + Greek *kotulē* (see COTYLEDON).

epicure *n.* a person devoted to sensual pleasures, esp. those of food and drink. WH: 14–15C. Medieval Latin *epicurus*, from *Epicurus*, from Greek *Epikouros* Epicurus, 341–270 BC, Greek philosopher who held that the highest good is pleasure.

epicycle *n.* a small circle the centre of which is carried round upon another circle. WH: 14–15C. Old French *épicycle* or Late Latin *epicyclus*, from Greek *epikuklos*, from EPI- + *kuklos* circle.

epideictic *a.* showing off. WH: 18C. Greek *epideiktikos*, from EPI- + *deiknunai* to show. See also -IC.

epidemic *a.* affecting at once a large number in a community. *Also n.* WH: 17C. French *épidémique*, from Old French *épidémie*, from Late Latin *epidemia*, from Greek *epidēmia* prevalence of a disease, from *epidēmios* prevalent, from EPI- + *dēmos* people. See also -IC.

epidermis *n.* the cuticle or skin constituting the external layer in animals. WH: 17C. Late Latin, from Greek, from EPI- + *derma* skin.

epidiascope *n.* an optical projector which may be used for opaque objects or transparencies. WH: early 20C. EPI- + DIA- + -SCOPE. Cp. EPISCOPE.

epididymis *n.* a mass of sperm-carrying tubes at the back of the testes. WH: 17C. Greek *epididumis*, from EPI- + *didumos* testicle, twin, from *duo* two.

epidote *n.* a brittle mineral, a silicate of alumina and lime, of vitreous lustre and of various colours, mostly found in crystalline rocks. WH: 19C. French *épidote*, from Greek *epididonai* to give in addition, from EPI- + *didonai* to give. The mineral is so named with reference to the great length of its crystals by comparison with that of some related minerals, with which it was originally confused.

epidural *a.* situated on, or administered outside, the lower portion of the spinal canal. *Also n.* WH: 19C. EPI- + DURA MATER + -AL¹.

epifauna *n.* the animals which live on the surface of submerged ground, or attached to underwater objects etc. WH: early 20C. EPI- + FAUNA.

epifocal *a.* epicentral. WH: 19C. EPI- + *focal* (FOCUS).

epigastrium *n.* the upper part of the abdomen, esp. that part above the stomach. WH: 17C. Late Latin *epigastrion*, from neut. sing. (used as n.) of Greek *epigastrios* over the belly, from EPI- + *gastēr, gastros* belly.

epigeal *a.* growing close to the ground. WH: 19C. Greek *epigeios*, from EPI- + *gē* earth. See also -AL¹.

epigene *a.* originating on the surface of the earth. WH: 19C. French *épigène*, from Greek *epigenēs*. See EPI-, -GEN.

epigenesis *n.* the theory that in reproduction the organism is brought into being by the union of the male and female elements. WH: 17C. EPI- + GENESIS.

epiglottis *n.* a leaflike cartilage at the base of the tongue which covers the glottis during the act of swallowing. WH: 14–15C. Greek *epiglōttis*, from EPI- + *glōtta* tongue. Cp. GLOTTIS.

epigone *n.* a person belonging to a later and less noteworthy generation. WH: 18C. French *épigones* (pl.), from Latin *epigoni*, from Greek *epigonoi*, pl. of *epigonos* offspring, from EPI- + *-gonos*, from *gignesthai* to be born.

epigram *n.* a short poem or composition of a witty or pointed character. WH: 14–15C. French *épigramme* or Latin *epigramma*, from Greek. See EPI-, -GRAM.

epigraph *n.* a quotation, in verse or prose, placed at the beginning of a work, or of divisions in a work, as a motto. WH: 16C. Greek *epigraphē*, from *epigraphein* to write on, from EPI- + *graphein* to write.

epigynous *a.* (of the stamens or corolla) growing on the top of the ovary, with only the upper portions free. WH: 19C. Modern Latin *epigynus*. See EPI-, -GYNOUS.

epilate *v.t.* to remove hair by the roots, by any method. WH: 19C. French *épiler*, from *é-* (EX-) + Latin *pilus* hair, based on DEPILATE.

epilepsy *n.* a functional disorder of the brain which involves convulsions of varying intensity, with or without loss of consciousness. WH: 16C. French *épilepsie* or Late Latin *epilepsia*, from Greek *epilēpsia*, from *epilab-*, stem of *epilambanein* to seize, to attack, from EPI- + *lambanein* to take hold of.

epilimnion *n.* the upper, warmer layer of water in a lake. WH: early 20C. EPI- + Greek *limnion*, dim. of *limnē* lake.

epilogue *n.* the concluding part of a book, essay or speech, a peroration. WH: 14–15C. Old French *épilogue*, from Latin *epilogus*, from Greek *epilogos*, from EPI- + *logos* saying, speech. See -LOGUE. Cp. PROLOGUE.

epimer *n.* either one of the two differing isomers which can form around asymmetric carbon atoms. WH: early 20C. EPI- + -MER.

epinasty *n.* curving of an organ through more rapid growth of the upper surface. WH: 19C. EPI- + Greek *nastos* pressed together + -Y².

epinephrine *n.* adrenalin. WH: 19C. EPI- + Greek *nephros* kidney + -INE.

epipetalous *a.* (of stamens) growing separately on the corolla. WH: 19C. EPI- + *petalous* (PETAL).

epiphany *n.* the manifestation of Christ to the Magi at Bethlehem. WH: 12–14C. Ult. from Greek *epiphanein* to manifest, from EPI- + *phanein* to show. See also -Y².

epiphenomenon *n.* a phenomenon that is secondary and incidental, a mere concomitant of some effect, esp. a secondary symptom of a disease. WH: 17C. EPI- + PHENOMENON.

epiphragm *n.* the disclike secretion with which snails and other molluscs close their shells during hibernation. WH: 19C. Modern Latin *epiphragma*, from Greek lid, from EPI- + *phragma* fence. Cp. DIAPHRAGM.

epiphyllous *a.* growing on a leaf. WH: 19C. EPI- + Greek *phullon* leaf + -OUS.

epiphysis *n.* a process formed by a separate centre of ossification. WH: 17C. Modern Latin, from Greek *epiphusis*, from EPI- + *phusis* growth.

epiphyte *n.* a plant growing upon another, usu. not deriving its nourishment from this. WH: 19C. EPI- + -PHYTE.

episcopacy *n.* government of a Church by bishops, the accepted form in the Latin and Greek communions and the Church of England; prelacy. WH: 17C. Ecclesiastical Latin *episcopatus*, from *episcopus* BISHOP, based on *prelacy* (see PRELATE). See also -ACY.

episcope *n.* an optical projector used for projecting an enlarged image of an opaque object onto a screen. WH: early 20C. EPI- + -SCOPE.

episematic *a.* (of coloration) serving to facilitate recognition by animals of the same species. WH: 19C. EPI- + SEMATIC.

episiotomy *n.* the cutting of the perineum during childbirth in order to prevent its tearing. WH: 19C. Greek *epision* pubic region + -TOMY.

episode *n.* an incident or series of events in a story, separable though arising out of it. WH: 17C. Greek *epeisodion*, neut. (used as n.) of *epeisodios* coming in besides, from EP- + *eisodos* entrance, from *eis* into + *hodos* way, passage. In Greek tragedy, an episode was originally a passage of dialogue interpolated between two choric songs.

epispastic *a.* drawing, exciting action in the skin; blistering. *Also n.* WH: 17C. Modern Latin *epispasticus*, from Greek *epispastikos*, from *epispan* to attract, from EPI- + *span* to draw. See also -IC.

epistaxis *n.* bleeding from the nose. WH: 18C. Modern Latin, from Greek, from *epistazein* to bleed at the nose, from EPI- + *stazein* to drip.

epistemology *n.* the science which deals with the origin and method of knowledge. WH: 19C. Greek *epistēmo-*, comb. form of *epistēmē* knowledge, from *epistathai* to know (how to do) + -O- + -LOGY.

episternum *n.* the upper part of the sternum or breast-bone in mammals, or that portion of an articulate animal immediately adjoining the sternum. WH: 19C. EPI- + STERNUM.

epistle *n.* a written communication, a letter. *Also v.t.* WH: pre-1200. Latin *epistola*, from Greek *epistolē*, from EPI- + *stellein* to send.

epistrophe *n.* a rhetorical figure in which several sentences or clauses end with the same word. WH: 16C. Greek *epistrophē*, from *epistrephein* to turn about, from EPI- + *strephein* to turn.

epistyle *n.* the architrave. WH: 16C. French *épistyle* or Latin *epistylium*, from Greek *epistulion*, from EPI- + *stulos* column.

epitaph *n.* a commemorative inscription in prose or verse, as for a tomb or monument. *Also v.t.* WH: 14–15C. Old French *épitaphe*, from Latin *epitaphium* funeral oration, from Greek *epitaphion*, neut. (used as n.) of *epitaphios* over a tomb, from EPI- + *taphos* tomb, obsequies.

epitasis *n.* the portion of a classical drama in which the plot is developed, between the protasis and the catastrophe. WH: 16C. Modern Latin, from Greek, from *epiteinein* to intensify, from EPI- + *teinein* to stretch.

epitaxy *n.* the growth of one layer of crystals on another so that they have the same structure. WH: mid-20C. French *épitaxie*, from EPI- + Greek *-taxia* TAXIS.

epithalamium *n.* a song or poem celebrating a marriage. WH: 16C. Greek *epithalamion*, neut. (used as n.) of *epithalamios* nuptial, from EPI- + *thalamos* bridal chamber.

epithelium *n.* the cell tissues lining the alimentary canal and forming the outer layer of the mucous membranes. WH: 18C. Modern Latin, from EPI- + Greek *thēlē* teat, nipple + -IUM.

epithem *n.* any external application, except ointment or plasters. WH: 14–15C. Latin *epithema*, from Greek, from *epitithenai*. See EPITHET.

epithet *n.* an adjective or phrase denoting any quality or attribute. *Also v.t.* WH: 16C. French *épithète* or Latin *epitheton*, neut. (used as n.) of Greek *epithetos* attributed, p.p. of *epitithenai* to put on, to add, from EPI- + *tithenai* to place.

epitome *n.* a brief summary of a book, document etc. WH: 16C. Latin, from Greek *epitomē*, from *epitemnein* to cut into, to cut short, from EPI- + *temnein* to cut.

epizoon *n.* an animal parasitic upon the exterior surface of another. WH: 19C. EPI- + Greek *zōion* animal.

e pluribus unum *n.* one out of many (the motto of the USA). WH: 18C. Latin one out of many, from *e*, form of EX² + abl. pl. of *plus*, *pluris* more (see PLUS) + neut. sing. of *unus* one. The phrase was adapted from *e pluribus unus* in Virgil's *Minor Poems* and was adopted on June 20, 1782 for the motto on the face of the Great Seal of the United States.

epoch *n.* a fixed point from which succeeding years are numbered, a memorable date. WH: 17C. Modern Latin *epocha*, from Greek *epokhē* stoppage, fixed point of time, from *epekhein* to stop, from EP- + *ekhein* to hold, to be in a particular state.

epode *n.* (in Greek lyric poetry) the part after the strophe and antistrophe. WH: 17C. French *épode* or Latin *epodos*, from Greek *epōidos*, from EP- + *ōidē* ODE.

eponym *n.* a name given to a people, place or institution, after some person. WH: 19C. Greek *epōnumos* given as a name, from EP- + *ōnuma* -ONYM.

epopee *n.* an epic or heroic poem. WH: 17C. French *épopée*, from Greek *epopoiia*, from *epos* (see EPOS) + *poiein* to make.

EPOS *abbr.* electronic point-of-sale (a sales-recording system in which bar codes are read by a laser scanner). WH: Acronym of electronic *point-of-sale*.

epos *n.* an epopee. WH: 19C. Greek word, song, from *ep-*, stem of *eipein* to say.

epoxy *a.* containing oxygen plus two other atoms, frequently carbon, themselves already attached. *Also n.* WH: mid-20C. EP- + OXY-¹.

EPROM *n.* a kind of read-only memory which can be erased and reprogrammed. WH: Acronym of *erasable programmable read-only memory*. Cp. ROM.

epsilon *n.* the fifth letter of the Greek alphabet (Ε, ε). WH: 18C. Greek *epsilon*, lit. bare e, i.e. short e.

Epsom salts *n.pl.* sulphate of magnesia, a saline purgative. WH: 17C. *Epsom*, a town in Surrey, where salts were prepared from a mineral spring discovered in *c.*1618.

Epstein–Barr virus *n.* a virus which causes glandular fever, and is associated with several human cancers. WH: mid-20C. Sir Anthony *Epstein*, 1921– , English microbiologist + Yvonne M. *Barr*, 1932– , Irish-born virologist, who first isolated the virus in 1964.

epyllion *n.* a poem like an epic but shorter. WH: 19C. Greek *epullion*, dim. of *epos*. See EPOS.

equable *a.* characterized by evenness or uniformity. WH: 17C. Latin *aequabilis*, from *aequare* to make level, from *aequus* level, equal. See also -ABLE.

equal *a.* the same in size, number, quality, degree etc. *Also n.*, *v.t.* WH: 14–15C. Latin *aequalis*, from *aequus* level, even, equal. See also -AL¹.

equanimity *n.* evenness or composure of mind. WH: 17C. Latin *aequanimitas*, from *aequus* even + *animus* mind. See also -ITY.

equate *v.t.* to regard as equal (to). *Also v.i.* WH: 14–15C. Latin *aequatus*, p.p. of *aequare* to make equal, from *aequus* EQUAL. See also -ATE³.

equation *n.* the act of making equal. WH: 14–15C. Old French *équation* or Latin *aequatio*, *aequationis*, from *aequatus*. See EQUATE, also -ION.

equator *n.* a great circle on the earth's surface, equidistant from its poles, and dividing it into the northern and southern hemispheres. WH: 14–15C. Old French *équateur*, from Medieval Latin *aequator*, in full *circulus aequator diei et noctis* circle equalizing day and night. See EQUATE, also -OR. The term originally applied to the celestial equator. It was first applied to the terrestrial equator in the 17C.

equerry *n.* an officer of a royal household. WH: 16C. Obs. French *escurie* (now *écurie* stable), from Old French *escurie* company of squires, prince's stables, from *esquier* ESQUIRE. The word has come to be popularly associated with Latin *equus* horse. It originally applied to an officer in the service of a royal or noble person charged with the care of the horses.

equestrian *a.* of or relating to horses or horsemanship. *Also n.* WH: 17C. Latin *equester*, *equestris* belonging to a horseman, from *eques* horseman, knight, from *equus* horse. See also -IAN.

equi- *comb. form* equal. WH: Latin *aequi-*, from *aequus* EQUAL.

equiangular *a.* having or consisting of equal angles. WH: 17C. Late Latin *equiangulus*, from EQUI- + *angulus* ANGLE¹. See also -AR¹.

equidistant *a.* equally distant from some point or place. WH: 16C. French *équidistant* or Medieval Latin *equidistans*, *equidistantis*. See EQUI-, DISTANT.

equilateral *a.* having all the sides equal. *Also n.* WH: 16C. French *équilateral* or Late Latin *aequilateralis*, from *aequilaterus*, from *aequi-* EQUI- + Latin *latus*, *lateris* side. See also -AL¹.

equilibrate *v.t.* to balance (two things) exactly. *Also v.i.* WH: 17C. Late Latin *aequilibratus*, p.p. of *aequilibrare*, from *aequi-* EQUI- + *libra* balance. See also -ATE³.

equilibrium *n.* a state of equal balance, equipoise. WH: 17C. Latin *aequilibrium*, from *aequi-* EQUI- + *libra* balance.

equine *a.* of or relating to a horse or horses. WH: 18C. Latin *equinus*, from *equus* horse. See also -INE.

equinox *n.* the moment at which the sun crosses the equator and renders day and night equal throughout the world, now occurring (vernal equinox) on 21 March and (autumnal equinox) on 23 September. WH: 14–15C. Old French *équinoxe* or Latin *aequinoctium*, from *aequi-* EQUI- + *nox*, *noctis* night. Some languages refer to the equality of day with night rather than with day, e.g. Russian *ravnodenstviye*, where *ravno* is equal and *den-* day. German has *Tagundnachtgleiche*, lit. day and night equality.

equip *v.t.* to furnish, accoutre, esp. to supply with everything needed for some profession or activity. WH: 16C. French *équiper*, prob. from Old Norse *skipa* to man (a vessel), to fit up, from *skip* SHIP.

équipe *n.* (esp. in motor racing) a team. WH: mid-20C. French group, team. See EQUIP.

equipoise *n.* a state of equality of weight or force, equilibrium. *Also v.t.* WH: 17C. EQUI- + POISE¹, replacing phr. *equal poise*.

equipollent *a.* having equal force, power, significance etc. *Also n.* WH: 14–15C. Old French *equipolent* (Modern French *équipollent*), from Latin *aequipollens*, *aequipollentis* of equal value, from *aequi-* EQUI- + *pollere* to be strong.

equiponderate *v.t.* to counterpoise. WH: 17C. Medieval Latin *aequiponderatus*, p.p. of *aequiponderare*, from *aequi-* EQUI- + *ponderare* to weigh. See also -ATE³. An alternative origin is in PREPONDERATE, with EQUI- substituted for PRE-.

equipotential a. having the same, or being at the same, potential at all points (of a line, surface or region). *Also n.* WH: 17C. EQUI- + *potential* (POTENT).

equiprobable a. equally probable. WH: early 20C. EQUI- + PROBABLE.

equisetum n. a plant of the genus of cryptogams *Equisetum*, containing the horsetails and constituting the order Equisetaceae. WH: 17C. Modern Latin, from Latin *equisaetum*, from *equus* horse + *saeta* bristle.

equitable a. acting or done with equity; fair, just. WH: 16C. French *équitable*, from *équité* EQUITY. See also -ABLE. The suffix has an active sense, as in *charitable* (CHARITY).

equitant a. overlapping, astride or overriding (of leaves etc.). WH: 18C. Latin *equitans*, *equitantis*, pres.p. of *equitare*. See EQUITATION, also -ANT.

equitation n. the act or art of riding on horseback. WH: 16C. French *équitation* or Latin *equitatio*, *equitationis*, from *equitatus*, p.p. of *equitare*, from *eques*, *equitis* horseman, from *equus* horse. See also -ATION.

equity n. justice, fairness. WH: 12–14C. Old French *équité*, from Latin *aequitas*, from *aequus* EQUAL. See also -ITY.

equivalent a. of equal value, force or weight (to). *Also n.* WH: 14–15C. Old French *équivalent*, from Late Latin *aequivalens*, *aequivalentis*, pres.p. of *aequivalere*, from *aequi-* EQUI- + *valere* to be strong. See also -ENT.

equivocal a. doubtful of meaning, ambiguous, capable of a twofold interpretation. WH: 16C. Late Latin *aequivocus*, from Latin *aequus* equal + *vocare* to call. See also -AL[1].

equivocate v.i. to use words in an ambiguous manner. *Also v.t.* WH: 15C. Late Latin *aequivocatus*, p.p. of *aequivocare*, from *aequivocus*. See EQUIVOCAL, also -ATE[3].

equivoque n. an ambiguous term or phrase, an equivocation. WH: 14–15C. Old French *équivoque* or Late Latin *aequivocus*. See EQUIVOCAL.

ER abbr. Queen Elizabeth. WH: Abbr. of Latin *Elizabeth Regina* Elizabeth Queen. Cp. GR.

er int. used to express a hesitation in speech. WH: 19C. Imit. Cp. UM.

-er[1] suf. forming nouns, denoting an agent or doer, as in *hatter*, *player*, *singer*. WH: Old English *-ere*, from Germanic.

-er[2] suf. forming nouns, denoting a person or thing connected with, as in *butler*, *officer*, *teenager*. WH: Old French *-er*, from Latin *-aris* -AR[1], or from Anglo-French *-er* (Old French *-ier*), from Latin *-arius*, *-arium* (see -ARY[1]), or from Old French *-eüre* (Modern French *-oir*), from Latin *-atorium*, or var. of -OR (replacing *-our*).

-er[3] suf. forming adjectives, denoting the comparative, as in *dirtier*, *richer*, *taller*. WH: Old English *-ra* (a.), *-or* (adv.), both from Germanic.

-er[4] suf. forming nouns, denoting an action, as in *disclaimer*, *user*. WH: Anglo-French inf. ending of vv.

-er[5] suf. forming verbs, with a frequentative meaning, as in *chatter*, *slumber*, *twitter*. WH: Old English *-erian*, *-rian*, from Germanic.

-er[6] suf. forming nouns, with diminutive and colloquial meanings, as in *soccer*. WH: 19C. Orig. Rugby School slang, then widely adopted at Oxford University.

era n. a historical period or system of chronology running from a fixed point of time marked by an important event such as the birth of Christ, the Hegira etc. WH: 17C. Late Latin *aera* number as basis of reckoning, epoch from which time is reckoned, from pl. of Latin *aes*, *aeris* copper, money, counter.

eradiate v.i. to shoot out, as rays of light. *Also v.t.* WH: 17C. E- + RADIATE.

eradicate v.t. to root up. WH: 14–15C. Latin *eradicatus*, p.p. of *eradicare*, from E- + *radix*, *radicis* root. See also -ATE[3].

erase v.t. to rub out. WH: 16C. Latin *erasus*, p.p. of *eradere*, from E- + *radere* to scrape.

ERASMUS n. an exchange scheme for European Community university students. WH: Abbr. of *European Community Action for the Mobility of University Students*, punning on name of Desiderius *Erasmus*, c.1466–1536, Dutch scholar and humanist.

Erastian n. a person holding the opinions on ecclesiastical matters attributed to Erastus, that the State has supreme authority over the Church. *Also a.* WH: 17C. Thomas *Erastus*, 1524–83, Swiss physician and theologian + -IAN.

erbium n. a rare metallic element, at. no. 68, chem. symbol Er, forming a rose-coloured oxide. WH: 19C. *Ytterby*, a locality in Sweden (cp. YTTERBIUM) + -IUM. The name was coined in 1843 by the element's discoverer, the Swedish chemist Carl Gustaf Mosander.

ere prep. before, sooner than. *Also conj.* WH: pre-1200. Old English *ǣr*, from comp. of Germanic base. Cp. OR[2].

erect a. upright, vertical. *Also v.t.*, *v.i.* WH: 14–15C. Latin *erectus*, p.p. of *erigere* to set up, from E- + *regere* to direct.

eremite n. a hermit or recluse. WH: 12–14C. Old French. See HERMIT.

erethism n. undue excitation of an organ or tissue. WH: 19C. French *éréthisme*, from Greek *erethismos*, from *erethizein* to irritate. See also -ISM.

erg[1] n. the unit of work done in moving a body through 1 cm of space against the resistance of 1 dyne. WH: 19C. Greek *ergon* work. The term was proposed in 1873 by the British Association (for the Advancement of Science).

erg[2] n. an area of shifting sand dunes, esp. in the Sahara. WH: 19C. French, from Arabic *'irk*, *'erg*.

ergative a. of or relating to a case in some languages used to denote the doer of an action as the object of the verb. *Also n.* WH: mid-20C. Greek *ergatēs* worker + -IVE.

ergo adv. therefore. WH: 14–15C. Latin therefore.

ergocalciferol n. vitamin D₂, calciferol. WH: mid-20C. ERGOSTEROL + CALCIFEROL.

ergonomics n. the scientific study of the relationship between workers, their environment and machinery. WH: mid-20C. Greek *ergon* work + *economics* (ECONOMIC). The term was introduced in 1949 by the English industrial adviser K.F.H. Murrell.

ergosterol n. a plant sterol which is converted to vitamin D₂ by ultraviolet radiation. WH: early 20C. ERGOT + STEROL.

ergot n. a disease in various grains and grasses, esp. rye, caused by a fungus, *Claviceps purpurea*, whose presence can cause food poisoning. WH: 17C. French cock's spur, from Old French *argot*, of unknown orig. The reference is to the hard black sclerotia, resembling a cock's spur.

ergotism n. arguing, wrangling. WH: 17C. French *ergotisme*, from Latin ERGO, assoc. with French ERGOT. See also -ISM.

erica n. a member of the genus *Erica* of shrubby plants forming the heath family. WH: Modern Latin, or from Greek *ereikē* heath. The name is popularly derived from Greek *ereikō* I break, since an infusion of the plant's leaves was said to break bladder stones.

erigeron n. a member of the genus *Erigeron* of plants resembling the aster. WH: 17C. Latin groundsel, from Greek, from *ēri* early + *gerōn* old man. The plant flowers early and has a hoary appearance.

Erinys n. in Greek mythology, a Fury. WH: 17C. Latin, from Greek *Erinus* a Fury.

eristic a. of or relating to controversy or disputation. *Also n.* WH: 17C. Greek *eristikos*, from *erizein* to wrangle, from *eris* strife.

Eritrean a. of or relating to Eritrea. *Also n.* WH: early 20C. *Eritrea*, a country of NE Africa + -AN.

erk n. a naval rating. WH: early 20C. Orig. unknown. The word is popularly said to represent the pronunciation of *airc*, from *aircraftman* (AIR), but naval usage is earliest.

erl-king n. in German and Scandinavian folklore, a bearded goblin harmful to children. WH: 18C. Partial trans. of German *Erlkönig*, lit. alder king, mistranslating Danish *ellerkonge* king of the elves. The mistranslation was perpetrated by the German critic and poet Johann Gottfried Herder in his collection of folk songs, *Stimmen der Völker in Liedern* ('Voices of the Peoples in Songs') (1779).

ermine n. the stoat, *Mustela erminea*, hunted in winter for its fur, which then becomes snowy white, with the exception of the tip of the tail which is always black. WH: 12–14C. Old French, (Modern French *hermine*), prob. from Medieval Latin *(mus) Armenius* Armenian (mouse).

-ern suf. forming adjectives, as in *northern*, *southern*. WH: Old English, from Germanic, rel. to -ANEOUS.

erne n. an eagle, esp. the sea eagle. WH: pre-1200. Old English *earn*, from Germanic base. Cp Dutch *arend*.

Ernie n. the device employed for drawing the prize-winning numbers of Premium Bonds. WH: mid-20C. Acronym of *electronic number indicator equipment*, punning on male forename *Ernie*, pet form of *Ernest*, and prob. also on EARN.

erode *v.t.* to eat into or away. *Also v.i.* WH: 17C. French *éroder* or Latin *erodere*, from E- + *rodere* to gnaw.

erogenous *a.* sensitive to sexual stimulation. WH: 19C. Greek *erōs* sexual love + -GENOUS. Cp. EROTOGENIC (a better formation).

erotic *a.* of or relating to, caused by or causing sexual desire; amatory. *Also n.* WH: 17C. French *érotique* or Greek *erōtikos*, from *erōs, erōtos* sexual love. See also -IC. Greek *erōs* was personified in Eros, the god of love. Cp. CUPID.

eroto- *comb. form* erotic, eroticism. WH: Greek *erōs, erōtos* sexual love. See also -O-.

erotogenic *a.* erogenous. WH: early 20C. EROTO- + -GENIC.

erotology *n.* the study of eroticism or of sexual behaviour. WH: 19C. EROTO- + -LOGY.

erotomania *n.* abnormal or excessive sexual desire. WH: 19C. EROTO- + -MANIA.

err *v.i.* to blunder, to miss the truth, right or accuracy; to be incorrect. *Also v.t.* WH: 12–14C. Old French *errer*, from Latin *errare*, from base rel. to Gothic *airzei* error, Old High German *irri* astray. Cp. German *irren*.

errand *n.* a short journey to carry a message or perform some other commission, esp. on another's behalf. WH: pre-1200. Old English *ǣrende*, from Germanic base, ult. of unknown orig. The sense to the 18C was the message itself. The current sense of journey with a message arose in the 17C.

errant *a.* erring. WH: 12–14C. Old French, from Latin *errans, errantis*, pres.p. of *errare* ERR. See also -ANT. In the sense of wandering, roaming, the origin is in Old French *errer* to travel, from Late Latin *iterare*, from Latin *iter* journey. But both senses are ultimately of identical origin.

erratic *a.* irregular in movement, eccentric, unpredictable. *Also n.* WH: 14–15C. Old French *erratique*, from Latin *erraticus*, p.p. of *errare*. See ERR, also -IC.

erratum *n.* an error or mistake in printing or writing. WH: 16C. Latin error, neut. p.p. (used as n.) of *errare* ERR.

erroneous *a.* mistaken, incorrect. WH: 14–15C. Old French, or from Latin *erroneus*, from *erro, erronis* truant, vagabond, from *errare*. See ERR, also -EOUS.

error *n.* a mistake in writing, printing etc. WH: 12–14C. Old French *errur* (Modern French *erreur*), from Latin *error*, from *errare* ERR. See also -OR.

ersatz *a.* imitation. *Also n.* WH: 19C. German compensation, replacement.

†Erse *n.* the Gaelic dialect of Ireland or the Scottish Highlands. *Also a.* WH: 14–15C. Early Scottish var. of IRISH.

erst *adv.* once, formerly, of yore. WH: pre-1200. Old English *ǣrest*, superl. corr. to *ǣr* ERE. See also -EST[1].

erubescent *a.* reddening, blushing. WH: 18C. Latin *erubescens, erubescentis*, pres.p. of *erubescere* to blush, from E- + *rubescere* to redden, from *rubere* to be red. See also -escent (-ESCENCE).

eruca *n.* a member of the genus *Eruca*, herbs of the family Cruciferae. WH: 18C. Latin caterpillar, (garden) rocket, ? from *er* hedgehog (see URCHIN).

eructation *n.* the act or an instance of belching. WH: 14–15C. Latin *eructatio, eructationis*, from *eructatus*, p.p. of *eructare*, from E- + *ructare* to belch. See also -ATION.

erudite *a.* learned, well-read, well-informed. WH: 14–15C. Latin *eruditus*, p.p. of *erudire* to instruct, to train, from E- + *rudis* rude, untrained. See also -ITE[2].

erupt *v.t.* to emit violently, as a volcano, geyser etc. *Also v.i.* WH: 17C. Latin *eruptus*, p.p. of *erumpere*, from E- + *rumpere* to burst forth.

-ery *suf.* used with nouns and adjectives, and sometimes with verbs, to form nouns, generally abstract or collective, meaning a business, place of business, cultivation etc., conduct, things connected with or of the nature of etc., as in *foolery, grocery, pinery, rockery, tannery, witchery*. WH: French *-erie*, partly from Latin *-ario* + *-ia* -Y[2], partly from Old French *-ere, -eor* (Modern French *-eur*), from Latin *-ator* + *-ie* -Y[2]. The suffix was originally confined to Romance words, but is now widely used with those of Germanic origin.

eryngo *n.* any plant of the genus *Eryngium*, umbelliferous plants, including the sea holly. WH: 16C. Italian or Spanish *eringio*, from Latin *eryngion*, from Greek *ēruggion*, dim. of *ēruggos* sea holly.

erysipelas *n.* a streptococcal infection of the skin in which the affected parts are of a deep red colour, with a diffused inflammation of the underlying cutaneous tissue and cellular membrane. WH: 14–15C. Latin, from Greek *erusipelas*, prob. from base of *eruthros* red + *pel-* in *pella* skin.

erythema *n.* a superficial redness of the skin, occurring in patches. WH: 18C. Greek *eruthēma*, from *eruthainein* to be red, from *eruthros* red.

erythrism *n.* an abnormal red coloration, esp. of fur or plumage. WH: 19C. Greek *eruthros* red + -ISM.

erythrite *n.* a red or greenish-grey variety of feldspar. WH: 19C. Greek *eruthros* red + -ITE[1].

erythro- *comb. form* red. WH: Greek *eruthros* red. See also -O-.

erythroblast *n.* a cell in the bone marrow that will develop into an erythrocyte. WH: 19C. ERYTHRO- + -BLAST.

erythrocyte *n.* a red blood cell in vertebrates. WH: 19C. ERYTHRO- + -CYTE.

erythroid *a.* of or relating to erythrocytes. WH: 19C. ERYTHRO- + -OID.

erythromycin *n.* an antibiotic used to treat bacterial infections. WH: mid-20C. ERYTHRO- + -MYCIN.

erythropoiesis *n.* the formation of red blood cells. WH: early 20C. ERYTHRO- + Greek *poiēsis* creation.

-es[1] *suf.* forming the plural of nouns that end in a sibilant sound, as in *kisses, witches, axes*; also of some nouns that end in *-o*, as in *tomatoes*. WH: Var. of -S[1].

-es[2] *suf.* forming the 3rd person singular present of verbs that end in a sibilant sound, as in *kisses, watches*; also of some verbs that end in *-o*, as in *goes*. WH: Var. of -S[4].

escadrille *n.* a French squadron of aircraft. WH: early 20C. French flotilla (alt. influ. by French *escadre* squadron), from Spanish *escuadrilla*, dim. of *escuadra* SQUADRON, squad.

escalade *n.* an attack on a fortified place in which ladders are used to mount the ramparts etc. *Also v.t.* WH: 16C. French, from Spanish *escalada*, from Medieval Latin *scalare* SCALE[3]. See also -ADE.

escalate *v.i.* to increase (rapidly) in scale, intensity or magnitude. *Also v.t.* WH: early 20C. Back-formation from ESCALATOR.

escalator *n.* a conveyor for passengers consisting of a continuous series of steps on an endless chain, ascending or descending and arranged to give facilities for mounting or leaving at either end; a moving staircase. WH: early 20C. ESCALADE + -ATOR, based on *elevator* (ELEVATE). The word was originally the trade name of a moving staircase built by the Otis Elevator Company in 1900. Cp. TRAVOLATOR.

escallonia *n.* an evergreen shrub of the S American flowering genus *Escallonia*, of the saxifrage family. WH: 19C. Modern Latin, from *Escallon*, 18C Spanish traveller in S America + -IA.

escallop *n.* an escalope. WH: 15C. Old French *escalope* shell. Cp. SCALLOP.

escalope *n.* a thin boneless slice of meat, esp. veal or pork. WH: 19C. French, from Old French shell. Cp. ESCALLOP. The cut is so named from the shell-shaped pan in which it is cooked.

escapade *n.* an exciting or daring prank or adventure. WH: 17C. French, from Spanish or Provençal, from *escapar* ESCAPE. See also -ADE.

escape *v.t.* to get safely away from. *Also v.i., n.* WH: 12–14C. Old French *eschaper* (Modern French *échapper*), from *es-* (EX-) + Medieval Latin *cappa* cloak. See CAP. The original concept was of breaking free from a cloak. Cp. Mark xiv.51–2.

escargot *n.* an edible snail. WH: 19C. French, from Old French *escargol*, from Provençal *escaragol*.

escarp *n.* a steep slope below a plateau. *Also v.t.* WH: 17C. French *escarpe*, from Italian *scarpa* slope. Cp. SCARP[1].

-esce *suf.* forming inceptive verbs, as in *acquiesce, coalesce, effervesce*. WH: Latin *-escere*.

-escence *suf.* forming abstract nouns from inceptive verbs, as in *acquiescence, coalescence, opalescence*. WH: French *-escence* or Latin *-escentia*, from *-escens, -escentis*, pres.p. ending of vv. in *-escere*. See -ESCE, -ENT.

eschalot *n.* a shallot. WH: 18C. French *eschallote* (now *échalotte*), alt. of Old French *escalogne*. See SCALLION. Cp. SHALLOT.

eschatology *n.* the doctrine of the final issue of things, death, the last judgement, the future state etc. WH: 19C. Greek *eskhatos* last + -O- + -LOGY.

escheat *n.* the reverting of property to the Crown or the state, on the death of the owner intestate without heirs. *Also v.t., v.i.* WH: 12–14C. Old French *eschete*, ult. from Latin *excidere* to fall away, to escape, from EX- + *cadere* to fall.

eschew *v.t.* to avoid; to shun. WH: 14–15C. Old French *eschiver*, from Germanic base of Old High German *sciuhen*, German *scheuen* to shun. Cp. SHY[1].

eschscholtzia *n.* a member of the genus of flowering herbs, *Eschscholtzia*, comprising the California poppy. WH: 19C. Modern Latin, from Johann Friedrich *Eschscholtz*, 1793–1831, Russian-born German naturalist and traveller.

escort[1] *n.* an armed guard attending persons, baggage etc. which are being conveyed from one place to another, as a protection against attack or for compulsion or surveillance. WH: 16C. French *escorte*, from Italian *scorta*, fem. p.p. (used as n.) of *scorgere* to guide, to conduct, from Popular Latin *excorrigere*, from EX- + Latin *corrigere* to set right, CORRECT.

escort[2] *v.t.* to act as escort to. WH: 16C. French *escorter*, from *escorte*. See ESCORT[1].

escribe *v.t.* to draw (a circle) so as to touch one side of a triangle exteriorly and the other two internally. WH: 16C. From E- + Latin *scribere* to write.

escritoire *n.* a writing desk with drawers etc. for papers and stationery, a bureau. WH: 16C. Old French study, writing box (Modern French *écritoire* writing desk), from Latin *scriptorium* (see SCRIPT).

escrow *n.* a fully-executed deed or engagement to do or pay something, put into the custody of a third party until some condition is fulfilled. *Also v.t.* WH: 17C. Old French *escroe* scrap, scroll, from Medieval Latin *scroda*, from Germanic base of SHRED.

escudo *n.* the standard unit of currency in Portugal. WH: 19C. Spanish and Portuguese, from Latin *scutum* shield. Cp. ÉCU, SCUDO.

esculent *a.* fit or good for food. *Also n.* WH: 17C. Latin *esculentus*, from *esca* food, from *esse* to eat. See also -ULENT.

escutcheon *n.* a shield or shield-shaped surface charged with armorial bearings. WH: 15C. Old French *escusson* (Modern French *écusson*), from Latin *scutum* shield.

-ese *suf.* forming adjectives and nouns, meaning belonging to a country etc. as inhabitant(s) or language, as in *Maltese, Chinese*. WH: Old French *-eis* (Modern French *-ois, -ais*), from Latin *-ensis*.

esemplastic *a.* moulding, shaping or fashioning into one, unifying. WH: 19C. Greek *es* into + *hen* one, neut. of *heis* + *plastikos* PLASTIC, rendering German *Ineinsbildung* forming into one. The word was introduced in 1817 by the English poet Samuel Taylor Coleridge.

esker *n.* a bank or long mound of glacial drift such as are found abundantly in Irish river valleys. WH: 19C. Irish *eiscir*.

Eskimo *n.* a member of a group of peoples inhabiting Greenland and the adjacent parts of N America, the Aleutian Islands and Siberia. *Also a.* WH: 16C. Danish, from French *Esquimaux* (pl.), from Algonquian. Cp. Abnaki *askimo* eaters of raw meat.

Esky® *n.* in Australia, a portable container or chest for cooled drinks or food. WH: mid-20C. Prob. from ESKIMO + -Y[3].

esoteric *a.* of philosophical doctrines, religious rites etc., meant for or intelligible only to the initiated. WH: 17C. Greek *esōterikos*, from *esōterō* inner, comp. of *esō* within, from *es, eis* into. See also -IC. Cp. EXOTERIC.

espadrille *n.* a rope-soled shoe with a cloth upper. WH: 19C. French, from Provençal *espadilhos*, from *espart* ESPARTO.

espagnolette *n.* a bolt used for fastening a French window, one turn of the knob securing the sash both at top and bottom. WH: 19C. French, from *espagnol* Spanish. See also -ETTE. The bolt is so named as it is of Spanish origin.

espalier *n.* a lattice-work on which shrubs or fruit trees are trained flat against a wall. *Also v.t.* WH: 17C. French, from Italian *spalliera*, from *spalla* shoulder, from Latin SPATULA, shoulder blade.

esparto *n.* a kind of coarse grass or rush, *Stipa tenacissima*, growing in the sandy regions of N Africa and Spain, used largely for making paper, mats etc. WH: 19C. Spanish, from Latin *spartum*, from Greek *sparton* rope. Cp. SPARTINA.

especial *a.* distinguished in a certain class or kind. WH: 14–15C. Old French (Modern French *spécial*), from Latin *specialis*. See SPECIAL.

†esperance *n.* hope. WH: 14–15C. Old French *espérance*, from *espérer* to hope, from Latin *sperare*. See also -ANCE.

Esperanto *n.* an international artificial language invented in 1887, based on the chief European languages. WH: 19C. Dr *Esperanto* (Esperanto hoping one), pen name of its inventor, Lazarus Ludwig Zamenhof, 1859–1917, Polish oculist and philologist.

espiègle *a.* roguish, frolicsome. WH: 19C. French *Ulespiegle*, from Dutch *Uilenspiegel*, from *uil* OWL + *spiegel* mirror, from Latin *speculum*. The reference is to Till *Eulenspiegel*, a German peasant of the 14C whose practical jokes were the subject of a 16C collection of satirical tales. His name was translated as English *owlglass* to mean jester.

espionage *n.* the act or practice of spying. WH: 18C. French *espionage*, from *espionner* to spy, from *espion* SPY. See also -AGE.

esplanade *n.* a level space, esp. a level walk or drive by the seaside etc. WH: 16C. French, from Italian *spianata*, from fem. of Latin *explanatus*, flattened, levelled, p.p. of *explanare*. See EXPLAIN, also -ADE.

espouse *v.t.* to adopt, to support, defend (a cause etc.). WH: 14–15C. Old French *espouser* (Modern French *épouser*), from Latin *sponsare*, from *sponsus*, p.p. of *spondere* to betroth. Cp. SPOUSE. The original sense was to marry. The current sense emerged in the 17C.

espressivo *a.* with expression. WH: 19C. Italian, from Latin *expressus*. See EXPRESS[2].

espresso *n.* very strong black coffee made by a machine which uses steam pressure. WH: mid-20C. Italian (*caffè*) *espresso*, from *espresso* pressed out, from Latin *expressus*. See EXPRESS[2].

esprit *n.* wit. WH: 16C. French, from Latin *spiritus* SPIRIT.

espy *v.t.* to catch sight of. *Also v.i.* WH: 12–14C. Old French *espier* (Modern French *épier*). See SPY.

-esque *suf.* forming adjectives, meaning like, in the manner or style of, as in *arabesque, burlesque, picturesque*. WH: French, from Italian *-esco*, from Medieval Latin *-iscus*. Cp. -ISH[1].

esquire *n.* a title of respect, placed after a man's surname in the addresses of letters. *Also v.t.* WH: 14–15C. Old French *esquier* (Modern French *écuyer*), from Latin *scutarius* shield bearer, from *scutum* shield. See -ARY[1]. Cp. SQUIRE. A squire was originally a young nobleman who while training to be a knight acted as shield bearer and attendant to a knight. Later, the word was a title for a man ranking next below a knight.

ess *n.* the 19th letter of the alphabet, S, s. WH: 16C. Representation of the pronun. of *S* as letter's name.

-ess[1] *suf.* forming nouns, denoting the feminine, as in *empress, seamstress, songstress* (the last two are double feminines formed on the OE fem. *-ster*, as in *spinster*). WH: French *-esse*, from Late Latin *-issa*, from Greek. Cp. -STER.

-ess[2] *suf.* forming abstract nouns from adjectives, as in *largess, duress*. WH: Old French *-esse, -ece*, from Latin *-itia*. Cp. -ICE.

essay[1] *n.* a short informal literary composition or disquisition, usu. in prose. WH: 16C. Old French *essai*, from *essayer*. See ESSAY[2]. Cp. ASSAY. The sense literary composition derives from the title of Francis Bacon's *Essays* (1597), itself adopted from Montaigne's *Essais* (1580).

essay[2] *v.t.* to try, to attempt. *Also v.i.* WH: 15C. Alt. of ASSAY by assim. to Old French *essayer*, from Late Latin *exagium* weighing, from Latin *exag-*, base of *exigere*. See EXACT[1].

essence *n.* the distinctive quality of a thing. *Also v.t.* WH: 14–15C. Old French, from Latin *essentia*, from *esse* to be, itself based on Greek *ousia* being, from *ōn, ontos*, pres.p. of *einai* to be. See also -ENCE.

Essene *n.* a member of an ancient Jewish sect of religious mystics who cultivated poverty, community of goods and asceticism of life. WH: 14–15C. Latin *Esseni* (pl.), from Greek *Essēnoi*, ? from Aramaic.

essential *a.* important in the highest degree. *Also n.* WH: 12–14C. Late Latin *essentialis*, from Latin *essentia*. See ESSENCE, also -IAL.

Essex man *n.* the stereotypical southern English working man, lacking in style and cultural interests, but with a large disposable income. WH: late 20C. *Essex*, a county in SE England.

-est[1] *suf.* forming the superlative degree of adjectives and adverbs, as in *richest, tallest, liveliest*. WH: Old English *-ost-, -ust-, -ast-* and *-est-, -st-*, both from Germanic. Cp. Greek *-isto-*.

†-est[2] *suf.* forming the 2nd person singular of verbs, as in *givest, gavest, canst, didst*. WH: Old English *-est, -ast, -st*. Cp. Old High German *-ist*, German *-st*.

establish *v.t.* to set upon a firm foundation, to found, to institute. WH: 14–15C. Old French *establir*, *establiss-* (Modern French *établir*), from Latin *stabilire*, from *stabilis* STABLE[1]. See also -ISH[2].

estaminet *n.* a small cafe in which wine etc. is sold. WH: 19C. French, from Walloon *staminé* byre, from *stamo* pole to which a cow is tethered in a stall, ? from German *Stamm* stem, trunk.

estancia *n.* in Spanish America, a cattle-farm, ranch or country estate. WH: 17C. Spanish station, from Medieval Latin *stantia*, from Latin *stans*, *stantis*, pres.p. of *stare* to stand.

estate *n.* property, esp. a landed property. WH: 12–14C. Old French *estat* (Modern French *état*), from Latin *status*. See STATE.

esteem *v.t.* to hold in high estimation, to regard with respect; to prize. Also *n.* WH: 14–15C. Old French *estimer*, from Latin *aestimare* to estimate, to assess. The original sense (to the 18C) was identical to that of ESTIMATE[1]. The sense to think highly of arose in the 16C.

ester *n.* an organic compound derived by the replacement of hydrogen in an acid by an organic radical. WH: 19C. German, prob. from *Essig* vinegar (from Latin *acetum*) + *Äther* ether.

estimable *a.* worthy of esteem or regard. WH: 15C. Old French, from Latin *aestimabilis*, from *aestimare*. See ESTEEM, also -ABLE.

estimate[1] *v.t.* to compute the value of, to appraise. WH: 15C. Latin *aestimatus*, p.p. of *aestimare*. See ESTEEM, also -ATE[3].

estimate[2] *n.* an approximate calculation of the value, number, extent etc. of anything. WH: 14–15C. ESTIMATE[1] or prob. from Latin *aestimatus*, verbal n. from *aestimare*. See ESTEEM, also -ATE[1].

Estonian *a.* of or relating to Estonia, its people or their language. Also *n.* WH: 18C. Modern Latin *Esthonia*, *Estonia*, a country on the S side of the Gulf of Finland + -AN.

estop *v.t.* to bar, preclude, prevent (from). WH: 14–15C. Old French *estopper* (Modern French *étouper*) to stop up, to impede, from Late Latin deriv. of Latin *stuppa* oakum.

estovers *n.pl.* necessaries or supplies allowed by law, esp. wood which a tenant could take from a landlord's estate for repairs etc. WH: 15C. Pl. of Anglo-French *estover*, use as n. of *estover*, from Old French *estoveir* to be necessary, based on Latin *opus est* it is necessary. See also -ER[4].

estrade *n.* a slightly raised platform, a dais. WH: 17C. French, from Spanish *estrado*, from Latin STRATUM.

estrange *v.t.* to alienate, to make indifferent or distant in feeling. WH: 15C. Old French *estranger* (Modern French *étranger*), from Latin *extraneare* to treat as a stranger, from *extraneus*. See EXTRANEOUS. Cp. STRANGE.

estray *n.* a domestic animal, as a horse, ox etc. found straying or without an owner. Also *v.i.* WH: 16C. Anglo-French, from Old French *estraier* STRAY.

estreat *n.* a true copy of an original writing, esp. of penalties set down in a court record. Also *v.t.* WH: 12–14C. Old French *estraite*, fem. p.p. (used as n.) of *estraire* to extract, from Latin *extrahere*.

estuary *n.* the mouth of a river etc. in which the tide meets the current; a firth. WH: 16C. Latin *aestuarium* tidal part of a shore, from *aestus* heat, swell, tide. See also -ARY[1].

esurient *a.* hungry. WH: 17C. Latin *esuriens*, *esurientis*, pres.p. of *esurire* to be hungry, from *esus*, p.p. of *esse* to eat. See also -ENT.

-et[1] *suf.* forming diminutive nouns, as in *chaplet*, *coronet*, *dulcet*, *russet*, *violet*. WH: Old French, of uncertain (prob. not Latin) orig. Cp. Italian *-etto*.

-et[2] *suf.* forming nouns denoting a person involved in some activity as in *poet*, *athlete*. WH: Greek *-ētēs*.

ETA *n.* a Basque separatist terrorist organization. WH: Abbr. of Basque *Euzkadi ta Azkatasuna* Basque Homeland and Liberty. Cp. EUSKARIAN.

eta *n.* the seventh letter of the Greek alphabet (H, η). WH: 14–15C. Greek *ēta*.

étagère *n.* a stand with open shelves for ornaments etc. WH: 19C. French, from *étage* shelf, STAGE.

et al. *abbr.* and others. WH: Abbr. of Latin *et alii* and others, from *et* and + masc. pl. of *alius* other. The *al.* could also represent fem. *aliae* or neut. *alia*.

etalon *n.* a device which measures wavelengths by means of reflections from silvered glass or quartz plates. WH: early 20C. French *étalon* standard of measurement.

etcetera *adv.* and the rest, and so on. WH: 12–14C. Latin *et cetera* and the rest, from *et* and + *cetera*, neut. pl. of *ceterus* remaining over.

etch *v.t.* to produce or reproduce (a picture) on a metal plate, for printing copies, by engraving with an acid through the lines previously drawn with a needle on a coated surface. Also *v.i.* WH: 17C. Dutch *etsen*, from German *ätzen*, from Old High German *azzen*, from Germanic. Rel. to EAT. The acid 'eats' the surface of the metal.

eternal *a.* without beginning or end. Also *n.* WH: 14–15C. Old French (Modern French *éternel*), from Late Latin *aeternalis*, from Latin *aeternus*, contr. of *aeviternus*, from *aevum* age. See also -AL[1].

eternity *n.* eternal duration. WH: 14–15C. Old French *éternité*, from Latin *aeternitas*, from *aeternus* ETERNAL. See also -ITY.

etesian *a.* annual. WH: 17C. Latin *etesius*, from Greek *etēsios*, from *etos* year. See also -AN.

eth *n.* a letter (Ð, ð) used in Icelandic and in Old English (= th). WH: 19C. Icelandic, prob. representing the sound of the letter.

†-eth *suf.* forming the 3rd pers. sing. pres. of verbs, as in *goeth*, *saith*. WH: Old English *-eth*, *-ath*, *-th*. Cp. Old High German *-it*.

ethanal *n.* acetaldehyde. WH: mid-20C. ETHANE + ALDEHYDE.

ethane *n.* a colourless and odourless gaseous compound of the paraffin series. WH: 19C. ETHER + -ANE.

ethanoate *n.* a salt or ester of acetic acid, acetate. WH: mid-20C. *ethanoic* (from ETHANE + -O- + -IC) + -ATE[1].

ethanol *n.* a colourless liquid produced by fermenting sugars and constituting the intoxicating agent in various drinks, alcohol. WH: early 20C. ETHANE + -OL.

ethene *n.* a hydrocarbon gas found in petroleum and natural gas, used in the manufacture of polythene etc. WH: 19C. ETHYL + -ENE.

ether *n.* a light, volatile and inflammable fluid, produced by the distillation of alcohol with an acid, esp. sulphuric acid, and used as an anaesthetic or a solvent. WH: 14–15C. Old French *éther* or Latin *aether*, from Greek *aithēr* upper air, from base of *aithein* to kindle, to burn, to shine. The original sense was the clear sky, the region above the clouds, or the substance formerly believed to occupy it. Something of this sense survives in *ethereal*.

Ethernet® *n.* a type of LAN. WH: late 20C. ETHER + *net* (from *network*, from NET[1] + WORK).

ethic *n.* a moral principle or a set of principles. Also *a.* WH: 14–15C. Old French *éthique*, from Latin *ethice*, from Greek (*hē*) *ēthikē* (*tekhnē*) (the) ethic (art), from *ēthikos*. See ETHOS, also -IC.

Ethiopian *a.* of or relating to Ethiopia or its inhabitants. Also *n.* WH: 12–14C. Ethiopia, Aethiopia, a country in NE Africa, from Latin *Aithiops*, from Greek *Aithiops*, from *aithein* to burn + *ōps* face + -AN.

ethmoid *a.* resembling a sieve. Also *n.* WH: 18C. Greek *ēthmoeidēs*, from *ēthmos* sieve. See also -OID.

ethnarch *n.* the governor of a people or district in the Roman and Byzantine empires. WH: 17C. Greek *ethnarkhēs*, from *ethnos* nation + *arkhōn* ruler.

ethnic *a.* of, relating to or characteristic of a race, people or culture. Also *n.* WH: 14–15C. Ecclesiastical Latin *ethnicus* heathen, from Greek *ethnikos*, from *ethnos* nation. See also -IC.

ethno- *comb. form* ethnic, ethnological. WH: Greek *ethnos* nation. See also -O-.

ethnoarchaeology *n.* the scientific study of the cultural institutions of a society, through the examination of its buildings, artefacts etc. WH: mid-20C. ETHNO- + ARCHAEOLOGY.

ethnobotany *n.* (the study of) the knowledge and use of plants by traditional societies. WH: 19C. ETHNO- + BOTANY.

ethnocentrism *n.* the mental habit of viewing the world solely from the perspective of one's own culture. WH: early 20C. ETHNO- + *centrism* (CENTRE).

ethnography *n.* the scientific study and description of different human societies. WH: 19C. ETHNO- + -GRAPHY.

ethnology *n.* the science which treats of the varieties of the human race. WH: 19C. ETHNO- + -LOGY.

ethnomethodology *n.* the study of everyday human communication by speech. WH: mid-20C. ETHNO- + *methodology* (METHOD + -O- + -LOGY).

ethnomusicology *n.* the study of the music of different societies. WH: mid-20C. ETHNO- + *musicology* (MUSIC + -O- + -LOGY).

ethogram *n.* the typical behaviour and activities of an animal, noted in a list. WH: mid-20C. Greek *ēthos* nature or disposition of animals + -GRAM.

ethology *n.* the science of animal behaviour. WH: 17C. Latin *ethologia*, from Greek, from *ēthos*. See ETHOS, -LOGY.

ethos *n.* the characteristic spirit, character, disposition or genius of a people, community, institution, system etc. WH: 19C. Greek *ēthos* nature, disposition.

ethoxyethane *n.* ether, as used as an anaesthetic. WH: late 20C. ETHYL + OXY-[1] + ETHANE.

ethyl *n.* a monovalent fatty hydrocarbon radical of the paraffin series, forming the base of common alcohol and ether, acetic acid etc. WH: 19C. ETHER + -YL, based on German *Äther* + -YL.

ethyne *n.* acetylene. WH: 19C. ETHYL + -YNE.

-etic *suf.* forming nouns and adjectives, meaning (a person or thing) of the nature of or serving as, as in *ascetic, pathetic*. WH: Greek *-etikos, -ētikos*. Cp. -IC.

etiolate *v.t.* to blanch (a plant) by keeping in the dark. *Also v.i.* WH: 18C. French *étioler*, from Normandy French *étieuler* to grow into haulm, from *éteule*. See STUBBLE, also -ATE[3].

etiquette *n.* the conventional rules of behaviour in polite society. WH: 18C. French *étiquette* TICKET. The word is said to originate in the directions for behaviour on a soldier's billet (ticket) for lodgings.

Etonian *n.* a person educated or being educated at Eton College. *Also a.* WH: 17C. *Eton* College, a public school in Berkshire (now in Windsor and Maidenhead) + -IAN.

Etrurian *a.* of or relating to Etruria, an ancient country in central Italy. *Also n.* WH: 17C. Latin *Etruria*, an ancient region of central Italy + -AN. Cp. ETRUSCAN, TUSCAN.

Etruscan *a.* Etrurian. *Also n.* WH: 18C. Latin *Etruscus* + -AN. Cp. ETRURIAN, TUSCAN.

et seq. *abbr.* and the following (passage(s), page(s) etc.). WH: 12–14C. Abbr. of Latin *et sequens* and the following, from *et* and + pres.p. of *sequi* to follow, or of *et sequentes* (m. and fem. pl. of *sequens*), *et sequentia* (neut. pl. of *sequens*) and the following things.

-ette *suf.* forming nouns meaning diminutive, as in *cigarette, kitchenette*. WH: Old French fem. suf. Cp. -ET[1].

étude *n.* a short composition written mainly to test or develop a player's technical skill. WH: 19C. French STUDY.

etui *n.* a small case for pins, needles etc. WH: 17C. French *étui*, from Old French *estui* prison, from *estuier* to shut up, to keep. Cp. STEW[2], TWEEZERS.

-etum *suf.* forming nouns meaning (a place or garden containing) a collection of plants, as in *arboretum, pinetum*. WH: 17C. Latin, neut. of -etus.

etymology *n.* the branch of linguistics that treats of the origin and history of words. WH: 14–15C. Old French *ethimologie* (Modern French *étymologie*), from Latin *etimologia*, from Greek *etumologia*, from *etumologos* student of etymology, from *etumon*. See ETYMON, also -O- + -LOGY.

etymon *n.* the primitive or root form of a word. WH: 16C. Latin, from Greek *etumon*, neut. sing. (used as n.) of *etumos* true.

eu- *comb. form* good, well, pleasant, as in *eulogy, euphony*. WH: Greek, from *eu* well, from *eus* good.

eucaine *n.* a form of local anaesthetic. WH: 19C. EU- + -caine from COCAINE.

eucalyptus *n.* any evergreen myrtaceous tree belonging to the Australasian genus *Eucalyptus*, comprising the gum-trees. WH: 19C. Modern Latin, from Greek EU- + *kaluptos* covered, from *kaluptein* to cover, to conceal. It was so called in 1788 by the French botanist, Charles Louis Lhéritier, from the protective covering of the unopened flower.

eucharis *n.* a bulbous plant from S America of the genus *Eucharis*, cultivated in hothouses for its pure white bell-shaped flowers. WH: 19C. Greek *eukharis* gracious, from EU- + *kharis* grace.

Eucharist *n.* the sacrament of the Lord's Supper. WH: 14–15C. Old French *eucariste* (Modern French *eucharistie*), from Ecclesiastical Latin *eucharistia*, from Ecclesiastical Greek *eukharistia* giving of thanks, from Greek *eukharistos* grateful, from EU- + *kharizesthai* to show favour, to give freely, from *kharis* grace.

euchlorine *n.* a yellow explosive gas with bleaching properties,

obtained from a mixture of chlorate of potash and dilute hydrochloric acid. WH: 19C. EU- + CHLORINE.

euchre *n.* an orig. American card game for several persons, usu. four, with a pack from which the cards from the twos to the nines have been excluded. *Also v.t.* WH: 19C. German dial. *Juckerspiel*.

Euclidean *a.* of or relating to Euclid or to the axioms and postulates of his geometry. WH: 18C. Latin *Euclidius*, from Greek *Eukleideios*, from *Eukleidēs* Euclid, *fl.* 300 BC, Greek mathematician + -EAN.

eudemonism *n.* the system of ethics which makes the pursuit of happiness the basis and criterion of moral conduct. WH: 19C. Greek *eudaimōn* fortunate, happy (from EU- + *daimōn* genius, DEMON) + -ISM.

eudiometer *n.* an instrument, consisting of a graduated glass jar with wires for electric sparking, used to measure changes in volume of gases during chemical reactions. WH: 18C. Greek *eudios* fine (of weather) (from EU- + *dios* heavenly, gen. of *Zeus* god of the sky) + -O- + -METER.

eugenic *a.* of or relating to the development and improvement of offspring, esp. human offspring, through selective breeding. WH: 19C. EU- + -GEN + -IC. The term was coined in 1883 (together with the noun, *eugenics*) by the English scientist Francis Galton.

euglena *n.* a single-celled aquatic animal of the genus *Euglena*, with a single flagellum. WH: 19C. Modern Latin, from EU- + Greek *glēnē* eyeball, socket of joint.

euhemerism *n.* the theory formulated by Euhemerus of Messenia in Sicily (about 300 BC), that the classic gods are merely deified national kings and heroes, and their miraculous feats exaggerated traditions of actual events. WH: 19C. Latin *Euhemerus*, from Greek *Euēmeros*, from Euhemerus, *c.*316 BC, Sicilian writer + -ISM.

eukaryon *n.* a highly organized cell nucleus, with DNA in the form of chromosomes, characteristic of higher organisms. WH: mid-20C. EU- + Greek *karuon* nut, kernel.

eulachon *n.* the candlefish of the N Pacific. WH: 19C. Lower Chinook *úƚxan*.

eulogy *n.* praise, encomium, panegyric. WH: 14–15C. Medieval Latin *eulogium*, from Greek *eulogia*. See EU-, -LOGY.

eunuch *n.* a castrated man, esp. an attendant in a harem, or a state functionary in Oriental palaces and under the Roman emperors. *Also a., v.t.* WH: pre-1200. Latin *eunuchus*, from Greek *eunoukhos*, from *eunē* bed + stem of *ekhein* to keep. A eunuch was originally a guard of the bedchamber.

euonymus *n.* any tree or shrub of the genus *Euonymus*, containing the spindle tree. WH: 18C. Modern Latin, from Greek *euōnumos* having an auspicious name, from EU- + *onuma* name. According to Pliny, the flowering of the tree was a presage of pestilence. It was therefore named 'lucky' euphemistically.

eupatrid *n.* a member of the hereditary aristocracy of Attica, a patrician. WH: 19C. Greek *eupatridēs* person of noble ancestry, from EU- + *patēr* father.

eupeptic *a.* having a good digestion. WH: 17C. Greek *eupeptos* easy to digest, having a good digestion, from EU- + *peptein* to digest. See also -IC.

euphemism *n.* the use of a soft or pleasing term or phrase for one that is harsh or offensive. WH: 16C. Greek *euphēmismos*, from *euphēmizein* to speak well, from *euphēmos* fair of speech, from EU- + *phēmē* speaking. See also -ISM.

euphonium *n.* a brass instrument related to the tuba. WH: 19C. Greek *euphōnos*. See EUPHONY, -IUM.

euphony *n.* an agreeable sound. WH: 14–15C. French *euphonie*, from Late Latin *euphonia*, from Greek *euphōnia*, from *euphōnos* sounding well, from EU- + *phōnē* sound, voice. See also -Y[2].

euphorbia *n.* any plant of the genus *Euphorbia*, including the spurges, comprising about 700 species, many of which are poisonous while others have medicinal qualities. WH: 14–15C. Alt. (by assim. to -IA) of Latin *euphorbea*, from *Euphorbus*, *fl.*1C BC, physician to Juba II, King of Mauretania. Euphorbus used latex from some species of the plant for medicinal purposes.

euphoria *n.* a feeling of well-being, supreme content, esp. exaggerated or baseless. WH: 17C. Modern Latin, from Greek, from *euphoros* borne well, healthy, from EU- + *pherein* to bear. See also -IA.

euphrasy *n.* the eyebright, any plant of the genus *Euphrasia*. WH: 14–15C. Medieval Latin *euphrasia*, from Greek, lit. cheerfulness, from *euphrainein* to gladden, from EU- + *phrēn* mind.

euphuism *n.* a pedantic affectation of elegant and high-flown language. WH: 16C. *Euphues*, central character of John Lyly's work of the same name (1578–80), from Greek *euphuēs* well endowed by nature, from EU- + *phu-*, from *phuē* growth. See also -ISM. Lyly's work popularized the style.

Eurasian *a.* of mixed European and Asian descent; esp. formerly in British India etc., born of a European father and an Asian mother. *Also n.* WH: 19C. From EURO- + ASIAN, and also from *Eurasia* + -AN. *Eurasia*, as the name of Europe and Asia considered as a single continent, is first recorded in 1858, later than the adjective.

Euratom *n.* the European Atomic Energy Community of 1958 in which France, Belgium, W Germany, Italy, the Netherlands and Luxembourg united for the peaceful development of nuclear energy. WH: mid-20C. Abbr. of *Eur*opean *Atom*ic Energy Community.

eureka *int.* used to express exultation over a discovery. *Also n.* WH: 17C. Greek *heurēka* I have found (it), 1st pers. sing. perf. of *heuriskein* to find. The word represents an exclamation supposedly uttered by Archimedes when he hit on a method of establishing the purity of gold.

eurhythmics *n.* the scientific use or art of rhythmical movement, esp. as applied to dancing and gymnastic exercises. WH: early 20C. EU- + RHYTHM + -ICS. The term was popularized by the system of 'rhythmic gymnastics' introduced in *c*.1905 by the Swiss musician and educationalist Émile Jaques-Dalcroze.

Euro *n.* a European. *Also a.* WH: late 20C. Abbr. of EUROPEAN.

Euro- *comb. form* of or relating to Europe or Europeans, or the European Union. WH: Abbr. of *Europe* or EUROPEAN. See also -O-.

euro[1] *n.* a wallaby of S and central Australia, *Macropus robustus*. WH: 19C. Australian Aboriginal (Adnyamadhanha) *yuru*.

euro[2] *n.* the European Union unit of currency, introduced in 1999 (in use in member countries who have accepted European Monetary Union). WH: late 20C. Abbr. of EUROPEAN or EURO- as independent word. The name was objected to by some on the grounds that its pronunciation is identical to that of URO-[2].

Eurobond *n.* a bond issued in a European country, but in one of the other European currencies. WH: mid-20C. EURO- + BOND[1].

Eurocentric *a.* perceiving European culture, history etc. as of central importance in the world. WH: mid-20C. EURO- + *centric* (CENTRE).

Eurocheque *n.* a type of cheque able to draw on certain banks in other European countries on receipt of the appropriate card. WH: mid-20C. EURO- + CHEQUE.

Eurocommunism *n.* the form of Communism followed by western European Communist parties, more pragmatic than, and independent of, the Soviet version. WH: late 20C. EURO- + COMMUNISM.

Eurocrat *n.* an official involved in the administration of any part of the European Union. WH: mid-20C. EURO- + -CRAT.

Euro-currency *n.* currency of a country outside Europe held on deposit in a European bank. WH: mid-20C. EURO- + CURRENCY.

Eurodollar *n.* a US dollar held in European banks to ease the financing of trade. WH: late 20C. EURO- + DOLLAR.

Euro-election *n.* an election for the European Parliament. WH: late 20C. EURO- + *election* (ELECT).

Euromarket *n.* the money markets of the European Union collectively. WH: mid-20C. EURO- + MARKET.

European *a.* of or relating to, happening in, or extending over, Europe. *Also n.* WH: 16C. French *européen*, from Latin *europaeus*, from *Europa* Europe, from Greek *Eurōpē*. See also -EAN.

Europhile *n.* a person who is in favour of the European Union and its institutions. *Also a.* WH: late 20C. EURO- + -PHILE.

Europhobe *n.* a person who dislikes the European Union and its institutions and who is against further links with Europe. *Also a.* WH: late 20C. EURO- + -PHOBE.

europium *n.* an extremely rare metallic element, soft and silvery white, at. no. 63, chem. symbol Eu. WH: early 20C. *Europe* + -IUM. The element was discovered in 1896 by the French chemist Eugène-Anatole Demarçay and named by him for his native continent.

Euro-rebel *n.* a politician who disagrees with their party's official line on the European Union. WH: late 20C. EURO- + REBEL[1].

Eurosceptic *n.* a person who is sceptical about the benefits to the UK of membership of the European Union, and who is opposed to further integration into the Union. WH: late 20C. EURO- + SCEPTIC.

Eurotunnel *n.* the Channel tunnel. WH: late 20C. EURO- + TUNNEL. *Eurotunnel* is also the name of the Anglo-French company that built the Channel Tunnel in 1994.

Eurovision *n.* the network of European television production and relay run by the European Broadcasting Union. WH: mid-20C. EURO- + TELEVISION.

Euskarian *a.* Basque. *Also n.* WH: 19C. Basque *Euskara* BASQUE + -IAN.

Eustachian *a.* of or relating to Eustachius. WH: 18C. *Eustachius*, Latinized form of the name of Bartolomeo *Eustachio*, *c*.1500–74, Italian physician + -AN.

eustasy *n.* changes in the world shoreline level or sea level caused by melting ice, tectonic movements etc. WH: mid-20C. Back-formation from *eustatic* (from EU- + STATIC), based on Modern Latin *-stasis*, corr. to *-static*. See also -Y[2].

eutectic *a.* of or relating to the mixture of two or more substances with a minimum melting point. *Also n.* WH: 19C. Greek *eutēktos* easily melting, from EU- + *tēkein* to melt. See also -IC.

euterpe *n.* a palm of the S American genus *Euterpe*. WH: 19C. *Euterpē*, one of the Muses (the goddess of music), from EU- + *terpein* to please.

euthanasia *n.* easy, painless death. WH: 17C. Greek, from EU- + *thanatos* death. See also -IA.

euthenics *n.* the study of the improvement of human living standards by control of the environment. WH: early 20C. Greek *euthēneein* to thrive + -ICS. The term was introduced in *c*. 1905 by the US chemist Ellen H. Richards.

eutherian *n.* a member of the subclass of mammals, Eutheria, which nourish their unborn young through a placenta. *Also a.* WH: 19C. Modern Latin *Eutheria*, from EU- + Greek *thēria*, pl. of *thērion* wild animal. See also -AN.

eutrophic *a.* (of a body of water) rich in dissolved nutrients and supporting an abundance of plant life whose decomposition deoxygenates the water, harming the animal populations. WH: 19C. Greek *eutrophia*. See EU-, -TROPHY, also -IC.

evacuate *v.t.* to remove inhabitants from (a danger zone). WH: 14–15C. Latin *evacuatus*, p.p. of *evacuare* to empty (bowels), from E- + *vacuus* empty. See also -ATE[3]. The original sense was to empty one's bowels or other bodily organ. The sense to remove inhabitants from an area arose in the 17C.

evade *v.t.* to avoid or elude by artifice, stratagem or sophistry. *Also v.i.* WH: 15C. French *évader*, from Latin *evadere*, from E- + *vadere* to go.

evaginate *v.t.* to turn inside out, to unsheathe (as a tubular organ). WH: 17C. Latin *evaginatus*, p.p. of *evaginare* to unsheath, from E- + *vagina* sheath. See also -ATE[3].

evaluate *v.t.* to determine the value or worth of, to appraise. WH: 19C. Back-formation from *evaluation*, from Old French *évaluation*, from *évaluer*, from *é-* (EX-) + *value*. See VALUE, also -ATION.

evanesce *v.i.* to disappear, to vanish. WH: 19C. Latin *evanescere*, from E- + *vanus* empty. See also -ESCE.

evangel *n.* the Gospel. WH: 12–14C. Old French *évangile*, from Ecclesiastical Latin *evangelium*, from Greek *euaggelion* good news, from *euaggelos*, from EU- + *aggelein* to announce. Cp. GOSPEL.

evangelical *a.* of or relating to the Gospel. *Also n.* WH: 16C. Ecclesiastical Latin *evangelicus*, from Ecclesiastical Greek *euaggelikos*, from Greek *euaggelos*. See EVANGEL, also -IC, -AL[1].

evangelism *n.* the preaching of the Gospel. WH: 17C. *evangelic* (EVANGELICAL) + -ISM.

evanish *v.i.* to vanish, to disappear. WH: 12–14C. Old French *evanir*, *evaniss-*. See E-, VANISH.

evaporate *v.t.* to convert into vapour, to vaporize. *Also v.i.* WH: 14–15C. Latin *evaporatus*, p.p. of *evaporare*, from E- + *vapor* steam. See also -ATE[3].

evasion *n.* the act of evading or escaping (as from a question, argument or charge). WH: 14–15C. Old French *évasion*, from Latin *evasio*, *evasionis*, from *evasus*, p.p. of *evadere* EVADE. See also -ION.

eve *n.* the evening before a holiday or other event or date. WH: 12–14C. Orig. a two-syl. var. of EVEN[1]. For a similar loss of *n*, cp. CLEW, GAME[1], MAID.

evection *n.* an inequality in the longitude of the moon, due to the action of the sun. WH: 17C. Latin *evectio, evectionis*, from *evectus*, p.p. of *evehere* to carry out, to elevate, from E- + *vehere* to carry.

even[1] *n.* evening. WH: pre-1200. Old English *æfen*, from Germanic. Cp. German *Abend*.

even[2] *a.* level, smooth, uniform. WH: pre-1200. Old English *efen*, from Germanic, of unknown orig. Cp. German *eben*.

even[3] *v.t.* to make smooth or level. *Also v.i.* WH: pre-1200. Old English *efnan*. See EVEN[2].

even[4] *adv.* to a like degree, equally. WH: pre-1200. Old English *efne*, from Germanic. Cp. German *eben*.

evening *n.* the close or latter part of the day. *Also a., int.* WH: pre-1200. Old English *æfnung*, from *æfnian* to grow towards night. See EVEN[1], -ING[1]. The original sense (to the 16C) was the process of dusk falling. The current sense emerged in the 14–15C. Cp. MORNING.

event *n.* anything that happens, as distinguished from a thing that exists. *Also v.i.* WH: 16C. Latin *eventus*, from p.p. of *evenire* to come out, from E- + *venire* to come.

eventual *a.* finally resulting, ultimate, final. WH: 17C. Latin *eventus* EVENT + -*ual*, from Latin -*ualis*, based on ACTUAL.

ever *adv.* at all times; always. WH: pre-1200. Old English *æfre*, ult. of unknown orig. ? Rel. to Old English *ā* always. Cp. NEVER.

evert *v.i.* to turn outwards, to turn inside out. WH: 16C. Latin *evertere*, from E- + *vertere* to turn.

every *a.* each of a group or collection, all separately. WH: pre-1200. Old English *æfre ælc*, lit. ever each. See EVER, EACH.

evict *v.t.* to eject from lands, tenements or property by law. WH: 14–15C. Latin *evictus*, p.p. of *evincere*, from E- + *vincere* to conquer.

evidence *n.* anything that makes clear or obvious; grounds for knowledge, indication, testimony. *Also v.t.* WH: 12–14C. Old French *évidence*, from Latin *evidentia*, from *evidens, evidentis*, from E- + *pres.p.* of *videre* to see. See also -ENCE.

evil *a.* bad, injurious, mischievous, worthless, morally bad, wicked. *Also adv., n.* WH: pre-1200. Old English *yfel*, from Germanic. Cp. German *Übel*.

evince *v.t.* to show clearly, to indicate, to make evident. *Also v.i.* WH: 16C. Latin *evincere*. See EVICT.

eviscerate *v.t.* to disembowel. WH: 16C. Latin *evisceratus*, p.p. of *eviscerare*, from E- + VISCERA. See also -ATE[3].

evitable *a.* that can be avoided. WH: 16C. Old French *évitable* (from *éviter*, from Latin *evitare*) or Latin *evitabilis*, from *evitare*, from E- + *vitare* to shun. See also -ABLE.

evoke *v.t.* to call up, to summon forth (a memory etc.) esp. from the past. WH: 17C. Latin *evocare*, from E- + *vocare* to call. The original sense was to call up a spirit by the use of a magic charm. The current sense evolved in the 19C.

evolute *n.* a curve from which another is described by the end of a thread gradually wound upon or unwound from the former, thus forming the locus of the centres of curvature of the other (the *involute*). WH: 18C. Latin *evolutus*, p.p. of *evolvere* EVOLVE.

evolution *n.* the gradual cumulative change in the characteristics of organisms over many generations, which results in new species. WH: 17C. Latin *evolutio, evolutionis* unrolling (of a papyrus roll), from *evolutus*, p.p. of *evolvere* EVOLVE. See also -ION.

evolve *v.t.* to unfold, to expand. *Also v.i.* WH: 17C. Latin *evolvere* to unroll, to unfold, from E- + *volvere* to roll.

evulsion *n.* the act of forcibly plucking or extracting. WH: 14–15C. Latin *evulsio, evulsionis*, from *evulsus*, p.p. of *evellere* to pluck out, from E- + *vellere* to pluck.

evzone *n.* a member of an elite Greek infantry regiment. WH: 19C. Modern Greek *euzōnas*, from Greek *euzōnos* dressed for exercise, from EU- + *zōnē* girdle.

ewe *n.* a female sheep. WH: pre-1200. Old English *ēowu*, from Germanic, from Indo-European word also represented by Latin *ovis* (cp. OVINE) and Greek *ois*. Cp. German *Aue*.

ewer *n.* a kind of pitcher or large jug for water with a wide mouth. WH: 14–15C. Anglo-French, from Old French *aiguière*, from fem. of Latin *aquarius*, from *aqua* water. See also -ER[2].

ex[1] *n.* the 24th letter of the alphabet, X, x. WH: mid-20C. Representation of pronun. of *X* as letter's name.

ex[2] *prep.* from, out of, sold from. WH: 19C. Latin out of.

ex[3] *n.* a former spouse, boyfriend or girlfriend. WH: 19C. EX- as independent word.

ex- *pref.* out, forth, out of, as in *exceed, exclude, exit, extend, extol*. WH: Latin pref., from prep. *ex* out of, or from Greek. In Latin and French derivatives *x* is often dropped or assimilated to a subsequent consonant. See E-, EF-. Cp. EX[3].

exa- *pref.* a factor of 10^{18}. WH: HEXA-, based on pair TERA-/ TETRA-. Cp. PETA-. 10^{18} is $(10^3)^6$.

exacerbate *v.t.* to irritate, to exasperate, to embitter. WH: 17C. Latin *exacerbatus*, p.p. of *exacerbare*, from EX- + *acerbare* to make bitter, from *acerbus* harsh, bitter. See also -ATE[3].

exact[1] *a.* precisely agreeing in amount, number or degree. WH: 16C. Latin *exactus*, p.p. of *exigere* to complete, to bring to perfection, to ascertain, from EX- + *agere* to perform.

exact[2] *v.t.* to compel (money etc.) to be paid or surrendered. *Also v.i.* WH: 14–15C. Latin *exactus*, p.p. of *exigere*. See EXACT[1].

exaggerate *v.t.* to heighten, to overstate, to represent as greater than is in fact the case. *Also v.i.* WH: 16C. Latin *exaggeratus*, p.p. of *exaggerare*, from EX- + *aggerare* to heap up, from *agger* heap, mound. See also -ATE[3].

exalbuminous *a.* (of seeds) without albumen. WH: 19C. EX- + Latin ALBUMEN, *albuminis* + -OUS.

exalt *v.t.* to raise in dignity, rank, power or position. WH: 14–15C. Latin *exaltare*, from EX- + *altus* high.

exam *n.* an examination. WH: 19C. Abbr. of *examination* (EXAMINE).

examine *v.t.* to inquire into, to investigate, scrutinize. *Also v.i.* WH: 12–14C. Old French *examiner*, from Latin *examinare* to weigh accurately, from *examen, examinis* tongue of a balance, from *exigere*. See EXACT[1].

example *n.* a sample, a specimen. *Also v.t.* WH: 14–15C. Old French (Modern French *exemple*), alt. based on Latin of *essample* (see ENSAMPLE), from Latin *exemplum*, from *eximere* to take out (see EXEMPT).

exanimate *a.* lifeless, dead. WH: 16C. Latin *exanimatus*, p.p. of *exanimare* to deprive of life, from EX- + *anima* breath of life. See also -ATE[2].

ex ante *a.* based on the prediction of results. WH: mid-20C. Modern Latin, from EX[2] + ANTE.

exanthema *n.* a skin rash accompanying a disease. WH: 17C. Late Latin, from Greek *exanthēma* eruption, from EX- + *anthein* to blossom, from *anthos* flower.

exarch *n.* in the Greek Church, a grade in the ecclesiastical hierarchy instituted by Constantine the Great, formerly equivalent to patriarch or metropolitan, later a bishop in charge of a province, and also a legate of a patriarch. WH: 16C. Ecclesiastical Latin *exarchus*, from Greek leader, chief, from EX- + *arkhos* chief.

exasperate *v.t.* to irritate to a high degree; to provoke. WH: 16C. Latin *exasperatus*, p.p. of *exasperare*, from EX- + *asper* rough. See also -ATE[3].

ex cathedra *a.* authoritative, to be obeyed. *Also adv.* WH: 17C. Latin from the (teacher's) chair, from EX[1] + abl. sing. of CATHEDRA.

excaudate *a.* having no tail. WH: 19C. Modern Latin *excaudatus*, from EX- + Medieval Latin *caudatus*, from Latin *cauda* tail. See also -ATE[2].

excavate *v.t.* to hollow out. *Also v.i.* WH: 16C. Latin *excavatus*, p.p. of *excavare*, from EX- + *cavare* to make hollow, from *cavus* hollow. See also -ATE[3].

exceed *v.t.* to go or pass beyond. *Also v.i.* WH: 14–15C. Old French *excéder*, from Latin *excedere* to go away, to go out, to surpass, from EX- + *cedere* to go.

excel *v.t.* to surpass in qualities. *Also v.i.* WH: 14–15C. Latin *excellere*, from EX- + *celsus* lofty.

excelsior *int.* used to express an intention of climbing higher. *Also a.* WH: 18C. Latin, comp. of *excelsus*, from EX- + *celsus* lofty. See -IOR.

except *v.t.* to leave out, to omit, to exclude. *Also v.i., prep., conj.* WH: 14–15C. Latin *exceptus*, p.p. of *excipere*, from EX- + *capere* to take.

excerpt[1] *v.t.* to make an extract of or from. WH: 16C. Latin *excerptus*, p.p. of *excerpere*, from EX- + *carpere* to pluck.

excerpt[2] *n.* an extract or selection from a book, play, film etc. WH: 17C. Latin *excerptum*, neut. p.p. (used as n.) of *excerpere*. See EXCERPT[1].

excess *n.* that which exceeds what is usual or necessary. *Also a.* WH: 14–15C. Old French *excès*, from Latin *excessus*, from p.p. of *excedere* EXCEED.

exchange *v.t.* to give or receive in return for something else. *Also v.i., n.* WH: 14–15C. Old French *eschangier* (Modern French *échanger*), from *é-* EX- + *changer* CHANGE.

exchequer *n.* a State treasury. *Also v.t.* WH: 12–14C. Old French *eschequier* (Modern French *échiquier*), from Medieval Latin *scaccarium* chessboard, from *scaccus* CHECK[1], with *ex-* by assoc. with EX-. An exchequer is so called from the chequered tablecloth, resembling a chessboard, on which accounts were originally kept by means of counters. Cp. CHEQUER.

excide *v.t.* to cut out. WH: 18C. Latin *excidere* EXCISE[3].

excimer *n.* a dimer in an excited state, consisting of an excited and an unexcited molecule. WH: mid-20C. Blend of *excited* (see EXCITE) + DIMER.

excise[1] *n.* a tax or duty on certain articles produced and consumed in a country. WH: 15C. Middle Dutch *excijs*, ? from Latin *accensare* to tax, from AC- + *census* tax, CENSUS, influ. by EXCISE[3].

excise[2] *v.t.* to impose an excise duty on (goods). WH: 17C. EXCISE[1].

excise[3] *v.t.* to cut out (part of a book or of the body). WH: 16C. Latin *excisus*, p.p. of *excidere*, from EX- + *caedere* to cut.

excite *v.t.* to rouse, to stir into action, energy or agitation. WH: 12–14C. Old French *exciter* or Latin *excitare*, freq. of *exciere* to call out, from EX- + *ciere* to move, to call. The current sense evolved only in the 19C.

exciton *n.* a mobile entity in a crystal, formed by an excited electron bound to its associated hole. WH: mid-20C. From *excitation* (EXCITE) + -ON.

exclaim *v.i.* to cry out abruptly or passionately. *Also v.t., n.* WH: 16C. French *exclamer* or Latin *exclamare*, from EX- + *clamare*. See CLAIM.

exclamation *n.* the act of exclaiming. WH: 14–15C. Old French, or from Latin *exclamatio, exclamationis*, from *exclamatus*, p.p. of *exclamare*. See EXCLAIM, also -ATION.

exclave *n.* part of a country disjoined from the main part and surrounded by foreign territory, where it is considered an enclave. WH: 19C. EX- + *-clave* from ENCLAVE.

exclosure *n.* an area shut off from entry or intrusion, esp. a forested area fenced to keep out animals. WH: early 20C. EX- + CLOSURE, based on *enclosure* (ENCLOSE).

exclude *v.t.* to shut out, to prevent from coming in. WH: 14–15C. Latin *excludere*, from EX- + *claudere* to shut.

excogitate *v.t.* to think out. WH: 16C. Latin *excogitatus*, p.p. of *excogitare* to find out by thinking. See EX-, COGITATE.

excommunicate[1] *v.t.* to exclude from the communion and privileges of the Church. WH: 14–15C. Ecclesiastical Latin *excommunicatus*, p.p. of *excommunicare*, from EX- + Latin *communis* COMMON, based on *communicare* COMMUNICATE. See also -ATE[3].

excommunicate[2] *a.* excommunicated. *Also n.* WH: 16C. Ecclesiastical Latin *excommunicatus*, p.p. of *excommunicare*. See EXCOMMUNICATE[1], also -ATE[2].

ex-con *n.* an ex-convict, a person who has served their sentence and been released from prison. WH: early 20C. Abbr. of *ex-convict*, from EX- + CONVICT[2].

excoriate *v.t.* to strip the skin from. WH: 14–15C. Latin *excoriatus*, p.p. of *excoriare*, from EX- + *corium* skin, hide. See also -ATE[3].

excrement *n.* refuse matter discharged from the body after digestion, faeces. WH: 16C. French *excrément* or Latin *excrementum*, from base of *excretus*, p.p. of *excernere* EXCRETE. See also -MENT.

excrescence *n.* an abnormal, useless or disfiguring outgrowth. WH: 14–15C. Latin *excrescentia*, from *excrescens, excrescentis*, pres.p. of *excrescere* to grow out, from EX- + *crescere* to grow. See also -ESCE.

excrete *v.t., v.i.* to separate and discharge (superfluous matter) from the organism. WH: 17C. Latin *excretus*, p.p. of *excernere*, from EX- + *cernere* to sift.

excruciate *v.t.* to inflict severe pain or mental agony upon. WH: 16C. Latin *excruciatus*, p.p. of *excruciare* to torment, from EX- + *crux, crucis* cross. See also -ATE[3]. The reference is to the cross as an instrument of torture.

exculpate *v.t.* to clear from a charge. WH: 17C. Medieval Latin *exculpatus*, p.p. of *exculpare*, from EX- + Latin *culpa* blame. See also -ATE[3].

excurrent *a.* running or passing out. WH: 17C. Latin *excurrens, excurrentis*, pres.p. of *excurrere* to run out, from EX- + *currere* to run. See also -ENT.

excursion *n.* a journey or ramble for health or pleasure. WH: 16C. Latin *excursio, excursionis*, from *excursus*, p.p. of *excurrere*. See EXCURRENT, also -ION.

excursive *a.* rambling, deviating, exploring. WH: 17C. Latin *excursus* (see EXCURSION) + -IVE, ? based on DISCURSIVE.

excursus *n.* a dissertation appended to a work, containing an exposition of some point raised or referred to in the text. WH: 19C. Latin excursion, from *excursus*. See EXCURSION.

excuse[1] *v.t.* to free from blame or guilt, to lessen the blame or guilt attaching to. *Also v.i.* WH: 12–14C. Old French *escuser* (Modern French *excuser*), from Latin *excusare* to flee from blame, from EX- + *causa* accusation.

excuse[2] *n.* a plea offered in extenuation of a fault or for release from an obligation, duty etc. WH: 14–15C. French, from *excuser*. See EXCUSE[1].

ex-directory *a.* (of a telephone number) not listed in a telephone directory and not revealed to inquirers. WH: mid-20C. EX[2] + DIRECTORY.

ex div. *abbr.* ex dividend. WH: 19C. Abbr. of EX DIVIDEND.

ex dividend *a., adv.* not including the next dividend. WH: 19C. EX[2] + DIVIDEND.

exeat *n.* leave of absence, as to a student at school or university. WH: 18C. Latin let him go out, 3rd pers. sing. pres. subj. of *exire* EXIT[2]. Cp. EXEUNT.

exec *n.* an executive. WH: 19C. Abbr. of *executive* (EXECUTE).

execrate *v.t.* to curse, to imprecate evil upon. *Also v.i.* WH: 16C. Latin *execratus*, p.p. of *execrari* to curse, from EX- + *sacrare* to devote religiously, from *sacer, sacri* holy. See also -ATE[3].

execute *v.t.* to carry into effect, to put in force. *Also v.i.* WH: 14–15C. Old French *exécuter*, from Medieval Latin *executare*, from Latin *executus*, p.p. of *exequi* to follow up, to carry out, to punish, from EX- + *sequi* to follow.

executor *n.* a person who executes, esp. one appointed by a testator to carry out the provisions of their will. WH: 12–14C. Anglo-French *executur*, from Latin *executor*, from *executus*. See EXECUTE, also -OR.

exedra *n.* the portico of the Grecian palaestra in which discussions were held. WH: 18C. Latin, from Greek, from EX- + *hedra* seat.

exegesis *n.* exposition, interpretation, esp. of the Scriptures. WH: 17C. Greek *exēgēsis*, from *exēgeisthai*, from EX- + *hēgeisthai* to guide.

exemplar *n.* a pattern or model to be copied. *Also a.* WH: 14–15C. Old French *exemplaire*, from Late Latin *exemplarium*, from Latin *exemplum* EXAMPLE. See also -AR[1]. Cp. SAMPLE.

exemplify *v.t.* to illustrate by example. WH: 14–15C. Medieval Latin *exemplificare*, from Latin *exemplum* EXAMPLE. See also -FY.

exemplum *n.* an example. WH: 19C. Latin EXAMPLE.

exempt *a.* free (from). *Also n., v.t.* WH: 14–15C. Latin *exemptus*, p.p. of *eximere* to take out, to deliver, from EX- + *emere* to take.

exenterate *v.t.* to disembowel, eviscerate. WH: 17C. Latin *exenteratus*, p.p. of *exenterare*, based on Greek *exenterizein*, from EX- + *enteron* intestine. See also -ATE[3].

exequatur *n.* a written recognition of a consul or commercial agent, given by the government to which he is accredited. WH: 17C. Latin let him perform, 3rd pers. sing. pres. subj. of *exequi* (see EXECUTE).

exequies *n.pl.* funeral rites; the ceremony of burial. WH: 14–15C. Old French, from Latin (acc.) *exsequias* (nom. *exsequiae*) funeral procession, from *exsequi* to follow after. See EXECUTE. Cp. OBSEQUIES.

exercise *n.* systematic exertion of the body for the sake of health. *Also v.t., v.i.* WH: 12–14C. Old French *exercice* or Latin *exercitum*, from *exercere* to keep busy, to practise, from EX- + *arcere* to keep in, to keep away. The sense of physical exercise emerged through military training. Cp. Latin *exercitus* army.

exercitation *n.* exercise, practice. WH: 14–15C. Latin *exercitatio, exercitationis*, from *exercitatus*, p.p. of *exercitare*, freq. of *exercere*. See EXERCISE, also -ATION.

exergonic *a.* (of a biochemical reaction) accompanied by the release of energy, and therefore able to occur spontaneously. **WH:** mid-20C. EX- + Greek *ergon* work + -IC.

exergue *n.* the small space beneath the base line of a subject engraved on a coin or medal. **WH:** 17C. French, from Medieval Latin *exergum*, from Greek EX- + *ergon* work.

exert *v.t.* to apply or use (strength, power, ability etc.) with effort, to put in action or operation. **WH:** 17C. Latin *exertus*, p.p. of *exerere* to put forth, from EX- + *serere* to bind, to entwine.

exes *n.pl.* (reimbursable) expenses. **WH:** 19C. Abbr. of *expenses* (EXPENSE).

exeunt *v.i.* they go off the stage, they retire (stage direction). **WH:** 15C. Latin they go out, 3rd pers. pl. pres. ind. of *exire* EXIT[2].

exfiltrate *v.t.* to withdraw (spies etc.) secretly, as distinct from *infiltrate. Also v.i.* **WH:** late 20C. Back-formation from *exfiltration*, from EX- + *filtration* (FILTRATE). ? Based on *infiltration* (INFILTRATE).

exfoliate *v.i.* (of skin, rocks etc.) to shed or come off in flakes or scales. *Also v.t.* **WH:** 17C. Late Latin *exfoliatus*, p.p. of *exfoliare* to strip of leaves, from Latin EX- + *folium* leaf. See also -ATE[3].

ex gratia *a., adv.* as an act of favour, and with no acceptance of liability. **WH:** 18C. Latin from grace, from EX[2] + abl. sing. of *gratia* GRACE.

exhalation *n.* the act or process of exhaling. **WH:** 14–15C. Latin *exhalatio, exhalationis*, from *exhalatus*, p.p. of *exhalare* EXHALE. See also -ATION.

exhale *v.t.* to breathe out. *Also v.i.* **WH:** 14–15C. Old French *exhaler*, from Latin *exhalare*, from EX- + *halare* to breathe.

exhaust *v.t.* to use up the whole of, to consume. *Also n.* **WH:** 16C. Latin *exhaustus*, p.p. of *exhaurire*, from EX- + *haurire* to draw (water), to drain.

exhibit *v.t.* to offer to public view. *Also n.* **WH:** 14–15C. Latin *exhibitus*, p.p. of *exhibere*, from EX- + *habere* to hold.

exhilarate *v.t.* to gladden, to enliven, to animate. **WH:** 16C. Latin *exhilaratus*, p.p. of *exhilarare*, from EX- + *hilaris* cheerful. See also -ATE[3].

exhort *v.t.* to incite by words (to good deeds). *Also v.i., n.* **WH:** 14–15C. Old French *exhorter* or Latin *exhortari*, from EX- + *hortari* to encourage.

exhume *v.t.* to dig out, esp. a corpse from its grave. **WH:** 14–15C. Medieval Latin *exhumere*, from EX- + *humus* ground.

ex hypothesi *adv.* according to the hypothesis stated; following the hypothesis. **WH:** 17C. Modern Latin, from Latin *ex* by + abl. of Late Latin HYPOTHESIS.

exigeant *a.* exacting. **WH:** 18C. French, pres.p. of *exiger*, from Latin *exigere*. See EXACT[1].

exigence *n.* urgent need, demand, necessity. **WH:** 14–15C. Old French, or from Late Latin *exigentia*, from Latin *exigens, exigentis*. See EXIGENT, also -ENCE.

exigent *a.* urgent, pressing. *Also n.* **WH:** 17C. Latin *exigens, exigentis*, pres.p. of *exigere*. See EXACT[1], also -ENT.

exiguous *a.* small, slender, scanty. **WH:** 17C. Latin *exiguus*, from *exigere* to weigh exactly. See EXACT[1], also -OUS.

exile *n.* banishment, expatriation. *Also v.t.* **WH:** 12–14C. Old French *exil*, Latinized alt. of earlier *essil*, from Latin *exilium*, from *exul* banished person.

eximious *a.* excellent, illustrious. **WH:** 16C. Latin *eximius* set apart, select, from *eximere*. See EXEMPT, also -OUS.

ex int. *a., adv.* ex interest. **WH:** 19C. Abbr. of EX INTEREST.

ex interest *a., adv.* not including interest. **WH:** 19C. EX[2] + INTEREST[1].

exist *v.i.* to be, to have actual being. **WH:** 17C. Prob. back-formation from *existence* (14–15C) from Old French, or from Late Latin *existentia*, from *existens, existentis*, pres.p. of *existere* to emerge, to come into being, from EX- + *sistere* to take a stand.

exit[1] *n.* a passage or door, a way out. **WH:** 16C. Latin *exitus*, p.p. of *exire*. See EXIT[2].

exit[2] *v.i.* to depart, to leave a place. *Also v.t.* **WH:** 16C. Latin he goes out, 3rd pers. sing. pres. ind. of *exire* to go out, from EX- + *ire* to go. Cp. EXEAT.

ex-lib. *n.* an ex-libris. **WH:** early 20C. Abbr. of EX-LIBRIS.

ex-libris *n.* a bookplate, a label bearing an owner's name, crest, device etc. **WH:** 19C. Latin out of the books, from EX[2] + abl. pl. of *liber, libri* book.

ex nihilo *adv.* out of nothing. **WH:** 16C. Latin out of nothing, from EX[2] + abl. of *nihil* nothing.

exo- *comb. form* of or relating to the outside of anything, external. **WH:** Greek *exō* outside. See also -O-.

exobiology *n.* the branch of biology which studies the possibility of extraterrestrial life, and what forms this might take. **WH:** mid-20C. EXO- + BIOLOGY.

exocarp *n.* the outer layer of a pericarp. **WH:** 19C. EXO- + -CARP.

Exocet® *n.* a French-built surface-skimming missile that can be launched from surface or air. **WH:** late 20C. French flying fish, from Latin *exocetus*, from Greek *exōkoitos* sleeping out, fish that comes out (onto the beach), from EXO- + *koitos* bed.

exocrine *a.* (of a gland) producing secretions that are released through a duct. *Also n.* **WH:** early 20C. EXO- + Greek *krinein* to separate.

exoderm *n.* the epidermis, the outer layer of the blastoderm. **WH:** 19C. EXO- + -DERM.

exodus *n.* a departure, esp. of a large group of people. **WH:** pre-1200. Ecclesiastical Latin *exodus*, from Greek *exodos*, from EX- + *hodos* way. The sense of departure, emigration arose in the 17C.

ex off. *adv.* ex officio. **WH:** 19C. Abbr. of EX OFFICIO.

ex officio *adv.* by virtue of one's office. *Also a.* **WH:** 16C. Latin out of duty, from EX[2] + abl. sing. of *officium* duty, OFFICE.

exogamy *n.* the custom of marrying outside one's own tribe. **WH:** 19C. EXO- + -GAMY.

exogenous *a.* of or relating to aa plant whose stem increases by an annual layer growing on the outside of the wood. **WH:** 19C. Modern Latin *exogena* exogen (see EXO-, -GEN). + -OUS.

exon[1] *n.* any one of the four officers of the Yeomen of the Guard ranking as corporals. **WH:** 18C. Representation of pronun. of French EXEMPT.

exon[2] *n.* any segment of a gene which consists of codons. **WH:** late 20C. Abbr. of *expressed*, p.p. of EXPRESS[2] + -ON.

exonerate *v.t.* to free from a charge or blame, to exculpate. **WH:** 14–15C. Latin *exoneratus*, p.p. of *exonerare*, from EX- + *onus, oneris* burden. See also -ATE[3].

exoparasite *n.* an ectoparasite. **WH:** 19C. EXO- + PARASITE.

exophagy *n.* cannibalism in which only persons of a different tribe are eaten. **WH:** 19C. EXO- + -phagy (-PHAGE).

exophthalmia *n.* abnormal protrusion of the eyeball. **WH:** 17C. Greek *exophthalmos*, from EX- + *ophthalmos* eye. See also -IA.

exoplasm *n.* the denser outer layer of the cuticular protoplasm of certain protozoans, ectoplasm. **WH:** 19C. EXO- + -plasm (PLASMA).

exorable *a.* that can be persuaded by pleading. **WH:** 16C. Latin *exorabilis*, from *exorare* to implore, from EX- + *orare* to pray. See also -ABLE.

exorbitant *a.* out of all bounds, inordinate, extravagant. **WH:** 14–15C. Latin *exorbitans, exorbitantis*, pres.p. of *exorbitare* to go out of the track, from EX- + *orbita* ORBIT. See also -ANT.

exorcize *v.t.* to expel (as an evil spirit) by prayers and ceremonies. **WH:** 14–15C. Old French *exorciser* or Ecclesiastical Latin *exorcizare*, from Greek *exorkizein*, from EX- + *orkos* oath. See also -IZE.

exordium *n.* the beginning of anything, esp. the introductory part of a literary work or discourse. **WH:** 16C. Latin, from *exordiri* to begin, from EX- + *ordiri* to begin.

exoskeleton *n.* an external skeleton, e.g. in arthropods, formed by a hardening of the integument. **WH:** 19C. EXO- + SKELETON.

exosmosis *n.* passage of a liquid through a porous membrane from within outwards to mix with an external fluid. **WH:** 19C. French *exosmose*, from Greek EX- + *ōsmos* pushing. See also -OSIS.

exosphere *n.* the outermost layer of the earth's atmosphere. **WH:** mid-20C. EXO- + SPHERE.

exospore *n.* the outer layer of the wall of a spore. **WH:** 19C. EXO- + SPORE.

exostosis *n.* a tumour of a bony nature growing upon and arising from a bone or cartilage. **WH:** 16C. Greek *exostōsis* outgrowth of bone, from EX- + *osteon* bone. See also -OSIS.

exoteric *a.* external, public, fit to be imparted to outsiders. *Also n.* **WH:** 17C. Latin *exotericus*, from Greek *exōterikos*, from *exōterō* outer, comp. of *exō* outside. See also -IC.

exothermic *a.* involving the evolution of heat. **WH:** 19C. French *exothermique*. See EXO-, THERMAL, also -IC.

exotic *a.* introduced from a foreign country. *Also n.* WH: 16C. Latin *exoticus*, from Greek *exōtikos*, from *exō* outside.

exotoxin *n.* a toxin released from within a living bacterium into the surrounding medium. WH: early 20C. EXO- + TOXIN.

expand *v.t.* to open or spread out. *Also v.i.* WH: 14–15C. Latin *expandere*, from EX- + *pandere* to spread.

expanse *n.* a wide, open extent or area. WH: 17C. Modern Latin *expansum* firmament, use as n. of neut. of Latin *expansus*, p.p. of *expandere* EXPAND.

expansion *n.* the act, or an instance, of expanding. WH: 17C. Late Latin *expansio, expansionis*, from Latin *expansus*. See EXPANSE, also -ION.

expansive *a.* having the power of expanding. WH: 17C. Latin *expansus*. See EXPANSE, also -IVE.

ex parte *adv.* proceeding from one side only. WH: 17C. Latin from the side, from EX² + abl. sing. of *pars, partis* side.

expatiate *v.i.* to dilate. WH: 16C. Latin *expatiatus*, p.p. of *expatiari*, from EX- + *spatiari* to walk, from *spatium* space.

expatriate¹ *v.t.* to exile. *Also v.i.* WH: 18C. Latin *expatriatus*, p.p. of *expatriare*, from EX- + *patria* native land. See also -ATE³.

expatriate² *n.* a person living away from their own country. *Also a.* WH: 19C. Latin *expatriatus*. See EXPATRIATE¹.

expect *v.t.* to look forward to. *Also v.i., n.* WH: 16C. Latin *expectare*, from EX- + *spectare* to look.

expectorate *v.t.* to discharge from the lungs or throat by coughing, hawking or spitting. *Also v.i.* WH: 17C. Latin *expectoratus*, p.p. of *expectorare*, from EX- + *pectus, pectoris* breast. See also -ATE³.

expedient *a.* promoting the object in view. *Also n.* WH: 14–15C. Latin *expediens, expedientis*, pres.p. of *expedire*. See EXPEDITE, also -ENT.

expedite *v.t.* to facilitate, to assist or accelerate the progress of. *Also a.* WH: 15C. Latin *expeditus*, p.p. of *expedire* to extricate (lit. to free the feet), to put in order, from EX- *pes, pedis* foot. See also -ITE².

expedition *n.* any journey or voyage by an organized body for some definite object. WH: 14–15C. Old French *expédition*, from Latin *expeditio, expeditionis*, from *expeditus*. See EXPEDITE, also -ITION.

expel *v.t.* to drive or force out. WH: 14–15C. Latin *expellare*, from EX- + *pellere* to drive, to thrust.

expend *v.t.* to spend, to lay out. WH: 14–15C. Latin *expendere*, from EX- + *pendere* to weigh, to pay. Cp. SPEND.

expense *n.* a laying out or expending. WH: 14–15C. Anglo-French, alt. of Old French *espense*, from Late Latin *expensa*, fem. of p.p. of Latin *expendere* EXPEND.

experience *n.* practical acquaintance with any matter. *Also v.t.* WH: 14–15C. Old French *expérience*, from Latin *experientia*, from *experiri* to try. See also -ENCE.

experiential *a.* of, relating to or derived from experience. WH: 19C. EXPERIENCE + -IAL, based on *inferential* (INFER) etc.

experiment *n.* a trial, proof or test of anything. *Also v.i., v.t.* WH: 12–14C. Old French, or from Latin *experimentum*, from *experiri*. See EXPERIENCE, also -MENT.

expert *a.* experienced, adept from use and experience. *Also n., v.t.* WH: 14–15C. Old French *espert*, based on Latin *expertus*, p.p. of *experiri* to try.

expiate *v.t.* to atone for. WH: 16C. Latin *expiatus*, p.p. of *expiare*, from EX- + *piare* to seek to appease (by sacrifice), from *pius* PIOUS. See also -ATE³.

expire *v.t.* to breathe out from the lungs. *Also v.i.* WH: 14–15C. Old French *expirer*, from Latin *expirare* to breathe out, from EX- + *spirare* to breathe. The original sense was to die. The sense to breathe out dates from the 16C. Cp. INSPIRE.

explain *v.t.* to make clear, plain or intelligible. *Also v.i.* WH: 14–15C. Latin *explanare*, from EX- + *planus* flat, PLAIN¹. The spelling has been assimilated to *plain*.

explanation *n.* the act, or an instance, of explaining. WH: 14–15C. Latin *explanatio, explanationis*, from *explanatus*, p.p. of *explanare* EXPLAIN. See also -ATION.

explant¹ *v.t.* to remove (living tissue) to a medium for tissue culture. WH: 16C. Modern Latin *explantare*, from Latin EX- + *plantare* to plant.

explant² *n.* a piece of living tissue removed for culture. WH: early 20C. EXPLANT¹.

expletive *a.* serving to fill out or complete. *Also n.* WH: 14–15C. Late Latin *expletivus*, from *explere* to fill out, from EX- + *plere* to fill. See also -IVE. The sense of oath emerged in the 19C.

explicate *v.t.* to unfold the meaning of. WH: 16C. Latin *explicatus*, p.p. of *explicare* to unfold, from EX- + *plicare* to fold. See also -ATE³.

explicit¹ *a.* plainly expressed, distinctly stated, as distinct from *implicit*. WH: 17C. French *explicite* or Latin *explicitus*, p.p. of *explicare*. See EXPLICATE.

explicit² *n.* a word formerly written at the end of manuscript books, and equivalent to 'finis', 'the end'. WH: 12–14C. Late Latin, either *explicit* (3rd pers. sing.) here ends, or abbr. of *explicitus est liber* the book is unrolled. See EXPLICIT¹.

explode *v.t.* to cause to burst with a loud noise. *Also v.i.* WH: 16C. Latin *explodere* to drive out by clapping, to hiss off the stage, from EX- + *plaudere* to clap. The original sense (to the 19C) was to hiss off the stage (lit. 'to clap out'). The sense to cause to burst evolved in the 18C. Cp. APPLAUD. Clapping originally denoted derision as well as approval. Cp. Job xxvii.23.

exploit¹ *n.* a feat, a great or noble achievement. WH: 12–14C. Old French *espleit* (Modern French *exploit*), from Latin *explicitum*, neut. p.p. of *explicare* EXPLICATE.

exploit² *v.t.* to make use of, derive benefit from. WH: 14–15C. Old French *espleiter* (Modern French *exploiter*), to accomplish, to en-- joy, from Latin *explicare* EXPLICATE. The sense to utilize (for one's own ends) derives direct from French *exploiter* and dates from the 19C.

explore *v.t.* to search or inquire into. WH: 16C. French *explorer*, from Latin *explorare* to search out, from EX- + *plorare* to utter a cry.

explosion *n.* a bursting or exploding with a loud noise. WH: 17C. Latin *explosio, explosionis*, from *explosus*, p.p. of *explodere* EXPLODE. See also -ION.

Expo *n.* a large public exhibition. WH: mid-20C. Abbr. of *exposition* (EXPOSE).

exponent *a.* setting forth or explaining. *Also n.* WH: 16C. Latin *exponens, exponentis*, pres.p. of *exponere*. See EXPOUND, also -ENT.

export¹ *v.t.* to carry or send (goods) to foreign countries. *Also v.i.* WH: 15C. Latin *exportare*, from EX- + *portare* to carry.

export² *n.* the act or process of exporting, exportation. *Also a.* WH: 17C. EXPORT¹.

expose *v.t.* to lay bare or open. *Also n.* WH: 14–15C. Old French *exposer*, based on Latin *exponere* (see EXPOUND) but re-formed on Latin p.p. *expositus* and Old French *poser*. See POSE¹.

ex post *a.* based on actual results. WH: mid-20C. Modern Latin, from EX² + Latin *post* after.

ex post facto *a., adv.* having retrospective force. WH: 17C. Misdivision of Latin *ex postfacto* in the light of subsequent events, from EX² + abl. of *postfactum* that which is done subsequently (cp. POST-, FACTUM).

expostulate *v.i.* to reason earnestly (with a person), to remonstrate. *Also v.t.* WH: 16C. Latin *expostulatus*, p.p. of *expostulare*, from EX- + *postulare* to demand. See also -ATE³.

expound *v.t.* to set out the meaning of in detail. WH: 12–14C. Old French *espondre*, from Latin *exponere* to expose, to publish, to explain, from EX- + *ponere* to place.

express¹ *a.* set forth or expressed distinctly. *Also adv., n., v.t.* WH: 14–15C. Old French *exprès*, from Latin *expressus* distinctly presented, p.p. of *exprimere* (cp. EXPRESS²). An express train was originally a special one, running expressly to a particular destination.

express² *v.t.* to set out, to represent, to put into words or symbolize by gestures etc. WH: 14–15C. Old French *expresser*, from Latin EX- + *pressare* PRESS¹, in its use representing Latin *exprimere*. Both the literal and figurative senses arose simultaneously, although the sense to represent in words evolved later, in the 16C.

expropriate *v.t.* (of the state) to take from an owner, esp. for public use. WH: 16C. Medieval Latin *expropriatus*, p.p. of *expropriare*, from EX- + PROPRIUM. See also -ATE³.

expulsion *n.* the act, or an instance, of expelling. WH: 14–15C. Latin *expulsio, expulsionis*, from *expulsus*, p.p. of *expellere* EXPEL. See also -ION.

expunge *v.t.* to blot or rub out. WH: 17C. Latin *expungere* to mark for deletion by points set above or below, from EX- + *pungere* to prick. Not rel. to SPONGE.

expurgate *v.t.* to free from anything offensive, obscene or noxious (used esp. of books). WH: 17C. Latin *expurgatus*, p.p. of *expurgare*, from EX- + *purgare*. See PURGE, also -ATE³.

exquisite *a.* fine, delicate, dainty. *Also n.* WH: 14–15C. Latin *exquisitus*, p.p. of *exquirere* to search out, from EX- + *quaerere* to search, to seek. The original sense (to the 18C) was careful, precise. The sense of delicately beautiful arose in the 16C, of intensely pleasurable or painful in the 17C.

exsanguinate *v.t.* to drain of blood. WH: 19C. Latin *exsanguinatus* drained of blood, from EX- + *sanguis*, *sanguinis* blood. See also -ATE³.

exscind *v.t.* to cut off or out, to sever, to excise. WH: 17C. Latin *exscindere* to cut out, from EX- + *scindere* to cut.

exsect *v.t.* to cut out. WH: 17C. Latin *exsectus*, p.p. of *exsecare* to cut out, from EX- + *secare* to cut.

exsert *v.t.* to thrust out, to protrude. WH: 17C. EXERT.

ex-service *a.* having formerly been a member of one of the armed forces. WH: early 20C. EX- + SERVICE¹.

exsiccate *v.t.* to dry up. WH: 14–15C. Latin *exsiccatus*, p.p. of *exsiccare*, from EX- + *siccare*, from *siccus* dry. See also -ATE³.

ex silentio *a.*, *adv.* based on a lack of contrary evidence. WH: early 20C. Latin from silence, from EX² + abl. of *silentium* silence.

exstipulate *a.* without stipules. WH: 19C. EX- + STIPULE. See also -ATE².

extant *a.* (of a species, document etc.) still existing. WH: 16C. Latin *extans*, *extantis*, pres.p. of *extare* to be prominent, to exist, from EX- + *stare* to stand. See also -ANT.

extemporaneous *a.* uttered, made, composed or done without preparation. WH: 17C. Late Latin *extemporaneus*, from Latin *extemporalis* arising out of the moment, from *ex tempore*. See EXTEMPORE, also -ANEOUS.

extempore *adv.* without premeditation or preparation. *Also a.* WH: 16C. Latin *ex tempore* on the spur of the moment, from EX² + abl. sing. of *tempus*, *temporis* time.

extend *v.t.* to stretch out; to make larger in space, time or scope. *Also v.i.* WH: 12–14C. Latin *extendere* to stretch out, from EX- + *tendere* to stretch.

extension *n.* the act or process of extending. WH: 14–15C. Late Latin *extensio*, *extensionis*, from Latin *extensus*, p.p. of *extendere*. See EXTEND, also -ION.

extensive *a.* widely spread or extended, large. WH: 14–15C. French *extensif* or Late Latin *extensivus*, from Latin *extensus*. See EXTENSION, also -IVE.

extensometer *n.* an instrument which measures small changes in length etc. of metal under stress. WH: 19C. Latin *extensus* (see EXTENSION) + -METER.

extensor *n.* a muscle which serves to extend or straighten any part of the body. WH: 18C. Late Latin, from Latin *extensus* (see EXTENSION). See also -OR.

extent *n.* the space, dimension or degree to which anything is extended. WH: 12–14C. Anglo-French *extente*, from Medieval Latin *extenta*, use as n. of fem. of Latin *extentus*, p.p. of *extendere* EXTEND.

extenuate *v.t.* to lessen, to diminish the seriousness of, by showing mitigating circumstances. WH: 14–15C. Latin *extenuatus*, p.p. of *extenuare* to thin, to reduce, from EX- + *tenuis* thin. See also -ATE³.

exterior *a.* external, outer. *Also n.* WH: 16C. Latin, comp. of *exter* external. See also -IOR.

exterminate *v.t.* to eradicate, to destroy utterly, esp. living creatures. WH: 14–15C. Latin *exterminatus*, p.p. of *exterminare*, from EX- + *terminus* boundary. See also -ATE³. The original sense (to the 17C) was to drive beyond the boundaries of a state etc., i.e. to banish. The current sense arose in the 16C.

extern *n.* a student or pupil who does not reside in a college or seminary. *Also a.* WH: 16C. French *externe* or Latin *externus*, from *exter*. See EXTERIOR.

external *a.* situated on the outside. *Also n.* WH: 14–15C. Medieval Latin, from Latin *exter*. See EXTERN, also -AL¹.

exteroceptor *n.* a sensory organ which receives impressions from outside the body, e.g. the eye. WH: early 20C. Prob. from EXTERIOR or EXTERNAL + -O- + *receptor* (RECEPTION).

extinct *a.* having died out. *Also v.t.* WH: 14–15C. Latin *extinctus*, p.p. of *extinguere*, from EX- + *stinguere* to quench.

extinction *n.* the act of extinguishing or of making extinct. WH: 14–15C. Latin *extinctio*, *extinctionis*, from *extinctus*. See EXTINCT, also -ION.

extine *n.* the outer coat of a grain of pollen. WH: 19C. Latin *extimus* outermost + -INE.

extinguish *v.t.* to put out, to quench (as a light, hope, passion, life etc.). WH: 16C. Latin *extinguere*. See EXTINCT, also -ISH². Cp. DISTINGUISH.

extirpate *v.t.* to root out, to destroy utterly, to exterminate. WH: 16C. Latin *extirpatus*, p.p. of *extirpare*, from EX- + *stirps* stem, stock (of a tree). See also -ATE³.

extol *v.t.* to praise in the highest terms, to glorify. WH: 14–15C. Latin *extollere*, from EX- + *tollere* to raise.

extort *v.t.* to wrest or wring (from) by force, threats, importunity etc. WH: 16C. Latin *extortus*, p.p. of *extorquere*, from EX- + *torquere* to twist.

extra *a.* beyond what is absolutely necessary. *Also adv.*, *n.* WH: 17C. Prob. from EXTRAORDINARY, based on similar forms in French and German.

extra- *comb. form* on the outside, without. WH: Latin *extra* outside, beyond.

extracanonical *a.* not part of the canon of the Bible. WH: 19C. EXTRA- + *canonical* (CANON).

extracellular *a.* situated or occurring outside a cell or cells. WH: 19C. EXTRA- + CELLULAR.

extracorporeal *a.* outside the body. WH: 19C. EXTRA- + CORPOREAL.

extract¹ *v.t.* to draw or pull out. WH: 14–15C. Latin *extractus*, p.p. of *extrahere*, from EX- + *trahere* to draw.

extract² *n.* that which is extracted by distillation, solution etc. WH: 14–15C. Latin *extractum*, use as n. of neut. of *extractus*, p.p. of *extrahere*. See EXTRACT¹.

extra-curricular *a.* (of an activity) outside or in addition to the normal course of study. WH: early 20C. EXTRA- + *curricular* (CURRICULUM).

extradition *n.* the surrender of fugitives from justice by a government to the authorities of the country where the crime was committed. WH: 19C. French. See EX-, TRADITION.

extrados *n.* the exterior curve of an arch, esp. measured on the top of the voussoirs (cp. INTRADOS). WH: 18C. French, from Latin *extra* outside + French *dos* back.

extragalactic *a.* being or occurring outside the Milky Way. WH: 19C. EXTRA- + GALACTIC.

extrajudicial *a.* taking place outside the court, not legally authorized. WH: 17C. Medieval Latin *extraiudicialis*. See EXTRA-, JUDICIAL.

extralinguistic *a.* outside the area of language or of linguistics. WH: early 20C. EXTRA- + *linguistic* (LINGUIST).

extramarital *a.* (esp. of sexual relations) outside marriage. WH: early 20C. EXTRA- + MARITAL.

extramundane *a.* of, relating to or existing in a region outside our world or outside the material universe. WH: 17C. Late Latin *extramundanus*, from *extra mundum* outside the world.

extramural *a.* situated beyond or outside the walls or boundaries of a place. WH: 19C. Latin *extra muros* outside the walls + -AL¹.

extraneous *a.* foreign, not belonging to a class, subject etc. WH: 17C. Latin *extraneus*, from *extra* outside + -OUS. Cp. STRANGE.

extranuclear *a.* situated or occurring outside the nucleus of a cell. WH: 19C. EXTRA- + NUCLEAR.

extraordinary *a.* beyond or out of the ordinary course, unusual. *Also n.* WH: 14–15C. Latin *extraordinarius*, from *extra ordinem* out of order, exceptionally. See also -ARY¹.

extraparochial *a.* beyond, outside of or not reckoned within the limits of, any parish. WH: 17C. EXTRA- + PAROCHIAL.

extra-physical *a.* not subject to or bound by physical laws or processes. WH: 19C. EXTRA- + PHYSICAL.

extrapolate *v.t.* to estimate (the value of a function etc.) beyond the known values by the extension of a curve. WH: 19C. EXTRA- + -*polate* from INTERPOLATE.

extra-professional *a.* not coming within the ordinary duties of a profession. WH: 19C. EXTRA- + *professional* (PROFESSION).

extrasensory *a.* beyond the ordinary senses. WH: mid-20C. EXTRA- + *sensory* (SENSORIUM).

extra-spectral *a.* lying outside the visible spectrum. WH: 19C. EXTRA- + *spectral* (SPECTRUM).

extraterrestrial *a.* situated or occurring outside the earth or its atmosphere. *Also n.* WH: 19C. EXTRA- + TERRESTRIAL.

extraterritorial *a.* beyond the jurisdiction of the laws of the country in which one is living. WH: 19C. Modern Latin *extra territorium* outside the territory + -AL[1].

extra-tropical *a.* beyond or outside of the tropics, north or south. WH: 18C. EXTRA- + *tropical* (TROPIC).

extra-uterine *a.* outside the uterus. WH: 18C. EXTRA- + *uterine* (UTERUS).

extravagant *a.* exceeding due bounds, unrestrained by reason, immoderate. WH: 14–15C. Medieval Latin *extravagans*, *extravagantis*, from Latin EXTRA- + *vagans*, *vagantis*, pres.p. of *vagari* to wander. See also -ANT. The original sense (to the 17C) was unusual, abnormal. The current sense dates from the 16C.

extravaganza *n.* a fantastic composition in drama, fiction, poetry, music or other literary form. WH: 18C. Alt. (based on EXTRA-) of Italian *estravaganza*, from *estravagante* EXTRAVAGANT.

extravasate *v.t.* to force or let out of the proper vessels (as blood). *Also v.i.* WH: 17C. EXTRA- + Latin *vas* vessel + -ATE[3].

extravascular *a.* outside the vascular system. WH: 19C. EXTRA- + VASCULAR.

extravehicular *a.* taking place outside a vehicle, esp. a spacecraft. WH: mid-20C. EXTRA- + *vehicular* (VEHICLE).

extreme *a.* of the highest degree, most intense. *Also n.* WH: 14–15C. Old French *extrême*, from Latin *extremus*, from *exter* outer.

extremum *n.* the maximum or the minimum value of a function. WH: early 20C. Latin, neut. of *extremus* EXTREME.

extricate *v.t.* to disentangle, to set free from any perplexity, difficulty or embarrassment. WH: 17C. Latin *extricatus*, p.p. of *extricare*, from EX- + *tricae* perplexities. See also -ATE[3].

extrinsic *a.* being outside or external. WH: 16C. Late Latin *extrinsecus* outer, from Latin *extrinsecus* outwardly, from *exter* external + *-im* adv. suf., as in *interim* + *secus* alongside of. See also -IC.

extrorse *a.* (of anthers) turned outwards from the axis of growth. WH: 19C. Late Latin *extrorsus* in an outward direction, from Latin *extra* outside + *versus* towards, p.p. of *vertere* to turn.

extrovert *n.* a person having a type of temperament which is predominantly engaged with the external world. *Also a.* WH: early 20C. Var. of *extravert* (from *extraversion*, from EXTRA- + VERSION), based on INTROVERT[1]. The prefix *extro-* is an alteration of EXTRA- used to express the opposite of INTRO-, as in the pair *extrospective*/ *introspective* (INTROSPECTION).

extrude *v.t.* to thrust or push out or away. *Also v.i.* WH: 16C. Latin *extrudere*, from EX- + *trudere* to thrust.

exuberant *a.* overflowing with vitality, spirits or imagination. WH: 14–15C. French *exubérant*, from Latin *exuberans*, *exuberantis*, pres.p. of *exuberare*, from EX- + *uberare* to be fruitful, from *uber* fruitful. See also -ANT.

exude *v.t.* to emit or discharge through pores, as sweat, moisture or other liquid matter. *Also v.i.* WH: 16C. Latin *exudare*, from EX- + *sudare* to sweat.

exult *v.i.* to rejoice greatly. WH: 16C. Latin *exultare*, freq. of *exsilire* to leap up, from EX- + *salire* to leap.

exurbia *n.* residential areas outside the suburbs of a town or city. WH: mid-20C. EX- + -*urbia*, based on *suburbia* (SUBURB).

exuviae *n.pl.* the cast or shed skin, shells, teeth etc. of animals. WH: 17C. Latin clothing stripped off, skins of animals, from *exuere* to divest oneself of.

ex-voto *adv.* in pursuance of a vow. *Also n.* WH: 18C. Latin *ex voto* from a vow, from EX[2] + abl. sing. of *votum* vow. See VOTE.

ex works *a.*, *adv.* direct from the factory. WH: mid-20C. EX[2] + *works* (WORK).

eyas *n.* an unfledged hawk. *Also a.* WH: 15C. Old French *niais* bird taken from the nest, (now) silly person, from Latin *nidus* nest. The initial *n* has been lost by misdivision as in *a nadder*/ *an adder* (see ADDER).

eye[1] *n.* the organ of vision. WH: pre-1200. Old English *ēage*, from Germanic. Cp. German *Auge*.

eye[2] *v.t.* to watch, to observe (fixedly, suspiciously, jealously etc.). *Also v.i.* WH: 16C. EYE[1].

eyelet *n.* a small hole or opening, an aperture like an eye, for a cord etc. to pass through. *Also v.t.* WH: 14–15C. Old French *oillet* (Modern French *œillet*), dim. of *oil* eye (Modern French *œil*), from Latin *oculus*. See also -ET[1]. The word is not from EYE[1] + -LET, although the sense is the same.

Eyetie *n.*, *a.* (an) Italian. WH: early 20C. Abbr. of *Eyetalian*, representing non-standard (or facetious) pronun. of ITALIAN + -*ie* (-Y[3]).

eyra *n.* a reddish-coloured variety of jaguarundi. WH: 17C. Spanish, from Tupi-Guarani *irára*.

eyre *n.* a journey or circuit. WH: 12–14C. Old French *eire*, from Latin *iter* journey.

eyrie *n.* the nest of any bird of prey, esp. of an eagle. WH: 15C. Medieval Latin *area*, *aeria*, *eyria*, prob. from Old French *aire*, from Latin *area* level piece of ground (cp. AREA), nest of a bird of prey. The spelling with *ey* arose in the 16C from an association with Middle English *ey* egg, in the belief that the word meant repository for eggs.

fab *a.* wonderful, very good. WH: mid-20C. Abbr. of FABULOUS.

fabaceous *a.* leguminous, beanlike. WH: 18C. Late Latin *fabaceus*, from *faba* bean. See also -EOUS.

Fabian *a.* cautious, avoiding open conflict. *Also n.* WH: 16C. Latin *Fabianus* of the Fabian gens of ancient Rome. The name specifically relates to Q. *Fabius* Maximus, d.203 BC, nicknamed *Cunctator* (Delayer) for his stalling tactics in the Second Punic War.

fable *n.* a story, esp. one in which animals are represented as endowed with speech in order to convey a moral lesson. *Also v.i., v.t.* WH: 12–14C. Old French, from Latin *fabula* story, from *fari* to speak. Rel. to BAN. The association with animals is due to Aesop's fables.

fabliau *n.* a metrical tale, dealing usually with ordinary life, composed by the trouvères in the 12th and 13th cents., and intended for recitation. WH: 19C. French, from Old French (Picard) *fabliaux*, pl. of *fablel*, dim. of *fable*. See FABLE.

Fablon® *n.* an adhesive-backed plastic sheeting used for covering shelves, table mats etc. WH: mid-20C. Prob. blend of FABRIC and NYLON.

fabric *n.* felted or knitted material. WH: 15C. Old French *fabrique*, from Latin *fabrica* trade, manufactured object, forge, from *faber* worker in metal etc. Cp. FORGE[1].

fabricate *v.t.* to build, to construct. WH: 14–15C. Latin *fabricatus*, p.p. of *fabricari*, from *fabrica*. See FABRIC, also -ATE[3].

fabulist *n.* a writer or inventor of fables. WH: 16C. French *fabuliste*, from Latin *fabula* FABLE. See also -IST.

fabulous *a.* wonderful, very good. WH: 14–15C. French *fabuleux* or Latin *fabulosus*, from *fabula* FABLE. See also -ULOUS.

façade *n.* the front of a building. WH: 17C. French, from Old French *face* (see FACE), based on Italian *facciata*. See -ADE.

face *n.* the front part of the head, from the chin to the top of the forehead. *Also v.t., v.i.* WH: 12–14C. Old French, from alt. of Latin *facies* form, appearance, visage, prob. rel. to *fax* torch.

facet *n.* an aspect or part of something. *Also v.t.* WH: 17C. French *facette*, dim. of *face* FACE. See -ET[1].

facetiae *n.pl.* humorous or witty sayings. WH: 16C. Latin, pl. of *facetia* jest, from *facetus* graceful, witty. Cp. FACETIOUS.

facetious *a.* given to or characterized by levity; flippant. WH: 16C. French *facétieux*, from *facétie*, from Latin *facetia*. See FACETIAE, also -OUS.

facia *n.* the instrument board of a car. WH: 18C. Var. of FASCIA.

facial *a.* of or relating to the face. *Also n.* WH: 17C. Medieval Latin *facialis*, from Latin *facie*. See FACE, also -AL[1].

-facient *comb. form* added to the stems of Latin and English verbs to give the sense of producing the action expressed in the verb, as in *calefacient*, *febrifacient*. WH: Latin *-faciens*, *-facientis* making, pres.p. of *facere* to do, to make.

facies *n.* the general aspect of an assembly of organisms characteristic of a particular locality. WH: 17C. Latin. See FACE.

facile *a.* easily done; easily surmountable. WH: 15C. French, or from Latin *facilis*, from *facere* to do, to make. See also -IL.

facilitate *v.t.* to make easy or less difficult. WH: 17C. French *faciliter*, from Italian *facilitare*, from *facile*, from Latin *facilis* (see FACILE), based on Latin *debilitare* DEBILITATE etc.

facility *n.* easiness in performing or in being performed. WH: 14–15C. French *facilité* or Latin *facilitas*, from *facilis*. See FACILE, also -ITY.

facing *n.* a covering in front for ornament, strength or other purposes. WH: 14–15C. FACE + -ING[1].

façon de parler *n.* manner of speaking; phrase, phrasing. WH: 19C. French way of speaking, from *façon* FASHION + *de* of + *parler* to speak (see PARLEY).

facsimile *n.* an exact copy of printing, a picture etc. *Also v.t.* WH: 16C. Modern Latin, from Latin *fac*, imper. of *facere* to do, to make + *simile*, neut. of *similis* SIMILAR. Cp. FAX.

fact *n.* something that has really occurred or is known to be true or existing, as distinct from an inference or conjecture. WH: 15C. Latin *factum*, neut. (used as n.) of p.p. of *facere* to do, to make. The original meaning (to the 19C) was an action, a deed. The current sense dates from the 17C. The word replaced native DEED.

factice *n.* a rubber-like material made by treating vegetable oils with sulphur. WH: 19C. German *Factis*, *Faktis*, from Latin *facticius* artificial, from *facere* to do, to make.

faction[1] *n.* a body of persons combined or acting in union, esp. a party within a party combined to promote their own views or purposes. WH: 15C. Old French, from Latin *factio*, *factionis*, from *factus*, p.p. of *facere* to do, to make. See also -ION. The original sense was the action of doing something. The current sense emerged in the 16C.

faction[2] *n.* literary etc. work which blends factual events and characters with fiction. WH: mid-20C. Blend of FACT and FICTION.

-faction *comb. form* denoting making, turning or converting, as in *rarefaction*, *satisfaction*, *tumefaction*. WH: Latin *-factio*, *-factionis*. See FACTION[1].

factitious *a.* artificial, not natural. WH: 17C. Latin *facticius*, from *factus*. See FACTION[1], also -ITIOUS[2].

factitive *a.* causing, effecting. WH: 19C. Modern Latin *factitivus*, from Latin *factitare*, freq. of *facere* to do, to make. See also -IVE.

factoid *n.* an item of information that is considered to be true because it is repeated frequently. *Also a.* WH: late 20C. FACT + -OID.

factor *n.* any circumstance, fact or influence which contributes to a result. *Also v.t., v.i.* WH: 14–15C. French *facteur* or Latin *factor*, from *factus*. See FACTION[1], also -OR. The original sense (to the 19C) was a doer, a maker. The current sense arose in the 19C.

factory *n.* a building in which any manufacture is carried out. WH: 16C. Late Latin *factorium* (recorded in sense oil press), from Latin FACTOR + -Y[2].

factotum *n.* a person employed to do all sorts of work, a handyman. WH: 16C. Medieval Latin, from Latin *fac*, imper. of *facere* to do, to make + *totum* the whole. Cp. FAINÉANT.

factual *a.* concerned with or containing facts; actual. WH: 19C. FACT, based on ACTUAL.

factum *n.* a thing done; an act or deed. WH: 18C. Latin. See FACT.

facula *n.* a luminous spot or streak on the sun's disc. WH: 18C. Latin, dim. of *fax, facis* torch. See also -ULE.

faculty *n.* a natural power of the mind; a capacity for any natural action, such as seeing, feeling, speaking. WH: 14–15C. Old French *faculté*, from Latin *facultas*, from *facilis* FACILE. See also -TY[1]. The sense branch of knowledge (to the 19C) gave university faculty, originally especially theology, law, medicine or the arts.

fad *n.* a passing fancy or fashion. WH: 19C. Prob. second element of earlier *fidfad* fusspot, trifle, contr. of *fiddle-faddle* (FIDDLE).

fade *v.i.* to grow pale or indistinct. *Also v.t., n.* WH: 12–14C. Old French *fader*, from *fade* vapid, dull, prob. blending Latin *fatuus* FATUOUS and *vapidus* VAPID.

fadge †*v.i.* to suit, to fit. *Also n.* WH: 16C. Orig. unknown. Cp. FUDGE[2].

fado *n.* a type of esp. melancholy Portuguese folk song. WH: early 20C. Portuguese, lit. fate.

faeces *n.pl.* excrement from the bowels. WH: 14–15C. Latin, pl. of *faex* dregs.

†faerie *n.* fairyland. *Also a.* WH: 16C. Archaic var. of FAIRY, introduced by Spenser in *The Faerie Queene* (1590, 1596). Cp. FAY.

Faeroese *a.* of or relating to the Faeroes. *Also n.* WH: 19C. *Faeroes*, a group of islands in the N Atlantic between the Shetland Islands and Iceland + -ESE.

faff *v.i.* to dither, to fuss (often with *about*). *Also n.* WH: 18C. Imit.

fag[1] *n.* a cigarette. *Also v.i., v.t.* WH: 15C. Orig. unknown. In the sense cigarette, the word is an abbreviation of *fag-end*, from obsolete *fag* something hanging loose, flap + END. In the sense fatigue, it is perhaps related to FLAG[2] (rather than to FATIGUE itself).

fag[2] *n.* a male homosexual. WH: early 20C. Abbr. of FAGGOT.

faggot *n.* a cake or ball of chopped liver, herbs etc. *Also v.t., v.i.* WH: 12–14C. Old French *fagot*, from Italian *fagotto*, dim. of a back-formation from Greek *phakelos* bundle. The sense male homosexual (early 20C) may have originated in FAG[1], although this word (as FAG[2]) is now regarded as an abbr. of *faggot*.

fagotto *n.* a bassoon. WH: 19C. Italian bassoon. See FAGGOT.

fah *n.* the fourth note of a major scale in the tonic sol-fa system of notation. WH: 12–14C. Latin *famuli*. See UT.

Fahrenheit *a.* of or relating to the temperature scale on which the freezing point of water is marked at 32° and the boiling point at 212°. WH: 18C. Gabriel Daniel *Fahrenheit*, 1686–1736, German physicist who invented the mercury thermometer.

faience *n.* tin-glazed earthenware of a particular kind. WH: 17C. French *faïence*, from *Faïence* Faenza, city in N Italy, where it was originally made.

fail[1] *v.i.* not to succeed (in). *Also v.t., n.* WH: 12–14C. Old French *faillir* to be wanting, alt. of Latin *fallere* to disappoint the expectations of, to deceive. Cp. FALLACY.

fail[2] *n.* a turf, sod. WH: 14–15C. Orig. unknown.

†fain *a.* glad, well-pleased; desirous. *Also adv., v.i.* WH: pre-1200. Old English *fægn*, from Germanic, from base represented by Old English *gefēon* to rejoice. Rel. to FAIR[1]. The sense may have been influenced by Old French *avoir faim* (Modern French *avoir faim*) to be hungry. Cp. the story of the Prodigal Son who 'would fain have filled his belly' (Luke xv.16).

fainéant *a.* do-nothing; idle, sluggish. *Also n.* WH: 17C. French, from *fait*, 3rd pers. sing. of *faire* to do + *néant* nothing. Cp. FACTOTUM.

faint *a.* (of sound or brightness) dim, indistinct. *Also v.i., n.* WH: 12–14C. Old French, p.p. of *faindre* FEIGN.

fair[1] *a.* just, reasonable. *Also adv., n., v.t., v.i.* WH: pre-1200. Old English *fæger*, from Germanic. Rel. to FAIN and FAWN[2]. The sense blond (of hair) evolved in the 12–14C on the basis that dark hair was regarded unfavourably (i.e. as 'foul'). The same applied to a light (as opposed to dark) complexion.

fair[2] *n.* a usu. outdoor show with rides, sideshows, games of skill and other amusements. WH: 12–14C. Old French *feire* (Modern French *foire*), from Late Latin *feria* holiday, from Latin (sing. of) *feriae* religious festivals, holy days. Cp. FERIAL.

Fair Isle *a.* applied to woollen articles knitted in coloured patterns typical of Fair Isle. WH: 19C. One of the Shetland Islands. The island name does not come from FAIR[1] but from Old Norse *faar* sheep, whose wool is used for the articles.

fairy *n.* an imagined small supernatural being having magical powers. *Also a.* WH: 12–14C. Old French *faerie* (Modern French *féerie*). See FAY, -ERY. Cp. FAERIE. The original sense was fairyland. The current sense evolved in the 14–15C. The word is not related to FAIR[1].

fait accompli *n.* an accomplished fact. WH: 19C. French accomplished fact, from *fait* FACT + *accompli*, p.p. of *accomplir* ACCOMPLISH.

faith *n.* firm and earnest belief, complete confidence. *Also int., v.t.* WH: 12–14C. Old French *feid*, from Latin *fides*, from var. of base also of *fidus* trustworthy, from *fidere* to trust (cp. FIDELITY).

fajita *n.* a kind of tortilla wrapped around meat, chillies, onions etc. WH: late 20C. Mexican Spanish, lit. little strip, little belt.

fake[1] *v.t.* to pretend, to simulate. *Also n., a.* WH: 19C. Orig. uncertain. ? Var. of *feague* to beat, to whip, ? from German *fegen* to cleanse, to sweep. Cp. FIG[2]. An early sense was to rob, to steal. The current sense emerged only in the mid-20C.

fake[2] *n.* one of the coils in a rope or cable when laid up. *Also v.t.* WH: 14–15C. Orig. unknown.

fakir *n.* a Muslim religious mendicant. WH: 17C. Arabic *faḳīr* poor (man).

Falange *n.* the Fascist movement in Spain, founded in 1933. WH: mid-20C. Spanish PHALANX.

Falasha *n.* a member of an Ethiopian people who practise a form of Judaism. WH: 18C. Amharic exile, immigrant.

falbala *n.* a trimming, a flounce. WH: 18C. French, of unknown orig. Cp. FURBELOW. According to some sources, the word is from Provençal *farbello*, related to Italian *faldella* carded cotton (for linings).

falcate *a.* hooked; bent or curved like a sickle or scythe. WH: 19C. Latin *falcatus*, from *falx, falcis* sickle. See also -ATE[2]. Cp. FALCHION.

falchion *n.* a short, broad sword with a slightly curved blade. WH: 12–14C. Old French *fauchon*, from Latin *falx, falcis* sickle.

falciform *a.* having the form of a sickle. WH: 18C. Latin *falx, falcis* sickle + -*i*- + -FORM.

falcon *n.* any diurnal bird of prey of the family *Falconidae* having pointed wings, esp. the peregrine falcon and others trained to hawk game. WH: 12–14C. Old French *faucon*, oblique case of *fauc*, from Late Latin *falco, falconis*, from *falx, falcis* sickle, or from Germanic base of Old High German *falco* (cp. German *Falke* falcon). Latin *falx* presumably refers to the bird's curved talons, or else to its sword-like wings.

falderal *n.* a trifle, a gewgaw. WH: 19C. Meaningless refrain in songs, of imit. orig.

faldstool *n.* a portable folding seat, stool or chair, used by a bishop. WH: pre-1200. Old English *fældestōl*, from Germanic, from base of FOLD[2] + STOOL. Cp. FAUTEUIL.

fall *v.i.* to descend from a higher to a lower place or position by the force of gravity. *Also v.t., n.* WH: pre-1200. Old English *feallan*, *fallan*, from Germanic. Cp. FELL[1].

fallacy *n.* a prevalent but mistaken belief. WH: 15C. Latin *fallacia*, from *fallax, fallacis*, from *fallere* to deceive. See also -ACY. An early sense (to the 18C) was deception, guile.

fallal *n.* a gaudy ornament or trinket, a gewgaw. WH: 18C. Prob. from FALBALA.

fallible *a.* liable to make mistakes. WH: 14–15C. Medieval Latin *fallibilis*, from Latin *fallere* to deceive. See also -IBLE.

Fallopian tube *n.* either of two ducts or canals in female mammals by which ova are conveyed to the uterus. WH: 18C. *Fallopius*, Latinized name of Gabriello *Fallopio*, 1523–62, Italian anatomist. See also -AN.

fallow[1] *a.* (of land) ploughed and tilled but not sown. *Also n., v.t.* WH: 12–14C. Prob. from Old English v. *fealgian*, from Germanic. Cp. German *Felge* ploughed up land. The word is popularly associated with FALLOW[2], with reference to the colour of upturned earth.

fallow[2] *a.* of a pale brownish or reddish-yellow colour. WH: pre-1200. Old English *falu*, from Germanic. Ult. rel. to PALE[1].

false *a.* not conformable to fact; incorrect. *Also adv., n., v.t.* WH: pre-1200. Latin *falsum*, neut. of *falsus*, orig. p.p. of *fallere* to deceive. The current form of the word developed from Old French *fals* (Modern French *faux, fausse*), from Latin *falsus*.

falsetto *n.* a pitch or range of (usu. the male) voice higher than the natural register. *Also a.* WH: 18C. Italian, dim. of *falso* FALSE.

falsify *v.t.* to make false. WH: 14–15C. Old French *falsifier*, from Medieval Latin *falsificare*, from Latin *falsificus* making false, from *falsus* FALSE. See also -FY.

Falstaffian *a.* fat; coarsely humorous; convivial; dissolute. WH: 19C. *Falstaff*, name of Sir John Falstaff, fat, jolly and dissipated knight in Shakespeare's plays *Henry IV* (1597–8), *Henry V* (1598) and *The Merry Wives of Windsor* (1600) + -IAN.

falter *v.i.* to stumble, to be unsteady. *Also v.t.* WH: 14–15C. ? From FOLD[2] (in sense to falter of the legs or tongue) + -*ter* from TOTTER.

fame *n.* the state of being well-known, celebrity. *Also v.t.* WH: 12–14C. Old French, from Latin *fama* report, fame, rel. to Greek *phēmē* voice, report.

familiar *a.* of one's own acquaintance, well-known. *Also n.* WH: 12–14C. Old French *familier*, from Latin *familiaris*, from *familia* FAMILY. See also -AR[1].

famille *n.* a Chinese enamelled porcelain. WH: 19C. French family.

family *n.* a group of people related to one another, esp. parents and their children. *Also a.* WH: 14–15C. Latin *familia* household, from *famulus* servant. See also -Y[2].

famine *n.* extreme shortage of food. WH: 14–15C. Old French, from *faim* hunger, from Latin *fames*.

famish *v.i.* to suffer extreme hunger; to die of hunger. *Also v.t.* WH: 14–15C. Obs. fame to starve, shortening of Old French *afamer* (Modern French *affamer*), from Latin AF- + *fames* hunger + -ISH².

famous *a.* very well-known; renowned. WH: 14–15C. Old French *fameus* (Modern French *fameux*), from Latin *famosus*, from *fama* FAME. See also -OUS.

famulus *n.* an assistant or servant of a magician or scholar. WH: 19C. Latin servant (cp. FAMILY).

fan¹ *n.* an apparatus with revolving blades to give a current of air for ventilation. *Also v.t., v.i.* WH: pre-1200. Latin *vannus* winnowing fan. Cp. VAN³.

fan² *n.* an enthusiastic admirer; a devotee. WH: 17C. Abbr. of FANATIC, ? influ. by FANCY.

fanatic *a.* enthusiastic in the extreme. *Also n.* WH: 16C. French *fanatique*, or from Latin *fanaticus* pertaining to a temple, inspired by a god, frenzied, from *fanum* temple. Cp. FANE. See also -ATIC.

fancy *v.t.* to want to have or do. *Also v.i., int., n., a.* WH: 14–15C. Contr. of FANTASY.

fandangle *n.* a gaudy trinket, a gewgaw. WH: 19C. ? Alt. of FANDANGO based on NEWFANGLED.

fandango *n.* a lively Spanish dance in triple time, for two people who beat time with castanets. WH: 18C. Spanish, of unknown orig.

fane *n.* a temple, a place of worship, a sanctuary. WH: 14–15C. Latin *fanum* temple.

fanfare *n.* a short, loud sounding of trumpets, bugles etc. WH: 18C. French, ult. of imit. orig. Cp. *tarantara*.

fanfaronade *n.* arrogant boasting, swaggering or blustering. *Also v.i.* WH: 17C. French *fanfaronnade*, from *fanfaron* (see also -OON), from *fanfare* FANFARE. See also -ADE.

fang *n.* a large pointed tooth, esp. the canine tooth of a dog or wolf. *Also v.t.* WH: pre-1200. Old Norse capture, grasp, from Germanic base also of Old English *fōn* to take, to seize, rel. to Latin *pangere* to fix. Cp. VANG. The original sense was something caught or taken, booty, spoils. The sense of canine tooth arose in the 16C.

fanny *n.* the female genitals. WH: 19C. Orig. unknown. The word is attributed by some to *Fanny* Hill, heroine of John Cleland's pornographic novel *Memoirs of a Woman of Pleasure* (1748–9). But there is a long gap between the novel date and that of the earliest record of the word in its current sense.

Fanny Adams *n.* nothing at all (euphem. for *fuck all*). WH: 19C. *Fanny Adams*, young girl murdered at Alton, Hampshire, 1867.

fanon *n.* in the Roman Catholic Church, a maniple or napkin used by the officiating priest at Mass; an embroidered band attached to the wrist of the celebrant. WH: 14–15C. Old French, from Frankish, rel. to Old High German *fano*, Latin *pannus* (piece of) cloth. Cp. GONFALON.

fan-tan *n.* a Chinese gambling game involving guessing a number of objects. WH: 19C. Chinese *fān tān*, from *fān* kind + *tān* to spread out, to take a share. The name alludes to the payment of stakes so many times the original number of objects.

fantast *n.* a dreamer or visionary. WH: 16C. Orig. from Medieval Latin, from Greek *phantastēs* boaster. Later through German *Phantast*.

fantastic *a.* wonderful, very good. *Also n.* WH: 14–15C. Old French *fantastique*, from Medieval Latin *fantasticus*, from Late Latin *phantasticus*, from Greek *phantastikos*, from *phantazein* to make visible, from *phantos* visible, from *phan-*, base of *phanein* to show. See also -IC.

fantasy *n.* a fanciful mental image or daydream. *Also v.t.* WH: 14–15C. Old French *fantasie* (Modern French *fantaisie*), from Latin *phantasia*, from Greek appearance, from *phantazein* to make visible. See FANTASTIC, also -Y². Cp. FANCY.

Fanti *n.* a member of a Ghanaian people. WH: 19C. Fante.

far *a.* distant, a long way off. *Also adv., n.* WH: pre-1200. Old English *feorr*, from Germanic comp. form of Indo-European base also of Sanskrit *para*, Greek *pera* further.

farad *n.* the derived SI unit of capacitance, the capacity of a capacitor in which the electrical potential is raised 1 volt by the presence of 1 coulomb of charge on each plate. WH: 19C. FARADAY. The word was originally proposed as the term for a unit of electrical charge.

faraday *n.* a quantity of electric charge numerically equal to Faraday's constant. WH: 19C. Michael *Faraday*, 1791–1867, English scientist.

farandole *n.* a lively Provençal dance. WH: 19C. French, from Provençal *farandoulo*.

farce *n.* a humorous play in which the actors are involved in ridiculously complex and improbable situations. WH: 16C. Old French stuffing, from Latin *farcire* to stuff. The word was originally used metaphorically of interludes 'stuffed' between the acts of a mystery play. Cp. INTERLARD.

farceur *n.* a joker, a jester, a wag. WH: 17C. French, from obs. *farcer* to act farces (see FARCE) + -*eur* -OR.

farcy *n.* a disease in horses, closely allied to glanders, in which the lymph vessels become inflamed and form nodules. WH: 14–15C. Old French *farcin*, from Late Latin *farciminum*, from *farcire* to stuff. The reference is to the appearance of the swollen nodules.

†farded *a.* rouged, painted with cosmetics. WH: 14–15C. P.p. of *fard*, from *fard* white paint (for the face), from Old French *farder*, from Frankish *farwidhon*, from *farwjan* to tint (cp. German *Farbe* colour).

fare *n.* the sum of money to be paid by a passenger for a journey by bus, train etc. *Also v.i.* WH: pre-1200. Old English *fær*, from base of *faran* to journey, from Germanic, from Indo-European. Cp. German *fahren* to travel. The original sense (to the 18C) was journey, voyage, then road, way, path. Cp. *wayfarer* (WAY). The sense then narrowed to a journey for which a price was paid, then to the cost of the journey itself.

farewell *int.* goodbye, adieu. *Also n., a.* WH: 14–15C. Imper. of FARE + WELL¹. Cp. BON VOYAGE.

farina *n.* flour or meal of cereal; the powder obtained by grinding nuts, roots etc. WH: 14–15C. Latin, from *far* corn.

farl *n.* a thin cake of oatmeal or flour, orig. a quarter of such a cake. WH: 17C. Contr. of obs. *fardel* fragment, from source of FOURTH + DEAL¹.

farm *n.* an area of land together with its buildings, used for growing crops or rearing animals. *Also v.t., v.i.* WH: 12–14C. Old French *ferme*, from Medieval Latin *firma* fixed payment, from Latin *firmare* to fix, to settle, from Latin *firmus* firm FIRM¹. The original sense was a fixed annual sum payable as rent, then a tract of leased land (in the 16C).

faro *n.* a game of cards in which players bet against the dealer. WH: 18C. French PHARAOH, ? as one of the names of the king of hearts.

farouche *a.* unsociable, shy, sullen. WH: 18C. French, alt. of Old French *faroche*, from Medieval Latin *forasticus*, from Latin *foras* out of doors. The original sense was wild, savage, shunning human activity.

farrago *n.* a confused mixture, a medley. WH: 17C. Latin mixed fodder for cattle, from *far* spelt, corn.

farrier *n.* a person who shoes horses. *Also v.i.* WH: 16C. Old French *ferrier*, from Latin *ferrarius*, from *ferrum* horseshoe, iron. See also -IER.

farrow *n.* a litter of pigs. *Also v.t., v.i.* WH: pre-1200. Old English *færh*, from Germanic, from Indo-European base also of Latin *porcus*, Greek *porkos*. See PORK.

farruca *n.* a type of flamenco dance. WH: early 20C. Spanish, fem. of *farruco*, from *Farruco*, pet form of male forename *Francisco* Francis. *Farruco* is a nickname for someone from Galicia or Asturias, where the dance originated.

Farsi *n.* modern Persian, the Indo-European language of Iran. WH: 19C. Arabic *fārsī*, from *Fārs*, from Persian *Pārs* Persian, PARSEE.

fart *v.i.* to break wind through the anus. *Also n.* WH: pre-1200. Old English *fearting* (verbal n.), from Germanic, rel. to Greek *perdein*, Russian *perdet'* to break wind. The word is not related to Latin *pedere*. See PETARD.

farthing *n.* a quarter part of an old penny, the smallest British copper coin (withdrawn in 1961). WH: pre-1200. Old English *fēorthing*, from *fēortha* FOURTH.

farthingale *n.* (esp. in the 16th cent.) a woman's hooped skirt used to extend the wide gown and petticoat. WH: 16C. Old French *verdugale*, alt. of Spanish *verdugado*, from *verdugo* rod, stick, from *verde* green. The skirt is so named as it was originally extended by cane hoops or rods inserted underneath. These were later replaced by whalebone or steel.

fartlek *n.* a method of athletic training, mixing fast and slow running. WH: mid-20C. Swedish, from *fart* speed + *lek* play.

fasces *n.pl.* the ancient insignia of the Roman lictors, consisting of a bundle of elm or birch rods, in the middle of which was an axe. WH: 16C. Latin, pl. of *fascis* bundle. Cp. FASCISM.

fascia *n.* a flat surface in an entablature or elsewhere. WH: 16C. Latin band, fillet, casing of a door. Rel. to FASCES.

fascicle *n.* any one of the parts of a book that is published in instalments. WH: 15C. Latin *fasciculus*, dim. of *fascis*. See FASCES, also -ULE.

fasciitis *n.* inflammation of the fascia of a muscle. WH: 19C. FASCIA + -ITIS.

fascinate *v.t.* to exercise an irresistible influence over; to captivate. WH: 16C. Latin *fascinatus*, p.p. of *fascinare*, from *fascinum* spell, witchcraft. See also -ATE³. The original meaning of the verb (to the 17C) was to bewitch, to put under a spell.

fascine *n.* a cylindrical faggot of brushwood used in building earthworks, for filling trenches, protecting riverbanks etc. WH: 17C. French, from Latin *fascina*, from *fascis* bundle.

Fascism *n.* the extreme right-wing theory of government introduced into Italy by Benito Mussolini in 1922, the object of which was to oppose socialism and communism by controlling every form of national activity. WH: early 20C. Italian *fascismo*, from *fascio* bundle, group, from Popular Latin *fascium*, from Latin *fascis* bundle. See also -ISM. The Fascists adopted the FASCES as their symbol.

fashion *n.* the activity or business concerned with the style of clothes. *Also v.t.* WH: 12–14C. Old French *façon*, from Latin *factio*, *factionis*, from *factus*, p.p. of *facere* to do, to make. See also -ION.

fast¹ *a.* moving quickly. *Also adv., n.* WH: pre-1200. Old English *fæst*, from Germanic. The original sense was firmly fixed, not easily moved. The sense swift, rapid, evolved in the 12–14C from the concept of determination. Cp. FAST².

fast² *v.i.* to abstain from food, esp. as a religious observance for the mortification of the body or as a sign of grief or penitence. *Also n.* WH: pre-1200. Old English *fæstan*, from Germanic base of FAST¹. Cp. German *fast* almost. The concept is of determination and resolve.

fasten *v.t.* to fix firmly, to make secure. *Also v.i.* WH: pre-1200. Old English *fæstnian*, from Germanic base also of FAST². See also -EN⁵.

fastidious *a.* extremely refined, esp. in matters of taste; fussy. WH: 14–15C. Latin *fastidiosus*, from *fastidium* loathing. See also -IOUS. The original sense (to the 17C) was disagreeable, distasteful. The current sense emerged in the 17C.

fastigiate *a.* tapering to a point like a pyramid. WH: 17C. Latin *fastigium* tapering point, gable + -ATE².

fat *a.* having a lot of flesh and overweight. *Also n., v.t., v.i.* WH: pre-1200. Old English *fætt*, p.p. of *fætan* to cram, to stuff, from Germanic. The original sense was plump, as distinct from current overplump. The original meaning is still present in *fatstock*, animals fattened up for slaughter.

fatal *a.* causing death, destruction or ruin. WH: 14–15C. Old French, or from Latin *fatalis*, from *fatum* FATE. See also -AL¹.

fata Morgana *n.* a mirage observed from the harbour of Messina and adjacent places, and supposed by Sicilians to be the work of the fairy Morgana. WH: 19C. Italian fairy Morgan, sister of King Arthur. The legend of King Arthur was brought to Sicily by Norman settlers.

fate *n.* a power considered to control and decide events unalterably. *Also v.t.* WH: 14–15C. Italian *fato*, from Latin *fatum*, lit. that which has been spoken, neut. p.p. of *fari* to speak.

father *n.* a male parent. *Also v.t.* WH: pre-1200. Old English *fæder*, from Germanic, from Indo-European source also of Latin *pater*, Greek *patēr*, Sanskrit *pitṛ*.

fathom *n.* a measure of length, six ft. (1.8 m) used principally in nautical and mining measurements. *Also v.t.* WH: pre-1200. Old English *fæthm* length of the outstretched arms, from Germanic. The original sense was embracing arms, bosom. The distance from the end of one outstretched arm to that of the other became standardized at 6 feet.

fatigue *n.* exhaustion from bodily or mental exertion. *Also v.t.* WH: 17C. Old French *fatiguer*, from Latin *fatigare* to exhaust with

riding or working, from *ad fatim* to satiety, to bursting, rel. to *fatiscare* to burst open.

Fatiha *n.* the short first sura of the Koran, used by Muslims as a prayer. WH: 19C. Arabic *al-Fātiḥa* the opening (sura), use as n. of fem. part. *fātiḥa* opening, from *fataḥa* to open.

Fatimid *n.* a descendant of Fatima, daughter of Muhammad. *Also a.* WH: 19C. Arabic *Fātima* Fatima, *c.*605–33, daughter of Muhammad + -ID.

fatuous *a.* idiotic, inane. WH: 17C. Latin *fatuus* foolish, silly + -OUS.

fatwa *n.* a religious edict issued by a Muslim leader. WH: 17C. Arabic *fatwā*, from *'aftā* to decide a point of law. Cp. MUFTI.

faubourg *n.* a suburb of a city or town. WH: 15C. French, from Old French *fors borc* outside the town, from *fors* outside (Modern French *hors*), from Latin *foris* (cp. FOREIGN), + *borc* (Modern French *bourg*), from Late Latin *burgus* (cp. BOROUGH), influ. by French *faux* FALSE.

fauces *n.pl.* the area from the cavity at the back of the mouth to the pharynx. WH: 14–15C. Latin throat.

faucet *n.* a tap. WH: 14–15C. Old French *fausset*, from Provençal *falset*, from *falsar* to bore, rel. to Old French *fausser* to damage, to break into.

fault *n.* a defect, imperfection. *Also v.t., v.i.* WH: mid-20C. Old French *faut* (Modern French *faute*), from Popular Latin *fallita* falling, replacing Latin *falsus*, p.p. of *fallere* FAIL¹. Cp. FALSE.

faun *n.* one of a kind of rural deities, with a human body and the horns and legs of a goat, bearing a strong resemblance to the satyrs, with whom they are generally identified. WH: 14–15C. Old French *faune* or Latin *Faunus*, ancient Italian god worshipped by shepherds and farmers. Faunus was identified with the Greek god Pan. Cp. FAUNA.

fauna *n.* the animals found in or belonging to a certain region or time. WH: 18C. *Fauna*, ancient Italian rural goddess, sister of Faunus (see FAUN). The name of the goddess was adopted by Linnaeus for the title of his work *Fauna Suecica* ('Swedish Fauna') (1746), a companion volume to his *Flora Suecica* (1745). See FLORA.

faute de mieux *adv.* for lack of anything better. WH: 18C. French (for) want of (anything) better, from *faute* FAULT + *de* of + *mieux* better, comp. of *bien* well.

fauteuil *n.* an easy, upholstered armchair. WH: 18C. French, from Old French *faudestuel*. See FALDSTOOL.

fauvism *n.* a 20th-cent. art movement, characterized by vivid use of colour and a free treatment of form. WH: early 20C. French *fauvisme*, from *fauve* wild animal + -ISM. The name was coined by the French art critic Louis Vauxcelles at the Autumn Salon in 1905. Seeing a classical-style statue in the midst of works by Matisse and his contemporaries, he commented, 'Donatello au milieu des fauves' ('Donatello among the wild animals').

faux *a.* imitation, false. WH: late 20C. French FALSE.

faux pas *n.* a blunder, a slip. WH: 17C. French false step, from *faux* FALSE + *pas* step, PACE¹.

fave *n., a.* favourite. WH: mid-20C. Abbr. of FAVOURITE.

favela *n.* in Brazil, a shack or shanty town. WH: mid-20C. Portuguese.

favour *n.* a kind or indulgent act. *Also v.t.* WH: 12–14C. Old French (Modern French *faveur*), from Latin *favor*, from *favere* to regard with good will, rel. to *favere* to cherish.

favourite *a.* preferred before all others. *Also n.* WH: 16C. Obs. French *favorit* (now *favori*), from Italian *favorito*, p.p. of *favorire*, from *favore* FAVOUR.

favus *n.* a disease of the scalp, characterized by pustules succeeded by cellular crusts bearing some resemblance to a honeycomb. WH: 16C. Latin honeycomb.

fawn¹ *n.* a young deer; a buck or doe in its first year. *Also a., v.t., v.i.* WH: 14–15C. Old French *faon*, from Latin *fetus* offspring, FOETUS.

fawn² *v.i.* to court in a servile manner, to grovel, to cringe. *Also n.* WH: 12–14C. Var. (representing Old English *fagnian*) of obs. *fain* to be glad, to welcome. See FAIN.

fax *n.* a system for electronically scanning, transmitting and reproducing documents etc. via a telephone line. *Also v.t.* WH: mid-20C. Representation of abbr. of FACSIMILE.

fay *n.* a fairy. WH: 14–15C. Old French *faie* (Modern French *fée*), from Latin *fata* the Fates, pl. of *fatum* FATE, taken as fem. sing. Cp. FAIRY.

faze *v.t.* to disconcert, to put off one's stroke. WH: 19C. Var. of obs. *feeze* to drive away, to frighten, from Old English *fēsian*, of unknown orig.

FD *abbr.* Defender of the Faith. WH: Abbr. of Latin FIDEI DEFENSOR.

FDR *abbr.* Free Democratic Republic (the former W Germany). WH: Abbr. of German *Freie Demokratische Republik* Free Democratic Republic.

Fe *chem. symbol* iron. WH: Abbr. of Latin *ferrum* iron.

fealty *n.* fidelity of a vassal or feudal tenant to a lord. WH: 12–14C. Old French *feaulte* (Modern French *féauté*), from Latin *fidelitas*, from *fidelis* faithful, from *fides* faith. See also -TY[1].

fear *n.* an unpleasant feeling caused by impending danger, pain etc. *Also v.t., v.i.* WH: pre-1200. Old English *fǣr*, from Germanic. Cp. German *Gefahr* danger.

feasible *a.* that may or can be done, practicable. WH: 14–15C. Old French *faisable*, from *faire*, *fais-* to do. See also -IBLE.

feast *n.* a large and sumptuous meal enjoyed by a great number of people. *Also v.t., v.i.* WH: 12–14C. Old French *feste* (Modern French *fête*), from Latin *festa*, neut. pl. of *festus* festal, joyous. Cp. FÊTE.

feat[1] *n.* a notable act, esp. one displaying great skill or daring. WH: 14–15C. Old French *fet* (Modern French *fait*), from Latin *factum* FACT.

†feat[2] *a.* deft, skilful. WH: 12–14C. Old French *fet* (Modern French *fait*), from Latin *factus*, lit. made (for something). See FACT.

feather *n.* a plume or quill, one of the appendages growing from a bird's skin, forming collectively the soft covering of a bird. *Also v.t., v.i.* WH: pre-1200. Old English *fether*, from Germanic, from Indo-European base represented also in Sanskrit *patra* wing, Greek *pteron* wing, Latin *penna* PEN[1]. Cp. German *Feder*.

feature *n.* a distinctive or prominent part of anything. *Also v.t., v.i.* WH: 14–15C. Old French *feture*, from Latin *factura* formation, creature, from *factus*, p.p. of *facere* to do. See also -URE. The original sense (to the 17C) was form, shape, creation. The current sense evolved in the 17C.

febrifacient *a.* causing fever. *Also n.* WH: 19C. Latin *febris* fever + -FACIENT.

febrifuge *n.* a medicine which has the property of dispelling or mitigating fever. WH: 17C. French *fébrifuge*, from Latin *febris* fever. See -FUGE. Cp. FEVERFEW.

febrile *a.* of, relating to, proceeding from or indicating fever. WH: 17C. French *fébrile* or Medieval Latin *febrilis*, from Latin *febris* fever. See also -IL.

February *n.* the second month of the year, containing in ordinary years 28 days, and in leap years 29. WH: 12–14C. Old French *fevrier* (Modern French *février*), from Late Latin *febrarius*, from Latin *februarius*, from *februa* (neut. pl.) a Roman festival of purification held on 15 February.

fec. *abbr.* he/she made it. WH: Abbr. of Latin *fecit* he/ she made (it).

feck *n.* efficacy, strength, vigour. WH: 15C. Shortening of var. of EFFECT.

feckless *a.* weak, ineffective. WH: 16C. FECK + -LESS.

fecula *n.* lees, sediment, from vegetable infusions, esp. starch. WH: 17C. Latin *fecula* crust of wine, dim. of *faex* dregs, sediment. Cp. FAECES. See also -CULE.

feculent *a.* filthy, foul. WH: 15C. French *féculent* or Latin *faeculentus*. See FAECES, -ULENT.

fecund *a.* fertile, productive. WH: 14–15C. French *fécond* or Latin *fecundus*.

Fed *n.* The Federal Reserve. WH: 18C. Abbr. of FEDERAL.

fed[1] *a.* that has been fed. WH: 14–15C. P.p. of FEED.

fed[2] *n.* (in the US) a federal agent or official, esp. a member of the FBI. WH: early 20C. Abbr. of FEDERAL.

fedayee *n.* a member of an Arab commando group, esp. fighting against Israel. WH: 19C. Arabic and Persian *fidā'ī* one who gives his life for another, from *fadā* to ransom.

federal *a.* relating to, arising from or supporting a system of government formed by the union of several states. *Also n.* WH: 17C. Latin *foedus*, *foederis* covenant. See also -AL[1].

fedora *n.* a soft felt hat with a curled brim. WH: 19C. *Fédora*, title of a drama (1882) by the French dramatist Victorien Sardou.

fee *n.* payment or remuneration to a public officer, a professional person or an organization for the execution of official functions or for the performance of a professional service. *Also v.t.* WH: 12–14C. Old French *feu* (Modern French *fief*), var. of Medieval Latin *feodum*, from Frankish base rel. to obs. *fee* cattle, from Old English *feoh*, *fēo*, from Germanic var. of Indo-European base represented by Sanskrit *pasu*, Latin *pecu* cattle. Cp. PECULIAR. The original sense was tenure of an estate. The current sense evolved in the 14–15C.

feeble *a.* weak, destitute of physical strength. *Also n., v.t.* WH: 12–14C. Old French *feble*, var. of *fieble* (Modern French *faible*), from Latin *flebilis* that is to be wept over, from *flere* to weep. See also -BLE. Cp. FOIBLE.

feed *v.t.* to give food to. *Also v.i., n.* WH: pre-1200. Old English *fēdan*, from Germanic. See FOOD.

feedback *n.* the return of part of the output of a system, circuit or mechanical process to the input. WH: 20C. FEED + BACK[1].

feel *v.t.* to perceive by touch. *Also v.i., n.* WH: pre-1200. Old English *fēlan*, from Germanic. Rel. to PALP.

feign *v.t.* to pretend, to simulate. *Also v.i.* WH: 12–14C. Old French *feindre*, *feign-*, from Latin *fingere* to form, to conceive, to contrive.

feijoa *n.* any evergreen shrub or tree of the genus *Feijoa*. WH: 19C. Modern Latin, from J. da Silva *Feijó*, 1760–1824, Brazilian naturalist.

feint[1] *n.* a pretence of aiming at one point while another is the real object. *Also v.i., a.* WH: 17C. Old French *feinte*, fem. p.p. (used as n.) of *feindre* FEIGN.

feint[2] *a.* (of ruled lines on paper) light, faint. WH: 19C. Commercial var. of FAINT.

feisty *a.* spirited, tough. WH: 19C. From *feist*, var. of *fist* act of breaking wind + -Y[1].

felafel *n.* a spicy ball or cake of mashed chickpeas or beans. WH: mid-20C. Egyptian coll. Arabic *falāfil*, pl. of Arabic *fulfil*, *filfil* pepper.

feldspar *n.* any of a group of silicates of aluminium combined with a mineral, e.g. potassium, sodium or calcium, that are the most important group of rock-forming minerals and the major constituent of igneous rocks. WH: 18C. Alt. of German *Feldspath*, from *Feld* FIELD + *Spath* spath (see SPATHIC), with substitution of synonymous SPAR[3]. The false association with German *Fels* rock gave the variant spelling *felspar*.

felicity *n.* happiness, blissfulness. WH: 14–15C. Old French *félicité*, from Latin *felicitas*, from *felix*, *felicis* happy. See also -ITY.

felid *n.* a member of the Felidae, the cat family, containing lions, tigers, leopards, pumas and cats. WH: 19C. Modern Latin *Felidae*, from Latin *feles* cat. See also -ID.

feline *a.* of or relating to cats, catlike; belonging to the Felidae, the cat family. *Also n.* WH: 17C. Latin *felinus*, from *feles* cat. See also -INE.

fell[1] *v.t.* to cut down. *Also n.* WH: pre-1200. Old English *fellan*, from Germanic. Rel. to FALL.

fell[2] *n.* the hide or skin of an animal, esp. if covered with hair; a fleece. WH: pre-1200. Old English *fel*, from Germanic, from Indo-European base also of Latin *pellis* (cp. PELLICLE), Greek *pella* skin. Rel. to FILM.

fell[3] *n.* a rocky hill. WH: 12–14C. Old Norse *fjall* and *fell* hill, mountain, prob. rel. to German *Fels* rock.

fell[4] *a.* cruel, savage, fierce. *Also adv.* WH: 12–14C. Old French *fel*, from Medieval Latin *fello* villain, FELON[1].

fella *n.* fellow, man. WH: 19C. Representation of affected (or nonstandard) pronun. of FELLOW. Cp. FELLER.

fellah *n.* an Egyptian agricultural labourer or peasant. WH: 18C. Arabic *fallāh*, coll. pl. *fallāhīn*, tiller of the soil, from *falaha* to split, to till the soil.

fellatio *n.* oral stimulation of the penis. WH: 19C. Modern Latin, from Latin *fellatus*, p.p. of *fellare* to suck.

feller *n.* fellow, man. WH: 19C. Representation of affected (or nonstandard) pronun. of FELLOW. Cp. FELLA.

felloe *n.* any one of the curved segments of a wheel, to which the spokes are attached. WH: pre-1200. Old English *felg*, from Germanic, of unknown orig.

fellow *n.* a man, a boy. *Also a., v.t.* WH: pre-1200. Old English *fēolaga*, from Old Norse *félagi*, from *fé* FEE + Germanic base of LAY[1]. The literal meaning is a fee-layer, i.e. one who lays down money in a joint enterprise. Former meanings (both to the 17C) were sharer, female companion.

felo de se *n.* a person who commits felony by suicide. WH: 17C. Anglo-Latin FELON[1] of himself, from *felo* + *de* of + *se* himself.

felon[1] *n.* a person who has committed a felony. *Also a.* WH: 12–14C. Old French, oblique case of *fel*, from Medieval Latin *fello*, *fellonis*, of unknown orig. Cp. FELL[4]. Some derive the Old French word from Frankish *fillo*, from *filljo* one who beats (a slave), rel. to FELL[2]. Others regard it as originally a term of abuse, from Latin *fellare* to suck (cp. FELLATIO).

felon[2] *n.* a whitlow or abscess close to the nail. WH: 12–14C. Appar. from FELON[1]. Medieval Latin *fello* had the same specific sense.

felsite *n.* felstone. WH: 18C. FELDSPAR + -ITE[1].

felstone *n.* feldspar occurring in compact masses. WH: 19C. Partial trans. of German *Felsstein*, from *Fels* rock + *Stein* stone.

felt *n.* a kind of cloth made of wool or wool and cotton compacted together by rolling, beating and pressing; similar cloth or material made from other fibres. *Also a., v.t., v.i.* WH: pre-1200. Old English, from Germanic base rel. to that of FILTER.

felucca *n.* a small vessel used in the Mediterranean, propelled by oars or lateen sails or both. WH: 17C. Italian, prob. from obs. Spanish *faluca*, ? from Arabic word of unknown orig.

felwort *n.* a gentian with purple flowers, *Gentianella amarella*. WH: pre-1200. Old English *feldwyrt*, from *feld* FIELD + *wyrt* WORT.

female *a.* denoting the sex which gives birth to young or lays eggs from which new individuals are developed. *Also n.* WH: 12–14C. Old French *femelle*, from Latin *femella*, dim. of *femina* woman. The form of the current word is due to association with MALE.

feme *n.* a woman or wife. WH: 16C. Old French (Modern French *femme*), from Latin *femina* woman.

feminine *a.* of, relating to or characteristic of women or the female sex. WH: 14–15C. Old French *féminin* or Latin *femininus*, from *femina* woman. See also -INE.

femme *n.* a particularly feminine or effeminate person. WH: mid-20C. French woman. See FEME.

femme de chambre *n.* a chambermaid. WH: 18C. French woman of the bedroom, from FEMME + *de* of + *chambre* CHAMBER.

femme fatale *n.* a seductive woman, esp. one who lures men to their downfall. WH: early 20C. French fatal woman, from FEMME + fem. of *fatal* FATAL.

femto- *pref.* a thousand million millionth (10⁻¹⁵). WH: Danish or Norwegian *femten* fifteen. See also -O-.

femur *n.* the thigh bone. WH: 15C. Latin thigh.

fen[1] *n.* low, flat and marshy land. WH: pre-1200. Old English, from Germanic. Cp. German *Fenn*.

fen[2] *n.* a Chinese monetary unit worth one-hundredth of a yuan; a coin of this value. WH: 19C. Chinese *fēn* to divide, to distribute, fraction.

fence *n.* a structure, e.g. a line of posts, serving to enclose and protect a piece of ground. *Also v.t., v.i.* WH: 12–14C. Shortening of DEFENCE. The original sense (to the 16C) was the act of defending.

fencible *n.* a soldier enlisted for home defence. *Also a.* WH: 12–14C. Shortening of *defensible* (DEFEND).

fend *v.t.* to provide for, to support. *Also v.i.* WH: 12–14C. Shortening of DEFEND.

fender *n.* a piece of furniture, usu. of iron or brass, placed on the hearth to keep in falling coals, ashes etc. WH: 12–14C. FEND + -ER[1].

fenestella *n.* a niche on the south side of the altar containing the piscina, and often the credence. WH: 14–15C. Latin, dim. of *fenestra* window. See also -EL.

fenestra *n.* a window-like aperture in a bone. WH: 19C. Latin window.

feng shui *n.* in Chinese philosophy, a system of good and bad influences in the environment, used when deciding where to locate buildings etc. WH: 18C. Chinese *fēng* wind + *shuĭ* water.

Fenian *n.* a member of an Irish secret society which was formed in America in about 1858, having as its object the overthrow of the British government in Ireland, and the establishment of an independent republic. *Also a.* WH: 19C. Old Irish *féne* a name of the ancient population of Ireland, confused with *fian* the guard of legendary kings. Cp. FIANNA FÁIL.

fennec *n.* a small fox, *Vulpes zerda*, common in Africa. WH: 18C. Arabic *fanak*, from Persian.

fennel *n.* a fragrant umbelliferous plant with yellow flowers, *Foeniculum vulgare*, whose seeds and leaves are used as flavourings. WH: pre-1200. Old English *finugl*, from Latin *faeniculum*, dim. of *faenum* hay.

fent *n.* the opening left in a garment (as in a shirtsleeve) for convenience of putting it on. WH: 14–15C. Old French *fente* slit, from fem. p.p. (used as n.) of Latin *findere* to cleave, to split. Cp. VENT[2].

fenugreek *n.* a leguminous plant, *Trigonella foenum-graecum*, the seeds of which are used as a flavouring or in animal fodder. WH: pre-1200. Old English *fenogrecum*, from Latin *faenugraecum*, from *faenum Graecum* Greek hay. The Romans used the dried plant for fodder.

feoff *v.t.* to grant possession to, to enfeoff. *Also n.* WH: 12–14C. Old French *fieuffer*. See FIEF.

ferae naturae *a.* (of deer, hares, pheasants etc.) wild, as distinguished from domesticated. WH: 17C. Latin of wild nature, from gen. sing. of *fera natura*, from fem. of *ferus* wild + *natura* NATURE.

feral *a.* wild, savage. WH: 17C. Latin *fera* wild animal, use as n. of *ferus* wild + -AL[1].

fer de lance *n.* the yellow viper of Central and S America, *Bothrops atrox*. WH: 19C. French iron (head) of lance, from *fer* iron + *de* of + *lance* LANCE. The name alludes to the shape of the snake's head.

feretory *n.* the bier or shrine in which relics of saints were carried in procession. WH: 12–14C. Old French *fiertre*, from Latin *feretrum*, from Greek *pheretron* bier, from *pherein* to bear, assim. to words in -tory.

ferial *a.* in the Church calendar, of or relating to ordinary weekdays as opposed to festival or fast days. WH: 14–15C. Old French *férial* or Medieval Latin *ferialis*, from Latin *feria* holiday (cp. FAIR[2]). See also -AL[1].

ferine *a.* feral. WH: 17C. Latin *ferinus*, from *fera*. See FERAL, also -INE.

fermata *n.* a continuation of a note or rest beyond its usual length; pause. WH: 19C. Italian stop, pause, from *fermare* to stop.

ferment[1] *n.* agitation, uproar. WH: 14–15C. Old French, or from Latin *fermentum*, from *fervere* to boil. See also -MENT.

ferment[2] *v.t.* to excite fermentation in. *Also v.i.* WH: 14–15C. Old French *fermenter*, from Latin *fermentare*, from *fermentum*. See FERMENT[1]. The current general sense evolved in the 17C.

fermeture *n.* the mechanism for closing the breech of a gun or other firearm. WH: 19C. French closure, from *fermer* to close, from Latin *firmare*, from *firmus* FIRM[1].

fermi *n.* a unit of length equal to 10⁻¹⁵ metre. WH: early 20C. Enrico Fermi, 1901–54, Italian-born physicist.

fern *n.* a non-flowering plant springing from a rhizome, and having the reproductive organs on the lower surface of fronds or leaves, which are often divided in a graceful, feathery form. WH: pre-1200. Old English *fearn*, from Germanic. Cp. German *Farn*.

ferocious *a.* fierce, cruel. WH: 17C. Latin *ferox*, *ferocis* fierce. See also -IOUS.

-ferous *suf.* bearing, producing, having, as in *auriferous*, *glandiferous*. WH: French -*fère* or Latin -*fer* carrying, bearing, from *ferre* to carry, to bear. See also -OUS.

†ferrandine *n.* a mixed cloth of silk and other materials. WH: 17C. French, from Italian *ferrandina*, from *ferro* iron. The name refers to the cloth's light grey colour.

ferrara *n.* a broadsword of special excellence. WH: 18C. Of disputed orig. According to some, the word is from Andrea dei *Ferrara* of Belluno, Italy. According to others, it is from *Ferrara*, a city in N Italy, where it was originally made. Others again take it from Latin *ferrarius* smith. The sword is also known as *Andrew Ferrara*, hence the first theory.

ferrate *n.* a salt of the hypothetical ferric acid. WH: 19C. Latin *ferrum* iron + -ATE[1].

ferret[1] *n.* a partially tamed variety of polecat, *Mustela putorius furo*, used for killing rats and driving rabbits out of their holes. *Also v.t., v.i.* WH: 14–15C. Old French *fuiret* (Modern French *furet*), alt. of *fuiron*, from Late Latin *furo*, *furonis* thief, ferret, from Latin *fur* thief. See also -ET[1]. Cp. FURTIVE.

ferret[2] *n.* a tape made of silk or cotton. WH: 16C. Prob. from Italian *fioretti* floss-silk, pl. of *fioretto*, dim. of *fiore* FLOWER.

ferri- *comb. form* denoting a compound of iron in the ferric state. WH: Latin *ferrum* iron.

ferriage *n.* conveyance by a ferry. WH: 12–14C. FERRY + -AGE.

ferric *a.* of, relating to or extracted from iron. WH: 18C. Latin *ferrum* iron + -IC.

ferricyanic *a.* of or relating to a compound of iron in its ferric state with cyanogen. WH: 19C. FERRI- + CYANIC.

ferriferous *a.* yielding iron. WH: 19C. Latin *ferrum* iron + -FEROUS.

ferrimagnetism *n.* the spontaneous magnetization of a substance in which one group of magnetic atoms is arranged in an opposite direction to the other. WH: mid-20C. FERRI- + *magnetism* (MAGNET).

Ferris wheel *n.* a big, upright revolving fairground wheel with seats suspended from its rim. WH: 19C. George W. G. *Ferris*, 1859–96, US engineer + WHEEL. Ferris designed the wheel for the World's Columbian Exposition held in Chicago in 1893.

ferrite *n.* a sintered ceramic consisting of a mixture of ferric oxide and other metallic oxides, which possesses magnetic properties. WH: 19C. Latin *ferrum* iron + -ITE[1].

ferro- *comb. form* denoting a substance containing iron. WH: Latin *ferrum* iron. See also -O-.

ferrocalcite *n.* calcite containing carbonate of iron and turning brown on exposure. WH: 19C. FERRO- + CALCITE.

ferroconcrete *n.* concrete strengthened with iron bars, strips etc.; reinforced concrete. *Also a.* WH: early 20C. FERRO- + CONCRETE[1].

ferrocyanic *a.* of or relating to iron in the ferrous state and cyanogen. WH: 19C. FERRO- + CYANIC.

ferroelectric *a.* (of materials) showing spontaneous electric polarization, but not conducting electric current. *Also n.* WH: mid-20C. FERRO- + ELECTRIC.

ferromagnetism *n.* the magnetic properties of certain materials, e.g. iron and cobalt, that are easily magnetized, vary in their degree of magnetization depending on the strength of the applied magnetizing field, and in some cases retain their magnetization when that field is withdrawn. WH: 19C. FERRO- + *magnetism* (MAGNET).

ferrosilicon *n.* a compound of silicon and iron added to molten iron to give it a larger proportion of silicon. WH: 19C. FERRO- + SILICON.

ferrotype *n.* a positive photograph on a sensitized film laid on a thin iron plate. WH: 19C. FERRO- + TYPE.

ferrous *a.* containing iron. WH: 19C. Latin *ferrum* iron + -OUS.

ferruginous *a.* containing iron or iron rust. WH: 17C. Latin *ferrugo, ferruginis* iron rust, dark red, from *ferrum* iron + -OUS.

ferrule *n.* a metallic ring or cap on the handle of a tool, the end of a stick, the joint of a fishing rod, a post etc. to strengthen it. WH: 17C. Alt. (prob. by assim. to Latin *ferrum* iron and -ULE) of earlier *verrel*, from Old French *virelle* (Modern French *virole*), from Latin *viriola*, dim. of *viriae* bracelets.

ferry *v.t.* to transport over a river, strait or other narrow expanse of water, in a boat, barge etc. *Also v.i., n.* WH: pre-1200. Old English *ferian*, from Germanic, from base of FARE. The original noun sense was place where a boat regularly transports passengers. This sense was soon after transferred to the boat itself.

fertile *a.* able to support abundant growth. WH: 14–15C. French, from Latin *fertilis*, from *ferre* to bear. See also -IL.

ferula *n.* any umbelliferous plant of the Mediterranean genus *Ferula*, esp. the giant fennel *F. communis* with a thick stem. WH: 14–15C. Latin giant fennel, rod.

ferule *n.* a rod or cane formerly used to punish children in school. *Also v.t.* WH: 14–15C. Latin FERULA.

fervent *a.* ardent, vehement. WH: 12–14C. Old French, from Latin *fervens, ferventis*, pres.p. of *fervere* to boil, to glow. See also -ENT.

fescennine *a.* scurrilous, licentious. WH: 17C. Latin *Fescenninus* pertaining to Fescennia in Etruria, a town noted for its scurrilous dialogues in verse + -INE.

fescue *n.* a grass of the genus *Festuca*, important for pasture. WH: 14–15C. Old French *festu* (Modern French *fétu*), from Latin *festuca* stalk, stem, straw. The original sense (to the 17C) was straw, twig, and hence something trivial. In the 16C a fescue was a small stick used for pointing out letters to children learning to read.

fess[1] *n.* a broad band of metal or colour crossing a shield horizontally, and occupying one-third of it. *Also adv.* WH: 15C. Old French *fesse*, alt. of *faisse*, from Latin FASCIA.

fess[2] *v.i.* to confess. WH: 19C. Shortening of CONFESS.

-fest *comb. form* an event or gathering for a particular activity, as in *songfest*. WH: 19C. German *Fest* festival.

festal *a.* festive, joyous, gay, merry. WH: 15C. Old French, from Late Latin *festalis*, from *festum*. See FEAST, also -AL[1].

fester *v.i.* to become septic. *Also v.t., n.* WH: 14–15C. Old French *festrir*, from *festre*, from Latin FISTULA.

†festinate[1] *a.* hasty, hurried. WH: 17C. Latin *festinatus*, p.p. of *festinare* to hasten. See also -ATE[2].

†festinate[2] *v.i.* to hasten. *Also v.t.* WH: 16C. Latin *festinatus*, p.p. of *festinare* to hasten. See also -ATE[3].

festival *n.* a day or period of celebration or holiday, often with religious significance. *Also a.* WH: 14–15C. Old French, from Medieval Latin *festivalis*, from *festivus*, from *festum*. See FEAST, also -AL[1].

festoon *n.* a decorative chain or garland of flowers, foliage, drapery etc. suspended by the ends to hang as a curve. *Also v.t.* WH: 17C. French *feston*, from Italian *festone* festal ornament, from Latin *festa*. See FEAST, also -OON.

Festschrift *n.* a collection of learned writings by various authors, published in honour of a scholar. WH: early 20C. German, lit. celebration writing, from *Fest* celebration, FEAST + *Schrift* writing.

feta *n.* a firm white Greek cheese made from sheep's or goat's milk. WH: mid-20C. Modern Greek *pheta* slice (of cheese), from Italian *fetta*.

fetch[1] *v.t.* to go for and bring back. *Also v.i., n.* WH: pre-1200. Old English *feccan*, alt. of *fetian* (obs. English v. *fet*), prob. rel. to Old English *fatian*, rel. to German *fassen* to grasp, from base of VAT. As a noun, *fetch* formerly (in the 16C) meant contrivance, trick. Echoes of this sense remain in *far-fetched* (FAR).

fetch[2] *n.* a wraith or double. WH: 17C. Orig. unknown.

fête *n.* an outdoor event with stalls and entertainments, usu. locally organized to raise money for charity. *Also v.t.* WH: 14–15C. French, from Old French *feste* FEAST.

fetial *a.* of or relating to the priests in ancient Rome, who presided over the ceremonies connected with the ratification of peace or the formal declaration of war. *Also n.* WH: 16C. Latin *fetialis*, of unknown orig.

fetid *a.* having an offensive smell; stinking. WH: 14–15C. Latin *fetidus*, from *fetere* to stink. See also -ID.

fetish *n.* an object providing sexual gratification. WH: 17C. French *fétiche*, from Portuguese *feitiço* charm, sorcery, use as n. of a. meaning made as art, from Latin *facticius* FACTITIOUS.

fetlock *n.* the back projecting part of a horse's leg, between the pastern and the cannon-bone. WH: 12–14C. From Germanic (cp. German *Fessel* fetlock), from Indo-European base of FOOT. Cp. FETTER. The second element is a diminutive suffix (see -OCK) but was assimilated to LOCK[2].

fetter *n.* a chain for the feet. *Also v.t.* WH: pre-1200. Old English *feter*, from Germanic (cp. German *Fesser* fetter), from Indo-European base of FOOT. Cp. FETLOCK.

fettle *v.t.* to clean, trim or put right. *Also v.i., n.* WH: pre-1200. Old English *fetel*, from Germanic base meaning to grasp, to hold. Cp. German *Fessel* chain, band.

fettuccine *n.* tagliatelle. WH: early 20C. Italian, pl. of *fettuccina*, dim. of *fetta* slice. Cp. FETA.

feu *n.* a perpetual lease at a fixed rent. *Also v.t.* WH: 15C. Old French FEE.

feud[1] *n.* hostility between two tribes or families in revenge for an injury, often carried on for several generations. *Also v.i.* WH: 12–14C. Old French *fede*, from Germanic, from base of FOE. Cp. Old English *fǣhth* enmity.

feud[2] *n.* land held on condition of performing certain services; a fief. WH: 12–14C. Medieval Latin *feudum*. See FEE.

feu de joie *n.* the firing of guns in token of public rejoicing. WH: 17C. French fire of joy, from *feu* FIRE + *de* of + *joie* JOY. The original sense was bonfire. The current sense arose in the 18C.

fever *n.* an abnormally high body temperature and quickened pulse, often accompanied by delirium. *Also v.t., v.i.* WH: pre-1200. Old English *fēfer*, from Latin *febris*. The current form has been influenced by French *fièvre*, from Latin.

feverfew *n.* a bushy strong-scented plant, *Tanacetum parthenium*. WH: pre-1200. Latin *febrifuga*, from *febris* fever + *fugare* to drive away. Cp. FEBRIFUGE. The plant is so called as it was formerly used as a febrifuge.

few a. not many. *Also pron., n.* WH: pre-1200. Old English *fēawe*, from Germanic, from Indo-European base also of Latin *paucus* (cp. PAUCITY), Greek *pauros* small.

fewter n. a rest for the lance attached to the saddle (orig. lined with felt). WH: 14–15C. Old French *feutre*, from Medieval Latin *filtrum*. See FILTER.

fey a. eccentric, odd in a whimsical, other-worldly way. WH: pre-1200. Old English *fǣge*, from Germanic. Cp. German *feige* cowardly. Not rel. to FAY.

Feynman diagram n. a graphical representation of the interactions between subatomic particles. WH: mid-20C. Richard P. *Feynman*, 1918–88, US nuclear physicist who devised it + DIAGRAM.

fez n. a flat-topped conical usu. red cap without a brim, fitting close to the head, with a tassel of silk, wool etc., worn by men in the Middle East. WH: 19C. Turkish *fes*, from *Fez* (now Fès), a town in Morocco, where it was originally made.

fiacre n. a small four-wheeled horse-drawn carriage. WH: 17C. French, from the Hôtel de St *Fiacre*, rue St Antoine, Paris, where the vehicles were first hired out. St Fiacre, d. *c*.670, was an Irish saint who settled as a hermit near Meaux, east of Paris.

fiancé n. the man to whom a woman is engaged to be married. WH: 19C. French, from Old French *fiancer* to betroth, from *fiance* promise, engagement, from *fier* to trust. Cp. AFFIANCE.

fianchetto n. in chess, the development of a bishop to a long diagonal of the board. *Also v.t.* WH: 19C. Italian, dim. of *fianco* FLANK.

Fianna Fáil n. one of the major political parties in the Republic of Ireland. WH: early 20C. Irish, from *fianna*, pl. of *fian* band of warriors + *Fáil*, gen. of *Fál*, an ancient name of Ireland, lit. defensive fortification, rel. to Latin VALLUM and WALL. The party name is conventionally interpreted as Warriors of Destiny. *Fál* itself is an ancient 'stone of destiny' (Irish *lia fáil*) at Tara, Co. Meath. Cp. FENIAN.

fiar n. a person who has the fee simple or reversion of property. WH: 15C. FEE + -AR[3].

fiasco n. a complete and humiliating failure. WH: 19C. Italian bottle, FLASK. The current sense derives from the Italian phrase *far fiasco* literally to make a bottle, with an unexplained allusion.

fiat n. an order, command, decree, esp. an arbitrary one. WH: 14–15C. Latin let it be done, 3rd pers. sing. pres. subj. of *fieri* to be made, to come about.

fib n. a harmless lie. *Also v.i.* WH: 16C. ? Abbr. of obs. *fible-fable* nonsense, redupl. of FABLE. Cp. coll. sense of STORY.

Fibonacci series n. a series of numbers, e.g. 1, 1, 2, 3, 5, in which each number is the sum of the preceding two numbers. WH: 17C. Leonardo *Fibonacci*, *c*.1170–1250, Tuscan mathematician.

fibre n. a slender filament; a thread, string or filament, of which the tissues of animals and plants are made. WH: 14–15C. Old French, from Latin *fibra*.

fibril n. a little fibre. WH: 17C. Modern Latin *fibrilla*, dim. of *fibra* FIBRE.

fibrillate[1] v.i. (of a fibre) to split into fibrils. *Also v.t.* WH: 19C. Latin *fibrilla* (see FIBRIL) + -ATE[3].

fibrillate[2] a. of or relating to fibrils or a fibrous structure. WH: 19C. Latin *fibrilla* (see FIBRIL) + -ATE[2].

fibrin n. a protein contained in the blood, causing it to clot. WH: 19C. FIBRE + -IN[1].

fibro n. a cement mixed with asbestos fibre, used in sheets for building. WH: mid-20C. Abbr. of *fibro-cement*. See FIBRO-, CEMENT.

fibro- comb. form denoting a substance consisting of or characterized by fibres. WH: Latin, from *fibra* FIBRE. See also -O-.

fibroblast n. a cell that contributes to the formation of connective tissue fibres. WH: 19C. FIBRO- + -BLAST.

fibroid a. of the nature or form of fibre or fibrous tissue. *Also n.* WH: 19C. FIBRE + -OID.

fibroin n. the protein that is the chief constituent of silk, cobwebs, the horny skeleton of sponges etc. WH: 19C. FIBRO- + -IN[1].

fibroline n. a yarn spun from waste in hemp, flax and jute, used for backing carpets, rugs etc. WH: mid-20C. FIBRO- + -/- + -INE.

fibroma n. a benign fibrous tumour. WH: 19C. Latin *fibra* FIBRE + -OMA.

fibrosis n. scarring and thickening of fibrous connective tissue, often resulting from an injury. WH: 19C. Latin *fibra* FIBRE + -OSIS.

fibrositis n. the inflammation of fibrous tissue, muscular rheumatism. WH: early 20C. *fibrose* (FIBRE, -OSE[1]) + -ITIS. The term was coined in 1904 by the English physician William R. Gowers.

fibula n. the outer and smaller bone of the leg. WH: 16C. Latin brooch, ? from base of *figere* to fix. The bone is so named from its resemblance to the tongue of a clasp, with the tibia forming the other part.

-fic suf. forming adjectives from nouns, verbs etc., as in *honorific, malefic, terrific*. WH: French -*fique*, from Latin -*ficus* making, doing, from base of *facere* to make, to do.

-fication suf. forming nouns from verbs in -FY, as in *purification*. WH: French, or from Latin -*ficatio*, -*ficationis*, from vv. with p.p. in -*ficatus*. Cp. -FY.

fichu n. a light shawl or scarf worn by women over the neck and shoulders. WH: 18C. Orig. unknown. According to some, the word is from the past participle of *ficher* to put (on in a hurry), from Latin *figere* to fix. Cp. THROW as a term for a shawl or stole.

fickle a. changeable, inconstant. WH: pre-1200. Old English *ficol*, rel. to *gefic* deceit and *fǣcne* deceitful.The original meaning was deceitful, false. The sense changeable, inconstant evolved in the 12–14C.

†fico n. a fig; a worthless thing. WH: 16C. Italian, from Latin *ficus* FIG[1].

fictile a. capable of being moulded; moulded by art. WH: 17C. Latin *fictilis*, from *fictus*. See FICTION, also -IL.

fiction n. an invented narrative; a story. WH: 14–15C. Old French, from Latin *fictio, fictionis*, from *fictus*, p.p. of *fingere* to fashion. See also -ION. Cp. FEIGN.

ficus n. any plant of the genus *Ficus*, including the fig tree and the rubber plant. WH: 14–15C. Latin fig tree, fig.

fid n. a bar of wood or iron to support a topmast. WH: 17C. Orig. unknown.

-fid comb. form divided into parts. WH: Latin -*fidus* split.

Fid. Def. abbr. Defender of the Faith. WH: Abbr. of Latin FIDEI DEFENSOR.

fiddle n. a violin or stringed instrument with a bow. *Also v.i., v.t.* WH: pre-1200. Old English *fithele*, from Germanic, from Latin *vitulari* to celebrate a festival, to be joyful. *Vitula* was the Roman goddess of victory and jubilation. The sense of the verb *fiddle* runs: to play on the fiddle (14–15C), to make restless movements with the hands (16C), to cheat, to swindle (17C).

fiddley n. the iron framework enclosing the deckhatch leading to the stokehole of a steamer. WH: 19C. Orig. unknown.

fideicommissum n. a testator's bequest to trustees. WH: 18C. Latin *fidei-commissum*, neut. p.p. of *fidei-committere* to entrust something to a person's good faith, from *fidei*, dat. of *fides* FAITH + *committere* to entrust, COMMIT.

Fidei Defensor n. Defender of the Faith. WH: 16C. Latin Defender of the Faith, from *fidei*, gen. of *fides* FAITH + *defensor* defender, from *defendere* DEFEND + -OR. The title was first given to Henry VIII in 1521 by Pope Leo X for writing his *Assertio septem sacramentorum* (Declaration of the seven sacraments) against Luther. It was authorized as a royal title in 1544.

fideism n. the religious doctrine that knowledge can be attained only by faith not by reason. WH: 19C. Latin *fides* FAITH + -ISM.

fidelity n. careful and loyal observance of duty; faithful adherence to an agreement, a set of beliefs etc. WH: 14–15C. French *fidélité*, from Latin *fidelitas* faithful, from *fides* FAITH. See also -ITY.

fidget v.i. to move about restlessly. *Also v.t., n.* WH: 17C. dial. *fidge* to move about restlessly, ? rel. to obs. *fig* to move briskly, var. of dial. *fyke*, from Old Norse *fikja* to move briskly, to be restless.

Fido n. an apparatus that allows aircraft to land by dispersing fog, using petrol burners positioned on the ground. WH: mid-20C. Acronym of *fog investigation dispersal operation*, punning on dog's name *Fido*, from Latin *fido* I trust.

fiducial a. denoting a fixed point or line used as a basis for measurement or comparison. WH: 16C. Late Latin *fiducialis*, from Latin *fiducia* trust, from *fidere* to trust. See also -AL[1], -IAL.

fidus Achates n. a trusty friend, a faithful companion. WH: 17C. Latin faithful Achates, from *fidus* faithful + *Achates*, the name of the faithful friend of Aeneas in Virgil's *Aeneid* (1C BC).

fie *int.* used to express contempt, irony, disgust, shame or impatience. WH: 12–14C. Old French *fi*, from Latin exclamation of disgust at a foul smell. Cp. PHEW.

fief *n.* an estate held under the feudal system or in fee. WH: 17C. Old French. See FEE. Cp. FEOFF.

field *n.* a piece of land, esp. one enclosed for crops or pasture. *Also v.t., v.i.* WH: pre-1200. Old English *feld*, from Germanic. Cp. VELD. The word is not from *felled* (FELL[1]) as if land cleared of trees.

fieldfare *n.* a species of thrush, *Turdus pilaris*, a winter visitant in England. WH: pre-1200. Old English *feldefare*, prob. from *feld* FIELD + base of FARE. According to some, the second element of the Old English name is an alteration of *-ware* dwellers, related to Old English *warian* to guard (see WARE[2]). The bird would thus be a 'field dweller' rather than a 'field farer'.

fiend *n.* an evil spirit. WH: pre-1200. Old English *fēond*, from pres.p. of a Germanic v. that gave Old High German *fīen* to hate. Cp. German *Feind* enemy. The formation of the word is similar to that of FRIEND.

fierce *a.* furiously aggressive; violent. WH: 12–14C. Old French *fiers*, nom. of *fer* (Modern French *fier* proud), from Latin *ferus* untamed. Cp. FERAL.

fieri facias *n.* a writ to a sheriff to order a levy on the goods and chattels of a defendant in order to pay a sum or debt. WH: 14–15C. Latin cause (it) to be made, from *fieri* to come into being + 2nd pers. sing. pres. subj. of *facere* to make, to do.

fiery *a.* on fire, flaming with fire. WH: 12–14C. FIRE + -Y[1].

fiesta *n.* a holiday or festivity. WH: 19C. Spanish FEAST.

FIFA *abbr.* International Football Federation. WH: Abbr. of French *Fédération Internationale de Football Association* International Federation of Association Football.

fi. fa. *abbr.* fieri facias. WH: Abbr. of FIERI FACIAS.

fife *n.* a small flutelike pipe, chiefly used in military music. *Also v.i., v.t.* WH: 16C. German *Pfeife* PIPE, or from French *fifre*, from Swiss German *Pfifre*.

fifish *a.* disturbed in one's mind, cranky. WH: 19C. Appar. from *Fife*, a county in SE Scotland + -ISH[1].

fifteen *n.* the number or figure 15 or xv. *Also a.* WH: pre-1200. Old English *fiftēne*, from Germanic base of FIVE + -TEEN.

fifth *n.* any one of five equal parts. *Also a., n.* WH: pre-1200. Old English *fifta*, from Germanic, from Indo-European base also of Latin *quintus* (cp. QUINT), Greek *pemptos*. See also -TH[1].

fifty *n.* the number or figure 50 or l. *Also a.* WH: pre-1200. Old English *fiftig*, from Germanic. See FIVE, also -TY[2].

fig[1] *n.* the pear-shaped fleshy fruit of the genus *Ficus*, esp. *F. carica*. *Also v.t.* WH: 12–14C. Old French *figue*, from Provençal *figa*, alt. of Latin *ficus* fig tree, fig.

fig[2] *v.t.* to dress, deck, rig (up or out). *Also n.* WH: 17C. Var. of obs. *feague* to beat, to set going briskly, ? from *feak* to wipe the beak (of a falcon) after feeding, from German *fegen* to cleanse.

fight *v.i.* to contend in arms or in battle, or in single combat (with, against). *Also v.t., n.* WH: pre-1200. Old English *feohtan*, from Germanic, from Indo-European base also of Greek *pugmē* fist (cp. PYGMY). Cp. German *fechten* to fence, to fight.

figment *n.* an invented statement, something that exists only in the imagination. WH: 14–15C. Latin *figmentum*, from base of *fingere* to fashion. See also -MENT. Cp. FICTION.

figuline *a.* made of clay; earthenware. *Also n.* WH: 17C. Latin *figulinus*, from *figulus* potter. See also -INE.

figura *n.* a person or thing that is representative or symbolic. WH: mid-20C. Latin. See FIGURE.

figure *n.* the external form of a person or thing. *Also v.t., v.i.* WH: 12–14C. Old French, from Latin *figura*, from base of *fingere* to fashion. See also -URE.

Fijian *n.* a native or inhabitant of the Fiji islands. *Also a.* WH: 19C. *Fiji*, an island state in the S Pacific + -AN.

†filaceous *a.* consisting of threads. WH: 17C. Latin *filum* thread + -ACEOUS.

filament *n.* a slender, threadlike fibre or fibril, such as those of which animal and vegetable tissues are composed. WH: 16C. French, or from Modern Latin *filamentum*, from Late Latin *filare* to spin, from Latin *filum* thread. See also -MENT.

filar *a.* of or relating to a thread. WH: 19C. Latin *filum* thread + -AR[1].

filaria *n.* any of the genus of threadlike parasitic nematode worms producing live embryos which find their way into the bloodstream of the human host. WH: 19C. Modern Latin former genus name, from Latin *filum* thread + *-aria* -ARY[1].

filature *n.* the reeling of silk from cocoons. WH: 18C. French, from Italian *filatura* to spin, from Late Latin *filare*. See also -URE.

filbert *n.* the nut of the cultivated hazel, *Corylus maxima*. WH: 14–15C. Anglo-French *philbert*, from St *Philibert* c.608–c.685, Frankish abbot. The nut was regarded as being ripe about St Philibert's day, 20 August.

filch *v.t.* to steal, to pilfer. *Also n.* WH: 12–14C. Orig. unknown.

file[1] *n.* a box or folder etc. in which documents are kept in order, for preservation and convenience of reference. *Also v.t., v.i.* WH: 16C. French *filer* to string on a thread, from Late Latin *filare* to spin, from Latin *filum* thread. The noun *file* derives from the earlier verb *file*, 14–15C.

file[2] *n.* a steel instrument with a ridged surface, used for cutting and smoothing metals, ivory, wood, fingernails etc. *Also v.t.* WH: pre-1200. Old English *fīl*, from Germanic, from Indo-European base also of Greek *pikros* sharp.

filet *n.* a kind of net or lace having a square mesh. WH: 19C. French. See FILLET.

filial *a.* of or relating to a son or daughter. WH: 14–15C. Old French, or from Ecclesiastical Latin *filialis*, from Latin *filius* son, *filia* daughter. See also -AL[1].

filibeg *n.* a kilt. WH: 18C. Gaelic *feileadh-beag* little kilt, from *feileadh* plaid + *beag* little.

filibuster *n.* a parliamentary obstructionist, a person who seeks to hinder legislation by prolonged speeches. *Also v.i., v.t.* WH: 16C. Orig. from Dutch *vrijbuiter* FREEBOOTER, then (in the 18C) from French *filibustier*, and finally (in the 19C) from Spanish *filibustero*, from French.

filiform *a.* having the form of a thread. WH: 18C. Latin *filum* thread + *-i-* + -FORM.

filigree *n.* ornamental work, executed in fine gold or silver wire, plaited, and formed into delicate openwork or tracery. *Also a.* WH: 17C. Alt. of obs. *filigreen*, var. of *filigrane*, from French, from Italian *filigrana*, from Latin *filum* thread + *granum* seed.

filings *n.pl.* the fine particles cut or rubbed off with a file. WH: 14–15C. Pl. of *filing*, from FILE[2] + -ING[1].

Filipino *n.* a native or inhabitant of the Philippine Islands. *Also a.* WH: 19C. Spanish, from (*las Islas*) *Filipinas* (the) Philippine (Islands).

fill *v.t.* to put or pour into until all the space is occupied. *Also v.i., n.* WH: pre-1200. Old English *fyllan*, from Germanic, from base of FULL[1].

fille de joie *n.* a prostitute. WH: 18C. French, lit. girl of pleasure, from *fille* girl + *de* of + *joie* pleasure, JOY.

fillet *n.* a fleshy portion or slice of meat. *Also v.t.* WH: 12–14C. Old French *filet*, from dim. of Latin *filum* thread. See FILE[1], also -ET[1]. The original sense was a ribbon or band worn on the head, then a strip of anything. The sense fleshy portion of meat arose in the 14–15C with reference to the strip of meat beneath an animal's ribs.

fillip *n.* a stimulus, an incentive, a boost. *Also v.t., v.i.* WH: 16C. Imit. Cp. FLIP.

fillis *n.* a kind of loosely-twisted string used to tie up plants etc. WH: early 20C. French *filasse* tow, from Latin *filum* thread.

fillister *n.* the rabbet on the outer edge of a sash bar. WH: 19C. ? French *feuilleret* in same sense.

filly *n.* a female foal. WH: 14–15C. Old Norse *fylja*, from Germanic base of FOAL. Not rel. to French *fille* girl, Latin *filia* daughter.

film *n.* a series of connected moving images projected on a screen; a story represented in this way. *Also v.t., v.i.* WH: pre-1200. Old English *filmen*, from Germanic, ult. from base of FELL[2]. The original sense (to the 18C) was membrane. The photographic sense evolved in the 19C with reference to the coating of emulsion on the photographic plate.

filo *n.* a kind of flaky pastry, usually layered in thin leaves. WH: mid-20C. Modern Greek *phullo* leaf.

Filofax® *n.* a small ring-binder with a leather or similar cover into which the owner can insert sheets at will to make up e.g. a diary, an address list etc., intended as a personal, portable compendium of information. **WH:** mid-20C. FILE[1] + -O- + pl. of FACT, representing *file of facts*.

filoplume *n.* a thread feather, one having an almost invisible stem. **WH:** 19C. Modern Latin *filopluma*, from Latin *filum* thread + *pluma* feather. See also -O-.

filose *a.* having or ending in a threadlike process. **WH:** 19C. Latin *filum* thread + -OSE[1].

filoselle *n.* floss silk. **WH:** 17C. French, from Italian *filosello*, from Popular Latin *fillicellus* little bug, influ. by Italian *filo* thread.

fils[1] *n.* a monetary unit of Bahrain, Iraq, Jordan, Kuwait and Yemen. **WH:** 19C. Coll. pronun. of Arabic *fals* small copper coin, from Greek *phollis* follis, small coin introduced by Diocletian, 296 AD.

fils[2] *n.* the son; junior; added to a French surname to distinguish a son from a father with the same name. **WH:** 19C. French son, from Latin *filius*. Cp. PÈRE.

filter *n.* an apparatus for straining liquids and freeing them from impurities, usu. by means of layers of material through which they are passed. *Also v.t., v.i.* **WH:** 14–15C. Old French *filtre*, var. of *feltre* (Modern French *feutre* felt), from Medieval Latin *filtrum*, from Germanic base rel. to that of FELT.

filth *n.* anything dirty or foul. **WH:** pre-1200. Old English *fylth*, from Germanic base of FOUL. See also -TH[1]. The original sense (to the 17C) was rotting or purulent matter.

filtrate *n.* any liquid that has passed through a filter. *Also v.t., v.i.* **WH:** 19C. Modern Latin *filtratus*, p.p. of *filtrare* to filter. See also -ATE[1].

fimbria *n.* the radiated fringe of the Fallopian tube. **WH:** 18C. Late Latin border, fringe.

fin *n.* the organ by which fish propel, balance and steer themselves, consisting of a membrane supported by rays. *Also v.t., v.i.* **WH:** pre-1200. Old English, from Germanic, prob. ult. rel. to Latin *pinna* feather, wing.

finagle *v.i.* to behave dishonestly. *Also v.t.* **WH:** early 20C. From obs. *fainaigue* to cheat, prob. from Old French *fornier* to deny, ult. from Latin *foris* outside, away + *negare* to deny.

final *a.* of, occurring at or relating to the end or conclusion. *Also n.* **WH:** 12–14C. Old French, or from Latin *finalis*, from *finis* end. See also -AL[1].

finale *n.* the last section or movement of a musical composition. **WH:** 18C. Italian, n. of a. from Latin *finalis*. See FINAL.

finance *n.* the system of management of (esp. public) revenue and expenditure. *Also v.t., v.i.* **WH:** 14–15C. Old French end, payment, money, from *finer* to make an end, to settle, from *fin* end.

finch *n.* any songbird of the family Fringillidae, including the bull-finch, chaffinch and canary, with a short conical beak that is used to crack seeds. **WH:** pre-1200. Old English *finc*, from Germanic, prob. imit. of its cry. Cp. dial. names of the bird, *pink, spink*.

find *v.t.* to chance on, to meet with. *Also v.i., n.* **WH:** pre-1200. Old English *findan*, from Germanic. Cp. German *finden*.

fin de siècle *a.* of, relating to or characteristic of the close of the nineteenth century. *Also n.* **WH:** 19C. French end of the century, from *fin* end + *de* of + *siècle* century.

fine[1] *a.* excellent in quality or appearance. *Also adv., v.t., v.i., n., int.* **WH:** 12–14C. Old French *fin*, from Latin *finire* FINISH.

fine[2] *n.* a sum of money imposed as a penalty for an offence. *Also v.t., v.i.* **WH:** 12–14C. Old French *fin*, from Latin *finis* end.

fine[3] *n.* old liqueur brandy. **WH:** early 20C. French, abbr. of *fine champagne* fine (brandy from) Champagne. The brandy comes from the Grande Champagne and Petite Champagne vineyards in the Charente region of France.

Fine Gael *n.* one of the major political parties in the Republic of Ireland. **WH:** mid-20C. Irish tribe of Gaels, from *fine* family group, race + *Gael* GAEL.

finery[1] *n.* fine clothes, showy decorations. **WH:** 17C. FINE[1] + -ERY, based on *bravery* (BRAVE).

finery[2] *n.* a hearth for converting cast iron into wrought iron. **WH:** 16C. French *finerie*, from Old French *finer* to refine. See also -ERY.

fines herbes *n.pl.* a mixture of chopped herbs used as flavouring. **WH:** 19C. French fine herbs, from fem. pl. of *fin* FINE[1] + pl. of *herbe* HERB. They are so called because finely chopped.

finesse *n.* elegance, refinement. *Also v.i., v.t.* **WH:** 12–14C. French, from base of *fin* FINE[1]. See also -ESS[1].

finger *n.* any of the five digits or parts at the end of the hand; any of the four longer digits as distinguished from the thumb. *Also v.t., v.i.* **WH:** pre-1200. Old English, from Germanic, prob. ult. rel. to FIVE.

fingering *n.* a thick, loose, woollen yarn used for knitting. **WH:** 17C. ? Alt. of French *fin grain* fine grain. Cp. GROGRAM.

finial *n.* a terminal ornament on top of the apex of a gable, pediment, roof, canopy etc. **WH:** 14–15C. Old French *fin*, from Latin *finis* end. See also -AL[1].

finical *a.* fussy, fastidious. **WH:** 16C. Prob. from FINE[1] + -ical (from -IC + -AL[1]). The word was originally university slang.

finis *n.* the end, finish, conclusion (printed at the end of a book). **WH:** 14–15C. Latin end.

finish *v.t.* to bring to an end. *Also v.i., n.* **WH:** 12–14C. Old French *fenir, feniss-* (Modern French *finir, finiss-*), from Latin *finire*, from *finis* end. See also -ISH[2].

finite *a.* having limits or bounds. **WH:** 14–15C. Latin *finitus*, p.p. of *finire* finish.

fink *n.* an informer. *Also v.t.* **WH:** 19C. Orig. unknown. Proposed origins include *Pink*, abbreviation of *Pinkerton*, referring to a member of the US Pinkerton detective force, or German *Fink* finch, a student nickname for one who did not join in duelling and drinking societies.

Finn *n.* a native inhabitant of Finland. **WH:** pre-1200. Old English *Finnas* (pl.), a name recorded as Latin *Fenni* by Tacitus, Greek *phinnoi* by Ptolemy. The Finns' own name for themselves is *Suomi*.

finnan haddock *n.* a kind of smoke-dried haddock. **WH:** 18C. *Findon*, a fishing village near Aberdeen, E Scotland + HADDOCK.

finnesko *n.* a boot made of the tanned skin of reindeer, having the hair on the outside. **WH:** 19C. Norwegian *finnsko*, from *Finn* FINN + *sko* shoe.

fino *n.* a light-coloured very dry sherry. **WH:** 19C. Spanish FINE[1].

fiorin *n.* white bent grass, *Agrostis stolonifera*. **WH:** 19C. Appar. from Irish *fiorthann* long coarse grass.

fioritura *n.* a decorative phrase or turn, a flourish added by the performer. **WH:** 19C. Italian, from *fiorire* to flower.

fipple *n.* an arrangement of a block and a sharp edge, the sound-producing mechanism in e.g. a recorder. **WH:** 17C. Orig. unknown. Cp. Icelandic *flipi* horse's lip.

fir *n.* any coniferous tree of the genus *Abies* with single needle-like leaves. **WH:** 14–15C. Prob. from Old Norse *fyri-*, from Germanic, from base also of Old English *furh-, fyrh-* as in *furhwudu* firwood.

fire *n.* the production of heat and light by combustion. *Also v.t., v.i., int.* **WH:** pre-1200. Old English *fyr*, from Germanic, from Indo-European base also of Greek *pur* fire. Cp. German *Feuer*.

firkin *n.* a measure of capacity; one quarter of a barrel or nine gallons (about 41 l). **WH:** 14–15C. Prob. from Middle Dutch dim. of *vierde* fourth. See also -KIN.

†firlot *n.* a dry measure, one quarter part of a boll. **WH:** 15C. Anglo-Latin *firlota*, prob. from Old Norse *fjórthi hlotr* fourth part. See FOURTH, LOT.

firm[1] *a.* stable, steady. *Also adv., v.t., v.i.* **WH:** 12–14C. Old French *ferme*, from Latin *firmus*.

firm[2] *n.* a business partnership. **WH:** 16C. Spanish and Italian *firma*, from Medieval Latin (cp. FARM), from Latin *firmare* to strengthen, from *firmus* FIRM[1].

firmament *n.* the sky regarded as an arch or vault. **WH:** 12–14C. Old French, from Latin *firmamentum*, from *firmare*. See FIRM[1], also -MENT.

firman *n.* a decree, mandate or order of an Eastern monarch, issued for any purpose, such as a passport, grant, licence etc. **WH:** 17C. Persian *firmān*. Cp. Sanskrit *pramāṇa* measure, standard, authority.

firn *n.* névé, snow on the higher slopes of lofty mountains, not yet consolidated into ice. **WH:** 19C. German, from Old High German *firni* old, rel. to Old Norse *forn* ancient.

first *a.* foremost in order, importance or excellence. *Also adv., n.* **WH:** pre-1200. Old English *fyrst*, from Germanic superl., from Indo-European base also of Latin *primus* (cp. PRIME[1]), Greek *prōtos* (cp. PROTON), Sanskrit *prathama*. Cp. German *Fürst* prince.

firth *n.* an estuary, a narrow inlet of the sea. **WH:** 14–15C. Old Norse *fjǫrthr* FJORD.

fisc *n.* the treasury of the State, the public purse or exchequer. WH: 16C. French, or from Latin *fiscus* rush basket, purse, treasury.

fiscal *a.* of or relating to the public revenue or exchequer or to taxes, financial. *Also n.* WH: 16C. French, or from Latin *fiscalis*, from *fiscus* treasury. See FISC.

fish[1] *n.* a cold-blooded vertebrate animal with gills and fins, living wholly in water. *Also v.i., v.t.* WH: pre-1200. Old English *fisc*, from Germanic, from Indo-European base also of Latin *piscis* fish. Cp. German *Fisch*.

fish[2] *n.* a flat piece of wood or iron etc. used to strengthen a beam etc. *Also v.t.* WH: 16C. French *fiche*, from *ficher* to fix, from Latin *figere* to fix.

fisk[1] *n.* the Crown Treasury of Scotland. WH: 16C. Scottish var. of FISC.

†fisk[2] *v.i.* to bustle. WH: 14–15C. ? Freq. of Old English *fȳsan* to hurry or *fēsian* to drive away (see FAZE), with *k* as in WALK or TALK.

fissi- *comb. form* divided; dividing; by division, as in *fissidactyl*, *fissiped*. WH: Latin *fissus*, p.p. of *findere* to split + *-i-*.

fissidactyl *a.* having the digits divided. WH: 19C. FISSI- + Greek *daktulos* finger.

fissile *a.* capable of undergoing nuclear fission. WH: 17C. Latin *fissilis*, from *fissus*, p.p. of *findere* to split. See also -IL.

fission *n.* the act or process of cleaving, splitting or breaking up into parts. WH: 17C. Latin *fissio, fissionis*, from *fissus*. See FISSILE, also -ION.

fissiparous *a.* reproducing by fission. WH: 19C. FISSI- + -PAROUS, based on VIVIPAROUS.

fissiped *a.* having the toes separate. *Also n.* WH: 17C. FISSI- + -PEDE.

fissirostral *a.* having a deeply cleft beak; belonging to the group of birds, Fissirostres. WH: 19C. FISSI- + Latin *rostrum* beak + -AL[1].

fissure *n.* a cleft made by the splitting or parting of any substance. *Also v.t., v.i.* WH: 14–15C. Old French, or from Latin *fissura*, from *fissus*. See FISSILE, also -URE.

fist *n.* the clenched hand, esp. in readiness to strike a blow. *Also v.t.* WH: pre-1200. Old English *fȳst*, from Germanic. Cp. German *Faust*.

fistula *n.* an abnormal or surgically made opening between a hollow organ and the skin surface or between two hollow organs. WH: 14–15C. Latin pipe, flute. Cp. FESTER.

fit[1] *a.* adapted, suitable. *Also v.t., v.i., n., adv.* WH: 14–15C. Orig. unknown. The original sense (to the 18C) was specifically (of an object) having the right measurements or size. The sense of the verb *fit* as used of clothes (to *fit* well) may owe something to confusion with SIT (to *sit* well), since handwritten *f* was similar to old 'long *s*' (like *f* without the crossbar).

fit[2] *n.* a sudden attack of epilepsy or other disease characterized by unconsciousness or convulsions. WH: pre-1200. Old English *fitt*, ? rel. to FIT[3].

†fit[3] *n.* a short canto or division of a poem. WH: pre-1200. Old English *fitt*, ? rel. to Old High German *fizza* border of cloth (cp. German *Fitze* skein of yarn) and Old Norse *fit* hem, but cp. FIT[2].

fitch *n.* a polecat. WH: 14–15C. Early Dutch *fisse, visse*. Cp. FITCHEW.

fitchew *n.* a polecat. WH: 14–15C. Old French *ficheau*, dial. var. of *fissel*, later *fissau*, dim. of a word occurring in early Dutch as *fisse*. See FITCH.

FitzGerald contraction *n.* the contraction that a moving body shows when its speed comes close to that of light. WH: early 20C. G. F. *FitzGerald*, 1851–1901, Irish physicist.

five *n.* the number or figure 5 or v. *Also a.* WH: pre-1200. Old English *fíf*, from Germanic, from Indo-European base also of Latin *quinque* (cp. QUINARY), Greek *pente* (cp. PENTA-), Sanskrit *pañca* (cp. PUNCH[2]).

fix *v.t.* to fasten, to secure firmly. *Also v.i., n.* WH: 14–15C. Medieval Latin *fixare*, from Latin *fixus*, p.p. of *figere* to fix, to fasten.

fixate *v.t.* to render fixed. WH: 19C. Latin *fixus* (see FIX) + -ATE[3].

fixity *n.* coherence of parts. WH: 17C. Partly from obs. *fix* fixed, from Old French, from Latin *fixus* (see FIX) + -ITY, partly from French *fixité*.

fixture *n.* anything fixed in a permanent position. WH: 16C. Alt. of obs. *fixure* fixed condition (from Late Latin *fixura*, from Latin *figere* FIX), based on MIXTURE. See also -URE.

fizgig *n.* a gadding, flirting girl. *Also a.* WH: 16C. Prob. from FIZZ + *gig* flighty girl, prob. of imit. orig.

fizz *v.i.* to make a hissing or spluttering sound. *Also n.* WH: 17C. Imit. Cp. HISS.

fizzle *v.i.* to fizz. *Also v.t., n.* WH: 14–15C. Imit. See FIZZ, also -LE[4]. The word originally (to the 18C) had the sense to break wind quietly. The current sense dates from the 19C.

fjord *n.* a long, narrow inlet of the sea, bounded by high cliffs, as in Norway. WH: 17C. Norwegian, from Old Norse *fjǫrthr*. Cp. FIRTH, FORD.

flabbergast *v.t.* to overwhelm with wonder and amazement; to astound, to stagger with surprise. WH: 18C. Orig. unknown. ? Based on FLABBY and AGHAST.

flabby *a.* hanging loosely. WH: 17C. Alt. of *flappy* (FLAP).

flabellate *a.* fan-shaped. WH: 19C. Latin *flabellum* fan + -ATE[2].

flabellum *n.* a fan, esp. one used in the Greek Church to drive away flies from the chalice or in the Roman Catholic Church to carry in religious processions. WH: 19C. Latin, from *flabrum* gust, from *flare* to blow + -ellum (see also -LE[2]).

flaccid *a.* lacking firmness or vigour. WH: 17C. French *flaccide* or Latin *flaccidus*, from *flaccus* flabby. See also -ID.

flack *n.* a publicity agent. WH: mid-20C. Orig. unknown. According to some, the word comes from the name of Gene *Flack*, a US film publicity agent.

flacon *n.* a small bottle, esp. a scent-bottle. WH: 19C. French. See FLAGON.

flag[1] *n.* a piece of cloth, usu. square or oblong, and plain or bearing a design, attached by one edge to a staff or rope by which it can be hoisted on a pole or mast, and displayed as a banner, ensign or signal. *Also v.t.* WH: 16C. ? From obs. *flag* drooping (of hair, animal's tail), of unknown orig. Cp. FLAG[2].

flag[2] *v.i.* to lose strength or vigour. *Also v.t.* WH: 16C. Rel. to obs. *flag* drooping. See FLAG[1].

flag[3] *n.* a broad flat stone used for paving. *Also v.t.* WH: 14–15C. Prob. from Scandinavian. Cp. Icelandic *flag* place where turf has been cut out, Old Norse *flaga* stone slab.

flag[4] *n.* any of various herbaceous plants with long bladelike leaves growing in moist places, chiefly belonging to the genus *Iris*. WH: 14–15C. Rel. to Dutch *flag*, Danish *flæg*, ult. of unknown orig.

flag[5] *n.* a quill-feather of a bird's wing. WH: 15C. Orig. unknown.

flagellate[1] *v.t.* to whip, to beat, to scourge. WH: 17C. Latin *flagellatus*, p.p. of *flagellare* to whip, from *flagellum*, dim. of *flagrum* scourge. See also -ATE[3].

flagellate[2] *a.* having whiplike outgrowths or flagella. *Also n.* WH: 19C. Latin *flagellum* (see FLAGELLATE[1]) + -ATE[2].

flageolet[1] *n.* a small wind instrument blown from a mouthpiece at the end, with two thumb holes and producing a shrill sound similar to but softer than that of the piccolo. WH: 17C. French, dim. of Old French *flagol*, from Provençal *flaujol*, of unknown orig. See also -ET[1]. Cp. FLUTE.

flageolet[2] *n.* a kind of French bean. WH: 19C. French, ult. from Latin *phaseolus* bean. See also -ET[1].

flagitate *v.t.* to demand with importunity. WH: 17C. Latin *flagitatus*, p.p. of *flagitare* to demand earnestly. See also -ATE[3].

flagitious *a.* heinous, flagrant, villainous. WH: 14–15C. Latin *flagitosus*, from *flagitium* importunity, from *flagitare*. See FLAGITATE, also -IOUS.

flagon *n.* a large squat bottle usually holding about 2 pints (1.13 l), in which wine is sold. WH: 14–15C. Old French *flacon*, from Late Latin *flasco, flasconis* FLASK.

flagrant *a.* openly outrageous. WH: 15C. French, or from Latin *flagrans, flagrantis*, pres.p. of *flagrare* to burn, to blaze. See also -ANT.

flail *n.* a wooden instrument consisting of a short heavy bar hinged to a longer staff or handle, used for threshing grain by hand. *Also v.t., v.i.* WH: pre-1200. Old English **flegel*, from Germanic, prob. from Latin *flagellum* scourge, flail.

flair *n.* a natural aptitude or gift; talent. WH: 19C. French, from *flairer* to smell, from Latin *fragrare*. See FRAGRANT.

flak *n.* fire from anti-aircraft guns. WH: mid-20C. German, abbr. of *Fliegerabwehrkanone*, lit. aviator defence gun.

flake[1] *n.* a fleecy particle (as of snow). *Also v.t., v.i.* WH: 12–14C. Prob. of Germanic orig. Cp. FLAW[1], FLAUGHT.

flake[2] *n.* a rack for drying fish. WH: 12–14C. ? Old Norse *flaki* wicker shield. Cp. Danish *flage* hurdle.

flam *n.* a false pretext, a sham, a deception, a lie. *Also a., v.t.* WH: 17C. Orig. uncertain. ? Abbr. of FLIMFLAM or obs. *flamfew* bauble, from obs. French *fanfelue* (now *fanfreluche*), from Medieval Latin *famfaluca* bubble, lie, appar. from Greek *pompholux* bubble.

flambé *v.t.* to sprinkle with brandy etc. and ignite. *Also a.* WH: 19C. French, p.p. of *flamber* to singe, to pass through flame, ult. from Latin *flamma* FLAME. Cp. FLAMBEAU.

flambeau *n.* a torch, esp. one made of thick wicks covered with wax or pitch. WH: 17C. French, dim. of *flambe*, from Latin *flammula*, dim. of *flamma* FLAME.

flamboyant *a.* exuberant, showy. WH: 19C. French, pres.p. of *flamboyer* to blaze, to flame, from *flambe*. See FLAMBEAU.

flame *n.* a mass or stream of vapour or gas in a state of combustion. *Also v.t., v.i.* WH: 12–14C. Old French *flamme*, from Latin *flamma*. The original Old English word for flame was *līeg*, related to LIGHT[1].

flamen *n.* an ancient Roman priest devoted to some special deity. WH: 12–14C. Latin.

flamenco *n.* a kind of music played on the guitar or sung by gypsies. WH: 19C. Spanish FLEMING, FLAMINGO. The word is said to have first applied to the music and dancing of gypsies of Andalusia, whose colourful show suggested the ruddy complexion of the Flemings and the bright pink plumage of the flamingo.

flamingo *n.* a long-necked web-footed wading bird, with a small body and very long legs, its feathers rose or scarlet in colour, belonging to the family Phoenicopteridae. WH: 16C. Var. of Spanish *flamenco* FLEMING, from the assoc. of the bird's colouring with the ruddy complexion of the Flemish or Dutch. Cp. FLAMENCO.

flammable *a.* that can catch fire and burn easily. WH: 19C. Latin *flammare*, from *flamma* flame. See also -ABLE. Cp. INFLAMMABLE.

flan *n.* an open pastry or sponge base with fruit or savoury filling. WH: 19C. French round cake, from Old French *flaon*, from Medieval Latin *flado*, *fladonis*, from Frankish, from Germanic.

flanch[1] *n.* a flange. WH: 18C. ? Old French *flanche* (fem.), *flanc* (m.) FLANK.

flanch[2] *v.i.* to slope inwards towards the top of a chimney. *Also v.t.* WH: 18C. FLANCH[1].

flaneur *n.* a lounger, an idler. WH: 19C. French *flâneur*, from *flâner* to lounge, to saunter idly, from Scandinavian *flana* to wander about.

flange *n.* a projecting rib or rim affixed to a wheel, tool, pipe etc., for strength, as a guide, or for attachment to something else. *Also v.t.* WH: 17C. Orig. uncertain. Rel. to FLANCH[1].

flank *n.* the fleshy or muscular part of the side between the hips and the ribs. *Also v.t., v.i.* WH: pre-1200. Old French *flanc*, from Frankish base meaning side. Rel. to LANK.

flannel *n.* a soft woollen fabric, with a light nap. *Also v.t., v.i.* WH: 12–14C. Prob. from Welsh *gwlanen* woollen article, from *gwlân* wool.

flap *v.t.* to move (wings, one's arms etc.) rapidly up and down or to and fro. *Also v.i., n.* WH: 12–14C. Prob. imit. Cp. CLAP[1].

flare *v.i.* to open or spread outwards at one end. *Also v.t., n.* WH: 16C. ? Scandinavian. The sense to blaze, to flame up arose in the 17C.

flash *v.i.* to send out a quick, sudden or regular gleam. *Also v.t., n., a.* WH: 12–14C. Appar. imit. Cp. DASH, PLASH[2], SLASH, SPLASH.

flask *n.* a small bottle or similar vessel. WH: 17C. French *flasque*, from Old French *flasche*, from Medieval Latin *flasca*, or from Italian *fiasco*, from Medieval Latin *flasco*. Cp. FLAGON.

flasket *n.* a long shallow basket with two handles. WH: 12–14C. Old French *flasquet*, dim. of *flasque*. See FLASK, also -ET[1].

flat[1] *a.* having a level and even surface. *Also adv., n., v.i.* WH: 12–14C. Old Norse *flatr*, from Germanic, from Indo-European base also of Greek *platus* flat, broad. Prob. rel. to PLATE.

flat[2] *n.* a set of rooms on one floor forming a separate residence. *Also v.i.* WH: 19C. Alt. of obs. *flet* floor, dwelling, house, ult. from Germanic base of FLAT[1]. The original sense of the word was floor, storey.

flatter *v.t.* to praise falsely or unduly. *Also v.i.* WH: 12–14C. Orig. uncertain. ? Back-formation from *flattery*, from Old French *flaterie*, from *flater*, prob. ult. from Germanic base of FLAT[1], meaning to pat, to smooth.

flatulent *a.* affected with or troubled by wind or gases generated in the alimentary canal. WH: 16C. French, from Modern Latin *flatulentus*, from Latin *flatus* blowing, blast, from *flare* to blow. See also -ULENT.

flaught *n.* a flapping, a commotion. WH: 12–14C. Prob. Old English or Old Norse, from Germanic, from base of FLAKE[1], FLAW[1].

flaunt *v.i.* to make an ostentatious or gaudy show. *Also v.t., n.* WH: 16C. Orig. unknown. The form of the word suggests a French origin, but no French source is known.

flautist *n.* a player of the flute. WH: 19C. Italian *flautista*, from *flauto* flute. See also -IST.

flavescent *a.* yellowish. WH: 19C. Latin *flavescens*, *flavescentis*, pres.p. of *flavescere*, from *flavus* yellow. See also -escent (-ESCENCE).

flavin *n.* any of various chemical compounds containing nitrogen that form the nucleus of certain natural yellow pigments. WH: 19C. Latin *flavus* yellow + -IN[1].

flavour *n.* that quality in any substance which affects the taste, or the taste and smell. *Also v.t.* WH: 14–15C. Old French *flaor* (influ. by *savour*), ? from blending of Latin *flatus* blowing, breath and *foetor* stench.

flaw[1] *n.* a defect, an imperfection. *Also v.t., v.i.* WH: 12–14C. Prob. from Old Norse *flaga* slab of stone, from Germanic base rel. to that of FLAKE[1]. Cp. FLAUGHT.

flaw[2] *n.* a sudden puff or gust. WH: 16C. Prob. from Middle Low German *vlāge* in basic sense stroke.

flax *n.* a plant of the genus *Linum*, esp. *L. usitatissimum*, the common flax, the fibre of which is made into yarn, and woven into linen cloth. WH: pre-1200. Old English *flæx*, from Germanic, prob. from Indo-European base found also in Greek *plekein*, Latin *plectare*, German *flechten* to plait.

flay *v.t.* to strip the skin from. WH: pre-1200. Old English *flēan*, from Germanic.

flea *n.* a small wingless blood-sucking insect belonging to the order Siphonaptera, parasitic on mammals and birds and noted for its leaping powers. WH: pre-1200. Old English *flēah*, from Germanic, prob. from same base as that of FLEE.

fleam *n.* a lancet for bleeding horses and cattle. WH: 14–15C. Old French *flieme* (Modern French *flamme*), from alt. of Late Latin *phlebotomus*, from Greek *phlebotomon*. See PHLEBOTOMY.

flèche *n.* a spire, esp. a slender one, usu. of wood covered with lead, over the intersection of the nave and transepts of a church. WH: 12–14C. Old French arrow, from Frankish. Cp. German *fliegen* to fly.

fleck *n.* a dot or patch of colour or light. *Also v.t.* WH: 14–15C. Orig. unknown. Cp. Old Norse *flekkr*, German *Fleck*.

fledge *v.t.* to provide with feathers or plumage. *Also v.i.* WH: 14–15C. Prob. back formation from Old English base of *unfligge*, rendering Latin *implumes* unfledged, from Germanic, from base of FLY[2].

flee *v.i.* to run away, as from danger to a place of safety. *Also v.t.* WH: pre-1200. Old English *flēon*, from Germanic. Prob. rel. to FLY[2].

fleece *n.* the woolly covering of a sheep or similar animal. *Also v.t.* WH: pre-1200. Old English *flēos*, from Germanic, prob. ult. from same base as that of Latin *pluma* feather.

fleech *v.t.* to flatter. WH: 14–15C. Orig. unknown. Cp. German *flehen* to beseech, Dutch *vleien* to flatter.

fleecy[1] *a.* woolly, wool-bearing. WH: 16C. FLEECE + -Y[1].

fleecy[2] *n.* a person whose job is to pick up fleeces after shearing. WH: 19C. FLEECY[1].

fleer *v.i.* to grin or laugh in contempt or scorn. *Also v.t., n.* WH: 14–15C. Prob. from Scandinavian. Cp. Norwegian and Swedish dial. *flira*, Danish dial. *flire* to grin, to laugh derisively.

fleet[1] *n.* a number of ships or smaller vessels with a common object, esp. a body of warships under one command. WH: pre-1200. Old English *flēot*, from *flēotan* to float, to swim. See FLEET[2].

fleet[2] *a.* rapid, speedy. *Also v.i., v.t.* WH: 16C. Prob. from Old Norse *fljótr*, from Germanic base of Old English *flēotan* to float, to swim. Cp. German *fliessen* to flow.

fleet[3] *a.* shallow. *Also adv.* WH: 17C. Prob. from an Old English word rel. to Dutch *vloot* shallow, from Germanic base of FLEET[2].

fleet[4] *n.* a creek, an inlet. WH: pre-1200. Old English *flēot*, from Germanic base of FLEET[2]. London's *Fleet* Street takes its name from the *Fleet* river (now channelled underground), its own name deriving from the Old English word.

Fleming *n.* a native of Flanders. WH: pre-1200. Old English *Flæmingi*, partly from Old Norse, partly from Middle Dutch *Vlaminc*, from *Vlām-*, base of *Vlaanderen* Flanders. See also -ING[3]. Cp. FLAMENCO, FLAMINGO.

flense *v.t.* to strip the blubber or the skin from (a whale or seal). WH: 19C. Danish *flensa*.

flesh *n.* the soft part of an animal body, esp. the muscular tissue, between the bones and the skin. *Also v.t.* WH: pre-1200. Old English *flæsc*, from Germanic. Cp. German *Fleisch*.

†fletch *v.t.* to feather (as an arrow). WH: 17C. Alt. of FLEDGE, prob. influ. by *fletcher* person who makes arrows, from Old French *flechier*, from *fleche* arrow, ult. of unknown orig.

fleur-de-lis *n.* the iris flower. WH: 12–14C. Old French *flour de lys*, from *flour* FLOWER + *de* of + *lys* LILY.

fleuret *n.* an ornament like a small flower. WH: 19C. French *fleurette*, dim. of *fleur* FLOWER. See also -ET[1].

fleuron *n.* a flower-shaped ornament, used for a tailpiece, in architecture, on coins etc. WH: 14–15C. Old French *floron* (Modern French *fleuron*), from *flour* FLOWER.

flews *n.pl.* the large lips of a deep-mouthed hound. WH: 16C. Pl. of *flew*, of unknown orig.

flex[1] *v.t.* to bend or cause to bend. *Also v.i.* WH: 16C. Latin *flexus*, p.p. of *flectere* to bend.

flex[2] *n.* flexible insulated wire. WH: early 20C. Abbr. of FLEXIBLE.

flexible *a.* pliant, easily bent. WH: 14–15C. Old French, or from Latin *flexibilis*, from *flexus*. See FLEX[1], also -IBLE.

flexitime *n.* a system of working which allows workers some freedom to choose the times when they arrive for and leave work, usu. so long as they are present during a stipulated period (core time). WH: late 20C. FLEXIBLE + TIME.

flexography *n.* a form of letterpress printing that uses flexible rubber or plastic plates and synthetic inks, used for printing on paper, packaging, plastics etc. WH: mid-20C. Latin *flexus* (see FLEX[1]) + -O- + -GRAPHY.

fley *v.t.* to frighten. WH: 12–14C. Old Norse *fleygja*, ult. from Germanic base of FLY[2].

flibbertigibbet *n.* a chatterer. WH: 14–15C. Prob. imit. of meaningless chatter, although the latter half of the word may have been suggested by GIBBET.

flick *n.* a smart, light blow or flip. *Also v.t., v.i.* WH: 14–15C. Imit.

flicker[1] *v.i.* to shine unsteadily. *Also n.* WH: pre-1200. Old English *flicorian*, from Germanic imit. base. Cp. German *flackern*.

flicker[2] *n.* any N American woodpecker of the genus *Colaptes*. WH: 19C. Imit. of bird's call.

flight[1] *n.* the act, manner or power of flying through the air. *Also v.t.* WH: pre-1200. Old English *flyht*, from Germanic, from base of FLY[2].

flight[2] *n.* the act of running away. WH: 12–14C. From Germanic base of FLEE. Cp. German *Flucht*. The word was probably in Old English but has not been recorded.

flimflam *n.* nonsense, rubbish. *Also v.t.* WH: 16C. Imit. redupl. Cp. *whim-wham* (WHIM).

flimsy *a.* without strength or solidity. *Also n.* WH: 18C. Prob. based on FLIMFLAM. See also -SY.

flinch *v.i.* to shrink from (an undertaking, suffering etc.). *Also n.* WH: 16C. Old French *flenchir* to turn aside, from Germanic. Rel. to LANK. Cp. FLANK.

flinder *n.* a fragment, a piece, a splinter. WH: 14–15C. Prob. from Scandinavian. Cp. Norwegian *flindra* thin chip, splinter.

fling *v.t.* to cast or throw with sudden force. *Also v.i., n.* WH: 12–14C. Prob. rel. to Old Norse *flengja* to flog.

flint *n.* a variety of quartz, usu. grey, smoke-brown or brownish-black and encrusted with white, easily chipped into a sharp cutting edge. WH: pre-1200. Old English, from Germanic. Rel. to SPLIT, SPLINTER and ? PLINTH.

flip *v.t.* to flick or toss (e.g. a coin) quickly to make it spin in the air. *Also v.i., n., a.* WH: 16C. Prob. contr. of FILLIP.

flippant *a.* trifling, lacking in seriousness. WH: 17C. FLIP + -ANT.

flirt *v.i.* to make sexual advances for amusement or self-gratification. *Also v.t., n.* WH: 16C. Appar. imit. Cp. FLICK, SPURT. The original sense (to the 18C) was to sneer, to scoff. The current sense dates from the 17C.

flisk *v.i.* to frisk. *Also n.* WH: 16C. Imit.

flit *v.i.* to pass from place to place. *Also n.* WH: 12–14C. Old Norse *flytja*, from base of *fljóta*. See FLEET[2]. The original sense was to change, to alter. The current sense dates from the 14–15C.

flitch *n.* a side of pork salted and cured. *Also v.t.* WH: pre-1200. Old English *flicce*, from Germanic.

flite *v.i.* to contend. *Also n.* WH: pre-1200. Old English *flītan*, from Germanic. Cp. German *sich befliessen* to busy oneself.

flitter *v.i.* to flit about. WH: 14–15C. FLIT + -ER[5].

flivver *n.* a cheap small motor car or aircraft. WH: early 20C. Orig. unknown.

flix *n.* fur, esp. the down of the beaver. WH: 17C. Orig. unknown.

flixweed *n.* a plant *Descurainia sophia*, formerly supposed to cure dysentery. WH: 16C. Obs. *flix*, var. of FLUX + WEED. The plant was said to be a remedy for dysentery.

float *v.i.* to be supported on the surface of or in a fluid. *Also v.t.* WH: pre-1200. Old English *flotian*, from Germanic base of FLEET[2].

floatel *n.* a boat or platform providing accommodation for offshore oil-rig workers. WH: mid-20C. Blend of FLOAT and HOTEL. Cp. MOTEL.

floc *n.* matter in woolly or loose floating masses precipitated in a solution. WH: early 20C. Shortening of Modern Latin *flocculus*, dim. of FLOCCUS. Cp. FLOCK[2].

floccus *n.* a tuft of woolly hair. WH: 19C. Latin FLOCK[2].

flock[1] *n.* a group of animals, esp. sheep, goats or birds. *Also v.i., v.t.* WH: pre-1200. Old English *flocc*, from Germanic, ult. of unknown orig.

flock[2] *n.* a lock or tuft of wool, cotton, hair etc. WH: 12–14C. Old French *floc*, from Latin FLOCCUS.

floe *n.* a large sheet of floating ice. WH: 19C. Prob. from Norwegian *flo*, from Old Norse *fló* layer, stratum. Cp. FLAW[1].

flog *v.t.* to beat with a whip or stick as punishment. *Also v.i.* WH: 17C. Prob. imit., or from Latin *flagellare* FLAGELLATE[1].

flong *n.* prepared paper used for the matrices in stereotyping. WH: 19C. French *flan* FLAN.

flood *n.* an abundant flow of water. *Also v.t., v.i.* WH: pre-1200. Old English *flōd*, from Germanic, from Indo-European base also of Greek *ploein* to swim.

floor *n.* the bottom surface of a room, on which people walk and which supports the furniture. *Also v.t.* WH: pre-1200. Old English *flōr*, from Germanic. Cp. German *Flur* open fields, meadow. Rel. to PLAIN[1].

floozie *n.* a woman who is attractive in a common sort of way and thought to be free with her company and favours. WH: early 20C. Orig. unknown. ? Rel. to *flossy* (FLOSS).

flop *v.i.* to tumble about or fall loosely. *Also v.t., n., adv.* WH: 17C. Var. of FLAP.

-flop *comb. form* floating-point operations per second, as in *megaflop*. WH: Acronym of *floating point*.

floptical *a.* of, relating to or designed for a kind of floppy disk drive that uses a laser to set the read-write head. WH: late 20C. Blend of *floppy* (FLOP) and *optical* (OPTIC).

flora *n.* the whole vegetation of a country, district or geological period. WH: 16C. Latin, from *Flora*, the Roman goddess of flowers and gardens, from *flos*, *floris* FLOWER. Cp. FAUNA.

Floréal *n.* the eighth month of the French revolutionary calendar, from 21 April to 20 May. WH: 19C. French, from Latin *floreus* flowery, from *flos*, *floris* FLOWER. See also -AL[1].

floreat *v.i.* may (a person, situation etc.) flourish. WH: 19C. Latin may he flourish, 3rd pers. sing. pres. subj. of *florere* to flower, to flourish. Cp. FLORUIT.

Florence *n.* a kind of red wine from Florence. WH: 12–14C. Old French, name of the chief city of Tuscany, W Italy, from Latin *Florentia*.

Florentine *a.* of or relating to Florence. *Also n.* WH: 12–14C. Old French *Florentin* or Latin *Florentinus*, from *Florentina*. See FLORENCE, also -INE.

florescence *n.* the flowering of a plant. WH: 18C. Modern Latin *florescentia*, from Latin *florescens*, *florescentis*, pres.p. of *florescere* to come into flower, from *florere* to flower. See also -ENCE.

floret *n.* a small flower. WH: 17C. Latin *flos*, *floris* flower + -ET[1].

floriate *v.t.* to adorn with floral ornaments or designs. WH: 19C. Latin *flos*, *floris* flower + -ATE[3].

floribunda *n.* a plant, esp. a rose, whose flowers grow in dense clusters. WH: 19C. Modern Latin, use as n. of fem. of *floribundus* flowering profusely, from Latin *flos*, *floris* flower + -bundus as in *moribundus* (see MORIBUND), influ. by *abundus* copious.

floriculture *n.* the cultivation of flowers or flowering plants. WH: 19C. Latin *flos, floris* flower + CULTURE, based on HORTICULTURE.

florid *a.* flushed with red, ruddy. WH: 17C. French *floride*, from Latin *floridus*, from *flos, floris* flower or *florere* to flower. See also -ID.

floriferous *a.* bearing many flowers. WH: 17C. Latin *florifer* (from *flori-*, comb. form of *flos* flower) + -OUS. See also -FEROUS.

floriform *a.* having the shape of a flower. WH: 19C. Latin *flori-*, comb. form of *flos* flower + -FORM.

florilegium *n.* an anthology. WH: 17C. Modern Latin, lit. bouquet, from Latin *flori-*, comb. form of *flos* flower + *legere* to gather, translating Greek *anthologion* ANTHOLOGY.

florin *n.* a former British coin, orig. silver, worth the equivalent of 10p. WH: 12–14C. Old French, from Italian *fiorino*, from *fiore* flower. The original coin was so named as it had a lily (fleur-de-lis) on the reverse as the national badge of FLORENCE.

florist *n.* a person who sells flowers. WH: 17C. Latin *flos, floris* flower + -IST, based on French *fleuriste* or Italian *florista*.

floruit *v.i.* (he or she) was alive and actively working; flourished, used to express the period during which a person, e.g. a painter or writer, was most active (in the absence of exact dates of birth and death). *Also n.* WH: 19C. Latin he flourished, 3rd pers. sing. perf. ind. of *florere* to flourish. Cp. FLOREAT.

floscular *a.* having little flowers. WH: 17C. Latin *flosculus*, dim. of *flos* flower + -AR[1].

flos ferri *n.* a spicular variety of aragonite. WH: 18C. Latin, lit. flower of iron, from *flos* flower + gen. of *ferrum* iron.

floss *n.* the exterior rough silk envelope of a silkworm's cocoon. *Also v.t., v.i.* WH: 18C. Old French *flosche* down, pile on velvet (Modern French *floche*), ult. of unknown orig.

flotant *a.* floating, as a flag, bird, or anything swimming. WH: 17C. French *flottant*, pres.p. of *flotter* to float.

flotation *n.* the floating of a company on the Stock Exchange. WH: 19C. FLOAT + -ATION, based on French *flottaison*.

flotilla *n.* a small fleet. WH: 18C. Spanish, dim. of *flota* fleet.

flotsam *n.* goods lost in shipwreck and found floating. WH: 17C. Anglo-French *floteson*, from *floter* FLOAT. Cp. JETSAM.

flounce[1] *v.i.* to move abruptly or violently. *Also n.* WH: 16C. Orig. uncertain. ? Rel. to Norwegian *flunsa* to hurry, Swedish dial. *flunsa* to fall with a splash, or ? of imit. orig. (cp. BOUNCE, POUNCE[1]).

flounce[2] *n.* a gathered or pleated strip of cloth sewed to a petticoat, dress etc., with the lower border hanging loose. *Also v.t.* WH: 18C. Alt. of earlier *frounce* wrinkle, crease, from Old French *fronce*, from Frankish, prob. assim. to FLOUNCE[1].

flounder[1] *n.* a flatfish, *Pleuronectes flesus*, resembling the plaice, but with paler spots. WH: 12–14C. Old French *flondre*, prob. of Scandinavian orig.

flounder[2] *v.i.* to struggle or stumble about violently, as when stuck in mud. *Also n.* WH: 16C. Imit., ? blend of FOUNDER and BLUNDER. Many words beginning *fl-* express an impatient or clumsy movement. Cp. FLING, FLOUNCE[1].

flour *n.* the finer part of meal, esp. of wheatmeal. *Also v.t.* WH: 12–14C. Orig. form of FLOWER, as finest part of meal. The spelling *flower* was in use in this sense to the 19C.

flourish *v.i.* to grow in a strong and healthy way. *Also v.t., n.* WH: 12–14C. Old French *florir, floriss-* (Modern French *fleurir*), from alt. of Latin *florere*, from *flos, floris* FLOWER. See also -ISH[2].

flout *v.t.* to mock, to insult. *Also v.i., n.* WH: 16C. ? Dutch *fluiten* to whistle, to play the flute. Cp. coll. German *pfeifen auf* to pipe at.

flow *v.i.* (of a fluid) to move or spread. *Also v.t., n.* WH: pre-1200. Old English *flōwan*, from Germanic base of FLOOD. Not rel. to FLUID.

flower *n.* the organ or growth comprising the organs of reproduction in a plant. *Also v.i., v.t.* WH: 12–14C. Old French *flor, flour* (Modern French *fleur*), from Latin *flos, floris*. Cp. FLOUR.

fl. oz. *abbr.* fluid ounce. WH: Abbr. of FLUID + OZ.

FLQ *n.* a terrorist group seeking independence for Quebec from the rest of Canada. WH: Abbr. of French *Front de Libération du Québec* Quebec Liberation Front.

flu *n.* influenza. WH: 19C. Abbr. of INFLUENZA.

flub *v.t., v.i.* to botch or bungle. *Also n.* WH: early 20C. Orig. unknown.

fluctuate *v.i.* to vary, to change irregularly in degree. *Also v.t.* WH: 17C. Latin *fluctuatus*, p.p. of *fluctuare* to undulate, from *fluctus* current, flow, from stem of *fluere* to flow. See also -ATE[3].

flue[1] *n.* a passage or tube by which smoke can escape or hot air be conveyed. WH: 14–15C. Orig. unknown. No connection proven with FLOW.

flue[2] *n.* light down or fur. WH: 16C. Appar. from Flemish *vluwe* in same sense. Cp. FLUFF.

flue[3] *n.* a kind of fishing net. WH: 14–15C. Middle Dutch *vluwe* fishing net.

flue[4] *v.i.* to widen or spread out. *Also v.t.* WH: 18C. Appar. from obs. *flue* shallow, of unknown orig.

fluence *n.* influence. WH: early 20C. Shortening of INFLUENCE.

fluent *a.* able to speak a foreign language easily, accurately and without hesitation. *Also n.* WH: 16C. Latin *fluens, fluentis*, pres.p. of *fluere* to flow. See also -ENT. The original sense (to the 17C) was giving freely, generous.

fluff *n.* light down or fur. *Also v.t., v.i.* WH: 18C. Prob. dial. var. of FLUE[2]. Cp. Flemish *vluwe* fluff, Dutch *fluweel* velvet.

flugelhorn *n.* a valved brass instrument resembling, but slightly larger than, a cornet. WH: 19C. German *Flügelhorn*, from *Flügel* wing + *Horn* horn. The instrument is so named because it was originally used to signal the flanking riders in a hunt, especially when drawing game.

fluid *n.* a liquid or gas, not a solid. *Also a.* WH: 14–15C. Old French *fluide* or Latin *fluidus*, from *fluere* to flow. See also -ID.

fluke[1] *n.* an accidentally successful stroke; any lucky chance. *Also v.i., v.t.* WH: 19C. Orig. uncertain. ? Of dial. orig.

fluke[2] *n.* a parasitic worm belonging to the Trematoda, found chiefly in the livers of sheep. WH: pre-1200. Old English *flōc*, of Germanic orig., rel. to German *flach* flat.

fluke[3] *n.* the broad holding portion of an anchor. WH: 16C. ? From FLUKE[2], ref. to the shape.

flume *n.* an artificial channel for conveying water to a mill or for some other industrial use. *Also v.t., v.i.* WH: 12–14C. Old French *flum*, from Latin *flumen* river, from *fluere* to flow.

flummery *n.* nonsense, humbug. WH: 17C. Welsh *llymru*, ? rel. to *llymrig* bare, soft, slippery. The word was originally used for a dish of oatmeal etc. The current sense evolved in the 18C.

flummox *v.t.* to perplex, to confound. WH: 19C. Prob. dial., imit. Cp. LUMMOX.

flump *v.i.* to fall down heavily. *Also v.t., n.* WH: 17C. Imit.

flunk *v.t.* to (cause to) fail (a subject, course etc.). *Also v.i., n.* WH: 19C. Of uncertain orig. Cp. FUNK[1].

flunkey *n.* a servant in livery, a footman. WH: 18C. ? Rel. to *flanker* (FLANK) in sense of person who stands at one's flank + -Y[3].

fluor *n.* an isometric, transparent or subtranslucent brittle mineral, having many shades of colour, composed of calcium fluoride. WH: 17C. Latin flow, from *fluere* to flow. See also -OR. The English word translates German *Fluss* flow.

fluorescence *n.* a quality existing in certain substances of giving out light of a different colour from their own or that of the light falling upon them. WH: 19C. *fluorspar* (FLUOR + SPAR[3]) + -ESCENCE. Cp. *phosphorescence* (PHOSPHOR). *Fluorspar* exhibits the described quality. The word was coined in 1852 by the Irish mathematician and physicist Sir George G. Stokes.

fluorine *n.* a non-metallic gaseous element, at. no. 9, chem. symbol F, forming with chlorine, bromine and iodine the halogen group. WH: 19C. FLUOR + -INE. The name was coined in 1810 by Ampère (see AMPERE), who suggested it to the English chemist Sir Humphry Davy.

fluoro- *comb. form* fluorine. WH: Comb. form of FLUORINE (less commonly *fluoride* (FLUORINE + -IDE)) or FLUORESCENCE. See also -O-.

fluorocarbon *n.* any of a series of compounds of fluorine and carbon, which are chemically inert and highly resistant to heat. WH: mid-20C. FLUORO- + CARBON.

fluoroscope *n.* an apparatus consisting of a lightproof box with a fluorescent screen, for observing the effects of X-rays. WH: 19C. FLUORO- + -SCOPE.

fluorosis *n.* poisoning by fluorine or its compounds. WH: early 20C. FLUORO- + -OSIS.

flurry *n.* a squall. *Also v.t.* WH: 17C. From obs. *flurr* to scatter, to fly up, of imit. orig., prob. based on HURRY.

flush[1] *v.i.* to colour as if with a rush of blood, to blush. *Also v.t., n.* WH: 12–14C. Prob. imit., ? influ. by FLASH. The sense to colour arose in the 16C, influenced by BLUSH. The sense to cleanse by a flow of water dates from the 18C.

flush² *v.i.* to flow swiftly. *Also v.t., n.* WH: 16C. FLUSH¹.

flush³ *a.* on the same plane (with). *Also v.t.* WH: 16C. Prob. rel. to FLUSH¹.

flush⁴ *n.* a hand of cards all of one suit. WH: 16C. Obs. French *flus*, from Latin *fluxus* FLUX.

flush⁵ *v.i.* to take wing. *Also v.t., n.* WH: 14–15C. FLUSH¹.

fluster *v.t.* to flurry or confuse. *Also v.i., n.* WH: 17C. Orig. uncertain. Prob. rel. to Icelandic *flaustr* to hurry, *flaustra* to bustle.

flustra *n.* a sea-mat, an individual of the genus of Polyzoa called *Flustridae*. WH: 18C. Modern Latin. The name was introduced by Linnaeus in 1761 but he did not give its origin.

flute *n.* a tubular wind instrument with a blowhole near the end and holes stopped by the fingers or with keys for producing variations of tone, esp. a transverse flute. *Also v.i., v.t.* WH: 12–14C. Old French *flahute*, *flëute* (Modern French *flûte*), prob. from Provençal *flaüt*, of unknown orig.

flutter *v.i.* to flap the wings rapidly. *Also v.t., n.* WH: pre-1200. Old English *floterian*, freq. of Germanic base of FLEET². See also -ER⁵.

fluvial *a.* of or belonging to a river. WH: 14–15C. Latin *fluvialis*, from *fluvius* river, from *fluere* to flow. See also -AL¹.

fluvio- *comb. form* relating to a river or rivers. WH: Latin *fluvius* river. See also -O-.

fluvioglacial *a.* of, relating to or caused by rivers from glacial ice or rivers and glaciers. WH: 19C. FLUVIO- + GLACIAL.

fluviomarine *a.* of, relating to or produced by the joint action of a river and the sea (as deposits at a river mouth). WH: 19C. FLUVIO- + MARINE.

fluviometer *n.* an apparatus for measuring the rise and fall in a river. WH: 19C. FLUVIO- + -METER.

flux *n.* the act or state of flowing. *Also v.t., v.i.* WH: 14–15C. Old French, or from Latin *fluxus*, from p.p. of *fluere* to flow.

fly¹ *n.* a two-winged insect of the order Diptera, esp. the housefly *Musca domestica*. WH: pre-1200. Old English *flÿge*, from Germanic, from base of FLY². Cp. German *Fliege*.

fly² *v.i.* to move through the air with wings. *Also v.t., n.* WH: pre-1200. Old English *flēogan*, from Germanic. Cp. German *fliegen*.

fly³ *a.* clever, sharp, wide-awake. WH: 19C. Orig. uncertain. ? Rel. to FLY².

flying *a.* fluttering in the air, streaming, loose. WH: pre-1200. FLY² + -ING².

foal *n.* the young of a horse or related animal; a colt, a filly. *Also v.i., v.t.* WH: pre-1200. Old English *fola*, from Germanic, rel. to Latin *pullus* (see PULLET), Greek *pōlos*. Cp. FILLY.

foam *n.* a mass of bubbles produced in liquids by violent agitation or fermentation. *Also v.i., v.t.* WH: pre-1200. Old English *fām*, from Germanic, from Indo-European, rel. to Latin *pumex* PUMICE and *spuma* SPUME.

fob¹ *n.* a chain by which a pocket watch is carried in a waistband pocket. *Also v.t.* WH: 17C. Prob. of German orig. Cp. German dial. *Fuppe* pocket.

fob² *v.t.* to cheat, to impose upon. WH: 14–15C. Of Germanic orig. Cp. German *foppen* to cheat, to deceive.

focaccia *n.* a kind of Italian bread sprinkled before baking with olive oil, salt and often herbs. WH: mid-20C. Italian.

focus *n.* a point at which rays of light, heat, electrons etc. meet after reflection, deflection or refraction, or from which they appear to diverge. *Also v.t., v.i.* WH: 17C. Latin fireplace, domestic hearth.

fodder *n.* food such as straw or hay fed to cattle. *Also v.t.* WH: pre-1200. Old English *fōdor*, from Germanic, from base rel. to that of FOOD.

foe *n.* a personal enemy; an opponent. *Also v.t.* WH: pre-1200. Old English *fāh* (a.) and *gefā* (n.), orig. use as n. of a. meaning at feud (with), both words rel. to Old High German *gifēh* at feud, odious, from Germanic. Cp. FEUD¹.

foetus *n.* the young of animals in the womb, and of vertebrates in the egg, after the parts are distinctly formed, esp. an unborn human more than eight weeks after conception. WH: 14–15C. Latin *fetus*, *foetus* pregnancy, giving birth, young offspring, n. parallel to a. *fetus* pregnant, productive.

fog¹ *n.* a dense watery vapour rising from land or water and suspended near the surface of land or sea, reducing or obscuring visibility. *Also v.t., v.i.* WH: 16C. Appar. back-formation from *foggy*, from FOG², of unknown orig. The sense link between FOG¹ and FOG² is hard to see, although both cover the ground. There may be a similar relationship between MIST and German *Mist* dung.

fog² *n.* a second growth of grass after first cutting, aftermath. *Also v.t., v.i.* WH: 14–15C. Orig. unknown.

fogey *n.* an old-fashioned eccentric person. WH: 18C. Rel. to obs. *fogram* old-fashioned person, of unknown orig. According to some, the word is from *foggy* (see FOG¹) in its obsolete sense of fat, flabby (16C).

föhn *n.* the warm south wind in the Alps. WH: 19C. German, ult. from Latin (*ventus*) *Favonius* mild west wind, rel. to *fovere* to warm. Cp. FOMENT.

foible *n.* a weak point in a person's character. WH: 16C. French, obs. var. of *faible* FEEBLE.

foil¹ *n.* very thin sheet metal. *Also v.t.* WH: 12–14C. Partly from Old French *foil*, from Latin *folium* leaf, partly from Old French *foille* (Modern French *feuille*), from Latin *folia*, neut. pl. (treated as sing.) of *folium*.

foil² *v.t.* to baffle, to frustrate. *Also v.i., n.* WH: 12–14C. ? Anglo-French var. of Old French *fouler* to full cloth, to trample, ult. from Latin *fullo* fuller (see FULL²).

foil³ *n.* a straight thin sword, blunted by means of a button on the point, used in fencing. WH: 16C. Orig. unknown. ? Rel. to FOIL² in sense of weapon that has been made ineffective by blunting.

†foin *v.t.* to thrust at. *Also v.i., n.* WH: 14–15C. Old French *foine* three-pronged fish spear (Modern French *fouine*), from Latin *fuscina* trident.

†foison *n.* plenty, abundance. WH: 12–14C. Old French, from Latin *fusio*, *fusionis* outpouring. See FUSE¹.

foist *v.t.* to impose (an unwelcome thing or person) (on). *Also n.* WH: 16C. Dutch dial. *vuisten* FIST. Two early senses were to palm a false die, to pick a pocket.

fold¹ *n.* a pen or enclosure for sheep. *Also v.t.* WH: pre-1200. Old English *fald*, from Germanic, of unknown orig. Not rel. to FOLD².

fold² *v.t.* to double or lay one part of (a flexible thing) over another. *Also v.i., n.* WH: pre-1200. Old English *faldan*, from Germanic, from base also of Latin *plicare* to fold, to bend (cp. PLIABLE). Cp. German *falten*.

-fold *suf.* forming adjectives and adverbs denoting multiplication or composition of a number of parts, as in *sixfold*, *manifold*. WH: Old English *-fald*, from Germanic, rel. to FOLD² and ult. to *-plex* in DUPLEX (twofold), *triplex* (threefold) (see TRIPLE).

folder *n.* a person who or thing that folds. WH: 17C. FOLD² + -ER¹.

foliaceous *a.* having the texture, structure or organs of or as of leaves. WH: 17C. Latin *foliaceus*, from *folium* leaf. See also -ACEOUS.

foliage *n.* leaves in the aggregate. *Also v.t.* WH: 14–15C. Alt. (based on Latin *folium*) of Old French *feuillage*, from *feuille* leaf. See FOIL¹, also -AGE.

foliate¹ *v.i.* to split or disintegrate into thin laminae. *Also v.t.* WH: 17C. Latin *folium* leaf + -ATE³.

foliate² *a.* leaflike, leaf-shaped. WH: 17C. Latin *foliatus* leaved, from *leaved* leaf. See also -ATE².

folic acid *n.* a vitamin of the vitamin B complex found esp. in green vegetables and liver and used in the treatment of anaemia. WH: mid-20C. Latin *folium* leaf + -IC.

folie *n.* madness, folly. WH: 19C. French. See FOLLY.

folio *n.* a leaf of paper or other material for writing etc., numbered on the front. *Also a.* WH: 14–15C. Medieval Latin, from Latin (abl. of) *folium* leaf, or Latinization of Italian *foglio*. The Medieval Latin sense meant literally at leaf (so-and-so). In the sense of book size (16C) the origin is in the phrase *in folio*, from Italian *in foglio*.

foliole *n.* a leaflet, one of the separate parts of a compound leaf. WH: 18C. French, from Latin *foliolum*, dim. of *folium* leaf. See also -OLE².

folk *n.* people collectively. *Also a.* WH: pre-1200. Old English *folc*, from Germanic. Cp. VOLK. The term *folklore* was coined in 1846 by the English antiquary William J. Thoms.

follicle *n.* a small cavity, sac or gland. WH: 14–15C. Latin *folliculus* little bag, dim. of *follis* bellows. See also -CULE.

follow *v.t.* to go or come after. *Also v.i.* WH: pre-1200. Old English *folgian*, from Germanic, of unknown orig. Cp. German *folgen*.

folly *n.* foolishness, lack of judgement. WH: 12–14C. Old French *folie* madness, from *fol* mad, foolish. See FOOL¹, also -Y². The sense ornamental building arose in the 16C and may owe something to an association, through French, with Latin *folium* leaf, as if a leafy retreat. A number of country houses in N France are named *La Folie*, mostly from Old French *folie* madness but sometimes from Old French *foille* leaf. Cp. FOLIAGE.

foment *v.t.* to cause (trouble or a riot) to develop. WH: 14–15C. Old French *fomenter*, from Late Latin *fomentare*, from Latin *fomentum* lotion, poultice, from *fovere* to heat, to cherish.

fomes *n.* a substance of a porous kind liable to absorb and retain contagious substances and so spread disease. WH: 17C. Latin tinder.

fond *a.* doting on, delighting in. *Also v.t., v.i.* WH: 14–15C. From obs. *fon* foolish, of unknown orig. Cp. FUN. The original sense (to the 19C) was insipid, sickly. The current sense evolved in the 16C.

fondant *n.* a sweet paste made of sugar and water. WH: 19C. French, use as n. of pres.p. of *fondre* to melt. See FOUND², also -ANT.

fondle *v.t.* to caress. *Also v.i.* WH: 17C. Back-formation from *fondling* foolish person, from FOND + -LING¹. The original sense (to the 18C) was to pamper.

fondue *n.* a dish consisting of a hot sauce (usu. of cheese and white wine) into which pieces of bread etc. are dipped, or of cubes of meat which are cooked by dipping into hot oil at table and eaten with a variety of spicy sauces. WH: 19C. French, fem. p.p. of *fondre* to melt. See FOUND².

font¹ *n.* the vessel or basin to contain water for baptism. WH: pre-1200. Latin *fons*, *fontis* spring, fountain, in Ecclesiastical Latin phr. *fons baptismi* waters of baptism.

font² *n.* a set of type of one face and size. WH: 16C. French *fonte*, from *fondre* to melt. See FOUND².

fontanelle *n.* an interval between the bones of the infant cranium. WH: 16C. French, from Modern Latin *fontanella*, Latinization of Old French *fontanelle*, dim. of *fontaine* FOUNTAIN. See also -EL. The word originally denoted a hollow of skin between muscles, then (in the 17C) an outlet for bodily fluids. The current sense dates from the 18C.

food *n.* any substance, esp. solid in form, which, taken into the body, assists in sustaining or nourishing the living being. WH: pre-1200. Old English *fōda*, from Germanic. Cp. FEED, FODDER. The word has no exact counterparts in other Germanic languages.

fool¹ *n.* a person without common sense or judgement. *Also a., v.t., v.i.* WH: 12–14C. Old French *fol*, from Latin *follis* bellows, inflated ball, windbag.

fool² *n.* a dish made of fruit, esp. gooseberries, stewed and crushed with cream etc. WH: 16C. ? From FOOL¹. Not from French *fouler* to crush. The dish is perhaps so called because it was regarded as superficial or frivolous. Cp. TRIFLE.

foolhardy *a.* daring without sense or judgement. WH: 12–14C. Old French *folhardi*, from *fol* foolish (see FOOL¹) + *hardi* HARDY.

foolscap *n.* a size of writing paper 17 × 13½ in. (43.2 × 34.3 cm) or of printing paper 13½ × 8½ in. (34.3 × 21.6 cm), quarto, 8½ × 6¾ in. (21.6 × 17.1 cm), octavo, 6¾ × 4¼ in. (17.1 × 10.8 cm). WH: 17C. FOOL¹ + -'S + CAP. The paper so named was originally water-marked with a cap worn by court jesters.

foot *n.* the part of the leg which treads on the ground in standing or walking, and on which the body is supported; the part below the ankle. *Also v.i., v.t.* WH: pre-1200. Old English *fōt*, from Germanic, from Indo-European base represented also by Sanskrit *pad*, *pāda*, Greek *pous*, *podos*, Latin *pes*, *pedis* foot.

football *n.* any of several games played between two teams with a ball that is kicked, or handled and kicked, to score goals or points. WH: 14–15C. FOOT + BALL¹.

footing *n.* a place for standing or putting the feet on. WH: 14–15C. FOOT + -ING¹.

footle *v.i.* to trifle; to potter about aimlessly. *Also n.* WH: 19C. Prob. from obs. *footer* worthless person, to potter about, var. of *foutre* valueless thing, from Old French, use as n. of inf., from Latin *futuere* to have sexual intercourse with, with substitution of suf. -LE⁴ for -*er*.

Footsie *n.* the Financial Times–Stock Exchange 100 Index. WH: late 20C. Alt. of acronym *FT–SE 100*, based on *footsie* (FOOT). The two zeros of *100* serve as the -*oo*- of *Footsie*, while the *1* is the *i*. There may also be an implied pun on *to play the market*, alluding to the amorous play of *footsie*.

foo yong *n.* a Chinese dish made with egg mixed with chicken, meat and other ingredients, cooked like an omelette. WH: mid-20C. Chinese *foô yung*, lit. hibiscus.

foozle *v.i.* to waste time, to fool about. *Also v.t., n.* WH: 19C. German (dial.) *fuseln* to work badly. Cp. FUSEL OIL.

fop *n.* a man overfond of dress. WH: 14–15C. Orig. unknown. ? Rel. to FOB².

for *prep.* in the place of, instead of. *Also conj.* WH: pre-1200. Old English, prob. reduced form of Germanic prep. meaning before, represented by Old English FORE.

for- *pref.* away, off, as in *forget*, *forgive*. WH: Old English, or from Germanic base of FOR, corr. to Greek *peri-*, *para-*, Latin *per-*, *por-*, Sanskrit *pari*, *parā*, from Indo-European.

forage *n.* food for horses and cattle. *Also v.i., v.t.* WH: 12–14C. French *fourrage*, from Old French *fuerre* straw, from Frankish, from Germanic base of FODDER. See also -AGE.

foramen *n.* a small natural opening, passage or perforation in parts of plants and animals. WH: 17C. Latin *foramen*, *foraminis*, from *forare* to bore.

†forasmuch as *conj.* seeing that; since; in consideration that. WH: 12–14C. Orig. 3 words, *for as much* (*as*), translating Old French *por tant que* for as much as.

foray *n.* a sudden attacking expedition. *Also v.t., v.i.* WH: 14–15C. Back-formation from *forayer* person who forays, raider, from Old French *forrier* (Modern French *fourrier* quartermaster). Rel. to FORAGE.

forbear *v.t.* to refrain or abstain from. *Also v.i.* WH: pre-1200. Old English *forbearan*, from base of FOR-, BEAR². The original sense (to the 16C) was to bear, to endure. The current sense dates from the 12–14C.

forbid *v.t.* to order not to do. WH: pre-1200. Old English *forbēodan*, from base of FOR-, BID. Cp. VERBOTEN.

forbye *prep.* besides, in addition to. *Also adv.* WH: 12–14C. for-, var. of FORE- + BY. Cp. German *vorbei*.

force¹ *n.* strength, active power. *Also v.t.* WH: 12–14C. Old French, from Latin *fortis* strong.

force² *n.* a waterfall. WH: 14–15C. Old Norse *fors*. Not rel. to FORCE¹.

force majeure *n.* superior power. WH: 19C. French superior strength, from *force* strength, FORCE¹ + fem. of *majeur* superior, greater (cp. MAJOR).

forceps *n.* a surgical instrument in the form of a pair of tongs, pincers or pliers for holding or extracting anything. WH: 16C. Latin, from *formus* hot + base of *capere* to take.

ford *n.* a shallow part of a river where it may be crossed by wading or in a vehicle. *Also v.t., v.i.* WH: pre-1200. Old English, from Germanic base of FARE, ult. rel. to WADE.

†fordo *v.t.* to destroy, to ruin, to kill, to put an end to. WH: pre-1200. Old English *fordōn*, from base of FOR-, DO.

fore *a.* being in front. *Also n., int., prep., adv.* WH: 15C. Independent use of FORE-.

fore- *pref.* before, in front, beforehand, chiefly with verbs, as in *forebode*, *foreordain*, *foresee*. WH: Old English *fore* beforehand, from Germanic, rel. to Sanskrit *pra*, *purā*, Greek *pro*, *para*, Latin *pro*, *prae*, *per*.

forearm¹ *v.t.* to prepare beforehand for attack or defence. WH: 16C. FORE- + ARM².

forearm² *n.* the anterior part of the arm, between the wrist and elbow. WH: 18C. FORE- + ARM¹.

forebear *n.* an ancestor. WH: 15C. FORE- + var. of *beer* one who is (from BE + -ER¹). Not. rel. to BEAR².

forebode *v.t.* to foretell, to predict. *Also v.i.* WH: 17C. FORE- + BODE.

fore-body *n.* that part of a vessel's hull forward of midship. WH: 17C. FORE- + BODY.

forebrace *n.* a rope on the fore yardarm for shifting the sail. WH: 19C. FORE- + BRACE.

forebrain *n.* the front part of the brain, including the cerebrum, thalamus and hypothalamus. WH: 19C. FORE- + BRAIN.

forecabin *n.* a forward cabin, usu. for second-class passengers. WH: 19C. FORE- + CABIN.

forecast *v.t.* to foresee, to predict. *Also v.i., n.* WH: 14–15C. FORE- + CAST.

forecastle *n.* in merchant ships, a forward space below deck where the crew live. WH: 14–15C. FORE- + CASTLE.

foreclose *v.t.* to shut out, exclude or bar. WH: 12–14C. Old French *forclos*, p.p. of *forclore*, from *for-* out (from Latin *foris* outside) + *clore* CLOSE².

forecourt *n.* an open or paved area in front of a building, esp. a filling station. WH: 16C. FORE- + COURT.

foredeck *n.* the forepart of a deck. WH: 16C. FORE- + DECK.

foredoom *v.t.* to doom beforehand. WH: 16C. FORE- + DOOM.

fore-edge *n.* the front or outer edge of a book or of a leaf in a book. WH: 17C. FORE- + EDGE.

forefather *n.* an ancestor. WH: 12–14C. FORE- + FATHER. Cp. Old Norse *forfathir*.

forefinger *n.* the finger next to the thumb. WH: 14–15C. FORE- + FINGER.

forefoot *n.* either of the front feet of a quadruped. WH: 14–15C. FORE- + FOOT, ? based on Dutch *voorvoet*. Cp. German *Vorderfuss*.

forefront *n.* the extreme front. WH: 14–15C. FORE- + FRONT.

foregather *v.i.* to meet together, to assemble. *Also v.t.* WH: 15C. Dutch *vergadern* to meet, to assemble, assim. to FOR-, GATHER.

forego *v.t., v.i.* to go before, to precede in time, order or place. WH: pre-1200. FORE- + GO¹.

foreground *n.* the nearest part of a view. *Also v.t.* WH: 17C. FORE- + GROUND¹, based on Dutch *voorgrond*. Cp. German *Vordergrund*.

forehand *n.* a stroke made with the palm of the hand facing in the direction of the stroke. *Also a.* WH: 16C. FORE- + HAND.

forehead *n.* the part of the face which reaches from the eyebrows upwards to the hair. WH: pre-1200. Old English *forhēafod*, from *for-*, var. of FORE- + *hēafod* HEAD¹.

forehock *n.* a foreleg cut of pork or bacon. WH: early 20C. FORE- + HOCK¹.

forehold *n.* the forepart of a ship's hold. WH: 17C. FORE- + HOLD³.

forehorse *n.* the foremost horse in a team. WH: 15C. FORE- + HORSE.

foreign *a.* belonging to, connected with or derived from a country or nation other than one's own. *Also adv.* WH: 12–14C. Old French *forein*, from Latin *foris, foras*, from **fora*, rel. to *fores* door. The spelling with *-eign* arose as for SOVEREIGN. The original sense was out of doors, but the current sense soon followed.

forejudge *v.t.* to judge before trial or decide before hearing the evidence. WH: 16C. FORE- + JUDGE, based on French *préjuger* or Latin *praeiudicare* PREJUDGE.

foreknow *v.t.* to know beforehand. WH: 14–15C. FORE- + KNOW.

†**forel** *n.* a kind of parchment used for book covers. WH: 12–14C. Old French (Modern French *fourreau* sheath), from *fuerre*, from Frankish, from Germanic, rel. to Sanskrit *pātra* receptacle, from *pāti* it protects.

forelady *n.* a forewoman. WH: 19C. FORE- + LADY. Cp. FOREMAN.

foreland *n.* a point of land extending into the sea, a promontory. WH: 12–14C. FORE- + LAND. Cp. Dutch *voorland*.

foreleg *n.* a front leg of an animal, chair etc. WH: 14–15C. FORE- + LEG.

forelock¹ *n.* a lock of hair growing over the forehead. WH: pre-1200. FORE- + LOCK².

forelock² *n.* a pin or wedge passing through the end of a bolt to prevent this from being withdrawn. *Also v.t.* WH: 12–14C. FORE- + LOCK¹.

foreman *n.* a worker supervising others. WH: 12–14C. FORE- + MAN, prob. based on Old Norse *formathr* leader, or direct from Dutch *voorman*. Cp. German *Vormann*.

foremast *n.* the mast nearest the bow of a vessel. WH: 15C. FORE- + MAST¹.

forementioned *a.* already mentioned. WH: 16C. FORE- + p.p. of MENTION. Cp. *aforementioned* (AFORE).

foremost *a.* first in time, place or importance. *Also adv.* WH: pre-1200. Old English *formest*, from *forma* first, with additional superl. suf. (see -EST¹), later assim. to FORE- + -MOST.

foremother *n.* a female ancestor or predecessor. WH: 15C. FORE- + MOTHER¹. Cp. FOREFATHER.

forename *n.* a name preceding the surname, a Christian name. WH: 16C. FORE- + NAME, based on French *prénom* or Latin *praenomen*. Cp. Dutch *voornam*.

forenamed *a.* named or mentioned before. WH: 12–14C. FORE- + p.p. of NAME.

forenight *n.* the evening. WH: 12–14C. FORE- + NIGHT.

forenoon *n.* the early part of the day, from morning to noon. WH: 14–15C. FORE- + NOON.

forensic *a.* of or relating to courts of law, crime detection or to public debate. *Also n.* WH: 17C. Latin *forensis* of or in the forum, public. See FORUM, also -IC.

foreordain *v.t.* to ordain beforehand, to predestine. WH: 14–15C. FORE- + ORDAIN.

forepart *n.* the first or most advanced part. WH: 14–15C. FORE- + PART.

forepaw *n.* either of the front paws of a four-footed animal. WH: 19C. FORE- + PAW.

forepeak *n.* the part of a vessel's hold in the angle of the bow. WH: 17C. FORE- + PEAK¹. Cp. Dutch *voorpiek*.

foreplay *n.* sexual stimulation preceding intercourse. WH: early 20C. FORE- + PLAY.

forequarter *n.* the front half of the side of a carcass, as of beef. WH: 14–15C. FORE- + QUARTER.

forerank *n.* the foremost rank. WH: 16C. FORE- + RANK¹.

forereach *v.t.* to gain upon, to get ahead of. *Also v.i.* WH: 17C. FORE- + REACH¹.

foreread *v.t.* to tell beforehand. WH: 17C. FORE- + READ.

forerun *v.t.* to precede, to go before. WH: pre-1200. FORE- + RUN.

foresail *n.* the principal sail on the foremast. WH: 15C. FORE- + SAIL.

foresee *v.t.* to see beforehand. WH: pre-1200. Old English *foresēon*, from FORE- + *sēon* SEE¹.

foreshadow *v.t.* to show or be a sign or warning of beforehand. *Also n.* WH: 16C. FORE- + SHADOW.

foresheet *n.* the rope holding the lee corner of a foresail. WH: 17C. FORE- + SHEET¹.

foreship *n.* the forepart of a ship, the prow. WH: pre-1200. FORE- + SHIP.

foreshock *n.* a comparatively small earthquake that precedes a much larger earthquake. WH: early 20C. FORE- + SHOCK¹.

foreshore *n.* the part of the shore lying between high- and low-water marks. WH: 18C. FORE- + SHORE¹.

foreshorten *v.t.* in drawing or painting, to represent (figures or parts of figures that project towards the spectator) so as to give a correct impression of form and proportions. WH: 16C. FORE- + *shorten* (SHORT), prob. based on Dutch *verkorten*.

foreshow *v.t.* to predict, to represent beforehand. WH: pre-1200. FORE- + SHOW.

foresight *n.* consideration beforehand, forethought. WH: 12–14C. FORE- + SIGHT.

foreskin *n.* the prepuce, the loose skin covering the end of the penis. WH: 16C. FORE- + SKIN, based on German *Vorhaut*. Cp. PREPUCE.

†**forespeak** *v.t.* to predict, to foretell. WH: 12–14C. FORE- + SPEAK.

forest *n.* an extensive wood or area of wooded country. *Also v.t.* WH: 12–14C. Old French (Modern French *forêt*), from Late Latin *forestis silva*, lit. outside wood (a royal forest reserved for hunting), from *foris* out of doors, outside.

forestall *v.t.* to act beforehand in order to prevent. WH: pre-1200. Old English *foresteall*, from FORE- + *steall* position taken up, STALL¹.

forestay *n.* a strong rope, reaching from the foremast head to the bowsprit end, to support the mast. WH: 12–14C. FORE- + STAY².

foretaste¹ *n.* experience or enjoyment (of) beforehand. WH: 14–15C. FORE- + TASTE.

foretaste² *v.t.* to taste beforehand. WH: 14–15C. FORE- + TASTE.

foretell *v.t.* to predict, to prophesy. WH: 12–14C. FORE- + TELL¹.

forethought *n.* consideration beforehand. WH: 12–14C. FORE- + THOUGHT.

foretime *n.* time past. WH: 15C. FORE- + TIME.

foretoken¹ *v.t.* to foreshadow, to prognosticate. WH: pre-1200. FORE- + TOKEN.

foretoken² *n.* a token beforehand, an omen. WH: pre-1200. FORE- + TOKEN.

foretooth *n.* a front tooth. WH: pre-1200. FORE- + TOOTH.

foretop *n.* the top or platform at the head of the foremast. WH: 15C. FORE- + TOP[1].

forever *adv.* for all future time, eternally. *Also n.* WH: 12–14C. Orig. two words, from FOR + EVER.

forewarn *v.t.* to warn or caution beforehand. WH: 12–14C. FORE- + WARN.

forewind *n.* a favourable wind. WH: 16C. FORE- + WIND[1]. Cp. Dutch *voorwind*.

forewoman *n.* a woman who supervises other workers. WH: 18C. FORE- + WOMAN. Cp. FOREMAN.

foreword *n.* a short introduction at the beginning of a book, often written by someone other than the author. WH: 19C. FORE- + WORD, based on German *Vorwort*.

foreyard *n.* the lowest yard on a foremast. WH: 15C. FORE- + YARD[1].

forfeit *n.* a fine, esp. a stipulated sum to be paid in case of breach of contract. *Also a., v.t.* WH: 12–14C. Old French *forfet* crime (Modern French *forfait*), from p.p. of *forfaire* to transgress, from *for-* out (from Latin *foris* outside) + *faire* to do. The original sense (to the 19C) was crime, transgression. The sense penalty evolved in the 17C.

forfend *v.t.* to avert, to ward off. WH: 14–15C. FOR- + FEND.

forfex *n.* a pair of scissor-like anal appendages in earwigs. WH: 18C. Latin scissors.

forge[1] *v.t.* to invent or imitate fraudulently. *Also v.i., n.* WH: 12–14C. Old French *forger*, from Latin *fabricare* FABRICATE.

forge[2] *v.i.* to move steadily (forward or ahead). WH: 18C. ? Alt. of FORCE[1].

forget *v.t., v.i.* to lose remembrance of. WH: pre-1200. Old English *forgietan*, from Germanic, from base of FOR- + GET[2]. The original sense was probably to lose generally, but this is not recorded in any Germanic language. The *forget-me-not* has equivalent names in many languages, eg. French *ne-m'oubliez-pas*, German *Vergissmeinnicht*, Italian *nontiscordardime*, Spanish *nomeolvides*, Russian *nezabudka*. Those wearing it were said to ensure against being forgotten by their lovers.

forgive *v.t.* to cease to feel anger or resentment towards. *Also v.i.* WH: pre-1200. Old English *forgiefan*, from Germanic, from base of FOR- + GIVE. An early sense (to the 15C) was to give, to grant, but the current sense also dates from Old English times.

forgo *v.t.* to go without, to refrain from. WH: pre-1200. FOR- + GO[1].

forint *n.* the monetary unit of Hungary since 1946, equivalent to 100 fillér. WH: mid-20C. Hungarian, from Italian *fiorino*. See FLORIN.

forjudge *v.t.* to deprive, dispossess or exclude by a judgement. WH: 14–15C. Old French *forjugier*, from *for-* out (from Latin *foris* outside) + *jugier* JUDGE.

fork *n.* an instrument with two or more prongs, used in eating or cooking. *Also v.t., v.i.* WH: pre-1200. Old English *forca*, from Germanic, from Latin *furca* pitchfork, forked stake. The fork as an eating implement evolved in the 14–15C.

forlorn *a.* lonely and sad. WH: pre-1200. P.p. of obs. *forlese* to lose, to kill, from Old English *forlēosan*, from Germanic, from bases of FOR-, LOSE. Cp. German *verlieren* to lose, p.p. *verloren*.

forlorn hope *n.* a bold, desperate enterprise. WH: 16C. Dutch *verloren hoop*, from *verloren*, p.p. of *verliezen* + *hoop* company (see HEAP). Cp. FORLORN. The original sense was a picked troop sent to the front to begin an attack. As such, they were likely to lose the initial encounter. The phrase became associated with HOPE[1] to give the sense faint hope in the 17C.

form *n.* the shape or external appearance of anything apart from its colour. *Also v.t., v.i.* WH: 12–14C. Old French *forme*, from Latin *forma* mould, shape, beauty. The sense of school class evolved in the 16C and is associated with the earlier sense bench (14–15C).

form- *comb. form* containing the radical formyl, which theoretically constitutes the base of formic acid. WH: formyl (FORMIC).

-form *suf.* like, having the shape of, as in *cruciform*. WH: French *-forme*, Latin *formis*, from *forma* FORM.

formal *a.* made, performed, held or done according to established forms. *Also n.* WH: 14–15C. Latin *formalis*, from *forma*. See FORM, also -AL[1].

formaldehyde *n.* formic aldehyde, a colourless gas generated by the partial oxidation of methyl alcohol, and used as an antiseptic and disinfectant. WH: 19C. FORMIC + ALDEHYDE.

formalin *n.* a solution of formaldehyde used as an antiseptic, for the destruction of disease germs, and as a food preservative. WH: 19C. FORMALDEHYDE + -IN[1].

formant *n.* a component of a sound, esp. which gives it its particular tone, colour or quality. WH: early 20C. German, from Latin *formans, formantis*, pres.p. of *formare* FORM. See also -ANT.

format *n.* the external form and size of a book, magazine etc. *Also v.t.* WH: 19C. French, from German, from Latin *formatus* (*liber*) shaped (book), p.p. of *formare* FORM.

formation *n.* the act or process of forming or creating. WH: 14–15C. Old French, or from Latin *formatio, formationis*, from *formatus*, p.p. of *formare* FORM. See also -ATION.

forme *n.* a body of type composed and locked in a chase for printing. WH: 15C. Var. of FORM.

former[1] *a.* preceding in time. WH: 12–14C. Obs. *forme* earlier, from Old English *forma*, superl. from base of FORE + -ER[3]. Cp. FOREMOST.

former[2] *n.* a person or thing that forms. WH: 14–15C. FORM + -ER[1].

formic *a.* of, relating to or produced by ants. WH: 18C. Latin *formica* ant. See also -IC.

Formica® *n.* a hard, long-lasting laminated plastic used for surfacing materials and other purposes. WH: early 20C. *for mica*. See FOR, MICA. The name was coined in 1913 by two US scientists who were instrumental in discovering a natural resin substitute *for mica* as an insulation material for electrical wiring.

formidable *a.* tending to excite fear or respect. WH: 14–15C. French, or from Latin *formidabilis*, from *formidare* to fear. See also -ABLE.

formula *n.* an expression by means of symbols of the elements of a compound. WH: 17C. Latin, dim. of *forma* FORM. See also -ULE.

fornent *prep.* right opposite to. *Also adv.* WH: 14–15C. FORE + ANENT.

fornicate *v.i.* to have sexual intercourse while unmarried or with someone other than one's spouse. WH: 16C. Ecclesiastical Latin *fornicatus*, p.p. of *fornicari*, from Latin FORNIX, *fornicis* brothel, (orig.) arch. See also -ATE[3].

fornix *n.* the arch of the vagina. WH: 17C. Latin arch, vaulted chamber.

forrader *a., adv.* more or further forward. WH: 18C. Alt. of *forwarder*, comp. of FORWARD. See also -ER[3].

forsake *v.t.* to leave, to abandon. WH: pre-1200. Old English *forsacan*, from Germanic, from base of FOR- + Old English *sacan* to quarrel, to accuse. See SAKE[1]. The original sense (to the 17C) was to decline, to refuse (something offered). The sense to abandon developed in the 12–14C.

forsooth *adv.* in truth, certainly, doubtless. WH: pre-1200. Old English *forsōth*. See FOR-, SOOTH.

†**forspeak** *v.t.* to forbid, to speak against. WH: pre-1200. FOR- + SPEAK.

†**forspend** *v.t.* to wear out, to exhaust with toil. WH: pre-1200. FOR- + SPEND.

forswear *v.t.* to renounce upon oath or with protestations. *Also v.i.* WH: pre-1200. FOR- + SWEAR.

forsythia *n.* any oleaceous shrub of the genus *Forsythia* bearing numerous yellow flowers in early spring before the leaves. WH: 19C. Modern Latin, from William *Forsyth*, 1737–1804, Scottish botanist, said to have introduced the shrub from China. See also -IA.

fort *n.* a fortified place, esp. a detached outwork or an independent fortified work of moderate extent. WH: 14–15C. Old French, or from Italian *forte*, use as n. of *fort, forte* strong, from Latin *fortis* strong.

fortalice *n.* an outwork of a fortification. WH: 14–15C. Medieval Latin *fortalitia*, from Latin *fortis* strong. Cp. Portuguese *fortaleza*, which gave the name of *Fortaleza*, a city and port in NE Brazil.

forte[1] *n.* a person's strong point. WH: 17C. French *fort*, use as n. of *fort* (FORT). The French feminine form was substituted for the masculine in English, as in LOCALE, MORALE. The pronunciation has been partly influenced by that of FORTE[2].

forte[2] *adv.* with loudness or force. *Also a., n.* WH: 18C. Italian strong, loud, from Latin *fortis* strong.

forth *adv.* forward in place, time or order. *Also prep.* WH: pre-1200. Old English, from Germanic, from Indo-European base represented by FORE-.

fortify *v.t.* to strengthen by forts, ramparts etc. *Also v.i.* WH: 14–15C. Old French *fortifier*, from Late Latin *fortificare*, from Latin *fortis* strong. See also -FY.

fortissimo *adv.* very loudly. *Also a., n.* WH: 18C. Italian, superl. of FORTE[2].

fortitude *n.* the strength of mind which enables one to meet danger or endure pain with calmness. WH: 12–14C. Old French, from Latin *fortitudo*, *fortitudinis*, from *fortis* strong. See also -TUDE.

fortnight *n.* a period of two weeks or 14 days. WH: pre-1200. Old English *fēowertīene niht*. See FOURTEEN, NIGHT. Cp. SENNIGHT.

Fortran *n.* a high-level computer language used esp. for mathematical and scientific purposes. WH: mid-20C. Abbr. of *formula translation*. The name was coined in 1953 by the US mathematician and computer expert John Backus, head of the IBM team.

fortress *n.* a fortified place, esp. a strongly fortified town accommodating a large garrison and forming a permanent stronghold. *Also v.t.* WH: 12–14C. Old French *fortresse* strong place, from Latin *fortis* strong. Cp. FORT.

fortuitous *a.* happening by chance. WH: 17C. Latin *fortuitus*, from *forte* by chance, from *fors* chance, luck. See also -OUS.

fortunate *a.* lucky, prosperous. WH: 14–15C. Latin *fortunatus*, from *fortuna*. See FORTUNE, also -ATE[2].

fortune *n.* wealth. *Also v.t., v.i.* WH: 12–14C. Old French, from Latin *fortuna* chance (as a divinity), (good) luck. An early sense (to the 18C) was chance, accident, and also (15–17C) mishap, disaster. The sense of wealth arose in the 16C.

forty *n.* the number or figure 40 or xl. *Also a.* WH: pre-1200. Old English *fēowertig*, from Germanic. See FOUR, also -TY[2].

forum *n.* a place of assembly for public discussion or judicial purposes. WH: 14–15C. Latin, rel. to *fores* (outside) door, orig. an enclosure surrounding a house.

forward *a.* at or near the forepart of anything. *Also n., v.t., adv.* WH: pre-1200. Old English *forweard*, var. of *forthweard*, from FORTH + -WARD.

fossa *n.* a shallow depression, pit or cavity. WH: 17C. Latin ditch, fem. p.p of *fodere* to dig. Cp. FOSSIL.

fosse *n.* a ditch, a trench, esp. around a fortification, commonly filled with water. WH: pre-1200. Old French, from Latin *fossa*. See FOSSA. The Roman road known as the *Fosse Way*, probably originally running from Devon to Lincolnshire, was so called from the ditch either side of it.

fossick *v.i.* to search for gold or precious stones, esp. in abandoned workings. WH: 19C. English dial., to obtain by asking, to ferret out, of unknown orig. ? Rel. to FUSS.

fossil *n.* the hardened remains of a prehistoric animal or plant found inside a rock etc. *Also a.* WH: 16C. French *fossile*, from Latin *fossilis* dug up, from *fossus*, p.p. of *fodere* to dig. See also -IL.

fossor *n.* a member of an order of inferior clergy charged with the burial of the dead. WH: 19C. Latin digger, miner, from *fossus*. See FOSSIL, also -OR.

foster *v.t.* to promote the growth of. *Also v.i., a., n.* WH: pre-1200. Old English *fōstrian*, from Germanic base of FOOD + instr. suf.

fou *a.* drunk. *Also n.* WH: 16C. Var. of FULL[1].

foudroyant *a.* (of a disease) beginning in a sudden and intense form. WH: 19C. French, pres.p. of *foudroyer* to strike (as if) by lightning, from *foudre*, from Latin *fulgur* lightning. See also -ANT.

fouetté *n.* a step in ballet in which the dancer stands on one foot and makes a whiplike movement with the other. WH: 19C. French, p.p. of *fouetter* to whip.

foul *a.* dirty, filthy. *Also adv., n., v.t., v.i.* WH: pre-1200. Old English *fūl*, from Germanic, from Indo-European base also of Latin PUS, *putere* to stink. Cp. German *faul* rotten, lazy.

foulard *n.* a soft, thin material of silk or silk mixed with cotton. WH: 19C. French, of unknown orig. According to some, the word is from Provençal *foulat* fulled (cloth).

foumart *n.* the polecat. WH: 12–14C. FOUL + form of Old English *mearth* (see MARTEN). The foumart is noted for its fetid smell. Cp. French *putois* polecat, from Latin *putere* to stink.

found[1] *v.t.* to set up or establish (an institution, organization etc.) by providing the necessary money. *Also v.i.* WH: 12–14C. Old French *fonder*, from Latin *fundare*, from *fundus* bottom, foundation.

found[2] *v.t.* to cast by melting (metal) or fusing (material for glass) and pouring it into a mould. WH: 14–15C. Old French *fondre*, from Latin *fundere* to pour, to melt.

foundation *n.* the natural or artificial base of a structure. WH: 14–15C. Old French *fondation*, from Latin *fundatio*, *fundationis*, from *fundatus*, p.p. of *fundare*. See FOUND[1], also -ATION.

founder *v.i.* (of a ship) to fill with water and sink. *Also v.t., n.* WH: 12–14C. Old French *fondrer*, *esfondrer* to send to the bottom, to collapse, from alt. of Latin *fundus* bottom. The earliest senses relate to a horse or its rider falling to the ground. The sense of a ship sinking evolved in the 17C.

foundling *n.* a deserted child of unknown parents. WH: 12–14C. P.p. of FIND + -LING[1], prob. based on Middle Dutch *vondeling*.

fount *n.* a spring, a fountain, a well. WH: 16C. Prob. back-formation from FOUNTAIN, based on pair MOUNT[2]/ MOUNTAIN.

fountain *n.* an ornamental jet of water driven high into the air by pressure. WH: 12–14C. Old French *fontaine*, from Late Latin *fontana*, use as n. of *fontanus*, from *fons*, *fontis* spring.

four *n.* the number or figure 4 or iv. *Also a.* WH: pre-1200. Old English *fēower*, from Germanic, from Indo-European base also of Sanskrit *catvārah̬*, Greek *tessares*, Latin *quattuor*.

fourchette *n.* a thin fold of skin at the back of the vulva. WH: 18C. French, dim. of *fourche*. See FORK, also -ETTE.

fourgon *n.* a French baggage-wagon. WH: 19C. French, of unknown orig. The wagon may originally have been known as a *charrette à fourgon*, from *fourgon* poker (from Popular Latin *furicare*, from Latin *furari* to steal), with reference to its slatted sides, resembling pokers.

Fourier analysis *n.* the analysis of periodic function into its harmonic components, using an infinite trigonometric series. WH: 19C. Jean-Baptiste Joseph *Fourier*, 1768–1830, French mathematician.

Fourierism *n.* a system of social reorganization advocated by Fourier, based on the principle of natural affinities. WH: 19C. French *Fouiérisme*, from Charles *Fourier*, 1772–1837, French socialist + -ISM.

fourteen *n.* the number or figure 14 or xiv. *Also a.* WH: pre-1200. Old English *fēowertīene*, from Germanic. See FOUR, -TEEN.

fourth *n.* any one of four equal parts, a quarter. *Also n., a.* WH: pre-1200. Old English *fēowertha*, from Germanic, from Indo-European base also of Latin *quartus*, Greek *tetartos*, Sanskrit *caturtha*. See also -TH[1].

fovea *n.* a small pit or depression. WH: 17C. Latin small pit.

foveola *n.* a small depression. WH: 19C. Latin, dim. of FOVEA.

fowl *n.* a cock or hen of the domestic or poultry kind, kept mainly for its eggs and flesh. *Also v.i.* WH: pre-1200. Old English *fugol*, from Germanic, from base of FLY[2]. Cp. German *Vogel* bird. This was the general word for bird until at least the 15C. It still has the general sense as the second element in combinations such as *waterfowl* (WATER), *wildfowl* (WILD).

fox *n.* any of various doglike mammals of the genus *Vulpes* or a related genus with a pointed snout, erect ears and a straight bushy tail, esp. the reddish brown *V. vulpes*. *Also v.t., v.i.* WH: pre-1200. Old English, from Germanic. Cp. VIXEN.

foyer *n.* the entrance hall or other large public area where people meet or wait in a hotel, theatre etc. WH: 18C. French hearth, home, from Latin *focus* fire. See also -ER[2].

Fra *n.* brother, a title given to an Italian monk or friar. WH: 16C. Abbr. of Italian *frate* monk, friar, from Latin *frater* brother.

frabjous *a.* joyous. WH: 19C. Word invented by Lewis Carroll, appar. intended to suggest a blend of FAIR[1], FABULOUS and *joyous* (JOY).

fracas *n.* a disturbance, a row, an uproar, a noisy quarrel. WH: 18C. French, from *fracasser* from Italian *fracassare* to make an uproar.

fractal *n.* a computer-generated figure produced from a simpler figure by applying a fixed set of rules, and itself giving rise to more complex figures by repeated application of the same rules. *Also a.* WH: late 20C. French, from Latin *fractus*. See FRACTION, also -AL[1].

fraction *n.* a number that is not a whole number, e.g. ¼, 0.7. WH: 14–15C. Old French, from Late Latin *fractio*, *fractionis*, from Latin *fractus*, p.p. of *frangere* to break. See also -ION.

fractious *a.* apt to quarrel. WH: 17C. FRACTION + -OUS, prob. based on *factious* (FACTION[1]).

fracture *n.* the act of breaking by violence. *Also v.t., v.i.* WH: 14–15C. Old French, or from Latin *fractura*, from *fractus*. See FRACTION, also -URE.

fraenum *n.* a band or ligament restraining the action of an organ, as that of the tongue. WH: 18C. Latin bridle.

fragile *a.* brittle, easily broken. WH: 15C. Old French, or from Latin *fragilis*, from base of *frangere* to break. See also -IL. The original sense (to the 16C) was morally weak, liable to sin. Cp. FRAIL[1].

fragment[1] *n.* a piece broken off. WH: 14–15C. French, or from Latin *fragmentum*, from base of *frangere* to break. See also -MENT.

fragment[2] *v.i.* to break into fragments. *Also v.t.* WH: 19C. FRAGMENT[1].

fragrant *a.* emitting a pleasant perfume, sweet-smelling. WH: 14–15C. French, or from Latin *fragrans, fragrantis*, pres.p. of *fragrare* to smell sweet. See also -ANT.

frail[1] *a.* fragile, delicate. *Also n.* WH: 12–14C. Old French *fraile* (Modern French *frêle*), from Latin *fragilis* FRAGILE. The original sense was morally weak.

frail[2] *n.* a rush basket used for packing figs etc. WH: 14–15C. Old French *fraiel*, of unknown orig.

fraise *n.* a ruff. WH: 17C. French mesentery of a calf.

Fraktur *n.* a style of typeface formerly used for typesetting German. WH: 19C. German, from Latin *fractura* a breaking. Cp. FRACTION. The name refers to the curlicues that broke up the continuous line of a word.

framboesia *n.* the yaws, a contagious eruption characterized by swellings like raspberries. WH: 19C. Modern Latin, from French *framboise* raspberry, from Latin *fraga ambrosia* ambrosian strawberry.

frame *n.* a case or border to enclose or surround a picture, a pane of glass etc. *Also v.t.* WH: pre-1200. Old English *framian* to profit, to make progress, from base of FROM. The noun evolved from the verb in the 12–14C.

franc *n.* the standard unit of currency in France, Belgium, Switzerland and various other countries. WH: 14–15C. Old French, from Latin *Francorum rex* King of the Franks. This was the legend on gold coins first struck in the reign of Jean le Bon (1350–64). Cp. FRANK.

franchise *n.* the right to vote. *Also v.t.* WH: 12–14C. Old French, from *franc*, fem. *franche* free, FRANK + -*ise*, representing Latin -*itia* -ESS[2].

Franciscan *a.* of or relating to St Francis of Assisi, or the Franciscan order of friars. *Also n.* WH: 16C. French *franciscain*, from Modern Latin *Franciscanus*, from *Franciscus* (St) Francis, *c.*1181–1226, Italian founder in 1209 of the order of friars named for him.

francium *n.* a radioactive chemical element of the alkali metal group, at. no. 87, chem. symbol Fr. WH: mid-20C. *France* + -IUM. The element was so named in 1939 after the country of Marguerite Percy, the French chemist who discovered it in Paris.

Franco- *comb. form* of or relating to France or the French, as in *Franco-German, Franco-Russian*. WH: Medieval Latin *Francus* FRANK + -O-.

francolin *n.* a partridge of the genus *Francolinus*. WH: 17C. French, from Italian *francolino*, of unknown orig. The partridge is said to be so named from Italian *franco* free as it was a privileged (protected) bird which the commons were forbidden to kill.

Francophile *n.* an admirer of France or the French. WH: 19C. FRANCO- + -PHILE.

Francophobe *n.* a disliker or fearer of France or the French. WH: 19C. FRANCO- + -PHOBE.

Francophone *a.* French-speaking, having French as the native or an official language. *Also n.* WH: early 20C. FRANCO- + -PHONE.

franc-tireur *n.* a French light-infantry soldier belonging to an irregular corps. WH: 19C. French free shooter, from *franc* free, FRANK + *tireur*, from *tirer* to shoot + -*eur* -OR. The soldier was so called because he was free to shoot with any group of fighters.

frangible *a.* that may be easily broken. WH: 14–15C. Old French, or from Medieval Latin *frangibilis*, from *frangere* to break. See also -IBLE.

frangipane *n.* a kind of pastry made with cream, almonds and sugar; a flan filled with this. WH: 17C. French, from FRANGIPANI. The word was originally the name of the perfume, then (19C) that of the pastry or, more properly, the cream with which it is made. The pastry name is sometimes popularly said to mean Frank's bread, as if from Latin *Franci panis*. Cp. MARZIPAN.

frangipani *n.* a shrub or tree of the tropical American genus *Plumeria* with clusters of fragrant white or pink flowers. WH: 19C.

Mazio *Frangipani*, 16C Italian nobleman who invented a perfume made from the plant for scenting gloves.

franglais *n.* an informal version of French which contains a high proportion of English words. WH: mid-20C. French, blend of *français* French and *anglais* English. The word was popularized by René Étiemble in his book *Parlez-vous Franglais?* (1964). Cp. Spanglish (*Spanish* and *English*) and similar formations.

Frank *n.* a member of the ancient Germanic peoples or tribes who conquered France in the 6th cent. WH: pre-1200. Old English *Franca*, ? so named after a weapon. Cp. Old English *franca* javelin. According to some sources, the word is from Old High German *franka* brave. It is not from Old French *franc* free (FRANK).

frank *a.* candid, sincere. *Also v.t., n.* WH: 12–14C. Old French *franc*, from Medieval Latin *francus* free. The word was originally identical with the ethnic name *Francus*. See FRANK.

frankalmoign *n.* a tenure by which a religious body holds lands with no obligations except such as prayers, almsgiving etc. WH: 16C. Anglo-French *fraunke almoigne*, from Old French *franc* free, FRANK + *almone* ALMS (Modern French *aumône*).

Frankenstein *n.* a work that brings disaster to its creator. WH: 19C. *Frankenstein*, title of a novel (1818) by Mary Shelley. The novel's eponymous main character created a human monster who subsequently came to be popularly associated with the name of its creator.

frankfurter *n.* a small, smoked sausage of beef and pork. WH: 19C. German *Frankfurter Wurst* sausage of Frankfurt, a city in central Germany. Cp. HAMBURGER.

frankincense *n.* a gum or resin burning with a fragrant smell, used as incense, obtained from trees of the genus *Boswellia*. WH: 14–15C. Old French *franc encens*, lit. high-quality (see FRANK) incense.

franklin *n.* in the 14th and 15th cents., an English freeholder, not liable to feudal service. WH: 12–14C. Anglo-Latin *francalanus*, from *francalis* held without fees, from *francus* free. See FRANK, also -AL[1], -AN.

frantic *a.* wildly excited or desperately worried. *Also n.* WH: 14–15C. Old French *frénétique*, from Latin *phreneticus* FRENETIC. The original sense was mentally deranged. The current sense evolved in the 17C.

frap *v.t.* to draw together by ropes crossing each other, to secure and strengthen, to bind the end of a rope with string. WH: 12–14C. Old French *fraper* to strike (Modern French *frapper*). The original sense was to strike. The current nautical sense evolved in the 16C.

frappé *a.* iced. *Also n.* WH: 19C. French, p.p. of *frapper* to ice (drinks) (lit. to strike).

frascati *n.* an esp. white wine from the Frascati region of Italy. WH: mid-20C. *Frascati*, a district in Latium, Italy, south-east of Rome.

frass *n.* excrement of larvae. WH: 19C. German, from *fressen* to devour. See FRET[1].

fratch *v.i.* to quarrel. *Also n.* WH: 14–15C. Prob. imit. The original sense (to the 15C) was to make a harsh noise. The current sense dates from the 18C.

†frater *n.* a refectory in a monastery. WH: 12–14C. Old French *fraitur*, shortening of *refreitor*, from Late Latin *refectorium* REFECTORY.

fraternal *a.* brotherly. WH: 14–15C. Medieval Latin *fraternalis*, from Latin *fraternus*, from *frater* brother. See also -AL[1].

fratricide *n.* the murder of a brother or sister. WH: 15C. Old French, from Latin *fratricida* killer of a brother, and from Late Latin *fratricidium* killing of a brother, from *frater, fratris* brother. See -CIDE.

Frau *n.* a German woman, wife or widow; Mrs. WH: 19C. German. Cp. FROW. Ult. rel. to FREE[1].

fraud *n.* an act or course of deception deliberately practised to gain unlawful or unfair advantage. *Also v.t.* WH: 12–14C. Old French *fraude*, from Latin *fraus, fraudis* deceit, injury.

fraught *a.* involving, filled (with). *Also n.* WH: 14–15C. P.p. of obs. *fraught* to load, from Middle Dutch *vrachten*. See FREIGHT.

Fräulein *n.* a young lady, a German spinster; Miss. WH: 17C. German, dim. of FRAU. German -*lein* corresponds to English -LING[1].

Fraunhofer lines *n.pl.* the dark lines in spectra of the sun or stars. WH: 19C. Joseph von *Fraunhofer*, 1787–1826, Bavarian optician and physicist.

fraxinella n. a kind of rue or dittany, esp. *Dictamnus albus*, cultivated for its leaves and flowers which give off an inflammable vapour. WH: 17C. Modern Latin, from dim. of Latin *fraxinus* ash tree. The name alludes to the plant's pinnate leaves, like those of the ash.

fray[1] v.t. to wear away by rubbing. *Also v.i., n.* WH: 14–15C. French *frayer*, from Latin *fricare* to rub.

fray[2] n. a noisy quarrel, fighting. *Also v.t., v.i.* WH: 12–14C. Shortening of AFFRAY.

frazil n. ice crystals formed in turbulent water. WH: 19C. Canadian French *frasil* snow floating on water. Cp. French *fraisil* cinders.

frazzle v.t. to reduce to a state of physical or nervous exhaustion. *Also v.i., n.* WH: 19C. Orig. uncertain. Prob. blend of FRAY[1] and obs. *fazle* to unravel, rel. to German *fasern* to fray.

freak n. an abnormal or deformed person or thing. *Also a., v.t., v.i.* WH: 16C. Orig. unknown. Prob. from a dial. word. According to some, the word is related to Old English *frīcian* to dance.

freckle n. a yellowish or light-brown spot on the skin, caused by sunburn or other causes. *Also v.t., v.i.* WH: 14–15C. Old Norse *freknur* (pl.), from an Indo-European base meaning to break out.

free[1] a. at liberty; not under restraint. *Also adv.* WH: pre-1200. Old English *frēo*, from Germanic, from Indo-European, from base meaning to love. The Germanic sense evolved from the application of the word to members of a household connected by family ties to its head, as distinct from slaves. Cp. FRIEND.

free[2] v.t. to set at liberty, to emancipate. WH: pre-1200. Old English *frēon*, from Germanic, from base of FREE[1].

freebie n. something given for which a person does not have to pay. WH: mid-20C. Arbitrary expansion of FREE[1].

freebooter n. a pirate or buccaneer, an adventurer who makes a business of plundering. WH: 16C. Dutch *vrijbuiter*. See FREE[1], BOOTY, also -ER[1]. Cp. FILIBUSTER.

freedom n. the state of being free, liberty. WH: pre-1200. Old English *frēodōm*. See FREE[1], also -DOM.

freehold n. an estate held in fee simple, fee tail or for life. *Also a.* WH: 14–15C. Trans. of Anglo-French *fraunc tenement* free holding. See FRANK, TENEMENT.

freeman n. a person who is not a slave or serf. WH: pre-1200. FREE[1] + MAN.

freemartin n. a sexually imperfect cow, usu. born as twin with a bull calf. WH: 17C. Orig. unknown. Cp. Irish, Gaelic *mart* cow fattened for the market.

Freemason n. a member of an association of 'Free and Accepted Masons', a secret order or fraternity (probably originating as a fraternity of skilled masons, with right of free movement, about the 14th cent.). WH: 14–15C. FREE[1] + MASON.

freesia n. any of a southern African genus of bulbous flowering plants allied to the iris. WH: 19C. Modern Latin, from Friedrich H.T. *Freese*, d.1876, German physician. See also -IA. Some sources take the name from E.M. *Fries*, a Swedish botanist.

freeze v.i. to be turned from a fluid to a solid state by cold. *Also v.t., n.* WH: pre-1200. Old English *frēosan*, from Germanic, from Indo-European base represented by Latin *pruina* hoarfrost, Sanskrit *pruṣvā*.

freight n. the transportation of goods by road, railway, sea or air. *Also v.t.* WH: 14–15C. Middle Low German and Middle Dutch *vrecht*, var. of *vracht*. See FRAUGHT.

fremitus n. a movement or vibration perceptible externally, as on the walls of the chest when a patient speaks. WH: 19C. Latin, from *fremere* to roar.

French a. of or relating to France, its inhabitants or language. *Also n.* WH: pre-1200. Old English *frencisc*, from Germanic, from base of FRANK. See also -ISH[1].

frenetic a. frantic, frenzied. WH: 14–15C. Old French *frénétique*, from Latin *phreneticus*, from Late Greek *phrenētikos*, from *phrenitis* delirium, from *phrēn*, *phrenos* heart, mind. See also -ITIS, -IC. Cp. FRANTIC. The original sense was mental derangement. The current sense evolved in the 14–15C.

frenzy n. a violent bout of wild or unnatural agitation or fury. *Also a., v.t.* WH: early 20C. Old French *frénésie*, from Medieval Latin *phrenesia*, from Latin *phrenesis*, from Greek *phrēn*, *phrenos* mind. See FRENETIC, also -Y[2].

Freon® n. any of various gaseous and liquid fluorine-containing chemicals used in aerosols, refrigerants etc. WH: mid-20C. Orig. unknown. The name is perhaps from letters of *fluorinated hydrocarbon*.

frequency n. the quality of occurring frequently. WH: 16C. Latin *frequentia*, from *frequens*, *frequentis*. See FREQUENT[1], also -ENCY.

frequent[1] a. occurring often, common. WH: 14–15C. Old French *fréquent*, from Latin *frequens*, *frequentis* crowded, frequent, of unknown orig.

frequent[2] v.t. to visit or resort to often or habitually. WH: 15C. Old French *fréquenter*, or from Latin *frequentare*, from *frequens*, *frequentis*. See FREQUENT[1].

fresco n. a kind of watercolour painting on fresh plaster or on a wall covered with mortar not quite dry. *Also v.t.* WH: 16C. Italian cool, fresh. Cp. ALFRESCO. The English word first occurs in the phrase *in fresco*, representing Italian *al fresco* on the fresh (plaster).

fresh a. new. *Also adv., n., v.t., v.i.* WH: pre-1200. Old English *fersc*, from Germanic, influ. by Old French *freis* (Modern French *frais*), from same Germanic base. Cp. German *frisch*.

fresnel n. a photographic lens that has a surface of stepped concentric circles which are thinner and flatter than an ordinary lens of equivalent focal length. WH: 19C. Augustin Jean *Fresnel*, 1788–1827, French physicist.

fret[1] v.i. to be worried or troubled. *Also v.t., n.* WH: pre-1200. Old English *fretan*, from Germanic bases of FOR-, EAT. Cp. German *fressen* to eat (of animals). The original sense was (of animals) to eat, to devour. The current sense evolved in the 16C.

fret[2] v.t. to ornament, to decorate. *Also n.* WH: 14–15C. Prob. from Old French *freté*, p.p. of *freter*, rel. to *frete* trellis, interlaced work, of unknown orig.

fret[3] n. any of several small pieces of metal, wood, or ivory placed upon the fingerboard of certain stringed instruments to regulate the pitch of the notes. *Also v.t.* WH: 16C. Orig. unknown. ? Rel. to FRET[2].

Freudian a. of or relating to the psychological theories of Freud. *Also n.* WH: early 20C. Sigmund *Freud*, 1856–1939, Austrian neurologist and founder of psychoanalysis. See also -IAN.

friable a. capable of being easily reduced to powder. WH: 16C. French, or from Latin *friabilis*, from *friare* to crumble into small pieces. See also -ABLE.

friar n. a member of a monastic order, esp. one of the four mendicant orders, Augustinians or Austin Friars, Franciscans or Grey Friars, Dominicans or Black Friars, and Carmelites or White Friars. WH: 12–14C. Old French *frère*, from Latin *frater*, *fratris* brother.

fribble v.i. to act frivolously. *Also v.t., a., n.* WH: 17C. Prob. imit., partly based on FRIVOLOUS.

fricandeau n. a larded veal cutlet, braised or roasted and glazed. *Also v.t.* WH: 18C. French, ? from source of FRICASSEE.

fricassee n. small pieces of meat, esp. chicken or veal, fried, stewed and served in a usu. white sauce. *Also v.t.* WH: 16C. French *fricassée*, fem. p.p. of *fricasser* to cut up and stew in sauce, ? from Popular Latin *frigicare*, from Latin *frigere* FRY[1], or a blend of French *frire* to fry and *casser* to break.

fricative n. a consonant, such as *f*, *sh*, *th*, produced by the friction of the breath issuing through a narrow opening. *Also a.* WH: 19C. Modern Latin *fricativus*, from Latin *fricare* to rub. See also -ATIVE.

friction n. the act of two bodies rubbing together. WH: 16C. French, from Latin *frictio*, *frictionis*, from *frictus*, p.p. of *fricare* to rub. See also -ION.

Friday n. the sixth day of the week, following Thursday. *Also adv.* WH: pre-1200. Old English *Frīgedæg Frīg's* day, from *Frigg*, wife of Odin in Norse mythology, translating Late Latin *Veneris dies* day of Venus (cp. French *vendredi*), based on Greek *Aphroditēs hēmera* day of Aphrodite. Frigg's name comes from the Germanic base of FREE[1].

friend n. a person known well to another and regarded with affection, usually excluding sexual or familial relationships. *Also v.t.* WH: pre-1200. Old English *frēond*, from Germanic pres.p. of v. meaning to love, from base of FREE[1]. Cp. German *Freund*.

Friesian n. any of a breed of large black and white dairy cattle originally from Friesland. *Also a.* WH: early 20C. Alt. of FRISIAN.

frieze[1] *n.* the middle division of an entablature, between the architrave and the cornice, usu. enriched by sculpture. WH: 16C. French *frise*, from Medieval Latin *frisium*, var. of *frigium*, from Latin *Phrygium* (*opus*) Phrygian (work).

frieze[2] *n.* a coarse woollen cloth, with a rough nap on one side. WH: 14–15C. French *frise*, from Medieval Latin *frisium* Frisian (wool). Cp. FRIEZE[1].

frig *v.t.*, *v.i.* to masturbate. Also *n.* WH: 14–15C. ? Imit. Cp. obs. *fridge* to move restlessly, to fidget. According to some, the word is related to FRICTION. Cp. FROTTAGE.

frigate *n.* a naval escort vessel between a corvette and a destroyer in size. WH: 16C. French *frégate*, from Italian *fregata*, ult. of unknown orig.

frigatoon *n.* a Venetian vessel with a square stern, and only a mainmast and mizzen-mast. WH: 18C. Italian *fregatone*, augm. of *fregata* FRIGATE. See also -OON.

fright *n.* sudden and violent fear or alarm. Also *v.t.* WH: pre-1200. Old English *fryhto*, alt. of *fyrhto*, from Germanic, from base meaning afraid. Cp. German *Furcht* fear.

frigid *a.* lacking warmth or feeling or ardour. WH: 14–15C. Latin *frigidus*, from *frigere* to be cold, from *frigus* cold. See also -ID.

frigorific *a.* producing cold (from an old theory that cold is due to an imponderable substance called *frigoric* (cp. CALORIC)). WH: 17C. Latin *frigorificus*, from *frigus*, *frigoris* cold. See also -FIC.

frijol *n.* a bean resembling the kidney bean, used in Mexican cookery. WH: 16C. Spanish bean, ult. from Latin *phaseolus*. Cp. FLAGEOLET[2].

frill *n.* a pleated or fluted strip of cloth sewn upon one edge only. Also *v.t.*, *v.i.* WH: 16C. Orig. uncertain. ? From (or rel. to) Flemish *frul*.

Frimaire *n.* the third month of the French revolutionary calendar, from 22 November to 21 December. WH: 19C. French, from *frimas* hoarfrost, from Frankish *hrim*. Cp. RIME.

fringe *n.* an ornamental border to dress or furniture, consisting of loose threads or tassels. Also *v.t.*, *a.* WH: 12–14C. Old French *frenge* (Modern French *frange*), alt. of Late Latin FIMBRIA.

fringilline *a.* finchlike, belonging to the genus *Fringilla* or family Fringillidae of small singing birds containing the finches. WH: 19C. Latin *fringilla* finch + -INE.

frippery *n.* worthless, needless or showy adornments. Also *a.* WH: 16C. French *friperie* or Old French *freperie*, from *frepe* rag, old clothes, ult. of unknown orig. See also -ERY.

Frisbee® *n.* a plastic disc, used in throwing and catching games. WH: mid-20C. The name is said to come from the *Frisbie* bakery in Bridgeport, Connecticut, USA, whose pie tins could be used similarly.

frisée *n.* ENDIVE. WH: late 20C. French, from *chicorée frisée* curly chicory. See CHICORY, FRISETTE.

frisette *n.* a front or band of artificial curls worn on the forehead. WH: 19C. French, from *friser* to curl, to frizz. See also -ETTE.

friseur *n.* a hairdresser. WH: 18C. French, from *friser* (see FRISETTE) + *-eur* -OR.

Frisian *a.* of or relating to Friesland. Also *n.* WH: 16C. Latin *Frisii* Frisians, from Old Frisian *Frīsa*. See also -IAN.

frisk *v.i.* to leap or gambol about. Also *v.t.*, *n.* WH: 14–15C. Old French *frisque* vigorous, alert, lively, var. of *friche*, earlier *frique*, prob. ult. rel. to Old High German *frisc* fresh, lively, and so to FRESH.

frisket *n.* a light frame by which a sheet of paper to be printed is held in place. WH: 17C. French *frisquette*, from Provençal *frisqueto*, from Spanish *frasqueta*.

frisson *n.* a shudder, a thrill. WH: 18C. French shiver, thrill, from Late Latin *frictio*, *frictionis*, from *frictus*, p.p. of *frigere* FRY[1], assoc. with *frigere* to be cold (cp. FRIGID).

frit[1] *n.* a calcined mixture of sand and fluxes ready to be melted in a crucible to form glass. Also *v.t.* WH: 17C. Italian *fritta*, fem. p.p. (used as n.) of *friggere* FRY[1].

frit[2] *a.* frightened. WH: 19C. P.p. of dial. v. *fright*, from Germanic base of FRIGHT.

frit-fly *n.* a small fly, *Oscinella frit*, that arrests the growth of wheat and other cereals by boring into the bud. WH: 19C. Latin *frit* small particle in ear of corn + FLY[1].

fritillary *n.* any plant of the liliaceous genus *Fritillaria*, esp. snake's

head (*F. meleagris*), with drooping bell-like flowers speckled with dull purple. WH: 17C. Modern Latin *Fritillaria*, from Latin *fritillus* dice box + *-aria* -ARY[1]. The name probably refers to the chequered corolla of *F. meleagris*.

frittata *n.* an Italian dish made with fried beaten eggs. WH: mid-20C. Italian, from *frittare* to fry, from *fritto*, p.p. of *friggere* FRY[1]. Cp. FRITTER[1].

fritter[1] *n.* a piece of fruit, meat etc. dipped in a light batter and fried. WH: 14–15C. Old French *friture*, from Latin *frictus*, p.p. of *frigere* FRY[1]. See also -ER[2].

fritter[2] *n.* fragments, bits, shreds. Also *v.t.* WH: 17C. Alt. of *flitters* fragments, itself alt. of *fitters*, from obs. *fitter*, prob. rel. to Middle High German *vetze* (German *Fetzen*) rag, scrap. See also -ER[5].

fritto misto *n.* a dish of fried food, esp. seafood. WH: early 20C. Italian mixed fry, from *fritto* (see FRITTATA) + *misto* mixed.

fritz *n.* the process of failing (only in the phrase *on the fritz*). WH: early 20C. Orig. unknown.

frivolous *a.* trifling, of little or no importance. WH: 14–15C. Latin *frivolus* silly, trifling + -OUS.

frizz *v.t.* to curl, to crisp. Also *v.i.*, *n.* WH: 14–15C. Old French *friser*, ? from *frire*, *fris-* FRY[1] (cp. FRISSON).

frizzle[1] *v.t.*, *v.i.* to form (into) crisp, tight curls. Also *n.* WH: 16C. FRIZZ + -LE[4].

frizzle[2] *v.t.* to fry (bacon etc.) with a hissing noise. Also *v.i.* WH: 18C. FRY[1] with imit. ending. See also -LE[4]. Cp. FIZZLE, SIZZLE.

fro *adv.* away, backwards (only in the phrase *to and fro*). WH: 12–14C. Old Norse *frá*. Cp. FROM, FROWARD.

frock *n.* a woman's or girl's dress. Also *v.t.* WH: 14–15C. Old French *froc*, from Frankish. Cp. German *Rock* skirt.

froe *n.* a cleaving tool, with a handle set at right angles to the wedge-shaped blade. WH: 16C. Use as n. of FROWARD in sense turned away.

Froebel system *a.* a form of kindergarten in which the child's senses are developed by handwork etc. WH: 19C. Friedrich W.A. *Fröbel*, 1782–1852, German teacher and educationalist.

frog[1] *n.* a squat, smooth-skinned, tailless amphibian of the order Anura with the back legs developed for jumping. WH: pre-1200. Old English *frogga*, pet form rel. to Old English *forsc*, *frosc*, from Germanic. Cp. German *Frosch*.

frog[2] *n.* a spindle-shaped button or toggle used for fastening military cloaks and coats. WH: 18C. Orig. unknown.

frog[3] *n.* a tender horny substance in the middle of the sole of a horse's foot. WH: 17C. Orig. uncertain. Appar. from FROG[1], influ. by Italian *forchetta* or French *fourchette*, both in same sense, respectively dims. of *forca* and *fourche*. See FORK.

froideur *n.* coolness in a relationship between people. WH: early 20C. French coolness, from *froid* cold, from Latin *frigidus* FRIGID.

frolic *v.i.* to play pranks. Also *a.*, *n.* WH: 16C. Dutch *vrolijk* (a.), from Middle Dutch *vro* glad, joyous + *-lijk* -LY[1]. Cp. German *fröhlich* happy.

from *prep.* away, out of (expressing separation, departure, point of view, distinction or variation). WH: pre-1200. Old English *fram*, from Germanic base meaning forward, corresponding to PRO-[1] + suf. *-m*.

fromage blanc *n.* a kind of soft French cheese made from cow's milk, with a creamy sour taste. WH: late 20C. French white cheese, from *fromage* cheese (from Popular Latin *formaticum*, from Latin *forma* FORM) + *blanc* white (cp. BLANK).

fromage frais *n.* a kind of smooth low-fat soft cheese with a light texture. WH: late 20C. French fresh cheese, from *fromage* (see FROMAGE BLANC) + *frais* FRESH.

frond *n.* a leaflike expansion in which the functions of stem and foliage are not entirely differentiated, often bearing the organs of fructification, as in many cryptogams, esp. the ferns. WH: 18C. Latin *frons*, *frondis* leaf.

Fronde *n.* the French party, 1648–57, who attacked Mazarin and the Court during the minority of Louis XIV. WH: 18C. French, lit. sling. The name refers to a children's game played in the streets of Paris in defiance of the civil authorities.

front *n.* the forward part or side of anything. Also *a.*, *v.t.*, *v.i.*, *int.* WH: 12–14C. Old French, from Latin *frons*, *frontis* forehead, front.

frontier *n.* that part of a country which fronts or borders upon another. Also *a.*, *v.i.*, *v.t.* WH: 14–15C. Old French *frontière*, deriv. of Latin *frons*, *frontis* FRONT.

frontispiece *n.* a picture facing the title-page of a book. *Also v.t.* WH: 16C. French *frontispice* or Late Latin *frontispicium* façade of a building, from Latin *frons, frontis* FRONT + *-spicium* as in *auspicium* AUSPICE, assim. to PIECE.

frontlet *n.* a small band or fillet worn on the forehead. WH: 15C. Old French *frontelet*, dim. of *frontel* (Modern French *frontal*), from Latin *frontale*, from *frons, frontis* FRONT. See also -AL¹, -LET.

fronto- *comb. form* of or relating to the forehead, the frontal bone of the forehead, or the frontal region. WH: Latin *frons, frontis* forehead, FRONT. See also -O-.

fronton *n.* a pediment, frontal. WH: 17C. French, from Italian *frontone*, augm. of *fronte* forehead. See FRONT, also -OON.

†frore *a.* frozen, frosty. *Also adv.* WH: 12–14C. Orig. p.p. of FREEZE.

frost *n.* minute crystals of frozen dew or vapour, rime or hoar frost, esp. covering the ground at night. *Also v.i., v.t.* WH: pre-1200. Old English, from Germanic, from base of FREEZE. Cp. German *Frost*.

froth *n.* the mass of small bubbles caused in liquors by shaking or fermentation. *Also v.t., v.i.* WH: 14–15C. Old Norse *frotha*, from Germanic. Cp. Old English *āfrēothan* to froth.

frottage *n.* the technique of producing images or textures by rubbing with e.g. a pencil on a sheet of paper placed on top of an object. WH: mid-20C. French rubbing, friction, from *frotter* to rub, from Old French *freter*, from Popular Latin *frictare*, freq. of Latin *fricare* to rub.

frou-frou *n.* a rustling, as of a silk dress. WH: 19C. French, imit.

frow *n.* a Dutchwoman. WH: 14–15C. Dutch *vrouw* woman. Cp. FRAU.

†froward *a.* not willing to comply, refractory, perverse, mutinous. *Also prep., adv.* WH: pre-1200. Old English *frāward*. See FRO, -WARD. Cp. TOWARD.

frown *v.i.* to express displeasure, worry or seriousness by contracting the brows. *Also v.t., n.* WH: 14–15C. Old French *frognier*, from *frogne* surly look, of Celtic orig. Cp. Welsh *ffroen* nostril.

frowst *n.* stuffiness. *Also v.i.* WH: 19C. Back-formation from *frowsty*, of uncertain orig. Cp. Old French *frouste* ruinous.

frowzy *a.* musty, fusty, close. WH: 17C. Orig. uncertain. Prob. rel. to obs. *froughy* musty, stale and *frowsty* (FROWST).

frozen *a.* preserved by freezing. WH: 12–14C. P.p. of FREEZE.

Fructidor *n.* in the French Revolutionary calendar, the 12th month of the republican year from 18 August to 16 September. WH: 18C. French, from Latin *fructus* fruit + Greek *dōron* gift.

fructify *v.t.* to make fruitful or productive. *Also v.i.* WH: 12–14C. Old French *fructifier*, from Latin *fructificare*, from *fructus* fruit. See also -FY.

frugal *a.* thrifty, sparing. WH: 16C. Latin *frugalis*, from *frugi* economical. See also -AL¹. Latin *frugi* is an indeclinable adjective formed from the dative of *frux, frugis* fruit.

frugiferous *a.* bearing fruit, fruitful. WH: 17C. Latin *frugifer* (from *frux, frugis* fruit) + -OUS. See -FEROUS.

fruit *n.* the edible succulent product of a plant or tree in which the seeds are enclosed. *Also v.i., v.t.* WH: 12–14C. Old French, from Latin *fructus* (enjoyment of) the produce of the soil, harvest, fruit, from *frui* to enjoy, from base of *fruges* fruits of the earth.

fruition *n.* the bearing of fruit. WH: 14–15C. Old French, from Late Latin *fruitio, fruitionis*, from Latin *fruitus*, p.p. of *frui* to enjoy. See FRUIT, also -ION.

frumentaceous *a.* of the nature of, resembling or composed of wheat or other cereal. WH: 17C. Late Latin *frumentaceus*, from Latin *frumentum* corn. See also -ACEOUS.

frumenty *n.* a dish made of wheat boiled in milk and flavoured with spices. WH: 14–15C. Old French *frumentee*, from *frument, fourment* (Modern French *froment* wheat), from Latin *frumentum* corn. See also -Y².

frump *n.* an old-fashioned, unattractive or dowdy-looking woman. *Also v.t.* WH: 16C. Prob. shortening of obs. *frumple* to wrinkle, to crumple, from Middle Dutch *verrompelen*, from *ver-* FOR- + *rompelen* RUMPLE.

frustrate¹ *v.t.* to make ineffective. WH: 14–15C. Latin *frustratus*, p.p. of *frustrari*, from *frustra* in vain. See also -ATE³.

frustrate² *a.* vain, of no effect. WH: 15C. Latin *frustratus*. See FRUSTRATE¹, also -ATE².

frustule *n.* the covering or shell, usu. in two valves, of a diatom. WH: 19C. Latin *frustulum*, dim. of FRUSTUM. See also -ULE.

frustum *n.* the part of a regular solid next to the base, formed by cutting off the top. WH: 17C. Latin piece cut off.

frutex *n.* a woody plant smaller than a tree, a shrub. WH: 17C. Latin.

fry¹ *v.t.* to cook with hot fat or oil in a pan. *Also v.i., n.* WH: 12–14C. Old French *frire*, from Latin *frigere*, rel. to Greek *phrugein*, Sanskrit *bhṛjjati* to grill.

fry² *n.pl.* young fish, esp. those fresh from the spawn, also yearling salmon. WH: 12–14C. Old Norse *frjó*, of unknown orig. According to some, the word is related to FRAY¹, referring to the way some fish spawn by rubbing their belly on the sand.

ft lb *abbr.* foot-pound. WH: See LB.

FT–SE *abbr.* Financial Times–Stock Exchange. WH: Cp. FOOTSIE.

fubsy *a.* fat, squat. WH: 18C. Obs. *fub* small chubby person, ? blend of FAT and CHUB. See also -SY.

fuchsia *n.* any garden plant of the genus *Fuchsia*, with hanging purple, red or white funnel-shaped flowers. WH: 18C. Modern Latin, from Leonard *Fuchs*, 1501–66, German botanist. See also -IA.

fuchsine *n.* a magenta dye of the rosaniline series. WH: 19C. German *Fuchs* fox, translating French *Renard*, name of the chemical company that first produced it commercially + -INE.

fuck *v.i., v.t.* to have sexual intercourse (with). *Also n., int.* WH: 16C. Orig. unknown. ? Rel. to German *ficken* to strike, to copulate with.

fucus *n.* a genus of algae, containing some of the commonest seaweeds. WH: 17C. Latin rock lichen, red dye, from Greek *phukos* seaweed.

fuddle *v.t.* to make stupid with drink, to intoxicate. *Also v.i., n.* WH: 16C. Orig. unknown.

fuddy-duddy *a.* old-fogeyish, old-fashioned. *Also n.* WH: early 20C. Orig. unknown.

fudge¹ *n.* a soft sweet of chocolate, candy etc. *Also int.* WH: 18C. FUDGE².

fudge² *v.t.* to deal with in a makeshift, careless way. *Also v.i., n.* WH: 17C. ? Alt. of obs. FADGE.

fuel *n.* combustible matter, such as wood, coal or peat burnt to provide heat or power. *Also v.t., v.i.* WH: 12–14C. Old French *fouaille*, from Popular Latin *focalia*, from Latin *focus* hearth.

fuero *n.* in Spain, a code, charter, grant of privileges or custom having the force of law. WH: early 20C. Spanish, from Latin FORUM.

fug *n.* the close atmosphere of an unventilated room. *Also v.i.* WH: 19C. Orig. unknown.

fugacious *a.* fleeting, lasting only a short time, transitory, ephemeral. WH: 17C. Latin *fugax, fugacis*, from *fugere* to flee. See also -ACIOUS.

-fuge *comb. form* expelling, driving out, as in *febrifuge*. WH: Modern Latin *-fugus*, from Latin *fugare* to put to flight.

fugitive *a.* fleeing, running away. *Also n.* WH: 14–15C. Old French *fugitif*, from Latin *fugitivus*, from *fugitus*, p.p. of *fugere* to flee. See also -IVE.

fugleman *n.* a soldier who takes up a position in front of a company as a guide to the others in their drill. WH: 19C. German *Flügelmann* flank man, from *Flügel* wing + *Mann* man.

fugue *n.* a musical composition on one or more short subjects, which are repeated by successively entering voices and developed contrapuntally. *Also v.i.* WH: 16C. French, or from Italian *fuga*, from Latin *fuga* flight, rel. to *fugere* to flee.

führer *n.* a leader, esp. one who exerts tyrannical authority. WH: mid-20C. German leader. The word became widely known as Adolf Hitler's title in World War II.

-ful *suf.* full of, abounding in, having, able to, as in *artful, beautiful, sinful, mournful, wilful*. WH: FULL¹.

Fulah *n.* a member of one of the peoples of W and central Africa. WH: 18C. Indigenous name. Cp. Fulfulde *pulo* Fulah person.

fulcrum *n.* the fixed point on which the bar of a lever rests or about which it turns. WH: 17C. Latin post or foot of a couch, from base of *fulcire* to prop up, to support.

fulfil *v.t.* to accomplish, to carry out. WH: pre-1200. Old English *fullfyllan*, from FULL¹ + *fyllan* FILL. The original sense was to fill full, to pervade.

fulgent *a.* shining, dazzling, exceedingly bright. WH: 14–15C. Latin *fulgens, fulgentis*, pres.p. of *fulgere* to shine. See also -ENT.

fuliginous *a.* sooty, smoky, soot-coloured. WH: 16C. Late Latin *fuliginosus*, from *fuligo, fuliginis* soot. See also -OUS.

full¹ *a.* filled up, replete. *Also adv., n., v.t., v.i.* WH: pre-1200. Old English, from Germanic, from Indo-European, rel. to Greek *polus*, Latin *plenus*.

full² *v.t.* to cleanse and thicken (cloth). WH: 12–14C. Prob. back-formation from *fuller* person who fulls cloth, from Latin *fullo* (of unknown orig.) + -ER¹.

fuller *n.* a blacksmith's tool for making grooves. *Also v.t.* WH: 19C. Orig. unknown.

fullerene *n.* a molecule consisting of 60 carbon atoms arranged in spherical shape, with possible uses as a lubricant, superconductor etc., also called a *Bucky ball.* WH: late 20C. Abbr. of BUCKMINSTER-FULLERENE.

fulmar *n.* a seabird of the genus *Fulmarus glacialis*, allied to the petrels, abundant in the Arctic seas. WH: 17C. Hebridean Norn dial., (Gaelic *fulmair*), from Old Norse *fúll* FOUL + *már* gull (cp. MEW²). The name refers to the bird's habit of regurgitating its oily stomach contents when disturbed.

fulminate¹ *v.i.* to lighten or thunder. *Also v.t.* WH: 14–15C. Latin *fulminatus*, p.p. of *fulminare* to strike with lightning, from *fulmen, fulminis* lightning. See also -ATE³.

fulminate² *n.* a salt of fulminic acid. WH: 19C. From *fulminic* (from Latin *fulmen, fulminis* lightning + -IC) + -ATE¹.

fulsome *a.* (esp. of compliments, flattery etc.) excessive, satiating. WH: 12–14C. FULL¹ + -SOME¹. The original sense was plentiful. The current sense appears to have evolved by associated with FOUL. The mid-20C saw the re-emergence of the original sense, as e.g. *fulsome* praise.

fulvous *a.* tawny, reddish-yellow. WH: 17C. Latin *fulvus* + -OUS.

fumarole *n.* a hole in the ground in a volcanic region forming an exit for subterranean vapours. WH: 19C. Obs. Italian *fumaruolo*, from Late Latin *fumarolium* vent, hole for smoke, dim. ult. of Latin *fumus* smoke + -arium -ARY¹. See also -OLE².

fumatorium *n.* a room or apparatus for fumigating. WH: 19C. Latin, from *fumare* to smoke + -ORIUM.

fumatory *n.* a place for smoking or fumigation. WH: 18C. Latin FUMATORIUM.

fumble *v.i.* to grope about. *Also v.t., n.* WH: 14–15C. Low German *fummeln, fommeln*, rel. to Danish *famle* to grope.

fume *n.* a smoke, vapour or gas, esp. an unpleasant or toxic one. *Also v.i., v.t.* WH: 14–15C. Old French *fum*, from Latin *fumus* smoke, and from Old French *fume*, from *fumer*, from Latin *fumare* to smoke.

fumet *n.* the smell of game or meat when high. WH: 18C. French, from *fumer* FUME.

fumigate *v.t.* to subject to the action of smoke or vapour, esp. for the purpose of disinfection. WH: 16C. Latin *fumigatus*, p.p. of *fumigare*, from *fumus* FUME. See also -ATE³.

fumitory *n.* a herb belonging to the genus *Fumaria*, esp. *F. officinalis*, formerly used for skin diseases. WH: 14–15C. Old French *fumeterre*, from Medieval Latin *fumus terrae*, lit. smoke of the earth. The name alludes to the plant's diffuse grey-coloured foliage.

fun *n.* (a source of) amusement, enjoyment. *Also a.* WH: 17C. Prob. orig. dial. var. of obs. *fon* to be foolish, of uncertain orig. Cp. FOND.

funambulist *n.* a rope-walker or rope-dancer; a performer on the tight or slack rope. WH: 18C. French *funambule* or Latin *funambulus*, from *funis* rope + *ambulare* to walk.

function *n.* a specific purpose of any animal or plant organ. *Also v.i.* WH: 16C. Old French *fonction*, from Latin *functio, functionis*, from *functus*, p.p. of *fungi* to perform. See also -ION.

fund *n.* a sum of money or stock of anything available for use or enjoyment. *Also v.t.* WH: 17C. Latin *fundus* bottom. The earliest senses (to the 18C) were bottom, basis.

fundament *n.* the lower part of the body, the buttocks. WH: 12–14C. Old French *fondement*, from Latin *fundamentum*, from *fundare* FOUND¹. See also -MENT. An earlier sense (to the 17C) was foundation (of a building), but the current sense also dates from the first.

fundamental *a.* of, relating to or serving as a foundation or base. *Also n.* WH: 14–15C. French *fondamental* or Late Latin *fundamentalis*. See FUNDAMENT, also -AL¹.

fundus *n.* the base of an organ or the part furthest away from its opening. WH: 18C. Latin bottom.

funeral *n.* the ceremony held at the burial or cremation of a dead person. *Also a.* WH: 14–15C. Old French *funeraille*, from Medieval Latin *funeralia*, neut. pl. of Late Latin *funeralis*, from Latin *funus, funeris* funeral, death, corpse. See also -AL¹.

fungible *a.* of such a nature that it may be replaced by another thing of the same class. *Also n.pl.* WH: 17C. Medieval Latin *fungibilis*, from *fungi* to perform, to enjoy. See also -IBLE.

fungus *n.* a mushroom, toadstool, mould, mildew, or other cryptogamous plant, without chlorophyll and feeding on organic matter. WH: 14–15C. Latin, prob. from Greek *sphoggos, spoggos* SPONGE.

funicular *a.* of, relating to, consisting of, or depending on a rope or cable. *Also n.* WH: 17C. Latin *funiculus*, dim. of *funis* rope. See also -CULE, -AR¹.

funk¹ *n.* a state of fear or panic. *Also v.i., v.t.* WH: 18C. Orig. uncertain. ? From FUNK².

funk² *n.* a stink. *Also v.t., v.i.* WH: Prob. from dial. French *funkier*, from a Popular Latin word represented also by Italian *fumicare*, from Late Latin *fumigare*, from Latin *fumus* smoke.

funnel *n.* a conical vessel usu. terminating below in a tube, for pouring liquids etc. into vessels with a small opening. *Also v.t., v.i.* WH: 14–15C. Appar. from Old French, from Provençal *fonill*, from Latin *infundibulum, fundibulum*, from *infundere* to pour in. Cp. INFUSE.

funny¹ *a.* amusing, causing laughter. *Also n.* WH: 18C. FUN + -Y¹.

funny² *n.* a narrow, clinker-built pleasure boat, for a pair of sculls. WH: 18C. Orig. uncertain. ? From FUNNY¹.

fur *n.* the soft fine hair growing thickly upon certain animals, distinct from ordinarily longer hair. *Also v.t., v.i.* WH: 12–14C. Anglo-French, alt. of Old French *forrer* to line, to encase (Modern French *fourrer*), from *forre* sheath, from Germanic. Cp. German *Futter* lining.

furbelow *n.* a piece of material, plaited and puckered, used as trimming on skirts and petticoats, a flounce. *Also v.t.* WH: 17C. Alt. of FALBALA, influ. by FUR, BELOW.

furbish *v.t.* to rub so as to brighten, to polish up. WH: 14–15C. Old French *forbir, forbiss-* (Modern French *fourbir*), from Germanic. See also -ISH².

furcate¹ *a.* forked, dividing into branches like the prongs of a fork. WH: 19C. Late Latin *furcatus* cloven, from Latin *furca* FORK. See also -ATE².

furcate² *v.i.* to fork, to divide into branches. WH: 19C. FURCATE¹. See also -ATE³.

furcula *n.* the two clavicles of birds joined together so as to form one V-shaped bone, the wishbone. WH: 19C. Latin, dim. of *furca* FORK. See also -CULE.

furfur *n.* scurf or dandruff. WH: 14–15C. Latin bran.

furfurol *n.* an oil formed in the dry distillation of sugar, or by distilling bran with dilute sulphuric acid. WH: 19C. Latin FURFUR + -OL.

furioso *adv.* with fury or vehemence. *Also n.* WH: 17C. Italian, from Latin *furiosus* FURIOUS.

furious *a.* extremely angry. WH: 14–15C. Old French *furieus* (Modern French *furieux*), from Latin *furiosus*, from *furia* FURY. See also -OUS.

furl *v.t.* to roll up (a sail) and wrap about a yard, mast or stay. *Also v.i.* WH: 16C. Old French *ferler*, earlier *fermlier*, from *ferm* FIRM¹ + *lier* to bind (from Latin *ligare*).

furlong *n.* a measure of length, the eighth part of a mile, 220 yd. (201 m). WH: pre-1200. Old English *furlang*, from *furh* FURROW + *lang* LONG¹. The original sense was the length of a furrow in a common field (regarded as a square of 10 acres).

furlough *n.* leave of absence, esp. from military duty or from missionary service. *Also v.t., v.i.* WH: 17C. Dutch *verlof*, based on German *Verlaub*, from *ver-* FOR- + Germanic base of LEAVE².

furnace *n.* a chamber or structure containing a chamber in which fuel is burned for the production of intense heat, esp. for melting ores, metals etc. *Also v.t.* WH: 12–14C. Old French *fornais* (Modern French *fournaise*), from Latin *fornax, fornacis*, from *fornus* oven.

furnish *v.t.* to equip, to fit up, esp. (a house or room) with movable furniture. *Also v.i.* WH: 14–15C. Old French *furnir, furniss-* (Modern French *fournir*), from Germanic v. meaning to promote, to accommodate, from base of FRAME, FROM. See also -ISH².

furniture *n.* movable articles, e.g. beds, chairs, tables etc. with which a house or room is furnished. WH: 16C. French *fourniture*, from *fournir* FURNISH. English has developed a specialized sense that Romance languages do not have. French *fourniture* thus means simply supply, provision.

furore *n.* an outburst of public indignation. WH: 18C. Italian, from Latin *furor*, from *furere* to rage.

furphy *n.* a groundless rumour, a false report. WH: early 20C. *Furphy* carts, manufactured by the Furphy family at Shepparton, Victoria, Australia, in World War I. 'In Egypt the various rumours were brought into the camps by the drivers of the water carts. As those water carts were branded Furphy, it is easy to see the origin of the slang meaning' (Robert Graves, *On Gallipoli*, 1915).

furrow *n.* a trench in the earth made by a plough. *Also v.t., v.i.* WH: pre-1200. Old English *furh*, from Germanic, from Indo-European base also of Latin *porca* ridge between furrows. Cp. German *Furche*.

further¹ *a.* more remote. *Also adv.* WH: pre-1200. Old English *furthra*, from Germanic base of FORTH. See also -ER³.

further² *v.t.* to help forward, to advance. WH: pre-1200. Old English *fyrthrian*, from *furthor*, *furthra* FURTHER¹.

furtive *a.* stealthy, sly. WH: 17C. Old French *furtif* or Latin *furtivus*, from *furt-*, stem in *furtum* theft. See also -IVE.

furuncle *n.* a superficial inflammatory tumour, with a central core, a boil. WH: 14–15C. Latin *furunculus*, lit. petty thief, dim. of *fur* thief. See also -UNCLE. Cp. FERRET¹. Latin *furunculus* was the word for the secondary branch of a vine that robbed the main branches of sap.

fury *n.* vehement, uncontrollable anger. WH: 14–15C. Old French *furie*, from Latin *furia*, from *furiosus* FURIOUS, from *furere* to rage. See also -Y².

furze *n.* gorse. WH: pre-1200. Old English *fyrs*, of unknown orig.

fusarole *n.* a moulding placed immediately under the echinus in Doric, Ionic or composite capitals. WH: 17C. French *fusarolle*, from Italian *fusaruola*, ult. from Latin *fusus* spindle. See also -OLE².

fuscous *a.* brown tinged with grey or black; dingy. WH: 17C. Latin *fuscus* dusky + -OUS.

fuse¹ *v.t.* to melt. *Also v.i., n.* WH: 16C. Latin *fusus*, p.p. of *fundere* to pour, to melt. Cp. FOUND².

fuse² *n.* a tube, cord or casing filled or saturated with combustible material, and used for igniting a charge in a mine or projectile. *Also v.t.* WH: 17C. Italian *fuso* spindle, from Latin *fusus*.

fusee *n.* the cone round which the chain is wound in a clock or watch. WH: 16C. French *fusée* spindleful, ult. from Latin *fusus* spindle.

fuselage *n.* the main body of an aeroplane. WH: early 20C. French, from *fuseler* to shape like a spindle, from *fuseau* spindle. See FUSIL².

fusel oil *n.* a poisonous oily product, composed chiefly of amyl alcohol, formed during the manufacture of corn, potato or grape spirits. WH: 19C. German *Fusel* bad brandy (cp. FOOZLE) + OIL.

fusiform *a.* shaped like a spindle, tapering at both ends. WH: 18C. Latin *fusus* spindle + *-i-* + -FORM.

fusil¹ *n.* an obsolete firelock, lighter than a musket. WH: 16C. French, ult. from Latin FOCUS hearth.

fusil² *n.* a bearing resembling a lozenge, longer in proportion to breadth. WH: 14–15C. Old French (Modern French *fuseau*), dim. of Latin *fusus* spindle.

fusilli *n.pl.* pasta in the form of short, thick spirals. WH: mid-20C. Italian, pl. of *fusillo*, dim. of *fuso* spindle.

fuss *n.* excessive activity or trouble, taken or exhibited. *Also v.i., v.t.* WH: 18C. Orig. uncertain. ? Anglo-Irish, or imit.

fustanella *n.* a type of short white kilt worn by men in Greece and Albania. WH: 19C. Italian, from Modern Greek *phoustani*, *phoustanela*, and from Albanian *fustan*, ? from Italian *fustagno* FUSTIAN.

fustian *n.* a coarse twilled cotton or cotton and linen cloth, with short velvety pile. *Also a.* WH: 12–14C. Old French *fustaigne* (Modern French *futaine*), from Medieval Latin *fustaneum*, (*pannus*) *fustaneus* (cloth) of *Fostat*, suburb of Cairo, Egypt.

fustic *n.* a yellow wood used in dyeing, from either of two kinds of tree, esp. *old fustic*. WH: 14–15C. French *fustoc*, from Spanish, from Arabic *fustuk*, from Greek *pistakē* pistachio tree.

†fustigate *v.t.* to beat with a cudgel. WH: 17C. Late Latin *fustigatus*, p.p. of *fustigare* to cudgel to death, from *fustis* cudgel. See also -ATE³.

fusty *a.* mouldy, musty. WH: 15C. Old French *fusté*, from *fust* wine cask (Modern French *fût*), from Latin *fustis* cudgel. See also -Y¹.

futchel *n.* any of the timbers set lengthwise in the framework of a carriage, to support the splinter-bar and the shafts or pole. WH: 18C. Orig. unknown.

futhorc *n.* the runic alphabet. WH: 19C. From the first six letters, *f, u, th, o* or *a, r, k*.

futile *a.* useless, of no effect. WH: 16C. Latin *futilis* that easily pours out, leaky, from *fut-*, appar. from *fundere* to pour. See also -IL.

futon *n.* a Japanese floor-mattress used as a bed. WH: 19C. Japanese bedding.

futtock *n.* any of the timbers in the compound rib of a vessel. WH: 12–14C. Orig. uncertain. ? From FOOT + HOOK, or from Middle Low German.

future *a.* that will be. *Also n.* WH: 14–15C. Old French *futur*, from Latin *futurus*, future p. of *esse* to be, from *fu-*.

fuzz *v.i.* to fly off in minute particles. *Also v.t., n.* WH: 16C. Prob. of Low Dutch orig. Cp. Dutch *voos*, Low German *fussig* spongy.

FX *abbr.* (visual) effects. WH: Representation of pronun. of *effects*.

-fy *suf.* forming verbs, meaning to bring into a certain state, to make, to produce, as in *beatify, deify, horrify, petrify, sanctify*. WH: French *-fier*, from Latin *-ficare* and *-facere*. Cp. -FICATION, -FACTION.

fyke *n.* a fish trap consisting of a net that is open at one end so as to allow fish to enter but opposing their exit. WH: 19C. Dutch *fuik* fish trap.

fylfot *n.* a swastika. WH: 15C. Orig. uncertain. ? From *fill-foot* a pattern for filling the foot of a painted window.

fyrd *n.* a militia at the command of the king in Anglo-Saxon times, able to bear arms. WH: pre-1200. Old English *ferd*, *fyrd*, from Germanic base of FARE. Cp. German *Fahrt* journey.

G

gab *n.* idle talk, chatter. *Also v.i.* WH: 18C. ? Abbr. of GABBLE.

gabardine *n.* a cloth with a corded effect, used largely for raincoats. WH: 16C. Old French *gauvardine*, prob. from Middle High German *wallevart* pilgrimage.

gabble *v.i.* to utter inarticulate sounds rapidly. *Also v.t., n.* WH: 16C. Middle Dutch *gabbelen*, of imit. orig. Cp. BABBLE.

gabbro *n.* (a) rock composed of feldspar and diallage, sometimes with serpentine or mica. WH: 19C. Italian (Tuscan), from Latin *glaber, glabris* smooth. Cp. GLABROUS.

gabelle *n.* a tax or duty, esp. the tax on salt in France before the Revolution, 1789. WH: 14–15C. French, or from Italian *gabella*, rel. to Spanish *alcabula*, from Arabic *al-kabāla* the tax.

gabion *n.* a cylindrical basket of wickerwork or metal, filled with earth or stones, used for foundations etc. in engineering work and (esp. formerly) for shelter against an enemy's fire while trenches are being dug. WH: 16C. French, from Italian *gabbione*, augm. of *gabbia* CAGE.

gable *n.* the triangular upper portion of the end of a building, between the sloping sides of the roof. WH: 14–15C. Old French, from Old Norse *gafl*, rel. to words in other Germanic languages meaning fork. Cp. German *Gabel* fork.

gad¹ *v.i.* to rove or wander idly (about, out etc.). *Also n.* WH: 14–15C. Back-formation from obs. *gadling* companion, fellow, from Germanic base represented by Old English *gǣd* fellowship, rel. to GATHER.

gad² *int.* used to express surprise etc. WH: 15C. Alt. of GOD. Cp. BEGAD, EGAD.

gad³ *n.* a miner's iron wedge sharply pointed for splitting stone etc. WH: 12–14C. Old Norse *gaddr* goad, spike, sting, rel. to YARD¹.

Gadarene *a.* involving or taking part in a chaotic or suicidal rush, flight etc. WH: 19C. Late Latin *Gadarenus*, from Greek *Gadarēnos* inhabitant of Gadara, a town of ancient Palestine near the sea of Galilee. The reference is to the biblical story of the herd of swine near Gadara that were possessed by devils and plunged into the sea (Matt. viii.28–34).

gadfly *n.* a bloodsucking insect of the genus *Tobanidae* or *Oestrus*, which bites cattle and other animals, a horsefly. WH: 16C. GAD³ + FLY¹. In the obsolete sense gadabout the origin is in GAD¹.

gadget *n.* a small tool, an appliance. WH: 19C. ? French *gâchette* piece of a mechanism, dim. of *gâche* staple of a lock, wall staple. See also -ETTE. Cp. GIZMO.

gadoid *n.* any fish of the cod family Gadidae. *Also a.* WH: 19C. Modern Latin *gadus*, from Greek *gados*. Cp. French *gade*.

gadolinite *n.* a black, vitreous silicate of yttrium, beryllium and iron, formed in crystals. WH: 19C. Johan Gadolin, 1760–1852, Finnish mineralogist + -ITE¹. The silicate was so named in 1802.

gadroon *n.* an ornament consisting of a series of convex curves, used in architecture and metalwork for edgings, mouldings etc. WH: 17C. French *gadron*, prob. rel. to *goder* to pucker, to crease. See also -OON.

gadwall *n.* a large freshwater duck, *Anas strepera*, of N Europe and America. WH: 17C. Orig. uncertain. ? Imit. of its cry.

Gael *n.* a Scottish Celt. WH: 18C. Gaelic *Gàidheal*, rel. to Irish *Gaedheal*, from Old Irish *Goídel* GOIDEL.

gaff¹ *n.* a stick with a metal hook at the end, used by anglers to land heavy fish. *Also v.t.* WH: 12–14C. Provençal *gaf*. Cp. French *gaffe* boathook.

gaff² *n.* foolish talk, nonsense, outcry. WH: 19C. Orig. unknown.

gaff³ *n.* a person's home. WH: mid-20C. Orig. unknown. The word originally denoted a fair, then (in the 19C) any public place of entertainment. The current sense dates from the mid-20C.

gaff⁴ *v.i.* to gamble. WH: 19C. Orig. unknown.

gaffe *n.* a social blunder, esp. a tactless comment. WH: early 20C. French, lit. boathook, from Provençal *gafar*, from Gothic *gaffôn* to seize.

gaffer *n.* a foreman, an overseer. WH: 16C. Prob. contr. of godfather (GOD). Cp. GAMMER.

gag *v.t.* to stop the mouth of (a person) by thrusting something into it or tying something round it, so as to prevent speech. *Also v.i., n.* WH: 12–14C. Orig. uncertain. ? Imit. of choking sound or rel. to Old Norse *gagháls* with the neck thrown back.

gaga *a.* foolish, senile, fatuous. WH: early 20C. French, of imit. orig. Cp. GABBLE, GAGGLE.

gage¹ *n.* something laid down as security, to be forfeited in case of non-performance of some act; a pledge, a pawn. *Also v.t.* WH: 14–15C. Old French, from Germanic base rel. to Latin *vas, vadis* surety. Cp. WAGE.

gage² *n.* a greengage. WH: 19C. Abbr. of GREENGAGE.

gaggle *v.i.* to make a noise like a goose. *Also n.* WH: 12–14C. Imit. Cp. CACKLE, GOBBLE.

Gaia *n.* the earth as a self-regulating organism. WH: late 20C. Greek (the) earth.

gaiety *n.* mirth, merriment. WH: 17C. Old French *gaieté* (Modern French *gaîté*), from *gai* GAY. See also -TY¹, -ITY.

gaijin *n.* in Japan, a foreigner. *Also a.* WH: mid-20C. Japanese, contr. of *gaikoku-jin*, from *gaikoku* foreign country + *jin* person.

gaillardia *n.* any plant of the genus *Gaillardia*, the daisy family. WH: 19C. Modern Latin, from *Gaillard* de Marentonneau, 18C French amateur botanist. See also -IA.

gain *n.* anything obtained as an advantage or in return for labour. *Also v.t., v.i.* WH: 15C. Old French, from *gaigner* (Modern French *gagner*), from Germanic v. represented also in Old High German *weidenen* to graze, to pasture, to hunt, to fish, from a v. represented also in Old English *wāth* hunting. The original sense (to the 16C) was booty, spoils.

gaine *n.* a metal tube containing explosive which is screwed to a fuse. WH: early 20C. French sheath, ult. from Latin VAGINA.

gainly *a.* suitable, gracious. WH: 12–14C. GAIN + -LY¹. Cp. UNGAINLY.

gainsay *v.t.* to contradict, to deny. *Also n.* WH: 12–14C. Obs. *gain* straight, direct, from Old Norse *gagn*, from Germanic + SAY.

gait *n.* a manner of walking or going, carriage. WH: 14–15C. Special use of GATE². The spelling *gait* was orig. Scottish.

gaiter *n.* a covering for the ankle or the leg below the knee, usu. fitting down upon the shoe. *Also v.t.* WH: 18C. French *guêtre*, obs. *guestre*, ? from alt. of Germanic base of WRIST.

gal¹ *n.* a girl. WH: 18C. Representation of a pronun. of GIRL. Cp. 'upper-class' *gel*.

gal² *n.* a unit of acceleration equal to 1 cm per second per second. WH: early 20C. Abbr. of *Galileo*. See GALILEAN.

gala *n.* a festivity, a fête. *Also a.* WH: 17C. French, or from Italian, from Spanish, from Old French *gale* merrymaking. See GALLANT¹.

galactagogue *a.* promoting the flow of milk. *Also n.* WH: 19C. GALACTO- + Greek *agōgos* leading, eliciting.

galactic *a.* of or relating to a galaxy, esp. the Milky Way. *Also n.* WH: 19C. Greek *galaktias*, var. of *galaxias* GALAXY + -IC.

galacto- *comb. form* milk or milky. WH: Greek *gala, galaktos* milk. See also -O-.

galactometer *n.* a lactometer. WH: 19C. GALACTO- + -METER.

galactophorous *a.* producing milk. WH: 18C. GALACTO- + -*phorous* (-PHORE).

galactopoietic *a.* increasing the flow of milk. *Also n.* WH: 17C. GALACTO- + Greek *poietikos* capable of producing.

galactorrhoea *n.* an excessive flow of milk. WH: 19C. GALACTO- + -RRHOEA.

galactose *n.* a sweet crystalline glucose obtained from milk-sugar by treatment with dilute acid. WH: 19C. GALACTO- + -OSE².

galago *n.* the bushbaby, one of an African genus of lemurs. WH: 19C. Modern Latin.

galah *n.* the grey, rose-breasted cockatoo, *Eulophus roseicapillus.* WH: 19C. Australian Aboriginal (Yuwaalaraay) *gilaa.*

Galahad *n.* a chivalrous person, noted for courtesy, integrity etc. WH: 19C. *Galahad,* the noblest knight of the Round Table in Arthurian legend.

galantine *n.* a dish of white meat, freed from bone, tied up, sliced, boiled, covered with jelly and served cold. WH: 12–14C. Old French, alt. of *galatine,* from Medieval Latin *galatina,* dial. var. of *gelatina* GELATIN.

galatea *n.* a blue-and-white striped cotton fabric. WH: 19C. HMS *Galatea,* warship commanded 1867 by Duke of Edinburgh. The fabric was based on the ship's crew's uniform and was used initially for children's 'sailor suits'. The ship herself was named after the sea nymph of Greek mythology.

Galatian *a.* belonging to Galatia. *Also n.* WH: 16C. *Galatia,* an ancient country of Asia Minor + -AN.

galaxy *n.* a star system held together in a symmetrical or asymmetrical shape by gravitational attraction. WH: 14–15C. Old French *galaxie,* from Medieval Latin *galaxia,* from Late Latin *galaxias,* from Greek *galaxias* (*kuklos*) (circle) of milk, from *gala, galaktos* milk. The myriad stars packed densely together have a white appearance, like milk. See MILKY WAY.

galbanum *n.* a bitter, odorous gum resin obtained from Persian species of *Ferula,* esp. *F. galbaniflua,* an ingredient in the anointing oil used by Jewish people. WH: 12–14C. Latin, from Greek *khalbanē,* of Semitic orig. Cp. Hebrew *ḥelbĕnāh.* 'Take unto thee sweet spices, stacte, and onycha, and galbanum' (Exod. xxx.34).

gale¹ *n.* a wind stronger than a breeze but less violent than a storm. WH: 16C. Orig. uncertain. ? Orig. an *a.* in *gale wind* and of Scandinavian orig. Cp. Old Norse *galenn* mad, frantic. A poetic sense gentle breeze evolved in the 17C.

gale² *n.* the bog myrtle, *Myrica gale,* a twiggy shrub growing on marshy ground, sweet-gale. WH: pre-1200. Old English *gagel.* The present form of the word is unexplained.

gale³ *n.* a periodic payment of rent. WH: 17C. Contr. of GAVEL².

galea *n.* a helmet-like organ or part. WH: 19C. Latin helmet.

Galen *n.* a physician. WH: 16C. Anglicized from Latin *Galenus,* from Greek *Galēnos,* Claudius *Galenus,* *c.*130–*c.*201 AD, Greek physician.

galena *n.* native sulphide of lead or lead-ore. WH: 17C. Latin lead ore.

galeopithecus *n.* a flying lemur. WH: 19C. Modern Latin, from Greek *galeē* weasel + *pithēkos* ape.

galette *n.* a flat, round cake. WH: 18C. French, dim. of Old French *gal* pebble. See also -ETTE. The cake is so named for its round shape.

galia melon *n.* a small round melon with orange flesh and rough skin. WH: mid-20C. Hebrew personal name *Galia* + MELON.

Galibi *n.* a member of an Indian people of French Guiana. *Also a.* WH: 19C. Carib, lit. strong man.

Galician *a.* of or relating to either of the regions called Galicia, one in NW Spain, the other in central Europe. *Also n.* WH: 14–15C. *Galicia,* a region of NW Spain + -AN. *Galician,* from *Galicia* in E central Europe (+ -AN), dates from the 19C.

Galilean *a.* of or according to Galileo, esp. applied to the simple telescope developed and used by him. WH: 18C. *Galileo* Galilei, 1564–1642, Italian astronomer + -AN.

galilee *n.* a porch or chapel at the entrance of a church. WH: 14–15C. Old French *galilée,* from Medieval Latin *galilea,* from *Galilee,* a Roman province in N ancient Palestine between the Mediterranean and the Jordan. Cp. GALLERY. The name either alludes to Galilee as an outlying region of the Holy Land or refers to 'Galilee of the Gentiles' (Matt. iv.15).

galingale *n.* the aromatic rootstock of certain E Asian plants of the ginger family and of the genus *Alpinia* and *Kaempferia,* used for culinary purposes. WH: pre-1200. Old French *galingal,* from Arabic *kalanjān,* ? from Chinese *gāoliángjiāng,* from *gāoliáng* a district in Guangdong province, China + *jiāng* ginger.

galipot *n.* a yellowish-white, sticky resin exuding from the pine tree *Pinus maritimus* and hardening into a kind of turpentine, called, after refining, white, yellow or Burgundy pitch. WH: 18C. French, of unknown orig. Cp. Provençal *garapot* pine tree resin.

galium *n.* bedstraw, a genus of slender herbaceous plants, containing goosegrass, lady's bedstraw etc. WH: 16C. Modern Latin, or from Greek *galion* bedstraw.

gall¹ *n.* self-assurance, cheek, impudence. WH: pre-1200. Old English *gealla,* from Germanic. Rel. to Greek *kholē* bile (see CHOLER). The original sense was bile. The current sense evolved in the 19C.

gall² *n.* an abnormal growth on plants, esp. the oak, caused by the action of some insect. *Also v.t.* WH: 14–15C. Old French *galle,* from Latin *galla* oak-apple, gall.

gall³ *n.* a sore, swelling, or blister, esp. one produced by friction or chafing on a horse. *Also v.t., v.i.* WH: pre-1200. Old English *gealle,* from Germanic. ? Ident. to GALL¹.

gallant¹ *a.* brave, high-spirited, courageous, chivalrous. WH: 14–15C. Old French *galant,* pres.p. of *galer* to make merry, to make a show, from *gale* merrymaking, rejoicing. See also -ANT. Cp. GALA. The sense polite and attentive to women emerged in the 17C.

gallant² *n.* a man of fashion, a beau. *Also a., v.t., v.i.* WH: 14–15C. GALLANT¹.

galleass *n.* a heavy, low-built type of galley propelled by both sails and oars, usu. with three masts and about 20 guns. WH: 16C. Old French *galleasse* (Modern French *galéace*), from Italian *galeaza,* augm. of *galea* GALLEY¹.

galleon *n.* a large ship, with three or four decks, much used in 15th–17th cents., esp. by the Spaniards in trade with their American possessions. WH: 16C. Either Middle Dutch *galjoen,* from Old French *galion,* augm. of *galie* GALLEY¹, or from Spanish *galeón.* See also -OON.

galleria *n.* a number of small independent shops in one building, on one floor or arranged in galleries on several floors. WH: 19C. Italian GALLERY.

gallery *n.* an elevated floor or platform projecting from the wall toward the interior of a church, hall, theatre, or other large building, commonly used for musicians, singers or part of the congregation or audience. *Also v.t.* WH: 14–15C. Old French *galerie,* from Italian *galleria,* from Medieval Latin *galeria,* ? alt. of *galilea* GALILEE. A gallery was originally a covered passageway or a long, narrow balcony. The sense of picture gallery arose in the 16C.

galley¹ *n.* the cook-house on board a ship, boat or aircraft. WH: 12–14C. Old French *galie* (Modern French *galée*), from Medieval Latin *galea,* from Medieval Greek, of unknown orig. A galley was originally a type of slave ship. The sense cook-house on board a ship evolved in the 18C. Cp. GALLEY².

galley² *n.* in the traditional method of printing by hot-metal composition, an oblong tray on which compositors placed type as it was set up. WH: 17C. French *galée.* See GALLEY¹.

galley-west *adv.* to put (somebody or something) into a state of confusion, unconsciousness or inaction, esp. in *to knock galley-west.* WH: 19C. Alt. of dial. *Colly-west* awry, askew, from *Collyweston,* a village in Northamptonshire. The allusion is presumably to the slates for which the village is famous.

galliambic *n.* a literary metre, technically a tetrameter catalectic composed of Ionics, a minore (˘ ˘) with variations and substitutions – the metre of the *Attis* of Catullus and of Tennyson's *Boadicea.* *Also a.* WH: 19C. Latin *galliambus* song of the *Galli* (priests of Cybele), from *Gallus* + IAMBUS. See also -IC.

galliard *n.* a lively dance, common in the 16th and 17th cents. *Also a.* WH: 14–15C. Old French *gaillard,* ? from a *n.* meaning strength, power, of Celtic orig. Cp. Irish *gal* vigour, Welsh *gallu* to have power. See also -ARD.

Gallic *a.* French; characteristic of the French. WH: 17C. Latin *Gallicus,* from *Gallus, Gallia* Gaul. See also -IC.

gallic *a.* of, relating to or from plant galls. WH: 18C. Latin *galla* oak gall + -IC.

Gallican *a.* of or relating to the ancient Church of Gaul or France. *Also n.* WH: 14–15C. French, or from Latin *Gallicanus,* from *Gallicus.* See GALLIC, also -AN.

galligaskins *n.pl.* loose breeches popular in the 16th and 17th cents. WH: 16C. Prob. ult. from obs. French *gargesque,* infl. by GALLEY¹ and GASCON. The origin of the initial *galli-* is unknown.

gallimaufry *n.* a hash, a hotchpotch. **WH:** 16C. French *galimafrée*, of unknown orig. According to some, the word is from Picardian *mafrer* to eat a lot, a variant of *bâfrer* to guzzle, to gobble + *galer* to make merry (cp. GALA).

gallinaceous *a.* of or relating to the order Galliformes of birds, containing pheasants, partridges, grouse, turkeys, domestic fowls, and allied forms. **WH:** 18C. Latin *gallinaceus*, from *gallina* hen, from *gallus* cock + -OUS. See also -ACEOUS.

gallinule *n.* any bird of the genus *Gallinula*, esp. *G. chloropus*, the moorhen. **WH:** 18C. Modern Latin *Gallinula* genus name, dim. of Latin *gallina* hen. See also -ULE.

galliot *n.* a small, swift galley propelled by sails and oars. **WH:** 12–14C. Old French *galiote*, from Italian *galeotta*, dim. of Medieval Latin *galea* GALLEY[1]. See also -OT[1].

gallipot *n.* a small glazed earthenware pot used to contain ointments, medicines, preserves etc. **WH:** 14–15C. Prob. from GALLEY[1] + POT[1]. The pot is probably so named as it was brought in galleys from the Mediterranean.

gallium *n.* a soft, grey metallic element of extreme fusibility, at. no. 31, chem. symbol Ga, used in semiconductors. **WH:** 19C. Latin *Gallia* France + -IUM. The element was discovered in 1875 by the French chemist Paul-Émile *Lecoq* de Boisbaudran and probably puns on his name: French *coq* and Latin *gallus* both mean cock. (The cockerel that is a symbol of France puns on the same association of words.)

gallivant *v.i.* to gad about, to go around seeking pleasure. **WH:** 19C. Orig. uncertain. ? Alt. of GALLANT[1].

galliwasp *n.* a small harmless W Indian lizard, *Diploglossus monotropis*, erroneously reputed to be venomous. **WH:** 17C. Orig. unknown.

Gallo- *comb. form* French. **WH:** Latin *Gallus*, *Gallia* Gaul. See GAUL, also -O-.

gallo- *comb. form* of or relating to gallic acid, gallic. **WH:** GALLIC + -O-.

galloglass *n.* an armed soldier or retainer of an ancient Irish chieftain. **WH:** 15C. Irish *gallóglach*, from *gall* foreigner + *óglach* youth, servant, warrior, from *óg* young + abstract suf. *-lach*.

Gallomania *n.* a mania for French fashions, habits, or practices, literature etc. **WH:** 19C. GALLO- + -MANIA.

gallon *n.* a British liquid measure of capacity equal to eight pints (4.55 l). **WH:** 12–14C. Anglo-French *galon*, var. of Old French *jalon*, from base of Medieval Latin *galleta*, ? of Celtic orig. Cp. Old English *gellet* dish, basin, German *Gelte* bucket.

galloon *n.* a narrow braid of silk, worsted or cotton, with gold or silver thread interwoven, for binding uniforms, dresses etc. **WH:** 17C. French *galon*, from *galonner* to trim with braid, of unknown orig. See also -OON. According to some, the word is related to Old French *galer* to make merry. Cp. GALA, GALLANT[1].

gallop *v.i.* to run in a series of springs, as a horse at its fastest pace. *Also v.t., n.* **WH:** 16C. Old French *galoper*. See WALLOP.

Gallophile *n.* a devotee of French customs etc., a Francophile. **WH:** 19C. GALLO- + -PHILE.

Gallophobe *n.* a person who hates French ways or fears the French. **WH:** 19C. GALLO- + -PHOBE.

Gallovidian *a.* of or belonging to Galloway in SW Scotland. *Also n.* **WH:** 17C. Medieval Latin *Gallovidia* Galloway (see GALLOWAY) + -AN.

galloway *n.* a black breed of cattle, orig. bred in Galloway. **WH:** 16C. *Galloway*, a region of SW Scotland, now part of Dumfries and Galloway.

gallows *n.sing.* a framework, usu. consisting of timber uprights and a crosspiece, on which criminals are executed by hanging. **WH:** pre-1200. Old English *gealga*, from Germanic, from Indo-European base meaning branch, pole. Cp. GALLUSES.

Gallup poll *n.* a method of ascertaining the trend of public opinion by questioning a representative cross-section of the population. **WH:** mid-20C. George H. *Gallup*, 1901–84, US statistician.

galluses *n.pl.* braces for trousers. **WH:** 19C. Pl. of *gallus*, var. of GALLOWS.

galoot *n.* an awkward, uncouth person. **WH:** 19C. Orig. unknown. ? Ult. from Spanish *galeoto* galley slave.

galop *n.* a lively dance in 2/4 time. *Also v.i.* **WH:** 19C. French. See GALLOP.

galore *adv.* in plenty, abundantly. **WH:** 17C. Irish *go leór* to sufficiency. The word's use in modern English may be due to Sir Walter Scott, who probably took it from the Gaelic equivalent, *gu leòr*.

galoshes *n.pl.* a pair of waterproof overshoes, usu. of vulcanized rubber, for protecting a person's boots or shoes in wet weather. **WH:** 14–15C. Old French *galoche*, from Late Latin *gallicula*, dim. of Latin *gallica*, use as n. of *Gallicus* GALLIC. A galosh was originally a clog or wooden sole attached by a strap to an undershoe, as worn in ancient Gaul. (An earlier derivation from Greek *kalon* wood and *pous* foot is now rejected.)

galtonia *n.* any plant of the genus *Galtonia* of the lily family, native to S Africa, esp. *G. candicans*, with lanceolate leaves, waxy white flowers and a fragrant scent. **WH:** 19C. Modern Latin, from Sir Francis *Galton*, 1822–1911, British scientist who travelled in S Africa.

galumph *v.i.* to move noisily and clumsily. **WH:** 19C. Coined by Lewis Carroll as a blend of GALLOP and TRIUMPH.

galvanism *n.* electricity produced by chemical action, esp. that of acids on metals. **WH:** 18C. French *galvanisme*, from Luigi *Galvani*, 1737–98, Italian physiologist. See also -ISM.

galvanize *v.t.* to rouse into life or activity as by a galvanic shock. **WH:** 19C. French *galvaniser*, from *Galvani*. See GALVANISM.

galvano- *comb. form* galvanic current. **WH:** *galvanic* (GALVANISM). See also -O-.

galvanometer *n.* a delicate apparatus for determining the existence, direction, and intensity of electric currents. **WH:** 19C. GALVANO- + -METER.

galvanoscope *n.* an instrument for detecting the presence and showing the direction of electric currents. **WH:** 19C. GALVANO- + -SCOPE.

galvanotropism *n.* the directional movement in a growing plant induced by an electric stimulus. **WH:** 19C. GALVANO- + TROPISM.

Galwegian *a.* of or belonging to Galloway, SW Scotland; Gallovidian. *Also n.* **WH:** 18C. From GALLOWAY, based on pair NORWEGIAN/ *Norway*.

gam[1] *n.* a group, or school, of whales. *Also v.i., v.t.* **WH:** 19C. Orig. unknown.

gam[2] *n.* a human leg, esp. female. **WH:** 18C. Prob. var. of GAMB.

gama grass *n.* a fodder grass, *Tripsacum dactyloides*, with culms from 4–7 ft. (1–2 m) high, growing in the south of the US. **WH:** 19C. ? Alt. of *grama grass* (GRAMA).

gamb *n.* a figure of an animal's leg on a coat of arms. **WH:** 17C. Old French *gambe*, var. of *jambe* JAMB.

gamba *n.* a viola da gamba. **WH:** 16C. Shortening of *viola da gamba* (VIOLA[1]), an instrument held between the player's legs (Italian *gamba* leg).

gambade *n.* a bound or spring of a horse. **WH:** 16C. French, from Italian *gambata*, from *gamba* leg. See also -ADE. Cp. GAMBADO, GAMBOL. The form *gambado* is from Spanish (from *gamba* leg) and dates from the 19C.

gambado *n.* a leather legging or large boot for horse riders. **WH:** 17C. Italian *gamba* leg + -ADO.

Gambian *a.* of or relating to The Gambia. *Also n.* **WH:** early 20C. *The Gambia*, a country in W Africa + -AN.

gambier *n.* an extract from the leaves of *Uncaria gambir*, used in medicine as an astringent, and also for dyeing and tanning. **WH:** 19C. Malay *gambir*, name of the plant.

gambit *n.* an opening in chess, in which a pawn is sacrificed in order to obtain a favourable position for attack. **WH:** 17C. Italian *gambetto*, lit. tripping up, from *gamba* leg, with *-it* from French equivalent *gambit*.

gamble *v.i.* to play, esp. a game of chance, for money. *Also v.t., n.* **WH:** 18C. Obs. *gamel* to play games, as freq. of GAME[1], or direct from GAME[1]. See also -LE[4].

gamboge *n.* a gum resin, from E Asia, used as a yellow pigment and in medicine. **WH:** 17C. Modern Latin *gambaugium*, var. of *cambugium*, from *Cambodia*, a country in SE Asia.

gambol *v.i.* to frisk or skip about; to frolic. *Also n.* **WH:** 16C. Alt. of GAMBADE, with sense assoc. with GAME[1].

gambrel *n.* a horse's hock. **WH:** 16C. Old French *gamberel*, from *gambier* forked stick, from *gambe*, var. of *jambe* leg. See JAMB. Cp. CAMBREL.

game[1] *n.* an exercise for diversion, usu. with other players, a pastime. *Also a., v.i., v.t.* WH: pre-1200. Old English *gamen*, from Germanic bases of Y-, MAN. The original sense was amusement, fun, play. The current senses of competitive sport and wild animals, birds or fish formerly (or still) hunted for food or sport both evolved in the 12–14C.

game[2] *a.* lame, crippled. WH: 18C. Orig. unknown. The colloquial form *gammy* (19C) is a dialect variant.

gamelan *n.* a SE Asian percussion instrument similar to a xylophone. WH: 19C. Javanese.

gametangium *n.* a cell or organ in which gametes are formed. WH: 19C. GAMETE + Greek *aggeion* vessel + -IUM.

gamete *n.* a sexual reproductive cell, either of the two germ cells that unite to form a new organism – in the male, a spermatozoon, in the female an ovum. WH: 19C. Modern Latin *gameta*, from Greek *gametē* wife, *gametēs* husband, from *gamos* marriage.

gameto- *comb. form* gamete. WH: GAMETE. See also -O-.

gametocyte *n.* a cell that breaks up into gametes. WH: 19C. GAMETO- + -CYTE.

gametogenesis *n.* the formation of gametes. WH: early 20C. GAMETO- + GENESIS.

gametophyte *n.* a plant of the generation that produces gametes in plant species which show alternation of generations. WH: 19C. GAMETO- + -PHYTE.

gamic *a.* of or relating to sex, sexual, sexually produced. WH: 19C. Greek *gamikos*, from *gamos* marriage. See also -IC.

gamin *n.* a homeless child, an urchin. WH: 19C. French, ? from base *gamm-* meaning good-for-nothing.

gamine *n.* a small boylike girl or woman. *Also a.* WH: 19C. French, fem. of GAMIN.

gamma *n.* the third letter of the Greek alphabet (Γ, γ). WH: 14–15C. Latin, from Greek.

gammadion *n.* an ornament composed of the gamma singly or in combination, formerly used in sacerdotal vestments in the Greek Church. WH: 19C. Late Greek, from GAMMA.

†**gammer** *n.* an old woman. WH: 16C. Prob. contr. of *godmother* (GOD), with *ga-* by assoc. with *grandmother* (GRAND). Cp. GAFFER.

gammon[1] *n.* the buttock or thigh of a hog salted and dried. *Also v.t.* WH: 15C. Old French *gambon* (Modern French *jambon*), from *gambe* leg. Cp. JAMB.

gammon[2] *n.* nonsense, humbug. *Also int., v.t., v.i.* WH: 18C. ? From source of GAMMON[3].

gammon[3] *n.* a defeat at backgammon in which the winner's score is equivalent to two games. *Also v.t.* WH: 18C. ? Old English *gamnian* GAME[1] (v.) or *gamen* GAME[1] (n.).

gammon[4] *v.t.* to make fast (the bowsprit) to the stem of a ship. *Also n.* WH: 17C. ? From GAMMON[1], ref. to the tying up of a ham.

gamo- *comb. form* sexual. WH: Greek *gamos* marriage. See also -O-.

gamogenesis *n.* sexual reproduction. WH: 19C. GAMO- + GENESIS.

gamopetalous *a.* having the petals united. WH: 19C. GAMO- + *petalous* (PETAL).

gamophyllous *a.* having the leaves united. WH: 19C. GAMO- + Greek *phullon* leaf. See also -OUS.

gamosepalous *a.* having the sepals united. WH: 19C. GAMO- + *sepalous* (SEPAL).

gamp *n.* an umbrella, esp. a large and clumsy one. WH: 19C. Sarah *Gamp*, monthly nurse in Dickens's *Martin Chuzzlewit* (1843), who carried a large cotton umbrella.

gamut *n.* the whole range, compass or extent. WH: 14–15C. Contr. of Medieval Latin *gamma ut*, from GAMMA + UT. The Greek letter *gamma* represented a note one tone lower than A in medieval times, while *ut* was the first of the six notes forming a hexachord.

-gamy *comb. form* marriage or kind of marriage, as in *bigamy*, *endogamy*, *misogamy*. WH: Greek *gamos* marriage + -Y[2].

gander *n.* the male of the goose. *Also v.i.* WH: pre-1200. Old English *ganra*, from Germanic base also of GANNET.

gang[1] *n.* a number of persons associated for a particular purpose (often in a bad sense). *Also v.i.* WH: pre-1200. Old Norse *gangr* walking motion, course, from a German n. of action rel. to base of GO[1]. The original sense was an action or manner of going, then (12–14C) a set of things or persons. The current sense group of

criminals developed in the 14–15C. The original sense is still present in *gangway* (WAY).

gang[2] *v.i.* to go. WH: pre-1200. Old English *gangan*, from Germanic. See GANG[1].

gangling *a.* loosely built, lanky, awkward. WH: 19C. GANG[2] + -LE[4] + -ING[2].

ganglion *n.* in pathology, a globular growth in the sheath of a tendon. WH: 17C. Greek *gagglion* tumour under the skin.

gangrene *n.* death or decay in a part of the body, the first stage of mortification, as a result of poor blood supply to the part. *Also v.t., v.i.* WH: 16C. French *gangrène*, from Latin *gangraena*, from Greek *gaggraina*. Cp. Greek *goggros* growth on trees.

gangue *n.* the earthy matter or matrix in which ores are embedded. WH: 19C. French, from German *Gang* way, course, vein of metal. Cp. GANG[1].

ganister *n.* a kind of grit or hard sandstone from the lower coal-measures. WH: 19C. Orig. unknown.

ganja *n.* marijuana, a dried preparation of *Cannabis sativa* or Indian hemp, smoked as an intoxicant and narcotic. WH: 19C. Hindi *gãjā*.

gannet *n.* a seabird, *Sula bassana*, also called *solan goose*. WH: pre-1200. Old English *ganot*, from Germanic base also of GANDER.

ganoid *a.* (of fish scales) bright, smooth, like enamel. *Also n.* WH: 19C. French *ganoïde*, from Greek *ganos* brightness. See also -OID.

gansey *n.* a woollen pullover or jersey. WH: 19C. Representation of a pronun. of GUERNSEY.

gantry *n.* a structure surrounding a rocket on the launch pad, for carrying railway signals, a travelling crane etc. WH: 14–15C. Prob. from dial. *gawn* gallon, bucket (contr. of GALLON) + TREE. According to some, the word is from Old Northern French *gantier* (Modern French *chantier* building site), from Latin *cantherius* trellis, rafter, gelding, related to the source of Greek *kanthēlios* pack ass.

gap *n.* an opening, a breach, as in a hedge, a fence etc. *Also v.t.* WH: 12–14C. Old Norse chasm, rel. to *gapa* GAPE.

gape *v.i.* to stare with open mouth in wonder, surprise or perplexity. *Also n.* WH: 12–14C. Old Norse *gapa*, from Germanic. Cp. GAP. The original sense of the verb was to open the mouth wide to bite or swallow something.

gar *n.* any fish of the family Belonidae with a long pointed snout, esp. *Belone belone*. WH: 18C. Abbr. of *garfish* (14–15C) appar. from Old English *gār* spear + FISH[1]. Cp. MARLIN, PIKE[1], *swordfish* (SWORD).

garage *n.* a building for housing or repairing motor vehicles. *Also v.t., a.* WH: early 20C. French, from *garer* to shelter. Rel. to WARE[2].

garam masala *n.* a mixture of spices often used in Indian cookery. WH: early 20C. Urdu *garam maṣālaḥ* hot MASALA.

garb[1] *n.* dress, costume. *Also v.t.* WH: 16C. Obs. French *garbe* (now *galbe*), from Italian *garbo*, ult. from Germanic. Rel. to GEAR, YARE. The original sense of the word was grace, elegance. The sense of dress, costume evolved in the 17C.

garb[2] *n.* a sheaf of grain. WH: 16C. Old French *garbe* (Modern French *gerbe*), from Frankish. See GERBE.

garbage *n.* kitchen waste. WH: 14–15C. Anglo-French, of unknown orig. The original sense (to the 19C) was offal of an animal used as food. The sense domestic waste arose in the 16C.

garble *v.t.* to jumble, give a confused version of (a story, quotation etc.). WH: 14–15C. Anglo-Latin and Italian *garbellare* to sift, to sort, from Arabic *ġarbala* to sift, to select, ? from Late Latin *cribellare*, from *cribellum*, dim. of Latin *cribrum* sieve. The original sense (to the 19C) was to sift out extraneous matter or refuse from spice etc. The current sense to distort, to jumble arose in the 17C.

garbo *n.* a refuse collector. WH: mid-20C. GARBAGE + -O-.

garboard *n.* the first plank fastened on either side of a ship's keel. WH: 17C. Obs. Dutch *gaarboord*, ? from *garen*, contr. of *gadern* GATHER + *boord* BOARD.

garbologist *n.* a refuse collector. WH: mid-20C. GARBAGE + -O- + -LOGIST.

garçon *n.* a waiter (usu. used as a form of address: *Garçon!*). WH: 17C. French boy, (male) servant, from Frankish.

garden *n.* an enclosed piece of ground appropriated to the cultivation of fruit, flowers or vegetables, often with a lawn. *Also a., v.i.* WH: 12–14C. Old French *gardin*, var. of *jardin*, from Germanic. Cp. GARTH, YARD[2].

gardenia *n.* any shrub or tree of the tropical genus *Gardenia*, usu. cultivated in greenhouses for its large fragrant flowers. WH: 18C. Modern Latin, from Alexander *Garden*, c.1730–91, Scottish-American naturalist + -IA.

garganey *n.* a small duck of Europe and Asia, *Anas querquedula*, the male of which has a white stripe over each eye. WH: 17C. Italian *garganei*, of imit. orig. Cp. GAGGLE.

gargantuan *a.* immense, enormous, incredibly big. WH: 16C. *Gargantua*, the large-mouthed voracious giant in Rabelais's book of the same name (1534) + -AN. Gargantua's name derives from Spanish and Portuguese *gargantua* gullet, throat. Cp. GARGLE, GARGOYLE.

garget *n.* an inflammation of the throat in cattle. WH: 12–14C. Old French *gargate* throat, from Provençal *gargata*. See GARGOYLE. *Garget* was originally the word for the throat in cattle. The current sense dates from the 16C.

gargle *v.t.* to rinse (the mouth or throat) with some medicated liquid, which is prevented from passing down the throat by the breath. *Also v.i., n.* WH: 16C. French *gargouiller* to gurgle, to bubble, from *gargouille* throat. See GARGOYLE.

gargoyle *n.* a grotesque spout, usu. carved to represent a human or animal figure, projecting from Gothic buildings, esp. churches, to throw rainwater clear of the wall. WH: 12–14C. Old French *gargouille* throat, rel. to Latin *gargarizare* to gargle, from Greek *gargarizein*, of imit. orig. The water passes through a gargoyle's 'throat' to be ejected from its mouth.

garibaldi *n.* a loose kind of blouse worn by women or children and popular in the 1860s, like the red shirts worn by Garibaldi and his men. WH: 19C. Giuseppe *Garibaldi*, 1807–82, Italian patriot, general and statesman.

garish *a.* gaudy, showy, flashy. WH: 16C. Orig. unknown.

garland *n.* a wreath or festoon of flowers, leaves etc. worn round the neck or hung up. *Also v.t.* WH: 12–14C. Old French *garlande* (Modern French *guirlande*), of uncertain orig. ? From Middle High German *wieren* to adorn, rel. to WEAR¹.

garlic *n.* any of various bulbous-rooted plants of the genus *Allium*, esp. *A. sativum*, with a strong odour and a pungent taste, used in cookery. WH: pre-1200. Old English *gārlēac*, from *gār* spear + *lēac* LEEK. The 'spears' of the plant are its cloves.

garment *n.* an article of clothing, esp. one of the larger articles, such as a coat or gown. *Also v.t.* WH: 12–14C. Old French *garnement* equipment, from *garnir* GARNISH. See also -MENT.

garner *v.t.* to store in or as in a granary, to gather. *Also n.* WH: 12–14C. Old French *gernier* (Modern French *grenier*), from Latin *granarium* GRANARY. See also -ER².

garnet *n.* a vitreous mineral of varying composition, colour and quality, the deep red, transparent kinds of which are prized as gems. WH: 12–14C. Prob. from Middle Dutch *gernate*, from Old French *grenat*, from Medieval Latin *granatus*, ? transferred use of *granatum* pomegranate.

garni *a.* in cooking, garnished, trimmed, esp. with salad. WH: early 20C. French, p.p. of *garnir* GARNISH.

garnish *v.t.* to adorn; to embellish (as a dish of food) with something laid round it. *Also n.* WH: 14–15C. Old French *garnir*, *garniss-*, from a Germanic v. prob. rel. to base of WARN. See also -ISH².

garniture *n.* ornamental appendages, trimmings, ornament, embellishment. WH: 15C. French, from *garnir* GARNISH.

garret *n.* an upper room or storey immediately under the roof, an attic. WH: 12–14C. Old French *garite* watchtower (Modern French *guérite*), from *garir*. See GARRISON. A garret was originally (to the 16C) a turret projecting from the top of a tower or from the parapet of a fortification.

garrison *n.* a body of troops stationed in a fort or fortified place. *Also v.t.* WH: 12–14C. Old French *garison* defence, safety, from *garir* to defend, to furnish, from Germanic. The original sense was store, treasure, then (to the 17C) defence, safety. The current sense arose in the 14–15C.

garron *n.* a small horse bred in Galloway, the Highlands and Ireland. WH: 16C. Gaelic *gearran*, Irish *gearrán*.

garrotte *n.* a method of execution in which the victim was fastened by an iron collar to an upright post, and a knob operated by a screw or lever dislocated the spinal column, or a small blade severed the spinal cord at the base of the brain (orig. the method was strangulation by a cord twisted with a stick). *Also v.t.* WH: 17C. Spanish *garrote* cudgel, from a base ? of Celtic orig.

garrulous *a.* talkative, loquacious, chattering. WH: 17C. Latin *garrulus*, from *garrire* to chatter, to prattle. See also -ULOUS.

garter *n.* a band round the leg for holding a stocking up. *Also v.t.* WH: 12–14C. Old French *gartier*, var. of *jartier* (Modern French *jarretière*), from *jaret* bend of the knee, calf of the leg, prob. of Celtic orig. Cp. GARROTTE.

garth *n.* the grass plot surrounded by the cloisters of a cathedral, monastery etc. WH: 12–14C. Old Norse *garthr*, rel. to Old English *geard* YARD².

gas *n.* a substance in the form of air, possessing the condition of perfect fluid elasticity. *Also a., v.i., v.t.* WH: 17C. Invented by J.B. van Helmont, 1577–1644, Flemish chemist, based on Greek *khaos* chaos, Dutch *g* representing Greek *kh*. The word is not from Dutch *geest* spirit, as formerly supposed. Van Helmont also invented obsolete *blas*, a term for a supposed 'flatus' or influence of the stars, affecting the weather, based on the Germanic source of BLAST.

Gascon *n.* a native of Gascony, France. *Also a.* WH: 12–14C. Old French, from Latin *Vasco*, *Vasconis*. Cp. BASQUE.

gaselier *n.* an ornamental metalwork pendant with branches carrying gas burners for lighting a room etc. WH: 19C. GAS + CHANDELIER.

gash¹ *n.* a long, deep, open cut, esp. in flesh; a flesh wound. *Also v.t.* WH: 12–14C. Old French **garce*, from *garcer* (Modern French *gercer* to chap, to crack), prob. from Popular Latin *charissare*, var. of *charassare*, from Greek *kharassein* to engrave. Cp. CHARACTER. The *r* was lost as with BASS², DACE.

gash² *a.* spare, extra, surplus to requirements. *Also n.* WH: early 20C. Orig. unknown.

gash³ *v.i.* to gossip, to tattle. WH: 18C. Orig. unknown.

gasket *n.* a strip of tough but flexible material for packing or caulking joints in pipes, engines etc. to make them airtight or watertight. WH: 17C. ? Alt. of French *garcette* little girl, thin rope, dim. of *garce*, fem. of *gars* boy. The term is of nautical origin and was first used of a rope securing a sail. The current sense evolved in the early 20C.

gaskin *n.* the part of a horse's hind leg between the stifle and the hock, lower thigh. WH: 16C. ? From GALLIGASKINS or GASCON.

gaso- *comb. form* of, relating to or using gas. WH: GAS. See also -O-.

gasoline *n.* a volatile inflammable product of the distillation of petroleum, used for heating and lighting. WH: 19C. GAS + -OL + -INE.

gasometer *n.* an apparatus for measuring, collecting, preserving or mixing different gases. WH: 18C. French *gazomètre*, from *gaz* gas + -*mètre* -METER.

gasoscope *n.* an instrument for detecting the presence of carburetted hydrogen in mines, buildings etc. WH: 19C. GASO- + -SCOPE.

gasp *v.i.* to breathe in a convulsive manner, as from exhaustion or astonishment. *Also v.t., n.* WH: 14–15C. Old Norse *geispa* to yawn, from base of *geip* idle talk. The sense to pant for air arose in the 16C.

Gastarbeiter *n.* a person with temporary permission to work in a foreign country. WH: mid-20C. German, from *Gast* guest + *Arbeiter* worker.

gasthaus *n.* a German guest house or small hotel. WH: 19C. German, from *Gast* GUEST + *Haus* HOUSE¹.

gasthof *n.* a (relatively large) German hotel. WH: 19C. German, from *Gast* GUEST + *Hof* hotel, large house.

gastralgia *n.* pain in the stomach. WH: 19C. GASTRO- + -ALGIA.

gastrectomy *n.* the surgical removal of (part of) the stomach. WH: 19C. GASTRO- + -ECTOMY.

gastric *a.* of or relating to the stomach. WH: 17C. Modern Latin *gastricus*, from Greek *gastēr*, *gastros* stomach. See also -IC.

gastro- *comb. form* stomach. WH: Greek *gastēr*, *gastros* stomach. See also -O-.

gastrocnemius *n.* the large muscle in the calf of the leg which helps to extend the foot. WH: 17C. Modern Latin, from Greek *gastroknēmia* calf of the leg, from *gastēr* stomach, belly + *knēmē* leg. The muscle is so called because it bulges ('bellies') like a stomach.

gastroenteric *a.* of or relating to the stomach and the intestines. WH: 19C. GASTRO- + ENTERIC.

gastrointestinal *a.* of or relating to the stomach or the intestines. WH: 19C. GASTRO- + *intestinal* (INTESTINE).

gastrolith *n.* a small stone swallowed by birds, reptiles and fish to aid digestion in the gizzard. WH: 19C. GASTRO- + -LITH.

gastronomy *n.* the art or science of good eating, epicurism. WH: 19C. French *gastronomie*, from Greek *gastronomia*, alt. of *gastrologia*. See GASTRO-, -LOGY, -NOMY.

gastrophile *n.* a lover of their stomach or of good eating. WH: 19C. GASTRO- + -PHILE.

gastropod *n.* an individual of the Gastropoda, a class of molluscs usu. inhabiting a univalve shell (as the snails), of which the general characteristic is a broad muscular ventral foot. *Also a.* WH: 19C. French *gastéropode*, from Modern Latin *Gastropoda*. See GASTRO-, -POD.

gastroscope *n.* a medical instrument for examining the interior of the stomach. WH: 19C. GASTRO- + -SCOPE.

gastrostomy *n.* a surgical operation to introduce food directly into the stomach, where it cannot be taken by mouth. WH: 19C. GASTRO- + Greek *stoma* mouth + -Y².

gastrotomy *n.* the surgical operation of cutting into or opening the abdomen. WH: 17C. GASTRO- + -TOMY.

gastrovascular *a.* of or relating to the vascular system and the stomach. WH: 19C. GASTRO- + VASCULAR.

gastrula *n.* an embryonic form or stage in the development of a metazoon, consisting of a double-walled sac enclosing a cuplike cavity. WH: 19C. Modern Latin, from Greek *gastēr, gastros* stomach. See also -ULE.

gat¹ *n.* a narrow passage between sandbanks, a strait, a channel. WH: 16C. Appar. from Old Norse hole, opening. See GATE¹.

gat² *n.* a revolver. WH: early 20C. Abbr. of GATLING.

gate¹ *n.* a movable barrier, consisting of a frame of wood or iron, swinging on hinges or sliding, to close a passage or opening, usu. distinguished from a door by openwork instead of solid panels. *Also v.t.* WH: pre-1200. Old English *gæt, geat*, from Germanic. Cp. Old Norse *gat* hole, opening. The word was originally a term for an opening in a wall as well as the barrier that closed it.

gate² *n.* a street (*usu. in comb.*, as in *Boargate, Friargate*). WH: 12–14C. Old Norse *gata*, from Germanic. Cp. German *Gasse* street, lane. Some street names in *-gate* derive from GATE¹, especially when referring to the entrance to a town. Typical examples are *Northgate, Eastgate, Southgate, Westgate*, common in southern England.

-gate *comb. form* added to the name of a place or person to denote a scandal connected with that place or person, as in *Billygate, Irangate* etc. WH: late 20C. WATERGATE.

gateau *n.* a rich cake filled with cream and decorated with icing etc. WH: 19C. French *gâteau* cake, from Old French *gastel*, from Popular Latin *wastellum*, from Germanic. Cp. Frankish *wastil* food.

gather *v.t.* to bring together, to collect, to cause to assemble. *Also v.i., n.* WH: pre-1200. Old English *gaderian*, from Germanic base of TOGETHER.

Gatling *n.* a machine-gun with a series of parallel barrels each having its own lock actuated by a crank at the breech, capable of firing more than 1000 shots a minute. WH: 19C. Richard J. *Gatling*, 1818–1903, US inventor.

gator *n.* an alligator. WH: 19C. Abbr. of ALLIGATOR.

gauche *a.* awkward, clumsy. WH: 18C. French, lit. left-handed. Cp. GAWK.

gaucho *n.* a cowboy of the pampas of Uruguay and Argentina, noted for their horse-riding skills. WH: 19C. American Spanish, prob. from Araucanian *kaucu*.

gaudeamus igitur *int.* let us therefore rejoice. WH: 18C. Latin let us be merry therefore, 1st pers. pl. pres. subj. of *gaudere* to rejoice + *igitur* therefore. Cp. GAUDY¹, GAUDY². The words open the Modern Latin students' song with the first line *Gaudeamus igitur, iuvenes dum sumus* Let us be merry therefore while we are still young.

gaudy¹ *a.* vulgarly and tastelessly brilliant and ornate, garish, flashy. WH: 15C. From obs. *gaud* trick, jest, ? from Old French *gaudir*, from Latin *gaudere* to rejoice + -Y¹.

gaudy² *n.* a grand festival or entertainment, esp. one held annually at an English college in commemoration of some event. WH: 14–15C. Latin *gaudium* joy, from *gaudere* to rejoice, or *gaude*, imper. of this v. The specific sense of college feast evolved in the 17C.

gauge *v.t.* to ascertain the dimensions, quantity, content, capacity or power of. *Also n.* WH: 12–14C. Old French var. of *jauge*, ult. of unknown orig. The pronunciation evolved as for that of SAFE from French *sauf*.

Gaul *n.* a native or inhabitant of the ancient Roman province of Gaul (at the centre of which was France). WH: 14–15C. Latin *Gallus*, prob. from Celtic. Cp. GALLIC. The word is probably related to Old English *wealh* foreigner. See WELSH.

gauleiter *n.* the chief official of a district in Germany under the Nazi regime. WH: mid-20C. German, from *Gau* administrative district + *Leiter* leader.

Gaullist *n.* a person who adheres to the policies and principles associated with General Charles de Gaulle, president of France 1959–69. WH: mid-20C. French *Gaulliste*, from Charles de *Gaulle*, 1890–1970, French military and political leader. See also -IST.

gault *n.* a series of geological beds of stiff dark-coloured clay and marl between the upper and lower greensand. WH: 16C. Orig. unknown. ? Rel. to Old Swedish *galt*, neut. of *galder* barren.

gaultheria *n.* a plant of the genus *Gaultheria*, evergreen aromatic shrubs of the heath family, containing the wintergreen, *Gaultheria procumbens*. WH: 19C. Modern Latin, from Jean-François *Gaulthier*, c.1708–56, Canadian botanist. See also -IA.

gaunt *a.* thin, emaciated, haggard, pinched, attenuated. WH: 14–15C. Orig. unknown. A sense to the 18C was slender, slim.

gauntlet¹ *n.* a long stout glove covering the wrists. WH: 14–15C. Old French *gantelet*, dim. of *gant* glove, from Germanic base seen also in Swedish and Danish *vante* glove. See also -LET.

gauntlet² *n.* a military (and sometimes a naval) punishment, in which a prisoner had to run between two files of men armed with sticks, knotted cords or the like, with which they struck him as he passed. WH: 17C. Alt. of obs. *gantlope*, from Swedish *gantlopp* (from *gata* lane, GATE² + *lopp* course), assim. to GAUNTLET¹.

gaur *n.* a large fierce Indian ox, *Bos gaurus*. WH: 19C. Sanskrit *gaura*, from base also of COW¹.

gauss *n.* the cgs unit of magnetic flux density. WH: 19C. Karl F. *Gauss*, 1777–1855, German mathematician. The name was proposed by the British physicist Silvanus P. Thompson.

Gaussian distribution *n.* in statistics, normal distribution. WH: 19C. *Gauss* (see GAUSS) + -IAN.

gauze *n.* a surgical dressing of an openwork mesh such as muslin. WH: 16C. French *gaze*, ? from *Gaza*, a town in Palestine.

gavage *n.* the fattening of poultry by forced feeding. WH: 19C. French, from *gaver* to force feed, from Provençal *gavar*, from base of Old French *gave* throat.

gavel¹ *n.* a small mallet, esp. one used by a chairman for demanding attention or by an auctioneer. *Also v.i., v.t.* WH: 19C. Orig. unknown.

gavel² *n.* partition of land among the whole tribe or clan at the holder's death. WH: 19C. Shortening of *gavelkind* (12–14C), from obs. *gavel* payment, rent, from Old English *gafol*, from Germanic, from base of GIVE + KIND.

gavotte *n.* a dance of a lively yet dignified character resembling the minuet. WH: 17C. French, from Provençal *gavoto*, from *Gavot* an inhabitant of the Alps. The *Gavots* are so named from Provençal *gava* throat, goitre, with reference to the goitrous condition from which many mountain dwellers suffered.

Gawd *n., int.* God. WH: 19C. Alt. of GOD.

gawk *n.* a clumsy, awkward, shy person. *Also v.i.* WH: 17C. Prob. from dial. *gawk-handed* left-handed, appar. contr. of dial. *gallack* in same sense, of unknown orig.

gawky *a.* awkward, clownish. *Also n.* WH: 18C. GAWK + -Y¹.

gawp *v.i.* to gape, esp. in astonishment. WH: 17C. ? Alt. of GAPE.

gay *a.* full of mirth; light-hearted, cheerful, merry. *Also n.* WH: 12–14C. Old French *gai*, of unknown orig. ? From Frankish *wāhi* impetuous. A sense dissolute, immoral evolved in the 14–15C. The sense homosexual became established in the mid-20C.

gayal *n.* an ox, *Bos frontalis*, with horns depressed at the base and extended outwards, widely domesticated in Asia. WH: 18C. Bengali.

gazania *n.* any plant of the southern African genus *Gazania*, with bright yellow or orange flowers that close up in the afternoon. WH: 19C. Modern Latin, from Theodorus *Gaza*, 1398–1478, Greek scholar.

gazar *n.* a stiff gauzy silk fabric. WH: 19C. French, from *gaze* GAUZE.

gaze *v.i.* to fix the eye intently (at or upon). *Also v.t., n.* WH: 14–15C. ? Scandinavian. Cp. Old Norse *gá* to heed. The original sense was to stare vacantly or curiously rather than fixedly, as now.

gazebo *n.* an ornamental turret, lantern or summer house with a wide prospect, often erected in a garden. WH: 18C. ? From GAZE with pseudo-Latin ending based on a word such as LAVABO. According to some, the word is a corruption of some oriental (possibly Chinese) word.

gazelle *n.* a swift and very graceful antelope of Africa and Asia, esp. *Gazella dorcas*, noted for its large, soft black eyes. WH: 17C. Old French *gazel*, prob. from Spanish *gacel*, from Arabic *ghazāl*.

gazette *n.* an official journal containing lists of appointments to any public office or commission, legal notices, lists of bankrupts etc. *Also v.t.* WH: 17C. French, or from Italian *gazzetta*, orig. Venetian *gazeta de la novità* 'ha'p'orth of news', from *gazeta*, a Venetian coin of small value. See also -ETTE.

gazpacho *n.* a spicy Spanish soup made with tomatoes, chopped onion, cucumber, green peppers, garlic etc. and usu. served cold. WH: 19C. Spanish, from Arabic word meaning soaked bread.

gazump *v.t., v.i.* to raise the price of a property etc. after accepting an offer from (a buyer) but before contracts have been signed, usu. because other parties have made a subsequent higher offer. WH: early 20C. Yiddish *gezumph* to overcharge.

gazunder *v.t., v.i.* to lower the sum offered to (a seller) on a property etc. just before the contracts are signed. WH: late 20C. GAZUMP (punningly, as if from *gaz-* and UP) + UNDER.

gean *n.* the wild cherry, *Prunus avium*. WH: 16C. Old French *guine* (Modern French *guigne*), ult. of unknown orig.

gear *n.* apparatus, tools, mechanical appliances, harness, tackle, equipment, dress. *Also v.t., v.i.* WH: 12–14C. Old Norse *gervi*, from Germanic. Cp. YARE.

†geck *n.* a dupe, a fool. *Also v.i.* WH: 16C. Of Low Dutch orig. Cp. German *Geck* fop, dandy.

gecko *n.* any of various lizards with adhesive toes, by which means they can walk on a wall or ceiling. WH: 18C. Malay (dial.) *geko*, *gekok*, ult. imit. Cp. TOKAY.

geddit *int.* (do you) get it?, do you see the joke etc.? WH: late 20C. Representation of coll. pronun. of (*do you*) *get it*?

gee[1] *int.* go on, move faster (a command to a horse etc.). *Also v.t.* WH: 17C. Orig. unknown.

gee[2] *n.* the letter G . WH: mid-20C. Representation of pronun. of G as letter's name. Cp. CEE, DEE. The word is used for a thousand dollars etc. as the first letter of GRAND.

gee[3] *int.* an exclamation expressing surprise, delight etc. WH: 19C. ? Alt. of JESUS.

geebung *n.* any shrub or tree of the proteaceous genus *Persoonia*, or its fruit. WH: 19C. Australian Aboriginal (Dharuk) *jibung*.

geek *n.* an odd or eccentric person, a misfit, an inept person. WH: 19C. Var. of GECK.

geep *n.* a cross between a goat and a sheep produced artificially by combining genetic material from both. WH: late 20C. Blend of GOAT and SHEEP.

geezer *n.* a man. WH: 19C. Representation of dial. pronun. of *guiser* (GUISE).

gefilte fish *n.* in Jewish cookery, cooked chopped fish mixed with matzo meal, egg and seasonings and then poached, either stuffed back into the skin of the fish or as dumplings. WH: 19C. Yiddish stuffed fish, from *gefilte*, inflected p.p. of *filn* FILL + FISH[1].

gegenschein *n.* a faint glow in the night sky at a position opposite to that of the sun, counterglow. WH: 19C. German *gegen* opposite + *Schein* shine, glow.

Gehenna *n.* hell, a place of torment. WH: 15C. French *gehenne*, or from Ecclesiastical Latin, from Hellenistic Greek *geenna*, from Hebrew *gē' hinnōm* hell. The Hebrew word literally means valley of *Hinnom*, a place near Jerusalem where children were sacrificed (II Kgs. xxiii.10).

gehlenite *n.* a green mineral silicate of aluminium and calcium occurring in tetragonal crystalline form. WH: 19C. Adolf F. *Gehlen*, 1775–1815, German chemist + -ITE[1]. The mineral was so named in 1815 by the German mineralogist Johann Fuchs.

Geiger counter *n.* a device for the detection and counting of particles from radioactive materials. WH: early 20C. Hans *Geiger*, 1882–1945, German physicist, its inventor.

geisha *n.* a Japanese girl or woman trained in the art of being a hostess for men, with skills in conversation, dancing, music. WH: 19C. Japanese entertainer, from *gei* (performing) arts + *sha* person.

Geissler tube *n.* a sealed, gas-filled glass or quartz tube with electrodes at each end, producing visible or ultraviolet light, used in spectroscopy. WH: 19C. Heinrich *Geissler*, 1814–79, German glass-blower.

Geist *n.* the spirit, principle or tendency of an age, time-spirit. WH: 19C. German. See GHOST.

gel *n.* the jelly-like material formed when a colloidal solution is left standing. *Also v.i., v.t.* WH: 19C. Abbr. of GELATIN.

gelada *n.* a baboon from NE Africa, *Theropithecus gelada*, with long mane, bare red chest and ridged muzzle. WH: 19C. Amharic *č'āllada*.

gelatin *n.* a transparent substance forming a jelly in water, obtained from connective animal tissue, such as skin, tendons, bones, horns etc. WH: 19C. French *gélatine*, from Italian *gelatina*, from *gelata* JELLY. See -IN[1], -INE. Cp. GALANTINE.

gelation *n.* solidification into a gel by cooling or freezing. WH: 19C. Latin *gelatio*, *gelationis*, from *gelatus*, p.p. of *gelare* to freeze. See also -ATION.

geld[1] *v.t.* to castrate (esp. a horse), to emasculate, to spay. WH: 12–14C. Old Norse *gelda*, from *geldr* barren.

geld[2] *n.* the tax paid by landholders to the Crown under the Saxon and early Norman kings. WH: 15C. Medieval Latin *geldum*, from Old English *geld*, from Germanic base of GUILD, YIELD.

gelid *a.* extremely cold. WH: 17C. Latin *gelidus*, form *gelu* frost. See also -ID.

gelignite *n.* an explosive containing nitroglycerin. WH: 19C. Prob. from GELATIN + Latin *lignum* wood + -ITE[1]. According to some, the middle element represents Latin *ignis* fire. But gelignite has always (usually) contained wood pulp.

gelsemium *n.* any plant of the genus of climbing shrubs *Gelsemium*, which contains three species, of which the best known is the American yellow jasmine, *Gelsemium sempervirens*, the poisonous root of which yields a medicinal substance. WH: 19C. Modern Latin, from Italian *gelsomino* JASMINE.

gelt *n.* money, cash. WH: 16C. German *Geld*.

gem *n.* a precious stone, such as the diamond, ruby, emerald etc. *Also v.t., v.i.* WH: pre-1200. Old English *gim*, from Latin *gemma* bud, jewel. The word was readopted in the 14–15C and based on Old French *gemme*.

Gemara *n.* the second portion of the Talmud, consisting of a commentary on the first part of the Mishna, or text. WH: 17C. Aramaic *gěmārā* completion.

gemeinschaft *n.* a social group united by kinship, common beliefs etc. WH: mid-20C. German, from *gemein* common, general + -*schaft* -SHIP.

gemel *n.* a pair of parallel bars. WH: 14–15C. Old French, from Latin *gemellus*, dim. of *geminus* twin.

geminal *a.* (of molecules) having two functional groups attached to the same atom. WH: late 20C. Latin *geminus* twin + -AL[1].

geminate[1] *a.* united or arranged in pairs. WH: 14–15C. Latin *geminatus*, p.p. of *geminare*. See GEMINATE[2], also -ATE[2].

geminate[2] *v.t.* to double, to arrange in pairs. *Also v.i.* WH: 17C. Latin *geminatus*, p.p. of *geminare*, from *geminus* twin. See also -ATE[3].

Gemini *n.* a constellation, the Twins, containing the two conspicuous stars, Castor and Pollux. WH: pre-1200. Latin, pl. of *geminus* twin.

gemma *n.* a budlike outgrowth in polyps, ascidians etc., which separates from the parent organism and develops into an individual. WH: 18C. Latin bud, jewel.

gemmate *a.* reproducing by gemmation. *Also v.i.* WH: 19C. Latin *gemmatus*, p.p. of *gemmare* to put forth buds, from *gemma* bud, jewel. See also -ATE[2].

gemmiferous *a.* producing gems. WH: 17C. Latin *gemmifer*, from *gemma* GEM + -OUS. See -FEROUS.

gemmiparous *a.* propagating by gemmation. WH: 18C. Modern Latin *gemmiparus*, from *gemma* GEM + -OUS.

gemmule *n.* any one of the small reproductive bodies thrown off by sponges. **WH:** 19C. French, from Latin *gemmula*, dim. of GEMMA. See also -ULE.

gemote *n.* a public meeting or assembly, esp. the court held in Anglo-Saxon England in each shire or hundred before the Norman Conquest. **WH:** pre-1200. Old English *gemōt*, from *ge-* -Y[1] + *mōt* MOOT.

gemsbok *n.* a large antelope of W and E Africa, *Oryx gazella*, with long straight horns. **WH:** 18C. Afrikaans, from Dutch *chamois*, from *gems* chamois + *bok* buck. Cp. BLESBOK, BONTEBOK, GRYSBOK, RHEBOK, SPRINGBOK, STEENBOK etc.

gemütlich *a.* comfortable, cosy. **WH:** 19C. German.

gen *n.* full particulars (of), information (about). *Also v.i.* **WH:** mid-20C. ? From first syl. of *general information*.

-gen *comb. form* producing. **WH:** French *-gène*, from Greek *-genēs* born, of a specified kind, from *gen-*, base of *gignesthai* to be born, to become, and *genos* kind (n.) etc.

genco *n.* a company generating and selling power, esp. electricity. **WH:** late 20C. Abbr. of *generating company*.

gendarme *n.* an armed policeman, in France and some other Continental countries. **WH:** 16C. French, sing. n. from pl. *gens d'armes* men of arms. The word is popularly regarded as the general French word for policeman, which is really *agent* (*de police*).

gender *n.* any one of the classes (usually *masculine*, *feminine* and *common* or *neuter*) into which words referring to people or things are divided, often coinciding with their sex or sexlessness. *Also v.t.*, *v.i.* **WH:** 14–15C. Old French *gendre* (Modern French *genre*), from Latin *genus*, *generis*. See GENUS.

gene *n.* the unit of heredity, one of the units of DNA occupying a fixed linear position on the chromosome. **WH:** early 20C. German *Gen*, from *Pangen*, obs. Eng. *pangene*, from PAN- + stem of Greek *genos* kind, race.

genealogy *n.* the history or investigation of the descent of families. **WH:** 12–14C. Old French *généalogie*, from Late Latin *genealogia*, from Greek *genealogia*, from *genealogos* genealogist, from *genea* race, generation. See also -LOGY.

general *a.* common, universal. *Also n.* **WH:** 12–14C. Old French *général*, from Latin *generalis*, from *genus*, *generis* class, race, kind. See GENUS, also -AL[1].

generalissimo *n.* the chief commander of a force furnished by several powers, or military and naval in combination. **WH:** 17C. Italian, superl. of *generale* GENERAL.

generate *v.t.* to produce or bring into existence; to cause to be. **WH:** 16C. Latin *generatus*, p.p. of *generare* to beget, from *genus*, *generis* stock, race. See also -ATE[3].

generic *a.* of or relating to a class or kind, as opposed to specific. **WH:** 17C. French *générique*, from Latin *genus*, *generis* GENUS. See also -IC.

generous *a.* open-handed, bountiful, liberal, munificent. **WH:** 16C. Old French *généreux*, from Latin *generosus* noble, magnanimous, from *genus*, *generis* GENUS. See also -OUS. The original sense was high-born. The current sense dates from the 17C.

genesis *n.* the act of begetting, producing or giving origin to. **WH:** pre-1200. Latin, from Greek generation, creation, from base of *gignesthai* to be born, to be produced. The biblical book of Genesis is so named as it describes the origin of the universe and of the nation of Israel, both the creations of God.

genet *n.* a small mammal, *Genetta vulgaris*, related to the civet. **WH:** 14–15C. Old French *genete* (Modern French *genette*).

genetic *a.* of or relating to genes or genetics. **WH:** 19C. GENESIS, based on pairs such as ANTITHESIS/ *antithetic*.

Geneva *a.* of, originating from or relating to Geneva, Switzerland. **WH:** 16C. *Geneva*, a city in Switzerland.

genever *n.* Dutch gin. **WH:** 18C. Dutch, or from Old French *genevre* (Modern French *genièvre*), from alt. of Latin *iuniperus* JUNIPER. Cp. GIN[1].

genial[1] *a.* of a cheerful and kindly disposition, cordial, sympathetic, enlivening. **WH:** 16C. Latin *genialis* nuptial, productive, joyous, from GENIUS. See also -AL[1]. The original sense was pertaining to marriage or to reproduction. The current sense dates from the 18C.

genial[2] *a.* of, relating to or near the chin. **WH:** 19C. Greek *geneion* chin, from *genus* jaw. See also -AL[1].

-genic *comb. form* of or relating to generation, as in *antigenic*. **WH:** -GEN + -IC.

geniculate *a.* having knee joints. *Also v.t.* **WH:** 17C. Latin *geniculatus*, from *geniculum* joint in a plant stem, small knee, dim. of *genu* knee. See also -CULE, -ATE[2].

genie *n.* in fairy stories etc., a magical being who appears suddenly to carry out a person's wishes. **WH:** 17C. French *génie*, from Latin GENIUS. The French word was adopted by the French translators of the *Arabian Nights' Entertainments* because of its similarity in sound and sense to Arabic *jinnī* JINNEE.

genio- *comb. form* chin. **WH:** Greek *geneion* chin. See GENIAL[2], also -O-.

genipap *n.* the fruit of the W Indian tree *Genipa americana*, about the size of an orange, with a winy taste. **WH:** 17C. Portuguese *jenipapo*, from Tupi *ianipaba*.

genista *n.* any shrub of the genus *Genista* with few, simple leaves and yellow flowers. **WH:** 17C. Latin (the plant) broom. Cp. PLANTAGENET.

genital *a.* of or relating to the reproductive organs. **WH:** 14–15C. Old French *génital* or Latin *genitalis*, from *genitus*, p.p. of *gignere* to beget. See also -AL[1].

genitive *a.* denoting a grammatical case indicating origin, possession or the like, applied to a case in inflected languages and also to the Eng. possessive. *Also n.* **WH:** 14–15C. Old French *génitif* or Latin *genitivus*, from *genitus*, p.p. of *gignere* to beget, to produce. See also -IVE. Latin *genitivus casus* mistranslated Greek *genikē ptōsis* which properly means generic case.

genito- *comb. form* genital. **WH:** Latin *genitus* GENITAL. See also -O-.

genitor *n.* a biological father, sire. **WH:** 14–15C. Old French *géniteur* or Latin *genitor*, from base of *gignere* to beget. See also -OR.

genito-urinary *a.* of or relating to the genital and urinary organs. **WH:** 19C. GENITO- + *urinary* (URINE).

genius *n.* a person of extraordinary intellectual, imaginative, expressive or inventive ability. **WH:** 14–15C. Latin, from base of *gignere* to beget and Greek *gignesthai* to be born. The earliest sense is a tutelary spirit allotted to every person at their birth. The current sense of person of extraordinary intellectual power dates from the 17C.

genizah *n.* a room attached to a synagogue for storing old books, documents etc. **WH:** 19C. Hebrew, lit. a hiding, from *gānaz* to set aside, to hide.

genoa *n.* in yachting, a large triangular jib sail. **WH:** 16C. *Genoa*, a city and seaport in NW Italy. Cp. JEAN.

genocide *n.* the (attempted) intentional and systematic destruction of a national, ethnic or religious group, e.g. the Jews by the Nazi Germans during World War II. **WH:** mid-20C. Greek *genos* offspring, race + -O- + -CIDE. The word was coined in 1944 by the US jurist Raphael Lemkin with reference to the extermination of the Jews under the Nazis in World War II.

genome *n.* the complete set of chromosomes that is contained in any single cell. **WH:** mid-20C. Greek *genos* offspring, race + -O- + CHROMOSOME.

genotype *n.* the basic genetic structure of an organism. **WH:** early 20C. German *Genotypus*, from Greek *genos* offspring, race + -O-. See TYPE.

-genous *comb. form* born. **WH:** -GEN + -OUS.

genre *n.* a kind, sort, class, particularly in the field of the arts. **WH:** 19C. French kind. See GENDER.

genro *n.pl.* elder statesmen in Japan who were on occasion consulted by the Emperor. **WH:** 19C. Japanese principal elders, from *gen* origin + *rō* old.

gens *n.* in anthropology, a tribe, clan or group of families. **WH:** 19C. Latin, from base of *gignere* to beget.

gent *n.* a gentleman. **WH:** 16C. Abbr. of GENTLEMAN.

genteel *a.* gentlemanly or ladylike. *Also n.* **WH:** 16C. Re-adoption of French *gentil*, which had earlier given GENTLE. Cp. JAUNTY.

gentian *n.* any plant of the genus *Gentiana* or *Gentianella* of bitter herbs, usu. having blue flowers, common in mountain regions. **WH:** 14–15C. Latin *gentiana*, according to Pliny from *Gentius*, 2C BC, King of ancient Illyria. See also -IAN. Gentius is said to have discovered the medicinal properties of the roots of *Gentiana lutea*, the yellow gentian.

gentile *a.* Christian, as opposed to Jewish. *Also n.* WH: 14–15C. Latin *gentilis*, from *gens*, *gentis* clan, race, from base of *gignere* to beget.

gentility *n.* social superiority, polite good breeding. WH: 12–14C. Old French *gentilité*, from *gentil*. See GENTLE, also -ITY.

gentle *a.* mild, tender, kindly. *Also n.*, *v.t.* WH: 12–14C. Old French *gentil* high-born (Modern French pleasant, agreeable), from Latin *gentilis* of the same clan, belonging to a good family. Cp. GENTEEL, GENTILE, JAUNTY.

gentleman *n.* a man of good breeding, kindly feelings and high principles, a man of honour. WH: 12–14C. GENTLE + MAN, based on Old French *gentilz homme* (Modern French *gentilhomme*).

gentlewoman *n.* a woman of good birth or breeding. WH: 12–14C. GENTLE + WOMAN.

gentoo *n.* a penguin, *Pygoscelis papua*, found esp. in the Falkland Islands. WH: 19C. Appar. from Portuguese *gentio* GENTILE, orig. term for Hindu in S India.

gentry *n.* people of high birth and social standing. WH: 14–15C. Old French *genterie*. See GENTLE.

genu *n.* the knee. WH: 19C. Latin.

genuflect *v.i.* to bend the knee, esp. in worship. WH: 17C. Ecclesiastical Latin *genuflectere*, from *genu* knee + *flectere* to bend.

genuine *a.* natural, belonging to or coming from the true source. WH: 16C. Latin *genuinus*, ? from *genu* knee. The Latin word probably refers to the Roman custom of a father acknowledging the paternity of a newborn child by placing the baby on his knee.

genus *n.* a class or kind of objects containing several subordinate classes or species. WH: 16C. Latin birth, family, nation.

-geny *comb. form* production or mode of production, as in *ontogeny*, *philogeny*. WH: French *-génie*, or Greek *-geneia*, forming nn. from aa. in *-genēs*, from base of *gignesthai* to be born, to come into being.

geo *n.* a narrow inlet, a creek, esp. in Orkney and Shetland. WH: 17C. Old Norse *gjá*.

geo- *comb. form* of or relating to the earth. WH: Greek *gēo-*, from *gē* earth. See also -O-.

geobotany *n.* the study of the geographical distribution of plants. WH: early 20C. GEO- + BOTANY.

geocarpy *n.* the ripening of a plant's fruit below the ground. WH: 19C. GEO- + Greek *karpos* fruit. See also -Y².

geocentric *a.* having the earth as centre. WH: 17C. GEO- + -CENTRIC. See also -AL¹.

geochemistry *n.* the study of the chemical composition of the crust of the earth. WH: early 20C. GEO- + CHEMISTRY.

geochronology *n.* the measuring of geological time. WH: 19C. GEO- + CHRONOLOGY.

geode *n.* a hollow nodule of any mineral substance, often lined with crystals. WH: 17C. Latin *geodes*, from Greek *geōdēs* earthy, from *gē* earth. See also -ODE¹.

geodesy *n.* the science or art of measuring the earth's surface or large portions of it, as distinguished from surveying, which deals only with limited tracts. WH: 16C. Modern Latin *geodaesia*, from Greek *geōdaisia*, from *daiein* to divide. See GEO-, also -Y².

geodynamic *a.* relating to the latent forces of the earth. WH: 19C. GEO- + DYNAMIC.

geogeny *n.* the science or study of the formation of the crust of the earth. WH: 19C. GEO- + -GENY.

geognosy *n.* knowledge of the structure of the earth, structural geology. WH: 18C. French *géognosie*, from Greek *gēo-* GEO- + *gnōsis* knowledge.

geogony *n.* the science of the formation of the earth. WH: 19C. Greek *gēo-* GEO- + *gonia* production.

geography *n.* the science of the surface of the earth, its physical features, natural productions, inhabitants, political divisions, commerce etc. WH: 15C. Latin *geographia*, from Greek *geōgraphia*. See GEO-, -GRAPHY.

geoid *n.* the shape of the earth, an oblate spheroid. WH: 19C. Greek *geoeidēs* earthlike. See GEO-, also -OID.

geology *n.* the science of the earth's crust, its composition, its structure, and the history of its development. WH: 18C. Modern Latin *geologia*. See GEO-, -LOGY.

geomagnetism *n.* the magnetic field of the earth. WH: mid-20C. GEO- + *magnetism* (MAGNET).

geomancy *n.* the art of siting buildings by a form of divination. WH: 14–15C. Medieval Latin *geomantia*. See GEO-, -MANCY.

geometry *n.* the branch of mathematics concerned with the properties and relationships of points, lines, curves, surfaces and solids. WH: 12–14C. Old French *géométrie*, from Latin *geometria*, from Greek. See GEO-, -METRY.

geomorphic *a.* of or relating to the form of the earth or the solid features of its surface. WH: 19C. GEO- + *-morphic* (-MORPH).

geomorphology *n.* the study of the origin, development and characteristics of land forms. WH: 19C. GEO- + MORPHOLOGY.

geophagy *n.* the act or habit of eating earth. WH: 19C. GEO- + *-phagy* (-PHAGE).

geophones *n.pl.* a device for deflecting sound waves, shock waves etc. in the ground. WH: early 20C. GEO- + -PHONE + -S¹.

geophysics *n.* the science that deals with the physical characteristics of the earth. WH: 19C. GEO- + PHYSICS.

geophyte *n.* a perennial plant that propagates by having buds (i.e. bulbs, corms etc.) below the surface of the soil. WH: 19C. GEO- + -PHYTE.

geopolitics *n.* the study of how the political views and aims of a nation are affected by its geographical position. WH: early 20C. GEOGRAPHY + POLITICS.

geoponics *n.* the art and science of agriculture. WH: 17C. Greek *gēoponikos*, from *gēoponos* farmer. See also -ICS.

Geordie *n.* a native of Tyneside, NE England. *Also a.* WH: 19C. Dim. of GEORGE. The word is popularly said to have been adopted from the name of George Stephenson, 1781–1848, English railway pioneer (the Stockton and Darlington railway opened in 1825). The earliest records of the name date from the 1860s.

George *n.* an automatic aircraft pilot. WH: 16C. Male forename.

georgette *n.* a plain semi-transparent dress material usually of silk or crêpe. WH: early 20C. Mme *Georgette* de la Plante, *fl. c.*1900, French dressmaker.

Georgian¹ *a.* relating to the period of George I–IV in Great Britain, 1714–1830. WH: 18C. GEORGE + -IAN. The term relates specifically to the reigns of George I, 1714–27, II, 1727–60, III, 1760–1820 and IV, 1820–30, although the *Georgian* poets relate to the reign of George V, 1910–36.

Georgian² *a.* of or relating to Georgia, a republic of SE Europe. *Also n.* WH: 14–15C. *Georgia*, a republic of SE Europe + -AN.

georgic *n.* a poem on husbandry or rural affairs. *Also a.* WH: 16C. Latin *georgicus*, from Greek *geōrgikos*, from *geōrgos* farmer. See also -IC.

geoscience *n.* any of the sciences that are concerned with the earth, e.g. geology, geophysics or geodesy. WH: mid-20C. GEO- + SCIENCE.

geosphere *n.* the solid part of the earth, the lithosphere. WH: 19C. GEO- + SPHERE.

geostatic *a.* able to resist or support the pressure of earth from all sides. WH: 19C. GEO- + STATIC.

geostationary *a.* (of a satellite) orbiting the earth at the same speed as the earth rotates so remaining above the same spot on the earth's surface. WH: mid-20C. GEO- + *stationary* (STATION).

geostrophic *a.* of or caused by the force produced by the rotation of the earth. WH: early 20C. GEO- + Greek *strophē* a turning + -IC.

geosyncline *n.* a part of the earth's crust that has sunk inwards, resulting in a usu. long and broad depression containing deep thicknesses of rock or sediment. WH: 19C. Back-formation from *geosynclinal*, from GEO- + SYNCLINAL.

geotaxis *n.* the response of an organism or a plant to the stimulus of gravity. WH: 19C. GEO- + TAXIS.

geotectonic *a.* of or relating to the structure of the earth. WH: 19C. GEO- + TECTONIC.

geothermal *a.* of or relating to the internal heat of the earth. WH: 19C. GEO- + THERMAL.

geothermometer *n.* an instrument for measuring the earth's heat at different depths, as in mines or wells. WH: 19C. GEO- + THERMOMETER.

geotropism *n.* the tendency exhibited by the organs of a plant to turn towards the centre of the earth. WH: 19C. GEO- + Greek *tropē* a turning + -ISM.

gerah *n.* the smallest ancient Hebrew weight and coin, equivalent to one twentieth of a shekel. WH: 16C. Hebrew *gērāh*.

geraniol *n.* an alcohol with the odour of roses, found in many essential oils and used in perfumery. WH: 19C. GERANIUM + -OL.

geranium *n.* any hardy herbaceous plant or shrub of the genus *Geranium*, natives of all temperate regions, such as the cranesbill. WH: 16C. Latin, from Greek *geranion*, from *geranos* crane. See also -IUM. The plant is so named from its seed pod, supposedly resembling the bill of a crane.

geratology *n.* the branch of knowledge dealing with the phenomena of ageing and decay. WH: 19C. Greek *gēras*, *gēratos* old age + -O- + -LOGY.

gerbe *n.* a figure resembling a wheatsheaf. WH: 16C. French wheatsheaf, from Frankish *garbe*, from Germanic. Cp. German *Garbe*.

gerbera *n.* any plant of the genus *Gerbera*, esp. *G. jamesonii*, the Transvaal daisy from S Africa. WH: 19C. Modern Latin, from Traugott *Gerber*, d.1743, German naturalist.

gerbil *n.* any of numerous small, burrowing, mouselike rodents of the subfamily Gerbillinae, from desert regions of Asia and Africa, often kept as pets. WH: 19C. French *gerbille*, from Modern Latin *gerbillus*, dim. of *gerboa* JERBOA.

gerenuk *n.* an antelope, *Litocranius walleri*, of E Africa, characterized by a long neck and long legs. WH: 19C. Somali.

geriatrics *n.* the branch of medicine dealing with old age and its diseases. WH: early 20C. Greek *gēras* old age + *iatrikos* (see IATRIC), based on PAEDIATRICS. The term was coined in 1909 by the US physician I.L. Nascher.

germ *n.* a micro-organism, esp. the type that is supposed to cause disease, a microbe. WH: 14–15C. Old French *germe*, from Latin *germen* seed, sprout.

German *a.* of or relating to Germany or its inhabitants. *Also n.* WH: 14–15C. Latin *Germanus*, naming a group of related peoples in N and central Europe. Cp. JERRY. The Germans' name for themselves is *deutsch* (cp. DUTCH, TEUTON), while the French name is *allemand* (cp. ALLEMANDE).

german *a.* having both parents the same. *Also n.* WH: 12–14C. Old French *germain*, from Latin *germanus* having the same parents, genuine. Cp. Latin *germanus* brother, *germana* sister.

germander *n.* any plant of the genus *Teucrium*. WH: 14–15C. Medieval Latin *germandra*, alt. of *gamandrea*, ult. from Greek *khamaidrus*, lit. ground oak, from *khamai* on the ground + *drus* oak.

germane *a.* relevant (to), appropriate. WH: 12–14C. Var. of GERMAN.

germanium *n.* a metallic element of a greyish-white colour, at. no. 32, chem. symbol Ge, used in the construction of transistors because of its electrical properties. WH: 19C. Latin *Germanus* GERMAN + -IUM. The element was named in 1886 by Clemens Winkler, the German chemist who discovered it.

Germano- *comb. form* German. WH: GERMAN + -O-.

Germanomania *n.* enthusiasm for Germany or German things. WH: 19C. GERMANO- + -MANIA.

Germanophile *n.* an admirer of Germany and the Germans. WH: 19C. GERMANO- + -PHILE.

Germanophobe *n.* a hater of Germany or Germans. WH: early 20C. GERMANO- + -PHOBE.

germen *n.* the ovary or rudimentary seed-vessel of a plant. WH: 17C. Latin seed, sprout, GERM.

germinate *v.i.* to sprout, to shoot, to bud. *Also v.t.* WH: 16C. Latin *germinatus*, p.p. of *germinare*, from *germen*, *germinis* seed, sprout, GERM. See also -ATE³.

germon *n.* ALBACORE. WH: 19C. French, of unknown orig.

Geronimo *int.* used to express excitement, bravado etc. when about to leap, go into energetic action etc. WH: mid-20C. *Geronimo*, 1829–1909, Apache Indian chief. Geronimo's name was adopted as a slogan in World War II by US paratroops.

geronto- *comb. form* of or relating to old age. WH: Greek *gerōn*, *gerontos* old man. See also -O-.

gerontocracy *n.* government by old men or old people. WH: 19C. GERONTO- + -CRACY.

gerontology *n.* the science dealing with old age, the ageing process and the problems special to old people. WH: early 20C. GERONTO- + -O- + -LOGY.

geropiga *n.* a mixture sometimes added to port wine, made of unfermented grape juice with brandy, sugar and colouring matter. WH: 19C. Portuguese *jeropiga*.

-gerous *comb. form* bearing, having, as in *armigerous*. WH: Latin *-ger* bearing, from base of *gerere* to bear, to carry + -OUS.

gerrymander *v.t.* to tamper with the boundaries of (an electoral district or constituency) so as to secure unfair advantages for a particular candidate, party or class. *Also n.* WH: 19C. Elbridge *Gerry*, 1744–1814, US governor + SALAMANDER. The word alludes to the supposed resemblance to the shape of a salamander of an electoral district in Massachusetts formed by Gerry in 1812 to enable his political party to retain its majority.

gerund *n.* a form of a verb acting as a noun: in English a form ending in *-ing*, in Latin, a part of the verb used as a noun instead of the infinitive in cases other than the nominative. WH: 16C. Late Latin *gerundium*, from *gerundum*, var. of *gerendum*, ger. of Latin *gerere* to carry on.

gesellschaft *n.* a social group, held together by practical concerns and not by ties of kinship, as distinct from *gemeinschaft*. WH: 19C. German, from *Gesell* companion + *-schaft* -SHIP.

gesso *n.* plaster of Paris used for painting, sometimes used for sculpture. WH: 16C. Italian, from Latin GYPSUM.

†gest *n.* a deed, an exploit, an achievement. *Also v.i.* WH: 12–14C. Old French *geste*, *jeste*, from Latin *gesta* actions, exploits, neut. pl. (used as n.) of p.p. of *gerere* to bear, to carry, to perform. Cp. JEST.

gestalt *n.* an organized whole in which each part affects every other part. WH: early 20C. German form, shape.

Gestapo *n.* the body of secret police formed to secure strict obedience to the government of Nazi Germany. WH: mid-20C. German, acronym of *Geheime Staatspolizei* Secret State Police.

gestation *n.* the process of being carried in the uterus from the time of conception to that of birth. WH: 16C. Latin *gestatio*, *gestationis*, from *gestatus*, p.p.o of *gestare* to carry (in the womb), freq. of *gerere* to bear, to carry. See also -ATION.

gesticulate *v.i.* to make expressive gestures or motions, as in speaking or instead of speaking. *Also v.t.* WH: 17C. Latin *gesticulatus*, p.p. of *gesticulari*, from *gesticulus*, dim. of *gestus* action, gesture. See also -ATE³.

gesture *n.* a motion of the face, body or limbs, used to express emotion or to illustrate or enforce something that is said. *Also v.i.*, *v.t.* WH: 14–15C. Medieval Latin *gestura*, from Latin *gerere* to bear, to carry, to perform. See also -URE.

gesundheit *int.* your health (said after someone has sneezed). WH: early 20C. German health.

get¹ *v.t.* to procure, to obtain, to gain possession of by any means, to acquire. *Also v.i.* WH: 12–14C. Old Norse *geta* to obtain, to beget, from Germanic, from Indo-European base also of Latin *praeda* booty, PREY, *praedium* estate, *praehendere* to lay hold of, Greek *khandanein* to hold, to contain. Cp. BEGET, FORGET.

get² *n.* the act of begetting. WH: 12–14C. GET¹. Cp. GIT.

geta *n.* a Japanese wooden sandal. WH: 19C. Japanese.

geum *n.* any plant of the genus *Geum*, the rose family, comprising the avens or herb-bennet. WH: 16C. Modern Latin, var. of Latin *gaeum*.

gewgaw *n.* a showy trifle; a toy, a bauble. *Also a.* WH: 12–14C. Orig. uncertain. ? Redupl. of Old French *gogue* game, joke. Cp. AGOG. According to some, the word has been influenced by French *joujou* toy, plaything. Cp. JU-JU.

gey *a.* considerable, middling (in amount). *Also adv.* WH: 18C. Var. of GAY. Cp. JOLLY¹.

geyser *n.* a hot spring throwing up a column of water at intervals (as in SW Iceland, the Yellowstone region in N America, and New Zealand). WH: 18C. Icelandic *Geysir*, name of a particular hot spring in Iceland, rel. to *geysa* to gush.

Ghanaian *n.* a native or inhabitant of Ghana in W Africa. *Also a.* WH: mid-20C. *Ghana*, a country in W Africa + -IAN.

gharial *n.* a large Indian crocodile, *Gavialis gangeticus*, with a long, slender muzzle. WH: 19C. Hindi *ghaṛiyāl*.

gharry *n.* a variety of wheeled carriage in the Indian subcontinent. WH: 19C. Hindi *gāṛī*.

ghastly *a.* horrible, frightful, shocking. *Also adv.* WH: 12–14C. Obs. *gast* to frighten, from Old English *gæstan*, from Germanic base of GHOST + -LY¹. The earlier spelling was *gastly*. The spelling with *gh-* (based on GHOST) was introduced by Spenser in the 16C. The original meaning was causing real terror.

ghat *n.* a flight of steps descending to a river, a landing-place. WH: 17C. Hindi *ghāṭ*.

ghazal *n.* an Oriental lyric poem, usu. erotic, convivial or religious in subject, having a limited number of couplets, all with the same rhyme. WH: 18C. Persian, from Arabic *ǧazal*.

Ghazi *n.* a person who has fought for Islam against non-Muslims. WH: 18C. Arabic *al-ǧāzī*, active part. of *ǧazā* to raid, to invade.

ghee *n.* butter, usu. prepared from buffalo-milk, clarified into an oil, which can be kept for a long time. WH: 17C. Hindi *ghī*, from Sanskrit *ghṛta*, p.p. of *ghṛ-* to sprinkle.

gherao *n.* in the Indian subcontinent, a form of industrial action in which a person, e.g. an employer, is imprisoned in a room, building etc. until certain demands are met. WH: mid-20C. Hindi *ghernā* to surround, to besiege.

gherkin *n.* a young and green small variety of cucumber, used for pickling. WH: 17C. Dutch *augurkje*, dim. of *augurk*, *gurk*, ult. from a Slavonic word. Cp. Polish *ogórek*, Russian *ogurets* cucumber.

ghetto *n.* a poor, densely populated area of a city, esp. inhabited by an ethnic minority. *Also v.t.* WH: 17C. Orig. uncertain. ? Abbr. of Italian *borghetto*, dim. of *borgo* BOROUGH, or from Italian *getto* foundry (where first ghetto in Venice was sited, 1516). According to some, the word is from Latin *Aegyptus*. Cp. GYPSY.

Ghibelline *n.* a person who sided with the German Emperors in their contests with the Guelphs or partisans of the Popes, in Italy during the Middle Ages. WH: 16C. Italian *Ghibellino*, supposedly from German *Waiblingen*, an estate of the Hohenstaufen family, said to have been used as a war cry by partisans of the Hohen-staufen emperor Conrad III at the Battle of Weinsberg in 1140.

ghost *n.* the spirit or soul of a dead person appearing to the living, an apparition. *Also v.i., v.t.* WH: pre-1200. Old English *gāst*, from Germanic. Cp. German *Geist*. The spelling with *gh-*, established in the 16C, is probably from Flemish *gheest*.

ghoul *n.* an evil spirit supposed, in Eastern tales, to devour human corpses. WH: 18C. Arabic *ǧūl*, from *ǧāla* he seized. The evil spirit was said to rob graves and feed on corpses.

GI *n.* a soldier in the US Army, esp. a private. *Also a.* WH: mid-20C. Abbr. of *government issue* or *general issue*, designating equipment and supplies issued to members of the US armed forces.

giant *n.* a mythical being of human form but superhuman size. *Also a.* WH: 12–14C. Old French *géant*, from var. of Latin *gigas*, *gigantis*, from Greek.

giaour *n.* a non-Muslim, esp. a Christian. WH: 16C. Turkish *gâvur*, from Persian *gaur*, var. of *gabr*, prob. from Arabic *kāfir* KAFFIR.

giardiasis *n.* stomach infection with the protozoa of the genus *Giardia*, esp. *G. lamblia* causing nausea, diarrhoea etc., often caused by drinking contaminated water. WH: early 20C. Modern Latin *Giardia* genus name, from Alfred M. *Giard*, 1848–1908, French biologist. See also -IA, -IASIS.

Gib *n.* Gibraltar. WH: 19C. Abbr. of *Gibraltar*. See GIBRALTARIAN.

gib¹ *n.* a metal wedge, pin or bolt to hold a machine part etc. in place. *Also v.t.* WH: 18C. Orig. unknown.

†gib² *n.* a cat, esp. a tom-cat. WH: 14–15C. Abbr. of male forename *Gilbert*.

gibber¹ *v.i.* to jabber, to talk rapidly and inarticulately. *Also n.* WH: 17C. Imit. Cp. JABBER. *Gibberish* is recorded in the 16C and may not be related to *gibber*.

gibber² *n.* a stone, a boulder. WH: 18C. Australian Aboriginal (Dharuk) *giba*.

gibberellic acid *n.* a product extracted from the fungus *Gibberella fujikuroi*, used to stimulate plant growth. WH: mid-20C. Modern Latin *Gibberella*, dim. of *Gibbera* genus name, from Latin *gibber* hump. See also -IC.

gibbet *n.* an upright post with a crosspiece from which the bodies of executed criminals were formerly hung on display. *Also v.t.* WH: 12–14C. Old French *gibet* staff, cudgel, gallows, dim. of *gibe* staff, club, prob. ult. from Germanic.

gibbon *n.* any individual of the genus *Hylobates*, long-armed anthropoid apes from E Asia. WH: 18C. French, of unknown orig.

gibbous *a.* protuberant, convex, swelling into inequalities. WH: 14–15C. Late Latin *gibbosus*, from Latin *gibbus* hump. See also -OUS.

gibe *v.i.* to use sneering or taunting expressions. *Also v.t., n.* WH: 16C. ? Old French *giber* to handle roughly. Cp. JIB³.

Gibeonite *n.* any of the inhabitants of Gibeon, condemned for their duplicity to be 'hewers of wood and drawers of water' (Josh. ix.23). WH: 14–15C. *Gibeon* (mod. Al-Jīb), a city in ancient Palestine northwest of Jerusalem which made a league with Joshua to avoid the fate of Jericho + -ITE¹.

giblets *n.pl.* the feet, neck, and internal eatable parts of a fowl, such as the heart, liver, gizzard etc., which are removed before cooking. WH: 12–14C. Old French *gibelet* game stew, ? from *gibier* game. Cp. French *gibelotte* rabbit stew.

Gibraltarian *n.* an inhabitant of Gibraltar. *Also a.* WH: 19C. *Gibraltar*, a fortified town and rocky headland at S tip of Spain + -IAN. Gibraltar has been a British colony since 1704.

†Gibson girl *n.* a girl conforming to the tastes in fashion and beauty of around 1900. WH: 19C. Charles Dana *Gibson*, 1867–1944, US artist and illustrator, who drew such girls.

gibus *n.* a crush-hat, an opera hat. WH: 19C. *Gibus*, 19C French inventor of this type of hat.

gid *n.* a disease causing vertigo in sheep, sturdy. WH: 17C. Back-formation from GIDDY.

giddy *a.* having a whirling, swimming or dizziness in the head. *Also v.t., v.i.* WH: pre-1200. Old English *gidig*, from Germanic, from base of GOD. See also -Y¹. The basic sense of the word is possessed by a god. Cp. ENTHUSIASM.

giddy-up *int.* used as a command to a horse to make it start moving or go faster. WH: early 20C. Var. of *giddap*, representing a pronun. of *get up*. Cp. *gee-up* (GEE¹).

gidgee *n.* a small Australian tree, *Acacia cambagei*. WH: 19C. Australian Aboriginal (Nyungar) *giji*.

gie *v.t., v.i.* to give. WH: 14–15C. Var. of GIVE.

gift *n.* a thing given, a present, a contribution. *Also v.t.* WH: 12–14C. Old Norse *gipt*, rel. to Old English *gift* payment for a wife, from Germanic base of GIVE.

gig¹ *n.* a light two-wheeled vehicle drawn by one horse. WH: 18C. Appar. from *gig* whirling thing. Cp. *whirligig* (WHIRL).

gig² *n.* a job, esp. a booking for a musician to perform. *Also v.i.* WH: early 20C. Orig. unknown.

gig³ *n.* a type of fishing spear. WH: 18C. Abbr. of obs. *fishgig* or *fizgig*, prob. ult. from Spanish *fisga* harpoon.

giga- *comb. form* denoting 10⁹, as in *gigawatt*, or 2³⁰, as in *gigabyte*. WH: mid-20C. Greek *gigas* giant.

gigabyte *n.* a unit of computer memory capacity equal to 1,024 megabytes. WH: late 20C. GIGA- + BYTE.

giga-electron-volt *n.* a unit of energy equal to 1,000 million electron-volts. WH: late 20C. GIGA- + *electron-volt* (ELECTRON, VOLT¹).

gigaflop *n.* a unit of computer processing speed equal to 1,000 million floating-point operations per second. WH: late 20C. Back-formation from *gigaflops*, from GIGA- + acronym of *f*loating-point *op*erations per *s*econd, with -*s* taken as -S¹.

gigahertz *n.* a unit of frequency equal to 10⁹ hertz. WH: mid-20C. GIGA- + HERTZ.

gigametre *n.* a unit of distance equal to 10⁹ metres. WH: mid-20C. GIGA- + METRE¹.

gigantic *a.* huge, enormous, giant-like; immense, extraordinary. WH: 17C. Latin *gigas*, *gigantis* (see GIANT) + -IC.

gigawatt *n.* a unit of power equal to 10⁹ watts. WH: mid-20C. GIGA- + WATT.

giggle *v.i.* to laugh in a silly or affected manner, to titter. *Also n.* WH: 16C. Imit. Cp. Dutch *gichelen*, Low German *giggeln*, Russian *khikhikat'*.

giglet *n.* a flighty, giddy girl. *Also a.* WH: 12–14C. ? From obs. *gig* in same sense (prob. imit.), later assoc. with GIGGLE. See also -LET.

gigolo *n.* a young man paid by an older woman to be a sexual partner or escort. WH: early 20C. French, formed as m. of *gigole* dance hall woman. Rel. to JIG.

gigot *n.* a leg of mutton or lamb. WH: 16C. French, dim. of dial. *gigue* leg, from *giguer* to hop, to jump. Rel. to JIG.

gigue *n.* a piece of dance music, usu. in 6/8 time. WH: 17C. French, from JIG.

Gila monster *n.* a large poisonous lizard, *Heloderma suspectum*, found in Arizona and New Mexico. WH: 19C. *Gila*, a river in New Mexico and Arizona.

gilbert *n.* the cgs unit for measuring magnetomotive force. WH: 19C. William *Gilbert*, 1544–1603, English physician and natural philosopher.

Gilbertian *a.* absurdly topsy-turvy. WH: 19C. W.S. *Gilbert*, 1836–1911, librettist of Gilbert and Sullivan operas + -IAN.

gild *v.t.* to coat, overlay or wash thinly with gold. WH: pre-1200. Old English *gyldan*, from Germanic base of GOLD.

gilet *n.* a woman's light sleeveless top resembling a waistcoat. WH: 19C. French *waistcoat*, from Spanish *gileco*, from Spanish Arabic *jalaco*, from Turkish *yelek*.

gilgai *n.* in Australia, a saucer-shaped depression containing a pool of water, a water hole. WH: 19C. Australian Aboriginal (Wiradhuri and Kamilaroi) *gilgaay*.

gill[1] *n.* each of the organs of respiration, or branchiae, of fishes and some amphibia. WH: 12–14C. Old Norse, from a base rel. to Greek *khelunē* lip, jaw, *kheilos* lip.

gill[2] *n.* a deep and narrow ravine, often wooded. WH: 12–14C. Old Norse *gil* deep glen. A variant form *ghyll* was introduced in the 18C by Wordsworth and is mainly found in Lake District tourist literature.

gill[3] *n.* a liquid measure, usu. one quarter of a pint (about 140 cl). WH: 12–14C. Old French *gille*, from Medieval Latin *gillo*, from Late Latin *gello* water pot.

gill[4] *n.* a girl, a lass; a sweetheart. WH: 14–15C. Abbr. of female forename *Gillian*. Cp. JACK[1].

gillie *n.* a man or boy who attends a person fishing or hunting, esp. in the Scottish highlands. WH: 17C. Gaelic *gille*, rel. to Irish *giolla* lad, servant. This is the source of the first syllable of surnames such as *Gillespie*, *Gilmore*, respectively meaning servant of the bishop, servant of (the Virgin) Mary.

gillion *n.* in Britain, one thousand million, now superseded by the term *billion*. WH: mid-20C. Shortening of GIGA- + MILLION.

gillyflower *n.* the clove-scented pink, *Dianthus caryophyllus*. WH: 12–14C. Alt. (by assim. to FLOWER) of Old French *gilofre*, *girofle*, from Medieval Latin *caryophyllum* clove, from Greek *karuophullon*, form *karuon* nut + *phullon* leaf. Cp. CLOVE[1].

gilt[1] *a.* gilded. *Also n.* WH: 12–14C. P.p. of GILD.

gilt[2] *n.* a young sow. WH: 12–14C. Old Norse *gyltr*.

gimbals *n.pl.* forms of universal joint for securing free motion in suspension, or for suspending anything, such as a lamp, a compass, a chronometer etc., so that it retains a horizontal or other required position, or is in equilibrium. WH: 16C. Var. of *gimmal*, alt. of GEMEL + -S[1].

gimcrack *n.* a pretty but useless or flimsy article, a worthless knick-knack. *Also a.* WH: 12–14C. Orig. unknown. According to some, the word is from Old French *giber* to rattle, to shake + CRACK.

gimlet *n.* a small boring-tool with a worm or screw for penetrating wood, and a wooden crosspiece for a handle. *Also v.t.* WH: 12–14C. Old French *guimbelet*, dim. of *guimble*, from Germanic.

gimme *n.* in golf, a small putt that is unlikely to be missed and that an opponent would normally concede without the necessity of one playing it. WH: 19C. Representation of a pronun. of *give me*. Cp. LEMME.

gimmick *n.* a trick, device or oddity of behaviour used to attract extra interest, attention or publicity. WH: early 20C. Orig. unknown. ? Alt. of GIMCRACK. According to some, the word is an approximate anagram of MAGIC.

gimp[1] *n.* silk, wool, or cotton twist interlaced with wire or coarse cord. *Also v.t.* WH: 17C. Dutch, of unknown orig.

gimp[2] *n.* a lame or crippled person, esp. an old one. WH: early 20C. Orig. uncertain. ? Ult. from *gammy* (GAME[2]).

gin[1] *n.* an alcoholic drink, distilled usu. from grain, and flavoured with juniper berries. WH: 18C. Abbr. of *geneva*, GENEVER.

gin[2] *n.* a trap, a snare for small mammals and birds. *Also v.t.* WH: 12–14C. Shortening of Old French *engin* ENGINE.

gin[3] *n.* an Aboriginal woman of Australia. WH: 19C. Australian Aboriginal (Dharuk) *diyin*.

ginger *n.* the hot spicy root of the ginger plant used, either whole or powdered, in cookery, as a preserved sweet, in drinks or in medicine. *Also v.t.* WH: pre-1200. Old English *gingifer*, *gingiber*, conflating in the 12–14C with Old French *gingimbre* (Modern French *gingembre*), from Medieval Latin *gingiber*, *zingeber*, from Latin *zingiber*, from Greek *ziggiberis*, from Pali *singivera*, from Dravidian.

gingerbread *n.* a dark-coloured cake or biscuit made of flour, treacle or molasses, ground ginger and other spices. *Also a.* WH: 12–14C. Old French *gingembras*, from Medieval Latin *gingibratum*, from *gingiber* GINGER + *-atum* -ATE[1]. The word was subsequently assimilated to GINGER + BREAD.

gingerly *adv.* daintily, fastidiously, cautiously, so as to move without noise or risk of hurting oneself or anything trodden upon. *Also a.* WH: 16C. ? Old French *gensor*, *genzor* pretty, delicate, comp. of *gent* graceful, from Latin *genitus* well-born. See also -LY[2].

gingham *n.* a kind of linen or cotton fabric woven of dyed yarn, usu. in stripes or checks. WH: 17C. Dutch *gingang*, from Malay *genggang* striped. The word is not from *Guingamp*, a town in Brittany, France, despite the origin of many fabric names in town names. Cp. CALICO, CAMBRIC, DENIM, FUSTIAN, GAUZE, LAWN[2], LISLE, MUSLIN, TULLE, WORSTED etc.

gingili *n.* sesame, *Sesamum orientale*. WH: 18C. Hindi and Marathi *jiñjalī*, from Arabic dial. *jonjolīn*, from Arabic *juljulān*.

gingival *a.* of or relating to the gums. WH: 17C. Modern Latin *gingivalis*, from *gingiva* gum. See also -AL[1].

ginglymus *n.* a hinge joint admitting only of flexion and extension in one plane, such as the elbow. WH: 16C. Modern Latin, from Greek *gigglumos* hinge.

gink *n.* an awkward, clumsy or foolish person. WH: early 20C. Orig. unknown. Cp. GECK.

ginkgo *n.* a Japanese tree, *Ginkgo biloba*, with fan-shaped leaves, also called *maidenhair tree*. WH: 18C. Japanese *ginkyō*, from Chinese *yínxìng*, from *yín* silver + *xìng* apricot.

ginnel *n.* a narrow passage, alley. WH: 17C. ? French *chenel* CHANNEL[1].

ginormous *a.* huge, enormous. WH: mid-20C. Blend of GIGANTIC and ENORMOUS.

ginseng *n.* any of several herbs belonging to the genus *Panax*, esp. *P. schinseng* of China and *P. quinquefolius* of N America, the root of which has a sharp, aromatic taste, and is highly esteemed as a medicine or tonic by the Chinese and others. WH: 17C. Chinese *rénshēn*, from *rén* man + *shēn* kind of herb. The herb has a forked root suggesting a human body and resembling the Chinese ideogram for human being, man.

giocoso *adv., a.* (played) in a lively, joking manner. WH: 19C. Italian merry, from Latin *iocosus* JOCOSE.

Giottesque *a.* in the style of or after Giotto. *Also n.* WH: 19C. *Giotto* di Bondone, *c.*1267–1337, Italian painter + -ESQUE.

gip *v.t.* to take out the entrails of (herrings etc.). WH: 17C. Orig. unknown.

gippo *n.* a gypsy or similar person. WH: early 20C. Alt. of *gippy* (see also -O), from GYPSY.

gippy tummy *n.* an upset stomach, diarrhoea etc. WH: early 20C. Abbr. of EGYPTIAN (see -Y[3]) + TUMMY, prob. influ. by GYP[3].

giraffe *n.* an African ruminant, *Giraffa camelopardalis*, with an extremely long neck, and two bony excrescences on the head, light fawn in colour with darker spots. WH: 16C. Italian *giraffa*, from Arabic *zarāfa*, prob. of African orig.

girandole *n.* a revolving firework discharging rockets. WH: 17C. French, from Italian *girandola*, from *girare*, from Late Latin *gyrare* to gyrate.

girasol *n.* a variety of opal with reddish refractions, also called *fire-opal*. WH: 16C. French, or from Italian *girasole*, from *girare* (see GIRANDOLE) + *sole* sun. Cp. HELIOTROPE.

gird[1] *v.t.* to bind round (usu. the waist) with some flexible band, esp. in order to secure or confine the clothes. WH: pre-1200. Old English *gyrdan*, from Germanic. Cp. GIRDLE[1], GIRTH.

gird[2] *v.i.* to sneer, to mock (at). *Also n.* WH: 12–14C. Orig. unknown. Cp. GRIDE.

girder *n.* a principal beam, esp. a compound structure of iron, steel, wood or metal, spanning the distance from wall to wall, or pier to pier, used to support joints, walls, roof, roadway, or other similar load. WH: 17C. GIRD[1] + -ER[1].

girdle[1] *n.* a lightweight elasticated undergarment worn by women about the hips and thighs. *Also v.t.* WH: pre-1200. Old English *gyrdel*, from Germanic base of GIRD[1]. See also -LE[1].

girdle[2] *n.* a round flat plate of iron for baking cakes etc. WH: 14–15C. Alt. of GRIDDLE.

girl *n.* a female child, a young, unmarried woman. WH: 12–14C. ? Rel. to Low German *gör* boy, girl. Cp. GAL[1]. The word was originally used of a child or young person of either sex. The sense female child evolved in the 16C.

giro *n.* in the UK, a system operated by banks and post offices whereby, when the required instructions have been issued, payments can be made by transfers from one account to another. *Also v.t.* WH: 19C. German, from Italian circulation (of money), from Latin GYRUS.

Girondist *n.* in French history, a member of the moderate Republican party in the French Assembly (1791–3) (so named because its leaders represented the department of the Gironde). *Also a.* WH: 18C. French *Girondiste*, from *Gironde*, a department of SW France + -iste -IST.

girt *a.* girded, bound. WH: 17C. P.p. of GIRD[1].

girth *n.* the measurement round anything, the circumference e.g. of one's waist, of a tree. *Also v.t.* WH: 12–14C. Old Norse *gjörth* girdle, girth, hoop, from Germanic. Cp. GIRD[1], GIRDLE[1].

gisarme *n.* a long-shafted battleaxe with a point on the back of the axe head, carried by foot soldiers. WH: 12–14C. Old French, from Frankish *wīs-arm*, lit. guide-arm. Cp. WISE[1], ARM[1].

gist *n.* the essence or main point of a question. WH: 18C. Old French (Modern French *gît*), 3rd pers. sing. pres. ind. of *gésir* to lie (from Latin *iacere*), as in the French legal phr. *cest action gist* this action lies.

git *n.* an unpleasant or worthless person; a bastard. WH: mid-20C. Var. of GET[2].

gitano *n.* a male gypsy. WH: 19C. Spanish, alt. of *Egiptano* Egyptian, from Popular Latin *Aegyptanus*. Cp. GYPSY.

gîte *n.* in France, a privately-owned, self-contained, self-catering apartment or cottage available for holiday lets. WH: 18C. French. See GIST. The original sense was stopping place, lodging. The current sense evolved in the mid-20C.

gittern *n.* a medieval instrument like a guitar, a cittern. WH: 14–15C. Old French *guiterne*, rel. to CITTERN and GUITAR.

giusto *a., adv.* (of musical tempo) regular(ly), strict(ly), accurate(ly). WH: 19C. Italian regular, from Latin *iustus* JUST.

give *v.t.* to hand over or transfer the possession of or right to without price or compensation. *Also v.i., n.* WH: pre-1200. Old English *giefan*, from Germanic. Cp. German *geben*.

gizmo *n.* a gadget. WH: mid-20C. Orig. unknown. ? Rel. to GIMMICK.

gizzard *n.* a strong muscular division of the stomach, esp. the second stomach in birds. WH: 14–15C. Old French *giser* (Modern French *gésier*), from alt. of Latin *gigeria* cooked entrails of a fowl.

glabella *n.* the smooth flat area of bone between the eyebrows. WH: 19C. Modern Latin, use as n. of Latin a., dim. of *glaber*. See GLABROUS.

glabrous *a.* smooth. WH: 17C. Latin *glaber*, *glabris* hairless, smooth + -OUS.

glacé *a.* (of fruit etc.) preserved in sugar, candied (and usu. glossy). WH: 19C. French, p.p. of *glacer* to ice, to give a gloss to, from *glace* ice. The sense has apparently been influenced by GLASS, GLOSS[1].

glacial *a.* (of geological formations) due to or characterized by glaciers, ice sheets or floating ice. WH: 17C. French, or from Latin *glacialis* icy, from *glacies* ice. See also -AL[1].

glacier *n.* a streamlike mass of ice, formed by consolidated accumulations of snow at high altitudes, slowly descending to lower regions. WH: 18C. French (earlier *glacière*), from *glace* ice, from alt. of Latin *glacies* ice. See also -IER.

glacio- *comb. form* glacial. WH: GLACIER. See also -O-.

glaciology *n.* the study of glacial action and its geological effects. WH: 19C. GLACIO- + -LOGY.

glaciometer *n.* an apparatus or device for measuring the rate of movement of glaciers. WH: 19C. GLACIO- + -METER.

glacis *n.* a sloping bank in a fortification, e.g. in front of a rampart, where assailants would be exposed to fire. WH: 17C. French, from Old French *glacier* to slip, to slide, from *glace*. See GLACIER.

glad[1] *a.* pleased, gratified. *Also v.t., v.i.* WH: pre-1200. Old English *glæd*, from Germanic base rel. to Latin *glaber* smooth, GLABROUS. The original sense (to the 15C) was bright, shining, beautiful.

glad[2] *n.* a gladiolus. WH: early 20C. Abbr. of GLADIOLUS.

gladdon *n.* a purple iris, *Iris foetidissima*, also called *stinking iris* because of its unpleasant odour when bruised. WH: pre-1200. Old English *glædene*, from Popular Latin alt. of Latin GLADIOLUS.

glade *n.* an open space in a wood or forest. WH: 14–15C. Orig. uncertain. Cp. GLAD[1].

gladiate *a.* sword-shaped. WH: 18C. Latin *gladius* sword + -ATE[2].

gladiator *n.* in Roman times, a man employed to fight in the amphitheatre. WH: 14–15C. Latin, from *gladius* sword. See also -ATOR.

gladiolus *n.* any iridaceous plant of the genus *Gladiolus*, with a fleshy bulb, sword-shaped leaves and spikes of bright-coloured flowers. WH: pre-1200. Latin, dim. of *gladius* sword. The plant's leaves are sword-shaped.

Gladstone *n.* a light leather bag with flexible sides, opening along the middle and secured with a clasp and straps. WH: 19C. W.E. *Gladstone*, 1809–98, English statesman, who travelled with a bag of this type.

Glagolitic *a.* of or relating to the earliest Slavonic alphabet, principally used in Istria and Dalmatia, in the offices of the Roman Catholic Church. WH: 19C. Modern Latin *glagoliticus*, from Serbo-Croat *glagòljica* the Glagolitic alphabet, from Old Church Slavonic *glagolŭ* word.

glair *n.* white of egg, or a preparation made with this, used as size or varnish. *Also v.t.* WH: 12–14C. Old French *glaire*, from Medieval Latin *glarea*, from var. of Medieval Latin use as n. of Latin *clarus* clear.

glam *a.* glamorous. *Also v.t.* WH: mid-20C. Abbr. of *glamorous* (GLAMOUR).

glamour *n.* fascinating attractiveness due largely to grooming, expensive clothes or other artifice, or to unfamiliarity. *Also v.t.* WH: 18C. Alt. of GRAMMAR in the sense of its var. *gramarye* occult learning, magic. The original sense was magic, enchantment.

glance[1] *v.i.* to give a quick or cursory look (at). *Also v.t., n.* WH: 14–15C. Prob. alt. of obs. *glace* to glance off (of a weapon), from Old French *glacer* to glide, to slip, ult. from Latin *glacies* ice.

glance[2] *n.* any mineral with a metallic lustre, usu. a sulphide, selenide or telluride. WH: 14–15C. German *Glanz* lustre.

gland *n.* an organ secreting certain constituents of the blood, either for extraction and specific use or for elimination as waste products. WH: 17C. French *glande*, alt. of Old French *glandre*. See GLANDERS.

glanders *n.pl.* a very dangerous and contagious disease in horses, characterized by a running discharge from the nostrils, and enlargement and hardening of the glands of the lower jaw. WH: 15C. Old French *glandre*, from Latin *glandulae* (pl.) throat glands, swollen glands in the neck.

glandiferous *a.* bearing acorns or other nutlike fruits. WH: 17C. Latin *glandifer*, from *glans*, *glandis* acorn + -OUS. See -FEROUS.

glans *n.* the nutlike fruit of some forest trees, an acorn, a beech-nut, a chestnut etc. WH: 17C. Latin acorn.

glare[1] *v.i.* to shine with a dazzling or overpowering light. *Also v.t., n.* WH: 12–14C. Middle Low German and Middle Dutch *glaren* to gleam, to glare. The sense to look or stare fixedly evolved in the 17C.

glare[2] *a.* smooth and glassy (as ice). WH: 19C. Orig. uncertain. Prob. rel. to GLARE[1].

glasnost *n.* esp. of the USSR government of the later 1980s, a willingness to be more open and accountable. WH: late 20C. Russian *glasnost'* the state of being public, openness, from Old Church Slavonic *glasŭ* voice + Russian *-nost'* -NESS.

glass *n.* a hard, brittle, transparent substance, formed by fusing together mixtures of the silicates of potash, soda, lime, magnesia, alumina and lead in various proportions, according to the quality or kind required. *Also v.t., v.i.* WH: pre-1200. Old English *glæs*, from a Germanic word prob. rel. to Old English *glær* amber.

Glaswegian *n.* a native or inhabitant of Glasgow in Scotland. *Also a.* WH: 19C. *Glasgow*, a city in S Scotland, based on GALWEGIAN etc. See also -IAN.

Glauber's salt *n.* sodium sulphate, a strong laxative. WH: 18C. Johann Rudolf *Glauber*, 1604–88, German chemist.

glaucescent *a.* tending to become or becoming glaucous. WH: 19C. See GLAUCOUS, also *-escent* (-ESCENCE).

glaucoma *n.* a disease of the eye in which the pressure within the eyeball causes dimness and ultimately loss of vision. WH: 17C. Greek *glaukōma*, from *glaukos*. See GLAUCOUS, also -OMA.

glauconite *n.* an amorphous green hydrous silicate of iron, potassium etc. WH: 19C. German *Glaukonit*, from Greek *glaukon*, neut. of *glaukos*. See GLAUCOUS, also -ITE[1].

glaucous *a.* sea-green, pale greyish-blue. WH: 17C. Latin *glaucus*, from Greek *glaukos* bluish-green, bluish-grey. See also -OUS.

glaze *v.t.* to furnish, fit or cover with glass. Also *v.i., n.* WH: 14–15C. From GLASS, as GRAZE[1] from GRASS.

gleam *n.* a flash, a beam, a ray, esp. one of a faint or transient kind. Also *v.i.* WH: pre-1200. Old English *glǣm*, from Germanic. Cp. GLIMMER.

glean *v.t.* to collect bit by bit, to pick up here and there. Also *v.i., n.* WH: 12–14C. Old French *glener* (Modern French *glaner*), from Late Latin *glenare*, ult. from Celtic base represented by Old Irish *do-glenn* (he) gathers.

glebe *n.* the land furnishing part of the revenue of an ecclesiastical benefice. WH: 14–15C. Latin *gleba, glaeba* clod, land, soil.

glede *n.* the kite, *Milvus regalis*. WH: pre-1200. Old English *glida*, from Germanic base of GLIDE.

glee *n.* joy, mirth, gladness, delight. WH: pre-1200. Old English *glēo*, from Germanic. The original sense (to the 17C) was entertainment, play, fun. The sense of part-song evolved in the 17C.

gleet *n.* a viscous discharge from the urethra in gonorrhoea. Also *v.i.* WH: 12–14C. Old French *glette* slime, filth, secretion, of unknown orig.

Gleichschaltung *n.* the enforced standardization of political, cultural, economic institutions etc. in authoritarian states. WH: mid-20C. German coordination, from *gleich* like + *schalten* to govern.

glen *n.* a narrow valley, esp. in Scotland, a dale. WH: 14–15C. Gaelic and Irish *gleann* valley. Cp. Welsh *glyn*. The word is familiar in the names of Scotch whiskies, e.g. *Glenfiddich, Glenlivet, Glenmorangie*, where the second part of the name is usually that of a river.

glene *n.* the ball or pupil of the eye. WH: 18C. Modern Latin, from Greek *glēnē* ball or pupil of the eye.

glengarry *n.* a woollen cap, high in front with ribbons hanging down behind, worn by some Highland regiments. WH: 19C. *Glengarry*, a valley in Highland, Scotland. The cap was popularized by the Highland chief Macdonnell of Glengarry during the visit of George IV to Edinburgh in 1822.

gley *n.* a sticky, waterlogged clay, bluish-grey in colour. WH: early 20C. Ukrainian *gleĭ* sticky bluish clay, rel. to CLAY.

gliadin *n.* gluten. WH: 19C. French *gliadine*, from Greek *glia* glue. See also -IN[1].

glib *a.* voluble, fluent, not very weighty or sincere. Also *adv.* WH: 16C. From Germanic base prob. of imit. orig. Cp. Dutch *glibberig* slippery.

glide *v.i.* to move smoothly and gently. Also *v.t., n.* WH: pre-1200. Old English *glīdan*, from Germanic, ult. of unknown orig. Cp. German *gleiten*.

glim *n.* a faint light. WH: 14–15C. ? Abbr. of GLIMMER or GLIMPSE.

glimmer *v.i.* to emit a faint or feeble light. Also *n.* WH: 14–15C. Prob. of Scandinavian orig. Cp. GLEAM. The original sense (to the 16C) was to shine brightly, to glitter.

glimpse *n.* a momentary look, a rapid and imperfect view (of). Also *v.t., v.i.* WH: 12–14C. From base of GLIMMER, ult. from Germanic.

glint *v.i.* to gleam, to flash. Also *v.t., n.* WH: 14–15C. Alt. of dial. *glent* to move quickly, to glance, prob. of Scandinavian orig. Cp. Swedish dial. *glinta* to slip, to slide.

glissade *n.* a method of sliding down a steep snow slope, usu. with an ice axe or alpenstock held as rudder and support. Also *v.i.* WH: 19C. French, from *glisser* to slip, to slide. See also -ADE.

glissando *a., n.* (of) an esp. rapid sliding up and down the musical scale. WH: 19C. Italian, from French *glissant*, pres.p. of *glisser* to slip, to slide.

glissé *n.* in ballet, a sliding step esp. using the flat of the foot. WH: early 20C. French, p.p. of *glisser* to slip, to slide.

glisten *v.i.* to gleam, to sparkle, usu. by reflection. Also *n.* WH: pre-1200. Old English *glisnian*, from base of *glissian*, from Germanic. See also -EN[5]. Cp. GLISTER.

†glister *v.i.* to glitter, to sparkle. Also *n.* WH: 14–15C. Prob. from Middle Low German *glistern*, from Germanic. See also -ER[5]. Cp. GLISTEN.

glitch *n.* an unexpected problem, malfunction etc., technical hitch, hiccup. WH: mid-20C. Orig. unknown. Cp. HITCH and Yiddish *glitsh* slippery place.

glitter *v.i.* to gleam, to sparkle. Also *n.* WH: 14–15C. Old Norse *glitra*, from Germanic. Cp. German *gleissen*. See also -ER[5].

glitterati *n.pl.* fashionable people, such as media personalities, artists, jet-setters etc., as a social group. WH: mid-20C. Blend of GLITTER and *literati* (LITERATE).

glitz *n.* ostentation, conspicuous showiness. Also *v.i.* WH: late 20C. Back-formation from *glitzy*, prob. from GLITTER, based on RITZY.

gloaming *n.* evening twilight. WH: pre-1200. Old English *glōmung*, from *glōm* twilight, prob. from Germanic base of GLOW. Not rel. to GLOOM.

gloat *v.i.* to look or dwell (on or over) with exultant feelings of malignity, lust, greed etc. Also *n.* WH: 16C. ? Scandinavian. Cp. Old Norse *glotta* to grin, Swedish dial. *glotta* to peep.

glob *n.* a rounded lump of something soft, a dollop. WH: early 20C. ? Blend of BLOB and GOB[1].

globe *n.* a ball, a sphere, a round or spherical body. Also *v.t., v.i.* WH: 14–15C. Old French, or from Latin *globus* spherical body.

globin *n.* a colourless protein of the blood. WH: 19C. Abbr. of HAEMOGLOBIN.

globule *n.* a particle of matter in the form of a small globe. WH: 17C. French, or from Latin *globulus*, dim. of *globus* GLOBE. See also -ULE.

glochidium *n.* any of the barbed hairs among the spores of some ferns and on certain plants. WH: 19C. Modern Latin, from Greek dim. of *glōkhis* arrowhead.

glockenspiel *n.* a musical instrument consisting of hanging metal bars or tubes, to be struck with a hammer. WH: 19C. German bell-play, chimes.

glom *v.t.* to snatch, seize. WH: early 20C. Var. of Scottish *glaum* to snatch at, of unknown orig.

glomerate *a.* compactly clustered (as glands, vessels etc.). WH: 18C. Latin *glomeratus*, p.p. of *glomerare*, from *glomus, glomeris* ball of yarn. See also -ATE[2].

glomerule *n.* a flower-cluster forming a compact head. WH: 18C. French *glomérule*, from Modern Latin *glomerulus*, dim. of Latin *glomus, glomeris* ball of yarn. See also -ULE.

gloom *n.* obscurity, partial darkness. Also *v.i., v.t.* WH: 14–15C. Orig. unknown. Cp. GLUM. The original sense was to look sullen, to frown, to scowl.

gloop *n.* a thick, sticky liquid. WH: late 20C. Imit. Cp. GLOP.

glop *n.* a soft, gooey mush, esp. unpalatable food of this consistency. WH: early 20C. Imit.

Gloria *n.* a song or versicle of praise, forming part of the English Church service or the Mass, or the music to this, esp. *Gloria in excelsis Deo*. WH: 12–14C. Latin GLORY.

gloria *n.* a halo. WH: 18C. GLORIA.

glorify *v.t.* to make glorious, to pay honour and glory to in worship, to praise, to extol (God). WH: 12–14C. Old French *glorifier*, from Ecclesiastical Latin *glorificare*, from Late Latin *glorificus*, from Latin *gloria*. See GLORY, also -FY.

gloriole *n.* a glory, halo or nimbus. WH: 19C. French, from Latin *gloriola*, dim. of *gloria* GLORY. See also -OLE[2].

glory *n.* high honour, honourable distinction. Also *v.i., v.t.* WH: 12–14C. Old French *glorie*, from Latin *gloria* fame, praise, renown.

gloss[1] *n.* the brightness or lustre from a polished surface. Also *v.t.* WH: 16C. Orig. unknown. The word is one of many in gl- rel. to GLEAM, GLISTEN etc.

gloss[2] *n.* an explanatory word or note in the margin or between the lines of a book, as an explanation of a foreign or strange word. Also *v.t., v.i.* WH: 16C. Alt. of GLOZE based on Medieval Latin *glossa* explanation of difficult word, from Greek *glōssa* word needing explanation. Cp. GLOSSA.

glossa *n.* tongue. WH: 19C. Greek *glōssa* tongue.

glossary *n.* a list, vocabulary or dictionary of explanations of technical, obsolete, rare or dialectal words or forms. WH: 14–15C. Latin *glossarium*, from *glossa*. See GLOSS², also -ARY¹.

glosseme *n.* a unit or feature of a language which has a meaning but which cannot be analysed in terms of any smaller unit. WH: early 20C. Greek *glōssēma* word requiring explanation, from *glōssa*. See GLOSSO-, also -EME.

glosso- *comb. form* of or relating to the tongue. WH: Greek *glōsso-*, comb. form of *glōssa* tongue, language, word requiring an explanation (cp. GLOSS²). See also -O-.

glossography *n.* the writing of glosses or comments. WH: 17C. GLOSSO- + -GRAPHY.

glossolalia *n.* speech in an unknown language, occurring in religious ecstasy, trances etc. WH: 19C. GLOSSO- + Greek *lalia* speech, chatter. The reference is to the 'speaking with tongues' described in Acts x.46, I Cor. xiv.6,23.

glossology *n.* the explanation of technical terms, as of a science. WH: 18C. GLOSSO- + -LOGY.

glossopharyngeal *a.* of or relating to the tongue and the pharynx. *Also n.* WH: 19C. GLOSSO- + *pharyngeal* (PHARYNX).

glottis *n.* the mouth of the windpipe forming a narrow aperture covered by the epiglottis when one holds the breath or swallows, contributing, by its dilatation and contraction, to the modulation of the voice. WH: 16C. Modern Latin, from Greek *glōttis*, from *glōtta*, Attic form of *glōssa*. See GLOSSO-.

glove *n.* a covering for the hand, usu. with a separate division for each finger. *Also v.t.* WH: pre-1200. Old English *glōf*, from Germanic, ? from base of Y- + base of Old Norse *lófi*, Gothic *lofa* hand.

glow *v.i.* to radiate light and heat, esp. without flame. *Also v.t., n.* WH: pre-1200. Old English *glōwan*, from Germanic. Rel. to GLARE¹, GLOAMING etc.

glower *v.i.* to scowl, to stare fiercely or angrily. *Also n.* WH: 15C. ? Scottish var of obs. *glore* in same sense, or from obs. *glow* to stare (? rel. to GLOW) + -ER⁵. The original sense was to stare with wide open eyes (at). The current sense dates from the 18C.

gloxinia *n.* any tropical plant of the genus *Gloxinia*, with large bell-shaped flowers, from tropical America. WH: 19C. Modern Latin, from Benjamin Peter *Gloxin*, German physician and botanist who described it in 1785.

gloze *v.t.* to explain away, to palliate, to extenuate. *Also v.i., n.* WH: 12–14C. Old French *gloser*, from Medieval Latin *glosa*, from Latin *glossa*. See GLOSS².

glucagon *n.* a hormone produced in the pancreas which aids the breakdown in the liver of glycogen to glucose. WH: early 20C. Greek *glukus* sweet + *agōn*, pres.p. of *agein* to lead, to bring. Cp. GLYCO-.

glucinum *n.* beryllium (from the sweet taste of the salts). WH: 19C. Modern Latin, from French *glucine*, from Greek *glukus* sweet. See GLYCO-, also -IN¹, -IUM.

glucose *n.* a fermentable sugar, less sweet than cane sugar, obtained from dried grapes and other fruits, dextrin etc. and occurring in the urine of persons suffering from glucosuria. WH: 19C. French, from Greek *gleukos* sweet wine, rel. to *glukus* sweet. See also -OSE².

glucosuria *n.* one form of diabetes, the principal characteristic of which is the occurrence of sugar in the urine. WH: 19C. Greek *glukus* sweet (see GLYCO-) + -URIA.

glue *n.* an adhesive or sticky substance. *Also v.t., v.i.* WH: 12–14C. Old French *glu*, from Late Latin *glus*, *glutis*, from Latin *gluten* glue. Cp. GLUTEN.

glug *n.* the sound of liquid being poured, esp. out of or into a narrow opening. WH: 17C. Imit. Cp. GURGLE.

glühwein *n.* hot, spiced sweetened red wine, mulled wine, as prepared in Germany. WH: 19C. German, from *glühen* to mull, GLOW + *wein* WINE.

glum *a.* sullen, moody, dejected, dissatisfied. *Also v.i.* WH: 14–15C. Var. of GLOOM. The original sense was to look sullen, to frown. The current adjectival sense arose in the 16C.

glume *n.* a chafflike scale or bract forming part of the inflorescence in grasses. WH: 18C. Latin *gluma* hull, husk, rel. to *glubere* to shell, to peel.

gluon *n.* a hypothetical subatomic particle, thought of as passing between quarks, binding them together to form particles. WH: late 20C. GLUE + -ON.

glut *n.* an oversupply of a market. *Also v.t.* WH: 12–14C. Prob. from Old French *gloutir* to swallow, from Latin *gluttire*. See GLUTTON.

glutamate *n.* a salt or ester of glutamic acid, esp. a sodium salt used as a flavour enhancer in some foods. WH: 19C. GLUTAMIC ACID + -ATE¹.

glutamic acid *n.* an amino acid occurring in proteins which plays an important part in the nitrogen metabolism of plants and animals. WH: 19C. GLUTEN + AMINE + -IC (+ ACID).

glutamine *n.* an amino acid present in many proteins. WH: 19C. GLUTAMIC ACID + AMINE.

gluten *n.* a yellowish-grey, elastic albuminous substance, left in wheat flour which has been washed in water. WH: 16C. French, from Latin glue.

gluteus *n.* each of the three large muscles forming the buttock. WH: 17C. Modern Latin, from Greek *gloutos* buttock.

glutinous *a.* viscous, gluey, sticky. WH: 14–15C. Old French *glutineux* or Latin *glutinosus*, from *gluten*, *glutinis* glue. See also -OUS.

glutton *n.* a person who eats to excess. *Also v.i.* WH: 12–14C. Old French *gluton* (Modern French *glouton*), from Latin *glutto*, *gluttonis*, rel. to *gluttire* to swallow, *gluttus* greedy, *gula* throat. The word was applied to the wolverine in the 17C.

glycerol *n.* a sticky, sweet, colourless liquid obtained from animal and vegetable fats and oils, used in the manufacture of soaps, medicines, confectionery, antifreeze etc. WH: 19C. *glycerine* (see GLYCEROL) + -OL. Cp. GLYCO-, LIQUORICE.

glycine *n.* a crystalline, sweetish amino acid occurring in proteins, glycocoll. WH: 19C. Greek *glukus* sweet + -INE.

glyco- *comb. form* containing glycerol or compounds producing sugars. WH: Greek *glukus* sweet. See also -O-.

glycogen *n.* a white insoluble, starchlike compound occurring in animal tissues such as the liver and convertible into dextrose. WH: 19C. GLYCO- + -GEN.

glycol *n.* a diatomic alcohol of the fatty group typified by ethyl glycol, used as an antifreeze in car engines and for de-icing aircraft wings. WH: 19C. *glycerine* (GLYCEROL) + -OL.

glycolysis *n.* the breakdown of glucose by enzymes into acids, with the release of energy. WH: 19C. GLYCO- + -*lysis* (LYSIS).

glyconic *a.* applied to varieties of classic verse consisting of three trochees and a dactyl. *Also n.* WH: 17C. *Glukōn*, a Greek lyric poet of unknown date + -IC.

glycoprotein *n.* any of a group of complex proteins containing a carbohydrate mixed with a simple protein. WH: early 20C. GLYCO- + PROTEIN.

glyph *n.* in a computer or word processor, a character or symbol beyond the normal range of characters. WH: 18C. French *glyphe*, from Greek *gluphē* carving, rel. to *gluphein* to carve.

glyphography *n.* the process of making engravings for printing in which an electrotype with the design in relief is obtained from an intaglio etching. WH: 19C. Greek *gluphē* (see GLYPH) + -O- + -GRAPHY.

glyptal *n.* an alkyd resin used for surface coatings, esp. one formed from glycerol and phthalic acid or anhydride. WH: early 20C. ? From GLYCEROL + (letters in) PHTHALIC.

glyptic *a.* relating to carving or engraving, esp. on gems. *Also n.* WH: 19C. French *glyptique*, or from Greek *gluptikos*, from *gluptēs* carver, from *gluptein* to carve. See also -IC.

glyptodont *n.* any extinct edentate mammal of the genus *Glyptodon* from S America, similar to but larger than the armadillo. WH: 19C. Greek *gluptos* carved + -ODONT. The mammal was named in 1838 by the English palaeontologist Richard Owen from 'the fluted or sculptured form of the tooth'.

glyptography *n.* the art of engraving on gems. WH: 18C. Greek *gluptos* carved + -O- + -GRAPHY.

glyptotheca *n.* a room or building for the preservation of sculpture. WH: 19C. Greek *gluptos* carved + *thēkē* repository. Cp. BIBLIOTHECA, DISCOTHEQUE.

gnamma *n.* a waterhole in a rock. WH: 19C. Australian Aboriginal (Nyungar) *ngamar*.

gnaphalium *n.* any woolly plant of the genus *Gnaphalium*, typified by the cudweed, having a small sessile flower-head. WH: 19C. Modern Latin, from Greek *gnaphallion*, from *gnaphallon* flock of wool. See also -IUM.

gnarled *a.* rugged, lined, weather-beaten, twisted. WH: 17C. Var. of *knurled* (KNURL).

gnash *v.t.* to strike or grind (the teeth) together. *Also v.i.* WH: 14–15C. ? Imit., or alt. of obs. *gnast* in same sense, from base of Old Norse *gnastan* gnashing of teeth, *gneista* to emit sparks, *gnesta* clatter.

gnat *n.* any small two-winged fly of the genus *Culex*, the females of which have a blood-sucking proboscis, esp. *C. pipiens*, the common gnat. WH: pre-1200. Old English *gnætt*, from Germanic. Cp. German *Gnitze*. Ult. rel. to GNAW.

gnathic *a.* of or relating to the jaw. WH: 19C. Greek *gnathos* jaw + -IC.

gnatho- *comb. form* of or relating to the jaw or cheek. WH: Greek *gnathos* jaw. See also -O-.

†gnathonic *a.* flattering, sycophantic, parasitical. WH: 17C. Latin *Gnathonicus*, from *Gnatho*, *Gnathonis* a sycophantic character in Terence's *Eunuchus*, from Greek *gnathōn* parasite, from *gnathos* jaw. See also -IC.

gnathoplasty *n.* the formation of a cheek by plastic surgery. WH: mid-20C. GNATHO- + -PLASTY.

gnathopod *n.* the foot-jaw of crustaceans. WH: 19C. GNATHO- + -POD.

-gnathous *comb. form* having a jaw of a certain kind, as in *prognathous*. WH: Greek *gnathos* jaw + -OUS.

gnaw *v.t.* to bite or eat away by degrees. *Also v.i.* WH: pre-1200. Old English *gnagan*, from Germanic, of imit. orig. ? Rel. to NAG[1].

gneiss *n.* a laminated metamorphic rock consisting of feldspar, quartz and mica. WH: 18C. German, from Old High German *gneisto* spark, from Germanic.

gnocchi *n.* an Italian dish consisting of small potato or semolina dumplings, served with a sauce or used to garnish soup etc. WH: 19C. Italian, pl. of *gnocco*, from *nocchio* knot (in wood).

gnome[1] *n.* an imaginary being, a kind of misshapen sprite, dwarf, goblin, supposed to inhabit the interior of the earth, and to be the guardian of mines, quarries etc. WH: 17C. French, from Modern Latin *gnomus*, said to be coined by Paracelsus as a synonym of *Pygmaeus* (see PYGMY) from a putative Greek form *gēnomos* earth dweller (? based on Greek *thalassonomos* sea dweller). There may have been an intentional association with GNOME[2], as gnomes are said to be intelligent and 'knowing'.

gnome[2] *n.* a pithy saying expressing a general truth, a maxim, an aphorism. WH: 16C. Greek *gnōmē* thought, judgement, from *gnō-*, base of *gignōskein* KNOW.

gnomo- *comb. form* of or relating to a maxim or saying. WH: Greek *gnōmē* thought, pl. *gnōmai* sayings, maxims. See GNOME[2], also -O-.

gnomology *n.* a collection of maxims or sententious reflections or sayings. WH: 17C. GNOMO- + -LOGY.

gnomon *n.* a rod, pillar, pin or plate on a sundial, indicating the time of day by its shadow. WH: 16C. French, or from Latin, from Greek *gnōmōn* inspector, indicator, from *gnō-*. See GNOME[2].

gnosiology *n.* the philosophy dealing with cognition, the theory of knowledge, or the operation of the cognitive faculties. WH: 19C. Greek *gnōsis* (GNOSIS) + -O- + -LOGY.

gnosis *n.* knowledge, esp. of mysteries. WH: 16C. Greek *gnōsis* investigation, knowledge, from *gno-*. See GNOME[2].

-gnosis *comb. form* esp. in medicine, recognition, as in *diagnosis*. WH: Greek *gnōsis*. See GNOSIS.

gnostic *a.* relating to knowledge or cognition, intellectual. *Also n.* WH: 16C. Ecclesiastical Latin *gnosticus*, from Greek *gnōstikos*, from *gnōstos* known, from *gnō-*. See GNOME[2], also -IC.

gnu *n.* any large-horned antelope of the genus *Connochaetes*, native to southern Africa, also called *wildebeest*. WH: 18C. Khoisan.

go[1] *v.i.* to move, to move from one place, condition, or station to another. WH: pre-1200. Old English *gān*, from Germanic. Cp. German *gehen*. The original past tense (Old English *ēode*) was superseded by forms from WEND from the 15C. Hence *went*.

go[2] *n.* a turn, a bout (of doing something). WH: 17C. GO[1].

go[3] *n.* a Japanese board game for two people, its aim being to capture one's opponent's counters (or stones) in order to occupy a greater amount of the board. WH: 19C. Japanese.

goa *n.* a Tibetan gazelle, *Procapra picticaudata*, grey-brown in colour with backward-curving horns. WH: 19C. Tibetan *dgoba*.

goad *n.* a pointed instrument to urge oxen to move faster. *Also v.t.* WH: pre-1200. Old English *gād*, rel. to Lombard *gaida* arrowhead, from Germanic.

goal *n.* in football, hockey etc., the posts connected by a crossbar between which the ball must be driven to win a point. WH: 12–14C. Orig. unknown. According to some, the word is from Old English **gāl* obstacle, barrier. Cp. Old English *gǣlan* to hinder.

goanna *n.* a large monitor lizard. WH: 19C. Alt. of *guana*, shortening of IGUANA.

goat *n.* a hairy, horned and bearded domesticated ruminant belonging to the genus *Capra*, esp. *C. hircus*, of which there are many varieties. WH: pre-1200. Old English *gāt*, from Germanic base rel. to Latin *haedus* kid. Cp. German *Geiss*.

goatee *n.* a small beard like a goat's on the point of the chin. WH: 19C. GOAT + -EE.

gob[1] *n.* the mouth. *Also v.i.* WH: 16C. ? Gaelic and Irish beak, mouth. Prob. rel. to earlier *gob* mass, lump (14–15C), from Old French *gobe* mouthful, lump (Modern French *gobbe* ball of food, pill), from *gober* to swallow, to gulp, itself ? from Celtic. Cp. GOBBET.

gob[2] *n.* a US sailor. WH: early 20C. Orig. uncertain. ? From GOB[1] in sense lump.

gobang *n.* a game played on a chequer-board, with 50 coloured counters, the object being to get five into a row. WH: 19C. Japanese *goban* board for playing GO[3].

gobbet *n.* a mouthful, a lump, a piece, esp. of meat. WH: 12–14C. Old French *gobet*, dim. of *gobe* GOB[1].

gobble *v.t.* to swallow down hastily and greedily or noisily. *Also v.i., n.* WH: 17C. Prob. from GOB[1] + -LE[4], but partly imit.

gobbledegook *n.* pretentious, esp. unintelligible, language characterized by jargon and circumlocution. WH: mid-20C. Imit., based on GOBBLE. The word was coined in 1944 by the US lawyer Maury Maverick in imitation of the gobbling of a turkey.

Gobelin *a.* applied to a superior kind of French tapestry made at the Gobelins or imitated from this. WH: 18C. *Gobelins*, French state-owned carpet and tapestry factory in Paris, named after its founders (15C), the Gobelin family of weavers and dyers.

gobemouche *n.* a gullible, credulous person, someone who will believe anything. WH: 19C. French *gobe-mouches* flycatcher, from *gober* to swallow + *mouche* fly.

gobioid *a.* of or relating to the Gobiidae family of fishes that includes the goby. WH: 19C. Modern Latin *Gobioides*. See GOBY, also -OID.

goblet *n.* a drinking vessel, usu. of glass, with a stem, a foot and without a handle. WH: 14–15C. Old French *gobelet*, dim. of *gobel* cup. See also -ET[1].

goblin *n.* a mischievous spirit of ugly or grotesque shape; an elf, a gnome. WH: 12–14C. Prob. from French *gobelin*, dim. of name *Gobel* (now *Gobeau*), appar. rel. to KOBOLD, COBALT. Latin *gobelinus* is recorded for an evil spirit that haunted Évreux, France in the 12C.

gobo *n.* in television, film etc., a shield placed around a camera to exclude unwanted light. WH: mid-20C. Orig. unknown. ? From *go between*.

goby *n.* a small fish belonging to the genus *Gobius*, characterized by the union of the ventral fins into a disc or sucker. WH: 18C. Latin *gobius*, from Greek *kōbios* some kind of small fish. Cp. GUDGEON[1].

god *n.* a superhuman or supernatural being regarded as controlling natural forces and human destinies and worshipped or propitiated by humans. *Also v.t.* WH: pre-1200. Old English, from Germanic, prob. ult. from Indo-European, represented by Sanskrit *hū-* to invoke the gods.

godet *n.* in dressmaking, a piece of cloth inserted in a skirt, so that it hangs in folds suggestive of a flare. WH: 12–14C. Old French, ? from Middle Dutch *kudde* wooden cylinder, or from Provençal *got* glass, from Latin *guttus* narrow-necked flask. The original sense (to the 17C) was drinking cup. The current sense arose in the 19C.

godetia *n.* any plant of the genus *Godetia*, a flowering herb allied to the evening primroses. WH: 19C. Modern Latin, from Charles H. *Godet*, 1797–1879, Swiss botanist + -IA.

godown *n.* an E Asian or Indian warehouse. WH: 16C. Portuguese *gudão*, from Tamil *kiṭaṅku*, Malayalam *kiṭaṅṅu*, Kannada *gaḍaṅgu* store.

godwit *n.* a marsh or shore bird of the genus *Limosa*, resembling the curlew but having a slightly upturned bill. WH: 16C. Orig. unknown. Prob. orig. imit. of its call.

Godwottery n. affected, over-elaborate, archaic speech or writing. WH: mid-20C. *God wot*, words in a line from T.E. Brown's poem *My Garden* (1876): 'A garden is a lovesome thing, God wot!' For *wot* see WIT[2].

goer n. a person who attends regularly (usu. in comb. as in church-goer). WH: 12–14C. GO[1] + -ER[1].

Goethian a. of, relating to or characteristic of Goethe. Also n. WH: 19C. Johann Wolfgang von *Goethe*, 1749–1832, German writer. See also -IAN.

gofer[1] n. a person employed to run errands, give general assistance etc. WH: mid-20C. Representation of a pronun. of *go for*.

gofer[2] n. a waffle, a thin batter cake baked between two hinged plates that imprint a honeycomb pattern on both sides. WH: 18C. French *gaufre* honeycomb. See GOFFER.

goffer v.t. to plait, to crimp (edges of lace etc.) with a heated iron. Also n. WH: 16C. French *gaufrer* to stamp with a patterned tool, from *gaufre* honeycomb, from Germanic. Cp. WAFFLE[1], WAFER.

goggle v.i. to strain or roll the eyes. Also v.t., a., n. WH: 14–15C. Prob. freq., from imit. base *gog*, as for pair JOG/ JOGGLE. See also -LE[4].

goglet n. an earthenware vessel, a water-cooler used esp. in the Indian subcontinent. WH: 17C. Portuguese *gorgoleta*, dim. of *gorja* throat. Cp. GORGE.

go-go a. active, lively. WH: mid-20C. Redupl. of GO[1], ? influ. by À GOGO.

Goidel n. a member of the Celtic people of Ireland, Scotland and the Isle of Man. WH: 19C. Old Irish. See GAEL.

going n. the act of moving or walking. Also a. WH: 12–14C. GO[1] + -ING[1].

goitre n. a morbid enlargement of the thyroid gland, causing an unsightly deformity of the neck. WH: 17C. French, either from Old French *goitron*, from Provençal, from Latin *guttur* throat, or back-formation from French *goitreux* goitred, from Latin a. from *guttur*.

Golconda n. an inexhaustible mine of wealth. WH: 19C. *Golconda*, a ruined city near Hyderabad, India, famous for its diamonds.

gold n. a precious metallic element, at. no. 79, chem. symbol Au, of a bright yellow colour, the most ductile, malleable, and one of the heaviest of metals, much used for coins, jewellery etc. Also a. WH: pre-1200. Old English, from Germanic, ult. from Indo-European base of YELLOW.

golden a. of the colour or lustre of gold. WH: 12–14C. GOLD + -EN[3], superseding obs. *gilden*, from Old English *gylden*, from Germanic base of GOLD.

goldilocks n. a person with golden hair. WH: 16C. *goldy* (from GOLD + -Y[1]) + LOCK[2] + -S[1].

golem n. in Jewish legend, a figure constructed in the form of a human being and brought to life by supernatural means. WH: 19C. Yiddish *goylem*, from Hebrew *gōlem* shapeless mass.

golf n. a game played by two persons or couples with clubs and small hard balls on commons, moorlands, fields or links with short grass, consisting of hitting the balls into a series of small holes in the ground in as few strokes as possible. Also v.i. WH: 14–15C. ? Rel. to Dutch *kolf* club.

Golgi body n. a structure of vesicles, vacuoles and folded membranes within the cytoplasm of most cells, involved esp. in the secretion and transport of substances. WH: 19C. Camillo *Golgi*, 1844–1926, Italian histologist.

†Golgotha n. a burial place, a charnel house. WH: 17C. Late Latin, from Greek, from Aramaic *gōgolṭā*, ? influ. by Hebrew *gulgōleṯ*. See CALVARY.

†goliard n. any of various authors of satirical and ribald Latin verses (12th–13th cents.), some of which were signed by a mythical *Golias*. WH: 15C. Old French glutton, from *gole* (Modern French *gueule*), from Latin *gula* gluttony. See also -ARD.

Goliath n. a giant. WH: 16C. Ecclesiastical Latin, from Hebrew *golyaṯ*, name of the giant slain by David (I Sam. xvii).

golliwog n. a black-faced doll with fuzzy hair and bright clothes. WH: 19C. *Golliwogg*, the name of a doll character in books (1890s) by US writers Florence and Bertha Upton, ? from GOLLY[1] + POLLIWOG.

gollop v.t. to swallow greedily and hurriedly. Also n. WH: 19C. ? Var. of GULP, influ. by GOBBLE.

golly[1] int. used to express surprise. WH: 18C. Alt. of GOD.

golly[2] n. a golliwog. WH: mid-20C. Abbr. of GOLLIWOG.

gombeen n. usury. WH: 19C. Irish *gaimbín*.

gombroon n. Persian semi-transparent white pottery imitated in Chelsea ware. WH: 17C. *Gambroon* (now Bandar-e 'Abbās), a seaport in S Iran.

gomeril n. a simpleton. WH: 19C. Orig. unknown.

Gomorrah n. a dissolute town. WH: 16C. *Gomorrah*, one of five biblical 'cities of the plain', destroyed together with SODOM by 'brimstone' and fire because of their wickedness (Gen. xix.24).

gomphosis n. a kind of articulation by which the teeth are firmly implanted in their sockets. WH: 16C. Greek, from *gomphoun* to bolt together, from *gomphos* bolt. See also -OSIS.

gomuti n. a black hairlike fibre, not decaying in water, obtained from the sago palm, and used for cordage, thatching etc. WH: 19C. Malay *gemuti*.

-gon comb. form used to form nouns denoting a figure with a number of angles, as in *hexagon, octagon, pentagon*. WH: Greek *-gōnos* angled, from *gōnia* angle.

gonads n.pl. undifferentiated sex glands, the embryonic sexual apparatus, with rudiments of both sexes which later develop into either ovaries or testes. WH: 19C. Modern Latin, pl. *gonades*, from Greek *gonē, gonos* generation, seed. See also -AD[1].

gondola n. a long, narrow Venetian boat with peaked ends, propelled by one oar. WH: 16C. Venetian Italian, from Old Italian *gondula*, of uncertain orig. ? From Greek *kondu* vase, drinking cup.

gone a. past. WH: 16C. P.p. of GO[1].

gonfalon n. an ensign or banner, usu. displayed from a crossyard on a pole, with streamers, such as the standard of certain Italian republics. WH: 16C. Italian *gonfalone*, from French *gonfanon*, from Frankish *gundfano* war flag, from Germanic. Cp. GUN, VANE.

gong n. a tambourine-shaped metal instrument which when struck with a padded stick emits a loud sonorous note, used as a signal for meals etc. Also v.t. WH: 17C. Malay, of imit. orig.

gongoozler n. a person who stares idly or curiously at something. WH: early 20C. Orig. unknown. ? From Lincolnshire dial. *gawn* + *gooze* to stare, to gape.

Gongorism n. a florid and affected style of writing somewhat analogous to euphemism, introduced by Góngora. WH: 19C. Luis de *Góngora* y Argote, 1561–1627, Spanish poet + -ISM.

goniatite n. any extinct cephalopod mollusc of the Palaeozoic genus *Goniatites*, similar to an ammonite. WH: 19C. Modern Latin *Goniatites*, from Greek *gōnia* angle. See also -ITE[1]. The molluscs are so named from their angular suture lines.

gonidium n. a reproductive cell produced asexually in algae. WH: 19C. Modern Latin, from Greek *gonos* offspring + Latin dim. ending *-idium*.

goniometer n. an instrument for measuring angles, esp. of crystals. WH: 18C. French *goniomètre*, from Greek *gōnia* angle. See also -METER.

gonk n. a soft round toy with arms and legs, popular in the 1960s. WH: mid-20C. Arbitrary.

gonna contr. going to. WH: early 20C. Representation of a pronun. of *going to*.

gono- comb. form sexual or reproductive, as in *gonorrhoea*. WH: Greek *gonos, gonē* generation, offspring. See also -O-.

gonococcus n. the organism that causes gonorrhoea. WH: 19C. GONORRHOEA + COCCUS.

gonocyte n. a germ cell. WH: early 20C. GONO- + -CYTE.

gonophore n. a stalk holding the pistil and stamens above the floral envelope in certain plants. WH: 19C. GONO- + -PHORE.

gonorrhoea n. a venereal disease affecting the urethra and other mucous surfaces, accompanied by inflammation and purulent discharge. WH: 16C. Late Latin, from Greek *gonorrhoia*, from *gonos* semen. See -RRHOEA.

gonzo a. bizarre, crazy, esp. of exaggerated journalistic writing style. WH: late 20C. ? Italian foolish, or from Spanish *ganso* goose, fool.

goo n. sticky matter. WH: early 20C. Orig. uncertain. ? Abbr. of BURGOO.

good a. having such qualities as are useful, proper, and satisfactory. Also n. WH: pre-1200. Old English *gōd*, from Germanic, from a base meaning to bring together, to unite represented also in GATHER. Not rel. to GOD.

goodbye *int.* farewell. *Also n.* WH: 16C. Contr. of *God be with you*, with substitution of GOOD for GOD, based on *good day, good night* (GOOD). The etymological sense of the word was used by the US Congregational minister J.E. Rankin as the basis of his hymn 'God be with you till we meet again' (1880), traditionally sung at partings and farewells.

goof *n.* a foolish mistake, a blunder. *Also v.i., v.t.* WH: early 20C. Orig. unknown. ? Rel. to GAFFE.

goog *n.* an egg. WH: early 20C. Orig. uncertain. According to some, the word is from Scottish dialect *goggie*, a child's word for an egg.

googly *n.* in cricket, a ball bowled in a disguised manner to break a different way from that expected, an off-break ball bowled with a leg-break action. WH: early 20C. Orig. unknown.

googol *n.* ten raised to the power of one hundred, 10^{100}. WH: mid-20C. Arbitrary. The word was coined in 1940 by the 9-year-old nephew of US mathematician Edward Kasner, perhaps suggested by the cartoon character Barney *Google*.

gook *n.* a foreigner, esp. a person from E Asia. WH: early 20C. Orig. unknown. ? From some Oriental word.

goolie *n.* a testicle. WH: early 20C. Hindi *golī* ball, bullet.

goombah *n.* a member of a criminal gang. WH: mid-20C. Prob. from Italian dial. alt. of *compare* godfather, friend, accomplice.

goon *n.* a stupid person. WH: 19C. ? From *goony*, alt. of dial. *gony* simpleton, of unknown orig., but also influ. by name of Alice the *Goon*, a subhuman cartoon character invented by US illustrator E.C. Segar in the comic strip *Thimble Theatre* (1910). As applied to German guards by prisoners-of-war in World War II, the word was perhaps influenced by HUN.

goonda *n.* a desperado, a hooligan. WH: early 20C. Hindi *guṇḍā* rascal.

goop[1] *n.* a rude or foolish person. WH: early 20C. Appar. arbitrary. Cp. GOOF.

goop[2] *n.* a thick, sticky liquid, gloop. WH: late 20C. Var. of GLOOP.

goosander *n.* a large diving duck, *Mergus merganser*. WH: 17C. Prob. blend of GOOSE and GANDER.

goose *n.* a web-footed bird intermediate in size between the duck and the swan, belonging to the family Anatidae. *Also v.t.* WH: pre-1200. Old English *gōs*, from Germanic, from Indo-European base also of Latin *anser* (cp. ANSERINE), Greek *khēn*, Sanskrit *haṃsá*.

gooseberry *n.* the thorny shrub *Ribes grossularia*. WH: 16C. ? From GOOSE + BERRY. The first part of the word may have been assimilated to GOOSE from some other form. Cp. French *groseille* currant, German *Krauselbeere* gooseberry, from *kräuseln* to make frizzy, to crimp.

goosegog *n.* a gooseberry. WH: 19C. Alt. of GOOSEBERRY, with -*gog* from GOB[1].

gopak *n.* a folk dance from Ukraine characterized by high leaps, performed by men. WH: early 20C. Russian, from Ukrainian *hopak*, from *hop!*, interjection used in lively dances. Cp. *gee-up* (GEE[1]), *hoopla* (HOOP).

gopher[1] *n.* any of various American burrowing animals of the family Geomyidae. WH: 18C. ? Canadian French *gaufre* honeycomb, ref. to animal's burrowing habits. Cp. GOFER[2].

gopher[2] *n.* the wood of which Noah's ark was made. WH: 17C. Hebrew *gōper*.

goral *n.* a Himalayan goatlike antelope, *Nemorhaedus goral*. WH: 19C. Local name.

gorblimey *int.* used to express surprise, indignation etc. *Also n.* WH: 19C. Alt. of *God blind me*. Cp. BLIMEY.

gorcock *n.* the moorcock or male of the red grouse. WH: 17C. Orig. unknown.

Gordian *a.* intricate, complicated. WH: 16C. Latin *Gordius* or *Gordium*, from Gordius, King of Gordium, Phrygia, who tied an intricate knot cut through by Alexander the Great.

Gordon setter *n.* a black and tan breed of setter, used as gun dogs. WH: 19C. Alexander *Gordon*, 4th Duke of Gordon, 1743–1827, promoter of the breed.

gore[1] *n.* blood from a wound, esp. thick, clotted blood. WH: pre-1200. Old English *gor*, from Germanic, rel. to Old Irish *gor*, Welsh *gôr* matter, pus.

gore[2] *v.t.* to pierce, to stab. WH: 14–15C. Orig. unknown. According to some, the word is from Old English *gār* spear. Cp. GORE[3].

gore[3] *n.* a triangular piece in a dress, sail, balloon, umbrella etc. *Also v.t.* WH: pre-1200. Old English *gāra*, from Germanic, prob. rel. to Old English *gār* spear.

gorge *n.* a narrow pass between cliffs or hills. *Also v.t., v.i.* WH: 14–15C. Old French throat, from alt. of Latin *gurges* whirlpool, of imit. orig. Cp. GURGLE. The verb *gorge* dates from the 12–14C.

gorgeous *a.* splendid, richly decorated, magnificent. WH: 15C. Old French *gorgias* fine, stylish, elegant, of unknown orig., with -*ias* assim. to -EOUS.

gorget *n.* a piece of armour for defending the throat or neck. WH: 14–15C. Old French *gorgete*, from *gorge* throat. See also -ET[1].

Gorgio *n.* (among gypsies) someone who is not a gypsy. WH: 19C. Romany *gorjo*.

gorgon *n.* in Greek mythology, any one of three snake-haired female monsters so terrible in appearance that the sight of them was fabled to turn beholders to stone. WH: 14–15C. Latin *Gorgo, Gorgonis*, from Greek *Gorgō*, from *gorgos* terrible.

gorgonian *n.* any brightly-coloured horny coral of the order Gorgonacea, having flexible polyps growing in the form of shrubs, feathers etc., such as the sea fan. *Also a.* WH: 19C. Modern Latin *Gorgonia*, fem. of *gorgonius*, from Latin *Gorgo* GORGON. See also -IAN. The coral is so named from its petrifaction: those who caught the Gorgon's gaze were turned to stone.

Gorgonzola *n.* a soft blue-veined Italian cheese. WH: 19C. *Gorgonzola*, a village near Milan, Italy, where orig. made.

gorilla *n.* a large vegetarian African anthropoid ape, *Gorilla gorilla*, growing to about 5½ ft. (1.6 m) in height. WH: 19C. Modern Latin, from an alleged African word meaning wild man or hairy man.

gormandize *v.t.* to eat greedily, to gorge. *Also v.i., n.* WH: 14–15C. French *gourmandise* gluttony, from GOURMAND.

gormless *a.* witless, clumsy, stupid. WH: 18C. Obs. *gaum* heed, wit, from Old Norse *gaumr* care, heed + -LESS.

gorse *n.* any yellow-flowered, prickly shrub of the genus *Ulex*, furze, whin. WH: pre-1200. Old English *gors*, from Indo-European base meaning rough, prickly, seen also in Latin *hordeum* barley. Cp. German *Gerste* barley.

Gorsedd *n.* a meeting of bards and Druids in Wales, esp. associated with the eisteddfod. WH: 18C. Welsh mound, throne, assembly.

gosh *int.* used to express surprise. WH: 18C. Alt. of GOD.

goshawk *n.* a large, short-winged hawk, *Accipiter gentilis*. WH: pre-1200. Old English *gōshafoc*, from *gōs* GOOSE + *hafoc* HAWK[1]. The bird is said to be so called because it was originally flown by falconers against geese.

Goshen *n.* a land of plenty. WH: 17C. Hebrew, name of the fertile land allotted to the Israelites in Egypt in which 'all the children of Israel had light' (Exod. x.23) during the plague of darkness.

gosling *n.* a young goose. WH: 12–14C. Old Norse *gæslingr*, from *gás* GOOSE. See also -LING[1].

gospel *n.* the teaching or revelation of Jesus Christ. *Also v.t.* WH: pre-1200. Old English *gōdspel*, lit. good news, from *gōd* GOOD + *spel* news, tidings (see SPELL[2]), translating Ecclesiastical Latin *bona annuntiatio* or *bonus nuntius*, used as lit. translations of Ecclesiastical Latin *evangelium*, Greek *euaggelion* EVANGEL. The word was later associated with GOD.

gossamer *n.* the slender cobweb-like threads floating in the air in calm weather, produced by small spiders. WH: 12–14C. Appar. from GOOSE + SUMMER[1], ref. to time of year (around 'St Martin's summer') when geese were eaten, which is when gossamer is most likely to be seen.

gossip *n.* idle talk, tittle-tattle. *Also v.t., v.i.* WH: pre-1200. Old English *godsibb* godparent (see GOD, SIB). The current sense evolved in the 19C and originated in the familiarity that arose between a baptized person and his or her sponsors.

gossoon *n.* a boy, a lad. WH: 17C. Old French *garçon* boy. See GARÇON.

gossypium *n.* a tropical genus of herbs and shrubs belonging to the Malvaceae or mallow family, including three species from which commercial cotton is obtained. WH: 19C. Modern Latin genus name, from Latin *gossypinum* cotton plant, of unknown orig.

got *a.* dressed up, disguised, prepared for effect or to take in. WH: 16C. P.p. of GET[1].

Goth *n.* a member of an ancient Germanic tribe which invaded southern Europe in the 3rd–5th cents., establishing kingdoms in Italy, southern France and Spain. WH: pre-1200. Old English *Gota*, from base of Gothic *Gutthiuda* the Gothic people.

†**Gothamist** *n.* a foolish person, someone easily taken in. WH: 16C. *Gotham*, a village in Nottinghamshire, proverbial for its foolish inhabitants + -IST.

Gothic *a.* in the style of architecture characterized by pointed arches, clustered columns etc. *Also n.* WH: 16C. French *gothique* or Late Latin *Gothicus*, from *Gothi*. See GOTH, also -IC.

gotta *contr.* have got to. WH: early 20C. Representation of a pronun. of *got to*.

Götterdämmerung *n.* in German mythology, the final destruction of the world. WH: early 20C. German, lit. twilight of the gods, from *Götter*, pl. of *Gott* god + *Dämmerung* twilight, from *dämmern* to fall (of dusk). The term was popularized as the title of Wagner's opera (1876).

gouache *n.* a method of painting with opaque colours mixed with water, honey and gum. WH: 19C. French, from Italian *guazzo*, ult. from Latin *aqua* water.

Gouda *n.* a round mild cheese originally made at Gouda, in the Netherlands. WH: 19C. *Gouda*, a town in the Netherlands, where orig. made.

gouge *n.* a chisel with a concave blade, used to cut holes or grooves. *Also v.t.* WH: 14–15C. Old French, from Late Latin *gubia*, ? from Celtic. Cp. Old Irish *gulba* beak, Welsh *gylf* sharp-pointed instrument.

goujon *n.* a small strip of chicken or fish, usu. deep-fried in a coating of breadcrumbs etc. WH: 19C. French. See GUDGEON[1].

goulash *n.* a stew of meat and vegetables highly seasoned with paprika. WH: 19C. Hungarian *gulyáshús*, from *gulyás* herdsman + *hús* meat.

gourami *n.* a nest-building Oriental fish, *Osphronemus guramy*, much valued for food. WH: 19C. Malay *gurami*.

gourd *n.* a large fleshy fruit of climbing or trailing plants belonging to the Cucurbitaceae, the hard outer coat of which can serve as a container for water, wine etc. WH: 12–14C. Old French *gourde*, ult. from Latin *cucurbita*. Cp. COURGETTE.

gourmand *n.* a glutton. *Also a.* WH: 14–15C. Old French, of unknown orig. Cp. GOURMET.

gourmet *n.* a connoisseur of good food, an epicure. *Also a.* WH: 19C. French, orig. wine-taster, from Old French *gromme* wine merchant, of uncertain orig., ? from Old English **grom* manservant. Cp. GROOM.

gout *n.* a disease affecting the joints, esp. the big toe and foot, with inflammation, pain and irritability being the leading symptoms. WH: 12–14C. Old French *gote* (Modern French *goutte*), or from Medieval Latin *gutta*, lit. drop. The name alludes to the medieval theory that the disease was caused by the dropping of diseased matter from the blood.

goût *n.* taste, relish. WH: 16C. French, earlier *goust*, from Latin *gustus* taste. Cp. GUSTO.

govern *v.t.* to direct and control. *Also v.i.* WH: 12–14C. Old French *governer* (Modern French *gouverner*), from Latin *gubernare* to steer, to direct, to rule, from Greek *kubernan* to steer.

governess *n.* a woman employed to teach children in a private household. WH: 14–15C. Old French *governeresse*, fem. of *governëor*. See GOVERNOR, also -ESS[1].

government *n.* control, direction, regulation, exercise of authority, esp. authoritative administration of public affairs. WH: 14–15C. Old French *governement* (Modern French *gouvernement*). See GOVERN, also -MENT.

governor *n.* a person who governs, esp. someone invested with authority to execute the laws and administer the affairs of a state, province etc. WH: 12–14C. Old French *governëor* (Modern French *gouverneur*), from Latin *gubernator*, from *gubernare*. See GOVERN, also -OR.

gowan *n.* the daisy or similar white or yellow field-flower. WH: 16C. Prob. alt. of obs. *gollan*, ? rel. to *-gold* of MARIGOLD.

gowk *n.* a fool, a simple or awkward person. WH: 12–14C. Old Norse *gaukr*, rel. to Old English *gēac* cuckoo, from Germanic, of imit. orig. Cp. CUCKOO.

gown *n.* a woman's loose, long, outer garment, a dress, esp. a handsome or stylish one. WH: 12–14C. Old French *goune*, from Late Latin *gunna* fur garment.

gowpen *n.* a handful, a double handful, as much as can be held in the hollow of the two hands. WH: 12–14C. Old Norse *gaupn*, from Germanic.

goy *n.* among Jews, a name for a non-Jewish person. WH: 19C. Hebrew *gōy* people, nation.

GR *abbr.* King George. WH: Abbr. of Latin *Georgius Rex* George King.

Graafian follicle *n.* a small sac in which the ova are matured in the ovary of mammals. WH: 19C. Regnier de *Graaf*, 1641–73, Dutch anatomist + -IAN.

grab *v.t.* to seize, snatch or grasp suddenly. *Also v.i., n.* WH: 16C. Middle Low German and Middle Dutch *grabben*, ? from alt. of base of GRIP[1], GRIPE, GROPE.

grabble *v.i.* to grope, to feel about (for). WH: 16C. Prob. from Dutch or Low German *grabbeln* to scramble (for), freq. of *grabben*. See GRAB, also -LE[1].

graben *n.* an elongated depression where the earth's surface has subsided between two fault lines. WH: 19C. German, orig. ditch.

grace *n.* the quality which makes form, movement, expression or manner elegant, harmonious, refined and charming. *Also v.t.* WH: 12–14C. Old French (Modern French *grâce*), from Latin *gratia*, from *gratus* pleasing. Cp. GRATEFUL.

gracile *a.* slender, lean, thin, esp. in an anthropological sense. WH: 17C. Latin *gracilis*.

gracious *a.* exhibiting grace, favour or kindness. WH: 12–14C. Old French (Modern French *gracieux*), from Latin *gratiosus*, from *gratia*. See GRACE, also -OUS.

grackle *n.* any American oriole of the genus *Quiscalus*, also called *blackbird* in N America. WH: 18C. Modern Latin *Gracula*, from Latin *graculus*, jackdaw.

grad *n.* a graduate. WH: 19C. Abbr. of GRADUATE[2]. Cp. *undergrad*.

gradation *n.* an orderly arrangement, succession or progression step by step. WH: 16C. Latin *gradatio, gradationis* from *gradus* step. See GRADE, also -ATION.

grade *n.* a degree or step in rank, quality, value, order etc. *Also v.t.* WH: 16C. French, or from Latin *gradus* step.

-grade *comb. form* of a kind or manner of movement or progression, as in *retrograde*. WH: Latin *gradus* step.

gradely *a.* decent, respectable, worthy. *Also adv.* WH: 12–14C. Old Norse *greithligr*, from *greithr*, obs. English *graith* ready, direct. See also -LY[1].

gradient *n.* the rate of ascent or descent in a railway or road, degree of slope, inclination. WH: 19C. Prob. from GRADE, based on SALIENT.

gradine *n.* each in a series of rising steps or a tier of seats. WH: 19C. Italian *gradino*, dim. of *grado* step.

gradual *a.* regular and slow, as opposed to abrupt, steep, rapid. *Also n.* WH: 14–15C. Medieval Latin *gradualis*, from *gradus* step. See also -AL[1].

graduate[1] *v.i.* to be awarded a first degree from a university. *Also v.t.* WH: 14–15C. Medieval Latin *graduatus*, p.p. of *graduare* to take a degree, from Latin *gradus* degree, step. See also -ATE[3].

graduate[2] *n.* a person who has received a degree from a university. WH: 14–15C. Medieval Latin *graduatus*, p.p. (used as n.) of *graduari* GRADUATE[1]. See also -ATE[1].

gradus *n.* a dictionary of Greek or Latin prosody formerly used in public schools. WH: 18C. Latin *gradus* step, in *Gradus ad Parnassum* Step (Steps) to Parnassus, title of a manual of Latin prosody (1687).

Graecism *n.* a Greek idiom, style or mode of expression. WH: 15C. French *grécisme* or Medieval Latin *Graecismus*, from *Graecus* Greek. See also -ISM.

Graeco- *comb. form* Greek. WH: Latin *Graecus* Greek. See also -O-.

graffiti *n.pl.* drawings or words, sometimes obscene, sometimes political, painted or written on walls etc. in public view. WH: 19C. Italian, pl. of *graffito*, from *graffio* scratching.

graft[1] *n.* a small shoot of a tree or plant inserted into another tree of a different stock which supplies the sap to nourish it. *Also v.t., v.i.* WH: 15C. Alt. of obs. *graff*, from Old French *grafe* (Modern French *greffe*), from Latin *graphium*, from Greek *graphion* stylus, from *graphein* to write. The altered spelling may have occurred from the confusion of written *-ff* and *-ft* at the end of a word.

graft² *n.* acquisition of money etc. by taking advantage of an official position. WH: 19C. ? From *graft* hard work or rel. to GRAFT¹ in sense of excrescence.

Grail *n.* a dish or cup said to have been used by Christ at the Last Supper, and employed by Joseph of Arimathea to collect Christ's blood while on the cross. WH: 12–14C. Old French *graal*, from Medieval Latin *gradalis* dish, of unknown origin. ? Ult. from Latin *crater* bowl.

grain *n.* a single seed of a plant, particularly of food plants. *Also v.t., v.i.* WH: 12–14C. Old French, from Latin *granum* grain, seed.

graith *n.* equipment, attire. *Also a., v.t.* WH: 12–14C. Old Norse *greithi*, rel. to Old English *geræde* trappings, equipage, from German bases of Y-, READY. Cp. GEAR. Rel. to GRADELY.

grallatorial *a.* of or relating to long-legged wading birds such as storks, flamingoes etc. WH: 19C. Modern Latin *grallatorius*, from Latin *grallator* walker on stilts, from *grallae* stilts. See also -ATOR, -IAL.

gralloch *n.* the entrails of a deer. *Also v.t.* WH: 19C. Gaelic *grealach* entrails.

gram¹ *n.* the standard unit of mass in the metric system, defined as the mass of one cubic centimetre of distilled water at its maximum density weight equalling a thousandth of a kilogram (about 0.04 oz.). WH: 18C. French *gramme*, from Late Latin *gramma* small weight, from Greek.

gram² *n.* the chick-pea, *Cicer arietinum*, or other kinds of pulse, used esp. in Asia as food. WH: 18C. Portuguese *grão*, from Latin *granum* grain.

-gram *comb. form* forming compounds with prepositional prefixes, numerals etc., to denote something written, as in *epigram*, *monogram*, *anagram*. WH: Greek *gramma*, *grammatos* something written, letter of the alphabet, from *graphein* to write.

grama *n.* any of various species of low pasture grass in the western and south-western US. WH: 19C. Spanish grass.

†gramercy *int.* used to express thanks or surprise. *Also n.* WH: 12–14C. Old French *grant merci* (God give you) great reward. See GRAND, MERCY.

graminaceous *a.* of or relating to grass or the tribe of grasses. WH: 17C. Latin *gramen*, *graminis* grass + -ACEOUS.

grammalogue *n.* in shorthand writing, a word represented by a single sign. WH: 19C. Greek *gramma* written character + *logos* word, based on CATALOGUE etc. See -LOGUE.

grammar *n.* a system of principles and rules for speaking and writing a language. WH: 14–15C. Old French *gramaire* (Modern French *grammaire*), ult. from Latin *grammatica*, from Greek *grammatikē* (*tekhnē*) (art) of letters, from *gramma*, *grammatos* letter, written character.

gramophone *n.* a record-player. WH: 19C. Inversion of the two elements of PHONOGRAM.

grampus *n.* the dolphin *Grampus griseus*, characterized by a blunt snout and pointed black flippers. WH: 16C. Alt. (by assim. to GRAND) of obs. *grapeys*, from Old French *grapois*, from Medieval Latin *crapiscis*, from Latin *crassus piscis* fat fish.

Gram stain *n.* a technique used to classify bacteria, based on their ability to retain or lose a violet stain. WH: 19C. Hans C.J. *Gram*, 1853–1938, Danish physician.

gran *n.* grandmother. WH: 19C. Abbr. of *grandmother*. See GRAND.

granary *n.* a storehouse for grain. WH: 16C. Latin *granarium*, from *granum* grain. See also -ARY¹.

grand *a.* great or imposing in size, character or appearance. *Also n.* WH: 14–15C. Old French, from Latin *grandis* fully grown, big, great. Latin *grandis* superseded earlier *magnus*.

grand cru *n., a.* (a wine) from a top-ranking vineyard. WH: 19C. French great growth. See GRAND, CRU.

grande dame *n.* an aristocratic lady. WH: 18C. French great lady, from fem. of *grand* + *dame* DAME.

grandee *n.* a Spanish or Portuguese nobleman of the highest rank. WH: 16C. Spanish and Portuguese *grande*, use as n. of a. *grande*, with ending assim. to -EE.

grandeur *n.* the quality of being grand. WH: 16C. Old French *grand* great, GRAND + *eur* -OR.

Grand Guignol *n.* a theatrical programme consisting of short sensational blood-curdling pieces. WH: early 20C. French Great Punch, name of a theatre in Paris. *Guignol* is an alteration of the puppet name *Chignol*, itself so called because its owner came from the village of *Chignolo*. The name is apparently not related to French *guigner* to eye surreptitiously.

grandiflora *a.* (of a plant etc.) bearing large flowers. WH: early 20C. Modern Latin, from Latin *grandis* great + *flos*, *floris* flower + fem. adjectival suf. -A¹.

grandiloquent *a.* using lofty or pompous language. WH: 16C. Latin *grandiloquus*, from *grandis* great + *loquus* speaking, from *loqui* to speak, with ending assim. to that of *eloquent* (ELOQUENCE).

grandiose *a.* imposing, impressive, producing the effect of grandeur. WH: 19C. French, from Italian *grandioso*, from *grande* grand. See also -OSE¹.

grand mal *n.* a major epileptic attack, as opposed to *petit mal*. WH: 19C. French, lit. great sickness, from *grand* great + *mal* sickness. Cp. GRAND, MALADY.

Grand Marnier® *n.* a French liqueur with an orange flavour, based on brandy. WH: early 20C. French, from *grand* great, fine + *Marnier-Lapostolle*, name of orig. manufacturer.

Grand Prix *n.* any of several international motor or motorcycle races taking place annually in locations round the world. WH: 19C. French great prize, from *grand* great, GRAND + *prix* prize, PRICE.

grand seigneur *n.* a person of high rank. WH: 17C. French great lord. See GRAND, SEIGNEUR.

grand siècle *n.* the golden age, esp. the 17th cent. in France. WH: 19C. French great century, great age. Cp. GRAND, SECULAR.

grange *n.* a farmhouse with the outbuildings etc., esp. if occupied as a country residence. WH: 12–14C. Old French, from Medieval Latin *granica* pertaining to grain, from Latin *granum* GRAIN. The original sense was granary, barn.

grangerize *v.i., v.t.* to add illustrations to (a book) that have been taken from other books. WH: 19C. James *Granger*, 1723–76, English biographer + -IZE.

graniferous *a.* bearing grain or seed of grainlike form. WH: 17C. Latin *granum* GRAIN + -FEROUS.

granite *n.* a granular, igneous rock consisting of feldspar, quartz and mica, confusedly crystallized. WH: 17C. Italian *granito*, lit. grained, granular, from *grano* GRAIN.

grannom *n.* a four-winged fly frequenting streams. WH: 18C. Orig. unknown.

granny *n.* a grandmother. WH: 17C. From obs. *grannam*, representing coll. pronun. of *grandam* (i.e. grandmother) + -Y³.

granodiorite *n.* a coarse-grained igneous rock with elements of granite and diorite in its composition. WH: 19C. GRANITE + -O- + DIORITE.

granolith *n.* artificial stone consisting of crushed granite and cement. WH: 19C. Latin *grano-*, comb. form of *granum* grain + -LITH.

grant *v.t.* to bestow, concede or give, esp. in answer to a request. *Also v.i., n.* WH: 12–14C. Old French *granter*, alt. of *creanter* to guarantee, to assure, from Latin *credens*, *credentis*, pres.p. of *credere* to believe, to trust.

Granth *n.* the sacred scriptures of the Sikhs. WH: 18C. Sanskrit *grantha* tying, literary composition, from *granth* to tie.

granule *n.* a little grain. WH: 17C. Ecclesiastical Latin *granulum*, dim. of Latin *granum* GRAIN. See also -ULE.

granulo- *comb. form* of or relating to granules. WH: 19C. GRANULE + -O-.

granulocyte *n.* a white blood cell that ingests bacteria etc. and that has granular cytoplasm. WH: early 20C. GRANULO- + -CYTE.

granulometric *a.* relating to the distribution of grain sizes in sand etc. WH: 20C. French *granulométrique*. See GRANULO-, -METRIC.

grape *n.* a berry, the fruit of the vine. WH: 12–14C. Old French (Modern French *grappe* bunch of grapes), from *graper* to gather (grapes), from *grape* hook, from Germanic. Rel. to CRAMP¹.

graph¹ *n.* a diagram representing a mathematical or scientific relationship and based on two graduated scales. *Also v.t.* WH: 19C. Abbr. of *graphic formula*. See GRAPHIC.

graph² *n.* in linguistics, a visual symbol, usu. a letter or letters that represents a unit of spoken sound etc. WH: mid-20C. Greek *graphē* writing.

-graph 262 **grazier**

-graph *comb. form* written, writing, writer, as in *autograph, lithograph, seismograph, tachograph*. WH: French *-graphe*, from Latin *-graphus*, from Greek *-graphos* written, writing.

grapheme *n.* a letter or combination of letters representing a unit of spoken sound, e.g. *sh* in *shut*. WH: mid-20C. GRAPH² + -EME.

graphic *a.* of or relating to the art of writing, delineating, engraving, painting etc. *Also n.* WH: 17C. Latin *graphicus*, from Greek *graphikos*, from Latin *graphē* drawing, writing. See also -IC.

graphite *n.* a form of carbon used in pencils, as a lubricant and in nuclear reactors, blacklead, plumbago. WH: 18C. German *Graphit*, from Greek *graphein* to write. See also -ITE¹. Graphite is so called from its use as the 'lead' in pencils.

grapho- *comb. form* of, relating to or for writing. WH: Greek *graphē* writing. See also -O-.

graphology *n.* the study of handwriting. WH: 19C. GRAPHO- + -LOGY.

graphomania *n.* a psychological urge to write or scribble (sometimes senseless) words. WH: 19C. GRAPHO- + -MANIA.

-graphy *comb. form* denoting a particular style of writing, drawing etc., as in *lithography*. WH: French and German *-graphie*, from Latin and Greek *-graphia* writing.

grapnel *n.* an instrument with several flukes or claws for seizing, grasping or lifting. WH: 14–15C. Old French *grapon* (Modern French *grappin*), from Germanic base of GRAPE. See also -EL.

grappa *n.* a coarse Italian brandy distilled from the residue of a wine press. WH: 19C. Italian, from Italian dial. grape stalk. See GRAPE.

grapple *v.i.* to contend or struggle (with or together) in close fight. *Also v.t., n.* WH: 12–14C. Old French *grapil*, from Provençal, from *grapa* hook, from Germanic base of GRAPE. The verb evolved from the noun in the 16C.

graptolite *n.* an extinct marine invertebrate with a solid axis somewhat resembling a pencil or quill pen, found as a fossil. WH: 19C. Greek *graptos* painted or marked with letters + -LITE.

grasp *v.t.* to seize and hold fast. *Also v.i., n.* WH: 14–15C. Orig. unknown. ? Ult. from Germanic base related to that of GROPE.

grass *n.* the green-bladed herbage on which cattle, sheep etc. feed. *Also v.t., v.i.* WH: pre-1200. Old English *græs*, ult. from Germanic base of GREEN, GROW.

grasshopper *n.* a grass-eating, chirping insect of the order Orthoptera, with hind legs formed for leaping. *Also a.* WH: 14–15C. Var. of obs. *grasshop*, from Old English *gærshoppa*, from *gærs* GRASS + *hoppa*, from *hoppian* HOP¹.

grate¹ *n.* a frame of iron bars for holding fuel for a fire. *Also v.t.* WH: 12–14C. Old French, or from Spanish *grada* hurdle, ult. from Latin *cratis* wickerwork, hurdle.

grate² *v.t.* to rub against a rough surface so as to reduce to small particles. *Also v.i.* WH: 14–15C. Old French *grater* (Modern French *gratter*), from Germanic. Cp. German *kratzen* to scratch.

grateful *a.* thankful, marked by or indicative of gratitude. WH: 16C. From obs. *grate* pleasing, thankful, from Latin *gratus* (GRACE) + -FUL.

graticule *n.* a grid of intersecting lines in a telescope or other optical instrument to aid viewfinding or to measure the scale of the object viewed. WH: 19C. French, from Medieval Latin *graticula*, from Latin *craticula* small gridiron, dim. of *cratis* hurdle.

gratify *v.t.* to please, to delight. WH: 14–15C. French *gratifier*, or from Latin *gratificari* to do a favour to, to make a present of, from *gratus* pleasing + *-i-* + -FY. The original sense (to the 17C) was to make pleasing, to grace. The current sense evolved in the 16C.

gratin *n.* in cookery, a light crust on a dish, usu. made by browning breadcrumbs and cheese. WH: 17C. French, from *gratter*, earlier *grater* GRATE². Cp. AU GRATIN.

grating *n.* an open framework or lattice of metal bars or wooden slats, parallel or crossed. WH: 17C. GRATE¹ + -ING¹.

gratis *adv.* for nothing, without charge, free. *Also a.* WH: 14–15C. Latin, contr. of *gratiis* out of kindness, abl. pl. of *gratia* grace, favour. Cp. GRATUITOUS.

gratitude *n.* thankfulness, appreciation of kindness. WH: 14–15C. French, or from Latin *gratitudo*, from *gratus* pleasing, agreeable. See also -TUDE.

gratuitous *a.* uncalled for, unnecessary. WH: 17C. Old French *gratuiteus* (obs. Modern French *gratuiteux*), from Latin *gratuitus* freely given. See also -OUS.

gratuity *n.* a gift, a present voluntarily given in return for a service, a tip. WH: 15C. Old French *gratuité* or Medieval Latin *gratuitas* gift, from *gratus* pleasing, agreeable. See also -ITY. The original sense (to the 17C) was graciousness, favour. The current sense dates from the 16C.

gratulatory *a.* congratulatory, complimentary, expressing joy. WH: 16C. Late Latin *gratulatorius*, from Latin *gratulatus*, p.p. of *gratulari* from *gratus* pleasing, agreeable. See also -ORY².

graunch *v.i.* to make a crunching, grating or grinding sound. *Also v.t.* WH: 19C. Imit. Cp. CRUNCH.

graupel *n.* soft hail, snow pellets. WH: 19C. German, dim. of *Graupe* peeled grain, prob. from Slavonic. Cp. Russian *krupa* peeled grain.

gravamen *n.* the most serious part of a charge. WH: 17C. Ecclesiastical Latin physical inconvenience, from Latin *gravare* to weigh on, to oppress, from *gravis* GRAVE².

grave¹ *n.* a hole in the earth for burying a dead body in. *Also v.t.* WH: pre-1200. Old English *græf*, from Germanic, ult. from base of GROOVE. As a verb (Old English *grafan*) the original sense was to carve, to sculpt, then (to the 17C) to engrave.

grave² *a.* important, serious, momentous. WH: 15C. Old French, or from Latin *gravis* heavy, important.

grave³ *v.t.* to clean (a ship's bottom) by scraping or burning, and (formerly) by covering it with pitch and tallow. WH: 14–15C. Prob. from dial. French *grave*, var. of Old French *grève* shore, from Celtic. Cp. GRAVEL.

gravel *n.* small water-worn stones or pebbles mixed with sand etc. *Also v.t.* WH: 12–14C. Old French, dim. of *grave* gravel, coarse sand. See GRAVE³, also -EL.

†graveolent *a.* (of plants) smelling strongly and offensively. WH: 17C. Latin *graveolens, graveolentis* from *grave*, use as adv. of neut. of *gravis* heavy (see GRAVE²) + *olens, olentis*, pres.p. of *olere* to have a smell. See also -ENT.

Graves *n.* a light usu. white wine, pressed in the Graves district. WH: 17C. *Graves*, a district of SW France.

Graves' disease *n.* a disease characterized by an overactive thyroid gland, resulting in swelling of the neck and protruding eyes. WH: 19C. Robert J. *Graves*, 1796–1853, Irish physician.

gravid *a.* pregnant. WH: 16C. Latin *gravidus* laden, pregnant, from *gravis* heavy. See GRAVE², also -ID.

gravimeter *n.* an instrument for determining variations in gravity at different points of the earth's surface. WH: 18C. French *gravimètre*, from Latin *gravis* heavy. See -METER.

gravitate *v.i.* to be powerfully drawn (towards). WH: 17C. Modern Latin *gravitatus*, p.p. of *gravitare*, from Latin *gravitas* gravity. See also -ATE³.

gravity *n.* the force causing bodies to tend towards the centre of the earth. WH: 15C. Old French *gravité*, from Latin *gravitas*, from *gravis* heavy. See also -ITY.

gravlax *n.* dry-cured salmon marinated in salt, sugar, herbs and spices, originally from Scandinavia. WH: mid-20C. Swedish, from *grav* pit, GRAVE¹ + *lax* salmon. The dish is so named because the salmon was originally marinated in a hole in the ground. A variant form *gravadlax* has *gravad-* from *gravad*, p.p. of Swedish *grava* to dig, to bury.

gravure *n.* (short for) photogravure. WH: 19C. Abbr. of PHOTOGRAVURE.

gravy *n.* the fat and juice from meat during and after cooking. WH: 12–14C. ? From a misreading as *gravé* of Old French *grané*, probably from *grain* spice. See GRAIN, also -Y¹. The word was originally used for a dressing of broth, milk of almonds, spices and wine or ale for white meats, fish and vegetables. The current sense dates from the 16C.

grayling *n.* any freshwater fish of the genus *Thymallus* with a large dorsal and an adipose fin. WH: 12–14C. From *gray*, var. of GREY + -LING¹.

graze¹ *v.i.* to eat growing grass. *Also v.t.* WH: pre-1200. Old English *grasian*, from *græs* GRASS.

graze² *v.t.* to touch, rub or brush slightly in passing. *Also v.i., n.* WH: 16C. ? From GRAZE¹, in sense to take off the grass close to the ground.

grazier *n.* a person who pastures cattle, and rears and fattens them for market. WH: 12–14C. From GRASS. See also -IER. The word was formerly associated with French *graissier* fattener.

grazioso *a.* graceful, elegant. WH: 19C. Italian graceful, GRACIOUS.

grease[1] *n.* oily or fatty matter of any kind. WH: 12–14C. Old French *graisse*, from Latin *crassus*. See CRASS.

grease[2] *v.t.* to smear, lubricate or soil with grease. WH: 14–15C. GREASE[1].

greasy *a.* smeared, saturated or soiled with grease. WH: 16C. GREASE[1] + -Y[1].

great *a.* large in bulk, number, amount, extent or degree. *Also n.* WH: pre-1200. Old English *grēat*, from Germanic, of unknown orig. Cp. German *gross*. Not rel. to GROSS.

greave *n.* armour for the legs. WH: 12–14C. Old French *greve* calf of the leg, skin, of unknown orig.

greaves *n.pl.* fibrous scraps or refuse of melted tallow. WH: 17C. Low German *greven* (pl.), of unknown orig. Cp. German *Griebe* refuse of lard.

grebe *n.* a diving bird of the family Podicipedidae with lobed feet and no tail. WH: 18C. French *grèbe*, of unknown orig.

Grecian *a.* of or relating to Greece. *Also n.* WH: 14–15C. Old French *grecien*, from Latin *Graecia* Greece. See also -IAN.

grecque *n.* an ornamental Greek fret. WH: 19C. French, fem. of *grec* Greek.

greed *n.* avarice, insatiable desire or covetousness. WH: 16C. Back-formation from GREEDY.

greedy *a.* having an inordinate desire for food or drink, gluttonous. WH: pre-1200. Old English *grēdig*, from Germanic, from base meaning hunger, greed, of unknown orig.

Greek *n.* a native or inhabitant of Greece. *Also a.* WH: pre-1200. Old English *Grēcas* (pl.), from Germanic, from Latin *Graecus*, from Greek *Graikos*. The Greeks' name for themselves is HELLENE.

green *a.* having a colour like growing herbage, of the colour in the spectrum between blue and yellow. *Also n., v.i., v.t.* WH: pre-1200. Old English *grēne*, from Germanic, from base of GRASS, GROW.

greengage *n.* a green, sweet variety of plum, *Prunus domestica italica.* WH: 18C. GREEN + Sir William *Gage*, 1657–1727, who introduced the fruit to England in *c.*1725.

Greenwich Mean Time *n.* mean time for the meridian of Greenwich, adopted as the standard time in Great Britain and several other countries. WH: 19C. *Greenwich*, a borough of SE London, the former site of the Royal Observatory + MEAN[2] + TIME.

greet[1] *v.t.* to address with a salutation at meeting. *Also v.i.* WH: pre-1200. Old English *grētan*. Cp. German *grüssen* to salute, to greet. The original sense was to assail, to attack (to the 14–15C).

greet[2] *v.i.* to weep, to cry, to lament. *Also n.* WH: pre-1200. Partly from Old English *grētan*, from Germanic base rel. to that of GREET[1], partly from Old English *grēotan*, ? from Germanic base of Y- + v. represented by Old English *rēotan* in same sense.

gregarious *a.* tending to associate with others, sociable. WH: 17C. Latin *gregarius*, from *grex, gregis* flock, herd, + -OUS. See also -ARIOUS.

Gregorian *a.* of, relating to, produced or established by Gregory. *Also n.* WH: 16C. Partly from Medieval Latin *Gregorianus*, from Late Latin *Gregorius*, from Greek *Grēgorius*, partly from the English name *Gregory*. See also -IAN.

Gregory powder *n.* the compound powder of rhubarb, magnesium carbonate and ginger, used as a laxative. WH: 19C. James *Gregory*, 1758–1822, Scottish physician.

greige *a.* of a colour midway between grey and beige. WH: early 20C. French *grège* in *soie grège* raw silk, from Italian *greggio* raw, crude, unprocessed.

gremial *n.* in the Roman Catholic Church, an episcopal vestment covering the lap, orig. to prevent drops of chrism falling on the vestments during ordination etc. *Also a.* WH: 16C. Medieval Latin *gremialis* alumnus, *gremiale* bishop's apron, from Latin *gremium* lap, bosom. See also -IAL.

gremlin *n.* an imaginary mischievous sprite, jokingly held to be responsible for problems in mechanical, electronic equipment, systems etc. WH: early 20C. Prob. based on GOBLIN.

grenade *n.* a small explosive shell thrown by hand (also known as a *hand grenade*) or fired from a rifle. WH: 16C. French, alt. of *(pome)grenate* POMEGRANATE, based on Spanish *granada*.

grenadier *n.* the Grenadier Guards, the first regiment of the royal household infantry. WH: 17C. French GRENADE. See also -IER.

grenadilla *n.* any of various species of passion flower, *Passiflora.* WH: 16C. Spanish, dim. of *granada* pomegranate.

grenadine[1] *n.* a pomegranate syrup. WH: 19C. French (*sirop de*) *grenadine*, from *grenade* GRENADE.

grenadine[2] *n.* a thin, gauzy, silk or woollen fabric for women's dresses etc. WH: 19C. French silk of a grained texture, from *grenu* grained, from *grain* GRAIN. See also -INE.

Gresham's law *n.* the tendency for currency superior in intrinsic worth to be hoarded and to circulate less than currency of lower intrinsic worth. WH: 19C. Sir Thomas *Gresham*, 1519–79, English financier.

gressorial *a.* adapted for walking, applied to the feet of birds having three toes in front (two of them connected) and one behind. WH: 19C. Modern Latin *gressorius*, from *gressus*, p.p. of *gradi* to proceed, to walk. See also -AL[1].

grey *a.* of a colour between white and black, ash-coloured. *Also n., v.t., v.i.* WH: pre-1200. Old English *grǣg*, from Germanic. Cp. German *grau*.

greyhound *n.* a variety of dog characterized by its tall slender form, keen sight, and swiftness. WH: pre-1200. Old English *grīghund*, from Germanic base also of Old Norse *grey* bitch (orig. unknown) + *hund* HOUND. Not rel. to GREY.

greywacke *n.* a gritstone or conglomerate, usu. consisting of small fragments of quartz, flinty slate etc. cemented together, occurring chiefly in Silurian strata. WH: 18C. German *Grauwacke*, from *grau* grey + WACKE.

grice *n.* a young or sucking pig. WH: 12–14C. Old Norse *gríss* young pig.

grid *n.* a grating of parallel bars. WH: 19C. Back-formation from GRIDIRON.

griddle *n.* a heated metal plate for cooking, usu. commercially, eggs, burgers etc. *Also v.t.* WH: 12–14C. Old French *gredil* gridiron, from dim. of Latin *cratis.* See CRATE, GRATE[1]. Cp. GRILLE.

gride *v.i.* to grind, scrape or jar (along, through etc.). *Also v.t., n.* WH: 14–15C. Alt. of *gird* to strike, to smite, of unknown orig.

gridelin *n.* a colour of mixed white and red, a grey-violet or purple. WH: 17C. French *gris-de-lin*, lit. grey of flax.

gridiron *n.* a grated iron utensil for broiling fish, meat etc. WH: 12–14C. Alt. of GRIDDLE, with assim. of second syl. to IRON. Cp. ANDIRON.

gridlock *n.* a large-scale traffic jam where a whole area of intersecting roads is at a standstill. WH: late 20C. GRID + LOCK[1].

grief *n.* deep sorrow or mental distress due to loss, disaster or disappointment. WH: 12–14C. Old French, from *grever* GRIEVE[1].

grievance *n.* a cause for complaint. WH: 12–14C. Old French *grevance*, from *grever*. See GRIEVE[1], also -ANCE.

grieve[1] *v.t.* to lament, to sorrow over. *Also v.i.* WH: 12–14C. Old French *grever* to burden, to encumber, from alt. of Latin *gravare*, from *gravis* GRAVE[2].

grieve[2] *n.* an overseer, steward or bailiff. WH: pre-1200. Old English *grǣfa.* See REEVE[1].

griffin *n.* a fabulous creature, with the body and legs of a lion, the head and wings of an eagle and listening ears, emblematic of strength, agility and watchfulness. WH: 12–14C. Old French *grifoun* (Modern French *griffon*), from augm. form of Late Latin *gryphus*, from *gryps, grypos*, from Greek *grups, grupos.* Cp. GRIFFON[1], GRIFFON[2].

griffon[1] *n.* a variety of dog like a terrier, with short, coarse hair. WH: 18C. French GRIFFIN. The dog is so named from its fanciful resemblance to a GRIFFIN.

griffon[2] *n.* a vulture, *Gyps fulvus*, of Eurasia and N Africa. WH: 14–15C. Var. of GRIFFIN. The bird is so named from its supposed resemblance to a GRIFFIN.

grift *v.i.* to swindle. WH: early 20C. ? Alt. of GRAFT[2].

grig *n.* a sand eel or a young eel. WH: 14–15C. Orig. unknown. According to some, the word is from *Grig*, a pet form of *Gregory*.

Grignard reagent *n.* any of a class of organic magnesium compounds used in the synthesis of organic compounds. WH: early 20C. Victor *Grignard*, 1871–1934, French chemist.

grike *n.* a vertical fissure in an exposed limestone surface, formed by the action of rainwater. WH: 18C. Orig. unknown.

grill *v.t.* to cook under a grill, broil on a gridiron. *Also n.* WH: 17C. French *griller*, from *gril* GRILL. See GRILLE.

grillage n. a structure of sleepers and cross-beams forming a foundation in marshy soil for a pier, wharf or the like. WH: 18C. French GRILLE + -AGE.

grille n. an open grating, railing or screen of lattice-work, to enclose or shut a sacred or private place, or to fill an opening in a door etc. WH: 17C. Old French, earlier *graille*, from Medieval Latin *graticula*, *craticula*, from Latin *craticula*, dim. of *cratis*. See CRATE, GRATE[1]. Cp. GRIDDLE.

grilse n. a young salmon when it first returns from the sea, usu. in its second year. WH: 14–15C. Orig. unknown.

grim a. stern, relentless, severe, unyielding. WH: pre-1200. Old English, from Germanic. Cp. German *grimm*. The original meaning was fierce, cruel, savage.

grimace n. a distortion of the features, a wry face, expressing disgust, contempt, affectation etc. Also v.i. WH: 17C. French, earlier *grimache*, from Spanish *grimazo* caricature, from *grima* fright. Rel. to GRIME.

†**grimalkin** n. an old cat, esp. a she-cat. WH: 16C. GREY + MALKIN.

grime n. dirt, smut. Also v.t. WH: 12–14C. Germanic. Cp. Flemish *grijmen*, Low German *gremen* to begrime.

Grimm's law n. a law formulated by Grimm concerning the modification of consonants in the most important of the Indo-European languages. WH: 19C. Jakob *Grimm*, 1785–1863, German philologist.

grin v.i. to show the teeth as in laughter, derision or pain. Also v.t., n. WH: pre-1200. Old English *grennian*, from German. Cp. GROAN, GURN. A sense to smile broadly evolved in the 15C.

grind v.t. to reduce to powder or fine particles by crushing and friction. Also v.i., n. WH: pre-1200. Old English *grindan*. Cp. Latin *frendere* to rub away, to gnash. The verb has no equivalent in other Germanic languages.

gringo n. an English-speaking foreigner. WH: 15C. Spanish foreign, foreigner, gibberish, of uncertain orig. ? From *griego* Greek (in sense gibberish).

grip[1] v.t. to seize hold of. Also v.i., n. WH: pre-1200. Old English *grippe*, from Germanic. Cp. GRIPE.

grip[2] n. a small ditch or furrow. Also v.t. WH: pre-1200. Old English *grypa*, rel. to *grēop* burrow, from Germanic base meaning to hollow out.

gripe v.i. to complain, esp. in a persistent, peevish way. Also v.t., n. WH: pre-1200. Old English *grīpan*, from Germanic. Cp. GRIP[1], GROPE.

Griqua n. a member of a people descended from Dutch settlers and the Nama of southern Africa. WH: 18C. Nama.

grisaille n. a style of painting or staining in grey monochrome, esp. on stained glass, representing solid bodies in relief, such as ornament of cornices etc. WH: 19C. French, from *gris* grey + *-aille* -AL[1].

griseofulvin n. an antibiotic used to treat fungal infections. WH: mid-20C. Modern Latin (*Penicillium*) *griseofulvum*, from Medieval Latin *griseus* grey + Latin *fulvus* reddish-yellow.

griseous a. bluish-grey. WH: 19C. Medieval Latin *griseus* grey + -OUS.

grisette n. a lively and attractive girl or young woman of the French working classes. WH: 18C. French, from *gris* grey. See also -ETTE. The name refers to the cheap grey dress fabric formerly worn by French working girls.

griskin n. the lean part of the loin of a bacon pig. WH: 17C. GRICE + KIN.

grisly a. horrible, terrible, fearful, grim. Also adv. WH: pre-1200. Old English *grislic*, from base of *-grīsan* in *agrīsan* to terrify, from Germanic. See also -LY[1].

grison n. any carnivorous mammal of the genus *Galactis*, like a large weasel with grey fur and a white stripe across the forehead. WH: 18C. French, use as n. of a. from *gris* grey. See also -OON.

grist[1] n. corn to be ground. WH: pre-1200. Old English *grīst* action of grinding. See GRIND.

grist[2] n. a size of rope as denoted by the number and thickness of the strands. WH: 18C. ? Rel. to GIRD[1].

gristle n. cartilage, esp. when found in meat. WH: pre-1200. Old English, from Germanic. Ult. of unknown orig.

grit[1] n. coarse rough particles such as sand or gravel. Also v.i., v.t. WH: pre-1200. Old English *grēot*, from Germanic base also of GRITS, GROATS, GROUT[1].

grit[2] a. great. WH: 14–15C. Var. of GREAT.

grits n.pl. coarsely-ground grain, esp. corn. WH: pre-1200. Old English *grytt*, from Germanic base also of GRIT[1], GROATS + -S[1].

grizzle[1] v.i. (usu. of a child) to cry, complain etc. in a fretful way. Also n. WH: 18C. Orig. unknown.

grizzle[2] n. a grey colour. WH: 12–14C. Old French *grisel*, from *gris* grey. See also -EL.

groan v.i. to utter a deep moaning sound, as in pain or grief. Also v.t., n. WH: pre-1200. Old English *grānian*, from Germanic. Cp. GRIN.

groat n. a small silver coin, value 4 old pence. WH: 14–15C. Middle Dutch *groot*, from Middle Low German *grōte* GREAT, use as n. of a. here meaning thick. Cp. GROSCHEN.

groats n.pl. husked oats or wheat. WH: pre-1200. Old English *grotan*, rel. to GRIT[1], GROUT[1].

Gro-bag® n. a large plastic bag, containing a growing medium (such as compost) in which seeds can be germinated and plants grown to full size. WH: late 20C. GROW + BAG.

grocer n. a dealer in food and miscellaneous household supplies. WH: 12–14C. Old French *grossier*, from Medieval Latin *grossarius*, from *grossus* GROSS. The original sense (to the 17C) was a person buying and selling in large quantities, 'in the gross'. The current more specialized sense evolved in the 14–15C.

grockle n. a tourist (as described by a resident of the host region). WH: mid-20C. Orig. unknown. ? Arbitrary. See also -LE[2]. The word is said to derive from a fantastic creature in a children's comic, popularized by the film *The System* (1962).

grog n. a mixture of rum and cold water, orig. issued in the Royal Navy. Also v.t., v.i. WH: 18C. Appar. abbr. of GROGRAM, as nickname ('Old Grog') of Admiral Vernon, 1684–1757, who wore a grogram cloak and ordered the mixture to be served out to sailors instead of rum.

grogram n. a coarse cloth of silk and mohair or silk and wool. Also a. WH: 16C. French *gros grain*, lit. coarse grain. See GROSS, GRAIN. Cp. GROSGRAIN. The final n has changed to m as with BUCKRAM, VELLUM.

groin n. the hollow in the human body where the thigh and the trunk unite. Also v.t. WH: 14–15C. ? From Old English *grynde* depression.

Grolier n. a book or binding from Grolier's collection. WH: 19C. Jean *Grolier* de Servin, Vicomte d'Aiguisy, 1479–1565, French book collector.

grommet n. a ring or eyelet of metal, rubber or plastic designed to strengthen or protect the opening of a hole. WH: 17C. Obs. French *gourmette* curb chain, from *gourmer* to curb, to bridle, of unknown orig.

gromwell n. any trailing herb of the genus *Lithospermum* of the borage family, esp. *L. officinale*, the hard stony seeds of which were formerly used in medicine. WH: 12–14C. Old French *gromil* (Modern French *grémil*), from *grès* sandstone + *mil* millet. The name refers to the hardness of the seeds.

groom n. a person in charge of horses or a stable. Also v.t. WH: 12–14C. Orig. uncertain. Prob. rel. to GROW. Cp. GOURMET. The original sense (to the 17C) was male child, boy. The sense bridegroom evolved in the 17C.

groove n. a channel, furrow or long hollow, esp. cut with a tool for something to fit into or work in. Also v.t., v.i. WH: 12–14C. Obs. Dutch *groeve* furrow, ditch (now *groef*), from Germanic, rel. to base of GRAVE[1].

grope v.i. to search (after) something as in the dark, by feeling about with the hands. Also v.t. WH: pre-1200. Old English *grāpian*, from Germanic base of GRIPE.

grosbeak n. any of several finches and cardinals having thick bills and bright plumage. WH: 17C. French *grosbec*, from *gros* GROSS + *bec* BEAK.

groschen n. an Austrian coin worth one-hundredth of a schilling. WH: 17C. German, from Middle High German *gros*, from Medieval Latin *denarius grossus* thick penny. See GROSS, GROAT.

groset n. a gooseberry. WH: 18C. Alt. of *groser* (16C), from French *groseille*. See GOOSEBERRY.

grosgrain n. a heavy ribbed silk, rayon etc. fabric or ribbon. WH: 19C. French. See GROGRAM.

gros point n. a stitch in embroidery covering two horizontal and two vertical threads, as distinct from *petit point*. WH: 19C. French large stick. See GROSS, POINT.

gross *a.* big, rank. *Also n., v.t.* WH: 12–14C. Old French *gros*, from Late Latin *grossus*, of similar formation to *bassus* BASE², *crassus* CRASS.

grossular *a.* of or belonging to a gooseberry. *Also n.* WH: 19C. Modern Latin *grossularia*, from French *groseille*. See GOOSEBERRY.

grot *n.* rubbish, junk, dirt, filth. *Also a.* WH: mid-20C. Abbr. of GROTTY.

grotesque *a.* distorted, irregular, extravagant or fantastic in appearance. *Also n.* WH: 16C. French *crotesque*, from Italian *grottesca*, from *pittura grottesca* painting resembling a grotto, from *grotta* GROTTO. The original sense was a style of decorative painting with a fantastic interweaving of human and animal figures with flowers and foliage. The current sense dates from the 18C.

grotto *n.* a small cave, esp. one that is picturesque. WH: 17C. Italian *grotta*, from var. of Latin *crypta*, from Greek *kruptē* vault, CRYPT.

grotty *a.* unattractive. WH: mid-20C. Shortening of GROTESQUE + -Y¹.

grouch *v.i.* to grumble, to grouse. *Also n.* WH: 19C. Var. of obs. *grutch*, from Old French *groucier*, *grouchier* to grumble, to murmur, of unknown orig. Rel. to GRUDGE.

ground¹ *n.* the surface of the earth as distinct from the air or the sea. *Also v.t., v.i.* WH: pre-1200. Old English *grund*, from Germanic. Cp. German *Grund*. No related words outside Germanic are known.

ground² *a.* having been ground. WH: 14–15C. P.p. of GRIND.

groundsel *n.* any plant of the genus *Senecio* with pinnatifid leaves and small yellow flowers, esp. the common weed, *S. vulgaris*, which is used for feeding cage birds. WH: pre-1200. Old English *grundeswylige*, earlier *gundæswelgæ*, prob. from *gund* pus + base of SWALLOW¹, assim. to GROUND¹. The plant was formerly used in poultices as a 'pus swallower'.

group *n.* the combination of several figures or objects to form a single mass. *Also v.t., v.i.* WH: 17C. French *groupe*, from Italian *gruppo*, from Germanic. Rel. to CROP. The original basic sense is lump, mass.

grouper *n.* any marine fish of the family Serranidae, characterized by heavy body, big head and large mouth. WH: 17C. Portuguese *garoupa*, probably from a S American name. The form of the word has altered as for BREAKER.

grouse¹ *n.* any gallinaceous game bird of the family Tetraonidae with a plump body and feet more or less feathered, esp. *Lagopus scoticus*, the red grouse, moor fowl or moor game, *Lyrurus tetrix*, the black game or heath fowl, *Tetrao urogallus*, the capercaillie, wood or great grouse, and *Lagopus mutus*, the ptarmigan or rock grouse. *Also v.i.* WH: 16C. Prob. orig. a pl. form of a word rel. to Latin *gruta*, or Old French *grue*, from Latin *grus* crane.

grouse² *v.i.* to grumble. *Also n.* WH: 19C. Orig. unknown. Cp. GROUCH.

grout¹ *n.* a thin, coarse mortar to run into the joints of masonry and brickwork. *Also v.t.* WH: pre-1200. Old English *grūt*, from Germanic base of GRIT¹, GROATS. The original sense was coarse meal. The sense of fluid mortar arose in the 17C as a technical application of the earlier 16C sense of coarse porridge.

grout² *v.t.* (of a pig) to turn (up) with the snout. *Also v.i.* WH: 18C. GROUT¹ or var. of earlier obs. *grout* in same sense, probably rel. to GRIT¹, GROATS.

grove *n.* a small wood. WH: pre-1200. Old English *grāf*, rel. to *græfa* brushwood, thicket, from Germanic. Not rel. to GRAVE¹, and with no known Germanic or Indo-European rel. words.

grovel *v.i.* to make an abject apology. WH: 14–15C. Back-formation from *grovelling* face downward, from obs. *groof* (from Old Norse *grúfa* in *á grúfu* face downwards) + -LING². *Grovelling* is now regarded as a pres.p. of GROVEL.

grow *v.i.* to increase in bulk by the assimilation of new matter into the living organism. *Also v.t.* WH: pre-1200. Old English *grōwan*, from Germanic base also of GRASS, GREEN.

growl *v.i.* to make a deep guttural sound as of anger. *Also v.t., n.* WH: 17C. Prob. imit. Cp. CUR.

groyne *n.* a structure of piles, concrete etc., acting as a breakwater on a foreshore, and causing sand and shingle to be retained. *Also v.t.* WH: 16C. Transferred use of obs. *groin* animal's snout, from Old French *groign* (Modern French *groin*), from Late Latin *grunium*, from Latin *grunnire* to grunt like a pig. Cp. GRUNT.

grub *v.i.* to dig by scratching or tearing up the ground superficially. *Also v.t., n.* WH: 12–14C. Orig. uncertain. Cp. Old High German *grubilōn* to dig, to search closely, Middle Dutch *grobben* to scrape together, Dutch *grobbelen* to root out, from Germanic base rel. to that of GRAVE¹.

Grub Street *n.* the work and milieu of hack writers. *Also a.* WH: 17C. *Grub Street* in London where many struggling writers lived. Cp. GRUB (hack). Grub Street, now Milton Street near the Barbican, may have been named for its infestation of maggots, although it could have been named from the surname Grub (Grubbe).

grudge *v.t.* to feel discontent or envy at. *Also v.i., n.* WH: 14–15C. Var. of obs. *grutch* in same sense. See GROUCH.

grue *v.i.* to shudder. WH: 12–14C. From Scandinavian word represented by Old Swedish *grua* and Old Danish *grue* to be awed, to shudder, from Germanic. Cp. German *grauen* to be awed.

gruel *n.* semi-liquid food made by boiling oatmeal or other meal in water or milk. WH: 12–14C. Old French (Modern French *gruau*), from dim. (represented by Medieval Latin *grutellum*) of a Frankish word. See also -EL.

gruesome *a.* frightful, horrible, repulsive. WH: 16C. GRUE + -SOME¹.

gruff *a.* of a rough, surly or harsh aspect. WH: 15C. Flemish and Dutch *grof*, from Germanic. Cp. German *grob* coarse. Ult. rel. to ROUGH.

grumble *v.i.* to murmur with discontent. *Also v.t., n.* WH: 16C. Freq. of obs. *grumme* in same sense (orig. uncertain) + -b- + -LE¹. Cp. Dutch *grommen*, Middle Low German *grommelen*, from imit. Germanic.

grume *n.* a fluid of a thick, sticky consistency. WH: 16C. Latin *grumus* little heap. Cp. obs. French *grume* (now *grumeau*) clot.

grumpy *a.* surly, cross, peevish, ill-tempered. WH: 18C. From *grump*, imit. of sound denoting displeasure (cp. HUMPH) + -Y¹.

Grundyism *n.* prudishness. WH: 19C. Mrs *Grundy*, narrow-minded and censorious character in Thomas Morton's play *Speed The Plough* (1798) + ISM. In the play, Dame Ashfield frequently asks 'What will Mrs Grundy say?'

grunge *n.* a style of rock music, fashion etc. emphasizing discordant, often ugly elements, the music being characterized by raucous, distorted guitar, the fashion by loose-fitting uncoordinated outfits. WH: mid-20C. Appar. arbitrary, based on *grubby* (GRUB), DINGY. Cp. GUNGE.

grunion *n.* a small Californian sea fish, *Leuresthes tenuis*, that spawns on shore. WH: early 20C. Prob. from Spanish *gruñón* grunter.

grunt *v.i.* to make a deep guttural noise like a pig. *Also v.t., n.* WH: pre-1200. Old English *grunnettan*, from Germanic imit. base rel. to that of Latin *grunnire* to grunt.

Gruyère *n.* a Swiss or French cheese made from cows' milk, pale-coloured, firm and full of cavities. WH: 19C. *Gruyère*, a town in Switzerland.

grysbok *n.* any small, straight-horned antelope of the genus *Raphicerus*, found in central and southern Africa. WH: 18C. Afrikaans, from Dutch *grijs* grey + *bok* BUCK¹.

GT *abbr.* gran turismo, a touring car, usu. a fast sports car. WH: Abbr. of Italian *gran turismo*, lit. grand touring.

GTi *abbr.* gran turismo injection, a GT car with fuel injection. WH: GT + initial of *injection*.

guacamole *n.* a Mexican dish of mashed avocado, citrus juice and seasonings. WH: early 20C. American Spanish, from Nahuatl *ahuacamolli*, from *ahuacatl* avocado + *molli* sauce.

guaco *n.* a tropical American plant, *Mikania guaco*, and others, said to cure snake-bites. WH: 19C. American Spanish.

guaiacum *n.* any tree of the genus *Guaiacum*, W Indian and tropical N American trees, one of which, *G. officinale*, furnishes lignum vitae, while its bark, wood and resin, with those of *G. sanctum*, are used in medicine. WH: 16C. Modern Latin, from Spanish *guayaco*, from Taino *guayacan*.

guan *n.* a bird similar to a pheasant of the family Cracidae, esp. of the genus *Penelope*, found in the tropical rainforests of S America. WH: 17C. American Spanish, from Miskito *kwamu*.

guanaco *n.* a wild mammal, *Lama guanicoe*, related to the llama and inhabiting the chain of the Andes to their most southerly point. WH: 17C. Spanish, from Quechua *huanacu*.

guano *n.* a valuable manure, composed chiefly of the excrement of seabirds found esp. on islands off S America and in the Pacific. *Also v.t.* WH: 17C. Spanish, or from American Spanish *huano*, from Quechua *huanu* dung.

guarana *n.* the powdered seeds of *Paullinia cupana*, a Brazilian shrub. WH: 19C. Portuguese, from Tupi *guaraná*.

Guarani *n.* a member of a S American Indian people of Paraguay, S Brazil and Bolivia. *Also a.* WH: 18C. Spanish.

guarantee *n.* a formal promise to see an agreement, duty or liability fulfilled, esp. with regard to the quality etc. of a bought product. *Also v.t.* WH: 17C. Prob. orig. from Spanish *garante*, later influ. by French *garantie* GUARANTY. Cp. WARRANT.

guaranty *n.* the act of guaranteeing, esp. an undertaking to be responsible for a debt or obligation of another person. WH: 16C. Old French *garantie*, fem. p.p. (used as n.) of *garantir* to guarantee, from Germanic base of WARRANT.

guard *v.t.* to watch over, to protect, to defend (from or against). *Also v.i., n.* WH: 14–15C. Old French *garder*, from Germanic base of WARD.

guardian *n.* a person who has the charge, care or custody of any person or thing. *Also a.* WH: 14–15C. Old French *garden* (Modern French *gardien*), from Frankish, from Germanic base of WARD. Cp. WARDEN.

guava *n.* the luscious fruit of various species of the tropical American myrtaceous genus *Psidium*, esp. *P. guajava*. WH: 16C. Spanish *guayaba*, of S American orig.

guayule *n.* a silver-leaved Mexican shrub, *Parthenium argentatum*. WH: early 20C. American Spanish, from Nahuatl *cuauhuli*.

gubbins *n.* a small device, gadget etc. WH: 16C. Var. of obs. *gobbon* piece, slice (from Old French, appar. rel. to GOB[1], GOBBET) + -S[1]. Not rel. to surname *Gubbins*, which is var. of *Gibbon*.

gubernatorial *a.* of or relating to a governor, esp. of a US state. WH: 18C. Latin *gubernator* (see GOVERNOR) + -IAL.

guddle *v.i.* to grope for fish with the hands. *Also v.t., n.* WH: 17C. Orig. unknown.

gudgeon[1] *n.* a small freshwater fish, *Gobio gobio*, easily caught and largely used as bait. WH: 14–15C. Old French *goujon*, from Latin *gobio, gobionis*, from *gobius* GOBY.

gudgeon[2] *n.* any of several types of pivot at the centre of a wheel, bell mechanism etc. WH: 12–14C. Old French *goujon*, dim. of *gouge* GOUGE.

guelder rose *n.* a shrubby plant, *Viburnum opulus*, bearing ball-shaped bunches of white flowers, also called the *snowball tree*. WH: 16C. Dutch *geldersche roos*, from *Gelderland*, a Dutch province (or its capital, *Gelders*).

Guelph *n.* a member of the popular party in medieval Italy which aimed at national independence, and supported the Pope against the Ghibellines. WH: 16C. Italian *Guelfo*, from Middle High German *Welf*, name of family of one of two great rival dynasties (12–13C).

guenon *n.* any of various long-tailed African monkeys of the genus *Cercopithecus*. WH: 19C. French, of unknown orig.

guerdon *n.* a reward, a recompense. *Also v.t.* WH: 14–15C. Old French, from Medieval Latin *widerdonum*, from Germanic source of Old English *witherlēan*, from *wither* again + *lēan* payment, with assim. of 2nd element to Latin *donum* gift.

guereza *n.* a black Ethiopian monkey, of the genus *Colobus*, with a fringe of white hair and a bushy tail. WH: 19C. Prob. African.

guerite *n.* a small loopholed tower, usu. on the point of a bastion, to hold a sentinel. WH: 18C. French *guérite*. See GARRET.

Guernsey *n.* a Guernsey cow. WH: 16C. *Guernsey*, the second largest of the Channel Islands. Cp. GANSEY.

guerrilla *n.* a member of a small independent fighting band carrying out irregular warfare, esp. against an army, and usu. politically motivated. WH: 19C. Spanish, dim. of *guerra* war. The word was introduced into English during the Peninsular War (1808–14).

guess *v.t.* to judge or estimate on imperfect grounds, to conjecture. *Also v.i., n.* WH: 12–14C. ? Of naut. orig., from vars. with *-e-* of Middle Low German and Middle Dutch *gissen*, or from Old Swedish *gissa*, Old Danish *gitse*, all ult. from base of GET[1]. The spelling with *gu-* dates from the 16C. Cp. GUEST.

guest *n.* a person invited by another to a meal, party etc. or to stay

at their house. *Also v.t., v.i.* WH: 12–14C. Old Norse *gestr*, superseding Old English *giest*, *gest*, from Germanic, from Indo-European base seen also in Latin *hostis* enemy, (orig.) stranger. Cp. HOST[1], HOST[2].

guest-rope *n.* a hawser carried by a boat to a distant object for warping a vessel towards this. WH: 17C. First element of unknown orig. + ROPE.

guffaw *n.* a burst of loud or coarse laughter. *Also v.i., v.t.* WH: 18C. Imit. Cp. *haw-haw*.

guide *v.t.* to direct, lead or conduct. *Also n.* WH: 14–15C. Old French *guider*, alt. of *guier*, from Germanic, from alt. base of WIT[2]. Cp. GUY[2].

guidon *n.* the forked or pointed pennant of a troop of light cavalry. WH: 16C. French, from Italian *guidone*, from *guida* guide. See also -OON.

guild *n.* a society or corporation belonging to the same class, trade or pursuit, combined for mutual aid and protection of interests. WH: pre-1200. Prob. from Middle Low German or Middle Dutch *gilde*, from Germanic, rel. to Old English *gild* payment, offering, sacrifice, guild, also from Germanic. Cp. German *Geld* money.

guilder *n.* the chief monetary unit of the Netherlands. WH: 14–15C. Alt. of Dutch GULDEN.

guile *n.* deceit, craft, cunning. *Also v.t.* WH: 12–14C. Old French, from Old Norse. See WILE.

guillemot *n.* any swimming seabird of the genus *Uria* or *Cepphus*, with a short tail and pointed wings. WH: 17C. French, dim. of *Guillaume* William, in turn prob. of imit. orig.

guilloche *n.* an ornament of intertwisted or interlaced bands. WH: 19C. French *guillochis* guilloche, or *guilloche* the tool used in making it.

guillotine *n.* an apparatus for beheading a person at a stroke, consisting of an upright frame, down which a weighted blade slides in grooves. *Also v.t.* WH: 18C. French, from Joseph-Ignace *Guillotin*, 1738–1814, French physician, who recommended it for executions in 1789.

guilt *n.* the state of having committed a crime or offence. WH: pre-1200. Old English *gylt*, ult. of unknown orig.

guinea *n.* a gold coin formerly current in Great Britain, with the nominal value of 20s. (£1) until 1717, when this was fixed at 21s. WH: 17C. *Guinea*, a region bordering the W coast of Africa (now a state). Gold from Guinea was used for striking coins for the African trade, first in 1663.

guipure *n.* a lace without a ground or mesh, the pattern being held in place by threads. WH: 19C. French from *guiper* to cover with silk, wool, etc, from Germanic base meaning to wind round. Cp. WIPE.

guise *n.* external appearance. *Also v.t., v.i.* WH: 12–14C. Old French, from Frankish, from Germanic base represented also by WISE[2].

guitar *n.* a (usu. six-)stringed instrument, somewhat like the violin in shape, but larger, with frets stopped by one hand, the strings being plucked with the fingers of the other or with a plectrum. WH: 17C. Orig. from Spanish *guitarra*, later from French *guitare*, both ult. from Greek *kithara*. Cp. CITHARA, CITTERN, CITOLE, GITTERN, KIT[2], ZITHER.

guiver *n.* plausible talk. WH: 19C. Orig. unknown.

Gujarati *n.* the language of Gujarat in W India. *Also a.* WH: 19C. Hindi, from *Gujarāt*. See also -I[3].

gula *n.* a large plate on the underside of the head in some insects. WH: 14–15C. Latin throat.

gulag *n.* the system of forced labour camps in the former USSR, esp. as used to correct dissidents. WH: 20C. Russian acronym, from Glavnoe upravlenie ispravitel'no-trudovykh *lagerei* (Chief Administration for Corrective Labour Camps). The camps were first popularized by Aleksandr Solzhenitsyn's account, *The Gulag Archipelago* (Russian *Arkhipelag Gulag*) (1973–6).

gulch *n.* a deep ravine caused by the action of water. *Also v.t.* WH: 19C. ? From obs. *gulch* to swallow greedily, of imit. orig. Cp. GULP.

gulden *n.* any of various gold coins of Germany or the Netherlands. WH: 15C. Dutch and German, use as n. of a. corr. to obs. *gilden* (see GULDEN). Cp. GUILDER.

gules *n.* a red colour, represented on an engraved escutcheon by vertical lines. *Also a.* WH: 12–14C. Old French *goles* (Modern French *gueules*), pl. of *gule* throat (Modern French *gueule* mouth). Old

French *goles*, like related Medieval Latin *gulae* (pl.), was used as a term for pieces of red-dyed fur serving as a neck ornament.

gulf *n.* an inlet of the sea, deeper and narrower proportionately than a bay. Also *v.t.*, *v.i.* WH: 14–15C. Old French *golfe*, from Italian *golfo*, from Greek *kolpos* bosom, fold, gulf.

gull *n.* any long-winged, web-footed bird of the family Laridae, mostly marine in habitat. Also *v.t.* WH: 14–15C. Of Celtic orig. Cp. Welsh *gwylan*, Breton *gouelan*, *gwelan* (giving French *goéland*).

Gullah *n.* a member of a black people living on the coast of S Carolina and neighbouring islands. Also *a.* WH: 18C. Orig. uncertain. ? From *Angola*.

gullet *n.* the throat. WH: 14–15C. Old French *goulet*, dim. of *goule*, *gole*. See GULES, also -ET¹.

gullible *a.* credulous, easily deceived. WH: 19C. From *gull* (16C) to dupe, to trick (see GULL) + -IBLE.

gully¹ *n.* a channel or ravine worn by water. Also *v.t.* WH: 16C. French *goulet*. See GULLET.

gully² *n.* a large knife. WH: 16C. Orig. unknown.

†**gulosity** *n.* gluttony, greediness. WH: 15C. Late Latin *gulositas*, from *gulosus* gluttonous, from Latin GULA. See also -ITY.

gulp *v.t.* to swallow (down) eagerly or in large draughts. Also *v.i.*, *n.* WH: 14–15C. Prob. from Middle Dutch *gulpen* to swallow, to guzzle, ult. of imit. orig.

gum¹ *n.* the fleshy tissue around the roots of the teeth. WH: pre-1200. Old English *gōma*, from Germanic. Cp. German *Gaumen* roof of the mouth.

gum² *n.* a sticky substance which exudes from certain trees, and hardens, but is more or less soluble in water, used for sticking things together. Also *v.t.*, *v.i.* WH: 12–14C. Old French *gomme*, from Latin *gummi*, var. of *cummi*, from Greek *kommi*, from Egyptian *kemai*.

gumbo *n.* the okra, *Abelmoschus esculentus*. WH: 19C. Of African orig. Cp. Bantu (Angolan) *kingombo* (with pref. ki-) okra.

gumma *n.* a tumour with gummy contents, usu. due to syphilis. WH: 18C. Modern Latin, from Latin *gummi* GUM².

gumption *n.* common sense, practical shrewdness, acuteness, tact, capacity for getting on. WH: 18C. Orig. unknown.

gun *n.* a tubular weapon from which projectiles are shot by means of gunpowder or other explosive force, a cannon, musket, rifle or carbine. Also *v.t.*, *v.i.*, *a.* WH: 12–14C. From pet form (in Swedish dial. *Gunne*) of Scandinavian female name *Gunnhildr*, from *gunnr* + *hildr*, both meaning war.

gunge *n.* an unpleasant sticky substance, a dirty encrustation. WH: mid-20C. Orig. uncertain. ? Partly imit. Cp. GOO, GUNK.

gung-ho *a.* uninhibited, over-eager. WH: mid-20C. Chinese *gōnghé* to cooperate, from *gōng* work + *hé* to join, to combine. The term was adopted as a slogan by US marines in World War II.

gunk *n.* an unpleasant sticky or slimy substance, gunge. WH: mid-20C. Orig. uncertain. ? From GUNGE.

gunnel *n.* any small eel-like sea fish of the family Pholidae, esp. *Pholis gunnellus*, the butterfish, common on the British coasts and on the N American shores of the Atlantic. WH: 17C. Orig. unknown.

gunnera *n.* any plant of the genus *Gunnera*, a large-leaved ornamental herb. WH: 18C. Modern Latin, from J.E. *Gunnerus*, 1718–73, Norwegian botanist.

gunny *n.* a heavy coarse sackcloth, usu. of jute or hemp, of which bags etc. are made. WH: 18C. Marathi *gōnī*, from Sanskrit *goṇī* sack.

Gunter *n.* a Gunter's scale. WH: 17C. Edmund *Gunter*, 1581–1662, English mathematician.

gunwale *n.* the upper edge of a ship's side next to the bulwarks. WH: 14–15C. GUN + WALE. The gunwale is so called as it was originally used to support guns.

gunyah *n.* an Aboriginal bush hut, usu. built of twigs and bark. WH: 19C. Australian Aboriginal (Dharuk) *ganyi*.

guppy *n.* a small brightly-coloured W Indian freshwater fish, now a common aquarium fish. WH: early 20C. R.J.L. *Guppy*, 19C clergyman of Trinidad, who presented the first specimen to the British Museum.

gurdwara *n.* a Sikh temple. WH: early 20C. Panjabi *gurduārā*, from Sanskrit GURU + *dvāra* door.

gurgitation *n.* the movement of a liquid in a whirlpool or in boiling. WH: 16C. Late Latin *gurgitatus*, p.p. of *gurgitare* to engulf, from Latin *gurges*, *gurgis* whirlpool. See also -ATION.

gurgle *v.i.* to make a bubbling sound, as water poured from a bottle or running over a stony stream bottom. Also *v.t.*, *n.* WH: 14–15C. Prob. imit., or poss. from words such as Middle Low German *gorgelen*, German *gurgeln*, Medieval Latin *gurgulare*, all ult. from Latin *gurgulio* gullet. Cp. GARGOYLE, GLUG.

Gurkha *n.* a member of the dominant ethnic group in Nepal, of Hindu descent, expelled from Rajputana by the Muslim invasion. WH: 19C. *Gurkha*, a town in central Nepal, from Sanskrit *gorakṣa* cowherd, from *go* cow + *raks-* to protect, as epithet of local deity, Gorakhnāth.

gurn *v.i.* to pull a face. WH: 14–15C. Alt. of GRIN.

gurnard *n.* any sea fish of the family Triglidae, characterized by a large angular head, covered with bony plates, and three free pectoral rays. WH: 12–14C. Old French *gornart*, from *gronir*, var. of *grondir*, from Latin *grundire*, *grunnire* GRUNT. See also -ARD.

guru *n.* a Hindu spiritual teacher or guide. WH: 17C. Sanskrit elder, teacher.

gush *v.i.* to flow or rush out copiously or with violence. Also *v.t.*, *n.* WH: 14–15C. Prob. of imit. orig.

gusset *n.* a small triangular piece of cloth inserted in a dress to enlarge or strengthen some part. WH: 14–15C. Old French *gousset*, dim. of *gousse* pod, shell, of unknown orig.

gussy *v.t.* to smarten (up), to dress (up). WH: early 20C. ? From *Gussie*, pet form of male first name *Augustus*. See also -Y³.

gust *n.* a short but violent rush of wind, a squall. WH: 16C. Old Norse *gustr*, from base of *gjósa* to gush.

gustation *n.* the act of tasting. WH: 16C. French, or from Latin *gustatio*, *gustationis*, from *gustatus*, p.p. of *gustare* to taste. See also -ATION.

gusto *n.* zest, enjoyment, pleasure. WH: 17C. Italian, from Latin *gustus* taste. Cp. GOÛT, DISGUST.

gut *n.* the intestinal canal. Also *v.t.*, *a.* WH: pre-1200. Old English *guttas* (pl.), prob. from base of *gēotan* to pour.

gutta *n.* a drop. WH: 14–15C. Latin drop. Cp. GOUT.

gutta-percha *n.* a tough, waterproof rubber substance obtained from the latex of various Malaysian trees. WH: 19C. Malay *getah perca*, from *getah* gum + *perca* strips of cloth (which it resembles).

gutter *n.* a channel at the side of a street or a trough below eaves for carrying away water. Also *v.t.*, *v.i.* WH: 12–14C. Old French *gotiere* (Modern French *gouttière*), from Latin GUTTA. See also -ER².

guttural *a.* (of a sound, voice etc.) throaty, harsh, raucous. Also *n.* WH: 16C. French, or from Medieval Latin *gutturalis*, from *guttur* throat. See also -AL¹.

gutturo- *comb. form* of the throat. WH: Latin *guttur* throat. See also -O-.

guv *n.* used as a term of address to a man (usu. in authority). WH: 19C. Abbr. of GOVERNOR, representing pronun. of its first syl.

guy¹ *n.* a man, a fellow, a person. Also *v.t.*, *v.i.* WH: 19C. *Guy* Fawkes, 1570–1606, English Catholic, hanged for his part in the Gunpowder Plot.

guy² *n.* a rope, chain etc., to steady a load in hoisting or to act as a stay. Also *v.t.* WH: 14–15C. Old French *guie* guide, from *guier* (see GUIDE), from Germanic. The sense of rope, chain may come direct from Germanic. Cp. Dutch *gei* brail, *geiblok* pulley, German *Geitau* clewline.

guzzle *v.i.* to drink or eat greedily. Also *v.t.*, *n.* WH: 16C. ? Old French *gosillier* to chatter, to vomit, from Old French *gosier* throat, from Late Latin *geusiae* cheeks.

gwyniad *n.* a freshwater salmonoid fish, *Coregonus pennantii*, found in Lake Bala, Wales and the Lake District. WH: 17C. Welsh, from *gwyn* white.

gybe *v.i.* to take the wind on the other quarter (of a sailing boat). Also *v.t.*, *n.* WH: 17C. Obs. Dutch *gijben* (now *gijpen*). Cp. JIB².

gym *n.* a gymnasium. WH: 19C. Abbr. of GYMNASIUM.

gymkhana *n.* a meeting for equestrian sports and games, orig. a place for athletic sports. WH: 19C. Alt. (by assim. to GYMNASIUM) of Urdu *gendḵānah* racket court, from Hindi *gẽd* ball + Persian *ḵānah* house.

gymnasium *n.* a building or room where gymnastics, indoor sports etc. are done. WH: 16C. Latin, from Greek *gumnasion*, from *gumnazein* to exercise naked, from *gumnos* naked.

gymnastics *n.* a course of instruction, discipline or exercise for the development of body or mind. WH: 16C. Latin *gumnasticus*, from Greek *gumnastikos*, from *gumnazein* + -S[1]. See GYMNASIUM, also -IC.

gymno- *comb. form* naked, destitute of protective covering. WH: Greek *gumnos* naked. See also -O-.

gymnosophist *n.* a member of an ancient Hindu sect of philosophic hermits who wore little or no clothing and lived a life of contemplation and asceticism. WH: 14–15C. French *gymnosophiste*, from Latin *gymnosophistae* (pl.), from Greek *gumnosophistai* (pl.), from *gumnos* GYMNO- + *sophistēs* sophist (SOPHISM).

gymnosperm *n.* any one of a class of plants having naked seeds, such as the pine. WH: 19C. Modern Latin *gymnospermus*, from Greek *gumnospermos*, from *gumnos* GYMNO- + *sperma* seed.

gynaeco- *comb. form* of or relating to women. WH: Greek *gunaiko-*, from *gunē*, *gunaikos* woman, female. See also -O-.

gynaecocracy *n.* government by women or a woman. WH: 17C. French *gynécocratie*, or from Modern Latin *gynaecocratia*, from Greek *gunaikokratia*. See GYNAECO-, -CRACY.

gynaecology *n.* the science dealing with the functions and diseases of women and girls. WH: 19C. GYNAECO- + -O- + -LOGY.

gynaecomastia *n.* the enlargement of a man's breasts usu. due to hormone imbalance or hormone therapy. WH: 19C. GYNAECO- + Greek *mastos* breast. See also -IA.

gynandrous *a.* (of a plant) having the stamens and pistil together in a single column. WH: 19C. Greek *gunandros* of doubtful sex, from *gunē* woman, female + -ANDROUS. Cp. *androgynous* (ANDROGYNE).

gyniolatry *n.* excessive devotion to women. WH: 19C. Greek *gunē* woman, female + -O- + -LATRY.

gyno- *comb. form* distinctively feminine. WH: Greek *gunē* woman, female. See also -O-. Rel. to QUEEN.

gynoecium *n.* the female organs in a plant. WH: 19C. Modern Latin, from GYNO- + Greek *oikos* house.

gynophobia *n.* an abnormal fear of women. WH: 19C. GYNO- + *-phobia* (-PHOBE).

gynophore *n.* a stalk supporting an ovary above the level of other parts of the flower, as in the passion flower. WH: 19C. GYNO- + -PHORE.

-gynous *comb. form* of or relating to women, as in *androgynous*, *misogynous*. WH: Modern Latin *-gynus*, from Greek *-gunos*. See GYNO-, also -OUS.

gyp[1] *n.* a male servant in some colleges at Cambridge and Durham Universities. WH: 18C. ? Abbr. of obs. *gippo* scullion, from obs. French *jupeau*, earlier *jupel*. Cp. JUPON. A gyp is so named from the short tunic that he formerly wore.

gyp[2] *v.t.* to cheat, swindle. *Also n.* WH: 19C. Orig. unknown.

gyp[3] *n.* pain. WH: 19C. Appar. contr. of *gee-up* (GEE[1]).

gypsophila *n.* any plant of the genus *Gypsophila*, a hardy perennial with small white and pink flowers, related to the pinks. WH: 18C. Modern Latin, from Greek *gupsos* chalk, gypsum + *-philos* -loving. The plant is so named because some species grow on alkaline soils.

gypsum *n.* a mineral consisting of hydrous sulphate of lime, used to make plaster, paint, glass, fertilizer etc. *Also v.t.* WH: 14–15C. Latin, from Greek *gupsos* chalk, gypsum.

gypsy *n.* a member of a nomad people (calling themselves Romany), prob. of Hindu extraction, dark in complexion and hair. *Also v.i.* WH: 16C. Shortening of EGYPTIAN, prob. influ. in spelling by Latin *Aegyptius*. Cp. GITANO. Gypsies were originally thought to have come from Egypt. Cp. BOHEMIAN.

gyrate *v.i.* to rotate, revolve, whirl, in either a circle or a spiral. *Also a.* WH: 19C. Late Latin *gyratus*, p.p. of *gyrare*, from Latin *gyrus*. See GYRUS, also -ATE[3].

gyrfalcon *n.* a large and powerful falcon of northern regions, *Falco rusticolus*. WH: 12–14C. Old French *gerfaucon* (Modern French *gerfaut*), from Frankish, from Germanic. The first element probably means spear, from Old High German *gēr*, Old English *gār*. The second is FALCON. The spelling with *gyr-* arose by (false) association with Latin *gyrare* GYRATE.

gyro *n.* a gyroscope. WH: early 20C. Abbr. of GYROSCOPE.

gyro- *comb. form* round, curved. WH: Greek *guros* ring, circle. See also -O-.

gyrocompass *n.* a navigating compass consisting of an electrically driven gyroscope, the axle of which orientates the sensitive element. WH: early 20C. GYROSCOPE + COMPASS.

gyromagnetic *a.* of or caused by the magnetic and mechanical properties resulting from the spin of a rotating charged particle. WH: early 20C. GYRO- + *magnetic* (MAGNET).

gyromancy *n.* divination performed by walking round in a circle or ring until one falls from dizziness. WH: 16C. Old French *gyromancie*. See GYRO-, -MANCY.

gyron *n.* a triangular charge formed by two lines meeting at the fesse-point. WH: 16C. Old French *giron* gusset. See GORE[3].

gyropilot *n.* a gyrocompass used in ships, aircraft etc. for automatic steering. WH: early 20C. GYROCOMPASS + PILOT.

gyroplane *n.* an aeroplane deriving its lift from the reaction of the air on freely rotating rotors in a horizontal plane, an autogiro. WH: early 20C. GYRO- + PLANE[4].

gyroscope *n.* a heavy flywheel rotated (usu. electrically) at very high speed and supported on an axis at right angles to the plane of the wheel, used as a controlling or stabilizing device or as a compass in ships, aeroplanes etc. WH: 19C. French. See GYRO-, -SCOPE. The gyroscope was so named in 1852 by the French physicist J.B.L. Foucault, its inventor.

gyrostabilizer *n.* a gyroscopic device for steadying the roll of a vessel. WH: early 20C. GYRO- + *stabilizer* (STABLE[1]).

gyrostat *n.* Lord Kelvin's modification of the gyroscope, for illustrating the dynamics of rotating bodies. WH: 19C. GYRO- + -STAT.

gyrus *n.* a fold, a ridge between two grooves, esp. of the brain. WH: 19C. Latin, from Greek *guros* ring, circle.

gyte[1] *a.* mad, crazy. WH: 18C. Orig. unknown.

gyte[2] *n.* a child. WH: 19C. ? Alt. of GET[2]. Cp. GIT.

gytrash *n.* a ghost, spectre, apparition. WH: 19C. Orig. unknown.

gyttja *n.* a usu. black organic sediment deposited in a lake. WH: 19C. Swedish mud, ooze.

gyve *n.* a fetter, shackle. *Also v.t.* WH: 12–14C. Orig. unknown.

ha *int.* used to express surprise, joy, suspicion or other sudden emotion. *Also v.i.* WH: Natural exclamation. Cp. AH, AHA, HO.

haaf *n.* a deep-sea fishing ground (off Orkney and Shetland). WH: 18C. Old Norse *haf* sea, ocean.

haar *n.* a wet mist, esp. a sea-fog. WH: 17C. ? Old Norse *hárr* hoar, hoary. Cp. HOAR.

habanera *n.* a Cuban dance in slow duple time. WH: 19C. Spanish short for *danza habanera* Havanan dance, fem. of *habanero* of Havana, the capital of Cuba.

habdabs *n.pl.* a feeling of anxiety, apprehension or irritation. WH: mid-20C. Orig. unknown. Cp. HEEBIE-JEEBIES.

habeas corpus *n.* a writ to produce a prisoner before a court, with details of the day and cause of the arrest and detention, in order that the justice of this may be determined. WH: 14–15C. Latin thou (shalt) have the body, 2nd pers. sing. pres. subj. of *habere* to have + acc. sing. of *corpus* body. The fuller version of the formula is *habeas corpus ad subiiciendum* thou (shalt) have the body to be subjected (to examination).

haberdasher *n.* a seller of small articles of apparel, as ribbons, laces, silks etc. WH: 12–14C. Prob. from an alt. of Anglo-French *hapertas* small wares, petty merchandise, of unknown orig., ? the name of a fabric. See also -ER[1]. The altered form has not been recorded but cp. recorded Anglo-Latin *habardasshator*. The original sense was a dealer in household articles, then from the 16C a dealer in hats and caps. The current sense followed in the 17C.

habergeon *n.* a sleeveless coat of mail or armour to protect the neck and breast. WH: 12–14C. Old French *haubergeon*, from *hauberc* (Modern French *haubert*). See HAUBERK, also -OON.

habiliment *n.* an item of clothing. WH: 14–15C. Old French *abillement* (Modern French *habillement*), from *habiller* to make fit, to fit out (hence, by assoc. with *habit*), to clothe, to dress, from *habile* suitable, from Latin *habilis* (which gave ABLE). See also -MENT.

habilitate *v.i.* to become qualified (for). *Also v.t.* WH: 17C. Medieval Latin *habilitatus*, p.p. of *habilitare*, from *habilitas* ABILITY. See also -ATE[3].

habit *n.* a permanent tendency to perform certain actions. *Also v.t.* WH: 12–14C. Old French *abit* (Modern French *habit*), from Latin *habitus*, p.p. of *habere* to have, to hold. The sense bearing, demeanour, posture became obsolete in the 17C.

habitable *a.* that may be lived in or inhabited. WH: 14–15C. Old French *abitable* (Modern French *habitable*), from Latin *habitabilis*, from *habitare* to have possession of, to inhabit, from *habitus* (see HABIT), also -ABLE.

habitat *n.* the natural home or locality of an animal or plant. WH: 18C. Latin, lit. it inhabits, 3rd pers. sing. pres. ind. of *habitare*. See HABITABLE. The term evolved from the first word of Latin descriptions in Floras and Faunas, such as (of the primrose): *Habitat in silvis sepibus et ericetis ubique* It inhabits woods, hedges and heaths everywhere (1762).

habitual *a.* formed or acquired by habit. WH: 14–15C. Medieval Latin *habitualis*, from *habitus*. See HABIT, also -AL[1].

habitué *n.* a person who habitually frequents a place, esp. a place of amusement. WH: 19C. French, p.p. of *habituer*, from Latin *habituare*, from *habitus*. See HABIT.

háček *n.* a diacritical mark (ˇ) placed above a letter to modify its pronunciation, esp. in Slavonic languages. WH: mid-20C. Czech, dim. of *hák* hook.

hachure *n.* any one of a series of short lines employed to represent half-tints and shadows, and on maps to denote hill slopes. *Also v.t.* WH: 19C. French, from *hacher* HATCH[3]. See also -URE.

hacienda *n.* in Spain, Latin America etc., an estate, a farm or plantation, an establishment in the country for stock-raising etc.,

esp. with a residence for the proprietor. WH: 18C. Spanish, from Latin *facienda* things to be done, from *facere* to do.

hack[1] *v.t.* to cut irregularly or into small pieces. *Also v.i., n.* WH: pre-1200. Old English *haccian* to cut in pieces, ult. from Germanic deriv. of imit. base. Cp. Old English *hæccan* in same sense.

hack[2] *n.* a hackney, a horse for hire. *Also v.t., v.i., a.* WH: 12–14C. Abbr. of HACKNEY.

hack[3] *n.* a rack or grated frame, a hatch. *Also v.t.* WH: 15C. Var. of HATCH[1].

hackamore *n.* a rope with a loop used instead of a bit on a horse unused to a bridle. WH: 19C. ? Spanish *jaquima*, earlier *xaquima* halter.

hackberry *n.* a N American tree of the genus *Celtis*, related to the elms. WH: 18C. Var. of HAGBERRY.

hackbut *n.* a harquebus. WH: 16C. French *haquebut*, alt. of *haquebusche*, from Middle Dutch *hakebus* (Dutch *haakbus*) and Middle Low German *hakebusse*, from *hake* hook + *busse* gun, firearm (cp. BLUNDERBUSS). Cp. HARQUEBUS.

hackery *n.* in the Indian subcontinent, a simple two-wheeled car, drawn by bullocks. WH: 17C. Hindi *chakṛā* two-wheeled cart.

hackle[1] *n.* a long shining feather on or from a cock's neck. *Also v.t.* WH: 14–15C. Var. of HATCHEL. The sense of flax comb arose in the 15C, originally in the form HECKLE. The application of the word in the plural to erectile hairs on a dog's back arose in the 19C.

hackle[2] *v.t.* to hack, to mangle. WH: 16C. Dim. or freq. of HACK[1]. See also -LE[4]. Cp. HAGGLE.

hackney *n.* a horse kept for riding or driving. *Also v.t.* WH: 12–14C. Anglo-French *hakeney*, probably from *Hackney* (formerly *Hakenei*) in E London, where horses were pastured. The sense passed to the vehicle plying for hire in the 17C. It remains current in *hackney carriage*, the official term for a taxi.

haddock *n.* a sea fish, *Melanogrammus aeglefinus*, allied to the cod and fished for food. WH: 12–14C. Anglo-French *hadoc*, from Old French *hadot*, of unknown orig.

hade *n.* the inclination of a fault or vein from the vertical, complementary to the dip. *Also v.i.* WH: 16C. Orig. unknown.

Hades *n.* in Greek mythology, the lower world, the abode of the spirits of the dead. WH: 16C. Greek *haidēs* (orig. *aidēs*), of unknown orig. In biblical Greek the word translates Hebrew *šĕ'ôl* SHEOL.

Hadith *n.* tradition, esp. the body of tradition relating to the sayings and doings of Muhammad. WH: 18C. Arabic *ḥadīt* statement, tradition.

hadji *n.* (a title conferred on) a Muslim who has performed the pilgrimage to Mecca. WH: 17C. Persian, from Turkish *ḥājjī* pilgrim, from Arabic *al-ḥajj* the pilgrimage.

hadron *n.* an elementary particle taking part in strong nuclear interactions. WH: mid-20C. Greek *hadros* bulky + -ON.

hadrosaur *n.* a gigantic fossil saurian of the family Hadrosauridae, from the Cretaceous strata of N America. WH: 19C. Modern Latin *Hadrosaurus* genus name, from Greek *hadros* thick, stout + *sauros* lizard.

hae *v.t.* to have. WH: 12–14C. Alt. of HAVE.

haecceity *n.* the quality of being a particular thing, individuality. WH: 17C. Medieval Latin *haeccitas*, from Latin *haec*, fem. of *hic* this + -*itas* -ITY. Cp. QUIDDITY.

haem *n.* a red organic compound containing iron, found in haemoglobin. WH: early 20C. Back-formation from *haemoglobin* (see HAEMO-).

haema- *comb. form* blood. WH: Greek *haima* blood. Cp. HAEMO-.

haemal *a.* of or relating to the blood. WH: 19C. Greek *haima* blood + -AL[1].

haematemesis *n.* a vomiting of blood. WH: 19C. HAEMATO- + Greek *emesis* vomiting.

haematic *a.* of or relating to the blood. *Also n.* WH: 19C. Greek *haimatikos*, from *haima, haimatos* blood. See also -IC.

haematin *n.* an amorphous substance associated with haemoglobin in the blood. WH: 19C. Greek *haima, haematos* blood + -IN¹.

haematite *n.* a native sesquioxide of iron, occurring in two forms, red and brown, a valuable iron ore. WH: 14–15C. Latin *haematites*, from Greek *haimatītēs* (*lithos*) bloodlike (stone), from *haima, haimatos* blood. See also -ITE¹.

haemato- *comb. form* blood. WH: Greek *haima, haematos* blood. See also -O-.

haematuria *n.* the presence of blood in the urine. WH: 19C. HAEMATO- + -URIA.

haemo- *comb. form* blood. WH: Greek *haima* blood + -O-.

haemoglobin *n.* the colouring matter of the red corpuscles of the blood. WH: 19C. Abbr. of *haematoglobulin*, from HAEMATO- + *globulin*, from Latin *globulus* (GLOBULE) + -IN¹.

haemorrhage *n.* an abnormal discharge of blood from the heart, arteries, veins or capillaries. *Also v.i., v.t.* WH: 17C. Alt. of obs. *haemorrhagy*, from Old French *emorogie* (Modern French *hémorrhagie*), from Latin *haemorrhagia*, from Greek *haimorrhagia*, from *haima* blood + base of *rhēgnunai* to break, to burst.

haemorrhoids *n.pl.* swollen veins around the anus. WH: 14–15C. Old French *emeroyde*, later *hémorrhoides*, from Latin *haemorrhoida*, from Greek *haimorrhois, haemorrhoidos* discharging blood, from *haemorrhoides phlebes* veins discharging blood, bleeding piles, from *haimorrhoos*, from *haima* blood + *rhoos* stream, a flowing, from *rhein* to flow. Cp. EMERODS.

haeremai *int.* welcome! WH: 18C. Maori, lit. come hither.

hafiz *n.* (a Muslim title for) a person knowing the Koran by heart. WH: 17C. Persian, from Arabic *ḥāfiẓ*, pres.p. of *ḥāfiẓa* to guard, to know by heart.

hafnium *n.* a metallic element occurring in zirconium ores, symbol Hf, at. no. 72. WH: early 20C. *Hafnia*, Latinized form of Danish *Havn* harbour, orig. name of Copenhagen, capital of Denmark. See also -IUM. The element is so named from the city in which it was discovered in 1923.

haft *n.* a handle, esp. of a dagger, knife or tool. *Also v.t.* WH: pre-1200. Old English *hæft*, from Germanic base of HEAVE.

hag¹ *n.* a witch. *Also v.t.* WH: 12–14C. ? Abbr. of Old English *hægtesse* fury, witch, from Germanic, of unknown orig. Cp. HEX¹.

hag² *n.* a break or soft place in a bog. *Also v.t., v.i.* WH: 12–14C. Old Norse *hogg* gap, breach. Cp. HEDGE. A hag was originally a break or gap in a crag or cliff. The current sense dates from the 17C.

hagberry *n.* the bird cherry, *Prunus padus.* WH: 16C. Of Scandinavian orig. Cp. Danish *hægebær*, Norwegian *heggebær*, with first element rel. to HEDGE. Cp. HACKBERRY.

Haggadah *n.* the legendary part of the Talmud. WH: 18C. Hebrew *Haggāḏāh* tale, from biblical Hebrew *higgīḏ* to declare, to tell.

haggard¹ *a.* anxious, care-worn or gaunt from fatigue, trouble etc. *Also n.* WH: 16C. Old French *hagard*, ? from Germanic word meaning hedge, bush. Later influ. by HAG¹. The original sense was (of a hawk) wild, untamed. The current sense evolved in the 17C.

haggard² *n.* a stack-yard. WH: 12–14C. Old Norse *heygarthr*, from *hey* hay + *garthr* GARTH.

haggis *n.* a Scottish dish traditionally made of liver, lights, heart etc. minced with onions, suet, oatmeal etc., enclosed in a sheep's stomach. WH: 14–15C. Prob. from Scottish *hag* to hack, to hew, from Old Norse *hoggva* to strike with a sharp weapon. The reference would be to the minced contents.

haggle *v.i.* to wrangle, esp. over a bargain. *Also v.t., n.* WH: 16C. Scottish *hag* (see HAGGIS) + -LE⁴. Cp. HACKLE². The original sense was to hack, to mangle. The sense to wrangle evolved in the 17C.

hagiarchy *n.* government by priests. WH: 19C. HAGIO- + -ARCHY.

hagio- *comb. form* of or relating to saints or to holy things. WH: Greek *hagios* holy, saintly. See also -O-.

hagiocracy *n.* government by priests or holy persons. WH: 19C. HAGIO- + -CRACY.

hagiography *n.* the writing of the biography of saints. WH: 19C. HAGIO- + -GRAPHY.

hagiolatry *n.* the worship of saints. WH: 19C. HAGIO- + -LATRY.

hagiology *n.* literature relating to the lives and legends of saints. WH: 19C. HAGIO- + -LOGY.

hagioscope *n.* an oblique opening in the wall of a church to enable people in the transept or aisles to see the high altar. WH: 19C. HAGIO- + -SCOPE. Cp. SQUINT.

ha-ha *n.* a hedge, fence or wall sunk between slopes. WH: 18C. French, ? from the cry of surprise of one coming across it. See HA. According to some, the word is from a reduplication of French *haie* hedge, or from a hunting cry to rally hounds over the obstacle.

hahnium *n.* the name formerly proposed by the American Chemical Society for DUBNIUM. WH: late 20C. Otto *Hahn*, 1879–1968, German physicist + -IUM.

Haida *n.* a member of a N American Indian people of British Columbia. *Also a.* WH: 19C. Haida, people.

haiduk *n.* a member of a class of mercenaries in Hungary who were granted lands and the rank of nobles in 1605. WH: 17C. Czech, Polish and Serbo-Croat *hajduk*, from Hungarian *hajdú* robber, pl. *hajdúk.*

haik *n.* a strip of woollen or cotton cloth worn as an upper garment by Arabs over the head and body. WH: 18C. Arabic *ḥā'ik.*

haiku *n.* a Japanese verse of 17 syllables, in 3 parts. WH: 19C. Japanese, abbr. of *haikai no ku* unserious verse.

hail¹ *n.* frozen rain or particles of frozen vapour falling in showers. *Also v.i., v.t.* WH: pre-1200. Old English *hagol, hægl*, from Germanic, rel. to Greek *kakhlēx* pebble.

hail² *v.t.* to call or signal to (a person, taxi etc.) from a distance. *Also v.i., int., n.* WH: 12–14C. Var. of obs. *hale* health, safety, from Old Norse *heill* health, good luck, assim. to HALE¹. Cp. WASSAIL. The original sense was to salute or greet someone with a cry of 'hail!'. The sense to come from a place emerged in the 19C.

hair *n.* a filament composed of a tube of horny, fibrous substance, with a central medulla enclosing pigment cells, growing from the skin of an animal. WH: pre-1200. Old English *hær, hēr*, ult. rel. to Greek *keras* horn (cp. KERATIN) and so to HORN.

haka *n.* a ceremonial Maori dance. WH: 19C. Maori.

hake¹ *n.* a fish belonging to the genus *Merluccius*, allied to the cod. *Also v.i.* WH: 12–14C. ? Old English *haca* hook. Cp. Old English *hacod* pike.

hake² *n.* a wooden frame for drying. WH: 14–15C. Var. of HACK³.

hakenkreuz *n.* the swastika, the Nazi symbol. WH: mid-20C. German, from *Haken* hook + *Kreuz* cross.

hakim¹ *n.* (in Muslim countries) a physician. WH: 17C. Arabic *ḥakīm* wise man, philosopher, physician. Cp. HAKIM².

hakim² *n.* (in Muslim countries) a governor. WH: 17C. Arabic *ḥakīm* ruler, governor, judge, from *ḥakama* to pass judgement.

Halachah *n.* a body of traditional laws, supposed to be of Mosaic origin, included in the Mishna. WH: 19C. Hebrew *hălāḵāh* law.

halal *n.* meat which is prepared in accordance with Muslim law. *Also v.t., a.* WH: 19C. Arabic *ḥalāl* according to religious law.

halation *n.* a blurring in a photographic negative caused by the reflection of a strong light from the back of the plate during exposure. WH: 19C. HALO + -ATION.

halberd *n.* a weapon consisting of a combination of spear and battleaxe, mounted on a pole 5 to 7 ft. (1.5 to 2m) in length. WH: 15C. French *hallebarde*, from Italian *alabarda*, from Middle High German *helmbarde*, from *helm* handle, HELM¹ + *barde* hatchet.

halcyon *n.* a tropical (esp. Australasian) kingfisher of the genus *Halcyon. Also a.* WH: 14–15C. Latin, from Greek *alkuōn* kingfisher. Greek *alkuōn* had a variant form *halkuōn*, as if from *hals* sea + *kuōn* conceiving. Hence the sense of the English word for a bird said to make a nest floating on the sea at the time of the winter solstice and to charm the wind and waves so that the sea was calm for it to breed.

hale¹ *a.* (esp. of an elderly man) sound and vigorous, robust. WH: pre-1200. N dial. representation of Old English *hāl* WHOLE. Cp. HAIL².

hale² *v.t.* to drag, to draw violently. WH: 12–14C. Old French *haler*, from Old Norse *hala*, from Germanic. Cp. German *holen* to fetch. Rel. to HAUL.

haler *n.* a unit of currency of the Czech Republic. WH: mid-20C. Czech *haléř*, from Middle High German *haller*, from (*Schwäbisch*) *Hall*, town in Germany where the *heller* was first minted. See also -ER¹.

half *n.* either of two equal parts into which a thing or quantity is or may be divided. *Also a., adv., v.t.* WH: pre-1200. Old English *healf*, from Germanic, with basic sense side. The original sense (to the 16C) was one or other of two sides of an object, its right or left side.

halibut *n.* a large flat fish of the N Atlantic, *Hippoglossus hippoglossus*, sometimes weighing from 300 to 400 lb. (135–180 kg), used for food. WH: 14–15C. Alt. of HOLY + BUTT⁵. The fish is so called because it was eaten on holy days.

halide *n.* a binary salt of halogen. WH: 19C. HALOGEN + -IDE.

halieutic *a.* of or relating to fishing. *Also n.* WH: 17C. Latin *halieuticus*, from Greek *halieutikos*, from *halieutēs* fisher. See also -IC.

haliotis *n.* any gastropod belonging to the genus *Haliotis*, having a shell lined with mother-of-pearl. WH: 18C. Greek *hals*, *hali-* sea + *ous*, *ōtos* ear.

halite *n.* rock salt. WH: 19C. Greek *hals* salt + -ITE¹.

halitosis *n.* offensive breath. WH: 19C. Latin *halitus* breath, from *halare* to breathe + -OSIS.

hall *n.* a large room, esp. one in which public meetings or concerts are held, the large public room in a palace, castle etc. WH: pre-1200. Old English, from Germanic base meaning to cover, to conceal. Cp. HELL. The sense large residence dates from the beginning. The sense entrance passage of a house evolved in the 17C.

hallmark *n.* an official stamp stamped by the Goldsmiths' Company and Government assay offices on gold and silver articles to guarantee the standard. *Also v.t.* WH: 18C. HALL + MARK¹. The stamp is so called because it is used at Goldsmiths' *Hall* in London.

halloo *v.i.* to cry, to call attention. *Also v.t., n., int.* WH: 16C. Prob. var. of HOLLO. Cp. HELLO.

hallow *v.t.* to make sacred or worthy of reverence. *Also n.* WH: pre-1200. Old English *hālgian*, from Germanic base of HOLY.

Hallstatt *a.* denoting the first period of the Iron Age, typified by weapons found in the necropolis of Hallstatt which illustrate the transition from the use of bronze to that of iron. WH: 19C. *Hallstatt*, a village in Upper Austria, the site of a prehistoric burial ground. More than 2000 graves were found at Hallstatt between 1846 and 1899.

hallucinate *v.i.* to have hallucinations. *Also v.t.* WH: 17C. Latin *hallucinatus*, p.p. of *hallucinari*, late form of *alucinari*, to wander in thought or speech, from Greek *alussein* to be distraught. See also -ATE³.

hallux *n.* the big toe. WH: 19C. Modern Latin, alt. of Medieval Latin *allex*, from Latin *hallus*.

halma *n.* a game for two or four played on a board with 256 squares. WH: 19C. Greek leap. Pieces advance on the board by moving over ('leaping') other pieces. The game was invented in *c.*1880.

halo *n.* a luminous circle round the sun or moon caused by the refraction of light through mist. *Also v.t., v.i.* WH: 16C. Medieval Latin, from Latin *halos*, from Greek *halōs* threshing floor, disc of the sun or moon.

halo- *comb. form* of or relating to salt or the sea. WH: Greek *hals*, *halos* salt, sea. See also -O-.

halogen *n.* an element or other radical which by combination with a metal forms a salt (fluorine, chlorine, bromine, iodine and astatine). WH: 19C. Greek *hals*, *halos* salt + -GEN.

haloid *a.* resembling common salt. *Also n.* WH: 19C. HALO- + -OID.

halon *n.* any of various halogens, used in fire extinguishers. WH: mid-20C. HALOGEN + -ON.

haloperidol *n.* a drug used in the treatment of mania and other psychotic disorders. WH: late 20C. HALOGEN + PIPERIDINE + -OL.

halophyte *n.* a plant suited to growing in salty conditions. WH: 19C. HALO- + -PHYTE.

halothane *n.* a volatile liquid used as a general anaesthetic. WH: mid-20C. HALOGEN + ETHANE.

halt¹ *n.* a stop or interruption in activity or motion. *Also v.i., v.t.* WH: 16C. From phr. *to make halt*, translating German *halt machen* or Spanish *alto hacer*. In the German phrase *halt* was probably originally based on the imperative, meaning stop, stand still, of *halten* HOLD¹.

halt² †*a.* limping, lame, crippled. *Also v.i., n.* WH: pre-1200. Old English, from Germanic base of unknown orig.

halter *n.* a headstall and strap or rope by which an animal is fastened. *Also v.t.* WH: pre-1200. Old English *hælfter*, from Germanic base represented also by HELVE. Not rel. to HALT¹.

haltere *n.* either of two modified hind wings on dipterous insects, used for maintaining balance in flight. WH: 16C. Greek *halterēs* (pl.), from *hallesthai* to jump. The original sense is a weight held in the hand to give an impetus in jumping. The entomological sense dates from the 19C.

halva *n.* a sweet made from sesame seeds and honey, typically from the E Mediterranean. WH: 17C. Yiddish, also mod. Hebrew *ḥalbāh*, mod. Greek *khalbas*, Turkish *helva* etc., from Arabic and Persian *ḥalwā* sweetmeat.

halve *v.t.* to divide into two equal parts. WH: 12–14C. HALF.

halyard *n.* a rope or tackle for hoisting or lowering yards, sails or flags. WH: 14–15C. HALE² + -IER, alt. (18C) by assoc. with YARD¹. Cp. LANYARD.

ham¹ *n.* the hind part of the thigh. *Also v.t., v.i.* WH: pre-1200. Old English, from a Germanic v. meaning to be crooked. The original sense was hollow or bend of the knee. The sense back of the thigh evolved in the 15C.

ham² *n.* a village, a town (now only in place names, as *Egham*, *Horsham*). WH: 19C. Old English *hām* HOME¹. Many place names ending *-ham*, as *Buckingham*, *Cheltenham*, are in fact from Old English *hamm* land in a river bend, land hemmed in by higher ground. Cp. HEM¹.

hamadryad *n.* in Greek and Roman mythology, a dryad or wood nymph, who lived and died with the tree in which she lived. WH: 14–15C. Latin *Hamadryas*, from Greek *Hamadruas*, from *hama* together + *drus* tree. Cp. DRYAD.

hamadryas *n.* an Arabian and NE African baboon, *Papio hamadryas*. WH: 19C. HAMADRYAD.

hamamelis *n.* a shrub, such as the witch hazel, belonging to the genus *Hamamelis*. WH: 18C. Modern Latin, from Greek *hamamēlis* medlar, lit. together with fruit, from *hama* with + *mēlon* apple, fruit.

hamartia *n.* the tragic flaw which destroys the principal character in a Greek tragedy. WH: 18C. Greek fault, failure, guilt.

hamartiology *n.* the doctrine of sin. WH: 19C. Greek HAMARTIA + -O- + -LOGY.

hamate *a.* hook-shaped. WH: 18C. Latin *hamatus* hooked, from *hamus* hook. See also -ATE².

hamba *int.* go away. WH: 19C. Nguni, imper. of *ukuhamba* to go.

hamburger *n.* a flat cake of minced beef, fried or grilled and often served in a bun. WH: 19C. German of *Hamburg*, a city in N Germany. Cp. BURGER. A hamburger was originally a type of German sausage, named after the city where it was first made.

hame¹ *n.* either of the pair of curved bars of wood or metal fixed on the collar of a draught horse, to which the traces are connected. WH: 12–14C. Middle Dutch (cp. Dutch *haam*), from Germanic, of unknown orig.

hame² *n.* home. WH: 12–14C. Var. of HOME¹.

hamesucken *n.* the crime or felony of assaulting someone in their own house. WH: pre-1200. Old English *hāmsōcn*, from *hām* home, dwelling + *sōcn* seeking, attack, assault. Cp. SOC.

Hamite *n.* a member of a group of peoples in Egypt and N Africa, supposedly descended from Noah's son Ham. WH: 17C. *Ham* (formerly *Cham*), the second son of Noah (Gen. vi.10) + -ITE¹. Cp. SEMITE.

hamlet *n.* a small village, a little cluster of houses in the country. WH: 12–14C. Old French *hamelet*, dim. of *hamel* (Modern French *hameau*), itself dim. of *ham* village. See also -EL, -ET¹. Cp. HAM².

hammal *n.* an Oriental porter. WH: 18C. Arabic *ḥammāl*, from *ḥamala* to carry.

hammam *n.* an Oriental bathhouse. WH: 17C. Turkish, from Arabic *ḥammām* bath, from *ḥamma* to heat.

hammer *n.* a tool for driving nails, beating metals etc., consisting of a head, usu. of steel, fixed at right angles on a handle. *Also v.t., v.i.* WH: pre-1200. Old English *hamor*, *hamer*, from Germanic. Cp. Old Norse *hamarr* hammer, back of an axe, crag.

hammock *n.* a swinging or suspended bed made of canvas or netting, and hung by hooks from a roof, ceiling, tree etc. WH: 16C. Spanish *hamaca*, from Taino *hamaka*, with ending assim. to -OCK.

hamper[1] *n.* a large wickerwork basket, with a cover. *Also v.t.* WH: 12–14C. Contr. of obs. *hanaper* basket for a *hanap* drinking vessel, wine cup, from Old French, from Frankish. Cp. Old English *hnæp*, German *Napf* bowl. See also -ER[5]. A hamper was originally a large case or basket in general.

hamper[2] *v.t.* to impede the movement or free action of. *Also n.* WH: 14–15C. Of uncertain orig. Cp. German *hemmen* to restrain, also -ER[5].

hamshackle *v.t.* to fasten the head of (an ox, horse etc.) to one of its forelegs. WH: 19C. Orig. uncertain. 1st element prob. rel. to HAMPER[2]. 2nd element is SHACKLE.

hamster *n.* a ratlike rodent of the subfamily Cricetinae, with large cheek pouches in which it carries grain for food during hibernation. WH: 17C. German, from Old High German *hamustro*, rel. to *hamustra* corn weevil.

hamstring *n.* any of the tendons of the thigh muscle behind the knee. *Also v.t.* WH: 16C. HAM[1] + STRING.

hamulus *n.* a hooklike process. WH: 18C. Latin, dim. of *hamus* hook. See also -ULE.

hamza *n.* the sign used for a glottal stop in Arabic script. WH: 19C. Arabic, lit. compression (i.e. of the larynx).

Han *n.* a member of one of the peoples indigenous to China, as distinct from Manchus, Mongols etc. WH: 18C. Chinese *Hàn*.

hance *n.* the haunch of an arch. WH: 16C. Anglo-French, alt. of Old French *hauce* (Modern French *hausse*), from *haucer* (Modern French *hausser*), from base seen also in ENHANCE.

hand *n.* the part of the body used for grasping and holding, consisting of the palm and fingers, at the extremity of the human arm. *Also v.t.* WH: pre-1200. Old English, from Germanic, of unknown orig. No related words are known outside Germanic.

handicap *n.* any physical or mental disability. *Also v.t.* WH: 17C. Appar. from phr. *hand i' cap* (hand in the cap), ref. to the drawing of lots etc. out of a cap. A handicap was originally a game in which players showed acceptance or rejection of a disputed object's valuation by bringing their hands either full or empty out of a cap in which money had been deposited. In the 18C a similar practice was used to signify agreement or disagreement with an allocation of additional weight to be carried in horse races. The general current sense of disability arose in the 19C.

handicraft *n.* skill in working with the hands. *Also a.* WH: 12–14C. Alt. of *handcraft* (from HAND + CRAFT), based on HANDIWORK.

handiwork *n.* work done by the hands. WH: pre-1200. Old English *handgeweorc*, from *hand* HAND + *geweorc*, from *ge-* Y- + WORK. A variant form *handywork* arose in the 16C, as if from HANDY + WORK.

handkerchief *n.* a piece of cloth, silk, linen or cotton, carried for wiping the nose, face etc. WH: 16C. HAND + KERCHIEF. A handkerchief was originally a piece of material worn around the neck as well as being used in the modern manner.

handle *v.t.* to touch, to feel with, to wield or use with the hands. *Also v.i., n.* WH: pre-1200. Old English *handlian*, from Germanic. See HAND, also -LE[1].

†**handsel** *n.* a gift for luck, esp. on the first Monday in the New Year. *Also v.t.* WH: 12–14C. Old English *handselen* delivery into the hand, or from Old Norse *handsal* giving of the hand, ult. from HAND + base of SELL. Cp. Swedish *handsöl* gratuity, Danish *handsel* earnest money.

handsome *a.* good-looking, well formed, finely featured. WH: 14–15C. HAND + SOME. The original sense (to the 16C) was easy to handle, HANDY. The current sense dates from the 16C.

handy *a.* useful and easy to use. WH: 12–14C. HAND + -Y[1].

hang *v.t.* to attach to a point of support higher than its own height. *Also v.i., n.* WH: pre-1200. Old English *hangian*, from Germanic. Ult. rel. to Latin *cunctari* to delay (see CUNCTATION).

hangar *n.* a large shed, esp. for aircraft. WH: 17C. French, orig. uncertain. ? From Frankish words rel. to HOME[1] + GUARD. A hangar was originally a shed or shelter in general.

Hang Seng index *n.* an indicator giving relative prices of major shares on the Hong Kong Stock Exchange. WH: mid-20C. *Hang Seng*, a bank in Hong Kong + INDEX.

hank *n.* a coil or skein. *Also v.t.* WH: 12–14C. Old Norse *hǫnk*, from Germanic source also of HANG.

hanker *v.i.* to have strong desire or longing (after). WH: 17C. Prob. from Flemish *hankeren*, rel. to HANK and so to HANG. Not rel. to HUNGER.

hanky *n.* a handkerchief. WH: 19C. Contr. of HANDKERCHIEF. See also -Y[3].

Hanoverian *a.* of or relating to Hanover or the Hanoverians. *Also n.* WH: 18C. *Hanover*, a N German state, or the town of the same name, its former capital. See also -IAN.

Hansard *n.* the official report of the proceedings of the British Parliament (from the name of the compilers and printers, 1774–1889). WH: 19C. Luke *Hansard*, 1752–1828, English printer.

Hanse *n.* a corporation or guild of merchants. WH: 12–14C. Medieval Latin *hansa*, from Old High German troop, company, from Germanic. Cp. Finnish *kansa* people, company.

Hansen's disease *n.* leprosy. WH: early 20C. G.H.A. *Hansen*, 1841–1912, Norwegian physician.

hansom *n.* a two-wheeled horse-drawn cab in which the driver's seat is behind the body, the reins passing over the hooded top. WH: 19C. Joseph Aloysius *Hansom*, 1803–82, English architect, who registered a patent safety cab in 1834.

Hanta virus *n.* an often-fatal virus whose symptoms are similar to those of flu. WH: mid-20C. *Hantaan* river, Korea, where the virus was first isolated.

Hanukkah *n.* the Jewish festival of lights in commemoration of the rededication of the temple (165 BC). WH: 19C. Hebrew *ḥănukkāh* consecration.

hanuman *n.* a lemur, *Presbytis entellus*, sacred to Hindus. WH: 19C. Sanskrit *hanumant*, nom. *hanumān* large-jawed.

†**hap**[1] *n.* chance, luck. *Also v.i.* WH: 12–14C. Old Norse *happ*, rel. to Old English *gehæplic* fitting, convenient. Cp. HAPPEN, HAPPY, PERHAPS.

hap[2] *v.t.* to cover over. *Also n.* WH: 12–14C. Prob. from Scandinavian.

hapax legomenon *n.* a word or expression that has only been used once; a nonce-word. WH: 17C. Greek (thing) said only once, from *hapax* once + *legomenon* said, from *legein* to say.

haphazard *a.* happening by chance. *Also n., adv.* WH: 16C. HAP[1] + HAZARD, in sense hazard of chance.

hapless *a.* unhappy, unfortunate, luckless. WH: 14–15C. HAP[1] + -LESS.

haplo- *comb. form* single, simple. WH: Greek *haploos* single, simple. See also -O-. Cp. DIPLO-.

haplography *n.* inadvertent writing of a word or letter once which should be written twice, as *superogatory* for *supererogatory*. WH: 19C. HAPLO- + -GRAPHY. Cp. *dittography* (DITTO).

haploid *a.* having half the usual number. *Also n.* WH: early 20C. Greek *haploos* single + -OID. The word was coined in 1905 by the German botanist Eduard Adolf Strasburger.

haplology *n.* the omission in speech of one or more similar sounds or syllables. WH: 19C. HAPLO- + -LOGY.

happen *v.i.* to occur. *Also adv.* WH: 14–15C. HAP[1] + -EN[5], superseding obs. *hap* (v.).

happi *n.* a loose casual coat worn in Japan. WH: 19C. Japanese *happi* kind of coat formerly worn by the followers of nobles + COAT.

happy *a.* enjoying pleasure from something good. *Also v.t.* WH: 14–15C. HAP[1] + -Y[1]. The original sense was favoured by good fortune. The current sense evolved in the 16C.

haptic *a.* relating to the sense of touch. WH: 19C. Greek *haptikos*, from *haptesthai* to grasp, to touch, middle voice of *haptein* to fasten.

hapuka *n.* a New Zealand fish, the grouper. WH: 19C. Maori.

hara-kiri *n.* a Japanese method of suicide by disembowelling. WH: 19C. Japanese, from *hara* belly + *kiri* cutting. The Japanese v. meaning to commit hara-kiri is *seppuku*. *Hara-kiri* itself was long popularly understood to mean happy dispatch, a misinterpretation that may have arisen as a joke.

harangue *n.* a declamatory address to a large assembly. *Also v.i., v.t.* WH: 14–15C. French, earlier *arenge*, from Medieval Latin *harenga*, ? ult. from Germanic.

harass *v.t.* to torment. *Also n.* WH: 17C. French *harasser*, pejorative deriv. of *harer* to set a dog on, from *hare* cry used for this.

harbinger *n.* a person who announces the approach of another. *Also v.t.* WH: 12–14C. Old French *herbergere*, from *herbergier* to provide lodging for, from *herberge* lodging, from Old Saxon *heriberga*, shelter for an army, from *heri* host, army (see HARRY) + Germanic base meaning to protect (cp. BOROUGH). Cp. AUBERGE, HARBOUR. The *-n-* appeared as in MESSENGER, PASSENGER.

harbour *n.* a refuge, esp. a refuge or shelter for ships. *Also v.t., v.i.* WH: pre-1200. Old English *hereborg*, from Germanic bases of HARBINGER. See also -OUR. A harbour was originally any place of shelter, refuge or lodging. The current sense dates from the 12–14C.

hard *a.* firm, solid, compact. *Also adv., n.* WH: pre-1200. Old English, from Germanic, from Indo-European base also of Greek *kratus* strong, powerful (see -CRACY).

harden *v.t.* to make hard or harder. *Also v.i.* WH: 12–14C. HARD + -EN[5], based on Old Norse *harthna*, superseding obs. *hard* (v.), from Old English *heardian.*

hardly *adv.* scarcely, not quite. WH: 12–14C. HARD + -LY[2]. The original sense (to the 19C) was with energy, vigorously, also (to the 17C) boldly, daringly, and (to the 16C) firmly. The current sense dates from the 16C.

hards *n.pl.* the coarse or refuse part of flax or wool. WH: pre-1200. Old English *heordan* (pl.), orig. unknown.

hardship *n.* that which is hard to bear, as privation, suffering, toil, fatigue, oppression, injury, injustice. WH: 12–14C. HARD + -SHIP.

hardy *a.* unaffected by fatigue; robust. *Also n.* WH: 12–14C. Old French *hardi* bold, p.p. of *hardir* to become, from Germanic, from base of HARD.

hare *n.* a long-eared short-tailed mammal of the genus *Lepus*, similar to but larger than the rabbit and with longer hind legs. *Also v.i.* WH: pre-1200. Old English *hara*, from Germanic. Cp. German *Hase.*

Hare Krishna *n.* a sect devoted to the Hindu god Krishna. WH: late 20C. *Hare Krishna*, words of a Sanskrit devotional chant, from Hindi *hare Krishnā* O Lord Krishna.

harem *n.* the apartments reserved for the women in a Muslim household. WH: 17C. Turkish, from Arabic *ḥaram* (that which is) prohibited, (hence) inviolable place, sanctuary, women's apartments, wives, women, from *ḥarama* to be prohibited.

harewood *n.* stained sycamore, used for furniture. WH: 17C. Obs. *hare*, from German dial. *Ehre*, from Latin *acer* maple + WOOD.

haricot *n.* the kidney or French bean, often dried. WH: 17C. French, prob. from Aztec *ayacotli.*

Harijan *n.* a member of a class of people in India, formerly considered to be inferior and untouchable. WH: mid-20C. Sanskrit *harijana* person devoted to the Hindi god Vishnu, from *Hari* Vishnu + *jana* person.

hark †*v.i.* to listen (*usu. in imper.*). *Also v.t.* WH: 12–14C. From Germanic source of HEARKEN. Cp. German *horchen* to listen.

harl[1] *n.* filaments of flax or hemp. WH: 17C. Appar. from Middle Low German *herle*, Low German *harl*, fibre of flax or hemp.

harl[2] *v.t.* to drag along the ground. *Also v.i., n.* WH: 12–14C. Orig. unknown.

harlequin *n.* a leading character in a pantomime or harlequinade, dressed in a mask and parti-coloured and spangled clothes. *Also a., v.i., v.t.* WH: 16C. Obs. French (Modern French *arlequin*, from Italian *arlecchino*), later var. of *Herlequin, Hellequin*, leader of a legendary nocturnal troop of demon horsemen known in Medieval Latin as *familia Hellequini* or *familia Herlethingi*, ? ult. from Old English *Herla cyning* King Herla, a mythical character sometimes identified with Woden.

†**harlot** *n.* a prostitute; a promiscuous woman. *Also v.i.* WH: 12–14C. Old French young fellow, knave, from Medieval Latin *harlotus* vagabond, beggar. The original sense (to the 17C) was vagabond, beggar, rogue, also generally fellow. The current sense dates from the 14–15C.

harm *n.* hurt, injury, damage. *Also v.t.* WH: pre-1200. Old English *hearm*, from Germanic. Cp. German *Harm* grief, harm.

harmattan *n.* a dry hot wind blowing from the interior of Africa to the western coast in December, January and February. WH: 17C. Twi *haramata.*

harmonic *a.* of or relating to harmony or music. *Also n.* WH: 16C. Latin *harmonicus*, from Greek *harmonikos*, from *harmonia* HARMONY. See also -IC.

harmonium *n.* a keyed musical wind instrument whose tones are produced by the forcing of air through free reeds. WH: 19C. French,

from Latin *harmonia* HARMONY, or from Greek *harmonios* harmonious. The name was coined by Alexandre Debain, a French manufacturer of keyboard instruments, who invented it in *c*.1842.

harmony *n.* the adaptation of parts to each other, so as to form a complete, symmetrical or pleasing whole. WH: 14–15C. Old French *harmonie*, from Latin *harmonia* agreement, concord, from Greek *harmos* joint, *harmozein* to fit together.

harmotome *n.* a vitreous hydrous silicate of aluminium and barium characterized by cross-shaped crystals. WH: 19C. French, from Greek *harmos* joint + *-tomos* (-TOME) cutting. The silicate is apparently so named from the way the octohedral crystal divides.

harness *n.* the working gear of a horse or other draught animal. *Also v.t.* WH: 12–14C. Old French *harneis* military equipment (Modern French *harnais*), from Old Norse *hernest* provisions for an army, from *herr* army (see HARRY) + *nest* provisions. The original sense was equipment of a horse for riding, driving etc. The sense subsequently narrowed to mean the equipment by which a horse is fastened to a cart, etc.

harp *n.* a musical instrument of triangular shape, with strings which are plucked by the fingers with the frame upright. *Also v.i.* WH: pre-1200. Old English *hearpe*, from Germanic. Cp. German *Harfe.*

harpings *n.pl.* the strengthening planks that encompass the bow or extensions of the rib-bands of a vessel. WH: 14–15C. Old French *harpon* clamp (see HARPOON) + -S[1].

harpoon *n.* a barbed, spearlike missile weapon with a line attached, used for striking and killing whales etc. *Also v.t.* WH: 17C. French *harpon*, from *harpe* dog's claw, clamp, from Latin, from Greek *harpē* sickle.

harpsichord *n.* a stringed instrument with a keyboard moving quills that pluck instead of hammers that strike, similar in form to the pianoforte. WH: 17C. Obs. French *harpechorde*, from Modern Latin *harpichordium* and Ecclesiastical Latin *harpa* HARP + *chorda* string (see CORD). The *-s-* is unexplained.

harpy *n.* in Greek and Roman mythology, a monster represented with the face of a woman, the body of a vulture and fingers armed with sharp claws. WH: 14–15C. Old French *harpie*, from Latin *harpyia*, pl. *harpyiae*, from Greek *harpuiai* snatchers, rel. to *harpazein* to seize.

harquebus *n.* an old kind of musket fired from a forked hand rest or tripod. WH: 16C. French *arquebuse*, ult. from Middle Low German *hakebusse* (German *Haakbus*), or from Middle High German *hakebühse* (German *Hakenbüchse*). See also HACKBUT.

harridan *n.* an ill-tempered or bullying (old) woman. WH: 17C. ? Alt. of French *haridelle* old horse, ult. of unknown orig.

harrier[1] *n.* a variety of dog, smaller than the foxhound, orig. used for hare-hunting. WH: 14–15C. HARE + -ER[1], based on Old French *lévrier*, from Medieval Latin *leporarius* greyhound, with assim. to HARRIER[2].

harrier[2] *n.* a person who harries or plunders. WH: 16C. HARRY + -ER[1].

Harris Tweed® *n.* a type of tweed woven in the Outer Hebrides. WH: 19C. *Harris*, an island (with Lewis) in the Outer Hebrides, NW Scotland + TWEED.

Harrovian *a.* of or relating to Harrow School. *Also n.* WH: 19C. Modern Latin *Harrovia*, Harrow(-on-the-Hill), a town in Middlesex (now a unitary authority). See also -AN, -IAN. Harrow School was founded in 1572.

harrow[1] *n.* a large rake or frame with teeth, drawn over ground to level it, stir the soil, destroy weeds or cover seed. *Also v.t.* WH: 12–14C. Old Norse *herfi*, rel. to Middle Dutch *harke* (Dutch *hark*) rake.

†**harrow**[2] *v.t.* to plunder, to spoil, to harry, to pillage. WH: 12–14C. Var. of HARRY.

harrumph *v.i.* to make a sound as if clearing one's throat, often to indicate disapproval. *Also v.t.* WH: mid-20C. Imit. Cp. HEM[2], HUM[2], HUMPH.

harry *v.t.* to plunder, to pillage, to lay waste. *Also v.i.* WH: pre-1200. Old English *hergian*, from Germanic, from base meaning host, army. Cp. HARROW[2].

harsh *a.* rough to the touch or other senses. WH: 12–14C. Middle Low German and German *harsch* rough, lit. hairy, from Middle Low German *haer* (German *Haar*) hair. See also -ISH[1].

hart *n.* a stag, esp. a male red deer, from its fifth year onwards. WH: pre-1200. Old English *heort*, from Germanic. Ult. rel. to Greek *keras* horn, Latin *cervus* stag, deer.

hartal *n.* a boycott or protest carried out by closing shops. WH: early 20C. Hindi *haṛtāl*, var. of *haṭṭal*, lit. locking of shops, from Sanskrit *haṭṭa* shop + *tāla* lock.

hartebeest *n.* a large African antelope of the genus *Alcephalus*, with horns that bend at the tips. WH: 18C. Afrikaans (now *hartebees*), from Dutch *hert* hart + *beest* beast. Cp. WILDEBEEST.

†hartshorn *n.* a preparation from shavings or chippings of the horns of the hart. WH: pre-1200. HART + -S[1] + HORN.

harum-scarum *a.* giddy, hare-brained, reckless. *Also n.* WH: 17C. Rhyming comb., appar. from HARE + SCARE. Cp. HELTER-SKELTER.

haruspex *n.* an ancient Etruscan or Roman soothsayer who divined the will of the gods by inspecting the entrails of victims. WH: 15C. Latin, from base seen in Sanskrit *hirā* artery + Latin *-spex*, from *specere* to look at.

Harvard classification *n.* a system for classifying stars based on their spectral type. WH: 19C. *Harvard* University, Cambridge, Massachusetts, where the system evolved in the 1880s.

harvest *n.* the process of reaping and gathering crops, esp. of corn. *Also v.t.* WH: pre-1200. Old English *hærfest* autumn, from Germanic, from Indo-European base represented by Latin *carpere* to pluck, Greek *karpos* fruit. Cp. German *Herbst* autumn. Old English *hærfestmōnath* harvest month was an old name for September.

has-been *n.* a person or idea that is no longer important, influential or useful. WH: 17C. From *has*, 3rd pers. sing. pres. ind. of HAVE + *been*, p.p. of BE. The sense is of a person or a thing that *has been* important, etc., but no longer is.

hash[1] *n.* a dish of meat that has already been cooked, cut into small pieces and recooked, often mixed with vegetables etc. *Also v.t.* WH: 17C. From v. *hash* (16C), replacing earlier obs. *hachy*, from Old French *haché*, p.p. of *hacher* to hash.

hash[2] *n.* hashish. WH: mid-20C. Abbr. of HASHISH.

hashish *n.* the tender tops and sprouts of Indian hemp, *Cannabis indica*, used as a narcotic for smoking, chewing etc. WH: 16C. Arabic *ḥašīš* dry herb, hay, powdered hemp leaves. Cp. ASSASSIN.

Hasid *n.* a member of any of several mystical Jewish sects. WH: 19C. Hebrew *ḥāsīḏ* pious, pietist.

haslet *n.* mixed pieces of the entrails, liver, heart etc. of an animal, usu. a hog, cooked and pressed into a loaf. WH: 14–15C. Old French *hastelet* (Modern French *hâtelet*), dim. of *haste* (Modern French *hâte*) spit, roast meat, from Germanic. See also -LET.

hasp *n.* a fastening, esp. a clamp or bar hinged at one end, the other end passing over a staple, where it is secured by a pin, key or padlock. *Also v.t.* WH: pre-1200. Old English *hæpse*, *hæsp*, from Germanic. ? Ult. rel. to Latin *capsa* container. Cp. CAPTIVE.

hassium *n.* a synthetic element, chem. symbol Hs, atom. no. 108, produced by a heavy-ion accelerator. WH: late 20C. Modern Latin *Hassia* Hesse, a state of central Germany + -IUM. The element was discovered in Darmstadt, the capital of Hesse, in 1984.

hassle *n.* something causing difficulty or problems. *Also v.t., v.i.* WH: 19C. Orig. uncertain. ? Blend of HAGGLE and TUSSLE, or rel. to HAZE[2].

hassock *n.* a small stuffed footstool or cushion for kneeling on in church. WH: pre-1200. Orig. unknown. The original sense was a firm tuft or clump of grass in marshy ground (hence *Hassocks*, a town in W Sussex). The current sense dates from the 16C.

hastate *a.* triangular, like the head of a spear. WH: 18C. Latin *hastatus*, from *hasta* spear. See also -ATE[2].

haste *n.* hurry, speed of movement or action; urgency, precipitance. *Also v.i.* WH: 12–14C. Old French (Modern French *hâte*), from Germanic, of unknown orig. Cp. Old English *hǣst* violence, fury, Old Norse *heifst* hate, revenge, Gothic *haifsts* strife.

hat *n.* a covering for the head, usu. having a crown or top and a continuous brim. *Also v.t.* WH: pre-1200. Old English *hætt*, rel. to Old Norse *hǫttr* hood, cowl, from Germanic, from base of HOOD[1].

hatch[1] *n.* an opening in a wall between two rooms. *Also v.t.* WH: pre-1200. Old English *hæcc*, from Germanic. Cp. HACK[3], HECK[2]. A hatch was originally a small gate. The sense gate remains in place names such as *Brands Hatch*, *Colney Hatch*, etc.

hatch[2] *v.t.* to produce (young) from eggs by incubation or artificial heat. *Also v.i., n.* WH: 12–14C. Germanic, of unknown orig. Cp. Middle High German *hecken*, Swedish *häcka*, Danish *hække*.

hatch[3] *v.t.* to mark with fine lines, parallel or crossing each other. *Also n.* WH: 15C. Old French *hacher*, from *hache* axe. See HATCHET.

hatchel *v.t.* to dress (flax). WH: 12–14C. Ult. from Germanic base represented also by HOOK. Cp. HACKLE[1], HECKLE.

hatchet *n.* a small axe with a short handle for use with one hand. WH: 12–14C. Old French *hachette*, dim. of *hache* axe, from Medieval Latin *hapia*, from Germanic. See also -ET[1].

hatchment *n.* a funeral escutcheon or panel bearing the coat of arms of a deceased person placed on the front of the person's house, in a church etc. WH: 16C. Prob. from obs. French *hachement*, from Old French *acesmement* adornment.

hate *n.* extreme dislike or aversion, hatred. *Also v.t.* WH: pre-1200. Old English *hete*, from Germanic. Cp. German *Hass*.

hatha yoga *n.* a form of yoga involving physical exercises and breathing control. WH: early 20C. Sanskrit, from *haṭha* force + YOGA.

hatto- *comb. form* denoting a factor of 10^{-18}. WH: Danish or Norwegian *atten* eighteen. See also -O-.

hauberk *n.* a coat of mail, sometimes without sleeves, formed of interwoven steel rings. WH: 12–14C. Old French *hauberc*, from Frankish, from base of Scottish dial. *hause* neck (cp. HAWSE) + Germanic base meaning to protect (cp. BOROUGH). The hauberk was originally armour for the neck and shoulders.

haughty *a.* proud, arrogant, disdainful, supercilious. WH: 16C. Obs. *haught* in the same sense, from French *haut*, from Old French *hault*, from Latin *altus*, influ. by Germanic base of HIGH + -Y[1]. The basic sense is high in one's own estimation.

haul *v.t.* to pull or drag with force. *Also v.i., n.* WH: 16C. Var. of HALE[2].

haulm *n.* a stem, a stalk. WH: pre-1200. Old English *halm*, from Germanic, from Indo-European base represented also by Latin *culmus*, Greek *kalamos* reed.

haunch *n.* the part of the body between the ribs and the thigh; the buttock, the basal joint. WH: 12–14C. Old French *hanche*, of Germanic orig. Cp. Low German *hanke* hind leg of a horse.

haunt *v.t.* to visit (a place or person) frequently as a ghost or spirit. *Also v.i., n.* WH: 12–14C. Old French *hanter*, from Germanic base also of HOME[1]. Cp. Old English *hāmettan* to provide with a home, Old Norse *heimta* to get home. The sense of visiting as a ghost dates from the 16C and is first found in Shakespeare.

Hausa *n.* a member of a people of W Africa and central Sudan. *Also a.* WH: 19C. Hausa.

hausfrau *n.* a German housewife. WH: 18C. German, from *Haus* house + *Frau* wife, woman.

haustellum *n.* the sucking organ of certain insects and crustaceans. WH: 19C. Modern Latin, dim. of *haustrum* bucket, scoop, from *haustus*, p.p. of *haurire* to draw water.

haustorium *n.* a rootlet or sucker of a parasitic plant. WH: 19C. Latin *haustor* drawer of water, from *haurire* to draw water. See also -ORIUM.

hautboy *n.* an oboe. WH: 16C. French *hautbois*, from *haut* high + *bois* wood. Cp. OBOE.

haute couture *n.* the designing and making of exclusive trend-setting fashions. WH: early 20C. French, lit. high dressmaking, from fem. of *haut* high + COUTURE.

haute cuisine *n.* cooking of a very high standard. WH: early 20C. French, lit. high cooking, from fem. of *haut* high + CUISINE.

haute école *n.* difficult feats of horsemanship. WH: 19C. French, lit. high school, from fem. of *haut* high + *école* SCHOOL[1].

hauteur *n.* haughtiness, lofty manners or demeanour. WH: 17C. French *haut* high + *-eur* -OR.

haut monde *n.* high society. WH: 19C. French, lit. high world, from *haut* high + *monde* world. Cp. *beau monde* (BEAU).

haut-relief *n.* high relief. WH: 19C. French, lit. high relief, from *haut* + *relief* RELIEF[1]. Cp. ALTO-RELIEVO.

Havana *n.* a cigar made at Havana or elsewhere in Cuba. WH: 19C. *Havana*, the capital of Cuba.

have *v.t.* to possess, to hold as owner. *Also v.i., v.aux., n.* WH: pre-1200. Old English *habban*, from Germanic base prob. rel. to HEAVE.

havelock *n.* a light covering for the cap hanging over the neck, worn as a protection against sunstroke. WH: 19C. Sir Henry *Havelock*, 1795–1857, British major-general serving in India, who wore one.

haven *n.* a port, a harbour. *Also v.t.* WH: pre-1200. Old Norse *hofn*, from Germanic. Cp. German *Haven*.

haver[1] *v.i.* to talk nonsense. *Also n.* WH: 18C. Orig. unknown.

haver[2] *n.* a person who holds a deed or document. WH: 14–15C. HAVE + -ER[1].

haversack *n.* a strong bag carried over the shoulder or on the back to hold provisions etc. when walking. WH: 18C. French *havresac*, from obs. German *Habersack* bag in which cavalry carried oats for their horses, from *Haber* oats + *Sack* SACK[1].

Haversian canal *n.* any one of the canals forming a network in bone, conveying and protecting the blood vessels. WH: 19C. Clopton *Havers*, d.1702, English physician and anatomist + -IAN.

haversine *n.* a value equal to half of a versed sine. WH: 19C. Contr. of *half versed sine*.

havildar *n.* a sergeant of an Indian regiment of infantry. WH: 17C. Urdu *hawildār*, from Persian *hawāldār* charge holder, from *hawāl*, from Arabic *hawal* charge, assignment + Persian -*dār* holding, holder.

havoc *n.* widespread destruction; devastation, waste. *Also v.t.* WH: 14–15C. Anglo-French *havok*, alt. of Old French *havot* pillage, ult. of unknown orig. The word was originally a signal cry to an army to seize spoil.

haw[1] *n.* the berry or fruit of the hawthorn. WH: pre-1200. Old English *haga*, from Germanic base also of HEDGE.

haw[2] *int., n.* a sound expressive of hesitation in speaking. *Also v.i.* WH: 17C. Imit. Cp. HUM[2], ER.

haw[3] *n.* the nictitating membrane or third eyelid (of a horse etc.). WH: 14–15C. Orig. unknown. ? From HAW[1], ref. to its shape.

Hawaiian *a.* of or relating to Hawaii, its people or their language. *Also n.* WH: 19C. *Hawaii*, an island and archipelago in the N Pacific + -AN.

hawfinch *n.* a large European finch, *Coccothraustes coccothraustes*, with a sturdy beak. WH: 17C. HAW[1] + FINCH. The bird is so called because it feeds largely on the berries of the hawthorn. Cp. CHAFFINCH.

hawk[1] *n.* a bird of prey belonging to the family Accipitridae, having a long tail, short rounded wings and a curved beak. *Also v.i., v.t.* WH: pre-1200. Old English *hafoc, haefoc*, from Germanic. Cp. German *Habicht*.

hawk[2] *v.i.* to clear or try to clear the throat in a noisy manner. *Also v.t., n.* WH: 16C. Prob. imit. Cp. COUGH.

hawk[3] *v.t.* to carry about for sale, to try to sell. WH: 15C. Back-formation from HAWKER[2].

hawk[4] *n.* a plasterer's board with handle underneath, for carrying plaster, mortar etc. WH: 14–15C. Orig. unknown.

hawker[1] *n.* a person who practises the sport of hawking. WH: pre-1200. HAWK[1] + -ER[1].

hawker[2] *n.* a person who travels around selling goods in the street or from house to house. WH: 16C. Prob. from Low Dutch. See HUCKSTER.

hawse *n.* that part of the bow in which the hawse-holes are situated. WH: 14–15C. ? Old Norse *hals* neck, ship's bow, rope's end.

hawser *n.* a cable, used in towing and mooring. WH: 12–14C. Anglo-French *haucer*, from Old French *haucier* (Modern French *hausser*) to hoist, from Latin *altus* high. See also -ER[2]. The word was associated early with HAWSE.

hawthorn *n.* a thorny, rosaceous shrub or tree belonging to the genus *Crataegus*, bearing white or pink flowers which develop into haws. WH: pre-1200. Old English *hagathorn*, from *haga* HAW[1] + THORN.

hay[1] *n.* grass cut and dried for fodder. *Also v.t., v.i.* WH: pre-1200. Old English *hēg, hīeg*, from a Germanic base meaning to cut down, HEW.

hay[2] *n.* a country dance with a winding movement. WH: 16C. Obs. French *haie* a kind of dance, of unknown orig.

hazard *n.* a danger, a risk. *Also v.t., v.i.* WH: 12–14C. Old French *hasard*, from Spanish *azar*, from coll. Arabic *az-zahr*, from *az-*, form of *al-* the + Persian *zār* gaming die or Turkish *zar* die, dice, chance.

haze[1] *n.* lack of transparency in the air, a very thin mist or vapour, usu. due to heat. *Also v.t.* WH: 18C. Prob. back-formation from *hazy*

(17C), of unknown orig. According to some, the word is related to German *Hase* hare and of folklore origin.

haze[2] *v.t.* to harass or punish with overwork. WH: 17C. Orig. uncertain. Cp. obs. French *haser* to tease, to anger.

hazel *n.* a shrub or small tree of the genus *Corylus*, esp. the European *C. avellana*, bearing the hazelnut. *Also a.* WH: pre-1200. Old English *hæsel*, from Germanic, from Indo-European base represented also by Latin *corylus* hazel.

-hazia *comb. form* used to denote a person who is clumsy or tactless, as in *Glenhazia*. WH: late 20C. ? From HAZE[2] + -IA.

he *pron.* the male person or animal referred to. *Also n.* WH: pre-1200. Old English, from Germanic demonstrative stem that is also base of HIM, HIS and prob. HERE, HENCE.

head[1] *n.* the foremost part of the body of an animal, the uppermost in a human, consisting of the skull, with the brain and the special sense organs. *Also a.* WH: pre-1200. Old English *hēafod*, from Germanic, prob. rel. to Latin *caput*, Greek *kephalē*, Sanskrit *kapāla* skull.

head[2] *v.t.* to lead, to be the leader to, to direct. *Also v.i.* WH: 12–14C. HEAD[1].

-head *suf.* denoting state or quality, as in *godhead, maidenhead*. WH: Var. of -HOOD. *Godhead* (GOD) is now distinguished from *godhood* the state of being God or a god, and *maidenhead* (see MAIDEN) from *maidenhood*. The latter share the sense the state of being a maiden or virgin, but *maidenhead* has the additional sense hymen, which *maidenhood* does not have. Both *godhead* and *maidenhead* (in its additional sense) have further been influ. by HEAD[1].

header *n.* an act of heading a ball. WH: 14–15C. HEAD[1] + -ER[1].

heading *n.* an inscription at the head of an article, chapter etc. WH: 12–14C. HEAD[2] + -ING[1].

headquarters *n.* the residence of the commander-in-chief of an army. WH: 17C. HEAD[1] + QUARTER + -S[1].

heal *v.t.* to make sound or whole again, to restore to health; to cure of (disease etc.). *Also v.i.* WH: pre-1200. Old English *hǣlan*, from Germanic, from base seen also in WHOLE.

heald *n.* a heddle. WH: pre-1200. Old English *hefel, hefeld*, from base meaning to raise. Cp. HEDDLE.

health *n.* a state of bodily or organic soundness, freedom from bodily or mental disease or decay. WH: pre-1200. Old English *hǣlth*, from Germanic base also of WHOLE. See also -TH[2].

heap *n.* a pile or accumulation of many things placed or thrown one on another. *Also v.t.* WH: pre-1200. Old English *hēap*, from Germanic, from Indo-European base also of HIGH. Cp. FORLORN HOPE.

hear *v.t.* to perceive by the ear, to perceive the sound of. *Also v.i.* WH: pre-1200. Old English *hēran*, from Germanic. Cp. German *hören*.

†hearken *v.i.* to listen attentively (to). *Also v.t.* WH: pre-1200. Old English *hercnian*. See HARK, also -EN[5]. The spelling with -*ea*- arose by association with HEAR.

hearsay *n.* common talk, report or gossip. *Also a.* WH: 14–15C. Orig. in phr. *by hearsay*, translating Old French *par ouïr dire* (Modern French *ouï-dire*), from *par* by + *ouïr* to hear + *dire* to say.

hearse *n.* a vehicle in which the dead are taken to the place of burial or cremation. *Also v.t.* WH: 12–14C. Old French, lit. harrow, from Medieval Latin *erpica*, from Latin *hirpex* type of harrow, from Samnite *hirpus* wolf (with ref. to the teeth). Cp. REHEARSE. A hearse was originally a flat framework something like a harrow for candles and decorations, hung or placed over a coffin. The current sense evolved in the 17C.

heart *n.* the muscular central organ of the circulation of the blood, which keeps going by its rhythmical contraction and dilation. *Also v.i., v.t.* WH: pre-1200. Old English *heorte*, from Germanic, from Indo-European base represented also by Greek *kēr, kardia*, Latin *cor, cordis*. Cp. CARDIAC, CORDIAL.

hearten *v.t.* to encourage, to inspire, to stir up. *Also v.i.* WH: 16C. HEART + -EN[5], superseding obs. *heart*, from Old English *hiertan*.

hearth *n.* the floor of a fireplace; the area around a fireplace. WH: pre-1200. Old English *heorth*, from Germanic. Cp. German *Herd*.

heartsease *n.* the wild pansy, *Viola tricolor*. WH: 14–15C. HEART + -'S + EASE. The earliest sense was peace of mind (ease of heart). The flower name dates from the 16C and presumably refers to the 'ease of heart' that its scent gives.

hearty *a.* proceeding from the heart, sincere. *Also n.* WH: 14–15C. HEART + -Y¹. The original sense was courageous and bold. The sense robust, hale dates from the 16C.

heat *n.* a form of energy capable of melting and decomposing matter, and transmissible by means of radiation, conduction or convection. *Also v.t., v.i.* WH: pre-1200. Old English *hǣtu*, from Germanic, from base of HOT. The sense of a single course or round in a race arose in the 17C and developed from the figurative sense of vehemence of feeling, passion. Racers in a heat are often both physically and emotionally heated.

heath *n.* an open space of country, esp. one covered with shrubs and coarse herbage. WH: pre-1200. Old English *hǣth*, from Germanic. Cp. German *Heide*.

heathen *n.* a person who is not Christian, Jewish or Muslim. *Also a.* WH: pre-1200. Old English *hǣthen*, from Germanic base of HEATH. See also -EN⁴. The original literal sense was person inhabiting open country, a savage, perhaps as a loose rendering of Latin *paganus* PAGAN.

heather *n.* a low-growing ericaceous plant, *Calluna vulgaris*, with narrow leaves, wiry stems and purple, pink or white flowers. WH: pre-1200. Old English *hadre*, of unknown orig. The word is not related to HEATH but has been assimilated to it, as the plant grows there.

Heath Robinson *a.* (of a device) ingenious and extremely complex. WH: early 20C. W. *Heath Robinson*, 1872–1944, English humorous illustrator, whose drawings depicted such contraptions.

†theaume *n.* a large helmet coming down to the shoulders. WH: 16C. French, from Latin *helme*. See HELM².

heave *v.t.* to lift, to raise, with effort. *Also v.i., n.* WH: pre-1200. Old English *hebban*, from a Germanic word rel. to Latin *capere* to take. Cp. HAVE.

heaven *n.* the sky, the firmament; the atmosphere enveloping the earth regarded as the region in which the clouds float, the winds blow etc. *Also int.* WH: pre-1200. Old English *heofon*, earlier *hefen*, from Germanic, ult. of unknown orig. Cp. German *Himmel*. The word is popularly related to HEAVE, seeing heaven as a region 'lifted up'.

heaves *n.pl.* an asthmatic disease in horses, broken wind. WH: 18C. HEAVE + -S¹.

Heaviside layer *n.* a layer in the upper atmosphere that reflects radio waves, thus enabling reception round the curved surface of the earth, the E-layer. WH: early 20C. Oliver *Heaviside*, 1850–1925, English physicist.

heavy *a.* having great weight, weighty, ponderous. *Also n., adv.* WH: pre-1200. Old English *hefig*, from Germanic, from base of HEAVE.

hebdomad *n.* a week, a period of seven days (alluding to Daniel's prophecy (Dan. ix.27)). WH: 16C. Late Latin, from Greek *hebdomas*, *hebdomados* the number seven, period of seven days, from *hepta* seven. See also -AD¹.

hebe *n.* an evergreen shrub of the genus *Hebe*, with spikes of purple or white flowers. WH: 17C. Greek *hēbē* youthful beauty, *Hēbē* the goddess of youth and spring. The original sense was a young woman resembling Hebe. The shrub was so named in the mid- 20C, presumably because it is 'ever green', like the goddess.

hebetate *v.t.* to make blunt or dull. *Also v.i.* WH: 16C. Latin *hebetatus*, p.p. of *hebetare*, from *hebes*, *hebetis* blunt, dull. See also -ATE³.

hebetic *a.* of or relating to youth or pubescence. WH: 19C. Greek *hēbētikos* youthful, from *hēbē* youth, pubes. See also -IC.

Hebraic *a.* of or relating to the Hebrews. WH: 14–15C. Ecclesiastical Latin *Hebraicus*, from Late Greek *Hebraikos*, from *Hebra-*, based on Aramaic *'ibrāy*. See HEBREW, also -IC.

Hebrew *n.* the Semitic language of the ancient Jews and, in a modern form, of the State of Israel. *Also a.* WH: 12–14C. Old French *ebreu* (Modern French *hébreu*), from Medieval Latin *Ebreus*, from Latin *Hebraeus*, from Late Greek *Hebraios*, from Aramaic *'ibrāy*, from Hebrew *'ibrī*, interpreted as one from the other side (of the river), as if from *'ēber* the region on the other side, from *'ābar* to cross over, to pass over. The reference would be to the river Euphrates.

Hebridean *n.* a native or inhabitant of the Hebrides. *Also a.* WH: 17C. *Hebrides*, a group of islands off the W coast of Scotland + -AN.

hecatomb *n.* in ancient Greece or Rome, the sacrifice of 100 oxen or other beasts. WH: 16C. Latin *hecatombe*, from Greek *hekatombē*, from *hekaton* hundred + *bous* ox. Cp. HOLOCAUST.

heck¹ *int.* used to express irritation, dismay etc. *Also n.* WH: 19C. Alt. of HELL.

heck² *n.* a grated contrivance in a stream, used as a fish trap or to obstruct the passage of fish. WH: 12–14C. Var. of HATCH¹. Cp. HACK³.

heckelphone *n.* a baritone oboe. WH: early 20C. Wilhelm *Heckel*, 1856–1909, German instrument maker + -PHONE.

heckle *v.t.* to interrupt and worry (a public speaker) by deliberately inconvenient questions, taunts etc. *Also n.* WH: 12–14C. Var. of HACKLE¹. The original sense was to dress flax or hemp with a heckle. The sense to interrupt with questions arose in the 17C.

hectare *n.* a measure of area equal to 10,000 sq. metres or 2.471 acres. WH: 19C. French, from Greek *hekaton* hundred + ARE. See HECTO-.

hectic *a.* full of excitement, exciting; very busy. *Also n.* WH: 14–15C. Old French *etique*, from Late Latin *hecticus*, from Greek *hektikos* habitual, hectic, consumptive, from *hexis* habit, state of body or mind. See also -IC. The earliest sense is the medical one of consumptive. The current general sense evolved in the early 20C.

hecto- *comb. form* a hundred. WH: French, contr. of Greek *hekaton* hundred.

hector *v.t.* to bully, to treat with insolence. *Also v.i., n.* WH: 14–15C. Latin *Hector*, Greek *Hektōr*, son of Priam and Hecuba in Greek mythology, a Trojan hero. The word came to be applied in the 17C to gangs of unruly young men on the streets of London. In Homer's *Iliad*, Hector is described as challenging the Greeks to combat in a belligerent way.

heddle *n.* one of the sets of parallel cords or wires forming loops for the warp threads of a loom. WH: 16C. Appar. ult. from Old English alt. of *hefeld* HEALD.

hedera *n.* a climbing plant of the genus *Hedera*, an ivy. WH: 17C. Latin ivy.

hedge *n.* a fence of bushes or small trees. *Also v.t., v.i.* WH: pre-1200. Old English *hegg*, from Germanic base rel. to HAG², HAW¹.

hedgehog *n.* a small insectivorous mammal, *Erinaceus europaeus*, covered above with spines, and able to roll itself up into a ball. WH: 14–15C. HEDGE + HOG. The animal is so called as it bears some resemblance to a pig and hibernates in hedges. Most languages name the hedgehog from its spines, as French *hérisson* (see URCHIN) and German *Igel*, related to Old English *igil*, its earlier English name. (Cp. ECHIDNA.)

hedonism *n.* the doctrine or belief that pleasure is the chief good. WH: 19C. Greek *hēdonē* pleasure + -ISM.

-hedron *comb. form* a solid figure having the specified number of sides. WH: Greek *hedra* seat, base.

heebie-jeebies *n.pl.* nervous anxiety, apprehension. WH: early 20C. Orig. uncertain. Cp. HABDABS. The word is said to have been coined by a US cartoonist named Billy De Beck.

heed *v.t.* to pay attention to, to take notice of. *Also v.i., n.* WH: pre-1200. Old English *hēdan*, from Germanic. ? Ult. rel. to HOOD¹. Cp. German *Hut* care, keeping.

hee-haw *v.i.* to bray like a donkey. *Also n.* WH: 19C. Imit. Cp. French *hi-han*, German *iah*, donkey *Eeyore* in A.A. Milne's *Winnie the Pooh* books (1926) etc.

heel¹ *n.* the rounded hinder part of the human foot. *Also v.t., v.i., int.* WH: pre-1200. Old English *hēla*, from Germanic base of Old English *hōh* heel. See HOCK¹.

heel² *v.i.* of a ship, to incline or cant over to one side. *Also v.t., n.* WH: 16C. Prob. from obs. *hield* to bend to one side, to incline, from Old English *hieldan*, from Germanic base of Old English *heald* inclined. Cp. German *Halde* slope.

heel³ *v.t.* to plant in the ground and cover the roots. WH: pre-1200. Old English *helian*, from Germanic base meaning to conceal rel. to Latin *celare*, Greek *kaluptein*. See HOLE.

heft *v.t.* to try the weight of by lifting. *Also n.* WH: 14–15C. Prob. from HEAVE on analogy with pairs CLEAVE¹/CLEFT¹, WEAVE¹/WEFT¹, etc.

hefty *a.* strong, muscular, powerful. WH: 19C. HEFT + -Y¹.

Hegelian *a.* of or relating to Hegel or his philosophy. *Also n.* WH: 19C. Georg *Hegel*, 1770–1831, German philosopher + -IAN.

hegemony n. leadership, predominance, esp. applied to the relation of one state to another or to a confederation. WH: 16C. Greek *hēgemonia* , from *hēgemōn* leader. See -MONY.

Hegira n. the flight of Muhammad from Mecca to Medina, in AD 622, from which the Muslim era is computed. WH: 16C. Medieval Latin, from Arabic *hijra* departure from one's home and friends, from *hajara* to separate, to emigrate.

hegumen n. the head of a monastery in the Greek Church. WH: 17C. Late Latin *hegumenus*, from Greek *hēgoumenos*, pres.p. (used as n.) of *hēgeisthai* to lead, to command.

heifer n. a young cow that has not yet calved. WH: pre-1200. Old English *heahfore*, *heafru*, of unknown orig.

heigh int. used to call attention or express enquiry or encouragement. WH: 12–14C. Natural exclamation. Cp HEY, HI.

height n. the distance of the top above the foot, basis or foundation. WH: pre-1200. Old English *hēhthu*, from Germanic. Cp. HIGH, also -TH². A former spelling was *heighth*, with -*th* sounded (as still by some even now). Cp. LENGTH, BREADTH, WIDTH, DEPTH.

heinous a. abominable, flagrant, atrocious; wicked in the highest degree. WH: 14–15C. Old French *haïneus* (Modern French *haineux*), from *haïne* (Modern French *haine*), from Old French *haïr*, from Frankish, rel. to HATE. See also -OUS.

heir n. a person who by law succeeds or is entitled to succeed another in the possession of property or rank. *Also v.t.* WH: 12–14C. Old French *eir*, *heir*, from Late Latin *herum*, var. of *heredem*, acc. of *heres* heir.

Heisenberg uncertainty principle n. the principle that the position and velocity of a subatomic particle cannot both be ascertained at the same time. WH: mid-20C. Werner *Heisenberg*, 1901–76, German physicist.

heist n. a burglary, a robbery. *Also v.t.* WH: 19C. Representation of US local pronun. of HOIST.

hei-tiki n. a neck decoration made of greenstone. WH: 19C. Maori, from *hei* to hang + TIKI.

HeLa cell n. a human cultured epithelial cell used in virological research. WH: mid-20C. *Henrietta Lacks*, patient whose cervical carcinoma provided the original tissue in 1951.

Heldentenor n. (a singer with) a strong tenor voice, suitable for Wagnerian roles. WH: early 20C. German hero tenor, from *Held* hero + *Tenor* TENOR.

helenium n. any plant belonging to the genus *Helenium*, having daisy-like flowers and often growing up to 5 ft (1.6 m) tall. WH: 14–15C. Modern Latin, from Greek *helenion*, prob. commemorating Helen of Troy, renowned for her beauty.

heli- comb. form helicopter. WH: HELICOPTER.

heliacal a. closely connected with the sun. WH: 16C. Medieval Latin *heliacus*, from Greek *hēliakos*, from *hēlios* sun + -AL¹.

helianthemum n. any low-growing evergreen plant of the genus *Helianthemum*, having yellow or orange saucer-shaped flowers. WH: 19C. Modern Latin, from Greek *hēlios* sun + *anthemon* flower.

helianthus n. any plant, such as the sunflower, belonging to the genus *Helianthus*, typically having large daisy-like flowers. WH: 18C. Modern Latin, from Greek *hēlios* sun + *anthos* flower. Cp. *sunflower* (SUN, FLOWER).

helical a. like a helix; spiral. WH: 16C. Latin HELIX, *helic-* + -AL¹.

helichrysum n. any plant of the genus *Helichrysum*, having daisy-like flowers with papery petals. WH: 16C. Latin, from Greek *helikhrusos*, from HELIX + *khrusos* gold.

helicon n. a bass tuba that coils behind the player's head. WH: 15C. Latin, from Greek *Helikōn*, mountain in Boeotia, Greece, formerly sacred to the gods. The name was often confused by 16C and 17C writers with the springs of Aganippe and Hippocrene which rose in the mountain. Hence the original sense of source of inspiration. The name of the tuba dates from the 19C and is associated with HELIX.

Heliconian a. of or relating to Helicon or the Muses. WH: 16C. HELICON + -IAN.

helicopter n. an aircraft with one or more power-driven airscrews mounted on vertical axes with the aid of which it can take off and land vertically. *Also v.t., v.i.* WH: 19C. French *hélicoptère*, from HELIX + *pteron* wing.

helio- comb. form of or relating to the sun. WH: Greek *hēlios* sun. See also -O-.

heliocentric a. having reference to the sun as centre. WH: 17C. HELIO- + -CENTRIC.

Heliochrome® n. a photograph representing an object in the natural colours. WH: 19C. HELIO- + Greek *khrōma* colour.

heliograph n. an apparatus for signalling by reflecting flashes of sunlight. *Also v.i., v.t.* WH: 19C. HELIO- + -GRAPH.

heliogravure n. photogravure. WH: 19C. French *héliogravure*. See HELIO-, GRAVURE.

heliolatry n. sun-worship. WH: 19C. HELIO- + -LATRY.

heliolithic a. of or relating to a civilization known for sun-worship and the erection of megaliths. WH: early 20C. HELIO- + Greek *lithikos* (LITHIC), based on *Eolithic* (EOLITH), etc.

heliology n. the science of the sun. WH: 19C. HELIO- + -LOGY.

heliometer n. an instrument for measuring small angles in the heavens, such as the angular distance between stars, the diameter of stars etc. (orig. for measuring the diameter of the sun). WH: 18C. HELIO- + -METER.

heliophilous a. attracted by or turning towards the sunlight. WH: 19C. HELIO- + -*philous* (-PHILE).

heliophobic a. disliking or turning away from the sunlight. WH: 19C. HELIO- + -*phobic* (-PHOBE).

heliostat n. an instrument, comprising a mirror turned by clockwork, by which the rays of the sun are continuously reflected in a fixed direction. WH: 18C. Modern Latin *heliostata*, or from French *héliostat*. See HELIO-, -STAT.

heliotherapy n. curative treatment by exposing the body to the rays of the sun. WH: early 20C. HELIO- + *therapy* (THERAPEUTIC).

heliothermometer n. a thermometer with a blackened bulb for registering the effect of atmospheric absorption on solar radiation. WH: 19C. HELIO- + THERMOMETER.

heliotrope n. any plant of the borage family belonging to the genus *Heliotropium*, having scented purple flowers. *Also a.* WH: pre-1200. Latin *heliotropium*, from Greek *hēliotropion*, from *hēlios* sun + -*tropos* turning, from *trepein* to turn. The name alludes to the belief that the flower heads turn to follow the sun. Cp. *sunflower* (SUN).

heliotype n. a picture obtained by printing from a gelatin surface in the same way as from a lithographic stone. WH: 19C. HELIO- + -*type* (TYPE).

heliozoan a. of or relating to the order Heliozoa, a group of protozoans with threadlike radiating processes. *Also n.* WH: 19C. Modern Latin *Heliozoa* (pl.), from Greek *hēlios* sun + *zōion* animal. See also -AN.

helipad n. a helicopter pad. WH: mid-20C. HELI- + PAD¹.

heliport n. an airport for the landing and departure of helicopters. WH: mid-20C. HELI- + *airport* (AIR).

heli-skiing n. skiing from a starting point reached by helicopter. WH: late 20C. HELI- + *skiing* (SKI).

helispheric a. winding round a globe spirally. WH: 19C. Greek HELIX + *spheric*, *spherical* (SPHERE).

helium n. a gaseous inert element, chem. symbol He, at. no. 2. WH: 19C. Greek *hēlios* sun + -IUM. The name was coined by the English astronomer Joseph Norman Lockyer who inferred the element's existence in 1868 on observing a yellow line in the solar spectrum not accountable by any element then known on earth.

helix n. a spiral or coiled curve, as of wire or rope. WH: 16C. Latin *helix*, *helicis*, from Greek *helix*, *helikos* spiral.

hell n. the place of punishment for the wicked after death in Christianity, Judaism and Islam; the place or state of the dead. *Also int.* WH: pre-1200. Old English, from Germanic base meaning to cover, to conceal. Cp. HEEL³, HELM².

hellebore n. any plant of the ranunculaceous genus *Helleborus*, containing *H. niger*, the Christmas rose, and the hellebore of the ancients, *H. officinalis*. WH: pre-1200. Old French *ellebre*, *elebore*, from Medieval Latin *eleborus*, from Latin *helleborus*, from Greek *helleboros*, of uncertain orig. According to some, the original meaning was eaten by fawns, from Greek *hellos* fawn + *bora* food.

Hellene n. an ancient Greek, a person of Greek descent whether inhabiting Europe or Asia Minor. WH: 17C. Greek *Hellēn* a Greek.

hellgrammite n. the aquatic larva of the dobsonfly *Corydalus cornutus*, used as bait in fishing. WH: 19C. Orig. unknown.

hellion *n.* a naughty child; a mischievous person. WH: 19C. Prob. var. of dial. *hallion* (? rel. to French *haillon* rag), assim. to HELL.

hello *int.* an informal greeting. Also *n.*, *v.i.* WH: 19C. Prob. var. of HOLLO. Cp. HALLOO, HOLLA.

helm[1] *n.* the instrument or apparatus by which a vessel is steered; the rudder and its operative parts, such as the tiller or wheel; the tiller. Also *v.t.* WH: pre-1200. Old English *helma*, from Germanic base also of HELVE. Cp. Old Norse *hjamvǫlr* rudder stick.

helm[2] *n.* a helmet. WH: pre-1200. Old English, from Germanic, from Indo-European base meaning to cover, to conceal. Cp. HEEL[3], HELL.

helmet *n.* a piece of defensive armour for the head. WH: 14–15C. Old French, from *helme*. See HELM[2], also -ET[1].

helminth *n.* a worm, esp. a parasitic intestinal worm. WH: 19C. Greek *helmins, helminthos* intestinal worm.

helot *n.* a serf or bond slave in ancient Sparta. WH: 16C. Latin *Helotes* (pl.), from Greek *Heilōtes* (pl. of *Heilōs*), usu. derived from *Helos*, a town in Laconia whose inhabitants were enslaved.

help *v.t.* to provide with something needed or wanted to achieve an end; to assist, to aid. Also *v.i.*, *n.* WH: pre-1200. Old English *helpan*, from Germanic. Cp. German *helfen*.

helpmate *n.* a helper. WH: 18C. HELP + MATE[1], prob. influ. by *help-meet* suitable helper, from *help meet* two words taken as one. The quoted phrase refers to Eve with regard to Adam: 'an help meet for him' (Gen. ii.18), i.e. a companion fitting for him.

helter-skelter *adv.* in great hurry and confusion. Also *a.*, *n.* WH: 16C. Rhyming comb. Cp. (earlier) HARUM-SCARUM, (later) HURRY-SCURRY.

helve *n.* the handle of a weapon or tool. Also *v.t.* WH: pre-1200. Old English *helfe*, from Germanic, rel. to HALTER. Cp. HELM[1].

Helvetian *a.* Swiss. Also *n.* WH: 16C. Latin *Helvetia* Switzerland, from *Helvetius* pertaining to the Helvetii. See also -IAN.

hem[1] *n.* the edge or border of a garment or piece of cloth, esp. when doubled and sewn in to strengthen it. Also *v.t.* WH: pre-1200. Old English, rel. to Old Frisian enclosed land. Cp. HAM[2].

hem[2] *int.*, *n.* a voluntary short cough, uttered by way of warning, encouragement etc. Also *v.i.*, *v.t.* WH: 15C. Imit. Cp. AHEM, HUM[2].

hemeralopia *n.* a pathological condition in which the eyes see badly by daylight and better by night or artificial light. WH: 18C. Modern Latin, from Greek *hēmeralōps*, from *hēmera* day + *alaos* blind + *ōps* eye. See also -IA. Cp. NYCTALOPIA.

hemerocallis *n.* the day lily. WH: 17C. Greek *hēmerokallis* a lily that flowers for one day only, from *hēmera* day + *kallos* beauty.

hemi- *comb. form* half, halved. WH: Greek *hēmi-*, comb. element rel. to Latin *semi-* SEMI-, from Indo-European base also of Old English *sam-* (cp. SAND-BLIND).

hemianopsia *n.* blindness over half the field of vision. WH: 19C. HEMI- + Greek AN-[3] + *opsis* vision. See also -IA.

hemicellulose *n.* any of a group of polysaccharides occurring chiefly in the cell wall. WH: 19C. HEMI- + CELLULOSE.

hemichordate *n.* any small wormlike marine animal of the phylum Hemichordata, having numerous gill slits in the pharynx. Also *a.* WH: 19C. HEMI- + *chordate* (CHORD[2]).

hemicycle *n.* a semicircle. WH: 15C. French *hémicycle*, from Latin *hemicyclium*, from Greek *hēmikuklion*. See HEMI-, CYCLE.

hemihedral *a.* in crystallography, having only half the normal number of planes or facets. WH: 19C. HEMI- + Greek *hedra* seat, base (cp. -HEDRON). See also -AL[1].

hemiplegia *n.* paralysis of one side of the body. WH: 17C. Modern Latin, from Greek *hēmiplēgia*. See HEMI-, -PLEGIA.

hemipterous *a.* of or belonging to the order Hemiptera of insects with piercing or sucking mouthparts, and usu. having four wings, the upper pair partly horny and partly membranous, comprising bugs, lice etc. WH: 19C. Modern Latin *Hemiptera*, neut. pl. of *hemipterus*. See HEMI-, -PTERA, also -OUS. The name refers to the partly formed forewings of the insects.

hemisphere *n.* the half of a sphere or globe, divided by a plane passing through its centre. WH: 14–15C. Old French *emispere* (Modern French *hémisphère*), or from Latin *hemisphaerium*, from Greek *hēmisphairion*. See HEMI-, SPHERE.

hemistich *n.* half a verse, usu. as divided by the cæsura. WH: 16C. Late Latin *hemistichium*, from Greek *hēmistikhion*. See HEMI-, STICH.

hemitrope *a.* (of a crystal) looking as if one half were turned round upon the other. Also *n.* WH: 19C. HEMI- + -TROPE.

hemlock *n.* any poisonous umbelliferous plant of the genus *Conium*, esp. *C. maculatum*, having finely divided leaves, spotted stems and small white flowers. WH: pre-1200. Old English *hymlic, hemlic*, of unknown orig. The second syl. became -*lock* (14–15C) as for CHARLOCK.

hemp *n.* an Asian herbaceous plant, *Cannabis sativa*. WH: pre-1200. Old English *henep*, from a Germanic word rel. to Greek *kannabis* (see CANNABIS). See CANVAS.

hen *n.* the female of any bird, esp. the domestic fowl. WH: pre-1200. Old English *henn*, from a deriv. of Germanic base of Old English *hana* cock, rel. to Latin *canere* to sing.

hence *adv.* from this time. Also *int.* WH: 12–14C. Obs. *hen* in the same sense, from Old English *heonan*, from Germanic pronominal base of HE + -S[2]. The spelling -*ce* is phonetic, representing the earlier unvoiced -*s*.

henchman *n.* a faithful follower or supporter. WH: 12–14C. Old English *hengest* stallion, gelding + MAN. The original sense was groom, then squire or page of honour to a person of rank. The sense attendant of a Highland chief evolved in the 18C, and of a political supporter in the 19C. The Old English word gave the name of *Hengest* (*Hengist*), legendary founder of the kingdom of Kent together with his brother Horsa (horse).

hendeca- *comb. form* eleven. WH: Greek *hendeka* eleven (from *hen*, neut. of *heis* one + *deka* ten).

hendecagon *n.* a plane figure of 11 sides and angles. WH: 18C. HENDECA- + -GON.

hendecasyllable *n.* a verse or line of 11 syllables. WH: 17C. Alt. (based on SYLLABLE) of Latin *hendecasyllabus*, from Greek *hendekasullabos*, use as n. of a., eleven-syllabled. Cp. HENDECA-, SYLLABLE.

hendiadys *n.* a rhetorical figure representing one idea by two words connected by a conjunction rather than with subordination, e.g. 'go and find' rather than 'go to find'. WH: 16C. Medieval Latin, from Greek *hen dia duoin* one through two.

henequen *n.* an agave plant, *Agave fourcroydes*, from Mexico. WH: 17C. Spanish *jeniquen, geniquen*, from the Mexican name.

henge *n.* a circle of stones or staves of prehistoric date. WH: 18C. Shortening of *Stonehenge*.

henna *n.* a tropical shrub, *Lawsonia inermis*, having white or red fragrant flowers. Also *v.t.* WH: 17C. Arabic *ḥinnā'*. Cp. ALKANET.

henotheism *n.* worship of or ascription of supreme power to one out of several gods. WH: 19C. Greek *heno-* stem of *heis* one + *theos* god + -ISM.

henry *n.* a unit of inductance of a circuit in which a change of current of 1 ampere per second induces an emf of 1 volt. WH: 19C. Joseph *Henry*, 1797–1878, US physicist.

heparin *n.* a polysaccharide, containing sulphate groups, present in most body tissues; an anticoagulant used in the treatment of thrombosis. WH: early 20C. Greek *hēpar* liver + -IN[1].

hepatic *a.* of or relating to the liver. Also *n.* WH: 14–15C. Latin *hepaticus*, from Greek *hēpatikos*, from *hēpar, hēpatos* liver. See also -IC.

hepatitis *n.* inflammation or congestion of the liver. WH: 18C. Modern Latin *hēpar, hēpatos* liver + -ITIS.

Hepplewhite *a.* belonging to a school of light and graceful furniture design characterized by the use of curves esp. in shield-shaped chair-backs. WH: 19C. George *Hepplewhite*, 1727–86, English cabinetmaker.

hepta- *comb. form* consisting of seven. WH: Greek *hepta* seven.

heptachord *n.* a series of seven notes. WH: 18C. HEPTA- + CHORD[1].

heptad *n.* a sum or group of seven. WH: 17C. Greek *heptas, heptad-*, from *hepta* seven. See also -AD[1].

heptagon *n.* a plane figure having seven sides and seven angles. WH: 16C. French *heptagone*, or from Medieval Latin *heptagonum*, neut. sing. (used as n.) of Late Latin *heptagonus*, a. from Greek *heptagonos* seven-cornered. See HEPTA-, -GON.

heptahedron *n.* a solid figure having seven sides. WH: 17C. HEPTA- + -HEDRON.

heptamerous *a.* having seven parts or members. WH: 19C. HEPTA- + Greek *meros* part + -OUS.

heptameter *n.* a line or verse of seven metrical feet. **WH:** 19C. Late Latin *heptametrum*, from Greek *heptametron*, from HEPTA- + *metron* measure, metre.

heptane *n.* a liquid hydrocarbon of the alkane series, obtained from petroleum. **WH:** 19C. HEPTA- + -ANE.

heptarchy *n.* government by seven rulers. **WH:** 16C. HEPTA- + -ARCHY, based on *tetrarchy* (TETRARCH).

heptastich *n.* a poem or stanza of seven lines. **WH:** 19C. HEPTA- + STICH.

Heptateuch *n.* the first seven books of the Bible. **WH:** 17C. Late Latin *heptateuchus*, from Greek *heptateukhos*, from *hepta* seven + *teukhos* book. Cp. PENTATEUCH.

heptathlon *n.* an athletic contest in which competitors take part in seven events. **WH:** late 20C. HEPTA- + Greek *athlon* contest, based on PENTATHLON etc.

heptavalent *a.* having a valency of seven. **WH:** 19C. HEPTA- + -*valent* (VALENCE), from Latin *valens, valentis*, pres.p. of *valere* to be strong. See also -ENT.

her *pron.* objective (accusative and dative) of SHE. *Also a.* **WH:** pre-1200. Old English *hire* (pron.), *hiere, hire* (a.), respectively dat. and gen. of *hīo, hēo,* fem. of HE. See SHE.

Heraclean *a.* of or relating to Heracles. **WH:** 19C. Latin *Heracleus*, from Greek *Hērakleos*, from *Hēraklēs* Heracles (see HERCULES) + -AN.

herald *n.* a messenger. *Also v.t.* **WH:** 12–14C. Old French *herault* (Modern French *héraut*), from Germanic bases of obs. *here* host, army (cp. HARRY, HARBOUR, HERIOT) and WIELD. The original literal sense is army commander. The sense precursor evolved in the 16C.

herb *n.* a plant producing shoots of only annual duration. **WH:** 12–14C. Old French *erbe* (Modern French *herbe*), from Latin *herba* grass, green crops, herb.

herbivore *n.* an animal, esp. a mammal, that feeds on grass or plants. **WH:** 18C. French or Modern Latin *herbivorus*, from Latin *herba* HERB + -*i*- + *vorare* to devour (see -VORE).

Hercules *n.* a man of enormous strength. **WH:** 12–14C. Latin, alt. of Greek *Hēraklēs*, from *Hēra* wife of Zeus + *kleos* glory, lit. having the glory of Hera. Hercules (Heracles) was a mythological hero of super-human strength, famous for accomplishing twelve great tasks or 'labours' imposed on him by Hera. After his death he was ranked among the gods.

Hercynian *a.* denoting a period of mountain building in Europe in the late Palaeozoic age. **WH:** 16C. Latin *Hercynia* (*silva*) Hercynian (forest). See also -AN. The Latin name is that of a vaguely defined area of forest-covered mountains between the Rhine and the Carpathians.

herd *n.* a number of beasts or cattle feeding, kept or driven together. *Also v.i., v.t.* **WH:** pre-1200. Old English *heord*, from Germanic. Cp. German *Herde*.

herdic *n.* a small horse-drawn carriage, with a low-hung body, back entrance and side seats. **WH:** 19C. Peter *Herdic*, 1824–88, US inventor.

Herdwick *n.* a hardy breed of sheep orig. raised in the mountainous parts of Cumbria. **WH:** 12–14C. HERD (in sense herdsman) + WICK[2]. The original sense (as common n. not name) was pasturage. The name of the sheep breed dates from the 19C.

here *adv.* in or at this place or position. *Also n.* **WH:** pre-1200. Old English *hēr*, appar. from Germanic base meaning this (see HE).

hereditable *a.* that may be inherited. **WH:** 14–15C. Obs. French *héréditable* or Medieval Latin *hereditabilis*, from Ecclesiastical Latin *hereditare* to inherit, from *heres, heredis* HEIR. See also -ABLE.

hereditament *n.* any property that may be inherited. **WH:** 20C. Medieval Latin *hereditamentum*, from Ecclesiastical Latin *hereditare*. See HEREDITABLE, also -MENT.

hereditary *a.* descending or passing by inheritance. **WH:** 14–15C. Latin *hereditarius*, from *hereditas*. See HEREDITY, also -ARY[1].

heredity *n.* the tendency to transmit individual characteristics to one's offspring. **WH:** 16C. Old French *hérédité* or Latin *hereditas*, from *heres, heredis* HEIR. See also -ITY.

Hereford *n.* a breed of red and white beef cattle. **WH:** 19C. *Hereford*, a city and county in the west of England.

heresiarch *n.* a leader of a sect of heretics. **WH:** 16C. Ecclesiastical Latin *haeresiarcha*, from early Greek *hairesiarkhēs* leader of a sect. See HERESY, ARCH-.

heresiographer *n.* a writer on heresies. **WH:** 17C. Greek *hairesis* HERESY + -O- + -*grapher* (-GRAPH).

heresiology *n.* the study of the history of heresy. **WH:** 19C. Greek *hairesis* HERESY + -O- + -LOGY.

heresy *n.* departure from what is held to be true doctrine, esp. when such opinions lead to division in the Christian Church. **WH:** 12–14C. Old French *heresie* (Modern French *hérésie*), from Ecclesiastical Latin *haeresis*, from early Greek *hairesis* heretical sect, from Ecclesiastical Greek *haireomai* to choose, from *hairein* to take.

heretic *n.* a person who holds unorthodox opinions, esp. in religious matters. **WH:** 12–14C. Old French *hérétique*, from Ecclesiastical Latin *haereticus*, from Ecclesiastical Greek *haeretikos* heretical, from Greek *haireomai*. See HERESY, also -IC.

heriot *n.* a tribute, such as a live animal, paid to a lord on the decease of a tenant. **WH:** pre-1200. Old English *heregeatwa*, from *here* host, army + *geatwa* trappings.

heritable *a.* capable of being inherited. **WH:** 14–15C. Old French *héritable*, from *hériter*, from Ecclesiastical Latin *herediture*. See HEREDITABLE.

heritage *n.* land or other property that passes by descent or course of law to an heir. **WH:** 12–14C. Old French (Modern French *héritage*), from *hériter*. See HERITABLE, also -AGE.

herm *n.* in ancient Greece, a statue of a head, usu. of Hermes, placed on a square pillar and set as a boundary etc. **WH:** 16C. Latin *Herma*, from Greek *Hermēs* Hermes, the son of Zeus and Maia in Greek mythology, represented as the god of commerce and the messenger of the gods. The Romans identified him as MERCURY.

hermaphrodite *n.* a human being or an animal abnormally combining in itself both male and female reproductive organs. *Also a.* **WH:** 14–15C. Latin *hermaphroditus*, from Greek *hermaphroditos*, orig. in Greek mythology the name of the son of Hermes and Aphrodite, who became joined in one body with the nymph Salmacis.

hermeneutic *a.* interpreting, explaining, explanatory. **WH:** 17C. Greek *hermēneutikos*, from *hermēneutēs* one who interprets, from *hermēneuein* to interpret, from *hermeneus* interpreter. See also -IC.

hermetic *a.* having an airtight closure. **WH:** 17C. Modern Latin *hermeticus*, from *Hermes Trismegistus* Hermes thrice greatest. See also -IC. *Hermes Trismegistus* was the name given by alchemists to Thoth, the Egyptian god regarded as the founder of alchemy and the supposed inventor of the process of making a glass tube airtight by means of a secret seal. The original sense was pertaining to Hermes Trismegistus or his writings. The sense airtight dates from the 18C.

hermit *n.* an early Christian recluse. **WH:** 12–14C. Old French *ermite, eremite* (Modern French *ermite*) or Late Latin *eremita*, from Greek *erēmitēs*, from *erēmia* desert, from *erēmos* solitary, deserted.

hernia *n.* the protrusion of any organ, or part of an organ, from its natural place; a rupture. **WH:** 14–15C. Latin rupture, rel. to *hira* intestine.

hero *n.* a person of extraordinary valour, fortitude or enterprise. **WH:** 16C. Back-formation from *heroes* (pl.), from Latin pl. of *heros*, from Greek *hērōs*, (pl.) *hērōes*.

heroic *a.* of, relating to or becoming a hero. **WH:** 14–15C. Old French *héroïque* or Latin *heroicus*, from Greek *hērōikos* pertaining to heroes, from *hērōs*. See HERO, also -IC.

heroin *n.* a derivative of morphine, used in medicine and by drug addicts. **WH:** 19C. German, from HERO + -IN[1]. The drug is so called from the effect on the user's self-esteem.

heron *n.* a long-legged, long-necked wading bird of the family Ardeidae, esp. *Ardea cinerea*, the common European heron. **WH:** 12–14C. Old French (Modern French *héron*), from Germanic base of imit. orig. Cp. CROW[1], ROOK[1], etc.

herpes *n.* a viral infection producing vesicles grouped on an inflamed skin surface such as the lip. **WH:** 14–15C. Latin shingles, from Greek, lit. creeping, from *herpein* to creep. Rel. to SERPENT.

herpetology *n.* the study of reptiles and amphibians. **WH:** 19C. Greek *herpeton* creeping thing + -O- + -LOGY.

herptile *n.* a reptile or amphibian. *Also a.* **WH:** early 20C. HERPET-OLOGY + REPTILE.

Herr *n.* the German title corresponding to the English Mr. **WH:** 17C. German, from Old High German *hērro*, comp. of *hēr* exalted.

Herrenvolk *n.* the supposed Aryan race as conceived by Nazi ideology as a master race. WH: mid-20C. German *master race*. See HERR, FOLK.

herring *n.* a soft-finned marine fish, *Clupea harengus*, of the N Atlantic, moving in large shoals and spawning near the coast. WH: pre-1200. Old English *hæring*, from Germanic, of unknown orig.

Herrnhuter *n.* a Moravian, a member of the sect calling themselves the United Brethren. WH: 18C. German *Herrnhut* (the Lord's keeping), name of the first settlement of the Moravian Church + -ER[1]. A group of the earlier Bohemian Brethren fled Moravia in 1722 and settled on the estate of Count Nikolaus Ludwig von Zinzendorf in Saxony, naming their new settlement Herrnhut.

hers *pron.* something which belongs to or is associated with her. WH: 12–14C. HER (pron.) + -S[1].

herself *pron.* SHE or HER (objective), used to give emphasis (usu. in apposition). WH: pre-1200. HER (pron.) + SELF, but long taken as HER (a.) + SELF.

herstory *n.* in feminist jargon, history emphasizing the role of women or told from a woman's point of view. WH: late 20C. HER + STORY, punningly based on HISTORY (as if *his story*).

hertz *n.* a standard unit of frequency equal to one cycle per second. WH: 19C. Heinrich *Hertz*, 1857–94, German physicist.

Hertzian *a.* of or relating to Hertz or the phenomena of electromagnetic vibrations discovered by him. WH: 19C. HERTZ + -IAN.

Heshvan *n.* the second month of the Jewish civil year and the eighth month of the Jewish ecclesiastical year. WH: 19C. Hebrew *ḥeshwān*, from earlier *marḥeshwān*, from Akkadian *araḥ samna* eighth month.

hesitate *v.i.* to stop or pause in action. WH: 17C. Latin *haesitatus*, p.p. of *haesitare* to stick fast, to be undecided, from *haesus*, p.p. of *haerare* to stick, to hold fast. See also -ATE[3].

hesperidium *n.* a citrus fruit, e.g. the orange, with a tough rind and a pulp divided into sections. WH: 19C. Greek *Hesperides* (HESPERUS) + -IUM. The name refers to the mythical golden apples of the Hesperides, the islands guarded by nymphs and believed to be located at the western border of Oceanus, the river that encircles the world.

Hesperus *n.* the evening star, Venus. WH: 14–15C. Latin, from Greek *hesperos* western.

Hessian *n.* a native or inhabitant of Hesse. *Also a.* WH: 17C. *Hesse*, a former grand duchy (now a state) in SW Germany + -IAN.

†hest *n.* a command, an injunction, a behest. WH: pre-1200. Old English *hæs*, from Germanic base of *hātan* to call (see HIGHT), assim. to nn. ending in -t.

hetaera *n.* one of a class of highly educated courtesans in ancient Greece. WH: 19C. Greek *hetaira*, fem. of *hetairos* companion.

hetero *n.* a heterosexual person. WH: mid-20C. Abbr. of HETEROSEXUAL. Cp. HOMO.

hetero- *comb. form* different, dissimilar. WH: Greek *heteros* the other of two, other. See also -O-.

heteroblastic *a.* derived from unlike cells, as distinct from *homoblastic*. WH: 19C. HETERO- + -blastic (-BLAST).

heterocercal *a.* (of fishes) having the upper lobe of the tail longer than the lower. WH: 19C. HETERO- + Greek *kerkos* tail. See also -AL[1].

heterochromatic *a.* of different colours. WH: 19C. HETERO- + CHROMATIC. See also -OUS.

heteroclite *a.* deviating from the ordinary rules or forms. *Also n.* WH: 15C. Medieval Latin *ethroclitus* or Late Latin *heteroclitus*, from Greek *heteroklitos*, from HETERO- + Greek -*klitos* bent, inflected, from *klinein* to lean, to bend. See also -ITE[2].

heterocyclic *a.* (of an organic chemical compound) having a ring structure of atoms of different kinds in the molecules. WH: 19C. HETERO- + *cyclic* (CYCLE).

heterodactyl *a.* (of some birds) having the first and second toes directed backwards and the other two forwards. WH: 19C. HETERO- + Greek *daktulos* finger.

heterodont *a.* having teeth of different forms. *Also n.* WH: 19C. HETERO- + -ODONT.

heterodox *a.* contrary to received or established doctrines, principles or standards; heretical, not orthodox. WH: 17C. Late Latin *heterodoxus*, from Greek *heterodoxos*, from HETERO- + *doxa* opinion.

heterodyne *a.* of or relating to a beat frequency caused in a radio receiver by the interplay of two alternating currents of similar frequencies. *Also v.i.* WH: early 20C. HETERO- + Greek *dunamis* power.

heteroecious *a.* (of parasitic fungi) developing at different times on different hosts. WH: 19C. HETERO- + Greek *oikia* house. See also -OUS.

heterogamous *a.* having flowers or florets sexually different, as in certain Compositae, where the disc florets are male and the ray florets neuter or female. WH: 19C. HETERO- + Greek *gamos* marriage + -OUS.

heterogeneous *a.* diverse in character or structure. WH: 17C. Medieval Latin *heterogeneus*, from Greek *hetergenēs* of different kinds, from HETERO- + *genos* kind. See also -OUS.

heterogenesis *n.* the production of offspring differing in kind from the parent. WH: 19C. HETERO- + GENESIS.

heterogonous *a.* (of certain flowers) having stamens and styles or pistils on different plants of the species differing in length so as to promote cross-fertilization. WH: 19C. HETERO- + Greek -*gonia* generation + -OUS.

heterograft *n.* a tissue graft obtained from a member of one species for a member of another. WH: early 20C. HETERO- + GRAFT[1].

heterography *n.* the employment of the same letters to represent different sounds, as *g* in *go* and *gin*. WH: 18C. HETERO- + -GRAPHY, based on ORTHOGRAPHY.

heterologous *a.* differing in structure from normal tissue. WH: 19C. HETERO- + Greek *logos* relation, ratio. See LOGOS, also -OUS.

heteromerous *a.* differing in number, form or character of parts; not isomerous. WH: 19C. HETERO- + -MEROUS. See also -OUS.

heteromorphic *a.* differing from the normal form. WH: 19C. HETERO- + -*morphic* (-MORPH).

heteronomous *a.* subject to the law or rule of another, not autonomous. WH: 19C. HETERO- + Greek *nomos* law. See also -OUS.

heteronym *n.* a word spelt the same way as another but differing in sound and meaning, as *gill* (gil), a breathing-organ, and *gill* (jil), a measure. WH: 19C. HETERO- + -ONYM.

Heteroousian *a.* of or relating to the Heteroousians. *Also n.* WH: 17C. Greek *heteroousios*, from HETERO- + *ousia* essence, substance. See also -IAN.

heteropathic *a.* allopathic. WH: 19C. HETERO- + Greek *pathos* suffering. See also -IC.

heterophyllous *a.* having leaves of different form on the same plant. WH: 19C. HETERO- + Greek *phullon* leaf. See also -OUS.

heteropolar *a.* having dissimilar (magnetic) poles. WH: 19C. HETERO- + POLAR.

heteropteran *n.* an insect of the suborder Heteroptera, including bugs in which the wings are of dissimilar parts. *Also a.* WH: 19C. Modern Latin *Heteroptera*, from HETERO- + Greek *pteron* wing. See also -AN.

heterosexual *a.* feeling sexual attraction to the opposite sex. *Also n.* WH: 19C. HETERO- + SEXUAL.

heterosis *n.* abnormal vigour or strength typical of a hybrid plant or animal. WH: 19C. Greek *heterōsis* alteration, from *heteros* different. See also -OSIS.

heterosporous *a.* having two kinds of spores. WH: 19C. HETERO- + Greek *spora* spore. See also -OUS.

heterostyled *a.* heterogonous. WH: 19C. HETERO- + STYLE + -ED.

heterotaxy *n.* deviation of organs or parts from ordinary arrangement. WH: 19C. HETERO- + Greek -*taxia* TAXIS.

heterotopy *n.* displacement of a bodily organ etc. WH: 19C. Modern Latin *heterotopia*, from HETERO- + Greek -*topia*, from *topos* place. See also -Y[2].

heterotrophic *a.* obtaining nourishment from organic compounds. WH: 19C. HETERO- + -TROPHIC.

hetman *n.* a commander or leader of Cossacks or Poles. WH: 20C. Polish, ? from German *Hauptmann* (earlier *Heubtman*) headman, captain. Cp. ATAMAN.

het up *a.* excited, agitated, annoyed. WH: 19C. Dial. p.p. of HEAT + UP.

heuchera *n.* a herbaceous plant of the genus *Heuchera* of the saxifrage family, with roundish leaves and stalks of red, white or green flowers rising directly from the rootstock. WH: 18C. Modern Latin, from J.H. *Heucher*, 1677–1747, German botanist.

heulandite *n.* a monoclinic, transparent brittle mineral, consisting chiefly of silica, alumina and lime, occurring chiefly in amygdaloid rock. WH: 19C. Henry *Heuland*, 1777–1856, English mineralogist + -ITE[1].

heuristic *a.* serving or tending to find out; not correct or provable, but aiding the discovery of truth. *Also n.* WH: 19C. Greek *heuriskein* to find, based on words in *-istic* from vv. in *-izein* -IZE.

hevea *n.* any tree of the S American genus *Hevea*, having a milky sap which provides rubber. WH: 19C. Modern Latin, from Quechua *hyeve*.

hew *v.t.* to cut (down, away, off etc.) with an axe etc. *Also v.i., n.* WH: pre-1200. Old English *hēawan*, from Germanic. Cp. German *hauen*.

hex[1] *v.i.* to practise witchcraft. *Also v.t., n.* WH: 19C. Pennsylvanian German *hexe*, from German *hexen*, from *Hexe* witch. Cp. HAG[1].

hex[2] *n.* the hexadecimal number system; hexadecimal notation. WH: late 20C. Abbr. of HEXADECIMAL.

hexa- *comb. form* six. WH: Greek *hex*, *hexa-* six.

hexachord *n.* a scale or diatonic series of six notes with a semitone between the third and the fourth. WH: 17C. HEXA- + CHORD[1].

hexad *n.* a group of six. WH: 17C. Greek *hexas*, *hexados* group of six, from *hex* six. See also -AD[1].

hexadecimal *a.* (of a number system) having 16 as its base. *Also n.* WH: mid-20C. HEXA- + DECIMAL.

hexaemeron *n.* a period of six days, esp. the six days of the Creation in the biblical account. WH: Ecclesiastical Latin, from Greek use as n. of a. *hexaēmeros*, from HEXA- + *hēmera* day.

hexagon *n.* a plane figure having six sides. WH: 16C. Late Latin *hexagonum*, from Greek *hexagōnon*, use as n. of *hexagōnos* six-cornered. See HEXA-, -GON.

hexagram *n.* a figure formed by two equilateral triangles whose points coincide with those of a regular hexagon. WH: 19C. HEXA- + -GRAM.

hexahedron *n.* a solid body of six sides, esp. a regular cube. WH: 16C. Greek *hexaedron*, neut. sing. of *hexaedros*. See HEXA-, -HEDRON.

hexameter *n.* a line or verse consisting of six metrical feet. WH: 14–15C. Latin, from Greek *hexametros* of six measures. See HEXA- + -METER.

hexane *n.* a liquid hydrocarbon of the alkane series. WH: 19C. HEXA- + -ANE.

hexangular *a.* having six angles. WH: 17C. HEXA- + ANGULAR.

hexapla *n.* an edition of a book, esp. of the Bible, having six versions in parallel columns. WH: 17C. Greek (*ta*) *hexapla* (the) sixfold (texts), neut. pl. of *hexaplous* sixfold. *Hexapla* was the title of Origen's edition of the Old Testament in six versions arranged in parallel columns (3C AD).

hexapod *n.* an animal having six legs; a member of the order Hexapoda or Insecta, an insect. *Also a.* WH: 17C. Greek *hexapous*, *hexapodos*. See HEXA-, -POD.

hexastich *n.* a poem or poetical passage of six lines or verses. WH: 16C. HEXA- + Greek *stikhos* line of verse. See STICH.

hexastyle *n., a.* (a portico or temple) having six columns. WH: 18C. HEXA- + Greek *stulos* column. See STYLE.

Hexateuch *n.* the first six books of the Old Testament. WH: 19C. HEXA- Greek *teukhos* book. Cp. HEPTATEUCH, PENTATEUCH.

hexavalent *a.* having a valency of six. WH: 19C. HEXA- + *-valent*, from Latin *valens*, *valentis*, pres.p. of *valere* to be strong. See also -ENT.

hexose *n.* a monosaccharide, such as glucose, that contains six carbon atoms per molecule. WH: 19C. HEXA- + -OSE[2].

hey *int.* used to express joy, surprise, interrogation, encouragement etc. WH: 12–14C. Natural exclamation. Cp. HEIGH.

heyday *n.* the time of greatest spirits, vigour, prosperity etc. WH: 16C. Obs. *hey-day*, interjection of joy, surprise etc. Cp. Low German *heida*, lit. hi there. Not from *high day* (HIGH). The original sense was a state of high spirits. The sense of the full bloom of youth etc. dates from the 18C.

Hg *chem. symbol* mercury. WH: Abbr. of HYDRARGYRUM.

hi *int.* used as a greeting or to call attention. WH: 14–15C. Natural exclamation. Cp. HEY.

hiatus *n.* a gap, a break, a lacuna in a manuscript, connected series etc. WH: 16C. Latin gaping, opening, from *hiare* to gape.

Hib *n.* a bacterium, *Haemophilus influenzae* type B, causing meningitis in children. WH: late 20C. Acronym of *H*aemophilus *i*nfluenzae (type) *B*.

hibernaculum *n.* the winter quarters of a hibernating animal. WH: 17C. Latin, from *hibernare* HIBERNATE. See also -CULE.

hibernate *v.i.* (of some animals) to pass the winter in sleep or torpor. WH: 19C. Latin *hibernatus*, p.p. of *hibernare*, from *hiberna* winter quarters, neut. pl. (used as n.) of *hibernus* wintry. See also -ATE[3].

Hibernian *a.* of or relating to Ireland. *Also n.* WH: 16C. Latin *Hibernia* Ireland, alt. of *Iuverna*, *luberna*, from Greek *Iernē*, from Celtic. See also -AN, -IAN.

Hiberno- *comb. form* of or relating to Ireland, Irish. WH: Medieval Latin *Hibernus* Irish. See HIBERNIAN, also -O-.

hibiscus *n.* a mallow of the mostly tropical genus *Hibiscus* with large brightly coloured flowers. WH: 18C. Latin, from Greek *hibiskos* marsh mallow.

hic *int.* used to represent a sound like a hiccup, denoting interruption, as in the speech of a drunken person. WH: 19C. Imit. Cp. HICCUP.

hiccup *n.* a short, audible catching of the breath due to spasmodic contraction of the diaphragm and the glottis. *Also v.i., v.t.* WH: 16C. Imit. The alternative spelling *hiccough* has been assimilated to COUGH.

hic jacet *n.* an epitaph. WH: 17C. Latin here lies, first two words of a Latin epitaph, from *hic* here + 3rd pers. sing. pres. of *iacere* to lie. Cp. CI-GÎT.

hick *n.* a country bumpkin, a farmer, a yokel; an unsophisticated person. *Also a.* WH: 16C. *Hick*, pet form of male forename *Richard*. Cp. DICK[1], HODGE.

hickey *n.* a device, a gadget. WH: early 20C. Orig. unknown.

hickory *n.* any of several N American trees of the genus *Carya*, allied to the walnuts, esp. *C. alba*, the timber of which is tough and elastic. WH: 17C. Abbr. of obs. *pohickory*, from Virginia Algonquian *pawcohiccora*.

hidalgo *n.* a Spanish nobleman of the lowest class, a gentleman by birth. WH: 16C. Spanish, formerly also *hijo dalgo*, contr. of *hijo de algo*, lit. son of something.

hide[1] *v.t.* to put out of or withhold from sight or observation. *Also v.i., n.* WH: pre-1200. Old English *hȳdan*, from Germanic.

hide[2] *n.* the skin of an animal, esp. when dressed. *Also v.t.* WH: pre-1200. Old English *hȳd*, from Germanic, from Indo-European base also of Latin *cutis*, Greek *kutos* skin, hide. Cp. German *Haut* skin.

hide[3] *n.* a certain portion of land variously estimated at from 60 to 120 acres (24 to 48 ha), orig. enough to support a family and its dependants. WH: pre-1200. Old English *hīd*, earlier *hīgid*, from Germanic, from base of Latin *civis* citizen. Cp. HIND[3].

hideous *a.* exceedingly ugly, repulsive. WH: 12–14C. Old French *hidos*, *hideus* (Modern French *hideux*), from *hide* fear, ult. of unknown orig. See also -EOUS.

hidrosis *n.* (esp. excessive) sweating, perspiration. WH: 19C. Greek *hidrōsis*, from *hidrōs sweat*. See also -OSIS.

†hie *v.i., v.refl.* to hasten, to hurry. *Also v.t., n.* WH: pre-1200. Old English *hīgian* to strive, to hasten, from Germanic.

Hieland *a.* Highland. WH: 14–15C. Var. of HIGHLAND.

hierarchy *n.* a system of persons or things arranged in a graded order. WH: 14–15C. Old French *ierarchie* (Modern French *hiérarchie*), from Medieval Latin *hierarchia*, from Greek *hierarkhia*, from *hierarkhēs* high priest, from *hieros* sacred + *arkhēs* ruling. See also -Y[2].

hieratic *a.* of or relating to the priesthood, priestly. WH: 17C. Latin *hieraticus*, from Greek *hieratikos* priestly, from *hierasthai* to be a priest, from *hiereus* priest, *hieros* sacred. See also -IC.

hiero- *comb. form* sacred; of or relating to sacred things. WH: Greek *hieros* sacred, holy. See also -O-.

hierocracy *n.* government by priests, hierarchy. WH: 18C. HIERO- + -CRACY.

hieroglyph *n.* the figure of an animate or inanimate object used in writing to represent a word, sound etc., as practised by the ancient Egyptians, the Aztecs and others. *Also v.t.* WH: 16C. Back-formation from *hieroglyphic*, from French *hiéroglyphique* or Late Latin *hieroglyphicus*, from Greek *hierogluphikos*, from *hieros* (see HIERO-) + *gluphē* carving. See also -IC.

hierogram *n.* a sacred writing, character or symbol. WH: 17C. HIERO- + -GRAM.

hierolatry *n.* the worship of sacred persons or things, esp. the worship of saints. WH: 19C. HIERO- + -LATRY.

hierology *n.* religious or sacred literature or lore. WH: 19C. HIERO + -LOGY.

hierophant *n.* a person who teaches or explains the mysteries of religion. WH: 17C. Late Latin *hierophanta*, from Greek *hierophantēs*, from *hieros* (see HIERO-) + *phan-*, base of *phanein* to reveal. See also -ANT.

hi-fi *n.* any equipment for high-quality sound reproduction. *Also a.* WH: mid-20C. *hi*, representation of pronun. of HIGH + abbr. of FIDELITY, representing *high fidelity*.

higgle *v.i.* to haggle or dispute over terms when bargaining. WH: 17C. Var. of HAGGLE.

higgledy-piggledy *adv.* in confusion, topsy-turvy. *Also a.*, *n.* WH: 16C. Rhyming jingle based on PIG, ref. to pigs herding together (or huddling together).

high *a.* rising or extending upwards for or to a great extent. *Also adv.*, *n.* WH: pre-1200. Old English *hēah*, from Germanic. Cp. German *hoch*.

highland *n.* high or mountainous ground. WH: pre-1200. HIGH + LAND.

high-muck-a-muck *n.* a self-important person. WH: 19C. Said to be from Chinook Jargon *hiyu muckamuck* plenty of food, from Nootka *ḥayo* ten + *ma·ho·maq-* choice whalemeat, with assim. to HIGH and MUCK. Cp. *Lord Muck*.

†**thight** *v.i.* to be named or called. *Also v.t.* WH: pre-1200. Old English *hātan*, from Germanic, from a base represented by Latin *ciere* to summon, CITE. Cp. German *heissen* to be called.

highway *n.* a public road open to all passengers. WH: pre-1200. HIGH + WAY. The road is so called, like *high street*, not for its elevation but for its importance as a main throughfare.

hijack *v.t.* to take over (a vehicle, aircraft etc.) by force, esp. to divert it from its route. *Also n.* WH: early 20C. Orig. uncertain. ? From HIGHWAY + JACK¹ (in sense man, fellow). Cp. *highwayman* (HIGHWAY).

hike *n.* a ramble, a long country walk. *Also v.i.*, *v.t.* WH: 19C. Orig. unknown. Not rel. to HITCH despite similarity of sense in e.g. *hike/hitch up one's trousers* and assoc. of both words in *hitch-hike* (see HITCH).

hilarious *a.* extremely funny. WH: 19C. Latin *hilaris*, from Greek *hilaros* cheerful + -OUS.

Hilary term *n.* the spring term at Oxford and Dublin universities and the Inns of Court. WH: 14–15C. *Hilarius* (Hilary), *c.*315–*c.*368, bishop of Poitiers, whose feast day is 13 January.

hill *n.* a noticeable natural elevation on the surface of the earth, less high and abrupt than a mountain. *Also v.t.* WH: pre-1200. Old English *hyll*, from Germanic, from Indo-European base also of Latin *collis*, Greek *kolōnos* hill. Cp. HOLM¹.

hilt *n.* the handle of a sword, dagger etc. *Also v.t.* WH: pre-1200. Old English, from Germanic, of unknown orig.

hilum *n.* the spot on a seed where it was attached to the seed vessel. WH: 17C. Latin little thing, trifle.

him *pron.* objective (accusative and dative) of HE. WH: pre-1200. Old English, from Germanic base of HE.

Himalayan *a.* of or relating to the Himalayas, a range of high mountains in Nepal. WH: 19C. *Himalaya*, mountains in Nepal (from Sanskrit *hima* snow + *ālaya* abode) + -AN.

himation *n.* the ordinary outer garment in ancient Greece, an oblong piece of cloth thrown over the left shoulder. WH: 19C. Greek, dim. of *heima*, *heimatos* garment.

himbo *n.* a man who looks good but lacks depth or intelligence, a male bimbo. WH: late 20C. Blend of HIM + BIMBO.

himself *pron.* HE or HIM (objective), used to give emphasis (usu. in apposition). WH: pre-1200. HIM + SELF.

hin *n.* a Hebrew measure for liquids, equal to 12 pints or 3.5 litres. WH: 14–15C. Biblical Hebrew *hīn*.

hind¹ *a.* of, relating to or situated at the back or rear. WH: 12–14C. ? Abbr. of Old English *behindan* BEHIND.

hind² *n.* the female of the deer, esp. the red deer. WH: pre-1200. Old English, from Germanic, from Indo-European base meaning hornless. Cp. Greek *kemas* young deer.

hind³ *n.* an agricultural labourer, a farm worker, esp. one in charge of two horses and allotted a house on the farm. WH: pre-1200. Old

English *hīna*, gen. pl. of *hīgan* (cp. HIDE³), as in *hīna fæder* paterfamilias. The *-d* was added as for SOUND¹.

hinder *v.t.* to obstruct, to impede, to prevent from proceeding or moving. *Also v.i.* WH: pre-1200. Old English *hindrian*, from Greek, from a base represented by Old English *hinder* below.

Hindi *n.* the group of Indo-European languages spoken in northern India. *Also a.* WH: 19C. Urdu *hindī*, from *Hind* India. Cp. HINDU.

Hindu *n.* a follower of Hinduism. *Also a.* WH: 17C. Urdu, from Persian *hindū*, formerly *hindō*, from *Hind* India.

hinge *n.* the joint or mechanical device on which a door or lid turns. *Also v.t.*, *v.i.* WH: 12–14C. From base of HANG.

hinny¹ *n.* the offspring of a male horse and female donkey. WH: 17C. Latin *hinnus*, from Greek *hinnos*, assim. to HINNY².

hinny² *v.i.* to neigh, to whinny. WH: 14–15C. Old French *hennir*, from Latin *hinnire* to neigh, of imit. orig. Cp. WHINNY.

hinny³ *n.* sweetheart, darling. WH: 19C. Var. of HONEY.

hint *n.* a slight or distant allusion. *Also v.t.*, *v.i.* WH: 17C. Prob. alt. of obs. *hent* to seize, to reach, to get, from Old English *hentan*, from Germanic base of HUNT. The original sense (to the 19C) was occasion, opportunity.

hinterland *n.* the region situated behind something, esp. a coast or the shore of a river. WH: 19C. German, from *hinter-* behind + *Land* land.

hip¹ *n.* the projection of the articulation of the femur and the thigh bone; the projecting fleshy part covering a hip joint. *Also v.t.* WH: pre-1200. Old English *hype*, from Germanic base rel. to HOP¹.

hip² *n.* the fruit of a rose plant. WH: pre-1200. Old English *hēope*, from Germanic. Cp. German *Hiefe*.

hip³ *int.* used to introduce cheers. WH: 18C. Orig. unknown.

hip⁴ *a.* aware, in the know. WH: early 20C. Orig. uncertain. According to some, the word comes from the drillmaster's *hep*, *hep*, to a marching column, keeping them in step. It evolved from the American jazz scene, and early jazz musicians often marched in parades.

hippic *a.* of or relating to horses or horseracing. WH: 19C. Greek *hippikos*, from *hippos* horse. See also -IC.

hippo *n.* a hippopotamus. WH: 19C. Abbr. of HIPPOPOTAMUS.

hippo- *comb. form* of, relating to or resembling a horse. WH: Greek *hippos* horse. See also -O-.

hippocampus *n.* a sea horse of the genus *Hippocampus*. WH: 16C. Latin, from Greek *hippokampos*, from *hippos* horse + *kampos* sea monster.

hippocras *n.* a cordial made of wine and spices. WH: 14–15C. Old French *ipocras*, from Latin *Hippocrates* (see HIPPOCRATIC), used in Medieval Latin *vinum Hippocraticum* wine strained through a filter known as Hippocrates' sleeve, a conical bag of cotton, linen or flannel used as a filter.

Hippocratic *a.* of or relating to Hippocrates. WH: 17C. Medieval Latin *Hippocraticus*, from *Hippocrates*, *c.*460–*c.*377 BC, Greek physician. See also -IC.

Hippocrene *n.* poetic inspiration. WH: 17C. Latin, from Greek *Hippokrēnē* or *Hippou krēnē*, lit. fountain of the horse. The name is that of a fountain on Mount Helicon sacred to the Muses, said to have been produced by a stamp of the hoof of Pegasus.

hippodrome *n.* a music hall, variety theatre or circus. WH: 16C. Old French, or from Latin *hippodromus*, from Greek *hippodromos*, from *hippos* horse + *dromos* race, course.

hippogriff *n.* a fabulous winged creature, half horse and half griffin. WH: 17C. French *hippogriffe*, from Italian *ippogrifo*, from *ippo* HIPPO- + *grifo* griffin, from Late Latin *gryphus* GRIFFIN.

hippopotamus *n.* a massive African thick-skinned quadruped, *Hippopotamus amphibius*, of amphibious habits, with a heavy body, short, blunt muzzle and short limbs and tail. WH: 12–14C. Old French *ypotame*, Medieval Latin *ypotamus*, or from Latin *hippopotamus*, ult. from Greek *hippopotamos*, earlier *hippos ho potamios* horse of the river.

hippy *n.* a member of the youth culture of the 1960s, which stressed universal love and brotherhood, rejection of middle-class values, the wearing of long hair and colourful clothes, and the use of drugs. WH: mid-20C. HIP⁴ + -Y³.

hiragana *n.* the cursive form of Japanese syllabic writing. WH: 19C. Japanese, from *hira* plain + KANA. Cp. KATAKANA.

hircine *a.* of or like a goat esp. in smell. WH: 17C. Latin *hircinus*, from *hircus* he-goat. See also -INE.

hire *n.* the act of hiring or the state of being hired. *Also v.t.* WH: pre-1200. Old English *hÿr*, from Germanic.

hirsute *a.* rough or hairy. WH: 17C. Latin *hirsutus* rough, shaggy.

hirudin *n.* a substance secreted by the salivary gland of the leech, preventing blood-clotting. WH: early 20C. Latin *hirudo* leech + -IN[1].

hirundine *n.* a bird of the swallow family Hirundinidae. *Also a.* WH: 19C. Latin *hirundo* swallow + -INE.

his *a.* possessive of HE. *Also pron.* WH: pre-1200. Old English, gen. of HE, IT[1].

Hispanic *a.* of or relating to Spain or Spain and Portugal. *Also n.* WH: 16C. Latin *Hispanicus*, from Hispania Spain. See also -IC.

hispid *a.* rough, bristly. WH: 17C. Latin *hispidus*. See also -ID.

hiss *v.i.* (of a person or animal) to make a sound like that of the letter *s*, to make a sibilant sound. *Also v.t., n.* WH: 14–15C. Imit. Cp. WHISTLE, WHISPER.

†hist *int.* used to attract attention or as a warning to be silent, behave etc. *Also v.t.* WH: 16C. Natural exclamation. Cp. PSST, WHISHT.

histamine *n.* an amine formed from histidine and released by the body tissues in allergic reactions. WH: early 20C. HISTIDINE + AMINE.

histic *a.* of or relating to tissue. WH: 19C. Greek *histos* tissue + -IC.

histidine *n.* an amino acid derived from proteins. WH: 19C. Greek *histos* tissue, web + -IDE + -INE.

histo- *comb. form* of or relating to organic tissues. WH: Greek *histos* tissue. See also -O-.

histochemistry *n.* the application of chemistry to organic tissue. WH: 19C. HISTO- + CHEMISTRY.

histocompatibility *n.* the compatibility of tissues that allows one to be grafted successfully onto another. WH: mid-20C. HISTO- + *compatibility* (COMPATIBLE).

histogen *n.* an area of tissue on a plant from which a specific part develops. WH: early 20C. HISTO- + -GEN.

histogenesis *n.* the formation of tissues and organs from undifferentiated cells. WH: 19C. HISTO- + GENESIS.

histogram *n.* a pictorial method of showing the distribution of various quantities, e.g. rainfall month by month. WH: 19C. Greek *histos* mast, web + -GRAM. The word was coined in 1891 by the English mathematician and scientist Karl Pearson.

histology *n.* the (microscopic) study of the tissues of plants or animals. WH: 19C. HISTO- + -LOGY.

histolysis *n.* the decay and dissolution of organic tissue. WH: 19C. HISTO- + -*lysis* (LYSIS).

histone *n.* any of various water-soluble proteins found in cell nuclei. WH: 19C. German *Histon*, ? from Greek *histonai* to arrest or *histos* web, tissue. See also -ONE.

histopathology *n.* (the study of) changes in tissue caused by disease. WH: 19C. HISTO- + PATHOLOGY.

historian *n.* a writer of history, esp. one who is an authority on it. WH: 14–15C. Old French *historien*, from Latin *historia*. See also -AN, -IAN.

historiated *a.* ornamented with figures (as illuminated capitals etc.). WH: 19C. French *historié*, p.p. of *historier*, from Medieval Latin *historiare*. See HISTORY, also -ATE[3], -ED.

historic *a.* celebrated in history, associated with historical events. WH: 17C. French *historique* or Latin *historicus*, from Greek *historikos*, from *historia* HISTORY. See also -IC.

historiographer *n.* a writer of history, esp. an official historian. WH: 15C. Old French *historiographe* or Late Latin *historiographus*, from Greek *historiographos*, from *historia* HISTORY. See also -O-, -*grapher* (-GRAPH).

history *n.* a systematic record of past events, esp. those of public importance. *Also v.t.* WH: 14–15C. Latin *historia*, from Greek learning by enquiry, narrative, from *histōr* learned, wise man, ult. from Indo-European base also of WIT[1].

histrionic *a.* of or relating to actors or acting. *Also n.* WH: 17C. Late Latin *histrionicus*, from Latin *histrio, histrionis* actor. See also -IC.

hit *v.t.* to strike or touch with a blow or missile, esp. after taking aim. *Also v.i., n.* WH: pre-1200. Old Norse *hitta* to light upon, to meet with, from Scandinavian, ult. of unknown orig. Cp. Swedish *hitta*, Danish *hitte* to find.

hitch *v.t.* to fasten with a hook or knot, esp. temporarily. *Also v.i., n.* WH: 12–14C. Orig. unkown. Not rel. to HIKE.

hither *adv.* to this place, end or point. *Also a.* WH: pre-1200. Old English *hider*, from Germanic demonstrative base of HE, HENCE, HERE + suf. as in Latin *citra* on this side (see CIS-). Cp. THITHER, WHITHER, etc.

Hitler *n.* a person resembling Hitler. WH: mid-20C. Adolf *Hitler*, 1889–1945, German Nazi dictator, Chancellor of the German Reich.

Hittite *a.* of or relating to the Hittites, a people of uncertain origin inhabiting parts of Asia Minor and Syria before 1000 BC. *Also n.* WH: 16C. Hebrew *Ḥittīm*, Hittite *Ḥatti* + -ITE[1].

hive *n.* an artificial structure for housing bees, a beehive. *Also v.t., v.i.* WH: pre-1200. Old English *hÿf*, from Germanic base of Old Norse *húfr* ship's hull. Cp. Latin *cupa* barrel.

hives *n.pl.* nettle-rash or a similar inflammation of the skin. WH: 18C. Orig. unknown.

hiya *int.* used as a greeting. WH: mid-20C. Appar. contr. of *how are you*, influ. by HI.

ho *int.* used to call attention, or to express exultation, surprise etc. WH: 12–14C. Natural exclamation. Cp. HA, O.

hoactzin *n.* a S American bird, *Opisthocomus hoazin*, with a brownish plumage and a harsh hissing cry. WH: 17C. American Spanish, from Nahuatl *uatzin*, prob. imit.

hoar *a.* grey with age. *Also v.i., v.t., n.* WH: pre-1200. Old English *hār* grey, from Germanic, from Indo-European stem meaning to shine. Cp. German *hehr* august, sacred.

hoard *n.* an accumulated store (often of valuables) hidden away for future use. *Also v.t., v.i.* WH: pre-1200. Old English *hord* store, valuable stock, from Germanic.

hoarding *n.* a large screen for posting bills on. WH: 19C. Obs. *hoard* (prob. ult. from Anglo-French *hourdis*, from Old French *hourd*, from Frankish, rel. to Old High German *hurt* HURDLE + -*is* from Latin -*itius* -ICE) + -ING[1].

hoarse *a.* (of the voice) harsh, rough or husky. WH: pre-1200. Old English *hās*, from Germanic, ult. of unknown orig. Not rel. to HARSH. The -*r*- is unexplained.

hoary *a.* white or whitish-grey as with age. WH: 14–15C. HOAR + -Y[1].

hoast *v.i.* to cough. *Also n.* WH: 12–14C. Old Norse *hóste*, from Germanic.

hoax *n.* a deception meant as a practical joke. *Also v.t.* WH: 18C. Prob. contr. of HOCUS.

hob[1] *n.* the flat top part of a cooking stove containing hotplates or burners. WH: 16C. Alt. of HUB.

hob[2] *n.* a hobgoblin or an elf, a sprite. WH: 14–15C. *Hob*, var. of *Rob*, pet form of male forename *Robert* or *Robin*.

Hobbesian *a.* of or relating to the philosopher Hobbes or his political philosophy. WH: 18C. Thomas *Hobbes*, 1588–1679, English political philosopher + -IAN.

hobbit *n.* a member of a fictional race of small people living in holes. WH: mid-20C. Invented word. The word was coined by the English writer J.R.R. Tolkien, 1892–1973, who said it meant hole builder. It became widely known following the publication of his tale *The Hobbit* (1937).

hobble *v.i.* to walk lamely or awkwardly. *Also v.t., n.* WH: 12–14C. Prob. of Low German orig. Cp. early Dutch *hobbelen* to toss, to rock from side to side, to halt. The sense to tie the legs of horses arose in the 18C as a variant of HOPPLE.

hobbledehoy *n.* a clumsy, awkward youth. WH: 16C. Orig. unknown. ? First element from HOB[2]. The word has been derived by some from French *hobereau* (HOBBY[2]) which also means country squire.

hobby[1] *n.* any recreation or pursuit. WH: 12–14C. Var. of *Robbie*, abbr. of male forename *Robert*. The original sense was small horse, pony, whether real or as a figure (*hobbyhorse*) worn by a performer in a morris dance, pantomime, etc. The sense children's toy horse arose in the 16C and this (as *hobbyhorse*) gave the sense topic of obsessive interest (17C), then (as *hobby*) favourite recreation or pursuit (19C).

hobby[2] *n.* a small species of falcon, *Falco subbuteo*. WH: 14–15C. Old French *hobé, hobet*, dim. of *hobe* falcon, prob. rel. to *hobeler*, from Middle Dutch *hobbelen* to turn, to roll (see HOBBLE). Cp. HOBBLEDEHOY.

hobday *v.t.* to perform a surgical operation on (a horse) to improve breathing. WH: mid-20C. Sir Frederick T.G. *Hobday*, 1869–1939, British veterinary surgeon.

hobgoblin *n.* a kind of goblin, elf or fairy, esp. one of a frightful appearance. WH: 16C. HOB² + GOBLIN.

hobnail *n.* a short thick nail with a large head, used for heavy boots. *Also v.t.* WH: 16C. HOB¹ + NAIL.

hobnob *v.i.* to associate familiarly (with). *Also adv.* WH: 19C. From phr. *hob and nob* or *hob or nob* expressing good wishes to another person before drinking, from *hob*, var. of obs. *hab* (from Old English *hæbbe*, pres. subj. of HAVE) and corr. neg. form *nab* (Old English *næbbe*). The sense is thus may you have or not have (whichever you wish).

hobo *n.* a wandering worker, vagrant or tramp. WH: 19C. Of unknown orig.

Hobson-Jobson *n.* the practice of assimilating foreign words and modifying them to approximate to familiar sounds in the native language. WH: 19C. Title of Henry Yule and A.C. Burnell's *Hobson-Jobson* (1886), a dictionary of Anglo-Indian words. The title itself represents a British corruption of Arabic *Yā Ḥasan! Yā Ḥusayn!* O Hasan! O Husain!, a cry used by Muslims at the Muharram festival as an expression of mourning for Hasan and Husain, grandsons of Muhammad. Hasan died in AD 669, perhaps poisoned, while Husain was killed in the struggle between the Sunni and Shia parties in AD 680.

Hobson's choice *n.* no alternative. WH: 17C. Thomas *Hobson*, 1554–1631, Cambridge carrier who gave his customers a choice between the next available horse or none at all.

hock¹ *n.* the joint between the knee and the fetlock in the hind leg of quadrupeds. *Also v.t.* WH: 15C. *Hock*, var. of *hough* (pre-1200), from Old English *hōh*, from Germanic. The word is related to obsolete *hoe* projecting ridge of land, as in Plymouth *Hoe*.

hock² *n.* a kind of light wine, still or sparkling, made at Hochheim in Nassau. WH: 17C. Abbr. of obs. *Hockamore*, alt. of German *Hochheimer* (*Wein*) (wine) of Hochheim, a town on the river Main, Germany.

hock³ *v.t.* to pawn. *Also n.* WH: 19C. Dutch *hok* hutch, hovel, prison, credit, debt.

hockey¹ *n.* a team ball game played with a club having a curved end. WH: 16C. Orig. uncertain. ? Rel. to Old French *hocquet* stick, crook, or to HOOK.

hockey² *n.* harvest home, or the feast celebrating this. WH: 16C. Alt. of obs. *horkey*, of unknown orig.

Hocktide *n.* a festival held on the second Monday and Tuesday after Easter. WH: 12–14C. Orig. unknown.

hocus *v.t.* to take in, to hoax. *Also n.* WH: 17C. Abbr. of *hocus-pocus*, from pseudo-Latin *hax pax max Deus adimax*, used as magical formula, ? ult. from *Hoc est corpus meum* This is my body, phr. from Latin mass. According to some, *hocus-pocus* is a variant form of HOTCHPOTCH.

hod *n.* a wooden holder shaped like a trough and fixed on a long handle, for carrying mortar or bricks on the shoulder. WH: 16C. Var. of obs. *hot* kind of basket, from Old French *hotte*, prob. of Germanic orig.

hodden *n.* a coarse woollen cloth such as would be produced by a handloom. *Also a.* WH: 16C. Orig. unknown.

Hodge *n.* a typical member of the agricultural labouring class. WH: 14–15C. Form of male forename *Roger*. Cp. HICK.

hodgepodge *n.* a dish of mixed ingredients. WH: 14–15C. Var. of HOTCHPOTCH.

Hodgkin's disease *n.* a malignant disease characterized by progressive anaemia and enlargement of the liver, lymph glands etc. WH: 19C. Thomas *Hodgkin*, 1798–1866, English physician.

hodiernal *a.* of or relating to the present day. WH: 17C. Latin *hodiernus*, from *hodie* today. See also -AL¹.

hodograph *n.* the curve traced by the end of lines, drawn from a fixed point, representing in magnitude and direction the velocity of a moving point. WH: 19C. Greek *hodos* way + -GRAPH.

hodoscope *n.* any device for tracing the path of a charged particle. WH: early 20C. Greek *hodos* way + -SCOPE.

hoe *n.* a tool used to scrape or stir up earth around plants, cut weeds

up from the ground etc. *Also v.t., v.i.* WH: 12–14C. Old French *houe*, from Frankish, from Germanic. Rel. to HEW.

hog *n.* a swine, esp. a castrated boar meant for killing. *Also v.t., v.i.* WH: pre-1200. ? Celtic. Cp. Welsh *hwch*, Cornish *hoch* pig, sow.

hogget *n.* a yearling sheep. WH: 14–15C. HOG + -ET¹. The original sense was a young boar in its second year.

hoggin *n.* screened gravel for footpaths. WH: 19C. Orig. unknown.

hogmanay *n.* in Scotland, the last day of the year, New Year's Eve. WH: 17C. Rel. in sense and use to Old French *aguillanneuf* last day of the year, new year gift (as cried on this day), with Norman form of this, *hoguinané*, ? source of English word. The Old French word has been analysed as *au gui l'an neuf* to the mistletoe the new year, though only the second half of this seems plausible.

hogshead *n.* a large cask. WH: 14–15C. HOG + -'S + HEAD¹. The reason for the name is unknown.

ho-hum *int.* used to express a feeling of tedium, lack of interest, resignation etc. WH: early 20C. HO + HUM², representing the sound of a yawn.

hoick *v.t.* to pull up or out of something, esp. abruptly. WH: 19C. ? Var. of HIKE.

hoi polloi *n.* the common herd, the masses. WH: 17C. Greek the many, from *hoi*, pl. of *ho* the + *polloi* many, pl. of *polus* much (see POLY-). To speak of 'the hoi polloi' is strictly speaking a tautology.

hoist *v.t.* to raise up. *Also n.* WH: 15C. Alt. of obs. *hoise* in same sense, prob from, from obs. Dutch *hijschen* (now *hijsen*), or from Low German *hissen*, from Germanic. Cp. HEIST. The final -*t* may have come from the past participle of the original verb.

hoity-toity *int.* used to express astonishment mixed with disapproval and contempt. *Also a., n.* WH: 17C. Redupl. of obs. *hoit* to behave riotously, of unknown orig. The original sense was riotous conduct. The current sense followed soon after.

hokey *a.* sentimental, corny or phoney. WH: mid-20C. HOKUM + -Y¹.

hokey-cokey *n.* a dance in which a group forms a circle and moves and shakes arms and legs in accordance with the song to which it is danced. WH: mid-20C. Orig. unknown. ? From refrain of a song. The word is related by some to *hocus-pocus* (HOCUS).

hokey-pokey *n.* ice cream formerly sold by street vendors. WH: 19C. Orig. unknown. The original sense was deception, trickery, as an altered form of *hocus-pocus* (HOCUS). The sense ice cream followed soon after but is probably from a different source. Some derive it from the cry of Italian ice cream sellers, *O che poco!* Oh how little!, referring to the cost.

hoki *n.* an edible fish of New Zealand coasts, *Macruronus novaezelandiae*, related to the hake. WH: 19C. Maori.

hokum *n.* bunkum. WH: early 20C. Orig. unknown. ? Blend of HOCUS and BUNKUM.

Holarctic *a.* of or relating to the entire northern region of the globe. *Also n.* WH: 19C. HOLO- + ARCTIC.

hold¹ *v.t.* to grasp and retain. *Also v.i.* WH: pre-1200. Old English *haldan*, from Germanic v. orig. with senses to watch (cp. BEHOLD), to look after, to pasture (cattle). Cp. German *halten* to hold. Rel. to HALT¹.

hold² *n.* the act of seizing or grasping in the hands. WH: pre-1200. Partly from HOLD¹, partly from Old Norse *hald* hold, support, custody.

hold³ *n.* a cavity in the lower part of a ship or aircraft, in which the cargo is stowed. WH: 16C. Alt. of obs. *hull*, from Old English *hol* HOLE, assim. to HOLD¹. Cp. HULL¹.

holding *n.* tenure or occupation. WH: 12–14C. HOLD¹ + -ING¹.

hole *n.* a hollow place or cavity. *Also v.t., v.i.* WH: pre-1200. Old English *hol*, from Germanic, ult. from Indo-European base meaning to cover, to conceal. Cp. HALL, HEEL³, HELL, HELM², HOLD³, HOLLOW, HOWE, HULL².

holiday *n.* a period away from work, school or one's usual duties; an extended period spent away from home for recreation. *Also a., v.i.* WH: pre-1200. Old English *hāligdæg*, from *hālig* HOLY + *dæg* DAY. The original sense was holy day, i.e. a day set apart for religious observance, a religious festival. The current sense dates from the 12–14C.

holism *n.* the tendency in nature to evolve wholes that are more than the sum of the parts. WH: early 20C. HOLO- + -ISM. The variant *wholism* (from WHOLE) arose in the mid-20C. *Holism* itself was coined in 1926 by the S African statesman General J.C. Smuts.

holla *int.* used to call attention. *Also n., v.i., v.t.* WH: 16C. French *holà*, from *ho* + *là* there. Cp. HOLLO. The original sense was stop! cease!

holland *n.* coarse unbleached linen with a glazed surface, first made in Holland. WH: 12–14C. *Holland*, a former province of the Netherlands (now also an alt. name for the whole country). See also NETHERLANDER.

hollandaise sauce *n.* a sauce made with butter, egg yolk and lemon juice etc. often served with fish. WH: 19C. French, fem. of *hollandais* Dutch, from *Hollande* Holland.

Hollander *n.* a native of Holland. WH: 14–15C. HOLLAND + -ER[1].

holler *v.i.* to shout loudly, to cry out. *Also v.t., n.* WH: 17C. Var. of HOLLO.

hollo *int.* used to call attention. *Also n., v.i., v.t.* WH: 14–15C. Prob. var. of obs. *hallow* to pursue with shouting, from Old French *halloer*, of imit. orig. Cp. HALLOO, HELLO, HOLLER.

hollow *a.* containing a cavity or empty space. *Also n., v.t.* WH: pre-1200. Old English *holh* (n.), rel. to *hol* HOLE. The modern noun *hollow* was re-formed in the 16C from the adjective.

holly *n.* a shrub or tree of the genus *Ilex*, esp. *I. aquifolium*, a tree with glossy, prickly leaves and scarlet or, more rarely, yellow berries. WH: 12–14C. Reduced form of Old English *holegn*, obs. *hollin*, from Germanic source of French *houx* holly. Rel. to Welsh *celyn*. Cp. HOLM[2].

hollyhock *n.* a tall garden plant, *Alcea rosea*, with red, pink and yellow flowers. WH: 12–14C. HOLY + obs. *hock*, name of various plants of mallow family, of unknown orig. Cp. Welsh *hocys bendigaid* hollyhock, lit. blessed mallow.

Hollywood *n.* the films, styles and practices of the big US cinema studios. WH: early 20C. *Hollywood*, district of Los Angeles, California, leading centre of US film industry.

holm[1] *n.* flat ground, liable to flooding, along the side of a river. WH: pre-1200. Old Norse *holmr* islet, meadow by water.

holm[2] *n.* an evergreen oak, *Quercus ilex*. WH: 12–14C. Alt. of obs. *hollin* (HOLLY).

holmium *n.* a metallic element of the rare-earth group, chem. symbol Ho, at. no. 67. WH: 19C. *Holmia*, Latinized form of *Stockholm*, capital of Sweden. See also -IUM. The name was coined by the Swedish chemist Per Cleve, who discovered the element in 1879 and named it for his native city.

holo- *comb. form* complete or completely. WH: Greek *holos* whole, entire.

holoblastic *a.* (of an ovum) undergoing segmentation throughout. WH: 19C. HOLO- + -BLAST + -IC.

holocaust *n.* a wholesale sacrifice of life, or general destruction, esp. by fire or nuclear weapons. WH: 12–14C. Old French *holocauste*, from Late Latin *holocaustum*, from Greek *holokauston*, from HOLO- + *kaustos*, var. of *kautos* burnt, from *kau-*, base of *kaiein* to burn. A holocaust was originally a sacrifice consumed by fire, then a wholesale sacrifice (15C). The sense wholesale massacre evolved in the 17C and the name of the mass murder of Jews by the Nazis in the mid-20C (World War II). The latter retains something of the original Greek sense as the bodies of the victims were burnt in crematoria.

Holocene *n.* the most recent period of geological time. *Also a.* WH: 20C. French *holocène*. See HOLO-, -CENE.

holocryptic *a.* wholly secret, unintelligible, or indecipherable. WH: 19C. HOLO- + CRYPTIC.

holoenzyme *n.* the active complex of an enzyme and its coenzyme. WH: mid-20C. HOLO- + ENZYME.

hologram *n.* (a photographic reproduction of) a pattern produced by the interference between a beam of coherent light (e.g. from a laser) and a direct beam of such light reflected off an object. WH: mid-20C. HOLO- + -GRAM. The word was coined in 1947 by the British physicist Dennis Gabor.

holograph *a.* wholly in the handwriting of the author or signatory. *Also n.* WH: 17C. French *holographe* or Late Latin *holographus*, from Greek *holographos*. See HOLO-, -GRAPH.

holohedral *a.* (of crystals) having the full possible number of planes symmetrically arranged. WH: 19C. HOLO- + -*hedral* (-HEDRON).

holometabolism *n.* complete metamorphosis (in insects). WH: 19C. HOLO- + METABOLISM.

holomorphic *a.* having the properties of an entire function, being finite, continuous and one-valued for all finite values of the variable. WH: 19C. HOLO- + -*morphic* (-MORPH).

holophotal *a.* utilizing the whole of the available light (applied to the illuminating apparatus in lighthouses). WH: 19C. HOLO- + Greek *phōs, phōtos* light + -AL[1].

holophrasis *n.* the expression of a whole sentence in a single word. WH: 19C. HOLO- + Greek *phrasis* speech, phrase.

holophyte *n.* a plant that obtains food like a green plant, esp. by photosynthesis. WH: 19C. HOLO- + -PHYTE.

holothurian *a.* belonging to the Holothuroidea, a class of echinoderms comprising the sea slugs. *Also n.* WH: 19C. Modern Latin *Holothuria* genus name, from Latin *holothurion* name of some marine creature, from Greek, of unknown orig. + -AN.

holotype *n.* the original specimen from which a new species is derived or described. WH: 19C. HOLO- + TYPE.

hols *n.pl.* holidays. WH: early 20C. Abbr. of *holidays* (HOLIDAY). Cp. VAC[1].

holster *n.* a leather case, usu. on a belt or attached to a saddle bow, to hold a pistol or revolver. WH: 17C. Corr. to Dutch *holster*, ? ult. from Germanic base of HOLE. See also -STER.

†holt[1] *n.* a wood, a grove, a copse. WH: pre-1200. Old English, from Germanic, from Indo-European base also of Greek *klados* twig.

holt[2] *n.* the burrow of an animal, esp. an otter. WH: 14–15C. Var. of HOLD[2].

holus-bolus *adv.* all at once, at one gulp. WH: 19C. Orig. uncertain. Appar. pseudo-Latin meaning whole bolus, or from assumed Greek *holos bōlos* whole lump (see BOLUS).

holy *a.* of high spiritual excellence. WH: pre-1200. Old English *hālig*, from Germanic base of WHOLE.

holystone *n.* a soft sandstone used for scrubbing the decks of vessels. *Also v.t.* WH: 19C. Prob. from HOLY + STONE. The stone was probably so called as it was used when kneeling, or perhaps because it was 'holey' or hollow.

hom *n.* a sacred plant of the Parsees and ancient Persians. WH: 19C. Obs. Persian *hōm*, rel. to Sanskrit *soma* SOMA[2].

homage *n.* a public show of respect or honour to someone or something. *Also v.t.* WH: 12–14C. Old French (Modern French *hommage*), from Medieval Latin *hominaticum*, from Latin *homo, hominis* man. See also -AGE. A homage was originally a formal public acknowledgement of allegiance to a king or lord by a tenant or vassal.

hombre *n.* man. WH: 19C. Spanish man, from Latin *homo, hominis* human being. Cp. OMBRE.

Homburg *n.* a man's hat of soft felt with a dented crown and a depression in the top. WH: 19C. *Homburg*, a town near Wiesbaden, W Germany.

home[1] *n.* the place where one lives. *Also a., adv.* WH: pre-1200. Old English *hām*, from Germanic. Cp. HAM[2].

home[2] *v.i.* (of birds, esp. pigeons and other animals) to reach home accurately from a distance. *Also v.t.* WH: 17C. HOME[1].

homelyn *n.* the spotted ray, *Raja montagui*, a European sea fish used for food. WH: 17C. Orig. unknown.

homeo- *comb. form* like or similar. WH: Greek *homoios* like, similar. See also -O-.

homeomorphous *a.* similar in form and structure (esp. of crystals differing in chemical composition). WH: 19C. HOMEO- + -*morphous* (-MORPH).

homeoplastic *a.* (of tumours etc.) similar in structure to the surrounding tissue. WH: 19C. HOMEO- + -PLAST + -IC.

homeostasis *n.* the keeping of an even level within an animal's body by a tendency to compensate for disrupting changes. WH: early 20C. HOMEO- + Greek *stasis* standing still.

homeotherm *n.* an organism that maintains the same body temperature. WH: 19C. HOMEO- + Greek *thermē* heat.

homeozoic *a.* (of regions of the earth) containing similar forms of life. WH: 19C. HOMEO- + -ZOIC.

homer *n.* a Hebrew liquid measure of 75 5/8 gal. (343.8 l). WH: 16C. Hebrew *ḥōmer*, lit. heap. 'The seed of an homer shall yield an ephah' (Isa. v.10).

Homeric *a.* of, relating to, or resembling Homer or his poems. WH: 17C. Latin *Homericus*, from Greek *Homērikos*, from *Homēros*

Homer, traditional author of two ancient epics, the *Iliad* and the *Odyssey*. The traditional date of Homer's life is between 12C and 7C BC, now often narrowed down to 9C or 8C.

homicide *n.* the act of killing a human being. WH: 12–14C. Old French, from Latin *homicidium* killing of a human being, or *homicida* killer of a human being, both from *homo*, *hominis* human being. See -CIDE.

homiletic *a.* of or relating to homilies. WH: 17C. Late Latin *homileticus*, from Greek *homilētikos*, from *homilētos*, verbal a. of *homilein* to consort with, from *homilos* crowd. See also -IC.

homily *n.* a discourse or sermon on a moral or religious topic. WH: 14–15C. Old French *omelie* (Modern French *homélie*), from Ecclesiastical Latin *homilia*, from Greek converse, discourse, from *homilos* crowd. See -Y².

hominid *n.* a creature of the family Hominidae, comprising humans and their precursors. *Also a.* WH: 19C. Modern Latin *Hominidae*, from *homo*, *hominis* human being. See also -ID.

hominoid *a.* of or like man. *Also n.* WH: early 20C. Latin *homo*, *hominis* human being + -OID.

hominy *n.* maize hulled and coarsely ground, boiled with water or milk for food. WH: 17C. Contr. of Virginia Algonquian *uskatahomen*.

Homo *n.* any primate of the genus *Homo*, of which man is the only living species. WH: 16C. Latin man, human being.

homo *n.* a homosexual. WH: early 20C. Abbr. of HOMOSEXUAL. Cp. HETERO.

homo- *comb. form* alike, similar, identical. WH: Greek *homos* same. See also -O-.

homoblastic *a.* derived from the same kind of cells, as distinct from *heteroblastic*. WH: 19C. HOMO- + -BLAST + -IC.

homocentric *a.* concentric, having the same centre. WH: 17C. Modern Latin *homocentricus*, from HOMO- + Greek *kentrikos*. See -CENTRIC.

homocercal *a.* (of fishes) having the upper and lower lobes of the tail of the same length. WH: 19C. HOMO- + Greek *kerkos* tail. See also -AL¹.

homochromy *n.* the resemblance of an animal's colour to the colour of its surroundings. WH: 19C. HOMO- + Greek *khrōma* colour. See also -Y².

homocyclic *a.* (of an organic compound) having a closed chain of atoms of the same kind. WH: early 20C. HOMO- + *cyclic* (CYCLE).

homodont *a.* having teeth that are all of the same type, as opposed to heterodont. WH: 19C. HOMO- + -ODONT.

homoeopathy *n.* the system which aims at curing diseases by administering in small doses medicines which would produce in healthy persons symptoms similar to those they are designed to remove. WH: 19C. *homoeo-* (HOMEO-) + -PATHY. The term was coined in 1796 by the German physician Samuel Hahnemann.

homoerotic *a.* of or concerning sexual attraction to the same sex. WH: early 20C. HOMO- + EROTIC.

homogametic *a.* of or relating to the sex that possesses two chromosomes of the same sex. WH: early 20C. HOMO- + *gametic* (GAMETE).

homogamous *a.* having all the florets of a capitulum hermaphrodite. WH: 19C. HOMO- + Greek *gamos* marriage + -OUS.

homogeneous *a.* composed of the same or similar parts or elements. WH: 17C. Latin *homogeneus*, from Greek *homogenēs* of the same kind, from HOMO- + *genos* kind. See also -OUS.

homograft *n.* a tissue graft from one organism to a member of the same species. WH: early 20C. HOMO- + GRAFT¹.

homograph *n.* a word having the same spelling as another, but differing in pronunciation, origin or meaning. WH: 19C. HOMO- + -GRAPH.

homoiousian *a.* having a similar nature or substance. *Also n.* WH: 17C. Ecclesiastical Latin *homoeusius*, from Greek *homoiousios* of like essence, from *homoios* like, similar + *ousia* essence, substance. See also -IAN. Cp. HOMOOUSIAN.

homologate *v.t.* to admit, to concede. WH: 16C. Medieval Latin *homologatus*, p.p. of *homologare* to agree, based on Greek *homologein* to confess, to acknowledge. See also -ATE³.

homologous *a.* having the same relative position, proportion, value, structure etc. WH: 17C. Medieval Latin *homologus*, from

Greek *homologos* agreeing, consonant, from *homos* same + *logos* relation, ratio. See LOGOS, also -OUS.

homologumena *n.pl.* those books of the New Testament the canonicity of which was accepted at once. WH: 17C. Greek *homologoumena*, neut. pl. p.p. of *homologein* (see HOMOLOGATE).

homomorphic *a.* analogous, identical or closely similar in form. WH: 19C. HOMO- + *-morphic* (-MORPH).

homonomous *a.* subject to the same law of growth. WH: 19C. HOMO- + Greek *nomos* law + -OUS.

homonym *n.* a word having the same sound or spelling as another, but differing in meaning; a homograph or homophone. WH: 17C. Latin *homonymum*, from Greek *homōnumon*, neut. of *homōnumos*, from HOMO- + *onuma* name. See also -OUS.

homoousian *a.* consubstantial, of the same substance or essence, as distinct from homoiousian. *Also n.* WH: 16C. Latin *homousianus*, from *homousius*, from Greek *homoousios*, from HOMO- + *ousia* essence, substance. See also -IAN. Cp. HOMOIOUSIAN.

homophobia *n.* a hatred or fear of homosexuals or homosexuality. WH: mid-20C. HOMOSEXUAL + *-phobia* (-PHOBE).

homophone *n.* a word having the same sound as another, but differing in meaning or spelling, as *heir* and *air*. WH: 17C. Greek *homophōnos*. See HOMO-, -PHONE.

homoplastic *a.* similar in structure though not homogenetic. WH: 19C. HOMO- + Greek *plastos* moulded + -IC.

homopolar *a.* having an equal distribution of charge; covalent. WH: 19C. HOMO- + POLAR.

homopteran *n.* any insect of the suborder Homoptera having wings of a uniform texture. WH: 19C. Modern Latin *Homoptera*, from HOMO- + Greek *pteron* wing. See also -AN.

homosexual *a.* feeling sexual attraction to one's own sex. *Also n.* WH: 19C. HOMO- + SEXUAL. The first element is not from Latin *homo*, *hominis* man, human being.

homotaxis *n.* arrangement of strata in different localities in the same relative position in the geological series. WH: 19C. HOMO- + Greek *taxis* arrangement (TAXIS).

homotonous *a.* of the same tenor or tone. WH: 18C. HOMO- + Greek *tonos* TONE + -OUS.

homotype *n.* a part or organ having the same structure or relative position to that of another. WH: 19C. HOMO- + TYPE.

homozygote *n.* an animal or plant that has two identical alleles for any one gene and so breeds true to type. WH: early 20C. HOMO- + ZYGOTE.

homunculus *n.* a little man; a dwarf; a manikin. WH: 17C. Latin, dim. of *homo* man. See also -CULE.

honcho *n.* a boss, leader or manager. *Also v.t.* WH: mid-20C. Japanese *hanchō* group leader.

hone¹ *n.* a whetstone esp. for sharpening razors. *Also v.t.* WH: pre-1200. Old English *hān*, from Germanic.

hone² *v.i.* to moan, to whine. WH: 14–15C. Old French *hagner* to grumble.

honest *a.* upright, fair, truthful, trustworthy in dealings, business or conduct. *Also adv.* WH: 12–14C. Old French *oneste* (Modern French *honnête*), from Latin *honestus*, from *honos*, *honor* HONOUR. The original sense to the 17C was held in honour, respected.

honey *n.* a sweet viscid product collected from plants by bees, and largely used as food. *Also v.t.*, *v.i.* WH: pre-1200. Old English *hunig*, from Germanic. Cp. German *Honig*.

honeymoon *n.* a holiday taken by a newly married couple. *Also v.i.* WH: 16C. HONEY + MOON. The original sense was the first month (moon) after marriage, when the affections are sweetest (like honey). According to some, a honeymoon is so called because the affections may wane, like the moon.

hong *n.* in China, a foreign factory, warehouse or other mercantile establishment. WH: 18C. Chinese *háng* row, trade.

Honiton *n.* a kind of lace with floral sprigs. WH: 19C. *Honiton*, a town in Devon, where orig. made.

honk *n.* the cry of the wild goose. *Also v.i.*, *v.t.* WH: 19C. Imit.

honky *n.* a white person. WH: mid-20C. Orig. uncertain. ? Var. of *hunky*, from *bohunk* immigrant from central or E Europe, appar. from BOHEMIAN + HUNGARIAN.

honky-tonk *n.* a disreputable nightclub, bar etc. WH: 19C. Orig. uncertain.

honnête homme *n.* a decent, sophisticated man of the world; a gentleman. WH: 17C. French honest man, from *honnête* decent, HONEST + *homme* man.

honorand *n.* a person receiving an honour such as an honorary degree. WH: mid-20C. Latin *honorandus*, ger. of *honorare* HONOUR. See also -AND.

honorarium *n.* a fee or payment for the services of a professional person. WH: 17C. Latin gift made on being admitted to a post of honour, use as n. of neut. of *honorarius* HONORARY. See also -ARIUM.

honorary *a.* done, made or conferred as a mark of honour. WH: 17C. Latin *honorarius*, from *honor* HONOUR. See also -ARY[1].

honorific *a.* conferring or showing honour. *Also n.* WH: 17C. Latin *honorificus*, from *honor*. See HONOUR, also -FIC.

honoris causa *adv.* (esp. of an honorary degree) as a token of esteem. WH: 17C. Latin for the sake of honour, from *honoris*, gen. of *honor* HONOUR + abl. of *causa* sake, CAUSE.

honour *n.* respect, esteem, reverence. *Also v.t.* WH: 12–14C. Old French *honor*, *honur*, earlier *enor* (Modern French *honneur*), from Latin *honor*, *honoris*. See also -OUR.

honourable *a.* worthy of honour. WH: 12–14C. Old French, from Latin *honorabilis*, from *honorare*. See HONOUR, also -ABLE.

hooch *n.* crude alcoholic liquor. WH: 19C. Abbr. of *Hoochinoo*, name of a Tlingit Indian people of Admiralty Island, Alaska, who made such liquor.

hood[1] *n.* a loose covering for the head and back of the neck, separate, or part of a cloak etc. *Also v.t.* WH: pre-1200. Old English *hōd*, from Germanic base rel. to that of HAT. Cp. German *Hut* hat.

hood[2] *n.* a hoodlum, a gangster. WH: mid-20C. Abbr. of HOODLUM.

hood[3] *n.* a neighbourhood. WH: late 20C. Shortening of *neighbourhood* (NEIGHBOUR).

-hood *suf.* denoting a state or quality, as in *childhood*, *parenthood*. WH: Old English *-hād*, from a Germanic n. meaning person, sex, condition, rank, represented by Old English *hād* honour, worth. Cp. -HEAD.

hoodlum *n.* a street rowdy, a hooligan, orig. esp. one of a gang of street ruffians who flourished in San Francisco during the 1870s and 1880s. WH: 19C. Orig. unknown. The word is popularly said to derive from dialect German *Huddellump* ragamuffin, although some claim it to be a reversal of the Irish name *Muldoon* (with *h* for *n*). Cp. similar HOOLIGAN.

hoodoo *n.* bad luck. *Also v.t.* WH: 19C. Appar. alt. of VOODOO.

hooey *n., int.* rubbish, nonsense. WH: early 20C. Orig. uncertain. ? Based on PHOOEY.

hoof *n.* the horny sheath covering the feet of horses, oxen. etc. *Also v.t., v.i.* WH: pre-1200. Old English *hōf*, from Germanic base related to Sanskrit *śapha*, Avestan *safa* with same meaning. Cp. German *Huf*.

hooh-ha *n.* fuss, noisy commotion or excitement. WH: mid-20C. Orig. unknown. Cp. BROUHAHA.

hook *n.* a curved piece of metal or other material by which an object is caught or suspended. *Also v.t., v.i.* WH: pre-1200. Old English *hōc* corner, angle, point of land, rel. to *haca* bolt, from Germanic.

hookah *n.* a tobacco pipe in which the smoke passes through water. WH: 18C. Urdu, from Arabic *ḥuḳḳa* small box, container, jar.

hooker[1] *n.* a person or thing that hooks. WH: 16C. HOOK + -ER[1]. The original sense was a thief who snatched things using a hook. The sense prostitute dates from the 19C.

hooker[2] *n.* a two-masted Dutch or Irish coasting or fishing vessel. WH: 17C. Dutch *hoeker*, from *hoek* HOOK. See also -ER[1].

Hooke's law *n.* the principle expressing the proportionality of strain to the stress causing it. WH: 19C. Robert *Hooke*, 1635–1703, English inventor and natural philosopher.

hookey *n.* truant. WH: 19C. ? From HOOK (in sense to run away) + *-ey* -Y[3].

Hoolee *n.* the great Hindu festival in honour of Krishna. WH: 17C. Hindi *holī*.

hooley *n.* a lively party usu. with singing and dancing. WH: 19C. Orig. unknown. ? From *hurly* commotion, uproar (cp. HURLEY, HURLY-BURLY).

hooligan *n.* any of a gang of street ruffians given to violent attacks on people. WH: 19C. ? From *Hooligan*, surname of fictional rowdy Irish family in music hall song, also character in a cartoon. The word first appeared in print in 1898 and was originally understood to refer to *Hooley's gang*, from an Irishman of this name. Cp. HOOLEY.

hoop *n.* a strip of wood or metal bent into a band or ring to hold the staves of casks etc. together or for forming part of a framework. *Also v.t.* WH: pre-1200. Old English *hōp*, from Germanic, rel. to Old Norse *hóp* small land-locked bay.

hoopoe *n.* a bird, *Upupa epops*, a rare British visitor with large crest and fine plumage. WH: 17C. Alt. of obs. *hoop*, from French *huppe*, from Latin *upupa*, imit. of bird's cry.

hoosegow *n.* a prison. WH: early 20C. S American or Mexican Spanish *juzgao*, from *juzgado* tribunal, from Latin *iudicatum*, p.p. of *iudicare* JUDGE.

hoot *v.i.* (of an owl) to utter its hollow cry. *Also v.t., n.* WH: 12–14C. ? Imit. Cp. Dutch *huie* to shout, to cry, to halloo. The word was not applied to the cry of the owl until the 15C.

hootenanny *n.* an informal concert with folk music and sometimes dancing. WH: early 20C. Orig. unknown Prob. a fanciful invention, with *hoo-* ? from WHO.

hoots *int.* used to express disgust, impatience etc. WH: 16C. Natural exclamation. The *-s* arose in the 19C and represents -S[2].

Hoover® *n.* a type of vacuum cleaner. WH: early 20C. W.H. *Hoover*, 1849–1932, US industrialist.

hop[1] *v.i.* to spring, leap or skip on one foot. *Also v.t., n.* WH: pre-1200. Old English *hoppian*, from Germanic. Cp. German *hüpfen*.

hop[2] *n.* a perennial climbing plant, *Humulus lupulus*, the mature cones of which are used in brewing. *Also v.t., v.i.* WH: 14–15C. Middle Low German and Middle Dutch *hoppe*, from Germanic. Cp. German *Hopfen*.

hope[1] *n.* an expectant desire; confidence in a future event. *Also v.i., v.t.* WH: pre-1200. Old English *hopa*, from Germanic, ult. of unknown orig. Cp. German *hoffen* to hope.

hope[2] *n.* a small enclosed valley, the upper part of a dale (often used in place names). WH: pre-1200. Old English *hop*, from Germanic, of unknown orig. The names of the towns of *Bacup* and *Worksop* contain the Old English word.

hoplite *n.* in ancient Greece, a heavily-armed soldier. WH: 18C. Greek *hoplitēs*, from *hoplon* weapon, *hopla* arms. See also -ITE[1].

hopple *v.t.* to fetter (a horse, cattle etc.) by tying the feet together. *Also n.* WH: 16C. Prob. of Low German orig. Cp. Middle Dutch *hobelen* to jump, to dance. See HOBBLE.

Hoppus foot *n.* a unit of volume for timber equal to 1.27 cu. ft. (0.034 cu. m). WH: 19C. Edward *Hoppus*, 18C English surveyor.

hopscotch *n.* a children's game in which a stone is driven by the foot of a player hopping from one compartment to another of a figure traced on the ground. WH: 19C. HOP[1] + SCOTCH[1].

horal *a.* of or relating to hours. WH: 18C. Late Latin *horalis*, from Latin *hora* HOUR. See also -AL[1].

Horatian *a.* of, relating to or resembling Horace or his poetry. WH: 17C. Latin *Horatianus*, from Quintus *Horatius* Flaccus (*Horace*), 65–8 BC, Roman poet. See also -AN.

horde *n.* a gang, a multitude. *Also v.i.* WH: 16C. Polish *horda*, rel. to Russian *orda*, Italian and Romanian *orda*, all ult. from Turkish *ordu* (royal) camp. Cp. URDU.

hordein *n.* a protein found in barley grains. WH: 19C. Latin *hordeum* barley + -IN[1].

horehound *n.* a labiate herb, *Marrubium vulgare*, with woolly stem and leaves and aromatic juice, used as a tonic and a remedy for colds etc.; white horehound. WH: pre-1200. HOAR + Old English *hūne* the plant *Marrubium*, of unknown orig. The added *-d* is as for BOUND[4], SOUND[1].

horizon *n.* the circular line where the sky and the earth seem to meet. WH: 14–15C. Old French *orizon* (Modern French *horizon*), from Late Latin *horizon*, *horizontis*, from Greek *horizōn*, pres.p. (used as n.) of *horizein* to bound, to limit, to define, from *horos* boundary. The Greeks referred to the horizon as *horizōn kuklos* bounding circle.

horizontal *a.* of or relating to the horizon. *Also n.* WH: 16C. French, or from Modern Latin *horizontalis*, from Late Latin *horizon*, *horizontis*. See HORIZON, also -AL[1].

hormone *n.* a secretion from an internal gland having the property of stimulating vital and functional physiological activity. WH: early 20C. Greek *hormōn*, pres.p. of *horman* to set in motion (from *hormē* impulse, onset), assim. to -ONE. The word was coined in 1905 by the English physiologist Ernest Henry Starling.

horn *n.* a projecting bony growth, usu. pointed and in pairs on the heads of certain animals. *Also v.t.* WH: pre-1200. Old English, from Germanic, rel. to Latin *cornu*, Greek *keras*.

hornblende *n.* a dark-coloured mineral consisting of silica, magnesia, lime and iron. WH: 18C. German, from *Horn* HORN + BLENDE.

hornet *n.* a large social wasp, *Vespa crabro*, with a severe sting. WH: pre-1200. Old English *hyrnet*, from Germanic, ? ult. from base of HORN.

hornfels *n.* a compact rock formed by the action of heat on clay rocks. WH: 19C. German horn rock, from *Horn* HORN + *Fels* rock.

hornito *n.* a small smoking mound or fumarole produced by volcanic action. WH: 19C. American Spanish, dim. of *horno* (from Latin *furnus*) oven, furnace.

hornswoggle *v.t.* to cheat, deceive. WH: 19C. Orig. unknown.

horo- *comb. form* of or relating to times or seasons, or to the measurement of time. WH: Greek *hōra* time, HOUR.

horography *n.* the art of constructing clocks, watches etc. WH: 18C. French *horographie*. See HORO-, -GRAPHY.

†horologe *n.* a timepiece. WH: 14–15C. Old French *orloge* (Modern French *horloge*), from Latin *horologium* timepiece, from Greek *hōrologion*, dim. of *hōrologos*. See HORO-, -LOGUE.

horometry *n.* the art or practice of measuring time. WH: 16C. HORO- + -METRY.

horoscope *n.* the prediction of a person's future based on a map showing the relative position of the stars and planets at that person's birth. WH: pre-1200. Latin *horoscopus*, from Greek *hōroskopos* nativity, horoscope. See HORO-, -SCOPE.

horrendous *a.* awful; horrifying. WH: 17C. Latin *horrendus*, ger. of *horrere*. See HORRIBLE, also -OUS.

horrent *a.* bristling. WH: 17C. Latin *horrens*, *horrentis*, pres.p. of *horrere*. See HORRIBLE, also -ENT.

horrible *a.* causing or tending to cause horror; dreadful, shocking, harrowing. WH: 12–14C. Old French *orrible* (Modern French *horrible*), from Latin *horribilis*, from *horrere* to stand on end (of hair), to tremble, to shudder. See also -IBLE.

horrid *a.* horrible, repellent. WH: 16C. Latin *horridus*, from *horrere*. See HORRIBLE, also -ID. The original sense was rough, bristling. The current sense evolved in the 17C.

horrify *v.t.* to strike with horror. WH: 18C. Latin *horrificare*, from *horrificus*, from *horrere*. See HORRIBLE, also -FY.

horripilation *n.* goose-flesh, a sensation of a creeping or motion of the hair of the body, caused by disease, terror etc. WH: 17C. Late Latin *horripilatio*, *horripilationis*, from *horripilatus*, p.p. of *horripilare* to become bristly, from *horrere* (see HORRIBLE) + *pilus* hair. See also -ATION.

horrisonant *a.* having a dreadful sound. WH: 16C. Latin *horrere* (see HORRIBLE) + *sonans*, *sonantis* sounding, from *sonare* to sound. See also -ANT.

horror *n.* dread or terror. *Also a.* WH: 12–14C. Old French *horrour* (Modern French *horreur*), from Latin *horror*, from *horrere*. See HORRIBLE, also -OR.

hors *prep.* out of, beyond. WH: 18C. French out of, outside, var. of *fors*, from Latin *foris* outside. See FOREIGN.

horse *n.* a solid-hoofed quadruped, with mane and tail of long coarse hair, domesticated and employed as a beast of draught and burden. *Also v.t., v.i.* WH: pre-1200. Old English *hors*, from Germanic. Cp. German *Ross* steed. The word is related to Latin *currere* to run, Gaulish *carros* wagon, and so to COURSE, CART.

horst *n.* a raised block of land separated by faults from the surrounding land. WH: 19C. German heap, mass.

hortative *a.* giving or containing advice or encouragement. WH: 17C. Latin *hortativus*, from *hortatus*, p.p. of *hortari* to exhort. See also -IVE.

hortensia *n.* a type of hydrangea, *Hydrangea macrophylla*, having large infertile flower heads. WH: 18C. Modern Latin, from *Hortense*, name of the wife of J.-A. Lepaute, 1720–c.1787, French clockmaker. Perhaps intentionally, the name suggests an origin in Latin *hortensis* of the garden. The name itself was given by Philibert Commerson, 1722–73, French botanist.

horticulture *n.* the art of cultivating or managing gardens. WH: 17C. Latin *hortus* garden + -*culture*, based on AGRICULTURE.

hortus siccus *n.* a collection of dried plants arranged systematically; a herbarium. WH: 17C. Latin dry garden, from *hortus* garden + *siccus* dry.

hosanna *n.*, *int.* an acclamatory prayer for blessing. WH: pre-1200. Ecclesiastical Latin *osanna*, from Greek *hōsanna*, from Rabbinic Hebrew *hôšaʿnā*, abbr. of biblical *hôšîʿā-nnā* save, (we) pray (Ps. cxviii.25).

hose *n.* (a piece of) flexible tubing for water or other fluid, as that used by firefighters. *Also v.t.* WH: pre-1200. Old English *hosa*, from Germanic. Cp. German *Hosen* trousers. The original sense was an article of clothing for the leg. The sense flexible tubing for water evolved in the 12–14C.

hospice *n.* a nursing home or hospital for the terminally ill, needy or afflicted. WH: 19C. Old French, from Latin *hospitium* hospitality, lodgings, from *hospes*, *hospitis* HOST[1].

hospitable *a.* entertaining or disposed to entertain strangers or guests with kindness. WH: 16C. French, from obs. *hospiter* to receive a guest, from Medieval Latin *hospitare*, from Latin *hospes*, *hospitis* HOST[1]. See also -ABLE.

hospital *n.* an institution for the reception and treatment of the sick or injured. WH: 12–14C. Old French (Modern French *hôpital*), from Medieval Latin *hospitale*, use as n. of Latin *hospitalis* hospitable, from *hospes*, *hospitis* HOST[1]. See also -AL[1]. A hospital was originally a house for the reception of pilgrims, travellers or strangers, then a charitable institution for the infirm, aged and needy. The current sense evolved in the 16C.

hospitaller *n.* one of a religious brotherhood whose office was to relieve the poor, strangers and the sick. WH: 12–14C. Old French *hospitalier*, from Medieval Latin *hospitalarius*, from *hospitale*. See HOSPITAL, also -ER[2].

hospitium *n.* a hospice. WH: 17C. See HOSPICE.

hospodar *n.* a prince or governor of Wallachia and Moldavia under the Ottomans. WH: 16C. Romanian *hospodár*, from Ukrainian *hospodar*, rel. to Russian *gospodar*, from *gospod'* lord, in turn rel. to Latin *hospes* HOST[1].

host[1] *n.* a person who entertains another. *Also v.t., v.i.* WH: 12–14C. Old French *oste* (Modern French *hôte*), from Latin *hospes*, *hospitis* host, prob. from *hostis*. See HOST[2].

host[2] *n.* a great number, a multitude. WH: 12–14C. Old French *ost*, from Latin *hostis* stranger, enemy. Cp. GUEST.

host[3] *n.* the consecrated bread or wafer used in the Eucharist. WH: 12–14C. Old French *hoiste*, from Latin *hostia* sacrificial animal, victim.

hosta *n.* any plant of the genus *Hosta* having green decorative leaves and blue, lilac and white flowers. WH: 19C. Modern Latin, from Nicolaus Thomas *Host*, 1761–1834, Austrian physician. See also -A[1].

hostage *n.* a person given or seized in pledge for the performance of certain conditions or for the safety of others. WH: 12–14C. Old French *ostage* (Modern French *otage*), from Ecclesiastical Latin *obsidatus* hostageship, from *obses*, *obsidis* hostage, from *ob* OB- + base of *sedere* to sit. See also -AGE. A hostage is literally 'one sitting against', and originally (to the 18C) was a person handed over in security for the fulfilment of an undertaking. The current sense also dates from the beginning.

hostel *n.* a house or extra-collegiate hall for the residence of students etc. WH: 12–14C. Old French *ostel* (Modern French *hôtel* HOTEL), from Medieval Latin *hospitale* HOSPITAL.

hostie *n.* the host. WH: 14–15C. Old French, from Latin *hostia*. See HOST[3].

hostile *a.* of or relating to an enemy. WH: 16C. French, or from Latin *hostilis*, from *hostis* stranger, enemy. See also -IL.

hostler *n.* an ostler. WH: 14–15C. Contr. of *hosteler*, from HOSTEL + -ER[1].

hot *a.* having a high temperature. *Also adv., v.t., v.i., n.* WH: pre-1200. Old English *hāt*, from Germanic. Cp. German *heiss*. Rel. to HEAT.

hotchpot *n.* a general commixture of property in order to secure equal division (among heirs of an intestate person etc.). WH: 14–15C.

Old French *hochepot*, from *hocher* to shake, prob. from Low German + POT[1]. Cp. HOTCHPOTCH.

hotchpotch *n.* a confused mixture, a jumble. WH: 14–15C. Alt. of HOTCHPOT by rhyming assim. Cp. HODGEPODGE.

hotel *n.* a commercial establishment providing accommodation, meals etc. WH: 17C. French *hôtel*, later form of *hostel*. See HOSTEL.

Hottentot *n.* NAMA. WH: 17C. Dutch, prob. orig. a repetitive formula in a Nama dancing song, applied by Dutch seamen to the people themselves.

Houdini *n.* a clever escape. WH: early 20C. Harry *Houdini* (professional name of Erich Weiss), 1874–1926, US escapologist.

hound *n.* a dog used in hunting (*bloodhound, deerhound, foxhound*). Also *v.t.* WH: pre-1200. Old English *hund*, from Germanic, from Indo-European base represented also by Irish *cú*, Greek *kuōn* dog. The original sense was dog in general. The sense of hunting dog evolved in the 12–14C.

hour *n.* the 24th part of a natural day, the space of 60 minutes. WH: 12–14C. Old French *ore, eure* (Modern French *heure*), from Latin *hora*, from Greek *hōra* season, time of day, hour. Rel. to YEAR. The Old English word for hour was *tīd* TIDE.

houri *n.* a nymph of the Muslim paradise. WH: 18C. French, from Persian *ḥūrī*, from Arabic *ḥūr*, pl. of *'aḥwar*, fem. *ḥawrā'* having eyes with marked contrast of black and white.

house[1] *n.* a building for shelter or residence, a dwelling, a place of abode. WH: pre-1200. Old English *hūs*, from Germanic, ult. of unknown orig. Cp. German *Haus*.

house[2] *v.t.* to place or store in a building. Also *v.i.* WH: pre-1200. Old English *hūsian*, from Germanic base of HOUSE[1].

household *n.* those who live together under the same roof and compose a domestic unit. Also *a.* WH: 14–15C. HOUSE[1] + HOLD[2].

†**housel** *n.* the Eucharist. Also *v.t.* WH: pre-1200. Old English *hūsl*, rel. to Gothic *hunsl* sacrifice, offering, ult. of unknown orig.

housewife *n.* a married woman who stays at home to run a household rather than having a full-time paid job. WH: 12–14C. HOUSE[1] + WIFE. Cp. HUSSY.

housey-housey *n.* the game of bingo. WH: mid-20C. HOUSE[1] + -Y[3].

housing[1] *n.* lodging, shelter, accommodation. WH: 12–14C. HOUSE[1] + -ING[1].

†**housing**[2] *n.* a cloth covering for a horse. WH: 14–15C. Old French *houce* (Modern French *housse*), from Medieval Latin *hultia*, from Germanic + -ING[1].

houting *n.* a European freshwater whitefish *Coregonus lavaretus*. WH: 19C. Dutch, from Middle Dutch *houtic*, of unknown orig.

hovel *n.* a miserable dwelling. Also *v.t.* WH: 14–15C. ? Low German.

hover *v.i.* to hang or remain (over or about) fluttering in the air or on the wing. WH: 14–15C. Obs. *hove*, of unknown orig. + -ER[5].

how[1] *adv.* in what way or manner. Also *n.* WH: pre-1200. Old English *hū*, from Germanic, from base of WHO, WHAT.

how[2] *int.* used as a N American Indian greeting. WH: 19C. Sioux *háo* or Omaha *hou*.

howdah *n.* a seat, usu. canopied, carried on an elephant's back. WH: 18C. Urdu *haudah*, from Arabic *hawdaj* a litter carried by a camel.

howdy[1] *int.* hello. WH: 19C. Alt. of *how d'ye* (*do*)?

howdy[2] *n.* a midwife. WH: 17C. Orig. unknown.

howe *n.* a hollow, a valley, a dell. WH: 14–15C. Var. of obs. *holl*, from Old English *hol* HOLE. Cp. HOLLOW.

howff *n.* a resort, a haunt. Also *v.i.* WH: 16C. Orig. unknown. The word was originally the name of the main burial ground at Dundee, then any cemetery in general. The sense meeting-place, haunt dates from the 18C.

howitzer *n.* a short, light or heavy field gun with a high trajectory and low muzzle velocity. WH: 17C. Dutch *houwitser*, from German *Haubitze*, from Czech *houfnice* sling, catapult. See also -ER[1].

howk *v.t.* to dig (up or out). Also *v.i.* WH: 14–15C. Of Germanic orig., from base of obs. *holl* (see HOWE) + dim. formative -*k* (as in TALK).

howl *v.i.* to utter a protracted hollow cry, as a dog or wolf. Also *v.t., n.* WH: 12–14C. Of Germanic orig., ? from OWL. Cp. Latin *ululare* to howl, Greek *hulan* to bark.

howlet *n.* an owlet. WH: 15C. Dim. of OWL with assim. to HOWL. See also -ET[1].

hoy[1] *int.* used to draw attention etc. Also *n.* WH: 14–15C. Natural exclamation. Cp. AHOY, OI.

hoy[2] *v.t.* to throw. WH: 19C. Orig. unknown.

hoy[3] *n.* a one-masted coasting vessel. WH: 12–14C. Middle Dutch *hoei*, var. of *hoede* (Modern Dutch *heu*), of unknown orig.

hoya *n.* any tropical climbing shrub of the genus *Hoya* with pink, white or yellow flowers, called by gardeners wax flowers. WH: 19C. Modern Latin, from Thomas *Hoy*, d.1821, English gardener.

hoyden *n.* a boisterous girl, a tomboy. Also *a., v.i.* WH: 16C. Prob. from Dutch *heiden* HEATHEN, gypsy. The word originally meant a rude or ignorant young man. The current sense developed in the 17C.

Hoyle *n.* an authoritative source (only in the phrase *according to Hoyle*). WH: early 20C. Edmond *Hoyle*, 1672–1769, English author of works on card games.

hozzle *v.i.* (of rain) to come down very heavily. WH: 18C. Orig. unknown.

hrumble *v.i.* to make a low, heavy, continuous sound, as of thunder, heavy vehicles etc. Also *v.t., n.* WH: 14–15C. Prob. from Middle Dutch *rommelen, rummelen*, of imit. orig.

hub *n.* the central part of a wheel from which the spokes radiate. WH: 16C. Orig. unknown. Cp. HOB[1].

hubble-bubble *n.* a type of pipe in which the smoke is drawn through water, making a bubbling noise, a kind of hookah. WH: 17C. Imit. redupl. of BUBBLE.

Hubble's constant *n.* the ratio of the velocity at which a galaxy recedes to the distance of that galaxy from the observer. WH: mid-20C. Edwin P. *Hubble*, 1889–1953, US astronomer.

hubbub *n.* a confused noise. WH: 16C. ? Irish. Cp. Irish *ababú!* used in battle cries.

hubby *n.* husband. WH: 17C. Abbr. of HUSBAND.

hubris *n.* insolent pride or security, arrogance. WH: 19C. Greek insolence, outrage.

huckaback *n.* a coarse linen or cotton cloth, with a rough surface, used for towels. WH: 17C. Orig. unknown.

huckle *n.* the hip, the haunch. WH: 16C. Dim. of obs. *huck* in same sense, of uncertain orig. ? Rel. to Middle Low German, Middle Dutch *hūken* to sit bent, to crouch, from Germanic base meaning to be bent. See also -LE[1].

huckleberry *n.* any low shrub of the genus *Gaylussacia* of N America. WH: 16C. ? From HUCKLE + BERRY.

huckster *n.* a retailer of small goods, a pedlar, a hawker. Also *v.i.* WH: 12–14C. Prob. of Low German orig. and rel. to HAWK[3]. See also -STER.

huddle *v.t.* to throw or crowd (together, up etc.) closely. Also *v.i., n.* WH: 16C. ? Of Low German orig. and ult. from Germanic base of HIDE[1].

Hudibrastic *a.* mock-heroic, resembling *Hudibras* in style or metre. WH: 18C. *Hudibras*, mock-satirical poem by Samuel Butler (1663–78), based on FANTASTIC, etc.

hue *n.* colour, tint. WH: pre-1200. Old English *hēw, hīw*, rel. to Old Norse *hý* down on plants, from Germanic base of unknown orig.

hue and cry *n.* a clamour or outcry (against). WH: 14–15C. Anglo-French *hu e cri*, from *hu* outcry (from Old French *huer* to shout as in battle or hunting, of imit. orig.) + *e* and + *cri* CRY.

huff *v.t.* to blow or puff (up). Also *v.i., n.* WH: 16C. Imit. Cp. PUFF.

hug *v.t.* to embrace closely. Also *v.i., n.* WH: 16C. ? Scandinavian. Cp. Old Norse *hugga* to comfort, to console, rel. to *hugr* thought, interest, feeling.

huge *a.* very large, enormous, immense. WH: 12–14C. Shortening of Old French *ahuge*, of unknown orig.

hugger-mugger *n.* secrecy, privacy. Also *a., adv., v.i., v.t.* WH: 16C. Redupl., with first element prob. rel. to HUDDLE and second to obs. *mucker* to hoard (money or goods), ? from MUCK + -ER[5]. Cp. obs. *hudder-mudder* (14–15C) in same sense.

Huguenot *n.* a French Protestant. WH: 16C. French, alt. (by assim. to name of Besançon *Hugues*, *c.*1491–1532, a Geneva burgomaster) of obs. *eiguenot*, pl. *aignos, hugenaulx*, from Dutch *eedgenot*, from Swiss German *Eidgenoss* confederate, from *Eid* OATH + *Genoss* associate.

huh *int.* used to express surprise, contempt, disbelief etc. WH: 17C. Natural exclamation.

huia *n.* an extinct New Zealand bird, *Heteralocha acutirostris*, of the starling family. WH: 19C. Maori, imit.

hula *n.* a Hawaiian dance performed by women. WH: 19C. Hawaiian.

hulk *n.* the hull or body of a ship, esp. an unseaworthy one. WH: pre-1200. Old English *hulc*, prob. of Mediterranean orig. Cp. Greek *holkas* cargo ship. A hulk was originally a trading ship or warship. The current sense dates from the 17C.

hull¹ *n.* the body of a ship. *Also v.t., v.i.* WH: 14–15C. ? Var. of obs. *holl* (see HOLD³) or same as HULL².

hull² *n.* the outer covering of a nut or seed, the pod, shell or husk. *Also v.t.* WH: pre-1200. Old English *hulu*, from *helan* to cover. Cp. HOLE.

hullabaloo *n.* an uproar. WH: 18C. Redupl. of HELLO, *hullo*, etc., ? influ. by HURLY-BURLY.

hum¹ *v.i.* to make a prolonged murmuring sound like a bee. *Also v.t., n.* WH: 14–15C. Imit. Cp. German *summen*, Dutch *brommen*.

hum² *int.* used to express hesitation, disapproval etc. WH: 14–15C. Rel. to or from HUM¹.

†**hum**³ *v.t.* to impose upon. *Also n.* WH: 18C. Abbr. of HUMBUG.

human *a.* of or relating to people or humankind. *Also n.* WH: 14–15C. Old French *humain*, from Latin *humanus*, rel. to *homo, hominis* man.

humane *a.* having the feelings proper to humans. WH: 14–15C. Earlier form of HUMAN. Cp. pair URBAN/URBANE.

humanism *n.* a moral or intellectual system that regards the interests of humankind as of supreme importance, as distinct from individualism or theism. WH: 19C. Back-formation from *humanist* (16C), from French *humaniste*, from Italian *humanista*, from *umano*, from Latin *humanus*. See HUMAN, also -IST.

humanitarian *a.* humane. *Also n.* WH: 19C. HUMANITY + -ARIAN, based on *equalitarian* (EQUAL), *Unitarian* (UNIT), etc.

humanity *n.* human nature. WH: 14–15C. Old French *humanité*, from Latin *humanitas*, from *humanus*. See HUMAN, also -ITY.

humble *a.* having or showing a sense of lowliness or inferiority, modest. *Also v.t.* WH: 12–14C. Old French *umble* (Modern French *humble*), from Latin *humilis* low, lowly, base, from *humus* ground, earth, rel. to *homo* man. Cp. *lowly* (LOW¹).

humble-bee *n.* a bumble-bee. WH: 14–15C. Prob. from Middle Low German *hummelbē*, from *hummel* hum, buzz + *bē* BEE. Cp. *bumblebee* (BUMBLE).

humbug *n.* a boiled sweet highly flavoured with peppermint. *Also int., v.t., v.i.* WH: 18C. Orig. unknown. The original sense was hoax, trick. The sense deception, pretence arose in the 19C as did that of the boiled sweet (perhaps in a sense similar to that of TRIFLE).

humdinger *n.* an excellent person or thing. WH: early 20C. Prob. from HUM¹ + *dinger* in same sense (from DING¹ + -ER¹).

humdrum *a.* dull, commonplace, tedious. *Also n., v.i.* WH: 16C. Prob. redupl. of HUM¹, influ. by DRUM¹.

humectant *a.* moistening. *Also n.* WH: 17C. Latin *humectans, humectantis*, pres.p. of *humectare*, from *humectus* moist, wet, from *humere* to be moist.

humerus *n.* the long bone of the upper arm, articulating above with the scapula and below with the radius and the ulna. WH: 14–15C. French *humide* or Latin *humidus*, from *humere* to be moist. See also -ID.

humid *a.* moist, damp. WH: 14–15C. French *humide* or Latin *humidus*, from *humere* to be moist. See -ID.

humiliate *v.t.* to lower in self-esteem, to mortify. WH: 16C. Late Latin *humiliatus*, p.p. of *humiliare*, from *humilis* HUMBLE. See also -ATE³.

humility *n.* the state of being humble. WH: 12–14C. Old French *humilité*, from Latin *humilitas*, from *humilis* HUMBLE. See also -ITY.

Humism *n.* the philosophical doctrines of David Hume. WH: 19C. David *Hume*, 1711–76, Scottish philosopher and historian + -ISM.

hummel *a.* (of cattle) hornless. *Also v.t.* WH: 15C. Low German *hummel* hornless animal, prob. rel. to English *hamble* to mutilate, to maim, from Old English *hamelian*, from Germanic (cp. German *Hammel* castrated sheep).

hummock *n.* a mound or hillock, a protuberance formed by pressure in an ice field. *Also v.t., v.i.* WH: 16C. Orig. unknown. The original form was *hammock*.

hummus *n.* a kind of Middle Eastern hors d'œuvre consisting of puréed chickpeas, sesame oil, garlic and lemon. WH: mid-20C. Arabic *ḥummuṣ*.

humongous *a.* huge, enormous. WH: late 20C. Orig. uncertain. ? Blend of HUGE and MONSTROUS.

humoral *a.* of or relating to bodily fluids, esp. with regard to a type of immune response from antibodies in the blood. WH: 14–15C. Old French, or from Medieval Latin *humoralis*, from Latin *humor* HUMOUR. See also -AL¹.

humoresque *n.* a composition of a humorous or capricious character. *Also a.* WH: 19C. German *Humoreske*, from *Humor* humour + -eske -ESQUE.

humorist *n.* a person who displays humour in their conversation, writings etc. WH: 16C. HUMOUR + -IST.

humorous *a.* full of humour. WH: 14–15C. HUMOUR + -OUS.

humour *n.* the quality of being amusing, comical, witty etc. *Also v.t.* WH: 12–14C. Old French *umor* (Modern French *humeur*), from Latin *humor*, from *humere*. See HUMID, also -OUR. A humour was originally one of the four body fluids (the cardinal humours), then (in the 15C) mental disposition, which was believed to be determined by these. The current sense dates from the 16C.

hump *n.* a swelling or protuberance, esp. on the back. *Also v.t., v.i.* WH: 17C. Prob. rel. to Low German *humpe*, Dutch *homp* lump, hunk (giving orig. English sense, now obs., of complaint). Otherwise abbr. of *humpback*, from *hump* (in orig. sense) + BACK¹, ? influ. by *hunchback* (HUNCH).

humph *int.* used to express doubt, disapproval etc. WH: 16C. Natural exclamation. Cp. HARRUMPH.

humpty-dumpty *n.* a short, squat person. *Also a.* WH: 18C. ? From *humpy* (from HUMP + -Y¹) + DUMPY. The added -t- is unexplained. The word was originally the name of a nursery rhyme character (whose name is taken to refer to an egg), adopted by Lewis Carroll as a character in *Through the Looking-Glass* (1871).

humpy *n.* a hut, shack, lean-to. WH: 19C. Australian Aboriginal (Jagara) *yumpi*, influ. by HUMP.

humus *n.* soil or mould, esp. that largely composed of decayed vegetation. WH: 18C. Latin, rel. to Greek *khamai* on the ground (cp. CHAMELEON).

Hun *n.* a member of an ancient Tartar people from Asia that overran Europe in the 4th and 5th cents. and gave their name to Hungary. WH: pre-1200. Old English *Hūne*, from Late Latin *Hunni* (pl.), from Greek *Hounni*, from Sogdian *xwn*.

hunch *n.* an intuitive feeling or premonition. *Also v.t., v.i.* WH: 15C. Rel. to *hunchback, hunchbacked*, of unknown orig. The original sense was the verb meaning to give a push to, to shove. The sense of hump (protuberance on the back) arose in the 19C as did that of intuitive feeling. The latter relates in sense to the original meaning of the verb. The sense of lump, thick piece may related to HUNK.

hundred *n.* 10 times 10, the number or figure 100 or c. *Also a.* WH: pre-1200. Old English, from Germanic, from base rel. to Latin *centum* + base meaning number (cp. Gothic *rathjō* number, account).

hung *a.* (of an election) not resulting in a clear majority for any party. WH: 14–15C. P.p. of HANG.

Hungarian *a.* of or relating to Hungary. *Also n.* WH: 16C. Medieval Latin *Hungaria*, from *Hungarī, Ungrī, Ugrī* (cp. UGRIC), name applied to the people. See also -AN. The Hungarians' own name for themselves is MAGYAR.

hunger *n.* a craving for food. *Also v.i., v.t.* WH: pre-1200. Old English *hungor*, from Germanic. Cp. German *Hunger*.

hungry *a.* feeling a sensation of hunger. WH: pre-1200. Old English *hungrig*, from Germanic, from base of HUNGER. See also -Y¹.

hunk *n.* a large piece. WH: 19C. Prob. from Low Dutch. Cp. HUNCH.

hunker *v.i.* to squat on the calves or heels. *Also n.pl.* WH: 18C. Appar. rel. to Middle Dutch *hucken*, Middle Low German *hūken* (Dutch *huiken*, German *hocken*), Old Norse *húko*. Not rel. to HAUNCH, but ? influ. by it.

hunky-dory *a.* satisfactory, fine. WH: 19C. *hunky* (from *hunk* 'home' in former New York children's game + -Y¹) + *dory*, of unknown orig.

hunt *v.t.* to search for, to seek after. *Also v.i., n.* WH: pre-1200. Old English *huntian*, from Germanic base of obs. *hent* to seize, to grasp, from Old English *hentan*.

Huntington's chorea n. a rare hereditary type of chorea accompanied by progressive dementia. WH: 19C. George *Huntington*, 1851–1916, US neurologist.

Huon pine n. a large yew, *Dacrydium franklinii*, orig. from Tasmania, valued for its finely-marked wood, used in cabinetmaking, boat-building etc. WH: 19C. *Huon*, a river in S Tasmania + PINE[1].

hurdies n. the buttocks, the haunches. WH: 16C. Orig. unknown.

hurdle n. a movable framework of withes or split timber serving for gates, enclosures etc. *Also v.t.* WH: pre-1200. Old English *hyrdel*, from Germanic, from Indo-European base also of Latin *cratis* hurdle, Greek *kartalos* basket. See also -LE[1].

hurdy-gurdy n. a barrel organ, or other similar instrument which is played with a handle. WH: 18C. Imit. of sound of instrument. Cp. dial. *hirdy-girdy* uproar, disorder.

hurl v.t. to throw with violence. *Also v.i., n.* WH: 12–14C. Prob. imit. Cp. Low German *hurreln* to toss, to throw.

Hurler's syndrome n. a condition caused by a defect in metabolism resulting in bone deformity, an abnormally large head, a protruding abdomen and mental retardation. WH: mid-20C. Gertrud *Hurler*, 1889–1965, Austrian paediatrician.

hurley n. an Irish game resembling hockey in which two teams of 15 players each equipped with sticks try to score goals. WH: 19C. HURL + -ey -Y[3].

hurly-burly n. commotion, uproar, boisterous activity. WH: 12–14C. Redupl. of HURL.

hurrah int. used to express joy, welcome, applause etc. *Also v.i., v.t., n.* WH: 17C. Alt. of HUZZA.

hurricane n. a storm with a violent wind of force 12, i.e. having a mean velocity of over 75 mph (120 kph). WH: 16C. Spanish *huracán* and Portuguese *furacão*, prob. from Taino *hurakán*. The spelling may owe something to the folk etymology of a derivation in *hurry cane*, as the storm agitated the canes in sugar plantations.

hurry v.i. to hasten. *Also v.t., n.* WH: 16C. Imit. Cp. obs. *hurr* to make a vibrating sound, WHIR, German *hurren* to move quickly.

hurry-scurry a., adv. in a hurry or bustle. *Also n., v.i.* WH: 18C. Redupl. of HURRY, ? influ. by SCUD or SCUTTLE[3].

hurst n. a wood, a thicket. WH: pre-1200. Old English *hyrst*, from Germanic.

hurt v.t. to cause pain, injury, loss or detriment to. *Also v.i., n.* WH: 12–14C. Old French *hurter* (Modern French *heurter*), ? of Germanic orig. The original sense was to knock, to strike, without necessarily wounding or injuring.

hurter n. a concrete block, beam etc. placed to protect a building, kerb etc. from damage by vehicles. WH: 12–14C. Anglo-French *hurtour*. See HURT, also -OUR, -ER[2].

hurtle v.i. to rush with great force and noise. *Also v.t.* WH: 18C. HURT + -LE[4].

hurtleberry n. the whortleberry. WH: 14–15C. First element of unknown orig. + BERRY. The word is earlier than dialect *hurt* in the same sense and also than WHORTLEBERRY.

husband n. a married man in relation to his wife. *Also v.t.* WH: pre-1200. Old Norse *húsbóndi* master of a house, husband, from *hús* HOUSE[1] + *bóndi* occupier and tiller of the soil (see BOND[2]).

husbandry n. the business of a farmer, agriculture. WH: 12–14C. HUSBAND + -RY. Cp. ECONOMY.

hush[1] v.t. to make silent, to repress the noise of. *Also v.i., n., int., a.* WH: 16C. Prob. back-formation from obs. *husht* silent, still, quiet (from *husht*, natural exclamation; cp. WHISHT), regarded as a p.p.

hush[2] n. a smooth, swift rush of water. *Also v.t.* WH: 18C. Imit.

husk n. the dry external covering of certain fruits or seeds. *Also v.t.* WH: 14–15C. Prob. from Low German *hūske* little house, core of fruit, dim. of *hūs* HOUSE[1].

husky n. a powerful breed of Arctic sledge dog with a thick coat and a curled tail. WH: 19C. Abbr. of *Ehuskemay* or Newfoundland dial. *Huskemaw*, ? from Creek *a:yaskime·w* or a rel. form. Cp. ESKIMO.

huss n. the flesh of various kinds of dogfish. WH: 14–15C. Orig. unknown.

hussar n. a soldier of a light cavalry regiment in European armies. WH: 16C. Hungarian *huszár* freebooter, light horseman, from Old Serbian *husar, gusar*, from Italian *corsaro* CORSAIR.

hussif n. the pocket sewing kit of a soldier or sailor, a housewife. WH: 18C. Contr. of HOUSEWIFE. Cp. HUSSY.

Hussite n. a follower of John Huss, a Bohemian religious reformer. WH: 16C. Modern Latin *Hussita*, from John *Huss* or *Hus*, c.1372–1415, Bohemian religious reformer. See also -ITE[1]. Huss was named from his native village, *Husinec*.

hussy n. a pert, forward girl. WH: 14–15C. Contr. of HOUSEWIFE. Cp. *goody* for *goodwife* (GOOD).

hustings n. proceedings at a parliamentary election. WH: pre-1200. Old Norse *husthing* house of assembly. See HOUSE[1], THING[2]. The Old Norse word was used for a house of assembly held by a king with his immediate followers, as distinct from a general assembly. The parliamentary sense, with the word in the plural, evolved in the 18C.

hustle v.t. to hurry or cause to move quickly. *Also v.i., n.* WH: 17C. Middle Dutch *husselen, hutselen* to shake, to toss, freq. of *hutsen*, from Germanic imit. base. The original sense (to the 19C) was to shake to and fro, to toss money in gambling. The current sense dates from the 18C.

hut n. a small, simple house. *Also v.t., v.i.* WH: 16C. French *hutte*, from Middle High German *hütte*, prob. ult. rel. to HOUSE[1].

hutch n. a coop or boxlike pen for small animals. *Also v.t.* WH: 12–14C. Old French *huche*, from Medieval Latin *hutica*, of unknown orig.

Hutu n. a member of a people of Rwanda and Burundi. *Also a.* WH: mid-20C. Bantu.

†huzza int. used to express joy, applause etc., hurray. *Also v.i., v.t., n.* WH: 16C. Prob. orig. a sailor's cry when hauling (cp. HOIST). See HURRAH.

hwyl n. passion or fervour, esp. in speech, recitation etc. WH: 19C. Welsh.

hyacinth n. any plant of the genus *Hyacinthus*, esp. *H. orientalis*, a bulbous-rooted flowering plant of the order Lilaceae. WH: 16C. French *hyacinthe*, from Latin *hyacinthus*, from Greek *huakinthos*, of pre-Hellenic orig. Cp. JACINTH.

Hyades n.pl. a cluster of stars, including Aldebaran, in the constellation Taurus, supposed by the ancients to bring rain when they rose with the sun. WH: 14–15C. Greek *Huades*, supposedly from *huein* to rain but prob. really from *hus* pig, SWINE. Cp. HYENA. The Latin name of the Hyades is *Suculae* little pigs.

hyalin n. a glossy translucent nitrogenous compound, the chief constituent of hydatid cysts, similar to chitin. WH: 19C. Latin *hyalinus*. See HYALINE.

hyaline a. glassy, transparent, crystalline. *Also n.* WH: 17C. Latin *hyalinus*, from Late Greek *hualinos*, from *hualos* glass. See also -INE.

hyalo- comb. form colourless, transparent, crystalline. WH: Greek *hualos* glass. See also -O-.

hyaloid a. glassy, vitriform. *Also n.* WH: 19C. French *hyaloïde* or Late Latin *hyaloïdes*, from Greek *hualoeidēs* like glass, from *hualos* glass. See also -OID.

hyaloplasm n. the clear, fluid constituent of cytoplasm. WH: 19C. HYALO- + *plasm* (PLASMA).

hyaluronic acid n. a viscous fluid carbohydrate with important lubricating properties found in synovial fluid, the vitreous humour of the eye etc. WH: mid-20C. HYALOID + *uronic* (from URO-[2] + -n- + -IC).

hybrid a. produced by the union of two distinct species, varieties etc. *Also n.* WH: 17C. Latin *hybrida*, var. of *ibrida* mongrel, of unknown orig.

hydatid n. a watery cyst occurring in animal tissue, esp. one resulting from the development of the embryo of a tapeworm. WH: 17C. Medieval Latin *hydatis, hydatidis*, from Greek *hudatis, hudatidos* drop of water, watery vesicle, from *hudōr, hudatos* water. See also -ID.

hydra n. any freshwater polyp of the genus *Hydra*, with a slender body and tentacles round the mouth, which multiplies when divided. WH: 14–15C. Old French *ydre, idre*, from Latin *hydra*, from Greek *hudra* water snake.

hydracid n. an acid containing hydrogen but no oxygen. *Also a.* WH: 19C. HYDRO- + ACID.

hydrangea n. any flowering shrub of the genus *Hydrangea*, from Asia and America. WH: 18C. Modern Latin, from Greek *hudōr* water + *aggeion* vessel. The name refers to the plant's cup-shaped seed capsule.

hydrant *n.* a spout or discharge pipe, usu. with a nozzle for attaching a hose, connected with a water main for drawing water, esp. in emergencies. WH: 19C. HYDRO- + -ANT.

hydranth *n.* a polyp in a hydroid colony specialized for feeding. WH: 19C. HYDRA + Greek *anthos* flower.

†hydrargyrum *n.* mercury, quicksilver. WH: 16C. Modern Latin, from Latin *hydrargyrus*, from Greek *hudrarguros* artificial quicksilver, from *hudr-* HYDRO- + *arguros* silver.

hydrastine *n.* a bitter alkaloid prepared from the root of a N American plant, *Hydrastis canadensis*, used as a tonic, to reduce fever and arrest haemorrhage. WH: 19C. Modern Latin *hydrastis*, of unknown orig. + -INE.

hydrate *n.* a compound of water with an element or another compound. *Also v.t.* WH: 19C. French, from Greek *hudōr*, *hudr-* water. See also -ATE².

hydraulic *a.* of or relating to fluids in motion, or to the power exerted by water conveyed through pipes or channels. WH: 17C. Latin *hydraulicus*, from Greek *hudraulikos*, from *hudr-* HYDRO- + *aulos* pipe. See also -IC.

hydrazine *n.* a colourless corrosive liquid that is a strong reducing agent, used esp. in rocket fuel. WH: 19C. HYDRO- +AZO- + -INE.

hydric *a.* of or containing hydrogen in chemical combination. WH: 19C. HYDROGEN + -IC.

hydro *n.* an establishment such as a hotel or clinic orig. offering hydropathic treatment. WH: 19C. Abbr. of *hydropathic* (HYDROPATHY).

hydro- *comb. form* of, relating to or connected with water. WH: Greek *hudr-*, comb. form of *hudōr* water. See also -O-.

hydro-barometer *n.* an instrument for determining the depth of the sea by its pressure. WH: 19C. HYDRO- + BAROMETER.

hydrobromic *a.* composed of hydrogen and bromine. WH: 19C. HYDRO- + *bromic* (BROMINE).

hydrocarbon *n.* a compound of carbon and hydrogen. WH: 19C. HYDRO- + CARBON.

hydrocele *n.* an accumulation of fluid, often swollen and painful, in a saclike cavity, esp. in the scrotum. WH: 15C. French *hydrocèle*, from Latin *hydrocele*, from Greek *hydrokēlē*, from *hudro-* HYDRO- + *kēlē* tumour.

hydrocephalus *n.* an accumulation of water on the brain, resulting in an enlargement of the head and possible brain damage. WH: 17C. Modern Latin, from Greek *hudrokephalon*, from *hudr-* HYDRO- + *kephalē* head.

hydrochloric acid *n.* a solution of hydrogen chloride in water, a strong corrosive acid. WH: 19C. HYDRO- + CHLORIC.

hydrochloride *n.* a compound of hydrochloric acid, esp. with an organic base. WH: 19C. HYDRO- + CHLORIDE.

hydrocortisone *n.* the steroid hormone naturally secreted by the adrenal cortex, synthesized to treat inflammatory conditions. WH: mid-20C. HYDRO- + CORTISONE.

hydrocyanic acid *n.* a poisonous volatile liquid formed by the combination of hydrogen and cyanogen in aqueous solution, having a faint odour of bitter almonds; *also called prussic acid, hydrogen cyanide.* WH: 19C. HYDRO- + CYANIC.

hydrodynamics *n.* the science which deals with water and other liquids in motion, hydromechanics. WH: 18C. Modern Latin *hydrodynamica*, from HYDRO- + Greek *dunamikos* DYNAMIC. See also -ICS.

hydroelectric *a.* of or relating to electricity generated from water-power. WH: 19C. HYDRO- + ELECTRIC.

hydrofluoric acid *n.* a colourless solution of hydrogen fluoride in water. WH: 19C. HYDRO- + *fluoric* (FLUORINE).

hydrofoil *n.* a fast vessel with one or more pairs of vanes attached to its hull which lift it out of the water at speed. WH: early 20C. HYDRO- + FOIL¹, based on AEROFOIL.

hydrogel *n.* protoplasm comprising gelatine or albumen in a jelly-like state with water filling the interstices. WH: 19C. HYDRO- + GELATIN.

hydrogen *n.* an invisible, flammable, gaseous element, the lightest of all known elements, which in combination with oxygen produces water. WH: 18C. French *hydrogène*, from Greek *hudr-* HYDRO-. See -GEN. Hydrogen was discovered by the English chemist Henry Cavendish 1706 and at first called PHLOGISTON. It was given its present name in 1787 by the French chemist Antoine Laurent Lavoisier, himself the discoverer of OXYGEN.

hydrogeology *n.* the branch of geology concerned with the geological effects of underground and surface water. WH: 19C. HYDRO- + GEOLOGY.

hydrography *n.* the science and art of studying, surveying and mapping seas, lakes, rivers and other waters, and their physical features, tides, currents etc. WH: 16C. HYDRO- + -GRAPHY, based on GEOGRAPHY.

hydrokinetic *a.* relating to the motion of liquids. WH: 19C. HYDRO- + KINETIC.

hydrolase *n.* any enzyme serving as a catalyst in the hydrolysis of a substrate. WH: early 20C. HYDROLYSIS + -ASE.

hydrology *n.* the science of water, its properties, phenomena, laws and distribution. WH: 17C. Modern Latin *hydrologia*. See HYDRO-, -LOGY.

hydrolysis *n.* the formation of an acid and a base from a salt by the action of water. WH: 19C. HYDRO- + -*lysis* (LYSIS).

hydromagnetic *a.* relating to the behaviour of fluids within magnetic fields. WH: mid-20C. HYDRO- + *magnetic* (see MAGNET).

†hydromancy *n.* divination by means of water. WH: 14–15C. Old French *hydromancie* or Late Latin *hydromantia*. See HYDRO-, -MANCY.

hydromania *n.* morbid craving for water. WH: 18C. HYDRO- + -MANIA.

hydromechanics *n.* the mechanics of liquids, hydrodynamics. WH: 19C. HYDRO- + *mechanics* (MECHANIC).

†hydromel *n.* a drink consisting of honey diluted with water, mead. WH: 14–15C. Latin, from Greek *hudromeli*, from *hudro-* HYDRO- + *meli* honey.

hydrometallurgy *n.* extraction of metal from ore by treatment with fluid. WH: 19C. HYDRO- + METALLURGY.

hydrometeor *n.* a meteorological phenomenon produced by water vapour, such as rain, snow etc. WH: 19C. HYDRO- + METEOR.

hydrometer *n.* an instrument for determining the specific gravity of liquids or solids by means of flotation. WH: 18C. HYDRO- + -METER.

hydronaut *n.* a person trained to operate vessels for exploring the ocean's depths. WH: mid-20C. HYDRO- + -*naut* as in *astronaut* (ASTRONAUTICS).

hydropathy *n.* the treatment of disease by the internal and external application of water. WH: 19C. HYDRO- + -PATHY.

hydrophane *n.* an opal which becomes translucent when immersed in water. WH: 18C. HYDRO- + Greek -*phanēs* apparent, from *phainein* to show.

hydrophilic *a.* having a great affinity for water. WH: early 20C. HYDRO- + -*philic* (-PHILE).

hydrophobia *n.* an unnatural dread of water, esp. as a symptom of rabies resulting from the bite of a rabid animal. WH: 14–15C. Late Latin, from Greek *hudrophobia*, from *hudrophobos*, from *hudro-* HYDRO- + -*phobia* (-PHOBE).

hydrophone *n.* an instrument for detecting sound by water, used to locate submarines etc. WH: 19C. HYDRO- + -PHONE.

hydrophyte *n.* an aquatic plant or one which grows in very moist conditions. WH: 19C. HYDRO- + -PHYTE.

hydroplane *n.* a light motor boat capable of rising partially above the surface of water. *Also v.i.* WH: early 20C. HYDRO- + PLANE¹, based on AEROPLANE.

hydroponics *n.* the cultivation of plants without soil in water containing chemicals. WH: mid-20C. HYDRO- + Greek *ponos* work + -ICS. The term was coined in 1937 by the US botanist William Gericke on the suggestion of a colleague, Dr. W.A. Setchell, of the University of California.

hydropower *n.* hydroelectric power. WH: mid-20C. HYDROELECTRIC + POWER.

hydroquinone *n.* a compound derived from benzoquinone, employed in the development of photographs. WH: 19C. HYDRO- + QUINONE.

hydroscope *n.* an instrument for viewing underwater. WH: 17C. Greek *hudroskopos* water-seeking. See HYDRO-, -SCOPE.

hydrosome *n.* the colonial organism of a hydrozoan. WH: 19C. HYDRO- + -SOME².

hydrosphere *n.* the watery part of the surface of the earth, the sea and oceans. WH: 19C. HYDRO- + SPHERE.

hydrostat *n.* an electrical contrivance for detecting the presence of water esp. one used to prevent the explosion of steam boilers. WH: 19C. HYDRO- + -STAT.

hydrostatics n. the science concerned with the pressure and equilibrium of liquids at rest. WH: 17C. HYDRO- + statics (STATIC).

hydrotherapy n. the therapeutic application of water, usu. the use of swimming pools etc. for the treatment of muscular conditions, arthritis etc. WH: 19C. HYDRO- + therapy (THERAPEUTIC).

hydrothermal a. relating to the action of heated water, esp. on the materials of the earth's crust. WH: 19C. HYDRO- + Greek thermos hot + -AL[1].

hydrothorax n. an abnormal accumulation of fluid in the chest. WH: 18C. HYDRO- + THORAX.

hydrotropism n. the tendency in the growing parts of plants to turn towards or away from moisture. WH: 19C. HYDRO- + TROPISM.

hydrous a. containing water. WH: 19C. Greek hudr- HYDRO- + -OUS.

hydrovane n. a vane on a seaplane to aid take-off or increase stability. WH: early 20C. HYDRO- + VANE.

hydroxide n. a compound formed by the union of a basic oxide with the molecules of water. WH: 19C. HYDRO- + OXIDE.

hydroxonium ion n. the hydrated hydrogen in H_2O^+. WH: early 20C. HYDRO- + oxonium (from OXY-[1], based on AMMONIUM).

hydroxy- comb. form containing the radical hydroxyl. WH: HYDROXYL.

hydroxyl n. the monad radical formed by the combination of one atom of hydrogen and one of water occurring in many chemical compounds. WH: 19C. HYDRO- + OXY-[1] + -YL.

hydrozoan n. any aquatic coelenterate of the class Hydrozoa, including the hydra, medusa, jellyfish etc. Also a. WH: 19C. Modern Latin Hydrozoa, from HYDRO- + Greek zōia, pl. of zōion animal.

hyena n. any carnivorous quadruped of the family Hyaenidae, allied to the dog, with three modern species, the striped Hyena striata, the spotted H. crocuta, and the brown hyena, H. brunnea (the first is also called the laughing hyena). WH: 12–14C. Old French hyene, from Latin hyaena, from Greek huaina, use of fem. of hus, hu- pig, SWINE with ending as in leaina lioness, etc. The hyena was perhaps so called from its bristly back, rather like that of a pig.

hyetal a. of or belonging to rain. WH: 19C. Greek huetos rain + -AL[1].

hyeto- comb. form of or relating to rain or rainfall. WH: Greek huetos rain. See also -O-.

hyetograph n. an automatic instrument that registers rainfall. WH: 19C. HYETO- + -GRAPH.

hyetology n. the branch of meteorology concerned with the study of rainfall. WH: 19C. HYETO- + -LOGY.

hyetometer n. a rain gauge. WH: 18C. HYETO- + -METER.

Hygeian a. relating to Hygeia, the Greek goddess of health. WH: 18C. Greek Hugieia Hygeia, the goddess of health, from hugiēs healthy. See also -AN.

hygiene n. the science of the prevention of disease. WH: 16C. French hygiène, from Modern Latin hygieina, from Greek hugieinē (tekhnē) healthful (art), from hugieinos, from hugiēs health.

hygristor n. an electronic component whose resistance varies with humidity. WH: mid-20C. HYGRO- + resistor (RESIST).

hygro- comb. form of, relating to or denoting the presence of moisture. WH: Greek hugro-, comb. form of hugros wet, moist. See also -O-.

hygrograph n. an automatic hygrometer. WH: 19C. HYGRO- + -GRAPH.

hygrology n. the branch of physics relating to humidity, esp. of the atmosphere. WH: 18C. HYGRO- + -LOGY.

hygrometer n. an instrument for measuring the moisture of the air etc. WH: 17C. HYGRO- + -METER.

hygrophilous a. (of a plant) living or growing in moist places. WH: 19C. HYGRO- + -philous (-PHILE).

hygrophyte n. a hydrophyte. WH: early 20C. HYGRO- + -PHYTE.

hygroscope n. an instrument for indicating the degree of moisture in the atmosphere. WH: 17C. HYGRO- + -SCOPE.

hygrostat n. a device for maintaining constant humidity, a humidistat. WH: early 20C. HYGRO- + -STAT.

hylic a. of or relating to matter, material. WH: 19C. Late Latin hylicus, from Greek hulikos, from hulē wood, timber, material, matter. See also -IC.

hylo- comb. form of matter, as opposed to spirit. WH: Greek hulo-, comb. form of hulē. See HYLIC, also -O-.

hylomorphism n. the theory that matter is the cause of the universe. WH: 19C. HYLO- + -morphism (-MORPH).

hylophagous a. (of insects etc.) feeding on wood. WH: 19C. HYLO- + -PHAGOUS.

hylotheism n. the system which regards God and matter as identical, pantheism. WH: 19C. HYLO- + THEISM.

hylozoism n. the doctrine that matter is necessarily endowed with life. WH: 17C. HYLO- + Greek zōē life + -ISM.

hymen n. a membrane stretched across the vaginal entrance. WH: 16C. Latin, from Greek humēn membrane. Hymen was the Greek god of marriage.

hymeneal a. of or relating to marriage. Also n. WH: 17C. Latin hymenaeus, from Greek humenaios. See also -AL[1].

hymenium n. the spore-bearing stratum or surface in fungi. WH: 19C. Greek humenion, dim. of humēn. See HYMEN.

hymeno- comb. form membranous. WH: Greek humēn membrane. See also -O-.

hymenopteran n. any insect of the order Hymenoptera, having four membranous wings, such as the bee, wasp, ant etc. Also a. WH: 18C. Modern Latin Hymenoptera, from neut. pl. of Greek humenopteros, from humēn, humenos (see HYMEN) + -O- + pteron wing. See also -A[2], -AN.

hymn n. a song or ode in praise or adoration of God, esp. in Christian worship. Also v.t., v.i. WH: pre-1200. Old French ymne, from Latin hymnus, from Greek humnos song in praise of a god or hero. The Greek word is used in the Septuagint to render various Hebrew words, and is thus found in the New Testament and other Christian writings from Augustine onwards.

hyoid a. U-shaped. Also n. WH: 19C. French hyoïde, from Modern Latin hyoides, from Greek huoeidēs shaped like the letter upsilon, from hu (name of) the letter u. See also -OID.

hyoscyamine n. a white crystalline alkaloid obtained from the seeds of henbane, Hyoscyamus niger, highly poisonous, used as a sedative. WH: 19C. Modern Latin hyoscyamus, from Greek huoskuamos, from huos, gen. of hus swine + kuamos bean + -INE.

hypabyssal a. (of igneous rock) formed at a moderate distance below the surface of the earth. WH: 19C. HYPO- + abyssal (ABYSS).

hypaesthesia n. reduced capacity for sensation, esp. of the skin. WH: 19C. hyp- (HYPO-) + Greek aisthēsis sensation. See also -IA.

hypaethral a. (esp. of a temple or sanctuary not intended to be roofed) open to the sky, roofless. WH: 18C. Latin hypaethrus, from Greek hupaithros, from hupo- HYPO- + aithēr air, ETHER. See also -AL[1].

hypalgesia n. reduction of or freedom from pain. WH: 19C. HYPO- + Greek algēsis sense of pain + -IA.

hypallage n. the interchange of natural or grammatical relations between terms in a sentence, e.g. 'the clock's ticking time'. WH: 16C. Late Latin, from Greek hupallagē, from hupo- HYPO- + allag-, stem of allassein to exchange, from allos other.

hype[1] n. exaggerated or false publicity used to sell or promote. Also v.t. WH: early 20C. Orig. uncertain. ? Partly from HYPERBOLE, partly from underworld slang.

hype[2] n. a drug addict. WH: early 20C. Abbr. of HYPODERMIC.

hyper- comb. form above, beyond. WH: Greek huper-, from huper over, beyond, overmuch. Ult. rel. to OVER.

hyperacidity n. excessive acidity in the digestive tract, esp. in the stomach. WH: 19C. HYPER- + acidity (ACID).

hyperactive a. abnormally active. WH: 19C. HYPER- + ACTIVE.

hyperaesthesia n. excessive sensibility to stimuli, esp. of the nerves and the skin. WH: 19C. HYPER- + Greek aisthēsis sensation. See also -IA.

hyperbaric a. (esp. of oxygen) at higher than normal pressure. WH: mid-20C. HYPER- + Greek baros heavy + -IC.

hyperbaton n. a figure by which words are transposed or inverted from their natural and grammatical order. WH: 16C. Latin, from Greek huperbaton overstepping, from huperbainein, from huper- HYPER- + bainein to walk.

hyperbola n. a plane curve formed by cutting a cone when the intersecting plane makes a greater angle with the base than the side of the cone makes. WH: 17C. Modern Latin, from Greek huperbolē. See HYPERBOLE.

hyperbole *n.* a figure of speech expressing much more than the truth, rhetorical exaggeration. WH: 14–15C. Latin, from Greek *huperbolē* excess, exaggeration, from *huper-* HYPER- + *ballein* to throw.

hyperborean *a.* belonging to or inhabiting the extreme north. *Also n.* WH: 14–15C. Late Latin *hyperboreanus*, from Latin *hyperboreus*, from Greek *huperboreios*, from *huper-* HYPER- + *boreios* northern (cp. BOREAL). See also -AN.

hypercatalectic *a.* (of a line of verse) having an extra syllable or extra syllables at the end. WH: 17C. Ecclesiastical Latin *hypercatalecticus*, from Greek *huperkatalēktikos*, from *huper-* HYPER- + *katalēktikos* (CATALECTIC).

hypercharge *n.* an interaction between elementary particles that is a weak force tending to oppose gravitational attraction between objects. WH: mid-20C. *hyperonic* (from HYPERON + -IC) + CHARGE.

hypercholesterolaemia *n.* an excess of cholesterol in the blood. WH: early 20C. HYPER- + CHOLESTEROL + -AEMIA.

hypercolour *n.* a process for dyeing fabric so that it changes colour when exposed to raised temperatures. WH: late 20C. HYPER- + COLOUR.

hyperconscious *a.* acutely or excessively aware (of). WH: mid-20C. HYPER- + CONSCIOUS.

hypercritical *a.* unreasonably critical. WH: 17C. HYPER- + *critical* (CRITIC).

hypercube *n.* a theoretical solid in four or more dimensions, analogous to a cube in three dimensions. WH: late 20C. HYPER- + CUBE.

hyperdulia *n.* in the Roman Catholic Church, the particular veneration made to the Virgin Mary, as distinct from that paid to the saints and from the worship paid to God. WH: late 20C. Medieval Latin. See HYPER-, DULIA.

hyperfocal distance *n.* the distance beyond which objects appear sharply defined through a lens focused at infinity. WH: early 20C. HYPER- + *focal* (FOCUS).

hyperglycaemia *n.* an excessive level of sugar in the blood. WH: 19C. HYPER- + GLYCO- + -AEMIA.

hypergolic *a.* (of a rocket fuel) able to ignite spontaneously on contact with an oxidizer. WH: mid-20C. German *Hypergol* (prob. from Greek *ergon* work + -OL) + -IC.

hypericum *n.* any herbaceous plant or shrub of the genus *Hypericum* typified by the St John's wort. WH: 14–15C. Latin, from Greek *hupereikon*, from *huper* over + *ereikē* heath.

hyperinflation *n.* a very high level of inflation in an economy. WH: mid-20C. HYPER- + *inflation* (INFLATE).

hyperinosis *n.* an excess of fibrin in the blood. WH: 19C. HYPER- + Greek *is, inos* fibre + -OSIS.

hyperkinesis *n.* excessive movement, as in a muscle spasm. WH: 19C. HYPER- + KINESIS.

hypermarket *n.* a very large self-service store selling a wide range of household and other goods, usu. on the outskirts of a town or city. WH: late 20C. HYPER- + MARKET, translating French *hypermarché*, from *marché* market, based on *supermarché* SUPERMARKET.

hypermedia *n.* multimedia. WH: mid-20C. HYPER- + MEDIA[1].

hypermetrical *a.* (of a line of verse) having an extra syllable or extra syllables. WH: 18C. HYPER- + *metrical* (METRIC).

hypermetropia *n.* an abnormal state of the eye characterized by long-sightedness, as opposed to myopia. WH: 19C. Greek *hupermetros* beyond measure, from *huper-* HYPER- + *metron* measure + -OPIA.

hypernym *n.* a word representing a general class or family which is applicable to more specific related words (e.g. *tree* is a hypernym for *ash* and *beech*). WH: late 20C. HYPER- + -ONYM, based on HYPONYM.

hyperon *n.* an elementary particle of the baryon group with a greater mass than a proton or a neutron. WH: mid-20C. HYPER- + -ON.

hyperphysical *a.* supernatural. WH: 17C. HYPER- + PHYSICAL.

hyperplasia *n.* excessive growth due to abnormal multiplication of cells. WH: 19C. HYPER- + -PLASIA.

hypersensitive *a.* excessively sensitive. WH: 19C. HYPER- + SENSITIVE.

hypersonic *a.* (of speeds) higher than Mach 5. WH: mid-20C. HYPER- + SONIC, based on SUPERSONIC, *ultrasonic* (ULTRA-).

hyperspace *n.* space that has more than three dimensions. WH: 19C. HYPER- + SPACE.

hypersthene *n.* an orthorhombic, foliated, brittle mineral, magnesium iron silicate, allied to hornblende, with a beautiful pearly lustre. WH: 19C. French *hypersthène*, from HYPER- + Greek *sthenos*

strength. The mineral was so named in 1803 by the French mineralogist René-Just Haüy because it is harder than hornblende.

hypertension *n.* abnormally high blood pressure. WH: 19C. HYPER- + TENSION.

hypertext *n.* a system of hardware and software that allows easy movement between related text, sound and graphics. WH: mid-20C. HYPER- + TEXT. The term was coined in 1965 by the US computer engineer T.H. Nelson.

hyperthermia *n.* abnormally high body temperature. WH: 19C. HYPER- + Greek *thermē* heat + -IA.

hyperthyroidism *n.* excessive activity of the thyroid gland, causing an accelerated metabolic rate, rapid heartbeat, nervousness etc. WH: early 20C. HYPER- + THYROID + -ISM.

hypertonic *a.* (of muscles) being excessively tense. WH: 19C. HYPER- + TONIC.

hypertrophy *n.* excessive development or enlargement of an organ or tissue. *Also v.t., v.i.* WH: 19C. HYPER- + -TROPHY.

hyperventilation *n.* excessive breathing, causing excessive loss of carbon dioxide in the blood. WH: early 20C. HYPER- + *ventilation* (VENTILATE).

hypha *n.* any of the filaments in the mycelium of a fungus. WH: 19C. Modern Latin, from Greek *huphē* web.

hyphen *n.* a short stroke (-) joining two words or parts of words. *Also v.t.* WH: 17C. Late Latin, from Late Greek *huphen* the sign ˜, use as n. of *huphen* together, from *huph-, hupo-* HYPO- + *hen*, neut. of *heis* one.

hypnagogic *a.* of or concerning the state of drowsiness before sleep. WH: 19C. French *hypnagogique*, from HYPNO- + Greek *agōgos* leading, from *agein* to lead. See also -IC.

hypno- *comb. form* relating to sleep or hypnosis. WH: Greek *hupnos* sleep. See also -O-.

hypnogenesis *n.* inducement of hypnotic sleep. WH: 19C. HYPNO- + GENESIS.

hypnology *n.* the study of the phenomena of sleep. WH: 19C. HYPNO- + -LOGY.

hypnopaedia *n.* learning by hearing during sleep. WH: mid-20C. HYPNO- + Greek *paideia* education.

hypnopompic *a.* of or concerning the state of drowsiness between sleep and waking. WH: early 20C. HYPNO- + Greek *pompē* sending away + -IC.

hypnosis *n.* a state resembling sleep in which the subconscious mind responds to external suggestions and forgotten memories are recovered. WH: 19C. HYPNO- + -OSIS.

hypnotherapy *n.* treatment by hypnotism. WH: 19C. HYPNO- + *therapy* (THERAPEUTIC).

hypnotic *a.* of, relating to or inducing hypnotism. *Also n.* WH: 17C. French *hypnotique*, from Late Latin *hypnoticus*, from Greek *hupnōtikos* putting to sleep, narcotic, from *hupnoun* to put to sleep, from *hupnos* sleep. See also -IC.

hypnotism *n.* the practice of inducing hypnosis. WH: 19C. Shortened form of *neuro-hypnotism*, from NEURO- + HYPNOTIC + -ISM. The original word was coined in 1842 by Dr. James Braid of Manchester as a term for 'the state or condition of nervous sleep'. He shortened it the following year.

hypnum *n.* any moss of the genus *Hypnum*. WH: 18C. Modern Latin, from Greek *hupnon* a kind of lichen.

hypo[1] *n.* sodium thiosulphate, the normal fixing solution in photography. WH: 19C. Abbr. of HYPOSULPHITE.

hypo[2] *n.* a hypodermic needle. WH: early 20C. Abbr. of HYPODERMIC. Cp. HYPE[2].

hypo[3] *n.* an attack of hypoglycaemia. WH: mid-20C. Abbr. of HYPOGLYCAEMIA.

hypo- *comb. form* under, below. WH: Greek *hupo-*, from *hupo* under.

hypo-allergenic *a.* not likely to cause an allergic reaction. WH: mid-20C. HYPO- + *allergenic* (ALLERGY).

hypoblast *n.* the innermost membrane of the blastoderm, the endoderm. WH: 19C. HYPO- + -BLAST.

hypobole *n.* a mode of reasoning in which several things seemingly opposed to the argument are mentioned and then refuted. WH: 18C. Greek *hupobolē*, from *hupoballein* to throw under, to suggest.

hypocaust *n.* in ancient Roman buildings, a space or series of channels under the floor by which heat was conducted from a furnace to heat a building, room, bath etc. WH: 17C. Latin *hypocaustum*, from Greek *hupokauston* room heated from below, from *hupo-* HYPO- + *kau-*, *kaiein* to burn.

hypochlorite *n.* a salt or ester of hypochlorous acid. WH: 19C. HYPO- + CHLORITE².

hypochondria *n.* a condition characterized by excessive anxiety with regard to one's health. WH: 14–15C. Ecclesiastical Latin (pl.), from Greek *hupokhondria* (pl.), from *hupokhondrion* (sing.), use as n. of *hupokhondrios* (a.), from *hupo-* HYPO- + *khondros* gristle, cartilage, esp. that of the breast bone.

hypocorism *n.* a pet name. WH: 19C. HYPO- + Greek *korē* child + -ISM.

hypocotyl *n.* the part of the stem of an embryo plant between the cotyledons and the top of the radicle. WH: 19C. HYPO- + COTYLEDON.

hypocrisy *n.* dissimulation, pretence, a feigning to be what one is not. WH: 12–14C. Old French *ypocrisie* (Modern French *hypocrisie*), from Ecclesiastical Latin *hypocrisis*, from Greek *hupokrisis* acting of a theatrical part, from *hupokrinesthai* to answer, to play a part, to pretend, from *hupo-* HYPO- + *krinein* to decide, to judge.

hypocycloid *n.* a curve generated by a point on the circumference of a circle rolling round the inside of the circumference of another circle. WH: 19C. HYPO- + CYCLOID.

hypodermic *a.* of or relating to the layers beneath the skin. *Also n.* WH: 19C. HYPO- + Greek *derma* skin + -IC.

hypogastrium *n.* the middle part of the lowest zone into which the abdomen is divided. WH: 17C. Modern Latin, from Greek *hupogastrion*, from *hupo-* HYPO- + *gastēr*, *gastros* belly. See also -IUM.

hypogeal *a.* existing or growing underground. WH: 17C. Late Latin *hypogeus*, from Greek *hupogeios* underground, from *hupo-* HYPO- + *gē* earth. See also -AL¹.

hypogeum *n.* (a part of) a building below the level of the ground. WH: 17C. Latin, from Greek *hupogeion*, neut. sing. (used as n.) of *hupogeios*. See HYPOGEAL.

hypoglossal *a.* under the tongue. WH: 19C. HYPO- + Greek *glōssa* tongue + -AL¹.

hypoglycaemia *n.* an abnormally low level of sugar in the blood. WH: 19C. HYPO¹ + GLYCO- + -AEMIA.

hypognathous *a.* having a lower mandible longer than the upper. WH: 19C. HYPO- + -GNATHOUS.

hypogynous *a.* (of stamens) growing from below the base of the ovary. WH: 19C. Modern Latin *hypogynus*, from HYPO- + Greek *gunē* woman (here, pistil). See also -OUS.

hypoid *n.* a type of bevel gear having a tooth form based on a hypocycloidal curve in which the pinion is offset from the centre line of the wheel to connect non-intersecting shafts and to withstand high surface loading. WH: early 20C. Orig. uncertain. ? From *hyperboloid* (HYPERBOLA) or *hyperbolic paraboloid* (PARABOLA).

hypolimnion *n.* the lower, colder layer of water below the thermocline of a lake. WH: early 20C. HYPO- + Greek *limnion*, dim. of *limnē* lake.

hypomania *n.* the mental state of overexcitability. WH: 19C. HYPO- + -MANIA.

hyponasty *n.* more active growth of a plant organ on the underside causing a tendency to upward curvature. WH: 17C. HYPO- + Greek *nastos* pressed + -Y².

hyponym *n.* a word with a more specific meaning that is included in the scope of another word (e.g. *ash* is a hyponym of *tree*). WH: early 20C. HYPO- + -ONYM.

hypophosphate *n.* a salt of hypophosphoric acid. WH: 19C. HYPO- + PHOSPHATE.

hypophysis *n.* the pituitary gland. WH: 17C. Modern Latin, from Greek *hupophusis* offshoot, outgrowth, from *hupo-* HYPO- + *phusis* growth.

hypoplasia *n.* underdevelopment of an organ or part. WH: 19C. HYPO- + -PLASIA.

hyposensitize *v.t.* to reduce the sensitivity of, to desensitize. WH: mid-20C. HYPO- + *sensitize* (SENSITIVE).

hypostasis *n.* that which forms the basis of anything. WH: 16C. Ecclesiastical Latin, from Greek *hupostasis* sediment, foundation, subject matter, from *hupo-* HYPO- + *stasis* standing.

hypostyle *a.* having the roof supported by pillars. *Also n.* WH: 19C. HYPO- + Greek *stulos* pillar, STYLE.

hyposulphite *n.* a thiosulphate, a salt of hyposulphurous acid. WH: 19C. HYPO- + SULPHITE.

hypotaxis *n.* subordinate construction in syntax, as opposed to *parataxis*. WH: 19C. Greek *hupotaxis* subjection, from *hupotassein* to arrange under, from *hupo-* HYPO- + *tassein* to arrange.

hypotension *n.* abnormally low blood pressure. WH: 19C. HYPO- + TENSION.

hypotenuse *n.* the side of a right-angled triangle opposite to the right angle. WH: 16C. Latin *hypotenusa*, from Greek *hupoteinousa* subtending, fem. pres.p. of *hupoteinein* to stretch under, from *hupo-* HYPO- + *teinein* to stretch.

hypothalamus *n.* a region at the base of the brain controlling autonomic functions, e.g. hunger and thirst. WH: 19C. HYPO- + THALAMUS.

hypothec *n.* a security in favour of a creditor over the property of their debtor, while the property continues in the debtor's possession. WH: 16C. French *hypothèque*, from Late Latin *hypotheca*, from Greek *hupothēkē* deposit, pledge, from *hupotithenai* to deposit as a pledge, from *hupo-* HYPO- + *tithenai* to place.

hypothermia *n.* subnormal body temperature, esp. when induced for surgical purposes. WH: 19C. HYPO- + Greek *thermē* heat + -IA.

hypothesis *n.* a proposition assumed for the purpose of an argument. WH: 16C. Late Latin, from Greek *hupothesis* foundation, base, from *hupo-* HYPO- + *thesis* placing.

hypothyroidism *n.* underactivity of the thyroid gland. WH: early 20C. HYPO- + THYROID + -ISM.

hypotonic *a.* (of muscles) deficient in tension. WH: 19C. HYPO- + TONIC.

hypoventilation *n.* abnormally slow breathing, causing an excessive amount of carbon dioxide in the blood. WH: mid-20C. HYPO- + *ventilation* (VENTILATE).

hypoxia *n.* a deficiency of oxygen reaching the body tissues. WH: mid-20C. HYPO- + OXYGEN + -IA.

hypso- *comb. form* height. WH: Greek *hupso-*, from *hupsos* height. See also -O-.

hypsography *n.* the branch of geography concerned with the study and mapping of altitudes above sea level. WH: 19C. HYPSO- + -GRAPHY.

hypsometer *n.* an instrument for measuring heights above sea level by observing the boiling point of water with a delicate thermometer and so determining the relative atmospheric pressure. WH: 19C. HYPSO- + -METER. The word was coined in 1817 by the instrument's inventor, the English chemist and physicist William Hyde Wollaston. Cp. PALLADIUM¹, RHODIUM¹.

hyrax *n.* any small harelike quadruped of the order Hyracoidea, including the Syrian rock rabbit (the dassie) and the S African rock badger. WH: 19C. Modern Latin, from Greek *hurax* shrew-mouse.

hyssop *n.* any small labiate aromatic herb of the genus *Hyssopus*, esp. *H. officinalis*, with blue flowers. WH: pre-1200. Old English *ysope*, from Latin *hyssopus*, from Greek *hussōpos*, of Semitic orig. Cp. Hebrew *'ēzōb*.

hysterectomy *n.* the removal of the womb by surgery. WH: 19C. HYSTERO- + -ECTOMY.

hysteresis *n.* the tendency of a magnetic substance to remain in a certain magnetic condition, the lag of magnetic effects behind their causes. WH: 19C. Greek *husterēsis* shortcoming, deficiency, from *husterein* to be behind, to come late, from *husteros* late.

hysteria *n.* an outbreak of frenzied uncontrollable emotion. WH: 19C. Latin *hystericus*, from Greek *husterikos* pertaining to the uterus, from *hustera* uterus. See also -IA. Hysteria was originally regarded as a disease of women caused by a disturbance of the uterus.

hystero- *comb. form* the womb. WH: Greek *hustera* uterus, womb. See also -O-.

hysterogenic *a.* producing hysteria. WH: 19C. HYSTERO- + -GENIC.

hysteroid *a.* resembling hysteria. WH: 19C. HYSTERIA + -OID.

hysteron proteron *n.* a figure of speech in which what should follow comes first, an inversion of the natural or logical order. WH: 16C. Ecclesiastical Latin, from Greek *husteron proteron* latter (put in place of) former, from *husteron*, neut. of *husteros* latter + *proteron*, neut. of *proteros* before, former. Cp. PREPOSTEROUS.

hysterotomy *n.* delivery of a child through the walls of the abdomen, a Caesarean section. WH: 19C. HYSTERO- + -TOMY.

I

I *pron.* in speaking or writing denotes oneself. *Also n.* WH: pre-1200. Old English *ic*, from Germanic, rel. to Latin EGO, Greek *egō*, Sanskrit *aham*, Old Church Slavonic *jazŭ* (Russian *ya*), Lithuanian *eo*. Cp. ME[1], MY.

-i[1] *suf.* forming the plural of L nouns in *-us*, as in *fungi, hippopotami*. WH: Latin *-i*.

-i[2] *suf.* forming the plural of It. nouns in *-o* or *-e*, as in *banditti, timpani*. WH: Italian *-i*.

-i[3] *suf.* forming adjectives and nouns from names of Eastern countries or regions, as in *Bangladeshi, Yemeni*. WH: Semitic *-i*.

-ia *suf.* forming abstract nouns, as in *mania, militia*. WH: Greek and Latin *-ia*.

-ial *suf.* forming adjectives, as in *celestial, terrestrial*. WH: French *-iel* or Latin *-ialis, -iale*.

iambus *n.* a poetic foot of one short and one long, or one unaccented and one accented syllable. WH: 16C. Latin, from Greek *iambos* iambus, lampoon, from *iaptein* to assail in words. The iambic trimeter was first used by Greek satirists.

-ian *suf.* forming nouns or adjectives, as in *Athenian, Baconian, Cantabrigian*. WH: Latin *-ianus*, from *-anus* -AN added to n. stems in *-i-*.

-iasis *comb. form* indicating a disease, as in *elephantiasis, psoriasis*. WH: *-i-* + Latin or Greek *-asis* used to form nn. of state or process.

iatric *a.* of or relating to physicians or medicine. WH: 19C. Greek *iatrikos*, from *iatros* physician, from *iasthai* to heal. See also -IC.

Iberian *a.* of or relating to ancient Iberia in SW Europe, comprising modern Spain and Portugal. *Also n.* WH: 16C. Latin *Iberia*, the country of the *Iberi* or *Iberes*, from Greek *Ibēres*, name of either the Spaniards or a people of the S Caucasus. See also -IAN.

iberis *n.* a plant of the genus *Iberis*, including the candytufts. WH: 18C. Modern Latin, prob. from Greek *ibēris* a kind of pepperwort.

Ibero- *comb. form* Iberian. WH: IBERIAN. See also -O-.

ibex *n.* a wild goat of any of several species inhabiting the mountain regions of Europe, N Africa and Asia, of which the best known is *Capra ibex*. WH: 17C. Latin.

ibidem *adv.* in the same place (when referring to a book, page etc. already cited). WH: 18C. Latin in the same place, from *ibi* there + demonstrative suf. *-dem*. Cp. IDEM, TANDEM.

ibis *n.* any of the heron-like wading birds belonging to the family Threskiornithidae, esp. *Threskiornis aethiopica*, the sacred ibis, which was venerated by the ancient Egyptians. WH: 14–15C. Latin, from Greek, from Egyptian *hab* a sacred bird of Egypt.

-ible *suf.* forming adjectives, able to be, that may, as in *forcible, terrible*. WH: Latin a. suf. *-ibilis*, the form taken by *-bilis* (-BLE) when added to Latin consonantal stems and some *e-* and *i-* stems.

Ibo *n.* a black African people living in SE Nigeria. *Also a.* WH: 18C. African name.

ibuprofen *n.* a drug used esp. for relieving arthritic pain and reducing inflammation. WH: mid-20C. ISO- + BUTYL + PROPIONIC ACID + alt. of PHENYL, all elements from the full chemical name 2-(4-isobutylphenyl)propionic acid.

-ic *suf.* forming adjectives, of or relating to, like, as in *alcoholic, algebraic, domestic, Miltonic, plutonic*. WH: French *-ique*, or from Latin *-icus*, from Greek *-ikos*.

ice *n.* frozen water. *Also v.t., v.i.* WH: pre-1200. Old English *īs*, from Germanic, rel. to Avestan *isu-* icy. Cp. German *Eis*.

-ice *suf.* forming nouns, as in *justice, malice, novice, service*. WH: Old French (Modern French *-ise*), from Latin *-itia, -itius, -itium*.

iceberg *n.* a large mass of ice floating in the sea, usu. formed by detachment from a glacier. WH: 18C. Middle Dutch *ijsberg*. See ICE, BARROW[1]. The Dutch word also gave German *Eisberg*, Swedish *isberg*, Danish *isbjerg*.

Icelander *n.* a native or inhabitant of Iceland, an island in the N Atlantic between Scandinavia and Greenland. WH: 17C. *Iceland*, an island republic in the N Atlantic near the Arctic Circle + -ER[1].

I Ching *n.* an ancient Chinese method of divination employing a set of symbols, 8 trigrams and 64 hexagrams, together with the text known as the *I Ching* which serves to interpret them. WH: 19C. Chinese, lit. Book of Changes, from *yì* change + *jīng* classics.

ichneumon *n.* a small carnivorous animal, *Herpestes ichneumon*, related to the mongoose, found in Egypt, where it was formerly held sacred on account of its devouring crocodiles' eggs. WH: 15C. Latin, from Greek *ikhneumōn*, lit. tracker, from *ikhneuein* to track, from *ikhnos* track, footprint. Cp. COCKATRICE. The animal was presumably so named as it searches out crocodiles' eggs.

ichnography *n.* the art of drawing ground plans etc. WH: 16C. French *ichnographie*, or from Latin *ichnographia*, from Greek *ikhnographia*, from *ikhnos* track, footprint. See -GRAPHY.

ichnolite *n.* a stone with the impression of a footprint. WH: 19C. Greek *ikhnos* footprint + -LITE.

ichnology *n.* the department of palaeontology that treats of and classifies fossil footprints. WH: 19C. Greek *ikhnos* track, footprint + -LOGY.

ichor *n.* in Greek mythology, the ethereal fluid which flowed in place of blood in the veins of the gods. WH: 17C. Greek *ikhōr*.

ichthyic *a.* of or relating to fish. WH: 19C. Greek *ikhthuïkos* fishy, from *ikhthus* fish. See also -IC.

ichthyo- *comb. form* of or relating to fish. WH: Greek *ikhthus* fish. See also -O-.

ichthyoid *a.* resembling fish. *Also n.* WH: 19C. ICHTHYO- + -OID.

ichthyolatry *n.* the worship of fishes, or of a fish god such as Dagon. WH: 19C. ICHTHYO- + -LATRY.

ichthyolite *n.* a fossil fish. WH: 19C. ICHTHYO- + -LITE.

ichthyology *n.* the study of fishes. WH: 17C. ICHTHYO- + -LOGY.

ichthyophagy *n.* the practice of eating fish; the having of a fish diet. WH: 17C. French *ichthyophagie*, from Greek *ikhthuophagia* fish diet, from *ikhthuophagos*. See ICHTHYO-, -PHAGE + -Y[2].

ichthyornis *n.* an extinct Cretaceous seabird of the genus *Ichthyornis*, having biconcave vertebrae and socketed teeth. WH: 19C. Modern Latin, from ICHTHYO- + Greek *ornis* bird. The name was coined in 1872 by the US palaeontologist O.C. Marsh.

ichthyosaurus *n.* any extinct marine reptile of the order Ichthyosauria, shaped like a fish, with flippers and a long head. WH: 19C. Modern Latin, from ICHTHYO- + Greek *sauros* lizard.

ichthyosis *n.* a hereditary skin disease, marked by thick, hard, overlapping grey scales. WH: 19C. Modern Latin, from ICHTHYO- + -OSIS.

ichthys *n.* a symbol in the form of a fish, connected with Christ. WH: 18C. Greek *ikhthus* fish. The Greek letters ΙΧΘΥΣ give the initials of the Greek words meaning 'Jesus Christ, Son of God, Saviour'. It is uncertain whether the symbol gave the acrostic or the acrostic the symbol.

-ician *suf.* indicating a specialist in a subject, as in *beautician*. WH: Old French *-icien*, from *-ique* -IC + *-ien* -IAN or directly from -IC + -IAN.

icicle *n.* a hanging conical point of ice, formed when dripping water freezes. WH: 12–14C. ICE + obs. *ickle* in same sense, from Old English *gicel*, rel. to Old Norse *jökull* icicle, glacier, from Germanic.

-icist *suf.* forming nouns indicating a specialist in a subject from adjectives in *-ic* or nouns in *-ics*, as in *classicist*. WH: -IC or -ICS + -IST.

-icity *suf.* forming abstract nouns from adjectives in *-ic* etc., as in *publicity*. WH: French *-icité*, from Latin *-icitas, -icitatis*, suf. combining *-tat-* (see -TY[1]) with adjectival stems in *-ic-* or *-ici-*.

icky *a.* cloying; over-sentimental. WH: early 20C. Orig. uncertain. ? From *sickly* (SICK[1]) or *sticky* (STICK[2]), or blend of both.

-icle *suf.* forming diminutive nouns, as in *particle, versicle.* WH: French *-icule,* or from Latin *-iculus, -icula, -iculum.* See -CLE, -CULE.

icon *n.* in the Eastern Church, a sacred image, picture, mosaic, or monumental figure of a holy personage. WH: 16C. Latin, from Greek *eikōn* likeness, image, similitude.

icono- *comb. form* of or relating to images or idols. WH: Greek *eikono-,* from *eikōn* ICON. See also -O-.

iconoclasm *n.* active hostility towards or disregard of established opinions, practices etc. WH: 18C. Back-formation from *iconoclast* (from Medieval Latin *iconoclastes,* from Ecclesiastical Greek *eikon-oklastēs,* from *eikōn* ICON + *klan* to break), based on pairs such as *enthusiast*/ENTHUSIASM. The original iconoclasts were the image breakers in the Orthodox Church in the 8C and 9C. Later equivalents were the Puritans of the 16C and 17C.

iconography *n.* the study of portraits, pictures, statues, symbolism etc. WH: 17C. Greek *eikonographia* sketch, description. See ICONO-, -GRAPHY.

iconolatry *n.* the adoration of images. WH: 17C. Ecclesiastical Greek *eikonolatreia.* See ICONO-, -LATRY.

iconology *n.* the study of images, pictures etc. WH: 18C. ICONO- + -LOGY.

iconomatic *a.* denoting a kind of writing in which pictures represent the sounds of the names of objects rather than the objects themselves, as in a stage of writing intermediate between picture-writing and phonetic writing. WH: 19C. Contr. of **icono-nomatic,* from Greek *eikōn* ICON + *onoma, onomatos* name + -IC. The word was coined in 1886 by the US anthropologist Daniel G. Brinton.

iconometer *n.* an instrument for measuring the size or distance of an object. WH: 19C. ICONO- + -METER.

iconophile *n.* a connoisseur of pictures, prints etc. WH: 19C. ICONO- + -PHILE.

iconoscope *n.* a type of electron camera. WH: 19C. ICONO- + -SCOPE.

iconostasis *n.* in the Eastern Church, a screen on which icons are placed, separating the sanctuary from the rest of the church. WH: 19C. Modern Greek *eikonostasis.* See ICONO-, *-stasis* (STASIS).

icosahedron *n.* a solid figure having 20 plane sides. WH: 16C. Late Latin *icosahedrum,* from Greek *eikosaedron,* from *eikosi* twenty + -HEDRON.

-ics *suf.* indicating a science or art, as in *linguistics.* WH: -IC + -S[1], representing French *-iques,* Medieval Latin *-ica,* Greek *-ika.*

icterus *n.* jaundice. WH: 18C. Latin, from Greek *ikteros.*

ictus *n.* the stress, or rhythmical accent on a syllable in a line of verse. WH: 18C. Latin, from *ictus,* p.p. of *icere* to strike.

id *n.* the instinctive impulses in the unconscious mind of the individual. WH: early 20C. Latin it, translating German *es.* Cp. EGO. The word was popularized by Freud (see FREUDIAN) in *Das Ich und das Es* (1923), translated as *Ego and Id.*

-id *suf.* forming adjectives denoting the quality orig. expressed by a L verb, as in *acid, frigid, morbid, tepid.* WH: French *-ide* and Latin *-idus* or *-id, -is* (from Greek *-ida, -is*) or *-ides* (pl. *-idae, -ida*) (from Greek *-idēs*).

ide *n.* a northern European fish, *Leuciscus idus,* of the carp family. WH: 19C. Modern Latin *idus,* from Swedish *id.*

-ide *suf.* indicating chemical compounds of an element with another element or a radical, as in *chloride, fluoride, oxide.* WH: From OXIDE, the first compound to be so classified.

idea *n.* a mental image or representation of anything. WH: 14–15C. Latin, from Greek look, semblance, kind, nature, from base of *idein* to see.

ideal *a.* reaching one's standard of perfection; perfect. *Also n.* WH: 14–15C. Late Latin *idealis,* from Latin IDEA. See also -AL[1].

idée fixe *n.* a fixed idea, an obsession. WH: 19C. French fixed idea, from *idée* IDEA + *fixe* fixed (see FIX).

idée reçue *n.* a generally accepted idea. WH: mid-20C. French received idea, from *idée* IDEA + *reçue,* fem. p.p. of *recevoir* RECEIVE.

idem *n.* the same (word, author, book etc.). *Also adv.* WH: 14–15C. Latin the same.

identic *a.* (of diplomatic communications etc.) identical. WH: 17C. Medieval Latin *identicus,* from *ident-.* See IDENTITY, also -IC.

identical *a.* (of one thing viewed or found under different conditions) absolutely the same, not different. WH: 16C. Medieval Latin *identicus,* from *ident-.* See IDENTITY, also -IC, -AL[1].

identify *v.t.* to determine or prove the identity of. *Also v.i.* WH: 17C. Medieval Latin *identificare,* from *ident-.* See IDENTITY, also -FY. The original sense (to the 19C) was to be identical.

Identikit® *n.* a set of facial features on transparent slips, used to compose a likeness, esp. of a criminal suspect. *Also a.* WH: mid-20C. Blend of IDENTITY and KIT[1]. Cp. E-FIT.

identity *n.* the condition of being a particular person or thing. WH: 16C. Late Latin *identitas,* from Latin *idem* same, prob. based on *entitas* ENTITY, but ? assoc. with *identidem* repeatedly. Latin *ident-* became established as the combining form of *idem.*

ideo- *comb. form* of, relating to or expressing ideas. WH: Greek IDEA. See also -O-.

ideograph *n.* a symbol, figure etc., suggesting or conveying the idea of an object, without expressing its name. WH: 19C. IDEO- + -GRAPH.

ideology *n.* the political or social philosophy of a nation, movement, group etc. WH: 18C. French *idéologie.* See IDEO-, -LOGY.

ideomotor *a.* denoting unconscious muscular movements due to the concentration of attention on an idea. WH: 19C. IDEO- + MOTOR.

ides *n.pl.* in the ancient Roman calendar, the 15th of March, May, July, October, and 13th of the other months. WH: pre-1200. Old French, from Latin *idus* (pl.), of unknown orig.

idio- *comb. form* individual, peculiar. WH: Greek *idios* own, personal, private, distinct. See also -O-.

idiograph *n.* a private mark or signature, esp. a trademark. WH: 17C. IDIO- + -GRAPH.

idiolect *n.* a form of speech or language peculiar to an individual. WH: mid-20C. IDIO- + DIALECT.

idiom *n.* a phrase etc. whose meaning cannot be deduced simply from the meaning of each of its words. WH: 16C. French *idiome* or Late Latin *idioma,* from Greek property, peculiar phraseology, from *idiousthai* to make one's own, from *idios* own, private.

idiomorphic *a.* (of a mineral) having a distinctive form of its own, esp. having distinctive faces of crystallization. WH: 19C. IDIO- + *-morphic* (-MORPH).

idiopathy *n.* a primary disease, one not occasioned by another. WH: 17C. IDIO- + -PATHY.

idiophone *n.* a percussion instrument, such as a cymbal, made out of a naturally resonant material. WH: mid-20C. IDIO- + -PHONE. The term was devised in 1914 as one of four classifications of instruments by the German musicologists Curt Sachs and E.M. von Hornbostel.

idioplasm *n.* the portion of protoplasm derived from the parent organism and supposed to determine the character of the individual, distinct from that due to the development of the individual. WH: 19C. IDIO- + *plasm* (PLASMA).

idiosyncrasy *n.* a characteristic or habit peculiar to an individual. WH: 17C. Greek *idiosugkrasia,* from *idios* IDIO- + *sugkrasis* commixture, tempering, from *sun-* SYN- + *krasis* CRASIS.

idiot *n.* a stupid, silly person. *Also a.* WH: 12–14C. Old French, from Latin *idiota* ignorant person, from Greek *idiotēs* private person, lay man, ignorant person, from *idios* private, peculiar. A former meaning (to the 17C) was layman, from the original Greek.

idiot savant *n.* a person who is considered to be mentally retarded but who has an outstanding ability in a specific area, such as mental arithmetic. WH: early 20C. French clever idiot, from *idiot* IDIOT + *savant* clever, learned, SAVANT.

idle *a.* averse to work, lazy. *Also v.i., v.t., n.* WH: pre-1200. Old English *īdel,* from Germanic, ult. of unknown orig. Cp. German *eitel* bare, mere, Dutch *ijdel* vain, useless, frivolous. The original basic sense was empty, vacant, vain, useless, preserved in Tennyson's 'Tears, idle tears' (1847).

Ido *n.* an artificial international language based on Esperanto. WH: 19C. Ido offspring. Ido is so called as the 'offspring' of Esperanto, its parent language. The name actually represents the Esperanto suffix *-ido* meaning derived from. Cp. -ID.

idocrase *n.* vesuvianite. WH: 19C. Greek *eidos* form + *krasis* mixture.

idol *n.* an image, esp. one worshipped as a god. WH: 12–14C. Old French *idole,* from Latin *idolum* image, form, apparition, from Greek *eidōlon,* from *eidos* form, shape.

idolum *n.* an image. WH: 17C. Latin, from Greek *eidōlon* IDOL.

idyll *n.* a brief, artistic, and picturesque narrative or description of rustic life, either in verse or prose. WH: 16C. Latin *idyllium*, from Greek *eidullion*, dim. of *eidos* form, picture.

i.e. *abbr.* id est, that is to say. WH: Abbr. of Latin *id est* that is, from *id* that + *est*, 3rd pers. sing. pres. of *esse* to be.

-ier *suf.* denoting occupation, profession etc., as in *bombardier*, *brigadier*, *chevalier*, *financier*. WH: French, from Latin *-arius*. See -ARY¹. Cp. -EER.

if *conj.* providing that; in the case that. *Also n.* WH: pre-1200. Old English *gif, gyf*, from Germanic, ult. of unknown orig. Cp. German *ob*, Dutch *of*.

iff *conj.* used to express *if and only if*. WH: mid-20C. Written abbr. of *if and only if*.

iffy *a.* doubtful, uncertain. WH: mid-20C. IF + -Y¹.

igloo *n.* an Eskimo (Inuit) hut, often built of snow. WH: 19C. Eskimo (Inuit) *iglu* house.

igneous *a.* of or like fire. WH: 17C. Latin *igneus*, from *ignis* fire + -OUS. See also -EOUS.

ignescent *a.* emitting sparks when struck, as with steel. *Also n.* WH: 19C. Latin *ignescens, ignescentis*, pres.p. of *ignescere* to catch fire, from *ignis* fire. See also -ENT.

ignimbrite *n.* a volcanic rock formed by the consolidation of the lava fragments and dust of a nuée ardente. WH: mid-20C. Latin *ignis* fire + *imber, imbris* shower of rain, storm cloud + -ITE¹.

ignis fatuus *n.* an apparent flame, probably due to the spontaneous combustion of inflammable gas, floating above the ground in marshes etc. WH: 16C. Modern Latin foolish fire, from *ignis* fire + *fatuus* foolish, FATUOUS. The phenomenon is so called because it flits erratically from place to place.

ignite *v.t.* to set on fire. *Also v.i.* WH: 17C. Latin *ignitus*, p.p. of *ignire* to set on fire, from *ignis* fire.

ignoble *a.* mean, base, dishonourable. *Also v.t.* WH: 14–15C. French, from Latin *ignobilis*, from *i-* IN-² + *gnobilis* NOBLE.

ignominy *n.* public disgrace or shame; dishonour. WH: 16C. French *ignominie*, from Latin *ignominia*, from *i-* IN-² + (var. of) *nomen* name, reputation. See also -Y².

ignoramus *n.* an ignorant person. *Also a.* WH: 16C. Latin we do not know, we take no notice of (it), 1st pers. pl. pres. ind. of *ignorare* IGNORE. The sense of ignorant person arose in the 17C and may originate in *Ignoramus*, the title of a comedy by George Ruggle (1615) satirizing lawyers. The word was originally used as an endorsement by a grand jury on an indictment which they rejected as it was not backed by sufficient evidence to bring before a petty jury.

ignorance *n.* the state of being ignorant, lack of knowledge (of). WH: 12–14C. Old French, from Latin *ignorantia*, from *ignorans, ignorantis*, pres.p. of *ignorare*. See IGNORE, also -ANCE.

ignore *v.t.* to pass over without notice, to disregard. WH: 15C. Old French *ignorer*, from Latin *ignorare*, *i-* IN-² + base *gno-* to know. The original sense, as still with French *ignorer*, was to be ignorant of, not to know. The current sense dates from the 19C.

iguana *n.* any large lizard of the American genus *Iguana*, esp. *I. iguana*, of S and Central America and the W Indies. WH: 16C. Spanish, from Arawak *iwana*.

iguanodon *n.* a large, bipedal, herbivorous dinosaur of the Cretaceous period. WH: 19C. IGUANA + *-odon* (see -ODONT). The animal was so named in *c.*1830 by the English geologist W.D. Conybeare from its supposed resemblance to the iguana. Cp. MASTODON.

IHS *abbr.* Jesus, often used as a Christian symbol. WH: Abbr. (first two and last letters) of Greek *Iesous* Jesus. The letters have been popularly interpreted as an abbreviation of various Latin phrases, e.g. *Iesus Hominum Salvator* Jesus Saviour of Men, *In Hoc Signo* (*vinces*) in this sign (thou shalt conquer), *In Hac Salus* in this (cross is) salvation. These take the second letter of the original Greek, eta, as a Roman H.

ikebana *n.* the Japanese art of arranging flowers. WH: early 20C. Japanese, from *ikeru* to arrange + *hana* (*bana*) flower.

il-¹ *pref.* in, into, within, on, against, towards, as in *illustrate, illuminate*. WH: Latin pref., from IN-¹ with *n* assim. to *l*.

il-² *pref.* not, without, as in *illiterate, illegal*. WH: Latin pref., from IN-² with *n* assim. to *l*.

-il *suf.* that may be, capable of being, of or relating to etc., as in *civil, fossil, docile, fragile, Gentile, puerile, senile*. WH: Latin *-ilis*. The variant *-ile* usually occurs in adoptions through French.

ileum *n.* the portion of the small intestine communicating with the larger intestine. WH: 17C. Medieval Latin, var. of ILIUM, appar. by confusion with ILEUS.

ileus *n.* a painful obstruction of the intestine. WH: 17C. Latin, from Greek *ileos, eileos* colic, appar. from *eilein* to roll.

ilex *n.* the holm-oak. WH: 14–15C. Latin holm-oak.

ilium *n.* the upper part of the hip bone. WH: 14–15C. Latin *ilia* (pl.) flanks, sides, entrails. Cp. ILEUM.

ilk *n.* a class, sort or kind. WH: pre-1200. Old English *ilca* (m.), *ilce* (fem. and neut.), from Germanic pron. stem found also in Gothic *is*, Old High German *ir*, German *er* he, Latin *is* that, *idem* same + base of ALIKE. Cp. SUCH, WHICH. The current sense dates from the 18C.

ilka *a.* each, every. WH: 12–14C. Old English *ælc* EACH + A. Not rel. to ILK.

ill *a.* unwell, diseased. *Also adv., n.* WH: 12–14C. Old Norse *illr* (a.), *illa* (adv.), ult. of unknown orig.

illation *n.* deduction. WH: 16C. Latin *illatio, illationis*, from *illatus*, p.p. of *inferre* INFER.

Illawarra shorthorn *n.* a noted breed of Australian dairy cattle. WH: early 20C. *Illawara*, a district in New South Wales, Australia.

illegal *a.* not according to law. WH: 17C. Old French *illégal* or Medieval Latin *illegalis*, or from Latin IL-² + *legalis* legal.

illegible *a.* that cannot be read or deciphered. WH: 17C. IL-² + LEGIBLE.

illegitimate¹ *a.* born of parents not married to each other. *Also n.* WH: 16C. Late Latin *illegitimus*, based on LEGITIMATE¹. See IL-², also -ATE³. The sense born out of wedlock is the oldest.

illegitimate² *v.t.* to render or declare illegitimate. WH: 17C. ILLEGITIMATE¹.

illiberal *a.* narrow-minded. WH: 16C. Old French *illibéral*, from Latin *illiberalis* mean, sordid, from IL-² + *liberalis* LIBERAL.

illicit *a.* not allowed or permitted. WH: 16C. Old French *illicite* or Latin *illicitus*, from IL-² + LICIT.

illimitable *a.* boundless, limitless. WH: 16C. IL-² + *limitable* (LIMIT).

†illinium *n.* promethium. WH: early 20C. *Illinois* University, USA. See also -IUM. The element is named for the university where it was mistakenly reported to have been identified in 1926.

illiquid *a.* (of assets) not easily convertible into cash. WH: 17C. IL-² + LIQUID.

illiterate *a.* unable to read or write. *Also n.* WH: 14–15C. Latin *illiteratus*. See IL-², LITERATE.

illness *n.* the state of being ill. WH: 16C. ILL + -NESS.

illogical *a.* contrary to reason. WH: 16C. IL-² + *logical* (LOGIC).

illude *v.t.* to deceive, to cheat. WH: 14–15C. Latin *illudere*. See ILLUSION.

illume *v.t.* to illuminate, to lighten or brighten up. WH: 14–15C. Contr. of *illumine*, from Old French *illuminer*, from Latin *illuminare* ILLUMINATE¹.

illuminate¹ *v.t.* to light up. *Also v.i., a.* WH: 14–15C. Orig. p.p., from Latin *illuminatus*, from p.p. of *illuminare*, from IL-¹ + *lumen, luminis* light. See also -ATE³. Cp. ILLUME.

illuminate² *n.* a person who claims to possess special enlightenment. WH: 17C. ILLUMINATE¹. See also -ATE¹.

illuminati *n.pl.* a group of people claiming to possess knowledge or gifts. WH: 16C. Pl. of Italian *illuminato* enlightened, or of Latin *illuminatus*. See ILLUMINATE¹.

illusion *n.* deception. WH: 12–14C. Old French, from Latin *illusio, illusionis*, from *illusus*, p.p. of *illudere* to mock, to jest at, from IL-¹ + *ludere* to play. See also -ION.

illustrate *v.t.* to embellish (a book, etc.) with pictures. WH: 16C. Latin *illustratus*, p.p. of *illustrare*, from IL-¹ + *lustrare* to illuminate. See also -ATE³.

illustrious *a.* distinguished, famous. WH: 16C. Latin *illustris* clear, bright, evident, famous + -OUS.

Illyrian *a.* of or relating to Illyria, and roughly corresponding to parts of present-day Albania, Slovenia and Croatia. *Also n.* WH: 16C. Latin *Illyrius*, from *Illyria*, a region on the E coast of the Adriatic + -AN.

illywhacker *n.* a confidence trickster. WH: mid-20C. Orig. unknown. The word was popularized by Peter Carey's novel *Illywhacker* (1985).

ilmenite *n.* a black mineral that is found in igneous rocks and is the principal ore of titanium. WH: 19C. *Ilmen* Mountains in S Urals + -ITE¹. The mineral is named from the location where it was discovered in 1827.

-ily *suf.* forming adverbs from adjectives ending in -y, as in *happily, noisily.* WH: -i- (from -Y¹) + -LY².

im-¹ *pref.* in, into, within, on, against, towards, as in *imbibe, imbrue.* WH: Latin pref., from IN-¹ with *n* assim. to *b, m, p.*

im-² *pref.* not, without, as in *immaculate, impossible.* WH: Latin pref., from IN-² with *n* assim. to *b, m, p.*

image *n.* a visible representation or likeness of a person or thing, esp. in sculpture. *Also v.t.* WH: 12–14C. Old French, from Latin *imago, imaginis,* rel. to *imitari* IMITATE.

imagine *v.t.* to form an image of in the mind. *Also v.i.* WH: 12–14C. Old French *imaginer,* from Latin *imaginare* to form an image of, to represent, or *imaginari* to picture to oneself, to fancy, from *imago, imaginis.* See IMAGE.

imago *n.* the adult, fully-developed insect after its metamorphoses. WH: 18C. Latin. See IMAGE.

imam *n.* a person who leads congregational prayer in a mosque. WH: 17C. Arabic *'imām* leader from *'amma* to lead the way.

IMAX® *n.* a system of wide-screen motion-picture presentation, that produces an image much larger than that from standard 35mm film. WH: mid-20C. IMAGE + MAXIMUM.

imbalance *n.* a lack of balance or proportion. WH: 19C. IM-² + BALANCE.

imbecile *a.* mentally weak, half-witted. *Also n.* WH: 16C. Obs. French *imbécille* (now *imbécile*), from Latin *imbecillus* lit. without support, from IM-² + var. of *baculum* stick, staff. The original sense was physically weak, impotent. The current sense of mentally weak arose in the 19C.

imbibe *v.t.* to drink. *Also v.i.* WH: 14–15C. Latin *imbibere,* from IM-¹ + *bibere* to drink.

imbricate¹ *v.t.* to lap (leaves, scales on fish etc.) one over the other like tiles. *Also v.i.* WH: 18C. Latin *imbricatus,* p.p. of *imbricare* to cover with rain tiles, from *imbrex, imbricis* roof tile, from *imber* rain shower. See also -ATE³.

imbricate² *a.* arranged in an imbricated fashion. WH: 17C. Latin *imbricatus.* See IMBRICATE¹, also -ATE².

imbroglio *n.* a perplexing or confused state of affairs. WH: 18C. Italian, from *imbrogliare* to confuse, rel. to EMBROIL.

imbrue *v.t.* to steep, to soak or moisten (in or with blood). WH: 14–15C. Old French *embruer, embrouer* to bedaub, to bedabble, from EM- + *breu, bro,* ult. from Germanic base of BROTH.

imbue *v.t.* to inspire, to impregnate (with). WH: 14–15C. French *imbu,* obs. *imbut,* p.p., from Latin *imbutus,* p.p. of *imbuere* to moisten, to stain.

imburse *v.t.* to provide with money. WH: 16C. Medieval Latin *imbursare* to put in one's purse, to appropriate, from IM-¹ + Late Latin *bursa* purse.

imide *n.* a compound derived from ammonia by the replacement of two atoms of hydrogen by a metal or organic radical. WH: 19C. French, arbitrary alt. of AMIDE.

imine *n.* a compound derived from ammonia by the replacement of two atoms of hydrogen by other groups. WH: 19C. Alt. of AMINE, based on that of IMIDE from AMIDE.

imitate *v.t.* to follow the example of. WH: 16C. Latin *imitatus,* p.p. of *imitari* to copy, rel. to *imago* image. See also -ATE³.

immaculate *a.* spotlessly clean or tidy. WH: 14–15C. Latin *immaculatus,* from IM-² + *maculate* (MACULA). The word was first used in English in reference to the Virgin Mary, who was conceived and born free from original sin. (The religious feast of the Immaculate Conception relates to her own birth, not that of Christ.)

immanent *a.* remaining within, inherent; indwelling. WH: 16C. Late Latin *immanens, immanentis,* pres.p. of *immanere,* from IM-¹ + Latin *manere* to remain, to dwell. See also -ENT.

immaterial *a.* irrelevant, unimportant. WH: 14–15C. Late Latin *immaterialis,* from IM-² + *materialis* MATERIAL.

immature *a.* not fully developed. WH: 16C. Latin *immaturus* untimely, unripe, from IM-² + *maturus* MATURE.

immeasurable *a.* that cannot be measured. WH: 14–15C. IM-² + *measurable* (see MEASURE).

immediate *a.* done or occurring at once, instant. WH: 14–15C. Old French *immédiat* or Late Latin *immediatus,* from IM-² + *mediatus* MEDIATE².

immedicable *a.* that cannot be healed; incurable. WH: 16C. Latin *immedicabilis,* from IM-² + *medicabilis* curable, *medicable* (MEDICAL).

immemorial *a.* beyond memory or record. WH: 17C. Medieval Latin *immemorialis,* from IM-² + Latin *memorialis* MEMORIAL.

immense *a.* huge, vast. WH: 14–15C. Old French, from Latin *immensus* immeasurable, from IM-² + *mensus,* p.p. of *metiri* to measure (cp. METER).

immensurable *a.* immeasurable. WH: 15C. French or Late Latin *immensurabilis,* from IM-² + *mensurabilis* MENSURABLE.

†immerge *v.t.* to immerse. *Also v.i.* WH: 17C. Latin *immergere.* See IMMERSE.

immerse *v.t.* to plunge, to dip (into or under water or other fluid). WH: 17C. Latin *immersus,* p.p. of *immergere,* from IM-¹ + *mergere* to dip, MERGE.

immethodical *a.* not methodical. WH: 16C. IM-² + *methodical* (METHOD).

immigrate *v.i.* to enter a foreign country for settlement there. *Also v.t.* WH: 17C. Latin *immigratus,* p.p. of *immigrare,* from IM-¹ + *migrare* MIGRATE. See also -ATE³.

imminent *a.* impending; close at hand. WH: 14–15C. Latin *imminens, imminentis,* pres.p. of *imminere* to project, to be impending, from IM-¹ + *minere* to project. See also -ENT.

immiscible *a.* not capable of being mixed (with). WH: 17C. Late Latin *immiscibilis,* from IM-² + MISCIBLE.

immitigable *a.* incapable of being mitigated. WH: 16C. Late Latin *immitigabilis,* from IM-² + *mitigable* (MITIGATE).

immittance *n.* electrical admittance or impedance. WH: mid-20C. Blend of *impedance* (IMPEDE) and *admittance* (ADMIT).

†immix *v.t.* to mix or mingle together. WH: 14–15C. Orig. p.p., from Latin *immixtus,* p.p. of *immiscere,* from IM-¹ + *miscere* to mix. The verb dates from the 16C, either as a back-formation from the original past participle form *immixt, immixed,* or direct from IM-¹ + MIX.

immobile *a.* not moving. WH: 12–14C. Old French, from Latin *immobilis,* from IM-² + *mobilis* MOBILE.

immoderate *a.* excessive. WH: 14–15C. Latin *immoderatus,* from IM-² + *moderatus* MODERATE¹.

immodest *a.* not modest, forward. WH: 16C. French *immodeste* or Latin *immodestus.* See IM-², MODEST.

immolate *v.t.* to kill or offer up in sacrifice. WH: 16C. Latin *immolatus,* p.p. of *immolare* to sprinkle with (sacrificial) meal, from IM-¹ + *mola* meal. See also -ATE³.

immoral *a.* not moral. WH: 17C. IM-² + MORAL.

immortal *a.* not mortal, not subject to death. *Also n.* WH: 14–15C. Latin *immortalis* not dying, from IM-² + *mortalis* MORTAL.

immortelle *n.* an everlasting flower, esp. a helichrysum. WH: 19C. French, from *fleur immortelle* everlasting flower. The flowers so named have a papery texture and retain their colour after being dried.

immovable *a.* that cannot be moved. WH: 14–15C. IM-² + *movable* (MOVE).

immune *a.* protected against a particular disease, infection etc. owing to inoculation or the body's natural resistance. *Also n.* WH: 14–15C. Latin *immunis* exempt from service, from IM-² + *munis* ready for service. The original sense was exempt, free from a liability. The medical sense evolved in the 19C.

immuno- *comb. form* immunity. WH: IMMUNE, *immunity,* IMMUNOLOGY. See also -O-.

immunoassay *n.* the identification of a substance, esp. a protein, through its behaviour as an antigen or antibody. WH: mid-20C. IMMUNO- + ASSAY.

immunochemistry *n.* the chemical study of antigens, antibody reactions etc. WH: early 20C. IMMUNO- + CHEMISTRY.

immunocompromised *a.* having an impaired immune system. WH: late 20C. IMMUNO- + COMPROMISE + -ED.

immunodeficiency *n.* a deficiency in a person's immune response. WH: mid-20C. IMMUNO- + *deficiency* (DEFICIENT).

immunogenic *a.* causing or able to produce an immune response. WH: mid-20C. IMMUNO- + -GENIC.

immunoglobulin *n.* any one of five classes of proteins showing antibody activity. WH: mid-20C. IMMUNO- + *globulin* (GLOBULE).

immunology *n.* the scientific study of immunity. WH: early 20C. *immunity* (IMMUNE) + -O- + -LOGY.

immunosuppressive *a.* (of a drug) that minimizes the body's natural reactions to a foreign substance, e.g. a transplanted organ. *Also n.* WH: mid-20C. IMMUNO- + *suppressive* (SUPPRESS).

immunotherapy *n.* the treatment of disease through the stimulation of the patient's own natural immunity. WH: early 20C. IMMUNO- + *therapy* (THERAPEUTIC).

immure *v.t.* to surround as with a wall; to confine. *Also n.* WH: 16C. French *emmurer* or Medieval Latin *immurare*, from IM-¹ + *murus* wall.

immutable *a.* unchangeable. WH: 14–15C. Latin *immutabilis*, from IM-² + *mutabilis*, MUTABLE.

imp *n.* a mischievous child. *Also v.t.* WH: pre-1200. Old English *impa* young shoot, from *impian* to graft, from Medieval Latin *impotus* graft, from Greek *emphutos* implanted, verbal a. of *emphuein*, from EN- + *phuein* to plant. The original sense was the young shoot of a plant, sapling, scion, then descendant, offspring. The sense then developed in the 16C to lad, boy (to the 19C), and in the 17C to mischievous child, as now.

impact¹ *n.* a forcible striking (upon or against). WH: 18C. Latin *impactus*, p.p. of *impingere* IMPINGE.

impact² *v.t.* to press or drive firmly together, to pack firmly in. *Also v.i.* WH: 17C. Partly from Latin *impactus*, p.p. of *impingere* IMPINGE, partly back-formation from *impacted* (from *impactus* + -ED).

impair *v.t.* to damage or weaken in quality, strength etc. *Also v.i.* WH: 12–14C. Old French *empeirier*, from EM- + Late Latin *peiorare*, from Latin *peior* worse.

impala *n.* an antelope, *Aepyceros melampus*, of southern and eastern Africa, that has lyre-shaped horns and is able to move with long high leaps. WH: 19C. Zulu *i-mpala*, rel. to Setswana *phala* gazelle.

impale *v.t.* to transfix, esp. to put to death by transfixing with a sharp stake. WH: 16C. French *impaler* or Medieval Latin *impalare*, from IM-¹ + *palus* stake, PALE². The original sense was to surround with a palisade. The sense to transfix a body with a stake dates from the 17C.

impalpable *a.* not able to be readily apprehended by the mind. WH: 16C. French, or from Late Latin *impalpabilis*. See IM-², PALPABLE.

impaludism *n.* a disease carried by insects, affecting those living in marshy regions. WH: 19C. IM-¹ + Latin *palus, paludis* marsh + -ISM.

impanate *a.* embodied in bread. *Also v.t.* WH: 16C. Medieval Latin *impanatus*, p.p. of *impanare*, from IM-¹ + *panis* bread. See also -ATE².

imparadise *v.t.* to put in a place or state of perfect happiness. WH: 16C. IM-¹ + PARADISE.

imparipinnate *a.* pinnate with an odd terminal leaflet. WH: 19C. Latin *impar* uneven, based on PARIPINNATE.

imparisyllabic *a.* (of a noun or verb) not having the same number of syllables in the different inflected forms. *Also n.* WH: 18C. Latin *impar* unequal, based on PARISYLLABIC.

imparity *n.* disparity, inequality. WH: 16C. Late Latin *imparitas*, from *impar* unequal, uneven, from IM-² + *par* equal. Cp. PARITY¹.

†**impark** *v.t.* to form (land) into a park. WH: 14–15C. Old French *emparquer*, from EM- + *parc* PARK.

impart *v.t.* to communicate (knowledge, information). *Also v.i.* WH: 14–15C. Old French *impartir*, from Latin *impartire*, from IM-¹ + *pars, partis* PART.

impartial *a.* not favouring one party or one side more than another. WH: 16C. IM-² + PARTIAL.

impartible *a.* not subject to or capable of partition. WH: 16C. Late Latin *impartibilis*, from IM-² + *partibilis* partible (PART).

impassable *a.* that cannot be passed or travelled through. WH: 16C. IM-² + *passable* (PASS).

impasse *n.* an insurmountable obstacle; deadlock. WH: 19C. French, from *im-* IM-² + stem of *passer* PASS. The word was adopted by Voltaire in 1761 as a euphemistic synonym for CUL-DE-SAC.

impassible *a.* impassive. WH: 12–14C. Old French, from Ecclesiastical Latin *impassibilis*. See IM-², PASSIBLE.

impassion *v.t.* to rouse the deepest feelings of, to stir to ardour or passion. WH: 16C. Obs. Italian *impassionare* (now *impassionnare*), from *im-* IM-¹ + *passione* PASSION.

impassive *a.* not showing or affected by pain, feeling or passion. WH: 17C. IM-² + PASSIVE.

impaste *v.t.* in painting, to lay colours thickly and boldly on. WH: 16C. Italian *impastare*, from *im-* IM-¹ + *pasta* PASTE.

impatiens *n.* any plant of the genus *Impatiens*, including the busy Lizzie and balsam. WH: 18C. Modern Latin, from Latin IM-PATIENT. The plant is so called because its capsules readily burst when touched.

impatient *a.* not able to wait or to endure. *Also n.* WH: 14–15C. Latin *impatiens, impatientis*. See IM-², PATIENT.

impeach *v.t.* to charge with a crime, esp. treason. WH: 14–15C. Old French *empecher* (Modern French *empêcher* to prevent), from Late Latin *impedicare* to catch, to entangle, from IM-¹ + *pedica* FETTER.

impearl *v.t.* to form into pearls or pearl-like drops. WH: 16C. French *emperler* or Italian *impelare*. See EM-, IM-¹, PEARL.

impeccable *a.* (of manners, behaviour etc.) faultless. WH: 16C. Latin *impeccabilis*, from IM-² + *peccare* to sin. See also -ABLE.

impecunious *a.* having no money. WH: 16C. IM-² + *pecunious* (PECUNIARY).

impede *v.t.* to hinder, to obstruct. WH: 16C. Latin *impedire*, lit. to shackle the feet, from IM-¹ + *pes, pedis* foot.

impel *v.t.* to drive or urge (to an action or to do). WH: 14–15C. Latin *impellere*, from IM-¹ + *pellere* to drive.

impend *v.i.* to threaten, to be imminent. WH: 16C. Latin *impendere*, from IM-¹ + *pendere* to hang.

impenetrable *a.* that cannot be penetrated or pierced. WH: 14–15C. Old French *impénétrable*, from Latin *impenetrabilis*, from IM-² + *penetrabilis*, penetrable (PENETRATE).

impenitent *a.* not penitent, not contrite. *Also n.* WH: 14–15C. Ecclesiastical Latin *impaenitens, impaenitentis*, from IM-² + *paenitens, paenitentis*. See PENITENT.

impennate *a.* (of birds) wingless; having short wings adapted for swimming. *Also n.* WH: 19C. IM-² + PENNATE. The word was coined in 1811 by the German naturalist Johann Illiger.

imperative *a.* urgent. *Also n.* WH: 14–15C. Late Latin *imperativus*, from Latin *imperatus*, p.p. of *imperare* to command, to rule. See EMPEROR, also -ATIVE. In the grammatical sense, Late Latin *imperativus* translated Greek *prostaktikē* (*egklisis*), literally ordered (mood), from *prostassein* to give orders (cp. TACTICS).

imperator *n.* a title originally bestowed upon a victorious Roman general. WH: 16C. Latin, from *imperatus*. See IMPERATIVE, also -OR.

imperceptible *a.* not able to be perceived. WH: 14–15C. French, or from Medieval Latin *imperceptibilis*, from IM-² + Late Latin *perceptibilis* perceptible (PERCEPTION).

impercipient *a.* not perceiving; not having power to perceive. *Also n.* WH: 19C. IM-² + PERCIPIENT.

imperfect *a.* not perfect, defective. *Also n.* WH: 12–14C. Old French *imparfait*, from Latin *imperfectus*, from IM-² + *perfectus* PERFECT¹.

imperforate *a.* not perforated. WH: 17C. IM-² + PERFORATE².

imperial *a.* of or relating to an empire, an emperor, or other supreme ruler. *Also n.* WH: 14–15C. Old French *impérial*, from Latin *imperialis*, from *imperium* rule, EMPIRE. See also -AL¹, -IAL.

imperil *v.t.* to endanger. WH: 14–15C. IM-¹ + PERIL, prob. based on ENDANGER.

imperious *a.* dictatorial, overbearing. WH: 16C. Latin *imperiosus*, from *imperium* rule, EMPIRE + -OUS.

imperishable *a.* enduring permanently. WH: 17C. IM-² + *perishable* (PERISH).

imperium *n.* absolute command, authority or rule. WH: 17C. Latin. See EMPIRE.

impermanent *a.* not permanent. WH: 17C. IM-² + PERMANENT.

impermeable *a.* not allowing passage, esp. of a fluid; impervious. WH: 17C. French *imperméable*, from Late Latin *impermeabilis*, from IM-² + *permeabilis* permeable (PERMEATE).

impermissible *a.* not permissible. WH: 19C. IM-² + *permissible* (PERMIT¹).

imperscriptible *a.* not derived from written authority. WH: 19C. IM-² + Latin *perscriptus*, p.p. of *perscribere* to write at length, to register, from PER- + *scribere* to write + -IBLE.

impersonal *a.* without personality. *Also n.* WH: 14–15C. Late Latin *impersonalis*, from IM-² + *personalis* personal (PERSON).

impersonate *v.t.* to pretend to be (someone) in order to entertain or deceive. WH: 17C. IM-¹ + Latin *persona* PERSON + -ATE³, based on INCORPORATE¹.

impertinent *a.* impudent, insolent. *Also n.* WH: 14–15C. Old French, or from Late Latin *impertinens, impertinentis* not pertinent. See IM-², PERTINENT. The original sense was unconnected, irrelevant, i.e. not pertinent. The current sense dates from the 17C.

imperturbable *a.* not easily disturbed or excited. WH: 14–15C. Late Latin *imperturbabilis*, from IM-² + *perturbare* PERTURB. See also -ABLE.

impervious *a.* not receptive or open (to). WH: 17C. Latin *impervius*. See IM-², PERVIOUS.

impetigo *n.* a contagious bacterial skin infection marked by the formation of pustules and yellow crusty sores. WH: 14–15C. Latin, from *impetere* to assail, to attack. See IMPETUS.

impetrate *v.t.* to obtain by petition, esp. by prayer. WH: 15C. Latin *impetratus*, p.p. of *impetrare*, from IM-¹ + *patrare* to bring to pass. See also -ATE³. Cp. PERPETRATE.

impetuous *a.* acting hastily or suddenly. WH: 14–15C. Old French *impétueux*, from Late Latin *impetuosus*. See IMPETUS, also -OUS.

impetus *n.* an impulse or driving force. WH: 17C. Latin assault, force, from *impetere* to assail, from IM-¹ + *petere* to seek.

impi *n.* a group of Zulu fighters. WH: Zulu regiment, army, military force.

impiety *n.* the quality of being impious. WH: 12–14C. Old French *impiété* or Latin *impietas*, from *impius*. See IMPIOUS, also -TY¹.

impinge *v.i.* to have an effect (on). WH: 16C. Latin *impingere*, from IM-¹ + *pangere* to drive in.

impious *a.* lacking reverence, esp. towards God. WH: 16C. Latin *impius*. See IM-², PIOUS, also -IOUS.

implacable *a.* not to be appeased. WH: 14–15C. Latin *implacabilis*, from IM-² + *placabilis* PLACABLE.

implacental *a.* (of marsupials and monotremes) without a placenta. WH: 19C. IM-² + *placental* (PLACENTA).

implant¹ *v.t.* to plant for the purpose of growth. WH: 14–15C. Late Latin *implantare* to engraft, from IM-¹ + *plantare* PLANT.

implant² *n.* something implanted, esp. something grafted or inserted into the body. WH: 19C. IMPLANT¹.

implausible *a.* not having an appearance of truth and credibility. WH: 17C. IM-² + PLAUSIBLE.

implead *v.t.* to prosecute or bring an action against. *Also v.i.* WH: 14–15C. Old French *empleidier, emplaidier*, from EM- + *plaidier* PLEAD.

impledge *v.t.* to pledge, to pawn. WH: 16C. IM-¹ + PLEDGE.

implement *n.* a tool, a utensil. *Also v.t.* WH: 14–15C. Partly from Medieval Latin *implementa* (pl.), from *implere* to employ, to spend, partly from Late Latin *implementum*, filling up, from Latin *implere* to fill up, to fulfil, from IM-¹ + *plere* to fill. See also -MENT.

implex *a.* involved, complicated. WH: 18C. Latin *implexus*, p.p. of *implectere* to entwine, from IM-¹ + *plectere* to twist, to plait.

implicate *v.t.* to show (a person) to be involved (in). *Also n.* WH: 14–15C. Latin *implicatus*, p.p. of *implicare*, from IM-¹ + *plicare* to fold. See also -ATE³. Cp. IMPLY. The current sense dates from the 18C.

implicit *a.* implied rather than directly stated. WH: 16C. French *implicite*, or from Latin *implicitus* entangled, entwined, later form of *implicatus*. See IMPLICATE.

implode *v.i.* to burst inwards. *Also v.t.* WH: 19C. IM-¹ + Latin *plodere, plaudere*, to clap, based on EXPLODE.

implore *v.t.* to supplicate or beg (someone to do something). *Also v.i.* WH: 16C. French *implorer* or Latin *implorare* to invoke with tears, from *in-*, IM-¹ + *plorare* to weep.

imply *v.t.* to indicate strongly the truth or existence of (something) in an indirect way. WH: 14–15C. Old French *emplier*, from Latin *implicare*. See IMPLICATE. Cp. EMPLOY.

impolder *v.t.* to form into a polder. WH: 19C. Dutch *impolderen*, from *im-* IM-¹ + POLDER.

impolicy *n.* an act of or the quality of being impolitic or inexpedient. WH: 18C. IM-² + POLICY¹, based on IMPOLITIC.

impolite *a.* not polite, ill-mannered. WH: 17C. Latin *impolitus*, from IM-² + *politus* POLITE.

impolitic *a.* not politic, injudicious, inexpedient. WH: 16C. IM-² + POLITIC.

imponderable *a.* incalculable. *Also n.* WH: 18C. IM-² + *ponderable* (PONDER).

imponent *a.* that imposes. *Also n.* WH: 19C. Latin *imponens, imponentis*, pres.p. of *imponere*. See IMPOSE, also -ENT.

import¹ *v.t.* to bring (goods) from a foreign country (into). *Also v.i.* WH: 14–15C. Latin *importare* to carry in, to bring in, from IM-¹ + *portare* to carry.

import² *n.* something which is imported from abroad. WH: 16C. IMPORT¹.

importance *n.* the quality of being important. WH: 16C. French, from Medieval Latin *importantia* significance, consequence, from *importans, importantis*, pres.p. of *importare* to be of consequence. See IMPORT¹, also -ANT.

importunate *a.* unreasonably insistent or demanding. WH: 16C. Latin *importunus* (IMPORTUNE) + -ATE², ? based on OBSTINATE.

importune *v.t.* to solicit insistently or urgently. *Also v.i., a.* WH: 16C. French *importuner* or Medieval Latin *importunari*, from Latin *importunus* inconvenient, unsuitable, from IM-² + *Portunus* the protecting god of harbours. Cp. OPPORTUNE.

impose *v.t.* to lay (e.g. a burden, tax, toll etc.) upon. *Also v.i.* WH: 15C. Old French *imposer*, based on Latin *imponere* to place onto, to inflict (see IM-¹) but re-formed on Latin p.p. *impositus* and Old French *poser*. See POSE¹.

imposition *n.* the act of imposing or placing upon. WH: 14–15C. Old French, or from Latin *impositio, impositionis*, from IM-¹ + *positio, positionis* POSITION.

impossible *a.* not possible. *Also n.* WH: 12–14C. Old French, or from Latin *impossibilis*, from IM-² + *possibilis* POSSIBLE.

impost¹ *n.* something which is imposed or levied as a tax, tribute or duty (esp. on imported goods). WH: 16C. French (now *impôt*), from Medieval Latin *impostus, impostum*, use as n. of m. or neut. of Latin *impostus, impositus*, p.p. of *imponere* IMPOSE.

impost² *n.* the upper member of a pillar or entablature on which an arch rests. WH: 15C. Italian *imposta*, fem. p.p. (used as n.) of *imporre*, from Latin *imponere* IMPOSE.

impostor *n.* a person who falsely assumes a character. WH: 16C. French *imposteur*, from Late Latin contr. of *impositor*, from Latin *impositus*, p.p. of *imponere* IMPOSE. See also -OR.

†impostume *n.* an abscess. *Also v.i.* WH: 14–15C. Old French *empostume*, alt. of *apostume*, from Latin *apostema*, from Greek *apostēma* separation (of pus into an abscess), from *apostēnai* to withdraw.

impotent *a.* powerless; helpless. *Also n.* WH: 14–15C. Old French, from Latin *impotens, impotentis*. See IM-², POTENT.

impound *v.t.* to take possession of or confiscate (a document etc.). WH: 14–15C. IM-¹ + POUND².

impoverish *v.t.* to make poor. WH: 14–15C. Old French *empoverir, empoveriss-* (Modern French *empauvrir*), from EM- + *povre* POOR. See also -ISH².

impracticable *a.* not able to be carried out in practice. WH: 17C. IM-² + PRACTICABLE.

impractical *a.* not practical. WH: 19C. IM-² + PRACTICAL.

imprecate *v.t.* to invoke (as an evil on). *Also v.i.* WH: 17C. Latin *imprecatus*, p.p. of *imprecari*, from IM-¹ + *precari* PRAY. See also -ATE³.

imprecise *a.* not precise. WH: 19C. IM-² + PRECISE.

impregnable *a.* (of a castle or defences) that cannot be taken by assault. WH: 14–15C. Old French *imprenable*, from IM-² + *prenable* takeable, from *prendre, pren-* to take, from Latin *prehendre*. See also -ABLE. The *-g-* was probably added under the influence of PREGNANT.

impregnate *v.t.* to make pregnant. *Also a.* WH: 17C. Late Latin *impregnatus*, p.p. of *impregnare*, from IM-¹ + *pregnare* to be pregnant. See also -ATE³.

impresa *n.* a heraldic device. WH: 16C. Italian undertaking, device. See EMPRISE. Cp. IMPRESARIO.

impresario *n.* a person who organizes musical or theatrical performances. WH: 18C. IMPRESA + -*ario* -ARY¹.

imprescriptible *a.* (of rights) that cannot be lost or impaired by usage or claims founded on prescription. **WH:** 16C. Medieval Latin *imprescriptibilis*, from IM-² + *prescriptibilis* prescriptible (PRESCRIBE).

impress¹ *v.t.* to produce a favourable effect on. **WH:** 14–15C. Old French *empresser*, from EM- + *presser* PRESS¹, based on Latin *imprimere* (IMPRESSION).

impress² *n.* the act of marking by pressure or with a stamp, seal etc. **WH:** 16C. IMPRESS¹.

impress³ *v.t.* to compel (men) to enter government service. **WH:** 16C. IM-¹ + PRESS².

impression *n.* an effect produced upon the senses, feelings etc. **WH:** 14–15C. Old French, from Latin *impressio, impressionis*, from *impressus*, p.p. of *imprimere*, from IM-¹ + *primere* PRESS¹. See also -ION.

imprest *n.* an advance of money, esp. for carrying out some public service. **WH:** 16C. IM-¹ + PREST.

imprimatur *n.* a licence to print a book, granted by the Roman Catholic Church. **WH:** 17C. Latin let it be printed, 3rd pers. sing. pres. subj. pass. of *imprimere* IMPRINT¹.

imprimatura *n.* a coloured transparent glaze used as a primer in painting. **WH:** mid-20C. Italian *imprimatura*, from *imprimere* IMPRESS¹.

imprimis *adv.* in the first place. **WH:** 14–15C. Latin, assim. form of *in primis* among the first (things), from *in* IN + *primis*, abl. pl. of *primus* first.

imprint¹ *v.t.* to impress, to stamp. **WH:** 14–15C. Old French *empreinter*, from *empreint*, p.p. of *empreindre*, ult. from Latin *imprimere* IMPRESS¹.

imprint² *n.* a mark or impression. **WH:** 14–15C. Old French *empreinte*, fem. p.p. (used as n.) of *empreindre*. See IMPRINT¹.

imprison *v.t.* to put into prison. **WH:** 12–14C. Old French *emprisoner* (Modern French *emprisonner*), from EM- + PRISON.

impro *n.* improvisation. **WH:** late 20C. Abbr. of *improvisation* (IMPROVISE).

improbable *a.* not likely to be true. **WH:** 16C. French, or from Latin *improbabilis* hard to prove, from IM-² + *probabilis* PROBABLE.

improbity *n.* lack of probity; wickedness. **WH:** 14–15C. Latin *improbitas*, from IM-² + *probitas* PROBITY.

impromptu *adv.* off-hand, without previous study. *Also a., n.* **WH:** 17C. French, from Latin *in promptu* at hand, in readiness, from *in* IN + abl. of *promptus* readiness. See PROMPT.

improper *a.* unbecoming, indecent. **WH:** 14–15C. Old French *impropre* or Latin *improprius*, from IM-² + *proprius* PROPER.

impropriate *v.t.* to convert (esp. ecclesiastical property) to one's own or to private use. *Also a.* **WH:** 16C. Anglo-Latin *impropriatus*, p.p. of *impropriare*, from Latin IM-¹ + *proprius* PROPER. See also -ATE³.

impropriety *n.* the quality of being improper, indecency. **WH:** 17C. French *impropriété* or Latin *improprietas*, from *improprius* IMPROPER. See also -ITY.

improve *v.t.* to make better. *Also v.i.* **WH:** 16C. Anglo-French *emprower*, *emprouer*, from Old French EM- + *prou* profit, later influ. by PROVE. Cp. APPROVE. The original sense was to profit, to turn to advantage, surviving in 'improve the shining hour'.

improvident *a.* neglecting to make provision for the future. **WH:** 15C. IM-² + *provident* (PROVIDENCE), or from Late Latin *improvidens, improvidentis*, from IM-² + *providens, providentis*, pres.p. of *providere* PROVIDE. See also -ENT.

improvise *v.t., v.i.* to play, sing or perform, composing as one goes along. **WH:** 19C. French *improviser*, or from Italian *improvvisare*, from *improvviso* extempore, from Latin *improvisus* unforeseen, from IM-² + *provisus*, p.p. of *providere* PROVIDE.

imprudent *a.* rash, incautious. **WH:** 14–15C. Latin *imprudens, imprudentis*, from IM-² + *prudens, prudentis* PRUDENT.

impudent *a.* rude and disrespectful. **WH:** 14–15C. Latin *impudens, impudentis*, from IM-² + *pudens, pudentis*, ashamed, modest, orig. pres.p. of *pudere* to feel ashamed. See also -ENT. The original sense (to the 18C) was lacking in modesty, indelicate. The current sense dates from the 16C.

impugn *v.t.* to call in question, to contradict, to gainsay. **WH:** 14–15C. Latin *impugnare*, from IM-¹ + *pugnare* to fight. The original sense (to the 17C) was to fight against, to attack.

impuissant *a.* powerless, impotent. **WH:** 17C. French, from *im-* IM-² + *puissant* (PUISSANCE).

impulse *n.* a sudden desire or whim. **WH:** 17C. Latin *impulsus*, use as n. of p.p. of *impellere* IMPEL.

impunity *n.* exemption from punishment or the unpleasant consequences of an action. **WH:** 16C. Latin *impunitas*, from *impunis* unpunished, from IM-² + *poena* penalty, punishment, *punire* to punish. See also -ITY.

impure *a.* not pure; mixed with other substances. **WH:** 14–15C. Latin *impurus*, from IM-² + *purus* pure.

impute *v.t.* to ascribe or attribute (esp. something dishonourable) to a person. **WH:** 14–15C. Old French *imputer*, from Latin *imputare*, to bring into the reckoning, from IM-¹ + *putare* to reckon.

in *prep.* denoting presence or situation within the limits of time, place, circumstance etc. *Also adv., a., v.t.* **WH:** pre-1200. Old English, from Germanic, rel. to Latin *in*, Greek *en*, Welsh *yn*, Russian *v*, from Indo-European.

in-¹ *pref.* in, into, within, on, against, towards, as in *indicate, induce.* **WH:** Latin pref., from prep. *in* IN, into. For reasons of pronunciation *n* is often assimilated to a subsequent consonant. See IL-¹, IM-¹, IR-¹.

in-² *pref.* not, without, as in *incomprehensible, inequality.* **WH:** Latin pref., corresponding to Greek *a-, an-* A-³, Germanic *un-* UN-¹.

-in¹ *suf.* denoting neutral compounds, and usu. distinct from alkaloids and basic compounds in -INE, as in *albumin, casein.* **WH:** Alt. of -INE.

-in² *comb. form* indicating a gathering for common activity, as in *love-in, sit-in.* **WH:** IN.

-ina¹ *suf.* denoting the feminine in titles and proper names, as in *Tsarina, Thomasina.* **WH:** early 20C. Latin fem. suf. as in *regina* queen, extended in Italian or Spanish, and hence in English.

-ina² *suf.* forming names of groups of animals, usu. from the name of a genus, as in *Globigerina.* **WH:** Latin, neut. pl. of aa. in -*inus*. See also -INE.

inability *n.* the state of being unable (to do, understand etc.). **WH:** 15C. IN-² + ABILITY.

inaccessible *a.* that cannot be reached, attained, or approached. **WH:** 14–15C. Old French, or from Late Latin *inaccessibilis*. See IN-², *accessible* (ACCESS).

inaccurate *a.* not accurate. **WH:** 18C. IN-² + ACCURATE.

inaction *n.* inactivity; a lack of action. **WH:** 17C. IN-² + ACTION.

inadequate *a.* not adequate; insufficient. **WH:** 17C. IN-² + ADEQUATE.

inadmissible *a.* (of evidence) that cannot be allowed or received. **WH:** 18C. IN-² + ADMISSIBLE.

inadvertent *a.* (of an action) unintentional, accidental. **WH:** 17C. IN-² + Latin *advertens, advertentis*, pres.p. of *advertere* ADVERT. See also -ENT.

inadvisable *a.* not advisable. **WH:** 19C. IN-² + *advisable* (ADVISE).

inalienable *a.* that cannot be alienated or transferred. **WH:** 17C. IN-² + *alienable* (ALIENATE).

inalterable *a.* incapable of alteration. **WH:** 16C. IN-² + *alterable* (ALTER).

inamorato *n.* a man who is in love or is beloved. **WH:** 16C. Italian (now *innamorato*), p.p. of *inamorare* to fall in love, from *in-* IN-¹ + *amore* love.

inane *a.* silly, fatuous. *Also n.* **WH:** 16C. Latin *inanis* empty, vain.

inanga *n.* a small fish, *Galaxias maculatus*, whose young are eaten as whitebait. **WH:** 19C. Maori.

inanimate *a.* not living; lacking any sign of life. **WH:** 14–15C. Late Latin *inanimatus* lifeless. See IN-², ANIMATE².

inappellable *a.* beyond appeal; absolute, final. **WH:** 19C. Obs. French *inappelable*, from *appeler* APPEAL. See IN-², also -ABLE.

inappetence *n.* lack of desire or appetite. **WH:** 17C. IN-² + APPETENCE.

inapplicable *a.* not applicable. **WH:** 17C. IN-² + *applicable* (APPLY).

inapposite *a.* not apposite; not pertinent. **WH:** 17C. IN-² + APPOSITE.

inappreciable *a.* not perceptible; too insignificant to be considered. **WH:** 18C. IN-² + *appreciable* (APPRECIATE).

inapprehensible *a.* that cannot be apprehended or understood. **WH:** 17C. Late Latin *inapprehensibilis*. See IN-², *apprehensible* (APPREHEND).

inapproachable *a.* inaccessible; unapproachable. **WH:** 19C. IN-² + *approachable* (APPROACH).

inappropriate *a.* not appropriate, unsuitable. WH: 19C. IN-[2] + APPRO-PRIATE[2].

inapt *a.* not apt; unsuitable. WH: 17C. IN-[2] + APT. Cp. INEPT.

inarch *v.t.* to graft (a plant) by inserting a scion, without separating it from the parent tree, into a stock. WH: 17C. IN-[2] + ARCH[1].

inarguable *a.* that cannot be disputed. WH: 19C. IN-[2] + *arguable* (ARGUE).

inarticulate *a.* unable to express oneself clearly. WH: 17C. IN-[2] + ARTICULATE[2].

inartificial *a.* artless, simple, natural. WH: 16C. IN-[2] + ARTIFICIAL.

inartistic *a.* not designed, done etc., according to the principles of art. WH: 19C. IN-[2] + *artistic* (ARTIST).

inasmuch *adv.* seeing that; since; in so far as. WH: 12–14C. Orig. three words, from IN + AS[1] + MUCH, translating French *en tant* (*que*), or from Latin *in tantum* (*ut*). Cp. INSOMUCH.

inattention *n.* lack of attention; negligence. WH: 17C. IN-[2] + ATTEN-TION.

inaudible *a.* that cannot be heard. WH: 14–15C. Late Latin *in-audibilis*. See IN-[2], AUDIBLE.

inaugurate *v.t.* to install or induct into office solemnly or with appropriate ceremonies. WH: 16C. Latin *inauguratus*, p.p. of *inaugurare* to take omens from the flight of birds. See IN-[1], AUGUR, also -ATE[3].

inauspicious *a.* unlucky, unfortunate. WH: 16C. IN-[2] + *auspicious* (AUSPICE).

inauthentic *a.* not authentic. WH: 16C. IN-[2] + AUTHENTIC.

inbeing *n.* inherence; inherent existence. WH: 16C. IN + BEING.

inboard *adv.* within the sides or towards the middle of a ship, aircraft or vehicle. Also *a.*, *prep.* WH: 19C. IN + BOARD.

inborn *a.* innate, naturally inherent. WH: pre-1200. IN-[1] + BORN, based on Late Latin *innatus* INNATE.

inbound *a.* coming in. WH: 19C. IN + BOUND[4].

inbreathe *v.t.* to draw in (breath). WH: 14–15C. IN-[1] + BREATHE, based on Latin *inspirare*.

inbred *a.* innate, inborn, natural. WH: 16C. IN + *bred* (BREED).

inbreed *v.t.* to develop or produce within something. WH: 16C. IN-[1] + BREED.

inbuilt *a.* that is included as a part of something. WH: early 20C. IN + *built* (BUILD).

Inca *n.* a member of a S American Indian people in Peru until the Spanish conquest in 1531. WH: 16C. Quechua lord, king, royal person.

incalculable *a.* that cannot be reckoned or estimated in advance. WH: 18C. IN-[2] + *calculable* (CALCULATE).

incalescent *a.* becoming warm. WH: 17C. Latin *incalescens, incalescentis*, pres.p. of *incalescere*, from IN-[1] + *calescere* to grow warm. See also -ENT.

incandesce *v.i.* to glow with heat. Also *v.t.* WH: 19C. Back-formation from *incandescent*, from French, from Latin *incandescens, incandescentis*, pres.p. of *incandescere* to glow, from IN-[1] + *candescere* to become white. See CANDID, -escent (-ESCENCE).

incantation *n.* a formula, said or sung, supposed to add force to magical ceremonies. WH: 14–15C. Old French, from Late Latin *incantatio, incantationis*, from *incantus*, p.p. of *incantare* to chant, to charm, from IN-[1] + *cantare* to sing.

incapable *a.* not physically, intellectually, or morally capable (of). Also *n.* WH: 16C. French, or from Late Latin *incapabilis*, from IN-[2] + *capabilis* CAPABLE.

incapacious *a.* not capacious; not roomy. WH: 17C. Late Latin *incapax, incapacis*. See IN-[2], CAPACIOUS.

incapacitate *v.t.* to render incapable; to disable. WH: 17C. IN-CAPACITY + -ATE[3].

incapacity *n.* a lack of power or capacity; inability. WH: 17C. French *incapacité* or Late Latin *incapacitas*, from IN-[2] + *capacitas* CAPACITY.

incarcerate *v.t.* to imprison. Also *a.* WH: 16C. Medieval Latin *incarceratus*, p.p. of *incarcerare*, from IN-[1] + *carcer* prison. See also -ATE[3].

incardinate *v.t.* in the Roman Catholic Church, to institute as principal priest, deacon etc., of a particular church or diocese. WH: 17C. Late Latin *incardinatus*, p.p. of *incardinare* to ordain to the first rank (in a church), from IN-[1] + *cardo, cardinis* hinge, *cardinalis* chief presbyter. See CARDINAL, also -ATE[3].

incarnadine *a.* red or flesh-coloured. Also *n.*, *v.t.* WH: 16C. French *incarnadin*, from Italian *incarnadino*, var. of *incarnatino* carnation, flesh-colour, from *incarnato*. See INCARNATE[1], also -INE.

incarnate[1] *a.* invested or clothed with flesh, embodied in flesh, esp. in human form. WH: 14–15C. Ecclesiastical Latin *incarnatus*, p.p. of *incarnari* to be made flesh, from IN-[1] + *caro, carnis* flesh. See also -ATE[2].

incarnate[2] *v.t.* to embody in flesh. WH: 16C. Ecclesiastical Latin *incarnari*, p.p. of *incarnari*, to be made flesh. See INCARNATE[1], also -ATE[3].

incautious *a.* lacking in caution; rash. WH: 17C. IN-[2] + *cautious* (CAUTION), based on Latin *incautus*.

incendiary *a.* of or relating to the malicious burning of property. Also *n.* WH: 14–15C. Latin *incendarius*, from *incendium* conflagration, from *incendere* to set fire to. See INCENSE[1], also -ARY[1].

incense[1] *n.* a mixture of fragrant gums, spices etc. used for producing perfumes when burnt, esp. in religious rites. Also *v.t.* WH: 12–14C. Old French *encens*, from Ecclesiastical Latin *incensum*, neut. (used as n.) of *incensus*, p.p. of *incendere* to set fire to, from IN-[1] + root of *candere* to glow.

incense[2] *v.t.* to inflame, to enrage. WH: 12–14C. Old French *encenser*, from *encens*, or from Ecclesiastical Latin *incensare*, from *incensum*. See INCENSE[1].

incentive *n.* something which acts as a motive, incitement or spur (to action). Also *a.* WH: 14–15C. Latin *incentivum*, neut. (used as n.) of *incentivus* setting the tune, from *incent-*, var. of *incant-* (see INCANTATION). See also -IVE.

incept *v.t.* (of an organism) to receive, to take in. Also *v.i.* WH: 16C. Latin *inceptus* (INCEPTION).

inception *n.* a beginning. WH: 14–15C. Old French, or from Latin *inceptio, inceptionis*, from *inceptus*, p.p. of *incipere* to begin. See INCIPIENT.

inceptor *n.* a person at the point of taking a master's or doctor's degree. WH: 15C. Latin beginner. See INCEPT, also -OR.

incertitude *n.* uncertainty. WH: 14–15C. Old French, from Late Latin *incertitudo*. See IN-[2], CERTITUDE.

incessant *a.* unceasing, continual. WH: 14–15C. Old French, from Late Latin *incessans, incessantis*, from IN-[2] + Latin *cessans, cessantis*, pres.p. of *cessare* CEASE. See also -ANT.

incest *n.* sexual intercourse between persons who are considered to be too closely related to marry. WH: 12–14C. Latin *incestus*, from *in-* IN-[2] + *castus* chaste.

inch[1] *n.* the 12th part of a linear foot (2.54 cm). Also *v.t.*, *v.i.* WH: pre-1200. Old English *ynce*, rel. to Old High German *unza*, from Latin *uncia* twelfth part. See OUNCE[1].

inch[2] *n.* an island. WH: 12–14C. Gaelic *innis*, rel. to Old Irish *inis*, Welsh *ynys* and prob. to Latin *insula* island.

-in-chief *comb. form* leading, most important, as in *commander-in-chief*. WH: 17C. Old French *en chief*, or from Medieval Latin *in capite*. See IN, CHIEF.

inchoate *a.* only begun, commenced. Also *v.t.* WH: 16C. Latin *inchoatus*, p.p. of *inchoare*, var. of *incohare* to begin. See also -ATE[2]. The sense confused, incoherent arose early in the 20C, perhaps through a wrong association with *chaotic* (CHAOS). However, something that has only just begun could equally be 'chaotic' if it is not yet definably formed. The sense development could thus be natural.

incident *n.* an event or occurrence. Also *a.* WH: 14–15C. Old French, use as n. of *a.*, from Latin *incidens, incidentis*, pres.p. of *incidere* to fall upon, to happen to, from IN-[1] + *cadere* to fall. See also -ENT. The sense episode in a war, public disturbance dates from the early 20C.

incinerate *v.t.* to burn completely; to reduce to ashes. WH: 15C. Medieval Latin *incineratus*, p.p of *incinerare*, from IN-[1] + *cinis, cineris* ashes. See also -ATE[3]. Cp. CINERARY.

incipient *a.* beginning; in the first stages. WH: 16C. Latin *incipiens, incipientis*, pres.p. of *incipere* to undertake, to begin, from IN-[1] + *capere* to take. See also -ENT.

incise *v.t.* to cut into. WH: 16C. French *inciser*, from Latin *incisus*, p.p. of *incidere*, from IN-[1] + *caedere* to cut.

incisor *n.* a pointed tooth at the front of the mouth, adapted for cutting or dividing food. WH: 17C. Medieval Latin, in *dens incisor* incisor tooth, from Latin, lit. cutter, from *incisus*. See INCISE, also -OR.

incite *v.t.* to stir up; to prompt (to action). WH: 15C. Old French *inciter*, from Latin *incitare*, from IN + *citare* to set in rapid motion, to raise. See CITE.

incivility *n.* rudeness, impoliteness. WH: 16C. French *incivilité* or Late Latin *incivilitas*, from Latin *incivilis*, from IN-² + *civilis* CIVIL.

inclement *a.* (of weather) rough, stormy. WH: 17C. French *inclément* or Latin *inclemens*, *inclementis*. See IN-², CLEMENT. The sense to the 19C was also pitiless, severe, not merciful.

incline¹ *v.i.* to be disposed (to). *Also v.t.* WH: 12–14C. Old French *encliner*, from Latin *inclinare*, from IN-¹ + *clinare* to bend.

incline² *n.* a slope, a gradient. WH: 17C. INCLINE¹.

include *v.t.* to contain as a part, member etc. WH: 14–15C. Latin *includere*, from IN-¹ + *claudere* to shut.

incogitable *a.* unthinkable. WH: 16C. Latin *incogitabilis*. See IN-², *cogitable* (COGITATE).

incognito *a.*, *adv.* with one's real name or identity disguised or kept secret. *Also n.* WH: 17C. Italian, from Latin *incognitus* unknown, from IN-² + *cognitus*, p.p. of *cognoscere* to know.

incognizant *a.* unaware (of). WH: 19C. IN-² + *cognizant* (COGNIZANCE).

incoherent *a.* inarticulate, unable to express oneself intelligibly. WH: 17C. IN-² + *coherent* (COHERE).

incombustible *a.* incapable of being burnt or consumed by fire. *Also n.* WH: 15C. Medieval Latin *incombustibilis*, from IN-² + *combustibilis* (COMBUST).

income *n.* the amount of money (usu. annual) accruing as payment, profit, interest etc. from labour, business, profession or property. WH: 12–14C. Orig. from Old Norse *innkoma* arrival; later from IN + COME. The original literal sense was arrival, entrance. The current sense of money earned from work etc. dates from the 16C. *Income tax* was introduced in 1799 as a war tax.

incomer *n.* a person who comes in. WH: 14–15C. IN-¹ + COMER.

-incomer *comb. form* having an income of a specified type or level. WH: late 20C. INCOME + -ER¹.

incommensurable *a.* having no common standard and not able to be compared. *Also n.* WH: 16C. Late Latin *incommensurabilis*. See IN-², COMMENSURABLE.

incommode *v.t.* to cause trouble or inconvenience to. WH: 16C. French *incommoder* or Latin *incommodare*, from IN-² + *commodus* convenient. See COMMODIOUS.

incommunicable *a.* that cannot be communicated to or shared with another. WH: 16C. Late Latin *incommunicabilis* not to be imparted, from IN-² + *communicabilis*. See *communicable* (COMMUNICATE).

incommunicado *a.* with no means of communication with the outside world. WH: 19C. Spanish *incomunicado*, p.p. of *incomunicar* to deprive of communication.

incommutable *a.* not commutable. WH: 14–15C. Latin *incommutabilis*. See IN-², *commutable* (COMMUTE).

incomparable *a.* not to be compared (to or with). WH: 14–15C. Old French, from Latin *incomparabilis*, from IN-² + *comparabilis* comparable (COMPARE).

incompatible *a.* opposed in nature; discordant. *Also n.* WH: 14–15C. Medieval Latin *incompatibilis*, from IN-² + *compatibilis* COMPATIBLE.

incompetent *a.* lacking in ability or fitness for a task. *Also n.* WH: 16C. French *incompétent*, from Ecclesiastical Latin *incompetens*, *incompetentis*, from IN-² + *competens*, *competentis* COMPETENT.

incomplete *a.* not complete; not perfect. WH: 14–15C. Late Latin *incompletus*, from IN-² + Latin *completus* COMPLETE.

incompliant *a.* not yielding or flexible. WH: 17C. IN-² + *compliant* (COMPLIANCE).

incomposite *a.* not composite; not properly composed. WH: 17C. Latin *incompositus*, from IN-² + *compositus* COMPOSITE¹.

incomprehensible *a.* that cannot be conceived or understood. WH: 14–15C. Latin *incomprehensibilis*, from IN-² + *comprehensibilis* comprehensible (COMPREHEND).

incompressible *a.* not compressible; strongly resisting compression. WH: 18C. IN-² + *compressible* (COMPRESS¹).

incomputable *a.* not computable; incalculable. WH: 17C. IN-² + Latin *computabilis* computable (COMPUTE).

inconceivable *a.* not conceivable; incomprehensible. WH: 17C. IN-² + *conceivable* (CONCEIVE).

inconclusive *a.* (of evidence, a discussion etc.) not decisive. WH: 17C. IN-² + *conclusive* (CONCLUDE).

incondensable *a.* not condensable; not reducible to a liquid or solid condition. WH: 19C. IN-² + *condensable* (CONDENSE).

incondite *a.* ill-composed. WH: 16C. Latin *inconditus*, from IN-² + *conditus*, p.p. of *condere* to put together.

incongruous *a.* improper, out of place. WH: 17C. Latin *incongruus*. See IN-², *congruous* (CONGRUENT), also -OUS.

inconsecutive *a.* not consecutive, not in regular order. WH: 19C. IN-² + CONSECUTIVE.

inconsequent *a.* irrelevant. WH: 16C. Latin *inconsequens*, *inconsequentis* not logically consequent, from IN-² + *consequens*, *consequentis* CONSEQUENT.

inconsiderable *a.* small. WH: 16C. Obs. French *inconsidérable* or Late Latin *inconsiderabilis*. See IN-², *considerable* (CONSIDER).

inconsiderate *a.* hasty, incautious. WH: 14–15C. Latin *inconsideratus*. See IN-², *considerate* (CONSIDER).

inconsistent *a.* not in keeping; incompatible (with). WH: 17C. IN-² + *consistent* (CONSIST).

inconsolable *a.* (of a person, grief etc.) not to be consoled. WH: 16C. French, or from Latin *inconsolabilis*, from IN-² + *consolabilis*, from *consolari* CONSOLE¹.

inconsonant *a.* not consonant, discordant (with). WH: 17C. IN-² + CONSONANT.

inconspicuous *a.* not conspicuous; not easy to see. WH: 17C. Latin *inconspicuus*. See IN-², CONSPICUOUS, also -OUS.

inconstant *a.* not constant, changeable. WH: 14–15C. Old French, and from Latin *inconstans*, *inconstantis*, from IN-² + *constans*, *constantis* CONSTANT.

inconsumable *a.* not consumable; indestructible. WH: 17C. IN-² + *consumable* (CONSUME).

incontestable *a.* indisputable, unquestionable. WH: 17C. French, or from Medieval Latin *incontestabilis*, from IN-² + *contestabilis*, from *contestari* CONTEST¹. See also -ABLE.

incontinent¹ *a.* unable to restrain one's desires, esp. sexual desires. *Also n.* WH: 14–15C. Old French, or from Latin *incontinens*, *incontinentis*. See IN-², CONTINENT². The medical sense of lacking voluntary control over excretion dates from the 19C.

†incontinent² *adv.* straightaway, immediately. WH: 14–15C. Old French *incontenant*, from Late Latin *in continenti* (*tempore*), in continuous (time), without an interval. Cp. CONTINENT².

incontrollable *a.* not controllable. WH: 16C. IN-² + *controllable* (CONTROL).

incontrovertible *a.* incontestable, indisputable. WH: 17C. IN-² + *controvertible* (CONTROVERT).

inconvenience *n.* the quality or state of being inconvenient. *Also v.t.* WH: 14–15C. Old French (Modern French *inconvenance*), from Latin *inconvenientia* incongruity, inconsistency. See IN-², *convenience* (CONVENIENT).

inconvertible *a.* incapable of being converted into or exchanged for something else, esp. money. WH: 17C. French, or from Late Latin *inconvertibilis*, from IN-² + Latin *convertibilis* convertible (CONVERT¹).

incoordinate *a.* not coordinate. WH: 19C. IN-² + COORDINATE¹.

incorporate¹ *v.t.* to unite or combine into one body (with). *Also v.i.* WH: 14–15C. Late Latin *incorporatus*, p.p. of *incorporare*, from IN-¹ + *corporare* (CORPORATE). See also -ATE³.

incorporate² *a.* (of a society, company etc.) made into a corporation. WH: 14–15C. Late Latin *incorporatus*, p.p. of *incorporare*. See INCORPORATE¹, also -ATE².

†incorporate³ *a.* incorporeal, not embodied in matter. WH: 14–15C. Late Latin *incorporatus* not embodied, from IN-² + *corporatus* CORPORATE.

incorporeal *a.* not having a body or material form. WH: 14–15C. Latin *incorporeus* (from IN-² + *corporeus*, from *corpus*, *corporis* body) + -AL¹.

incorrect *a.* wrong, inaccurate. WH: 14–15C. French, or from Latin *incorrectus*. See IN-², CORRECT.

incorrigible *a.* bad beyond hope of amendment. *Also n.* WH: 12–14C. Old French, or from Latin *incorrigibilis*, from IN-² + *corrigibilis* CORRIGIBLE.

incorrupt *a.* not corrupt; pure. WH: 14–15C. Latin *incorruptus*, from IN-[2] + *corruptus* CORRUPT.

incrassate *a.* thick, thickened (in form). *Also v.t., v.i.* WH: 15C. Late Latin *incrassatus*, p.p. of *incrassare*, from IN-[1] + *crassare* to make thick, from *crassus* thick. See also -ATE[2].

increase[1] *v.i.* to become greater in quantity, degree etc. *Also v.t.* WH: 12–14C. Old French *encreistre*, *encreis-*, from Latin *increscere*, from IN-[1] + *crescere* to grow.

increase[2] *n.* the act, state or process of increasing; growth. WH: 14–15C. INCREASE[1].

incredible *a.* not credible; difficult to believe. WH: 14–15C. Latin *incredibilis*. See IN-[2], CREDIBLE.

incredulous *a.* indisposed to believe, sceptical (of). WH: 16C. Latin *incredulus* (IN-[2], CREDULOUS) + -OUS.

increment *n.* an increase, esp. one of a series. WH: 14–15C. Latin *incrementum*, from stem of *increscere* INCREASE[1]. See also -MENT.

increscent *a.* increasing, growing. *Also n.* WH: 16C. Latin *increscens*, *increscentis*, pres.p. of *increscere* INCREASE[1]. See also -ENT.

incriminate *v.i.* to make seem guilty. WH: 18C. Late Latin *incriminatus*, p.p. of *incriminare* to accuse, from IN-[1] + *criminare* CRIMINATE. See also -ATE[3].

incrustation *n.* the act or process of encrusting. WH: 17C. French, or from Latin *incrustatio*, *incrustationis*, from *incrustus*, p.p. of *incrustare*, from IN-[1] + *crustare* to form a crust (from *crusta* crust). See also -ATION.

incubate *v.t.* to sit on or artificially heat (eggs) until the young birds etc. emerge. *Also v.i.* WH: 17C. Latin *incubatus*, p.p. of *incubare* to lie on, from IN-[1] + *cubare* to lie. See also -ATE[3].

incubus *n.* a demon supposed to have sexual intercourse with women at night. WH: 12–14C. Late Latin, from Latin *incubo* nightmare, from *incubare*. See INCUBATE. Cp. SUCCUBA.

inculcate *v.t.* to impress upon the mind by emphasis or frequent repetition. WH: 16C. Latin *inculcatus*, p.p of *inculcare* to stamp with the heel, to press in, from IN-[1] + *calcare* to tread, from *calx*, *calcis* heel. See also -ATE[3].

inculpate *v.t.* to charge with participation in a crime. WH: 18C. Late Latin *inculpatus*, p.p. of *inculpare*, from IN-[1] + Latin *culpare* to blame, from *culpa* fault. See also -ATE[3].

incumbent *a.* imposed (upon) as a duty or obligation. *Also n.* WH: 15C. Latin *incumbens*, *incumbentis*, pres.p. of *incumbere* to lie on, to apply oneself to, from IN-[1] + nasalized stem corresponding to *cubare* (see INCUBATE). See also -ENT. The original sense (to the 18C) was impending, imminent.

incunable *n.* an early printed book, an incunabulum. WH: 19C. French. See INCUNABULUM.

incunabulum *n.* an early printed book, esp. one printed before AD 1500. WH: 19C. Latin *incunabula* (neut. pl.) swaddling clothes, cradle, from IN-[1] + *cunae* cradle. The reference is to books produced in the infancy of printing.

incur *v.t.* to bring upon oneself (risk, injury, punishment etc.). WH: 14–15C. Latin *incurrere*, from IN-[1] + *currere* to run.

incurable *a.* that cannot be cured or healed. *Also n.* WH: 12–14C. Old French, or from Late Latin *incurabilis*, from IN-[2] + *curabilis* curable (CURE).

incurious *a.* not curious or inquisitive. WH: 16C. Partly from Latin *incuriosus* careless, from IN-[2] + *curiosus* careful (CURIOUS) + -OUS, partly from IN-[2] + CURIOUS.

incursion *n.* a sudden raid. WH: 14–15C. Latin *incursio*, *incursionis*, from *incursus*, p.p. of *incurrere* INCUR. See also -ION.

incurvate *v.t.* to cause to curve inwards. *Also a.* WH: 16C. Latin *incurvatus*, p.p. of *incurvare*, from IN-[1] + *curvare* CURVE. See also -ATE[3].

incus *n.* one of the small bones of the ear, shaped rather like an anvil and connected to the malleus and stapes. WH: 17C. Latin *incus*, *incudis* anvil. The bone is so named from its shape. Cp. MALLEUS.

incuse *v.t.* to impress (a design etc.) on a coin by stamping. *Also a., n.* WH: 19C. Latin *incusus*, p.p. of *incudere* to forge.

indaba *n.* a council; a conference. WH: 19C. Zulu discussion.

indebted *a.* being under a debt or obligation (to or for). WH: 12–14C. Old French *endetté*, p.p. of *endetter* to involve in debt, based on Medieval Latin *indebitare*. See IN-[1], DEBT, also -ED.

indecent *a.* offensive to modesty or propriety. WH: 16C. Old French *indécent*, or from Latin *indecens*, *indecentis*. See IN-[2], DECENT.

indecipherable *a.* not decipherable, illegible. WH: 19C. IN-[2] + *decipherable* (DECIPHER).

indecision *n.* lack of decision; irresolution. WH: 18C. French *indécision*. See IN-[2], DECISION.

indeclinable *a.* having no inflections. *Also n.* WH: 14–15C. French *indéclinable*, from Latin *indeclinabilis*, from IN-[2] + *declinare* DECLINE. See also -ABLE.

indecorous *a.* violating propriety or good manners. WH: 17C. Latin *indecorus*. See IN-[2], DECOROUS, also -OUS.

indeed *adv.* in reality, in truth. *Also int.* WH: 12–14C. Orig. two words, from IN + DEED. Cp. *in fact* (FACT), still two words.

indefatigable *a.* not yielding to fatigue; unwearied. WH: 17C. Obs. French *indéfatigable* (now *infatigable*) or Latin *indefatigabilis*, from IN-[2] + DE- + *fatigare* to exhaust. See also -ABLE.

indefeasible *a.* incapable of being annulled or forfeited. WH: 16C. IN-[2] + *defeasible* (DEFEASANCE).

indefectible *a.* not liable to defect, decay or failure. WH: 17C. IN-[2] + *defectible* (DEFECT[1], also -IBLE).

indefensible *a.* incapable of being defended, excused or justified. WH: 16C. IN-[2] + *defensible* (DEFEND).

indefinable *a.* that cannot be defined. WH: 17C. IN-[2] + *definable* (DEFINE).

indefinite *a.* not limited or defined. WH: 16C. Latin *indefinitus*. See IN-[2], DEFINITE.

indehiscent *a.* (of fruits) not opening to set free the seeds. WH: 19C. IN-[2] + *dehiscent* (DEHISCE).

indelible *a.* that cannot be blotted out or effaced. WH: 15C. French *indélébile* or Latin *indelebilis*. See IN-[2], *delible* (DELE).

indelicate *a.* lacking delicacy or tact. WH: 18C. IN-[2] + DELICATE.

indemnify *v.t.* to secure from damage, loss or penalty. WH: 17C. Latin *indemnis* unhurt + -FY. See INDEMNITY.

indemnity *n.* security against damage, loss or penalty. WH: 14–15C. Old French *indemnité*, from Late Latin *indemnitas*, from *indemnis* free from loss, from IN-[2] + *damnum*. See DAMAGE, also -ITY.

indemonstrable *a.* that cannot be demonstrated; assumed as self-evident, axiomatic. WH: 16C. IN-[2] + *demonstrable* (DEMONSTRATE).

indent[1] *v.t.* to set (a line of text) further in from the margin than the rest of the paragraph. *Also v.i.* WH: 14–15C. Anglo-French *endenter*, from Medieval Latin *indentare*, from IN-[1] + Latin *dens*, *dentis* tooth.

indent[2] *n.* an indented line of text. WH: 15C. INDENT[1].

indent[3] *v.t.* to dent; to make a dent in. *Also n.* WH: 14–15C. IN-[1] + DENT[1].

indenture *n.* an agreement or contract under seal, esp. one binding an apprentice to a master. *Also v.t., v.i.* WH: 14–15C. Anglo-French *endenture*, from Medieval Latin *indentura*, from *indentus*, p.p. of *indenture*. See INDENT[1], also -URE. The agreement was so called because it was originally written in identical versions on a sheet that was then cut in two along a zigzag or notched line. If the notched edges of the two copies could be subsequently fitted together the document was proved to be genuine.

independence *n.* the quality or state of being independent (from, of). WH: 17C. From *independent* (from IN-[2] + *dependent*; see DEPEND), partly based on French *indépendance*. See also -ENCE.

indescribable *a.* too fine, bad etc. to be described. WH: 18C. IN-[2] + *describable* (DESCRIBE).

indesignate *a.* indefinite in quantity. WH: 19C. IN-[2] + DESIGNATE[2].

indestructible *a.* incapable of being destroyed. WH: 17C. IN-[2] + *destructible* (DESTRUCTION).

indeterminable *a.* that cannot be determined or defined. WH: 15C. Late Latin *indeterminabilis*, from IN-[2] + *determinabilis* finite. See *determinable* (DETERMINE).

indeterminate *a.* not fixed or limited in scope, nature etc. WH: 14–15C. Late Latin *indeterminatus*. See IN-[2], DETERMINATE.

indetermination *n.* lack of determination, vacillation. WH: 17C. INDETERMINATE + -ATION.

indeterminism *n.* the theory that conduct is not solely determined by motives, esp. that the will is able to choose between motives. WH: 19C. IN-[2] + *determinism* (DETERMINE).

index *n.* a list of names, subjects, places etc. in alphabetical order, with page references, usu. at the back of a book. *Also v.t.* WH: 14–15C. Latin *index, indicis* forefinger, informer, from IN-¹ + *-dex, -dicis*, from base represented by *dicere* to say. The earliest meaning was the forefinger, used in pointing. The sense list of names, etc. dates from the 16C.

Indian *a.* of or relating to India or the Indian subcontinent (India, Pakistan and Bangladesh). *Also n.* WH: 12–14C. *India*, a subcontinent of S Asia + -AN.

Indic *a.* originating or existing in India. *Also n.* WH: 19C. Latin *Indicus*, from Greek *Indikos*, from *India*. See INDIAN, also -IC.

indican *n.* the natural glucoside contained in the indigo plant and from which indigo is obtained. WH: 19C. Latin *indicum* INDIGO + -AN.

indicant *a.* indicating. *Also n.* WH: 17C. Latin *indicans, indicantis*, pres.p. of *indicare* INDICATE. See also -ANT.

indicate *v.t.* to show, to point out. *Also v.i.* WH: 17C. Latin *indicatus*, p.p. of *indicare*, from IN-¹ + *dicere* to proclaim. See also -ATE³.

indicia *n.pl.* distinguishing marks. WH: Pl. of Latin *indicium*. See INDEX.

indict *v.t.* to charge (a person) with a crime or misdemeanour, esp. by means of an indictment. WH: 12–14C. Old French *enditier*, from Latin *indictus*, p.p of *indicere* to proclaim, to appoint, from IN-¹ + *dicere* to pronounce, to utter.

indiction *n.* a period of 15 years arbitrarily fixed by Constantine the Great as a fiscal arrangement, beginning 1 September 312, adopted by the Popes as part of their chronological system. WH: 14–15C. Latin *indictio, indictionis*, from *indictus*. See INDICT, also -ION.

indie *a.* (of pop music) produced by a small independent record company. *Also n.* WH: early 20C. Abbr. of *independent* (INDEPENDENCE). See also -Y³.

Indies *n.pl.* India and the neighbouring regions. WH: 16C. Pl. of obs. *Indy*, var. of *India* (INDIAN).

indifferent *a.* unconcerned, apathetic. *Also n.* WH: 14–15C. Old French *indifférent* or Latin *indifferens, indifferentis*. See IN-², DIFFERENT. The original sense was impartial, unimportant.

indigenous *a.* (of plants and animals) naturally existing in a region, not exotic. WH: 17C. Latin *indigena* (a) native, from *indi-*, strengthened form of IN-¹ + *-gena*, from base of *gignere* to beget. See also -OUS.

indigent *a.* in want, poor, needy. WH: 14–15C. Old French, from Latin *indigens, indigentis*, pres.p. of *indigere* to lack, from *indi-* (INDIGENOUS) + *egere* to be in want, to need. See also -ENT.

indigest *a.* shapeless. *Also n., v.t.* WH: 14–15C. Latin *indigestus* unarranged, from IN-² + *digestus*, p.p. of *digerere* DIGEST¹.

indignant *a.* feeling or showing indignation, esp. at meanness, injustice etc. WH: 16C. Latin *indignans, indignantis*, pres.p. of *indignari* to regard as unworthy, from *indignus*, from IN-² + *dignus* worthy. See also -ANT.

indignity *n.* undeserved contemptuous treatment. WH: 16C. French *indignité* or Latin *indignitas*, from *indignus* unworthy. See INDIGNANT, also -ITY.

indigo *n.* a violet-blue dye obtained from the indigo plant. *Also a.* WH: 16C. Spanish *indico*, from Latin *indicum*, from Greek *indikon*, from *indikos*. See INDIC.

indirect *a.* not direct, deviating from a direct line. WH: 14–15C. Old French, or from Medieval Latin *indirectus*. See IN-², DIRECT.

indiscernible *a.* not discernible, not distinguishable. *Also n.* WH: 17C. IN-² + *discernible* (DISCERN).

indiscipline *n.* lack of discipline. WH: 18C. IN-² + DISCIPLINE.

indiscreet *a.* not discreet. WH: 14–15C. Latin *indiscretus* (INDISCRETE).

indiscrete *a.* not discrete or separated. WH: 17C. Latin *indiscretus* unseparated, undistinguished. See IN-², DISCRETE.

indiscriminate *a.* not discriminating or making distinctions. WH: 16C. Latin IN-² + *discriminatus* DISCRIMINATE².

indispensable *a.* that cannot be dispensed with; absolutely necessary. *Also n.pl.* WH: 16C. Medieval Latin *indispensabilis*. See IN-², DISPENSABLE.

indispose *v.t.* to make disinclined or unfavourable (to or towards). WH: 17C. IN-² + DISPOSE.

indisputable *a.* that cannot be disputed or doubted. WH: 16C. Late Latin *indisputabilis*, from IN-² + *disputabilis* disputable (DISPUTE).

indissociable *a.* not to be separated or disassociated. WH: 17C. IN-² + *dissociable* (DISSOCIATE).

indissoluble *a.* that cannot be dissolved or disintegrated. WH: 15C. Latin *indissolubilis*, from IN-² + *dissolubilis* DISSOLUBLE.

indistinct *a.* not distinct, obscure. WH: 16C. Latin *indistinctus*. See IN-², DISTINCT.

indistinguishable *a.* not distinguishable (from). WH: 17C. IN-² + *distinguishable* (DISTINGUISH).

indite *v.t.* to put into words, to compose. WH: 12–14C. Old French *enditier*. See INDICT.

indium *n.* a soft, silver-white metallic element, at. no. 49, chem. symbol In, occurring in minute quantities in zinc ores. WH: 19C. INDIGO + -IUM. The element was discovered in 1863 by the German chemists Ferdinand Reich and Theodor Richter, who named it from the indigo-coloured lines in its spectrum.

individual *a.* existing as a single indivisible entity. *Also n.* WH: 14–15C. Medieval Latin *individualis*, from Latin *individuus*, from IN-² + *dividuus* divisible (DIVIDE).

indivisible *a.* not divisible. *Also n.* WH: 14–15C. Late Latin *indivisibilis*, from IN-² + *divisibilis* DIVISIBLE.

Indo- *comb. form* Indian. WH: Latin *Indus*, from Greek *Indos* Indian. See also -O-.

Indo-Aryan *a.* of or relating to the Aryan peoples of India or the Indic languages. *Also n.* WH: 19C. INDO- + ARYAN.

Indo-Chinese *a.* of or relating to Indo-China, its people or their languages. *Also n.* WH: 19C. INDO- + CHINESE.

indocile *a.* not docile; unwilling to be instructed or disciplined. WH: 17C. French, or from Latin *indocilis*, from *docilis* DOCILE, or from IN-² + DOCILE.

indoctrinate *v.t.* to teach (someone) to accept, esp. without questioning, a set of beliefs. WH: 17C. Old French *endoctriner* (see EN-, DOCTRINE) + -ATE³, or IN-¹ + obs. English *doctrinate* to teach, from Medieval Latin *doctrinatus*, p.p. of *doctrinare* to teach, from *doctrina* DOCTRINE. The original sense was to teach, to instruct. The sense to brainwash dates from the 19C.

Indo-European *a.* of or relating to the family of languages spoken over most of Europe and over Asia as far as northern India. *Also n.* WH: 19C. INDO- + EUROPEAN.

Indo-Iranian *a.* of or relating to the Indic and Iranian languages, constituting a subfamily of Indo-European. *Also n.* WH: early 20C. INDO- + IRANIAN.

indole *n.* a white or yellowish crystalline heterocyclic compound derived from coal tar. WH: 19C. INDIGO + -OLE¹.

indoleacetic acid *n.* a natural growth hormone in plants. WH: 19C. INDOLE + ACETIC (+ ACID).

indolent *a.* habitually idle or lazy. WH: 17C. Late Latin *indolens, indolentis*, from IN-² + *dolens, dolentis*, pres.p. of *dolere* to suffer, to give pain. See also -ENT.

Indology *n.* the study of Indian history, philosophy, literature etc. WH: 19C. INDO- + -LOGY.

indomitable *a.* untameable, unconquerable. WH: 17C. Late Latin *indomitabilis*, from IN-² + *domitare*. See DAUNT, also -ABLE.

Indonesian *a.* of or relating to Indonesia, its people or language. *Also n.* WH: 19C. *Indonesia*, an island group in SE Asia, from INDO- + Greek *nēsos* island + -IA. See also -AN.

indoor *a.* being or done inside a building or under cover. WH: 18C. IN + DOOR, superseding earlier *within-door*.

indraught *n.* the act of drawing in. WH: 16C. IN-¹ + DRAUGHT.

indrawn *a.* drawn in. WH: 14–15C. P.p. of *indraw*, from IN-¹ + DRAW.

indri *n.* a Madagascan lemur, *Indri indri*. WH: 19C. Malagasy *indry!* lo! behold!, or *indry izy!* there he is! The Malagasy words were taken to be the name of the animal by the French naturalist Pierre Sonnerat when he sighted it in *c.*1780 and asked local people what it was called. Its actual native name is *babakoto* (BABACOOTE).

indubitable *a.* that cannot be doubted or questioned. WH: 14–15C. Latin *indubitabilis*, from *dubitabilis* dubitable (DUBITATION), or from IN-² + dubitable.

induce *v.t.* to lead by persuasion or reasoning (to do something). WH: 14–15C. Latin *inducere*, from IN-¹ + *ducere* to lead, or from French *enduire* (ENDUE).

induct v.t. to put in possession of an ecclesiastical benefice or of any office, with the customary forms and ceremonies. WH: 14–15C. Latin inductus, p.p. of inducere INDUCE.

inductile a. not ductile. WH: 18C. IN-² + DUCTILE.

indulge v.t. to yield to (a desire, whim etc.). Also v.i. WH: 17C. Latin indulgere to allow space or time for, to give rein to.

induline a. any one of a series of blue, blue-black and grey dyestuffs related to aniline. WH: 19C. INDIGO + -ULE + -INE.

indult n. a license or privilege granted by the Pope, or authorizing something not normally permitted by the Church's common law. WH: 15C. French, from Late Latin indultum grant, concession, use as n. of neut. of Latin indultus, p.p. of indulgere INDULGE.

indumentum n. a covering of hairs on a plant or leaf. WH: 19C. Latin garment, from induere to put on. See also -MENT.

induna n. a leader or tribal councillor, esp. of an impi. WH: 19C. Zulu, from nominal pref. in- + duna councillor, headman, overseer.

induplicate a. (of leaves and flowers in bud) having the edges folded in. WH: 19C. IN-¹ + DUPLICATE¹.

indurate v.t. to make hard, to harden. Also v.i., a. WH: 16C. Latin induratus, p.p. of indurare to make hard, from IN-¹ + durus hard. See also -ATE³.

indusium n. a membranous covering that protects the developing spores of a fern. WH: 18C. Latin tunic, from induere to put on (a garment).

industry n. mechanical and manufacturing work as distinct from agriculture and commerce. WH: 14–15C. Old French industrie or Latin industria diligence, from earlier *industruia, from indostruus diligent, from indu, in within + stem of struere to build.

indwell v.t. (of a spirit, principle etc.) to abide in or inhabit. Also v.i. WH: 14–15C. IN-¹ + DWELL, orig. translating Latin inhabitare to inhabit.

Indy n. a kind of motor racing, practised chiefly in the US, in which cars race at very high speeds around oval circuits. WH: mid-20C. Abbr. of Indianapolis, the state capital of Indiana, USA. The name derives from the Indianapolis 500 (colloquially Indy 500), the annual 500-mile circuit race for rear-engined cars held since 1909 at the Indianapolis Motor Speedway.

-ine suf. forming adjectives meaning of or relating to or of the nature of, as in crystalline, divine, equine, hyacinthine, marine. WH: French -in, -ine, or from Latin -inus, -ina, -inum (from Greek -inos).

inebriate¹ v.t. to make drunk. WH: 14–15C. Orig. p.p., from Latin inebriatus, p.p. of inebriare, from IN-¹ + ebriare to intoxicate, from ebrius drunk. See also -ATE³.

inebriate² a. intoxicated, drunk. Also n. WH: 18C. INEBRIATE¹. See also -ATE².

inedible a. not edible; not suitable for eating. WH: 19C. IN-² + EDIBLE.

inedited a. not edited. WH: 18C. IN-² + EDIT + -ED.

ineducable a. incapable of being educated, esp. because of mental handicap. WH: 19C. IN-² + educable (EDUCATE).

ineffable a. unutterable, beyond expression. WH: 14–15C. Old French, or from Latin ineffabilis, from IN-² + effabilis, from effari to speak out, from EF- + fari to speak. See also -ABLE.

ineffaceable a. that cannot be rubbed out or obliterated. WH: 19C. IN-² + effaceable (EFFACE).

ineffective a. not having an effect. WH: 17C. IN-² + effective (EFFECT).

ineffectual a. not producing any effect or the desired effect. WH: 14–15C. Medieval Latin ineffectualis; later from IN-² + effectual (EFFECT).

inefficacious a. not efficacious; producing no result or effect. WH: 17C. IN-² + EFFICACIOUS.

inefficient a. not efficient. WH: 18C. IN-² + EFFICIENT.

inelastic a. not elastic. WH: 18C. IN-² + ELASTIC.

inelegant a. lacking grace, refinement etc. WH: 16C. French inélégant, from Latin inelegans, inelegantis, from IN-² + elegans, elegantis. See ELEGANT.

ineligible a. not eligible. WH: 18C. IN-² + ELIGIBLE.

ineluctable a. that cannot be escaped. WH: 17C. Latin ineluctabilis, from IN-² + eluctari to struggle out. See also -ABLE. Cp. RELUCTANT.

inept a. clumsy, incompetent. WH: 16C. Latin ineptus, from IN-² + aptus APT. Cp. INAPT.

inequable a. unfair. WH: 18C. Latin inequabilis. See IN-², EQUABLE.

inequality n. a lack of equality. WH: 14–15C. Old French inequalité (Modern French inégalité) or Latin inaequalitas, from inaequalis. See IN-², EQUAL, also -ITY.

inequitable a. not equitable, not fair or just. WH: 17C. IN-² + EQUIT-ABLE.

ineradicable a. that cannot be eradicated. WH: 19C. IN-² + eradic-able (ERADICATE).

inerrable a. infallible. WH: 16C. Latin inerrabilis, from IN-² + errare to err, to wander. See also -ABLE.

inert a. lacking inherent power of motion. WH: 17C. Latin iners, inertis unskilled, inactive, from IN-² + ars, artis skill, ART.

inescapable a. inevitable, that cannot be escaped or avoided. WH: 18C. IN-² + escapable (ESCAPE).

inescutcheon n. a small escutcheon borne within a shield. WH: 17C. IN-¹ + ESCUTCHEON.

inessential a. not essential or necessary. Also n. WH: 17C. IN-² + ESSENTIAL.

inestimable a. too valuable, great, excellent etc. to be estimated. WH: 14–15C. Old French, from Latin inaestimabilis, from IN-² + aestimabilis ESTIMABLE.

inevitable a. that cannot be avoided or prevented. WH: 14–15C. Latin inevitabilis, from IN-² + evitabilis EVITABLE.

inexact a. not exact, not precisely accurate. WH: 19C. IN-² + EXACT¹.

inexcusable a. that cannot be excused or justified. WH: 14–15C. Latin inexcusabilis, from IN-² + excusabilis excusable (EXCUSE¹).

inexhaustible a. that cannot be exhausted. WH: 17C. IN-² + exhaust-ible (EXHAUST).

inexistent a. not existing, non-existent. WH: 17C. IN-² + existent (EXIST).

inexorable a. relentless. WH: 16C. French, or from Latin in-exorabilis. See IN-², EXORABLE.

inexpedient a. not expedient; inadvisable, disadvantageous. WH: 16C. IN-² + EXPEDIENT.

inexpensive a. not expensive, cheap. WH: 19C. IN-² + expensive (EXPENSE).

inexperience n. lack of experience or of knowledge gained by experience. WH: 16C. French inexpérience, from Late Latin inexperientia, from IN-² + experientia EXPERIENCE.

inexpert a. not expert, unskilful. WH: 14–15C. Old French, from Latin inexpertus untried, inexperienced, from IN-² + expertus EXPERT.

inexpiable a. that cannot be expiated or atoned for. WH: 14–15C. Latin inexpiabilis, from IN-² + expiabilis expiable (EXPIATE).

inexplicable a. that cannot be explained. Also n.pl. WH: 14–15C. French, or from Latin inexplicabilis that cannot be unfolded, from IN-² + explicabilis explicable (EXPLICATE).

inexplicit a. not definitely or clearly stated. WH: 17C. IN-² + EXPLICIT¹.

inexpressible a. incapable of being expressed or described. Also n.pl. WH: 17C. IN-² + expressible (EXPRESS¹).

inexpugnable a. impregnable. WH: 14–15C. Old French, from Latin inexpugnabilis, from IN-² + expugnabilis, from expugnare to take by storm, from EX- + pugnare to fight. See also -ABLE.

inexpungible a. that cannot be expunged. WH: 19C. IN-² + EXPUNGE + -IBLE.

in extenso adv. at full length. WH: 19C. Latin, from in IN + extenso, abl. of extensus, p.p. of extendere EXTEND.

inextinguishable a. incapable of being extinguished, quenched or repressed. WH: 16C. IN-² + extinguishable (EXTINGUISH).

in extremis a. in desperate circumstances, in extremity. WH: 16C. Latin, from in IN + extremis, abl. pl. of extremus. See EXTREME.

inextricable a. that cannot be disentangled or solved. WH: 16C. Latin inextricabilis, from IN-² + extricare EXTRICATE. See also -ABLE.

infallible a. exempt from liability to error or to failure. WH: 15C. French infaillible or Late Latin infallibilis, from IN-² + Latin fallere to deceive. See also -IBLE.

infamous a. having a very bad reputation. WH: 14–15C. Medieval Latin infamosus, from IN-² + fama FAME. See also -OUS.

infant n. a child during the earliest years of its life. Also a., v.t. WH: 14–15C. Old French enfant, from Latin infans, infantis, use as n. of infans unable to speak, from IN-² + pres.p. of fari to speak. See also -ANT.

infanta *n.* in Spain and (formerly) Portugal, any royal princess (usu. the eldest) except an heiress apparent. WH: 16C. Spanish and Portuguese, fem. of *infante*, from Latin *infans, infantis*. See INFANT. An infanta is so called because although the oldest she is junior to the heir to the throne. In 1998 the heir to the Spanish throne was thus Infante Felipe, b.1968, but the eldest child of King Juan Carlos I was Infanta Elena, b.1963.

infanticide *n.* murder of a newborn infant. WH: 17C. French, from Late Latin *infanticidium*, from Latin *infans, infantis*. See INFANT, also -CIDE.

infantry *n.* foot-soldiers, usu. armed with small arms or rifle and bayonet; a branch of an army made up of such soldiers. WH: 16C. French *infanterie*, from Italian *infanteria*, from *infante* youth, foot soldier, from Latin *infans, infantis*. See INFANT, also -ERY. The infantry was originally a force of low-ranking soldiers, too inexperienced for the cavalry. They were thus the 'infants' as against the 'adult' horsemen.

infarct *n.* an area of tissue that is dying from lack of blood supply. WH: 19C. Modern Latin *infarctus*, from p.p. of *infarcire* to stuff into, from IN-[1] + *farcire* to stuff.

infatuate *v.t.* to inspire with an extravagant and usu. transitory passion. *Also a.* WH: 16C. Latin *infatuatus*, p.p. of *infatuare*. See IN-[1], FATUOUS, also -ATE[3].

infauna *n.* the animal life that exists in the sediments of the ocean floor and river beds. WH: early 20C. IN-[1] + FAUNA.

infeasible *a.* not feasible. WH: 16C. IN-[2] + FEASIBLE.

infect *v.t.* to contaminate (water, food etc.) with a bacterium, virus etc., and so cause disease. *Also a.* WH: 14–15C. Latin *infectus*, p.p. of *inficere* to dip in, to stain, to spoil, from IN-[1] + *facere* to put, to do.

infecund *a.* not fecund; barren. WH: 16C. Latin *infecundus*, from IN-[2] + *fecundus* FECUND.

infelicitous *a.* unfortunate. WH: 19C. IN-[2] + *felicitous* (FELICITY).

infer *v.t.* to deduce as a fact, consequence or result. *Also v.i.* WH: 16C. Latin *inferre* to bear in, to bring in, to cause, from IN-[1] + *ferre* BEAR[2].

inferior *a.* lower in rank, value, ability etc. *Also n.* WH: 14–15C. Latin, comp. of *inferus* low. See also -IOR.

infernal *a.* of or relating to hell or the lower regions. WH: 14–15C. Old French, or from Ecclesiastical Latin *infernalis*, from *infernus* below, subterranean, hell. See also -AL[1].

infertile *a.* not fertile; unfruitful. WH: 16C. French, or from Late Latin *infertilis*, from IN-[2] + *fertilis* FERTILE.

infest *v.t.* (of vermin, parasites) to swarm over in large numbers. WH: 14–15C. Old French *infester* or Latin *infestare*, from *infestus* hostile, unsafe.

infeudation *n.* the granting of or putting in possession of an estate in fee. WH: 15C. Medieval Latin *infeudatio, infeudationis*, from *infeudatus*, p.p. of *infeudare* to enfeoff, from *feudum*. See FEE, also -ATION.

infibulate *v.t.* to carry out infibulation on. WH: 17C. Latin *infibulatus*, p.p. of *infibulare*. See IN-[1], FIBULA, also -ATE[3].

infidel *a.* disbelieving in religion or a particular religion. *Also n.* WH: 15C. French *infidèle*, or from Latin *infidelis* unfaithful, unbelieving, from IN-[2] + *fidelis* faithful, from *fides* FAITH.

infield *n.* in cricket, the part of the field close to the wicket. WH: 15C. IN-[1] + FIELD.

infighting *n.* behind-the-scenes squabbling or jockeying for power within a group or organization. WH: 19C. IN-[1] + *fighting* (FIGHT).

infill *v.t.* to fill in. *Also n.* WH: 19C. IN-[1] + FILL.

infiltrate *v.t.* to secretly gain or cause to gain access or entrance to. *Also v.i.* WH: 18C. IN-[1] + FILTRATE. The sense to penetrate enemy lines, etc. dates only from the mid-20C (World War II).

infinite *a.* having no bounds or limits. WH: 14–15C. Latin *infinitus* unbounded, unlimited. See IN-[2], FINITE.

infinitive *a.* unlimited. *Also n.* WH: 14–15C. Latin *infinitivus* unlimited, indefinite, from IN-[2] + *finitivus* definite. See FINITE, also -IVE.

infirm *a.* lacking bodily strength or health, esp. through age or disease. *Also v.t.* WH: 14–15C. Latin *infirmus*, from IN-[2] + *firmus* FIRM[1].

infix[1] *v.t.* to fasten or fix in. WH: 16C. Partly from Latin *infixus*, p.p. of *infigere* to fix in, from IN-[1] + *figere* to fasten, partly from IN-[1] + FIX.

infix[2] *n.* a modifying element in the body of a word. WH: 17C. INFIX[1], based on PREFIX[1], SUFFIX[1].

in flagrante *adv.* whilst actually committing the misdeed. WH: 18C. Latin in the heat (of the crime), from *in* IN + abl. of *flagrans, flagrantis*. Cp. FLAGRANT.

inflame *v.t.* to stir up strong feelings in (someone). *Also v.i.* WH: 12–14C. Old French *enflammer*, from Latin *inflammare*, from IN-[1] + *flamma* FLAME.

inflammable *a.* that may be easily set on fire. *Also n.* WH: 14–15C. Medieval Latin *inflammabilis*, from *inflammare*. See INFLAME, also -ABLE. The synonymous adjective FLAMMABLE is now generally preferred in official notices etc. to avoid misinterpretation of *in-* (IN-[1]) as IN-[2], i.e. as a negative prefix.

inflammation *n.* an abnormal physical condition characterized by heat, redness, swelling, pain and loss of function in the part affected. WH: 14–15C. Latin *inflammatio, inflammationis*, from *inflammatus*, p.p. of *inflammare*. See INFLAME, also -ATION.

inflate *v.t.* to cause (a balloon, mattress etc.) to expand by filling with air. WH: 14–15C. Latin *inflatus*, p.p. of *inflare*, from IN-[1] + *flare* to blow. See also -ATE[3].

inflect *v.t.* to modulate (the voice). WH: 14–15C. Latin *inflectere*, from IN-[1] + *flectere* to bend.

inflexible *a.* incapable of being bent or curved. WH: 14–15C. Latin *inflexibilis*, from IN-[2] + *flexibilis* FLEXIBLE.

inflict *v.t.* to impose (suffering, a penalty, oneself) on. WH: 16C. Latin *inflictus*, p.p. of *infligere*, from IN-[1] + *fligere* to strike down.

inflorescence *n.* the flower head of a plant. WH: 18C. Modern Latin *inflorescentia*, from Late Latin *inflorescere* to come into flower. See IN-[1], FLORESCENCE.

inflow *n.* a flowing in; an influx. *Also v.i.* WH: 19C. IN-[1] + FLOW.

influence *n.* power to move, direct or control, ascendancy (over). *Also v.t.* WH: 14–15C. Old French, or from Medieval Latin *influentia*, from Latin *influens, influentis*, pres.p. of *influere* to flow in, from IN-[1] + *fluere* to flow. See also -ENCE. The word was originally applied to the 'flowing in' of ethereal fluid from the stars in astrology.

influent *a.* flowing in. *Also n.* WH: 14–15C. Latin *influens, influentis*. See INFLUENCE, also -ENT.

influenza *n.* a highly contagious virus infection, often occurring in epidemics, often characterized by muscular aches and pains, catarrh and fever. WH: 18C. Italian, lit. influence, from Medieval Latin *influentia* INFLUENCE. Cp. FLU. The word originated from the epidemic that broke out in Italy in the 1740s and that spread to the rest of Europe. The Italians regarded it as a 'visitation' by some evil force and named it accordingly.

influx *n.* the arrival of a large number of people or things. WH: 16C. French, from Late Latin *influxus*, from Latin *influere* to flow in. See IN-[1], FLUX.

info *n.* information. WH: early 20C. Abbr. of *information* (see IN-FORM[1]). This abbreviation facilitated the formation of later blends such as INFOMERCIAL, INFOPRENEURIAL, INFOTAINMENT.

infomercial *n.* a short film advertising something. WH: late 20C. Blend of *information* (INFORM[1]) and COMMERCIAL.

infopreneurial *a.* of or relating to the manufacture and sale of electronic equipment for the distribution of information. WH: late 20C. Blend of *information* (INFORM[1]) and *entrepreneurial* (ENTRE-PRENEUR).

inform[1] *v.t.* to communicate knowledge to, to tell (of, about). *Also v.i.* WH: 12–14C. Old French *enformer* (Modern French *informer*), from Latin *informare* to shape, to form an idea of, to describe, from IN-[1] + *forma* FORM. The original sense was to give form to, to shape. In the sense of imparting knowledge this meant to form the mind of the person receiving it.

†inform[2] *a.* without regular form. WH: 16C. French *informe* or Latin *informis*, from IN-[2] + *forma* FORM.

informal *a.* without formality; relaxed. WH: 14–15C. IN-[2] + FORMAL.

in forma pauperis *adv.* allowed on account of poverty to sue without paying costs. WH: 16C. Latin in the form of a poor person. See FORM, PAUPER.

infotainment *n.* the presentation of news and current affairs as entertainment. WH: late 20C. Blend of *information* (INFORM[1]) and *entertainment* (ENTERTAIN).

infra *adv.* (in a passage of a book etc.) below, further on. WH: 19C. Latin below. Cp. SUPRA.

infra- *pref.* below, beneath, as in *inframarginal*, *infraorbital*. WH: Latin *infra* below, underneath, beneath.

infraclass *n.* a taxonomic category below a subclass. WH: mid-20C. INFRA- + CLASS.

infracostal *a.* situated below the ribs. WH: 19C. INFRA- + *costal* (COSTA).

infraction *n.* a violation, an infringement. WH: 14–15C. Latin *infractio*, *infractionis*, from *infractus*, p.p. of *infringere* INFRINGE.

infradian *a.* (of a biological cycle, rhythm) having a period of recurrence longer than 24 hours. WH: mid-20C. INFRA- + *-dian*, based on CIRCADIAN.

infra dig *a.* beneath one's dignity. WH: 19C. Abbr. of Latin *infra dignitatem* beneath (one's) dignity. The colloquial abbreviation may to some extent pun on DIG, as an action 'beneath' one. Cp. the biblical parable of the unjust steward: 'I cannot dig: to beg I am ashamed' (Luke xvi.3).

infralapsarian *n.* a Calvinist holding that God decreed the salvation of the elect after the Fall, as opposed to *supralapsarian*. Also *a.* WH: 18C. INFRA- + Latin *lapsus* fall, LAPSE + -ARIAN. Cp. SUPRALAPSARIAN.

infrangible *a.* that cannot be broken. WH: 16C. French, or from Medieval Latin *infrangibilis*, from IN-² + *frangibilis* FRANGIBLE.

infraorbital *a.* situated below the orbit of the eye. WH: 19C. INFRA- + *orbital* (ORBIT).

infra-red *a.* of, relating to or using electromagnetic radiation having a wavelength longer than that of the red end of the visible spectrum but shorter than that of microwaves. Also *n.* WH: 19C. INFRA- + RED.

infrasonic *a.* having a frequency below the usual limit of human audibility. WH: early 20C. INFRA- + SONIC.

infrastructure *n.* an underlying structure or basic framework. WH: early 20C. INFRA- + STRUCTURE.

infrequent *a.* rare, uncommon. WH: 16C. Latin *infrequens*, *infrequentis*, from IN-² + *frequens*, *frequentis* FREQUENT¹.

infringe *v.t.* to break or violate (a law, contract etc.). Also *v.i.* WH: 16C. Latin *infringere*, from IN-¹ + *fringere* to break.

infula *n.* either of the two ribbons hanging from a bishop's mitre. WH: 17C. Latin.

infundibular *a.* funnel-shaped. WH: 18C. Latin *infundibulum* funnel, from *infundere* to pour in. See INFUSE, also -AR¹.

infuriate¹ *v.t.* to provoke to fury. WH: 17C. Medieval Latin *infuriatus*, p.p. of *infuriare*, from IN-¹ + *furiare* to madden, from *furia* FURY. See also -ATE³.

infuriate² *a.* infuriated, enraged. WH: 17C. Medieval Latin *infuriatus*, p.p. of *infuriare*. See INFURIATE¹, also -ATE².

infuscate *a.* tinged with brown. Also *v.t.* WH: 19C. Latin *infuscatus*, p.p. of *infuscare*, from IN-¹ + *fuscus* dark brown. See also -ATE².

infuse *v.t.* to pervade or fill (with). Also *v.i.* WH: 14–15C. Latin *infusus*, p.p. of *infundere*, from IN-¹ + *fundere* to pour.

infusible *a.* that cannot be fused or melted. WH: 16C. IN-² + *fusible* (FUSE¹).

†infusoria *n.pl.* microscopic organisms of the former class Infusoria (mainly ciliate protozoa), found in infusions of decaying organic matter. WH: 18C. Pl. of *infusorium*, use as n. of neut. of Modern Latin *infusorius*. See INFUSE.

-ing¹ *suf.* forming verbal nouns denoting an action or its result, as in *cleansing*, *hunting*, *painting*, *washing*. WH: Old English *-ung*, *-ing*, from Germanic.

-ing² *suf.* forming the present participle of verbs, as in *standing*, *talking*. WH: Alt. of Old English *-ende*, corresponding to Latin *-ent-*, Greek *-ont-*, Sanskrit *-ant-*.

-ing³ *suf.* forming nouns with the sense of belonging to or having the quality of, as *sweeting*, *shilling*, *atheling*. WH: Old English, from Germanic. Cp. -LING¹.

ingathering *n.* the act of gathering or collecting, esp. of getting in the harvest. WH: 16C. IN-¹ + *gathering* (GATHER).

ingeminate *v.t.* to repeat, to reiterate. WH: 16C. Latin *ingeminatus*, p.p. of *ingeminare*. See IN-¹, GEMINATE².

ingenerate¹ *v.t.* to generate or produce within; to engender. WH: 16C. Latin *ingeneratus*, p.p. of *ingenerare*. See IN-¹, GENERATE.

ingenerate² *a.* inborn, innate. WH: 17C. Ecclesiastical Latin *ingeneratus*. See INGENERATE¹, also -ATE².

ingenious *a.* skilful, clever, esp. at inventing. WH: 14–15C. French *ingénieux*, from Latin *ingeniosus*, from *ingenium* mind, intellect. See also -OUS.

ingénue *n.* an ingenuous or naive girl, esp. such a character on the stage. WH: 19C. French, fem. of *ingénu* INGENUOUS. There is no corresponding male *ingénu*.

ingenuous *a.* innocent or artless. WH: 16C. Latin *ingenuus*, lit. native, inborn, from IN-¹ + base of *gignere* to beget. See also -OUS.

ingest *v.t.* to take (food) into the stomach. WH: 17C. Latin *ingestus*, p.p. of *ingerere* to carry in, to bring in, from IN-¹ + *gerere* to bear, to carry.

ingle *n.* a fire on the hearth. WH: 16C. ? Gaelic *aingeal* fire, light, Irish *aingeal* live ember, rel. to Latin *ignis* fire, and so to IGNITE.

inglorious *a.* shameful, ignominious. WH: 16C. Latin *inglorius* (from *gloria* GLORY) + -OUS, or from IN-² + *glorious* (GLORY).

ingoing *a.* going in, entering. Also *n.* WH: 19C. IN-¹ + GOING.

ingot *n.* a mass of metal, esp. steel, gold or silver, cast in a mould. WH: 14–15C. ? From IN-¹ + Old English *goten*, p.p. of *geotan* to pour, to cast in metal.

ingrain¹ *v.t.* to cause (a dye etc.) to permeate something. WH: 14–15C. IN-¹ + GRAIN.

ingrain² *a.* dyed in the grain or yarn before manufacture. Also *n.* WH: 16C. From *in grain* (GRAIN).

†ingrate *a.* ungrateful. Also *n.* WH: 14–15C. Latin *ingratus* unpleasant, ungrateful, from IN-² + *gratus* pleasing, grateful.

ingratiate *v.t.* to insinuate (oneself) into goodwill or favour (with) another. WH: 17C. Latin *in gratiam* into favour + -ATE³, based on obs. Italian *ingratiare*.

ingratitude *n.* lack of gratitude. WH: 12–14C. Old French or Late Latin *ingratitudo*. See INGRATE, also -TUDE.

ingravescent *a.* (of an illness) becoming worse. WH: 19C. Latin *ingravescens*, *ingravescentis*, pres.p. of *ingravescere* to grow heavy, to grow worse, from IN-¹ + *gravescere*, from *gravis* heavy, severe. See -escent (-ESCENCE).

ingredient *n.* an element or a component part in a compound, recipe, mixture etc. Also *a.* WH: 14–15C. Latin *ingrediens*, *ingredientis*, pres.p. of *ingredi* to enter, from IN-¹ + *gradi* to proceed, to walk. See also -ENT.

ingress *n.* the act of entering, entrance. WH: 14–15C. Latin *ingressus*, from p.p. of *ingredi*. See INGREDIENT.

ingrowing *a.* growing inwards. WH: 19C. IN-¹ + GROW + -ING².

inguinal *a.* of, relating to or situated near the groin. WH: 14–15C. Latin *inguinalis*, from *inguen*, *inguinis* groin. See also -AL¹.

ingurgitate *v.t.* to swallow down greedily. Also *v.i.* WH: 16C. Latin *ingurgitatus*, p.p. of *ingurgitare*, from IN-¹ + *gurges*, *gurgitis* whirlpool, gulf. See also -ATE³.

inhabit *v.t.* to live or dwell in (a house, town etc.). Also *v.i.* WH: 14–15C. Old French *enhabiter* or Latin *inhabitare*, from IN-¹ + *habitare*. See HABIT.

inhale *v.t.* to breathe in. Also *v.i.* WH: 18C. Latin *inhalare*, from IN-¹ + *halare* to breathe.

inharmonious *a.* not harmonious; unmusical. WH: 18C. IN-² + *harmonious* (HARMONY).

inhere *v.i.* to be an essential or necessary part (in). WH: 16C. Latin *inhaerare*, from IN-¹ + *haerare* to stick.

inherit *v.t.* to receive (property, a title etc.) by legal succession upon the death of a former possessor. Also *v.i.* WH: 12–14C. Old French *enheriter* to make heir, from Late Latin *inhereditare* to appoint as heir, from IN-¹ + *heres*, *heredis* heir.

inhesion *n.* inherence. WH: 17C. Late Latin *inhaesio*, *inhaesionis*, from Latin *inhaesus*, p.p. of *inhaerere*. See INHERE, also -ION.

inhibit *v.t.* to restrain, to hinder. WH: 14–15C. Latin *inhibitus*, p.p. of *inhibere* to hold in, to hinder, from IN-¹ + *habere* to hold.

inhospitable *a.* not inclined to show hospitality to strangers. WH: 16C. French. See IN-², HOSPITABLE.

inhuman *a.* brutal; savage. WH: 14–15C. Latin *inhumanus*, from IN-² + *humanus* HUMAN. The word was originally the opposite of HUMANE, not of HUMAN.

inhumane *a.* lacking in humanity. WH: 14–15C. Orig. var. of INHUMAN. Later from IN-² + HUMANE.

inhume *v.t.* to bury, to inter. WH: 17C. Latin *inhumere*, from IN-¹ + *humus* ground.

inimical *a.* hostile. WH: 16C. Late Latin *inimicalis*, from *inimicus* ENEMY. See also -AL[1].

inimitable *a.* that cannot be imitated; unique. WH: 15C. French, or from Latin *inimitabilis*, from IN-[2] + *imitabilis* imitable (IMITATE).

inion *n.* the most prominent part of the occipital bone. WH: 19C. Greek nape of the neck.

iniquity *n.* a lack of equity, gross injustice. WH: 12–14C. Old French *iniquité*, from Latin *iniquitas*, from *iniquus*, from *in-* IN-[2] + *aequus* equal, just. See also -ITY.

initial *a.* of or relating to the beginning. *Also n., v.t.* WH: 16C. Latin *initialis*, from *initium* beginning. See also -AL[1].

initiate[1] *v.t.* to begin or originate. *Also v.i.* WH: Latin *initiatus*, p.p. of *initiare* to begin, from *initium* beginning. See also -ATE[3].

initiate[2] *a.* initiated. *Also n.* WH: 17C. Latin *initiatus*, p.p. of *initiare*. See INITIATE[1], also -ATE[2].

inject *v.t.* to introduce (a fluid) into the body by or as if by a syringe. WH: 16C. Latin *iniectus*, p.p. of *iniicere* to throw in, from IN-[1] + *iacere* to throw.

injudicious *a.* done without judgement. WH: 17C. IN-[2] + *judicious* (JUDICIAL).

Injun *n.* an American Indian. WH: 17C. Representation of coll. and dial. pronun. of INDIAN.

injunction *n.* a writ or process whereby a party is required to refrain from doing certain acts. WH: 14–15C. Late Latin *iniunctio, iniunctionis*, from Latin *iniunctus*, p.p. of *iniungere* ENJOIN. See also -ION.

injure *v.t.* to hurt, to damage. WH: 14–15C. Back-formation from INJURY.

injury *n.* damage, harm. WH: 14–15C. Anglo-French *injurie* (Modern French *injure* insult), from Latin *iniuria*, use as n. of fem. of *iniurius* unjust, wrongful, from IN-[2] + *ius, iuris* right. See also -Y[2].

injustice *n.* the quality of being unjust; unfairness. WH: 14–15C. Old French, from Latin *iniustitia*, from *iniustus*, from IN-[2] + *iustus* JUST. See also -ICE.

ink *n.* a coloured liquid or viscous material used in writing or printing. *Also v.t.* WH: 12–14C. Old French *enque* (Modern French *encre*), from Late Latin *encaustum*, from Greek *egkauston* purple ink, from *egkaiein* to burn in. Cp. ENCAUSTIC.

†**inkle** *n.* a broad linen tape. WH: 16C. Orig. unknown.

inkling *n.* a hint; a slight suspicion or intimation (of). WH: 14–15C. Obs. *inkle* to give a hint of, of unknown orig. + -ING[1].

inland *a.* situated in the interior of a country away from the sea. *Also adv., n.* WH: pre-1200. IN-[1] + LAND.

in-law *n.* a relation by marriage. WH: 19C. IN + LAW[1], based on Old French *en loi* (*de mariage*) in law (of marriage).

inlay[1] *v.t.* to lay or insert in. WH: 16C. IN-[1] + LAY[1].

inlay[2] *n.* material inlaid or prepared for inlaying. WH: 17C. INLAY[1].

inlet *n.* a small arm of the sea; a creek. *Also a.* WH: 12–14C. IN-[1] + LET[1]. Not from -LET.

inlier *n.* an isolated portion of an underlying bed, which has become surrounded by a later formation. WH: 19C. IN-[1], based on *outlier* (OUT-).

in loco parentis *adv.* in the place of a parent (used esp. of a teacher). WH: 18C. Latin in place of a parent. See LOCUS, PARENT.

inly *adv.* inwardly, internally. *Also a.* WH: pre-1200. IN + -LY[2].

inlying *a.* situated inside or near a centre. WH: 19C. IN-[1] + *lying* (LIE[2]).

inmate *n.* a resident or occupant, esp. of a prison or institution. *Also a.* WH: 16C. Prob. orig. from INN, but later assoc. with IN + MATE[1].

in medias res *adv.* in or into the middle of things or of a story. WH: 18C. Latin into the midst of things. See MEDIUM, RES.

in memoriam *prep.* in memory of. *Also n.* WH: 19C. Latin to the memory (of), from *in* IN + acc. of *memoria* MEMORY. The phrase was popularized by Tennyson's poem, *In Memoriam A.H.H.* (1850).

inmost *a.* remotest from the surface; most inward. WH: pre-1200. IN + -MOST.

inn *n.* a public house providing alcoholic drink and sometimes food and lodging. *Also v.i., v.t.* WH: pre-1200. Old English, from Germanic, from base of IN.

innards *n.pl.* entrails. WH: 19C. Representation of a pronun. of *inwards*, pl. of obs. n. *inward* (INWARD).

innate *a.* inborn, natural. WH: 14–15C. Latin *innatus*, p.p. of *innasci*, from IN-[1] + *nasci* to be born.

inner *a.* interior; nearer the centre. *Also n.* WH: pre-1200. Old English *innera* (comp. of IN), from Germanic. See -ER[3].

innervate *v.t.* to supply (an organ) with nerves or nerve filaments. WH: 19C. IN-[1] + NERVE + -ATE[3].

innings *n.* in cricket, the time or turn for batting of a player or a side. WH: 18C. IN + -ING[1] + -S[1].

innocent *a.* free from moral guilt; blameless. *Also n.* WH: 12–14C. Old French, or from Latin *innocens, innocentis*, from IN-[2] + *nocens, nocentis*, pres.p. of *nocere* to hurt, to injure. See also -ENT.

innocuous *a.* having no injurious qualities, harmless. WH: 16C. Latin *innocuus*, from IN-[2] + *nocuus*, from *nocere* to hurt + -OUS.

innominate *a.* not named; nameless. WH: 17C. Late Latin *innominatus*, from IN-[2] + Latin *nominatus* (NOMINATE).

innovate *v.i.* to introduce alterations (in). *Also v.t.* WH: 16C. Latin *innovatus*, p.p. of *innovare* to renew, to alter, from IN-[1] + *novare* to make new, from *novus* new. See also -ATE[3].

innoxious *a.* harmless, innocuous. WH: 17C. Latin *innoxius*. See IN-[2], NOXIOUS, also -OUS.

innuendo *n.* an indirect or oblique hint, esp. one that is disapproving. *Also v.t., v.i.* WH: 16C. Latin by nodding at, by intimating, abl. ger. of *innuere* to nod, to signify, from IN-[1] + *nuere* to nod.

innumerable *a.* countless, numberless. WH: 12–14C. Latin *innumerabilis*. See IN-[2], *numerable* (NUMERAL).

innumerate *a.* ignorant of or unskilled in mathematics or science. WH: mid-20C. IN-[2] + NUMERATE[1].

innutrition *n.* lack of nutrition or nourishment. WH: 18C. IN-[2] + *nutrition* (NUTRIENT).

inobservant *a.* not observant. WH: 17C. Late Latin *inobservans, inobservantis*. See IN-[2], OBSERVE, also -ANT.

inobtrusive *a.* unobtrusive. WH: 18C. IN-[2] + *obtrusive* (OBTRUDE).

inoculate *v.t.* to inject (a person or animal) with a mild form of a disease in order to induce immunity against the disease. *Also v.i.* WH: 14–15C. Latin *inoculatus*, p.p. of *inoculare* to engraft, to implant, from IN-[1] + *oculus* eye, bud. See also -ATE[3]. Not rel. to INNOCUOUS.

inodorous *a.* without smell, odourless. WH: 17C. Latin *inodorus* (from IN-[2] + *odorus* odorous; see ODOUR) + -OUS, or from IN-[2] + *odorous*.

inoffensive *a.* giving no offence; harmless. WH: 17C. IN-[2] + *offensive* (OFFEND).

inofficious *a.* regardless of natural obligation and duty. WH: 17C. Latin *inofficiosus* (from IN-[2] + *officiosus* OFFICIOUS), or from IN-[2] + OFFICIOUS.

inoperable *a.* that cannot be operated on. WH: 19C. IN-[2] + *operable* (OPERATE).

inoperative *a.* not in operation. WH: 17C. IN-[2] + *operative* (OPERATE).

inopportune *a.* not opportune; unseasonable. WH: 16C. Late Latin *inopportunus* unfitting, from IN-[2] + *opportunus* OPPORTUNE.

inordinate *a.* excessive, immoderate. WH: 14–15C. Latin *inordinatus*, from IN-[2] + *ordinatus*, p.p. of *ordinare* ORDAIN. See also -ATE[2].

inorganic *a.* not organic, not having the organs or characteristics of living organisms. WH: 18C. IN-[2] + ORGANIC.

inosculate *v.i.* (e.g. of two blood vessels) to become united by the mouth of one fitting into the mouth of the other, or by a duct. *Also v.t.* WH: 17C. IN-[1] + Latin *osculare* to furnish with a mouth, from *osculum*, dim. of *os* mouth, based on Greek *anastomoun* (ANASTOMOSE). See also -ATE[3].

inositol *n.* a member of the vitamin B complex, found in most plant and animal tissues. WH: 19C. From obs. *inosite* (from Greek *is, inos* fibre, muscle + -O- + -OSE[2] + -ITE[1]) + -OL.

inotropic *a.* of or controlling contraction of the heart muscles. WH: early 20C. Greek *is, inos* fibre, muscle + -O- + *tropic* (-TROPE). See also -IC.

in propria persona *adv.* in person. WH: 17C. Latin in (one's) own person. See PROPER, PERSON.

input *n.* something that is put into a machine, the body etc. *Also a., v.t.* WH: 16C. IN-[1] + PUT.

inquest *n.* a judicial inquiry or investigation, esp. a coroner's inquest, usu. held before a jury. WH: 12–14C. Old French *enqueste* (Modern French *enquête*), from Medieval Latin *inquesta*, fem. p.p. (used as n.) of var. of Latin *inquirere* INQUIRE.

inquietude *n.* restlessness, uneasiness. WH: 14–15C. Old French *inquiétude* or Late Latin *inquietudo*, from Latin *inquietus*. See IN-[2], QUIET, also -TUDE.

inquiline *n.* an animal living in the abode of another, as certain beetles in ants' nests, or certain insects in the galls of other insects. WH: 17C. Latin *inquilinus* sojourner, from *incolere* to inhabit, from IN-[1] + *colere* to dwell. See -INE.

inquire *v.i.* to ask questions (of). *Also v.t.* WH: 12–14C. Old French *enquire* (Modern French *enquérir*), from var. of Latin *inquirere*, from IN-[1] + *quaerere* to ask.

inquirendo *n.* authority given to inquire into something for the benefit of the Crown. WH: 17C. Latin by inquiring, abl. ger. of *inquirere* INQUIRE.

inquisition *n.* a thorough search or investigation. WH: 14–15C. Old French, from Latin *inquisitio, inquisitionis*, from *inquisitus*, p.p. of *inquirere* INQUIRE. See also -ION.

inquorate *a.* not having enough people to constitute a quorum. WH: late 20C. IN-[2] + *quorate* (QUORUM).

in re *prep.* RE. WH: 17C. Latin, from *in* IN + abl. of *res* thing.

INRI *abbr.* Jesus of Nazareth King of the Jews. WH: Abbr. of Latin *Iesus Nazarenus Rex Iudaeorum* Jesus of Nazareth, King of the Jews. The reference is to the superscription on Christ's cross (John xix.19), which was 'written in Hebrew, and Greek, and Latin' (xix.20).

inroad *n.* an encroachment (on). WH: 16C. IN + ROAD[1] (in sense riding). Cp. RAID. The original sense was hostile incursion, invasion. The current sense dates from the 17C.

inrush *n.* a sudden rush in; an influx. WH: 19C. IN-[1] + RUSH[1].

insalivate *v.t.* to mix (food) with saliva during eating. WH: 19C. IN-[1] + *salivate* (SALIVA).

insalubrious *a.* unhealthy. WH: 17C. Latin *insalubris*, from IN-[2] + *salubris* SALUBRIOUS. See also -OUS.

insane *a.* deranged in mind; mad. WH: 16C. Latin *insanus*. See IN-[2], SANE.

insanitary *a.* not sanitary. WH: 19C. IN-[2] + SANITARY.

insatiable *a.* that cannot be satisfied or appeased. WH: 14–15C. Old French *insaciable* or Latin *insatiabilis*. See IN-[2], SATIATE, also -ABLE.

inscape *n.* the unique essence of a person, object etc. WH: 19C. ? From IN + -SCAPE. The word was coined in 1868 by the English poet Gerard Manley Hopkins.

inscribe *v.t.* to write or engrave (words, a design etc.) on a stone, paper or some other surface. WH: 14–15C. Latin *inscribere*, from IN-[1] + *scribere* to write.

inscription *n.* the art or act of inscribing. WH: 14–15C. Latin *inscriptio, inscriptionis*, from *inscriptus*, p.p. of *inscribere* INSCRIBE. See also -ION.

inscrutable *a.* unfathomable, mysterious. WH: 14–15C. Ecclesiastical Latin *inscrutabilis*, from IN-[2] + *scrutari* to search. See SCRUTINY, also -ABLE.

insect *n.* a member of the Insecta, a class of articulate, usu. winged animals, with three pairs of legs. WH: 17C. Latin *(animal) insectum*, from *insectus*, p.p. of *insecare* to cut up, to cut into, from IN-[1] + *secare* to cut, translating Greek *(zōion) entomon*. See ENTOMO-. An insect is 'cut up' into three distinct segments: head, thorax and abdomen.

insectivore *n.* any mammal of the order Insectivora, including moles, shrews and hedgehogs. WH: 19C. Modern Latin *Insectivora*, from *insectivorus*, based on Latin *carnivorus* carnivorous (CARNIVORE). See INSECT, also -VORE.

insecure *a.* lacking in self-confidence; apprehensive. WH: 17C. Medieval Latin *insecurus* unsafe, or from IN-[2] + SECURE.

inselberg *n.* an isolated steep rocky hill in a flat plain. WH: early 20C. German, from *Insel* island + *Berg* mountain.

inseminate *v.t.* to impregnate, esp. by artificial means. WH: 17C. Latin *inseminatus*, p.p. of *inseminare*, from IN-[1] + *seminare* to sow. See also -ATE[3].

insensate *a.* lacking sensation; inanimate or unconscious. WH: 15C. Ecclesiastical Latin *insensatus*, from IN-[2] + *sensatus* sensate (a.) (SENSATION).

insensible *a.* not having the power of feeling or perceiving, unconscious. WH: 14–15C. Partly from Old French, or from Latin *insensibilis*, partly from IN-[2] + SENSIBLE.

insensitive *a.* unfeeling, unsympathetic (to). WH: 16C. IN-[2] + SENSITIVE.

insentient *a.* not sentient, inanimate. WH: 18C. IN-[2] + SENTIENT.

inseparable *a.* incapable of being separated. *Also n.* WH: 14–15C. Latin *inseparabilis*. See IN-[2], *separable* (SEPARATE[1]).

insert *v.t.* to set or place (a thing) into another. *Also n.* WH: 15C. Latin *insertus*, p.p. of *inserere*, from IN-[1] + *serere* to plant, to put into.

insessorial *a.* (of feet, claws) adapted for perching. WH: 19C. Modern Latin *Insessores* perchers, pl. of Late Latin *insessor*, from *insidere* to sit upon, from IN-[1] + *sedere* to sit. See also -IAL. Cp. INSIDIOUS.

inset[1] *n.* a piece let into a dress etc. WH: 16C. IN-[1] + SET[2].

inset[2] *v.t.* to set or fix (in), to insert (in). WH: pre-1200. IN-[1] + SET[1].

inset[3] *abbr.* in-service education and training (for teachers). WH: late 20C. Acronym of *in-*service education and training, ? punning on INSET[1]. The word is popularly taken as an acronym of *in-*service training.

inshallah *int.* if Allah wills it. WH: 19C. Arabic *in šā' Allāh* if God (Allah) wills it. Cp. *deo volente*.

inshore *a., adv.* on, near or towards the shore. WH: 18C. IN-[1] + SHORE[1].

inside[1] *a.* situated within; interior, inner. *Also n.* WH: 14–15C. IN-[1] + SIDE.

inside[2] *adv.* in or into the interior, within; indoors. *Also prep.* WH: 14–15C. INSIDE[1].

insidious *a.* treacherous, sly. WH: 16C. Latin *insidiosus* cunning, deceitful, from *insidiae* ambush, trick, from *insidere* to sit on. See also -OUS.

insight *n.* the capacity to discern the real character of things. WH: 12–14C. Prob. from Scandinavian and Low German. Cp. Swedish *insikt*, German *Einsicht*. See IN-[1], SIGHT.

insignia *n.pl.* badges of office or honour. WH: 17C. Latin, pl. of *insigne* mark, sign, badge of office, use as n. of neut. of *insignis* distinguished, differentiated, from IN-[1] + *signum* sign. See -IA. Cp. ENSIGN.

insignificant *a.* unimportant, trivial. WH: 17C. IN-[2] + *significant* (SIGNIFY).

insincere *a.* not sincere; false. WH: 17C. Latin *insincerus*, from IN-[2] + *sincerus* SINCERE.

insinuate *v.t.* to indicate indirectly or obliquely. WH: 16C. Latin *insinuatus*, p.p. of *insinuare*, from IN-[1] + *sinuare* to curve. See also -ATE[3].

insipid *a.* tasteless, savourless. WH: 17C. French *insipide* or Late Latin *insipidus*, from IN-[2] + *sapidus* SAPID. Rel. to SAVOUR.

insist *v.i.* to be emphatic, positive, urgent or persistent (on or upon). *Also v.t.* WH: 16C. Latin *insistere*, from IN-[1] + *sistere* to stand.

in situ *adv.* in its place. WH: 18C. Latin in (its) place. See SITE.

insobriety *n.* lack of sobriety; intemperance (usu. in drinking). WH: 17C. IN-[2] + *sobriety* (SOBER).

insofar *adv.* in so far (as). WH: 16C. IN + SO + FAR.

insolate *v.t.* to expose to the sun's rays, e.g. for bleaching, or as a form of medical treatment. WH: 17C. Latin *insolatus*, p.p. of *insolare*, from IN-[1] + *sol* sun. See also -ATE[3].

insole *n.* the inner sole of a boot or shoe. WH: 19C. IN + SOLE[1].

insolent *a.* showing overbearing contempt; impudent. WH: 14–15C. Latin *insolens, insolentis*, from IN-[2] + *solens, solentis*, pres.p. of *solere* to be accustomed. See also -ENT.

insoluble *a.* that cannot be solved. WH: 14–15C. Old French, or from Latin *insolubilis*, from IN-[2] + *solubilis* SOLUBLE.

insolvable *a.* that cannot be solved, insoluble. WH: 17C. IN-[2] + *solvable* (SOLVE).

insolvent *a.* not able to discharge all debts or liabilities. *Also n.* WH: 16C. IN-[2] + *solvent* (SOLVE).

insomnia *n.* sleeplessness; chronic inability to sleep or sleep well. WH: 17C. Latin *insomnis* sleepless (from IN-[2] + *somnus* sleep) + -IA.

insomuch *adv.* to such a degree (that). WH: 14–15C. Orig. three words, from IN + SO + MUCH, translating Old French *entant (que)*. The word was at first an alternative to INASMUCH but was subsequently differentiated.

insouciant *a.* carefree or unconcerned. WH: 19C. French, from IN- + *souciant*, pres.p. of *soucier* to care, from Latin *sollicitare* to disturb. See also -ANT.

inspan *v.t.* to yoke (horses, oxen etc.) to a wagon etc. *Also v.i.* WH: 19C. Afrikaans, from Dutch *inspannen*, from *in-* IN-[1] + *spannen* (see SPAN[2]).

inspect *v.t.* to look closely into or at; to scrutinize carefully. *Also v.i.* WH: 17C. Latin *inspectus*, p.p. of *inspicere*, from IN-[1] + *specere* to look, or Latin *inspectare*, freq. of *inspicere*.

inspire *v.t.* to stimulate (a person) to some activity, esp. creative activity. *Also v.i.* WH: 12–14C. Old French *inspirer*, from Latin *inspirare*, from IN-[1] + *spirare* to breathe. The verb was originally used of a divine agency imparting a truth. 'All scripture is given by inspiration of God' (II Tim. iii.16).

inspirit *v.t.* to infuse spirit, life or animation into. WH: 17C. IN-[1] + SPIRIT.

inspissate *v.t.* to thicken by boiling or evaporation. *Also a.* WH: 17C. Late Latin *inspissatus*, p.p. of *inspissare*, from IN-[1] + *spissus* thick, dense. See also -ATE[3].

instability *n.* lack of stability or firmness. WH: 14–15C. French *instabilité*, from Latin *instabilitas*, from *instabilis*. See INSTABLE, also -ITY.

instable *a.* unstable. WH: 14–15C. Old French, or from Latin *instabilis*, from IN-[2] + *stabilis* STABLE[1], or IN-[2] + STABLE[1].

install *v.t.* to put (apparatus, equipment etc.) in position for use. WH: 14–15C. Medieval Latin *installare*, from IN-[1] + *stallum* STALL[1]. The literal meaning is to put in a stall, as of a person invested with a particular rank or office by being given a special seat (like the stalls of canons in a cathedral).

instalment *n.* each one of the parts into which a sum of money owed is divided, each part being paid at intervals over an agreed period of time. WH: 18C. Alt. of obs. *estalment*, from Old French *estaler* to place, to fix. See STALL[1], also -MENT.

instance *n.* an example, illustrative case. *Also v.t.* WH: 12–14C. Old French, from Latin *instantia* (translating Greek *enstasis* objection), from *instans*, *instantis*. See INSTANT, also -ANCE.

instant *a.* immediate. *Also n.* WH: 14–15C. Old French, from Latin *instans*, *instantis*, pres.p. of *instare* to be present, to apply oneself to, from IN-[1] + *stare* to stand. See also -ANT.

instanter *adv.* at once, immediately. WH: 17C. Latin immediately. See INSTANT.

instar *n.* a stage in the development of an insect or other arthropod between two moults. WH: 19C. Latin form, figure, likeness.

instate *v.t.* to put in a certain place, office etc., to install. WH: 17C. IN-[1] + STATE.

in statu pupillari *a.* in a state of wardship, esp. as a pupil. WH: 19C. Latin in a state of guardianship. See STATE, PUPIL[1].

instauration *n.* renewal, restoration. WH: 17C. Latin *instauratio*, *instaurationis*, from *instauratus*, p.p. of *instaurare* to restore, from IN-[1] + stem also of *restaurare* RESTORE. See also -ATION.

instead *adv.* in the place (of). WH: 12–14C. Orig. two words, from IN + STEAD. Cp. *in someone's stead* (STEAD).

instep *n.* the arched upper side of the human foot, near the ankle. WH: 14–15C. Orig. unknown. Cp. W Frisian *ynstap* opening in a shoe for the foot to be inserted. Prob. not rel. to STEP, but ? rel. to STEEP[1].

instigate *v.t.* to provoke or bring about (an action). WH: 16C. Latin *instigatus*, p.p. of *instigare*, from IN-[1] + *stigare* to prick, to incite. See also -ATE[3].

instil *v.t.* to introduce slowly and gradually (into the mind of a person). WH: 14–15C. Latin *instillare*, from IN-[1] + *stillare*, from *stilla* a drop.

instinct[1] *n.* a natural impulse present in most animals, leading them without reasoning or conscious design to perform certain actions. WH: 14–15C. Latin *instinctus* instigation, impulse, from p.p. of *instinguere* to incite, to impel, from IN-[1] + *stinguere* to prick.

instinct[2] *a.* animated or impelled from within. WH: 16C. Latin *instinctus*, p.p. of *instinguere*. See INSTINCT[1].

institute *v.t.* to set up, to establish. *Also n.* WH: 12–14C. Latin *institutus*, p.p. of *instituere* to establish, to arrange, to teach, from IN-[1] + *statuere* to set up.

instruct *v.t.* to teach, to educate (in a subject). WH: 14–15C. Latin *instructus*, p.p. of *instruere* to set up, to furnish, to teach, from IN-[1] + *struere* to pile up, to build.

instrument *n.* a tool or implement, esp. one for scientific or delicate operations. *Also v.t.* WH: 12–14C. Old French, from Latin *instrumentum*, from *instruere*. See INSTRUCT, also -MENT.

insubordinate *a.* not submissive to authority; disobedient. WH: 19C. IN-[2] + SUBORDINATE[1].

insubstantial *a.* unreal. WH: 17C. Late Latin *insubstantialis*, from IN-[2] + *substantialis* SUBSTANTIAL.

insufferable *a.* not able to be borne or endured. WH: 14–15C. IN-[2] + *sufferable* (SUFFER).

insufficient *a.* not sufficient; inadequate. WH: 14–15C. Old French, from Late Latin *insufficiens*, *insufficientis*, from IN-[2] + *sufficiens*, *sufficientis* sufficient (SUFFICE).

insufflate *v.t.* to blow or breathe (air, vapour, powder etc.) into an opening, cavity etc. WH: 17C. Late Latin *insufflatus*, p.p. of *insufflare*, from IN-[1] + Latin *sufflare*, from SUF- + *flare* to blow. See also -ATE[3].

insular *a.* of or relating to an island. WH: 16C. Late Latin *insularis*, from *insula* island. See also -AR[1].

insulate *v.t.* to separate from other bodies by a non-conductor, so as to prevent the passage of electricity or heat. WH: 16C. Latin *insula* island or *insulatus*. See also -ATE[3]. Cp. ISOLATE.

insulin *n.* a protein hormone produced in the pancreas which regulates the metabolism of sugar and fat, and the lack of which causes diabetes. WH: early 20C. Latin *insula* island + -IN[1]. The hormone is produced by the islets of Langerhans. Hence the name.

insult[1] *v.t.* to treat or speak to rudely or contemptuously. *Also v.i.* WH: 16C. Latin *insultare*, from IN-[1] + *saltare*, freq. of *salire* to leap, to jump.

insult[2] *n.* an insulting act or remark. WH: 17C. French, or from Ecclesiastical Latin *insultus*, from IN-[1] + Latin *saltus* leap, based on *insultare*. See INSULT[1].

insuperable *a.* impossible to overcome. WH: 12–14C. Old French, from Latin *insuperabilis*. See IN-[2], SUPERABLE.

insupportable *a.* insufferable, intolerable. WH: 16C. Old French. See IN-[2], SUPPORT, also -ABLE.

insuppressible *a.* that cannot be suppressed. WH: 17C. IN-[2] + *suppressible* (SUPPRESS).

insure *v.t.* to secure compensation, whole or partial, in the event of loss or injury to (property, life etc.) by paying a periodical premium. *Also v.i.* WH: 14–15C. Alt. of ENSURE, with substitution of IN-[1] for EN-. Cp. ASSURE.

insurgent *a.* rising up in revolt; rebellious. *Also n.* WH: 18C. Obs. French, from Latin *insurgens*, *insurgentis*, pres.p. of *insurgere*, from IN-[1] + *surgere* to rise. See also -ENT.

insurmountable *a.* that cannot be surmounted or overcome. WH: 17C. IN-[2] + *surmountable* (SURMOUNT).

insurrection *n.* the act of rising in open opposition to established authority. WH: 14–15C. Old French, from Late Latin *insurrectio*, *insurrectionis*, from Latin *insurrectus*, p.p. of *insurgere*. See INSURGENT, also -ION.

insusceptible *a.* not susceptible (of, to); incapable of being moved by any feeling or impression. WH: 17C. IN-[2] + SUSCEPTIBLE.

intact *a.* untouched. WH: 14–15C. Latin *intactus*, from IN-[2] + *tactus*, p.p. of *tangere* to touch.

intaglio *n.* a figure cut or engraved in a hard substance. *Also v.t.* WH: 17C. Italian, from *intagliare* to engrave, from *in-* IN-[1] + *tagliare* to cut.

intake *n.* the act of taking in. WH: 12–14C. From phr. *take in*. See IN, TAKE[1].

intangible *a.* not tangible; imperceptible to the touch. *Also n.* WH: 17C. French, or from Medieval Latin *intangibilis*, or from IN-[2] + TANGIBLE.

intarsia *n.* the practice or art of using wood to make decorative mosaics, as developed in 15th-cent. Italy. WH: 19C. Italian *intarsio*, from *intarsiare* to inlay, from *in-* IN-[1] + *tarsiare* to inlay. Cp. TARSIA.

integer *n.* a whole number as distinguished from a fraction. WH: 16C. Latin intact, from IN-[2] + *tag-*, *teg-*, base of *tangere* to touch.

integral *a.* whole, complete. *Also n.* WH: 16C. Late Latin *integralis*. See INTEGER, also -AL[1].

integrand *n.* an expression to be integrated. WH: 19C. Latin *integrandus*, ger. of *integrare* INTEGRATE[1].

integrant *a.* making part of a whole; necessary to constitute an entire entity. **WH:** 17C. French *intégrant*, from *intégrer*, from Latin *integrare*. See INTEGRATE[1], also -ANT.

integrate[1] *v.t.* to make into a whole, to complete by adding parts. *Also v.i.* **WH:** 17C. Latin *integratus*, p.p. of *integrare*. See INTEGER, also -ATE[3].

integrate[2] *a.* made up of integrant parts. **WH:** 14–15C. Latin *integratus*, p.p. of *integrare*. See INTEGRATE[1], also -ATE[2].

integrity *n.* honesty; high principle. **WH:** 14–15C. French *intégrité* or Latin *integritas*. See INTEGER, also -ITY.

integument *n.* a covering, esp. a natural one, such as a skin, husk, rind or shell. **WH:** 17C. Latin *integumentum*, from *integere* to cover in, from IN-[1] + *tegere* to cover. See also -MENT.

intellect *n.* the faculty of understanding, thinking and reasoning, as distinguished from the faculty of feeling or wishing. **WH:** 14–15C. Old French, or from Latin *intellectus* perception, discernment, meaning, from p.p.p. of *intellegere*. See INTELLIGENT.

intelligence *n.* the exercise of the understanding; intellectual power. **WH:** 14–15C. Old French, from Latin *intelligentia*. See INTELLIGENT, also -ENCE.

intelligent *a.* endowed with understanding. **WH:** 16C. Latin *intelligens, intelligentis*, earlier *intellegens, intellegentis*, pres.p. of *intellegere*, lit. to choose among, from *inter-* INTER- + *legere* to pick up, to gather, to choose, to read. See also -ENT.

intelligible *a.* capable of being understood, comprehensible. **WH:** 14–15C. Latin *intellegibilis, intelligibilis*, from *intellegere*. See INTELLIGENT, also -IBLE.

Intelpost *n.* the electronic transmission of messages internationally by fax, telex etc. **WH:** late 20C. Abbr. of *International Electronic Post*.

Intelsat *n.* an international body which operates a system of communications satellites. **WH:** mid-20C. Abbr. of *International Telecommunications Satellite* (*Consortium*).

intemperate *a.* not exercising due moderation or self-restraint; immoderate. **WH:** 14–15C. Latin *intemperatus*. See IN-[2], TEMPERATE.

intend *v.t.* to propose, to plan. *Also v.i.* **WH:** 12–14C. Old French *entendre*, from Latin *intendere* to extend, to direct, to intend, from IN-[1] + *tendere* to stretch.

intense *a.* extreme in degree. **WH:** 14–15C. Old French *intens*, from Latin *intensus* stretched tight, strained, from p.p of *intendere* INTEND.

intension *n.* intense exertion or concentration (of the mind, will etc.). **WH:** 17C. Latin *intensio, intensionis*, from *intensus*, p.p. of *intendere*. See INTEND, also -ION. Cp. INTENTION.

intensive *a.* concentrated, thorough. *Also n.* **WH:** 14–15C. Old French *intensif* or Medieval Latin *intensivus*. See INTENSE, also -IVE.

intent *n.* purpose, intention. *Also a.* **WH:** 14–15C. Old French *entent*, from Latin *intentus*, from *intendere* INTEND.

intention *n.* purpose, intent. **WH:** 14–15C. Old French *entencion* (Modern French *intention*), from Latin *intentio, intentionis*, from *intentus*, p.p. of *intendere*. See INTEND, also -ION. Cp. INTENSION.

inter *v.t.* to bury; to place in a grave or tomb. **WH:** 12–14C. Old French *enterrer*, from *en-* IN-[1] + Latin *terra* earth.

inter- *pref.* among or between, as in *interstate*. **WH:** Old French *inter-, entre-*, or from Latin *inter-*, from *inter* between, among, amid, in the midst. Cp. INTRA-, INTRO-.

interact *v.i.* to act reciprocally; to act on each other. **WH:** 19C. INTER- + ACT.

inter alia *adv.* among other things. **WH:** 17C. Latin among other (things), from *inter* among + *alia*, acc. neut. pl. of *alius* another.

inter-allied *a.* among or relating to two or more allies. **WH:** early 20C. INTER- + *allied* (ALLY[1]).

interarticular *a.* between the surfaces of a joint. **WH:** 19C. INTER- + ARTICULAR.

interatomic *a.* between or among atoms. **WH:** 19C. INTER- + *atomic* (ATOM).

interbank *a.* operating, existing etc. between banks. **WH:** mid-20C. INTER- + BANK[2].

interbed *v.t.* to interstratify. **WH:** 19C. INTER- + BED.

interblend *v.t.* to mingle with one another. *Also v.i.* **WH:** 16C. INTER- + BLEND[1].

interbreed *v.i.* to breed with members of a different species, race etc. *Also v.t.* **WH:** 19C. INTER- + BREED.

intercalary *a.* (of a day, month) inserted in the calendar to make it correspond with the solar year. **WH:** 17C. Latin *intercalarius*, from *intercalare* to proclaim the insertion of a day etc. into the calendar, from *inter-* INTER- + *calare* to proclaim solemnly. See also -ATE[3]. Rel. to CALENDAR.

intercede *v.i.* to plead (with someone) in favour of another. **WH:** 16C. Old French *intercéder* or Latin *intercedere*, from *inter-* INTER- + *cedere* to go.

intercellular *a.* occurring or situated between or among cells. **WH:** 19C. INTER- + CELLULAR.

intercensal *a.* of or relating to the interval between two censuses. **WH:** 19C. INTER- + CENSUS + -AL[1].

intercept[1] *v.t.* to stop, take or seize on the way from one place to another. **WH:** 14–15C. Latin *interceptus*, p.p. of *intercipere* from *inter-* INTER + *capere* to take, to seize.

intercept[2] *n.* the part of a line that is intercepted. **WH:** 19C. INTERCEPT[1].

intercession *n.* the act of interceding. **WH:** 14–15C. Old French, or from Latin *intercessio, intercessionis*, from *intercessus*, p.p. of *intercedere*. See INTERCEDE, also -ION.

interchange[1] *v.t.* (of two people) to exchange with each other. *Also v.i.* **WH:** 14–15C. Old French *entrechangier*, from *entre-* INTER- + *changier* CHANGE.

interchange[2] *n.* reciprocal exchange. **WH:** 14–15C. Partly from INTERCHANGE[1], partly from Old French *entrechange*, from *entre-* INTER- + *change* CHANGE.

intercity *a.* existing, carried on or travelling between different cities. *Also n.* **WH:** early 20C. INTER- + CITY.

inter-class *a.* existing or carried on between different classes. **WH:** early 20C. INTER- + CLASS.

interclavicle *n.* a median bony plate attached to the clavicles, present in many reptiles. **WH:** 19C. INTER- + CLAVICLE.

intercollegiate *a.* existing or carried on between colleges or universities. **WH:** 19C. INTER- + COLLEGIATE.

intercolonial *a.* existing or carried on between colonies. **WH:** 19C. INTER- + COLONIAL.

intercolumnar *a.* placed between columns. **WH:** 19C. INTER- + *columnar* (COLUMN).

intercom *n.* a system of intercommunication by telephone in aircraft, within a building etc. **WH:** mid-20C. Abbr. of *intercommunication* (INTERCOMMUNICATE).

intercommunicate *v.i.* to hold or enjoy mutual communication. *Also v.t.* **WH:** 16C. Anglo-Latin *intercommunicatus*, p.p. of *intercommunicare*. See INTER-, COMMUNICATE.

intercommunity *n.* the quality of being common to various people, groups etc. or of holding things in common. **WH:** 16C. INTER- + COMMUNITY.

interconnect *v.i., v.t.* to connect with each other. **WH:** 19C. INTER- + CONNECT.

intercontinental *a.* existing or travelling between or connecting different continents. **WH:** 19C. INTER- + *continental* (CONTINENT[1]).

interconvert *v.t., v.i.* to convert into each other. **WH:** mid-20C. INTER- + CONVERT[1].

intercooler *n.* a heat exchanger used e.g. in a supercharged internal-combustion engine to cool gas between successive compressions. **WH:** early 20C. INTER- + *cooler* (COOL).

intercorrelate *v.i.* to correlate with each other. *Also v.t.* **WH:** early 20C. INTER- + CORRELATE.

intercostal *a.* situated between the ribs. *Also n.pl.* **WH:** 16C. INTER- + *costal* (COSTA).

intercounty *a.* existing or carried on between counties. **WH:** 19C. INTER- + COUNTY.

intercourse *n.* association, communication etc., between people, nations etc. **WH:** 14–15C. Old French *entrecours* exchange, commerce, from Latin *intercursus*, from p.p.p. of *intercurrere* to intervene, from *inter-* INTER- + *currere* to run. The specific sense of sexual intercourse arose in the 18C.

intercrop *n.* a crop raised between the rows of another crop. *Also v.t., v.i.* **WH:** 19C. INTER- + CROP.

intercross *v.t.* to lay (things) across each other. *Also v.i., n.* **WH:** 18C. INTER- + CROSS.

intercrural *a.* between the legs. **WH:** 17C. INTER- + CRURAL.

intercurrent *a.* occurring between or among; intervening. WH: 17C. Latin *intercurrens*, *intercurrentis*, pres.p. of *intercurrere*. See INTERCOURSE, also -ENT.

intercut *v.t.* to alternate (contrasting camera shots) by cutting. WH: 17C. INTER- + CUT[1].

interdenominational *a.* existing or carried on between different religious denominations. WH: 19C. INTER- + *denominational* (DENOMINATE).

interdental *a.* situated between the teeth. WH: 19C. INTER- + DENTAL.

interdepartmental *a.* involving more than one department. WH: 19C. INTER- + *departmental* (DEPARTMENT).

interdepend *v.i.* to depend upon each other. WH: 19C. INTER- + DEPEND.

interdict[1] *n.* an official prohibition. WH: 12–14C. Old French *entredit*, from Latin *interdictum*, neut. p.p. (used as n.) of *interdicere* to interpose by speech, to forbid by decree, from *inter*- INTER- + *dicere* to say.

interdict[2] *v.t.* to forbid; to prohibit. WH: 12–14C. INTERDICT[1], based on Old French *entredire*, from Latin *interdicere*.

interdigital *a.* situated between the fingers or toes. WH: mid-20C. INTER- + DIGIT + -AL[1].

interdisciplinary *a.* involving two or more disciplines or fields of study. WH: early 20C. INTER- + DISCIPLINE + -ARY[1].

interest[1] *n.* lively, sympathetic or curious attention. WH: 14–15C. Alt. of obs. *interess*, from Medieval Latin *interesse*, use as n. of Latin inf. *interesse* to differ, to be of importance, from *inter*- INTER- + *esse* to be. The altered form came about partly by the addition of *-t*, partly by association with Old French *interest* damage, loss (Modern French *intérêt*), apparently a noun use of Latin *interest* it makes a difference, it matters, 3rd person singular present indicative of *interesse*.

interest[2] *v.t.* to arouse or hold the attention or curiosity of. WH: 17C. Alt. of obs. *interess*, from French *intéresser* to concern, from Latin *interesse*. See INTEREST[1].

interface *n.* a surface lying between two spaces. *Also v.t.*, *v.i.* WH: 19C. INTER- + FACE.

interfaith *a.* of, relating to or occurring between different religious faiths or their representatives. WH: mid-20C. INTER- + FAITH.

interfemoral *a.* situated or extending between the thighs. WH: 19C. INTER- + *femoral* (FEMUR).

interfere *v.i.* to hinder or obstruct a process, activity etc. WH: 14–15C. Old French *s'entreferir* to strike each other, from *entre*- INTER- + *ferir* (Modern French *férir*), from Latin *ferire* to strike. In the 16C the word was used of a horse that knocked its feet together when trotting, a sense still current in N America.

interferon *n.* an antiviral protein substance produced in living cells in humans and other creatures in response to infection from a virus. WH: mid-20C. INTERFERE + -ON. The protein was discovered in 1957 by the Scottish biologist Alick Isaacs and Swiss virologist Jean Lindenmann, who named it from its ability to inhibit or interfere with the replication of viruses.

interfibrillar *a.* between fibrils. WH: 19C. INTER- + *fibrillar* (FIBRIL).

interfile *v.t.* to file (two sets of items) together. WH: mid-20C. INTER- + FILE[1].

interflow *v.i.* to flow into each other; to merge. *Also n.* WH: 16C. INTER- + FLOW.

interfluent *a.* flowing together or into each other. WH: 17C. Latin *interfluens*, *interfluentis*, pres.p. of *interfluere*, from *inter*- INTER- + *fluere* to flow.

interfuse *v.t.* to intersperse (with). *Also v.i.* WH: 16C. Latin *interfusus*, p.p. of *interfundere*, from *inter*- INTER + *fundere* to pour.

intergalactic *a.* between galaxies. WH: early 20C. INTER- + GALACTIC.

interglacial *a.* occurring or formed between two of the glacial periods. *Also n.* WH: 19C. INTER- + GLACIAL.

intergovernmental *a.* involving or concerning two or more governments. WH: early 20C. INTER- + *governmental* (GOVERNMENT).

intergrade *n.* an intermediate grade or stage. *Also v.i.* WH: 19C. INTER- + GRADE.

intergrowth *n.* a growing into each other. WH: 19C. INTER- + *growth* (GROW).

interim *n.* the intervening time or period. *Also a.*, *adv.* WH: 16C. Latin, from *inter*- between + adverbial ending *-im*.

interior *a.* internal, inner. *Also n.* WH: 15C. Latin inner, comp. a. from *inter* between. See also -IOR.

interjacent *a.* lying between or among; intervening. WH: 16C. Latin *interiacens*, *interiacentis*, pres.p. of *interiacere*, from *inter*- INTER- + *iacere* to lie. See also -ENT.

interject *v.t.* to insert (a remark etc.) abruptly. WH: 16C. Latin *interiectus*, p.p. of *interiicere* to interpose, from *inter*- INTER- + *iacere* to throw, to cast.

interknit *v.t.*, *v.i.* to knit together. WH: 16C. INTER- + KNIT.

interlace *v.t.* to lace or weave together; to interweave. *Also v.i.* WH: 14–15C. Old French *entrelacier*, from *entre*- INTER- + *lacier* LACE.

interlanguage *n.* a language having characteristics of two or more other languages, e.g. Pidgin English. WH: early 20C. INTER- + LANGUAGE.

interlap *v.i.* to overlap. WH: 19C. INTER- + LAP[2].

interlard *v.t.* to diversify (a conversation, passage in a book etc.) with unusual phrases etc. WH: 14–15C. Old French *entrelarder*, from *entre*- INTER- + *larder* LARD.

interleaf *n.* a leaf, usu. blank, inserted between the leaves of a book, e.g. in order to protect an illustration. WH: 18C. INTER- + LEAF.

interleukin *n.* any of a number of proteins that are produced by white blood cells and stimulate activity against infection. WH: late 20C. INTER- + *leukocyte* (LEUCOCYTE) + -IN[1].

interlibrary *a.* between libraries. WH: 19C. INTER- + LIBRARY.

interline[1] *v.t.* to write or print between the lines of. WH: 14–15C. Medieval Latin *interlineare*, from *inter*- INTER- + Latin *linea* LINE[1].

interline[2] *v.t.* to insert an extra lining between the outer fabric and the lining of (a garment). WH: 15C. INTER- + LINE[2].

Interlingua *n.* an artificial language based on Latin roots. WH: early 20C. INTER- + Latin *lingua* tongue, language.

interlink *v.t.*, *v.i.* to link together. *Also n.* WH: 16C. INTER- + LINK[1].

interlobular *a.* situated or occurring between the lobes of a gland or other organ. WH: 19C. INTER- + *lobular* (LOBULE).

interlock[1] *v.t.* to connect firmly together by reciprocal engagement of parts; to link or lock together. *Also v.i.* WH: 17C. INTER- + LOCK[1].

interlock[2] *a.* (of a fabric) closely knitted. *Also n.* WH: 19C. INTERLOCK[1].

interlocution *n.* conversation, dialogue, discussion. WH: 16C. Latin *interlocutio*, *interlocutionis*, from *interlocutus*, p.p. of *interloqui*, from *inter*- INTER- + *loqui* to speak. See also -ION.

interloper *n.* an intruder. WH: 16C. INTER- + *loper* as in *landloper* vagabond (from Middle Dutch *landlooper*, from *land* LAND + *loopen* to run). Rel. to LEAP. Cp. ELOPE.

interlude *n.* a pause or a short entertainment between the acts of a play. WH: 12–14C. Medieval Latin *interludium*, from *inter*- INTER- + *ludus* play. Cp. ENTR'ACTE[1], INTERMEZZO.

interlunar *a.* of or relating to the time when the moon, about to change from old to new, is invisible. WH: 16C. Appar. from obs. French *interlunaire*, from Latin *interlunium*, based on *lunaire*. INTER-, LUNAR.

intermarriage *n.* marriage between people of different families, tribes, castes or nations. WH: 16C. INTER- + MARRIAGE.

intermeddle *v.i.* to meddle. *Also v.t.* WH: 14–15C. Anglo-French *entremedler*, from Old French *entremesler*, from *entre*- INTER- + *mesler* MEDDLE.

intermediary *a.* being, coming or acting between; intermediate. *Also n.* WH: 18C. French *intermédiaire*, from Italian *intermediario*, from Latin *intermedius*. See INTERMEDIATE[1].

intermediate[1] *a.* coming between two things, extremes, places etc. *Also n.* WH: 14–15C. Medieval Latin *intermediatus*, from Latin *intermedius*, from *inter*- INTER- + *medius* middle. See also -ATE[2].

intermediate[2] *v.i.* to act as intermediary; to mediate (between). WH: 17C. INTER- + MEDIATE[1].

intermesh *v.i.* to become meshed together. *Also v.t.* WH: early 20C. INTER- + MESH.

intermezzo *n.* a short movement connecting the main divisions of an opera or a large musical composition. WH: 18C. Italian, from Late Latin *intermedium*, neut. sing. (used as n.) of Latin *intermedius*. See INTERMEDIATE[1]. Cp. MEZZO.

intermigration *n.* reciprocal migration. WH: 17C. INTER- + *migration* (MIGRATE).

interminable *a.* endless or seeming to have no end. WH: 14–15C. Old French, or from Late Latin *interminabilis*, from IN-² + *terminare*. See TERMINATE, also -ABLE.

intermingle *v.t.* to mingle together, to intermix. *Also v.i.* WH: 15C. INTER- + MINGLE.

intermit *v.t.* to cause to cease for a time; to suspend. *Also v.i.* WH: 16C. Latin *intermittere*, from *inter-* INTER- + *mittere* to let go.

intermix *v.t., v.i.* to mix together. WH: 16C. Orig. p.p., from Latin *intermixtus*, p.p. of *intermiscere*, from *inter-* INTER- + *miscere* to mix.

intermodal *a.* (of a transport system) involving two or more modes of conveyance. WH: mid-20C. INTER- + MODE + -AL¹.

intermolecular *a.* between molecules. WH: 19C. INTER- + *molecular* (MOLECULE).

intern¹ *v.t.* to confine (aliens, political opponents etc.), esp. during wartime. WH: 17C. French *interner*, from Latin *internus* inward, internal, from *in* IN + suf. *-ternus*.

intern² *n.* an assistant surgeon or physician resident in a hospital. *Also v.i.* WH: 16C. Old French *interne*, from Latin *internus*. See INTERN¹.

internal *a.* of or relating to or situated on the inside. *Also n.pl.* WH: 16C. Modern Latin *internalis*, from Latin *internus*. See INTERN¹, also -AL¹.

international *a.* of or relating to, subsisting or carried on between, different nations. *Also n.* WH: 18C. INTER- + NATIONAL. The word was apparently coined by the English philosopher and writer on jurisprudence Jeremy Bentham, in reference to the 'law of nations'.

internecine *a.* mutually destructive. WH: 17C. Latin *internecinus*, from *internecio*, *internecionis* general slaughter, extermination, from *internecare* to slaughter, to exterminate, from *inter-* INTER- + *necare* to kill. See also -INE. The current sense (mutually destructive) is due to Dr. Johnson, who took *inter-* in its common sense of mutual (as in INTERCHANGE¹) instead of its actual force as an intensive, as here.

Internet *n.* an international computer network via which business, academic and private users can exchange information and communicate. WH: late 20C. INTER- + *net* (from *network*, from NET¹ + WORK). The word is popularly understood as an abbreviation of *international network*.

internist *n.* a specialist in internal medicine. WH: early 20C. INTERNAL + -IST.

internode *n.* a part between two nodes or joints. WH: 17C. Latin *internodium*. See INTER- + NODE.

internuclear *a.* between nuclei. WH: 19C. INTER- + NUCLEAR.

internuncio *n.* a messenger between two parties. WH: 17C. Italian *internunzio*, from Latin *internuntius*, from *inter-* INTER- + *nuntius* messenger.

interoceanic *a.* situated between or connecting two oceans. WH: 19C. INTER- + *oceanic* (OCEAN).

interoceptive *a.* of or relating to stimuli developing inside the viscera. WH: early 20C. INTERIOR + -O- + *receptor* (RECEPTION) + -IVE.

interoperable *a.* able to operate jointly. WH: mid-20C. INTER- + *operable* (OPERATE).

interorbital *a.* situated between the orbits of the eyes. WH: 19C. INTER- + *orbital* (ORBIT).

interosseal *a.* situated between bones. WH: 18C. INTER- + Latin *os*, *ossis* bone, *osseus* bony + -AL¹.

interpage *v.t.* to insert (pages) between other pages in a book. WH: 19C. INTER- + PAGE¹.

interparietal *a.* situated between the parietal bones of the skull. *Also n.* WH: 19C. INTER- + PARIETAL.

interpellate *v.t.* to interrogate, esp. to interrupt discussion in a parliament in order to demand a statement or explanation from (a minister). WH: 16C. Latin *interpellatus*, p.p. of *interpellare* to interrupt by speaking, from *inter-* INTER- + *-pellare* to thrust oneself.

interpenetrate *v.t.* to penetrate thoroughly, to permeate. *Also v.i.* WH: 19C. INTER- + PENETRATE.

interpersonal *a.* involving communication between people. WH: 19C. INTER- + *personal* (PERSON).

interphase *n.* the period between one division of a cell and the next. WH: early 20C. INTER- + PHASE.

interplait *v.i., v.t.* to plait together. WH: 19C. INTER- + PLAIT.

interplanetary *a.* of or relating to travel between the planets. WH: 17C. INTER- + *planetary* (PLANET).

interplay *n.* reciprocal action between parts or things. WH: 19C. INTER- + PLAY.

interplead *v.i.* to take legal proceedings in order to discuss and determine an incidental issue. *Also v.t.* WH: 16C. Anglo-French *entrepleder*. See INTER-, PLEAD.

Interpol *n.* the International Police Commission, that ensures co-operation between police forces in the suppression and detection of crime. WH: mid-20C. Abbr. of *International Police* (Commission).

interpolate *v.t.* to insert (esp. a word or passage) in (a book or document). *Also v.i.* WH: 17C. Latin *interpolatus*, p.p. of *interpolare* to refurbish, to alter, from *inter-* INTER- + *-polare*, rel. to *polire* POLISH.

interpose *v.t.* to place between or among. *Also v.i.* WH: 16C. Old French *interposer*, based on Latin *interponere* (from *inter-* INTER- + *ponere* to place), but re-formed on Latin p.p. *interpositus* and Old French *poser*. See POSE¹.

interpret *v.t.* to explain the meaning of. *Also v.i.* WH: 14–15C. Old French *interpréter* or Latin *interpretari* to explain, to translate, from *interpres*, *interpretis* agent, interpreter, from *inter-* INTER- + base corresponding to Sanskrit *prath-* to spread about.

interprovincial *a.* existing, carried on etc. between different provinces. WH: 19C. INTER- + *provincial* (PROVINCE).

interracial *a.* existing, carried on etc. between different races. WH: 19C. INTER- + *racial* (RACE²).

interradial *a.* situated between radii or rays. *Also n.* WH: 19C. INTER- + RADIAL.

interregnum *n.* the period between two reigns, ministries or governments. WH: 16C. Latin, from *inter-* INTER- + *regnum* REIGN.

interrelate *v.t.* to relate (things) to each other. *Also v.i.* WH: 19C. INTER- + RELATE.

interrex *n.* a person who governs during an interregnum; a regent. WH: 16C. Latin *inter-* INTER- + *rex* king.

interrogate *v.t.* to put questions to, esp. in a formal or thorough way. *Also v.i.* WH: 15C. Latin *interrogatus*, p.p. of *interrogare*, from *inter-* INTER- + *rogare* to ask. See also -ATE³.

interrupt *v.t.* to stop or obstruct by breaking in upon. *Also v.i., a., n.* WH: 14–15C. Latin *interruptus*, p.p. of *interrumpere*, from *inter-* INTER- + *rumpere* to break.

intersect *v.t.* to divide by cutting or passing across. *Also v.i.* WH: 17C. Latin *intersectus*, p.p. of *intersecare* to cut asunder, from *inter-* INTER- + *secare* to cut. See also -ATE³.

interseptal *a.* situated between or of or relating to septa or partitions. WH: 19C. INTER- + *septal* (a.) (SEPTUM).

intersex *n.* an individual developing characteristics of both sexes. WH: early 20C. INTER- + SEX.

interspace¹ *n.* intervening space. WH: 14–15C. INTER- + SPACE.

interspace² *v.t.* to put a space or spaces between. WH: 17C. INTER- + SPACE.

interspecific *a.* subsisting between different species. WH: 19C. INTER- + *specific* (SPECIFY).

intersperse *v.t.* to scatter here and there (among etc.). WH: 16C. Latin *interspersus*, p.p. of *interspergere*, from *inter-* INTER- + *spargere* to scatter, to sprinkle.

interspinal *a.* situated between spines or spinal processes. WH: 19C. INTER- + *spinal* (SPINE).

interstadial *n.* a period of ice retreat during a glacial period. *Also a.* WH: early 20C. INTER- + Latin *stadialis* (see STADIUM, also -AL¹).

interstate *a.* subsisting, maintained or carried on between states, esp. the states of the US. *Also n.* WH: 19C. INTER- + STATE.

interstellar *a.* situated between or passing through the regions between the stars. WH: 17C. INTER- + STELLAR.

interstice *n.* a space, opening, crevice etc. between things near together or between the component parts of a body. WH: 14–15C. Latin *interstitium*, from *intersistere* to stand between, from *inter-* INTER- + *sistere* to stand.

interstratify *v.t.* to stratify between or among other strata. WH: 19C. INTER- + STRATIFY.

intertextuality *n.* the relationship between literary texts. WH: mid-20C. INTER- + *textuality* (TEXT). The term was coined in 1967 by the French critic Julia Kristeva.

intertidal *a.* of or relating to the area between the low-water and high-water marks. WH: 19C. INTER- + *tidal* (TIDE).

intertribal *a.* occurring or carried on between different tribes. WH: 19C. INTER- + TRIBAL.

intertrigo *n.* (an) inflammation caused by the rubbing of one part of the skin against another. WH: 18C. Latin sore place caused by chafing, from *inter-* INTER- + *-trigo*, from *terere* to rub.

intertwine *v.t.* to entwine or twist together. *Also v.i., n.* WH: 17C. INTER- + TWINE.

intertwist *v.t.* to twist together. WH: 17C. INTER- + TWIST.

interval *n.* an intervening space or time. *Also v.t.* WH: 12–14C. Old French *entreval* (Modern French *intervalle*), ult. from Latin *intervallum*, lit. space between ramparts, from *inter-* INTER- + *vallum* rampart.

intervale *a.* a tract of low ground between hills or along the banks of rivers. WH: 17C. Var. of INTERVAL by assoc. with VALE[1].

interveined *a.* intersected as with veins. WH: 17C. INTER + VEIN + -ED.

intervene *v.i.* to happen or break in so as to interrupt or disturb. WH: 16C. Latin *intevenire*, from *inter-* INTER- + *venire* to come.

intervertebral *a.* situated between vertebrae. WH: 18C. INTER- + *vertebral* (VERTEBRA).

interview *n.* a meeting in which an employer questions a candidate for a job, college place etc. in order to test the candidate's suitability. *Also v.t., v.i.* WH: 16C. Obs. French *entreveue*, from *entrevoir* to have a glimpse of, *s'entrevoir* to see each other (from *entre-* INTER- + *voir* to see), based on *vue* VIEW.

intervocalic *a.* pronounced or occurring between vowels. WH: 19C. INTER- + Latin *vocalis* vocal, vowel + -IC.

inter-war *a.* occurring in the period between two wars, esp. World Wars I and II. WH: mid-20C. INTER- + WAR.

interweave *v.t.* to weave together (with). WH: 16C. INTER- + WEAVE[1].

interwind *v.t., v.i.* to wind together. WH: 17C. INTER- + WIND[2].

interwork *v.t.* to work (things) together or into each other. *Also v.i.* WH: 17C. INTER- + WORK.

intestate *a.* dying without having made a will. *Also n.* WH: 14–15C. Latin *intestatus*, from IN-[2], TESTATE.

intestine *n.* the part of the alimentary canal from the stomach to the anus. *Also a.* WH: 14–15C. Latin *intestinum*, use as n. of *intestinus*, from *intus* within. See also -INE.

intifada *n.* the Palestinian uprising in the Israeli-occupied West Bank and Gaza Strip, that began in 1987. WH: late 20C. Arabic *intifāḍa* a shaking off, a jumping up (in response to some external stimulus).

intimate[1] *a.* close in friendship; familiar. *Also n.* WH: 17C. Late Latin *intimatus*, p.p. of *intimare*, from *intimus* close friend, innermost. See also -ATE[2].

intimate[2] *v.t.* to make known, to announce. WH: 16C. Late Latin *intimatus*, p.p. of *intimare* to announce. See INTIMATE[1], also -ATE[3].

intimidate *v.t.* to frighten or to influence with threats or aggressive behaviour. WH: 17C. Medieval Latin *intimidatus*, p.p. of *intimidare*, from Latin IN-[1] + *timidus* TIMID. See also -ATE[3].

intinction *n.* the method of administering the Eucharist by dipping the bread in the wine. WH: 16C. Late Latin *intinctio, intinctionis*, from Latin *intinctus*, p.p. of *intingere* to dip in. See also -ION.

intitule *v.t.* to entitle (esp. an Act of Parliament). WH: 15C. Old French *intituler* ENTITLE.

into *prep.* expressing motion or direction within or against. WH: pre-1200. Old English *intō*, from IN + TO.

intolerable *a.* not tolerable, unendurable. WH: 14–15C. French *intolérable* or Latin *intolerabilis*, from IN-[2] + *tolerabilis* tolerable (TOLERATE).

intolerant *a.* not tolerant (of); not enduring or allowing difference of opinion, teaching, worship etc. *Also n.* WH: 18C. Latin *intolerans, intolerantis*, from IN-[2] + *tolerans, tolerantis*, pres.p. of *tolerare* TOLERATE. See also -ANT.

intone *v.i.* to recite or chant prayers etc., esp. in a monotone. *Also v.t.* WH: 15C. Medieval Latin *intonare*, from IN-[1] + *tonus* TONE.

intorsion *n.* a winding or twisting. WH: 18C. French, from Late Latin *intorsio, intorsionis*, from IN-[1] + *torsio, torsionis* TORSION.

in toto *adv.* completely. WH: 19C. Latin in entirety. See TOTAL.

intoxicate *v.t.* to make drunk. *Also a.* WH: 14–15C. Medieval Latin

intoxicatus, p.p. of *intoxicare*, from Latin *in-* IN-[1] + *toxicum* poison. See TOXIC, also -ATE[3].

intra- *pref.* within or inside, as in *intrauterine*. WH: Latin *intra* on the inside, within. Cp. INTER-, INTRO-.

intra-abdominal *a.* situated inside the abdomen. WH: 19C. INTRA- + *abdominal* (ABDOMEN).

intra-arterial *a.* occurring within an artery. WH: 19C. INTRA- + *arterial* (see ARTERY).

intracapsular *a.* situated or occurring inside a capsule. WH: 19C. INTRA- + *capsular* (CAPSULE).

intracardiac *a.* situated or occurring inside the heart. WH: 19C. INTRA- + CARDIAC.

intracellular *a.* in a cell or cells. WH: 19C. INTRA- + CELLULAR.

intracranial *a.* within the skull. WH: 19C. INTRA- + *cranial* (CRANIUM).

intractable *a.* unmanageable. WH: 15C. Latin *intractabilis*. See IN-[2], TRACTABLE.

intrados *n.* the inner surface or curve of an arch, as opposed to the *extrados*. WH: 18C. French, from *intra-* INTRA- + *dos* back.

intramolecular *a.* within a molecule. WH: 19C. INTRA- + *molecular* (MOLECULE).

intramural *a.* situated or happening within walls or boundaries. WH: 19C. INTRA- + Latin *murus* wall + -AL[1].

intranet *n.* a computer networking link restricted to a specific group of users. WH: late 20C. INTRA- + *network* (NET[1]), based on INTERNET.

intransigent *a.* uncompromising, inflexible. *Also n.* WH: 19C. French, from Spanish *los intransigentes*, lit. the uncompromising ones, name of party of the extreme left in the Spanish Cortes (1873–4), ult. from IN-[2] + pres.p. of Latin *transigere* to come to an understanding. See TRANSACT, also -ENT.

intransitive *a.* (of a verb) denoting action confined to the agent and so not requiring a direct object. WH: 17C. Late Latin *intransitivus* not passing over. See IN-[2], TRANSITIVE.

intrant *n.* a person who enters, esp. a person who enters a college, society etc. WH: 16C. Latin *intrans, intrantis*, pres.p. of *intrare* to enter. See also -ANT.

intranuclear *a.* situated or occurring within the nucleus of a cell. WH: 19C. INTRA- + NUCLEAR.

intraocular *a.* situated or occurring within the eyeball. WH: 19C. INTRA- + OCULAR.

intrapreneur *n.* a person who initiates or manages a new business or division within an existing firm. WH: late 20C. INTRA- + *-preneur*, based on ENTREPRENEUR.

intrauterine *a.* situated or occurring inside the womb. WH: 19C. INTRA- + *uterine* (UTERUS).

intravenous *a.* into a vein or veins. WH: 19C. INTRA- + *venous* (VENOSE).

intrepid *a.* fearless, bold. WH: 17C. French *intrépide* or Latin *intrepidus*, from IN-[2] + *trepidus* agitated, alarmed.

intricate *a.* involved, complicated. WH: 14–15C. Latin *intricatus*, p.p. of *intricare* to entangle, to perplex, from IN-[1] + *tricae* trifles, tricks, from *tricari* to make difficulties. See also -ATE[2].

intrigant *n.* an intriguer. WH: 18C. Var. of *intriguant*, from French pres.p. of *intriguer*. See INTRIGUE[2], also -ANT.

intrigue[1] *v.i.* to carry on a plot to effect some object by underhand means. *Also v.t.* WH: 17C. French *intriguer*, from Italian *intrigare*. See INTRIGUE[2].

intrigue[2] *n.* the act of intriguing. WH: 17C. French, from Italian *intrigo*, from *intrigare* to entangle, from Latin *intricare*. See INTRICATE.

intrinsic *a.* inherent; belonging to the nature of a thing. WH: 15C. Old French *intrinsèque*, from Late Latin *intrinsecus*, from Latin inwardly, inwards. See also -IC.

intro *n.* an introduction. WH: 19C. Abbr. of *introduction* (INTRODUCE).

intro- *comb. form* in, into, as in *introspection*. WH: Latin, from *intro*, lit. to the inside. Cp. INTER-, INTRA-.

introduce *v.t.* to make (a person, oneself) known in a formal way to another. WH: 14–15C. Latin *introducere*, from INTRO- + *ducere* to lead, to bring.

†introgression *n.* the introduction of the genes of one species into the gene pool of another. WH: 17C. Latin *introgredi* to step in, from

INTRO- + *gradi* to proceed, to walk, based on pairs EGRESS / *egression*, INGRESS / *ingression*.

introit *n.* a psalm or antiphon sung or recited as the priest approaches the altar to begin the Mass or Eucharist. WH: 14–15C. Old French *introït*, from Latin *introitus* entrance, from *introire* to enter, from INTRO- + *ire* to go.

introject *v.t.* to assimilate unconsciously into one's personality. WH: early 20C. Back-formation from *introjection* (19C), from INTRO- + *-jection*, based on *projection* (PROJECT[1]).

intromit *v.t.* to admit, to allow to enter. *Also v.i.* WH: 14–15C. Latin *intromittere* to introduce, from INTRO- + *mittere* to send.

intron *n.* a section of a nucleic acid that does not carry coded information for protein synthesis. WH: late 20C. *intragenic* (from INTRA- + *genic*; see GENE) + -ON.

introrse *a.* turned towards the axis. WH: 19C. Latin *introrsus*, from *introversus* (turned) inwards, from INTRO- + *versus*, p.p. of *vertere* to turn.

introspection *n.* the analysis and observation of the workings of one's own mind. WH: 17C. Latin *introspectus*, p.p. of *introspicere* to look into (from INTRO- + *specere* to look) + -ION.

introvert[1] *n.* a person who is interested chiefly in their own feelings and mental processes rather than in the outside world. WH: 19C. INTROVERT[2].

introvert[2] *v.t.* to turn (one's mind or thoughts) inwards. WH: 17C. Modern Latin *introvertere*, from INTRO- + *vertere* to turn.

intrude *v.t.* to thrust or force (on to, into). *Also v.i.* WH: 16C. Latin *intrudere*, from IN-[1] + *trudere* to thrust.

intrusion *n.* the act of intruding. WH: 14–15C. Old French, or from Medieval Latin *intrusio*, *intrusionis*, from *intrusus*, p.p. of *intrudere*. See INTRUDE, also -ION.

intrusive *a.* tending to intrude or characterized by intrusion. WH: 17C. Latin *intrusus* (INTRUSION) + -IVE.

intubate *v.t.* to insert a tube into (the larynx), as in a case of diphtheria. WH: 17C. IN-[1] + Latin *tuba* tube + -ATE[3].

intuition *n.* immediate perception by the mind without reasoning. WH: 14–15C. Late Latin *intuitio*, *intuitionis*, from Latin *intuitus*, p.p. of *intueri* to look upon, to consider, from IN-[1] + *tueri* to look. See also -ION.

intumesce *v.i.* to swell up. WH: 18C. Latin *intumescere* to swell up, from IN-[1] + *tumescere* to begin to swell, from *tumere* to be swollen. See also -ESCE.

intussuscept *v.t.* to turn or fold (an organ or part) within itself; to invaginate. WH: 19C. Latin *intus* within + *susceptus*, p.p. of *suscipere* to take up (from SUS- + *capere* to take).

Inuit *n.* a Canadian Eskimo. *Also a.* WH: 18C. Eskimo (Inuit), pl. of *inuk* person.

inulin *n.* a soluble, white starchy powder, obtained from the roots of elecampane and other composite plants. WH: 19C. Latin *inula* (see ELECAMPANE) + -IN[1].

inunction *n.* anointing or smearing with ointment, oil etc. WH: 15C. Latin *inunctio*, *inunctionis*, from *inunctus*, p.p. of *inunguere*, from IN-[1] + *unguere* to smear, to anoint. See also -ION.

inundate *v.t.* to overflow, to flood. WH: 16C. Latin *inundatus*, p.p. of *inundare*, from IN-[1] + *undare* to flow. See also -ATE[3].

Inupiaq *n.* a member of an Inuit people of northern Alaska. *Also a.* WH: mid-20C. Eskimo (Inuit), from *inuk* person + *piaq* genuine.

inurbane *a.* discourteous, rude, unpolished. WH: 17C. Latin *inurbanus*, from IN-[2] + *urbanus* URBANE.

inure *v.t.* to accustom, to habituate, to harden (to). *Also v.i.* WH: 14–15C. Anglo-French *en ure*, from *en* IN + *ure* custom, practice (Modern French OEUVRE).

inurn *v.t.* to place in a cinerary urn. WH: 17C. IN-[1] + URN.

in utero *adv.* in the womb. WH: 18C. Latin in the womb. See UTERUS.

inutile *a.* useless. WH: 14–15C. Old French, from Latin *inutilis*, from IN-[2] + *utilis* useful (USE[1]).

in vacuo *adv.* in a vacuum. WH: 17C. Latin in a vacuum. See VACUUM.

invade *v.t.* to enter (a country) by force, as an enemy. *Also v.i.* WH: 14–15C. Latin *invadere*, from IN-[1] + *vadere* to go.

invaginate *v.t.* to put into or as into a sheath. WH: 17C. Back-formation from *invagination*, from Modern Latin *invaginatio*, *invaginationis*. See IN-[1], VAGINA, also -ATION, -ATE[3].

invalid[1] *a.* having no force or cogency. WH: 16C. Latin *invalidus*, from IN-[2] + *validus* VALID.

invalid[2] *a.* infirm or disabled through ill health or injury. *Also n., v.t., v.i.* WH: 17C. INVALID[1].

invalidity *n.* the fact or condition of being without validity. WH: 16C. French *invalidité* or Medieval Latin *invaliditas*. See INVALID[1], also -ITY.

invaluable *a.* precious above estimation; priceless. WH: 16C. IN-[2] + *valuable* (VALUE).

Invar® *n.* a nickel-steel alloy with a small coefficient of expansion, used in the manufacture of balance springs for clocks etc. WH: early 20C. Abbr. of INVARIABLE.

invariable *a.* uniform; not liable to change. *Also n.* WH: 14–15C. Old French, or from Late Latin *invariabilis*, from IN-[2] + *variabilis* VARIABLE.

invasion *n.* the act of invading. WH: 14–15C. Old French, or from Late Latin *invasio*, *invasionis*, from Latin *invasus*, p.p. of *invadere*. See INVADE, also -ION.

invective *n.* a violent expression of censure or abuse. *Also a.* WH: 14–15C. Old French *invectif*, from Late Latin *invectivus*, from p.p. of *invehere*. See INVEIGH, also -IVE.

inveigh *v.i.* to speak censoriously and abusively (against). WH: 15C. Latin *invehi* to attack with words, pass. form of *invehere*, to carry in, from IN-[1] + *vehere* to carry.

inveigle *v.t.* to entice; to entrap (into). WH: 15C. Anglo-French *enveigler*, alt. of Old French *aveugler* to blind, from *aveugle* blind, from Medieval Latin *ab oculis* deprived of eyes.

invent *v.t.* to devise or contrive (a new means, instrument etc.). WH: 15C. Latin *inventus*, p.p. of *invenire* to come upon, to discover, from IN-[1] + *venire* to come. The original sense was to find out, to discover. The current sense dates from the 16C.

inventory *n.* a detailed list or catalogue of goods, possessions etc. *Also v.t.* WH: 11–12C. Medieval Latin *inventorium*, alt. of Late Latin *inventarium*, lit. list of what is found. See INVENT, also -ORY[1].

inveracity *n.* untruthfulness. WH: 16C. IN-[2] + *veracity* (VERACIOUS).

Inverness *n.* a kind of sleeveless cloak with a cape hanging loosely over the shoulders. WH: 19C. *Inverness*, a town in NE Scotland.

inverse *a.* opposite in order or relation. *Also n.* WH: 14–15C. Latin *inversus*, p.p. of *invertere* INVERT[1].

inversion *n.* the act of inverting. WH: 16C. Latin *inversio*, *inversionis*, from *inversus*, p.p. of *invertere*. See INVERT[1], also -ION.

invert[1] *v.t.* to turn upside down. WH: 16C. Latin *invertere*, from IN-[1] + *vertere* to turn. The literal sense is to turn outside in, i.e. inside out, and so upside down.

invert[2] *n.* an inverted arch, esp. such as forms the bottom of a sewer etc. WH: 19C. INVERT[1].

invertebrate *a.* (of an animal) not having a backbone or vertebral column. *Also n.* WH: 19C. Modern Latin *Invertebrata*, from French *invertébrés*, from IN-[2] + VERTEBRA.

invest *v.t.* to employ (money) in remunerative property, business, stocks etc. *Also v.i.* WH: 16C. Old French *investir* or Latin *investire* to clothe, to surround, from IN-[1] + *vestis* clothing. The earliest sense was to clothe with a garment. The sense to employ money in a remunerative enterprise (as if giving it a new 'clothing') dates from the 17C.

investigate *v.t.* to examine or inquire into closely. *Also v.i.* WH: 16C. Latin *investigatus*, p.p. of *investigare*, from IN-[1] + *vestigare* to track, to trace out. See also -ATE[3].

investiture *n.* the ceremony of investing with office, rank etc. WH: 14–15C. Medieval Latin *investitura*, from Latin *investitus*, p.p. of *investire* INVEST. See also -URE.

inveterate *a.* determinedly settled in a habit. WH: 14–15C. Latin *inveteratus*, p.p. of *inveterare* to make old, from IN-[1] + *vetus, veteris* old. See also -ATE[2].

invidious *a.* tending to incur or provoke envy, ill will or indignation. WH: 17C. Latin *invidiosus*, from *invidia* ill will. See ENVY, also -IOUS.

invigilate *v.i.* to supervise students during an examination. *Also v.t.* WH: 16C. Latin *invigilatus*, p.p. of *invigilare*, from IN-[1] + *vigilare* to watch, from *vigil* watchful. See also -ATE[3].

invigorate *v.t.* to give vigour or strength to. WH: 17C. Medieval Latin *invigoratus*, p.p. from IN-[1] + Latin *vigorare* to make strong, from *vigor*. See VIGOUR, also -ATE[3].

invincible *a.* that cannot be conquered. WH: 14–15C. Old French, from Latin *invincibilis*, from IN-[2] + *vincibilis*, from *vincere* to conquer. See also -IBLE.

inviolable *a.* not to be violated, profaned or dishonoured. WH: 14–15C. Old French, or from Latin *inviolabilis*, from IN-[2] + *violabilis* violable (VIOLATE).

invisible *a.* not visible; imperceptible to the eye. Also *n.* WH: 12–14C. Old French, or from Latin *invisibilis*, from IN-[2] + *visibilis* VISIBLE.

invitatory *a.* containing or using invitation. Also *n.* WH: 12–14C. Late Latin *invitatorius*, from Latin *invitare* to invite. See also -ORY[2].

invite[1] *v.t.* to ask (someone) courteously to do something, come to an event etc. Also *v.i.* WH: 16C. French *inviter*, or from Latin *invitare*, from IN-[1] + *vitus* pleasant.

invite[2] *n.* an invitation. WH: 17C. INVITE[1].

in vitro *a., adv.* (of biological processes etc.) taking place outside a living organism, e.g. in a test tube. WH: 19C. Latin in glass. See VITREOUS.

in vivo *a., adv.* (of biological processes) occurring within a living organism. WH: early 20C. Latin in the living (body). See VIVID.

invocation *n.* the act of invoking. WH: 14–15C. Old French, from Latin *invocatio, invocationis*, from *invocatus*, p.p. of *invocare* INVOKE. See also -ATION.

invoice *n.* a list of goods dispatched, with particulars of quantity and price, sent to a consignee. Also *v.t.* WH: 16C. Orig. pl. of obs. *invoy*, from obs. French *envoy* ENVOI. An invoice is sent or dispatched as an ENVOY or messenger is.

invoke *v.t.* to address in prayer. WH: 15C. Old French *invoquer*, from Latin *invocare*, from IN-[1] + *vocare* to call.

involucre *n.* a whorl of bracts surrounding the flowers of certain plants. WH: 16C. French, or from Latin *involucrum*, from *involvere* INVOLVE.

involuntary *a.* done unintentionally, not from choice. WH: 16C. IN-[2] + VOLUNTARY.

involute *a.* complicated, involved. Also *n.* WH: 17C. Latin *involutus*, p.p. of *involvere* INVOLVE.

involution *n.* the act of involving. WH: 14–15C. Latin *involutio, involutionis*, from *involutus*, p.p. of *involvere* INVOLVE. See also -ION.

involve *v.t.* to cause to take part (in); to include (in). WH: 14–15C. Latin *involvere*, from IN-[1] + *volvere* to roll.

invulnerable *a.* incapable of being wounded or injured. WH: 16C. Latin *invulnerabilis*, from IN-[2] + *vulnerare* to wound. See also -ABLE.

invultuation *n.* the practice of pricking or stabbing the wax or clay image of an enemy, in the belief that their death will thereby be magically brought about. WH: 19C. Medieval Latin *invultuatio, invultuationis*, from *invultuare* to make a likeness, from IN-[1] + *vultus* visage, likeness. See also -ATION.

inward *a.* internal; situated or being within. Also *adv.* WH: pre-1200. Old English *innanweard, inweard*, from base of IN + *-weard* -WARD.

inweave *v.t.* to weave in or together. WH: 14–15C. IN-[1] + WEAVE[1].

inwrought *a.* (of a pattern etc.) wrought or worked in. WH: 17C. IN + *wrought*, p.p. of WORK.

iodine *n.* a non-metallic bluish-black element, at. no. 53, chem. symbol I, yielding violet fumes when heated, and resembling bromine and chlorine in chemical properties, used in medicine and photography. WH: 19C. French *iode*, from Greek *iōdēs* violet-coloured, from *ion* violet + *-eidēs* like. See also -OID, -INE. The name was coined in 1814 by the English chemist Sir Humphry Davy from French *iode*, the name given earlier (1812) by the French chemist and physicist Joseph Louis Gay-Lussac. Davy added *-ine* to blend with CHLORINE and FLUORINE, also named by him.

iolite *n.* a blue orthorhombic transparent or translucent silicate of aluminium, iron and magnesium. WH: 19C. German *Iolit*, from Greek *ion* violet + *lithos* stone. See -LITE.

ion *n.* an electrically charged atom or group of atoms formed by the loss or gain of electrons. WH: 19C. Greek, neut. pres.p. of *ienai* to go. The term was coined in 1834 by the English scientist Michael Faraday with reference to the fact that ions move towards the electrode of opposite charge. Cp. ANION, CATION.

-ion *suf.* forming nouns indicating an action, process or resulting state or product, as in *distribution, celebration, aspiration*. WH: French *-ion*, Latin *-ionis* (gen. of nn. in *-io*).

Ionian *a.* of or relating to Ionia, or to the Ionians. Also *n.* WH: 16C. Latin *Ionius*, from Greek *Iōnios*, from *Iōnia* Ionia, a region of W Asia Minor + -AN.

ionosphere *n.* the region surrounding the earth at a height of approx. 60–1000 km, in which ionized layers of gas occur. WH: 20C. ION + -O- + SPHERE. The term was coined in 1926 by the Scottish physicist Robert Watson-Watt, who based it on STRATOSPHERE and TROPOSPHERE.

-ior *suf.* forming comparative adjectives, as in *junior, superior*. WH: Latin comp. suf.

iota *n.* the ninth letter of the Greek alphabet (I, ι). WH: 14–15C. Greek *iōta*, of Phoenician orig. Cp. JOT, YOD. The sense smallest part dates from the 17C. Iota is the smallest letter of the Greek alphabet.

IOU *n.* a formal acknowledgement of debt, bearing these letters, the sum involved and the debtor's signature. WH: 18C. Representation of pronun. of *I owe you*.

-iour *suf.* forming nouns, as in *behaviour, saviour, warrior*. WH: -i- + -OUR, -OR.

-ious *suf.* characterized by, full of, as in *ambitious, cautious, suspicious*. WH: -i- + -OUS, representing Latin *-iosus*, French *-ieux*.

ipecacuanha *n.* the dried root of *Cephaelis ipecacuanha*, a cinchonaceous plant from Brazil, used in medicine as an emetic and purgative. WH: 17C. Portuguese, from Tupi-Guarani *ipekaaguéne*, from *ipe* small + *kaa* leaves + *guíne* to vomit.

ipomoea *n.* any twining plant of the genus *Ipomoea*, including the morning glory and jalap. WH: 18C. Modern Latin, from Greek *ips, ipos* woodworm + *homoios* like.

ipse dixit *n.* a mere assertion. WH: 16C. Latin (he) himself said (it), translating Greek *autos epha*, a phr. used of Pythagoras by his followers.

ipsilateral *a.* on or occurring on the same side of the body. WH: early 20C. Latin *ipse* self + LATERAL.

ipsissima verba *n.pl.* the precise words. WH: 19C. Latin the very words, neut. pl. of *ipsissimus*, superl. of *ipse* self (cp. IPSE DIXIT) + pl. of *verbum* word (VERB).

ipso facto *adv.* by that very fact. WH: 16C. Latin by the fact itself, abl. of *ipse* self + abl. of *factum* deed, FACT.

ir-[1] *pref.* in, into, within, on, against, towards, as in *irradiate*. WH: Latin pref., from IN-[1] with *n* assim. to *r*.

ir-[2] *pref.* not, without, as in *irrelevant, irreligion*. WH: Latin pref., from IN-[2] with *n* assim. to *r*.

iracund *a.* easily angered. WH: 19C. Latin *iracundus*, from *ira* anger + *-cundus* inclining to.

irade *n.* a written decree of a Muslim ruler. WH: 19C. Turkish *irade*, from Arabic *'irāda* will, decree, from *'arāda* to intend.

Iranian *a.* of or belonging to Iran. Also *n.* WH: 18C. *Iran* (formerly Persia), a country in SW Asia + -IAN.

Iraqi *a.* of or relating to Iraq. Also *n.* WH: 19C. *Iraq*, a country in SW Asia + -I[3].

irascible *a.* easily excited to anger; irritable. WH: 14–15C. Old French, from Late Latin *irascibilis*, from Latin *irasci* to grow angry, from *ira* anger, IRE. See -IBLE.

irate *a.* angry, enraged. WH: 19C. Latin *iratus*, from *ira* anger, IRE. See also -ATE[2].

ire *n.* anger. WH: 12–14C. Old French, from Latin *ira* anger.

irenic *a.* pacific; promoting peace. WH: 19C. Greek *eirēnikos*, from *eirēnē* peace. See also -IC.

iridacious *a.* of or relating to the Iridaceae family of plants which grow from bulbs, corms or rhizomes and include the iris. WH: 19C. Modern Latin *iridaceus*, from Latin IRIS, *iridis*. See also -ACEOUS.

iridescent *a.* exhibiting a spectrum of luminous or shimmering colours. WH: 18C. Latin IRIS, *iridis* + *-escent* (-ESCENCE).

iridium *n.* a shining white metallic element belonging to the platinum group, at. no. 77, chem. symbol Ir. WH: 19C. Latin *iris, iridis* rainbow + -IUM. The name was coined in 1803 by the English chemist Smithson Tennant, with reference to the various colours of the element's compounds.

irido- *comb. form* of or relating to the iris of the eye. WH: Greek IRIS, *iridos*. See also -O-.

iridology *n.* a diagnostic technique in alternative medicine involving studying the iris of the eye. WH: early 20C. IRIDO- + -LOGY.

iridosmine *n.* a native alloy of iridium and osmium, used for the points of gold pens. WH: 19C. IRIDIUM + OSMIUM + -INE.

iris *n.* the flat circular coloured membrane surrounding the pupil of the eye. WH: 14–15C. Latin, from Greek *iris*, *iridos* rainbow, iris.

Irish *a.* of or relating to Ireland or its inhabitants or Celtic language. *Also n.* WH: 12–14C. Old English *Iras* inhabitants of *Írland* Ireland, an island (divided into the Republic of Ireland and N Ireland) lying west of Great Britain + -ISH[1].

iritis *n.* inflammation of the iris of the eye. WH: 19C. Latin IRIS + -ITIS.

irk *v.t.* to annoy or irritate. *Also v.i.* WH: 12–14C. ? Old Norse *yrkja* WORK. Cp. Swedish *yrka* to claim, to demand, to insist.

iroko *n.* either of two African trees of the genus *Chlorophora*. WH: 19C. Yoruba.

iron *n.* a malleable ductile metallic element, at. no. 26, chem. symbol Fe, widely used for tools etc. *Also a., v.t.* WH: pre-1200. Old English *íren*, prob. alt. of *ísen*, from Germanic, prob. from Celtic and rel. to Latin *aes* bronze, Old English *ār* ORE. Cp. German *Eisen* iron.

irony *n.* an expression, often humorous or slightly sarcastic, intended to convey the opposite of its usual meaning. WH: 16C. Latin *ironia*, from Greek *eirōneia* simulated ignorance, from *eirōn* dissembler. See also -Y[2].

Iroquois *n.* the American Indian confederacy of the Mohawk, Oneida, Seneca, Onondaga, Cayuga and Tuscarora. WH: 17C. French, from Algonquian.

irradiate *v.t.* to subject to sunlight or ultraviolet rays. *Also v.i., a.* WH: 16C. Latin *irradiatus*, p.p. of *irradiare*, from IR-[1] + *radiare* to shine, from *radius* ray. See also -ATE[3].

irrational *a.* without reason or understanding. *Also n.* WH: 14–15C. Latin *irrationalis*, from IR-[2] + *rationalis* RATIONAL.

irreclaimable *a.* incapable of being reclaimed; obstinate; inveterate. WH: 17C. IR-[2] + *reclaimable* (RECLAIM).

irreconcilable *a.* incapable of being reconciled; implacably hostile. *Also n.* WH: 16C. IR-[2] + *reconcilable* (RECONCILE).

irrecoverable *a.* that cannot be recovered; irreparable. WH: 14–15C. IR-[2] + *recoverable* (RECOVER).

irrecusable *a.* not to be refused or rejected. WH: 18C. French *irrécusable* or Late Latin *irrecusabilis*, from IR-[2] + *recusabilis*, from *recusare* to refuse. See RECUSANT, also -ABLE.

irredeemable *a.* not redeemable. WH: 17C. IR-[2] + *redeemable* (REDEEM).

irredentist *n.* a person who advocates the reclaiming of territory that once belonged to their country. WH: 19C. Italian *irredentista*, from (*Italia*) *irredenta* unredeemed (Italy) + -*ista* -IST.

irreducible *a.* not reducible; not to be lessened or lowered. WH: 17C. IR-[2] + *reducible* (REDUCE).

irrefragable *a.* incapable of being refuted; undeniable, unanswerable. WH: 16C. Late Latin *irrefragabilis*, from IR-[2] + *refragari* to oppose, to contest. See also -ABLE.

irrefrangible *a.* not to be broken, inviolable. WH: 18C. IR-[2] + RE-FRANGIBLE.

irrefutable *a.* incapable of being refuted. WH: 17C. Late Latin *irrefutabilis*, from IR-[2] + *refutabilis*, from *refutare* REFUTE. See also -ABLE.

irregular *a.* not according to rule or established principles or custom. *Also n.* WH: 14–15C. Old French *irreguler* (Modern French *irrégulier*), from Medieval Latin *irregularis*. See IR-[2], REGULAR.

irrelative *a.* unconnected (to). *Also n.* WH: 17C. IR-[2] + RELATIVE.

irrelevant *a.* not applicable or pertinent; having no application (to the matter in hand). WH: 16C. IR-[2] + RELEVANT.

irreligion *n.* indifference or hostility to religion. WH: 16C. French *irréligion* or Late Latin *irreligio*, *irreligionis*, from Latin IR-[2] + *religio*, *religionis* RELIGION.

irremediable *a.* incapable of being remedied or corrected. WH: 14–15C. Latin *irremediabilis*, from IR-[2] + *remediabilis* remediable (REMEDY).

irremissible *a.* that cannot be remitted or pardoned. WH: 14–15C. Old French *irrémissible*, or from Ecclesiastical Latin *irremissibilis*, from Latin IR-[2] + *remissibilis* remissible (REMISSION). See also -IBLE.

irremovable *a.* that cannot be removed or displaced. WH: 16C. IR-[2] + *removable* (REMOVE).

irreparable *a.* incapable of being repaired, remedied or restored. WH: 14–15C. Old French *irréparable*, from Latin *irreparabilis*, from IR-[2] + *reparabilis* reparable (REPARATION).

irrepealable *a.* incapable of being repealed, irrevocable. WH: 17C. IR-[2] + *repealable* (REPEAL).

irreplaceable *a.* that cannot be replaced. WH: 19C. IR-[2] + *replaceable* (REPLACE).

irrepressible *a.* that cannot be repressed. WH: 19C. IR-[2] + REPRESS + -IBLE. *Irrepressible* predates *repressible* (mid-20C).

irreproachable *a.* blameless, faultless. WH: 17C. French *irréprochable*, from IR-[2] + *réprochable* reproachable (REPROACH).

irresistible *a.* that cannot be resisted or withstood. WH: 16C. Medieval Latin *irresistibilis*, or from IR-[2] + *resistible* (RESIST).

irresoluble *a.* incapable of being resolved into its elements; insoluble. WH: 17C. Latin *irresolubilis* indissoluble. See IR-[2], RE-, SOLUBLE.

irresolute *a.* not resolute. WH: 16C. Latin *irresolutus* not loosened, or from IR-[2] + RESOLUTE.

irresolvable *a.* incapable of being resolved, insoluble. WH: 17C. IR-[2] + *resolvable* (RESOLVE).

irrespective *a.* regardless of, without reference to. *Also adv.* WH: 17C. IR-[2] + *respective* (RESPECT).

irrespirable *a.* (of air) not fit to be breathed. WH: 19C. IR-[2] + *respirable* (RESPIRE), or from French *irrespirable*.

irresponsible *a.* performed or acting without a proper sense of responsibility. WH: 17C. IR-[2] + RESPONSIBLE.

irresponsive *a.* not responsive (to). WH: 19C. IR-[2] + *responsive* (RESPONSE).

irretentive *a.* not retentive. WH: 18C. IR-[2] + *retentive* (RETENTION).

irretrievable *a.* not to be retrieved; irreparable. WH: 17C. IR-[2] + *retrievable* (RETRIEVE).

irreverent *a.* lacking in reverence; disrespectful. WH: 14–15C. Latin *irreverens*, *irreverentis*, from IR-[2] + *reverens*, *reverentis*, pres.p. of *revereri* REVERE. See also -ENT.

irreversible *a.* not reversible; irrevocable. WH: 17C. IR-[2] + *reversible* (REVERSE).

irrevocable *a.* incapable of being revoked or altered. WH: 14–15C. Old French *irrévocable*, from Latin *irrevocabilis*, from IR-[2] + *revocabilis* revocable (REVOKE).

irrigate *v.t.* to water (land) by causing a stream to flow over it. WH: 17C. Latin *irrigatus*, p.p. pf *irrigare*, from IR-[1] + *rigare* to wet, to water. See also -ATE[3].

irritate *v.t.* to annoy; to exasperate. WH: 16C. Latin *irritatus*, p.p. of *irritare*. prob. freq. of *irrire, rel. to Greek *orinein* to rouse to anger. The original sense (to the 19C) was to excite, to rouse. The current sense dates from the 17C.

irruption *n.* a bursting in. WH: 16C. Latin *irruptio*, *irruptionis*, from *irruptus*, p.p. of *irrumpere* to break in, from IR-[1] + *rumpere* to break.

Isabel *a., n.* greyish-yellow. WH: 17C. *Isabel*, *Isabella*, female forename, French *Isabelle*, of uncertain orig. The name is popularly said to be that of Isabella of Austria (1566–1633), daughter of Philip II of Spain, who vowed not to change her underwear until Ostend was taken (1604). But the colour is mentioned in 1600, a year before the siege began. Chronologically the reference could be to Isabella of Castile (1451–1504), queen of Spain, about whom a similar story is told, but the legend is unsubstantiated.

isagogic *a.* introductory. WH: 19C. Latin *isagogicus*, from Greek *eisagōgikos*, from *eisagōgē*, from *eis* into + *agein* to lead.

isatin *n.* a yellowish-red crystalline compound obtained by oxidizing indigo, used for making dyes. WH: 19C. Latin *isatis* woad, from Greek. See also -IN[1].

ischaemia *n.* a shortage of blood in part of the body. WH: 19C. Modern Latin, from Greek *iskhaimos* stopping blood, from *iskhein* to hold + *haima* blood. See also -IA.

ischium *n.* either of the posterior bones of the pelvic girdle. WH: 17C. Latin, from Greek *iskhion* hip joint.

-ise[1] *suf.* forming abstract nouns, as in *franchise*, *merchandise*. WH: Old French -*ise*, -*ice*, either from Latin -*itia*, -*itium*, or formed independently. Cp. -ICE.

-ise[2] *suf.* forming verbs, as in *advertise*. WH: Var. of -IZE.

isentropic *a.* having equal entropy. WH: 19C. ISO- + *entropic* (ENTROPY).

-ish¹ *suf.* of the nature of, of or relating to, as in *childish*. WH: Old English *-isc*, from Germanic, rel. to Greek *iskos*, dim. n. suf. Cp. German *-isch*.

-ish² *suf.* forming verbs, as in *cherish, finish, punish*. WH: French *-iss-*, lengthened stem of vv. in *-ir*, from Latin *-isc-*.

Ishmael *n.* an outcast. WH: 17C. *Ishmael*, son of Abraham and Hagar (Gen. xvi.15). Ishmael and his mother were exiled by Abraham after the birth of Isaac (Gen. xxi) and he became the archetype of the outcast. When the narrator of Herman Melville's *Moby Dick* (1851) opens his story with the words 'Call me Ishmael' he is recalling the biblical description of Ishmael: 'He will be a wild man; his hand will be against every man, and every man's hand against him' (Gen. xvi.12).

isinglass *n.* a gelatinous substance prepared from the swimming-bladders of the sturgeon, cod, and other fish, used for making jellies, glue etc. WH: 16C. Alt. of early Dutch *huysenblas*, from *huysen* sturgeon + *blas* bladder. Not rel. to GLASS but assim. to it.

Islam *n.* the Muslim religion, that teaches that there is only one God and that Muhammad is his prophet. WH: 17C. Arabic *'islām*, from *'aslama* to submit, to surrender (i.e. to God). Cp. MUSLIM, SALAAM.

island *n.* a piece of land surrounded by water. *Also v.t.* WH: pre-1200. Old English *ēgland, īegland*, later *īland*, from *īeg, īg* island, sea + LAND. Cp. AIT. The spelling with *-s-* arose by association with unrelated ISLE. Cp. AISLE.

isle *n.* an island, esp. a small island. *Also v.t.* WH: 12–14C. Old French *ile*, earlier *isle* (Modern French *île*), from Latin *insula* island.

ism *n.* a doctrine or system of a distinctive kind. WH: 17C. -ISM used independently.

-ism *suf.* forming abstract nouns denoting a doctrine, theory or system, as in *Conservatism, Socialism*. WH: Partly from French *-isme*, mainly from Latin *-ismus*, from Greek *-ismos*, forming nn. of action of vv. in *-izein*, partly also from Latin *-isma*, from Greek, forming nn. expressing something done.

Ismaili *n.* a member of a sect of Shiite Muslims whose spiritual leader is the Aga Khan. WH: 19C. Arabic *'Ismā'īl* (d.762), eldest son of Ja'far ibn Muḥammad, the sixth Shiite imam + -I³. The Ismailis hold that at the death (765) of Ja'far, the imamate should have descended to the posterity of his deceased eldest son, 'Ismā'īl, whereas it actually passed to his younger son, Mūsā al-Kāẓim (d.799).

iso- *comb. form* equal, having the same number of parts, as in *isodynamic*. WH: Greek, from *isos* equal.

isobar *n.* a line on a map connecting places having the same mean barometric pressure, or the same pressure at a given time. WH: 19C. Greek *isobaros* of equal weight, from ISO- + *baros*, bare- weight.

isocheim *n.* a line on a map connecting places having the same mean winter temperature. WH: 19C. ISO- + Greek *kheima* winter weather.

isochor *n.* on a diagram representing relations between pressure and temperature, a line connecting the points denoting equal volumes. WH: early 20C. ISO- + Greek *khōra* space.

isochromatic *a.* of the same colour. WH: 19C. ISO- + CHROMATIC.

isochronal *a.* denoting or occupying equal spaces of time. WH: 17C. Modern Latin *isochronus*, from Greek *isokhronos*, from ISO- + *khronos* time. See also -AL¹.

isochroous *a.* having a uniform colour throughout. WH: 19C. ISO- + Greek *khroa* colour. See also -OUS.

isoclinal *a.* having the same inclination or dip. WH: 19C. ISO- + Greek *klinein* to lean, to slope + -AL¹.

isodiametric *a.* equal in diameter. WH: 19C. ISO- + *diametric* (DIAMETER).

isodimorphism *n.* isomorphism between substances that are dimorphous. WH: 19C. ISO- + *dimorphism* (DIMORPHIC).

isodynamic *a.* having equal force, esp. magnetic force. WH: 19C. Greek *isodunamos* equal in power, from ISO- + *dunamis* power + -IC.

isoelectric *a.* having identical electric potential. WH: 19C. ISO- + ELECTRIC.

isoenzyme *n.* any of two or more enzymes with identical activities but different structure. WH: mid-20C. ISO- + ENZYME.

isogamy *n.* the sexual fusion of two gametes of similar size and form. WH: 19C. ISO- + -GAMY.

isogeny *n.* general similarity of origin. WH: 19C. ISO- + -GENY.

isogeotherm *n.* an imaginary line below the surface of the earth connecting places having the same mean temperature. WH: 19C. ISO- + GEO- + Greek *thermē* heat, *thermos* hot.

isogloss *n.* a line on a map separating off a region that has a specific dialectal feature. WH: early 20C. ISO- + Greek *glōssa* tongue, word.

isogon *n.* a geometrical figure in which all the angles are equal. WH: 17C. Greek *isogōnos* equiangular. See ISO-, -GON.

isohel *n.* a line on a map connecting places having equal amounts of sunshine. WH: early 20C. ISO- + Greek *hēlios* sun.

isohyet *n.* a line on a map connecting places having equal amounts of rainfall. WH: 19C. ISO- + Greek *huetos* rain.

isokinetic *a.* not involving any change in speed. WH: mid-20C. ISO- + KINETIC.

isolate *v.t.* to place apart; to detach. WH: 19C. Back-formation from *isolated* (18C), from French *isolé*, from Italian *isolato*, from Late Latin *insulatus* made an island, from Latin *insula* island. See also -ATE³, -ED. Cp. INSULATE. *Isolated* is now regarded as the past participle of *isolate*.

isoleucine *n.* an essential amino acid. WH: early 20C. ISO- + *leucine* (LEUCIN).

isomer *n.* any of two or more compounds with the same molecular composition but a different structure and different properties. WH: 19C. Greek *isomerēs* sharing equally, from ISO- + *meros* part, share.

isometric *a.* of equal measure. WH: 19C. Greek *isometria* equality of measure, from ISO- + *-metria* -METRY. See also -IC.

isomorph *n.* an organism or substance exhibiting isomorphism. WH: 19C. ISO- + -MORPH.

-ison *suf.* forming nouns, as in *comparison, orison*. WH: Old French *-aison, -eison, -eson, -ison*, Latin *-ationis* (cp. -ATION), *-etionis, -itionis*.

isonomy *n.* equality of political or legal rights. WH: 17C. Italian *isonomia*, from Greek, from ISO- + *nomos* law. See also -Y².

isophote *n.* a line where the light intensity is constant. WH: early 20C. ISO- + Greek *phōs, phōtos* light.

isopleth *n.* a line on a map connecting points at which a variable such as humidity has a constant value. WH: early 20C. Greek *isoplēthēs* equal in quantity, from ISO- + *plēthos* multitude, quantity.

isopod *n.* any of the Isopoda or sessile-eyed crustaceans characterized by seven pairs of thoracic legs almost of the same length, including woodlice and many aquatic species. *Also a.* WH: 19C. Modern Latin *Isopoda*, from Greek ISO- + *pous, podos* foot.

isoprene *n.* a hydrocarbon of the terpene group used esp. in synthetic rubber. WH: 19C. Appar. from ISO- + *propylene* (PROPYL).

isorhythmic *a.* (of medieval motets) consisting of the constant repetition of the same rhythm. WH: 19C. ISO- + *rhythmic* (RHYTHM).

isosceles *a.* (of a triangle) having two sides equal. WH: 16C. Late Latin, from Greek *isoskelēs*, from ISO- + *skelos* leg.

isoseismal *a.* connecting points at which an earthquake has been of the same intensity. *Also n.* WH: 19C. ISO- + *seismal* (SEISMIC).

isosmotic *a.* equal in osmotic pressure. WH: 19C. ISO- + *osmotic* (OSMOSIS).

isostatic *a.* in equilibrium owing to equality of pressure on every side, as that normally prevailing in the crust of the earth. WH: ISO- + Greek *stasis* station + -IC.

isothere *n.* a line on a map connecting points having the same mean summer temperature. WH: 19C. French *isothère*, from ISO- + Greek *theros, there-* summer.

isotherm *n.* a line on a globe or map passing over places having the same mean temperature. WH: 19C. French *isotherme*, from iso- ISO- + Greek *thermē* heat, *thermos* hot.

isotonic *a.* having equal tones. WH: 19C. Greek *isotonos* of equal tension, of equal tone, from ISO- + *tonos* TONE. See also -IC.

isotope *n.* each of two or more atoms of a chemical element having the same atomic number but differing in atomic mass. WH: early 20C. ISO- + Greek *topos* place. The term was coined in 1913 by the English chemist Frederick Soddy, with reference to the fact that the forms of the element have the same chemical properties and the same atomic number, although different weights.

isotropic *a.* manifesting the same physical properties in every direction. WH: 19C. ISO- + Greek *tropos* turn + -IC.

I spy *n.* a children's game in which one player specifies the initial letter of a visible object, which the other players then try to guess. WH: 18C. I + SPY. I spy was originally a game of hide and seek, with the seeker calling 'I spy' on discovering the hider. An educational version of the modern game was created in a popular series of *I-Spy* books from the 1950s.

Israeli *a.* of or relating to the modern state of Israel. *Also n.* WH: mid-20C. *Israel*, a country in SW Asia (formerly the northern kingdom of the ancient Jewish nation) + -I[3].

issue *n.* the act of sending, giving out or putting into circulation. *Also v.i., v.t.* WH: 12–14C. Old French, fem. p.p. of *issir* to go out, from Latin *exire* (EXIT[1]).

-ist *suf.* forming nouns and corresponding adjectives denoting an adherent or follower, as in *Baptist, fatalist, Socialist*. WH: French *-iste*, Latin *-ista*, Greek *-istēs*. Cp. -IZE.

-ister *suf.* denoting an agent etc., as in *chorister, sophister*. WH: Old French *-istre*, var. of -IST.

isthmus *n.* a neck of land connecting two larger portions of land. WH: 16C. Latin, from Greek *isthmos*, of unknown orig.

istle *n.* a species of Mexican agave, or the tough wiry fibre of its leaves, used for cord, nets etc. WH: 19C. American Spanish *ixtle*, from Nahuatl *ixtli*.

it[1] *pron.* the thing, or sometimes the animal or small child, mentioned or referred to. WH: pre-1200. Old English *hit*, neut. nom. and acc. of Germanic demonstrative stem represented also in HE. The *h* of Old English *hit* was lost in everyday speech, as it is (although still written) in *him* and *her* in e.g. *Give him the money, Ask her to come*.

it[2] *n.* Italian vermouth. WH: Abbr. of ITALIAN.

itacolumite *n.* a granular micaceous sandstone which in thin slabs is sometimes flexible. WH: 19C. *Itacolumi*, a mountain in SE Brazil + -ITE[1].

Italian *a.* of or relating to Italy, its people or language. *Also n.* WH: 14–15C. Italian *italiano*, from *Italia* Italy, a country in S Europe. See also -AN.

italic *a.* applied to a sloping type (*thus*), often used for emphasis or for foreign words. *Also n.pl.* WH: 14–15C. Latin *Italicus*, from Greek *Italikos*, from *Italia* Italy, from Latin. See ITALIAN, also -IC. The type so called was introduced by the Italian printer Aldus Manutius (see ALDINE) and was first used in an edition of Virgil (1501) dedicated to Italy.

Italiot *a.* of or relating to the Greek colonies in Italy. *Also n.* WH: 17C. Greek *Italiōtēs*, from *Italia* Italy. See also -OT[2].

Italo- *comb. form* Italian, as in *Italophile*. WH: ITALIAN + -O-.

ITAR-Tass *n.* the official Russian news agency. WH: late 20C. Abbr. of Russian *Informatsionnoe telegrafnoe agentstvo Rossii* Information Telegraph Agency of Russia + TASS.

itch *v.i.* to have an uncomfortable and irritating sensation in the skin causing a desire to scratch. *Also n.* WH: pre-1200. Old English *giccan*, from Germanic. Cp. German *jucken*.

-ite[1] *suf.* denoting a follower of, as in *Pre-Raphaelite, Hitlerite*. WH: French *-ite*, Latin *-ita (-ites)*, from Greek *-itēs*.

-ite[2] *suf.* forming nouns, as in *infinite*. WH: Latin *-itus*, p.p. ending of vv. in *-ire, -ere*.

item *n.* any of a series of things listed or enumerated. *Also adv., v.t.* WH: 14–15C. Latin just so, similarly, moreover, from *ita* thus, so. The word was originally used as an introductory word in a list or formal document. The sense then passed (16C) to an individual component of the list itself.

iterate *v.t.* to repeat; to say over and over again. WH: early 20C. Latin *iteratus*, p.p. of *iterare* to repeat, from *iterum* again. See also -ATE[3].

ithyphallic *a.* of or relating to the erect phallus carried in ancient bacchic processions. *Also n.* WH: 17C. Late Latin *ithyphallicus*, from Greek *ithuphallikos*, from *ithuphallos*, from *ithus* straight + *phallos* PHALLUS. See also -IC.

-itic *suf.* forming adjectives from nouns ending in *-ite, -itis* etc., as in *arthritic*. WH: French *-itique*, Latin *-iticus*, Greek *-itikos*. See also -IC. Cp. -ITE[1], -ITIS.

itinerant *a.* passing or moving from place to place. *Also n.* WH: 16C. Late Latin *itinerans, itinerantis*, pres.p. of *itinerari*, from Latin *iter, itineris* journey. See ITINERARY, also -ANT.

itinerary *n.* a route taken or to be taken. *Also a.* WH: 14–15C. Late Latin *itinerarium*, use as n. of neut. of *itinerarius*, from Latin *iter, itineris* journey, way, road. See also -ARY[1].

-ition *suf.* forming nouns, as in *proposition, contrition*. WH: French *-ition*, Latin *-itio, -itionis*, suf. forming nn. from vv. with p.p. in *-itus*. Cp. -ION.

-itious[1] *suf.* forming adjectives that correspond to nouns ending in *-ition*, as in *ambitious, nutritious*. WH: Latin *-itiosus*, from *-itio, -itionis* -ITION + *-osus* -OUS. Cp. -IOUS.

-itious[2] *suf.* having the nature of, as in *adventitious, factitious*. WH: Late Latin *-itius*, alt. of Latin *-icius*. Cp. -OUS.

-itis *suf.* denoting inflammation, as in *gastritis, peritonitis*. WH: Greek, forming fem. of aa. in *-itēs*, combined with *nosos* disease, to form names of diseases affecting a particular part of the body.

-itive *suf.* forming adjectives, as in *genitive*. WH: French *-itif, -itive*, Latin *-itivus*. Cp. -ATIVE, -IVE.

-itor *suf.* forming nouns denoting an agent, as in *editor*. WH: Latin. Cp. -OR.

-itory *suf.* forming adjectives involving an action, as in *prohibitory*. WH: Latin *-itorius*.

-itous *suf.* forming adjectives that correspond to nouns ending in *-ity*, as in *serendipitous*. WH: -ITY + -OUS, or based on French *-iteux*, Latin *-itosus*.

its *a.* possessive of IT[1]. *Also pron.* WH: 16C. IT[1] + -'S.

itself *pron.* IT[1], used to give emphasis (usu. in apposition). WH: pre-1200. IT[1] + SELF.

itsy-bitsy *a.* tiny. WH: mid-20C. Childish form of LITTLE + *bitsy*, from BIT[1] or *bitty* (BIT[1]) + -SY.

-ity *suf.* denoting a state or condition, as in *equality, fragility*. WH: French *-ité*, from Latin *-itas, -itatis*. Cp. -TY[1].

-ium *suf.* used to form names of metals, as in *aluminium, lithium, sodium*. WH: Modern Latin, from Latin, representing Greek *-ion*.

-ive *suf.* disposed, serving or tending; of the nature or quality of, as in *active, massive, pensive, restive, talkative*. WH: Old French *-if, -ive*, from Latin *-ivus*.

ivory *n.* the hard white substance composing the tusks of the elephant, the narwhal etc. *Also a.* WH: 12–14C. Old French *yvoire* (Modern French *ivoire*), from Latin *ebur, eboris* ivory, rel. to Egyptian *āb, ābu*, Coptic *ebou, ebu* elephant.

ivy *n.* an evergreen climbing plant, *Hedera helix*, usu. having five-angled leaves, and adhering by aerial rootlets. WH: pre-1200. Old English *ifig*, from Germanic, of unknown orig. Cp. German *Efeu* (influ. by *Heu* HAY[1]).

†iwis *adv.* certainly (often spelt erron. *I wis*). WH: pre-1200. Old English *gewis*, from Germanic, from base also of WISE[1]. Cp. WIS.

ixia *n.* any southern African bulbous flowering plant of the genus *Ixia* of the iris family. WH: 16C. Latin, from Greek.

Iyar *n.* in the Jewish calendar, the eighth month of the civil year and the second month of the religious year. WH: 18C. Hebrew *'iyyār*.

izard *n.* a kind of antelope related to the chamois, inhabiting the Pyrenees. WH: 18C. French *isard*, Gascon *isart*, ? of Iberian orig.

-ize *suf.* forming verbs meaning to follow or practise some principle, policy etc., as in *economize*. WH: French *-iser*, from Late Latin *-izare*, from Greek *-izein*.

†izzard *n.* the letter z. WH: 18C. Alt. of ZED.

J

jab *v.t.* to poke violently. *Also n.* WH: 19C. Var. (orig. Scottish) of JOB[2].

jabber *v.i.* to talk volubly and incoherently. *Also v.t., n.* WH: 15C. Imit. Cp. GABBLE, GIBBER[1], JABBLE.

jabberwocky *n.* nonsense, gibberish; an instance of this. WH: early 20C. Title of pseudo-nonsensical poem in Lewis Carroll's *Through the Looking-Glass* (1871). ? Based on JABBER + Old English *wŏcor* offspring, as if the result of meaningless chatter.

jabble *v.i.* to splash, to dash in wavelets. *Also n.* WH: 18C. Appar. imit. See also -LE[4].

jabiru *n.* a bird of the genus *Ephippiorhynchus*, esp. *E. mycteria*, S American storklike wading birds. WH: 18C. Tupi-Guarani *jabirú*, from *j* that which has + *abirú* swollen (ref. to its large neck).

jaborandi *n.* any shrub of the genus *Pilocarpus*. WH: 17C. Portuguese, from Tupi-Guarani *jaburandi*, lit. person who makes saliva, one who spits. The leaves of the shrub promote salivation when chewed.

jabot *n.* a lace frill worn at the neck of a woman's bodice. WH: 19C. French bird's crop, shirt frill, ? from Latin *gaba* cheek.

jacamar *n.* any bird of the tropical American family Galbulidae, resembling the kingfisher. WH: 19C. French, appar. from Tupi.

jacana *n.* any bird of the family Jacanidae, from the warmer parts of N and S America. WH: 18C. Portuguese *jaçaña*, from Tupi-Guarani *jasañã*.

jacaranda *n.* a tropical American tree, esp. of the genus *Jacaranda*, yielding fragrant and ornamental wood. WH: 18C. Portuguese, from Tupi-Guarani *jakara'nda*.

jacinth *n.* a variety of zircon. WH: 12–14C. Old French *iacinte* (Modern French *jacinthe*), or from Medieval Latin *iacintus*, alt. of Latin *hyacinthus* HYACINTH.

jack[1] *n.* a contrivance for lifting heavy weights. *Also v.t.* WH: 14–15C. *Jack*, pet form of male forename *John*. Cp. JOHN.

jack[2] *n.* a jacket, usu. of leather, formerly worn by foot soldiers. WH: 14–15C. Old French *jaque*, ? from Spanish or Portuguese *jaco*, or from Arabic.

jack[3] *n.* a tropical Asian tree of the genus *Artocarpus*. WH: 16C. Portuguese *jaca*, from Malayalam *chakka*.

jackal *n.* a gregarious animal, *Canis aureus*, closely allied to the dog. WH: 17C. Turkish *çakal*, from Persian *šagāl*, rel. to Sanskrit *sṛgāla*, assim. to JACK[1].

†jackanapes *n.* a pert fellow. WH: 16C. Prob. from a playful name for an ape, from JACK[1] + APE, with *n* as in early *an ewt* for *a newt* and *s* as in surname such as *Hobbs*.

jackaroo *n.* a newcomer, a novice. WH: 19C. JACK[1] + KANGAROO.

jackass *n.* a male ass. WH: 18C. JACK[1] + ASS.

jackdaw *n.* the smallest of the British crows, *Corvus monedula*. WH: 16C. JACK[1] + DAW. Cp. MAGPIE.

jacket *n.* a short coat or sleeved outer garment for men or women. *Also v.t.* WH: 14–15C. Old French *jacquet*, dim. of *jaque*. See JACK[2], also -ET[1]. Modern French *jaquette* means (man's) morning coat, (woman's) jacket.

Jacobean *a.* belonging to the reign of James I. *Also n.* WH: 18C. Modern Latin *Jacobaeus*, from Ecclesiastical Latin *Iacobus* James. See also -EAN. Cp. JACOBIN, JACOBITE. The reference is to James I of England, reigned 1603–25, or the apostle St James, or the Epistle of St James.

Jacobin *n.* a member of a revolutionary republican club, 1789–94. WH: 12–14C. Old French, from Medieval Latin *Iacobinus*, from Ecclesiastical Latin *Iacobus* James (French *Jacques*). The revolutionaries so named met in the hall of the Jacobin friars, in the Rue St Jacques, Paris, their own name coming from the church of St Jacques (St James).

Jacobite *n.* a partisan of James II after his abdication, or of the Stuart pretenders to the throne. *Also a.* WH: 17C. Ecclesiastical Latin *Iacobus* James + -ITE[1]. The reference is to James II of England, reigned 1685–8.

Jacob's ladder *n.* a garden plant, *Polemonium caeruleum*, with closely pinnate leaves. WH: 18C. Ref. is to Jacob's dream of a ladder reaching to heaven (Gen. xxviii.12). The plant is so named from its long leaves with closely spaced leaflets, like rungs.

Jacob's staff *n.* a surveyor's rod. WH: 16C. Ref. is to St James (Ecclesiastical Latin *Iacobus*), whose symbols are a pilgrim's staff and a scallop shell. Cp. also: 'And Jacob took him rods of green poplar' etc (Gen. xxx.37–43) and Jacob's words, 'With my staff I passed over this Jordan' (Gen. xxxii.10).

jacobus *n.* a gold coin struck in the reign of James I. WH: 17C. Ecclesiastical Latin *Iacobus* James. The reference is to James I of England (JACOBEAN).

jaconet *n.* a fine, close, white cotton cloth, rather heavier than cambric. WH: 18C. Hindi *Jagannāthpurī* (now Puri), a town and port in E India, its place of orig. See JUGGERNAUT.

jacquard *n.* an apparatus with perforated cards used to weave intricate designs. WH: 19C. J.M. *Jacquard* 1752–1834, French inventor.

Jacquerie *n.* a revolt of the peasants against the nobles in France, in 1357–8. WH: 16C. Old French, from male forename *Jacques*. French *Jacques* equates to English *James* as a name, but here corresponds in meaning to JACK[1]. The similarity between the names is unexplained.

jactation *n.* the act of throwing. WH: 16C. Latin *iactatio, iactationis*, from *iactatus*, p.p. of *iactare*, freq. of *iacere* to throw. See also -ATION.

Jacuzzi® *n.* a type of bath or small pool with a mechanism which makes the water swirl round. WH: mid-20C. Candido *Jacuzzi*, c.1903–86, US inventor.

jade[1] *n.* a broken-down, worthless horse. *Also v.t., v.i.* WH: 14–15C. Orig. unknown.

jade[2] *n.* a green, massive, sometimes crypto-crystalline, silicate of lime and magnesia, used for ornamental purposes. WH: 16C. French *lejade* (from *l'ejade*), from Spanish *ijada* (in *piedra de ijada*, lit. stone of colic), from Latin *ilia* flanks, pl. of ILIUM. The mineral is so called because it was believed to cure the colic. Cp. NEPHRITE.

j'adoube *int.* in chess, used as a notification that a piece is being adjusted rather than moved. WH: 19C. French I adjust, from *je, j'* I + 1st pers. sing. pres. ind. of *adouber* (DUB[1]).

Jaeger® *n.* a woollen material used in clothes-making, orig. one containing no vegetable fibre. WH: 19C. Dr. Gustav *Jaeger*, 1832–1917, German naturalist, its orig. manufacturer.

jaeger *n.* a seabird of the skua family esp. of the genus *Stercoraria*. WH: 19C. German *Jäger* hunter.

Jaffa *n.* a type of orange from Jaffa in Israel. WH: 19C. *Jaffa*, a city and port in Israel (the biblical *Joppa*).

jag[1] *n.* a notch. *Also v.t.* WH: 14–15C. Var. of JOG.

jag[2] *n.* a bout of drinking or drug-taking. WH: 16C. Orig. unknown.

jaggery *n.* a coarse dark-brown kind of sugar made in India from the juice of certain palms. WH: 16C. Portuguese *xagara, jagara*, from Malayalam *cakkarā*, from Sanskrit *śarkarā* SUGAR.

jaguar *n.* a S American feline animal, *Panthera onca*, resembling the leopard. WH: 17C. Portuguese, from Tupi-Guarani *yaguára*.

jaguarundi *n.* a wild cat, *Felis yagouaroundi*, of Central and S America. WH: 19C. Portuguese, from Tupi-Guarani, from *yaguára* JAGUAR + *undi* dark.

jai alai *n.* a game played by two or four players on a court, who wear woven baskets tied to their wrists and using these hurl a ball at the walls. WH: early 20C. Spanish, from Basque *jai* festival + *alai* merry.

jail *n.* a prison, a public place of confinement for persons charged with or convicted of crime. *Also v.t.* WH: 12–14C. Old French *jaiole, geole* (Modern French *geôle*) prison, from Popular Latin *gaviola,* dim. of Latin *cavea* CAGE.

Jain *n.* an adherent of a non-Brahminical Indian religion. *Also a.* WH: 18C. Hindi, from Sanskrit *jaina* pertaining to a Jina, from *jina,* lit. victor, overcomer, from *ji-* to conquer or *jyā-* to overcome.

jake *a.* honest. WH: early 20C. Orig. unknown.

jalap *n.* the dried tubercles of *Exogonium purga,* used as a purgative. WH: 17C. French, from Spanish *jalapa,* in full *purga de jalapa,* from *Jalapa, Xalapa,* a city in Mexico.

jalapeño *n.* a very hot green chilli pepper. WH: mid-20C. Mexican Spanish (*chile*) *jalapeño* Jalapa chilli. See JALAP.

jalopy *n.* a much-worn motor vehicle. WH: early 20C. Orig. unknown.

jalouse *v.t.* to suspect. WH: 17C. French *jalouser* to regard with jealousy, from *jaloux* JEALOUS.

jalousie *n.* a louvre blind, a Venetian shutter. WH: 18C. French, lit. jealousy. One can see (jealously) through the blind without being seen.

jam[1] *v.t.* to wedge or squeeze (in or into). *Also v.i., n.* WH: 18C. ? Imit., otherwise of unknown orig. Cp. CHAMP[1], JUMBLE.

jam[2] *n.* a conserve of fruit made by boiling with sugar. *Also v.t.* WH: 18C. ? From JAM[1]. The reference would be to the fruit being pressed or crushed.

Jamaican *a.* of or relating to Jamaica. *Also n.* WH: 17C. *Jamaica,* an island in the W Indies + -AN.

jamb *n.* any one of the upright sides of a doorway, window, or fireplace. WH: 12–14C. Old French *jambe* leg, vertical support, from Late Latin *gamba* hoof, from Greek *kampē* joint.

jambalaya *n.* a S US dish consisting of meat, seafood, rice, onions etc. WH: 19C. Louisiana French, from Provençal *jambalaia* chicken and rice stew.

jamboree *n.* a Scout rally. WH: 19C. Orig. unknown. ? From JAM[1]. Cp. *shivaree* from CHARIVARI.

jampan *n.* a sedan chair borne on two bamboo poles by four people. WH: 19C. Bengali *jhāmpān,* Hindi *jhappān.*

jane *n.* a woman. WH: early 20C. *Jane,* female forename.

jangle *v.i.* to sound harshly or discordantly. *Also v.t., n.* WH: 12–14C. Old French *jangler,* prob. from Germanic. Cp. Dutch *jangelen,* ult. of imit. orig. The original sense was to chatter, to babble. The current sense dates from the 15C.

janitor *n.* a doorkeeper. WH: 16C. Latin, from *janua* door, entrance. See also -OR.

janizary *n.* a soldier of the old Turkish infantry forming the Sultan's bodyguard (orig. young prisoners trained to arms), disbanded in 1826. WH: 16C. French *janissaire,* ult. from Turkish *yeniçeri,* from *yeni* new + *çeri* troops.

jankers *n.* punishment, detention. WH: early 20C. Orig. unknown. ? From JANGLE, ref. to chains.

jannock[1] *n.* oaten bread, an oaten loaf. WH: 15C. Orig. unknown.

jannock[2] *a., adv.* fair, straightforward. WH: 19C. Orig. unknown.

January *n.* the first month of the year. WH: pre-1200. Latin *Januarius,* use as n. of a. from *Janus.* See JANUS-FACED.

Janus-faced *a.* two-faced, deceitful, hypocritical. WH: 17C. Latin *Janus,* name of a god in Roman mythology who guarded doors and gates and was represented with two faces, one looking forward, the other back + -faced (FACE).

japan *n.* an intensely hard varnish, or varnishing liquid, made from linseed oil, resin, shellac etc. *Also v.t.* WH: 17C. *Japan* (JAPANESE), whence it originated.

Japanese *a.* of or relating to Japan or its inhabitants. *Also n.* WH: 17C. *Japan,* a country in the Far East + -ESE.

jape *v.i.* to jest, to play tricks. *Also v.t., n.* WH: 14–15C. Old French *japer* (Modern French *japper*) to yelp, to yap, influ. in sense by Old French *gaber* to mock.

Japlish *n.* a blend of Japanese and English. WH: mid-20C. Blend of JAPANESE and ENGLISH. Cp. FRANGLAIS. Japanese contains many words adopted from English, e.g. *bijinesu* business, *doraibā* screwdriver, *nekkuresu* necklace, *terebijon* television. Cp. KARAOKE.

japonica *n.* any flowering shrub of the genus *Chaenomeles,* esp. *C. speciosa,* the Japanese quince. WH: 19C. Modern Latin, fem. of *Japonicus* from Japan.

jar[1] *v.i.* to emit a harsh or discordant sound. *Also v.t., n.* WH: 16C. Prob. imit.

jar[2] *n.* a vessel of glass or earthenware of various shapes and sizes, used for various domestic purposes. WH: 16C. French *jarre,* from Arabic *jarra.*

jar[3] *n.* a state of partial closure (only in the expression *on the jar*). WH: 17C. Var. of CHAR[3]. Cp. AJAR[1].

jardinière *n.* an ornamental pot or stand for growing flowers in a room etc. WH: 19C. French, lit. female gardener.

jargon[1] *n.* any professional, technical or specialized language. *Also v.i.* WH: 14–15C. Old French *jargoun, gergon,* ult. of unknown orig. The original meaning was twittering of birds, chattering. The current sense evolved in the 17C.

jargon[2] *n.* a transparent, colourless or smoky variety of zircon found in Sri Lanka. WH: 18C. French, from Italian *giargone,* prob. ult. rel. to ZIRCON.

jargonelle *n.* a kind of early pear. WH: 17C. French, dim. of JARGON[2]. The word was originally the name of a gritty kind of pear.

jarl *n.* a Norse or Dutch nobleman or chieftain, an earl or count. WH: 19C. Old Norse. See EARL.

jarrah *n.* the W Australian mahogany gum tree, *Eucalyptus marginata.* WH: 19C. Australian Aboriginal (Nyunga) *jarrily.*

jasmine *n.* any plant of the genus *Jasminum,* many of which are climbers with sweet-scented white or yellow flowers, esp. the common white *J. officinale.* WH: 16C. French *jasmin,* obs. *jessemin,* from Arabic *yāsamīn,* from Persian *yāsaman.*

jaspé *a.* (of ceramics) having an appearance like jasper. WH: 19C. French, p.p. of *jasper* to marble. See JASPER.

jasper *n.* an impure variety of quartz, of many colours and shades, opaque even in thin splinters. WH: 12–14C. Old French *jaspre,* var. of *jaspe,* from Latin *iaspis,* from Greek, of Semitic orig.

Jat *n.* a member of an Indo-Aryan people of NW India. *Also a.* WH: 17C. Hindi *Jāt.*

jato *n.* jet assisted take-off. WH: Acronym of *jet assisted take-off.*

jaundice *n.* a condition due to obstruction of the bile or absorption of the colouring matter into the blood, characterized by yellowness of the skin, diarrhoea and general debility. *Also v.t.* WH: 12–14C. Old French *jaunice* (Modern French *jaunisse*) yellowness, from *jaune* yellow. See also -ICE. The *d* has entered as with SOUND[1].

jaunt *n.* a ramble, an excursion, a short journey, a trip. *Also v.i.* WH: 16C. Orig. unknown. The original sense was tiring or troublesome journey. The current sense arose in the 17C.

jaunty *a.* sprightly, airy, self-satisfied, perky. WH: 17C. French *gentil.* See GENTLE, GENTEEL. Not rel. to JAUNT. The original sense was well-bred, gentlemanly, elegant. The sense lively, brisk, dates from the 18C.

Javanese *a.* of or relating to Java. *Also n.* WH: 18C. *Java,* an island in the Malay archipelago (now in Indonesia) + -n- + -ESE.

javelin *n.* a light spear thrown by the hand, used as a weapon or in field events. *Also v.t.* WH: 14–15C. Old French *javeline,* alt. of *javelot,* ? from Celtic. Cp. Old Irish *gabul,* Welsh *gafl* fork.

Javelle water *n.* a solution of sodium hypochlorite used in disinfecting and bleaching. WH: 19C. *Javel,* a village in N France (now a suburb of Paris), where first used.

jaw *n.* either of two bones or bony structures in which the teeth are fixed, forming the framework of the mouth. *Also v.i., v.t.* WH: 14–15C. Old French *joe* (Modern French *joue*) cheek, jaw, of unknown orig.

jay[1] *n.* a chattering bird, *Garrulus glandarius,* with brilliant plumage. WH: 15C. Old French (Modern French *geni*), from Late Latin *gaius,* ? from male praenomen *Gaius.*

jay[2] *n.* the letter J. WH: 17C. Representation of pronun. of *J* as letter's name.

jazerant *n.* a light coat of armour composed of small plates of metal, usu. fastened to a flexible lining. WH: 14–15C. Old French *jaserant,* orig. an a., in *osberc* (*hauberc*) *jazerant* (see HAUBERK), of unknown orig. According to some authorities, the word comes ultimately from *al-Jaza'ir,* the Arabic name of Algiers, where the armour was originally made.

jazz *n.* syncopated music of African-American origin. *Also v.i.* WH: early 20C. Orig. unknown. ? Rel. to earlier *jasm* energy, drive, appar. of African orig.

JCB® *n.* a type of construction machine with a hydraulically operated shovel at the front and an excavator at the back. WH: mid-20C. Initials of Joseph Cyril Bamford, 1916–, its British manufacturer.

J cloth® *n.* a type of cloth used esp. for cleaning, wiping work surfaces etc. WH: mid-20C. Initial of Johnson and Johnson, its US manufacturers.

jealous *a.* suspicious or apprehensive of being supplanted in the love or favour (of a wife, husband, lover or friend). WH: 12–14C. Old French *gelos* (Modern French *jaloux*), from Medieval Latin *zelosus*, from Ecclesiastical Latin *zelus*, from Greek *zēlos* ZEAL. See also -OUS.

Jeames *n.* a footman, a flunkey. WH: 17C. Var. of *James*, male forename. The word was popularized by Thackeray in *The Diary of C. Jeames de la Pluche, Esq.* (1846), the central character being a former footman whose real name is James Plush.

jean *n.* a twilled undressed cloth with cotton warp. WH: 15C. Old French *Janne* (Modern French *Gênes*), from Medieval Latin *Janna* Genoa, a city and port in NW Italy, where orig. made. Cp. JEANS.

jeans *n.pl.* close-fitting casual trousers usu. made of denim or other cotton fabric. WH: 19C. JEAN + -S[1].

Jeep® *n.* a fast, light car for military use. WH: mid-20C. Representation of initials GP general purpose, but influ. by name of Eugene the Jeep, a versatile cartoon character with a cry of 'Jeep' introduced in E.C. Segar's comic strip *Thimble Theatre* in 1936.

jeepers *int.* used to express surprise etc. WH: early 20C. Alt. of JESUS (Christ).

jeer *v.i.* to scoff, to mock (at). Also *v.t., n.* WH: 16C. Orig. unknown. Prob. not rel. to CHEER.

jeez *int.* used to express surprise etc. WH: early 20C. Abbr. of JESUS.

jeffersonite *n.* a greenish-black variety of pyroxene. WH: 19C. Thomas *Jefferson*, 1743–1826, US president + -ITE[1]. The mineral was so named in 1822.

Jehoshaphat *int.* used as a mild expletive, esp. in *jumping Jehoshaphat*. WH: 19C. *Jehoshaphat*, a king of Judah (II Sam. viii.16 etc.). The name was seized on for its sonority and has no personal or historical allusion.

Jehovah *n.* the most sacred name given in the Old Testament to God, esp. regarded as the God of the Jewish people. WH: 16C. Medieval Latin *Iehoua*, from Hebrew *yhwh, jhvh*, representing the Tetragrammaton or divine name, too sacred to be spoken, with insertion of the vowels of *'ăḏōnāy* my lord. Cp. ADONAI, YAHWEH.

Jehu *n.* a coachman, a driver, esp. one who drives fast or furiously. WH: 17C. *Jehu*, a king of Israel who 'driveth furiously' (II Kgs. ix.20).

jejune *a.* bare, meagre, scanty. WH: 17C. Latin *ieiunus* fasting, barren. The original sense was fasting, hungry. The sense shallow, simplistic evolved in the 17C and that of puerile, naive in the 19C, perhaps in the belief that the word derives from Latin *iuvenis* young or French *jeune* young.

jejunum *n.* the second portion of the small intestine between the duodenum and the ileum. WH: 16C. Medieval Latin, from Latin *ieiunum* (*intestinum*) fasting (intestine). The jejunum is usually found to be empty after death.

Jekyll and Hyde *n.* a person with a split personality, one side evil, the other good. WH: 19C. From R.L. Stevenson's story *The Strange Case of Dr Jekyll and Mr Hyde* (1886), in which the central character, Dr Henry Jekyll, brews a potion that turns him into the villainous Edward Hyde.

jell *v.i.* to turn into jelly. WH: 18C. Back-formation from JELLY.

jelly *n.* any gelatinous substance, esp. that obtained by decoction from animal matter. Also *v.i., v.t.* WH: 14–15C. Old French *gelée* frost, jelly, from use as n. of Latin *gelata*, fem. p.p. of *gelare* to freeze, from *gelu* frost.

jemadar *n.* in the Indian subcontinent, an army officer. WH: 18C. Urdu *jama'dār*, from Persian, from Arabic *jama', jamā'at* to muster + Persian *-dār* holder.

jemima *n.* an elastic-sided boot. WH: 19C. *Jemima*, female forename. The word was originally a commercial name, initially for a type of made-up tie.

jemmy[1] *n.* a short, stout crowbar, used by burglars. Also *v.t.* WH: 18C. Pet form of the male forename *James*. See also -Y[3]. Cp. JIMMY.

jemmy[2] *a.* spruce, neat. WH: 19C. Var. of obs. *gim*, ? itself var. of dial. *jimp*, of unknown orig.

je ne sais quoi *n.* an indefinable something. WH: 17C. French, lit. I do not know what.

jennet *n.* a small Spanish horse. WH: 14–15C. French *genet*, from obs. Spanish *ginete* (now *jinete*) light horseman, from Spanish Arabic *Genētī*, from *Zanāta*, a Berber tribe famed for their horsemanship.

jenneting *n.* an early kind of apple. WH: 17C. French *Jeannet*, pet form of *Jean* JOHN. See also -ING[3]. The apple is so named as it is ripe by St John's Day, 24 June. Popular etymology explains the name as representing *June-eating*.

jenny *n.* a female ass, animal, bird etc. WH: 17C. Pet form of female forenames *Janet, Jennifer* or *Jane*, serving as a fem. equivalent of JACK[1].

jeopardy *n.* exposure to danger, loss or injury. WH: 12–14C. Old French *iu parti*, later *ieu parti* divided play, even game, uncertain chance. The word originally denoted a chess problem, then a trick or stratagem, then (to the 19C) a daring deed. The current sense dates from the first, however.

jequirity *n.* a tropical twining shrub, *Abrus precatorius*, with parti-coloured seeds or beans which are used for ornaments and for medicinal purposes. WH: 19C. French *jéquirity*, from Tupi-Guarani *jekiriti*.

jerboa *n.* a small mouselike rodent of the family Dipodidae, with long hind legs adapted for leaping. WH: 17C. Modern Latin, from Arabic *yarbū'a*. Cp. GERBIL.

jereed *n.* a javelin, used in Iran and Turkey, esp. in games. WH: 17C. Arabic *jarīd* palm branch stripped of its leaves, javelin.

jeremiad *n.* a lamentation, esp. over modern degeneracy, in the style of the prophet Jeremiah. WH: 18C. French *jérémiade*, from *Jérémie*, from Ecclesiastical Latin *Jeremias* Jeremiah (JEREMIAH), with ref. to the biblical Lamentations of Jeremiah. See also -AD[1].

Jeremiah *n.* a prophet of doom. WH: 18C. *Jeremiah*, a Hebrew prophet noted for his calls for moral reform, his predictions of the fall of Jerusalem, and the poems grieving for the fall of Jerusalem in Lamentations, ascribed to him.

jerk[1] *v.t.* to pull, push, or thrust sharply. Also *v.i., n.* WH: 16C. Prob. imit. The original sense was to strike with a whip.

jerk[2] *v.t.* to cure (beef) by cutting it into long pieces and drying it in the sun. WH: 18C. American Spanish *charquear*, from *charqui*, from Quechua *echarqui* dried flesh in long strips. Cp. CHARQUI.

jerkin *n.* a short coat or jacket, formerly often made of leather. WH: 16C. Orig. unknown.

jerkinhead *n.* a combination of truncated gable and hipped roof. WH: 19C. ? Alt. of *jerking*, pres.p. of JERK[1] + HEAD[1].

jeroboam *n.* a wine bottle holding 10–12 quarts (about 12 l). WH: 19C. *Jeroboam*, a king of Israel who was 'a mighty man of valour' (I Kgs. xi.28) 'who made Israel to sin' (xiv.16).

jerque *v.t.* to search (a vessel or her papers) for unentered goods. WH: 19C. ? Italian *cercare* to search.

Jerry *n.* a German soldier. WH: early 20C. Alt. of GERMAN + -Y[3].

jerry *a.* cheaply and badly built, flimsy. Also *n.* WH: 19C. Abbr. of *jerry-built*, of unknown orig. The word has been related by some to obsolete *jerry* (18C) to shake (someone) about, probably from a pet form of the male forename *Jeremy, Jeremiah, Gerald* or *Gerard*.

jerrycan *n.* a can for petrol, water etc., orig. German. WH: mid-20C. JERRY + CAN[2]. Such cans were first used in Germany and subsequently adopted by the Allies in World War II.

jersey *n.* a knitted garment, as a pullover, worn on the upper part of the body. WH: 16C. *Jersey*, the largest of the Channel Islands.

Jerusalem artichoke *n.* a species of sunflower, *Helianthus tuberosus*, the tuberous roots of which are edible. WH: 17C. Alt. of Italian *girasole* sunflower (GIRASOL) + ARTICHOKE.

jess *n.* in falconry, a short leather or silk ribbon for tying round each leg of a hawk, to which the leash may be attached. Also *v.t.* WH: 12–14C. Old French *ges*, nom. sing. and acc. pl. of *get* (Modern French *jet* cast), from var. of Latin *iactus* a throw, from *iacere* to throw.

jessant *a.* issuing or springing (from). WH: 16C. Prob. from French *issant*, pres.p. of Old French *issir* to go out, ISSUE.

Jesse *n.* a genealogical tree representing the genealogy of Christ, esp. in the form of a large brass candlestick with many branches. WH: 14–15C. *Jesse*, the father of David and an ancestor of Jesus (I Sam. xvi.12, Isa. xi.1).

jest n. a joke, something ludicrous said or done to provoke mirth. Also v.i. WH: 14–15C. Var. of obs. GEST. The original sense (to the 17C) was satirical comment. The current sense evolved in the 16C.

Jesuit n. a member of the Society of Jesus, a Roman Catholic order founded in 1534 by Ignatius Loyola. WH: 16C. French *jésuite* or Modern Latin *Jesuita*, from JESUS + -ITA -ITE¹.

Jesus n. the Saviour of Christian belief. Also int. WH: 12–14C. Ecclesiastical Latin *Iesus*, from Greek *Iēsous*, from late Hebrew or Aramaic *Yēšûă'*, var. of *Yĕhôšûā'* Joshua.

jet¹ n. a black compact variety of lignite capable of being brilliantly polished, formerly much used for articles of personal ornament. Also a. WH: 12–14C. Old French *jaiet* (Modern French *jais*), from Latin *Gagates*, from Greek *Gagatēs*, from *Gagai*, a town in Lycia in south-west Asia Minor.

jet² v.i. to spurt or shoot out, to come out in a jet or jets. Also v.t., n. WH: 16C. Old French *jeter* to throw, from var. of Latin *iactare*. Cp. JUT. The original sense was to project, to protrude. The current sense dates from the 17C.

jeté n. a leap from one foot to another in ballet. WH: 19C. French, p.p. of *jeter* to throw.

jetsam n. goods, cargo etc., thrown overboard in order to lighten a ship in distress, and subsequently washed ashore. WH: 16C. Contr. of JETTISON.

jettison n. the casting of goods overboard to lighten a vessel in distress. Also v.t. WH: 14–15C. Old French *getaison*, from Latin *iactatio*, *iactationis*, from *iactare* to throw. See also -ISON.

jetton n. a stamped or engraved counter used in card-playing, or as a coin in a machine. WH: 18C. French *jeton*, from *jeter* to cast up (accounts), to calculate. See JET².

jetty¹ n. a structure of stone or timber projecting into water and serving as a mole, pier, or wharf. WH: 14–15C. Old French *jetee*, fem. p.p. (used as n.) of *jeter* to throw. See JET². Cp. JUT.

jetty² a. of the nature of jet. WH: 15C. JET¹ + -Y¹.

jeu n. a game, a play, a jest. WH: 18C. French play, game, from Latin *iocus* JOKE.

jeunesse dorée n. gilded youth. WH: 19C. French, lit. gilded youth, from *jeunesse* youth + fem. p.p. of *dorer* to gild (cp. DORY¹).

Jew n. a person of Hebrew descent or whose religion is Judaism. WH: 12–14C. Old French *giu*, earlier *juiu* (Modern French *juif*), from Latin *Iudaeus*, from Greek *Ioudaios*, from Aramaic *yĕhūḏāy*, Hebrew *yehūḏī*, from *yĕhūḏāh* Judah, a son of the Hebrew patriarch Jacob, the tribe descended from Judah.

jewel n. a precious stone, a gem. Also v.t. WH: 12–14C. Old French *joel* (Modern French *joyau*), from Medieval Latin *iocale*, from Latin *iocus* pastime, sport, JOKE.

Jewry n. the Jews or the land where they dwell or dwelt. WH: 12–14C. Old French *juierie* (Modern French *juiferie*). See JEW, also -ERY.

jewstone n. a black basalt found in the Clee Hills, Shropshire. WH: 17C. Trans. of Medieval Latin *lapis Iudaicus* (cp. JUDAIC).

Jezebel n. a wicked, bold, or vicious woman, esp. a woman who paints her face. WH: 16C. *Jezebel*, wife of Ahab, king of Israel (I Kgs. xxi.5–15) who 'painted her face' (II Kgs. ix.30).

jib¹ n. a large triangular sail set on a stay between the fore-topmast-head and bowsprit or jib-boom in large vessels and between the masthead and the bowsprit in smaller ones. WH: 17C. Orig. unknown.

jib² v.t. to shift (a boom, yard or sail) from one side of a vessel to the other. Also v.i. WH: 17C. Orig. unknown. Cp. GYBE.

jib³ v.i. (of a horse etc.) to move restively sideways or backwards. WH: 19C. ? Var. of GIBE.

jibba n. a long, loose coat worn by Muslims. WH: 19C. Var. of *jubba* (16C), from Arabic. Cp. JUMPER¹.

jibe v.i. to agree, accord (with). WH: 19C. Orig. unknown.

jiff n. a moment, an instant, an extremely short time. WH: 18C. Orig. unknown.

Jiffy bag® n. a padded envelope. WH: mid-20C. *jiffy* (JIFF) + BAG.

jig n. a lively dance for one or more performers. Also v.i., v.t. WH: 16C. Orig. unknown. Cp. GIGUE.

jigger¹ n. a small tackle used for holding on to the cable as it is heaved in, and similar work. WH: 16C. JIG + -ER¹.

jigger² n. the flea *Tunga penetrans*, a chigger. WH: 18C. Alt. of CHIGOE.

jiggered a. very surprised, confounded. WH: 19C. P.p. of *jigger*, from JIG, JIGGER¹, prob. influ. by *buggered* (BUGGER).

jiggery-pokery n. underhand goings-on. WH: 19C. Appar. alt. of Scottish *joukery-pawkery*, from dial. *jouk* to bend oneself, to dodge, to duck, of uncertain orig. (? rel. to DUCK²).

jiggle v.t. to jerk or rock lightly to and fro. Also v.i., n. WH: 19C. Partly from JIG + -LE⁴, partly alt. of JOGGLE.

jig-jog n. a jogging, jolting motion. WH: 17C. Imit. Cp. JIG, JOG.

jihad n. a holy war proclaimed by Muslims against unbelievers or the enemies of Islam. WH: 19C. Arabic *jihād*, lit. effort.

jillaroo n. a female newcomer or novice. WH: mid-20C. Female forename *Jill* + -*aroo*, based on JACKAROO.

jilt v.t. to throw over or discard (one's lover). Also v.i., n. WH: 17C. Orig. unknown. ? Rel. to female forename *Gillian*. Cp. Scottish *jillet* frivolous young woman, wench.

Jim Crow n. a black person. WH: 19C. Name of black character in plantation song.

jiminy n.pl. meteoric bodies radiating, usu. in early December, from the constellation Gemini. WH: 19C. Alt. of GEMINI, euphem. used for JESUS.

jim-jams¹ n.pl. delirium tremens. WH: 16C. Fanciful redupl. Cp. FLIMFLAM, *whim-wham* (WHIM).

jim-jams² n.pl. pyjamas. WH: early 20C. Redupl. of second element of PYJAMAS.

Jimmy n. an act of urination. WH: mid-20C. Rhyming slang, *Jimmy Riddle*, PIDDLE.

jimmy n. a short crowbar, a jemmy. WH: 19C. Alt. of JEMMY¹.

Jimmy Woodser n. a drink one pays for oneself. WH: 19C. *Jimmy Wood*, name of character in a poem by Barcroft Boake (1892). The poem has the line: 'Who drinks alone, drinks toast to Jimmy Wood, sir'. There may have been an actual person of the name.

jimson n. a poisonous weed, *Datura stramonium*, the thorn apple. WH: 17C. Alt. of *Jamestown*, a town in Virginia, USA.

jingle v.i. to make a clinking or tinkling sound like that of small bells, bits of metal etc. Also v.t., n. WH: 14–15C. Imit. Cp. JANGLE.

jingo n. a person given to (excessive) belligerent patriotism. Also a. WH: 17C. Orig. unknown. The sense of blustering patriot arose in the 19C from the phrase *by jingo* in a music hall song at the time of Disraeli's decision in 1878 to send a British fleet into Turkish waters to resist the advance of Russia. The two relevant lines ran: 'We don't want to fight; But, by Jingo! if we do, / We've got the ships, we've got the men, we've got the money too'.

jink v.i. to move nimbly. Also v.t., n. WH: 18C. Orig. uncertain. ? Imit.

jinker n. a sort of two-wheeled bogey for transporting heavy logs and timber. WH: 19C. Var. of Scottish dial. *janker* long pole on wheels for carrying logs, of unknown origin.

jinnee n. any of a race of spirits or demons in Muslim mythology supposed to have the power of assuming human or animal forms. WH: 19C. Arabic *jinnī* (m. sing), *jinn* (pl.). Cp. GENIE.

jinrickshaw n. a rickshaw. WH: 19C. Japanese *jin-riki-sha*, from *jin* man + *riki* strength, power + *sha* vehicle. Punsters equate the name with *Pullman car* (PULLMAN).

jinx n. a person or thing that brings ill luck. Also v.t. WH: early 20C. Prob. alt. of *jynx* wryneck, from Modern Latin *iynx*, Greek *iugx*.

jit n. a type of beat music that originated in Zimbabwe. WH: mid-20C. Orig. unknown.

jitney n. a small bus that carries passengers for a low fare, orig. five cents. WH: early 20C. Orig. unknown.

jitter v.i. to be nervous, behave in a nervous way. WH: early 20C. Orig. unknown. ? Alt. of CHITTER.

jive n. a style of lively, jazz-style music. Also v.i. WH: early 20C. Orig. unknown. Prob. of African orig.

jizz n. the characteristic features, appearance, behaviour etc. which distinguish a bird or other animal or plant from other species. WH: early 20C. Orig. unknown. ? Representation of second syl. of SPECIES.

jo n. one's sweetheart. WH: 16C. Scottish from of JOY.

joanna n. a piano. WH: 19C. Rhyming slang, female forename *Joanna*, PIANO¹.

Job n. an uncomplaining sufferer or victim. WH: 16C. *Job*, a patriarch who is the subject of the biblical book that bears his name. He was a wealthy and devout man who was visited with grim afflictions by God to demonstrate the strength of his piety. Although losing his wealth, his family and friends, and suffering a painful disease, he refused to 'curse God and die' (Job ii.9).

job[1] *n.* a piece of work, esp. one done for a stated price. *Also a., v.t., v.i.* WH: 16C. Orig. unknown. ? Var. of GOB[1].

job[2] *v.t.* to stab, poke or prod with a sharp instrument. *Also v.i., n.* WH: 16C. JOB[1].

jobbernowl *n.* a blockhead. WH: 16C. French *jobard*, from Old French *jobe* stupid, silly + NOLL.

Jock *n.* a soldier of a Scottish regiment. WH: 16C. Scottish form of JACK[1].

jock[1] *n.* a jockey. WH: 18C. Abbr. of JOCKEY.

jock[2] *n.* an athlete. WH: early 20C. Abbr. of JOCKSTRAP.

jockey *n.* a professional rider in horse races. *Also v.t., v.i.* WH: 16C. Dim. of pet form of JOCK[1]. See also -Y[3]. The original sense was horse dealer, cheat. The current sense dates from the 17C.

jocko *n.* a chimpanzee. WH: 18C. Bantu. Cp. *còkó* a kind of monkey. Assim. to JOCK[1] + -O.

jockstrap *n.* a support for the genitals worn by men engaged in athletic or sporting activity. WH: 19C. From *jock* the genitals, of unknown orig. + STRAP.

jocose *a.* humorous, facetious. WH: 17C. Latin *iocosus*, from *iocus* JOKE. See also -OSE[1].

jocular *a.* addicted to jesting. WH: 17C. Latin *iocularis*, from *ioculus*, dim. of *iocus* JOKE. See also -AR[1].

jocund *a.* sportive, merry. WH: 14–15C. Old French *jocond*, from Latin *iocundus*, var. of *iucundus* pleasant, agreeable, assoc. with *iocus* JOKE.

jodhpurs *n.pl.* long riding-breeches fitting closely from the knee to the ankle. WH: 19C. *Jodhpur*, a town and district in NW India.

joe *n.* a fourpenny or threepenny bit. WH: 19C. *Joseph* Hume, 1777–1855, English politician and financial expert. See also -Y[3].

Joe Bloggs *n.* a typical or ordinary person. WH: mid-20C. Arbitrary nickname.

joey *n.* a young kangaroo. WH: 19C. Australian Aboriginal *joè*.

jog *v.t.* to push or jerk lightly, usu. with the hand or elbow. *Also v.i., n.* WH: 14–15C. Var. of JAG[1].

joggle *v.t.* to shake, push, nudge or jerk slightly. *Also v.i., n.* WH: 16C. Dim. or freq. of JOG. See also -LE[4].

Johannisberger *n.* a white Rhine wine. WH: 19C. German, from *Johannisberg*, a vineyard near Wiesbaden, W Germany.

john *n.* a lavatory. WH: 14–15C. Male forename *John*. Cp. JACK[1] and (prob.) rel. *jakes* (16C) lavatory.

johnny *n.* a condom. WH: 17C. Dim. of JOHN. See also -Y[3].

Johnsonian *a.* of or relating to Dr Samuel Johnson. WH: 18C. Dr Samuel *Johnson*, 1709–84, English man of letters and lexicographer + -IAN.

joie de vivre *n.* joy of living; exuberance. WH: 19C. French joy of living. See JOY, VIVID. Cp. German *Lebenslust*.

join *v.t.* to connect, to fasten together, to unite. *Also v.i., n.* WH: 12–14C. Old French *joindre*, *joign-*, from Latin *iungere*, from Indo-European base represented also by YOKE.

joint *n.* a junction or mode of joining parts together. *Also a., v.t.* WH: 14–15C. Old French, use as n. of p.p. of *joindre*. See JOIN.

joist *n.* any of a series of parallel horizontal timbers to which floor-boards or the laths of a ceiling are nailed. *Also v.t.* WH: 14–15C. Old French *giste* beam supporting a bridge (Modern French *gîte*), from neut. p.p. of Latin *iacere* to lie down. Cp. GIST.

jojoba *n.* a desert shrub, *Simmondsia chinensis*, native to Arizona, Mexico and California, whose edible seeds provide waxy oil similar to spermaceti, used in cosmetics, toiletries etc. WH: early 20C. Mexican Spanish, from native Indonesian *hohohwi*.

joke *n.* something said or done to excite laughter or merriment. *Also v.i., v.t.* WH: 17C. Prob. from Latin *iocus* jest, wordplay.

jolie laide *n.* a fascinating ugly woman. WH: 19C. French, from *jolie* pretty + *laide* ugly (fem. aa.).

jolly[1] *a.* happy and cheerful. *Also adv., v.i., v.t., n.* WH: 12–14C. Old French *jolif* (Modern French *joli*), orig. merry, pleasant, then pretty, ? from Old Norse *jól* midwinter festival, YULE. See also -Y[1].

jolly[2] *n.* a small boat for the general work of a ship. WH: 17C. Orig. uncertain. ? rel. to YAWL[1].

jolt *v.t.* to shake with sharp, sudden jerks, as in a vehicle along a rough road. *Also v.i., n.* WH: 16C. Orig. unknown.

Jonah *n.* a bringer of bad luck. WH: 16C. *Jonah*, a Hebrew prophet, the subject of a biblical book named after him. He is thrown overboard by his shipmates in a storm that they attribute to him (Jonah i.15).

Jonathan *n.* the American people collectively. WH: 18C. Male forename. The reference is probably to *Jonathan* Trumbull, 1710–85, Governor of Connecticut, called Brother Jonathan by George Washington when turning to him for advice (cp. II Sam. i.26).

jongleur *n.* an itinerant minstrel or reciter of the Middle Ages, esp. in N France. WH: 18C. French, alt. of *jougleur*, from Latin *ioculator* jester. See JUGGLE.

jonquil *n.* a narcissus, *Narcissus jonquilla*, with two to six yellow or white flowers on a stem. WH: 17C. Modern Latin *jonquilla*, or from French *jonquille*, from Spanish *junquillo*, dim. of *junco*, from Latin *iuncus* rush, reed.

Jordanian *n.* a native or inhabitant of Jordan. *Also a.* WH: mid-20C. *Jordan*, a kingdom in the Middle East, also a river running into the Dead Sea + -IAN.

jorum *n.* a large bowl or drinking vessel. WH: 18C. ? From *Joram*, a son of King Toi of Hamath in the Old Testament. 'Joram brought with him vessels of silver, and vessels of gold, and vessels of brass' (II Sam. viii.10).

Joseph *n.* a man of invincible chastity. WH: 16C. Male forename *Joseph*. The reference is to the Old Testament patriarch, the son of Jacob and Rachel (Gen. xxx.23).

josh *v.t.* to make fun of, to ridicule. *Also v.i., n.* WH: 19C. Orig. unknown.

Joshua tree *n.* a yucca, *Yucca brevifolia*, with sword-shaped leaves and greenish-white flowers, of the south-western US. WH: 19C. *Joshua*, prophet and leader of the Israelites, whose story is told in the biblical book named after him. The tree name has a specific reference: 'And Joshua stretched out the spear that he had in his hand' (Josh. viii.18). The branching shape of the tree resembles a man brandishing a spear.

joskin *n.* a bumpkin, a yokel. WH: 18C. Orig. unknown. Cp. BUMPKIN.

joss *n.* a Chinese idol. WH: 18C. ? Ult. from obs. Portuguese *deos*, from Latin *deus* god.

jostle *v.t.* to push against, to hustle. *Also v.i., n.* WH: 14–15C. Obs. *just*, var. of JOUST + -LE[4].

jot *n.* a tittle, an iota. *Also v.t.* WH: 15C. Latin *iota*, from Greek *iōta* IOTA.

joule *n.* the SI unit of work and energy, equal to the work done when a force of 1 newton advances its point of application 1 metre. WH: 19C. James Prescott *Joule*, 1818–89, English physicist.

jounce *v.t., v.i.* to jolt or shake. *Also n.* WH: 14–15C. Prob. imit. Cp. FLOUNCE[1].

journal *n.* a record of events or news; any newspaper or other periodical published at regular intervals. WH: 14–15C. Old French *jurnal* (Modern French *journal*), use as n. of a. *journal*, from Late Latin *diurnalis* DIURNAL. Cp. DIARY.

journey *n.* passage or travel from one place to another, esp. by land or at a long distance. *Also v.i.* WH: 12–14C. Old French *jornee* (Modern French *journée* day), from var. of Latin *diurnum* daily portion, use as n. of neut. of *diurnus* DIURNAL. The original sense was day, also (to the 16C) distance that can be travelled in a day, hence travel in general.

joust *v.i.* to tilt, to encounter on horseback with lances. *Also n.* WH: 12–14C. Old French *juster* (Modern French *jouter*) to bring together, to engage on horseback, from Latin *iuxta* near together.

Jove *n.* Jupiter, the chief of the Roman divinities. WH: 14–15C. Latin *Jov-*, stem of oblique cases of JUPITER.

jowl *n.* the (lower) jaw. *Also v.t.* WH: pre-1200. Old English *ceafl*, from Germanic. The sense throat or neck of a double-chinned person comes from Old English *ceole*, from Germanic. Cp. German *Kehle*.

joy *n.* the emotion produced by gratified desire, success, happy fortune etc.; gladness, happiness, delight. *Also v.i., v.t.* WH: 12–14C. Old French *joie*, from Latin *gaudia*, pl. of *gaudium*, from *gaudere* to rejoice. Cp. GAUDY[2].

Joycean *a.* of or characteristic of James Joyce. *Also n.* WH: early 20C. James *Joyce*, 1882–1941, Irish writer + -AN.

juba[1] *n.* a mane, as of a horse. WH: 17C. Latin.

juba[2] *n.* a characteristic dance developed by black people in the southern US. WH: 19C. Orig. unknown.

jube[1] *n.* a rood-loft or gallery dividing the choir from the nave. WH: 18C. French *jubé*, from Latin *iube*, imper. of *iubere* to bid, to order. The Latin word is the first word of the formula *Jube, domine, benedicere* Sir, bid a blessing, addressed by a deacon to a priest before the reading of the Gospel, which in some churches was done in the rood-loft.

jube[2] *n.* a jujube. WH: mid-20C. Abbr. of JUJUBE.

jubilant *a.* exultant, rejoicing, shouting for joy. WH: 17C. Latin *iubilans, iubilantis*, pres.p. of *iubilare* JUBILATE[1]. See also -ANT.

jubilate[1] *v.i.* to exult. WH: 17C. Latin *iubilatus*, p.p. of *iubilare* to call, to shout for joy. See also -ATE[3].

jubilate[2] *n.* the 100th Psalm used as a canticle in the morning service of the Church of England, from its Latin commencing words *Jubilate Deo*. WH: 12–14C. Latin shout for joy!, imper. of *iubilare* (JUBILATE[1]). More fully, as the opening words of Psalm 100, *Jubilate Deo*, translated in the Prayer Book as 'O be joyful in the Lord' and in the Bible as 'Make a joyful noise unto the Lord'.

jubilee *n.* a season of great public rejoicing or festivity. WH: 14–15C. Old French *jubilé*, from Ecclesiastical Latin *iubilaeus* (*annus*) jubilee (year) (with assim. to *iubilare* JUBILATE[1]), from Ecclesiastical Greek *iōbēlaios*, from *iōbēlos*, from Hebrew *yōbēl* jubilee, orig. ram, (hence) ram's horn (with which the jubilee year was proclaimed).

Judaeo- *comb. form* of or relating to the Jews or Judaism. WH: Latin *Iudaeus* Judaean, Jewish. See JEW, also -O-.

Judaic *a.* of or relating to the Jews, Jewish. WH: 17C. Latin *Iudaicus*, from Greek *Ioudaïkos*, from *Ioudaios* JEW. See also -AL[1].

Judas *n.* a traitor. WH: 14–15C. *Judas* Iscariot, the disciple who betrayed Jesus to the religious authorities for thirty pieces of silver (Matt. xxxvi.15).

judder *v.i.* to wobble. *Also n.* WH: mid-20C. Imit. Cp. SHUDDER.

judge *n.* a civil officer invested with power to hear and determine causes in a court of justice. *Also v.t., v.i.* WH: 12–14C. Old French *juge*, from Latin *iudex, iudicis*, from *ius* right, law + -*dicus* saying, speaking.

judicature *n.* the administration of justice by trial and judgement. WH: 16C. Medieval Latin *iudicatura*, from Latin *iudicatus*, p.p. of *iudicare* JUDGE. See also -URE.

judicial *a.* of, relating to or proper to courts of law or the administration of justice. WH: 14–15C. Latin *iudicialis*, from *iudicium* legal proceedings, judgement, from *iudex, iudicis* JUDGE. See also -IAL.

judicium Dei *n.* the judgement of God. WH: 17C. Latin judgement of God, from *iudicium* (JUDICIAL) + gen. of *Deus* God.

judo *n.* a modern sport derived from a form of ju-jitsu. WH: 19C. Japanese *jū* gentle + *dō* way. Cp. JU-JITSU.

Judy *n.* Punch's wife in the Punch and Judy show. WH: 19C. Pet form of female forename *Judith*.

jug[1] *n.* a vessel, usu. with a swelling body, narrow neck, and handle, for holding liquids. *Also v.t.* WH: 16C. Prob. from *Jug*, pet form of female forename *Joan, Joanna* or *Judith*.

jug[2] *v.i.* (of the nightingale etc.) to make a sound like 'jug'. WH: 16C. Imit.

jugal *a.* of or relating to the cheekbone. WH: 16C. Latin *iugalis*, from *iugum* YOKE. See also -AL[1].

jugate *a.* having leaflets in pairs. WH: 19C. Latin *iugatus*, p.p. of *iugare* to join together. See also -ATE[3].

Jugendstil *n.* art nouveau in Germany, Austria etc. WH: early 20C. German, from *Jugend* youth + *Stil* style. *Jugend* was a German satirical magazine, first published in 1896, in which the designs appeared.

juggernaut *n.* a very large articulated lorry (causing damage to the environment). WH: 17C. Sanskrit *Jagannātha*, from *jagat* world + *nātha* lord, protector, a title of the Hindu god Krishna, whose image was carried in an enormous wagon or cart in an annual procession at Puri in E India. Many of Krishna's devotees are said to have sacrificed themselves by being crushed beneath the wheels of the cart as it passed.

juggins *n.* a blockhead, a dolt. WH: 19C. ? From surname *Juggins*, influ. by MUGGINS.

juggle *v.i.* to play tricks by sleight of hand, to conjure. *Also v.t., n.* WH: 14–15C. Back-formation from *juggler* (JONGLEUR), or from Old French *jogler*, from Latin *ioculari* to jest, from *ioculus*, dim. of *iocus* JOKE. The original sense was to entertain with jesting, buffoonery, etc. The current sense to toss and catch objects dates from the 19C.

jugular *a.* belonging to the neck or throat. *Also n.* WH: 16C. Late Latin *iugularis*, from Latin *iugulum* collarbone, throat, dim. of *iugum* YOKE. See also -AR[1].

juice *n.* the watery part of fruits etc. or the fluid part of animal bodies. WH: 12–14C. Old French *jus*, from Latin *ius* broth, sauce, vegetable juice.

ju-jitsu *n.* the Japanese art of wrestling, based on the principle of making one's opponent exert their strength to their own disadvantage. WH: 19C. Japanese *jūjutsu*, from *jū* gentle + *jutsu* skill. Cp. JUDO.

ju-ju *n.* a fetish, an idol credited with supernatural power. WH: 17C. W African, prob. from French *joujou* plaything, redupl. formation from *jouer* to play, from Latin *iocare*.

jujube *n.* the berry-like fruit of *Zizyphus vulgaris* or *Z. jujuba*, spiny shrubs of the buckthorn family, dried as a sweetmeat. WH: 14–15C. French, or from Medieval Latin *iuiuba*, ult. from Latin *zisyphum*, from Greek *zizuphos*.

jukebox *n.* an automatic record or disc player, usu. in a public place, in which coins are inserted and buttons pressed to select the relevant tunes. WH: mid-20C. From *juke* roadhouse (prob. from Gullah *juke* disorderly, wicked, of W African orig.) + BOX[1].

julep *n.* a sweet drink, esp. a preparation with some liquid used as a vehicle for medicine. WH: 14–15C. Old French, or from Medieval Latin *iulapium*, from Arabic *julāb*, from Persian *gulāb* rose water, from *gul* rose + *āb* water.

Julian *a.* of, relating to or originated by Julius Caesar. WH: 16C. Latin *Iulianus*, from *Iulius*, Gaius *Julius* Caesar, d.44 BC, Roman statesman. See also -AN.

julienne *n.* a clear soup made from meat with chopped or shredded vegetables. WH: 18C. French, from male forename *Jules* or *Julien*. The identity of the man of this name is unknown.

Juliet cap *n.* a small close-fitting cap worn esp. by brides. WH: early 20C. *Juliet*, heroine of Shakespeare's play *Romeo and Juliet* (1595) + CAP. A cap of this type is a traditional part of Juliet's costume.

July *n.* the seventh month of the year. WH: 12–14C. Anglo-French *julie*, from Latin *Iulius* of Julius. See JULIAN. The name is that of Julius Caesar, who was born in this month (earlier called *Quintilis* fifth).

jumble *v.t.* to mix confusedly. *Also v.i., n.* WH: 16C. Appar. imit. base + -LE[4].

jumbo *n.* a huge, unwieldy person, animal or thing, esp. a large elephant. *Also a.* WH: 19C. Prob. second element of MUMBO-JUMBO. The word was popularized by an elephant of this name, acquired by the London Zoo in 1865 and sold to P.T. Barnum's circus in 1882.

jumbuck *n.* a sheep. WH: 19C. Orig. unknown.

jumelle *a.* twin, paired. *Also n.* WH: 15C. French, fem. of *jumeau* twin, from Latin *gemellus*, dim. of *geminus*. Cp. GEMINI.

jump *v.i.* to throw oneself from the ground or other base by a sudden movement of the muscles of the legs and feet. *Also v.t., adv., n.* WH: 16C. Prob. imit. of sound of two feet landing. Cp. BUMP[1], THUMP.

jumper[1] *n.* a knitted or crocheted woollen upper garment. WH: mid-20C. Prob. from obs. *jump* man's short coat, woman's underbodice (alt. of *jupe* man's or woman's jacket, from Old French, from Arabic *jibba*) + -ER[1]. Cp. JUPON.

jumper[2] *n.* a person who, or animal or thing which jumps or leaps. WH: 17C. JUMP + -ER[1].

juncaceous *a.* of or resembling rushes. WH: 19C. Modern Latin *Juncaceae*, from Latin *iuncus* rush + -OUS. See also -ACEOUS.

junco *n.* any small American bunting of the genus *Junco*, which has a greyish plumage. WH: 18C. Spanish, from Latin *iuncus* rush.

junction *n.* the act of joining or the state of being joined, a combination. WH: 18C. Latin *iunctio, iunctionis*, from *iunctus*, p.p. of *iungere* JOIN. See also -ION.

juncture *n.* a junction, a union. WH: 14–15C. Latin *iunctura* joint, from *iunctus*. See JUNCTION, -URE.

June *n.* the sixth month of the year. WH: 12–14C. Old French *juin*, from Latin *Iunius*, var. of *Iunonius* sacred to JUNO.

Jungian *a.* of or relating to the psychoanalytical system of Carl Jung. *Also n.* WH: mid-20C. Carl Gustav *Jung*, 1875–1961, Swiss leader of the school of analytic psychology + -IAN.

jungle *n.* land covered with forest trees or dense, matted vegetation. WH: 18C. Hindi *jaṅgal*, from Sanskrit *jāṅgala* rough and arid (of terrain).

junior *a.* the younger (esp. as distinguishing a son from his father of the same name, or two of the same surname). *Also n.* WH: 12–14C. Latin, comp. of *iuvenis* young. See -IOR. Cp. SENIOR.

juniper *n.* any evergreen shrub or tree of the genus *Juniperus*, esp. *J. communis*, the berries of which are used to flavour gin. WH: 14–15C. Latin *iuniperus*, of unknown orig.

junk[1] *n.* rubbish, valueless odds and ends. *Also v.t.* WH: 14–15C. Orig. unknown. ? Rel. to French *junc* rush (cp. JUNKET). The original sense (to the 18C) was old rope. The current sense of rubbish dates from the 19C.

junk[2] *n.* a flat-bottomed vessel with lugsails, used in the Chinese seas. WH: 16C. Portuguese *junco*, or from obs. French *juncque* (now *jonque*), from Malay *jong*, partly also from Dutch *jonk*.

junk[3] *n.* a lump or chunk of anything. WH: 18C. JUNK[1].

junker *n.* a young German noble. WH: 16C. German, earlier *Junkherr*, from Middle High German *junc* YOUNG + *herre* (modern German *Herr*) lord, HERR. Cp. YOUNKER.

junket *n.* a dish of curds sweetened and flavoured, and served with cream. *Also v.i., v.t.* WH: 14–15C. Old French *jonquette*, from *jonc* rush, from Latin *iuncus*. The word originally denoted a type of cream cheese made in a rush basket or served on a rush mat. The sense feast, banquet dates from the 16C.

Juno *n.* a beautiful queenly woman. WH: 17C. Latin *Iuno*, the Roman goddess of marriage and childbirth, the wife of Jupiter. Cp. JUNE. Juno was later identified by the Greeks with Hera, the wife of Zeus.

junta *n.* a group, esp. of military officers who take control of a country e.g. after a coup. WH: 17C. Spanish and Portuguese, from Italian *giunta*, from Latin *iuncta*, fem. p.p. of *iungere* JOIN.

junto *n.* a secret political or other council. WH: 17C. Alt. of JUNTA, based on Spanish nn. in -O.

jupati palm *n.* a S American palm, *Raphia taedigera*, yielding a fibre resembling raffia. WH: 19C. Portuguese, from Tupi-Guarani *yupáti* + PALM[1].

Jupiter *n.* the largest planet of the solar system, the fifth from the sun. WH: 12–14C. Latin, from *Iovis-pater*, lit. JOVE Father, corr. to Sanskrit *dyauṣpitṛ* heaven father.

jupon *n.* a skirt or petticoat. WH: 14–15C. Old French *juppon* (Modern French *jupon*), from *jupe*. See JUMPER[1], also -OON.

jural *a.* of or relating to law or jurisprudence, esp. with regard to rights and obligations. WH: 17C. Latin *ius, iuris* right, law + -AL[1].

Jurassic *a.* belonging to the oolitic limestone formation well developed in the Jura Mts. *Also n.* WH: 19C. French *Jurassique*, from *Jura*, a range of mountains on the border between France and Switzerland, based on *Liassic* (LIAS), *Triassic* (TRIAS).

jurat[1] *n.* a person under oath. WH: 14–15C. Medieval Latin *iuratus*, lit. sworn man, m. p.p. (used as n.) of Latin *iurare* to swear.

jurat[2] *n.* an official statement of the circumstances in which an affidavit is made. WH: 18C. Latin *iuratum*, neut. p.p. (used as n.) of *iurare* to swear.

juridical *a.* of or relating to the administration of justice, to courts of justice, or to jurisprudence. WH: 16C. Latin *iuridicus*, from *ius, iuris* right, law + -*dicus* saying, speaking, from *dicere* to say. See also -IC, -AL[1].

jurisconsult *n.* a person learned in law, esp. civil or international law. WH: 17C. Latin *iurisconsultus*, from *iuris*, gen. of *ius* right, law + *consultus* skilled (CONSULT).

jurisdiction *n.* the legal power or right of administering justice, making and enforcing laws, or exercising other authority. WH: 12–14C. Old French *jurediction* (Modern French *juridiction*), from Latin *iurisdictio, iurisdictionis*, from *iuris*, gen. of *ius* right, law + *dictio, dictionis* (DICTION).

jurisprudence *n.* the science or philosophy of law. WH: 17C. Late Latin *iurisprudentia*, from *iuris*, gen. of *ius* right, law + *prudentia* skill, proficiency.

jurist *n.* a person learned in the law. WH: 15C. French *juriste* or Medieval Latin *iurista*, from Latin *ius, iuris* right, law. See also -IST.

juror *n.* a person who serves on a jury. WH: 14–15C. Old French *jureor* (Modern French *jureur*), from Latin *iuratus*, p.p. of *iurare* to swear, from *ius, iuris* right, law. See also -OR.

jury *n.* a body of persons selected according to law and sworn to try, and give a true verdict upon, questions put before them. WH: 14–15C. Old French *juree* oath, from Anglo-Latin *iurata*, fem. p.p. (used as n.) of Latin *iurare* to swear, from *ius, iuris* right, law.

jury- *comb. form* makeshift, temporary. WH: 17C. Prob. ult. from Old French *ajurie* aid, from *aju-*, pres.p. stem of *aidier* AID + -*rie* -RY.

jussive *a.* expressing command. *Also n.* WH: 19C. Latin *iussus*, p.p. of *iubere* to command + -IVE. Cp. IMPERATIVE.

just *a.* acting according to what is right and fair. *Also adv.* WH: 14–15C. Old French *juste*, from Latin *iustus*, from *ius* right, law.

justice *n.* the quality of being just. WH: pre-1200. Old French, from Latin *iustitia*, from *iustus* JUST. See also -ICE.

justify *v.t.* to prove or show to be just or right. *Also v.i.* WH: 12–14C. Old French *justifier*, from Ecclesiastical Latin *iustificare* to do justice to, to vindicate, from Latin *iustus* JUST. See also -FY. The original sense (to the 17C) was to administer justice, to rule. The current sense dates from the 16C.

jut *v.i.* to project, to protrude, to stick (out). *Also n.* WH: 16C. Var. of JET[2], by assim. to obs. *jutty*, itself var. of JETTY[1].

Jute *n.* a member of a Germanic people orig. from Jutland, who settled in southern Britain in the 5th–6th cents. WH: pre-1200. Old English *Eotas*, *Iotas* (pl.). Cp. Icelandic *Jótar* people of Jutland (Old Norse *Jótland*), region of Denmark. The Old English name was subsequently altered under the influence of Medieval Latin *Jutae* or *Juti*.

jute *n.* the fibre from the inner bark of two Asian plants, *Corchorus capsularis* and *C. olitorius*, from which fabrics, paper and cordage are prepared. WH: 18C. Bengali *jhuṭo*, from Prakrit *juṣṭi*.

juvenescent *a.* growing or being young. WH: 19C. Latin *iuvenescens, iuvenescentis*, pres.p. of *iuvenescere* to reach the age of youth. See -escent (-ESCENCE).

juvenile *a.* young, youthful. *Also n.* WH: 17C. Latin *iuvenilis*, from *iuvenis* (a) young (person). See also -IL.

juxtapose *v.t.* to place (things) side by side. WH: 19C. French *juxtaposer*, from Latin *iuxta* near to, by the side of + French *poser* POSE[1].

K *chem. symbol* potassium. WH: Abbr. of Latin *kalium*.

ka *n.* the spirit of a person or statue in ancient Egyptian mythology, born with but surviving the individual. WH: 19C. Ancient Egyptian.

Kaaba *n.* a sacred building in Mecca, containing the black stone, which Muslims face when they pray. WH: 17C. Arabic (*al*) *ka'ba*, lit. the square house.

kaama *n.* the hartebeest. WH: 19C. Nama.

kabuki *n.* a highly-stylized, traditional and popular form of Japanese drama, based on legend and acted only by men, in elaborate costumes. WH: 19C. Japanese, orig. (as v.) to act dissolutely, but later interpreted as from *ka* song + *bu* dance + *ki* art, skill.

Kabyle *n.* a member of an agricultural branch of the Berber people inhabiting the highlands of Algeria and Tunisia. WH: 18C. Prob. from Arabic *ḳabā'il*, pl. of *ḳabīla* tribe.

kachina *n.* any of the spirits of the ancestors of the Pueblo Indians. WH: 19C. Hopi *kacina* supernatural, from Keresan.

Kaddish *n.* a form of thanksgiving and prayer used by the Jews, esp. in mourning. WH: 17C. Aramaic *qaddīš* holy.

Kaffir *n.* a member of the S African Xhosa-speaking people. *Also a.* WH: 16C. Arabic *kāfir* unbeliever, from active p. of *kafara* to be unbelieving.

Kafir *n.* a native of Kafiristan in E Afghanistan. WH: 19C. KAFFIR.

Kafkaesque *a.* of or like the ideas and work of Kafka, esp. his ideas on the alienation of man. WH: mid-20C. Franz *Kafka*, 1883–1924, Czech writer + -ESQUE.

kaftan *n.* a long belted tunic worn in the East. WH: 16C. Turkish, from Persian *ḳaftān*.

kahawai *n.* a large marine perch, *Arripis trutta*, that resembles a salmon, found in Australian and New Zealand coastal waters. WH: 19C. Maori.

kai *n.* food. WH: 19C. Maori.

kainite *n.* hydrous chlorosulphate of magnesium and potassium, used as a fertilizer. WH: 19C. German *Kainit*, from Greek *kainos* new, recent. See also -ITE[1]. The mineral was named in 1865 by the German mineralogist C.F. Zincken, with regard to its recent formation.

kaiser *n.* an emperor. WH: pre-1200. Old English *cāsere*, from Germanic, from Greek *kaisar*, from Latin CAESAR. Cp. TSAR. In modern use, referring to Austrian or German emperors, the immediate source is German *Kaiser*.

kaizen *n.* the concept of constant improvement in Japanese business and industry. WH: late 20C. Japanese improvement, from *kai* revision, change + *zen* (the) good.

kajawah *n.* a pannier or frame carried in pairs on a camel, horse or mule, used as a litter by women and children in some Eastern countries. WH: 17C. Urdu *kajāwah*.

kaka *n.* a New Zealand parrot of the genus *Nestor*. WH: 18C. Maori.

kakemono *n.* a Japanese wall-picture mounted on rollers for putting away. WH: 19C. Japanese, from *kake-* to hang + *mono* thing.

kaki *n.* an Asian persimmon, *Diospyros kaki*. WH: 18C. Japanese.

kakistocracy *n.* government by the worst citizens. WH: 19C. Greek *kakistos* worst + -CRACY, based on ARISTOCRACY.

kala-azar *n.* a chronic tropical disease with a high mortality, caused by a protozoan *Leishmania donovani*. WH: 19C. Assamese, from *kālā* black + *āzār* disease.

kalanchoe *n.* a succulent plant of the genus *Kalanchoe*, often grown indoors or in a greenhouse, with pink, red or yellow flowers. WH: 19C. Modern Latin, from French, ult. from Chinese *gāláncài*.

Kalashnikov *n.* a type of sub-machine gun made in Russia. WH: late 20C. Mikhail T. *Kalashnikov*, 1919–, Russian weapons designer.

kale *n.* a variety of cabbage with crinkled leaves. WH: 12–14C. Northern form of COLE.

kaleidophone *n.* an instrument for exhibiting the character of sound waves by means of a vibrating bar or plate armed with a reflector. WH: 19C. KALEIDOSCOPE + -PHONE[1].

kaleidoscope *n.* an instrument showing by means of bits of coloured glass, paper etc. and a series of reflecting surfaces, an endless variety of symmetrical forms. WH: 19C. Greek *kalos* beautiful + *eidos* form + -SCOPE. The instrument was named in 1817 by its inventor, the Scottish physicist Sir David Brewster.

kali *n.* a glasswort, *Salsola kali*, from which soda ash was obtained. WH: 16C. Coll. Arabic *ḳalī* calcined ashes of Salsola, etc. Cp. ALKALI.

kalian *n.* an Iranian form of hookah. WH: 19C. Persian *ḳalyān*, from Arabic *ġalayān*.

kalmia *n.* an evergreen N American flowering shrub of the genus *Kalmia*. WH: 18C. Modern Latin, from Pehr *Kalm*, 1716–79, Swedish botanist + -IA.

Kalmuck *n.* a member of a Mongolian people living in a region extending from W China to the Volga. *Also a.* WH: 17C. Russian *kalmyk*.

kalong *n.* a flying fox, *Pteropus edulis*. WH: 19C. Javanese.

kalpa *n.* a day of Brahma, or a period of 4,320,000 years, constituting the age or cycle of a world. WH: 18C. Sanskrit.

Kama *n.* the god of love in the puranas. WH: 19C. Sanskrit *kāma* love, desire.

kamala *n.* an Indian and SE Asian tree, *Mallotus philippinensis*, of the the spurge family. WH: 19C. Sanskrit, prob. of Dravidian orig.

kame *n.* a long mound of glacial detritus, an esker. WH: 14–15C. Var. of COMB.

kameez *n.* a type of loose tunic with tight sleeves worn esp. by Muslim women in the Indian subcontinent and S Asia. WH: 19C. Arabic *ḳamīṣ*, ? from Late Latin *camisia*. See CHEMISE.

kamerad *int.* comrade, a German form of surrender or appeal for quarter. *Also v.i.* WH: early 20C. German, lit. friend, from French *camerade*, *camarade*. See COMRADE.

kami *n.* a Japanese title, equivalent to lord, given to nobles, ministers, governors etc. WH: 17C. Japanese.

kamikaze *n.* a Japanese airman or plane performing a suicidal mission in World War II. *Also a.* WH: 19C. Japanese divine wind, from KAMI + *kaze* wind. In Japanese tradition, the original 'divine wind' was the gale that destroyed the fleet of invading Mongols in 1281.

kampong *n.* a Malay village. WH: 18C. See COMPOUND[3].

Kampuchean *n.* a native or inhabitant of Kampuchea, a Cambodian. *Also a.* WH: late 20C. *Kampuchea*, Khmer name of Cambodia (CAMBODIAN) + -AN. Kampuchea was the official name of Cambodia from 1975 to 1989.

kana *n.* a Japanese syllabic system of writing. WH: 18C. Japanese. Cp. HIRAGANA, KATAKANA.

kanaka *n.* an indigenous Hawaiian. WH: 19C. Hawaiian person, human being.

Kanarese *n.* a member of the Dravidian people living largely in Kanara. *Also a.* WH: 19C. *Kanara*, a district in SW India + -ESE.

kanban *n.* the Japanese system of printing orders on cards during manufacturing processes. WH: late 20C. Japanese billboard, sign.

kanga *n.* a piece of brightly coloured cotton worn as a woman's dress in E Africa. WH: mid-20C. Kiswahili.

kangaroo *n.* any of several marsupial quadrupeds of the genus *Macropus*, native to Australia, Tasmania, New Guinea and adjacent islands, distinguished by their large hind limbs, used for leaping, and short front limbs. *Also v.i.* WH: 18C. Australian Aboriginal (Guugu Yimidhirr) *gangurru*.

kanji *n.* a script for representing Japanese syllables derived from Chinese orthography. WH: early 20C. Japanese *kan* Chinese + *ji* letter, character.

Kannada *n.* the Kanarese language. WH: 19C. Kannada *Kannaḍa*.

kanoon *n.* a kind of dulcimer or zither with 50 or 60 strings. WH: 19C. Persian *ḵānūn*, from Arabic, ult. from Greek *kanōn*.

kantar *n.* an Oriental measure of weight, varying from 100 to 130 lb. (45.4–59.0 kg). WH: 16C. Arabic *ḳinṭār*, pl. *ḳanāṭīr*, from Latin *centenarius* centenary (CENTENARIAN). Cp. QUINTAL.

Kantian *a.* of or relating to the philosophy of Kant. Also *n.* WH: 18C. Immanuel *Kant*, 1724–1804, German philosopher + -IAN.

kantikoy *n.* a N American Indian ceremonial dance. WH: 17C. Delaware *kéntke:w*, lit. he dances.

kaolin *n.* a porcelain clay (also used medicinally as a poultice or internally) derived principally from the decomposition of feldspar, China clay. WH: 18C. French, from Chinese *gāolíng*, lit. high hill, a place in the Jiangxi province where it is found.

kaon *n.* an unstable type of meson, a K-meson. WH: mid-20C. *ka* (representing pronun. of letter *k*) + -ON.

kapellmeister *n.* the musical director of a choir, band or orchestra, esp. a German one. WH: 19C. German, from *Kapelle* court orchestra, from Medieval Latin *capella* CHAPEL + *Meister* master.

kapok *n.* a fine woolly or silky fibre enveloping the seeds of a tropical tree, *Ceiba pentandra*, used for stuffing cushions etc. WH: 18C. Malay *kapuk*.

Kaposi's sarcoma *n.* a type of skin cancer often found in people with Aids. WH: 19C. Moritz K. *Kaposi*, 1837–1902, Hungarian dermatologist.

kappa *n.* the tenth letter of the Greek alphabet (Κ, κ). WH: 14–15C. Greek.

kaput *a.* finished, done for, smashed up. WH: 19C. German *kaputt*, from French (*être*) *capot* (to be) without tricks (in piquet etc.). Cp. CAPOT.

karabiner *n.* a metal clip with a spring inside it, for attaching to a piton, used in mountaineering. WH: mid-20C. Abbr. of German *Karabinerhaken* spring hook. Cp. CARBINE, HOOK.

Karaite *n.* a member of a Jewish sect who hold by the literal inspiration of the Scriptures, rejecting rabbinical tradition. WH: 18C. Hebrew *Qārā'īm* scripturalists, from *qārā'* to read. See also -ITE[1].

karakul *n.* a breed of sheep from the Bukhara district of central Asia. WH: 19C. Russian *karakul'*, name of an oasis in Uzbekistan and of two lakes in Tajikistan.

karaoke *n.* a leisure activity in which members of an audience can sing solo with pre-recorded backing music. WH: late 20C. Japanese, from *kara* empty + *oke*, abbr. of *ōkesutora* orchestra. The orchestra is 'empty' until complemented by the singers.

karate *n.* a traditional Japanese martial art, based on blows and kicks. WH: mid-20C. Japanese, from *kara* empty + *te* hand. Karate is a form of unarmed combat.

Karen *n.* a member of a Thai people living in eastern and southern Burma (Myanmar). WH: 18C. Burmese *ka-reng* wild unclean man.

karma *n.* in Buddhism and Hinduism, the results of action, ethical causation as determining future existence, esp. the cumulative consequence of a person's acts in one stage of existence as controlling their destiny in the next. WH: 19C. Sanskrit *karman* action, effect, fate.

Karoo *n.* any of the waterless S African tablelands, esp. the Great and the Little Karoo in S Cape Province. WH: 18C. Nama dry.

kaross *n.* a traditional S African garment made of skins with the hair left on. WH: 18C. Afrikaans *karos*, ? from Nama *caro-s* skin blanket.

karri *n.* a W Australian timber tree, *Eucalyptus diversicolor*. WH: 19C. Australian Aboriginal (Nyungar).

karst *n.* the characteristic scenery of a limestone region with underground streams, caverns and potholes forming a drainage system. WH: 19C. German *der Karst*, a limestone plateau region in Slovenia, SE Europe.

kart *n.* a go-kart. WH: mid-20C. Abbr. of *go-kart* (GO[1]).

karyo- *comb. form* relating to the nucleus of an animal or vegetable cell. WH: Greek *karuon* nut. See also -O-.

karyogamy *n.* the fusion of cell nuclei in fertilization. WH: 19C. KARYO- + -GAMY.

karyokinesis *n.* the series of changes that take place in indirect or mitotic cell division. WH: 19C. KARYO- + KINESIS.

karyolymph *n.* the liquid part of a cell nucleus. WH: 19C. KARYO- + LYMPH.

karyoplasm *n.* the protoplasm in the nucleus of a cell. WH: 19C. KARYO- + *plasm* (PLASMA).

karyosome *n.* the nucleus of a cell. WH: 19C. KARYO- + -SOME[2].

karyotype *n.* the chromosomes of a cell. WH: early 20C. KARYO- + TYPE. The term was coined in 1924 by the Russian geneticist G.A. Levitsky.

kasbah *n.* the castle or fortress in a N African city. WH: 18C. French *casbah*, from Maghribi pronun. of Arabic *ḳaṣaba* fortress.

Kashmiri *n.* a native or inhabitant of Kashmir. Also *a.* WH: 19C. *Kashmir*, a territory (divided between India and Pakistan) in the W Himalayas + -I[3].

kashruth *n.* the state of being kosher. WH: early 20C. Hebrew legitimacy (in religion). See KOSHER.

kata *n.* a martial arts exercise consisting of a sequence of movements. WH: mid-20C. Japanese.

katabasis *n.* a military retreat. WH: 19C. Greek *kata* down + *basis* going.

katabatic *a.* (of wind) blowing downhill. WH: 19C. Greek *katabatikos*, from *katabainein* to go down. See -IC.

katakana *n.* an angular form of Japanese syllabary. WH: 18C. Japanese from *kata* side + KANA.

kathak *n.* a type of Indian classical dance involving mime. WH: mid-20C. Sanskrit *kathaka* professional storyteller, from *kathā* story.

kathakali *n.* a type of S Indian drama consisting of dance and mime. WH: early 20C. Malayalam *kathakaḷi*, from Sanskrit *kathā* story + Malayalam *kaḷi* play.

katharevusa *n.* a literary form of modern Greek, based on ancient Greek. WH: early 20C. Modern Greek *kathareuousa*, fem. of *kathareuōn*, pres.p. of Greek *kathareuein* to be pure, from *katharos* pure.

katipo *n.* a venomous spider found in New Zealand and Australia. WH: 19C. Maori.

katydid *n.* any of various large green grasshoppers of the genus *Microcentrum* and related genera, common in N America. WH: 18C. Imit. The word imitates the sound made by the male when rubbing its front wings together. It predates (but perhaps in some way influenced) the title of Susan Coolidge's popular children's novel *What Katy Did* (1872).

katzenjammer *n.* a hangover. WH: 19C. German, from *Katzen* (comb. form of *Katze* cat) + *Jammer* distress, wailing.

kauri *n.* a New Zealand coniferous forest tree, *Agathis australis*. WH: 19C. Maori.

kava *n.* a Polynesian shrub, *Piper methysticum*. WH: 18C. Tongan.

kawakawa *n.* an aromatic New Zealand shrub, *Macropiper excelsum*. WH: 19C. Hawaiian.

kayak *n.* the Eskimo (Inuit) and Alaskan canoe, made of sealskins stretched on a light wooden framework. Also *v.i.* WH: 18C. Eskimo (Inuit) *qayaq*. Cp. UMIAK.

kayo *n.* a knockout. Also *v.t.* WH: early 20C. Latin. Representation of pronun. of *KO*, abbr. of *knockout*.

Kazakh *n.* a member of a Turkic people inhabiting Kazakhstan. Also *a.* WH: 19C. Russian. See COSSACK.

kazoo *n.* a tube of metal or plastic with a membrane covering a hole in the side, through which a player sings or hums to produce sound. WH: 19C. Appar. imit. of sound produced. According to some, the word is an altered form of *bazoo*. See BAZOOKA.

kea *n.* a brownish green mountain parrot, *Nestor notabilis*, of New Zealand whose diet includes carrion. WH: 19C. Maori.

keb *v.i.* to cast a lamb prematurely or dead. Also *n.* WH: 14–15C. Orig. unknown.

kebab *n.* small pieces of meat, vegetables etc. cooked on skewers. WH: 17C. Arabic *kabāb*, ? ult. from Persian.

keck *v.i.* to retch, to heave. WH: 17C. Imit. Cp. COUGH.

ked *n.* a tick infesting sheep, esp. *Melophagus ovinus*. WH: 16C. Orig. unknown.

kedge *n.* a small portable anchor, used in warping. Also *v.t., v.i.* WH: 15C. ? Var. of CADGE.

kedgeree *n.* a stew of rice, pulse, onions, eggs etc., a common Indian dish. WH: 17C. Hindi *khichṛī*, from Sanskrit *khiccā* dish of boiled rice and sesame.

keek *v.i.* to peep, to pry. *Also n.* WH: 14–15C. ? Rel. to Middle Dutch and Low German *kīken* to look, to peep. Cp. PEEK.

keel[1] *n.* the principal timber or steel structure of a ship, extending from bow to stern and supporting the whole structure. *Also v.i., v.t.* WH: 12–14C. Old Norse *kjǫlr*, from Germanic.

keel[2] *n.* a lighter or flat-bottomed barge, esp. one of those used for loading colliers in the Tyne. WH: 12–14C. Middle Low German *kēl*, Middle Dutch *kiel* ship (modern Dutch *keel*), from Germanic. Despite the similarity in source and sense, the word is not related to KEEL[1].

keelie *n.* a kestrel. WH: 14–15C. ? From same source as GILLIE.

keelson *n.* a longitudinal piece placed along the floor-timbers of a ship binding them to the keel. WH: 12–14C. Rel. to (and prob. from) Low German *kielswīn*, from *kiel* KEEL[1] + (prob.) *swin* SWINE. The second element of the Low German word uses an animal name for a timber in the same way as *cat*, *dog*, *horse*, etc. in e.g. *cathead* (CAT[1]), *dogshore* (DOG).

keen[1] *a.* enthusiastic, eager, ardent. WH: pre-1200. Old English *cēne*, from Germanic. Cp. German *kühn* bold, brave. The original sense was (to the 17C) brave, daring.

keen[2] *n.* a wailing lamentation over the body of a dead person. *Also v.i., v.t.* WH: 19C. Irish *caoinim* I wail, I weep.

keep[1] *v.t.* to hold for a significant length of time, to retain. *Also v.i.* WH: pre-1200. Old English *cēpan*, of unknown orig. The original sense was to seize, to snatch, to take.

keep[2] *n.* subsistence, maintenance. WH: 12–14C. KEEP[1].

keeshond *n.* a Dutch breed of dog, with a heavy coat, pointed muzzle, and erect ears. WH: early 20C. Dutch *kees*, pet form of male forename *Cornelius* + *hond* dog.

kef *n.* the drowsy, dreamy, trancelike condition produced by the use of marijuana etc. WH: 19C. Arabic *kayf*.

keffiyeh *n.* a Bedouin Arab's kerchief headdress. WH: 19C. Arabic *kūffiyya*, *keffiyya*.

keg *n.* a small cask or barrel. WH: 17C. Var. of obs. *cag*, from Old Norse *kaggi*.

keister *n.* the buttocks. WH: 19C. Orig. unknown. According to some, the word is from German *Kiste* chest, box (cp. CIST[2]), referring either to the back pocket where a wallet, etc. may be kept or to the use of the rectum for concealing drugs, etc.

keloid *n.* a hard, pinkish growth of scar tissue, usu. occurring in dark-skinned people. WH: 19C. French *chéloïde*, from Greek *khēlē* claw of a crab. See also -OID.

kelp *n.* any large, coarse seaweed. WH: 14–15C. Orig. unknown.

kelpie *n.* a water-spirit usu. in the form of a horse, supposed to haunt fords, and to rejoice in the drowning of wayfarers. WH: 17C. ? Gaelic *cailpeach* bullock, colt. The Australian breed of sheepdog so called was apparently named in *c*.1870 after a particular bitch, *King's Kelpie*.

kelt *n.* a salmon or sea trout after spawning. WH: 12–14C. Orig. unknown.

kelvin *n.* the basic SI unit of temperature. WH: 19C. Sir William Thomson, Lord *Kelvin*, 1824–1907, British physicist and inventor.

kemp *n.* the coarse rough hairs of wool. WH: 14–15C. Old Norse *kampr* beard, moustache, whisker.

kempt *a.* (of hair) combed, neat. WH: pre-1200. P.p. of obs. *kemb* to comb, from Old English *cemban*, from Germanic base of COMB. Cp. UNKEMPT.

ken *n.* range of sight or knowledge, apprehension. *Also v.t., v.i.* WH: pre-1200. Old English *cennan* to make known, to declare, from Germanic, from Indo-European base also of CAN[1], KNOW. Cp. German *kennen* to know.

kenaf *n.* the fibre from an Asian hibiscus, used in ropes. WH: 19C. Persian, var. of *kanab* HEMP.

Kendal green *n.* green cloth, orig. made at Kendal for foresters. WH: 14–15C. *Kendal*, a town in Cumbria + GREEN.

kendo *n.* the Japanese martial art of fencing, usu. with pliable bamboo staves, occasionally with swords. WH: early 20C. Japanese, from *ken* sword + *dō* way.

kennel[1] *n.* a house or shelter for a dog or hounds. *Also v.i., v.t.* WH: 12–14C. Dial. Old French *kenil*, from Old French *chenil*, from Latin *canis* dog.

kennel[2] *n.* a gutter, the watercourse at the side of a street. WH: 16C. Var. of obs. *cannel*, from Old French *chanel*. Cp. CANAL, CHANNEL[1].

kenosis *n.* Christ's relinquishment of the divine nature at the Incarnation. WH: 19C. Greek *kenōsis* an emptying. The reference is to Phil. ii.7, where Paul says that Christ 'made himself of no reputation'. In the Revised Version, the original Greek words, *heauton ekonōse*, are translated 'emptied himself'.

kenspeckle *a.* conspicuous, easily recognized. WH: 16C. Dial. *kenspeck*, of Scandinavian orig. (cp. Norwegian *kjennespak* quick at recognizing, from Old Norse *kenna* KEN + *spak-* wise) + -LE[2].

Kentish *a.* of or relating to Kent. WH: pre-1200. Old English *Cent* Kent, a county in SE England, from Latin *Cantium*, from Celtic + -ISH[1].

kentledge *n.* pig-iron used for permanent ballast. WH: 17C. Old French *quintelage* ballast, assim. to *kentle*, obs. var. of QUINTAL. See also -AGE.

Kenyan *n.* a native or inhabitant of Kenya. *Also a.* WH: mid-20C. *Kenya*, a country in E Africa + -AN.

kep *v.t.* to catch. *Also n.* WH: 14–15C. Var. of KEEP[1]. Cp. *kept*, p.p. of *keep*.

kepi *n.* a French flat-topped military hat with a horizontal peak. WH: 19C. French *képi*, from Swiss German *Käppi*, dim. of *Kappe* cap.

Kepler's laws *n.pl.* three laws formulated by Kepler concerning the revolution of planets round the sun. WH: 18C. Johann *Kepler*, 1571–1630, German astronomer.

keratin *n.* a nitrogenous substance, the chief constituent of hair, feathers, claws and horns. WH: 19C. Greek *keras*, *keratos* horn + -IN[1].

kerb *n.* a row of stones set as edging to a pavement etc. WH: 17C. Var. of CURB.

kerchief *n.* a cloth to cover the head. WH: 12–14C. Old French *cuevre-chief* (Modern French *couvre-chef*), from *couvrir* COVER + *chief* head (CHIEF). Cp. HANDKERCHIEF.

kerf *n.* the slit, notch or channel made by a saw or axe in cutting. WH: pre-1200. Old English *cyrf*, from Germanic, from base of CARVE.

kerfuffle *n.* a commotion, a fuss. WH: 19C. Prob. from Irish *cíor thuathail* confusion, disorder, from *cíor* row, comb, mane, teeth + *tuathal* turn to the left, wrong direction. According to some the origin may be in the Gaelic prefix *car-* to twist, to bend + Scottish dialect *fuffle* to throw into disorder.

kermes *n.* the dried bodies of the females of an insect, *Kermes ilicis*, yielding a red or scarlet dye. WH: 16C. French *kermès*, from Arabic *ḳirmiz*. Cp. CRIMSON.

kermis *n.* in the Netherlands, a fair or outdoor festival or merry-making, orig. a church festival. WH: 16C. Dutch, from *kerk* CHURCH + *misse* MASS. The word was originally the term for a mass held on the annual anniversary of a church's dedication, with an accompanying fair.

kern[1] *n.* the part of a letter which overhangs the main body of type. *Also v.t.* WH: 17C. Prob. from French *carne* corner, var. of Old French *charne*, from Latin *cardo*, *cardinis* hinge.

kern[2] *n.* a light-armed Irish foot soldier. WH: 14–15C. Irish *ceithearn*, from Old Irish *ceithern* band of foot soldiers. Cp. CATERAN.

kernel *n.* the substance, usu. edible, contained in the shell of a nut or the stone of a fruit. *Also v.i.* WH: pre-1200. Old English *cyrnel*, dim. of *corn* seed. See CORN[1], also -EL.

kerosene *n.* an oil distilled from petroleum, coal or bituminous shale, used for burning in jet engines and oil lamps. WH: 19C. Greek *kēros* wax + -ENE. The reference to wax alludes to the fact that kerosene contains paraffin in some stages of its preparation.

Kerry *n.* any of a breed of small black dairy cattle, from Ireland. WH: 18C. *Kerry*, a county in SW Ireland.

kersey *n.* a coarse woollen cloth, usu. ribbed. *Also a.* WH: 14–15C. Prob. from *Kersey*, a village in Suffolk.

kerseymere *n.* a fine twilled woollen cloth used esp. for suits. WH: 18C. Alt. of CASSIMERE, by assoc. with KERSEY.

kerygma *n.* in the early Christian Church, the teaching of the Gospel. WH: 19C. Greek *kērugma*, from *kērussein* to proclaim.

kestrel *n.* a small species of hawk, *Falco tinnunculus*. WH: 14–15C. ? French *casserelle*, dial. var. of *crécerelle*, from *crécelle*, lit. rattle, of imit. orig. Cp. the bird's Latin name: *tinnunculus* is from *tinnire* to ring (cp. TINNITUS).

ketamine *n.* an anaesthetic drug, also used as a hallucinogenic recreational drug. WH: mid-20C. KETONE + AMINE.

ketch *n.* a fore-and-aft rigged two-masted sailing boat. WH: 17C. Var. of obs. catch, prob. from CATCH.

ketchup *n.* a sauce, usu. prepared from mushrooms, tomatoes etc., used as a condiment. WH: 17C. Malay *kēchap*. The variant forms *catchup* and *catsup* have been influenced by *catch* and *up*, *cat* and *sup*.

ketone *n.* any of a class of organic compounds, usu. formed by oxidation of a secondary alcohol. WH: 19C. German *Keton*, alt. of *Aketon* ACETONE.

kettle *n.* a vessel, usu. of metal and with a lid, handle and spout, for heating water or other liquid. WH: pre-1200. Old English *cetel*, from Germanic, from Latin *catillus*, dim. of *catinus* deep vessel for serving or cooking food. Cp. German *Kessel*.

kevel *n.* a belaying cleat, usu. fixed in pairs. WH: 12–14C. Old Northern French *keville*, from Old French *cheville* pin, leg.

Kevlar® *n.* a strong synthetic fibre, used in the manufacture of tyres. WH: late 20C. Orig. unknown. Cp. *Mylar*, a polyester used to make heat-resistant films.

Kewpie doll® *n.* a plump baby doll with hair in a topknot. WH: early 20C. CUPID + -*ie* (-Y³). The dolls are so called 'because they look like little Cupids' (Rose C. O'Neill, their US illustrator, 1909). The name also suggests *cutie* (CUTE).

kex *n.* any of various umbelliferous plants, such as the hemlock, the hogweed or the angelica. WH: 12–14C. ? Celtic. Cp. Welsh *cegid*, Cornish *kegaz*, Breton *kegid*.

key¹ *n.* a portable instrument, usu. of metal, for working the bolt of a lock to and fro. Also *a.*, *v.t.* WH: pre-1200. Old English *cǣg*, *cǣge*, of unknown orig. Cp. CLEF. The sense system of musical notes evolved in the 14–15C.

key² *n.* a low island, esp. of coral, such as off the coast of Florida. WH: 17C. Var. of CAY, influ. by pronun. of QUAY.

Keynesian *a.* of or relating to the philosophy that governments should control the economy through monetary and fiscal policies. Also *n.* WH: mid-20C. John Maynard *Keynes*, 1883–1946, English economist + -IAN.

KGB *abbr.* the former Soviet secret police. WH: Abbr. of Russian *Komitet gosudarstvennoĭ bezopasnosti* Committee of State Security.

khaddar *n.* Indian hand-woven cloth. WH: early 20C. Punjabi.

khaki *a.* dust-coloured, dull brownish yellow. Also *n.* WH: 19C. Urdu *ḳāḳī* dust-coloured, from *ḳāk* dust, from Persian.

khalasi *n.* a labourer or servant in the Indian subcontinent. WH: 18C. Urdu *ḳalāṣī*.

Khalka *n.* the official language of the Mongolian People's Republic. WH: 19C. Orig. unknown.

khamsin *n.* a hot southerly wind blowing in Egypt for some 50 days in March to May. WH: 17C. Arabic *ḳamāsīn*, from *ḳamsīn* fifty.

khan¹ *n.* a title given to officials and rulers in central Asia etc., equivalent to 'esquire'. WH: 14–15C. Old French *chan* or Medieval Latin *canus*, from Turkic *ḳān* lord, prince. The title was originally popularized in Europe by the Mongol warrior Genghis Khan, *c.*1162–1227, and was later associated with the Aga Khan as spiritual head of the Ismaili Muslim sect. (Aga Khan I was granted his title in 1818.)

khan² *n.* a caravanserai. WH: 14–15C. Persian *ḳān*.

khat *n.* an evergreen shrub, *Catha edulis*, grown in Africa and Arabia. WH: 19C. Arabic *ḳāt*.

Khedive *n.* the official title of the governor of Egypt under the Turks, 1867–1914. WH: 19C. French *khédive*, from Ottoman Turkish *ḳedıv*, from Persian *ḳadiw* prince, var. of *ḳudaiw* petty god, from *ḳudā* god.

Khmer *n.* a member of a people inhabiting Cambodia. Also *a.* WH: 19C. Khmer.

Khoisan *n.* a family of African languages which includes the Nama and Bushman languages. Also *a.* WH: mid-20C. Nama *Khoikhoi*, lit. men of men + *San*, from Nama *sān* aborigines, settlers proper.

khus-khus *n.* the fibrous, aromatic root of an Indian grass, used for making fans, baskets etc. WH: 19C. Urdu, from Persian *ḳaskas*.

kiang *n.* an Asian wild ass, *Equus hemionus*. WH: 19C. Tibetan *kyang*.

kia ora *int.* greetings!, your health! WH: 19C. Maori. The phrase is familiar as the brand name of a fruit squash, originally sold in Australia.

kibble¹ *n.* a strong iron (formerly wooden) bucket for raising ore from a mine. WH: 14–15C. Germanic, from Medieval Latin *capellus* corn measure, drinking vessel, from *cuppa* CUP. Cp. German *Kübel*.

kibble² *v.t.* to grind (grain, beans etc.) coarsely. Also *n.* WH: 18C. Orig. unknown.

kibbutz *n.* a communal agricultural settlement in Israel. WH: mid-20C. Modern Hebrew *qibbūṣ* gathering.

kibe *n.* a chap occasioned by cold, an ulcerated chilblain. WH: 14–15C. Orig. unknown.

kibitka *n.* a Russian wheeled vehicle with a tentlike covering, used as a sledge in snowy weather. WH: 18C. Russian, from Turkic *kebit*, *kibit* + Russian suf. -*ka*.

kibitzer *n.* an interfering looker-on, esp. at a card game. WH: early 20C. From *kibitz*, from Yiddish, from German *kiebitzen*, from *Kiebitz* lapwing, peewit + -ER¹. The lapwing is a noisy, 'fussy' bird.

kiblah *n.* the direction of the Kaaba at Mecca, to which Muslims turn during prayer. WH: 17C. Arabic *kibla* that which is opposite.

kibosh *n.* bosh, humbug. WH: 19C. ? Yiddish, influ. by BOSH.

kick¹ *v.t.* to strike with the foot or hoof etc. Also *v.i.*, *n.* WH: 14–15C. Orig. unknown.

kick² *n.* the pushed-in base of a glass bottle. WH: 19C. Orig. uncertain. ? From KICK¹.

kickshaw *n.* something fantastical, a trifle, a trinket. WH: 16C. French *quelque chose* something.

kid¹ *n.* the young of the goat. Also *v.i.* WH: 12–14C. Old Norse *kith*, rel. to Old High German *chizzī*, from Germanic. Cp. German *Kitze*.

kid² *v.t.* to humbug, to hoax, to pretend. Also *v.i.*, *n.* WH: 19C. ? From KID¹ in sense of to make a goat of, to make a child of.

kid³ *n.* a small wooden tub, esp. one used at mess by sailors. WH: 18C. ? Var. of KIT¹.

kidder KID¹. WH: 16C. Orig. unknown.

Kidderminster *n.* a reversible two-ply ingrain carpet of a type originally made at Kidderminster. Also *a.* WH: 17C. *Kidderminster*, a town in Worcestershire.

kiddle *n.* a weir or dam in a river with traps or nets for catching fish. WH: 12–14C. Anglo-French *kidel*, from Old French *quidel* (Modern French *guideau*), of unknown orig.

kidnap *v.t.* to carry off (a person) by force or illegally, to abduct. WH: 17C. Back-formation from *kidnapper*, from KID¹ + obs. *napper* thief, prob. rel. to NAB. The original kidnappers carried off children to work as servants or labourers in the American colonies. Such white servants were called (KID¹). In R.L. Stevenson's novel *Kidnapped* (1886) David Balfour, in his late teens, is carried off to sea with the aim of being sold into slavery in America.

kidney *n.* an oblong flattened glandular organ embedded in fatty tissue in the lumbar region on each side of the spine, and serving to secrete urine and remove nitrogenous matter from the blood. WH: 12–14C. Orig. uncertain. ? Rel. to COD² + obs. *ey* EGG¹, ref. to shape.

kiekie *n.* a New Zealand climber, *Freycinetia banksii*, the berries of which are eaten and the leaves used for baskets etc. WH: 19C. Maori.

kieselguhr *n.* a type of diatomite. WH: 19C. German, from *Kiesel* gravel + *Guhr* fermentation.

kike *n.* a Jew. Also *a.* WH: early 20C. Orig. unknown. ? From *ikey*, coll. abbr. of Jewish male forename *Isaac*.

Kikuyu *n.* a member of a Bantu-speaking people of Kenya. Also *a.* WH: 19C. Bantu.

kilderkin *n.* a small barrel, usu. of 18 gals. (81.8 l). WH: 14–15C. Middle Dutch *kinderkin*, var. of *kinnekin*, dim. of *kintal* QUINTAL. See also -KIN.

kilerg *n.* a unit of measurement of work, 1000 ergs. WH: 19C. KILO- + ERG¹.

kilim *n.* a pileless woven carpet made in the Middle East. WH: 19C. Turkish *kilim*, from Persian *gelīm*.

kill *v.t.* to deprive of life, to put to death. Also *v.i.*, *n.* WH: 12–14C. Prob. from Germanic word rel. to QUELL. An original Old English verb *cyllan* is postulated.

killdeer *n.* a N American plover, *Charadrius vociferus*. **WH:** 18C. Imit. of the bird's call.

killick *n.* a stone or small anchor used for mooring a fishing boat. **WH:** 17C. Orig. unknown.

killifish *n.* any minnow-like fish of the genus *Fundulus* and related genera, used as bait and to control mosquitoes. **WH:** 19C. Appar. from *kill* stream, creek (from Dutch *kil* river bed) + FISH[1].

kiln *n.* a furnace, oven or stove for calcining, drying, hardening etc., esp. one for calcining lime or firing pottery etc. *Also v.t.* **WH:** pre-1200. Latin *culina* kitchen, cooking stove.

kilo *n.* a kilogram. **WH:** 19C. French, abbr. of *kilogramme* KILOGRAM.

kilo- *comb. form* denoting a factor of one thousand, esp. in the metric system. **WH:** French, from Greek *khilioi* thousand. See also -O-. The term was introduced in France in 1795 on the official adoption of the metric system.

kilobit *n.* a unit of computer information equal to 1024 bits. **WH:** mid-20C. KILO- + BIT[3].

kilobyte *n.* a unit of computer storage equal to 1024 bytes. **WH:** late 20C. KILO- + BYTE.

kilocalorie *n.* a unit of heat equalling 1000 (small) calories, used in measuring the energy content of food. **WH:** 19C. KILO- + CALORIE.

kilocycle *n.* a unit for measuring the frequency of alternating current, equal to 1000 cycles per second. **WH:** early 20C. KILO- + CYCLE.

kilogram *n.* a measure of weight, 1000 grams or 2.2046 lb. av., the SI base unit of mass. **WH:** 18C. French *kilogramme*. See KILO-, GRAM[1].

kilohertz *n.* a unit used to measure the frequency of radio waves, equal to 1000 hertz. **WH:** early 20C. KILO- + HERTZ.

kilojoule *n.* a unit of energy equal to 1000 joules. **WH:** 19C. KILO- + JOULE.

kilolitre *n.* a liquid measure, 1000 litres. **WH:** 19C. French. See KILO-, LITRE.

kilometre *n.* a measure of distance, equal to 1000 metres or 0.621 miles. **WH:** 18C. French *kilomètre*. See KILO-, METRE[1].

kiloton *n.* a measure of explosive power, equal to 1000 tons of TNT. **WH:** mid-20C. KILO- + TON[1].

kilovolt *n.* a unit of electromotive force equal to 1000 volts. **WH:** 19C. KILO- + VOLT[1].

kilowatt *n.* a unit of measurement of electrical energy, equal to 1000 watts. **WH:** 19C. KILO- + WATT.

kilt *n.* a kind of short skirt usu. of tartan cloth gathered in vertical pleats, worn as part of male dress by the highlanders of Scotland. *Also v.t.* **WH:** 12–14C. Of Scandinavian orig. Cp. Swedish dial. *kilta* to swathe, Danish *kilte* (*op*) to tuck (up), Old Norse *kilting* skirt. The noun dates from the 18C.

kilter *n.* good condition, fitness, form. **WH:** 17C. Orig. unknown.

kimberlite *n.* a diamond-bearing claylike bluish rock, found in southern Africa and Siberia. **WH:** 19C. *Kimberley*, a diamond-mining town in S Africa + -ITE[1]. The rock was so named in 1887. Kimberley arose as a mining camp in 1873 following the discovery of diamonds on farms in the area in the period after 1869.

kimono *n.* a loose robe fastened with a sash, the principal outer garment of Japanese costume. **WH:** 17C. Japanese, from *ki* wearing + *mono* thing.

kin *n.* one's blood relations or family connections collectively, kindred. *Also a.* **WH:** pre-1200. Old English *cyn*, from Germanic, from Indo-European base also of Greek *genos*, Latin *genus* race, GENUS.

-kin *suf.* forming diminutive nouns. **WH:** From (or based on) Middle Dutch *-kijn*, German *-chen*, as respectively in *husekijn*, *Häuschen* little house. The suffix is familiar in surnames such as *Jenkinson*, *Watkinson*, meaning respectively son of little John, son of little Walter.

kina *n.* the standard monetary unit of Papua New Guinea. **WH:** late 20C. Tolai, lit. clam, mussel (orig. used as currency).

kinaesthesia *n.* the brain's sense of the body's positioning, the perception of muscular movement. **WH:** 19C. Greek *kinein* to move + *aisthēsis* sensation. See also -IA. The term was coined in 1880 by the English biologist H.C. Bastian.

kinase *n.* a chemical in the body which converts a zymogen into an enzyme. **WH:** early 20C. Greek *kinein* to move + -ASE.

kincob *n.* a rich Indian fabric interwoven with gold or silver thread. **WH:** 18C. Urdu and Persian *kamḵāb* gold or silver brocade, alt. of *kamḵā* damask silk, from Chinese.

kind *n.* a genus, a species, a natural group. *Also a., v.t.* **WH:** pre-1200. Old English *cynd*, earlier *gecynd*, from Germanic, from bases of Y-, KIN.

kindergarten *n.* a school for infants and children below official school age, in which knowledge is imparted chiefly by simple object lessons, by toys, games, singing and work. **WH:** 19C. German, lit. children's garden, from pl. of *Kind* child + *Garten* garden. The word was originally the term for a school teaching young children according to the principles proposed by Friedrich Froebel (FROEBEL SYSTEM), and it was he who coined it in 1840.

kindle *v.t.* to set fire to, to light. *Also v.i.* **WH:** 12–14C. Old Norse *kynda* + -LE[4], based on Old Norse *kindill* candle, torch.

kindred *n.* relatives, kin. *Also a.* **WH:** 12–14C. KIN + -RED. The *d* appeared between *n* and *r* as in THUNDER.

kinematics *n.* the science of pure motion, admitting conceptions of time and velocity but excluding that of force. **WH:** 19C. Greek *kinēma, kinēmatos* movement (from *kinein* to move) + -ICS.

kinesi- *comb. form* movement. **WH:** Greek *kinēsis* movement.

kinesiology *n.* the study of human movement and anatomy. **WH:** 19C. KINESI- + -O- + -LOGY.

kinesis *n.* movement. **WH:** 17C. Greek *kinēsis* movement.

kinetic *a.* of or producing motion. **WH:** 19C. Greek *kinētikos*, from *kinein* to move. See also -IC.

kinetin *n.* a synthetic kinin used to promote cell division in plants. **WH:** mid-20C. Greek *kinētos* movable + -IN[1].

king *n.* the male sovereign of a nation, esp. a hereditary sovereign of an independent state. *Also v.t., v.i.* **WH:** pre-1200. Old English *cyning*, later *cyng*, from Germanic, prob. from bases of KIN, -ING[3]. Cp. German *König*.

kinin *n.* any of a group of polypeptides formed in the body which cause dilation of the blood vessels. **WH:** mid-20C. Greek *kinein* to set in motion + -IN[1].

kink *n.* a twist or abrupt bend in a rope, thread, wire etc. *Also v.i., v.t.* **WH:** 17C. Low German *kinke*, from a base meaning to bend. Cp. Icelandic *kikna* to bend at the knees.

kinkajou *n.* an arboreal fruit-eating quadruped, *Potos flavus*, of S and Central America, allied to the raccoon, with long body and prehensile tail. **WH:** 18C. French *quincajou*, alt. of CARCAJOU. The name was wrongly transferred from the glutton by the French naturalist Georges-Louis Leclerc, Comte de Buffon.

kino *n.* an astringent gum used for tanning or dyeing and in medicine, obtained from certain Indian, African and Australian trees. **WH:** 18C. Appar. from a W African language.

-kins *suf.* added to nouns to show affection, as in *mummykins*, *daddykins* etc. **WH:** Extension of -KIN.

kiosk *n.* an open-fronted structure for the sale of newspapers etc. **WH:** 17C. French *kiosque*, from Turkish *köşk*, from Persian *kušk* pavilion.

kip[1] *n.* a sleep. *Also v.i.* **WH:** 18C. Orig. uncertain. Cp. Danish *kippe* hovel, tavern. The word originally meant a brothel, then a cheap lodging house, then (in the 19C) a sleep.

kip[2] *n.* the hide of a calf or of small cattle, used for leather. **WH:** 14–15C. Orig. uncertain. ? Rel. to Middle Dutch *kip, kijp* pack of hides.

kip[3] *n.* the standard monetary unit of Laos. **WH:** mid-20C. Thai.

kip[4] *n.* a wooden bat for tossing coins in the game of two-up. **WH:** 19C. Orig. uncertain. ? From KEP.

kipper *n.* a salmon or herring split open, salted and dried in smoke or the open air. *Also v.t.* **WH:** pre-1200. Old English *cypera*, ? rel. to COPPER, ref. to colour of male salmon.

kipsie *n.* a home, house or shelter. **WH:** early 20C. KIP[1] + -SY.

Kir® *n.* a drink made from white wine and cassis. **WH:** mid-20C. Canon Félix Kir, 1876–1968, mayor of Dijon, France, said to have devised its recipe.

kirby grip *n.* a type of hairgrip. **WH:** early 20C. *Kirby*, Beard & Co Ltd, its orig. manufacturers + GRIP[1].

kirk *n.* a church. **WH:** 12–14C. Old Norse *kirkja*, from Old English *cirice* CHURCH.

kirn *n.* a harvest home. **WH:** 16C. Orig. unknown.

kirsch *n.* an alcoholic liqueur distilled from the fermented juice of the black cherry. **WH:** 19C. German, abbr. of *Kirschenwasser*, from *Kirsche* cherry + *Wasser* water.

†**kirtle** n. a woman's gown or petticoat. Also v.t. WH: pre-1200. Old English cyrtel, from Germanic, ult. prob. from Latin curtus short. See CURT, also -LE².

kiskadee n. a S and central American flycatcher, Pitangus sulphuratus. WH: 19C. Imit. of the bird's call.

kismet n. fate, destiny. WH: 19C. Turkish kısmet, from Arabic ḳismat division, portion, lot, fate.

kiss n. a touch with the lips, esp. in affection or as a salutation. Also v.t., v.i. WH: pre-1200. Old English coss, from Germanic base of cyssan to kiss, from Germanic, ult. of imit. orig.

Kiswahili n. a widely-spoken Bantu language, Swahili. WH: 19C. Bantu, from pref. ki- + SWAHILI. In Bantu the prefix ki- denotes an abstract or inanimate object. Hence also KiKongo as an alternative name of KONGO, etc.

kit¹ n. the equipment needed for a particular job, sport etc. Also v.t. WH: 12–14C. Middle Dutch kitte, of unknown orig. A kit was originally a type of wooden tub. All current senses of the word arose in or after the 18C.

kit² n. a type of small violin esp. used by dancing masters. WH: 16C. Orig. uncertain. ? From first syl. of Latin cithara, Greek kithara CITHARA.

kit³ n. a kitten. WH: 16C. Abbr. of KITTEN.

kit-cat n. a portrait of a particular size, rather less than half-length but showing one hand. WH: 18C. Kit (i.e. Christopher) Cat or Catling, keeper of the pie house near Temple Bar in London where the Kit-Cat Club of Whig politicians met from 1688. Its members had their portraits painted in a size less than half length, allegedly because the dining room where they were hung was too low for half-length portraits.

kitchen n. a room or area in a house etc. where food is cooked. Also v.t. WH: pre-1200. Old English cycene, from Germanic, from Late Latin coquina, from coquere to cook. Cp. German Küche.

kite n. a device consisting of a light frame of wood covered with fabric or paper, constructed to fly in the air by means of a string. Also v.i., v.t. WH: pre-1200. Old English cȳta, from base also of Middle High German kūze screech owl and other words imit. of various cries. The word was originally the name of the bird. It was first applied to the child's flying toy in the 17C.

kith n. kindred. WH: pre-1200. Old English cȳthth, from Germanic, rel. to COUTH. A prime sense to the 19C was knowledge, information, specifically knowledge of how to behave, rules of etiquette.

kitsch n. art or literature that is inferior or in bad taste, esp. that designed to appeal to popular sentimentality. WH: early 20C. German, prob. from German dial. kitschen to smear.

kitten n. the young of the cat. Also v.i., v.t. WH: 14–15C. Anglo-French var. of Old French chitoun (Modern French chaton), dim. of chat CAT¹, with ending assim. to -EN¹. Cp. CHICKEN.

kittiwake n. a seagull of the genus Rissa, esp. R. tridactyla, common on the British coasts. WH: 17C. Imit. of the bird's cry.

kittle a. ticklish, awkward to deal with, intractable. Also v.t. WH: 16C. Scottish dial., from Germanic. Cp. German kitzeln to tickle.

kitty n. the pool into which each player puts a stake in poker, and other games. WH: 19C. Orig. unknown. ? Rel. to KIT¹.

kiwi n. a New Zealand wingless bird of the genus Apteryx. WH: 19C. Maori, imit. of male bird's shrill call.

Klan n. the Ku Klux Klan. WH: 19C. Abbr. of KU KLUX KLAN.

Klaxon® n. a loud horn or hooter, formerly used on cars. WH: early 20C. Name of orig. US manufacturers, itself prob. from Greek klagksō I will make a loud noise, from the same imit. base as CLANG.

Kleenex® n. a soft paper tissue used as a handkerchief etc. WH: early 20C. Invented name, prob. from CLEAN + EX².

Klein bottle n. a one-sided surface surrounding a three-dimensional space, formed by putting the narrow end of tapered tube through the surface of the tube, then stretching it to fit into the other end. WH: mid-20C. Felix Klein, 1849–1925, German mathematician.

klepht n. any of the Greeks who refused to submit to the Turks after the conquest (15th cent.), and took refuge in the mountains. WH: 19C. Modern Greek klephtēs, from Greek kleptēs thief.

kleptomania n. a form of mental illness displaying itself in an irresistible urge to steal. WH: 19C. Greek kleptēs thief + -O- + -MANIA.

klieg n. a powerful arc lamp used as floodlighting in a film studio. WH: early 20C. Anton T. and John H. Kliegl, 1872–1927 and 1869–1959, US inventors.

klipspringer n. a small southern African antelope, Oreotragus oreotragus. WH: 18C. Afrikaans, from Dutch klip rock + springer springer (SPRING).

Klondike n. a source of wealth. Also v.t., v.i. WH: 19C. Klondike, a region and river in the Yukon, NW Canada, the scene of a gold rush in 1896.

klong n. a canal in Thailand. WH: 19C. Thai.

kloof n. a ravine, gully or mountain gorge. WH: 18C. Dutch cleft, rel. to CLEAVE¹.

kludge n. an untidy mixture of things. WH: mid-20C. Prob. imit. Cp. FUDGE².

klutz n. a clumsy or foolish person. WH: mid-20C. Yiddish, from German Klotz wooden block. Cp. CLOT.

klystron n. an electron tube used to amplify or generate microwaves. WH: mid-20C. Greek klus-, stem of kluzein to wash, to break over + -TRON. The electrons are made to 'bunch' through a narrow gap, their passage suggesting the breaking of waves on the shore. The name was coined in 1939 by the US physicists R.H. and S.F. Varian.

knack n. a trick or an adroit way of doing a thing. WH: 14–15C. Prob. from Dutch knak, from Low German, ult. of imit. orig. In English words beginning kn-, the k was formerly pronounced but has been silent from the 17C.

knacker n. a buyer of worn-out horses, cattle etc. for slaughter; a horse-slaughterer. Also v.t. WH: 16C. Orig. uncertain. ? From KNACK + -ER².

knackwurst n. a type of short fat spicy German sausage. WH: mid-20C. German, from knacken to make a cracking noise + Wurst sausage (WURST).

knag n. a knot in wood. WH: 14–15C. German Knagge knot, peg.

knap¹ n. a hill crest, rising ground. WH: pre-1200. Old English cnæp, prob. rel. to Old Norse knappr knob. Cp. KNOP.

knap² v.t. to break into pieces, esp. with a sharp snapping noise, to break, flake, or chip (flint). Also v.i. WH: 14–15C. Imit. Cp. Dutch and German knappen to crack, to crackle.

knapsack n. a case or bag for clothes, food etc., carried on the back by soldiers on a march or by hikers etc. WH: 17C. Middle Low German, from Dutch knapzak (German Knappsack), prob. from German knappen to bite + zak SACK¹.

knapweed n. any of various composite plants with purple globular flowers, of the genus Centaurea, esp. C. nigra, and C. scabiosa. WH: 14–15C. KNOP + WEED, with change of vowel as in pair STROP / STRAP.

knar n. a knot in wood, a protuberance on the trunk or branch of a tree. WH: 12–14C. Middle Low German and Middle Dutch knorre knobbly protuberance.

knave n. a deceitful, cunning person, a rogue. WH: pre-1200. Old English cnafa, from Germanic. Cp. German Knabe boy. The original sense was boy in general, then boy servant, then (12–14C) rogue. Cp. BOY, which originally meant a male servant, then gained a general sense.

knawel n. any of several short plants of the genus Scleranthus. WH: 16C. German Knauel.

knead v.t. to work up (flour, clay etc.) into a plastic mass by pressing and folding it with the hands. WH: pre-1200. Old English cnedan, from Germanic. Cp. German kneten.

knee n. the joint of the thigh or femur with the lower leg. Also v.t. WH: pre-1200. Old English cnēow, from Germanic, from Indo-European, from base also of Latin GENU, Greek gonu.

kneel v.i. to bend or incline the knees. WH: pre-1200. Old English cnēowlian, from cnēow KNEE.

knell v.i. to ring, to toll, as for a death or funeral. Also v.t., n. WH: pre-1200. Old English cnyllan, from Germanic, of unknown orig. Cp. KNOLL². The present spelling probably arose by association with BELL¹.

Knesset n. the single-chamber parliament of the modern state of Israel. WH: mid-20C. Hebrew, lit. gathering.

knickerbocker n. loose breeches gathered in below the knee. WH: 19C. Diedrich Knickerbocker, supposed author of Washington

Irving's humorous *History of New York* (1809). The trousers are said to be so called from their resemblance to the knee breeches worn by the Dutchmen in Cruikshank's illustrations to Irving's book. Irving took his alias from a friend, Herman Knickerbocker. The surname itself means baker of knickers (clay marbles).

knickers *n.pl.* women's underpants; also called *pair of knickers. Also int.* WH: 19C. Abbr. of *knickerbockers* (KNICKERBOCKER).

knick-knack *n.* any little ornamental article. WH: 15C. Redupl. of KNACK with variation of vowel.

knife *n.* a blade with one edge sharpened, usu. set in a handle. *Also v.t., v.i.* WH: pre-1200. Old English *cnīf*, from Old Norse *knīfr*, from Germanic word of unknown orig. French *canif* penknife comes from the same source.

knight *n.* a man who holds a non-hereditary dignity conferred by the sovereign or their representative, and entitling the possessor to the title of 'Sir' prefixed to his name. *Also v.t.* WH: pre-1200. Old English *cniht*, from Germanic word of unknown orig. Cp. German *Knecht*. The original sense was boy, then boy employed as servant, then male servant to a person of high rank. Cp. KNAVE, where the sense went from neutral to bad.

kniphofia *n.* any of various tall plants of the genus *Kniphofia*, native to southern and E Africa and having spikes of red, orange or yellow flowers, esp. the red-hot poker. WH: 19C. Modern Latin, from Johann Hieronymus *Kniphof*, 1704–63, German botanist + -IA.

knish *n.* a filled dumpling that is baked or fried. WH: mid-20C. Yiddish, from Russian, kind of bun or dumpling.

knit *v.t.* to form into a fabric or form (a fabric, garment etc.) by looping or knotting a continuous yarn or thread, by hand with knitting needles or on a knitting machine. *Also v.i., n., a.* WH: pre-1200. Old English *cnyttan*, from Germanic, from base of KNOT[1]. The original sense was to tie with a knot.

knob *n.* a rounded protuberance, usu. at the end of something. *Also v.t., v.i.* WH: 14–15C. Middle Low German *knobbe* knot, knob, bud. Cp. KNOP, NOB[2].

knobkerrie *n.* the round-headed club used as a weapon by S African tribesmen. WH: 19C. KNOB + Nama *kierie* short club, knobbed stick.

knock *v.t.* to strike so as to make a sound, to hit, to give a hard blow to. *Also v.i., n.* WH: 12–14C. Old English *cnocian*, of imit. orig. Cp. Middle High German *knochen*, Old Norse *knoka*.

knoll[1] *n.* a rounded hill, a mound, a hillock. WH: pre-1200. Old English *cnoll*, from Germanic. Cp. German *Knolle* clod, lump.

knoll[2] *v.t.* to ring or toll (a bell). *Also v.i., n.* WH: 12–14C. Prob. imit. alt. of KNELL.

knop *n.* a knob, a button. WH: 12–14C. Middle Low German and Middle Dutch *knoppe*, from Germanic. Cp. German *Knopf* knob, knot, button.

knot[1] *n.* the interlacement or intertwining of a rope or ropes, cords etc., so as to fasten one part to another part of the rope etc. or to another object. *Also v.t., v.i.* WH: pre-1200. Old English *cnotta*, from Germanic. Cp. Dutch *knot*.

knot[2] *n.* a small sandpiper, *Calidris canutus*. WH: 14–15C. Orig. uncertain. ? Imit. of the bird's call. The bird's Latin name wrongly implies that it was so called after King *Canute* (Cnut), *c.*995–1035.

know *v.t.* to have a clear and certain perception of. *Also v.i., n.* WH: pre-1200. Old English *cnāwan*, from Germanic, from Indo-European base also of CAN[1], KEN and Latin *cognoscere* (cp. COGNITION), Greek *gignōskein* (cp. GNOME[2]).

knowledge *n.* familiarity or understanding gained by experience or study or from instruction; an instance of this. WH: 12–14C. Old English *cnāwelǣcing*, verbal n., from *cnāwan* KNOW + -lǣcan from -lac, -lock as in WEDLOCK.

knuckle *n.* the bone at each one of the joints of a finger, esp. at the base. *Also v.t., v.i.* WH: 12–14C. Middle Low German *knökel*, dim. of base of *knoke* bone, prob. ult. rel. to KNEE. Cp. German *Knochen* bone.

knur *n.* a hard swelling on the trunk of a tree, a knot. WH: 14–15C. Var. of KNAR.

knurl *n.* a knot, a lump, an excrescence. *Also v.t.* WH: 17C. Appar. from KNUR. Cp. GNARLED.

koala *n.* an Australian marsupial, *Phascolarctos cinereus*, not unlike a small bear, with dense fur, which feeds on eucalyptus leaves. WH: 19C. Australian Aboriginal (Dharuk) *gula*.

kob *n.* an African antelope, *Kobus kob.* WH: 18C. Wolof *kooba.*

kobold *n.* in Germanic folklore, an elf or sprite frequenting houses; also a gnome or goblin haunting mines and hidden lodes. WH: 19C. German. See COBALT. Cp. GOBLIN.

Köchel number *n.* a number given to the works of Mozart in the Köchel catalogue of his compositions. WH: 19C. Ludwig von *Köchel*, 1800–77, Austrian cataloguer of Mozart's works. Köchel's first thematic catalogue was published in Leipzig in 1862.

kochia *n.* any annual, ornamental plant of the genus *Kochia*, with purple-red foliage in the late summer. WH: 19C. Modern Latin, from W.D.J. *Koch*, 19C German botanist + -IA.

KO'd *a.* knocked out. WH: early 20C. *KO*, abbr. of *knockout* + -'d (-ED).

Kodiak *n.* a brown bear, *Ursus arctos*, found in Alaska and the neighbouring Aleutian Islands, esp. Kodiak Island. WH: 19C. *Kodiak*, an island off Alaska.

koeksister *n.* a cake made with sweetened dough. WH: early 20C. Afrikaans, ? from *koek* cake + *sissen* to sizzle.

koel *n.* any of several SE Asian and Australasian cuckoos of the genus *Eudynamys*, esp. *E. scolopacea*. WH: 19C. Hindi *koël*, from Sanskrit *kokila*.

kofta *n.* in Indian cookery, a spiced ball of meat, vegetables etc. WH: 19C. Urdu and Persian *koftah* pounded meat.

kohl *n.* fine black powder, usu. of antimony or lead sulphide used to darken the eyelids. WH: 18C. Arabic *kuḥl*. See ALCOHOL.

kohlrabi *n.* a variety of cabbage, *Brassica oleracea caulorapa*, with an edible swollen stem resembling a turnip. WH: 19C. German, from (with assim. to *Kohl* COLE) Italian *cauli rape* or *cavoli rape*, pl. of *cavolo rapa*, from Medieval Latin *caulorapa*. See COLE, RAPE[2].

koi *n.* a large Japanese variety of carp. WH: 18C. Japanese.

koine *n.* a Greek dialect used as a common language in the E Mediterranean during the Hellenistic and Roman periods. WH: 19C. Greek *koinē*, fem. sing. of *koinos* common, ordinary.

kokanee *n.* a salmon, *Oncorhynchus nerka kennerlyi*, from one of the land-locked lakes in NW America. WH: 19C. Shuswap.

kolinsky *n.* a type of Asian mink, *Mustela sibirica.* WH: 19C. *Kola*, a peninsula in NW Russia + pseudo-Russian ending *-insky*. The actual Russian adjective from *Kola* is *kol'skiĭ*.

kolkhoz *n.* a cooperative or collective farm in the former USSR. WH: early 20C. Russian, abbr. of *kollektivnoe khozyaĭstvo* collective farm.

Kol Nidre *n.* the service marking the beginning of Yom Kippur. WH: 19C. Aramaic *kol niḍrē* all the vows (the first words of the opening prayer).

Komodo dragon *n.* the largest known lizard, *Veranus komodoensis*, from Indonesia. WH: early 20C. *Komodo*, an island in Indonesia.

Komsomol *n.* the Young Communist League of the former USSR. WH: mid-20C. Russian, abbr. of *Kommunicheskiĭ soyuz molodëzhi* Communist Union of Youth.

Kongo *n.* a member of a Bantu-speaking central African people. *Also a.* WH: 19C. Kikongo. Cp. CONGOLESE.

konimeter *n.* an instrument for indicating the amount of dust in the atmosphere. WH: early 20C. Greek *konis* dust + -METER.

kook *n.* an eccentric, mad or foolish person. *Also a.* WH: mid-20C. Prob. abbr. of CUCKOO.

kookaburra *n.* any large Australian kingfisher of the genus *Dacelo*, also called the laughing jackass. WH: 19C. Australian Aboriginal (Wiradhuri) *gugubarra*, imit. of its call.

kop *n.* a prominent hill. WH: 19C. Afrikaans, from Dutch head. Cp. COP[2].

kopi *n.* powdered gypsum. WH: 19C. Australian Aboriginal (Bagandji) *yabi*.

kopje *n.* a small hill. WH: 19C. Afrikaans, from Dutch, dim. of *kop* head. Cp. KOP.

koradji *n.* an Aboriginal medicine man. WH: 18C. Australian Aboriginal (Dharuk) *garraaji*.

Koran *n.* the Muslim sacred scriptures consisting of the revelations delivered orally by Muhammad and collected after his death. WH: 17C. Arabic *ḳur'ān* recitation, reading, from *ḳara'a* to read, to recite.

Korean *a.* of or relating to Korea, its people or its language. *Also n.* WH: 17C. *Korea*, a country in E Asia (now divided into the Republic of Korea, or S Korea, and the Korean People's Republic, or N Korea) + -AN.

korfball *n.* a game not unlike basketball, with teams each consisting of six men and six women. WH: early 20C. Dutch *korfbal*, from *korf* basket + *bal* ball.

korma *n.* an Indian dish composed of braised meat or vegetables cooked in spices and a yoghurt or cream sauce. WH: 19C. Urdu *kormā*, from Turkish *kavurma*, lit. cooked meat.

koruna *n.* the standard monetary unit of the Czech Republic and Slovakia, equal to 100 haleru. WH: early 20C. Czech crown.

kosher *a.* (of food or a shop where it is sold) fulfilling the requirements of the Jewish law. *Also n., v.t.* WH: 19C. Hebrew *kāšēr* fit, proper.

koto *n.* a Japanese stringed instrument with a wooden body and 13 silk strings. WH: 18C. Japanese.

kotuku *n.* a white heron found in New Zealand, *Egretta alba*. WH: 19C. Maori.

kouprey *n.* a rare Indo-Chinese ox, *Bos sauveli*. WH: mid-20C. Khmer.

kourbash *n.* a hide whip used as an instrument of punishment in Turkey and Egypt. WH: 19C. Arabic *kurbāj*, from Turkish *kırbaç* whip.

kowhai *n.* a small shrub with clusters of golden flowers, *Sophora tetraptera*, found in Australasia and Chile. WH: 19C. Maori.

kowtow *n.* the ancient Chinese method of obeisance by kneeling or prostrating oneself, and touching the ground with the forehead. *Also v.i.* WH: 19C. Chinese *kētóu*, from *kē* to knock, to strike + *tóu* head.

KP *n.* enlisted soldiers detailed to help in the kitchen. WH: Abbr. of *kitchen police*.

kraal *n.* a S African village or group of huts enclosed by a palisade. WH: 18C. Afrikaans, from Portuguese *curral*, from Nama. Cp. CORRAL, CRAWL[2].

kraft *n.* strong, brown, wrapping paper. WH: early 20C. Swedish strength, from *kraftpapper* kraft paper.

krait *n.* any poisonous Asian rock snake of the genus *Bungarus*. WH: 19C. Hindi *karait*.

kraken *n.* a fabulous sea monster, said to have been seen at different times off the coast of Norway. WH: 18C. Norwegian dial., from *krake* kraken + Norwegian *-n*, definite article suf.

krans *n.* a precipitous upward slope, esp. of crags walling in a valley. WH: 18C. Afrikaans, from Dutch coronet, chaplet, from Germanic base meaning ring. Cp. German *Kranz* coronet, circle.

Kraut *n.* a German. WH: 19C. German vegetable, cabbage. Cp. SAUERKRAUT.

Krebs cycle *n.* a sequence of biochemical reactions in living organisms in which acetate is broken down to provide energy. WH: mid-20C. Sir Hans Adolf *Krebs*, 1900–81, German-born British biochemist.

kremlin *n.* the citadel of a Russian town. WH: 17C. French, from Russian *kreml'* citadel.

kreuzer *n.* a copper coin (earlier silver), formerly current in Germany and Austria. WH: 16C. German *Kreuz* CROSS. See also -ER[1]. The coin is so named from the two crosses with which it was originally stamped.

kriegspiel *n.* a war game played on maps. WH: 19C. German, from *Krieg* war + *Spiel* game.

krill *n.* tiny shrimplike crustaceans, the main food of whales. WH: early 20C. Norwegian *kril* small fish fry.

krimmer *n.* the tightly curled black or grey fleece from a type of lamb found in the Crimea. WH: 19C. German, from *Krim* Crimea, a peninsula between the sea of Azov and the Black Sea. See also -ER[1].

kris *n.* a Malaysian or Indonesian dagger with a wavy edge. WH: 16C. Malay *keris*.

Krishnaism *n.* the worship of Krishna, a Hindu deity (a form of Vishnu). WH: 19C. Sanskrit *kŕṣṇa* Krishna, a Hindu god (an incarnation of Vishnu) + -ISM.

kromesky *n.* a roll or ball of minced meat or fish wrapped in bacon, then fried. WH: 19C. Polish *kromeczka* small slice, dim. of *kromka* slice.

krona *n.* the basic monetary unit of Sweden. WH: 19C. Swedish CROWN.

krone *n.* the monetary unit of Denmark and Norway. WH: 19C. Danish and Norwegian, from German CROWN.

Kru *n.* a member of a W African people on the coast of Liberia, famous for their skill as seamen. *Also a.* WH: 19C. W African.

krugerrand *n.* a coin minted in S Africa containing 1 troy oz. of gold. WH: mid-20C. Stephanus Johannes Paulus *Kruger*, 1825–1904, President of the Transvaal (1883–99) + RAND[1].

krummhorn *n.* a medieval wind instrument with a curved tube and a tone like that of a clarinet. WH: 17C. German, from *krumm* crooked, curved + *Horn* HORN.

krypton *n.* an inert gaseous element, at no. 38, chem. symbol Kr. WH: 19C. Greek *krupton*, neut. of *kruptos* hidden, concealed (cp. CRYPTO-). The element was discovered in 1898 by the British chemists Sir William Ramsay and Morris W. Travers and so named because it is a rare gas, forming only a minute portion (1 part in about 900,000) of the atmosphere.

Kshatriya *n.* a member of the warrior caste in the Hindu caste system. WH: 18C. Sanskrit *kṣatriya*, from *kṣatra* rule.

K/T boundary *n.* the boundary between the Cretaceous and Tertiary periods. WH: K, symbol for Cretaceous + T, symbol for Tertiary.

kudos *n.* glory, fame, credit. WH: 18C. Greek praise, renown.

kudu *n.* either of two southern African antelopes, *Tragelaphus strepsericos* or *T. imberbis*, with white stripes. WH: 18C. Afrikaans *koedoe*, from Xhosa *i-qudu*.

kudzu *n.* an ornamental plant with edible tubers, *Pueraria lobata*, native to China and Japan. WH: 19C. Japanese *kuzu*.

Kufic *n.* an early form of the Arabic alphabet. *Also a.* WH: 18C. *Kufa*, an ancient city of Iraq + -IC.

Ku Klux Klan *n.* a secret society in the S States of the US, aiming to repress the black population, orig. formed after the American Civil War of 1861–65 and though suppressed by the US government in 1871 since revived with the aim of preserving white supremacy. WH: 19C. Prob. from Greek *kuklos* circle + alt. of CLAN.

kukri *n.* a curved knife broadening at the end, used by the Gurkhas. WH: 19C. Nepali *khukuri*.

kulak *n.* a prosperous Russian peasant of the class owning their own farms. WH: 19C. Russian, lit. fist, i.e. tight-fisted person, from Turkic *kol* hand.

kulan *n.* a SW Asian wild ass, related to the kiang. WH: 18C. Turkic.

Kultur *n.* German culture, esp. in its authoritarian and militaristic aspects. WH: early 20C. German, from Latin *cultura* or French *culture* CULTURE.

kumara *n.* the sweet potato. WH: 18C. Maori.

kumiss *n.* a spirituous liquor made by Tartars from fermented mare's milk. WH: 16C. French *koumis*, Russian *kumys*, from Tartar *kumiz*.

kümmel *n.* a liqueur flavoured with caraway seeds made in Germany and Russia. WH: 19C. German, representing Middle High German, Old High German *kumil*, var. of *kumîn* CUMIN.

kumquat *n.* a small orangelike fruit with acid pulp and a sweet rind. WH: 17C. Chinese (Cantonese dial.) *kam kwat*, little orange.

kung fu *n.* a Chinese martial art resembling karate. WH: 19C. Chinese *gōngfù* skill, from *gōng* merit + *fù* man.

Kuomintang *n.* the Chinese Nationalist party founded by Sun Yat Sen and holding power from 1928 until replaced by the Communist Party in 1949. WH: early 20C. Chinese *guómíndǎng* national people's party, from *guó* nation + *mín* people + *dǎng* party.

Kuo-yü *n.* a form of Mandarin taught all over China. WH: mid-20C. Chinese *guó* nation + *yǔ* language.

kurchatovium *n.* a name proposed in the former USSR for the element now called RUTHERFORDIUM. WH: mid-20C. I.V. *Kurchatov*, 1903–60, Russian nuclear physicist + -IUM. The name was coined in 1967 by the Russian physicist G.N. Flёrov.

Kurd *n.* a native or inhabitant of Kurdistan. WH: 17C. Kurdish.

kurdaitcha *n.* in some Australian Aboriginal tribes, the practice of using a bone to cast spells. WH: 19C. Australian Aboriginal (Aranda) *gwedaje*.

kuri *n.* a mongrel dog. WH: 19C. Maori dog.

kurrajong *n.* any of several trees and shrubs with fibrous bark, esp. *Brachychiton populneum*. WH: 19C. Australian Aboriginal (Dharuk) *garrajung*.

kursaal *n.* a public room for the use of visitors, esp. at German health resorts. WH: 19C. German *Kur* cure + *Saal* hall, room.

kurta *n.* a loose tunic worn by Hindus. WH: early 20C. Urdu and Persian *kurtah*.

kurtosis *n.* in statistics, the distribution and density of points around the mean. WH: early 20C. Greek *kurtōsis* bulge, convexity, from *kurtos* bulging, convex. See also -OSIS.

kuru *n.* a disease, usu. fatal, of the nervous system occurring in the inhabitants of eastern New Guinea. WH: mid-20C. New Guinea name.

kvass *n.* beer made from rye, esp. in Russia. WH: 16C. Russian *kvas*, rel. to *kislyĭ* sour, Latin *caseus* CHEESE[1].

kvetch *v.i.* to whine, to complain. WH: mid-20C. Yiddish *kvetsh* (n.), *kvetschn* (v.), from German *Quetsche* crusher, presser, *quetschen* to crush, to press.

Kwa *n.* a group of languages spoken in W Africa from the Ivory Coast to Nigeria. *Also a.* WH: 19C. Kwa.

kwacha *n.* the standard monetary unit in Zambia and Malawi. WH: mid-20C. Bantu dawn.

kwanza *n.* the standard monetary unit of Angola. WH: late 20C. Prob. from River *Kuranza* (now *Cuanza*), Angola.

kwashiorkor *n.* a nutritional disease caused by lack of protein. WH: mid-20C. Local name in Ghana. The word is said to mean deposed child (i.e. deposed from the mother's breast by a newborn sibling) in one African dialect and red boy in another. The latter would refer to the reddish-orange discoloration of the hair that the disease causes.

kwela *n.* a type of jazzlike pop music of central and southern Africa. WH: mid-20C. Afrikaans, from Zulu *khwela* to climb, to mount.

kyanite *n.* a hard, translucent mineral, often blue, occurring in flattened prisms in gneiss and mica-schist. WH: 18C. Greek *kuanos* dark blue + -ITE[1].

kyanize *v.t.* to impregnate (wood) with a solution of mercuric chloride (corrosive sublimate) to prevent dry rot. WH: 19C. J.H. *Kyan*, 1774–1850, Irish inventor + -IZE.

kyat *n.* the basic monetary unit of Burma (Myanmar). WH: mid-20C. Burmese.

kyle *n.* a narrow channel in Scotland, between an island and another island or the mainland. WH: 16C. Gaelic *caol* narrow.

kylie *n.* a boomerang. WH: 19C. Australian Aboriginal (Nyungar) *garli*.

kylin *n.* a mythical animal of composite form, shown on Chinese and Japanese pottery. WH: 19C. Chinese *qílín*, from *qí* male + *lín* female.

kyloe *n.* a small highland breed of cattle. WH: 19C. Gaelic *gaidhealach* Gaelic, Highland.

kymograph *n.* an instrument for recording wavelike oscillations, as of the pulsation of the blood in a living body. WH: 19C. Greek *kuma* wave + -O- + -GRAPH. The instrument was invented in 1846 by the German physiologist Karl Ludwig and named in 1850 by A.W. Volkmann.

kyphosis *n.* a condition of the spine resulting in a hunched back. WH: 19C. Greek *kuphōsis* humpbacked condition, from *kuphos* bent, hunchbacked. See also -OSIS.

Kyrgyz *n.* a member of a Mongolian people inhabiting central Asia, mainly Kyrgyzstan. *Also a.* WH: 17C. Russian *Kirgiz*, from Turkish *Kirğiz*.

Kyrie *n.* this phrase used as a short petition in the liturgies of the Eastern and Western Churches, esp. at the beginning of the Eucharist or Mass. WH: 12–14C. Medieval Latin, from Greek *kuriē eleēson* Lord, have mercy.

kyu *n.* each of the grades for beginners in judo, karate etc. WH: mid-20C. Japanese *kyū* class.

L

†**la** *int.* lo! see! behold! (*derisively etc.*) really! WH: 16C. Natural exclamation. Cp. LO.

laager *n.* in S Africa, a defensive encampment, esp. one formed by wagons drawn into a circle. *Also v.t., v.i.* WH: 19C. Afrikaans. Cp. German *Lager* camp, LAIR¹, LEAGUER.

labarum *n.* the imperial standard of Constantine the Great (bearing the cross and a monogram of the Greek name of Christ), adopted by him after his conversion to Christianity. WH: 17C. Late Latin, of unknown orig.

labefaction *n.* weakening, decay. WH: 17C. Latin *labefactus*, p.p. of *labefacere* to weaken, from *labi* to fall + *facere* to make. See -FACTION.

label *n.* a piece of cloth, paper, plastic or other material attached to an object to indicate contents, destination, ownership or other particulars. *Also v.t.* WH: 12–14C. Old French ribbon, fillet, prob. from a Germanic word rel. to LAP¹ with dim. suf.

labellum *n.* the lower lip-shaped part of the corolla in an orchidaceous flower. WH: 19C. Latin, dim. of *labrum* lip.

labial *a.* of or relating to the lips or the labium. *Also n.* WH: 16C. Medieval Latin *labialis*, from Latin *labia* lips. See also -AL¹.

labile *a.* unstable, liable to chemical or other change. WH: 14–15C. Late Latin *labilis*, from *labi* to fall. See also -IL.

labio- *comb. form* labial. WH: Latin *labium* lip + -O-.

labiodental *a.* produced by the agency of the lips and teeth. *Also n.* WH: 17C. LABIO- + DENTAL.

labium *n.* a lip or liplike structure or part. WH: 16C. Latin lip. Cp. LABRUM.

laboratory *n.* a room or building in which scientific experiments and research are conducted. WH: 17C. Medieval Latin *laboratorium*, from Latin *laboratus*, p.p. of *laborare*. See LABOUR, also -ORY¹.

labour *n.* physical or mental exertion, esp. to obtain the means of subsistence, the performance of work. *Also a., v.i., v.t.* WH: 12–14C. Old French (Modern French *labeur* ploughing), from Latin *labor* toil, trouble, suffering.

Labrador *n.* a Labrador retriever. WH: 19C. *Labrador*, a peninsula in E Canada.

labrum *n.* a lip or liplike part, as in insects, crustaceans etc. WH: 18C. Latin lip, rel. to *labium*, in turn rel. to Greek *laptein* LAP³.

laburnum *n.* a poisonous tree or shrub of the genus *Laburnum*, that has racemes of yellow flowers. WH: 16C. Latin bean trefoil.

labyrinth *n.* a structure composed of intricate winding passages, paths, tunnels etc., a maze. *Also v.t.* WH: 14–15C. French *labyrinthe* or Latin *labyrinthus*, from Greek *laburinthos*, of unknown orig. According to some, the Greek word is related to Lydian *labrus* double-edged axe. Such an axe was a symbol of royal power, so a labyrinth may originally have been a royal palace.

lac *n.* a resinous incrustation secreted, chiefly on the banyan tree, by parasitic lac insects and used in the making of shellac. WH: 14–15C. Medieval Latin, from Portuguese *laca*, from Hindi *lākh*, Persian *lāk*. Cp. LACQUER, LAKE², SHELLAC.

Lacanian *a.* of or relating to Jacques Lacan. *Also n.* WH: mid-20C. Jacques *Lacan*, 1901–81, French psychoanalyst and structuralist, who reinterpreted Freud + -IAN.

laccolith *n.* an intrusive mass of lava penetrating between strata and raising the surface into domes. WH: 19C. Greek *lakkos* reservoir + -LITH.

lace *n.* a kind of ornamental network of threads of linen, cotton, silk, gold or silver wire or other suitable material, forming a fabric of open texture. *Also v.t., v.i.* WH: 12–14C. Old French *laz, las* (Modern French *lacs* noose), or from Latin *laqueus* noose. The original meaning to the 17C was net, noose, snare. The current sense dates from the 16C.

lacerate¹ *v.t.* to tear, to mangle. WH: 14–15C. Latin *laceratus*, p.p. of *lacerare*, from *lacer* mangle, torn. See also -ATE³.

lacerate² *a.* having the edge in irregular segments, as if torn. WH: 16C. Latin *laceratus*, p.p. of *lacerare*. See LACERATE¹, also -ATE².

lacertian *n.* any reptile of the suborder Lacertilia that includes lizards. *Also a.* WH: 19C. Modern Latin *Lacertilia*, from Latin *lacerta* lizard + -IAN.

laches *n.* remissness or unreasonable delay in performing a legal duty, seeking a legal remedy, asserting a right etc. WH: 14–15C. Old French *laschesse* (Modern French *lâchesse* cowardice), from *lasche* (Modern French *lâche*), from var. of Latin *laxus* LAX. Cp. LUSH¹.

lachryma Christi *n.* a wine from S Italy, orig. a sweet white wine made from grapes grown on the slopes of Mt. Vesuvius. WH: 17C. Modern Latin Christ's tear, from *lachryma* (LACHRYMAL) + gen. of *Christus* CHRIST. Cp. LIEBFRAUMILCH.

lachrymal *a.* of or relating to tears. *Also n.* WH: 14–15C. Medieval Latin *lachrymalis*, from Latin *lacrima* tear, rel. to Greek *dakru* tear. See also -AL¹.

laciniate *a.* divided into long, narrow lobes; fringed. WH: 18C. Latin *lacinia* fringe, hem, rag + -ATE².

lack *n.* deficiency, need (of). *Also v.t.* WH: 12–14C. Old Frisian *lek* blame, Middle Low German *lak* deficiency, fault, blame. Prob. in Old English but not recorded. The original meaning (to the 16C) was defect, moral failing, crime. The current sense evolved in the 16C.

lackadaisical *a.* careless, slipshod, inattentive. WH: 18C. Extended form of LACKADAY + -IC + -AL¹. Cp. UPSYDAISY.

†**lackaday** *int.* alas. WH: 17C. Shortening of *alackaday*. See ALACK.

lackey *n.* a servile political follower or hanger-on. *Also v.t., v.i.* WH: 16C. French *laquais*, obs. *alaquais*, rel. to Catalan *alacay*. See ALCAYDE.

Laconian *a.* of or relating to Laconia or Sparta, its inhabitants or their dialect. *Also n.* WH: 16C. Latin *Laconia* (from Greek *Lakōn*), a territory of ancient Greece + -AN.

laconic *a.* using few words, concise. WH: 16C. Latin *Laconicus*, from Greek *Lakōnikos*, from *Lakōn*. See LACONIAN, -IC. The Lacedaemonians (Spartans) were known for their terse speech.

lacquer *n.* a varnish composed of shellac dissolved in alcohol and often coloured with gold, gamboge, saffron etc., that dries hard and is used to coat articles of metal or wood. WH: 16C. Obs. French *lacre* sealing wax, from Portuguese *laca*. See LAC.

lacrosse *n.* a ball game of N American Indian origin resembling hockey, but played with a crosse or stringed bat with which the players throw and catch the ball. WH: 19C. French (*le jeu de*) *la crosse* (the game of) the hooked stick. Cp. CROSIER.

lactase *n.* an enzyme that acts on lactose to produce glucose and galactose. WH: 19C. LACTOSE + -ASE.

lactate¹ *v.i.* to secrete or produce milk. WH: 19C. Back-formation from *lactation* (17C), from Late Latin *lactatio, lactationis*, from *lactatus*, p.p. of *lactare* to suckle, from *lac, lactis* milk. See also -ATION, -ATE³.

lactate² *n.* a salt of lactic acid. WH: 18C. LACTIC + -ATE¹.

lacteal *a.* of or relating to milk; milky. WH: 17C. Latin *lacteus* (from *lac, lactis* milk) + -AL¹.

lactescent *a.* having a milky appearance or consistency. WH: 17C. Latin *lactescens, lactescentis*, pres.p. of *lactescere* to be milky, from *lac, lactis* milk. See -escent (-ESCENCE).

lactic *a.* of, relating to or derived from milk. WH: 18C. Latin *lac, lactis* milk + -IC.

lactiferous *a.* carrying or producing milk or milky juice. WH: 17C. Latin *lac, lactis* milk + -i- + -FEROUS.

lacto- *comb. form* of or relating to milk. WH: Latin *lac*, *lactis* milk. See also -O-.

lactobacillus *n.* any rod-shaped bacterium of the family Lactobacillaceae which ferments carbohydrates to produce lactic acid. WH: early 20C. LACTO- + BACILLUS.

lactoflavin *n.* an earlier name for riboflavin. WH: mid-20C. LACTO- + FLAVIN.

lactogenic *a.* inducing lactation. WH: mid-20C. LACTO- + -GENIC.

lactometer *n.* a kind of hydrometer for showing the specific gravity and consequent value of different samples of milk. WH: 19C. LACTO- + -METER.

lactone *n.* any cyclic ester formed from a hydroxycarboxylic acid by the elimination of water. WH: 19C. LACTO- + -ONE.

lactoprotein *n.* any protein that is present in milk. WH: 19C. LACTO- + PROTEIN.

lactoscope *n.* an instrument for determining the quality of milk by ascertaining its relative opacity. WH: 19C. LACTO- + -SCOPE.

lactose *n.* the form in which sugar occurs in milk, a glucose and a galactose monomer. WH: 19C. LACTO- + -OSE[2].

lacuna *n.* a gap, blank or hiatus, esp. in a manuscript or text. WH: 17C. Latin, from *lacus* LAKE[1].

lacustrine *a.* of, relating to or living on or in a lake. WH: 19C. Latin *lacus* LAKE[1], based on *palustris* marshy (PALUDAL).

lad *n.* a boy, a youth. WH: 12–14C. Orig. unknown.

ladanum *n.* an odorous, resinous substance, which exudes from the leaves and twigs of various kinds of cistus. WH: 16C. Latin, from Greek *ladanon*, *lēdanon*, from *lēdon* mastic.

ladder *n.* a device of wood, iron, rope etc. for going up or down by, often portable and consisting of two long uprights, connected by rungs or cross-pieces, which form steps. *Also v.t.*, *v.i.* WH: pre-1200. Old English *hlæder*, from Germanic. Cp. German *Leiter*.

lade *v.t.* to put a cargo or freight on board. *Also v.i.* WH: pre-1200. Old English *hladan*, from Germanic base also of LAST[4].

la-di-da *a.* affectedly genteel, pretentious and precious in speech or manners. *Also n.* WH: 19C. Imit. of style described.

Ladin *n.* the Rhaeto-Romance language spoken in the Engadine and part of the Tyrol. WH: 19C. Latin *Latinus* LATIN.

ladino *n.* a white clover, *Trifolium repens*, used as fodder. WH: early 20C. Italian.

ladle *n.* a large spoon, usu. with a deep bowl at right angles to a long handle, with which liquids are lifted out or served from a vessel. *Also v.t.* WH: pre-1200. Old English *hlædel*, from *hladan* LADE. See also -EL.

lady *n.* a woman regarded as being of refinement or social standing. WH: pre-1200. Old English *hlæfdīge*, from *hlāf* LOAF[1] + Germanic base meaning to knead. Cp. DAIRY. The original Old English sense was mistress of a household, wife of a lord, literally one who kneads loaves. Cp. LORD.

laevo- *comb. form* left, as opposed to right. WH: Latin *laevus* left + -O-.

laevogyrate *a.* laevorotatory. WH: 19C. LAEVO- + GYRATE.

laevorotatory *a.* turning the plane of polarization to the left. WH: 19C. LAEVO- + *rotatory* (ROTATE[1]).

laevulose *n.* a sugar or glucose distinguished from dextrose by its turning the plane of polarization to the left, fructose. WH: 19C. LAEVO- + -ULE + -OSE[2].

lag[1] *a.* last. *Also v.i.*, *n.* WH: 16C. ? dial. alt. of LAST[1].

lag[2] *n.* a convict. *Also v.t.* WH: 19C. Orig. unknown.

lag[3] *n.* the non-heat-conducting jacket of a boiler or cylinder. *Also v.t.* WH: 17C. Prob. of Scandinavian orig. Cp. Icelandic *lagger*, Swedish *lagg* stave, from Germanic base of LAY[1].

lagan *n.* wreckage or goods lying at the bottom of the sea, usu. marked by a float or buoy. WH: 16C. Old French, or ? from Old Norse *lagn-*, as in *lagn*, gen. *lagnar* dragnet, from Germanic base of LAY[1].

lager *n.* a light beer, blond in colour and effervescent, the ordinary beer of Germany. WH: 19C. German *Lager-Bier* beer brewed for keeping, from *Lager* storehouse. Cp. LAIR[1].

lagniappe *n.* a small gift, esp. to a customer. WH: 19C. Louisiana French, from Spanish *la ñapa* the gift, from Quechua *yapa* something given extra.

lagomorph *n.* any gnawing mammal with two pairs of upper incisors (e.g. hares, rabbits). WH: 19C. Greek *lagōs* hare + -MORPH.

lagoon *n.* a shallow lake near a river or the sea, due to the infiltration or overflow of water from the larger body. WH: 17C. Italian and Spanish *laguna*, from Latin LACUNA. See also -OON.

Lagrangian point *n.* any one of the five points in the plane of orbit of one body around another where the combined gravitational forces of the two bodies are zero and a third body, of negligible mass, can remain at rest. WH: 19C. Joseph Louis *Lagrange*, 1736–1813, Italian-born mathematician working in Prussia and France + -IAN.

lah *n.* the sixth note of a major scale in the tonic sol-fa system of notation. WH: 12–14C. Latin *labii*. See UT.

lahar *n.* a landslide or mudflow consisting mainly of volcanic debris and usu. occurring after heavy rain. WH: early 20C. Javanese.

laid *a.* lying down. WH: 16C. P.p. of LAY[1].

lair[1] *n.* the den or retreat of a wild animal. *Also v.i.*, *v.t.* WH: pre-1200. Old English *leger*, from Germanic base of LIE[2]. Cp. German *Lager* bed, camp. The original meaning (to the 18C) was the action (or fact) of lying down. The sense of animal's den dates from the 14–15C.

lair[2] *n.* mire, mud. *Also v.i.* WH: 12–14C. Old Norse *leir*.

lair[3] *n.* an over-dressed man; a show-off. WH: mid-20C. Back-formation from *lairy*, var. of *leery*, knowing, streetwise, ? rel. to LEER.

laird *n.* the owner of a landed estate. WH: 14–15C. Scottish var. of LORD.

lake[1] *n.* a large sheet of water entirely surrounded by land. WH: pre-1200. Old French *lac*, from Latin *lacus* lake, pool, pit, ? assim. to Old English *lacu* stream, from Germanic.

lake[2] *n.* a crimson pigment, orig. derived from lac or cochineal. WH: 17C. Var. of LAC.

lakh *n.* in the Indian subcontinent, the number 100,000 (usu. of a sum of rupees). WH: 17C. Hindi *lākh*, from Sanskrit *laksa* mark, token, 100,000.

Lallans *n.* the Lowland Scots dialect, esp. in its modern literary use. WH: 18C. Representation of a pronun. of *lowland* (LOW[1]).

lallation *n.* pronunciation of *r* as *l*. WH: 17C. Latin *lallatio*, *lallationis*, from *lallatus*, p.p. of *lallare* to sing lullaby. See also -ATION.

lallygag *v.i.* to loiter aimlessly. WH: 19C. Orig. unknown.

lam[1] *v.t.* to thrash, to wallop. WH: 16C. ? Of Scandinavian orig. Cp. Norwegian and Danish *lamme* to lame, to paralyse.

lam[2] *n.* a quick escape, a hasty flight, esp. from the law. *Also v.i.* WH: 19C. LAM[1].

lama *n.* a Tibetan or Mongolian Buddhist priest or monk. WH: 17C. Tibetan *bla-ma* (with silent *b*), lit. superior. Cp. DALAI LAMA.

lamantin *n.* the manatee. WH: 17C. French MANATEE.

Lamarckian *a.* of or relating to Lamarck. *Also n.* WH: 19C. Jean Baptiste *Lamarck*, 1744–1829, French naturalist + -IAN.

lamb *n.* the young of a sheep. *Also v.i.*, *v.t.* WH: pre-1200. Old English, from Germanic. No related words are known outside Germanic.

lambada *n.* an erotic Brazilian dance performed by couples in close contact with one another who gyrate their hips in synchronized movements. WH: late 20C. Portuguese, lit. beating, lashing, from *lambar* to beat, to whip.

lambast *v.t.* to beat. WH: 17C. LAM[1] + BASTE[2].

lambda *n.* the 11th letter of the Greek alphabet (Λ, λ) transliterated as Roman *l*. WH: 17C. Greek.

lambent *a.* (of flame or light) playing or moving about, touching slightly without burning. WH: 17C. Latin *lambens*, *lambentis*, pres.p. of *lambere* to lick. See also -ENT.

lambert *n.* a former measure of the luminous intensity or brightness of a surface, one lumen for every square centimetre. WH: 19C. Johann Heinrich *Lambert*, 1728–77, German mathematician.

Lambeth Walk *n.* a line dance popular in Britain in the 1930s. WH: mid-20C. *Lambeth Walk*, a street in Lambeth, S London.

lambrequin *n.* an ornamental strip of drapery over a door, window, mantelshelf etc. WH: 18C. French, from Dutch dim. of *lamper* veil. See also -KIN.

lame[1] *a.* disabled in one or more of the limbs, esp. the foot or leg. *Also v.t.* WH: pre-1200. Old English *lama*, from a Germanic n. meaning weak in the limbs, rel. to Old High German *luomi* dull, slack, gentle.

lame[2] *n.* a thin plate, overlapping with others, esp. in a suit of armour. WH: 16C. Old French, from Latin *lamina*, *lamna*. Cp. LAMINA.

lamé *n.* a fabric containing metallic, usu. gold or silver threads. *Also a.* WH: early 20C. French, lit. laminated, from *lame* metal leaf, from Latin *lamina*.

lamella *n.* a thin plate, layer, scale or membrane, esp. in bone tissue. WH: 17C. Latin, dim. of LAMINA. See LAME².

lamelli- *comb. form* of or relating to thin layers, scales etc. WH: Latin LAMELLA + *-i-*.

lamellibranch *n.* any of the Lamellibranchiata, a class of molluscs breathing by two pairs of platelike gills. WH: 19C. LAMELLI- + Greek *bragkhia* gills.

lamellicorn *a.* of or relating to the superfamily Scarabaeoidia (formerly Lamellicornia) a group of beetles, including the stag beetle and cockchafer, having short antennae terminated by a short lamellated club. *Also n.* WH: 19C. LAMELLI- + Latin *cornu* horn.

lamellirostral *a.* of or relating to the Lamellirostres, a group of birds, including ducks and geese, having bills with a fringe of thin plates along the inside edge. WH: 19C. LAMELLI- + Latin *rostrum* beak + -AL¹.

lament *v.i.* to mourn, to wail. *Also v.t., n.* WH: 14–15C. French *lamenter* or Latin *lamentari*, from *lamenta* (pl.) wailing, weeping.

lamia *n.* in classical mythology, a lascivious evil spirit in the form of a serpent with a woman's head. WH: 14–15C. Latin, from Greek mythical monster, carnivorous fish.

lamina *n.* a thin layer, plate, flake esp. of mineral or bone. WH: 17C. Latin. Cp. LAME².

Lammas *n.* 1 August, the day on which first-fruits were offered in Anglo-Saxon times. WH: pre-1200. Old English *hlāfmæsse*, from *hlāf* LOAF¹ + *mæsse* MASS. The name was subsequently taken to derive from LAMB + MASS.

lammergeier *n.* the great bearded vulture, *Gypaetus barbatus*, an inhabitant of the high mountains of S Europe, Asia and N Africa. WH: 19C. German *Lämmergeier*, from *Lämmer*, pl. of *Lamm* lamb + *Geier* vulture. Cp. OSPREY.

lamp *n.* a device for the production of artificial light, which may be fixed or portable and usu. has a glassed container enclosing the light source which may be an electric bulb, gas-jet or wick. *Also v.i., v.t.* WH: 12–14C. Old French *lampe*, from Late Latin *lampada*, from acc. of Latin *lampas*, from Greek *lampas*, *lampados* torch, rel. to *lampein* to shine.

lampas¹ *n.* a swelling of the roof of the mouth in horses. WH: 16C. Old French, prob. from dial. *lāpá* throat, *lāpé* gums, from a nasalized var. of Germanic base of LAP³.

lampas² *n.* a flowered silk or woollen cloth used in upholstery. WH: 14–15C. French, of uncertain orig. ? Rel. to *lambeau* rag, itself rel. to LABEL.

lampern *n.* the river lamprey, *Lampetra fluviatilis*. WH: 12–14C. Old French *lampreion*, dim. of *lampreie* LAMPREY.

lampion *n.* an oil lamp with a small coloured globe or cup, used in illuminations. WH: 19C. French, from Italian *lampione*, augm. of *lampa* (from French *lampe*) LAMP.

lampoon *n.* a satire, often a scurrilous personal one. *Also v.t.* WH: 17C. French *lampon*, ? from *lampons* let us drink (used as a refrain), 1st pers. pl. imper. of *lamper* to gulp down, to guzzle, nasalized var. of *laper* LAP³. See also -OON.

lamprey *n.* a blood-sucking eel-like fish belonging to the family Petromyzontidae, with a suctorial mouth with which it clings to its prey or to rocks. WH: 12–14C. Old French *lampreie* (Modern French *lamproie*), from Medieval Latin *lampreda*, prob. alt. of *lampetra*, from Latin *lambere* to lick + *petra* stone. The name would allude to the lamprey's ability to attach itself to stones by means of its mouth.

LAN *n.* a network of computers in close proximity to one another so that a high rate of data transfer is possible. WH: late 20C. Abbr. of *local area network*.

lanate *a.* woolly, covered with curly hairs. WH: 18C. Latin *lanatus*, from *lana* wool. See also -ATE².

Lancastrian *a.* of or relating to Lancashire or Lancaster. *Also n.* WH: 16C. *Lancaster*, a city in NW England, formerly the county town of Lancashire + -IAN.

lance *n.* a thrusting weapon consisting of a long shaft with a sharp point. *Also v.t.* WH: 12–14C. Old French, from Latin *lancea*, prob. of Celtic orig. Cp. LAUNCH¹.

lancelet *n.* a small transparent fishlike non-vertebrate of the family Branchiostomidae, esp. *Amphioxus lanceolatus*, that burrows in the sand. WH: 16C. LANCE + -LET.

lanceolate *a.* tapering to a point at each end. WH: 18C. Late Latin *lanceolatus*, from Latin *lanceola*, dim. of *lancea* LANCE. See also -ATE².

lancet *n.* a sharp surgical instrument with a two-edged blade, used in making incisions, opening abscesses etc. *Also a.* WH: 14–15C. Old French *lancette*, dim. of *lance* LANCE. See also -ET¹.

lancinate *v.t.* to tear, to lacerate. WH: 17C. Latin *lancinatus*, p.p. of *lancinare* to tear, rel. to *lacer*. See LACERATE¹, also -ATE³.

Land *n.* a federal state in Germany; a province in Austria. WH: early 20C. German LAND.

land *n.* the solid portion of the earth's surface, as distinct from the oceans and seas. *Also v.t., v.i., a.* WH: pre-1200. Old English, from German.

landammann *n.* the chairman of the governing body in some of the Swiss cantons. WH: 17C. Swiss German, from *Land* LAND + *Ammann*, var. of German *Amtmann*, from *Amt* office + *Mann* man.

landau *n.* a four-wheeled horse-drawn carriage with folding hoods at the front and back which can be raised to cover the occupants. WH: 18C. *Landau*, a town in W Germany, where orig. made.

landdros *n.* a district magistrate, civil commissioner, fiscal agent etc., in S Africa. WH: 18C. Afrikaans, from Dutch *land* LAND + *drost* bailiff.

landgrave *n.* a German title, dating from the 12th cent., orig. used to distinguish a governor of a province from inferior counts. WH: 14–15C. Middle Low German, from *land* LAND + *grave* count (cp. BURGRAVE, MARGRAVE).

ländler *n.* an Austrian or S German dance, similar to a slow waltz, in which the couples spin and clap. WH: 19C. German, from *Landel*, a district of Austria north of the River Ems.

landscape *n.* an extensive area of ground, esp. in the country, regarded as a setting or scenery, as a visual whole, or in relation to its particular topography. *Also a., v.t., v.i.* WH: 16C. Middle Dutch *lantscap* landscape, province. See LAND, -SHIP. Not rel. to SCOPE¹.

landsknecht *n.* a mercenary foot soldier, esp. a German pikeman, in the late 15th, 16th and 17th cents. WH: 17C. German, from gen. of *Land* LAND + *Knecht* soldier (cp. KNIGHT).

Landsturm *n.* the legislative assembly in a German-speaking country. WH: 19C. German, lit. land storm.

Landtag *n.* the legislative assembly of a German or Austrian Land. WH: 16C. German, lit. land day (cp. DIET²).

Landwehr *n.* the army reserve in German-speaking countries. WH: 19C. German, lit. land defence.

lane¹ *n.* a narrow road, way or passage, esp. between hedges. WH: pre-1200. Old English, from Germanic, ult. of unknown orig.

lane² *a.* lone. WH: 14–15C. Scottish var. of LONE.

lang *a.* long. WH: 14–15C. Scottish var. of LONG¹.

langlauf *n.* cross-country skiing; a cross-country skiing race. WH: early 20C. German, lit. long run.

Langobard *n.* a member of one of the founding tribes or an early inhabitant of Lombardy. WH: 18C. Late Latin *Langobardus*. See LOMBARD.

langouste *n.* the spiny lobster. WH: 19C. French, from Old Provençal *lagosta*, from Popular Latin alt. of Latin *locusta* LOCUST.

language *n.* the communication of ideas by articulate sounds or words of agreed meaning. WH: 12–14C. Old French *langage*, from Latin *lingua* tongue, language. See also -AGE.

langue *n.* (in linguistics) language regarded as an abstract system tacitly shared by a speech community. WH: 12–14C. French, from Latin *lingua* tongue, language.

languet *n.* a tongue-shaped part. WH: 14–15C. Old French *languete* (Modern French *languette*), dim of *langue* tongue. See also -ET¹.

languid *a.* lacking energy; indisposed to exertion. WH: 16C. French *languide* or Latin *languidus*, from *languere*. See LANGUISH, also -ID.

languish *v.i.* to become weak, feeble or sluggish. *Also n.* WH: 12–14C. Old French *languir*, *languiss-*, from var. of Latin *languere* to languish, rel. to *laxus* LAX. See also -ISH².

languor *n.* lack of energy. WH: 12–14C. Old French (Modern French *langueur*), from Latin, from *languere*. See LANGUISH.

langur *n.* any of several Asian monkeys, esp. of the genus *Presbytis*, having long tails and a circle of long hair around the face. **WH:** 19C. Hindi *laṅgūr*, from Sanskrit *lāṅgūla* having a tail.

laniary *a.* (of a tooth) adapted for tearing. *Also n.* **WH:** 19C. Latin *laniarius* pertaining to a butcher, from *lanius* butcher, from *laniare* to tear, to rend. See also -ARY[1].

laniferous *a.* bearing wool. **WH:** 17C. Latin *lanifer*, from *lana* wool. See -FEROUS.

lank *a.* lean, long and thin. *Also v.i.* **WH:** pre-1200. Old English *hlanc*, from Germanic base seen also in Middle High German *lenken* to bend, to turn, Old English *hlanca* hip, loin. Cp. FLINCH, LINK[1].

lanner *n.* (the female of) a large falcon, *Falco biarmicus*. **WH:** 14–15C. Old French *lanier*, ? use as n. of a. *lanier* cowardly, from derog. use of *lanier* weaver, from Latin *lanarius* wool merchant, from *lana* wool. See also -ER[2].

lanolin *n.* an oily, viscous substance forming the basis of ointments etc., extracted from wool. **WH:** 19C. Latin *lana* wool + *oleum* oil + -IN[1]. The word was coined in 1885 by the German physician Oscar Liebreich.

lantana *n.* an evergreen shrub of the tropical American genus *Lantana* of the verbena family, able to bloom continuously with spikes of yellow or orange flowers. **WH:** 18C. Modern Latin. The shrub is so called from the specific name of the wayfaring tree, *Viburnum lantana*, which it to some extent resembles.

lantern *n.* a light enclosed in a case with transparent sides or panes. *Also v.t.* **WH:** 12–14C. Old French *lanterne*, from Latin *lanterna*, from Greek *lamptēr* torch, lamp (from *lampein* to shine), based on *lucerna* lamp. Cp. LAMP.

lanthanum *n.* a metallic divalent element, at. no. 57, chem. symbol La, usu. occurring with didymium and cerium in cerite and used in the making of alloys and electronic devices. **WH:** 19C. Greek *lanthanein* to lie hidden + -IUM. The element was so named by the Swedish chemist Carl Gustaf Mosander, who discovered it in 1839, from the fact that it was found concealed in oxide of cerium.

lanugo *n.* pre-natal hair. **WH:** 14–15C. Latin down, from *lana* wool.

lanyard *n.* cord, esp. one worn round the neck, to which a whistle or knife is attached. **WH:** 14–15C. Old French *lanière*, earlier *lasniere*, from *lasne*, ? blend of *laz* LACE and *nasle*, from Germanic. (Cp. German *Nestel* string, lace.) The final syllable came to be associated with YARD[1]. Cp. HALYARD.

Lao *n.* a member of a Buddhist people of Laos and NE Thailand. *Also a.* **WH:** 18C. Lao.

Laodicean *a.* lukewarm or half-hearted in religion, politics etc. *Also n.* **WH:** 17C. Latin *Laodicea* (from Greek *Laodikeia*), a city in Asia Minor + -AN.

lap[1] *n.* the part of the body from the waist to the knees in a sitting position, esp. as a place for holding an object, a child etc. **WH:** pre-1200. Old English *læppa*, from Germanic. Cp. German *Lappen* rag, cloth. The original sense was the part of a garment that hangs down and that can be folded over, otherwise a flap. Cp. LAPEL.

lap[2] *n.* one circuit of a racecourse, running track etc. *Also v.t., v.i.* **WH:** 17C. LAP[1]. The original sense was a bundle of hay or straw. The current sense dates from the 19C.

lap[3] *v.i.* to drink by lifting with the tongue. *Also v.t., n.* **WH:** pre-1200. Old English *lapian*, from Germanic, rel. to Latin *lambere*, Greek *laptein* to lick, to lap.

laparoscope *n.* a fibre-optical instrument for the internal examination of the abdominal organs after insertion in the wall of the abdomen. **WH:** 19C. Greek *lapara* soft part of the body (between ribs and hip), flank, from *laparos* slack, loose + -O- + -SCOPE.

laparotomy *n.* incision into the cavity of the abdomen for examination or diagnosis. **WH:** 19C. Greek *lapara* (LAPAROSCOPE) + -O- + -TOMY.

lapel *n.* that part of a garment made to lap or fold over, esp. the fold on the front of a coat or jacket below the collar. **WH:** late 20C. LAP[1] + -EL.

lapicide *n.* a person who cuts or engraves stones. **WH:** 17C. Latin *lapicida*, from *lapidicida*, from *lapis, lapidis* stone. See -CIDE.

lapidary *n.* a person who cuts, polishes or engraves gems. *Also a.* **WH:** 14–15C. Latin *lapidarius*, from *lapis, lapidis* stone. See also -ARY[1].

lapilli *n.pl.* volcanic ashes, consisting of small, angular, stony or slaggy fragments. **WH:** 18C. Latin, pl. of *lapillus*, dim. of *lapis* stone.

lapis lazuli *n.* a rich blue mineral, used as a gemstone, containing sodium aluminium silicate and sulphur. **WH:** 14–15C. Latin *lapis* stone + Medieval Latin *lazuli*, gen. of *lazulum*, from Persian *lāžward* lapis lazuli. Cp. AZURE.

Lapp *n.* a member of a nomadic tribe inhabiting the region of Lapland in the far north of Europe. *Also a.* **WH:** 16C. Swedish. The Lapps' name for themselves is *Sami*.

lappet *n.* a little lap, fold or loose part of a garment or headdress; a flap. **WH:** 14–15C. LAP[1] + -ET[1].

lapsang souchong *n.* a smoky type of souchong tea. **WH:** 19C. Invented first word + SOUCHONG.

lapse *v.i.* to slide, to glide, to pass insensibly or by degrees. *Also v.t., n.* **WH:** 14–15C. Latin *lapsare*, from *lapsus*, p.p. of *labi* to slip, to fall, rel. to *labor* LABOUR.

lapsus *n.* a lapse, a slip. **WH:** 17C. Latin. See LAPSE.

lapwing *n.* a bird of the genus *Vanellus*, of the plover family, esp. *V. vanellus*, a British bird with black and white plumage, a backward-pointing crest and a shrill cry; the peewit. **WH:** pre-1200. Old English *hlēapewince*, from *hlēapan* LEAP + base (meaning to move from side to side) of WINK, assim. to LAP[2], WING. The bird is so named from its irregular flapping flight.

lar *n.* an ancient Roman tutelary god, usu. a deified ancestor or hero. **WH:** 16C. Latin, pl. *lares*.

larboard *n.* the port or left side of a vessel to a person standing on deck and facing the bow. *Also a.* **WH:** 14–15C. ? From LADE + BOARD, based on STARBOARD. The term would have referred to the side of the vessel on which cargo was received.

larceny *n.* the unlawful taking away of another's personal goods with intent to convert them for one's own use. **WH:** 15C. Old French *larcin*, from Latin *latrocinium*, from *latro, latronis* brigand, robber, mercenary soldier, from Greek *latron* pay.

larch *n.* a tree of the coniferous genus *Larix*, having deciduous bright-green foliage and tough, durable timber and yielding Venetian turpentine. **WH:** 16C. Middle High German *larche*, var. of *lerche*, from Old High German, from Latin *larix, laricis*, prob. from a local Alpine language of Indo-European orig. The name was introduced to English in 1548 by the English naturalist William Turner.

lard *n.* the rendered fat of pigs, esp. in solid white form for use in cooking. *Also v.t., v.i.* **WH:** 12–14C. Old French bacon, from Latin *laridum*, rel. to Greek *larinos* fat.

larder *n.* a room where meat and other provisions are kept, a pantry. **WH:** 12–14C. Old French *lardier*, from Medieval Latin *lardarium*, from Latin *laridum* LARD. See also -ER[2]. The original sense (to the 15C) was a store of meat. The more general sense evolved in the 14–15C.

large *a.* great in size, number, quantity, extent or capacity. *Also adv.* **WH:** 12–14C. Old French (Modern French *broad, wide*), from Latin *larga*, fem. of *largus* abundant, bountiful. The original sense (to the 17C) was abundant, ample.

largesse *n.* a present, a reward, a generous bounty (usu. from a superior to inferiors). **WH:** 12–14C. Old French, from Latin *largus*. See LARGE, also -ESS[2].

largo *adv.* slowly, broadly, in an ample, dignified style. *Also n.* **WH:** 17C. Italian broad, from Latin *largus*. See LARGE.

lariat *n.* a lasso. *Also v.t.* **WH:** 19C. Spanish *la reata*, from *la* the + *reata*, from *reatar* to tie again, from *re-* RE- + *atar*, from Latin *aptare* to adjust, from *aptus*. See APT.

larine *a.* of, relating to or like a gull. **WH:** 19C. Modern Latin *Larinae*, from *larus* gull. See also -INE.

lark[1] *n.* any bird of the family Alaudidae, with five British species, esp. the skylark, *Alauda arvensis*. **WH:** pre-1200. Old English *lāferce*, earlier *lǣwerce*, from Germanic, ult. of unknown orig. Cp. German *Lerche*. The name may ultimately imitate the bird's trilling song.

lark[2] *n.* a prank. *Also v.i.* **WH:** 19C. Orig. uncertain. ? from Old English *lācan* to play. Cp. earlier *skylark* (17C) from SKY + LARK[1].

larn *v.i.* to learn. *Also v.t.* **WH:** 18C. Dial. form of LEARN.

larrigan *n.* a high leather boot worn by woodsmen etc. **WH:** 19C. Orig. unknown.

larrikin _n._ a rowdy youngster, a young hooligan. WH: 19C. Orig. unknown.

larrup _v.t._ to thrash, to flog, to lash. WH: 19C. Orig. uncertain. ? Rel. to LATHER or LEATHER.

†larum _n._ an alarm. WH: 14–15C. Shortening of _alarum_ (ALARM).

larva _n._ the first condition of an insect on its issuing from the egg, when it is usu. in the form of a grub, caterpillar or maggot. WH: 17C. Latin ghost, mask. The stage was so called by Linnaeus because it is a 'ghost' form of the fully developed imago.

laryngeal _a._ of or relating to the larynx. WH: 18C. Modern Latin _laryngeus_, from _larynx, laryngis_ (LARYNX) + -AL[1].

laryngitis _n._ inflammation of the larynx. WH: 19C. Modern Latin _larynx, laryngis_ (LARYNX) + -ITIS.

laryngo- _comb. form_ of or relating to the larynx. WH: Modern Latin _larynx, laryngis_ LARYNX. See also -O-.

laryngology _n._ the branch of medical science dealing with the larynx and its diseases. WH: 19C. LARYNGO- + -LOGY.

laryngoscope _n._ an instrument with a reflecting mirror for obtaining a view of the larynx; any instrument for examining, or inserting a tube through the larynx. WH: 19C. LARYNGO- + -SCOPE.

laryngotomy _n._ the operation of making an incision into the larynx in order to provide an artificial channel for breathing. WH: 17C. Greek _laruggotomia_, from _larugx, laruggos_ LARYNX. See also -TOMY.

larynx _n._ a hollow muscular organ, situated in the upper part of the windpipe and containing the vocal cords in humans and higher vertebrates, the voice box. WH: 16C. Modern Latin, from Greek _larugx, laruggos_, prob. alt. of _laimos_ throat by assoc. with _pharunx_ PHARYNX.

lasagne _n._ pasta in the form of wide flat strips. WH: 19C. Italian, pl. of _lasagna_, ult. from Latin _lasanum_ chamber pot, ? also cooking pot.

Lascar _n._ a sailor from SE Asia or India. WH: 17C. Persian and Urdu _laškarī_ soldier, from _laškar_ army, camp.

lascivious _a._ lewd, wanton. WH: 14–15C. Late Latin _lasciviosus_, from Latin _lascivia_ licentiousness, from _lascivus_ sportive, lustful, wanton. See also -OUS.

laser _n._ an instrument which amplifies light waves by stimulation to produce a powerful, coherent beam of monochromatic light, an optical maser. WH: mid-20C. Acronym of _l_ight _a_mplification by _s_timulated _e_mission of _r_adiation, based on MASER.

lash _n._ a stroke with a whip. _Also v.t., v.i._ WH: 12–14C. ? Imit. Many words ending in _-ash_ are imit. Cp. BASH[1], CRASH[1], DASH, FLASH, GNASH, MASH[1], SLASH, SMASH, etc.

lasket _n._ a loop of line at the foot of a sail by which an additional piece of sail is attached. WH: 18C. ? Alt. of French _lacet_ (LATCHET) in same sense, based on GASKET.

lass _n._ a young woman, a girl. WH: 12–14C. Ult. from Old Norse _laskura_ (fem.) unmarried, from base seen in Old Swedish _løsk kona_ unmarried woman. The word is not from _*ladess_, as if a feminine form of LAD, as sometimes popularly explained.

Lassa fever _n._ an often fatal tropical viral disease symptomized by fever and muscle pain and transmitted by rats etc. WH: late 20C. _Lassa_, a village in NW Nigeria, where first reported in 1969.

lassitude _n._ weariness. WH: 14–15C. French, from Latin _lassitudo_, from _lassus_ weary. See also -TUDE.

lasso _n._ a rope, esp. of untanned hide, with a running noose, used for catching cattle, horses etc. _Also v.t._ WH: 18C. Spanish _lazo_, rel. to Old French _laz_ LACE.

last[1] _a._ coming after all others or at the end, final. _Also n., adv._ WH: pre-1200. Old English _latost_, from Germanic superl. of base of LATE. See also -EST[1]. _Latest_ is thus a more recent superl. of LATE. The original sense is preserved in _last word_. Cp. French _dernier cri_ (DERNIER).

last[2] _v.i._ to continue in existence, to go on. _Also n._ WH: pre-1200. Old English _læstan_, from Germanic, from base also of LAST[3]. The original sense (to the 15C) was to follow, to pursue. The current sense dates from the 12–14C.

last[3] _n._ a shaped wooden block on which boots and shoes are fashioned or repaired. WH: pre-1200. Old English _læst_, from Germanic base meaning to follow. Cp. LAST[2]. The original sense (to the 15C) was footprint, track, hence boot, hence shoemaker's model of a

foot for shaping and repairing boots and shoes. All these senses existed in Old English.

last[4] _n._ a certain weight or quantity, varying for different commodities (commonly 2 tons, 80 bushels or 640 gallons). WH: pre-1200. Old English _hlæst_, from Germanic base also of LADE.

latch _n._ a fastening for a door, gate etc., consisting of a bolt and catch. _Also v.t., v.i._ WH: 12–14C. Old English _læccan_ to grasp, to seize, from Germanic, from base rel. to those of Greek _lazesthai_ to grasp, Latin _laqueus_ noose.

†latchet _n._ a string for a shoe or sandal. WH: 14–15C. Old French _lachet_, var. of _lacet_, from _laz_ LACE. See also -ET[1].

late _a._ coming after the proper, usual or agreed time. _Also adv., n._ WH: pre-1200. Old English _læt_, from Germanic, from Indo-European base represented also by Latin _lassus_ weary. Rel. to LET[2]. For _latest_, see LAST[1]. Cp. LATTER. The sense recently deceased dates from the 14–15C.

lateen _a._ a term applied to a triangular sail, inclined at an angle of about 45°, used principally in the Mediterranean. _Also n._ WH: 16C. French _latine_, fem. of _Latin_ LATIN. The French _voile latine_ Latin sail was so called as it was used in the Mediterranean, at the centre of the former Roman Empire.

latent _a._ hidden or concealed. WH: 14–15C. Latin _latens, latentis_, pres.p. of _latere_ to lie hidden. See also -ENT.

-later _comb. form_ a person who worships a particular thing, as in _idolater_. WH: Greek _-latrēs_ worshipper.

lateral _a._ of or relating to, at, from or towards the side. _Also n._ WH: 14–15C. Latin _lateralis_, from _latus, lateris_ side. See also -AL[1].

Lateran _n._ a cathedral church at Rome, dedicated to St John the Baptist. _Also a._ WH: 12–14C. Latin _Laterana_, from the ancient Roman family of the Plautii _Laterani_.

laterigrade _a._ walking sideways (like a crab). WH: 19C. Latin _latus, lateris_ side + -I- + -GRADE.

laterite _n._ a red porous rock, composed of silicate of alumina and oxide of iron, found in extensive beds in India and SW Asia. WH: 19C. Latin _later_ brick + -ITE[1].

lateroversion _n._ sideways displacement of an organ or part, esp. the uterus. WH: 19C. Latin _latus, lateris_ side + -O- + _versus_ turned. See VERSION, also -ION.

latex _n._ the juice of milky plants, esp. rubber trees. WH: 17C. Latin liquid, fluid, prob. from Greek _latox_ drops of wine in the bottom of a cup, dregs.

lath _n._ a thin strip of wood, esp. one nailed to rafters to support tiles or to the studs of partitions to support plastering. _Also v.t._ WH: pre-1200. Old English _lætt_, from Germanic. Cp. German _Latte_.

lathe[1] _n._ a machine for cutting, shaping and polishing wood, ivory, metal etc. by rotating it against a fixed tool. _Also v.t._ WH: 12–14C. Prob. from Old Danish _lad_ stand, supporting framework, from Old Norse _hlath_, rel. to _hlatha_ LADE.

lathe[2] _n._ a former division of Kent. WH: pre-1200. Old English _læth_, rel. to Old Norse _láth_ landed possession, land, from Germanic.

lather _n._ froth or foam made by soap moistened with water or caused by profuse sweating. _Also v.t._ WH: pre-1200. Old English _læthor_, from Germanic, from Indo-European base also of Greek _loutron_ bath. Rel. to LYE. The earliest Old English sense was washing soda, or its froth.

lathi _n._ a long, heavy stick used as a weapon in India, esp. by police. WH: 19C. Hindi _lāṭhī_.

laticlave _n._ a broad purple stripe worn on the front of the tunic, as a mark of senatorial rank in ancient Rome. WH: 17C. Late Latin _laticlavium_, from _latus_ broad + _clavus_ purple stripe.

latifundium _n._ a large landed or agricultural estate, esp. in ancient Rome. WH: 17C. Latin, from _latus_ broad + _fundus_ landed estate.

Latin _a._ of, relating to or expressed in the language of the ancient Romans. _Also n._ WH: pre-1200. Latin _Latinus_, from _Latium_, an area of central Italy including Rome. See also -INE.

latitude _n._ angular distance on a meridian, angular distance of a place north or south of the equator. WH: 14–15C. Latin _latitudo, latitudinis_, from _latus_ broad. See also -TUDE.

latria _n._ in the Roman Catholic Church, that supreme worship which can lawfully be offered to God alone. WH: 16C. Ecclesiastical Latin, from Greek _latreia_, from _latreuein_ to wait on, to serve with prayer.

latrine *n.* a lavatory, a toilet, esp. in a camp or barracks. WH: 12–14C. French, from Latin *latrina*, contr. of *lavatrina*, from *lavare* to wash. Cp. LAVATORY.

-latry *comb. form* worship or excessive devotion, as in *bibliolatry*, *idolatry*, *zoolatry*. WH: Greek *-latreia* worship. Cp. LATRIA.

latten *n.* a finer kind of brass, of which the incised plates for sepulchral monuments, crosses etc., were made. *Also a.* WH: 12–14C. Old French *laton* (Modern French *laiton*), of unknown orig.

latter *a.* (of two) second, second-mentioned. WH: pre-1200. Old English *lætra*, comp. of *læt* LATE. *Later* is a more recent comp., formed on LATE.

lattice *n.* a structure of laths or strips of metal or wood crossing and forming openwork. *Also a., v.t.* WH: 12–14C. French *lattis*, from *latte* LATH.

Latvian *n.* a native or inhabitant of Latvia, a Lett. *Also a.* WH: early 20C. *Latvia*, a Baltic state between Estonia and Lithuania + -AN.

laud *v.t.* to praise, to extol. *Also n.* WH: 14–15C. Latin *laudare*, from *laus*, *laudis* praise.

laudanum *n.* opium prepared in alcohol, tincture of opium, formerly used as a painkiller. WH: 16C. Modern Latin, word invented by Paracelsus. Paracelsus used the word as the name of a costly medical preparation in which opium was early thought to be the active ingredient. He may have based it on Latin LADANUM or on *laudare* LAUD, or perhaps a blend of both.

laugh *v.i.* to express amusement, scorn or exultation by inarticulate sounds and the convulsive movements of the face and body. *Also v.t., n.* WH: pre-1200. Old English *hlæhhan*, from Germanic, ult. from Indo-European imit. base. Cp. CLUCK.

launce *n.* a sand eel. WH: 17C. ? Var. of LANCE. Cp. LANCELET.

launch[1] *v.t.* to cause to glide into the water (e.g. a vessel), or take off from land (e.g. a space rocket). *Also v.i., n.* WH: 12–14C. Old Northern French *lancher*, var. of Old French *lancier* LANCE. The original sense (to the 17C) was to pierce, to wound.

launch[2] *n.* a large open pleasure-boat propelled by steam, electricity or internal-combustion engine. WH: 17C. Spanish *lancha* pinnace, ? of Malay orig. Not rel. to LAUNCH[1].

launder *v.t.* to wash and iron (clothing, linen etc.). *Also v.i., n.* WH: 12–14C. Contr. of LAVENDER. The original sense (as a noun) was a person who washes linen. The verb evolved from the noun in the 16C.

lauraceous *a.* of or relating to the family Lauraceae which includes the laurels and avocado. WH: 19C. Modern Latin *Lauraceae*, from *laurea* LAUREL. See also -OUS.

Laurasia *n.* the supercontinent thought to have existed in the northern hemisphere after the first division of Pangaea 200 million years ago, comprising what is now N America, Greenland, Europe and Asia apart from the Indian subcontinent. WH: mid-20C. Modern Latin, from *Laurentia*, the ancient land mass corresponding to N America (see LAURENTIAN) + *Eurasia* (EURASIAN).

laureate *a.* crowned or decked with laurel. *Also n.* WH: 14–15C. Latin *laureatus*, from *laurea* laurel tree, laurel crown, use as n. of fem. of *laureus*, from *laurus* LAUREL.

laurel *n.* a glossy-leaved evergreen shrub, *Laurus nobilis*, also called the bay tree. WH: 12–14C. Old French *lorier* (Modern French *laurier*), from Provençal *laurier*, from *laur*, from Latin *laurus*, prob. of Mediterranean orig.

Laurentian *a.* of, relating to or in the style of D.H. Lawrence or T.E. Lawrence. WH: 19C. Latin *Laurentius* Laurence, Lawrence + -AN.

laurustinus *n.* an ornamental evergreen shrub, *Viburnum tinus*, with pinkish-white winter flowers and dark-blue berries. WH: 17C. Modern Latin *laurus tinus*, from Latin *laurus* laurel + *tinus* laurustinus.

lav *n.* a lavatory. WH: early 20C. Abbr. of LAVATORY.

lava *n.* molten matter flowing in streams from volcanic vents. WH: 18C. Italian (orig. Neapolitan dial.), from Latin *lavare* to wash. Italian etymologists derive the word from Latin *labes* a fall, from *labi* to fall.

lavabo *n.* the washing of the celebrant's hands, in the Roman Catholic and other Churches, after the offertory and before the Eucharist. WH: 18C. Latin I will wash, 1st pers. sing. fut. of *lavare* to wash. The word comes from the opening sentence of Ps. xxvi.6, *Lavabo inter innocentes manus meas*, I will wash mine hands in innocency.

lava-lava *n.* a rectangular piece of printed cloth worn as a shirtlike garment by both sexes in Polynesia. WH: 19C. Samoan.

lavatera *n.* a plant of the genus *Lavatera*, closely related to the mallows, grown usu. for its large white, pink or purple flowers. WH: 18C. Modern Latin, from J.R. *Lavater*, 17C Swiss physician and naturalist.

lavatory *n.* a receptacle for urinating or defecating into, usu. connected by pipes to a sewer and flushed with water; a toilet. WH: 14–15C. Late Latin *lavatorium*, from Latin *lavatus*, p.p. of *lavare* to wash. See also -ORY[1]. A lavatory was originally a vessel for washing (cp. LAVABO), then a room with washing facilities. The current sense dates from the 17C.

lave *v.t.* to wash; to bathe. *Also v.i.* WH: pre-1200. Old English *lafian*, from Germanic, from Latin *lavare* to wash.

lavender *n.* a sweet-scented flowering shrub, *Lavandula vera*, cultivated for its scent, its mauve or blue flowers, and its oil which is used in perfumery. *Also a., v.t.* WH: 12–14C. Anglo-French *lavendre*, from Medieval Latin *lavendula*, of unknown orig. ? from Latin *lividus* bluish, LIVID. The word is popularly derived from Latin *lavare* to wash, from the plant's use as a perfume in washing and laundering.

laver *n.* any of various types of seaweed, esp. *Porphyra umbilicaulis*, *P. vulgaris* and other edible species. WH: pre-1200. Latin, orig. a water plant mentioned by Pliny. The sense seaweed dates from the 17C.

lavish *a.* spending or giving with profusion. *Also v.t.* WH: 14–15C. Old French *lavasse* deluge of rain, from *laver* to wash, to pour. See also -ISH[1].

lavolta *n.* an old Italian dance for two persons, with much high leaping, popular in the 16th cent. WH: 16C. Italian, from *la* the + *volta* turn. Cp. VOLTA as an alternative name for the same dance.

law[1] *n.* a rule of conduct imposed by authority or accepted by the community as binding. *Also v.i.* WH: pre-1200. Old English *lagu*, from Old Norse pl. of *lag* something laid down, ult. from Germanic base of LAY[1], LIE[2].

†law[2] *n.* a hill, esp. a rounded or conical hill of moderate size. WH: 12–14C. Var. of dial. *low*, from Old English *hlāw*, *hlǣw*, from Germanic, ult. from Indo-European base meaning slope.

lawks *int.* an old exclamation of surprise or wonder. WH: 18C. Alt. of LORD, ? also rel. to ALACK.

lawn[1] *n.* a grassy space kept smooth and closely mown in a garden, park etc. WH: 16C. Alt. of dial. *laund* open space among trees, glade, from Old French *launde* (Modern French *lande*) wooded district, heath, from Gaulish *landa*, rel. to Welsh *llan* clearing, enclosure, church (in place names such as Llandudno).

lawn[2] *n.* a cotton or linen fabric, finer than cambric (e.g. used for the sleeves of an Anglican bishop's rochet). WH: 14–15C. Prob. from *Laon*, a city in N France, long a centre of linen manufacture.

lawrencium *n.* a radioactive element, at. no. 103, chem. symbol Lr, with a short half-life, orig. produced in America. WH: mid-20C. Ernest O. *Lawrence*, 1901–58, US physicist + -IUM. The element was so named in 1961 by four nuclear physicists in memory of the founder of their laboratory.

lax *a.* not strict; careless. WH: 14–15C. Latin *laxus* loose, rel. to SLACK[1].

lay[1] *v.t.* to cause to lie, to place in a horizontal position. *Also v.i., n.* WH: pre-1200. Old English *lecgan*, from Germanic base also of LIE[2].

lay[2] *a.* of or relating to the people as distinct from the *clergy*. WH: 12–14C. Old French *lai* (Modern French *laïque*), from Late Latin *laicus*, from Greek *laikos*, from *laos* people.

lay[3] *n.* a lyric song or ballad. WH: 12–14C. Old French *lai*, of uncertain orig. ? from Celtic. Cp. Irish *laid* song, poem.

layer *n.* a thickness or anything spread out (usu. one of several), a stratum. *Also v.t., v.i.* WH: 12–14C. LAY[1] + -ER[1].

layette *n.* the outfit for a newborn infant. WH: 19C. French, dim. of Old French *laie* drawer, box, from Dutch *laege*. See also -ETTE.

lay figure *n.* a jointed figure of the human body used by artists for hanging drapery etc. WH: 18C. From obs. *layman*, from Dutch *leeman* (from *led* (now *lid*) limb, joint + *man* MAN) + FIGURE.

†**lazar** *n.* a person infected with a loathsome disease, esp. a leper. WH: 12–14C. Medieval Latin *lazarus*, from name of *Lazarus* in biblical parable of the rich man and the leper. 'There was a certain beggar named Lazarus ... full of sores' (Luke xvi.20).

lazaretto *n.* a hospital (chiefly abroad) for persons suffering from some contagious disease, esp. leprosy. WH: 16C. Italian, dim. of *lazzaro* LAZAR.

lazulite *n.* an azure-blue to pale greenish-blue mineral, composed of phosphate of aluminium and magnesium. WH: 19C. *lazuli* (from LAPIS LAZULI) + -ITE[1].

lazurite *n.* a rare blue mineral composed of sodium aluminium silicate and sulphide, used as the gemstone lapis lazuli. WH: 19C. Medieval Latin *lazur*, from Arabic *lāzaward* (AZURE). See also -ITE[1].

lazy *a.* idle, disinclined to labour or exertion. WH: 16C. ? Of Low Dutch orig. Cp. Low German *lasich* languid, idle. Not rel. to LASSITUDE or LEISURE.

lb *abbr.* pound(s). WH: Latin LIBRA.

L.Ch. *abbr.* Licentiate in Surgery. WH: Abbr. of Latin *Licentiatus Chirurgiae* Licenciate in Surgery.

-**le**[1] *suf.* forming nouns esp. denoting appliances or instruments as in *handle*, *thimble* or animals and plants, as in *beetle*, *thistle*. WH: Old English *-el*, *-ela*, *-ele*, from Germanic.

-**le**[2] *suf.* forming nouns which orig. had a diminutive sense, as in *angle*, *castle*, *puddle*, *novel*, *tunnel*. WH: Old French *-el*, from Latin *-ellum*, or from Old French *-el*, from Latin *-ale*, neut. sing. of *-alis*, or from Old French *-aille*, from Latin *-alia*, neut. pl. of *-alis*, or from Old French *-eille*, from Latin *-icula*.

-**le**[3] *suf.* forming adjectives, often with, or orig. with, the sense 'likely or liable to', as in *brittle*, *fickle*, *little*. WH: As -LE[1].

-**le**[4] *suf.* forming verbs, esp. expressing repeated action or having a diminutive sense, as in *crackle*, *tickle*, *wriggle*. WH: Old English *-lian*, from Germanic.

lea[1] *n.* a meadow. WH: pre-1200. Old English *lēah*, from Germanic, from Indo-European base also of Latin *lucus* grove.

lea[2] *n.* land left untilled, fallow land, land under grass. Also *a.* WH: pre-1200. ? From base of LAY[1], LIE[2].

lea[3] *n.* a length of yarn which varies for different materials, usu. 80 yards for wool, 120 for cotton and silk, 300 for linen. WH: 14–15C. ? From French *lier* to bind, to tie, from Latin *ligare*.

leach *v.t.* to wash out or separate (a soluble constituent) by percolation. Also *v.i.*, *n.* WH: pre-1200. Old English *leccan*, from Germanic, from base also Old English *lacu* small stream (LAKE[1]). The original meaning (to the 16C) was to water, to wet. The current sense dates from the 19C.

lead[1] *v.t.* to conduct, to guide by taking by the hand or halter or by showing the way. Also *v.i.*, *n.*, *a.* WH: pre-1200. Old English *lǣdan*, from Germanic, from base also of LOAD.

lead[2] *n.* a soft malleable and ductile, bluish-grey, toxic heavy metal, at. no. 82, chem. symbol Pb, occurring naturally in galena and used in building, in alloys and paints and as a shield against radiation. Also *a.*, *v.t.* WH: pre-1200. Old English *lēad*, from Germanic. Cp. German *Lot* plummet, solder.

leader *n.* a person who or something which leads. WH: 12–14C. LEAD[1] + -ER[1].

leading *a.* main, principal. Also *n.* WH: 12–14C. LEAD[1] + -ING[2].

leaf *n.* any of the usu. flat, green, lateral organs of plants which aid in the assimilation of food-materials and the transpiration and absorption of carbon dioxide from the atmosphere. Also *v.i.* WH: pre-1200. Old English *lēaf*, from Germanic. Cp. German *Laub* foliage.

leaflet *n.* a handbill, circular. Also *v.i.* WH: 18C. LEAF + -LET.

league[1] *n.* a combination or union for mutual help or the pursuit of common interests. Also *v.i.* WH: 14–15C. Partly from French *ligue*, from Italian *liga*, Latinized form of *lega*, from *legare* to bind, from Latin *ligare*, partly directly from Italian *lega*.

league[2] *n.* an old measure of distance, varying in different countries (in England usu. about three land or nautical miles, about 4.8 km). WH: 14–15C. Late Latin *leuca*, *leuga*, from Late Greek *leugē*, from Gaulish, or from Provençal *lega*.

†**leaguer** *n.* a siege. Also *v.t.* WH: 16C. Dutch *leger* camp, rel. to LAIR[1]. Cp. LAAGER.

leak *v.i.* to let liquid, gas etc. pass in or out through a hole, crevice or fissure. Also *v.t.*, *n.* WH: 14–15C. Prob. from Middle Dutch *leken* to drip, ult. from Germanic var. of base of LACK.

leal *a.* loyal, true. WH: 12–14C. Old French *leel* LOYAL.

lean[1] *v.i.* to incline one's body from an erect attitude. Also *v.t.*, *n.* WH: pre-1200. Old English *hleonian*, *hlinian*, from Germanic base rel. to that of Greek *klimax* ladder, CLIMAX, Latin *clivus* declivity. Rel. to INCLINE[1].

lean[2] *a.* thin, without surplus fat or flesh. Also *n.* WH: pre-1200. Old English *hlǣne*, from Germanic, of uncertain orig. ? Rel. to LEAN[1]. Cp. Old English *hlǣnan* to cause to lean.

leap *v.i.* to jump, to spring upwards or forward. Also *v.t.*, *n.* WH: pre-1200. Old English *hlēapan*, from Germanic. Cp. German *laufen* to run.

learn *v.t.* to acquire knowledge of or skill in by study, experience or instruction. Also *v.i.* WH: pre-1200. Old English *leornian*, from Germanic, from base also of LORE[1]. Cp. German *lernen*.

lease *n.* a letting or renting of land, houses, offices etc. for a specified period. Also *v.t.* WH: 14–15C. Old French *lais*, *leis*, from *lesser*, *laissier* (Modern French *laisser*) to let, to leave, from Latin *laxare*, from *laxus* loose, LAX.

leash *n.* a lead for a dog or other animal. Also *v.t.* WH: pre-1200. Old French *lesse* (Modern French *laisse*), from *lesser*, *laissier*. See LEASE. The Old French verb had the special sense to let run on a slack lead. The original application of the English word was to a hound or hunting dog.

least *a.* smallest, slightest. Also *adv.*, *n.* WH: pre-1200. Old English *lǣst*, contr. of *lǣsest*, from Germanic, from bases of LESS, -EST[1].

leat *n.* a watercourse conveying water to a mill etc. WH: 16C. From base of Old English *lǣtan* LET[1].

leather *n.* the tanned or dressed skin or hide of an animal. Also *a.*, *v.t.* WH: pre-1200. Old English *lether*, from Germanic, from Indo-European base also of Old Irish *lethar* (modern Irish *leathar*), Welsh *lledr*, Breton *ler*. Cp. German *Leder*.

leave[1] *v.t.* to go or depart from. Also *v.i.* WH: pre-1200. Old English *lǣfan*, from a Germanic v. meaning to remain. Cp. German *bleiben* to remain, to stay. Not rel. to LEAVE[2].

leave[2] *n.* permission. WH: pre-1200. Old English *lēaf*, from Germanic base also of LIEF. Cp. German *erlauben* to permit, *Urlaub* leave, furlough. The earliest sense was permission in general. The sense permission to be absent from work or duty dates from the 18C.

leave[3] *v.i.* to produce leaves. WH: 12–14C. LEAF.

leaven *n.* fermenting dough or any other substance (e.g. yeast) mixed with other dough, a batter etc. in order to cause fermentation and make it lighter. Also *v.t.* WH: 12–14C. Old French *levain*, from Latin *levamen*, lit. means of raising, from *levare* to lighten, to relieve, to raise, from *levis* light.

Lebanese *a.* of, relating or belonging to Lebanon. Also *n.* WH: early 20C. *Lebanon*, a coastal country in the E Mediterranean + -ESE.

Lebensraum *n.* territory considered necessary for a country's expanding population in terms of trade and settlement. WH: early 20C. German, lit. living room, from gen. of *Leben* life + *Raum* space, ROOM.

lechaim *int.* a drinking toast. Also *n.* WH: mid-20C. Hebrew *lĕ-ḥayyīm* to life!

lecher *n.* a man who continually lusts after or seduces women. Also *v.i.* WH: 12–14C. Old French *lichiere*, from *lecher* to live in debauchery (Modern French *lécher* to lick), from Frankish, from Germanic base of LICK. Cp. LICKERISH.

lecithin *n.* a nitrogenous fatty substance containing phosphorus found in the cellular tissue of animal and vegetable bodies. WH: 19C. Greek *lekithos* yolk + -IN[1].

Leclanché cell *n.* a primary electric cell consisting of a carbon cathode covered with manganese dioxide, all in a porous pot, and a zinc anode dipping into ammonium chloride solution. WH: 19C. Georges *Leclanché*, 1839–82, French chemist.

lectern *n.* a reading desk or stand for a book from which parts of a church service, esp. the lessons, are said or sung. WH: 12–14C. Old French *letrun*, from Medieval Latin *lectrum*, from Latin *legere* to read.

lectin *n.* any of various usu. plant-derived proteins that bind to specific carbohydrate groups and cause agglutination of specific cell types. WH: mid-20C. Latin *lectus*, p.p. of *legere* to choose, to select + -IN¹.

lection *n.* a reading or variation in a text. WH: 12–14C. Latin·*lectio*, *lectionis*, from *lectus*, p.p. of *legere* to read. See also -ION.

lector *n.* a person whose duty it is to read the lessons in church services. WH: 14–15C. Latin, from *lectus*. See LECTION, also -OR.

lecture *n.* a formal expository or instructive discourse on any subject, before an audience or a class. *Also v.i.*, *v.t.* WH: 14–15C. Old French, or from Medieval Latin *lectura*, from *lectus*. See LECTION, also -URE. The original meaning (to the 17C) was a particular way of reading a text or interpreting it. The current sense dates from the 16C.

lecythus *n.* in ancient Greece, a narrow-necked vase or flask for oil, unguents etc. WH: 19C. Late Latin, from Greek *lēkuthos*.

lederhosen *n.pl.* leather shorts with braces, the traditional male dress of Austria and Bavaria. WH: mid-20C. German, from *Leder* leather + pl. of *Hose* trouser.

ledge *n.* a shelf or shelflike projection. WH: 12–14C. Orig. uncertain. ? An early form of LAY¹.

ledger *n.* the principal book in a set of account-books, in which a record of all trade transactions is entered. *Also a., v.i.* WH: 14–15C. Prob. from early form of LAY¹ corr. to Dutch *leggen* LAY¹, *liggen* LIE². See also -ER¹. The basic sense is a book that lies permanently in a particular place. Originally (to the 17C) this was a large Bible or breviary. The current sense dates from the 16C.

lee *n.* shelter, protection. *Also a.* WH: pre-1200. Old English *hlēo*, *hlēow*, from Germanic.

leech¹ *n.* an aquatic annelid worm of the suctorial order Hirudinea, employed for the local extraction of blood. *Also v.t.* WH: pre-1200. Old English *lǣce*, from Germanic, of unknown orig. The Germanic origin was early assimilated to identical Old English *lǣce* physician, from Germanic, from Indo-European. Cp. Irish *liaigh* (now *lia*) doctor.

leech² *n.* the perpendicular edge of a square sail. WH: 15C. ? Rel. to Old Norse *lík*, a nautical term of uncertain meaning. Cp. Swedish *lik*, Danish *lig* bolt rope.

leek *n.* a culinary vegetable, *Allium porrum*, allied to the onion, with a straight green stem that unfurls as overlapping leaves and a small, white cylindrical bulb, the national emblem of Wales. WH: pre-1200. Old English *lēac*, from Germanic base also of Finnish *laukka*, Old Church Slavonic *lukŭ* (Russian *luk*). Cp. GARLIC.

leer *n.* an oblique or sly look. *Also v.i.* WH: 16C. Prob. from obs. *leer* face, cheek, from Old English *hlēor*, from Germanic. A leer can be seen as a glance over one's cheek.

lees *n.pl.* the sediment of liquor which settles to the bottom. WH: 14–15C. Pl. of obs. *lee*, from Old French *lie*, from Gaulish. Cp. Old Irish *lige* bed, rel. to LIE².

†leet¹ *n.* a court leet; a court of record. WH: 12–14C. Anglo-French *lete*, of unknown orig.

leet² *n.* a list of candidates for any office. WH: 14–15C. Prob. from Old French *litte*, var. of *liste* LIST¹.

left¹ *a.* of, relating to or situated on the side that is to the west when a person faces north, as opposed to *right*. *Also adv.*, *n.* WH: pre-1200. Old English *lyft*- weak, in words such as *lyftādl* paralysis (lit. weak disease), from Germanic, ult. of unknown orig. The Old English sense of weak probably arose from the fact that the left hand is usually weaker than the right. Cp. GAUCHE.

left² *a.* that has been discarded or laid aside. WH: pre-1200. Old English *gelǣfed*, p.p. of *lǣfan* LEAVE¹.

leg *n.* each of the limbs by which humans and other mammals walk, esp. the part from the knee to the ankle. *Also a., v.t.* WH: 12–14C. Old Norse *leggr*, from Germanic. Cp. Latin *lacertus* muscles. The original Old English word was *sceanca* SHANK.

legacy *n.* a bequest, money or property bequeathed by will. WH: 14–15C. Old French *legacie*, from Medieval Latin *legatia* legateship, from *legatus* LEGATE. See also -CY. The sense bequest also represents Medieval Latin *legantia*, from *legare* to bequeath. An early sense to the 18C was the function or office of a delegate or deputy, especially a papal legate.

legal *a.* of, relating to, or according to law. WH: 14–15C. Old French *légal* or Latin *legalis*, from *lex*, *legis* law. See also -AL¹. Cp. LEAL, LOYAL.

legate *n.* a papal emissary. WH: pre-1200. Old French *légat*, from Latin *legatus*, p.p. (used as n.) of *legare* to bequeath. See also -ATE¹. A legate originally deputized for the Pope and was granted his authority.

legato *adv.*, *a.* in an even gliding manner without a break. *Also n.* WH: 18C. Italian, p.p. of *legare* to bind, from Latin *ligare*.

legend *n.* a traditional story, esp. one popularly accepted as true. WH: 12–14C. Old French *légende*, from Medieval Latin *legenda*, lit. things to be read, neut. pl. of ger. of *legere* to read, taken as fem. sing. See also -END. The word was originally the term for a collection of saints' lives, like the 13C *Golden Legend*. The current general sense dates from the 17C.

legerdemain *n.* sleight of hand, a trick in which the eye is deceived by the quickness of the hand, conjuring. WH: 14–15C. French *léger-demain*, from *léger* light + *de* of + *main* hand.

leghorn *n.* a plait of the straw of bearded Italian wheat cut green and bleached, used for bonnets and hats. WH: 18C. *Leghorn*, anglicized form of *Legorno*, now *Livorno*, a city and port in NW Italy.

legible *a.* clear enough to be read. WH: 14–15C. Late Latin *legibilis*, from *legere* to read. See also -IBLE.

legion *n.* a division of the ancient Roman army, varying, at different periods, from 3000 to 6000 men. WH: 12–14C. Old French (Modern French *légion*), from Latin *legio*, *legionis*, from *legere* to choose, to levy. See also -ION.

legislate *v.i.* to make or enact a law or laws. WH: 18C. Back-formation from *legislator* (15C) or *legislation* (17C), the former from Latin *legis lator*, i.e. *legis*, gen. of *lex* law + *lator* proposer, mover, from *latus*, p.p. of *tollere* to raise.

legist *n.* a person learned in the law. WH: 14–15C. Old French *légiste* or Medieval Latin *legista*, from Latin *lex*, *legis* law. See also -IST.

legit *a.* legitimate. *Also n.* WH: 19C. Abbr. of LEGITIMATE¹.

legitimate¹ *a.* lawful, properly authorized. *Also n.* WH: 14–15C. Medieval Latin *legitimatus*, p.p. of *legitimare* to legitimate, from Latin *lex*, *legis* law. See also -ATE².

legitimate² *v.t.* to make, pronounce or prove legitimate or legitimately born. WH: 15C. Medieval Latin *legitimatus*, p.p. of *legitimare*. See LEGITIMATE¹, also -ATE³.

Lego® *n.* a building toy mainly consisting of connecting plastic bricks. WH: mid-20C. Danish *leg godt* play well, from *lege* to play + *godt* GOOD.

legume *n.* the fruit or pod of a leguminous plant, usu. dehiscent along its face and back, and bearing its seeds on either margin of the ventral suture (as the pod of the pea). WH: 17C. French *légume*, from Latin *legumen*, from *legere* to gather. The fruit is so called because it is gathered by hand.

lehr *n.* a tunnel-shaped furnace for annealing glass. WH: 17C. Orig. unknown.

lei *n.* a garland or necklace of flowers. WH: 19C. Hawaiian.

Leicester *n.* a type of usu. orange-coloured cheese resembling cheddar. WH: 18C. *Leicester*, a city in Leicestershire, central England.

leishmania *n.* any of a genus, *Leishmania*, of parasitic flagellate protozoans that cause skin diseases in humans and animals. WH: early 20C. Modern Latin, from W.B. *Leishman*, 1865–1926, British pathologist + -IA.

leister *n.* a pronged fishing-spear, esp. for salmon. *Also v.t.* WH: 16C. Old Norse *ljóstr*, from *ljósta* to strike.

leisure *n.* freedom from business, occupation or hurry. *Also a.* WH: 12–14C. Old French *leisir* (Modern French *loisir*), from Latin *licere* to be allowed. Cp. LICENCE.

leitmotiv *n.* a leading, representative or recurring theme in a composition, orig. a musical theme invariably associated with a certain person, situation or idea throughout an opera etc. WH: 19C. German, from *leit*- leading + *Motiv* MOTIVE. The term was first used in *c.*1865 by the Austrian composer A.W. Ambros in an article about Wagner's operas.

lek¹ *n.* the chief currency of Albania. WH: early 20C. Abbr. of Albanian *Aleksandr* Alexander, from Alexander III (the Great), 356–323 BC, King of Macedonia.

lek² *n.* an area where certain species of birds (esp. black grouse) assemble for sexual display and courtship. WH: 19C. ? Swedish *leka* to play.

†leman *n.* a sweetheart of either sex. WH: 12–14C. LIEF + MAN.

lemma *n.* an auxiliary proposition taken to be valid in order to demonstrate some other proposition. WH: 16C. Latin, from Greek *lēmma* something taken for granted, theme, argument, from base also of *lambanein* to take.

lemme *contr.* let me. WH: 19C. Contr. of *let me.* Cp. GIMME, LUMME.

lemming *n.* a small Arctic volelike rodent of the genus *Lemmus* and related genera, esp. the Scandinavian variety *L. lemmus* which migrates in very large numbers when its population reaches a peak, often attempts to cross large areas of water and is popularly supposed to be prone to mass suicide. WH: 18C. Norwegian and Danish, rel. to Swedish *lämmel*, Old Norse *lómundr*, of uncertain orig. The meaning may be barker, from a word related to Latin *latrare*, Old Slavonic *lajati* (Russian *layat'*) to bark.

Lemnian *a.* of or relating to Lemnos. *Also n.* WH: 18C. Latin *Lemnius*, Greek *Lēmnios*, from *Lēmnos* Lemnos, an island in the Aegean sea + -AN.

lemniscate *n.* a curve of the general form of a figure 8, ∞. WH: 18C. Modern Latin *lemniscata*, fem. of Latin *lemniscatus* adorned with ribbons. See LEMNISCUS, also -ATE[1].

lemniscus *n.* a bundle of fibres or ribbon-like appendages in the brain connected to the thalamus. WH: 19C. Latin, from Greek *lēmniskos* ribbon.

lemon *n.* the oval, acid, yellow-skinned fruit of the lemon tree. *Also a.* WH: 14–15C. Old French *limon* (French *lime*), from Medieval Latin *limo, limonis*, from Arabic *līmūn, laymūn* fruits of the citron kind.

lemon sole *n.* a flatfish, *Microstomus kitt*, with brown markings, valued as a food. WH: 19C. French *limande*, from Old French *lime*, ? rel. to *lime* rasp, in sense prickly fish. Not rel. to LEMON.

lempira *n.* the standard monetary unit of Honduras, equivalent to 100 centavos. WH: mid-20C. *Lempira*, 1497–1537, an Indian chieftain killed when leading an army against the Spanish conquistadors.

lemur *n.* any member of a genus of arboreal nocturnal animals allied to the monkeys, having pointed snouts, long tails and occurring naturally only in Madagascar. WH: 16C. Modern Latin, from Latin *lemures* (pl.) shades of the dead. The animal is so called because of its nocturnal habits and ghostly appearance.

lend *v.t.* to grant for temporary use. *Also v.i.* WH: pre-1200. Old English *lǣnan*, from Germanic base also of LOAN. The *-d* appeared on an analogy with verbs such as BEND and SEND that have a similar p.p. (*bent, sent*).

length *n.* measure or extent from end to end, as distinct from breadth or thickness. WH: pre-1200. Old English *lengthu*, from Germanic, from base also of LONG[1]. See also -TH[2].

lenient *a.* merciful, tending not to be strict or punish severely. *Also n.* WH: 17C. Latin *leniens, lenientis*, pres.p. of *lenire* to soothe, from *lenis* soft, mild, smooth. See also -ENT. The original sense was soothing, relaxing. The current sense arose in the 18C.

Leninism *n.* the political and economic theories of Lenin; Marxism as modified by Lenin. WH: early 20C. *Lenin*, assumed name of Vladimir Il'ich Ulyanov, 1870–1924, Russian Bolshevik leader and founder of the Soviet Union + -ISM.

lenis *n.* a consonant, such as English *b* or *v*, articulated without muscular tension or force of breath. *Also a.* WH: early 20C. Latin. See LENIENT.

leno *n.* an open cotton fabric resembling fine muslin. WH: 18C. French *linon*, from *lin* flax. Cp. LINE[1], LINEN.

lens *n.* a piece of transparent substance, usu. glass, with one or both surfaces curved so as to change the direction of rays of light, and diminish or increase the apparent size of objects viewed through it. WH: 17C. Latin lentil. The lens is so named from its shape.

Lent *n.* a period of 40 days (excluding Sundays) from Ash Wednesday to Easter Eve, observed in the Christian Church as a season of penitence and fasting in commemoration of Christ's fasting in the wilderness. WH: 12–14C. Abbr. of *Lenten*, from Old English *lencten* spring, from Germanic base of LONG[1]. The reference is to the lengthening of the days in spring. *Lenten* was originally a noun but is now an adjective interpreted as deriving from *Lent* + -EN[3].

-lent *suf.* forming adjectives, as in *violent, redolent.* WH: Latin *-lentus*-ful.

lenticel *n.* a lens-shaped mass of cells in the bark of a plant, through which respiration takes place. WH: 19C. Modern Latin *lenticella*, dim. of Latin *lens, lentis* lentil.

lenticular *a.* resembling in shape a lentil or doubly convex lens. WH: 14–15C. Latin *lenticularis*, from *lenticula*. See LENTIL, also -CULE.

lentiform *a.* shaped like a lens. WH: 18C. Latin *lens, lentis* lentil + -*i-* + -FORM.

lentigo *n.* a freckle, freckly eruption. WH: 14–15C. Latin, from *lens, lentis* lentil.

lentil *n.* a small branching leguminous plant, *Lens culinaris*. WH: 12–14C. Old French *lentille*, from Latin *lenticula*, dim of *lens, lentis* lentil.

lentivirus *n.* any of a family of viruses that includes the Aids virus and others which affect cattle, goats and sheep. WH: late 20C. Latin *lentus* slow + -*i-* + VIRUS. The virus is so called as the symptoms are slow to appear.

lento *a., adv.* (to be played) slowly. *Also n.* WH: 18C. Italian slow, from Latin *lentus*.

Leo *n.* one of the 12 zodiacal constellations, the Lion. WH: pre-1200. Latin. See LION.

leone *n.* the standard monetary unit of Sierra Leone, equivalent to 100 cents. WH: mid-20C. Sierra *Leone*, a country on the coast of W Africa.

leontiasis *n.* a form of leprosy in which the victim's face takes on a lionlike appearance. WH: 18C. Modern Latin, from Greek, from *leōn, leontos* LION. See also -IASIS.

leontopodium *n.* a plant of the Eurasian alpine genus *Leontopodium* that includes the edelweiss. WH: 19C. Modern Latin, from Latin *leontopodion* (the plant) lion's foot, from Greek, from *leōn, leontos* LION + *podion*, dim. of *pous, podos* foot.

leopard *n.* a large mammal, *Panthera pardus*, of the cat family from Africa and S Asia, having a pale fawn to tan coat with dark spots; the panther. WH: 12–14C. Old French (Modern French *léopard*), from Late Latin *leopardus*, from Late Greek *leopardos*, from *leōn, leontos* LION + *pardos* PARD[2]. The leopard was originally thought to be a hybrid animal, half lion, half panther.

leotard *n.* a close-fitting garment resembling a swimsuit, though sometimes having legs and sleeves, worn during exercise, dance practice etc. WH: 19C. Jules *Léotard*, 1830–70, French trapeze artist, who wore one.

leper *n.* a person affected with leprosy. *Also a.* WH: 14–15C. Old French *lèpre* leprosy, from Late Latin *lepra*, from Latin *leprae* (pl.), from Greek *lepra*, use as n. of fem. of *lepros* scaly, from *lepos, lepis* scale. The original meaning was leprosy. The word then became an adjective (as in *leper folk*) and soon after a noun in the sense person with leprosy.

lepido- *comb. form* having scales. WH: Greek *lepis, lepidos* scale. See also -O-.

lepidolite *n.* a pinky-violet mica containing lithium. WH: 18C. LEPIDO- + -LITE.

lepidopteran *n.* any member of an order of insects, Lepidoptera, characterized by having four wings clothed with minute powder-like scales, containing the butterflies and moths. *Also a.* WH: 19C. Modern Latin *Lepidoptera*, from LEPIDO- + Greek *pteron* wing. See also -A[2], -AN.

lepidosiren *n.* a dipnoan fish of a genus, *Lepidosiren*, with one species, *L. paradoxa*, the S American mudfish from the river Amazon. WH: 19C. LEPIDO- + SIREN.

lepidote *a.* scaly; covered with scaly spots or leaves. WH: 19C. Modern Latin *lepidotus*, from Greek *lepidōtos*, from *lepis, lepidos* scale.

leporine *a.* of or relating to hares, having the nature or form of a hare. *Also n.* WH: 17C. Latin *leporinus*, from *lepus, leporis* hare. See also -INE.

leprechaun *n.* in Irish folklore, a brownie or dwarfish sprite who performs domestic tasks, mends shoes etc. WH: 17C. Irish *leipreachán*, alt. of Medieval Irish *luchrupán*, alt. in turn of Old Irish *luchorpán*, from *lu* small + *corp* body.

-lepsy *comb. form* forming nouns denoting a seizure or sudden attack. WH: Greek *lēpsis* seizure, from *lambanein* to take, to seize.

lepto- *comb. form* fine, thin, delicate, slender. WH: Greek *leptos* fine, small, thin, delicate. See also -O-.

leptocephalic *a.* having a long and narrow skull. WH: 19C. LEPTO- + -CEPHALIC.

leptocercal *a.* slender-tailed. WH: 19C. LEPTO- + Greek *kerkos* tail.

leptodactyl *a.* having long, slender toes. *Also n.* WH: 19C. LEPTO- + Greek *daktulos* toe.

lepton[1] *n.* a modern Greek coin and monetary unit worth one-hundredth of a drachma. WH: 18C. Greek, neut. of *leptos* small.

lepton[2] *n.* any of various elementary particles (e.g. electron, muon) that participate only in weak interaction. WH: mid-20C. Greek *leptos* small + -ON.

leptorrhine *a.* having a long, narrow nose. WH: 19C. LEPTO- + Greek *rhis, rhinos* nose.

leptosome *n.* a person who is of slender build, narrow-chested etc. WH: mid-20C. LEPTO- + Greek *sōma* body.

leptospirosis *n.* any of various infectious diseases that can be transmitted by animals to humans and are caused by spirochaete bacteria of the genus *Leptospira*. WH: early 20C. LEPTO- + Greek *speira* coil. See also -OSIS.

leptotene *n.* the first stage of the prophase of meiosis in which long, single-stranded chromosomes develop. WH: early 20C. LEPTO- + Greek *tainia* band, ribbon.

lesbian *n.* a female homosexual. *Also a.* WH: 16C. Latin *Lesbius,* Greek *Lesbios,* from *Lesbos,* an island in the N Aegean sea + -AN. The reference is to Sappho, *c.*610–*c.*580 BC, a poetess of Lesbos, noted for her alleged homosexuality. Cp. SAPPHIC.

lese-majesty *n.* an offence against the sovereign power or its representative, high treason. WH: 14–15C. French *lèse-majesté,* from Latin *laesa maiestas* hurt majesty, from *laesa,* fem. p.p. pf *laedere* to injure, to hurt + *maiestas* MAJESTY.

lesion *n.* physical change in a tissue or organ due to injury. WH: 14–15C. Old French *lésion,* from Latin *laesio, laesionis,* from *laesus,* p.p. of *laedere* to injure, to hurt. See also -ION.

less *a.* not so much. *Also prep., adv., n., conj.* WH: pre-1200. Old English *læssa,* from Germanic, from Indo-European base also of Greek *loisthos* last. Cp. LEAST. The word is used as a comparative form of LITTLE but is not related to it.

-less *suf.* devoid of, free from, as in *fearless, godless, sinless, tireless.* WH: Old English -*lēas* devoid (of), free (from), from Germanic base also of LOOSE. Not rel. to LESS.

lessee *n.* a person to whom a lease is granted. WH: 15C. Old French *lessé,* p.p. of *lesser* (Modern French *laisser*). See LEASE, also -EE.

lesson *n.* the amount or duration of instruction given to a pupil or pupils at one time. *Also v.t.* WH: 12–14C. Old French *leçon,* from Latin *lectio, lectionis.* See LECTION. The original sense of reading survives in ecclesiastical *first lesson, second lesson.*

lessor *n.* a person who grants a lease. WH: 14–15C. Old French *lesser* (Modern French *laisser*). See LEASE, also -OR.

lest *conj.* for fear that, in case, so that (one may) not. WH: pre-1200. Old English *thȳ læs the* whereby less that (from *thȳ* THE + *læs* less + *the* relative particle), later *the læste,* the first word subsequently being lost.

let[1] *v.t.* to permit, to allow (to be or do). *Also v.aux., v.i., n.* WH: pre-1200. Old English *lætan,* from a Germanic v. from base rel. to that of LATE. Cp. German *lassen.*

let[2] *n.* in tennis etc., a stoppage, hindrance etc., requiring the ball to be served again. *Also v.t., v.i.* WH: 12–14C. Old English *lettan* to hinder, to delay, from Germanic base of LATE.

-let *suf.* forming nouns, usu. diminutives, as in *booklet, tartlet,* or items of dress or ornament, as in *anklet.* WH: Orig. from Old French -*elette,* from -ET[1] added to words in -EL.

lethal *a.* deadly, fatal. WH: 16C. Latin *lethalis,* from *lethum,* var. of *letum* death, by assoc. with Greek *lēthē.* See LETHE, also -AL[1].

lethargy *n.* a state of apathy or inactivity. *Also v.t.* WH: 14–15C. Old French *litargie* (Modern French *léthargie*), from Late Latin *lethargia,* from Greek *lēthargia,* from *lēthargos* forgetful, from *lēth-,* base of *lanthanesthai* to forget.

Lethe *n.* in Greek mythology, a river of Hades whose waters produced forgetfulness in those who drank them. WH: 16C. Latin, from Greek *lēthē* forgetfulness, oblivion, from *lēth-.* See LETHARGY.

†Lett *n.* a member of a people largely inhabiting Latvia (Lettland), a Latvian. WH: 16C. German *Lette,* from Latvian *Latvi.*

letter *n.* a mark or character employed to represent a sound in speech. *Also v.t.* WH: 12–14C. Old French *lettre,* from Latin *littera* letter of the alphabet, *litterae* (pl.) epistle, document, literature, culture.

lettre de cachet *n.* a royal warrant for the imprisonment or exile of a person without trial, in France before the Revolution. WH: 18C. French, lit. letter of seal, from *lettre* LETTER + *de* of + *cachet* seal (CACHET).

lettuce *n.* a crisp-leaved garden plant of the genus *Lactuca,* esp. *L. sativa,* much used for salad. WH: 12–14C. Old French *letuës, laituës,* pl. of *laituë* (Modern French *laitue*), from Latin *lactuca,* from *lac, lactis* milk. The name alludes to the plant's milky juice.

leu *n.* the basic monetary unit of Romania, equal to 100 bani. WH: 19C. Romanian LION.

leucin *n.* an essential amino acid present in many proteins. WH: 19C. Greek *leukos* white + -IN[1].

leucite *n.* a dull, glassy silicate of aluminium and potassium, occurring at Mt. Vesuvius and Monte Somma. WH: 18C. Greek *leukos* white + -ITE[1].

leuco- *comb. form* white, pale. WH: Greek *leukos* white. See also -O-.

leucocyte *n.* a white corpuscle or blood cell. WH: 19C. LEUCO- + -CYTE.

leucoma *n.* a white opaque spot in the cornea, due to a wound, inflammation etc. WH: 18C. Modern Latin, from Greek *leukōma.* See LEUCO-, -OMA.

leucorrhoea *n.* a mucous discharge from the vagina, commonly called whites. WH: 18C. LEUCO- + -RRHOEA.

leucotomy *n.* a surgical operation to cut white nerve fibres within the brain, esp. a prefrontal lobotomy. WH: 18C. LEUCO- + -TOMY.

leukaemia *n.* any of various acute and often fatal diseases of the bone marrow in which leucocytes multiply inordinately causing loss of red corpuscles, hypertrophy of the spleen etc. WH: 19C. *leuko-* (LEUCO-) + -AEMIA.

lev *n.* the basic monetary unit of Bulgaria, equal to 100 stotinki. WH: 19C. Bulgarian, var. of *lăv* lion.

Levant *n.* the eastern part of the Mediterranean with its adjoining countries. WH: 15C. French, pres.p. of *lever* to raise. See also -ANT. The region is so named as the east is the point where the sun rises.

levant *v.i.* to abscond, to run away, esp. with gambling liabilities undischarged. WH: 14–15C. French, pres.p. of *lever* to raise, *se lever* to rise. See also -ANT.

levator *n.* a muscle that raises some part of the body. WH: 17C. Latin one who lifts, from *levatus,* p.p. of *levare* to raise. See also -OR.

levee[1] *n.* a general reception or assembly of visitors. WH: 17C. French *levé,* var. of *lever* rising, use as n. of *lever* to rise.

levee[2] *n.* an artificial bank to prevent overflow and flooding. WH: 18C. French *levée,* fem. of *levé,* p.p. of *lever* to raise. See LEVY.

level *n.* a horizontal line or plane or plane surface. *Also a., v.t., v.i.* WH: 12–14C. Old French *livel* (later *nivel,* Modern French *niveau*), from var. of Latin *libella,* dim. of *libra* balance, scales.

lever *n.* a bar of wood, metal, or other rigid substance resting on a fixed point of support, used to lift a certain weight. *Also v.t., v.i.* WH: 12–14C. Old French *levier,* alt. of *leveor,* from *lever* to raise.

leveret *n.* a young hare, esp. one in its first year. WH: 14–15C. Anglo-French, dim. of *levre,* from Old French *lièvre,* from Latin *lepus, leporis* hare. See also -ET[1].

leviathan *n.* a huge sea monster. WH: 14–15C. Late Latin, from Hebrew *liwyāṯān* dragon, serpent, prob. from base of *lāwāh* he twisted. 'Leviathan the piercing serpent, even leviathan that crooked serpent' (Isa. xxvii.1).

levigate *v.t.* to grind or rub down to a fine powder. *Also a.* WH: 16C. Latin *levigatus,* p.p. of *levigare* to make smooth, to polish. See also -ATE[3].

†levin *n.* lightning. WH: 12–14C. Prob. Old Norse, ? from 1st element of Old Swedish *liughnelder* lightning flash, from Germanic base of LIGHT[1].

levirate *n.* an ancient law of the Hebrews and others binding a man to marry the widow of his dead brother if the orig. marriage was childless. *Also a.* WH: 18C. Latin *levir* brother-in-law + -ATE[1].

Levis® *n.pl.* a type of (blue) denim jeans. **WH:** early 20C. *Levi* Strauss, 1829–1902, US clothing manufacturer, who first produced them in the 1850s.

levitate *v.t., v.i.* to (cause to) rise or float in the air, esp. a body through supernatural causes. **WH:** 17C. Latin *levis* light, based on GRAVITATE. See also -ATE³.

Levite *n.* a member of the tribe or family of Levi, esp. one of those who acted as assistants to the priests in the Jewish temple. **WH:** 12–14C. Ecclesiastical Latin *levita*, *levites*, from Greek *leuitēs*, from Hebrew *lēwī* Levi, a son of Jacob and Leah, who became father of the ancient Hebrew tribe named after him.

levity *n.* lack of seriousness or earnestness, frivolity. **WH:** 16C. Latin *levitas*, from *levis* light. See also -ITY.

levodopa *n.* L-dopa, the laevorotatory form of dopa. **WH:** late 20C. *levo-*, var. of LAEVO- + DOPA.

levy *n.* the act of raising or collecting (e.g. a tax, a fee). *Also v.t.* **WH:** 12–14C. Old French *levée*, use as n. of fem. p.p. of *lever*, from Latin *levare* to raise, from *levis* light.

lewd *a.* lascivious, indecent. **WH:** pre-1200. Old English *lǣwede*, of unknown orig. The original sense (to the 19C) was lay, not in holy orders, then (to the 17C) unlearned, unlettered. Hence (from the 14–15C) the current sense.

lewis *n.* a hoisting device for heavy stone blocks employing metal, usu. curved pieces which fit into and grasp the stone. **WH:** 14–15C. Prob. from Old French *lous*, pl. of *loup* wolf, a kind of siege engine.

Lewis gun *n.* a portable gas-operated machine-gun. **WH:** early 20C. Colonel Isaac Newton *Lewis*, 1858–1931, US soldier who invented it.

lewisite *n.* a poisonous liquid used in chemical warfare obtained from arsenic and acetylene. **WH:** early 20C. Winford Lee *Lewis*, 1878–1943, US chemist + -ITE¹.

lex *n.* a body of law. **WH:** 16C. Latin law.

lexeme *n.* in linguistics, an irreducible unit of meaning in a language; a particle, word or phrase whose meaning cannot be deduced from the sum of its separate constituents. **WH:** mid-20C. LEXICON + -EME.

lexicon *n.* a dictionary. **WH:** 17C. Modern Latin, from Greek *lexikon*, neut. sing. of *lexikos* pertaining to words, from *lexis* phrase, word, diction, from *legein* to speak.

ley *n.* arable land laid down (temporarily) to grass. *Also a.* **WH:** 14–15C. Dial. form of *lea* fallow, ? from base of LAY¹, LIE².

Leyden jar *n.* a glass bottle or jar coated inside and out with tinfoil used as an electrical condenser. **WH:** 18C. *Leyden* (now *Leiden*), a city in the Netherlands, where it was invented in *c.*1745.

lhasa apso *n.* a breed of small Tibetan terrier with a thick, long, straight coat and a feathered tail that curls up over its back. **WH:** early 20C. *Lhasa*, the capital of Tibet + Tibetan *apso* (breed of) dog.

li *n.* a Chinese measure of distance, rather more than one-third of a mile (0.5 km). **WH:** 16C. Chinese *lǐ*.

liable *a.* tending or likely (to). **WH:** 14–15C. ? Anglo-French, from Old French *lier* to bind (LIAISON). See also -ABLE.

liaison *n.* communication and contact between units, groups etc., esp. between military units. **WH:** 17C. French, from *lier* to bind, from Latin *ligare*. See also -ISON.

liana *n.* any of the climbing and twining plants common in the forests of tropical America. **WH:** 18C. French *liane*, orig. clematis, ? from dial. French *liener* to bind sheaves.

liang *n.* a Chinese weight, equal to about 1/13 oz. av. (38 g). **WH:** 19C. Chinese *liǎng*.

liar *n.* a person who knowingly utters a falsehood, esp. someone addicted to lying. **WH:** pre-1200. Old English *lēogere*, from *lēogan* LIE¹ + -ER¹. See also -AR⁴.

Lias *n.* the lowest series of rock strata of the Jurassic system. **WH:** 14–15C. Old French *liais* hard limestone, prob. from *lie* (LEES).

lib¹ *n.* liberation. **WH:** mid-20C. Abbr. of *liberation* (LIBERATE).

lib² *v.t.* to castrate, to geld. **WH:** 14–15C. ? From Germanic base represented also by Middle Dutch *lubben* to maim, to geld.

libation *n.* a sacrificial offering to a deity involving the pouring of oil or wine. **WH:** 14–15C. Latin *libatio*, *libationis*, from *libatus*, p.p. of *libare* to pour out, rel. to Greek *leibein* to pour drop by drop. See also -ATION.

libber *n.* a liberationist. **WH:** late 20C. LIB¹ + -ER¹.

Lib. Dem. *abbr.* Liberal Democrat. **WH:** late 20C. Abbr. of *Liberal Democrat* (LIBERAL).

libeccio *n.* the south-west wind, esp. blowing on to the W coast of Corsica. **WH:** 17C. Italian, from Latin *Libs*, *Libis*, from Greek *Lips*, *Libos*.

libel *n.* a publication of any kind containing false statements or representations tending to bring any person into ridicule, contempt or disrepute. *Also v.t., v.i.* **WH:** 12–14C. Old French (Modern French *libelle*), from Latin *libellus*, dim. of *liber* book. See also -EL.

liber *n.* the bast or phloem. **WH:** 18C. Latin inner bark, parchment, book.

liberal *a.* favourable to individual freedom, democratic government, progress and moderate reform. *Also n.* **WH:** 12–14C. Old French *libéral*, from Latin *liberalis*, from *liber* free. See also -AL¹.

liberate *v.t.* to set at liberty. **WH:** 16C. Latin *liberatus*, p.p. of *liberare*, from *liber* free. See also -ATE³.

libero *n.* in football, a sweeper. **WH:** mid-20C. Italian, abbr. of *battitore libero*, from *battitore*, lit. beater (i.e. defender) + *libero* free.

libertine *n.* a licentious or dissolute person. *Also a.* **WH:** 14–15C. Latin *libertinus*, from *liberus* freedman, from *liber* free. The current sense dates from the 16C. The change of meaning from freedman may have resulted from a misunderstanding of 'Libertines' in Acts vi.9 as the 'freed men' who opposed Stephen.

liberty *n.* the quality or state of being free from captivity or despotic control. **WH:** 14–15C. Old French *liberté*, from Latin *libertas*, *libertatis*, from *liber* free. See also -TY¹.

libidinous *a.* characterized by lewdness or lust. **WH:** 14–15C. Latin *libidinosus*, from LIBIDO, *libidinis* lust. See also -OUS.

libido *n.* the sexual drive. **WH:** early 20C. Latin desire, lust, from *libere* to be pleasing.

Lib-Lab *a.* in the UK, involving or uniting the Liberal or Liberal Democrat and Labour Parties. **WH:** early 20C. *Lib.* + *Lab.*.

Libra *n.* one of the 12 zodiacal constellations, the Scales and Balance. **WH:** pre-1200. Latin *libra* pound, balance, Libra.

libra *n.* an ancient Roman pound, equal to about 12 oz. (240 gr). **WH:** 14–15C. Latin *libra* pound.

library *n.* a collection of books, esp. one that is classified and catalogued, or otherwise organized, to facilitate its use either by the public or by private persons. **WH:** 14–15C. Old French *librairie* (Modern French bookshop), from alt. of Latin *libraria* bookshop, use as n. of *librarius* concerned with books, from *liber*, *libris* book. See also -ARY¹, -Y².

librate *v.i.* to move like a balance, to oscillate, to swing or sway. **WH:** 17C. Latin *libratus*, p.p. of *librare*, from *libra* balance. See also -ATE³.

libretto *n.* the words of an opera, oratorio etc. **WH:** 18C. Italian, dim. of *libro* book. Cp. LIBEL.

Librium® *n.* a tranquillizing drug containing chlordiazepoxide. **WH:** mid-20C. Orig. unknown. ? From EQUILIBRIUM.

Libyan *a.* of or relating to Libya, its language or its people. *Also n.* **WH:** 15C. *Libya*, a country in N Africa + -AN.

licence *n.* a document certifying consent or permission granted by a constituted authority (to marry, drive a motor vehicle etc.). **WH:** 14–15C. Old French, from Latin *licentia* liberty, freedom, from *licens*, *licentis*, pres.p. of *licere* to be allowed. See also -ENCE.

license *v.t.* to authorize by a legal permit. **WH:** 14–15C. LICENCE. The spelling with -s- is based on such pairs as PRACTICE/ PRACTISE.

licentious *a.* immoral, dissolute. **WH:** 14–15C. Latin *licentiosus*, from *licentia*. See LICENCE, also -OUS.

lichen *n.* a cryptogamic thallophytic plant of the order Lichenaceae, parasitic fungi on algal cells covering rocks, tree trunks etc., with variously coloured crusts. **WH:** 17C. Latin, from Greek *leikhēn*, lit. that eats around itself, prob. from *leikhein* LICK.

lich-gate *n.* a churchyard gate with a roof, under which a coffin used to be placed while the introductory portion of the burial service was read. **WH:** 15C. From obs. *lich* dead body, from Old English *līc*, from Germanic (cp. German *Leiche* corpse) + GATE¹.

licit *a.* lawful, allowed. **WH:** 15C. Latin *licitus*, p.p. of *licere* to be allowed.

lick *v.t.* to draw or pass the tongue over. *Also v.i., n.* **WH:** pre-1200.

Old English *liccian*, from Germanic, from Indo-European base represented also by Greek *leikhein*, Latin *lingere*.

lickerish *a.* lecherous. **WH:** 15C. Alt. of obs. *lickerous*, from Old French *lecheros* lecherous (LECHER). See also -OUS. Not rel. to LIQUOR.

lickety-split *adv.* very quickly. **WH:** 19C. Fanciful extension of LICK + SPLIT.

lictor *n.* in ancient Rome, a civil officer who attended the chief magistrates, and bore the fasces as a sign of authority. **WH:** 14–15C. Latin, ? rel. to *ligare* to bind.

lid *n.* a hinged or detachable cover or cap, usu. for shutting a vessel, container or aperture. **WH:** pre-1200. Old English *hlid*, from Germanic, from base meaning to cover.

lido *n.* a bathing beach, an outdoor swimming pool. **WH:** 17C. Italian *Lido*, a bathing beach near Venice, from *lido* shore, beach, from Latin *litus* (cp. LITTORAL).

lie¹ *v.i.* to say or write anything with the deliberate intention of deceiving. *Also v.t., n.* **WH:** pre-1200. Old English *lēogan*, from Germanic. Cp. German *lügen*.

lie² *v.i.* to rest or place oneself in a reclining or horizontal posture. *Also n.* **WH:** pre-1200. Old English *licgan*, from Germanic, from Indo-European base represented also by Greek *lektron*, Latin *lectus* bed.

Liebfraumilch *n.* a light white wine from the Rhine region of Germany. **WH:** 19C. German, from *lieb* dear + *Frau* lady + *Milch* MILK. The 'dear lady' is the Virgin Mary, patroness of the convent where it was first made. The 'milk' is the white wine that she (it) produces.

lied *n.* a type of German song, often a poem set to music and usu. for solo voice with piano accompaniment. **WH:** 19C. German *Lied* song, rel. to LAUD.

†lief *adv.* willingly, gladly, freely. *Also a., n.* **WH:** pre-1200. Old English *lēof*, from Germanic, rel. to LEAVE², LOVE.

liege *a.* bound by some feudal tenure, either as a vassal or as a lord. *Also n.* **WH:** 12–14C. Old French *lige*, from Medieval Latin *leticus*, from *letus, litus*, prob. from Germanic base also of LET¹.

lien *n.* a right to detain the goods of another until some claim has been satisfied. **WH:** 16C. French, from Old French *loien*, from Latin *ligamen* bond, from *ligare* to tie.

lientery *n.* diarrhoea in which the food passes rapidly through the bowels undigested. **WH:** 14–15C. Old French *lientérie*, or from Medieval Latin *lienteria*, from Greek *leienteria*, from *leios* smooth + *entera* bowels. See also -Y².

lierne *n.* a cross-rib connecting the main ribs in Gothic vaulting, introduced about the middle of the 14th cent. **WH:** 14–15C. French, ? from *lierne* clematis, dial. var. of *liane*. See LIANA.

lieu *n.* place, stead. **WH:** 12–14C. Old French, from Latin LOCUS place.

lieutenant *n.* an officer acting as deputy or substitute to a superior. **WH:** 14–15C. Old French. See LIEU, TENANT. Cp. *locum tenens* (LOCUM). The original sense was an officer acting for a superior.

life *n.* the state or condition which distinguishes animate beings from dead ones and from inorganic matter and involves the ability to grow, change, respond to stimuli, reproduce etc. *Also a.* **WH:** pre-1200. Old English *līf*, from Germanic, from base of LIVE¹. Cp. German *Leib* body.

lift¹ *v.t.* to raise to a higher position, to elevate. *Also v.i., n.* **WH:** 12–14C. Old Norse *lypta*, from Germanic base of LIFT².

lift² *n.* the sky, the upper regions of the air. **WH:** pre-1200. Old English *lyft*, from Germanic. Cp. German *Luft* air. See LOFT.

ligament *n.* a short band of fibrous tissue by which bones are bound together. **WH:** 14–15C. Latin *ligamentum*, from *ligare* to bind, to tie. See also -MENT.

ligand *n.* a single atom, molecule, radical or ion attached to a central atom to form a coordination complex. **WH:** mid-20C. Latin *ligandus*, ger. of *ligare* to bind. See also -AND.

ligate *v.t.* to tie with a ligature. **WH:** 16C. Latin *ligatus*, p.p. of *ligare* to tie, to bind. See also -ATE³.

liger *n.* a cross between a lion and a tigress. **WH:** mid-20C. Blend of LION and TIGER. Cp. TIGON.

light¹ *n.* the brightness from a light, the sun etc. that allows one to see things; electromagnetic radiation acting on the retina. *Also a., v.t., v.i.* **WH:** pre-1200. Old English *lēoht*, from Germanic, ult. from Indo-European base represented also by Greek *leukos* white, Latin *lux* light. Cp. German *Licht*.

light² *a.* of little weight, not heavy. *Also adv.* **WH:** pre-1200. Old English *lēocht*, from Germanic, from Indo-European base represented also by LUNG. Cp. German *leicht*.

light³ *v.i.* (of a bird) to descend as from flight, to settle. *Also v.t.* **WH:** pre-1200. Old English *līhtan*, from Germanic base also of LIGHT². Cp. ALIGHT¹.

lighten¹ *v.i.* to become light, to brighten. *Also v.t.* **WH:** 12–14C. LIGHT¹ + -EN⁵.

lighten² *v.t.* to reduce in weight. *Also v.i.* **WH:** 14–15C. LIGHT² + -EN⁵.

lighter¹ *n.* a pocket appliance for lighting cigarettes, a pipe etc. **WH:** 16C. LIGHT¹ + -ER¹.

lighter² *n.* a large, open, usu. flat-bottomed boat, used in loading and unloading ships. *Also v.t.* **WH:** 14–15C. LIGHT² + -ER¹, or from Dutch *lichter*. A lighter lightens the load of the ship whose cargo it takes.

lightning *n.* the dazzling flash caused by the discharge of electricity between clouds or from a cloud to the earth. *Also a.* **WH:** 12–14C. Var. of *lightening*, from LIGHTEN¹ + -ING².

lights *n.pl.* the lungs of animals, esp. as food for cats etc. **WH:** 12–14C. Use as n. of LIGHT². See also -S¹. Cp. LUNG. The lungs are distinguished from other organs of the body by their lightness.

lightsome¹ *a.* light-hearted, playful. **WH:** 12–14C. LIGHT² + -SOME¹.

†lightsome² *a.* luminous, light-giving. **WH:** 14–15C. LIGHT¹ + -SOME¹.

lignaloes *n.* the fragrant wood of an Asian tree *Aquilaria agallocha*, also called *eaglewood*. **WH:** 14–15C. Late Latin *lignum aloes* wood of the aloe, from *lignum* wood + gen. of *aloe* ALOE.

ligneous *a.* made or consisting of wood. **WH:** 17C. Latin *ligneus*, from *lignum* wood. See also -OUS, -EOUS.

ligni- *comb. form* of or relating to wood. **WH:** Latin *lignum* wood + -i-.

lignin *n.* a complex organic material which forms the woody cell walls of certain plants. **WH:** 19C. Latin *lignum* wood + -IN¹.

ligniperdous *a.* destructive of wood, as certain insects. **WH:** 19C. LIGNI- + Latin *perdere* to destroy. See also -OUS.

lignite *n.* a partially carbonized coal showing fibrous woody structure, usu. of Cretaceous or Tertiary age. **WH:** 19C. Latin *lignum* wood + -ITE¹.

lignivorous *a.* feeding on wood. **WH:** 19C. LIGNI- + -vorous (-VORE).

lignocaine *n.* a local anaesthetic, usu. administered by injection. **WH:** mid-20C. *ligno-* (from Latin *lignum* wood + -o-) + COCAINE. *Ligno-* relates to its earlier name, *xylocaine*. See XYLO-.

lignum vitae *n.* the very hard and heavy wood of various tropical American trees, esp. *Guaiacum officinale*. **WH:** 16C. Latin wood of life. The wood is so called because the resin obtained from it was at one time believed to have medicinal properties.

ligroin *n.* a volatile fraction of petroleum used as a solvent. **WH:** 19C. Orig. unknown.

ligule *n.* a membranous process at the top of the sheath beneath the blade of a grass. **WH:** 17C. Latin *ligula* strap, spoon, var. of LINGULA. See also -ULE.

like¹ *prep.* similar to, resembling. *Also a., adv., conj., n.* **WH:** 12–14C. Old Norse *líkr*, shortening of *glíkr*. See ALIKE.

like² *v.t.* to find pleasure or satisfaction in, to enjoy. *Also v.i., n.* **WH:** pre-1200. Old English *līcian*, from Germanic, from base also of LIKE¹.

-like *suf.* forming adjectives, as in *saintlike, warlike*. **WH:** LIKE¹.

lilac *n.* a shrub of the genus *Syringa*, esp. *S. vulgaris*, with very fragrant pale violet or purple flowers, white in cultivated varieties. *Also a.* **WH:** 17C. Obs. French (now *lilas*), ult. from Persian *līlak*, var. of *nīlak* bluish, from *nīl* blue + dim. suf. -*ak*.

Lilliputian *a.* of or relating to Lilliput. *Also n.* **WH:** 18C. *Lilliput*, an imaginary country in Jonathan Swift's *Gulliver's Travels* (1726) peopled by pygmies six inches high + -IAN.

Lilo® *n.* a type of inflatable mattress used in camping, on the beach etc. **WH:** mid-20C. Alt. of *lie low*.

lilt *n.* a jaunty, springing rhythm or movement. *Also v.i., v.t.* **WH:** 14–15C. Rel. to Low German and Dutch *lul* pipe, of unknown orig.

lily *n.* a flower or plant of the bulbous genus *Lilium*, producing white or coloured trumpet-shaped flowers of great beauty, esp. the Madonna lily, *L. candidum*. *Also a.* **WH:** pre-1200. Latin *lilium*, from Greek *leirion*, prob. of non-Indo-European orig.

lima bean *n.* a tropical American climbing bean plant, *Phaseolus lunatus*. **WH:** 18C. *Lima*, the capital of Peru.

limaceous *a.* of or relating to the genus *Limax* or the family Limacidae which contains the slugs. WH: 17C. Latin *limax, limacis* slug, snail + -ACEOUS.

limb¹ *n.* each of the articulated extremities of an animal, an arm, leg or wing. *Also v.t.* WH: pre-1200. Old English *lim*, from Germanic. Cp. Old Norse *limr*.

limb² *n.* the outermost edge of the sun, moon etc. WH: 14–15C. Old French *limbe* or Latin *limbus* edge, border. Cp. LIMBO¹.

limber¹ *a.* lithe, agile. WH: 16C. ? From LIMBER². The reference would be to the flexible movements of the shafts of a cart.

limber² *n.* the detachable part of a gun carriage consisting of two wheels and ammunition box. *Also v.t., v.i.* WH: 14–15C. ? Old French *limon* shaft of a cart, of unknown orig.

limber³ *n.* a gutter on each side of the keelson for draining. WH: 17C. Old French *lumière* light, limber, from Latin *luminare* to light, from *lumen, luminis* light.

limbo¹ *n.* the edge or uttermost limit of hell, the abode of those who died unbaptized through no fault of their own, such as the just before Christ and infants. WH: 14–15C. Latin, abl. sing. of *limbus* edge, border, in phrs. such as *in limbo* on the edge, *e limbo* from the edge. The edge or border referred to is that of Hell.

limbo² *n.* a W Indian dance in which the participants bend backwards and pass under a bar. WH: mid-20C. LIMBER¹.

Limburger *n.* a white cheese with a strong taste and smell. WH: 19C. Dutch and German, from *Limburg*, a province of NE Belgium. See also -ER¹.

lime¹ *n.* a white caustic alkaline substance, calcium oxide, obtained by burning calcium carbonate (usu. in limestone form), used in building and agriculture; quicklime. *Also v.t.* WH: pre-1200. Old English *līm*, from Germanic base of LOAM, ult. rel. to Latin *limus* mud.

lime² *n.* any tree of the genus *Tilia*, esp. *T. europaea*, with soft timber, heart-shaped leaves, and small clusters of delicately-scented flowers. WH: 17C. Alt. of *line*, var. of obs. *lind*. See LINDEN.

lime³ *n.* a small tropical citrus tree, *Citrus aurantifolia*. WH: 17C. French, from Spanish *lima*, from Arabic *līma*. Cp. LEMON.

limen *n.* the stage of consciousness at which a given stimulus begins to produce sensation and below which it is imperceptible. WH: 17C. Latin threshold.

limerick *n.* a nonsense verse, usu. of five lines, the first, second and fifth having three feet and rhyming together, and the third and fourth having two feet and a different rhyme. WH: 19C. *Limerick*, the chief town of County Limerick, Ireland. The word is said to derive from the refrain 'Will you come up to Limerick?' sung at convivial parties following each recitation of improvised nonsense verses.

limes *n.* the fortified boundary of the Roman Empire. WH: 16C. Latin LIMIT.

limit *n.* a line, point or edge marking termination or utmost extent. *Also v.t.* WH: 14–15C. Latin *limes, limitis* boundary, border.

limitrophe *a.* on the border, adjacent (to). WH: 16C. French, from Late Latin *limitrophus*, from *limes, limitis* LIMIT + Greek *-trophos* supporting, from *trephein* to support.

limivorous *a.* mud-eating. WH: 19C. Latin *limus* mud + -vorous (-VORE).

limn *v.t.* to paint or draw, to depict, to portray, esp. in watercolour. WH: 14–15C. Alt. of obs. *lumine* to illuminate, from Old French *luminer*, from Latin *luminare*, from *lumen, luminis* light. The original sense was to illuminate (a manuscript, etc.). The current sense dates from the 16C.

limnology *n.* the study of the physical, biological, geographical etc. features of lakes, ponds and other freshwater bodies. WH: 19C. Greek *limnē* pool, marshy lake + -O- + -LOGY.

limo *n.* a limousine. WH: mid-20C. Abbr. of LIMOUSINE.

limonite *n.* a common mineral consisting of hydrated ferric oxides, a source of iron. WH: 19C. German *Limonat*, prob. from Greek *leimōn* meadow, based on the earlier German name *Wiesenerz*, lit. meadow ore. See also -ITE¹.

limousine *n.* a large opulent car (orig. having a closed body with a separate driver's seat), esp. one with a glass partition dividing the driver from the passengers. WH: early 20C. French, fem. of *limousin* of Limousin, a province centred on Limoges, central France. French

limousine was originally the word for a caped cloak worn in Limousin by cart drivers. The car is said to be so called because its closed compartment protected the driver like a cloak.

limp¹ *v.i.* to walk lamely, esp. dragging one injured leg. *Also n.* WH: 14–15C. Prob. back-formation from obs. *limphalt* lame, limping, from Germanic, from Indo-European base of Sanskrit *lámbate* (it) hangs down + HALT².

limp² *a.* not stiff, flexible. WH: 18C. Prob. of dial. orig. and ult. rel. to LIMP¹. Something limp hangs loose like the leg of a person who limps.

limpet *n.* any individual of the genus of gastropods *Patella*, having an open conical shell, found adhering firmly to rocks. WH: pre-1200. Old English *lempedu*, from Medieval Latin *lampreda*. See LAMPREY.

limpid *a.* clear, transparent. WH: 14–15C. Latin *limpidus*, prob. rel. to *lympha* LYMPH.

limpkin *n.* a tropical American wading bird, *Aramus guarauna*, similar to a rail, with dark brown plumage and white markings. WH: 19C. LIMP¹ + -KIN. The name refers to the bird's limping gait.

limulus *n.* a horseshoe crab of the genus *Limulus*. WH: 19C. Modern Latin, from Latin *limulus* rather oblique, from *limus* oblique.

linage *n.* amount of printed matter reckoned by lines. WH: 19C. LINE¹ + -AGE.

linchpin *n.* a pin serving to hold a wheel on the axle. WH: 14–15C. Obs. *linch* linchpin, from Old English *lynis*, from Germanic + PIN.

Lincoln green *n.* bright green cloth formerly made at Lincoln. WH: 12–14C. *Lincoln*, the county town of Lincolnshire, a county in E England.

lincrusta *n.* a type of thick wallpaper with designs embossed in bold relief. WH: 19C. Latin *linum* flax + *crusta* rind, bark, based on LINOLEUM. The paper was named in *c.*1882 by its manufacturer, Frederick Walton, following his invention of linoleum.

linctus *n.* a syrupy cough medicine. WH: 17C. Medieval Latin (Latin licking, from *lingere* to lick), based on Late Latin *electuarium* ELECTUARY.

linden *n.* a tree of the genus *Tilia*, a lime tree. WH: 16C. Partly from obs. a. *linden* (from obs. *lind* lime tree + -EN³), partly from Dutch *lindeboom* or German *Lindenbaum*, from *linde* + *boom*, *Baum* tree.

line¹ *n.* a threadlike mark; such a mark drawn by a pencil, pen, graver or other instrument. *Also v.t., v.i.* WH: pre-1200. Old English *līne*, prob. from Germanic, from Latin *linea* (cp. German *Leine* cord), or from Old French *ligne*, from var. of Latin *linea*, orig. use as n. of fem. of *lineus* pertaining to flax, from *linum* flax.

line² †*n.* the fine long fibre of flax separated from the tow. *Also v.t.* WH: 14–15C. LINE¹, ref. to use of linen as a lining material.

lineage *n.* descendants in a direct line from a common progenitor, ancestry. WH: 12–14C. Old French *lignage*, from Latin *linea* LINE¹. See also -AGE.

lineal *a.* ascending or descending in the direct line of ancestry, as opposed to *collateral*. WH: 14–15C. Old French *linéal*, from Late Latin *linealis*, from Latin *linea* LINE¹. See also -AL¹.

lineament *n.* characteristic lines or features. WH: 14–15C. Latin *lineamentum*, from *lineare* to make straight, from *linea* LINE¹. See also -MENT.

linear *a.* composed of or having the form of lines. WH: 17C. Latin *linearis*, from *linea* LINE¹. See also -AR¹.

lineate *a.* (of leaves) marked with lines, esp. long straight lines. WH: 17C. Latin *lineatus*, p.p. of *lineare* to reduce to a line, from *linea* LINE¹. See also -ATE².

linen *n.* a cloth made of flax. *Also a.* WH: pre-1200. Old English *līnen*, from Germanic, from base also of LINE¹. See also -EN³.

lineolate *a.* marked with minute lines. WH: 19C. Latin *lineola*, dim. of *linea* LINE¹ + -ATE².

liner *n.* each of a regular line of passenger ships or aircraft. WH: 14–15C. LINE¹ + -ER¹.

ling¹ *n.* a long slender food fish, *Molva molva*, found in the northern seas. WH: 12–14C. Prob. of Dutch or Low German orig. and rel. to LONG¹.

ling² *n.* heather or heath, *Calluna vulgaris*. WH: 12–14C. Old Norse *lyng*, of unknown orig.

-ling *suf.* forming nouns denoting a person or thing, as in *grayling*, *sibling*. WH: Old English, from Germanic, from source of -LE¹ + that of -ING³.

-ling[2] *suf.* forming adverbs and adjectives, as in *darkling*. **WH:** Old English, from Germanic base meaning to extend, rel. to LONG[1]. In many words *-ling* has now been replaced by *-long*. Cp. *headlong* (HEAD[1]), *sidelong* (SIDE).

lingam *n.* the phallus, representative of the god Siva in Hindu mythology. **WH:** 18C. Sanskrit *liṅga* sign, (sexual) characteristic, influ. by Tamil *iliṅkam*.

linger *v.i.* to delay going, to be slow to leave. *Also v.t.* **WH:** 12–14C. Freq. of obs. *ling* to lengthen, to linger, from Old English *lengan*, from Germanic, from base also of LONG[1]. See also -ER[5].

lingerie *n.* women's underwear and nightclothes. **WH:** 19C. French, from *linge* linen. See also -ERY. The original sense was linen articles in general, or all such articles in a woman's wardrobe or trousseau.

lingo *n.* a foreign language, peculiar dialect or technical phraseology. **WH:** 17C. Prob. from Portuguese *lingoa*, var. of *língua*, from Latin LINGUA.

lingua *n.* the tongue. **WH:** 17C. Latin tongue, language.

lingua franca *n.* a language serving as a medium of communication between different peoples. **WH:** 17C. Italian Frankish tongue. 'Frankish' probably meant European to Arabs and other users of the original lingua franca.

lingual *a.* of or relating to the tongue. *Also n.* **WH:** 14–15C. Medieval Latin *lingualis*, from Latin *lingua* tongue + -AL[1].

linguine *n.pl.* pasta in the form of long flat ribbons. **WH:** mid-20C. Italian, pl. of *linguina*, dim. of *lingua* tongue, from Latin.

linguist *n.* a person who is skilled in languages. **WH:** 16C. Latin *lingua* tongue, language + -IST.

lingula *n.* a tongue-shaped part. **WH:** 17C. Latin, partly from *lingere* to lick, partly from Latin dim. of *lingua* tongue. See also -ULE. Cp. LIGULE.

linhay *n.* a shed, usu. a lean-to open at the sides, for cattle or carts. **WH:** 17C. Orig. unknown.

liniment *n.* a liquid preparation, usu. with oil, for rubbing on bruised or inflamed parts. **WH:** 14–15C. Late Latin *linimentum*, from Latin *linire* to smear, to anoint. See also -MENT.

link[1] *n.* a ring or loop of a chain. *Also v.t., v.i.* **WH:** 14–15C. Old Norse *hlekkr*, from Germanic, rel. to Middle Low German *lenkhake* pot hook, German *Gelenk* joint, link.

link[2] *n.* a torch made of tow and pitch, used for lighting people in the streets. **WH:** 16C. ? Medieval Latin *linchinus*, alt. of *lichinus* wick, match, from Greek *lukhnos* light.

links *n.pl.* a golf course. **WH:** pre-1200. Old English *hlinc*, ? from base of LEAN[1]. The plural form dates from the 14–15C.

linn *n.* a waterfall, a torrent. **WH:** pre-1200. Old English *hlynn*, but primarily from Gaelic *linne*, Irish *linn*, rel. to Welsh *llyn* lake, pool.

Linnaean *a.* of or relating to Linnaeus or his system of classification and naming of plants and animals. *Also n.* **WH:** 18C. *Linnaeus*, Latinized name of Carl von *Linné*, 1707–78, Swedish naturalist + -AN.

linnet *n.* a finch, *Acanthis cannabina*, with brownish plumage. **WH:** 16C. Old French *linette*, earlier *linot*, from *lin* flax, from Latin *linum*. The bird is so called because much of its diet depends on flaxseed.

lino *n.* linoleum. **WH:** early 20C. Abbr. of LINOLEUM.

linoleic acid *n.* a colourless oily polyunsaturated fatty acid occurring as a glyceride in linseed and other natural oils, used in making soaps and emulsifiers and essential to the human diet. **WH:** 19C. Latin *linum* flax + OLEIC.

linolenic acid *n.* a fatty acid similar in its properties and provenance to linoleic acid but with one more double bond. **WH:** 19C. German *Linolensäure*, from *Linolsäure* LINOLEIC ACID, with added *-en* -ENE. See also -IC.

linoleum *n.* a preparation of oxidized linseed oil mixed with ground cork and laid upon fabric, used as a floor covering. **WH:** 19C. Latin *linum* flax + *oleum* oil. The word was coined by the English inventor Frederick Walton, who patented the covering in 1863 and formed the Linoleum Manufacturing Company the following year. Cp. LINCRUSTA.

Linotype® *n.* a typesetting machine for producing castings or slugs of whole lines of words. **WH:** 19C. Alt. of *line o' type*. The machine was created by the German-born US inventor Ottmar Mergenthaler and patented in 1884.

linsang *n.* a kind of civet cat common in Borneo and Java. **WH:** 19C. Javanese *lingsang*, *wlinsang*, Malay *linsang*.

linseed *n.* the seed of the flax plant. **WH:** pre-1200. Old English *līnsǣd*, from *līn* flax, LINEN + *sǣd* SEED.

linsey-woolsey *n.* a coarse fabric of linen or cotton warp with wool filling. **WH:** 15C. *linsey* (14–15C), prob. from *Lindsey*, a village in Suffolk, E England, where said to have been first manufactured + WOOL + *-sey* jingling ending. Cp. WINCEY. Cp. also KERSEY. Lindsey and Kersey are only two miles apart.

linstock *n.* a forked staff to hold a lighted match for firing a gun. **WH:** 16C. Dutch *lontsok*, from *lont* match + *stok* stick, assim. to LINT.

lint *n.* absorbent cotton cloth with the nap raised on one side, used for dressing wounds etc. **WH:** 14–15C. ? Old French *linette* linseed, from *lin* flax. See also -ETTE, -ET[1].

lintel *n.* the horizontal beam or stone over a door or window. **WH:** 12–14C. Old French (Modern French *linteau*), of uncertain orig. Prob. alt. of *lintier*, from Popular Latin *limitaris* threshold, from Latin *limitaris*, from *limes, limitis* edge, border, LIMIT.

lintie *n.* a linnet. **WH:** 18C. Abbr. of *lintwhite* (from Old English *līn* flax, LINEN + *-twige* as in Old High German *zwigōn* to pluck) + *-ie* (-Y[3]).

lion *n.* a large and powerful carnivorous quadruped, *Panthera leo*, usu. brown or tawny, with tufted tail and (in the adult male) a long mane, inhabiting southern Asia and Africa. **WH:** 12–14C. Old French, from Latin *leo, leonis*, from Greek *leōn*, of unknown orig.

lip *n.* either of the two fleshy parts enclosing the opening of the mouth. *Also v.t., v.i.* **WH:** pre-1200. Old English *lippa*, from Germanic, from Indo-European base also of Latin *labia, labra* lips.

lipase *n.* any enzyme which decomposes fats. **WH:** 19C. LIPO- + -ASE.

lipid *n.* any of various organic compounds which are esters of fatty acids, insoluble in water but soluble in other substances, and important structural components of living cells. **WH:** early 20C. French *lipide*. See LIPO-, also -IDE.

Lipizzaner *n.* a breed of horses (usu. white or grey in colour) used esp. by the Spanish Riding School in Vienna for dressage displays. **WH:** early 20C. German *Lippizaner*, from *Lippiza*, the location of the original stud near Trieste.

lipo- *comb. form* fat, fatty. **WH:** Greek *lipos* fat. See also -O-.

lipogenesis *n.* the formation of fat from the synthesis of fatty substances. **WH:** 19C. LIPO- + GENESIS.

lipography *n.* the accidental omission of a letter or letters in writing. **WH:** 19C. Greek *lip-*, stem of *leipein* to leave, to be lacking + -O- + -GRAPHY.

lipohaemia *n.* prevalence of fatty matter in the blood. **WH:** 19C. LIPO- + Greek *haima* blood. See also -IA.

lipoid *a.* fatlike. **WH:** 19C. LIPO- + -OID.

lipoma *n.* a fatty tumour. **WH:** 19C. LIPO- + -OMA.

lipoprotein *n.* a soluble protein which carries lipids in the bloodstream. **WH:** early 20C. LIPO- + PROTEIN.

liposome *n.* a minute synthetic sac made of a lipid substance containing an aqueous droplet, used to convey drugs to specific tissues. **WH:** early 20C. LIPO- + -SOME[2].

liposuction *n.* a surgical process for the cosmetic removal of excess fat from beneath the skin by suction. **WH:** late 20C. LIPO- + SUCTION.

liquate *v.t.* to liquefy (metals) in order to purify. *Also v.i.* **WH:** 17C. Latin *liquatus*, p.p. of *liquare* to make liquid, rel. to LIQUOR. See also -ATE[3].

liquefy *v.t.* to convert from a solid (or gaseous) to a liquid form. *Also v.i.* **WH:** 14–15C. Old French *liquéfier*, from Latin *liquefacere* to make liquid, to melt, from *liquere*, rel. to LIQUOR. See also -FY.

liqueur *n.* an alcoholic cordial sweetened or flavoured with an aromatic substance and drunk in small quantities, usu. after a meal. *Also v.t.* **WH:** 18C. French LIQUOR.

liquid *a.* flowing or capable of flowing, like water or oil. *Also n.* **WH:** 14–15C. Latin *liquidus*, from *liquere*, rel. to LIQUOR. See also -ID.

liquidambar *n.* any tropical tree of the genus *Liquidambar*, several species of which yield a fragrant resin or balsam called storax. **WH:** 16C. Modern Latin, appar. from Latin *liquidus* LIQUID + Medieval Latin *ambar* AMBER.

liquor *n.* an alcoholic drink, usu. not including wine or beer; such drinks collectively. *Also v.t.* WH: 12–14C. Old French *licur* (Modern French LIQUEUR), from Latin *liquor*, rel. to *liquare* to liquefy, to filter, *liqui* to flow, *liquere* to be fluid.

liquorice *n.* a black extract from the root of the leguminous plant *Glycyrrhiza glabra*, used in medicine and confectionery. WH: 12–14C. Old French *licoresse*, from (with assim. to *licor* LIQUOR) Late Latin *liquiritia*, from Greek *glukurrhiza*, from *glukus* sweet + *rhiza* root.

lira *n.* the standard monetary unit of Italy. WH: 17C. Italian, from Provençal *liura*, from Latin *libra* pound. Cp. LIVRE.

liriodendron *n.* a N American tree of the genus *Liriodendron* of the Magnoliaceae and containing the tulip tree. WH: 19C. Modern Latin, from Greek *leirion* lily + *dendron* tree.

liripipe *n.* the long tail attached to a graduate's hood. WH: 16C. Medieval Latin *liripipium*, of unknown orig.

lisle *n.* a fine, strong cotton thread, esp. for stockings. WH: 16C. *Lisle* (now *Lille*), a town in NE France, where orig. made.

LISP *n.* a high-level computer programming language used in artificial intelligence research. WH: mid-20C. Abbr. of *list* processing.

lisp *v.i.* to pronounce *s* and *z* with the sound of *th* or *dh*. *Also v.t., n.* WH: pre-1200. Old English *wlyspian*, from *wlisp* (a.) lisping, from Germanic, of imit. orig. Cp. German *lispeln*.

lissom *a.* lithe, supple, nimble. WH: 18C. Contr. of *lithesome*, from LITHE + -SOME[1].

list[1] *n.* a record or catalogue of items, names etc. which are related in some way or to be used for some specific purpose, usu. entered one below the other. *Also v.t., v.i.* WH: 16C. French *liste*, prob. from LIST[2]. The reference would be to a strip of paper, originally one torn from the edge of a sheet.

list[2] *n.* the border, edge or selvage of cloth. *Also v.t.* WH: pre-1200. Old English *līste*, from Germanic. Cp. German *Leiste*.

list[3] *n.* the fact of leaning over to one side (of a ship, building etc.). *Also v.i., v.t.* WH: 17C. Orig. unknown.

†list[4] *v.t.* to please, to be pleasing to. *Also v.i., n.* WH: pre-1200. Old English *lystan*, from Germanic, from base of LUST.

†list[5] *v.i.* to listen. *Also v.t.* WH: pre-1200. Old English *hlystan*, ult. from Germanic base represented also by LISTEN.

listen *v.i.* to make an effort to hear. *Also n., v.t.* WH: pre-1200. Old English *hlysnan*, from Germanic. Cp. LIST[5].

listeria *n.* any bacterium of a genus, *Listeria*, found in certain foods, esp. poultry and soft cheese, and capable of affecting the central nervous system and causing meningitis, encephalitis or miscarriage if not killed by cooking. WH: mid-20C. Joseph *Lister*, 1827–1912, English surgeon. See also -IA.

listless *a.* lacking the will or energy to do anything. WH: 14–15C. LIST[4] + -LESS.

litany *n.* a solemn form of supplicatory prayer, used in public worship, consisting of a series of short invocations followed by fixed responses. WH: 12–14C. Old French *letanie* (Modern French *litanie*), from Ecclesiastical Latin *litania*, from Greek *litaneia* prayer, entreaty, from *litaneuein* to pray, from *litanos* suppliant, from *litē* supplication. See also -Y[2].

lit crit *abbr.* literary criticism. WH: 19C. Abbr. of *literary criticism*.

lite *a.* low in fat, calories or alcoholic content. *Also n.* WH: 16C. Var. of LIGHT[1] or LIGHT[2]. Cp. *nite* for NIGHT. In the late 20C the word was adopted as a deliberate respelling of the original.

-lite *suf.* forming names of minerals and fossils as in *aerolite*, *coprolite*, *radiolite*. WH: French *-lite*, German *-lit*, *-lith*, from Greek *lithos* stone. Cp. -LITH.

literae humaniores *n.* at Oxford University, a faculty and honours course concerned with Greek and Latin literature, ancient history and philosophy. WH: 18C. Latin, lit. more humane letters. The course is secular, devoted to humans, as opposed to divinity (theology), devoted to God.

literal *a.* according or limited to the primary or explicit meaning, not figurative or metaphorical. *Also n.* WH: 14–15C. Old French *litéral* or Late Latin *literalis*, from *litera* LETTER. See also -AL[1].

literary *a.* of or relating to literature or writing. WH: 17C. Latin *literarius*, from *litera* LETTER. See also -ARY[1].

literate *a.* able to read and write. *Also n.* WH: 14–15C. Latin *literatus*, from *litera* LETTER. See also -ATE[2].

literatim *adv.* letter for letter, literally. WH: 17C. Medieval Latin, from *litera* LETTER. Cp. VERBATIM.

-lith *suf.* denoting a type of stone, as in *monolith*. WH: Greek *lithos* stone. Cp. -LITE.

litharge *n.* a red or yellow mineral form of lead monoxide. WH: 12–14C. Old French *litarge* (Modern French *litharge*), from Latin *lithargyrus*, from Greek *litharguros*, from *lithos* stone + *arguros* silver.

lithe *a.* flexible, supple. WH: pre-1200. Old English *līthe*, from Germanic, from Indo-European. Cp. German *lind* soft, gentle. The original sense was gentle, meek, mild.

lithia *n.* oxide of lithium. WH: 19C. Alt. of obs. *lithion* (from Greek *lithios* stony, from *lithos* stone), based on SODA, etc.

lithic *a.* of, relating to or composed of stone or calculi. WH: 18C. Greek *lithikos*, from *lithos* stone. See also -IC.

lithium *n.* a soft, silver-white element, the lightest metallic element, at. no. 3, chem. symbol Li, a member of the alkali series, used, esp. in alloys and batteries. WH: 19C. LITHIA. See also -IUM. The element was discovered in 1817 by the Swedish chemist Johan Arfvedson and named in 1818 (originally as *lithion*) by the Swedish chemist J.J. Berzelius to emphasize its mineral origin. (Previously discovered alkalis were of vegetable origin.) Cp. CERIUM, SELENIUM, THORIUM, all discovered and named by Berzelius.

litho *n.* a lithograph. *Also a., adv., v.t.* WH: 19C. Abbr. of LITHOGRAPH.

litho- *comb. form* of or relating to stone. WH: Greek *lithos* stone. See also -O-.

lithogenous *a.* stone-producing. WH: 19C. LITHO- + -GENOUS.

lithograph *v.t.* to print by lithography. *Also n.* WH: 19C. Backformation from *lithography* (18C), from German *Lithographie*. See LITHO-, -GRAPHY.

lithoid *a.* resembling a stone in nature or structure. WH: 19C. Greek *lithoeidēs*. See LITHO-, also -OID.

lithology *n.* the science of the composition, structure and classification of rocks, petrology. WH: 18C. LITHO- + -LOGY.

lithomarge *n.* a hydrated silicate of alumina related to or identical with kaolin. WH: 18C. Modern Latin *lithomarga*, from LITHO- + Latin *marga* marl.

lithophyte *n.* a plant that grows on stone. WH: 18C. LITHO- + -PHYTE.

lithopone *n.* a white pigment made from a mixture of zinc sulphide, barium sulphate and zinc oxide. WH: 19C. LITHO- + Greek *ponos* (thing produced by) work.

lithosphere *n.* the outer, rocky shell of the earth, the crust of the earth. WH: 19C. LITHO- + SPHERE.

lithotomy *n.* the surgical removal of a stone in the bladder. WH: 17C. Late Latin *lithotomia*, from Greek. See LITHO-, -TOMY.

lithotripsy *n.* the use of ultrasound to pulverize stones in the bladder, kidney or gall bladder so that they can be passed out through the urethra. WH: 19C. LITHO- + Greek *tripsis* rubbing, grinding + -Y[2].

lithotype *n.* a stereotype made with shellac, sand, tar and linseed oil, pressed hot on a plaster mould taken from type. *Also v.t.* WH: 19C. LITHO- + TYPE.

Lithuanian *a.* of or relating to Lithuania, an independent republic (formerly part of the USSR) on the Baltic Sea. *Also n.* WH: 16C. *Lithuania*, the southernmost of the three Baltic states + -AN.

litigate *v.t.* to contest in a court of law. *Also v.i.* WH: 17C. Latin *litigatus*, p.p. of *litigare*, from *lis*, *litis* strife, lawsuit. See also -ATE[3].

litmus *n.* a substance obtained from *Roccella tinctoria* or other lichens, that is turned red by acids or blue by alkalis. WH: 12–14C. Old Norse *lit-mosi*, from *litr* dye + *mosi* MOSS.

litotes *n.* an understatement by which an affirmative is expressed by negation of its contrary, as in 'not a little' for 'very' or a weaker expression used to suggest a stronger one. WH: 16C. Late Latin, from Greek *litōtēs*, from *litos* single, simple, meagre.

litre *n.* the unit of capacity in the metric system, equal to a cubic decimetre, or about 1.75 pints. WH: 18C. French, alt. of *litron*, from Medieval Latin *litra*, from Greek *litra* a Sicilian monetary unit.

Litt. B. *abbr.* Bachelor of Letters, Bachelor of Literature. WH: Abbr. of Latin *Litterarum Baccalaureus* Bachelor of Letters.

Litt. D. *abbr.* Doctor of Letters, Doctor of Literature. WH: Abbr. of Latin *Litterarum Doctor* Doctor of Letters.

litter *n.* rubbish, esp. waste paper, scattered about in a public place. Also *v.t.*, *v.i.* WH: 12–14C. Old French *litière*, from Medieval Latin *lectaria*, from Latin *lectus*. The original sense (to the 15C) was bed, then straw used as bedding, then (from the 18C) scatterings of discarded material. The sense bedding gave that of a group of young animals (14–15C) who were born on such a bedding.

littérateur *n.* an author, a professional writer. WH: 19C. French, from Latin *litterator* teacher of letters, grammarian, from *litera* LETTER. See also -ATOR.

little *a.* small, not great in size, amount or quantity. Also *adv.*, *n.* WH: pre-1200. Old English *lȳtel*, from Germanic. Cp. German dial. *lützel* little.

littoral *a.* of or relating to the shore, esp. the zone between high- and low-water marks. Also *n.* WH: 17C. Latin *littoralis*, var. of *litoralis*, from *litus*, *litoris* shore. See also -AL[1].

liturgy *n.* a form of public worship laid down by a Church. WH: 16C. French *liturgie* or Late Latin *liturgia*, from Greek *leitourgia* public service, worship of the gods, from *leitourgos* public servant, minister, from var. of *lēitos* public, from *lēos*, Ionic form of *lāos* people + -*ergos* performing.

live[1] *v.i.* to have life, to be alive. Also *v.t.* WH: pre-1200. Old English *libban*, *lifian*, from Germanic base rel. to that of LIFE, LEAVE[1]. Cp. German *leben*.

live[2] *a.* alive, living. Also *adv.* WH: 16C. Shortening of ALIVE.

livelihood *n.* means of subsistence; occupation. WH: pre-1200. Old English *līflād*, from *līf* LIFE + *lād* course, way (see LOAD, LODE). The word was assimilated in the 16C to LIVELY and -HOOD.

livelong[1] *a.* long-lasting. WH: 14–15C. Orig. from LIEF + LONG[1] but in 16C interpreted as from LIVE[1] or LIVE[2] + LONG[1]. Cp. German *die liebe lange Nicht*, lit. the dear long night.

livelong[2] *n.* ORPINE. WH: 16C. LIVE[1] + LONG[1]. The plant retains its form or greenness for a long time.

lively *a.* full of life, active. WH: pre-1200. LIFE + -LY[1]. The original sense (to the 17C) was living, live.

liver[1] *n.* a glandular organ in the abdominal cavity of vertebrates which secretes bile and purifies the blood. Also *a.* WH: pre-1200. Old English *lifer*, from Germanic. ? Rel. to Greek *lipos* fat, and so to LIPID. Cp. German *Leber*.

liver[2] *n.* a fabulous bird, supposed to have given its name to Liverpool, and still commemorated in the arms of that city. WH: 17C. Back-formation from *Liverpool*, a city and port in NW England. The bird was originally intended to be the eagle of St John the Evangelist, patron saint of the city corporation.

Liverpudlian *n.* a native or inhabitant of Liverpool. WH: 19C. *Liverpool*, a city and port in NW England, with humorous substitution of -*puddle* for -*pool*.

livery *n.* a distinctive dress worn by the servants of a particular person or the members of a city company. Also *v.t.* WH: 12–14C. Old French *livrée*, fem. p.p. (used as n.) of *livrer* to dispense, to deliver, from Latin *liberare* LIBERATE. See also -Y[2]. The original sense was the dispensing of food, provisions or clothing to retainers and servants, then the clothing itself worn by such servants.

livid *a.* furious, very angry. WH: 14–15C. French *livide* or Latin *lividus*, from *livere* to be bluish. See also -ID. The sense furiously angry arose in the early 20C. An angry person can be white-faced.

living *a.* alive, having life. Also *n.* WH: pre-1200. LIVE[1] + -ING[2].

livre *n.* an old French coin, replaced by the franc in 1795. WH: 16C. French, from Latin *libra* pound. Cp. LIRA.

lixiviate *v.t.* to leach, to dissolve out by washing or filtering. WH: 17C. Modern Latin *lixiviatus*, p.p. of *lixiviare*, from Late Latin *lixivium*, use as n. of Latin *lixivius* made into lye, from *lix* ashes, lye. See also -ATE[3].

lizard *n.* any member of the reptilian order Lacertilia, esp. of the typical genus *Lacerta*, having a long, scaly body and tail, and four limbs, each with five toes of unequal length. WH: 14–15C. Old French *lesard* (Modern French *lézard*), from Latin *lacertus*, appar. same word as *lacertus* muscle. See also -ARD. Cp. ALLIGATOR.

llama *n.* a domesticated Peruvian wool-bearing animal, *Lama glama*, resembling a camel, but humpless and smaller, used as a beast of burden. WH: 17C. Spanish, from Quechua.

llano *n.* a level, treeless steppe or plain in the northern part of S America. WH: 17C. Spanish, from Latin *planum* PLANE[1]. Cp. PLAIN[1].

LL B *abbr.* Bachelor of Laws. WH: Abbr. of Latin *Legum Baccalareus* Bachelor of Laws.

LL D *abbr.* Doctor of Laws. WH: Abbr. of Latin *Legum Doctor* Doctor of Laws.

LL M *abbr.* Master of Laws. WH: Abbr. of Latin *Legum Magister* Master of Laws.

Lloyd's *n.* a corporation, with offices in the City of London, esp. dealing with marine insurance, the classification and registration of vessels etc. WH: 19C. Edward *Lloyd*, d. *c*.1730, English coffee-house keeper, who supplied shipping information to merchants and ship-owners from 1688 to 1726.

lo *int.* see! behold! look! WH: pre-1200. Old English *lā*, natural exclamation, later assoc. with LOOK.

loach *n.* any of the Cobitidae, a group of the carp family, esp. *Nemachilus barbatulus*, a small British river fish. WH: 14–15C. Old French *loche*, of unknown orig.

load *n.* a burden. Also *v.t.*, *v.i.* WH: pre-1200. Old English *lād* way, course, from Germanic, from base also of LEAD[1]. The original sense was carriage, carrying. The current sense evolved in the 12–14C.

loadsa *a.* short for *loads of*. WH: late 20C. Representation of a pronun. of *loads of*.

loaf[1] *n.* a shaped mass of bread, esp. of a standard size or weight. WH: pre-1200. Old English *hlāf*, from Germanic. Cp. German *Laib*. The original sense was bread or loaf. Cp. LORD, LADY.

loaf[2] *v.i.* to lounge or idle about. Also *v.t.*, *n.* WH: 19C. Prob. back-formation from *loafer*, from German *Landläufer* tramp, from *Land* LAND + *laufen* to run. Cp. *landloper* (LAND).

loam *n.* soil consisting of sand and clay loosely coherent, with admixture of organic matter or humus. Also *v.t.* WH: pre-1200. Old English *lām*, from Germanic, from var. of base of LIME[1], rel. to Latin *limus* mud.

loan *n.* something which is lent, esp. a sum of money lent at interest. Also *v.t.* WH: 12–14C. Old Norse *lán*, from Germanic base also of LEND. The Old English equivalent, *lǣn*, did not survive into Middle English except in the obsolete legal term *laen*, an estate held as a benefice in Anglo-Saxon England.

loath *a.* unwilling, reluctant. WH: pre-1200. Old English *lāth*, from Germanic. Cp. German *Leid* sorrow, pain, *leider* unfortunately. The original sense was hostile, angry, then (to the 16C) repulsive, loathsome. The current sense dates from the 12–14C.

loathe *v.t.* to feel disgust at. Also *v.i.* WH: pre-1200. Old English *lāthian*, from Germanic, from base of LOATH. The original sense (to the 16C) was to be hateful, to be displeasing. The current sense dates from the 12–14C.

lob *n.* in tennis, a ball struck in a high arc, usu. over one's opponent's head; a stroke that sends the ball on this trajectory. Also *v.t.*, *v.i.* WH: 16C. Prob. from various Low Dutch words. Cp. Dutch *lubbe* hanging lip, *lobbes* bumpkin. The current sense dates from the 19C.

lobby *n.* a passage or vestibule, usu. opening into several apartments. Also *v.i.*, *v.t.* WH: 16C. Medieval Latin *lobia*. See LODGE.

lobe *n.* any rounded and projecting or hanging part. WH: 14–15C. Late Latin *lobus*, from Greek *lobos* lobe of the ear, capsule, pod.

lobelia *n.* any of a genus, *Lobelia*, of herbaceous and brilliant flowering plants. WH: 18C. Matthias de *Lobel*, 1538–1616, Flemish botanist to James I + -IA.

loblolly *n.* any of various US pine trees. WH: 16C. Orig. unknown. The word originally denoted a type of thick gruel. The sense of pine tree dates from the 18C, the name referring to the swampy soil in which it grows.

lobola *n.* a southern African custom whereby the bridegroom's family makes a payment of cash or cattle to the bride's family shortly before a marriage. WH: 19C. Bantu (Nguni) *ukulobola* to give a dowry.

lobotomy *n.* a surgical incision into the lobe of an organ or gland. WH: mid-20C. LOBE + -O- + -TOMY.

lobscouse *n.* a hash of meat with vegetables of various kinds and ship's biscuit. WH: 18C. Rel. to Dutch *lapskous*, Danish and Norwegian *lapskaus*, ult. of unknown orig. Cp. LOBLOLLY. See also SCOUSE.

lobster *n.* a large marine long-tailed and stalk-eyed decapod crustacean with large pincers, of the genus *Homarus*. WH: pre-1200. Old English *loppestre*, from Latin *locusta* crustacean, LOCUST, with -*stre* based on nn. in -STER.

lobule *n.* (a subdivision of) a small lobe. WH: 17C. LOBE + -ULE, based on GLOBULE, etc.

lobworm *n.* a large earthworm, used as bait by anglers. WH: 17C. Obs. or dial. *lob* (LOB) + WORM.

local *a.* existing in or peculiar to a particular place or places. *Also n.* WH: 14–15C. Old French, from Late Latin *localis*, from Latin LOCUS. See also -AL[1].

locale *n.* a place, site, esp. with reference to an event taking place there. WH: 18C. French *local* (LOCAL), respelt to indicate the stress. Cp. MORALE.

locate *v.t.* to discover or determine the site of. *Also v.i.* WH: 16C. Latin *locatus*, p.p. of *locare* to place, to let for hire, from LOCUS place. See also -ATE[3].

loc. cit. *adv.* in the place cited. WH: 19C. Abbr. of Latin *loco citato* or *locus citatus* (in) the place cited.

loch *n.* a lake or a narrow or land-locked arm of the sea in Scotland. WH: 14–15C. Gaelic LAKE[1]. Cp. LOUGH.

lochia *n.pl.* the uterine evacuations which follow childbirth. WH: 17C. Modern Latin, from Greek *lokhia*, neut. pl. (used as n.) of *lokhios* pertaining to childbirth, from *lokhos* childbirth.

lock[1] *n.* a device for fastening doors etc., usu. having a bolt moved by a key of a particular shape. *Also v.t., v.i.* WH: pre-1200. Old English *loc*, from Germanic. Cp. German *Loch*.

lock[2] *n.* a number of strands of hair curled or hanging together, a tress. WH: pre-1200. Old English *locc*, from Germanic. ? Identical with LOCK[1]. Cp. German *Locke*.

locker *n.* a cupboard, chest or other closed receptacle, with lock and key, esp. one of a number for public use e.g. at a swimming pool or railway station. WH: 12–14C. LOCK[1] + -ER[1].

locket *n.* a small gold or silver case, worn as an ornament and adapted to contain hair, a miniature etc. WH: 14–15C. Old French *locquet* (Modern French *loquet* latch), dim. of *loc* latch, lock, from Germanic base also of LOCK[1]. See also -ET[1]. The original sense (to the 16C) was an iron crossbar in a window. The current sense dates from the 17C.

loco[1] *n.* a locomotive. WH: 19C. Abbr. of *locomotive* (LOCOMOTION).

loco[2] *a.* insane, mad. *Also n.* WH: 19C. Spanish insane.

locomotion *n.* the act or power of moving from place to place. WH: 17C. Latin *loco*, abl. of LOCUS place + *motio, motionis* MOTION.

loculus *n.* a small cavity, a cell, esp. any one of a large number of such. WH: 14–15C. Latin, dim. of LOCUS place. See also -CULE.

locum *n.* a deputy or substitute, esp. one acting in the place of a doctor or member of the clergy. WH: early 20C. Abbr. of *locum tenens* 17C, from Medieval Latin, from Latin *locum*, acc. of *locus* place + *tenens*, pres.p. of *tenere* to hold. Cp. LIEUTENANT.

locus *n.* the exact place, the locality (of). WH: 18C. Latin place.

locust *n.* a winged insect of various species allied to the grasshopper, which migrates in vast swarms and is very destructive to vegetation. WH: 12–14C. Old French *locuste*, from Latin *locusta* locust, crustacean (cp. LOBSTER).

locution *n.* a phrase or expression considered with regard to style or idiom. WH: 14–15C. Old French, or from Latin *locutio, locutionis*, from *locutus*, p.p of *loqui* to talk, to speak. See also -ION.

locutory *n.* a conversation room or parlour in a monastery. WH: 15C. Medieval Latin *locutorium*, from Latin *locutus*. See LOCUTION, also -ORY[1].

lode *n.* a vein in rock bearing precious ore. WH: pre-1200. Old English *lād*. See LOAD. The original sense was course, way, journey. The sense vein of ore evolved in the 17C.

loden *n.* a thick soft waterproof woollen cloth used for making coats. WH: early 20C. German, from Old High German *lodo* thick cloth.

lodge *n.* a small house at the entrance to or in a park, esp. for a gatekeeper or gardener. *Also v.t., v.i.* WH: 12–14C. Old French *loge* arbour, summer house, hut, from Medieval Latin *laubia, lobia*, from Germanic, ? from base of LEAF. Cp. LOBBY.

lodicule *n.* any of two or three minute green or white scales below the ovary of a grass flower. WH: 19C. Latin *lodicula*, dim. of *lodix, lodicis* coverlet. See also -CULE.

loess *n.* a wind-borne deposit of loam, sand etc., in the Rhine, Mississippi and other river valleys. WH: 19C. German *Löss*, from Swiss German *lösch* loose, from *lösen* to loosen.

loft *n.* the room or air space under a roof. *Also v.t.* WH: pre-1200. Old Norse *lopt* air, sky, upper room, from Germanic. Cp. ALOFT, LIFT[2].

log[1] *n.* a bulky piece of unhewn timber. *Also v.t., v.i.* WH: 12–14C. Orig. unknown. The sense device for ascertaining the speed of a ship arose in the 16C and originally referred to the piece of wood with a line attached that was used for the purpose. This sense in turn gave that of log book (19C) and hence of any record of things done, found, etc. (early 20C).

log[2] *n.* a logarithm. WH: 17C. Abbr. of LOGARITHM.

logan *n.* a rocking-stone. WH: 18C. Var. of *logging*, part. a. of dial. *log* to rock, of unknown orig.

loganberry *n.* a permanent hybrid plant obtained by crossing the raspberry and a species of the blackberry. WH: 19C. J.H. *Logan*, 1841–1928, US horticulturalist + BERRY.

logaoedic *a.* in ancient prosody, applied to lines consisting of a mixture of dactyls and trochees to give the effect of prose. *Also n.* WH: 19C. Late Latin *logaoedicus*, from Greek *logaoidikos*, from *logos* saying, speech (see LOGOS) + *aoidē* song. See also -IC.

logarithm *n.* the exponent of the power to which a fixed number, called the base, must be raised to produce a given number (tabulated and used as a means of simplifying arithmetical processes by enabling addition and subtraction to be substituted for multiplication and division). WH: 17C. Modern Latin *logarithmus*, from Greek *logos* relation, ratio (see LOGOS) + *arithmos* number. The word was coined in 1614 by John Napier (see NAPIER'S BONES).

loge *n.* a box in the theatre. WH: 18C. French. See LODGE.

loggerhead *n.* a large marine turtle, *Caretta caretta*. WH: 16C. Prob. from dial. *logger* heavy block of wood, from LOG[1] + HEAD[1].

loggia *n.* an open corridor, gallery or arcade along the front of a large building. WH: 18C. Italian LODGE.

logic *n.* the science of reasoning, correct thinking. WH: 14–15C. Old French *logique*, from Late Latin *logica*, from Greek *logikē* (*tekhnē*) (art) of reason, from *logos* reasoning, discourse. See LOGOS, also -IC.

-logic *comb. form* forming adjectives from nouns ending in -logy. WH: Greek -*logikos*, from aa. and nn. in -*logos*, -*logia* -LOGY. See also -IC.

logion *n.* a traditional saying, revelation or truth, esp. one of those ascribed to Christ but not recorded in the Gospels. WH: 19C. Greek oracle, from *logos* word (LOGOS).

-logist *comb. form* forming nouns meaning a person versed in or working in, as in *anthropologist, astrologer*. WH: -LOGY + -IST.

logistics *n.pl.* the branch of strategy concerned with the moving and supply of troops. WH: 19C. French *logistique*, from *loger* to quarter, LODGE. See also -ICS.

loglog *n.* the logarithm of a logarithm. WH: early 20C. Redupl. of LOG[2].

logo *n.* a symbol or simple design used to identify a company, organization etc. WH: mid-20C. Abbr. of LOGOGRAM.

logo- *comb. form* of or relating to words. WH: Greek *logos* word. See also -O-.

logogram *n.* a sign representing a word, esp. in shorthand. WH: 19C. LOGO- + -GRAM.

logography *n.* a method of printing in which a type represents a word instead of a letter. WH: 18C. LOGO- + -GRAPHY.

logogriph *n.* a word puzzle, esp. one based on transposing the letters of a word. WH: 16C. French *logogriphe*, from Greek *logos* (LOGOS) + *griphos* fishing basket, riddle.

logomachy *n.* contention about words, a controversy hingeing on verbal matters. WH: 16C. Greek *logomakhia*, from *logos* word (LOGOS) + -*makhia*, from *makhē* battle. See also -Y[2].

logorrhoea *n.* excessive or uncontrollable talkativeness. WH: early 20C. LOGO- + -RRHOEA, prob. based on DIARRHOEA.

Logos *n.* in Greek philosophy, the divine reason implicit in and governing the cosmos. WH: 16C. Greek account, relation, reasoning, argument, discourse, saying, speech, word, rel. to *legein* to choose, to collect, to gather, to say. The word was used in a mystic sense by Hellenistic and Neoplatonist philosophers and by St John, in whose Gospel and Book of Revelation it is translated in English by 'Word' as a title of Christ.

logotype *n.* a type having two or more letters cast in one piece, but not as a ligature, as *are, was* etc. WH: 19C. LOGO- + TYPE.

-logue *comb. form* forming nouns relating to discourse, as in *epilogue*, *prologue*. WH: French, or from Greek *-logos*, *-logon* speaking of, treating of, from *logos*. See LOGOS.

-logy *comb. form* forming names of sciences and departments of knowledge, and nouns denoting modes of speaking or discourses, as *astrology*, *eulogy*, *tautology*. WH: French *-logie*, from Medieval Latin *-logia*, from Greek *logos*. See LOGOS, also -Y².

†**loimic** *a.* of or relating to the plague or to contagious diseases. WH: 19C. Greek *loimikos*, from *loimos* plague.

loin *n.* the part of the body of a human being or quadruped lying between the lower ribs and the hip joint. WH: 12–14C. Old French *loigne*, var. of *longe* (Modern French loin of veal), from Latin *lumbus* loin.

loiter *v.i.* to linger, to dawdle. *Also v.t.* WH: 14–15C. ? Middle Dutch *loteren* to wag about, Dutch *leuteren* to shake, to totter, from base also of Middle Dutch *lutsen* to wag about. Cp. German *lottern*.

Lok Sabha *n.* the lower chamber of the Indian parliament. WH: mid-20C. Sanskrit *lok* people + *sabhā* assembly, council.

loll *v.i.* to stand, sit or lie in a lazy attitude. *Also v.t.* WH: 14–15C. Imit. Cp. LULL.

lollapalooza *n.* something first-rate, excellent etc. WH: 19C. Orig. uncertain. ? Fanciful creation based on LULU.

Lollard *n.* any one of a sect of English religious reformers in the 14th and 15th cents., followers of John Wyclif (?1330–84). WH: 14–15C. Middle Dutch *lollaerd*, lit. mumbler, mutterer, from *lollen* to mumble. See also -ARD. The name arose as a contemptuous nickname for the sect members, who were seen as heretics pretending to be pious and humble by mumbling prayers without any thought of the content.

lollipop *n.* a flat or round boiled sweet on the end of a stick. WH: 18C. ? From dial. *lolly* tongue (? from LOLL) + POP¹. The word was originally used for a particular kind of sweet or (in the plural) for sweets in general.

lollop *v.i.* to move with an ungainly bouncing gait. WH: 18C. Prob. from LOLL, by assoc. with TROLLOP.

lolly *n.* a lollipop, a sweet on a stick. WH: 19C. Abbr. of LOLLIPOP.

Lombard *n.* any of a Germanic people who conquered Italy in the 6th cent. *Also a.* WH: 12–14C. Middle Dutch and Middle Low German *lombaerd*, or from French *lombard*, from Italian *lombardo*, from Late Latin *Langobardus*, *Longobardus*, from Latin *langobardi*, from Germanic, from base of LONG¹ + ethnic name *Bardi*. Cp. LUMBER².

loment *n.* an indehiscent legume, that separates when ripe by means of a transverse articulation between each seed. WH: 14–15C. Latin *lomentum* bean meal (orig. a cosmetic made from bean meal), from *lavare* to wash.

London clay *n.* a formation of a lower Eocene age in SE England. WH: 12–14C. *London*, the capital of England and now also of the UK + CLAY.

lone *a.* solitary, without company or a comrade. WH: 14–15C. Shortening of ALONE.

lonely *a.* sad through lacking company or companionship. WH: 16C. LONE + -LY¹.

long¹ *a.* of considerable or relatively great linear extent. *Also adv., n.* WH: pre-1200. Old English *lang*, *long*, from Germanic. Cp. German *lang*.

long² *v.i.* to have an earnest desire (for). WH: pre-1200. Old English *langian*, from Germanic, from base of LONG¹. Cp. German *langen* to reach, to extend, to suffice.

longanimity *n.* long-suffering, forbearance. WH: 14–15C. Late Latin *longanimitas*, from *longanimus*, from *longus* LONG¹ + *animus* mind, rendering Greek *makrothumia* (from *makros* long + *thumos* soul, spirit).

longeron *n.* a longitudinal spar of an aeroplane's fuselage. WH: early 20C. French longitudinal girder, from *allonger* to make long, from *long* LONG¹.

longevity *n.* great length of life. WH: 17C. Late Latin *longaevitas*, from Latin *longaevus*, from *longus* LONG¹ + *aevum* age. See also -ITY.

longi- *comb. form* long. WH: Latin *longus* LONG¹ + *-i-*.

longicorn *a.* of or relating to the Longicornes, a division of beetles with large filiform antennae. *Also n.* WH: 19C. Modern Latin *Longicornia*, from Latin *longus* LONG¹ + *-i-* + Latin *cornu* horn.

longipennate *a.* having long wings or feathers. WH: 19C. LONGI- + PENNATE.

longitude *n.* angular distance of a place east or west of a given meridian, usu. that of Greenwich. WH: 14–15C. Latin *longitudo*, from *longus* LONG¹. See also -TUDE.

longshore *a.* of or belonging to, existing or working on the shore. WH: 19C. Shortening of *alongshore*. See ALONG, SHORE¹.

lonicera *n.* a dense evergreen shrub of the genus, *Lonicera*, used for hedging. WH: 18C. Modern Latin, from Adam *Lonicer*, 1528–86, German botanist.

Lonsdale belt *n.* a broad ornamental metal belt, awarded as a trophy to British professional boxing champions who retain it as a personal possession if they win it three times. WH: early 20C. Hugh Cecil Lowther, 5th earl of *Lonsdale*, 1857–1944, who presented the first trophy in 1909.

loo¹ *n.* a lavatory. WH: mid-20C. Orig. unknown. ? From *Waterloo*, a district of London, with pun on WATER and French *l'eau* the water and ref. to French *water* water closet, lavatory.

loo² *n.* a round game at cards. *Also v.t.* WH: 17C. Abbr. of obs. *lanterloo*, from French *lanterlu*, orig. meaningless refrain of a pop. 16C song.

looby *n.* an awkward, clumsy person, a lubber. WH: 14–15C. Orig. uncertain. ? Rel. to LOB.

loofah *n.* a tropical gourdlike climbing plant, *Luffa cylindrica*, with an edible fruit. WH: 19C. Arabic *lūfa* the plant, *lūf* the species.

look *v.i.* to direct the eyes (towards, at etc.) in order to see an object. *Also v.t., n., int.* WH: pre-1200. Old English *lōcian*, from Germanic. Cp. German dial. *lugen* to look, to peep.

loom¹ *n.* a machine in which yarn or thread is woven into a fabric. WH: pre-1200. Old English *gelōma* utensil, tool.

loom² *v.i.* to appear indistinctly or faintly in the distance. *Also n.* WH: 16C. Prob. of Dutch orig. Cp. E Frisian *lōmen* to move slowly.

†**loom³** *n.* a diver (the bird). WH: 17C. Old Norse *lómr*. Cp. LOON².

loon¹ *n.* a daft or eccentric person. WH: 14–15C. Orig. unknown.

loon² *n.* a diver, any bird of the Gaviidae family. WH: 17C. Prob. from same source as LOOM³, assim. to LOON¹.

loony *n.* a lunatic; a foolish person. *Also a.* WH: 19C. Abbr. of LUNATIC, assoc. with LOON¹.

loop¹ *n.* a folding or doubling of a string, rope, thread etc. across itself to form a curve or eye. *Also v.t., v.i.* WH: 14–15C. Orig. uncertain. Cp. Irish *lúb*, Gaelic *lub* loop, bend.

†**loop²** *n.* a loophole in a wall. WH: 12–14C. Orig. unknown.

loophole *n.* an aperture in a wall for shooting or looking through or for admission of light. *Also v.t.* WH: 16C. LOOP² + HOLE.

loose *a.* not tied, fastened or confined. *Also v.t., v.i., n.* WH: 12–14C. Old Norse *lauss*, from Germanic, from base also of -LESS.

loosestrife *n.* any of a genus of plants of the primrose family, esp. *Lysimachia vulgaris* with yellow flowers; yellow loosestrife. WH: 16C. LOOSE + STRIFE, mistranslating Latin *lysimachia*, as if from Greek *lusimakhos* loosing (i.e. ending) strife, from *lusis* loosening (LYSIS) + *makhē* strife, battle (cp. LOGOMACHY), instead of from *Lusimakhos* Lysimachus, *c.*355–281 BC, king of Thrace, the plant's discoverer.

loot *n.* booty, plunder, esp. from a conquered city. *Also v.t., v.i.* WH: 19C. Hindi *lūṭ*, *lūṭṇā*, from Sanskrit *luṇṭ* to rob.

lop¹ *v.t.* to cut off the top or extremities of (a tree, body etc.). *Also v.i., n.* WH: 16C. Orig. uncertain. ? Ult. rel. to Lithuanian *lūpti* to strip, to peel.

lop² *v.i.* to hang down limply, to flop, to droop. *Also v.t., n.* WH: 16C. Prob. imit. Cp. LOB.

lope *v.i.* to gallop, swing or move (along) with long strides or leaps. *Also n.* WH: 12–14C. Var. of LOUP. The original sense was to jump, to leap. The current sense dates from the 19C.

lopho- *comb. form* having a crest, crested. WH: Greek *lophos* crest. See also -O-.

lophobranch *n.* a teleost fish of the suborder Lophobranchii, comprising the seahorses or pipefishes, that have their gills in tufts. WH: 19C. LOPHO- + Greek *bragkhia* gills.

lophodont *a.* having ridges on the crowns of the crowns of the molar teeth. *Also n.* WH: 19C. LOPHO- + -ODONT.

lophophore *n.* a ring or horseshoe or ciliated tentacles round the mouth of some minute sessile sea creatures. WH: 19C. LOPHO- + -PHORE.

lopolith *n.* a saucer-shaped body of igneous rock formed by the intrusion of magma into existing rock layers. WH: early 20C. Greek *lopas* basin + -O- + -LITH.

loquacious *a.* talkative, chattering. WH: 17C. Latin *loquax, loquacis,* from *loqui* to speak. See also -ACIOUS.

loquat *n.* a Chinese and Japanese tree, *Eriobotrya japonica.* WH: 19C. Chinese dial. *luh* rush + *kwat* orange.

lor *int.* Lord. WH: 19C. Alt. of LORD.

loran *n.* a system of navigation in which position is determined by the intervals between pulses received from widely spaced radio transmitters. WH: mid-20C. Acronym of *long-range navigation.*

lord *n.* a ruler, a master. *Also v.t., int.* WH: pre-1200. Old English *hlāford,* contr. of *hlāfweard,* from Germanic, from base of LOAF[1] + WARD. The literal sense is one who guards loaves. Cp. LADY. *Lord* is used in the Old Testament to translate Hebrew words for God, and in the New Testament, as a title of Christ, to translate Latin *dominus* or Greek *kurios* (KYRIE).

lordosis *n.* curvature of a bone, esp. of the spine, forward. WH: 18C. Modern Latin, from Greek *lordōsis,* from *lordos* bent backwards. See also -OSIS.

lore[1] *n.* the collective traditions and knowledge relating to a given subject. WH: pre-1200. Old English *lār,* from Germanic base also of LEARN.

lore[2] *n.* a straplike part, the surface between the eye and the beak in birds. WH: 17C. Latin *lorum* strap, thong.

lorgnette *n.* a pair of eyeglasses or opera glasses with a long handle. WH: 19C. French, from *lorgner* to squint, to ogle. See also -ETTE.

lorica *n.* the carapace of a crustacean, the sheath of certain infusoria and rotifers. WH: 18C. Latin breastplate. Rel. to LORE[2].

lorikeet *n.* any of various brightly-coloured parrots of the subfamily Lorunae, belonging to Australasia and SE Asia. WH: 18C. LORY + -keet, based on PARAKEET.

†**lorimer** *n.* a maker of bits and spurs, a spurrier. WH: 12–14C. Old French *lorenier, loremier,* from *lorain* strap of a harness, from Latin *lorum* strap, thong. See also -ER[2].

loris *n.* a slow-moving, nocturnal primate with small ears and a short tail, of S India and Sri Lanka, *Nycticebus coucang.* WH: 18C. French, ? from obs. Dutch *loeris* clown, booby.

†**lorn** *a.* lost, abandoned, forlorn. WH: 12–14C. P.p. of obs. *lese* to lose, representing Old English *-lēosan* as in *forlēosan* (FORLORN).

lorry *n.* a large motor vehicle for carrying heavy loads. WH: 19C. ? From pers. name *Laurie.* The word was originally used for a truck or wagon on a railway. The sense road vehicle dates from the early 20C.

lory *n.* a brilliantly coloured parrot-like bird of various genera of Loriinae, found in SE Asia and Australia. WH: 17C. Malay *lori, luri,* dial. var. of *nuri.*

lose *v.t.* to be deprived of. *Also v.i.* WH: pre-1200. Old English *losian,* from *los* LOSS. The original meaning was to perish, to be lost, to be missing. The later senses were influenced by related obsolete *lese* (LORN), and the pronunciation by LOOSE.

†**losel** *n.* a worthless person, a scamp, a ne'er-do-well. *Also a.* WH: 14–15C. Appar. from *los-,* stem of obs. *lese* (see LORN) + -EL.

loss *n.* the act of losing or the state of being deprived of something. WH: pre-1200. Old English *los* death, destruction, from Germanic base also of obs. *lese* (LORN), LOOSE. The current noun resulted as a back-formation from *lost,* the past participle of LOSE.

lot *n.* a considerable quantity or amount, a great deal. *Also v.t.* WH: pre-1200. Old English *hlot,* from Germanic. Cp. German *Los.* The original sense was a set of objects used at random to decide on a dispute, etc. The general sense large amount dates from the 16C. The sense plot of land evolved in the 17C, and that of an item for sale at an auction in the 18C. Cp. ALLOT, LOTTERY.

Lothario *n.* a libertine, a seducer. WH: 18C. *Lothario,* the main character in Nicholas Rowe's play *The Fair Penitent* (1703), who seduces Calista, the 'fair penitent'.

lotic *a.* associated with or living in fast-flowing water. WH: early 20C. Latin *lotus* washing, from p.p. of *lavare* to wash. See also -IC.

lotion *n.* a medicinal or cosmetic liquid application for external use.

WH: 14–15C. Old French, or from Latin *lotio, lotionis* washing, from *lotus, lautus,* p.p. of *lavare* to wash. See also -ION.

lottery *n.* a method of allotting valuable prizes by chance or lot among purchasers of tickets. WH: 16C. Prob. from Dutch *loterij,* from *lot* LOT + -*erij* -ERY.

lotus *n.* in Greek legend, any of several plants the fruit of which was said to induce a dreamy languor in those who ate it. WH: 15C. Latin, from Greek *lōtos,* prob. from Semitic.

louche *a.* morally suspect. WH: 19C. French cross-eyed, squinting, from Latin *luscus* one-eyed.

loud *a.* powerful in sound, sonorous. WH: pre-1200. Old English *hlūd,* from Germanic, from Indo-European, from base meaning to hear represented also in Greek *kluein* to hear, Latin *cluere* to be famous.

lough *n.* a lake, an arm of the sea in Ireland. WH: pre-1200. Irish *loch.* Cp. LOCH.

louis *n.* an old French gold coin issued from Louis XIII to Louis XVI, worth at different times 20 or 23 francs, superseded by the 20-franc piece. WH: 17C. French, from *Louis* XIII, 1601–43, in whose reign it was first issued (1640). The coin retained the name through the reigns of subsequent kings Louis until that of Louis XVI (1774–93). It was withdrawn following his execution in 1793.

lounge *v.i.* to loll or recline. *Also v.t., n.* WH: 16C. ? Imit. The word is related by some to French *s'allonger* to lounge about, to stretch out, from *allonger* to extend, from long LONG[1].

loup *v.t., v.i.* to leap. WH: 14–15C. Old Norse *hlaup.* See LEAP.

loupe *n.* a small magnifying glass used by jewellers, watchmakers etc. WH: 14–15C. Old French, prob. from Frankish *luppa* mass of congealed liquid.

lour *v.i.* (of clouds, weather etc.) to appear dark or gloomy. *Also n.* WH: 12–14C. Orig. unknown. Not rel. to LOWER.

louse *n.* a blood-sucking insect of the genus *Pediculus,* three species of which are parasitic on man. *Also v.t.* WH: pre-1200. Old English *lūs,* from Germanic. Cp. German *Laus.*

lout[1] *n.* a rough, crude, ill-mannered person. *Also v.t.* WH: 16C. Orig. unknown. ? From LOUT[2]. According to some, the word is an altered form of LEWD.

lout[2] *v.i.* to bend, to bow, to stoop. WH: pre-1200. Old English *lūtan,* from Germanic.

louvre *n.* a louvre-board. WH: 12–14C. Old French *lover* skylight, prob. from a Germanic word rel. to base of LODGE.

lovage *n.* a European umbelliferous herb, used in salads and for flavouring food, *Levisticum officinale.* WH: 14–15C. Alt. (by assoc. with LOVE and obs. *ache* parsley) of Old French *levesche* (Modern French *livèche*), from Late Latin *ligusticum,* neut. of *ligusticus* Ligurian. The plant was said to originate in Liguria, formerly a country extending from NE Spain to NW Italy and including Switzerland and SE Gaul.

lovat *n.* a muted bluish-grey-green colour, usu. found in tweed or woollen cloth. *Also a.* WH: early 20C. *Lovat,* a place near Inverness, Scotland.

love *n.* a feeling of deep regard, fondness and devotion (for, towards etc.). *Also v.t., v.i.* WH: pre-1200. Old English *lufu,* from Germanic, from Indo-European base also of Latin *lubet* it is pleasing, *lubido* desire, LIBIDO, Old Church Slavonic *ljubŭ* dear (Russian *lyubit'* to love), Sanskrit *lubhyati* (he) desires.

low[1] *a.* not reaching or situated far up. *Also adv., n.* WH: 12–14C. Old Norse *lágr,* from Germanic base rel. to that of LIE[2].

low[2] *v.i.* to utter the moo of cow. *Also v.i., n.* WH: pre-1200. Old English *hlōwan,* from Germanic, from Indo-European base also of Latin *clamare* to shout.

lower *a.* situated at a less high level than, or below, another thing. *Also adv., v.t., v.i.* WH: 12–14C. LOW[1] + -ER[3].

lox[1] *n.* a kind of smoked salmon. WH: mid-20C. Yiddish *laks,* from German *Lachs* salmon.

lox[2] *n.* liquid oxygen, used in rocket fuels. WH: early 20C. Orig. abbr. of *l*iquid *ox*ygen explosive, but later interpreted as abbr. of *l*iquid *ox*ygen.

loxodromic *a.* of or relating to the rhumb lines or to map projections, such as Mercator's, in which rhumb lines appear straight. WH: 17C. French *loxodromique,* from Greek *loxos* oblique + *dromos* course. See also -IC.

loyal *a.* faithful, in a trust or obligation (to). *Also n.* WH: 16C. French, from Old French *loial*, var. of *leial*, *leel*, from French *legalis* LEGAL. Cp. LEAL.

lozenge *n.* a rhombus or oblique-angled parallelogram. WH: 12–14C. Old French *losenge* (Modern French *losange*), prob. deriv. of word represented by Provençal *lausa*, Spanish *losa*, Portuguese *lousa* slab, tombstone, and Late Latin *lausiae* (*lapides*) stone slabs, ult. of Gaulish or Iberian orig. The original sense was a diamond-shaped figure, such as a heraldic charge. This was extended to a cake so shaped and (in the 16C) to a medicinal sweet.

LP *n.* a long-playing record, usu. 12 in. (30 cm) in diameter and designed to rotate at 33.3 revolutions per minute. WH: Abbr. of *long-playing*.

L.S.D. *abbr.* of Latin *librae*, *solidi*, *denarii*, pounds, shillings and pence. WH: See LIBRA, SOLIDUS, DENARIUS.

lubber *n.* a lazy, clumsy person, an awkward lout. WH: 14–15C. ? Old French *lobeor* swindler, parasite, from *lober* to deceive, to sponge on.

lubra *n.* an Aboriginal woman. WH: 19C. Australian Aboriginal, of unknown orig.

lubricate *v.t.* to cover or treat with grease, oil or similar substance, in order to reduce friction. WH: 17C. Latin *lubricatus*, p.p. of *lubricare*, from *lubricus* slippery. See also -ATE³.

lubricious *a.* lewd, lascivious. WH: 16C. Latin *lubricus* slippery + -IOUS.

Lucan *a.* of or relating to the evangelist St Luke. WH: 19C. Ecclesiastical Latin *Lucas*, Greek *Loukas* Luke + -AN.

lucarne *n.* a dormer or garret window, a light in a spire. WH: 16C. Old French, from Provençal *lucana*, of unknown orig.

luce *n.* a pike (the fish), esp. when full-grown. WH: 14–15C. Old French *lus*, *luis*, from Late Latin *lucius*.

lucent *a.* shining, bright, luminous, resplendent. WH: 14–15C. Latin *lucens*, *lucentis*, pres.p. of *lucere* to shine. See also -ENT.

lucerne *n.* alfalfa. WH: 17C. French *luzerne*, from Provençal *luzerno* glow worm. The name refers to the plant's shiny seeds.

lucid *a.* clear, easily understood. WH: 16C. French *lucide* or Italian *lucido*, from Latin *lucidus*, from *lucere* to shine, to be evident, from *lux*, *lucis* light. See also -ID.

Lucifer *n.* the morning star. WH: pre-1200. Latin light-bringing, from *lux*, *lucis* light + *-fer*, from *ferre* to bring, based on Greek *phōsphoros* (PHOSPHORUS).

lucifugous *a.* (of certain animals) shunning the light. WH: 17C. Latin *lucifugus*, from *lux*, *lucis* light + *fugere* to flee. See also -OUS.

luck *n.* chance, as bringer of fortune, whether good or bad. WH: 15C. Low German *luk*, shortened form of *geluk* (cp. German *Glück* good fortune, happiness), from *ge-* Y- + base of unknown orig. The word probably originated as a gambling term.

lucrative *a.* producing gain, profitable. WH: 14–15C. Latin *lucrativus*, from *lucratus*, p.p. of *lucrari* to gain, from *lucrum* gain. See also -ATIVE.

lucre *n.* pecuniary gain or advantage, usu. as an object of greed. WH: 14–15C. French, or from Latin *lucrum* gain. 'Filthy lucre' (I Tim. iii.3) is William Tyndale's translation of Greek *aiskhron kerdos*, from *aiskhros* shameful + *kerdos* gain, profit.

lucubrate *v.i.* to study by lamplight. *Also v.t.* WH: 17C. Latin *lucubratus*, p.p. of *lucubrare*, from *lux*, *lucis* light. See also -ATE³.

luculent *a.* clear, lucid, plain, manifest. WH: 14–15C. Latin *luculentus*, from *lux*, *lucis* light. See also -ENT.

Lucullan *a.* lavish, sumptuous. WH: 19C. Latin *Lucullanus*, from Licinius *Lucullus*, *c.*110–57 BC, a Roman general famous for his lavish banquets. See also -AN.

lud *n.* lord, as in *m'lud*, *my lud*, phrases used to address a judge in court. WH: 18C. Representation of a pronun. of LORD.

Luddite *n.* a member of a band of workmen who organized riots, 1811–16, for the destruction of machinery as a protest against unemployment. WH: 19C. ? from Ned *Lud*, an insane person who destroyed two stocking frames in *c.*1779. See also -ITE¹.

ludicrous *a.* liable to excite laughter or derision; ridiculous. WH: 17C. Latin *ludicrus*, from *ludicrum* source of fun, theatrical show, from *ludere* to play, from *ludus* sport. See also -OUS. The original senses were sportive, jesting, frivolous. The current sense dates from the 18C.

ludo *n.* a game played with counters on a specially chequered board. WH: 19C. Latin I play, 1st pers. sing. pres. ind. of *ludere* to play.

lues *n.* plague, contagious disease, infection, contagion, now used only for syphilis. WH: 17C. Latin plague.

luff *n.* the weather edge of a fore-and-aft sail. *Also v.i., v.t.* WH: 12–14C. Old French *lof*, prob. from Low German or Dutch.

lug¹ *v.t.* to pull, esp. roughly or with exertion. *Also v.i., n.* WH: 14–15C. Prob. of Scandinavian orig. Cp. Swedish *lugga* to pull someone's hair and LUG². Cp. LUGGAGE.

lug² *n.* a projecting part, esp. a projecting part of a machine made to hold or grip another part. WH: 15C. Prob. of Scandinavian orig. Cp. Swedish *lugg* forelock, nap of cloth.

luge *n.* a small toboggan for one or two people. *Also v.i.* WH: 19C. Swiss French, ult. rel. to SLIDE.

Luger *n.* a type of German automatic pistol. WH: early 20C. George *Luger*, 1849–1923, German engineer and firearms specialist.

luggage *n.* a traveller's suitcases, trunks etc. WH: 16C. LUG¹ + -AGE, based on BAGGAGE.

lugger *n.* a small vessel with two or three masts, a running bowsprit and lugsails. WH: 18C. LUGSAIL + -ER¹.

lugsail *n.* a four-cornered sail bent to a yard lashed obliquely to the mast. WH: 17C. Prob. from LUG² + SAIL.

lugubrious *a.* mournful, dismal. WH: 17C. Latin *lugubris*, from *lugere* to mourn. See also -IOUS.

lugworm *n.* any large marine worm of the genus *Arenicola*, burrowing in the sand, used for bait. WH: 19C. *lug*, of unknown orig. + WORM.

lukewarm *a.* moderately warm, tepid. *Also n.* WH: 14–15C. Dial. *luke*, prob. rel. to LEE (cp. Old Norse *hlyr* warm, mild) + WARM.

lull *v.t.* to soothe to sleep, to calm. *Also v.i., n.* WH: 12–14C. Imit. (of sounds used to send a child to sleep). Cp. Latin *lallare* to sing to sleep.

lulu *n.* an extremely good or bad person or thing. WH: 19C. Orig. uncertain. ? From. earlier *looly* beautiful girl, of unknown orig., influ. by *Lulu*, pet form of female forename *Louise*. Cp. LOLLAPALOOZA.

lum *n.* a chimney. WH: 16C. ? Old French *lum* light (from Latin *lumen*). Cp. French *lumière* light, aperture, passage.

lumbago *n.* rheumatism in the lumbar region. WH: 17C. Latin, from *lumbus* loin.

lumbar *a.* of or relating to the portion of the body between the lower ribs and the upper part of the hip bone. *Also n.* WH: 14–15C. Medieval Latin *lumbaris*, from Latin *lumbus* loin. See also -AR¹.

lumber¹ *v.i.* to move heavily or clumsily. WH: 14–15C. ? Imit., influ. by LAME¹.

lumber² *n.* discarded articles of furniture and other rubbish taking up room. *Also v.t., v.i.* WH: 16C. ? From LUMBER¹, but at one time assoc. with *lumber*, alt. of LOMBARD, in sense of pawnbroker.

lumbrical *a.* of, relating to or resembling a worm. WH: 16C. Modern Latin *lumbricalis*, from *lumbricus* worm. See also -AL¹.

lumen *n.* the SI unit of luminous flux, being the quantity of light emitted per second in a solid angle of one steradian by a uniform point-source having an intensity of one candela. WH: 19C. Latin light, opening. Cp. LUMINOUS. The term was coined in 1894 by the French physicist André Blondel. Cp. LUX.

luminaire *n.* a light fitting. WH: early 20C. French. See LUMINARY.

Luminal® *n.* phenobarbitone. WH: early 20C. Prob. from Latin LUMEN (rendering *phen-* of PHENOBARBITONE) + -AL².

luminary *n.* a famous person. WH: 14–15C. Old French *luminarie* (Modern French *luminaire*), from Late Latin *luminarium*, from Latin LUMEN, *luminis*. See also -ARY¹.

luminesce *v.i.* to exhibit luminescence. WH: 19C. Back-formation from *luminescent*, from Latin LUMEN, *luminis* + *-escent* (-ESCENCE).

luminiferous *a.* giving, yielding or transmitting light. WH: 19C. Latin LUMEN, *luminis*. See -FEROUS.

luminous *a.* emitting light. WH: 14–15C. Old French *lumineux* or Latin *luminosus*, from LUMEN, *luminis*. See also -OUS.

lumme *int.* used to express surprise. WH: 19C. Alt. of (*Lord*) *love me*.

lummox *n.* a clumsy person. WH: 19C. Orig. unknown. Cp. German *Lümmel* lout.

lump¹ *n.* a small mass of matter of no definite shape. *Also v.t., v.i.* WH: 12–14C. Poss. from Dutch. Cp. Dutch *lomp*, obs. *lompe* rag, rel. to German *Lumpen* rag.

lump² *v.t.* to put up with. WH: 16C. Imit. Cp. DUMP¹, GRUMPY, MUMP, etc.

lumpen *a.* stupid, oafish. WH: mid-20C. Back-formation from *lumpenproletariat*, from German *Lumpen* rag (cp. LUMP¹) + *Proletariat* (PROLETARIAN). German *Lumpenproletariat* was coined by Karl Marx in 1850 from *Lumpenvolk* rabble + *Proletariat* as a term for the proletariat that lacked class-consciousness.

lumpfish *n.* a suctorial fish, *Cyclopterus lumpus*, of northern seas, with a globular body covered in tubercles and pelvic fins modified as a sucker. WH: 17C. Obs. *lump* lumpfish, prob. from same source as LUMP¹ + FISH¹.

lunacy *n.* unsoundness of mind, insanity. WH: 16C. LUNATIC. See also -ACY.

luna moth *n.* a large N American moth, *Actias luna*, with crescent-shaped markings on its forewings. WH: 19C. Latin moon.

lunar *a.* of or relating to, caused or influenced by the moon. *Also n.* WH: 14–15C. Latin *lunaris*, from *luna* moon. See also -AR¹.

lunatic *a.* insane. *Also n.* WH: 12–14C. Old French *lunatique*, from Late Latin *lunaticus*, from Latin *luna* moon. See also -ATIC. Insanity was formerly thought to be caused by the changes of the moon.

lunch *n.* a midday meal. *Also v.i., v.t.* WH: 16C. Abbr. of *luncheon*, of uncertain orig. ? Alt. of dial. *nuncheon* light meal, from Old English *nōn* NOON + *scenc* drink, influ. by obs. *liunch* thick piece, hunk (of bread or cheese), ? from Spanish *lonja* slice.

lune *n.* a figure enclosed by two intersecting arcs. WH: 18C. French, from Latin *luna* moon.

lunette *n.* a semicircular aperture in a concave ceiling. WH: 16C. French, dim. of *lune* moon, from Latin *luna*. See also -ETTE.

lung *n.* either of the two organs of respiration in vertebrates, situated on each side of the chest. WH: pre-1200. Old English *lungen*, from Germanic, from Indo-European base represented also by LIGHT². The lungs are so called from their lightness. Cp. LIGHTS.

lunge¹ *n.* a sudden thrust with a sword etc., esp. an attacking move in fencing. *Also v.i., v.t.* WH: 18C. Shortening of *allonge*, from French *lengthening*, from *allonger*, from *long* LONG¹.

lunge² *n.* a long rope or rein used in training horses. *Also v.t.* WH: 17C. Old French *longe*, var. of *loigne*, itself var. of *longe*, shortening of *allonge*. See LUNGE¹.

lungi *n.* a long cloth used as a loincloth or sash, sometimes as a turban. WH: 17C. Hindi *lungī*.

lunisolar *a.* of, relating to, or compounded of the revolutions of, the sun and the moon. WH: 17C. Latin *luna* moon + -*i*- + SOLAR.

lunitidal *a.* of or relating to the tidal phenomena governed by the moon. WH: 19C. Latin *luna* moon + -*i*- + *tidal* (TIDE).

lunula *n.* a crescent-shaped mark, spot or part, esp. at the base of a fingernail. WH: 16C. Latin, dim. of *luna* moon. See also -ULE.

Lupercal *n.* a Roman fertility festival in honour of Lupercus, celebrated on 15 February. *Also a.* WH: 16C. Latin *lupercale*, neut. of *lupercalis* pertaining to *Lupercus*, a Roman equivalent of the Greek god Pan.

lupin *n.* a leguminous plant of the genus *Lupinus*, with spikes of white or coloured flowers, grown in flower-gardens and for fodder. WH: 14–15C. Latin *lupinus* LUPINE. The reason for the association with wolves is uncertain, but it may be because the plant destroys the ground it grows on, as wolves destroy their prey.

lupine *a.* of or relating to wolves. WH: 17C. Latin *lupinus*, from *lupus* wolf.

lupulin *n.* the bitter essence of hops. WH: 19C. Modern Latin *lupulus*, from Latin, a plant mentioned by Pliny (? wild hops). See also -IN¹.

lupus *n.* a spreading tuberculous or ulcerous inflammation of the skin, esp. lupus vulgaris. WH: 16C. Latin wolf.

lur *n.* a trumpet with long, curved tube, of prehistoric origin and used in Scandinavia for calling cattle home. WH: 19C. Danish, Norwegian and Swedish.

lurch¹ *v.i.* (of a ship) to roll suddenly to one side. *Also n.* WH: 17C. Orig. unknown.

lurch² *n.* a losing position in the game of cribbage and some other games. WH: 16C. Appar. from obs. French *lourche* a game resembling backgammon, of Germanic orig. Cp. German dial. *lurtsch* left, wrong.

†lurch³ *v.i.* to lie in wait; to prowl about suspiciously. *Also v.t.* WH: 14–15C. ? Var. of LURK, influ. in meaning by LURCH².

lurcher *n.* a dog, usu. a cross between a retriever or collie and a greyhound. WH: 16C. LURCH³ + -ER¹. The lurcher was originally used by poachers for pursuing hares and rabbits.

†lurdan *a.* stupid, lazy, useless. *Also n.* WH: 12–14C. Old French *lourdin*, from *lourd* heavy, *lort* foolish, from Latin *luridus* LURID.

lure *n.* an enticement, an allurement. *Also v.t., v.i.* WH: 12–14C. Old French *luere* (Modern French *leurre*), from Germanic, prob. rel. to German *Luder* bait. A lure was originally a falconer's device for recalling a hawk while training it.

Lurex® *n.* (a fabric made from) a thin plastic-coated metallic thread. WH: mid-20C. ? From ALLURE (rather than LURID).

lurgy *n.* an unspecified (horrible) illness, usu. in *the dreaded lurgy*. WH: mid-20C. Orig. unknown. ? From *allergic* (ALLERGY), influ. by LURK.

lurid *a.* shockingly or glaringly bright. WH: 17C. Latin *luridus*, from base of *luror* wan. See also -ID. The original sense was pale and dismal, then (in the 18C) vivid and glowing. The current sense dates from the 19C.

lurk *v.i.* to move about furtively. *Also n.* WH: 12–14C. ? From LOUR + freq. -*k* as in TALK. Cp. Norwegian *lurka* to sneak away.

luscious *a.* very sweet, delicious. WH: 14–15C. ? Alt. of shortened form of DELICIOUS. Cp. LUSH¹.

lush¹ *a.* luxuriant in growth. WH: 14–15C. ? Alt. of obs. *lash* soft, tender, from Old French *lasche* (Modern French *lâche*), from var. of Latin *laxus* LAX, by assoc. with LUSCIOUS.

lush² *n.* a heavy drinker, an alcoholic. *Also v.i., v.t.* WH: 18C. Orig. uncertain. ? From LUSH¹.

lush³ *a.* luscious. WH: 19C. Abbr. of LUSCIOUS.

lust *n.* a powerful desire for sexual pleasure. *Also v.i.* WH: pre-1200. Old English, from Germanic base represented also by LIST⁴. The original sense (to the 17C) was pleasure, delight, but the current sense was also in use from the first.

lustre¹ *n.* bright light, reflected light. *Also v.t.* WH: 16C. French, from Italian *lustro*, from *lustrare*, from Latin to illuminate, from *lustrum* (LUSTRE²). There are two Latin verbs *lustrare*, respectively meaning to illuminate and to purify (by means of a propitiatory offering). They were formerly thought to derive from unrelated sources, but are now generally held to represent an identical base.

lustre² *n.* a period of five years. WH: 16C. Latin *lustrum*, orig. purificatory sacrifice after a quinquennial census, later, period of five years, ult. of unknown orig. Cp. LUSTRE¹.

†lustring *n.* a glossy silk fabric. WH: 17C. French *lustrine*, or from Italian *lustrino*, from *lustro* lustre, with assim. to -ING³.

lute¹ *n.* a stringed instrument with a pear-shaped body and a long fretted fingerboard. *Also v.t., v.i.* WH: 12–14C. Old French *leüt* (Modern French *luth*), prob. from Provençal *laüt*, from Arabic *al-'ūd* the wood.

lute² *n.* a composition of clay or cement used to secure the joints of vessels and tubes, or as a covering to protect crucibles etc. from fire. *Also v.t.* WH: 14–15C. Old French *lut* or Medieval Latin *lutum*, from Latin mud, potter's clay.

luteal *a.* of or relating to the corpus luteum. WH: early 20C. Latin *luteus* yellow + -AL¹.

luteo- *comb. form* orange-coloured. WH: Latin *luteus* yellow. See also -O-.

lutetium *n.* an extremely rare metallic element, at. no. 71, symbol Lu, one of the lanthanides. WH: early 20C. French *lutécium*, from *Lutèce*, from *Lutetia*, an ancient city on the site of modern Paris, used as a name for Paris itself. The element was discovered independently in 1906–7 by the Austrian chemist Carl Aller von Welsbach and the French chemist Georges Urbain. Urbain named it after his native city, Paris. The name was widely accepted except in Germany where the element was called *cassiopeium* (after Cassiopeia, the mother of Andromeda in Greek mythology) until the 1950s.

Lutheran *a.* of or belonging to Luther or his doctrines. *Also n.* WH: 16C. Martin *Luther*, 1483–1546, German Protestant theologian + -AN.

luthier *n.* a maker of lutes, guitars and other stringed instruments. WH: 19C. French, from *luth* LUTE¹. See also -IER.

Lutine bell *n.* a bell recovered from the ship HMS *Lutine* and rung at Lloyd's in London before important announcements, such as the loss of a vessel. WH: 19C. HMS *Lutine*, a ship that sank off Holland in 1799 carrying £200,000 of bullion insured with Lloyd's. Its bell was recovered in 1859.

lutz *n.* in figure-skating, a jump from one skate with one, two or three rotations and a return to the other skate. WH: mid-20C. Prob. from Gustave *Lussi*, 1898–, Swiss figure skater, who introduced it.

luvvy *n.* a member of the acting profession, esp. one given to sentiment, effusiveness or camp. WH: mid-20C. Var. of *lovey* (LOVE). The theatrical sense evolved in the late 20C.

lux *n.* the SI unit of illumination equal to one lumen per square metre. WH: 19C. Latin light. The term was adopted in 1889 by the English physicist, William Preece.

luxate *v.t.* to put out of joint, to dislocate. *Also a.* WH: 17C. Latin *luxatus*, p.p. of *luxare*, from *luxus* dislocated. See also -ATE[3].

luxe *n.* luxury, sumptuousness, superfine elegance. WH: 16C. French, from Latin *luxus*. See LUXURY.

Luxembourger *n.* a native or inhabitant of Luxembourg. WH: early 20C. *Luxembourg*, a state lying between Belgium, Germany and France + -ER[1].

luxury *n.* great comfort with abundant provision of pleasant and delightful things. *Also a.* WH: 12–14C. Old French *luxurie*, var. of *luxure*, from Latin *luxuria*, from *luxus* abundance, rich provision. See also -Y[2]. The original sense (to the 19C) was lechery, lust. The current sense dates from the 17C.

LXX *abbr.* Septuagint. WH: Roman numerals for 70. See SEPTUAGINT.

-ly[1] *suf.* forming adjectives, esp. meaning having the qualities of, as in *godly*, *manly* or at intervals of, as in *hourly*, *weekly*. WH: Old English *-lic*, from Germanic, from base also of LIKE[1].

-ly[2] *suf.* forming adverbs from adjectives, as in *badly*, *heavily*, *mightily*. WH: Old English *-līce*, from Germanic base of -LY[1].

lycanthropy *n.* insanity in which patients believe themselves to be a wolf or some other animal, whose instincts and habits they assume. WH: 16C. Modern Latin *lycanthropia*, from Greek *lukanthrōpia*, from *lukanthrōpos*, from *lukos* wolf + *anthrōpos* man. See also -Y[2]. Cp. WEREWOLF.

lycée *n.* a French state secondary school. WH: 19C. French, from Latin LYCEUM. The French word was introduced in France in the early 19C, replaced by *collège royal* in 1815 following the Restoration, then readopted in 1848 in the Second Republic.

lyceum *n.* the garden at Athens in which Aristotle taught. WH: 16C. Latin, from Greek *Lukeion*, neut. of *Lukeios*, lit. wolfslayer, an epithet of Apollo. The original garden at Athens in which Aristotle taught philosophy was named from the neighbouring temple of Apollo Lukeios. Cp. ACADEMY, ATHENAEUM.

lychee *n.* the fruit of the Chinese tree, *Nephelium litchi*, which has a hard, scaly skin and a soft white pulp. WH: 16C. Chinese *lìzhī*, from *lì* (of no meaning) + *zhī* branch, twig.

lychnis *n.* any of a genus of plants, *Lychnis*, belonging to the family Silenaceae, comprising the campions. WH: 17C. Latin, from Greek *lukhnis* a red flower, *lukhnos* lamp.

lycopod *n.* a clubmoss, a member of the genus *Lycopodium*, or the order Lycopodiaceae. WH: 19C. Modern Latin *Lycopodium*, from Greek *lukos* wolf + *pous*, *podos* foot, -POD. The plant is so called from its rhizomes, which resemble a wolf's paws.

Lycra® *n.* a synthetic elastic fibre and material used in swimwear and other tight-fitting garments. WH: mid-20C. Orig. unknown.

lyddite *n.* a powerful explosive composed mainly of picric acid, used in shells. WH: 19C. *Lydd*, a town in Kent, where first tested + -ITE[1].

Lydian *a.* of or relating to Lydia, in Asia Minor, whose inhabitants were noted for effeminacy and voluptuousness. *Also n.* WH: 15C. Latin *Lydius*, Greek *Ludios* of Lydia, an ancient country in Asia Minor + -AN.

lye *n.* an alkaline solution leached from wood ashes or other alkaline substance. WH: pre-1200. Old English *lēag*, from Germanic base also of LATHER, from Indo-European.

lykewake *n.* a night watch over a dead body. WH: 14–15C. From *lyke*, var. of *lich* (see LICH-GATE) + WAKE[1].

Lyme disease *n.* a form of arthritis caused by spirochaetes of the genus *Borrelia* and transmitted by ticks. WH: late 20C. *Lyme*, a town in Connecticut, USA, where an outbreak occurred in 1975.

lyme grass *n.* a coarse grass of the genus *Elymus*, planted in sand in order to bind it. WH: 18C. ? From LIME[1]. See GRASS.

lymph *n.* the comparatively transparent, colourless, alkaline fluid in the tissues and organs of the body, consisting mainly of white blood corpuscles. WH: 16C. French *lymphe* or Latin *lympha* water nymph, water, prob. var. of *nympha*, Greek *numphē* NYMPH, or from Latin *lympha* water nymph.

lynch *v.t.* (of a mob) to execute, esp. by hanging, without a trial or after mock trial. WH: 19C. Captain William *Lynch*, 1742–1820, head of a self-constituted judicial tribunal in Virginia, USA, in 1780.

lynchet *n.* a ridge formed by ploughing or a cultivation terrace on the side of a steep hill. WH: 17C. Prob. from dial. *linch* rising ground, ridge, from Old English *hlinc* (LINKS).

lynx *n.* a feline mammal of Europe and N America, *Felis lynx*, characterized by tufted ear-tips, short tail and extremely sharp sight. WH: 12–14C. Latin, from Greek *lugx*, rel. to Old English *lox*, Old High German *luhs* (German *Luchs*), ult. from base of LIGHT[1]. The lynx is probably so called from its shining eyes.

Lyon *n.* the chief of the Scottish heralds. WH: 14–15C. Var. of LION. The title refers to the lion on the royal shield.

lyophilic *a.* (of a colloid) easily dispersed in a solvent. WH: early 20C. Greek *luein* to loose + -philic (-PHILE).

lyre *n.* an ancient Greek stringed instrument like a small harp, consisting of a resonating box with a pair of curved arms above it connected by a crossbar. WH: 12–14C. Old French (Modern French *lyre*), from Latin *lyra*, from Greek *lura*, of unknown orig.

lyric *a.* (of a poem) expressing the individual emotions of the poet. *Also n.* WH: 16C. Old French *lyrique* or Latin *lyricus*, from Greek *lurikos*, from *lura* lyre. See also -IC. The poetry was so called as it was originally meant to be sung to the lyre.

lysergic acid *n.* a crystalline compound derived from ergot. WH: mid-20C. -*lys*- (as in HYDROLYSIS) + ERGOT + -IC.

lysis *n.* the destruction of cells by the action of a lysin. WH: 16C. Latin, from Greek *lusis* loosening, from *luein* to untie.

ma *n.* mother. WH: 19C. Abbr. of MAMMA¹.

ma'am *n.* madam (used esp. in addressing a queen or a royal princess). WH: 17C. Contr. of MADAM. Cp. MEMSAHIB.

maar *n.* a volcanic crater without a cone of lava, caused by a single explosion. WH: 19C. German dial.

Mac *n.* a Scotsman. WH: 17C. *Mac-* or *Mc-*, patronymic pref. in many Scottish names, from Gaelic *mac* son.

mac *n.* a mackintosh, a raincoat. WH: early 20C. Abbr. of MACKINTOSH.

macabre *a.* gruesome. WH: 14–15C. Old French *macabré* (Modern French *macabre*), prob. alt. of *Macabé* Maccabaeus, Maccabee. The reference would be to a miracle play about the slaughter of the MACCABEES.

macaco *n.* any of various kinds of lemur, esp. *Lemur macaco*. WH: 18C. French *mococo*, ? ult. from Malagasy *maka*, *maki* lemur. Cp. MACAQUE.

macadam *n.* broken stone for road-making. *Also v.t.* WH: 19C. John Loudon *McAdam*, 1756–1836, British surveyor, its orig. inventor. Cp. TARMAC.

macadamia *n.* any evergreen tree of the genus *Macadamia* of Australia, esp. *M. integrifolia* and *M. tetraphylla*. WH: Modern Latin, from John *Macadam*, 1827–65, Scottish-born chemist.

macaque *n.* any monkey of the genus *Macaca*, including the rhesus monkey and the Barbary ape. WH: 17C. French *macaque*, from Portuguese *macaco*, from Bantu *makaku* some monkeys, from *ma-* numerical sign + *kaku* monkey. Cp. MACACO.

macaroni *n.* an Italian pasta made of fine wheat flour formed into long slender tubes. *Also a.* WH: 16C. Obs. Italian *maccaroni*, later *maccheroni*, pl. of obs. *maccarone*, from Late Greek *makaria* barley food.

macaronic *a.* consisting of a jumble of incongruous words, as of different languages, or of modern words Latinized or Latin words modernized, in burlesque poetry. *Also n.* WH: 17C. Modern Latin *macaronicus*, from obs. Italian *macaronico*, later *maccheronico*, from MACARONI. The words are jumbled like strands of macaroni. The word itself was popularized by the Mantuan poet Teofilo Folengo in his poem *Liber Macaronicus* (1517), in which he likened his work to macaroni.

macaroon *n.* a small sweet cake or biscuit made of flour, almonds, sugar etc. WH: 16C. French *macaron*, from dial. *maccarone*. See MACARONI, also -OON. The original meaning (to the 19C) was buffoon, dolt. The current sense dates from the 17C. The French meaning was apparently invented by Rabelais, who introduced the word in 1552.

Macassar *n.* an oil formerly used on the hair to make it shiny, orig. brought from Macassar in Indonesia. WH: 17C. *Macassar*, early form of *Makasar*, a district of the island of Sulawesi (Celebes), Indonesia. Macassar oil was originally made from ingredients obtained from Makasar. Hence also *antimacassar*, as a covering for chairs and sofas to prevent their soiling by macassar oil on the hair.

macaw *n.* any S and Central American parrot, of the genus *Ara* or *Anodorhynchus*, distinguished by their large size and bright, beautiful plumage. WH: 17C. Portuguese *macao*, of unknown orig.

macaw tree *n.* a palm of the genus *Acrocomia*, esp. *A. aculeata*. WH: 17C. Carib. Cp. Arawak *mocoya*, *macoya*.

Maccabees *a.* four books of Jewish history and theology, two of which are in the Apocrypha. WH: 14–15C. Latin *Maccabaeus*, Greek *Makkabaios*, epithet of Judas Maccabaeus ('Hammerer'), who led a religious revolt in Judaea against the Syrian Seleucid King Antiochus IV in 165 BC. Judas' epithet is perhaps from Hebrew *maqqebeṭ* hammer.

maccoboy *n.* a rose-scented snuff, orig. grown at Macouba. WH: 18C. *Macouba*, a district in Martinique.

Mace® *n.* a liquid causing the eyes to run and a feeling of nausea, used in self-defence, riot control etc. *Also v.t.* WH: mid-20C. Prob. from MACE¹, but also an acronym of the chemical compound name *M*ethylchloroform chlor*ace*tophenone.

mace¹ *n.* an ornamented staff of office. WH: 12–14C. Old French *masse*, *mace*, from Popular Latin *mattea*, from *mateola* a type of agricultural implement.

mace² *n.* a spice made from the dried covering of the nutmeg. WH: 12–14C. Old French *macis*, from Latin *macir* red spicy bark from India. *Mace* was formed as a singular noun from *macis*, wrongly taken to be a pl.

macédoine *n.* a dish of mixed vegetables. WH: 19C. French, from *Macédoine* Macedonia. The vegetables are mixed, like the mixed races in the Macedonian empire of Alexander the Great.

macerate *v.t.* to soften by steeping. *Also v.i.* WH: 16C. Latin *maceratus*, p.p. of *macerare*, prob. rel. to Greek *massein* to knead. See also -ATE³.

Mach *n.* a number representing the ratio of the velocity of a body in a certain medium to the velocity of sound in the same medium, used as an indicator of air speed. WH: early 20C. Ernst *Mach*, 1838–1916, Austrian physicist and philosopher.

machair *n.* a strip of land just above the high-water mark along a sandy shore, used for pasturage. WH: 17C. Gaelic.

machan *n.* an elevated platform for hunting or watching game. WH: 19C. Hindi *macān*, from Sanskrit *mañcaka*.

machete *n.* a broad knife or cutlass used in tropical America as a weapon, to cut down sugar canes etc. WH: 16C. Spanish, from *macho* hammer, from Latin *marcus*.

machiavellian *a.* unscrupulous, scheming. *Also n.* WH: 16C. Niccolò dei *Machiavelli*, 1469–1527, Florentine statesman who advised rulers to place advantage above morality + -IAN.

machicolation *n.* an opening (on a parapet etc.) between corbels for dropping stones etc. on attackers below. WH: 18C. Old French *machicoler*, from Provençal *machacol*, from *macar* to beat, to crush + *col* neck + -ATION.

machinate *v.i.* to plot, to intrigue. WH: 16C. Latin *machinatus*, p.p. of *machinari*, from *machina* MACHINE. See also -ATE³.

machine *n.* a mechanical apparatus by which motive power is applied. *Also v.t., v.i.* WH: 16C. Old French, from Latin *machina* device, contrivance, engine, from Greek *makhana*, *mēkhanē*, from *mēkhos* contrivance, ult. from Germanic base of MAY¹. The original sense (to the 18C) was scheme, plot. The current mechanical sense dates from the 17C.

macho *a.* masculine, virile, esp. in an ostentatious or exaggerated way. *Also n.* WH: early 20C. Mexican Spanish male animal, masculine, vigorous, from Latin *masculus* MASCULINE.

Machtpolitik *n.* power politics, esp. the advocacy of force by a state to attain its ends. WH: early 20C. German, from *Macht* power, strength + *Politik* policy, politics.

mackerel *n.* a marine fish, *Scomber scombrus*, moving in shoals in the N Atlantic and coming inshore in summer to spawn, valuable as a food. WH: 12–14C. Old French *maquerel* (Modern French *maquereau*), of unknown orig.

mackinaw *n.* a short heavy woollen jacket, usu. of plaid. WH: 19C. *Mackinaw* City, Michigan, USA, formerly an important trading post.

mackintosh *n.* a raincoat. WH: 19C. Charles *Macintosh*, 1766–1843, Scottish inventor of a waterproofing process.

mackle *n.* in printing, a blurred impression, causing printed matter to appear double. *Also v.t.* WH: 16C. French *macule*, from Latin MACULA spot.

macle *n.* a twin crystal. WH: 18C. French, from Latin MACULA spot, mesh.

macramé *n.* a fringe or trimming of knotted thread or cord. WH: 19C. Turkish *makrama* handkerchief, tablecloth, towel, from Arabic *miḳrama* bedcover, bedspread.

macro *n.* a single computer instruction that represents a sequence of instructions in performing a task. WH: mid-20C. Independent use of MACRO-.

macro- *comb. form* great, large (as distinct from small). WH: Greek *makro-*, from *makros* long, large. See also -O-.

macrobiotic *a.* (of a diet) consisting chiefly of whole grains or of vegetables grown without chemical additives. WH: 18C. Greek *makrobiotikos*, from *makro-* MACRO- + *biotos* life. See also -IC.

macrocarpa *n.* a large coniferous tree, *Cupressus macrocarpa*, often cultivated for hedges, shelter belts etc. WH: early 20C. Modern Latin, from Greek *makro-* MACRO- + *karpos* fruit.

macrocephalic *a.* large-headed. WH: 19C. MACRO- + -CEPHALIC.

macrocosm *n.* the world, the universe, as distinct from *microcosm*. WH: 17C. Medieval Latin *macrocosmus*, from Greek *makro-* MACRO- + *kosmos* world, prob. based on MICROCOSM.

macrocyte *n.* an abnormally large red blood cell. WH: 19C. MACRO- + -CYTE.

macrodactylic *a.* having long fingers or toes. WH: 19C. Greek *makro-* MACRO- + *daktulos* finger, toe. See also -IC.

macrodiagonal *n.* the longer diagonal of a rhombic prism. WH: 19C. MACRO- + DIAGONAL.

macroeconomics *n.* the study of economics on a large scale, e.g. of national economies. WH: mid-20C. MACRO- + *economics* (ECONOMIC).

macroevolution *n.* major evolutionary development, usu. over a long period of time. WH: mid-20C. MACRO- + EVOLUTION.

macrolepidoptera *n.* butterflies and larger moths. WH: 19C. MACRO- + *Lepidoptera* (LEPIDOPTERAN).

macromolecule *n.* a large complex molecule formed from a number of simple molecules. WH: 19C. MACRO- + MOLECULE.

macron *n.* a short horizontal line put over a vowel (as ē) to show that it is pronounced with a long sound or with stress. WH: 19C. Greek *makron*, neut. of *makros* long.

macronutrient *n.* any substance that is required in large amounts for the growth and development of organisms, such as carbon, hydrogen, oxygen. WH: mid-20C. MACRO- + NUTRIENT.

macrophage *n.* a large phagocytic white blood cell found in connective tissue. WH: 19C. MACRO- + Greek *phagein* to eat.

macrophotography *n.* close-up photography producing an image as large as or larger than the object. WH: 19C. MACRO- + *photography* (PHOTOGRAPH).

macropod *a.* long-footed. *Also n.* WH: 19C. Modern Latin *Macropodidae*, *Macropus* genus name, from Greek *makropous* big foot, from *makro-* MACRO- + *pous* foot. See -POD.

macropterous *a.* long-winged. WH: 19C. MACRO- + Greek *pteron* feather, wing. See also -OUS.

macroscopic *a.* large enough to be visible with the naked eye, as distinct from *microscopic*. WH: 19C. from MACRO- + *-scopic* (-SCOPE[1]), based on *microscopic* (MICROSCOPE).

macrosporangium *n.* a sporangium or capsule containing megaspores. WH: 19C. MACRO- + SPORANGIUM.

macrurous *a.* long-tailed. WH: 19C. Modern Latin *Macrura*, from Greek *makros* long + *oura* tale. See also -OUS.

macula *n.* a spot, as on the skin, the surface of the sun etc. WH: 14–15C. Latin spot.

MAD *abbr.* mutual assured destruction, a theory of nuclear deterrence based on the ability of each side to inflict an unacceptable level of damage on the other. WH: late 20C. Acronym of *mutual assured destruction*, punning on MAD. The term was coined in 1973 by the US military strategist and mathematician Donald G. Brennan.

mad *a.* disordered in mind, insane. *Also v.i., v.t.* WH: pre-1200. Old English *gemǣd*, *gemǣded*, p.p. of v. meaning to make insane, from *gemād* insane, from Germanic.

madam *n.* a polite form of address to a woman. WH: 12–14C. Old French *ma dame* (Modern French *madame*), lit. my lady.

Madame *n.* the French title for married women and polite form of address to a woman. WH: 12–14C. Old French. See MADAM.

madarosis *n.* loss of the hair, esp. of the eyebrows. WH: 17C. Modern Latin, from Greek *madarōsis*, from *madaros* bald. See also -OSIS.

madder *n.* a shrubby climbing-plant, *Rubia tinctorum*, the root of which is used in dyeing. WH: pre-1200. Old English *mædere*, from Germanic. Cp. Swedish *madra*, Norwegian *modra*.

made *a.* that has been made. WH: 14–15C. P.p. of MAKE[1].

Madeira *n.* a fortified white wine. WH: 16C. *Madeira*, an island in the Atlantic, where it is made.

madeleine *n.* a small sponge cake, often coated with jam and coconut. WH: 19C. Appar. from *Madeleine* Paulmier, 19C French pastry-cook.

Mademoiselle *n.* the French title for unmarried women or girls and polite form of address to an unmarried woman or a girl. WH: 14–15C. Old French. See MADAM, DEMOISELLE.

maderize *v.i.* (of white wine) to go reddish and flat-tasting through oxidation. WH: mid-20C. French *madériser*, from *Madère* MADEIRA. See also -IZE.

madge *n.* the barn owl. WH: 16C. Prob. from *Madge*, pet form of female name *Margaret*. Cp. MAG.

Madonna *n.* the Virgin Mary. WH: 16C. Italian, from *ma*, old unstressed form of *mia* my (from Latin *mea*) + *donna* lady (from Latin *domina*). Cp. MADAM.

madras *n.* a fine cotton or silk fabric. WH: 19C. *Madras*, a city and port on the E coast of India.

madrepore *n.* a perforated coral of the genus *Madrepora*. WH: 18C. French *madrépore* or Modern Latin *Madrepora*, from Italian *madrepora*, prob. from *madre* mother + *poro*, from Latin *porus* PORE[1] or Latin *porus*, from Greek *pōros* calcareous stone. The name appears to allude to the coral's prolific growth.

madrigal *n.* an unaccompanied vocal composition in five or six parts. WH: 16C. Italian *madrigale*, from Medieval Latin *matricalis* invented, original, of the womb (MATRIX). The work is probably so called from its simple, uncontrived form.

madroño *n.* a large evergreen tree, *Arbutus menziesii*, of N California, with hard wood, and edible berries. WH: 19C. Spanish.

maduro *n.* a type of dark, strong cigar. WH: 19C. Spanish ripe, mature.

Maecenas *n.* a munificent patron of literature or art. WH: 16C. Gaius *Maecenas*, d.8 BC, Roman friend of Augustus, statesman, and patron of Horace and Virgil.

maelstrom *n.* a dangerous whirlpool, dangerously swirling water. WH: 17C. Early Modern Dutch (now *maalstroom*), from *maalen* to grind, to whirl round + *stroom* STREAM. Cp. Swedish *malström*, Danish *malstrøm*.

maenad *n.* a woman who took part in the orgies of Bacchus, a bacchante. WH: 16C. Latin *Maenas*, *Maenadis*, from Greek *Mainas*, *Mainados*, from *mainesthai* to rave. Cp. MANIA.

maestoso *a., adv.* with dignity, grandeur and strength. *Also n.* WH: 18C. Italian majestic, from *maestà*, from Latin *maestas*, *maestatis* MAJESTY + Italian *-oso* -OUS.

maestro *n.* a master in any art, esp. in music. WH: 18C. Italian, from Latin *magister* MASTER.

Mae West *n.* an inflatable life jacket. WH: mid-20C. *Mae West*, 1892–1980, US film actress and entertainer, famous for her full figure.

Mafia *n.* a secret criminal society based on active hostility to the law and its agents, engaged in international organized crime, esp. in Sicily and the US. WH: 19C. Italian (Sicilian) bragging, bravado. The name alludes to the society's hostility to the law and those who uphold it, especially by means of vindictive crimes.

mag *n.* the magpie. *Also v.i.* WH: 14–15C. *Mag*, pet form of female forename *Margaret*. Cp. MADGE.

magalog *n.* a mail-order catalogue designed to look like a magazine. WH: late 20C. Blend of MAGAZINE and CATALOGUE.

magazine *n.* a periodical publication containing miscellaneous articles by different people. WH: 16C. French *magasin*, from Italian *magazzino*, from Arabic *makzan* storehouse, from *kazana* to store up. A magazine was originally regarded as a 'storehouse' of information. The original sense of storehouse in general soon came to apply to a storehouse of ammunition, hence (18C) to a chamber of cartridges in a rifle, machine gun, etc.

magdalen *n.* a reformed prostitute. WH: 14–15C. Ecclesiastical Latin (*Maria*) *Magdalena*, from Greek (*Mariaē*) *Magdalēnē* Mary Magdalene, lit. Mary of Magdala, a town in ancient Palestine. The reference is to Mary Magdalene, a follower of Jesus, commonly identified with the woman 'which was a sinner' (Luke vii.37) who anointed the feet of Jesus and wiped them with her hair, and who came to be regarded as representing a repentant sinner, or specifically a reformed prostitute. Cp. MAUDLIN.

Magdalenian a. of or relating to the period of Upper Palaeolithic culture, succeeding the Solutrian period, typified by the implements and weapons of bone, horn, ivory and stone, and carvings and engravings found at La Madeleine. *Also n.* WH: 19C. French *Magdalénien*, from *La Madeleine*, a site in the Dordogne, France, where such artefacts were found. The site is so named from its chapel, dedicated to St Mary Magdalene (MAGDALEN).

†mage n. a magician. WH: 14–15C. Anglicized form of Latin MAGUS.

Magellanic cloud n. either of two galaxies in the southern hemisphere, similar to portions of the Milky Way. WH: 17C. *Magellan*, anglicized form of name of Fernão de *Magalhães* (Spanish *Magallanes*), d.1521, Portuguese explorer + -IC. The galaxies are so named as they were discovered by Magellan's crew during their first voyage around the world in 1520.

magenta n. a brilliant crimson colour. WH: 19C. *Magenta*, site of a battle (1859) in N Italy. The dye that gives the colour was discovered shortly after the battle, in which the Austrians were defeated by the Italians and Sardinians, and was named after it, its crimson colour representing the blood shed.

maggot n. a grub, a worm, esp. the larva of the cheese-fly or flesh-fly. WH: 14–15C. Prob. Anglo-French alt. of obs. *maddock* earthworm, maggot, from Germanic base represented by German *Made* maggot + -OCK. Cp. MAWKISH.

magic n. the supposed art of employing supernatural power to influence or control events. *Also a., v.t.* WH: 14–15C. Old French *magique* (Modern French *magie*), from Late Latin *magica*, from Greek *magikē*, use as n. of a. *magikos*, from *magos* MAGUS. See also -IC.

Maginot Line n. a line of defensive fortifications in NE France built in 1929 against a German invasion. WH: mid-20C. André *Maginot*, 1877–1932, French minister of war + LINE[1].

magisterial a. authoritative, commanding. WH: 17C. Medieval Latin *magisterialis*, from Late Latin *magisterius*, from Latin *magister* MASTER. See also -IAL.

magistrate n. a public officer commissioned to administer the law. WH: 14–15C. Latin *magistratus*, from *magister* MASTER. See also -ATE[1].

Maglemosian a. of or relating to a Mesolithic culture, represented by finds at Maglemose in Denmark. *Also n.* WH: early 20C. *Maglemose*, a site near Mullerup on the W coast of Denmark. See also -IAN.

maglev n. a rapid transport system in which trains glide along a continuous magnetic field, supported by magnetic repulsion. WH: late 20C. Abbr. of *magnetic levitation*.

magma n. the molten semi-fluid matter below the earth's crust. WH: 14–15C. Latin, from Greek, from base of *massein* to knead.

Magna Carta n. the Great Charter of English liberties sealed by King John on 15 June 1215. WH: 15C. Medieval Latin, lit. great charter.

magna cum laude adv. with great distinction. WH: 19C. Latin, lit. with great praise, from fem. abl. sing. of *magnus* great + *cum* with + abl. of *laus*, *laudis* praise (LAUD).

magnanimous a. generous, great-minded. WH: 16C. Latin *magnanimus*, from *magnus* great + *animus* mind. See also -OUS.

magnate n. a person of great wealth and influence, esp. in business. WH: 14–15C. Late Latin *magnas*, *magnatis*, from Latin *magnus* great. See also -ATE[1].

magnesia n. magnesium oxide, a white alkaline antacid earth. WH: 14–15C. Medieval Latin, from Greek *magnēsia* mineral from Magnesia in Asia Minor.

magnesium n. a divalent metallic element, at. no.12, chem. symbol Mg, the base of magnesia, used in alloys and burned as a source of bright light. WH: 19C. MAGNESIA + -IUM. The element was named by the English chemist Sir Humphry Davy, who discovered it in 1808. He originally used the term to refer to manganese.

magnet n. a piece of iron or steel etc. having the properties of attracting iron and pointing to the poles. WH: 14–15C. Old French *magnete* or Latin *magnes*, *magnetis*, from Greek *Magnēs*, from *Magnētos lithos* stone of Magnesia (MAGNESIA).

magneto n. a magneto-electric machine (esp. the igniting apparatus of an internal-combustion engine). WH: 19C. Abbr. of *magneto-electric machine*. See MAGNETO-, ELECTRIC.

magneto- comb. form of a magnet or magnetism. WH: MAGNET. See also -O-.

magneto-electricity n. electricity generated by the inductive action of magnets. WH: 19C. MAGNETO- + *electricity* (ELECTRIC).

magnetograph n. an instrument for measuring magnetic forces, esp. terrestrial magnetism. WH: 19C. MAGNETO- + -GRAPH.

magnetometer n. a device for measuring the intensity or direction of a magnetic field, esp. of the earth. WH: 19C. MAGNETO- + -METER.

magnetomotive a. (of a force) being the sum of magnetic forces along an electric circuit. WH: 19C. MAGNETO- + MOTIVE, based on *electromotive* (ELECTROMOTION).

magneton n. the unit of magnetic moment. WH: early 20C. *magnetic* (MAGNET) + -ON.

magnetosphere n. the region surrounding the earth or other planet, star etc. in which its magnetic field has effect. WH: mid-20C. MAGNETO- + SPHERE.

magnetron n. a thermionic tube for generating very high frequency microwave oscillations. WH: early 20C. *magnetic* (MAGNET) + -TRON.

†magnific a. magnificent, grand, sublime. WH: 15C. Old French *magnifique* or Latin *magnificus*, from *magnus* great. See also -FIC.

Magnificat n. the song of the Virgin Mary. WH: 12–14C. Latin (it) magnifies, 3rd pers. sing. pres. ind. of *magnificare* MAGNIFY. The word opens the hymn of the Virgin Mary in Luke i.46–55, beginning in the Vulgate (Latin version) *Magnificat anima mea Dominum* My soul doth magnify the Lord.

magnificent a. grand in appearance, splendid. WH: 14–15C. Old French, or from Latin *magnificens*, *magnificentis*, from *magnificus* MAGNIFIC. See also -ENT.

magnifico n. a magnate, a grandee, orig. of Venice. WH: 16C. Italian magnificent, from Latin *magnificus* MAGNIFIC.

magnify v.t. to increase the apparent size of (an object) with an optical instrument. *Also v.i.* WH: 14–15C. Old French *magnifier* or Latin *magnificare*, from *magnificus*. See MAGNIFIC, also -FY. The original sense was to praise highly, to glorify. The current sense to increase the apparent size of something dates from the 17C, and that of to exaggerate from the 18C.

magniloquent a. using high-flown or bombastic language. WH: 17C. Latin *magniloquus* (from *magnus* great + *-loquus* speaking) + -ENT.

magnitude n. size, extent. WH: 14–15C. Latin *magnitudo*, from *magnus* great, large, rel. to Greek *megas* (MEGA-) and Germanic base of MUCH. See also -TUDE.

magnolia n. any flowering tree or shrub of the genus *Magnolia*, chiefly N American. WH: 18C. Modern Latin, from Pierre *Magnol*, 1638–1715, French botanist. See also -IA.

magnox n. any one of several magnesium-based alloys containing aluminium, used in nuclear reactors to enclose the uranium fuel elements. WH: mid-20C. Abbr. of *magnesium no oxidation*.

magnum n. a wine bottle containing the equivalent of two normal bottles (about 1½ litres). WH: 18C. Latin, use as n. of neut. sing. of *magnus* large.

magnum opus n. the greatest work of a writer, painter etc. WH: 18C. Latin great work. See MAGNUM, OPUS.

magot n. the tailless Barbary ape, *Macaca sylvana*, of Gibraltar and N Africa. WH: 17C. French, appar. from *Magog*, the name of a tribe, who, together with *Gog*, were deceived by or allied with Satan in Rev. xx.8.

magpie n. a chattering bird of the crow family, *Pica pica*, with black and white plumage. WH: 16C. MAG + PIE[2].

maguey n. a type of agave plant whose leaves yield fibre used to make an alcoholic drink. WH: 16C. Spanish, from Taino.

magus n. a member of the priestly caste among the Medes and Persians. WH: 12–14C. Latin, from Greek *magos*, from Old Persian *maguš*. Cp. MAGE.

Magyar n. a member of the Ural-Altaic people (entering Europe in 884), predominant in Hungary. *Also a.* WH: 18C. Hungarian.

maharaja n. a title assumed by some Indian princes. WH: 17C. Sanskrit *mahārājā*, from *mahā* great + *rājan* RAJA. Sanskrit *mahā* is ultimately related to MUCH.

maharishi n. a Hindu religious teacher. WH: 18C. Alt. of Sanskrit *maharṣi*, from *mahā* great + *ṛṣi* RISHI.

mahatma n. in the Indian subcontinent, a much revered person. WH: 19C. Sanskrit *mahātman*, from *mahā* great + *ātman* soul, ATMAN.

Mahayana n. the most widespread tradition of Buddhism, practised esp. in China, Japan and Tibet. WH: 19C. Sanskrit *mahāyāna*, from *mahā* great + *yāna* vehicle.

Mahdi n. the Muslim messiah, a title once assumed by leaders of insurrection in Sudan. WH: 19C. Arabic *(al-)mahdī*, lit. he who is rightly guided, from pass. part. of *hadā* to lead on the right way, to guide aright.

mah-jong n. a Chinese table game played with 136 or 144 pieces called tiles. WH: early 20C. Chinese dial. *ma jiang* sparrows (lit. hemp birds). The game is so called from a design on the tiles.

mahoe n. a small bushy New Zealand tree, *Melicytus ramiflorus*. WH: 19C. Maori.

mahogany n. the hard, fine-grained wood of *Swietenia mahagoni*, a tree of tropical America, largely used in making furniture. *Also a.* WH: 17C. Orig. unknown.

mahonia n. any evergreen shrub of the genus *Mahonia*, with small yellow flowers and spiny leaves. WH: 19C. Modern Latin, from Bernard McMahon, *c.*1775–1816, US botanist + -IA.

mahout n. an elephant driver or keeper. WH: 17C. Hindi *mahāut*, *mahāvat*, from Sanskrit *mahāmātra* high official, elephant keeper, from *mahā* great + *mātra* measure.

mahseer n. either of two large and powerful, edible Indian freshwater fish, *Barbus tor* or *B. putitora*, both somewhat like the barbel. WH: 19C. Hindi *mahāser*, from Sanskrit *mahā* great + *śaphara* carp.

maid n. a female servant. WH: 12–14C. Abbr. of MAIDEN. The *-n* has been lost as in CLEW, EVE, GAME[1]. The earliest sense was simply girl.

maidan n. an open space used as a sports or parade ground in India, Pakistan etc. WH: 17C. Urdu and Persian *maidān*, from Arabic *maydān*.

maiden n. a girl, an unmarried woman. *Also a.* WH: pre-1200. Old English *mægden*, dim. of *mægth*, from Indo-European base also of Gothic *magus* son. See also -EN[1]. Cp. German *Mädchen*, earlier *Magdchen*, dim. of *Magd* maiden. The earliest sense was simply girl. Cp. MAID. The use as an adjective to mean first of its kind (as *maiden speech*) dates from the 16C.

maidenhair n. a fern with delicate fronds, esp. *Adiantum capillus-veneris*. WH: 14–15C. MAIDEN + HAIR.

maieutic a. helping to bring out or develop (applied to the system pursued by Socrates, in which he endeavoured to bring out latent ideas by persistent questioning). WH: 17C. Greek *maieutikos*, from *maieuesthai* to act as midwife, from *maia* midwife. See also -IC.

maigre a. (of a day) that is designated a fast day in the Roman Catholic Church. *Also a.* WH: 16C. Old French. See MEAGRE.

mail[1] n. the letters etc. conveyed by the post. *Also v.t.* WH: 12–14C. Old French *male* (Modern French *malle* bag, trunk), from Germanic. The original sense was bag, pack, hence (17C) bag or packet of letters conveyed by post, hence (17C) the letters themselves, the post.

mail[2] n. defensive armour for the body, formed of rings, chains or scales. *Also v.t.* WH: 12–14C. Old French *maille*, from Latin *macula* spot, mesh, MACULA. The original sense (to the 18C) was one of the metal rings or plates in mail armour. The sense then passed to the armour itself.

†**mail**[3] n. rent, tribute, tax. WH: pre-1200. Old English *mæl*, prob. contr. of Old English *mæthel* meeting, discussion, from Germanic. Cp. *blackmail* (BLACK).

maillot n. tights for dancing, exercising etc. WH: 19C. French, from *maille*. See MAIL[2].

maim v.t. to deprive of the use of a limb. *Also n.* WH: 12–14C. Old French *mahaignier*, *mayner*, ult. of unknown orig. Cp. MAYHEM. The original sense was to disable, to wound.

main[1] a. chief, most important. WH: pre-1200. Old English *mægan-*, from Germanic base meaning to have power. Cp. MAY[1].

main[2] n. a chief conduit, electric cable etc. WH: pre-1200. Old English *mægen*. See MAIN[1]. The original meaning was force, power, now only in *with might and main* (MIGHT). The senses mainland, open ocean arose in the 16C, then chief matter, principal channel for water, gas, etc. in the 17C.

main[3] n. a throw at dice, or a number (5–9) called by the caster before throwing. WH: 16C. Prob. from *main chance* (MAIN[1]).

mainstream n. the most prevalent or widely accepted aspects of a culture, society etc. *Also a.* WH: 17C. MAIN[1] + STREAM, orig. as two words.

maintain v.t. to keep in order, proper condition or repair. WH: 12–14C. Old French *maintenir*, from Latin *manu*, abl. of *manus* hand + *tenere* to hold. The original meaning (to the 17C) was to practise habitually, to observe (a rule, etc.).

maiolica n. tin-glazed earthenware having metallic colours on a white ground (orig. from Italy). WH: 16C. Italian, former name of island of *Majorca* (MAJORCAN).

maisonette n. part of a house or block of flats let separately, usu. having two floors and with a separate entrance. WH: 18C. French *maisonnette*, dim. of *maison* house. See also -ETTE.

maître d'hôtel n. the manager, chief steward etc. of a hotel. WH: 16C. French, lit. master of house. The original meaning was majordomo, steward, butler. The sense hotel manager, head waiter evolved in the 19C.

maize n. a cereal plant from N America, *Zea mays*, also called Indian corn. WH: 16C. French *maïs* or Spanish *maíz*, from Taino *mahiz*.

majesty n. the quality of inspiring awe or reverence. WH: 12–14C. Old French *majesté*, from Latin *maiestas*, from var. of *maius, maior-* MAJOR. See also -TY[1]. The original sense was the greatness and glory of God.

Majlis n. the Iranian legislative assembly. WH: 19C. Arabic place of session, from *jalasa* to be seated.

major a. of considerable importance. *Also n.* WH: 12–14C. Latin *maior*, comp. of *magnus* great.

Majorcan n. a native or inhabitant of Majorca. *Also a.* WH: 17C. *Majorca*, one of the Balearic Islands in the W Mediterranean + -AN.

majuscule n. a capital or large letter, as in Latin manuscripts, before the introduction of minuscules. *Also a.* WH: 18C. French, from Latin *maiuscula*, fem. of *maiusculus*, dim. of *maior*. See MAJOR, also -CULE.

make[1] v.t. to construct, to produce. *Also v.i., n.* WH: pre-1200. Old English *macian*, from Germanic base meaning fitting. Rel. to MATCH[1]. Cp. MAKE[2].

†**make**[2] n. a person's equal, like or match. WH: pre-1200. Old English *gemaca*, from Germanic. Rel. to MATCH[1].

mako n. a small New Zealand tree, *Aristotelia racemosa*. WH: 19C. Maori.

mal- comb. form bad(ly). WH: French *mal*, from Latin *male* ill, badly.

malabsorption n. imperfect absorption of food into the small intestine caused by disease. WH: mid-20C. MAL- + *absorption* (ABSORB).

malacca n. the stem of a palm tree used as a walking stick. WH: 19C. *Malacca*, a town and state on the Malay peninsula, SE Asia.

malachite n. a bright green monoclinic carbonate of copper, often polished for ornamental use. WH: 14–15C. Old French *melochite* (Modern French *malachite*), from Latin *molochites*, from Greek *molokhitis*, from *molokhē*, var. of *malakhē* MALLOW.

malaco- comb. form soft. WH: Greek *malakos* soft. See also -O-.

malacology n. the natural history of molluscs. WH: 19C. MALACO- + -LOGY.

malacopterygian a. belonging to the Malacopterygii, a group of soft-finned fishes, including salmon and herring. *Also n.* WH: 19C. MALACO- + Greek *pterugion* fin, dim. of *pterux* wing.

malacostracan n. any crustacean of the class Malacostraca, a division containing crabs, lobsters etc. *Also a.* WH: 19C. Modern Latin *Malacostraca*, from Greek *malakostraka*, from *malakos* soft + *ostrakon* shell. See also -AN.

maladaptation n. imperfect adaptation to the prevailing environment. WH: 19C. MAL- + *adaptation* (ADAPT).

maladjusted a. imperfectly adjusted. WH: 19C. MAL- + *adjusted*, p.p. of ADJUST.

maladministration n. defective or dishonest management, esp. of public affairs. WH: 17C. MAL- + *administration* (ADMINISTER).

maladroit *a.* awkward, clumsy. WH: 17C. French. See MAL-, ADROIT.

malady *n.* a disease, esp. a lingering or deep-seated disorder. WH: 12–14C. Old French *maladie*, from *malade* sick, ill, from Latin *male* badly + *habitus*, p.p. of *habere* to have, to hold.

mala fide *a., adv.* (acting or done) in bad faith. WH: 17C. Latin with bad faith, abl. of *mala fides* bad faith.

Malaga *n.* sweet, fortified white wine imported from Málaga. WH: 17C. *Málaga*, a seaport in S Spain.

Malagasy *a.* of or relating to Madagascar or its inhabitants or language. Also *n.* WH: 19C. Var. of *Madagascar*, an island state off the E coast of Africa.

malagueña *n.* a Spanish dance or folk tune similar to the fandango. WH: 19C. Spanish of *Málaga* (MALAGA).

malaise *n.* a feeling of uneasiness, esp. as premonition of a serious malady. WH: 18C. French, from Old French *mal* bad, ill (from Latin *malus*) + *aise* EASE.

malamute *n.* a powerful dog used to pull sledges in Arctic regions. WH: 19C. Eskimo (Inuit) *malimiut*, a people of the Kotzebue Sound, Alaska, who developed the breed.

†malapert *a.* pert, impudent, saucy, forward. Also *n.* WH: 12–14C. Old French, from *mal-* (indicating the opposite) + *apert*, var. of *espert* EXPERT, but taken as if from MAL- + *apert* bold, pert.

malapropism *n.* grotesque misapplication of words. WH: 19C. Mrs *Malaprop* (from MALAPROPOS), a character who grotesquely confuses words in R.B. Sheridan's play *The Rivals* (1775). See also -ISM.

malapropos *adv.* unseasonably, unsuitably, out of place. Also *a., n.* WH: 17C. French *mal à propos*, from *mal* ill + *à* to + *propos* purpose. See MAL-, APROPOS.

malar *a.* of or relating to the cheek or cheekbone. Also *n.* WH: 18C. Modern Latin *malaris*, from Latin *mala* jaw, cheekbone. See also -AR[1].

malaria *n.* a fever of an intermittent and remittent nature caused by a parasite of the genus *Plasmodium* introduced by the bite of mosquitoes. WH: 18C. Italian *mal' aria*, from *mala* bad + *aria* air. The disease was originally thought to be caused by the bad air in swampy areas.

malarkey *n.* foolish or insincere talk, nonsense. WH: early 20C. Orig. unknown.

malassimilation *n.* imperfect assimilation, esp. of nutriment. WH: 19C. MAL- + *assimilation* (ASSIMILATE).

malathion *n.* an insecticide used for houseflies and garden pests. WH: mid-20C. *maleate*, a salt or ester of MALEIC ACID + -*a*- + THIO- + -ON.

Malay *a.* of or relating to a people of Malaysia and Indonesia. Also *n.* WH: 16C. Obs. Malay *Malayu* (now *Melayu*).

Malayalam *n.* the Dravidian language of Kerala in S India, related to Tamil. WH: 19C. Malayalam *Malayālam*, from *mala* mountain + *āḷ* man.

Malaysian *n.* a native or inhabitant of Malaysia in SE Asia. Also *a.* WH: 17C. *Malaysia*, a name for the Malay archipelago, from root of Malay *Melaya* (MALAY) based on *Asia* (ASIAN). See also -AN.

malcontent *n.* a person who is discontented, esp. with the government. Also *a.* WH: 16C. Old French. See MAL-, CONTENT[1].

mal de mer *n.* seasickness. WH: 18C. French, from *mal* sickness + *de* of + *mer* sea.

maldistribution *n.* imperfect, unequal or unfair distribution. WH: 19C. MAL- + *distribution* (DISTRIBUTE).

male *a.* of or relating to the sex that begets young or has organs for impregnating ova. Also *n.* WH: 14–15C. Old French *masle* (Modern French *mâle*), from Latin *masculus*, from *mas* male person. Cp. MASCULINE.

malediction *n.* a curse, an imprecation. WH: 14–15C. Latin *maledictio, maledictionis*, from *maledictus*, p.p. of *maledicere* to speak evil of, from *male* ill, badly + *dicere* to say. See also -ION.

malefactor *n.* an evildoer, a criminal. WH: 14–15C. Latin, from *male facere* to do evil (to). See also -OR.

malefic *a.* mischief-making, harmful, hateful. WH: 17C. Latin *maleficus*, from *male* ill, badly. See also -FIC.

maleic acid *n.* a colourless, crystalline acid used in making synthetic compounds. WH: 19C. French *maléique*, alt. of *malique* malic (MALIC ACID).

malevolent *a.* malicious, wishing evil on others. WH: 16C. Old French *malivolent* or Latin *malevolens, malevolentis*, from *male* ill, badly + *volens, volentis*, pres.p. of *velle* to will, to wish. See also -ENT.

malfeasance *n.* evildoing, esp. illegal conduct by a public official. WH: 17C. Anglo-French *malfaisance*, from *mal-* MAL- + Old French *faisance*, from *fais-*, pres. stem of *faire* to do. See also -ANCE.

malformation *n.* faulty formation. WH: 19C. MAL- + FORMATION.

malfunction *n.* a failure to function. Also *v.i.* WH: early 20C. MAL- + FUNCTION.

malgré *prep.* in spite of. WH: 16C. French. See MAUGRE.

mali *n.* a member of the gardener caste in the Indian subcontinent. WH: 18C. Hindi *mālī*, from Sanskrit *mālin*, from *mālā* garland.

malic acid *n.* an organic acid derived from unripe apples and other fruit. WH: 18C. Latin *malum* apple + -IC.

malice *n.* the desire to harm others deliberately, active malevolence. Also *v.t.* WH: 12–14C. Old French, from Latin *malitia*, from *malus* bad. See also -ICE.

malign *a.* unfavourable, hurtful. Also *v.t., v.i.* WH: 12–14C. Old French *maligne*, fem. of *malin*, or from Latin *malignus*, from *malus* bad.

malignant *a.* (of a disease, tumour etc.) threatening life. Also *n.* WH: 16C. Late Latin *malignans, malignantis*, pres.p. of *malignare* to contrive maliciously, from *malignus*. See MALIGN, also -ANT.

malinger *v.i.* to exaggerate or pretend illness in order to avoid work or other responsibility. WH: 19C. Back-formation from *malingerer*, appar. from Old French *malingre*, prob. ult. from *mal-* MAL- + *haingre* weak, thin, prob. of Germanic orig. Not rel. to LINGER.

malism *n.* the doctrine that on the whole this is a bad world. WH: 19C. Latin *malus* bad + -ISM, based on PESSIMISM.

†malison *n.* a curse, a malediction. WH: 12–14C. Old French *maleïson*, from Late Latin *maledictio, maledictionis* MALEDICTION.

†malkin *n.* a female servant who works in a kitchen. WH: 12–14C. Dim. of *Malde*, early form of female forenames *Maud* or *Matilda*. See also -KIN. Cp. GRIMALKIN.

mall *n.* an enclosed street or area of shops reserved for pedestrians. WH: 12–14C. Earlier form of MAUL. Cp. PALL-MALL. The original sense (as MAUL) was heavy hammer. The present spelling arose in the 17C when meanings were successively the mallet in game of pall-mall, the game itself, the alley where the game was played, a walk by such an alley (as London's *The Mall* originally was), then finally shopping precinct (mid-20C).

mallard *n.* a wild duck or drake. WH: 12–14C. Old French (Modern French *malart*), prob. from same source as MALE + -ARD.

malleable *a.* capable of being rolled out or shaped by hammering without being broken. WH: 14–15C. Old French, from Medieval Latin *malleabilis*, from Latin *malleare* to hammer. See MALLEUS, also -ABLE.

mallee *n.* any of various dwarf species of eucalyptus growing in the deserts of Victoria and S Australia. WH: 19C. Australian Aboriginal (Wemba-Wemba) *mali*.

mallenders *n.pl.* a scaly eruption at the back of the knee in horses. WH: 14–15C. Old French *malandre*, from Latin *malandria* (pl.) pustules on the neck.

malleolus *n.* either of two hammer-shaped bony projections extending either side of the ankle. WH: 17C. Latin, dim. of MALLEUS.

mallet *n.* a light hammer, usu. of wood. WH: 14–15C. Old French *maillet*, from *mailler* to hammer, from *mail* hammer, MAUL. See also -ET[1]. Cp. MALL.

malleus *n.* one of the small bones of the middle ear or tympanum. WH: 17C. Latin hammer. The bone is so named from its shape. Cp. INCUS.

mallow *n.* a plant of various species belonging to the genus *Malva*, usu. with pink or mauve flowers and hairy stems and foliage, and having emollient properties. WH: pre-1200. Latin *malva*, rel. to Greek *malakhē*, *molokhē* mallow. Cp. MAUVE. According to some, the Greek name relates to *malakos* soft, gentle, soothing, referring to the plant's emollient properties.

malm *n.* a soft, friable chalky rock or loam, used with clay and sand for brick-making. Also *v.t.* WH: pre-1200. Old English *mealm-* (in *mealmstān* malmstone), from Germanic base of MEAL[2].

malmsey *n.* a strong sweet white wine now chiefly made in Madeira. WH: 14–15C. Middle Dutch and Middle Low German *malmesie*, from Medieval Latin *malmasia*, from Greek *Monemvasia*, a port in SE Greece. Cp. MALVOISIE.

malnourished *a.* suffering from malnutrition. WH: early 20C. MAL- + *nourished*, p.p. of NOURISH.

malnutrition *n.* insufficient or defective nutrition. WH: 19C. MAL- + *nutrition* (NUTRIENT).

malocclusion *n.* a defect in the position of the teeth in the lower jaw relative to those of the upper jaw. WH: 19C. MAL- + *occlusion* (OCCLUDE).

malodorous *a.* having an unpleasant smell. WH: 19C. MAL- + *odorous* (ODOUR).

Malpighian *a.* applied to certain corpuscles, layers and other structures, in the spleen and kidneys. WH: 19C. Marcello *Malpighi*, 1628–94, Italian anatomist + -AN.

malpractice *n.* illegal or immoral conduct, esp. improper treatment of a case by a physician, lawyer etc. WH: 17C. MAL- + PRACTICE.

malpresentation *n.* an abnormal position of the foetus at birth. WH: 19C. MAL- + PRESENTATION.

malt *n.* grain, usu. barley, steeped in water and fermented, then dried in a kiln, usu. used for brewing and distilling. *Also a., v.t., v.i.* WH: pre-1200. Old English, from Germanic, rel. to base of MELT.

Malta fever *n.* brucellosis, a fever formerly common in Malta and other places in the Mediterranean, said to be conveyed by goat's milk. WH: 17C. *Malta*, an island and republic in the central Mediterranean.

Maltese *a.* of or relating to Malta or its inhabitants. *Also n.* WH: 17C. *Malta* (see MALTA FEVER) + -ESE.

maltha *n.* an ancient form of bituminous cement, mineral tar. WH: 14–15C. Latin, from Greek.

Malthusian *a.* of or relating to or supporting the teachings of Malthus. *Also n.* WH: 19C. Thomas Robert *Malthus*, 1766–1834, English clergyman and economist + -IAN.

maltose *n.* a sugar obtained by the action of malt or diastase on starch paste. WH: 19C. MALT + -OSE².

maltreat *v.t.* to ill-treat, to abuse. WH: 18C. French *maltraiter*. See MAL-, TREAT.

malvaceous *a.* belonging to or resembling the genus *Malva* or the family Malvaceae, including the mallows. WH: 17C. Latin *malvaceus*, from *malva* MALLOW. See also -ACEOUS.

malversation *n.* fraudulent conduct or corruption in a position of trust, esp. corrupt administration of public funds. WH: 16C. French, from *malverser*, from Latin *male versari* to behave badly. See also -ATION.

malvoisie *n.* malmsey. WH: 14–15C. French form of *Monemvasia*. See MALMSEY.

mam *n.* mother. WH: 16C. Prob. imit. of infants' first speech. See MAMMA¹. Cp. MUM¹.

mamba *n.* any of various African poisonous snakes of the genus *Dendroaspis*. WH: 19C. Zulu *imamba*.

mambo *n.* a W Indian syncopated dance or dance tune, like the rumba. *Also v.i.* WH: mid-20C. American Spanish, prob. from Haitian creole, from Yoruba, lit. to talk.

mamelon *n.* a small rounded hill or mound. WH: 19C. French nipple, from Latin MAMILLA. The hill is so called from its supposed resemblance to a woman's breast.

Mameluke *n.* any of the mounted soldiers of Egypt (orig. Circassian slaves) who formed the ruling class in that country, destroyed by Mehmet Ali in 1811. WH: 16C. French *mammeluk*, from Arabic *mamlūk* object of possession, slave, pass. part. (used as n.) of *malaka* to possess.

mamilla *n.* a nipple or teat. WH: 17C. Latin, dim. of *mamma* breast, teat. Cp. MAMMA².

mamma¹ *n.* mother (used by or to children). WH: 16C. Redupl. of *ma* in the first natural speech of infants. Cp. MA, MOMMA, MOMMY, MUMMY². Rel. to MAMMA².

mamma² *n.* the milk-secreting organ in female mammals. WH: pre-1200. Latin breast, mother. Cp. MAMMAL.

mammal *n.* any vertebrate of the class Mammalia, having milk-secreting organs for suckling their young, the highest division of vertebrates. WH: 19C. Modern Latin *Mammalia*, neut. pl. of Late Latin *mammalis*, from *mamma*. See MAMMA². The Modern Latin class name was coined by Linnaeus.

mammee *n.* a tropical American tree, *Mammea americana*, bearing edible pulpy fruit. WH: 16C. Spanish *mamei*, from Taino.

†**mammock** *n.* a shapeless piece. *Also v.t.* WH: 16C. First element of unknown orig. + -OCK.

Mammon *n.* riches personified as an idol or an evil influence. WH: 14–15C. Late Latin *mammona*, *mammon*, from New Testament Greek *mammōnas*, from Hebrew *māmōn* money, wealth. Cp. Matt. vi.24, Luke xvi.9,11,13.

mammoth *n.* a large extinct species of elephant of the genus *Mammuthus*. *Also a.* WH: 18C. Russian *mamont*, prob. of Siberian orig., prob. from a Nenets word meaning devourer. The name would refer to the mammoth's supposed habit of burrowing into the earth by 'devouring' it.

mammy *n.* mother (used by or to children). WH: 16C. MAM + -Y³.

man *n.* an adult male of the human race. *Also v.t.* WH: pre-1200. Old English, from Germanic bases rel. to Sanskrit *manu* human being, man. The basic sense is human being, irrespective of sex or age, otherwise person. In all the Germanic languages the word came to mean both human being and adult male, and many Germanic languages still retain the former sense, as German *Mensch* person. English lost this sense, however.

mana *n.* spiritual power exerted through man or inanimate objects. WH: 19C. Maori.

manacle *n.* a handcuff, shackle. *Also v.t.* WH: 12–14C. Old French *manicle* handcuff, gauntlet, from Latin *manicula*, dim. of *manus* hand.

manage *v.t.* to direct, to carry on. *Also v.i., n.* WH: 16C. Italian *maneggiare*, from Latin *manus* hand. The original sense was to handle or train a horse, especially by putting it through the exercises of the MANÈGE. The current sense emerged in the 18C.

manakin *n.* any small bird of the family Pipridae of tropical Central and S America. WH: 17C. Var. of MANIKIN.

mañana *n., adv.* tomorrow. WH: 19C. Spanish morning, tomorrow, ult. from Latin *mane* in the morning. The Spanish sense tomorrow derives from Old Spanish *cras mañana*, lit. tomorrow early.

manatee *n.* a large herbivorous aquatic mammal of the genus *Trichechus*, a sea cow. WH: 16C. Spanish *manatí*, from Carib *manáti*.

manche *n.* a sleeve, with long hanging ends. WH: 14–15C. Old French, from Latin *manica*, from *manus* hand.

†**Manchester goods** *n.pl.* cotton textiles. WH: 16C. *Manchester*, a large city formerly in Lancashire, historically the chief centre of cotton manufacture in Britain.

manchineel *n.* a W Indian tree, *Hippomane mancinella*, with a poisonous sap and apple-like fruit. WH: 17C. French *mancenille*, from Spanish *manzanilla*, dim. of *manzana* apple, alt. form of Old Spanish *mazana*, from Latin *matiana* (neut. pl.) a kind of apple. Cp. MANZANILLA.

Manchu *n.* a member of a Chinese people which governed China, 1644–1912. *Also a.* WH: 17C. Manchu pure.

mancipate *v.t.* under Roman law, to hand over (property), to deliver possession of, by the formal method of mancipation. WH: 15C. Latin *mancipatus*, p.p. of *mancipare*, from *manceps* purchaser, from *manus* hand + base of *capere* to take. See also -ATE³.

manciple *n.* a steward, a buyer of stores, esp. for a college, Inn of Court etc. WH: 12–14C. Old French var. of *mancipe*, from Latin *mancipium* purchase, slave, from *manceps*. See MANCIPATE.

Mancunian *n.* a native or inhabitant of Manchester. *Also a.* WH: early 20C. Latin *Mancunio*, alt. of *Mamucio*, Roman name of Manchester + -AN.

-mancy *comb. form* divination by, as in *necromancy*, *pyromancy*. WH: Old French *-mancie*, from Late Latin *-mantia*, from Greek *manteia* divination, from *manteuesthai* to prophesy, from *mantis* prophet, diviner. See also -CY. Cp. MANTIS.

Mandaean *n.* a member of a Gnostic sect of Iraq. *Also a.* WH: 18C. Mandaean Aramaic *mandaia*, from *manda* knowledge + -AN.

mandala *n.* any of various symbols used to represent the universe in Buddhism or Hinduism, used as an aid to meditation. WH: 19C. Sanskrit *maṇḍala* disc, circle.

mandamus *n.* a writ or (now) order issued from a higher court directed to a person, corporation or inferior court, requiring them to do a particular thing relating to their office or duty. WH: 16C. Latin we command, 1st pers. pl. pres. ind. of *mandare* to command. Cp. MANDATE.

mandarin¹ *n.* a mandarin orange. WH: 18C. French *mandarine*, fem. of *mandarin* Mandarin. See MANDARIN². The fruit is probably so called from the colour of the costume worn by Mandarins.

mandarin² *n.* Chinese official. WH: 16C. Portuguese *mandarim*, alt. of Malay *menteri*, from Sanskrit *mantrī*, *mantrin* counsellor, minister.

mandate *n.* an authoritative charge or order. WH: 16C. Latin *mandatum*, neut. p.p. (used as n.) of *mandare* to command, to send out, from *manus* hand + base of *dare* to give. See also -ATE¹.

Mandelbrot set *n.* a set of complex numbers which, when plotted, has a convoluted fractal boundary. WH: late 20C. Benoit *Mandelbrot*, 1924–, Polish-born US mathematician, who investigated the concept.

mandible *n.* the jaw, the lower jaw in vertebrates, the upper or lower in birds, and the pair in insects. WH: 14–15C. Old French, from Late Latin *mandibula*, from *mandere* to chew.

mandolin *n.* a musical instrument with a deep almond-shaped body and two or three pairs of metal strings. WH: 18C. French *mandoline*, from Italian *mandolino*, dim. of *mandola*, *mandora*, alt. of Late Latin *pandura* three-stringed lute, from Greek *pandoura*, prob. of Oriental orig.

mandorla *n.* an area of light, oval but pointed in shape, surrounding a painting or sculpture of the risen Christ or of the Virgin at the Assumption. WH: 19C. Italian almond.

†mandragora *n.* the mandrake. WH: pre-1200. Old French *mandragore*, from Medieval Latin *mandragora*, from Latin *mandragoras*, from Greek, prob. of pre-Hellenic orig. See MANDRAKE.

mandrake *n.* the poisonous plant *Mandragora officinarum*, having emetic and narcotic properties, the root of which was anciently believed to be like the human form and to shriek when pulled up. WH: 12–14C. Prob. from Middle Dutch *mandragre*, from Medieval Latin MANDRAGORA, influ. by MAN (alluding to the shape of the root) and DRAKE².

mandrel *n.* an arbor or axis of a lathe on which work is fixed for turning. WH: 16C. Orig. unknown.

mandrill *n.* a W African baboon, *Mandrillus sphinx*, which has a brightly-coloured face and blue hindquarters. WH: 18C. Appar. from MAN + DRILL³.

manducate *v.t.* to chew, to eat. WH: 17C. Latin *manducatus*, p.p. of *manducare* to chew. See also -ATE³.

mane *n.* the long hair on the neck of some animals, such as the horse or (male) lion. WH: pre-1200. Old English *manu*, from Germanic.

manège *n.* a school for training horses or teaching horsemanship. *Also v.t.* WH: 17C. French. See MANAGE.

manes *n.pl.* the spirits of the dead, esp. of ancestors worshipped as guardian divinities. WH: 14–15C. Latin, ? rel. to *manus* good.

mangabey *n.* a small long-tailed African monkey of the genus *Cercocebus*. WH: 18C. *Mangabey*, a region in Madagascar. The name was wrongly given by the French naturalist Georges-Louis Leclerc, Comte de Buffon, to a species of *Cercocebus* that actually inhabits the W coast of Africa.

manganese *n.* a metallic element, at. no. 25, chem. symbol Mn, of a greyish-white colour. WH: 17C. French *manganèse*, from Italian *manganese*, alt. of Medieval Latin *magnesia* MAGNESIA. Cp. MAGNESIUM.

mange *n.* a skin disease caused by a mite, occurring in cattle, dogs etc. WH: 14–15C. Old French *manjue* itch, from stem of *mangier* (Modern French *manger*) to eat, from Latin *manducare*. See MANDUCATE.

mangel-wurzel *n.* a large-rooted variety of the common beet, *Beta vulgaris*, cultivated as fodder for cattle. WH: 18C. German *Mangoldwurzel*, from *Mangold* beet + *Wurzel* root.

manger *n.* a trough for horses or cattle to eat out of. WH: 12–14C. Old French *mangeoire*, from *mangeure*, from Latin *manducatus*. See MANDUCATE.

mangetout *n.* a type of pea which is eaten complete with the pod. WH: 19C. French, lit. eat-all, from *manger* to eat + *tout* all,

everything. The pea is so called because the pod is edible as well as the peas.

mangle¹ *v.t.* to mutilate, to disfigure by hacking. WH: 14–15C. Anglo-French *mangler*, prob. freq. of *mahaignier* MAIM. See also -LE⁴.

mangle² *n.* a rolling machine for pressing water out of washing, damp sheets etc. *Also v.t.* WH: 17C. Dutch *mangel*, abbr. of *mangelstok* mangle, from *mangelen* to mangle + *stok* staff, roller, STOCK, ult. from Greek *magganon*. See MANGONEL. Not rel. to MANGLE¹.

mango *n.* the fruit of an Indian tree, *Mangifera indica*. WH: 16C. Portuguese *manga*, from Malay *mangga*, from Tamil *māṅkāy*, from *mā* mango tree + *kāy* fruit.

mangonel *n.* a medieval engine for throwing missiles. WH: 12–14C. Old French (Modern French *mangonneau*), from Medieval Latin *manganellus*, dim. of Late Latin *manganum*, from Greek *magganon* engine of war, pulley axis, rel. to *manganeuein* to deceive.

mangosteen *n.* a Malaysian tree, *Garcinia mangostana*. WH: 16C. Malay *manggustan*, dial. var. of *manggis*. Not rel. to MANGO.

mangrove *n.* any tropical tree of the genus *Rhizophora*, growing in muddy places by the coast, the bark of which is used for medicine and in tanning. WH: 17C. Prob. ult. from Portuguese *mangue* or Spanish *mangle*, from Taino, with second element assim. to GROVE.

manhattan *n.* a cocktail containing whisky, vermouth and sometimes a dash of bitters. WH: 19C. *Manhattan*, a borough of New York City.

mania *n.* a form of mental disorder characterized by hallucination, emotional excitement and violence. WH: 14–15C. Late Latin, from Greek, rel. to *mainesthai* to be mad, ult. from Indo-European base of MIND. See also -IA.

-mania *comb. form* denoting special kinds of derangement, hallucination, infatuation or excessive enthusiasm, as in *erotomania*, *kleptomania*, *megalomania*, *monomania*. WH: MANIA.

Manichaean *a.* of or relating to Manichaeism. *Also n.* WH: 16C. Late Latin *Manichaeus*, from *Mani*, *Manes*, *c.*216–76, Persian founder of the system named after him. See also -AN.

manicure *n.* the care of the hands, fingernails etc. *Also v.t.* WH: 19C. French, from Latin *manus* hand + *cura* care. Cp. PEDICURE.

manifest¹ *a.* plainly apparent, obvious. *Also v.t.*, *v.i.* WH: 12–14C. Old French *manifeste* or Latin *manifestus*, earlier *manufestus*, from *manus* hand + *-festus* struck, from base of *defendere* DEFEND, *offendere* OFFEND.

manifest² *n.* a list of a ship's cargo for the use of customs officers. WH: 16C. Italian MANIFESTO. The original sense was manifestation, then (in the 17C) manifesto. The current sense dates from the 18C.

manifesto *n.* a public declaration, esp. by a political party, government, sovereign or other authoritative body, of opinions, motives or intentions. *Also v.i.* WH: 16C. Italian, from *manifestare*, from Latin *manifestus*. See MANIFEST¹.

manifold *a.* of various forms or kinds. *Also n.*, *v.t.* WH: pre-1200. Old English *manigfeald*, from Germanic. See MANY, -FOLD.

manikin *n.* a little man or a dwarf. WH: 16C. Dutch *manneken*, dim. of *man* MAN. See also -KIN. Cp. MANNEQUIN.

Manila *n.* a kind of cigar or cheroot made in Manila. WH: 17C. *Manila*, the capital and chief port of the Philippines.

manilla *n.* a metal ring worn by some Africans on the legs or arms. WH: 16C. Spanish, prob. dim. of *mano* hand, from Latin *manus*.

manille *n.* in ombre or quadrille, the highest but one trump or honour. WH: 17C. French, from Spanish *malilla*, dim. of *mala*, fem. of *malo* bad. The second best trump card is not the best, and is relatively thus a *mala carta*, Spanish bad card.

manioc *n.* the cassava, *Manihot esculenta*, *M. dulcis* etc. WH: 16C. French, from Tupi *manioca*.

maniple *n.* a strip worn as a Eucharistic vestment on a priest's left arm. WH: 12–14C. Old French (Modern French *manipule*) or Latin *manipulus* handful, troop of soldiers, from *manus* hand + element of unknown orig. The ecclesiastical garment originated as a handkerchief held in the left hand.

manipulate *v.t.* to operate on with the hands, to handle. *Also v.i.* WH: 19C. Back-formation from *manipulation* (18C), from French, from Latin *manipulus*. See MANIPLE, also -ATE³.

manitou *n.* among certain N American Indians, a spirit or being endowed with supernatural power. WH: 16C. Narragansett *manittówock* (pl.) or Delaware *manét:u* supernatural being.

manky *a.* dirty, unpleasant, bad. WH: mid-20C. Prob. from obs. *mank* maimed, mutilated, from Old French *manc*, from Latin *mancus* maimed + -Y[1], ? influ. by French MANQUÉ.

manna *n.* the food miraculously supplied to the Israelites in the wilderness. WH: pre-1200. Late Latin, from Hellenistic Greek, from Aramaic *mannā*, from Hebrew *mān*, rel. to Arabic *mann* exudation of the tamarisk (*Tamarix mannifera*).

mannequin *n.* a woman employed to wear and display clothes. WH: 18C. French, from Dutch *manneken* MANIKIN. A mannequin was originally a dummy figure for the display of clothes. The current sense dates from the early 20C.

manner *n.* the way in which something is done or happens, method. WH: 12–14C. Old French *manière*, from use as n. of fem. of Latin *manuarius* pertaining to the hand, from *manus* hand. See also -ER[2].

mannite *n.* a sweetish substance obtained from manna. WH: 19C. MANNA + -ITE[1].

manoeuvre *n.* a tactical movement or change of position by troops or warships. *Also v.i., v.t.* WH: 15C. French *manœuvre*, from *manœuvrer*, from Medieval Latin *manuoperare*, from Latin *manu operari* to work with the hand, from *manus* hand. Cp. MANURE.

manometer *n.* an instrument for measuring the pressure of a gas or liquid. WH: 18C. French *manomètre*, from Greek *manos* thin, rare. See also -METER.

ma non troppo *adv.* but not too much. WH: early 20C. Italian but not too much, from *ma* but + *non* not + TROPPO[1].

manor *n.* a large country house, usu. with an estate. WH: 12–14C. Old French *maneir* (Modern French *manoir*) dwelling, habitation, use as n. of inf. of *maneir* to dwell, from Latin *manere* to remain.

manqué *a.* having the potential to be, but not actually being, something specified. WH: 18C. French, p.p. of *manquer* to fall short of, to lack, to fail.

mansard roof *n.* a roof with four sloping sides, the lower sections of which slope more steeply, giving space for attics. WH: 18C. Latin (*toit en*) *mansarde* mansard (roof), from François *Mansard*, 1598–1666, French architect.

manse *n.* the residence of a clergyman, esp. a Presbyterian minister. WH: 15C. Medieval Latin *mansus*, p.p. of *manere*. See MANSION.

-manship *comb. form* used to form nouns indicating skill, expertise or daring in a particular field, as in *penmanship, brinkmanship*. WH: MAN + -SHIP, based on *churchmanship* (CHURCH), *craftsmanship* (CRAFT), etc. The current specific senses originate from *gamesmanship* (middle 20C) (GAME[1]).

mansion *n.* a residence of considerable size and pretensions. WH: 12–14C. Old French, from Latin *mansio, mansionis* stay, station, quarters, from *mansus*, p.p. of *manere* to remain, to stay. Cp. MAISONETTE, MANSE.

†mansuete *a.* tame, gentle, meek. WH: 14–15C. Latin *mansuetus*, from *manus* hand + *suetus* accustomed. Cp. MASTIFF.

manta *n.* any of various very large fish of the family Mobulidae, esp. *Manta birostris*, with wide, winglike fins and feeding on plankton. WH: 17C. Spanish blanket.

mantel *n.* the ornamental facing round a fireplace with the shelf above it. WH: 15C. Var. of MANTLE.

mantelet *n.* a short sleeveless cloak worn by women. WH: 14–15C. Old French, dim. of *mantel* MANTLE. See also -ET[1].

mantic *a.* of or relating to prophecy or divination. WH: 19C. Greek *mantikos*, from *mantis* prophet, from *man-* as in MANIA. See also -IC.

manticore *n.* a fabulous monster with a human head, a lion's body and the tail of a scorpion. WH: 12–14C. Latin *manticora*, from Greek *mantikhōras*, a corrupt reading in Aristotle for *martikhoras*, from an Old Persian word meaning man-eater.

mantilla *n.* a veil for the head and shoulders, worn in Spain and Italy. WH: 18C. Spanish, dim. of *manta* MANTLE.

mantis *n.* any carnivorous orthopterous insect of the family Mantidae, esp. *Mantis religiosa*. WH: 17C. Modern Latin, from Greek, lit. prophet. See MANTIC. The mantis holds its forelegs doubled up as if praying like a prophet.

mantissa *n.* the decimal or fractional part of a logarithm. WH: 17C. Latin makeweight, ? from Etruscan.

mantle *n.* a sleeveless cloak or loose outer garment. *Also v.t., v.i.* WH: pre-1200. Latin *mantellum*, var. of *mantelum*, rel. to *mantelium* towel, napkin, tablecloth. Cp. MANTEL.

Mantoux test *n.* a test for past or present tuberculosis carried out by injecting tuberculin beneath the skin. WH: mid-20C. Charles *Mantoux*, 1877–1947, French physician.

mantra *n.* a word or phrase chanted inwardly in meditation, orig. a Hindu formula or charm. WH: 18C. Sanskrit, lit. thought, from *man* to think.

mantua *n.* a woman's loose gown worn in the 17th and 18th cents. WH: 16C. Alt. of French *manteau* gown, cloak, from Old French *mantel*, from Latin *mantellum* (MANTLE), influ. by name of *Mantua*, a city in N Italy.

manual *a.* of or performed with the hands. *Also n.* WH: 14–15C. Old French *manuel*, from Latin *manualis*, from *manus* hand. See also -AL[1].

manubrium *n.* any handle-shaped part or process, such as the presternum in mammals or the peduncle hanging down from medusae such as the jellyfish. WH: 17C. Latin handle, from *manus* hand.

manufacture *n.* the making of articles by means of labour or machinery, esp. on a large scale. *Also v.t., v.i.* WH: 16C. French, from Italian *manifattura*, re-formed after Latin *manu factum* made by hand. See FACT, also -URE.

manuka *n.* a New Zealand tea-tree, *Leptospermum scoparium*. WH: 19C. Maori.

manumit *v.t.* to release from slavery. WH: 14–15C. Latin *manumittere*, from *manu emittere*, lit. to send out from one's hand.

manure *n.* animal dung, esp. that of horses, used to fertilize land for cultivation. *Also v.t.* WH: 14–15C. Old French *manoeuvrer* (Modern French *manœuvrer*). See MANOEUVRE. The original sense of the verb was to hold or occupy land, to administer. Hence to till land, and hence to enrich it with manure.

manus *n.* the hand or a corresponding part in an animal. WH: 16C. Latin hand.

manuscript *n.* a book or document written by hand, not printed. *Also a.* WH: 16C. Medieval Latin *manuscriptus*, from Latin *manu* by hand + *scriptus*, p.p. of *scribere* to write.

Manx *a.* of or relating to the Isle of Man, its inhabitants or its language. *Also n.* WH: 16C. Old Norse, from Old Irish *Manu* Isle of Man + -skr -ISH[1].

many *a.* numerous, comprising a great number. *Also n.* WH: pre-1200. Old English *manig, monig*, from Germanic. Cp. German *manch* many a.

manyplies *n.* the third stomach of a ruminant, the omasum. WH: 18C. MANY + *plies*, pl. of PLY[1]. The word refers to the organ's many folds.

manzanilla *n.* a very dry sherry. WH: 19C. Spanish, lit. camomile, dim. of *manzana* apple.

manzanita *n.* any of several evergreen shrubs of the genus *Arctostaphylos*, esp. *A. manzanita* of California. WH: 19C. Spanish, dim. of *manzana* apple.

Maoism *n.* the political thought expounded by the Chinese communist leader Mao Zedong. WH: mid-20C. *Mao* Zedong (Tse-Tung), 1893–1976, chairman of the Central Committee of the Chinese Communist Party + -ISM.

Maori *n.* any of the Polynesian original inhabitants of New Zealand. *Also a.* WH: 19C. Maori.

map *n.* a representation of a portion of the earth's surface or the heavens or the surface of a planet etc. on a two-dimensional surface. *Also v.t.* WH: 16C. Medieval Latin *mappa* (*mundi*), lit. sheet (of the world), from Latin *mappa* tablecloth, napkin + *mundi*, gen. of *mundus* world.

maple *n.* a tree or shrub of the genus *Acer*. WH: pre-1200. Old English *mapel-* in *mapeltrēow* maple tree, from Germanic.

maquette *n.* a sculptor's preliminary model in clay, wax etc. WH: early 20C. French, from Italian *macchietta* speck, little spot, dim. of *macchia* spot, from *macchiare* to spot, to stain, from Latin *maculare* maculate (MACULA).

maqui *n.* a Chilean evergreen shrub, *Aristotelia chilensis*, the berries of which produce a medicinal wine. WH: 18C. Spanish *maquí*, from Mapuche.

maquillage *n.* make-up, cosmetics. WH: 19C. French, from *maquiller* to make up one's face, from Old French *masquiller* to stain, alt. of *mascurer* to darken. See also -AGE.

Maquis *n.* those surreptitiously resisting the German invaders of France etc., in 1940–45. WH: 19C. French, from Corsican Italian *macchia* thicket, from Latin *macula* spot.

mar *v.t.* to spoil, to disfigure. *Also n.* WH: pre-1200. Old English *merran*, from Germanic. Cp. Old High German *marren* to hinder, Old Norse *merja* to bruise.

marabou *n.* a W African stork, *Leptoptilos crumeniferus*, the downy feathers from under the wings and tail of which are used for trimming hats etc. WH: 19C. French, from Arabic *murābiṭ* holy man (MARABOUT). The bird is so called either because it appears meditative or because it is solitary, like a hermit.

marabout *n.* a Muslim hermit or saint, esp. one of a priestly caste in N Africa. WH: 17C. French, from Portuguese *marabuto*, from Arabic *murābiṭ*, from *ribāṭ* frontier station. Cp. MARAVEDI. The holy man is so called because he could win merit by fighting the infidel at the frontier.

maraca *n.* a hollow gourd or shell containing beads, shot etc. shaken, usu. in a pair, as a percussive accompaniment to music, esp. in Latin America. WH: 17C. Portuguese *maracá*, from Tupi *maráka*.

maraschino *n.* a cordial or liqueur distilled from bitter cherries grown in Dalmatia. WH: 18C. Italian, from *marasca* variety of cherry (from *amarasca*, from *amaro* bitter) + *-ino* -INE.

marasmus *n.* wasting away of the body. WH: 17C. Modern Latin, from Greek *marasmos*, from *marainein* to waste away.

Maratha *n.* a member of a people of SW India, esp. the state of Maharashtra. WH: 18C. Marathi *Marāṭhā*, Hindi *Marhaṭṭā*, from Sanskrit *Mahārāṣṭra* great kingdom.

marathon *n.* a long-distance race, usu. a running race, of 26 miles 385 yards (42.195 km). WH: 19C. *Marathōn* in Greece, site of an Athenian victory over an invading Persian army (490 BC). News of the victory is said to have been brought to Athens by a messenger who ran all the way from the battlefield and dropped dead on arrival.

maraud *v.i.* to make a plundering raid (on). *Also v.t., n.* WH: 17C. French *marauder*, from *maraud* rogue, vagabond, scoundrel, orig. tomcat, prob. imit. of the purring or yowling of a cat (cp. French *ronron* purr).

maravedi *n.* a former Spanish copper coin of low value. WH: 14–15C. Spanish *maravedí*, from Arabic *murābiṭīn*, oblique case of *murābiṭ* (MARABOUT). The coin is named after the N African Berber rulers of Muslim Spain, 1087–1145.

marble *n.* a fine-grained or crystalline limestone often polished for decorative use in sculpture or building. *Also v.t., a.* WH: 12–14C. Old French var. of *marbre*, from Latin *marmor*, from Greek *marmaros* shining stone, orig. (block of) stone, but later assoc. with *marmairein* to shine.

marc *n.* the compressed residue of grapes left after pressing, in the making of wine or oil. WH: 17C. French from *marcher* (MARCH¹) in its orig. sense to tread, to trample.

Marcan *a.* of or relating to St Mark. WH: early 20C. Latin *Marcus* Mark + -AN.

marcasite *n.* pyrites, esp. a white orthorhombic form of iron pyrites, used for making ornaments. WH: 14–15C. Medieval Latin *marcasita*, from Arabic *marḳašīṭa*, from Persian, assoc. with -ITE¹.

marcato *a.* (of notes) heavily accented. *Also adv.* WH: 19C. Italian, p.p. of *marcare* to mark, to accent, of Germanic orig.

marcel *n.* a style of permanent wave in hairdressing. *Also v.t.* WH: 19C. François *Marcel* Grateau, 1852–1936, French hairdresser.

marcescent *a.* (of blooms, leaves etc.) withering without falling. WH: 18C. Latin *marcescens, marcescentis*, pres.p. of *marcescere* to begin to fade, from *marcere* to wither, to be faint. See *-escent* (-ESCENCE).

March *n.* the third month of the year. WH: 12–14C. Old French *marche*, north-eastern var. of *marz, mars*, from Latin *Martius* (*mensis*) (month) of Mars.

march¹ *v.i.* to move with regular steps like a soldier. *Also v.t., n.* WH: 14–15C. Old French *marcher* to walk (orig. to tread, to trample), from Late Latin *marcus* hammer.

march² *n.* the frontier or boundary of a territory. *Also v.i.* WH: 12–14C. Old French *marche*, from Medieval Latin *marca*, from Germanic base of MARK¹. Cp. MARQUIS.

marchioness *n.* the wife or widow of a marquess. WH: 16C. Medieval Latin *marchionissa*, from *marchio, marchionis* captain of the marches, from *marca* MARK¹. See also -ESS¹.

Mardi Gras *n.* Shrove Tuesday. WH: 17C. French, lit. fat Tuesday, from *Mardi* Tuesday + *gras* fat. Mardi Gras is so named as the last day before Ash Wednesday and the start of Lent, the 'feast before the fast'.

mardy *a.* spoilt, sulky, lacking in toughness. WH: early 20C. Dial. *mard* spoilt, representing pronun. of *marred*, p.p. of MAR + -Y¹.

mare¹ *n.* the female of the horse or other equine animal. WH: pre-1200. Old English *mearh*, from Germanic, from base represented also by Gaelic *marc*, Welsh *march* stallion.

mare² *n.* any of the darkish areas on the moon or other planets etc. WH: 19C. Latin sea. The word existed earlier from the 17C in the Modern Latin names of areas on the moon such as *Mare Imbrium* Sea of Rains, *Mare Tranquillitatis* Sea of Tranquillity, etc.

maremma *n.* a marshy and usu. unhealthy region by the seashore. WH: 19C. Italian, from Latin *maritima*, fem. of *maritimus* MARITIME.

margaric *a.* resembling pearl, pearly. WH: 19C. French *margarique*, from Greek *margaron* pearl. *Margaric* acid is so called from the pearly lustre of its crystals. Cp. MARGARINE. It was named by the French biochemist Michel-Eugène Chevreul after a fatty acid that he (wrongly) believed to be one of the constituents of animal fats.

margarine *n.* an emulsion of edible oils and fat with water, skimmed milk or other substances with or without the addition of colouring matter, used for the same purposes as butter. WH: 19C. French, from *margarique* margaric acid + -INE. See MARGARIC. Margarine was invented in 1869 by the French food technologist Hippolyte Mège-Mouries, and originally made from clarified beef fat.

margarita *n.* a cocktail made from tequila and lemon (or other fruit) juice. WH: early 20C. Spanish *Margarita* Margaret.

margarite *n.* pearl mica, a hydrous silicate. WH: 12–14C. Old French (Modern French *marguerite*), from Latin *margarita*, from Greek *margaritēs*, from *margaron* pearl. See also -ITE¹. The name of the silicate dates from the 19C.

margay *n.* a Brazilian wildcat, *Felis wiedii*. WH: 18C. French, from Tupi *marakaya*.

marge¹ *n.* margarine. WH: early 20C. Abbr. of MARGARINE.

marge² *n.* a margin. WH: 16C. Old French MARGIN.

margin *n.* an edge, a border. *Also v.t., v.i.* WH: 14–15C. Latin *margo, marginis*, rel. to MARK¹.

marginal *a.* of or relating to or at the margin. *Also n.* WH: 16C. Medieval Latin *marginalis*, from *margo, marginis* MARGIN. See also -AL¹.

margrave *n.* a German title of nobility, orig. a lord or governor of a march or border province. WH: pre-1200. Middle Dutch *markgrave*, from Old High German *marca* MARK¹ + *grāve* count (cp. German *Graf*).

marguerite *n.* the ox-eye daisy and other wild or cultivated varieties of chrysanthemum. WH: 17C. French, from Old French *margarite* daisy, pearl, from Latin *margarita* (MARGARITE). The plant is named from its white flower. The name was originally that of the common daisy.

mariage de convenance *n.* a marriage of convenience. WH: 19C. French marriage of convenience, from *mariage* MARRIAGE + *de* of + *convenance* convenience (CONVENIENT).

Marian *a.* of or relating to the Virgin Mary. *Also n.* WH: 17C. Latin *Maria* Mary + -AN. The name can relate to the Virgin Mary, to Mary I of England, 1516–68, or to Mary, Queen of Scots, 1542–87.

mariculture *n.* the cultivation of marine organisms in their own natural environment. WH: early 20C. Latin *mare, maris* sea + CULTURE.

marigold *n.* any plant of the genus *Calendula* or *Tagetes*, usu. bearing bright yellow or orange flowers. WH: 12–14C. *Mary* (prob. ref. to Virgin Mary) + GOLD.

marijuana *n.* dried leaves, flowering tops and stems of Indian hemp, usu. used to make cigarettes smoked as a narcotic. WH: 19C. American Spanish, of unknown orig.

marimba *n.* a musical instrument similar to a xylophone. WH: 18C. Congolese.

marina *n.* a system of sheltered moorings designed mainly for pleasure boats. WH: 19C. Mayan and Spanish, fem. of *marino*, from Latin *marinus* MARINE.

marinade *n.* a mixture of vinegar, oil etc. flavoured with wine, spices etc. for soaking fish or meat prior to cooking. *Also v.t.* WH: 18C. French, from Spanish *marinada*, from *marinar* to pickle in brine, from *marino* (MARINA).

marine *a.* found in or produced by the sea. *Also n.* WH: 12–14C. Old French, fem. of *marin*, from Latin *marinus*, from *mare*, *maris* sea. See also -INE.

mariner *n.* a sailor. WH: 12–14C. Old French *marinier*, from Medieval Latin *marinaritus*, from Latin *marinus*. See MARINE, also -ER[2].

Mariolatry *n.* idolatrous worship of the Virgin Mary. WH: 17C. Latin *Maria* Mary + -*o*- + -LATRY.

marionette *n.* a puppet moved by strings. WH: 17C. French *marionnette*, from *Marion*, dim. of *Marie* Mary. See also -ETTE. *Marie* was a common name for female characters in old French plays.

†marish *n.* a marsh. *Also a.* WH: 12–14C. Old French *marais*, from Medieval Latin *mariscus* MARSH.

Marist *n.* a member of the Roman Catholic order of Mary for teaching and foreign missions. *Also a.* WH: 19C. French *Mariste*, from *Marie* Mary. See also -IST.

marital *a.* of or relating to marriage. WH: 15C. Latin *maritalis*, from *maritus* husband. See also -AL[1].

maritime *a.* of or relating to the sea. WH: 16C. French, from Latin *maritimus*, from *mare*, *maris* sea + -*timus*, as in *finitimus* neighbouring, etc.

marjoram *n.* an aromatic herb of the mint family, esp. wild or sweet marjoram. WH: 14–15C. Old French *marjorane* (Modern French *marjolaine*), from Medieval Latin *majorana*, of unknown orig.

mark[1] *n.* a visible sign or impression, such as a stroke or dot. *Also v.t., v.i.* WH: pre-1200. Old English *merc*, *mearc*, from a Germanic n. rel. to Latin *margo* MARGIN. Cp. MARCH[2]. The original sense was boundary, border, limit, although the general sense sign, token also dates from the first.

mark[2] *n.* a German unit of currency, the Deutschmark or (formerly) Ostmark. WH: pre-1200. Old English *marc*, prob. from Medieval Latin *marcus* and ult. identical with MARK[1]. A mark was originally a unit of weight or money marked with a sign or imprint.

market *n.* an open space or large building in which commodities are offered for sale. *Also v.i., v.t.* WH: pre-1200. Old Northern French var. of Old French *marchiet* (Modern French *marché*), from Latin *mercatus* trading, trade, market, from *mercari* to trade, to buy, from *merx*, *mercis* wares, merchandise.

markhor *n.* a wild Himalayan mountain goat, *Capra falconeri*. WH: 19C. Persian *mār-kwār*, lit. serpent-eater.

markka *n.* the standard unit of currency in Finland. WH: early 20C. Finnish. Cp. MARK[2].

Markov chain *n.* a sequence of events in which the probability of each event is dependent on the event immediately preceding it. WH: mid-20C. A.A. *Markov*, 1856–1922, Russian mathematician.

marksman *n.* a person who shoots well. WH: 17C. MARK[1] + -S[1] + MAN.

marl[1] *n.* soil containing clay and lime, much used as a fertilizer. *Also v.t.* WH: 12–14C. Old French *marle* (Modern French *marne*), from Medieval Latin *margila*, from Latin *marga*, ? from Gaulish.

marl[2] *n.* a yarn with different coloured threads, used to make a mottled fabric. WH: 19C. Contr. of *marbled* (MARBLE).

marlin *n.* any of various large oceanic fishes of the genera *Makaira* and *Tetrapterus*, with a long upper jaw. WH: early 20C. Appar. from *marlin-spike* pointed iron tool, appar. from *marling*, pres.p. of *marl* to tie, to noose (from Dutch *marlen*) + SPIKE[1], but later taken to come from *marline* two-stranded rope, from Dutch *marlijn* (from *marren* to bind + *lijn* LINE[1]) and *marling* (from *marlen*, freq. of Middle Dutch *marren* + -*ing* -ING[1]).

marmalade *n.* a jam or preserve prepared from fruit, esp. oranges or lemons, boiled with the sliced rind. WH: 15C. French *marmelade*, from Portuguese *marmelada*, from *marmelo* quince, from Latin *melimelum*, from Greek *melimēlon* kind of apple grafted on a quince, from *meli* honey + *mēlon* apple. Marmalade was originally made from quinces.

Marmite® *n.* a savoury yeast extract used as a spread or for flavouring. WH: early 20C. French MARMITE.

marmite *n.* an earthenware cooking pot. WH: 19C. French, orig. meaning hypocrite, from blend of base of *marmouser* to murmur + *mite*, name of the cat in the *Roman de Renart* (12–13C), of imit. orig. Both a hypocrite and a cooking pot conceal their content.

marmoreal *a.* made of marble. WH: 18C. Latin *marmorus*, from *marmor* MARBLE. See also -AL[1].

marmoset *n.* a small tropical American monkey of various species belonging to the family Callithricidae, called squirrel-monkeys from their bushy tails. WH: 14–15C. Old French *marmouset* grotesque image, young boy, of unknown orig.

marmot *n.* any burrowing squirrel-like rodent of the genus *Marmota*, in N America the woodchuck. WH: 17C. French *marmotte*, prob. alt. of Romansch *murmont*, from a word meaning mountain mouse.

marocain *n.* a cloth similar in structure to crêpe de Chine, but made from coarser yarns. WH: early 20C. French from *Maroc* Morocco (MOROCCAN) + -*ain* -AN. Cp. MAROQUIN.

Maronite *n.* a member of a Christian sect whose home is the Lebanon region. WH: 16C. Medieval Latin *Maronita*, from *Maron*, supposed founder of the sect in 5C AD. See also -ITE[1].

maroon[1] *a.* of a brownish-crimson colour. *Also n.* WH: 17C. French *marron* chestnut, from Italian *marrone*, from Medieval Greek *maraon*. Cp. MARRON GLACÉ. The sense detonating device arose in the 19C and refers to the popping of a roast chestnut.

maroon[2] *v.t.* to put ashore and abandon on a desolate island. *Also n.* WH: 17C. French *marron*, from Spanish *cimarrón* runaway slave, from *cima* peak. The literal sense of the Spanish word is a runaway who lives in the mountains. A person abandoned on a desert island lives in similar conditions.

maroquin *n.* morocco leather. WH: 16C. French alt. (prob. based on Spanish *marroquín*) of *Maroc* Morocco (MOROCCAN) + -*in* -INE. Cp. MAROCAIN.

marque[1] *n.* a brand, esp. a make of motor car as distinct from a specific model of car. WH: early 20C. French, back-formation from *marquer* to mark, to brand, alt. of Old French *merchier*, from *merc* limit, of Scandinavian orig. Rel. to MARK[1].

marque[2] *n.* reprisals. WH: 14–15C. French, from Provençal *marca*, from *marcar* to seize as a pledge, ? ult. from Germanic base of MARK[1].

marquee *n.* a large tent used for social or commercial purposes. WH: 17C. From *marquise* (MARQUIS), taken as a pl. and assim. to -EE. A large tent would be suitable for a noble lady.

marquess *n.* a title or rank of nobility in England, ranking next below a duke and above an earl. WH: 14–15C. Var. of MARQUIS.

marquetry *n.* work inlaid with different pieces of fine wood, ivory, plates of metal, steel etc. WH: 16C. French *marquetrie*, from *marqueter* to variegate. See MARQUE[1], also -ERY.

marquis *n.* a foreign title or rank of nobility between a duke and a count. WH: 12–14C. Old French *marchis* (later *marquis*), from base of MARCH[2].

marram *n.* a seaside grass, *Ammophila arenaria*, frequently used to stabilize sand dunes. WH: 17C. Old Norse *marálmr*, from *marr* sea + *hálmr* HAULM.

marriage *n.* the legal union of a man and a woman. WH: 12–14C. Old French *mariage*, from *marier* MARRY[1]. See also -AGE.

marron glacé *n.* a preserved chestnut coated with sugar. WH: 16C. French, lit. iced chestnut, from *marron* chestnut (see MAROON[1]) + GLACÉ.

marrow[1] *n.* a large edible gourd with white flesh from the plant *Cucurbita pepo*. WH: pre-1200. Old English *mærh*, from Germanic. The original sense was fatty substance in the cavities of the bones, regarded as providing rich and nutritious food. The application to the vegetable (properly, *vegetable marrow*) evolved in the 19C. Its flesh is a plant's equivalent of bone marrow.

†marrow[2] *n.* a match, a mate, a partner. WH: 14–15C. Prob. from Old Norse *margr* many, i.e. friendly, sociable.

marry[1] *v.t.* to take as one's husband or wife. *Also v.i.* WH: 12–14C. Old French *marier*, from Latin *maritare*, from *maritus* married, husband, prob. from Indo-European.

†marry[2] *int.* indeed, forsooth. WH: 16C. Alt. of (the Virgin) *Mary*.

Mars *n.* the fourth planet from the sun. WH: 12–14C. Latin *Mars*, *Martis*, Roman god of war.

Marsala *n.* a sweet white fortified dessert wine. WH: 19C. *Marsala*, a town and port on the W coast of Sicily.

Marseillaise *n.* the national anthem of the French Republic. WH: 18C. French, fem. of *Marseillais* of Marseilles, from *Marseille* Marseilles, a city and port in SE France + *-ais* -ESE. The Marseillaise was composed in 1792 on the declaration of war against Austria and first sung in Paris by patriots from Marseilles.

marseille *n.* a stiff and heavy cotton fabric quilted in the loom. WH: 18C. French *Marseille* Marseilles (MARSEILLAISE).

marsh *n.* a tract of low land covered wholly or partially with water. WH: pre-1200. Old English *mersc*, from Germanic base also of Latin *mariscus*. Cp. MARISH.

marshal *n.* an officer regulating ceremonies and directing processions, races etc. *Also v.t., v.i.* WH: 12–14C. Old French *mareschal* (Modern French *maréchal*), from Frankish Latin *mariscalcus*, from Germanic, from two words meaning horse (represented by MARE[1]) and servant (represented by Old English *scealc*). The original sense (to the 18C) was person who tends horses, smith. Various titles and ranks have evolved since then. Cp. CONSTABLE.

marsipobranch *n.* a vertebrate with sacciform gills, a cyclostome. WH: 19C. Modern Latin *Marsipobranchii*, from Greek *marsipos* (MARSUPIAL) + *bragkhia* gills.

marsupial *n.* any individual of the order Marsupialia, mammals carrying the young in a pouch, such as the kangaroos and opossums. *Also a.* WH: 17C. Modern Latin *marsupialis*, from Latin *marsupium*, from Greek *marsupion*, dim. of *marsipos* purse.

mart *n.* a trade centre, market, market place etc. WH: 12–14C. Obs. Dutch, var. of *markt* MARKET.

martagon *n.* the Turk's-cap lily, *Lilium martagon*. WH: 15C. French, from Ottoman Turkish *martagān* form of turban worn by Sultan Mehmed I, d.1421.

Martello *n.* a circular, isolated tower of masonry, erected on the coast to oppose the landing of invaders. WH: 19C. Alt. (by assoc. with Italian *martello* hammer) of Cape *Mortella*, Corsica, where such a tower proved difficult for the English to capture in 1794.

marten *n.* a small carnivorous mammal, of the genus *Martes*, allied to the weasel, with a valuable fur. WH: 12–14C. Middle Dutch *martren*, from Old French *martrine*, use as n. of *martrin*, from *martre*, from Germanic base of Old English *mearth*, Old Norse *morthr* marten. The original sense was the fur of the marten. The word was then applied to the animal itself.

martensite *n.* a constituent of steel that has been rapidly cooled, a solid solution of carbon in iron. WH: 19C. Adolf *Martens*, 1850–1914, German metallurgist + *-ITE*[1].

martial *a.* of or suited to war. WH: 14–15C. Old French, or from Latin *martialis*, from *Mars, Martis* MARS. See also *-AL*[1], *-IAL*.

Martian *n.* a supposed inhabitant of the planet Mars. *Also a.* WH: 14–15C. Old French *martien* or Latin *Martianus*, from MARS, *Martis*. See also *-IAN*.

martin *n.* any swallow of the family Hirundinidae, esp. the house martin or sand martin. WH: 14–15C. *Martin*, male forename, prob. from St *Martin* of Tours. The bird migrates at about the time of MARTINMAS, 11 November.

martinet *n.* a strict disciplinarian. WH: 17C. Appar. from Colonel Jean *Martinet*, 17C French drillmaster notorious for his strictness.

martingale *n.* a strap or straps fastened to a horse's girth to keep the head down. WH: 16C. French, in *chausse à la martingale* kind of hose fastening at the back, ? from Provençal *martelago*, fem. of *martegal* inhabitant of Martigues in Provence. According to some, the word is from Spanish *almartaga* check, rein, from Arabic *rāta'* to shackle, to fetter.

Martini® *n.* a type of Italian vermouth. WH: 19C. *Martini* and Rossi, Italian firm selling vermouth. The name of the cocktail may have a different origin.

Martinmas *n.* the feast of St Martin, 11 November. WH: 12–14C. St *Martin*, 4C bishop of Tours and patron saint of France + MASS.

martlet *n.* a swallow-like bird without feet. WH: 14–15C. French *martelet*, alt. of *martinet* MARTIN, dim. of male forename *Martin*. See also *-ET*[1].

martyr *n.* a person who suffers death or persecution in defence of their faith or principles, esp. one of the early Christians who suffered death for their religion. *Also v.t.* WH: pre-1200. Old English *martir*, from Ecclesiastical Latin *martyr*, from Greek *martur*, prob. rel. to *mermēra* care, trouble. Cp. MEMORY.

marvel *n.* a wonderful or astonishing thing. *Also v.i.* WH: 12–14C. Old French *merveille*, from use as sing. n. of Latin *mirabilia*, neut. pl. of *mirabilis* wonderful, from *mirari* to wonder at.

Marxism *n.* the theory that human and political motives are at root economic, and that class struggle explains the events of history and will inevitably lead to the overthrow of capitalism. WH: 19C. Karl *Marx*, 1818–83, German political theorist + *-ISM*.

marzipan *n.* a confection of ground almonds, sugar and white of egg. *Also v.t.* WH: 15C. German, earlier *marcipan*, alt. (as if Latin *Marci panis* Mark's bread) of *marczapan*, from Italian *marzapone* sweet box. The word was formerly thought to derive from Arabic *mauṭabān* seated king, the name of a coin bearing the image of a seated Christ. This was then said to have given the name of a weight or capacity, and to have been transferred to a small box of such a capacity, and so to the sweetmeats it contained.

Masai *n.* a member of a mainly Hamitic people inhabiting Kenya and Tanzania. *Also a.* WH: 19C. *Masai*.

masala *n.* any of several spice mixtures used in Indian cookery. WH: 18C. Urdu *maṣālaḥ*, from Persian and Urdu *masālih*, from Arabic *maṣāliḥ*.

mascara *n.* a dark cosmetic for eyelashes. WH: 19C. Italian *mascara*, *maschera* MASK.

mascarpone *n.* a soft mild cream cheese made in Italy. WH: mid-20C. Italian, earlier *mascarpa* a type of ricotta + *-one* -OON. According to some, the derivation may be in Latin *manuscarpere* to take in the hand, to masturbate, as an analogy with the S Italian phrase *far ricotta* to masturbate, literally to make ricotta.

mascle *n.* a lozenge with a lozenge-shaped hole in the middle. WH: 12–14C. Anglo-French, from Anglo-Latin *mascula*, alt. of Latin *macula* MAIL[2] by assoc. with MASK. The original meaning (to the 17C) was mesh of a net.

mascon *n.* any of the concentrations of dense material just beneath the moon's surface. WH: mid-20C. Abbr. of *mass concentration*.

mascot *n.* an object or person that acts as a talisman and is thought to bring luck. WH: 19C. French *mascotte*, from Provençal *mascotto*, fem. of *mascot*, dim. of *masco* witch. See also *-OT*[1]. The word was popularized by the French composer Edmond Audran's opera *La Mascotte* (1880), in which a goose girl is sent as a good luck mascot to a farmer.

masculine *a.* belonging to or having the characteristic qualities of the male sex. *Also n.* WH: 12–14C. Old French *masculin*, from Latin *masculinus*, from *masculus* MALE. See also *-INE*.

maser *n.* a device similar to a laser used for amplifying microwave radiation. WH: mid-20C. Acronym of *microwave amplification by stimulated emission of radiation*. Cp. LASER.

MASH *abbr.* mobile army surgical hospital. WH: Acronym of *mobile army surgical hospital*, prob. (blackly) punning on MASH[1].

mash[1] *n.* a mass of ingredients crushed and mixed into a pulp. *Also v.t., v.i.* WH: pre-1200. Old English *māsc*, from Germanic, prob. ult. rel. to Old English *miscian* to mix. Cp. MUSH[1].

†mash[2] *v.t.* to ogle, to flirt with. *Also n.* WH: 19C. Back-formation from *masher*, orig. (15C) person who mashes or mixes wine, from MASH[1].

mashie *n.* in golf, an iron club with a deep short blade for lofted shots, a number five iron. WH: 19C. Orig. uncertain. ? From French *massue* club.

masjid *n.* a mosque. WH: 19C. Arabic. See MOSQUE.

mask *n.* a covering for the face, for protection or to conceal one's identity. *Also v.t., v.i.* WH: 16C. French *masque*, from Italian *maschera*, ? from Arabic *maskara* buffoon, from *saḳira* to ridicule.

maslin *n.* a mixture of grain, esp. wheat and rye. *Also a.* WH: 12–14C. Old French *mesteillon*, from Latin *mistus*, p.p. of *miscere* MIX.

masochism *n.* a variety of sexual perversion in which a person takes delight in being dominated or cruelly maltreated by another. WH: 19C. Leopold von Sacher-*Masoch*, 1835–95, Austrian novelist, who described the practice + *-ISM*.

mason *n.* a craftsman who works in stone. *Also v.t.* WH: 12–14C. Old French *masson* (Modern French *maçon*), prob. from Germanic, ? rel. to MATTOCK. Cp. German *Steinmetz* stonemason.

Mason–Dixon line *n.* the boundary drawn between Pennsylvania and Maryland, regarded as the dividing line between the Northern states and the Southern slave states prior to the American Civil War. WH: 18C. Charles *Mason*, 1730–87, and Jeremiah *Dixon*, d.1777, English astronomers, who surveyed the line in 1763–67.

Masorah *n.* a mass of traditional information and illustrative matter on the text of the Hebrew Bible, compiled before the 10th cent. WH: 17C. Hebrew, var. of *māsōreṭ* bond, from 'ā*sar* to bind, but later interpreted as meaning tradition, as if from *māsar* to hand down. The biblical ref. is to Ezek. xx.37: 'I will bring you into the bond of the covenant'.

masque *n.* a play or dramatic entertainment, usu. presented by amateurs at court or in noblemen's houses, the performers wearing masks, orig. in dumb show, later with dialogue, poetical and musical accompaniments. WH: 16C. French *masque*. See MASK. The word was originally the same as MASK, but was retained in its French form to denote the play or entertainment presented in noblemen's houses.

masquerade *n.* a ball or assembly at which people wear masks. *Also v.i.* WH: 16C. French *mascarade*, from Italian *mascherata*, from *maschera* MASK. See also -ADE.

Mass *n.* (the celebration of) the Eucharist, esp. in the Roman Catholic Church. WH: pre-1200. Old English *mæsse*, from Ecclesiastical Latin *missa*, verbal n. from *missus*, p.p. of *mittere* to send (away), ? from the formula at the end of the service, *Ite missa est* Go, you are dismissed. Not rel. to MASS.

mass *n.* a body of matter formed into a coherent whole of indefinite shape. *Also v.t., v.i., a.* WH: 14–15C. Old French *masse*, from Latin *massa*, from Greek *maza* barley cake, ? rel. to *massein* to knead.

massacre *n.* indiscriminate slaughter, wholesale murder. *Also v.t.* WH: 16C. Old French shambles, butchery, of unknown orig.

massage *n.* treatment by rubbing or kneading the muscles and body, usu. with the hands. *Also v.t.* WH: 19C. French, from *masser* to apply massage to, ? from Portuguese *amassar* to knead.

massé *n.* in billiards, a stroke with the cue held almost vertically. WH: 19C. French, p.p. of *masser* to play a massé stroke, from *masse* MACE[1].

masseter *n.* either of the two muscles which raise the lower jaw. WH: 16C. Greek *masētēr*, from *masasthai* to chew.

massicot *n.* yellow lead monoxide, used as a pigment. WH: 15C. French, appar. rel. to Italian *marzacotto* unguent, Spanish *mazacote* kali, mortar, prob. ult. from Arabic.

massif *n.* the main or central mass of a mountain or range. WH: 16C. French, use as n. of a. *massif* MASSIVE.

massive *a.* heavy, bulky. WH: 14–15C. French *massif*, alt. of Old French *massiz* solid and weighty, from Popular Latin, from Latin *massa* MASS.

mast[1] *n.* a long pole of timber, or a metal tube, placed upright in a ship to support the yards, sails etc. WH: pre-1200. Old English *mæst*, from Germanic, from Indo-European source prob. also of Latin *malus* mast.

mast[2] *n.* the fruit of the oak, beech or other forest trees. WH: pre-1200. Old English *mæst*, from Germanic, prob. from base of MEAT.

mastaba *n.* an ancient Egyptian tomb or chapel covering a sepulchral pit, used for the deposit of offerings. WH: 17C. Arabic *maṣṭaba*.

mastectomy *n.* surgical removal of the breast. WH: early 20C. Greek *mastos* breast + -ECTOMY.

master *n.* a person thoroughly acquainted with or skilled in an art, craft etc. *Also a., v.t.* WH: pre-1200. Old English *mægister*, a Germanic adoption from Latin *magister*, from *magis* more, comp. of *magnus* great. Latin *magister* originally meant a more important person by contrast with MINISTER, a less important person.

mastic *n.* a putty-like preparation used for bedding window frames etc. in buildings. WH: 14–15C. Old French, from Late Latin *mastichum*, var. of *mastiche*, from Greek *mastikhē*, prob. from *mastikhan*. See MASTICATE.

masticate *v.t.* to grind and crush with the jaw, to chew. WH: Late Latin *masticatus*, p.p of *masticare*, from Greek *mastikhan* to grind the teeth, rel. to *masathai* to chew. See also -ATE[3].

mastiff *n.* a breed of large dog of great strength and courage, characterized by drooping ears, often used as a watchdog. WH: 12–14C. Old French *mastin* (Modern French *mâtin*), from Latin *mansuetus* tamed, tame. See MANSUETE. The ending of *mastiff* was influenced by Old French *mestif* mongrel, from Late Latin *misticius* mingled, from Latin *mixtus*, past particple of *miscere* MIX.

mastitis *n.* inflammation of the breast or udder. WH: 19C. Greek *mastos* breast + -ITIS.

mastodon *n.* an extinct mammal of the genus *Mammut*, closely allied to the elephant. WH: 19C. Greek *mastos* breast + *odōn, odontos* tooth. The mammal is so named for the nipple-like projections on its teeth. The word was introduced in 1806 by the French zoologist Georges Cuvier.

mastodynia *n.* pain in the breast. WH: 19C. Greek *mastos* breast + *odunē* pain.

mastoid *n.* a conical prominence of bone behind the ear. *Also a.* WH: 18C. French *mastoïde* or Modern Latin *mastoides*, from Greek *mastoeidēs*, from *mastos* breast. See also -OID. The bone is so named from its shape.

masturbate *v.i.* to excite one's genitals, usu. with the hand, to obtain sexual pleasure. *Also v.t.* WH: 19C. Latin *masturbatus*, p.p. of *masturbari*, of unknown orig. See also -ATE[3]. According to some, the word is an altered form of Latin **manstuprare*, from *manus* hand + *stuprare* to defile, influenced by *turbare* to stir up.

mat[1] *n.* a piece of coarse fabric of fibre, rushes, hemp, wire etc. or of perforated rubber etc., used as a carpet, to wipe shoes on, for packing etc. *Also v.t., v.i.* WH: pre-1200. Old English *matt*, from Germanic, from Late Latin *matta*, prob. from Phoenician. Cp. Hebrew *mittāh* bed, couch.

mat[2] *n.* a matrix, a mould. WH: early 20C. Abbr. of MATRIX.

matador *n.* in Spanish bullfights, the person who has to kill the bull. WH: 17C. Spanish, from *matar* to kill.

Mata Hari *n.* a beautiful female spy. WH: mid-20C. *Mata Hari*, name taken by Margaretha Geertruida Zelle, 1876–1917, Dutch courtesan and spy, from Malay *matahari* sun, from *mata* eye + *hari* day. It may not be a coincidence that the name *Margaretha* (*Margaret*) has the French equivalent *Marguerite* which gave MARGUERITE as the word for a daisy, and that this flower's English name literally means day's eye (DAISY), the exact equivalent of Malay *matahari*.

match[1] *n.* a person or thing, equal, like, or corresponding to another. *Also v.t., v.i.* WH: pre-1200. Old English *gemæcca*, from Germanic, rel. to base of *gemaca* MAKE[2].

match[2] *n.* a small strip of wood or taper tipped with combustible material for producing or communicating fire. WH: 14–15C. Old French *meiche* (Modern French *mèche*), from Popular Latin *micca*, alt. (influ. by *muccus* MUCUS) of Latin *myxa*, from Greek *muxa* lamp wick. The original meaning (to the 17C) was candle wick, lamp wick, then a wick used to light a trail of gunpowder. The current meaning dates from the 19C.

mate[1] *n.* a companion, an equal. *Also v.t., v.i.* WH: 12–14C. Middle Low German, from Germanic bases of Y- (denoting association), MEAT. The literal sense of the word is messmate, one who eats with another. Cp. COMPANION[1].

mate[2] *v.t.* to checkmate. *Also a., n.* WH: 12–14C. Old French *mat* mated at chess, from Persian *māt* in phr. *šāh māt*. See CHECKMATE.

maté *n.* an infusion of the leaves of *Ilex paraguayensis*, a Brazilian holly. WH: 18C. Spanish *mate*, from Quechua *mati*.

matelassé *a.* having a raised pattern as in quilting. *Also n.* WH: 19C. French, p.p of *matelasser* to quilt, from *matelas* MATTRESS.

matelot *n.* a sailor. WH: early 20C. French sailor, from Middle Dutch *mattenoot*, lit. bed companion, from *matte* MAT[1], bed + *noot* companion.

matelote *n.* a dish of fish with wine, onions etc. WH: 18C. French, from *matelot* sailor. See MATELOT.

mater *n.* a mother (see also DURA MATER, PIA MATER). WH: 19C. Latin mother.

materfamilias *n.* the mother of a family, the female head of a household. WH: 18C. Latin, from MATER + *familias*, old gen. of *familia* FAMILY.

material *n.* the substance or matter from which anything is made. *Also a.* WH: 12–14C. Old French *matérial*, from Late Latin *materialis*, from Latin *materia* matter. See also -AL[1].

materia medica *n.* the different substances employed in medicine. WH: 17C. Modern Latin, translating Greek *hulē iatrikē* healing material.

materiel *n.* the material, supplies, machinery or instruments, as distinct from the personnel, employed in an art, business, military or naval activity etc. WH: 19C. French *matériel*, use as n. of a. See MATERIAL.

maternal *a.* motherly. WH: 15C. Old French *maternel* or Latin *maternus*, from *mater* MOTHER[1]. See also -AL[1].

math *n.* mathematics. WH: 19C. Abbr. of MATHEMATICS. Cp. MATHS.

mathematical *a.* of or relating to mathematics. WH: 14–15C. Old French *mathématique* or Latin *mathematicus*, from Greek *mathēmatikos*, from *mathēmat-* something learned, science, from base of *manthanein* to learn. See also -IC, -AL[1].

mathematics *n.* the science of quantity or magnitude as expressed by numbers. WH: 16C. Pl. of *mathematic* (MATHEMATICAL), prob. based on French *mathématiques*, representing Latin *mathematica* (neut. pl.), Greek *mathēmatika*. See also -ICS.

maths *n.* mathematics. WH: early 20C. Abbr. of MATHEMATICS.

Matilda *n.* a bushman's bag of belongings, a swag. WH: 19C. *Matilda*, female forename. The reason for the adoption of this particular name is unknown.

matinal *a.* of, relating to or occurring in the morning. WH: 19C. Old French, from *matin* morning. See also -AL[1].

matinée *n.* an afternoon performance of a play, film etc. WH: 19C. French morning, that which occupies a morning, from *matin* morning. Cp. SOIRÉE.

matins *n.pl.* the daily office of morning prayer in the Anglican Church. WH: 12–14C. Old French *matines*, pl. of *matin* morning, from Ecclesiastical Latin *matutinas*, fem. acc. pl. (used as n.) of *matutinus* MATUTINAL.

matrass *n.* a round or oval glass vessel with a long neck, used for distilling etc. WH: 17C. French *matras*, ? from Old French *materas* quarrel, bolt for a crossbow (alluding to its shape), influ. by Arabic *maṭra* leather bottle, or ult. from Greek *metrētēs* a liquid measure.

matri- *comb. form* mother. WH: Latin *mater, matris* MOTHER[1] + -*i-*.

matriarch *n.* the female head of a family, tribe etc. WH: 17C. MATRI- + -*arch* from PATRIARCH. The analogy is false, since *patri-* in PATRIARCH does not come from Latin *pater, patris* father.

matric *n.* matriculation. WH: 19C. Abbr. of *matriculation* (MATRICULATE[1]).

matricide *n.* the murder of one's mother. WH: 16C. Latin *matricidium, matricida*, from *mater, matris* mother. See -CIDE.

matriculate[1] *v.i.* to be admitted as a member or student at a university, college etc. *Also v.t.* WH: 16C. Medieval Latin *matriculatus*, p.p. of *matriculare*, from Late Latin *matricula*, dim. of Latin MATRIX. See also -ATE[3].

matriculate[2] *a.* matriculated. *Also n.* WH: 15C. Medieval Latin *matriculatus*, p.p. of *matriculare*. See MATRICULATE[1], also -ATE[2].

matrilineal *a.* of, relating to, or based on succession through the mother. WH: early 20C. MATRI- + LINEAL.

matrilocal *a.* of or relating to a pattern in marriage in which the man moves to live in the woman's community. WH: early 20C. MATRI- + LOCAL.

matrimony *n.* the act of marrying. WH: 12–14C. Old French *matremoine*, from Latin *matrimonium*, from *mater, matris* MOTHER[1]. See also -MONY.

matrix *n.* a mould in which anything is cast or shaped. WH: 14–15C. Latin breeding animal, register, womb, from *mater, matris* MOTHER[1]. See also -TRIX.

matron *n.* a married woman, esp. an elderly one. WH: 14–15C. Old French *matrone*, from Latin *matrona*, from *mater, matris* MOTHER[1]. The original sense was married woman. The sense woman in charge of nurses in a hospital or domestic arrangements of a school dates from the 16C.

matt *a.* dull, lustreless, not glossy. *Also n., v.t.* WH: 17C. French *mat*, ? rel. to Old French *mat* MATE[2].

mattamore *n.* an underground storage place for grain. WH: 17C. French *matamore*, from Arabic *maṭmūra*, from *ṭamara* to put underground, to bury.

matte[1] *n.* an impure metallic product containing sulphur, from the smelting of ore, esp. copper. WH: 19C. French, use as n. of fem. of *mat* MATT.

matte[2] *n.* in film-making etc., a mask used to obscure part of an image to allow the superimposition of another image. WH: 19C. MATTE[1].

matter *n.* that which constitutes the substance of physical things, as distinguished from thought, mind, spirit etc. *Also v.i.* WH: 12–14C. Old French *matière*, from Latin *materia* timber, stuff of which something is made, subject of discourse, from *mater, matris* MOTHER[1].

mattock *n.* a kind of pick with one broad adze-edged end, for loosening ground, severing roots etc. WH: pre-1200. Orig. unknown. See also -OCK.

mattoid *a.* semi-insane. *Also n.* WH: 19C. Italian *mattoide*, from *matto* insane. See also -OID.

mattress *n.* a case, usu. of padding, springs etc., used for the bottom of a bed. WH: 12–14C. Old French *materas* (Modern French *matelas*), rel. to (or from) Italian *materasso*, ult. from Arabic (*al-*) *maṭraḥ* (the) carpet, cushion, seat, bed, lit. thing thrown down, from *ṭaraḥa* to throw.

maturate *v.t.* to bring to maturity. *Also v.i.* WH: 16C. Latin *maturatus*, p.p. of *maturare*. See MATURE, also -ATE[3].

maturation *n.* the attainment of maturity or ripeness, the completion of growth. WH: 14–15C. Old French, or from Medieval Latin *maturatio, maturationis*, from Latin *maturatus*. See MATURATE, also -ATION.

mature *a.* ripe, ripened. *Also v.t., v.i.* WH: 14–15C. Latin *maturus* ripe, timely, early, ? rel. to *mane* early, in the morning. Cp. MATUTINAL.

matutinal *a.* of, relating to or occurring in the morning. WH: 16C. Late Latin *matutinalis*, from Latin *matutinus*, from *Matuta* goddess of the dawn, rel. to *maturus* MATURE. See also -AL[1].

matzo *n.* (a thin wafer of) unleavened bread, eaten esp. at the Passover. WH: 19C. Yiddish *matse*, from Hebrew *maṣṣāh*.

maud *n.* a grey-striped plaid worn by shepherds etc., or used as a travelling rug. WH: 18C. Orig. unknown.

maudlin *a.* characterized by sickly sentimentality. *Also n.* WH: 12–14C. Old French *Madeleine*, from Ecclesiastical Latin *Magdalena* (MAGDALEN). The reference is to pictures in which Mary Magdalene is portrayed as a weeping penitent. 'A woman in the city ... stood at his feet behind him weeping, and began to wash his feet with tears' (Luke vii.37–38).

†maugre *prep.* in spite of. WH: 12–14C. Old French *maugré* (Modern French *malgré*), from *mal*, from Latin *malum* bad, evil + *gré* pleasure, from Latin *gratum*, use as n. of neut. of *gratus* pleasing.

maul *v.t.* to handle roughly. *Also n.* WH: 12–14C. Old French *mail*, from Latin MALLEUS. The original meaning (to the 17C) was to strike with a heavy weapon, to knock down. The current sense dates from the 17C. Cp. MALL.

maulstick *n.* a light stick with a round pad at the end used as a rest for the right hand by painters, signwriters etc. WH: 17C. Dutch *maalstok*, from *malen* to paint + *stok* stick.

maund *n.* a measure of weight of western Asia and the Indian subcontinent, varying from place to place. WH: 16C. Arabic *mann*, from Akkadian *mana*.

maunder *v.i.* to grumble, to mutter. *Also v.t.* WH: 17C. ? Freq. of obs. *maund* to beg, ? from Old French *mendier* to beg, from Latin *mendicare*. See MENDICANT, also -ER[5].

Maundy *n.* the ceremony of washing the feet of poor people on the Thursday before Easter, in commemoration of Christ's performing this office for his disciples. WH: 12–14C. Old French *mandé*, from Latin *mandatum* commandment, MANDATE. The reference is to Latin *mandatum novum* a new commandment, in the words 'A new commandment I give unto you, that ye love one another' (John xiii.34) opening the first antiphon sung at the Maundy ceremony.

Mauser® *n.* a variety of German magazine rifle. WH: 19C. Paul von Mauser, 1838–1914, German inventor.

mausoleum *n.* a sepulchral monument of considerable size or architectural pretensions. WH: 14–15C. Latin, from Greek *Mausōleion*, from *Mausōlos* Mausolos, king of Caria, whose magnificent tomb was erected in the 4C BC at Halicarnassus by his queen, Artemisia.

mauvais quart d'heure *n.* a brief unpleasant experience. WH: 18C. French, lit. bad quarter of an hour. The phrase was formerly associated with the time between the arrival of guests and the start of dinner.

mauve *n.* a pale purple colour. *Also a.* WH: 19C. French, from Latin *malva* MALLOW.

maven *n.* an expert, a connoisseur. WH: mid-20C. Hebrew *mēḇīn* understanding.

maverick *n.* an individualist, a determined non-conformer. *Also v.t.* WH: 19C. Samuel A. *Maverick*, 1803–70, Texas engineer, who did not brand his cattle.

mavis *n.* the songthrush. WH: 14–15C. Old French *mauvis*, rel. to MEW[2].

mavourneen *n.* my dear one, darling. WH: 19C. Irish *mo mhuirnín*, from *mo* my + *muirnín*, dim. of *muirn* affection. See also -EEN.

maw *n.* the stomach of lower animals, esp. the fourth stomach of ruminants. WH: pre-1200. Old English *maga*, from Germanic. Cp. German *Magen*.

mawkish *a.* falsely or feebly sentimental. WH: 17C. From obs. *mawk* maggot (from Old Norse *mathkr*) + -ISH[1]. The original sense was inclined to sickness, lacking appetite.

max *n.* maximum. *Also a., adv., v.i.* WH: 19C. Abbr. of MAXIMUM.

maxi *a.* very large, long etc. for its type. *Also n.* WH: mid-20C. Independent adoption of MAXI-.

maxi- *comb. form* very large or long. WH: mid-20C. Abbr. of MAXIMUM. Cp. MINI-.

maxilla *n.* a jaw-bone, esp. the upper jaw in mammals. WH: 14–15C. Latin jaw, dim. of *mala* cheekbone, of unknown orig.

Maxim *n.* an automatic single-barrelled quick-firing machine-gun, invented in 1884. WH: 19C. Sir Hiram S. *Maxim*, 1840–1916, US-born British inventor.

maxim *n.* a general principle of a practical kind. WH: 14–15C. French *maxime* or Medieval Latin *maxima*, use as n. of fem. of *maximus*. See MAXIMUM.

maximal *a.* of the greatest, largest etc. size, rate etc. WH: 19C. MAXIMUM + -AL[1].

maximin *n.* the highest value of a set of minima, esp. of minimum gains in game theory. WH: mid-20C. MAXIMUM + MINIMUM, based on MINIMAX.

maximum *n.* the greatest quantity or degree attainable in any given case. *Also a.* WH: 16C. French, from Modern Latin use as n. of neut. of Latin *maximus*, superl. of *magnus* great.

maxwell *n.* a unit of magnetic flux in the cgs system. WH: 19C. James Clerk *Maxwell*, 1831–79, Scottish physicist.

May *n.* the fifth month of the year. *Also v.i.* WH: pre-1200. Old French *mai*, from Latin *Maius*, pertaining to the Roman earth goddess *Maia*. The Old English name of the month was *thrimilce* (MILCH).

may[1] *v.aux.* expressing possibility, ability, permission, desire, obligation, contingency or uncertainty. WH: pre-1200. Old English *mæg*, from a Germanic v. with basic meaning to have power. Cp. MIGHT.

†may[2] *n.* a maiden, a girl. WH: pre-1200. Old English *mæg*, from Germanic fem. of base of Gothic *magus* boy. Cp. MAIDEN.

Maya *n.* a member of an ancient Indian people of Yucatan, Honduras and other parts of central America. *Also a.* WH: 19C. Spanish, from Maya.

maya *n.* in Hinduism, the world as perceived by the senses, regarded as illusory. WH: 18C. Sanskrit *māyā*, from *mā* to create.

mayday *n.* an international distress signal used by ships and aircraft. WH: early 20C. French *m'aider*, from *venez m'aider* come and help me.

mayhem *n.* a state of disorder or confusion. WH: 15C. Old French *mahaing* MAIM.

mayonnaise *n.* a thick sauce or salad dressing made of egg yolk, vinegar etc. WH: 19C. French, ? fem. of *mahonnais* (a.), from *Mahon*, the capital of Minorca. Mahon was captured in 1756 by the Duc du Richelieu, and his cook is said to have created the sauce in honour of his master's victory.

mayor *n.* the chief officer of a city or borough, or a district council with the same status. WH: 12–14C. Old French *maire*, from Latin MAJOR, used as n. in Late Latin.

mayweed *n.* a wild camomile of Eurasia, often found as a weed. WH: 16C. From obs. *maythe* a kind of mayweed (from Old English *magothe*, of unknown orig.) + WEED.

mazard *n.* a small kind of European black cherry, *Prunus avium*. WH: 16C. Prob. from obs. *mazard* cup, bowl, alt. of MAZER, by assoc. of -er with -ARD.

mazarine *n., a.* (of) a deep rich blue. WH: 17C. ? From Cardinal Jules *Mazarin*, 1602–61, or the Duchesse de *Mazarin*, d.1699.

maze *n.* a network of paths and hedges etc. designed as a puzzle. *Also v.t., v.i.* WH: 12–14C. Shortening of AMAZE.

mazer *n.* a large cup or drinking vessel, orig. made of maple wood. WH: 12–14C. Old French *masere*, of Germanic orig., ? influ. by Middle Dutch *maeser* maple.

mazuma *n.* money, cash. WH: early 20C. Yiddish, from Hebrew *mēzummān*, from *zimmēn* to prepare.

mazurka *n.* a lively Polish dance like the polka. WH: 19C. French, or from German *Masurka*, from Polish *mazurka* woman from (the province of) Mazovia.

MB *abbr.* Bachelor of Medicine. WH: Abbr. of Latin *Medicinae Baccalaureus* Bachelor of Medicine.

MC *n.* the lead vocalist in a rap-music group. WH: Abbr. of *Master of Ceremonies*.

McCarthyism *n.* the hunting down of suspected Communists and their dismissal from public employment. WH: mid-20C. Joseph R. *McCarthy*, 1908–57, US senator + -ISM.

McCoy *n.* used only in the phrase *the real McCoy*. WH: 19C. Orig. unknown. Said to be alt. of *McKay* or *MacKay* in Scottish phr. *the real McKay* (*Mackay*). Among derivations proposed are: (1) from *Mackay*, a Scotch whisky distilled by A. and M. Mackay of Glasgow; (2) from Kid *McCoy*, a former welterweight boxing champion (1898–1900); (3) from a northern branch of the Scots clan *MacKay*, whose chief, Lord Reay, was nicknamed *the Reay MacKay* (later the *real MacKay*) for distinction from other Mackay branches.

M.Ch. *abbr.* Master of Surgery. WH: Abbr. of Latin *Magister Chirurgiae* Master of Surgery.

McNaughten rules *n.pl.* rules governing the degree of criminal responsibility of a mentally disturbed defendant. WH: 19C. Daniel *M'Naghten*, acquitted of murder in 1843. The rules arose from the consideration of his case by the House of Lords.

me[1] *pron.* objective (accusative and dative) of I. WH: pre-1200. Old English *mē*, from Germanic, from Indo-European. Cp. German *mich* (acc.), *mir* (dat.), Latin *me* (acc.), *mihi* (dat.).

me[2] *n.* the third note of a major scale in the tonic sol-fa system of notation. WH: 14–15C. Latin *mira*. See UT.

mea culpa *int.* used to acknowledge responsibility for a mistake. *Also n.* WH: 14–15C. Latin, lit. (through) my fault. The words come from the prayer of confession in the Latin liturgy of the Church, more fully: *Mea culpa, mea culpa, mea maxima culpa* Through my fault, through my fault, through my most grievous fault.

mead[1] *n.* a fermented liquor made from honey, water and spices. WH: pre-1200. Old English *medu*, from Germanic, from Indo-European base also of Greek *methu* wine, Sanskrit *madhu* honey. Cp. German *Med*.

mead[2] *n.* a meadow. WH: pre-1200. Old English *mǣd*. See MEADOW.

meadow *n.* a tract of land under grass, esp. if grown for hay. WH: pre-1200. Old English *mǣdwe* (etc.), oblique case of *mǣd*, from Germanic, from base also of MOW[1].

meagre *a.* thin, lacking flesh. *Also v.t.* WH: 12–14C. Old French *maigre*, from Latin *macer*, *macris*, rel. to Greek *makros* long, *makethnos* tall, slender. Cp. MAIGRE.

meal[1] *n.* food taken at one of the customary times of eating. *Also v.i.* WH: pre-1200. Old English *mǣl* appointed time, mealtime, meal, from Germanic, from Indo-European base meaning to measure. Cp. German *Mal* time, *Mahl* meal.

meal[2] *n.* the edible portion of grain or pulse ground into flour. WH: pre-1200. Old English *melu*, from Germanic, from Indo-European base also of Latin *molere* to grind. Not rel. to MEAL[1].

mealie *n.* maize. WH: 19C. Afrikaans *mielie*, from Portuguese *milho* maize, millet, from Latin *milium*. Not rel. to MEAL[2].

mean[1] *v.t.* to intend, to have in mind. *Also v.i.* WH: pre-1200. Old English *mǣnan*, from Germanic, from Indo-European base of MIND. Cp. German *meinen* to have an opinion.

mean² *a.* occupying a middle position. *Also n.* WH: 12–14C. Old French *meien* (Modern French *moyen*), from Latin *medianus* MEDIAN.

mean³ *a.* low in quality, rank etc. WH: pre-1200. Old English *gemǽne*, from Germanic, from *ge-* Y- + base represented also by a form of Latin *communis* COMMON. Cp. German *gemein*.

meander *v.i.* to wind or flow in a tortuous course. *Also n.* WH: 16C. French *méandre*, from Latin *maeander*, from Greek *maiandros*, from *Maiandros*, the name of a winding river in SW Asia Minor.

means *n.pl.* that by which anything is done or a result attained. WH: 12–14C. Partly from MEAN², partly from Old French *meien*, use as n. of a. See MEAN². The plural form came into general use in the current sense in the 16C.

measles *n.pl.* a contagious viral disease, indicated by red spots on the skin, usu. attacking children. WH: 12–14C. Prob. from Middle Low German *masele*, or from Middle Dutch *masel* pustule, spot on the skin, from Germanic. The plural form has been in use from the first because there are many spots.

measure *n.* the extent or dimensions of a thing as determined by measuring. *Also v.t., v.i.* WH: 12–14C. Old French *mesure*, from Latin *mensura*, from *mensus*, p.p. of *metiri* to measure. See also -URE.

meat *n.* the flesh of animals, usu. excluding fish and fowl, used as food. WH: pre-1200. Old English *mete*, from Germanic, from base of METE¹. The original sense was food in general. The sense flesh of animals as food arose in the 12–14C.

meatus *n.* a passage, channel or tubular canal. WH: 14–15C. Latin, lit. passage, course, from *meare* to go, to pass.

Mecca *n.* a place frequently visited. WH: 19C. Arabic *Makka*, birthplace of Muhammad in Saudi Arabia, an important place of pilgrimage for Muslims.

Meccano® *n.* a set of toy engineering parts that can be built up into various mechanical models. WH: early 20C. Invented word based on MECHANICAL.

mechanic *n.* a person who is employed or skilled in repairing or maintaining machines. *Also a.* WH: 14–15C. Old French *mécanique*, from Latin *mechanicus*, from Greek *mēkhanikos*, from *mēkhanikē* MACHINE. See also -IC.

mechanical *a.* of or relating to machinery or mechanisms. *Also n.* WH: 14–15C. MECHANIC. See also -IC, -AL¹.

mechanism *n.* the structure or correlation of parts of a machine. WH: 17C. Modern Latin *mechanismus*, from Greek *mēkhanē* MACHINE. See also -ISM.

mechanize *v.t.* to make mechanical. WH: 17C. MECHANIC + -IZE.

mechano- *comb. form* of or relating to mechanics or machinery. WH: Greek *mēkhano-*, comb. form of *mēkhanē* MACHINE. See also -O-.

mechanoreceptor *n.* a sensory receptor, as in the skin, that responds to mechanical stimuli such as pressure, sound etc. WH: early 20C. MECHANO- + *receptor* (RECEPTION).

mechanotherapy *n.* the treatment of disease through the agency of mechanical appliances. WH: 19C. MECHANO- + *therapy* (THERAPEUTIC).

mechanotropism *n.* the bending of tendrils or other plant organs through reaction to contact or other mechanical stimulus. WH: 19C. MECHANO- + TROPISM.

mechatronics *n.* technology that combines electronics with mechanical engineering in design and manufacture. WH: late 20C. From *mechanics* (MECHANIC) + *electronics* (ELECTRONIC).

Mechlin *n.* a light lace made at Mechlin (Malines), near Brussels. WH: 15C. *Mechlin*, former name of *Mechelen* (Malines), a town in Belgium.

meconic *a.* contained in or derived from the poppy. WH: 19C. Greek *mēkōn* poppy + -IC.

Med *n.* the Mediterranean Sea. WH: mid-20C. Abbr. of MEDITERRANEAN.

medal *n.* a piece of metal, often in the form of a coin, stamped with a figure and inscription to commemorate some illustrious person, event or achievement. WH: 16C. French *médaille*, from Italian *medaglia*, from Popular Latin *medalia* small coin.

meddle *v.i.* to interfere (in) officiously. WH: 12–14C. Old French *medler*, var. of *mesler* (Modern French *mêler*), from Latin *miscere* to mix. The original meaning (to the 17C) was to mix, to mingle, to combine. The current sense dates from the 14–15C.

Mede *n.* a member of an Indo-European people who established an empire in Media, now NW Iran, in the 7th and 6th cents. BC. WH: 14–15C. Latin *Medi* (pl.), from Greek *Mēdoi*.

media¹ *n.pl.* the means of communication with large numbers of people, i.e. radio, TV, Internet, newspapers etc. WH: early 20C. Pl. of MEDIUM.

media² *n.* the middle coat or tunic of a vessel. WH: mid-20C. Latin, fem. of *medius* MID².

medial *a.* of, relating to or situated in the middle, intermediate. *Also n.* WH: 16C. Late Latin *medialis*, from *medius* MID². See also -AL¹.

median *a.* situated in the middle, esp. in the plane dividing the body longitudinally into two equal halves. *Also n.* WH: 14–15C. French (*veine*) *médiane*, or from Medieval Latin *medianus* (in *mediana vena*), from Latin, from *medius* MID². See also -AN. The original meaning was anatomical, referring to the median vein.

mediant *n.* the third tone of any scale. WH: 18C. French *médiante*, from Italian *mediante*, from *mediare* to come between, from Late Latin *mediare* to be in the middle, from *medius* MID².

mediastinum *n.* a membranous septum or cavity between the two main parts of an organ etc., esp. the folds of the pleura between the right and left lung. WH: 14–15C. Neut. of Medieval Latin *mediastinus* medial, from Latin, orig. a low class of slave, from *medius* MID².

mediate¹ *v.t.* to interpose between (parties) in order to reconcile them. *Also v.i.* WH: 16C. Latin *mediatus*, p.p. of *mediare*, from *medius* MID². See also -ATE³. The original meaning (to the 17C) was to divide in two. The current meaning dates from the 17C.

mediate² *a.* situated in the middle or between two extremes. WH: 14–15C. Latin *mediatus*, p.p. of *mediare*. See MEDIATE¹, also -ATE².

mediatize *v.t.* to make dependent. WH: 19C. French *médiatiser*, from *médiat*, from Latin *mediatus*. See MEDIATE², also -IZE.

medic *n.* a medical student. WH: 17C. Latin *medicus*, from *mederi* to heal. See also -IC. Partly also abbr. of MEDICAL.

Medicaid *n.* in the US, government-sponsored health insurance for the needy. WH: mid-20C. MEDICAL + AID. Cp. MEDICARE.

medical *a.* of or relating to medicine. *Also n.* WH: 17C. French *médical* or Medieval Latin *medicalis*, from Latin *medicus* physician, from *mederi* to heal. See also -AL¹.

Medicare *n.* in the US, government-sponsored health insurance for the elderly. WH: mid-20C. MEDICAL + CARE. Cp. MEDICAID.

Medicean *a.* of or relating to the wealthy Medici family. WH: 17C. Modern Latin *Mediceus*, from Italian *Medici*, the family who were rulers of Florence in the 15C + -AN.

medicine *n.* a substance, usu. taken internally, used for the alleviation or removal of disease. *Also v.t.* WH: 12–14C. Old French *medecine* (Modern French *médecine*), from Latin *medicina*, from *medicus*. See MEDIC, also -INE.

medick *n.* any plant of the genus *Medicago*, allied to the clover, esp. *M. sativa*, alfalfa. WH: 14–15C. Latin *medica*, from Greek *Mēdikē* (*poa*), lit. Median (grass).

medico *n.* a physician, a doctor. WH: 17C. Italian, from Latin *medicus* MEDIC.

medico- *comb. form* medical. WH: 17C. Latin *medicus* MEDIC + -O-.

medieval *a.* of or relating to, or characteristic of the Middle Ages. *Also n.* WH: 19C. Modern Latin *medium aevum* middle age + -AL¹.

medina *n.* the ancient Arab quarter of N African cities. WH: early 20C. Arabic, lit. town. The Arabic word gave the name of *Medina*, the second of the two most sacred cities of Islam (cp. MECCA), in W Saudi Arabia.

medio- *comb. form* situated in, of or relating to the middle. WH: 19C. Latin *medius* MID² + -O-.

mediocre *a.* of middling quality. WH: 16C. French *médiocre*, from Latin *mediocris* of middle height, of middle degree, from *medius* MID² + *ocris* rugged mountain.

meditate *v.i.* to engage in contemplation, esp. on religious or spiritual matters. *Also v.t.* WH: 16C. Latin *meditatus*, p.p. of *meditari*, freq. from Indo-European stem meaning to measure. See also -ATE³. Cp. METE¹, MODE.

Mediterranean *a.* denoting, of or relating to the sea between Europe and Africa or the countries surrounding it. *Also n.* WH: 16C.

Latin *mediterraneus* inland, from *medius* MID[2] + *terra* land, earth, in Late Latin used for the name of the Mediterranean Sea, *Mare Mediterraneum*. See also -AN, -EAN.

medium *n.* anything serving as an agent or instrument. *Also a.* WH: 16C. Latin, lit. middle, midst, Medieval Latin means, neut. (used as n.) of *medius* MID[2]. Cp. MEDIA[1].

Medjidie *n.* a Turkish order of knighthood established by Sultan Abdul-Medjid in 1851. WH: 19C. Turkish *mecidiye* silver coins, from Sultan Abdul-*Medjid*, 1823-61.

medlar *n.* a rosaceous tree, *Mespilus germanica*. WH: 14–15C. Old French *medler*, from var. of *mesle*, from Latin *mespila*, from Greek *mespilē*. The ending *-ar* has been influenced by CEDAR, POPLAR.

medley *n.* a musical or literary miscellany. *Also a., v.t.* WH: 12–14C. Old French *medlee*, var. of *meslee* MÊLÉE, from use as n. of fem p.p. of Medieval Latin *misculare* to mix. Cp. MEDDLE. The original sense was mixture rather than miscellany, as now.

Medoc *n.* a red claret wine. WH: 19C. Latin *Médoc*, an area along the left bank of the Gironde estuary, SW France.

medulla *n.* the inner part of certain organs, as the kidneys. WH: 17C. Latin pith, marrow, ? from *medius* MID[2].

medusa *n.* a jellyfish. WH: 14–15C. Latin, from Greek *Medousa*, the only mortal Gorgon of three in Greek mythology, with snakes for hair and a gaze that turned anyone who saw her to stone. Some jellyfish have feelers resembling hair. The Latin genus name was coined by Linnaeus.

meed *n.* reward, recompense, esp. for merit. WH: pre-1200. Old English *mēd*, from Germanic, rel. to Greek *misthos* reward. Cp. German *Miete* rent, hire. The original meaning was something given in return for labour or service.

meek *a.* mild, forbearing. WH: 12–14C. Old Norse *mjúkr* soft, pliant, gentle. Rel. to MUCUS. The original meaning (to the 17C) was courteous, kind, merciful.

meerkat *n.* a small, carnivorous mongoose of southern Africa, esp. the grey meerkat. WH: 15C. Dutch, from Middle Low German *meerkatte*, lit. seacat, prob. orig. alt. of an Oriental name. Cp. Sanskrit *markaṭa* ape.

meerschaum *n.* a white compact hydrous magnesium silicate, used for tobacco pipes. WH: 18C. German, from *Meer* sea (MERE[1]) + *Schaum* foam (SCUM), translating Persian *kef-i-daryā* foam of sea. The reference is to the mineral's lightness and whiteness, evoking froth in the sea or surf.

meet[1] *v.t.* to come face to face with. *Also v.i., n.* WH: pre-1200. Old English *mētan*, from Germanic base also of MOOT.

†meet[2] *a.* fit, proper, suitable. WH: pre-1200. Old English *gemǣte*. See Y-, METE[1]. The original meaning was commensurate.

mega *a.* very large in number. WH: late 20C. Independent adoption of MEGA-.

mega- *comb. form* great, large. WH: Greek comb. form of *megas* great. Cp. MEGALO-.

megabit *n.* one million bits. WH: mid-20C. MEGA- + BIT[3].

megabuck *n.* a million dollars. WH: mid-20C. MEGA- + BUCK[1].

megabyte *n.* one million bytes. WH: late 20C. MEGA- + BYTE.

megacephalic *a.* large-headed. WH: 19C. MEGA + -CEPHALIC.

megadeath *n.* one million deaths, esp. in nuclear war. WH: mid-20C. MEGA- + DEATH.

megaflop *n.* a measure of processing speed equal to one million floating-point operations per second. WH: late 20C. MEGA- + -FLOP.

megahertz *n.* a unit of frequency equal to one million hertz. WH: mid-20C. MEGA- + HERTZ.

megalith *n.* a great stone. WH: 19C. Back-formation from *megalithic*, from MEGA- + LITHIC.

megalo- *comb. form* great. WH: Greek comb. form of *megas*, *megalou* great. See also -O-. Cp. MEGA-.

megalomania *n.* a form of mental disorder characterized by delusions of grandeur or power. WH: 19C. MEGALO- + -MANIA.

megalopolis *n.* a large, densely-populated urban area. WH: 19C. MEGALO- + -POLIS.

megalosaurus *n.* an extinct carnivorous lizard of the genus *Megalosaurus*. WH: 19C. Modern Latin, from MEGALO- + Greek *sauros* lizard. The name was coined in 1824 by the English geologist and clergyman William Buckland in consultation with William D. Conybeare.

Megan's Law *n.* a law requiring that a community be notified of paedophiles and other sex offenders living in the area. WH: late 20C. *Megan* Kanka, a seven-year-old child raped and murdered by a convicted paedophile in New Jersey in 1994; her mother campaigned for the introduction of the law.

megaphone *n.* a hand-held apparatus for amplifying the voice. WH: 19C. MEGA- + -PHONE.

megapode *n.* an Australian or Malaysian bird of the family Megapodiidae, which builds mounds to incubate its eggs in. WH: 19C. Modern Latin *Megapodius* genus name, from MEGA- + -POD. The birds are so called from their unusually large legs and feet.

megaron *n.* the central room of a large Mycenaean house. WH: 19C. Greek, from *megas* great, large.

megaspore *n.* any one of the larger kind of spores in some cryptogams, from which female gametophytes develop. WH: 19C. MEGA- + SPORE.

megass *n.* fibrous residue after sugar has been extracted from the cane, bagasse. WH: 19C. Orig. unknown. Cp. BAGASSE.

megastar *n.* a very popular, internationally-known star of the cinema, theatre etc. WH: late 20C. MEGA- + STAR.

megastore *n.* a large usu. out-of-town store selling many different products. WH: late 20C. MEGA- + STORE.

megathere *n.* an extinct gigantic slothlike edentate of the genus *Megatherium*, from S America. WH: 19C. Modern Latin *Megatherium*, as if from Greek *mega thērion* great animal. See also MEGA-.

megaton *n.* one million tons. WH: mid-20C. MEGA- + TON[1].

megavolt *n.* one million volts. WH: 19C. MEGA- + VOLT[1].

megawatt *n.* one million watts. WH: early 20C. MEGA- + WATT.

Megger® *n.* an instrument for measuring high electrical resistances. WH: early 20C. Orig. uncertain. ? From MEGOHM.

megilp *n.* a mixture of linseed oil and mastic varnish added to oil paints. WH: 18C. Orig. unknown.

megohm *n.* one million ohms. WH: 19C. MEGA- + OHM.

megrim[1] *n.* a migraine. WH: 14–15C. Var. of MIGRAINE.

megrim[2] *n.* either of two deep-water flatfishes *Lepidorhombus whiffiagonis* and *Arnoglossus laterna*, the sail-fluke. WH: 19C. Orig. unknown.

†meinie *n.* a household. WH: 12–14C. Old French *meinée*, from Provençal *mesnada*, from Latin *mansio*, *mansionis* MANSION. See also -Y[2]. Later influ. by MANY.

meiosis *n.* the diminution of the number of chromosomes in the cell nucleus. WH: 16C. Modern Latin, from Greek *meiōsis*, from *meioun* to lessen, from *meiōn* less. See also -OSIS.

Meissen *n.* a type of fine German porcelain. WH: 19C. *Meissen*, a town near Dresden in Germany. Cp. DRESDEN CHINA.

meistersinger *n.* a German burgher poet and musician of the 14th–16th cents., one of the successors of the minnesingers. WH: 19C. German, from *Meister* MASTER + *Singer* singer (SING).

meitnerium *n.* a synthetic element, chemical symbol Mt, atom. no. 109, produced by a heavy-ion accelerator. WH: late 20C. Lise *Meitner*, 1878–1968, Austrian-born Swedish physicist.

melamine *n.* a white crystalline compound used for making synthetic resins. WH: 19C. German *Melam*, of arbitrary foundation + AMINE. The name was coined in 1834 by the German chemist Justus von Liebig.

melan- *comb. form* dark, black. WH: Greek *melas*, *melanos* black. In many scientific terms the origin is MELANIN.

melanaemia *n.* a condition in which the blood contains an excessive proportion of melanin. WH: 19C. MELAN- + -AEMIA.

melancholia *n.* a mental disorder, often preceding mania, characterized by depression, frequently with suicidal tendencies. WH: 17C. Late Latin. See MELANCHOLY.

melancholy *n.* a gloomy, dejected state of mind. *Also a.* WH: 12–14C. Old French *mélancolie*, from Late Latin *melancholia*, from Greek *melankholia*, from *melas*, *melanos* black + *kholē* bile. See also -Y[2]. The condition was originally thought to have been caused by an excess of black bile.

Melanesian *a.* of or relating to Melanesia, the group of islands in the Pacific Ocean lying to the east of New Guinea. *Also n.* WH: 19C. *Melanesia*, an island group in the SW Pacific + -IA, based on *Polynesia* (POLYNESIAN). See also -AN.

mélange *n.* a mixture, medley or miscellany. WH: 17C. French, from *mêler* to mix. Cp. MÊLÉE.

melanin *n.* a black or dark brown pigment occurring in the hair, skin and iris of the eye. WH: 19C. Greek *melas, melanos* black + -IN[1].

melanite *n.* a black variety of garnet. WH: 19C. Greek *melas, melanos* black + -ITE[1]. The term was coined in 1799 by the German geologist Abraham G. Werner.

melanochroi *n.pl.* a postulated subdivision of the Caucasian race comprising those with dark hair and pale complexion. WH: 19C. MELAN- + Greek *ōkhros* pale. The term was coined in 1866 by the English biologist T.H. Huxley. The name has subsequently also been interpreted as if from MELAN- + -O- + Greek *khroa* skin.

melanoma *n.* a malignant tumour with dark pigmentation, esp. on the skin. WH: 19C. MELAN- + -OMA.

melatonin *n.* a hormone produced by the pineal gland. WH: mid-20C. MELAN- + SEROTONIN.

Melba toast *n.* very thin crisp toast. WH: early 20C. Nellie *Melba*, stage name of the Australian opera singer Helen Mitchell, 1861–1931.

meld[1] *v.t., v.i.* in the card games, rummy, canasta etc., to declare (one's cards) for a score. *Also n.* WH: 19C. German *melden* to announce, to declare (at cards).

meld[2] *v.t., v.i.* to mix, blend, combine. WH: mid-20C. ? Blend of MELT + WELD[1].

mêlée *n.* a confused hand-to-hand fight, an affray. WH: 17C. French, from Old French *mellée*, p.p. of *meller*, var. of *mesler* MEDDLE. Cp. MEDLEY.

melic *a.* (esp. of certain Greek lyric poetry) intended to be sung. WH: 17C. Latin *melicus*, from Greek *melikos*, from *melos* song. See also -IC.

melilot *n.* a plant of the leguminous genus *Melilotus*. WH: 14–15C. Old French *mélilot*, from Latin *melilotos*, from Greek *melilōtos*, from *meli* honey + *lōtos* LOTUS.

melinite *n.* a French explosive containing picric acid. WH: 19C. Greek *mēlinos* of (the colour of) quince, from *mēlon* quince, apple. See also -ITE[1]. The name was coined in 1884 by the French chemist Eugène Turpin, the explosive's inventor.

meliorate *v.t.* to make better. *Also v.i.* WH: 16C. Late Latin *melioratus*, p.p. of *meliorare* to improve, from Latin *melior* better. See also -ATE[3].

meliphagous *a.* eating honey. WH: 19C. Greek *meli* honey + *phagos* eater + -OUS.

melisma *n.* a melodic embellishment, consisting of a group of notes sung to a single syllable. WH: 19C. Greek, lit. song.

melliferous *a.* producing or yielding honey. WH: 17C. Latin *mellifer*, from *mel, mellis* honey. See -FEROUS.

mellifluous *a.* flowing smoothly and sweetly (usu. of a voice, words etc.). WH: 14–15C. Old French *melliflue*, or from Late Latin *mellifluus*, from Latin *mel, mellis* honey + *-fluus* flowing, from *fluere* to flow. See also -OUS.

mellophone *n.* a brass musical instrument similar in tone to a French horn. WH: early 20C. MELLOW + -PHONE.

mellow *a.* (of fruit) fully ripe. *Also v.i., v.t.* WH: early 20C. ? Old English *melu* MEAL[2].

melodeon *n.* a small German accordion. WH: 19C. Alt. of *melodium*, from MELODY, based on HARMONIUM.

melodrama *n.* a sensational play, film, novel etc. with a plot characterized by startling situations, crude sentimentality and a happy ending. WH: 19C. Alt. of obs. *melodrame* (from French *mélodrame*, from Greek *melos* song, music + French *drame* DRAMA), based on DRAMA.

melody *n.* an agreeable succession of sounds, esp. of simple tones in the same key. WH: 12–14C. Old French *mélodie*, from Late Latin *melodia*, from Greek *melōidia* singing, choral song, from *melōides* musical, from *melos* song, music + *ōidē* ODE. See also -Y[2]. The word's connotation of 'sweetness' is probably due to its popular association with Latin *mel* honey.

melon *n.* the edible fruit of various plants of the gourd family, usu. large and round with pulpy flesh and many seeds. WH: 14–15C. Old French, from Late Latin *melo, melonis*, contr. of Latin *melopepo*, from Greek *mēlopepōn*, from *mēlon* apple + *pepōn* a kind of gourd.

melt *v.i.* to pass from a solid to a liquid state by heat. *Also v.t., n.* WH: pre-1200. Old English *meltan*, from Germanic base also of MALT, from Indo-European base also of Greek *meldein* to melt, Latin *mollis*, Sanskrit *mṛdu* soft. Cp. MILD, SMELT[1].

melton *n.* a jacket worn in hunting. WH: 19C. *Melton* Mowbray, a town in Leicestershire, central England.

member *n.* a person belonging to a society or body. *Also a.* WH: 12–14C. Old French *membre*, from Latin *membrum* limb.

membrane *n.* a thin sheet of tissue lining or covering parts of an organism. WH: 14–15C. French, from Latin *membrana* skin covering part of the body, use as n. of fem. a. from *membrum* limb, MEMBER.

†**membrum virile** *n.* the penis. WH: 19C. Latin male member. See MEMBER, VIRILE.

memento *n.* a souvenir. WH: 14–15C. Latin remember!, imper. of *meminisse* to remember, with redupl. of base of MIND.

memo *n.* a memorandum. WH: 18C. Abbr. of MEMORANDUM.

memoir *n.* an account of events or transactions in which the narrator took part. WH: 16C. French *mémoire*, from Latin *memoria* MEMORY.

memorabilia *n.pl.* souvenirs of past events, people etc. WH: 18C. Latin, neut. pl. of *memorabilis*. See MEMORABLE, also -IA.

memorable *a.* worthy to be remembered. WH: 14–15C. French *mémorable* or Latin *memorabilis*, from *memorare*. See MEMORANDUM, also -ABLE.

memorandum *n.* a note to help the memory. WH: 14–15C. Latin, neut. sing. of *memorandus*, ger. of *memorare* to bring to mind, from *memor* mindful.

memorial *a.* intended to preserve the memory of a past event, person etc. *Also n.* WH: 14–15C. Old French *mémorial*, from Latin *memorialis* (a.), from *memoria* MEMORY. See also -AL[1]. The original sense as a noun (to the 18C) was remembrance, recollection.

memorize *v.t.* to learn by heart. WH: 16C. MEMORY + -IZE.

memory *n.* the mental faculty that retains and recalls previous ideas and impressions. WH: 12–14C. Old French *memorie* (Modern French *mémoire*), from Latin *memoria*, from *memor* mindful. See also -Y[2].

memsahib *n.* a term of address formerly applied by Indians in speaking to or of European married women living in the Indian subcontinent. WH: 19C. *mem*, var. of MA'AM + SAHIB.

menace *n.* a threat. *Also v.t.* WH: 12–14C. Latin *minacia*, from *minax, minacis* threatening, from base of *minari* to threaten.

ménage *n.* a household. WH: 12–14C. Old French *menaige* (Modern French *ménage*), from Latin *mansio, mansionis*. See MANSION, -AGE.

menagerie *n.* a collection of wild animals. WH: 17C. French *ménagerie*, from *ménage*. See MÉNAGE, also -ERY.

menaquinone *n.* one of the K vitamins, produced by bacteria of the intestine and essential for blood-clotting, vitamin K_2. WH: mid-20C. METHYL + *naphthalene* (NAPHTHA) + QUINONE.

menarche *n.* the first onset of menstruation. WH: early 20C. Greek *mēn* month + *arkhē* beginning. The term was coined in 1895 by the German physiologist E.H. Kisch.

mend *v.t.* to repair, to restore. *Also v.i., n.* WH: 12–14C. Anglo-French *mender*, shortening of *amender* AMEND.

mendacious *a.* given to lying, untruthful. WH: 17C. Latin *mendax, mendacis* lying, deceitful, from *mendum* defect, fault + -OUS.

mendelevium *n.* an artificially-produced transuranic element, at. no. 101, chem. symbol Md. WH: mid-20C. Dmitri Ivanovich *Mendeleev*, 1834–1907, Russian chemist + -IUM. The element was named in 1955 by its discoverers, a team of five US scientists (Albert Ghiorso, Bernard G. Harvey, Gregory R. Choppin, Stanley G. Thompson, Glenn T. Seaborg).

Mendelism *n.* a theory of heredity based on the observation that the characters of the parents of cross-bred offspring reappear by certain proportions in successive generations according to definite laws. WH: early 20C. Gregor Johann *Mendel*, 1822–84, Moravian monk and botanist + -ISM.

mendicant *n.* a beggar. *Also a.* WH: 14–15C. Latin *mendicans, mendicantis*, pres.p. of *mendicare* to beg, from *mendicus* beggar, from *mendum* defect, fault. See also -ANT.

menfolk *n.pl.* the men, esp. of a particular family or community. WH: 19C. *men*, pl. of MAN + FOLK.

menhaden *n.* a N American sea fish of the genus *Brevoortia*, allied to the herring. WH: 18C. Algonquian, ? from a base meaning to fertilize.

menhir *n.* a prehistoric monument consisting of a tall upright stone. WH: 19C. Breton *maen-hir*, from *maen* stone + *hir* long.

menial *a.* servile, degrading. *Also n.* WH: 14–15C. Anglo-French *menial*, from *meinie* MEINIE. See also -AL¹.

meningitis *n.* inflammation of the meninges owing to infection. WH: 19C. Modern Latin, from *mening-* (MENINX) + -ITIS.

meninx *n.* each of the three membranes that envelop the brain and spinal cord. WH: 17C. Modern Latin, from Greek *mēnigx, mēniggos* membrane.

meniscus *n.* the top of a liquid column made convex or concave by capillarity (as mercury in a barometer). WH: 17C. Modern Latin, from Latin *mēniskos* crescent, dim. of *mēnē* moon.

menisperm *n.* any tropical or sub-tropical plant of the family Menispermaceae, most of which are woody climbers. WH: 19C. Modern Latin *Menispermum*, from Greek *mēnē* moon + *sperma* seed. The plant is so named from its crescent-shaped seeds.

Mennonite *n.* a member of a Protestant sect originating in Friesland in the 16th cent., with principles similar to those of the Anabaptists. WH: 16C. *Menno* Simons, 1496–1561, the sect's early leader + -ITE¹.

meno- *comb. form* of or relating to menstruation. WH: Greek *mēn, mēnos* month. See also -O-.

menology *n.* a calendar of months, esp. the martyrology of the Greek Church. WH: 17C. Modern Latin *menologium*, from Ecclesiastical Greek *mēnologion*, from *mēn* month + *logos* (LOGOS) account.

menopause *n.* final cessation of menstruation, the change of life. WH: 19C. MENO- + Greek *pausis* cessation, PAUSE.

menorah *n.* a candelabrum with several branches, used in Jewish worship. WH: 19C. Hebrew *mĕnōrāh* candlestick.

menorrhagia *n.* excessively heavy bleeding at menstruation. WH: 18C. Modern Latin, from MENO- + -RRHAGIA.

menorrhoea *n.* the bleeding at menstruation. WH: 19C. Back-formation from AMENORRHOEA.

mensal¹ *a.* of, relating to or used at the table. WH: 14–15C. Late Latin *mensalis*, from *mensa* table. See also -AL¹.

mensal² *a.* monthly. WH: 15C. Latin *mensis* month + -AL¹.

menses *n.pl.* the flow of blood etc. from the uterus of women at menstruation, the period. WH: 16C. Latin, pl. of *mensis* month.

Menshevik *n.* a member of the moderate party in the Russian Revolution, as distinct from *Bolshevik*. WH: early 20C. Russian *men'shevik* member of the minority, from *men'shiï* less, comp. of *malyĭ* little.

mens rea *n.* criminal intent, the knowledge that an act is wrong. WH: 19C. Latin guilty mind.

menstruum *n.* any fluid that dissolves a solid, a solvent. WH: 14–15C. Latin, use as n. of *menstruus* monthly, from *mensis* month.

mensurable *a.* measurable, having defined limits. WH: 14–15C. French, or from Late Latin *mensurabilis*, from *mensurare*. See MENSURATION, also -ABLE.

mensuration *n.* the act or practice of measuring. WH: 16C. Late Latin *mensuratio, mensurationis*, from *mensuratus*, p.p. of *mensurare*, from Latin *mensura* MEASURE. See also -ATION.

menswear *n.* clothing for men. WH: mid-20C. *men*, pl. of MAN + -'S + WEAR¹. The earlier form was as two words, *men's wear*.

-ment *suf.* forming nouns denoting result, state, action etc., as in *agreement, bereavement, enticement, impediment, ornament*. WH: French, or from Latin *-mentum*.

mental¹ *a.* of or relating to the mind. WH: 14–15C. Old French, from Late Latin *mentalis*, from *mens, mentis* mind. See also -AL¹.

mental² *a.* of or relating to the chin. WH: 18C. French, from Latin *mentum* chin. See also -AL¹.

menthol *n.* a waxy crystalline substance obtained from oil of peppermint, used as a flavouring and as a local anaesthetic for neuralgia etc. WH: 19C. Latin *mentha* MINT² + -OL. The term was coined in 1861 by the German chemist Friedrich Oppenheim.

mention *n.* a concise notice (of), an allusion. *Also v.t.* WH: 12–14C. Old French, from Latin *mentio, mentionis*, from base of *meminisse* to remember, ult. redupl. of base of MIND. See also -ION.

mentor *n.* an experienced adviser. WH: 18C. French, from Latin *Mentor*, from Greek *Mentōr*, the guide and advisor of Telemachus,

son of Odysseus. Mentor himself was probably so named from a Greek base meaning to remember, to think, to advise. Cp. Greek *menos* intent, purpose, spirit.

menu *n.* a list of dishes available at a restaurant etc. WH: 17C. French detailed list, use as n. of *a.* meaning small, from Latin *minutus* MINUTE².

mepacrine *n.* the drug quinacrine. WH: mid-20C. *methoxy-* (from METHYL + OXY-¹) + -*p*- (? from PENTANE) + ACRIDINE.

meperidine *n.* the drug pethidine. WH: mid-20C. METHYL + PIPERIDINE.

Mephistopheles *n.* a tempter. WH: 16C. *Mephistopheles*, the evil spirit to whom Faust sold his soul in German legend. Mephistopheles was widely made known from his representation in Marlowe's play *Doctor Faustus* (*c*.1590) and Goethe's version of this, *Faust* (1808–32). His name has been popularly interpreted as 'hating light', i.e. 'liking dark', from Greek *mē* not + *phōs, phōtos* light + *philos* loving.

mephitis *n.* a foul, offensive or poisonous stench. WH: 18C. Latin, from Oscan.

-mer *comb. form* a substance of a specified type, as in *polymer, elastomer*. WH: Greek *meros* part, based on ISOMER, POLYMER.

meranti *n.* hardwood timber from a tree of the genus *Shorea*, found in Malaysia and Indonesia. WH: 18C. Malay.

mercantile *a.* of or relating to buying and selling. WH: 17C. French, from Italian, from *mercante* MERCHANT.

Mercator projection *n.* a projection of a map of the surface of the earth on to a plane so that the lines of latitude are represented by horizontal lines and the meridians by parallel lines at right angles to them. WH: 17C. Gerhardus *Mercator*, Latinized name of Gerhard Kremer, 1512–94, Flemish cartographer.

mercenary *a.* done from or actuated by motives of gain. *Also n.* WH: 14–15C. Latin *mercenarius*, from *merces, mercedis* reward, wages. See MERCY, also -ARY¹.

mercer *n.* a person who deals in silk, cotton, woollen and linen goods. WH: 12–14C. Old French *mercier*, from Latin *merx, mercis* merchandise. See also -ER².

mercerize *v.t.* to treat (cotton fabrics) with an alkaline solution before dyeing, to impart strength and lustre. WH: 19C. John *Mercer*, 1791–1866, English discoverer of the process (1844) + -IZE.

merchandise *n.* goods for sale and purchase. *Also v.i., v.t.* WH: 12–14C. Old French *marchandise*, from *marchand* MERCHANT. See also -ISE¹.

merchant *n.* a person who carries on trade on a large scale, esp. with foreign countries. *Also a.* WH: 12–14C. Old French *marchant* (Modern French *marchand*), from Popular Latin *mercatans, mercatantis*, pres.p. of *mercatare*, freq. of Latin *mercari* to trade, from *merx, mercis* merchandise. See also -ANT.

Mercury *n.* the planet nearest the sun. WH: 12–14C. Latin *Mercurius*, the Roman god of commerce and the messenger of the gods. Mercury's name derives from Latin *merx, mercis* merchandise.

mercury *n.* a liquid, silvery, toxic, metallic element, at. no. 80, chem. symbol Hg. WH: 14–15C. Medieval Latin *mercurius*, from Latin *Mercurius* MERCURY. The element is so called from its mobility. The god Mercury was famed for his fleetness as a messenger. Cp. *quicksilver* (QUICK, SILVER).

mercy *n.* a disposition to temper justice with mildness. WH: 12–14C. Old French *merci*, from Latin *merces, mercedis* reward, wages. The Latin word was often used in Ecclesiastical Latin in the same sense as Latin *misericordia* (MISERICORD).

†mere¹ *n.* a lake, a pool. WH: pre-1200. Old English, from Germanic, from Indo-European base also of Old Church Slavonic *morje* (Russian *more*), Latin *mare* sea. The original meaning was sea. Cp. *mer-* in MERMAID.

mere² *a.* such and no more. WH: 14–15C. Old French *mier* or Latin *merus* unmixed, pure, bare. The original meaning (to the 19C) was pure, unmixed, undiluted. The current sense dates from the 16C.

mere³ *n.* a boundary. *Also v.t.* WH: pre-1200. Old English *gemǣre*, from Germanic, ? rel. to Latin *murus* wall.

mere⁴ *n.* a short flat Maori war club, esp. one made of greenstone. WH: 19C. Maori.

-mere *comb. form* part, segment, as in *blastomere*. WH: Greek *meros* part.

meretricious *a.* alluring by false or empty show. WH: 17C. Latin *meretricius*, from *meretrix*, *meretricis* prostitute, from *mereri* to serve for hire. See MERIT, also -OUS. The original sense was pertaining to a prostitute. The current sense arose soon after.

merganser *n.* any diving or fish-eating duck belonging to the genus *Mergus*, the sawbill. WH: 17C. Modern Latin, from *mergus* diver + *anser* goose.

merge *v.i.* to be absorbed or swallowed up (with). *Also v.t.* WH: 17C. Latin *mergere* to dip, to plunge.

mericarp *n.* one of the two carpels forming the fruit of umbelliferous plants. WH: 19C. French *méricarpe*, from Greek *meros* part + *karpos* fruit.

meridian *a.* of or relating to midday. *Also n.* WH: 14–15C. Old French *méridien*, or from Latin *meridianus*, from *meridies* midday, south, from *medius* middle + *dies* day. See also -AN.

meringue *n.* a baked confection of white of eggs, sugar etc. WH: 18C. French, of unknown orig.

merino *n.* a breed of sheep valuable for their fine wool. *Also a.* WH: 18C. Spanish, of unknown orig.

meristem *n.* vegetable tissue or cells in process of growth. WH: 19C. Greek *meristos* divided, divisible, from *merizein* to divide into parts, from *meros* part + ending based on PHLOEM, XYLEM.

merit *n.* the quality of deserving. *Also v.t., v.i.* WH: 12–14C. Old French *mérite*, from Latin *meritum* price, value, service rendered, neut. p.p. (used as n.) of *merere* to earn, to deserve, rel. to Greek *meiresthai* to obtain as a share, *moira* share, fate, *meros* part.

merle *n.* the blackbird. WH: 14–15C. Old French, from Latin *merula*.

merlin *n.* the smallest of the European falcons, *Falco columbarius*. WH: 12–14C. Anglo-French *merilun*, shortened form of Old French *esmirillon* (Modern French *émirillon*), augm. of *esmiril*, from a Frankish word corr. to Old High German *smerlo*, German *Schmerl*.

merlon *n.* the solid part of an embattled parapet between two embrasures. WH: 18C. French, from Italian *merlone*, augm. of *merlo* battlement.

Merlot *n.* a black grape used in wine-making. WH: 19C. French, dim. of *merle* blackbird (see MERLE). See also -OT[1].

mermaid *n.* an imaginary marine creature, having the upper half like a woman and the lower like a fish. WH: 12–14C. MERE[1] + MAID.

mero- *comb. form* partly, partial. WH: Greek *meros* part, fraction. See also -O-.

meroblast *n.* an ovum only a part or portion of which is directly germinal. WH: 19C. MERO- + BLAST.

meroistic *a.* (of the ovaries of certain insects) secreting yolk-forming cells as well as ova. WH: 19C. MERO- + Greek *ōion* egg + -*istic* (-IST, -IC).

-merous *comb. form* having so many parts, as in *dimerous*. WH: From DIMEROUS, etc.

Merovingian *a.* of or relating to the Frankish dynasty reigning in Gaul and Germany, founded by Clovis in AD 486. *Also n.* WH: 17C. French *mérovingien*, from Medieval Latin *Merovingi* (pl.), from Latin *Meroveus*, their supposed founder. See also -ING[3], -IAN.

merry *a.* cheerful, happy. WH: pre-1200. Old English *myrge*, from Germanic base also of MIRTH. The original basic sense was pleasant, agreeable, as still in *merry England* (though now understood here as joyous, full of fun and laughter).

merycism *n.* a disorder in which food is brought back from the stomach and chewed again. WH: 19C. Modern Latin *merycismus*, from Greek *mērukismos* rumination, from *mērukizein* to ruminate. See also -ISM.

mesa *n.* a plateau with steep sides, a tableland. WH: 18C. Spanish table, from Latin *mensa*.

mesail *n.* the visor of a helmet, esp. if made in two parts. WH: 19C. French *mésail*, appar. from Old French *muçaille* concealment, from *mucier* to hide.

mésalliance *n.* marriage with a person of inferior social position. WH: 18C. French from *més-* MIS-[1] + *alliance* ALLIANCE.

mesaraic *a.* mesenteric. WH: 14–15C. Medieval Latin *mesaraïcus*, from Greek *mesaraïkos*, from *mesaraïon*, from *meson* middle + *araia* flank, belly. See also -IC.

mescal *n.* a small globular cactus, *Lophophora williamsii*, the peyote, of the southern US and Mexico, the tubercles of which are chewed for their hallucinogenic effects. WH: 18C. Spanish *mezcal*, from Nahuatl *mexcalli* a fermented drink made from maguey, from *metl* maguey + *ixcalli* stew.

mesembryanthemum *n.* any succulent plant of the genus *Mesembryanthemum*, with thick, fleshy leaves and brilliant flowers, including the ice plant. WH: 18C. Modern Latin, from Greek *mesēmbria* noon + *anthemon* flower. The *-y-* should properly be *-i-*. The name refers to the fact that many plants of the genus open their flowers only for a short time at midday.

mesencephalon *n.* the midbrain. WH: 19C. MESO- + ENCEPHALON.

mesentery *n.* a fold of the peritoneum supporting the small intestines and connecting them with the wall of the abdomen. WH: 14–15C. Modern Latin *mesenterium*, from Greek *mesenterion*, from *mesos* middle + *enteron* intestine. See also -Y[2].

mesh *n.* a fabric or structure of network. *Also v.t., v.i.* WH: 14–15C. Prob. from Middle Dutch *maesche*, from Germanic. Cp. German *Masche*.

mesial *a.* of or relating to, situated or directed towards the middle, esp. the middle line of the body. WH: 19C. Greek *mesos* middle + -IAL.

mesmerism *n.* the art or power of inducing an abnormal state of the nervous system, in which the will of the patient is controlled by that of the agent. WH: 18C. Friedrich (or Franz) A. *Mesmer*, 1734–1815, Austrian physician, who developed the practice + ISM.

mesne *a.* middle, intermediate. WH: 14–15C. French, legal var. of Anglo-French *meen* MEAN[2]. The *-s-* has appeared as for DEMESNE.

meso- *comb. form* intermediate, in the middle. WH: Greek *mesos* middle. See also -O-.

mesoblast *n.* the intermediate germ layer of an embryo. WH: 19C. MESO- + -BLAST.

mesocarp *n.* the middle layer of the pericarp of a fruit. WH: 19C. MESO- + -CARP.

mesocephalic *a.* having a medium-sized head, intermediate between dolichocephalic and brachycephalic. WH: 19C. MESO- + -CEPHALIC.

mesoderm *n.* the middle germ layer of an animal embryo. WH: 19C. MESO- + -DERM.

mesolithic *a.* of or relating to the phase of the Stone Age between the Neolithic and Palaeolithic phases. *Also n.* WH: 19C. MESO- + LITHIC.

mesomorphic *a.* having a compact muscular physique. WH: early 20C. MESO- + -*morphic* (-MORPH). *Mesomorph* was coined in 1940 by the US psychologist William H. Sheldon. Cp. ECTOMORPH, ENDOMORPH.

meson *n.* a particle intermediate in mass between a proton and an electron. WH: mid-20C. MESO- + -ON. The original name was *mesotron*, from MESO- + -*tron*, based on ELECTRON, neuron (NEURONE), coined in 1938 by the US physicists Carl Anderson and Seth Neddermeyer.

mesopause *n.* the zone between the mesosphere and the thermosphere, at which the temperature has fallen to its lowest and begins to rise again. WH: mid-20C. MESO- + PAUSE.

mesophyll *n.* the inner spongy tissue of a leaf. WH: 19C. MESO- + -PHYLL.

mesophyte *n.* a plant that grows in conditions where there is a moderate supply of water. WH: 19C. MESO- + -PHYTE.

mesosphere *n.* the region of the earth's atmosphere extending for about 80 km above the stratosphere. WH: mid-20C. MESO- + SPHERE.

mesothelioma *n.* a tumour of the lining of the lungs, heart or stomach, often caused by blue asbestos dust. WH: early 20C. MESO- + EPITHELIUM + -OMA.

mesothorax *n.* in insects, the middle segment of the thorax bearing the anterior legs and the middle wings. WH: 19C. MESO- + THORAX.

Mesozoic *a.* belonging to the second great geological epoch, Secondary. *Also n.* WH: 19C. MESO- + -ZOIC. The name was coined in 1840 by the English geologist John Phillips as a term appropriate for an epoch between the PALAEOZOIC and CENOZOIC.

mesquite *n.* any leguminous shrub or tree of the genus *Prosopis* growing in the SW United States and as far south as Peru, yielding the pods used for fodder. WH: 18C. Mexican Spanish *mezquite*, from Nahuatl *mizquitl*.

mess *n.* a state of dirt and disorder. *Also v.i., v.t.* WH: 12–14C. Old French *mes* portion of food (Modern French *mets*), from Late Latin *missus* course of a meal, from Latin *missus*, p.p. of *mittere* to send (out). Cp. MUSS.

message *n.* a communication, oral or written, from one person to another. *Also v.t.* WH: 12–14C. Old French, from Latin *missus*, p.p. of *mittere* to send. See also -AGE.

messenger *n.* a person who carries a message. WH: 12–14C. Old French *messanger*. See MESSAGE, also -ER². The *-n-* has entered as with PASSENGER, SCAVENGER, etc.

Messiah *n.* an expected saviour or deliverer. WH: 12–14C. Old French *Messie*, from Popular Latin *Messias*, from Greek, from Aramaic *mĕšīḥā*, Hebrew *māšīāḥ* anointed, from *māšaḥ* to anoint. The form *Messiah* was created by the 1560 Geneva Bible translators as looking more Hebraic than *Messias*. Cp. the many Old Testament names ending in *-iah*, as *Isaiah, Jeremiah, Josiah, Nehemiah*, etc.

Messieurs *n.pl.* sirs, gentlemen. WH: 18C. French, pl. of MONSIEUR.

messuage *n.* a dwelling house with the adjacent buildings and land for the use of the household. WH: 14–15C. Anglo-French, prob. orig. a misreading of *mesnage* MÉNAGE. See also -AGE.

mestee *n.* the offspring of a white person and a quadroon, an octoroon. WH: 17C. Abbr. of Spanish MESTIZO.

mestizo *n.* a person of mixed Spanish or Portuguese and American Indian blood. WH: 16C. Spanish, from Latin *mixtus*, p.p. of *miscere* to mix.

met *a.* meteorological. *Also n.* WH: mid-20C. Abbr. of *meteorological* (METEOROLOGY).

met- *comb. form* beyond, above, as in *metamathematics*. WH: Greek *met-*, *meta-*, from *meta* with, after.

metabolism *n.* the continuous chemical change going on in living matter. WH: 19C. Greek *metabolē* change, from *metaballein* to change, from *meta-* MET- + *ballein* to throw + -ISM.

metacarpus *n.* the part of the hand between the wrist and the fingers. WH: 14–15C. Modern Latin, alt. of Greek *metakarpion*, based on CARPUS. See MET-.

metacentre *n.* the point in a floating body slightly out of equilibrium where the vertical drawn through the centre of gravity when it is in equilibrium intersects the vertical passing through the centre of buoyancy. WH: 18C. French *métacentre*. See MET-, CENTRE.

metachrosis *n.* change of colour, as in certain lizards. WH: 19C. *meta-* (MET-) + Greek *khrōsis* colouring.

metagalaxy *n.* the universe beyond our galaxy. WH: mid-20C. *meta-* (MET-) + GALAXY.

metage *n.* official measurement, esp. of coal. WH: 16C. METE¹ + -AGE.

metagenesis *n.* alternation of like and unlike generations. WH: 19C. *meta-* (MET-) + GENESIS.

metal *n.* any of a class of elementary substances which usu. present in various degrees certain physical characters, such as lustre, malleability and ductility, possessed by the six metals known to the ancients, viz. gold, silver, copper, iron, lead and tin. *Also v.t.* WH: 12–14C. Old French *métal* or Latin *metallum* mine, quarry, metal, from Greek *metallon* metal, ore.

metalanguage *n.* a language or system of symbols used to speak about another language. WH: mid-20C. *meta-* (MET-) + LANGUAGE.

metalepsis *n.* a form of metonymy, the substitution of one word for another that is itself figurative, or the union of two or more tropes of a different kind in one word. WH: 16C. Latin, from Greek *metalēpsis*, from *metalambanein* to substitute, from *meta-* MET- + *lambanein* to take.

metalinguistics *n.* the branch of linguistics dealing with metalanguages. WH: mid-20C. *meta-* (MET-) + *linguistics* (LINGUIST).

metallize *v.t.* to coat with a metal. WH: Greek *metallon* METAL + -IZE.

metallo- *comb. form* metal. WH: Greek *metallon* METAL. See also -O-.

metallography *n.* the science of metals, esp. the microscopic study of their internal structure. WH: 18C. METALLO- + -GRAPHY.

metallophone *n.* any musical instrument like the xylophone with metal bars, such as the vibraphone and glockenspiel. WH: 19C. METALLO- + -PHONE.

metallurgy *n.* the science of metals. WH: 18C. Greek *metallon* METAL + -*ourgia* work, working (as in *kheirourgia* SURGERY).

metamere *n.* each of a series of similar parts of a body. WH: 19C. *meta-* (MET-) + Greek *meros* part.

metamorphose *v.t.* to change into a different form. *Also v.i.* WH: 16C. French *métamorphoser*, from *métamorphose* (n.), from Latin *metamorphosis*, from Greek *metamorphōsis*, from *meta-* morphoun to transform, from *meta-* MET- + *morphē* form. See also -OSIS.

metaphase *n.* the second stage of meiotic cell division at which the chromosomes become attached to the spindle fibres, forming the equatorial plate. WH: 19C. Greek, from *meta-* MET- + PHASIS.

metaphor *n.* a figure of speech by which a word is transferred in application from one object to another, so as to imply comparison. WH: 15C. Old French *métaphore* or Latin *metaphora*, from Greek, from *metapherein* to transfer, from *meta-* MET- + *pherein* to bear.

metaphrase *v.t.* to translate literally. *Also n.* WH: 16C. Greek *metaphrazein* to translate, from *meta-* MET- + *phrazein* to tell.

metaphysics *n.* the philosophy of being and knowing. WH: 16C. Pl. of *metaphysic* (n.), from Medieval Latin *metaphysica* (neut. pl.), from Medieval Greek (*ta*) *metaphusika*, from earlier *ta meta ta phusika* the (works of Aristotle) after the Physics. The latter Greek title meant that the works in question were placed after those on physics. It was wrongly taken to mean, however, that they were 'beyond' physics, i.e. transcended physics.

metaplasia *n.* the change of one form of tissue into another. WH: 19C. Greek *metaplassein* to mould into a new form, from *meta-* MET- + *plassein* to mould. See -PLASIA.

metapsychology *n.* the body of theory on psychological matters. WH: early 20C. *meta-* (MET-) + PSYCHOLOGY.

metastable *a.* seeming stable because passing slowly from one state to another. WH: 19C. *meta-* (MET-) + STABLE¹.

metastasis *n.* a change in the seat of a disease, esp. cancer, from one organ to another. WH: 16C. Late Latin, from Greek removal, change, from *methistanai* to remove, to change.

metatarsus *n.* that part of the foot between the tarsus and the toes, in humans consisting of five long bones. WH: 14–15C. Modern Latin. See MET-, TARSUS.

metatheory *n.* a theory used to discuss the nature of another theory or theories. WH: mid-20C. *meta-* (MET-) + THEORY.

metathesis *n.* the transposition of sounds or letters in a word. WH: 16C. Late Latin, from Greek, from *metatithenai* to transpose, from *meta-* MET- + *tithenai* to put, to place.

metathorax *n.* the posterior segment of the thorax in an insect. WH: 19C. *meta-* (MET-) + THORAX.

metazoan *n.* any animal of the subkingdom Metazoa, which includes all animals that have many-celled bodies and differentiated tissues, as distinct from protozoan. *Also a.* WH: 19C. Modern Latin *Metazoa*, from *meta-* (MET-) + Greek *zōia*, pl. of *zōion* animal. See also -AN.

mete¹ *v.t.* to allot, to apportion (out). *Also v.i.* WH: pre-1200. Old English *metan*, from Germanic, from Indo-European base represented also by Latin *meditari* MEDITATE, Greek *medesthai* to care for.

mete² *n.* a limit, a boundary, a boundary stone. WH: 14–15C. Old French, from Latin *meta* boundary work, limit, goal.

metempirics *n.* the philosophy of things lying beyond the bounds of experience. WH: 19C. *meta-* (MET-) + *empiric* (EMPIRICAL) + -S¹.

metempsychosis *n.* the supposed passage of the soul after death from one animal body to another. WH: 16C. Late Latin, from Greek *metempsukhōsis*, from *meta-* MET- + *en* in + *psukhē* soul. See also -OSIS.

meteor *n.* a luminous body appearing for a few moments in the sky and then disappearing, a shooting star. WH: 15C. Modern Latin *meteorum*, from Greek *meteōron*, use as n. of neut. of *meteōros* raised up, lofty, from *meta-* MET- + alt. of base of *aeirein* to raise.

meteorology *n.* the science of the atmosphere and its phenomena, esp. for the purpose of forecasting the weather. WH: 17C. Greek *meteōrologia*, from *meteōron*. See METEOR, -O- +-LOGY.

meter *n.* a person who or something which measures, esp. an instrument for registering the quantity of gas, water, electric energy etc. supplied. *Also v.t.* WH: 12–14C. METE¹ + -ER¹.

-meter *comb. form* a measuring instrument, as in *barometer, thermometer*. WH: Greek *metron* measure.

methadone *n.* a synthetic drug similar to morphine, often used in the treatment of addiction. WH: mid-20C. METHYL + AMINE + -O- + DI-[2] + -ONE. The elements represent the drug's full chemical name, b-di*methyl*amino-4,4-*di*phenyl-3-heptan*one*.

methamphetamine *n.* a variety of amphetamine used as a stimulant. WH: mid-20C. METHYL + AMPHETAMINE.

methanal *n.* formaldehyde. WH: 19C. METHANE + -AL[2].

methane *n.* a light, colourless gas produced by the decomposition or dry distillation of vegetable matter, one of the chief constituents of coal gas, and also of firedamp and marsh gas. WH: 19C. METHYL + -ANE.

methanoic acid *n.* formic acid. WH: 19C. METHANE + -O- + -IC + ACID.

methanol *n.* a colourless, volatile liquid used as a solvent or as fuel, methyl alcohol. WH: 19C. METHANE + -OL.

Methedrine® *n.* METHAMPHETAMINE. WH: mid-20C. METHYL + BENZEDRINE.

metheglin *n.* a variety of mead, orig. Welsh. WH: 16C. Welsh *meddyglyn*, from *meddyg* medicinal (from Latin *medicus*; see MEDIC) + *llyn* liquor.

methinks *v.i.* it seems to me, I think. WH: pre-1200. Orig. two words, ME[1] (dat.) + 3rd pers. sing. of THINK.

methionine *n.* an amino acid containing sulphur, occurring in many proteins. WH: early 20C. METHYL + *thion*- (THIO-) + -INE.

metho *n.* methylated spirits. WH: mid-20C. Abbr. of *methylated spirits* (METHYL) + -O.

method *n.* a mode of procedure, way or order of doing. WH: 14–15C. Latin *methodus*, from Greek *methodos* pursuit of knowledge, mode of investigation, from *meta* (MET-) + *hodos* way.

Methodist *n.* a member of any of the religious bodies that have grown out of the evangelical movement begun in the middle of the 18th cent. by John Wesley, 1703–91, his brother Charles, and George Whitefield, 1714–70. WH: 16C. Modern Latin *methodista*, from Latin *methodus* METHOD. See also -IST. The reason for the name is uncertain. The allusion may be to those who are methodical in their religious practices.

meths *n.pl.* methylated spirits. WH: mid-20C. Abbr. of *methylated spirits* (METHYL).

Methuselah *n.* a very old person; a very old thing. WH: 14–15C. Hebrew *mĕṯūšelaḥ*, a biblical patriarch said to have lived 969 years (Gen. v.27).

methyl *n.* the hypothetical radical of wood spirit, formic acid and many other organic compounds. WH: 19C. French *méthyle*, German *Methyl*, back-formation from French *méthylène*, German *Methylen* methylene (METHYL), from Greek *methu* wine + *hulē* wood. See also -YL, -ENE.

metic *n.* in ancient Greece, an immigrant, a resident alien. WH: 19C. Greek *metoikos*, from *meta*- MET- + *oikos* dwelling, from *oikein* to dwell. See also -IC.

meticulous *a.* very careful. WH: 16C. Latin *meticulosus*, from *metus* fear. See also -ULOUS. The original sense (to the 17C) was fearful, timid. The current sense dates from the 19C.

métier *n.* trade, profession. WH: 18C. French, from alt. of Latin *ministerium* service, ministry (MINISTER), prob. influ. by *mysterium* MYSTERY[1].

Metis *n.* a person of mixed blood, esp. (in Canada) the offspring of a person of European descent and an American Indian. WH: 19C. French *métis*, from Old French *mestis*, from Latin *mixtus*. See MESTIZO.

metol *n.* a white soluble organic substance derived from phenol, used as photographic developer. WH: 19C. Arbitrary.

Metonic cycle *n.* the cycle of 19 Julian years at the end of which the new and full moons recur on the same dates. WH: 17C. Greek *Metōn*, 5C BC Athenian astronomer + -IC.

metonymy *n.* a figure of speech in which one word is used for another with which it is associated, as the effect for the cause, the material for the thing made etc., e.g. 'bench' for 'magistrates'. WH: 16C. Late Latin *metonymia*, from Greek *metōnumia*, lit. change of name, from *meta*- MET- + *onuma* name. See also -Y[2].

metope[1] *n.* the space between the triglyphs in a Doric frieze. WH: 16C. Latin *metopa*, from Greek *metopē*, from *meta* between + *opē* hole in a frieze for a beam-end.

metope[2] *n.* the face or front. WH: 19C. Greek *metōpon* forehead.

metre[1] *n.* the standard measure of length in the metric system, orig. the ten-millionth part of the quadrant of a meridian, 39.37 in., now defined as the distance travelled by light in a vacuum in 1/299,792,458 of a second. WH: 18C. French *mètre*, from Latin *metrum*. See METRE[2].

metre[2] *n.* the rhythmical arrangement of syllables in verse. WH: pre-1200. Old French *mètre*, from Latin *metrum*, from Greek *metron* measure, from Indo-European base + instr. suf.

metric *a.* of or relating to the metre as a unit of measurement or the metric system. *Also n.* WH: 15C. Latin *metricus*, from Greek *metrikos*, from *metron* METRE[2]. See also -IC.

-metric *comb. form* forming adjectives denoting measurement, as in *geometric*. WH: French *-métrique*, from Latin *metricus* METRIC.

metritis *n.* inflammation of the womb. WH: 19C. Greek *mētra* womb + -ITIS.

metro *n.* an underground railway network in a city. WH: early 20C. French *métro*, abbr. of (*Chemin de Fer*) *Métropolitain* Metropolitan (Railway).

metro- *comb. form* measuring. WH: Greek *metron* measure. See also -O-.

metrology *n.* the study of measurement. WH: 19C. METRO- + -LOGY.

metromania *n.* a passion for writing verses. WH: 18C. METRO- + -MANIA.

metronome *n.* an instrument for indicating and marking time in music by means of a pendulum. WH: 19C. METRO- + Greek *nomos* law, rule. The word was coined in 1814 by J.N. Maelzel, the instrument's German inventor.

metronymic *a.* (of names) derived from the name of a mother or maternal ancestor. *Also n.* WH: 19C. Greek *mētēr*, *mētros* mother, based on PATRONYMIC.

metropolis *n.* the chief town or capital of a country. WH: 16C. Late Latin, from Greek *mētropolis*, from *mētēr*, *mētros* mother + *polis* city.

metropolitan *a.* of or relating to a capital or large city. *Also n.* WH: 14–15C. Late Latin *metropolitanus*, from Greek *mētropolitēs*, from *mētropolis*. See METROPOLIS, also -AN.

metrorrhagia *n.* excessive bleeding from the womb. WH: 19C. Greek *mētra* womb + -O- + -RRHAGIA.

-metry *comb. form* science of measuring, as in *geometry*, *trigonometry*. WH: Greek *-metria*, from *-metrēs* measurer, from *metron* METRE[2]. See also -Y[2].

mettle *n.* quality of temperament or disposition. WH: 16C. Var. of METAL.

meu *n.* the plant spignel. WH: 16C. Latin *meum*, from Greek *mēon*.

meunière *a.* (of fish) cooked or served in butter with lemon juice and herbs, esp. parsley. WH: 19C. French (*à la*) *meunière*, lit. (in the manner of a) miller's wife.

mew[1] *v.i.* to make a characteristic high-pitched cry, as a cat or seagull. *Also n.* WH: 12–14C. Imit. Cp. MIAOW.

mew[2] *n.* a kind of seagull, esp. *Larus canus*. WH: pre-1200. Old English *mǣw*, from Germanic, prob. of imit. orig. Cp. German *Möwe*.

mew[3] *n.* a cage for hawks, esp. whilst moulting. *Also v.t., v.i.* WH: 12–14C. Old French *mue*, from *muer*, from Latin *mutare*. See MUTATE.

mewl *v.i.* to cry, whine or whimper, as a child. WH: 14–15C. Imit. Cp. MIAUL.

mews *n.* stabling, orig. for carriage-horses etc. WH: 14–15C. Pl. of MEW[3]. The word originally referred to the royal stables at Charing Cross, London, built on the site of the royal hawk mews. The sense row of houses built in the style of (or converted from) stables arose in the 19C.

Mexican *a.* of or relating to Mexico. *Also n.* WH: 17C. Spanish *mexicano* (now *mejicano*), from *Mexico*, a country in southern N America + -AN.

mezereon *n.* a small ornamental shrub, *Daphne mezereum*. WH: 15C. Medieval Latin, from Arabic *māzaryūn*.

mezuzah *n.* a small case containing extracts from religious texts fixed to the doorpost by Jews as a sign of their piety. WH: 17C. Hebrew *mĕzūzāh*, lit. doorpost. 'And thou shalt write them [God's commandments] upon the post of thy house' (Deut. vi.9).

mezzanine *n.* a storey intermediate in level between two main storeys, usu. between the ground and first floors. *Also a.* WH: 18C. French, from Italian *mezzanino*, dim. of *mezzano* middle, medium, from Latin *medianus* MEDIAN.

mezza voce *a., adv.* (singing or sung) softly. WH: 18C. Italian *mezza*, fem. of MEZZO + *voce* voice.

mezzo *a.* half or medium. *Also n.* WH: 18C. Italian middle, half, from Latin *medius* MEDIUM.

mezzotint *n.* a process of engraving in which a copper plate is uniformly roughened so as to print a deep black, tones and half-tones being then produced by scraping away the burr. *Also v.t.* WH: 18C. Anglicized form of Italian *mezzotinto*, lit. half-tint. See MEZZO, TINT.

mho *n.* a unit of electrical conductivity, now the *siemens*. WH: 19C. Reversal of OHM.

miaow *n.* the cry of a cat. *Also v.i.* WH: 16C. Imit. Cp. MEW[1], MIAUL.

miasma *n.* an infectious or poisonous vapour. WH: 17C. Greek defilement, pollution, rel. to *miainein* to pollute.

miaul *v.i.* (of a cat) to cry 'miaow'. *Also v.t.* WH: 17C. French *miauler*, of imit. orig.

mica *n.* any of a group of silicates having a perfect basal cleavage into thin, tough and shining plates, formerly used instead of glass. WH: 18C. Latin grain, crumb. The present sense may have arisen by (false) association with Latin *micare* to shine.

micelle *n.* an aggregate of molecules of colloidal size in a solution such as detergent. WH: 19C. German *Micell*, formed as dim. of Latin *mica* crumb.

Michaelmas *n.* the feast of St Michael the Archangel, 29 September. WH: 12–14C. Contr. of *St Michael's mass*. See MASS.

mick *n.* an Irishman. WH: 19C. Pet form of male forename *Michael*. Cp. MICKEY, MIKE.

mickey *n.* an Irish lad. WH: 19C. Pet form of male forename *Michael*. Cp. MICK, MIKE.

Mickey Finn *n.* a doped drink. WH: early 20C. Appar. a pers. name, of unknown orig.

Mickey Mouse *a.* of poor quality, suitable for play only, as distinct from the real thing. WH: mid-20C. A mouselike cartoon character created in 1928 by the US cartoonist Walt Disney.

mickle *a.* much, great. *Also n.* WH: pre-1200. Old English *micel*, from Germanic. Cp. MUCH.

micro *n.* a microcomputer. WH: 19C. Independent adoption of MICRO-.

micro- *comb. form* of or relating to small things (as opposed to large ones). WH: Greek *mikro-*, from *mikros* small. See also -O-.

microanalysis *n.* the chemical analysis of substances using a very small sample. WH: 19C. MICRO- + ANALYSIS.

microbe *n.* any minute organism, esp. a bacterium or microzyme causing disease or fermentation. WH: 19C. French from MICRO- + Greek *bios* life. The word was coined in 1878 by the French physician and surgeon Charles E. Sédillot. Greek *mikrobios* would actually mean short-lived, not small life, as Sédillot intended.

microburst *n.* a particularly strong downward movement of turbulent air, esp. during a thunderstorm. WH: late 20C. MICRO- + BURST.

microcephalic *a.* having an unusually small skull in relation to the rest of the body. *Also n.* WH: 19C. MICRO- + -CEPHALIC.

microchip *n.* a chip of silicon etc. bearing many integrated circuits. WH: late 20C. MICRO- + CHIP.

microcircuit *n.* a very small integrated circuit on a semiconductor. WH: mid-20C. MICRO- + CIRCUIT.

microclimate *n.* the climate of a very small area, as distinct from that of the area around. WH: early 20C. MICRO- + CLIMATE.

micrococcus *n.* any minute spherical bacterium of the genus *Micrococcus*. WH: 19C. MICRO- + COCCUS.

microcode *n.* a microinstruction. WH: mid-20C. MICRO- + CODE.

microcomputer *n.* a small computer with one or more microprocessors. WH: late 20C. MICRO- + COMPUTER.

microcopy *n.* a very small copy of printed matter on microfilm or microfiche. *Also v.t.* WH: mid-20C. MICRO- + COPY.

microcosm *n.* a representation (of) in miniature form. WH: 12–14C. French *microcosme* or Medieval Latin *microcosmus*, from Greek *mikros kosmos* little world.

microcyte *n.* an abnormally small red blood corpuscle, such as appear in cases of anaemia. WH: 19C. MICRO- + -CYTE.

microdot *n.* a photographic image reduced to the size of a dot, e.g. for espionage purposes. WH: mid-20C. MICRO- + DOT[1].

microeconomics *n.* the branch of economics concerned with individual commodities, firms etc. and the economic relationships between them. WH: mid-20C. MICRO- + *economics* (ECONOMIC).

microelectronics *n.* electronics as applied to microcircuits. WH: mid-20C. MICRO- + *electronics* (ELECTRONIC).

microevolution *n.* evolution taking place within a species or small group of organisms, esp. over a short period of time. WH: mid-20C. MICRO- + EVOLUTION.

microfarad *n.* a unit of electrical capacitance, one-millionth of a farad. WH: 19C. MICRO- + FARAD.

microfiche *n.* a sheet of film bearing miniature photographs of documents etc. WH: mid-20C. MICRO- + French *fiche* slip of paper, index card.

microfilm *n.* a strip of film on which successive pages of a document or book are photographed for purposes of record. *Also v.t.* WH: mid-20C. MICRO- + FILM.

microfloppy *n.* a small floppy disk, usu. 3.5 inches in diameter. WH: late 20C. MICRO- + *floppy* (FLOP).

microform *n.* a method of storing symbolic information using microphotographic techniques. WH: mid-20C. MICRO- + FORM.

microgeology *n.* the department of geology dealing with microscopic structures. WH: 19C. MICRO- + GEOLOGY.

microgram *n.* one-millionth of a gram. WH: 19C. MICRO- + GRAM[1].

micrograph *n.* a very small picture, photograph etc. taken by using a microscope. WH: 19C. MICRO- + -GRAPH.

microgravity *n.* a state of weak or no gravity. WH: late 20C. MICRO- + GRAVITY.

microgroove *n.* the groove of a long-playing gramophone record. WH: mid-20C. MICRO- + GROOVE.

microinstruction *n.* a computer instruction that activates a particular circuit to execute part of an operation specified by a machine instruction. WH: mid-20C. MICRO- + *instruction* (INSTRUCT).

microlepidoptera *n.pl.* small moths. WH: 19C. MICRO- + *Lepidoptera* (LEPIDOPTERAN).

microlight *n.* a very small light aircraft, usu. for one person. WH: late 20C. MICRO- + LIGHT[2].

microlite *n.* a native salt of calcium found in small crystals. WH: 19C. MICRO- + -LITE.

microlith *n.* a small mesolithic flint tool, forming part of a composite tool. WH: 19C. MICRO- + -LITH.

micrology *n.* the branch of science dealing with microscopic objects. WH: 17C. MICRO- + -LOGY.

micromesh *n., a.* (material) made of a fine mesh, esp. nylon. WH: mid-20C. MICRO- + MESH.

micrometer *n.* an instrument used to measure small distances or objects. WH: 17C. French *micromètre*. See MICRO-, -METER.

micrometre *n.* one-millionth of a metre, a micron. WH: 19C. MICRO- + METRE[1].

microminiaturization *n.* the production of very small electronic components and circuitry by using integrated circuits. WH: mid-20C. MICRO- + *miniaturization* (MINIATURE).

micron *n.* one-millionth of a metre, the unit of length in microscopic research. WH: 19C. Greek *mikron*, neut. of *mikros* small.

Micronesian *a.* of or relating to Micronesia. *Also n.* WH: 19C. *Micronesia*, a group of small islands in the W Pacific, based on *Polynesia* (POLYNESIAN). See also -AN.

micronutrient *n.* a substance, chemical element etc. required in very small amounts for the survival and development of living organisms. WH: mid-20C. MICRO- + NUTRIENT.

micro-organism *n.* an organism of microscopic size. WH: 19C. MICRO- + ORGANISM.

microphone *n.* an instrument for converting sound into electrical waves. WH: 17C. MICRO- + -PHONE.

microphotography *n.* the production of microscopic photographs. WH: 19C. MICRO- + *photography* (PHOTOGRAPH).

microphyte *n.* a microscopic vegetable organism, esp. a bacterium. WH: 19C. MICRO- + -PHYTE.

microprocessor *n.* an integrated circuit operating as the central processing unit of a microcomputer. WH: late 20C. MICRO- + *processor* (PROCESS[1]).

microprogram *n.* a sequence of microinstructions controlling the central processing unit of a computer. WH: mid-20C. MICRO- + *program* (PROGRAMME).

micropsia *n.* a state of vision in which objects appear unnaturally small. WH: 19C. MICRO- + Greek *-opsia* seeing.

micropterous *a.* having small wings or fins. WH: 19C. MICRO- + Greek *pteron* wing. See also -OUS.

micropyle *n.* a minute opening in the external membrane of the ovum by which spermatozoa may enter. WH: 19C. French, from *micro-* MICRO- + Greek *pulē* gate.

microscope *n.* an optical instrument by which objects are so magnified that details invisible to the naked eye are clearly seen. WH: 17C. Modern Latin *microscopium*. See MICRO-, -SCOPE.

microsecond *n.* one-millionth of a second. WH: early 20C. MICRO- + SECOND[1].

microseism *n.* a slight tremor or vibration of the earth's crust. WH: 19C. MICRO- + Greek *seismos* earthquake.

microsome *n.* any of the minute granules in the endoplasm of protoplasmic cells. WH: 19C. MICRO- + -SOME[2].

microsporangium *n.* a sporangium containing microspores. WH: 19C. MICRO- + SPORANGIUM.

microspore *n.* any one of the smaller kind of spores in some cryptogams, from which male gametophytes develop. WH: 19C. MICRO- + SPORE.

microstructure *n.* the arrangement of crystals etc. esp. within metals and alloys, as made visible by a microscope. WH: 19C. MICRO- + STRUCTURE.

microsurgery *n.* surgery performed using a microscope and special small instruments. WH: early 20C. MICRO- + SURGERY.

microswitch *n.* a very small electronic switch, operated by very slight movement or pressure. WH: mid-20C. MICRO- + SWITCH.

microtome *n.* an instrument for cutting thin sections of tissue etc. for microscopic examination. WH: 19C. MICRO- + -TOME.

microtone *n.* any interval smaller than a semitone. WH: early 20C. MICRO- + TONE.

microtubule *n.* a very small rigid structure of protein occurring in the cytoplasm of many plants and animal cells. WH: mid-20C. MICRO- + *tubule* (TUBULAR).

microwave *n.* a microwave oven. *Also v.t.* WH: mid-20C. MICRO- + WAVE.

micrurgy *n.* the manipulation, examination etc. of single cells under a microscope. WH: early 20C. MICRO- + *-urgy*, based on METALLURGY.

micturition *n.* a frequent desire to urinate. WH: 18C. Latin *micturire*, from *mictus*, p.p. of *meiere* to urinate. See also -ITION.

mid[1] *prep.* amid. WH: 14–15C. Shortening of AMID.

mid[2] *a.* middle. *Also n.* WH: pre-1200. Old English *midd*, from Germanic, from Indo-European base also of Latin *medius*, Greek *mesos* MESO-.

mid- *comb. form* middle, medium. WH: MID[2].

Midas *n.* a fabulously rich man. WH: 16C. Latin and Greek *Midas*, a legendary king of Phrygia whose touch was said to turn everything to gold.

midden *n.* a dunghill. WH: 12–14C. Of Scandinavian orig. Cp. Danish *Mødding*, earlier *møgdyng*, from *møg* MUCK + *dynge* heap (cp. DUNG).

middle *a.* placed equally distant from the extremes. *Also n., v.t.* WH: pre-1200. Old English *middel*, from Germanic base of MID[2]. See also -LE[2].

middy[1] *n.* a midshipman. WH: 19C. From obs. *mid* (18C), abbr. of *midshipman* (MID-) + -Y[3].

middy[2] *n.* a glass of beer. WH: mid-20C. MID[2] + -Y[3].

midge *n.* a gnat or other minute fly, esp. of the families Chironomidae and Ceratopogonidae. WH: pre-1200. Old English *mycg*, from Germanic, rel. to Latin *musca* fly. Cp. German *Mücke*.

MIDI *n.* an electronic system to link musical instruments with computer technology for composition and performance. WH: late 20C. Acronym of *m*usical *i*nstrument *d*igital *i*nterface.

midi- *comb. form* of middle size. WH: mid-20C. MID[1], MIDDLE, based on MAXI-, MINI-.

midinette *n.* a shop girl in Paris, esp. in a milliner's shop. WH: early 20C. French, from *midi* midday + *dînette* light dinner. The girls are so called because they originally had a light meal at midday.

midland *a.* situated in the middle or interior of a country. *Also n.* WH: 14–15C. MID[2] + LAND.

midnight *n.* the middle of the night, twelve o'clock at night. *Also a.* WH: pre-1200. MID[2] + NIGHT.

Midrash *n.* a commentary on part of the Hebrew scriptures. WH: 17C. Hebrew *miḏrāš* commentary, from *dāraš* to study, to expound.

midriff *n.* the middle part of the front of the body, between waist and chest. WH: pre-1200. Old English *midhrif*, from *mid-* MID[2] + *hrif* belly, of unknown orig.

midst *n.* the middle (now only in idioms below). *Also prep., adv.* WH: 14–15C. From obs. *mids* middle (from MID[2] + -S[2]) + *t* as in AGAINST, *amongst* (AMONG), etc.

midwife *n.* a person who assists at childbirth. *Also v.i., v.t.* WH: 12–14C. Prob. from obs. *mid* with, from Germanic (cp. German *mit*), rel. to Greek *meta* (MET-) + WIFE. A midwife is so called as she is with the mother at the birth.

mien *n.* air or manner, appearance, deportment, demeanour, bearing, carriage. WH: 16C. Prob. shortened form of DEMEAN[2], later assim. to French *mine* look, aspect.

miff *n.* a petty quarrel. *Also v.i., v.t.* WH: 17C. Prob. imit. of an expression of disgust.

might *n.* strength, force. WH: pre-1200. Old English *miht*, from Germanic, from base also of MAY[1]. Cp. German *Macht* (as in WEHRMACHT).

mignon *a.* delicate and small, dainty. WH: 16C. French. See MINION.

mignonette *n.* any annual plant of the genus *Reseda*, esp. *R. odorata*, which has fragrant greenish flowers. WH: 18C. French *mignonette*, dim. of MIGNON. See also -ETTE.

migraine *n.* a recurrent severe headache, esp. on one side of the head only, often accompanied by nausea and visual disturbances. WH: 14–15C. Old French, from Late Latin *hemicrania*, from Greek *hēmikrania*, from *hēmi-* half, HEMI- + *kranion* skull.

migrate *v.i.* to move permanently from one place to another. WH: 17C. Latin *migratus*, p.p. of *migrare* to move from one place to another. See also -ATE[3].

mihrab *n.* a niche etc. in a mosque indicating the direction of Mecca. WH: 19C. Arabic *miḥrāb*.

mikado *n.* the emperor of Japan. WH: 18C. Japanese, from *mi* august + *kado* gate.

Mike *n.* a person's name, only in the phrase *for the love of Mike*. WH: 19C. Pet form of male forename *Michael*. Cp. MICK, MICKEY.

mike[1] *n.* a microphone. WH: early 20C. Abbr. of MICROPHONE.

mike[2] *v.i.* to shirk, to be idle. *Also n.* WH: 19C. Orig. unknown.

mil *n.* a unit of length, a thousandth part of an inch (0.0254 mm), in measuring wire. WH: 17C. Abbr. of Latin *millesimum* thousandth part. Cp. MILL[2]. In pharmacy, *mil* (early 20C) is an abbreviation of MILLILITRE.

miladi *n.* an English gentlewoman or noblewoman. WH: 18C. French, from English *my lady*. Cp. MILORD.

Milanese *a.* of or relating to Milan. *Also n.* WH: 15C. *Milan* (Italian *Milano*), the chief city of Lombardy, N Italy + -ESE.

milch *a.* (of a farm animal) giving milk. WH: 12–14C. From 2nd element of Old English *thrimilce* May (when cows could be milked thrice daily), from Germanic base of MILK.

mild *a.* gentle in manners or disposition. *Also n.* WH: pre-1200. Old English *milde*, from Germanic, from Indo-European base also of Latin *mollis*, Greek *malakos* soft.

mildew *n.* a harmful fungoid growth on plants, cloth, paper, food etc. after exposure to damp. *Also v.t., v.i.* WH: pre-1200. Old English *mildēaw*, from Germanic, from base also of Latin *mel*, Greek *meli* honey + base of DEW. The original meaning (to the 17C) was honeydew. The current sense dates from the 12–14C.

mile *n.* a measure of length or distance, 1760 yds. (1.609 km). WH: pre-1200. Old English *mīl*, from Germanic, from Latin *millia*, pl. of *mille* thousand. The original sense was a Roman unit of distance of 1000 paces.

Milesian *a.* Irish. *Also n.* WH: 16C. *Milesias*, a mythical Spanish king whose sons were said to have conquered the ancient kingdom of Ireland in *c.*1300 BC + -AN.

milfoil *n.* the yarrow, *Achillea millefolium*, named because the leaves are finely divided. WH: 12–14C. Old French *milfoil* (Modern French MILLEFEUILLE), from Latin *milefolium*, from Latin *mille* thousand + *folium* leaf, based on Greek *muriophullon* (from *murios* myriad + *phullon* leaf).

miliary *a.* like millet seed. WH: 17C. Latin *miliarius* pertaining to millet, from *milium* millet. See also -ARY[1].

milieu *n.* environment, surroundings. WH: 19C. French, from *mi* (from Latin *medius* MID[2]) + LIEU place.

militant *a.* combative, aggressive. *Also n.* WH: 14–15C. Old French, or from Latin *militans, militantis*, pres.p. of *militare*. See MILITATE, also -ANT.

military *a.* of or relating to soldiers, arms or warfare. *Also n.* WH: 14–15C. Old French *militaire*, or from Latin *militaris*, from *miles, militis* soldier + -aris -ARY[1].

militate *v.i.* to have weight or influence. WH: 16C. Latin *militatus*, p.p. of *militare* to serve as a soldier, from *miles, militis* soldier. See also -ATE[3].

militia *n.* a supplementary military force consisting of the body of citizens not enrolled in the regular army. WH: 16C. Latin military service, warfare, from *miles, militis* soldier.

milk *n.* the whitish fluid secreted by female mammals for the nourishment of their young. *Also v.t., v.i.* WH: pre-1200. Old English *milc, meolc*, from Germanic, from Indo-European base also of Latin *mulgere* (EMULSION). Cp. German *Milch*.

Milky Way *n.* a luminous zone of innumerable stars, stretching across the heavens, being the galaxy of which our solar system is a part. WH: Translation of Latin *via lactea*. The earliest sense was that of GALAXY.

mill[1] *n.* a machine for grinding corn to a fine powder. *Also v.t., v.i.* WH: pre-1200. Old English *mylen*, from Germanic, from Late Latin *molinum*, from Latin *mola* grindstone, mill, rel. to *molere* to grind (see MEAL[2]). The final *n* has been lost as with ELL.

mill[2] *n.* a money of account in the US, the thousandth part of a dollar or tenth of a cent. WH: 18C. Abbr. of Latin *millesimum* thousandth part, based on CENT. Cp. MIL.

millefeuille *n.* a cake of puff pastry filled with jam and cream. WH: 19C. French, lit. thousand leaves, from *mille* thousand + *feuille* leaf. Cp. MILFOIL. The name refers to the many layers of puff pastry.

millennium *n.* a period of 1000 years. WH: 17C. Modern Latin, from Latin *mille* thousand, based on *biennium* (BIENNIAL). The original sense was the period of one thousand years during which Christ was expected to reign on earth, as apparently implied in Rev. xx.1–5.

millepore *n.* any coral of the order *Milleporina*, the surface of which is full of minute pores. WH: 18C. Modern Latin, from Latin *mille* thousand + *porus* passage, PORE[1].

millesimal *a.* consisting of thousandth parts. *Also n.* WH: 19C. Latin *millesimus* thousandth + -AL[1].

millet *n.* the cereal plant *Panicum miliaceum*. WH: 14–15C. Old French dim. of dial. *mil*, from Latin *milium*.

milli- *comb. form* one-thousandth. WH: Latin *mille* thousand + -i-.

milliammeter *n.* an instrument for measuring electrical current in milliamperes. WH: early 20C. MILLI- + AMMETER.

milliamp *n.* a unit of electrical current equal to one-thousandth of an ampere. WH: early 20C. Abbr. of MILLIAMPERE.

milliampere *n.* a unit of electrical current equal to one-thousandth of an ampere. WH: 19C. MILLI- + AMPERE.

milliard *n.* one thousand million. WH: 18C. French, from *mille* thousand.

†milliary *a.* of, relating to or denoting a mile, esp. a Roman mile. *Also n.* WH: 17C. Latin *milliarius*, from *mille* thousand. See MILE, also -ARY[1].

millibar *n.* a unit of atmospheric pressure, one-thousandth of a bar, equivalent to 100 pascals, the pressure exerted by a column of mercury about 0.03 in. (0.762 mm) high. WH: early 20C. MILLI- + BAR[2].

milligram *n.* one-thousandth of a gram, 0.0154 of an English grain. WH: 19C. MILLI- + GRAM[1].

millilitre *n.* one-thousandth of a litre, 0.06103 cu. in. WH: 19C. MILLI- + LITRE.

millimetre *n.* one-thousandth of a metre, 0.03937 in. WH: 19C. MILLI- + METRE[1].

milliner *n.* a person who makes and sells hats for women. WH: 14–15C. *Milan* (MILANESE) + -ER[1]. Milan was at one time famous for the straw work in hats made there. Such hats were regarded as fashionable and were exported to England, among other countries.

million *n.* one thousand thousand, i.e. 1,000,000 or 10[6]. *Also a.* WH: 14–15C. Old French, prob. from. obs. Italian *millione* (now *milione*), from *mille* thousand + augm. suf. *-one* -OON.

millipede *n.* any arthropod of the class Diplopoda, having a cylindrical body made up of many segments, each with two pairs of legs. WH: 17C. Latin *millepeda* woodlouse, from *mille* thousand + *pes, pedis* foot.

millisecond *n.* one-thousandth of a second. WH: early 20C. MILLI- + SECOND[1].

millivolt *n.* one-thousandth of a volt. WH: early 20C. MILLI- + VOLT[1].

Mills bomb *n.* a type of hand grenade. WH: early 20C. Sir William *Mills*, 1856–1932, English engineer, its inventor in 1915.

milord *n.* my lord (formerly applied to rich Englishmen). WH: 16C. French, from *my lord*. Cp. MILADI.

milt *n.* the spleen in mammals. *Also v.t.* WH: pre-1200. Old English, from Germanic, ? rel. to base of MELT. Cp. German *Milz*.

Miltonic *a.* of or resembling the style of Milton. WH: 18C. John *Milton*, 1608–74, English poet + -IC.

mim *a.* prim, demure, quiet, precise. WH: 16C. Imit. of pursing of the mouth.

mimbar *n.* the pulpit of a mosque. WH: 19C. Arabic *minbar*, from *nabara* to raise.

mime *n.* communication through facial expression, gesture etc. and without words. *Also v.i., v.t.* WH: 17C. Latin *mimus*, from Greek *mimos*, of unknown orig.

mimeograph *n.* a duplicating apparatus in which a paraffin-coated sheet is used as a stencil for reproducing written or typewritten matter. *Also v.t.* WH: 19C. Greek *mimeomai* I imitate + -GRAPH.

mimesis *n.* mimicry, imitation of or close natural resemblance to the appearance of another animal or of a natural object. WH: 16C. Greek *mimēsis*, from *mimeisthai* to imitate, from *mimos* MIME.

mimetite *n.* a native arsenate of lead. WH: 19C. Greek *mimētēs* imitator + -ITE[1]. The mineral is so called because it resembles pyromorphite.

mimic *n.* a person who mimics. *Also a., v.t.* WH: 16C. Latin *mimicus*, from Greek *mimikos*, from *mimos* MIME. See also -IC.

miminy-piminy *a.* too fastidious, finicky. *Also n.* WH: 19C. Imit. of fastidiousness. Cp. MIM, NIMINY-PIMINY.

mimosa *n.* any leguminous shrub of the genus *Mimosa*, including the sensitive plant, *M. pudica*. WH: 18C. Modern Latin, appar. from Latin *mimus* MIME + -osa, fem. of -osus -OSE[1]. The shrub is so called because some species seem to imitate animal reactions by folding their leaves at the slightest touch.

mimulus *n.* any flowering plant of the genus *Mimulus* having a masklike corolla, including the monkey flower. WH: 18C. Modern Latin, appar. dim. of Latin *mimus* MIME. The plant is apparently so called because the flowers resemble a face.

Min *n.* any of several Chinese dialects or forms of Chinese spoken in the Fukien province. WH: early 20C. *Min*, a district of Fukien province, SE China.

mina *n.* an ancient Greek weight of 100 drachmae, or about 1 lb. avoirdupois (0.454 kg). WH: 16C. Latin, from Greek *mna*, prob. ult. from Akkadian.

minacious *a.* threatening. WH: 17C. Latin *minax, minacis*, from *minari* to threaten + -OUS.

minaret *n.* a lofty slender turret on a mosque, from which the muezzin summons the people to prayers. WH: 17C. French, or from Spanish *minarete*, Italian *minaretto*, Turkish *mināre*, from Arabic *manāra* lighthouse, minaret, from *nāra* to shine.

minatory *a.* threatening, menacing. WH: 16C. Late Latin *minatorius*, from Latin *minatus*, p.p. of *minari* to threaten. See also -ORY[2].

mince *v.t.* to cut or chop into very small pieces. *Also v.i., n.* WH: 14–15C. Old French *mincier*, from Latin MINUTIA. The senses to walk in an affected manner, to walk with affected preciseness, arose in the 16C.

mind *n.* the intellectual powers of a human being, the understanding. *Also v.t., v.i.* WH: pre-1200. Old English *gemynd*, from Germanic, from base of Y- + stem of Indo-European v. meaning to think, rel. to Latin *mens* mind (MENTAL¹), Greek *menos* intent, spirit, purpose (see MENTOR).

mine¹ *pron.* something which belongs to or is associated with me. *Also a.* WH: pre-1200. Old English *mīn*, from Germanic, from Indo-European loc. base of ME¹ + adjectival suf.

mine² *v.t.* to dig into or burrow in. *Also v.i., n.* WH: 12–14C. Old French *miner*, prob. deriv. of Celtic word represented by Irish *méin*, Gaelic *mèinn* ore, mine, Welsh *mwyn* ore. Cp. MINERAL.

mineral *n.* an inorganic body, homogeneous in structure, with a definite chemical composition, found in the earth. *Also a.* WH: 14–15C. Old French, or from Medieval Latin *minerale*, neut. sing (used as n.) of *mineralis*, from *minera* ore, from Old French *miniere* mine, ? ult. from same source as MINE². See also -AL¹.

minestrone *n.* a thick soup of mixed vegetables with pasta or rice. WH: 19C. Italian, from *minestra* vegetable soup, from *minestrare* to serve, to dish out + augm. suf. -one -OON.

Ming *n.* the imperial dynasty of China 1368–1644. WH: 18C. Chinese *míng* bright, clear.

minge *n.* the female genitals. WH: early 20C. Orig. unknown. ? From Romany.

mingle *v.t.* to mix up together. *Also v.i., n.* WH: 14–15C. Freq. of obs. *meng* to mix, to mingle, from Old English *mengan*, from Germanic, from base represented also in AMONG. See also -LE⁴.

mingy *a.* mean, stingy. WH: early 20C. ? Blend of MEAN³ and STINGY.

mini *n.* a miniskirt. WH: mid-20C. Independent adoption of MINI-.

mini- *comb. form* smaller than the usual size. WH: 19C. MINIATURE (influ. by MINIMUM). Cp. MAXI-.

miniature *n.* a small-sized painting, esp. a portrait on ivory, vellum etc., orig. a small picture in an illuminated manuscript. *Also a., v.t.* WH: 16C. Italian *miniatura*, from Medieval Latin, from *miniare* to rubricate, to illuminate, from MINIUM. See also -URE. Cp. MINI- (to which it is not rel.). The reference is to a small-sized illuminated picture in a medieval manuscript, which was painted in minium (vermilion). The reduced image subsequently became associated with Latin MINIMUS.

minibar *n.* a selection of drinks placed in a hotel room for guests' possible use. WH: late 20C. MINI- + BAR¹.

minibus *n.* a small bus for about 10–15 passengers. WH: 19C. MINI- + BUS, based on OMNIBUS.

minicab *n.* a taxi that can be ordered by telephone, but may not cruise in search of passengers. WH: mid-20C. MINI- + CAB¹.

minicomputer *n.* a computer of medium capacity and power. WH: mid-20C. MINI- + COMPUTER.

minify *v.t.* to make little or less. WH: 17C. Latin *minor* less, *minimus* least, based on MAGNIFY.

minigolf *n.* a small version of the game of golf, played on a lawn etc. WH: mid-20C. Abbr. of *miniature golf*. See MINIATURE, GOLF.

minikin *a.* tiny, delicate. *Also n.* WH: 16C. Dutch *minneken*, from *minne* love + -*ken* -KIN. Not rel. to MINI-.

minim *n.* a note of the value of two crotchets or half a semibreve. WH: 14–15C. Latin *minimus* least, smallest, superl. of *parvus* small. See MINOR.

minimal *a.* least possible. WH: 17C. Latin *minimus* (MINIM) + -AL¹.

minimax *n.* the lowest of a set of maximum values. WH: mid-20C. MINIMUM + MAXIMUM. Cp. MAXIMIN.

minimize *v.t.* to reduce to the smallest possible amount or degree. *Also v.i.* WH: 19C. Latin *minimus* (MINIM) + -IZE.

minimum *n.* the smallest amount or degree possible or usual. *Also a.* WH: 17C. Latin, use as n. of neut. of *minimus*. See MINIM.

minimus *a.* denoting the youngest of several boys of the same name in a (public) school. *Also n.* WH: 16C. Latin. See MINIM. Cp. MINOR.

minion *n.* a servile dependant. WH: 16C. French *mignon*, from Old French *mignot*, ? from Celtic (cp. Old Irish *mīn* tender, soft), or from Germanic (cp. Old High German *minna* love). See also -OT¹. Cp. MIGNON. The original sense was lover, mistress, hence favourite, hence follower, hence servile dependant, slave.

minipill *n.* a low-dose oral contraceptive pill without oestrogen. WH: mid-20C. MINI- + PILL.

miniseries *n.* a short series of television programmes. WH: late 20C. MINI- + SERIES.

miniskirt *n.* a skirt with the hem far above the knees. WH: mid-20C. MINI- + SKIRT.

minister *n.* a person entrusted with the direction of a state department. *Also v.i., v.t.* WH: 12–14C. Old French *ministre*, from Latin *minister*, from *minus* less. The original sense was agent, servant, underling. The sense person in charge of a government department, Secretary of State, evolved in the 17C. The basic concept is 'one who serves'. A servant serves his master, a minister of religion his God and his flock, a government minister his country and its people.

†minium *n.* red oxide of lead vermilion, red lead. WH: 14–15C. Latin. Cp. MINIATURE.

miniver *n.* a white fur used for ceremonial robes. WH: 16C. Anglo-French *menuver*, from Old French *menu vair*, from *menu* little (MENU) + VAIR.

mink *n.* either of two amphibious stoatlike animals of the genus *Mustela*, esteemed for their fur. *Also a.* WH: 14–15C. Orig. uncertain. Rel. to Swedish *menk*, *mänk*. Cp. Low German *mink* otter.

minke *n.* a small whale, *Balaenoptera acutorostrata*. WH: mid-20C. Norwegian, appar. from *Meincke*, a 19C whaling gunner, who mistook it for the larger blue whale.

minnesinger *n.* any of a body of German lyric poets and singers, 1138–1347, whose chief theme was love. WH: 19C. German, from *Minne* love + obs. *Singer* (now *Sänger*) singer.

minnow *n.* a small fish of the carp family common all over Europe, *Phoxinus phoxinus*. WH: 14–15C. Prob. from an Old English word rel. to Old High German *muniwa*, but influ. by Old French *menu* small (MENU).

Minoan *a.* of or relating to ancient Crete or its people or the Bronze Age civilization of which it was the centre. *Also n.* WH: 19C. Latin *Minos*, Greek *Minōs*, a legendary king of Crete to whom a palace excavated at Knossos is attributed + -AN.

minor *a.* less, smaller (not used with *than*). *Also n., v.i.* WH: 12–14C. Latin, comp. of *parvus* small, rel. to *minuere* to lessen.

Minorcan *a.* of or relating to Minorca. *Also n.* WH: 18C. *Minorca*, Spanish *Menorca*, the easternmost of the Balearic Islands in the W Mediterranean + -AN.

Minotaur *n.* in Greek mythology, a monster having the head of a bull and the rest of the body human, devouring human flesh. WH: 14–15C. Old French (Modern French *Minotaure*), from Latin *Minotaurus*, from Greek *minōtauros*, from *Minōs* (MINOAN) + *tauros* bull. The Minotaur was the offspring of a bull and Pasiphaë, wife of Minos.

minster *n.* a cathedral or other large and important church. WH: pre-1200. Old English *mynster*, from Germanic, rel. to Ecclesiastical Latin *monasterium* MONASTERY. Cp. German *Münster*. Not rel. to MINISTER.

minstrel *n.* any of a class of men in the Middle Ages who lived by singing and reciting, a travelling musician or entertainer. WH: 12–14C. Old French *menestral* servant, from Provençal *menestral* officer, attendant, musician, from Late Latin *ministerialis* official, officer, from Latin *ministerium*. See MINISTER, also -AL¹.

mint¹ *n.* a place where money is coined, usu. under state authority. *Also v.t., a.* WH: pre-1200. Old English *mynet*, from Germanic, from Latin *moneta*. See MONEY.

mint² *n.* any plant of the aromatic genus *Mentha*, many of which are used for flavouring, esp. spearmint, *M. spicata*. WH: pre-1200. Old English *minte*, from Latin *mentha*, from Greek *minthē*, *minthos*, prob. of Mediterranean orig. Cp. MENTHOL.

minuend *n.* the quantity from which another is to be subtracted. WH: 18C. Latin *minuendus*, ger. of *minuere* to diminish. See also -END.

minuet *n.* a slow stately dance in triple time. *Also v.i.* WH: 17C. French *menuet*, use as n. of a. *menuet* small, fine, delicate, dim. of *menu* small. See MENU, also -ET¹.

minus *a., prep.* less by, with the deduction of. *Also n.* WH: 15C. Latin, use as adv. of neut. of *minor*. See MINOR.

minuscule *a.* very small. *Also n.* WH: 18C. French, from Latin *minuscula*, fem. of *minusculus* rather less, dim. of MINOR. See also -CULE. A variant spelling *miniscule* has arisen by association with MINI-.

minute[1] *n.* the 60th part of an hour. *Also v.t.* WH: 14–15C. Old French, from Late Latin use as n. of Latin *minuta*, fem. of *minutus* (see MINUTE[2]). The time and degree division was originally Medieval Latin *pars minuta prima* first minute part, the second being the *pars minuta secunda* second minute part.

minute[2] *a.* very small. WH: 14–15C. Latin *minutus*, p.p. of *minuere* to make small, to diminish.

minutia *n.* a small and precise or trivial particular. WH: 18C. Latin smallness, from *minutus* MINUTE[2].

minx *n.* a flirtatious, pert or scheming young woman. WH: 16C. Orig. unknown. The original sense was pet dog.

Miocene *a.* denoting the middle division of the Tertiary strata or period. *Also n.* WH: 19C. Greek *meiōn* less + *kainos* new, recent. The name was coined in 1831 by the English mineralogist William Whewell with reference to the fact that the epoch contains the remains of fewer modern species than the Pliocene. Cp. PLIOCENE.

miosis *n.* abnormal constriction of the pupil of the eye. WH: 19C. Greek *muein* to shut the eyes + -OSIS.

MIPS *n.* a unit of computing speed, equal to a million instructions per second. WH: Acronym of *million instructions per second*.

mirabelle *n.* a European plum tree, *Prunus institia*, bearing small firm yellow fruit. WH: 18C. French, alt. (influ. by female forename *Mirabelle*, from Latin *mirabilis* wonderful, lovely) of Latin *myrobalanus* MYROBALAN.

miracidium *n.* the flat cilial first-stage larva of a trematode. WH: 19C. Greek *meirakidion*, dim. of *meirakion* boy, stripling.

miracle *n.* a marvellous event or act attributed to a supernatural agency. *Also v.i.* WH: 12–14C. Old French, from Latin *miraculum* object of wonder, from *mirari* to look at, to wonder, from *mirus* wonderful.

mirador *n.* a belvedere turret or gallery, commanding an extensive view. WH: 17C. Spanish, from *mirar* to look, to observe. Cp. BELVEDERE, GAZEBO.

mirage *n.* an optical illusion by which images of distant objects are seen as if inverted, esp. in a desert where the inverted sky appears as a sheet of water. WH: 19C. French from *se mirer* to be reflected, to be mirrored, from Latin *mirari*. See MIRACLE, also -AGE.

MIRAS *abbr.* mortgage interest relief at source. WH: Acronym of *mortgage interest relief at source*.

mire *n.* swampy ground, a bog. *Also v.t., v.i.* WH: 12–14C. Old Norse *mýrr*, ult. from Germanic base of MOSS.

mirepoix *n.* a sauce of sautéd chopped vegetables. WH: 19C. French, from the Duc de *Mirepoix*, 1699–1757, French diplomat and general. The sauce was reputedly devised by the duke's cook.

mirid *n.* a heteropteran bug of the family Miridae, including various plant pests. *Also a.* WH: mid-20C. Modern Latin *Miridae*, from *Miris* genus name, from Latin *mirus* wonderful, extraordinary. See also -ID.

mirific *a.* wonderful, marvellous. WH: 15C. French *mirifique*, from Latin *mirificus*, from *mirus* wonderful. See also -FIC.

mirror *n.* an appliance with a polished surface for reflecting images. *Also v.t.* WH: 12–14C. Old French *mirour* (Modern French *miroir*), from Latin *miratus*, p.p. of *mirari*. See MIRACLE, also -OR.

mirth *n.* merriment, jollity. WH: pre-1200. Old English *myrgth*, from Germanic base also of MERRY. See also -TH[2].

MIRV *n.* a missile with two or more warheads designed to strike separate targets. WH: mid-20C. Acronym of *multiple independently-targeted re-entry vehicle*, punning on *Merv*, pet form of male forename *Mervyn* (*Mervin*).

mirza *n.* an Iranian title for a doctor, scholar or other learned person. WH: 17C. Persian *mīrzā*, from *mīr* prince (from Arabic *'amīr* AMIR) + *zād* son.

mis-[1] *pref.* wrongly, badly, amiss, unfavourably. WH: Partly Old English, from Germanic, partly from Old French *mes-* (Modern French *més-*, *mé*), ult. from Latin *minus* (MINUS), assim. to the Old English form.

mis-[2] *comb. form* dislike, hatred. WH: Greek *miso-*, from base of *misein* to hate, *misos* hatred.

misaddress *v.t.* to direct (a letter etc.) to the wrong address. WH: 17C. MIS-[1] + ADDRESS.

misadventure *n.* an unlucky chance or accident. WH: 12–14C. Old French *mesaventure*, from *mesavenir* to turn out badly (from *mes-*,

MIS-[1] + *avenir*, from Latin *advenire*; see ADVENT), based on *aventure* ADVENTURE.

misadvise *v.t.* to advise wrongly. WH: 14–15C. MIS-[1] + ADVISE.

misalign *v.t.* to align wrongly. WH: mid-20C. MIS-[1] + ALIGN.

misalliance *n.* an improper alliance, esp. by marriage. WH: 18C. MIS-[1] + ALLIANCE, based on French MÉSALLIANCE.

misandry *n.* a hatred of men. WH: early 20C. MIS-[2] + ANDRO- + -Y[2], based on MISOGYNY.

misanthrope *n.* a hater of humankind. WH: 16C. French, from Medieval Latin *misanthropus*, from Greek *misanthrōpos*, from *mis-* MIS-[2] + *anthrōpos* man.

misapply *v.t.* to apply wrongly. WH: 16C. MIS-[1] + APPLY.

misappreciate *v.t.* to fail to appreciate rightly or fully. WH: 19C. MIS-[1] + APPRECIATE.

misapprehend *v.t.* to misunderstand. WH: 17C. MIS-[1] + APPREHEND.

misappropriate *v.t.* to apply to a wrong use or purpose (esp. funds to one's own use). WH: 19C. MIS-[1] + APPROPRIATE[1].

misbegotten *a.* illegitimate. WH: 15C. MIS-[1] + *begotten*, p.p. of *beget* to procreate, from Old English *begietan*. See BE-, GET[1].

misbehave *v.i.* to behave badly or improperly. WH: 15C. MIS-[1] + BEHAVE.

misbelief *n.* false or erroneous belief. WH: 12–14C. MIS-[1] + BELIEF.

miscalculate *v.t.* to calculate wrongly. WH: 17C. MIS-[1] + CALCULATE.

miscall *v.t.* to call by a wrong or unsuitable name. WH: 14–15C. MIS-[1] + CALL.

miscarry *v.i.* to have a miscarriage. WH: 12–14C. Old French *mescarier*. See MIS-[1], CARRY.

miscast *v.t.* to cast (a play or an actor) inappropriately. WH: 14–15C. MIS-[1] + CAST.

miscegenation *n.* intermarriage or interbreeding between people of different races. WH: 19C. Latin *miscere* MIX + *genus* race + -ATION.

miscellaneous *a.* consisting of several kinds, mixed. WH: 17C. Latin *miscellaneus*, from *miscellus* mixed, from *miscere* MIX. See also -EOUS.

mischance *n.* misfortune, bad luck. *Also v.i.* WH: 12–14C. Old French *meschance*, from *mescheoir*, from *mes-* MIS-[1] + *cheoir* to befall. See CHANCE.

mischief *n.* irritating behaviour that is non-malicious, esp. practical jokes etc. *Also v.t.* WH: 12–14C. Old French *meschef* (Modern French *méchef*), from *meschever*, from *mes-* MIS-[1] + *chever* to come to an end (of), from *chef* head.

misch metal *n.* an alloy of cerium with other rare earth metals, used for cigarette-lighter flints. WH: early 20C. German *Mischmetall*, from *mischen* to mix + *Metall* metal.

miscible *a.* capable of being mixed (with). WH: 16C. Medieval Latin *miscibilis*, from Latin *miscere* MIX. See also -IBLE.

miscompute *v.t.* to calculate wrongly, to miscalculate. *Also n.* WH: 17C. MIS-[1] + COMPUTE.

misconceive *v.t.* to have a wrong idea of. WH: 14–15C. MIS-[1] + CONCEIVE.

misconduct[1] *n.* improper conduct, e.g. adultery. WH: 18C. MIS-[1] + CONDUCT[1].

misconduct[2] *v.t.* to mismanage. WH: 18C. MIS-[1] + CONDUCT[2].

misconstrue *v.t.* to put a wrong interpretation or construction upon. WH: 14–15C. MIS-[1] + CONSTRUE.

miscopy *v.t.* to copy incorrectly. WH: 19C. MIS-[1] + COPY.

miscount[1] *v.t.* to count wrongly. *Also v.i.* WH: 14–15C. MIS-[1] + COUNT[1].

miscount[2] *n.* a mistake in counting, esp. of votes. WH: 16C. MIS-[1] + COUNT[1].

miscreant *n.* a vile wretch, a scoundrel. *Also a.* WH: 12–14C. Old French *mescreant* (Modern French *mécréant*) misbelieving, unbelieving, pres.p. of *mescroire* (Modern French *mécroire*) to disbelieve, from *mes-* MIS-[1] + *croire*, from Latin *credere* to believe. See also -ANT. The original sense was misbeliever, heretic. The current sense dates from the 16C.

miscreate[1] *v.t.* to create wrongly or badly. WH: 17C. MIS-[1] + CREATE.

†miscreate[2] *a.* deformed, shapeless. WH: 16C. MIS-[1] + obs. *create* created, from Latin *creatus*, p.p. of *creare*. See CREATE, also -ATE[2].

miscue *n.* in billiards, snooker etc., failure to strike a ball properly with the cue. *Also v.i.* WH: 19C. MIS-[1] (or stem of MISS[1]) + CUE[2].

misdate *v.t.* to date wrongly. *Also n.* WH: 16C. MIS-[1] + DATE[1].

misdeal *v.t.* to deal wrongly (as cards). *Also v.i., n.* WH: 15C. MIS-[1] + DEAL[1].

misdeed *n.* a crime. WH: pre-1200. Old English *misdǣd*, from Germanic base of MIS-[1], DEED.

misdemeanour *n.* misbehaviour, misconduct. WH: 15C. MIS-[1] + *demeanour* (DEMEAN[2]).

misdescribe *v.t.* to describe wrongly. WH: 19C. MIS-[1] + DESCRIBE.

misdiagnose *v.t.* to diagnose incorrectly. WH: early 20C. MIS-[1] + *diagnose* (DIAGNOSIS).

misdial *v.t., v.i.* to dial (a telephone number) incorrectly. WH: mid-20C. MIS-[1] + DIAL.

misdirect *v.t.* to direct (a person, letter etc.) wrongly. WH: 17C. MIS-[1] + DIRECT.

misdivision *n.* wrong or erroneous division. WH: 19C. MIS-[1] + DIVISION.

misdoing *n.* a misdeed, a wrong action. WH: 12–14C. MIS-[1] + DOING.

†**misdoubt** *v.t.* to have doubts or misgivings as to the truth or fact of. *Also v.i., n.* WH: 12–14C. MIS-[1] + DOUBT.

†**mise** *n.* a treaty, esp. a settlement by arbitration or compromise. WH: 14–15C. Old French action of setting, expenses, wages, from *mis*, p.p. of *mettre* to place, to set, from Latin *mittere* to send, (later) to put, to place.

miseducate *v.t.* to educate wrongly. WH: 19C. MIS-[1] + EDUCATE.

mise en scène *n.* the settings, properties etc. of a play, film etc. WH: 19C. French *mise en scène*, lit. (a) putting onto the stage, from fem. p.p. (used as n.) of *mettre* to put + *en* on + *scène* stage, SCENE.

misemploy *v.t.* to misapply, to misuse. WH: 17C. MIS-[1] + EMPLOY.

miser *n.* a person who denies themselves the comforts of life for the sake of hoarding. WH: 15C. Latin wretched, unfortunate. The original sense (to the 19C) was miserable or wretched person.

miserable *a.* very wretched or unhappy. *Also n.* WH: 14–15C. Old French *misérable*, from Latin *miserabilis* pitiable, from *miserari* to be pitiful, from *miser*. See MISER, also -ABLE.

misère *n.* a declaration in solo whist etc. by which a player undertakes not to take a single trick. WH: 19C. French poverty, misery.

miserere *n.* a prayer or cry for mercy. WH: 12–14C. Latin have mercy!, imper. sing. of *misereri* to have pity, to have mercy, from *miser* MISER. The word begins the Latin version of Ps. li, more fully: *Miserere mei Deus* Have mercy upon me, O God.

misericord *n.* a bracketed projection on the underside of the seat of a choir stall, to allow a person standing to rest. WH: 12–14C. Old French *miséricorde*, from Latin *misericordia*, from *misericors* pitiful, from *miser*, stem of *misereri* (MISERERE) + *cor, cordis* heart. The original meaning was compassion, mercy. The sense projection on a choir stall seat evolved in the 16C. Such a projection 'pities' the person standing in the stall and enables him to rest.

misery *n.* great unhappiness or wretchedness of mind or body. WH: 14–15C. Anglo-French, var. of Old French *misère*, or from Latin *miseria*, from *miser*. See MISER, also -Y[2].

misfeasance *n.* a trespass, a wrong, esp. negligent or improper performance of a lawful act. WH: 17C. Old French *mesfaisance*, from pres.p. of *mesfaire* (Modern French *méfaire*), from *mes-* MIS-[1] + *faire* to do. See also -ANCE. Cp. MALFEASANCE.

misfield[1] *v.t.* to field (a cricket ball, baseball etc.) badly. WH: 19C. MIS-[1] + FIELD.

misfield[2] *n.* an act of misfielding a cricket ball, baseball etc. WH: 19C. MIS-[1] + FIELD.

misfire *n.* failure to go off or explode (of a gun, charge etc.). *Also v.i.* WH: 18C. MIS-[1] + FIRE.

misfit[1] *n.* a bad fit. WH: 19C. MIS-[1] + FIT[1].

misfit[2] *v.t., v.i.* to fail to fit. WH: 19C. MIS-[1] + FIT[1].

misfortune *n.* bad luck, calamity. WH: 14–15C. MIS-[1] + FORTUNE.

misgive *v.t.* to fill (one's mind) with doubt or suspicion. WH: 16C. MIS-[1] + GIVE.

misgovern *v.t.* to govern badly. WH: 14–15C. MIS-[1] + GOVERN.

misguided *a.* mistaken in thought, foolish. WH: 15C. *misguide* (from MIS-[1] + GUIDE) + -ED.

mishandle *v.t.* to deal with (a matter etc.) ineffectively or incorrectly. WH: 14–15C. MIS-[1] + HANDLE.

mishap *n.* an unfortunate accident, a mischance. WH: 12–14C. MIS-[1] + HAP[1].

mishear *v.t.* to hear incorrectly. WH: pre-1200. MIS-[1] + HEAR.

mishit[1] *v.t.* to hit wrongly. WH: early 20C. MIS-[1] + HIT.

mishit[2] *n.* an instance of hitting wrongly. WH: 19C. MIS-[1] + HIT.

mishmash *n.* a hotchpotch, a jumble. WH: 15C. Redupl. of MASH[1].

Mishnah *n.* the second or oral Jewish law, the collection of traditions etc. forming the text of the Talmud. WH: 17C. Post-biblical Hebrew *mišnāh* repetition, instruction.

misidentify *v.t.* to identify wrongly. WH: 19C. MIS-[1] + IDENTIFY.

misinform *v.t.* to give erroneous information to. WH: 15C. MIS-[1] + INFORM[1].

misinterpret *v.t.* to interpret wrongly. WH: 16C. MIS-[1] + INTERPRET.

misjoin *v.t.* to join or connect badly or improperly. WH: 16C. MIS-[1] + JOIN.

misjudge *v.t.* to form an erroneous opinion of. WH: 14–15C. MIS-[1] + JUDGE.

miskey *v.t.* to enter (data) wrongly from a keyboard. WH: late 20C. MIS-[1] + KEY[1].

miskick[1] *v.t.* to kick (a ball) badly. WH: 19C. MIS-[1] + KICK[1].

miskick[2] *n.* an instance of miskicking a ball. WH: 19C. MIS-[1] + KICK[1].

Miskito *n.* a member of a people of the Atlantic coast of Honduras and Nicaragua. *Also a.* WH: 18C. American Indian name.

mislay *v.t.* to put in a wrong place or in a place that cannot be remembered. WH: 14–15C. MIS-[1] + LAY[1].

mislead *v.t.* to deceive, to delude. WH: pre-1200. Old English *mislǣdan*. See MIS-[1], LEAD[1].

†**mislike** *v.t.* to dislike. *Also v.i., n.* WH: pre-1200. Old English *mislīcian*. See MIS-[1], LIKE[2].

mismanage *v.t., v.i.* to manage badly or wrongly. WH: 17C. MIS-[1] + MANAGE.

mismarriage *n.* an unsuitable, incongruous or unfortunate marriage. WH: 19C. MIS-[1] + MARRIAGE.

mismatch[1] *v.t.* to match unsuitably. WH: 16C. MIS-[1] + MATCH[1].

mismatch[2] *n.* an unsuitable match. WH: 17C. MIS-[1] + MATCH[1].

mismated *a.* mated or matched unsuitably. WH: 19C. MIS-[1] + MATE[1] + -ED.

mismeasure *v.t.* to measure wrongly. WH: 18C. MIS-[1] + MEASURE.

misname *v.t.* to call by a wrong or unsuitable name. WH: 18C. MIS-[1] + NAME.

misnomer *n.* a mistaken or misapplied name or designation. WH: 14–15C. Anglo-French, use as n. of Old French *mesnomer*, from *mes-* MIS-[1] + *nommer*, from Latin *nominare*, from *nomen* name. See also -ER[4].

misogamy *n.* hatred of marriage. WH: 17C. Modern Latin *misogamia*, from Greek *misogamos* hating marriage. See MIS-[2], -GAMY.

misogyny *n.* hatred of women. WH: 17C. Modern Latin *misogynia*, from Greek *misogunia*, from *miso-* MIS-[2] + *gunē* woman. See also -Y[2].

misology *n.* hatred of reason or knowledge. WH: 19C. MIS-[2] + -LOGY.

misoneism *n.* hatred of what is new. WH: 19C. MIS-[2] + Greek *neos* new. See also -ISM.

mispickel *n.* a mineral composed of iron, arsenic and sulphur, arsenical pyrites. WH: 17C. German *Misspickel*, of unknown orig.

misplace *v.t.* to mislay. *Also v.i.* WH: 16C. MIS-[1] + PLACE.

misplay *v.t.* to play (a card, ball etc.) wrongly or ineffectively. *Also n.* WH: 19C. MIS-[1] + PLAY.

misplead *v.t., v.i.* to plead wrongly. WH: 17C. MIS-[1] + PLEAD.

misprint[1] *v.t.* to print incorrectly. WH: 15C. MIS-[1] + PRINT.

misprint[2] *n.* a mistake in printing. WH: 19C. MIS-[1] + PRINT.

misprision[1] *n.* an offence involving the concealment or neglect of one's knowledge of a crime. WH: 14–15C. Old French *mesprison* error, wrong action, from *mesprendre* (Modern French *méprendre*), from *mes-* MIS-[1] + *prendre* to take.

misprision[2] *n.* undervaluing. WH: 16C. MISPRIZE, based on MISPRISION[1].

misprize *v.t.* to undervalue, to slight, to despise. *Also n.* WH: 14–15C. Old French *mesprisier* (Modern French *mépriser*), from *mes-* MIS-[1] + *priser*, from *pris-*. See also PRIZE[1].

mispronounce *v.t.* to pronounce wrongly. WH: 16C. MIS-[1] + PRONOUNCE.

mispunctuate *v.t., v.i.* to punctuate wrongly. WH: 19C. MIS-[1] + PUNCTUATE.

misquote *v.t.* to quote erroneously. WH: 16C. MIS-[1] + QUOTE.

misread *v.t.* to read incorrectly. WH: 19C. MIS-[1] + READ.

misrelate *v.t.* to relate inaccurately. WH: 17C. MIS-[1] + RELATE.

misremember *v.t.* to remember imperfectly. WH: 16C. MIS-[1] + REMEMBER.

misreport *v.t.* to report wrongly. *Also n.* WH: 14–15C. MIS-[1] + REPORT.

misrepresent *v.t.* to represent falsely or incorrectly. WH: 17C. MIS-[1] + REPRESENT.

misrule *n.* bad government. *Also v.t.* WH: 14–15C. MIS-[1] + RULE.

miss[1] *v.t.* to fail to reach, hit or meet. *Also v.i.*, *n.* WH: pre-1200. Old English *missan*, from Germanic. See also MIS-[1].

miss[2] *n.* a title of address for an unmarried woman or girl. WH: 17C. Abbr. of MISTRESS. Cp. MRS, MS.

missal *n.* in the Roman Catholic Church, the book containing the service of the Mass for the whole year. WH: 12–14C. Ecclesiastical Latin *missale*, neut. sing. of *missalis*, from *missa* MASS.

misshape *v.t.* to give a bad shape to. *Also n.* WH: 14–15C. MIS-[1] + SHAPE.

missile *n.* a weapon or other object projected or propelled through the air, esp. a rocket-propelled weapon. *Also a.* WH: 17C. Latin *missilis*, from *missus*, p.p. of *mittere* to send (out).

mission *n.* the commission or charge of a messenger, agent etc. WH: 16C. French, or from Latin *missio, missionis*, from *missus*, p.p. of *mittere* to send (out). See also -ION.

missis *n.* a wife. WH: 18C. Representation of an informal pronun. of MISTRESS. Cp. MRS.

missive *n.* a message, a letter. *Also a.* WH: 14–15C. Medieval Latin *missivus*, from Latin *missus*. See MISSION, also -IVE.

misspell *v.t.* to spell incorrectly. WH: 17C. MIS-[1] + SPELL[1].

misspend *v.t.* to spend wastefully or inadvisedly. WH: 14–15C. MIS-[1] + SPEND.

misstate *v.t.* to state wrongly. WH: 17C. MIS-[1] + STATE.

misstep *n.* a wrong step, action, speech etc. WH: 18C. MIS-[1] + STEP.

missuit *v.t.* to be ill-suited or unbecoming to. WH: 17C. MIS-[1] + SUIT.

mist *n.* visible water vapour in the atmosphere at or near the surface of the earth. *Also v.t., v.i.* WH: pre-1200. Old English, from Germanic, from Indo-European base represented also by Greek *omikhlē* mist, fog.

mistake *v.t.* to understand wrongly. *Also v.i., n.* WH: 12–14C. Old Norse *mistaka* to take in error, from *mis-* MIS-[1] + *taka* TAKE[1].

misteach *v.t.* to teach wrongly or incorrectly. WH: pre-1200. MIS-[1] + TEACH.

mister *n.* the common form of address prefixed to untitled men's names or certain official titles (abbr. in writing to Mr). *Also v.t.* WH: 15C. Var. of MASTER. Cp. MISTRESS.

misterm *v.t.* to misname. WH: 16C. MIS-[1] + TERM.

mistico *n.* a small coasting vessel used in the Mediterranean. WH: 19C. Spanish, ? ult. from Arabic *musaṭṭaḥ* armed vessel.

mistigris *n.* the joker or a blank card used as a wild card in a form of draw poker. WH: 19C. French *mistigri* jack of clubs, orig. a pop. cat name, from *miste*, var. of *mite*, of imit. orig + *gris* grey.

mistime *v.t.* to say or do at an inappropriate time. WH: pre-1200. Old English *mistimian*. See MIS-[1], TIME. The original sense was to cause or suffer misfortune. The current sense dates from the 17C.

mistitle *v.t.* to call (someone) by a wrong title. WH: 17C. MIS-[1] + TITLE.

mistle thrush *n.* the largest of the European thrushes, *Turdus viscivorus*, that feeds on mistletoe berries. WH: pre-1200. Old English *mistel*, from Germanic, from Germanic, ult. of unknown orig. The original meaning (to the 17C) was mistletoe. The thrush name dates from the 17C.

mistletoe *n.* a plant, *Viscum album*, parasitic on the apple and other trees, bearing white glutinous berries. WH: pre-1200. Old English *misteltān*, from *mistel* (MISTLE THRUSH) + *tān* twig. The final *-n* of the original Old English word was dropped because *-tān* was taken to be the plural of *tā* toe.

mistral *n.* a cold dry NW wind of S France. WH: 17C. French, from Provençal, from Latin *magistralis* (*ventus*) dominant (wind). See MAGISTERIAL.

mistranslate *v.t.* to translate wrongly. WH: 16C. MIS-[1] + TRANSLATE.

mistreat *v.t.* to ill-treat. WH: 14–15C. MIS-[1] + TREAT.

mistress *n.* a woman with whom a man has a long-term extra-marital relationship. WH: 12–14C. Old French *maistresse* (Modern French *maîtresse*), from *maistre* MASTER + *-esse* -ESS[1]. The first vowel was subsequently shortened. Cp. MISTER. The original sense was a woman in charge of a child.

mistrial *n.* an abortive or inconclusive trial. WH: 17C. MIS-[1] + TRIAL.

mistrust *v.t.* to regard with doubt or suspicion. *Also n.* WH: 14–15C. MIS-[1] + TRUST, prob. based on Old French *mesfier* (Modern French *méfier*).

mistype *v.t.* to type (a character, number etc.) incorrectly. WH: mid-20C. MIS-[1] + TYPE.

misunderstand *v.t.* to mistake the meaning or sense of. WH: 12–14C. MIS-[1] + UNDERSTAND.

misuse[1] *v.t.* to use or treat improperly. WH: 14–15C. MIS-[1] + USE[2].

misuse[2] *n.* improper use. WH: 14–15C. MIS-[1] + USE[1].

misword *v.t.* to word incorrectly. WH: 17C. MIS-[1] + WORD.

miswrite *v.t.* to write incorrectly. WH: pre-1200. MIS-[1] + WRITE.

mite[1] *n.* any minute arachnid of the order Acarida occurring in terrestrial or aquatic habitats. WH: pre-1200. Old English *mīte*, from Germanic.

mite[2] *n.* a very small coin, orig. Flemish. WH: 14–15C. Middle Low German and Middle Dutch *mīte*, from Germanic, prob. identical with MITE[1].

Mithraism *n.* the worship of the ancient Persian god Mithra, the god of light and the sun. WH: 19C. *Mithra*, from Latin *Mithras*, from Greek, from Old Persian *Mithra*, an ancient Persian god identified with the sun + -ISM.

mithridatism *n.* immunity to poison brought about by the administering of gradually increasing doses of it. WH: 19C. *Mithridates* VI, d.63 BC, king of Pontus, who reputedly made himself immune to poisons by constantly using antidotes + -ISM.

mitigate *v.t.* to make less rigorous or harsh. *Also v.i.* WH: 14–15C. Latin *mitigatus*, p.p. of *mitigare*, from *mitis* mild, gentle. See also -ATE[3].

mitochondrion *n.* a spherical or rodlike organism, found in cytoplasm, whose function is energy production. WH: early 20C. Greek *mitos* thread + *khondrion*, dim. of *khondros* granule, lump (of salt).

mitogenetic *a.* productive of mitosis. WH: mid-20C. MITOSIS + GENETIC.

mitosis *n.* indirect cell division. WH: 19C. Greek *mitos* thread of a warp + -OSIS.

mitrailleuse *n.* a breech-loading machine-gun consisting of several barrels united, for firing simultaneously or in succession. WH: 19C. French, fem. of *mitrailleur*, from *mitrailler* to fire mitraille, from *mitraille* small money, pieces of metal, from *mite*, rel. to MITE[2].

mitral *a.* of or resembling a mitre. WH: 17C. Modern Latin *mitralis*, from Latin *mitra* MITRE. See also -AL[1].

mitre *n.* a tall ornamental cap shaped like a cleft cone rising into two peaks, worn as a symbol of office by bishops and abbots. *Also v.t., v.i.* WH: 12–14C. Old French, from Latin *mitra*, from Greek *mitra* belt, turban, ? of Asian orig.

mitt *n.* a mitten. WH: 18C. Abbr. of MITTEN.

mitten *n.* a glove with a thumb but no fingers. WH: 12–14C. Old French *mitaine*, from *mite* mitten, ? from Old High German *mittamo* middle, midmost. The original literal sense was probably glove cut off at the middle.

mittimus *n.* a warrant of commitment to prison. WH: 14–15C. Latin we send, 1st pers. plur. pres. ind. of *mittere* to send, first word of the writ in Latin.

mitzvah *n.* in Judaism, a commandment or rule. WH: 17C. Hebrew *miṣwāh* commandment. Cp. BAR MITZVAH, BAT MITZVAH.

mix *v.t.* to put together or blend into one mass or compound. *Also v.i., n.* WH: 15C. Back-formation from *mixed*, from Old French *mixte*, from Latin *mixtus*, p.p. of *miscere* to mingle, to mix. See also -ED.

mixen *n.* a dunghill. WH: pre-1200. Old English, from Germanic, ult. from Germanic base meaning to urinate. Cp. German *Mist* dung, Old English *mīgan* to urinate.

mixture *n.* something which is being or has been mixed. WH: 14–15C. French, or from Latin *mixtura*, from *mixtus*, p.p. of *miscere* MIX. See also -URE.

mizzen *n.* a fore-and-aft sail set on the mizzen-mast of a sailing ship. WH: 14–15C. French *misaine* (now foresail, foremast), from Italian *mezzana*, use as n. of fem. of *mezzano* middle.

mizzle[1] *v.i.* to rain in very fine drops, to drizzle. *Also n.* WH: 14–15C. Prob. from German *miseln*, freq. of the Low German base represented by Dutch dial. *miesregen* to drizzle, Low German *misig* drizzling. See also -LE[4].

mizzle[2] *v.i.* to run away, decamp. WH: 18C. Orig. unknown.

M.Litt. *abbr.* Master of Letters. WH: Abbr. of Latin *Magister Litterarum* Master of Letters.

mnemonic *n.* an aid to memory. *Also a.* WH: 18C. Medieval Latin *mnemonicus*, from Greek *mnēmonikos*, from *mnēmon* mindful, from *mna-* base of *mnasthai* to remember. See also -IC.

mo[1] *n.* moment. WH: 19C. Abbr. of MOMENT.

†mo[2] *n., a., adv.* more. WH: pre-1200. Old English *mā*, from Germanic comp., from Indo-European. Cp. German *mehr* more.

-mo *suf.* used to form nouns denoting book size. WH: Final syllable of terms derived from the abl. sing. masc. of Latin ordinal numerals.

moa *n.* an extinct, flightless bird of the genus *Dinornis*. WH: 19C. Maori.

moan *n.* a low prolonged sound expressing pain or sorrow. *Also v.i., v.t.* WH: 12–14C. Ult. from Germanic base also of obs. *mean* to complain, to lament, from Old English *mǣnan*.

moat *n.* a ditch round a castle, fort etc., usu. filled with water. *Also v.t.* WH: 14–15C. Var. of obs. *mote* mound, embankment, from Old French *mote* hillock, mound, castle. See MOTTE.

mob *n.* a gang of criminals engaged in organized crime. *Also v.t., v.i.* WH: 17C. Abbr. of obs. *mobile*, from Latin *mobile* (*vulgus*), lit. the excitable (crowd).

mob cap *n.* a plain indoor cap or headdress for women, usu. tied under the chin. WH: 17C. Var. of obs. *mab* slattern, promiscuous woman, of unknown orig. The original meaning was prostitute. The sense of cap evolved in the 18C.

mobile *a.* movable, free to move. *Also n.* WH: 15C. Old French, from Latin *mobilis*, from *movere* MOVE. See also -IL.

Möbius strip *n.* a long, rectangular strip of paper twisted through 180° and joined at the ends, to form a one-sided surface bounded by one continuous curve. WH: early 20C. August Ferdinand *Möbius*, 1790–1868, German mathematician, who discovered it in 1858.

moccasin *n.* a bedroom slipper of soft leather made of one piece. WH: 17C. Virginia Algonquian *mockasin*.

mocha *n.* a choice quality of coffee, orig. from Mocha. WH: 18C. *Mocha*, a port in Yemen on the Red Sea.

mock *v.t.* to deride, to laugh at. *Also v.i., a., n.* WH: 14–15C. Old French *moquer* (Modern French *se moquer de* to laugh at) to deride, to jeer, from base represented also by Italian dial. *moka*, Spanish *mueca* grimace, Portuguese *moca* derision, prob. ult. of imit. orig. The word has also been related to the Old French verb *moucher* to blow the nose (related to MUCUS), alluding to a contemptuous gesture or action.

mod[1] *a.* modern. *Also n.* WH: mid-20C. Abbr. of MODERN.

mod[2] *prep., adv.* modulo. WH: 19C. Abbr. of *modulo* (MODULUS).

mod[3] *n.* a Highland gathering analogous to a Welsh eisteddfod. WH: 19C. Gaelic *mòd* assembly, court, from Old Norse *mót*. See MOOT.

modal *a.* of or relating to mode, form or manner, as opposed to substance. *Also n.* WH: 16C. Medieval Latin *modalis*, from Latin *modus*. See MODE, also -AL[1].

mod cons *n.pl.* modern devices or appliances that give comfort, convenience etc. WH: mid-20C. Abbr. of *modern conveniences*.

mode *n.* method, way of doing, existing etc. WH: 14–15C. French, from Latin *modus* measure, from Indo-European base also of METE[1]. Cp. MOOD[2]. Many of the technical senses, e.g. in music, logic and philosophy, derive direct from Latin *modus*.

model *n.* a representation or pattern in miniature, in three dimensions, of something made on a larger scale. *Also a., v.t., v.i.* WH: 16C. Obs. French *modelle* (now *modèle*), from Italian *modello*, from alt. of Latin MODULUS.

modem *n.* a device used to transmit and receive data, esp. between computers over a telephone line. WH: mid-20C. *modulator* (MODULATE) + *demodulator* (DEMODULATE). A modem is a combined modulator and demodulator.

modena *n.* a deep crimson or purple. WH: 19C. *Modena*, a city in N Italy.

moderate[1] *a.* temperate, reasonable. *Also n.* WH: 14–15C. Latin *moderatus*, p.p. of *moderari*. See MODERATE[2], also -ATE[2].

moderate[2] *v.t.* to reduce to a calmer or less intense condition. *Also v.i.* WH: 14–15C. Latin *moderatus*, p.p. of *moderari* to reduce, to control. See also -ATE[3].

modern *a.* of or relating to the present or recent time. *Also n.* WH: 14–15C. Old French *moderne* or Late Latin *modernus*, from Latin *modo* just now, based on *hodiernus* of today (from *hodie* today).

modest *a.* humble, unassuming in regard to one's merits or importance. WH: 16C. Old French *modeste*, from Latin *modestus* keeping due measure, from base of MODERATE[2] + p.p. suf.

modicum *n.* a little, a small amount, a scanty allowance. WH: 15C. Latin little way, short time, neut. sing. of *modicus* moderate, from *modus* MODE.

modify *v.t.* to alter, to make different. WH: 14–15C. Old French *modifier*, from Latin *modificari*, from *modus* MODE. See also -FY.

modillion *n.* an ornamental bracket beneath a cornice, esp. in the Corinthian order. WH: 16C. French *modillion*, from Italian *modiglione*, ult. from Latin *mutulus* MUTULE.

modiolus *n.* the central column round which the cochlea of the ear winds. WH: 17C. Latin nave of a wheel, dim. of MODUS.

modish *a.* fashionable, stylish. WH: 17C. MODE + -ISH[1].

modiste *n.* a milliner. WH: 19C. French, from *mode* fashion, MODE + -*iste* -IST.

Mods *n.pl.* Moderations, the first public examination for a degree at Oxford University. WH: 19C. Abbr. of *Moderations* (MODERATE[2]).

modular *a.* of or relating to a module, consisting of modules. WH: 18C. Modern Latin *modularis*, from Latin MODULUS. See also -AR[1].

modulate *v.t.* to adjust, to regulate. *Also v.i.* WH: 16C. Latin *modulatus*, p.p. of *modulari* to measure, to adjust to rhythm, to make melody, from MODULUS. See also -ATE[3].

module *n.* any element or unit that forms part of a larger system, e.g. of a spacecraft, an educational course. WH: 16C. French, or from Latin MODULUS. See also -ULE.

modulus *n.* a constant number or coefficient expressing a force, effect, function, etc. WH: 16C. Latin, dim. of *modus* MODE.

modus *n.* mode, manner, way. WH: 16C. Latin MODE.

modus operandi *n.* a method of working. WH: 17C. Latin mode of operating, from MODUS + gen. of *operandum*, ger. of *operare* OPERATE.

modus vivendi *n.* a way of living, or life. WH: 19C. Latin mode of living, from MODUS + gen. of *vivendum*, ger. of *vivere* to live.

mofette *n.* a fissure in the earth giving vent to noxious gas, a fumarole. WH: 19C. French, from Neapolitan Italian *mofetta*, from *muffa* mould, mildew, from Germanic base *muff-*, of imit. orig. (cp. SNIFF).

mog *n.* a cat. WH: 17C. Var. of *Maggie*, pet form of female forename *Margaret*. The original sense of *maggie* was girl, wench. The term for a cat evolved in the early 20C, when the short form *mog* is also first recorded.

Mogadon® *n.* a drug used to treat insomnia. WH: mid-20C. Orig. unknown. ? Anagram of *Goodman* or *good man*.

mogul[1] *n.* a powerful and influential entrepreneur. WH: 16C. Urdu *mugal*, from Persian and Urdu *muġul*, alt. of MONGOL.

mogul[2] *n.* a mound of packed snow on a ski slope. WH: mid-20C. Prob. from S German dial. *Mugel, Mugl*.

mohair *n.* the hair of the angora goat. WH: 16C. Arabic *mukayyar* cloth of goat's hair, lit. select, choice, pass. part. of *kayyara* to prefer. Not rel. to HAIR although later assim. to this. Cp. MOIRE.

Mohawk *n.* a member of a N American Indian people. *Also a.* WH: 17C. Narragansett *mohowawog*, lit. man-eaters. Not rel. to HAWK[1].

Mohican *n.* a member of a N American Indian people living in the Hudson river valley. *Also a.* WH: 17C. Mohegan.

Moho *n.* the boundary between the earth's crust and mantle, the Mohorovičić discontinuity. WH: mid-20C. Abbr. of *Mohorovičić discontinuity*, from Andrija *Mohorovičić*, 1857–1936, Croatian seismologist and meteorologist.

Mohock *n.* any set of aristocratic ruffians who roamed the streets of London at night early in the 18th cent. WH: 17C. Var. of MOHAWK.

Mohs scale *n.* a scale of 1–10 by which the hardness of minerals is measured. WH: 19C. Friedrich *Mohs*, 1773–1839, German mineralogist.

moidore *n.* a Portuguese gold coin. WH: 18C. Portuguese *moeda d'ouro* money of gold.

moiety *n.* a half. WH: 14–15C. Old French *moité* (Modern French *moitié*), from Latin *medietas, medietatis*, from *medius* MID[2]. See also -ITY.

†moil *v.i.* to toil, to drudge, to work hard. *Also v.t.* WH: 14–15C. Old French *moillier* to wet, to moisten, to paddle in mud (Modern French *mouiller*), from Latin *mollis* soft. The original meaning was to wet, to bedaub. The sense to toil evolved in the 16C.

moire *n.* watered silk. WH: 17C. French, later form of *mouaire* MOHAIR.

moist *a.* moderately wet, damp. WH: 14–15C. Old French *moiste* (Modern French *moite*), ? from Latin *mucidus* mouldy, alt. by assoc. with *musteus* new, fresh, from *mustum* MUST[3].

moke *n.* a donkey. WH: 19C. Prob. from a pers. name. Cp. MOG.

moki *n.* a New Zealand sea fish, either *Latridopsis ciliaris* or *Chironemus spectabilis*. WH: 19C. Maori.

moko *n.* the Maori method of tattooing. WH: 19C. Maori.

moksha *n.* in Hindu and Jain religions, release from the cycle of rebirth. WH: 18C. Sanskrit *mokṣa*, from *muc* to set free, to release.

molar[1] *n.* any of the back or grinding teeth. *Also a.* WH: 14–15C. Latin *molaris* of a mill, grindstone, from *mola* mill. See also -AR[1].

molar[2] *a.* of or relating to mass. WH: 19C. Latin *moles* mass + -AR[1].

molasses *n.* the sticky, dark-brown uncrystallizable syrup drained from sugar during the refining process. WH: 16C. Portuguese *melaço*, from Late Latin *mellaceum* must, use as n. of neut. sing. of *mellaceus* of the nature of honey, from Latin *mel, mellis* honey.

mole[1] *n.* a spot on the human skin, usu. dark-coloured and sometimes covered with hair. WH: pre-1200. Old English *māl*, from Germanic, rel. to Old English *mǣlan* to stain.

mole[2] *n.* a small soft-furred burrowing mammal of the family Talpidae, esp. *Talpa europaea*. *Also v.t.* WH: 12–14C. Prob. from Middle Dutch *mol*, ? rel. to MOULD[3] and so to MEAL[2].

mole[3] *n.* a pile of masonry, such as a breakwater or jetty by a port. WH: 14–15C. French *môle*, from Latin *moles* mass.

mole[4] *n.* the basic SI unit of substance, being the amount of substance of a system which contains as many specified elementary entities as there are atoms in 0.012 kg of carbon-12. WH: early 20C. German *Mol*, from *Molekül* molecule.

mole[5] *n.* an abnormal fleshy growth in the uterus. WH: 14–15C. Latin *mola*.

molecule *n.* any of the structural units of which matter is built up, the smallest quantity of substance capable of separate existence without losing its chemical identity with that substance. WH: French *molécule*, from Modern Latin *molecula*, dim. of Latin *moles* MOLE[3]. See also -CULE.

molest *v.t.* to trouble, to harm. WH: 14–15C. Old French *molester* or Latin *molestare*, from *molestus* troublesome, ? rel. to *moles* MOLE[3].

moline *a.* (of the arms of a cross) shaped like the support for a millstone, with broad backward-curving extremities. *Also n.* WH: 16C. Prob. from Anglo-French, from *molin* (Modern French *moulin*) mill.

Molinism *n.* the doctrine that the efficacy of divine grace depends on free acceptance by the human will. WH: 17C. Luis de *Molina*, 1535–1600, Spanish Jesuit + -ISM.

moll *n.* a gangster's girlfriend. WH: 17C. Pet form of female forename *Mary*. Cp. MOLLY[1].

mollify *v.t.* to soften, to assuage. WH: 14–15C. French *mollifier*, or from Latin *mollificare*, from *mollis* soft. See also -FY.

mollusc *n.* any invertebrate of the Mollusca. WH: 18C. French *mollusque*, from Modern Latin *mollusca*, neut. pl. of Latin *molluscus*, from *mollis* soft.

molly[1] *n.* an effeminate man or boy, a person who likes to be coddled, a milksop. WH: 18C. Pet form of female forename *Mary*. Cp. MOLL.

molly[2] *n.* any brightly-coloured freshwater fish of the genus *Poecilia*, esp. *P. sphenops*. WH: mid-20C. Abbr. of *Mollienisia*, from Count F.N. *Mollien*, 1758–1850, French statesman. See also -IA.

mollymawk *n.* any fulmar, petrel or albatross of the genus *Diomedea*. WH: 17C. Dutch *mallemok*, from *mal* foolish + *mok* gull.

Moloch *n.* an idol of the Phoenicians to which human sacrifices were offered. WH: 17C. Late Latin, from Greek *Molokh*, from Hebrew *mōleḵ*, a Canaanite idol to whom children were sacrificed as burnt offerings. The name is said to be an alteration of Hebrew *meleḵ* king, by substitution of the vowels of *bōšeṯ* shame. 'And thou shalt not let any of thy seed pass through the fire to Molech' (Lev. xviii.21).

Molotov cocktail *n.* a home-made incendiary device consisting of a bottle containing an inflammable liquid, with a rag for a wick. WH: mid-20C. Vyacheslav Mikhailovich *Molotov*, 1890–1936, Soviet Minister for Foreign Affairs, 1939–49.

molten *a.* made of melted metal. WH: 12–14C. P.p. of MELT.

molto *adv.* much, very. WH: 19C. Italian, from Latin *multus* much.

moly *n.* wild garlic, *Allium moly*, with small yellow flowers. WH: 16C. Latin, from Greek *mōlu*, ? rel. to Sanskrit *mūla* root.

molybdenum *n.* a rare metallic element, at. no. 42, chem. symbol Mo, found in combination as molybdenite. WH: 19C. Obs. *molybdena* ore or salt of lead (from Latin *molybdaena*, from Greek *molubdaina* angler's plummet, from *molubdos* lead) + *-um* based on the names of other chemical elements (usu. in -IUM).

mom *n.* mother. WH: Partly var. of MAM, MUM[1], partly abbr. of MOMMA.

moment *n.* a very brief portion of time. WH: 12–14C. Old French, from Latin *momentum* movement, importance, moment of time, from *movere* MOVE. See also -MENT.

momentum *n.* impetus, power of overcoming resistance to motion. WH: 17C. Latin. See MOMENT.

momma *n.* mother. WH: 19C. Alt. of MAMMA[1]. Cp. MOM, MOMMY.

mommy *n.* mummy, mother. WH: early 20C. Alt. of MAMMY. Cp. MOM, MUMMY[2].

Momus *n.* a fault-finding or querulous person. WH: 16C. Latin, from Greek *Mōmos*, the god of ridicule in Greek mythology.

monachal *a.* monastic. WH: 16C. Old French *monacal*, or from Ecclesiastical Latin *monachalis*, from Latin *monachus* MONK. See also -AL[1].

monactinal *a.* (of a sponge) having single-rayed, rod-shaped spicules. WH: 19C. MONO- + Greek *aktis, aktinos* ray + -AL[1].

monad *n.* a simple, indivisible unit. WH: 16C. French *monade* or Late Latin *monas, monadis*, from Greek, from *monos* alone. See also -AD[1].

monadelphous *a.* having the stamens united by their filaments. WH: 19C. MONO- + Greek *adelphos* brother + -OUS. 'Brother' because a flower's stamen is a male organ.

monadnock *n.* a steep, isolated hill of hard rock rising from a plain of softer rock. WH: 19C. *Monadnock*, a hill in New Hampshire, USA.

monandry *n.* the form of marriage in which one woman has only one husband at a time. WH: 19C. From MONOGAMY, based on pair POLYGAMY/ POLYANDRY.

monanthous *a.* bearing only one flower (on each stalk). WH: 19C. MONO- + Greek *anthos* flower + -OUS.

monarch *n.* a sole ruler. WH: 14–15C. Old French *monarque* or Late Latin *monarcha*, from Greek *monarkhēs*, more usu. *monarkhos*, from *monos* alone. See MONO-, ARCH-.

monastery *n.* a residence for a community, esp. of monks, living under religious vows of seclusion. WH: 14–15C. Ecclesiastical Latin *monasterium*, from Ecclesiastical Greek *monastērion*, from Greek *monazein* to live alone, from *monos* alone. Cp. MONK.

monatomic *a.* having one atom in the molecule, monovalent. WH: 19C. MONO- + *atomic* (ATOM).

monaural *a.* (of recorded sound) monophonic as distinct from stereophonic. WH: 19C. MONO- + AURAL.

monazite *n.* a mineral consisting of a phosphate of thorium, cerium and lanthanum. WH: 19C. Greek *monazein* to be solitary + -ITE[1]. The name was coined in 1829 by the German mineralogist Johann F.A. Breithaupt, with reference to the mineral's rarity.

mondaine *a.* of fashionable society. *Also n.* WH: 19C. French, fem. of *mondain*. See MUNDANE. Cp. DEMI-MONDAINE.

Monday *n.* the second day of the week, following Sunday. *Also adv.* WH: pre-1200. Old English *mōnandæg*, from Germanic. See MOON, DAY. The Germanic compound translates Latin *lunae dies* day of the moon, which itself translates Greek *selēnēs hēmera*.

Monegasque *a.* of or relating to the principality of Monaco. *Also n.* WH: 19C. French *monégasque* of Monaco, an independent principality forming an enclave on the S coast of France, from Provençal *mounegasc*, from *Mounegue* Monaco.

Monel *n.* an alloy of nickel and copper with high tensile strength and resistance to corrosion. WH: early 20C. Ambrose *Monell*, d.1921, US president of the International Nickel Company, New York, which introduced the alloy.

monergism *n.* the Lutheran doctrine that regeneration is entirely the work of the Holy Spirit, as distinct from *synergism*. WH: 19C. Modern Latin *monergismus*, from Greek *monos* (MONO-) + *ergon* work. See also -ISM.

monetary *a.* of or relating to money or coinage. WH: 19C. French *monétaire* or Late Latin *monetarius*, from Latin *moneta* MINT[1]. See also -ARY[1].

money *n.* coin or other material used as medium of exchange. WH: 12–14C. Old French *moneie* (Modern French *monnaie* change), from Latin *moneta* mint (in Rome), money. *Moneta* was an epithet of the Roman goddess Juno, in whose temple the mint was housed.

monger *n.* a trader, a dealer (now only in comb., as in *ironmonger*, *scandalmonger*). WH: pre-1200. Old English *mongere*, from *mongian* to deal, to trade, from Germanic, from Latin *mango* dealer, trader. See also -ER[1].

Mongol *n.* a member of an Asian people now inhabiting Mongolia. *Also a.* WH: 17C. Mongolian, said to come from *mong* brave. Cp. MOGUL[1].

mongoose *n.* any of various small civet-like mammals of the family Viverridae, esp. of the genus *Herpestes*, found in Africa, S Europe and SE Asia, which feed on venomous snakes. WH: 17C. Marathi *maṅgūs*, from Telugu *muṅgisi*, Kannada *muṅgisa*. Not rel. to GOOSE.

mongrel *n.* anything, esp. a dog, of mixed breed. *Also a.* WH: 14–15C. Appar. from base meaning to mix (cp. AMONG) + dim. or derog. suf. -rel (cp. COCKEREL, DOGGEREL, SCOUNDREL).

'mongst *prep.* among. WH: 16C. Shortening of *amongst* (AMONG).

monial *n.* a mullion. WH: 12–14C. Old French *moinel* (Modern French *meneau*), use as n. of a., middle, from *moien*. See MEAN[2], also -AL[1].

moniker *n.* a name. WH: 19C. Orig. unknown. According to some, the word is an altered form of MONOGRAM.

moniliform *a.* shaped like a necklace or string of beads. WH: 19C. French *moniliforme* or Modern Latin *moniliformis*, from Latin *monile* necklace. See -FORM.

monism *n.* the doctrine that all existing things and activities are forms or manifestations of one ultimate principle or substance. WH: 19C. Modern Latin *monismus*, from Greek *monos* single. See also -ISM.

monition *n.* a warning (of). WH: 14–15C. Old French, from Latin *monitio*, *monitionis*, from *monitus*, p.p. of *monere* to advise, to warn. See also -ITION.

monitor *n.* a television screen used e.g. with a computer for displaying and checking pictures or information. *Also v.t., v.i.* WH: 16C. Latin, from *monitus*. See MONITION, also -OR. The original sense was school pupil assigned disciplinary duties. The lizard of the name is so called as it is supposed to give warning of crocodiles nearby.

monk *n.* a member of a religious community of men, living apart under vows of poverty, chastity and obedience. WH: pre-1200. Old English *munuc*, from Germanic, from Popular Latin var. of Late Latin *monachus*, from Late Greek *monakhos*, use as n. of a., single, solitary, from *monos* alone. Cp. MONASTERY.

monkey *n.* a long-tailed quadrumanous mammal of various species and families ranging from the anthropoid apes to the lemurs. *Also v.i., v.t.* WH: 16C. Orig. uncertain. ? From Low German dim. of Italian *monna*, or from Spanish *mona* monkey + (dim. suf.) -key. According to some, the word is from *Moneke*, the son of Martin the Ape in the medieval beast epic *Reynard the Fox*.

mono *n., a.* monophonic (sound). WH: mid-20C. Independent adoption of MONO-.

mono- *comb. form* alone, single, as in *monograph*, *monosyllable*. WH: Greek, from *monos* alone, only, single. See also -O-.

monoacid *a.* capable of saturating one molecule of monobasic acid, having only one hydroxide ion per molecule. WH: 19C. MONO- + ACID.

monobasic *a.* (of an acid) with one base or replaceable atom. WH: 19C. MONO- + *basic* (BASE[1]).

monocardian *a.* having a single undivided heart. WH: 19C. MONO- + Greek *kardia* heart. See also -AN.

monocarpic *a.* bearing fruit only once, and dying after fructification. WH: 19C. MONO- + Greek *karpos* fruit + -IC.

monocausal *a.* attributing or assuming a single cause. WH: mid-20C. MONO- + *causal* (CAUSE).

monocephalous *a.* having one head. WH: 19C. MONO- + -*cephalous* (-CEPHALIC).

monoceros *n.* a one-horned creature, the unicorn. WH: 12–14C. Old French, from Latin, from Greek *monokerōs*, from *monos* MONO- + *keras* horn. Cp. UNICORN.

monochlamydeous *a.* (of a flower) having a single floral envelope, as a calyx, but no corolla. WH: 19C. MONO- + Greek *khlamus*, *khlamudos* cloak. See also -EOUS.

monochord *n.* a musical instrument with one string for determining the ratios of musical intervals. WH: 14–15C. Old French *monocorde*, from Late Latin *monochordon* or Greek *monokhordon*, use as n. of neut. of *monokhordos* having a single string. See MONO-, CORD.

monochromatic *a.* (of light) presenting rays of one colour only. WH: 19C. MONO- + CHROMATIC.

monocle *n.* an eyeglass for one eye. WH: 19C. French, from Late Latin *monoculus*, from Greek MONO- + Latin *oculus* eye.

monoclinal *a.* (of strata) dipping continuously in one direction. WH: 19C. MONO- + Greek *klinein* to lean, to slope + -AL[1].

monoclinous *a.* having male and female reproductive organs on the same flower, as distinct from *diclinous*. WH: 19C. French *monocline* or Modern Latin *monoclinus*, or from Greek MONO- + *klinē* bed. See also -OUS.

monoclonal *a.* forming a single clone, deriving from a single cell. WH: early 20C. MONO- + *clonal* (CLONE).

monocoque *n.* in an aircraft, a form of streamlined fuselage shaped like an elongated egg. WH: early 20C. French, from *mono-* MONO- + *coque* eggshell.

monocotyledon *n.* a plant having a single cotyledon. WH: 18C. Modern Latin *monocotyledones* (pl.). See MONO-, COTYLEDON.

monocracy *n.* government by a single person. WH: 17C. MONO- + -CRACY.

monocular *a.* one-eyed. WH: 17C. Late Latin *monoculus* (MONOCLE) + -AR[1].

monoculture *n.* the cultivation of a single type of crop. WH: early 20C. MONO- + CULTURE.

monocycle *n.* a unicycle. WH: 19C. MONO- + CYCLE, based on BICYCLE, TRICYCLE.

monocyte *n.* the largest white blood cell in vertebrate blood. WH: early 20C. MONO- + -CYTE.

monodactylous *a.* having one finger, toe or claw. WH: 19C. Greek *monodaktulos*, from MONO- + *daktulos* finger. See also -OUS.

monodrama *n.* a dramatic piece for one performer only. WH: 18C. MONO- + DRAMA.

monody *n.* in Greek tragedy, an ode, usu. of a mournful character, for a single actor. WH: 17C. Late Latin *monodia*, from Greek *monōdia*, from *monōdos* singing alone, from MONO- + *ōdē* ODE. See also -Y[3].

monoecious *a.* belonging to the Monoecia, a class comprising plants in which the stamens and pistils are in distinct flowers. WH: 18C. Modern Latin *Monoecia*, from MONO- + Greek *oikos* house. See also -IOUS.

monofil *n.* a single strand of synthetic fibre. WH: mid-20C. MONO- + -*fil*, abbr. of FILAMENT.

monogamy *n.* marriage to one wife or husband only at a time. WH: 17C. French *monogamie*, from Ecclesiastical Latin and Greek *monogamia*, from Greek *monogamos*. See MONO-, -GAMY.

monogenesis *n.* generation from one parent, asexual reproduction. WH: 19C. MONO- + GENESIS.

monoglot *a.* speaking only one language. *Also n.* WH: 19C. Greek *monoglōttos*, from MONO- + *glōtta* tongue.

monogony *n.* asexual propagation. WH: 19C. MONO- + Greek -*gonia* begetting + -Y[2].

monogram *n.* a character composed of two or more letters interwoven. WH: 17C. French *monogramme*, from Late Latin *monogramma*, from Greek. See MONO-, -GRAM.

monograph *n.* a treatise on a single thing or class of things. *Also v.t.* WH: 19C. MONO- + -GRAPH, replacing *monography* (18C), from Modern Latin *monographia*, from *monographus* writer of a specialized treatise. See also -Y².

monogynous *a.* having only one wife at a time. WH: 19C. MONO- + -GYNOUS.

monohull *n.* a vessel with a single hull as distinct from a catamaran, trimaran etc. WH: mid-20C. MONO- + HULL¹.

monohybrid *n.* the offspring of two parents that differs with respect to the alleles of one gene. WH: early 20C. MONO- + HYBRID.

monohydric *a.* containing one hydroxyl group per molecule. WH: 19C. MONO- + HYDRIC.

monokini *n.* a one-piece beach garment for a woman, usu. similar to the bottom half of a bikini. WH: mid-20C. MONO- + -*kini* from BIKINI, as if its *bi*- came from BI-.

monolatry *n.* worship of one god, esp. among many. WH: 19C. MONO- + -LATRY.

monolayer *n.* a single layer of atoms or molecules adsorbed on a surface. WH: mid-20C. MONO- + LAYER.

monolingual *a.* using or expressed in only one language. WH: mid-20C. MONO- + LINGUAL.

monolith *n.* a monument or other structure formed of a single stone. WH: 19C. French *monolithe*, from Greek *monolithos*, from MONO- + *lithos* stone.

monologue *n.* a dramatic scene in which a person speaks by themselves, a soliloquy. WH: 17C. French. See MONO-, -LOGUE.

monomania *n.* an obsession of the mind on one subject only. WH: 19C. MONO- + -MANIA.

monomark *n.* any of a system of combinations of numbers serving to identify property or manufactured goods. WH: early 20C. MONO- + MARK¹.

monomer *n.* a compound that can undergo polymerization. WH: early 20C. MONO- + -MER.

monometallism *n.* a one-metal standard of value for coinage. WH: 19C. MONO- + *metallic* (METAL) + -ISM, based on BIMETALLISM.

monometer *n.* a verse consisting of one foot. WH: 19C. Late Latin, from Greek *monometros*, from MONO- + *metron* METRE².

monomial *n.* a mathematical expression consisting of a single term. *Also a.* WH: 18C. MONO- + -*mial*, based on BINOMIAL.

monomolecular *a.* only one molecule in thickness. WH: 19C. MONO- + *molecular* (MOLECULE).

monomorphic *a.* having the same structure or morphological character, esp. throughout successive stages of development. WH: 19C. MONO- + -*morphic* (-MORPH).

mononuclear *a.* having only one nucleus. WH: 19C. MONO- + NUCLEAR.

mononucleosis *n.* the presence of an abnormally large number of monocytes in the blood. WH: early 20C. MONONUCLEAR + -OSIS.

monopetalous *a.* having the petals coherent in a single corolla. WH: 17C. MONO- + PETAL + -OUS.

monophagous *a.* feeding on only one type of food. WH: 19C. MONO- + -PHAGOUS.

monophobia *n.* morbid dread of being alone. WH: 19C. MONO- + -*phobia* (-PHOBE).

monophone *n.* a monophonous sound. WH: 19C. MONO- + Greek *phonē* sound.

monophthong *n.* a simple or single vowel sound. WH: 17C. Greek *monophthoggos*, from MONO- + *phthoggos* voice, sound.

monophyletic *a.* of or relating to a single family or race or descended from one parental form. WH: 19C. MONO- + Greek *phuletikos*, from *phulē* tribe. See also -IC.

monophyllous *a.* having or formed of one leaf. WH: 18C. MONO- + Greek *phullon* leaf. See also -OUS.

Monophysite *n.* a member of an Eastern 5th-cent. sect affirming that there is only one nature in the person of Christ. WH: 17C. Ecclesiastical Latin *Monophysita*, from Ecclesiastical Greek *monophusitēs*, from MONO- + Greek *phusis* nature. See also -ITE¹.

monoplane *n.* an aircraft with one set of wings. WH: early 20C. MONO- + PLANE⁴.

monoplegia *n.* paralysis of a single part or limb. WH: 19C. MONO- + -PLEGIA.

monopod *n.* a structure with only one foot, e.g. a shooting stick.

WH: 19C. Latin *monopodius*, from Late Greek *monopodios*, from MONO- + *pous*, *podos* foot. See also -POD.

monopole¹ *n.* a single electrical charge or a magnetic pole considered in isolation. WH: mid-20C. MONO- + POLE².

monopole² *n.* champagne supplied exclusively to or by one shipper. WH: 16C. Old French, or from Late Latin *monopolium* MONOPOLY.

monopoly *n.* an exclusive trading right in a certain commodity or class of commerce or business. WH: 16C. Latin *monopolium*, from Greek *monopōlion*, from MONO- + *pōlein* to sell.

monopteros *n.* a temple composed of a single circle of columns supporting a roof. WH: 17C. Use as n. of Latin a. from Greek, having one wing, from MONO- + *pteron* wing.

monorail *n.* a railway, usu. elevated, with a track consisting of a single rail. *Also a.* WH: 19C. MONO- + RAIL¹.

monorchid *a.* having only one testicle. WH: 19C. MONO- + Greek *orkhis*, *orkhidos* testicle.

monorhyme *n.* a composition in which all the lines end in the same rhyme. *Also a.* WH: 18C. French *monorime*, from *mono-* MONO- + *rime* RHYME.

monosaccharide *n.* a sugar that cannot be hydrolysed to form simpler sugars. WH: 19C. MONO- + *saccharide* (SACCHAR-).

monosepalous *a.* having one sepal. WH: 19C. MONO- + *sepalous* (SEPAL).

monoski *n.* a single ski on which both the skier's feet are placed. *Also v.i.* WH: mid-20C. MONO- + SKI.

monosodium glutamate *n.* a salt of glutamic acid used as a flavour-enhancing food additive. WH: early 20C. *monosodium* (19C) (from MONO- + SODIUM) + GLUTAMATE.

monospermous *a.* having only one seed. WH: 18C. MONO- + Greek *sperma* seed, SPERM + -OUS.

monostich *n.* a single metrical line forming a complete composition, such as an epigram. *Also a.* WH: 16C. Late Latin *monostichum*, from Greek *monostikhon*, use as n. of neut. of *monostikhos*, from MONO- + *stikhos* vow, line of verse.

monostrophic *a.* in prosody, having only one form of strophe. WH: 17C. Greek *monostrophikos*, from *monostrophos*. See MONO-, STROPHE.

monostyle¹ *a.* consisting of a single shaft. WH: 19C. MONO- + STYLE.

monostyle² *a.* built in the same style throughout. WH: 19C. MONO- + STYLE.

monosyllable *n.* a word of one syllable. WH: 16C. MONO- + SYLLABLE.

monosymmetric *a.* (of a crystal) monoclinic. WH: 19C. MONO- + *symmetric* (SYMMETRY).

monothalamous *a.* possessing a single chamber, as some shells. WH: 19C. MONO- + Greek *thalamos* chamber + -OUS.

monotheism *n.* the doctrine that there is only one God. WH: 17C. MONO- + Greek *theos* god + -ISM.

monotint *n.* a picture or other representation in one colour. WH: 19C. MONO- + TINT.

monotone *n.* continuance of or repetition in the same tone. *Also a., v.t., v.i.* WH: 17C. Modern Latin *monotonus*, from Late Greek *monotonos*, from MONO- + *tonos* TONE.

monotreme *n.* any mammal of the sub-class Monotremata, having only one aperture or vent for the genital organs and the excretions. *Also a.* WH: 19C. MONO- + Greek *trēma*, *trēmatos* hole, perforation.

monotype *n.* an impression on paper produced by inking glass or metal. WH: 19C. MONO- + TYPE.

monotypic *a.* (of a genus etc.) having only one type of animal or plant. WH: 19C. Modern Latin *monotypus*. See MONO-, TYPE, also -IC.

monounsaturated *a.* (of a compound, esp. oils, fats etc.) saturated except for one multiple bond. WH: mid-20C. MONO- + *unsaturated*. See UN-¹, SATURATE¹.

monoxide *n.* an oxide containing one atom of oxygen in combination with a radical. WH: 19C. MONO- + OXIDE.

monozygotic *a.* from a single zygote. WH: early 20C. MONO- + *zygotic* (ZYGOTE).

Monroe doctrine *n.* the principle that non-American powers should not intervene in affairs in either of the American continents, formulated by Monroe in 1823. WH: 19C. James *Monroe*, 1758–1831, US president, 1816–25.

Monseigneur *n.* a French title of honour given to high dignitaries, esp. in the Church. WH: 17C. French, from *mon* my + *seigneur* lord.

Monsieur *n.* the French title of address, Mr or Sir. WH: 16C. French, from *mon* my + *sieur* lord.

Monsignor *n.* a title given to Roman Catholic prelates, officers of the Pope's court and others. WH: 16C. Italian, based on French MONSEIGNEUR.

monsoon *n.* a wind in SW Asia and the Indian Ocean. WH: 16C. Early Modern Dutch *monssoen* (Modern Dutch *moesson*), from Portuguese *monção*, from Arabic *mawsim* season, fixed period, from *wasama* to brand, to mark.

mons pubis *n.* the mound of subcutaneous fatty tissue lying over the joint of the pubic bones. WH: 19C. Latin mount of the pubes.

monster *n.* something misshapen, a deformed creature. Also *a.*, *v.t.* WH: 12–14C. Old French *monstre*, from Latin *monstrum*, orig. divine portent, warning, from *monere* to warn.

monstera *n.* any climbing plant of the genus *Monstera*, esp. *M. deliciosa*, the Swiss cheese plant. WH: early 20C. Modern Latin, appar. from Latin MONSTER. The name probably refers to the odd appearance of the leaves in some species.

monstrance *n.* an open or transparent vessel in which the Host is carried in procession or exposed for adoration, esp. in a Roman Catholic church. WH: 12–14C. Medieval Latin *monstrantia*, from Latin *monstrans*, *monstrantis*, pres.p. of *monstrare* to show, from *monstrum*. See MONSTER, also -ANCE.

monstrous *a.* unnatural in form. Also *adv.* WH: 14–15C. Old French *monstreux* or Latin *monstrosus*, from *monstrum* MONSTER. See also -OUS.

mons Veneris *n.* the pad of fatty tissue over the pubic bone of the human female. WH: 17C. Latin mount of Venus. Cp. VENUS.

montage *n.* the cutting and assembling of shots taken when making a film, video etc. WH: early 20C. French, from *monter* to mount.

montagnard *n.* an inhabitant of mountain country. WH: 19C. French, from *montagne* MOUNTAIN. See also -ARD.

Montagu's harrier *n.* a migratory Eurasian bird of prey, *Circus pygargus*, having long wings and tail. WH: 19C. George *Montagu*, 1751–1815, British naturalist.

montane *a.* of or relating to mountainous regions. WH: 19C. Latin *montanus*, from *mons*, *montis* mountain. See MOUNT[2], also -ANE.

montbretia *n.* a bulbous-rooted plant with orange flowers of the genus *Crocosmia*. WH: 19C. Modern Latin, former genus name, from A.F.E. Coquebert de *Montbret*, 1780–1801, French botanist. See also -IA.

monte *n.* a Spanish game of chance with 45 cards, resembling faro. WH: 19C. Spanish mountain, pile of cards left after dealing.

Monte Carlo method *n.* in statistics, the use of random sampling of numbers to estimate the solution to mathematical problems. WH: mid-20C. *Monte Carlo*, a town in Monaco, famous for its casino.

montero *n.* a Spanish huntsman's cap with flaps and a round crown. WH: 17C. Spanish mountaineer, hunter, from *monte* MOUNT[2].

Montessori method *n.* a system of teaching the very young, in which physical activity, individual tuition and early attention to writing are main features. WH: early 20C. Maria *Montessori*, 1870–1952, Italian physician and educationist.

Montezuma's revenge *n.* acute diarrhoea, esp. as suffered by travellers in Mexico. WH: mid-20C. *Montezuma* II, 1466–1526, last Aztec emperor of Mexico. The 'revenge' would be for the conquest of Mexico by the Spanish.

month *n.* each of the twelve parts into which the year is divided, orig. the period of one revolution of the moon round the earth, a calendar month. WH: pre-1200. Old English *mōnath*, from Germanic, rel. to MOON.

monticule *n.* a little hill, a mound, a hillock, esp. a small volcanic cone. WH: 18C. French, from Late Latin *monticulus*, dim. of *mons*, *montis* MOUNT[2]. See also -CULE.

montmorillonite *n.* a soft clayey mineral, a hydrated aluminium silicate, the chief constituent of bentonite and fuller's earth. WH: 19C. *Montmorillon*, a town in France + -ITE[1].

monument *n.* anything by which the memory of persons or things is preserved, esp. a building or permanent structure. WH: 12–14C. Old French, from Latin *monumentum*, from *monere* to remind. See also -MENT. The original meaning (to the 17C) was burial place.

-mony *suf.* forming nouns, esp. denoting abstract concepts, as in *ceremony*, *matrimony*, *parsimony*. WH: Latin *-monia*, *-monium*, French *-monie*.

moo *v.i.* to make the vocal noise of cattle, to make a noise like a cow. Also *n.* WH: 16C. Imit.

mooch *v.i.* to wander aimlessly, amble. Also *v.t.* WH: 14–15C. Prob. from Old French *muchier* to hide, to skulk.

mood[1] *n.* a state of mind, disposition. Also *a.* WH: pre-1200. Old English *mōd*, from Germanic. Cp. German *Mut*.

mood[2] *n.* a verb form expressing the manner in which the act, event or fact is conceived, whether as actual, contingent, possible, desirable etc. WH: 16C. Alt. of MODE, by assoc. with MOOD[1].

Moog® *n.* an electronic keyboard instrument producing a variety of sounds. WH: mid-20C. Robert A. *Moog*, 1934–, US engineer, its inventor in 1965.

moolah *n.* money. WH: mid-20C. Orig. unknown.

mooli *n.* a large white root vegetable like a radish. WH: mid-20C. Hindi *mūlī*, from Sanskrit *mūlika*, from *mūla* root.

moolvi *n.* a Muslim doctor of law. WH: 17C. Urdu *maulvī*, from Arabic *mawlawī* judicial, from *mawlā* MULLAH.

moon *n.* the earth's satellite revolving round it monthly. Also *v.i.*, *v.t.* WH: pre-1200. Old English *mōna*, from a Germanic word rel. to base of MONTH, ult. from Indo-European base represented also by Latin *metiri* MEASURE. The phases (changes) of the moon are used to measure time.

Moonie *n.* a member of the Unification Church, whose followers give all their possessions to it and live in communes. WH: late 20C. Sun Myung *Moon*, 1920–, S Korean religious leader, founder of the Church in 1954 + -ie (-Y[3]).

moonshee *n.* a secretary, teacher of languages or interpreter in the Indian subcontinent. WH: 18C. Persian and Urdu *munšī*, from Arabic *munši'* writer, author, active p. of *'anša'a* to write (a book).

Moor *n.* a member of a mixed Berber and Arab people inhabiting Morocco and the adjoining parts of NW Africa. WH: 14–15C. Old French *More* (Modern French *Maure*), from Latin *Maurus*, from Greek *Mauros*.

moor[1] *v.t.* to secure (a ship, boat etc.) with cable and anchor. Also *v.i.* WH: 15C. Prob. from Low German *mōren*. Cp. Old English *mǣrels* mooring-rope, Middle Dutch *māren* (Dutch *meren*) to tie up, to moor.

moor[2] *n.* a tract of wild open land, esp. if overgrown with heather. WH: pre-1200. Old English *mōr*, from Germanic, prob. rel. to MERE[1].

moose *n.* the elk, *Alces alces*, inhabiting the colder parts of N America. WH: 17C. Abnaki *mos*.

moot *v.t.* to raise for discussion, to suggest. Also *v.i.*, *a.*, *n.* WH: pre-1200. Old English *mōtian*, from Germanic, from base also of MEET[1]. Cp. MOD[3], GEMOTE.

mop[1] *n.* a bundle of rags or a pad of synthetic material fastened to a long handle, and used for cleaning floors etc. Also *v.t.* WH: 15C. Orig. uncertain. ? Ult. rel. to Latin *mappa* (MAP).

†mop[2] *v.i.* to make wry faces or grimaces. Also *n.* WH: 16C. ? Imit. of movement of the lips. Cp. Dutch *moppen* to pout.

mope *v.i.* to be dull or dispirited. Also *v.t.*, *n.* WH: 16C. ? Of Scandinavian orig. Cp. Swedish dial. *mopa* to sulk, Danish *maabe* to be stupid.

moped *n.* a motorized pedal cycle, of less than 50cc. WH: mid-20C. Swedish, from *trampcykel med motor och pedaler*, pedal cycle with engine and pedals.

mopoke *n.* a small brown spotted owl, *Ninox novaeseelandiae*, the boobook, native to Australia and New Zealand. WH: 19C. Imit. of bird's call. Cp. BOOBOOK.

moppet *n.* a pet, a darling (applied to children, young girls etc.). WH: 17C. Obs. *mop* baby, toddler, of uncertain orig. (? rel. to MOPE) + -ET[1].

moquette *n.* a woven fabric of wool and hemp or linen with a velvety pile, used for carpets and upholstery. WH: 19C. French, of unknown orig. ? Rel. to (or from) obs. Italian *mocaiardo* mohair.

mor *n.* acidic humus formed where decomposition is slow. WH: mid-20C. Danish humus.

mora *n.* in prosody, a unit of time equal to a short syllable. WH: 16C. Latin delay.

moraine n. the debris of rocks brought down by glaciers. WH: 18C. French, from Savoyard Italian *morena*, from southern French *mor*, *morre* muzzle, snout, from a word rel. to MORION.

moral a. of or relating to character and conduct in terms of the distinction between right and wrong. Also n., v.i. WH: 14–15C. Latin *moralis* (translating Greek *ēthikos* ethical), from *mos*, *moris* custom (MORES). See also -AL¹.

morale n. mental or moral condition. WH: 18C. French *moral*, from Latin *moralis* (MORAL), respelt to indicate the stress. Cp. LOCALE.

morass n. anything that is confused or complicated, esp. when it impedes progress. WH: 14–15C. Middle Low German *moras* and Dutch *moeras*, alt. (by assim. to *moer* MOOR¹) of Middle Dutch *maras*, from Old French *marais*. See MARISH.

moratorium n. a deferment, delay or temporary suspension. WH: 19C. Modern Latin, neut. sing. (used as n.) of Late Latin *moratorius* that which delays, from *moratus*, p.p. of *morari* to delay. See also -ORIUM.

Moravian a. of or relating to Moravia, the Moravians or their dialect of Czech. Also n. WH: 16C. Medieval Latin *Moravia*, a region around the River *Morava*, now part of the Czech Republic. See also -AN.

moray n. any brightly-patterned coastal eel of the family Muraenidae, esp. *Muraena helena*. WH: 17C. Portuguese *moréia*, from Latin MURAENA.

morbid a. unhealthily preoccupied with unpleasant matters, esp. with death. WH: 17C. Latin *morbidus*, from *morbus* disease. See also -ID.

morbilli n.pl. measles. WH: 16C. Medieval Latin, pl. of *morbillus* pustule, spot characteristic of measles, dim. of Latin *morbus* disease.

morceau n. a small piece. WH: 18C. French. See MORSEL.

mordant a. caustic, pungent. Also n. WH: 14–15C. Old French, pres.p. of *mordre* to bite, from alt. of Latin *mordere*. See also -ANT.

mordent n. a rapid alternation of a note with the one immediately below it, a kind of trill. WH: 19C. German, from Italian *mordente*, use as n. of verbal a. from *mordere* to bite. See MORDANT.

more a. greater in quantity, extent, importance etc. Also adv., n. WH: pre-1200. Old English *māra*, from Germanic base of MO². Cp. MOST¹.

moreen n. a stout woollen or wool and cotton fabric for hangings etc. WH: 17C. Orig. unknown.

morel¹ n. an edible fungus, *Morchella esculenta*, and other species of *Morchella*. WH: 17C. French *morille*, from Dutch, rel. to Old High German *morhila*. Cp. German *Morchel* fungus.

morel² n. the black nightshade, *Solanum nigrum*, and other nightshades of the family Solanaceae. WH: 12–14C. Old French *morele* (Modern French *morelle*), from Medieval Latin *morellus*. See MORELLO.

morello n. a bitter dark-red cherry. WH: 17C. Appar. from Italian *morello* blackish, from Medieval Latin *morellus*, *maurelus* dark brown (of a horse), dim. of Latin *Maurus* MOOR. Cp. MOREL².

moreover adv. besides, in addition. WH: 12–14C. MORE + OVER. Orig. two words.

mores n.pl. the customs and conduct which embody the fundamental values of a social group. WH: 19C. Latin, pl. of *mos*, *moris* manner, custom. Cp. MORAL.

Moresque a. Moorish in style and decoration. Also n. WH: 14–15C. French, from Italian *moresco*, from *Moro* MOOR + -esco -ESQUE. Cp. MORISCO.

morganatic a. of or relating to a marriage between a person of high rank and one of lower rank, by virtue of which the latter does not acquire the spouse's rank and, along with any children of the marriage, is not entitled to inherit the spouse's title or possessions. WH: 16C. French *morganatique*, German *morganatisch*, or from Medieval Latin *morganaticus*, in *matrimoniam ad morganaticam* morganatic marriage, lit. marriage of the morning, in which *morganaticam* prob. derives from Old High German **morgangeba* morning gift, from bases of MORN, GIVE. The 'morning gift' is that of the husband to the wife after consummation, relieving him of any further liability or financial responsibility for possible children.

morgen n. in SE Africa, the Netherlands and parts of the US, a unit of land measurement, about 0.8 ha (just over 2 acres). WH: 17C. Dutch and German (MORN), appar. meaning the area of land that can be ploughed in a morning.

morgue n. a mortuary. WH: 19C. French, proper name of a Paris mortuary, orig. a place in a Paris prison where bodies were viewed to establish their identity, prob. from *morgue* haughtiness, orig. sad expression, solemn look, of unknown orig.

moribund a. in a dying state. Also n. WH: 18C. Latin *moribundus*, from *mori* to die.

morion n. a helmet having no beaver or visor. WH: 16C. French, from Spanish *morrión*, from *morro* round object. Cp. MORAINE.

Moriori n.pl. the original inhabitants of New Zealand before the arrival of the Maoris. WH: 19C. Polynesian.

+**Morisco** n. a Moor, esp. one of the Moors remaining in Spain after the conquest of Granada. Also a. WH: 16C. Spanish, from *Moro* MOOR + -isco -ESQUE. Cp. MORESQUE.

Mormon n. a member of an American religious body, founded by Joseph Smith in 1830, now calling themselves the Latter-Day Saints, who claim continuous divine revelation through their priesthood, and formerly practised polygamy. WH: 19C. *Mormon*, the name of the prophet said to be the author of the Book of Mormon, a text that the Mormons accept as Scripture together with the Bible.

morn n. morning. WH: pre-1200. Old English *morgen*, from Germanic. Cp. German *Morgen*.

mornay a. served with a cheese sauce. WH: early 20C. ? Philip de *Mornay*, 1549–1623, French Huguenot writer. According to some, the name is that of Mornay, the French cook and eldest son of Joseph Voiron, chef of the restaurant Durand at the end of the 19C, and inventor of the sauce.

morning n. the first part of the day, esp. from dawn to midday. Also int., a. WH: 12–14C. MORN + -ING¹, based on EVENING.

Moro n. a member of a Muslim people of the S Philippines. Also a. WH: 19C. Spanish MOOR.

Moroccan a. of or relating to Morocco or its inhabitants. Also n. WH: 18C. *Morocco*, a country in NW Africa + -AN. The name of Morocco ultimately derives from an Arabic variant of *Marrākeš* Marrakesh. Cp. MAROQUIN.

moron n. a very stupid or foolish person. WH: early 20C. Greek *mōron*, neut. of *mōros* foolish. The word was coined in 1910 (in the medical sense) by H.H. Goddard of the American Association for the Study of the Feeble-minded.

morose a. sullen, gloomy. WH: 14–15C. Late Latin *morosus*, from Latin *mos*, *moris* manner. See MORAL. The original sense (to the 17C) was slow, deliberate, painstaking. The current sense evolved in the 16C.

morph n. the phonological representation of a morpheme, an allomorph. WH: mid-20C. MORPHEME.

-morph comb. form denoting shape or structure. WH: Greek *morphē* form.

morpheme n. a linguistic element that can carry meaning and cannot be divided into smaller elements of this kind. WH: 19C. French *morphème*, from Greek *morphē* form, based on *phonème* PHONEME.

morphic a. morphological. WH: 19C. Greek *morphē* form + -IC.

morphine n. the alkaloid derived from opium, used in medicine as a sedative and analgesic. WH: 19C. *Morpheus*, name of the Roman god of dreams + -INE. The drug is so called from its sleep-inducing properties. Morpheus is popularly regarded as the god of sleep.

morphing n. in a film, video etc. the transformation of one image to another by means of computer technology. WH: late 20C. From *morph*, from *metamorphosis* (METAMORPHOSE) + -ING¹.

morpho- comb. form of or relating to form. WH: Greek *morphē* form. See also -O-.

morphogenesis n. the development of the form of an organism during its growth to maturity. WH: 19C. MORPHO- + GENESIS.

morphology n. the branch of biology dealing with the form of organisms. WH: 19C. MORPHO- -LOGY.

morphosis n. the mode or order of development of an organ or organism. WH: 17C. Greek *morphōsis* a shaping, from *morphoun* to shape, from *morphē* form. See also -OSIS.

Morris chair n. an armchair with an adjustable back. WH: 19C. William *Morris*, 1834–96, English poet and craftsman.

morris dance *n.* a style of folk dance performed by groups in colourful rustic costume, often using bells, sticks, handkerchiefs etc. and accompanied by the concertina or fiddle. WH: 14–15C. Var. of *Moorish* (MOOR). Cp. Flemish *mooriske dans*, Dutch *moors dans*.

Morrison shelter *n.* an indoor air-raid shelter in the form of a steel table. WH: mid-20C. Herbert S. *Morrison*, 1888–1965, UK Secretary of State for Home Affairs and Home Security, 1940–45, when the shelter was adopted.

morrow *n.* the day next after the present, the following day. WH: 12–14C. Var. of MORN (Old English *morgen*), with *-w* evolving from the orig. Old English *-g-*. Cp. TOMORROW.

Morse *n.* a system of sending messages by telegraph in which letters are represented by combinations of dots and dashes. WH: 19C. Samuel F.B. *Morse*, 1791–1872, US inventor of the electric telegraph (1837) and a code for using it.

morsel *n.* a bite, a small piece of food. WH: 12–14C. Old French (Modern French MORCEAU), dim. of *mors*, from Latin *morsus*, p.p. of *mordere* to bite. See also -EL.

mort *n.* a note sounded on a hunting horn at the death of the deer. WH: 12–14C. Old French, from Latin *mors, mortis* death.

mortadella *n.* a type of large spicy pork sausage, sold ready to eat. WH: 17C. Italian, from Latin *murtatum* (sausage) seasoned with myrtle berries, from *murtus* myrtle.

mortal *a.* liable to die; human. Also *n., adv.* WH: 14–15C. Old French, from Latin *mortalis*, from *mors, mortis* death. See also -AL¹.

mortar *n.* a cement, made of lime, sand and water, for joining bricks etc. in building. Also *v.t.* WH: pre-1200. Partly from Old French *mortier*, from Latin *mortarium* vessel for pounding or grinding, partly from Low German. The meaning was transferred from the vessel to the substance prepared in it.

mortgage *n.* the conditional conveyance of a house, estate or other property into the ownership of a building society etc. as security for the repayment of a loan, to be voided on the discharge of the debt or loan. Also *v.t.* WH: 14–15C. Old French lit. dead pledge, from *mort* dead + *gage* pledge, GAGE¹. A mortgage is so called because the debt becomes void ('dead') when the pledge is redeemed.

mortician *n.* an undertaker. WH: 19C. Latin *mors, mortis* death + -ICIAN.

mortify *v.t.* to humiliate, to wound. Also *v.i.* WH: 14–15C. Old French *mortifier*, from Ecclesiastical Latin *mortificare* to kill, to subdue (the flesh), from Latin *mors, mortis* death. See also -FY.

mortise *n.* a hole cut in timber etc. to receive the end of another part, esp. a tenon. Also *v.t.* WH: 14–15C. Old French *mortoise* (Modern French *mortaise*), ? from Arabic *murtaj* locked, place of locking.

mortmain *n.* inalienable possession or tenure of lands or tenements by an ecclesiastical or other corporation. WH: 14–15C. Old French *mortemain*, from Medieval Latin *mortua manus* dead hand, from fem. of Latin *mortuus* dead + *manus* hand. The reference is probably to the impersonal ownership.

mortuary *n.* a building for the temporary reception of the dead. Also *a.* WH: 14–15C. Anglo-French *mortuarie*, from Medieval Latin *mortuarium*, neut. sing. of Latin *mortuarius*, from *mortuus* dead. See also -ARY¹. The original sense was a gift claimed by a parish priest from the estate of a deceased parishioner. The current sense dates from the 19C and replaces the earlier *dead-house*.

morula *n.* the stage of development in which an ovum has become completely segmented. WH: 19C. Modern Latin, dim. of *morum* mulberry.

morwong *n.* an edible fish of the family Cheilodactylidae, found off the coasts of Australia and New Zealand. WH: 19C. Prob. from Australian Aboriginal.

Mosaic *a.* of or relating to Moses or to the law given through him. WH: 17C. French *mosaïque* or Modern Latin *Mosaicus*, from Ecclesiastical Latin *Moses*, Ecclesiastical Greek *Mōsēs*, from Hebrew *Mōšeh* Moses, the Hebrew prophet who led the Israelites out of slavery in Egypt and passed on to them the Ten Commandments. See also -IC.

mosaic *n.* a pattern, picture etc. produced by the arrangement of small pieces of coloured marble, glass or stone. Also *a., v.t.* WH: 14–15C. Old French *mosaicq* (Modern French *mosaïque*), from Italian *mosaico*, from Modern Latin *mosaicus*, from Late Greek *mouseion* (MUSEUM). A mosaic is so called from the decorations of medieval grottoes dedicated to the Muses.

mosasaurus *n.* a large fossil marine reptile of the Cretaceous period esp. of the genus *Mosasaurus*, first found near Maastricht on the Meuse. WH: 19C. Modern Latin genus name, from Latin *Mosa* (the river) Meuse, near which the first remains were found + Greek *sauros* lizard.

moschatel *n.* a small perennial herb, *Adoxa moschatellina*, with yellowish-green flowers and a musky scent. WH: 18C. French *moscatelle*, from Italian *moscatella*, from *moscato* musk.

Moselle *n.* a white wine made in the valley of the river Moselle. WH: 17C. *Moselle*, a river of NE France and W Germany. *Moselle* is the French form of the name, *Mosel* the German.

mosey *v.i.* to walk, amble. WH: 19C. Orig. uncertain. ? Shortened form of Spanish *vamos* let's go (VAMOOSE).

moshav *n.* a co-operative association of small farms in Israel. WH: mid-20C. Hebrew *mōšāḇ* dwelling, colony.

mosque *n.* a Muslim place of worship. WH: 14–15C. French *mosquée*, from Italian *moschea*, ult. from Arabic *masjid*, lit. place of prostration.

mosquito *n.* an insect of the family Culicidae, esp. of the genera *Culex*, *Anopheles* or *Aedes*, with a proboscis for piercing the skin of animals and sucking their blood. WH: 16C. Spanish and Portuguese, dim. of *mosca* fly, from Latin *musca*.

moss *n.* a low, tufted, herbaceous plant of the cryptogamous class Musci, usually growing on damp soil or the surface of stones, trees etc. Also *v.t.* WH: pre-1200. Old English *mos*, from a Germanic word rel. to Old Norse *mosi* bog, moss, and ult. to Latin *muscus* moss.

mosso *adv.* with liveliness and speed. WH: 19C. Italian, p.p. of *muovere* to move.

most¹ *a.* greatest in amount, number, extent, quality, degree etc. Also *adv., n.* WH: pre-1200. Old English *māst*, from Germanic, from bases of MO², -EST¹. Cp. MORE.

most² *adv.* almost. WH: 19C. Shortening of ALMOST.

-most *suf.* forming superlatives of adjectives and adverbs denoting position, order etc., as in *hindmost*, *inmost*, *utmost*. WH: Old English *-mest*, from Germanic superl. suf. with *-m-* + base of -EST¹. The suffix has long been regarded as if from MOST¹.

mot *n.* a witty or pithy saying. WH: 16C. French word, saying, from alt. of Popular Latin *muttum*, rel. to Latin *muttire* to murmur. Cp. MOTTO.

mote¹ *n.* a particle of dust, a speck, a spot. WH: pre-1200. Old English *mot*, from Germanic, of unknown orig.

†mote² *v.t.* may, must. WH: pre-1200. Old English *mōt* (MUST¹).

motel *n.* a roadside hotel or furnished cabins providing accommodation for motorists. WH: early 20C. Blend of MOTOR and HOTEL.

motet *n.* a vocal composition in harmony, of a sacred character. WH: 14–15C. Old French, dim. of MOT. See also -ET¹.

moth *n.* any of a group of nocturnal or crepuscular insects of the order Lepidoptera, distinct from butterflies by not having knotted antennae and folding the wings flat when at rest. WH: pre-1200. Old English *moththe*, from Germanic. The word was originally used for the larva of a clothes moth, then for a clothes moth itself. The general use of the name for the night-flying insects dates from the 18C.

mother¹ *n.* a female parent. Also *v.t., a.* WH: pre-1200. Old English *mōdor*, from Germanic, from Indo-European base also of Latin *mater*, Greek *mētēr*, Old Church Slavonic *mati* (Russian *mat'*), Old Irish *máthir* (Irish *máthair*), Sanskrit *mātr*.

mother² *n.* a thick slimy substance forming in various liquids during fermentation. Also *v.i.* WH: 14–15C. Prob. from MOTHER¹. Cp. French *mère* (*de vinaigre*) mother (of vinegar).

motif *n.* the dominant feature or idea in a literary, musical or other artistic composition. WH: 19C. French. See MOTIVE.

motile *a.* capable of motion. WH: 19C. Latin *motus* motion + -IL, based on MOBILE.

motion *n.* the act, process or state of moving. Also *v.t., v.i.* WH: 14–15C. Old French, from Latin *motio, motionis*, from *motus*, p.p. of *movere* MOVE.

motive *n.* that which incites to action, or determines the will. *Also a., v.t.* WH: 14–15C. Old French *motif*, from Late Latin *motivus*, from Latin *motus*, p.p. of *movere* MOVE. See also -IVE.

motley *a.* of varied character, heterogeneous. *Also n.* WH: 14–15C. Orig. uncertain. ? Ult. from MOTE¹. The word was formerly derived from MEDLEY, and its current sense has been apparently influenced by this. Cp. MOTTLE.

motmot *n.* a S American and Mexican bird of the family Momotidae allied to the kingfishers. WH: 19C. American Spanish. Imit.

motocross *n.* the sport of racing on motorcycles over rough ground. WH: mid-20C. French *moto-cross*, from *moto* motorcycle (from *motocyclette*) + *cross*, shortening of *cross-country*, from English (CROSS).

moto perpetuo *n.* a short fast-moving instrumental piece. WH: 19C. Italian perpetual motion. Cp. PERPETUUM MOBILE.

motor *n.* something that imparts motive power, esp. a machine imparting motion to a vehicle or vessel (usu. excluding steam engines). *Also a., v.i., v.t.* WH: 14–15C. Latin mover; later, partly from *motus* (MOTIVE) + -OR, partly from French *moteur*.

Motown *n.* a form of music associated with Detroit, Michigan, containing elements of rhythm and blues and pop, often combined with the rhythm of gospel music. WH: mid-20C. Contr. of *Motor Town*, nickname of Detroit, Michigan, USA, an important motor-manufacturing city.

motte *n.* a mound on which a castle, camp etc. is situated. WH: 19C. French mound, from Old French *mote* hillock, mound, castle.

mottle *v.t.* to blotch, to variegate with spots of different colours or shades of colour. *Also n.* WH: 17C. Prob. back-formation from MOTLEY.

motto *n.* a short pithy sentence or phrase expressing a sentiment. WH: 16C. Italian, from Latin *muttum* grunt, word. See MOT.

moue *n.* a small pouting grimace. WH: 19C. French. See MOW³.

mouflon *n.* a wild sheep, *Ovis orientalis*, of Sardinia and Corsica. WH: 18C. French, from Italian *muflone*, from Popular Latin dial. *mufro*.

mouillé *a.* (of a consonant) palatalized (as *gn* in *lasagne*, *ñ* in *señor*). WH: 19C. French, p.p. of *mouiller* to wet, to moisten.

moulage *n.* the taking of plaster casts of footprints etc. WH: early 20C. French moulding, moulded reproduction, from *mouler* to mould. See also -AGE.

mould¹ *n.* a hollow shape into which molten metal etc. is poured in a fluid state to cool into a permanent shape. *Also v.t.* WH: 12–14C. Appar. from Old French *modle* (Modern French *moule*), from Latin MODULUS.

mould² *n.* a minute fungoid growth forming a woolly or furry coating on matter left in the damp. WH: 14–15C. Prob. from p.p. of obs. *moul* to grow mouldy, ult. from an Old Norse v. rel. to *mygla* to grow mouldy.

mould³ *n.* fine soft earth, easily pulverized, suitable for cultivation. WH: pre-1200. Old English *molde*, from Germanic base meaning to pulverize, to grind. Cp. MEAL².

moulder *v.i.* to turn to dust by natural decay. WH: 16C. ? From MOULD³ + -ER⁵, but cp. Norwegian dial. *muldra*.

moulin *n.* a vertical pit in a glacier created and maintained by a constant stream of water from the surface. WH: 19C. French, lit. mill.

moult *v.i.* to shed the feathers, hair, skin, horns etc. (of certain birds and animals). *Also v.t., n.* WH: 12–14C. Old English -*mūtian* (as in *bīmūtian* to exchange), from Germanic, from Latin *mutare* to change. The -*l*- entered as for ASSAULT, FAULT, where it was originally inserted to achieve a supposedly correct spelling.

mound¹ *n.* an artificial elevation of earth, stones etc. *Also v.t.* WH: 16C. Orig. unknown, but with meanings subsequently assoc. with MOUNT². The original meaning was hedge, fence. The sense pile of earth, etc. dates from the 18C, natural elevation from the 19C.

mound² *n.* a ball or globe representing the earth, usu. of gold and surmounted by a cross, used as part of regalia, an orb. WH: 12–14C. Old French *monde*, from Latin *mundus* world.

mount¹ *v.t.* to ascend, to climb. *Also v.i., n., int.* WH: 12–14C. Old French *munter* (Modern French *monter*), from Latin *mons, montis* MOUNT². Cp. AMOUNT.

mount² *n.* a high hill, a mountain (in poetry, or as first part of a proper name). WH: pre-1200. Latin *mons, montis* mountain, influ. by Old French *mont*.

mountain *n.* a natural elevation of the earth's surface rising high above the surrounding land. WH: 12–14C. Old French *montaigne* (Modern French *montagne*), from Popular Latin *montanea*, use as n. of fem. of *montaneus*, from Latin *montanus* mountainous, from *mons, montis* MOUNT².

mountant *n.* an adhesive for mounting photographs etc. WH: 19C. MOUNT¹ + -ANT, based on French *montant*, pres.p. of *monter* MOUNT¹.

mountebank *n.* a swindler, a boastful pretender, a charlatan. *Also v.t.* WH: 16C. Italian *montambanco*, from *monta in banco* mount on a bench! See BANK³. The word was originally used for an itinerant quack who appealed to potential buyers of his medicines from a raised platform, entertaining them with stories, juggling, etc.

mourn *v.i.* to express or feel sorrow or grief. *Also v.t.* WH: pre-1200. Old English *murnan*, from Germanic, ult. rel. to MEMORY.

mouse¹ *n.* a small rodent quadruped of various species belonging to the family Muridae. WH: pre-1200. Old English *mūs*, from Germanic, from Indo-European base represented also by Latin *mus*, Greek *mus*.

mouse² *v.i.* to hunt for or catch mice. *Also v.t.* WH: 12–14C. MOUSE¹.

mousquetaire *n.* a musketeer. WH: 18C. French, from *mousquet* MUSKET + -*aire* -EER. Cp. MUSKETEER.

moussaka *n.* a Greek dish of minced meat, aubergines and tomatoes, topped with a cheese sauce. WH: mid-20C. Turkish *musakka*, from Arabic *musakkā*.

mousse *n.* a dish of flavoured cream whipped and frozen. WH: 19C. French moss, froth.

mousseline *n.* fine French muslin. WH: 17C. French. See MUSLIN.

moustache *n.* the hair on the upper lip, esp. the hair of men when left to grow. WH: 16C. French, from Italian *mostaccio*. See MUSTACHIO.

Mousterian *n.* the main culture of the palaeolithic period, from *c.*80,000–35,000 BC, characterized by flint flake tools and associated with Neanderthal man. *Also a.* WH: 19C. French *moustérien*, from *Le Moustier*, a cave in the Dordogne, SW France, where the remains were first found. See also -IAN.

mouth¹ *n.* the opening through which food is taken into the body. WH: pre-1200. Old English *mūth*, from Germanic, from Indo-European, corr. to Latin *mentum* chin. Cp. German *Mund*.

mouth² *v.t.* to utter pompously or in an elaborate or constrained manner, to declaim. *Also v.i.* WH: 12–14C. MOUTH¹.

move *v.t.* to cause to change position or posture. *Also v.i., n.* WH: 12–14C. Old French *moveir* (Modern French *mouvoir*), from Latin *movere*.

movie *n.* a cinema film. WH: early 20C. Abbr. of *moving picture* (MOVE).

mow¹ *v.t.* to cut down (grass, corn etc.) with a mower, scythe etc. *Also v.i.* WH: pre-1200. Old English *māwan*, from Germanic base also of MEAD², MEADOW. Cp. German *mähen*.

mow² *n.* a heap or pile of hay, corn or other field produce, a stack. *Also v.t.* WH: pre-1200. Old English MOW¹.

†mow³ *n.* a wry face, a grimace. *Also v.i.* WH: 12–14C. Prob. from Old French *moe* (Modern French *moue*) pouting, or from Middle Dutch *mouwe*, ult. imit. of movement of mouth.

moxa *n.* a downy material obtained from the dried leaves of *Crossostephium artemisioides*, burnt on the skin in oriental medical treatments such as acupuncture, or as a counterirritant. WH: 17C. Japanese *mogusa*, contr. of *moe kusa* burning herb.

moxie *n.* vigour, courage, force of character, wit. WH: mid-20C. *Moxie*, proprietary name for a bitter-tasting non-alcoholic drink that originated as a patent medicine. The original preparation was advertised as a drink 'that will build up your nerve'.

Mozarab *n.* any of those Christians in Spain after the Moorish conquest who were allowed the exercise of their religion in return for allegiance to the Moors. WH: 17C. Spanish *mozárabe*, from Arabic *musta'rib*, lit. making oneself an Arab.

mozzarella *n.* a soft white unsalted Italian curd cheese. WH: early 20C. Italian, dim. of *mozza* a kind of cheese, from *mozzare* to cut off.

mozzetta *n.* a short cape with a small hood worn by cardinals, bishops, abbots etc. in the Roman Catholic Church. WH: 18C. Italian, shortening of *almozzetta*, from Medieval Latin *almucia* AMICE² + -*etta* -ET¹.

mpingo *n.* a leguminous tree, *Dalbergia melanoxylon* native to E Africa. WH: late 20C. Kiswahili.

Mr mister. WH: 14–15C. Abbr. of MASTER, (now) MISTER.

mRNA *abbr.* messenger RNA. WH: Abbr. of *messenger RNA* (MESSENGER).

Mrs *n.* the title of a married woman. WH: 17C. Abbr. of MISTRESS. Cp. MISSIS.

Ms *n.* the title of a woman of unknown or undisclosed marital status. WH: mid-20C. Contr. of MRS, MISS².

mu *n.* the twelfth letter of the Greek alphabet (M, μ). WH: 12–14C. Greek.

mucedinous *a.* mouldy, mildewy. WH: 19C. Modern Latin *mucedo*, *mucedinis* mould (from *mucere* to be mouldy) + -OUS.

much *a.* great in quantity or amount. *Also adv., n.* WH: 12–14C. Shortening of *muchel*, *michel*, from Old English *micel*. See MICKLE.

mucic *a.* denoting an acid formed by the oxidation of milk, sugar and various gums. WH: 19C. French *mucique*, from *mucus* MUCUS. See also -IC.

mucilage *n.* a sticky or viscous substance from the seeds, bark or roots of various plants. WH: 14–15C. Old French, from Late Latin *mucilago* musty juice. See MUCUS, also -AGE.

muck *n.* dung or manure. *Also v.t.* WH: 12–14C. Prob. of Scandinavian orig. Cp. Old Norse *myki* dung, from a Germanic word meaning soft.

muco- *comb. form* mucus, mucous. WH: MUCUS. See also -O-.

mucopolysaccharide *n.* any of a group of polysaccharides whose molecules contain two sugars, often found as components of connective tissue. WH: mid-20C. MUCO- + POLYSACCHARIDE.

mucro *n.* a sharp point, process, or organ. WH: 17C. Latin point.

mucus *n.* the slimy secretion of the mucous membrane. WH: 17C. Latin, rel. to Greek *mussesthai* to blow the nose, *mukter* nose, nostril.

mud *n.* moist, soft earth, or earthy matter. *Also v.t.* WH: 14–15C. Prob. from Middle Low German *mudde*. Cp. Dutch *modden* to dabble in mud, Middle High German *mot* bog, peat.

muddle *v.t.* to confuse, to bewilder. *Also v.i., n.* WH: 12–14C. Prob. from Middle Dutch *moddelen*, freq. of *modden* to dabble in mud (cp. MUD). See also -LE⁴. The original meaning was to bathe or wallow in mud or muddy water. The current sense dates from the 17C.

mudir *n.* a governor of a village or canton in Turkey. WH: 19C. Turkish *mudır*, from Arabic *mudīr* active part. of *'adāra* to direct, to manage.

muesli *n.* a dish of crushed cereals, dried fruit and nuts, usu. eaten as a breakfast cereal. WH: mid-20C. Swiss German, dim. of *mus* pulpy food, purée, rel. to Old English *mōs* food.

muezzin *n.* a Muslim crier of the hour of prayer. WH: 16C. Arabic, dial. var. of Arabic *mu'aḏḏin*, active p. of *'aḏḏana* to call to prayer, from *'uḏn* ear.

muff¹ *n.* a covering, usu. cylindrical, of fur or other material, in which the hands are placed to keep them warm. WH: 16C. Dutch *mof*, abbr. of Middle Dutch *moffel*, *muffel*, from Medieval Latin *muffala* glove, of unknown orig.

muff² *v.t.* to bungle or fail in. *Also v.i., n.* WH: 19C. Orig. unknown. According to some, the word is from MUFF¹. One who bungles is like a person with their hands in a muff.

muffin *n.* a plain, round cake made with yeast dough, usu. toasted and eaten hot with butter. WH: 18C. Orig. unknown.

muffle¹ *v.t.* to wrap or cover (up) closely and warmly. *Also n.* WH: 14–15C. ? Old French *enmoufler*, from *en-* EN- + *moufle* MUFF¹.

muffle² *n.* the thick, naked upper lip and nose of ruminants and rodents. WH: 17C. French *mufle*, of unknown orig.

mufti *n.* an official interpreter or expounder of the Koran and Muslim law. WH: 16C. Arabic *muftī*, active part. of *'aftā* to decide a point of law, rel. to FATWA. The sense ordinary dress, 'civvies' dates from the 19C and may allude to the costume formerly traditional for the stage role of a mufti, viz. dressing gown, cap, and slippers.

mug¹ *n.* a drinking vessel, usu. cylindrical without a lip, used without a saucer. *Also v.i.* WH: 16C. Prob. of Scandinavian orig., ult. of unknown orig. Cp. Norwegian *mugge*, Swedish *mugg* pitcher with a handle. The sense face, mouth arose in the 18C and alludes to the practice of representing faces on mugs.

mug² *v.t.* to rob (someone) violently or by threatening violence, esp. in the street. WH: 19C. MUG¹. The allusion is to striking someone in the face.

mug³ *v.i.* to study hard, to grind. *Also v.t., n.* WH: 19C. Orig. unknown.

mugger *n.* an Indian crocodile, *Crocodylus palustris*, with a broad snout. WH: 19C. Hindi *magar*.

muggins *n.* a fool, a simpleton, used esp. of oneself. WH: 19C. Prob. surname *Muggins*, alluding to MUG¹ in sense dupe. Cp. JUGGINS.

muggy *a.* damp and close. WH: 18C. From obs. *mug* to drizzle, prob. of Scandinavian orig. + -Y¹. Cp. Old Norse *mugga* mist, drizzle, Norwegian and Swedish dial. *mugg* mould, mildew, prob. rel. to MUCUS.

Mughal *n.* a Mongolian. WH: 16C. Urdu *mugal*. See MOGUL¹.

mugwort *n.* any of several herbs of the genus *Artemisia*, esp. *A. vulgaris*, the motherwort. WH: pre-1200. Old English *mucgwyrt*, from Germanic bases of MIDGE, WORT.

mugwump *n.* a person of importance, a leader, a consequential person. *Also v.i.* WH: 19C. Algonquian *mugquomp* great chief.

Muhammadan *a.* of or relating to Muhammad or Islam. *Also n.* WH: 17C. Arabic *Muḥammad*, c.570–632, Arabian prophet of Islam + -AN.

Muharram *n.* the first month (30 days) of the Muslim year. WH: 19C. Arabic *muḥarram* inviolable.

mujahedin *n.pl.* fundamentalist Muslim guerrilla fighters. WH: mid-20C. Persian and Arabic *mujāhidīn*, collect. pl. of *mujāhid* person who fights a jihad.

mulatto *n.* the offspring of a white person and a black person. *Also a.* WH: 16C. Spanish and Portuguese *mulato* young mule, mulatto, from *mulo* MULE¹.

mulberry *n.* any tree of the genus *Morus*, bearing a collective fruit like a large blackberry. WH: pre-1200. Old English *mōrberie*, from Germanic, from Latin *morum* mulberry + BERRY. Cp. German *Maulbeere*.

mulch *n.* a surface layer of dead vegetable matter, manure etc. to keep the ground or the roots of plants moist. *Also v.t.* WH: 17C. Prob. from use as n. of obs. *mulsh* soft, from Germanic, rel. to Latin *mollis* soft.

mulct *n.* a fine, esp. for an offence or misdemeanour. *Also v.t.* WH: 15C. Latin *mulcta* fine.

mule¹ *n.* the offspring of a male donkey and a female horse. WH: pre-1200. Old English *mūl*, prob. from Germanic, from Latin *mulus*, prob. of Mediterranean orig.

mule² *n.* a backless shoe or slipper. WH: 14–15C. French *mule* slipper, from Latin *mulleus* (*calceus*) red high-soled (shoe) (worn by Roman patricians), rel. to Greek *melas* black.

muley *n.* a hornless cow. *Also a.* WH: 16C. ? Rel. to Irish *maol*, Welsh *moel*, lit. bald.

mulga *n.* the tree *Acacia aneura*. WH: 19C. Australian Aboriginal (Yuwaalaraay) *malga*.

muliebrity *n.* womanhood. WH: 16C. Late Latin *muliebritas*, from Latin *muliebris*, from *mulier* woman. See also -ITY.

mull¹ *v.t.* to ponder, consider (*usu. followed by* over). WH: 19C. ? Var. of MILL¹.

mull² *v.t.* to warm (wine, beer etc.), sweeten and flavour with spices. WH: 17C. Orig. unknown.

mull³ *n.* a layer of humus formed rapidly in non-acid conditions. WH: early 20C. Danish *muld* MOULD³.

mull⁴ *n.* a promontory. WH: 12–14C. Rel. to Gaelic *maol*, Old Irish *mael* (Modern Irish *maol*) bare, blunt.

mull⁵ *n.* a thin soft muslin. WH: 17C. Abbr. of *mulmull*, from Hindi *malmal*.

mullah *n.* an honorary title among Muslims for persons learned in theology and sacred law, and for Muslim ecclesiastical and civil dignitaries. WH: 17C. Persian and Urdu *mullā*, Turkish *molla*, from Arabic *mawlā* master.

mullein *n.* any herbaceous plant of the genus *Verbascum*, such as *V. thapsus*, having woolly leaves and tall spikes of yellow flowers, sometimes called Aaron's rod. WH: 14–15C. Old French *moleine* (Modern French *molène*), from a Gaulish base corr. to Breton *melen*, Cornish and Welsh *melyn* yellow.

muller *n.* a stone with a flat surface, used to grind and mix pigment etc. on a slab. WH: 14–15C. ? Anglo-French, from *moldre* to grind. Cp. -ER².

Müllerian mimicry *n.* a form of mimicry in which two harmful or inedible creatures develop similar appearance etc. as a protection from predators. WH: 19C. Johann F.T. *Müller*, 1821–97, German zoologist + -IAN.

mullet[1] *n.* a fish living near coasts and ascending rivers, belonging either to the genus *Mullus* and family Mullidae (red mullet) or the genus *Mugil* and the family Mugilidae (grey mullet). WH: 14–15C. Old French *mulet*, from Latin *mullus* red mullet, from Greek *mullos*, rel. to *melos* black. See also -ET[1].

mullet[2] *n.* the figure of a five-pointed star, supposed to resemble the rowel of a spur, the mark of cadency indicating a third son. WH: 14–15C. Old French *molette* rowel, dim. of *meule* millstone, from Latin *mola* grindstone. See also -ET[1].

mulligatawny *n.* a highly-flavoured curry soup. WH: 18C. Tamil *miḷaku-taṇṇi*, lit. pepper-water.

mullion *n.* a vertical bar separating the compartments of a window. Also *v.t.* WH: 16C. Var. of MONIAL. Cp. var. *munnion*.

mullock *n.* rock containing no gold. WH: 14–15C. *mull* dust, ashes, particles, from Middle Dutch *mul*, from Germanic base also of MEAL[2] + -OCK. Cp. MOULD[3].

mulloway *n.* a large edible Australian seafish, *Argyrosomos hololepidotus*. WH: 19C. Australian Aboriginal (Yaralde) *malowe*.

multangular *a.* having many angles. WH: 19C. MULTI- + ANGULAR.

multarticulate *a.* many-jointed. WH: 19C. MULTI- + ARTICULATE[2].

multi- *comb. form* many, several. WH: Latin *multus* much, many + -*i*-.

multi-access *n.* a system in which several users have simultaneous connection to the same computer. WH: mid-20C. MULTI- + ACCESS.

multiaxial *a.* having many axes or lines of growth. WH: 19C. MULTI- + *axial* (AXIS[1]).

multicellular *a.* many-celled. WH: 19C. MULTI- + CELLULAR.

multichannel *a.* having or using many communication or television channels. WH: mid-20C. MULTI- + CHANNEL[1].

multicipital *a.* having many heads. WH: 19C. MULTI- + -*cipital*, based on *bicipital* (BICEPS).

multicolour *a.* of or in many colours, many-coloured. WH: 19C. MULTI- + COLOUR.

multicultural *a.* (of a society) made up of many cultural and ethnic groups. WH: mid-20C. MULTI- + *cultural* (CULTURE).

multidimensional *a.* having more than three dimensions. WH: 19C. MULTI- + *dimensional* (DIMENSION).

multidirectional *a.* extending in several directions. WH: mid-20C. MULTI- + *directional* (DIRECTION).

multi-ethnic *a.* composed of, or relating to several ethnic groups. WH: mid-20C. MULTI- + ETHNIC.

multifaced *a.* (of some crystals) having many faces. WH: 19C. MULTI- + -*faced* (FACE).

multifaceted *a.* (of a gem) having many facets. WH: 19C. MULTI- + *faceted* (FACET).

multifarious *a.* having great multiplicity or diversity. WH: 16C. Latin *multifarius* varied, diverse, from *multifariam* in many parts, from *multi* MULTI- + -*fariam* parts, ? rel. to *fari* to tell (cp. FABLE). See also -OUS. Cp. OMNIFARIOUS.

multifid *a.* having many divisions, cleft into parts, lobes, segments etc. WH: 18C. MULTI- + -FID.

multifoil *a.* having more than five foils. Also *n.* WH: 19C. MULTI- + FOIL[1].

multiform *a.* having many forms. WH: 17C. French *multiforme* or Latin *multiformis*. See MULTI-, -FORM.

multifunctional *a.* having many functions. WH: mid-20C. MULTI- + *functional* (FUNCTION).

multigrade *a., n.* (of) an engine oil with a viscosity that matches several standard grades. WH: mid-20C. MULTI- + GRADE.

multigym *n.* a single piece of apparatus with weights, levers etc. for improving muscular fitness in a variety of ways. WH: mid-20C. MULTI- + GYM.

multihull *n.* a vessel with more than one hull. WH: mid-20C. MULTI- + HULL[1].

multilateral *a.* of an agreement or treaty in which more than two states participate. WH: 17C. Late Latin *multilaterus* + -AL[1]. See MULTI-, LATERAL.

multilingual *a.* able to speak, or speaking, several languages. WH: 19C. MULTI- + Latin *lingua* tongue + -AL[1].

multimedia *a.* using different media. Also *n.pl.* WH: mid-20C. MULTI- + MEDIA[1].

multimillionaire *n.* a person who possesses several million pounds, dollars etc. WH: 19C. MULTI- + *millionaire* (MILLION).

multinational *n., a.* (a company) operating in several countries. WH: early 20C. MULTI- + NATIONAL.

multinomial *a.* having many terms, polynomial. Also *n.* WH: 17C. MULTI- + -*nomial*, based on BINOMIAL. Cp. POLYNOMIAL.

multinucleate *a.* (of cells) having several nuclei. WH: 19C. MULTI- + NUCLEATE[1].

multipack *n.* a pack containing a number of items of a foodstuff etc., sold at less than the price of that number of individual items. WH: mid-20C. MULTI- + PACK.

multiparous *a.* giving birth to many at one time. WH: 17C. Modern Latin *multiparus*. See MULTI-, -PAROUS.

multipartite *a.* divided into many parts. WH: 18C. Latin *multipartitus*. See MULTI-, PARTITE.

multi-party *a.* (of a state etc.) having several political parties. WH: early 20C. MULTI- + PARTY[1].

multiped *a.* having many feet. Also *n.* WH: 14–15C. Latin *multipeda*, from *multi-* MULTI- + *pes, pedis* foot.

multiphase *a.* (of an electrical device etc.) polyphase. WH: 19C. MULTI- + PHASE. Cp. POLYPHASE.

multiplane *n.* an aeroplane having more than one pair of wings. WH: early 20C. MULTI- + PLANE[4].

multiple *a.* having many parts, components or relations. Also *n.* WH: 17C. French, from Late Latin *multiplus*, alt. of Latin MULTIPLEX.

multiplex *a.* multiple, manifold. Also *n., v.t.* WH: 14–15C. Latin, from *multi-* MULTI- + -*plex*, from *plicare* to fold. Cp. -FOLD.

multiply *v.t.* to add (a quantity called the multiplicand) to itself a certain number of times (called the multiplier) so as to produce a quantity called the product. Also *v.i.* WH: 12–14C. Old French *multiplier*, from Latin *multiplicare*, from MULTIPLEX, *multiplicis*.

multipolar *a.* having more than two poles. Also *n.* WH: 19C. MULTI- + POLAR.

multiprocessing *n.* processing by a number of central processing units working together in parallel. WH: mid-20C. MULTI- + PROCESS[1] + -ING[1].

multiserial *a.* having many series or rows. WH: 19C. MULTI- + SERIAL.

multiskill *v.t.* to train in a range of skills, esp. relating to the same manufacturing process. WH: late 20C. MULTI- + SKILL.

multi-stage *a.* (of a rocket) having several sections which fall off in series at set points during flight. WH: early 20C. MULTI- + STAGE.

multi-storey *a.* (esp. of a car park) having several storeys. Also *n.* WH: early 20C. MULTI- + STOREY.

multitasking *n.* the carrying out by a computer or system of several tasks simultaneously. WH: mid-20C. MULTI- + TASK + -ING[1].

multi-track *a.* (of a sound recording) using several different tracks blended to produce the final sound. WH: late 20C. MULTI- + TRACK.

multitude *n.* the state of being numerous. WH: 12–14C. Old French, from Latin *multitudo, multitudinis*, from *multus* many. See also -TUDE.

multi-user *a.* (of a computer system) designed for use by several people simultaneously. WH: mid-20C. MULTI- + *user* (USE[2]).

multivalent *a.* having several degrees of valency. WH: 19C. MULTI- + -*valent*, from Latin *valens, valentis*, pres.p. of *valere* to be strong. See also -ENT. Cp. VALENCE.

multivalve *a.* (of a shell) having many valves. Also *n.* WH: 18C. MULTI- + VALVE.

multivariate *a.* having two or more variable quantities. WH: early 20C. MULTI- + *variate* (VARIATION).

multiversity *n.* a university with many departments and affiliated institutions. WH: mid-20C. MULTI- + UNIVERSITY.

multivitamin *n.* a pill etc. containing doses of several vitamins. WH: mid-20C. MULTI- + VITAMIN.

multivocal *a.* having several possible interpretations, ambiguous. Also *n.* WH: 19C. MULTI- + Latin *vocare* to call + -AL[1].

multi-way *a.* having several paths of communication etc. WH: mid-20C. MULTI- + WAY.

multum in parvo *n.* much in little, a lot in a small space. WH: 18C. Latin much in little.

multungulate *a.* (of an ungulate) having more than two separate toes on each foot. *Also n.* WH: 19C. Modern Latin *multungulatus*. See MULTI-, *ungulate* (UNGULA).

mum[1] *n.* mother. WH: 17C. Partly var. of MAM, partly abbr. of MUMMY[2]. Cp. MOM.

mum[2] *a.* silent. *Also int., v.i.* WH: 14–15C. Imit.

mumble *v.i.* to speak indistinctly, to mutter. *Also v.t., n.* WH: 12–14C. MUM[2] + -LE[4]. Cp. Low German *mummelen*, Dutch *mommelen*, *mummelen*.

mumbo-jumbo *n.* incomprehensible or nonsensical language. WH: 18C. ? From Mande *mama dyumbo*, from *mama* ancestor + *dyumbo* pompon-wearer.

mummer *n.* an actor in a mime, esp. one of a number of people who formerly went from house to house at Christmas in fantastic disguises performing a folk play. WH: 14–15C. Old French *momeur*, from *momer* to act in dumb show, rel. to *momon* mask, Spanish *momo* grimace, ? of Germanic orig. Cp. MUM[2]. See also -ER[2].

mummy[1] *n.* a body of a person or animal preserved from decay by embalming, esp. after the manner of the ancient Egyptians. *Also v.t.* WH: 14–15C. Old French *mumie* (Modern French *momie*), from Medieval Latin *mumia*, from Arabic *mūmiyā* pissasphalt, embalmed body, ? from Persian *mūm* wax.

mummy[2] *n.* mother. WH: 18C. Representation of pronun. of MAMMY. Cp. MOMMY.

mump *v.i.* to sulk, to mope. *Also v.t.* WH: 16C. Imit. of movements of mouth. Cp. MOW[3].

mumps *n.* a contagious disease characterized by a swelling and inflammation in the parotid and salivary glands. WH: 16C. Pl. of obs. *mump* grimace. Cp. MUMP.

mumsy *a.* maternal, drab, homely, unfashionable. *Also n.* WH: 19C. MUM[1] + -SY.

munch *v.t.* to chew audibly. *Also v.i.* WH: 14–15C. Appar. imit. Cp. CRUNCH, SCRUNCH.

Münchausen's syndrome *n.* a syndrome in which the patient repeatedly simulates illness in order to obtain hospital treatment. WH: 19C. Baron *Munchausen* (in German form *Münchhausen*), the hero of a supposed autobiographical account of impossible adventures, written in English by the German author Rudolf Eric Raspe (1785).

mundane *a.* everyday, banal. WH: 14–15C. Old French *mondain*, from Late Latin *mondanus*, from Latin *mundus* world. See also -ANE.

mung *n.* (the seed of) an E Asian bean plant of the genus *Vigna*, used as a forage plant and as the main source of beansprouts. WH: 19C. Hindi *mūng*.

mungo *n.* woollen cloth made of second-hand material (of rather higher grade than shoddy). WH: 19C. ? From Scottish male forename *Mungo*, alluding to obs. *mong*, *mung* mingling, mixture, rel. to AMONG.

municipal *a.* of or relating to the government of a town or city or to local government in general. WH: 16C. Latin *municipalis*, from *municipium* town having self-government, from *municeps*, *municipis*, from *munia* civic offices + *capere* to take. See also -AL[1].

munificent *a.* generous, bountiful. WH: 16C. Latin *munificens*, *munificentis*, from *munificus*, from *munus* gift. See also -FIC, -ENT.

muniment *n.* a title deed, charter or record kept as evidence or defence of a title. WH: 14–15C. Old French, from Latin *munimentum* fortification, from *munire* to fortify, to secure. See also -MENT.

munition *n.* military ammunition and stores of all kinds. *Also v.t.* WH: 14–15C. Old French, from Latin *munitio*, *munitionis*, from *munitus*, p.p. of *munire* to fortify, to secure. See also -ION.

munt *n.* a black African. WH: mid-20C. Bantu *umuntu* person, sing. of *abantu* (BANTU).

muntin *n.* a vertical strip dividing panels in a door or panes in a sash window, a glazing bar. WH: 17C. Var. of obs. *montant*, from French, use as n. of pres.p. of *monter* to mount. See also -ANT.

muntjac *n.* a small SE Asian deer of the genus *Muntiacus*. WH: 18C. Sundanese *minchek*.

Muntz metal *n.* a type of brass alloy (60% copper, 40% zinc) used for casting, extrusion, sheathing ships etc. WH: 19C. George Frederick *Muntz*, 1794–1857, English metallurgist.

muon *n.* a subatomic particle, an unstable lepton with a mass approx. 207 times that of the electron. WH: mid-20C. Contr. of *mu-meson*. See MU, also -ON. Cp. MESON.

muraena *n.* the moray, an edible marine eel-like fish of the genus *Muraena*. WH: 16C. Latin sea-eel, lamprey, from Greek *muraina*, from *muros* sea-eel.

murage *n.* a toll for the repair or maintenance of the walls of a town. WH: 14–15C. Old French. See MURE, also -AGE.

mural *n.* a large painting, mosaic etc. on a wall. *Also a.* WH: 15C. Old French *muraille*, from Latin *muralia*, neut. pl. of *muralis* (from *murus* wall), taken as fem. sing. See also -AL[1].

murder *n.* homicide with malice aforethought, a premeditated killing of another person. *Also v.t.* WH: pre-1200. Old English *morthor*, from Germanic, from Indo-European base also of Latin *mors*, *mortis* death, *mori* to die (see MORTAL).

†mure *v.t.* to immure, to shut up. *Also n.* WH: 14–15C. Old French *murer*, from *mur*, from Latin *murum*, acc. of *murus* wall.

murex *n.* any marine gastropod mollusc of the genus *Murex*, used as a source of a purple dye. WH: 16C. Latin, ? rel. to Greek *muax* sea-mussel.

muriatic acid *n.* hydrochloric acid. WH: 17C. Latin *muriaticus* pickled in brine, from *muria* brine. See also -ATIC.

muricate *a.* having sharp points or prickles. WH: 17C. Latin *muricatus* shaped like a murex, from MUREX, *muricis*. See also -ATE[2].

muriform *a.* arranged like bricks in a wall. WH: 19C. Latin *murus* wall + -i- + FORM.

murine *a.* of or related to, or similar to a mouse. WH: 17C. Latin *murinus*, from *mus*, *muris* mouse. See also -INE.

murk *n.* darkness. *Also a.* WH: pre-1200. Old English *mirce*, *myrce*, from Germanic, of Scandinavian orig. Cp. Old Norse *myrkr* darkness.

murmur *n.* a low, confused, continuous or repeated sound, as of running water. *Also v.i., v.t.* WH: 14–15C. Manchu *murmure* or Latin *mumur* a humming, muttering, roaring, rushing, prob. of imit. orig.

murphy *n.* a potato. WH: 19C. *Murphy*, Irish surname.

Murphy's Law *n.* the maxim that if something can go wrong, it *will* go wrong. WH: mid-20C. Surname MURPHY.

murrain *n.* an infectious disease among cattle. *Also a.* WH: 12–14C. Old French *morine*, from stem of *mourir*, from Latin *mori* to die.

murre *n.* an awk or guillemot. WH: 16C. Orig. unknown.

†murrey *a.* of a dark-red colour. *Also n.* WH: 12–14C. Old French *moré*, from Medieval Latin *moratus*, from Latin *morum* mulberry.

murrhine *a.* denoting a delicate kind of Eastern ware made of fluorspar. WH: 16C. Latin *murrhinus*, from *murra*, Greek *morria* substance for making valuable vases, etc.

Mus.B. *abbr.* Bachelor of Music. WH: Abbr. of Latin *Musicae Baccalaureus* Bachelor of Music.

musca *n.* any dipterous insect of the genus *Musca*, which includes the houseflies. WH: 18C. Latin fly.

Muscadet *n.* a light dry white wine from the Loire region of France. WH: early 20C. French, from *muscade* nutmeg, from *musc* MUSK. See also -ET[1].

muscardine *n.* a disease fatal to silkworms, caused by a fungoid or parasitic growth. WH: 19C. French from *muscadin*, *muscardin*, lit. musk-comfit, from Italian *moscado* MUSK. The disease is so called because the fungus resembles *muscadin*.

muscarine *n.* an alkaloid poison from the fungus *Amanita muscaria*. WH: 19C. Modern Latin *muscaria*, fem. of Latin *muscarius* pertaining to a fly, from *musca* fly. See also -INE. The named fungus is fly agaric.

muscatel *n.* a kind of rich wine made from muscadine grapes. WH: 14–15C. Old French *muscadel*, *muscatel*, from Provençal dim. of *muscat* a variety of grape, from *musc* MUSK. See also -EL.

muscle *n.* an organ consisting of a band or bundle of contractile fibrous tissue serving to move or hold in place some part of an animal body. WH: 14–15C. French, from Latin *musculus*, from *mus* mouse. See also -CULE. The shape and movement of some muscles resemble those of a mouse. (Both can be observed well in the biceps.)

muscoid *a.* resembling moss. *Also n.* WH: 19C. Latin *muscus* moss. See also -OID.

muscovado *n.* a moist, dark-coloured, unrefined sugar left after evaporation from the juice of sugar cane and the draining off from the molasses. **WH:** 17C. Portuguese *mascabado*, use as n. of p.p. of *mascabar* to make badly. See -ADO.

Muscovite *n.* a native or inhabitant of Moscow. *Also a.* **WH:** 16C. Modern Latin *Muscovita*, from *Muscovia*, from Russian *Moskva* Moscow, the capital of Russia and formerly of the principality of Muscovy.

muscovite *n.* a silver-grey form of mica, used for electrical insulation. **WH:** 19C. From *Muscovy glass* (MUSCOVITE) + -ITE¹.

muscular *a.* of or relating to the muscles. **WH:** 17C. From obs. *musculous*, from Old French *musculeux* or Latin *musculosus*, from *musculus* MUSCLE (see also -ULOUS), with substitution of -AR¹ for -ous.

Mus.D. *abbr.* Doctor of Music. **WH:** Abbr. of *Musicae Doctor* Doctor of Music.

muse¹ *n.* in Greek mythology, each of nine goddesses, daughters of Zeus and Mnemosyne, who presided over the liberal arts. **WH:** 14–15C. Old French, or from Latin *musa*, from Greek *mousa*, of unknown orig.

muse² *v.i.* to ponder, to meditate (upon). *Also v.t., n.* **WH:** 12–14C. Old French *muser*, ? ult. from Medieval Latin *musum* muzzle.

musette *n.* a small bagpipe formerly used in France. **WH:** 14–15C. Old French, dim. of *muse* bagpipe. See also -ETTE.

museum *n.* a room or building for the preservation or exhibition of objects illustrating antiquities, art, natural science etc. **WH:** 17C. Latin library, study, from Greek *mouseion* seat of the Muses, use as n. of neut. of *mouseios*, from *mousa* MUSE¹.

mush¹ *n.* a mash, a soft pulp, pulpy mass. **WH:** 17C. Appar. var. of MASH¹.

mush² *v.i.* a command to a team of sled dogs to move forward. *Also n.* **WH:** 19C. Alt. of French *marchez!* go! or *marchons!* let's go!, imper. forms of *marcher* to go, MARCH¹.

mushroom *n.* a quick-growing edible fungus, esp. *Agaricus campestris*, the field mushroom. *Also a., v.i.* **WH:** 14–15C. Old French *mousseron*, from Late Latin *mussirio, mussirionis*, of unknown orig.

music *n.* the art of combining vocal and instrumental tones in a rhythmic form for the expression of emotion and pleasing of the aesthetic sense. **WH:** 12–14C. Old French *musique*, from Latin *musica*, from Greek *mousikē* (*tekhnē*) (art) of the Muses, from fem. (used as n.) of *mousikos*, from *mousa* MUSE¹. See also -IC.

musique concrète *n.* concrete music, consisting of pieces of pre-recorded music or other sound put together and electronically modified. **WH:** mid-20C. French concrete music (CONCRETE¹).

musk *n.* an odoriferous, resinous substance obtained from a sac in the male musk deer. **WH:** 14–15C. Late Latin *muscus*, from Persian *mušk*, ? from Sanskrit *muṣka* scrotum. The reference would be to the shape of the musk deer's musk-bag.

muskeg *n.* an undrained level area of mossy bog or swamp in Canada. **WH:** 19C. Cree *maske:k*.

muskellunge *n.* a large N American pike, *Esox masquinongy*, found esp. in the Great Lakes. **WH:** 18C. Ojibwa.

musket *n.* the old firearm of the infantry superseded by the rifle. **WH:** 16C. French *mousquet*, from Italian *moschetto*, (orig.) bolt from a crossbow, from *mosca* fly, from Latin *musca*. See also -ET¹.

musketeer *n.* a soldier armed with a musket. **WH:** 16C. MUSKET + -EER, based on French MOUSQUETAIRE.

Muslim *n.* a person of the Islamic faith. *Also a.* **WH:** 17C. Arabic *muslim*, active p. of *'aslama*. See ISLAM.

muslin *n.* a fine, thin, cotton fabric used for dresses, curtains etc. *Also a.* **WH:** 17C. French MOUSSELINE, from Italian *mussolina*, from *Mussolo* Mosul, a city in N Iraq, where formerly made. See also -INE.

musmon *n.* the mouflon. **WH:** 17C. Latin *musimo, musimonis*, Late Greek *mousimōn*.

muso *n.* a musician. **WH:** mid-20C. Abbr. of *musician* (MUSIC). See also -O.

muss *n.* a state of confusion or disorder, a mess. *Also v.t.* **WH:** 19C. Appar. alt. of MESS.

mussel *n.* any mollusc of the bivalve genus *Mytilus*, esp. the edible *M. edulis.* **WH:** pre-1200. Old English *muscle, musle*, from alt. of Latin *musculus*. See MUSCLE.

†Mussulman *n.* a Muslim. *Also a.* **WH:** 16C. Persian *musulmān*, var. of MUSLIM. Not rel. to MAN.

must¹ *v.aux.* to be obliged to, to be under a necessity to. *Also n.* **WH:** pre-1200. Old English *mōste*, past tense of *mōt* MOTE², from Germanic.

must² *n.* mustiness, mould. *Also v.t., v.i.* **WH:** 17C. Back-formation from MUSTY.

must³ *n.* new wine, the expressed juice of the grape before fermentation. **WH:** pre-1200. Old English, from Latin *mustum*, use as n. of neut. of *mustus* new, fresh.

must⁴ *a.* (of male elephants and camels) in a dangerous state of frenzy, connected with the mating season. *Also n.* **WH:** 19C. Urdu *mast*, from Persian, lit. intoxicated.

mustachio *n.* a moustache, esp. a large one. **WH:** 16C. Italian *mostaccio*, ult. from Greek *mustax, mustakos* upper lip, moustache.

mustang *n.* the wild horse of the American prairies. **WH:** 19C. Appar. blend of Spanish *mestengo* (now *mesteño*) and *mostrenco*, both meaning wild cattle, ownerless cattle, with *mestengo* from *mesta* (from Latin *mixta*, use as n. of fem. p.p. of *miscere* to mix) association of graziers who divided strays or unclaimed animals.

mustard *n.* the seeds of *Sinapis alba* ground and used esp. as a condiment. *Also a.* **WH:** 12–14C. Old French *moustarde* (Modern French *moutarde*), from *mourt*, from Latin *mustum* MUST³. The condiment is so called because it was originally prepared by adding new wine or must to mustard seeds.

mustelid *n.* a small mammal of the family Mustelidae which contains the weasels, martens, skunks, badgers etc. *Also a.* **WH:** early 20C. Modern Latin *Mustelidae*, from *Mustela* genus name, from Latin *mustela* weasel.

muster *v.t.* to summon (up) (strength, courage etc.). *Also v.i., n.* **WH:** 12–14C. Old French *moustrer* (Modern French *montrer*), from Latin *monstrare* to show. The original meaning (to the 17C) was to show, to display, to exhibit. This then gave the sense to assemble soldiers for inspection (14–15C) and so to summon one's own personal resources (16C).

musty *a.* mouldy. **WH:** 16C. ? Alt. of *moisty* (from MOIST + -Y¹), based on MUST³. Cp. MUST².

mutable *a.* liable to change. **WH:** 14–15C. Latin *mutabilis*, from *mutare* to change. See also -ABLE.

mutagen *n.* something that causes or assists genetic mutation. **WH:** mid-20C. From *mutation* (MUTATE) + -GEN.

mutant *n.* an organism that has undergone mutation. *Also a.* **WH:** early 20C. Latin *mutans, mutantis*, pres.p. of *mutare* to change. See also -ANT.

mutate *v.i.* to change. *Also v.t., a., n.* **WH:** 19C. Back-formation from *mutation* (14–15C), from Latin *mutatio, mutationis*, from *mutatus*, p.p. of *mutare* to change. See also -ATION.

mutatis mutandis *adv.* the necessary alterations having been made. **WH:** 15C. Latin, lit. things being changed that have to be changed, abl. pl. respectively of p.p. and ger. of *mutare* to change.

mutch *n.* a close-fitting woman's cap. **WH:** 14–15C. Middle Dutch *mutse*, rel. to Middle High German *mütze*, shortening of Medieval Latin *almucia* AMICE². Cp. German *Mütze* cap.

mutchkin *n.* a Scottish measure of about three-quarters of a pint (426 ml). **WH:** 14–15C. Early Modern Dutch *mudseken* (now *mutsje*), dim. of *mudde*. See also -KIN.

mute¹ *a.* uttering no sound, speechless. *Also n., v.t.* **WH:** 12–14C. Old French *muet*, dim. of *mu*, from Latin *mutus*, ult. imit. of a dull sound made with tightly pressed lips.

†mute² *v.i.* (of birds) to excrete. *Also v.t., n.* **WH:** 14–15C. Old French *meutir*, later *mutir*, shortening of *esmeutir* (Modern French *émeutir*), ? from a Frankish v. meaning to smelt.

mutilate *v.t.* to maim, to mangle. **WH:** 16C. Latin *mutilatus*, p.p. of *mutilare*, from *mutilus* maimed. See also -ATE³.

mutineer *n.* a person who mutinies. *Also v.i.* **WH:** 17C. French *mutinier*, from Old French *mutin* mutiny, from *muete* (Modern French *meute*), from Popular Latin *movita*, from Latin *movere* MOVE. See also -EER.

muton *n.* the smallest element of genetic material capable of giving rise to a new form by mutation. **WH:** mid-20C. From *mutation* (MUTATE) + -ON.

mutt n. a fool, a stupid or inept person. WH: 19C. Abbr. of *mutton-head* (MUTTON).

mutter v.i. to speak, in a low voice or with compressed lips. *Also* v.t., n. WH: 12–14C. From base represented also by MUTE[1]. See also -ER[5].

mutton n. the flesh of sheep used as food. WH: 12–14C. Old French *moton* (Modern French *mouton*), from Medieval Latin *multo, multonis*, prob. of Gaulish orig. Cp. Irish *molt* castrated ram, Gaelic *mult*, Welsh *mollt*, Cornish *mols* wether, Breton *maout* sheep.

mutual a. reciprocally given and received. WH: 15C. Old French *mutuel*, from Latin *mutuus* borrowed, mutual, rel. to *mutare* to change. See also -AL[1].

mutule n. one of the projecting blocks under the corona of a Doric cornice, a modillion. WH: 17C. French, from Latin *mutulus*.

†mutuum n. a contract under which goods are lent for consumption, to be repaid in property of the same kind and quantity. WH: 15C. Latin loan, use as n. of neut. of *mutuus* borrowed. See MUTUAL.

muu-muu n. a loose brightly-coloured dress worn by women in Hawaii. WH: early 20C. Hawaiian *mu'u mu'u*, lit. cut off. The dress is so called because the yoke was originally omitted.

Muzak® n. recorded background music played in shops, restaurants etc. WH: mid-20C. Alt. of MUSIC, prob. based on a proprietary name such as *Kodak*.

muzhik n. a Russian peasant, a serf. WH: 16C. Russian, dim. of *muzh* man, husband. Russian peasants were called 'little men' because they were regarded as minors under old Russian law.

muzzle n. the projecting mouth and nose of an animal, as of a horse, dog etc., the snout. *Also* v.t. WH: 14–15C. Old French *musel* (Modern French *museau*), from dim. of Medieval Latin *musum*, of unknown orig. The word was formerly derived from Latin *morsus* bite, but this origin is not sustainable.

muzzy a. muddled, dazed. WH: 18C. Orig. unknown. Cp. *fuzzy* (FUZZ).

my a. possessive of I. *Also* int. WH: 12–14C. Reduced form of MINE[1]. Cp. ME[1].

myalgia n. a morbid state of the muscles characterized by pain and cramp, muscular rheumatism. WH: 19C. MYO- + -ALGIA.

myalism n. a kind of witchcraft practised in the W Indies. WH: 19C. ? From Hausa *mayl* sorcerer + -ISM.

myall n. any tree of the genus *Acacia*, esp. *A. pendula*, yielding scented wood used in making tobacco pipes. WH: 19C. Australian Aboriginal, ? rel. to Dharuk *mayal* stranger.

Myanman a. of or relating to Myanmar (Burma) in SE Asia. *Also* n. WH: late 20C. Burmese *myanma* of Myanmar + -AN.

myasthenia n. a condition causing loss of muscle power. WH: 19C. MYO- + ASTHENIA.

mycelium n. the vegetative parts of fungi, mushroom spawn. WH: 19C. Greek *mukēs* fungus + -*elium*, based on EPITHELIUM.

Mycenaean a. of or relating to the late Bronze Age civilization of Mycenae, an ancient city of Argolis, Greece. *Also* n. WH: 18C. Latin *Mycenaeus*, from *Mycenae* Mycenae, an ancient city in the Argive plain, Greece + -AN.

-mycete comb. form used to form the names of fungi, as in *myxo-mycete*. WH: Greek *mukēs, mukētos* fungus.

myceto- comb. form used to form words denoting a connection with fungi, as in *mycetophagous, mycobacterium*. WH: Greek *mukēs, mukētos* fungus. See also -O-. Cp. MYCO-.

mycetoma n. a fungoid disease affecting the bones of the feet or hand. WH: 19C. MYCETO- + -OMA.

-mycin comb. form used to form the names of antibiotic compounds developed from fungi, as in *streptomycin*. WH: *myco-* (MYCETO-) + -IN[1].

myco- comb. form used to from words denoting a connection with fungi, as in *mycoplasma, mycosis*. WH: Greek *mukēs* fungus + -O-. Cp. MYCETO-.

mycology n. the study of fungi. WH: 19C. MYCO- + -LOGY.

mycophagy n. the eating of fungi. WH: 19C. MYCO- + -PHAGE + -Y[2].

mycoplasma n. any of a group of prokaryotic mainly parasitic micro-organisms of the genus *Mycoplasma*. WH: mid-20C. Modern Latin *Mycoplasma* genus name. See MYCO-, PLASMA.

mycoprotein n. protein obtained from fungi, esp. that produced for human consumption. WH: 19C. MYCO- + PROTEIN.

mycorrhiza n. a fungoid growth supplying the roots of a plant with material from humus. WH: 19C. MYCO- + Greek *rhiza* root.

mycosis n. the presence of parasitic fungi in the body. WH: 19C. MYCO- + -OSIS.

mycotoxin n. a poisonous substance produced by a fungus. WH: mid-20C. MYCO- + TOXIN.

mycotrophy n. the condition of a plant in a symbiotic association with its mycorrhizae. WH: early 20C. MYCO- + -TROPHY.

mydriasis n. an abnormal dilation of the pupil of the eye. WH: 19C. Latin, from Greek *mudriasis*. See also -IASIS.

myelin n. a soft, white, fatty tissue forming a sheath round certain nerve fibres. WH: 19C. MYELO- + -IN[1].

myelitis n. inflammation of the spinal cord. WH: 19C. MYELO- + -ITIS.

myelo- comb. form of or relating to the spinal cord. WH: Greek *muelos, muelon* marrow, spinal cord. See also -O-.

myeloid a. of or relating to the spinal cord. WH: 19C. MYELO- + -OID.

myeloma n. a usu. malignant tumour of the bone marrow. WH: 19C. MYELO- + -OMA.

mylodon n. a gigantic Pleistocene slothlike edentate of the genus *Mylodon*. WH: 19C. Modern Latin, from Greek *mulē, mulos* molar (lit. millstone) + *odōn*, var. of *odous, odontos* tooth. The sloth is so called as its teeth are more or less cylindrical molars, resembling millstones.

mylohyoid a. of or relating to the molar teeth and the hyoid bone. WH: 17C. Medieval Latin *mylohyoideus*, from Greek *mulē, mulos*. See MYLODON, HYOID.

mynah n. any of various SE Asian passerine birds, esp. *Gracula religiosa*, known particularly for its ability to imitate the human voice. WH: 18C. Hindi *mainā*.

mynheer n. the Dutch title of address equivalent to Mr or Sir. WH: 17C. Dutch *mijnheer*, from *mijn* my + *heer* lord, master.

myo- comb. form of or relating to muscles. WH: Greek *mus, muos* muscle. See also -O-.

myocardium n. the muscular substance of the heart. WH: 19C. MYO- + -*cardium*, based on PERICARDIUM.

myofibril n. any of the elongated contractile threads that make up striated muscle cells. WH: 19C. MYO- + FIBRIL.

myogenic a. originating in the muscles. WH: 19C. MYO- + -GENIC.

myoglobin n. a protein containing iron that stores oxygen in muscle. WH: early 20C. MYO- + GLOBIN, based on *haemoglobin* (HAEMO-).

myography n. the recording of muscular contractions. WH: 18C. MYO- + -GRAPHY.

myology n. the study of the muscles. WH: 17C. MYO- + -LOGY.

myopia n. short-sightedness. WH: 18C. Modern Latin, from Late Greek *muōpia*, from Greek *muōps* short-sighted, from *muein* to blink, to shut (an eye). See also -OPIA.

myosin n. a protein in the contractile muscular tissue. WH: 19C. MYO- + -OSE[2] + -IN[1].

myositis n. inflammation of a muscle. WH: 19C. Greek *muos*, gen. of *mus* muscle + -ITIS.

myosotis n. any hardy plant of the genus *Myosotis*, esp. the forget-me-not. WH: 17C. Latin, from Greek *muosōtis*, from *muos*, gen. of *mus* mouse + *ous, ōtos* ear.

myotonia n. the inability to relax muscles after vigorous effort, muscle stiffness or spasm. WH: 19C. MYO- + Greek *tonos* TONE + -IA.

myriad a. innumerable, countless. *Also* n. WH: 16C. Late Latin *myrias, myriadis*, from Greek *murias, muriados*, from *murios* countless, innumerable, pl. *murioi* ten thousand. See also -AD[1].

myriapod n. any terrestrial arthropod of the class Myriapoda, including the centipedes and millipedes and characterized by a very large indeterminate number of jointed feet. *Also* a. WH: 19C. Modern Latin *Myriapoda*, from Greek *murias* very numerous (MYRIAD) + *pous, podos* foot.

myrica n. the tamarisk. WH: 18C. Latin, from Greek *murikē*.

myrmeco- comb. form of or relating to ants. WH: Greek *murmēx, murmēkos* ant. See also -O-.

myrmecology n. the study of ants. WH: 19C. MYRMECO- + -LOGY.

myrmecophile n. an organism living in a symbiotic relationship with ants. WH: 19C. MYRMECO- + -PHILE.

myrmidon n. a faithful follower, esp. an unscrupulous underling, a hired ruffian. WH: 14–15C. Latin *Myrmidones* (pl.), from Greek *Murmidones*, from *murmēkes* ants. The *Murmidones* were a warlike people of ancient Thessaly whom Achilles led to the siege of Troy. They were said to have been created from ants.

myrobalan n. the cherry plum. WH: 14–15C. Old French *myrobolan* or Latin *myrobalanum*, from Greek *murobalanon*, from *muron* balsam, unguent + *balanos* acorn, date, ben nut.

myrrh[1] n. a gum resin from trees of the genus *Commiphora* or other trees growing in the Near East, used in the manufacture of incense, perfumes etc. WH: pre-1200. Old English *myrra*, from Germanic, from Latin *myrrha*, from Greek *murra*, of Semitic orig. Cp. Arabic *murr* bitter.

myrrh[2] n. an umbelliferous plant, *Myrrhis odorata*, also called *sweet cicely*. WH: 16C. Latin *myrris*, from Greek *murris*.

myrtle n. a tree or shrub of the genus *Myrtus*, esp. *M. communis*, a tall shrub with glossy evergreen leaves and sweet-scented white or rose-coloured flowers, anciently sacred to Venus. WH: 14–15C. Medieval Latin *myrtilla*, dim. of Latin *myrtus*, from Greek *murtos*.

myself pron. I or ME[1] (objective) used to give emphasis (usu. in apposition). WH: pre-1200. ME[1] + SELF, but long interpreted as MY + SELF.

mystagogue n. a person who interprets or initiates into divine mysteries, esp. an initiator into the Eleusinian and other ancient Greek mysteries. WH: 16C. French, or from Latin *mystagogus*, from Greek *mustagōgos*, from *mustēs* (MYSTIC) + *agōgos* leading, from *agein* to lead.

mystery[1] n. a secret or obscure matter. WH: 12–14C. Anglo-French equiv. of Old French *mistere* (Modern French *mystère*), or direct from Latin *mysterium*, from Greek *mustērion* secret thing, secret ceremony, from base also of *mustikos* secret, MYSTIC. *Mystery plays*, as medieval religious plays based on the Bible, were often performed by members of craft guilds, so came to be associated with MYSTERY[2].

†mystery[2] n. a handicraft, trade or occupation. WH: 14–15C. Medieval Latin *misterium*, contr. of Latin *ministerium* ministry (MINISTER), by assoc. with *mysterium* (MYSTERY[1]).

mystic a. of or relating to mystery or mysticism. *Also* n. WH: 12–14C. Old French *mystique* or Latin *mysticus*, from Greek *mustikos*, from *mustēs* initiated person, from *muein* to close (the eyes or the lips), to initiate. See also -IC.

mystify v.t. to bewilder, to puzzle. WH: 19C. French *mystifier*, from *mystère* MYSTERY[1] or *mystique* MYSTIC. See also -FY.

mystique n. professional skill or technique that impresses the layperson. WH: 19C. French. See MYSTIC.

myth n. a fictitious legend or tradition, accepted as historical, usu. embodying the beliefs of a people on the creation, the gods, the universe etc. WH: 19C. Modern Latin *mythus*, Late Latin *mythos*, from Greek *muthos*.

mytho- comb. form of or relating to myth. WH: Greek *muthos* or direct from MYTH. See also -O-.

mythogenesis n. the creation or production of myths. WH: 19C. MYTHO- + GENESIS.

mythography n. the writing or narration of myths, fables etc. WH: 19C. Greek *muthographia*. See MYTHO-, -GRAPHY.

mythology n. a system of myths in which are embodied the beliefs of a people concerning their origin, deities, heroes etc. WH: 14–15C. French *mythologie* or Late Latin *mythologia*, from Greek *muthologia*. See MYTHO-, -LOGY.

mythomania n. an abnormal tendency to lie or exaggerate. WH: early 20C. MYTHO- + -MANIA.

mythopoeia n. the making of myths. WH: mid-20C. Greek *muthopoiia*, from *mutho-* MYTHO- + *poiein* to make. See also -IA.

mythos n. myth. WH: 18C. Greek *muthos* MYTH.

mythus n. myth. WH: 19C. Modern Latin MYTH. Cp. MYTHOS.

myxo- comb. form of, relating to or living in slime. WH: Greek *muxa* slime, mucus. See also -O-.

myxoedema n. a condition characterized by underactivity of the thyroid gland and consequent weight gain, mental sluggishness, thickening of the skin, listlessness and sensitivity to cold. WH: 19C. MYXO- + OEDEMA.

myxoma n. a benign tumour composed of mucous or gelatinous tissue. WH: 19C. MYXO- + -OMA.

myxomatosis n. a contagious and fatal virus disease in rabbits. WH: early 20C. *myxomat-* (taken as stem of MYXOMA) + -OSIS. The term was coined in 1898 by the Italian bacteriologist Giuseppe Sanarelli.

myxomycete n. a slime mould of the class Myxomycetes. WH: 19C. Modern Latin *Myxomycetes*, from *myxo-* MYXO- + Greek *mukētes*, pl. of *mukēs* fungus.

myxovirus n. any of a group of viruses causing such illnesses as influenza, mumps etc. WH: mid-20C. MYXO- + VIRUS.

'n *conj.* and. **WH:** 19C. Reduced form of AND.

Na *chem. symbol* sodium. **WH:** Abbr. of Latin *natrium*.

na *adv.* not. **WH:** 18C. Var. of NO².

NAAFI *n.* an organization running canteens for the Services. **WH:** early 20C. Acronym of *Navy, Army* and *Air Force Institutes*.

nab *v.t.* to catch, to seize, to apprehend. **WH:** 17C. Orig. unknown.

nabob *n.* a deputy-governor or prince under the Mughal empire in India. **WH:** 17C. Portuguese *nababo*, or from Spanish *nabab*, from Urdu *nawwāb*, *nawāb* deputy governor. See NAWAB.

nacarat *n.* a pale-red colour tinged with orange. **WH:** 18C. French, ? from Spanish and Portuguese *nacarado*, from *nacar* nacre.

nacho *n.* a crisp corn chip used as an appetizer in Mexican cuisine, often served with melted cheese, a chilli dip etc. **WH:** mid-20C. Orig. uncertain. ? Mexican Spanish *Nacho*, pet form of male forename *Ignacio*. The name of the dish may be that of the chef who created it.

nacre *n.* mother-of-pearl. **WH:** 16C. French, ? from Italian *naccaro*, from Arabic *naḳḳāra* small drum, NAKER. According to some, the word is from the related Arabic *nāḳūr* hunting horn, which the mollusc resembles in shape.

nadir *n.* the point of the heavens directly opposite to the zenith or directly under our feet. **WH:** 14–15C. Old French, from Arabic *naẓīr* (*as-samt*) opposite (the zenith).

naevus *n.* a congenital discoloration of the skin, a birthmark or mole. **WH:** 19C. Latin.

naff¹ *a.* unfashionable, lacking in taste, style or credibility. **WH:** mid-20C. Orig. unknown.

naff² *v.i.* to go away. **WH:** mid-20C. Prob. euphemistic substitute for FUCK. Cp. EFF.

nag¹ *v.i.* to be continually finding fault. *Also v.t., n.* **WH:** 19C. ? Ult from Scandinavian, or from Low German. Cp. Swedish *nagga*, Norwegian *nagge* to gnaw, to nibble, to irritate, Low German *naggen* to irritate, to provoke.

nag² *n.* a small horse or pony for riding. **WH:** 14–15C. Orig. unknown. ? Rel. to NEIGH.

Nagari *n.* Devanagari. **WH:** 18C. Sanskrit *nāgarī* , from *nagara* town. Cp. DEVANAGARI.

nagor *n.* the reedbuck. **WH:** 18C. Arbitrary, based on earlier *nanguer*. The animal was named in 1764 by the French naturalist Georges-Louis Leclerc, Comte de Buffon, from the resemblance of its horns to those of the *nanguer*, a species of antelope.

Nahuatl *n.* a member of any of various peoples native to Central America and Mexico. *Also a.* **WH:** 19C. Spanish, from Nahuatl.

naiad *n.* a water nymph. **WH:** 14–15C. Latin *Naïas, Naïadis*, from Greek, rel. to *naein* to flow.

naiant *a.* swimming, natant. **WH:** 16C. Old French *naiant*, pres.p. of *noier* to swim, from alt. of Latin *natare*. Cp. NATANT.

nail *n.* a small, pointed spike, usu. of metal, with a head, for hammering into wood or other material to fasten things together, or for use as a peg etc. *Also v.t.* **WH:** pre-1200. Old English *nægel*, from Germanic, from Indo-European base also of Latin *unguis*, Greek *onux*. The Old English word was used for both the horny finger and toe covering and the metal spike.

nainsook *n.* a thick muslin, formerly made in India. **WH:** 18C. Urdu (Hindi) *nainsukh*, from *nain* eye + *sukh* pleasure.

naira *n.* the standard monetary unit of Nigeria. **WH:** late 20C. Orig. uncertain. ? Ult. from *Nigeria* (NIGERIAN).

naissant *a.* rising or coming forth, from a fesse or other ordinary. **WH:** 16C. Old French, pres.p. of *naître*, from Latin *nasci* to be born. See also -ANT.

naive *a.* ingenuous, simple, unaffected. **WH:** 17C. Old French *naïve*, fem. of *naïf*, from Latin *nativus* NATIVE.

naked *a.* without clothing, uncovered, nude. **WH:** pre-1200. Old English *nacod*, from Germanic, rel. to Latin *nudus* NUDE, Sanskrit *nagna*. Cp. German *nackt*.

†naker *n.* a kind of kettledrum. **WH:** 12–14C. Old French *nacaire*, *nacre*, from Italian *nacchera*, from Arabic *naḳḳāra* drum.

Nama *n.* a member of a people of S Africa and Namibia. *Also a.* **WH:** 19C. Nama.

namby-pamby *a.* weakly and insipidly sentimental. *Also n.* **WH:** 18C. Fanciful formation based on name of *Ambrose* Philips, 1674–1749, English poet. Philips was the author of pastorals ridiculed by Pope and Henry Carey, the latter in the farce *Namby-Pamby* (1726). Many of Philips' verses were addressed to infants, in lines such as 'Dimply damsel, sweetly smiling' (*Ode to Miss Charlotte Pulteney*, 1727). Carey's work contained the following: 'Namby-Pamby is your guide, / Albion's joy, Hibernia's pride. / Namby-Pamby Pilly-pis, / Rhimy-pim'd on missy-mis'.

name *n.* a word denoting any object of thought, esp. one by which a person, animal, place or thing is known, spoken of or addressed. *Also v.t., a.* **WH:** pre-1200. Old English *nama*, from Germanic, from Indo-European, rel. to Latin NOMEN, Greek *onoma* (cp. ONOMASTIC), Sanskrit *nāman*.

Namibian *n.* a native or inhabitant of Namibia. *Also a.* **WH:** mid-20C. *Namibia*, a country in SW Africa + -AN.

nan *n.* a grandmother. **WH:** mid-20C. From GRAN, or abbr. of NANNY.

nana¹ *n.* a fool. **WH:** mid-20C. Shortening of BANANA¹.

nana² *n.* a grandmother. **WH:** 19C. From GRAN, or var. of NANNY.

nancy *n.* an effeminate young man. *Also a.* **WH:** early 20C. Earlier *Miss Nancy* (19C), from female forename *Nancy*, ? influ. by NAMBY-PAMBY.

nanism *n.* dwarfishness; being stunted. **WH:** 19C. French *nanisme*, from Latin *nanus* (Greek *nanos*) dwarf. See also -ISM.

nankeen *n.* a cotton fabric, usu. of a buff or yellow colour, exported from Nanjing. **WH:** 18C. *Nanking* (Nanjing), the capital of Kiangsu province, E central China.

nanny *n.* a children's nurse. *Also v.t.* **WH:** 18C. Pet form of female forename *Ann* (Anne). See also -Y³.

nannygai *n.* an edible red fish, *Centroberyx affinis*, found in Australian rivers. **WH:** 19C. Australian Aboriginal.

nano- *comb. form* one thousand-millionth. **WH:** Greek *nanos*, Latin *nanus* dwarf. See also -O-.

nanogram *n.* one thousand-millionth of a gram. **WH:** mid-20C. NANO- + GRAM¹.

nanometre *n.* one thousand-millionth of a metre. **WH:** mid-20C. NANO- + METRE¹.

nanosecond *n.* one thousand-millionth of a second. **WH:** mid-20C. NANO- + SECOND¹.

nanotechnology *n.* the branch of technology which deals with measuring, making or manipulating extremely small objects. **WH:** late 20C. NANO- + TECHNOLOGY.

naos *n.* in ancient Greece, the inner part of a temple. **WH:** 18C. Greek temple.

nap¹ *v.i.* to sleep lightly or briefly, to doze. *Also n.* **WH:** pre-1200. Old English *hnappian*, from Germanic, ult. of unknown orig.

nap² *n.* the smooth and even surface produced on cloth or other fabric by cutting and smoothing the fibre or pile. *Also v.t.* **WH:** 14–15C. Middle Low German and Middle Dutch *noppe*, rel. to *noppen* to trim by shearing the nap.

nap³ *n.* a card-game in which five cards are dealt to each player, the one engaging to take the highest number of tricks playing against the others. *Also v.t.* **WH:** 19C. Abbr. of NAPOLEON.

napalm *n.* a thickening agent which is produced from naphthenic acid, other acids and aluminium. *Also v.t.* WH: mid-20C. *naphthenic* (NAPHTHA) + *palmitate* (PALMITIC).

nape *n.* the back of the neck. WH: 12–14C. Orig. unknown.

napery *n.* linen, esp. table linen. WH: 12–14C. Old French *naperie*, from *nappe* tablecloth. See NAPKIN, also -ERY.

naphtha *n.* an inflammable oil produced by dry distillation of organic substances, such as bituminous shale or coal. WH: 14–15C. Latin, from Greek, of Oriental orig. Cp. Persian *naft* naphtha.

Napier's bones *n.pl.* a contrivance invented by John Napier for facilitating the multiplication and division of high numbers by means of slips of bone or other material divided into compartments. WH: 17C. John *Napier*, 1550–1617, Scottish mathematician.

napiform *a.* turnip-shaped. WH: 19C. Latin *napus* turnip, NEEP + -*i*- + -FORM.

napkin *n.* a small square of linen or paper, esp. one used at table to wipe the hands, protect the clothes, or serve fish etc., on; a serviette. WH: 14–15C. Old French *nappe* tablecloth, from Latin *mappa* MAP. See also -KIN.

Naples yellow *n.* a yellow pigment made from antimony. WH: 17C. *Naples*, a city in S Italy.

napoleon *n.* a French gold coin of 20 francs issued by Napoleon I. WH: 19C. *Napoleon*, forename of certain French emperors, esp. *Napoléon* I (Bonaparte), 1769–1821.

Napoleonic *a.* of or relating to Napoleon I or his times. WH: 19C. NAPOLEON + -IC.

nappa *n.* a soft leather made from sheepskin or goatskin. WH: 19C. *Nappa*, a county, town and valley in California, USA.

nappe *n.* a large sheet of rock which has been moved from its original position by thrusting. WH: 19C. French, lit. tablecloth.

napper *n.* the head. WH: 18C. Orig. unknown.

nappy[1] *n.* a piece of soft absorbent material fastened round a baby's bottom to absorb urine and faeces. WH: early 20C. Abbr. of NAPKIN. See also -Y[3].

nappy[2] *a.* (of ale or beer) foaming, strong, heady. *Also n.* WH: 14–15C. Prob. from *nappy* (from NAP[2] + -Y[1]).

narc *n.* a narcotics agent. WH: mid-20C. Abbr. of NARCOTIC.

narceine *n.* a bitter crystalline alkaloid contained in opium after the extraction of morphine. WH: 19C. French *narcéine*, from Greek *narkē* numbness. See also -INE.

narcissism *n.* a state of self-love. WH: 19C. Latin *Narcissus*, from Greek *Narkissos* Narcissus, a youth in Greek mythology who fell in love with his own reflection in a spring and pined away. See also -ISM. Cp. NARCISSUS.

narcissus *n.* any bulbous plant of the genus *Narcissus*, containing the daffodils and jonquils, esp. the white *N. poeticus*. WH: 16C. Latin, from Greek *narkissos*, prob. from *narkē* numbness, with ref. to its narcotic effects. Cp. NARCISSISM.

narco- *comb. form* of or relating to torpor or narcotics. WH: Greek *narkē* numbness, deadness, or from NARCOTIC. See also -O-.

narcolepsy *n.* a nervous disease characterized by fits of irresistible drowsiness. WH: 19C. NARCO- + -*lepsy*, based on EPILEPSY.

narcosis *n.* narcotic poisoning, the effect of continuous use of narcotics. WH: 17C. Greek *narkōsis*, from *narkoun* to make numb. See also -OSIS.

narcoterrorism *n.* terrorism involving illegal drugs. WH: late 20C. NARCO- + *terrorism* (TERROR).

narcotherapy *n.* the treatment of mental disorder by drug-induced sleep. WH: mid-20C. NARCO- + *therapy* (THERAPEUTIC).

narcotic *a.* allaying pain and causing sleep or dullness. *Also n.* WH: 14–15C. Old French *narcotique* or Medieval Latin *narcoticus*, from Greek *narkōtikos*, from *narkoun* to make numb, from *narkē* numbness. See also -OTIC.

nard *n.* any of various plants of the valerian family, esp. *Valeriana celtica*. WH: pre-1200. Latin *nardus*, from Greek *nardos*, ult. from Sanskrit *nalada*, *narada*.

nardoo *n.* an Australian plant, *Marsilea quadrifolia*, the spore case of which is pounded and eaten by the Aborigines. WH: 19C. Australian Aboriginal (Kamilaroi) *nhaaduu*.

nares *n.pl.* the nostrils. WH: 17C. Latin, pl. of *naris* nose, nostril.

nark *n.* a police spy, a decoy. WH: 19C. Romany *nāk* nose. Cp. NOSE.

Narragansett *n.* an almost extinct Algonquian language of Rhode Island. WH: 17C. Narragansett.

narrate *v.t.* to tell, to relate, to give an account of the successive particulars of in speech or writing. WH: 17C. Latin *narratus*, p.p. of *narrare*, or back-formation from *narration* (NARRATE). See also -ATE[3]. Latin *narrare* is related to *gnarus* knowing.

narrow *a.* of little breadth or extent from side to side. *Also v.i., v.t., n.* WH: pre-1200. Old English *nearu*, from Germanic. Cp. German *Narbe* scar.

narthex *n.* a vestibule or porch across the west end in early Christian churches, to which catechumens, women and penitents were admitted. WH: 17C. Latin, from Greek *narthēx* giant fennel, stick, casket, narthex.

nartjie *n.* a small sweet orange like a mandarin. WH: 18C. Afrikaans *naarjie*, from Tamil *nārattai* citrus.

narwhal *n.* an Arctic delphinoid cetacean, *Monodon monoceros*, with a long tusk or tusks developed from one or both of its teeth. WH: 17C. Dutch *narwal*, Danish *narhval*, rel. to Old Norse *náhvalr*, from *nár* corpse + *hval* WHALE[1]. The narwhal is said to be so called because its whitish colour resembles that of a corpse.

nary *a.* not one single. WH: 18C. Alt. of *ne'er a*. See NE'ER.

nasal *a.* of or relating to the nose. *Also n.* WH: 14–15C. French, or Medieval Latin *nasalis*, from *nasus* nose. See also -AL[1].

nascent *a.* coming into being; beginning to develop; immature. WH: 17C. Latin *nascens*, *nascentis*, pres.p. of *nasci* to be born. See also -ENT.

naseberry *n.* a sapodilla. WH: 17C. Spanish and Portuguese *néspera* medlar, assim. to BERRY.

naso- *comb. form* of or relating to the nose. WH: Latin *nasus* nose. See also -O-.

nasofrontal *a.* of or relating to the nose and frontal bone. WH: 19C. NASO- + *frontal* (FRONT).

nasogastric *a.* of or relating to the nose and stomach. WH: mid-20C. NASO- + GASTRIC.

nasolacrymal *a.* of or relating to the nose and tears. WH: 19C. NASO- + *lacrymal* (LACHRYMAL).

nastic *a.* (of movement) not related to the direction of the stimulus. WH: early 20C. Greek *nastos* pressed together + -IC.

nasturtium *n.* a trailing plant, *Tropaeolum majus*, with vivid orange flowers. WH: pre-1200. Latin *nasturcium*, appar. from *naris* nose + *torquere* to twist. The nasturtium has a rather pungent smell.

nasty *a.* extremely unpleasant. *Also n.* WH: 14–15C. Orig. unknown. According to some, the word is from Old French *nastre* bad, a shortened form of *villenastre* infamous, bad, ignoble, from *vilein* VILLAIN + pejorative suf. -*astre* -ASTER. See also -Y[1]. The original meaning was foul, filthy, dirty. The current general sense emerged in the 18C.

natal[1] *a.* of, from or relating to one's birth. WH: 14–15C. Latin *natalis*, from *natus*, p.p of *nasci* to be born. See also -AL[1].

natal[2] *a.* of or relating to the buttocks. WH: 19C. NATES + -AL[1].

natant *a.* swimming. WH: 14–15C. Latin *natans*, *natantis*, pres.p. of *natare*, freq. of *nare* to swim, to float. See also -ANT.

natch[1] *int.* of course. WH: mid-20C. Abbr. of *naturally* (NATURAL).

natch[2] *n.* the part of an ox between the loins, the rump. WH: 12–14C. Old French *nache*, pl. *naches*, from Late Latin *naticas*, acc. pl. of *naticae*, from Latin *natis* buttock. See NATES. Cp. AITCHBONE.

nates *n.pl.* the buttocks. WH: 17C. Latin, pl. of *natis* rump, buttock.

†nathless *adv.* nevertheless. WH: pre-1200. Obs. *na* not, no (from Old English *ne* no + *ā* ever; see AYE[2]) + THE + LESS.

nation *n.* a people under the same government and inhabiting the same country. WH: 12–14C. Old French, from Latin *natio*, *nationis* birth, race, from *natus*, p.p. of *nasci* to be born. See also -ION.

national *a.* of or relating to the nation, esp. to the whole nation. *Also n.* WH: 16C. French. See NATION, also -AL[1].

native *n.* a person born in a specified place. *Also a.* WH: 14–15C. Anglo-Latin *nativus*, use as n. of Latin produced by birth, innate, natural, from *natus*, p.p. of *nasci* to be born. See also -IVE.

nativity *n.* birth, esp. that of Jesus Christ, the Virgin Mary or St John the Baptist. WH: 12–14C. Old French *nativité*, from Late Latin *nativitas*, from Latin *nativus*. See NATIVE, also -ITY.

natron *n.* a mineral consisting of hydrated sodium carbonate. WH: 17C. French, from Spanish *natrón*, from Arabic *naṭrūn*, *niṭrūn*, from Greek *nitron* NITRE.

natter *v.i.* to chatter idly; to chat, exchange gossip. *Also n.* WH: 19C. Imit. See also -ER[5].

natterjack *n.* a European toad, *Bufo calamita*, with a yellow stripe down the back. WH: 18C. Orig. unknown. Cp. JACK[1].

nattier blue *n.* a soft blue. *Also a.* WH: early 20C. Jean Marc *Nattier*, 1685–1766, French painter.

natty *a.* neat, tidy, spruce. WH: 18C. Appar. rel. to NEAT[1]. See also -Y[1].

natural *a.* of, relating to, produced by or constituted by nature. *Also adv., n.* WH: 12–14C. Old French *naturel*, from Latin *naturalis*, from *natura* NATURE. See also -AL[1].

nature *n.* the essential qualities of anything. WH: 12–14C. Old French, from Latin *natura*, from *natus*, p.p. of *nasci* to be born. See also -URE.

naught *n.* nothing. *Also a., adv.* WH: pre-1200. Old English *nāwiht*, from obs. *na* (see NATHLESS) + *wiht* WIGHT. Cp. NOUGHT.

naughty *a.* perverse, mischievous; disobedient, badly behaved. WH: 14–15C. NAUGHT + -Y[1]. The original sense was possessing nothing. The current sense dates from the 17C.

naumachia *n.* in ancient Rome, a naval combat, esp. a mock battle shown as a spectacle. WH: 16C. Latin, from Greek *naumakhia*, from *naus* ship + *makhē* fight. See also -IA.

nauplius *n.* a larval stage of development in some of the lower crustaceans. WH: 19C. Modern Latin, from Latin a kind of shellfish, or from Latin *Nauplius*, Greek *Nauplios* a son of Poseidon in Greek mythology.

Nauruan *n.* a native or inhabitant of Nauru. *Also a.* WH: early 20C. *Nauru*, an island in the W Pacific + -AN.

nausea *n.* a feeling of sickness, with a propensity to vomit. WH: 14–15C. Latin, from Greek seasickness, nausea, from *naus* ship.

nautical *a.* of or relating to ships, navigation or sailors; naval. WH: 16C. French *nautique* or Latin *nauticus*, from Greek *nautikos*, from *nautēs* sailor, from *naus* ship + -IC + -AL[1].

nautilus *n.* any cephalopod of the genus *Nautilus*, esp. the pearly nautilus. WH: 17C. Latin, from Greek *nautilos* sailor, nautilus, from *nautēs*. See NAUTICAL.

Navajo *n.* a member of an American Indian people of New Mexico and Arizona. *Also a.* WH: 18C. Spanish *Apaches de Navajó*, from Tewa *navahu:* fields adjoining arroyo.

naval *a.* consisting of or relating to ships or a navy. WH: 14–15C. Latin *navalis*, from *navis* ship. See also -AL[1].

navarin *n.* a lamb casserole with vegetables. WH: 19C. French, prob. from *Navarin* Navarino, from name of battle (1827) in which a Turkish-Egyptian fleet was destroyed by the allied naval forces of Britain, France and Russia. The battle was fought in the Bay of Navarin in the SW Peloponnese.

nave[1] *n.* the body of a church, extending from the main doorway to the choir or chancel, distinct, and usually separated by pillars, from the aisles. WH: 17C. Medieval Latin, from Latin *navis* ship. Cp. NEF. A nave is said to be so called because the Christian church is regarded as a ship buffeted by waves, or simply because the long area of the church resembles the hull of a ship. According to some, the origin is actually in Greek *naos* temple.

nave[2] *n.* the central block of a wheel in which the axle and spokes are inserted, the hub. WH: pre-1200. Old English *nafu*, from Germanic, from Indo-European base represented also by Sanskrit *nābhis* nave, navel. Cp. NAVEL.

navel *n.* the scar of the umbilical cord, forming a depression on the surface of the abdomen. WH: pre-1200. Old English *nafela*, from Germanic, from Indo-European base represented also by Latin *umbo* boss of a shield (cp. UMBILICAL), Greek *omphalos* navel, boss. Cp. NAVE[2].

navew *n.* a turnip. WH: 16C. Old French *navel* (Modern French *naveau*), from Latin *napus* turnip, NEEP.

navicert *n.* a certificate authorizing the passage in wartime of approved seaborne merchandise to neutral ports. WH: early 20C. Latin *navis* ship + CERTIFICATE[1].

navicular *a.* shaped like a boat. *Also n.* WH: 14–15C. French *naviculaire* or Late Latin *navicularis*, from Latin *navicula*, dim. of *navis* ship. See also -AR[1].

navigate *v.i.* to sail, to pass from place to place by water or air. *Also v.t.* WH: 16C. Latin *navigatus*, p.p. of *navigare*, from *navis* ship + -ig-, comb. stem of *agere* to drive. See also -ATE[3].

navvy *n.* a labourer in any kind of excavating work, esp. construction of railways etc. WH: 19C. Abbr. of *navigator* (NAVIGATE). Navvies are so called from their work in the construction of canals and artificial waterways for inland navigation.

navy *n.* the warships of a nation. *Also a.* WH: 12–14C. Old French *navie* ship, fleet, from var. of Popular Latin *navia*, from Latin *navis* ship. See also -Y[2].

nawab *n.* in Pakistan, a distinguished Muslim. WH: 18C. Urdu *nawāb*, from Urdu and Persian *nawwāb*, var. of *nuwwāb*, pl. (used as sing.) of Arabic *nā'ib* deputy. Cp. NABOB.

nay *adv.* not only so, not this alone, more than that, and even. *Also n., v.t., v.i.* WH: 12–14C. Old Norse *nei*, from *né* not + *ei* ever, AYE[2].

Nazarene *n.* a native or inhabitant of Nazareth. *Also a.* WH: 12–14C. Ecclesiastical Latin *Nazarenus*, from Greek *Nazarēnos*, from *Nazaret* Nazareth, the town in N Palestine that was the home of Joseph and Mary and the child Jesus, now a city in N Israel. See also -ENE.

Nazarite *n.* a Hebrew who had taken certain vows of abstinence (specified in Num. vi). WH: 16C. Ecclesiastical Latin *Nazareus*, from Hebrew *nāzīr*, from *nāzar* to separate oneself + -ITE[1]. Not rel. to NAZARENE.

naze *n.* a promontory, a headland. WH: 18C. Var. of NESS found mainly in place names, such as *The Naze* in Essex. Cp. NOSE.

Nazi *n.* a member of the German National Socialist Party. *Also a.* WH: mid-20C. German, representation of the pronun. of the first two syls. of *Nationalsozialist* National Socialist. The full name of the party was *Nationalsozialistiche Deutsche Arbeiterpartei* National Socialist German Workers' Party, in power under Hitler in Germany, 1933–45.

nazir *n.* a non-European official formerly employed in Anglo-Indian courts. WH: 17C. Persian and Urdu *nāzir*, from Arabic *nāzir* superintendent, inspector, from *nazar* sight, vision.

NB *abbr.* note well. WH: Abbr. of Latin NOTA BENE.

-nd *suf.* used to form nouns, as in *friend*. WH: Old English *-ond*, orig. part. ending.

Ndebele *n.* a member of a Nguni people. *Also a.* WH: 19C. Bantu, from Ndebele *n-*, sing. pref. + SeSotho *tèbèlè* Nguni.

né *a.* born (used with a man's original name), as in *Elton John, né Reginald Dwight*. WH: mid-20C. French born, m. p.p. of *naître* to be born. Cp. NÉE.

Neanderthal *a.* of or relating to a Palaeolithic species of man whose remains were first found in the Neanderthal valley. WH: 19C. *Neanderthal*, from *Neander*, a river near Düsseldorf, W Germany + German *Tal* (earlier *Thal*) valley.

neap *a.* low or lowest (applied to the tides which happen in the middle of the second and fourth quarters of the moon, when the rise and fall are least). *Also n., v.i., v.t.* WH: pre-1200. Old English *nēp* in *nēpflōd* (see FLOOD), of unknown orig.

Neapolitan *a.* of or relating to Naples. *Also n.* WH: 14–15C. Latin *Neapolitanus*, from *Neapolites*, from Greek *Neapolis* new town, Naples. See also -ITE[1], -AN.

near *adv.* at or to a short distance, at hand; not far off, not remote in place, time or degree. *Also prep., a., v.t., v.i.* WH: pre-1200. Old Norse *nær*, orig. comp. of *ná*, rel. to Old English *nēah* NIGH. The original Old English meaning was nearer, but the word came to be used as a positive form, and a new comparative form, *nearer*, developed from it.

near- *comb. form* almost, as *near-fatal*. WH: 16C. NEAR.

nearby[1] *a.* situated close at hand. WH: 19C. NEARBY[2].

nearby[2] *adv.* close at hand. WH: 14–15C. NEAR + BY.

Nearctic *a.* of or relating to the N (Arctic and temperate) part of N America. *Also n.* WH: 19C. NEO- + ARCTIC.

neat[1] *a.* tidy, trim. WH: 16C. Old French *net*, from Latin *nitidus* shining, clean, from *nitere* to shine. Cp. NET[2]. The original sense (to the 18C) was clean, clear, bright.

†neat[2] *n.* cattle of the bovine kind. *Also a.* WH: pre-1200. Old English *nēat*, from Germanic, rel. to Old English *nēotan* to enjoy. Cp. German *geniessen* to enjoy, to make use of.

neath *prep.* beneath. WH: 14–15C. Shortening of dial. *aneath*, var. of BENEATH.

neb *n.* a beak, a bill. WH: pre-1200. Old English *nebb*, from Germanic. Cp. NIB.

nebbish *n.* a timid person. *Also a.* WH: 19C. Yiddish *nebekh* poor thing.

nebbuk *n.* a thorny shrub, *Ziziphus spina-christi*, supposed to have supplied the thorns for Christ's crown. WH: 19C. Arabic *nabk̜, nibk̜* the shrub's fruit.

Nebuchadnezzar *n.* a large wine bottle which holds 20 times as much as a standard bottle. WH: early 20C. *Nebuchadnezzar*, 605–562 BC, a king of Babylon, who captured and destroyed Jerusalem in 586 BC and deported its leaders.

nebula *n.* a cloudy patch of light in the heavens produced by groups of stars or by a mass of gaseous or stellar matter. WH: 17C. Latin mist, vapour.

nebuly *a.* represented by, shaped in or ornamented with wavy lines. WH: 16C. French *nébulé*, from Medieval Latin *nebulatus*, p.p. of *nebulare* to cloud, from Latin NEBULA.

necessary *a.* needful, requisite, indispensable, requiring to be done. *Also n.* WH: 12–14C. Old French *nécessaire*, or from Latin *necessarius*, from *necesse* (*esse, habere*) (to be, to consider) necessary. See also -ARY[1].

neck *n.* the narrow portion of the body connecting the trunk with the head. *Also v.i., v.t.* WH: pre-1200. Old English *hnecca*, from Germanic, from Indo-European. Cp. German *Nacken* neck, *Genick* nape. The word originally denoted the back part of the body connecting the head and shoulders, then later the whole of this part. The sense narrow part of a bottle dates from the 16C.

necklace *n.* a string of beads or gems worn round the neck. *Also v.t.* WH: 16C. NECK + LACE.

necro- *comb. form* of or relating to dead bodies or the dead. WH: Greek *nekros* dead person, corpse.

necrobiosis *n.* decay of living tissue, as in old age. WH: 19C. Modern Latin, from *necro-* NECRO- + Greek *bios* life. See also -OSIS.

necrolatry *n.* worship of the dead, esp. ancestors. WH: 19C. Ecclesiastical Greek *nekrolatreia*. See NECRO-, -LATRY.

necrology *n.* a register of deaths. WH: 18C. Medieval Latin *necrologium*. See NECRO-, -LOGY.

necromancy *n.* the supposed art of revealing future events by communication with the dead. WH: 12–14C. Old French *nigromancie*, from Medieval Latin *nigromantia*, alt. (by assoc. with Latin *niger, nigris* black) of Late Latin *necromantia*, from Greek *nekromanteia*. See NECRO-, -MANCY.

necrophagous *a.* eating or feeding on carrion. WH: 19C. NECRO- + -PHAGOUS.

necrophilia *n.* an obsession with, and usu. erotic interest in, corpses. WH: NECRO- + -PHILIA.

necrophobia *n.* revulsion from or fear of anything to do with the dead. WH: 19C. NECRO- + *-phobia* (-PHOBE).

necropolis *n.* a cemetery, esp. one on a large scale. WH: 19C. Greek. See NECRO-, -POLIS.

necropsy *n.* an autopsy, a post-mortem examination. WH: 19C. NECRO- + *-psy*, based on AUTOPSY.

necroscopy *n.* a post-mortem examination. WH: 19C. NECRO- + *-scopy* (-SCOPE).

necrosis *n.* the mortification of part of the body, esp. of bone. WH: 17C. Modern Latin, from Greek *nekrōsis* state of death, from *nekroun* to kill, to mortify. See NECRO-, also -OSIS.

nectar *n.* in Greek and Roman mythology, the drink of the gods. WH: 16C. Latin, from Greek *nektar*, of uncertain orig. (poss. from *nek-* death + *-tar* overcoming; cp. AMBROSIA).

nectarine *n.* a smooth-skinned, firm variety of peach. WH: 17C. NECTAR + -INE.

nectocalyx *n.* the bell-shaped swimming organ in the Hydrozoa. WH: 19C. Modern Latin *necto-*, from Greek *nēktos* swimming (from *nēkhein* to swim) + CALYX.

Neddy *n.* the National Economic Development Council. WH: mid-20C. NEDDY, from *NEDC* + -Y[3].

neddy *n.* a donkey (used by or to children). WH: 16C. Dim. of *Ned*, pet form of male forename *Edward*. See also -Y[3].

née *a.* born (used with the maiden name of a married woman), as in *Joan Murphy, née Smith*. WH: French born, fem. p.p. of *naître* to be born. Cp. NÉ.

need *v.t.* to be in want of, to require. *Also v.i., n.* WH: pre-1200. Old English *nēodian*, from *nēd*, from Germanic. Cp. German *Not* need, want.

needle *n.* a small, thin, rod-shaped, pointed steel instrument with an eye for carrying a thread, used in sewing. *Also v.t., v.i.* WH: pre-1200. Old English *nǣdl*, from Germanic, from Indo-European base also of Latin *nere* to spin, Greek *nēma* thread. Cp. German *Nadel*.

neem *n.* a tree, *Azadirachta indica*, found in India, whose leaves and bark are used for medicinal purposes. WH: 19C. Hindi *nīm*, from Sanskrit *nimba*.

neep *n.* a turnip, a swede. WH: pre-1200. Latin *napus* turnip. Cp. TURNIP.

ne'er *adv.* never. WH: 12–14C. Contr. of NEVER.

†neeze *v.i.* to sneeze. *Also n.* WH: 12–14C. Old Norse *hnjósa*, of imit. orig. Cp. SNEEZE.

nef *n.* an ornamental piece of plate shaped like a boat or ship, formerly used for holding the salt cellars, table napkins etc. of people of great distinction. WH: 17C. French ship, nave. See NAVE[1].

nefandous *a.* unspeakable, atrocious. WH: 17C. Latin *nefandus*, from *ne-* not + *fandus*, ger. of *fari* to speak. See also -OUS.

nefarious *a.* wicked, abominable, infamous. WH: 17C. Latin *nefarius*, from *nefas* wrong, wickedness, from *ne-* not + *fas* divine permission, divine law. See also -OUS.

neg *n.* a photographic negative. WH: 19C. Abbr. of *negative* (NEGATE).

negate *v.t.* to render negative, to nullify. WH: 17C. Latin *negatus*, p.p. of *negare* to say no, to deny, from *neg-*. See NEGLECT, also -ATE[3].

neglect *v.t.* to treat carelessly. *Also n.* WH: 14–15C. Latin *neglectus*, p.p. of *neglegere* to disregard, to slight, from *neg-*, var. of *nec* not + *legere* to choose.

negligée *n.* a woman's loose dressing gown of flimsy material. WH: 18C. French *négligé*, p.p. of *négliger* to neglect. The word was originally used for a kind of loose gown worn by women in the 18C. The current sense dates from the middle 20C only.

negligence *n.* disregard of appearances, conventions etc., in conduct, literature etc. WH: 12–14C. Old French *négligence* or Latin *negligentia*, from *negligens, negligentis*, pres.p. of *negligere*, var. of *neglegere*. See NEGLECT, also -ENCE.

negotiate *v.i.* to discuss a matter with other people in order to make a bargain, agreement, compromise etc. *Also v.t.* WH: 16C. Latin *negotiatus*, p.p. of *negotiari* to carry on business, from *negotium* business, from *neg-*, var. of *nec* not + *otium* leisure. See also -ATE[3].

Negrillo *n.* a member of a black people of small stature in central and southern Africa. WH: 19C. Spanish, dim of NEGRO.

Negrito *n.* a member of a black people in some islands of the Malay Archipelago etc. WH: 19C. Spanish, dim. of NEGRO.

Negritude *n.* the state of belonging to a black race. WH: mid-20C. French *négritude*. See NIGRITUDE.

Negro *n.* a person belonging to, or descended from, one of the dark-skinned African peoples. *Also a.* WH: 16C. Spanish and Portuguese, from Latin *niger, nigris* black, of unknown orig.

negro *a.* black, dark. WH: 19C. NEGRO.

Negus *n.* the sovereign of Ethiopia. WH: 16C. Amharic *n'gus* kinged, king.

negus *n.* a beverage of wine, hot water, sugar and spices. WH: 18C. Colonel Francis *Negus*, d.1732, its first maker.

neigh *v.i.* to utter the cry of a horse; to whinny. *Also v.t., n.* WH: pre-1200. Old English *hnǣgan*, from Germanic, of imit. orig. Cp. WHINNY.

neighbour *n.* a person who lives near, a person living in the same street, village, community etc. *Also a., v.t., v.i.* WH: pre-1200. Old English *nēahgebūr*, from *nēah* NIGH + *gebūr* dweller (cp. BOWER[1]), from Germanic. Cp. German *Nachbar*.

neither *a.* not either. *Also pron., conj., adv.* WH: pre-1200. Old English *nawther, nauther*, contr. of *nāhwæther*, from *nā* NO[2] + *hwæther* which of two, WHETHER, with later form based on EITHER.

nek *n.* a mountain pass. WH: 19C. Dutch NECK.

nekton *n.* all forms of organic life found in various depths of salt and fresh water. WH: 19C. Greek *nēkton*, neut. of *nēktos* swimming, from *nēkhein* to swim. The word was coined in 1890 by the German naturalist Ernst Haeckel.

nelly *n.* a foolish or weak person. WH: mid-20C. Pet form of female forenames *Helen*, *Eleanor*.

nelson *n.* a wrestling hold in which one or both arms are passed under the opponent's arm or arms from behind, and the hands joined so that pressure can be exerted with the palms on the back of the opponent's neck. WH: 19C. Appar. from pers. name *Nelson*.

Nelson touch *n.* a skilful approach to a problem. WH: 19C. Horatio *Nelson*, 1758–1805, British admiral.

nelumbo *n.* any water lily of the genus *Nelumbo*, esp. the sacred lotus, *N. nucifera*. WH: 18C. Modern Latin *nelumbium*, from Sinhalese *neḷumba*.

nemathelminth *n.* a threadworm or nematode. WH: 19C. Greek *nēma, nēmatos* thread + *helmins, helminthos* worm.

nematic *a.* denoting a liquid crystal state in which the molecules are parallel but not arranged in distinct planes. *Also n.* WH: early 20C. Greek *nēma, nēmatos* thread + *-IC*.

nemato- *comb. form* threadlike; filamentous. WH: Greek *nēma, nēmatos* thread.

nematocyst *n.* a thread cell in jellyfish and other coelenterates from which the stinging thread is projected. WH: 19C. NEMATO- + CYST.

nematode *n.* a worm of the phylum Nematoda, which includes the parasitic roundworm and the threadworm. *Also a.* WH: 19C. NEMATO- + -ODE[1].

Nembutal® *n.* sodium ethyl methylbutyl barbiturate, used as a sedative, hypnotic and antispasmodic. WH: mid-20C. NA + ETHYL + METHYL + BUTYL + -AL[2]. The name was coined in 1930.

nem. con. *adv.* with no one dissenting. WH: 16C. Abbr. of Latin *nemine contradicente* (with) no one contradicting, abl. of *nemo* no one + abl. of *contradicens*, pres.p. of *contradicere* CONTRADICT.

Nemean *a.* of or relating to Nemea. WH: 16C. Latin *Nemaeus*, *Nemeus*, from Greek *Nemaios* of Nemea, a wooded district near Argos in ancient Greece.

nemertean *a.* belonging to the phylum Nemertea, comprising flat-worms and ribbonworms, chiefly marine. *Also n.* WH: 19C. Modern Latin *Nemertes* genus name, from Greek *Nēmertēs* the name of a sea nymph. See also -AN.

nemesia *n.* any plant of the southern African genus *Nemesia*, grown for their brightly coloured flowers. WH: 19C. Modern Latin, from Greek *nemesion* catchfly. See also -IA.

nemesis *n.* retributive justice. WH: 16C. Greek righteous indigna-tion, personified as *Nemesis*, the goddess of retribution or ven-geance, from *nemein* to deal out what is due, rel. to *nomos* custom, law.

nemophila *n.* an annual trailing plant with blue-and-white flowers. WH: 19C. Modern Latin, from Greek *nemos* wooded pasture, glade + *-philos* -PHILE.

nenuphar *n.* the white water lily, *Nymphaea alba*. WH: 12–14C. Medieval Latin, from Arabic *nīlūfar*, Persian *nīnūfar*, from Sanskrit *nīlotpala*, from *nīla* blue (see ANIL) + *utpala* water lily, lotus. Cp. NUPHAR.

neo- *comb. form* new, recent, modern, later, revived. WH: Greek *neos* new. See also -O-.

neo-Catholic *a.* of or relating to the Puseyite school in the Church of England, or to the school of Liberal Catholicism headed by Lamennais and Lacordaire in the Church of France. WH: 19C. NEO- + CATHOLIC.

neo-Christian *a.* of or relating to rationalized Christianity. WH: 19C. NEO- + CHRISTIAN.

neoclassical *a.* of or relating to the 18th-cent. revival of classicism. WH: 19C. NEO- + CLASSICAL.

neocolonialism *n.* the policy of a strong nation gaining control over a weaker one through economic pressure etc. WH: mid-20C. NEO- + *colonialism* (COLONIAL).

Neocomian *a.* of or relating to the lower division of the Cretaceous strata typically exhibited near Neuchâtel in Switzerland. WH: 19C. French *Néocomien*, from *Neocomium* (from Greek *neos* new + *kōmē* village), Latinized name of Neuchâtel, a town in Switzer-land.

Neo-Darwinism *n.* Darwinism as modified by later investi-gators, esp. to take account of the findings of genetics. WH: 19C. NEO- + *Darwinism* (DARWINIAN).

neodymium *n.* a silver-grey metallic element, at. no. 60, chem. symbol Nd, of the cerium group of rare earth elements. WH: 19C. NEO- + DIDYMIUM.

neo-fascism *n.* a movement attempting to reinstate the policies of fascism. WH: mid-20C. NEO- + FASCISM.

neo-Georgian *a.* of or relating to a revival of the Georgian style. WH: early 20C. NEO- + GEORGIAN[1].

neogothic *n.* the Gothic revival of the mid-19th cent. *Also a.* WH: 19C. NEO- + GOTHIC.

neogrammarian *n.* any one of a modern school of grammarians insisting upon the invariability of the laws governing phonetic change. WH: 19C. NEO- + *grammarian* (GRAMMAR).

Neohellenism *n.* the revival of Greek ideals in art and liter-ature, as in the Italian Renaissance. WH: 19C. NEO- + *Hellenism* (HELLENE).

Neo-Kantian *a.* of or relating to the teaching of Kant as modified by later interpreters. *Also n.* WH: 19C. NEO- + KANTIAN.

Neo-Lamarckian *a.* of or relating to the teaching of Lamarck on organic evolution, as revived in a modified form by those who believe in the inheritance of acquired characters. WH: 19C. NEO- + LAMARCKIAN.

neolithic *a.* of or relating to the later Stone Age, characterized by ground and polished implements and the introduction of agri-culture. *Also n.* WH: 19C. NEO- + LITHIC.

neologism *n.* a new word or phrase, or a new sense for an old one. WH: 19C. French *néologisme*. See NEO-, -LOGY, also -ISM.

neomycin *n.* an antibiotic effective against some infections that resist ordinary antibiotics. WH: mid-20C. NEO- + -MYCIN.

neon *n.* a colourless gaseous element, at. no. 10, chem. symbol Ne, existing in minute quantities in the air, isolated from argon in 1898. WH: 19C. Greek, neut. of *neos* new. The element was named in 1898 by its joint discoverers, the Scottish chemist Sir William Ramsay and the English chemist Morris W. Travers. It was so called as it was instantly recognized as a new element by its unique glow when electrically stimulated.

neonatal *a.* of or relating to the first few weeks after birth in human babies. WH: 19C. NEO- + NATAL[1].

neo-Nazi *n.* a person belonging to an organization attempting to reinstate the policies of Naziism. *Also a.* WH: mid-20C. NEO- + NAZI.

neopaganism *n.* a revived form of paganism. WH: 19C. NEO- + *paganism* (PAGAN).

neophobia *n.* a fear of anything new. WH: 19C. NEO- + -*phobia* (-PHOBE).

neophyte *n.* a person who is newly converted or newly baptized. *Also a.* WH: 14–15C. Ecclesiastical Latin *neophytus*, from Greek *neo-phutos* newly planted, from *neo-* NEO- + *phuton* plant. The Greek word is translated as 'novice' in the Authorized Version (I Tim. iii.6) but was 'neophyte' in the earlier Rheims Bible (1582).

neoplasm *n.* an abnormal growth of new tissue in some part of the body, a cancer. WH: 19C. NEO- + *plasm* (PLASMA).

neoplasty *n.* restoration of a part by granulation, adhesive inflam-mation etc. WH: mid-20C. NEO- + -PLASTY.

Neoplatonism *n.* a system of philosophy combining the Platonic ideas with the theosophy of the East, originating in Alexandria in the 3rd cent. AD. WH: 19C. NEO- + *platonism* (PLATONIC).

neoprene *n.* a synthetic rubber-like polymer, used in waterproof products. WH: mid-20C. NEO- + -*prene*, based on ISOPRENE.

neoteny *n.* the retention of juvenile characteristics in the adult. WH: 19C. NEO- + Greek *teinein* to keep. See also -Y[2].

neoteric *a.* new; of recent origin. *Also n.* WH: 16C. Late Latin *neo-tericus*, from Greek *neōterikos*, from *neōteros*, comp. of *neos* new. See also -IC.

neotropical *a.* of, relating to or characteristic of tropical and S America. WH: 19C. NEO- + *tropical* (TROPIC).

Neozoic *a.* belonging to the later or post-Palaeozoic period, in-cluding both Mesozoic and Cenozoic, or corresponding to Cenozoic. WH: 19C. NEO- + -*zoic*, based on PALAEOZOIC. The term was coined in 1854 by the British naturalist Edward Forbes.

Nepali *n.* a native or inhabitant of Nepal, or a descendant of one. *Also a.* WH: 19C. *Nepal*, a country in S Asia, bordered by Tibet to the north and India to the south + -I[3].

nepenthes *n.* a drug or potion that drives away sorrow or grief. WH: 16C. Latin, from Greek *nēpenthes*, neut. of *nēpenthēs* banishing pain, from *nē-* not + *penthos* grief.

nephalism *n.* total abstinence from intoxicants, teetotalism. WH: 19C. Late Greek *nēphalismos*, from *nēphalios* sober. See also -ISM.

nepheline *n.* a vitreous silicate of aluminium and sodium found in volcanic rocks. WH: 19C. French *néphéline*, from Greek *nephelē* cloud. See also -INE. The mineral is so called because its fragments are made cloudy when immersed in nitric acid.

nephelometer *n.* an instrument for measuring cloudiness esp. in liquids. WH: 19C. Greek *nephelē* cloud + -O- + -METER.

nephew *n.* the son of a brother or sister. WH: 12–14C. Old French *neveu*, from Latin *nepos, nepotis* grandson, nephew, descendant, rel. to Germanic. Cp. Dutch *neef*, German *Neffe* nephew.

nephology *n.* the scientific study of clouds. WH: 19C. Greek *nephos* cloud + -LOGY.

nephoscope *n.* an instrument for observing the elevation, direction and velocity of clouds. WH: 19C. Greek *nephos* cloud + -SCOPE.

nephralgia *n.* pain or disease in the kidneys. WH: 19C. NEPHRO- + -ALGIA.

nephrectomy *n.* removal of a kidney by surgical means. WH: 19C. NEPHRO- + -ECTOMY.

nephric *a.* of or relating to the kidney. WH: 19C. NEPHRO- + -IC.

nephrite *n.* jade. WH: 18C. Greek *nephros* kidney + -ITE[1]. The mineral is so called because it was supposed to cure kidney disease.

nephritic *a.* of or relating to the kidneys. *Also n.* WH: 14–15C. Late Latin *nephriticus*, from Greek *nephritikos*, from *nephritis* (NEPHRO-, -ITIS). See also -IC.

nephro- *comb. form* of or relating to the kidneys. WH: Greek *nephros* kidney. See also -O-.

nephroid *a.* of or relating to the kidneys. WH: 19C. NEPHRO- + -OID.

nephrology *n.* the scientific study of the kidneys. WH: 19C. NEPHRO- + -LOGY.

nephrotomy *n.* surgical incision of the kidney. WH: 17C. NEPHRO- + -TOMY.

ne plus ultra *n.* the most perfect or uttermost point. WH: 17C. Latin not further beyond. The Latin words were said to be inscribed on the Pillars of Hercules (Strait of Gibraltar) to prohibit ships from passing through.

nepotism *n.* favouritism towards one's relations, for example in business. WH: 17C. French *népotisme*, from Italian *nepotismo*, from *nipote* nephew + -ISM.

Neptune *n.* the eighth planet from the sun. WH: 14–15C. French, or from Latin *Neptunus* Neptune, the Roman god of the sea.

neptunium *n.* a radioactive metallic element, at. no. 93, chem. symbol Np, obtained by the bombardment of uranium with neutrons. WH: 19C. NEPTUNE + -IUM, based on URANIUM. The name is said to have been coined for the element in c.1940 by the US physicist Edward M. McMillan, its codiscoverer, because it followed uranium (atomic number 92) in the same way that the planet Neptune comes after Uranus. The name was earlier in use for a supposed element similar to tantalum.

nerd *n.* an ineffectual or socially awkward person, a fool. WH: mid-20C. Orig. unknown. ? Alt. of NUT.

nereid *n.* a sea nymph. WH: 14–15C. Latin *Nereis, Nereidis*, from Greek *Nērēis, Nērēidos*, from *Nēreus* a sea god. See also -ID.

nerine *n.* any southern African plant of the genus *Nerine*, with scarlet or rose-coloured flowers, including the Guernsey lily. WH: 19C. Modern Latin, from Latin, from Greek *Nērēis* a water nymph. Cp. NEREID.

neroli *n.* an essential oil distilled from the flowers of the bitter or Seville orange, used as a perfume. WH: 17C. French *néroli*, from Italian *neroli*, from Anne-Marie de La Trémoille, 1635–1722, wife of Flavio Orsini, prince of *Nerola*, who popularized the perfume.

Neronian *a.* of, relating to or like the Emperor Nero. WH: 16C. Latin *Neronianus*, from *Nero* Claudius Caesar, AD 37–68, Roman emperor. See also -IAN.

nerve *n.* any of the fibres or bundles of fibres conveying sensations and impulses to and from the brain or other organs. *Also v.t.* WH: 14–15C. Latin *nervus* sinew, bowstring, rel. to Greek *neuron* sinew, nerve, Latin *nere* to spin.

nescient *a.* ignorant, having no knowledge (of). *Also n.* WH: 14–15C. Latin *nesciens, nescientis*, pres.p. of *nescire*, from *ne* not + *scire* to know. See also -ENT.

nesh *a.* soft, friable. WH: pre-1200. Old English *hnesce*, from Germanic, of unknown orig.

ness *n.* a promontory, a cape. WH: pre-1200. Old English *næs, nes*, rel. to NOSE. Cp. NAZE.

-ness *suf.* forming nouns denoting state, condition, as *happiness*. WH: Old English *-nes, -nis*, from Germanic. The initial *-n-* was originally part of the stem of the preceding word, as in Gothic, where the suf. is *-assus*. Cp. Gothic *ibnassus* evenness, from *ibn* even + *-assus* -ness.

nest *n.* the bed or shelter constructed or prepared by a bird for laying its eggs and rearing its young. *Also v.t., v.i.* WH: pre-1200. Old English, from Indo-European, from base meaning down + base of SIT. Cp. Latin *nidus*, Irish *nead*, Welsh *nyth*, Sanskrit *nīḍa* resting place.

nestle *v.i.* to settle oneself (down, in etc.). *Also v.t.* WH: pre-1200. Old English *nestlian*, from Germanic. See NEST, also -LE[4]. The current general sense evolved in the 17C. The original sense, still current, relates to birds nesting.

Nestor *n.* a wise counsellor; a sage; a venerable senior. WH: 16C. Greek *Nestōr*, a Homeric hero famous for his age and wisdom.

Nestorian *a.* of or relating to Nestorius or his doctrines. *Also n.* WH: 14–15C. Late Latin *Nestorianus*, from *Nestorius*, d.451, Syrian ecclesiastic, patriarch of Constantinople. See also -AN.

net[1] *n.* a fabric of twine, cord etc., knotted into meshes, for catching fish, birds, or other animals, or for covering, protecting, carrying etc. *Also v.t., v.i.* WH: pre-1200. Old English, from Germanic, rel. to Latin *nodus* knot.

net[2] *a.* free from all deductions. *Also v.t.* WH: 12–14C. French *net*, fem. *nette* NEAT[1]. The original sense (to the 19C) was neat, trim, smart. The current sense evolved in the 14–15C.

†nether *a.* lower. WH: pre-1200. Old English *neothera, nithera*, from Germanic base meaning down, downwards. See also -ER[3]. Cp. German *nieder*.

Netherlander *n.* a native or inhabitant of the Netherlands, or a descendant of one. WH: 17C. From the *Netherlands*, based on Dutch *Nederlander*, from *Nederland* (from *neder* NETHER + *land* LAND), a country in W Europe bordering the N Sea. See also -ER[1].

netsuke *n.* a small piece of carved wood or ivory worn or attached to various articles, as a toggle or button, by the Japanese. WH: 19C. Japanese.

nettle *n.* any plant of the genus *Urtica*, with two European species, the great or common and the small nettle, with inconspicuous flowers and minute stinging hairs. *Also v.t.* WH: pre-1200. Old English *netele, netle, netel*, from Germanic deriv. (see -LE[1]) of base of Old High German *nazza*. Cp. German *Nessel*.

Neufchâtel *n.* a soft white cheese, similar to cream cheese but with less fat. WH: 19C. *Neufchâtel*, a town in N France near Rouen.

neume *n.* a sequence of notes to be sung to one syllable in plainsong. WH: 14–15C. Old French, from Medieval Latin *neuma*, from Greek *pneuma* breath.

neural *a.* of or relating to the nerves or the nervous system. WH: 19C. Greek *neuron* nerve + -AL[1].

neuralgia *n.* an acute pain in a nerve or series of nerves, esp. in the head or face. WH: 19C. NEURO- + -ALGIA.

neurasthenia *n.* weakness of the nervous system, nervous debility. WH: 19C. NEURO- + ASTHENIA.

neuration *n.* the arrangement of the nervures, as in an insect's wings. WH: 19C. Greek *neuron* nerve + -ATION.

neurectomy *n.* excision of a nerve, or part of it. WH: 19C. NEURO- + -ECTOMY.

neurilemma *n.* the membranous sheath encasing a nerve. WH: 19C. Orig. from Greek *neuron* nerve + *eilēma* covering, but later taken as if from Greek *lemma* husk, skin.

neurility *n.* the power of a nerve to convey stimuli. WH: 19C. NEURO- + -IL + -ITY.

neurine *n.* a poisonous ptomaine derived from putrefying organic matter. WH: 19C. NEURO- + -INE.

neuritis *n.* inflammation of a nerve. WH: 19C. NEURO- + -ITIS.

neuro- *comb. form* of or relating to a nerve cell. WH: Greek *neuron* nerve. See also -O-.

neuroanatomy *n.* the anatomy of the nervous system. WH: early 20C. NEURO- + ANATOMY.

neurobiology *n.* the biology of the nervous system. WH: early 20C. NEURO- + BIOLOGY.

neurocomputer *n.* a computer using a neural network. WH: late 20C. NEURO- + COMPUTER.

neurogenesis *n.* the development of nervous tissue. WH: early 20C. NEURO- + GENESIS.

neurogenic *a.* originating in nervous tissue. WH: early 20C. NEURO- + -GENIC.

neuroglia *n.* the supporting tissue of the central nervous system. WH: 19C. NEURO- + Greek *glia* glue.

neurohormone *n.* a hormone produced by nerve cells. WH: mid-20C. NEURO- + HORMONE.

neurolinguistics *n.* the branch of linguistics which deals with the relationship between language and the functioning of the brain. WH: mid-20C. NEURO- + *linguistics* (LINGUIST).

neurology *n.* the scientific study of the anatomy, physiology and pathology of nerves. WH: 17C. Modern Latin *neurologia*. See NEURO-, -LOGY.

neuroma *n.* a tumour consisting of nerve tissue. WH: 19C. NEURO- + -OMA.

neuromuscular *a.* of or relating to nerves and muscles. WH: 19C. NEURO- + MUSCULAR.

neurone *n.* a nerve cell with its processes and ramifications, one of the structural units of the nervous system. WH: 19C. Greek *neuron* sinew, cord, nerve. The term was coined in 1891 by the German histologist Wilhelm Waldeyer-Hertz.

neuropath *n.* a person suffering from a nervous disorder or having abnormal nervous sensibility. WH: 19C. NEURO- + -PATH.

neurophysiology *n.* the physiology of the nervous system. WH: 19C. NEURO- + PHYSIOLOGY.

neuropsychology *n.* psychology based upon the study of the nervous system. WH: 19C. NEURO- + PSYCHOLOGY.

neuropteran *n.* any insect of the order Neuroptera, having four reticulated membranous wings. WH: 19C. Modern Latin *Neuroptera*, from NEURO- + Greek *pteron* wing. See also -A², -AN.

neuroradiology *n.* a method of diagnosis of such conditions as cerebral tumours, aneurysms etc. by X-ray examination. WH: mid-20C. NEURO- + RADIOLOGY.

neuroscience *n.* the study of the structure and function of the brain and the nervous system. WH: mid-20C. NEURO- + SCIENCE.

neurosis *n.* functional disorder of the nervous system. WH: 18C. Modern Latin, from NEURO- + -OSIS.

neurosurgery *n.* the branch of surgery dealing with the nervous system. WH: early 20C. NEURO- + SURGERY.

neurotomy *n.* an incision in a nerve, usu. to produce sensory paralysis. WH: 18C. NEURO- + -TOMY.

neurotoxin *n.* any poison which acts on the nervous system. WH: early 20C. NEURO- + TOXIN.

neurotransmitter *n.* a chemical substance by means of which nerve cells communicate with each other. WH: mid-20C. NEURO- + *transmitter* (TRANSMIT).

neuter *a.* neither masculine nor feminine. *Also n., v.t.* WH: 14–15C. Old French *neutre* or Latin *neuter*, from *ne* not + *uter* either of two.

neutral *a.* taking no part with either side, esp. not assisting either of two belligerents. *Also n.* WH: 14–15C. Obs. French *neutral* or Latin *neutralis*, from *neutr-* NEUTER. See also -AL¹.

neutrino *n.* any of a class of subatomic particles with almost zero mass and zero charge but specified spin. WH: mid-20C. NEUTRAL + Italian dim. suf. *-ino*. The term was coined in 1933 by the Italian physicist Enrico Fermi.

neutron *n.* a particle that is neutral electrically with approximately the same mass as a proton. WH: early 20C. NEUTRAL + -ON. The term was coined in 1930 by the British physicist Ernest Rutherford, but the particle remained hypothetical until discovered in 1932 by the British physicist James Chadwick. The term was in use earlier in other scientific contexts, e.g. in 1921 for a 'hydrogen atom'.

névé *n.* consolidated snow above the glaciers, in the process of being converted into ice. WH: 19C. Swiss French, from Latin *nix, nivis* snow.

never *adv.* not ever, at no time. *Also int.* WH: pre-1200. Old English *næfre*, from *ne* NOT + *æfre* EVER.

new *a.* not formerly in existence. *Also adv.* WH: pre-1200. Old English *nēowe*, from Germanic, from Indo-European base represented also by Greek *neos*, Latin *novus*, Sanskrit *nava*. Cp. NEO-.

Newcastle disease *n.* an acute, highly contagious disease of chickens and other birds. WH: 18C. *Newcastle* (*upon Tyne*), a city in NE England where first recorded, 1926.

newel *n.* the central column from which the steps of a winding stair radiate. WH: 14–15C. Old French *nouel* knob, from Medieval Latin *nodellus*, dim. of *nodus* knot. See also -EL.

newfangled *a.* new-fashioned; different from the accepted fashion. WH: 14–15C. From dial. *newfangle* (from NEW + *-fangle*, from an Old English word rel. to FANG; see -LE⁴) + -ED.

Newfoundland *n.* a large breed of dog, famous for swimming powers, orig. from Newfoundland. WH: 17C. *Newfoundland*, a large island on the E coast of Canada, forming a province with mainland Labrador.

Newfoundlander *n.* a native or inhabitant of Newfoundland. WH: 17C. NEWFOUNDLAND + -ER¹.

Newmarket *n.* a gambling card game in which players try to match cards with cards laid out. WH: 17C. *Newmarket*, a town in Suffolk, famous for horse racing.

news *n.* recent or fresh information. WH: 14–15C. Pl. of NEW, based on Old French *noveles*, pl. of *novele* (Modern French *nouvelle*) NOVEL, or on Medieval Latin *nova*, pl. of *novum*, use as n. of neut. of Latin *novus* NEW. The word was long popularly said to represent the letters of the four points of the compass (N + E + W + S) on the basis that news comes from all directions.

newt *n.* a small, tailed amphibian of the genus *Tritunus*, like the salamander. WH: 14–15C. Misdivision of *an ewt* (see EFT) as *a newt*. Cp. APRON, NICKNAME, UMPIRE.

newton *n.* a unit of force equal to 100,000 dynes. WH: 19C. Sir Isaac *Newton*, 1642–1727, English scientist and philosopher.

Newtonian *a.* of or relating to Sir Isaac Newton or his theories. *Also n.* WH: 18C. NEWTON + -IAN.

New Yorker *n.* a native or inhabitant of New York. WH: 18C. *New York*, a city and state in E USA + -ER¹.

New Zealander *n.* a native or inhabitant of New Zealand, or a descendant of one. WH: 18C. *New Zealand*, a country consisting of two large islands and several smaller ones in the SW Pacific + -ER¹.

next *a.* nearest in place, time or degree. *Also adv., n., prep.* WH: pre-1200. Old English *nēhsta*, from Germanic superl. of HIGH. See also -EST¹.

nexus *n.* a connected group. WH: 17C. Latin, from *nexus*, p.p. of *nectere* to bind.

ngaio *n.* a New Zealand tree, *Myoporum laetum*, noted for its fine white wood. WH: 19C. Maori.

ngultrum *n.* the chief monetary unit of Bhutan, central Asia. WH: late 20C. Bhutanese, from *ngul* silver + *trum*, shortening of *tram-ka*, dim. of *tram* tram (cp. DRACHM).

Nguni *n.* a member of a group of peoples of southern Africa. *Also a.* WH: early 20C. Zulu.

niacin *n.* nicotinic acid. WH: mid-20C. Abbr. of *nicotinic acid* (NICOTINE) + -IN¹.

nib *n.* the point of a pen. *Also v.t., v.i.* WH: 16C. Prob. from Middle Dutch and Middle Low German *nibbe*, var. of *nebbe* beak. See NEB.

nibble *v.t.* to bite little by little. *Also v.i., n.* WH: 14–15C. Prob. from Low Dutch. Cp. Low German *nibbeln* to gnaw.

niblet *n.* a small piece (of food). WH: 19C. NIB or NIBBLE. See also -LET.

niblick *n.* a golf club with a small cup-shaped iron head. WH: 19C. Orig. unknown.

nicad *n.* a battery which has a nickel anode and a cadmium cathode. WH: mid-20C. NICKEL + CADMIUM.

Nicam *n.* a sound system in which audio signals are converted into digital form and transmitted along with a standard television signal. WH: late 20C. Acronym of *near instantaneously companded* (i.e. compressed and expanded) *audio multiplex*.

Nicaraguan *n.* a native or inhabitant of Nicaragua. *Also a.* WH: 19C. *Nicaragua*, a republic of Central America + -AN.

niccolite *n.* arsenide of nickel. WH: 19C. Modern Latin *niccolum* nickel + -ITE[1].

nice *a.* pleasing or agreeable. WH: 12–14C. Old French, from Latin *nescius* ignorant, from *nescire*. See NESCIENT. The original meaning (to the 16C) was foolish, stupid. Several now mainly obsolete meanings then arose in Middle English including wanton, showy, dainty, strange, pampered, coy. The sense discriminating arose in the 16C, and the senses pleasing, agreeable, kind, friendly in the 18C.

Nicene *a.* of or relating to Nicaea. WH: 14–15C. Late Latin *Nicenus, Nicaenus*, from *Nicea, Nicaea*, Greek *Nikaia*, a town of ancient Bithynia, Asia Minor.

niche *n.* a recess in a wall for a statue, vase etc. *Also v.t.* WH: 17C. Old French from *nichier* (Modern French *nicher*) to make a nest, to nestle, from Latin *nidus* nest.

Nichrome® *n.* a nickel-chromium alloy with high electrical resistance and an ability to withstand high temperature. WH: early 20C. NICKEL + CHROME.

nick[1] *n.* a small notch, cut or dent, esp. used as a guide or a tally or score for keeping account. *Also v.t., v.i.* WH: 14–15C. Orig. unknown.

nick[2] *v.i.* to go quickly or furtively. WH: 19C. NICK[1] (in sense to steal). Cp. STEAL (in sense to go or come furtively).

nickel *n.* a lustrous silvery-white ductile metallic element, at. no. 28, chem. symbol Ni, usu. found in association with cobalt, used in the manufacture of German silver and in other alloys. *Also v.t.* WH: 18C. Abbr. of German *Kupfernickel* copper-nickel, niccolite, from *Kupfer* copper + *Nickel* dwarf, mischievous demon. The element is so called because the ore in which it was first found resembled copper but yielded none. Cp. COBALT. The name was coined in 1754 by the metal's discoverer, the Swedish mineralogist and chemist Baron Axel Fredrik Cronstedt.

nickelodeon *n.* an early form of jukebox, esp. one operated by a 5-cent piece. WH: early 20C. NICKEL + MELODEON. The original meaning was a theatre or cinema with an admission price of one nickel. The sense jukebox dates from the mid-20C.

nicker[1] *n.* a pound (money). WH: early 20C. Orig. unknown.

nicker[2] *v.i.* to neigh. *Also n.* WH: 16C. Imit. Cp. WHICKER.

nickname *n.* a name given in derision or familiarity. *Also v.t.* WH: 14–15C. Misdivision of *an eke-name* (from *eke* addition, from Old English *ēaca*, from base also of EKE) as *a neke-name*. Cp. NEWT.

nicol *n.* a crystal of calcium carbonate so cut and cemented as to transmit only the extraordinary ray, used for polarizing light. WH: 19C. William *Nicol, c.*1768–1851, Scottish physicist and geologist.

nicotine *n.* an acrid, poisonous alkaloid contained in tobacco. WH: 19C. Modern Latin *nicotiana* (NICOTINE), from Jacques *Nicot, c.*1530–1600, French ambassador at Lisbon, who introduced tobacco to France in 1560 + -INE.

nictate *v.i.* to nictitate. WH: 17C. Latin *nictatus*, p.p. of *nictare* to wink. See also -ATE[3]. Cp. NICTITATE.

nictitate *v.i.* to wink, esp. to open and shut the eyes rapidly. WH: 19C. Back-formation from *nictitating*, from Medieval Latin *nictitatus*, p.p. of *nictitare*, freq. of Latin *nictare* to wink. Cp. NICTATE.

niddle-noddle *v.i.* to wag the head. *Also v.t., a.* WH: 18C. Redupl. of NOD.

†nide *n.* a collection of pheasants. WH: 17C. French *nid* or Latin *nidus* NEST. A variant spelling *nye* (14–15C) is from Old French *ni* (Modern French *nid*).

nidify *v.i.* to build a nest or nests. WH: 17C. Latin *nidificare*, from *nidus* nest. See also -FY.

nid-nod *v.i.* to keep nodding, as if sleepy. WH: 18C. Redupl. of NOD. Cp. NIDDLE-NODDLE.

nidus *n.* a nest, a place for the deposit of eggs laid by birds, insects etc. WH: 18C. Latin nest.

niece *n.* the daughter of one's brother or sister, or one's brother-in-law or sister-in-law. WH: 12–14C. Old French *nièce*, from Popular Latin *neptia*, from Latin *neptis* granddaughter, niece, rel. to *nepos* grandson, NEPHEW. The borrowed word replaced related Old English *nift*, from Germanic.

niello *n.* a black alloy used to fill the lines of incised designs on metal plates. WH: 19C. Italian, from Latin *nigellus*, dim. of *niger* black.

Niersteiner *n.* a white Rhenish wine. WH: 19C. *Nierstein*, a town in W Germany + *-er* -ER[1].

Nietzschean *a.* of or relating to Nietzsche, or his philosophy. *Also n.* WH: early 20C. Friedrich *Nietzsche*, 1844–1900, German philosopher. See also -EAN.

niff *n.* a stink, a bad smell. *Also v.i.* WH: early 20C. ? From SNIFF.

nifty *a.* quick, slick. WH: 19C. Orig. unknown. According to some, the word is a shortening and alteration of MAGNIFICENT + -Y[1].

nigella *n.* a plant of the genus *Nigella*, of ranunculaceous plants comprising love-in-a-mist. WH: 14–15C. Modern Latin, fem. of Latin *nigellus*, dim. of *niger* black. The plant is so named from its black seeds.

Nigerian *n.* a native or inhabitant of Nigeria. *Also a.* WH: 19C. *Nigeria*, a republic in W Africa. See also -AN.

Nigerien *n.* a native or inhabitant of Niger, Africa. *Also a.* WH: mid-20C. Var. of NIGERIAN.

niggard *n.* a stingy person, a miser; a person who is grudging. *Also a., v.t., v.i.* WH: 14–15C. Alt. of obs. *nigon* (from obs. *nig*, prob. of Scandinavian orig. + suf. of unknown orig.), with substitution of -ARD for *-on*.

nigger *n.* a black person. WH: 17C. Var. of obs. *neger*, from French *nègre*, from Spanish *negro* NEGRO.

niggle *v.i.* to busy oneself with petty details. *Also v.t., n.* WH: 17C. Appar. from Scandinavian. Cp. Norwegian *nigla*.

†nigh *adv.* near. *Also a., prep., v.t., v.i.* WH: pre-1200. Old English *nēah*, from Germanic. Cp. NEAR, NEXT.

night *n.* the time of darkness from sunset to sunrise. *Also int.* WH: pre-1200. Old English *niht*, from Indo-European base also of Latin *nox, noctis*, Greek *nux, nuktos*, Sanskrit *nak*.

nightingale[1] *n.* a small, brownish migratory bird, *Luscinia megarhynchos*, singing at night as well as by day. WH: pre-1200. Old English *nihtegala*, from Germanic base of NIGHT + base meaning to sing (cp. YELL). The subsequently inserted -*n*- has no etymological significance.

nightingale[2] *n.* a jacket or wrap worn by invalids sitting up in bed. WH: 19C. Florence *Nightingale*, 1820–1910, British nurse and medical reformer.

nightshade *n.* any of several plants of the genus *Solanum*, esp. the black nightshade or woody nightshade. WH: pre-1200. Old English *nihtscada*, from Germanic, appar. from bases of NIGHT and SHADE. The name probably alludes to the narcotic or poisonous properties of the berries.

nigrescent *a.* blackish. WH: 18C. Latin *nigrescens, nigrescentis*, pres.p. of *nigrescere* to grow black, from *niger, nigris* black. See also -escent (-ESCENCE).

nigrify *v.t.* to blacken. WH: 17C. Latin *niger, nigris* black + -FY.

nigritude *n.* blackness. WH: 17C. Latin *nigritudo*, from *niger, nigris*. See also -TUDE. Cp. NEGRITUDE.

nigrosine *n.* a blue-black dyestuff obtained from aniline hydrochlorates. WH: 19C. Latin *niger, nigris* black + -OSE[1] + -INE.

nihil *n.* nothing. WH: 16C. Latin nothing. Cp. NIL.

-nik *comb. form* a person who practises something, as in *beatnik, kibbutznik, peacenik*. WH: mid-20C. Russian (as SPUTNIK), Hebrew and Yiddish.

nikau *n.* the New Zealand palm, *Rhopalostylis sapida*. WH: 19C. Maori.

Nikkei index *n.* an index of the relative prices of stocks and shares on the Tokyo Stock Exchange. WH: late 20C. Japanese, abbr. of *Nihon Keizai Shimbun* Japanese Economic Journal. The named publication is Japan's principal financial daily newspaper.

nil *n.* nothing; zero. WH: 19C. Latin, contr. of NIHIL.

nil desperandum *int.* do not despair. WH: 17C. Latin, opening words of a quotation from Horace's *Odes: Nil desperandum Teucro duce et auspice Teucro* No need to despair with Teucer as your leader and Teucer to protect you.

Nile *n.* a pale greenish-blue or pale green. *Also a.* WH: 19C. *Nile*, a river flowing north from E central Africa through Egypt to the Mediterranean.

nilgai *n.* a large Indian antelope, *Boselaphus tragocamelus.* WH: 18C. Hindi *nīlgāe*, *nīlgao*, from Sanskrit *nīla* blue + *-gāvī*, *-gavī* cow. The male nilgai is blue-grey, the female tawny.

Nilometer *n.* an instrument for measuring the rise of the River Nile during its floods. WH: 18C. NILE + -O- + -METER, based on Greek *Neilometrion.*

Nilotic *a.* of or relating to the Nile etc. WH: 17C. Latin *Niloticus*, from Greek *Neilōtikos*, from *Neilos* NILE. See also -OTIC.

nim *n.* an ancient game for two players in which a number of counters are used. WH: early 20C. Orig. uncertain. ? From German *nimm* take!, imper. of *nehmen* to take.

nimble *a.* light and quick in motion; agile, swift, dexterous. WH: pre-1200. Old English *næmel*, from *niman* to take, from Germanic, rel. to Greek *nemein* to deal out, to distribute, to possess. See also -LE³. The *-b-* entered as with THIMBLE. The original sense (to the 15C) was quick to seize or grasp at, wise.

nimbostratus *n.* a dense, grey, rain- or snow-bearing cloud. WH: 19C. NIMBUS + -O- + STRATUS.

nimbus *n.* a halo or glory surrounding the heads of divine or sacred personages in paintings etc. WH: 17C. Latin cloud, rain, aureole.

Nimby *a.* supporting the dumping of nuclear waste, the construction of ugly buildings etc., as long as one's own property is not affected. *Also n.* WH: late 20C. Acronym of *not in my backyard.*

niminy-piminy *a.* affecting niceness or delicacy; mincing; affected. WH: 18C. Fanciful formation based on NAMBY-PAMBY. Cp. MIMINY-PIMINY.

Nimrod *n.* a great hunter. WH: 16C. Hebrew *Nimrōd*, a great-grandson of Noah, the traditional founder of the Babylonian dynasty and famous as 'a mighty hunter' (Gen. x.9).

nincompoop *n.* an idiot, a fool. WH: 17C. Orig. uncertain. Prob. from male forename *Nicholas* or *Nicodemus* (cp. French *nicodème* simpleton), with *n-* from assoc. with NINNY, + obs. *poop* to deceive, to cheat, of uncertain orig. (cp. Dutch *poep* clown). The word is popularly derived from NON COMPOS MENTIS, but this does not tally with early spellings.

nine *n.* the number or figure 9 or ix. *Also a.* WH: pre-1200. Old English *nigon*, from var. of a Germanic word represented by Old High German *niun*, German *neun*, from Indo-European base represented also by Latin *novem*, Greek *ennea*, Sanskrit *nava.*

ninja *n.* a person who is skilled in ninjutsu. WH: mid-20C. Japanese spy, from *nin* stealth, invisibility + *ja* person.

ninjutsu *n.* a Japanese martial art involving stealth and camouflage. WH: mid-20C. Japanese, from *nin* stealth, invisibility + *jutsu* art, science.

ninny *n.* a fool, a simpleton. WH: 16C. Orig. uncertain. ? From INNOCENT with prefixed *n-*. See also -Y³.

ninon *n.* a lightweight silk material. WH: early 20C. French *Ninon*, female forename.

ninth *n.* any one of nine equal parts. *Also n., a.* WH: pre-1200. Old English *nigotha*, replaced in Middle English by forms from NINE + -TH¹.

niobium *n.* a grey-blue metallic element, at. no. 41, chem. symbol Nb, occurring in tantalite etc. WH: 19C. *Niobe*, the legendary daughter of Tantalus + -IUM. The element was named in 1844 by Heinrich Rose, the German chemist who discovered it, with reference to its occurrence in nature with tantalum.

Nip *n.* a Japanese person. WH: mid-20C. Abbr. of NIPPONESE.

nip¹ *v.t.* to pinch, to squeeze or compress sharply. *Also v.i., n.* WH: 14–15C. Prob. from Low Dutch.

nip² *n.* a small drink of spirits. *Also v.i., v.t.* WH: 18C. Prob. abbr. of *nipperkin* small vessel for liquor, rel. to Low Dutch *nippen* to sip. See also -ER¹, -KIN.

nipa *n.* a palm tree of tropical SE Asia and the islands of the Indian Ocean, *Nipa fruticans*, with feathery leaves used in thatching, basket-weaving etc., and for packing bunches of fruit. WH: 16C. Malay *nipah.*

nipple *n.* the small prominence in the breast of female mammals, by which milk is sucked or drawn. WH: 16C. Orig. uncertain. ? Dim. of NEB. See also -LE¹.

Nipponese *n.* a Japanese person. *Also a.* WH: 19C. Japanese *Nippon* Japan, lit. land of the rising sun, from *nichi* the sun + *pon, hon* source. See also -ESE.

NIREX *abbr.* Nuclear Industry Radioactive Waste Executive, a government body which oversees the disposal of nuclear waste in the UK. WH: Acronym of *N*uclear *I*ndustry *R*adioactive Waste *Ex*ecutive.

nirvana *n.* absorption of individuality into the divine spirit with extinction of personal desires and passions, the Buddhist state of beatitude. WH: 19C. Sanskrit *nirvāṇa*, p.p. (used as n.) of *nirvā-* to be extinguished, from *nis-* out + *vā-* to blow.

†nis *v.i.* is not. WH: pre-1200. Old English *ne* NOT + *is* (see BE).

nisei *n.* a person of Japanese descent born in the US. WH: mid-20C. Japanese, from *ni* second + *sei* generation.

nisi *a.* taking effect on certain conditions. WH: 14–15C. Latin unless.

Nissen hut *n.* a long hut of corrugated iron with a semicircular roof. WH: early 20C. Lieutenant-Colonel Peter Norman *Nissen*, 1871–1930, its British inventor.

nisus *n.* an effort, striving. WH: 17C. Latin *niti* to strive, to endeavour.

nit¹ *n.* the egg of a louse or other small, esp. parasitic, insect. WH: pre-1200. Old English *hnitu*, from Germanic, from Indo-European. Cp. German *Nisse.*

nit² *int.* used to express warning of someone's approach. WH: 19C. Orig. unknown. According to some, the word is an alteration of NIX³.

nit³ *n.* a fool. WH: 16C. NIT¹.

nit⁴ *n.* the unit of luminance, one candela per square metre. WH: mid-20C. French, from Latin *nitere* to shine.

nit⁵ *n.* a unit of information in computing (1.44 bits). WH: mid-20C. Abbr. of Napierian *digit* (see NAPIER'S BONES).

nitid *a.* shining; bright, gay. WH: 17C. Latin *nitidus*, from *nitere* to shine. See also -ID.

nitinol *n.* an alloy of nickel and titanium. WH: mid-20C. *Ni* (chemical symbol for NICKEL) + *Ti* (chemical symbol for TITANIUM) + initial letters of *Naval Ordnance Laboratory*, Maryland, USA, workplace of the metallurgists who discovered the alloy and coined its name in *c.*1968.

niton *n.* radon. WH: Latin *nitere* to shine + -ON.

nitrate¹ *n.* a salt of nitric acid. WH: 18C. French. See NITRE, also -ATE¹.

nitrate² *v.t.* to treat or combine with nitric acid. WH: 19C. NITRE + -ATE³.

nitre *n.* saltpetre, potassium nitrate, occurring as an orthorhombic mineral. WH: 14–15C. Old French, from Latin *nitrum*, from Greek *nitron*, of Semitic orig. or from Egyptian *ntrj*. Cp. NATRON.

nitric *a.* of or relating to nitre. WH: 18C. NITRE + -IC.

nitride *n.* a compound of nitrogen with phosphorus, boron, silicon etc. WH: NITROGEN + -IDE.

nitrile *n.* any organic compound consisting of an alkyl radical bound to a cyanide radical. WH: 19C. NITRE + *-ile*, alt. of -YL.

nitro- *comb. form* nitric. WH: NITRE or Greek *nitron*. See also -O-.

nitrobenzene *n.* an oily compound of benzene with nitric acid, having an odour of oil of bitter almonds, used for flavouring perfumes and confectionery. WH: 19C. NITRO- + BENZENE.

nitrocellulose *n.* an extremely flammable material made by treating cellulose with nitric acid, used to make explosives and celluloid. WH: 19C. NITRO- + CELLULOSE.

nitro compound *n.* a compound obtained by treatment with nitric acid. WH: 19C. NITRO- + COMPOUND¹.

nitrogen *n.* a colourless, tasteless, gaseous element, at. no. 7, chem. symbol N, forming 80% of the atmosphere, the basis of nitre and nitric acid. WH: 18C. French *nitrogène*. See NITRO-, -GEN. The name was coined in 1790 by the French chemist J.A. Chaptal, although the gas was first produced in 1772 by the Scottish physicist Daniel Rutherford.

nitroglycerine *n.* a highly explosive colourless oil, obtained by adding glycerine to a mixture of nitric and sulphuric acids. WH: 19C. NITRO- + *glycerine* (GLYCEROL).

nitrometer *n.* an instrument for determining nitrogen in some of its combinations. WH: 19C. NITRO- + -METER.

nitrosamine *n.* any carcinogenic substance containing the chemical group :N-N:O. WH: 19C. Latin *nitrosus* nitrous + AMINE.

nitrous *a.* obtained from, impregnated with, or resembling nitre. WH: 17C. NITRE + -OUS.

nitroxyl *n.* a radical composed of one atom of nitrogen in chemical combination with two of oxygen. WH: 19C. NITRO- + OXY-¹ + -YL.

nitty-gritty *n.* the basic facts, the realities of a situation. WH: mid-20C. Orig. unknown. ? Ult. rel. to NIT[1] and GRIT[1].

nitwit *n.* a foolish or stupid person. WH: early 20C. ? From NIT[1] + WIT[1].

nival *a.* growing in or under snow. WH: 17C. Latin *nivalis*, from *nix, nivis* snow. See also -AL[1].

nix[1] *n.* nothing, nobody. *Also v.t.* WH: 18C. German, dial. and coll. var. of *nichts* nothing.

nix[2] *n.* a water sprite. WH: 19C. German, from Middle High German *niches*, from Old High German *nichus*, from Germanic base also of obs. *nicker* water demon, from Old English *nicor*.

nix[3] *int.* look out! WH: 19C. NIX[1].

nizam *n.* a soldier in the Turkish regular army. WH: 18C. Turkish, Persian and Urdu *nizām*, from Arabic *niẓām* good order, disposition, arrangement. In the sense soldier, the word is an abbreviation of *nizām askeri* regular soldier; as a title of the ruler of Hyderabad, of *nizām-al-mulk* administrator of the realm.

No. *abbr.* number. WH: Contr. of Latin *numero*, abl. of *numerus* number.

no[1] *a.* not any. WH: pre-1200. Reduced form of NONE[1].

no[2] *adv.* a word of denial or refusal, the categorical negative. *Also n.* WH: pre-1200. Old English *ne* NOT + *ō*, var. of *ā* ever (AYE[2]).

Noachian *a.* of or relating to Noah or his times. WH: 17C. *Noach*, Noah, a biblical patriarch (Gen. vi–x) + -IAN.

Noah's ark *n.* the vessel in which Noah and his family were saved from the Deluge. WH: 16C. *Noah* (NOACHIAN) + -'S + ARK.

nob[1] *n.* a person of rank or distinction. WH: 17C. Orig. unknown.

nob[2] *n.* the head. *Also v.t.* WH: 17C. ? Var. of KNOB.

nobble *v.t.* to dose, lame or otherwise tamper with (a horse) to prevent its winning a race. WH: 19C. Prob. var. of *knobble*, var. of dial. *knubble* to strike with the knuckles, from dial. *knub*, rel. to KNOB + -LE[2]. Cp. NUB.

Nobelist *n.* a Nobel prizewinner. WH: mid-20C. Alfred *Nobel*, 1833–96, Swedish inventor of dynamite.

nobelium *n.* an artificially produced, radioactive element, at. no. 102, chem. symbol No. WH: mid-20C. *Nobel* (NOBELIST) + -IUM. The name was coined in 1957 with reference both to Alfred Nobel and to the Nobel Institute for Physics, Stockholm, where work on the element was carried out.

Nobel Prize *n.* any of six prizes awarded annually by the will of Alfred Nobel for excellence in various branches of learning and the furtherance of universal peace. WH: early 20C. Alfred *Nobel* (NOBELIST). The first prizes were awarded in 1901.

nobility *n.* the quality of being noble. WH: 14–15C. Old French *nobilité* or Latin *nobilitas*, from *nobilis*. See NOBLE, also -ITY.

noble *a.* lofty or illustrious in character, worth or dignity; magnanimous, high-minded, morally elevated. *Also n.* WH: 12–14C. Old French, from Latin *nobilis*, earlier *gnobilis*, from Indo-European base represented also by KNOW. See also -BLE.

noblesse *n.* the nobility (of a foreign country). WH: 12–14C. Old French. See NOBLE.

nobody *pron.* no one, no person. *Also n.* WH: 12–14C. NO[1] + BODY. Orig. two words.

nock *n.* the notched tip at each end of a bow. *Also v.t.* WH: 14–15C. Middle Dutch *nocke* (Dutch *nok*), from Germanic.

noctambulism *n.* somnambulism. WH: 19C. Latin *nox, noctis* night + *ambulare* to walk + -ISM.

nocti- *comb. form* nocturnal, by night. WH: Latin *nox, noctis* night.

noctiluca *n.* a phosphorescent marine animalcule. WH: 14–15C. Modern Latin, from Latin lantern, moon, from NOCTI- + Latin *lucere* to shine. The word was originally used as a name for the glow-worm. The current sense dates from the 19C.

noctilucent *a.* shining by night. WH: 19C. NOCTI- + Latin *lucere* to shine + -ENT.

noctivagant *a.* wandering by night. WH: 17C. Latin *noctivagus*, from NOCTI- + *vagari* to wander. See also -ANT.

noctuid *n.* any nocturnal moth of the family Noctuidae. *Also a.* WH: 19C. Modern Latin *Noctua* genus name, from Latin night owl + -ID.

noctule *n.* a large European bat, *Nyctalus noctula*. WH: 18C. French, from Italian *nottola* bat.

nocturn *n.* in the Roman Catholic Church, one of the divisions of matins, usually said at night. WH: 12–14C. Old French *nocturne* or Ecclesiastical Latin *nocturnus*, use as n. of Latin of the night, from *nox, noctis* night. Cp. NOCTURNE.

nocturnal *a.* relating to or occurring in the night, performed or active by night. WH: 15C. Late Latin *nocturnalis*, from *nocturnus*. See NOCTURN, also -AL[1].

nocturne *n.* a dreamy piece of music suited to the night or evening. WH: 19C. French. See NOCTURN. The term was invented, and the form popularized, in *c.*1814 by the Irish pianist and composer John Field.

nocuous *a.* hurtful, noxious. WH: 17C. Latin *nocuus*, from *nocere* to hurt. See also -OUS. Cp. earlier INNOCUOUS.

nod *v.i.* to incline the head with a slight, quick motion in token of assent. *Also v.t., n.* WH: 14–15C. ? Low German. Cp. Middle High German *notten* to move about, to shake.

noddle[1] *n.* the head. WH: 14–15C. Orig. unknown. The original sense was back of the head.

noddle[2] *v.t.* to nod, to wag. WH: 18C. Freq. of NOD. See also -LE[4].

noddy *n.* a simpleton, a fool. WH: 16C. ? From NOD + -Y[1].

node *n.* a knot, a knob. WH: 14–15C. Latin *nodus* knot.

Noel *n.* Christmas. WH: 14–15C. Old French *nouel* (Modern French *noël*), var. of *nael*, based on Latin *natalis* (*dies*) NATAL[1] (day). The word was originally shouted or sung as an expression of joy, with reference to the birth of Jesus.

noetic *a.* of or relating to the intellect. *Also n.* WH: 17C. Greek *noētikos*, from *noētos* intellectual, from *noein* to think, to perceive, from *nous* mind, thought. See also -IC.

nog[1] *n.* a pin, treenail or peg. *Also v.t.* WH: 17C. Orig. unknown.

†**nog**[2] *n.* a strong ale brewed in E Anglia. WH: 17C. Orig. unknown.

noggin *n.* a small mug. WH: 17C. Orig. unknown.

nogging *n.* a timber frame filled with bricks. WH: 19C. NOG[1] + -ING[1].

Noh *n.* the Japanese drama developed out of religious dance. WH: 19C. Japanese talent, faculty, accomplishment.

noil *n.* tangles and knots of wool removed by a comb. WH: 17C. Prob. from Old French *noel*, from Medieval Latin *nodellus*, dim. of Latin *nodus* knot.

noise *n.* a sound of any kind, esp. a loud, discordant, harsh or disagreeable one. *Also v.t., v.i.* WH: 12–14C. Old French, prob. from Latin NAUSEA.

noisette[1] *n.* a small round piece of mutton, veal, etc. WH: 19C. French, dim. of *noix* nut. See also -ETTE.

noisette[2] *n.* a variety of rose, a cross between the China rose and the musk-rose. WH: 19C. Philippe *Noisette*, brother of Louis Claude *Noisette*, d.1849, French gardener.

noisome *a.* hurtful, noxious. WH: 14–15C. Obs. *noy* annoyance, shortening of ANNOY + -SOME[1].

nolens volens *adv.* willingly or unwillingly, willy-nilly. WH: 16C. Latin, pres.pp. of *nolo, nolle* to be unwilling, *volo, velle* to be willing.

noli-me-tangere *n.* the touch-me-not, any of several plants of the genus *Impatiens*, whose ripe seed pods burst open when touched. WH: 14–15C. Latin do not touch me. The words are those spoken by Christ to Mary Magdalene immediately after the Resurrection: 'Touch me not' (John xx.17).

noll *n.* the head. WH: pre-1200. Old English *hnoll*, from Germanic.

nolle prosequi *n.* the act by a plaintiff discontinuing a suit. WH: 17C. Latin to be unwilling to pursue.

nolo contendere *n.* I will not contest it, a plea which accepts conviction without pleading guilt. WH: 19C. Latin I do not wish to contend.

noma *n.* a destructive ulceration of the cheek, esp. affecting debilitated children. WH: 19C. Modern Latin, alt. of Latin *nome*, Greek *nomē*, from *nemein* to feed.

nomad *n.* a member of a people that wanders about seeking pasture for their flocks. *Also a.* WH: 16C. French *nomade*, from Latin *Nomades* (pl.), *Nomas* (sing.), from Greek *nomas, nomados* roaming about (in order to pasture), from base of *nemein* to feed, to pasture. See also -AD[2].

nomarch *n.* a ruler or governor of an Egyptian nome or Greek nomarchy. WH: 17C. Greek *nomarkhēs* or *nomarkhos*, from *nomos* NOME. See ARCH-.

nombril *n.* the point of an escutcheon between the fess point and the base point. WH: 16C. French navel, from Popular Latin *umbiliculus*, from Latin *umbilicus* (UMBILICAL).

nom de guerre *n.* an assumed name, a pseudonym. WH: 17C. French war name.

nom de plume *n.* a pen-name. WH: 19C. French pen name, based on NOM DE GUERRE.

nome *n.* a province of a country, esp. modern Greece or Egypt. WH: 18C. Greek *nomos*, from *nemein* to divide.

nomen *n.* in ancient Rome, a person's second name, designating the gens. WH: 18C. Latin name.

nomenclator *n.* a person who gives names to things, esp. in classification of natural history etc. WH: 16C. Latin, from *nomen* name + *calare* to call.

nomenclature *n.* a system of names for the objects of study in any branch of science. WH: 17C. French, from Latin *nomenclatura*, from NOMENCLATOR.

nomic *a.* (of spelling) ordinary, customary. *Also n.* WH: 19C. Greek *nomikos*, from *nomos* law. See also -IC.

nominal *a.* existing in name only, as distinct from *real*. WH: 15C. French, or from Latin *nominalis*, from *nomen, nominis* name. See also -AL[1].

nominate *v.t.* to propose as a candidate. WH: 17C. Latin *nominatus*, p.p. of *nominare*, from *nomen, nominis* name. See also -ATE[3].

nominative[1] *n.* the case of the subject of a verb. *Also a.* WH: 16C. Old French *nominatif* or Latin *nominativus*, from *nominatus* (NOMINATE). See also -ATIVE.

nominative[2] *a.* appointed by nomination, rather than by election. WH: 17C. NOMINATIVE[1].

nomistic *a.* of or based on law. WH: 19C. Greek *nomos* law + -IST + -IC.

nomo- *comb. form* of or relating to law. WH: Greek *nomos* law. See also -O-.

nomocracy *n.* a system of government according to a code of laws. WH: 19C. NOMO- + -CRACY.

nomogeny *n.* origination of life according to natural law, rather than by miracle. WH: 19C. NOMO- + -GENY.

nomogram *n.* a chart with scales of quantities arranged side by side, which can be used to carry out rapid calculations. WH: early 20C. NOMO- + -GRAM.

nomology *n.* the science of law. WH: 19C. NOMO- + -LOGY.

nomothetical *a.* legislative. WH: 17C. Greek *nomothetikos*, from *nomothetēs* lawgiver, legislator, from *nomos* law. See also -IC, -AL[1].

-nomy *comb. form* an area of knowledge. WH: Greek *-nomia*, rel. to *nomos* law, *nemein* to distribute. See also -Y[2].

non- *pref.* not. WH: Anglo-French *noun-*, Old French *non-, nom-* (Modern French *non-*) or Latin *non-*, use as pref. of *non* not.

nona- *comb. form* nine. WH: Latin *nonus* ninth, based on TETRA-, PENTA-, etc.

nonage *n.* the state of being under age; minority. WH: 14–15C. Old French. See NON-, AGE.

nonagenarian *n.* a person aged between 90 and 100. *Also a.* WH: 19C. Latin *nonagenarius*, from *nonageni* ninety each, from *nonaginta* ninety. See also -ARIAN.

nonagesimal *a.* of or relating to 90. *Also n.* WH: 18C. Latin *nonagesima* ninetieth, from *nonaginta* ninety. See also -AL[1].

nonagon *n.* a figure having nine sides and nine angles. WH: 17C. NONA- + -GON.

nonary *a.* (of a scale of notation) based on the number nine. *Also n.* WH: 17C. Latin *nonus* ninth + -ARY[1], based on DENARY, etc.

nonce *n.* the present time, occasion, purpose etc. WH: 12–14C. Misdivision (in Middle English) of *than anes* the one (occasion). Cp. NEWT. In derivation, *than* is the dative singular neuter of *the* THE; *anes* is an alteration of *ane*, the dative singular neuter of *an* ONE.

nonchalant *a.* careless, cool, unmoved, indifferent. WH: 18C. Old French, from NON- + *chalant*, pres.p. of *chaloir* to be concerned.

non compos mentis *a.* not in one's right mind. WH: 17C. Latin not master of one's mind. See NON-, COMPOSE, MENTAL[1].

nondescript *a.* not easily described or classified; neither one thing nor another. *Also n.* WH: 17C. NON- + obs. *descript* described, from Latin *descriptus*, p.p. of *describere* DESCRIBE.

none[1] *pron.* no one, no person. *Also a., adv.* WH: pre-1200. Old English *nān*, from *ne* not + *ān* ONE.

none[2] *n.* in the Roman Catholic Church, the nones. WH: 17C. French, from Latin *nona* (*hora*) ninth (hour). See NOON. Cp. NONES.

nonentity *n.* an unimportant person or thing. WH: 16C. Medieval Latin *nonentitas*, from *non* not + *entitas* ENTITY.

nones *n.pl.* in ancient Rome, the ninth day before the ides of a month. WH: 14–15C. Old French, from Latin *nonas*, fem. acc. pl. (used as n.) of *nonus* ninth, from *novem* nine. The ecclesiastical sense of the word dates from the 18C and originates from NONE[2] + -S[1], based on MATINS, etc.

nonet *n.* a musical composition for nine players or singers. WH: 19C. Italian *nonetto*, from *nono* ninth. See also -ET[1].

nong *n.* a stupid person, a fool. WH: mid-20C. Orig. unknown. ? From *ning-nong*, presumably rel. to *nig-nog*, of unknown orig.

nonillion *n.* a million raised to the ninth power, denoted by a unit with 54 zeros annexed. WH: 17C. French, from Latin *nona* nine + *-illion* based on MILLION, BILLION, etc.

nonpareil *a.* having no equal; peerless, unrivalled, unique. *Also n.* WH: 14–15C. French, from *non-* NON- + *pareil* like, equal, from Popular Latin *pariculus*, dim. of Latin PAR[1].

non placet *n.* the formula used in university and ecclesiastical assemblies in giving a negative vote. WH: 16C. Latin, lit. it does not please, from *non* not + 3rd pers. sing. pres. ind. of *placere* please.

nonplus *v.t.* to puzzle, to confound, to bewilder. *Also n.* WH: 16C. Latin *non plus* not more, no further.

non possumus *n.* a plea of inability. WH: 19C. Latin, lit. we cannot, from *non* not + 2nd pers. pl. pres. ind. of *potere* to be able.

nonsense *n.* unmeaning words, ideas etc. WH: 17C. NON- + SENSE.

non sequitur *n.* an inference not warrantable from the premisses. WH: 14–15C. Latin, lit. it does not follow, from *non* not + 3rd pers. sing. pres. ind. of *sequi* to follow.

nonsuch *n.* a person who or something which is without an equal, a paragon, a nonpareil. WH: 17C. Var. of *nonesuch* 16C (based on NONPAREIL), from NONE[1] + SUCH.

nonsuit *n.* the stoppage of a suit during trial through insufficient evidence or non-appearance of the plaintiff. *Also v.t.* WH: 14–15C. Anglo-French. See NON-, SUIT.

noodle[1] *n.* a strip or ring of pasta. WH: 18C. German *Nudel*, of unknown orig.

noodle[2] *n.* a simpleton, a fool. WH: 18C. Orig. unknown. Cp. NODDLE[1].

nook *n.* a corner. WH: 12–14C. Orig. unknown. ? From Scandinavian.

nooky *n.* sexual intercourse. WH: early 20C. Orig. uncertain. ? From NOOK + -Y[3].

noology *n.* the science of the understanding. WH: 19C. Greek *noos* mind + -LOGY.

noon *n.* the middle of the day, twelve o'clock. *Also a.* WH: pre-1200. Old English *nōn*, from Latin *nona* (*hora*) ninth (hour), fem. of *nonus* ninth. Cp. NONE[2], NONES. The original meaning was the ninth hour from sunrise, viz. about 3 p.m. This then changed to 12 o'clock when the time of nones was put back three hours to follow the main Mass of the day.

noose *n.* a loop with a running knot binding the closer the more it is pulled, as in a snare or a hangman's halter. *Also v.t.* WH: 14–15C. Orig. uncertain. ? From Old French *nos, nous*, nom. sing. and acc. pl. of *no, nou*, from Latin *nodus* knot.

Nootka *n.* the language of an Indian people of Vancouver. WH: 19C. *Nootka* Sound, an inlet on the coast of Vancouver Island, British Columbia, Canada.

nopal *n.* any American cactus of the genus *Nopalea*, esp. *N. cochinellifera*, grown for the support of the cochineal insect. WH: 18C. French, from Spanish, from Nahuatl *nopalli* cactus.

nope *adv.* no. WH: 19C. Extended form of NO[2]. Cp. YEP.

nor *conj.* and not (a word marking the second or subsequent part of a negative proposition; occasionally used without the correlative). *Also adv.* WH: 12–14C. Contr. of obs. *nother*, from Old English, from *ne* not + contr. of var. of *āhwæther*, from *ā* ever (AYE[2]) + *hwæther* WHETHER.

nor' *n., a., adv.* north. WH: 14–15C. Contr. of NORTH.

noradrenalin *n.* an amine related to adrenalin, used as a heart resuscitant. WH: mid-20C. NORMAL + ADRENALIN.

Nordic *a.* of or relating to a tall, blond physical type inhabiting Scandinavia, parts of Scotland and other parts of N Europe. *Also n.* WH: 19C. French *nordique*, from *nord* north. See also -IC.

norepinephrine *n.* noradrenalin. WH: mid-20C. NORMAL + EPI-NEPHRINE.

Norfolk jacket *n.* a man's loose jacket with vertical pleats in the back and front, and a waistband. WH: 14–15C. *Norfolk*, a county in E England, forming the northern part of E Anglia.

noria *n.* an endless chain of buckets on a wheel for raising water from a stream or similar. WH: 18C. Spanish, from Arabic *nāy'ūra*.

nork *n.* a woman's breast. WH: mid-20C. Orig. unknown. According to some, the word is from the *Norco* Co-operative Ltd, a New South Wales, Australia, butter manufacturer.

norland *n.* northland. WH: 16C. Contr. of *northland* (NORTH).

norm *n.* a standard, model, pattern or type. WH: 19C. Anglicized form of Latin *norma* carpenter's square, pattern, rule.

normal *a.* according to rule, standard, or established law; regular, typical, usual. *Also n.* WH: 15C. French, or from Latin *normalis* made according to a square, right(-angled). See also -AL[1]. Cp. NORM.

Norman *n.* a native or inhabitant of Normandy. *Also a.* WH: 12–14C. Old French *Normans*, *Normanz*, pl. of *Normant* (Modern French *Normand*), or from Old Norse *Northmathr*, pl. *Northmenn*, from *northr* NORTH + *mathr* MAN.

norman *n.* a bar inserted in a capstan or bitt for fastening the cable. WH: 18C. Dutch *noorman*, German *Normann*, ? rel. to NORMAN.

normative *a.* of, relating to or establishing a norm. WH: 19C. French *normatif*, from Latin *norma*. See NORM, also -ATIVE.

Norn *n.* any one of the Norse Fates. WH: 18C. Orig. unknown.

Norroy *n.* the third King of Arms, having jurisdiction north of the Trent. WH: 14–15C. Old French *nord* north + *roi* king.

Norse *n.* the Norwegian language. *Also a.* WH: 16C. Dutch *noordsch*, from *noord* north + -SCH -ISH[1].

north *n.* one of the four cardinal points, the one to the right of a person facing the setting sun at the equinox. *Also a., adv., v.i., v.t.* WH: pre-1200. Old English, from Germanic. Cp. German *Nord*.

Northumbrian *n.* a native or inhabitant of ancient Northumbria (England north of the Humber) or of Northumberland. *Also a.* WH: 16C. *Northumbria*, Latinized form of *Northumber*, from NORTH + (the river) *Humber* (in NE England). See also -AN.

Norway lobster *n.* a small European lobster, *Nephrops norvegicus*. WH: 17C. *Norway*, a country in Scandinavia.

Norwegian *n.* a native or inhabitant of Norway. *Also a.* WH: 17C. Medieval Latin *Norvegia*, from Old Norse *Norvegr* Norway (NORWAY LOBSTER). See also -AN.

Nos. *abbr.* numbers. WH: NO. + -S[1].

nose *n.* the projecting part of the face between the forehead and mouth, containing the nostrils and the organ of smell. *Also v.t., v.i.* WH: pre-1200. Old English *nosu*, from Germanic, rel. to Latin *nasus* nose, *nares* nostrils. Cp. NESS.

nosegay *n.* a bunch of flowers, esp. fragrant flowers. WH: 15C. NOSE + GAY.

nosh *n.* food. *Also v.t., v.i.* WH: early 20C. Yiddish. Cp. German *naschen* to nibble.

noso- *comb. form* of or relating to diseases. WH: Greek *nosos* disease. See also -O-.

nosocomial *a.* of or relating to hospitals. WH: 19C. Greek *nosokomos* person who tends the sick, from NOSO- + -*komos*, rel. to *kamnein* to work. See also -AL[1].

nosography *n.* the scientific description of diseases. WH: 17C. NOSO- + -GRAPHY.

nosology *n.* a systematic classification of diseases. WH: 18C. NOSO- + -LOGY.

nosophobia *n.* morbid fear of disease. WH: 19C. NOSO- + -*phobia* (-PHOBE).

nostalgia *n.* a yearning for the past. WH: 18C. Modern Latin, translating German *Heimweh* homesickness (cp. HOME[1], WOE), from Greek *nostos* homecoming + *algos* pain. See also -IA.

nosto- *comb. form* of or relating to a return. WH: Greek *nostos* homecoming. See also -O-.

nostoc *n.* any gelatinous freshwater alga of the genus *Nostoc*. WH: 17C. Name invented by Paracelsus.

nostology *n.* gerontology. WH: 19C. NOSTO- + -LOGY.

nostomania *n.* an abnormal anxiety to go back to a familiar place. WH: 19C. NOSTO- + -MANIA.

nostophobia *n.* an abnormal fear of going back to a familiar place. WH: 19C. NOSTO- + -*phobia* (-PHOBE).

Nostradamus *n.* a person who predicts or professes to predict. WH: 17C. Latinized form of the name of Michel de *Nostredame*, 1503–66, French physician who published a book of prophecies in 1555.

nostril *n.* either of the two apertures of the nose. WH: pre-1200. Old English *nosthyrl*, from *nosu* NOSE + *thyrel* hole, THIRL.

nostrum *n.* a medicine based on a secret formula; a quack remedy. WH: 17C. Latin *nostrum* (*remedium*) our (remedy), from *nostrum* neut. sing. of *noster* our. The medicine was so called as it was presumably prepared by the person recommending it.

not *adv.* a particle expressing negation, denial, prohibition or refusal. WH: 12–14C. Contr. of NOUGHT.

nota bene *v.t.* note well, take note. WH: 18C. Latin note well!, from *nota*, 2nd pers. sing. imper. of *notare* NOTE + *bene* well.

notable *a.* worthy of note; remarkable, memorable, distinguished. *Also n.* WH: 12–14C. Old French, from Latin *notabilis*, from *notare* NOTE. See also -ABLE.

notandum *n.* something to be noted, a memorandum. WH: 17C. Latin, neut. ger. of *notare* NOTE.

notary *n.* a public official appointed to attest deeds, contracts etc., and administer oaths etc. WH: 12–14C. Latin *notarius* shorthand writer, clerk, from *nota* NOTE. See also -ARY[1].

notation *n.* the act or process of representing by signs, figures etc. WH: 16C. Old French, or from Latin *notatio*, *notationis*, from *notatus*, p.p. of *notare* NOTE. See also -ATION.

notch *n.* a nick, a cut, a V-shaped indentation. *Also v.t.* WH: 16C. Anglo-French *noche*, from a v. rel. to *anoccer* to add a notch to. Cp. Latin *inoccare* to harrow in, Old French *oche* (Modern French *hoche*) nick, notch.

note *n.* a brief record, a memorandum. *Also v.t.* WH: 12–14C. Old French, from Latin *nota* mark.

nothing *n.* no thing. *Also a., adv.* WH: pre-1200. NO[1] + THING[1]. Orig. two words.

notice *n.* observation, regard, attention. *Also v.t.* WH: 14–15C. Old French, from Latin *notitia* being known, acquaintance, knowledge, notice, from *notus* known. See also -ICE.

notify *v.t.* to give notice to, to inform (of or that). WH: 14–15C. Old French *notifier*, from Latin *notificare*, from *notus* known. See also -FY.

notion *n.* an idea, a conception. *Also v.t.* WH: 14–15C. Latin *notio*, *notionis* conception, idea, from *notus*, p.p. of *gnoscere* to know. See also -ION.

notitia *n.* a list, register, or catalogue. WH: 18C. Latin knowledge, from *notus* known.

noto- *comb. form* of or relating to the back. WH: Greek *nōton* back.

notochord *n.* the elastic cartilaginous band constituting a rudimentary form of the spinal column in the embryo and some primitive fishes. WH: 19C. NOTO- + CHORD[2].

notonectal *a.* of or relating to the genus *Notonecta* of hemipterous insects. WH: 17C. Modern Latin *Notonecta*, from Greek *nōton* back + *nēktēs* swimmer. See also -AL[1].

notorious *a.* widely or publicly or commonly known for something bad. WH: 16C. Medieval Latin *notorius*, from Latin *notus* known. See also -IOUS.

notornis *n.* a gigantic flightless New Zealand bird, *Porphyrio mantelli*, now very rare. WH: 19C. Modern Latin, from Greek *notos* south + *ornis* bird.

nototherium *n.* an extinct Australian gigantic marsupial of the genus *Nototherium*. WH: 19C. Modern Latin, from Greek *notos* south + *thērion* beast.

notum *n.* the back of the thorax in insects. WH: Greek *nōton* back.

notwithstanding *prep.* in spite of, despite. *Also adv., conj.* WH: 14–15C. NOT + *withstanding*, pres.p. of WITHSTAND, based on Old French *non obstant*, Medieval Latin *non obstante* not being in the way, from *non* not + *obstante*, abl. pres.p. of *obstare* to be in the way (cp. OBSTINATE).

nougat *n.* a confection made of nuts and sugar. WH: 19C. French, from Provençal *nogat*, from *noga* nut, from Latin *nux* + *-at*, from Latin *-atum* -ATE[1].

nought *n.* zero. WH: pre-1200. Old English *nōwiht*, from *ne* not + *ōwiht*, var. of *āwiht* AUGHT. Cp. NAUGHT, OUGHT[2].

noumenon *n.* the substance underlying a phenomenon. WH: 18C. German, from Greek neut. pres.p. pass. (used as n.) of *noein* to apprehend, to conceive. The term was introduced by the German philosopher Immanuel Kant in contrast to PHENOMENON.

noun *n.* a word used as the name of anything. WH: 14–15C. Old French *nun*, *num* (Modern French *nom*), from Latin *nomen* name.

nourish *v.t.* to feed, to sustain, to support. *Also v.i.* WH: 12–14C. Old French *norir*, *noriss-* (Modern French *nourrir*), from Latin *nutrire* to feed, to foster, to cherish. See also -ISH[2].

nous *n.* sense, wit, intelligence. WH: 17C. Greek.

nouveau *a.* new. WH: early 20C. French new, from Latin *novus*.

nova *n.* a star which flares up to great brightness and subsides after a time. WH: 17C. Latin, fem. of *novus* new. The word was originally used for a new star or nebula.

novaculite *n.* a fine-grained slate used for hones. WH: 18C. Latin *novacula* razor + -ITE[1].

novalia *n.pl.* waste lands newly brought into cultivation. WH: 19C. Latin, pl. of *novale*, from *novus* new.

Novatian *n.* a follower of Novatianus, who taught that the Church had no power to absolve the lapsed or to admit them to the Eucharist. *Also a.* WH: 14–15C. Ecclesiastical Latin *Novatiani* (pl.), from *Novatianus*, 3C AD Roman presbyter.

novation *n.* the substitution of a new obligation or debt for an old one. WH: 16C. Late Latin *novatio*, *novationis*, from Latin *novatus*, p.p. of *novare* to make new, from *novus* new. See also -ATION.

novel *n.* a fictitious narrative in prose, usu. of sufficient length to fill a volume. *Also a.* WH: 14–15C. Old French (Modern French *nouvel*, *nouveau*), from Latin *novellus*, from *novus* new. See also -EL. The sense fictitious narrative derives direct from Italian *novella* (*storia*) new (story), from fem. of *novello*, from Latin *novellus*.

November *n.* the 11th month of the year. WH: pre-1200. Old French *novembre*, from Latin *November*, from *novem* nine. The month was originally the ninth of the Roman year. The meaning of *-ber* is unknown. Cp. SEPTEMBER, OCTOBER, DECEMBER.

novena *n.* in the Roman Catholic Church, a devotion consisting of a prayer or service repeated on nine successive days. WH: 19C. Medieval Latin, from *novem* nine, based on Latin *novenarius* of nine days. See NOVENARY.

novenary *n.* a group or set of nine. *Also a.* WH: 16C. Latin *novenarius*, from *novem* nine. See also -ARY[1].

novercal *a.* of, relating to or suitable to a stepmother. WH: 17C. Latin *novercalis*, from *noverca* stepmother, from *novus* new. See also -AL[1].

novice *n.* a person entering a religious house on probation before taking the vows. *Also a.* WH: 12–14C. Old French, from Late Latin *novicius*, from Latin *novus* new. See also -ICE.

Novocaine® *n.* a synthetic produce derived from coal tar, used as a local anaesthetic. WH: early 20C. Latin *novo-*, comb. form of *novus* new + COCAINE.

now *adv.* at the present time. *Also conj.*, *n.*, *a.* WH: pre-1200. Old English *nū*, from Germanic, from Indo-European adv. of time also represented also by Latin *num*, *nunc*, Greek *nu*, *nun*, Sanskrit *nu*. Cp. German *nun*.

nowhere *adv.* not in, at, or to any place or state. *Also pron.* WH: pre-1200. NO[1] + WHERE.

nowt[1] *n.* nothing. WH: 12–14C. Var. of NOUGHT.

†nowt[2] *n.* cattle or a bullock. WH: 12–14C. Old Norse *naut*, rel. to Old English *nēat* NEAT[1].

nowy *a.* having a convex projection in the middle. WH: 16C. Old French *noé* (Modern French *noué*), p.p. of *noer* (Modern French *nouer*) to knot, from Latin *nodare*, from *nodus* knot.

noxious *a.* hurtful, harmful, unwholesome. WH: 15C. Latin *noxius*, from *noxa* damage, hurt. See also -OUS.

noyade *n.* a mode of executing political prisoners by drowning, esp. during the Reign of Terror in France in 1794. WH: 19C. French from *noyer* to drown, from Latin *necare* to kill without a weapon, to drown, from *nex*, *necis* slaughter. See also -ADE.

noyau *n.* brandy cordial flavoured with bitter almonds etc. WH: 18C. French, earlier *noiel* kernel, from Popular Latin *nodellus*, from Late Latin *nucalis*, from *nux*, *nucis* nut.

nozzle *n.* a spout, a projecting mouthpiece, or end of pipe or hose. WH: 17C. NOSE + -LE[1].

nu *n.* the thirteenth letter of the Greek alphabet (N, ν). WH: 14–15C. Greek, of Semitic orig. Cp. Hebrew *nūn*.

nuance *n.* a delicate gradation in colour or tone. *Also v.t.* WH: 18C. French, from *nuer* to show cloudlike variations in colour, from *nue* cloud, from Popular Latin var. of Latin *nubes*. See also -ANCE.

nub *n.* the pith or gist (of). WH: 16C. Var. of dial. *knub*, from Middle Low German *knubbe*, var. of *knobbe* KNOB. The original sense was small lamp, protuberance, knob. The sense pith, gist dates from the 18C.

nubecula *n.* one of the two southern nebulae called the Magellanic clouds. WH: 17C. Latin, dim. of *nubes* cloud. See also -CULE.

nubiferous *a.* producing or bringing clouds. WH: 17C. Latin *nubifer*, from *nubes* cloud. See -FEROUS.

nubile *a.* (of a woman) marriageable. WH: 17C. Latin *nubilis*, from *nubere* to be married to (a man). See also -IL. The original sense was marriageable, sexually mature. The sense sexually attractive dates from the mid-20C.

nucellus *n.* the nucleus of an ovule. WH: 19C. Modern Latin, appar. dim. of *nucleus*.

nuchal *a.* of or relating to the nape of the neck. WH: 19C. Medieval Latin *nucha*, from Arabic *nuḵā'* spinal marrow, medulla.

nuci- *comb. form* of or relating to nuts. WH: Latin *nux*, *nucis* nut + *-i-*.

nuciferous *a.* bearing nuts. WH: 17C. NUCI- + -FEROUS.

nucivorous *a.* eating or feeding on nuts. WH: 19C. NUCI- + *-vorous* (-VORE).

nuclear *a.* of or relating to atomic nuclei. WH: 19C. NUCLEUS + -AR[1].

nuclease *n.* any of a group of enzymes which catalyse the breakdown of nucleic acids. WH: early 20C. *nucleic* (NUCLEIC ACID) + -ASE.

nucleate[1] *a.* having a nucleus, nucleated. WH: 19C. NUCLEUS + -ATE[2].

nucleate[2] *v.t.* to form into a nucleus. *Also v.i.* WH: 19C. NUCLEUS + -ATE[3].

nucleic acid *n.* either of two complex organic acids forming part of nucleoproteins. WH: 19C. NUCLEUS + -IC (+ ACID).

nuclein *n.* the protein forming the chief constituent of cell nuclei. WH: 19C. NUCLEUS + -IN[1].

nucleo- *comb. form* of or relating to a nucleus. WH: NUCLEUS, NUCLEAR, NUCLEIC ACID. See also -O-.

nucleolus *n.* a nucleus of or within another nucleus. WH: 19C. Late Latin, dim. of NUCLEUS.

nucleon *n.* a proton or neutron. WH: early 20C. NUCLEUS + -ON.

nucleonics *n.* the science of the nucleus of the atom. WH: mid-20C. NUCLEON + -ICS, based on *electronics* (ELECTRONIC).

nucleoprotein *n.* a complex of nucleic acid and protein. WH: early 20C. NUCLEO- + PROTEIN.

nucleoside *n.* an organic compound containing a purine or pyrimidine base linked to a sugar. WH: early 20C. NUCLEO- + *glycoside* (from GLYCO- + *-side*, based on *glucoside*; see GLUCOSE).

nucleosynthesis *n.* the cosmic formation of heavier elements from lighter by nuclear fusion. WH: mid-20C. NUCLEO- + SYNTHESIS.

nucleotide *n.* an organic compound containing a nucleoside linked to a phosphate group. WH: early 20C. NUCLEO- + *-t-* + -IDE.

nucleus *n.* a central part about which aggregation, accretion or growth goes on. WH: 18C. Latin nut, kernel, inner part, var. of *nuculeus*. See NUCULE. The sense central body of a cell arose in the 19C. The sense charged centre of an atom was introduced in 1912 by the British physicist Ernest Rutherford.

nuclide *n.* a kind of atom characterized by a specific number of protons and neutrons. WH: mid-20C. NUCLEUS + *-ide* (from Greek *eidos* form, kind).

nucule *n.* a small nut or nutlike fruit or seed. WH: 19C. Latin *nucula*, dim. of *nux*, *nucis* nut. See also -ULE.

nuddy *n.* a state of nudity. WH: mid-20C. Prob. from NUDE + -Y[3].

nude *a.* bare, naked, uncovered, unclothed. *Also n.* WH: 14–15C. Latin *nudus* bare, naked. The original sense (to the 17C) was mere, plain, especially in a legal sense. The current sense of naked arose in the 19C, mainly as a euphemistic term in art.

nudge *v.t.* to push gently, esp. with the elbow. *Also n.* WH: 17C. ? Rel. to Norwegian dial. *nugga, nyggja* to push, to rub.

nudi- *comb. form* bare, naked. WH: Latin *nudus* NUDE + *-i-*.

nudibranch *n.* a mollusc of the order Nudibranchia, characterized by naked gills or the absence of a shell. *Also a.* WH: 19C. Modern Latin *Nudibranchia.* See NUDI-, BRANCHIA.

nuée ardente *n.* a hot cloud of ash, gas and lava fragments ejected from a volcano. WH: early 20C. French, lit. burning cloud. The term was introduced in 1903 by the French mineralogist Alfred Lacroix, who said that by *ardent* he meant *brûlant* burning rather than *incandescent* glowing. The term is usually rendered in English as glowing cloud rather than burning cloud.

nuevo sol *n.* the standard unit of currency of Peru. WH: late 20C. Spanish *new sol,* from *nuevo* new + *sol,* lit. sun.

nugae *n.pl.* trifles, esp. literary compositions of a trifling kind. WH: 18C. Latin jests, trifles.

nugatory *a.* trifling, insignificant, futile. WH: 17C. Latin *nugatorius,* from *nugatus,* p.p. of *nugari* to trifle, from NUGAE. See also -ORY[2].

nuggar *n.* a broad, strongly built boat used on the upper Nile. WH: 19C. Prob. from Arabic *nuḵur,* pl. of *naḵīra* nuggar.

nugget *n.* a lump of metal, esp. of gold. WH: 19C. Appar. dim. of dial. *nug* lump, piece, of unknown orig. See also -ET[1].

nuisance *n.* anything that annoys, irritates or troubles. WH: 14–15C. Old French from *nuire, nuis-* to injure, from Latin *nocere.* See also -ANCE. The original sense was injury, harm, hurt. The current general sense dates from the 17C.

nuke *n.* a nuclear weapon. *Also v.t.* WH: mid-20C. Abbr. of NUCLEAR.

null *a.* having no legal force or validity. *Also n., v.t.* WH: 14–15C. Old French *nulle* or Latin *nullus,* from *ne* not + *ullus* any, from *unus* one.

nullah *n.* a ravine, gully or watercourse. WH: 18C. Hindi *nālā.*

nulla-nulla *n.* a club-shaped weapon of hard wood used by the Australian Aborigines. WH: 19C. Australian Aboriginal (Dharuk) *ngala ngala.*

nullifidian *n.* a person who has no religion. *Also a.* WH: 16C. Medieval Latin *nullifidius,* from *nulli-, nullus* no, none + *fides* faith. See also -AN, -IAN.

nullify *v.t.* to make void. WH: 16C. NULL + *-i-* + -FY.

nullipara *n.* a woman who has never given birth to a child. WH: 19C. Modern Latin, or from Latin *nulli-, nullus* no, none + *-para,* fem. of *-parus* (-PAROUS).

nullipore *n.* a seaweed with calcareous fronds. WH: 19C. Latin *nulli-, nullus* no, none + PORE[1].

nullity *n.* invalidity. WH: 16C. French *nullité* or Medieval Latin *nullitas,* from Latin *nullus* no, none. See also -ITY.

numb *a.* deprived of sensation and motion. *Also v.t.* WH: 14–15C. From *num,* p.p. of obs. *nim* to take, from Old English *niman,* from Germanic, rel. to Greek *nemein* to deal out, to distribute.

numbat *n.* a small marsupial, *Myrmecobius fasciatus,* of Australia, with a bushy tail. WH: early 20C. Australian Aboriginal (Nyungar) *numbad.*

number *n.* a measure of discrete quantity. *Also v.t.* WH: 12–14C. Old French *nombre,* from Latin *numerus.*

numbles *n.pl.* certain inner parts of a deer used as food. WH: 12–14C. Old French, ult. from Latin *lumbulus,* dim. of *lumbus* loin. Cp. UMBLES.

numdah *n.* an embroidered felt rug from India etc. WH: 19C. Urdu *namdā,* from Persian *namad* felt, carpet, rug. Cp. NUMNAH.

numen *n.* a deity or spirit presiding over a place. WH: 17C. Latin, rel. to *nuere* to nod, Greek *neuein* to incline the head.

numeral *n.* a word, symbol or group of symbols denoting number. *Also a.* WH: 14–15C. Late Latin *numeralis,* from Latin *numerus* NUMBER. See also -AL[1].

numerate[1] *a.* able to count; competent in mathematics. WH: 14–15C. Latin *numeratus,* p.p. of *numerare* NUMBER. See also -ATE[2]. The original sense, now obsolete, was numbered, counted. The current sense, able to count, dates from the mid-20C and derives from Latin *numerus* NUMBER, based on LITERATE.

numerate[2] *v.t.* to reckon, to number. WH: 18C. Latin *numeratus,* p.p. of *numerare* NUMBER. See also -ATE[3].

numerology *n.* the study of the alleged significance of numbers. WH: early 20C. Latin *numerus* NUMBER + -O- + -LOGY.

numerous *a.* many in number. WH: 14–15C. Latin *numerosus,* from *numerus* NUMBER. See also -OUS.

numinous *a.* of or relating to divinity. WH: 17C. Latin *numin-,* stem of NUMEN + -OUS.

numismatic *a.* of or relating to coins or medals. WH: 18C. French *numismatique,* from Late Latin *numisma, numismatis* coin, currency, var. of *nomisma,* from Greek current coin, from *nomisein* to have in use. See also -ISM, -ATIC.

nummary *a.* of or relating to coins. WH: 17C. Latin *nummarius,* from *nummus* coin. See also -ARY[1].

nummulite *n.* a fossil foraminifer resembling a coin. WH: 19C. Modern Latin *Nummulites,* from Latin *nummulus,* dim. of *nummus* coin. See also -ITE[1].

numnah *n.* a fabric or sheepskin pad placed under a saddle to prevent chafing. WH: 19C. Var. of NUMDAH.

numskull *n.* a stupid person. WH: 18C. NUMB + SKULL.

nun *n.* a woman devoted to a religious life and living in a convent under certain vows, usu. of poverty, chastity and obedience. WH: pre-1200. Old English *nunne,* from Late Latin *nonna,* fem. of *nunnus* monk, orig. a term of address to an elderly person, prob. orig. from children's speech (cp. NANA[2]).

nunatak *n.* a mountain peak which projects through an ice sheet. WH: 19C. Eskimo (Inuit) *nunataq.*

nun-buoy *n.* a buoy shaped like two cones united at the base. WH: 18C. From obs. *nun* child's top, of uncertain orig. (? rel. to NUN) + BUOY.

Nunc Dimittis *n.* the Song of Simeon (Luke ii.29–32). WH: 16C. Latin now you let (your servant) depart, opening words of the canticle, in the Vulgate (Latin version of the Bible) beginning: *Nunc dimittis servum tuum, Domine, secundum verbum tuum in pace,* (AV) Lord, now lettest thou thy servant depart in peace: according to thy Word.

nuncio *n.* a papal envoy or ambassador to a foreign power. WH: 16C. Obs. Italian *nuncio* (now *nunzio*), from Latin *nuncius,* from *nunciare* to announce.

nuncupate *v.t.* to declare (a will, vow etc.) orally, rather than in writing. WH: 16C. Latin *nuncupatus,* p.p. of *nuncupare* to name, to designate, to declare. See also -ATE[3].

nundinal *a.* of or relating to fairs or markets. WH: 17C. French, from *nundine,* from Latin *nundinae,* from *novem* nine + *dies* day. See also -AL[1]. The original reference was to a market held every eighth day (i.e., by inclusive reckoning, every ninth day).

nunnation *n.* the addition of final *n* to words, in the declension of Arabic nouns etc. WH: 18C. Modern Latin *nunnatio, nunnationis,* from *nun,* Arabic name of letter *n.* See also -ATION.

Nupe *n.* a member of a Negroid people of W central Nigeria. *Also a.* WH: 19C. *Nupe,* a former kingdom at the junction of the Niger and Benue rivers in W Africa.

nuphar *n.* the yellow water lily, of the genus *Nuphar.* WH: 19C. Arabic, from Persian *nūfar,* reduced form of *nīnūphar* NENUPHAR.

nuptial *a.* of or relating to a wedding. WH: 15C. Old French, or from Latin *nuptialis,* from *nuptiae* wedding, from *nuptus,* p.p. of *nubere.* See NUBILE, also -IAL.

nurdle *v.i.* to score runs in cricket by gently pushing the ball with the bat. WH: late 20C. Orig. unknown. ? Var. of NUDGE + -LE[4].

nurse *n.* a person who tends to the sick, wounded or infirm. *Also v.t., v.i.* WH: 14–15C. Alt. of obs. *nourice,* from Old French *nurice* (Modern French *nourrice*), from Late Latin *nutricia,* fem. of Latin *nutricius,* from *nutrix, nutricis* wet-nurse, from *nutrire* NOURISH.

nursery *n.* a room set apart for young children. WH: 14–15C. Prob. from Anglo-French, from *norice,* from Old French *nurice* (NURSE). See also -ERY.

nurture *n.* the act of bringing up, training, fostering. *Also v.t.* WH: 12–14C. Old French *nourture,* contr. of *noureture* (Modern French *nourriture*), from *norir.* See NOURISH.

nut *n.* the fruit of certain trees, containing a kernel in a hard shell which does not open to set free the seeds. *Also v.i., v.t.* WH: pre-1200. Old English *hnutu,* from Germanic. Cp. German *Nuss.* The sense small piece of metal with a threaded hole arose in the 17C, and that of a crazy person in the early 20C.

nutate *v.i.* to nod, to bend forward, to droop. WH: 19C. Latin *nutatus,* p.p. of *nutare* to nod, from base of *-nuere* to nod. See also -ATE[3].

nutmeg *n.* an evergreen tree, *Myristica fragrans*, whose hard aromatic seed is used for flavouring and in medicine. WH: 12–14C. Partial trans. of Anglo-French alt. of Old French *nois muguede* (Modern French *noix muscade*), from Medieval Latin *nux muscata*, lit. musk-scented nut.

nutria *n.* the coypu. WH: 19C. Spanish otter.

nutrient *n.* a nutritious substance. *Also a.* WH: 17C. Latin *nutriens*, *nutrientis*, pres.p. of *nutrire* to nourish. See also -ENT.

nux vomica *n.* a S Asian tree, *Strychnos nux-vomica*. WH: 14–15C. Medieval Latin, lit. emetic nut, from Latin *nux* nut + a. from *vomere* to vomit.

nuzzle *v.t.* to rub or press the nose against. *Also v.i.* WH: 14–15C. NOSE + -LE⁴. The sense to cuddle up to dates from the 16C and may have been influenced by NESTLE or NURSE.

nyala *n.* a large southern African antelope, *Tragelaphus angasi*, with spiral horns. WH: 19C. Zulu *i-nyala*.

nyctalopia *n.* a disease of the eyes in which vision is worse in shade or twilight than in daylight, night-blindness. WH: 17C. Late Latin, from Greek *nuktalōps*, *nuktalōpos*, from *nux*, *nuktos* night + *alaos* blind + -*ōps* eye. See also -IA.

nyctitropic *a.* (of leaves) changing position or direction at night. WH: 19C. Greek *nux*, *nuktos* night + *tropikos* turning. See also -IC.

nyctophobia *n.* a morbid fear of darkness. WH: early 20C. Greek *nux*, *nuktos* night + -O- + *phobos* fear. See -PHOBE, also -IA.

nylon *n.* any of various thermoplastics, used largely for tights, shirts, dress fabrics, imitation furs, ropes, brushes etc. *Also a.* WH: mid-20C. Invented word based on RAYON, COTTON. The inital *ny-* is popularly said to derive from the initials of *New York*. The word was coined in 1938 by chemists working for the Du Pont company, USA, who have stated that the first element is entirely arbitrary.

nymph *n.* any one of a class of mythological youthful female divinities inhabiting groves, springs, mountains, the sea etc. WH: 14–15C. Old French *nimphe* (Modern French *nymphe*), from Latin *nympha*, from Greek *numphē* bride, nymph, rel. to Latin *nubere* to be married to (a man). Cp. NUBILE.

nymphalid *a.* of or relating to the family Nymphalidae of butterflies. *Also n.* WH: 19C. Modern Latin *Nymphalidae*, from *Nymphalis* genus name, from *nympha* nymph. See also -ID.

nympho *n.* a nymphomaniac. WH: mid-20C. Abbr. of *nymphomaniac* (NYMPHOMANIA).

nympholepsy *n.* a state of ecstasy or frenzy supposed to affect someone who has gazed on a nymph. WH: 18C. Greek *numpholēptos* caught by nymphs, from *numphē* NYMPH + *lambanein* to take hold of, based on EPILEPSY.

nymphomania *n.* excessive sexual desire in a woman. WH: 18C. Modern Latin, from Latin *nympha* NYMPH + -O- + -MANIA.

nystagmus *n.* a spasmodic movement of the eyeballs, a condition affecting miners and others working in a dim light. WH: 19C. Modern Latin, from Greek *nustagmos* nodding, drowsiness, from *nustazein* to nod, to be sleepy.

nystatin *n.* an antibiotic used for fungal infections. WH: mid-20C. From letters of *New York State* (where developed) + -IN¹.

Nyungar *n.* an extinct Aboriginal language of SW Australia. WH: 19C. Australian Aboriginal (Nyungar) *nyungar* an Aboriginal person.

O *int.* an exclamation of earnest or solemn address, entreaty, invocation, pain, surprise, wonder etc. WH: 12–14C. Natural exclamation. See OH.

O' *pref.* descendant of, in Irish surnames. WH: 18C. Irish *ó, ua* grandson.

o' *prep.* of, on. WH: 12–14C. Reduced form of OF, ON.

o- *pref.* straight. WH: Abbr. of ORTHO-.

-o *suf.* serving as a diminutive, as in *cheapo, wino.* WH: Prob. from O, reinforced by the final syl. of abbrs. such as COMPO[1], HIPPO, PHOTO, etc.

-o- *suf.* used as the terminal vowel in combining forms, as in *Russo-, petro-.* WH: Greek *-o-* as stem vowel or connective.

oaf *n.* a silly, stupid person. WH: 17C. Old Norse *álfr,* rel. to Old English *ælf* ELF. The original sense was the child of an elf or goblin, or in human terms a deformed or idiot child.

oak *n.* any tree or shrub of the genus *Quercus,* esp. *Q. robur,* a forest tree much valued for its timber. *Also a.* WH: pre-1200. Old English *āc,* from Germanic. Cp. German *Eiche.*

oakum *n.* old rope, untwisted and pulled into loose fibres, used for caulking seams, stopping leaks etc. in ships. WH: pre-1200. Old English *ācumbe,* lit. off-combings, from *ā-* out, off + *camb-* stem of *cemban,* from Germanic base of COMB. The original sense was tow, also trimmings, shreds. The current sense dates from the 15C.

oar *n.* a long pole with a flattened blade, for rowing, sculling or steering a boat. *Also v.i., v.t.* WH: pre-1200. Old English *ār,* from Germanic, prob. rel. to Greek *eretmos* oar, *eretēs* rower, *eressein* to row.

oasis *n.* a fertile spot in a waste or desert. WH: 17C. Late Latin, from Greek, appar. of Egyptian orig. Cp. Coptic *wahe, ouahe* dwelling-place, oasis.

oast *n.* a kiln for drying hops. WH: pre-1200. Old English *āst,* from Germanic, from Indo-European base meaning to burn. The original meaning was kiln in general.

oat *n.* a cereal plant of the genus *Avena,* esp. *A. sativa.* WH: pre-1200. Old English *āte,* of unknown orig. The word is peculiar to English. The common Germanic word for the cereal is **habran-.* Cp. HAVERSACK.

oath *n.* a solemn appeal to God or some revered person or thing, in witness of the truth of a statement or of the binding nature of a promise, esp. in a court of law. WH: pre-1200. Old English *āth,* from Germanic. Cp. German *Eid.*

ob. *abbr.* obiit, he/she died. WH: Abbr. of Latin *obiit* (he) died. See OBIT.

ob- *pref.* toward, to, meeting, in, facing, as in *obvious.* WH: Latin pref., from prep. *ob* towards, against, in the way of.

obang *n.* an oblong gold coin formerly current in Japan. WH: 17C. Japanese *ō-ban,* from *ō* great, major + *ban* part, share, division.

obbligato *a.* not to be omitted. *Also n.* WH: 18C. Italian obliged, obligatory. See OBLIGE.

obconic *a.* inversely conical. WH: 19C. OB- + CONIC. See also -AL[1].

obcordate *a.* inversely heart-shaped. WH: 18C. OB- + CORDATE.

obdurate *a.* stubborn. *Also v.t.* WH: 14–15C. Latin *obduratus,* p.p. of *obdurare,* from OB- + *durare* to harden, from *durus* hard. See also -ATE[2].

obeah *n.* a form of sorcery practised by blacks, esp. in the W Indies. WH: 18C. Twi *o-bayifo* sorcerer, from *bayi* sorcery.

obedience *n.* the act or practice of obeying. WH: 12–14C. Old French *obédience,* from Latin *oboedientia,* from *oboediens, oboedientis,* pres.p. of *oboedire* OBEY. See also -ENCE.

obeisance *n.* a bow or any gesture signifying submission, respect or salutation. WH: 14–15C. Old French *obéissance,* from *obéissant,* pres.p. of *obéir* OBEY. See also -ANCE. The original basic meaning (to the 17C) was obedience.

obelion *n.* the part of the skull between the two parietal foramina where the sagittal suture becomes simple. WH: 19C. Greek *obeliaios* sagittal + *-ion,* based on INION.

obelisk *n.* a quadrangular stone shaft, usually monolithic and tapering, with a pyramidal apex. WH: 16C. Latin *obeliscus,* from Greek *obeliskos,* dim. of *obelos* spit, pointed pillar.

obelus *n.* a mark (-, ÷, or †), used to mark spurious or doubtful passages in ancient manuscripts. WH: 14–15C. Latin spit, critical obelus, from Greek *obelos.* See OBELISK.

obese *a.* excessively fat, corpulent. WH: 17C. Latin *obesus* having eaten oneself fat, from OB- + *esus,* p.p. of *edere* to eat.

obex *n.* a band of white matter in the medulla oblongata. WH: 17C. Latin barrier, bolt, from *obicere* to cast in front of, from OB- + *iacere* to throw.

obey *v.t.* to perform or carry out (a command, instruction or direction). *Also v.i.* WH: 12–14C. Old French *obéir* or Latin *oboedire,* from OB- + *audire* to hear.

obfuscate *v.t.* to darken, to obscure. WH: 14–15C. Late Latin *obfuscatus,* p.p. of *obfuscare,* from OB- + *fuscare* to darken, from *fuscus* dark. See also -ATE[3].

obi *n.* a coloured sash worn around a Japanese kimono. WH: 19C. Japanese belt.

obit *n.* a memorial service or commemoration of a death. WH: 14–15C. Old French, from Latin *obitus* going down, setting, death, from *obitus,* p.p. of *obire* to perish, to die (from phr. *mortem obire* to meet death), from OB- + *ire* to go. The sense obituary partly derives from the abbreviation of OBITUARY.

obiter *adv.* incidentally, by the way. WH: 16C. Latin *ob itur* by the way.

obituary *a.* relating to or recording a death or deaths. *Also n.* WH: 18C. Medieval Latin *obituarius,* from *obitus.* See OBIT.

object[1] *v.t.* to oppose. *Also v.i.* WH: 14–15C. Latin *obiectus,* p.p. of *obiectare,* freq. of *obicere,* from OB- + *iacere* to throw. The original sense (to the 19C) was literal: to place so as to interrupt, to put in the way.

object[2] *n.* anything presented to the senses or the mind, esp. anything visible or tangible. WH: 14–15C. Partly from use as n. of *object,* obs. p.p. of OBJECT[1], partly from Medieval Latin *obiectum* thing presented to the mind, neut. p.p. (used as n.) of Latin *obicere.*

objective *a.* proceeding from the object of knowledge or thought as opposed to the perceiving or thinking subject. *Also n.* WH: 17C. Medieval Latin *obiectivus,* from *obiectum.* See OBJECT[2], also -IVE.

objet *n.* an object. WH: 19C. French OBJECT[2].

objurgate *v.t., v.i.* to chide, to reprove. WH: 17C. Latin *obiurgatus,* p.p. of *obiurgare,* from OB- + *iurgare* to quarrel, to scold, from *iurgium* quarrel. See also -ATE[3].

oblanceolate *a.* inversely lanceolate. WH: 19C. OB- + LANCEOLATE.

oblast *n.* an administrative district or province in Russia. WH: 19C. Russian *oblast'* power, province, from Old Church Slavonic *obvlost',* from *ob-* around + *volst'* possession.

oblate[1] *a.* flattened at the poles, as opposed to *prolate.* WH: 18C. Modern Latin *oblatus,* from OB- + *-latus,* based on Latin *prolatus* PROLATE.

oblate[2] *n.* a person not under vows but dedicated to monastic or religious life or work. WH: 17C. French *oblat,* from Medieval Latin *oblatus,* use as n. of p.p. of Latin *offerre* OFFER.

obligation *n.* the binding power of a promise, contract, vow, duty, law etc. WH: 12–14C. Old French, from Latin *obligatio, obligationis,* from *obligatus,* p.p. of *obligare.* See OBLIGE, also -ATION.

oblige *v.t.* to constrain by legal, moral or physical force. *Also v.i.* WH: 12–14C. Old French *obliger*, from Latin *obligare*, from OB- + *ligare* to bind.

oblique *a.* deviating from the vertical or horizontal. *Also n., v.i.* WH: 14–15C. Old French, from Latin *obliquus*, from OB- + second element of unknown orig. (? rel. to Latin *licinus* bent upward).

obliterate *v.t.* to efface, to erase. WH: 16C. Latin *obliteratus*, p.p. of *obliterare* to strike out, to erase, from OB- + *littera* LETTER. See also -ATE³.

oblivion *n.* forgetfulness, unawareness. WH: 14–15C. Old French, from Latin *oblivio, oblivionis*, from *obliv*-, stem of *oblivisci* to forget. See also -ION.

oblong *a.* longer than broad, of greater breadth than height esp. of rectangles with adjoining sides unequal. *Also n.* WH: 14–15C. Latin *oblongus* rather long, oblong, from OB- + *longus* LONG¹.

obloquy *n.* censorious language. WH: 14–15C. Late Latin *obloquium* contradiction, from OB- + *loqui* to talk, to speak.

obmutescence *n.* loss of speech. WH: 17C. Latin *obmutescere*, from OB- + *mutescere* to grow mute. See also -ESCENCE.

obnoxious *a.* offensive, objectionable. WH: 16C. Latin *obnoxiosus* or *obnoxius* exposed to harm, liable, from OB- + *noxa* hurt, injury. See also -IOUS. The original sense was subject to injury. The current sense emerged in the 17C.

obnubilate *v.t.* to cloud, to obscure. WH: 16C. Latin *obnubilatus*, p.p. of *obnubilare* to cover with clouds, from OB- + *nubilare* to make cloudy, to be cloudy, from *nubila* (neut. pl.), from *nubes* cloud. See also -ATE³.

oboe *n.* a woodwind instrument with a double reed, usu. of soprano pitch. WH: 18C. Italian, from French *haut bois*. See HAUTBOY.

obol *n.* a small coin of ancient Greece weighing and worth one-sixth of a drachma. WH: 14–15C. Latin *obolus*, from Greek *obolos*, var. of *obelos* OBELISK.

obovate *a.* inversely ovate. WH: 18C. OB- + *ovate* (OVARY).

obreption *n.* acquisition or attempted acquisition of gifts etc. by falsehood. WH: 14–15C. French, or from Latin *obreptio, obreptionis*, from *obreptus*, p.p. of *obrepere* to creep up to, to steal up on, from OB- + *repere* to creep (cp. REPTILE). See also -ION.

obscene *a.* indecent, disgusting. WH: 16C. French *obscène* or Latin *obscaenus* ill-omened, abominable, from OB- + *caenum* filth. A sense inauspicious was current in the 17–19C.

obscurant *n.* an opponent of intellectual progress. WH: 18C. German, from Latin *obscurans, obscurantis*, pres.p. of *obscurare*. See OBSCURE, also -ANT.

obscure *a.* dark, dim. *Also v.t., v.i., n.* WH: 14–15C. Old French *obscur*, from Latin *obscurus* dark.

obsecration *n.* the act of imploring, entreaty. WH: 14–15C. Latin *obsecratio, obsecrationis*, from *obsecratus*, p.p. of *obsecrare* to entreat, to beseech (orig. in the name of the gods), from OB- + *sacrare* to hold sacred. See also -ATION.

obsequent *a.* (of a stream) flowing in the opposite direction to the original slope of the land. WH: 19C. OB- + *-sequent*, based on CONSEQUENT, etc.

obsequies *n.pl.* funeral rites. WH: 14–15C. Anglo-French, from Old French *obsèques*, from Medieval Latin *obsequiae*, prob. alt. of Latin *exequiae* (EXEQUIES) by assoc. with *obsequium* dutiful service (see OBSEQUIOUS).

obsequious *a.* fawning, over-ready to comply with the desires of others. WH: 15C. Latin *obsequiosus*, from *obsequium* compliance, from OB- + *sequi* to follow. See also -IOUS.

observe *v.t.* to regard attentively, to take notice of. *Also v.i.* WH: 14–15C. Old French *observer*, from Latin *observare* to watch, to attend to, from OB- + *servare* to watch, to keep.

obsess *v.t.* to beset, to trouble (as an evil spirit). *Also v.i.* WH: 14–15C. Latin *obsessus*, p.p. of *obsidere* to sit down before, to besiege, from OB- + *sedere* to sit. A sense to besiege was current in the 16–17C.

obsidian *n.* a black or dark-coloured vitreous lava. WH: 17C. Latin (*lapis*) *obsidianus* obsidian (stone), from erron. form of *obsianus*, from Greek *opsianos* (*lithos*) Obsian (stone), a black stone named after *Obsius*, its supposed discoverer. According to Pliny, Obsius was a Roman who was supposed to have found the rock in Ethiopia.

obsidional *a.* of or relating to a siege. WH: 14–15C. Latin *obsidionalis*, from *obsidio, obsidionis* siege, from *obsidere*. See OBSESS, also -AL¹.

obsign *v.t.* to seal, to ratify. WH: 16C. Latin *obsignare* to seal, to seal up, from OB- + *signare* to mark, to seal, SIGN. See also -ATE³.

obsolescent *a.* becoming obsolete. WH: 18C. Latin *obsolescens, obsolescentis*, pres.p. of *obsolescere*, from OB- + *solere* to be accustomed. See also *-escent* (-ESCENCE).

obstacle *n.* an impediment, an obstruction. *Also a.* WH: 12–14C. Old French, from Latin *obstaculum*, from *obstare* to stand in the way, from OB- + *stare* to stand.

obstetric *a.* of or relating to childbirth or obstetrics. WH: 18C. Modern Latin *obstetricus*, from Latin *obstetricius*, from *obstetrix* midwife, from *obstare* + -TRIX. See OBSTACLE. Latin *obstetrix* literally means one who stands opposite to (the woman giving birth).

obstinate *a.* stubbornly adhering to one's opinion or purpose. WH: 12–14C. Latin *obstinatus*, p.p. of *obstinare*, to persist, from OB- + deriv. of *stare* STAND. See also -ATE².

obstipation *n.* extreme constipation. WH: 16C. Alt. of *constipation* (CONSTIPATE). See OB-.

obstreperous *a.* noisy, clamorous. WH: 16C. Latin *obstreperus*, from *obstrepere* to make a noise against. See also -OUS.

obstriction *n.* the state of being legally constrained. WH: 17C. Medieval Latin *obstrictio, obstrictionis*, from *obstrictus*, p.p. of *obstringere*, from OB- + *stringere* to tie, to bind. See also -ION.

obstruct *v.t.* to block up, to close by means of obstacles. *Also v.i.* WH: 16C. Latin *obstructus*, p.p. of *obstruere* to build against, to block up, from OB- + *struere* to pile, to build.

obtain *v.t.* to gain, to acquire. *Also v.i.* WH: 14–15C. Old French *obtenir*, from Latin *obtinere*, from OB- + *tenere* to hold. Among the many former senses, now all obsolete, were to win (a victory), to attain, to manage (to do), to hold, to possess. The sense to be prevalent evolved in the 17C.

obtect *a.* (of the pupae of some insects) protected, encased by a chitinous covering. WH: 19C. Latin *obtectus*, p.p. of *obtegere* to cover over, from OB- + *tegere* to cover.

obtest *v.t.* to beseech, to supplicate, to adjure. *Also v.i.* WH: 16C. Latin *obtestari* to call to witness, to protest by, from OB- + *testari* to bear witness, to call upon as witness.

obtrude *v.t.* to thrust out, forward or upon. *Also v.i.* WH: 16C. Latin *obtrudere*, from OB- + *trudere* to thrust.

obtund *v.t.* to blunt, to deaden. WH: 14–15C. Latin *obtundere*, from OB- + *tundere* to beat.

obturate *v.t.* to stop up or close (esp. the breech of a gun). WH: 17C. Latin *obturatus*, p.p. of *obturare* to stop up, from OB- + *turare* to close up. See also -ATE³.

obtuse *a.* blunt or rounded, not pointed or acute. WH: 14–15C. Latin *obtusus*, p.p. of *obtundere* OBTUND. The figurative sense of dull, stupid dates from the 16C.

obverse *a.* turned towards one. *Also n.* WH: 17C. Latin *obversus*, p.p. of *obvertere* to turn towards, from OB- + *vertere* to turn.

obviate *v.t.* to clear away, to remove, to overcome, counteract or neutralize (dangers, difficulties etc.). WH: 16C. Late Latin *obviatus*, p.p. of *obviare* to meet in the way, to prevent, from OB- + *via* way. See also -ATE³. Cp. OBVIOUS.

obvious *a.* plain to the eye, immediately evident. *Also n.* WH: 16C. Latin *obvius*, from *obviam* in the way, from OB- + *via* way. See also -IOUS. Cp. OBVIATE. An early sense (to the 18C) was frequently encountered, commonly occurring.

obvolute *a.* folded together so that the alternate margins are respectively exposed or covered. WH: 18C. Latin *obvolutus*, p.p. of *obvolvere* to wrap around, from OB- + *volvere* to roll.

oc- *pref.* toward, to, meeting, in, facing, as in *occasion, occur*. WH: Latin pref., from OB- with *b* assim. to *c*.

oca *n.* any of various S. American herbaceous plants of the genus *Oxalis*, which have edible tubers. WH: 17C. American Spanish, from Quechua *ócca*.

ocarina *n.* a musical instrument of terracotta with finger-notes and a mouthpiece, giving a mellow whistling sound. WH: 19C. Italian, from *oca* goose. See also -INA¹. The instrument is so called with reference to its shape.

Occamism *n.* the doctrines of William of Occam. WH: 19C. William of *Occam*, *c.*1285–*c.*1349, English scholastic philosopher. See also -ISM. Occam is *Ockham*, a village in Surrey.

occasion *n.* an event, circumstance or position of affairs, giving an opportunity, reason, or motive for doing something. *Also v.t.* WH: 14–15C. Old French, from Latin *occasio*, *occasionis* juncture, opportunity, motive, cause, from *occasus*, p.p. of *occidere* to go down, to set, from OC- + *cadere* to fall. See also -ION. The sense occurrence, event, incident (rather than the time of an occurrence) was current until the 17C.

Occident *n.* the West. WH: 14–15C. Old French, from Latin *occidens*, *occidentis* setting, sunset, west, pres.p. (used as n.) of *occidere* to go down, to set. See OCCASION, also -ENT.

occiput *n.* the back part of the head. WH: 14–15C. Latin, from OC- + *caput* head.

Occitan *n.* the Provençal language. WH: mid-20C. French, from Medieval Latin (*lingua*) *occitana* Occitan (language), Latinized form of *langue d'oc* (LANGUE).

occlude *v.t.* to shut or stop up. WH: 16C. Latin *occludere*, from OC- + *claudere* to close.

occult *a.* supernatural, mystical. *Also v.t., v.i., n.* WH: 15C. Latin *occultus*, p.p. of *occulere*, prob. from OC- + *celare* to conceal. The current sense dates from the 17C. The earliest basic sense, now obsolete, was hidden from sight.

occupant *n.* a person who occupies. WH: 16C. French, or from Latin *occupans*, *occupantis*, pres.p. of *occupare*. See OCCUPY, also -ANT.

occupy *v.t.* to take possession of. WH: 12–14C. Anglo-French var. of Anglo-French var. of Old French *occuper*, from Latin *occupare*, from OC- + *capere* to take, to seize. The original meaning was to take possession of, to seize. A sense to have sexual intercourse with was current in the 16–17C.

occur *v.i.* to happen, to take place. WH: 15C. Latin *occurrere* to run to meet, to befall, from OC- + *currere* to run.

ocean *n.* the vast body of water covering about two-thirds of the surface of the globe. *Also a.* WH: 12–14C. Old French *ocean* (Modern French *océan*), from Latin *oceanus*, from Greek *ōkeanos* (*potamos*) the great river (Greek *potamos*) encompassing the earth, the great sea, personified as *Ōkeanos*, the god of the sea, the son of Uranus (Heaven) and Gaea (Earth) and husband of Tethys.

ocellus *n.* a simple eye, as opposed to the compound eye of insects. WH: 19C. Latin, dim. of *oculus* eye.

ocelot *n.* a small American feline, *Felis pardalis*, which has a yellow or orange coat marked with black stripes and spots. WH: 18C. French, from Nahuatl *tlatlocelotl*, lit. field tiger.

och *int.* used to express impatience, contempt, regret, surprise etc. WH: 16C. Gaelic and Irish. Cp. OHONE.

oche *n.* in darts, the line or mark behind which a player must stand when throwing at the dartboard. WH: mid-20C. Orig. uncertain. ? Ult. rel. to Old French *ocher* to cut a deep notch in. Cp. NOTCH.

ochlocracy *n.* mob rule. WH: 16C. French *ochlocratie* or Modern Latin *ochlocratia*, from Greek *okhlokratia*, from *okhlos* crowd. See also -CRACY.

ochre *n.* a native earth consisting of hydrated peroxide of iron with clay in various proportions, used as a red or yellow pigment. *Also a.* WH: 12–14C. Old French *ocre*, from Latin *ochra*, from Greek *ōkhra*, from *ōkhros* pale yellow, paleness.

-ock *suf.* indicating smallness or youngness, as in *bullock*, *hillock*. WH: Old English *-oc*, *-uc*.

ocker *n.* a boorish, chauvinistic Australian. *Also a.* WH: late 20C. Alt. of pers. name *Oscar*, used as a nickname for a character devised and played by Ron Fraser in a television series, *The Mavis Bramston Show*, 1965–8.

o'clock *adv.* of the clock. WH: 15C. Contr. of *of the clock*.

ocotillo *n.* a cactus-like shrub, *Fouquiera splendens*, of Mexico and the south-western US. WH: 19C. American Spanish, dim. of *ocote*, from Nahuatl *ocotl* torch.

ocrea *n.* a sheath formed by the union of two stipules round a stem. WH: 19C. Latin *ochrea* greave, protective legging.

octa- *comb. form* having eight. WH: Greek *okta-*, comb. form of *oktō* eight. Cp. OCTO-.

octachord *n.* a musical instrument with eight strings. WH: 18C. Latin *octachordos*, from Greek *oktakhordos*, from *okta-* + *khordē* string (see CORD).

octad *n.* a group or series of eight. WH: 19C. Greek *oktas*, *oktados* group of eight, from *oktō* eight. See also -AD[1].

octagon *n.* a plane figure of eight sides and angles. WH: 16C. Latin *octagonum*, from Greek *oktagōnon*, use as n. of neut. *oktagōnos* eight-cornered. See OCTA-, -GON.

octahedron *n.* a solid figure contained by eight plane faces. WH: 16C. Greek *oktaedron*, use as n. of *oktaedros* eight-sided. See OCTA-, -HEDRON.

octal *a.* referring to or based on the number eight. WH: mid-20C. OCTA- + -AL[1].

octamerous *a.* having parts in eights or in series of eight. WH: 19C. OCTA- + -MEROUS.

octameter *n.* in verse, a line of eight metrical feet. WH: 19C. OCTA- + -METER, based on HEXAMETER, PENTAMETER.

octandrous *a.* having eight stamens. WH: 19C. OCTA- + -ANDROUS.

octane *n.* a colourless liquid hydrocarbon of the alkane series that occurs in petroleum. WH: 19C. OCTA- + -ANE. The name refers to the number of carbon atoms (C_8) in the hydrocarbon.

octangular *a.* having eight angles. WH: 17C. Latin *octangulus* (from OCTO- + *angulus* ANGLE[1]) + -AR[1].

octant *n.* an arc comprising the eighth part of a circle's circumference. WH: 17C. Latin *octans*, *octantis* half-quadrant, from OCTO-. Cp. QUADRANT, SEXTANT.

octapodic *a.* containing eight metrical feet. WH: early 20C. OCTA- + -POD + -IC.

octastich *n.* a strophe, stanza or series of eight lines of verse. WH: 16C. Greek *oktastikhos*, from *okta-* OCTA- + *stikhos* vow, line of verse.

octastrophic *a.* consisting of eight strophes. WH: early 20C. OCTA- + *strophic* (STROPHE).

octastyle *n.* a building having eight columns in front. *Also a.* WH: 18C. Latin *octastylus*, from Greek *oktastulos*, from *okta-* OCTA- + *stulos* column.

octateuch *n.* the first eight books of the Old Testament. WH: 17C. Late Latin *octateuchus*, from Greek *oktateukhos* containing eight books, from *okta-* OCTA- + *teukhos* book. Cp. PENTATEUCH, HEXATEUCH, HEPTATEUCH.

octavalent *a.* having a valency of eight. WH: early 20C. OCTA- + -*valent*, from Latin *valens*, *valentis*, pres.p. of *valere* to be strong. See also -ENT. Cp. VALENCE.

octave *n.* the interval between any musical note and that produced by twice or half as many vibrations per second (lying eight notes away inclusively). WH: 12–14C. Old French, from Latin *octava*, fem. of *octavus* eighth, from *octo* eight. The earliest sense was ecclesiastical: the seventh day after a festival. The musical sense dates from the 16C.

octavo *n.* a book in which a sheet is folded into 8 leaves or 16 pages. *Also a.* WH: 16C. Latin (*in*) *octavo* (in) an eighth (of a sheet), from *octavus* eighth.

octennial *a.* recurring every eighth year. WH: 17C. Late Latin *octennium* period of eight years, from *octo* eight + *annus* year. See also -AL[1].

octet *n.* a musical composition of eight parts or for eight instruments or singers. WH: 19C. Italian *ottetto* or German *Oktett*, assim. to OCTA-, -ET[1], based on DUET, QUARTET.

octile *n.* an eighth part. WH: 17C. Modern Latin *octilis*, from Latin *octo* eight + -*ilis* -IL, based on DECILE, etc.

octillion *n.* the number produced by raising a million to the eighth power of a thousand, represented by 1 followed by 48 zeros. WH: 17C. OCTA- + -*illion*, based on MILLION, BILLION, etc.

octingenary *n.* an 800th anniversary, an octocentenary. WH: 19C. Latin *octingenti* eight hundred, based on *centenary* (CENTENARIAN).

octo- *comb. form* having eight. WH: Latin *octo* eight. See also -O-. Cp. OCTA-.

October *n.* the tenth month of the year. WH: pre-1200. Latin *October*, from *octo* eight. Cp. SEPTEMBER, NOVEMBER, DECEMBER. The month was originally the eighth in the Roman year.

octobrachiate *a.* having eight limbs, arms or rays. WH: 19C. OCTO- + *brachiate* (BRACHIAL).

octocentenary *n.* an 800th anniversary. *Also a.* WH: 19C. OCTO- + *centenary* (CENTENARIAN).

octodecimo *n.* a book having 18 leaves to the sheet. *Also a.* WH: 19C. Latin (*in*) *octodecimo* (in) an eighteenth (of a sheet), from *octodecimus* eighteenth.

octodentate *a.* having eight teeth. WH: 19C. OCTO- + Latin *dens, dentis* tooth. See also -ATE².

octofid *a.* having eight segments. WH: 18C. OCTO- + Latin -*fidus* cleft.

octogenarian *n.* a person who is 80, or between 80 and 90 years old. *Also a.* WH: 19C. Latin *octogenarius*, from *octogeni* eighty each, from *octoginta* eighty. See also -ARIAN.

octogynous *a.* having eight pistils. WH: 19C. OCTO- + -GYNOUS.

octonary *a.* relating to, computing or proceeding by the number eight. *Also n.* WH: 16C. Latin *octonarius* containing eight, from *octoni* eight each, from *octo* eight. See also -ARY¹.

octonocular *a.* having eight eyes. WH: 18C. Latin *octoni* eight each + *oculus* eye. See also -AR¹.

octoped *n.* an eight-footed animal. WH: 19C. OCTO- + -*ped* (-PEDE).

octopetalous *a.* having eight petals. WH: 18C. OCTO- + *petalous* (PETAL).

octopod *a.* having eight feet. *Also n.* WH: 19C. Greek *oktōpod-*, stem of *oktōpous*. See OCTOPUS, -POD.

octopus *n.* any cephalopod mollusc of the genus *Octopus*, having eight arms furnished with suckers. WH: 18C. Modern Latin, from Greek *oktōpous*, from *oktō* eight + *pous* foot.

octoroon *n.* the offspring of a quadroon and a white person (having one-eighth black ancestry). WH: 19C. OCTO- + -*roon*, based on QUADROON.

octosepalous *a.* having eight sepals. WH: 19C. OCTO- + *sepalous* (SEPAL).

octospermous *a.* having eight seeds. WH: 19C. OCTO- + Greek *sperma* seed. See also -OUS.

octosporous *a.* eight-spored. WH: 19C. OCTO- + Greek *spora* SPORE. See also -OUS.

octosyllabic *a.* having eight syllables. *Also n.* WH: 18C. OCTO- + *syllabic* (SYLLABLE).

octroi *n.* a tax levied at the gates of some European, esp. French, towns on goods brought in. WH: 16C. French, from *octroyer* to grant, from Medieval Latin *auctorizare* AUTHORIZE.

octuple *a.* eightfold. *Also n., v.t., v.i.* WH: 17C. French, or from Latin *octuplus*, from OCTO- + -*plus* as in *duplus* double.

octyl *n.* the hypothetical organic radical of a hydrocarbon series. WH: 19C. OCTA- + -YL.

ocular *a.* of, relating to, by or with the eye or eyes, visual. *Also n.* WH: 16C. French *oculaire*, from Late Latin *ocularis*, from Latin *oculus* eye. See also -AR¹.

OD *n.* an overdose of a drug. *Also v.i.* WH: Abbr. of *overdose*.

†od¹ *int., n.* a minced form of 'God' used as an expletive or asseveration. WH: 16C. Alt. of GOD.

od² *n.* a natural force once thought to pervade the universe and to produce the phenomena of magnetism, crystallization, hypnotism etc. WH: 19C. Arbitrary formation, selected by the German scientist Baron von Reichenbach in 1850 as a good word-forming element.

odalisque *n.* an Oriental female slave or concubine, esp. in a harem. WH: 17C. French, from Turkish *ōdalık*, from *ōda* chamber, hall + -*lık*, suf. expressing a function.

odd *a.* remaining after a number or quantity has been divided into pairs. *Also n.* WH: 12–14C. Old Norse *odda-* in *odda-mathr* third man, odd man (giving a casting vote), from *oddi* point, angle.

ode *n.* a lyric poem in an elevated style, rhymed or unrhymed, of varied and often irregular metre, usu. in the form of an address or invocation. WH: 16C. French, from Latin *oda*, from Greek *ōidē*, Attic form of *aoidē* song, singing, from *aeidein* to sing. The original sense was a poem intended to be sung. Cp. ODEON.

-ode¹ *suf.* denoting a thing resembling or of the nature of, as in *geode*, *sarcode*. WH: Modern Latin -*odium*, from Greek -*ōdēs*, -*ōdes*, contr. of -*oeidēs*. See also -OID.

-ode² *suf.* denoting a path or way, as in *anode*, *cathode*. WH: Greek *hodos* way, path.

odeon *n.* in ancient Greece or Rome, a theatre in which poets and musicians contended for prizes. WH: 17C. French *odéum* or Latin *odeum*, from Greek *ōideion*, from *ōidē*. See ODE. The word was popularized by the chain of cinemas so named from the 1930s.

odious *a.* hateful, repulsive. WH: 14–15C. Old French (Modern French *odieux*), from Latin *odiosus*, from *odium* hatred, from *odi* I hate. See also -OUS.

odometer *n.* an instrument attached to a vehicle for measuring and recording the distance travelled. WH: 18C. French *odomètre*, from Greek *hodos* way + -METER.

-odont *comb. form* -toothed. WH: Greek *odous, odontos* tooth.

odontalgia *n.* toothache. WH: 17C. Greek. See ODONTO-, -ALGIA.

odontiasis *n.* cutting of teeth, dentition. WH: 18C. Modern Latin, from Greek *odontian* to cut teeth (from *odous, odontos* tooth). See also -IASIS.

odontic *a.* dental. WH: 17C. Greek *odontikos* fit for the teeth, from *odous, odontos* tooth. See also -IC.

odonto- *comb. form* having teeth or processes resembling teeth. WH: Greek *odous, odontos* tooth. See also -O-.

odontoblast *n.* a cell producing dentine. WH: 19C. ODONTO- + -BLAST.

odontocete *n.* a toothed whale. WH: 19C. ODONTO- + Greek *kētos* whale.

odontogeny *n.* the origin and development of teeth. WH: 19C. ODONTO- + -GENY.

odontoglossum *n.* any of various orchids of the tropical American genus *Odontoglossum*, with finely coloured flowers which have jagged edges. WH: 19C. Modern Latin, from Greek *odous, odontos* tooth + *glōssa* tongue.

odontography *n.* the description of teeth. WH: 19C. ODONTO- + -GRAPHY.

odontoid *a.* toothlike. WH: 19C. Greek *odontoeidēs*. See ODONTO-, also -OID.

odontology *n.* the science dealing with the structure and development of teeth. WH: 19C. ODONTO- + -LOGY.

odontoma *n.* a small tumour or excrescence composed of dentine. WH: 19C. French *odontome*. See ODONTO-, also -OMA.

odontophore *n.* a ribbon-like organ covered with teeth, used for mastication by certain molluscs. WH: 19C. Greek *odontophoros* bearng teeth. See ODONTO-, -PHORE.

odontorhyncous *a.* having toothlike serrations in the bill or beak. WH: 19C. ODONTO- + Greek *rhunkos* snout. See also -OUS.

odontotherapia *n.* the treatment and care of the teeth; dental hygiene or therapeutics. WH: late 20C. ODONTO- + Greek *therapeia* therapy (THERAPEUTIC).

odontotoxia *n.* unevenness of the teeth. WH: 19C. ODONTO- + Greek *toxon* bow. See also -IA.

odontotrypy *n.* the operation of perforating a tooth to draw off pus from an abscess in the internal cavity. WH: 19C. ODONTO- + Greek *trupē* hole, *trupan* to pierce (cp. TREPAN¹). See also -Y².

odour *n.* a smell, whether pleasant or unpleasant. WH: 12–14C. Old French *odor* (Modern French *odeur*), from Latin *odor* smell, scent.

odyssey *n.* (a story of) a long journey containing a series of adventures and vicissitudes. WH: 19C. *Odyssey*, the title of a Greek epic poem attributed to Homer, describing the adventures of Odysseus (Ulysses) on his way home to Ithaca after the fall of Troy, from Latin *Odyssea*, from Greek *Odusseia*, from *Odusseus* Odysseus.

oedema *n.* swelling due to accumulation of serous fluid in the cellular tissue; dropsy. WH: 14–15C. Late Latin, from Greek *oidēma*, from *oidein* to swell.

Oedipus complex *n.* a psychical impulse in offspring characterized by excessive love or sexual desire for the parent of the opposite sex and hatred for the parent of the same sex. WH: 16C. Greek *Oidipous*, a legendary Theban king who unknowingly killed his father and married his mother + COMPLEX.

oenanthic *a.* possessing a vinous odour. WH: 19C. Latin *oenanthe*, from Greek *oinanthē* vine shoot, vine blossom (from *oinē* vine + *anthē* blossom). See also -IC.

oeno- *comb. form* wine. WH: Greek *oinos* wine.

oenothera *n.* any plant of the genus *Oenothera*, which includes the evening primrose. WH: 17C. Modern Latin, from Greek *oinothēras* name of an unknown narcotic plant, lit. wine trap, from *oinos* wine + -*thēras* -catcher, from *thēra* hunting. Greek *oinothēras* was probably a misreading of *onothēras*, from *onos* ass.

o'er *prep., adv.* over. **WH:** 15C. Contr. of OVER.

oersted *n.* a unit of magnetic field or magnetizing force. **WH:** 19C. Hans Christian *Oersted*, 1777–1851, Danish physicist.

oesophagus *n.* the gullet, the canal by which food passes to the stomach. **WH:** 14–15C. Medieval Latin *ysophagus*, from Greek *oisophagos*, from obscure first element + (appar.) *-phagos* eating, eater. According to some, the first element is perhaps from Greek *oisein*, used as the future infinitive of *pherein* to carry. The overall meaning might thus be that which carries and eats.

oestrogen *n.* any of the female sex hormones which induce oestrus and encourage the growth of female secondary sexual characteristics. **WH:** early 20C. OESTRUS + -O- + -GEN.

oestrus *n.* the cyclical period of sexual receptivity in some female mammals, heat. **WH:** 17C. Latin, from Greek *oistros* gadfly, breeze, sting, frenzy. The word was originally the name of a biting fly. The current physiological sense dates from the 19C.

œuvre *n.* the works of an author, painter etc. **WH:** 19C. French work, from Latin *opera* (OPERA). Cp. CHEF-D'ŒUVRE.

of *prep.* denoting connection with or relation to in situation, origin or point of departure. **WH:** pre-1200. Old English, from Germanic, from Indo-European, represented also by Latin *ab*, Greek *apo*, Sanskrit *apa* away from. Rel. to OFF.

of- *pref.* toward, to, meeting, in, facing, as in *offence*. **WH:** Latin pref., from OB- with *b* assim. to *f*.

ofay *n.* (esp. used by blacks) a white person. *Also a.* **WH:** early 20C. Orig. unknown.

off *adv.* away, at a distance or to a distance in space or time (expressing removal, separation, suspension, discontinuance or termination). *Also prep., a., n., v.i., int.* **WH:** pre-1200. Old English *of*. The original preposition of, in the spelling *off*, came to be used as the emphatic form, i.e. as an adverb.

offal *n.* parts of the carcass of an animal, including the head, tail, kidneys, heart, liver etc. (used as food). **WH:** 14–15C. OFF + FALL, prob. based on Middle Dutch *afval*. The original sense was the refuse or waste from some process, such as milling grain, dressing wood, etc.

offend *v.t.* to wound the feelings of, to hurt. *Also v.i.* **WH:** 14–15C. Old French *offendre*, or from Latin *offendere*, from OF- + *-fendere* to strike. The sense was literal (to attack, to assault) to the 18C.

OFFER *abbr.* Office of Electricity Regulation. **WH:** Cp. OFGAS (Office of Gas Supply), OFTEL (Office of Telecommunications), OFWAT (Office of Water Services) etc.

offer *v.t.* to present, to tender for acceptance or refusal. *Also v.i., n.* **WH:** pre-1200. Old English *offrian*, from Germanic, from Latin *offerre*, from OF- + *ferre* to bring. The original sense was specifically to offer to God or a saint as an act of worship.

office *n.* a room, building or other place where business is carried on. **WH:** 12–14C. Old French, from Latin *officium* service, duty, function, from *opus* work + *facere*, *fic-* to do. The sense of room or building for business evolved in the 18C.

officinal *a.* (of a pharmaceutical product) ready-prepared. *Also n.* **WH:** 17C. Medieval Latin *officinalis*, from *officina* storeroom for medicines, from Latin workshop, contr. of *opificina*, from *opifex*, *opificis* workman, maker, doer.

officious *a.* aggressively interfering. **WH:** 15C. Latin *officiosus*, from *officium* OFFICE. See also -OUS. The original sense (to the 19C) was performing an office, efficacious. The current sense dates from the 16C.

often *adv.* frequently, many times. *Also a.* **WH:** 12–14C. Extended form of *oft* (pre-1200) (from Old English, from Germanic), prob. based on Middle English *selden* SELDOM.

ogdoad *n.* a set of eight. **WH:** 17C. Late Latin *ogdoad*, *ogdoadis*, from Greek, from *ogdoos* eighth, *oktō* eight. See also -AD[1].

ogee *n.* a wavelike moulding having an inner and outer curve like the letter S, a talon. *Also a.* **WH:** 12–14C. Prob. reduced form of OGIVE.

Ogen melon *n.* a variety of small sweet melon resembling a cantaloupe. **WH:** mid-20C. *Ogen*, the kibbutz in Israel where it was developed.

ogham *n.* an ancient Celtic system of writing consisting of an alphabet of twenty characters derived from the runes. **WH:** 18C. Old Irish *ogam*, modern Irish *ogham*, Gaelic *oghum*, from *Ogma*, its mythical inventor.

ogive *n.* a diagonal rib of a vault. **WH:** 14–15C. French, of unknown orig.

ogle *v.t.* to look or stare at with admiration, wonder etc., esp. amorously. *Also v.i., n.* **WH:** 17C. Prob. from Low Dutch. See also -LE[4]. Cp. Middle Dutch *ōghe* EYE[1].

ogre *n.* a fairy-tale giant living on human flesh. **WH:** 18C. French, of unknown orig. ? From Old French **orc*, from Latin *Orcus*, god of the infernal regions. Cp. ORC. The word first appears in the fairy tales of Charles Perrault, published in 1697, and may have been coined by him.

Ogygian *a.* of great or obscure antiquity, primeval. **WH:** 19C. *Ogyges*, a mythical Attic or Boeotian king + -IAN.

oh *int.* O. **WH:** 16C. Var. of O, influ. by French and Latin *oh*. Cp. AH.

ohm *n.* the unit of electrical resistance, that between two points on a conductor when a potential difference of one volt produces a current of one amp. **WH:** 19C. Georg Simon *Ohm*, 1787–1854, German physicist. The original form of the word was *ohma*.

oho *int.* used to express surprise, irony or exultation. **WH:** 12–14C. O + HO. Cp. AHA.

ohone *int., n.* a Scottish and Irish cry of lamentation. **WH:** 14–15C. Irish *ochón*, Gaelic *ochòin*.

oi *int.* used to give warning, attract attention etc. *Also n., a.* **WH:** mid-20C. Representation of a pronun. of HOY[1].

-oid *comb. form* forming adjectives and nouns denoting resemblance, as in *colloid*, *cycloid*, *rhomboid*. **WH:** Modern Latin *-oides*, Greek *-oidēs*, from *-o-* of the preceding element or as a connective + *-eidēs* having the form of, like, from *eidos* form. Cp. -ODE[1]. The Latin equivalent is *-formis*. See -FORM.

-oidea *comb. form* denoting zoological classes or families. **WH:** Modern Latin, from Latin *-oides* -OID + *-ea*, neut. pl. of *-eus* -EOUS.

oidium *n.* any of various fungal spores. **WH:** 19C. Modern Latin, from Greek *ōion* egg + *-idium*, Modern Latin dim. ending corr. to -IUM.

oik *n.* a stupid or uncouth person. **WH:** early 20C. Orig. unknown. ? Imit. of derision or dislike. Cp. YUCK.

oil *n.* an unctuous liquid, insoluble in water, soluble in ether and usually in alcohol, obtained from various animal and vegetable substances. *Also v.t., v.i.* **WH:** 12–14C. Old French *oile* (Modern French *huile*), from Latin *oleum* (olive) oil.

oink *n.* the grunt of a pig. *Also v.i.* **WH:** mid-20C. Imit.

ointment *n.* a soft unctuous preparation applied to diseased or injured parts or used as a cosmetic. **WH:** 12–14C. Alt. of Old French *oignement*, from Popular Latin *unguimentum*, var. of Latin *unguentum* UNGUENT. See also -MENT.

Oireachtas *n.* the legislature of the Republic of Ireland. **WH:** early 20C. Irish assembly, convocation.

Ojibwa *n.* a member of a N American people living in the westerly region of the Great Lakes. *Also a.* **WH:** 18C. Ojibwa *ojibwe*, said to mean puckered. The reference would be to the puckered moccasins worn by the people.

OK *a.* quite correct, all right. *Also adv., int., v.t., n.* **WH:** 19C. Appar. the initials of *orl korrect*, a fanciful respelling of *all correct*. The term was popularized as a slogan in the US 1840 election campaign. Hence a rival proposed origin from the initials of *Old Kinderhook*, a nickname (derived from his birthplace) of President Martin van Buren, 1782–1862, who then sought re-election.

okapi *n.* a ruminant mammal, *Okapia johnstoni*, with a dark chestnut coat and stripes on the hindquarters. **WH:** early 20C. African name.

okra *n.* an African plant, *Abelmoschus esculentus*, cultivated for its green pods used in curries, soups, stews etc.; also called *gumbo* and *ladies' fingers*. **WH:** 18C. Appar. W African. Cp. Igbo *okuro* okra, Twi *nkrakra* broth.

-ol *suf.* denoting a chemical compound containing an alcohol, or (loosely) an oil, as in *benzol*, *menthol*, *phenol*. **WH:** From ALCOHOL, or Latin *oleum* oil. Cp. -OLE[1].

old *a.* advanced in years or long in existence. **WH:** pre-1200. Old English *ald*, *eald*, from Germanic, a p.p. formation from Germanic base of Old English *alan* to grow, to nourish, appar. with sense grown up, adult. Cp. ELDER[1].

olé *int.* used to express approval or victory at a bullfight. **WH:** 19C. Spanish, from Arabic *wa-llāh*, from *wa-* and + *allāh* God, ALLAH.

-ole¹ *comb. form* forming names of organic compounds, esp. heterocyclic ones. **WH:** Latin *oleum* oil.

-ole² *suf.* indicating something small. **WH:** Latin dim. ending *-olus.*

oleaceous *a.* of the plant family Oleaceae, which includes ash, privet, olive, jasmine and lilac. **WH:** 19C. Modern Latin *Oleaceae,* from Latin *olea* olive tree. See also -ACEOUS.

oleaginous *a.* oily, greasy, unctuous. **WH:** 14–15C. Old French *oléagineux,* from Latin *oleaginus* oily, from *oleum* oil. See also -OUS.

oleander *n.* a poisonous evergreen shrub, *Nerium oleander,* with lanceolate leaves and pink or white flowers. **WH:** 16C. Medieval Latin, prob. alt. of Late Latin *lorandrum,* in turn alt. of Latin *rhododendron* RHODODENDRON, influ. by *laurea* laurel tree. The leaves of the oleander are similar to those of the laurel.

oleaster *n.* any shrub or tree of the genus *Elaeagnus,* esp. *E. angustifolia,* also called *Russian olive.* **WH:** 14–15C. Latin, from *olea* olive tree. See also -ASTER.

oleate *n.* a salt or ester of oleic acid. **WH:** 19C. OLEIC + -ATE¹.

olecranon *n.* the bony projection of the ulna at the elbow. **WH:** 18C. Greek *ōlekranon,* contr. of *ōlenokranon* head or point of the elbow, from *ōlenē* elbow + *kranion* head.

olefin *n.* any one of a group of hydrocarbons containing two atoms of hydrogen to one of carbon. **WH:** 19C. French *oléfiant* (formed as pres.p. of v. in *-fier* -FY, from Latin *oleum* oil; see also -ANT) + -IN¹.

oleic *a.* of, relating to or derived from oil. **WH:** 19C. Latin *oleum* oil + -IC.

olein *n.* an oily compound, chief constituent of fatty oils, triolene. **WH:** 19C. French *oléine,* from Latin *oleum* oil + *-ine* -IN¹, based on *glycerine* (GLYCEROL).

olent *a.* smelling, yielding fragrance. **WH:** 17C. Latin *olens, olentis,* pres.p. of *olere* to smell. See also -ENT.

oleo *n.* oleomargarine. **WH:** 19C. Abbr. of OLEOMARGARINE.

oleo- *comb. form* oil. **WH:** Latin *oleum* oil. See also -O-.

oleograph *n.* a picture printed in oil colours to resemble a painting. **WH:** 19C. OLEO- + -GRAPH.

oleomargarine *n.* a yellow fatty substance from beef tallow, used in margarine. **WH:** 19C. OLEO- + MARGARINE.

oleometer *n.* an instrument for determining the relative densities of oils. **WH:** 19C. OLEO- + -METER.

oleon *n.* an oily liquid obtained by the dry distillation of oleic acid with lime. **WH:** 19C. Latin *oleum* oil + -ON.

oleoresin *n.* a mixture of an essential oil and a resin. **WH:** 19C. OLEO- + RESIN.

oleraceous *a.* of the nature of a pot-herb. **WH:** 17C. Latin *oleraceus,* from *olus, oleris* pot-herb. See also -OUS, -ACEOUS.

oleum *n.* fuming sulphuric acid. **WH:** early 20C. Latin oil.

olfactory *a.* of, relating to or used in smelling. *Also n.* **WH:** 17C. Latin *olfactor-* (in *olfactoria* nosegay), from *olfactare,* freq. of *olfacere* to smell, from *olere* to smell + *facere* to make. See also -ORY².

olibanum *n.* a gum resin from certain species of *Boswellia,* formerly used in medicine, now as incense; frankincense. **WH:** 14–15C. Medieval Latin, ult. from Greek *libanos* frankincense tree, incense (of Semitic orig.), prob. through Arabic *al-lubān* storax.

olid *a.* rank, stinking. **WH:** 17C. Latin *olidus* smelling, from *olere* to smell. See also -ID.

oligarch *n.* a member of an oligarchy. **WH:** 17C. Greek *oligarkhēs,* from *oligos* few. See ARCH-.

oligo- *comb. form* denoting few, small. **WH:** Greek *oligos* small, little, few. See also -O-.

oligocarpous *a.* having few fruits. **WH:** 19C. OLIGO- + Greek *karpos* fruit. See also -OUS.

Oligocene *a.* of or relating to the age or strata between the Eocene and Miocene. *Also n.* **WH:** 19C. OLIGO- + Greek *kainos* new, recent.

oligochaete *n.* an annelid worm of the division Oligochaeta having bristles along its length to aid locomotion. *Also a.* **WH:** 19C. Modern Latin *Oligochaeta,* from *oligo-* OLIGO- + Greek *khaitē* mane (here, bristle).

oligochrome *a.* painted or decorated in few colours. **WH:** 19C. OLIGO- + Greek *khrōma* colour.

oligoclase *n.* a soda-lime feldspar resembling albite. **WH:** 19C. OLIGO- + Greek *klasis* breaking, cleavage. The mineral is so called as it was thought to have a less perfect cleavage than albite.

oligopod *a.* having few legs or feet. **WH:** early 20C. OLIGO- + -POD.

oligopoly *n.* a situation in the market in which a few producers control the supply of a product. **WH:** 19C. OLIGO- + Greek *pōlein* to sell, based on MONOPOLY.

oligopsony *n.* a situation in the market in which purchase is in the hands of a small number of buyers. **WH:** mid-20C. OLIGO- + Greek *opsōnein* to buy provisions, based on *monopsony* (MONO-).

oligosaccharide *n.* any carbohydrate consisting of a few monosaccharide units linked together. **WH:** mid-20C. OLIGO- + *saccharide* (SACCHAR-).

oligotrophic *a.* (of lakes etc. in rocky terrain) being nutritionally poor, sparsely vegetated, but rich in oxygen. **WH:** mid-20C. OLIGO- + Greek *trophē* nourishment. See also -IC.

olio *n.* a mixed dish. **WH:** 17C. Alt. of Spanish *olla,* from Latin *olla* pot, jar. Cp. OLLA.

olive *n.* an evergreen tree of the genus *Olea,* with narrow leathery leaves and clusters of oval drupes which when ripe and eaten unripe as a relish, esp. *O. europaea* and *O. africana.* *Also a.* **WH:** 12–14C. Old French, from Latin *oliva,* from Greek *elaia* olive tree, olive.

oliver *n.* a small trip-hammer worked by the foot, used in making nails etc. **WH:** 19C. ? From male forename *Oliver.*

Oliverian *a.* of or relating to the Protector Oliver Cromwell. *Also n.* **WH:** 17C. *Oliver* Cromwell, 1599–1658, English soldier, statesman and Puritan leader of the Parliamentary forces in the English Civil War + -IAN.

olla *n.* an olio. **WH:** 17C. Spanish, from Latin.

ollamh *n.* among the ancient Irish, a learned man, a doctor, a scholar. **WH:** 18C. Irish and Old Irish *ollam* learned man, doctor.

olm *n.* a blind, cave-dwelling type of European salamander, *Proteus anguinus.* **WH:** early 20C. German, from Old High German.

ology *n.* a science. **WH:** 19C. Independent adoption of *-ology,* from -O- + -LOGY.

oloroso *n.* a medium-sweet golden sherry. **WH:** 19C. Spanish fragrant. Cp. OLFACTORY.

Olympiad *n.* a period of four years, being the interval between the celebrations of the Olympic Games, a method of chronology used from 776 BC to AD 394. **WH:** 14–15C. French *Olympiade* or Latin *Olympias, Olympiadis,* or from Greek *Olumpias, Olumpiados,* from *olumpios,* a. of *Olumpos* Olympus. See also -AD¹. The original Olympic Games were held in Olympia, a district of Elis in S Greece. Olympus, the mountain that was the traditional home of the 12 greater gods of Greek mythology, is in N Thessaly.

-oma *comb. form* denoting a tumour or growth. **WH:** Greek *-ōma,* suf. of many nn. from vv. in *-ousthai.* Cp. -OME.

omadhaun *n.* a fool, a simpleton. **WH:** 19C. Irish *amadán.*

omasum *n.* the third stomach of a ruminant. **WH:** 18C. Latin bullock's tripe.

ombre *n.* a game of cards, for two, three or five players, popular in the 17th and 18th cents. **WH:** 17C. Spanish HOMBRE.

ombré *a.* (of a fabric etc.) with colours shading into each other from light to dark. **WH:** 19C. French, p.p. of *ombrer* to shade.

ombro- *comb. form* denoting rain. **WH:** Greek *ombros* shower of rain. See also -O-.

ombrology *n.* the branch of meteorology concerned with rainfall. **WH:** 19C. OMBRO- + -LOGY.

ombrometer *n.* a rain gauge. **WH:** 18C. OMBRO- + -METER.

ombudsman *n.* an official investigator of complaints against government bodies or employees; in the UK, the Parliamentary Commissioner for Administration. **WH:** mid-20C. Swedish, from *ombud* commissioner, from Old Norse *umboth* charge, commission, *umbothsmathr* commissary, manager. The office of ombudsman originated in Sweden in 1809 and was subsequently introduced to other countries, including Britain in 1967.

-ome *comb. form* denoting a mass or part. **WH:** Anglicized form of -OMA.

omega *n.* the last letter of the Greek alphabet (Ω, ω). **WH:** 16C. Greek *ō mega,* lit. great O. Cp. OMICRON.

omelette *n.* a flat dish made with beaten eggs cooked in fat, eaten plain or seasoned and filled with herbs, cheese etc. **WH:** 17C. French, earlier *amelette,* alt. of *alemette,* from *alemelle* knife-blade (with *la lemelle* misdivided as *l'alemelle*), from Latin LAMELLA. The reference is probably to the thin flat shape that an omelette has.

omen *n.* a sign taken as indicating a good or evil event or outcome. *Also v.t.* WH: 16C. Latin *omen, ominis*. Cp. OMINOUS.

omentum *n.* a fold of the peritoneum connecting the viscera with each other. WH: 14–15C. Latin.

omer *n.* a Hebrew measure of capacity, 5 1/16 pts (about 2.8 l). WH: 17C. Hebrew *'ōmer*.

omertà *n.* a conspiracy of silence, part of the Mafia code of honour. WH: 19C. Italian, dial. var. of *umiltà* humility. The term originally referred to the Mafia code which obliged members to submit to their leader.

omicron *n.* the 15th letter of the Greek alphabet (O, o), the short o. WH: 17C. Greek *o mikron*, lit. little O. Cp. OMEGA.

ominous *a.* threatening, portending evil. WH: 16C. Latin *ominosus*, from *omen, ominis* OMEN. See also -OUS.

omit *v.t.* to leave out, not to include. WH: 14–15C. Latin *omittere*, from OB- + *mittere* to send, to let go.

ommateum *n.* a compound eye. WH: 19C. Modern Latin, from Greek *omma, ommatos* eye.

omni- *comb. form* universally, in all ways, of all things. WH: Latin *omnis* all, every + -*i*-.

omnibus *n.* a bus. *Also a.* WH: 19C. French, also *voiture omnibus* carriage for all (from Latin *omnibus*, dat. pl. of *omnis* all). Cp. BUS.

omnicompetence *n.* competence in all areas or matters. WH: early 20C. OMNI- + *competence* (COMPETENT).

omnidirectional *a.* (capable of) moving, sending or receiving in every direction (of radio waves, a radio transmitter or receiver). WH: early 20C. OMNI- + *directional* (DIRECTION).

omnifarious *a.* of all kinds. WH: 17C. Latin *omnifarius*, from *omni-* OMNI- + -*farium* parts, as in *bifariam* in two parts. See also -OUS. Cp. MULTIFARIOUS.

OMNIMAX® *a.* (of a film) shot for showing through a special lens on a hemispheral screen. WH: late 20C. OMNI- + MAXIMUM, based on IMAX®.

omnipotent *a.* almighty. WH: 12–14C. Old French, from Latin *omnipotens, omnipotentis*. See OMNI-, POTENT.

omnipresent *a.* present in every place at the same time. WH: 17C. Medieval Latin *omnipresens, omnipresentis*. See OMNI-, PRESENT[1].

omniscience *n.* infinite knowledge. WH: 17C. Medieval Latin *omniscientia*, from *omni-* OMNI- + *scientia* knowledge (SCIENCE).

omnium *n.* in the Stock Exchange, the aggregate value of the different stocks in which a loan is funded. WH: 18C. Latin, lit. of all (things), gen. pl. of *omnis* all.

omnivore *n.* a creature that eats any type of available food (i.e. vegetable matter and meat). WH: 19C. French, from Latin *omnivorus*, or back-formation from *omnivorous*, from same source. See OMNI-, -VORE.

omo- *comb. form* of or relating to the shoulder. WH: Greek *ōmos* shoulder. See also -O-.

omohyoid *a.* of or relating to the shoulder blade and the hyoid bone. *Also n.* WH: 19C. OMO- + HYOID.

omophagic *a.* eating raw flesh. WH: 19C. Greek *ōmophagia*, from *ōmos* raw + -*phagia* (-PHAGE). See also -IC.

omoplate *n.* the shoulder blade. WH: 16C. Greek *ōmoplatē*, from *ōmo-* OMO- + *platē* broad surface, blade.

omosternum *n.* an ossified process at the anterior extremity of the sternum, in certain animals. WH: 19C. OMO- + Modern Latin *sternum*, Greek *sternon* breast.

omphacite *n.* a green variety of pyroxene. WH: 19C. Greek *omphakinos* made of unripe grapes, from *omphax* unripe + -ITE[1].

omphalo- *comb. form* relating to the navel. WH: Greek *omphalos* navel. See also -O-.

on *prep.* in or as in contact with, esp. as supported by, covering, encircling or suspended from the upper surface or level of. *Also adv., a., n.* WH: pre-1200. Old English, unstressed var. of *an*, from Germanic, rel. to Greek *ana* on, upon, Sanskrit *anu* along, Old Church Slavonic *na* on. Cp. German *an*.

-on *suf.* denoting a chemical compound, as in *interferon*. WH: From ending of ION, influ. by Greek *ōn* being (cp. -ONT), -*on* ending of neut. nn., or ending of COTTON, NYLON, or German -*on* -ONE.

onager *n.* a wild ass, esp. *Equus hemionus* of Asian deserts. WH: 12–14C. Latin, from Greek *onagros*, from *onos* ass + *agrios* wild.

onanism *n.* masturbation. WH: 18C. French *onanisme*, from Modern Latin *onanismus*, from *Onan*, the son of Judah, who 'spilled it [his seed] on the ground' (Gen. xxxviii.9), i.e. practised coitus interruptus.

once *adv.* one time. *Also n., a., conj.* WH: 12–14C. ONE + -S[2].

onchocerciasis *n.* a disease caused by infestation with parasitic threadworms of the genus *Onchocerca*, esp. river blindness. WH: early 20C. Modern Latin *Onchocerca*, from Greek *ogkos* barb + *kerkos* tail. See also -IASIS.

onco- *comb. form* denoting a tumour. WH: Greek *ogkos* mass, bulk, swelling. See also -O-.

oncogene *n.* any of several genes capable of causing cancer. WH: mid-20C. ONCO- + GENE.

oncology *n.* the study of tumours and cancers. WH: 19C. ONCO- + -LOGY.

oncotomy *n.* the opening of an abscess or the excision of a tumour. WH: 18C. ONCO- + -TOMY.

ondes martenot *n.* an electronic keyboard instrument producing one note of variable pitch. WH: mid-20C. French *ondes* (*musicales*) (musical) waves + Maurice *Martenot*, 1898–1980, French inventor. The instrument was patented in 1922 by Martenot, who himself named it *ondes musicales*.

on dit *n.* hearsay, gossip. WH: 19C. French they say, from *on* one + 3rd pers. sing. pres. of *dire* to say.

one *a.* single, undivided. *Also pron., n., v.t.* WH: pre-1200. Old English *ān*, from Germanic, from Indo-European base also of Latin *unus*. Cp. German *ein*. The pronunciation with an initial 'w' evolved in the 15C.

-one *suf.* denoting certain chemical compounds, esp. hydrocarbons, as in *acetone, ketone, ozone*. WH: Greek -*ōnē*, a fem. suf.

oneiric *a.* of or relating to dreams. WH: 19C. Greek *oneiros* dream + -IC.

oneiro- *comb. form* of or relating to dreams. WH: Greek *oneiros* dream. See also -O-.

oneirodynia *n.* nightmare, disturbed sleep. WH: 19C. ONEIRO- + Greek *odunē* pain. See also -IA.

oneirology *n.* the science of dreams. WH: 19C. ONEIRO- + -LOGY.

oneiromancy *n.* divination by dreams. WH: 17C. ONEIRO- + -MANCY.

onerous *a.* heavy, troublesome. WH: 14–15C. Old French *onéreux* or Latin *onerosus*, from *onus, oneris* load, burden. See also -OUS.

oneself *pron.* the reflexive and emphatic form *one*. WH: 16C. Orig. *one's* (from ONE + -'S) + SELF, but later assim. to HIMSELF, HERSELF, etc.

onion *n.* a plant, *Allium cepa*, with an underground bulb of several coats and a pungent smell and flavour, much used in cookery. WH: 12–14C. Old French *oignon*, from alt. of Latin *unionis* a kind of onion, of unknown orig.

onkus *a.* bad, no good. WH: early 20C. Orig. unknown.

only *a.* single or alone in its or their kind. *Also adv., conj.* WH: 12–14C. Old English *ānlic*, var. of *ǣnlic*, from Germanic bases of ONE, -LY[1].

onomastic *a.* of or relating to a name. WH: 16C. Greek *onomastikos* pertaining to naming, from *onoma* name. See also -IC.

onomato- *comb. form* of or relating to a name or word. WH: Greek *onoma, onomatos* name. See also -O-.

onomatopoeia *n.* the formation of words in imitation of the sounds associated with or suggested by the things signified. WH: 16C. Late Latin, from Greek *onomatopoiia* making of words, from *onomatopoios*, from *onoma, onomatos* word, name + -*poios* making, from *poiein* to make, to create. See also -IA.

-ont *comb. form* denoting an individual of a specified type, as in *symbiont*. WH: Greek *ōn, ontos* being, pres.p. of *einai* to be, to exist.

onto- *comb. form* being. WH: Greek *ōn, ontos* being. See -ONT.

ontogenesis *n.* the origin and development of the individual organism. WH: 19C. ONTO- + -GENESIS.

ontology *n.* the branch of metaphysics dealing with the theory of pure being or reality. WH: 18C. Modern Latin *ontologia*. See ONTO-, -LOGY.

onus *n.* a duty or obligation. WH: 19C. Latin load, burden.

onychia *n.* inflammation of or near the nail, a whitlow. WH: 19C. Greek *onux, onukhos* nail, claw. See also -O-.

onychophoran n. a soft-bodied arthropod of the class Onychophora, which have segmented bodies and are intermediate in evolution between annelids and arthropods. *Also a.* WH: 19C. Modern Latin *Onychophora*, from Greek *onux, onukhos* nail, claw + *-phoros* bearing. See also -AN.

-onym *comb. form* denoting a name or word, as in *pseudonym, antonym.* WH: -O- + Greek *onuma, onoma* name, later taken from HOMONYM, SYNONYM.

onyx n. a variety of quartz resembling agate, with variously-coloured layers. WH: 12–14C. Old French *oniche*, from Latin *onyx, onychis*, from Greek *onux, onukhos* nail, claw, onyx.

oo- *comb. form* of or relating to ova or an egg. WH: Greek *ōo-*, from *ōion* egg, ovum. See also -O-. Cp. OVI-[1].

oocyte n. the unfertilized ovum or egg cell. WH: 19C. OO- + -CYTE.

oodles n.pl. a great quantity, superabundance. WH: 19C. Orig. unknown. Cp. BOODLE, CABOODLE.

oof n. money. WH: 19C. Abbr. of *ooftish*, from Yiddish *ooftisch*, from German *auf (dem) Tische* on (the) table, i.e. (money) laid on the table.

oogamous a. reproducing by the union of male and female cells. WH: 19C. OO- + Greek *gamos* marriage. See also -OUS.

oogenesis n. the origin and development of an ovum. WH: 19C. OO- + GENESIS.

ooh *int.* used to express delight, surprise, pain, admiration etc. *Also v.i.* WH: early 20C. Natural exclamation. Cp. O.

oolite n. a limestone composed of grains or particles of sand like the roe of a fish. WH: 19C. French *oölithe*, Modern Latin *oolites*. See OO-, -LITE.

oology n. the study of birds' eggs. WH: 19C. French *oölogie*, Modern Latin *oologia*. See OO-, -LOGY.

oolong n. a kind of China tea. WH: 19C. Chinese *wūlóng*, from *wū* black + *lóng* dragon.

oompah n. an imitation or representation of the sound of a large brass musical instrument. *Also v.i.* WH: 19C. Imit.

oomph n. vigour, energy. WH: mid-20C. Orig. uncertain. ? Imit.

-oon *suf.* forming nouns, as in *balloon, poltroon.* WH: French *-on*, Italian *-one*, Spanish *-on*, from Latin *-on-*.

oopak n. a variety of black tea. WH: 19C. Chinese dial. *upak*, from *Hupeh*, a central province of China.

oophorectomy n. a surgical operation to remove an ovary. WH: 19C. Greek *ōophoron* ovary (use as n. of neut. of *ōophoros* egg-bearing, from *ōo-* OO- + *-phoros* -PHORE) + -ECTOMY.

oops *int.* used to express surprise, dismay, apology, esp. on having dropped something. WH: mid-20C. Natural exclamation. Cp. *oops-a-daisy* (UPSYDAISY).

Oort cloud n. a cloud of small frozen bodies orbiting the solar system. WH: mid-20C. Jan Hendrik *Oort*, 1900–92, Dutch astronomer.

oosperm n. a fertilized egg. WH: 19C. OO- + -SPERM.

oospore n. a fertilized ovum. WH: 19C. OO- + Greek *spora* SPORE.

ooze n. wet mud, slime. *Also v.i., v.t.* WH: pre-1200. Old English *wāse*, from Germanic. Cp. German *Wasen* turf.

op n. (an) operation. WH: early 20C. Abbr. of *operation* (OPERATE).

op- *pref.* toward, to, meeting, in, facing, as in *oppose, oppress.* WH: Latin pref., from OB- with *b* assim. to *p*.

opah n. a rare Atlantic fish, *Lampris guttatus*, of the mackerel family, having brilliant colours. WH: 18C. W African.

opal n. an amorphous, transparent, vitreous form of hydrous silica, several kinds of which are characterized by a play of iridescent colours and used as gems. *Also a.* WH: 16C. French *opale* or Latin *opalus*, prob. ult. from Sanskrit *upala* stone, precious stone.

opaque a. impervious to rays of light, not transparent. *Also n.* WH: 14–15C. Latin *opacus* shaded dark, influ. in spelling by French *opaque*.

op art n. a type of abstract art employing shapes arranged to produce an optical illusion, esp. that of movement. WH: mid-20C. Abbr. of *optical* (OPTIC) + ART.

op. cit. *abbr. opere citato*, in the work cited. WH: 19C. Abbr. of OPERE CITATO.

ope a., v.t., v.i. (to) open. WH: 14–15C. Reduced form of OPEN.

opeidoscope n. an instrument for exhibiting sound vibrations by means of reflections of light. WH: 19C. Greek *ōps, opos* voice + *eidos* form, image + -SCOPE.

open a. not closed, not obstructed. *Also n., v.t., v.i.* WH: pre-1200. Old English, from Germanic base having the form of a p.p. from UP.

opera n. a dramatic entertainment in which music forms an essential part. WH: 17C. Italian, from Latin labour, work produced, rel. to *opus, operis* work, OPUS. Cp. OEUVRE.

operate v.t. to work or control the working of. *Also v.i.* WH: 17C. Latin *operatus*, p.p. of *operari* to work, to expend labour on, from *opus, operis* work. See also -ATE[3].

operculum n. a lid or cover as of the leaf of the pitcher plant, *Nepenthes*, or of the spore vessel in mosses. WH: 18C. Latin lid, covering, from *operire* to cover. See also -CULE.

opere citato *adv.* in the work cited. WH: 19C. Latin in the work cited, abl. of *opus citatum* the work quoted. See OPUS, CITE.

operetta n. a short opera of a light character. WH: 18C. Italian, dim. of OPERA.

operettist n. a performer in an operetta. WH: early 20C. OPERETTA + -IST.

operon n. a group of genes controlled by another gene. WH: mid-20C. French *opéron*, from *opérer* to effect, to work. See also -ON.

operose a. done with or requiring much labour, laborious, wearisome. WH: 17C. Latin *operosus*, from *opus, operis* work. See also -OSE[1].

ophicleide n. a musical wind instrument, consisting of a wide conical tube with usu. eleven finger-levers and a bass or alto pitch. WH: 19C. French *ophicléide*, from Greek *ophis* snake + *kleis, kleidos* key. The U-shaped instrument was a development of the serpent.

ophidian n. a reptile of the suborder Serpentes (formerly Ophidia). *Also a.* WH: 19C. Modern Latin *Ophidia*, from Greek *ophis, ophidos* snake. See also -IA, -IAN.

ophio- *comb. form* of or relating to a snake. WH: Greek *ophis* snake. See also -O-.

ophiolatry n. worship of snakes. WH: 19C. OPHIO- + -LATRY.

ophiology n. the study of snakes. WH: 19C. OPHIO- + -LOGY.

ophiophagous a. feeding on snakes. WH: 17C. OPHIO- + -PHAGOUS.

ophite n. serpentine, serpentine marble. WH: 17C. Latin *ophites*, from Greek *ophitēs* serpentine stone, from *ophis* snake. See also -ITE[1].

ophthalmia n. inflammation of the eye. WH: 14–15C. Late Latin, from Greek, from *ophthalmos* eye. See also -IA.

ophthalmic a. of or relating to the eye. WH: 17C. Latin *ophthalmicus*, from Greek *ophthalmikos*, from *ophthalmos* eye. See also -IC.

ophthalmitis n. ophthalmia, esp. inflammation involving all the structures of the eye. WH: 19C. Greek *ophthalmos* eye + -ITIS.

ophthalmo- *comb. form* of or relating to the eye. WH: Greek *ophthalmos* eye. See also -O-.

ophthalmology n. the science of the eye, its structure, functions and diseases. WH: 19C. OPHTHALMO- + -LOGY.

ophthalmoscope n. an instrument for examining the inner structure of the eye. WH: 19C. OPHTHALMO- + -SCOPE.

-opia *comb. form* denoting a condition or defect of the eye, as in *myopia, diplopia.* WH: Greek *-ōpia*, from *ōps, ōpos* eye, face. See also -IA.

opiate[1] n. a medicine compounded with opium. *Also a.* WH: 14–15C. Medieval Latin *opiatus*, from p.p. of *opiare*, from Latin *opium*. See OPIUM, also -ATE[2].

opiate[2] v.t. to treat with opium. WH: 16C. Medieval Latin *opiatus*, p.p. of *opiare*. See OPIATE[1], also -ATE[3].

opine v.i., v.t. to think, to suppose (that). WH: 14–15C. Latin *opinari* to think, to believe.

opinion n. a judgement or belief falling short of positive knowledge. WH: 12–14C. Old French, from Latin *opinio, opinionis*, from stem of *opinari* to think, to believe. See also -ION.

opistho- *comb. form* behind. WH: Greek *opisthen* behind. See also -O-.

opisthobranchiate a. belonging to the Opisthobranchiata, an order of gastropods having the gills behind the heart. WH: 19C. Modern Latin *Opisthobranchiata*, from *Opistho-* OPISTHO- + Greek *bragkhia* gills. See also -ATE[2].

opisthognathous a. having receding jaws or teeth. WH: 19C. OPISTHO- + Greek *gnathos* jaw. See also -OUS.

opisthograph *n.* a manuscript or tablet having writing on the back as well as the front. WH: 17C. Greek *opisthographos*. See OPISTHO-, -GRAPH.

opium *n.* an addictive narcotic drug prepared from the dried exudation of the unripe capsules of the poppy, esp. the opium poppy. WH: 12–14C. Latin, from Greek *opion* poppy juice, opium, dim. of *opos* vegetable juice, from Indo-European base meaning water.

opoponax *n.* the resinous juice from the root of *Opoponax chironium*, formerly used as a stimulant and in medicine. WH: 14–15C. Latin, from Greek, from *opos* juice + *panax*. See PANACEA.

opossum *n.* an American marsupial quadruped of the family Didelphidae, with a prehensile tail and a thumb on the hind foot, most species of which are arboreal and one aquatic. WH: 17C. Virginia Algonquian *opassom*, from *op* white + *assom* dog, doglike animal. Cp. POSSUM.

opotherapy *n.* the treatment of diseases with prepared extracts of glands or organs. WH: 19C. Greek *opos* juice + *therapy* (THERAPEUTIC).

oppilate *v.t.* to block up, to obstruct. WH: 14–15C. Latin *oppilatus*, p.p. of *oppilare* to stop up, from OP- + *pilare* to ram down, to stop up. See also -ATE³.

oppo *n.* a colleague or friend. WH: mid-20C. Abbr. of *opposite number* (OPPOSITE).

opponent *n.* a person who opposes, esp. in a debate or contest. *Also a.* WH: 16C. Latin *opponens*, *opponentis*, pres.p. of *opponere* to set against, from OP- + *ponere* to place. See also -ENT.

opportune *a.* occurring, done etc. at a favourable moment. WH: 14–15C. Old French *opportun*, from Latin *opportunus* (of wind) driving towards the harbour, (hence) seasonable, from OP- + *portus* harbour. *Portunus* was a Roman protecting god of harbours.

oppose *v.t.* to set against as an obstacle or contrast (to). *Also v.i.* WH: 14–15C. Old French *opposer*, blend of *poser* to place, to lay down, and Latin *opponere* to oppose, to object to, to set against. Cp. OPPONENT. The original meaning (to the 17C) was to confront with objections, to examine, to interrogate.

opposite *a.* situated in front of or contrary in position (to). *Also n., adv., prep.* WH: 14–15C. Old French, from Latin *oppositus*, p.p. of *opponere*. See OPPONENT.

opposition *n.* the act or state of opposing. WH: 14–15C. Old French, from Latin *oppositio*, *oppositionis*, from *oppositus*, p.p. of *opponere*. See also OPPONENT, also -ION.

oppress *v.t.* to tyrannize over, to keep subservient. WH: 12–14C. Old French *oppresser*, from Medieval Latin *oppressare*, from Latin *oppressus*, p.p. of *opprimere*, from OP- + *premere* PRESS¹. The original meaning (to the 19C) was to put down, to suppress. The current sense dates from the 14–15C.

opprobrium *n.* disgrace, infamy, ignominy, obloquy. WH: 17C. Latin infamy, reproach, from OP- + *probrum* shameful deed, disgrace, use as n. of neut. of *probus* disgraceful.

oppugn *v.t.* to oppose, to dispute, to call in question. WH: 14–15C. Latin *oppugnare*, from OP- + *pugnare* to fight.

opsimath *n.* a person who acquires education late in life. WH: 19C. Back-formation from *opsimathy* (17C), from Greek *opsimathia*, from *opsimathēs* late in learning, from *opsi-* late + *math-* to learn. See also -Y².

opsomania *n.* an abnormal craving for some special kind of food. WH: 19C. Modern Latin, from Greek *opson* cooked meat, relish, rich fare + -MANIA.

opsonin *n.* an antibody in the blood which renders germs more vulnerable to destruction by phagocytes. WH: early 20C. Latin *opsonare* to buy provisions, to cater, from Greek *opsōnein*. See also -IN¹.

opt *v.i.* to make a choice (for, between). WH: 19C. French *opter*, from Latin *optare* to choose, to desire. Cp. ADOPT.

optative *a.* expressing a wish or desire. *Also n.* WH: 16C. French *optatif*, from Late Latin *optativus*, from *optatus*, p.p. of *optare* to choose. See also -IVE.

optic *a.* of or relating to vision or the eye. *Also n.* WH: 14–15C. Old French *optique* or Medieval Latin *opticus*, from Greek *optikos*, from *optos* seen, visible. See also -IC.

optimism *n.* a sanguine temperament, disposition to take a hopeful view of things. WH: 18C. French *optimisme*, from Latin OPTIMUM.

Cp. PESSIMISM. The French word was based on Latin *optimum* as used by Leibniz in 1710 in connection with his theory that this is the 'best of all possible worlds'. He presumably based it on MAXIMUM and MINIMUM.

optimum *n.* the most favourable condition. *Also a.* WH: 19C. Latin, use as n. of neut. of *optimus* best. Cp. OPTIMISM.

option *n.* the right, power or liberty of choosing. WH: 16C. French, or from Latin *optio*, *optionis*, from *opt-*, stem of *optare*. See OPT, also -ION.

opto- *comb. form* of or relating to sight or optics. WH: Greek *optos* seen, visible. See also -O-.

optoelectronics *n.* the branch of technology concerned with visual and electronic signals. WH: mid-20C. OPTO- + *electronics* (ELECTRONIC).

optometer *n.* an instrument for ascertaining the range of vision and other powers of the eye. WH: 18C. OPTO- + -METER.

optophone *n.* a device for enabling the blind to read by sound. WH: early 20C. OPTO- + -PHONE.

opulent *a.* rich, wealthy. WH: 16C. Latin *opulens*, *opulentis*, from *opes*, resources, wealth. See also -ULENT.

opuntia *n.* a cactus of the genus *Opuntia*, the prickly pear. WH: 17C. Latin from *Opus*, *Opuntis*, from *Opus*, a city of Locris, Greece, where it was said to grow. See also -IA.

opus *n.* a work, esp. a musical composition. WH: 18C. Latin work. Cp. OPERA.

or¹ *conj.* a disjunctive introducing an alternative. WH: 12–14C. Reduced form of OTHER.

†or² *prep.* ere, before, sooner than. WH: pre-1200. Old English *ār* or (later) Old Norse *ár*, rel. to Old English *ær* ERE.

or³ *n.* gold. *Also a.* WH: 14–15C. Old French, ult. from Latin *aurum* gold.

-or *suf.* denoting agency or condition, as in *actor*, *author*, *creator*, *equator*. WH: Either Old French *-or*, *-ur* (Modern French *-eur*) or from Latin *-or*, or from Old French *-ëor*, *-ëur* (Modern French *-eur*), or from Latin *-ator*, *-etor*, *-itor*. In some cases var. of -ER¹, -ER², or from Old French *-oir*. American *-or* is often var. of -OUR.

orache *n.* a plant, *Atriplex hortensis*, sometimes used as a vegetable; also called *saltbush*. WH: 12–14C. Old French *arache* (Modern French *arroche*), from Latin *atriplex*, *atriplicis*, from Greek *atraphaxus*, *atraphaxis*.

Oracle® *abbr.* the teletext service of British Independent Television, replaced by Teletext in 1993. WH: late 20C. ORACLE, later analysed as acronym of *optimal reception of announcements by coded line electronics*.

oracle *n.* the answer of a god or inspired priest to a request for advice or prophecy. *Also v.i., v.t.* WH: 14–15C. Old French, from Latin *oraculum*, from *orare* to speak, to plead, to pray. See also -CLE.

oracy *n.* skill in spoken communication and self-expression. WH: mid-20C. Latin *os*, *oris* mouth + -ACY, based on *literacy* (LITERATE).

oral *a.* spoken, not written; by word of mouth. *Also n.* WH: 17C. Late Latin *oralis*, from Latin *os*, *oris* mouth. See also -AL¹.

Orange *a.* of or relating to the Orangemen. WH: 17C. *Orange*, a town and principality in S France. The Orangemen arose as a Protestant political society formed in 1795 to defend and uphold Protestant supremacy in Ireland, taking their name from William III of England (William of Orange), who won a victory over the deposed Catholic king James II at the Battle of the Boyne in 1690.

orange *n.* the large roundish cellular pulpy fruit of *Citrus aurantium* or *C. sinensis*. *Also a.* WH: 14–15C. Old French *orenge* in *pomme d'orenge*, ult. from Arabic *nāranj*, from Persian *nārang*, from Sanskrit *nāraṅga*. The word is popularly associated with Old French *or* gold (OR³) and with *Orange* (ORANGE), the town in S France through which oranges were shipped north.

orang-utan *n.* a large, red-haired, arboreal anthropoid ape, *Pongo pygmaeus*, of Borneo and Sumatra. WH: 17C. Malay *orang hutan* forest person.

orarium *n.* a scarf sometimes wound round the handle of the medieval crozier. WH: 18C. Latin napkin, from *os*, *oris* mouth, face. See also -ARIUM.

oration *n.* a formal speech, dealing with some important subject in elevated language. WH: 14–15C. Latin *oratio, orationis* speech, discourse, from *oratus,* p.p. of *orare* to speak, to plead. See also -ATION.

oratorio *n.* a musical composition for voices and instruments, usually semi-dramatic in character, having a scriptural theme. WH: 17C. Italian, from Ecclesiastical Latin *oratorium* ORATORY. The form of composition originated in the musical services held in the church of the Oratory of St Philip Neri in Rome.

oratory *n.* a small chapel, esp. one for private devotions. WH: 12–14C. Old French *oratoire,* from Ecclesiastical Latin *oratorium,* use as n. of neut. of *oratorius* pertaining to an orator, from *orator* orator + *-ius.* See ORATION, also -ORY¹. Cp. ORATORIO.

orb *n.* a sphere, a globe. *Also v.t., v.i.* WH: 14–15C. Latin *orbis* circle, disc, ring, of unknown orig.

orbit *n.* the path of a celestial body around another. *Also v.t., v.i.* WH: 16C. Latin *orbita* wheel-track, orbit, from *orbis* wheel, circle.

orc *n.* a whale of the genus *Orca,* esp. *O. gladiator,* a grampus. WH: 16C. French *orque* or Latin *orca* large sea creature (prob. killer whale).

Orcadian *a.* of or relating to the Orkney Islands. *Also n.* WH: 17C. Latin *Orcades* Orkney Islands, off the N coast of mainland Scotland + -IAN.

orchard *n.* an enclosure containing fruit trees, or a plantation of these. WH: pre-1200. Old English *ortgeard, orcgeard,* from bases of Latin *hortus* garden + YARD² (both of which are rel. to each other and to GARDEN).

orchestra *n.* a body of musicians playing a variety of instruments, performing in a theatre, concert room etc. WH: 16C. Latin, from Greek *orkhēstra,* from *orkheisthai* to dance. The original sense was the area in front of the stage in the Greek theatre where the chorus danced and sang.

orchid *n.* any of a large order of monocotyledonous plants, the Orchidaceae, of which the genus *Orchis* is the type, characterized by tuberous roots and flowers usually of a fantastic shape and brilliant colours in which the pistils and stamens are united with the floral axis. WH: 19C. Modern Latin *Orchidaceae,* from *orchid-,* wrongly taken as stem of Latin *orchis* a kind of orchid, from Greek *orkhis* orchid, testicle. See ORCHIDO-, also -ID. The reference is to the shape of the plant's root. The English word was introduced by the botanist John Lindley in the third edition of his *School Botany* (1845).

orchidectomy *n.* the surgical removal of one or both testicles. WH: 19C. ORCHIDO- + -ECTOMY.

orchido- *comb. form* denoting a testicle or testicles. WH: Greek *orkhis* orchid, testicle. See also -O-. For the element *-id,* see ORCHID. The genitive of Greek *orkhis* is actually *orkheōs,* so that the proper combining form should be *orchio-.*

orchil *n.* a violet, purple or red dye obtained from various lichens, esp. *Roccella tinctoria.* WH: 15C. Spanish *orchilla,* of unknown orig.

orchitis *n.* inflammation of the testicles. WH: 18C. Greek *orkhis* testicle + -ITIS.

orcin *n.* a colourless crystalline compound obtained from several species of lichen, yielding colours used for dyeing on treatment with various reagents. WH: 19C. Modern Latin *orcina,* Italian *orcello* ORCHIL. See also -IN¹.

ordain *v.t.* to set apart for an office or duty, to appoint and consecrate, to confer holy orders on. WH: 12–14C. Old French *ordener* (Modern French *ordonner*), from Latin *ordinare,* from *ordo, ordinis* ORDER. The original meaning (to the 16C) was to arrange in rows, to draw up in order of battle, also (to the 19C) to appoint (a person) to an official position. The current ecclesiastical sense dates from the first, however.

ordeal *n.* an experience testing endurance, patience etc. WH: pre-1200. Old English *ordāl* judgement, verdict, from Germanic base meaning to share out. Cp. German *Urteil* judgement, verdict. An ordeal was originally a test of guilt or innocence by means of pain or torture, the outcome being regarded as the judgement of God.

order *n.* regular or methodical disposition or arrangement. *Also v.t., v.i.* WH: 12–14C. Old French *ordre,* earlier *ordene,* from Latin *ordo, ordinis* row, series, course, regular arrangement, of unknown orig.

orderly *n.* a soldier who attends on an officer to carry orders, messages etc. WH: 16C. ORDER + -LY¹. The sense of a soldier who carries orders developed in the 18C from the adjective of ORDER, as did that of a hospital attendant in the 19C.

ordinaire *n.* everyday drinking wine, *vin ordinaire.* WH: 19C. French ORDINARY.

ordinal *a.* denoting order or position in a series. *Also n.* WH: 14–15C. Late Latin *ordinalis* denoting order in a series, from *ordo, ordinis* ORDER. See also -AL¹. The sense of a book setting out the order for church services dates from the 12–14C and has its origin in Medieval Latin *ordinale,* neuter singular (used as noun) of *ordinalis.*

ordinance *n.* an order or regulation laid down by a constituted authority. WH: 12–14C. Old French *ordenance* (Modern French *ordonnance*), from Medieval Latin *ordinantia,* from Latin *ordinare* ORDAIN. See also -ANCE. Cp. ORDNANCE.

ordinary *a.* normal, not exceptional or unusual. *Also n.* WH: 14–15C. Latin *ordinarius* orderly, usual, from *ordo, ordinis* ORDER. See also -ARY¹. The original sense (as a noun) was rule, ordinance, dating from the 12–14C, with a source in Old French *ordinarie* (Modern French *ordinaire*) from Medieval Latin *ordinarius* (masculine) or *ordinarium* (neuter).

ordinate *a.* arranged in a row or rows. *Also n.* WH: 14–15C. Latin *ordinatus,* p.p. of *ordinare.* See ORDAIN, also -ATE².

ordnance *n.* heavy guns, cannon, artillery. WH: 14–15C. Contr. of Old French *ordenance* ORDINANCE.

ordonnance *n.* the arrangement of the elements of a picture, building, literary composition etc. WH: 17C. French, alt. of Old French *ordenance,* based on French *ordonner.* See ORDINANCE.

Ordovician *n.* the middle period of the lower Palaeozoic era, which followed the Cambrian period. *Also a.* WH: 19C. Latin *Ordovices,* an ancient British tribe in N Wales + -IAN. The term was coined in 1879 by the English geologist Charles Lapworth.

ordure *n.* excrement, dung, filth. WH: 12–14C. Old French, from *ord* filthy, from Latin *horridus* HORRID. See also -URE. The original sense was filth, dirt in general. The sense excrement evolved in the 14–15C.

ore *n.* a natural mineral substance from which metal may be profitably extracted. WH: pre-1200. Partly from Old English *ōra* ore, unworked metal, partly from Old English *ār* brass, copper, bronze, both from Germanic with *ār* rel. to Latin *aes* crude metal, bronze, money.

öre *n.* a monetary unit in Sweden. WH: 17C. Swedish, from Old Norse *aurar* (pl.), prob. from Latin *aureus* golden.

øre *n.* a monetary unit in Norway and Denmark. WH: 17C. Norwegian and Danish, from Old Norse *aurar* (ÖRE).

oread *n.* a mountain nymph. WH: 14–15C. Latin *Oreas, Oreadis* or Greek *Oreias, Oreiados,* from *oros* mountain. See also -AD¹.

orectic *a.* of or relating to appetite or desire. WH: 17C. Greek *orektikos* appetitive, from *orektos,* from *oregein* to stretch out, to grasp after, to desire. See also -IC.

oregano *n.* the (usu. dried) leaves of wild marjoram, *Origanum vulgare,* used as a culinary herb. WH: 18C. Spanish and American Spanish var. of ORIGANUM.

orfe *n.* a small yellow or golden-coloured fish, *Leuciscus idus,* of the carp family. WH: 19C. German, from Latin *orphus,* from Greek *orphos* sea-perch.

organ *n.* a musical wind instrument composed of an assemblage of pipes sounded by means of a bellows and played by keys. WH: pre-1200. Old French *organe* (Modern French *orgue*), from Latin *organum* instrument, engine, musical instrument, from Greek *organon,* from Indo-European base also of WORK. Cp. ORGY. The sense musical instrument (of any kind) predates that of organ of the body (14–15C). The sense of church organ dates from the 12–14C.

organdie *n.* a stiff, light transparent muslin. WH: 19C. French *organdi,* of unknown orig. According to some, the word is an alteration of *Organzi,* a variant form of *Urgench,* a city in Uzbekistan in central Asia, where it was produced. Cp. ORGANZA.

organelle *n.* a unit in a cell having a particular structure and function. WH: early 20C. Modern Latin *organella,* from *organum.* See ORGAN.

organic *a.* of or relating to a bodily organ or organs. **WH:** 14–15C. French *organique*, from Latin *organicus*, from Greek *organikos* pertaining to an organ, from *organon* ORGAN. See also -IC.

organism *n.* an organized body consisting of mutually dependent parts fulfilling functions necessary to the life of the whole. **WH:** 18C. French *organisme*. See ORGANIZE, also -ISM.

organize *v.t.* to put into proper working order. *Also v.i.* **WH:** Old French *organiser*, from Medieval Latin *organizare*, from *organum*. See ORGAN, also -IZE.

organo- *comb. form* organ. **WH:** Greek *organon* ORGAN, or ORGANIC. See also -O-.

organogenesis *n.* the development of organs in animals and plants. **WH:** 19C. ORGANO- + GENESIS.

organography *n.* a description of the organs of plants and animals. **WH:** 16C. ORGANO- + -GRAPHY.

organoleptic *a.* affecting the bodily or sense organs. **WH:** 19C. French *organoleptique*, from ORGANO- + Greek *lēptikos*, from *lambanein* to apprehend by the senses. See also -IC.

organology *n.* the branch of biology or physiology concerned with the organs of the body. **WH:** 19C. ORGANO- + -LOGY.

organometallic *a.* of, being or relating to a compound containing linked carbon and metal atoms. **WH:** 19C. ORGANO- + *metallic* (METAL).

organon *n.* a system of principles and rules of investigation, deduction and demonstration regarded as an instrument of knowledge. **WH:** 16C. Greek instrument, organ. See ORGAN.

organophosphate *n.* an organic compound that contains phosphate. **WH:** mid-20C. ORGANO- + PHOSPHATE.

organotherapy *n.* the treatment of disease by the administration of one or more hormones in which the body is deficient. **WH:** 19C. ORGANO- + *therapy* (THERAPEUTIC).

organum *n.* in medieval music, a part sung a fourth or fifth below or above a plainsong melody. **WH:** 17C. Latin, from Greek ORGANON.

organza *n.* a thin transparent fabric of silk, rayon or nylon. **WH:** 19C. Prob. alt. of trademark *Lorganza*, prob. itself based on ORGANZINE. According to some accounts, the word is an alteration of the name *Organzi*. See ORGANDIE.

organzine *n.* silk thread made of several threads twisted together in a direction contrary to that of the strands; thrown silk. **WH:** 17C. French *organsin*, from Italian *organzino*, of unknown orig.

orgasm *n.* the culminating excitement in the sexual act. *Also v.i.* **WH:** 17C. French *orgasme* or Modern Latin *orgasmus*, from Greek *orgasmos*, from *organ* to swell as with moisture, to be excited.

orgeat *n.* a liquor made from barley or sweet almonds and orange flower water. **WH:** 14–15C. French, from Provençal *orjat*, from *ordi* barley, from Latin *hordeum*.

†**orgulous** *a.* proud, haughty. **WH:** 12–14C. Old French *orguillus* (Modern French *orgueilleux*), from *orgoill*, *orguill*, from Frankish *urgôli* pride. See also -ULOUS.

orgy *n.* a wild revel, esp. involving indiscriminate sexual activity. **WH:** 16C. Orig. in pl. from French *orgies*, from Latin *orgia* (neut. pl.) secret rites, from Indo-European base also of WORK. Cp. ORGAN. See also -Y².

oribi *n.* a small fawn-coloured antelope, *Ourebia ourebi*, of southern and E Africa. **WH:** 18C. Afrikaans, appar. from Nama.

oriel *n.* a projecting polygonal recess with a window or windows, usu. built out from an upper storey and supported on corbels or a pier. **WH:** 14–15C. Old French *oriol* passage, gallery, of unknown orig. Cp. Medieval Latin *oriolum* porch, anteroom, chamber. The Medieval Latin word may have been borrowed from the Old French.

orient *n.* the East, the countries east of S Europe and the Mediterranean. *Also a., v.t., v.i.* **WH:** 14–15C. Old French, from Latin *oriens*, *orientis*, pres.p. of *oriri* to rise. See also -ENT.

orienteering *n.* a sport in which the contestants race cross-country following checkpoints located by a map and compass. **WH:** mid-20C. Swedish *orientering* orienteering, orig. orientating. Cp. ORIENT, also -ING¹.

orifice *n.* an opening or aperture, esp. of the body. **WH:** 14–15C. Old French, from Late Latin *orificium*, from *os*, *oris* mouth + -*fic*-, var. of *fac*-, stem of *facere* to make.

oriflamme *n.* the ancient royal banner of France, orig. the red silk banderole of the Abbey of St Denis handed to the early kings in setting out for war. **WH:** 14–15C. Old French *oriflambe*, from Medieval Latin *auriflamma*, from *aurum* gold + *flamma* FLAME.

origami *n.* the (traditionally Japanese) art of paper folding. **WH:** mid-20C. Japanese, from *oru*, *orori* to fold + *kami* paper.

origanum *n.* any plant of the genus *Origanum*, esp. wild marjoram. **WH:** 12–14C. Latin, from Greek *origanon*, prob. from *oros* mountain + *ganos* brightness, joy. Cp. OREGANO.

origin *n.* the beginning, commencement (of anything). **WH:** 16C. French *origine* or Latin *origo*, *originis*, from *oriri* to rise.

Orimulsion® *n.* a mixture of bitumen, water and detergents, used in fossil-fuelled power stations. **WH:** late 20C. *Orinoco*, a river in Venezuela + EMULSION. The bitumen was originally extracted from the Orinoco oil belt.

orinasal *a.* of, relating to or sounded by the mouth and nose. *Also n.* **WH:** 19C. Latin *ori-*, comb. form of *os*, *oris* mouth + NASAL.

oriole *n.* any bird of the genus *Oriolus*, esp. *O. oriolus*, the golden oriole. **WH:** 18C. Medieval Latin *oriolus*, from Old French *oriol*, from Latin *aureolus*, dim. of *aureus* golden, from *aurum* gold. See also -OLE².

Orion *n.* one of the best-known constellations, a group of stars seen as representing a hunter with belt and sword. **WH:** 14–15C. Latin, from Greek *Oriōn*, a mighty hunter in Greek mythology.

orismology *n.* the branch of science concerned with definitions and the explanation of technical terms. **WH:** 19C. Greek *horismos* definition + -O- + -LOGY.

orison *n.* a prayer, a supplication. **WH:** 12–14C. Old French (Modern French *oraison*), from Latin *oratio*, *orationis* speech, oration. See ORATION.

-orium *suf.* denoting a place where something specific is done, as in *sanatorium*. **WH:** Latin neut. sing. ending of aa. in -*orius* -ORY².

Oriya *n.* a member of a people living in Orissa in India. **WH:** 19C. Oriya *Oṛiyā*, Bengali, Hindi *Uṛiyā*, ult. from Sanskrit *Oḍra* Odra, an ancient region of India corr. to modern Orissa.

orle *n.* a bearing in the form of a narrow band round the edge of a shield. **WH:** 16C. Old French, from *ourler* to hem, from dim. of Latin *ora* edge, border, prob. from *os*, *oris* mouth.

orleans *n.* a cloth of cotton and wool used for women's dresses. **WH:** 17C. French *Orléans*, a city in N central France.

Orlon® *n.* (a fabric made from) acrylic fibre. **WH:** mid-20C. Invented name. Cp. NYLON.

orlop *n.* the lowest deck of a vessel having three or more decks. **WH:** 14–15C. Middle Dutch *overloop*, from *overloopen* to run over. See OVER, LEAP.

ormer *n.* an edible mollusc, esp. *Haliotis tuberculata*; also called sea-ear. **WH:** 17C. Channel Islands French (French *ormier*), from Latin *auris maris* ear of the sea. The mollusc is so called from its resemblance to the ear.

ormolu *n.* a gold-coloured alloy of copper, zinc and tin, used for cheap jewellery. **WH:** 18C. French *or moulu*, lit. powdered gold.

ornament¹ *n.* a thing or part that adorns; a decoration. **WH:** 12–14C. Old French *ornement*, from Latin *ornamentum* equipment, ornament, from *ornare* to adorn. See also -MENT.

ornament² *v.t.* to decorate, to embellish. **WH:** 18C. ORNAMENT¹.

ornate *a.* ornamented, richly decorated. **WH:** 14–15C. Latin *ornatus*, p.p. of *ornare* to adorn. See also -ATE².

ornery *a.* mean, low. **WH:** 19C. Dial. var. of ORDINARY.

ornithic *a.* relating to birds. **WH:** 19C. Greek *ornithikos* birdlike, from *ornis* bird. See also -IC.

ornithischian *a.* of or relating to the order Ornithischia, an order of dinosaurs. *Also n.* **WH:** early 20C. Modern Latin *Ornithischia*, from ORNITHO- + ISCHIUM. See also -IA, -IAN.

ornitho- *comb. form* of or relating to birds. **WH:** Greek *ornis*, *ornithos* bird. See also -O-.

ornithodelphian *a.* of the order Ornithodelphia, comprising monotremes and prototherians. **WH:** 19C. Modern Latin *Ornithodelphia*, from ORNITHO- + Greek *delphus* womb. See also -IA, -IAN. The order is so named from the ornithic nature of the reproductive organs.

ornithology n. the branch of zoology dealing with birds. WH: 17C. Modern Latin *ornithologia*, from Greek *ornithologos* treating of birds. See ORNITHO-, -LOGY.

ornithopod n. any bipedal herbivorous dinosaur of the suborder Ornithopoda, including the iguanodon. *Also a.* WH: 19C. Modern Latin *Ornithopoda*. See ORNITHO-, -POD.

ornithopter n. an aeroplane driven by power supplied by the aviator and not by an engine. WH: early 20C. French *ornithoptère*, coined to replace *orthoptère* (ORTHOPTERAN). See ORNITHO-. The machine was designed to fly by means of flapping wings powered by the aviator.

ornithorhyncus n. the duck-billed platypus, *Ornithorhyncus anatinus*, an Australian aquatic oviparous mammal. WH: 19C. Modern Latin, from ORNITHO- + Greek *rhugkhos* bill.

ornithoscopy n. observation of birds for purposes of divination. WH: 19C. ORNITHO- + *-scopy* (-SCOPE).

ornithosis n. a disease similar to psittacosis that occurs in birds other than parrots. WH: mid-20C. ORNITHO- + -OSIS.

oro- comb. form of or relating to mountains. WH: Greek *oros* mountain. See also -O-.

orogenesis n. the process of forming mountains. WH: 19C. ORO- + GENESIS.

orography n. the branch of physical geography concerned with mountains and mountain systems. WH: 19C. Greek *oros* mountain + -GRAPHY.

orohippus n. a fossil quadruped considered to be the ancestor of the horse. WH: 19C. ORO- + Greek *hippos* horse.

oroide n. an alloy of copper and zinc, resembling gold in appearance, used for cheap jewellery. WH: 19C. French *or* gold (from Latin *aurum*) + Greek *eidos* form. See also -OID.

orology n. the scientific study of mountains. WH: 18C. Greek *oros* mountain + -LOGY.

orometer n. an instrument for measuring the height of mountains. WH: 19C. ORO- + -METER.

oropesa float n. a float used in minesweeping to support the sweeping wire between two trawlers. WH: mid-20C. *Oropesa*, name of the trawler that first tested the float.

orotund a. characterized by fullness and resonance. WH: 18C. Contr. of Latin *ore rotundo*, lit. with round mouth, from abl. of *os, oris* mouth + abl. of *rotundus* round, ROTUND. The Latin phrase itself comes from Horace's *Ars Poetica*, more fully: *Grais ingenium, Grais dedit ore rotundo / Musa loqui* It was the Greeks who had the Muse's native gift, the Greeks who had speech in rounded phrases.

orphan n. a child bereft of one parent, or of both. *Also a., v.t.* WH: 14–15C. Late Latin *orphanus*, from Greek *orphanos* without parents, bereft, rel. to Latin *orbus* bereft.

Orphean a. of or relating to Orpheus, or his music. WH: 16C. Latin *Orpheus*, from Greek *Orpheios*, from *Orpheus*, a musician and poet of Greek mythology, whose lyre-playing was said to have the power to move rocks and trees. See also -AN, -EAN.

orphrey n. a band of gold and silver embroidery decorating an ecclesiastical vestment. WH: 12–14C. Old French *orfreis* (Modern French *orfroi*), from Medieval Latin *aurifrisium*, alt. of *auriphrygium* gold embroidery, i.e. *aurum Phrygium* Phrygian gold.

orpiment n. native yellow trisulphide of arsenic, used as a pigment and a dyestuff. WH: 14–15C. Old French, from Latin *auripigmentum*, from *aurum* gold + *pigmentum* PIGMENT.

orpine n. a fleshy-leaved plant, *Sedum telephium*, of the stonecrop family, with purple flowers. WH: 12–14C. Old French *orpin*, presumably contr. of *orpiment*. See ORPIMENT.

Orpington n. a variety of domestic fowl. WH: 19C. *Orpington*, a town in Kent (now in Bromley).

orra a. odd, extra, left over. WH: 16C. Orig. unknown.

orrery n. a mechanical model for illustrating the motions, magnitudes and positions of the planetary system. WH: 18C. Charles Boyle, 4th earl of *Orrery*, 1676–1731, for whom one of the first such devices was made. Orrery is in County Cork, Ireland.

orris[1] n. any plant of the genus *Iris*, esp. *I. florentina*. WH: 16C. Appar. alt. of IRIS.

orris[2] n. a kind of gold or silver lace. WH: 18C. ? Alt. of obs. var. of ORPHREY.

ort n. refuse, fragments, odds and ends, leavings. WH: 14–15C. Middle Low German *orte* refuse of food, rel. to obs. early Modern Dutch *ooræte*, ? from Dutch *oor* out (as in ORDEAL) + *eten* EAT.

ortanique n. a citrus fruit, a cross between an orange and a tangerine. WH: mid-20C. ORANGE + TANGERINE + UNIQUE.

ortho- comb. form straight. WH: Greek, from *orthos* straight, right. See also -O-.

orthocentre n. the point of intersection of two altitudes of a triangle. WH: 19C. ORTHO- + CENTRE.

orthocephalic a. having a breadth of skull from 70 to 75 per cent of the length, between brachycephalic and dolichocephalic. WH: 19C. ORTHO- + -CEPHALIC.

orthochromatic a. giving the correct values of colours in relations of light and shade. WH: 19C. ORTHO- + CHROMATIC.

orthoclase n. common or potash feldspar having a rectangular cleavage. WH: 19C. ORTHO- + Greek *klasis* breaking down.

orthodontics n. dentistry dealing with the correction of irregularities of the teeth. WH: early 20C. ORTHO- + Greek *odous, odontos* tooth + -ICS.

orthodox a. holding right or accepted views, esp. in matters of faith and religious doctrine. WH: 14–15C. Ecclesiastical Latin *orthodoxus*, from Greek *orthodoxos*, from ORTHO- + *doxa* opinion.

orthodromic a. (of a nerve impulse) moving in the normal direction in the nerve fibre. WH: 18C. ORTHO- + Greek *dromos* course + -IC.

orthoepy n. the branch of grammar dealing with the pronunciation of words. WH: 17C. Greek *orthoepeia* correctness of diction, from ORTHO- + *epos, epe-* word. See also -IA, -Y[2].

orthogenesis n. a theory of evolution that postulates that variation is determined by the action of environment. WH: 19C. ORTHO- + GENESIS.

orthognathous a. straight-jawed, having little forward projection of the jaws. WH: 19C. ORTHO- + Greek *gnathos* jaw + -OUS.

orthogon n. a rectangular figure. WH: 16C. Late Latin *orthogonium*, neut. of *orthogonius*, from Greek *orthogōnios* right-angled. See ORTHO-, -GON.

orthography n. correct spelling. WH: 14–15C. Old French *ortografie*, later *ortographie* (Modern French *orthographie*), from Latin *orthographia*, from Greek. See ORTHO-, -GRAPHY.

orthometry n. the art of correct versification. WH: 18C. ORTHO- + -METRY.

orthopaedics n. the branch of medicine concerned with bones and joints; the act or art of curing muscular or skeletal deformities by surgery, esp. in children. WH: 19C. French *orthopédique*, from *orthopédie*, from ORTHO- + Greek *paideia* rearing of children + -S[1]. See also -IC.

orthophosphate n. any salt or ester of orthophosphoric acid. WH: 19C. ORTHO- + PHOSPHATE.

orthopnoea n. difficulty of breathing except in an upright posture, a form of asthma. WH: 17C. Latin, from Greek *orthopnoia*, from ORTHO- + *pnoē* breathing. See also -A[1].

orthopraxy n. orthodox procedure or behaviour, correct practice. WH: 19C. ORTHO- + Greek *praxis* action. See also -Y[2].

orthopsychiatry n. the study and treatment of mental disorders, esp. the prevention of mental illness in childhood. WH: mid-20C. ORTHO- + PSYCHIATRY.

orthopteran n. any insect of the order *Orthoptera*, with two pairs of wings, the hind wings membranous and those in front coriaceous and usually straight; any orthopterous insect. WH: 19C. Modern Latin *Orthoptera*, neut. pl. of *orthopterus*, from Greek ORTHO- + *pteron* wing. See also -A[2], -AN.

orthoptic a. relating to correct vision with both eyes. *Also n.* WH: 19C. ORTHO- + OPTIC.

orthorhombic a. (of a crystal) having three planes of dissimilar symmetry at right angles to each other. WH: 19C. ORTHO- + *rhombic* (RHOMB).

orthoscope n. an instrument for examining the interior of the eye, the refraction of the cornea being corrected by a body of water. WH: 19C. ORTHO- + -SCOPE.

orthostichy n. an imaginary straight line connecting a row of leaves on a stem. WH: 19C. ORTHO- + Greek *-stikhia*, from *stikhos* row, rank.

orthotics *n.* the provision and use of aids to assist the movement of weak joints and muscles. **WH:** mid-20C. Greek *orthōsis* making straight, from *orthoun* to set straight. See -OTIC, also -S¹.

orthotone *a.* (of a Greek word) having its own accent, independently accented. *Also n.* **WH:** 19C. Greek *orthotonos*, from ORTHO- + *tonos* tone, accent.

orthotropal *a.* (of ovules, embryos etc.) turned or growing straight. **WH:** 19C. ORTHO- + Greek *tropos* turn. See also -AL¹.

ortolan *n.* a small bunting, *Emberiza hortulana*, formerly esteemed as a delicacy. **WH:** 16C. French, from Provençal *gardener*, from Latin *hortulanus*, from *hortulus*, dim. of *hortus* garden. See also -AN. The ortolan is apparently so called because it frequents gardens. (But so do many birds, and this origin may be a folk etymology.)

Orwellian *a.* relating to or in the style of George Orwell. *Also n.* **WH:** mid-20C. George *Orwell*, 1903–50, English writer + -IAN.

-ory¹ *suf.* denoting place where or instrument, as in *dormitory*, *lavatory*, *refectory*. **WH:** Latin *-oria*, *-orium*, Old French *-oire*.

-ory² *suf.* forming adjectives, as in *amatory*, *admonitory*, *illusory*. **WH:** Latin *-orius*, Old French *-oir*, *-oire*.

oryx *n.* any straight-horned antelope of the genus *Oryx*, of Africa and Arabia. **WH:** 14–15C. Latin, from Greek *orux*, lit. stonemason's pickaxe. The animal is so named for its pointed horns.

oryza *n.* a grass of the genus *Oryza*, esp. *O. sativa*, rice. **WH:** 19C. Latin, from Greek *oruza* rice.

os *n.* a bone. **WH:** 14–15C. Latin bone.

Osage orange *n.* a thorny N American tree, *Maclura pomifera*. **WH:** 17C. Alt. of Osage *Wazhazhe*, one of three groups comprising the N American people who formerly inhabited the Osage River valley, Missouri. The tree's fruit, the size of a large orange, is actually yellow-green in colour but its wood is yellow-orange.

Oscan *n.* a member of an ancient Italian people. *Also a.* **WH:** 16C. Latin *Oscus*, sing. of *Osci*, a people inhabiting Campania in S Italy + -AN.

Oscar *n.* a gold-plated statuette awarded by the American Academy of Motion Picture Arts and Sciences to the actor, director, filmwriter etc. whose work is adjudged the best of the year. **WH:** mid-20C. Appar. from the supposed resemblance of the statuette to an employee's uncle named *Oscar*.

oscillate *v.i.* to swing, to move like a pendulum. *Also v.t.* **WH:** 18C. Latin *oscillatus*, p.p. of *oscillare* to swing. See also -ATE³.

oscine *a.* of or relating to the suborder Oscines of passerine birds that includes most of the songbirds. **WH:** 19C. Latin *oscen*, *oscinis* singing or divining bird, from OB- + *canere* to sing. The name was originally that of the birds (especially ravens or owls) from whose voices the Romans took auguries.

oscitation *n.* yawning, sleepiness. **WH:** 16C. Latin *oscitatio*, *oscitationis*, from *oscitatus*, p.p. of *oscitare* to gape. See also -ATION.

osculate *v.t.* to kiss. *Also v.i.* **WH:** 17C. Latin *osculatus*, p.p. of *osculari* to kiss, from *osculum*, dim. of *os*, *oris* mouth. See also -ATE³.

-ose¹ *suf.* forming adjectives denoting fullness, abundance, as in *grandiose*, *jocose*, *verbose*. **WH:** Latin *-osus*. Cp. -OUS.

-ose² *suf.* forming nouns denoting carbohydrates and isomeric compounds. **WH:** From GLUCOSE.

osier *n.* any of various willows, esp. *Salix viminalis*, the pliable shoots of which are used for basket-making. **WH:** 12–14C. Old French, m. form corr. to fem. (dial.) *osière*, from Medieval Latin *auseria*, said to derive from a Gaulish word meaning river bed.

-osis *comb. form* denoting conditions, esp. morbid states, as in *chlorosis*, *necrosis*. **WH:** Latin, or from Greek *-ōsis*.

-osity *suf.* forming nouns, as in *grandiosity*, *luminosity*. **WH:** -OSE¹ or -OUS + -ITY, from (or based on) French *-osité*, or from Latin *-ositas*.

Osmanli *a.* of or relating to the Ottoman Empire, the W branch of the Turkish peoples or their language. *Also n.* **WH:** 18C. Turkish *Osmānli*, from *Osman* (from Arabic *'Uṭmān*; see OTTOMAN) + adjectival suf. *-li*.

osmazome *n.* the portion of the aqueous product of meat in which are found those constituents of the flesh which decide its taste and smell. **WH:** 19C. French *osmazôme*, from Greek *osmē* scent + *zōmos* soup, sauce.

osmic *a.* of or relating to odours or the sense of smell. **WH:** mid-20C. Greek *osmē* smell + -IC.

osmiridium *n.* a very hard natural alloy of osmium and iridium used esp. in pen nibs. **WH:** 19C. OSMIUM + IRIDIUM.

osmium *n.* the heaviest known metallic element, at. no. 76, chem. symbol Os, usu. found in association with platinum. **WH:** 19C. Greek *osmē* odour + -IUM. The element's name refers to the distinctive pungent smell of the tetroxide. It was coined by the English chemist Smithson Tennant, who discovered it in 1804. Cp. IRIDIUM.

osmograph *n.* an instrument for measuring osmotic pressures. **WH:** 19C. Greek *ōsmos* push, thrust + -GRAPH.

osmoregulation *n.* the adjustment of osmotic pressure in a cell in relation to the surrounding fluid. **WH:** mid-20C. Greek *ōsmos* push, shove + *regulation* (REGULATE).

osmosis *n.* the diffusion of a solvent through a semipermeable membrane into a more concentrated solution. **WH:** 19C. Latinized form of *osmose*, from common element in *endosmose* (ENDOSMOSIS) and *exosmose* (EXOSMOSIS), itself from Greek *ōsmos* push, shove.

osmund *n.* the flowering fern, *Osmunda regalis*; also called *royal fern*. **WH:** 14–15C. Old French *osmonde*, of unknown orig.

osnaburg *n.* a coarse kind of linen. **WH:** 16C. Alt. of *Osnabrück*, a town in N Germany.

osprey *n.* a large bird, *Pandion haliaetus*, preying on fish; also known as the *sea eagle* or *fish-hawk*. **WH:** 14–15C. Old French *ospres*, appar. ult. from Latin *ossifraga* ossifrage, a bird of prey mentioned by Pliny, from *ossifragus*, lit. bone-breaking, from *os*, *ossis* bone + base of *frangere* to break. According to some, the word derives from Medieval Latin *avis prede* bird of prey, from Latin *avis praedae*. See AVIAN, PREY. Pliny's ossifrage has been identified with the lammergeier, which feeds on carrion and drops the bones from a height onto flat rocks below in order to break them and extract the marrow. Cp. LAMMERGEIER.

ossein *n.* the gelatinous tissue left when mineral matter is eliminated from a bone. **WH:** 19C. Latin *osseus* bony + -IN¹.

osselet *n.* an ossicle. **WH:** 17C. French, from *os* bone, from Latin OS. See also -LET.

osseous *a.* of the nature of or like bone, bony. **WH:** 14–15C. Latin *osseus*, from OS. See also -EOUS.

ossicle *n.* a small bone. **WH:** 16C. Latin *ossiculum*, dim. of OS. See also -CULE.

ossiferous *a.* (of cave deposits etc.) containing or yielding bones. **WH:** 19C. Latin OS + -*i*- + -FEROUS.

ossify *v.t.* to turn into bone. *Also v.i.* **WH:** 18C. French *ossifier*, from Latin OS. See also -FY.

osso bucco *n.* a stew made from knuckle of veal and marrowbone. **WH:** mid-20C. Italian *ossobuco* marrowbone, from *osso* bone + *buco* hole.

ossuary *n.* a charnel house. **WH:** 17C. Late Latin *ossuarium*, from *ossu*, var. of *os* OS. See also -ARY¹.

osteal *a.* osseous, bony. **WH:** 19C. OSTEO- + -AL¹.

ostealgia *n.* pain in a bone. **WH:** 19C. OSTEO- + -ALGIA.

osteitis *n.* inflammation of bone. **WH:** 19C. OSTEO- + -ITIS.

ostensible *a.* put forward for show or to hide the reality. **WH:** 18C. French, from Medieval Latin *ostensibilis*, from Latin *ostensus*, p.p. of *ostendere* to stretch out to view, from OB- + *tendere* to stretch. See also -IBLE.

osteo- *comb. form* bone. **WH:** Greek *osteon* bone. See also -O-.

osteoarthritis *n.* degenerative arthritis, esp. of the weight-bearing joints of the spine, hips and knees. **WH:** 19C. OSTEO- + *arthritis* (ARTHRITIC).

osteoblast *n.* a cell concerned in the development of bone. **WH:** 19C. OSTEO- + -BLAST.

osteoclasis *n.* the operation of breaking a bone to remedy a deformity etc. **WH:** early 20C. OSTEO- + Greek *klasis* breaking.

osteocolla *n.* an incrustation of carbonate of lime on the roots and stems of plants growing in sandy ground. **WH:** 17C. OSTEO- + Greek *kolla* glue. The deposit is so called from its supposed ability to knit broken bones.

osteogenesis *n.* the formation of bone. **WH:** 19C. OSTEO- + GENESIS.

osteoid *a.* like bone. **WH:** 19C. OSTEO- + -OID.

osteology *n.* the branch of anatomy treating of bones, osseous tissue etc. **WH:** 17C. OSTEO- + -LOGY.

osteomalacia *n.* softening of the bones. **WH:** 19C. OSTEO- + Greek *malakos* soft. See also -IA.

osteomyelitis *n.* inflammation of the marrow of the bones. WH: 19C. OSTEO- + MYELITIS.

osteopathy *n.* a method of treating diseases by eliminating structural derangement by manipulation, mainly of the spinal column. WH: 19C. OSTEO- + -PATHY.

osteoplasty *n.* transplantation of bone with its periosteum. WH: 19C. OSTEO- + -PLASTY.

osteoporosis *n.* development of porous or brittle bones due to lack of calcium in the bone matrix. WH: 19C. OSTEO- + PORE[1] + -OSIS.

osteosarcoma *n.* a disease of the bones due to the growth of medullary or cartilaginous matter within them. WH: 19C. OSTEO- + SARCOMA.

osteotome *n.* an instrument used in the dissection of bones. WH: 19C. OSTEO- + -TOME.

ostinato *n.* a musical figure continuously reiterated throughout a composition. WH: 19C. Italian obstinate, persistent.

ostium *n.* the mouth or opening of a passage. WH: 17C. Latin door, opening, river mouth.

ostler *n.* a man who looks after horses at an inn, a stableman. WH: 14–15C. Var. of HOSTLER. The term has long been popularly associated with HORSE, or more precisely with its dialect form, *hoss*.

Ostmark *n.* the standard unit of currency in the former Democratic Republic of Germany. WH: mid-20C. German, from *Ost* east + *Mark* MARK[2].

Ostpolitik *n.* the foreign policy of establishing normal relations with the Communist bloc. WH: mid-20C. German, from *Ost* east + *Politik* POLICY[1].

ostracize *v.t.* to exclude from society, to ban, to send to Coventry. WH: 17C. Greek *ostrakizein*, from *ostrakon* shell, potsherd. See also -IZE. Temporary banishment in ancient Greece was determined by popular ballot, cast by potsherds or tiles.

ostre- *comb. form* oyster. WH: Latin *ostrea*, Greek *ostreon* oyster. See also -O-.

ostreiculture *n.* the artificial breeding of oysters. WH: 19C. OSTRE- + -*i*- + CULTURE.

ostreophagous *a.* eating or feeding on oysters. WH: 19C. OSTRE- + -O- + -PHAGOUS.

ostrich *n.* a large African bird, *Struthio camelus*, having rudimentary wings, but capable of running with great speed, and valued for its feathers, which are used as plumes, and for its meat. WH: 12–14C. Old French *ostrice*, *ostriche* (Modern French *autruche*), from Latin *avis* bird + Late Latin *struthio*, from Greek *strouthiōn* ostrich, from *strouthos* sparrow, ostrich. The fuller Greek name for the bird was *ho megas strouthos*, literally the big sparrow.

Ostrogoth *n.* an eastern Goth, a member of the division of the Gothic peoples who conquered Italy in the 5th cent. WH: 14–15C. Late Latin *Ostrogothi* (pl.), from Germanic base of EAST + Latin *Gothus* Goth.

ot- *comb. form* of or relating to the ear. WH: Assim. form of OTO-.

-ot[1] *suf.* forming nouns, originally diminutives, as in *parrot*. WH: Old French.

-ot[2] *suf.* forming nouns denoting persons, as in *patriot*. WH: French -*ote*, Latin -*ota*, Greek -*otēs*, suf. meaning nativity.

otalgia *n.* earache. WH: 17C. Greek *ōtalgia*. See OT-, -ALGIA.

otarian *a.* of or relating to the Otariidae, a family of pinnipeds with external ears, including the fur seals and sea lions. WH: 19C. Modern Latin *Otariidae*, from *Otaria* genus name, from Greek *ous*, *ōtos* ear. See also -ID, -AN.

other *a.* not the same as one specified or implied. *Also n., pron., adv.* WH: pre-1200. Old English *ōther*, from Germanic, from Indo-European base also of Latin *alter* (ALTER), Sanskrit *ántara*. Cp. German *ander*.

otic *a.* of or relating to the ear. WH: 17C. Greek *ōtikos*, from *ous*, *ōtos* ear. See also -IC.

-otic *suf.* forming adjectives corresponding to nouns ending in -OSIS, as in *neurotic*, *osmotic*. WH: French -*otique*, Latin -*oticus*, from Greek -*ōtikos*, from nn. in -*ōtēs* or aa. in -*ōtos* + -*ikos* -IC.

otiose *a.* not wanted, useless, superfluous. WH: 18C. Latin *otiosus*, from *otium* leisure. See also -OSE[1].

otitis *n.* inflammation of the ear. WH: 18C. OT- + -ITIS.

oto- *comb. form* of or relating to the ear. WH: Greek *ous*, *ōtos* ear. See also -O-.

otolaryngology *n.* the study of diseases of the ear and throat. WH: 19C. OTO- + LARYNGOLOGY.

otolith *n.* a calcareous concretion found in the inner ear of vertebrates and some invertebrates. WH: 19C. OTO- + -LITH.

otology *n.* the science of the ear or of diseases of the ear. WH: 19C. OTO- + -LOGY.

otorhinolaryngology *n.* ear, nose and throat medicine. WH: early 20C. OTO- + RHINO- + LARYNGOLOGY.

otorrhoea *n.* purulent discharge from the ear. WH: 19C. OTO- + -RRHOEA.

otoscope *n.* an instrument for inspecting the ear and eardrum. WH: 19C. OTO- + -SCOPE.

ottava rima *n.* a form of versification consisting of stanzas of eight lines, of which the first six rhyme alternately, and the last two form a couplet (as in Byron's *Don Juan*). WH: 18C. Italian eighth rhyme.

otter *n.* any of several semiaquatic mammals of the genus *Lutra* with dense fur and webbed feet. WH: pre-1200. Old English *otr*, *otor*, from Germanic, from Indo-European word represented by Sanskrit *udra*, Greek *hudros* watersnake, *hudra* HYDRA.

Ottoman *a.* of or relating to the dynasty of Othman or Osman I. *Also n.* WH: 16C. French, or from Latin *Ottomano*, Medieval Latin *Ottomanus*, Medieval Greek *Othōmanoi*, from Arabic '*Uṭmāni*, a. of pers. name '*Uṭmān* Othman (Osman), *c*.1259–*c*.1326, founder of the Turkish dynasty in *c*.1300. Cp. OSMANLI.

ottoman *n.* a cushioned seat or sofa without back or arms, introduced from Turkey. WH: 19C. French *ottomane*, fem. of *ottoman* (n.) OTTOMAN. The seat was probably so called to suggest its oriental style.

ouabain *n.* a poisonous white crystalline glycoside extracted from certain trees. WH: 19C. French, from Somali *wabayo* tree yielding arrow poison containing ouabain. See also -IN[1].

oubit *n.* a hairy caterpillar. WH: 14–15C. Appar. from WOOL + unexplained 2nd element.

oubliette *n.* an underground dungeon in which persons condemned to perpetual imprisonment or secret death were confined. WH: 18C. French, from *oublier* to forget. See also -ETTE. The French word itself dates from the 14C. Its use in England was popularized by Sir Walter Scott, e.g. in *Ivanhoe* (1819).

ouch[1] *int.* used to express sudden pain. WH: 17C. Natural exclamation. Cp. OW.

†ouch[2] *n.* the setting of a gem. WH: 12–14C. Old French *nosche*, *nouche*, from Old Frankish *nuskja* buckle, clasp, ? from Celtic. The initial *n*- was lost by misdivision, as with ADDER, APRON, etc.

ought[1] *v.aux.* to comply with duty or rightness. *Also n.* WH: pre-1200. Old English *āhte*, past tense of OWE.

ought[2] *n.* a figure denoting nothing; nought. WH: 19C. From NOUGHT, with *a nought* misdivided as *an ought*, as with ADDER, APRON, etc., and influ. by AUGHT.

Ouija® *n.* a board inscribed with the letters of the alphabet, used for receiving messages etc. in spiritualistic manifestations. WH: 19C. French *oui* yes + German *ja* yes. The name implies that a positive message may be received in any language.

ounce[1] *n.* a unit of weight, of one-sixteenth of a pound avoirdupois (about 28 g). WH: 12–14C. Old French *unce* (Modern French *once*), from Latin *uncia* twelfth part (cp. INCH[1]), from *unus* ONE, prob. orig. intended to denote a unit.

ounce[2] *n.* a wild cat, *Panthera uncia*, of Asia; also called *mountain panther* and *snow leopard*. WH: 12–14C. Old French *once*, *lonce* (the *l*- taken to be *l'* the), from Latin LYNX, *lyncis*.

our *a.* possessive of WE. WH: pre-1200. Old English *ūre*, gen. of WE, from Germanic. Cp. German *unser*.

-our *suf.* forming nouns, as in *ardour*, *clamour*, *favour*. WH: Earlier form of -OR.

ourie *a.* shivering, chilly. WH: 12–14C. Orig. unknown.

ours *pron.* something which belongs to or is associated with us. WH: 12–14C. OUR + -'S.

ourselves *pron.* WE or US (objective), used to give emphasis. WH: 15C. *ourself* (from OUR + SELF) + -S[1].

-ous *suf.* full of, abounding in, as in *dubious*, *glorious*. WH: Old French -*os*, -*us*, -*ous*, from Latin -*osus*. Cp. -OSE[1].

oust *v.t.* to eject, to expel, to turn out (from). WH: 16C. Old French *oster* (Modern French *ôter*) to take away, to remove, from Latin *obstare* to oppose, to hinder, from OB- + *stare* to stand.

out *adv.* from the inside or within. *Also prep., n., a., int., v.t., v.i.* WH: pre-1200. Old English *ūt*, from Germanic, rel. to Sanskrit pref. *ud-* out. Cp. German *aus*.

out- *pref.* out, towards the outside, external. WH: OUT.

†outfangthief *n.* the right of a lord to try a thief who was his own man in his own court. WH: pre-1200. OUT + p.p. of obs. *fang* to seize, to capture (from Old English *fōn*, from Germanic base of FANG) + THIEF, based on *infangthief* (IN) right of a lord to try a thief caught within the limits of his demesne.

outlandish *a.* strange, extraordinary. WH: pre-1200. *outland* (from Old English *ūtland* foreign land) + -ISH[1]. The original sense was foreign, alien. The current sense arose in the 16C.

outlaw *n.* a lawless person. *Also v.t.* WH: pre-1200. Old Norse *útlagi*, from *útlagr* outlawed, banished, from *út* out (of) + pl. of *lag* law. See OUT, LAW[1].

output *n.* the produce of a factory, mine etc. *Also v.t.* WH: 19C. OUT + PUT.

outrage *n.* wanton injury to or violation of the rights of others. *Also v.t., v.i.* WH: 12–14C. Old French, from *outrer* to exceed, to exaggerate, from *outre* beyond, from Late Latin ULTRA-. See also -AGE. Cp. OUTRÉ. Not rel. to RAGE.

outré *a.* extravagant, exaggerated, eccentric. WH: 18C. French, p.p. of *outrer*. See OUTRAGE.

outside *n.* the external part or surface, the exterior. *Also a., adv., prep.* WH: 16C. OUT- + SIDE.

outward *a.* exterior, outer. *Also adv., n.* WH: pre-1200. OUT- + -WARD.

ouzel *n.* a thrush, *Turdus torquatus*, the ring ouzel. WH: pre-1200. Old English *ōsle*, rel. to Old High German *amusla, amsala*. Cp. German *Amsel* blackbird.

ouzo *n.* an aniseed-flavoured spirit from Greece. WH: 19C. Modern Greek, of unknown orig. According to some, the word is derived from Italian *uso Massalia* for the (commercial) use of Marseilles, words formerly stamped on packages of silkworm cocoons exported from Greece. The designation came to imply superior quality, which the spirit claimed to possess. But this is probably a popular etymology.

oval *a.* egg-shaped, roughly elliptical. *Also n.* WH: 16C. Medieval Latin *ovalis*. See OVUM, also -AL[1].

ovary *n.* each of the organs (two in number in the higher vertebrates) in a female in which the ova are produced. WH: 17C. Modern Latin *ovarium*, from Latin OVUM. See also -ARY[1].

ovation *n.* enthusiastic applause. WH: 16C. Latin *ovatio, ovationis*, from *ovatus*, p.p. of *ovare* to celebrate a lesser triumph. See also -ATION. The word was originally the term for a processional (but not triumphal) entrance into Rome by a victorious commander. The current sense dates only from the 19C.

oven *n.* a close chamber in which substances are baked etc. WH: pre-1200. Old English *ofen*, from Germanic. Cp. German *Ofen*.

over *prep.* above, in a higher position than. *Also adv., a., int., n.* WH: pre-1200. Old English *ofer*, from Germanic; from Indo-European comp. formation rel. to Sanskrit *upari*, Greek *huper* (HYPER-), Latin *super* (SUPER-), the Indo-European positive being represented by Latin *sub* (SUB-). Cp. German *über*.

over- *pref.* above. WH: OVER.

overt *a.* plain, apparent. WH: 12–14C. Old French (Modern French *ouvert*), p.p. of *ovrir* (Modern French *ouvrir*), from Latin *aperire*.

overture *n.* an introductory piece for instruments, a prelude to an opera, oratorio etc. *Also v.t.* WH: 14–15C. Old French (Modern French *ouverture*), from Latin *apertura* APERTURE, influ. by French *ouvrir* to open. The original sense (to the 18C) was aperture, orifice, hole. The musical sense dates from the 17C.

ovi-[1] *comb. form* of or relating to an egg or ovum. WH: Latin *ovum* egg + -i-.

ovi-[2] *comb. form* of or relating to sheep. WH: Latin *ovis* sheep + -i-.

ovibovine *a.* having characteristics intermediate between those of sheep and oxen. *Also n.* WH: early 20C. Modern Latin *Ovibovinae* (fem. pl.), from *Ovibos* musk ox, from OVI-[2] + Latin *bos* ox.

Ovidian *a.* of or in the manner of Ovid. WH: 17C. Latin *Ovidius* Ovid (Publius Ovidius Naso), 43 BC–AD 17, Roman poet. See also -IAN.

oviduct *n.* a passage through which ova pass from the ovary, esp. in oviparous animals. WH: 18C. OVI-[1] + DUCT.

oviferous *a.* egg-bearing. WH: 19C. OVI-[1] + -FEROUS.

oviform *a.* egg-shaped. WH: 17C. OVI-[1] + -FORM.

ovigerous *a.* egg-bearing, carrying eggs. WH: 19C. OVI-[1] + -GEROUS.

ovine *a.* of, relating to, or like sheep. WH: 19C. Late Latin *ovinus*. See OVI-[2], -INE.

oviparous *a.* producing young by means of eggs that are expelled and hatched outside the body. WH: 17C. OVI-[1] + -PAROUS.

oviposit *v.i.* to deposit eggs, esp. with an ovipositor. WH: 19C. OVI-[1] + Latin *positus*, p.p. of *ponere* to place (cp. DEPOSIT).

ovisac *n.* a closed receptacle in the ovary in which ova are developed. WH: 19C. OVI-[1] + SAC[1].

ovo- *comb. form* of or relating to an egg or ovum. WH: Latin *ovum* egg. See also -O-.

ovoid *a.* egg-shaped, oval with one end larger than the other, ovate. *Also n.* WH: 19C. French *ovoïde*, from Medieval Latin *ovoides*, from Latin *ovum* egg. See also -OID.

ovolo *n.* a convex moulding, in Roman architecture a quarter-circle in outline in Greek, elliptical with the greatest curve at the top. WH: 17C. Italian, dim. of *uovo*, obs. *ovo*, from Latin *ovum* egg.

ovotestis *n.* an organ producing both ova and spermatozoa. WH: 19C. OVO- + TESTIS.

ovoviviparous *a.* producing young by ova hatched within the body of the parent. WH: 19C. OVO- + VIVIPAROUS.

ovulate *v.i.* to produce or discharge ovaries or ovules. WH: 19C. OVULE + -ATE[3].

ovule *n.* the rudimentary seed. WH: 19C. French, and from Medieval and Modern Latin *ovulum*, dim. of Latin *ovum* egg. See also -ULE.

ovum *n.* the female egg cell, or gamete, produced within the ovary and capable, usu. after fertilization by the male, of developing into a new individual. WH: 17C. Latin egg.

ow *int.* used to express pain. WH: early 20C. Natural exclamation. Cp. OUCH[1].

owe *v.t.* to be indebted to for a specified amount. *Also v.i.* WH: pre-1200. Old English *āgan*, from Germanic, ult. from Indo-European base represented also in Sanskrit *īs* to possess, to own. Cp. OUGHT[1], OWN[1].

ower *prep., adv., a.* over. WH: 14–15C. Var. of OVER.

owl *n.* any nocturnal raptorial bird of the order Strigiformes, with large head, short neck and short hooked beak, including barn owls, tawny owls etc. WH: pre-1200. Old English *ūle*, from Germanic, ult. imit. of bird's characteristic cry. Cp. German *Eule*.

own[1] *a.* belonging to, individual, not anyone else's (usu. appended as an intensive to the poss. pronoun, adjective etc.). WH: pre-1200. Old English *āgen*, p.p. of OWE, from Germanic. Cp. German *eigen*.

own[2] *v.t.* to possess. *Also v.i.* WH: pre-1200. Old English *āgnian*, from *āgen* OWN[1]. Cp. OUGHT[1].

owt *n.* anything. WH: 12–14C. Var. of AUGHT.

ox *n.* any bovine animal, esp. of domesticated species, large cloven-hoofed ruminants, usu. horned. WH: pre-1200. Old English *oxa*, from Germanic, from Indo-European base represented also by Sanskrit *ukṣán* bull. Cp. German *Ochse*.

oxalis *n.* any plant of the genus *Oxalis*, e.g. wood sorrel. WH: 17C. Latin, from Greek sorrel, from *oxus* sour, acid. The plant is so called from its sour-tasting leaves.

Oxbridge *n.* the Universities of Oxford and Cambridge, esp. seen as elitist educational establishments conferring social, economic and political advantages. *Also a.* WH: 19C. Blend of Ox*ford* and Cam*bridge*, as two of Britain's oldest universities.

Oxfam *abbr.* Oxford Committee for Famine Relief. WH: mid-20C. Abbr. of *Ox*ford Committee for *Fam*ine Relief.

Oxford *a.* of, relating to, or derived from Oxford. WH: 16C. *Oxford*, a city in the SE Midlands, famous for its university.

oxide *n.* a binary compound of oxygen with another element or an organic radical. WH: 18C. French (now *oxyde*), from *oxygène* OXYGEN + -*ide* based on *acide* ACID. The term was coined in 1787 by the French chemists Louis Bernard, Baron Guyton de Morveau and Antoine Lavoisier.

Oxonian *n.* a student or graduate of Oxford University. *Also a.* WH: 16C. *Oxonia*, Latinized form of Old English *Oxnaford* OXFORD. See also -AN, -IAN.

oxter *n.* the armpit. WH: pre-1200. Old English *ōxta, ōhsta*, from Germanic, rel. to Latin *axilla* (AXIL). Cp. German *Achsel*. The word was extended in Middle English by the *-er* suffix.

oxy-¹ *comb. form* sharp, keen. WH: Greek *oxu-*, comb. form of *oxus* sharp, acute, acid.

oxy-² *comb. form* denoting the presence of oxygen or its acids or of an atom of hydroxyl substituted for one of hydrogen. WH: Comb. form of OXYGEN.

oxyacetylene *a.* yielding a very hot blowpipe flame from the combustion of oxygen and acetylene, used for welding metals etc. WH: early 20C. OXY-² + ACETYLENE.

oxyacid *n.* an acid containing oxygen as distinguished from one formed with hydrogen. WH: 19C. OXY-² + ACID.

oxycarpous *a.* having pointed fruit. WH: 19C. OXY-¹ + Greek *karpos* fruit. See also -OUS.

oxygen *n.* a colourless, tasteless, odourless divalent element, at. no. 8, chem. symbol O, existing in a free state in the atmosphere, combined with hydrogen in water, and with other elements in most mineral and organic substances. WH: 18C. French *oxygène* acidifying principle. See OXY-¹, -GEN. Oxygen was originally supposed to be essentially composed of acids. The term was coined in 1786 by the French chemist Antoine Laurent Lavoisier, who originally called the element *principe oxigine*, then *principe oxygène*. Oxygen was first discovered *c.*1772 by the Swedish chemist Carl Wilhelm Scheele, then independently in 1774 by the English chemist Joseph Priestley, who called it *dephlogisticated air* (see PHLOGISTON).

oxyhaemoglobin *n.* the bright red product formed when oxygen from the lungs combines with haemoglobin. WH: 19C. OXY-² + HAEMOGLOBIN.

oxyhydrogen *a.* consisting of a mixture of oxygen and hydrogen (used to create an intense flame for welding). WH: 19C. OXY-² + HYDROGEN.

oxymoron *n.* a rhetorical figure in which an epithet of a quite contrary signification is added to a word for the sake of point or emphasis, e.g. a clever fool, a cheerful pessimist. WH: 17C. Greek *oxumōron*, neut. sing. (used as n.) of *oxumōros* pointedly foolish, from *oxus* (see OXY-¹) + *mōros* foolish (MORON).

oxytetracycline *n.* a broad-spectrum antibiotic. WH: mid-20C. OXY-² + *tetracycline* (TETRACYCLIC).

oxytocin *n.* a hormone secreted by the pituitary gland that stimulates uterine muscle contraction during childbirth. WH: early 20C. Greek *oxutokia* sudden delivery (from *oxu-* OXY-¹ + *tokos* childbirth) + -IN¹.

oxytone *a.* having an acute accent on the last syllable. *Also n.* WH: 18C. Greek *oxutonos*, from *oxu-* OXY-¹ + *tonos* pitch, accent, TONE.

oyer *n.* a hearing or trial of causes under writ of oyer and terminer. WH: 14–15C. Anglo-French, from Old French *oïr*. See OYEZ, also -ER⁴.

oyez *int.* repeated three times as introduction to any proclamation made by an officer of a court of law or public crier. WH: 14–15C. Old French hear ye! imper. pl. of *oïr* (Modern French *ouïr*), from Latin *audire* to hear. Not rel. to YES or its French equivalent, *oui*.

oyster *n.* any of various bivalve molluscs of the families Ostreidae and Aviculidae, esp. *Ostrea edulis*, found in salt or brackish water, eaten as food. WH: 12–14C. Old French *oistre, uistre* (Modern French *huître*), from Latin *ostrea, ostreum*, from Greek *ostreon*, rel. to *osteon* bone, *ostrakon* shell (cp. OSTRACIZE).

Oz *n.* Australia. *Also a.* WH: early 20C. Representation of pronun. of abbr. of *Australia*.

oz *abbr.* ounce(s). WH: Abbr. of Italian *onza* ounce.

ozocerite *n.* a fossil resin like spermaceti in appearance, used for making candles, insulators etc. WH: 19C. German *Ozokerit*, from Greek *ozein* to smell + *kēros* beeswax. See also -ITE¹. The word was coined in 1833 by the German mineralogist Ernst Friedrich Glocker.

ozone *n.* an allotropic form of oxygen, having three atoms to the molecule, with a slightly pungent odour, found in the atmosphere, probably as the result of electrical action. WH: 19C. Greek *ozein* to smell + -ONE. The gas was named in 1840 by its discoverer, the German chemist Christian Friedrich Schönbein.

pa[1] *n.* father (used by or to children). WH: 19C. Shortening of PAPA[1].

pa[2] *n.* a Maori settlement. WH: 18C. Maori *pà*, from *pā* to block up.

pa'anga *n.* the standard unit of currency of Tonga, in the SW Pacific. WH: mid-20C. Tongan (coin-shaped) seed, money.

pabulum *n.* food; nourishment. WH: 17C. Latin, from stem of *pascere* to feed. Cp. PASTURE. The sense bland intellectual fare arose in the late 20C, perhaps partly influenced by *Pablum*, the proprietary name of a children's breakfast cereal, itself from PABULUM.

paca *n.* a large Central and S American tailless rodent, of the genus *Agouti*. WH: 17C. Spanish and Portuguese, from Tupi *páca*.

pace[1] *n.* a step, the space between the feet in stepping (about 30 in., 76 cm). *Also v.i., v.t.* WH: 12–14C. Old French *pas*, from Latin *passus* step, pace, lit. stretch (of the leg), from *pandere* to stretch, to spread out. Cp. EXPAND.

pace[2] *prep.* with the permission of; with due respect to (someone who disagrees). WH: 18C. Latin, abl. sing. of *pax* peace, as in *pace tua* by your leave.

pachinko *n.* a Japanese form of pinball. WH: mid-20C. Japanese.

pachisi *n.* an Indian game played on a board with cowries for dice, named after the highest throw. WH: 19C. Hindi *pacīsī* (throw of) twenty-five (the highest throw in the game), ult. from Sanskrit *pañcaviṃśati* twenty-five.

pachy- *comb. form* denoting thickness. WH: Greek *pakhus* thick, large.

pachydactyl *a.* having thick toes. WH: 19C. PACHY- + Greek *daktulos* finger, toe.

pachyderm *n.* any large, thick-skinned mammal, esp. an elephant, rhinoceros or hippopotamus. WH: 19C. French *pachyderme*, from Greek *pakhudermos* thick-skinned, from *pakhu-* PACHY- + *derma* skin. The word was coined in 1797 by the French comparative anatomist Baron Cuvier.

pachymeter *n.* an instrument for determining the thickness of glass, paper etc. WH: 19C. PACHY- + -METER.

Pacific *a.* of or relating to the Pacific Ocean. *Also n.* WH: 17C. Medieval Latin (*Mare*) *Pacificum* PACIFIC (sea), Pacific Ocean, between America to the east and Asia to the west. The ocean was so named in 1520 by the Portuguese explorer Ferdinand Magellan (as Portuguese *mar pacifico*) because he had encountered no storms when crossing it on his voyage from Tierra del Fuego to the Philippines.

pacific *a.* inclined or tending to peace. WH: 16C. Old French *pacifique*, from Latin *pacificus*, from *pax*, *pacis* peace. See also -FIC.

pack *n.* a bundle of things tied or wrapped together for carrying. *Also v.t., v.i.* WH: 12–14C. Rel. to Flemish, Dutch, Low German *pak*, of unknown orig.

packet *n.* a small package. *Also v.t.* WH: 16C. PACK + -ET[1], ? based on an Anglo-French formation. Cp. Anglo-Latin *paccettum*. The original sense was a parcel of letters or dispatches, especially official mail to or from foreign countries.

paco *n.* the alpaca. WH: 17C. Spanish, from Quechua *pako* red, reddish yellow.

pact *n.* an agreement, a compact. WH: 14–15C. Old French *pacte*, from Latin *pactum*, use as n. of (neut. of) p.p. of *pacisci* to make a covenant, from base also of *pax* PEACE.

pad[1] *n.* a soft cushion. *Also v.t.* WH: 16C. Prob. of Dutch orig. Cp. obs. Flemish *pad*, Low German *pad* sole of the foot. The original sense (to the 18C) was a bundle of straw to lie on. The sense soft cushion arose in the 17C and that of an animal's cushion-like paw in the 18C.

pad[2] *v.i.* to trudge. *Also v.t., n.* WH: 16C. Low German and Dutch *pad* PATH, or from Low German *padden* to tread, to tramp.

paddle[1] *n.* a broad short oar used without a rowlock. *Also v.t., v.i.* WH: 14–15C. Orig. uncertain. Cp. PATTLE. ? Rel. to PATELLA, PATEN. Not rel. to PADDLE[2]. A paddle was originally a spadelike implement: 'And thou shalt have a paddle [and] thou shalt dig therewith' (Deut. xxiii.13). The current sense dates from the 17C.

paddle[2] *v.i.* to wade in shallow water. *Also n.* WH: 16C. Prob. of Low Dutch orig. Cp. Low German *paddeln* to tramp about, freq. of *padden* PAD[2]. See also -LE[4].

paddock *n.* a small field or enclosure, usu. under pasture and near a stable. *Also v.t.* WH: 17C. Alt. of dial. *parrock*, from Old English *pearruc*. See PARK.

Paddy *n.* an Irishman. WH: 18C. Pet form of Irish male forename *Pádraig* Patrick. See also -Y[3].

paddy[1] *n.* a paddy field. WH: 17C. Malay *pādī*, corr. to Javanese *pari*, Kannada *bhatta*.

paddy[2] *n.* a rage, a temper. WH: 19C. PADDY. The Irish are popularly reputed to have a quick temper.

padella *n.* a shallow dish containing oil etc. in which a wick is set, used esp. in Italy for illuminations. WH: 19C. Italian, from Latin PATELLA.

pademelon *n.* a small bush kangaroo or wallaby of the genus *Thylogale*. WH: 19C. Alt. of Australian Aboriginal (Dharuk) *budimaligan*.

Padishah *n.* the title of the Shah of Iran, also in India of the British sovereign and of the Great Mogul. WH: 17C. Persian *pādišāh*, Pahlavi *pātakšāh*, from *pati* lord + *šāh* SHAH.

padlock *n.* a detachable lock with a bow or loop for fastening to a staple etc. *Also v.t.* WH: 15C. 1st element of unknown orig. + LOCK[1]. The lock is perhaps so called as it was originally shaped like a *pad*, a dialect word for a frog or toad.

padouk *n.* a leguminous tree of the genus *Pterocarpus*, of Africa and Asia. WH: 19C. Burmese.

padre *n.* father (used in addressing a priest in Italy, Spain and Spanish America). WH: 16C. Italian, Spanish and Portuguese, from Latin *pater*, *patris* FATHER.

padrone *n.* a master, an Italian employer or house-owner. WH: 17C. Italian, from Latin *patronus*. See PATRON.

paduasoy *n.* a kind of silk material, frequently used in the 18th cent. WH: 16C. French *pou-de-soie* (earlier *pout de soie*), of unknown orig., by assoc. with earlier *Padua say* say (a cloth resembling serge) from Padua, Italy. French *pou-de-soie* has become associated with *soie* silk. Cp. PEAU-DE-SOIE.

paean *n.* a choral song addressed to Apollo or some other deity. WH: 16C. Latin, from Greek *paian*, *paiōn* hymn to Apollo evoked by the name of *Paian*, *Paiōn*, orig. the Homeric name of the physician of the gods. Cp. PAEON, PEONY.

paedeutics *n.* the science of education. WH: 19C. Greek *paideutikos* of teaching, from *paideutikē* education. See also -ICS.

paediatrics *n.* the branch of medicine dealing with children's diseases. WH: 19C. *paediatric*, from PAEDO- + Greek *iatrikos* (IATRIC). See also -ICS.

paedo- *comb. form* of or relating to children. WH: Greek *pais*, *paidos* child, boy. See also -O-.

paedobaptism *n.* infant baptism, as opposed to adult baptism. WH: 17C. PAEDO- + *baptism* (BAPTIZE).

paedomorphosis *n.* the retention of juvenile features in the adult. WH: early 20C. PAEDO- + MORPHOSIS.

paedophilia *n.* the condition of being sexually attracted to children. WH: early 20C. PAEDO- + -PHILIA.

paella *n.* a Spanish dish of rice, seafood, meat and vegetables, flavoured with saffron. WH: 19C. Catalan, from Old French *paele* (Modern French *poêle*), from Latin *patella* pan, dish. Cp. PATELLA.

paeon *n.* a metrical foot of four syllables, one long and the others short in different order. WH: 17C. Latin, from Greek *paiōn*. See PAEAN.

pagan *n.* a heathen; a barbarous or unenlightened person. *Also a.* WH: 14–15C. Latin *paganus* villager, rustic, civilian, as opp. to *miles* soldier, from *pagus* (rural) district, the country. See also -AN. Cp. HEATHEN. In Christian terms, Latin *paganus* was the heathen, as opposed to *miles Christi*, the soldier of Christ.

page[1] *n.* a leaf or either side of a leaf of a book etc. *Also v.t., v.i.* WH: 16C. Old French, reduced form of *pagene*, from Latin *pagina* vine trellis, column of writing, page, from *pangere* to fasten, to fix in, to fix together.

page[2] *n.* a young male attendant on people of rank. *Also v.t.* WH: 12–14C. Old French, ? from Italian *paggio*, from Greek *paidion*, dim. of *pais*, *paidos* boy. The original meaning (to the 16C) was simply boy. Some authorities dispute the Greek origin.

pageant *n.* a brilliant display or spectacle, esp. a parade. *Also v.t.* WH: 14–15C. Orig. unknown. According to some, the word is from Latin *pagina* PAGE[1], with the addition of *-t* as in ANCIENT[1]. The manuscript page of a play thus came to denote the play itself that formed part of the cycle of mystery plays staged in the original medieval pageant.

pagoda *n.* a sacred temple, usu. in the form of a pyramidal tower in many receding storeys, all elaborately decorated, in China, Japan and other Eastern countries. WH: 16C. Portuguese *pagode*, prob. ult. from Persian *butkada* idol temple, from *but* idol + *kada* habitation, alt. by assoc. with Prakrit *bhagodī* divine, holy.

pagurian *n.* any decapod crustacean of the family Paguridae, a hermit crab. *Also a.* WH: 19C. Modern Latin *Paguridae*, from Latin *pagurus*, Greek *pagouros* a kind of crab. See also -IAN.

pah *int.* used to express disgust or contempt. WH: 16C. Natural exclamation. Cp. BAH.

Pahlavi *n.* the system of characters used for the sacred writings of the Iranians. WH: 18C. Persian *pahlawī*, from *pahlav*, from *parthava* Parthia (PARTHIAN). See also -I[3].

pahoehoe *n.* hardened lava forming smooth, undulating masses. WH: 19C. Hawaiian.

paigle *n.* the cowslip, oxlip or buttercup. WH: 14–15C. Orig. unknown.

pail *n.* an open vessel, usu. round, of metal or plastic, for carrying liquids. WH: pre-1200. Old English *pægel*, from Germanic, of unknown orig. ? Rel. to Latin PATELLA.

paillette *n.* a small piece of metal or foil used in enamel painting. WH: 19C. French, dim. of *paille* straw, chaff. See also -ETTE. Cp. PAILLON.

paillon *n.* a bright metal backing for enamel or painting in translucent colours. WH: 19C. French, deriv. of *paille* scale of chaff. Cp. PAILLETTE.

pain *n.* bodily or mental suffering. *Also v.t.* WH: 12–14C. Old French *peine*, from Latin *poena* penalty, punishment. Cp. PINE[2]. The original sense was suffering or loss inflicted as a punishment.

paint *n.* a solid colouring substance or pigment, usu. dissolved in a liquid vehicle, used to give a coloured coating to surfaces. *Also v.t., v.i.* WH: 12–14C. Old French *peint*, p.p. of *peindre*, from Latin *pingere* to embroider, to tattoo, to paint, to embellish.

painter *n.* a bow-rope for fastening a boat to a ring, stake etc. WH: 12–14C. Appar. from Old French *penteur* rope running from masthead. Not rel. to PAINT.

pair *n.* two things or people of a kind, similar in form, or applied to the same purpose or use. *Also v.t., v.i.* WH: 12–14C. Old French *paire*, from Latin *paria*, neut. pl. of *par* equal. Cp. PAR[1].

paisa *n.* a monetary unit of countries of the Indian subcontinent, equal to one hundredth of a rupee or taka. WH: 19C. Hindi *paisā*. Cp. PICE.

Paisley *n.* (a fabric with) a colourful pattern of small intricate curves. *Also a.* WH: 19C. *Paisley*, a town in central Scotland, where orig. made.

pakeha *n.* a white person, as distinct from a Maori. *Also a.* WH: 19C. Maori.

Paki *n.* a Pakistani. WH: mid-20C. Abbr. of PAKISTANI.

Pakistani *n.* a native or inhabitant of Pakistan, or a descendant of one. *Also a.* WH: mid-20C. *Pakistan*, a country in the N part of the Indian subcontinent, orig. comprising W and E Pakistan (now Bangladesh) + -I[3].

pakora *n.* an Indian dish of pieces of vegetable, chicken etc. dipped in spiced batter and deep-fried. WH: mid-20C. Hindi *pakoṛā* a dish of vegetables in gram flour.

paktong *n.* a Chinese alloy of zinc, nickel and copper, like silver. WH: 18C. Chinese *bái tóng* white copper.

pal *n.* a friend. *Also v.i.* WH: 17C. English Romany pal, brother, rel. to Turkish *pral*, ult. from Sanskrit *bhrātṛ* brother.

palace *n.* the official residence of a monarch, emperor, bishop or other distinguished personage. WH: 12–14C. Old French *paleis* (Modern French *palais*), from Latin *palatium*, from *Palatium* the Palatine Hill in Rome. The original name was transferred from the hill to the house of Augustus built on it, then to the palace of the Caesars which covered it. Cp. PALATINE.

paladin *n.* any one of Charlemagne's 12 peers. WH: 16C. French, from Italian *paladino*, from Latin *palatinus*. See PALATINE.

Palaearctic *a.* of or relating to the Arctic and northern parts of the Old World. *Also n.* WH: 19C. PALAEO- + ARCTIC.

palaeichthyology *n.* the branch of palaeontology concerned with extinct fishes. WH: 19C. PALAEO- + ICHTHYOLOGY.

palaeo- *comb. form* ancient, old, prehistoric. WH: Greek *palaios* ancient. See also -O-.

palaeoanthropology *n.* the branch of anthropology concerned with fossil hominids. WH: early 20C. PALAEO- + ANTHROPOLOGY.

palaeobotany *n.* the botany of extinct or fossil plants. WH: 19C. PALAEO- + BOTANY.

Palaeocene *a., n.* (of or relating to) the oldest epoch of the Tertiary period. WH: 19C. PALAEO- + Greek *kainos* new, recent, based on EOCENE, MIOCENE, etc.

palaeoclimatology *n.* the science of the climates of the geological past. WH: early 20C. PALAEO- + *climatology* (CLIMATE).

palaeoecology *n.* the ecology of extinct and prehistoric organisms. WH: 19C. PALAEO- + ECOLOGY.

palaeogeography *n.* the study of geographical features of the geological past. WH: 19C. PALAEO- + GEOGRAPHY.

palaeography *n.* the art or science of deciphering ancient inscriptions or manuscripts. WH: 19C. French *paléographie*, from Modern Latin *palaeographia*. See PALAEO-, -GRAPHY.

palaeolithic *a.* of or relating to the earlier Stone Age. *Also n.* WH: 19C. PALAEO- + -LITH + -IC. The term was introduced by the English politician and biologist Sir John Lubbock in *Prehistoric Times* (1865).

palaeomagnetism *n.* the study of the magnetic properties of rocks. WH: 19C. PALAEO- + *magnetism* (MAGNET).

palaeontology *n.* the science or the branch of biology or geology dealing with fossil animals and plants. WH: 19C. PALAEO- + Greek *onta*, neut. pl. of *ōn* being, pres. p. of *einai* to be. See also -LOGY. The term was introduced by the Scottish geologist Sir Charles Lyell in *The Elements of Geology* (1838).

palaeotherium *n.* a pachydermatous mammal, chiefly from the Eocene strata. WH: 19C. Modern Latin, from PALAEO- + Greek *thērion* wild animal.

Palaeozoic *a.* of or relating to the lowest fossiliferous strata and the earliest forms of life. *Also n.* WH: 19C. PALAEO- + -ZOIC. The term was introduced in 1838 by the English geologist Adam Sedgwick.

palaestra *n.* in ancient Greece, a place where athletic exercises were taught and practised; a gymnasium or wrestling school. WH: 14–15C. Latin, from Greek *palaistra*, from *palaiein* to wrestle.

palafitte *n.* a prehistoric house built on piles, a lake-dwelling. WH: 19C. French, from Italian *palafitta* fence of stakes, from *palo* stake + *fitto* fixed.

palais *n.* a dance hall. WH: early 20C. French PALACE.

palama *n.* the webbing of the feet of aquatic birds. WH: 19C. Modern Latin, from Greek *palamē* PALM[2].

palampore *n.* a decorated chintz bedspread, formerly made in India. WH: 17C. Prob. from Portuguese *palangapuzes* (pl.), from Urdu and Persian *palangpoš* bed cover (cp. Hindi *palang* bed, Persian *poš* cover), or from *Pālanpur*, a town and former market centre in Gujarat, India.

palanquin *n.* a couch or litter in India and the East carried by four or six people on their shoulders. WH: 16C. Portuguese *palanquim*, from Oriya *pālaṅki*, Hindi *pālkī*, prob. through Malay *palangki*, ult. from Sanskrit *palyaṅka* bed, litter.

palatable *a.* pleasing to taste. WH: 17C. PALATE + -ABLE.

palate *n.* the roof of the mouth. Also *v.t.* WH: 14–15C. Latin *palatum*, of unknown orig.

palatial *a.* magnificent or splendid like a palace. WH: 18C. Latin *palatium* (PALACE) + -AL[1].

palatine *a.* of, relating to or connected with a palace, orig. the palace of the Caesars, later of the German Emperors. Also *n.* WH: 14–15C. Old French *palatin*, from Latin *palatinus* of the palace, from *palatium*. See PALACE, also -INE.

palaver *n.* unnecessary fuss and bother, tedious activity. Also *v.i.*, *v.t.* WH: 18C. Portuguese *palavra*, from Latin *parabola* PARABLE. The original sense was talk, conference, parley, especially between tribespeople and traders or travellers. The sense fuss, bother arose in the 19C.

palay *n.* a small Indian tree with hard, close-grained wood used for turnery. WH: 19C. Tamil.

palberry *n.* a type of currant. WH: 19C. Australian Aboriginal *palbri*, with assim. to BERRY.

pale[1] *a.* ashen, lacking in colour. Also *v.t.*, *v.i.* WH: 12–14C. Old French *palle*, *pale* (Modern French *pâle*), from Latin *pallidus* PALLID.

pale[2] *n.* a pointed stake. Also *v.t.* WH: 12–14C. Old French *pal*, from Latin *palus* stake. Cp. PALLET[2], PEEL[3].

palea *n.* a bract or scale resembling chaff, at the base of the florets in composite flowers, enclosing the stamens and pistil in grass flowers, or on the stems of ferns. WH: 14–15C. Latin chaff.

Palestinian *a.* of or relating to Palestine, a region on the E Mediterranean coast. Also *n.* WH: 19C. *Palestine*, a territory in SW Asia on the E Mediterranean coast + -IAN.

paletot *n.* a loose overcoat for men or women. WH: 19C. French, of unknown orig. ? From Middle English *paltok* a kind of jacket.

palette *n.* a flat board used by artists for mixing colours on. WH: 18C. French. See PALLET[2].

palfrey *n.* a small horse, esp. to be ridden by a woman. WH: 12–14C. Old French *palefrei* (Modern French *palefroi*), from Medieval Latin *palefredus*, alt. of Late Latin *paraveredus*, from Greek *para* beside, extra (PARA-[1]) + Latin *veredus* light horse, of Gaulish orig.

Pali *n.* the canonical language of Buddhist literature, related to Sanskrit. Also *a.* WH: 18C. Pali *pāli* (the) canonical text (as opposed to the commentary).

†palification *n.* the driving of piles for a foundation etc. WH: 17C. Medieval Latin *palificatio*, *palificationis*, from *palificare* to make a foundation of piles, from *palus* pile, stake + *-ficare* to make. See also -ATION.

palimony *n.* alimony paid to an unmarried partner after the end of a long-term relationship. WH: early 20C. Blend of PAL and ALIMONY.

palimpsest *n.* a manuscript on parchment or other material from which the original writing has been erased to make room for another record. Also *a.*, *v.t.* WH: 17C. Latin *palimpsestus*, from Greek *palimpsestos*, from *palin* again + *psestos*, p.p. formation from *psēn* to rub smooth.

palindrome *n.* a word, verse or sentence that reads the same backwards and forwards, e.g. 'Madam I'm Adam' (Adam's alleged self-introduction to Eve). WH: 17C. Greek *palindromos* running back again, from *palin* back, again + *drom-*, *dramein* to run.

palingenesia *n.* a new birth, a regeneration. WH: 17C. French *palingénésie*, from Medieval Latin *palingenesia*, from Greek *paliggenesia* rebirth, from *palin* again + *genesis* birth. See also -Y[2].

palingenesis *n.* the form of ontogenesis in which the development of the ancestors is exactly reproduced. WH: 19C. Greek *palin* again + *genesis* birth.

palinode *n.* a poem in which a previous poem, usu. satirical, is retracted. Also *v.t.* WH: 16C. Obs. French, from Latin *palinodia*, from Greek *palinōidia*, from *palin* again + *ōidē* song, ode.

palisade *n.* a fence or fortification of stakes, timbers or iron railings. Also *v.t.* WH: 17C. French *palissade*, from Provençal *palissada*, from *palissa* fence of pales, from Latin *palus* PALE[2]. See also -ADE.

pall[1] *n.* a large cloth, thrown over a coffin. Also *v.t.* WH: pre-1200. Latin PALLIUM covering, Greek mantle, philosopher's cloak. The

original sense was a fine or rich (often purple) cloth for robes. The current sense evolved in the 12–14C.

pall[2] *v.i.* to become insipid; to become boring. Also *v.t.* WH: 14–15C. Shortening of APPAL (in its orig. sense of to grow pale, to fade). The original sense (to the 19C) was to become pale, to become dim. The sense to become uninteresting dates from the 18C.

Palladian *a.* of or relating to Andrea Palladio, or his school of architecture. WH: 18C. Andrea *Palladio*, 1518–80, Italian architect + -IAN.

palladium[1] *n.* a greyish-white metallic element of the platinum group, at. no. 46, chem. symbol Pd, used as an alloy with gold and other metals. WH: 19C. *Pallas* (PALLADIUM[2]) + -IUM. The metal was named by its discoverer, the English chemist William H. Wollaston, and given in 1803 for the asteroid *Pallas* discovered in 1802. Cp. CERIUM.

palladium[2] *n.* a defence, a safeguard. WH: 14–15C. Latin, from Greek *palladion*, from *Pallas*, *Pallados* an epithet of Athene, the Greek goddess of wisdom. See also -IUM. An image of the goddess Pallas Athene was in the citadel of Troy and the safety of the city was supposed to depend on it. The goddess also gave the name of the asteroid *Pallas* (see PALLADIUM[1]).

pallescent *a.* growing pale. WH: 17C. Latin *pallescens*, *pallescentis*, pres.p. of *pallescere* to become pale, from *pallere* to be pale. See also -escent (-ESCENCE).

pallet[1] *n.* a straw mattress. WH: 12–14C. Anglo-French *paillete*, from *paille* straw, from Latin *palea* chaff. See also -ET[1]. Cp. PALLIASSE.

pallet[2] *n.* a flat wooden structure on which boxes, crates etc. are stacked or transported. WH: 14–15C. Old French *palette*, dim. of *pale* spade, blade, from Latin *pala* spade, shovel, rel. to *palus* stake. Cp. PALE[2], PEEL[3]. The word was originally used for a flat wooden blade used in pottery. The sense small platform on which goods can be stacked and stored dates only from the early 20C.

palliasse *n.* a mattress of straw. WH: 16C. Old French *paillasse*, from Italian *pagliaccio*, from Latin *palea* straw, chaff.

palliate *v.t.* to excuse; to extenuate. WH: 14–15C. Late Latin *palliatus*, p.p. of *palliare* to cover, to hide, to conceal, from Latin PALLIUM. See also -ATE[3].

pallid *a.* pale, wan. WH: 16C. Latin *pallidus*, rel. to *pallere* to be pale. See also -ID.

pallium *n.* a scarflike vestment of white wool with red crosses, worn by the Pope and certain metropolitans and archbishops. WH: 12–14C. Latin. Cp. PALL[1].

pall-mall *n.* an old game in which a ball was driven with a mallet through an iron ring. WH: 16C. Obs. French *pallemaille*, from Italian *pallamaglio*, from *palla*, var. of *balla* BALL[1] + *maglio* mallet. Cp. MALL, MALLET. Not rel. to PELL-MELL.

pallone *n.* an Italian game like tennis, in which the ball is struck with the arm protected by a wooden guard. WH: 19C. Italian, augm. of *palla* ball.

pallor *n.* paleness, lack of healthy colour. WH: 14–15C. Latin, rel. to *pallere* to be pale. See also -OR.

palm[1] *n.* a tree of the Palmae, a family of tropical or subtropical endogens, usu. with a tall branched stem and head of large fan-shaped leaves. WH: pre-1200. Old English, from Germanic, from Latin *palma* PALM[2]. The leaf of the palm tree is like a spread hand.

palm[2] *n.* the inner part of the hand. Also *v.t.* WH: 12–14C. Old French *paume*, from Latin *palma*.

palmer *n.* a pilgrim who carried a palm branch as a token of having been to the Holy Land. WH: 12–14C. Old French *palmier*, from Medieval Latin *palmarius*, from Latin *palma* PALM[1]. See also -ER[2].

palmette *n.* a carved or painted ornament in the form of a palm leaf. WH: 19C. French, dim. of *palme* PALM[1]. See also -ETTE.

palmetto *n.* a small palm, esp. *Sabal palmetto*, a fan palm of the southern US. WH: 16C. Spanish *palmito* dwarf fan palm, dim. of *palma* PALM[1], later assim. to Italian dims. in *-etto*.

palmier *n.* a sweet pastry shaped like a palm leaf. WH: early 20C. French, lit. palm tree.

palmification *n.* a method, employed by the Babylonians, of artificially fertilizing the female flowers of the date palm by suspending clusters of male flowers of the wild date above them. WH: 19C. Latin *palma* PALM[1], based on CAPRIFICATION.

palmiped *a.* (of a bird) having palmate or webbed feet. *Also n.* WH: 17C. Latin *palmipes, palmipedis,* from *palma* PALM² + *pes, pedis* foot.

palmitic *a.* of or derived from palm oil. WH: 19C. French *palmitique,* from *palme* PALM¹. See also -IC.

palmyra *n.* an Asian palm, *Borassus flabellifer,* with fan-shaped leaves used for mat-making. WH: 17C. Portuguese *palmeira* palm tree, with spelling influ. by *Palmyra,* an ancient city in Syria.

palomino *n.* a cream, yellow or gold horse with a white mane and tail. WH: early 20C. American Spanish, from Spanish, from Latin *palumbinus* like a dove, from *palumba* ring dove. The horse is so called because of its dovelike colouring.

paloverde *n.* any yellow-flowered American tree of the genus *Cercidium.* WH: 19C. American Spanish green tree, from *palo* tree + *verde* green.

palp *n.* a jointed sense organ developed from the lower jaw of an insect etc., a feeler. WH: 19C. French *palpe,* from Latin *palpus,* from *palpare.* See PALPATE.

palpable *a.* easily perceived, obvious. WH: 14–15C. Late Latin *palpabilis,* from Latin *palpare.* See PALPATE, also -ABLE.

palpate *v.t.* to feel, to handle, to examine by touch. WH: 19C. Latin *palpatus,* p.p. of *palpare* to touch gently. See also -ATE³.

palpebral *a.* of or relating to the eyelid. WH: 19C. Latin *palpebra* eyelid + -AL¹.

palpitate *v.i.* (of the heart) to beat rapidly. WH: 17C. Latin *palpitatus,* p.p. of *palpitare,* freq. of *palpare.* See PALPATE.

palsgrave *n.* a Count Palatine, orig. one who had the super-intendence of a prince's palace. WH: 16C. Early Dutch *paltsgrave* (Middle Dutch *paltsgraaf*), from *palts* palatinate + *grave* count.

palstave *n.* a bronze chisel shaped like an axe head, made to fit into a handle instead of being socketed. WH: 19C. Dutch *paalstav,* from Old Norse *pálstavr,* from *páll* hoe, spade (from Latin *palus* stake, PALE²) + *stafr* STAFF¹.

palsy *n.* paralysis. *Also v.t.* WH: 12–14C. Old French *paralisie,* from alt. of Latin PARALYSIS.

palter *v.i.* to equivocate, to shuffle, to haggle. WH: 16C. Orig. unknown. The original sense was to speak indistinctly, to mumble. The current sense dates from the 17C.

paltry *a.* petty, trivial. WH: 16C. Appar. from a var. of dial. *pelt* trash, rubbish + -RY. Cp. Middle Low German *palter-* in *palterlappen* rags, Low German *paltrig* ragged, torn.

paludal *a.* of or relating to marshes or fens, marshy. WH: Latin *palus, paludis* marsh + -AL¹. See also -OUS.

paludament *n.* a cloak worn by an ancient Roman general and his chief officers. WH: 17C. Latin *paludamentum.*

Paludrine® *n.* a synthetic quinine substitute for the treatment of malaria. WH: mid-20C. Latin *palus, paludis* marsh + -*rine,* based on *Atabrine* (ATEBRIN®), MEPACRINE.

palynology *n.* the study of pollen grains and other spores. WH: mid-20C. Greek *palunein* to sprinkle + -O- + -LOGY.

pam *n.* in cards, the knave of clubs, esp. in the game loo, where this is the highest trump. WH: 17C. Appar. from French *pamphile,* from Greek *Pamphilos* beloved of all. Cp. PAMPHLET.

pampas *n.pl.* the open, far-extending, treeless plains in S America, south of the Amazon. WH: 18C. Spanish, pl. of *pampa,* from Quechua plain.

pamper *v.t.* to indulge (a person, oneself), often excessively. WH: 14–15C. Prob. of Low German or Low Dutch orig. Cp. German dial. *pampen, pampfen* to cram, to gorge, prob. nasalized var. of base of PAP¹.

pampero *n.* a violent westerly or south-westerly wind blowing over the pampas. WH: 18C. Spanish from *pampa* (PAMPAS) + -*ero.*

pamphlet *n.* a small unbound booklet of a few sheets. *Also v.t.* WH: 14–15C. *Pamphilet,* short name of a 12C Latin love poem, *Pamphilus, seu de Amore,* Pamphilus, or about Love, from Greek *pamphilos* beloved by all, from *pan-* all + -*philos* loving. Not rel. to -LET.

pamplegia *n.* general paralysis. WH: 19C. Modern Latin from Greek *pam-,* assim. form of PAN- + *plēgē* stroke.

pan¹ *n.* a broad shallow vessel of metal or earthenware, usu. for cooking. *Also v.t., v.i.* WH: pre-1200. Old English *panne,* from Germanic, ? from pop. var. of Latin *patina* (PATEN).

pan² *n.* a betel leaf. WH: 17C. Hindi *pān* betel leaf, from Sanskrit *parna* leaf.

pan- *comb. form* all. WH: Greek, from *pan,* neut. of *pas* all.

panacea *n.* a universal remedy. WH: 16C. Latin, from Greek *panakeia,* from *panakēs* all-healing, from PAN- + base of *akos* remedy. See also -A¹.

panache *n.* show, swagger, bounce; style; airs. WH: 16C. French, from Italian *pennacchio,* from Late Latin *pinnaculum,* dim. of *pinna* feather. The original sense was a tuft or plume of feathers, especially as headdress. The current sense dates from the 19C.

panada *n.* a paste made of flour, water etc. WH: 16C. Spanish and Portuguese, from deriv. of Latin *panis* bread. See also -ADE.

panaesthesia *n.* the whole sum of perceptions by an individual at any given time. WH: 19C. Greek PAN- + *aisthēsis* perception (cp. AESTHESIA).

Pan-African *a.* of or relating to the whole of the African continent. WH: early 20C. PAN- + AFRICAN.

panama *n.* a hat made from the undeveloped leaves of a pine tree. WH: 19C. *Panama,* a country in Central America. Panama hats were originally made in S America, not Central America.

Panamanian *n.* a native or inhabitant of the Republic of Panama, Central America, or a descendant of one. *Also a.* WH: 19C. PANAMA + -*n-* + -IAN. The -*n-* is purely for euphony.

Pan-American *a.* of or relating to the whole of N, S and Central America. WH: 19C. PAN- + AMERICAN.

Pan-Arabic *a.* of or relating to all the Arab nations. WH: mid-20C. PAN- + *Arabic* (ARAB).

panarthritis *n.* inflammation involving the whole structure of a joint. WH: 19C. PAN- + *arthritis* (ARTHRITIC).

panatella *n.* a type of long, slender cigar. WH: 19C. American Spanish *panatela* long thin biscuit, sponge cake, from Spanish, from Italian *panatella* small loaf, dim. of *panata.* See PANADA, also -EL.

Panathenaea *n.* in ancient Greece, the chief annual festival of the Athenians, celebrating with games and processions the union of Attica under Theseus. WH: 17C. Greek *panathēnaia,* neut. pl. a., from PAN- + *Athēnaios* Athenian, from *Athēnai* Athens or *Athēnē* Athene.

panchayat *n.* a village council in India. WH: 19C. Hindi *pañcāyat,* prob. from Sanskrit *pañcāyatta,* from *pañca* five + *āyatta* depending on.

Panchen Lama *n.* a Grand Lama of Tibet, next in rank after the Dalai Lama. WH: 18C. Tibetan, abbr. of *pandi-tachen-po* great learned one (cp. PUNDIT) + LAMA.

pancheon *n.* a large earthenware pan, used for standing milk in etc. WH: 17C. Appar. from PAN¹. Cp. *luncheon* (LUNCH).

panchromatic *a.* uniformly sensitive to all colours. WH: early 20C. PAN- + CHROMATIC.

pancratium *n.* in ancient Greece, an athletic contest including both boxing and wrestling. WH: 17C. Latin, from Greek *pagkration,* from PAN- + *kratos* strength. See also -IUM.

pancreas *n.* a gland near the stomach secreting a fluid that aids digestive action. WH: 16C. Modern Latin, from Greek *pagkreas,* from PAN- + *kreas* flesh.

panda *n.* a large, black-and-white, bearlike mammal, *Ailuropoda melanoleuca,* from China and Tibet, a giant panda. WH: 19C. Local word in Nepal.

pandanus *n.* a tropical tree or bush of the genus *Pandanus,* containing the screw pines. WH: 19C. Modern Latin, from Malay *pandan.*

Pandean *a.* of or relating to the god Pan. WH: 19C. *Pan,* a rural god of Greek mythology + -*dean,* adjectival suf. based on some spurious classical analogy.

pandect *n.* the digest of the Roman civil law made by direction of the emperor Justinian in the 6th cent. WH: 16C. French *pandecte,* from Latin *pandecta,* from Greek *pandektēs* all-receiver, from PAN- + *dekhesthai* to receive.

pandemic *a.* affecting a whole country or the whole world. *Also n.* WH: 17C. Greek *pandēmos* public, from PAN- + *dēmos* people. See also -IC.

pandemonium *n.* confusion, uproar. WH: 17C. Modern Latin *Pandaemonium,* from PAN- + Greek *daimōn* DEMON. See also -IUM. The word was originally the name of the abode of all demons, otherwise Hell, and specifically that of the capital of Hell in Milton's *Paradise Lost* (1667). The current sense dates from the 19C.

pander *v.i.* to do something that someone wants. *Also v.t., n.* WH: 14–15C. *Pandarus*, a character in Chaucer's *Troilus and Criseyde* (*c.*1385) who procures for Troilus the love of Criseyde, from Italian *Pandaro*, a similar character in Boccaccio, from Latin *Pandarus*, from Greek *Pandaros*. The original sense was a go-between in an illicit love affair. The current sense (as a verb) dates from the 17C.

pandiculation *n.* a stretching of the body and limbs in drowsiness or in certain nervous disorders. WH: 17C. Latin *pandiculatus*, p.p. of *pandiculari* to stretch oneself, from *pandus* bent (with dim. element), from *pandere* to stretch, to spread. See also -ATION.

Pandora's box *n.* an action which triggers a series of problems. WH: 16C. Greek *Pandōra*, lit. all-gifted, the name in Greek mythology of the first mortal woman, on whom all the gods and goddesses bestowed gifts, from PAN- + *dōron* gift. Pandora's box enclosed all human ills or blessings, which flew out when she opened it out of curiosity, with the exception of hope.

pandore *n.* a lutelike musical instrument, a bandore. WH: 16C. Italian *pandora*, from Latin *pandura*, from Greek *pandoura*, of unknown orig.

pandour *n.* any one of a body of Croatian foot soldiers, noted for their ferocity, who were enrolled in the Austrian army. WH: 18C. French and German *Pandur*, from Serbo-Croat *pandur* constable, bailiff, prob. from Medieval Latin *banderius* guard of cornfields and vineyards.

pandowdy *n.* a deep-dish dessert of sweetened apple slices topped with a cake crust. WH: 19C. Orig. unknown. 1st element may be PAN[1].

panduriform *a.* fiddle-shaped. WH: 18C. Latin *pandura* PANDORE + -*i*- + -FORM.

pane *n.* a sheet of glass in a window. *Also v.t.* WH: 12–14C. Old French *pan*, from Latin *pannus* (piece of) cloth. Cp. PANEL. The original meaning was a piece of cloth. The sense sheet of glass in a window arose in the 14–15C.

panegyric *n.* a eulogy written or spoken in praise of some person, act or thing. *Also a.* WH: 17C. French *panégyrique*, from Latin *panegyricus* public eulogy, use as n. of a. from Greek *panēgurikos*, from *panēguris* general assembly, from PAN- + *aguris* AGORA[1]. See also -IC.

panel *n.* a rectangular piece (orig. of cloth). *Also v.t.* WH: 12–14C. Old French *piece of cloth, saddle cushion (Modern French *panneau*), from dim. of Latin *pannus*. See PANE, also -EL. The sense piece of cloth transferred to piece of parchment in the 14–15C. Hence written list, as of jurors (14–15C), game participants (16C), doctors (early 20C).

pang *n.* a sudden paroxysm of extreme pain, either physical or mental. *Also v.t.* WH: 15C. Alt. of PRONG.

panga *n.* a broad, heavy, African knife. WH: mid-20C. E African name.

pangenesis *n.* reproduction from every unit of the organism, a theory of heredity provisionally suggested by Darwin. WH: 19C. PAN- + GENESIS. The word was coined in 1868 by the English naturalist Charles Darwin.

Pan-German *a.* of or relating to Germans collectively or to Pan-Germanism. WH: 19C. PAN- + GERMAN.

pangolin *n.* a scaly anteater, of various species belonging to the genus *Manis* or *Phataginus*. WH: 18C. Malay *peng-guling*, lit. roller. The animal is so called from its habit of rolling itself up.

panhandle *n.* a strip of territory belonging to one political division extending between two others. *Also v.t., v.i.* WH: 19C. PAN[1] + HANDLE.

panharmonicon *n.* a mechanical musical instrument. WH: 19C. PAN- + Greek *harmonikon*, neut. sing. of *harmonikos* HARMONIC.

Panhellenic *a.* of, characteristic of, including or representing all Greeks. WH: 19C. PAN- + *Hellenic* (HELLENE).

panic[1] *n.* sudden, overpowering fear, esp. when many people are affected. *Also a., v.t., v.i.* WH: 17C. French *panique*, from Modern Latin *panicus*, from Greek *panikos*, from *Pan*, the Greek god of nature. Woodland sounds were attributed to Pan, and his appearance or unseen presence was said to cause terror in herds and crowds.

panic[2] *n.* any of several species of the genus *Panicum*. WH: 14–15C. Latin *panicum*, rel. to *panus* thread wound on a bobbin, swelling, ear of millet, from Greek *pēnos* web. Cp. PANICLE. Latin *panicum* foxtail millet was adopted by Linnaeus as a genus name.

panicle *n.* a loose and irregular compound flower cluster. WH: 16C. Latin *pannicula*, dim. of *panus*. See PANIC[2], also -CLE.

panification *n.* the process of making or converting into bread. WH: 18C. French, from *panifier* to make into bread, from Latin *panis* bread. See also -FICATION.

Pan-Islam *n.* the whole of Islam. WH: 19C. PAN- + ISLAM.

panjandrum *n.* a mock title for a self-important or arrogant person. WH: 19C. Invented word, occurring as *Grand Panjandrum* in a nonsense verse (1755) by the English playwright and actor Samuel Foote. The title simulates grandiose words beginning *pan*- (Greek *all*).

panlogism *n.* the doctrine that the universe is the outward manifestation of the inward idea or logos. WH: 19C. PAN- + Greek *logos* speech, word, reason. See also -ISM.

panmixia *n.* fortuitous mingling of hereditary characters due to the cessation of the influence of natural selection with regard to organs that have become useless. WH: 19C. Modern Latin, from German *Panmixie*, from *Pan-* PAN- + Greek *mixia*, from *mixis* mixing, mingling.

panne *n.* a soft, long-napped fabric. WH: 18C. French, of unknown orig. ? From Latin *penna* feather.

pannier[1] *n.* a large basket, esp. one of a pair slung over the back of a beast of burden. WH: 12–14C. Old French *panier*, from Latin *panarium* bread basket, from *panis* bread. See also -IER.

pannier[2] *n.* any of the robed waiters in the dining hall at the Inns of Court. WH: 19C. Orig. unknown.

pannikin *n.* a small drinking cup of metal. WH: 19C. PAN[1], based on CANNIKIN.

pannose *a.* like cloth in texture. WH: 19C. Latin *pannosus* ragged, raglike, from *pannus* cloth. See also -OSE[1].

pannus *n.* an opaque vascular state of the cornea. WH: 14–15C. ? Latin cloth.

panoistic *a.* (of the ovaries of some insects) producing ova only, as distinct from *meroistic*. WH: 19C. PAN- + Greek *ōion* egg + -*istic* (-IST, -IC).

panophobia *n.* excessive or irrational fear. WH: 18C. Greek *Pan*, gen. *Panos* (PANIC[1]) + -*phobia* (-PHOBE).

panoply *n.* a full, impressive array. WH: 16C. French *panoplie*, or from Modern Latin *panoplia* full armour of a hoplite, from *pan-* PAN- + *hopla* arms. See also -Y[2]. The original meaning was a complete defence or protection, with senses often implying a biblical allusion to 'the whole armour of God' (Eph. vi.11) (in the original Greek, *tēn panoplian tou Theou*). The sense full, impressive array evolved in the 19C.

panoptic *a.* viewing all aspects. WH: 19C. Greek *panoptos* seen by all, *panoptēs* all-seeing, from PAN- + *optos* visible. See also -IC.

panorama *n.* a continuous picture of a complete scene on a sheet unrolled before the spectator or on the inside of a large cylindrical surface viewed from the centre. WH: 18C. PAN- + Greek *orama* view.

pan pipes *n.pl.* a musical instrument made of a number of pipes or reeds, a mouth organ, originally associated with Pan, the chief rural divinity of the Greeks. WH: 19C. *Pan*, the Greek rural god said to have invented it (see PANIC[1]) + PIPE + -S[1].

Pan-Presbyterian *a.* of or relating to all Presbyterians. WH: 19C. PAN- + *Presbyterian* (PRESBYTER).

Pan-Slavism *n.* a movement for the union of all the Slavic peoples. WH: 19C. PAN- + SLAV + -ISM, based on German *Pansclavismus*.

pansophy *n.* universal knowledge. WH: 17C. PAN- + Greek *sophia* wisdom. See also -Y[2].

panspermatism *n.* the theory that the atmosphere is pervaded by invisible germs which develop on finding a suitable environment. WH: 19C. Greek *panspermos* containing all kinds of seed, from PAN[1] + *sperma, spermatos* seed, SPERM. See also -ISM.

pansy *n.* any of various garden plants of the genus *Viola*, with flowers of various rich colours. WH: 14–15C. Old French *pensée* thought, pansy, from *penser* to think, from Latin *pensare* to weigh, to consider. Cp. *forget-me-not* (FORGET).

pant[1] *v.i.* to breathe quickly, to gasp for breath. *Also v.t., n.* WH: 12–14C. Rel. to Old French *pantaisier* to be agitated, to gasp, to pant, from Greek *phantasioun* to cause to imagine, to make sport of, from *phantasia*. See FANTASY.

pant[2] *n.* pants. WH: 19C. Back-formation from PANTS.

pantagamy *n.* a system of communistic marriage in which all the men are married to all the women, as practised in the Oneida Community in Idaho, from 1838 onwards. WH: 19C. Alt. of PANTO- + -GAMY.

Pantagruelism *n.* coarse and boisterous burlesque and buffoonery, esp. with a serious purpose, like that of Pantagruel. WH: 19C. *Pantagruel*, a giant in Rabelais's *Gargantua and Pantagruel* (1532–64), represented as a coarse and extravagant humorist + -ISM.

pantalets *n.pl.* loose drawers extending below the skirts, with frills at the bottom, worn by children and women in the early 19th cent. WH: 19C. Dim. of PANTALOONS. See also -ET[1], -S[1].

pantaloons *n.pl.* tight trousers fastened below the shoe, as worn in the Regency period. WH: 16C. French *pantalon*, from Italian *pantalone*. See also -OON, -S[1]. Cp. PANTS. *Pantalone* was the name of a Venetian character in the Italian *commedia dell'arte*, portrayed as a lean and foolish old man, wearing spectacles, pantaloons and slippers. The English garment was first worn in the 17C.

pantechnicon *n.* a pantechnicon van. WH: 19C. PAN- + Greek *tekhnikon*, neut. of *tekhnikos* (TECHNIC). The word was originally the name of a large building in London. It originally housed artistic work but was subsequently converted into a furniture repository.

pantheism *n.* the doctrine that God and the universe are identical. WH: 18C. PAN- + Greek *theos* god + -ISM.

pantheon *n.* a building dedicated to the illustrious dead. WH: 12–14C. Latin, from Greek *pantheion*, from PAN- + *theios* divine, *theos* god.

panther *n.* a black leopard. WH: 12–14C. Old French *pantere* (Modern French *panthère*), from Latin *panthera*, from Greek *panthēr*. The Greek name was long popularly understood as *pan* all + *thēr* beast, giving rise to many fanciful stories about the animal and its origins.

panties *n.pl.* women's or girls' short knickers. WH: 19C. Dim. of PANTS. See also -Y[3], -S[1].

pantile *n.* a tile having an S-shaped cross-section. WH: 17C. PAN[1] + TILE, prob. based on Dutch *dakpan* roof pan. Cp. German *Dachpfanne*, *Pfannenziegel* pantile.

pantisocracy *n.* a Utopian scheme of communism in which all are equal in rank, and all are ruled by all. WH: 18C. PANTO- + *isocracy* equality of power (see ISO-, -CRACY).

panto *n.* a (Christmas) pantomime. WH: 19C. Abbr. of PANTOMIME.

panto- *comb. form* all. WH: Greek, comb. form of *pan*. See PAN-, also -O-.

pantograph *n.* a drawing instrument used to enlarge, copy or reduce plans etc. WH: 18C. PANTO- + -GRAPH.

pantomime *n.* a theatrical entertainment for children, usu. based on a fairy tale and produced at Christmas time. *Also v.t., v.i.* WH: 16C. French, or from Latin *pantomimus*, from Greek *pantomimos*. See PANTO-, MIME. The word was originally the term for a mimic actor in ancient Rome. The sense was transferred to that of a mimed performance to music in the 17C and to the traditional Christmas entertainment in the 18C.

pantophagist *n.* a person or animal that eats all kinds of food, an omnivore. WH: 19C. PANTO- + Greek *phagein* to eat (-PHAGOUS) + -IST. Cp. OMNIVORE.

pantoscope *n.* a panoramic camera. WH: 19C. PANTO- + -SCOPE.

pantothenic acid *n.* an oily acid, a member of the vitamin B complex. WH: mid-20C. Greek *pantothen* from every side + -IC.

pantry *n.* a room or cupboard in which dishes, cutlery etc. are kept. WH: 12–14C. Old French *panetrie*, from *panetier*, from Late Latin *panarius* bread-seller, from *panis* bread. See also -RY. The pantry, where the bread was kept, was originally under the charge of the *panter*, the officer of the household who supplied the bread.

pants *n.pl.* underpants for men and boys. WH: 19C. Abbr. of PANTALOONS. The original sense (as still in N America) was trousers. The sense underpants developed in the early 20C.

panty girdle *n.* a girdle shaped like pants. WH: mid-20C. From *panty*, sing. of PANTIES + GIRDLE[1].

pantyhose *n.pl.* women's tights. WH: mid-20C. From *panty*, sing. of PANTIES + HOSE.

panzer *n.* armoured troops, esp. an armoured division, in the German army. *Also a.* WH: mid-20C. German mail, coat of mail, ult. rel. to PAUNCH.

pap[1] *n.* soft or semi-liquid food for infants etc. WH: 14–15C. Prob. from Low German *pappe*, prob. from Medieval Latin, from Latin *pappare* to eat. Cp. German *Pappe*.

pap[2] *n.* a teat, a nipple. WH: 12–14C. Prob. from Scandinavian base imit. of sound of sucking. Cp. Latin *papilla* nipple.

†papa[1] *n.* father (used by or to children). WH: 17C. French, from Late Latin *papa*, from Greek *pappas*, *papas* father. Cp. POPPA.

papa[2] *n.* the pope. WH: pre-1200. Ecclesiastical Latin bishop, and specifically the Bishop of Rome. See POPE[1]. The sense priest of the Greek church derives from Greek *papas* father.

papa[3] *n.* a blue clay found in New Zealand. WH: 19C. Maori.

papabile *a.* suitable for high office. WH: mid-20C. Italian suitable to be a pope. See PAPA[2].

papacy *n.* the office, dignity or tenure of office of a pope. WH: 14–15C. Medieval Latin *papatia*. See PAPA[2], also -ACY.

papain *n.* a protein compound found in the milky juice of the pawpaw, used to tenderize meat and to aid digestion. WH: 19C. From *papaya*, var. of PAWPAW + -IN[1].

paparazzo *n.* a freelance professional photographer who specializes in photographing celebrities at private moments, usu. without their consent. WH: mid-20C. Italian, from *Paparazzo*, name of a freelance photographer in the Italian film *La Dolce Vita* (1959). The word has become popularly associated with PAPER (i.e. newspaper).

papaveraceous *a.* of or relating to the poppy family Papaveraceae. WH: 19C. Modern Latin *Papaveraceae*, from Latin *papaver* poppy. See also -ACEOUS.

papaverous *a.* resembling or allied to the poppy. WH: 17C. Latin *papaver* poppy + -OUS.

paper *n.* a thin flexible substance made of wood pulp or similar material, used for writing and printing on, wrapping etc. *Also a., v.t.* WH: 12–14C. Old French *papier*, from Latin *papyrus* PAPYRUS.

papeterie *n.* an ornamental case for writing materials. WH: 19C. French paper manufacture, stationer's shop, writing case, from *papetier* paper-maker. See PAPER.

Paphian *a.* of or relating to Paphos. *Also n.* WH: 16C. Latin *Paphius*, from *Paphos*, a city of Cyprus formerly sacred to Aphrodite or Venus. See also -AN.

papier mâché *n.* a material made from pulped paper, moulded into trays, boxes etc. *Also a.* WH: 18C. French, lit. chewed paper, from *papier* PAPER + *mâché*, p.p. of *mâcher* to chew, from Latin *masticare* (cp. MASTICATE). The material was promoted commercially under this name in Britain apparently in the belief that it meant mashed paper. It may thus not actually have been of French origin.

papilionaceous *a.* resembling a butterfly (used of plants with butterfly-shaped flowers, such as the pea). WH: 17C. Modern Latin *papilionaceus*, from Latin *papilio*, *papilionis* butterfly. See also -ACEOUS.

papilla *n.* a small pap, nipple or similar process; a small protuberance on an organ or part of the body or on plants. WH: 17C. Latin nipple, dim. of *papula* PAPULE. Cp. PAP[2].

papillon *n.* a breed of toy spaniel. WH: early 20C. French butterfly. The dog is so named from its butterfly-shaped ears.

papillote *n.* a paper frill round a cutlet etc. WH: 18C. French, from *papillot*, dim. of *papillon* butterfly.

papist *n.* a Roman Catholic. *Also a.* WH: 16C. French *papiste*, or from Modern Latin *papista*, from Ecclesiastical Latin *papa* POPE[1]. See PAPA[2], also -IST.

papoose *n.* a young N American Indian child. WH: 17C. Algonquian *papoos*.

pappus *n.* the calyx of composite plants, consisting of a tuft of down or fine hairs or similar agent for dispersing the seed. WH: 18C. Latin, from Greek *pappos*, lit. grandfather.

paprika *n.* a sweet variety of red pepper. WH: 19C. Hungarian, from Serbo-Croat *pàpar* pepper, from Latin *piper* PEPPER.

Pap test *n.* a test for the early diagnosis of cervical cancer in which cells are scraped from the cervix, and examined under a microscope. WH: mid-20C. Abbr. of name of George N. *Papanicolaou*, 1883–1962, Greek-born US anatomist.

Papua New Guinean *a.* of or relating to Papua New Guinea. *Also n.* WH: late 20C. *Papua New Guinea*, an island country in the SW Pacific + -AN.

papule *n.* a pimple. WH: 18C. Latin *papula*. See also -ULE.

papyrology *n.* the study of ancient papyri. WH: 19C. Greek *papuros* PAPYRUS + -O- + -LOGY.

papyrus *n.* a rushlike plant of the genus *Cyperus papyrus*, formerly common on the Nile and still found in Ethiopia, Syria etc. WH: 14–15C. Latin, from Greek *papuros* paper-reed, of unknown orig. Cp. PAPER.

par[1] *n.* average or normal condition, rate etc. WH: 16C. Latin equal, equality.

par[2] *n.* in journalism, a paragraph. WH: 19C. Abbr. of PARAGRAPH.

para-[1] *comb. form* denoting closeness of position, correspondence of parts, situation on the other side, wrongness, irregularity, alteration etc. WH: Greek, from *para* beside, by, beyond.

para-[2] *comb. form* of or relating to protection. WH: 19C. French, from Italian, imper. of *parare* to defend, to shield, to cover from, from Latin *parare*, to prepare.

parabaptism *n.* irregular or uncanonical baptism. WH: 18C. Late Greek *parabaptisma* irregular baptism, from PARA-[1] + *baptisma* baptism (BAPTIZE).

parabasis *n.* a choral part in ancient Greek comedy in which the chorus addressed the audience, in the name of the poet, on personal or public topics. WH: 19C. Greek from *parabainein* to go aside, to step forward, from *parabainein* to go aside, to step forward, from PARA-[1] + *bainein* to step, to walk.

parabiosis *n.* the anatomical union of two organisms with shared physiological processes. WH: early 20C. PARA-[1] + Greek *biōsis* way of life, from *bios* life.

parablast *n.* the peripheral nutritive yolk of an ovum, or a germ layer supposed to be developed from this and to produce the blood etc. WH: 19C. PARA-[1] + -BLAST.

parable *n.* an allegorical narrative of real or fictitious events from which a moral is drawn. *Also v.t.* WH: 12–14C. Old French *parabole*, from Latin *parabola* comparison, allegory, proverb, speech, from Greek *parabolē* comparison, analogy, proverb, from *paraballein* to put alongside, to compare, from PARA-[1] + *ballein* to cast, to throw. The original Old English word was *bīspell*, from *bī* BY + *spell* SPELL[2], story, narration.

parabola *n.* a plane curve formed by the intersection of the surface of a cone with a plane parallel to one of its sides. WH: 16C. Modern Latin, from Greek *parabolē* application. Cp. PARABLE. The curve is so called because it is produced by the 'application' of a given area to a given straight line.

Paracelsian *a.* of, relating to or characteristic of the philosophical teaching or medical practice of Paracelsus. *Also n.* WH: 16C. *Paracelsus*, *c.*1493–1541, Swiss physician, chemist and natural philosopher + -IAN.

paracentesis *n.* the operation of perforating a cavity of the body, or tapping, for the removal of fluid etc. WH: 16C. Latin couching of a cataract, from Greek *parakentēsis*, from *parakentein* to pierce at the side, from PARA-[1] + *kentein* to prick, to stab.

paracetamol *n.* a painkilling drug. WH: mid-20C. Abbr. of chemical name *para*-*acetyl*aminophen*ol*. See PARA-[1], ACETYL, AMINE, PHENOL.

parachronism *n.* an error in chronology, esp. post-dating of an event. WH: 17C. PARA-[1] + Greek *khronos* time + -ISM, or alt. of ANACHRONISM.

parachute *n.* an umbrella-shaped contrivance by which a safe descent is made from a height, esp. from an aircraft. *Also a., v.t., v.i.* WH: 18C. French from *para-* PARA-[2] + *chute* fall. The word was coined by the French pioneer balloonist Jean-Pierre Blanchard and gained popular currency when he put a dog in a basket attached to a parachute and dropped it from a balloon in 1785.

Paraclete *n.* an advocate, esp. as a title of the Holy Ghost, the Comforter. WH: 12–14C. Old French *paraclet*, from Ecclesiastical Latin *paracletus*, from Greek *paraklētos* advocate, intercessor, from *parakalein* to call to one's aid, from PARA-[1] + *kalein* to call.

paracme *n.* a point past the acme or highest development. WH: 17C. Greek *parakmē* the time at which the peak is past, from PARA-[1] + *akmē* peak, ACME.

paracrostic *n.* a poetic composition in which the first verse contains, in order, all the letters which commence the remaining verses. WH: 19C. PARA-[1] + ACROSTIC.

paracyanogen *n.* a porous brown substance obtained from cyanide of mercury when heated. WH: 19C. PARA-[1] + CYANOGEN.

parade *n.* a muster of troops for inspection etc. *Also v.i., v.t.* WH: 17C. French, from Spanish *parada*, Italian *parata* display, parry, pulling-up of a horse, from use as n. of fem. p.p. of Latin *parare* to prepare. See also -ADE.

paradiddle *n.* a simple drumming pattern consisting of four beats played either *left*, *right*, *left*, *right* or *right*, *left*, *right*, *left*. WH: early 20C. Imit.

paradigm *n.* an example, a pattern. WH: 15C. Late Latin *paradigma*, from Greek *paradeigma* example, from *paradeiknunai* to show side by side, from PARA-[1] + *deiknunai* to show.

paradise *n.* heaven. WH: 12–14C. Old French *paradis*, from Ecclesiastical Latin *paradisus*, from Greek *paradeisos* royal park, garden, enclosure, paradise, from Avestan *pairidaēza* enclosure, from *pairi* around (cp. PERI-) + *diz* to mould, to form. Cp. PARVIS.

parador *n.* a Spanish state-owned hotel. WH: 19C. Spanish inn, hostel.

parados *n.* a rampart or earthwork to protect against fire from the rear. WH: 19C. French from *para-* PARA-[2] + *dos* back.

paradox *n.* a statement, view or doctrine contrary to received opinion. WH: 16C. Late Latin *paradoxum*, use as n. of neut. of *paradoxus*, from Greek *paradoxos*, from PARA-[1] + *doxa* opinion.

paradoxure *n.* the palm-civet. WH: 19C. Modern Latin *Paradoxurus*, from Greek *paradoxos* (PARADOX) + *oura* tail. The animal is so called because of its unusually long curving tail.

paraenesis *n.* an exhortation. WH: 16C. Late Latin, from Greek *parainesis*, from *parainein* to exhort, from PARA-[1] + *ainein* to speak of, to praise.

paraesthesia *n.* disordered perception or hallucination. WH: 19C. PARA-[1] + Greek *aisthēsis* sensation. See also -ADE.

paraffin *n.* a mixture of liquid paraffins used as a lubricant or fuel. WH: 19C. German, from Latin *parum* too little, barely + *affinis* related. The mixture is so called because of its low affinity for other substances. The name was coined by the German chemist Karl von Reichenbach in 1830.

paragenesis *n.* the production in an organism of characteristics of two different species. WH: 19C. PARA-[1] + GENESIS.

paragliding *n.* the sport of gliding while attached to a device like a parachute, in which one is pulled by an aircraft etc., then allowed to drift to the ground. WH: mid-20C. PARACHUTE + GLIDE + -ING[1].

paraglossa *n.* either of the two appendages of the ligula in insects. WH: 19C. PARA-[1] + Greek *glōssa* tongue.

paragoge *n.* the addition of a letter or syllable to a word. WH: 16C. Late Latin, from Greek *paragōgē* derivation, addition to the end of a syllable, from PARA-[1] + *agōgē* carrying, leading.

paragon *n.* a pattern of perfection. *Also v.t.* WH: 16C. Obs. French (now *parangon*), from Italian *paragone* touchstone, comparison, from Medieval Greek *parakonē* whetstone.

paragraph *n.* a distinct portion of a discourse or writing marked by a break in the lines. *Also v.t.* WH: 15C. Old French *paragraphe*, or from Medieval Latin *paragraphus*, from Greek *paragraphos* short horizontal stroke written below the beginning of a line in which there is a break of sense, a passage so marked, from PARA-[1] + -*graphos* -GRAPH.

paragraphia *n.* the habitual writing of words or letters other than those intended, often a sign of brain disorder. WH: 19C. PARA-[1] + Greek -*graphia* writing.

Paraguayan *n.* a native or inhabitant of Paraguay. *Also a.* WH: 17C. *Paraguay*, a country in S America + -AN.

Paraguay tea *n.* an infusion of the leaves of *Ilex paraguayensis*, maté. WH: 18C. *Paraguay*, a river and country of S America + TEA.

paraheliotropic *a.* (of leaves) turning so that the surfaces are parallel to the rays of sunlight. WH: 19C. PARA-[1] + *heliotropic* (HELIOTROPE).

para-influenza virus *n.* any of various viruses causing influenza-like symptoms. WH: mid-20C. PARA-¹ + INFLUENZA + VIRUS.

parakeet *n.* any one of the smaller long-tailed parrots. WH: 16C. Old French *paroquet* (Modern French *perroquet* parrot), Italian *parrocchetto*, Spanish *periquito*, prob. ult. based on a dim. (French *Pierrot*, Spanish *Perico*) of the name Peter (French *Pierre*, Spanish *Pedro*). Cp. PARROT.

paralanguage *n.* elements such as intonation, nods and gestures, which accompany language. WH: mid-20C. PARA-¹ + LANGUAGE.

paraldehyde *n.* a hypnotic used in asthma, respiratory and cardiac diseases and epilepsy. WH: 19C. PARA-¹ + ALDEHYDE.

paralegal *a.* of or relating to auxiliary aspects of the legal profession. *Also n.* WH: late 20C. PARA-¹ + LEGAL.

paralipomena *n.pl.* things omitted in a work. WH: 12–14C. Ecclesiastical Latin (pl.), from Greek *paraleipomena* (things) left out, from *paraleipein* to leave on one side, to omit, from PARA-¹ + *leipein* to leave. As a title of the Books of Chronicles, the word comes from Greek *Paraleipomenōn biblia*, literally books of things left out.

paralipsis *n.* a rhetorical figure by which a speaker pretends to omit mention of what at the same time they really call attention to. WH: 16C. Late Latin, from Greek *paraleipsis* passing by, omission, from *paraleipein*. See PARALIPOMENA.

parallax *n.* apparent change in the position of an object due to change in the position of the observer. WH: 16C. French *parallaxe*, from Modern Latin *parallaxis*, from Greek change, alternation, angle between two lines, from *parallassein* to alter, to alternate, from PARA-¹ + *allassein* to exchange, from *allos* other.

parallel *a.* (of lines etc.) having the same direction and equidistant everywhere. *Also n., v.t.* WH: 16C. French *parallèle*, from Latin *parallelus*, from Greek *parallēlos*, from PARA-¹ + *allēlos* one another.

parallelepiped *n.* a regular solid bounded by six parallelograms, the opposite pairs of which are parallel. WH: 16C. Greek *parallēlepipedon*, from *parallēlos* PARALLEL + *epipedon* plane, surface, use as n. of neut. of *epipedos* plane, flat, from EPI-² + *pedon* ground.

parallelogram *n.* a four-sided rectilinear figure whose opposite sides are parallel and equal. WH: 16C. French *parallélogramme*, from Late Latin *parallelogrammum*, from Greek *parallēlogrammon*, from *parallēlos* PARALLEL. See -GRAM.

paralogism *n.* a fallacious argument, esp. one of which the reasoner is unconscious. WH: 16C. French *paralogisme* or Latin *paralogismus*, from Greek *paralogismos*, from *paralogizesthai* to reason falsely, from *paralogos* contrary to reason, from PARA-¹ + *logos* reasoning, discourse. See LOGOS, also -ISM.

Paralympics *n.pl.* an international sporting event for disabled people, modelled on the Olympic Games. WH: mid-20C. From *paraplegic* (PARAPLEGIA) + *Olympics* (OLYMPIAD). The word was perhaps intentionally coined to suggest a first element PARA-¹ (in the sense distinct from, but parallel to). Not all participants in Paralympics are actually paraplegics.

paralyse *v.t.* to affect with paralysis. WH: 14–15C. French *paralyser*, from *paralysie*. See PALSY.

paralysis *n.* total or partial loss of the power of muscular contraction or of sensation in the whole or part of the body; palsy. WH: pre-1200. Latin, from Greek *paralusis*, from *paraluesthai* to be disabled at the side, pass. of *paraluein*, from PARA-¹ + *luein* to loosen. Cp. PALSY.

paramagnetic *a.* having the property of being attracted by the poles of a magnet; magnetic, as distinct from *diamagnetic*. WH: 19C. PARA-¹ + *magnetic* (MAGNET).

paramastoid *a.* situated near the mastoid process of the temporal bone. *Also n.* WH: 19C. PARA-¹ + MASTOID.

paramecium *n.* any member of a genus, *Paramecium*, of protozoa. WH: 18C. Modern Latin, from Greek *paramēkēs* oval, from PARA-¹ + *mēkos* length. See also -IUM.

paramedic *n.* a person who is trained to help doctors, e.g. an ambulance operative. WH: late 20C. Back-formation from *paramedical*, from PARA-¹ + MEDICAL. Cp. MEDIC. The word is liable to confusion with *paramedic* (mid-20C), person trained to be dropped by parachute to give medical aid, from PARACHUTE + MEDIC.

parameter *n.* a quantity remaining constant for a particular case,

esp. a constant quantity entering into the equation of a curve etc. WH: 17C. Modern Latin, from PARA-¹ + Greek *metron* measure. See also -METER.

paramilitary *a.* having a similar nature or structure to military forces. *Also n.* WH: mid-20C. PARA-¹ + MILITARY.

paramnesia *n.* déjà vu. WH: 19C. PARA-¹ + Greek -*mnēsis* memory. See also -IA.

paramo *n.* a high plateau with no trees in S America. WH: 18C. Spanish and Portuguese *páramo*, from Latin *paramus* plain.

paramorph *n.* a pseudomorph having the same chemical composition but differing in molecular structure. WH: 19C. PARA-¹ + -MORPH.

paramount *a.* pre-eminent, most important. *Also n.* WH: 16C. Anglo-French *paramont*, use as n. of *paramont* above, from Old French *par* by + *amont*. See AMOUNT.

paramour *n.* a lover, usu. an illicit one. WH: 12–14C. Old French *par amour* through love.

parang *n.* a heavy sheath knife. WH: 19C. Malay.

paranoia *n.* mental derangement, esp. in a chronic form characterized by delusions etc. WH: 19C. Modern Latin, from Greek from *paranoos* distracted, from PARA-¹ + *noos, nous* mind.

paranormal *a.* not rationally explicable. *Also n.* WH: early 20C. PARA-¹ + NORMAL.

paranthelion *n.* a diffuse image of the sun at the same altitude and at an angular distance of 120° due to reflection from ice-spicules in the air. WH: 19C. PARA-¹ + ANTHELION.

parapet *n.* a low or breast-high wall at the edge of a roof, bridge etc. WH: 16C. French, from Italian *parapetto*, lit. breast-high wall, from *para-* PARA-² + *petto* breast, from Latin *pectus*.

paraph *n.* a flourish after a signature, orig. intended as a protection against forgery. *Also v.t.* WH: 14–15C. French *paraphe*, from Medieval Latin *paraphus*, contr. of *paragraphus* PARAGRAPH.

paraphernalia *n.pl.* miscellaneous belongings, equipment. WH: 17C. Medieval Latin, neut. pl. (used as n.) of *paraphernalis*, from Latin *parapherna*, from Greek, from PARA-¹ + *phernē* dowry. See also -IA. The word originally denoted articles of personal property which a married woman was allowed to keep and deal with. The current general sense evolved in the 18C.

paraphimosis *n.* permanent retraction of the prepuce. WH: 17C. Modern Latin, from PARA-¹ + PHIMOSIS.

paraphrase *n.* a free translation or rendering of a passage. *Also v.t., v.i.* WH: 16C. French, from Latin *paraphrasis*, from Greek, from *paraphrazein* to tell in other words, from PARA-¹ + *phrazein* to tell.

paraphrenia *n.* a type of schizophrenia characterized by ideas of persecution, grandeur etc. WH: 19C. French *paraphrénie*, from PARA-¹ + Greek *phrēn* mind. See also -IA.

paraphysis *n.* a sterile filament accompanying sexual organs in some cryptogams. WH: 19C. Modern Latin, from PARA-¹ + Greek *phusis* growth.

paraplegia *n.* paralysis of the lower limbs and the lower part of the body. WH: 17C. Modern Latin, from Greek *paraplēgia* stroke on one side, from *paraplēssein* to strike at the side, from PARA-¹ + *plēssein* to strike. See also -IA.

parapodium *n.* any one of the jointless lateral locomotory organs of an annelid. WH: 19C. Modern Latin, from PARA-¹ + Greek *pous, podos* foot. See also -IUM.

parapophysis *n.* a process on the side of a vertebra, usu. serving as the point of articulation of a rib. WH: 19C. Modern Latin, from PARA-¹ + *apophysis* (from APO- + Greek *phusis* growth).

parapsychical *a.* denoting phenomena such as hypnotism or telepathy which appear to be beyond explanation by the ascertained laws of science. WH: early 20C. PARA-¹ + *psychical* (PSYCHIC).

parapsychology *n.* the study of mental phenomena which are beyond the sphere of ordinary psychology. WH: early 20C. PARA-¹ + PSYCHOLOGY.

paraquat *n.* a very poisonous weedkiller. WH: mid-20C. PARA-¹ + QUATERNARY. The herbicide is so called because the bond between the two rings of the molecule is in the *para-* position (see PARA-¹) relative to their quaternary nitrogen atoms.

parasailing *n.* the sport of gliding through the air attached to the back of a motor boat while wearing an open parachute. WH: mid-20C. PARACHUTE + *sailing* (SAIL).

parasang *n.* an ancient Persian measure of length, about 3¼ miles (5.25 km). WH: 16C. Latin *parasanga*, from Greek *parasaggēs*, from Persian.

parascending *n.* paragliding. WH: late 20C. PARACHUTE + *ascending* (ASCEND).

parasceve *n.* the day of preparation for the Jewish Sabbath. WH: 16C. Late Latin, from Greek *paraskeuē* (day of) preparation, from PARA-¹ + *skeuē* equipment, outfit, attire. The parasceve was the day before the Sabbath, in Christian terms Good Friday: 'And now when the even was come, because it was the preparation, that is, the day before the sabbath' (Mark xv.42).

paraselene *n.* a mock moon appearing in a lunar halo. WH: 17C. Modern Latin, from PARA-¹ + Greek *selēnē* moon.

parasite *n.* an animal or plant subsisting at the expense of another organism. WH: 16C. Latin *parasitus*, from Greek *parasitos*, lit. feeding beside, person who eats at the table of another, from PARA-¹ + *sitos* food.

parasol *n.* a small umbrella used to give shelter from the sun, a sunshade. WH: 17C. French, from Italian *parasole*, from *para-* PARA-² + *sole* sun. Cp. French *parapluie* umbrella (from *para-* PARA-² + *pluie* rain).

parastatal *a.* esp. in some African countries, having some political authority, but indirectly controlled by the State. *Also n.* WH: mid-20C. PARA-¹ + STATE + -AL¹.

parasuicide *n.* an apparent attempt at suicide without any genuine intention of killing oneself. WH: mid-20C. PARA-¹ + SUICIDE.

parasympathetic *a.* of or relating to the part of the autonomic nervous system which slows the heartbeat, stimulates the smooth muscles of the digestive tract, constricts the bronchi of the lungs etc. and thus counteracts the sympathetic nervous system. WH: early 20C. PARA-¹ + *sympathetic* (SYMPATHY). The part is so called because some of the nerves involved run alongside sympathetic nerves.

parasynthesis *n.* the principle or process of forming derivatives from compound words. WH: 19C. PARA-¹ + SYNTHESIS.

parataxis *n.* an arrangement of clauses, sentences etc., without connectives indicating subordination etc. WH: 19C. Greek placing side by side, from *paratassein* to place side by side, from PARA-¹ + *tassein* to arrange. See TAXIS.

paratha *n.* in Indian cookery, a piece of flat, round, unleavened bread fried on a griddle. WH: mid-20C. Hindi *parāṭhā*.

parathesis *n.* apposition. WH: 17C. Modern Latin, from German a putting beside, from *paratithenai* to put beside, from PARA-¹ + *tithenai* to put. See THESIS.

parathion *n.* a highly toxic insecticide. WH: mid-20C. PARA-¹ + THIO- + -ON.

parathyroid *n.* a small endocrine gland, one of which is situated on each side of the thyroid. *Also a.* WH: 19C. PARA-¹ + THYROID.

paratonic *a.* (of a plant-movement) due to external stimuli. WH: 19C. PARA-¹ + TONIC. The term was coined in 1868 by the German botanist Julius von Sachs.

paratrooper *n.* a soldier belonging to a unit transported in aircraft and dropped by parachute, with full equipment, usu. behind enemy lines. WH: mid-20C. *paratroop* (from PARACHUTE + *troops*, pl. of TROOP) + -ER¹, influ. by *trooper* (17C) (TROOP).

paratyphoid *n.* an infectious fever of the enteric group, similar in symptoms to typhoid but of milder character. *Also a.* WH: early 20C. PARA-¹ + TYPHOID.

paravane *n.* a mine-sweeping appliance for severing the moorings of submerged mines. WH: early 20C. PARA-¹ + VANE. *Para-* here has the sense protector (of the ship employing it). The paravane was invented, and presumably named, in World War I by Lieutenant (later Commander) Dennistoun Burney.

par avion *adv.* by airmail. WH: early 20C. French by aeroplane. French *avion* comes from the name of two early aircraft, *Avion I* and *Avion II*, first flown in 1890 by the French engineer Clément Ader (1841–1925). The name itself is from Latin *avis* bird.

parazoan *n.* a member of the subkingdom Parazoa, the multicellular invertebrates, such as sponges. WH: early 20C. Modern Latin *Parazoa*, from PARA-¹ + Greek *zōia*, pl. of *zōion* animal. See also -AN. Cp. METAZOAN, PROTOZOAN.

parboil *v.t.* to boil partially. WH: 14–15C. Old French *parbouillir*, from Late Latin *perbullire* to boil thoroughly, from Latin PER-

+ *bullire* BOIL¹. The original meaning (to the 17C) was to boil thoroughly. This soon became to boil partially because the initial *par-* was taken as PART.

parbuckle *n.* a double sling usu. made by passing the two ends of a rope through a bight for hoisting or lowering a cask or gun. *Also v.t.* WH: 17C. Orig. unknown. Later assoc. with BUCKLE.

Parcae *n.pl.* in Roman mythology, the Fates. WH: 16C. Latin, sing. of *Parcae*, prob. from *parere* to produce, rather than *parcere* to spare.

parcel *n.* a quantity of things wrapped up together. *Also v.t., adv.* WH: 12–14C. Old French *parcelle*, from Latin *particula* PARTICLE. The original sense (to the 17C) was item, detail. The current sense dates from the 17C.

parcenary *n.* joint heirship, coparcenary. WH: 14–15C. Old French *parçonier*, from Latin *partitio* PARTITION. See also -ER², -ARY¹. Cp. PARTNER.

parch *v.t.* to scorch or roast partially dry, to dry up. *Also v.i.* WH: 12–14C. Orig. unknown.

Parcheesi® *n.* a modern board game based on pachisi. WH: 19C. Var. of PACHISI.

parchment *n.* the skin of calves, sheep, goats etc., prepared for writing upon, painting etc. *Also a.* WH: 12–14C. Old French *parchemin*, ult. from blend of Latin *pergamina* writing material from Pergamum (cp. PERGAMENEOUS) and *Parthica pellis* Parthian skin (see PARTHIAN) (a kind of scarlet leather). Not rel. to PARCH, -MENT. Pergamum (now Bergama, western Turkey) was the capital of an ancient kingdom in Asia Minor.

parclose *n.* a screen or railing enclosing an altar, tomb etc. in a church. WH: 12–14C. Old French, fem. p.p. (used as n.) of *parclore*, from *par-* PER- + *clore*, from Latin *claudere* to close.

pard¹ *n.* a partner. WH: 19C. Abbr. of *pardner*, representing a pronun. of PARTNER.

†pard² *n.* a panther, a leopard. WH: 12–14C. Old French, from Latin *pardus*, from Greek *pardos*, earlier *pardalis*, of Indo-Iranian orig.

pardalote *n.* any small, spotted Australian bird of the genus *Pardalotus*. WH: 19C. Modern Latin *Pardalotus*, from Greek *pardolōtos* spotted like a leopard, from *pardalis* (PARD²).

pardon *n.* the act of excusing or forgiving. *Also v.t.* WH: 12–14C. Old French *pardun, perdun* (Modern French *pardon*), from *pardoner* (Modern French *pardonner*), from Medieval Latin *perdonare*, from Latin PER- + *donare* to give.

pare *v.t.* to cut or shave (away or off). WH: 12–14C. Old French *parer* to adorn, to arrange, to peel (fruit), from Latin *parare* to prepare.

paregoric *a.* assuaging or soothing pain. *Also n.* WH: 17C. Late Latin *paregoricus*, from Greek *parēgorikos* encouraging, soothing, from *parēgorein* to console, to soothe.

pareira *n.* a drug used in urinary disorders, obtained from the root of *Chondrodendron tomentosum*, a Brazilian climbing plant. WH: 18C. Portuguese *parreira* vine trained against a wall, from *parra* vine.

parella *n.* a crustaceous lichen, *Lecanora parella*, from which litmus and orchil are obtained. WH: 19C. Modern Latin, from French *parelle*, earlier *pareele*, from Medieval Latin *paratella* name of a plant.

paren *n.* a round bracket, a parenthesis. WH: early 20C. Abbr. of PARENTHESIS.

parenchyma *n.* the soft cellular tissue of glands and other organs, as distinct from connective tissue etc. WH: 17C. Greek *paregkhuma* something poured in besides, from PARA-¹ + *egkhuma* infusion.

parent *n.* a father or mother. *Also v.t.* WH: 14–15C. Old French, from Latin *parens, parentis*, father or mother (pl. *parentes* parents, progenitors, kinsfolk), use as n. of pres.p. of *parere* to bring forth. See also -ENT. The Old English word for parents was *ieldra* ELDER¹.

parenteral *a.* situated or occurring outside the digestive tract, esp. being the means of administering a drug other than via the digestive tract. WH: early 20C. PARA-¹ + Greek *enteron* intestine + -AL¹.

parenthesis *n.* a word, phrase or sentence inserted in a sentence that is grammatically complete without it, usu. marked off by brackets, dashes or commas. WH: 16C. Late Latin, from Greek, from *parentithenai* to place in besides, from PARA-¹ + EN- + *tithenai* to place. See THESIS.

parergon *n.* a subsidiary work. WH: 17C. Latin, from Greek, from PARA-[1] + *ergon* work.

paresis *n.* incomplete paralysis, affecting muscular movement but not sensation. WH: 17C. Modern Latin, from Greek letting go, paralysis, from *parienai*, from PARA-[1] + *hienai* to let go.

par excellence *adv.* above all others, pre-eminently. WH: 17C. French, from Latin *per excellentiam* by virtue of excellence.

parfait *n.* a rich, cold dessert made with whipped cream, eggs, fruit etc. WH: 19C. French, lit. perfect.

parfleche *n.* a hide, usu. of buffalo, stripped of hair and dried on a stretcher. WH: 19C. Canadian French *parflèche*, from French *parer* (PARRY) + *flèche* arrow.

pargana *n.* in India, a subdivision of a district. WH: 17C. Persian and Urdu *parganah* district.

pargasite *n.* a greenish variety of hornblende. WH: 19C. *Pargas*, a town in SW Finland + -ITE[1].

parget *v.t.* to plaster over. Also *n.* WH: 14–15C. Old French *pargeter* to fill up joints in masonry, from *par* through, all over + *jeter* to cast.

parhelion *n.* a mock sun or bright spot in a solar halo, due to ice crystals in the atmosphere. WH: 17C. Latin *parhelion*, Greek *parēlion*, from PARA-[1] + *hēlios* sun.

pariah *n.* a social outcast. WH: 17C. Tamil *paṛaiyar*, pl. of *paṛaiyan*, lit. hereditary drummer, from *parai* to drum. Cp. PYE-DOG. The original low caste in southern India had the hereditary task of drumming at festivals.

Parian *a.* of or relating to the island of Paros, Greece, celebrated for its white marble. Also *n.* WH: 16C. Latin *Parius* of Paros, a Greek island in the Aegean Sea famous for its white marble. See also -AN.

parietal *a.* of or relating to a wall or walls, esp. those of the body and its cavities. WH: 16C. French *pariétal*, or from Late Latin *parietalis*, from *paries*, *parietis* wall, partition. See also -AL[1].

parieto- *comb. form* of or relating to a wall or walls. WH: Greek *paries*, *parietis* wall, partition. See also -O-.

pari-mutuel *n.* a system of betting in which the winners divide the losers' stakes less a percentage for management. WH: 19C. French mutual stake, mutual wager, from *pari* stake, wager + *mutuel* MUTUAL.

pari passu *adv.* (esp. in legal contexts) with equal pace, in a similar degree, equally. WH: 16C. Latin, lit. with equal step, from abl. of *par passus* equal step.

paripinnate *a.* equally pinnate, without a terminal leaflet. WH: 19C. Latin *par*, *paris* equal + PINNATE.

Paris *a.* of or relating to Paris. WH: 15C. *Paris*, the capital of France.

parish *n.* an ecclesiastical district with its own church and clergyman. Also *a.* WH: 12–14C. Old French *paroche*, *paroisse*, from Ecclesiastical Latin *parochia*, alt. of *paroechia*, from Greek *paroikia* sojourning, from *para-* PARA-[1] + *oikos* dwelling, house.

Parisian *a.* of or relating to Paris, France. Also *n.* WH: 14–15C. Old French *parisien*. See PARIS, also -IAN.

parison *n.* a rounded mass of glass before it is shaped. WH: 19C. French *paraison*, from *parer*, from Latin *parare* to prepare. See also -ISON.

parisyllabic *a.* (of a Greek or Latin noun) having the same number of syllables, esp. in all the cases. WH: 17C. Latin *par*, *pari-* equal to + *syllaba* SYLLABLE + -IC.

parity[1] *n.* equality of rank, value etc. WH: 16C. Old French *parité* or Late Latin *paritas*, from *par*. See PAR[1], also -ITY.

parity[2] *n.* the condition of having given birth. WH: 19C. *parous* (back-formation from -PAROUS) + -ITY.

park *n.* a piece of ground, ornamentally laid out, enclosed for public recreation. Also *v.t.*, *v.i.* WH: 12–14C. Old French *parc*, from Medieval Latin *parricus*, from Germanic base represented by Old High German *pfarrih*, *pferrih* pen, fold, corr. to Old English *pearruc* (PADDOCK). Cp. German *Pferch* pen, fold. The word originally applied to an enclosed tract of land reserved for hunting, held by royal grant and stocked with deer, etc. Hence the presence of deer (though not for hunting) in many parks today. The sense ornamentally landscaped area in a city dates from the 17C.

parka *n.* a hooded jacket edged or lined with fur. WH: 18C. Aleutian, from Russian skin jacket.

parkin *n.* a biscuit made of gingerbread, oatmeal and treacle. WH: 19C. ? From surname *Parkin*, *Perkin*.

Parkinson's disease *n.* a chronic disorder of the central nervous system causing loss of muscle coordination and tremor. WH: 19C. James *Parkinson*, 1755–1824, English surgeon and palaeontologist.

Parkinson's law *n.* the supposed principle in office management etc. that work expands to fill the time available for its completion. WH: mid-20C. Cyril Northcote *Parkinson*, 1909–93, English historian and journalist.

parky *a.* chilly. WH: 19C. Orig. unknown.

parlance *n.* way of speaking, idiom. WH: 16C. Old French, from *parler* to speak, from Latin *parabola* PARABLE. See also -ANCE.

parlay *v.t.* to bet (one's winnings) on a further stake. Also *n.* WH: 19C. Alt. of *paroli* (18C), from French, from Italian, from *paro* like, from Latin *par* PAR[1]. In a gambling card game, *paroli* is the staking of double the amount previously staked.

parley *n.* a conference for discussing terms, esp. between enemies. Also *v.i.*, *v.t.* WH: 14–15C. ? Old French *parlée*, fem. p.p. (used as n.) of *parler* to speak. See PARLANCE, also -Y[2].

parleyvoo *v.i.* to speak French. Also *n.* WH: 18C. French *parlez-vous* (*français*)? do you speak (French)?

parliament *n.* a deliberative assembly. WH: 12–14C. Old French *parlement*, from *parler*. See PARLANCE, also -MENT. The spelling with -*ia*- was influenced by Anglo-Latin *parliamentum*. The original sense was the action of speaking, speech, conference, discussion. Hence the council called by a monarch to discuss some matter of general importance.

parlour *n.* the family sitting-room in a private house. Also *a.* WH: 12–14C. Old French *parleor*, *parleur* (Modern French *parloir*), from *parler* to speak. See PARLANCE, also -OUR. The original sense was a room for conversation in a monastery or convent. The sense sitting-room in a private house dates from the 14–15C.

†**parlous** *a.* perilous, awkward, trying. Also *adv.* WH: 14–15C. Alt. of *perilous* (PERIL).

Parma ham *n.* a type of ham eaten uncooked. WH: 19C. *Parma*, a city and province in N Italy + HAM[1]. Cp. PARMESAN.

Parma violet *n.* a variety of violet with a strong scent and lavender-coloured flowers. WH: 19C. *Parma* (see PARMA HAM) + VIOLET.

Parmesan *n.* a kind of hard, dry cheese made at Parma and elsewhere in N Italy, used grated as a topping for pasta dishes. WH: 16C. French, from Italian *parmigiano*, from Parma (PARMA HAM).

Parnassian *a.* of or relating to Mount Parnassus. Also *n.* WH: 17C. Latin *Parnassius*, from PARNASSUS. See also -AN, -IAN.

Parnassus *n.* poetry, literature. WH: 14–15C. Latin, from Greek *Parnassos*, a mountain in central Greece, sacred in ancient times to Apollo and the Muses.

Parnellism *n.* the political views and tactics of C.S. Parnell. WH: 19C. Charles Stewart *Parnell*, 1846–91, Irish Nationalist leader and advocate of Home Rule for Ireland.

parochial *a.* of or relating to a parish. WH: 14–15C. Old French, from Ecclesiastical Latin *parochialis*, from *parochia*. See PARISH, also -AL[1].

parody *n.* a literary composition imitating an author's work for the purpose of humour. Also *v.t.* WH: 16C. Late Latin *parodia* or Greek *parōidia* burlesque song or poem, from PARA-[1] + *ōidē* ODE. See also -Y[2].

parol *a.* given orally. Also *n.* WH: 15C. Var. of Old French PAROLE.

parole *n.* the release of a prisoner under certain conditions, esp. good behaviour. Also *v.t.* WH: 15C. Old French, from Latin *parabola* PARABLE. The basic sense is a person's word of honour. Hence the current sense of a prisoner's promise of good behaviour in return for early release.

paronomasia *n.* a play on words, a pun. WH: 16C. Latin, from Greek from PARA-[1] + *onomasia* naming.

paronym *n.* a paronymous word. WH: 19C. Greek *parōnumon*, use as n. of neut. *parōnumos*, from PARA-[1] + *onuma* name.

parotid *a.* situated near the ear. Also *n.* WH: 17C. French *parotide*, from Latin *parotis*, *parotidis*, from Greek *parōtis*, *parōtidos*, from PARA-[1] + *ous*, *ōtos* ear. See also -ID.

-parous *comb. form* producing, bringing forth, as in *oviparous*. WH: Latin *-parus* bearing, from *parere* to bring forth. See also -OUS.

Parousia n. Christ's second coming, to judge the world. WH: 19C. Greek presence (of persons), from *pareinai* to be present, from PARA-[1] + *einai* to be.

paroxysm n. a sudden and violent fit. WH: 14–15C. Medieval Latin *paroxysmus* irritation, exasperation, from Greek *paroxusmos*, from *paroxunein* to goad, to exasperate, from PARA-[1] + *oxunein* to sharpen.

paroxytone a. (in classical Greek, of a word) having an acute accent on the penultimate syllable. Also n. WH: 18C. Modern Latin *paroxytonus*, from Greek *paroxutonos*, from PARA-[1] + OXYTONE.

parpen n. a stone going through a wall. WH: 12–14C. Old French *parpain* (Modern French *parpaing*), from Medieval Latin *parpanus*, prob. from Latin *per* through + *pannus* (PANE).

parquet n. a flooring of parquetry. Also a., v.t. WH: 19C. Old French small marked-off space, dim. of *parc* PARK. See also -ET[1].

parr n. a young salmon. WH: 18C. Orig. unknown.

parramatta n. a light twilled dress fabric of merino wool and cotton. WH: 19C. *Parramatta*, a settlement (now a city) in New South Wales, Australia, where orig. made.

parrhesia n. freedom or boldness in speaking. WH: 16C. Medieval Latin, from Greek *parrhēsia* free-spokenness, from PARA-[1] + *rhēsis* speech.

parricide n. the murder of a parent or other close relative, or of a revered person. WH: 16C. Old French, or from Latin *parricida*, *parricidium*, assoc. with *pater* FATHER, *parens* PARENT. See also -CIDE. Cp. PATRICIDE.

parrot n. any of various tropical birds with brilliant plumage of the order Psittaciformes, remarkable for their faculty of imitating the human voice. Also v.t., v.i. WH: 16C. Prob. from French (now dial.) *perrot* parrot, dim of *Pierre* Peter. See also -OT[1]. Cp. PARAKEET, PIERROT.

parry v.t. to ward off (a blow or thrust). Also n. WH: 17C. Prob. from French *parez*, imper. of *parer*, from Italian *parare* to ward off (orig. to make ready, to prepare). Cp. PARA-[2], PARADE.

parse v.t. to describe or classify (a word) grammatically, its inflectional forms, relations in the sentence etc. Also v.i. WH: 16C. ? Old French *pars*, pl. of *part* PART, influ. by Latin *pars* part. Orig. uncertain. The reference would be to parts of speech.

parsec n. a unit of length in calculating the distance of the stars, being 1.9×10^{13} miles (3×10^{13} km) or 3.26 light years. WH: early 20C. PARALLAX + SECOND[1]. The unit is equal to the distance at which a star would have a heliocentric parallax of one second of arc.

Parsee n. a Zoroastrian, a descendant of the Persians who fled to India from the Muslim persecution in the 7th and 8th cents. WH: 17C. Persian *Pārsē* Persian, from *Pārs* Persia.

parsimonious a. careful in the expenditure of money. WH: 16C. Latin *parsimonia*, from *parsus*, p.p. of *parcere* to refrain, to spare. See -MONY, also -OUS.

parsley n. an umbelliferous herb, *Petroselinum crispum*, cultivated for its aromatic leaves used for seasoning and garnishing dishes. WH: early 20C. Old English *petersilie*, from var. of Latin *petroselinum*, from Greek *petrosilenon*, from *petra* rock + *selinon* parsley. Cp. German *Petersilie*, French *persil*.

parsnip n. an umbelliferous plant, *Pastinaca sativa*, with an edible root used as a vegetable. WH: 14–15C. Old French *pasnaie* (Modern French *panais*), assim. to NEEP. Cp. TURNIP.

parson n. a rector, vicar or other clergyman holding a benefice. WH: 12–14C. Law French *parsone*, var. of Old French *persone*. See PERSON. The parson was originally the legal 'person' by whom the property of God or the church in the parish was actually held. He was the person to sue or be sued accordingly.

part n. a piece or amount of a thing or number of things. Also v.t., v.i., adv., a. WH: pre-1200. Latin *pars*, *partis*, later assoc. with Old French *part*, from Latin.

partake v.i. to take or have a part or share (of or in, with another or others). Also v.t. WH: 16C. Back-formation from *partaker* or *partaking*, respectively from PART and *taker* or *taking* (TAKE[1]).

parterre n. an ornamental arrangement of flower beds, with intervening walks. WH: 17C. French, use as n. of *par terre* on the ground, along the ground.

parthenogenesis n. generation without sexual union. WH: 19C. Greek *parthenos* virgin + GENESIS.

Parthian a. of or relating to Parthia. WH: 12–14C. *Parthia*, an ancient kingdom in the NE of modern Iran + -AN.

parti n. a person regarded as eligible for marriage. WH: 18C. French choice. See PARTY[1].

partial a. affecting a part only, incomplete. Also n. WH: 14–15C. Old French *parcial* (Modern French *partial*, *partiel*), from Late Latin *partialis*, from Latin *pars*, *partis* PART. See also -IAL.

participate v.i. to have or enjoy a share, to partake (in). Also v.t. WH: 15C. Latin *participatus*, p.p. of *participare*, from *particeps*, *participis* taking part, from *pars*, *partis* PART + *cip-*, var. of *cap-*, stem of *capere* to take. See also -ATE[3].

participle n. a word partaking of the nature of a verb and of an adjective, a verbal adjective qualifying a noun. WH: 14–15C. Old French, var. of *participe*, from Latin *participium*, from *particeps* (see PARTICIPATE), based on Greek *metokhē*, from *metekhein* to partake. The *-l-* appears as with PRINCIPLE, TREACLE. The part of speech is so called as it partakes of the nature of both verb and adjective.

particle n. an atom. WH: 14–15C. Latin *particula*, dim. of *pars*, *partis* PART. See also -CLE.

particoloured a. partly of one colour, partly of another; variegated. WH: 16C. PARTY[2] + *coloured* (COLOUR).

particular a. of or relating to a single person or thing as distinct from others. Also n. WH: 14–15C. Old French *particuler* (Modern French *particulier*), from Latin *particularis*, from *particula* PARTICLE. See also -AR[1]. The original sense (to the 17C) was belonging to or affecting a part.

partim adv. partly. WH: 18C. Latin in part.

parting n. a departure, leave-taking. Also a. WH: 14–15C. PART + -ING[1].

parti pris n. a preconceived view, bias, prejudice. Also a. WH: 19C. French, lit. side taken, from *parti* (PARTI) + *pris*, p.p. of *prendre* to take.

partisan[1] n. an adherent of a party, faction, cause etc., esp. one showing unreasoning devotion. Also a. WH: 16C. French, from Italian dial. *partezan*, *partisano*, Tuscan *partigiano*, from Italian *parte*, from Latin *pars*, *partis* PART.

partisan[2] n. a pike or long-handled spear like a halberd. WH: 16C. Obs. French *partisane* (now *pertuisane*, based on *pertuiser* to bore through), from obs. Italian *partesana*, dial. var. of *partigiana*, use as n. of fem. of *partigiano*. Cp. PARTISAN[1]. The weapon is presumably so called as it was carried by partisans.

partita n. a suite of music. WH: 19C. Italian, fem. pp. of *partire* to divide, from Latin *partiri* PART. The suite is so called as it is divided into parts, originally as a set of variations.

partite a. divided (usu. in comb. as *bipartite*). WH: 16C. Latin *partitus* divided, p.p. of *partiri* PART. See also -ITE[1].

partition n. division into parts, distribution. Also v.t. WH: 14–15C. Old French, from Latin *partitio*, *partitionis*, from *partitus*, p.p. of *partiri*. See PART, also -ION.

partly adv. in part. WH: 16C. PART + -LY[2].

partner n. a person who shares with another, esp. one associated with others in business; an associate. Also v.t. WH: 12–14C. Alt. of *parcener* (PARCENARY), by assoc. with PART.

parton n. an elementary particle postulated as a constituent of neutrons and protons. WH: mid-20C. PARTICLE + -ON. The name was coined in *c.*1969 by the US physicist Richard P. Feynman.

partridge n. any game bird of the genus *Perdix*, esp. *P. perdix*. WH: 12–14C. Old French *pertriz*, *perdriz* (Modern French *perdrix*), alt. of *perdix*, from Latin *perdix*, *perdicis*, from Greek *perdix*, prob. rel. to *perdesthai* to break wind. The Greek source would refer to the whirring of the bird's wings, suggesting the sound of someone breaking wind.

parturient a. about to give birth. WH: 16C. Latin *parturiens*, *parturientis*, pres.p. of *parturire* to be in labour (from *partus*, p.p. of *parere*; see PARENT). See also -ENT.

party[1] n. a social gathering, usually in someone's home, often to celebrate a special occasion such as a birthday. Also v.i., v.t. WH: 12–14C. Old French *partie* part, share, side in a contest, from use as n. of Latin *partita*, fem. p.p. of *partiri* PART. Cp. PARTY[2].

party[2] a. divided into compartments distinguished by different colours. WH: 14–15C. Old French *parti*, from Latin *partitus*, p.p. of *partiri* PART. Cp. PARTY[1].

parure *n.* a set of jewels or other personal ornaments. WH: 12–14C. Old French, from *parer*. See PARE, also -URE. The original sense was an ornament for an alb or amice, also a paring or peeling. The current sense dates from the 19C.

parvanimity *n.* smallness of mind, mean-spiritedness. WH: 17C. Latin *parvus* small + -*animity*, based on *magnanimity* (MAGNANIMOUS).

parvenu *n.* a person who has risen socially or financially. *Also a.* WH: 19C. French, use as n. of p.p. of *parvenir* to arrive, from Latin *pervenire*, from PER- + *venire* to come. Cp. ARRIVISTE.

parvis *n.* the vacant space in front of a church. WH: 14–15C. Old French, from Late Latin *paradisus* PARADISE. The Late Latin word was originally applied to the court in front of St Peter's, Rome, and from there passed to the corresponding area before other churches.

parvovirus *n.* any one of a group of very small viruses each of which affects a particular species, such as *canine parvovirus*. WH: mid-20C. Latin *parvus* small + -O- + VIRUS.

pas *n.* a dance step, esp. in ballet. WH: 18C. French step, PACE[1].

Pascal *n.* a computer language suitable for many applications. WH: late 20C. Blaise *Pascal*, 1623–62, French scholar and scientist. The language was named in 1971 by its developer, Niklaus Wirth, a Swiss computer scientist. The name is sometimes written in capitalized form *PASCAL*. Pascal devised and built a calculating machine in *c*.1642. Hence the relevance of the name.

pascal *n.* the SI unit of pressure, 1 newton per square metre. WH: mid-20C. Blaise *Pascal* (see PASCAL).

paschal *a.* of or relating to the Passover or to Easter. WH: 14–15C. Old French *pascal*, from Ecclesiastical Latin *paschalis*, from *pascha*, from Greek *pascha*, from Aramaic *pasḥa*, from Hebrew *pesaḥ* PASSOVER. Cp. PASKHA.

pash *n.* a violent infatuation, a crush. WH: early 20C. Abbr. of PASSION.

pasha *n.* a Turkish title of honour, usu. conferred on officers of high rank, governors etc. WH: 17C. Turkish *paşa*, from Persian *pādśāh*. See PADISHAH. According to some, the word is from Turkish *başa*, from *baş* head, chief.

pashm *n.* the under-fur of various Tibetan animals, esp. goats, used to make cashmere shawls. WH: 19C. Persian *pašm* wool.

Pashto *n.* a language spoken in Afghanistan and parts of Pakistan. *Also a.* WH: 18C. Pashto *pekhṭō*.

pasigraphy *n.* a universal system of writing, by means of signs representing ideas and not words. WH: 18C. Greek *pasi* for all (from *pas* all) + -GRAPHY.

paskha *n.* a Russian dessert made from curd cheese and dried fruit, traditionally eaten at Easter. WH: early 20C. Russian Easter. Cp. PASCHAL.

paso doble *n.* a Latin American ballroom dance in fast 2/4 time, based on a march step. WH: early 20C. Spanish double step.

pasque flower *n.* a plant of the buttercup family, *Pulsatilla vulgaris*, with bell-shaped purple flowers. WH: 16C. Orig. *passe-flower*, from French *passe-fleur* a variety of anemone, alt. by assoc. with *pasque* Easter (see PASCHAL). The plant is so called because it flowers early, around Easter (March–April).

pasquinade *n.* a lampoon, a satire. *Also v.t.* WH: 16C. Italian *pasquinata*, French *pasquinade*, from Italian *Pasquino*, the name of a statue in Rome on which abusive Latin verses were posted annually in the 16C. The name *Pasquino* (Pasquin) was the one popularly given to the statue when it was originally dug up in 1501. It is said to derive from that of a shopkeeper who lived near the spot where it was unearthed.

pass *v.i.* to move from one place to another, to go (along, on, quickly etc.). *Also v.t., n.* WH: 12–14C. Old French *passer*, from Latin *passus* FACE. Cp. PAST.

passacaglia *n.* an instrumental piece with a ground bass. WH: 17C. Italian, from Spanish *pasacalle*, from *pasar* to pass + *calle* street. The piece was originally one often played in the streets.

†passade *n.* in dressage, a turn or course of a horse backwards or forwards on the same spot. WH: 17C. French, from Italian *passata* or Provençal *passada*, from Medieval Latin *passare* PASS. See also -ADE.

passage[1] *n.* the act of passing. WH: 12–14C. Old French from *passer* PASS. See also -AGE.

passage[2] *v.i.* in dressage, to move sideways with diagonal pairs of legs lifted alternately. *Also v.t.* WH: 18C. French *passager*, alt. of *passéger*, from Italian *passeggiare* to walk, to pace, from Latin *passus* PACE[1].

passant *a.* walking and looking towards the dexter side with the dexter forepaw raised. WH: 12–14C. Old French, pres.p. of *passer* PASS. See also -ANT.

passé *a.* old-fashioned, behind the times. WH: 18C. French, p.p. of *passer* PASS. Cp. HAS-BEEN.

passementerie *n.* a trimming for dresses, esp. of gold and silver lace. WH: 17C. French, from *passement*, from *passer* PASS. See also -MENT, -ERY. The ornament is presumably so called from the passing of the thread.

passenger *n.* a person who travels on a public conveyance. *Also a.* WH: 12–14C. Old French *passager*, use as n. of a. meaning passing, from *passage* PASSAGE[1]. See also -ER[2]. The -*n*- entered as with HARBINGER, MESSENGER, etc. The original meaning was traveller on foot. The current sense dates from the 19C. (The original sense survives in *foot passenger*.)

passepartout *n.* a master key. WH: 17C. French, from *passer* PASS + *partout* everywhere.

passepied *n.* a Breton dance resembling a minuet, popular in the 17th cent. WH: 17C. French, from *passer* PASS + *pied* foot.

passerine *a.* of or relating to the order Passeriformes, which contains the great mass of the smaller perching birds, such as sparrows. *Also n.* WH: 18C. Latin *passer* sparrow + -INE.

passible *a.* capable of feeling or suffering, susceptible to impressions from external agents. WH: 12–14C. Old French, or Ecclesiastical Latin *passibilis*, from Latin *passus*, p.p. of *pati* to suffer. See also -IBLE.

passiflora *n.* any plant of the genus *Passiflora*, containing the passion flower. WH: 18C. Modern Latin, from Latin *passus* (see PASSION) + -*i*- + -*florus* flowering.

passim *adv.* here and there, throughout (indicating the occurrence of a word, allusion etc. in a cited work). WH: 19C. Latin, lit. scatteredly, from *passus* scattered, p.p. of *pandere* to spread out.

passimeter *n.* an automatic ticket-issuing machine. WH: early 20C. PASS or PASSENGER + -*i*- + -METER.

passing *a.* going by, occurring. *Also n., adv.* WH: 12–14C. PASS + -ING[2] (as n., + -ING[1]).

passion *n.* a deep and overpowering affection of the mind, such as grief, anger, hatred etc. *Also v.i.* WH: 12–14C. Old French, from Ecclesiastical Latin *passio, passionis* suffering, affliction, from Latin *passus*, p.p. of *pati* to suffer. See also -ION. The earliest sense was the suffering of Jesus on the Cross. The sense strong sexual feeling evolved in the 14–15C.

passive *a.* suffering, acted upon. *Also n.* WH: 14–15C. Old French *passif*, or from Latin *passivus*, from *passus*. See PASSION, also -IVE.

Passover *n.* a Jewish feast, on the 14th day of the month Nisan. WH: 16C. From *pass over* (see PASS), translating Hebrew *pesaḥ* (PASCHAL). The festival commemorates the sparing of the Israelites from the death of their first-born and their liberation from Egyptian bondage. 'For the Lord will pass through to smite the Egyptians; and ... will pass over the door and not suffer the destroyer to come in unto your houses' (Exod. xii.23).

passport *n.* an official document authorizing a person to travel in a foreign country and entitling them to legal protection. WH: 15C. French *passeport*, from *passer* PASS + *port* PORT[1]. The original sense was an authorization to pass from a port or leave a country.

past *a.* gone by, neither present nor future. *Also n., prep., adv.* WH: 12–14C. Obs. p.p. of PASS (now *passed*).

pasta *n.* a flour and water dough, often shaped and eaten fresh or in processed form, e.g. spaghetti. WH: 19C. Italian, from Late Latin. See PASTE.

paste *n.* a mixture of flour and water, usu. with butter, lard etc., kneaded and used for making pastry etc. *Also v.t.* WH: 12–14C. Old French (Modern French *pâte*), from Late Latin *pasta* small square piece of a medicinal preparation, from Greek *pastē*, pl. *pasta* barley porridge, from *pastos* sprinkled, from *passein* to sprinkle.

pastel *n.* a dry paste composed of a pigment mixed with gum water. *Also a.* WH: 16C. French, from Italian *pastello*, dim. of *pasta* paste, from Late Latin. See PASTE, also -EL.

pastern *n.* the part of a horse's leg between the fetlock and the hoof. WH: 12–14C. Old French *pasturon* (Modern French *pâturon*), from *pasture* hobble, ult. from Medieval Latin *pastoria, pastorium*, use as n. of fem. and neut. of Latin *pastorius* pertaining to a shepherd. See PASTOR.

pasteurism *n.* a method of preventing or curing certain diseases, esp. hydrophobia, by progressive inoculation. WH: 18C. Louis *Pasteur*, 1822–95, French scientist + -ISM.

pastiche *n.* a medley, musical work, painting etc. composed of elements drawn from other works or which imitates the style of a previous work. WH: 19C. French, from Italian *pasticcio* pie, pasty, from Late Latin *pasta* PASTE.

pastille *n.* an aromatic lozenge. WH: 17C. French, from Latin *pastillus* little loaf, roll, lozenge, dim. of *panis* loaf.

pastime *n.* something that makes time pass agreeably, a hobby. WH: 15C. PASS + TIME, based on French *passetemps*.

pastis *n.* an aniseed-flavoured alcoholic drink. WH: early 20C. French, orig. pie, pasty.

pastor *n.* a minister in charge of a church and congregation. WH: 12–14C. Old French *pastour* (Modern French *pasteur*), acc. of *pastre* (Modern French *pâtre* shepherd), from Latin *pastor*, from *pastus*, p.p. of *pascere* to feed, to graze. See also -OR. The literal (and earliest) sense is herdsman, shepherd. A church pastor looks after his 'flock' (congregation).

pastoral *a.* of or relating to shepherds. *Also n.* WH: 14–15C. Latin *pastoralis*, from PASTOR. See also -AL[1].

pastorale *n.* a simple rustic melody. WH: 18C. Italian, use as n. of a., pastoral.

pastrami *n.* a highly seasoned smoked beef. WH: mid-20C. Yiddish, from Romanian *pastramă*, prob. of Turkish orig.

pastry *n.* a dough of flour, fat and water, used baked to make pies. WH: 14–15C. PASTE + -RY, based on Old French *pastaierie*, from *pastaier* pastrycook.

pasture *n.* grass suitable for the grazing of cattle etc. *Also v.t., v.i.* WH: 12–14C. Old French (Modern French *pâture*), from Late Latin *pastura*, from Latin *pastus*, p.p. of *pascere* to feed, to pasture. See also -URE.

pasty[1] *a.* of or like paste. WH: 17C. PASTE + -Y[1].

pasty[2] *n.* a small pie, usu. of meat, baked without a dish. WH: 12–14C. Old French *pastée, pasté* (Modern French *pâté*), ult. from Late Latin *pasta* PASTE. See also -Y[3].

Pat *n.* an Irishman. WH: 19C. Abbr. of Irish male forename *Patrick*. Cp. PADDY.

pat *v.t.* to strike gently and quickly with something flat, esp. the fingers or hand. *Also v.i., n., a., adv.* WH: 16C. Orig. prob. imit.

pataca *n.* the standard unit of currency of Macao. WH: 19C. Spanish and Portuguese, from Portuguese *pataea* piece of eight, dollar.

patagium *n.* the wing membrane of a bat, flying lemur etc. WH: 19C. Latin gold edging on a tunic.

patch *n.* a piece of cloth, metal or other material put on to mend anything or to strengthen a fabric etc. *Also v.t., v.i.* WH: 14–15C. Prob. from Anglo-French var. of Old French *pieche*, dial. var. of *piece* PIECE.

patchouli *n.* an Indian shrub of the genus *Pogostemon*, yielding a fragrant oil. WH: 19C. Tamil *pacculi*.

pate *n.* the head, esp. the top of the head. WH: 12–14C. Orig. unknown. ? Latin *patena* dish, pan (see PATEN).

pâte *n.* the paste from which porcelain is made. WH: 19C. French PASTE.

pâté *n.* a spread made of cooked, diced meat, fish or vegetables blended with herbs etc. WH: 18C. French, from Old French *pasté*. See PASTY[2]. Cp. PATTY. The original sense was pie, pasty. The current sense dates from the 19C.

patella *n.* the kneecap. WH: 15C. Latin, dim. of *patina*. See PATEN.

paten *n.* a plate or shallow dish for receiving the Eucharistic bread. WH: 12–14C. Anglo-French var. of Old French *patène*, or from Latin *patena, patina* shallow dish, pan, from Greek *patanē* plate.

patent *n.* a grant from the Crown by letters patent of a title of nobility, or from the Crown or a government of the official exclusive right to make or sell a new invention. *Also a., v.t.* WH: 14–15C. Old French, from Latin *patens, patentis*, pres.p. of *patere* to lie open (see -ENT), orig. Old French *lettres patentes*, Medieval Latin *litterae*

patentes letters patent. The sense plain, open, manifest derives direct from Latin *patens, patentis*.

pater *n.* a father. WH: 12–14C. Latin father. The word was originally a shortening of PATERNOSTER. The current usage dates from the 17C, first in the sense spiritual father.

patera *n.* a round dish used for wine in ancient Rome. WH: 17C. Latin, from *patere* to be open.

paterfamilias *n.* the father of a family, the male head of a household. WH: 15C. Latin, from PATER + old gen. of *familia* family.

paternal *a.* of or relating to a father. WH: 14–15C. Late Latin *paternalis*, from Latin *paternus*, from PATER. See also -AL[1].

paternoster *n.* the Lord's Prayer, esp. in Latin. WH: pre-1200. Latin *pater noster*, lit. our father, the first two words of the Lord's Prayer in Latin. Cp. PATTER[2].

path *n.* a footway, esp. one beaten only by feet. *Also v.i., v.t.* WH: pre-1200. Old English *pæth*, from Germanic, of unknown orig. Cp. German *Pfad*.

-path *comb. form* a medical practitioner, as in *homoeopath*. WH: Greek *pathos* suffering, disease.

Pathan *n.* a member of a people of NW Pakistan and SE Afghanistan. WH: 17C. Hindi *Paṭhān*, from Pashto *Paštāna*, pl. of *Paštūn*.

pathetic *a.* affecting the feelings, esp. those of pity and sorrow. *Also n.* WH: 16C. French *pathétique*, from Late Latin *patheticus*, from Greek *pathētikos* sensitive, from *pathētos* liable to suffer, from *pathos* suffering. See PATHOS, also -ETIC. The original sense (to the 18C) was moving, stirring. The sense exciting pity or sadness arose in the 18C.

pathic *n.* a catamite. WH: 17C. Latin *pathicus*, from Greek *pathikos*, from *pathos* suffering, passive condition. See PATHOS, also -IC.

patho- *comb. form* disease. WH: Greek, from *pathos* suffering, disease. See -O-.

pathogen *n.* any disease-producing substance or micro-organism. WH: 19C. PATHO- + -GEN.

pathogenesis *n.* the origin and development of disease. WH: 19C. PATHO- + GENESIS.

pathognomy *n.* expression of the passions. WH: 18C. Greek *pathognōmonia* study of suffering, from PATHO- + *gnōmōn, gnōmonos* interpreter, based on PHYSIOGNOMY.

pathology *n.* the science of diseases, esp. of the human body. WH: 16C. French *pathologie* or Modern Latin *pathologia*. See PATHO-, -LOGY.

pathophobia *n.* a morbid fear of disease. WH: 19C. PATHO- + -phobia (-PHOBE).

pathos *n.* a quality or element in events or expression that excites emotion, esp. pity or sorrow. WH: 16C. Greek suffering, feeling, rel. to *paskhein* to suffer, *penthos* grief.

-pathy *comb. form* disease, treatment of this, as in *homoeopathy*. WH: Greek *patheia* suffering, feeling.

patience *n.* the quality of being patient. WH: 12–14C. Old French, from Latin *patientia*, from *patiens, patientis*, pres.p. of *pati* to suffer, to endure. See also -ENCE.

patient *a.* capable of bearing pain, suffering etc. without fretfulness. *Also v.t.* WH: 12–14C. Old French, from Latin *patiens, patientis*. See PATIENCE, also -ENT. The sense sick person (so called as one who suffers) arose in the 14–15C.

patina *n.* the green incrustation that covers ancient bronzes. WH: 18C. Latin shallow dish, pan.

patio *n.* a paved area beside a house, used for outdoor meals, sunbathing etc. WH: 19C. Spanish court of a house, prob. Old Provençal *patu, pati* untilled land, place of pasture, from Latin *pactum* agreement, PACT.

patisserie *n.* a pastry-cook's shop. WH: 16C. French *pâtisserie*, from Medieval Latin *pasticium*, from *pasta* PASTE.

Patna rice *n.* a variety of long-grain rice used for savoury dishes. WH: 19C. *Patna*, a district in N central Bihar, India.

patois *n.* a non-standard dialect of a district. WH: 17C. Old French rough speech, ? from *patoier* to handle roughly, to trample, from *patte* paw, of unknown orig.

patonce *a.* denoting a cross the four arms of which expand in curves from the centre and have floriated ends. WH: 16C. ? Rel. to POTENCE.

patri- *comb. form* father. WH: Latin, from *pater*, *patris* FATHER.

patrial *a.* legally entitled to reside in the UK. *Also n.* WH: 17C. French, or from Medieval Latin *patrialis*, from *patria* fatherland, from *pater*, *patris* father. See also -AL[1].

patriarch *n.* the head of a family or tribe, ruling by paternal right. WH: 12–14C. Old French *patriarche*, from Ecclesiastical Latin *patriarcha*, from Greek *patriarkhēs*, from *patria* family, clan + -*arkhēs*, from *arkhos* chief (ARCH-).

patrician *n.* a member of the Roman aristocracy. *Also a.* WH: 14–15C. Old French *patricien*, from use as n. of Latin *patricius* of a noble father, from *pater*, *patris* father. See also -ICIAN.

patricide *n.* (the act of) killing one's father. WH: 16C. Late Latin *patricida*, *patricidium*, alts. of *parricida*, *parricidium*. See PARRICIDE. Late Latin *patricida* is a person who kills their father; *patricidium* is the killing of one's father.

patrilineal *a.* by descent through the father. WH: early 20C. PATRI- + LINEAL.

patrimony *n.* an estate or right inherited from one's father or ancestors. WH: 12–14C. Old French *patrimoine*, from Latin *patrimonium*, from *pater*, *patris* father. See also -MONY.

patriot *n.* a person who loves their country and is devoted to its interests, esp. its freedom and independence. WH: 16C. French *patriote*, from Late Latin *patriota* fellow countryman, from Greek *patriōtēs*, from *patrios* of one's fathers, from *patris* fatherland. See also -OT[2].

patristic *a.* of or relating to the ancient Fathers of the Christian Church or their writings. WH: 19C. German *patristisch*, from Latin *pater*, *patris* father. See -IST, -IC.

patrol *n.* the action of moving around an area, esp. at night, for security. *Also v.i.*, *v.t.* WH: 17C. German *Patrolle*, from French *patrouille*, from *patrouiller* to paddle about in mud, from *patte* paw, foot + dial. *gadrouille* mud, dirty water. Patrolling originally involved tramping around in muck and mire.

patrology *n.* patristics. WH: 17C. Greek *patēr*, *patros* father + -O- + -LOGY.

patron *n.* a person who supports or fosters a person, cause etc. WH: 12–14C. Old French, from Latin *patronus* protector of clients, advocate, defender, from *pater*, *patris* father + *onuma* name. See also -IC.

patronymic *n.* a name derived from a father or ancestor; a family name. *Also a.* WH: 17C. Late Latin, from Greek *patrōnumikos*, from *patrōnumos*, from *patēr*, *patr-* father + *onuma* name. See also -IC.

patroon *n.* a proprietor of land with manorial privileges and right of entail under a Dutch grant, esp. in New York and New Jersey (abolished 1850). WH: 18C. Dutch PATRON.

patsy *n.* a person who is easily deceived, cheated etc., a sucker, a scapegoat. WH: 19C. Orig. unknown. ? Italian *pazzo* madman.

pattée *a.* (of a cross) having almost triangular arms widening outwards. WH: 15C. French, from *patte* paw, of unknown orig.

patten *n.* a clog or overshoe mounted on an iron ring etc., for keeping the shoes out of the mud or wet. WH: 14–15C. Old French *patin*, from *patte* paw, of unknown orig. Cp. -INE.

patter[1] *v.i.* (of rain) to fall with a quick succession of light, sharp sounds. *Also v.t.*, *n.* WH: 17C. Dim. and freq. of PAT. See also -ER[5]. Cp. PIT-A-PAT.

patter[2] *n.* rapid speech introduced impromptu into a song, comedy etc. *Also v.t.*, *v.i.* WH: 14–15C. PATER (in sense PATERNOSTER). The original sense (as v.) was to recite a prayer (such as the Lord's Prayer) mechanically or rapidly.

pattern *n.* a decorative design for a carpet, fabric etc. *Also v.t.* WH: 12–14C. Alt. of PATRON.

pattle *n.* an implement used for cleaning the earth from a ploughshare. WH: 14–15C. Orig. uncertain. Cp. PADDLE[1].

patty *n.* a little pie. WH: 17C. Alt. of French PÂTÉ by assoc. with PASTY[2].

patulous *a.* (of boughs etc.) spreading, expanding. WH: 17C. Latin *patulus* spreading, from *patere* to be open. See also -ULOUS.

patzer *n.* a poor chess player. WH: mid-20C. Orig. unknown. Cp. German *patzen* to bungle.

paua *n.* a large New Zealand shellfish of the genus *Haliotis*. WH: 19C. Maori.

paucity *n.* an insufficient amount; scarcity. WH: 14–15C. Old French *paucité* or Latin *paucitas*, from *paucus*, *pauci-* few. See also -ITY.

Pauli exclusion principle *n.* a law of quantum mechanics stating that two fermions cannot exist in identical states in the same atom. WH: early 20C. Wolfgang *Pauli*, 1900–58, Austrian-born US physicist.

Pauline *a.* of or relating to St Paul or his writings. *Also n.* WH: 14–15C. Medieval Latin *Paulinus*, from *Paulus* Paul. See also -INE. The reference is to St Paul, d. *c.*68 AD, Christian missionary and martyr, Apostle of the Gentiles.

Paul Jones *n.* a ballroom dance in which partners are exchanged several times. WH: early 20C. John *Paul Jones*, 1747–92, Scottish naval officer noted for his victories in the American War of Independence.

paulo-post-future *n.* the future-perfect tense in classical Greek. WH: 19C. Modern Latin *paulo post futurum*, translating Greek *ho met oligon mellōn* the future after a little.

paulownia *n.* any Chinese tree of the genus *Paulownia*, having purple flowers. WH: 19C. Modern Latin, from Anna *Paulowna* (Pavlovna), 1795–1865, daughter of Tsar Paul I of Russia and wife of William II of the Netherlands.

paunch *n.* the belly, the abdomen. *Also v.t.* WH: 14–15C. Old Northern French *panche*, var. of Old French *pance* (Modern French *panse*), from Latin *pantex*, *panticis* bowels, intestines.

pauper *n.* a person without means of support, a destitute person, a beggar. WH: 15C. Latin poor.

pause *n.* a cessation or intermission of action, speaking etc. *Also v.i.*, *v.t.* WH: 14–15C. Old French, or from Latin *pausa*, from Greek *pausis*, from *pausein* to stop, to cease.

pavane *n.* a slow and stately dance, usu. in elaborate dress, in vogue in the 16th and 17th cents. WH: 16C. French, prob. from Italian dial. *pavana*, fem. of *pavano* of Padua, from *Pavo*, dial. name of Padua (Italian *Padova*), a city in NE Italy. According to some, the word is from (or has been influenced by) Latin *pavo*, *pavonis* peacock.

pave *v.t.* to make a hard, level surface upon, with stone, bricks etc. WH: 12–14C. Old French *paver*, prob. back-formation from *pavement* pavement, from Latin *pavimentum* beaten floor, from *pavire* to beat, to tread down. See also -MENT.

pavé *n.* a pavement. WH: 14–15C. French, use as n. of p.p. of *paver* PAVE.

pavilion *n.* an ornamental building, usu. of light construction, for amusements etc., esp. one for spectators and players at a cricket ground etc. *Also v.t.* WH: 12–14C. Old French *pavillon* tent, canopy, from Latin *papilio*, *papilionis* butterfly, tent. The original reference is to a tent resembling a butterfly with outstretched wings.

pavlova *n.* a dessert consisting of a meringue base topped with fruit and whipped cream. WH: early 20C. Anna *Pavlova*, 1881–1931, Russian ballerina. The dessert was so named in the dancer's honour when she visited Australia and New Zealand in the 1920s.

Pavlovian *a.* of or relating to conditioned reflexes. WH: mid-20C. Ivan Petrovich *Pavlov*, 1849–1936, Russian physiologist + -IAN.

pavonazzo *n.* a variety of marble with brilliant markings like the colours of a peacock. *Also a.* WH: 19C. Italian, from Latin *pavonaceum*, from *pavo*, *pavonis* peacock. See also -ACEOUS.

pavonine *a.* of, relating to or resembling a peacock. *Also n.* WH: 17C. Latin *pavoninus*, from *pavo*, *pavonis* peacock. See also -INE.

paw *n.* the foot of an animal having claws, as distinct from a hoof. *Also v.t.*, *v.i.* WH: 12–14C. Old French *powe*, *poue*, from Frankish. Cp. Middle Dutch *pōte*, Dutch *poot*, German *Pfote*.

pawky *a.* humorous, arch. WH: 17C. Dial. *pawk* trick, of uncertain orig. + -Y[1].

pawl *n.* a hinged piece of metal or lever engaging with the teeth of a wheel etc., to prevent it from running back etc. *Also v.t.* WH: 17C. ? Low German or Dutch *pal*, rel. to a. *pal* immobile, fixed, ult. of unknown orig.

pawn[1] *n.* a piece of the lowest value in chess. WH: 14–15C. Old French *poön*, *peon*, from Medieval Latin *pedo*, *pedonis* foot-soldier, from Latin *pes*, *pedis* foot. Cp. PEON.

pawn[2] *v.t.* to deliver or deposit as a pledge for the repayment of a debt or loan, or the performance of a promise. *Also n.* WH: 15C. Old French *pan*, *pand* pledge, security, plunder, from Germanic. Cp. German *Pfand* pledge.

pawpaw *n.* a large, oblong, edible yellow fruit. WH: 16C. Spanish and Portuguese *papaya*, from Carib or Arawak. The change from *papaya* to *pawpaw* is unexplained.

pax *n.int.* the kiss of peace. *Also int.* WH: 14–15C. Latin peace.

paxwax *n.* a strong, stiff tendon from the dorsal vertebrae to the occiput in many mammals and, in a modified form, in humans. WH: 14–15C. Prob. alt. of obs. *fax* hair (from Old English *feax*) + base of WAX². Obsolete *fax* survives in the names *Fairfax* and *Halifax*.

pay¹ *v.t.* to hand over to (someone) what is due in discharge of a debt or for services or goods. *Also v.i., n.* WH: 12–14C. Old French *payer*, from Latin *pacare* to appease, to pacify, from *pax, pacis* PEACE. The original sense (to the 16C) was to appease, to pacify, to satisfy. The sense to give money for goods etc. evolved from the notion of pacifying a creditor.

pay² *v.t.* to coat, cover or fill with hot pitch for waterproofing. WH: 17C. Old French *peier*, from Latin *picare*, from *pix, picis* PITCH².

†paynim *n.* a pagan, a heathen. WH: 12–14C. Old French *painime*, from Ecclesiastical Latin *paganismus* heathenism, from Latin *paganus* PAGAN. See also -ISM.

payola *n.* clandestine reward paid for illicit promotion of a commercial product, e.g. of a record by a disc jockey. WH: mid-20C. PAY¹ + -ola, prob. from PIANOLA®.

†paysage *n.* a rural scene or landscape. WH: 17C. French, from *pays* country. See also -AGE.

Pb *chem. symbol* lead. WH: Abbr. of Latin *plumbum* lead.

pea *n.* a leguminous plant, *Pisum sativum*, the seeds of which are used as food. WH: 17C. Back-formation from PEASE, taken as pl. Cp. CHERRY.

peace *n.* a state of quiet or tranquillity. WH: 12–14C. Old French *pais* (Modern French *paix*), from Latin *pax, pacis*.

peach¹ *n.* a fleshy, downy stone fruit with sweet yellow flesh and a pinkish-orange skin. *Also a.* WH: 12–14C. Old French *pesche* (Modern French *pêche*), from Medieval Latin *persica*, from Latin *persicum* (*malum*), lit. Persian (apple).

peach² *v.i.* to turn informer against an accomplice, to inform (against or upon). *Also v.t.* WH: 14–15C. Shortening of *appeach* to charge, to accuse, to impeach, from Old French *empechier* IMPEACH.

peacock *n.* a male peafowl, having gorgeous plumage and a long tail capable of expanding like a fan. *Also v.t., v.i.* WH: 12–14C. Var. of obs. *po* peacock (from Old English *pāwa, pēa*, from Latin *pavo*) + COCK¹. Obsolete *po* survives in the surname *Pocock*.

pea-jacket *n.* a coarse, thick, loose overcoat worn by seamen. WH: 18C. Prob. from Dutch *pijjekker*, from *pij* coarse woollen cloth + *jekker* jacket, assim. to JACKET.

peak¹ *n.* a sharp point or top, esp. of a mountain. *Also v.i., a.* WH: 16C. Var. of PIKE¹, with sense mountain summit prob. partly var. of back-formation from *picked* (from PICK² + -ED). The original meaning was the projecting part of a garment, as of a hood. The sense pointed mountain top arose in the 17C.

peak² *v.i.* to pine away. WH: 14–15C. Orig. unknown.

peak³ *v.t.* to raise (a gaff or yard) until nearly vertical. *Also v.i.* WH: 17C. Prob. shortening of APEAK.

peal¹ *n.* a loud, esp. a prolonged or repercussive, sound, as of thunder, bells etc. *Also v.i., v.t.* WH: 12–14C. Shortening of APPEAL.

peal² *n.* a grilse or young salmon, usu. under 2 lb. (0.9 kg). WH: 16C. Orig. unknown.

pean *n.* a heraldic fur, represented by sable with or (golden) spots. WH: 16C. Orig. unknown.

peanut *n.* a plant, *Arachis hypogaea*, of the bean family with pods ripening underground, the seeds of which are edible and used for their oil. WH: 19C. PEA + NUT.

pear *n.* the fleshy yellow or greenish fruit of the pear tree. WH: pre-1200. Old English *pere*, from Popular Latin *pira*, fem. sing. var. of Latin *pirum*.

pearl¹ *n.* a smooth, white or bluish-grey, lustrous and iridescent, calcareous concretion, found in several bivalves, the best in the pearl-oyster, prized as a gem. *Also a., v.t., v.i.* WH: 14–15C. Old French *perle*, from Popular Latin *pernula*, dim. of Latin *perna* leg, ham, ham-shaped mollusc.

pearl² *n.* a picot. *Also v.t.* WH: 14–15C. Var. of PURL¹.

pearmain *n.* a kind of apple with firm, white flesh. WH: 12–14C. Old French *parmaine, permaine*, prob. from alt. of Latin *Parmensis* of Parma (see PARMA HAM). The original sense (to the 17C) was a variety of baking pear. The current sense, a variety of apple, dates from the 16C.

peart *a.* lively and cheerful, pert. WH: 12–14C. Var. of PERT.

peasant *n.* a rustic labourer. *Also a.* WH: 14–15C. Old French *païsant* (Modern French *paysan*), alt. of earlier *païsenc*, from *païs* (Modern French *pays*) country, from alt. of Latin *pagus* country district. See also -ANT. Cp. PAGAN.

pease *n.pl.* peas. WH: pre-1200. Old English *pise*, pl. *pisan*, from Late Latin *pisa*, pl. *pisae*, from *pisum*, pl. *pisa*, from Greek *pison*, pl. *pisa*, of unknown orig. Cp. PEA.

peat *n.* decayed and partly carbonized vegetable matter found in boggy places and used as fuel. WH: 12–14C. Anglo-Latin *peta*, ? from Celtic and rel. to PIECE. Cp. Old Irish *pit* portion.

peau-de-soie *n.* a rich, finely ribbed fabric of silk or rayon. WH: 19C. French, lit. silk skin, from *peau* skin + *de* of + *soie* silk. Cp. PADUASOY.

pebble *n.* a small stone rounded by the action of water. *Also a., v.t.* WH: pre-1200. Old English *papol-*, as in *papolstān* pebblestone, of unknown orig. The Old English element occurs in the place names *Papplewick*, (Newton) *Poppleford*.

pébrine *n.* an epidemic disease, characterized by black spots, attacking silkworms. WH: 19C. French, from Provençal *pebrino*, from *pebre* pepper.

pecan *n.* a N American hickory, *Carya illinoensis*, or its fruit or nut. WH: 18C. French *pacane*, from Illinois *pakani*.

peccable *a.* liable to sin. WH: 17C. Old French, from Medieval Latin *peccabilis*, from Latin *peccare* to sin. See also -ABLE.

peccadillo *n.* a minor sin or offence. WH: 16C. Spanish *pecadillo*, dim. of *pecado* sin.

peccant *a.* sinful, guilty. *Also n.* WH: 16C. Latin *peccans, peccantis*, pres.p. of *peccare* to sin.

peccary *n.* any American piglike mammal of the family Tayassuidae. WH: 17C. Carib *pakira*.

peccavi *int.* used to express contrition. *Also n.* WH: 16C. Latin I have sinned, 1st pers. sing. perf. ind. of *peccare* to sin.

pech *v.i.* to breathe hard, to pant. *Also n.* WH: 15C. Prob. imit. Cp. PUFF.

peck¹ *v.t.* to strike with a beak or pointed instrument. *Also v.i., n.* WH: 12–14C. Prob. from Middle Low German *pekken* to peck with the beak, of unknown orig.

peck² *n.* a measure of capacity for dry goods, 2 gallons (about 9l); the fourth part of a bushel. WH: 12–14C. Anglo-French *pek*, of unknown orig.

pecorino *n.* an Italian ewe's-milk cheese. WH: mid-20C. Italian, from *pecora* sheep.

pecten *n.* a comblike process forming a membrane in the eyes of birds and some reptiles. WH: 14–15C. Latin comb, wool-card, pubic hair, rel. to *pectere*, Greek *pektein* to comb.

pectin *n.* a white, amorphous compound found in fruits and certain fleshy roots, formed from pectose by the process of ripening. WH: 19C. Greek *pektos* fixed, congealed, curdled, from stem of *pēgnuein* to make firm, to make solid + -IN¹.

pectoral *a.* of, relating to or for the breast or chest. *Also n.* WH: 14–15C. Old French, from Latin *pectoralis*, from *pectus, pectoris* breast, chest. See also -AL¹.

peculate *v.t., v.i.* to appropriate (money or goods entrusted to one's care) to one's own use. WH: 18C. Latin *peculatus*, p.p. of *peculari*, rel. to *peculium*. See PECULIAR, also -ATE³.

peculiar *a.* strange, odd. *Also n.* WH: 14–15C. Latin *peculiaris* not held in common with others, from *peculium* property in cattle, private property, from *pecu* cattle, money. Cp. PECUNIARY. The original sense was particular, special. The sense strange, odd evolved in the 17C.

pecuniary *a.* of, relating to or consisting of money. WH: 16C. Latin *pecuniarius*, from *pecunia* money, orig. riches in cattle, from *pecu* cattle, money. See -ARY¹. Cp. PECULIAR.

pedagogue *n.* a teacher of young children, a schoolmaster (usu. in contempt, implying conceit or pedantry). *Also v.t.* WH: 14–15C.

Latin *paedagogus*, from Greek *paidagōgos* slave who took a child to school and back, from *pais, paidos* boy (cp. PAEDO-) + *agōgos* leading.

pedal[1] *n.* a lever acted on by the foot, e.g. on a bicycle or motor vehicle. *Also v.t., v.i.* WH: 17C. French *pédale*, from Italian *pedale* footstalk, tree trunk, from Latin *pedalis*, from *pes, pedis* foot. See -AL[1].

pedal[2] *a.* of or relating to a foot or footlike part (esp. of a mollusc). WH: 17C. Latin *pedalis*, from *pes, pedis* foot. See also -AL[1]. Cp. PEDAL[1].

pedant *n.* a person who makes a pretentious show of book-learning, or lays undue stress on rules and formulas. WH: 16C. French *pédant*, from Italian *pedante*, ? from 1st element of Latin *paedagogus* PEDAGOGUE.

pedate *a.* having feet. WH: 18C. Latin *pedatus* having feet, from *pes, pedis* foot. See also -ATE[2].

peddle *v.t.* to sell in small quantities, to retail as a pedlar. *Also v.i.* WH: 16C. Back-formation from PEDLAR. The sense to busy oneself with trifles is probably a variant of PIDDLE, by association with PEDDLE.

-pede *comb. form* a foot, as in *centipede, quadruped.* WH: Latin *pes, pedis* foot.

pederast *n.* a man who practises sodomy with a boy. WH: 17C. Greek *paiderastēs*, from *pais, paidos* boy + *erastēs* lover.

pedestal *n.* an insulated base for a column, statue etc. *Also v.t.* WH: 16C. French *piédestal*, from Italian *piedestallo*, from *piè* foot + *di* of + *stallo* STALL[1]. The English spelling has been influenced by Latin *pes, pedis* foot.

pedestrian *n.* a person who is walking. *Also a.* WH: 18C. French *pédestre*, or from Latin *pedester, pedestris* going on foot, written in prose, from *pes, pedis* foot. See also -IAN.

pedi- *comb. form* a foot. WH: Latin *pes, pedis* foot + *-i-*.

pedicab *n.* a rickshaw operated by pedals. WH: mid-20C. PEDI- + CAB[1].

pedicel *n.* the stalk supporting a single flower etc., as distinct from *peduncle.* WH: 17C. Modern Latin *pedicellus*, dim. of *pediculus* pedicle, from Latin *pes, pedis* foot. See also -CLE.

pedicular *a.* lousy, infested with lice. WH: 16C. French *pédiculaire*, from Latin *pedicularis*, from *pediculus* louse, from *pedis* louse. See also -CULE, -AR[1].

pedicure *n.* the surgical treatment of the feet. *Also v.t.* WH: 19C. French *pédicure*, from Latin *pes, pedis* foot + *curare* CURE. Cp. MANICURE.

pedigree *n.* genealogy, lineage, esp. of a domestic or pet animal. *Also a.* WH: 14–15C. Anglo-French *pé de grue* lit. foot of a crane, from *pé* (Old French *pie*, Modern French *pied*) foot + *de* of + *grue* crane. Not rel. to DEGREE. A pedigree is so called from the clawlike, three-branched mark used to show succession in genealogies.

pediment *n.* the triangular part surmounting a portico, in buildings in the Grecian style. WH: 16C. Orig. uncertain. ? Alt. of PYRAMID.

pedipalp *n.* an arachnid of the order Pedipalpi, characterized by pincer-like feelers, comprising the true scorpions. WH: 19C. Modern Latin *pedipalpi* (pl.), from PEDI- + Latin *palpus* PALP.

pedlar *n.* a travelling hawker of small wares, usu. carried in a pack. WH: 12–14C. Alt. of dial. *pedder*, appar. from dial. *ped* wicker pannier, of unknown orig. The ending is similar to that of dialect *tinkler* in its relationship to TINKER.

pedology *n.* the science of soils. WH: early 20C. Greek *pedon* ground + -O- + -LOGY.

pedometer *n.* an instrument for measuring the distance covered on foot by registering the number of steps taken. WH: 18C. Latin *pes, pedis* foot + -O- + -METER. A better form, with both elements from Greek, would be *podometer, as in the French equivalent, *podomètre.*

pedrail *n.* a contrivance for enabling a traction engine to move over rough ground. WH: early 20C. Latin *pes, pedis* foot + RAIL[1].

peduncle *n.* a flower stalk, esp. of a solitary flower or one bearing the subsidiary stalks of a cluster, as distinct from *pedicel.* WH: 18C. Modern Latin *pedunculus*, from *pes, pedis* foot. See also -UNCLE.

pedway *n.* a pedestrian footpath in a city. WH: mid-20C. PEDESTRIAN + WAY.

pee *v.i.* to urinate. *Also v.t., n.* WH: 18C. Euphem. for PISS (from its first letter).

peek *v.i.* to peer, to peep, to pry. *Also n.* WH: 14–15C. Orig. unknown. Cp. KEEK.

peel[1] *v.t.* to strip the skin, bark or rind off. *Also v.i., n.* WH: 12–14C. Var. of *pill* (PILLAGE), influ. by Old French *peler* to peel.

peel[2] *n.* a wooden shovel used by bakers. WH: 14–15C. Old French *pele* (Modern French *pelle*), from Latin *pala*, from base of *pangere* to fix, to plant.

peel[3] *n.* a square fortified tower, esp. those built about the 16th cent. in the border areas of Scotland and England for defence against raids. WH: 12–14C. Old French *pel* (Modern French *pieu*), from Latin *palus* stake. Cp. PALE[2], PALLET[2]. The sense square fortified tower arose in the 18C and is probably a shortening of *peel-house*, from the earlier (now obsolete) sense castle.

peeler *n.* a policeman, orig. a constable in the police organized by Sir Robert Peel. WH: 19C. Sir Robert *Peel*, 1788–1850, English statesman, who as Home Secretary organized the London police force in 1829. Cp. BOBBY[1]. The name was in use for some years before this for a member of the Irish constabulary, founded in 1822 following Peel's term in office as Secretary for Ireland, 1812–18.

Peelite *n.* an adherent of Sir Robert Peel. WH: 19C. Sir Robert *Peel* (see PEELER) + -ITE[1]. The name was used for a Conservative supporting Peel's measure for the repeal of the Corn Laws in 1846.

peen *n.* the point of a mason's hammer, opposite to the face. *Also v.t.* WH: 16C. Appar. of Scandinavian orig. Cp. Swedish dial. *pena*, Danish dial. *pene*, Norwegian dial. *penna* to beat thin with a hammer.

peep[1] *v.i.* to look through a crevice or narrow opening. *Also n.* WH: 14–15C. Imit. Cp. PEEK, PEER[1].

peep[2] *v.i.* (of a young bird, a mouse etc.) to cry, chirp or squeak. *Also n.* WH: 14–15C. Imit. Cp. CHEEP.

peeper *n.* a tree frog of the genus *Hyla.* WH: 16C. PEEP[2] + -ER[1].

peepul *n.* the bo tree. WH: 18C. Hindi *pīpal*, from Sanskrit *pippala.*

peer[1] *v.i.* to look very closely (at, into etc.). WH: 16C. Var. of obs. *pire* (from Low German *pīren* of unknown orig.), influ. by APPEAR. Cp. PORE[2].

peer[2] *n.* in the UK, a member of one of the degrees of nobility, comprising dukes, marquesses, earls, viscounts and barons. *Also v.t., v.i.* WH: 12–14C. Old French *per* (Modern French *pair*), from Latin *par, paris* equal. Cp. PAIR. The original meaning was a person of the same standing as another. This sense was then extended to a nobleman of the same rank as another.

peesweep *n.* the peewit. WH: 18C. Imit. of bird's call. Cp. PEEWIT.

peevers *n.* the game of hopscotch. WH: 19C. Orig. unknown. The *peever* is the stone, piece of pottery, etc. used in the game.

peevish *a.* irritable, expressing discontent. WH: 14–15C. Orig. unknown. According to some, the word comes from Latin *perversus* (PERVERSE).

peewee *n.* a lapwing. WH: 19C. Imit. of bird's call. Cp. PEWEE, PEEWIT.

peewit *n.* a lapwing. WH: 16C. Imit. of bird's call.

peg *n.* a pin or bolt, usu. of wood, for holding parts of a structure or fastening articles together, hanging things on, supporting, holding, marking etc. *Also v.t.* WH: 14–15C. Prob. from Low Dutch. Cp. Middle Dutch *pegge*, Dutch dial. *peg* plug, peg.

Pegasus *n.* poetic inspiration. WH: 14–15C. Latin *Pegasus*, from Greek *Pēgasos*, the winged horse of Greek mythology who sprang from the blood of the slain Medusa and was later represented as the favourite horse of the Muses, from *pēgē* spring, fount.

pegasus *n.* any member of the genus *Pegasus* of fishes, with broad pectoral fins. WH: 19C. PEGASUS.

pegmatite *n.* a coarse-grained variety of granite, with a little mica. WH: 19C. Greek *pēgma, pēgmatos* thing joined together + -ITE[1].

peignoir *n.* a loose robe or dressing gown worn by a woman. WH: 19C. French, from *peigner* to comb + -*oir* -ORY[1]. The garment was originally worn by a woman while her hair was being combed.

pejorative *a.* depreciatory, disparaging. *Also n.* WH: 19C. French *péjoratif*, from Late Latin *pejoratus*, p.p. of *pejorare* to make worse, from Latin *peior* worse. See also -ATIVE.

pekan *n.* a N American marten, *Martes pennanti*, of the weasel family, prized for its fur. WH: 18C. Canadian French, from Abnaki *pékané.*

Pekinese *a.* of or relating to Beijing (formerly Peking). *Also n.* WH: 19C. *Peking* (Beijing), the capital of China + -ESE.

pekoe *n.* a fine black tea. WH: 18C. Chinese (Amoy) *pekho*, from *pek* white + *ho* down, hair. The tea is so called because its leaves when picked are covered in white down.

pelage *n.* the coat or hair of an animal, esp. of fur. WH: 19C. French, from Old French *peil, pel* (Modern French *poil*) hair, down + -AGE.

Pelagian *n.* a follower of Pelagius, who denied the doctrine of original sin. *Also a.* WH: 14–15C. Ecclesiastical Latin *Pelagianus*, from *Pelagius*, *c.*360–*c.*420, British lay monk. See also -AN.

pelagian *a.* inhabiting the deep sea. *Also n.* WH: 17C. Latin *pelagius*, from Greek *pelagios* of the sea (see PELAGIC). See also -AN.

pelagic *a.* of or inhabiting the deep sea. WH: 17C. Latin *pelagicus*, from Greek *pelagikos*, from *pelagos* level surface of the sea. See also -IC.

pelargonium *n.* an ornamental plant of the genus *Pelargonium*, popularly called the geranium. WH: 19C. Modern Latin, from Greek *pelargos* stork, appar. based on earlier *geranion* GERANIUM. See also -IUM. The name was coined in 1787 by the French botanist Charles Louis L'Héritier.

Pelasgic *a.* of or relating to the Pelasgi, a widely diffused prehistoric race inhabiting the coasts and islands of the eastern Mediterranean and the Aegean. WH: 18C. Latin *Pelasgicus*, from Greek *Pelasgikos*, from *Pelasgoi* the Pelasgi, a pre-Hellenic people who inhabited the coasts and islands of the E Mediterranean and Aegean. See also -IC.

pelerine *n.* a lady's long narrow fur cape. WH: 18C. French *pèlerine*, fem. of *pèlerin* pilgrim. The garment is so called from its resemblance to the type of cape worn by pilgrims.

pelf *n.* money, wealth. WH: 14–15C. Old Northern French var. of Old French *pelfre, peufre* spoil, rel. to *pelfrer* to pillage, to rob, of unknown orig. Cp. PILFER.

pelham *n.* a horse's bit having a curb and a snaffle. WH: 19C. From surname *Pelham*.

pelican *n.* a large waterbird of the family Pelecanidae, with an enormous pouch beneath the mandibles for storing fish when caught. WH: pre-1200. Late Latin *pelicanus*, from Greek *pelekan*, prob. from *pelekus* axe, *pelekan* to hew with an axe. The name refers to the appearance or action (or both) of the bird's bill.

pelisse *n.* a woman's long cloak or mantle. WH: 18C. Old French, from Medieval Latin *pellicia* cloak, from Latin *pellicea*, fem. of *pelliceus* made of skin, from *pellis* skin.

pelite *n.* a rock made up of a claylike sediment. WH: 19C. Greek *pēlos* clay, earth, mud + -ITE[1].

pellagra *n.* a virulent disease attacking the skin and causing nervous disorders and mania, caused by deficiency of B vitamins. WH: 19C. Italian, from *pelle* skin (from Latin *pellis*) + -agra, based on PODAGRA.

pellet *n.* a little ball, esp. of bread, paper or something easily moulded. *Also v.t.* WH: 14–15C. Old French *pelote*, from dim. of Latin *pila* ball. See also -ET[1].

pellicle *n.* a thin skin, a membrane or film. WH: 16C. French *pellicule*, from Latin *pellicula*, dim. of *pellis* skin. See also -CLE.

pellitory *n.* a herb of the aster family, *Anacyclus pyrethrum*. WH: 14–15C. Old French *peletre*, alt. of *peretre*, from Latin PYRETHRUM. As the name of the *pellitory of the wall* (16C), the word is an alteration of obsolete *parietary*, from Old French *paritaire* (Modern French *pariétaire*), from Late Latin *parietaria*, from Latin *paries, parietis* wall, partition (cp. PARIETAL).

pell-mell *adv.* in disorderly haste. *Also a., n.* WH: 16C. French *pêle-mêle*, from Old French *pesle mesle*, redupl. of *mesle*, stem of *mesler* (Modern French *mêler*) to mix, MEDDLE. Cp. MÊLÉE.

pellucid *a.* clear, limpid, transparent. WH: 17C. Latin *pellucidus*, from *pellucere, perlucere* to shine through. See PER-, LUCID.

Pelmanism *n.* a system of training to improve the memory. WH: early 20C. Christopher Louis *Pelman*, founder in 1899 of the Pelman Institute for the Scientific Development of Mind, Memory and Personality in London + -ISM.

pelmet *n.* a canopy, built-in or detachable, which conceals the fittings from which curtains hang; a valance. WH: early 20C. Prob. alt. of French PALMETTE.

peloria *n.* symmetry or regularity in flowers that are normally irregular. WH: 19C. Modern Latin, from Greek *pelōros* monstrous, from *pelōr* monster. See also -IA.

pelorus *n.* a sighting device on a ship's compass. WH: 19C. *Pelorus*, said to be the name of Hannibal's pilot.

pelota *n.* a game similar to squash played with a ball and a curved racket fitting upon the hand, popular in Spain and the Basque country. WH: 19C. Spanish ball, augm. of *pella*, from Latin *pila* ball. Cp. PELLET.

pelotherapy *n.* treatment of disease by the application of mud. WH: mid-20C. Greek *pēlos* clay, mud + *therapy* (THERAPEUTIC).

pelt[1] *v.t.* to strike or assail by throwing missiles. *Also v.i., n.* WH: 15C. ? Contr. of PELLET. The original sense was to deliver repeated blows to. The sense to assail by throwing a missile dates from the 16C.

pelt[2] *n.* a hide or skin with the hair on, esp. of a sheep or goat. WH: 12–14C. Prob. var. of obs. *pellet* animal skin, from Old French *pelete*, dim. of *pel* (Modern French *peau*), from Latin *pellis* skin, leather, or shortening of *peltry* undressed skins, from Old French *peletrie* (Modern French *pelleterie*), from *peletier* furrier, from *pel*. See also -RY.

pelta *n.* a small light shield or target used by the ancient Greeks and Romans. WH: 17C. Latin, from Greek *peltē* a small light leather shield.

pelvis *n.* the lower portion of the great abdominal cavity. WH: 17C. Latin basin, laver.

pemmican *n.* dried meat, pounded, mixed with a large proportion of melted fat and pressed into cakes. WH: 18C. Cree *pimihka:n*, from *pimiy* grease.

pemphigus *n.* a disease characterized by the eruption of watery vesicles on the skin. WH: 18C. Modern Latin, from Greek *pemphix, pemphigos* bubble.

pen[1] *n.* an instrument for writing with ink. *Also v.t.* WH: 12–14C. Old French *penne*, from Latin *penna* feather. A pen was originally a feather, with its quill sharpened and split to make a nib. The basic word for pen is the same as that for feather in many languages. Cp. French *plume*, German *Feder*, Russian *pero*, etc. A penknife (14–15C) was originally used for making and mending quill pens.

pen[2] *n.* a small enclosure for cattle, sheep etc. *Also v.t.* WH: pre-1200. Old English *penn*, of unknown orig.

penal *a.* enacting, inflicting, of or relating to punishment. WH: 14–15C. Old French *pénal* or Latin *penalis, poenalis*, from *poena* PAIN. See also -AL[1].

penalty *n.* legal punishment for a crime, offence or misdemeanour. *Also a.* WH: 15C. Old French *pénalité*, from Medieval Latin *penalitas*, from Latin *penalis*. See PENAL, also -ITY.

penance *n.* sorrow for sin evinced by acts of self-mortification etc. *Also v.t.* WH: 12–14C. Old French, from Latin *poenitentia* penitence (PENITENT). See also -ANCE.

penannular *a.* nearly annular, almost a complete ring. WH: 19C. Latin *paene* almost + ANNULAR.

penates *n.pl.* the Roman household gods, orig. of the storeroom and kitchen. WH: 16C. Latin *Penates* (pl.), from *penus* provision of food, rel. to *penes* within.

pence *n.* plural of penny. WH: 12–14C. Contr. of *pennies* (PENNY).

penchant *n.* a strong inclination or liking. WH: 17C. French, use as n. of pres.p. of *pencher* to incline, to lean.

pencil *n.* a cylinder or slip of graphite, crayon etc., usu. enclosed in a casing of wood, used for writing, drawing etc. *Also a., v.t.* WH: 12–14C. Old French *pincel* (Modern French *pinceau*), from alt. of Latin *penicillus* paintbrush, dim. of *peniculus* brush, dim. of *penis* tail. The original sense was paintbrush. The current sense arose in the 16C by association with PEN[1]. The two words are unrelated.

pendant *n.* anything hanging down or suspended by way of ornament etc., such as an earring, a locket. *Also a.* WH: 12–14C. Old French, use of n. of pres.p. of *pendre* to hang, from Latin *pendere*. See also -ANT.

pendent *a.* hanging. WH: 14–15C. Old French *pendant* (PENDANT), later influ. by Latin *pendens, pendentis*, pres.p. of *pendere* to hang. See also -ENT.

pendente lite *adv.* while a suit is in progress. WH: 18C. Latin, lit. with the lawsuit pending, from abl. sing. of *pendens, pendentis* pres.p. of *pendere* to hang, be undecided + abl. sing. of *lis, litis* lawsuit.

pendragon *n.* a leader of the ancient Britons. WH: 14–15C. Welsh chief leader in war, from *pen* head, chief + *dragon* dragon, from Latin *draco, draconis,* the standard of a cohort.

pendulous *a.* hanging, suspended. WH: 17C. Latin *pendulus* pendent (from *pendere* to hang down) + -OUS. See also -ULOUS.

pendulum *n.* a body suspended from a fixed point and oscillating freely by the force of gravity, esp. the weighted rod regulating the movement of the works in a clock. WH: 17C. Modern Latin, from Medieval Latin something hanging down, ? based on Italian *pendolo,* use as n. of neut. of Latin *pendulus* PENDULOUS.

penelopize *v.t.* to undo (a piece of work) to cause delay. WH: 19C. Greek *Pēnelopē* Penelope, in Greek mythology the wife of Odysseus, who during his absence put off her suitors by saying she would marry only when she had finished her weaving, which she unravelled each night. See also -IZE.

peneplain *n.* an area of flat land produced by erosion. WH: 19C. Latin *paene* almost + PLAIN[1].

penetralia *n.pl.* the inner part of a house, palace, temple or shrine. WH: 17C. Latin (pl.) from *penetralis* interior, innermost, from stem of *penetrare* PENETRATE.

penetrate *v.t.* to pass into or through. *Also v.i.* WH: 16C. Latin *penetratus,* p.p. of *penetrare* to place within, to enter, from *penitus* inner, inmost, rel. to *penes* within.

penguin *n.* a black-and-white bird of the family Spheniscidae, belonging to the southern hemisphere, consisting of seabirds with rudimentary wings or paddles and scalelike feathers. WH: 16C. Orig. uncertain. Poss. from Welsh *pen* head + *gwyn* white. The name was originally applied to the great auk of Newfoundland, so that the Welsh source, if genuine, could apply not to the bird but to a 'white headland' where the great auk was found. Penguins in fact mostly have black heads. Moreover, Welsh *pen* + *gwyn* would give **penwyn* (white headland) with loss of the g.

penicillate *a.* furnished with, forming or consisting of a bundle of short close hairs or fibres. WH: 19C. Modern Latin *penicillus* (PENCIL) + -ATE[2].

penicillin *n.* an ether-soluble substance produced from the mould *Penicillium* and having an intense growth-inhibiting action against various bacteria. WH: early 20C. Modern Latin *penicillium* name of the mould from which penicillin was purified (from Latin *penicillus* paintbrush + -IUM) + -IN[1]. The antibiotic is so called from the resemblance of the cells of the mould to small brushes. The word was coined in 1929 by the British bacteriologist Sir Alexander Fleming, who discovered penicillin in 1928.

peninsula *n.* a piece of land almost surrounded by water, poss. connected to the mainland by an isthmus. WH: 16C. Latin *paeninsula,* from *paene* almost + *insula* island.

penis *n.* the copulatory and urethral organ of a male mammal. WH: 17C. Latin tail, penis.

penitent *a.* repentant, sorry. *Also n.* WH: 12–14C. Old French *pénitent,* from Latin *paenitens, paenitentis,* pres.p. of *paenitere* to cause want to, to make sorry. See also -ENT.

pennant *n.* a long narrow streamer borne at the masthead of a ship of war. WH: 14–15C. Blend of PENNON and PENDANT.

pennate *a.* winged, wing-shaped. WH: 19C. Latin *pennatus* winged, from *penna* feather. See also -ATE[2].

penne *n.* pasta quills, pasta in short, thick, ridged tube shapes. WH: late 20C. Italian, pl. of *penna* quill.

penniform *a.* having the form of a feather. WH: 18C. Latin *penna* feather + -*i*- + -FORM.

penniless *a.* without money, destitute. WH: 12–14C. PENNY + -LESS.

pennon *n.* a small pointed or swallow-tailed flag, formerly carried on the spears of knights and later as the ensign of a regiment of lancers. WH: 14–15C. Old French, from a deriv. of Latin *penna* PEN[1].

Pennsylvania Dutch *n.* a dialect of High German spoken by Pennsylvanian descendants of 17th- and 18th-cent. German and Swiss immigrants. WH: 18C. *Pennsylvania* (see PENNSYLVANIAN) + DUTCH.

Pennsylvanian *n.* a native or inhabitant of Pennsylvania. *Also a.* WH: 17C. *Pennsylvania,* an E state of the USA + -AN.

penny *n.* a bronze coin, a 100th part of a pound sterling. WH: pre-1200. Old English *penig,* earlier *penning,* from Germanic. Cp. German PFENNIG.

-penny *comb. form* denoting a specified number of pennies, esp. old pennies, as in *sixpenny.* WH: PENNY.

pennyroyal *n.* a kind of mint, *Mentha pulegium,* formerly and still popularly used for medicinal purposes. WH: 16C. Alt. of Anglo-French *puliol real,* from Old French *pouliol* (Modern French *pouliot),* from Popular Latin *puleium,* from Latin *pulegium* thyme + Old French *real* ROYAL. The mint is perhaps called 'royal' as it was regarded as a sovereign remedy.

penology *n.* the science of punishment and prison management. WH: 19C. Latin *poena* penalty + -O- + -LOGY.

pensée *n.* a thought, a reflection. WH: 14–15C. French thought, from Old French *pensee.* The original sense was thoughtfulness, anxiety, care. The current sense dates from the 19C.

pensile *a.* hanging, suspended, pendulous. WH: 17C. Latin *pensilis,* from *pensus,* p.p. of *pendere* to hang. See also -IL.

pension[1] *n.* a periodical allowance for past services paid by the government or an employer. *Also v.t.* WH: 14–15C. Old French, from Latin *pensio, pensionis* payment, rent, from *pensus,* p.p. of *pendere* to weigh, to pay. See also -ION.

pension[2] *n.* a boarding house. WH: 17C. French PENSION[1]. The current sense evolved from the payment made to keep a child at a boarding school.

pensive *a.* thoughtful. *Also v.t.* WH: 14–15C. Old French *pensif,* from *penser* to think, from Latin *pensare* to weigh, to balance, to consider. See POISE[1], also -IVE.

penstemon *n.* any herbaceous plant of the genus *Penstemon* with showy tubular flowers. WH: 18C. Modern Latin from *pen-* PENTA- + Greek *stēmōn* warp (in the thread of a loom), taken to mean stamen. The name refers to the plant's rudimentary fifth stamen in addition to the four perfect ones.

penstock *n.* a floodgate. WH: 17C. PEN[2] + STOCK.

pent *a.* penned in or confined, shut (up or in). WH: 16C. Obs. p.p. of PEN[2].

penta- *comb. form* five. WH: Greek comb. form of *pente* five.

pentachord *n.* a musical instrument with five strings. WH: 17C. PENTA- + CHORD[2].

pentacle *n.* a figure like a star with five points formed by producing the sides of a pentagon in both directions to their points of intersection. WH: 16C. Medieval Latin *pentaculum,* from *penta-* PENTA- + Latin *-culum* -CLE.

pentad *n.* the number five. WH: 17C. Greek *pentas, pentados,* from *pente* five. See also -AD[1].

pentadactyl *a.* having five fingers or toes. *Also n.* WH: 19C. PENTA- + Greek *daktulos* finger, toe.

pentadelphous *a.* having the stamens united in five sets. WH: 19C. PENTA- + Greek *adelphos* brother (here, stamen). See also -OUS.

pentagon *n.* a plane (usu. rectilineal) figure having five sides and five angles. WH: 16C. French *pentagone* or Late Latin *pentagonum,* from Greek *pentagōnon,* use as n. of neut. of a. *pentagōnos.* See PENTA-, -GON.

pentagram *n.* a pentacle. WH: 19C. Greek *pentagrammon,* use as n. of neut. of *pentagrammos* of five lines. See PENTA-, -GRAM.

pentagynian *a.* of or relating to the Linnaean order Pentagynia, containing plants with five pistils. WH: 19C. Modern Latin *pentagynia,* from *penta-* PENTA- + Greek *gunē* woman, female (here, pistil). See also -AN.

pentahedron *n.* a figure having five sides, esp. equal sides. WH: 18C. PENTA- + -HEDRON.

pentalpha *n.* a pentagram or pentacle. WH: 19C. PENTA- + ALPHA. The figure is so called because it presents the form of an alpha (a capital A) in five different positions.

pentamerous *a.* (of a flower-whorl) composed of five parts. WH: 19C. PENTA- + Greek *meros* part + -OUS.

pentameter *n.* a verse of five feet, such as the iambic verse of ten syllables. WH: 16C. Latin, from Greek *pentametron,* use as n. of neut. of a. *pentametros.* See PENTA-, -METER.

pentandrian *a.* of or relating to a Linnaean class containing plants with five stamens. WH: 19C. PENTA- + Greek *anēr, andros* man, male (here, stamen) + -IAN.

pentane *n.* a volatile, fluid, paraffin hydrocarbon contained in petroleum etc. WH: 19C. PENTA- + -ANE. The chemical is so called from its five carbon atoms. (Its chemical formula is C_5H_{12}.)

pentangle *n.* a pentagram. WH: 14–15C. ? Medieval Latin alt. of *pentaculum* PENTACLE, based on Latin *angulus* ANGLE[1].

pentanoic acid *n.* a colourless, liquid, carboxylic acid, used to make perfumes. WH: early 20C. PENTANE + -O- + -IC.

pentapody *n.* a verse or sequence of five natural feet. WH: 19C. Greek *pentapous* of five feet, from PENTA- + *pous, podos* foot.

pentapolis *n.* a group or confederacy of five towns. WH: 14–15C. PENTA- + -POLIS.

pentaprism *n.* a five-sided prism used in reflex cameras to invert the image by deflecting light from any direction through 90°. WH: mid-20C. PENTA- + PRISM.

pentarchy *n.* government by five rulers. WH: 16C. Greek *pentarkhia* rule of five. See PENTA-, -ARCHY.

pentastich *n.* a stanza or group of five lines of verse. WH: 17C. Modern Latin *pentastichus*, from Greek *pentastikhos*, from PENTA- + *stikhos* row, line of verse.

pentastyle *a.* (of a building) having five columns at the front or end. *Also n.* WH: 18C. PENTA- + Greek *stulos* pillar, column.

Pentateuch *n.* the first five books of the Old Testament, usu. ascribed to Moses. WH: 14–15C. Ecclesiastical Latin *pentateuchus*, from Ecclesiastical Greek *pentateukhos*, use as n. of a., from PENTA- + *teukhos* implement, vessel, book.

pentathlon *n.* a modern athletics contest comprising five events for each competitor. WH: 17C. Greek from PENTA- + *athlon* contest.

pentatomic *a.* containing five atoms in the molecule, esp. five replaceable atoms of hydrogen. WH: 19C. PENTA- + Greek *atomos* ATOM + -IC.

pentatonic *a.* consisting of five tones. WH: 19C. PENTA- + Greek *tonos* TONE + -IC.

pentavalent *a.* having a valency of five. WH: 19C. PENTA- + Latin *valens, valentis* having power, having value. See VALENCE, also -ENT.

Pentecost *n.* Whit Sunday. WH: pre-1200. Old English *pentecosten*, from acc. of Ecclesiastical Latin *Pentecoste*, from Greek *Pentēkostē*, use as n. of fem. ordinal a. of *pentēkonta* fifty. Cp. SHAVUOTH. The fifty days are the seven weeks following the Passover, otherwise those between Easter and Whit Sunday.

penthemimer *n.* in Greek prosody, a group of two and a half metrical feet, as a half of a pentameter. WH: 16C. Late Latin *penthemimeres*, from Greek *penthēmimerēs* consisting of five halves, from *pente* five + *hēmimerēs* halved (from *hēmi-* HEMI- + *meros* part).

penthouse *n.* a flat built on the rooftop of a tall building. *Also v.t., a.* WH: 12–14C. Orig. *pentis*, shortening of Old French *apentis*, from Medieval Latin *appendicium* appendage, from Latin *appendere* (APPEND), re-formed (16C) by assoc. with French *pente* slope + HOUSE[1], as if meaning sloping house. A penthouse was originally a subsidiary structure attached to a main building. The current sense arose in the 19C.

pentimento *n.* (a part of) a painting that has been painted over and later becomes visible. WH: early 20C. Italian, lit. repentance, regret. The work is so called because the artist has changed his mind or concealed a mistake.

pentobarbitone *n.* a barbiturate, formerly used as a sedative. WH: mid-20C. PENTANE + -O- + *barbitone* (BARBITURIC).

pentode *n.* a five-electrode thermionic valve. WH: 19C. PENTA- + -ODE[2].

pentose *n.* any of various sugars containing five carbon atoms in the molecule. WH: 19C. PENTA- + -OSE[2].

Pentothal® *n.* thiopentone. WH: mid-20C. Alt. of *thiopental*, from THIOPENTONE + -AL[2].

pent roof *n.* a lean-to roof. WH: 19C. PENTHOUSE + ROOF.

pentyl *n.* amyl. WH: 19C. PENTA- + -YL.

penult *n.* the last but one, esp. the last syllable but one of a word. *Also a.* WH: 15C. Abbr. of *penultimate*, from Latin *paenultimus* (from *paene* almost + *ultimus* last), based on ULTIMATE.

penumbra *n.* the partly shaded zone around the total shadow caused by an opaque body intercepting the light from a luminous body, esp. round that of the earth or moon in an eclipse. WH: 17C. Modern Latin, from Latin *paene* almost + *umbra* shadow. The word was coined in 1604 by the German astronomer Johannes Kepler.

penury *n.* extreme poverty, destitution. WH: 14–15C. Latin *penuria, paenuria*, ? rel. to *paene* almost. See also -Y[2].

peon *n.* a Spanish-American day labourer etc. WH: 17C. Spanish *peón*, from Medieval Latin *pedo, pedonis* foot-soldier. See PAWN[1].

peony *n.* any plant of the genus *Paeonia*, with large globular terminal flowers, usu. double in cultivated varieties. WH: pre-1200. Latin *peonia, paeonia*, from Greek *paiōnia*, from *Paiōn* the physician of the gods in Greek mythology (cp. PAEAN). The plant is so called from its use in medicine.

people *n.* the persons composing a nation, community or race. *Also v.t.* WH: 12–14C. Anglo-French *poeple*, from Old French (Modern French *peuple*), from Latin *populus* (cp. POPULACE). The native Old English word was *folc* FOLK.

pep *n.* vigour, spirit, energy. *Also v.t.* WH: early 20C. Abbr. of PEPPER.

peperino *n.* a porous volcanic rock, composed of sand, cinders etc. cemented together. WH: 18C. Italian, from *peper* (PEPPERONI) + dim. suf. *-ino*. The rock is so called because it consists of small grains.

peplum *n.* a flared extension attached to the waist of a tight-fitting jacket or bodice. WH: early 20C. Latin, from Greek *peplos*.

pepo *n.* any of various fruits of the gourd family, e.g. cucumber, melon, with a hard rind, watery pulp, and many seeds. WH: 14–15C. Latin *pepo, peponis* pumpkin, from Greek *pepōn*, use as n. of a., ripe.

pepper *n.* a pungent aromatic condiment made from the dried berries of *Piper nigrum* or other species of the genus *Piper*, used whole or ground into powder. *Also v.t.* WH: pre-1200. Old English *piper*, from Germanic, from Latin *piper*, from Greek *peperi*, from Sanskrit *pippalī* berry, peppercorn. Cp. German *Pfeffer*.

peppermint *n.* a pungent aromatic herb, *Mentha piperita*. WH: 17C. PEPPER + MINT[2].

pepperoni *n.* a dry sausage of pork and beef that is heavily seasoned, esp. with pepper. WH: mid-20C. Italian *peperone* chilli, from *pepe* pepper, from Latin *piper* (see PEPPER) + augm. suf. *-one*.

Pepsi-Cola® *n.* a cola-flavoured carbonated soft drink, dark brown in colour. WH: early 20C. Appar. from DYSPEPSIA (which it was orig. intended to relieve) + COLA, influ. by COCA-COLA®.

pepsin *n.* a protein-digesting enzyme contained in gastric juice. WH: 19C. Greek *pepsis* digestion + -IN[1]. The enzyme was so named in 1836 by the German physiologist Theodor Schwann, who discovered it.

peptone *n.* any of the soluble compounds into which the proteins in food are converted by the action of pepsin. WH: 19C. Greek *pepton*, neut. of *peptos* cooked, digested. See also -ONE.

per *prep.* for each. WH: 14–15C. Latin through, by. Cp. PER-. Ult. rel. to FOR.

per- *pref.* through, completely. WH: Latin pref., from PER.

peracute *a.* very acute or violent. WH: 14–15C. Latin *peracutus* very sharp. See PER-, ACUTE.

peradventure *adv.* perhaps. *Also n.* WH: 12–14C. Old French *per auenture*, from *per, par* by, PER + *auenture* ADVENTURE. Cp. PER-CHANCE. The word was assimilated to the Latin form in the 15–16C.

perambulate *v.t.* to walk over or through, esp. for the purpose of surveying or inspecting. *Also v.i.* WH: 14–15C. Latin *perambulatus*, p.p. of *perambulare*. See PER-, AMBULATE. Cp. PRAM[1].

per annum *adv.* yearly, each year. WH: 17C. Modern Latin, from PER + acc. of Latin *annus* year.

percale *n.* a closely woven cotton cambric. WH: 17C. Orig. unknown. The fabric was originally imported from India.

per capita *adv.* for each person. WH: 17C. Modern Latin, from PER + acc. pl. of Latin *caput* head.

perceive *v.t.* to observe, to see. WH: 12–14C. Old French *perçoivre* (Modern French *percevoir*), from Latin *percipere*, from PER- + *capere* to seize, to take.

per cent *adv.* in terms of 100 parts of a whole. *Also n.* WH: 16C. PER + obs. *cent* hundred (see CENT).

perception *n.* the act or an instance of perceiving. WH: 14–15C. Latin *perceptio, perceptionis*, from *perceptus*, p.p. of *percipere* PERCEIVE. See also -ION.

perch[1] *n.* a pole or bar used as a rest or roost for birds or anything serving this purpose. *Also v.i., v.t.* WH: 12–14C. Old French *perche*, from Latin *pertica* pole, measuring rod. Cp. PERK[4].

perch[2] *n.* a striped spiny-finned freshwater fish, *Perca fluviatilis, P. flavescens*, the yellow perch of the US. WH: 12–14C. Old French *perche*, from Latin *perca*, from Greek *perkē*.

†perchance *adv.* by chance. **WH:** 12–14C. Old French *par cheance*, from *par* by, PER + *cheance* CHANCE. Cp. PERADVENTURE, PERHAPS.

percheron *n.* a breed of heavy and powerful horses. **WH:** 19C. French, a. from *le Perche*, a region in N France, where the horse was orig. bred.

perchlorate *n.* a salt of perchloric acid. **WH:** 19C. PER- + CHLORATE.

percipient *a.* perceiving, apprehending, conscious. *Also n.* **WH:** 17C. Latin *percipiens, percipientis,* pres.p. of *percipere* PERCEIVE. See also -ENT.

percoct *a.* overdone, hackneyed. **WH:** 17C. Latin *percoctus,* p.p. of *percoquere,* from PER- + *coquere* COOK.

percolate *v.i.* to pass through small interstices. *Also v.t.* **WH:** 17C. Latin *percolatus,* p.p. of *percolare,* from PER- + *colare* to strain, from *colum* sieve, strainer (cp. COLANDER). See also -ATE³. Cp. PERK³.

per contra *adv.* on the opposite side. **WH:** 16C. Latin on the contrary.

percuss *v.t.* to strike quickly or tap forcibly in order to test or diagnose. **WH:** 16C. Latin *percussus,* p.p of *percutere* to strike through, to thrust through, from PER- + *quatere* to shake, to strike, to dash.

percussion *n.* the production of sound by striking on an instrument. **WH:** 14–15C. Old French, from Latin *percussio, percussionis,* from *percussus.* See PERCUSS, also -ION.

percutaneous *a.* acting or done through the skin. **WH:** 19C. Latin *per cutem* through the skin + -ANEOUS, based on CUTANEOUS.

per diem *a., adv.* by the day, for each day. *Also n.* **WH:** 16C. Modern Latin, from *per* PER + acc. of Latin *dies.*

perdition *n.* the loss of the soul or of happiness in a future state. **WH:** 12–14C. Old French *perdicium* (Modern French *perdition*) or Ecclesiastical Latin *perditio, perditionis,* from Latin *perditus,* p.p of *perdere* to destroy, from PER- + *dare* to give, to put. See also -ITION.

perdurable *a.* very lasting or durable, permanent, everlasting. **WH:** 14–15C. Old French, from Late Latin *perdurabilis,* from Latin *perdurare* to endure, from PER- + *durare* to harden, to endure, from *durus* hard. See also -ABLE.

père *n.* father, senior, as distinct from *fils.* **WH:** 17C. French father, from Latin *pater, patris* father.

Père David's deer *n.* a large deer, *Elaphurus davidianus,* with antlers. **WH:** 19C. *Père* Armand *David,* 1826–1900, French missionary and naturalist.

peregrination *n.* a sojourning in foreign countries. **WH:** 14–15C. Old French *pérégrination,* from Latin *peregrinatio, peregrinationis,* from *peregrinatus,* p.p. of *peregrinari* to travel abroad, to stay abroad, from *peregrinus.* See PEREGRINE, -ATION.

peregrine *n.* a peregrine falcon. *Also a.* **WH:** 14–15C. Old French *pérégrin,* from Latin *peregrinus* foreign, travelling, from *pereger* that is abroad, that is journeying, *peregre* abroad, from PER- + *ager* field. See -INE. Cp. PILGRIM. The bird's name translates Medieval Latin *falco peregrinus* pilgrim falcon, so called because it was caught full-grown in migration, not taken as a fledgling from the nest.

pereion *n.* the thorax in crustaceans. **WH:** 19C. Greek *peraioōn, peraiōn,* pres.p. of *peraioun* to transport.

peremptory *a.* precluding question or hesitation. **WH:** 14–15C. Old French *peremptoire,* from Latin *peremptorius* deadly, mortal, decisive, from *peremptus,* p.p. of *perimere* to take away entirely, to destroy, from PER- + *emere* to buy. See also -ORY². The original meaning (to the 18C) was decisive, definite, determined. The current sense dates from the 16C.

perennial *a.* lasting throughout the year. *Also n.* **WH:** 17C. Latin *perennis,* from PER- + *annus* year. See also -IAL.

perennibranchiate *a.* belonging to the Perennibranchiata, a division of amphibians retaining their gills through life. *Also n.* **WH:** 19C. Modern Latin *Perennibranchia* (pl.), from *perennis* PERENNIAL + BRANCHIA. See also -ATE².

perestroika *n.* in the former USSR, the policy of restructuring and reforming Soviet institutions initiated in the 1980s by Mikhail Gorbachev. **WH:** late 20C. Russian *perestroĭka* restructuring, from *pere-* again, across, PER- + *stroĭka,* from *stroit* to build.

perfect¹ *a.* complete in all its parts, qualities etc. *Also n.* **WH:** 12–14C. Old French *parfit* (Modern French *parfait*), from Latin *perfectus,* p.p. of *perficere* to accomplish, from PER- + *facere* to make. The current spelling has been assimilated to Latin *perfectus.*

perfect² *v.t.* to make perfect. **WH:** 14–15C. PERFECT¹.

perfecto *n.* a large cigar which tapers at both ends. **WH:** 19C. Spanish perfect.

perfervid *a.* very fervid. **WH:** 17C. Modern Latin *perfervidus.* See PER-, *fervid* (under FERVENT).

perfidy *n.* (a) violation of faith, allegiance or confidence. **WH:** 16C. Latin *perfidia,* from *perfidus* treacherous, from PER- + *fides* FAITH. See also -Y².

perfin *n.* a postage stamp perforated with an organization's initials. **WH:** mid-20C. From *perforated* (PERFORATE¹) + INITIAL.

perfoliate *a.* (of a plant) having leaves surrounding the stem so as to appear as if perforated by it. **WH:** 17C. Modern Latin *perfoliatus.* See PER-, FOLIATE².

perforate¹ *v.t.* to bore through, to pierce. *Also v.i.* **WH:** 16C. Latin *perforatus,* p.p. of *perforare,* from PER- + *forare* to bore, to pierce. See also -ATE³.

perforate² *a.* perforated. **WH:** 14–15C. Latin *perforatus,* p.p. of *perforare.* See PERFORATE¹, also -ATE².

†perforce *adv.* of necessity, compulsorily. **WH:** 12–14C. Old French *par force,* from *par* by + *force* FORCE¹. The original meaning (to the 17C) was by violence, forcibly. The current sense arose in the 16C.

perform *v.t.* to carry through, to accomplish. *Also v.i.* **WH:** 12–14C. Anglo-French *parfourmer,* alt. (based on *forme* FORM) of Old French *parfornir,* from *par-* PER- + *furnir* FURNISH. The sense to carry out publicly, to present (as of a play, piece of music, etc.) dates from the 17C.

perfume¹ *n.* a sweet smell. **WH:** 16C. French *parfum,* from *parfumer,* from obs. Italian *parfumare,* lit. to smoke through. See PER-, FUME. The word was originally used for the pleasant-smelling fumes or vapour given off when a substance is burned.

perfume² *v.t.* to fill or impregnate with a scent or sweet odour; to scent. **WH:** 16C. French *parfumer,* from obs. Italian *parfumare* (now *profumare*), lit. to smoke through. See PER-, FUME.

perfunctory *a.* done merely as a duty or in a careless manner. **WH:** 16C. Late Latin *perfunctorius* careless, negligent, from *perfunctus,* p.p. of *perfungi* to perform, to discharge, to get rid of, from PER- + *fungi.* See FUNCTION, also -ORY².

perfuse *v.t.* to besprinkle. **WH:** 14–15C. Latin *perfusus,* p.p. of *perfundere,* from PER- + *fundere* to pour out.

pergameneous *a.* (of skin etc.) having the texture of parchment. **WH:** 19C. Latin *pergamena* (see PARCHMENT) + -EOUS. The term was coined in 1826 by the English entomologist William Kirby.

pergola *n.* a covered walk or arbour with climbing plants trained over posts, trellis-work etc. **WH:** 17C. Italian, from Latin *pergula* projecting roof, vine arbour, from *pergere* to come forward, to go forward.

perhaps *adv.* possibly. **WH:** 15C. PER + HAP¹ + -S¹. The literal sense is through chances.

peri *n.* a being represented as a descendant of fallen angels, excluded from paradise until some penance is accomplished. **WH:** 18C. Persian *perī.*

peri- *pref.* around. **WH:** Greek pref., from *peri* round, around about, about.

perianth *n.* the outer part of a flower. **WH:** 18C. French *périanthe,* from Modern Latin *perianthium,* from *peri-* PERI- + Greek *anthos* flower, based on *pericarpium* PERICARP.

periapt *n.* something worn as a charm. **WH:** 16C. French *périapte,* from Greek *periapton,* from PERI- + *haptos* fastened, from *haptein* to fasten.

periblast *n.* the protoplasm around a cell nucleus. **WH:** 19C. PERI- + -BLAST.

pericardium *n.* the membrane enveloping the heart. **WH:** 14–15C. Medieval Latin, from Greek *perikardion,* from PERI- + *kardia* heart. See also -IUM.

pericarp *n.* the seed vessel or wall of the developed ovary of a plant. **WH:** 17C. French *péricarpe,* from Modern Latin *pericarpium,* from Greek *perikarpion* pod, husk, shell, from *peri-* PERI- + *karpos* wrist.

perichondrium *n.* the membrane investing the cartilages except at joints. **WH:** 18C. Modern Latin, from *peri-* PERI- + Greek *khondros* cartilage. See also -IUM.

periclase *n.* a greenish mineral composed of magnesia and protoxide of iron, from Vesuvius. **WH:** 19C. Modern Latin *periclasia,* from *peri-* PERI- + Greek *klasis* breaking. The mineral is so called from its perfect cleavage.

periclinal *a.* (of geological strata) sloping from a common centre. WH: 19C. Greek *periklinēs* sloping on all sides, from PERI- + *klinēs* sloping, from *klinein* to lean, to slope. See also -AL[1].

pericope *n.* an extract, a quotation, esp. a selection from the gospels or epistles read in public worship. WH: 17C. Late Latin, from Greek *perikopē* section, from PERI- + *kopē* cutting, from *koptein* to cut.

pericranium *n.* the membrane surrounding the skull. WH: 14–15C. Medieval Latin, from Greek *perikranion*, use as n. of *perikranios* round the skull, from PERI- + *kranion* skull.

pericycle *n.* a thin layer of cells surrounding the vascular tissue in roots and stems. WH: 19C. Greek *perikuklos* all round, spherical, *perikloun* to encircle.

pericynthion *n.* the point in the orbit of a body round the moon where the body is closest to the centre of the moon, the perilune. WH: mid-20C. PERI- + Greek *Kunthios*, a. naming Mount Cynthus on Delos, in Greek mythology the birthplace of Artemis, a goddess associated with the moon. Cp. PERILUNE.

periderm *n.* outer bark. WH: 19C. PERI- + Greek *derma* skin.

peridesmium *n.* the sheath of a ligament. WH: 18C. PERI- + Greek *desmos* band. See also -IUM.

peridium *n.* the outer envelope of certain fungi enclosing the spores. WH: 19C. Modern Latin, from Greek *pēridion*, dim of *pēra* wallet.

peridot *n.* a yellowish-green chrysolite, olivine. WH: 12–14C. Old French *peritot* (Modern French *peridot*), from Medieval Latin *peridotus*, of unknown orig.

peridrome *n.* the open space between the columns and the wall in an ancient temple. WH: 17C. Greek *peridromos* running round, surrounding gallery, from PERI- + *-dromos* running, from *dromos* race, course.

periegesis *n.* a travelling round, a perambulation. WH: 17C. Greek *periēgēsis*, from PERI- + *hēgēsis* leading, from *hēgeisthai* to lead, to guide.

perigastric *a.* surrounding the alimentary canal. WH: 19C. PERI- + Greek *gastēr* belly, stomach + -IC.

perigee *n.* the nearest point to the earth in the orbit of the moon, one of the planets or an artificial satellite, as distinct from *apogee*. WH: 16C. French *périgée*, from Modern Latin *perigeum*, from Late Greek *perigeion*, use as n. of neut. of *perigeios* close round the earth, from PERI- + *gaia*, *gē* earth.

perigenesis *n.* reproduction through rhythmic vibrations of protoplasmic molecules. WH: 19C. Modern Latin, from *peri-* PERI- + GENESIS.

periglacial *a.* of or relating to the region around a glacier. WH: early 20C. PERI- + GLACIAL.

perigone *n.* the outer part of a flower, the perianth. WH: 19C. French *périgone*, from Modern Latin *perigonium*, from *peri-* PERI- + Greek *gonos* offspring, seed.

perigynous *a.* (of stamens) growing upon some part surrounding the ovary. WH: 19C. Modern Latin *perigynus*, from *peri-* PERI- + Greek *gunē* woman, female (here, pistil) + -OUS.

perihelion *n.* the part of the orbit of a planet, comet etc. nearest the sun, as distinct from *aphelion*. WH: 17C. Graecized form of Modern Latin *perihelium*, from *peri-* PERI- + Greek *hēlios* sun.

perihepatic *a.* surrounding the liver. WH: 19C. PERI- + Greek *hēpar*, *hēpatos* liver + -IC.

peril *n.* danger, exposure to injury or destruction. Also *v.t.*, *v.i.* WH: 12–14C. Old French *péril*, from Latin *periculum* experiment, risk, danger, from base of *experiri* to try + *-culum* -CLE.

perilune *n.* the point in the orbit of a body round the moon where the body is closest to the centre of the moon, as distinct from *apolune*. WH: mid-20C. PERI- + Latin *luna* moon.

perilymph *n.* the clear fluid surrounding the labyrinth in the ear. WH: 19C. PERI- + LYMPH.

perimeter *n.* the bounding line of a plane figure. WH: 14–15C. Latin *perimetros*, from Greek, from PERI- + *metron* measure. See also -METER.

perimorph *n.* a mineral enclosing another. WH: 19C. PERI- + -MORPH.

perimysium *n.* the fibrous connective tissue surrounding muscle fibres. WH: 19C. PERI- + Greek *mus* muscle + -IUM.

perinatal *a.* of or relating to the period shortly before and after birth. WH: mid-20C. PERI- + NATAL[1].

perineum *n.* the part of the body between the genital organs and the anus. WH: 14–15C. Late Latin *perinaeum*, from Greek *perinaion* region of evacuation, from PERI- + *inan* to carry off by evacuation.

period *n.* any specified portion of time. Also *a.*, *v.t.* WH: 14–15C. Old French *période*, from Latin *periodus* cycle, sentence, from Greek *periodos* circuit, revolution, recurrence, course, orbit, from PERI- + *hodos* way, course.

periodontal *a.* (of tissue) around a tooth. WH: 19C. PERI- + Greek *odous*, *odontos* tooth + -AL[1].

perioperative *a.* occurring around the time of an operation. WH: mid-20C. PERI- + *operative* (OPERATE).

periosteum *n.* a dense membrane covering the bones. WH: 16C. Modern Latin, from Greek *periosteon*, from PERI- + *osteon* bone.

periotic *a.* surrounding the inner ear. Also *n.* WH: 19C. PERI- + Greek *ous*, *ōtos* ear + -IC.

peripatetic *a.* (of a teacher) working in several schools. Also *n.* WH: 14–15C. Old French *péripatétique* or Latin *peripateticus*, from Greek *peripatētikos*, from *peripatein* to walk up and down, from PERI- + *patein* to tread. See also -ETIC. The original sense related to a sect of philosophers holding the doctrines of Aristotle, who walked about while he taught.

peripatus *n.* any wormlike arthropod of the genus *Peripatus*, living in damp places in the southern hemisphere, and believed to represent an ancestral type of both insects and myriapods. WH: 17C. Modern Latin, from Greek *peripatos*, from PERI- + *patos* way, path.

peripeteia *n.* a reversal of circumstances or sudden change of fortune in a play or in life. WH: 16C. Greek, ult. from PERI- + *pet-*, stem of *piptein* to fall.

periphery *n.* the perimeter or circumference of a figure or surface. WH: 14–15C. Late Latin *peripheria*, from Greek *periphereia*, from *peripherēs* revolving round, from PERI- + *pherein* BEAR[2].

periphrasis *n.* roundabout speaking or expression, circumlocution. WH: 16C. Latin, from Greek, from *periphrazein*, from PERI- + *phrazein* to declare. Cp. CIRCUMLOCUTION.

periplast *n.* the main substance of a cell, as distinguished from the external coating of the nucleus. WH: 19C. PERI- + Greek *plastos* formed, moulded.

periplus *n.* a circumnavigation. WH: 18C. Latin, from Greek *periplous*, from PERI- + *plous* voyage. Cp. *circumnavigation* (CIRCUMNAVIGATE).

peripteral *a.* surrounded by a single row of columns. WH: 19C. Greek *peripteros*, from PERI- + *pteron* wing + -AL[1].

perique *n.* a strong, dark-coloured variety of tobacco grown and manufactured in Louisiana, used chiefly in mixtures. WH: 19C. Louisiana French, appar. from *Perique*, nickname (or pseudonym) of Pierre Chenet, who first grew it.

periscope *n.* an apparatus enabling people inside a submarine, trench etc. to look about above the surface of the water etc. WH: 19C. PERI- + -SCOPE.

perish *v.i.* to be destroyed, to come to nothing. Also *v.t.* WH: 12–14C. Old French *périr*, *périss-*, from Latin *perire* to pass away, to come to nothing, to die, from PER- + *ire* to go.

perisperm *n.* the mass of albumen outside the embryo-sac in certain seeds. WH: 19C. French *périsperme*, from Modern Latin *perispermum*, from Greek PERI- + *sperma* seed.

perispomenon *a.* (of a Greek word) having a circumflex accent on the last syllable. Also *n.* WH: 19C. Greek *perispōmenon*, neut. of pres.p. pass. of *perispan* to draw around, to mark with a circumflex, from PERI- + *span* to draw, to pull.

perissodactyl *a.* of or belonging to the order Perissodactyla of ungulates in which all the feet are odd-toed. Also *n.* WH: 19C. Modern Latin *Perissodactyla*, from Greek *perissos* uneven + *daktulos* finger, toe.

peristalith *n.* a group of stones standing round a burial mound etc. WH: 19C. Greek *peristatos* standing round + -LITH.

peristalsis *n.* the automatic, wavelike, contractile motion of the alimentary canal and similar organs by which the contents are propelled along. WH: 19C. Back-formation from *peristaltic*, from Greek *peristaltikos* clasping and compressing, from *peristallein* to wrap up, to wrap round, from PERI- + *stallein* to place. See also -IC.

peristeronic *a.* of or relating to pigeons. WH: 19C. Appar. from Greek *peristerōn* dovecot (from *peristera* dove, pigeon) + -IC.

peristome *n.* the fringe round the mouth of the capsule in mosses. WH: 18C. Modern Latin *peristoma*, from PERI- + Greek *stoma* mouth.

peristyle *n.* a row of columns surrounding a building, court etc. WH: 17C. French *péristyle*, from Latin *peristylum*, from Greek *peristulon*, use as n. of neut. of *peristulos* having pillars all round, from PERI- + *stulos* pillar, column.

peritoneum *n.* the serous membrane lining the abdominal cavity and enveloping all the abdominal viscera. WH: 14–15C. Late Latin, from Greek *peritonaion*, use as n. of neut. of *peritonaios*, from *peritonos* stretched around, from PERI- + -*tonos* stretched.

perityphlitis *n.* inflammation of the connective tissue surrounding the caecum or blind gut. WH: 19C. PERI- + Greek *tuphlon* caecum (from *tuphlos* blind) + -ITIS.

periwig *n.* a wig. WH: 16C. Var. of PERUKE, with the -*wi*- representing the sound of 'u' in French *perruque*. Cp. WIG[1].

periwinkle[1] *n.* any plant of the genus *Vinca*, comprising trailing evergreen shrubs with blue or white flowers. WH: pre-1200. Late Latin *pervinca*, from earlier *vincapervinca*, of unknown orig., assim. to PERIWINKLE[2].

periwinkle[2] *n.* a winkle. WH: 16C. Orig. unknown. Cp. WINKLE. According to some, the first element is from Latin *pina* mussel.

perjure *v.t.* to forswear (oneself), to lie under oath. *Also v.i., n.* WH: 15C. Old French *parjurer*, from Latin *periurare* to swear falsely, from PER- + *iurare* to swear.

perk[1] *v.t.* to hold or stick up. *Also v.i., a.* WH: 14–15C. ? Old French, dial. var. of *percher*. See PERCH[1].

perk[2] *n.* a benefit enjoyed by an employee over and above their salary. WH: 19C. Abbr. of PERQUISITE. The word is sometimes popularly associated with PERK[1].

perk[3] *v.i., v.t.* to percolate. WH: mid-20C. Abbr. of PERCOLATE. The word is sometimes popularly associated with PERK[1].

perk[4] *v.i.* to perch. *Also v.t.* WH: 14–15C. PERK[1].

perlite *n.* a glassy igneous rock characterized by spheroidal cracks formed by contractile tension in cooling. WH: 19C. French, from *perle* PEARL[1] + -ITE[1].

perm[1] *n.* a hairstyle in which hair is shaped and then set by chemicals, heat etc. *Also v.t.* WH: early 20C. Abbr. of PERMANENT.

perm[2] *n.* a forecast of a number of football match results selected from a larger number of matches. *Also v.t.* WH: mid-20C. Abbr. of PERMUTATION.

permaculture *n.* the development of self-sustaining agricultural ecosystems. WH: late 20C. PERMANENT + CULTURE.

permafrost *n.* a layer of permanently frozen earth in very cold regions. WH: mid-20C. PERMANENT + FROST.

permalloy *n.* an alloy with high magnetic permeability. WH: early 20C. From *permeable* (see PERMEATE) + ALLOY[1].

permanent *a.* lasting, remaining or intended to remain in the same state, place or condition, as distinct from *temporary*. WH: 14–15C. Old French, or from Latin *permanens*, *permanentis*, pres.p. of *permanere* to remain to the end, from PER- + *manere* to stay. See also -ENT.

permanganate *n.* a salt of permanganic acid. WH: 19C. PER- + MANGANESE + -ATE[1].

permeate *v.t.* to penetrate and pass through. *Also v.i.* WH: 17C. Latin *permeatus*, p.p. of *permeare* to pass through, from PER- + *meare* to go, to pass. See also -ATE[3].

permethrin *n.* a garden pesticide, esp. used against whitefly. WH: late 20C. PER- + *resmethrin* a synthetic pyrethroid, from unknown 1st element + -*ethrin*, based on *pyrethrin* (see PYRETHRUM).

Permian *a.* of or relating to the uppermost strata of the Palaeozoic series, consisting chiefly of red sandstone and magnesian limestone, which rest on the Carboniferous strata. *Also n.* WH: 19C. *Perm*, a city in W Russia to the west of the Urals + -IAN. The term was coined in 1841 by the British geologist Sir Roderick Murchison.

per mille *adv.* in every thousand. WH: 17C. PER + Latin *mille* thousand.

permit[1] *v.t.* to give permission to, to authorize. *Also v.i.* WH: 14–15C. Latin *permittere* to surrender, to allow, from PER- + *mittere* o let go. The original sense (to the 19C) was to submit, to hand over

(someone or something to another person). The sense to allow dates from the 15C.

permit[2] *n.* an order to permit something, a warrant, esp. a written authority to land or remove dutiable goods. WH: 16C. PERMIT[1].

permutation *n.* change of the order of a series of quantities. WH: 14–15C. Old French, or from Latin *permutatio*, *permutationis*, from *permutatus*, p.p. of *permutare*. See PERMUTE, also -ATION.

permute *v.t.* to change thoroughly. WH: 14–15C. Latin *permutare*, from PER- + *mutare* to change.

Permutit® *n.* an artificial zeolite used to soften water. WH: early 20C. German, from Latin *permutare* (PERMUTE) + German -*it* -ITE[1]. The ion-exchanging properties of zeolites are used to soften water.

pern *n.* a bird of the genus *Pernis*, a honey buzzard. WH: 19C. Modern Latin *Pernis*, from Greek *pternis* a kind of hawk.

pernicious *a.* destructive, very harmful. WH: 14–15C. Latin *perniciosus*, from *pernicies* destruction, from PER- + *nex*, *necis* death, destruction. See also -IOUS.

pernickety *a.* fastidious, fussy. WH: 19C. Orig. unknown. ? From PARTICULAR.

pernoctation *n.* a remaining out or watching all night. WH: 17C. Latin *pernoctatio*, *pernoctationis*, from *pernoctatus*, p.p. of *pernoctare*, from PER- + *nox*, *noctis* night. See also -ION.

Pernod® *n.* an aniseed-flavoured aperitif. WH: early 20C. Henri-Louis *Pernod*, French distiller, its orig. manufacturer in 1797. Pernod was originally a type of absinthe.

perone *n.* the fibula or small bone of the leg. WH: 17C. Modern Latin, from Greek *peronē* pin, buckle, fibula.

perorate *v.i.* to deliver an oration. *Also v.t.* WH: 17C. Latin *peroratus*, p.p. of *perorare* to speak at length, to speak to the close, from PER- + *orare* to speak. See also -ATE[3].

peroxide *n.* hydrogen peroxide. *Also a., v.t.* WH: 19C. PER- + OXIDE.

perpendicular *a.* at right angles to the plane of the horizon. *Also n.* WH: 14–15C. Latin *perpendicularis*, from *perpendiculum* plummet, plumbline, from PER- + *pendere* to hang. See also -CULE, -AR[1]. The word was adopted as an architectural term in 1812 by the English architect Thomas Rickman.

perpetrate *v.t.* to perform, to commit (a wrong). WH: 16C. Latin *perpetratus*, p.p. of *perpetrare* to perform, from PER- + *patrare* to bring about. See also -ATE[3].

perpetual *a.* unending, eternal. WH: 12–14C. Old French *perpétuel*, from Latin *perpetualis*, *perpetuus*, from *perpes*, *perpetis* continuous, uninterrupted, from PER- + *petere* to be directed towards. See also -AL[1].

perpetuate *v.t.* to make perpetual. WH: 16C. Latin *perpetuatus*, p.p. of *perpetuare*, from *perpetuus*. See PERPETUAL, also -ATE[3].

perpetuum mobile *n.* perpetual motion. WH: 17C. Latin perpetual motion, from *perpetuus* PERPETUAL + *mobilis* movable, MOBILE, based on PRIMUM MOBILE. Cp. MOTO PERPETUO.

perplex *v.t.* to puzzle, to bewilder. WH: 16C. Back-formation from *perplexed* (15C), from obs. a. *perplex* (from Old French *perflexe* or Latin *perplexus* involved, intricate, from per- PER- + *plexus*, p.p. of *plectere* to plait, to interweave, to involve) + -ED.

per pro. *abbr.* through the agency of. WH: 19C. Abbr. of Latin *pro procurationem* by procuration. See PROCURATION. The phrase is popularly taken to mean on behalf of. In a letter signature it properly denotes the person who signs it on behalf of the writer.

perquisite *n.* gain, profit or emolument, over and above regular wages or salary, a perk. WH: 14–15C. Medieval Latin *perquisitum* acquisition, neut. p.p. (used as n.) of Latin *perquirere* to search diligently for, from PER- + *quaerere* to seek.

perradial *a.* (in hydrozoons etc.) of, relating to or constituting a primary ray. WH: 19C. Modern Latin *perradius* (see PER-, RADIUS) + -AL[1].

Perrier® *n.* a sparkling mineral water. WH: early 20C. Louis Eugène *Perrier*, 1835–1912, French physician, its orig. producer. Perrier acquired the lease of the mineral springs at Vergèze, near Nîmes, France, in 1894, and set up his bottling plant there. The springs, originally named Bouillens ('bubbling'), were renamed after him as the *source Perrier*.

perron *n.* a platform with steps in front of a large building. WH: 14–15C. Old French, from augm. of Latin *petra* stone. Cp. Italian *petrone* large rock. See also -OON.

perry *n.* a fermented liquor made from the juice of pears. WH: 12–14C. Old French *peré*, from alt. of Latin *pirum* PEAR. See also -Y[2].

per se *adv.* by itself, in itself. WH: 16C. Latin by itself.

persecute *v.t.* to pursue in a hostile or malicious way; to afflict with suffering, esp. for adherence to a particular opinion or creed. WH: 12–14C. Old French *persécuter*, back-formation from *persécuteur* persecutor, from Latin *persecutus*, p.p. of *persequi*, from PER- + *sequi* to follow. See also -OR.

Perseid *n.* any one of a group of meteors appearing about 12 August, having their radiating point in Perseus. WH: 19C. Latin *Perseus*, the rescuer of Andromeda in Greek mythology + -ID. The constellation of Perseus lies between Andromeda and Auriga.

perseverate *v.i.* to persist in an action for a long time. WH: early 20C. Back-formation from *perseveration* (14–15C), from Old French *persévération*, from Latin *perseveratio, perseverationis*, from *perseveratus*, p.p. of *perseverare*. See PERSEVERE, also -ATION.

persevere *v.i.* to persist in or with any undertaking. WH: 14–15C. Old French *persévérer*, from Latin *perseverare* to abide by strictly, to persist, from *perseverus*, very strict. See PER-, SEVERE.

Persian *a.* of or relating to Persia (now Iran). *Also n.* WH: 12–14C. Old French *persien*, from Latin *Persia*, from Greek *Persis*, from Old Persian *pārsa* (modern Persian *pārs*, Arabic *fārs*). See also -AN.

persicaria *n.* a weed, *Polygonum persicaria*. WH: 14–15C. Medieval Latin, from Latin *persicum* PEACH[1]. The plant is so called because its leaves resemble those of the peach.

persicot *n.* a cordial made from peaches, nectarines etc., macerated in spirit and flavoured with their kernels. WH: 18C. French, dim. of Savoy dial. *perse* peach, from Latin *persicum*.

persienne *n.* an Oriental cambric or muslin. WH: 19C. French, fem. of *persien* PERSIAN.

persiflage *n.* banter, raillery, frivolous treatment of any subject. WH: 18C. French, from *persifler* to banter, from PER- + *siffler* to whistle. See also -AGE.

persimmon *n.* any evergreen tree of the genus *Diospyros*. WH: 17C. Alt. of Virginia Algonquian *pessemmins*.

persist *v.i.* to continue steadfastly, in the pursuit of any plan. WH: 16C. Latin *persistere*, from PER- + *sistere* to stand.

person *n.* a human being, an individual. WH: 12–14C. Old French *persone* (Modern French *personne*), from Latin *persona* mask used by an actor, person who plays a part. Cp. PARSON. The original sense was a part played in a play or in real life. Cp. DRAMATIS PERSONAE. The current sense of human being, individual arose from this.

persona *n.* a person's social façade, as distinct from *anima*. WH: early 20C. Latin. See PERSON.

personate[1] *v.t.* to assume the character or to act the part of. WH: 16C. Late Latin *personatus*, p.p. of *personare*, from *persona*. See PERSON, also -ATE[3].

personate[2] *a.* masklike (applied to a two-lipped corolla in which the mouth is closed by an upward projection of the lower part, as in the snapdragon). WH: 16C. Latin *personatus* masked, feigned, from *persona* mask. See PERSON, also -ATE[2]. The original sense (to the 19C) was personated, feigned. The botanical sense dates from the 18C and alludes to the masklike appearance.

personify *v.t.* to regard or represent (an abstraction) as possessing the attributes of a living being. WH: 18C. French *personnifier*, from *personne*. See PERSON, also -FY.

personnel *n.* the body of persons engaged in some service, esp. a public institution, military or naval enterprise etc. WH: 19C. French, use as n. of a., *personal* (PERSON), as distinct from MATERIEL.

perspective *n.* the art of representing solid objects on a plane surface exactly as regards position, shape and dimensions, as the objects themselves appear to the eye at a particular point. *Also a.* WH: 14–15C. Medieval Latin *perspectiva*, use as n. of fem. of Late Latin *perspectivus*, from Latin *perspectus*, p.p. of *perspicere* to look at closely, from PER- + *specere* to look. See also -IVE.

Perspex® *n.* a transparent plastic, very tough and of great clarity. WH: mid-20C. Latin *perspectus*, p.p. of *perspicere* to look through, from PER- + *specere* to look (at).

perspicacious *a.* mentally penetrating or discerning. WH: 17C. Latin *perspicax, perspicacis*, from *perspicere*. See PERSPECTIVE, also -ACIOUS.

perspicuous *a.* free from obscurity or ambiguity, clearly expressed, lucid. WH: 15C. Latin *perspicuus* transparent, clear, from *perspicere*. See PERSPECTIVE, also -OUS.

perspire *v.i./v.t.* to sweat. *Also v.t.* WH: 17C. From obs. French *perspirer*, from Latin *perspirare* to breathe everywhere, from PER- + *spirare* to breathe.

persuade *v.t.* to influence or convince by argument, entreaty etc. WH: 15C. Latin *persuadere*, from PER- + *suadere* to advise, to recommend.

persulphate *n.* a sulphate containing the greatest relative quantity of acid. WH: 19C. PER- + SULPHATE.

pert *a.* saucy, forward. WH: 12–14C. Old French *apert*, from Latin *apertus*, p.p. of *aperire* to open, partly blending with Old French *aspert*, from Latin *expertus* expert.

pertain *v.i.* to relate, to apply, to have reference (to). WH: 14–15C. Old French *partenir*, from Latin *pertinere* to extend, to tend to, to belong to, from PER- + *tenere* to hold.

pertinacious *a.* obstinate. WH: 17C. Latin *pertinax, pertinacis*, from PER- + *tenax* holding fast. See TENACIOUS.

pertinent *a.* relevant, apposite. *Also n.pl.* WH: 14–15C. Old French, or from Latin *pertinens, pertinentis*, pres.p. of *pertinere*. See PERTAIN, also -ENT.

perturb *v.t.* to throw into confusion or physical disorder. WH: 14–15C. Old French *pertourber*, from Latin *perturbare*, from PER- + *turbare* to disturb, to confuse.

pertuse *a.* (esp. of leaves) punched, pierced with holes. WH: 18C. Latin *pertusus*, p.p. of *pertundere* to punch a hole, to bore into a hole, from PER- + *tundere* to beat.

pertussis *n.* whooping cough. WH: 18C. Modern Latin, from PER- + *tussis* cough.

Peru balsam *n.* balsam from a tropical American tree, *Myroxylon pereirae*. WH: 18C. *Peru* (see PERUVIAN) + BALSAM.

peruke *n.* a wig. WH: 16C. French *perruque*, from Italian *perrucca, parrucca*, of unknown orig. Cp. PERIWIG.

peruse *v.t.* to read. WH: 15C. PER- + alt. of Latin freq. v. *usitari* to use often, from *usus* USE[1]. The original meaning (to the 16C) was to use up, to wear out by use. The sense to read dates from the 16C.

Peruvian *a.* of or relating to Peru. *Also n.* WH: 17C. Modern Latin *Peruvia* Peru, a country in S America + -AN.

pervade *v.t.* to pass through. WH: 17C. Latin *pervadere*, from PER- + *vadere* to go, to walk.

perve *n.* a sexual pervert. *Also v.i.* WH: mid-20C. Abbr. of PERVERT[2].

perverse *a.* wilfully or obstinately wrong. WH: 14–15C. Old French *pervers*, from Latin *perversus*, p.p. of *pervertere*. See PERVERT[1].

perversion *n.* the act of perverting. WH: 14–15C. Latin *perversio, perversionis*, from *perversus*, p.p. of *pervertere*. See PERVERT[1], also -ION.

pervert[1] *v.t.* to put to improper use. WH: 14–15C. Old French *pervertir* or Latin *pervertere* to turn around, to turn the wrong way, to overturn, to corrupt, from PER- + *vertere* to turn. The original meaning (to the 17C) was to turn upside down, to upset.

pervert[2] *n.* a person who has been perverted. WH: 17C. PERVERT[1].

pervicacious *a.* very obstinate, wilfully perverse. WH: 17C. Latin *pervicax, pervicacis*, from *pervic-*, base of *pervincere*, from PER- + *vincere* to conquer, to prevail against. See also -IOUS.

pervious *a.* permeable. WH: 17C. Latin *pervius*, from PER- + *via* way. See also -OUS.

Pesach *n.* Passover. WH: 17C. Hebrew *pesaḥ*. See PASSOVER.

pesade *n.* in dressage, the motion of a horse when raising the forequarters without advancing. WH: 18C. French, alt. of *posade*, from Italian *posata*, lit. pause, resting, from *posare* to pause, from Latin *pausare*. See also -ADE.

peseta *n.* the standard unit of currency of Spain and Andorra. WH: 19C. Spanish, dim. of *pesa* weight, from Latin *pensa*, pl. of *pensum*, neut. p.p. of *pendere* to weigh. Cp. PESO.

pesewa *n.* a unit of currency of Ghana, worth 100th of a cedi. WH: mid-20C. Fante and Twi penny.

Peshito *n.* the Syriac version of the Holy Scriptures. WH: 18C. Syriac *pšīṭtā*, lit. the simple, the plain.

peshwa *n.* the hereditary ruler of the Marathas. WH: 17C. Persian *pīšwā* chief.

pesky *a.* annoying, troublesome. *Also adv.* WH: 18C. ? Rel. to PEST.

peso *n.* the standard unit of currency of several Central and S American countries and the Philippines. WH: 16C. Spanish weight, from Latin *pensum*. See PESETA.

pessary *n.* a device inserted in the vagina to prevent or remedy prolapse of the womb or as a contraceptive. WH: 14–15C. Late Latin *pessarium*, var. of *pessulum*, dim. of *pessum*, from Greek *pessos* pessary, oval stone used in board games. See also -ARY¹. A pessary was originally a medicated plug inserted anywhere in the body. The current sense dates from the 18C.

pessimism *n.* the habit of taking a gloomy and despondent view of things. WH: 18C. Latin *pessimus* worst + -ISM, based on OPTIMISM. The original meaning (to the 19C) was the worst possible state or condition. The current sense dates from the 19C.

pest *n.* a person who or something which is extremely destructive or annoying. WH: 14–15C. French *peste*, or from Latin *pestis* plague, contagious disease.

pester *v.t.* to bother, to annoy. WH: 16C. French *empestrer* to place in an embarrassing situation (from Popular Latin *impastoriare* to hobble (an animal), from Latin IM-¹ + Medieval Latin *pastoria* rope to hobble an animal, shackle, use as n. of Latin *pastoria*, fem. of *pastorius* pertaining to a herdsman, from *pastor* herdsman, from *pascere* to graze), later influ. by PEST.

pestiferous *a.* pestilent. WH: 14–15C. Latin *pestifer*, from *pestis* plague + -fer. See -FEROUS.

pestilence *n.* any contagious disease that is epidemic and deadly, esp. bubonic plague. WH: 12–14C. Old French, from Latin *pestilentia*, from *pestilens*, *pestilentis*, from *pestis* plague. See also -ENCE.

pestle *n.* an implement used in pounding substances in a mortar. *Also v.t., v.i.* WH: 12–14C. Old French *pestel*, from Latin *pistillum*, from *pistus*, p.p. of *pinsere* to pound. See also -LE².

pesto *n.* an Italian sauce made of basil, garlic, pine nuts etc. WH: mid-20C. Italian, contr. of *pestato*, p.p. of *pestare* to pound, to crush.

pet¹ *n.* an animal kept in the house as a companion. *Also a., v.t., v.i.* WH: 16C. Orig. unknown. ? Rel. to PETTY.

pet² *n.* a fit of peevishness or bad temper. WH: 16C. Orig. unknown.

peta- *comb. form* a factor of 10 to the fifteenth power. WH: late 20C. Var. of PENTA-, based on the supposed relationship between TERA- and TETRA-. 10 to the fifteenth power (10^{15}) is (10^3)⁵.

petal *n.* any one of the divisions of a corolla of a flower. WH: 18C. Modern Latin *petalum*, from Late Latin metal plate, from Greek *petalon* lamina, leaf, use as n. of neut. of *petalos* outspread, from base *pet-* as in *petannusthai* to unfold.

pétanque *n.* a game similar to boules, played esp. in Provence. WH: mid-20C. French, from Provençal *pèd tanco*, lit. foot fixed (to the ground). The reference is to the start position.

petard *n.* a conical case or box of iron etc., formerly used for blowing open gates or barriers. WH: 16C. French *pétard*, from *péter* to break wind. See also -ARD.

petasus *n.* a broad-brimmed, low-crowned hat worn by the ancient Greeks. WH: 16C. Latin, from Greek *petasos*, from *pet-*. See PETAL.

Pete *n.* a person's name, only in the phrase *for Pete's sake*. WH: early 20C. Dim. of male forename *Peter*.

petechia *n.* a spot on the skin formed by extravasated blood etc., in malignant fevers etc. WH: 18C. Modern Latin, from Italian *petecchie* (pl.) skin eruption, from Popular Latin dim. of Latin *petigo* scab, eruption.

peter¹ *v.i.* in bridge, to play an echo. *Also n.* WH: 19C. Orig. uncertain. ? from male forename *Peter*.

peter² *n.* a prison cell. WH: 19C. See PETER¹.

Peter Pan *n.* a man who looks youthful or who behaves in a youthful manner. WH: early 20C. *Peter Pan*, the boy hero of J.M. Barrie's play *Peter Pan, the Boy Who Wouldn't Grow Up* (1904).

Peter Principle *n.* the theory that all members of a hierarchy rise to the level at which they are no longer competent. WH: mid-20C. Laurence Johnston *Peter*, 1919–90, US educationalist and writer, who propounded the principle.

petersham *n.* a thick corded-silk ribbon used for belts, hatbands etc. WH: 19C. Viscount *Petersham*, 1790–1851, English army officer, who wore a heavy greatcoat of his own design. The name passed to the cloth from which the coat was made, then to the ribbon.

Peter's pence *n.pl.* an annual tax of a penny from each householder, formerly paid to the Pope. WH: 14–15C. St *Peter* + -'S + PENCE. The name refers to the claim of the see of Rome to the patrimony of St Peter. The tax was probably introduced in the 8C and was discontinued by statute in 1534.

pethidine *n.* a synthetic analgesic drug with sedative effects similar to but less powerful than morphine, used esp. in childbirth. WH: mid-20C. Blend of PIPERIDINE and ETHYL.

pétillant *a.* (of wine) slightly sparkling. WH: 19C. French, from *pétiller*, dim. of *péter* to break wind. See also -ANT.

petiole *n.* the leaf-stalk of a plant. WH: 18C. French *pétiole*, from Modern Latin *petiolus*, from misspelling of Latin *peciolus* little foot, fruit-stalk. See also -OLE².

petit *a.* small, petty, inconsiderable, inferior. WH: 12–14C. Old French. See PETTY.

petite *a.* (of a woman) slight, dainty, graceful. WH: 16C. French, fem. of *petit*. See PETTY.

petition *n.* an entreaty, a request. *Also v.t., v.i.* WH: 12–14C. Old French *pétition*, from Latin *petitio*, *petitionis*, from *petitus*, p.p. of *petere* to aim at, to lay claim to, to ask, to seek. See also -ION.

petitio principii *n.* begging the question. WH: 16C. Latin assuming a principle, from *petitio* (PETITION) + gen. of *principium* principle.

Petrarchan *a.* denoting a sonnet which has an octave rhyming *abbaabba* and a sestet rhyming *cdcdcd* or *cdecde*. WH: 19C. *Petrarch* (Italian *Petrarca*), 1304–74, Italian poet + -AN.

petre *n.* saltpetre. WH: 16C. Abbr. of SALTPETRE.

petrel *n.* any member of the family Procellariidae or Hydrobatidae, small dusky seabirds, with long wings and great power of flight. WH: 17C. ? From male forename *Peter* + -el by assoc. with COCKEREL, DOTTEREL, etc. The allusion would be biblical: 'And when Peter was come down out of the ship, he walked on the water, to go to Jesus' (Matt. xiv.29).

Petri dish *n.* a shallow, circular, flat-bottomed dish used for cultures of micro-organisms. WH: 19C. Julius R. *Petri*, 1852–1922, German bacteriologist.

petrify *v.t.* to convert into stone or a stony substance. *Also v.i.* WH: 14–15C. Medieval Latin *petrificare*, from Latin *petra* stone. See also -FY.

Petrine *a.* of, relating to or derived from the apostle Peter. WH: 19C. Ecclesiastical Latin *Petrus* Peter + -INE. The reference is to the apostle St Peter. Cp. PAULINE.

petro- *comb. form* stone. WH: Greek *petros* stone, *petra* rock. See also -O-.

petrochemical *n.* any chemical obtained from petroleum. *Also a.* WH: early 20C. PETRO-, PETROLEUM + CHEMICAL.

petrochemistry *n.* the chemistry of rocks. WH: mid-20C. PETRO-, PETROLEUM + CHEMISTRY.

petrocurrency *n.* the currency of a country which exports significant quantities of petroleum. WH: late 20C. PETROLEUM + CURRENCY.

petrodollar *n.* a dollar earned from the exporting of petroleum. WH: late 20C. PETROLEUM + DOLLAR.

petroglyph *n.* a rock-carving. WH: 19C. French *pétroglyphe*, from *pétro-* PETRO- + Greek *gluphē* carving.

petrography *n.* descriptive petrology. WH: 17C. PETRO- + -GRAPHY.

petrol *n.* a refined form of petroleum used in motor cars etc. *Also a., v.t.* WH: 16C. French *pétrole*, from Medieval Latin PETROLEUM. The original sense (to the 19C) was petroleum. The current sense dates from the 19C.

petroleum *n.* an inflammable, oily liquid exuding from rocks or pumped from wells, used for lighting, heating and the generation of mechanical power. WH: 16C. Medieval Latin, from Latin *petra* rock + *oleum* oil.

pétroleur *n.* an arsonist who uses petroleum. WH: 19C. French, from *pétrole* PETROL + -eur -OR.

petrology *n.* the study of the origin, structure and mineralogical and chemical composition of rocks. WH: 19C. PETRO- + -LOGY.

petrosal *a.* of great hardness, like stone. *Also n.* WH: 18C. Latin *petrosus* stony, rocky, from *petra* stone. See also -OSE¹, -AL¹.

petrous *a.* denoting the hard part of the temporal bone. WH: 16C. Latin *petrosus* (PETROSAL) + -OUS.

pettichaps *n.* the garden warbler, *Sylvia borin*. WH: 17C. PETTY + *chaps*, pl. of CHAP² or CHAP³.

petticoat *n.* a loose underskirt. *Also a.* WH: 14–15C. PETTY + COAT. Orig. two words. The garment was originally (to the 16C) a small coat worn by men under the doublet. It was also a garment worn by women and young children, although not at first a skirt.

pettifog *v.i.* to do legal business in a mean or tricky way, to practise chicanery. WH: 17C. Back-formation from *pettifogger* (16C), from PETTY + *fogger* person given to underhand practices, ? from *Fugger*, surname of a family of merchants and financiers of Augsburg in the 15–16C.

pettitoes *n.pl.* the feet of a pig as food, pig's trotters. WH: 16C. Pl. of *pettitoe*, of uncertain orig. ? From French *petite oie* little goose, with assim. to PETTY and TOE. If the French origin is correct, the reference would be to a part of an animal cut off to be eaten. In the case of a goose, this would be the giblets. But the transference of sense is contrived.

petty *a.* trifling, insignificant. WH: 14–15C. Old French *petit* little, small, imit. of young children's speech. Cp. Late Latin *pitinnus* very small. English PRETTY is sometimes altered similarly in imitation of children's speech, perhaps through an association with *petty* or its French origin. Something pretty is often small, and something small often pretty. Cp. *Pitti-Sing* ('Pretty Thing') as one of the three sisters in Gilbert and Sullivan's *The Mikado* (1885).

petulant *a.* given to fits of bad temper. *Also n.* WH: 16C. Old French *pétulant*, from Latin *petulans*, *petulantis*, rel. to *petere* to seek, to aim at. See also -ANT.

petunia *n.* any member of the genus *Petunia* of S American plants, allied to the tobacco plant, cultivated in gardens for their showy funnel-shaped flowers. WH: 19C. Modern Latin, from French *petun* tobacco (from Guarani *petỹ*) + -IA. The petunia is so called from its close affinity to the tobacco plant. Its name was coined in 1789 by the French botanist Antoine-Laurent de Jussieu.

petuntse *n.* a fusible substance similar to feldspar used for the manufacture of porcelain. WH: 18C. Chinese *báidūnzĭ*, from *bái* white + *dūnzĭ* block of stone, mound of earth (from *dūn* block, heap + *zĭ* son).

pew *n.* a long bench with a back, for worshippers in church. *Also v.t.* WH: 14–15C. Old French *puye*, *puie*, from Latin *podia*, pl. of PODIUM.

pewee *n.* a N American flycatcher of the genus *Contopus*. WH: 18C. Imit. of bird's cry. Cp. PEEWEE.

pewter *n.* an alloy usu. of tin and lead, sometimes of tin with other metals. *Also a.* WH: 12–14C. Old French *peutre*, from Medieval Latin *peltrum*, of unknown orig.

peyote *n.* a Mexican cactus, *Lophophora williamsii*. WH: 19C. American Spanish, from Nahuatl *peyotl*.

pfennig *n.* a German unit of currency, worth one-hundredth of a mark. WH: 16C. German. See PENNY.

pH *n.* a measure of the acidity or alkalinity of a solution on a scale from 0 to 14, with 7 representing neutrality, figures below it denoting acidity and those above it alkalinity. WH: early 20C. Abbr. of German *Potenz* power + H·, symbol for the hydrogen ion.

phaenogam *n.* a phanerogam. WH: 19C. Modern Latin *phaenogama*, from Greek *phaino-* showing + *gamos* marriage, sexual union.

phaeton *n.* a light four-wheeled open carriage, usu. drawn by two horses. WH: 16C. French *pháeton*, from Latin *Phaethon*, from Greek *Phaethōn* (from *phaethōn* shining), in Greek mythology the son of Helios (the sun god) and Clymene, who was allowed to drive the sun's chariot for a day, with fatal consequences.

phage *n.* a bacteriophage. WH: early 20C. Abbr. of BACTERIOPHAGE.

-phage *comb. form* eater, as in *bacteriophage*. WH: Greek *-phagos*, from *phagein* to eat.

phago- *comb. form* eating. WH: Greek *phago-*, from *phagein* to eat. See also -O-.

phagocyte *n.* a leucocyte that absorbs microbes etc., protecting the system against infection. WH: 19C. PHAGO- + -CYTE.

-phagous *comb. form* eating, devouring, as in *anthropophagous*. WH: Latin *-phagus*, Greek *-phagos*, from Greek *phagein* to eat. See also -OUS.

phalange *n.* a phalanx. WH: 14–15C. French, from Latin PHALANX, *phalangis*.

phalanger *n.* any small, Australian, woolly-coated, arboreal marsupial of the family Phalangeridae, comprising the flying squirrel and flying opossum. WH: 18C. French and Modern Latin, from Greek *phalaggion* venomous spider. The animal is so called because its webbed hind toes resemble a spider's web.

phalanx *n.* the close order in which the heavy-armed troops of a Greek army were drawn up, esp. a compact body of Macedonian infantry. WH: 16C. Latin *phalanx*, *phalangis*, from Greek *phalagx* line of battle, finger bone, orig. trunk, log. Rel. to BAULK.

phalarope *n.* any small wading bird of the subfamily Phalaropodidae, related to the snipes. WH: 18C. French, from Modern Latin *Phalaropus* genus name, from Greek *phalaris* coot + -O- + *pous* foot.

phallus *n.* a penis. WH: 17C. Late Latin, from Greek *phallos*, rel. to *phallē* whale.

phanariot *n.* a member of the class of Greek officials under Turkey. WH: 19C. Modern Greek *phanariōtes*, from Greek *phanarion* lighthouse, lantern, dim. of *phanos* torch, lamp, lantern. The name comes from the *Phanar* (Fanar), the area of Istanbul that became the chief Greek quarter after the Ottoman conquest. Its own name comes from the lighthouse formerly there.

phanerogam *n.* a plant having pistils and stamens, a flowering plant. WH: 19C. French *phanérogame*, Modern Latin *phanerogamus*, from Greek *phaneros* visible, evident + *gamos* marriage, sexual union. The plant is so called because its reproductive organs (female pistils and male stamens) are readily seen.

phantasiast *n.* any one of those among the Docetae, who believed that Christ's body was not material but mere appearance. WH: 17C. Ecclesiastical Greek *phantasiastēs*, from Greek *phantasia*. See FANTASY.

phantasm *n.* a phantom, an optical illusion. WH: 12–14C. Old French *fantasme*, from Latin *phantasma*, from Greek, from *phantazein*. See FANTASY.

phantasmagoria *n.* a series of phantasms, fantastic appearances or illusions appearing to the mind as in nightmare, frenzy etc. WH: 19C. Prob. from French *fantasmagorie*, from *fantasme* PHANTASM with fanciful ending. Some relate the ending to Greek *agora* assembly (+ French *-ie* -Y²). *Phantasmagoria* was the name of an exhibition of optical illusions by means of magic lantern held in London in 1802.

phantom *n.* an apparition, a ghost. *Also a.* WH: 12–14C. Old French *fantosme* (Modern French *fantôme*), from Popular Latin *fantauma*, from *fantagma*, alt. of Latin *phantasma*, from Greek, from *phantazein*. See FANTASY.

Pharaoh *n.* any one of the ancient Egyptian kings. WH: 12–14C. Ecclesiastical Latin *Pharao*, *Pharaonis*, from Greek *Pharaō*, from Hebrew *par'ōh*, from *pr-'o* great house. The English final *-h* is from Hebrew.

phare *n.* a lighthouse. WH: 14–15C. Latin *pharus*, from Greek PHAROS.

Pharisee *n.* a member of an ancient Jewish sect who rigidly observed the rites and ceremonies prescribed by the written law, and were marked by their exclusiveness towards the rest of the people. WH: pre-1200. Ecclesiastical Latin *phariseus*, from Greek *pharisaios*, from Aramaic *prīšayyā*, emphatic pl. of *prīš*, corr. to Hebrew *pārūš* separated, separatist.

pharmaceutical *a.* of, relating to or engaged in pharmacy. *Also n.* WH: 17C. Late Latin *pharmaceuticus*, from Greek *pharmakeutikos*, from *pharmakeutēs*, var. of *pharmakeus* druggist, from *pharmakon*. See PHARMACY, also -IC, -AL¹.

pharmaco- *comb. form* of or relating to chemistry or drugs. WH: Greek *pharmako-*, comb. form of *pharmakon* drug, medicine, poison. See also -O-.

pharmacognosy *n.* the branch of pharmacology concerned with drugs of plant and animal origin. WH: 19C. PHARMACO- + Greek *gnōsis* investigation, knowledge.

pharmacology *n.* the science of drugs and medicines. WH: 18C. Modern Latin *pharmacologia*. See PHARMACO-, -LOGY.

pharmacopoeia *n.* a book, esp. an official publication, containing a list of drugs, formulas, doses etc. WH: 17C. Modern Latin, from Greek *pharmakopoiia* art of preparing drugs, from *pharmakopoios* preparer of drugs, from *pharmako-* PHARMACO- + *-poios* making, maker.

pharmacy *n.* the art or practice of preparing, compounding and dispensing drugs, esp. for medicinal purposes. WH: 14–15C. Old French *farmacie* (Modern French *pharmacie*), from Medieval Latin *pharmacia*, from Greek *pharmakeia* practice of a druggist, from *pharmakon* drug, medicine. See also -Y².

pharos *n.* a lighthouse, a beacon. WH: 16C. Latin and Greek *Pharos* name of a lighthouse built *c.*280 BC on the island of Pharos off Alexandria in Egypt. The island is now a peninsula forming part of the city. The lighthouse was still standing in the 12C but was already in ruins by the 15C.

pharyngo- *comb. form* of or relating to the pharynx. WH: Modern Latin PHARYNX, *pharyngis*. See also -O-.

pharyngoscope *n.* an instrument for inspecting the throat. WH: 19C. PHARYNGO- + -SCOPE.

pharyngotomy *n.* the surgical operation of cutting the pharynx. WH: 18C. PHARYNGO- + -TOMY.

pharynx *n.* the canal or cavity opening from the mouth into the oesophagus and communicating with the air passages of the nose. WH: 17C. Modern Latin *pharynx*, *pharyngis*, from Greek *pharugx* throat.

phase *n.* a stage of change or development. *Also v.t.* WH: 19C. Partly from French, from Modern Latin PHASIS, partly from a back-formation from *phases*, pl. of PHASIS.

-phasia *comb. form* speech disorder, as in *dysphasia*. WH: Modern Latin, from PHASIS.

†phasis *n.* a phase. WH: 17C. Modern Latin, from Greek, from base *pha-*, *phan-* of *phainein* to show, to appear.

phasmid *n.* any orthopterous insect of the family Phasmidae, comprising the stick insects etc. WH: 19C. Latin *phasma*, from Greek, from *phao* to shine or *phainein* to show, to appear + -ID. The insects are so called from their striking appearance.

phatic *a.* (of speech) used to express feelings, sociability etc., rather than to express meaning. WH: early 20C. Greek *phatos* spoken or *phatikos* assertory. See also -IC.

pheasant *n.* any game bird of the family Phasianidae, naturalized in Britain and Europe, noted for their brilliant plumage and delicate flesh. WH: 12–14C. Old French *faisan*, from Latin *phasianus*, from Greek *phasianos* (*ornis*) (bird) of Pharis, ancient name of the River Rioni in Georgia, from where the bird spread westwards. The *-t* was added as for TYRANT.

phellem *n.* a layer of cork cells formed by phellogen. WH: 19C. Greek *phelles* cask + -*em* as in PHLOEM.

phello- *comb. form* cork. WH: Greek *phellos* cork. See also -O-.

phelloderm *n.* a layer of parenchymatous tissue containing chlorophyll, sometimes formed on the inner side of a layer of phellogen. WH: 19C. PHELLO- + -DERM.

phellogen *n.* the layer of meristematic cells in the cortex of the stems and roots of woody plants, from which cork tissue is formed; cork tissue. WH: 19C. PHELLO- + -GEN.

phelloplastic *n.* a figure carved or modelled in cork. WH: 19C. PHELLO- + PLASTIC.

phenacetin *n.* a white crystalline compound used as an antipyretic. WH: 19C. PHENO- + ACETYL + -IN¹.

phenakistoscope *n.* a scientific toy in which a disc bearing figures in successive attitudes of motion was rapidly revolved so as to convey to the observer, by means of a mirror or a series of slits, the impression of continuous movement. WH: 19C. Greek *phenakistēs* cheat, from *phenakizein* to cheat + -SCOPE.

phencyclidine *n.* a hallucinogenic drug derived from piperidine. WH: mid-20C. PHENO- + CYCLO- + PIPERIDINE.

pheno- *comb. form* derived from coal tar, orig. in the production of coal gas for illuminating. WH: French *phényle* PHENYL. See also -O-. The prefix was introduced in chemical use in 1841 by the French chemist Auguste Laurent to denote substances that were originally by-products from the making of illuminating gas.

phenobarbitone *n.* a white, crystalline powder used as a sedative or hypnotic drug, esp. in cases of epilepsy. WH: mid-20C. PHENO- + barbitone (BARBITURIC).

phenocryst *n.* a large crystal in porphyritic rock. WH: 19C. French *phénocryste*, from *phéno-* PHENO- + Greek *krustallos* (CRYSTAL).

phenol *n.* carbolic acid. WH: 19C. French *phénole*. See PHENO-, -OL.

phenology *n.* the study of the times of recurrence of natural

phenomena, esp. of the influence of climate on plants and animals. WH: 19C. PHENOMENON + -O- + -LOGY.

phenom *n.* an exceptionally gifted person. WH: 19C. Abbr. of PHENOMENON.

phenomenon *n.* something which appears or is perceived by observation or experiment. WH: 16C. Late Latin *phaenomenon*, from Greek *phainomenon*, neut. pres.p. pass. (used as n.) of *phainein* to show. The sense notable occurrence dates from the 18C.

phenotype *n.* the observable characteristics of an organism produced by the interaction of the genotype and the environment. WH: early 20C. German *Phenotypus*. See PHENO-, TYPE.

phenyl *n.* the organic radical found in benzene, phenol, aniline etc. WH: 19C. French *phényle*, from Greek *phaino-* shining, *phainein* to show, *phainesthai* to appear. See also -YL. The radical is so called because it was first used in the names of compounds that were by-products of the manufacture of gas used for illumination.

pheon *n.* the barbed head of a dart, arrow or javelin, a broad arrow. WH: 15C. Orig. unknown.

pheromone *n.* any chemical substance secreted by an animal that stimulates responses from others of its species. WH: mid-20C. Greek *pherein* to convey + -O- + -*mone*, based on HORMONE.

phew *int.* used to express relief, surprise, disgust etc. WH: 17C. Imit. of puffing and whistling.

phi *n.* the 21st letter of the Greek alphabet (Φ, φ). WH: 14–15C. Greek.

phial *n.* a small glass vessel or bottle, esp. for medicine or perfume. *Also v.t.* WH: 12–14C. Old French *fiole*, from Latin *phiola*, *phiala* saucer, censer, from Greek *phialē* broad flat vessel. Cp. VESSEL.

Phi Beta Kappa *n.* a national honorary society for distinguished scholars. WH: 19C. Initial Greek letters (PHI, BETA, KAPPA) of *philosophia biou kubernētēs* philosophy the guide of life. See PHILOSOPHER, BIO-, CYBERNETICS.

philadelphus *n.* a strongly-scented flowering shrub of the genus *Philadelphus*. WH: 18C. Modern Latin, from Greek *philadelphos* loving one's brother, from *phil-* PHILO- + *adelphos* brother. The plant is presumably so called as a generally agreeable name.

philander *v.i.* (of a man) to have casual affairs with women, to flirt. WH: 18C. From obs. *philander* lover, from Greek *philandros* loving men, fond of one's husband, from *phil-* PHILO- + *anēr*, *andros* man, male, husband. The word was originally the name of a lover in literature, e.g. in Congreve's *The Way of the World* (1700). The name itself may have been popularly understood to mean a loving man.

philanthropy *n.* love of humankind. WH: 17C. Late Latin *philanthropia*, from Greek *philanthrōpia*, from *philanthrōpos*, from *phil-* PHILO- + *anthrōpos* man. See also -Y².

philately *n.* the collecting of postage stamps. WH: 19C. French *philatélie*, from Greek PHILO- + *atelēs* free of charge, *ateleia* exemption from payment. Greek *atelēs* was adopted to mean postage stamp since a stamp shows prepayment of the postal charge. The word was coined in 1864 by the French stamp collector George Herpin.

-phile *comb. form* a lover of, or loving, as in *bibliophile*, *Anglophile*. WH: Greek *philos* loving, dear.

philharmonic *a.* loving music. *Also n.* WH: 18C. French *philharmonique*, from Italian *filarmonico*. See PHILO-, HARMONY, also -IC.

philhellene *n.* a friend or lover of Greece and Greeks. *Also a.* WH: 19C. Greek *philellēn* loving the Greeks. See PHILO-, HELLENE.

-philia *comb. form* love of, as in *necrophilia*. WH: Greek *philia* friendship, fondness.

philippic *n.* a speech or declamation full of acrimonious invective. WH: 16C. Latin *philippicus*, from Greek *philippikos*, from *Philippos* Philip. The reference is to Philip II of Macedon, 382–336 BC, attacked by the orator Demosthenes in a series of speeches in an attempt to arouse Athenians to resist Philip's growing power.

Philippine *a.* of or relating to the Philippines. WH: 19C. Spanish FILIPINO of the Philippines, an island country in SE Asia.

Philistine *n.* a member of an ancient warlike people in S Palestine who were hostile to the Jews. *Also a.* WH: 12–14C. French *Philistin* or Late Latin *Philistinus*, from Late Greek *Philistinoi*, from Hebrew *pĕlištī*, rel. to *pĕlešet* Philistia, Palestine. The sense commonplace, uncultured arose in the 19C from German *Philister*, a name applied by German university students to townsmen or outsiders.

Phillips® *a.* denoting a screw having a cross-shaped slot in the head, or a screwdriver for use with such a screw. WH: mid-20C. Henry F. *Phillips* of Portland, Oregon, its US manufacturer.

phillipsite *n.* a monoclinic hydrous silicate of aluminium, potassium and calcium. WH: 19C. William *Phillips*, 1775–1828, English mineralogist and geologist + -ITE[1].

phillumeny *n.* the collecting of matchboxes or matchbox labels. WH: mid-20C. PHILO- + Latin *lumen* light + -Y[2].

Philly *n.* Philadelphia. WH: 19C. Abbr. of *Philadelphia*, a city and port of Pennsylvania, USA. See also -Y[3].

philo- *comb. form* fond of, affecting, inhabiting. WH: Greek, from *philein* to love, *philos* dear, friend. See also -O-.

philodendron *n.* any of various plants of the genus *Philodendron* (arum family), cultivated for their showy foliage. WH: 19C. Modern Latin, from Greek, neut. of *philodendros* fond of trees, from PHILO- + *dendron* tree. The plant is so called because it clings to trees.

philogyny *n.* devotion to women. WH: 17C. Greek *philogunia* love of women, from PHILO- + *gunē* woman.

philology *n.* the historical or comparative study of language. WH: 14–15C. French *philologie*, from Latin *philologia*, from Greek, love of learning or literature, from *philologos* fond of talking, fond of studying words. See PHILO-, LOGOS.

philomath *n.* a lover of learning, esp. of mathematics, a scholar. WH: 17C. Greek *philomathēs* fond of learning, from PHILO- + *math-*, base of *manthanein* to learn. Cp. MATHEMATICAL.

Philomel *n.* the nightingale. WH: 14–15C. Latin *philomela*, from Greek *philomēla* nightingale, from *Philomēla*, Procne's sister in Greek mythology, who was transformed into a nightingale. The name itself is popularly derived from Greek PHILO- + *melos* song.

philopena *n.* a game in which two people share the double kernel of a nut, the first being entitled to a forfeit, under certain conditions, on the next meeting with the other sharer. WH: 19C. Alt. of German *Vielliebchen*, dim. from *viellieb* very dear, from *viel* much + *lieb* dear, as if from *Philippchen* little Philip.

philoprogenitive *a.* prolific. WH: 19C. PHILO- + *progenitive* (PROGENITOR). The *n. philoprogenitiveness* was coined in 1815 by the German phrenologist Johann Spurzheim.

philosopher *n.* a person who studies philosophy. WH: 12–14C. Anglo-French *filosofre*, *philosophre*, var. of Old French *philosophe*, from Latin *philosophus*, from Greek *philosophos* lover of wisdom, from PHILO- + *sophos* wise.

philosophy *n.* the investigation of ultimate reality or of general principles of existence. WH: 12–14C. Old French *filosofie* (Modern French *philosophie*), from Latin *philosophia*, from Greek, from *philosophos* PHILOSOPHER. See also -Y[2].

philtre *n.* a love potion. *Also v.t.* WH: 16C. French, from Latin *philtrum*, from Greek *philtron* love potion, from *phil-*, stem of *philein* to love, *philos* loving + instr. suf. *-tron*.

-phily *comb. form* love of, as in *cartophily*. WH: Anglicized form of -PHILIA.

phimosis *n.* constriction of the opening of the foreskin. WH: 17C. Modern Latin, from Greek *phimōsis* muzzling.

phiz *n.* the face. WH: 17C. Abbr. of PHYSIOGNOMY.

phlebitis *n.* inflammation of the inner membrane of a vein. WH: 19C. PHLEBO- + -ITIS.

phlebo- *comb. form* a vein. WH: Greek *phleps*, *phlebos* vein. See also -O-.

phlebolite *n.* a calculus in a vein. WH: 19C. PHLEBO- + -LITE.

phlebotomy *n.* the opening of a vein, bloodletting. WH: 14–15C. Old French *flebothomi* (Modern French *phlébotomie*), from Late Latin *phlebotomia*, from Greek, from *phlebotomos* that which opens a vein. See PHLEBO-, -TOMY.

phlegm *n.* viscid mucus secreted in the air passages or stomach, esp. as a morbid product and discharged by coughing etc. WH: 12–14C. Old French *fleume* (Modern French *flegme*), from Late Latin *phlegma* clammy moisture of the body, from Greek inflammation, morbid state resulting from heat, from *phlegein* to burn. Phlegm was originally the name of one of the four bodily humours, here the one believed to cause indolence or apathy. The sense sluggishness, apathy arose in the 16C from the belief that such a condition was the result of a predominance of phlegm in the constitution.

phlegmon *n.* a tumour or inflammation of the cellular tissue.

WH: 14–15C. Latin, from Greek *phlegmonē* inflammation, boil, from *phlegein* to burn.

phloem *n.* the softer cellular portion of fibrovascular tissue in plants, the bark and the tissues closely connected with it, as opposed to *xylem*. WH: 19C. Greek *phloos* bark + pass. suf. *-ēma*.

phlogiston *n.* the principle of inflammability formerly supposed to be a necessary constituent of combustible bodies. WH: 18C. Greek, from *phlogizein* to set on fire, from *phlox*, *phlogos* flame, from *phleg-*, base of *phlegein* to burn.

phlox *n.* a plant of the genus *Phlox*, with clusters of showy flowers. WH: 18C. Modern Latin, from Latin flame-coloured flower, from Greek, lit. flame. Cp. PHLOGISTON.

phlyctena *n.* a vesicle, pimple or blister, esp. on the eyeball. WH: 17C. Modern Latin, from Greek *phluktaina* blister, from *phluein*, *phluzein* to swell.

-phobe *comb. form* a person who fears or hates, as in *homophobe*, *Francophobe*. WH: French, from Latin *-phobus*, from Greek *-phobos* fearing, from *phobos* fear.

phobia *n.* an irrational fear or hatred. WH: 18C. Independent adoption of *-phobia*, from Greek *-phobos*. See -PHOBE, also -IA.

phoca *n.* a seal. WH: 16C. Latin, from Greek *phōkē*.

phoebe *n.* any American flycatcher of the genus *Sayornis*. WH: 18C. Imit. of the bird's call, with assim. to *Phoebe*, name of Artemis or Diana in Greek mythology as goddess of the sun. See PHOEBUS.

Phoebus *n.* the sun. WH: 14–15C. Latin, from Greek *Phoibos*, name of Apollo in Greek mythology as the sun god, from *phoibos*, lit. bright, shining.

Phoenician *a.* of or relating to Phoenicia. *Also n.* WH: 14–15C. *Phoenicia*, an ancient country on the E Mediterranean approximating to modern Lebanon + -AN.

phoenix *n.* a mythical Arabian bird, the only one of its kind, said to live for 500 or 600 years in the desert, burn itself on a funeral pyre, and rise again in renewed youth. WH: pre-1200. Old French *fenix* (Modern French *phénix*), from Latin *phoenix*, from Greek *phoinix* phoenix, date palm, of unknown orig.

pholas *n.* a member of the genus *Pholas* of stone-boring bivalves, a piddock. WH: 17C. Modern Latin, from Greek *phōlas* that which lurks in a hole, from *phōleos* hole.

phon *n.* a unit of loudness. WH: mid-20C. Greek *phōnē* sound, voice.

phonate *v.i.* to make a vocal sound. *Also v.t.* WH: 19C. Greek *phōnē* sound, voice + -ATE[3].

phonautograph *n.* an apparatus for recording the vibrations of sounds. WH: 19C. French *phonautographe*. See PHONO-, AUTO-, -GRAPH.

phone[1] *v.t.*, *v.i.* to telephone. *Also n.* WH: 19C. Abbr. of TELEPHONE.

phone[2] *n.* an articulate sound, such as a simple vowel or consonant. WH: 19C. Greek *phōnē* sound, voice.

-phone *comb. form* sound, voice, a device producing sound, as in *telephone*. WH: Greek *phōnē* sound, voice, *phōnos* sounding.

phoneme *n.* any one of the smallest distinctive group of phones in a language. WH: 19C. French *phonème*, from Greek *phōnēma* sound, speech, from *phōnein* to speak.

phonendoscope *n.* a variety of stethoscope for enabling small sounds, esp. within the human body, to be distinctly heard. WH: 19C. PHONO- + ENDO- + -SCOPE.

phonetic *a.* of or relating to the voice or vocal sounds. WH: 19C. Modern Latin *phoneticus*, from Greek *phōnētikos*, from *phōnētos* to be spoken, p.p. formation from *phōnein* to speak, from *phōnē* sound, voice. See also -ETIC.

phoney *a.* false, counterfeit. *Also n.* WH: 19C. Orig. unknown. According to some, the word is perhaps an alteration of slang *fawney* finger ring used by swindlers, from Irish *fáinne* ring.

phonic *a.* of or relating to sounds, acoustic. WH: 19C. Greek *phōnē* sound, voice + -IC.

phono *a.* denoting a type of plug, and the socket with which it is used, in which one conductor is cylindrical and the other a longer, central part. WH: mid-20C. Abbr. of *phonograph* (see PHONOGRAM).

phono- *comb. form* sound. WH: Greek *phōnē* sound, voice. See also -O-.

phonogram *n.* a written character indicating a particular spoken sound. WH: 19C. PHONO- + -GRAM.

phonolite n. clinkstone. WH: 19C. PHONO- + -LITE. The rock is so called from its resonance when struck with a hammer.

phonology n. the science of the vocal sounds. WH: 18C. PHONO- + -O- + -LOGY.

phonometer n. an instrument for recording the number and intensity of vibrations, esp. of sound waves. WH: 19C. PHONO- + -METER.

phonon n. a quantum of vibrational energy in a crystal lattice. WH: mid-20C. PHONO- + -ON.

phonopore n. a device attached to a telegraph wire for allowing telephonic messages to be sent over the line at the same time as telegraphic messages, without interference from the current transmitting the latter. WH: 19C. PHONO- + Greek *poros* passage.

phonoscope n. an instrument of various kinds for translating sound vibrations into visible figures. WH: 19C. PHONO- + -SCOPE.

phonotype n. a character used in phonetic printing. WH: 19C. PHONO- + TYPE.

phooey int. used to express disbelief or dismissal. WH: early 20C. From *phoo* (17C), natural exclamation expressing rejection, dismissal, reproach, etc. + -Y[1]. Cp. POOH.

-phore comb. form bearer, as in *gonophore, semaphore*. WH: Modern Latin *-phorus*, from Greek *-phoros, -phoron* bearing, bearer, from *pherein* to bear.

-phoresis comb. form transmission, as in *electrophoresis*. WH: Greek *phorēsis* being carried.

phoresy n. an association in which one organism is carried by another without feeding on it. WH: early 20C. French *phorésie*, from Greek *phorēsis*. See -PHORESIS, also -Y[2].

phormium n. any plant of the New Zealand genus *Phormium*, having evergreen leaves and red or yellow flowers. WH: 19C. Modern Latin, from Greek *phormion*, dim. of *phormos* mat, basket. The plant is so called from the use to which its fibres are put.

phosgene n. gaseous carbon oxychloride, used as a poison gas. WH: 19C. Greek *phōs* light + -*gene*, var. of -GEN. The word was coined in 1812 by the British chemist John Davy.

phosphate n. any salt of phosphoric acid. WH: 18C. French. See PHOSPHO-, also -ATE[1].

phosphene n. a luminous image produced by pressure on the eyeball, caused by irritation of the retina. WH: 19C. Greek *phōs* light + *phainein* to show.

phosphide n. a combination of phosphorus with another element or radical. WH: 19C. PHOSPHO- + -IDE.

phosphine n. a colourless, fishy-smelling gas, which is slightly soluble. WH: 19C. PHOSPHO- + -INE, based on AMINE.

phosphite n. any salt of phosphorous acid. WH: 18C. French. See PHOSPHO-, also -ITE[1].

phospho- comb. form containing phosphorus. WH: PHOSPHORUS. See also -O-.

phospholipid n. any lipid which consists of a phosphate group and one or more fatty acids. WH: early 20C. PHOSPHO- + LIPID.

phosphor n. phosphorus. WH: 17C. Latin PHOSPHORUS.

phosphoroscope n. an apparatus for measuring the duration of phosphorescence. WH: 19C. From *phosphorescence* (from PHOSPHOR + -ESCENCE) + -O- + -SCOPE.

phosphorus n. a non-metallic element, at. no. 15, chem. symbol P, occurring in two allotropic forms, white phosphorus, which is waxy, poisonous, spontaneously combustible at room temperature and appears luminous, and red phosphorus which is non-poisonous and ignites only when heated. WH: 17C. Latin, from Greek *phōsphoros* light-bringing, from *phōs* light + -*phoros* -PHORE.

phosphorylate v.t. to introduce a phosphate group into (a compound etc.). WH: mid-20C. PHOSPHORUS + -YL + -ATE[3].

phossy jaw n. gangrene of the jaw caused by the fumes of phosphorus, esp. in the manufacture of matches. WH: 19C. From *phos*, abbr. of PHOSPHORUS + -Y[1] + JAW.

phot n. the unit of illumination, one lumen per square centimetre. WH: 19C. French, from Greek *phōs, phōtos* light.

photic a. of or relating to light. WH: 19C. Greek *phōs, phōtos* light + -IC.

photism n. a hallucinatory sensation of colour accompanying some other sensation. WH: 19C. Greek *phōtismos* illumination, from *phōtizein* to shine, to illuminate, from *phōs, phōtos* light. See also -ISM.

photo n. a photograph. Also v.t., a. WH: 19C. Abbr. of PHOTOGRAPH.

photo- comb. form of or relating to light or to photography. WH: From Greek *phōto-*, comb. form of *phōs, phōtos* light (see also -O-), or from *photographic, photography* (PHOTOGRAPH).

photobiology n. the study of the effect of light on living organisms. WH: mid-20C. PHOTO- + BIOLOGY.

photocall n. an occasion when someone is photographed by arrangement for publicity purposes. WH: mid-20C. PHOTO- + CALL.

photocell n. a photoelectric cell. WH: 19C. PHOTO- + CELL.

photochemical a. of, relating to or produced by the chemical action of light. WH: 19C. PHOTO- + CHEMICAL.

photochromic a. changing colour in response to the incidence of radiant energy. WH: mid-20C. PHOTO- + Greek *khrōma* colour + -IC.

photochronograph n. an instrument for taking a series of photographs, for example of moving objects, at regular intervals of time. WH: 19C. PHOTO- + CHRONOGRAPH.

photocomposition n. filmsetting. WH: early 20C. PHOTO- + COMPOSITION.

photoconductivity n. electrical conductivity that varies with the incidence of radiation, esp. light. WH: early 20C. PHOTO- + conductivity (CONDUCT[2]).

photocopy n. a photographic reproduction of matter that is written, printed etc. Also v.t. WH: early 20C. PHOTO- + COPY.

photodegradable a. capable of being decomposed by the action of sunlight. WH: late 20C. PHOTO- + *degradable* (DEGRADE).

photodiode n. a semiconductor diode, whose conductivity is controlled by incident illumination. WH: mid-20C. PHOTO- + DIODE.

photoelectric a. of or relating to photoelectricity, or to the combined action of light and electricity. WH: 19C. PHOTO- + ELECTRIC.

photoelectron n. an electron emitted during photoemission. WH: early 20C. PHOTO- + ELECTRON.

photoemission n. the emission of electrons from a substance on which radiation falls. WH: early 20C. PHOTO- + EMISSION.

photoengraving n. any process for producing printing blocks by means of photography. WH: 19C. PHOTO- + *engraving* (ENGRAVE).

photofit n. (a method of composing) a likeness of someone's face consisting of photographs of parts of faces, used for the identification of criminal suspects. WH: late 20C. PHOTO- + FIT[1].

photogen n. a light hydrocarbon obtained by distilling coal, shale, peat etc., used for burning in lamps. WH: 19C. PHOTO- + -GEN.

photogenic a. looking attractive in photographs or in cinema films. WH: 19C. PHOTO- + -GENIC. The original sense was produced by light. The current general sense evolved in the early 20C.

photogram n. an image produced with photographic material, but without a camera. WH: 19C. Alt. of PHOTOGRAPH, based on TELEGRAM.

photogrammetry n. the technique of taking measurements from photographs, e.g. making maps from aerial photographs. WH: 19C. PHOTO- + -GRAM + -METRY.

photograph n. a picture etc. taken by means of photography. Also v.t., v.i. WH: 19C. PHOTO- + -GRAPH. The word was introduced in 1839 by the English astronomer Sir John Herschel, together with *photographic* and *photography*.

photogravure n. the process of producing an intaglio plate for printing by the transfer of a photographic negative to the plate and subsequent etching. Also v.t. WH: 19C. French, from *photo-* PHOTO- + *gravure* engraving, from *graver* to engrave. See also -URE.

photojournalism n. journalism featuring photographs more than or instead of text. WH: mid-20C. PHOTO- + *journalism* (JOURNAL).

photolithography n. a mode of producing by photography designs upon stones etc., from which impressions may be taken at a lithographic press. WH: 19C. PHOTO- + *lithography* (LITHOGRAPH).

photolysis n. decomposition resulting from the incidence of radiation. WH: early 20C. PHOTO- + -*lysis* (LYSIS).

photomechanical a. of or relating to a process by which photographic images are reproduced or employed in printing by mechanical means. WH: 19C. PHOTO- + MECHANICAL.

photometer n. an instrument for measuring the relative intensity of light. WH: 18C. PHOTO- + -METER.

photomicrography n. the process of making magnified photographs of microscopic objects. WH: 19C. PHOTO- + MICRO- + *photography* (PHOTOGRAPH).

photomontage *n.* a means of producing pictures by the montage of many photographic images. WH: mid-20C. PHOTO- + MONTAGE.

photomultiplier *n.* a photocell with a series of electrodes, used to detect and amplify light from faint sources. WH: mid-20C. PHOTO- + *multiplier* (MULTIPLY).

photon *n.* the unit of light intensity. WH: early 20C. PHOTO- + -ON.

photonovel *n.* a novel presented as a series of photographs with speech bubbles. WH: late 20C. PHOTO- + NOVEL.

photo-offset *n.* offset printing from photolithographic plates. WH: early 20C. PHOTO- + *offset* (from OFF + SET[2]).

photoperiod *n.* the period of daylight in every 24 hours which an organism receives. WH: early 20C. PHOTO- + PERIOD.

photophobia *n.* abnormal shrinking from or intolerance of light. WH: 18C. PHOTO- + -*phobia* (-PHOBE).

photophone *n.* an instrument for transmitting sounds by the agency of light. WH: 19C. PHOTO- + -PHONE.

photophore *n.* any organ that emits light. WH: 19C. Greek *phōtophoros* light-bearing. See PHOTO-, -PHORE.

photopia *n.* vision in normal daylight. WH: early 20C. PHOTO- + -OPIA.

photo-process *n.* any photomechanical process. WH: 19C. PHOTO- + PROCESS[1].

photopsia *n.* a disorder of the eye causing the patient to see lines, flashes of light etc. WH: 19C. PHOTO- + Greek *opsis* vision. See also -IA.

photorealism *n.* meticulous realism in art, esp. depicting mundane or sordid subjects. WH: mid-20C. PHOTO- + REALISM.

photoreceptor *n.* a nerve ending receptive to light. WH: early 20C. PHOTO- + *receptor* (RECEPTION).

photo-relief *n.* an image in relief produced by a photographic process. *Also a.* WH: 19C. PHOTO- + RELIEF[2].

photosensitive *a.* sensitive to the action of light. WH: 19C. PHOTO- + SENSITIVE.

photosetting *n.* filmsetting. WH: mid-20C. PHOTO- + SET[1] + -ING[1].

photosphere *n.* the luminous envelope of the sun or a star. WH: 17C. PHOTO- + SPHERE, based on ATMOSPHERE.

Photostat® *n.* a type of photocopier. *Also v.t.* WH: early 20C. PHOTO- + -STAT.

photosynthesis *n.* the process by which carbohydrates are produced from carbon dioxide and water through the agency of light, esp. when it occurs in green plants. WH: 19C. PHOTO- + SYNTHESIS.

phototherapy *n.* the treatment of skin diseases by means of certain kinds of light rays. WH: 19C. PHOTO- + *therapy* (THERAPEUTIC).

phototransistor *n.* a transistor which responds to incident light by generating and amplifying an electric current. WH: mid-20C. PHOTO- + TRANSISTOR.

phototropism *n.* tropism due to the influence of light. WH: 19C. PHOTO- + TROPISM.

phototype *n.* a printing plate produced by photoengraving. WH: 19C. PHOTO- + TYPE.

photovoltaic *a.* of or relating to the production of electric current caused by electromagnetic radiation. WH: early 20C. PHOTO- + *voltaic* (VOLT[1]).

photoxylography *n.* engraving on wood from photographs printed on the block. WH: 19C. PHOTO- + *xylography* (XYLOGRAPH).

photozincography *n.* the process of producing an engraving on zinc by photomechanical means for printing in a manner analogous to photolithography. WH: 19C. PHOTO- + *zincography* (ZINC).

phrase *n.* an expression denoting a single idea or forming a distinct part of a sentence. *Also v.t.* WH: 16C. Latin *phrasis*, from Greek speech, manner of speaking, from *phrazein* to indicate, to declare, to tell.

phraseogram *n.* a character standing for a whole phrase, for example in shorthand. WH: 19C. PHRASE + -O- + -GRAM.

phraseology *n.* a choice or arrangement of words. WH: 17C. Modern Latin *phraseologia*, from Greek *phraseōn*, gen. pl. of *phrasis* PHRASE. See -LOGY.

phratry *n.* any tribal subdivision based on shared ancestry. WH: 19C. Greek *phratria*, from *phratēr* clansman. Cp. BROTHER.

phreak *n.* a phone freak. WH: late 20C. Alt. of FREAK, based on PHONE[1].

phreatic *a.* of or relating to groundwater. WH: 19C. Greek *phrear*, *phreatos* well, cistern + -IC.

phrenic *a.* of or relating to the diaphragm. *Also n.* WH: 18C. French *phrénique*, from Greek *phrēn*, *phrenos* diaphragm, mind. See also -IC. The mind was at one time thought to be located in the diaphragm.

phrenitis *n.* encephalitis. WH: 17C. Greek *phrēnitis* delirium, from *phren*-. See PHRENIC, also -ITIS.

phreno- *comb. form* the mind. WH: Greek *phrēn*, *phrenos* diaphragm, mind. See PHRENIC, also -O-.

phrenology *n.* the theory that the mental faculties and affections are located in distinct parts of the brain denoted by prominences on the skull. WH: 19C. PHRENO- + -LOGY. The word was coined in or shortly before 1815 by the German phrenologist Johann Spurzheim and his colleague Franz-Joseph Gall, a Viennese doctor.

phrontistery *n.* a place for thought or study. WH: 17C. Greek *phrontistēron*, from *phrontistēs* deep thinker, from *phrontizein* to be thoughtful, from *phrontis* thought.

Phrygian *a.* of or relating to Phrygia, an ancient country in Asia Minor. *Also n.* WH: 15C. Latin *Phrygianus*, from *Phrygia*, an ancient country of Asia Minor. See also -IAN.

phthalic *a.* of, relating to or derived from naphthalene. WH: 19C. From *naphthalic* (NAPHTHA).

phthiriasis *n.* a condition in which lice multiply on the skin. WH: 16C. Latin, from Greek *phtheiriasis*, from *phtheirian* to be infested with lice, from *phtheir* louse. See also -IASIS.

phthisic *a.* of or relating to phthisis. *Also n.* WH: 12–14C. Old French *tisike*, later *ptisique*, from use as n. of fem. of Latin *phthisicus*, from Greek *phthisikos* consumptive, from *phthisis*. See PHTHISIS, also -IC.

phthisis *n.* a wasting disease, esp. pulmonary tuberculosis. WH: 16C. Latin, from Greek, from *phthinein* to waste away.

phut *n.* a dull bang. WH: 19C. Imit., or from Hindi and Sanskrit *phaṭ* a crack, the sound of a slap.

phycology *n.* the botany of seaweeds or algae. WH: 19C. Greek *phukos* seaweed + -O- + -LOGY.

phycomycete *n.* any of various fungi which form a non-septate mycelium. WH: mid-20C. Anglicized sing. of Modern Latin *Phycomycetes*, from Greek *phukos* seaweed + *mukētes*, pl. of *mukēs* fungus. The fungi are so called from their resemblance to algae (seaweed).

phylactery *n.* a small leather box in which are enclosed slips of vellum inscribed with passages from the Pentateuch, worn on the head and left arm by Jews during morning prayer, except on the Sabbath. WH: 14–15C. Old French *filatiere*, from Late Latin *fylacterium*, *phylacterium* safeguard, amulet, from Greek *phulaktērion*, from *phulaktēr* guard, from *phulak*-, stem of *phulassein* to guard.

phyletic *a.* of or relating to a phylum, racial. WH: 19C. Greek *phuletikos*, from *phuletēs* tribesman, from *phulē* tribe, race. See also -ETIC.

-phyll *comb. form* a leaf, as in *chlorophyll*. WH: Greek *phullon* leaf.

phyllite *n.* an argillaceous schist or slate. WH: 19C. Greek *phullon* leaf + -ITE[1].

phyllo- *comb. form* a leaf. WH: Greek *phullon* leaf. See also -O-.

phyllobranchia *n.* a gill of a leaflike or lamellar structure, as in certain crustaceans. WH: 19C. Modern Latin, from PHYLLO- + Greek *bragkhia* gills.

phyllode *n.* a petiole having the appearance and functions of a leaf. WH: 19C. Modern Latin *phyllodium*, from Greek *phullōdēs* leaflike, from *phullon* leaf. See also -ODE[1].

phyllomania *n.* abnormal production of leaves. WH: 17C. PHYLLO- + -MANIA.

phyllome *n.* a leaf or organ analogous to a leaf. WH: 19C. Modern Latin *phylloma*, or from Greek *phullōma* foliage, from *phulloun* to clothe with leaves, from *phullon* leaf. See also -OME.

phyllophagous *a.* feeding on leaves. WH: 19C. PHYLLO- + -PHAGOUS.

phyllopod *n.* any crustacean of the order Phyllopoda, having at least four pairs of leaflike feet. WH: 19C. PHYLLO- + -POD.

phylloquinone *n.* a vitamin found in leafy green vegetables, and essential for blood-clotting; vitamin K_1. WH: mid-20C. PHYLLO- + QUINONE.

phyllotaxis *n.* the arrangement of the leaves etc. on the stem or axis of a plant. WH: 19C. PHYLLO- + Greek TAXIS arrangement, order.

phylloxera *n.* an aphid or plant-louse, *Daktulosphaira vitifoliae*, orig. from America, very destructive to grapevines. WH: 19C. Modern Latin , from PHYLLO- + Greek *xēros* dry. The term was coined in 1834 for a species of plant-louse that was observed to dry up the leaves of oak trees in Provence.

phylo- *comb. form* a tribe, a race. WH: Greek *phulē* tribe, race. See also -O-.

phylogeny *n.* the evolution of a group, species or type of plant or animal life. WH: 18C. PHYLO- + -GENY. The term was coined in 1866 by the German biologist Ernst Haeckel.

phylum *n.* a primary group consisting of related organisms descended from a common form. WH: 19C. Greek *phulon* tribe, race.

physalia *n.* any member of the genus *Physalia* of large oceanic hydrozoons, including the Portuguese man-of-war. WH: 19C. Modern Latin, from Greek *phusaleos* inflated with wind, from *phusallis* bladder.

physalis *n.* any plant of the genus *Physalis*, having fruit in lantern-like calyxes. WH: 19C. Modern Latin, from Greek *phusallis* bladder.

physic *n.* a medicine, esp. a purge or cathartic. *Also v.t.* WH: 12–14C. Old French *fisique* medicine (Modern French *physique*), from Latin *physica*, from Greek *phusikē*, use as n. of fem. of *phusikos* natural, from *phusis* nature. See also -IC.

physical *a.* bodily, corporeal, as opposed to *spiritual*. *Also n.* WH: 14–15C. Medieval Latin *physicalis*, from Latin *physica*. See PHYSIC, also -IC, -AL[1].

physician *n.* a person versed in or practising the art of healing, including medicine and surgery. WH: 12–14C. Old French *fisicien* (Modern French *physicien* physicist), from *fisique*. See PHYSIC, also -ICIAN.

physicist *n.* a person versed in physics. WH: 18C. PHYSIC, PHYSICS + -IST.

physico- *comb. form* physical. WH: PHYSIC, PHYSICS + -O-.

physico-chemical *a.* of or relating to physics and chemistry. WH: 17C. PHYSICO- + CHEMICAL.

physics *n.* the science dealing with the phenomena of matter, esp. as affected by energy, and the laws governing these, excluding biology and chemistry. WH: 15C. Pl. of PHYSIC (a. used as n.), translating Latin *physica* (neut. pl.), from Greek *ta phusika* the natural (things), collective title of Aristotle's treatises, from *phusis* nature. See also -ICS.

physio *n.* a physiotherapist. WH: mid-20C. Abbr. of *physiotherapist* (PHYSIOTHERAPY).

physio- *comb. form* of or relating to nature. WH: Partly from Greek *phusio-*, from *phusis* nature, partly from PHYSIOLOGY. See also -O-.

physiocracy *n.* government according to a natural order, taught by François Quesnay, 1694–1774, founder of the physiocrats, to be inherent in society. WH: 19C. French *physiocratie*. See PHYSIO-, -CRACY.

physiognomy *n.* the art of reading character from features of the face or the form of the body. WH: 14–15C. Old French *phisonomie* (Modern French *physionomie*), from Medieval Latin *phisonomia*, *physionomia*, Late Latin *physognomia*, from Late Greek *phusiognōmia*, contr. of Greek *phusiognōmonia*, from *phusis* nature + *gnōmōn*, *gnōmonos* interpreter. See also -Y[2]. The *g* entered the English word from the 16C.

physiography *n.* the scientific description of the physical features of the earth, and the causes by which they have been modified; physical geography. WH: 19C. PHYSIO- + -GRAPHY.

physiolatry *n.* nature-worship. WH: 19C. PHYSIO- + -LATRY.

physiology *n.* the science of the vital phenomena and the organic functions of animals and plants. WH: 16C. French *physiologie* or Latin *physiologia*, from Greek *phusiologia* natural philosophy. See PHYSIO-, -LOGY.

physiotherapy *n.* a form of medical treatment in which physical agents such as movement of limbs, massage, electricity etc. are used in place of drugs or surgery. WH: early 20C. PHYSIO- + *therapy* (THERAPEUTIC).

physique *n.* the physical structure or constitution of a person. WH: 19C. French, use as n. of a., physical. See PHYSIC.

physitheism *n.* deification of natural forces or phenomena. WH: 19C. Greek *phusis* nature + *theos* god + -ISM.

physoclistous *a.* having the air bladder closed and not connected with the intestines. WH: 19C. Greek *phusa* bladder + *kleistos* closed. See also -OUS.

physostomous *a.* having the air bladder connected by a duct with the intestinal canal. WH: 19C. Greek *phusa* bladder + *stoma* mouth + -OUS.

-phyte *comb. form* denoting a vegetable organism, as in *zoophyte*. WH: Greek *phuton* plant. See PHYTO-.

phyto- *comb. form* plant. WH: Greek *phuton* plant, from *phu-* BE, to grow. See also -O-.

phytochemistry *n.* the chemistry of plants. WH: 19C. PHYTO- + CHEMISTRY.

phytochrome *n.* a blue-green pigment found in most plants, which regulates many light-dependent processes. WH: 19C. PHYTO- + Greek *khrōma* colour.

phytogenesis *n.* the origin, generation or evolution of plants. WH: 19C. PHYTO- + GENESIS.

phytogeography *n.* the geographical distribution of plants. WH: 19C. PHYTO- + GEOGRAPHY.

phytography *n.* the systematic description and naming of plants. WH: 17C. PHYTO- + -GRAPHY.

phyton *n.* a plant unit. WH: 19C. French, from Greek *phuton*. See PHYTO-, also -ON.

phytopathology *n.* the science of the diseases of plants. WH: 19C. PHYTO- + PATHOLOGY.

phytophagous *a.* plant-eating. WH: 19C. PHYTO- + -PHAGOUS.

phytoplankton *n.* plant life as a constituent of plankton. WH: 19C. PHYTO- + PLANKTON.

phytotomy *n.* the dissection of plants. WH: 19C. PHYTO- + -TOMY.

phytotoxin *n.* any toxin derived from a plant. WH: early 20C. PHYTO- + TOXIN.

pi[1] *n.* the 16th letter of the Greek alphabet (Π, π). WH: 14–15C. Greek. As symbol representing the ratio of the circumference of a circle to its diameter, initial letter of Greek *periphereia* or English PERIPHERY. The mathematical symbol was adopted by the Swiss mathematician Leonhard Euler in his *Introductio in analysin infinitorum* (1748).

pi[2] *a.* pious. WH: 19C. Abbr. of PIOUS.

pia *n.* any Polynesian herb of the genus *Tacca*, esp. *T. leontopetaloides*, yielding a variety of arrowroot. WH: 19C. Polynesian.

piacular *a.* expiatory. WH: 17C. Latin *piacularis*, from *piaculum*, from *piare* to appease. See also -CLE, -AR[1].

piaffe *v.i.* (of a horse) to move at a piaffer. *Also n.* WH: 18C. French *piaffer* to strut, to make a show, of imit. orig.

pia mater *n.* a delicate membrane, the innermost of the three meninges enveloping the brain and spinal cord. WH: 14–15C. Medieval Latin tender mother, translating Arabic *al-'umm ar-raḳīḳa* thin mother, tender mother. See DURA MATER.

pianette *n.* a small piano. WH: 19C. PIANO[1] + -ETTE.

pianino *n.* a small piano. WH: 19C. Italian, dim. of *piano*. See PIANO[1].

pianissimo *adv.* very softly. *Also a., n.* WH: 18C. Italian, superl. of PIANO[2].

piano[1] *n.* a musical instrument, the sounds of which are produced by blows on the wire strings from hammers acted upon by levers set in motion by keys. WH: 19C. Italian, abbr. of PIANOFORTE or shortened form of *fortepiano* (FORTE[2]).

piano[2] *adv.* softly. *Also a., n.* WH: 17C. Italian, from Latin *planus* flat, later (of sound) soft, low.

pianoforte *n.* a piano. WH: 18C. Italian, earlier *piano e forte*, lit. soft and loud. The instrument is so called from its capacity to produce gradations of tone, as distinct from the unvarying tone of the harpsichord.

Pianola® *n.* a type of player-piano. WH: 19C. Appar. dim. of PIANO[1] formed by adding *-ola*, ? based on VIOLA[1].

piano nobile *n.* the main floor of a large house. WH: 19C. Italian, from *piano* floor, storey (PIANO[2]) + *nobile* noble, great.

piassava *n.* a coarse stiff fibre obtained from Brazilian palms, used esp. to make ropes and brushes. WH: 19C. Portuguese, from Tupi *piaçába*.

piastre *n.* a small coin of Turkey and several former dependencies. WH: 16C. French, from Italian *piastra* (*d'argento*) plate (of silver), from Latin *emplastra*, *emplastrum* PLASTER.

piazza *n.* a square open space, public square or market place, esp. in an Italian town. **WH:** 16C. Italian, rel. to French *place* PLACE. Cp. PLAZA. The sense was extended in the 17C to a covered gallery or walk around a square, as the Piazza, Covent Garden, London.

pibroch *n.* a series of variations, chiefly martial, played on the bagpipes. **WH:** 18C. Gaelic *pìobaireachd* the art of playing the bagpipes, from *pìobair* piper (from *pìob* pipe, from English *pipe*) + *-achd*, suf. of function.

pic *n.* a picture. **WH:** 19C. Abbr. of PICTURE.

pica[1] *n.* a unit of type size (one sixth of an inch). **WH:** 18C. Anglo-Latin book of rules for determining dates of holy days (supposed to have been printed in this type size), prob. from Latin *pica* magpie, PIE[2]. The book was so called from the colour and jumbled appearance of the black type, which looked 'pied' on the white paper.

pica[2] *n.* an appetite affected by illness etc. causing a person to crave for things unfit for food, such as coal and chalk. **WH:** 16C. Latin magpie, PIE[2], prob. translating Greek *kissa*, *kitta* magpie, false appetite.

picador *n.* in Spanish bullfights, a horseman with a lance who goads the bull. **WH:** 18C. Spanish, from *picar* to prick, to pierce.

picamar *n.* an oily compound, one of the products of the distillation of wood tar. **WH:** 19C. Latin *pix*, *picis* pitch + *amarus* bitter.

picaresque *a.* describing the exploits and adventures of rogues or vagabonds, of or relating to a style of fiction describing the episodic adventures of an errant rogue. **WH:** 19C. French, from Spanish *picaresco*, from *pícaro* roguish, knavish. See also -ESQUE. Cp. PICAROON.

†picaroon *n.* a rogue, a vagabond. **WH:** 17C. Spanish *picarón*, augm. of *pícaro*. See PICARESQUE, also -OON.

picayune *n.* a 5-cent piece or other small coin. *Also a.* **WH:** 19C. French *picaillon* old copper coin of Piedmont, cash, from Provençal *picaioun*, of unknown orig.

piccalilli *n.* a pickle of various chopped vegetables with pungent spices. **WH:** 18C. Prob. from PICKLE + CHILLI.

piccaninny *n.* a little black or Aboriginal child. *Also a.* **WH:** 17C. W Indian creole, from Spanish *pequeño*, or from Portuguese *pequeno* little, small, *pequenino* very small, tiny.

piccolo *n.* a small flute, with the notes one octave higher than the ordinary flute. **WH:** 19C. Italian small.

pice *n.* an Indian copper coin worth quarter of an anna. **WH:** 17C. Hindi *paisā*. Cp. PAISA.

piceous *a.* pitch-black, brownish-black. **WH:** 17C. Latin *piceus* pitchy, from *pix*, *picis* PITCH[2]. See also -EOUS.

pichiciago *n.* a small S American armadillo, esp. *Chlamyphorus truncatus*. **WH:** 19C. Spanish *pichiciego*, from Araucanian *pichi* small + Spanish *ciego* blind (from Latin *caecus*). American Spanish *pichi* is the name of the small armadillo *Zaedyus pichiy*.

pick[1] *v.t.* to choose, to select carefully. *Also v.i.*, *n.* **WH:** 12–14C. Orig. uncertain. Cp. French *piquer*, Dutch *pikken*, PICK[2], PIKE[1]. The original sense was to pierce, to indent, by striking with a pick or other pointed instrument. Hence the sense to detach and take, to pluck, to choose, also to steal.

pick[2] *n.* a tool with a long iron head, usu. pointed at one end and pointed or chisel-edged at the other, fitted in the middle on a wooden shaft, used for breaking ground etc. *Also v.t.* **WH:** 12–14C. Var. of PIKE[1].

pickaxe *n.* an instrument for breaking ground etc., a pick. *Also v.t.*, *v.i.* **WH:** 12–14C. Old French *picois*, later alt. by assoc. with AXE. Cp. PIKE[1].

pickeer *v.i.* to skirmish. **WH:** 17C. Appar. from Dutch *pickeren* to prick, to spur, from French *piquer*.

pickelhaube *n.* the spiked helmet of a German soldier. **WH:** 19C. German, alt. (influ. by *Pickel* pickaxe) of Middle High German *beckelhûbe* from *becken* basin + *hûbe* cap.

pickerel *n.* a young or small pike. **WH:** 12–14C. Dim. of PIKE[1]. The suffix *-rel* indicates a diminutive or derogatory sense, as in COCKEREL, DOGGEREL, MONGREL, etc.

picket *n.* a person or group of people set by a trade union to watch a shop, factory etc., during labour disputes. *Also v.t.*, *v.i.* **WH:** 17C. Old French *piquet*, from *piquer* to prick, to pierce, from *pic* pike. See also -ET[1]. The original basic sense was a pointed stake in a

military establishment. This was then extended to a group of soldiers or horsemen (18C), one of whose horses was originally tethered to the stake, and further to a group of workers outside a factory, etc. (19C).

pickle *n.* a liquid, such as brine, vinegar etc., for preserving fish, meat, vegetables etc. *Also v.t.* **WH:** 14–15C. Middle Low German and Middle Dutch *pekel*, of unknown orig. Cp. German *Pökel*. The sense plight, predicament evolved in the 16C, and mischievous child in the 18C.

Pickwickian *a.* of, relating to or characteristic of Mr Pickwick; plump and jovial. **WH:** 19C. Mr *Pickwick*, a generous, jovial and plump character in Dickens's *Pickwick Papers* (1837) + -IAN.

picnic *n.* an excursion into the country etc. with a packed lunch to be eaten outside. *Also v.i.* **WH:** 18C. French *pique-nique*, of unknown orig. ? rhyming redupl. of French *piquer* to pick, to peck.

pico- *comb. form* one millionth of a millionth part (10^{-12}). **WH:** early 20C. Spanish *pico* beak, peak, little bit. See also -O-.

picot *n.* a small loop of thread forming part of an ornamental edging. **WH:** 17C. French, dim. of *pic* peak, point, prick. See also -OT[1].

picotee *n.* a hardy garden variety of the carnation, with a spotted or dark-coloured margin. **WH:** 18C. French *picoté*, p.p. of *picoter* to mark with points, to prick. See PICOT. The flower's early variety was white with specks of colour.

picotite *n.* a variety of spinel containing chromium oxide. **WH:** 19C. Baron *Picot* de la Peyrouse, 1744–1818, French mining inspector and naturalist, who first described it. See also -ITE[1].

picric *a.* having an intensely bitter taste. **WH:** 19C. Greek *pikros* bitter + -IC.

picro- *comb. form* bitter. **WH:** Greek *pikros* bitter, or from PICRIC. See also -O-.

picrotoxin *n.* a bitter crystalline compound constituting the bitter principle of *Anamirta cocculus*. **WH:** 19C. PICRO- + TOXIN.

Pict *n.* a member of an ancient people who once inhabited parts of N Britain. **WH:** pre-1200. Late Latin *Picti*, ? from Latin *picti* painted (people), tattooed (people). Cp. PICTURE. This origin is disputed by some scholars. 'The pseudo-learned etymology which derives the name of the Picts from their supposed habit of tattooing or painting themselves is not acceptable from a linguistic point of view' (W.F.H. Nicolaisen, *Scottish Place-names*, 1976).

pictogram *n.* PICTOGRAPH. **WH:** early 20C. Latin *pictus* painted + -O- + -GRAM.

pictograph *n.* a picture standing for an idea, a pictorial character or symbol. **WH:** 19C. Latin *pictus* painted + -O- + -GRAPH.

pictorial *a.* of, relating to, containing, expressed in or illustrated by pictures. *Also n.* **WH:** 17C. Late Latin *pictorius*, from Latin *pictor* painter, from *pictus*. See PICTURE, also -IAL.

picture *n.* a painting or drawing representing a person, natural scenery or other objects. *Also a.*, *v.t.* **WH:** 14–15C. Latin *pictura*, from *pictus*, p.p. of *pingere* to paint.

picturesque *a.* having those qualities that characterize a good picture. *Also n.* **WH:** 18C. French *pittoresque*, from Italian *pittoresco*, from *pittore* painter, from Latin *pictor*. See PICTORIAL, also -ESQUE.

piddle *v.i.* to urinate (used by or to children). *Also n.* **WH:** 16C. Prob. based on PISS or PEE, by assoc. with PUDDLE. The sense to trifle is perhaps an alteration of PEDDLE, by association with Low German *piddeln*. The sense to urinate dates from the 18C.

piddock *n.* any bivalve mollusc of the family Pholadidae, used for bait. **WH:** 19C. Orig. unknown.

pidgin *n.* a language that is a combination of two or more languages, used esp. for trading between people of different native languages. **WH:** 19C. Chinese, alt. of English BUSINESS. The word is popularly associated with PIGEON[1]. See PIGEON[2].

pie[1] *n.* a pastry case filled with meat, fruit etc. **WH:** 12–14C. Prob. identical with PIE[2]. The mixed contents of a pie are similar to the miscellaneous objects collected by a magpie.

†pie[2] *n.* a magpie. **WH:** 12–14C. Old French, from Latin *pica* magpie, rel. to *picus* green woodpecker. Cp. MAGPIE.

pie[3] *n.* a confused mass of printers' type. *Also v.t.* **WH:** 17C. ? Trans. of Old French PÂTÉ pie, patty.

pie[4] *n.* an Indian copper coin worth one-twelfth of an anna. **WH:** 19C. Hindi *pāī*, from Sanskrit *pādikā*, from *pāda* quarter. Cp. PICE.

piebald a. (of a horse or other animal) having patches of two different colours, usu. black and white; particoloured, mottled. Also n. WH: 16C. PIE² + BALD. The animal is so called because its black and white colours are like those of a magpie. Cp. SKEWBALD.

piece n. a distinct part of anything. Also v.t., v.i. WH: 12–14C. Old French (Modern French pièce), from Popular Latin pettia, prob. of Gaulish orig. Cp. Welsh peth thing, Breton pez piece.

pièce de résistance n. an outstanding item. WH: 18C. French, lit. piece of resistance (orig. the most substantial dish in a meal).

pied a. particoloured, variegated, spotted. WH: 12–14C. PIE² + -ED.

pied-à-terre n. a flat or house for occasional use, e.g. a city apartment for a country dweller. WH: 19C. French, lit. foot to earth.

piedmont n. a gentle slope at the foot of a mountain or mountain range. WH: 19C. Piedmont, a region of the NE USA, based on Italian Piemonte, a region in NW Italy, from piede foot + monte mountain.

pier n. a structure projecting into the sea, used as a landing stage, promenade etc. WH: 12–14C. Anglo-Latin pera, of unknown orig.

pierce v.t. to penetrate or transfix with a pointed instrument. Also v.i. WH: 12–14C. Old French percer, from Latin pertusus, p.p. of pertundere to bore through, from PER- + tundere to thrust.

Pierian a. of or relating to Pieria, or to the Pierides or Muses. WH: 16C. Latin Pierius, from Pieria, a district in N Thessaly, the reputed home of the Muses + -AN.

pierrot n. a buffoon or itinerant minstrel, orig. French and usu. dressed in loose white costume with the face whitened. WH: 18C. French Pierrot, pet form of Pierre Peter. See also -OT¹. Cp. PARROT.

piet n. a magpie. WH: 12–14C. PIE² + -OT¹ (later -ET¹).

pietà n. a pictorial or sculptured representation of the Virgin Mary and the dead Christ. WH: 17C. Italian, from Latin pietas PIETY.

pietas n. respect due to an ancestor. WH: early 20C. Latin. See PIETY.

pietist n. a person who makes a display of strong religious feelings. WH: 17C. German, from Latin pietas. See PIETY, also -IST.

piety n. the quality of being pious. WH: 12–14C. Old French piete (Modern French piété), from Latin pietas dutifulness, from pius PIOUS. Cp. PITY.

piezo- comb. form pressure. WH: Greek piezein to press, to squeeze. See also -O-.

piezochemistry n. the study of the effect of high pressures on chemical reactions. WH: mid-20C. PIEZO- + CHEMISTRY.

piezoelectricity n. a property possessed by some crystals, e.g. those used in gramophone crystal pick-ups, of generating surface electric charges when mechanically strained. WH: 19C. PIEZO- + electricity (ELECTRIC).

piezometer n. an instrument for determining the compressibility of liquids or other forms of pressure. WH: 19C. PIEZO- + -METER. The term was coined in 1820 by the instrument's US inventor, Jacob Perkins.

piffero n. a small flute like an oboe. WH: 18C. Italian, rel. to Spanish pifaro, French fifre. See FIFE.

piffle n. trash, rubbish, twaddle. Also v.i. WH: 19C. Appar. imit., with dim. ending -LE⁴.

pig n. any ungulate, omnivorous mammal of the family Suidae, esp. the domesticated variety, Sus scrofa. Also v.i., v.t. WH: 12–14C. Orig. uncertain. Prob. from an unrecorded Old English word found only as element in picbrēd acorns (lit. swine bread).

pigeon¹ n. any grey-and-white bird of the family Columbidae, esp. Columbia livia; a dove. Also v.t. WH: 14–15C. Old French pijon young bird, (esp.) young pigeon (Modern French pigeon pigeon), from alt. of Late Latin pipio, pipionis, from imit. base rel. to PIPE. This word replaced the native Old English name, DOVE, as well as the earlier CULVER.

pigeon² n. a pidgin. WH: 19C. Alt. of PIDGIN, by assoc. with PIGEON¹, esp. in phr. not my pigeon.

piggin n. a small pail or vessel, usu. of wood, with a handle formed by one of the staves, for holding liquids. WH: 16C. ? From dial. pig, of unknown orig., in sense pitcher, jar, etc.

piggyback adv. on the back or shoulders, like a pack. Also v.i., v.t., n. WH: 16C. Orig. unknown. The earlier forms a pick-pack and on pick-pack appear to rule out an origin in PIG or even BACK¹.

pightle n. a small enclosure of land, a croft. WH: 12–14C. Orig. unknown. The word is the source of the Yorkshire surname Pickles.

pigment n. colouring matter used as paint or dye. WH: pre-1200. Latin pigmentum, from base of pingere PAINT + -MENT.

†pignoration n. the act of pledging or pawning. WH: 16C. Medieval Latin pignoratio, pignorationis from Latin pigneratus, p.p. of pignerare, from pignus, pigneris pledge. See also -ATION.

pi jaw n. a long, moralizing lecture. WH: 19C. PI² + JAW.

pika n. a small burrowing mammal of the genus Ochotona, related to the rabbit, a native of Asia and N America. WH: 19C. Tungus piika.

pike¹ n. a large slender voracious freshwater fish of the family Esocidae, with a long pointed snout. Also v.t. WH: pre-1200. Orig. unknown. Cp. PEAK¹, PICK¹, PICK². The fish is so called from its long, slender jaws. Cp. GAR.

pike² n. a toll gate. WH: 19C. Abbr. of turnpike (TURN), where pike refers to the orig. spiked barrier. See PIKE¹.

pikelet n. a round, thin crumpet. WH: 18C. Welsh (bara) pyglyd pitchy (bread).

pilaf n. a Middle Eastern or Indian mixed dish consisting of rice boiled with meat, poultry, or fish, together with raisins, spices etc. WH: 17C. Turkish pilâv cooked rice.

pilaster n. a rectangular column projecting from a wall or pier. WH: 16C. French pilastre, from Italian pilastro or Medieval Latin pilastrum, from Latin pila pillar, PILE¹. See also -ASTER.

pilchard n. a small sea fish, Sardina pilchardus, allied to the herring, and an important food fish. WH: 16C. Orig. unknown. The ending has been assimilated to -ARD.

pile¹ n. a heap, a mass of things heaped together. Also v.t., v.i. WH: 14–15C. Old French heap, pyramid, mass of masonry, from Latin pila pillar, pier, mole. The original meaning (to the 18C) was pillar.

pile² n. a heavy timber driven into the ground, esp. under water, to form a foundation. Also v.t. WH: pre-1200. Old English pīl, from Germanic, from Latin pilum javelin.

pile³ n. the nap of velvet, plush or other cloth, or of a carpet. WH: 12–14C. Prob. from Anglo-French peile, Old French poil, from Latin pilus hair.

piles n.pl. haemorrhoids. WH: 14–15C. Pl. of pile, prob. from Latin pila ball. The reference would be to the shape of an external pile.

pileum n. the top of the head, from the base of the bill to the nape, in a bird. WH: 19C. Latin, var. of PILEUS.

pileus n. the cap of a mushroom. WH: 18C. Latin felt cap.

pilfer v.t., v.i. to steal in small quantities. WH: 16C. Old French pelfrer to pillage, to rob, of unknown orig.

pilgrim n. a person who travels a distance to visit some holy place for religious reasons. Also v.i. WH: 12–14C. Provençal pelegrin, from Latin peregrinus foreign. See PEREGRINE. The change of n to m occurred as for BUCKRAM, GROGRAM.

piliferous a. bearing hairs. WH: 19C. Latin pilus hair + -i- + -FEROUS.

Pilipino n. the language of the Philippines. WH: mid-20C. Tagalog, from Spanish FILIPINO.

pill n. a little ball of some medicinal substance to be swallowed whole. Also v.i. WH: 14–15C. Middle Low German and Middle Dutch pille, prob. from Latin pilula PILULE.

pillage n. the act of plundering. Also v.t., v.i. WH: 14–15C. Old French, from piller, from Latin pilare to deprive of hair, from pilus hair. Cp. PEEL¹.

pillar n. an upright structure of masonry, iron, timber etc., of considerable height in proportion to thickness, used for support; a column, a post, a pedestal. Also v.t. WH: 12–14C. Old French pilier, from Latin pila PILE¹.

pillion n. a passenger seat on a motorcycle. Also a., adv. WH: 15C. Gaelic pillean, Irish pillín, dim. of pell couch, pallet, cushion, from Latin pellis skin.

pilliwinks n. an instrument of torture for squeezing the fingers and thumbs. WH: 14–15C. Orig. unknown.

pillock n. a stupid person. WH: 16C. Contr. of obs. pillicock penis, from 1st element prob. of Scandinavian orig. + COCK¹. The word was originally a dialect term for the penis. The current sense arose in the mid-20C.

pillory n. a wooden frame supported on a pillar and with holes through which the head and hands of a person were put, so as to expose them to public derision. Also v.t. WH: 12–14C. Anglo-Latin pillorium, from Old French pillorie (Modern French pilori), prob. from Provençal espilori, of unknown orig.

pillow *n.* a cushion filled with feathers or other soft material, used as a rest for the head of a person lying down, esp. in bed. *Also v.t., v.i.* WH: pre-1200. Old English *pyle*, from Germanic, from Latin *pulvinus* cushion, pillow, of unknown orig. Cp. German *Pfühl*.

pilocarpine *n.* a white crystalline or amorphous alkaloid from the jaborandi, a tropical American shrub of the genus *Pilocarpus*. WH: 19C. Modern Latin *Pilocarpus* (from Greek *pilos* wool, felt + *karpos* fruit) + -INE.

pilose *a.* covered with or consisting of hairs. WH: 18C. Latin *pilosus*, from *pilus* hair. See also -OSE¹.

pilot *n.* a person directing the course of an aeroplane, spacecraft etc. *Also a., v.t.* WH: 16C. French *pilote*, from Medieval Latin *pilotus*, var. of *pedota*, from Greek *pēdon* oar, rel. to *pous*, *pōdos* foot. The native Old English word was *lādmann*, from *lād* LODE + *mann* MAN.

Pilsner *n.* a pale beer with a strong flavour of hops. WH: 19C. German, from *Pilsen* (Czech *Plzeň*), a province and city in Bohemia (now in Czech Republic).

Piltdown man *n.* an early hominid postulated on the basis of fossil bones found in a gravel pit at Piltdown in 1912, but later found to be a hoax. WH: early 20C. *Piltdown*, a village near Uckfield, E Sussex.

pilule *n.* a pill, esp. a small pill. WH: 14–15C. Old French, from Latin *pilula*, dim. of *pila* ball. See also -ULE. Cp. PILL.

pimento *n.* a pimiento. WH: 17C. Spanish PIMIENTO.

pi-meson *n.* a pion. WH: mid-20C. PI¹ + MESON. Cp. PION.

pimiento *n.* a red pepper. WH: 17C. Spanish, from Latin *pigmentum* PIGMENT, paint, unguent (in Medieval Latin) scented confection or drink. Cp. DRINK.

pimp *n.* a man who finds customers for a prostitute or lives from her earnings. *Also v.i.* WH: 16C. Orig. unknown.

pimpernel *n.* any plant of the genus *Anagallis*, esp. the scarlet pimpernel. WH: 14–15C. Old French *pimpernelle* (Modern French *pimprenelle*), earlier *piprenelle*, from a. from Latin *piper* PEPPER. The word was originally the name of the great burnet, *Sanguisorba officinalis*, whose fruit resembles a peppercorn.

pimping *a.* small, puny. WH: 17C. Orig. unknown.

pimple *n.* a small pustule, or inflamed swelling on the skin. WH: 12–14C. Nasalized form of word rel. to Old English *piplian* to break out in pustules, and ult. also to Latin *papula* pustule.

PIN *n.* a personal identification number. WH: Abbr. of *personal identification number*.

pin *n.* a short, slender, pointed piece of metal, wood etc., used for fastening parts of clothing, papers etc., together. *Also v.t.* WH: pre-1200. Old English *pinn*, from Germanic, from Latin *pinna* feather, wing, but assoc. in meaning with *penna* PEN¹.

piña *n.* a pineapple. WH: 16C. S American Spanish, rel. to Portuguese *pinha* pineapple, (orig.) pine cone, from Latin *pinea* pine cone.

piña colada *n.* a cocktail made from rum, pineapple juice and coconut juice. WH: early 20C. Anglicized form of Spanish PIÑA pineapple + *colada* strained.

pinafore *n.* an apron or sleeveless overall worn to protect the front of clothes. WH: 18C. PIN + AFORE. The garment is so called because it is 'pinned afore' the dress.

pinaster *n.* a pine, *Pinus pinaster*, indigenous to the Mediterranean regions of Europe. WH: 16C. Latin, from *pinus* PINE¹. See also -ASTER.

pince-nez *n.* a pair of armless eyeglasses held in place by a spring clipping the nose. WH: 19C. French, from *pincer* PINCH + *nez* nose.

pincers *n.pl.* a tool with two limbs working on a pivot as levers to a pair of jaws, for gripping, crushing, extracting nails etc. WH: 12–14C. Old French *pincier* PINCH. See also -ER².

pincette *n.* a pair of small tweezers or forceps. WH: 16C. French, dim. of *pince* a pair of pincers.

pinch *v.t.* to press so as to cause pain or inconvenience. *Also v.i., n.* WH: 12–14C. Anglo-French *pincher*, var. of Old French *pincier* (Modern French *pincer*), ? from Popular Latin *pinctiare*, poss. a blend of *punctiare* to pierce (from Latin *punctum* POINT) and *piccare* to pierce (cp. PIKE¹).

pinchbeck *n.* an alloy of copper, zinc, etc., formerly used for cheap jewellery. *Also a.* WH: 18C. Christopher *Pinchbeck*, c.1670–1732, English watchmaker and inventor.

pindari *n.* a mounted marauder employed as an irregular soldier by princes in central India during the 17th and 18th cents. WH: 18C. Marathi *pēḍhārā* marauding band, Hindi *piṇḍārā*, Marathi *pēḍhārī* marauder.

Pindaric *a.* of, relating to or in the style of Pindar. *Also n.* WH: 17C. Latin *Pindaricus*, from Greek *Pindarikos*, from *Pindaros* Pindar, c.518–438 BC, Greek lyric poet + -IC.

pine¹ *n.* any tree of the coniferous genus *Pinus*, consisting of evergreen trees with needle-shaped leaves. *Also a.* WH: pre-1200. Latin *pinus*.

pine² *v.i.* to languish, waste away. *Also v.t., n.* WH: pre-1200. Old English *pīnian*, from Germanic, from Medieval Latin *pena*, from Latin *poena*. Cp. PAIN. The original sense was to suffer, to experience pain. The current sense dates from the 14–15C.

pineal *a.* shaped like a pine cone. WH: 17C. French *pinéal*, from Latin *pinea* pine cone. See also -AL¹. The pineal body is so called from its shape in humans.

pinfold *n.* a pound in which stray cattle were shut up. *Also v.t.* WH: pre-1200. Old English *pundfald*, from a base represented also by POND, POUND² + FOLD¹.

ping *n.* a sharp ringing sound, like the sound of a bullet flying through the air. *Also v.i., v.t.* WH: 18C. Imit.

pingo *n.* a mound of earth or gravel found in permafrost areas. WH: mid-20C. Eskimo (Inuit) *pinguq* nunatak.

ping-pong *n.* table tennis. WH: early 20C. Imit. of the sound made by the contact between bat and ball (*ping*) and ball and table (*pong*), ? based on DING-DONG.

pinguid *a.* fat, oily, greasy, unctuous. WH: 17C. Latin *pinguis* fat. See also -ID.

pinguin *n.* a W Indian plant, *Bromelia pinguin*, of the pineapple family, with a fleshy fruit. WH: 17C. Orig. unknown.

pinion¹ *n.* the joint of a bird's wing remotest from the body. *Also v.t.* WH: 12–14C. Old French *pignon* wing feather, wing, pinnacle, battlement, from Popular Latin *pinio*, *pinionis*, augm. form of Latin *pinna* PIN. Cp. PENNON.

pinion² *n.* the smaller of two cogwheels in gear with each other. WH: 17C. Old French *pignon*, alt. of obs. *pignol*, from Latin *pinea* pine cone, from *pinus* PINE¹.

pink¹ *n.* a pale rose colour or pale red slightly inclining towards purple. *Also a.* WH: 16C. Prob. short for *pink-eye* (PINK¹). Cp. French *œillet* pink (the plant), dim. of *œil* eye. The plant gave the name of the colour in the 17C. According to some, its own name is from PINK², with reference to its 'pinked' (jagged) petals.

pink² *v.t.* to pierce, to stab. WH: 12–14C. ? From Low Dutch. Cp. Low German *pinken* to strike, to peck.

pink³ *v.i.* (of an internal-combustion engine) to detonate prematurely, making a series of popping sounds. WH: 18C. Imit.

†pink⁴ *n.* a sailing ship with a very narrow stern, used chiefly in the Mediterranean. WH: 15C. Middle Dutch *pinke* small seagoing vessel, fishing boat, of unknown orig.

pink⁵ *n.* a yellow pigment obtained from quercitron bark or other vegetable sources. WH: 17C. Orig. unknown.

pink⁶ *n.* a young salmon. WH: 15C. Orig. unknown. The word was originally used for a minnow (now dialect). The sense young salmon dates from the 19C.

†pink⁷ *a.* small. WH: 16C. Orig. uncertain. ? Rel. to early Dutch *pinck* small, Dutch *pink* the little finger. Cp. PINKIE.

pinkie *n.* the little finger. WH: 16C. From PINK⁷, and also from Dutch *pink* the little finger. See also -Y³.

Pinkster *n.* Whitsuntide. WH: 18C. Dutch Pentecost, from Germanic, from Gothic *paintekuste* PENTECOST. Cp. German *Pfingsten*.

pinna *n.* the projecting upper part of the external ear. WH: 18C. Modern Latin, from Latin var. of *penna* feather, wing, fin.

pinnace *n.* a man-of-war's boat with six or eight oars. WH: 16C. French *pinace*, prob. ult. from Latin *pinus* PINE¹.

pinnacle *n.* the apex, the culmination (of). *Also v.t.* WH: 12–14C. Old French (Modern French *pinacle*), from Late Latin *pinnaculum*, dim. of Latin *pinna* feather, wing, pinnacle. See PIN, also -CULE.

pinnate *a.* having leaflets arranged featherwise along the stem. WH: 18C. Latin *pinnatus*, from *pinna*, *penna*. See PINNA, also -ATE².

pinner *n.* a person who pins. WH: 17C. PIN + -ER¹.

pinni- *comb. form* a wing, a fin. WH: Latin *pinna*, *penna* wing, fin + -*i-*.

pinniped *a.* having feet like fins. *Also n.* WH: 19C. Modern Latin *Pennipedia* (pl.), from Latin *pinna* fin, wing + *pes, pedis* foot.

pinnock *n.* a hedge sparrow. WH: 12–14C. 1st element appar. imit. See also -OCK.

pinnule *n.* any one of the smaller or ultimate divisions of a pinnate leaf. WH: 16C. Latin *pinnula*, dim. of PINNA. See also -ULE.

pinny *n.* a pinafore, an apron. WH: 19C. Abbr. of PINAFORE.

pinochle *n.* a card game similar to bezique, played with a 48-card pack by two or four players. WH: 19C. Orig. unknown.

pinocytosis *n.* the ingestion by cells of vesicles containing fluid. WH: 19C. Greek *pinein* to drink + *-cytosis*, based on *phagocytosis* (PHAGOCYTE).

pinole *n.* meal made from maize, mesquite beans etc. WH: 19C. American Spanish, from Aztec *pinolli*.

piñon *n.* any of various low-growing pines of the west of N America, esp. *Pinus edulis*. WH: 19C. Spanish, from Late Latin deriv. of Latin *pinea* pine cone.

pint *n.* a measure of capacity, the eighth part of a gallon (0.568 l). WH: 14–15C. Old French *pinte*, of unknown orig.

pintado *n.* a species of petrel. WH: 17C. Portuguese and Spanish guinea-fowl, use as n. of p.p. of *pintar* to paint, from var. of Latin *pictus*, p.p. of *pingere* to paint. Cp. PINTO.

pintle *n.* a pin or bolt, esp. one used as a pivot. WH: pre-1200. Old English *pintel*, dim. of a base represented by Low German, Dutch, German *pint* penis. See also -LE². The original sense was penis. The sense pin, bolt, dates from the 15C.

pinto *a.* piebald. *Also n.* WH: 19C. Spanish painted, mottled. Cp. PINTADO.

pinxit *v.i.* (he or she) painted it (in the signature to a picture). WH: 19C. Latin (he) painted, 3rd pers. sing. perf. ind. of *pingere* to paint.

Pinyin *n.* a system of romanized spelling used to transliterate Chinese characters. WH: mid-20C. Chinese *pīnyīn* transcription, from *pīn* to put together + *yīn* sound.

piolet *n.* a climber's ice axe. WH: 19C. French (Savoy dial.), dim. of *piolo*, appar. rel. to French *pioche, pic* pick, pickaxe.

pion *n.* a meson with positive or negative or no charge, chiefly responsible for nuclear force. WH: mid-20C. PI-MESON + -ON.

pioneer *n.* an early leader or developer of an enterprise. *Also v.t., v.i.* WH: 16C. French *pionnier*, from Old French *paonier*, from *paon, peon, pion* foot soldier. See PAWN¹, also -EER.

pious *a.* reverencing God, devout. WH: 14–15C. Latin *pius* dutiful, pious. See also -OUS.

pip¹ *n.* the seed of an apple, orange etc. *Also v.t.* WH: 14–15C. Abbr. of PIPPIN.

pip² *n.* a short, high-pitched sound. *Also v.i., v.t.* WH: early 20C. Imit. Cp. BEEP.

pip³ *n.* a spot on a playing card, domino, dice etc. WH: 16C. Orig. unknown.

pip⁴ *n.* a disease in poultry etc., causing a secretion of thick mucus in the throat. WH: 14–15C. Middle Low German *pip*, Middle Dutch *pippe*, prob. ult. alt. of Latin *pituita* slime (see PITUITARY).

pip⁵ *v.t.* to hit with a shot. WH: 19C. PIP¹ or PIP³.

†pip⁶ *n.* signallers' name for letter P. WH: early 20C. Arbitrary syllable containing the letter.

pipa *n.* the Suriname toad. WH: 18C. Prob. from Galibi.

pipe *n.* a long hollow tube or line of tubes, esp. for conveying liquids, gas etc. *Also v.t., v.i.* WH: pre-1200. Old English *pīpe*, from Germanic, ult. from Latin *pipare* to peep, to chirp, of imit. orig. Cp. German *Pfeife*. The original basic sense was wind instrument. The sense device for smoking tobacco arose in the 16C.

piperaceous *a.* of, relating to or derived from pepper. WH: 17C. Latin *piper* pepper + -ACEOUS.

piperidine *n.* a liquid which smells like pepper, formed by the reduction of pyridine. WH: 19C. Latin *piper* PEPPER + -IDE + -INE.

pipette *n.* a fine tube for removing quantities of a fluid, esp. in chemical investigations. *Also v.t.* WH: 19C. French, dim. of *pipe* PIPE. See also -ETTE.

piping *n.* the act of playing the pipes. *Also a.* WH: 12–14C. PIPE + -ING¹.

pipistrelle *n.* any small, reddish-brown bat of the genus *Pipistrellus*, the commonest British bat. WH: 18C. French, from Latin *pipistrello*, alt. of *vipistrello*, representing Latin *vespertilio* bat, from *vesper* evening.

pipit *n.* any larklike bird of the genus *Anthus*. WH: 18C. Prob. imit.

pipkin *n.* a small earthenware pot, pan or jar. WH: 16C. Orig. unknown.

pippin *n.* any of several varieties of apple. WH: 12–14C. Old French *pepin* (Modern French *pépin*), rel. to Spanish *pepita*, Italian *pippolo*, prob. from base **pipp-* expressing smallness.

pippy *a.* full of pips. WH: 19C. PIP¹ + -Y¹.

pipsqueak *n.* a small, contemptible or insignificant person. WH: early 20C. PIP³ + SQUEAK.

piquant *a.* having an agreeably pungent taste. WH: 16C. French, pres.p. of *piquer*. See PIQUE¹, also -ANT. Cp. POIGNANT, PUNGENT.

pique¹ *v.t.* to irritate. *Also n.* WH: 16C. French *piquer* to prick, to pierce, to sting, to irritate. Cp. PICK¹.

pique² *n.* in the game of piquet, the scoring of 30 points before one's opponent begins to count, entitling one to 30 more points. *Also v.t., v.i.* WH: 17C. French *pic*, of unknown orig.

piqué *n.* a heavy cotton fabric with a corded surface, quilting. WH: 19C. French, use as n. of p.p. of *piquer* to backstitch, PIQUE¹.

piquet *n.* a game of cards for two persons, with a pack of cards from which all below the seven have been withdrawn. WH: 17C. Orig. unknown.

piragua *n.* a pirogue. WH: 17C. Spanish, from Carib dug out. Cp. PIROGUE.

piranha *n.* a small, voracious, flesh-eating S American tropical fish, of the genus *Serrasalmus* which can attack and wound people and large animals. WH: 18C. Portuguese, from Tupi *piránye, piráya*, from *pirá* fish + *sainha* tooth.

pirate *n.* a robber on the high seas, a marauder. *Also a., v.t., v.i.* WH: 12–14C. Latin *pirata*, from Greek *peiratēs*, from *peiran* to attempt, to attack, *peira* attempt, trial. See also -ATE¹.

piripiri *n.* a plant of the rose family, *Acaena anserinifolia*, having prickly burs. WH: 19C. Maori.

pirogue *n.* a large canoe made from a hollowed trunk of a tree. WH: 17C. French, prob. from Carib. Cp. PIRAGUA.

pirouette *n.* a rapid whirling round on the point of one foot, in dancing. *Also v.i.* WH: 17C. French, of unknown orig. ? Influ. by *rouet*, dim. of *roue* wheel. See also -ET¹, -ETTE.

pis aller *n.* a makeshift, a last resort. WH: 17C. French, from *pis* worse + *aller* to go.

piscary *n.* right of fishing. WH: 15C. Medieval Latin *piscaria* fishing rights, use as n. of pl. of Latin *piscarius* pertaining to fishing, from *piscis* fish. See also -ARY¹.

piscatory *a.* of or relating to fishers or fishing. WH: 17C. Latin *piscatorius*, from *piscator* fisherman, from *piscatus*, p.p. of *piscari* to fish, from *piscis* fish. See also -ORY².

Pisces *n.* a large constellation representing two fishes joined to their tails. WH: pre-1200. Latin, pl. of *piscis* fish.

pisci- *comb. form* a fish. WH: Latin *piscis* fish.

pisciculture *n.* the artificial breeding, rearing and preserving of fish. WH: 19C. PISCI- + CULTURE, based on AGRICULTURE, etc.

pisciform *a.* like a fish in form. WH: 19C. PISCI- + -FORM.

piscina *n.* a stone basin with outlet beside the altar in some churches to receive the water used in purifying the chalice etc. WH: 16C. Latin fish pond, from *piscis* fish. The original sense was fish pond. The use of the word for a stone basin in a church dates from the 18C.

piscine *a.* of or relating to fish. WH: 18C. Latin *piscis* fish + -INE.

piscivorous *a.* living on fish. WH: 17C. PISCI- + -vorous (-VORE).

pisé *n.* rammed clay forming a wall. WH: 18C. French, use as n. of p.p. of *piser* to beat, to pound (earth), from Latin *pinsare*.

pish *int.* used to express contempt, disgust etc. *Also v.i.* WH: 16C. Natural exclamation. Cp. PSHAW, TUSH¹.

pishogue *n.* sorcery, witchery or enchantment of a sinister kind. WH: 19C. Irish *piseog, pisreog*, witchcraft, from Middle Irish *picseó, pisóc*.

pisiform *a.* pea-shaped. WH: 18C. Modern Latin *pisiformis*, from *pisum* PEA. See also -FORM.

pisky *n.* a pixie. WH: 17C. Var. of PIXIE.

pismire *n.* an ant. WH: 12–14C. PISS + MIRE. The insect is so called from the urinous smell of an anthill.

pisolite *n.* a variety of calcite made up of pealike concretions. WH: 18C. Modern Latin *pisolithus*, from Greek *pisos* pea. See also -LITE.

piss *v.i.* to urinate. *Also v.t., n.* WH: 12–14C. Old French *pisser*, from Popular Latin *pissiare*, of imit. orig.

pissoir *n.* a public urinal. WH: early 20C. French, from *pisser* PISS.

pistachio *n.* an Asian tree, *Pistacia vera*, having a reddish fruit with an edible pale greenish kernel. WH: 14–15C. Old French *pistace* (Modern French *pistache*), superseded by forms from Italian *pistaccio*, both from Latin *pistacium*, from Greek *pistakion*, *pistakē*.

pistareen *n.* a former Spanish-American silver coin. *Also a.* WH: 18C. Appar. alt. of PESETA.

piste *n.* a slope prepared for skiing. WH: 18C. French track, from Latin *pista* (*via*) beaten (track), from fem. p.p. of *pinsere* to pound, to stamp.

pistil *n.* the female organ in flowering plants, comprising the ovary and stigma, usu. with a style supporting the latter. WH: 18C. French *pistile* or Latin *pistillum* PESTLE. The organ is so called from its resemblance to a pestle.

pistol *n.* a small firearm for use with one hand. *Also v.t.* WH: 16C. Obs. French *pistole*, from German *Pistole*, from Czech *pišt'ala* fire-arm, (orig.) pipe, from *pišteti* to squeak, to whistle, of imit. orig. Some relate the word to *Pistoia*, a town in Tuscany, W Italy, formerly famous for its metal industry and gunsmithing.

pistole *n.* a foreign gold coin, esp. a 16th–17th cent. Spanish coin. WH: 16C. French, shortening of *pistolet*, of unknown orig.

piston *n.* a device fitted to occupy the sectional area of a tube and be driven to and fro by alternating pressure on its faces, so as to impart or receive motion, as in a steam engine or a pump. WH: 18C. French, from Italian *pistone*, var. of *pestone* pestle, rammer, augm. from *pest-* in *pestello*, from Latin *pistillum*. See PESTLE.

pit¹ *n.* a natural or artificial hole in the ground, esp. one of considerable depth in proportion to its width. *Also v.t., v.i.* WH: pre-1200. Old English *pytt*, from Germanic. Cp. German *Pfütze* pool, puddle.

pit² *n.* the stone of a fruit. *Also v.t.* WH: 19C. Appar. from Dutch *pit*, Middle Dutch *pitte*, from Germanic, ult. rel. to PITH.

pit-a-pat *n.* a tapping, a flutter, a palpitation. *Also adv.* WH: 16C. Imit. Similar *pitter-patter* (14–15C) is a redupl. of PATTER¹, PATTER².

pitch¹ *v.t.* to fix or plant in the ground. *Also v.i., n.* WH: 12–14C. Orig. uncertain. ? Rel. to Old English *picung* stigmata, ult. of unknown orig.

pitch² *n.* a dark brown or black resinous substance obtained from tar, turpentine and some oils, used for caulking, paving roads etc. *Also v.t.* WH: pre-1200. Old English *pic*, from Germanic, from Latin *pix*, *picis*.

pitcher¹ *n.* a large vessel, usu. of earthenware, with a handle and a spout, for holding liquids. WH: 12–14C. Old French *pichier*, *pechier* pot (Modern French *pichet*), from Frankish, rel. to BEAKER.

pitcher² *n.* a person who or something which pitches. WH: 18C. PITCH¹ + -ER¹.

piteous *a.* exciting or deserving pity, lamentable. WH: 12–14C. Old French *pitos*, *piteus*, from Medieval Latin *pietosus*, from Latin *pietas* PIETY, PITY. See also -EOUS.

pith *n.* the soft, white tissue under the skin of an orange, grapefruit etc. *Also v.t.* WH: pre-1200. Old English *pitha*, from Germanic, of unknown orig. Cp. Middle Low German, Middle Dutch *pitte*, *pit*.

†pithecanthropus *n. Homo erectus*, an extinct human species of which remains have been found in Java and elsewhere. WH: 19C. Modern Latin, from Greek *pithēkos* ape + *anthrōpos* man. The term was coined in 1868 by the German naturalist Ernst Haeckel as a word for the 'missing link' between apes and humans.

pithos *n.* in archaeology, a large storage jar. WH: 19C. Greek.

piton *n.* a bar, staff or stanchion used for fixing ropes on precipitous mountainsides etc. WH: 19C. French eye-bolt, of unknown orig.

Pitot tube *n.* a right-angled tube open at both ends used with a manometer to measure pressure in a flow of liquid or gas. WH: 19C. Henri Pitot, 1695–1771, French scientist.

pitpan *n.* a narrow, long, flat-bottomed dugout canoe, used in Central America. WH: 18C. Miskito *pitban* boat.

pitta¹ *n.* a flat, round, slightly leavened bread, hollow inside so that it can be filled with food. WH: mid-20C. Modern Greek *pētta*, *pitta* bread, cake, pie.

pitta² *n.* a brightly coloured bird of the family Pittidae. WH: 19C. Modern Latin, from Telugu *piṭṭa* (young) bird.

pittance *n.* a dole, an allowance, esp. of a meagre amount. WH: 12–14C. Old French *pietance*, from Medieval Latin *pitantia*, *pietantia*, from Latin *pietas* PITY. See also -ANCE. The original sense was a pious bequest to a religious house to provide an allowance of food and drink on specified occasions. The current general sense meagre allowance evolved in the 17C.

pittosporum *n.* any evergreen shrub of the Australasian genus *Pittosporum*, having small, sweet-scented flowers. WH: 18C. Modern Latin, from Greek *pitta* pitch + *sporos* seed. The shrub is so called from the resinous pulp that surrounds its seeds.

pituitary *a.* of or relating to the pituitary gland. *Also n.* WH: 17C. Latin *pituitarius*, from *pituita* gum, slime. See also -ARY¹. The pituitary gland is so called from the former belief that it channelled mucus to the nose.

pituri *n.* a solanaceous plant, *Duboisia hopwoodii*, the leaves of which are used medicinally and as a narcotic. WH: 19C. Australian Aboriginal (Pitta Pitta) *bijirri*.

pity *n.* a feeling of tenderness aroused by the distress of others. *Also v.t., v.i.* WH: 12–14C. Old French *pité* (Modern French *pitié*), from Latin *pietas*, *pietatis* PIETY. In Middle English, both *pity* and *piety* meant compassion, and subsequently (to the 17C) piety.

pityriasis *n.* squamous inflammation of the skin, dandruff. WH: 17C. Modern Latin, from Greek *pituriasis* scurf, from *pituron* bran. See also -IASIS.

più *adv.* more. WH: 18C. Italian more, from Latin PLUS.

pivot *n.* a shaft or bearing on which anything turns. *Also v.i., v.t.* WH: 14–15C. Old French, prob. from a base represented by French dial. *pue* tooth of a comb, harrow, etc, Provençal *pua*, Spanish *puya* point, of unknown orig.

pixel *n.* any one of the minute units which together form an image, e.g. on a cathode-ray tube. WH: mid-20C. From *pix* (a pl. form of PIC) + ELEMENT.

pixie *n.* a supernatural being akin to a fairy or an elf. WH: 17C. Orig. unknown. The association of pixies with the West Country and especially Cornwall suggests a possible Celtic origin.

pixilated *a.* mentally unbalanced, eccentric. WH: 19C. PIXIE + -*lated* as in *elated* (ELATE), *emulated* (EMULATE), etc., or var. of PIXIE-*led* (LEAD¹), in sense bewildered, confused, lit. led astray by pixies.

pizazz *n.* the quality of being exciting, lively and stylish. WH: mid-20C. Said to have been invented by Diana Vreeland, fashion editor of *Harper's Bazaar* in the 1930s. Cp. ZEST.

pizza *n.* a flat, round piece of baked dough covered with cheese and tomatoes, and also often with anchovies, mushrooms, slices of sausage etc. WH: 19C. Italian pie.

pizzicato *a.* played by plucking the strings of a violin etc. with the fingers. *Also adv., n.* WH: 19C. Italian, p.p. of *pizzicare* to pinch, to twitch, from *pizzare*, from *pizza* point, edge.

pizzle *n.* the penis of an animal, esp. a bull, used as a whip for flogging. WH: 15C. Low German *pēsel*, Flemish *pēzel*, dim. of Middle Low German *pēse*, Middle Dutch *pēze*. See also -LE¹.

placable *a.* able to be appeased, ready to forgive, mild, complacent. WH: 14–15C. Old French, or from Latin *placabilis*, from *placare*. See PLACATE, also -ABLE.

placard *n.* a written or printed paper posted up in a public place. *Also v.t.* WH: 15C. Obs. French *placquart* (now *placard*), from Old French *plaquier* (Modern French *plaquer*) to lay flat, to plaster, from Middle Dutch *placken*. See also -ARD.

placate *v.t.* to appease, to pacify. WH: 17C. Latin *placatus*, p.p. of *placare* to please, to appease. See also -ATE³.

place *n.* a particular portion of space. *Also v.t.* WH: pre-1200. Old French from alt. of Latin *platea* broad way, open space, from Greek *plateia* (*hodos*) broad (way), fem. of *platus* broad. The word superseded STEAD and obs. *stow* (in place names such as *Stow-on-the-Wold* and *Chepstow*) in general use.

placebo *n.* a medicine having no physiological action, given to humour the patient, to provide psychological comfort or as a control during experiments to test the efficacy of a genuine medicine. WH: 12–14C. Latin I shall please, I shall be acceptable, 1st pers. sing. fut. ind. of *placere* to please. The Latin word is the first word of the first antiphon in the Latin rite of Vespers of the Office of the Dead:

Placebo Domino in regione vivorum (Ps. cxiv.9) I will walk before the Lord in the land of the living (AV) (Ps. cxvi.9).

placenta *n.* the organ by which the foetus is nourished in the higher mammals. WH: 17C. Latin cake, from Greek *plakous, plakountos* flat cake, from base *plak-* of *plax* flat object.

placer *n.* an alluvial or other deposit containing valuable minerals. WH: 19C. American Spanish deposit, shoal, rel. to *placel* sandbank, from *plaza* place.

placet *n.* permission, assent, sanction. WH: 16C. Latin it pleases, 3rd pers. sing. pres. ind. of *placere* to please.

placid *a.* gentle, quiet. WH: 17C. French *placide*, or from Latin *placidus* pleasing, favourable, gentle, from *placere* to please. See also -ID.

†placitum *n.* a decree, judgement or decision, esp. in a court of justice or a state assembly. WH: 17C. Latin, neut. p.p. of *placere* to please, in Medieval Latin court sentence, trial, plea.

placket *n.* the opening or slit in a garment. WH: 17C. Alt. of PLACARD.

placoderm *a.* belonging to the class Placodermi, of fishes, having the head and pectoral region covered with large bony plates. *Also n.* WH: 19C. Greek *plax, plakos* tablet, flat plate + -O- + Greek *derma* skin.

placoid *a.* (of fish scales) plate-shaped. *Also n.* WH: 19C. Greek *plax, plakos* flat plate, tablet, + -OID.

plafond *n.* a ceiling, esp. one of a richly decorated kind. WH: 17C. French ceiling, from *plat* flat + *fond* bottom. As its source suggests, the original meaning of the French word was floor.

plagal *a.* (of the Gregorian modes) having the principal notes between the dominant and its octave. WH: 16C. Medieval Latin *plagalis*, from *plaga* plagal mode, from Latin *plagius*, from Medieval Greek *plagios* (in *plagios hēkhos* plagal mode), from Greek oblique, from *plagos* side. See also -AL[1].

plage *n.* a light or dark spot on a spectroheliogram, associated with hot or cool gas on the earth's surface. WH: 14–15C. Old French region (Modern French beach), from Medieval Latin *plaga* open space. The original sense (to the 17C) was region, district. The sense beach arose in the 19C, and the astronomical definition in the mid-20C, the latter with reference to a region usually associated with sunspots (as on a beach).

plagiarize *v.t., v.i.* to appropriate and give out as one's own (the writings or ideas of another). WH: 18C. Latin *plagiarius* kidnapper, literary thief, from *plagium* kidnapping, from Greek *plagion*. See also -ARY[1], -IZE.

plagio- *comb. form* slanting, oblique. WH: Greek *plagios* oblique, slanting, from *plagos* side. See also -O-.

plagiocephaly *n.* the condition of having the skull developed more on one side than the other. WH: 19C. PLAGIO- + Greek *kephalē* head + -Y[2].

plagioclastic *a.* having the cleavage oblique, as distinct from *orthoclastic*. WH: 19C. PLAGIO- + Greek *klastos* broken, cloven (from *klasis* breaking, cleavage) + -IC.

plagiostome *n.* any fish with the mouth placed transversely beneath the snout, such as a shark or ray. WH: 19C. PLAGIO- + Greek *stoma* mouth.

plagiotropic *a.* obliquely geotropic, the two halves (of plants, organs etc.) reacting differently to external influences. WH: 19C. PLAGIO- + -*tropic* (-TROPE).

plagium *n.* kidnapping. WH: 16C. Latin. See PLAGIARIZE.

plague *n.* a pestilence, an intensely malignant epidemic. *Also v.t.* WH: 14–15C. Latin *plaga* stroke, wound, pestilence, infection, prob. from Greek (Doric) *plaga*, (Attic) *plēgē*, from a v. meaning to strike rel. to Latin *plangere*.

plaice *n.* a European flatfish, *Pleuronectes platessa*, much used for food. WH: 12–14C. Old French *plaïz, plaïs*, later *plaise, pleisse*, from Late Latin *platessa*, from Greek *platus* broad.

plaid *n.* a long rectangular outer garment of tartan woollen cloth, worn by Scottish Highlanders. *Also a.* WH: 16C. Gaelic *plaide*, from Middle Irish, of unknown orig. Cp. *pluid, plaid* blanket.

plain[1] *a.* clear, evident. *Also adv., n.* WH: 12–14C. Old French *plain*, from Latin *planus*, from base meaning flat. Cp. PLANE[1].

†plain[2] *v.i.* to mourn, to lament, to complain. WH: 12–14C. Old French *plaindre, plaign-*, from Latin *plangere* to lament. Cp. COMPLAIN.

plaint *n.* an accusation, a charge. WH: 12–14C. Old French *plainte*, fem. p.p. (used as n.) of *plaindre*, or from Old French *plaint*, from Latin *planctus*, from *plangere* PLAIN[2].

plaintiff *n.* a person who brings a suit against another, a complainant, a prosecutor. WH: 14–15C. Law French *plaintif*, use as n. of Old French *plaintif*. See PLAINTIVE.

plaintive *a.* expressive of sorrow or grief. WH: 14–15C. Old French *plaintif*, from *plaint* PLAINT. See also -IVE.

plait *n.* a braid of several strands of hair, straw, twine etc. *Also v.t.* WH: 14–15C. Old French *pleit*, from Latin *plicitus*, p.p. of *plicare* to fold. See PLY[1]. Cp. PLEAT.

plan *n.* a drawing of a building, machine etc., by projection on a plane surface, showing the positions of the parts. *Also v.t., v.i.* WH: 17C. French plane surface, ground plan, alt. (based on *plan* PLANE[1]) of obs. *plant*, from *planter* PLANT, with sense based on that of Italian *pianta* plan of a building.

planarian *n.* any minute, flat, aquatic worm of the division Tricladida, found in salt or fresh water and in moist places. *Also a.* WH: 19C. Modern Latin *Planaria* genus name, from Latin *planarius* on level ground (here, flat). See also -AN.

planch *n.* a slab of metal, firebrick etc., used in enamelling. *Also v.t.* WH: 12–14C. Old French *planche*. See PLANK.

planchette *n.* a small, usu. heart-shaped, board resting on two castors, and a pencil which makes marks as the board moves under the hands of the person resting upon it (believed by spiritualists to be a mode of communicating with the unseen world). WH: 19C. French, dim. of *planche*. See PLANK, also -ETTE.

Planck's constant *n.* a constant (*h*) which expresses the ratio of a quantum of energy to its frequency. WH: early 20C. Max K.E.L. Planck, 1858–1947, German physicist.

plane[1] *n.* a surface such that a straight line joining any two points in it lies wholly within it. *Also a., v.i.* WH: 17C. Latin *planum* flat surface, use as n. of neut. of *planus* PLAIN[1]. As a., *plane* is a var. of PLAIN[1]. Cp. French *plan*, which similarly replaced *plain*.

plane[2] *n.* a tool for smoothing boards and other surfaces. *Also v.t.* WH: 12–14C. Old French, var. (influ. by *planer*) of obs. *plaine*, from Late Latin *plana* planing instrument, from *planare* to plane, to make smooth, from *planus* PLAIN[1].

plane[3] *n.* any tree of the genus *Platanus*, having large, spreading branches with broad angular leaves palmately lobed. WH: 14–15C. Old French, from Latin *platanus*, from Greek *platanos*, from *platus* broad. The tree is so called from its broad leaves.

plane[4] *n.* an aeroplane. WH: early 20C. Abbr. of AEROPLANE.

planet *n.* a heavenly body revolving round the sun, either as a primary planet in a nearly circular orbit or as a secondary planet or satellite revolving round a primary. WH: 12–14C. Old French *planète*, from Late Latin *planeta*, from Greek *planētēs* wanderer, from *planan* to wander. A planet is so called because it has an apparent motion of its own among the fixed stars.

plangent *a.* sounding noisily. WH: 19C. Latin *plangens, plangentis*, pres.p. of *plangere* to beat (the breast), to strike noisily. See also -ENT.

plani- *comb. form* level, flat, smooth. WH: Comb. form of PLANE[1], or of Latin *planus* flat, smooth, level + -i-.

planigraph *n.* an instrument for reproducing drawings on a different scale. WH: 19C. PLANI- + -GRAPH.

planimeter *n.* an instrument for measuring the area of an irregular plane surface. WH: 19C. French *planimètre*. See PLANI-, -METER.

planish *v.t.* to flatten, smooth, or toughen (metal) by hammering or similar means. WH: 14–15C. Old French *planir, planiss-* to smooth (Modern French *aplanir*), from *plain* PLAIN[1], PLANE[1]. See also -ISH[2].

planisphere *n.* a plane projection of a sphere, esp. of part of the celestial sphere. WH: 14–15C. Medieval Latin *planispherium*, from Latin *planus* PLAIN[1] + *sphaera*, Greek *sphaira* SPHERE.

plank *n.* a long piece of sawn timber thicker than a board. *Also v.t.* WH: 12–14C. Old Northern French *planke*, from Old French *planche*, from Late Latin *planca* plank, slab, use as n. of fem. of *plancus* flat, flat-footed.

plankton *n.* minute animals and plants or those of low organization, floating in water at any level. WH: 19C. German, from Greek *plagkton*, neut. of *plagktos* wandering, drifting, from base of *plazein* to cause to wander. Cp. PLANET. The word was coined in 1887 by the German physiologist and marine biologist Viktor Hensen.

plano- *comb. form* flat, level. WH: Latin *planus* flat, smooth, level. See also -O-. Cp. PLANI-.

planoconcave *a.* plane on one side and concave on the other. WH: 17C. PLANO- + CONCAVE.

planoconvex *a.* plane on one side and convex on the other. WH: 17C. PLANO- + CONVEX.

planographic *a.* of or relating to a process by which printing is done from a plane surface. WH: 19C. PLANO- + -GRAPHY + -IC.

planometer *n.* a plane plate used as a gauge for plane surfaces. WH: 19C. PLANO- + -METER.

plant *n.* any vegetable organism of the kingdom Plantae, usu. one of the smaller plants as distinct from shrubs and trees. *Also v.t., v.i.* WH: pre-1200. Latin *planta* sprout, slip, cutting, later influ. by French *plante*. The original sense was young tree, shrub, flower, etc. newly planted or intended for planting. The current general sense dates from the 16C.

Plantagenet *a.* of or relating to the kings of England from Henry II to Richard III. *Also n.* WH: 16C. Latin *planta genista*, lit. sprig of broom, worn as a crest by the Plantagenets, and the origin of their name. Henry II and his sons Richard I and John are usually referred to as the Angevin kings (see ANGEVIN) and the name Plantagenet was not used until *c.*1450 when Richard, Duke of York, adopted it to emphasize his descent from Edward III's fifth son, Edmund of Langley.

plantain[1] *n.* any plant of the genus *Plantago*, with broad flat leaves and a spike of dull green flowers. WH: 14–15C. Old French, from Latin *plantago, plantaginis*, from *planta* sole of the foot. The plant is so called from its broad leaves, which grow close to the ground.

plantain[2] *n.* a tropical American herbaceous tree, *Musa paradisiaca*, closely related to the banana, and bearing similar fruit. WH: 16C. Spanish *plántano*, prob. assim. of Central or S American name (such as Carib *balatana*) to Spanish *plátano* plane tree.

plantar *a.* of or relating to the sole of the foot. WH: 18C. Latin *plantaris*, from *planta* sole of the foot. See also -AR[1].

plantigrade *a.* walking on the sole of the foot as bears, badgers etc. *Also n.* WH: 19C. French, from Modern Latin *plantigradus*, from Latin *planta* sole of the foot + -*i*- + *gradus* walking. The term was coined in 1795 by the French anatomist Baron Georges Cuvier and French zoologist Étienne Geoffroy Saint-Hilaire.

planula *n.* the locomotory embryo of coelenterates. WH: 19C. Modern Latin, dim. of Latin *planus* PLANE[1]. See also -ULE.

planuria *n.* discharge of urine through an abnormal channel. WH: 19C. Greek *planos* wandering, straying + -URIA.

planxty *n.* a lively melody for the harp. WH: 18C. Orig. unknown.

plap *v.i.* to fall with a flat impact. *Also n.* WH: 19C. Imit. Cp. FLAP, SLAP.

plaque *n.* a plate, slab or tablet of metal, porcelain, ivory etc., usu. of an artistic or ornamental character. WH: 19C. French, from Dutch *plak* tablet, from *plakken* to stick. Cp. PLACARD.

plash[1] *n.* a large puddle, a marshy pool. WH: pre-1200. Old English *plæsc*, rel. to Middle Dutch *plasch* pool, of imit. orig. Cp. PLASH[2].

plash[2] *v.t.* to cause (water) to splash. *Also v.i., n.* WH: 16C. Imit. Cp. PLASH[1], SPLASH.

plash[3] *v.t.* to bend down or cut partly and intertwine (branches), to form a hedge. *Also n.* WH: 15C. Old French *plassier, plaissier*, from Latin *plectere* to weave, to plait. Cp. PLEACH.

-plasia *comb. form* growth, development, as in *hypoplasia*. WH: Greek *plasis* moulding, conformation, from *plassein* to form, to mould + -IA.

plasma *n.* the fluid part of the blood, lymph or milk. WH: 18C. Late Latin, from Greek *plasma, plasmatos* mould, image, from *plassein* to mould, to form. Cp. PLASTIC.

plasmo- *comb. form* plasma. WH: PLASMA + -O-.

plasmodesma *n.* a very fine thread of cytoplasm which passes through cell walls, providing communication between plant cells. WH: early 20C. German, from Greek *plasma* (PLASMO-) + *desma, desmos* bond, chain.

plasmodium *n.* any parasitic protozoan of the genus *Plasmodium*, found in the blood in malaria and quartan and tertian ague. WH: 19C. PLASMA + -ODE[1] + -IUM.

plasmolysis *n.* the contraction of the protoplasm in active cells under the influence of a reagent or of disease. WH: 19C. PLASMO- + -*lysis* (LYSIS).

-plast *comb. form* a living cell or subcellular particle, as in *protoplast*. WH: Greek *plastos* formed, moulded. See PLASTIC.

plasteel *n.* in science fiction, an extremely strong non-metallic material. WH: late 20C. PLASTIC + STEEL.

plaster *n.* a mixture of lime, sand etc., for coating walls etc. *Also a., v.t.* WH: pre-1200. Old English, from Germanic, from Medieval Latin *plastrum*, from Latin *emplastrum* (prob. influ. by Latin *plasticus* PLASTIC), from Greek *emplastron*, from *emplastos* daubed, plastered, from *emplassein*. See also -ER[2]. The original sense was a bandage or dressing spread with a curative substance. The sense mixture of lime, sand, etc. for coating walls arose in the 14–15C. The sense plaster of Paris (as applied to a broken limb) dates from the 19C.

plastic *n.* any of a group of synthetic, polymeric substances which, though stable in use at ordinary temperatures, are plastic at some stage in their manufacture and can be shaped by the application of heat and pressure. *Also a.* WH: 17C. French *plastique*, from Latin *plasticus*, from Greek *plastikos*, from *plastos*, p.p. of *plassein* to mould, to form. See also -IC. Cp. PLASMA.

Plasticine® *n.* a soft, modelling substance used esp. by children. WH: 19C. PLASTIC + -INE.

plastid *n.* a small particle in the cells of plants and some animals containing pigment, starch, protein etc. WH: 19C. German, from Greek *plastos* (-PLAST) + -ID.

plastron *n.* a padded leather shield worn by fencers to protect the breast. WH: 16C. French, from Italian *piastrone*, augm. of *piastra* breastplate, from Latin *emplastrum* PLASTER. Cp. PIASTRE.

-plasty *comb. form* formation or replacement by plastic surgery, as in *rhinoplasty*. WH: Greek *plastos*. See -PLAST, also -Y[2].

plat *n.* a small plot, patch or piece of ground. *Also v.t.* WH: 14–15C. Var. of PLOT, influ. by obs. *plat* flat thing, from Old French, from Popular Latin, from Greek *platus* broad, flat. The sense plan of a piece of ground arose in the 16C.

platan *n.* a plane tree. WH: 14–15C. Latin *platanus*, from Greek *platanos* PLANE[3].

platband *n.* a flat, rectangular, slightly projecting moulding. WH: 17C. French *platebande*, from *plate*, fem. of *plat* flat + *bande* BAND[1].

plat du jour *n.* the dish of the day on the menu of a restaurant etc. WH: early 20C. French dish of the day, from *plat* dish + *du* of the + *jour* day.

plate *n.* a small shallow dish for eating from. *Also v.t.* WH: 12–14C. Old French thin sheet of metal, from Medieval Latin *plata* plate armour, prob. from Popular Latin *plattus*, from Greek *platus* broad, flat. Cp. PLAT, PLATTER.

plateau *n.* a tableland, an elevated plain. *Also v.i.* WH: 18C. French, from Old French *platel*, from *plat* flat. See PLAT, also -EL.

platen *n.* the part of a printing press which presses the paper against the type to give the impression. WH: 14–15C. Old French *platine*, from *plat* flat (see PLAT, also -INE), partly also pop. alt. of *patène* PATEN.

plateresque *a.* in a richly ornamented style resembling silverware. WH: 19C. Spanish *plateresco*, from *platero* silversmith, from *plata* silver. See also -ESQUE.

platform *n.* any flat or horizontal surface raised above some adjoining level. *Also v.t., v.i.* WH: 16C. French *plateforme* ground plan, from *plate*, fem. of *plat* flat + *forme* FORM.

platinum *n.* a heavy, ductile and malleable metallic element of a silver colour, at. no. 78, chem. symbol Pt, fusing only at extremely high temperatures, immune to attack by most chemical reagents. WH: 19C. Alt. of obs. *platina*, from Spanish dim. of *plata* silver (see -INE), based on other metals in -*um* (e.g. TANTALUM). The term was coined in 1812 by the English chemist Sir Humphry Davy.

platitude *n.* a trite remark. WH: 19C. French from *plat* flat, based on CERTITUDE, *exactitude* (EXACT[1]), etc.

Platonic *a.* of or relating to Plato, or his philosophy or school. WH: 16C. Latin *Platonicus*, from Greek *Platōnikos*, from *Platōn* Plato, *c.*429–347 BC, Greek philosopher. See also -IC.

platoon *n.* a subdivision, usu. half, of a company, formerly a tactical unit under a lieutenant. WH: 17C. French *peloton* little ball, platoon, dim. of *pelote*. See PELLET, also -OON. The word was originally the term for a small body of foot soldiers operating independently.

platteland *n.* rural areas. WH: mid-20C. Afrikaans, from Dutch *plat* flat + *land* country.

platter *n.* a large shallow dish or plate. WH: 12–14C. Anglo-French *plater*, from *plat* dish, use as n. of Old French *plat* flat. See also -ER[1]. Cp. PLATE.

platy- *comb. form* broad, flat. WH: Greek *platu-*, comb. form of *platus* broad, flat.

platycephalous *a.* (of skulls) flat and broad relatively to length. WH: 19C. PLATY- + Greek *kephalē* head + -OUS.

platyhelminth *n.* the flatworm. WH: 19C. Modern Latin *Platyhelminthes* (pl.). See PLATY-, HELMINTH.

platypus *n.* a small, aquatic, egg-laying mammal of E Australia having a broad bill and tail, thick fur and webbed feet; also *duckbilled platypus*. WH: 18C. Modern Latin, from Greek *platupous* flatfooted, from *platus* flat + *pous* foot. Modern Latin *Platypus* was originally a genus name but was already in use for a genus of beetle.

platyrrhine *a.* (of monkeys) broad-nosed, as distinct from *catarrhine*. Also *n.* WH: 19C. Greek *platus* flat + *rhis, rhinos* nose. See also -INE.

plaudit *n.* an expression of applause. WH: 17C. Abbr. of obs. *plaudite* appeal for applause, from Latin, 2nd pers. pl. imper. of *plaudere* to clap.

plausible *a.* apparently reasonable, but specious. WH: 16C. Latin *plausibilis*, from *plausus*, p.p. of *plaudere* to clap. See also -IBLE.

plaustral *a.* of or relating to a wagon. WH: 18C. Latin *plaustrum* wagon + -AL[1].

play *n.* a series of actions engaged in for pleasure or amusement. Also *v.i., v.t.* WH: pre-1200. Old English *plegian* to exercise, to frolic, rel. to Middle Dutch *pleien* to dance, to leap for joy. Old English *plega* recreation, exercise, developed from the verb.

playa *n.* a dried-up lake in a desert basin. WH: 19C. Spanish shore, beach, coast, from Late Latin *plagia*. See PLAGE.

plaza *n.* a public square or open paved area. WH: 17C. Spanish, from Latin *platea* courtyard, broad street. Cp. PLACE.

plea *n.* an urgent entreaty. WH: 12–14C. Old French *plait, plaid* agreement, talk, lawsuit, from Latin *placitum* decision, decree, neut. p.p. (used as n.) of *placere* PLEASE.

pleach *v.t.* to interlace, to intertwine, to plash. WH: 14–15C. Old French (Modern French dial. *plêcher*), var. of *pleissier, plaissier* PLASH[3].

plead *v.i.* to speak or argue in support of a claim or in defence against a claim. Also *v.t.* WH: 12–14C. Old French *plaidier* (Modern French *plaider*), from *plaid* PLEA.

pleasance *n.* a pleasure ground, esp. a park or garden attached to a mansion. WH: 12–14C. Old French *plaisance*, from *plaisant*, pres.p. of obs. *plaisir* PLEASE. See also -ANCE.

pleasant *a.* pleasing, agreeable. WH: 12–14C. Old French *plaisant*, pres.p. of obs. *plaisir* (Modern French *plaire*) PLEASE. See also -ANT.

please *v.t.* to give pleasure to, to be agreeable to. Also *v.i., int.* WH: 12–14C. Old French *plaisir* (Modern French *plaire*), from Latin *placere* to be pleasing. The use of the verb as an imperative to make a polite request dates from the 17C.

pleasure *n.* the gratification of the mind or senses. Also *a., v.t., v.i.* WH: 14–15C. Old French *plesir* (Modern French *plaisir*), use as n. of *plaisir* PLEASE, with final syl. assim. to -URE.

pleat *n.* a flattened fold, a crease. Also *v.t.* WH: 14–15C. Var. of PLAIT.

pleb *n.* a common, vulgar person. WH: 17C. Orig. in pl. (*plebs*), from Latin *plebs* the common people, but later abbr. of PLEBEIAN.

plebeian *n.* a commoner in ancient Rome. Also *a.* WH: 16C. Latin *plebeius*, from *plebs*. See PLEB, also -IAN.

plebiscite *n.* a direct vote of the whole body of citizens in a state on a definite question, a referendum. WH: 16C. French *plébiscite*, from Latin *plebiscitum*, from *plebs* (PLEB) + *scitum* ordinance, decree, neut. p.p. (used as n.) of *sciscere* to approve, to vote for. See also -ITE[1].

plectognath *a.* of the Plectognathi, an order of teleostean fishes having the cheekbones united with the jaws. Also *n.* WH: 19C. Modern Latin *Plectognathi*, from Greek *plektos* twisted, plaited + *gnathos* jaw.

plectrum *n.* a small implement of ivory etc., with which players pluck the strings of the guitar, harp, lyre etc. WH: 14–15C. Latin, from Greek *plēktron* thing to strike with, from *plēssein* to strike.

pledge *n.* anything given as a guarantee of security for the repayment of money borrowed. Also *v.t.* WH: 12–14C. Old French *plege* (Modern French *pleige*), prob. from Frankish *plegan* to guarantee, from Germanic base of PLIGHT[2], influ. by Latin *praebere* to furnish, to supply.

pledget *n.* a compress of lint for laying over an ulcer, wound etc. WH: 16C. Orig. unknown.

-plegia *comb. form* paralysis, as in *paraplegia*. WH: Greek *plēgē* blow, stroke (from *plēssein* to strike) + -IA.

pleiad *n.* a cluster of brilliant persons, esp. seven. WH: 14–15C. Latin *Pleias*, pl. *Pleiades*, from Greek *Pleiades* (each of) the seven of daughters of Atlas and *Pleione* in Greek mythology. See also -AD[1]. The original sense (as *Pleiades*) was the name of a star cluster in the constellation Taurus. The sense cluster of brilliant persons evolved (as *pleiad*) in the 17C.

plein-air *a.* (done) out of doors, esp. in relation to the principles and practice of the Impressionist school of painting. WH: 19C. Shortening of French *en plein air* in the open air (lit. in full air).

pleiotropy *n.* the production of two or more apparently unrelated effects by a single gene. WH: mid-20C. From *pleio-* (PLIO-) + Greek *tropē* turn, turning. See also -Y[2].

Pleistocene *a.* of or relating to the strata or epoch overlying or succeeding the Pliocene formation. Also *n.* WH: 19C. Greek *pleistos* most + *kainos* new, recent. The epoch is so called as it contains the remains of the greatest number of modern species. Cp. PLIOCENE. The name was coined in 1839 by the Scottish geologist Charles Lyell to replace the earlier name *Newer Pliocene*.

plenary *a.* full, complete, entire, absolute. WH: 14–15C. Late Latin *plenarius*, from Latin *plenus* full. See also -ARY[1].

plenipotentiary *n.* an ambassador or envoy to a foreign court, with full powers. Also *a.* WH: 17C. Medieval Latin *plenipotentiaris*, from Latin *plenus* full + *potentia* power. See also -ARY[1].

plenist *n.* a person who maintains that all space is full of matter. WH: 17C. Latin PLENUM + -IST.

plenitude *n.* completeness, abundance, fullness. WH: 14–15C. Old French, from Late Latin *plenitudo*, from Latin *plenus* full. See also -TUDE.

plenty *n.* a large quantity or number, lots. Also *a., adv.* WH: 12–14C. Old French *plentet* (Modern French dial. *plenté*), from Latin *plenitas, plenitatis* fullness. See also -TY[1].

plenum *n.* a full meeting. WH: 17C. Latin, neut. of *plenus* full.

pleochroic *a.* (of a crystal etc.) showing different colours when looked at from different directions. WH: 19C. From *pleo-* (PLIO-) + Greek *khrōs* colour + -IC.

pleomorphism *n.* the occurrence of more than one different form in the life cycle of a plant or animal; polymorphism. WH: 19C. From Greek *pleo-* (PLIO-) + -MORPH + -ISM.

pleonasm *n.* redundancy of expression in speaking or writing. WH: 16C. Late Latin *pleonasmus*, from Greek *pleonasmos*, from *pleonazein* to be superfluous, from *pleiōn* more.

pleroma *n.* fullness, abundance. WH: 18C. Greek *plērōma* that which fills, from *plēroun* to make full, from *plērēs* full.

plesiosaurus *n.* any member of the genus *Plesiosaurus* of extinct marine saurian creatures with long necks, small heads and four paddles. WH: 19C. Modern Latin genus name, from Greek *plēsios* near + -O- + *sauros* lizard. The term was coined in 1821 by the English palaeontologist and geologist William D. Conybeare for a creature that he regarded as 'approximate to the Saurians'.

plethora *n.* superabundance, excess. WH: 16C. Late Latin, from Greek *plēthōrē* fullness, reputation, from *plēthein* to be full.

pleura *n.* a thin membrane covering the interior of the thorax and enveloping the lungs. WH: 14–15C. Medieval Latin, from Greek side, rib.

pleuro- *comb. form* of or relating to the side or ribs. WH: Greek *pleura* side, *pleuron* rib. See also -O-.

pleurodynia *n.* pain in the side due to chronic rheumatism of the walls of the chest. WH: 19C. PLEURO- + Greek *odunē* + -IA.

pleuron *n.* a pleura. WH: 18C. Greek rib, side.

pleuropneumonia *n.* inflammation of the lungs and pleurae, esp. as contagious disease among cattle. WH: 18C. PLEURO- + PNEUMONIA.

Plexiglas® *n.* a transparent plastic, the same as Perspex. WH: mid-20C. Greek *plēxis* percussion, from *plēssein* to strike + GLASS. According to some, the name is from Latin *plexus* intertwined, woven, p.p. of *plectere* to plait, to interweave, while others derive it from *plastic flexible glass*. The plastic is shock-resistant, however, which suggests the origin as given.

plexor *n.* an instrument used as a hammer to examine the chest by mediate percussion. WH: 19C. Greek *plēxis* percussion, from *plēssein* to strike + -OR.

plexus *n.* a network of veins, fibres or nerves. WH: 17C. Latin, p.p. of *plectere* to twine, to braid, to fold.

pliable *a.* easily bent, flexible. WH: 14–15C. French, from *plier* to bend. See PLY[1], also -ABLE.

plica *n.* a fold of membrane etc. WH: 17C. Modern Latin, from Medieval Latin *plica* fold, from Latin *plicare*. See PLY[1].

plicate *a.* plaited, folded like a fan. WH: 18C. PLICA + -ATE[2].

plié *n.* a ballet movement in which the knees are bent outwards while the back remains straight. WH: 19C. French, p.p. of *plier* to bend.

pliers *n.pl.* small pincers with long jaws for bending wire etc. WH: 16C. PLY[1] + -ER[1] + -S[1].

plight[1] *n.* condition, esp. one of distress. *Also v.t.* WH: 12–14C. Anglo-French *plit*, var. of Old French *ploit, pleit* fold, PLAIT.

†plight[2] *v.t.* to pledge, to promise, to engage (oneself, one's faith etc.). *Also n.* WH: pre-1200. Old English *plihtan*, from *pliht*, from Germanic. Cp. German *Pflicht* duty.

plim *v.i.* to fill out, to become plump. *Also v.t.* WH: 17C. Orig. unknown. ? Rel. to PLUMP[1].

plimsoll *n.* a rubber-soled canvas shoe worn for physical education etc. WH: 19C. PLIMSOLL LINE, from the resemblance to this of the side of the sole. A variant spelling *plimsole* has arisen by association with SOLE[1].

Plimsoll line *n.* a line, required to be placed on every British ship, marking the level to which the authorized amount of cargo submerges it. WH: 19C. Samuel *Plimsoll*, 1824–98, English politician and promoter of the Merchant Shipping Act of 1876. Cp. PLIMSOLL.

plinth *n.* a square member forming the lower division of a column etc. WH: 16C. French *plinthe* or Latin *plinthus*, from Greek *plinthos* tile, brick, stone squared for building.

plio- *comb. form* more. WH: Greek *pleiōn* more, comp. of *polus* much (see POLY-). See also -O-.

Pliocene *n.* the most modern epoch of the Tertiary. *Also a.* WH: 19C. Greek *pleiōn* more + *kainos* new, recent. The name was coined in 1831 by the English mineralogist and scholar William Whewell, with reference to the fact that the epoch contains more remains of modern species than the Miocene. Cp. EOCENE, MIOCENE.

plissé *a.* (of a fabric) having a wrinkled finish. *Also n.* WH: 19C. French, p.p. of *plisser* to pleat.

plod *v.i.* to walk slowly and laboriously. *Also v.t., n.* WH: 16C. Prob. imit.

-ploid *comb. form* denoting the number of sets of chromosomes in a cell, as in *polyploid*. WH: From the ending of HAPLOID or DIPLOID.

ploidy *n.* the number of sets of chromosomes in a cell. WH: mid-20C. From *haploidy, diploidy*, etc. See HAPLOID, DIPLOID.

plonk[1] *v.t., v.i.* to (be) put down or drop heavily, forcefully or with a plonk. *Also n.* WH: 19C. Imit. Cp. PLUNK.

plonk[2] *n.* cheap (and inferior) wine. WH: mid-20C. Prob. alt. of French *vin blanc* white wine.

plop *n.* the sound of something falling heavily into water. *Also adv., v.i., v.t.* WH: 19C. Imit. Cp. PLAP.

plosion *n.* in phonetics, the abrupt release of air in the pronunciation of a plosive. WH: early 20C. From EXPLOSION.

plosive *a.* in phonetics, produced by stopping and then suddenly releasing the airflow; explosive. *Also n.* WH: 19C. From *explosive* (EXPLOSION).

plot *n.* a small piece of ground. *Also v.t., v.i.* WH: pre-1200. Orig. unknown. Cp. PLAT. The sense to make a plan of dates from the 16C and is associated with obsolete *complot* conspiracy, from Old French *secret project*, of unknown origin.

plough *n.* an implement for cutting, furrowing and turning over land for tillage. *Also v.t., v.i.* WH: pre-1200. Old Norse *plógr*, from Germanic, from a northern Italic word represented by Lombardic Latin *plovus*, Rhaetian *plaumatorum*, and prob. Latin *plaustrum*. Cp. German *Pflug*. The native Old English word was *sulh*, related to Latin *sulcus* furrow.

plouter *v.i.* to dabble, to paddle, to flounder. *Also n.* WH: 19C. Appar. freq. of dial. *plout* to plunge, to splash, ? of imit. orig.

plover *n.* any one of several short-billed birds of the family Charadriidae, esp. the golden, yellow or green plover. WH: 12–14C. Old French *plovier, plouvier* (Modern French *pluvier*, influ. by *pluie* rain), from Latin *pluvia* rain. See also -ER[2]. The precise association with rain is uncertain, and accordingly some take the name to be of imitative origin, as for many birds. The plover's cry is melodious and far-reaching, like an extended *ploo*.

ploy *n.* a manoeuvre, a tactic, a stratagem. WH: 17C. Orig. unknown.

pluck *v.t.* to pull out, to pick. *Also v.i., n.* WH: pre-1200. Old English *ploccian, pluccian*, from Germanic, prob. from base of Old French *espeluchier* (Modern French *éplucher*) to pluck, itself ult. rel. to Latin *pilus* hair.

pluff *n.* a puff, a burst. *Also v.t., v.i.* WH: 16C. Imit.

plug *n.* a piece of wood or other substance used to stop a hole. *Also v.t.* WH: 17C. Middle Low German and Middle Dutch *plugge*, from Germanic, ult. of unknown orig. Cp. German *Pflock*.

plum *n.* a small, sweet, fleshy fruit with reddish or purple skin. *Also a.* WH: pre-1200. Old English *plūme*, from Germanic, from Medieval Latin *pruna*. See PRUNE[1]. Cp. German *Pflaume*.

plumb[1] *n.* a weight, usu. of lead, attached to a line, used to test perpendicularity. *Also adv., a., v.t.* WH: 12–14C. Prob. from Old French, from Latin *plumbum* lead, later assim. to Old French *plomb* lead.

plumb[2] *v.t.* to provide with plumbing. *Also v.i.* WH: 14–15C. PLUMB[1], prob. partly also based on French *plomber* to cover with lead, to weight with lead. The original sense was to weight with lead. The sense to measure the depth of water (with a plumb) evolved in the 16C. The sense to work as a plumber dates from the 19C, and to provide plumbing dates from the early 20C.

plumbago *n.* graphite. WH: 17C. Latin from *plumbum* lead. The Latin word translated Greek *molubdaina*, from *molubdos* lead. Cp. MOLYBDENUM. The original sense was lead ore. The current sense of graphite dates from the 18C.

plumber *n.* a person who fits and repairs cisterns, pipes, drains, gas fittings etc., in buildings. WH: 14–15C. Old French *plommier* (Modern French *plombier*), from Latin *plumbarius*, from *plumbum* lead. See also -ER[2]. The original sense was a person who works in lead.

plume *n.* a feather, esp. a large or conspicuous one. *Also v.t.* WH: 14–15C. Old French, from Latin *pluma* small soft feather, down.

plummer-block *n.* a pillow block. WH: 19C. 1st element of unknown orig. (? from the surname *Plummer*) + BLOCK.

plummet *n.* a weight attached to a line used for sounding. *Also v.i.* WH: 14–15C. Old French *plommet, plombet*, dim. of *plomb*. See PLUMB[1], also -ET[1].

plump[1] *a.* well-rounded, fat. *Also v.t., v.i.* WH: 15C. Middle Dutch *plomp*, Middle Low German *plomp*, *plump* blunt, obtuse, blockish, ? rel. to PLUMP[2]. The original sense was blunt, forthright, rude. The current sense arose in the 16C, ? influenced by PLUM.

plump[2] *v.i.* to plunge or fall suddenly and heavily. *Also v.t., n., adv., a.* WH: 12–14C. Low German *plumpen*, Middle Dutch *plompen* to fall into water, ult. of imit. orig. Cp. PLUMP[1].

plumularian *n.* any member of the genus *Plumularia* of plumelike hydroids. *Also a.* WH: 19C. Modern Latin *Plumularia*, from Latin *plumula*, dim. of *pluma* PLUME + -AN.

plumule *n.* the rudimentary stem in an embryo. WH: 18C. French, or from Latin *plumula*, dim. of *pluma* PLUME. See also -ULE.

plunder *v.t.* to pillage, to rob. *Also n.* WH: 17C. Low German *plündern*, from *plünderen*, lit. to rob of household effects, from Middle High German *plunder* bedclothes, household effects (German *Plunder* lumber, trash). The word was first current in English in connection with the Thirty Years' War, 1618–48.

plunge *v.t.* to force or thrust into water or other fluid. *Also v.i., n.* WH: 14–15C. Old French *plungier* (Modern French *plonger*), from Latin *plumbum* lead.

plunk *n.* a dull, metallic sound. *Also v.t., v.i.* WH: 18C. Prob. imit. Cp. PLONK[1], PLUMP[2].

pluperfect *a.* expressing action or time prior to some other past time. *Also n.* WH: 15C. Modern Latin *plusperfectum*, from Latin (*tempus praeteritum*) *plus quam perfectum* (past tense) more than perfect, translating Greek (*khronos*) *hupersuntelikos*.

plural *a.* consisting of more than one. *Also n.* WH: 14–15C. Old French *plurel* (Modern French *pluriel*), from Latin *pluralis*, from *plus, pluris* more. See PLUS, also -AL[1].

pluri- *comb. form* several, more, more than one. WH: Latin, from *plus, pluris* more, *plures* several + *-i-*.

pluriliteral *a.* in Hebrew grammar, containing more than the usual number of letters, i.e. more than three. *Also n.* WH: 19C. PLURI- + Latin *littera* letter. See also -AL[1].

plurilocular *a.* multilocular. WH: 19C. PLURI- + Latin *loculus* little place. See also -AR[1].

pluripara *n.* a woman who has given birth to more than one child. WH: 19C. Modern Latin, fem. of *pluriparus*, from PLURI- + *-parus* -PAROUS.

plus *prep.* with the addition of. *Also a., n., conj.* WH: 16C. Latin more.

plus ça change *int.* used to express the view that superficial changes cannot alter the essential nature of something, esp. human nature. WH: early 20C. French, in full *plus ça change, plus c'est la même chose* the more it changes, the more it stays the same. The expression is first recorded in the words of the French journalist Alphonse Karr in his satirical paper *Les Guêpes*: *On change quelquefois le prix, quelquefois le bouchon, mais c'est toujours la même piquette qu'on nous fait boire. – Plus ça change – plus c'est la même chose.* They sometimes change the price, sometimes the cork, but it's always the same plonk we're given to drink. The more they change it, the more it stays the same (1849).

plush *n.* a cloth of various materials with a pile or nap longer than that of velvet. *Also a.* WH: 16C. Obs. French *pluche*, contr. of *peluche*, or from Old French *peluchier* (PLUCK), from Italian *peluzzo*, dim. of *pelo*, from Latin *pilus* PILE[3].

plutarchy *n.* (a) plutocracy. WH: 17C. Greek *ploutos* wealth + -ARCHY.

pluteus *n.* a free-swimming larva of a sea urchin etc. WH: 14–15C. Latin. The original sense was a movable wooden wall or shed used by the Romans for besieging a city, then a barrier or wall placed between columns. The current sense dates from the 19C and refers to the larva's shape.

Pluto *n.* the smallest planet in the solar system, the furthest from the sun. WH: mid-20C. Latin, from Greek *Ploutōn* god of the underworld. The planet was discovered in 1930 and named partly from the initials of the US astronomer who had posited its existence, Percival Lowell, partly because, in Greek mythology, Pluto was the brother of Poseidon (Neptune) and Zeus (Jupiter), whose names already existed for planets. The name was also apt for the planet believed to be the outermost, and so in 'eternal darkness', like the god of the underworld.

pluto- *comb. form* of or relating to wealth. WH: Greek *ploutos* wealth. See also -O-.

plutocracy *n.* the rule of wealth or the rich. WH: 17C. Greek *ploutokratia*. See PLUTO-, -CRACY.

pluto-democracy *n.* (a) democracy dominated by wealth. WH: 19C. PLUTO- + DEMOCRACY.

plutolatry *n.* worship of wealth. WH: 19C. PLUTO- + -LATRY.

pluton *n.* a mass of plutonic rock. WH: mid-20C. German, back-formation from *plutonisch* plutonic (PLUTO).

plutonium *n.* a radioactive element, at. no. 94, chem. symbol Pu, formed by the radioactive decay of neptunium. WH: mid-20C. Latin, from Greek *Ploutōn* PLUTO + -IUM, based on URANIUM, NEPTUNIUM. The element is so called because it followed neptunium in the periodic table of elements, just as the planet Pluto orbits beyond Neptune. The name was coined by the element's discoverers in 1940, the US physicists Glenn T. Seaborg and Arthur C. Wahl. The name was earlier in use for a time in the 18C for a place where there were poisonous vapours.

pluvial *a.* of or relating to rain, rainy. WH: 17C. Latin *pluvialis* pertaining to rain, from *pluvia* rain, from *pluere* to rain. See also -AL[1].

ply[1] *n.* a thickness, a layer. WH: 14–15C. Old French *pli*, from *plier*, alt. of *pleier* (Modern French *ployer*), from Latin *plicare* to fold.

ply[2] *v.t.* to use (a tool) vigorously or busily. *Also v.i.* WH: 14–15C. Shortening of APPLY. The sense as applied to the course of a ship arose in the 16C: first to tack, then to cross a river in the 18C, then to travel regularly between specific ports or places in the 19C.

Plymouth Brethren *n.pl.* a strict evangelical group formed at Plymouth about 1830, having no regular ministry and formulating no creed. WH: 19C. *Plymouth*, a town and port in Devon + *brethren* (see BROTHER).

p.m. *abbr.* post meridiem (after noon). WH: Abbr. of Latin POST MERIDIEM.

pneuma *n.* breath, spirit, soul. WH: 14–15C. Greek wind, breath, spirit, that which is blown or breathed, from *pneein, pnein* to blow, to breathe.

pneumatic *a.* of, relating to or consisting of air, gaseous. *Also n.* WH: 17C. French *pneumatique*, or from Latin *pneumaticus*, from Greek *pneumatikos*, from *pneuma, pneumatos*. See PNEUMA, also -ATIC.

pneumato- *comb. form* air. WH: Greek, comb. form of *pneuma*. See PNEUMA, also -O-. Cp. PNEUMO-.

pneumatology *n.* the theory of spiritual existence. WH: Modern Latin *pneumatologia*. See PNEUMATO-, -LOGY.

pneumatometer *n.* an instrument for measuring the air exhaled at one expiration. WH: 19C. PNEUMATO- + -METER.

pneumatophore *n.* an air cavity of a compound hydrozoon. WH: 19C. PNEUMATO- + -PHORE.

pneumo- *comb. form* of or relating to the lungs. WH: Greek *pneumōn, pneumonos* lung. See also -O-.

pneumococcus *n.* a bacterium which causes pneumonia. WH: Modern Latin, from PNEUMONIA + COCCUS.

pneumoconiosis *n.* any disease of the lungs or bronchi caused by habitually inhaling metallic or mineral dust. WH: 19C. PNEUMO- + Greek *konis* dust + -OSIS.

pneumocystis carinii pneumonia *n.* a fatal lung infection common among Aids patients; PCP. WH: mid-20C. Modern Latin *Pneumocystis* (from *pneumo-* PNEUMO- + Late Latin *cystis*, from Greek *kustis* bladder) + *carinii*, gen. of *carinius* species name + PNEUMONIA.

pneumogastric *a.* of or relating to the lungs and the stomach. WH: 19C. PNEUMO- + GASTRIC.

pneumonectomy *n.* the surgical removal of a lung or part of a lung. WH: 19C. PNEUMO- + -ECTOMY.

pneumonia *n.* acute inflammation of a lung or the lungs. WH: 17C. Modern Latin, from Greek, from *pneumōn, pneumonos* lung. See also -IA.

pneumothorax *n.* accumulation of air in the pleural cavity, usu. associated with pleurisy. WH: 19C. PNEUMO- + THORAX.

po *n.* a chamber pot. WH: 19C. French *pot* (*de chambre*) (chamber) pot.

poa *n.* any plant of the genus *Poa* of grasses, meadow grass. WH: 18C. Modern Latin, from Greek grass.

poach[1] *v.t.* to cook (an egg, fish etc.) in simmering liquid. WH: 14–15C. Old French *pochier* (Modern French *pocher*), orig. to enclose in a bag, from *poche* bag, pocket. The white of a poached egg forms a 'pocket' round the yolk.

poach[2] *v.t.* to take (game, fish etc.) from another's lands or by illegitimate methods. *Also v.i.* WH: 16C. ? French *pocher* in special sense to pocket. See POACH[1]. The original sense was to ram or push together, to poke. The sense to steal game arose in the 17C.

pochard *n.* any European diving sea duck of the genus *Aythya*, esp. *A. ferina*. WH: 16C. Orig. uncertain. ? Var. of *poacher* (POACH[2]) or POKER[1] + *-ard* as in MALLARD.

pochette *n.* a small handbag shaped like an envelope. WH: 19C. French POCKET.

pock *n.* a pockmark. WH: pre-1200. Old English *poc*, from Germanic. Cp. POX.

pocket *n.* a small bag, esp. inserted in the clothing, to contain articles carried about the person. *Also a., v.t.* WH: 14–15C. Anglo-French *poket*, dim. of Old Northern French POKE[2], corr. to Old French *pochet* (Modern French POCHETTE), dim. of *poche* POUCH. See also -ET[1]. Cp. PUCKER.

poco *adv.* a little. WH: 18C. Italian (a) little, from Popular Latin *paucum*, neut. of Latin *paucus* few.

pococurante n. a careless or apathetic person. *Also a.* WH: 18C. Italian, from *poco* little + *curante* caring.

poculiform a. cup-shaped. WH: 19C. Latin *poculum* cup + -*i*- + -FORM.

pod[1] n. a long capsule or seed vessel, esp. of leguminous plants. *Also v.i., v.t.* WH: 17C. Back-formation from obs. *podware*, orig. field crops, of unknown orig.

pod[2] n. a flock, bunch or small herd of whales, seals etc. *Also v.t* WH: 19C. Orig. unknown.

-pod comb. form foot. WH: Greek *pous, podos* foot.

podagra n. gout, esp. in the foot. WH: 12-14C. Latin, from Greek *pous, podos* foot + *agra* seizure, trap, from a base meaning to chase, to catch.

poddy n. a hand-fed calf or foal. WH: 19C. POD[1] + -Y[1].

podestà n. a subordinate municipal judge in an Italian city. WH: 16C. Italian, from Latin *potestas, potestatis*, power, authority, magistrate.

podge n. a short and stout person. WH: 19C. Orig. unknown. Cp. PUDGE.

podiatry n. chiropody. WH: early 20C. PODO- + Greek *iatreia* healing + -Y[2].

podium n. a low projecting wall or basement supporting a building etc. WH: 18C. Latin elevated place, balcony, from Greek *podion*, dim. of *pous, podos* foot. See also -IUM.

podo- comb. form foot. WH: Greek, comb. form of *pous, podos* foot. See also -O-.

podophyllin n. a purgative resin extracted from the root of the mayapple. WH: 19C. Modern Latin *Podophyllum* (from Greek *podo*-PODO- + *phullon* leaf) + -IN[1].

podzol n. an infertile soil, with a greyish-white upper layer, like ash, and a brown subsoil. WH: early 20C. Russian, from *pod*- under + *zola* ash.

poem n. a metrical composition, esp. of an impassioned and imaginative kind. WH: 15C. Old French *poème* or Latin *poema*, from Greek *poēma*, var. of *poiēma* work, fiction, poem, from *poiein* to make, to create.

poesy n. the art of poetry. WH: 14-15C. Old French *poésie*, from Latin *poesis*, from Greek *poiēsis* creation, poetry, poem, from *poiein* to make, to create. Cp. POSY.

poet n. a writer of poems or metrical compositions, esp. one possessing high powers of imagination and rhythmical expression. WH: 12-14C. Old French *poète*, from Latin *poeta*, from Greek *poiētes* maker, author, poet, from *poiein* to make, to create.

po-faced a. deadpan. WH: mid-20C. Prob. from POH or PO + -*faced* (FACE), influ. by *poker-faced* (POKER[2]).

pogo n. a toy consisting of a strong pole attached to a spring and having a handle at the top and a crossbar on which one stands to bounce along. WH: early 20C. Orig. unknown. ? From POLE[1] + GO[1].

pogrom n. an organized attack, usu. with pillage and massacre, upon a class of the population, esp. Jews. WH: early 20C. Russian devastation, from *gromit'* to destroy by violent means, rel. to *grom* thunder.

poh int. used to express contempt or disgust. WH: 17C. Natural exclamation. Cp. PAH, POOH.

pohutukawa n. an evergreen myrtle, *Metrosideros excelsa*, with bright red flowers. WH: 19C. Maori.

poi n. a Hawaiian dish made of a paste of fermented taro root. WH: 19C. Polynesian.

poignant a. painful to the emotions, moving. WH: 14-15C. Old French, pres.p. of *poindre*, from Latin *pungere* to prick. See also -ANT. Cp. PUNGENT.

poikilothermal a. having a body temperature which varies with the surrounding temperature. WH: 19C. Greek *poikilos* variegated, various + *thermē* heat + -AL[1].

poilu n. a French private soldier. WH: early 20C. French hairy, virile, from *poil* hair, from Latin *pilus*.

poinciana n. any tree of the tropical genus *Caesalpinia* (formerly *Poinciana*) with bright red or orange flowers. WH: 18C. Modern Latin, from M. de *Poinci*, 17C French governor of the Antilles.

poind v.t. to distrain upon; to seize and sell (a debtor's goods). *Also n.* WH: 14-15C. Var. of obs. *pind* to enclose, to imprison, from Old English *gepyndan*, from base represented also by PINFOLD, POND, POUND[2].

poinsettia n. a shrub of the S American and Mexican genus *Poinsettia*, with red leaflike bracts and small greenish-yellow flowerheads. WH: 19C. Modern Latin, from Joel R. *Poinsett*, 1779-1851, first US minister to Mexico, where he is said to have found the shrub in 1828. See -IA.

point n. a mark made by the end of anything sharp. *Also v.t., v.i.* WH: 12-14C. Old French, from Latin *punctum*, neut. p.p. (used as n.) of *pungere* to pierce, to prick. The sense sharp end, salient part derives from Old French *pointe*, from Medieval Latin *puncta*, fem. p.p. (used as n.) of *pungere*.

pointe n. (in ballet) the extreme tip of the toe. WH: 19C. French POINT.

pointillism n. (in painting) delineation by means of dots of various pure colours which merge into a whole in the viewer's eye. WH: early 20C. French *pointillisme*, from *pointiller* to mark with dots, from *pointille*, from Italian *puntiglio*, dim. of *punto* point. See also -ISM.

poise[1] v.t. to balance to hold or carry in equilibrium. *Also v.i., n.* WH: 14-15C. Old French *pois*-, stem of *peser*, from Latin *pensare*, freq. of *pendere* to weigh. The original sense (to the 19C) was to weigh, both literally and in the mind. The current sense dates from the 17C.

poise[2] n. the cgs unit of viscosity. WH: early 20C. Abbr. of name of Jean L.M. *Poiseuille*, 1799-1869, French physiologist.

poison n. a substance that injures or kills an organism into which it is absorbed. *Also v.t* WH: 12-14C. Old French *puison* (Modern French *poison*), from Latin *potio, potionis* POTION. The original meaning was medicinal draught, potion, especially one prepared with a harmful ingredient.

Poisson distribution n. in statistics, a frequency distribution which gives the probability of events taking place in a fixed time. WH: early 20C. Siméon-Denis *Poisson*, 1781-1840, French mathematician and physicist.

poke[1] v.t. to push (in, out, through etc.) with the end of something. *Also v.i., n.* WH: 12-14C. Low German and Middle Dutch *poken*, of unknown orig.

poke[2] n. a bag, a sack. WH: 12-14C. Old Northern French *poque, poke*, var. of Old French *poche* POUCH. Cp. POCKET, PUCKER.

poke[3] n. a projecting front on a woman's hat or bonnet, formerly a detachable rim. WH: 18C. Prob. from POKE[1].

poker[1] n. an iron rod used to stir a fire. *Also v.t., v.i.* WH: 16C. POKE[1] + -ER[1].

poker[2] n. a card game in which the players bet on the value in their hands. WH: 19C. Orig. uncertain. ? Rel. to German *Pochspiel*, lit. bragging game, from *pochen* to brag.

pokeweed n. a N American herb, *Phytolacca americana*, with purple berries used medicinally. WH: 18C. From *poke*, Algonquian *poughkone* + WEED.

poky a. (of a room etc.) cramped, confined, stuffy. WH: early 20C. Alt. of *pogey*, of uncertain orig., ? influ. by *poky* (POKE[1]).

polacca n. a three-masted sailing boat used in the Mediterranean. WH: 17C. Var. of French *polacre*, Italian *polacra, polacca*. ? Rel. to POLACK.

Polack n. a Pole or a person of Polish origin. WH: 16C. French *Polaque*, German *Polack*, from Polish *Polak*.

polar a. of, relating to or situated near the poles of the earth or of the celestial sphere. *Also n.* WH: 16C. French *polaire* or Modern Latin *polaris*, from Latin *polus*. See POLE[2], also -AR[1].

polari- comb. form of or relating to poles or polarized light. WH: Comb. form of Medieval Latin *polaris* polar + -*i*-. See also -O-.

polarimeter n. an instrument for measuring the polarization of light, or the rotation of the plane of polarized light. WH: 19C. POLARI- + -METER.

Polaris n. the pole star. WH: 19C. Medieval Latin polar. See POLAR. The nuclear submarine so called dates from the mid-20C, its name indicating its ability to launch strikes against Russia from the Arctic polar region.

polariscope n. a polarimeter. WH: 19C. POLARI- + -SCOPE.

polarity n. the state of having two opposite poles, or of having different or opposing properties in opposite parts or directions. WH: 17C. POLAR + -ITY.

polarize v.t. to cause to acquire polarity or polarization. *Also v.i.* WH: 19C. POLAR + -IZE. The sense to restrict the vibrations of a light wave to one direction derives from French *polariser*, from *pôle* POLE[2].

polarography *n*. the analysis of a substance by measuring the current produced by electrolysing it at different voltages. WH: mid-20C. from *polarization* (POLARIZE) + -O- + -GRAPHY.

Polaroid® *n*. a light-polarizing material used esp. in sunglasses. WH: mid-20C. POLARIZE + -OID.

polder *n*. a tract of land below sea or river level, that has been drained and cultivated, esp. in the Netherlands. WH: 17C. Dutch, from Middle Dutch *poldre*.

Pole *n*. a native or inhabitant of Poland. WH: 16C. German, from Middle High German *Polān*, pl. *Polāne*, from Old Polish *Polanie*.

pole[1] *n*. a long slender piece of wood or metal, usu. rounded and tapering, esp. fixed upright in the ground as a flagstaff, support for a tent, telegraph wires etc. *Also v.t.* WH: pre-1200. Old English *pāl*, corr. to Old Frisian and Low German *pāl*, Middle Dutch *pael*, Old High German *pfāl*, Old Norse *páll*, from Germanic, from Latin *palus* stake, prop. Cp. German *Pfahl*.

pole[2] *n*. either of the extremities, north and south, of the axis on which a sphere or spheroid, esp. the earth, revolves. WH: 14–15C. Latin *polus* end of an axis, from Greek *polos* pivot, axis.

pole-axe *n*. a form of battleaxe consisting of an axe set on a long handle. *Also v.t.* WH: 12–14C. Middle Dutch *polaex*, Middle Low German *polexe*, from *pol* POLL[1] + *aex* AXE. The word is not related to POLE[1] but was later associated with it.

polecat *n*. a small carnivorous European weasel-like mammal, *Mustela putorius*, with two glands emitting an offensive smell. WH: 12–14C. ? Old French *pole* (Modern French *poule*) chicken, fowl. Orig. uncertain. See CAT[1]. The animal is perhaps so called because it preys on poultry. Cp. *hen harrier* (HEN).

polemarch *n*. in Greece, the third archon, orig. a military commander-in-chief, later a civil magistrate with varying functions. WH: 17C. Greek *polemarkhos*, from *polemos* war. See ARCH-.

polemic *n*. a controversy or controversial discussion. *Also a.* WH: 17C. Medieval Latin *polemicus*, from Greek *polemikos*, from *polemos* war. See also -IC.

polenta *n*. a kind of porridge made of maize meal, or less commonly from barley or chestnut meal, a common food in Italy. WH: pre-1200. Latin (later directly from Italian, from Latin) pearl barley.

poley *a*. (of cattle) without horns. WH: 19C. POLL[2] + -Y[1].

police *n*. a civil force organized by a state for the maintenance of order, the detection of crime, and the apprehension of offenders. *Also v.t.* WH: 15C. French, from Medieval Latin *politia*, from Latin. See POLICY[1], also -ICE. Cp. POLITY. The original meaning was civil administration. The current sense fully evolved only in the 19C.

policy[1] *n*. a course of action or administration adopted by a government, organization etc. WH: 14–15C. Old French *policie*, from Latin *politia*, from Greek *politeia* citizenship, government, from *politēs*, from *polis* city, state. Cp. POLICE, POLITY. The original meaning (to the 18C) was government, but this co-existed with the present sense.

policy[2] *n*. a contract of insurance. WH: 16C. French *police*, from Provençal *polissa*, Catalan *police*, prob. from Medieval Latin *apodissa*, alt. of Latin *apodoxis*, from Greek *apodeixis* demonstration, proof, from *apodeiknunai*. See APODICTIC.

policy[3] *n*. the pleasure grounds around a country house. WH: 14–15C. Latin *politus* polished, refined, influ. by POLICY[1].

poliomyelitis *n*. an acute infectious viral disease affecting the central nervous system, which can cause paralysis and muscle wasting. WH: 19C. Modern Latin, from Greek *polios* grey + *muelos* marrow + -ITIS. The disease is so called because it involves inflammation of the grey matter in the spinal cord.

polis *n*. a Greek city state. WH: 19C. Greek city.

-polis *comb. form* city. WH: Greek *polis* city.

Polish *a*. of or relating to Poland or to its inhabitants or their language. *Also n.* WH: 17C. POLE + -ISH[1].

polish *v.t.* to make smooth or glossy, usu. by friction. *Also v.i., n.* WH: 12–14C. Old French *polir*, from Latin *polire*. See also -ISH[1]. Cp. POLITE.

politburo *n*. the political bureau of the Central Committee of the Communist Party of the former USSR. WH: early 20C. Russian *politbyuro*, from *politicheskiĭ* political + *byuro* bureau.

polite *a*. refined in manners; courteous. WH: 14–15C. Latin *politus*, p.p. of *polire* to smooth, to polish. The original meaning (to the 18C) was smoothed, polished. The sense refined, elegant, cultivated dates from the 15C, and that of courteous, displaying good manners, from the 18C.

politesse *n*. formal politeness. WH: 18C. French, from Italian *pulitezza*, from *pulito* clean, neat, polished.

politic *a*. prudent and sagacious. WH: 14–15C. Old French *politique*, from Latin *politicus*, from Greek *politikos* civic, civil, political, from *politēs* citizen, from *polis* city, state. See also -IC.

political *a*. of or relating to civil government and its administration. *Also n.* WH: 16C. Latin *politicus* (POLITIC) + -AL[1].

politician *n*. a person experienced or skilled in politics. WH: 16C. French *politicien*, or directly from POLITIC. See also -IAN. The original sense (to the 18C) was shrewd person, schemer. The current sense dates from the 17C.

politicize *v.t.* to give a political tone or scope to. *Also v.i.* WH: 18C. POLITIC + -IZE.

politicking *n*. political activity, esp. vote-getting. WH: early 20C. POLITIC or POLITICS + -ING[1].

politico *n*. a politician. WH: 17C. Italian *politico*, Spanish *político* politic, politician.

politico- *comb. form* political and. WH: Greek *politikos* (POLITIC) + -O-.

politics *n*. the art or science of civil government. WH: 14–15C. POLITIC + -S[1], orig. from Greek *ta politika* affairs of state, politics, title of a treatise by Aristotle (4C BC).

polity *n*. the form, system or constitution of the civil government of a State. WH: 16C. Latin *politia*, from Greek *politeia*. See POLICY[1]. Cp. POLICE.

polka *n*. a lively round dance of Bohemian origin. *Also v.i.* WH: 19C. German and French, from Czech, ? rel. to *Polka*, fem. of *Polak* Pole. It is possible that Czech *polka* is an alteration of *půlka* half, referring to the half steps of the original Bohemian peasant dance.

poll[1] *n*. the voting at an election, the number of votes polled. *Also v.t., v.i.* WH: 12–14C. ? Of Low Dutch orig. and rel. to *bulla* bubble, knob (BULL[2]). The original sense was the head of a person or animal. Hence census (counting of heads) and counting of voters (both 17C) and so the action of voting itself (19C). The sense survey of public opinion evolved in the early 20C.

poll[2] *a*. (of cattle) having had the horns cut off. WH: 18C. Shortening of *polled*, p.p. of POLL[1]. The verb *poll* originally had the sense to cut the hair of a person or animal. The sense to cut off the horns of cattle evolved in the 17C.

poll[3] *n*. (used as a name for) a parrot. WH: 16C. Alt. of MOLL. *Polly*, a diminutive of *Poll*, evolved as a name for a parrot in the 19C.

pollack *n*. a sea fish, *Pollachius pollachius*, with a protruding lower jaw, used for food. WH: 14–15C. ? Celtic.

pollan *n*. a herring-like Irish freshwater fish, *Coregonus pollan*. WH: 18C. Irish *pollán*, ? from *poll* pool + formative suf. *-án*.

pollard *n*. a tree with its branches cut off so as to have a dense head of new young branches. *Also v.t.* WH: 16C. POLL[1] + -ARD.

pollen *n*. a powder of fine dustlike grains discharged from the anthers of flowers and able to fertilize in the ovules. WH: 16C. Latin *pollen*, *pollinis* fine flour, powder, rel. to POLENTA, *pulvis* powder, *puls* (PULSE[2]).

pollex *n*. in mammals, the first digit of the forelimb, in primates usu. the thumb. WH: Latin thumb, big toe.

polliwog *n*. a tadpole. WH: 14–15C. POLL[1] + WIGGLE. Cp. TADPOLE.

pollute *v.t.* to make foul or unclean. *Also a.* WH: 14–15C. Latin *pollutus*, p.p. of *polluere*, from base of PRO-[1] + base of *lutum* mud.

polly[1] *n*. (a drink of) Apollinaris water. WH: 19C. Abbr. of APOLLINARIS.

polly[2] *n*. a politician. WH: mid-20C. Abbr. of POLITICIAN.

Pollyanna *n*. an excessively or irritatingly cheerful and optimistic person. WH: early 20C. *Pollyanna*, girl heroine of stories for children by US author Eleanor H. Porter. The first novel featuring 11-year old Pollyanna Whittier is *Pollyanna* (1913). She has a permanently sunny disposition and her favourite word is 'glad'.

polo *n*. a game of Asian origin resembling hockey but played on horseback. WH: 19C. Tibetan *pholo*, lit. ball game. The game came to England from India.

polonaise n. a slow dance of Polish origin. *Also a.* WH: 18C. French, use as n. of fem. of *polonais* POLISH, from Medieval Latin *Polonia* Poland.

polonium n. a radioactive element, at. no. 84, chem. symbol Po. WH: 19C. Medieval Latin *Polonia* Poland + -IUM. The name was coined by the French physicists Marie Curie and Pierre Curie, who discovered the element in 1898 and named it after Poland, Marie Curie's homeland.

polony n. a sausage of partly-cooked pork. WH: 18C. Appar. alt. of BOLOGNA.

poltergeist n. an alleged spirit which makes its presence known by noises and moving objects. WH: 19C. German, from *poltern* to make a noise, to create a disturbance + *Geist* ghost. The word was popularized in English by spiritualists.

poltroon n. a contemptible coward. *Also a.* WH: 16C. French *poltron*, from Italian *poltrone* sluggard, coward, ? from obs. *poltro* bed (as if lie-abed).

poly[1] n. a polytechnic. WH: 19C. Abbr. of POLYTECHNIC.

poly[2] a. polythene, as in *poly bag*. WH: mid-20C. Abbr. of POLYTHENE.

poly- *comb. form* several, many. WH: Greek *polu-*, from *polus* much, *polloi* many.

polyact a. having several rays, as a sponge spicule. WH: 19C. POLY- + Greek *aktis* ray.

polyadelphous a. having many stamens arranged in three or more groups. WH: 19C. POLY- + Greek *adelphos* brother (here, stamen) + -OUS.

polyamide n. a synthetic, polymeric material such as nylon. WH: early 20C. POLY- + AMIDE.

polyandry n. the practice of a woman having more than one husband at a time. WH: 17C. Greek *poluandria*, from *polu-* POLY- + *anēr*, *andros* man, husband. See also -Y[2].

polyanthus n. a garden variety of primula, prob. a development from the cowslip or oxlip. WH: 18C. Modern Latin, lit. having many flowers, from Greek *poluanthos*, from *polu-* POLY- + *anthos* flower.

polyatomic a. (of elements) having more than one atom in their molecules, esp. replaceable atoms of hydrogen. WH: 19C. POLY- + *atomic* (ATOM).

polybasic a. (of acids etc.) having two or more replaceable hydrogen atoms per molecule. WH: 19C. POLY- + *basic* (BASE[1]).

polybasite n. an iron-black orthorhombic mineral. WH: 19C. POLY- + Greek *basis* BASE[1] + -ITE[1].

polycarbonate n. any of a class of strong thermoplastics, mostly used as moulding materials. WH: 19C. POLY- + *carbonate* (CARBON).

polycarpellary a. composed of several carpels. WH: 19C. POLY- + *carpellary* (CARPEL).

polycentric a. having more than one centre or focus. WH: 19C. POLY- + *centric* (CENTRE).

polychaete a. belonging to the Polychaeta, a class of marine worms with setae. *Also n.* WH: 19C. Modern Latin *Polychaeta*, from Greek *polukhaitēs* having much hair, from *polu-* POLY- + *khaitē* mane (here, bristle).

polychlorinated biphenyl n. any of various compounds with two benzene molecules in which chlorinated atoms have replaced hydrogens. WH: mid-20C. POLY- + *chlorinate* (CHLORINE) + -ED + BIPHENYL.

polychromatic a. exhibiting many colours or a play of colours. WH: 19C. POLY- + CHROMATIC.

polyclinic n. a clinic dealing with various diseases; a general hospital. WH: 19C. German *Poliklinik*, from Greek *polis* city + German *Klinik* clinic. The word was later assimilated to POLY-, as if referring to the many diseases dealt with.

polycotton n. a fabric made of a mixture of polyester and cotton fabrics. *Also a.* WH: mid-20C. POLYESTER + COTTON.

polycotyledon n. a plant with seeds having more than two cotyledons. WH: 19C. POLY- + COTYLEDON.

polycrystalline a. (of a solid substance) having constituent substances with differently-oriented crystals. WH: early 20C. POLY- + *crystalline* (CRYSTAL).

polycyclic a. having more than one ring of atoms in the molecule. WH: 19C. POLY- + *cyclic* (CYCLE).

polydactyl a. having more than the normal number of fingers or toes. *Also n.* WH: 19C. French *polydactyle*, from Greek *poludaktulos*, from *polu-* POLY- + *daktulos* finger, toe.

polyester n. any of a group of synthetic polymers made up of esters, used esp. in making fibres for cloth, plastics and resins. WH: early 20C. POLY- + ESTER.

polygamy n. the practice or condition of having more than one wife or husband at the same time. WH: 16C. French *polygamie*, from Late Latin *polygamia*, from Ecclesiastical Greek *polugamia*, from *polugamos* often married, polygamous. See POLY-, -GAMY.

polygene n. any of a group of genes that together control a single characteristic. WH: mid-20C. Back-formation from *polygenic*. See POLYGENISM.

polygenesis n. the theory that a race or species descends from several independent ancestral groups. WH: 19C. POLY- + GENESIS.

polygenism n. the theory that the different races of humankind are descended from different original ancestors, and therefore represent different species. WH: 19C. From *polygeny*. See POLY-, -GENY, also -ISM.

polyglot a. expressed in or speaking many languages. *Also n.* WH: 17C. French *polyglotte*, from Greek *poluglōttos*, from *polu-* POLY- + *glōtta* tongue.

polygon n. a closed plane figure, usu. rectilinear and of more than four angles or sides. WH: 16C. Late Latin *polygonum*, from Greek *polugōnon*, use as n. of neut. of *polugōnos*. See POLY-, -GON.

polygonum n. any plant of the genus *Polygonum*, comprising the knotgrass etc., with jointed stems. WH: 18C. Modern Latin *polugonon*, from *polu-* POLY- + *gonu* knee, joint. The plants are so called from their swollen joints.

polygraph n. an instrument which registers several small physiological changes simultaneously, e.g. in pulse rate, body temperature, often used as a lie detector. WH: 18C. POLY- + -GRAPH.

polygyny n. the practice or condition of having more than one wife at a time. WH: 18C. POLY- + Greek *gunē* woman. See also -Y[2].

polyhedron n. a solid bounded by many (usu. more than four) plane sides. WH: 16C. Greek *poluhedron*, use as n. of neut. of *poluedros*, from *polu-* POLY- + *hedra* base. See -HEDRON.

polyhistor n. a polymath. WH: 16C. Greek *poluistōr* very learned, from *polu-* POLY- + *histōr* (see HISTORY).

polymath n. a person of great and varied learning. WH: 17C. Greek *polumathēs* having learned much, from *polu-* POLY- + *math-*, stem of *manthanein* to learn.

polymer n. a compound, formed by polymerization, which has large molecules made up of many comparatively simple repeated units. WH: 19C. Greek *polumerēs* that has many parts, from *polu-* POLY- + *meros* part, share.

polymorphic a. having, assuming, or occurring in many forms. WH: 19C. POLY- + -morphic (-MORPH).

Polynesian a. of or relating to Polynesia. *Also n.* WH: 19C. *Polynesia*, a large collection of island groups in the central and W Pacific + -AN.

polyneuritis n. simultaneous inflammation of many nerves. WH: 19C. POLY- + NEURITIS.

polynomial a. multinomial. *Also n.* WH: 17C. POLY- + -nomial, based on BINOMIAL.

polynya n. an open place in water that is for the most part frozen over, esp. in the Arctic. WH: 19C. Russian, from base of *pole*, *polyana* field.

polyonymous a. having many different names. WH: 17C. Greek *poluōnumos*, from *polu-* POLY- + *onuma* name. See also -OUS.

polyp n. any one of various coelenterates, such as the hydra, the sea anemone etc., an individual in a compound organism of various kinds. WH: 14–15C. Old French *polipe* (Modern French *polype*), from Latin POLYPUS.

polypeptide n. any of a group of polymers made up of long amino-acid chains. WH: early 20C. POLY- + PEPTONE + -IDE.

polypetalous a. having many or separate petals. WH: 18C. POLY- + *petalous* (PETAL). See also -OUS.

polyphagous a. feeding on various kinds of food. WH: 19C. Greek *poluphagous* eating to excess. See POLY-, -PHAGOUS.

polyphase a. (of a circuit or system) having, producing or using two or more alternating voltages of equal frequency, the phases of which are cyclically displaced by fractions of a period. WH: 19C. POLY- + PHASE.

polyphone *n.* a symbol or letter standing for more than one sound. WH: 17C. Greek *poluphōnos* having many tones, from *polu-* POLY- + *phōnē* voice, sound.

polyphosphate *n.* any of several complex phosphates, used as food additives. WH: early 20C. POLY- + PHOSPHATE.

polyphyletic *a.* (of a group of organisms) descended from more than one ancestral group. WH: 19C. POLY- + PHYLETIC.

polyploid *a.* having more than twice the basic (haploid) number of chromosomes. *Also n.* WH: early 20C. POLY- + -PLOID.

polypod *a.* having numerous feet. *Also n.* WH: 18C. French *polypode*, from Greek *polupod-*, stem of *polupous* many-footed. See POLYPUS.

polypody *n.* a fern of the genus *Polypodium*, growing on rocks, walls, trees etc. WH: 14–15C. Latin *polypodium* a kind of fern, from Greek *polupodion*, from *polu-* POLY- + *pous, podos* foot + dim. suf. *-ion*.

polypoid *a.* like a polyp or polypus. WH: 19C. POLYP + -OID.

polypropylene *n.* any of various plastics or fibres that are polymers of propylene, used for laminates, pipes and various fibres. WH: mid-20C. POLY- + *propylene* (PROPYL).

polypus *n.* a usu. benign growth with ramifications growing in a mucous cavity; a polyp. WH: 14–15C. Latin, from Greek *polupous*, from *polu-* POLY- + *pous* foot.

polyrhythm *n.* the use of two or more different rhythms in the same piece. WH: early 20C. POLY- + RHYTHM.

polysaccharide *n.* any of a class of carbohydrates, e.g. starch, insulin etc., whose molecules contain chains of monosaccharides. WH: 19C. POLY- + *saccharide* (SACCHAR-).

polysemous *a.* having several meanings in one word. WH: 19C. Medieval Latin *polysemus*, from Greek *polusēma*, from *polu-* POLY- + *sēma* sign, *sēmainein* to signify. See also -OUS.

polysepalous *a.* having the sepals distinct. WH: 19C. POLY- + *sepalous* (SEPAL). See also -OUS.

polystyrene *n.* a thermoplastic polymer of styrene used esp. as a transparent plastic for moulded products or in expanded form, as a rigid white foam, for packaging and insulation. WH: early 20C. POLY- + *styrene* (STYRAX).

polysyllabic *a.* (of a word) consisting of many syllables. WH: 18C. POLY- + *syllabic* (SYLLABLE).

polysyndeton *n.* a rhetorical figure in which the conjunction or copulative is repeated several times. WH: 16C. Modern Latin, from POLY- + *-syndeton*, based on ASYNDETON.

polysynthetic *a.* compounded of several elements. WH: 19C. Greek *polusunthetos* much compounded, from *polu-* POLY- + *sunthetos* (SYNTHESIS).

polytechnic *a.* connected with, of or relating to, or giving instruction in many subjects, esp. technical ones. *Also n.* WH: 19C. French *polytechnique*, from Greek *polutekhnos* skilled in many arts, from *polu-* POLY- + *tekhnē* art. See also -IC. The educational establishment ultimately dates back to the French *École Polytechnique*, established in Paris in 1794 as the *École des Travaux Publiques* (School of Public Works) and renamed the following year.

polytetrafluoroethylene *n.* a tough, translucent plastic used esp. for moulded articles and as a non-stick coating. WH: mid-20C. POLY- + *tetrafluoroethylene* (from TETRA- + FLUORO- + *ethylene*; see ETHYL).

polytheism *n.* the belief in or worship of a plurality of gods. WH: 17C. French *polythéisme*, from Greek *polutheos* of many gods, from *polu-* POLY- + *theos* god. See also -ISM.

polythene *n.* any of various thermoplastics that are polymers of ethylene, used for packaging, domestic utensils, insulation etc. WH: mid-20C. Contr. of *polyethylene* (19C), from POLY- + *ethylene* (ETHYL). The word originated as the trade name of a thermoplastic produced by ICI in the 1930s.

polytonality *n.* the use of two or more keys at the same time in a piece. WH: early 20C. POLY- + *tonality* (TONAL).

polytypic *a.* having or existing in many forms. WH: 19C. POLY- + Greek *tupikos*, from *tupos* TYPE. See also -IC.

polyunsaturated *a.* (of certain animal and vegetable fats) having long carbon chains with many double bonds. WH: mid-20C. POLY- + *unsaturated*.

polyurethane *n.* any of a class of polymeric resins used esp. as foam for insulation and packing or in paints. WH: mid-20C. POLY- + URETHANE.

polyvinyl *n., a.* (of, related to or being) a polymerized vinyl compound. WH: mid-20C. POLY- + VINYL.

polyzoan *n.* any member of a class of invertebrate animals, mostly marine, existing in coral-like or plantlike colonies. *Also a.* WH: 19C. Modern Latin *Polyzoa*, from *poly-* POLY- + Greek *zōia*, pl. of *zōion* animal. See also -AN.

polyzonal *a.* (of lighthouse lenses) composed of many zones or annular segments. WH: 19C. POLY- + *zonal* (ZONE).

Pom *n.* a Pomeranian dog. WH: early 20C. Abbr. of POMERANIAN.

pomace *n.* the mashed pulp of apples crushed in a cider-mill, esp. the refuse after the juice has been pressed out. WH: 14–15C. Medieval Latin *pomacium* cider, from Latin *pomum* apple.

pomaceous *a.* of the nature of a pome or of trees producing pomes, such as the apple, pear, quince etc. WH: 18C. Latin *pomum* apple + -ACEOUS.

pomade *n.* a perfumed ointment for dressing the hair and the scalp. *Also v.t.* WH: 16C. French *pommade*, from Italian *pomata*, from Modern Latin POMATUM. The ointment is so called because it originally contained apple pulp.

pomander *n.* a perfumed ball or powder kept in a box, bag etc., used as a scent and formerly carried about the person to prevent infection. WH: 15C. Old French *pome d'embre*, from Medieval Latin *pomum ambrae, pomum de ambra* apple of amber.

pomatum *n.* pomade. *Also v.t.* WH: 16C. Modern Latin, from Latin *pomum* apple + *-atum* -ATE[1].

pome *n.* a compound fleshy fruit, composed of an enlarged receptacle enclosing carpels containing the seeds, such as the apple, pear, quince etc. WH: 14–15C. Old French (Modern French *pomme*) apple, from Popular Latin *poma*, fem. n. formed from Latin *poma*, neut. pl. of *pomum* apple.

pomegranate *n.* the fruit of a N African and W Asian tree, *Punica granatum*, resembling an orange, with a thick, tough rind and acid red pulp enveloping numerous seeds. WH: 12–14C. Old French *pome grenate*, from *pome* (see POME) apple + *grenate* (Modern French *grenade*) pomegranate, from var. of Latin (*malum*) *granatum*, lit. (apple) having many seeds.

pomelo *n.* a shaddock. WH: 19C. Orig. unknown.

Pomeranian *a.* of or relating to Pomerania. *Also n.* WH: 18C. *Pomerania*, a historical district on the Baltic sea in Germany and Poland + -AN.

pomfret *n.* any of various food-fishes of the Indian and Pacific oceans, of the family Stromateidae. WH: 18C. Appar. from Portuguese *pampo* + -LET, assim. to POMFRET-CAKE. Cp. POMPANO.

pomfret-cake *n.* a flat cake of liquorice, orig. made in Pontefract. WH: 19C. *Pomfret* (now *Pontefract*), a town in Wakefield + CAKE.

pommel *n.* a round ball or knob, esp. on the hilt of a sword. *Also v.t.* WH: 12–14C. Old French *pomel* (Modern French *pommeau*), from dim. of Latin *pomum* fruit, apple.

Pommy *n.* a British person, esp. an immigrant to Australia or New Zealand. *Also a.* WH: early 20C. Orig. uncertain. The word is said to derive from an abbreviation of POMEGRANATE + -Y[3], from a punning pronunciation of *immigrant* (IMMIGRATE).

pomp *n.* a pageant. WH: 12–14C. Old French *pompe*, from Latin *pompa* solemn procession, pomp, from Greek *pompē*, from *pempein* to send.

pompadour *n., a.* a method of wearing the hair brushed up from the forehead or (in women) turned back in a roll from the forehead. WH: 18C. Jeanne-Antoinette Poisson, marquise de *Pompadour*, 1721–64, mistress of Louis XV of France.

pompano *n.* a W Indian food-fish of various species belonging to the family Garangidae or Stromateidae. WH: 18C. Spanish *pámpano* butterfish, ? from *pámpana* vine leaf, with ref. to its shape.

Pompeian *a.* of or relating to Pompeii. WH: 19C. *Pompeii*, an Italian town buried by an eruption of Mount Vesuvius in AD 79 + -AN.

pom-pom *n.* an automatic quick-firing gun, usu. mounted for anti-aircraft defence. WH: 19C. Imit., from the sound of the discharge. The word arose as a nickname for the Maxim gun in the Boer War, 1899–1902.

pompon *n.* an ornament in the form of a tuft or ball of feathers, ribbon etc. worn on women's and children's hats, shoes etc., on the front of a soldier's shako, on a French sailor's cap etc. WH: 18C. French, of unknown orig. ? From Old French *pompe* POMP.

pompous *a.* exaggeratedly solemn, self-important. WH: 14–15C. Old French *pompeux*, from Latin *pomposus*, from *pompa* POMP. See also -OUS.

†'pon *prep.* upon. WH: 16C. Shortening of UPON.

ponce *n.* a prostitute's pimp. *Also v.i.* WH: 19C. ? From POUNCE[1].

poncho *n.* a woollen cloak, worn in S America, with a slit in the middle through which the head passes. WH: 18C. S American Spanish, from Araucanian.

pond *n.* a body of still water, often artificial, smaller than a lake. *Also v.t., v.i.* WH: 14–15C. Alt. of POUND[2]. A pond was originally a body of still water artificially created to preserve fish.

ponder *v.t.* to consider deeply, to reflect upon. *Also v.i., n.* WH: 12–14C. Old French *pondérer* to consider, from Latin *ponderare* to weigh, to reflect on, from *pondus, ponderis* weight, rel. to *pendere* to weigh. The original sense (to the 16C) was to estimate, to judge the value of, also (to the 17C) to weigh physically. The current sense dates from the 14–15C.

ponderosa *n.* a N American pine tree, *Pinus ponderosa*. WH: 19C. Modern Latin (*pinus*) *ponderosa*, fem. of Latin *ponderosus* of great weight, ponderous (see PONDER).

pone[1] *n.* a kind of bread made by N American Indians of maize meal. WH: 17C. Virginia Algonquian *pone, apone* bread.

pone[2] *n.* the player to the dealer's right who cuts the cards. WH: 19C. Latin, imper. sing. of *ponere* to place.

pong *n.* a bad smell, a stink. *Also v.i.* WH: early 20C. Orig. unknown. ? Imit. Cp. POOH.

pongal *n.* the Tamil festival celebrating New Year, in which new rice is cooked. WH: 18C. Tamil *poṅkal*, lit. swelling, boiling.

pongee *n.* a soft unbleached kind of Chinese silk. WH: 18C. Chinese *běnjī*, lit. own loom, or *běnzhì*, lit. home-woven.

pongid *n.* any ape of the family Pongidae, incl. orang-utans, gorillas and chimpanzees. *Also a.* WH: mid-20C. Modern Latin *Pongidae*, from *Pongo* genus name (PONGO). See also -ID.

pongo *n.* a large African anthropoid ape. WH: 17C. Congolese *mpongo, mpongi, impungu*.

poniard *n.* a small fine-bladed dagger. *Also v.t.* WH: 16C. French *poignard*, alt. of Old French *poignal*, from Medieval Latin *pugnale*, from Latin *pugnus* fist. See also -ARD.

pons *n.* a bridge. WH: 17C. Latin bridge.

pont *n.* a small ferry boat, esp. one guided across a river by a cable. WH: 17C. Dutch, from Middle Dutch *ponte*. See PUNT[1]. Cp. PONTOON[2].

Pontic *a.* of or relating to the Black Sea. WH: 14–15C. Latin *Ponticus*, from Greek *Pontikos*, from *Pontos* Pontos, an ancient region and kingdom on the Black Sea, the Black Sea itself, from *pontos* sea. See also -IC.

pontifex *n.* the Pope. WH: 16C. Latin *pons, pontis* bridge + *-fex*, from *facere* to make. Cp. PONTIFF. The word was originally a term for a chief priest, so called from his role as 'bridgemaker'.

pontiff *n.* the Pope. WH: 16C. French *pontife*, from Latin PONTIFEX.

pontificate *v.t.* to celebrate (Mass etc.) as a bishop. *Also v.i.* WH: 19C. Medieval Latin *pontificatus*, p.p. of *pontificare*, from Latin PONTIFEX. See also -ATE[3].

pontil *n.* an iron rod used for handling, twisting or carrying glass in process of manufacture. WH: 19C. French, appar. from Italian *pontello, puntello*, dim. of *punto* point. See also -IL. Cp. PUNTY.

pontoon[1] *n.* a card game in which the object is to make the aggregate number of the pips on the cards as nearly as possible 21, without exceeding this number. WH: early 20C. Prob. alt. of *vingt-un*, obs. var. of VINGT-ET-UN.

pontoon[2] *n.* a flat-bottomed boat, cylinder or other buoyant structure supporting a floating bridge. *Also v.t.* WH: 17C. Old French *ponton*, from Latin *ponto, pontonis* flat-bottomed ferry boat, from *pons, pontis* bridge. See also -OON. Cp. PONT, PUNT[1].

pony *n.* a horse of any small breed. WH: 17C. Prob. from French *poulenet*, dim. of Old French *poulain* foal, from Late Latin *pullanus*, from Latin *pullus* young animal, foal. See also -Y[3].

pooch *n.* a dog. WH: early 20C. Orig. unknown.

pood *n.* a Russian unit of weight of about 36 lb. (16 kg). WH: 16C. Russian *pud*, from Low German or Old Norse *pund* POUND[1].

poodle *n.* a breed of pet dog with long woolly hair, often clipped in a fanciful style. *Also v.i., v.t.* WH: 19C. German *Pudel*, short for *Pudelhund*, from Low German *puddeln* to splash in water. The poodle is a water dog.

poof[1] *n.* a male homosexual. WH: 19C. ? Alt. of PUFF.

poof[2] *int.* used to express rejection or contempt. WH: 19C. Imit. Cp. POOH, PUFF.

pooh *int.* used to express contempt or impatience. *Also n.* WH: 16C. Natural exclamation. Cp. PUFF.

Pooh-bah *n.* a person holding many offices. WH: 19C. *Pooh-Bah*, a character ('Lord High Everything Else') in Gilbert and Sullivan's light opera *The Mikado* (1885). The name itself represents POOH + BAH, exclamations of contempt.

pooka *n.* a hobgoblin, sometimes represented in the form of a horse. WH: 19C. Irish *púca*, corr. to Old English *pūca* PUCK[1].

pool[1] *n.* a small body of water. *Also v.i., v.t.* WH: pre-1200. Old English *pōl*, from Germanic. Cp. German *Pfuhl*.

pool[2] *n.* a group of people, vehicles, tools etc. available for use when required. *Also v.t.* WH: 17C. French *poule* stake, (orig.) hen (see PULLET), assoc. with POOL[1]. The association with POOL[1] was not only with the collected water into which one can 'dip' but, in the card game, with the identification of the *fish* (in the pool) with the *fiche*, the counter used in gaming (FISH[2]).

poon *n.* any large Indian tree of the genus *Calophyllum*. WH: 17C. Malayalam *punna*, Kannada *ponne*, Tamil *puṇṇai*.

poop[1] *n.* the stern of a ship. *Also v.t.* WH: 14–15C. Old French *pupe* (Modern French *poupe*), from var. of Latin *puppis* poop, stern.

poop[2] *v.t.* to render breathless, to exhaust. *Also v.i.* WH: mid-20C. Orig. unknown. ? Rel. to POOP[3].

poop[3] *v.i.* to defecate. *Also n.* WH: 14–15C. Imit. The original sense was to make a short blast of sound on a horn, etc. The current sense dates from the 18C.

poop[4] *n.* a stupid or ineffectual person. WH: early 20C. ? Abbr. of NINCOMPOOP.

poop[5] *n.* information, esp. useful or up-to-date. WH: mid-20C. Orig. unknown.

poor *a.* lacking enough money to live on, needy. *Also n.* WH: 12–14C. Old French *povre* (Modern French *pauvre*), from Latin *pauper*, from base of *paucus* little.

pootle *v.i.* to move along in a leisurely or lazy way. WH: late 20C. Blend of POODLE and TOOTLE.

pop[1] *v.i.* to make a short, explosive noise. *Also v.t., adv., n.* WH: 14–15C. Imit.

pop[2] *n.* pop music. *Also a.* WH: 19C. Abbr. of POPULAR.

pop[3] *n.* father. WH: 19C. Abbr. of POPPA.

pope[1] *n.* the bishop of Rome as the head of the Roman Catholic Church. WH: pre-1200. Ecclesiastical Latin *papa* bishop, from Ecclesiastical Greek *papas*, later form of *pappas* father. See PAPA[1].

pope[2] *n.* a priest in the Greek or Russian Orthodox Church. WH: 17C. Russian *pop*, or Old Church Slavonic *popŭ*, from Germanic, from Ecclesiastical Latin *papa*, from Ecclesiastical Greek *papas*. See POPE[1].

popinjay *n.* a conceited chattering fop. WH: 12–14C. Old French *papegay* (Modern French *papegai*), from Spanish *papagayo*, from Arabic *babbaḡā*, of imit orig. The final syllable has been assimilated to JAY[1]. The original sense was parrot. The current sense arose in the 16C and alludes both to the bird's gaudy plumage and to its mechanical repetition of words.

poplar *n.* a large tree of the genus *Populus*, of rapid growth, and having a soft, light wood. WH: 12–14C. Old French *poplier* (Modern French *peuplier*), from *pople*, from Latin *populus*, of unknown orig. The ending has been aligned with those of CEDAR, MEDLAR.

poplin *n.* a fine cotton fabric with a ribbed surface. WH: 18C. Obs. French *papeline*, ? from Italian *papalina*, use as n. of fem. of *papalino* papal. The fabric may be so called because it was originally made at Avignon, a town in S France which was the residence of the popes during their exile from Rome, 1309–77, and papal property, 1348–1791.

popliteal *a.* of or relating to the ham or hollow behind the knee joint. WH: 18C. Modern Latin *poples, poplitis* ham, hough + -AL[1].

poppa *n.* father (used esp. by children). WH: 19C. Alt. of PAPA[1]. Cp. POP[3].

poppadom n. a crisp, thin Indian bread, spiced and fried or roasted, often served with chutneys. WH: 19C. Tamil *pappaṭam*, ? from *paruppa aṭam* lentil cake.

poppet n. a darling, a term of endearment. WH: 12–14C. Orig. uncertain. Ult. based on Latin *pupa*, *puppa* girl, doll. See PUPPET, also -ET[1].

popple v.i. (of floating bodies or water) to bob up and down, to toss, to heave. *Also a.* WH: 12–14C. Prob. from Middle Dutch *popelen* to murmur, to babble, to quiver, to throb, of imit. orig. The original sense (to the 16C) was a bubble that rises and breaks in boiling water.

poppy n. any of various plants or flowers of the genus *Papaver*, containing plants with large showy flowers chiefly of scarlet colour, with a milky juice having narcotic properties. WH: pre-1200. Old English *popæg*, *papæg*, later *popig*, ult. from Popular Latin *papavum*, alt. of Latin *papaver* poppy.

poppycock n. nonsense, balderdash. WH: 19C. Dutch dial. *pappekak*, from *pap* soft + *kak* dung. Cp. CRAP[1], SHIT.

Popsicle® n. an ice lolly. WH: early 20C. Prob. from LOLLIPOP + ICICLE.

popsy n. an attractive young woman. WH: 19C. Prob. from abbr. of POPPET + -SY.

populace n. the common people. WH: 16C. French, from Italian *popolaccio*, *popolazzo*, from *popolo* PEOPLE + -*accio*, pejorative suf.

popular a. pleasing to or esteemed by the general public or a specific group. WH: 14–15C. Old French *populeir* (Modern French *populaire*) or Latin *popularis*, from *populus* people. See also -AR[1].

populate v.t. to furnish with inhabitants. WH: 16C. Medieval Latin *populatus*, p.p. of *populare*, from Latin *populus* people. See also -ATE[3].

populist n. a person claiming to represent the interests of the common people. *Also a.* WH: 19C. Latin *populus* people + -IST.

populous a. densely populated. WH: 14–15C. Late Latin *populosus*, from *populus* people. See also -ULOUS.

porbeagle n. a large shark of the genus *Lamna*, a mackerel shark. WH: 18C. Appar. Cornish dial., ? from Cornish *porth* harbour, cove + *bugel* shepherd.

porcelain n. a fine kind of earthenware, white, thin, and semitransparent. *Also a.* WH: 16C. French *porcelaine*, from Italian *porcellana* cowrie shell, polished surface of such a shell, (hence) chinaware, from *porcella*, dim. of *porca* sow, from Latin, fem. of *porcus* pig. The curved shape of the cowrie shell is similar to the curve in a pig's back, and both shell and pig are similar in colour.

porch n. a covered structure in front of, or extending from the entrance to, a building. WH: 12–14C. Old French *porche*, from Latin *porticus* colonnade, gallery, from *porta* gate, PORT[2].

porcine a. of, relating to or resembling a pig. WH: 17C. French *porcin* or Latin *porcinus*, from *porcus* pig. See also -INE.

porcupine n. any individual of the families Hystricidae or Erethizontidae, rodent quadrupeds covered with erectile, quill-like spines. WH: 14–15C. Old French *porc espin* (Modern French *porc-épic*), from Provençal *porc espin*, from Latin *porcus* pig, PORK + *spina* SPINE. Cp. German *Stachelschwein*, lit. prickle pig.

pore[1] n. a minute opening, esp. a hole in the skin. WH: 14–15C. Old French, from Latin *porus*, from Greek *poros* passage, pore.

pore[2] v.i. to gaze at or study with steady attention. *Also v.t.* WH: 12–14C. Orig. uncertain. ? From base of PEER[1].

porgy n. any one of a number of N American sea-fishes used for food, esp. of the genus *Calamus*. WH: 17C. Alt. of Spanish and Portuguese *porgo*, *pargo*, appar. from Latin *phager*.

poriferan n. any aquatic invertebrate animal of the phylum Porifera, the sponges. *Also a.* WH: 19C. Modern Latin *Porifera*, neut. pl. of *porifer*, from Latin *porus* PORE[1] + -*fer* bearing. See also -AN.

porism n. a proposition dealing with the conditions rendering certain problems indeterminate or capable of innumerable solutions. WH: 14–15C. Late Latin *porisma*, from Greek, from *porizein* to find, to obtain. See also -ISM.

pork n. the flesh of pigs, esp. fresh, as food. WH: 12–14C. Old French *porc*, from Latin *porcus* pig.

porky n. a porcupine. WH: early 20C. Abbr. of PORCUPINE.

porn n. pornography. *Also a.* WH: mid-20C. Abbr. of PORNOGRAPHY.

pornocracy n. the rule or domination of prostitutes, as in the government of Rome during the 10th cent. WH: 19C. Greek *pornē* prostitute. See also -CRACY.

pornography n. the obscene and exploitative depiction of erotic acts. WH: 19C. Greek *pornographos* (from *pornē* prostitute + *graphein* to write) + -Y[2]. See also -GRAPHY. The original sense was the description of the life or activities of prostitutes.

poro- comb. form of or relating to pores. WH: Greek *poros* PORE[1]. See also -O-.

poromeric a. permeable to water vapour, as certain synthetic leathers. *Also n.* WH: mid-20C. From *porous* (PORE[1]) + POLYMER + -IC.

porphyria n. any one of a group of inborn metabolic disorders characterized by an abnormal pigment in the urine, severe pain, photosensitivity, and periods of mental confusion. WH: early 20C. From *porphyrin* (from *haematoporphyrin*, from HAEMATO- + Greek *porphuros* purple + -IN[1]) + -IA.

porphyrogenitism n. succession to the throne of a younger son born while his father was actually monarch, in preference to an older son born before his father's accession. WH: 19C. Medieval Latin *porphyrogenitus* (based on Late Greek *porphurogennētos*, from *porphuros* purple + *gennētos* born) + -ISM. The original reference was to a member of the imperial family at Constantinople, reputedly born in a purple-hung or porphyry chamber.

porphyry n. an igneous rock consisting of a felsitic or cryptocrystalline groundmass full of feldspar or quartz crystals. WH: 14–15C. Ult. from Medieval Latin *porphyreum*, from Latin *porphyrites*, from Greek *porphuritēs*, from *porphura* purple dye, from *porphuros* purple. See PURPLE. The rock is so named from its colour.

porpoise n. any small whale of the genus *Phocaena*, as an adult about 5 ft. (1.5 m) long, with a blunt snout. WH: 12–14C. Old French *porpois*, *porpeis*, from comb. of Latin *porcus* pig and *piscis* fish.

porrect v.t. to stretch forward horizontally (esp. a part of the body, such as the palpi of moths). *Also a.* WH: 14–15C. Latin *porrectus*, p.p. of *porrigere*, from *por-* PRO-[1] + *regere* to stretch, to direct.

porridge n. a dish made by boiling oatmeal etc. in water or milk till it thickens. WH: 16C. Alt. of POTTAGE. The original sense was a broth of vegetables, meat, etc. thickened with barley or some other cereal. The current sense dates from the 17C.

porringer n. a small basin or bowl out of which soup etc. is eaten. WH: 14–15C. Alt. of dial. *pottinger*, from Old French *potager*, from POTAGE + -ER[2].

port[1] n. a sheltered piece of water into which vessels can enter and remain in safety. WH: pre-1200. Latin *portus* haven, harbour, rel. to *porta* (PORT[2]).

port[2] n. an opening in the side of a ship, allowing access to the holds etc. WH: pre-1200. Latin *porta* door, gate, rel. to *portus* (PORT[1]) or *porticus* porch.

port[3] n. a fortified dessert wine (usu. dark-red or tawny) made in Portugal. WH: 17C. *Oporto*, a city in W Portugal, the chief port of shipment for that country's wines.

port[4] n. the left-hand side of a ship, aircraft etc., as one looks forward, as distinct from *starboard*. *Also a., v.t., v.i.* WH: 16C. Prob. from PORT[1], towards which the ship's side was turned when loading or unloading cargo.

port[5] v.t. to carry or hold (a rifle etc.) in a slanting position across the body in front. *Also n.* WH: 16C. Old French *porter*, from Latin *portare* to bear, to carry, from *portus* PORT[1].

port[6] n. a suitcase, a travelling bag. WH: early 20C. Abbr. of PORTMANTEAU.

port[7] v.t. to transfer (software) from one system to another. WH: late 20C. PORT[5].

porta n. the aperture where veins, ducts etc. enter an organ, esp. the transverse fissure of the liver. WH: 14–15C. Modern Latin, from Latin gate.

portable a. capable of being easily carried, esp. about the person. *Also n.* WH: 14–15C. Old French, or from Late Latin *portabilis*, from *portare* to bear, to carry. See PORT[5], also -ABLE.

portage n. the act or an instance of carrying, carriage. *Also v.t., v.i.* WH: 14–15C. French, from *porter* (PORT[5]). See also -AGE.

Portakabin® n. a portable building delivered intact to, or speedily erected on, a site as temporary offices etc. WH: mid-20C. PORTABLE + CABIN.

portal[1] *n.* a door, a gate, a gateway, an entrance, esp. one of an ornamental or imposing kind. WH: 14–15C. Old French, from Medieval Latin *portale*, use as n. of neut. of *portalis*, from Latin *porta* gate. See PORT[2], also -AL[1].

portal[2] *a.* of, relating to or connected with the porta. WH: 17C. Modern Latin *portalis*, from Latin *porta* PORT[2]. See also -AL[1].

portamento *n.* a smooth, continuous glide from one note to another across intervening tones. WH: 18C. Italian, lit. a carrying, from *portare* to carry.

portative *a.* capable of carrying or supporting. WH: 14–15C. Old French *portatif*, appar. alt. of *portatil*, from Medieval Latin *portatilis* that may be carried, from Latin *portatus*, p.p. of *portare* PORT[5]. See also -IVE.

portcullis *n.* a strong timber or iron grating, sliding in vertical grooves over a gateway, and let down to close the passage in case of assault. WH: 12–14C. Old French *porte coleïce*, from *porte* door + *coleïce, coulice*, fem. of *couleïs* gliding, sliding, from Latin *colare* to filter. Cp. COULISSE.

Porte *n.* the old Imperial Turkish Government in Constantinople; also *Sublime Porte, Ottoman Porte.* WH: 17C. French (*la Sublime*) *Porte* (the exalted) gate, translating Turkish Arabic *bāb i-āli* high gate, eminent gate, official title of the central office of the Ottoman government.

porte cochère *n.* a carriage-entrance leading into a courtyard. WH: 18C. French, from *porte* PORT[2] + *cochère*, fem. a. fr. *coche* COACH.

portend *v.t.* to indicate by previous signs, to presage, to foreshadow. WH: 14–15C. Latin *portendere*, from Popular Latin *por-* PRO-[1] + *tendere* to stretch, TEND[1].

porter[1] *n.* a person employed to carry loads, esp. parcels, luggage etc. at a railway station, airport or hotel, or goods in a market. WH: 12–14C. Old French *portour* (Modern French *porteur*), from Medieval Latin *portator*, from *portatus*, p.p. of *portare* to bear, to carry. See PORT[5], also -ER[2], -OUR.

porter[2] *n.* a gatekeeper, a doorkeeper esp. of a large building, who usu. regulates entry and answers enquiries. WH: 12–14C. Old French *portier*, from Late Latin *portarius*, from *porta*. See PORT[2], also -ER[2].

portfire *n.* a slow-burning fuse, formerly used for firing guns, now chiefly in mining etc. WH: 17C. Partial Anglicization of French *porte-feu*, from *porte-*, stem of *porter* to carry, PORT[5] + *feu* fire.

portfolio *n.* a portable case for holding papers, drawings etc. WH: 18C. Italian *portafogli*, from *porta*, imper. of *portare* to carry + *fogli* leaves, sheets of paper, pl. of *foglio*, from Latin *folium* leaf.

portico *n.* a colonnade, a roof supported by columns. WH: 17C. Italian, from Latin *porticus* porch.

portière *n.* a door-curtain. WH: 19C. French, from *porte* door (PORT[2]) + *-ière* (from Latin *-aria*, -ARY[1]).

portion *n.* a share, a part assigned. *Also v.t.* WH: 12–14C. Old French *porcion* (Modern French *portion*), from Latin *portio, portionis*, gen. of a n. first found only in the phr. *pro portione* in proportion.

Portland *a.* of or derived from Portland. WH: 19C. (Isle of) *Portland*, a peninsula in Dorset.

portly *a.* stout, corpulent. WH: 15C. PORT[5] + -LY[1]. The original sense was stately, dignified, handsome, imposing. The sense stout, corpulent evolved in the 16C.

portmanteau *n.* a travelling bag which opens out flat, for carrying clothes. *Also a.* WH: 16C. French *portemanteau*, from *porte-*, stem of *porter* to carry, PORT[5] + *manteau* MANTLE.

portolan *n.* a sailing manual containing charts, descriptions of ports, coastlines etc. WH: 18C. Italian *portolano*, from PORT[1].

portrait *n.* a likeness or representation of a person or animal. *Also a.* WH: 16C. French p.p. (used as n.) of Old French *portraire* portray, from *por-* (PRO-[1]) + *traire* draw, from alt. of Latin *trahere*.

Port Salut *n.* a type of mild cheese, made in a round flat shape. WH: 19C. *Port Salut*, a Trappist monastery in NW France. The monastery name (properly *Port-du-Salut*) means haven of salvation.

Portuguese *a.* of or relating to Portugal, its people or its language. *Also n.* WH: 16C. Portuguese *Portuguez*, from Medieval Latin *Portugalensis*, from *Portus Cale* Portugal, a country in the W part of the Iberian peninsula, SW Europe. See also -ESE.

portulaca *n.* any plant of the genus *Portulaca*, low succulent herbs with flowers opening only in direct sunshine, comprising the purslane. WH: 16C. Modern Latin, use as genus name of Latin purslane.

posada *n.* an inn, in a Spanish-speaking country. WH: 18C. Spanish, from *posar* to lodge.

posaune *n.* a rich and powerful reed-stop in an organ. WH: 18C. German trombone, ult. from Old French *buisine*, from Latin *buccina* trumpet.

pose[1] *v.t.* to cause (an artist's model etc.) to take a certain attitude. *Also v.i., n.* WH: 12–14C. Old French *poser*, from Late Latin *pausare* to cease, PAUSE. The verb acquired the sense of Latin *ponere* to put, to place, by association with *pos-*, the perfect stem of *ponere* (as in the past tense *posui*, and the past participle *positus*) and essentially came to be identified with it, taking many of its compounds. These coexist in English as COMPOSE, DISPOSE, EXPOSE, etc.

pose[2] *v.t.* to puzzle (a person), to cause to be at a loss. WH: 16C. Shortening of obs. *appose*, from Old French *aposer*, var. of *oposer* OPPOSE.

posh *a.* smart, fashionable. *Also adv.* WH: early 20C. Orig. uncertain. ? From obs. *posh* money, ? Romany, lit. half. The word is popularly derived from the initial letters of *port out starboard home*, with reference to the better-class accommodation (avoiding the heat of the sun) on ships plying between England and India. But evidence to support such an origin is lacking.

posit *v.t.* to place, to set in position. *Also n.* WH: 17C. Latin *positus*, p.p. of *ponere* to place.

position *n.* the place occupied by a person or thing. *Also v.t.* WH: 14–15C. Old French, or from Latin *positio, positionis* a putting, a placing, from *positus*, p.p. of *ponere* to put, to place, translating Greek THESIS, *thema* THEME. See also -ITION.

positive *a.* definitely affirmed. *Also n.* WH: 12–14C. Old French *positif* or Latin *positivus*, from *positus*. See POSIT, also -IVE.

positron *n.* a subatomic particle having the same mass as an electron, but a positive charge. WH: mid-20C. POSITIVE + *-tron*, based on ELECTRON. The term was introduced in 1933 by the US physicist Carl David Anderson, who discovered the particle in 1932.

posology *n.* the science treating of doses or the quantities of medicines to be administered. WH: 19C. French *posologie*, from Greek *posos* how much. See also -LOGY.

posse *n.* a body or force (of persons). WH: 17C. Abbr. of Medieval Latin *posse comitatus* force of the county. The word was originally the term for the body of men in a county who could be summoned by the sheriff to repress a riot or for some other purpose.

possess *v.t.* to own as property, to have full power over. WH: 14–15C. Old French *possesser*, from Latin *possessus*, p.p. of *possidere*, from *potis* (POTENT) + *sedere* to sit.

possession *n.* the act or state of possessing. WH: 12–14C. Old French, or from Latin *possessio, possessionis*, from *possessus*. See POSSESS, also -ION.

possessive *a.* of or relating to possession. *Also n.* WH: 14–15C. Latin *possessivus*, from *possessus*. See POSSESS, also -IVE. In the grammatical sense, Latin *possessivus* (*casus*) translated Greek *ktētikē* (*ptōsis*) possessive (case).

posset *n.* a drink made of hot milk curdled with ale, wine etc. *Also v.t., v.i.* WH: 14–15C. Orig. unknown.

possible *a.* that may happen or be done. *Also n.* WH: 12–14C. Old French, or from Latin *possibilis*, from *posse* to be able. See also -IBLE.

possie *n.* a place, position. WH: early 20C. Abbr. of POSITION + *-ie* (-Y[3]).

possum *n.* an opossum. WH: 17C. Shortening of OPOSSUM.

post[1] *n.* a piece of timber, metal etc., set upright, and intended as a support to something, or to mark a boundary. *Also v.t.* WH: pre-1200. Old English, from Latin *postis*, ? from *por-* PRO-[1] + *stare* to stand.

post[2] *n.* a fixed place or position. *Also v.t.* WH: 16C. French *poste*, from Italian *posto*, from contr. of Popular Latin *positum*, neut. p.p. of *ponere* to place. Cp. POST[3].

post[3] *n.* an established system of conveyance and delivery of letters and parcels; orig. one of a series of men stationed at points along a road whose duty was to ride forward to the next man with letters. *Also adv., v.t., v.i.* WH: 16C. French *poste*, from Italian *posta*, from contr. of Latin *posita*, fem. p.p. of *ponere* to place. Cp. POST[2]. The word was originally used for a series of riders stationed in stages along certain roads, each conveying mail (originally from the monarch) to the next stage. The current sense, a system of carrying and delivering mail, evolved in the 17C.

post- *pref.* after, in time or order. WH: Latin *post* after, behind.

postage *n.* the fee for sending a letter etc. by post. WH: 16C. POST³ + -AGE. The original sense was carriage of mail by a postal messenger. The current sense arose in the 17C.

postal *a.* of or relating to the mail service. *Also n.* WH: 19C. French *poste* POST³. See also -AL¹.

poster *n.* a large placard or advertising bill. WH: 19C. POST¹ + -ER¹. The original sense was a person who puts up notices (at first on a post). The current sense evolved soon after.

poste restante *n.* a department in a post office where letters are kept until called for. WH: 18C. French post remaining. The term was originally a direction written on a letter indicating that it was to remain at a particular post office until called for. The name passed to the department itself in the 19C.

posterior *a.* coming or happening after. *Also n.* WH: 16C. Latin, comp. of *posterus* following, future, from *post* after. See also -IOR.

posterity *n.* those proceeding in the future from any person, descendants. WH: 14–15C. Old French *postérité*, from Latin *posteritas*, from *posterus*. See POSTERIOR, also -ITY.

postern *n.* a small doorway or gateway at the side or back. *Also a.* WH: 12–14C. Old French *pasterne* (Modern French *poterne*), alt. of *posterle*, from Late Latin *posterula*, dim. of *posterus*. See POSTERIOR.

post hoc *n.* the fallacy of assuming that if something happened after something else, it must have happened because of it. WH: 19C. Latin after this. The full form of the Latin term is *post hoc, ergo propter hoc* after this, therefore because of this.

posthumous *a.* (of a child) born after the death of the father. WH: 17C. Latin *postumus* last, superl. from *post* after, altered in Late Latin to *posthumus*, as if from Latin *humus* earth, i.e. after (the father has been put in) the ground.

postiche *n.* a hairpiece. *Also a.* WH: 18C. French, from Italian *posticcio* counterfeit, feigned.

posticous *a.* posterior. WH: 19C. Latin *posticus* hinder, posterior, from *post* behind. See also -IC, -OUS.

†postil *n.* a marginal note in a Bible. *Also v.i., v.t.* WH: 14–15C. Old French *postille*, from Medieval Latin *postilla*, prob. from Latin *post illa* (*verba*) after these (words), as a direction to a scribe.

postilion *n.* the rider on the near horse of the leaders or of a pair drawing a carriage. WH: 16C. French *postillon*, from Italian *postiglione* post boy, from *posta* POST³.

Post-it (note)® *n.* a small sheet of paper for writing messages, with a strip of adhesive along one edge which allows the note to be stuck to a surface and removed again without damaging the surface. WH: mid-20C. POST¹ + IT¹.

postliminy *n.* in Roman law, the right of resumption of former rights and privileges by an exile or captive returning to their own country. WH: 17C. Latin *postliminium*, from POST- + *limen, liminis* threshold. See also -Y².

postlude *n.* a closing piece or voluntary. WH: 19C. POST- + -*lude*, based on PRELUDE, INTERLUDE.

post meridiem *adv.* after noon. WH: 17C. Latin after midday. See MERIDIAN.

post-mortem *adv.* after death. *Also a., n.* WH: 18C. Latin after death.

post-obit *a.* taking effect after death; post-mortem. *Also n.* WH: 18C. Latin *post obitum* after decease. See OBIT.

post-partum *a.* of or relating to the period immediately after childbirth. WH: 19C. Latin after childbirth.

postpone *v.t.* to put off, to delay. *Also v.i.* WH: 15C. Latin *postponere*, from *post* after + *ponere* to place.

postposition *n.* the act of placing after. WH: 16C. Late Latin *postpositio, postpositionis*, from *postpositus*, p.p. of *postponere* POSTPONE.

postscenium *n.* the back part of a theatre behind the scenes. WH: 18C. Latin *postscaenium*, from *post* after, behind + *scaena, scena* SCENE.

postscript *n.* a paragraph added to a letter after the writer's signature. WH: 16C. Latin *postscriptum*, neut. p.p. (used as n.) of *postscribere* to write after, from *post* after + *scribere* to write.

postulant *n.* a candidate for entry into a religious order or for an ecclesiastical office. WH: 18C. French, or from Latin *postulans, postulantis*, pres.p. of *postulare* POSTULATE². See also -ANT.

postulate¹ *n.* a position assumed without proof as being self-evident. WH: 16C. Latin *postulatum*, neut. p.p. (used as n.) of *postulare*. See POSTULATE², also -ATE¹.

postulate² *v.t.* to suggest, to claim. WH: 14–15C. Latin *postulatus*, p.p. of *postulare* to ask, to demand, to request. See also -ATE³.

posture *n.* a pose, attitude or arrangement of the parts of the body. *Also v.t., v.i.* WH: 16C. French, from Italian *postura*, from Latin *positura* position, situation, from *positus*. See POSIT, also -URE.

posy *n.* a bunch of flowers, a nosegay. WH: 14–15C. Contr. of POESY. The original sense was a short motto (usually a line of verse) inscribed inside a ring, etc. The current sense evolved in the 15C.

pot¹ *n.* a round vessel of earthenware, metal or glass, usu. deep relative to the breadth, for holding liquids etc. *Also v.t., v.i.* WH: pre-1200. Old English *pott*, from Popular Latin *pottus*, of uncertain orig. (prob. not rel. to Late Latin *potus* drinking cup).

pot² *n.* marijuana. WH: mid-20C. Prob. from Mexican Spanish *potiguaya* marijuana leaves.

pot³ *n.* a drop goal in rugby. *Also v.t.* WH: 19C. Abbr. of *pot-shot* (POT¹).

potable *a.* drinkable. *Also n.* WH: 14–15C. Old French, or from Late Latin *potabilis*, from *potare* to drink. See also -ABLE.

potage *n.* thick soup. WH: 12–14C. Orig. from Old French, lit. that which is put in a pot, from *pot* POT¹ (see also -AGE), later readopted from French. Cp. POTTAGE.

potager *n.* a vegetable garden. WH: 17C. French (*jardin*) *potager* (garden) for the kitchen.

potamic *a.* of or relating to rivers. WH: 19C. Greek *potamos* river + -IC.

potash *n.* a powerful alkali, consisting of potassium carbonate in a crude form, orig. obtained from the ashes of plants. WH: 17C. Obs. Dutch *potasschen* (now *potasch*). See POT¹, ASH¹. Potash was originally obtained by leaching the ashes of burnt plant material and evaporating the solution in iron pots.

potassium *n.* a bluish or pinkish white metallic element, at. no. 19, chem. symbol K. WH: 19C. Modern Latin *potassa* POTASH + -IUM. The element is so called because potassium is the basis of potash. The term was coined in 1807 by the English chemist Sir Humphry Davy, who first separated potassium from potash.

potation *n.* the act, or an instance, of drinking. WH: 14–15C. Old French, from Latin *potatio, potationis*, from *potatus*, p.p. of *potare* to drink. See also -ATION.

potato *n.* a plant, *Solanum tuberosum*, with edible farinaceous tubers. WH: 16C. Spanish *patata*, var. of BATATA.

pot-au-feu *n.* a traditional French stew of beef and vegetables. WH: 18C. French, lit. pot on the fire.

potch *n.* an opal of inferior quality. WH: 19C. Orig. unknown.

poteen *n.* Irish whiskey illicitly distilled. WH: 19C. Irish (*fuisce*) *poitín* little hot (whiskey). See also -EEN.

potence *n.* a cross with ends resembling the head of a crutch or a T. WH: 14–15C. Old French, from Latin *potentia*, from *potens, potentis*. See POTENT. The original sense was a crutch.

potent *a.* powerful, mighty. *Also n.* WH: 14–15C. Latin *potens, potentis*, pres.p. of *posse* to be powerful, to be able, from *potis* powerful. See also -ENT.

potentilla *n.* any plant or shrub of the genus *Potentilla*, comprising the cinquefoil, tormentil etc. WH: 16C. Medieval Latin, from Latin *potens, potentis* (POTENT) + dim. suf. -*illa*. The plant is so called from the medicinal properties of some of the species.

pother *n.* bustle, confusion. *Also v.i., v.t.* WH: 16C. Orig. uncertain. ? Rel. to BOTHER.

potiche *n.* a kind of oriental pot or vase, round or polygonal, narrowing towards the top and with a detachable lid. WH: 19C. French, deriv. of *pot* POT¹.

potion *n.* a liquid mixture intended as a medicine or a magic charm. *Also v.t.* WH: 12–14C. Old French, from Latin *potio, potionis* drink, poisonous draught, from *potus*, p.p. of *potare* to drink. See also -ION.

potlatch *n.* a ceremonial feast among Indians of the northwestern US involving emulation in the giving of extravagant gifts. WH: 19C. Chinook Jargon, from Nootka *p'acitl* to make a gift (at a potlatch).

potometer *n.* an instrument which measures the rate at which a plant takes in water. WH: 19C. Greek *poton* drink + -METER.

potoroo *n.* the marsupial rat kangaroo. WH: 18C. Australian Aboriginal (Dharuk) *badaru*.

pot-pourri *n.* a mixture of dried flower-petals and spices, usu. kept in a bowl for perfuming a room. WH: 17C. French, lit. rotten pot, from *pot* POT¹ + *pourri*, p.p. of *pourrir* to rot, translating Spanish *olla podrida* (OLLA). The word was originally used for a stew made of different kinds of meat. The current sense dates from the 18C.

potrero *n.* a paddock or pasture for horses etc. WH: 19C. Spanish, from *potro* colt, pony.

pottage *n.* a kind of soup or stew. WH: 16C. Anglicized form of POTAGE. Cp. PORRIDGE.

potter¹ *n.* a maker of pottery. WH: pre-1200. POT¹ + -ER¹.

potter² *v.i.* to busy oneself in a desultory but generally agreeable way. *Also v.t.* WH: 16C. Freq. of obs. *pote* to push, to thrust, of unknown orig. Cp. PUT. See also -ER⁵.

pottle *n.* a vessel or basket for holding fruit. WH: 12–14C. Old French *potel*, dim. of *pot* POT¹. See also -EL.

potto *n.* a W African lemuroid, *Perodicticus potto*. WH: 18C. Appar. a W African word.

Pott's fracture *n.* a fracture of the leg, at the lower end of the fibula, usu. with dislocation of the ankle. WH: 19C. Sir Percival *Pott*, 1713–88, English surgeon.

potty¹ *a.* crazy, foolish. WH: 19C. Orig. unknown.

potty² *n.* a chamber pot, esp. one for use by small children. WH: mid-20C. POT¹ + -Y³.

pouch *n.* a small bag. *Also v.t., v.i.* WH: 12–14C. Old Northern French *pouche*, var. of Old French *poche* bag, pouch (Modern French pocket). Cp. POKE².

pouf *n.* a large, solid cushion used as a seat or a footstool. WH: 19C. French, ult. imit.

Poujadism *n.* a reactionary political movement aiming to protect the interests of small businesses. WH: mid-20C. Pierre *Poujade*, 1920–, French publisher and bookseller, who founded a movement for the protection of artisans and small shopkeepers in 1954.

poulard *n.* a hen that has been spayed and fattened for eating. WH: 18C. French *poularde*, from *poule* hen + -*arde* -ARD.

poult *n.* paduasoy. WH: mid-20C. Abbr. of *poult-de-soie*, alt. of French *pou-de-soie*. See PADUASOY.

poultice *n.* a heated and medicated composition, for applying to sore or inflamed parts of the body to reduce inflammation, a cataplasm. *Also v.t.* WH: 14–15C. Latin *pultes* (pl.), from *puls, pultis* thick pottage, pap. See PULSE².

poultry *n.* domestic fowls, including chickens, geese, ducks, turkeys etc. WH: 12–14C. Old French *pouletrie*, from *pouletier* dealer in domestic fowls, from *poulet* PULLET. See also -ER², -RY.

pounce¹ *n.* an abrupt swoop, spring etc. *Also v.i., v.t.* WH: 14–15C. ? Shortening of PUNCHEON¹ or from Old French *poinson, poinchon*. Cp. PUNCH¹. The original sense was a stamp or punch for impressing marks on metal. The sense to seize with claws or talons developed from this in the 17C (as a noun, in the 19C).

pounce² *n.* a fine powder formerly used to dry up ink on manuscript. *Also v.t.* WH: 18C. Old French *ponce*, from Popular Latin form of Latin *pumex, pumicis* PUMICE.

pound¹ *n.* an avoirdupois unit of weight divided into 16 ounces and equal to approx. 0.454 kg. *Also v.t.* WH: pre-1200. Old English *pund*, from Germanic, from Latin (*libra*) *pondo* (pound) by weight. Cp. German *Pfund*. Both the unit of weight and the unit of money date from pre-1200. The pound sign (£) represents the letter *L*, for Latin *libra*.

pound² *n.* an enclosure for confining stray cattle etc. *Also v.t.* WH: pre-1200. Orig. uncertain. Cp. POND.

pound³ *v.t.* to crush, to pulverize. *Also v.i.* WH: pre-1200. Old English *pūnian*, rel. to Dutch *puin* rubbish, rubble.

pour *v.t.* to cause (liquids etc.) to flow downwards. *Also v.i., n.* WH: 12–14C. Orig. unknown.

pourboire *n.* a gratuity, a tip. WH: 19C. French, lit. for drinking, from *pour* for + *boire* to drink. Cp. German *Trinkgeld*.

pour-parler *n.* a preliminary discussion with a view to formal negotiation. WH: 18C. French, use as n. of Old French *porparler*, from *por-* PRO-¹ + *parler* to speak.

pour-point *n.* a quilted doublet. WH: 12–14C. Old French *pourpoint*, orig. p.p. of *pourpoindre* to perforate, to quilt, from *pour-* PRO-¹ + *poindre* to prick, ult. from Latin *per* through + *pungere* to prick.

poussette *v.i.* (of partners in a country dance) to move up or down the set with hands joined. *Also n.* WH: 19C. French, dim. of *pousse* push. See also -ETTE.

poussin *n.* a young chicken reared for eating. WH: mid-20C. French chick, from Popular Latin *pullicinus*, dim. of Latin *pullus* PULLET.

pout¹ *v.i.* to thrust out the lips in displeasure or contempt. *Also v.t., n.* WH: 12–14C. ? From base of Swedish dial. *puta* to be inflated, Danish *pude* cushion. Cp. POUT². The ultimate origin is probably imitative. Cp. French *bouder* to pout, to sulk (see BOUDOIR).

pout² *n.* any one of various fishes that have a pouting appearance, esp. the eelpout and the bib or whiting-pout. WH: pre-1200. Appar. from source of POUT¹.

poverty *n.* the state of being poor. WH: 12–14C. Old French *poverte, poverté*, from Latin *paupertas*, from *pauper* poor. See also -TY¹.

pow *int.* used to express the sound of an impact, blow etc. WH: 19C. Imit.

powan *n.* a freshwater fish, *Coregonus clupeoides*, found in Loch Lomond etc. WH: 17C. Scottish form of POLLAN.

powder *n.* any dry, dustlike substance or fine particles. *Also v.t., v.i.* WH: 12–14C. Old French *poudre*, earlier *poldre*, from Latin *pulvis, pulveris* dust.

power *n.* the ability to do or act so as to effect something. *Also a., v.t., v.i.* WH: 12–14C. Old French *poier* (Modern French *pouvoir*), from alt. of Latin *posse* to be able.

powwow *n.* a meeting, talk or conference, orig. among N American Indians. *Also v.i., v.t.* WH: 17C. Narragansett *powah, powwaw* shaman. Cp. CAUCUS.

pox *n.* any disease characterized by the formation of pustules that leave pockmarks. WH: 14–15C. POCK + -S¹.

Pozidriv® *n.* a type of cross-head screwdriver. WH: mid-20C. Prob. from POSITIVE + *screwdriver* (SCREW). The head of the screw driven in is in the form of a plus sign (+), indicating a positive electrical charge.

pozzolana *n.* a volcanic ash used in hydraulic cements. WH: 18C. Italian *pozzuolana* (*terra*) (earth) belonging to Pozzuoli, a town near Naples, where the ash is found.

practicable *a.* capable of being done, feasible. WH: 17C. French, from *pratiquer* to put into practice, to use, from *pratique*, from Old French *practique*, from Medieval Latin *practica*, from Greek *praktikē*, use as n. of fem. of *praktikos*, from *prattein* to do. See also -IC, -ABLE.

practical *a.* of or relating to action not theory or speculation. *Also n.* WH: 16C. From obs. *practic* pertaining to practice, from Old French *practique* (PRACTICABLE) + -AL¹.

practice *n.* habitual or customary action or procedure. WH: 14–15C. From PRACTISE, based on such pairs as ADVICE/ ADVISE, DEVICE/ DEVISE.

practise *v.t.* to perform habitually; to carry out. *Also v.i.* WH: 14–15C. Old French *practiser* or Medieval Latin *practizare*, alt. of *practicare*, from *practica*. See PRACTICABLE.

practitioner *n.* a person who regularly practises any profession, esp. medicine. WH: 16C. Extended form (with -ER¹) of obs. var. of *practician* (PRACTICE).

praecipe *n.* a writ requiring something to be done, or a reason for its non-performance. WH: 14–15C. Latin, imper. of *praecipere*. See PRECEPT.

praemunire *n.* a writ or process against a person charged with obeying or maintaining the papal authority in England. WH: 14–15C. Latin to fortify or protect in front. See PREMUNITION. In Medieval Latin the word was confused with and used instead of *praemonere* to forewarn, to admonish. The words in the 1393 writ were: *precipimus quod per bonos et legales homines de balliua tua premunire facias prefatum propositum [A.B.] quod tunc sit coram nobis* We command that through good and loyal men of thy jurisdiction thou do [or cause to] warn the aforesaid [A.B.] that he appear before us.

praepostor *n.* a prefect in some public schools. WH: 18C. Contr. of Latin *praepositor*, from *praepositus*, p.p. of *praeponere* to put in charge. See also -OR. Cp. PREFECT.

praetor *n.* a Roman magistrate; orig. a consul as leader of the army, later a curule magistrate elected yearly to perform various judicial and consular duties. WH: 14–15C. French *préteur*, or from Latin *praetor*, ? from *prae-* PRE- + *itus*, p.p. of *ire* to go. See also -OR.

pragmatic *a.* concerned with practicalities rather than principles. *Also n.* WH: 16C. Late Latin *pragmaticus* (in *pragmatica sanctio* pragmatic sanction), from Greek *pragmatikos*, from *pragma*, *pragmatos* act, deed, affair, from *prak-*, stem of *prattein* to do.

prairie *n.* an extensive tract of level or rolling grassland, usu. destitute of trees, esp. in N America. WH: 18C. French, from Old French *praerie*, from Latin *pratum* meadow. See also -RY.

praise *v.t.* to express approval and commendation of. *Also n.* WH: 12–14C. Old French *preisier* to price, to value, to prize, to praise, from Late Latin *pretiare*, from Latin *pretium* price. Cp. PRICE, PRIZE[1].

Prakrit *n.* any of a group of N and central Indian languages or dialects no longer used, based on Sanskrit. WH: 18C. Sanskrit *prākṛta* natural, unrefined, vernacular. Cp. SANSKRIT.

praline *n.* a confection of almond or other nut with a brown coating of sugar. WH: 18C. French, from Marshal de Plessis-*Praslin*, 1598–1675, French soldier, whose cook invented it.

pralltriller *n.* an ornament in which a note is preceded by itself and the note immediately before it, an inverted mordent. WH: 19C. German, from *prallen* to bounce + *Triller* trill.

pram[1] *n.* a four-wheeled conveyance for a baby, with a cradle-like body and pushed by a person walking. WH: 19C. Abbr. of *perambulator* (PERAMBULATE), ? punning on PRAM[2].

pram[2] *n.* a flat-bottomed barge or lighter used in the Netherlands and the Baltic. WH: 14–15C. Middle Dutch *prame*, Middle Low German *prāme*, ? from Czech *prám*.

prana *n.* in Hinduism, the breath of life. WH: 19C. Sanskrit *prāṇa*.

prance *v.i.* to spring or caper on the hind legs, as a horse. *Also n.* WH: 14–15C. Orig. unknown. ? Rel. to PRANK[2].

prandial *a.* relating to lunch or dinner. WH: 19C. Latin *prandium* late breakfast + -AL[1].

prang *v.t.* to crash. *Also n.* WH: mid-20C. Prob. imit. According to some, a blend of PASTE and BANG (Eric Partridge, *A Dictionary of RAF Slang*, 1945).

prank[1] *n.* a wild frolic. WH: 16C. Orig. unknown.

prank[2] *v.t.* to dress up in a showy fashion; to deck (out). *Also v.i.* WH: 14–15C. Rel. to Middle Low German *prank* pomp, display, Dutch *pronk* show, finery, German *Prunk* pomp, ostentation.

prase *n.* a dull leek-green translucent quartz. WH: 18C. French, from Latin *prasius*, from Greek *prasios* leek-green, from *prason* leek.

praseodymium *n.* a rare metallic element, at. no. 59, chem. symbol Pr, occurring in certain rare-earth minerals. WH: 19C. German *Praseodym*, from Greek *prasios* leek-green + German *Didym* DIDYMIUM. See PRASE, also -IUM. The element was named in 1885 by its discoverer, the Austrian chemist Carl A. von Welsbach, who so called it from the colour of its salts and because the supposed element didymium was found to consist of two elements, neodymium and praseodymium.

prat *n.* a stupid or contemptible person. WH: 16C. Orig. unknown. The original meaning was buttock. The sense stupid person emerged in the mid-20C.

prate *v.i.* to chatter; to talk a lot and without purpose or reason. *Also v.t., n.* WH: 14–15C. Low German and Middle Dutch *praten*, prob. of imit. orig. Cp. PRATTLE.

pratie *n.* a potato. WH: 18C. Irish *prátaí*, pl. of *práta* potato, ult. from same source as POTATO.

pratincole *n.* any of a genus, *Glareola*, of birds related to the plover, living near water. WH: 18C. Modern Latin *pratincola*, from Latin *pratum* meadow + *-cole* (-COLOUS). The Modern Latin name was coined in 1756 by the Austrian naturalist Johann Kramer.

pratique *n.* a licence to a ship to hold communication with a port after quarantine, or upon certification that the vessel has not come from an infected place. WH: 17C. French practice, intercourse, corr. to (or from) Italian *pratica*, from Medieval Latin *practica*, use as n. of fem. of *practicus*, from Greek *praktikos*, from *prattein* to do.

prattle *v.i.* to talk in a childish or foolish manner. *Also v.t., n.* WH: 16C. Middle Low German *pratelen*, from *praten* PRATE. See also -LE[4]. Cp. TATTLE.

prawn *n.* any of several small decapod crustaceans, like large shrimps. *Also v.t.* WH: 14–15C. Orig. unknown.

praxis *n.* use, practice, accepted practice. WH: 16C. Medieval Latin, from Greek, from *prattein* to do.

pray *v.t.* to ask for with earnestness or submission. *Also v.i., int.* WH: 12–14C. Old French *preier* (Modern French *prier*), from Late Latin *precare*, alt. of Latin *precari* to entreat.

prayer *n.* the act of praying. WH: 12–14C. Old French *preiere* (Modern French *prière*), from use as n. of fem. of Latin *precarius* obtained by entreaty.

pre *prep.* before. WH: mid-20C. Independent use of PRE-.

pre- *pref.* before, earlier than; in advance. WH: Latin *prae* before, in front, in advance.

preach *v.i.* to deliver a sermon or public discourse on some religious subject. *Also v.t., n.* WH: 12–14C. Old French *prechier* (Modern French *prêcher*), from Latin *praedicare* to proclaim. See PREDICATE[1].

preamble *n.* an introductory statement, esp. the introductory portion of a statute setting forth succinctly its reasons and intentions. *Also v.i.* WH: 14–15C. Old French *préamble*, from Medieval Latin *preambulum*, use as n. of neut. of Late Latin *praeambulus* going before, from *praeambulare*, from *prae-* PRE- + AMBLE.

prebend *n.* the stipend or maintenance granted to a canon of a cathedral or collegiate church out of its revenue. WH: 14–15C. Old French *prébende*, from Late Latin *praebenda*, lit. things to be supplied, neut. pl. of ger. of *praebere* to supply, from *prae-* PRE- + *habere* to have, to hold. See also -END.

precarious *a.* not well-established, unstable. WH: 17C. Latin *precarius*, from *prex*, *precis* prayer, entreaty. See also -ARIOUS. A thing obtained or gained by the favour of another is necessarily insecure.

precative *a.* expressing a wish or entreaty. WH: 17C. Late Latin *precativus*, from Latin *precatus*, p.p. of *precari* to entreat.

precaution *n.* a measure taken beforehand to guard against something. *Also v.t.* WH: 16C. French *précaution*, from Late Latin *praecautio*, *praecautionis*, from *praecautus*, p.p. of *praecavere*, from *prae-* PRE- + *cavere* to take heed.

precede *v.t.* to go before in time or order. *Also v.i.* WH: 14–15C. Old French *précéder*, from Latin *praecedere*, from *prae-* PRE- + *cedere* CEDE.

precentor *n.* a cleric who directs choral services in a cathedral. WH: 17C. French *précenteur* or Latin *praecentor*, from *praecentus*, p.p. of *praecinere*, from *prae-* PRE- + *canere* to sing. See also -OR.

precept *n.* a command, a mandate. WH: 14–15C. Latin *praeceptum*, use as n. of p.p. of *praecipere* to take beforehand, to warn, to instruct, from *prae-* PRE- + *capere* to take.

precession *n.* precedence in time or order. WH: 12–14C. Late Latin *praecessio*, *praecessionis*, from Latin *praecessus*, p.p. of *praecedere* PRECEDE. See also -ION.

precinct *n.* the space enclosed by the walls or boundaries of a place, esp. a church. WH: 14–15C. Medieval Latin *praecinctum*, neut. p.p. (used as n.) of *praecingere* to gird about, to encircle, from *prae-* PRE- + *cingere* to gird.

precious *a.* of great price or value. *Also adv.* WH: 12–14C. Old French *precios* (Modern French *précieux*), from Latin *pretiosus*, from *pretium* PRICE. See also -OUS.

precipice *n.* a vertical or very steep cliff. WH: 16C. French *précipice* or Latin *praecipitium*, from *praeceps*, *praecipitis* headlong, steep, or *praecipitare* PRECIPITATE[1].

precipitate[1] *v.t.* to throw headlong. *Also v.i.* WH: 16C. Latin *praecipitatus*, p.p. of *praecipitare* to throw headlong, from *praeceps*, *praecipitis* headlong, from *prae-* PRE- + *caput* head. See also -ATE[3].

precipitate[2] *a.* headlong. *Also n.* WH: 17C. Latin *praecipitatus*, p.p. of *praecipitare*. See PRECIPITATE[1], also -ATE[2].

precipitin *n.* an antibody that produces a precipitation when mixed with its antigen. WH: early 20C. PRECIPITATE[1] + -IN[1].

precipitous *a.* like or of the nature of a precipice. WH: 17C. Obs. French *précipiteux*, from Latin *praecipitatus*. See PRECIPITATE[1], also -OUS.

précis *n.* an abstract, a summary. *Also v.t.* WH: 18C. French, use as n. of *précis* PRECISE.

precise *a.* definite, well-defined. WH: 14–15C. French *précis*, from Latin *praecisus*, p.p. of *praecidere* to cut short, to abridge, from *prae-* PRE- + *caedere* to cut.

preclude v.t. to shut out, to exclude. WH: 15C. Latin praecludere, from prae- PRE- + claudere to shut. The original sense was to close or bar a route physically. The current sense arose in the 17C.

precocial a. (having young which are) hatched with a complete covering of down and capable of leaving the nest within a very short time. Also n. WH: 19C. Modern Latin Praecoces, a former division of birds, pl. of Latin praecox. See PRECOCIOUS, also -IAL.

precocious a. prematurely developed intellectually. WH: 17C. Latin praecox, praecocis, from praecoquere to boil beforehand, to ripen fully, from prae- PRE- + coquere to cook. See also -IOUS. Cp. APRICOT.

precognition n. foreknowledge; clairvoyance. WH: 14–15C. Late Latin praecognitio, praecognitionis, from prae- PRE- + cognitio, cognitionis (COGNITION).

preconceive v.t. to conceive or form (an opinion of) beforehand. WH: 16C. PRE- + CONCEIVE.

preconize v.t. to proclaim publicly. WH: 14–15C. Medieval Latin praeconizare, from Latin praeco, praeconis public crier, herald. See also -IZE.

precordia n.pl. the chest and the parts it contains, the region about the heart. WH: 17C. Latin pl., diaphragm, entrails, from prae- PRE- + cor, cordis heart.

precursor n. a forerunner, a harbinger. WH: 14–15C. Latin praecursor, from praecursus, p.p. of praecurrere to run before, to precede, from prae- PRE- + currere to run. See also -OR.

predacious a. living by prey, predatory. WH: 18C. Latin praeda booty, plunder + -ACIOUS.

predator n. a predatory animal. WH: early 20C. Latin praedator plunderer, from praedatus, p.p. of praedari to seize as plunder, to pillage, from praeda booty, plunder. See also -OR.

predecessor n. a person who precedes another in any position, office etc. WH: 14–15C. Old French prédécesseur, from Late Latin praedecessor, from Latin prae- PRE- + decessor retiring officer, from decedere to depart. See also -OR.

predella n. the platform on which an altar stands or the highest of a series of altar steps. WH: 19C. Italian stool.

predestine v.t. to appoint beforehand by irreversible decree. WH: 14–15C. Old French prédestiner or Ecclesiastical Latin praedestinare, from prae- PRE- + destinare to make fast, to establish. See DESTINE.

predetermine v.t. to determine or settle beforehand. Also v.i. WH: 17C. Late Latin praedeterminare, from prae- PRE- + Latin determinare DETERMINE.

predial a. consisting of lands or farms. Also n. WH: 14–15C. Medieval Latin praedialis, from Latin praedium farm, estate. See also -AL[1].

predicable a. capable of being predicated or affirmed. Also n. WH: 16C. Medieval Latin praedicabilis, from Latin praedicare. See PREDICATE[1], also -ABLE.

predicament n. a particular state, esp. a difficult one. WH: 14–15C. Late Latin praedicamentum (translating Greek katēgoria CATEGORY), from Latin praedicare. See PREDICATE[1], also -MENT.

predicant n. a preaching friar, esp. a Dominican. Also a. WH: 16C. Latin praedicans, praedicantis, pres.p. of praedicare. See PREDICATE[1], also -ANT.

predicate[1] v.t. to affirm, to assert as a property etc. Also v.i. WH: 16C. Latin praedicatus, p.p. of praedicare to declare, from prae- PRE- + dicare to make known, rel. to dicere to say. See also -ATE[3].

predicate[2] n. that which is predicated, that which is affirmed or denied of the subject. WH: 14–15C. Late Latin praedicatum (translating Greek katēgoreuomenon), neut. of praedicatus, p.p. of praedicare. See PREDICATE[1], also -ATE[1].

predict v.t. to forecast, to foretell. Also n., a. WH: 16C. Latin praedictus, p.p. of praedicere, from prae- PRE- + dicere to say.

predikant n. a minister of the Dutch Reformed Church, esp. in S Africa. WH: 19C. Dutch PREDICANT.

predilection n. a prepossession in favour of something, a preference, a partiality. WH: 18C. French prédilection, from Medieval Latin praedilectus, p.p. of praediligere to choose before others, from prae- PRE- + diligere. See DILIGENT, also -ION.

predispose v.t. to dispose or incline beforehand (to some course of action etc.). WH: 17C. PRE- + DISPOSE.

prednisone n. a drug similar to cortisone used to treat rheumatic and allergic conditions, and leukaemia. WH: mid-20C. Appar. from pregnane a synthetic saturated tetracyclic hydrocarbon (so called from the occurrence of its derivatives in pregnancy urine; see PREGNANT, -ANE) + DIENE + CORTISONE.

predominate v.i. to be superior in strength or authority. Also v.t. WH: 16C. Medieval Latin predominatus, p.p. of predominari. See PRE-, DOMINATE.

preemie n. a premature baby. WH: early 20C. Abbr. of PREMATURE + -ie (-Y[3]). Cp. PREM.

pre-eminent a. eminent beyond others. WH: 14–15C. Latin praeeminens, praeeminentis, pres.p. of praeeminere to tower above the rest, to excel, from prae- PRE- + eminere. See EMINENT.

pre-empt v.t. to secure by pre-emption. Also v.i. WH: 19C. Back-formation from pre-emption (17C), from Medieval Latin praeemptio, praeemptionis, from praeemptus, p.p. of praeemere, from prae- PRE- + emere to buy. See also -ION.

preen[1] v.t., v.i. to clean and arrange (feathers) using the beak. WH: 14–15C. ? Alt. of PRUNE[2], by assim. to PREEN[2], with ref. to the 'pricking' action of a bird's beak.

preen[2] n. a pin, a brooch. Also v.t. WH: pre-1200. Old English prēon, from Germanic. Cp. German Pfriem awl.

preface n. something spoken or written as introductory to a discourse or book. Also v.t., v.i. WH: 14–15C. Old French préface, from Medieval Latin praefatia, alt. of Latin praefatio, from praefatus, p.p. of praefari to say beforehand, from prae- PRE- + fari to speak.

prefect n. a Roman commander, a governor, a chief magistrate. WH: 14–15C. Old French (Modern French préfet), from Latin praefectus, use as n. of p.p. of praeficere to put in charge, from prae- PRE- + facere to make.

prefer v.t. to like better. WH: 14–15C. Old French préférer, from Latin praeferre, from prae- PRE- + ferre to bear.

prefigure v.t. to represent beforehand by figures, types or similitudes; to foreshadow. WH: 14–15C. Ecclesiastical Latin praefigurare, from Latin prae- PRE- + figurare FIGURE.

prefix[1] v.t. to put, place or set in front of. WH: 14–15C. Old French préfixer, from Latin prefixus. See PREFIX[2].

prefix[2] n. a letter, syllable or word put at the beginning of a word to modify the meaning. WH: 17C. Modern Latin praefixum, use as n. of neut. of Latin praefixus, p.p. of praefigere to fix in front, from prae- PRE- + figere FIX.

preggers a. pregnant. WH: mid-20C. PREGNANT. See also -ER[6].

pregnable a. capable of being taken by force. WH: 14–15C. Old French prenable, pregnable talkable, from pren-, stem of prendre to take, from Latin prehendere. See also -ABLE.

pregnant a. having a child or young developing in the womb. WH: 14–15C. French prégnant or Latin pregnans, pregnantis, alt. (by assim. to -ans, -antis -ANT) of praegnas, praegnatis, prob. from prae- PRE- + base of nasci, gnasci to be born.

prehensile a. adapted to seizing or grasping, as the tails of monkeys. WH: 18C. French préhensile, from Latin prehens, prehentis, pres.p. of prehendere to grasp, to seize, to catch, var. of praehendere, from prae- PRE- + Latinized form of Greek khandanein to take in, to hold.

prejudge v.t. to form a premature opinion about. WH: 16C. PRE- + JUDGE, based on French préjuger or Latin praeiudicare.

prejudice n. opinion or bias formed without due consideration of facts. Also v.t. WH: 12–14C. Old French préjudice, from Latin praeiudicium, from prae- PRE- + iudicium judgement.

prelate n. an ecclesiastical dignitary of the highest order, such as an archbishop, bishop etc., formerly including abbot and prior. WH: 12–14C. Old French prélat, from Medieval Latin praelatus, use as n. of p.p. corr. to Latin praeferre PREFER. See also -ATE[1].

prelect v.i. to read a lecture or discourse in public. WH: 17C. Latin praelectus, p.p. of praelegere to read to others, to lecture on, from prae- PRE- + legere to read.

prelibation n. a foretaste. WH: 16C. Late Latin praelibatio, praelibationis, from praelibatus, p.p. of praelibare to taste beforehand, from prae- PRE- + libare to sip, to taste. See also -ATION.

preliminary a. introductory. Also n. WH: 17C. French préliminaire or Modern Latin preliminaris, from prae- PRE- + limen, liminis threshold. See also -ARY[2].

prelude *n.* something done, happening etc., introductory to that which follows. *Also v.t., v.i.* WH: 16C. French *prélude* or Latin *praeludium*, from *praeludere* to play beforehand, to preface, from *prae-* PRE- + *ludere* to play, from *ludus* play.

prem *n.* a premature baby. WH: mid-20C. Abbr. of PREMATURE. Cp. PREEMIE.

premature *a.* ripe or mature too soon. *Also n.* WH: 14–15C. Latin *praematurus* very early, from *prae-* PRE- + *maturus* MATURE. The original sense was ripe, mature. The current sense dates from the 16C.

premeditate *v.t.* to meditate on beforehand. *Also v.i., a.* WH: 16C. Latin *praemeditatus*, p.p. of *praemeditari*, from *prae-* PRE- + *meditari* MEDITATE.

premier *a.* first, chief, principal. *Also n.* WH: 14–15C. Old French, from Latin *primarius* PRIMARY.

premiere *n.* a first performance of a play or film. *Also v.t., v.i.* WH: 19C. French *première*, fem. of *premier* (PREMIER).

premise[1] *n.* a statement from which another is inferred. WH: 14–15C. Old French *prémisse*, from Medieval Latin *praemissa*, fem. sing. and neut. pl. p.p. (used as n.) of Latin *praemittere* to send before, to set before, from *prae-* PRE- + *mittere* to put, to send.

premise[2] *v.t.* to put forward as preparatory to what is to follow. *Also v.i.* WH: 14–15C. PREMISE[1].

premiss *n.* a statement from which another is inferred. WH: 14–15C. Var. of PREMISE[1].

premium *n.* a payment (usu. periodical) made for insurance. *Also a.* WH: 17C. Latin *praemium* booty, profit, reward, from *prae-* PRE- + *emere* to buy, (orig.) to take.

premonition *n.* a foreboding, a presentiment. WH: 16C. French *prémonition* or Late Latin *praemonitio, praemonitionis*, from Latin *praemonitus*, p.p. of *praemonere* to forewarn, from *prae-* PRE- + *monere* to warn. Cp. PREMONITION.

Premonstratensian *n.* a member of an order of regular canons, founded by St Norbert, or of the corresponding order of nuns. *Also a.* WH: 15C. Medieval Latin *Praemonstratensis* belonging to Prémontré + -AN. The order was founded by St Norbert at Prémontré near Laon, N France in 1120. The Medieval Latin name of the site, (*locus*) *praemonstratus*, means (place) shown beforehand, so called because St Norbert had prophetically pointed it out.

premorse *a.* ending abruptly as if bitten off. WH: 18C. Latin *praemorsus*, p.p. of *praemordere* to bite off, from *prae-* PRE- + *mordere* to bite.

premunition *n.* the act of guarding beforehand, as against objections. WH: 14–15C. Latin *praemunitio, praemunitionis*, from *praemunire* to fortify or protect in front, from *prae-* PRE- + *munire* to fortify, to defend. Cp. PRAEMUNIRE. By confusion, the original sense was that of PREMONITION. The sense guarding beforehand dates from the 17C, and the medical sense resistance to disease from the mid-20C.

prenomen *n.* a Roman personal name, first name, corresponding to the modern Christian name. WH: 17C. Latin *praenomen* forename, from *prae-* PRE- + *nomen* name.

†prentice *n.* an apprentice. WH: 12–14C. Shortening of APPRENTICE.

preoccupy *v.t.* to pre-engage, to engross (the mind etc.). WH: 16C. PRE- + OCCUPY, based on Latin *praeoccupare* to occupy beforehand, from *prae-* PRE- + *occupare* OCCUPY.

prep *n.* preparation or private study done at home or outside lesson time. *Also a., v.t.* WH: 19C. Abbr. of *preparation* (PREPARE).

prepare *v.t.* to make ready. *Also v.i., n.* WH: 14–15C. French *préparer* or Latin *praeparare*, from *prae-* PRE- + *parare* to make ready.

prepense *a.* premeditated, deliberate. *Also v.t.* WH: 18C. Alt. of *prepensed*, p.p. of obs. *prepense* to plan beforehand, itself alt. of obs. *purpense* (16C) to think of, to meditate on, from Old French *purpenser*, from PUR- + *penser* to think.

†prepollent *a.* having superior power or influence, predominating. WH: 17C. Latin *praepollens, praepollentis*, pres.p. of *praepollere* to exceed in power, from *prae-* PRE- + *pollere* to be strong. See also -ENT.

preponderate *v.i.* to be superior or to outweigh in number, power, influence etc. *Also v.t.* WH: 17C. Latin *praeponderatus*, p.p. of *praeponderare*, from *prae-* PRE- + *ponderare*. See PONDER, also -ATE[3].

prepone *v.t.* to bring forward to an earlier date or time. WH: late 20C. PRE- + *-pone*, based on POSTPONE.

preposition *n.* a word or group of words, e.g. *at, by, in front of*, used to relate the noun or pronoun it is placed in front of to other constituent parts of the sentence. WH: 14–15C. Latin *praepositio, praepositionis* putting in front (translating Greek *prothesis*) preposition, from *praeponere*. See PRE-, POSITION.

prepossess *v.t.* to imbue (with an idea, feeling etc.). WH: 17C. PRE- + POSSESS, prob. based on Medieval Latin *praepossessus* seized beforehand. The original sense (to the 18C) was to take prior possession of.

preposterous *a.* contrary to reason or common sense. WH: 16C. Latin *praeposterus* reversed, from *prae-* PRE- + *posterus* coming after. See also -OUS. The original sense was having last what should be first, hence contrary. Cp. ARSY-VERSY.

prepotent *a.* very powerful. WH: 14–15C. Latin *praepotens, praepotentis*, from *prae-* PRE- + POTENT.

prepuce *n.* the foreskin, the loose covering of the glans penis. WH: 14–15C. French *prépuce*, from Latin *praeputium*, prob. from *prae-* PRE- + **putos* penis.

prequel *n.* a novel, film etc. which narrates the events leading up to those in an existing novel or film. WH: late 20C. PRE- + SEQUEL.

prerogative *n.* an exclusive right or privilege vested in a particular person or body of persons, esp. a sovereign, in virtue of their position or relationship. *Also a.* WH: 14–15C. Old French *prérogative*, from Latin *praerogativa* previous election, fem. of *praerogativus*, from *praerogatus*, p.p. of *praerogare* to ask first, from *prae-* PRE- + *rogare* to ask. See also -IVE. Latin *praerogativa* originally referred to the Roman centuria, a unit of 100 voters, who by lot voted first and so set the example for those that voted after.

presage[1] *n.* something that foretells a future event, an omen, a prognostic. WH: 14–15C. French *présage*, or from Latin *praesagium*, from *praesagire* to forebode.

presage[2] *v.t.* to foreshadow, to betoken. *Also v.i.* WH: 16C. French *présager* or Latin *praesagire* to forbode, from *prae-* PRE- + *sagire* to perceive keenly.

presbyopia *n.* a form of long-sightedness with indistinct vision of near objects, caused by alteration in the refractive power of the eyes with age. WH: 18C. Greek *presbus* old man + -OPIA.

presbyter *n.* an elder who had authority in the early Church. WH: 16C. Ecclesiastical Latin, from Greek *presbuteros* an elder, use as n. of comp. of *presbus* old (man). Cp. PRIEST.

prescient *a.* foreknowing, far-seeing. WH: 17C. Latin *praesciens, praescientis*, pres.p. of *praescire* to know before, from *prae-* PRE- + *scire* to know. See also -ENT.

prescind *v.t.* to cut off, to separate. *Also v.i.* WH: 17C. Latin *praescindere* to cut off in front, from *prae-* PRE- + *scindere* to cut.

prescribe *v.t.* to direct (a medicine etc.) to be used as a remedy. *Also v.i.* WH: 14–15C. Latin *praescribere* to write before, to direct in writing, from *prae-* PRE- + *scribere* to write.

presence *n.* the quality or state of being present. WH: 12–14C. Old French *présence*, from Latin *praesentia*, from *praesens, praesentis*. See PRESENT[1], also -ENCE.

present[1] *a.* being here or in a place referred to, as distinct from absent. *Also n.* WH: 12–14C. Old French *présent*, from Latin *praesens, praesentis*, pres.p. of *praeesse* to be before, to be at hand, from *prae-* PRE- + *esse* to be.

present[2] *v.t.* to introduce to the acquaintance of, esp. to introduce formally. *Also v.i., n.* WH: 12–14C. Old French *présenter*, from Latin *praesentare* to place before, from *praesens, praesentis*. See PRESENT[1].

present[3] *n.* something which is presented, a gift. WH: 12–14C. Old French, in phr. *en present* (to offer) in the presence of, from Late Latin *in praesenti* face to face, from Latin *in re praesenti* in the situation in question. See PRESENT[1].

presentation *n.* the act, or an instance, of presenting, or the process of being presented. WH: 14–15C. Old French *présentation* or Late Latin *praesentatio, praesentationis*, from Latin *praesentatus*, p.p. of *praesentare*. See PRESENT[2], also -ATION.

presentee *n.* a person receiving a present. WH: 15C. Anglo-French, from French *présenté*, p.p. of *présenter*. See PRESENT[2], also -EE.

presenter *n.* a person who presents. WH: 14–15C. PRESENT[2] + -ER[1].

presentient *a.* feeling or perceiving beforehand. WH: 19C. Latin *praesentiens, praesentientis*, pres.p. of *praesentire* to feel beforehand, to perceive beforehand, from *prae-* PRE- + *sentire* to feel.

presentiment *n.* apprehension or anticipation, more or less vague, of an impending event, esp. of evil, a foreboding. WH: 18C. Obs. French *présentiment* (Modern French *pressentiment*), from *pré-* PRE- + SENTIMENT.

presently *adv.* soon, shortly. WH: 14–15C. PRESENT[1] + -LY[2]. The original sense (to the 16C) was on the spot, in person. The sense just then was current in the 16–18C. The two senses now and soon have co-existed from the first.

presentment *n.* the act of presenting (information). WH: 12–14C. Old French *presentement*. See PRESENT[2], also -MENT.

preserve *v.t.* to keep safe, to guard, to protect. *Also v.i., n.* WH: 14–15C. Old French *préserver*, from Late Latin *praeservare*, from *prae-* PRE- + *servare* to keep, to protect.

preses *n.* a chairman, a president. WH: 17C. Latin *praeses* president, chief, guardian, from *praesidere* PRESIDE.

preside *v.i.* to be set in authority over others, esp. in charge of a meeting, ceremony etc. WH: 17C. French *présider*, from Latin *praesidere*, from *prae-* PRE- + *sedere* to sit.

presidio *n.* a fort or fortified settlement, in areas under Spanish control. WH: 18C. Spanish, from Latin *praesidium* garrison, fort, from *praesidere* PRESIDE.

presidium *n.* a permanent executive committee in a Communist country. WH: early 20C. Russian *prezidium*, from Latin *praesidium*. See PRESIDIO.

presignify *v.t.* to signify or intimate beforehand. WH: 16C. Obs. French *présignifier* or Latin *praesignificare*, from *prae-* PRE- + *significare* SIGNIFY.

press[1] *v.t.* to act steadily upon with a force or weight. *Also v.i., n.* WH: 12–14C. Old French *presser*, from Latin *pressare*, freq. of *pressus*, p.p. of *premere*.

press[2] *v.t.* to force into naval or military service. *Also v.i., n.* WH: 16C. Alt. of obs. *prest* to engage (a person), from PREST, influ. by *prest*, obs. p.p. of PRESS[1].

pressor *a.* causing an increase in blood pressure. *Also n.* WH: 19C. Latin, from *pressus*. See PRESS[1], also -OR.

pressure *n.* the act of pressing. *Also v.t.* WH: 14–15C. Latin *pressura*, from *pressus*. See PRESS[1], also -URE.

†prest *n.* an advance, a loan. *Also a.* WH: 14–15C. Old French (Modern French *prêt*) from *prester* to lend, from Latin *praestare* to stand before, to vouch for, from *prae-* PRE- + *stare* to stand.

Prestel® *n.* the British Telecom viewdata system. WH: late 20C. PRESS[1] or PRESTO + TELECOMMUNICATION.

prestidigitation *n.* sleight of hand, conjuring. WH: 18C. French *preste* nimble or Italian PRESTO + Latin *digitus* finger + -ATION.

prestige *n.* influence derived from excellence, achievements etc. *Also a.* WH: 17C. French, from Late Latin *praestigium* illusion, from Latin *praestigiae* (pl.), juggler's tricks, prob. alt. of *praestrigiae*, from *praestringere* to bind, to blindfold, to dazzle, from *prae-* PRE- + *stringere* to tie, to bind. The original sense (to the 18C) was illusion, conjuring trick, imposture. The current sense dates from the 19C.

presto *adv.* quickly. *Also a., n., int.* WH: 16C. Italian quick, quickly, from Late Latin *praestus* ready, from Latin *praesto* at hand.

presume *v.t.* to assume without previous inquiry. *Also v.i.* WH: 14–15C. Old French *présumer*, from Latin *praesumere*, from *prae-* PRE- + *sumere* to take.

prêt-à-porter *a.* (of clothes) ready-to-wear. *Also n.* WH: mid-20C. French ready to wear, from *prêt* ready + *à* to + *porter* to wear.

pretend *v.t.* to assume the appearance of; to feign to be. *Also v.i., a.* WH: 14–15C. French *prétendre* or Latin *praetendere* to stretch forth, to put forward, to allege, to claim, from *prae-* PRE- + *tendere* to stretch, TEND[1]. The original sense (to the 17C) was to present for consideration, to profess to be. The sense to make believe dates from the 16C.

preter- *comb. form* beyond. WH: Latin *praeter* past, beyond, besides, comp. of *prae* before.

preterhuman *a.* more than human, superhuman. WH: 19C. PRETER- + HUMAN.

†preterimperfect *a.* applied to the imperfect tense as expressing a past action that is described as still going on. WH: 16C. Latin *praeteritum imperfectum* uncompleted part, from *praeteritum*, use as n. of neut. sing. of *praeteritus* (PRETERITE) + *imperfectus* IMPERFECT.

preterist *n.* a person whose chief interest is in the past. WH: 19C. PRETER- + -IST.

preterite *a.* denoting completed action or existence in past time. *Also n.* WH: 12–14C. Old French *prétérite*, or from Latin *praeteritus*, p.p. of *praeterire* to go by, to pass, from *praeter-* PRETER- + *ire* to go. See also -ITE[2].

pretermit *v.t.* to pass by or over, to neglect, to omit (to mention, to do etc.). WH: 15C. Latin *praetermittere*, from *praeter-* PRETER- + *mittere* to let go, to send.

preternatural *a.* beyond what is natural; out of the regular course of nature. WH: 16C. Medieval Latin *praeternaturalis*, from Latin phr. *praeter naturam* beyond nature. See PRETER-.

†preterperfect *n.* the perfect tense. *Also a.* WH: 16C. Latin *praeteritum perfectum* complete past, from Latin *praeteritum*. See PRETERIMPERFECT, PERFECT[1].

pretext *n.* an excuse. WH: 16C. Latin *praetextus* outward display, from *praetextus*, p.p. of *praetexere* to weave in front, to border, to disguise, from *prae-* PRE- + *texere* to weave.

pretty *a.* good-looking, attractive. *Also adv., n., v.t.* WH: pre-1200. Old English *prættig*, from Germanic base meaning trick, ult. of unknown orig. The original sense was cunning, crafty, then clever, skilful. The current sense evolved in the 14–15C.

pretzel *n.* a crisp biscuit of wheaten flour flavoured with salt, usu. in the shape of a stick or a knot. WH: 19C. German, from Old High German *brezitella*, from Medieval Latin *brachitellum*, dim. of Latin *bracchiatus* having branches, from *bracchium* arm. The biscuit was probably so called from its resemblance to a pair of folded arms.

prevail *v.i.* to have the mastery or victory (over, against etc.). WH: 14–15C. Latin *praevalere* to have great power, from *prae-* PRE- + *valere* (VAIL[2]), with assim. to AVAIL.

prevaricate *v.i.* to quibble. WH: 16C. Latin *praevaricatus*, p.p. of *praevaricari* to go crookedly, to deviate from the right path, to transgress, from *prae-* PRE- + *varicare* to spread the legs apart, to straddle, from *varus* knock-kneed. See also -ATE[3].

prevenient *a.* going before, preceding, previous. WH: 17C. Latin *praeveniens, praevenientis*, pres.p. of *praevenire* to come before, to anticipate, from *prae-* PRE- + *venire* to come. See also -ENT.

prevent *v.t.* to keep from happening, to stop. WH: 14–15C. Latin *praeventus*, p.p. of *praevenire* to precede, to anticipate, to hinder. See PREVENIENT. The original sense (to the 19C) was to act or do in advance, to anticipate. The sense to keep something from happening evolved in the 16C, and that of to hinder in the 17C. The special sense (of God and his grace) to go before arose in the 16C.

preview *n.* an advance view, a foretaste. *Also v.t.* WH: 19C. PRE- + VIEW.

previous *a.* going before in time or order. *Also adv.* WH: 17C. Latin *praevius* going before, leading the way, from *prae-* PRE- + *via* way. See also -OUS.

previse *v.t.* to know beforehand, to foresee. WH: 14–15C. Latin *praevisus*, p.p. of *praevidere* to foresee, to anticipate, from *prae-* PRE- + *videre* to see.

prevue *n.* a television or cinema trailer. WH: early 20C. Alt. of PRE-VIEW.

prex *n.* a college president. WH: early 21C. Alt. of abbr. of *president* (PRESIDE) + -Y[3].

prey *n.* an animal which is or may be seized to be devoured by carnivorous animals. *Also v.i.* WH: 12–14C. Old French *preie* (Modern French *proie*), from Latin *praeda* booty.

prezzie *n.* a present, a gift. WH: mid-20C. Abbr. of PRESENT[3] + -ie (-Y[3]).

priapism *n.* lasciviousness. WH: 14–15C. Late Latin *priapismus*, from Greek *priapismos*, from *priapizein* to act Priapus (the Roman god of procreation, whose symbol was the phallus), to be lewd, from *Priapos* Priapus. See also -ISM.

price *n.* the amount asked for a thing or for which it is sold. *Also v.t.* WH: 12–14C. Old French *pres* (Modern French *prix*), from Latin *pretium* price, value, wages, reward. Cp. PRAISE.

prick *n.* the act, or an instance, of pricking. *Also v.t., v.i.* WH: pre-1200. Old English *prica, pricca*, from Germanic, of unknown orig. Cp. PRICKLE.

pricket *n.* a buck in its second year. WH: 14–15C. PRICK + -ET[1]. The animal is so called from its straight unbranched horns. Cp. BROCKET[1].

prickle *n.* a small, sharp point. *Also v.t., v.i.* WH: pre-1200. Old English *pricel*, from Germanic base of PRICK. See also -LE¹.

pride *n.* satisfaction arising out of some accomplishment or relationship. WH: pre-1200. Old English *pryde*, var. of *prȳte*, *prȳtu* from PROUD.

prie-dieu *n.* a kneeling-desk for prayers. WH: 18C. French, lit. pray God.

priest *n.* a person who officiates in sacred rites, esp. by offering sacrifice. *Also v.t.* WH: pre-1200. Old English *prēost*, from Germanic, ult. from Ecclesiastical Latin PRESBYTER.

prig *n.* a self-righteous, formal or moralistic person. *Also v.t.* WH: 16C. Orig. unknown. The original sense was tinker, then thief. The current sense evolved in the 17C.

prill *n.* a button or pellet of metal from an assay. *Also v.t.* WH: 18C. Orig. unknown.

prim *a.* affectedly proper, demure. *Also v.t., v.i.* WH: 18C. Orig. uncertain. ? Ult. from Old French *prin*, corr. to Provençal *prim* excellent, fine, delicate, from Latin *primus* PRIME¹.

prima *a.* first, chief, principal. WH: 18C. Italian, fem. of *primo* first.

primacy *n.* the dignity or office of a primate. WH: 14–15C. Old French *primatie* or Medieval Latin *primatia*, from Latin *primas*, *primatis*. See PRIMATE, also -ACY.

prima facie *adv.* at first sight, on the first impression. *Also a.* WH: 15C. Latin at first sight, from fem. abl. of *primus* PRIME¹ + abl. of *facies* FACE.

primage *n.* a percentage on the freight paid to the owner of a ship for care in loading or unloading cargo. WH: 15C. Anglo-Latin *primagium*, from Latin *primus* PRIME¹. See also -AGE.

primal *a.* primary, original, primitive. WH: 16C. Medieval Latin *primalis*, from Latin *primus* PRIME¹. See also -AL¹.

primary *a.* first in time or order; original. *Also n.* WH: 14–15C. Latin *primarius* chief, from *primus* PRIME¹. See also -ARY¹.

primate *n.* a member of the Primates, the highest order of mammals, comprising humans, apes, monkeys and lemurs. WH: 12–14C. Old French *primat*, from Medieval Latin, use as n. of Latin *primas*, *primatis* of the first rank, from *primus* PRIME¹. See also -ATE¹. The original sense was archbishop. The zoological sense dates from the 19C as an Anglicized form of Linnaeus's Modern Latin order name *Primatus* (18C), from Latin *primates*, plural of *primas* chief, related to *primus* first.

primavera *n.* a tree bearing yellow flowers, *Cybistax donellsmithii*, growing in central America. WH: 19C. Spanish springtime, from use as fem. sing. of Latin *prima vera*, pl. of *primum ver* first spring. The tree is so called from its early flowering. Cp. PRIMROSE, PRIMULA.

prime¹ *a.* first in time or importance. *Also n.* WH: 14–15C. Old French, from Latin PRIMUS.

prime² *v.t.* to prepare something, esp. a gun, for use. *Also v.i.* WH: 16C. Orig. uncertain. ? Rel. to PRIMAGE.

primer¹ *n.* an elementary reading book for children. WH: 14–15C. Anglo-French, from Medieval Latin *primarius*, use as n. of Latin PRIMARY. See also -ER². The original sense was prayer book, especially a small one used for teaching children to read.

primer² *n.* either one of two sizes of type, great primer and long primer. WH: 16C. PRIMER¹. The type is so called from its use for printing prayer books.

primero *n.* a game of cards fashionable in the 16th and 17th cents., the original of poker. WH: 16C. Alt. of Spanish *primera*, fem. of *primero* first, from Latin *primarius* PRIMARY.

primeval *a.* belonging to the earliest ages, ancient. WH: 17C. Latin *primaevus*, from PRIMUS + *aevum* age. See also -AL¹.

primigravida *n.* a woman who is pregnant for the first time. WH: 19C. Modern Latin, fem. a., from PRIMUS + *gravidus* pregnant, based on PRIMIPARA.

primine *n.* the outer coating of an ovule. WH: 19C. French, from Latin PRIMUS + -INE.

primipara *n.* a woman who is giving birth for the first time. WH: 19C. Modern Latin, fem. a., from *primus* PRIME¹ + *-parus* (from *parere* to bring forth).

primitive *a.* of or relating to the beginning or the earliest periods, ancient. *Also n.* WH: 14–15C. Old French *primitif* or Latin *primitivus* first of its kind, from *primitus* in the first place, from PRIMUS. See also -IVE.

primo *n.* the first part (in a duet etc.). WH: 18C. Italian first, from Latin PRIMUS. Cp. PRIMA.

primogeniture *n.* seniority by birth amongst children of the same parents. WH: 17C. Medieval Latin *primogenitura*, from Latin *primo* at first + *genitura*, from base of *gignere* to beget. See also -URE.

primordial *a.* first in order, primary, original, primitive. *Also n.* WH: 14–15C. Late Latin *primordialis* that is first of all, from Latin *primordius* original, from PRIMUS + *ordiri* to begin. See also -AL¹.

primp *v.t.* to prink; to tidy up or smarten (oneself). *Also v.i.* WH: 16C. Rel. to PRIM.

primrose *n.* any plant of the genus *Primula*, esp. *Primula vulgaris*, a common British wild plant, flowering in early spring. *Also a.* WH: 14–15C. Old French *primerose*, from Medieval Latin *prima rosa* first rose. The plant is apparently so called because it flowers in early spring. It is not, however, one of the very first flowers of spring, nor is it much like a rose. This suggests that the origin of the name may not be quite so straightforward as given here. Cp. PRIMULA.

primula *n.* any plant of the genus of herbaceous plants *Primula*, belonging to the family Primulaceae, comprising the primrose, cowslip etc. WH: 18C. Modern Latin, from Medieval Latin, fem. of Latin *primulus*, dim. of PRIMUS. Latin *primulus* originally occurs in the name *primula veris*, literally little firstling of spring, applied to several flowers of early spring, including the cowslip, daisy and PRIMROSE.

primum mobile *n.* the first source of motion, the mainspring of any action. WH: 15C. Medieval Latin, lit. first moving thing, from Latin, neut. of PRIMUS + *mobilis* MOBILE.

Primus® *n.* a portable paraffin cooking stove used esp. by campers. WH: early 20C. Latin PRIMUS, ? punningly as 'first in the field'.

primus *n.* the presiding bishop in the Scottish Episcopal Church. *Also a.* WH: 16C. Latin first. Cp. PRIME¹.

prince *n.* a male member of a royal family, other than a reigning king. WH: 12–14C. Old French, from Latin *princeps*, *principis* chief man, leading citizen, PRINCEPS, use as n. of a., first, chief, sovereign, from PRIMUS + *cip-*, comb. form of *capere* to take.

princeps *a.* first. *Also n.* WH: 17C. Latin. See PRINCE.

principal *a.* main, first in importance. *Also n.* WH: 12–14C. Old French, from Latin *principalis* first, chief, original, from *princeps*, *prinicipis*. See PRINCE, also -AL¹.

principality *n.* the territory or jurisdiction of a prince. WH: 12–14C. Old French *principalté*, var. of *principalité* (Modern French *principauté*), from Late Latin *principalitas*, from Latin *principalis*. See PRINCIPAL, also -ITY.

principate *n.* the form of government under the early Roman emperors when some republican features were retained. WH: 12–14C. Old French *principat* or Latin *principatus* first place, from *princeps*, *principis*. See PRINCE, also -ATE¹.

principia *n.pl.* beginnings, origins, elements, first principles. WH: 17C. Latin, pl. of *principium*, from *princeps*, *principis*. See PRINCE.

principle *n.* a fundamental cause or element. *Also v.t.* WH: 14–15C. Anglo-French var. of Old French *principe*, from Latin *princeps*, *principis*. See PRINCE.

prink *v.i.* to dress for show. *Also v.t.* WH: 16C. Rel. to PRANK².

print *n.* an indentation or other mark made by pressure. *Also v.t., v.i.* WH: 12–14C. Old French *priente*, *preinte*, fem. p.p. (used as n.) of *preindre* to press, from Latin *premere*.

prion¹ *n.* an infectious protein particle associated with diseases of the brain and nervous system in human beings and animals, such as BSE, Creutzfeldt–Jakob disease, scrapie etc. WH: late 20C. Abbr. (with reversal of vowels) of *proteinaceous infectious particle.

prion² *n.* any of various petrels of the genus *Pachyptila* with a serrated bill, living in the southern oceans. WH: 19C. Modern Latin *Prion*, former genus name, from Greek *priōn* saw.

prior¹ *a.* former, earlier. *Also adv.* WH: 18C. Latin former, elder, superior, comp. of *prue*. See also PRE-.

prior² *n.* a superior of a monastic house or order next in rank below an abbot. WH: pre-1200. Medieval Latin, use as n. of Latin PRIOR¹.

priority *n.* the fact or the state of going before, antecedence. *Also a.* WH: 14–15C. Old French *priorité*, from Medieval Latin *prioritas*, from Latin *prior*. See PRIOR¹, also -ITY.

†**prisage** *n.* a customs duty on wine. WH: 16C. Anglo-French, from Old French *prise*, fem. p.p. (used as n.) of *prendre* to take, to seize. See also -AGE.

prise *v.t.* to wrench. *Also n.* WH: 14–15C. Old French *prise*. See PRISAGE. Cp. PRY².

prisere *n.* a primary sere, a succession from bare ground to the community climax. WH: early 20C. PRIMARY + SERE.

prism *n.* a solid having similar, equal and parallel plane bases or ends, its sides forming similar parallelograms. WH: 16C. Late Latin *prisma*, from Greek, lit. things sawn off, from *prizein* to saw.

prison *n.* a place of confinement, esp. a public building for the confinement of criminals, persons awaiting trial etc. *Also v.t.* WH: pre-1200. Old French *prisun* (Modern French *prison*), from Latin *prensio, prensionis*, var. of *prehensio, prehensionis*, from *prehendere* to seize.

prissy *a.* prim, fussy, prudish. WH: 19C. ? Blend of PRIM and *sissy* (SIS).

pristine *a.* of or relating to an early or original state or time. WH: 16C. Latin *pristinus* former. See also -INE. The sense unspoilt, spotless, fresh as new dates from the early 20C.

†**prithee** *int.* pray, please. WH: 16C. Abbr. of (*I*) *pray thee*.

prittle-prattle *n.* foolish or idle chatter; babbling. WH: 16C. Redupl. of PRATTLE. Cp. TITTLE-TATTLE.

privatdozent *n.* in a German university, a recognized teacher or lecturer not on the regular staff. WH: 19C. German *private teacher*, from *privat* PRIVATE + *Dozent* teacher, lecturer, from Latin *docens, docentis*, pres.p. of *docere* to teach.

private *a.* kept or withdrawn from publicity or observation. *Also n.* WH: 14–15C. Latin *privatus* withdrawn from public life, peculiar to oneself, p.p. of *privare* to bereave, to deprive, from *privus* single, individual, private. See also -ATE².

privateer *n.* an armed ship owned and officered by private persons commissioned by Government by letters of marque to engage in war against a hostile nation, esp. to capture merchant shipping. *Also v.i.* WH: 17C. PRIVATE + -EER, based on VOLUNTEER.

privation *n.* deprivation or lack of what is necessary to a comfortable life. WH: 12–14C. Latin *privatio, privationis*, from *privatus*, p.p. of *privare*. See PRIVATE, also -ATION.

privet *n.* any evergreen, white-flowered shrub of the genus *Ligustrum*, esp. *L. vulgare*, largely used for hedges. WH: 16C. Orig. uncertain. Appar. rel. to obs. alt. name *primprint*. The current spelling may have evolved by association with PRIVATE, as a privet hedge makes a good screen.

privilege *n.* a right or advantage belonging to a person, class etc. *Also v.t.* WH: 12–14C. Old French *privilège*, from Latin *privilegium* law applying to one individual, prerogative, from *privus* (PRIVATE) + *lex, legis* law.

privy *a.* secluded, hidden, secret, clandestine, private. *Also n.* WH: 12–14C. Old French *privé*, from Latin *privatus* PRIVATE. See also -Y².

prix fixe *n.* in a restaurant, (a menu at) a fixed price. WH: 19C. French, lit. fixed price.

prize¹ *n.* something which is offered or won as the reward of merit or superiority in a competition. *Also a., v.t.* WH: 12–14C. Var. of PRICE.

prize² *n.* something which is taken from an enemy in war, esp. a ship or other property captured at sea. *Also v.t.* WH: 14–15C. Specialized use of Old French *prise* (see PRISAGE), later taken as PRIZE¹.

prn *abbr.* pro re nata, as the need arises. WH: Abbr. of Latin *pro re nata*, lit. for the affair born.

pro¹ *prep.* for. *Also adv., n., a.* WH: 14–15C. Latin before, in front of, for, on behalf of, instead of, in return for, on account of.

pro² *n.* a professional (actor, footballer etc.), or a person who behaves professionally. *Also a.* WH: mid-20C. Abbr. of *professional* (PROFESSION).

pro-¹ *pref.* in favour of. WH: Latin pref., from PRO¹.

pro-² *pref.* before in time or position; earlier than. WH: Greek, from *pro* before.

proa *n.* a long, narrow, swift Malay canoe, usu. equipped with both sails and oars. WH: 16C. Malay *prāŭ*.

proactive *a.* energetic, enterprising, taking the initiative. WH: mid-20C. PRO-² + ACTIVE. The original sense was restricted to psychology: affecting the remembering of what is learned later. The more general sense energetic, ready to take the initiative, dates from the late 20C.

pro-am *a.* involving both professionals and amateurs. *Also n.* WH: mid-20C. PRO² + AMATEUR.

prob *abbr.* problem. WH: mid-20C. Abbr. of PROBLEM.

probabilism *n.* in Roman Catholic theology, the doctrine that, in matters of conscience about which there is disagreement or doubt, it is lawful to adopt any course, at any rate if this has the support of any recognized authority. WH: 19C. Latin *probabilis*. See PROBABLE, also -ISM.

probabilistic *a.* of or relating to probability. WH: 19C. From *probabilist* (PROBABILISM) + -IC.

probability *n.* the quality of being probable. WH: 14–15C. Old French *probabilité*, from Latin *probabilitas*, from *probabilis*. See PROBABLE, also -ITY.

probable *a.* likely to happen or prove true. *Also n.* WH: 14–15C. Old French, from Latin *probabilis* provable, credible, from *probare* PROVE. See also -ABLE.

proband *n.* a person with a distinctive characteristic who serves as the starting point for a genetic study of a family etc. WH: early 20C. Latin *probandus*, ger. of *probare* PROVE. See also -AND.

probang *n.* a slender flexible rod with a piece of sponge, a button or ball at the end, for removing obstructions in the throat or applying medication. WH: 17C. Orig. unknown. Prob. influ. by PROBE. The instrument was originally called *provang* by its inventor in c.1657, the Welsh judge Walter Ramsey.

probate *n.* the official proving of a will. *Also v.t.* WH: 14–15C. Latin *probatum* thing proved, neut. p.p. (used as n.) of *probare* PROVE. See also -ATE¹.

probation *n.* a method of dealing with criminals by allowing them to go at large under supervision during their good behaviour. WH: 14–15C. Old French, from Latin *probatio, probationis*, from *probatus*, p.p. of *probare* PROVE. See also -ATION. The original sense was the testing of a person who has provisionally joined a religious body. The current legal sense, as a method of dealing with criminals, dates from the 19C.

probative *a.* proving or tending to prove. WH: 14–15C. Latin *probativus*, from *probatus*. See PROBATION, also -IVE.

probe *n.* a surgical instrument, for exploring cavities of the body, wounds etc. *Also v.t., v.i.* WH: 14–15C. Late Latin *proba* proof, from Latin *probare* PROVE.

probit *n.* a unit of probability in statistics. WH: mid-20C. PROBABILITY + UNIT.

probity *n.* honesty, sincerity or integrity. WH: 14–15C. French *probité*, from Latin *probitas*, from *probus* good, honest. See also -ITY.

problem *n.* a question proposed for solution. *Also a.* WH: 14–15C. Old French *problème*, from Latin *problema*, from Greek *problēma*, from *proballein* to put forth, from PRO-² + *ballein* to throw.

pro bono *a.* of or relating to legal work done without charge for poor clients, or to a lawyer who does such work. WH: mid-20C. Latin, shortening of *pro bono publico* for the public good.

proboscis *n.* the trunk of an elephant or the elongated snout of a tapir etc. WH: 17C. Latin, from Greek *proboskis*, lit. means of providing food, from *pro-* PRO-² + *boskein* to feed.

procaine *n.* a synthetic crystalline substance used as a local anaesthetic, esp. in dentistry. WH: early 20C. PRO-¹ + COCAINE.

pro-cathedral *n.* a church used temporarily as a substitute for a cathedral. WH: 19C. PRO-¹ + CATHEDRAL.

proceed *v.i.* to go in (a specified direction or to a specified place). WH: 14–15C. Old French *procéder*, from Latin *procedere*, from PRO-¹ + *cedere* to go.

pro-celebrity *a.* of or relating to a sporting event, esp. a golf tournament, involving professional players and showbusiness celebrities. WH: late 20C. PRO² + *celebrity* (CELEBRATE).

proceleusmatic *a.* (in poetry) of or relating to a metrical foot of four short syllables. *Also n.* WH: 18C. Late Latin *proceleusmaticus*, from Greek *prokeleusmatikos*, from *prokeleusma, prokeleusmatos* incitement, from *prokeleuein* to incite. See also -IC.

procephalic *a.* of or relating to the anterior part of the head, esp. in invertebrates. WH: 19C. PRO-² + -CEPHALIC.

process[1] *n.* a course or method of proceeding or doing, esp. a method of operation in manufacture, scientific research etc. *Also v.t.* WH: 12–14C. Old French *procès*, from Latin *processus*, from p.p. of *procedere* PROCEED.

process[2] *v.i.* to go in procession. WH: 19C. Back-formation from PROCESSION.

procession *n.* a group of persons, vehicles etc. proceeding in regular order for a ceremony, demonstration etc. *Also v.i., v.t.* WH: pre-1200. Old French, from Latin *processio, processionis*, from *processus*. See PROCESS[1], also -ION.

procès-verbal *n.* in French law, a written statement of particulars relating to a charge. WH: 17C. French, lit. verbal trial. See PROCESS[1], VERBAL.

pro-chancellor *n.* in some universities, a deputy to the vice-chancellor. WH: 19C. PRO-[1] + CHANCELLOR.

pro-choice *a.* in favour of a woman's right to choose whether or not to have an abortion. WH: late 20C. PRO-[1] + CHOICE.

prochronism *n.* an error in chronology dating an event before its actual occurrence. WH: 17C. PRO-[2] + Greek *khronos* time + -ISM.

proclaim *v.t.* to announce publicly. WH: 14–15C. Latin *proclamare* to cry out, from PRO-[1] + *clamare* to shout.

proclitic *a.* (of a monosyllable) attached to and depending in accent upon a following word. *Also n.* WH: 19C. Modern Latin *proclitus*, from Greek *proklinein*, to lean forward, based on Late Latin *encliticus* ENCLITIC. The term was coined in 1801 by the German classical scholar Gottfried Hermann.

proclivity *n.* a tendency, bent. WH: 16C. Latin *proclivitas*, from *proclivis, proclivus* sloping, from PRO-[1] + *clivus* slope. See also -ITY.

proconsul *n.* a Roman magistrate, usu. an ex-consul, exercising consular power as governor of a province or commander of an army. WH: 14–15C. Latin, from *pro consule* (person acting) for the consul, from PRO[1] + CONSUL.

procrastinate *v.i.* to put off action. *Also v.t.* WH: 16C. Latin *procrastinatus*, p.p. of *procrastinare*, from PRO-[1] + *crastinus* belonging to tomorrow, from *cras* tomorrow. See also -ATE[3].

procreate *v.t.* to generate, to beget. *Also v.i.* WH: 14–15C. Latin *procreatus*, p.p. of *procreare*, from PRO-[1] + *creare* CREATE. See also -ATE[3].

Procrustean *a.* reducing to strict conformity by violent measures. WH: 19C. *Procrustes*, from Greek *Prokroustēs*, lit. stretcher, Procrustes, a robber of Greek mythology who stretched the bodies or cut short the legs of his victims to make them fit his bed + -AN.

procrypsis *n.* protective colouring of a plant or animal. WH: early 20C. PRO-[1] + Greek *krupsis* concealment. The earlier a. *procryptic* (19C) (from PRO-[1] + Greek *kruptikos* CRYPTIC) was appar. based on *protective* (PROTECT).

proctal *a.* anal, rectal. WH: 19C. PROCTO- + -AL[1].

proctalgia *n.* pain in the anus. WH: 19C. PROCTO- + -ALGIA.

proctectomy *n.* excision of the rectum or anus. WH: 19C. PROCTO- + -ECTOMY.

proctitis *n.* inflammation of the anus or rectum. WH: 19C. PROCTO- + -ITIS.

procto- *comb. form* of or relating to the anus. WH: Greek *prōktos* anus. See also -O-.

proctology *n.* the branch of medicine concerned with the anus and the rectum. WH: 19C. PROCTO- + -O- + -LOGY.

proctor *n.* an English university official (usu. one of two elected annually) with the duty of maintaining order and discipline. WH: 12–14C. Contr. of PROCURATOR.

proctoscope *n.* an instrument for examining the rectum. WH: 19C. PROCTO- + SCOPE[1].

procumbent *a.* lying down on the face; leaning forward. WH: 17C. Latin *procumbens, procumbentis*, pres.p. of *procumbere* to fall forwards, from PRO-[1] + nasalized stem corr. to *cubare* to lie. See also -ENT.

procuration *n.* the act of procuring or obtaining. WH: 14–15C. Old French *procuracion* (Modern French *procuration*), from Latin *procuratio, procurationis*, from *procuratus*, p.p. of *procurare*. See PROCURE, also -ATION.

procurator *n.* a person who manages another's affairs, esp. those of a legal nature, an agent, a proxy, an attorney. WH: 12–14C. Old

French *procurateur*, from Latin *procurator* manager, agent, deputy, tax collector in a province, from *procuratus*. See PROCURATION.

procure *v.t.* to obtain, to get by some means or effort. *Also v.i.* WH: 12–14C. Old French *procurer*, from Latin *procurare* to take care of, to attend to, to manage, from PRO-[1] + *curare* to look after.

Prod *n.* a Protestant (esp. in Ireland). WH: mid-20C. Abbr. (based on pronun.) of PROTESTANT.

prod *n.* a pointed instrument, a goad. *Also v.t., v.i.* WH: 18C. Alt. of ROD.

prodigal *a.* given to extravagant expenditure. *Also n., adv.* WH: 14–15C. Late Latin *prodigalis*, from Latin *prodigus* lavish. See also -AL[1]. The earliest use of the word in English is with reference to the parable of the Prodigal Son (Luke xv.11–32), in the 1523 edition of the Vulgate (Latin version of the Bible) titled *parabola de filio prodigo*.

prodigy *n.* something wonderful or extraordinary. WH: 15C. Latin *prodigium*, from *prod*, earlier form of *pro* PRO-[1] + element ? from *dio* I say or *agere* to act. See also -Y[2].

prodrome *n.* a symptom of approaching disease. WH: 17C. French, from Modern Latin *prodromus* or Greek *prodromos* precursor, from PRO-[2] + *-dromos* -DROME.

produce[1] *v.t.* to bring into view, to bring forward. WH: 14–15C. Latin *producere*, from PRO-[1] + *ducere* to lead.

produce[2] *n.* goods produced or yielded. WH: 16C. PRODUCE[1].

product *n.* that which is produced by a manufacturing process. WH: 14–15C. Latin *productum*, neut. p.p. (used as n.) of *producere*. See PRODUCE[1].

pro-educational *a.* in favour of education. WH: 19C. PRO-[1] + *educational* (EDUCATE).

proem *n.* a preface, a preamble, an introduction, a prelude. WH: 14–15C. Old French *proeme* (Modern French *proème*) or Latin *prooemium*, from Greek *prooimion* prelude, from PRO-[2] + *oimē* song.

proembryo *n.* a cellular structure of various forms in plants from which the embryo is developed. WH: 19C. German. See PRO-[2], EMBRYO.

proenzyme *n.* an enzyme in its early, inactive form. WH: early 20C. PRO-[2] + ENZYME.

pro-European *n.* a person who is in favour of the European Union and of the UK's membership of it. *Also a.* WH: mid-20C. PRO-[1] + EUROPEAN.

prof *n.* a professor at a university etc. WH: 19C. Abbr. of *professor* (PROFESS).

profane *a.* not sacred; secular. *Also v.t.* WH: 14–15C. Old French *prophane* (Modern French *profane*) or Latin *profanus* not sacred, uninitiated, impious, lit. before the temple, from PRO-[1] + *fanum* temple. A person 'before the temple' would not have been admitted to the temple with the initiates.

profess *v.t.* to make open or public declaration of. *Also v.i.* WH: 12–14C. Orig. p.p. and part. a., from Old French *profès*, from Latin *professus*. Later from Latin *professus*, p.p. of *profiteri* to declare aloud, to declare publicly, from PRO-[1] + *fateri* to declare, to avow.

profession *n.* the act of professing; a declaration. WH: 12–14C. Old French, from Latin *professio, professionis* public declaration, from *professus*. See PROFESS, also -ION.

proffer *v.t.* to offer or tender for acceptance. *Also n.* WH: 12–14C. Old French *proffrir*, earlier *poroffrir*, from *por* (from Latin PRO-[1]) + *offrir* OFFER.

proficient *a.* (of a person) well versed or skilled in any art, science etc. *Also n.* WH: 16C. Latin *proficiens, proficientis*, pres.p. of *proficere* to advance, from PRO-[1] + *facere* to do, to make. See also -ENT.

profile *n.* an outline, a contour. *Also v.t.* WH: 17C. Obs. Italian *profilo* (now *proffilo*), from obs. *profilare* to draw in outline, from *pro-* PRO-[1] + *filare* to spin, (formerly) to draw a line, from Latin, from *filum* thread.

profit *n.* an advantage or benefit. *Also v.t., v.i.* WH: 12–14C. Old French, from Latin *profectus* progress, profit, from p.p. of *proficere*. See PROFICIENT.

profiterole *n.* a small, hollow ball of choux pastry with a sweet filling, usu. served with chocolate sauce. WH: 16C. French, dim. of *profit* PROFIT. See also -OLE[2]. The pastry is presumably so called as it was originally regarded as a small welcome addition, a 'bonus'.

profligate a. licentious, dissolute. Also n. WH: 16C. Latin profligatus ruined, dissolute, p.p. of profligare to overthrow, to ruin, from PRO-[1] + fligere to strike. See also -ATE[2]. The original sense was overwhelmed, overthrown. The current sense dates from the 17C.

profluent a. flowing out or onwards. WH: 14–15C. Latin profluens, profluentis, pres.p. of profluere, from PRO-[1] + fluere to flow. See also -ENT.

pro forma a., adv. (done) as a matter of form, as a formality. Also n. WH: 16C. Latin for the sake of form.

profound a. having great intellectual penetration or insight. Also n. WH: 12–14C. Old French profund (Modern French profond), from Latin profundus, from PRO-[1] + fundus bottom.

profuse a. poured out lavishly, exuberant. WH: 14–15C. Latin profusus, use as a. of p.p. of profundere to pour out, from PRO-[1] + fundere to pour.

prog[1] n. a radio or TV programme. WH: late 20C. Abbr. of PROGRAMME.

prog[2] v.i. to poke about, esp. for food. Also n. WH: 17C. Orig. unknown.

†prog[3] n. a proctor at Oxford and Cambridge universities. Also v.t. WH: early 20C. Alt. of PROCTOR.

progenitor n. an ancestor in the direct line, a forefather, a parent. WH: 14–15C. Old French progeniteur, from Latin progenitor ancestor, from progenitus, p.p. of progignere to beget, from PRO-[1] + gignere to create. See also -OR.

progeny n. the offspring of human beings, animals or plants. WH: 12–14C. Old French progenie, from Latin progenies descent, family, from PRO-[1] + gen-, base of gignere to create, to beget. See also -Y[2].

progeria n. a rare condition causing premature old age in children. WH: early 20C. Greek progēros prematurely old, from PRO-[2] + gēros old age. See also -IA.

progesterone n. a female steroid hormone that prepares and maintains the uterus for pregnancy. WH: mid-20C. German, blend of progestin (from PRO-[1] + GESTATION + -IN[1]) and its German synonym Luteosteron, from Luteo-, representing Latin corpus luteum, lit. yellow body + -steron, -sterone (from STEROL + KETONE).

proglottis n. each of the segments making up the body of a tapeworm, forming distinct organisms with a reproductive system. WH: 19C. Greek proglōssis, proglōssidos point of the tongue, from PRO-[2] + glōtta, glōssa tongue.

prognathic a. having the jaws projecting. WH: 19C. PRO-[2] + Greek gnathos jaw + -IC. The earlier form prognathous was coined in 1836 by the English ethnologist James C. Prichard.

prognosis n. a forecast of the probable course or result of an illness. WH: 17C. Late Latin, from Greek prognōsis, from progignōskein to know beforehand, from PRO-[2] + gignōskein KNOW.

prognostic n. a symptom on which a prognosis can be based. Also a. WH: 14–15C. Old French prognostique (Modern French prognostic), from Latin prognosticum, prognosticon, from Greek prognōstikon, use as n. of neut. of prognōstikos, from progignōskein. See PROGNOSIS.

programme n. (a paper, booklet etc. giving) a list of the successive items of any entertainment, public ceremony, conference, course of study etc. plus other relevant information. Also v.t. WH: 17C. Orig. from Late Latin programma, from Greek prographein to write publicly, from PRO-[2] + graphein to write. Later reintroduced from French programme.

progress[1] n. movement onward, advance. WH: 14–15C. Latin progressus, from p.p. of progredi to go forward, from PRO-[1] + gradi to proceed, to walk, from gradus step.

progress[2] v.i. to move forward, to advance. Also v.t. WH: 16C. PROGRESS[1].

pro hac vice adv. for this occasion only. WH: 17C. Latin for this occasion (only).

prohibit v.t. to forbid authoritatively. WH: 14–15C. Latin prohibitus, p.p. of prohibere, from PRO-[1] + habere to hold.

project[1] n. a plan, a scheme. WH: 14–15C. Latin proiectum, neut. (used as n.) of proiectus. See PROJECT[2].

project[2] v.t. to throw or shoot forward. Also v.i. WH: 14–15C. Latin proiectus, p.p. of proiicere to throw out, to expel, from PRO-[1] + iacere to throw.

prokaryote n. an organism whose cells have no distinct nucleus, their genetic material being carried in a single filament of DNA. WH: mid-20C. PRO-[2] + Greek karuon nut, kernel + -ōtēs -OT[2].

prolactin n. a hormone produced by the pituitary gland, which stimulates lactation. WH: mid-20C. PRO-[1] + lactation (LACTATE[1]) + -IN[1].

prolamine n. any one of a group of simple plant proteins, which are alcohol-soluble. WH: early 20C. PROLINE, with inserted am- (from AMIDE).

prolapse n. a falling down or slipping out of place of an organ or part, such as the uterus or rectum. Also v.i. WH: 16C. Modern Latin prolapsus, from Late Latin fall, from Latin, p.p. of prolabi to slip forward, to slip down. See PRO-[1], LAPSE.

prolate a. extended in the direction of the longer axis, elongated in the polar diameter, as distinct from oblate. WH: 17C. Latin prolatus, p.p. of proferre to carry forward, to extend, to prolong, from PRO-[1] + ferre to carry. See also -ATE[2].

prole n., a. a proletarian. WH: 19C. Abbr. of PROLETARIAN.

proleg n. any one of the soft, fleshy appendages or abdominal limbs of caterpillars etc., distinct from the true legs. WH: 19C. PRO-[1] + LEG.

prolegomenon n. an introductory or preliminary discourse prefixed to a book etc. WH: 17C. Latin, from Greek, use as n. of neut. pres.p. of prolegein to say beforehand, from PRO-[2] + legein to say.

prolepsis n. anticipation. WH: 14–15C. Late Latin, from Greek prolēpsis, from prolambanein to anticipate, from PRO-[2] + lambanein to take.

proletarian a. of or relating to the common people. Also n. WH: 17C. Latin proletarius a Roman citizen of the lowest class (too poor to serve the state except by providing it with offspring), from proles offspring. See also -AN.

pro-life a. favouring greater restrictions on the availability of legal abortions and/or a ban on the use of human embryos for experimental purposes. WH: mid-20C. PRO-[1] + LIFE.

proliferate v.i. to grow by budding or multiplication of parts. Also v.t. WH: 19C. Back-formation from proliferation, from French prolifération, from prolifère proliferous, from Latin proles offspring + -FEROUS.

prolific a. producing offspring, esp. abundantly. WH: 17C. Medieval Latin prolificus, from Latin proles offspring. See also -FIC.

proline n. an amino acid occurring in proteins, esp. collagen. WH: early 20C. Contr. of pyrrolidine (PYRROLE).

prolix a. long and wordy. WH: 14–15C. Old French prolixe or Latin prolixus extensive, extended, lit. poured forth, from PRO-[1] + p.p. formation on liquere to be liquid.

prolocutor n. a chairperson or speaker, esp. of the lower houses of convocation in the Church of England. WH: 14–15C. Latin, from prolocutus, p.p. of proloqui to speak out. See also -OR.

Prolog n. a high-level programming language used esp. in artificial intelligence and expert systems. WH: late 20C. From programming (PROGRAMME) + LOGIC.

prologue n. an introductory discourse, esp. lines introducing a play. Also v.t. WH: 12–14C. Old French, from Latin prologus, from Greek prologos, from PRO-[2] + logos saying, speech. See also -LOGUE.

prolong v.t. to extend in duration. WH: 14–15C. Orig. from Old French prolonger. Later from Late Latin prolongare, from PRO-[1] + longus LONG[1].

prolonge n. a rope in three pieces connected by rings with a hook at one end and a toggle at the other, used for moving a gun etc. WH: 19C. French, from prolonger PROLONG.

prolusion n. a prelude. WH: 17C. Latin prolusio, prolusionis, from prolusus, p.p. of proludere, from PRO-[1] + ludere to play. See also -ION.

prom n. a paved promenade. WH: 19C. Abbr. of PROMENADE.

pro-marketeer n. a person who is in favour of the Common Market (European Union) and the UK's membership of it. WH: mid-20C. PRO-[1] + marketeer (MARKET).

promenade n. a walk, drive, or ride for pleasure, exercise or display. Also v.i., v.t. WH: 16C. French, from se promener to walk, reflex. of promener to cause to walk. See also -ADE.

promethazine n. an antihistamine drug used to treat allergies, travel sickness etc. WH: mid-20C. PROPYL + METHYL + AZINE.

Promethean *a.* of, relating to or like Prometheus; original, creative, daring. *Also n.* WH: 16C. *Prometheus*, a demigod in Greek mythology who was worshipped by craftsmen, who stole fire from the gods and gave it to the human race, and who was punished for this by Zeus by being chained to a rock where an eagle fed daily on his liver. See also -AN.

prominent *a.* standing out, protuberant. *Also n.* WH: 14–15C. Latin *prominens, prominentis*, pres.p. of *prominere* to jut out. See also -ENT.

prominenti *n.pl.* distinguished or important people. WH: mid-20C. Italian, from *prominente* PROMINENT.

promiscuous *a.* indulging in casual indiscriminate sexual intercourse. WH: 17C. Latin *promiscuus*, from PRO-[1] + *miscere* to mix. See also -OUS.

promise *n.* a verbal or written engagement to do or forbear from doing some specific act. *Also v.t., v.i.* WH: 14–15C. Old French *promesse* or Latin *promissum*, neut. p.p. (used as n.) of *promittere* to send forth, to put forth, to promise, from PRO-[1] + *mittere* to send.

prommer *n.* a person who attends a promenade concert, esp. regularly. WH: mid-20C. PROM + -ER[1].

promo *n.* something used to promote a product, esp. a pop video. *Also a.* WH: mid-20C. Abbr. of *promotion, promotional* (PROMOTE).

promontory *n.* a headland, a point of high land projecting into the sea. WH: 16C. Medieval Latin *promontorium*, alt. (based on Latin *mons, montis* MOUNT[2]) of Latin *promunturium*, ? from PRO-[1] + *mont*-. See also -ORY[1]. According to some, the word is related to Latin *prominere* (PROMINENT).

promote *v.t.* to raise to a higher rank or position. WH: 14–15C. Latin *promotus*, p.p. of *promovere* to move forward, from PRO-[1] + *movere* to move.

prompt *a.* acting quickly. *Also adv., n., v.t., v.i.* WH: 14–15C. Old French, or from Latin *promptus*, p.p. of *promere* to bring forth, from PRO-[1] + *emere* to take.

promulgate *v.t.* to make known to the public; to disseminate; to announce publicly. WH: 16C. Latin *promulgatus*, p.p. of *promulgare* to expose to public view, from PRO-[1] + base of *mulgere* to milk, (hence) to cause to issue forth, to bring to light. See also -ATE[3].

promycelium *n.* a short tubular growth from some fungal spores, which itself produces spores. WH: 19C. PRO-[1] + MYCELIUM.

pronaos *n.* the area immediately before a Greek or Roman temple enclosed by the portico. WH: 17C. Latin, from Greek. See PRO-[2], NAOS.

pronate *v.t.* to lay (a hand or forelimb) prone so as to have the palm downwards, as distinct from *supinate*. WH: 19C. Back-formation from *pronation* (17C), from PRONE (or Latin *pronus*) + -ATION.

prone *a.* leaning or bent forward or downward. WH: 14–15C. Latin *pronus*, from *pro* forwards.

pronephros *n.* in vertebrates, the anterior part of the embryonic kidney, nonfunctional, or absent, in the adult. WH: 19C. PRO-[2] + Greek *nephros* kidney.

proneur *n.* a flatterer. WH: 19C. French *prôneur*, from *prôner* to address a congregation, to eulogize, from *prône* the grating or railing separating the chancel of a church from the nave (where notices were given and addresses delivered) + -eur -OR.

prong *n.* any one of the spikes of a fork. *Also v.t.* WH: 15C. ? Rel. to Middle Low German *prange* pinching instrument, Dutch *prang* pinching. Cp. PANG.

pronominal *a.* of, relating to or of the nature of a pronoun. WH: 17C. Late Latin *pronominalis* belonging to a pronoun, from Latin *pronomen, pronominis* PRONOUN. See also -AL[1].

pronotum *n.* the dorsal part of the prothorax of an insect. WH: 19C. Modern Latin, from PRO-[2] + Greek *nōton* back, NOTUM.

pronoun *n.* a word used in place of a noun to denote a person or thing already mentioned or implied. WH: 14–15C. PRO-[1] + NOUN, based on French *pronom*, Latin *pronomen*.

pronounce *v.t.* to utter articulately, to say correctly. *Also v.i., n.* WH: 12–14C. Old French *pronuncier* (Modern French *prononcer*), from Latin *pronuntiare* to proclaim, to narrate, from PRO-[1] + *nuntiare* to announce.

pronto *adv.* without delay; quickly. WH: early 20C. Spanish, from Latin *promptus* PROMPT.

pronuclear *a.* in favour of the use of nuclear power. WH: mid-20C. PRO-[1] + NUCLEAR.

pronucleus *n.* the nucleus of a germ cell before fertilization. WH: 19C. PRO-[2] + NUCLEUS.

pronunciamiento *n.* a manifesto, a proclamation, esp. one issued by revolutionaries in Spanish-speaking countries. WH: 19C. Spanish *pronunciamiento*, from *pronunciar* (from Latin *pronuntiare* PRONOUNCE) + *-miento* -MENT.

pro-nuncio *n.* a papal ambassador of lower status than a nuncio. WH: mid-20C. Italian *pro-nunzio*, from *pro-* PRO-[1] + *nunzio* NUNCIO.

pro-oestrus *n.* in mammals, the phase in the oestrus cycle immediately before oestrus. WH: early 20C. PRO-[2] + OESTRUS.

proof *n.* the act of proving. *Also a., v.t.* WH: 12–14C. Old French *preve, proeve* (Modern French *preuve*), from Late Latin *proba*, from Latin *probare* PROVE. Cp. PROBE.

-proof *comb. form* (to make) resistant, impervious, immune to, as in *rainproof, soundproof*. WH: 16C. PROOF.

pro-otic *a.* in front of the ear. *Also n.* WH: 19C. PRO-[2] + OTIC.

prop[1] *n.* a rigid support, esp. a loose or temporary one. *Also v.t.* WH: 14–15C. Prob. from Middle Dutch *proppe* vine-prop, support.

prop[2] *n.* a stage property. WH: 19C. Abbr. of PROPERTY.

prop[3] *n.* an aeroplane propeller. WH: early 20C. Abbr. of *propeller* (PROPEL).

prop[4] *v.i.* (of a horse) to come to a sudden halt, to pull up sharply. *Also n.* WH: 19C. PROP[1]. The horse's rigid forelegs are its 'props'.

propaedeutic *a.* of, relating to or of the nature of introductory or preparatory study. WH: 18C. PRO-[2] + PAEDEUTICS, based on Greek *propaideuein* to teach beforehand. See also -IC.

propaganda *n.* information, ideas, opinions etc. propagated as a means of winning support for, or fomenting opposition to, a government, cause, institution etc. WH: 18C. Italian, from Modern Latin *congregatio de propaganda fide* congregation for propagating the faith. The Modern Latin title was originally that of a committee of cardinals responsible for foreign missions, founded by Pope Gregory XV in 1622. The current general sense dates from the early 20C.

propagate *v.t.* to cause to multiply by natural generation or other means. *Also v.i.* WH: 14–15C. Latin *propagatus*, p.p. of *propagare* to multiply (plants) from shoots or layers, from *propago* young shoot, from PRO-[1] + base of *pangere* to fix. See also -ATE[3].

propagule *n.* a small part of a plant, esp. a bud, which becomes detached and grows into a new plant. WH: 19C. Modern Latin *propagulum*, dim. of Latin *propago* shoot, runner. See PROPAGATE, also -ULE.

propane *n.* a flammable, gaseous hydrocarbon used as fuel. WH: 19C. PROPIONIC ACID + -ANE.

proparoxytone *a.* (in ancient Greek) having an acute accent on the antepenultimate syllable. *Also n.* WH: 18C. Greek *proparoxutonos*. See PRO-[2], PAROXYTONE.

pro patria *adv.* for one's country. WH: 19C. Latin for one's country. The Latin phrase is best known in a line from Horace's *Odes*: *Dulce et decorum est pro patria mori* It is lovely and honourable to die for one's country (1C BC).

propel *v.t.* to cause to move forward or onward. WH: 14–15C. Latin *propellere* to drive before one, from PRO-[1] + *pellere* to drive.

†propend *v.t.* to incline, to have a leaning or propensity. WH: 16C. Latin *propendere* to hang forward, to hang down, from PRO-[1] + *pendere* to hang.

propene *n.* propylene. WH: 19C. Contr. of *propylene* (PROPYL).

propensity *n.* bent, natural tendency, inclination. WH: 16C. Latin *propensus*, p.p. of *propendere* PROPEND + -ITY.

proper *a.* belonging or pertaining exclusively or peculiarly (to). *Also n., adv.* WH: 12–14C. Old French *propre*, from Latin *proprius* one's own, special, peculiar.

properdin *n.* a protein found in blood serum which plays a part in the destruction of viruses, bacteria etc. WH: mid-20C. PRO-[1] + Latin *perdere* to destroy + -IN[1].

properispomenon *a.* (in ancient Greek) having the circumflex accent on the penultimate syllable. *Also n.* WH: 19C. Greek *properispōmenon*. See PRO-[2], PERISPOMENON.

property *n.* a possession, possessions. *Also v.t.* WH: 12–14C. Old French *propriété*. See PROPRIETY.

prophage *n.* a virus in a bacterial cell which undergoes division with the bacterium and does not destroy it. WH: mid-20C. PRO-[2] + PHAGE.

prophase *n.* the first stage of mitosis, or of meiosis. WH: 19C. PRO-[2] + PHASE.

prophecy *n.* a prediction, esp. one divinely inspired. WH: 12–14C. Old French *profecie* (Modern French *prophétie*), from Late Latin *prophetia*, from Greek *prophētia*, from *prophētēs* PROPHET. See also -CY.

prophesy *v.t.* to predict, to foretell. *Also v.i.* WH: 12–14C. Old French *prophecier*. See PROPHECY, also -Y[2].

prophet *n.* a person who foretells future events, esp. under divine inspiration. WH: 12–14C. Old French *prophète*, from Latin *propheta*, *prophetes*, from Greek *prophētēs* interpreter, spokesman (of the will of a god), from PRO-[2] + *phētēs* speaker, from *phēnai* to speak.

prophylactic *a.* protecting against disease. *Also n.* WH: 16C. French *prophylactique*, from Greek *prophulaktikos*, from PRO-[2] + *phulak-*. See PHYLACTERY, also -IC.

propinquity *n.* nearness in time, space or relationship. WH: 14–15C. Old French *propinquité* or Latin *propinquitas*, from *propinquus* neighbouring, from *prope* near. See also -ITY.

propionic acid *n.* a colourless carboxylic acid used esp. to inhibit the growth of mould in bread. WH: 19C. French *propionique*, from *pro-* PRO-[2] + Greek *piōn* fat (+ ACID). See also -IC. The chemical is so called as it is the first in the carboxylic acid series to form fatty compounds. An alternative form *propanoic* (early 20C) is from PROPANE + *-oic* (from -O- + -IC).

propitiate *v.t.* to appease, to conciliate. *Also v.i.* WH: 16C. Latin *propitiatus*, p.p. of *propitiare*, from *propitius* favourable, gracious. See also -ATE[3].

propolis *n.* a resinous substance obtained by bees from buds etc. and used to cement their combs, stop up crevices etc. WH: 17C. Latin, from Greek, from PRO-[2] + *polis* city.

propone *v.t.* to propose, put forward (esp. before a court of law). WH: 14–15C. Latin *proponere* to put forth, to set forth, from PRO-[1] + *ponere* to place.

proponent *a.* proposing or advocating. *Also n.* WH: 16C. Latin *proponens, proponentis*, pres.p. of *proponere*. See PROPONE, also -ENT.

proportion *n.* the comparative relation of one part or thing to another with respect to magnitude or number. *Also v.t.* WH: 14–15C. Old French, from Latin *proportio, proportionis*, from *pro portione* proportionally, from PRO-[1] + *portio, portionis*. See PORTION.

propose *v.t.* to present for consideration. *Also v.i.* WH: 12–14C. Old French *proposer*, based on Latin *proponere* (PROPONE), with substitution of *poser* for *ponere*. See POSE[1].

proposition *n.* something which is propounded. *Also v.t.* WH: 12–14C. Old French, or from Latin *propositio, propositionis*, from *propositus*, p.p. of *proponere*. See PROPONE, also -ITION.

propositus *n.* a proband. WH: 18C. Latin, p.p. of *proponere*. See PROPONE.

propound *v.t.* to state or set out for consideration, to propose. WH: 16C. Alt. of PROPONE. The *-d* was added as for COMPOUND[1], EXPOUND.

propraetor *n.* a praetor who at the expiration of his term of office was made governor of a province. WH: 16C. Latin, orig. *pro praetore* (person acting) for the praetor.

propranolol *n.* a drug used to treat angina, abnormal heart rhythm and high blood pressure. WH: mid-20C. PROPYL + *propanol* (PROPANE), with redupl. of *-ol*.

proprietor *n.* an owner, esp. of a business; a person who has the exclusive legal right or title to anything, whether in possession or not, a possessor in one's own right. WH: 15C. From *proprietary* (from Late Latin *proprietarius*, from *proprietas* PROPRIETY; see also -ARY[1]) with substitution of -OR for -ARY[1].

propriety *n.* the quality of being conformable to an acknowledged or correct standard or rule. WH: 14–15C. Old French *proprieté*, from Latin *proprietas* peculiarity, ownership, from *proprius* PROPER. See also -ITY. Cp. PROPERTY.

proprioception *n.* reception of, or activation by, stimuli from within the organism. WH: early 20C. Latin *proprius* own + -O- + RECEPTION.

proprium *n.* a property. WH: 16C. Latin, use as n. of neut. sing. of *proprius* PROPER.

proptosis *n.* displacement or protusion, esp. of an eye. WH: 17C. Late Latin, from Greek *proptōsis*, from *propiptein* to fall forwards.

propulsion *n.* the act, or an instance, of propelling, a driving forward. WH: 17C. From obs. *propulse* (from Latin *propulsare*, freq. of *propellere* PROPEL) + -ION.

propyl *n.* a hydrocarbon radical derived from propane. WH: 19C. PROPIONIC ACID + -YL.

propylaeum *n.* the entrance, esp. one of imposing architectural character, to a temple. WH: 18C. Latin, from Greek *propulaion*, use as n. of neut. from a. *propulaios* before the gate, from PRO-[2] + *pulē* gate. Cp. PROPYLON.

propylon *n.* a propylaeum, esp. to an Egyptian temple. WH: 19C. Latin, from Greek *propulon*, from PRO-[2] + *pulē* gate.

pro rata *a.* proportional. *Also adv.* WH: 16C. Latin according to the rate. See PRO[1], RATE[1].

prorate *v.t.* to distribute proportionally. WH: 19C. PRO RATA.

prorogue *v.t.* to put an end to the meetings of (Parliament) without dissolving it. *Also v.i.* WH: 14–15C. Old French *proroger* or Latin *prorogare* to prolong, to extend, from PRO-[1] + *rogare* to ask.

pros- *pref.* to, towards. WH: Greek, from *pros* to, towards.

prosaic *a.* of, relating to or resembling prose. WH: 16C. French *prosaïque* or Late Latin *prosaicus*, from Latin *prosa* PROSE. See also -IC.

proscenium *n.* the part of a stage between the curtain and the orchestra. WH: 17C. Latin, from Greek *proskēnion*, from PRO-[2] + *skēnē* SCENE.

prosciutto *n.* cured Italian ham, usu. eaten as an hors d'œuvre. WH: mid-20C. Italian ham.

proscribe *v.t.* to forbid. WH: 14–15C. Latin *proscribere* to publish in writing, from PRO-[1] + *scribere* to write. The original sense was literal: to write (something) in front of something already written. In a specialized sense, to proscribe was also to post up the name of a person condemned to death. Hence the current sense which arose in the 17C.

prose *n.* ordinary written or spoken language not in metre, as distinct from *verse*. *Also a., v.i., v.t.* WH: 12–14C. Old French, from Latin *prosa* (*oratio*) straightforward (discourse), use as n. of fem. of *prosus*, from earlier *prorsus* straightforward, direct.

prosector *n.* a dissector, esp. a person who dissects bodies in preparation for lectures, demonstrations etc. WH: 19C. Late Latin anatomist. See PRO-[1], SECTOR.

prosecute *v.t.* to take legal proceedings against. *Also v.i.* WH: 14–15C. Latin *prosecutus*, p.p. of *prosequi* to pursue, to accompany, from PRO-[1] + *sequi* to follow.

proselyte *n.* a new convert to some religion, party or system, esp. a gentile convert to Judaism. *Also v.t.* WH: 14–15C. Late Latin *proselytus*, from Greek *prosēluthos* stranger, convert to Judaism, from *prosēluth-*, aorist stem of *proserkhesthai* to come to, to approach, from PROS- + *erkhesthai* to come.

prosencephalon *n.* the anterior part of the brain comprising the cerebral hemispheres etc., and sometimes including the olfactory lobes. WH: 19C. Modern Latin, from Greek *prosō* forwards + *egkephalos* brain.

prosenchyma *n.* plant tissue composed of elongated thick-walled cells closely interpenetrating, esp. fibrovascular tissue. WH: 19C. Modern Latin, from *pros-* PROS- + Greek *egkhuma* infusion, based on PARENCHYMA.

prosilient *a.* outstanding. WH: early 20C. Latin *prosiliens, prosilientis*, pres.p. of *prosilire* to leap out, from PRO-[1] + *salire* to leap. See also -ENT.

prosimian *a.* of or relating to a primitive suborder of primates, Prosimii, which includes lemurs, lorises and tarsiers. *Also n.* WH: 19C. PRO-[2] + SIMIAN.

prosit *int.* used as a (German) drinking toast. WH: 19C. German, from Latin may it benefit, 3rd pers. sing. pres. subj. of *prodesse* to be useful, to benefit.

prosody *n.* the study of the art of versification, formerly regarded as a branch of grammar. WH: 15C. Latin *prosodia* accent of a syllable, from Greek *prosōidia* song sung to music, (mark indicating the) tone of a syllable, from PROS- + *ōidē* song, ODE. See also -Y[2].

prosopagnosia *n.* an inability to recognize the faces of people whom one knows well. WH: mid-20C. Modern Latin, from Greek *prosōpon* face + *agnōsia* ignorance.

prosopography *n.* a biographical sketch. WH: 16C. Modern Latin *prosopographia*, from Greek *prosōpon* face, person. See -GRAPHY.

prosopopoeia *n.* a rhetorical figure by which abstract things are represented as persons, or absent persons as speaking. WH: 16C. Latin, from Greek *prosōpopoiia* representation in human form, from *prosōpon* face, person + *poiein* to make. See -GRAPHY.

prospect[1] *n.* an extensive view of a landscape etc. WH: 14–15C. Latin *prospectus* view, from *prospicere* to look forward, from PRO-[1] + *specere* to look.

prospect[2] *v.i.* to explore a place, esp. for minerals. *Also v.t.* WH: 16C. Latin *prospectare*, freq. of *prospicere* (PROSPECT[1]). The sense to search for minerals arose in the 19C and derives direct from PROSPECT[1].

prospectus *n.* a descriptive circular announcing the main objects and plans of a commercial scheme, institution, literary work etc. WH: 18C. Latin view, prospect, use as n. of p.p. of *prospicere*. See PROSPECT[1].

prosper *v.i.* to succeed; to thrive. *Also v.t.* WH: 14–15C. Old French *prospérer* or Latin *prosperare*, from *prosperus* doing well, from *pro spere* in accordance with hope, from *pro* PRO-[1] + abl. of *spes* hope.

prostaglandin *n.* any of a group of hormone-like substances which have wide-ranging effects on body processes, e.g. muscle contraction. WH: mid-20C. PROSTATE + GLAND + -IN[1]. The term was coined in 1936 by the Swedish physiologist Ulf S. von Euler.

prostate *n.* the prostate gland. *Also a.* WH: 17C. French, or from Modern Latin *prostata*, from Greek *prostatēs* guardian, from PRO-[2] + *statos* placed, standing. The gland is so called because it 'stands before' the (base of the) bladder.

prosternum *n.* the ventral segment of the thorax of an insect. WH: 19C. Modern Latin, from *pro-* PRO-[2] + STERNUM.

prosthesis *n.* the addition of an artificial part for the body to supply a deficiency. WH: 16C. Late Latin or Greek, from *prostithenai* to add, from PROS- + *tithenai* to place.

prosthodontics *n.* the branch of dentistry concerned with the provision of false teeth, bridgework etc.; dental prosthetics. WH: mid-20C. From PROSTHESIS, based on ORTHODONTICS.

prostitute *n.* a person (esp. a woman or girl) who engages in sexual activity for money. *Also v.t., a.* WH: 17C. Latin *prostituta*, use as n. of fem. of *prostitutus*, p.p. of *prostituere* to expose publicly, to offer for sale, to prostitute, from PRO-[1] + *statuere* to set up, to place.

prostomium *n.* the part of a worm's head in front of the mouth, bearing tentacles etc. WH: 19C. Modern Latin, or from Greek *prostomion*, lit. fore-mouth, from PRO-[2] + *stoma* mouth.

prostrate[1] *a.* lying flat or prone. WH: 12–14C. Latin *prostratus*, p.p. of *prosternere*. See PROSTRATE[2], also -ATE[2].

prostrate[2] *v.t.* to lay (a person etc.) flat. WH: 14–15C. Latin *prostratus*, p.p. of *prosternere* to throw in front of, to cast down, from PRO-[1] + *sternere* to lay low. See also -ATE[3].

prostyle *a.* having a row of columns, usu. four, entirely in front of the building. *Also n.* WH: 17C. Latin *prostylos* having pillars in front. See PRO-[2], STYLE.

protactinium *n.* a radioactive metallic element, at. no. 91, chem. symbol Pa, yielding actinium on disintegration. WH: early 20C. PROTO- + ACTINIUM. The element is so called because its commonest isotope decays to form actinium.

protagonist *n.* an advocate, champion etc. (of a cause). WH: 17C. Greek *protagōnistēs*, from *prot-* PROTO- + *agōnistēs* contestant, actor.

protamine *n.* any of a group of simple proteins occurring in the sperm of some fish. WH: 19C. PROTO- + AMINE.

protandry *n.* in plants and hermaphrodite animals, the production of male gametes before female ones. WH: 19C. PROTO- + -andry (-ANDROUS).

protanopia *n.* a form of colour-blindness in which the retina does not respond well to red, and red and green are confused. WH: early 20C. PROTO- + *an-* A-[3] + -OPIA.

protasis *n.* the clause containing the condition in a conditional sentence. WH: 16C. Latin, from Greek, from *proteinein* to put forward, to tender, from PRO-[2] + *teinein* to stretch.

protea *n.* any member of a southern African genus of shrubs and small trees, *Protea*, with large cone-shaped flowers. WH: 18C. Modern Latin from PROTEUS. The genus is so called because it has many different forms.

protean *a.* readily assuming different shapes or aspects; variable, changeable. WH: 16C. PROTEUS + -AN.

protease *n.* any enzyme which can hydrolyse proteins; a proteolytic enzyme. WH: early 20C. PROTEIN + -ASE.

protect *v.t.* to defend or keep safe (from or against injury, danger etc.). WH: 14–15C. Latin *protectus*, p.p. of *protegere* to cover in front, from PRO-[1] + *tegere* to cover.

protector *n.* a person who protects against injury or evil etc.; a guardian or patron. WH: 14–15C. Old French *protecteur*, from Late Latin *protector*, from Latin *protectus*. See PROTECT, also -OR.

protégé *n.* a person under the protection, care, or patronage of another. WH: 18C. French, p.p. of *protéger*, from Latin *protegere* PROTECT.

protein *n.* any of a class of complex organic compounds, containing carbon, oxygen, hydrogen and nitrogen, usu. with some sulphur, found in all living organisms and forming an essential constituent of animal foods. WH: 19C. French *protéine*, German *Proteïn*, from Greek *prōteios* primary, from *prōtos* first. See PROTO-, also -IN[1]. The French term was originally coined in 1838 by the Dutch chemist Gerhardus Johannes Mulder as a name for a nitrogenous substance believed to be the primary constituent of all animals and plants. The current use of the word, from the German name, dates from 1907.

pro tem *a.* temporary. *Also adv.* WH: 19C. Abbr. of Latin *pro tempore* (14–15C) for the time.

proteolysis *n.* the resolution or splitting up of proteins or peptides by the process of digestion or the application of enzymes. WH: 19C. PROTEIN + -O- + -*lysis* (LYSIS).

protero- *comb. form* former, anterior. WH: Greek *proteros* former, anterior. See also -O-.

Proterozoic *a.* of or relating to the later part of the Precambrian era, when the earliest forms of life appeared. *Also n.* WH: early 20C. PROTERO- + Greek *zōē* life + -IC.

protest[1] *v.i.* to express dissent or objection. *Also v.t.* WH: 14–15C. Old French *protester*, from Latin *protestari* to declare formally, from PRO-[1] + *testari* to be a witness, to assert.

protest[2] *n.* the act, or an instance, of protesting. *Also a.* WH: 14–15C. Old French (Modern French *protêt*), from *protester* PROTEST[1].

Protestant *n.* a member of a Church upholding the principles of the Reformation, or (loosely) of any western Church not within the Roman communion. *Also a.* WH: 16C. Modern Latin *protestans*, *protestantis*, use as n. of pres.p. of Latin *protestari* PROTEST[1]. See also -ANT. The original German princes and free cities were so called because they protested (dissented from) the decision of the Diet of Spires (Speyer) of 1529. This had denounced the Reformation by reaffirming the edict of the Diet of Worms of 1521.

protestation *n.* a solemn affirmation or declaration. WH: 12–14C. Old French, or from Late Latin *protestatio*, *protestationis*, from *protestatus*, p.p. of *protestari* PROTEST[1]. See also -ATION.

Proteus *n.* a changeable, shifty or fickle person or thing. WH: 16C. Latin, from Greek *Prōteus*, a sea god in Greek and Roman mythology, the son of Oceanus and Tethys, who were capable of taking various forms at will.

prothalamion *n.* a song or poem celebrating a forthcoming wedding. WH: 16C. From *Prothalamion*, the title of a poem ('A Spousall Verse') by Spenser (1597), based on *epithalamion*, var. of EPITHALAMIUM. See PRO-[2].

prothallium *n.* a cellular structure bearing the sexual organs in vascular cryptogams. WH: 19C. Modern Latin, from *pro-* PRO-[2] + Greek *thallos*. See THALLUS.

prothallus *n.* a prothallium. WH: 19C. Modern Latin. See PROTHALLIUM.

prothesis *n.* the placing of the elements in readiness for use in the Eucharist, esp. in the Orthodox church. WH: 16C. Greek a placing before, from PRO-[2] + *thesis* placing.

prothonotary *n.* a chief clerk or notary. WH: 14–15C. Modern Latin *prothonotarius*, *protonotarius*, from Greek *prōtonotarios*, from PROTO- + *notarios* NOTARY.

prothorax *n.* the anterior segment of the thorax in insects. WH: 19C. Modern Latin, from PRO-[2] + THORAX.

prothrombin *n.* a substance like a protein found in blood plasma, the inactive precursor of thrombin. WH: 19C. PRO-[2] + *thrombin* (THROMBOSIS).

protist *n.* any organism of the kingdom Protista, microscopic organisms whose position (as animals or plants) is doubtful, incl. protozoans, algae and fungi. WH: 19C. Modern Latin *Protista* (pl.), from German *Protisten* (pl.), from Greek *prōtista* , neut. pl. of *prōtistos* very first (superl. of *prōtos* first).

protium *n.* the ordinary isotope of hydrogen, of atomic weight 1, as distinct from *deuterium, tritium.* WH: mid-20C. Greek *prōtos* first + -IUM.

proto- *comb. form* chief. WH: Greek *prōto-*, comb. form of *prōtos* first. See also -O-.

protochordate *n.* any chordate animal which is not a vertebrate, marine animals having a notochord but no skull or spinal cord, the sea squirts etc. WH: 19C. PROTO- + *chordate* (CHORD²).

protococcus *n.* any member of a genus of unicellular algae, *Protococcus,* such as form the familiar green layers on damp stones, trees, timber etc. WH: 19C. PROTO- + COCCUS.

protocol *n.* the original draft of an official document or transaction, esp. minutes or a rough draft of a diplomatic instrument or treaty, signed by the parties to a negotiation. *Also v.i., v.t.* WH: 14–15C. Old French *prothocole* (Modern French *protocole*), from Medieval Latin *protocollum,* from Greek *prōtokollon* first leaf of a volume, fly leaf, from PROTO- + *kolla* glue. Greek *prōtokollon* denoted the first sheet (containing date and contents) glued on to a manuscript and describing its origin. The sense original draft of a diplomatic document arose in the 17C and that of official etiquette (first in France) in the 19C.

protogalaxy *n.* a cloud of gas supposed to be slowly condensing to form the stars of a new galaxy. WH: mid-20C. PROTO- + GALAXY.

protogenic *a.* (of a compound) able to donate a hydrogen ion in a chemical reaction. WH: 19C. PROTO- + -GENIC.

protogine *n.* a variety of granite forming the central mass of Mont Blanc and other mountains in the Alps, having a foliated structure due to dynamic action. WH: 19C. French, from PROTO- + Greek *ginesthai* to be born, to come into being. The rock was assumed to be more ancient than any other, so was 'first-born'.

protogyny *n.* in plants and hermaphrodite animals, the production of female gametes before male ones. WH: 19C. PROTO- + Greek *gunē* woman, female. See also -Y².

protohistoric *a.* of or relating to the period of history at the end of prehistory and immediately before the development of written records. WH: 19C. PROTO- + HISTORIC.

protohuman *n.* any of various prehistoric primates, supposed ancestors of humans. *Also a.* WH: early 20C. PROTO- + HUMAN.

protolanguage *n.* a hypothetical language, the earliest ancestor of any group of modern languages and reconstructed from them. WH: mid-20C. PROTO- + LANGUAGE.

protolithic *a.* of or relating to the very earliest Stone Age. WH: 19C. PROTO- + Greek *lithos* stone + -IC, based on NEOLITHIC, etc. The term was coined in *c.*1897 by the US geologist and archaeologist William J. McGee.

protomartyr *n.* a first martyr (applied esp. to St Stephen). WH: 14–15C. PROTO- + MARTYR.

protomorphic *a.* primitive in form; primordial. WH: 19C. PROTO- + -*morphic* (-MORPH).

proton *n.* a particle occurring in atomic nuclei and identical with the nucleus of the hydrogen atom, having an electric charge equal and opposite to that of the electron, and a mass 1840 times as great. WH: 19C. Greek *prōton,* neut. sing. of *prōtos* first. See also -ON. The term was coined in 1920 by the English physicist Ernest Rutherford, perhaps partly with reference to the name of William *Prout,* 1785–1850, the English chemist who suggested that hydrogen was a constituent of all the elements. The word was in use earlier for a type of primitive cell structure.

protonema *n.* a branched threadlike structure that grows from a moss spore and develops into a moss plant. WH: 19C. PROTO- + Greek *nēma* thread.

protopathic *a.* of or relating to a sensory nerve that only reacts to coarse stimuli like pain. WH: 19C. PROTO- + Greek *pathos* suffering, feeling, disease + -IC.

protopectin *n.* pectose. WH: early 20C. PROTO- + PECTIN.

protophloem *n.* the first part of the phloem, or food-conducting tissue, to be formed. WH: 19C. PROTO- + PHLOEM.

protophyte *n.* a unicellular plant bearing gametes. WH: 19C. PROTO- + -PHYTE.

protoplasm *n.* the viscid semifluid substance composed of oxygen, hydrogen, carbon and nitrogen, constituting the living matter of a cell and its nucleus. WH: 19C. German *Protoplasma,* from PROTO- + Greek PLASMA. The word was coined in 1846 by the German botanist Hugo von Mohl or adopted by him from the same term used in 1839 in a slightly different sense by the Bohemian physiologist Johannes E. Purkinje.

protoplast *n.* a unit of protoplasm, the nucleus and cytoplasm of a cell, but not the cell wall. WH: 16C. French *protoplaste,* or from Late Latin *protoplastus* first created being (Adam), from Greek *prōtoplastos,* from PROTO- + *plastos* formed, moulded· from *plassein* to form, to mould. The original sense was the first formed thing or being of its kind. The biological sense unit of protoplasm dates from the 19C.

protostar *n.* a slowly-condensing cloud of interstellar gas or dust from which a star is thought to develop. WH: mid-20C. PROTO- + STAR.

protostele *n.* a simple sort of stele with a solid core of vascular tissue. WH: early 20C. PROTO- + STELE.

prototherian *n.* any mammal of the subclass Prototheria, comprising the Monotremata and their ancestors. *Also a.* WH: 19C. Modern Latin *Prototheria,* from *proto-* PROTO- + Greek *thērion* wild animal. See also -AN.

prototrophic *a.* (of bacteria) feeding solely on inorganic matter. WH: early 20C. PROTO- + -TROPHIC.

prototype *n.* an original or primary person or thing, an exemplar, an archetype. *Also v.t.* WH: 16C. French, from Late Latin *prototypus,* from Greek *prōtotupos.* See PROTO-, TYPE.

protoxide *n.* the compound of oxygen and an element containing the lowest proportion of oxygen of all such compounds. WH: 19C. PROTO- + OXIDE.

protoxylem *n.* the first part of the xylem, or water-conducting tissue, to be formed. WH: 19C. PROTO- + XYLEM.

protozoan *n.* any member of the phylum Protozoa, consisting of microscopic unicellular organisms, amoebas, ciliates etc. *Also a.* WH: 19C. PROTO- + Greek *zōion* animal + -AN. Modern Latin *Protozoa* was coined in 1818 by the German palaeontologist Georg August Goldfuss. The term originally included higher forms of life, such as sponges and corals, but was restricted to the current sense in 1845.

protract *v.t.* to extend in duration. WH: 16C. Latin *protractus,* p.p. of *protrahere* to prolong, to defer, from PRO-¹ + *trahere* to draw. Cp. PORTRAIT.

protrude *v.t.* to thrust forward or out. *Also v.i.* WH: 17C. Latin *protrudere,* from PRO-¹ + *trudere* to thrust.

protuberant *a.* swelling, bulging out, prominent. WH: 17C. Late Latin *protuberans, protuberantis,* pres.p. of *protuberare,* from PRO-¹ + *tuber* a swelling. See also -ANT.

protyle *n.* a hypothetical primal matter existing before the differentiation of the chemical elements. WH: 19C. PROTO- + Greek *hulē* matter.

proud *a.* haughty, arrogant. WH: pre-1200. Old English *prūd,* from Old French *prud,* nom. *pruz* (Modern French *preux*) valiant, gallant, from Latin *prodesse* to be of value, to be good, from *prod,* var. of *pro* (PRO-¹) + *esse* to be.

proustite *n.* a red mineral, sulphide of silver and arsenic. WH: 19C. Joseph-Louis *Proust,* 1754–1826, French chemist + -ITE¹. The mineral was so named in 1832.

prove *v.t.* to establish or demonstrate the truth of by argument or testimony. *Also v.i.* WH: 12–14C. Old French *prover* (Modern French *prouver*), from Latin *probare* to test, to approve, to demonstrate, from *probus* good.

provenance *n.* an origin or source. WH: 18C. French, from *provenant,* pres.p. of *provenir* to come out, from Latin *provenire,* from PRO-¹ + *venire* to come. See also -ANCE.

Provençal *n.* a native or inhabitant of Provence (France). *Also a.* WH: 16C. French, from Latin *provincialis* provincial (PROVINCE). Provence, a region and former province of SE France, derives its name from Latin *provincia* PROVINCE. This was a nickname for southern Gaul under Roman rule, as the first Roman province to be founded beyond the Alps. Its actual name was *Gallia Transalpina* Transalpine Gaul.

provender *n.* dry food for beasts, fodder. **WH:** 12–14C. Old French *provendre*, var. of *provende*, from alt. of Latin *praebenda* PREBEND. The original sense was the portion of food supplied to each inmate of a monastery. The sense was soon extended to animal fodder and food generally for human beings.

proventriculus *n.* in birds, the thin-walled first part of the stomach in front of the gizzard, where the gastric juices are secreted. **WH:** 19C. PRO-¹ + Latin *ventriculus* (VENTRICLE).

proverb *n.* a short, pithy sentence, containing some truth or wise reflection. *Also v.t.* **WH:** 12–14C. Old French *proverbe* or Latin *proverbium*, from PRO-¹ + *verbum* word + collect. suf. *-ium*.

proviant *n.* provisions, esp. for an army. **WH:** 17C. German, from Italian *provianda*, appar. alt. of *provenda*. See PROVENDER.

provide *v.t.* to procure or prepare beforehand. *Also v.i.* **WH:** 14–15C. Latin *providere*, from PRO-¹ + *videre* to see. The original sense (to the 17C) was to foresee.

providence *n.* the beneficent care or control of God or nature. **WH:** 14–15C. Old French, or from Latin *providentia*, from *providens, providentis*, pres.p. of *providere* PROVIDE. See also -ENCE.

Provie *n.* a member of the Provisional IRA. **WH:** late 20C. Abbr. of *Provisional* (PROVISION). Cp. PROVO.

province *n.* a large administrative division of a kingdom, country or state. **WH:** 12–14C. Old French, from Latin *provincia* charge, official duty, region of a conquered country, of unknown orig. Cp. PROVENÇAL. The word is traditionally derived from Latin PRO-¹ + *vincere* to conquer, but this does not account for the earliest known Latin meaning (charge, official duty, governorship).

provirus *n.* an inactive form of a virus within a host cell. **WH:** mid-20C. PRO-² + VIRUS.

provision *n.* the act, or an instance, of providing. *Also v.t.* **WH:** 14–15C. Old French, from Latin *provisio, provisionis*, from *provisus*, p.p. of *providere* PROVIDE. See also -ION.

proviso *n.* a provisional condition, a stipulation. **WH:** 14–15C. Latin, neut. abl. sing. of p.p. of *providere* PROVIDE, as in Medieval Latin *proviso ut* it being provided that.

provisor *n.* a bishop's or archbishop's deputy. **WH:** 14–15C. French *proviseur*, from Latin *provisor*, from *provisus*. See PROVISION, also -OR.

provisory *a.* conditional. **WH:** 17C. French *provisoire* or Medieval Latin *provisorius*, from *provisus*. See PROVISION, also -ORY².

provitamin *n.* a substance which can be converted into a vitamin within an organism after ingestion. **WH:** early 20C. PRO-² + VITAMIN.

Provo *n.* a member of the Provisional IRA. **WH:** late 20C. Abbr. of *Provisional* (PROVISION). Cp. PROVIE.

provocateur *n.* a political agitator. **WH:** early 20C. French, provoker. See PROVOKE.

provoke *v.t.* to incite to action, anger etc. **WH:** 14–15C. Old French *provoquer* or Latin *provocare*, from PRO-¹ + *vocare* to call. The original sense (to the 18C) was to invoke, to invite. The sense to be provocative dates from the 16C.

provolone *n.* a soft, pale yellow kind of Italian cheese made from cow's milk. **WH:** mid-20C. Italian, from *provola* buffalo's milk cheese.

provost *n.* a person appointed to superintend or hold authority. **WH:** pre-1200. Old English *profost*, corr. to Old French *provost* (Modern French *prévôt*), from Medieval Latin *propositus*, alt. of Latin *praepositus* chief, prefect. Cp. PRAEPOSTOR.

prow *n.* the fore part of a vessel, the bow. **WH:** 16C. Old French *proue*, from Provençal *proa* or Italian dial. *prua*, from Latin *prora*, from Greek *prōra*, from base represented by Latin *pro* before, in front.

prowar *a.* in favour of war, or of a particular war; belonging to a party or faction which favours war. **WH:** 19C. PRO-¹ + WAR.

prowess *n.* outstanding ability or skill. **WH:** 12–14C. Old French *proesce* (Modern French *prouesse*), from *prou*, earlier *prud*. See PROUD, also -ESS².

prowl *v.i.* to rove (about) stealthily as if in search of prey. *Also v.t., n.* **WH:** 14–15C. Orig. unknown. The original sense was to move about looking for something generally (not specifically prey or plunder).

proxemics *n.* the study of the spatial relationships of people in ordinary conditions and activities. **WH:** mid-20C. From *proximity* (PROXIMAL), based on *phonemics* (PHONEME), etc. See also -ICS.

proximal *a.* nearest the centre of the body or the point of attachment, as distinct from *distal*. **WH:** 18C. Latin *proximus* nearest + -AL¹.

proxime accessit *n.* the person who comes second in an examination, or who gains the second prize. **WH:** 19C. Latin, lit. (he) came very near.

proximo *a.* in or of the month succeeding the present, next month (in old commercial use). **WH:** 19C. Latin in the next (month).

proxy *n.* the agency of a substitute for a principal. *Also a.* **WH:** 14–15C. Contr. of *procuracy* (PROCURATOR).

prude *n.* a person who affects great modesty or propriety, esp. in regard to sexual matters. **WH:** 18C. French, back-formation from *prudefemme*, fem. corr. to *prud'homme* good man and true, earlier *prodome*, from *prod* (PROUD) + *ome* (Modern French *homme*) man.

prudent *a.* cautious, discreet. **WH:** 14–15C. Old French, or from Latin *prudens, prudentis*, contr. of *providens, providentis* provident (PROVIDENCE).

pruinose *a.* covered with a white powdery substance or bloom, frosted. **WH:** 19C. Latin *pruinosus*, from *pruina* hoar frost. See also -OSE¹.

prune¹ *n.* the dried fruit of various kinds of *Prunus domestica*, the common plum. **WH:** 12–14C. Old French, ult. from Latin *prunum*, from Greek *prounon*, earlier *proumnon*.

prune² *v.t.* to cut or lop off the superfluous branches etc. from (a shrub or tree). *Also n.* **WH:** 14–15C. Old French *proignier*, earlier *prooignier*, ult. from PRO-¹ + Latin *rotundus* round, ROTUND.

prunella¹ *n.* any plant of the labiate genus *Prunella*, with purplish, bluish or white flowers, the common self-heal. **WH:** 16C. Modern Latin, from Medieval Latin *brunella* an infectious disease with brown coating of the tongue, dim. of *brunus* brown. The plant is apparently so called because it reputedly cured the disease. English *prunella* was formerly an alternative name for typhus.

prunella² *n.* a smooth dark silk or woollen cloth, used for making the uppers of shoes and gaiters, and formerly for clergymen's and barristers' gowns. **WH:** 17C. Orig. uncertain. ? French *prunelle* sloe, ref. to its dark colour.

prunus *n.* any member of the genus *Prunus*, fruit trees and shrubs including plum, cherry, peach, almond etc. **WH:** 18C. Latin plum tree, from Greek *prounos*, earlier *proumnē*.

prurient *a.* disposed to, characterized by or arousing an unhealthy interest in sexual matters. **WH:** 16C. Latin *pruriens, prurientis*, pres.p. of *prurire* to itch, to be wanton. See also -ENT. The original sense was having a mental itching or a morbid craving. The current sense, relating specifically to sexual matters, evolved in the 18C.

prurigo *n.* a papular disease of the skin producing severe itching. **WH:** 17C. Latin itching, from *prurire* to itch.

prusik *n.* in mountaineering, a type of sliding knot, which locks when weight is put on it, used to make loops in a rope. *Also v.i., v.t.* **WH:** mid-20C. Dr Karl *Prusik*, Austrian climber, who devised it.

Prussian *a.* of or relating to Prussia, a former German state. *Also n.* **WH:** 16C. *Prussia*, a former Polish and later German duchy and kingdom in NE Europe + -AN.

pry¹ *v.i.* to look closely or inquisitively. *Also v.t., n.* **WH:** 12–14C. Orig. unknown.

pry² *v.t.* to prise. **WH:** 19C. PRISE, taken as 3rd pers. sing. pres.

prytaneum *n.* the public hall, esp. in ancient Athens, in which the duties of hospitality were exercised towards ambassadors and citizens honoured with special distinction. **WH:** 17C. Latin, from Greek *prutaneron*, from *prutanis* prince, ruler.

Przewalski's horse *n.* a wild horse of central Asia, having an erect mane and no forelock. **WH:** 19C. Nikolaĭ Mikhaĭlovich *Przheval'skiĭ* (in Polish spelling *Przewalski*), 1839–88, Russian explorer, who discovered it in W Mongolia in *c*.1870.

psalm *n.* a sacred song or hymn. **WH:** pre-1200. Old English, from Late Latin *psalmus*, from Greek *psalmos* song sung to a harp, from *psallein* to pluck, to twang.

psalter *n.* the Book of Psalms. **WH:** pre-1200. Old English *psaltere*, from Latin *psalterium*, from Greek *psaltērion* stringed instrument, Book of Psalms, from *psallein* to pluck, to twang.

psalterium *n.* the third stomach of a ruminant, the omasum. **WH:** 19C. Latin. See PSALTER. The organ is so called because its many folds resemble the pages of a book.

psaltery *n.* a medieval stringed instrument somewhat resembling the dulcimer, but played by plucking the strings. **WH:** 12–14C. Old French *sautere, sauterie*, from Latin *psalterium*. See PSALTER.

psammite *n.* sandstone. **WH:** 19C. Greek *psammos* sand + -ITE[1].

pschent *n.* the double crown of ancient Egypt, combining the white pointed mitre of Upper Egypt and the red crown with square front of Lower Egypt. **WH:** 19C. Greek *pskhent*, from Egyptian *p-skhent*, from *p* the + *skhent*, from (hieroglyphic) *sekhent, sekhet, sekhte* the double crown of ancient Egypt.

psephite *n.* a coarse rock containing pebbles or other fragments. **WH:** 19C. Greek *psēphos* pebble + -ITE[1].

psephology *n.* the statistical and sociological study of elections, voting patterns etc. **WH:** mid-20C. Greek *psēphos* pebble (for voting) + -O- + -LOGY. The word was coined in 1947 by the Scottish historian and scholar Robert B. McCallum. The ancient Greeks voted in a legal verdict by placing a pebble in an urn.

pseud *n.* an affected or pretentious person, a pretender, a sham. *Also a.* **WH:** mid-20C. Abbr. of PSEUDO.

pseudaesthesia *n.* an imaginary sense of feeling in organs that have been removed. **WH:** 19C. PSEUDO- + AESTHESIA.

pseudaxis *n.* a sympodium. **WH:** 19C. PSEUDO- + AXIS[1].

pseudepigrapha *n.pl.* spurious writings, esp. uncanonical writings ascribed to Scriptural authors etc. **WH:** 17C. Greek, use as n. of neut. pl. of *pseudepigraphos* with false title, from PSEUDO- + *epigraphein*. See EPIGRAPH.

pseudo *a.* false, sham, spurious. *Also n.* **WH:** 14–15C. Independent adoption of (Greek) PSEUDO-.

pseudo- *comb. form* false, counterfeit, spurious. **WH:** Greek, from *pseudēs*, from *pseudos* falsehood. See also -O-.

pseudocarp *n.* a fruit composed of other parts besides the ovary. **WH:** 19C. PSEUDO- + -CARP.

pseudocyesis *n.* a false pregnancy, a psychosomatic condition in which many of the physical signs of pregnancy are present. **WH:** 19C. PSEUDO- + Greek *kuēsis* conception.

pseudograph *n.* a spurious writing, a literary forgery. **WH:** 17C. Late Latin *pseudographus*, from Greek *pseudographos*, from PSEUDO- + *-graphos* -GRAPH.

pseudohermaphroditism *n.* a congenital condition in which a person has the reproductive organs of one sex and the external genitalia of the other. **WH:** 19C. PSEUDO- + *hermaphroditism* (HERMAPHRODITE).

pseudomonas *n.* any member of the genus *Pseudomonas* of rod-shaped bacteria which live in the soil or in decaying organic matter. **WH:** early 20C. Modern Latin, from PSEUDO- + Greek *monas* MONAD.

pseudomorph *n.* a mineral having the crystalline form of another. **WH:** 19C. PSEUDO- + Greek *morphē* form.

pseudonym *n.* a fictitious name, esp. a pen name. **WH:** 19C. French *pseudonyme*, from Greek *pseudōnumon*, neut. of *pseudōnumos*, from *pseudō-* PSEUDO- + *onuma* name.

pseudopod *n.* a pseudopodium. **WH:** 19C. PSEUDOPODIUM.

pseudopodium *n.* a temporary protrusion from the cell surface of a protozoan etc., used for movement or feeding. **WH:** 19C. PSEUDO- + PODIUM.

pseudo-random *a.* (of a set of numbers) generated by a computer or a mathematical process, and thus not truly random, but sufficiently so for most purposes. **WH:** mid-20C. PSEUDO- + RANDOM.

pseudo-science *n.* a spurious science, an untested set of beliefs that passes as a science. **WH:** 19C. PSEUDO- + SCIENCE.

pshaw *int.* used to express contempt, impatience, disdain or dislike. *Also n., v.i., v.t.* **WH:** 17C. Natural exclamation. Cp. PISH.

psi *n.* the twenty-third letter of the Greek alphabet (Ψ, ψ), equivalent to *ps*. **WH:** 14–15C. Greek *psei*.

psilocybin *n.* a hallucinogenic drug obtained from Mexican mushrooms of the genus *Psilocybe*. **WH:** mid-20C. Modern Latin *Psilocybe*, from Greek *psilos* bare, smooth + *kubē* head. See also -IN[1].

psilomelane *n.* a black mineral mainly consisting of oxide of manganese, an important source of manganese. **WH:** 19C. Greek *psilos* smooth + *melan*, neut. of *melas* black.

psilosis *n.* sprue. **WH:** 19C. Greek *psilōsis*, from *psiloun* to strip bare. See also -OSIS. In sprue, the oesophagus is denuded of epithelium.

psittaceous *a.* belonging or allied to the parrots. **WH:** 19C. Latin *psittacus*, from Greek *psittakos* parrot + -EOUS.

psoas *n.* either of the two large muscles involved in flexing and rotating the hip joint. **WH:** 17C. Pl. (taken as sing.) of Modern Latin *psoa*, from Greek, usu. in pl. *psoai*, acc. *psoas* the muscles of the loins.

psoriasis *n.* a dry, scaly skin disease. **WH:** 17C. Modern Latin, from Greek *psōriasis*, from *psōrian* to have the itch, from *psōra* itch, mange.

psst *int.* used as a whispered call to attract someone's attention surreptitiously. **WH:** early 20C. Imit.

psych *v.t.* to psychoanalyse. *Also v.i.* **WH:** 19C. Abbr. of PSYCHIATRY, PSYCHOLOGY, PSYCHIC, *psychoanalyse* (PSYCHOANALYSIS), etc.

psyche *n.* the soul, the spirit, the mind. **WH:** 17C. Latin, from Greek *psukhē* breath, life, soul, mind, rel. to *psukhein* to breathe.

psychedelic *a.* of or relating to new, altered or heightened states of consciousness and sensory awareness as induced by the use of certain hallucinatory drugs. *Also n.* **WH:** mid-20C. PSYCHE + Greek *dēloun* to make manifest, to reveal, from *dēlos* manifest, clear. See also -IC. The word was proposed in 1956 by Humphry Osmond, a British research scientist (then living in Canada), in a letter to the writer Aldous Huxley.

psychiatry *n.* the study and treatment of mental disorders. **WH:** 19C. Greek *psukhē* PSYCHE + *iatreia* healing, from *iatros* healer.

psychic *a.* of or relating to the human spirit or mind. *Also n.* **WH:** 19C. Greek *psukhikos* of the mind, of the soul, from *psukhē* PSYCHE. See also -IC.

psycho *n.* a psychopath. *Also a.* **WH:** early 20C. Abbr. of *psychological* (PSYCHOLOGY), *psychopathic* (PSYCHOPATH), etc.

psycho- *comb. form* mental. **WH:** Greek *psukho-*, from *psukhē* PSYCHE. See also -O-.

psychoactive *a.* (of drugs) capable of affecting the mind or behaviour. **WH:** mid-20C. PSYCHO- + ACTIVE.

psychoanalysis *n.* a method devised by Sigmund Freud for exploring and bringing to light concepts, experience etc. hidden in the unconscious mind as a form of treatment for functional nervous diseases or mental illness. **WH:** early 20C. PSYCHO- + ANALYSIS.

psychobabble *n.* the excessive or inappropriate use of psychological jargon, esp. in popular psychotherapy. **WH:** late 20C. PSYCHO- + BABBLE.

psychobiography *n.* a biography which concentrates on the psychological development of its subject. **WH:** mid-20C. PSYCHO- + BIOGRAPHY.

psychobiology *n.* the study of the relationship between biology and mental and behavioural phenomena. **WH:** early 20C. PSYCHO- + BIOLOGY.

psychodrama *n.* an improvised dramatization of events from a patient's past life, used as a form of mental therapy. **WH:** mid-20C. PSYCHO- + DRAMA.

psychodynamics *n.* the study of mental and emotional forces and their effect on behaviour. **WH:** 19C. PSYCHO- + *dynamics* (DYNAMIC).

psychogenesis *n.* (the study of) the origin or development of the mind. **WH:** 19C. PSYCHO- + GENESIS.

psychogenic *a.* (of symptoms or illnesses) having a mental, as opposed to physical, origin. **WH:** early 20C. PSYCHO- + -GENIC.

psychogeriatrics *n.* the study and treatment of the mental disorders associated with old age. **WH:** mid-20C. PSYCHO- + GERIATRICS.

psychographics *n.* the study of personalities, aspirations, attitudes etc., esp. in market research. **WH:** mid-20C. PSYCHO- + *-graphic* (GRAPHIC) + -S[1]. See also -ICS.

psychohistory *n.* history written from a psychological point of view. **WH:** mid-20C. PSYCHO- + HISTORY.

psychokinesis *n.* apparent movement or alteration in physical objects produced by mental effort alone. **WH:** early 20C. PSYCHO- + KINESIS.

psycholinguistics *n.* the study of the psychology of language, its acquisition, development, use etc. **WH:** mid-20C. PSYCHO- + *linguistics* (LINGUIST).

psychology *n.* the science of the human mind or soul. **WH:** 17C. Modern Latin *psychologia*. See PSYCHO-, -LOGY.

psychometrics *n.* the branch of psychology dealing with the measurement of mental capacities and attributes, esp. by the use of psychological tests and statistical methods. **WH:** mid-20C. From earlier *psychometry* (19C) (PSYCHO- + -METRY) + -ICS.

psychomotor a. of or relating to muscular action proceeding from mental activity. WH: 19C. PSYCHO- + MOTOR.

psychoneurosis n. a neurosis, esp. one due to emotional conflict. WH: 19C. PSYCHO- + NEUROSIS.

psychopath n. a person suffering from a severe personality disorder characterized by antisocial behaviour and a tendency to commit acts of violence. WH: 19C. PSYCHO- + -PATH.

psychopathology n. (the branch of psychology dealing with) mental and behavioural aberrance. WH: 19C. PSYCHO- + PATHOLOGY.

psychopharmacology n. the study of the effect of drugs on the mind. WH: early 20C. PSYCHO- + PHARMACOLOGY.

psychophysics n. the science of the relations between mind and body, esp. between physical stimuli and psychological sensation. WH: 19C. PSYCHO- + PHYSICS.

psychophysiology n. the branch of physiology which deals with mental phenomena. WH: 19C. PSYCHO- + PHYSIOLOGY.

psychoprophylaxis n. a method of training women for natural childbirth by teaching breathing and relaxation techniques for the management of pain. WH: mid-20C. PSYCHO- + prophylaxis (PROPHYLACTIC).

psychosexual a. of or relating to the psychological aspects of sex. WH: 19C. PSYCHO- + SEXUAL.

psychosis n. a severe mental disorder, not due to organic lesion, characterized by distortion of the sufferer's concept of reality. WH: 19C. PSYCHE + -OSIS, prob. based on NEUROSIS.

psychosocial a. of or relating to the interaction of social and psychological factors, esp. in illness. WH: 19C. PSYCHO- + SOCIAL.

psychosomatic a. denoting a physical disorder caused by or influenced by the patient's emotional condition. WH: 19C. PSYCHO- + somatic (SOMA[1]).

psychosurgery n. the use of brain surgery in the treatment of mental disorder. WH: mid-20C. PSYCHO- + SURGERY.

psychotherapy n. the treatment of mental disorder by psychological or hypnotic means. WH: 19C. PSYCHO- + therapy (THERAPEUTIC).

psychotropic a. psychoactive. WH: mid-20C. PSYCHO- + -tropic (-TROPE).

psychrometer n. the wet-and-dry bulb hygrometer for measuring the humidity of the atmosphere. WH: 18C. Greek psukhros cold + -O- + -METER. The term was originally applied to a thermometer, so that the current etymological sense is inappropriate.

ptarmigan n. any of various birds of the genus Lagopus, allied to the grouse, having grey or brown plumage in the summer and white in the winter, esp. Lagopus mutus, of subarctic regions. WH: 16C. Gaelic tarmachan, from tarm-, torm- to grumble, to croak. The initial pt- was introduced in the 17C by false association with Greek words such as pteron (PTERO-).

PT boat n. a motor torpedo boat. WH: Abbr. of patrol torpedo boat.

-ptera comb. form organisms having a certain number or type of wings. WH: Greek ptera, pl. of pteron. See PTERO-, also -A[2].

pteridology n. the scientific study of ferns. WH: 19C. Greek pteris, pteridos fern + -O- + -LOGY.

pteridophyte n. any member of the division Pteridophyta including ferns, clubmosses and horsetails. WH: 19C. Greek pteris, pteridos fern + -O- + -PHYTE.

pteridosperm n. a fossil plant of the group Pteridospermae, fern-like but producing seeds. WH: early 20C. Greek pteris, pteridos fern + -O- + -SPERM.

pterion n. the H-shaped suture where the frontal, parietal and sphenoid bones of the skull meet. WH: 19C. Modern Latin, from Greek pteron wing + -ion, based on gnathion (GNATHIC), INION, etc. The suture is so called from the wings of the sphenoid.

ptero- comb. form winged. WH: Greek pteron wing, feather. See also -O-.

pterodactyl n. an extinct winged reptile from the Mesozoic strata with membranous wings and a long birdlike head. WH: 19C. Modern Latin Pterodactylus, from Greek pteron wing + daktulos finger.

pteropod n. any individual of the Pteropoda, a subclass of Mollusca in which the foot is expanded into winglike lobes or paddles. WH: 19C. Modern Latin Pteropoda. See PTERO-, -POD.

pterosaur n. any individual of the Pterosauria, an order of flying reptiles of the Mesozoic age. WH: 19C. Modern Latin Pterosauria, from PTERO- + Greek saura, sauros lizard.

pteroylglutamic acid n. folic acid. WH: mid-20C. From pteroic (from Greek pteron wing + -IC) + -YL + GLUTAMIC ACID.

pterygium n. a varicose excrescence of the conjunctiva of the eye. WH: 17C. Modern Latin, from Greek pterugion, dim. of pterux wing.

pterygoid a. wing-shaped. Also n. WH: 18C. Modern Latin pterygoides (pl.), from Greek pterugion. See PTERYGIUM, also -OID.

pteryla n. any of the tracts or patches of feathers on the skin of a bird. WH: 19C. Modern Latin, from Greek pteron feather + hulē wood, forest.

ptochocracy n. government by the poor, as distinct from plutocracy. WH: 18C. Greek ptōkhos beggar + -CRACY.

Ptolemaic a. of or relating to Ptolemy. WH: 17C. Greek Ptolemaios Ptolemy, c.90–168 AD, Alexandrian astronomer who held that the planets, including the sun, revolved round the earth + -IC. (In the Ptolemaic system, the 'planets', in order of supposed distance from the earth, were the moon, Mercury, Venus, the sun, Mars, Jupiter and Saturn.)

ptomaine n. any one of a class of sometimes poisonous amines derived from decaying animal and vegetable matter. WH: 19C. French ptomaïne, from Italian ptomaina, from Greek ptōma corpse. See also -INE. The Italian word was coined in 1878 by the Italian toxicologist Francesco Selmi. Since the combining form of Greek ptōma is ptōmat-, a better formation would have been *ptomatina, giving English *ptomatine.

ptosis n. a drooping of the upper eyelid from paralysis of the muscle raising it. WH: 18C. Greek ptōsis falling, fall.

ptyalin n. an enzyme contained in saliva, which converts starch into dextrin. WH: 19C. Greek ptualon spittle + -IN[1].

pub[1] n. a public house. Also v.i. WH: 19C. Abbr. of public house (PUBLIC).

pub[2] n. publication. Also v.t. WH: early 20C. Abbr. of PUBLICATION.

puberty n. the period of life at which persons become capable of begetting or bearing children. WH: 14–15C. Latin pubertas, from pubes, puberis an adult, or pubes pubes, the pubic hair, the groin, the genitals. See also -TY[1].

public a. of, relating to or affecting the people as a whole, as distinct from personal or private. Also n. WH: 14–15C. Old French public, publique or Latin publicus, from pubes adult, influ. by poplicus, from populus PEOPLE. See also -IC.

publican n. a keeper of a public house. WH: 12–14C. Old French publicain, from Latin publicanus, from publicum public revenue, use as n. of neut. of publicus PUBLIC. See also -AN. The original sense was a tax-gatherer in the Roman Empire. The current sense evolved in the 18C.

publication n. the act, or an instance, of making publicly known. WH: 14–15C. Old French, from Latin publicatio, publicationis, from publicatus, p.p. of publicare. See PUBLISH, also -ATION.

publicist n. a writer on current social or political topics, esp. a journalist, a person who publicizes, esp. a press or publicity agent. WH: 18C. French publiciste (based on canoniste canonist; see CANON), from Latin (ius) publicum public (law), from neut. of publicus PUBLIC. See also -IST.

publicity n. the process of attracting public attention to a product, person etc. WH: 18C. French publicité, from public PUBLIC. See also -ICITY.

publicize v.t. to make known to the public; to advertise. WH: early 20C. PUBLIC + -IZE.

publish v.t. to make public, to announce publicly. Also v.i. WH: 12–14C. Old French *publir, publiss- (Modern French publier), from Latin publicare to make public, from publicus PUBLIC. See also -ISH[2]. The original sense was to make generally known. The sense to prepare and issue a book, etc. dates from the 16C.

puccoon n. any one of various N American plants yielding a red or yellow dye. WH: 17C. Algonquian poughkone.

puce n. a dark reddish purple colour. Also a. WH: 18C. Old French flea, from Latin pulex, pulicis flea. The colour is so called from that of a squashed flea which has fed on blood.

puck[1] n. a mischievous sprite, elf or fairy. WH: pre-1200. Old English pūca, corr. to Old Norse púki mischievous demon, of unknown orig. Cp. POOKA.

puck[2] n. a vulcanized rubber disc used instead of a ball in ice hockey. WH: 19C. Orig. unknown. ? Rel. to POKE[1].

pucker *v.t.* to gather into small folds or wrinkles. *Also v.i., n.* WH: 16C. Prob. freq. from base also of POKE[1], POCKET. See also -ER[5].

pud *n.* a pudding. WH: 18C. Abbr. of PUDDING.

puddening *n.* a pad of rope etc. used as a fender. WH: 18C. From *pudden*, var. of PUDDING + -ING[1].

pudding *n.* a sweet dish, usu. cooked, and usu. made with flour, eggs, milk etc. WH: 12–14C. Old French *boudin* black pudding, from Latin *botellus* pudding, sausage, small intestine. See BOWEL. The word originally applied to the stomach or intestine of a pig, sheep, etc., stuffed with minced meat, oatmeal, suet, etc. and boiled, i.e. similar to a modern haggis. The current sense as a sweet (or savoury) dish arose in the 16C.

puddle *n.* a small pool, esp. of rainwater. *Also v.i., v.t.* WH: 12–14C. Dim. of Old English *pudd* ditch, furrow. See also -LE[2]. Cp. German dial. *Pfudel* pool.

pudency *n.* modesty, shamefacedness. WH: 17C. Late Latin *pudentia*, from *pudens, pudentis*, pres.p. of *pudere* to be ashamed. See also -ENCY.

pudge *n.* a short, thick or fat person or figure. WH: 19C. Rel. to PODGE.

pudsy *a.* plump. WH: 18C. Perh. from PUD, based on FUBSY. See also -SY.

pueblo *n.* a village, town or settlement, esp. of the Indians of New Mexico etc. *Also a.* WH: 19C. Spanish, from Latin *populus* PEOPLE.

puerile *a.* childish, inane. WH: 16C. French *puéril* or Latin *puerilis*, from *puer* boy, child. See also -IL.

puerperal *a.* of, relating to or resulting from childbirth. WH: 18C. Latin *puerperus* parturient, from *puer* child + *-parus* bringing forth. See also -AL[1].

Puerto Rican *n.* a native or inhabitant of Puerto Rico. *Also a.* WH: 19C. *Puerto Rico*, an island in the Greater Antilles group of the W Indies + -AN.

puff *v.i.* to emit or expel air, steam etc. in short, sudden blasts. *Also v.t., n.* WH: 12–14C. Imit., ? representing Old English *pyffan*, corr. to Dutch *poffen*.

puffin *n.* any of various seabirds of the genus *Fratercula*, esp. the N Atlantic *F. arctica*, with black and white plumage and a brightly-coloured bill. WH: 12–14C. Appar. from PUFF + -ING[3]. The reference would be to the plump nestlings of the Manx shearwater.

pug[1] *n.* a pug-dog. WH: 16C. ? Of Dutch orig. The word was originally a term of endearment. Other obsolete senses include bargeman, ship's boy, prostitute and higher servant. The current sense as applied to a dog arose in the 18C.

pug[2] *n.* clay and other material mixed and prepared for making into bricks. *Also v.t.* WH: 19C. Orig. uncertain. ? Rel. to dial. *pug* to poke, to punch, to pack or fill a space, also of uncertain orig.

pug[3] *n.* the footprint or trail of an animal. *Also v.i.* WH: 19C. Abbr. of PUGILIST.

pugaree *n.* a light turban. WH: 17C. Hindi *pagrī* turban.

pugilist *n.* a boxer, a prizefighter. WH: 18C. Latin *pugil* boxer + -IST.

pugnacious *a.* inclined to fight; quarrelsome. *Also adv.* WH: 17C. Latin *pugnax, pugnacis*, from *pugnare* to fight, from *pugnus* fist. See also -ACIOUS.

puisne *a.* (of a judge) junior or inferior in rank. *Also n.* WH: 16C. Old French (Modern French *puîné*), from *puis* (from Latin *postea* afterwards) + *né* (from Latin *natus* born). Cp. PUNY.

puissance *n.* a showjumping event that tests a horse's power to jump high obstacles. WH: 14–15C. Old French, from Latin *posse* to be able. See POTENT, also -ANCE.

puja *n.* a Hindu act of worship. WH: 17C. Sanskrit *pūjā* worship.

puke *v.t., v.i.* to vomit. *Also n.* WH: 16C. Prob. imit. Cp. German *spucken* to spit, Flemish *spukken* to spew.

pukeko *n.* a wading bird, *Porphyrio porphyrio*, with bright plumage. WH: 19C. Maori.

pukka *a.* genuine. WH: 17C. Hindi *pakkā* cooked, ripe, substantial.

pulchritude *n.* beauty. WH: 14–15C. Latin *pulchritudo*, from *pulcher* beautiful. See also -TUDE.

pule *v.i.* to cry plaintively or querulously, to whine, to whimper. *Also v.t.* WH: 14–15C. Prob. imit. Cp. French *piauler*, dial. *piouler* to chirp, to whine.

pulicide *n.* any chemical agent used for killing fleas. WH: mid-20C. Latin *pulex, pulicis* flea + -CIDE.

Pulitzer prize *n.* any one of a series of prizes awarded annually in the US for literature, journalism and music. WH: early 20C. Joseph Pulitzer, 1847–1911, US newspaper publisher. The first Pulitzer prize was awarded in 1917.

pull *v.t.* to draw towards one by force. *Also v.i., n.* WH: pre-1200. Old English *pullican*, prob. rel. to Low German *pūlen* to shell, to strip, to pluck, Dutch *peul* husk, shell.

pullet *n.* a young fowl, esp. a hen less than a year old. WH: 14–15C. Old French *poulet*, dim. of *poule* hen, from Popular Latin *pulla*, fem. of Latin *pullus* young animal, foal, chicken. See also -ET[1].

pulley *n.* a wheel with a grooved rim, or a combination of such wheels, mounted in a block for changing the direction or for increasing the effect of a force. *Also v.t.* WH: 12–14C. Old French *polie* (Modern French *poulie*), prob. ult. from Medieval Greek dim. of *polos* pivot, axis, windlass. Cp. POLE[2]. Not rel. to PULL.

Pullman *n.* a Pullman car. WH: 19C. George M. *Pullman*, 1831–97, US inventor, designer of a railway carriage with folding upper and lower berths.

pullorum disease *n.* an acute bacterial disease of young chickens characterized by whitish diarrhoea, caused by *Salmonella gallinarum*. WH: early 20C. Modern Latin (*Bacterium*) *pullorum* (Latin of chickens), former name of *Salmonella gallinarum*.

pullulate *v.i.* (of a shoot etc.) to shoot, bud. WH: 17C. Latin *pullulatus*, p.p. of *pullulare* to sprout, to grow, from *pullulus*, dim. of *pullus* young animal, foal, chicken. See also -ATE[3].

pulmo- *comb. form* of or relating to the lungs. WH: Latin *pulmo* lung. See also -O-.

pulmonary *a.* of or relating to the lungs. WH: 17C. Latin *pulmonarius*, from *pulmo, pulmonis* lung + -arius -ARY[1].

pulp *n.* any soft, moist, coherent mass. *Also v.t., v.i.* WH: 14–15C. Latin *pulpa*, of unknown orig.

pulpit *n.* an elevated enclosed stand in a church from which a preacher delivers a sermon. *Also a., v.t., v.i.* WH: 12–14C. Latin *pulpitum* scaffold, platform, stage.

pulque *n.* a Mexican vinous beverage made by fermenting the sap of a species of agave. WH: 17C. American Spanish, from Nahuatl *puliúhki* decomposed.

pulsar *n.* an interstellar source of regularly pulsating radio waves, prob. a swiftly rotating neutron star. WH: mid-20C. Contr. of *pulsating star*, based on QUASAR. See PULSATE.

pulsate *v.i.* to move, esp. to expand and contract, with rhythmical alternation, to beat, to throb. *Also v.t.* WH: 18C. Latin *pulsatus*, p.p. of *pulsare*, freq. of *pellere* (p.p. *pulsus*) to drive, to beat. See also -ATE[3].

pulsatilla *n.* the pasque flower, *Pulsatilla vulgaris*. WH: 16C. Modern Latin, dim. of Latin *pulsatus* beaten about (by the wind).

pulse[1] *n.* the rhythmic beating of the arteries caused by the propulsion of blood along them from the heart. *Also v.i., v.t.* WH: 12–14C. Old French *pous*, later *pouls*, from Latin *pulsus (venarum)* beating (of the veins), from *pulsus*, p.p. of *pellere* to drive, to beat.

pulse[2] *n.* the edible seeds of leguminous plants. WH: 12–14C. Old French *pols*, from *puls, pultis* thick pottage of meat or pulse, rel. to POLLEN.

pulverize *v.t.* to reduce to fine powder or dust. *Also v.i.* WH: 14–15C. Late Latin *pulverizare*, from Latin *pulvis, pulveris* dust. See also -IZE.

pulvillus *n.* the pad or cushion of an insect's foot. WH: 18C. Latin, contr. of *pulvinulus*, dim. of *pulvinus* cushion.

pulvinate *a.* cushion-shaped, padlike. WH: 19C. Latin *pulvinatus*, from *pulvinus* cushion. See also -ATE[2].

puma *n.* the cougar, *Felis concolor*, a large feline carnivore of the Americas. WH: 18C. Spanish, from Quechua *púma*.

pumice *n.* a light, porous or cellular kind of lava, used as a cleansing and polishing material. *Also v.t.* WH: 14–15C. Old French *pomis*, from Latin dial. *pomex, pomicis*, var. of *pumex, pumicis*. Cp. POUNCE[2]. The spelling was assimilated to the Latin form in the 16C.

pummel *v.t.* to strike or pound repeatedly, esp. with the fists. *Also n.* WH: 16C. Var. of POMMEL.

pump[1] *n.* a device or machine usu. in the form of a cylinder and piston, for raising water or other liquid. *Also v.t., v.i.* WH: 14–15C. Prob. from Middle Dutch *pompe* (wood or metal) pipe, stone conduit, of Germanic orig., ? ult. imit. The word was originally in nautical use.

pump² *n.* a light low-heeled, slipper-like shoe worn with evening dress and for dancing. **WH:** 16C. Orig. unknown. ? Rel. to POMP or of imit. orig. Cp. *dap* light shoe.

pumpernickel *n.* German wholemeal rye bread. **WH:** 18C. German, orig. lout, stinker, said to be from *pumpern* to break wind + *Nickel* goblin, rascal (see NICKEL).

pumpkin *n.* any plant of the genus *Cucurbita*, creeping plants with large lobed leaves. **WH:** 17C. Alt. of *pumpion*, var. of obs. *pompion*, from obs. French *pompon*, nasalized form of *popon*, from Latin *pepo*, *peponis* large melon, from Greek *pepōn*, use as n. of *pepōn* ripe, with assim. of ending to -KIN.

pun¹ *n.* the playful use of a word in two different senses or of words similar in sound but different in meaning. *Also v.i.* **WH:** 17C. Orig. uncertain. Poss. abbr. of obs. *pundigron*, itself prob. a fanciful alt. of PUNCTILIO.

pun² *v.t.* to pound, to crush, to consolidate by ramming. **WH:** 16C. Dial. var. of POUND³.

puna *n.* a cold high plateau between the two ranges of the Andes. **WH:** 17C. American Spanish, from Quechua.

Punch *n.* the chief character in the popular puppet show of Punch and Judy, represented as a grotesque hook-nosed hump-backed man. **WH:** 17C. Abbr. of PUNCHINELLO. Cp. PUNCH³.

punch¹ *n.* a tool for making holes. *Also v.t.* **WH:** 14–15C. Abbr. of PUNCHEON¹ or var. of POUNCE¹.

punch² *n.* a beverage made of wine or spirits, water or milk, lemons, sugar, spice etc., usu. served hot. **WH:** 17C. Appar. from Sanskrit *pañca* five, as the drink orig. had five ingredients. This origin has been disputed on various grounds, but is still held as a possibility.

punch³ *n.* a Suffolk punch, a short-legged draught horse orig. bred in Suffolk. **WH:** 17C. Abbr. of PUNCHINELLO. Cp. PUNCH.

puncheon¹ *n.* a short upright timber, used for supporting the roof in a mine or as an upright in the framework of a roof. **WH:** 12–14C. Old French *poinson* (Modern French *poinçon*), of unknown orig. Cp. PUNCH¹, POUNCE¹, PUNCHEON².

puncheon² *n.* a large cask holding from 72 to 120 gallons (324–540 l). **WH:** 14–15C. Old French *poinson* (Modern French *poinçon*), ? from same source as PUNCHEON¹.

Punchinello *n.* a buffoon, a Punch, a grotesque person. **WH:** 17C. Alt. of Neapolitan dial. *Polecinella*, literary Italian *Pulcinella*, prob. from dim. of *pollecena*, young of the turkeycock, from *pulcino* chicken, from Latin *pullus* (PULLET). The turkeycock's hooked beak bears some resemblance to the character's nose. Like the modern PUNCH, the original stock character of the Italian *commedia dell'arte* had a hooked nose, humped back, and short, stout figure.

punctate *a.* covered with points, dots, spots etc. **WH:** 18C. Latin *punctum* point + -ATE².

punctilio *n.* a nice point in conduct, ceremony or honour. **WH:** 16C. Italian *puntiglio*, Spanish *puntillo*, dim. of *punto* POINT, later assim. to Latin *punctum*.

punctual *a.* exact in matters of time. **WH:** 14–15C. Medieval Latin *punctualis*, from Latin *punctum* POINT.

punctuate *v.t.* to mark (written matter) with stops, to divide into sentences, clauses etc. with stops. **WH:** 17C. Medieval Latin *punctuatus*, p.p. of *punctuare*, from Latin *punctum* POINT. See also -ATE³.

punctum *n.* a point, a speck, a dot, a minute spot of colour etc. **WH:** 16C. Latin, orig. neut. of *punctus*, p.p. of *pungere* to prick.

puncture *n.* a small hole made with something pointed. *Also v.t., v.i.* **WH:** 14–15C. Latin *punctura*, from *punctus*, p.p. of *pungere* to prick. See also -URE.

pundit *n.* a Hindu learned in the Sanskrit language and the science, laws and religion of India. **WH:** 17C. Sanskrit *paṇḍita* learned, conversant with.

punga *n.* a New Zealand tree fern, the pith of which is edible. **WH:** 19C. Var. of *ponga*, from Maori.

pungent *a.* sharply affecting the senses, esp. those of smell or taste. **WH:** 16C. Latin *pungens*, *pungentis*, pres.p. of *pungere* to prick. See also -ENT. Cp. POIGNANT.

Punic *a.* of or relating to ancient Carthage, the Carthaginians, or the Carthaginian language. *Also n.* **WH:** 14–15C. Latin *Punicus*, earlier *Poenicus*, from *Poenus*, from Greek *Phoinix* Phoenician, Carthaginian. See also -IC.

punish *v.t.* to inflict a penalty on (a person) for an offence. **WH:** 12–14C. Old French *punir, puniss-*, from Latin *punire*, earlier *poenire*, from *poena* PAIN. See also -ISH².

Punjabi *n.* a native or inhabitant of the state of Punjab in India or the province of Punjab in Pakistan, or the larger area comprising both of these, formerly a province of British India. *Also a.* **WH:** 19C. Urdu *panjābī*, from *Panjāb* Punjab, a region in the NW of the Indian subcontinent, now divided between India and Pakistan + -I³.

punk *n.* a worthless person or thing. *Also a.* **WH:** 17C. Orig. uncertain. ? Rel. to SPUNK. The original sense was crumbly wood rotted by fungal attack. The sense worthless person evolved from this in the early 20C, then a style of rock music in the late 20C.

punkah *n.* a large portable fan made from a palm leaf. **WH:** 17C. Hindi *paṅkhā* fan, from Sanskrit *pakṣaka*, from *pakṣa* wing.

punnet *n.* a small, shallow basket for fruit, flowers etc. **WH:** 19C. ? Dim. of dial. var. of POUND². See also -ET¹.

punt¹ *n.* a shallow, flat-bottomed, square-ended boat, usu. propelled by pushing against the bottom of the stream with a pole. *Also v.t., v.i.* **WH:** pre-1200. Latin *ponto, pontonis* PONTOON². Cp. PONT. The word was readopted (in the 16C) from Middle Low German *punte, punto*, from Latin.

punt² *v.i.* to stake against the bank in some card games. *Also n.* **WH:** 18C. French *ponter*, rel. to *ponte* or Spanish *ponto* point.

punt³ *v.t.* in ball games, to kick the ball after dropping it from the hand and before it touches the ground. *Also n.* **WH:** 19C. ? Ult. dial. var. of BUNT³.

punt⁴ *n.* the standard monetary unit of the Republic of Ireland. **WH:** late 20C. Irish *púnt* pound.

punto *n.* a thrust or pass in fencing. **WH:** 16C. Italian or Spanish, from Latin *punctum* POINT.

punty *n.* a pontil. **WH:** 17C. French PONTIL.

puny *a.* small and feeble, tiny. *Also n.* **WH:** 16C. Phonetic spelling of PUISNE.

pup *n.* a puppy. *Also v.t., v.i.* **WH:** 16C. Back-formation from PUPPY, as if it were a dim. in -Y³.

pupa *n.* an insect at the immobile, metamorphic stage between larva and imago. **WH:** 18C. Modern Latin, from Latin girl, doll.

pupil¹ *n.* a young person under the care of a teacher. **WH:** 14–15C. Old French *pupille* or Latin *pupillus, pupilla* orphan, ward, dim. of *pupus* boy, *pupa* girl.

pupil² *n.* the circular opening of the iris of the eye through which rays of light pass to the retina. **WH:** 14–15C. Old French *pupille* or Latin *pupilla*, dim. of *pupa* girl, doll, pupil of the eye. The pupil is so called from the tiny image of oneself that can be seen when looking into someone's eyes.

puppet *n.* an articulated toy figure moved by strings, wires or rods, a marionette. **WH:** 16C. Later form of POPPET.

puppy *n.* a young dog. **WH:** 15C. Old French *popée* (Modern French *poupée*) doll, lay figure, toy, plaything, ult. from Latin *pupa*. See POPPET. Cp. PUP. The original sense was a small dog used as a lady's pet or plaything, otherwise a toy dog. The current sense dates from the 16C.

pur- *pref.* a form of PRO-¹, as in *purchase*. **WH:** Anglo-French form of Old French *por-, pur-* (Modern French *pour-*), from Latin *por-, pro-*. See PRO-¹.

Purana *n.* any of a great class of Sanskrit poems comprising the whole body of Hindu mythology. **WH:** 17C. Sanskrit *purāṇa* belonging to former times, from *purā* formerly.

Purbeck *n.* Purbeck stone. **WH:** 18C. (Isle of) *Purbeck*, a peninsula on the Dorset coast.

purblind *a.* partially blind, near-sighted, dim-sighted. **WH:** 12–14C. Orig. two words, from PURE (assim. to PUR-) + BLIND. The original sense was completely blind.

purchase *v.t.* to obtain by payment. *Also n.* **WH:** 12–14C. Old French *pourchacier* (Modern French *pourchasser*) to seek to obtain, to procure, from *pour-* PUR- + *chacier* (Modern French *chasser*) CHASE¹.

purdah *n.* the custom in some Muslim and Hindu societies of secluding women from the view of strangers. **WH:** 19C. Persian and Urdu *parda* veil, curtain.

pure *a.* unmixed, unadulterated. *Also n., adv., v.t.* **WH:** 12–14C. Old French *pur*, fem. *pure*, from Latin *purus* clean, clear, chaste.

purée *n.* a smooth thick pulp of fruit, vegetables etc. obtained by liquidizing, sieving etc. *Also v.t.* WH: 18C. Old French, in form fem. p.p. of *purer*, from Medieval Latin *purare* to refine (ore, metal), from Latin *purus* PURE.

purfle *v.t.* to decorate with a wrought or ornamental border, to border. *Also n.* WH: 12–14C. Old French *porfiler*, from *por-* PRO-[1] + Latin *filum* thread. Cp. PROFILE.

purgation *n.* the act of purging, purification. WH: 14–15C. Old French, or from Latin *purgatio*, *purgationis*, from *purgatus*, p.p. of *purgare* PURGE. See also -ATION.

purgatory *n.* a place or state of spiritual purging, esp. a place or state succeeding the present life in which, according to the Roman Catholic Church, the souls of the faithful are purified from venial sins by suffering. *Also a.* WH: 12–14C. Old French *purgatoire*, from Medieval Latin *purgatorium*, use as n. of neut. of Late Latin *purgatorius* purifying, from Latin *purgatus*. See PURGATION, also -ORY[1].

purge *v.t.* to cleanse or purify. *Also v.i., n.* WH: 12–14C. Old French *purgier* (Modern French *purger*), from Latin *purgare* to purify, from *purus* PURE.

puri *n.* an unleavened wholewheat bread, deep-fried and sometimes containing a spicy vegetable etc. mixture. WH: mid-20C. Hindi *pūrī*, from Sanskrit *pūrikā*.

purify *v.t.* to make pure, to cleanse. WH: 12–14C. Old French *purifier*, from Latin *purificare*, from *purus* PURE. See also -FY.

Purim *n.* a Jewish festival instituted in commemoration of the deliverance of the Jews from the destruction threatened by Haman's plot. WH: 14–15C. Hebrew, pl. of *pūr*, a foreign word explained in the Old Testament as meaning LOT, with ref. to the casting of lots by Haman. 'In the first month … they cast Pur, that is, the lot, before Haman' (Esther iii.7); 'Because Haman … had devised against the Jews to destroy them, and had cast Pur, that is, the lot, to consume them' (Esther ix.24). The festival commemorates the defeat of Haman's plot.

purin *n.* a crystalline solid derivable from uric acid. WH: 19C. Blend of Latin *purum* pure and Modern Latin *uricum* URIC + -IN[1].

purist *n.* a person advocating or affecting purity, esp. in art or language. WH: 18C. French *puriste*, from *pur* PURE. See also -IST.

puritan *n.* any one of a party or school of English Protestants of the 16th and 17th cents., who aimed at purifying religious worship from all ceremonies etc. not authorized by Scripture, and at the strictest purity of conduct. *Also a.* WH: 16C. Latin *puritas* PURITY + -AN. Cp. CATHAR.

purity *n.* the state of being pure, cleanness. WH: 12–14C. Old French *pureté*, later assim. to Late Latin *puritas*, from Latin *purus* PURE. See also -ITY.

purl[1] *n.* an edging or fringe of twisted gold or silver wire. *Also a., v.t., v.i.* WH: 14–15C. ? Imit.

purl[2] *v.i.* to flow with a soft, bubbling, gurgling or murmuring sound and an eddying motion. *Also n.* WH: 16C. Prob. imit. Cp. Norwegian *purla* to bubble up, to gush out, Swedish dial. *porla* to ripple, to gurgle.

purl[3] *v.t., v.i.* to upset, to overturn. *Also n.* WH: 18C. PURL[2].

purler *n.* something which is very good of its kind. WH: mid-20C. PURL[3] + -ER[1]. Cp. *knockout* (KNOCK).

purlieu *n.* the bounds or limits within which one ranges, one's usual haunts. WH: 15C. Prob. alt. (by assim. to *leu* LIEU) of Old French *pourallee* a going around (to settle the boundaries), from *pouraler* to traverse, from *pour-* PUR- + *aller* to go.

purlin *n.* a horizontal timber resting on the principal rafters and supporting the common rafters or boards on which the roof is laid. WH: 14–15C. Anglo-Latin *perlio*, *perlionis*, ? from Latin *per* through + stem of *ligare* to bind. Cp. French *lien* tie in carpentry.

purloin *v.t.* to steal, to take by theft. *Also v.i.* WH: 12–14C. Old French *porloigner*, from PUR- + *loign* (Modern French *loin*) far.

purple *a.* of the colour of red and blue blended, the former predominating. *Also n., v.t., v.i.* WH: pre-1200. Latin *purpura* purple-dyed cloth, from Greek *porphura* (shellfish yielding) a purple dye. Cp. PURPURA. The second *r* of the Latin and Greek words became *l* as with MARBLE, TURTLE. The dye was traditionally used for the fabric worn by people of imperial or royal rank. Hence *born in the purple* etc.

purport[1] *v.t.* to convey as the meaning, to signify. WH: 14–15C. Old French *purporter*, from Medieval Latin *proportare*, from Latin PRO-[1] + *portare* to carry, to bear.

purport[2] *n.* meaning, sense. WH: 14–15C. Old French *purport*, *porport* produce, contents. See PURPORT[1].

purpose *n.* an end in view, an aim. *Also v.t., v.i.* WH: 12–14C. Old French *purpos*, *porpos* (Modern French *propos*), from *purposer*, *porposer* (Modern French *pourposer*, from *pur-*, *por-* PUR- + *poser*), var. of *proposer* PROPOSE.

purpura *n.* a skin rash consisting of small purple spots caused by internal bleeding from the small blood vessels. WH: 18C. Latin. See PURPLE.

purr *n.* a soft vibratory murmuring as of a cat when pleased. *Also v.i., v.t.* WH: 17C. Imit.

purse *n.* a small bag or pouch for money, usu. carried in the pocket. *Also v.t., v.i.* WH: pre-1200. Alt. of Late Latin *bursa*, var. of *byrsa*, from Greek *bursa* leather. Cp. BURSA.

purser *n.* an officer on board ship or on an aircraft in charge of the provisions, pay and the general welfare of the passengers. WH: 12–14C. PURSE + -ER[1]. Cp. *bursar* (BURSA). The original sense (to the 17C) was a maker of purses. The current sense dates from the 14–15C.

purslane *n.* any of various herbs of the genus *Portulaca*, esp. the succulent herb, *Portulaca oleracea*, used as a salad and pot-herb. WH: 14–15C. Old French *porcelaine*, prob. assim. of Latin *porcilaca* (var. of *portulaca*) to French *porcelaine* PORCELAIN. See PORTULACA.

pursue *v.t.* to follow with intent to seize, kill etc. *Also v.i.* WH: 12–14C. Old French *poursuir*, *porsuir*, var. of *poursivre* (Modern French *poursuivre*), from alt. of Latin *prosequi* PROSECUTE.

pursuivant *n.* an attendant on a herald, an officer of the College of Arms of lower rank than a herald. WH: 14–15C. Old French *pursivant*, use as n. of pres.p. of *pursivre* PURSUE. also -ANT.

pursy[1] *a.* short-winded, asthmatic. WH: 14–15C. Later form of *pursive*, from Anglo-French *porsif*, alt. of *polsif* (Modern French *poussif*), from *polser* to breathe with difficulty, to pant, from Latin *pulsare* to drive violently, to agitate (see PUSH).

pursy[2] *a.* like a purse, puckered up like the mouth of a purse. WH: 16C. PURSE + -Y[1].

purtenance *n.* an appurtenance. WH: 14–15C. Anglo-French alt. of Old French *partinance*, from *partenant*, pres.p. of *partenir*. See PERTAIN, also -ANCE. (Later prob. taken as shortening of APPURTENANCE.)

purty *a.* pretty. WH: 19C. Representation of a local pronun. of PRETTY.

purulent *a.* consisting of or discharging pus or matter. WH: 14–15C. French, or from Latin *purulentus*, from *pus*, *puris* PUS. See also -ULENT.

purvey *v.t.* to supply, esp. provisions. *Also v.i.* WH: 12–14C. Old French *porveeir* (Modern French *pourvoir*), from Latin *providere* PROVIDE.

purview *n.* extent, range, scope, intention. WH: 14–15C. Old French *porveii* (Modern French *pourvu*), p.p. of *porveeir*. See PURVEY. The word was originally used in the Anglo-French phrase *purveu est* it is provided, or *purveu que* provided that, introducing a provision or proviso in a statute.

pus *n.* the thick yellowish liquid secreted from inflamed tissues, the produce of suppuration. WH: 14–15C. Latin. Rel. to FOUL.

Puseyism *n.* the High Church tenets of the Oxford Movement, in the Church of England, Tractarianism. WH: 19C. Edward *Pusey*, 1800–82, English churchman, a leader of the movement + -ISM.

push *v.t.* to press against with force, tending to urge forward or away. *Also v.i., n.* WH: pre-1200. Old French *pousser*, from Latin *pulsare*, freq. of *pulsus*, p.p. of *pellere* to drive, to thrust.

pusillanimous *a.* lacking courage, faint-hearted. WH: 14–15C. Late Latin *pusillanimis* (translating Greek *olugopsukhos*), from *pusillus* very small, weak + *animus* mind. See also -OUS.

puss[1] *n.* a pet name for a cat, esp. in calling. WH: 16C. Prob. imit., from Germanic. Cp. Dutch *poes*.

puss[2] *n.* the face. WH: 19C. Irish *pus* lip, mouth.

pustule *n.* a small vesicle containing pus, a pimple. WH: 14–15C. Old French, or from Latin *pustula*. See also -ULE. Not rel. to PUS.

put *v.t.* to move so as to place in some position. *Also v.i.*, *n.* WH: pre-1200. Old English **putian* (implied in verbal. n. *putung*), with parallel forms *potian*, *pytian*, ult. of unknown orig.

putamen *n.* the hard bony stone or endocarp of a fruit such as a peach or cherry. WH: 19C. Latin, from *putare* to prune.

putative *a.* reputed, supposed. WH: 14–15C. Old French *putatif* or Late Latin *putativus*, from Latin *putatus*, p.p. of *putare* to think, to suppose. See also -ATIVE.

putlog *n.* a short horizontal piece of timber for the floor of a scaffold to rest on. WH: 17C. ? From *put*, p.p. of PUT + LOG[1].

put-put *v.i.* (of a petrol engine) to make a rapid popping sound. *Also n.* WH: early 20C. Imit.

putrefy *v.t.* to cause to rot or decay. *Also v.i.* WH: 14–15C. Latin *putrefacere*, from *puter*, *putris* rotten + *facere* to make. See also -FY.

putrid *a.* in a state of putrefaction, decomposition, or decay. WH: 14–15C. Latin *putridus*, from *putrere* to rot, from *puter*, *putris* rotten. See also -ID.

putsch *n.* a sudden rising, revolt; a coup d'état. WH: early 20C. Swiss German thrust, blow.

putt *v.i.* to strike a golf ball with a putter. *Also v.t.*, *n.* WH: 18C. Var. of PUT.

puttee *n.* a long strip of cloth wound spirally round the leg, usu. from ankle to knee, as a form of gaiter. WH: 19C. Hindi *paṭṭī* band, bandage, from Sanskrit *paṭṭikā*.

putter *v.i.* to put-put. *Also n.* WH: mid-20C. Imit.

putto *n.* a figure of a small boy, cherub or cupid in Renaissance and baroque art. WH: 17C. Italian, from Latin *putus* boy.

putty *n.* whiting and linseed oil beaten up into a tenacious cement, used in glazing etc. *Also v.t.* WH: 17C. Old French *potée*, orig. potful, from *pot* POT[1]. See also -Y[2]. The current sense dates from the 18C.

puy *n.* a conical hill of volcanic origin, esp. in the Auvergne, France. WH: 19C. French hill, from Latin PODIUM.

puzzle *n.* a perplexing problem or question. *Also v.t.*, *v.i.* WH: 16C. Orig. uncertain. ? Freq. of POSE[2] + -LE[4].

pyaemia *n.* blood poisoning, due to the spread of pus-forming bacteria in the system causing multiple abscesses. WH: 19C. PYO- + -AEMIA.

pycnidium *n.* a flask-shaped structure in certain fungi which contains spores. WH: 19C. Modern Latin or Greek *puknos* close, dense + -idium, Modern Latin dim. ending corr. to -IUM.

pycnite *n.* a columnar variety of topaz. WH: 19C. Greek *puknos* thick, dense + -ITE[1].

pycno- *comb. form* thick, dense. WH: Greek *puknos* thick, dense. See also -O-.

pycnometer *n.* a bottle or flask of known volume used in measuring the specific gravity of fluids. WH: 19C. PYCNO- + -METER.

pye-dog *n.* a stray mongrel dog, esp. in India. WH: 19C. Prob. contr. of *pariah-dog* (PARIAH).

pyelitis *n.* inflammation of the pelvis of the kidney. WH: 19C. Greek *puelos* trough + -ITIS.

pyelo- *comb. form* of or relating to the kidneys. WH: Greek *puelos* trough. See also -O-.

pyelography *n.* the branch of radiology dealing with the kidneys and the surrounding structures. WH: 20C. PYELO- + -GRAPHY.

pyelonephritis *n.* inflammation of the kidney and of the renal pelvis. WH: 19C. PYELO- + *nephritis* (NEPHRITIC).

pygidium *n.* the tail, or other end structure, of certain worms, insects or other invertebrates. WH: 19C. Modern Latin, from Greek *pugē* rump + -idium, Modern Latin dim. ending corr. to -IUM.

pygmy *n.* a member of any of various dwarf peoples living in Malaysia or central Africa. *Also a.* WH: 14–15C. Latin *pygmaei*, pl. of *pygmaeus*, from Greek *pugmaios* dwarfish, from *pugmē* measure of length from elbow to knuckles, fist.

pygo- *comb. form* rump. WH: Greek *pugē* rump. See also -O-.

pygostyle *n.* the vomer or ploughshare bone forming the end of the vertebral column in most birds. WH: 19C. PYGO- + Greek *stulos* column.

pyjamas *n.pl.* a sleeping suit consisting of a loose jacket and trousers. WH: 19C. Persian and Urdu *pāy-jāmah*, *pā-jāmah*, from *pāy* leg + *jāmah* garment. The word was originally used for loose trousers worn by both sexes in Turkey, India, etc.

pyknic *a.* (of a body type) characterized by short stature, relatively short arms and legs, a large abdomen and a short neck. *Also n.* WH: early 20C. Greek *puknos* thick, close-packed + -IC.

pylon *n.* a structure, usu. of steel, supporting an electric cable. WH: 19C. Greek *pulōn* gateway, from *pulē* gate. The word was originally the term for a monumental gateway to an Egyptian temple. The electricity pylon dates from the early 20C.

pylorus *n.* the contracted end of the stomach leading into the small intestine. WH: 17C. Late Latin, from Greek *pulōros*, *pulouros* gatekeeper, from *pulē* gate + *ouros* warder.

pyo- *comb. form* pus. WH: Greek *puon* pus. See also -O-.

pyoderma *n.* any skin rash characterized by the formation of pus-filled spots. WH: mid-20C. PYO- + Greek *derma* skin.

pyogenesis *n.* the formation of pus, suppuration. WH: 19C. PYO- + GENESIS.

pyoid *a.* of the nature of pus, purulent. WH: 19C. Greek *puoeidēs* like pus, from *puon* pus. See also -OID.

pyorrhoea *n.* inflammation of the gums leading to the discharge of pus and loosening of the teeth; periodontal disease. WH: 19C. PYO- + -RRHOEA.

pyosis *n.* suppuration. WH: 17C. Modern Latin, from Greek *puōsis*. See PYO-, also -OSIS.

pyracantha *n.* any evergreen thorny shrub of the genus *Pyracantha*, with white flowers and coral-red berries, also called the firethorn, commonly trained against walls as an ornamental climber. WH: 17C. Modern Latin, use as genus name of Greek *purakantha*, an unidentified plant, from *pur* fire + *akantha* thorn. The plant is so called from the spiny shoots and red berries of some species.

pyralid *n.* any of various moths of the family *Pyralidae*, small and slender with long legs. *Also a.* WH: 19C. Modern Latin *Pyralidae*, from *Pyralis*, use as genus name of Greek *puralis* a mythical fly said to live in fire, from *pur* fire. See also -ID.

pyramid *n.* a monumental structure of masonry, with a square base and triangular sloping sides meeting at the apex. *Also v.i.* WH: 14–15C. Latin *pyramis*, *pyramidis*, from Greek *puramis*, ult. of unknown orig.

pyrargyrite *n.* a dark red mineral consisting of sulphide of silver and antimony. WH: 19C. PYRO- + Greek *arguros* silver + -ITE[1].

pyre *n.* a funeral pile for burning a dead body. WH: 17C. Latin *pyra*, from Greek *pura*, from *pur* fire.

pyrene[1] *n.* an aromatic hydrocarbon obtained in the dry distillation of coal. WH: 19C. Greek *pur* fire + -ENE.

pyrene[2] *n.* the stone of a fruit such as a peach. WH: 19C. Modern Latin *pyrena*, from Greek *purēn*.

pyrethrum *n.* any of several plants of the genus *Tanacetum* of the Compositae, esp. *T. coccineum*. WH: 12–14C. Latin, from Greek *purethron* feverfew, prob. from *puretos* fever.

pyretic *a.* of, relating to or producing fever. *Also n.* WH: 18C. Modern Latin *pyreticus*, from Greek *puretos* fever. See also -IC.

Pyrex® *n.* a heat-resistant glass containing oxide of boron. *Also a.* WH: early 20C. ? Greek *pur* fire + commercial suf. *-ex*. According to some, the name comes from PIE[1] + euphonious *r* + *-ex*.

pyrexia *n.* fever, feverish condition. WH: 18C. Modern Latin, from Greek *purexis*, from *puressein* to be feverish, from *pur* fire. See also -IA.

pyrheliometer *n.* an instrument for measuring the intensity of solar radiation. WH: 19C. Greek *pur* fire + *hēlios* sun + -METER.

pyridine *n.* a liquid alkaloid obtained from bone oil, coal tar etc., used as a solvent etc. WH: 19C. Greek *pur* fire + -ID + -INE.

pyriform *a.* pear-shaped. WH: 18C. Medieval Latin *pyriformis*, from *pyrum*, misspelling of *pirum* pear. See also -FORM.

pyrimidine *n.* a cyclic organic nitrogenous base, with the formula $C_4H_4N_2$. WH: 19C. From PYRIDINE, with inserted *im-* from IMIDE.

pyrites *n.* a native sulphide of iron, one of two common sulphides, chalcopyrite, yellow or copper pyrites, or marcasite, usu. called iron pyrites. WH: 14–15C. Latin, from Greek *puritēs*, use as n. of a. from *pur* fire.

pyro *n.* pyrogallic acid. WH: 19C. Abbr. of PYROGALLIC.

pyro- *comb. form* fire, heat. WH: Greek *pur* fire. See also -O-.

pyroacetic *a.* of or derived from acetic acid by heat. WH: 19C. PYRO- + ACETIC.

pyrochemical *a.* of, relating to or involving chemical reactions at very high temperatures. WH: 19C. PYRO- + CHEMICAL.

pyroclastic *a.* formed from or consisting of the fragments broken up or ejected by volcanic action. WH: 19C. PYRO- + CLASTIC.

pyroelectric *a.* (of some minerals) becoming electrically charged on heating. WH: 19C. PYRO- + ELECTRIC.

pyrogallic *a.* produced from gallic acid by heat. WH: 19C. PYRO- + GALLIC.

pyrogen *n.* a substance, such as ptomaine, that produces fever on being introduced into the body. WH: 19C. PYRO- + -GEN.

pyrognostic *a.* of or relating to pyrognostics. WH: 19C. PYRO- + Greek *gnōstikos* pertaining to knowledge. See also -IC.

pyrography *n.* the art of making designs in wood by means of fire, pokerwork. WH: 17C. PYRO- + -GRAPHY.

pyroligneous *a.* derived from wood by heat. WH: 18C. PYRO- + LIGNEOUS.

pyrolusite *n.* native manganese dioxide, one of the most important of the ores of manganese. WH: 19C. PYRO- + Greek *lousis* washing + -ITE[1]. The mineral is so called from its use in decolouring glass.

pyrolysis *n.* the chemical decomposition of a substance by heat. WH: 19C. PYRO- + -*lysis* (LYSIS).

pyromagnetic *a.* thermomagnetic. WH: 19C. PYRO- + *magnetic* (MAGNET).

pyromancy *n.* divination by fire. WH: 14–15C. Old French *piromance, pyromancie*, from Late Latin *pyromantia*, from Greek *puromanteia*. See PYRO-, -MANCY.

pyromania *n.* an irresistible desire to set things on fire. WH: 19C. PYRO- + -MANIA.

pyrometer *n.* an instrument for measuring high temperatures. WH: 18C. PYRO- + -METER.

pyromorphite *n.* an ore of lead consisting of phosphate and chloride of lead. WH: 19C. PYRO- + -MORPH + -ITE[1].

†**pyronomics** *n.* the science of heat. WH: 19C. PYRO- + Greek *nomos* usage, custom, law + -ICS.

pyrope *n.* a deep-red garnet. WH: 12–14C. Old French *pirope*, from Latin *pyropus*, from Greek *purōpos* gold-bronze, lit. fiery-eyed, from *pur* fire + *ōps* eye, face.

pyrophoric *a.* (of a chemical) igniting spontaneously on contact with air. WH: 19C. Modern Latin *pyrophorus*, from Greek *purophorus* fire-bearing, from *pur* fire + *-phoros* -bearing + -IC.

pyrophosphoric *a.* derived by heat from phosphoric acid. WH: 19C. PYRO- + *phosphoric* (PHOSPHORUS).

pyrophyllite *n.* a mineral occurring in metamorphic rocks, a form of hydrated aluminium silicate. WH: 19C. PYRO- + PHYLLITE.

pyrosis *n.* heartburn. WH: 18C. Modern Latin, from Greek *purōsis*, from *puroun* to set on fire, from *pur* fire. See also -OSIS.

pyrostat *n.* a type of thermostat for use at high temperatures. WH: 19C. PYRO- + -STAT.

pyrosulphate *n.* a salt of pyrosulphuric acid. WH: 19C. PYRO- + SULPHATE.

pyrotechnic *a.* of or relating to fireworks or their manufacture. WH: 18C. French *pyrotechnie*, from Modern Latin *pyrotechnia*, from PYRO- + Greek *tekhnē* art. See also -IC.

pyroxene *n.* any of a group of silicates of lime, magnesium, iron or manganese, of various forms and origin. WH: 19C. PYRO- + Greek *xenos* stranger. The mineral group is so called because it was originally thought to be alien to igneous rocks. The name was coined in 1796 by the French crystallographer and mineralogist René Just Haüy.

pyroxylin *n.* a nitrocellulose, gun cotton, used in the manufacture of plastics and lacquers. WH: 19C. PYRO- + Greek *xulon* wood + -IN[1].

Pyrrhic *a.* of or relating to Pyrrhus. WH: 19C. Greek *purrikhos*, from *Purrhos*, Latin *Pyrrhus*, king of Epirus in Greece, who defeated the Romans at Asculum in 280 BC but lost so many men he was unable to attack Rome itself + -IC.

pyrrhic *n.* a metrical foot of two short syllables. *Also a.* WH: 17C. Latin *pyrrhicius*, from Greek *purrhikhios* pertaining to the *purrhikē*, an ancient Greek dance in armour said to have been named after its inventor, *Purrhikos*. The metrical foot was used in the warsong accompanying the dance.

Pyrrhonism *n.* the sceptical philosophy taught by Pyrrho of Elis. WH: 17C. Greek *Purrhōn* Pyrrho of Elis, *c.*365-270 BC, Greek founder of the first school of sceptic philosophy + -ISM.

pyrrole *n.* a colourless toxic liquid found in e.g. porphyrins and chlorophyll. WH: 19C. Greek *purrhos* reddish + Latin *oleum* oil. See also -OL.

pyruvic acid *n.* an organic acid occurring as an intermediate in the metabolism of proteins and carbohydrates. WH: 19C. PYRO- + Latin *uva* grape + -IC + -ACID.

Pythagorean *n.* a follower of Pythagoras. *Also a.* WH: 16C. Latin *Pythagoreus*, from Greek *Puthagoreios*, from *Puthagoras* Pythagoras, *c.*580–*c.*500 BC, Greek philosopher and mathematician + -EAN.

Pythian *a.* of or relating to Delphi, Apollo, or his priestess who delivered oracles at Delphi. *Also n.* WH: 16C. Latin *Pythius*, from Greek *Puthios*, from *Puthō* Delphi (DELPHIC) + -IAN.

python *n.* a large non-venomous serpent of the family Pythonidae, that crushes its prey. WH: 14–15C. Latin, from Greek *Puthōn*, the huge serpent of Greek mythology killed by Apollo near Delphi.

Pythonesque *a.* (of humour) surreal, extravagant, absurd. WH: late 20C. Monty *Python*'s Flying Circus, a British television comedy series of the 1970s noted for its absurdist or surrealist humour + -ESQUE.

pythoness *n.* the priestess of the temple of Apollo at Delphi who delivered the oracles. WH: 14–15C. Old French *phitonise* (Modern French *pythonisse*), from Medieval Latin *phitonissa*, alt. of Late Latin *pythonissa*, fem. of *pytho, pythonis*, from Late Greek *puthōn* PYTHON. See also -ESS[1].

pyuria *n.* the presence of pus in the urine. WH: 19C. PYO- + -URIA.

pyx *n.* the covered vessel, usu. of precious metal, in which the Eucharistic host is kept. *Also v.t.* WH: 14–15C. Latin *pyxis*, from Late Greek *puxis* BOX[1].

QED a formula used at the conclusion of a proof or demonstration. WH: Abbr. of QUOD ERAT DEMONSTRANDUM.

Q factor *n.* the difference between stored energy and the rate at which energy is being expended. WH: Abbr. of QUALITY.

Q fever *n.* an acute disease caused by rickettsiae, the symptoms of which include fever and pneumonia. WH: Abbr. of QUERY.

qindar *n.* a unit of Albanian currency equal to one hundredth of a lek. WH: early 20C. Albanian, from *qind* hundred.

Q-ship *n.* an armed navy vessel disguised as a merchant ship, employed as a decoy to lure and surprise enemy submarines. WH: Appar. abbr. of QUERY.

qua *conj.* in the character of, by virtue of being, as. WH: 17C. Latin, abl. sing. fem. of *qui* who.

quack[1] *v.i.* to make the harsh cry of a duck or a similar sound. *Also n.* WH: 19C. Imit.

quack[2] *n.* an unqualified practitioner of medicine, esp. one offering ineffectual remedies. *Also a.* WH: 17C. Abbr. of QUACKSALVER.

†quacksalver *n.* a person who brags of their medicines or salves. WH: 16C. Early modern Dutch (now *kwakzalver*), prob. from stem of obs. *quacken* to prattle + *salf* SALVE[1]. Cp. CHARLATAN.

quad[1] *n.* a quadrangle or court, as of a college etc. WH: 19C. Abbr. of QUADRANGLE. Cp. QUOD.

quad[2] *n.* each child of quadruplets. WH: 19C. Abbr. of *quadruplet* (QUADRUPLE).

quad[3] *n.* a block of type metal lower than the type, used for spacing out lines etc. *Also v.t.* WH: 19C. Abbr. of QUADRAT.

quad[4] *a.* quadraphonic. *Also n.* WH: late 20C. Abbr. of QUADRAPHONIC.

quad bike *n.* a four-wheeled motorcycle designed for off-road sporting, agricultural etc. use. WH: late 20C. Abbr. of QUADRUPLE + BIKE[1].

quadragenarian *n.* a person who is 40 or between 40 and 50 years old. *Also a.* WH: 19C. Late Latin *quadragenarius*, from Latin *quadrageni* forty each, from *quadraginta* forty. See also -ARIAN.

Quadragesima *n.* the first Sunday in Lent. WH: 14–15C. Late Latin, use as n. of fem. of Latin *quadragesimus* fortieth, from *quadraginta* forty. The day is so called because it is the first Sunday in the 40 days of Lent.

quadrangle *n.* a plane figure having four angles and four sides, esp. a square or rectangle. WH: 14–15C. Old French, or from Late Latin *quadrangulum*, use as n. of *quadrangulus*, from *quadr-* QUADRI- + Latin *angulus* ANGLE[1].

quadrant *n.* the fourth part of the circumference of a circle, an arc of 90°. WH: 14–15C. Latin *quadrans, quadrantis* quarter (orig. of an as), from *quadr-* QUADRI-.

quadraphonic *a.* of, relating to or being a system of recording and reproducing sound using four independent sound signals or speakers. WH: mid-20C. Alt. of earlier *quadriphonic*, from QUADRI- + *-phonic* (-PHONE), based on STEREOPHONIC, etc.

quadrat *n.* a square of vegetation marked out for ecological study. WH: 14–15C. Var. of QUADRATE[1].

quadrate[1] *a.* square; rectangular. *Also n.* WH: 14–15C. Latin *quadratus*, p.p. of *quadrare* to square, from *quadr-* QUADRI-. See also -ATE[2].

quadrate[2] *v.t.* to square. *Also v.i.* WH: 16C. Latin *quadratus*, p.p. of *quadrare*. See QUADRATE[1], also -ATE[3].

quadrella *n.* a form of betting where the person making the bet must pick the winners of four races. WH: mid-20C. Latin *quadr-* QUADRI- + dim. suf. *-ella*. Cp. QUINELLA.

quadrennial *a.* lasting four years. WH: 17C. Latin *quadriennium* period of four years (from *quadr-* QUADRI- + *annus* year) + -AL[1].

quadri- *comb. form* four. WH: Latin comb. form of *quattuor* four.

quadric *a.* of the second degree; quadratic. *Also n.* WH: 19C. Latin *quadra* square + -IC.

quadricentennial *n.* the 400th anniversary of an event. *Also a.* WH: 19C. QUADRI- + *centennial* (CENTENARIAN).

quadriceps *n.* a four-headed muscle at the front of the thigh, acting as extensor to the leg. WH: 16C. Latin QUADRI- + *-ceps*, from *caput* head.

quadricone *n.* a quadric cone. WH: 19C. QUADRI- + CONE.

quadrifarious *a.* arranged in four parts or rows. WH: 18C. QUADRI- + Latin *-farius*, prob. rel. to *fari* to speak. See also -OUS.

quadrifid *a.* cleft into four parts, segments or lobes. WH: 17C. QUADRI- + -FID.

quadrifoliate *a.* having four leaves or leaflets. WH: 19C. QUADRI- + FOLIATE[2].

quadriga *n.* an ancient Roman two-wheeled chariot drawn by four horses abreast. WH: 17C. Latin, sing. of *quadrigae* (pl.), contr. of *quadriiugae*, from QUADRI- + *iugum* yoke.

quadrigeminal *a.* of or relating to four medullary tubercles situated at the base of the brain. WH: 19C. QUADRI- + Latin *geminus* + -AL[1].

quadrijugate *a.* pinnate with four pairs of leaflets. WH: 19C. QUADRI- + Latin *iugum* yoke + -ATE[2].

quadrilateral *n.* a plane figure or area with four straight sides. *Also a.* WH: 17C. Late Latin *quadrilaterus* (from Latin QUADRI- + *latus, lateris* side) + -AL[1].

quadrilingual *a.* speaking four languages. WH: 19C. QUADRI- + LINGUAL.

quadriliteral *a.* consisting of four letters. *Also n.* WH: 18C. QUADRI- + LITERAL.

quadrille[1] *n.* a dance consisting of five figures executed by four sets of couples. *Also v.i.* WH: 18C. French, from Spanish *cuadrilla*, from *cuadro* square.

quadrille[2] *n.* a game of cards played by four persons with 40 cards, fashionable in the 18th cent. WH: 18C. French, ? from Spanish *cuartillo* (from *cuarto* fourth), assim. to QUADRILLE[1].

quadrillion *n.* the fifth power of a thousand, one followed by 15 zeros. WH: 17C. French, from Latin QUADRI- + *-illion*, based on MILLION, BILLION, etc.

quadrilobate *a.* having four lobes. WH: 19C. QUADRI- + *lobate* (LOBE).

quadrilocular *a.* having four cells or chambers. WH: 18C. QUADRI- + *locular* (LOCULUS).

quadringenarious *a.* consisting of 400. WH: 17C. Latin *quadringenarius*, from *quadringeni* four hundred each, from *quadringenti* four hundred.

quadrinomial *a.* consisting of four terms. *Also n.* WH: 18C. QUADRI- + Greek *nomos* part, portion + -AL[1].

quadripartite *a.* divided into or consisting of four parts. WH: 14–15C. Latin *quadripartitus*. See QUADRI-, PARTITE.

quadriplegia *n.* paralysis of all four limbs. WH: early 20C. QUADRI- + PARAPLEGIA.

quadrireme *n.* an ancient Roman galley having four banks of oars. WH: 17C. Latin *quadriremis*, from QUADRI- + *remus* oar.

quadrisection *n.* division into four usu. equal parts. WH: 17C. QUADRI- + SECTION.

quadrisyllabic *a.* consisting of four syllables. WH: 19C. QUADRI- + *syllabic* (SYLLABLE).

quadrivalent *a.* having a valency or combining power of four, tetravalent. WH: 19C. QUADRI- + *-valent* (from Latin *valens, valentis*, pres.p. of *valere* to be strong). See also -ENT.

quadrivium *n.* in the Middle Ages, an educational course consisting of arithmetic, music, geometry, and astronomy. WH: 19C. Latin place where four ways meet, from QUADRI- + *via* way. See also -IUM. Cp. TRIVIAL.

quadroon *n.* the offspring of a mulatto and a white person; a person of one quarter black and three-quarters white ancestry. WH: 18C. Spanish *cuarterón* quàrter, later assim. to words in QUADRI-. See also -OON.

quadrumanous *a.* of, relating to or belonging to a group of mammals in which the hind as well as the fore feet have an opposable digit and are used as hands, containing the monkeys, apes, baboons and lemurs. WH: 17C. Modern Latin *quadrumana*, from *quadru-*, var. of QUADRI- + *manus* hand. See also -OUS.

quadruped *n.* a four-footed animal, esp. a mammal. *Also a.* WH: 17C. French *quadrupède* or Latin *quadrupes, quadrupedis*, from *quadru-*, var. of QUADRI- + *pes, pedis* foot.

quadruple *a.* consisting of four parts. *Also n., v.i., v.t.* WH: 14–15C. Old French, from Latin *quadruplus*, from *quadru-*, var. of QUADRI- + *-plus* as in *duplus* DUPLE.

quadrupole *n.* a system of two associated dipoles. WH: early 20C. From *quadru-*, var. of QUADRI- + POLE[2].

quaere *int.* ask, inquire, it is a question. *Also n.* WH: 16C. Latin, imper. sing. of *quaerere*. See QUAESTOR.

quaestor *n.* an ancient Roman magistrate having charge of public funds, a public treasurer, paymaster etc. WH: 14–15C. Latin, from old form of *quaesitus*, p.p. of *quaerere* to ask, to inquire, to seek.

quaff *v.t.* to drink in large draughts. *Also v.i., n.* WH: 16C. ? Middle Low German *quassen* to eat or drink immoderately. The written *-ss-* of *quassen* may have given the *-ff* of *quaff*.

quag *n.* a piece of marshy or boggy ground. WH: 16C. Imit. Prob. not rel. to QUAKE.

quagga *n.* a southern African quadruped, *Equus quagga*, intermediate between the ass and the zebra, now extinct. WH: 18C. Dutch, from Nama *qua-ha'*, ? imit. of the animal's braying or rel. to Nguni *iqwara* striped thing.

quagmire *n.* an area of soft marshy ground that sinks under the feet. WH: 16C. QUAG + MIRE.

quahog *n.* a common edible clam, *Venus mercenaria*, of the Atlantic coast of N America. WH: 18C. Narragansett *poquaûhock*.

quaich *n.* a shallow drinking vessel, usu. of wood. WH: 16C. Gaelic *cuach* cup, ? from *cua* hollow. Cp. Latin *caucus*, Welsh *caurg* bowl.

quail[1] *v.i.* to shrink back with fear. *Also v.t.* WH: 14–15C. Orig. unknown. According to some, the word is from Middle Dutch *quelen* to suffer, to be ill, rel. to QUELL.

quail[2] *n.* a small migratory bird of the genus *Coturnix*, allied to the partridge, esp. a European game bird *C. coturnix*. WH: 12–14C. Old French *quaille* (Modern French *caille*), from Medieval Latin *coacula*, prob. of imit. orig.

quaint *a.* old-fashioned. WH: 12–14C. Old French *cointe, queinte*, from Latin *cognitus*, p.p. of *cognoscere* to ascertain, from CO- + *gnoscere* to know. The original sense (to the 18C) was wise, clever, then specifically skilled in the use of fine language. The current sense dates from the 18C.

quake *v.i.* to shake, to tremble. *Also v.t., n.* WH: pre-1200. Old English *cwacian*, rel. to *cweccan* to cause to shake, of unknown orig.

Quaker *n.* a member of the Society of Friends. *Also a.* WH: 17C. QUAKE + -ER[1]. The word was originally a derogatory nickname, perhaps in allusion to the founder George Fox's direction to his opponents to 'tremble at the word of the Lord', or to the fits that members supposedly suffered when moved by the Spirit. Cp. *Shaker* (SHAKE).

qualify *v.t.* to provide with the requisite qualities. *Also v.i.* WH: 14–15C. Old French *qualifier*, from Medieval Latin *qualificare*, from Latin *qualis* of what kind, from base of *qui, quis* who + -ALS[1]. See also -FY.

quality *n.* a distinctive property or attribute. *Also a.* WH: 12–14C. Old French *qualité*, from Latin *qualitas* (translating Greek *poiotēs*), from *qualis*. See QUALIFY, also -ITY.

qualm *n.* a sensation of fear or uneasiness. WH: 16C. Orig. uncertain. Cp. Old English *cwalm* pestilence, pain (rel. to QUELL), Middle Low German *quallem*, German *Qualm* thick vapour, smoke.

qualy *n.* a method of measuring the quality and length of the life given to a patient by medical treatment, used to assess the cost-effectiveness of treatment, and to compare different, expensive, treatments. WH: late 20C. Acronym of *quality-adjusted life year*.

quandary *n.* a state of difficulty or perplexity. WH: 16C. Orig. uncertain. ? Latin *quando* when + inf. ending *-are*. Cp. NONPLUS.

quandong *n.* a small Australian tree, *Fusanus acuminatus*, with edible drupaceous fruit. WH: 19C. Australian Aboriginal (Wiradhuri) *guwandhaang*.

quango *n.* a board set up by central government to supervise activity in a specific field, e.g. the Race Relations Board. WH: late 20C. Acronym of *quasi non-governmental organization*, later taken to be *quasi-autonomous non-governmental organization*.

quant *n.* a punting-pole with a flange at the end to prevent its sinking in the mud. *Also v.t., v.i.* WH: 14–15C. ? Latin *contus* (Greek *kontos*) boat pole.

quantic *n.* a rational, integrally homogeneous function of two or more variables. WH: 19C. Latin *quantus* how great + -IC.

quantify *v.t.* to determine the quantity of, to measure as to quantity. WH: 16C. Medieval Latin *quantificare*, from *quantus* how great. See QUANTITY, also -FY.

quantity *n.* that property by virtue of which anything may be measured. WH: 12–14C. Old French *quantité*, from Latin *quantitas* (translating Greek *posotēs*), from *quantus* how great, how much, from base of *qui, quis* who. See also -ITY.

quantivalence *n.* valency. WH: 19C. Latin *quanti-*, comb. form of *quantus* how great, how much + *-valence*, based on *equivalence* (EQUIVALENT). See VALENCE.

quantize *v.t.* to restrict or limit to a set of fixed discrete values or quanta. WH: early 20C. QUANTUM + -IZE.

quantum *n.* the smallest possible amount into which a physical property such as energy or momentum can be subdivided and by which the value of that property can change. WH: 16C. Latin, neut. of *quantus* how much.

quaquaversal *a.* pointing in every direction. WH: 18C. Late Latin *quaqua versus*, from Latin *quaqua* wheresoever + *versus* turned. See also -AL[1].

quarantine *n.* the enforced isolation, esp. of people and animals coming from places infected with contagious disease. *Also v.t.* WH: 16C. Medieval Latin *quarantena*, ult. from Latin *quadraginta* forty. The original sense was a period of 40 days in which a widow had the right to remain in her late husband's dwelling. The current sense arose in the 17C from Italian *quarantina* (from *quaranta* forty) and originally referred to the 40 days of isolation required.

quarant' ore *n.* in the Roman Catholic Church, 40 hours' exposition of the Blessed Sacrament. WH: 17C. Italian, contr. of *quaranta ore* forty hours.

quarenden *n.* a large red variety of apple, grown in Devon and Somerset. WH: 14–15C. Orig. uncertain. ? From a place name.

quark[1] *n.* any of several hypothetical particles thought to be the fundamental units of other subatomic particles. WH: mid-20C. Invented word, assoc. with the line 'Three quarks for Muster Mark' in James Joyce's *Finnegans Wake* (1939). It was adopted in 1964 by the US physicist Murray Gell-Mann with reference to his original theory that there were three types of quarks from which protons and other elementary particles were composed.

quark[2] *n.* a low-fat soft cheese made from skimmed milk. WH: mid-20C. German curds, cottage cheese.

quarrel[1] *n.* a noisy or violent contention or dispute. *Also v.i., v.t.* WH: 12–14C. Old French *querele* (Modern French *querelle*), from Latin *querella*, var. of *querela* complaint, from *queri* to complain.

quarrel[2] *n.* a short, heavy bolt or arrow with a square head, formerly used for shooting from crossbows or arbalests. WH: 12–14C. Old French (Modern French *carreau*), from dim. of Late Latin *quadrus* a square. Cp. QUARRY[3].

quarrian *n.* a cockatiel found in inland Australia. WH: early 20C. Australian Aboriginal (Wiradhuri) *guwarraying*.

quarry[1] *n.* a place from which building stone, slates etc. are dug, cut, blasted etc. *Also v.t.* WH: 12–14C. Medieval Latin *quarreia*, alt. of *quareria*, from Old French *quarriere* (Modern French *carrière*), ult. from Latin *quadrum* a square.

quarry² *n.* any animal pursued by hounds, hunters, a bird of prey etc. *Also v.i., v.t.* WH: 12–14C. Anglo-French var. of Old French *cuiree* (Modern French *curée*), alt., based on *cuir* leather, *curer* to disembowel, (lit.) to cleanse (from Latin *curare* CURE), of *couree*, from Latin *cor* heart. See also -EE, -Y². The word was originally the term for the entrails of a deer's body placed on a hide and given to the hounds as a reward. The current sense dates from the 15C.

quarry³ *n.* a square or diamond-shaped pane of glass, a quarrel. *Also v.t.* WH: 16C. Alt. of QUARREL², prob. based on obs. a. *quarry* square, from Old French *quarré* (Modern French *carré*), from Latin *quadratus* QUADRATE¹.

quart¹ *n.* a measure of capacity, the fourth part of a gallon, two pints (1.136 l). WH: 12–14C. Old French *quarte*, from Latin *quarta*, use as n. of fem. of *quartus* fourth, from *quattuor* four.

quart² *n.* a sequence of four cards of the same suit in piquet etc. WH: 17C. French *quarte*. See QUART¹.

quartan *a.* (esp. of a fever) occurring or recurring every third or (inclusively) fourth day. *Also n.* WH: 12–14C. Old French *quartaine* (*fièvre*), from Latin *quartana* (*febris*), fem. of *quartanus*, from *quartus* fourth. See QUART¹, also -AN.

quartation *n.* the addition of silver, usu. in the proportion of 3:1, in the process of separating gold from its impurities by means of nitric acid. WH: 17C. Latin *quartus* (QUART¹) + -ATION.

quarte *n.* the fourth of eight parrying or attacking movements in fencing. WH: 17C. French *quarte*. See QUART¹.

quarter *n.* a fourth part. *Also v.t., v.i.* WH: 12–14C. Old French *quartier*, from Latin *quartarius* fourth part (of a measure), from *quartus* fourth. See QUART¹, also -ER².

quartern *n.* a quarter or fourth part of various measures, esp. a pint, peck or pound. WH: 12–14C. Old French *quartron*, from *quarte* fourth (QUART¹) or *quartier* QUARTER.

quartet *n.* a musical composition for four voices or instruments. WH: 17C. French *quartette*, from Italian *quartetto*, from *quarto* fourth. See also -ET¹, -ETTE.

quartic *a.* of or relating to the fourth degree. *Also n.* WH: 19C. Latin *quartus* fourth + -IC.

quartile *a.* denoting the aspect of two heavenly bodies when distant from each other a quarter of a circle. *Also n.* WH: 14–15C. Old French *quartil*, from Latin *quartus* fourth. See also -IL.

quarto *n.* a size obtained by folding a sheet of paper twice, making four leaves or eight pages (usu. written *4to*). *Also a.* WH: 14–15C. Latin (*in*) *quarto* (in) a fourth (of a sheet), from *quartus* fourth.

quartz *n.* a mineral consisting of pure silica or silicon dioxide, either massive or crystallizing hexagonally. WH: 18C. German *Quarz*, from Polish dial. *kwardy*, from Polish *twardy* hard.

quasar *n.* any of a group of unusually bright, starlike objects outside our galaxy, that exhibit large red shifts and are a powerful source of radio waves and other energy emissions. WH: mid-20C. Contr. of *quasi-stellar* (*object*). See QUASI-, STELLAR.

quash *v.t.* to annul or make void. WH: 12–14C. Old French *quasser* (Modern French *casser*) to annul, from Late Latin *cassare*, from Latin *cassus* null, void. Cp. SQUASH¹.

Quashie *n.* a black person, esp. a simple-minded one. WH: 18C. Akan *Kwasi*, the name given to a boy born on Sunday.

quasi *adv.* as if; as it were. WH: 15C. Latin as if, almost.

quasi- *comb. form* apparently, seeming, not real, as in *quasi-scientific*. WH: QUASI.

Quasimodo *n.* the first Sunday after Easter, Low Sunday. WH: 18C. Latin *quasi modo* (*geniti infantes*) as (newborn babes), the first words of the introit for this day in the Latin Mass. The words come from I Pet. ii.2.

quassia *n.* a tree of a S American genus *Quassia*, esp. *Q. amara*, the bitter wood, bark and oil of which yield a tonic and insecticide. WH: 18C. Modern Latin, from the 18C Surinamese slave Graman *Quassi* (QUASHIE), who first discovered its medicinal properties. See also -IA.

quatercentenary *n.* a 400th anniversary. WH: 19C. Latin *quater* four times + *centenary* (CENTENARIAN).

quaternary *a.* consisting of four, having four parts, esp. being or composed of an atom bound to four other atoms or radicals. *Also n.* WH: 14–15C. Latin *quaternarius*, from *quaterni* four at once, set of four, from *quater* four times, from *quattuor* four. See also -ARY¹.

quaternion *n.* a set, group or system of four. *Also v.t.* WH: 14–15C. Late Latin *quaternio, quaternionis*, from Latin *quaterni*. See QUATERNARY.

quatorzain *n.* a poem or stanza of 14 lines, esp. a sonnet of an irregular form. WH: 16C. French *quatorzaine* set of fourteen, from *quatorze* fourteen, from Latin *quattuordecim*.

quatrain *n.* a stanza of four lines, usu. rhyming alternately. WH: 16C. French, from *quatre* four + -*ain* AN.

quatrefoil *n.* an opening, panel or other figure in ornamental tracery, divided by cusps into four foils. WH: 14–15C. Anglo-French, from Old French *quatre* four + *foil* leaf, FOIL¹.

Quattrocento *n.* the 15th cent., regarded as a distinctive period in Italian art and literature. WH: 19C. Italian four hundred (i.e. the 1400s).

quaver *v.i.* to tremble, to vibrate. *Also v.t., n.* WH: 14–15C. Freq. of obs. *quave*, prob. from Old English **cwafian*, rel. to *cwacian* QUAKE.

quay *n.* a landing place or wharf, usu. of masonry and stretching along the side of or projecting into a harbour, for loading or unloading ships. *Also v.t.* WH: 14–15C. Old French *kay, kai, cay* (CAY), later (from 18C) *quay*, based on French *quai*.

quean *n.* an impudent or disreputable woman, a slut, a hussy. WH: pre-1200. Old English *cwene*, from Germanic, from Indo-European base represented by Greek *gunē* woman. Cp. QUEEN.

queasy *a.* sick at the stomach, affected with nausea. WH: 14–15C. Orig. uncertain. ? Rel. to unrecorded Anglo-French or Old French aa. rel. to Old French *coisier* to hurt, to wound.

Quebecker *n.* a native or inhabitant of Quebec. WH: 19C. *Quebec*, a city and province in E Canada + -ER¹.

quebracho *n.* any of several S American trees with hard dense wood. WH: 19C. Spanish, from *quebrar* to break + *hacha* axe.

Quechua *n.* a member of any of various groups of S American Indian peoples, including the Incas. WH: 19C. Spanish, from Quechua *ghechwa* temperate valleys.

queen *n.* a female sovereign, esp. a hereditary sovereign of an independent state. *Also v.t., v.i.* WH: pre-1200. Old English *cwēn*, from Germanic, from Indo-European base of QUEAN.

Queensberry Rules *n.pl.* standard rules of boxing. WH: 19C. Sir John Sholto Douglas, 8th Marquis of *Queensberry*, 1844–1900, who supervised the preparation of the rules.

Queensland nut *n.* a macadamia tree or nut. WH: 19C. *Queensland*, a state in NE Australia.

queer *a.* strange, odd. *Also n., v.t.* WH: 16C. ? German *quer* cross, oblique, squint, perverse. Rel. to THWART.

quell *v.t.* to suppress, to subdue. *Also v.i., n.* WH: pre-1200. Old English *cwellan*, from Germanic base represented also by Old English *cwalu* death.

quench *v.t.* to extinguish, to put out, esp. with water. *Also v.i.* WH: pre-1200. Old English *-cwencan* in *ācwencan* to quench, from Germanic. Cp. Old Frisian *quinka* to disappear.

quenelle *n.* a ball of savoury paste made of meat or fish, usu. served as an entrée. WH: 19C. French, of unknown orig. According to some, the word is from German *Knödel* dumpling.

quercetum *n.* a collection of living oaks, an arboretum of oak trees. WH: 19C. Latin oak wood, from *quercus* oak. See also -ETUM.

quercitron *n.* a N American oak, *Quercus velutina*. WH: 18C. Blend of Latin *quercus* oak and CITRON.

querimonious *a.* complaining, querulous, discontented. WH: 17C. Medieval Latin *querimoniosus*, from Latin *querimonia*, from *queri* to complain. See also -OUS.

querist *n.* a person who asks questions, an enquirer. WH: 17C. Latin *quaerere* to inquire + -IST.

quern *n.* a simple hand-mill for grinding corn, usu. consisting of two stones resting one on the other. WH: pre-1200. Old English *cweorn*, from Germanic. Cp. Dutch *kweern*. The Old English word gave the name of the Leicestershire village of Quorndon. See QUORN®.

querulous *a.* complaining. WH: 15C. Late Latin *querulosus*, or from Latin *querulus*, from Latin *queri* to complain. See also -ULOUS.

query *n.* a question. *Also v.i., v.t.* WH: 17C. Anglicized form of *quere*, obs. var. of QUAERE.

quesadilla *n.* a tortilla filled, fried and topped with cheese. **WH:** mid-20C. Spanish, dim. of *quesada* cheese turnover, from *queso* cheese (from Latin *caseus*) + *-ada* -ADE.

quest *n.* the act of seeking, a search. *Also v.i., v.t.* **WH:** 12–14C. Old French *queste* (Modern French *quête*), from var. of Latin *quaesita*, fem. p.p. (used as n.) of *quaerere* to seek, to inquire.

question *n.* a sentence requiring an answer. *Also v.t., v.i.* **WH:** 12–14C. Old French, from Latin *quaestio, quaestionis*, from *quaestus*, p.p. of *quaerere* to seek, to inquire. See also -ION.

questor *n.* a pardoner. **WH:** 14–15C. Medieval Latin, or from Latin QUAESTOR.

quetzal *n.* a Central American bird, *Pharomachius mocino*, of the trogon family, with brilliantly coloured plumage. **WH:** 19C. Spanish, from Nahuatl *quetzalli* brilliant tail feather of the bird called *quetzaltototl*, from *quetzal-*, comb. form of *quetzalli* + *tototl* bird.

queue *n.* a line of people, vehicles etc. waiting their turn. *Also v.t., v.i.* **WH:** 16C. French, ult. from Latin *cauda* tail. The original sense was a heraldic term for the tail of an animal. The current sense arose in the 19C.

quey *n.* a young cow that has not yet had a calf, a heifer. **WH:** 14–15C. Old Norse *kviga*, appar. from *ku* cow.

quibble *n.* a trivial or petty objection, argument or distinction, esp. one exploiting a verbal ambiguity. *Also v.i.* **WH:** 17C. Dim. of obs. *quib*, prob. from Latin *quibus* by what (things), dat. and abl. of *qui, quae, quod* who, what, which. See also -LE⁴. Latin *quibus* would have frequently occurred in legal documents, and as such became associated with subtle verbal distinctions.

quiche *n.* a pastry shell filled with a savoury egg custard to which cheese, onion or other vegetables, bacon etc. have been added. **WH:** mid-20C. French, from Alsatian dial. *Küchen* (German *Kuchen* cake).

quick *a.* rapid in movement. *Also adv., int., n., v.t., v.i.* **WH:** pre-1200. Old English *cwic*, from Germanic, from Indo-European base represented also by Latin *vivus* living. The original sense was living, animate, alive, applied in specific instances to running water and mental agility. The current sense of rapid, swift, evolved in the 12–14C. The original sense of living exists in many compounds, e.g. *quicklime, quicksand, quickset, quicksilver*.

quicken *v.t.* to make faster. *Also v.i., n.* **WH:** 12–14C. QUICK + -EN⁵.

quid¹ *n.* a pound (sterling). **WH:** 17C. Orig. unknown. According to some, the word is from Latin *quid* what, as shortening of QUID PRO QUO.

quid² *n.* a piece of tobacco for chewing. **WH:** 18C. Var. of CUD.

quiddity *n.* the essence of a thing. **WH:** 14–15C. Medieval Latin *quidditas*, from *quid* what + *-itas* -ITY.

quidnunc *n.* a person who is curious to know or pretends to know everything that goes on, a newsmonger, a gossip. **WH:** 18C. Latin *quid nunc?* what now?

quid pro quo *n.* something in return or exchange (for something), an equivalent. **WH:** 16C. Latin something for something. Cp. QUID¹.

quiescent *a.* at rest, still, not moving, inert, inactive, dormant. *Also n.* **WH:** 17C. Latin *quiescens, quiescentis*, pres.p. of *quiescere* to be still, from *quies* quiet. See QUIET, also -ENT.

quiet *a.* making little or no noise. *Also n., v.t., v.i.* **WH:** 12–14C. Old French *quieté*, from Latin *quies, quietis* rest, repose, quiet.

quietus *n.* a final discharge or settlement. **WH:** 14–15C. Abbr. of Medieval Latin *quietus est*, lit. (he) is quit.

quiff *n.* a tuft of hair brushed up and back from the forehead. **WH:** 19C. Orig. unknown.

quill *n.* the hollow stem or barrel of a feather. *Also v.t., v.i.* **WH:** 14–15C. Prob. from Low German *quiele*, rel. to Middle High German *kil*, German *Kiel*.

quillet *n.* a quibble, a quirk. **WH:** 16C. ? Rel. to QUIDDITY.

quillon *n.* either of the arms forming the cross-guard of a sword. **WH:** 19C. French, appar. from *quille* ninepin.

quilt *n.* a bedcover or bedspread made by stitching one cloth over another with some soft warm material as padding between them. *Also v.t.* **WH:** 12–14C. Old French *coilte, cuilte*, from Latin *culcita* mattress, cushion. Cp. COUNTERPANE.

quim *n.* the female genitals. **WH:** 18C. Orig. unknown. According to some, the word is perhaps from obsolete *queme* pleasing, agreeable, from Old English *gecwēme*, from Germanic (cp. German *bequem* comfortable), ultimately related to COME.

quin *n.* each child of quintuplets. **WH:** mid-20C. Abbr. of *quintuplet* (QUINTUPLE).

quina *n.* cinchona. **WH:** 19C. Spanish, from Quechua *kina* bark.

quinacrine *n.* an anti-malarial drug based on acridine. **WH:** mid-20C. QUININE + ACRIDINE.

quinary *a.* consisting of or arranged in fives. **WH:** 17C. Latin *quinarius*, from *quini* five each, from *quinque* five. See also -ARY¹.

quince *n.* a hard, acid, yellowish fruit used in cookery for flavouring and for preserves etc. **WH:** 12–14C. Old French *cooin* (Modern French *coing*), from Latin (*malum*) *cotoneum*, var. of (*malum*) *Cydonium*, lit. (apple) of Cydonia (now Canea, in Crete), translating Greek *mēlon kudōnion*.

quincentenary *n.* a 500th anniversary. **WH:** 19C. Latin *quinque* five + *centenary* (CENTENARIAN).

quincunx *n.* an arrangement of five things in a square or rectangle, one at each corner and one in the middle, esp. such an arrangement of trees in a plantation. **WH:** 17C. Latin five twelfths, from *quinque* five + *uncia* twelfth. Cp. OUNCE¹. The Latin word originally denoted an arrangement of five dots or dashes in this pattern to represent five twelfths of an *as*, a coin originally of 12 ounces.

quindecagon *n.* a plane figure having 15 sides and 15 angles. **WH:** 16C. Latin *quindecim* fifteen + -GON, based on DECAGON.

quinella *n.* a form of betting where the person placing the bet must pick the first- and second-placed winners. **WH:** early 20C. American Spanish *quiniela*.

quingentenary *n.* a quincentenary. **WH:** 19C. Latin *quingenti* five hundred, based on *centenary* (CENTENARIAN), etc.

quinine *n.* a bitter alkaloid obtained from cinchona bark formerly widely used, esp. in the form of its salts, to relieve fever, in the treatment of malaria and as a tonic. **WH:** 19C. Spanish *quina* (QUINA) + -INE.

quinnat *n.* the chinook salmon of the Pacific coast of N America. **WH:** 19C. Lower Chinook *ikwanat*.

quinoa *n.* an annual plant, *Chenopodium quinoa*, the ground farinaceous seeds of which are made into cakes in Chile and Peru. **WH:** 17C. Spanish, from Quechua *kinua, kinoa*.

quinol *n.* hydroquinone. **WH:** 19C. QUINA + -OL.

quinone *n.* a yellow crystalline compound, usu. produced by the oxidation of aniline, used in the manufacture of dyes. **WH:** 19C. QUINA + -ONE.

quinquagenarian *n.* a person who is 50 or between 50 and 60 years old. *Also a.* **WH:** 16C. Latin *quinquagenarius*, from *quinquageni* fifty each, from *quinquaginta* fifty + -ARIAN.

Quinquagesima *n.* the Sunday before Lent. **WH:** 14–15C. Medieval Latin, use as n. of fem. of Latin *quinquagesimus* fiftieth, from *quinquaginta* fifty, based on QUADRAGESIMA. The day is so called as it falls (almost) 50 days before Easter.

quinquangular *a.* having five angles. **WH:** 17C. Late Latin *quinquangulum*, from Latin *quinque* five + *angulus* ANGLE¹ + -AR¹.

quinque- *comb. form* five. **WH:** Latin *quinque* five.

quinquecostate *a.* having five ribs. **WH:** 19C. QUINQUE- + *costate* (COSTA).

quinquefarious *a.* arranged in five parts or rows. **WH:** 19C. QUINQUE- + Latin *-farius*, prob. from *fari* to speak. See also -OUS.

quinquefoliate *a.* having five leaves or leaflets. **WH:** 17C. QUINQUE- + FOLIATE².

quinqueliteral *a.* consisting of five letters. *Also n.* **WH:** 18C. QUINQUE- + LITERAL.

quinquennial *a.* lasting five years. **WH:** 15C. Latin *quinquennis*, from *quinque* five + *annus* year + -AL¹.

quinquepartite *a.* divided into or consisting of five parts. **WH:** 16C. Latin *quinquepartitus*, from QUINQUE- + *partitus*, p.p. of *partiri* to divide.

quinquereme *n.* an ancient Roman galley having five banks of rowers. **WH:** 16C. Latin *quinqueremis*, from QUINQUE- + *remus* oar.

quinquevalent *a.* having a valency or combining power of five, pentavalent. **WH:** 19C. QUINQUE- + *-valent* (from Latin *valens, valentis*, pres.p. of *valere* to be strong). See VALENCE.

quinsy *n.* an inflammatory sore throat, esp. with suppuration of one tonsil or of both. WH: 12–14C. Old French *quinensie*, from Medieval Latin *quinancia*, from Greek *kunagkhē*, from *kuon, kunos* dog + *agkhein* to throttle. The condition is so called as it constricts the throat like a dog collar.

quint *n.* a sequence of five cards of the same suit in piquet etc. WH: 17C. Old French, from Latin *quintus* fifth.

quinta *n.* a country house or villa in Portugal, Madeira and Spain. WH: 18C. Spanish and Portuguese, from *quinta parte* fifth part. The word originally applied to a house and farm let out at a rent of one fifth of the farm's produce.

quintain *n.* a post, or a figure or other object set up on a post, in the Middle Ages, to be tilted at, often fitted with a sandbag, sword or other weapon that swung round and struck a tilter who was too slow. WH: 14–15C. Old French *quintaine*, Medieval Latin *quintana*, appar. from Latin *quintana* market of a camp, from *quintus*. See QUINTAN. Latin *quintana via* was the road running between the fifth and sixth maniples where the market of a camp was located. Presumably military exercises were practised there also.

quintal *n.* a weight of 100 or 112 lb. (45.36 or 50.8 kg). WH: 14–15C. Old French, from Medieval Latin *quintale*, from Arabic *ḳinṭār*, ult. from Latin *centenarius*. Cp. KANTAR.

quintan *a.* (esp. of a fever) occurring or recurring every fourth (or inclusively, fifth) day. *Also n.* WH: 17C. Medieval Latin *quintana*, use as n. of fem. of *quintanus*, from *quintus* fifth. See also -AN. Cp. QUARTAN.

quinte *n.* the fifth of eight parrying or attacking movements in fencing. WH: 18C. French. See QUINT.

quintessence *n.* the essential principle or pure embodiment (of a quality, class of things etc.). WH: 14–15C. French, from Medieval Latin *quinta essentia* fifth essence. The original sense, as applied to classical and medieval philosophy, was the fifth essence or element that was added to the four elements of water, earth, fire and air and that permeated all things and formed the substance of the heavenly bodies.

quintet *n.* a musical composition for five voices or instruments. WH: 18C. Italian *quintetto*, or from French *quintette*, from Italian *quinto* fifth. See also -ET[1].

quintic *a.* of or relating to the fifth degree. *Also n.* WH: 19C. Latin *quintus* fifth + -IC.

quintile *n.* the aspect of two heavenly bodies when distant from each other one-fifth of a circle or 72°. WH: 17C. Latin *quintilis* (*mensis*) fifth (month), July, from *quintus* fifth. See also -IL.

quintillion *n.* the sixth power of a thousand, one followed by 18 zeros. WH: 17C. Latin *quintus* fifth + -*illion*, based on MILLION, BILLION, etc.

quintroon *n.* the offspring of a white person and an octoroon; a person one-fifth (inclusively) in descent from a black person. WH: 18C. Spanish *quinterón*, from *quinto* fifth. See also -OON.

quintuple *a.* consisting of five parts. *Also n., v.i., v.t.* WH: 16C. French, from Medieval Latin *quintuplus*, from Latin *quintus* fifth + -*plus* as in *duplus* DUPLE.

quinze *n.* a card game of chance analogous to vingt-et-un, the object being to score nearest to 15 points without exceeding it. WH: 18C. French, from Latin *quindecim* fifteen.

quip *n.* a sarcastic jest or sally. *Also v.i., v.t.* WH: 16C. Orig. uncertain ? Latin *quippe* indeed, really.

quipu *n.* a contrivance of coloured threads and knots used by the ancient Peruvians in place of writing. WH: 18C. Quechua *khípu* knot.

quire *n.* 24, or now usu. 25, sheets of paper. WH: 12–14C. Old French *quaier* (Modern French *cahier* copybook), from Latin *quaterni* set of four. See QUATERNARY.

Quirites *n.pl.* the ancient Roman citizens in their civil capacity. WH: 18C. Latin, pl. of *Quiris* Roman citizen, prob. from *coviriom* assemblage of citizens, from CO- + -*virius*, from *vir* man.

quirk *n.* a mannerism. WH: 16C. Orig. unknown. The original sense was quibble, then quip.

quirt *n.* a riding whip with a short handle and a long, braided leather lash. *Also v.t.* WH: 19C. Spanish *cuerda* cord, or from Mexican Spanish *cuarta* whip.

quisling *n.* a person who openly allies themselves with their nation's enemies. WH: mid-20C. Major Vidkun *Quisling*, 1887–1945, Norwegian army officer and diplomat who collaborated with the German occupying force in Norway in World War II.

quit *v.t.* to give up, to abandon. *Also v.i., a.* WH: 12–14C. Old French *quitter*, earlier *quiter*, from Latin *quietus* QUIET.

qui tam *n.* an action brought by an informer under a penal statute. WH: 18C. Latin, lit. who as well (beginning the clause of the action).

quitch *n.* couch grass. WH: pre-1200. Old English *cwice*, ? rel. to QUICK.

quite *adv.* completely, to the fullest extent. WH: 12–14C. Adverbial use of obs. *quite*, var. of a. QUIT. The original sense, as now, was entirely, completely. The contrasting sense somewhat, fairly, evolved in the 19C.

quitter *n.* an ulcer or suppurating sore on the quarter of a horse's hoof. WH: 12–14C. ? Old French *quiture, cuiture* cooking.

quiver[1] *v.i.* to tremble or be agitated with a rapid tremulous motion. *Also v.t., n., a.* WH: pre-1200. Old English *cwifer-* as in *cwiferlice* actively, quickly, ? rel. to *cwic* alive. See QUICK.

quiver[2] *n.* a portable case for arrows. WH: 12–14C. Anglo-French var. of Old French *quivre, coivre*, from a Germanic word represented by Old English *cocor*, German *Köcher*.

qui vive *int.* who lives, who goes there? WH: 16C. French, lit. (long) live who? The French phrase is a sentry's challenge, made to discover the loyalty of an approaching person. A typical answer might be *vive le roi* (long) live the king, or *vive la France* (long) live France. Cp. VIVAT.

quixotic *a.* extravagantly romantic and chivalrous. WH: 18C. Don *Quixote*, the chivalrous, romantic and naively idealistic hero of Cervantes' romance of the same name (1605–15) + -IC.

quiz *n.* a set of questions designed to test knowledge. *Also v.t., v.i.* WH: 19C. Orig. unknown. According to some, the word is from Latin *qui es*? who are you?, the first question of an oral examination in Latin in grammar schools.

quod *n.* prison, jail. WH: 17C. Orig. uncertain. ? Abbr. of QUADRANGLE.

quod erat demonstrandum a formula used at the conclusion of a proof or demonstration. WH: 17C. Latin which was to be demonstrated. The phrase translates Greek *hoti edei deixai*.

quodlibet *n.* a fantasia, a medley of popular tunes. WH: 14–15C. Medieval Latin, from Latin, from *quod* what + *libet* it pleases. The original sense was a question proposed as an exercise in a philosophical or theological debate. The sense musical medley arose in the 19C.

quoin *n.* the external angle of a building. *Also v.t.* WH: 12–14C. Var. of COIN. Cp. COIGN.

quoit *n.* a flattish circular ring of iron, rope etc. for throwing at a peg or similar mark. *Also v.t.* WH: 14–15C. Orig. unknown. According to some, the word is from Old French *coite* flat stone, cushion, mattress, a variant of *coilte*. See QUILT. Early quoits were made of stone or metal and may have originally been slid rather than thrown, in the manner of the stone in curling.

quokka *n.* a small-tailed wallaby, *Setonix brachyurus*. WH: 19C. Australian Aboriginal (Nyungar) *gwaga*.

quondam *a.* having formerly been, sometime, former. WH: 16C. Latin formerly.

Quonset hut® *n.* a hut similar to a Nissen hut. WH: mid-20C. *Quonset* Point, Rhode Island, USA, where the buildings were first made.

Quorn® *n.* a textured vegetable protein used as a meat substitute. WH: late 20C. *Quorn* (now Quorndon), a village in Leicestershire. The food was originally manufactured by, and named after, the firm of Quorn Specialities Ltd. It is now made by Marlow Foods Ltd.

quorum *n.* the minimum number of officers or members of a society, committee etc. that must be present to transact business. WH: 14–15C. Latin, lit. of whom, as in phr. *quorum vos ... unum esse volumus* of whom we wish that you ... be one. The phrase was originally used in the wording of commissions specifying one or more persons as always to be included.

quota *n.* a proportional share, part or contribution. WH: 17C. Medieval Latin *quota* (*pars*) how great (a part), fem. of *quotus*, from Latin *quot* how many.

quote *v.t.* to adduce or cite from (an author, book etc.), esp. in illustration or support of a point, statement etc. *Also v.i., n.* WH: 14–15C. Medieval Latin *quotare* to number, from Latin *quot* how many or Medieval Latin QUOTA. The original sense (to the 17C) was to mark (a book) with numbers (as of chapters, etc). Hence to give the page, chapter etc. of a text, and so (16C) to repeat the text or passage itself.

†quoth *v.t.* (1*st and* 3*rd pers.*) said, spoke. WH: 12–14C. Past tense of obs. *quethe* to say, to tell, from Old English *cwethan*, from Germanic. Cp. BEQUEATH. Not rel. to QUOTE.

quotidian *a.* daily. *Also n.* WH: 12–14C. Old French *cotidien* (Modern French *quotidien*), assim. to Latin *quotidianus*, earlier *cotidianus*, from *cotidie* every day. See also -IAN.

quotient *n.* the result obtained by dividing one quantity by another. WH: 14–15C. Latin *quotiens* how many times (from *quot* how many), wrongly taken as a part. form in *-ens, -entis* -ENT.

quo warranto *n.* a writ requiring a person or body to show by what authority some office or franchise is claimed or exercised. WH: 16C. Law Latin by what warrant, abl. sing. of *quod* what + abl. sing. of *warrantum* warrant.

qwerty *a.* relating to the standard English typewriter or keyboard layout. WH: early 20C. The first six letters from the left on the top row of letters on a standard English language keyboard.

R

rabato *n.* a stiff collar worn by either sex in the early 17C. **WH:** 16C. French *rabat* collar, based on Italian words in *-ato*.

rabbet *v.t.* to cut a groove or slot along the edge of (a board) so that it may receive the edge of another piece cut to fit it. *Also n.* **WH:** 14–15C. Old French *rabat*, from *rabattre* to beat back, to beat down.

rabbi *n.* a Jewish doctor or teacher of the law, esp. one ordained and having certain legal and ritual functions. **WH:** pre-1200. Ecclesiastical Latin and Ecclesiastical Greek, from Hebrew *rabbī* my master, from *rab* master.

rabbit *n.* a burrowing mammal, *Oryctolagus cuniculus*, allied to the hare, killed for its flesh and fur and kept as a pet. *Also v.i.* **WH:** 14–15C. Orig. uncertain. ? From an Old French word represented by French dial. *rabbotte*, *rabouillet* young rabbit, ? of Dutch orig. Cp. Flemish *robbe*. Some authorities relate the name to the personal name *Robert*, partly on the basis that the latter is the source of the surname *Rabbitt*.

rabble¹ *n.* a noisy crowd of people. *Also v.t., v.i.* **WH:** 14–15C. Prob. from obs. *rabble* to gabble, itself prob. from Middle Dutch *rabbelen*, Low German *rabbeln*, of imit. orig. The original sense (to the 17C) was a long series of words having no meaning. The current sense evolved in the 16C.

rabble² *n.* an iron tool consisting of a bar with the end sharply bent, used for stirring molten metal. **WH:** 17C. French *râble* (earlier *roable*), from Medieval Latin *rotabulum*, from Latin *rutabulum* fire shovel, oven rake, from *ruere*, *rut-* to rake up.

Rabelaisian *a.* of, relating to or characteristic of Rabelais. *Also n.* **WH:** 19C. François *Rabelais*, *c.*1494–1553, French satirist noted for his vivid imagination, lively language and coarse humour + *-IAN*.

rabi *n.* the grain crop reaped in the spring, the chief of the three crops in India, Pakistan etc. **WH:** 19C. Persian and Urdu, from Arabic *rabī'* spring.

rabid *a.* mad, raging, furious, violent. **WH:** 17C. Latin *rabidus*, from *rabere* to be mad. See also *-ID*. Cp. RABIES, RAGE. The sense affected with rabies dates from the 19C.

rabies *n.* an often fatal viral disease of the nervous system transmitted through the saliva of a rabid animal and characterized by hydrophobia and convulsions. **WH:** 16C. Latin, from *rabere* to be mad. Cp. RAGE.

raccoon *n.* a greyish-black furry ring-tailed N American carnivore of the genus *Procyon*, esp. *P. lotor*. **WH:** 17C. Virginia Algonquian *aroughcun*.

race¹ *n.* a contest of speed between runners, motor vehicles etc. *Also v.i., v.t.* **WH:** pre-1200. Old Norse *rás*, corr. to Old English *rǣs* running, rush, Middle Low German *rās* current. The original sense was rapid forward movement. The sense contest of speed evolved in the 16C.

race² *n.* a major division of human beings descended from a common stock and distinguished by physical characteristics. **WH:** 16C. French, from Italian *razza*. Cp. RACY.

race³ *n.* a root of ginger. **WH:** 14–15C. Old French *rais*, *raiz*, from Latin *radix*, *radicis* root.

raceme *n.* a centripetal inflorescence in which the flowers are attached separately by nearly equal stalks along a common axis. **WH:** 18C. Latin *racemus* cluster of grapes. Cp. RAISIN.

rachis *n.* the axis of an inflorescence. **WH:** 18C. Modern Latin, from Greek *rhakhis* spine, ridge.

rachitis *n.* rickets. **WH:** 18C. Modern Latin, from Greek *rhakhitis*. See RACHIS, also *-ITIS*. The literal sense is inflammation of the spine, but the word was adopted as a learned form of RICKETS by the English anatomist and physician Francis Glisson in his study *De Rachitide* (1650).

Rachmanism *n.* the conduct of an unscrupulous landlord who exploits tenants and charges extortionate rents for slum property. **WH:** mid-20C. Peter *Rachman*, 1919–62, London landlord + *-ISM*.

rack¹ *n.* an open framework or set of rails, bars, woven wire etc. for placing articles on. *Also v.t.* **WH:** 12–14C. Dutch *rak*, Low German *rack*, prob. from Middle Dutch *recken* to stretch, rel. to Old English *reccan* to stretch, from Germanic.

rack² *n.* destruction. **WH:** 16C. Var. of WRACK. Cp. WRECK, WREAK.

rack³ *v.t.* to draw off (wine etc.) from the lees. **WH:** 15C. Provençal *arracar*, from *raca* the stem and husks of grapes.

rack⁴ *n.* a joint of lamb comprising the front rib section. **WH:** 16C. Orig. unknown. The word is apparently not related to RACK¹.

rack⁵ *n.* light vapoury clouds, cloud-drift. *Also v.i.* **WH:** 12–14C. Prob. of Scandinavian orig. Cp. Norwegian and Swedish dial. *rak* (Swedish *vrak*, Danish *vrag*) wreck, wreckage, refuse, from *reka* to drive. Cp. RAKE³.

rack⁶ *n.* a horse's gait in which both hoofs of one side are lifted from the ground almost or quite simultaneously, all four legs being off the ground entirely at times. *Also v.i.* **WH:** 16C. Orig. unknown.

racket¹ *n.* a bat with a network of catgut etc. instead of a blade, with which players at tennis, squash, badminton or rackets strike the ball. *Also v.t.* **WH:** 14–15C. French *racquette*, from Italian *racchetta*, from Arabic *rāḥat*, construct form of *rāḥa* palm of the hand. (In Semitic languages, the construct form is the form of a noun depending on another noun, where in Indo-European languages the other noun would be in the genitive case, e.g. in *house of God*, *house* would be in the construct form.)

racket² *n.* a clamour, a confused noise. *Also v.i.* **WH:** 16C. Prob. imit. of clattering noise.

racloir *n.* in archaeology, a flint implement used for scraping sideways. **WH:** 19C. French scraper.

racon *n.* a radar beacon. **WH:** mid-20C. RADAR + BEACON.

raconteur *n.* a (good, skilful etc.) storyteller. **WH:** 19C. French, from *raconter* to relate + *-eur -OR*.

racy *a.* lively, spirited. **WH:** 17C. RACE² + *-Y¹*. An early sense of RACE² was a class of wine or its characteristic flavour.

rad¹ *n.* a political radical. **WH:** 19C. Abbr. of RADICAL.

rad² *n.* a unit measuring the dosage of ionized radiation absorbed, equivalent to 0.01 joule of energy per kilogram of mass of irradiated material. **WH:** early 20C. Acronym of radiation *a*bsorbed *d*ose.

rad³ *n.* a radiator. **WH:** mid-20C. Abbr. of *radiator* (RADIATE).

rad⁴ *a.* excellent, very good. **WH:** late 20C. Prob. abbr. of RADICAL.

rad⁵ *abbr.* radian. **WH:** early 20C. Abbr. of RADIAN.

radar *n.* a system which employs reflected or retransmitted radio waves to locate the presence of objects and to determine their angular position and range. **WH:** mid-20C. Acronym of radio *de*tection *a*nd *ra*nging. The word 'reflects' (reads the same backwards as forwards), like the radio waves used in the system, which return to their point of transmission when reflected by the object they detect.

raddle¹ *n.* ruddle. *Also v.t.* **WH:** 16C. Rel. to RED. Cp. RUDDLE.

raddle² *n.* a lath, stick or branch interwoven with others to form a fence, usu. plastered over with clay etc. *Also v.t.* **WH:** 16C. Anglo-French *reidele*, Old French *reddalle* (Modern French *ridelle*), from Middle High German *reidel* stout stick.

radial *a.* of, relating to or resembling a ray, rays or radii. *Also n.* **WH:** 14–15C. Medieval Latin *radialis*, from Latin RADIUS. See also *-AL¹*.

radian *n.* an arc equal in length to the radius of its circle. **WH:** 19C. RADIUS + *-an*.

radiant *a.* emitting rays of light or heat. *Also n.* **WH:** 14–15C. Latin *radians*, *radiantis*, pres.p. of *radiare* to emit rays. See also *-ANT*.

radiata pine *n.* a pine tree, *Pinus radiata*, grown in Australia and New Zealand for timber. WH: mid-20C. Modern Latin *radiata*, fem. of *radiatus*. See RADIATE. The tree is so called from the radiating lines on its cone scales.

radiate *v.i.* to emit rays of light, heat or other electromagnetic radiation. *Also v.t.* WH: 17C. Latin *radiatus*, p.p. of *radiare* to emit rays, from *radius* ray. See also -ATE[3].

radical *a.* of or relating to the root, source or origin. *Also n.* WH: 14–15C. Late Latin *radicalis*, from Latin *radix, radicis* root. See also -AL[1].

radicand *n.* a number from which a root is to be extracted, usu. preceded by a radical sign, e.g. three is the radicand of Ö3. WH: 19C. Latin *radicandus*, ger. of *radicare*. See RADICATE, also -AND.

radicate *a.* having a root, rooted. WH: 17C. Latin *radicatus*, p.p. of *radicare* to take root, from *radix, radicis* root. See also -ATE[2].

radicchio *n.* a type of chicory from Italy with purple and white leaves eaten raw in salads. WH: late 20C. Italian chicory.

radicle *n.* the part of a plant embryo that develops into the main root. WH: 17C. Latin *radicula*, from *radix, radicis* root + dim. suf. *-ula*. See also -ULE.

radio *n.* electromagnetic waves used in two-way broadcasting. *Also v.t., v.i.* WH: early 20C. Independent use of RADIO-[1].

radio-[1] *comb. form* of or relating to radio, radio frequency or broadcasting. WH: Partly from RADIO, partly from early combinations such as *radio-telegraphy* (e.g. RADIO-TELEGRAM).

radio-[2] *comb. form* radiate. WH: From RADIUS, RADIOACTIVE or *radiation* (RADIATE). See also -O-.

radioactive *a.* of or exhibiting radioactivity. WH: 19C. RADIO-[2] + ACTIVE.

radio-assay *n.* a chemical assay based on the amounts and types of radiation from a sample. WH: mid-20C. RADIO-[2] + ASSAY.

radiobiology *n.* the study of the effects of radiation on the body using radioactive tracers. WH: early 20C. RADIO-[2] + BIOLOGY.

radiocarbon *n.* carbon-14, a radioactive carbon isotope. WH: mid-20C. RADIO-[2] + CARBON.

radiochemistry *n.* the chemistry of radioactive substances. WH: early 20C. RADIO-[2] + CHEMISTRY.

radio-element *n.* a radioactive chemical element. WH: early 20C. RADIO-[2] + ELEMENT.

radiogenic *a.* produced by radioactivity. WH: early 20C. RADIO-[2] + -GENIC. The sense suitable for radio broadcasting derives from RADIO-[1] + PHOTOGENIC.

radio-goniometer *n.* an apparatus used as a radio direction-finding system. WH: early 20C. RADIO-[1] + GONIOMETER.

radiogram *n.* a combined radio and record player. WH: early 20C. RADIO + GRAMOPHONE. The sense photograph produced by X-rays dates from the 19C and derives from RADIO-[2] + -GRAM. The sense radio-telegraphic message dates from the early 20C and derives from RADIO-[1] + -GRAM.

radiograph *n.* a negative produced by X-rays, gamma rays etc. *Also v.t.* WH: 19C. RADIO-[2] + -GRAPH.

radioimmunoassay *n.* an immunological assay which uses radioactive labelling of various levels, such as hormone levels. WH: mid-20C. RADIO-[2] + IMMUNO- + ASSAY.

radioimmunology *n.* immunology that employs the techniques of radiology. WH: late 20C. RADIO-[2] + IMMUNOLOGY.

radioisotope *n.* a radioactive isotope of a chemical element. WH: mid-20C. RADIO-[2] + ISOTOPE.

radiolarian *n.* a marine rhizopod protozoan of the superclass Actinopoda, having radiating filamentous pseudopodia and abounding in warm seas. *Also a.* WH: 19C. Modern Latin *Radiolaria*, from Late Latin *radiolus* faint ray, dim. of Latin RADIUS + -AN.

radiolocation *n.* the location by radar of the position of an object in space. WH: mid-20C. RADIO-[1] + *location* (LOCATE).

radiology *n.* the branch of medical science concerned with radioactivity, X-rays and other diagnostic or therapeutic radiations. WH: early 20C. RADIO-[2] + -O- + -LOGY.

radioluminescence *n.* luminous radiation emitted by radioactive material. WH: early 20C. RADIO-[2] + *luminescence* (LUMINESCE).

radiometer *n.* an instrument for measuring the intensity of radiant energy. WH: 18C. RADIO-[2] + -METER.

radiomicrometer *n.* an instrument for measuring minute variations of heat etc. WH: 19C. RADIO-[2] + MICROMETER.

radiomimetic *a.* of or relating to a chemical or substance which affects living tissue in a similar way to ionizing radiation. WH: mid-20C. RADIO-[2] + *mimetic* (MIMESIS).

radionics *n.* a form of complementary medicine that bases diagnoses on the analysis of energy supposedly emitted from items, e.g. hair, belonging to the patient. WH: mid-20C. RADIO-[2] + *electronics* (ELECTRONIC).

radionuclide *n.* a radioactive nuclide. WH: mid-20C. RADIO-[2] + NUCLIDE.

radiopaging *n.* a system for alerting a person, using a small device which emits a sound in response to a signal at a distance. WH: mid-20C. RADIO-[1] + PAGE[2] + -ING[1].

radiopaque *a.* not allowing X-rays or other radiation to pass through. WH: early 20C. RADIO-[2] + OPAQUE.

radiophonic *a.* of, relating to or being music or other sounds produced electronically. WH: 19C. RADIO-[1] + PHONIC.

radioscopy *n.* examination of bodies by means of X-rays. WH: 19C. RADIO-[2] + *-scopy* (-SCOPE).

radiosensitive *a.* liable to injury from radiation. WH: early 20C. RADIO-[2] + SENSITIVE.

radiosonde *n.* a miniature radio transmitter sent up in a balloon and dropped by parachute, for sending information of pressures, temperatures etc. WH: mid-20C. RADIO-[1] + SONDE.

radio-telegram *n.* a telegram transmitted using radio waves, esp. from a ship to land. WH: early 20C. RADIO-[1] + TELEGRAM.

radio-telephone *n.* an apparatus for sending telephone messages using radio waves. *Also v.t.* WH: early 20C. RADIO-[1] + TELEPHONE.

radio-teletype *n.* a teleprinter which can transmit or receive messages using radio waves. WH: mid-20C. RADIO-[1] + TELETYPE®.

radiotelex *n.* a telex sent using radio-teletype apparatus. WH: late 20C. RADIO-[1] + TELEX.

radiotherapy *n.* the treatment of disease by means of X-rays or other radiation, esp. from radioactive sources. WH: early 20C. RADIO-[2] + *therapy* (THERAPEUTIC).

radio-ulna *n.* a bone in the forelimb of amphibians, equivalent to the radius and ulna of more advanced vertebrates. WH: 19C. RADIO-[2] + ULNA.

radish *n.* a cruciferous plant, *Raphanus sativus*, cultivated for its pungent root, which is eaten as a salad vegetable. WH: pre-1200. Latin *radix, radicis* root, with *-ish* ? from French *radis*. Rel. to ROOT[1] and ult. to WORT.

radium *n.* a highly radioactive metallic element, at. no. 88, chem. symbol Ra, occurring in pitchblende, used in making luminous materials and in radiotherapy. WH: 19C. Latin RADIUS + -IUM. The element is so called because it was found to give off radioactive rays. The name was coined in 1898 by the element's discoverers, the French chemists Pierre Curie and Marie Curie. See CURIE.

radius *n.* a straight line from the centre of a circle or sphere to any point on the circumference. *Also v.t.* WH: 16C. Latin staff, spoke, ray.

radix *n.* a quantity or symbol taken as the base of a system of numbering, logarithms etc. WH: 16C. Latin *radix, radicis* root (of a plant).

radome *n.* a protective covering for radar antennae, through which radio waves can pass. WH: mid-20C. Blend of RADAR and DOME[1].

radon *n.* a gaseous radioactive element, at. no. 86, chem. symbol Rn, formed by the disintegration of radium. WH: early 20C. From RADIUM, based on ARGON. The element is so called because it is formed by the radioactive decay of radium. It was discovered in 1900 by the German physicist Friedrich Ernst Dorn, who originally called it *niton* (from Latin *nitere* to shine + -ON).

radula *n.* a ribbon-like band covered with minute teeth occurring in some molluscs, used for scraping up food and drawing it into the mouth. WH: 18C. Latin scraper, from *radere* to scrape. See also -ULE.

raff *n.* sweepings, refuse. WH: 12–14C. Last element of *riff and raff*. See RIFF-RAFF.

Rafferty's rules *n.pl.* no rules whatsoever. WH: early 20C. Prob. alt. of REFRACTORY.

raffia *n.* a Madagascan palm, *Raphia ruffia*, with a short stem and gigantic pinnate leaves. WH: 18C. Malagasy.

raffinate *n.* the liquid remaining after extraction of a solute with a solvent. WH: early 20C. German or French *raffinat*, from German *raffinieren* (French *raffiner*) to refine. See also -ATE².

raffish *a.* disreputable, disorderly, dissipated-looking, rakish. WH: 19C. RAFF + -ISH¹.

raffle¹ *n.* a lottery in which one or more articles are put up to be disposed of by drawing lots among a number of people buying tickets for the draw. *Also v.t., v.i.* WH: 14–15C. Old French (Modern French *rafle*), from Medieval Latin *raffla*, of unknown orig. The word was originally used for a game played with dice. The sense of lottery dates from the 18C.

raffle² *n.* rubbish, lumber, debris. WH: 14–15C. ? Old French *rafle*, in *rifle ou rafle* anything at all, *ne rifle ne rafle* nothing at all. Cp. RAFF, RIFF-RAFF.

rafflesia *n.* any of a genus, *Rafflesia*, of very large stemless parasitic plants from Java and Sumatra. WH: 19C. Modern Latin, from Sir T. Stamford *Raffles*, 1781–1826, British governor of Sumatra + -IA.

raft¹ *n.* a flat floating framework of planks or other material used for supporting or carrying people, goods etc. on water. *Also v.t., v.i.* WH: 14–15C. Old Norse *raptr*, rel. to Old High German *ravo*, Old Norse *ráfr*. Cp. RAFTER. The original sense was beam, spar, rafter. The current sense dates from the 15C.

raft² *n.* a large number, a crowd, a lot. WH: 19C. Alt. of RAFF, ? by assoc. with RAFT¹.

rafter *n.* any of the sloping pieces of timber supporting a roof or forming the framework on which the tiles etc. of the roof are laid. *Also v.t.* WH: pre-1200. Old English *ræfter*, from Germanic, rel. to RAFT¹.

rag¹ *n.* a torn or worn piece of cloth, esp. an irregular piece detached from a fabric by wear and tear. WH: 12–14C. Prob. back-formation from RAGGED. Cp. RUG.

rag² *v.t.* to tease, irritate or play rough practical jokes on. *Also v.i., n.* WH: 18C. Orig. unknown.

rag³ *n.* a piece of ragtime music. *Also v.t.* WH: 19C. ? From RAGGED. Cp. RAGTIME.

rag⁴ *n.* a hard, coarse, rough stone, usu. breaking up into thick slabs. WH: 12–14C. Orig. unknown. The word was later associated with RAG¹.

raga *n.* in traditional Indian music, a form or a mode which forms the basis for improvisation. WH: 18C. Sanskrit *rāga* colour, passion, melody.

ragamuffin *n.* a ragged unkempt person, esp. a child. WH: 12–14C. Prob. from RAG¹ with fanciful ending. The second part of the word may be related to Middle Dutch *muffe* mitten.

rage *n.* violent anger, fury. *Also v.i., v.t.* WH: 12–14C. Old French, from var. of Latin RABIES. The original sense was a fit of madness.

ragga *n.* a form of popular dance music incorporating elements of reggae and hip hop. WH: late 20C. Abbr. of RAGAMUFFIN, prob. influ. by Jamaican *raga-raga*, *ragga-ragga* old ragged clothes, redupl. of RAG¹. Cp. REGGAE. The reference is presumably to the scruffy appearance of the performers.

ragged *a.* worn into rags, tattered. WH: 12–14C. Old Norse, *roggvathr* tufted. Cp. RAG¹.

raggle-taggle *a.* unkempt, untidy. WH: early 20C. Fanciful extension of *ragtag* (RAG¹), ? influ. by TANGLE¹.

ragi *n.* an Indian food-grain, *Eleusine coracana*. WH: 18C. Sanskrit and Hindi *rāgī*, from Telugu *rāgi*.

raglan *n.* a loose overcoat with no seams on the shoulders, the sleeves going up to the neck. *Also a.* WH: 19C. Lord *Raglan*, 1788–1855, British army commander in the Crimean War, who wore such a coat.

ragout *n.* a highly seasoned dish of small pieces of stewed meat and vegetables. *Also v.t.* WH: 17C. French *ragoût*, from *ragoûter* to revive the taste of (from Old French *re-* back + *à* to + *goût* taste). Cp. GUSTO.

ragtime *n.* a style of jazz music popular esp. in the early 20C, characterized by a syncopated melody and played esp. on the piano. *Also a.* WH: 19C. Prob. from obs. *rag* dance, ball (? from RAGGED) + TIME.

raguly *a.* having projections like lopped branches at the sides. WH: 17C. ? From RAGGED, based on NEBULY.

rah *int.* hurrah. WH: 19C. Shortening of HURRAH.

rai *n.* a form of popular music originating in Algeria that incorporates elements of traditional Bedouin music and Western rock. WH: late 20C. Algerian French *raï*, of uncertain orig. According to some, the word is from the dialect Arabic expression *ha er-ray*, literally here is the view, that's the thinking, frequently found in songs.

raid *n.* a sudden hostile incursion as of armed troops, criminals etc. *Also v.t., v.i.* WH: 14–15C. Scottish var. of Old English *rād* ROAD¹. Cp. INROAD.

rail¹ *n.* a bar of wood or metal or series of such bars resting on posts or other supports, forming part of a fence, banisters etc. *Also v.t., v.i.* WH: 12–14C. Old French *reille* iron rod, from Latin *regula* staff, rod, RULE.

rail² *v.i.* to use abusive or derisive language. *Also v.t.* WH: 14–15C. French *railler*, from Provençal *ralhar* to jest, from Popular Latin *ragulare* to bray, from Late Latin *ragere* to roar. Rel. to RALLY².

rail³ *n.* a wading bird of the family Rallidae, esp. the water rail and the corncrake or landrail. WH: 14–15C. Norman-Picard *raille*, from Old French *raale*, rel. to French *râler* to rattle, ? ult. of imit. orig. Cp. RALE.

raiment *n.* dress, apparel, clothes. WH: 14–15C. Shortening of *arrayment*. See ARRAY, also -MENT.

rain *n.* the condensed moisture of the atmosphere falling in drops. *Also v.i., v.t.* WH: pre-1200. Old English *regn*, from Germanic. Cp. German *Regen*.

raise *v.t.* to move or put into a higher position. *Also n.* WH: 12–14C. Old Norse *reisa*. See REAR².

raisin *n.* a dried grape, the partially dried fruit of various species of vine. WH: 12–14C. Old French *grape*, from alt. of Latin *racemus* cluster of grapes.

raison d'être *n.* the reason for a thing's existence. WH: 19C. French reason for being.

raisonné *a.* (of a catalogue) arranged systematically. WH: 18C. French, p.p. of *raisonner* to reason, from *raison* REASON.

raita *n.* an Indian side dish of chopped cucumber or other salad vegetables in yogurt. WH: mid-20C. Hindi *rāytā*.

raj *n.* (in the Indian subcontinent) rule, government. WH: 19C. Hindi *rāj*, from Sanskrit *rājya*. Cp. RAJA.

raja *n.* an Indian king, prince or tribal chief, a dignitary or noble. WH: 16C. Prob. from Portuguese, from Sanskrit *rājan* king, from *rāj* to reign, to rule, rel. to Latin *rex*, *regis* king. Cp. RICH.

Rajput *n.* a member of a Hindu warrior caste who claim descent from the Kshatriyas. WH: 16C. Hindi *rājpūt*, from Sanskrit *rājan* king + *putra* son. See RAJ.

rake¹ *n.* an implement having a long handle with a crossbar set with teeth, used for drawing loose material together, smoothing soil etc. *Also v.t., v.i.* WH: pre-1200. Old English *raca*, from Germanic. Cp. German *Rechen*.

rake² *n.* a dissolute or immoral man. *Also v.i.* WH: 17C. Abbr. of *rakehell*, from RAKE¹ + HELL.

rake³ *n.* inclination, slope, esp. backward slope. *Also v.i., v.t.* WH: 17C. Prob. rel. to German *ragen* to project, of unknown orig.

raki *n.* an aromatic liquor made from spirit or grape juice, usu. flavoured with mastic, used in the E Mediterranean region. WH: 17C. Turkish *rāqī* (now *rakı*) brandy, spirits.

rakish *a.* with masts sharply inclined. WH: 19C. RAKE³ + -ISH¹.

raku *n.* Japanese lead-glazed pottery used esp. for tea bowls. WH: 19C. Japanese, lit. ease, relaxed state, enjoyment.

rale *n.* a rattling sound in addition to that of respiration, heard with the stethoscope in lungs affected by disease. WH: 19C. French *râle*, from *râler* to rattle in the throat, of unknown orig.

rallentando *adv., a.* gradually slower. *Also n.* WH: 19C. Italian, pres.p. of *rallentare* to slow down.

ralli car *n.* a two-wheeled horse-drawn carriage seating four. WH: 19C. *Ralli*, the name of its first purchaser, in 1885.

ralline *a.* of or relating to the Rallidae, a family of birds including rails. WH: 19C. Modern Latin *Rallus* RAIL³ + -INE.

rally¹ *v.t.* to reunite, to bring (disordered troops) together again. *Also v.i., n.* WH: 17C. French *rallier*, from *re-* RE- + *allier* ALLY¹. Cp. RELY.

rally[2] *v.t.* to ridicule or tease in a good-humoured way. *Also n.* WH: 17C. French *railler*. See RAIL[2].

RAM *n.* a temporary storage space in a computer from which data can be accessed directly in any order and altered. WH: Abbr. of random-*access memory*. There may have originally been a punning allusion, via RAM, to BUFFER (in its sense of short-term storage unit in a computer). Cp. BUFF[2].

ram *n.* an uncastrated male sheep, a tup. *Also v.t., v.i.* WH: pre-1200. Old English *ramm*, from Germanic word prob. rel. to Old Norse *ramr* strong. The Old English word meant both male sheep and battering ram.

Ramadan *n.* the ninth and holiest month of the Islamic year, the time of the great annual fast. WH: 15C. Arabic *ramaḍān*, from *ramida* to be parched, to be hot. The reason for the name is uncertain.

Raman effect *n.* the change in wavelength which light undergoes when it passes through a transparent medium and is scattered by molecules of the medium. WH: early 20C. Sir Chandrasekhara Venkata *Raman*, 1888–1970, Indian physicist.

ramble *v.i.* to walk or move about freely, as for recreation. *Also n.* WH: 14–15C. ? Middle Dutch *rammelen* to be on heat and wander about (of cats, rabbits etc.), freq. of *rammen* to copulate with, ult. from Old High German *ram* RAM. See also -LE[4]. The original sense was to write or talk incoherently. The sense to walk aimlessly or for pleasure dates from the 17C.

Ramboesque *a.* characterized by, using or advocating extreme force, violence or aggression. WH: late 20C. *Rambo*, hero of David Morell's novel *First Blood* (1972), a Vietnam war veteran bent on violent retribution, popularized in the films *First Blood* (1982) and *Rambo: First Blood Part II* (1985) + -ESQUE.

rambunctious *a.* unruly, boisterous, exuberant. WH: 19C. Orig. unknown. Cp. RUMBUSTIOUS.

rambutan *n.* the red, hairy, pulpy fruit of a Malaysian tree, *Nephelium lappaceum*. WH: 18C. Malay, from *rambut* hair, with ref. to the covering of the fruit.

ramekin *n.* a dish of cheese, eggs, breadcrumbs etc., baked in a small dish or mould. WH: 17C. French *ramequin*, of Low Dutch orig, ? from Middle Dutch. Cp. German *Rahm* cream, also -KIN.

ramentum *n.* any of the thin membranous scales formed on leaves and stems esp. of a fern. WH: 17C. Latin, from *radere* to scrape. See also -MENT.

ramie *n.* a bushy Chinese and E Asian plant, *Boehmeria nivea*, of the nettle family. WH: 19C. Malay *rami*.

ramification *n.* the act of ramifying, the state of being ramified. WH: 17C. French, from *ramifier*, from Medieval Latin *ramificare* to branch out, from Latin RAMUS. See also -FICATION.

rammish *a.* strong-smelling, rank. WH: 14–15C. Appar. from RAM + -ISH[1].

rammy *n.* a brawl, a fight, a free-for-all. WH: mid-20C. Orig. uncertain. ? From *rammle*, Scottish var. of RAMBLE.

ramp[1] *v.i.* to dash about, to rage, to storm. *Also v.t., n.* WH: 12–14C. Old French *ramper* to creep, to crawl, to climb, of Germanic orig., ? rel. to ROMP. The original sense (to the 16C) was to creep or crawl on the ground. The current sense arose in the 17C.

ramp[2] *v.t.* to force to pay large amounts of money, esp. by swindling. *Also v.i., n.* WH: 16C. Orig. unknown.

rampage[1] *v.i.* to rage, to behave violently. WH: 17C. Orig. uncertain. ? Based on RAMP[1] and RAGE.

rampage[2] *n.* boisterous, violent behaviour. WH: 19C. RAMPAGE[1].

rampant *a.* wild, violent. WH: 12–14C. Old French, pres.p. of *ramper*. See RAMP[1], also -ANT.

rampart *n.* an embankment, usu. surmounted by a parapet, round a fortified place, or such an embankment together with the parapet. *Also v.t.* WH: 16C. French *rempart*, from *remparer* to fortify, from re- RE- + *emparer* to take possession of, from Provençal *amparar*, from Popular Latin *anteparare*, from Latin ANTE + *parare* PREPARE.

rampion *n.* a bellflower, *Campanula rapunculus*, with red, purple or blue blossoms. WH: 16C. From var. of Medieval Latin *rapuncium*, *rapontium*, appar. from Latin *rapum* RAPE[2].

ramshackle *a.* (of a building, vehicle etc.) tumbledown, rickety. *Also v.t.* WH: 19C. Alt. of *ranshackled*, p.p. of obs. *ransackle*, from RANSACK + -LE[4].

ramsons *n.* the broad-leaved garlic, *Allium ursinum*, or its bulbous root, eaten as a relish. WH: pre-1200. Old English *hramsan*, pl. of *hramsa*, later taken as sing., with pl. -*s*.

ramus *n.* a branched or forked part or structure. WH: 17C. Latin branch.

ran *n.* a length of 20 cords of twine. WH: 18C. Prob. from French.

ranch *n.* a farm for rearing cattle and horses, esp. in western N America. *Also v.t.* WH: 19C. Anglicized form of Spanish *rancho*, orig. group of people who eat together, from *ranchar* to lodge, to station, from Old French *ranger*, from *rang* row, line. See RANK[1].

rancid *a.* having the taste or smell of stale oil or fat. WH: 17C. Latin *rancidus*. See also -ID.

rancour *n.* deep-seated malice. WH: 12–14C. Old French (Modern French *rancœur*), from Late Latin *rancor* rankness, rel. to Latin *rancidus* RANCID. See also -OUR.

rand[1] *n.* the standard monetary unit of S Africa. WH: 19C. Afrikaans, from Dutch *rand* edge. See RAND[2]. The specific reference is to *the Rand*, i.e. the Witwatersrand, the chief gold-mining area of the Transvaal.

rand[2] *n.* a strip of leather between the sole and heel-piece of a boot or shoe. WH: pre-1200. Old English, corr. to Old Frisian *rond*, Dutch *rand*, Old High German *rant* (German *Rand*), Old Norse *rond* edge, rim of shield, from Germanic.

randan[1] *n.* a boat worked by three rowers, the one amidships using two oars. WH: 19C. Orig. unknown.

randan[2] *n.* a spree. WH: 18C. ? Alt. of French *randon* RANDOM.

randem *a.* having three horses harnessed together. *Also adv., n.* WH: 19C. Prob. alt. of RANDOM, based on TANDEM.

random *a.* done, made etc. without calculation or method; occurring by chance. *Also n.* WH: 12–14C. Old French *randon* great speed, rel. to *randir* to run impetuously, to gallop.

randy *a.* lustful, on heat, sexually eager or excited. *Also n.* WH: 17C. Orig. uncertain. Prob. from obs. *rand* to rave, to rant (from obs. Dutch *randen*, var. of *ranten* RANT) + -Y[1]. The original sense was loud and coarse-spoken. The current sense evolved from dialect use in the 19C.

ranee *n.* a Hindu queen. WH: 17C. Hindi *rānī*, from Prakrit, from Sanskrit *rājñī*, fem. of *rājan* RAJA.

rangatira *n.* a Maori chief of either sex. WH: 19C. Maori.

range *n.* the extent of variation in something. *Also v.t., v.i.* WH: 12–14C. Old French, from *rangier* (Modern French *ranger*), from *rang* line, row. See RANK[1].

rangé *a.* orderly. WH: 18C. French, p.p. of *ranger* RANGE.

rangiora *n.* a broad-leaved shrub or small tree, *Brachyglottis repanda*, found in New Zealand. WH: 19C. Maori.

ranine *a.* of or relating to the underside of the tip of the tongue, where ranulas occur. WH: 19C. RANULA + -INE.

rank[1] *n.* relative degree of excellence etc. *Also v.t., v.i.* WH: 12–14C. Old French *ranc* (Modern French *rang*), from Germanic base also of RING[1]. Cp. RANCH. The original basic sense was row, line. The sense distinct class, professional position arose in the 16C.

rank[2] *a.* excessively luxuriant in growth. *Also adv.* WH: 19C. Old English *ranc*, from Germanic. The original sense (to the 16C) was proud, haughty, also fully grown, mature. The current sense dates from the 12–14C. The sense offensive, strong may have arisen (in the 16C) by association with RANCID.

rankle *v.i.* to continue to cause irritation, anger or bitterness. WH: 12–14C. Old French *raoncler*, var. of *draoncler*, from *raoncle*, var. of *draoncle* ulcer, festering sore, from Medieval Latin *draculus*, alt. of Latin *dracunculus*, dim. of *draco* DRAGON. The original sense was (of a wound, sore etc.) to fester. The current sense evolved in the 16C.

ransack *v.t.* to pillage, to plunder. WH: 12–14C. Old Norse *rannsaka*, from *rann* house + *-saka*, rel. to *sœkja* SEEK. The original sense was to search a person for a missing object.

ransom *n.* a sum of money demanded or paid for the release of a person from captivity. *Also v.t.* WH: 12–14C. Old French *ransoun* (Modern French *rançon*), from Latin *redemptio, redemptionis* REDEMPTION.

rant *v.i.* to use loud or violent language. *Also v.t., n.* WH: 16C. Dutch *ranten* to talk foolishly, to rave.

ranula *n.* a cystic tumour under the tongue. WH: 17C. Latin, dim. of *rana* frog. See also -ULE. The reference may be either to the resemblance of the tumour to a little frog or to the croaking sound it causes the sufferer to make.

ranunculus *n.* a plant of the genus *Ranunculus*, typified by the buttercup. WH: 16C. Latin, lit. little frog, dim. of *rana* frog. See also -CULE. The plant is so called as many species grow in wet places.

rap[1] *v.t.* to strike with a slight, sharp blow. *Also v.i., n.* WH: 12–14C. Prob. imit. Cp. CLAP[1], FLAP. ? Of Scandinavian orig.

rap[2] *n.* the least amount. WH: 18C. Contr. of Irish *ropaire* robber, counterfeit coin. The word was originally the name of a counterfeit coin in Ireland.

rapacious *a.* grasping, extortionate. WH: 17C. Latin *rapax, rapacis* grasping, from *rapere* RAPE[1]. See also -IOUS.

rape[1] *v.t.* to force to have sexual intercourse. *Also n.* WH: 14–15C. Anglo-French *raper*, from Latin *rapere* to take by force, to seize. The original sense was to seize, then to carry off (especially a woman) by force (in the 16C), then to force (her) to have sexual intercourse (16C).

rape[2] *n.* a plant, *Brassica napus*, allied to the turnip, grown as food for animals and for its seed which yields oil. WH: 14–15C. Latin *rapum, rapa* turnip.

rape[3] *n.* the refuse stems and skins of grapes after the wine has been expressed, used to make vinegar. WH: 17C. French *râpe*, from Medieval Latin *raspa*.

rape[4] *n.* any of six divisions of the county of Sussex. WH: pre-1200. Var. of ROPE. The division is so called because the land was originally fenced off with a rope.

Raphaelesque *a.* after the style of Raphael. WH: 18C. *Raphael* (Italian *Raffaello* Sanzio), 1483–1520, Italian Renaissance painter + -ESQUE.

raphania *n.* a form of the poisoning ergotism, supposed to be due to the use of grain containing seeds of wild radish. WH: 18C. Modern Latin, from *raphanus* radish + -IA.

raphe *n.* a seamlike suture or line of union. WH: 18C. Modern Latin, from Greek *rhaphē* seam, suture.

raphide *n.* any of numerous needle-shaped transparent crystals, usu. of calcium oxalate, found in the cells of plants. WH: 19C. Greek *rhaphis, rhaphidos* needle.

rapid *a.* very swift, quick. *Also n.* WH: 17C. Latin *rapidus*, from *rapere*. See RAPE[1], also -ID.

rapier *n.* a light, narrow sword, used only in thrusting. *Also a.* WH: 16C. Prob. from Dutch, or from Low German *rappir*, from obs. French *espee rapiere*, of unknown orig.

rapine *n.* the act of plundering or carrying off by force. WH: 14–15C. Old French, or from Latin *rapina*, from *rapere* RAPE[1]. See also -INE.

rapparee *n.* an Irish irregular soldier, freebooter or robber, esp. during the late 17C and the 18C. WH: 17C. Prob. partly from Irish deriv. of *rapaire* rapier, partly from *ropaire* robber.

rappee *n.* a coarse kind of snuff. WH: 18C. French (*tabac*) *râpé* rasped (tobacco), from *râper* RASP.

rappel *n.* abseiling. *Also v.i.* WH: 19C. French, from *rappeler* to recall. The original sense was a drum roll calling soldiers to arms. The sense abseil dates from the mid-20C. A climber who abseils is one 'recalled' to the ground.

rapport *n.* sympathetic relationship, harmony. WH: 16C. French, from *rapporter*, from *re-* RE- + *apporter* to bring.

rapprochement *n.* reconciliation, re-establishment of friendly relations, esp. between nations. WH: 19C. French, from *rapprocher*, from *re-* RE- + *approcher* APPROACH. See also -MENT.

rapscallion *n.* a rascal, a scamp, a good-for-nothing. *Also a.* WH: 17C. Alt. of *rascallion* (RASCAL).

rapt *a.* carried away by one's thoughts or emotions. WH: 14–15C. Latin *raptus*, p.p. of *rapere*, see RAPE[1]. Cp. RAVISH.

raptor *n.* a bird of prey. WH: 14–15C. Latin, from *raptus* (RAPT). See also -OR.

rapture *n.* ecstatic joy. WH: 16C. Obs. French, or from Medieval Latin *raptura*, partly influ. by RAPT. See also -URE.

rara avis *n.* a rarity, something very rarely met with. WH: 17C. Latin rare bird. The phrase comes from Juvenal: *Rara avis in terris*

nigroque simillima cycno A rare bird on earth, comparable to a black swan (*Satires* vi.165, 1C AD).

rare[1] *a.* seldom existing or occurring, unusual. WH: 14–15C. Latin *rarus*.

rare[2] *a.* (of meat) half-cooked, underdone. WH: 17C. Later form of obs. *rear*, of unknown orig. Not rel. to RARE[1].

rarebit *n.* cheese mixed with seasonings, melted and spread over toasted bread, Welsh rabbit. WH: 17C. Alt. of RABBIT in *Welsh rabbit* (WELSH). The word is not recorded independently until the 19C.

raree-show *n.* a show, a spectacle, a carnival. WH: 17C. Representation of Savoyard pronun. of *rare show* (RARE[1]).

rarefy *v.t.* to make rare, thin, porous or less dense and solid. *Also v.i.* WH: 14–15C. Old French *raréfier* or Medieval Latin *rareficare*, extended form of Latin *rarefacere*, from *rarus* RARE[1] + *facere* to make. See also -FY.

rareripe *a.* ripening early. *Also n.* WH: 18C. From obs. *rare* early (var. of RATHE) + RIPE.

raring *a.* ready, eager. WH: early 20C. Pres.p. of *rare*, dial. var. of REAR[2].

ras *n.* an Ethiopian governor or administrator. WH: 17C. Amharic *rās* head, from Arabic *ra's* (coll. *rās*).

rasbora *n.* any of a genus, *Rasbora*, of small, brightly coloured cyprinid fishes from tropical Asia and E Africa, popular for aquariums. WH: 19C. Modern Latin, from native name in E Indies.

rascal *n.* a mischievous person, esp. a child (used playfully or affectionately). *Also a.* WH: 12–14C. Old French *rascaille* (Modern French *racaille*), prob. from Old Northern French var. of Old French *rasche*, Provençal *rasca* scab, scurf, from Latin *rasus*, p.p. of *radere* to scrape, to scratch, to shave. The word was originally a collective adjective for the common soldiers or camp followers of an army, the rabble. The current sense evolved in the 16C.

raschel *n.* a type of knitted fabric, often with open patterns. WH: mid-20C. German *Raschelmaschine*, from Élisa *Rachel*, stage name of Élisa Félix, 1821–58, French actress. The word was originally the name of the knitting machine that produced the fabric.

rash[1] *a.* hasty, impetuous. WH: 14–15C. Corr. to Middle Dutch *rasch*, Old High German *rasc* (German *rasch*), Old Norse *rǫskr* doughty, brave, ult. from Germanic base rel. to RATHE.

rash[2] *n.* an eruption of spots or patches on the skin. WH: 18C. ? Rel. to Old French *rache* ringworm, from Popular Latin *rasicare* to scrape, to scratch, from Latin *rasus* (RASCAL).

rasher *n.* a thin slice of bacon or ham for frying. WH: 16C. Orig. unknown.

raskolnik *n.* a dissenter from the Orthodox or Greek Church in Russia. WH: 18C. Russian *raskol'nik*, from *raskol* separation, schism + -nik -NIK.

rasorial *a.* of, relating to or being a bird (e.g. the common fowl) having toes ending in strong claws for scratching up seeds etc. from the ground. WH: 19C. Modern Latin *Rasores*, pl. of *rasor*, from Latin *radere* to scrape, RAZE + -IAL.

rasp *v.t.* to scrape or grate with a rough implement. *Also v.i., n.* WH: 12–14C. Old French *rasper* (Modern French *râper*), from Germanic. Cp. Old High German *raspōn* to scrape together.

raspberry *n.* the fruit of various species of *Rubus*, esp. *R. idaeus*, consisting of red or sometimes white or yellow drupes set on a conical receptacle. WH: 17C. From dial. *rasp* (abbr. of obsolete *raspis* raspberry, of unknown orig.) + BERRY.

rasse *n.* a feline carnivore allied to the civet, inhabiting S and SE Asia. WH: 19C. Javanese *rase*.

Rastafarian *n.* a member of the religious and political, largely Jamaican, sect which believes Haile Selassie, the former Emperor of Ethiopia, to be the Messiah. *Also a.* WH: mid-20C. *Ras Tafari*, name by which Emperor Haile Selassie of Ethiopia, 1892–1975, was known from 1916 to his accession in 1930 + -AN. The name itself means Head Tafari (see RAS), the latter word from Amharic *teferi* to be feared.

raster *n.* the pattern of scanning lines which appears as a patch of light on a television screen and which reproduces the image. WH: mid-20C. Greek screen, frame, from Latin *rastrum* rake, from *rasus* (RASCAL).

rat *n.* any of several rodents of the genus *Rattus* that are similar to but larger than mice, esp. the black rat, *R. rattus*, and *R. norvegicus*, the grey, brown or Norway rat. *Also v.i.* WH: pre-1200. Old English *ræt*, prob. ult. rel. to Latin *radere* to gnaw (see RODENT).

rata *n.* either of two large New Zealand forest trees, *Metrosideros robusta* and *M. lucida*, belonging to the myrtle family, having beautiful crimson flowers and yielding hard red timber. WH: 18C. Maori.

ratafia *n.* a liqueur or cordial flavoured with the kernels of cherry, peach, almond or other kinds of fruit. WH: 17C. French, ? rel. to TAFIA.

rataplan *n.* a noise like the rapid beating of a drum. *Also v.t., v.i.* WH: 19C. French, of imit. orig. Cp. RUB-A-DUB.

ratatouille *n.* a vegetable casserole from Provence, France, made with aubergines, tomatoes, peppers etc., stewed slowly in olive oil. WH: 19C. French dial., appar. from *ratouiller*, var. of *touiller* to stir up, to stir round.

ratch *n.* a ratchet or ratchet-wheel. WH: 14–15C. ? German *Ratsche*, *Rätsche* ratchet-wheel.

rate[1] *n.* the proportional measure of something in relation to some other thing. *Also v.t., v.i.* WH: 14–15C. Old French, from Medieval Latin *rata* (from *pro rata*, abbr. of *pro rata parte* or *pro rata portione* according to the proportional share), use as n. of fem. of Latin *ratus*. See RATIFY.

rate[2] *v.t.* to chide angrily, to scold. *Also v.i.* WH: 14–15C. Orig. unknown.

ratel *n.* a nocturnal carnivore of the genus *Mellivora*, allied to the badger, esp. *M. capensis*, the honey badger of W and southern Africa which feeds on small animals and honey, and *M. indicus* from India. WH: 18C. Afrikaans, of unknown orig.

rath *n.* a prehistoric Irish hill fort or earthwork. WH: 14–15C. Irish, corr. to obsolete Gaelic *ráth*, Gaulish *rātin*, *-rātum*. The Gaulish element is found in place names such as *Argentoratum*, the Romano-Gallic name of Strasbourg.

rathe *adv.* early, soon, quickly. *Also a.* WH: pre-1200. Old English *hræth* (a.), *hrathe* (adv.), from Germanic base prob. rel. to base of RASH[1].

rather *adv.* preferably. WH: pre-1200. Old English *hrathor*, comp. of *hrathe*, *hræthe* RATHE. See also -ER[3]. The original basic sense was earlier, sooner.

ratify *v.t.* to establish or make valid (by formal approval). WH: 14–15C. Old French *ratifier*, from Medieval Latin *ratificare*, from Latin *ratus* fixed, established, from *reri* to reckon, to think. See also -FY.

rating[1] *n.* the act of assessing, judging, ranking etc. WH: 16C. RATE[1] + -ING[1].

rating[2] *n.* a scolding, a harsh reprimand. WH: 16C. RATE[2] + -ING[1].

ratio *n.* the relation of one quantity or magnitude to another of a similar kind, measured by the number of times one is contained by the other, either integrally or fractionally. WH: 17C. Latin *ratio*, *rationis* reason, reckoning, from *ratus*, p.p. of *reri*. See RATIFY.

ratiocinate *v.i.* to reason or argue. WH: 17C. Latin *ratiocinatus*, p.p. of *ratiocinari* to calculate, to deliberate, from *ratio*, *rationis*. See RATIO, also -ATE[3].

ration *n.* a fixed statutory allowance of provisions in a time of shortage (e.g. war). *Also v.t.* WH: 16C. French, from Latin *razione* or Spanish *ración*, from Latin *ratio*, *rationis*. See RATIO, also -ION. The original sense was reasoning, then (to the 19C) ratio. The current sense dates from the 18C. The word was formerly pronounced to rhyme with *nation*, as in 'Still, as I say, though you've found salvation, / ... / See if the best of you bars me my ration!' (Robert Browning, *Christmas-Eve*, 1850).

rational *a.* having the faculty of reasoning. *Also n.* WH: 14–15C. Latin *rationalis*, from *ratio*, *rationis*. See RATIO, also -AL[1].

ratite *a.* of or belonging to the group of flightless birds with a keel-less sternum and abortive wings, such as the ostrich, emu, cassowary, kiwi, moa etc. *Also n.* WH: 19C. Latin *ratis* raft + -ITE[1].

ratline *n.* any of the small ropes extended across the shrouds on each side of a mast, forming steps or rungs. WH: 14–15C. Orig. unknown. Prob. influ. by LINE[1]. Not rel. to RAT.

ratoon *n.* a sprout from the root of a sugar cane that has been cut down. *Also v.i., v.t.* WH: 17C. Spanish *retoño* a fresh shoot.

rattan[1] *n.* any of various species of Malaysian climbing palms of the genus *Calamus* with long, thin pliable stems. WH: 17C. Malay *rotan*, prob. from *raut* to pare, to trim, to strip.

rattan[2] *n.* the beat of a drum, a rataplan. WH: 18C. Imit. Cp. RATAPLAN, RUB-A-DUB.

rat-tat *n.* a rapid knocking sound as of a knocker on a door. WH: 17C. Imit. Cp. RATTLE.

ratteen *n.* a thick quilted or twilled woollen material. WH: 17C. French *ratine*, of unknown orig. ? From obsolete *raster* to scrape.

ratten *v.t.* to annoy or molest by destroying, injuring or taking away the tools or machinery of (a worker or employer) in a trade-union dispute etc. *Also v.i.* WH: 19C. Orig. unknown. ? Rel. to RAT.

rattle *v.i.* to make a rapid succession of sharp noises, as of things clattered together. *Also v.t., n.* WH: 12–14C. Prob. from Middle Low German and Middle Dutch *ratelen*, of imit. orig.

raucous *a.* hoarse or harsh in sound. WH: 18C. Latin *raucus* hoarse. See also -OUS.

raunchy *a.* earthy, sexual. WH: mid-20C. Orig. unknown. Some authorities derive the word from Italian *rancio* rancid, stale, rank. Cp. US slang *ranchy* dirty, disgusting, indecent.

raupo *n.* the giant bulrush, *Typha angustifolia*. WH: 19C. Maori.

rauwolfia *n.* any of several tropical flowering shrubs and trees of the SE Asian genus *Rauwolfia*. WH: 18C. Modern Latin, from Leonhard *Rauwolf*, d.1596, German physician and botanist + -IA.

ravage *n.* devastation, ruin. *Also v.t., v.i.* WH: 17C. Old French, alt. of *ravine* rush of water. See RAVIN, also -AGE.

rave[1] *v.i.* to wander in mind, to talk wildly. *Also v.t., n.* WH: 12–14C. Prob. from Old Northern French *raver*, rel. to Middle Low German *reven* to be senseless, to rave.

rave[2] *n.* a cart-rail. WH: 16C. Var. of dial. *rathe*, of unknown orig.

ravel *v.t.* to entangle, to confuse, to complicate. *Also v.i.* WH: 14–15C. ? Dutch *ravelen* to tangle, to fray out, to unweave. The converse sense, to disentangle, to unravel, evolved in the 16C.

ravelin *n.* a detached outwork of a fortification with a parapet and ditch forming a salient angle in front of the plain wall of a larger work. WH: 16C. French, from obsolete Italian *ravellina* (now *rivellino*), of unknown orig.

raven[1] *n.* a large, black, omnivorous bird, *Corvus corax*, of the crow family. *Also a.* WH: pre-1200. Old English *hræfn*, from Germanic. Cp. German *Rabe*. Prob. ult. of imit. orig. Cp. CROW[1].

raven[2] *v.t.* to devour with voracity. *Also v.i., n.* WH: 15C. Old French *raviner* to rush, to ravage, ult. from Latin *rapina* RAPINE. The original sense was to take by force, to seize as spoil. The sense to devour voraciously evolved in the 16C.

ravenous *a.* hungry, famished. WH: 14–15C. Old French *ravinos*, from *raviner* (RAVEN[2]). See also -OUS.

ravin *n.* plundering, rapine, spoliation, ravaging. WH: 12–14C. Old French *ravine*, from Latin *rapina* RAPINE. Cp. RAVINE.

ravine *n.* a long, deep hollow caused esp. by a torrent, a gorge, a narrow gully or cleft. WH: 14–15C. French violent rush of water, *ravine*, from *ravine* RAVIN. The original sense was impetus, violence. The current sense arose in the 18C.

ravioli *n.* small pasta cases with a savoury filling. WH: 19C. Italian, pl. of *raviolo*, dim. of some n. now unknown. Some authorities take *raviolo* as a diminutive of *rava* turnip, perhaps with reference to the shape of the cases rather than their contents.

ravish *v.t.* to violate, to rape. WH: 12–14C. Old French *ravir*, *raviss-*, from alt. of Latin *rapere* to seize. See RAPE[1], also -ISH[2]. As with RAPE[1], the original sense was to seize and carry off. The sense to violate, to rape, as well as that of to fill with ecstasy, dates from the 14–15C.

raw *a.* uncooked. *Also n.* WH: pre-1200. Old English *hrēaw*, from Germanic, from Indo-European base also of Greek *kreas* raw flesh.

rawinsonde *n.* a hydrogen balloon which carries meteorological instruments to measure wind velocity. WH: mid-20C. RADAR + WIND[1] + SONDE.

Rawlplug® *n.* a thin ridged or toothed tube, usu. of plastic, inserted in masonry to provide a fixing for a screw. WH: early 20C. John *Rawlings*, English electrical engineer, its inventor in *c.*1912 + PLUG.

ray[1] *n.* a beam of light proceeding from a radiant point. *Also v.t., v.i.* WH: 12–14C. Old French *rai*, from Latin RADIUS.

ray² *n.* any of several large cartilaginous fish allied to the sharks, with a broad flat body, the eyes on the upper surface and a long, slender tail. WH: 12–14C. Old French *raie*, from Latin *raia*, of unknown orig.

ray³ *n.* the second note of a major scale in the tonic sol-fa system of notation. WH: 12–14C. Latin *resonare*. See UT.

Rayah *n.* a non-Muslim subject in Turkey. WH: 19C. Turkish *râya*, from Arabic *ra'āyā*, pl. of *ra'iyya*. See RYOT.

Raynaud's disease *n.* a disorder of the circulatory system in which spasms in the blood vessels, often intensified by cold or stress, restrict the supply of blood to the fingers and toes resulting in discoloration, numbness and sometimes pain. WH: 19C. Maurice *Raynaud*, 1834–81, French physician.

rayon *n.* an artificial textile fibre or fabric made from cellulose. WH: early 20C. Arbitrary, but prob. influ. by French *rayon* ray, with *-on* prob. from COTTON. Cp. NYLON, ORLON®.

raze *v.t.* to demolish, to level to the ground. WH: 12–14C. Old French *raser* to shave, from Latin *rasus*, p.p. of *radere* to scrape, to scratch.

razee *n.* a vessel cut down to a fewer number of decks. *Also v.t.* WH: 18C. French *rasé*, p.p. of *raser* RAZE. See also -EE.

razoo *n.* an insignificant sum of money, a farthing. WH: mid-20C. Orig. unknown.

razor *n.* a sharp-edged cutting instrument for shaving off the hair of the beard, head etc. *Also v.t.* WH: 12–14C. Old French *rasor* (Modern French *rasoir*), from *raser* RAZE. See also -OR.

razz *n.* a sound of contempt, a raspberry. *Also v.t.* WH: early 20C. Abbr. of *razzberry*, alt. of RASPBERRY.

razzia *n.* a foray or incursion for the purpose of capturing slaves etc., as practised by African Muslims. WH: 19C. French, from Algerian Arabic *gāziya* raid, from Arabic *gazā* to go forth to fight, to make a raid.

razzle-dazzle *n.* bewilderment, excitement, stir, bustle. *Also v.t.* WH: 19C. Redupl. of DAZZLE.

razzmatazz *n.* colourful, noisy, lively atmosphere or activities, razzle-dazzle. WH: 19C. ? Alt. of RAZZLE-DAZZLE, or redupl. of *razz*, alt. of JAZZ.

re *prep.* in the matter of. WH: 18C. Latin, abl. of *res* thing. Cp. IN RE.

re- *pref.* again, again and again, afresh, anew, repeatedly. WH: Latin back, again.

reach¹ *v.t.* to stretch out, to extend. *Also v.i., n.* WH: pre-1200. Old English *rǣcan*, from Germanic. Cp. German *reichen*.

†reach² *v.i.* to retch. WH: pre-1200. Old English *hrǣcan*, from Germanic, of imit orig. Cp. RETCH.

react *v.i.* to act in response (to a stimulus etc.). *Also v.t.* WH: 17C. RE- + ACT, orig. based on Medieval Latin *reactus*, p.p. of *reagere*, from RE- + *agere* to do, to act.

reaction *n.* the response of an organ etc. to stimulation. WH: 17C. REACT, orig. based on Medieval Latin *reactio, reactionis*, from *reactus*. See REACT, also -ION.

read *v.t.* to perceive and understand the meaning of (printed, written or other characters, signs etc.). *Also v.i., n.* WH: pre-1200. Old English *rǣdan* to explain, to read, to advise, from Germanic. Cp. German *raten* to advise.

reading *n.* the act, practice or art of reading. *Also a.* WH: pre-1200. READ + -ING¹.

ready *a.* fit for use or action. *Also adv., n., v.t.* WH: 12–14C. Extended form (with -Y¹) of Old English *rǣde*, from Germanic base meaning to prepare, to arrange. Cp. German *bereit* ready.

reagent *n.* a substance in a chemical reaction, esp. used to detect the presence of other substances or in chemical synthesis. WH: 18C. RE- + AGENT, based on pair ACT/ REACT.

real¹ *a.* actually existing; not imaginary. *Also adv., n.* WH: 14–15C. Old French *réel* or Late Latin *realis*, from Latin *res* thing. See also -AL¹.

real² *n.* the standard monetary unit of Brazil. WH: 16C. Spanish, use as n. of *real* ROYAL. Cp. RIAL.

realgar *n.* an orange-red mineral consisting of a sulphide of arsenic, used as a pigment and in the manufacture of fireworks. WH: 14–15C. Medieval Latin, from Spanish *rejalgar*, from Arabic *rahj al-ġār* arsenic, lit. powder of the cave, from *rahj* powder + *al* the + *ġār* cave.

realism *n.* the practice of regarding, accepting and dealing with people, circumstances etc. as they are; concern with what is factual and practicable. WH: 19C. REAL¹ + -ISM.

reality *n.* the quality of being real, actuality, actual existence, being, that which underlies appearances. WH: 15C. Old French *réalité*, from Medieval Latin *realitas*, from Late Latin *realis* REAL¹. See also -ITY.

realize *v.t.* to perceive as a reality. WH: 17C. REAL¹ + -IZE, based on French *réaliser*. The earliest sense was to make real. The sense to conceive (or perceive) as real evolved in the 18C.

realm *n.* a kingdom. WH: 12–14C. Old French *reaume, realme* (Modern French *royaume*), from Latin *regimen, regiminis*. The addition of *l* arose through the influence of Old French *real, reiel*, variants of *roial* ROYAL.

realpolitik *n.* politics based on practical reality rather than moral or intellectual ideals. WH: early 20C. German *Realpolitik*, from *real* objective, practical + *Politik* politics.

realty *n.* real property. WH: 14–15C. REAL¹ + -TY¹. The original sense (to the 17C) was reality. The current sense dates from the 17C.

ream¹ *n.* 500 sheets of paper, formerly 480 sheets or 20 quires. WH: 14–15C. Old French *raime* (Modern French *rame*), ult. from Arabic *rizma* bundle.

ream² *v.t.* to enlarge the bore of (a hole in metal etc.). WH: 18C. Orig. unknown.

reap *v.t.* to cut (a crop) with a scythe, sickle or reaping-machine. *Also v.i.* WH: pre-1200. Old English *ripan, reopan*, of unknown orig.

rear¹ *n.* the back or hindmost part. *Also a.* WH: 12–14C. Old French *rere, rier*, from Latin *retro* back. See RETRO-.

rear² *v.t.* to bring up, to educate. *Also v.i.* WH: pre-1200. Old English *rǣran*, from Germanic base rel. to that of RAISE.

reason *n.* that which serves as a ground or motive for an act, opinion etc. *Also v.i., v.t.* WH: 12–14C. Old French *reisun* (Modern French *raison*), from var. of Latin *ratio, rationis* reckoning, account, from *ratus*, p.p. of *reri* to think, to reckon. See also -ION.

reata *n.* a lariat. WH: 19C. Var. of *riata*, from Spanish *reata*. See LARIAT.

Réaumur *a.* relating to, conforming to or denoting measurement on the Réaumur scale of temperature, on which 0° corresponds to the freezing point of water and 80° to the boiling point. WH: 18C. René-Antoine Ferchault de *Réaumur*, 1683–1757, French naturalist and physicist.

†reave *v.t.* to take (away or from) by force. *Also v.i.* WH: pre-1200. Old English *rēafian*, from Germanic base also of ROB. Cp. BEREAVE.

rebarbative *a.* repellent, grim, forbidding. WH: 19C. French *rébarbatif*, from *barbe* beard. See also -ATIVE. The concept is of a two-man contest 'beard to beard', each confronting the other with a show of strength.

rebate¹ *n.* a refund of part of an amount paid. *Also v.t.* WH: 14–15C. Old French *rabattre*, from re- RE- + *abattre* ABATE, with RE- later substituted for *ra-*.

rebate² *n.* a kind of hard freestone. WH: 19C. Orig. unknown.

rebec *n.* a medieval three-stringed musical instrument played with a bow. WH: 14–15C. French, alt. of *rebebe, rubebe*, from Arabic *rabāb* type of stringed instrument. The alteration of final *-b* to *-c* is unexplained.

rebel¹ *n.* a person who forcibly resists the established government or renounces allegiance to it. *Also a.* WH: 12–14C. Old French *rebelle*, from Latin *rebellis*, from RE- + *bellum* war. Latin *rebellis* originally referred to the defeated who declared war again.

rebel² *v.i.* to act in rebellion (against). WH: 12–14C. Old French *rebeller*, from Latin *rebellare*, from RE- + *bellare* to make war, from *bellum* war. See REBEL¹.

reboant *a.* loudly resounding or re-echoing. WH: 19C. Latin *reboans, reboantis*, pres.p. of *reboare*, from RE- + *boare* to roar, to resound. See also -ANT.

rebound *v.i.* to bound back, to recoil (from a blow etc.). *Also v.t.* WH: 14–15C. Old French *rebonder* (Modern French *rebondir*), from RE- + *bondir* BOUND¹.

rebuff *n.* a rejection (to an offer or a person who makes advances etc.). *Also v.t.* WH: 16C. Obs. French *rebuffer*, from Italian *ribuffare*, from *ri-* RE- + *buffo* gust, puff, of imit. orig.

rebuke *v.t.* to reprove, to reprimand. *Also n.* WH: 12–14C. Old French *rebuchier*, from RE- + *buchier* to beat, to strike (strictly, to cut down wood), from *busche* (Modern French *bûche*) log. The original sense (to the 17C) was to force back, to repulse, but the current sense was also in use from the first.

rebus *n.* a picture or figure enigmatically representing a word, name or phrase, usu. by objects suggesting words or syllables. WH: 17C. French *rébus*, from Latin *rebus*, abl. pl. of *res* thing. Latin *rebus* has its origin in *de rebus quae geruntur*, literally concerning the things that are taking place, a title given in 16C Picardy to satirical pieces containing riddles in picture form. The pieces were composed by clerics at the annual carnival and related to current topics, follies, etc.

rebut *v.t.* to contradict or refute by plea, argument or countervailing proof. WH: 12–14C. Old French *reboter*, from RE- + *boter* BUTT⁴.

rec *n.* a recreation ground. WH: early 20C. Abbr. of *recreation ground* (RECREATION).

recalcitrant *a.* refractory, obstinately resisting authority or control. *Also n.* WH: 19C. French *récalcitrant*, from Latin *recalcitrans*, *recalcitrantis*, pres.p. of *recalcitrare* to kick out, from RE- + *calcitrare* to kick out with the heels, from *calx*, *calcis* heel. See -ANT.

recalescence *n.* a sudden temporary increase in the temperature of iron, steel etc. which occurs at certain temperatures during the cooling process as a result of changes in crystal structure. WH: 19C. RE- + Latin *calescere* to grow warm + -ENCE.

recall¹ *v.t.* to call back, to summon to return. WH: 16C. RE- + CALL, based on Latin *revocare* or French *rappeler*.

recall² *n.* a summons to return. WH: 17C. RECALL¹.

recant *v.t.* to retract, to renounce, to abjure. *Also v.i.* WH: 16C. Latin *recantare* to sing in answer, to recall, to revoke, from RE- + *cantare* to sing, CHANT, based on Greek *palinōidein*.

recap *v.t.*, *v.i.* to recapitulate. *Also n.* WH: mid-20C. Abbr. of RECAPITULATE.

recapitulate *v.t.* to repeat in brief (as the principal points or headings of a discourse), to sum up, to summarize. *Also v.i.* WH: 16C. Latin *recapitulatus*, p.p. of *recapitulare*, from RE- + *capitulum*. See CAPITULATE.

recaption *n.* recovery of goods, a wife, child etc. by peaceful means from someone unlawfully withholding them. WH: 17C. Anglo-Latin *recaptio*, *recaptionis*, from RE- + Latin *captio*, *captionis* CAPTION.

recce *n.* a reconnaissance. *Also v.t.*, *v.i.* WH: mid-20C. Abbr. of RECONNAISSANCE.

recede *v.i.* to go back or away (from). WH: 15C. Latin *recedere*, from RE- + *cedere* CEDE. The original sense was to depart from a usual state or standard. The current sense evolved in the 17C.

receipt *n.* a written acknowledgement of money or goods received. *Also v.t.* WH: 14–15C. Anglo-French or Old Northern French *receite*, alt. of Old French *recete* (Modern French *recette*), from Medieval Latin *recepta*, fem. p.p. (used as n.) of Latin *recipere* RECEIVE. Cp. RECIPE. The spelling with *p*, from the Latin original, did not become established until the 18C.

receive *v.t.* to obtain or take as a thing due, offered or given. *Also v.i.* WH: 12–14C. Old French *receivre*, var. of *reçoivre* or *recevoir*, ult. from Latin *recipere*, from RE- + *capere* to take.

recension *n.* a critical revision of a text. WH: 17C. Latin *recensio*, *recensionis*, from *recensere*, from RE- + *censere* to assess.

recent *a.* of or relating to time not long past. *Also n.* WH: 14–15C. French *récent* or Latin *recens*, *recentis*, of unknown orig.

receptacle *n.* something which receives, holds or contains. WH: 14–15C. Old French *réceptacle* or Latin *receptaculum*, from *receptare*, from *receptus*, p.p. of *recipere* RECEIVE.

reception *n.* the act of receiving. WH: 14–15C. Old French *réception*, or from Latin *receptio*, *receptionis*, from *receptus*. See RECEPTACLE, also -ION.

recess *n.* a part that recedes, a niche. *Also v.t.*, *v.i.* WH: 16C. Latin *recessus*, from p.p. of *recedere* RECEDE.

recession¹ *n.* a slump, esp. in trade or economic activity. WH: 19C. RECESSION².

recession² *n.* the act of giving back to a former owner. WH: 17C. Latin *recessio*, *recessionis*, from *recessus*. See RECESS, also -ION.

Rechabite *n.* a total abstainer from alcohol, esp. a member of a society of the Independent Order of Rechabites, a society of abstainers. WH: 14–15C. Ecclesiastical Latin *Rechabita* (pl.), from Hebrew *rēkāḇī*, from *rēḵāḇ* Rechab. See also -ITE¹. A rechabite was originally a member of an Israelite family, descended from Rechab, who refused to drink wine, live in houses, or cultivate fields and vineyards (Jer. xxxv).

réchauffé *n.* a dish warmed up again. WH: 19C. French, p.p. of *réchauffer* to warm up again, from *re-* RE- + *échauffer* to warm up (see CHAFE).

recherché *a.* out of the common, rare, choice, exotic. WH: 17C. French, p.p. of *rechercher*, from *re-* RE- + *chercher* to seek.

recidivist *n.* a relapsed or inveterate criminal, usu. one serving or who has served a second term of imprisonment. WH: 19C. French *récidiviste*, from *récidiver*, from Medieval Latin *recidivare*, from Latin *recidivus*, from *recidere* to fall back, from RE- + *cadere* to fall. See also -IST. Cp. RELAPSE.

recipe *n.* a list of ingredients and directions for preparing a dish. WH: 14–15C. Latin, imper. sing. of *recipere* to take, RECEIVE. Cp. RECEIPT. The word was originally used at the beginning of medical prescriptions. It then became the term for the prescription itself. The current sense dates from the 18C.

recipient *n.* a person who receives something. *Also a.* WH: 16C. French *récipient*, from Italian *recipiente* or Latin *recipiens*, *recipientis*, pres.p. of *recipere* RECEIVE. See also -ENT.

reciprocal *a.* acting, done or given in return. *Also n.* WH: 16C. Latin *reciprocus* moving backwards and forwards, ult. from *re-* back, *pro-* forward. See also -AL¹.

reciprocate *v.i.* to return an equivalent, to make a return in kind. *Also v.t.* WH: 16C. Latin *reciprocatus*, p.p. of *reciprocare*, from *reciprocus*. See RECIPROCAL, also -ATE³.

recision *n.* the act of rescinding, annulment. WH: 17C. Latin *recisio*, *recisionis*, from *recisus*, p.p. of *recidere* to cut back. See also -ION.

recitative¹ *n.* a style of rendering vocal passages intermediate between singing and ordinary speaking, as in oratorio and opera. WH: 17C. Italian *recitativo*, from Latin *recitatus*, p.p. of *recitare* RECITE + -*ivo* -IVE.

recitative² *a.* relating to, suitable for or characteristic of recitative. *Also v.t.* WH: 17C. RECITATIVE¹.

recite *v.t.* to repeat aloud from memory, esp. before an audience. *Also v.i.* WH: 14–15C. Old French *réciter* or Latin *recitare* to read out, from RE- + *citare* CITE.

reck *v.t.* to care about, to heed. *Also v.i.* WH: pre-1200. Partly representing Old English unrecorded infin. (past tense *rōhte*), from Germanic, partly representing Old English *reccan* to care, to heed, of unknown orig. Cp. RECKLESS.

reckless *a.* heedless of the consequences or danger. WH: pre-1200. Old English *recceléas*, from Germanic bases of RECK, -LESS. Cp. German *ruchlos* careless, untroubled.

reckon *v.t.* to add (up), calculate. *Also v.i.* WH: pre-1200. Old English *gerecenian*, from Germanic. Cp. German *rechnen*. The original sense (to the 16C) was to recount, to relate. The sense to count dates from the 12–14C.

reclaim *v.t.* to claim or demand back, to claim the restoration of. *Also v.i.*, *n.* WH: 12–14C. Old French *reclamer*, *reclaim-*, from Latin *reclamare* to cry out, to exclaim. The original sense was to call back a hawk. The sense to bring marshland under cultivation dates from the 18C.

réclame *n.* public attention, publicity or notoriety. WH: 19C. French, from *réclamer* RECLAIM.

recline *v.i.* to assume or be in a leaning or recumbent posture, to lie down or lean back upon cushions or other supports. *Also v.t.* WH: 14–15C. Old French *recliner*, from Latin *reclinare*, from RE- + *clinare* to bend.

recluse *n.* a person who lives retired from the world, esp. a religious devotee who lives in a solitary cell and practises austerity and self-discipline, a hermit. *Also a.* WH: 12–14C. Old French *reclus*, p.p. of *reclure*, from Latin *recludere* to enclose (orig. to open), from RE- + *claudere* CLOSE².

recognition *n.* the act of recognizing. WH: 15C. Latin *recognitio*, *recognitionis*, from *recognitus*, p.p. of *recognoscere*, from RE- + *cognoscere* (COGNITION). See also -ION.

recognizance n. a bond or obligation entered into in a court or before a magistrate to perform a specified act, fulfil a condition etc. (such as to keep the peace or appear when called upon). WH: 12–14C. Old French *reconnissance* (Modern French *reconnaissance*). See RE-, COGNIZANCE.

recognize v.t. to to recall the identity of. Also v.i. WH: 14–15C. Old French *reconnaistre, reconniss-* (Modern French *reconnaître*), from Latin *recognoscere*, from RE- + *cognoscere* (COGNITION).

recoil[1] v.i. to shrink back, as in fear or disgust. Also v.t. WH: 12–14C. Old French *reculer*, from Popular Latin *reculare*, from RE- + Latin *culus* buttocks. Not related to COIL[1].

recoil[2] n. the act of recoiling. WH: 12–14C. RECOIL[1].

recollect v.t. to recall to memory, to remember. Also v.i. WH: 16C. Earlier form of *re-collect*, now differentiated by pronun.

recombinant a. found by or exhibiting genetic recombination. Also n. WH: mid-20C. From *recombine* (from RE- + COMBINE[1]) + -ANT.

recommend v.t. to commend to another's favour, esp. to represent as suitable for employment. WH: 14–15C. Medieval Latin *recommendare*. See RE-, COMMEND. The original sense was to commend (oneself or another) to someone's care, especially that of God. The current sense dates from the 15C with regard to things, and from the 18C with regard to a person.

recompense v.t. to make a return or give an equivalent for, to requite, to repay (a person, a service, an injury etc.). Also n. WH: 14–15C. Old French *récompenser*, from Late Latin *recompensare*, from RE- + *compensare* COMPENSATE.

reconcile v.t. to restore to friendship after an estrangement. WH: 14–15C. Old French *réconcilier* or Latin *reconciliare*, from RE- + *conciliare* CONCILIATE.

recondite a. out of the way, abstruse, little known, obscure. WH: 17C. Latin *reconditus*, p.p. of *recondere* to put away, to hide, from RE- + *condere* to put together, to compose, to hide. The original sense was hidden from view.

reconnaissance n. a preliminary examination or survey. WH: 19C. French, from *reconnaître, reconniss-*. See RECONNOITRE, also -ANCE.

reconnoitre v.t. to make a reconnaissance of. Also v.i., n. WH: 18C. Obs. French *reconnoître* (now *reconnaître*), from Latin *recognoscere* to look over, to inspect. See RECOGNIZE.

record[1] v.t. to write an account of, to set down permanent evidence of. Also v.i. WH: 12–14C. Old French *recorder* to bring to remembrance, from Latin *recordare* to think over, to remember, from RE- + *cor, cordis* heart. The original sense (to the 17C) was to recite or repeat with the aim of committing to memory, also (to the 18C) to relate or narrate orally. The current sense dates from the 16C.

record[2] n. a written or other permanent account of a fact, event etc. WH: 12–14C. Old French remembrance, from *recorder*. See RECORD[1].

recorder n. a person or thing which records. WH: 14–15C. Old French *recordeur*, from *recorder*. See RECORD[1], also -ER[1]. (Later, partly from RECORD[1] + -ER[1].) The musical instrument is apparently so called as it was originally used to record a tune, in the early sense of recalling it and repeating it.

recount v.t. to relate in detail, to narrate. WH: 14–15C. Old Northern French *reconter*, from re- RE- + *conter* COUNT[1].

recoup v.t. to reimburse, to indemnify for a loss or expenditure. Also v.i. WH: 14–15C. Old French *recouper* to retrench, to cut back, from re- RE- + *couper* to cut. The original sense was to cut short, to interrupt. The current sense to reimburse dates from the 17C.

recourse n. resorting or applying (to) as for help. Also v.i. WH: 14–15C. Old French *recours*, from Latin *recursus*, from RE- + *cursus* COURSE.

recover v.t. to regain, to win back. Also v.i., n. WH: 12–14C. Old French *recovrer* (Modern French *recouvrer*), from Latin *recuperare* RECUPERATE.

recreant a. craven, cowardly. Also n. WH: 12–14C. Old French, use as a. and n. of pres.p. of *recroire* to yield, to surrender, from Medieval Latin (*se*) *recredere* to surrender (oneself), from RE- + *credere* to entrust, to believe. See -ANT.

recreation n. the act or process of renewing one's strength after toil. WH: 14–15C. Old French *récréation*, from Latin *recreatio, recreationis*, from RE- + *creatio, creationis* CREATION.

recrement n. fluid separated from the blood and absorbed into it again, such as gastric juice, saliva etc. WH: 16C. French *récrément* or Latin *recrementum*, from RE- + *cretus*, p.p. of *cernere* to separate. See also -MENT. Cp. EXCREMENT.

recriminate v.i. to return an accusation, to bring countercharges. Also v.t. WH: 17C. Medieval Latin *recriminatus*, p.p. of *recriminari*, from Latin RE- + *criminare* (CRIMINATE).

recrudesce v.i. to break out or become active again. WH: 19C. Back-formation from *recrudescence* (18C), from Latin *recrudescere*, from RE- + *crudescere* to become raw, from *crudus*. See CRUDE, also -ESCENCE.

recruit v.t. to enlist (people) to join the armed forces. Also v.i., n. WH: 17C. French *recruter*, from obs. dial. *recrute*, from *recrue*, fem. p.p. (used as n.) of *recroître* to increase again, from Latin *recrescere*, from RE- + *crescere* to grow. Cp. CREW, ROOKIE. The original sense was to reinforce, to supplement. The sense to enlist dates from the 19C.

rectangle n. a plane quadrilateral figure with four right angles. WH: 16C. French, or from Medieval Latin *rectangulum*, earlier *rectiangulum*, use as n. of neut. sing. of Late Latin *rectiangulus* (translating Greek *orthogōnios*), from Latin *rectus* straight + *angulus* ANGLE[1].

recti- comb. form straight. WH: Latin *rectus* straight + -i-.

rectify v.t. to set right, to correct. WH: 14–15C. Old French *rectifier*, from Medieval Latin *rectificare*, from *rectus* right. See also -FY.

rectilinear a. consisting of, lying or proceeding in a straight line. WH: 17C. Late Latin *rectilineus*, from Latin *rectus* straight + *linea* LINE[1]. See also -AR[1].

rectiserial a. (of leaves) arranged in a straight line, esp. in vertical ranks. WH: 19C. RECTI- + SERIAL.

rectitude n. uprightness, rightness of moral principle, conformity to truth and justice. WH: 14–15C. Old French, or from Late Latin *rectitudo*, from Latin *rectus* right, straight. See also -TUDE.

recto n. the right-hand page of an open book (usu. bearing an odd number) as distinct from *verso*. WH: 19C. Latin, abl. of *rectus* right.

recto- comb. form of or relating to the rectum. WH: Latin RECTUM. See also -O-.

rectocele n. protrusion of the rectum into the vagina. WH: 19C. RECTO- + -CELE.

rector n. the incumbent of a Church of England parish in which tithes were formerly paid to the incumbent. WH: 14–15C. Old French *rectour* (Modern French *recteur*), from Latin *rector*, from *rectus*, p.p. of *regere* to rule. See also -OR. The earliest sense (to the 17C) was ruler, governor, but the current ecclesiastical sense also dates from the first years of the period. The rector was the 'ruler' of the parish, entitled to all the tithes. Where the tithes went to a monastery, however, the clergyman in the parish was merely the rector's vicar, i.e. his substitute. See VICAR.

rectrix n. the quill feathers in a bird's tail which guide its flight. WH: 17C. Latin, fem. of RECTOR. See also -TRIX.

rectum n. the lowest portion of the large intestine extending to the anus. WH: 16C. Latin, neut. of *rectus* straight, short for *intestinum rectum* straight gut. The organ is so called because it is straight, by contrast with the coils and curves of the rest of the large intestine.

rectus n. a straight muscle, esp. of the abdomen, thigh, neck or eyes. WH: 18C. Latin straight. Short for *musculus rectus* straight muscle.

recumbent a. lying down, reclining. Also n. WH: 17C. Latin *recumbens, recumbentis*, pres.p. of *recumbere* to recline, from RE- + nasalized stem corr. to *cubare* to lie. See also -ENT.

recuperate v.i. to recover from sickness, exhaustion etc. Also v.t. WH: 16C. Latin *recuperatus*, p.p. of *recuperare*, from RE- + *capere* to take, to seize. See also -ATE[3]. Cp. RECOVER. Despite the similarity of sound and sense, the word is not related to RECOUP.

recur v.i. to happen again, to happen repeatedly. WH: 14–15C. Latin *recurrere*, from RE- + *currere* to run.

recurve v.t., v.i. to bend backwards. WH: 16C. Latin *recurvare*, from RE- + *curvare* CURVE.

recusant a. obstinately refusing to conform. Also n. WH: 16C. Latin *recusans, recusantis*, pres.p. of *recusare* to refuse, from RE- + *causa* CAUSE. See -ANT. The word originally applied to a Roman Catholic who refused to attend the services of the Church of England.

red *a.* of a bright warm colour, such as blood, usu. including crimson, scarlet, vermilion etc.; of the colour at the least refracted end of the spectrum or that farthest from the violet. *Also n.* WH: pre-1200. Old English *rēad*, from Germanic, from Indo-European base also of Latin *rufus, ruber,* Greek *eruthros,* Sanskrit *rudhira* red. Cp. German *rot.*

-red *suf.* condition, as in *hatred, kindred.* WH: Old English *rǣden* condition, later shortened by dropping of final syl.

redaction *n.* reduction to order, esp. revising, rearranging and editing a literary work. WH: 17C. French *rédaction,* from Late Latin *redactio, redactionis,* from Latin *redactus,* p.p. of *redigere* to bring back, to collect, from RE- + *agere* to drive. See also -ION.

redan *n.* a fortification having two faces forming a salient angle towards the enemy. WH: 17C. French, var. of *redent* notching as of a saw, from *re-* RE- + *dent* tooth.

redd[1] *v.t.* to clear (up), to put in order, to tidy, to make ready or clear. WH: 14–15C. Orig. uncertain. Cp. RID.

redd[2] *n.* a hollow made in a river bed by a salmon, trout etc. for spawning. WH: 17C. Orig. unknown.

†rede *n.* counsel, advice. *Also v.t.* WH: pre-1200. Old English *rǣd,* from Germanic, from base also of READ. Cp. German *Rat* advice, counsel (e.g. as in BUNDESRAT).

redeem *v.t.* to buy back. WH: 14–15C. French *rédimer* or Latin *redimere,* from RE- + *emere* to buy.

redemption *n.* the act of redeeming or the state of being redeemed. WH: 12–14C. Old French *rédemption,* from Latin *redemptio, redemptionis,* from *redemptus,* p.p. of *redimere* REDEEM. See also -ION. Cp. RANSOM.

rediffusion *n.* a system of relaying radio or television programmes via cables. WH: early 20C. RE- + *diffusion* (DIFFUSE[2]).

redingote *n.* a woman's long double-breasted coat. WH: 18C. French, from English *riding-coat.*

redintegrate *v.t.* to restore to completeness, to make united or perfect again. *Also a.* WH: 14–15C. Latin *redintegratus,* p.p. of *redintegrare,* from RE- + *integrare* INTEGRATE[1]. See also -ATE[3].

†redivivus *a.* come to life again, revived (*usu. following its noun*). WH: 16C. Latin, from RE- + *vivus* living, alive.

redolent *a.* suggestive, reminding one (of). WH: 14–15C. Old French, or from Latin *redolens, redolentis,* pres.p. of *redolere,* from RE- + *olere* to emit a smell. See -ENT. The original sense was literal, having a strong odour. The current sense dates from the 19C.

redoubt *n.* a detached outwork or fieldwork enclosed by a parapet without flanking defences. WH: 17C. French *redoute,* obs. *ridotte,* from obs. Italian *ridotta* (now *ridotto*), from Medieval Latin *reductus* refuge, retreat, from p.p. of Latin *reducere* to draw off, to withdraw, REDUCE. The *b* was added by association with *redoubt* or fear, to dread (REDOUBTABLE).

redoubtable *a.* formidable. WH: 14–15C. French *redoutable,* from *redouter,* obs. *redoubter* to fear, to dread, from *re-* RE- + *douter* DOUBT.

redound *v.i.* to have effect, to contribute (to one's credit etc.). WH: 14–15C. Old French *redonder,* from Latin *redundare,* from RE- + *undare* to surge, from *unda* wave. See REDUNDANT.

redowa *n.* a Bohemian round dance of two forms, one resembling a waltz, the other a polka. WH: 19C. French or German, from Czech *rejdovák,* from *rejdovat* to turn round, to whirl.

redox *a.* of, relating to or being a chemical reaction where one agent is reduced and another oxidized. *Also n.* WH: early 20C. REDUCTION + *oxidation* (OXIDE).

redress *v.t.* to amend, to make reparation for. *Also n.* WH: 12–14C. Old French *redresser,* from *re-* RE- + *dresser* DRESS.

redstart *n.* a red-tailed migratory songbird, *Phoenicurus phoenicurus.* WH: 16C. RED + obs. *start* tail, from Old English *steort,* from Germanic.

reduce *v.t.* to make smaller or less in size, extent etc. *Also v.i.* WH: 14–15C. Latin *reducere* to bring back, to restore, from RE- + *ducere* to lead, to bring. The original sense (to the 17C) was to bring back to mind, to recall. The current sense dates from the 18C.

reductio ad absurdum *n.* proof of the falsity of a proposition by showing the absurdity of its logical consequence. WH: 18C. Latin, lit. reduction to the absurd.

reduction *n.* the act or process of reducing. WH: 14–15C. Old French *réduction* or Latin *reductio, reductionis,* from *reductus,* p.p. of *reducere* REDUCE.

redundant *a.* superfluous, unnecessary. WH: 16C. Latin *redundans, redundantis,* pres.p. of *redundare.* See REDOUND, also -ANT. The original sense was copious, abundant. The current sense evolved in the 17C.

reduplicate *v.t.* to double, to repeat. *Also a., n.* WH: 16C. Late Latin *reduplicatus,* p.p. of *reduplicare,* from Latin RE- + *duplicare* DUPLICATE[2].

reduviid *a.* belonging to the Reduviidae, a family of bloodsucking insects. *Also n.* WH: 19C. Modern Latin *Reduviidae,* from *Reduvius* genus name, from Latin *reduvia* hangnail. See also -ID.

ree *n.* the female ruff. WH: 14–15C. Orig. unknown. Cp. REEVE[3]. The word is recorded earlier than *ruff,* so perhaps originally denoted the male as well.

reed *n.* any of various water or marsh plants with long straight stems, esp. of the genera *Phragmites* or *Arundo. Also v.t.* WH: pre-1200. Old English *hrēod,* from Germanic. Cp. German *Ried.*

reef[1] *n.* a ridge of rock, coral, sand etc. in the sea at or near the surface of the water. WH: 16C. Middle Low German and Middle Dutch *rif, ref,* from Old Norse *rif* RIB[1]. Cp. REEF[2].

reef[2] *n.* any of the horizontal portions across the top of a square sail or the bottom of a fore-and-aft sail, which can be rolled up or wrapped and secured in order to shorten sail. *Also v.t.* WH: 12–14C. Middle Dutch *reef, rif,* from Old Norse *rif* RIB[1]. Cp. REEF[1].

reefer *n.* a marijuana cigarette. WH: 19C. REEF[2] + -ER[1] or ? from Mexican Spanish *grifo* (smoker of) marijuana.

reek *v.i.* to give off a strong disagreeable odour. *Also n.* WH: pre-1200. Old English *rēocan,* from Germanic. Cp. German *riechen* to smell, rel. to *rauchen* to smoke. The original sense was to emit smoke. The current sense dates from the 18C.

reel[1] *n.* a rotatory frame, cylinder or other device on which thread, cord, wire, paper etc. can be wound, either in the process of manufacture or for winding and unwinding as required. *Also v.t.* WH: pre-1200. Old English *hrēol,* with no known related forms.

reel[2] *v.i.* to stagger, to sway. *Also n.* WH: 14–15C. REEL[1].

reel[3] *n.* a lively esp. Scottish dance in which the couples face each other and describe figures of eight. *Also v.i.* WH: 16C. REEL[2]. The dance is so named as the dancers follow a 'weaving' pattern around each other, as if reeling.

reest[1] *v.t.* to dry or smoke (bacon, fish etc.), to cure. *Also v.i.* WH: 16C. Orig. uncertain. ? Scandinavian. Cp. Danish *riste* to grill, to broil, from Old Norse *rist* gridiron.

reest[2] *v.i.* (esp. of a horse) to stop, to refuse to go on, to balk. WH: 18C. Prob. alt. of REST[1] or shortening of ARREST.

reeve[1] *n.* a chief officer or magistrate of a town or district, holding office usu. under the monarch but sometimes by election. WH: pre-1200. Old English *rēfa,* shortened form of *gerēfa* GRIEVE[2], from *ge-* Y- + base of *secgrōf* host of men, *stæfrōf* alphabet. Cp. SHERIFF. The word is apparently not related to -*grave* in BURGRAVE, LANDGRAVE, MARGRAVE, PALSGRAVE, WALDGRAVE, despite the similarity of meaning.

reeve[2] *v.t.* to pass (the end of a rope, a rod etc.) through a ring, a hole in a block etc. WH: 17C. ? Dutch *reven* to reef (a sail).

reeve[3] *n.* the female of the ruff. WH: 17C. Var. of REE, of unknown orig.

ref[1] *n.* a referee. *Also v.t.* WH: 19C. Abbr. of REFEREE.

ref[2] *abbr.* reference. WH: early 20C. Abbr. of REFERENCE.

refectory *n.* a room or hall where meals are taken in colleges, religious houses etc. WH: 14–15C. Late Latin *refectorium,* from Latin *reficere* to remake, to renew, from RE- + *facere* to make. See -ORY[1]. Cp. RESTAURANT.

refer *v.t.* to assign (to a certain cause, place etc.). *Also v.i.* WH: 14–15C. Old French *référer,* from Latin *referre* to carry back, from RE- + *ferre* to bear, to carry.

referee *n.* an umpire in football, boxing etc. *Also v.i.* WH: 16C. REFER + -EE. A referee is so called as matters of dispute are referred to him. The sense sporting umpire dates from the 19C.

reference *n.* the act of referring. *Also v.t.* WH: 16C. REFER + -ENCE.

referendum *n.* the submission of a political question to the whole electorate for a direct decision by general vote. WH: 19C. Latin, ger. of *referre* REFER.

reffo *n.* a political refugee from Europe. WH: mid-20C. Abbr. of *refugee* (REFUGE) + -O.

refine *v.t.* to clear from impurities, defects etc. *Also v.i.* WH: 16C. RE- + FINE[1], partly based on French *raffiner.*

reflate *v.t.* to inflate again. WH: mid-20C. RE- + -*flate*, based on DEFLATE, INFLATE.

reflect *v.t.* to turn or throw back (light, heat, sound etc.) esp. in accordance with certain physical laws. *Also v.i.* WH: 14–15C. Old French *reflecter* or Latin *reflectere*, from RE- + *flectere* to bend. The original sense was to divert, to deflect.

reflet *n.* a metallic lustre or glow, esp. on pottery. WH: 19C. French reflection.

reflex *a.* involuntary, produced independently of the will under stimulus from impressions on the sensory nerves. *Also n.* WH: 16C. Latin *reflexus*, from p.p. of *reflectere* REFLECT.

refluent *a.* flowing back. WH: 14–15C. Latin *refluens, refluentis,* pres.p. of *refluere* to flow back, from RE- + -*fluere* to flow. See also -ENT.

reflux *n.* the boiling of liquid in a flask fitted with a condenser, so that the vapour condenses and flows back into the flask. *Also v.t., v.i.* WH: 14–15C. RE- + FLUX.

reform *v.t.* to change from worse to better by removing faults. *Also v.i., n.* WH: 12–14C. Old French *réformer* or Latin *reformare*, from RE- + *formare* FORM. The original sense (to the 16C) was to restore to an original form, i.e. to *re-form*. The current sense dates from the 14–15C.

refract *v.t.* (of water, glass etc.) to cause (a ray of light etc.) to undergo refraction. WH: 17C. Latin *refractus,* p.p. of *refringere,* from RE- + *frangere* to break.

refractory *a.* perverse, insubordinate, obstinate in opposition or disobedience, unmanageable. *Also n.* WH: 17C. Alt. of obs. *refractary,* from Latin *refractarius,* from *refractus* (REFRACT), with substitution of -ORY[2] for -ARY[1].

refrain[1] *v.i.* to abstain (from an act or doing). *Also v.t.* WH: 12–14C. Old French *refréner*, from Latin *refrenare* to bridle, from RE- + *frenum* bridle. The original sense was to restrain, to suppress, then (to the 17C) to curb, to check. The current sense dates from the 16C.

refrain[2] *n.* a recurring phrase or line, esp. repeated at the end of every stanza, a chorus. WH: 14–15C. Old French, prob. from Provençal *refranh* bird's song, from *refranhar,* from var. of Latin *refringere.* See REFRACT.

refrangible *a.* capable of being refracted. WH: 17C. Modern Latin *refrangibilis,* from *refrangere,* from Latin *refringere.* See REFRACT, also -IBLE.

refresh *v.t.* to make fresh again, to reinvigorate. *Also v.i.* WH: 14–15C. Old French *refreschier, refreschir* (Modern French *rafraîchir*), from RE- + *fres,* fem. *fresche.*

refrigerate *v.t.* to make cool or cold. *Also v.i.* WH: 14–15C. Orig. p.p., from Latin *refrigeratus,* p.p. of *refrigerare,* from RE- + *frigus, frigoris* cold. See also -ATE[3].

refringent *a.* refractive. WH: 18C. Latin *refringens, refringentis,* pres.p. of *refringere.* See REFRACT, also -ENT.

refuge *n.* shelter from danger or distress. *Also v.t., v.i.* WH: 14–15C. Old French, from Latin *refugium,* from RE- + *fugere* to flee.

refulgent *a.* shining brightly, brilliant, radiant, splendid. WH: 15C. Latin *refulgens, refulgentis,* pres.p. of *refulgere,* from RE- + *fulgere* to shine. See also -ENT.

refund[1] *v.t.* to pay back, to repay. *Also v.i.* WH: 14–15C. Old French *refonder* or Latin *refundere,* from RE- + *fundere* to pour. Later based on FUND. The original sense was to pour back. The sense to pay back dates from the 16C.

refund[2] *n.* an act of refunding money. WH: 19C. REFUND[1].

refurbish *v.t.* to freshen up by renovating, redecorating etc. WH: 17C. RE- + FURBISH.

refuse[1] *v.t.* to decline (to do, yield, grant etc.). *Also v.i.* WH: 12–14C. Old French *refuser,* from Popular Latin *refusare,* prob. alt. of Latin *recusare* to refuse (RECUSANT), based on *refutare* REFUTE.

refuse[2] *a.* rejected as valueless. *Also n.* WH: 12–14C. ? Old French *refusé,* p.p. of *refuser* REFUSE[1].

refute *v.t.* to prove (a statement, argument etc.) false or erroneous, to disprove. WH: 16C. Latin *refutare* to repel, to rebut.

reg *n.* registration mark. WH: late 20C. Abbr. of *registration mark* (REGISTER).

regain *v.t.* to recover possession of. WH: 16C. Old French *regagner.* See RE-, GAIN.

regal[1] *a.* of, relating to or fit for a king or queen. WH: 12–14C. Old French, or from Latin *regalis,* from *rex, regis* king. See also -AL[1].

regal[2] *n.* a small portable reed-organ held in the hands, in use in the 16th and 17th cents.; also called *pair of regals.* WH: 16C. French *régale,* of uncertain orig. ? From Latin *regalis* royal, REGAL[1].

regale *v.t.* to entertain sumptuously with food and drink. *Also v.i., n.* WH: 17C. French *régaler,* from *re-* RE- + Old French *gale* pleasure, rejoicing. Cp. GALLANT[1], GALLANT[2].

regalia[1] *n.pl.* the insignia of royalty, esp. the emblems worn or displayed in coronation ceremonies etc. WH: 16C. Medieval Latin royal residence, royal rights, use as n. of neut. pl. of Latin *regalis* REGAL[1].

regalia[2] *n.* a Cuban cigar of superior quality. WH: 19C. Spanish royal privilege.

regard *v.t.* to view in a specified way, to consider (as). *Also v.i., n.* WH: 12–14C. Old French *regarder,* from *re-* RE- + *garder* GUARD. Cp. REWARD.

regatta *n.* a sporting event comprising a series of yacht or boat races. WH: 17C. Obs. Italian (Venetian) *regatta, rigatta* fight, struggle, contest, from *regattare* to compete, to contend for mastery, to sell by haggling, ? from *recatare* to buy and sell in order to resell, from Popular Latin *recaptare* to capture, from RE- + *captare* to try to catch.

regenerate[1] *v.t.* to generate anew, to give new existence to. *Also v.i.* WH: 16C. Latin *regeneratus,* p.p. of *regenerare.* See RE-, GENERATE.

regenerate[2] *a.* regenerated, renewed. WH: 14–15C. Latin *regeneratus.* See REGENERATE[1], also -ATE[2].

regent *n.* a person appointed to govern a country during the minority, absence or disability of a monarch. *Also a.* WH: 14–15C. Old French *régent* or Latin *regens, regentis,* use as n. of pres.p. of *regere* to rule. See also -ENT.

reggae *n.* a form of rhythmical W Indian rock music in 4/4 time. WH: mid-20C. W Indian, ult. of uncertain orig. Cp. Jamaican *rege-rege* quarrel, row, var. of *raga-raga.* See RAGGA.

regicide *n.* the killing of a king. WH: 16C. Latin *rex, regis* king + -CIDE, prob. based on French *régicide.*

Régie *n.* the revenue department in some European countries having sole control of the importation of tobacco and sometimes of salt. WH: 18C. French, fem. p.p. of *régir* to rule.

regime *n.* a prevailing system of government or management. WH: 15C. French *régime,* from Latin REGIMEN.

regimen *n.* a systematic plan or course of diet, exercise etc. for the preservation or restoration of health. WH: 14–15C. Latin, from *regere* to rule.

regiment[1] *n.* a body of soldiers forming the largest permanent unit of the army, usu. divided into two battalions comprising several companies or troops, and commanded by a colonel. WH: 14–15C. Old French *régiment,* from Late Latin *regimentum* rule, from *regere* to rule. See also -MENT. The original sense was rule, government, especially by royal authority. The current military sense evolved in the 16C.

regiment[2] *v.t.* to force order or discipline on, harshly. WH: 17C. REGIMENT[1].

Regina *n.* a reigning queen. WH: 18C. Latin queen. Cp. REX.

region *n.* a tract of land, sea etc. of large but indefinite extent. WH: 12–14C. Old French *région,* from Latin *regio, regionis* direction, line, boundary, district, province, from *regere* to rule. See also -ION.

régisseur *n.* an official in a dance company whose responsibilities include directing. WH: 19C. French, from *régir, régiss-* to direct + -eur -OR.

register *n.* an official list of names, facts etc., as of births, marriages, deaths, people entitled to vote at elections etc. *Also v.t., v.i.* WH: 14–15C. Old French *registre* or Medieval Latin *registrum,* alt. of *regestum,* sing. of Late Latin *regesta* list, neut. pl. of p.p. of Latin *regerere* to enter, to transcribe, to record.

regius *a.* royal. WH: 17C. Latin royal, from *rex, regis* king.

reglet *n.* a strip of wood, less than type high, used for separating pages, filling blank spaces etc. WH: 16C. French *réglet, réglette,* dim.

of *règle* RULE. See also -ET[1], -ETTE. The architectural use of the word for a narrow strip separating mouldings arose in the 17C and derives from Italian *regoletto*, from *regola* rule.

regma *n.* a dry fruit made up of several cells that burst open when ripe. WH: 19C. Greek *rhēgma* break, fracture.

regnal *a.* of or relating to a reign. WH: 17C. Anglo-Latin *regnalis*, from Latin *regnum* kingdom. See also -AL[1].

rego *n.* motor vehicle registration. WH: mid-20C. Abbr. of *registration* (REGISTER) + -O.

regolith *n.* unconsolidated rock, soil etc. at the earth's surface. WH: 19C. Greek *rhēgos* blanket + -LITH. The term was coined in 1897 by the US geologist George P. Merrill.

regrate *v.t.* to buy up (corn, provisions etc.) and sell again in the same or a neighbouring market so as to raise the prices. WH: 14–15C. Old French *regrater*, prob. from *re-* RE- + *grater* (Modern French *gratter*) to scratch, of Germanic orig.

regrede *v.i.* to go back. WH: 19C. Latin *regredi* to turn back, from RE- + *gradi* to walk. Cp. REGRESSION.

regression *n.* a backward movement, a return. WH: 14–15C. Latin *regressio*, *regressionis*, from *regressus*, p.p. of *regredi*. See REGREDE.

regret *n.* distress or sorrow for a disappointment or loss. *Also v.t.* WH: 14–15C. Old French *regreter* to bewail (the dead) (Modern French *regretter*), ? from *re-* RE- + Germanic base of GREET[2]. The original sense was complaint, lament. The current sense evolved in the 16C.

regular *a.* methodical, consistent; conforming to rule. *Also n.* WH: 14–15C. Old French *reguler* (Modern French *régulier*), from Latin *regularis*, from *regula* RULE. See also -AR[1].

regulate *v.t.* to adjust or control by rule. WH: 14–15C. Late Latin *regulatus*, p.p. of *regulare*, from Latin *regula* RULE. See also -ATE[3].

regulo *n.* the temperature of a gas oven, expressed as a particular number. WH: early 20C. REGULATE + -O, or from Latin *regulo* I regulate, 1st pers. sing. pres. ind. of *regulare* to rule, to control.

regulus *n.* the purer mass of a metal that sinks to the bottom when ore is being smelted, an intermediate product retaining to a greater or lesser extent the impurities of the ore. WH: 16C. Latin, dim. of *rex*, *regis* king. The word was originally in *regulus of antimony* metallic antimony, apparently so called because it readily combined with gold.

regurgitate *v.t.* to bring back (partially digested food) into the mouth after swallowing. *Also v.i.* WH: 16C. Medieval Latin *regurgitatus*, p.p. of *regurgitare*, from RE- + Late Latin *gurgitare* to engulf (see GURGITATION).

rehab *n.* rehabilitation. WH: mid-20C. Abbr. of *rehabilitation* (REHABILITATE).

rehabilitate *v.t.* to make fit after disablement, illness, imprisonment etc. for making a living or playing a part in the life of society. WH: 16C. Medieval Latin *rehabilitatus*, p.p. of *rehabilitare*, from RE- + *habilitare* HABILITATE. The original sense was to restore formally to former privileges, rank and possessions, then to re-establish the good name or reputation of. The current sense to make fit after illness, injury or imprisonment dates only from the mid-20C.

rehearse *v.t.* to practise (a play, musical performance etc.) before public performance. *Also v.i.* WH: 12–14C. Old French *rehercier*, prob. from *re-* RE- + *hercer* to harrow (see HEARSE). The concept is of 'raking over' the prepared material to make it smooth ready for 'sowing the seed' at the first performance.

rehoboam *n.* a wine bottle, especially a champagne bottle, which holds six times the amount of a standard bottle, approximately 156 fl. oz. (about 4.6 l). WH: 19C. *Rehoboam*, son of Solomon, King of Judah (I Kgs. xii–xiv). Cp. JEROBOAM.

Reich *n.* the German realm considered as an empire made up of subsidiary states. WH: early 20C. German kingdom, empire, state. Rel. to RICH.

reify *v.t.* to make (an abstract idea) concrete, to treat as real. WH: 19C. Latin *res*, *rei* thing + -FY.

reign *n.* the period during which a sovereign rules. *Also v.i.* WH: 12–14C. Old French *reigne* (Modern French *règne*) kingdom, from Latin *regnum*, rel. to *rex*, *regis* king.

reimburse *v.t.* to repay (a person who has spent money). WH: 17C. RE- + IMBURSE, based on French *rembourser*.

rein *n.* a long narrow strip, usu. of leather, attached at each end to a bit for guiding and controlling a horse or other animal in riding or driving. *Also v.t.*, *v.i.* WH: 12–14C. Old French *rene*, *reigne*, earlier *resne* (Modern French *rêne*), from Latin *retinare* RETAIN.

reindeer *n.* a deer, *Rangifer tarandus*, now inhabiting the subarctic parts of the northern hemisphere, domesticated for the sake of its milk and as a draught animal. WH: 14–15C. Old Norse *hreindýri*, from *hreinn* reindeer + *dýr* DEER. Not rel. to REIN.

reinforce *v.t.* to add new strength or support to. *Also n.* WH: 14–15C. Alt., by assim. to RE- and *inforce*, var. of ENFORCE, of obs. *renforce*, from Old French *renforcer*, from *re-* RE- + *enforcier* ENFORCE. Cp. *re-enforce*. The military sense dates from the 15C and probably derives from Italian *rinforzare*.

†**reins** *n.pl.* the kidneys. WH: pre-1200. Old French, from Latin *renes*. Cp. RENAL.

reiterate *v.t.* to repeat again and again. WH: 14–15C. Latin *reiteratus*, p.p. of *reiterare*. See RE-, ITERATE.

reive *v.i.* to go on a raid, to plunder. WH: pre-1200. Var. of REAVE.

reject[1] *v.t.* to put aside, to discard. WH: 14–15C. Latin *reiectus*, p.p. of *reicere*, *reiicere* to throw back, from RE- + *iacere* to throw.

reject[2] *n.* someone who or something which has been rejected. WH: 14–15C. REJECT[1]. The original sense was refusal, denial, then (to the 17C) a person who has been rejected or cast out generally. The current sense, a person rejected by others as unsuitable, dates from the early 20C.

rejoice *v.i.* to feel joy or gladness in a high degree. *Also v.t.* WH: 12–14C. Old French *resjoir* (Modern French *réjouir*), from *re-* RE- + *esjoir* (Modern French *éjouir*), from *es-* (EX-) + *jouir* JOY. The original sense (to the 16C) was to enjoy by possessing, to have for oneself. The current sense evolved in the 14–15C.

rejoin *v.t.* to answer to a reply, to retort. *Also v.i.* WH: 14–15C. Old French *rejoindre*, *rejoign-*. See RE-, JOIN.

rejuvenate *v.t.* to make young again. *Also v.i.* WH: 19C. RE- + Latin *iuvenis* young + -ATE[3], based on French *rajeunir*.

relapse *v.i.* to fall or slip back (into a former bad state or practice). *Also n.* WH: 14–15C. Latin *relapsus*, p.p. of *relabi*, from RE- + *labi* to slip.

relate *v.t.* to tell, to narrate. *Also v.i.* WH: 15C. Latin *relatus*, p.p. of *referre* REFER. See also -ATE[3].

relation *n.* the condition of being related or connected. WH: 14–15C. Old French, or from Latin *relatio*, *relationis*, from *relatus*. See RELATE, also -ATION.

relative *a.* depending on relation to something else. *Also n.* WH: 14–15C. Old French *relatif*, or from Late Latin *relativus* having reference, from *relatus*. See RELATE, also -IVE.

relator *n.* an informer, a complainant, esp. one who institutes proceedings by way of a relation or information to the Attorney-General. WH: 16C. Latin, from *relatus*. See RELATE, also -OR.

relax *v.i.* to become less tense or severe. *Also v.t.* WH: 14–15C. Latin *relaxare*, from RE- + *laxus* LAX. The original sense (to the 17C) was to make less dense, to loosen by separating the parts. The sense as applied to the human body arose in the 17C.

relay[1] *n.* a supply of fresh horses, workers, hounds etc. to relieve others when tired. WH: 14–15C. Old French *relai* (Modern French *relais*), from *relayer*. See RELAY[2].

relay[2] *v.t.* to spread (information etc.) by relays. WH: 14–15C. RELAY[1], or from Old French *relayer*, from *re-* RE- + *laier*, ult. from Latin *laxare*. See LEASE.

release *v.t.* to set free from restraint or confinement. *Also n.* WH: 12–14C. Old French *relesser*, *relaisser*, from Latin *relaxare* RELAX. Cp. LEASE. The original sense (to the 17C) was to withdraw a punishment or revoke a sentence.

relegate *v.t.* to consign or dismiss (to some inferior position etc.). WH: 14–15C. Latin *relegatus*, p.p. of *relegare* to send away, to refer, from RE- + *legare* to send. See LEGATE, also -ATE[3].

relent *v.i.* to give way to compassion. *Also v.t.*, *n.* WH: 14–15C. Ult. from Latin RE- + *lentare* to bend, from *lentus* flexible. The original sense (to the 18C) was to melt under the influence of heat. The current sense evolved in the 16C.

relevant *a.* bearing on the matter in hand, apposite. WH: 16C. Medieval Latin *relevans*, *relevantis*, pres.p. of Latin *relevare* to raise up, to relieve. See also -ANT.

relic *n.* any ancient object of historical interest. WH: 12–14C. Old French *relique* (orig. pl.), from Latin RELIQUIAE.

relict *n.* a plant or animal existing as a remnant of a formerly widely distributed group in a previous geological era. *Also a.* WH: 14–15C. Latin *relictus*, p.p. of *relinquere* RELINQUISH. The original sense was a widow (who remains after the death of her husband). The biological and geological sense arose in the early 20C.

relief¹ *n.* alleviation of pain, discomfort etc. WH: 12–14C. Old French, from *relever* RELIEVE. The military sense replacement of one person on duty by another dates from the 16C. Hence Francisco's well-known words, 'For this relief much thanks', in Shakespeare's *Hamlet* (1601), usually misunderstood to mean alleviation of pain.

relief² *n.* the projecting of carved or moulded figures or designs from a surface in approximate proportion to the objects represented. WH: 17C. French, from Italian *rilievo*, obs. *rilevo*, from *rilevare* to raise, ult. from Latin *relevare* RELIEVE. Cp. RELIEVO.

relieve *v.t.* to alleviate, to lighten. WH: 12–14C. Old French *relever*, from Latin *relevare* to raise again, to alleviate, from RE- + *levare* to raise, from *levis* light.

relievo *n.* raised or embossed work, relief. WH: 17C. Italian *rilievo*. See RELIEF².

religieuse *n.* a nun. WH: 17C. French, fem. of *religieux* religious (RELIGION).

religio- *comb. form* religion. WH: RELIGION, *religious*. See also -O-.

religion *n.* belief in a superhuman being or beings, esp. a personal god, controlling the universe and entitled to worship and obedience. WH: 12–14C. Old French, from Latin *religio*, *religionis* obligation, bond, reverence, prob. from *religare*, from RE- + *ligare* LIGATE. Cp. RELY.

relinquish *v.t.* to give up a claim to, to surrender. WH: 14–15C. Old French *relinquir*, *relinquiss-*, from Latin *relinquere*, from RE- + *linquere* to leave. See also -ISH².

reliquary *n.* a depository for relics, a casket for keeping a relic or relics in. WH: 16C. Old French *reliquare*, from *relique* RELIC. See also -ARY¹.

reliquiae *n.pl.* remains. WH: 17C. Latin, use as n. of fem. pl. of *reliquus* remaining, from RE- + *liq-*, stem of *linquere* to leave.

relish *n.* great enjoyment, gusto. *Also v.t., v.i.* WH: 12–14C. Ult. from Old French *relais* remainder, from *relaisser* to leave behind, RE-LEASE. The original sense was odour, scent, taste, which remains after the initial touching or trying. The sense pleasing taste arose in the 17C, as did that of great enjoyment generally. The sense condiment, piquant sauce evolved in the 18C.

reluctant *a.* unwilling, disinclined (to). WH: 17C. Latin *reluctans*, *reluctantis*, pres.p. of *reluctari* to struggle against, from RE- + *luctari* to struggle. See also -ANT.

rely *v.i.* to trust or depend (on or upon) with confidence. WH: 12–14C. Old French *relier* to bind together, from Latin *religare* to bind closely, from RE- + *ligare* to bind. Cp. RALLY¹.

rem *n.* a unit of radiation dosage which has the same biological effect as one roentgen of X-ray or gamma radiation. WH: mid-20C. Acronym of *roentgen equivalent man*.

remain *v.i.* to stay behind or be left after use, separation etc. WH: 14–15C. Old French *remanoir*, *remain-*, from Latin *remanere*, from RE- + *manere* to remain, or from Old French *remaindre*, from Latin *remanere*.

remand *v.t.* to recommit to custody after a partial hearing. *Also n.* WH: 14–15C. Late Latin *remandere*, from Latin RE- + *mandare* to command. The original sense was to send back again, to order to return. The legal sense dates from the 17C.

remanent *a.* remaining, left behind, surviving. WH: 14–15C. Latin *remanens*, *remanentis*, pres.p. of *remanere* REMAIN. See also -ENT.

remark *v.t.* to comment (that). *Also v.i., n.* WH: 16C. French *remarquer*, from *re-* RE- + *marquer* MARK¹. The original sense was to take notice of. The sense to comment evolved in the 17C and to make a remark in the 19C.

remarkable *a.* worthy of special observation or notice. WH: 17C. French *remarquable*, from *remarquer*. See REMARK, also -ABLE.

remblai *n.* the material used to form a rampart or embankment. WH: 18C. French, from *remblayer* to embank, from *re-* RE- + *emblayer* to heap up.

Rembrandtesque *a.* in the style of or resembling the effects of Rembrandt, esp. in chiaroscuro. WH: 19C. *Rembrandt* Harmensz van Rijn, 1606–69, Dutch painter and etcher + -ESQUE.

remedy *n.* something which cures a disease. *Also v.t.* WH: 12–14C. Old French *remède*, from Latin *remedium* medicine, means of relief, from RE- + *med-*, stem of *mederi* to heal. Cp. MEDICAL.

remember *v.t.* to keep in mind, not to forget. *Also v.i.* WH: 12–14C. Old French *remembrer*, from Late Latin *rememorari* to call to mind, from RE- + *memor* mindful.

remex *n.* any of the quill feathers of a bird's wings. WH: 17C. Latin, from *remus* oar.

remind *v.t.* to put in mind (of). WH: 17C. RE- + MIND.

reminiscence *n.* the act or power of remembering or recalling past knowledge. WH: 16C. Late Latin *reminiscentia*, from Latin *reminisci* to remember, from RE- + base of MIND. See also -ENCE.

remise *v.t.* to surrender, to release or grant back (a right, claim, property etc.). *Also v.i., n.* WH: 15C. Old French, fem. p.p. of *remettre* to put back, to put up.

remiss *a.* careless or lax in the performance of duty or business, heedless, negligent. WH: 14–15C. Latin *remissus*, p.p. of *remittere* REMIT¹.

remission *n.* the act of remitting. WH: 12–14C. Old French *rémission* or Latin *remissio*, *remissionis*, from *remissus*. See REMISS, also -ION.

remit¹ *v.t.* to transmit (cash, payment etc.), esp. by post. *Also v.i.* WH: 14–15C. Latin *remittere* to send back, to slacken, to relax, from RE- + *mittere* to send.

remit² *n.* the extent of responsibility, authority or concern of a person, committee etc. WH: 14–15C. REMIT¹.

remnant *n.* that which is left after a larger part has been separated, used or destroyed. *Also a.* WH: 12–14C. Contr. of obs. *remenant*, from Old French pres.p. of *remenoir*, *remanoir* REMAIN. See also -ANT.

remonstrance *n.* the act of remonstrating. WH: 15C. Old French (Modern French *remontrance*) or Medieval Latin *remonstrantia*, from *remonstrans*, *remonstrantis*, pres.p. of *remonstrare*. See REMONSTRATE, also -ANCE.

remonstrate *v.i.* to make a protest, to argue or object forcibly. *Also v.t.* WH: 16C. Medieval Latin *remonstratus*, p.p. of *remonstrare* to demonstrate, from RE- + Latin *monstrare* to show. See also -ATE³.

remontant *a.* (esp. of a rose) blooming more than once in the season. *Also n.* WH: 19C. French, pres.p. of *remonter* remount. See also -ANT.

remora *n.* any of various spiny-finned fishes of the family Echeneidae having a suctorial disc for attaching larger fish. WH: 16C. Latin delay, hindrance, from RE- + *mora* delay. The fish are so called because they were formerly believed to hinder the progress of ships to which they attached themselves.

remorse *n.* the pain caused by a sense of guilt or bitter regret. WH: 14–15C. Old French *remors* (Modern French *remords*), from Medieval Latin *remorsus*, from Latin, p.p. of *remordere* to vex, to torment, from RE- + *mordere* to bite, to sting.

remote *a.* distant in time or space. WH: 14–15C. Latin *remotus*, p.p. of *removere* REMOVE.

rémoulade *n.* a sauce, often made with mayonnaise, flavoured with herbs, mustard and capers and served with fish, cold meat, salads etc. WH: 19C. French, from Italian *remolata*, of unknown orig. According to some, the word is from Picardy dialect *ramolas* horseradish, from Latin *armoracea*.

remove *v.t.* to move or take from a place or position. *Also v.i., n.* WH: 12–14C. Old French *removeir* (Modern French *remouvoir*), from Latin *removere*. See RE-, MOVE.

remunerate *v.t.* to reward, to recompense, to pay for a service etc. WH: 16C. Latin *remuneratus*, p.p. of *remunerari*, from RE- + *munerari*, from *munus*, *muneris* gift. See also -ATE³.

Renaissance *n.* the revival of art and letters in the 14th–16th cents. WH: 19C. French, from *re-* RE- + *naissance* birth, from Latin *nascentia*, from *nasci* to be born, or from French *naître*, *naiss-* to be born. See also -ANCE. Cp. *renascence* (RENASCENT).

renal *a.* of or relating to the kidneys. WH: 17C. French *rénal*, from Late Latin *renalis*, from Latin *renes* REINS. See also -AL¹.

renascent *a.* coming into being again, reborn, renewed. WH: 18C. Latin *renascens*, *renascentis*, pres.p. of *renasci*, from RE- + *nasci* to be born. See also -ENT.

rencounter *n.* an unexpected meeting or encounter. *Also v.t., v.i.* WH: early 20C. Old French *rencontre*, from *rencontrer*, from RE- + *encontrer*. See ENCOUNTER.

rend *v.t.* to tear, pull or wrench (off, away, apart, asunder etc.). *Also v.i.* WH: pre-1200. Old English *rendan*, from Germanic. Rel. to RIND.

render *v.t.* to make, to cause to be. *Also n.* WH: 14–15C. Anglo-French, from Old French *rendre*, from alt. of Latin *reddere* to give back, from RE- + *dare* to give. The French infinitive ending has (unusually) been retained in English (perhaps for distinction from REND) as with TENDER[2].

rendezvous *n.* a place agreed upon for meeting. *Also v.i.* WH: 16C. French, use as n. of *rendez-vous* present yourselves, from *rendre*. See RENDER. The earliest sense is military.

rendzina *n.* a dark rich soil containing lime, found in grassy regions overlying chalk. WH: early 20C. Russian, from Polish *rędzina*.

renegade *n.* a deserter. *Also a., v.i.* WH: 15C. Anglicized form of Spanish *renegado*, from Medieval Latin *renegatus*, use as n. of p.p. of *renegare*. See RENEGE, also -ADO.

renege *v.i.* to go back (on one's promise, commitments etc.). *Also v.t.* WH: 16C. Medieval Latin *renegare*, from RE- + *negare* to deny, NEGATE.

renew *v.t.* to make new again or as good as new. *Also v.i.* WH: 14–15C. RE- + NEW, based on earlier obs. *renovel*, from Old French *renoveler* (Modern French *renouveler*), from re- RE- + Latin *novellus* young, new, from *novus* new. See NOVEL.

reni- *comb. form* of or relating to the kidneys. WH: Latin *ren* kidney + -i-.

reniform *a.* kidney-shaped. WH: 18C. RENI- + -FORM.

renin *n.* a proteolytic enzyme secreted by the kidneys, which helps to maintain blood pressure. WH: 19C. Latin *ren* kidney + -IN[1].

renitence *n.* resistance, esp. of a body to pressure. WH: 17C. French *rénitence*, from *rénitent*, from Latin *renitens, renitentis*, pres.p. of *reniti* to struggle against, to resist. See -ENCE.

rennet[1] *n.* curdled milk containing rennin, obtained from the stomach of an unweaned calf etc. or an aqueous infusion of the stomach membrane of the calf, used to coagulate milk. WH: 14–15C. Prob. dial. representation of unrecorded Old English form rel. to RUN.

rennet[2] *n.* any of several varieties of apple, esp. the pippin. WH: 16C. French *reinette, rainette*, ? from *raine* tree frog (from Latin *rana* frog). The fruit is apparently so called from the spots in certain varieties.

renounce *v.t.* to surrender or give up (a claim, right etc.), esp. by formal declaration. *Also v.i., n.* WH: 14–15C. Old French *renoncer*, from Latin *renuntiare* to announce, to proclaim, to protest against, from RE- + *nuntiare* to bring news.

renovate *v.t.* to restore to a state of soundness or good condition, to repair. WH: 16C. Latin *renovatus*, p.p. of *renovare*, from RE- + *novare* to make new, from *novus* new. See also -ATE[3].

renown *n.* exalted reputation, fame. *Also v.t.* WH: 12–14C. Old French *renon* (Modern French *renom*), from *renomer* to make famous, from re- RE- + *nomer* to name, from Latin *nominare* NOMINATE.

rent[1] *n.* a sum of money payable periodically for the use of land, buildings etc. *Also v.t., v.i.* WH: 12–14C. Old French RENTE, from base represented also by RENDER.

rent[2] *n.* a tear, slit or breach, an opening made by or as if by rending or tearing asunder. WH: 16C. From obs. *rent* to tear, var. of REND, based on its past tense and p.p. *rent*.

rente *n.* annual income or revenue from capital investment. WH: 19C. French, from Old French, from Popular Latin *rendita*, fem. p.p. (used as n.) of Latin *rendere* RENDER. Cp. RENT[1].

renter *v.t.* to sew together the edges of two pieces of cloth without doubling them, so that the seam is scarcely visible; to fine-draw. WH: 18C. French *rentrer, rentraire*, from RE- + Old French *entraire*, from Latin *intrahere* to draw in, from IN-[1] + *trahere* to draw.

renunciation *n.* the act of renouncing. WH: 14–15C. Old French *renonciation* or Late Latin *renuntiatio, renuntiationis*, from Latin *renuntiatus*, p.p. of *renuntiare* to announce. See RENOUNCE, also -ATION.

renvoi *n.* referral of a legal question or dispute to another jurisdiction. WH: 19C. French, from *envoyer* to send back, from re- RE- + *envoyer* to send. See ENVOY.

rep[1] *n.* repertory. WH: early 20C. Abbr. of REPERTORY.

rep[2] *n.* a representative, esp. a sales representative. *Also v.i.* WH: 19C. Abbr. of *representative* (REPRESENT).

rep[3] *n.* a textile fabric of wool, cotton or silk, with a finely-corded surface. WH: 19C. French *reps*, of unknown orig. According to some, the word is from a French variant of the plural of English RIB[1].

rep[4] *n.* reputation. WH: 18C. Abbr. of REPUTATION.

repair[1] *v.t.* to restore to a sound state after dilapidation or wear. *Also n.* WH: 14–15C. Old French *reparer*, from Latin *reparare*, from RE- + *parare* to make ready, to put in order.

repair[2] *v.i.* to go, to betake oneself, to resort (to). *Also n.* WH: 12–14C. Old French *repairer* (Modern French *repérer*), from Late Latin *repatriare* to return to one's country. See REPATRIATE.

repand *a.* having an uneven, wavy or sinuous margin. WH: 18C. Latin *repandus* bent backwards, from RE- + *pandus* bent.

reparation *n.* the act of making amends. WH: 14–15C. Old French *réparation*, from Late Latin *reparatio, reparationis*, from Latin *reparatus*, p.p. of *reparare*. See REPAIR[1], also -ATION.

repartee *n.* sharp, witty remarks or retorts or conversation consisting of these. *Also v.i.* WH: 17C. Old French *repartie*, fem. p.p. (used as n.) of *repartir* to set out again, to reply readily, from re- RE- + *partir* PART.

repast *n.* a meal. *Also v.i.* WH: 14–15C. Old French (Modern French *repas*), from *repaistre* (Modern French *repaître*), from Late Latin *repascere*, from RE- + Latin *pascere* to feed. Cp. PASTURE.

repat *n.* a repatriate. WH: mid-20C. Abbr. of REPATRIATE.

repatriate *v.t.* to restore (someone) to their country. *Also v.i., n.* WH: 17C. Late Latin *repatriatus*, p.p. of *repatriare* to go back home, from RE- + Latin *patria* native land. See also -ATE[3].

repay *v.t.* to pay back, to refund. *Also v.i.* WH: 14–15C. Old French *repaier*. See RE-, PAY[1].

repeal *v.t.* to revoke, to annul (a law etc.). *Also n.* WH: 14–15C. Old French *rapeler* (Modern French *rappeler*), from re- RE- + *appeler* APPEAL.

repeat *v.t.* to do, make or say over again. *Also v.i., n.* WH: 14–15C. Old French *répéter*, from Latin *repetere*, from RE- + *petere* to attack, to make for, to seek.

repechage *n.* a heat, esp. in rowing or fencing, where contestants beaten in earlier rounds get another chance to qualify for the final. WH: early 20C. French *repêchage*, from *repêcher*, lit. to fish out, to rescue.

repel *v.t.* to drive or force back. WH: 14–15C. Latin *repellere*, from RE- + *pellere* to drive.

repent[1] *v.i.* to feel sorrow for something done or left undone, esp. to feel such sorrow for sin as leads to amendment. *Also v.t.* WH: 12–14C. Old French *repentir*, from re- RE- + *pentir*, from alt. of Latin *paenitere*. See PENITENT.

repent[2] *a.* (of a plant) creeping, esp. along the ground, and rooting. WH: 17C. Latin *repens, repentis*, pres.p. of *repere* to creep. See also -ENT.

repercussion *n.* an effect or consequence of an act, action or event, esp. one that is indirect and wide-ranging. WH: 14–15C. Old French *répercussion* or Latin *repercussio, repercussionis*, from *repercussus*, p.p. of *repercutere*, from RE- + *percutere* PERCUSS. See also -ION. The original sense (to the 18C) was medical: the repression of an infection or eruption. The current sense dates only from the early 20C.

repertoire *n.* a stock of plays, musical pieces, songs etc., that a person, company etc. is ready to perform. WH: 19C. French *répertoire*, from Late Latin *repertorium*. See REPERTORY.

repertory *n.* a repertoire. WH: 16C. Late Latin *repertorium* inventory, from Latin *repertus*, p.p. of *reperire* to discover. See also -ORY[1].

repetend *n.* something repeated, a recurring word or phrase. WH: 18C. Latin *repetendum*, ger. of *repetere* REPEAT. See also -END.

répétiteur *n.* a person who coaches opera singers. WH: mid-20C. French tutor, coach, from Latin *repetitus*, p.p. of *repetere* REPEAT + -*eur* -OR.

repetition *n.* the act of repeating, reiteration. WH: 14–15C. Old French *répétition* or Latin *repetitio, repetitionis*, from *repetitus*, p.p. of *repetere* REPEAT. See also -ION.

repine *v.i.* to fret, to be discontented (at). *Also n.* WH: 14–15C. RE- + PINE[2], based on REPENT[1].

repique *n.* in piquet, the scoring of 30 points on cards alone before playing. *Also v.t., v.i.* WH: 17C. French *repic*, from Italian *ripicco*. See RE-, PIQUE[2].

replace *v.t.* to put back again in place. WH: 16C. RE- + PLACE, prob. based on French *remplacer*.

replenish *v.t.* to fill up again. *Also v.i.* WH: 14–15C. Old French *replenir*, *repleniss-*, from *re-* RE- + *plenir* to fill, from Latin *plenus* full. See also -ISH[2].

replete *a.* abundantly supplied or stocked (with). WH: 14–15C. Old French *replet* or Latin *repletus*, p.p. of *replere*, from RE- + *plere* to fill.

replevy *v.t.* to recover possession of (distrained goods) upon giving security to submit the matter to a court and to surrender the goods if required. *Also n.* WH: 16C. Old French *replevir* to recover, from *re-* RE- + *plevir*, appar. from Germanic base also of PLEDGE.

replica *n.* a duplicate of a picture, sculpture etc. by the artist who executed the original. WH: 18C. Italian, from Latin *replicare*. See REPLICATE[1].

replicate[1] *v.t.* to repeat (e.g. an experiment) exactly. *Also v.i.* WH: 14–15C. Latin *replicatus*, p.p. of *replicare* to unfold, from RE- + *plicare* to fold. See also -ATE[3]. Cp. PLY[1], REPLY.

replicate[2] *a.* folded back on itself. *Also n.* WH: 19C. Latin *replicatus*, p.p. of *replicare*. See REPLICATE[1], also -ATE[2].

replum *n.* the central process or placenta remaining after the valves of a dehiscent fruit have fallen away. WH: 19C. Latin, appar. a covering moulding. The Latin word was originally taken to mean door frame.

reply *v.i.* to answer, to respond. *Also v.t., n.* WH: 14–15C. Old French *replier*, from Latin *replicare*. See REPLICATE[1].

report *v.t.* to give an account of. *Also v.i., n.* WH: 14–15C. Old French *reporter*, from Latin *reportare* to carry back, to bear away, from RE- + *portare* to carry. The original sense (to the 17C) was to commit (oneself) to a person or thing for support. The sense as noun, noise of an explosion, dates from the 16C and relates to the re-echoing of the sound.

repose[1] *n.* cessation of activity, excitement etc. *Also v.i., v.t.* WH: 14–15C. REPOSE[2] or from Old French *repos*, from *reposer* REPOSE[2].

repose[2] *v.t.* to place, to put (confidence etc. in). WH: 14–15C. Old French *reposer*, earlier *repauser*, from Late Latin *repausare*, from RE- + Latin *pausare* PAUSE.

reposit *v.t.* to store, to deposit, as in a place of safety. WH: 17C. Latin *repositus*, p.p. of *reponere* to replace, to restore, to store up, from RE- + *ponere* to place.

repository *n.* a place or receptacle in which things are deposited for safety or preservation. WH: 15C. Obs. French *repositoire* or Latin *repositorium*, from *repositus*. See REPOSIT, also -ORY[1].

repoussé *a.* (of ornamental metalwork) formed in relief by hammering from behind. *Also n.* WH: 19C. French, p.p. of *repousser*, from *re-* RE- + *pousser* PUSH.

reprehend *v.t.* to find fault with. WH: 12–14C. Latin *reprehendere*, from RE- + *prehendere* to seize.

represent *v.t.* to stand for, to correspond to. WH: 14–15C. Old French *représenter* or Latin *repraesentare*, from RE- + *praesentare* PRESENT[1].

repress *v.t.* to keep under restraint. WH: 12–14C. Latin *repressus*, p.p. of *reprimere* to repress. See RE-. Cp. PRESS[1].

reprieve *v.t.* to suspend the execution of (someone) for a time. *Also n.* WH: 15C. Old French *repris*, p.p. of *reprendre*. See REPRISE. The changed spelling may have arisen by association with ACHIEVE. The original sense (to the 16C) was to send back to prison, to remand. The current sense, essentially the opposite, dates from the 16C.

reprimand[1] *n.* a severe reproof, a rebuke. WH: 17C. French *réprimande*, from Spanish *reprimenda*, from Latin *reprimenda*, neut. pl. of ger. of *reprimere* REPRESS.

reprimand[2] *v.t.* to reprove severely, to rebuke. WH: 17C. French *réprimander*, from *réprimande*. See REPRIMAND[1].

reprisal *n.* an act of retaliation. WH: 14–15C. Anglo-French *reprisaille*, from Medieval Latin *reprisalia*, *represalia*, neut. pl. contr. of *repraehensalia*, *repraehensaliae*, from Latin *repraehensus*, p.p. of *repraehendere*, from RE- + *praehendere* to take. See also -AL[1].

reprise *n.* a repeated phrase, theme etc., a refrain. *Also v.t.* WH: 14–15C. Old French, fem. p.p. (used as n.) of *reprendre*, from *re-* RE- + *prendre* to take. The original sense was amount taken back, loss, expense. The musical sense dates from the 18C.

repro *n.* a reproduction, a copy. WH: mid-20C. Abbr. of *reproduction* (REPRODUCE).

reproach *v.t.* to censure, to upbraid. *Also n.* WH: 12–14C. Old French *reprochier* (Modern French *reprocher*), from Popular Latin *repropiare* to bring back near, from RE- + Latin *prope* near.

reprobate *n.* a wicked, depraved wretch. *Also a., v.t.* WH: 15C. Late Latin *reprobatus*, p.p. of Latin *reprobare* to disapprove, from RE- + *probare* to approve. See PROVE, also -ATE[1]. The earliest sense was a person rejected by God: 'But I trust that ye shall know that we are not reprobates' (II Cor. xiii.6).

reproduce *v.t.* to copy. *Also v.i.* WH: 17C. RE- + PRODUCE[1], based on French *reproduire*. The sense to produce offspring arose in the 19C, as did the sense to make an exact copy.

reprography *n.* the art or process of reproducing printed matter e.g. by photocopying. WH: mid-20C. German *Reprographie*, from *Reproduktion* reproduction (REPRODUCE) + *Photographie* photography (PHOTOGRAPH).

reproof *n.* censure, blame, reprehension. WH: 12–14C. Old French *reprove*, from *reprover* (Modern French *réprouver*) reprove, from Latin *reprobare*. See REPROBATE.

reptant *a.* creeping. WH: 17C. Latin *reptans*, *reptantis*, pres.p. of *reptare* to creep. See -ANT.

reptile *n.* a crawling animal; a member of the Reptilia, a class of animals comprising the snakes, lizards, turtles, crocodiles etc. *Also a.* WH: 14–15C. Old French, or from Late Latin, neut. of *reptilis*, p.p. of *repere* to creep, to crawl. See also -IL.

republic *n.* a state or a form of political constitution in which the supreme power is vested in the people or their elected representatives; a commonwealth. WH: 16C. French *république*, from Latin *respublica*, from *res* affair, thing + fem. of *publicus* PUBLIC.

repudiate *v.t.* to refuse to acknowledge, to disown. *Also v.i.* WH: 15C. Orig. p.p., from Latin *repudiatus*, p.p. of *repudiare*, from *repudium* divorce. See also -ATE[2], -ATE[3]. The original specific sense was (of a husband) to divorce (one's wife). The more general sense emerged in the 16C.

†repugn *v.i.* to oppose, to resist, to strive (against). *Also v.t.* WH: 14–15C. Latin *repugnare*, from RE- + *pugnare* to fight.

repugnance *n.* antipathy, dislike, distaste, aversion. WH: 14–15C. Old French *répugnance* or Latin *repugnantia*, from *repugnans*, *repugnantis*, pres.p. of *repugnare*. See REPUGN, also -ANCE.

repulse *v.t.* to beat or drive back. *Also n.* WH: 14–15C. Latin *repulsus*, p.p. of *repellere* REPEL.

reputable *a.* being of good repute, respectable, creditable. WH: 17C. Obs. French *reputable* or Medieval Latin *reputabilis*. See REPUTE, also -ABLE.

reputation *n.* the estimation in which one is generally held. WH: 12–14C. Latin *reputatio*, *reputationis* computation, consideration, from *reputatus*, p.p. of *reputare*. See REPUTE, also -ATION.

repute *n.* character attributed by public report; reputation, fame. *Also v.t.* WH: 14–15C. Old French *réputer* or Latin *reputare*, from RE- + *putare* to reckon.

request *n.* the act of asking for something to be granted or done. *Also v.t.* WH: 12–14C. Old French *requeste* (Modern French *requête*), from use as n. of Latin *requisita*, fem. p.p. of *requirere* REQUIRE.

requiem *n.* in the Roman Catholic Church, a mass for the repose of the soul of a dead person. *Also a.* WH: 12–14C. Latin, acc. of *requies* rest, first word of the introit in the Mass for the dead in the Latin liturgy. The introit begins: *Requiem aeternam dona eis, Domine: et lux perpetua lucent eis* Give them eternal rest, O Lord: and let light perpetual shine upon them.

requiem shark *n.* any shark of the family Carcharhinidae, including tiger sharks and whaler sharks. WH: 17C. French *requiem*, obs. var. of *requin* shark, influ. by REQUIEM.

requiescat *n.* a wish or prayer for the repose of the dead. WH: 19C. Latin, from *requiescat in pace* may he rest in peace. Cp. RIP.

require *v.t.* to have need of. *Also v.i.* WH: 14–15C. Old French *requere*, *requer-*, *requier-* (Modern French *requérir*), from Latin *requirere*, from RE- + *quaerere* to seek, to ask. The original sense (to the 17C) was to ask a person a question, to inquire.

requisite *a.* necessary for completion etc. *Also n.* WH: 14–15C. Latin *requisitus*, p.p. of *requirere* to search for, to be necessary. See REQUIRE, also -ITE[2].

requisition *n.* an authoritative order for the supply of provisions etc. *Also v.t.* WH: 14–15C. Old French *réquisition* or Latin *requisitio, requisitionis*, from *requisitus*. See REQUISITE, also -ION.

requite *v.t.* to make return for. WH: 16C. RE- + *quite*, var. of QUIT.

reredos *n.* the ornamental screen at the back of an altar. WH: 14–15C. Old French *areredos*, from *arere* behind (see ARREARS) + *dos* back.

res *n.* a thing, property. WH: 17C. Latin thing.

rescind *v.t.* to annul, to cancel, to withdraw. WH: 16C. Latin *rescindere*, from RE- + *scindere* to split, to divide.

rescript *n.* the answer or decision of a Roman emperor to a question or appeal, esp. on a point of jurisprudence. WH: 14–15C. Latin *rescriptum*, neut. p.p. of *rescribere*, from RE- + *scribere* to write.

rescue *v.t.* to save from danger or injury. *Also n.* WH: 12–14C. Old French *rescoure*, from RE- + Latin *excutere* to shake out, to discard, from EX- + *quatere* to shake.

research *n.* a course of critical investigation. *Also a., v.t., v.i.* WH: 16C. Obs. French *recerche* (now *recherche*), from *re-* RE- + *cerche* SEARCH.

resect *v.t.* to excise a section of (an organ or part). WH: 17C. Latin *resectus*, p.p. of *resecare* to cut off, from RE- + *secare* to cut.

reseda *n.* any plant of the genus *Reseda*, containing the mignonette and dyer's weed. *Also a.* WH: 18C. Latin, in classical times taken as imper. of *resedare* to assuage, to allay, with ref. to the plant's supposed curative powers.

resemble *v.t.* to be like, to be similar to; to have features, nature etc., like those of. *Also v.i.* WH: 12–14C. Old French *resembler* (Modern French *ressembler*), from *re-* RE- + *sembler* to seem, from Latin *similare*, from *similis* like.

resent *v.t.* to regard as an injury or insult. *Also v.i.* WH: 16C. Obs. French *resentir* (now *ressentir*), from *re-* RE- + *sentir* to feel. The original sense (to the 18C) was to feel an emotion or sensation. The specific sense to feel injured dates from the 17C.

reserpine *n.* an alkaloid extracted from plants of the *Rauwolfia* genus, used to treat high blood pressure and as a sedative. WH: mid-20C. Modern Latin *Rauwolfia serpentina*, with inserted *e*, + -INE.

reservation *n.* the act of reserving. WH: 14–15C. Old French *réservation* or Late Latin *reservatio, reservationis*, from Latin *reservatus*, p.p. of *reservare*. See RESERVE, also -ATION.

reserve *v.t.* to keep back for future use, enjoyment etc. *Also n.* WH: 12–14C. Old French *réserver*, from Latin *reservare*, from RE- + *servare* to keep, to save.

reservoir *n.* a receptacle of earthwork or masonry for the storage of water in large quantity. *Also v.t.* WH: 17C. French *réservoir*, from *réserver* (RESERVE) + -*oir* -ORY[1].

res gestae *n.pl.* achievements. WH: 17C. Latin things done.

reside *v.i.* to dwell permanently or for a considerable length of time, to have one's home (at). WH: 14–15C. Prob. back-formation from *resident* (RESIDE), from Old French *résident* or Latin *résidens, residentis*, pres.p. of *residere* to remain behind, to rest, from RE- + *sedere* to settle, to sit, later influ. by French *résider* or Latin *residere*.

residue *n.* what is left or remains over, the rest, the remainder. WH: 14–15C. Old French *résidu*, from Latin *residuum*, use as n. of neut. of *residuus* remaining, from *residere* RESIDE.

resign *v.i.* to give up office, to retire (from). *Also v.t.* WH: 14–15C. Old French *résigner*, from Latin *resignare* to unseal, to cancel, to give up, from RE- + *signare* SIGN.

resile *v.i.* to spring back, to rebound, to recoil, to resume the original shape after compression, stretching etc., to show elasticity. WH: 16C. Obs. French *resilir* or Latin *resilire* to leap back, to recoil, from RE- + *salire* to leap.

resilience *n.* elasticity. WH: 17C. Latin *resiliens, resilientis*, pres.p. of *resilire*. See RESILE, also -ENCE.

resin *n.* an amorphous inflammable vegetable substance secreted by plants and usu. obtained by exudation, esp. from the fir and pine.

Also v.t. WH: 14–15C. Latin *resina*, Medieval Latin *rosinum, rosina*, rel. to Greek *rhētinē* resin from a pine. Cp. ROSIN.

resist *v.t.* to strive against, to act in opposition to. *Also v.i., n.* WH: 14–15C. Old French *résister* or Latin *resistere*, from RE- + *sistere* to stop, redupl. of *stare* to stand.

res judicata *n.* an issue that has already been settled in court and cannot be raised again. WH: 17C. Latin thing judged.

resoluble *a.* able to be dissolved, resolved or analysed. WH: 17C. French *résoluble* or Late Latin *resolubilis*, from RE- + *solubilis* SOLUBLE.

resolute *a.* having a fixed purpose, determined. *Also n.* WH: 14–15C. Latin *resolutus*, p.p. of *resolvere* RESOLVE.

resolve *v.t.* to cause (someone) to decide. *Also v.i., n.* WH: 14–15C. Latin *resolvere*, from RE- + *solvere* to loosen, to dissolve. The original sense was to melt, to dissolve, as well as to answer, to solve. The current sense evolved in the 16C.

resonant *a.* (of a sound) prolonged or reinforced by vibration or reverberation. WH: 16C. Old French *résonant* or Latin *resonans, resonantis*, pres.p. of *resonare*. See RESOUND, also -ANT.

resorb *v.t.* to absorb again. WH: 17C. Latin *resorbere*, from RE- + *sorbere* to drink in.

resorcin *n.* a crystalline phenol used as a dyestuff in resins, adhesives and in medicine. WH: 19C. RESIN + ORCIN.

resort *n.* a place frequented by holidaymakers. *Also v.i.* WH: 14–15C. Old French, from *resortir* (Modern French *ressortir*), from *re-* RE- + *sortir* to go out.

resound *v.i.* to ring, to re-echo, to reverberate (with). *Also v.t., n.* WH: 14–15C. RE- + SOUND[1], based on Old French *resoner* or Latin *resonare*, from RE- + *sonare* to sound.

resource *n.* an expedient, a device. *Also v.t.* WH: 17C. French *ressource*, obs. *ressourse*, fem. p.p. (used as n.) of Old French dial. *resourdre* to rise again, to recover, from Latin *resurgere*. See RESURGENT.

respect *n.* esteem, deferential regard. *Also v.t.* WH: 14–15C. Old French, or from Latin *respectus*, from p.p. of *respicere* to look (back) at, to regard, to consider, from RE- + *specere* to look. The original sense was relation, connection, regard (as in *with respect to*). The sense deferential esteem dates from the 16C.

respire *v.i.* to breathe. *Also v.t.* WH: 14–15C. Old French *respirer*, or from Latin *respirare*, from RE- + *spirare* to breathe.

respite *n.* an interval of rest or relief. *Also v.t.* WH: 14–15C. Old French *respit* (Modern French *répit*), from Latin *respectus* RESPECT.

resplendent *a.* shining with brilliant lustre, vividly or gloriously bright. WH: 14–15C. Latin *resplendens, resplendentis*, pres.p. of *resplendere*, from RE- + *splendere* to shine.

respond *v.i.* to answer, to reply. *Also v.t., n.* WH: 16C. Latin *respondere*, from RE- + *spondere* to promise.

response *n.* the act of answering. WH: 12–14C. Old French *respons* (Modern French *répons*) or *response* (Modern French *réponse*), or from Latin *responsum*, from *responsus*, p.p. of *respondere* RESPOND.

responsible *a.* answerable, accountable (to or for). WH: 16C. Obs. French *responsible*, from Latin *responsus*. See RESPONSE, also -IBLE. The original sense was answering (to). The current sense answerable (to) dates from the 16C, and that of involving responsibility from the 19C.

rest[1] *v.i.* to cease from motion or activity. *Also v.t., n.* WH: pre-1200. Old English *ræstan, restan*, from Germanic. Cp. German *Rast* rest.

rest[2] *n.* the remaining part or parts. *Also v.i.* WH: 14–15C. Old French *reste*, from *rester*, from Latin *restare*, from RE- + *stare* to stand. Not rel. to REST[1].

restaurant *n.* a place for refreshment, a public eating house. WH: 19C. French, use as n. of pres.p. of *restaurer* RESTORE. See also -ANT.

rest-harrow *n.* any plant of the genus *Ononis* with a tough woody root. WH: 16C. From dial. *rest* to seize, shortening of ARREST + HARROW[1]. The plant is so called as its tough roots checked the passage of the harrow.

restiform *a.* (of two bundles of fibrous matter connecting the medulla oblongata with the cerebellum) ropelike or cordlike. WH: 19C. Modern Latin *restiformis*, from Latin *restis* cord. See -FORM.

restitution *n.* the act of restoring something taken away or lost. WH: 12–14C. Old French, or from Latin *restitutio, restitutionis,* from *restitutus,* p.p. of *restituere* to restore, from RE- + *statuere* to set up, to establish.

restive *a.* restless, fidgety. WH: 16C. Alt. of obs. *restiff,* from Old French *restif* (Modern French *rétif*), from Latin *restare* REST[2] + *-ive* -IVE. The original sense (to the 19C) was inclined to stay still. The current sense evolved in the 17C. The change of meaning from staying still to being restless relates to the behaviour of a stubborn horse, which may either stop and refuse to go forward or move stubbornly in different directions.

restore *v.t.* to bring back to a former state, to repair. WH: 12–14C. Old French *restorer* (Modern French *restaurer*), from Latin *restaurare,* from RE- + *-staurare* as in *instaurare* to renew.

restrain *v.t.* to hold back, to check. WH: 12–14C. Old French *restreindre, restrein-,* from Latin *restringere* to bind fast, to confine, from RE- + *stringere* to draw tight (see STRAIN[1]).

restrict *v.t.* to confine, to keep within certain bounds. WH: 14–15C. Orig. p.p., from Latin *restrictus,* p.p. of *restringere* RESTRAIN.

result *v.i.* to terminate or end (in). *Also n.* WH: 14–15C. Latin *resultare* to spring back, to reverberate, from RE- + *saltare* to leap.

resume *v.t.* to begin again, to go on with after interruption. *Also v.i.* WH: 14–15C. Old French *résumer* or Latin *resumere,* from RE- + *sumere* to take.

résumé *n.* a summary, a recapitulation, a condensed statement. WH: 19C. French, p.p. of *résumer* RESUME.

resumption *n.* the act of resuming. WH: 14–15C. Old French *résumption* or Late Latin *resumptio, resumptionis,* from Latin *resumptus,* p.p. of *resumere* RESUME. See also -ION.

resupinate *a.* inverted, apparently upside-down. WH: 18C. Latin *resupinatus,* p.p. of *resupinare* to bend back. See RE-, SUPINE, also -ATE[2].

resurgent *a.* rising again, esp. in popularity. *Also n.* WH: 18C. Latin *resurgens, resurgentis,* pres.p. of *resurgere,* from RE- + *surgere* to rise. See also -ENT.

resurrect *v.t.* to bring again into vogue or currency, to revive. *Also v.i.* WH: 18C. Back-formation from *resurrection,* from Old French *résurrection* or Late Latin *resurrectio, resurrectionis,* from Latin *resurrectus,* p.p. of *resurgere.* See RESURGENT, also -ION.

resuscitate *v.t.* to restore from apparent death. *Also v.i.* WH: 16C. Orig. p.p., from Latin *resuscitatus,* p.p. of *resuscitare,* from RE- + *suscitare* to raise, to revive. See also -ATE[3].

ret *v.t.* to steep (flax etc.) to loosen the fibre from the woody portions. *Also v.i.* WH: 14–15C. Rel. to ROT, corr. to Middle Dutch *reeten,* Middle Low German *rōten.*

retable *n.* a shelf, ledge or panelled frame above the back of an altar for supporting ornaments. WH: 19C. French *rétable, retable,* from Spanish *retablo,* from Medieval Latin *retrotabulum,* from Latin RETRO- + *tabula* TABLE.

retail[1] *n.* the sale of commodities in small quantities, as distinct from *wholesale. Also a., adv.* WH: 14–15C. Anglo-French, special use of Old French *retaille* piece cut off, shred, from *retaillier,* from *re-* RE- + *taillier* to cut (cp. TAILOR).

retail[2] *v.t.* to sell in small quantities. *Also v.i.* WH: 14–15C. RETAIL[1].

retain *v.t.* to hold or keep possession of. WH: 14–15C. Anglo-French *retein-,* stem of Old French *retenir,* from Latin *retinere,* from RE- + *tenere* to hold.

retaliate *v.i.* to repay an injury or result. *Also v.t.* WH: 17C. Latin *retaliatus,* p.p. of *retaliare,* from RE- + *talis* of such a kind. See also -ATE[3].

retard[1] *v.t.* to cause to move more slowly. *Also v.i., n.* WH: 15C. Old French *retarder,* from Latin *retardare,* from RE- + *tardus* slow.

retard[2] *n.* a mentally retarded person. WH: 20C. French, from *retarder.* See RETARD[1]. The original sense was retardation, delay. The sense of mentally retarded person arose in the late 20C.

retch *v.i.* to make an effort to vomit. *Also n.* WH: 16C. Var. of REACH[2].

rete *n.* a network of nerves or blood vessels. WH: 14–15C. Latin *rete.*

retention *n.* the act of retaining. WH: 14–15C. Old French, or from Latin *retentio, retentionis,* from *retentus,* p.p. of *retinere.* See RETAIN, also -ION.

retiarius *n.* a Roman gladiator armed with a net and trident. WH: 17C. Latin, from *rete* net + *-arius* -ARY[1].

reticent *a.* reserved in speech. WH: 19C. Latin *reticens, reticentis,* pres.p. of *reticere* to keep silent, from RE- + *tacere* to be silent. See also -ENT.

reticle *n.* a network of fine lines etc., drawn across the focal plane of an optical instrument. WH: 17C. Latin RETICULUM. Cp. RETICULE.

reticular *a.* having the form of a net or network. WH: 16C. Modern Latin *reticularis,* from Latin RETICULUM. See also -AR[1].

reticulate[1] *v.t.* to make, divide into or arrange in a network, to mark with fine, intersecting lines. *Also v.i.* WH: 18C. Back-formation from *reticulated,* from RETICULATE[2] + -ED.

reticulate[2] *a.* formed into or resembling a network. WH: 17C. Latin *reticulatus,* from RETICULUM. See also -ATE[2].

reticule *n.* a lady's handbag. WH: 18C. French *réticule,* from Latin RETICULUM.

reticulum *n.* a netlike or reticulated structure, membrane etc. WH: 17C. Latin, dim. of *rete* net. See also -CULE.

retiform *a.* netlike, reticulated. WH: 17C. Latin *rete* net + *-i-* + -FORM.

retina *n.* a netlike layer of sensitive nerve fibres and cells behind the eyeball in which the optic nerve terminates. WH: 14–15C. Medieval Latin, from Latin *rete* net.

retinaculum *n.* an apparatus by which the wings of insects are interlocked in flight. WH: 18C. Latin, from *retinere* to hold back. See also -CULE.

retinitis *n.* inflammation of the retina. WH: 19C. RETINA + -ITIS.

retinoscopy *n.* examination of the eye using an instrument that throws a shadow on to the retina. WH: 19C. RETINA + -O- + *-scopy* (-SCOPE).

retinue *n.* the group of attendants accompanying a distinguished person. WH: 14–15C. Old French *retenue,* fem. p.p. (used as n.) of *retenir* to restrain.

retire *v.i.* to withdraw, to retreat. *Also v.t., n.* WH: 16C. Old French *retirer,* from *re-* RE- + *tirer* to draw. Cp. WITHDRAW.

retort[1] *n.* the turning of a charge, taunt, attack etc. against the originator or aggressor. *Also v.t., v.i.* WH: 15C. Latin *retortus,* p.p. of *retorquere,* from RE- + *torquere* to twist.

retort[2] *n.* a container with a bulblike receptacle and a long neck bent downwards used for distillation of liquids etc. *Also v.t.* WH: 17C. French *retorte,* from Medieval Latin *retorta,* fem. p.p. (used as n.) of Latin *retorquere.* See RETORT[1]. The container is so called from its curving neck.

retract *v.t.* to take back, to revoke, to acknowledge to be false or wrong. *Also v.i.* WH: 14–15C. Latin *retractus,* p.p. of *retrahere,* from RE- + *trahere* to draw, to pull. The original sense was to draw or pull (a thing) back in. The sense to take back (a statement etc.) dates from the 16C and derives from Old French *rétracter* or Latin *retractare,* from RE- + *tractare,* frequentative of *trahere.*

retreat *v.i.* to move back, esp. before an enemy. *Also v.t., n.* WH: 14–15C. Old French *retraiter,* use as n. of p.p. of *retraire,* from Latin *retrahere* RETRACT. Cp. WITHDRAW.

retrench *v.t.* to cut down, to reduce, to curtail, to diminish. *Also v.t.* WH: 16C. Obs. French *retrencher,* var. of *retrancher,* from *re-* RE- + *trancher* to cut. See TRENCH.

retribution *n.* a suitable return, esp. for evil; a punishment. WH: 14–15C. Ecclesiastical Latin *retributio, retributionis,* from Latin *retributus,* p.p. of *retribuere,* from *re-* RE- + *tribuere* to assign. See TRIBUTE, also -ION.

retrieve *v.t.* (of a dog) to find and bring in (a stick, a ball etc.). *Also v.i., n.* WH: 14–15C. Old French *retrover, retroev-* (Modern French *retrouver*), from *re-* RE- + *trover* (Modern French *trouver*) to find. The earliest sense is (of a dog) to flush partridge a second time, but *retriever* as a breed of dog dates only from the 19C.

retro *n.* an object made in the style of a past era. *Also a.* WH: late 20C. French *rétro,* abbr. of *rétrograde,* influ. by RETRO-. See RETROGRADE.

retro- *comb. form* back, in return. WH: Latin *retro* backwards. See also -O-.

retroact *v.i.* to act backwards or in return; to react. WH: 18C. RETRO- + ACT.

retrocede *v.i.* to move backwards. *Also v.t.* WH: 17C. Latin *retrocedere.* See RETRO-, CEDE.

retrochoir *n.* a part of a cathedral or other large church beyond the high altar. WH: 19C. RETRO- + CHOIR.

retrofit *v.t.* to equip or modify (an aircraft, car etc.) with new parts or safety equipment after manufacture. WH: mid-20C. RETRO- + FIT[1].

retroflected *a.* turned or curved backward. WH: 18C. Latin *retroflectere* to bend back, from RETRO- + *flectere* to bend, or from *retroflexus*, p.p. of *retroflectere*. See also -ED.

retrofract *a.* bent back so as to look as if broken. WH: 18C. Modern Latin *retrofractus*. See RETRO-, REFRACT, also -ED.

retrograde *a.* going, moving, bending or directed backwards. *Also n., v.i., v.t.* WH: 14–15C. Latin *retrogradus*, from RETRO- + *gradus* step. See GRADE.

retrogress *v.i.* to go backward, to retrograde. WH: 19C. RETRO- + -*gress*, based on PROGRESS[2].

retroject *v.t.* to throw backwards, as distinct from *project*. WH: 19C. RETRO- + -*ject*, based on PROJECT[2].

retromingent *a.* discharging the urine backwards. *Also n.* WH: 17C. RETRO- + Latin *mingens*, *mingentis*, pres.p. of *mingere* to urinate.

retropulsion *n.* a symptom of locomotory disease in which the patient has a tendency to walk backwards. WH: 18C. RETRO- + -*pulsion*, based on PROPULSION.

retro-rocket *n.* a small rocket on a spacecraft, satellite etc. which produces thrust in the opposite direction to flight for deceleration or manoeuvring. WH: mid-20C. RETRO- + ROCKET[1].

retrorse *a.* turned or bent backwards, reverted. WH: 19C. Latin *retrorsus*, contr. of *retroversus*, from RETRO- + *versus* turned.

retrospect *n.* a looking back on things past. *Also v.i., v.t.* WH: 17C. RETRO- + -*spect*, based on PROSPECT[1].

retrosternal *a.* behind the breastbone. WH: 19C. RETRO- + Latin STERNUM + -AL[1].

retroussé *a.* (of the nose) turned up at the end. WH: 19C. French, p.p. of *retrousser* to turn up, from *re*- RE- + *trousser* TRUSS.

retrovert *v.t.* to turn back (esp. of the womb). WH: 17C. Late Latin *retrovertere*, from Latin RETRO- + *vertere* to turn.

retrovirus *n.* any of a group of viruses which use RNA to synthesize DNA; many cause cancer in animals and one is the cause of Aids in humans. WH: late 20C. Modern Latin, from *reverse transcriptase* + -O- + VIRUS. The virus is so called because it contains an enzyme (reverse transcriptase) that uses RNA instead of DNA to encode genetic information, thus reversing the usual pattern of encoding. (The first part of the word can also be taken as RETRO-.)

retsina *n.* a resin-flavoured white wine from Greece. WH: early 20C. Modern Greek, from *retsini*, from Greek *rētinē* pine resin.

return *v.i.* to come or go back, esp. to the same place or state. *Also v.t., n.* WH: 12–14C. Old French *retorner* (Modern French *retourner*), from Latin RE- + *tornare* TURN.

retuse *a.* having a round end with a depression in the centre. WH: 18C. Latin *retusus*, p.p. of *retundere*, from RE- + *tundere* to beat.

reunion *n.* the act of reuniting. WH: 17C. French *réunion*, from *réunir* to unite, or from Anglo-Latin *reunio, reunionis*, from *reunire*, from Latin RE- + *unire* UNITE.

rev *n.* a revolution in an engine. *Also v.t., v.i.* WH: early 20C. Abbr. of REVOLUTION.

revalenta *n.* lentil meal. WH: 19C. Arbitrary alt. of *ervalenta*, from *Ervum lens*, Linnaean name of the lentil, from Latin *ervum* bitter vetch + *lens, lentis* LENTIL.

revanche *n.* a policy directed towards restoring lost territory or possessions. WH: 19C. French, earlier *revenche*, from *revencher*. See REVENGE.

reveal[1] *v.t.* to allow to appear. *Also n.* WH: 14–15C. Old French *révéler* or Latin *revelare*, from RE- + *velum* VEIL.

reveal[2] *n.* the depth of a wall as revealed in the side of an aperture, doorway or window. WH: 17C. From obs. *revail* to lower, to bring down, from Old French *revaler*, from *re*- RE- + *avaler* to sink, to drop (from *à val* at the bottom, from Latin *ad vallem*), later alt. by assoc. with REVEAL[1]. Cp. VAIL[1].

reveille *n.* a morning signal by drum or bugle to awaken soldiers or sailors. WH: 17C. French *réveillez*, imper. pl. of *réveiller* to awaken, from *ré*- RE- + *veiller*, from Latin *vigilare* to keep watch.

revel *v.i.* to make merry. *Also v.t., n.* WH: 14–15C. Old French *reveler*, from Latin *rebellare* REBEL[2].

revelation *n.* the act of revealing, a disclosing of knowledge. WH: 12–14C. Old French *révélation* or Ecclesiastical Latin *revelatio, revelationis*, from Latin *revelatus*, p.p. of *revelare* REVEAL[1]. See also -ATION.

revenant *n.* a person who returns from the grave or from exile, esp. a ghost. WH: 19C. French, pres.p. of *revenir* to return. See REVENUE, also -ANT.

revendication *n.* a formal claim for the surrender of rights, esp. to territory. WH: 18C. French, from *revendiquer* to claim back, from *re*- RE- + *vendiquer*, from Latin *vindicare*. See VINDICATE, also -ATION.

revenge *n.* retaliation or spiteful return for an injury. *Also v.t., v.i.* WH: 14–15C. Old French *revenger, revencher* (Modern French *revancher*), from Late Latin *revendicare*, from Latin RE- + *vindicare*. See VINDICATE.

revenue *n.* income, esp. of a considerable amount. WH: 14–15C. Old French *revenu*, p.p. (used as n.) of *revenir*, from Latin *revenire*, from RE- + *venire* to come. The sense government income dates from the 17C.

reverb *n.* an electronic device which creates an artificial echo in recorded music. WH: mid-20C. Abbr. of *reverberation* (REVERBERATE).

reverberate *v.i.* (of sound, light or heat) to be driven back or to be reflected, to resound, to re-echo. *Also v.t.* WH: 15C. Latin *reverberatus*, p.p. of *reverberare*, from RE- + *verberare* to strike, to beat, from *verbera* rods, scourge. See also -ATE[3].

revere *v.t.* to regard with awe mingled with affection. WH: 17C. French *révérer* or Latin *revereri*, from RE- + *vereri* to be in awe, to fear.

reverie *n.* listless musing, a daydream, a loose or irregular train of thought. WH: 12–14C. Old French *reverie* rejoicing, revelry, from *rever* to be delirious (Modern French *rêver* to dream), of unknown orig. The original sense (to the 16C) was joy, delight, revelry. The current sense daydream dates from the 17C and derives from French *resverie* (now *rêverie*), from Old French *reverie*. See also -ERY.

revers *n.* a part of a coat, esp. a lapel, turned back so as to show the lining. WH: 19C. French, from Latin *reversus*. See REVERSE.

reverse *v.t.* to turn in the contrary direction. *Also v.i., a., n.* WH: 12–14C. Old French *reverser* (Modern French *renverser*), from Late Latin *reversare*, from Latin *reversus*, p.p. of *revertere* REVERT.

reversi *n.* a game played by two people on a draughtboard with pieces differently coloured above and below, which may be reversed. WH: 19C. French, alt., based on REVERS, of earlier *reversion*, from Italian *rovescina*, from *rovesciare* to reverse.

reverso *n.* the left-hand page of an open book, usu. even-numbered; the verso. WH: 19C. RE- + VERSO.

revert *v.i.* to go back, to fall back, to return (to a previous condition, habits, type etc., esp. to a wild state). *Also v.t., n.* WH: 12–14C. Old French *revertir* or Latin *revertere*, from RE- + *vertere* to turn.

revet *v.t.* to face (a wall, scarp, parapet etc.) with masonry. WH: 19C. French *revêtir*, from Old French *revestir*, from Late Latin *revestire*, from Latin RE- + *vestire* to clothe.

review *n.* an examination, esp. by people in authority. *Also v.t., v.i.* WH: 14–15C. Obs. French *revenue* (now *revue*), from *revoir*, from RE- + *voir*. See VIEW.

revile *v.t.* to abuse, to vilify. *Also v.i., n.* WH: 12–14C. Old French *reviler*, from *re*- RE- + *vil* VILE.

revise *v.t.* to re-examine for correction or emendation. *Also v.i., n.* WH: 16C. Old French *réviser* or Latin *revisere*, from RE- + *visere* to examine, freq. of *videre* to see. The original sense (to the 17C) was to look again at, to look repeatedly at. The current sense dates from the 17C.

revive *v.i.* to return to life or consciousness. *Also v.t.* WH: 14–15C. Old French *revivre* or Late Latin *revivere*, from Latin RE- + *vivere* to live.

reviviscent *a.* recovering life and strength, reviving. WH: 18C. Latin *reviviscens, reviviscentis*, pres.p. of *reviviscere* to begin to revive, from *revivere* REVIVE.

revoke *v.t.* to annul, to cancel (a law etc.). *Also v.i., n.* WH: 14–15C. Old French *révoquer* or Latin *revocare*, from RE- + *vocare* to call.

revolt *v.i.* to rise in rebellion. *Also v.t., n.* WH: 16C. French (*se*) *révolter*, from Italian *rivoltare*, from Popular Latin *revolvitare*, freq. of Latin *revolvere* REVOLVE.

revolute *a.* (of a leaf) rolled backwards from the edge. WH: 14–15C. Latin *revolutus*, p.p. of *revolvere* REVOLVE.

revolution *n.* a fundamental change in government, esp. by the forcible overthrow of the existing system. WH: 14–15C. Old French *révolution* or Late Latin *revolutio, revolutionis*, from Latin *revolutus*, p.p. of *revolvere* REVOLVE. See also -ION. The original sense was astronomical, relating to the orbiting of one celestial object by another. The political sense of the word evolved in the 17C.

revolve *v.i.* to turn round. *Also v.t.* WH: 14–15C. Latin *revolvere*, from RE- + *volvere* to roll, to turn. The *revolver* was so called in 1835 by its inventor, Samuel Colt (COLT®), with reference to its cartridge chambers, which revolve in succession when the pistol is fired.

revue *n.* a light entertainment with songs, dances etc., representing topical characters, events, fashions etc. WH: 19C. French REVIEW.

revulsion *n.* a strong feeling of disgust. WH: 16C. French *révulsion* or Latin *revulsio, revulsionis*, from *revulsus*, p.p. of *revellere*, from RE- + *vellere* to pull. See also -ION.

reward *n.* something which is given in return usu. for good done or received. *Also v.t.* WH: 12–14C. Anglo-French, from Old French *reguard, regard* REGARD.

rewarewa *n.* a tall tree, *Knightia excelsa*, of New Zealand, having red flowers. WH: 19C. Maori, from *rewa* to float.

Rex *n.* a reigning king (the official title used by a king, esp. on documents, coins etc.). WH: 17C. Latin king. Cp. REGINA.

Rexine® *n.* a kind of artificial leather used for bookbinding etc. WH: early 20C. Orig. uncertain. ? From Latin REX + -INE.

Reynard *n.* a proper name for a fox (esp. in stories). WH: 14–15C. Old French *renard*, the fox in the 12C beast epic *Roman de Renart*, influ. by Middle Dutch name *Reynaerd*. The current French word for a fox derives from the proper name. The original word was *goupil*, from Popular Latin *vulpiculus*, dim. of Latin *vulpes* fox. Cp. VULPINE.

Reynolds number *n.* a number which indicates the degree of turbulence of flow of a fluid in a system. WH: early 20C. Osborne *Reynolds*, 1842–1912, Irish engineer and physicist.

rhabdomancy *n.* divination by a rod, esp. the discovery of minerals, underground streams etc. with a divining rod. WH: 17C. Greek *rhabdomanteia*, from *rhabdos* rod + -O- + *manteia* -MANCY.

Rhadamanthine *a.* rigorously just and severe. WH: 17C. Latin *Rhadamanthus*, from Greek *Rhadamanthos*, in Greek mythology a son of Zeus and Europa and a judge in the underworld + -INE.

Rhaetian *n.* Rhaeto-Romance. *Also a.* WH: 16C. *Rhaetia*, a Roman province in what is now SE Switzerland, N Austria and NW Italy + -IAN.

rhamphoid *a.* beak-shaped. WH: 19C. Greek *rhamphos* beak + -OID.

rhapontic *n.* a species of rhubarb, *Rheum rhaponticum*. WH: 16C. Modern Latin *rha Ponticum* Pontic rhubarb, from Late Latin *rha* rhubarb (? from *Rha*, ancient name of the Volga) + neut. of Latin *Ponticus* PONTIC.

rhapsody *n.* a high-flown, enthusiastic composition or utterance. WH: 16C. Latin *rhapsodia*, from Greek *rhapsōidia*, from *rhapsōidos*, from *rhaptein* to stitch + *ōidē* song, ODE. See also -Y². Greek *rhapsōidos* literally means song stitcher, as the term for an itinerant minstrel who recited epic poetry, 'stitching together' extracts from memory and elements that he improvised.

rhatany *n.* a Peruvian shrub, *Krameria triandra*, or its root, from which an extract is obtained for use in medicine and for adulterating port wine. WH: 19C. Modern Latin *rhatania*, from Portuguese *ratânia*, Spanish *ratania*, prob. from Quechua *ratá[n]ya*.

rhea¹ *n.* any flightless bird of the family Rheidae of S America, smaller than ostriches and with three toes. WH: 19C. Modern Latin, use as a genus name of Latin and Greek *Rhea*, the mother of Zeus (Jupiter) in classical mythology.

rhea² *n.* the ramie plant. WH: 19C. Assamese *rihā*.

rhebok *n.* a small antelope of southern Africa, *Pelea capreolus*, having a long neck and short, straight horns. WH: 18C. Dutch *reebok* roebuck (ROE²).

rhematic *a.* of or relating to the formation of words, esp. verbs. WH: 19C. Greek *rhēmatikos*, from *rhēma, rhēmatos* word, verb. See also -IC.

Rhemish *a.* of or relating to Rheims (applied esp. to an English translation of the New Testament by Roman Catholic students in 1582). WH: 16C. *Rhemes*, former English spelling of *Rheims* (French *Reims*), a city in NE France + -ISH¹.

Rhenish *a.* of or relating to the Rhine or the Rhineland. *Also n.* WH: 14–15C. Old French *rinois, rainois*, from Medieval Latin alt. of Latin *Rhenanus*, from *Rhenus* Rhine (German *Rhein*), a river of W Europe flowing mainly through Germany. See also -ISH¹.

rhenium *n.* a metallic element, at. no. 75, chem. symbol Re, occurring in certain platinum and molybdenum ores. WH: early 20C. Latin *Rhenus* Rhine (RHENISH) + -IUM. The name of the element was coined by Walter and Ida Noddack and Otto Carl Berg, the German chemists who discovered it in 1925.

rheo- *comb. form* of or relating to a current or flow. WH: Greek *rheos* stream, current, flowing thing, from *rhein* to flow. See also -O-.

rheology *n.* the science dealing with the flow and deformation of matter. WH: early 20C. RHEO- + -LOGY.

rheostat *n.* a variable resistance for adjusting and regulating an electric current. WH: 19C. RHEO- + -STAT.

rheotropism *n.* the tendency in growing plant organs exposed to running water to dispose their longer axes either in the direction of or against the current. WH: 19C. RHEO- + TROPISM.

rhesus *n.* a macaque, *Macaca mulatta*, held sacred in some parts of India. WH: 19C. Modern Latin (*Simia*) *rhesus*, from Latin *Rhesus*, Greek *Rhēsos*, a mythical king of Thrace.

rhetor *n.* in ancient Greece, a teacher or professor of rhetoric. WH: 12–14C. Late Latin *rhethor*, var. of Latin *rhetor*, from Greek *rhētōr* orator.

rhetoric *n.* the art of effective speaking or writing, the rules of eloquence. WH: 12–14C. Old French *rethorique* (Modern French *rhétorique*), from Medieval Latin *rethorica*, var. of Latin *rhetorica*, from Greek *rhētorikē* (*tekhnē*) (art) of oratory, from *rhētōr* RHETOR. See also -IC.

rheum *n.* the thin serous fluid secreted by the mucous glands as tears, saliva or mucus. WH: 14–15C. Old French *reume* (Modern French *rhume*), from Late Latin *rheuma* bodily humour, flow, from Greek, from *rhein* to flow.

rheumatic *a.* of, relating to, suffering from or subject to rheumatism. *Also n.* WH: 14–15C. Old French *reumatique* (Modern French *rhumatique*) or Latin *rheumaticus*, from Greek *rheumatikos*, from *rheuma* RHEUM. See also -ATIC.

rheumatology *n.* the study of rheumatism. WH: mid-20C. From *rheumatism* (RHEUMATIC) + -O- + -LOGY.

rhinal *a.* of or relating to the nose or nostrils. WH: 19C. Greek *rhis, rhinos* + -AL¹.

rhinencephalon *n.* the olfactory lobe of the brain. WH: 19C. See RHINAL, ENCEPHALON.

rhinestone *n.* a colourless artificial gem cut to look like a diamond. WH: 19C. *Rhine* (RHENISH) + STONE, translating French *caillou du Rhin*, lit. pebble of the Rhine. The gem is so called because it was originally cut in Strasbourg, a city near the Rhine in NE France.

Rhine wine *n.* a wine made from grapes grown in the neighbourhood of the River Rhine. WH: 19C. *Rhine* (RHENISH) + WINE.

rhinitis *n.* inflammation of the mucous membrane of the nose. WH: 19C. RHINO- + -ITIS.

rhino¹ *n.* a rhinoceros. WH: 19C. Abbr. of RHINOCEROS.

rhino² *n.* money. WH: 17C. Orig. unknown. According to some, the word is an allusion to the value of rhinoceros horn, a supposed aphrodisiac, or to the animal itself, formerly a symbol of wealth and exoticism.

rhino- *comb. form* of or relating to the nose or nostrils. WH: Greek *rhis, rhinos* nose. See also -O-.

rhinobatid *n.* any bottom-dwelling fish of the family Rhinobatidae. WH: 19C. Modern Latin *Rhinobatidae*, from Greek *rhinē* shark + *batos* ray. See also -ID.

rhinoceros *n.* a large grey-coloured quadruped of the family Rhinocerotidae , now found only in Africa and S Asia, with one or two horns on the nose. WH: 12–14C. Latin, from Greek *rhinokerōs*, from *rhis, rhinos* nose + *keras* horn.

rhinolith *n.* a nasal calculus. WH: 19C. RHINO- + -LITH.

rhinology *n.* the branch of medical science dealing with the nose and nasal diseases. WH: 19C. RHINO- + -LOGY.

rhinopharyngeal *a.* of or relating to the nose and pharynx. WH: 19C. RHINO- + *pharyngeal* (PHARYNX).

rhinoplasty *n.* plastic surgery of the nose. WH: 19C. RHINO- + -PLASTY.

rhinorrhoea *n.* discharge of blood from the nose. WH: 19C. RHINO- + -RRHOEA.

rhinoscleroma *n.* a disease affecting the nose, lips etc. with a tuberculous growth. WH: 19C. RHINO- + SCLEROMA.

rhinoscope *n.* an instrument for examining the nasal passages. WH: 19C. RHINO- + -SCOPE.

rhizanthous *a.* flowering or seeming to flower from the roots. WH: 19C. RHIZO- + Greek *anthos* flower. See also -OUS.

rhizic *a.* of or relating to the root of an equation. WH: 19C. Greek *rhiza* root + -IC.

rhizo- *comb. form* of or relating to a root. WH: Greek *rhiza* root. See also -O-.

rhizobium *n.* a soil bacterium of the genus *Rhizobium*, occurring in the root nodules of leguminous plants. WH: early 20C. Modern Latin, from RHIZO- + Greek *bios* life + -IUM.

rhizocarp *n.* a plant having a perennial root but a flower which withers annually. WH: 19C. RHIZO- + -CARP.

rhizocephalan *n.* any member of the Rhizocephala, a suborder of parasitic crustaceans related to the barnacles. WH: late 20C. RHIZO- + Greek *kephalē* head + -AN.

rhizogenic *a.* root-producing. WH: 19C. RHIZO- + -GENIC.

rhizoid *a.* rootlike. *Also n.* WH: 19C. Greek *rhiza* root + -OID.

rhizoma *n.* a rhizome. WH: 19C. Latin, from Greek *rhizōma*, from *rhizousthai* to take root, from *rhiza* root. See also -OMA.

rhizome *n.* a prostrate, thickened, rootlike stem, sending roots downwards and producing aerial shoots etc. annually. WH: 19C. Greek *rhizōma*. See RHIZOMA.

rhizomorph *n.* a rootlike mycelial growth by which some fungi attach themselves to higher plants. WH: 19C. RHIZO- + -MORPH.

rhizophagous *a.* feeding on roots. WH: 19C. RHIZO- + -PHAGOUS.

rhizophore *n.* a rootlike structure bearing the roots in species of *Selaginella*. WH: 19C. RHIZO- + -PHORE.

rhizopod *n.* an animalcule of the class Rhizopoda, comprising those with pseudopodia for locomotion and the ingestion of food. *Also a.* WH: 19C. RHIZO- + -POD.

rho *n.* the 17th letter of the Greek alphabet (P, ρ). WH: 14–15C. Greek *rhō*.

rhodamine *n.* any of a group of fluorescent, usu. red dyestuffs. WH: 19C. Greek *rhodon* rose + AMINE.

rhodanic *a.* producing a rose-red colour with ferric salts. WH: 19C. Greek *rhodon* rose + -AN + -IC.

Rhode Island Red *n.* an American breed of domestic fowl with reddish-brown plumage. WH: 18C. *Rhode Island*, a state in NE USA + RED.

Rhodes scholarship *n.* a scholarship at Oxford founded under the will of Cecil Rhodes for students from the British Commonwealth and the US. WH: early 20C. Cecil John *Rhodes*, 1853–1902, British financier and S African statesman. The Rhodes scholarship was first awarded in 1902.

Rhodian *a.* of or relating to Rhodes. *Also n.* WH: 16C. Latin *Rhodius*, from Greek *Rhodos* Rhodes, largest of the Dodecanese Islands in the SE Aegean. See also -AN.

rhodium[1] *n.* a greyish-white metallic element, at. no. 45, chem. symbol Rh, belonging to the platinum group. WH: 19C. Greek *rhodon* rose + -IUM. The element is so called from the rosy colours of its salts. It was named in 1804 by its discoverer, the English chemist and physicist Willliam H. Wollaston.

rhodium[2] *n.* a W Indian rosewood, *Amyris balsamifera*. WH: 17C. Modern Latin *rhodium* (*lignum*) roselike (wood), neut. of *rhodius*, from Greek *rhodon* rose.

rhodo- *comb. form* rose. WH: Greek *rhodon* rose. See also -O-.

rhodochrosite *n.* a mineral form of manganese carbonate formed of rose-red crystals. WH: 19C. Greek *rhodokhrōs* rose-coloured + -ITE[1].

rhododendron *n.* any evergreen shrub of the genus *Rhododendron* akin to the azaleas, with brilliant flowers. WH: 17C. Latin, from Greek, from *rhodon* rose + *dendron* tree. The word was originally the name of the oleander, *Nerium oleander*.

rhodolite *n.* a pale pink or purple garnet used as a gemstone. WH: 19C. RHODO- + -LITE.

rhodonite *n.* a rose-pink silicate of manganese. WH: 19C. Greek *rhodon* rose + -ITE[1].

rhodopsin *n.* a purplish pigment found in the retina, visual purple. WH: 19C. RHODO- + Greek *opsis* sight, vision + -IN[1].

rhodora *n.* a N American flowering shrub, *Rhodora canadensis*, belonging to the family Ericaceae, growing in boggy ground. WH: 18C. Modern Latin, from Greek *rhodon* rose.

rhoeadine *n.* an alkaloid obtained from the red poppy, *Papaver rhoeas*. WH: 19C. Greek *rhoias, rhoiados* a kind of poppy + -INE.

rhomb *n.* a rhombus. WH: 16C. French *rhombe* or Latin RHOMBUS.

rhombohedron *n.* a solid figure bounded by six equal rhombuses. WH: 19C. RHOMB- + -O- + -HEDRON.

rhomboid *a.* having the shape or nearly the shape of a rhomboid. *Also n.* WH: 16C. French *rhomboïde* or Late Latin *rhomboides*, from Greek *rhomboeides*, from *rhombos* RHOMBUS. See also -OID.

rhomboideus *n.* a muscle which connects the shoulder blade to the vertebrae. WH: 19C. Modern Latin, from Late Latin *rhomboides*. See RHOMBOID.

rhombus *n.* an oblique parallelogram with equal sides. WH: 16C. Latin, from Greek *rhombos* spinning top, rhombus, from *rhembesthai* to spin, to whirl.

rhotacism *n.* exaggerated or erroneous pronunciation of the letter r, burring. WH: 19C. Modern Latin *rhotacismus*, ult. from Greek *rhōtakizein* to make excessive or wrong use of the letter r, from *rhō* RHO + -*izein* -IZE, with inserted *k* for ease of pronun. See also -ISM.

rhotic *a.* of or relating to a dialect of English in which the letter r is pronounced before a consonant and at the end of a word. WH: mid-20C. RHOTACISM + -IC.

rhubarb *n.* any herbaceous plant of the genus *Rheum*, esp. *R. rhaponticum*, the fleshy and juicy leaf-stalks of which are cooked and eaten. WH: 14–15C. Old French *rubarbe, reubarbe* (Modern French *rhubarbe*), from shortened form of Medieval Latin *rheubarbarum*, alt. of *rhabarbarum*, lit. foreign rhubarb, from Late Latin *rha* (see RHAPONTIC) + Latin *barbarus* foreign, barbarous (BARBARIAN).

rhumb *n.* any of the 32 principal points of the compass. WH: 16C. French *rumb*, earlier *ryn* (*de vent* of wind) point of the compass, prob. from Dutch *ruim* space, room, with later alt. by assoc. with Latin RHOMBUS.

rhyme *n.* a correspondence of sound in the final accented syllable or group of syllables of a line of verse with that of another line, consisting of identity of the vowel sounds and of all the consonantal sounds but the first. *Also v.i., v.t.* WH: 17C. Var. of *rime* (from Old French, from Medieval Latin *rithmus, rythmus*, from Latin *rhythmus* RHYTHM) by assoc. with its ult. Latin source. The older form *rime* dates from the 12–14C and persisted due to its former false association with Old English *rīm* number.

rhyncho- *comb. form* having a snout or snoutlike process. WH: Modern Latin, from Greek *rhugkhos* snout, beak. See also -O-.

rhynchocephalian *a.* of or relating to the Rhynchocephalia, an almost extinct order of reptiles. *Also n.* WH: 19C. Modern Latin *Rhynchocephalia*, from RHYNCHO- + Greek *kephalē* head. See -AN.

rhynchophore *n.* a member of the Rhynchophora (now Curculionoidea), a division of tetramerous beetles containing the weevils. WH: 19C. Modern Latin *Rhynchophora*. See RHYNCHO-, -PHORE.

rhyolite *n.* an igneous rock with a structure showing the effect of lava-flow, composed of quartz and feldspar with other minerals. WH: 19C. Greek *rhuax* stream (of lava) + -LITE.

rhyparographer *n.* a painter of squalid subjects. WH: 17C. Latin *rhyparographos*, from Greek *rhuparographos*, from *rhuparos* filthy. See -grapher (-GRAPH).

rhythm *n.* movement characterized by action and reaction or regular alternation of strong and weak impulse, stress, accent, motion, sound etc. WH: 16C. Var. of *rime* (RHYME), assim. to Latin *rhythmus* or French *rhythme*.

ria *n.* a long, narrow inlet into the sea coast. WH: 19C. Spanish *ría* estuary.

rial *n.* the standard unit of currency in Iran, Oman, Saudi Arabia, Qatar and Yemen. WH: mid-20C. Arabic *riyāl*, from Spanish *real* REAL[2].

riant *a.* smiling, cheerful. WH: 16C. French, pres.p. of *rire*, from Latin *ridere* to laugh. See also -ANT.

rib[1] *n.* any one of the bones extending outwards and forwards from the spine, and in human beings forming the walls of the thorax. *Also v.t., v.i.* WH: pre-1200. Old English *ribb*, from Germanic. Cp. German *Rippe*.

rib[2] *v.t.* to tease, make fun of. WH: 16C. RIB[1]. The original sense was to provide with ribs. The current colloquial sense arose in the mid-20C, perhaps from the notion of tickling the ribs to provoke laughter.

ribald *a.* (of language) coarse, lewd. *Also n.* WH: 12–14C. Old French *ribault* (Modern French *ribaud*), from *riber* to be wanton, from Germanic base represented by Old High German *hriba* prostitute. Cp. German *reiben* to rub.

ribband *n.* a piece of timber used in launching a ship, as a stop, guide etc., or in the construction of pontoons, gun-platforms etc. WH: 18C. RIB[1] + BAND[1], or from RIBBON.

ribble-rabble *n.* a rabble, a mob. WH: 14–15C. Redupl. of RABBLE[1].

ribbon *n.* a narrow woven strip or band of silk, satin etc., used for ornamenting dress etc. WH: 16C. Var. of *riband* (12–14C) from Old French *riban* (Modern French *ruban*), prob. from Germanic compound of BAND[1].

riboflavin *n.* a yellow vitamin of the B complex, found esp. in milk and liver, which promotes growth in children; vitamin B$_2$. WH: mid-20C. RIBOSE + FLAVIN.

ribonuclease *n.* any of several enzymes that catalyse the hydrolysis of ribonucleic acid. WH: mid-20C. RIBOSE + NUCLEASE.

ribonucleic acid *n.* any of a group of nucleic acids present in all living cells and playing an essential role in the synthesis of proteins. WH: mid-20C. RIBOSE + NUCLEIC ACID.

ribose *n.* a pentose sugar occurring in ribonucleic acid and riboflavin. WH: 19C. Arbitrary alt. of *arabinose*, from ARABICA + -IN[1] + -OSE[2]. Arabinose is so called as it was first obtained from gum arabic.

ribosome *n.* any of numerous minute granules containing ribonucleic acid and protein in a cell, which are the site for protein synthesis. WH: mid-20C. RIBONUCLEIC ACID + -SOME[2].

Ribston pippin *n.* a variety of apple first cultivated in England at Ribston Park. WH: 18C. *Ribston* Park, in N Yorkshire.

Ricardian *a.* of or relating to the reign of Richard I, II, or III of England. *Also n.* WH: mid-20C. Medieval Latin *Ricardus* Richard + -IAN. The word is applied to the reigns of Richard I (1189–99), II (1377–99) or III (1483–85), kings of England.

rice *n.* the white grain or seeds of *Oryza sativa*, an Asian aquatic grass extensively cultivated in warm climates for food. WH: 12–14C. Old French *ris* (Modern French *riz*), from Italian *riso*, from Latin *oryza*, from Greek *oruza*, of Oriental orig.

ricercar *n.* an elaborate, contrapuntal, instrumental composition in a slow tempo. WH: 18C. Italian *ricercare* to search out, to seek.

rich *a.* wealthy, having a lot of valuable possessions. *Also v.t.* WH: pre-1200. Old English *ríce*, from Germanic, from Celtic *rix*, corr. to Latin *rex*, Irish *rí* king. Cp. RAJA, REICH. Celtic *rix* is found in personal names such as that of the Gallic chieftain *Vercingetorix*, 72–46 BC, literally great king of a hundred heads.

†**richesse** *n.* abundant possessions, wealth, opulence, affluence. WH: 12–14C. Old French *richeise* (Modern French *richesse*), from *riche* RICH + *-esse* -ESS[2]. English *riches* as in *rags to riches* was originally a variant of RICHESSE, not a plural form of RICH.

Richter scale *n.* a logarithmic scale for registering the magnitude of earthquakes. WH: mid-20C. Charles Francis *Richter*, 1900–85, US seismologist.

ricin *n.* a toxic substance obtained from castor oil beans. WH: 19C. Modern Latin *Ricinus* + -IN[1].

ricinoleic *a.* derived from castor oil. WH: 19C. See RICIN, OLEIC.

rick[1] *n.* a stack of corn, hay etc., built in a regular shape and thatched. *Also v.t.* WH: pre-1200. Old English *hréac*, from Germanic, of unknown orig.

rick[2] *v.t.* to wrench or sprain. *Also n.* WH: 18C. Prob. var. of WRICK.

rickets *n.* a disease of children resulting in the softening of the bones, esp. the spine, bow-legs, emaciation etc., owing to lack of mineral matter in the bones. WH: 17C. Orig. uncertain. ? Orig. dial., or alt. of Greek *rhakhitis* RACHITIS.

rickettsia *n.* any of a group of microorganisms of the genus *Rickettsia* found in lice, ticks etc. which when transmitted to human beings cause serious diseases, e.g. typhus. WH: early 20C. Modern Latin, from Howard Taylor *Ricketts*, 1871–1910, US pathologist + -IA.

rickey *n.* a cocktail made from gin, lime juice and soda water. WH: 19C. Prob. from the surname *Rickey*.

rickshaw *n.* a light two-wheeled hooded carriage drawn by one or two people, or attached to a bicycle etc. WH: 19C. Abbr. of JINRICKSHAW. Cp. TRISHAW.

ricochet *n.* a rebounding or skipping of a stone, projectile or bullet off a hard or flat surface. *Also v.i., v.t.* WH: 18C. French the skipping of a shot or of a flat stone on water, of unknown orig.

ricotta *n.* a soft white Italian cheese made from sheep's milk. WH: 19C. Italian recooked, from Latin *recocta*, fem. p.p. of *recoquere*, from RE- + *coquere* to cook.

ricrac *n.* a zigzag braid for trimming garments. WH: 19C. Orig. uncertain. ? Redupl. of RACK[1] or RICK[2].

rictus *n.* the expanse of a person's or animal's open mouth, gape. WH: 18C. Latin, lit. open mouth, from *rictus*, p.p. of *ringi* to gape.

rid *v.t.* to clear, to disencumber (of). *Also a.* WH: 12–14C. Old Norse *rythja*. Cp. REDD[1].

-ridden *comb. form* oppressed, dominated by or excessively concerned with, as in *debt-ridden*. WH: 17C. RIDE + -EN[6].

riddle[1] *n.* a question or proposition put in ambiguous language to exercise ingenuity; a puzzle, conundrum or enigma. *Also v.i., v.t.* WH: pre-1200. Old English *rædels* opinion, conjecture, riddle, from Germanic base of READ, REDE. See also -LE[1]. Cp. German *Rätsel*. The final *-s* of the Old English word has disappeared as it did with BURIAL.

riddle[2] *v.t.* to pass through a riddle, to sift. *Also n.* WH: pre-1200. Alt. of dial. *ridder*, from Old English *hridder*, from Germanic. See also -ER[1]. Cp. German *Reiter* sieve.

ride *v.i.* to sit and be carried along, as on a horse, cycle, public conveyance etc., esp. to go on horseback. *Also v.t., n.* WH: pre-1200. Old English *rídan*, from Germanic. Cp. ROAD[1].

ridge *n.* the long horizontal angle formed by the junction of two slopes. *Also v.t., v.i.* WH: pre-1200. Old English *hrycg*, from Germanic. Cp. German *Rücken* back. The original sense was back, spine (of human or animal), but the current sense dates also from the first.

ridicule *n.* derision, mockery. *Also v.t.* WH: 17C. French, or from Latin *ridiculum*, neut. sing. (used as n.) of *ridiculus* laughable, from *ridere* to laugh.

riding *n.* each of the three former administrative divisions of Yorkshire. WH: pre-1200. Old Norse *thrithjungr* third part, from *thrithi* third, with early assim. of initial *th-* to the last consonant of *east*, *north*, *west*. See -ING[3]. The three administrative divisions lost their names in 1974 on the reorganization of local government, but the E Riding resumed its name in 1996 as a 'unitary authority' within Yorkshire.

ridotto *n.* an entertainment consisting of singing and dancing, esp. a masked ball. WH: 18C. Italian, corr. to French *réduit*, from Medieval Latin *reductus*, use as n. of p.p. of Latin *reducere* REDUCE. The entertainment was apparently so called as it was originally among select company, 'reduced' to the best.

riel *n.* the standard monetary unit of Cambodia. WH: mid-20C. Khmer.

riem *n.* a rawhide strap or thong. WH: 19C. Dutch.

Riesling *n.* a dry white wine, or the grape that produces it. WH: 19C. German, of unknown orig.

rifacimento *n.* a recast of a literary work etc. WH: 18C. Italian, from *rifac-*, stem of *rifare* to remake.

rife *a.* occurring in great quantity, number etc., current, prevalent. WH: pre-1200. Old English *rýfe*, prob. from Old Norse *rífr* good, acceptable, from Germanic. Cp. Old Norse *reifa* to enrich, *reifr* glad, cheerful.

riff *n.* a phrase or figure played repeatedly in jazz or rock music, usu. as background to an instrument solo. *Also v.i.* WH: early 20C. Abbr. of RIFFLE[1].

riffle[1] *v.t.* to ruffle, to flick through rapidly (the pages of a book etc.). *Also v.i., n.* WH: 17C. Prob. partly a var. of RUFFLE, partly from obs. French *riffler*, from Old French *rifler* RIFLE. Influ. by RIPPLE[1].

riffle² *n.* in gold mining, a groove, channel, slab, block or cleat set in an inclined trough, sluice or cradle for arresting the particles of auriferous sand etc. WH: 18C. RIFFLE¹.

riffler *n.* a file with curved ends for working in shallow depressions etc. WH: 18C. French *rifloir*, from *rifler* RIFLE. See also -ER².

riff-raff *n.* worthless people, rabble. WH: 15C. From *riff and raff*, from Old French *rif et raf*, ult. of Germanic orig. Cp. RAFF.

rifle *n.* a firearm having the barrel spirally grooved so as to give a rotary motion to the projectile. *Also v.t., v.i.* WH: 17C. Old French *rifler* to scrape, to scratch, to plunder, ult. of Germanic orig. The firearm is named from its rifled bore, originally made by scratching grooves inside the barrel.

rift *n.* a cleft, a fissure. *Also v.t., v.i.* WH: 12–14C. Scandinavian, rel. to RIVE. Cp. Old Norse *ript* breach of contract, Norwegian, Danish *rift* cleft.

rig¹ *v.t.* to furnish or fit (a ship) with spars, gear or tackle. *Also v.i., n.* WH: 15C. ? Scandinavian. Cp. Norwegian *rigga* to bind up, to wrap up.

rig² *v.t.* to manipulate fraudulently. *Also v.i., n.* WH: 19C. Orig. unknown.

rig³ *n.* a ridge. WH: 14–15C. Var. of RIDGE.

rigadoon *n.* a lively dance performed by one couple. WH: 17C. French *rigodon, rigaudon*, said to be from one *Rigaud*, the dancing master who devised it.

right *a.* being or done in accordance with justice. *Also adv., n., v.t., v.i., int.* WH: pre-1200. Old English *riht*, from Germanic base rel. to Latin *rectus*, from Indo-European. Cp. German *recht*.

righteous *a.* upright, morally good. WH: pre-1200. Old English *rihtwīs*, from *riht* RIGHT + *wīs* -WISE, assim. to *-eous* as in *bounteous* (BOUNTY), *plenteous* (PLENTY), etc.

rigid *a.* stiff, not easily bent. WH: 14–15C. French *rigide*, from Latin *rigidus*, from *rigere* to be stiff. See also -ID.

rigmarole *n.* a long, complicated procedure. *Also a.* WH: 18C. Appar. coll. alt. of *ragman roll* (14–15C) long list, catalogue, from obs. *ragman* a type of legal document (? from Old Norse) + ROLL.

rigor *n.* a feeling of chill, a shivering accompanied by stiffening, premonitory of fever etc. WH: 14–15C. Latin numbness, stiffness. Cp. RIGOUR.

rigour *n.* exactness in enforcing rules. WH: 14–15C. Old French (Modern French *rigueur*), from Latin RIGOR. See also -OUR.

Rigsdag *n.* the Danish parliament. WH: 19C. Danish, from gen. of *rige* realm + *dag* DAY. Cp. *Reichstag* (REICH), RIKSDAG.

Rig-Veda *n.* the oldest and most original of the Hindu Vedas. WH: 18C. Sanskrit *ṛgveda*, from *ṛc* sacred stanza + *veda* VEDA.

Riksdag *n.* the Swedish parliament. WH: 19C. Swedish, from gen. of *rike* realm + *dag* DAY. Cp. RIGSDAG.

rile *v.t.* to make angry, to vex, to irritate. WH: 19C. Var. of ROIL.

rill *n.* a small stream, a rivulet. *Also v.i.* WH: 19C. Prob. of Low Dutch orig. Cp. Dutch *ril*, German *Rille*.

rille *n.* a furrow, trench or narrow valley on Mars and the moon. WH: 19C. German. See RILL.

rim *n.* an outer edge or margin. *Also v.t.* WH: pre-1200. Old English *rima*, rel. to Old Norse *rimi* strip of land. No other related words are known.

rime *n.* a deposit of ice caused by freezing fog or low temperatures. *Also v.t.* WH: pre-1200. Old English *hrīm*, rel. to Old Norse *hrim*.

rimose *a.* (of the bark of trees) full of chinks or cracks. WH: 18C. Latin *rimosus*, from *rima* slit, fissure, crack. See also -OSE¹.

rimu *n.* the red pine of New Zealand, *Dacrydium cupressinum*. WH: 19C. Maori.

rind *n.* the outer coating of trees, fruits etc.; bark, peel, husk, skin. *Also v.t.* WH: pre-1200. Old English, from Germanic, of unknown orig. Cp. German *Rinde*. Rel. to REND.

rinderpest *n.* a malignant contagious disease attacking ruminants, esp. cattle. WH: 19C. German, from *Rinder* cattle (pl. of *Rind*) + *Pest* plague.

ring¹ *n.* a circlet. *Also v.t., v.i.* WH: pre-1200. Old English *hring*, from Germanic. Rel. to RANK¹.

ring² *v.i.* to give a clear vibrating sound, like a sonorous metallic body when struck. *Also v.t., n.* WH: pre-1200. Old English *hringan*, corr. to Old Norse *hringja*, prob. of imit. orig.

ringent *a.* (of a flower or corolla) irregular and gaping. WH: 18C. Latin *ringens, ringentis*, pres.p. of *ringi* to gape. See also -ENT. Cp. RICTUS.

ringgit *n.* the standard unit of currency of Malaysia, the Malaysian dollar. WH: late 20C. Malay, lit. serrated, jagged (with ref. to the coin's edge).

rink *n.* a prepared floor for roller skating or an area of artificially formed ice for ice-skating. WH: 14–15C. Orig. uncertain. ? Ult from Old French *renc* (Modern French *rang*) RANK¹. The original sense (to the 17C) was an area of ground for jousting or racing. The application to ice was originally for curling (18C), then skating (19C).

rinkhals *n.* a venom-spitting snake of southern Africa, *Hemachatus hemachatus*. WH: 18C. Afrikaans, from *ring* ring + *hals* neck.

rinse *v.t.* to wash, to cleanse with clean water. *Also n.* WH: 12–14C. Old French *rincer*, of unknown orig. According to some, the word is probably a variant of Old French *recincier*, from Popular Latin *recentiare*, from Latin *recens, recentis* RECENT (in sense fresh).

Rioja *n.* a Spanish table wine from Rioja. WH: early 20C. *Rioja*, a district of N Spain.

riot *n.* an outbreak of lawlessness. *Also a., v.i.* WH: 12–14C. Old French *riote* (Modern French *riotte*) debate, quarrel, from *rihoter* to quarrel.

RIP *abbr.* may he, she or they rest in peace. WH: Abbr. of Latin *requiescat in pace* (REQUIESCAT) or its pl. equivalent, *requiescant in pace*. The abbreviation is sometimes popularly taken to represent an acronym of rest in peace.

rip¹ *v.t.* to tear or cut forcibly (out, off, up etc.). *Also v.i., n.* WH: 14–15C. Orig. unknown. Cp. RIP².

rip² *n.* an eddy, a stretch of broken water, a rip tide. WH: 18C. Appar. rel. to RIP¹.

rip³ *n.* a disreputable person. WH: 18C. ? Var. of *rep*, abbr. of REPROBATE.

riparian *a.* of, relating to or dwelling on the banks of a river. *Also n.* WH: 19C. Latin *riparius*, from *ripa* bank. See also -ARIAN.

ripe *a.* ready for reaping or gathering. *Also v.t., v.i.* WH: pre-1200. Old English *rīpe*, from Germanic. Cp. German *reif*.

ripieno *a.* additional, supplementary. *Also n.* WH: 18C. Italian, from *ri-* RE- + *pieno* full.

riposte *n.* a quick reply, a retort. *Also v.i.* WH: 18C. French, from Latin *risposta*, fem. p.p. (used as n.) of *rispondere* RESPOND.

ripple¹ *v.i.* to run in small waves or undulations. *Also v.t., n.* WH: 17C. Orig. unknown. Later appar. regarded as freq. of RIP¹. See also -LE⁴.

ripple² *n.* a large comb for removing the seeds from flax. *Also v.t.* WH: 14–15C. Corr. to Frisian *ripel*, Dutch *repel*, Old High German *riffila* (German *Riffel*).

riprap *n.* a foundation of loose stones, e.g. in deep water or on a soft bottom. *Also v.t.* WH: 16C. Redupl. of RAP¹.

Ripuarian *a.* of or relating to the ancient Franks living near the Rhine. *Also n.* WH: 18C. Medieval Latin *Ripuarius*. See also -ARIAN. The word is probably not from Latin *ripa* bank.

riroriro *n.* a small grey New Zealand bird, *Gerygone igata*. WH: 19C. Maori, of imit. orig.

risaldar *n.* the captain of a troop of Indian cavalry. WH: 19C. Hindi *risāldār*, from Persian *risāladār*, from *risāla* troop + *-dār* holder.

RISC *n.* a computer which performs a limited number of operations at high speed. WH: late 20C. Acronym of *reduced instruction set computer*, prob. punning on RISK.

rise *v.i.* to move upwards, to soar. *Also n.* WH: pre-1200. Old English *rīsan*, from Germanic. Cp. German *reisen* to travel. No certain related forms are known outside Germanic. The original sense (to the 17C) was to make an attack. The current sense to move upwards dates from the 12–14C.

rishi *n.* a seer, a saint, an inspired poet, esp. each of the seven sages said to have communicated the Hindu Vedas to humankind. WH: 18C. Sanskrit *ṛṣi*.

risible *a.* exciting laughter. WH: 16C. Late Latin *risibilis*, from Latin *risus*, p.p. of *ridere* to laugh. See also -IBLE.

risk *n.* a chance of injury, loss etc. *Also v.t.* WH: 17C. French *risque*, from obs. Italian *risco*, from *rischiare* to run into danger.

Risorgimento *n.* the rising of the Italian peoples against Austrian and papal rule, culminating in the unification of Italy in 1870. **WH:** 19C. Italian renewal, renaissance.

risotto *n.* an Italian dish of rice cooked in butter and stock or broth, with onions, cheese, chicken, ham etc. **WH:** 19C. Italian, from *riso* rice.

risqué *a.* suggestive of indecency, indelicate. **WH:** 19C. French, p.p. of *risquer* RISK.

rissole *n.* a ball or flat cake of minced meat, fish etc., coated with breadcrumbs and fried. **WH:** 18C. French, later form of Old French *ruissole*, dial. var. of *roisole*, *roussole*, from use as n. of fem. of Late Latin *russeolus* reddish, from Latin *russus* red.

ritardando *adv., a., n.* (a) slowing down. **WH:** 19C. Italian, pres.p. of *ritardare* to slow down.

rite *n.* a religious or solemn prescribed act, ceremony or observance. **WH:** 12–14C. Old French *rit*, later *rite*, or from Latin *ritus* (religious) usage. The French phrase *rite du passage* rite of passage was coined in 1909 by the French ethnographer and folklorist Charles-Arnold Van Gennep.

ritenuto *a., adv.* restrained, held back. *Also n.* **WH:** 19C. Italian, p.p. of *ritenere*, from Latin *retinere* RETAIN.

ritornello *n.* a brief prelude, interlude or refrain. **WH:** 17C. Italian, dim. of *ritorno* RETURN.

ritual *n.* a prescribed manner of performing divine service. *Also a.* **WH:** 16C. Latin *ritualis*, from *ritus* RITE. See also -AL[1].

ritzy *a.* elegant, showy, luxurious, rich. **WH:** early 20C. *Ritz*, the name of some luxury hotels, from César *Ritz*, 1850–1918, Swiss-born hotelier + -Y[1].

rival *n.* one's competitor for something. *Also a., v.t.* **WH:** 16C. Latin *rivalis*, lit. person who uses the same stream as another, from *rivus* stream. See also -AL[1].

†**rive** *v.t.* to tear, split, cleave or rend asunder. *Also v.i.* **WH:** 12–14C. Old Norse *rifa*, of unknown orig.

river *n.* a large stream of water flowing in a channel over a portion of the earth's surface and discharging itself into the sea, a lake, a marsh or another river. *Also a.* **WH:** 12–14C. Old French *rivière* river, river bank, from Popular Latin *riparia*, use as n. of fem. of Latin *riparius*, from *ripa* bank. See also -ER[2].

rivet *n.* a short bolt, pin or nail, usu. with a flat head at one end, the other end being flattened out and clinched by hammering, used for fastening metal plates together. *Also v.t.* **WH:** 12–14C. Old French, from *river* to clinch, of unknown orig. See also -ET[1].

riviera *n.* a coastal strip with a subtropical climate. **WH:** 18C. Italian seashore, coast. The word was originally the name of the coast either side of Genoa, NW Italy (now known as the Italian Riviera, for distinction from the French Riviera, SE France).

rivière *n.* a necklace of gems, usu. of several strings. **WH:** 19C. French. See RIVER. The necklace is so called as it 'streams'.

rivulet *n.* a small stream. **WH:** 16C. Alt. of obs. *riveret* (from French dim. of *rivière* RIVER), ? based on Italian *rivoletto*, dim. of *rivolo*, itself dim. of *rivo*, from Latin *rivus* stream. See also -LET.

rizzer *v.t.* to dry (haddock etc.) in the sun. *Also n.* **WH:** 18C. Obs. French *ressoré* parched, from *re-* RE- + obs. *sorer* to smoke, to dry, from Old French *sor* yellowish. See SORREL[2].

roach[1] *n.* a freshwater fish, *Rutilus rutilus*, allied to the carp. **WH:** 12–14C. Old French *roche*, *roce*, of unknown orig.

roach[2] *n.* a cockroach. **WH:** 19C. Abbr. of COCKROACH.

roach[3] *n.* a curved part of a fore-and-aft sail projecting beyond an imaginary straight line between its corners. **WH:** 18C. ? A special use of *roach*, var. of obs. *roche* cliff, rock, from Old French. See ROCK[1].

road[1] *n.* a track or way for travelling on, esp. a broad strip of ground suitable for motor vehicles, forming a public line of communication between places, a highway. **WH:** pre-1200. Old English *rād*, from Germanic. Rel. to RIDE. Cp. RAID. The original sense (to the 17C) was a riding on horseback, a journey on horseback. The current sense dates from the 16C.

road[2] *v.t.* (of a dog) to follow (a game bird) by its scent. **WH:** 19C. Orig. unknown. Appar. not rel. to ROAD[1].

roam *v.i.* to wander about without any definite purpose. *Also v.t., n.* **WH:** 12–14C. Orig. unknown. The word is popularly derived from *Rome*, as a place of pilgrimage.

roan[1] *a.* (of an animal, esp. a horse) of a bay, sorrel or dark colour, with spots of grey or white thickly interspersed. *Also n.* **WH:** 16C. Old French (Modern French *rouan*), of unknown orig. According to some, the word is from Spanish *roano*, from Latin *ravus* dark grey.

roan[2] *n.* a soft flexible leather made of sheepskin tanned with sumac. *Also a.* **WH:** 12–14C. *Roan*, old name of Rouen, a city in N France, where the tanning method appar. originated.

roar *n.* a loud, deep, continued sound, as of a lion etc. *Also v.i., v.t.* **WH:** pre-1200. Old English *rārian*, from Germanic, of imit. orig. Cp. German *röhren* to bellow.

roast *v.t.* to cook by exposure to the direct action of radiant heat, esp. at an open fire or in an oven. *Also v.i., a., n.* **WH:** 12–14C. Old French *rostir* (Modern French *rôtir*), from Germanic, from base also of Old High German *rōst* grill, gridiron.

rob *v.t.* to take something by secret theft from. *Also v.i.* **WH:** 12–14C. Old French *rober*, from Germanic base represented also by REAVE. Cp. ROBE.

robe *n.* a long, loose outer garment. *Also v.t., v.i.* **WH:** 12–14C. Old French, from Germanic base of ROB. The original sense was booty, hence clothes regarded as booty.

robin *n.* a small brown European bird, *Erithacus rubecula*, the male adult having a red throat and breast. **WH:** 16C. Old French male forename *Robin*, alt. of *Robert*. The bird was originally known as *robin redbreast* (14–15C). The second word was dropped to leave the personal name alone. Cp. JACKDAW, MAGPIE, *tomtit* (TOM). It is possible that this name, together with similar names for red-flowering plants such as *ragged robin* and *herb Robert*, has been popularly associated with Latin *rubeus* red.

robinia *n.* any member of the genus *Robinia* of leguminous shrubs and trees including the false acacia. **WH:** 18C. Jean *Robin*, 1550–1629, French herbalist and botanist to Henry IV of France.

roble *n.* the Californian white oak, *Quercus lobata*. **WH:** 19C. Spanish and Portuguese, from Latin *robur* oak.

roborant *a.* (of a medicine, tonic etc.) strengthening. *Also n.* **WH:** 17C. Latin *roborans*, *roborantis*, pres.p. of *roborare* to strengthen, from *robur*, *roboris* strength. See also -ANT.

robot *n.* a machine capable of acting and speaking in a human manner; a humanoid, an automaton. **WH:** early 20C. Czech, from *robota* forced labour. Cp. Russian *rabota* work. The word originated as a term for the mechanical men in Karel Čapek's play *R.U.R.* (standing for *Rossum's Universal Robots*, the firm that manufactured the men) (1920).

robust *a.* strong, capable of endurance. **WH:** 16C. Old French *robuste*, from Latin *robustus* oaken, firm and hard, solid, from *robus*, older form of *robur* oak, strength.

robusta *n.* coffee beans from an American plant, *Coffea canephora*. **WH:** early 20C. Latin, fem. of *robustus* ROBUST, the original species (now variety) name.

roc *n.* a legendary bird of immense size and strength. **WH:** 16C. Spanish *rocho*, *ruc*, from Arabic *rukk*, from Persian *ruk*.

rocaille *n.* decorative work of rock, shell or a similar material. **WH:** 19C. French, from Old French *roche* ROCK[1]. Cp. ROCOCO.

rocambole *n.* a plant related to the leek, *Allium scorodoprasum*, Spanish garlic. **WH:** 17C. French, from German dial. *Rockenbolle*, from *Rocken* (German *Roggen*) rye + *Bolle* onion.

Rochelle powder *n.* Seidlitz powder. **WH:** 14–15C. La *Rochelle*, a seaport in W France.

roche moutonnée *n.* rock ground down by glacial action so as to present a rounded appearance on the side from which the flow came. **WH:** 19C. French, from Old French *roche* ROCK[1] + French *moutonnée*, from *mouton* sheep (see MUTTON). The rock is so called as it is rounded like a sheep's back.

rochet *n.* an open-sided vestment with tight sleeves, resembling a surplice, worn by bishops and abbots. **WH:** 12–14C. Old French, var. of *roquet*, corr. to Medieval Latin *rochetum*, dim. of Germanic base represented also by Old English *rocc* coat. Cp. German *Rock*. See also -ET[1].

rock[1] *n.* the solid matter constituting the earth's crust, or any portion of this. **WH:** 12–14C. Old French *rocque*, *roque*, var. of *roche*, from Medieval Latin *rocca*, *rocha*, of unknown orig.

rock[2] *v.t.* to move backwards and forwards. *Also v.i., n., a.* **WH:** pre-1200. Old English *roccian*, prob. from Germanic base meaning to move, to remove, represented also by Middle Low German, Middle Dutch *rukken, rocken*, Old Norse *rykkja* to pull, to tug. Cp. German *rücken* to move, to push.

rocket¹ *n.* a firework consisting of a cylindrical case of paper or metal filled with a mixture of explosives and combustibles, used for display, signalling, conveying a line to stranded vessels and in warfare. *Also v.t., v.i.* WH: 17C. Old French *roquette*, from Italian *rocchetto*, dim. of *rocca* distaff. See also -ET¹. The projectile is so called from its cylindrical shape.

rocket² *n.* any of various plants of the genus *Hesperis* or *Sisymbrium.* WH: 15C. French *roquette*, from Italian *rochetta*, var. of *ruchetta*, dim. of *ruca*, from Latin *eruca*, of unknown orig. See also -ET¹.

rococo *n.* a florid style of ornamentation (in architecture, furniture etc.) flourishing in the 18th cent. *Also a.* WH: 19C. French, fanciful alt. of ROCAILLE. The style is so called from its use of rocaille. The term arose as artists' jargon.

rod *n.* a straight, slender piece of wood. WH: pre-1200. Old English *rodd*, prob. rel. to Old Norse *rudda* club.

rode *v.i.* (of a woodcock or wildfowl) to fly in the evening. WH: 18C. Orig. unknown.

rodent *n.* any animal of the order Rodentia, having two (or sometimes four) strong incisors and no canine teeth, including the squirrel, beaver, rat etc. *Also a.* WH: 19C. Latin *rodens, rodentis,* pres.p. of *rodere* to gnaw. See also -ENT. Rel. to RAT.

rodeo *n.* a driving together or rounding-up of cattle. WH: 19C. Spanish, from *rodear* to go round, based on Latin *rotare* ROTATE¹.

rodham *n.* in the Fens, a raised bank on the course of a dry river. WH: mid-20C. Orig. unknown.

rodomontade *n.* brag, bluster. *Also a., v.i.* WH: 17C. French, from obs. Italian *rodomontada*, from *Rodomonte*, the boastful Saracen leader in Ariosto's *Orlando Furioso* (1516). The character's name itself means 'roll mountain'.

roe¹ *n.* the mass of eggs forming the spawn of fishes, amphibians etc. WH: 14–15C. Middle Low German and Middle Dutch *roge*, from Germanic. Cp. German *Rogen.*

roe² *n.* a small species of deer, *Capreolus capreolus.* WH: pre-1200. Old English *rā*, earlier *rāa*, from Germanic. Cp. German *Reh.*

roentgen *n.* the international unit of quantity of X- or gamma-rays. WH: 19C. Wilhelm Conrad *Roentgen*, 1845–1923, German physicist, discoverer of X-rays.

rogation *n.* a solemn supplication, esp. one chanted in procession on the Rogation Days. WH: 14–15C. Latin *rogatio, rogationis,* from *rogatus,* p.p. of *rogare* to ask. See also -ATION.

roger *int.* in radio communication, your message is received and understood. *Also v.t., v.i.* WH: 18C. Male forename *Roger,* from Old French, of Germanic orig. In radio communication, the word is the name of the letter *r,* for *received.*

rogue *n.* a dishonest person, a criminal. *Also a., v.t.* WH: 16C. Prob. from Latin *rogare* to ask. The earliest sense was vagrant, vagabond, who would beg for food, drink or money.

roil *v.t.* to make turbid, as by stirring or shaking up. WH: 16C. ? Old French *ruiler* to mix mortar, from Late Latin *regulare* REGULATE. Cp. RILE.

roister *v.i.* to behave uproariously, to revel boisterously. *Also n.* WH: 16C. Old French *rustre* ruffian, alt. of *ruste,* from Latin *rusticus* RUSTIC.

Roland *n.* used only in the phrase *a Roland for an Oliver,* meaning an effective retort. WH: 16C. *Roland,* the legendary nephew of Charlemagne, celebrated with his companion and comrade Oliver in the medieval romance *Chanson de Roland.*

role *n.* a part or character taken by an actor. WH: 17C. French *rôle* ROLL, orig. the roll or paper containing an actor's part.

roll *n.* anything rolled up, a cylinder of any flexible material formed by or as by rolling or folding over on itself. *Also v.t., v.i.* WH: 12–14C. Old French *rolle, roulle* (Modern French *rôle*), from Latin *rotulus,* var. of *rotula,* dim. of *rota* wheel. Cp. ROLE, SCROLL.

rollick *v.i.* to behave in a careless, merry fashion; to frolic, to revel, to be merry or enjoy life in a boisterous fashion. *Also n.* WH: 19C. Prob. of dial. orig. ? Blend of ROMP and FROLIC.

roly-poly *n.* a pudding made of a sheet of suet pastry, spread with jam, rolled up and baked or boiled. *Also a.* WH: 17C. Fanciful formation from ROLL. The earliest sense (only in the 17C) was rascal. The name of the pudding dates from the 19C.

ROM *n.* a data-storage device in computers which retains information in an unalterable state. WH: mid-20C. Acronym of read-only memory.

Rom *n.* a male gypsy, a Romany. WH: 19C. Romany man, husband.

Romaic *n.* the vernacular language of modern Greece. *Also a.* WH: 19C. Modern Greek *romaiikos,* from Greek *Rhōmaikos* Roman, from *Rhōmē* Rome. 'Rome' here refers to the eastern Roman Empire.

romaine *n.* a cos lettuce. WH: early 20C. French, fem. of *romain* Roman.

romaji *n.* a system of romanized spelling for the transliteration of Japanese. WH: early 20C. Japanese, from *rōma* Roman + *ji* letter.

romal *n.* a handkerchief worn as a headdress. WH: 17C. Persian, and from Urdu *rūmāl,* from *rū* face + *māl* (base of Persian *mālidan* to wipe) wiping.

Roman *a.* of or relating to the modern or ancient city of Rome or its territory or people. *Also n.* WH: pre-1200. Latin *Romanus,* from *Roma* ROME. See also -AN. The noun predates the adjective (12–14C), which came from Latin via Old French *Romain.*

roman-à-clef *n.* a novel in which a knowing reader is expected to identify real people under fictitious names, or actual events disguised as fictitious. WH: 19C. French, lit. novel with a key, from *roman* romance, novel + *à* at, with + *clef* key, CLEF.

Romance *n.* any one of a group of languages derived from Latin, e.g. French, Spanish or Romanian. *Also a.* WH: 14–15C. ROMANCE.

romance *n.* the spirit or atmosphere of imaginary adventure, chivalrous or idealized love. *Also v.i., v.t.* WH: 12–14C. Old French *romanz, romans* the vernacular tongue, a work composed in it, from Popular Latin *romanice* (*scribere*) (to write) in a Roman language (i.e. one evolved from Latin, not Frankish), from Latin *Romanicus* in the Roman style, from *Romanus* ROMAN. The original medieval story about the adventures of some hero in chivalry evolved (or devolved) to the love story of the 17C, and this gave the sense of a sentimental or idealized love affair (19C).

Romanes *n.* the Romany language. WH: 19C. Romany, adv. from *Romano.* See ROMANY.

Romanesque *a.* of the styles of architecture that succeeded the Roman and lasted till the introduction of Gothic. *Also n.* WH: 18C. French, from *roman* ROMANCE. See also -ESQUE.

roman-fleuve *n.* a novel sequence or saga chronicling a family history, and thereby a social period. WH: mid-20C. French, lit. river-novel, from *roman* novel (ROMANCE) + *fleuve* river. The sequence is so called because the narrative flows through a series of novels like a river.

Romanian *a.* of or relating to the country of Romania, its people or language. *Also n.* WH: 19C. *Romania,* a country in SE Europe + -AN.

Romano *n.* a strong-tasting, hard Italian cheese. WH: early 20C. Italian Roman.

Romansh *n.* the Rhaeto-Romance dialects of part of E Switzerland. *Also a.* WH: 17C. Romansh *Rumantsch, Romantsch,* from Medieval Latin *romanice,* from Latin *Romanicus* (ROMANCE).

romantic *a.* of, or relating to or given to romance. *Also n.* WH: 17C. French *romantique,* from Old French *romant,* var. of *romanz.* See ROMANCE, also -IC.

Romany *n.* a gypsy. *Also a.* WH: 19C. Romany *Romani,* fem. and pl. of *Romano,* a. from ROM.

Rome *n.* the Roman Catholic Church. WH: 12–14C. Old French, or Latin *Roma,* a city in (now the capital of) Italy.

Romeo *n.* a man who is an ardent lover. WH: 18C. *Romeo,* the hero of Shakespeare's *Romeo and Juliet* (1594). Romeo's name evokes many of his attributes, not least ROMANCE.

romer *n.* a small piece of card or plastic marked with graduations for measuring map references. WH: mid-20C. Carrol *Romer,* 1883–1951, the British barrister who invented it.

romneya *n.* any plant of the genus *Romneya,* having large, poppy-like flowers. WH: late 20C. Modern Latin, from Thomas *Romney* Robinson, 1792–1882, Irish astronomer.

romp *v.i.* to play or frolic roughly or boisterously. *Also n.* WH: 18C. ? Alt. of RAMP¹.

rondavel *n.* a round hut or building in S Africa. WH: 19C. Afrikaans *rondawel.*

ronde *n.* a dance in which the dancers move round in a circle. WH: 19C. French, fem. of *rond* ROUND.

rondeau *n.* a poem in iambic verse of eight or ten syllables and ten or thirteen lines, with only two rhymes, the opening words coming twice as a refrain. WH: 16C. Old French, later form of *rondel*, from *rond* ROUND. Cp. ROUNDEL.

rone *n.* a gutter, a pipe for channelling rainwater from a roof. WH: 16C. Orig. unknown.

Roneo® *n.* a duplicating machine using stencils. *Also v.t.* WH: early 20C. ROTARY + *Neostyle*, orig. name of manufacturing company.

ronin *n.* in Japan, a lordless samurai. WH: 19C. Japanese.

roo *n.* a kangaroo. WH: early 20C. Abbr. of KANGAROO.

rood *n.* the cross of Christ, a crucifix, esp. one set on a beam or screen in a church. WH: pre-1200. Old English *rōd* cross, pole, measure of land, from Germanic. Cp. German *Rute* switch, cane, rod.

roof *n.* the upper covering of a house or other building. *Also v.t.* WH: pre-1200. Old English *hrōf*, from Germanic. Cp. Dutch *roef* cabin, coffin lid.

rooibos *n.* an evergreen shrub of the genus *Aspalathus*, whose leaves are used to make tea. WH: early 20C. Afrikaans, from *rooi* red + *bos* bush.

rooinek *n.* an English-speaking S African. WH: 19C. Afrikaans, from *rooi* red + *nek* neck. British troops were highly susceptible to sunburn in S Africa.

rook[1] *n.* a gregarious bird, *Corvus frugilegus*, of the crow family with glossy black plumage. *Also v.t.* WH: pre-1200. Old English *hrōc*, from Germanic, prob. of imit. orig.

rook[2] *n.* the castle in chess. WH: 12–14C. Old French *rok*, *roc*, ult. from Arabic *rukk*, of unknown orig. meaning, but assoc. with ROC.

rookie *n.* a raw recruit or beginner. WH: 19C. Orig. uncertain. ? Alt. of RECRUIT, influ. by ROOK[1] in sense simpleton.

room *n.* space regarded as available for occupation, accommodation etc. *Also v.i., v.t.* WH: pre-1200. Old English *rūm*, from Germanic. Cp. German *Raum* space.

roop *n.* a respiratory disease of poultry caused by a virus. WH: 17C. Var. of ROUP[2].

roost[1] *n.* a pole or perch for birds to rest on. *Also v.i., v.t.* WH: pre-1200. Old English *hrōst*, from Germanic, of unknown orig. The related noun *rooster* dates from the 18C as a US euphemistic substitute for COCK[1].

roost[2] *n.* a powerful tidal current, esp. off the Orkney and Shetland Islands. WH: 17C. Var. of *roust*, from Old Norse *rǫst*.

root[1] *n.* the descending part of a plant which fixes itself in the earth and draws nourishment from it. *Also a., v.i., v.t.* WH: pre-1200. Old Norse *rót*, from Scandinavian base rel. to Latin *radix* root, *ramus* branch. Cp. WORT.

root[2] *v.t.* to dig or grub (up) with the snout, beak etc. *Also v.i.* WH: pre-1200. Old English *wrōtan*, from Germanic. Cp. German *Rüssel* snout. ? Ult. rel. to Latin *rodere* to gnaw, but not to ROOT[1].

root[3] *v.i.* to cheer, to shout encouragement to, to give support. WH: 19C. ? From ROUT[3].

rope *n.* a stout cord of twisted fibres of cotton, nylon etc., or wire. *Also v.t., v.i.* WH: pre-1200. Old English *rāp*, from Germanic. Cp. Dutch *reep* rope, German *Reifen* tyre, hoop.

Roquefort *n.* a French blue cheese made from ewes' milk. WH: 19C. *Roquefort*, a village in SW France.

roquelaure *n.* a short cloak for men worn in the 18th cent. WH: 18C. Antoine-Gaston, duc de *Roquelaure*, 1656–1738, Marshal of France.

roquet *v.t.* in croquet, to make one's ball strike (another ball). *Also v.i., n.* WH: 19C. Appar. arbitrary alt. of CROQUET.

†roral *a.* pertaining to or like dew, dewy. WH: 17C. Latin *ros, roris* dew + -AL[1].

ro-ro *a.* roll-on roll-off. WH: mid-20C. Acronym of *roll-on roll-off* (ROLL).

rorqual *n.* a baleen whale with dorsal fins, of the family Balaenopteridae, the finback. WH: 19C. French, from Norwegian *røyrkval*, from Old Norse *reytharhvalr*, from *reythr* rorqual (rel. to *rauthr* red) + *hvalr* whale.

Rorschach test *n.* a test for personality traits and disorders based on the interpretation of random ink blots. WH: early 20C. Hermann *Rorschach*, 1884–1922, Swiss psychiatrist.

rort *n.* a deception. WH: mid-20C. Back-formation from *rorty* rowdy, of unknown orig.

rosace *n.* a rose window. WH: 19C. French, from Latin *rosaceus*, from *rosa* ROSE.

rosaline *n.* fine needlepoint or pillow lace. WH: early 20C. Prob. from French.

rosaniline *n.* a compound having powerful basic properties, derived from aniline. WH: 19C. ROSE + ANILINE.

rosary *n.* a form of prayer in the Roman Catholic Church in which three sets of five decades of aves, each decade preceded by a paternoster and followed by a gloria, are repeated. WH: 12–14C. Latin *rosarium* rose garden, from *rosarius*, from *rosa* ROSE. The current sense form of prayer evolved in the 16C from the notion of a 'garden' of prayers. The word was at one time used as the title of a book of devotion. Cp. ANTHOLOGY, FLORILEGIUM.

Roscian *a.* of or in the manner of Quintus Roscius Gallus. WH: 17C. Quintus *Roscius* Gallus, d.62 BC, a famous Roman actor + -AN.

roscoe *n.* a gun. WH: early 20C. The surname *Roscoe*.

rose *n.* any plant or flower of the genus *Rosa*, consisting of prickly bushes or climbing and trailing shrubs bearing single or double flowers, usu. scented, of all shades of colour from white and yellow to dark crimson. *Also a., v.t.* WH: pre-1200. Old English *rōse*, from Germanic, from Latin *rosa*, rel. to Greek *rhodon* rose. The sense perforated nozzle on a hose or watering can dates from the 18C and may have been partly influenced by French *arroser* to water (from Latin *ros, roris* dew).

rosé *n.* a pink-coloured wine, having had only brief contact with red grape skins. WH: 19C. French pink, from *rose* ROSE.

rosella *n.* a variety of brightly-coloured parakeet, *Platycercus eximius*. WH: 19C. Appar. from *Rose-Hiller*, from *Rose Hill*, Parramatta, near Sydney, Australia.

roselle *n.* a hibiscus, *Hibiscus sabdariffa*, with a red calyx. WH: 19C. ? Alt. of French name *l'oseille de Guinée* sorrel of Guinea, influ. by ROSE.

rosemaling *n.* the art of painting furniture with flower motifs. WH: mid-20C. Norwegian rose-painting.

rosemary *n.* an evergreen fragrant shrub, *Rosmarinus officinalis*, of the mint family, with leaves which yield a perfume and oil and which are used in cooking etc. WH: 14–15C. Alt. of obs. *rosmarine*, from Old French *rosmarin* (Modern French *romarin*), from Latin *ros marinus*, lit. sea dew, by assoc. with ROSE and female forename *Mary* (esp. as that of Virgin Mary).

roseola *n.* a rash occurring in measles etc. WH: 19C. Latin *roseus* rose-coloured + dim. suf. *-ola*, based on *rubeola* (RUBELLA).

roset *n.* a rosin. *Also v.t.* WH: 14–15C. Prob. from ROSE.

Rosetta Stone *n.* a key to understanding something previously unattainable. WH: early 20C. Name of a stone discovered in 1799 near Rosetta (Rashīd), Egypt. It bore a 2C BC trilingual inscription in Greek, demotic Egyptian and Egyptian hieroglyphs which served as a key for deciphering hieroglyphs. It is now in the British Museum.

rosette *n.* a rose-shaped ornament, knot or badge. WH: 18C. French, dim. of *rose* ROSE. See also -ETTE.

Rosh Hashana *n.* the Jewish New Year. WH: 18C. Hebrew *rō'š haššānāh*, lit. head of the year.

Roshi *n.* the spiritual leader of a community of Zen Buddhist monks. WH: mid-20C. Japanese, from *rō* old + *shi* teacher.

Rosicrucian *n.* a member of a secret religious society devoted to the study of occult science, which became known to the public early in the 17th cent. *Also a.* WH: 17C. Modern Latin *rosa crucis*, translating German *Rosenkreuz*, the name of Christian Rosenkreuz, its alleged founder in 1484. See also -IAN. Rosenkreuz is said to have been born in 1378 and to have died in 1484, the year of the society's foundation, at the age of 106. He is now generally regarded as a legendary character. His name evokes Christ, Rose and Cross, the latter the twin symbols of Christ's Redemption and Resurrection.

rosin *n.* resin, esp. the solid residue left after the oil has been distilled from crude turpentine. *Also v.t.* WH: 12–14C. Alt. of RESIN.

Rosinante *n.* a worn-out horse, a nag. WH: 18C. Spanish *Rocinante* (from *rocín* horse, jade), Don Quixote's horse in Cervantes' romance (1605–15).

rosolio *n.* a cordial made from raisins, spirits etc. in Italy and S Europe. WH: 19C. Italian, var. of *rosoli*, from Latin *ros* dew + *solis*, gen. of *sol* sun.

rostellum *n.* an elevated portion of the stigma in orchids. WH: 18C. Latin small beak, dim. of ROSTRUM.

roster *n.* a list showing the order of rotation in which employees, officers, members etc. are to perform their turns of duty. *Also v.t.* WH: 18C. Dutch *rooster* gridiron, table, list, from *roosten* to roast. See also -ER[1]. The list is so called from its parallel lines, resembling a gridiron.

rostrum *n.* a platform, a pulpit. WH: 16C. Latin beak, beak-headed, from *rodere* to gnaw. The word was originally the term for a platform for speakers in the Forum at Rome that was decorated with the beak-heads of captured warships.

rosula *n.* a rosette of leaves. WH: 19C. Late Latin, dim. of *rosa* ROSE. See also -ULE.

rot *v.i.* to decompose through natural change. *Also v.t., n., int.* WH: pre-1200. Old English *rotian*, from Germanic. Cp. RET.

rota *n.* a list of names, duties etc., a roster. WH: 17C. Latin wheel. The word was originally the name of a political club, founded in 1659 by James Harrington, that advocated rotation in the offices of government. Harrington also first used *rotation* (ROTATE[1]) in this sense in 1656.

rotary *a.* acting or characterized by rotation. *Also n.* WH: 18C. Medieval Latin *rotarius*, from Latin *rota*. See ROTA, also -ARY[1].

rotate[1] *v.i.* to revolve round an axis or centre. *Also v.t.* WH: 17C. Latin *rotatus*, p.p. of *rotare*, from *rota*. See ROTA, also -ATE[3].

rotate[2] *a.* (of a calyx, corolla etc.) wheel-shaped. WH: 18C. Latin *rota* wheel + -ATE[2].

rote *n.* mere repetition of words, phrases etc. without understanding; mechanical, routine memory or knowledge. *Also v.t.* WH: 12–14C. Orig. unknown. Appar. not rel. to French *route* (ROUTE) or Latin *rota* (ROTA).

rotenone *n.* a crystalline substance obtained from the roots of derris, used as an insecticide. WH: early 20C. Japanese *roten* derris + -ONE.

roti *n.* unleavened bread, food. WH: early 20C. Hindi *roṭī*.

rotifer *n.* any member of the Rotifera, a phylum of minute aquatic animals with swimming organs appearing to have a rotary movement. WH: 18C. Modern Latin, from Latin *rota* wheel + -*i*- + -*fer*, from Latin *ferre* to carry, to bear.

rotisserie *n.* a device with a spit on which food, esp. meat, is roasted or barbecued. WH: 19C. French *rôtisserie*, from *rôtir* to roast.

rotogravure *n.* a process of photogravure printing on a rotary machine. WH: early 20C. From the name of the German company *Rotogravur* Deutsche Tiefdruck Gesellschaft, assim. to PHOTO- GRAVURE.

rotor *n.* the rotating part of an electric machine. WH: 19C. Contr. of *rotator* (ROTATE[1]).

rotten *a.* decomposed, decayed. WH: 12–14C. Old Norse *rotinn*, prob. p.p. of an unrecorded v. corr. to ROT.

Rottweiler *n.* a large German breed of dog with a smooth black-and-tan coat. WH: early 20C. *Rottweil*, a town in SW Germany. See also -ER[1].

rotula *n.* the kneecap or patella. WH: 14–15C. Latin, dim. of *rota* wheel. See also -ULE.

rotund *a.* circular or spherical. WH: 15C. Latin *rotundus*, from *rotare* ROTATE[1]. Cp. OROTUND.

roturier *n.* a plebeian. WH: 16C. French, from *roture* land tenure of a person not of noble birth, from Latin *ruptura*, from *ruptus*, p.p. of *rumpere* to break. See also -IER. The evolution of meaning here is: broken land (i.e. land recently cleared), tax due to a lord for such land, land subject to tax, land held by a person not of noble birth.

rouble *n.* the standard monetary unit of Russia, Belarus and Tajikistan. WH: 16C. French, from Russian *rubl'*, from *rubit'* to chop, to hack. The reference is to a coin originally 'chopped' from a silver bar.

roué *n.* a rake, a debauchee. WH: 19C. French, use as n. of p.p. of *rouer* to break on the wheel. The reference is to the punishment said to be deserved by such a person.

rouge *n.* a cosmetic used to colour the cheeks red. *Also v.t., v.i., a.* WH: 14–15C. Old French, from Latin *rubeus* red.

rough *a.* having an uneven or irregular surface. *Also adv., n., v.t.* WH: pre-1200. Old English *rūh*, from Germanic. Cp. RUFF[1].

roulade *n.* a rolled piece of veal or pork. WH: 18C. French, from *rouler* to roll. See also -ADE.

rouleau *n.* a small roll, esp. a pile of coins done up in paper. WH: 17C. French, from obs. *roule* (now *rôle*). See ROLE.

roulette *n.* a gambling game played with a ball on a table with a revolving disc. WH: 18C. French, dim. of *rouelle* wheel, from Late Latin *rotella*, dim. of *rota* wheel.

rounce *n.* in printing on a hand press, the handle by which the bed of the printing press is run in and out under the platen. WH: 17C. Dutch *ronse*, *rondse*.

round *a.* spherical, circular or approximately so. *Also n., adv., prep., v.t., v.i.* WH: 12–14C. Old French *rond*-, stem of *ront*, earlier *reont* (Modern French *rond*), from var. of Latin *rotundus* ROTUND.

roundel *n.* a round disc, panel, heraldic circular charge etc. WH: 12–14C. Old French *rondel*, from *rond*-. See ROUND, also -EL. Cp. RONDEAU.

roundelay *n.* a simple song, usu. with a refrain. WH: 14–15C. Old French *rondelet*, dim. of *rondel* ROUNDEL, with ending assim. to VIRELAY or LAY[3].

roup[1] *v.t.* to sell by auction. *Also n.* WH: 12–14C. Scandinavian. Cp. Old Norse *raupa* to boast, to brag.

roup[2] *n.* a respiratory viral disease of poultry. WH: 16C. ROUP[1].

rouse *v.t.* to wake. *Also v.i., n.* WH: 14–15C. Prob. from Anglo-French. Cp. AROUSE.

roust *v.t.* to rouse, to rout (out). WH: 17C. ? Alt. of ROUSE.

rout[1] *n.* an utter defeat and overthrow. *Also v.t.* WH: 16C. Old French *route*, from Latin *rupta*, use as n. of fem. p.p. of *rumpere* to break. Cp. ROUTE.

rout[2] *v.t.* to root (up or out). *Also v.i.* WH: 16C. Var. of ROOT[2].

rout[3] *v.i.* (of cattle etc.) to bellow, to roar. WH: 12–14C. Old Norse *rauta*, *rjóta*. Cp. ROOT[3].

route *n.* the way or road(s) travelled or to be travelled. *Also v.t.* WH: 12–14C. Old French *rute* (Modern French *route*), from Latin *rupta via*, lit. broken way (i.e. a road opened up by force), from fem. p.p. of *rumpere* to break + *via* way (cp. VIA). Cp. ROUT[1].

routine *n.* a course of procedure or official duties etc., regularly pursued. *Also a.* WH: 17C. French, from *route* way, path, course. See ROUTE.

roux *n.* a sauce base, the thickening element in a sauce made from melted fat (esp. butter) and flour cooked together. WH: 19C. French browned (i.e. butter).

rove[1] *v.i.* to wander, to ramble, to roam. *Also v.t., n.* WH: 15C. Prob. ult. from Scandinavian.

rove[2] *n.* a small metal plate through which a rivet is passed and clenched over. WH: 12–14C. Old Norse *ró*.

rove[3] *v.t.* to draw out and slightly twist (slivers of wool, cotton etc.) before spinning into thread. *Also n.* WH: 18C. Orig. unknown.

row[1] *n.* a series of persons or things in a straight or nearly straight line. WH: pre-1200. Old English *rāw*, prob. rel. to Middle Dutch *rīe* (Dutch *rij*), Middle High German *rīhe* (German *Reihe*), from Germanic. Cp. Sanskrit *rekhā* stroke, line.

row[2] *v.t.* to propel by oars. *Also v.i., n.* WH: pre-1200. Old English *rōwan*, from Germanic. Rel. to Latin *remus*, Greek *eretmon* oar. Cp. RUDDER.

row[3] *n.* a noisy disturbance, a commotion. *Also v.t., v.i.* WH: 18C. Orig. unknown.

rowan *n.* the mountain ash, *Sorbus aucuparia*. WH: 15C. Scandinavian. Cp. Old Norse *reynir*, Norwegian *rogn*.

rowdy *a.* rough, riotous. *Also n.* WH: 19C. Prob. from ROW[3].

rowel *n.* a spiked disc or wheel on a spur. *Also v.t.* WH: 12–14C. Old French *roele*, from Late Latin *rotella*, dim. of Latin *rota* wheel.

rowen *n.* a second growth of grass, an aftermath. WH: 12–14C. Old Northern French var. of Old French *regain*, from *regaaigner*, from RE- + *gaagnier* (see GAIN).

Rowton house *n.* a cheap lodging house for poor, single men. WH: 19C. Montague William Lowry-Corry, 1st Lord *Rowton*, 1838–1903, English social reformer.

Roxburghe *n.* a style of bookbinding comprising a plain leather back, usu. gilt-lettered, cloth or paper sides, gilt top and the other edges untrimmed. WH: 19C. 3rd Duke of *Roxburghe*, 1740–1804, Scottish book collector.

royal *a.* of or relating to a king or queen. *Also n.* WH: 14–15C. Old French *roial* (Modern French *royal*), from Latin *regalis* (REGAL[1]).

rozzer *n.* a police officer. WH: 19C. Orig. unknown. ? From a Romany word.

-rrhagia *comb. form* abnormal discharge, excessive flow, as in *menorrhagia*. WH: Modern Latin, from Greek, from base of *rhēgnunai* to break, to burst.

-rrhoea *comb. form* a discharge, a flow, as in *diarrhoea*. WH: Greek *rhoia* flux, flow, from *rhein* to flow.

RSVP *abbr.* please reply. WH: Abbr. of French *répondez, s'il vous plaît* reply, please.

rub[1] *v.t.* to apply friction to, to move one's hand or other object over the surface of. *Also v.i., n.* WH: 12–14C. ? Low German *rubben*, of unknown orig.

rub[2] *n.* a rubber of bridge. WH: 19C. Abbr. of RUBBER[2].

rub-a-dub *n.* the sound of a rapid drumbeat. *Also v.i.* WH: 18C. Imit.

rubaiyat *n.* in Persian poetry, a verse form consisting of quatrains. WH: 19C. Arabic *rubā'iyāt*, pl. of *rubā'ī* quadripartite.

rubato *n.* flexibility of rhythm, fluctuation of tempo within a musical piece. *Also a.* WH: 18C. Italian, lit. robbed. The feature is so called because the strict time is 'robbed' from a note or notes, to be 'paid back' later.

rubber[1] *n.* a soft, elastic substance obtained from the coagulated juice of several tropical plants. *Also a.* WH: 16C. RUB[1] + -ER[1]. The original sense was a hard brush for rubbing things clean. The name of the substance dates from the 18C, and the sense eraser from the early 20C. The latter was originally known as an *India rubber* (INDIAN) in the 18C.

rubber[2] *n.* a series of three games at whist, bridge, backgammon etc. WH: 16C. Orig. uncertain. ? A special use of RUBBER[1].

rubbish *n.* waste matter, refuse. *Also a., v.t.* WH: 14–15C. Anglo-French *rubbous*, ? alt. of pl. of Anglo-French deriv. of Old French *robe* spoils (see RUBBLE), assim. to -ISH[1].

rubble *n.* rough, broken fragments of stone, brick etc. WH: 14–15C. ? Anglo-French alt. of Old French *robe* spoils. See ROBE. Cp. RUBBISH.

rube *n.* an unsophisticated country dweller, a country bumpkin. WH: 19C. *Rube*, pet form of male forename *Reuben*.

rubefy *v.t.* to make red. WH: 14–15C. Old French *rubifier, rubefier* (Modern French *rubéfier*), from Medieval Latin *rubificare*, from Latin *rubefacere*, from *rubeus* red. See also -FY.

rubella *n.* a mild, infectious disorder resembling measles which, if contracted by a pregnant woman, may cause birth deformities in her unborn child; German measles. WH: 19C. Use as n. of neut. pl. of Latin *rubellus* reddish, from *rubeus* red. See also -EL. The disorder is so called from its characteristic red rash.

Rubicon *n.* an irrevocable step, a point of no return. *Also v.t.* WH: 17C. *Rubicon*, a stream in NE Italy marking the ancient boundary between Italy and Cisalpine Gaul. Julius Caesar took his army across it (i.e. outside his own province) in 49 BC, so committing himself to war against the Senate and Pompey.

rubicund *a.* ruddy, rosy, red-faced. WH: 14–15C. Latin *rubicundus*, from *rubere* to be red, from *ruber* red.

rubidium *n.* a silvery-white metallic element, at. no. 37, chem. symbol Rb, belonging to the potassium group. WH: 19C. Modern Latin, from Latin *rubidus* red. See also -IUM. The element is so called with reference to the two red lines in its spectrum. It was so named by R.W. Bunsen (see BUNSEN BURNER), who discovered it in 1860 together with the German physicist G.R. Kirchhoff.

rubiginous *a.* rusty or brownish-red in colour. WH: 17C. Latin *rubigo, rubiginis* rust, blight + -OUS.

Rubik's cube® *n.* a puzzle consisting of a cube, each face of which is divided into nine coloured segments which can be revolved to obtain the same colour on each face. WH: late 20C. Ernö *Rubik*, 1944–, Hungarian architectural designer, who invented it in 1974.

rubric *n.* a title, chapter heading, entry, set of rules, commentary or direction, esp. a liturgical direction in the Prayer Book etc. *Also a.* WH: 12–14C. Old French *rubrique* or Latin *rubrica* red ochre, use as

n. of fem. of *a.* from base of *rubeus, ruber* red. Cp. RUBY. A rubric was originally a written or printed text in distinctive red lettering, especially a direction for the conduct of a religious service or an entry of a saint's name in a calendar.

ruby *n.* a precious stone of a red colour, a variety of corundum. *Also a.* WH: 12–14C. Old French *rubi* (Modern French *rubis*), from Medieval Latin *rubinus*, use as n. of a. from base of Latin *rubeus, ruber* red.

ruche *n.* a pleated strip of gauze, lace, silk or the like used as a frill or trimming. *Also v.t.* WH: 19C. French, from Medieval Latin *rusca* tree bark, of Celtic orig.

ruck[1] *n.* a multitude, a crowd, esp. the mass of horses left behind by the leaders in a race. *Also v.i.* WH: 12–14C. Appar. of Scandinavian orig., corr. to Norwegian *ruka*.

ruck[2] *v.i., v.t.* to wrinkle, to crease. *Also n.* WH: 18C. Old Norse *hrukka*, rel. to Norwegian *rukla, rukka*.

ruckle *v.i.* to make a rattling or gurgling noise. *Also n.* WH: 16C. Scandinavian. Cp. Norwegian dial. *rukla*.

rucksack *n.* a bag carried on the back by means of straps by campers, hikers, climbers etc. WH: 19C. German, from *Rucken*, dial. var. of *Rücken* back + *Sack* SACK[1]. Cp. *backpack* (BACK[1]).

ruckus *n.* a row, a disturbance, an uproar. WH: 19C. Orig. uncertain. ? Rel. to RUCTION, RUMPUS.

ruction *n.* a commotion, a disturbance, a row. WH: 19C. Orig. unknown. According to some, the word is a shortening of INSURRECTION.

rudaceous *a.* (of rock) composed of fairly large fragments. WH: early 20C. Latin *rudus* rubble + -ACEOUS.

rudbeckia *n.* a plant of the genus *Rudbeckia* of N American plants of the aster family. WH: 18C. Modern Latin, from Olaf *Rudbeck*, 1660–1740, Swedish botanist + -IA.

rudd *n.* a fish, *Scardinius erythrophthalmus*, resembling a roach. WH: 16C. Appar. from dial. *rud* red, redness, from Old English *rudu*, rel. to RED. The fish is so called from its red fins and iris, which distinguish it from the roach. Hence its alternative name *red-eye* and its species name (from Greek *eruthros* red + *ophthalmos* eye).

rudder *n.* a flat wooden or metal framework or solid piece hinged to the sternpost of a boat or ship and serving as a means of steering. WH: pre-1200. Old English *röther*, from Germanic, rel. to ROW[2]. Cp. German *Ruder*.

ruddle *n.* a variety of red ochre used for marking sheep, raddle. *Also v.t.* WH: 14–15C. Rel. to dial. *rud* (RUDD). See also -LE[1]. Cp. RADDLE[1].

ruddock *n.* a robin (the bird). WH: pre-1200. Old English *rudduc*, rel. to dial. *rud* (RUDD), RUDDY. See also -OCK. Cp. *redbreast* (RED).

ruddy *a.* of a red or reddish colour. *Also v.t., v.i.* WH: pre-1200. Old English *rudig*, from base of dial. *rud* (RUDD). See also -Y[1].

rude *a.* impolite, insulting. WH: 12–14C. Old French, from Latin *rudis* unworked, uncultivated, rel. to *rudus* broken stone. Cp. RUDERAL.

ruderal *a.* (of a plant) growing on rubbish. *Also n.* WH: 19C. Latin *rudera*, pl. of *rudus*. See RUDE, also -AL[1].

rudiment *n.* an elementary or first principle of knowledge etc. WH: 16C. French, or from Latin *rudimentum*, from *rudis* RUDE, based on *elementum* ELEMENT.

rue[1] *v.t.* to grieve or be sorry for, to regret, to repent of. *Also v.i., n.* WH: pre-1200. Old English *hrēowan*, from Germanic. Cp. German *reuen*.

rue[2] *n.* a plant of the genus *Ruta*, esp. *R. graveolens*, a shrubby evergreen plant, having a strong smell and acrid taste, formerly used as a stimulant etc. in medicine. WH: 12–14C. Old French, from Latin *ruta*, from Greek *rhutē*.

rufescent *a.* reddish, tinged with red. WH: 19C. Latin *rufescens, rufescentis*, pres.p. of *rufescere*, from *rufus* reddish. See -escent (-ESCENCE).

ruff[1] *n.* a broad pleated or fluted collar or frill of linen or muslin worn by both sexes, esp. in the 16C. WH: 16C. Prob. use as n. of var. of ROUGH. According to some, the word is a shortening of RUFFLE.

ruff[2] *n.* a small freshwater fish, *Gymnocephalus cernua*, related to and resembling the perch. WH: 14–15C. RUFF[1], or more directly from ROUGH.

ruff[3] *n.* the act of trumping when one cannot follow suit. *Also v.t., v.i.* WH: 16C. Old French *roffle*, *rouffle*, earlier *ronfle*, corr. to Italian *ronfla*, ? alt. of *trionfo* TRUMP[1].

ruffian *n.* a low, lawless, brutal person, a bully, a violent hoodlum. *Also a.* WH: 15C. Old French (Modern French *rufien*) or Italian *ruffiano*, prob. from dial. *rofia* scab, scurf, from Germanic. The word is popularly associated, at least in sense, with ROUGH.

ruffle *v.t.* to disturb the smoothness or order of. *Also v.i., n.* WH: 12–14C. Orig. unknown. Cp. RIFFLE[1].

rufiyaa *n.* the standard unit of currency of the Maldives. WH: late 20C. Maldivian, from source of RUPEE.

rufous *a.* of a brownish-red. WH: 18C. Latin *rufus* red, reddish + -OUS.

rug *n.* a thick, heavy wrap, coverlet etc., usu. woollen with a thick nap, or of skin with the hair or wool left on. WH: 16C. Prob. of Scandinavian orig. and rel. to RAG[1]. Cp. Norwegian dial. *rugga* coverlet, Swedish *rugg* ruffled hair.

ruga *n.* a wrinkle, crease, fold or ridge. WH: 18C. Latin.

rugby *n.* a game of football in which players are allowed to use their hands in carrying and passing the ball and tackling their opponents. WH: 19C. *Rugby* School, in Rugby, Warwickshire, where the game was first played in 1841.

rugged *a.* having an extremely uneven surface full of inequalities. WH: 12–14C. Prob. of Scandinavian orig. Cp. RUG, Swedish *rugga* to roughen.

rugosa *n.* a Japanese rose, *Rosa rugosa*, having deep pink flowers. WH: 19C. Latin, fem. of *rugosus*, from *ruga* wrinkle, RUGA. The plant is so named from its wrinkled leaves.

ruin *n.* a state of wreck, a downfall. *Also v.t., v.i.* WH: 12–14C. Old French *ruine*, from Latin *ruina*, from *ruere* to fall. The original sense was the action of a structure giving way and falling down. This then passed to the sense of fallen remains in the 14–15C.

rule *n.* something which is established as a principle or guide of action. *Also v.t., v.i.* WH: 12–14C. Old French *riule*, *reule* (Modern French *règle*), from Latin *regula* straight stick, bar, pattern, rel. to *regere* to rule. Cp. REX.

rum[1] *n.* a spirit distilled from fermented molasses or cane juice. WH: 17C. ? Abbr. of obs. *rumbullion*, of unknown orig.

rum[2] *a.* strange, singular, odd, queer. WH: 18C. Orig. unknown. ? Rel. to ROM.

rumba *n.* a complex and rhythmic Cuban dance. *Also v.i.* WH: early 20C. American Spanish, orig. spree, carousal, party.

rumbustious *a.* boisterous, turbulent, cheerful and noisy. WH: 18C. Prob. alt. of obs. *robustious*, from ROBUST + -IOUS. Cp. RUMPUS.

rumen *n.* the first cavity of the complex stomach of a ruminant. WH: 18C. Latin *rumen*, *ruminis* throat, gullet.

ruminant *n.* any member of the division of cud-chewing animals with a complex stomach, including cattle, sheep, deer etc. *Also a.* WH: 17C. Latin *ruminans*, *ruminantis*, pres.p. of *ruminari* to chew the cud, from RUMEN.

rummage *v.t.* to make a search in or through, to ransack, esp. by throwing the contents about. *Also v.i., n.* WH: 15C. Old French *arrumage* (Modern French *arrimage*), from *arrumer*, var. of *arimer*, *ariner*, from AR- + *run* ship's hold, from Dutch *ruim* space (ROOM). See also -AGE. The verb came from the noun, and originally had the meaning (to the 18C) to arrange goods in the hold of a ship. Hence the current opposite sense, to disarrange by searching (16C).

rummer *n.* a large drinking glass. WH: 17C. Low Dutch. Cp. Dutch *roemen* to extol, to boast.

rummy *n.* any of several card games in which the object is to collect combinations and sequences of cards. WH: early 20C. Orig. unknown.

rumour *n.* popular report, hearsay. *Also v.t.* WH: 14–15C. Old French *rumur* (Modern French *rumeur*), from Latin *rumor* noise, din. See also -OUR. Cp. BRUIT.

rump *n.* the end of the backbone of a mammal with the adjacent parts, the posterior, the buttocks. WH: 14–15C. Prob. of Scandinavian orig. Cp. Danish *rumpe*, Swedish *rumpa*, Icelandic *rumpur*.

rumple *v.t.* to make uneven, to crease. *Also v.i., n.* WH: 16C. Middle Dutch *rompel*, from *rompe*, Middle Low German *rumpe*, or from Middle Dutch, Middle Low German *rumpelen*, *rompelen* to rumple. The verb came from the noun.

rumpus *n.* a disturbance, an uproar, a row. WH: 18C. Prob. fanciful alt. of obs. *robustious*. See RUMBUSTIOUS.

run *v.i.* to move or pass over the ground by using the legs with a springing motion, so that both feet are never on the ground at once. *Also v.t., n.* WH: pre-1200. Old English *rinnan*, from Germanic v. of unknown orig. The prevailing form of the verb until the 12–14C was *urn*, and *run* became fully current only from the 16C.

runcible *n.* a three-pronged fork hollowed out like a spoon and with one of the prongs having a cutting edge. WH: 19C. Invented word introduced by Edward Lear, 1812–88, English humorist. Lear may have based the adjective on the noun *rouncival* a variety of pea, perhaps itself from Spanish *Roncesvalles*, French *Roncevaux*, a village in N Spain. He applied the adjective not only to the spoon (in *The Owl and the Pussy-Cat*, who went to sea 'in a beautiful pea-green boat') (1871), but subsequently to a cat (1877), a hat (1888), and a goose and a wall (1895). Some etymologists relate the word to RUNCINATE.

runcinate *a.* (of a leaf) saw-toothed. WH: 18C. Modern Latin *runcinatus*, from Latin *runcina* carpenter's plane (formerly taken to mean saw) + -ATE[2].

rune *n.* a letter or character of the earliest Germanic alphabet, formed from the Greek alphabet by modifying the shape to suit carving, used chiefly by the Scandinavians and Anglo-Saxons. WH: pre-1200. Var. of obs. *roun* secret, mystery, from Old English *rūn*, from Germanic. In its sense letter of the alphabet, the word is not recorded between the 12–14C and the 17C. It was then reintroduced from Late Latin *runa*, influenced by Old Norse *rúnar*, *rúnir* (pl.), secret lore, runes, magical signs.

rung *n.* a stick or bar forming a step in a ladder. WH: pre-1200. Old English *hrung*, from Germanic. Cp. German *Runge*. The original sense was a rounded stick used as a rail in a cart, chair etc. The current sense evolved in the 12–14C.

runlet *n.* a small stream, a runnel. WH: 17C. RUN + -LET.

runnel *n.* a rivulet, a little brook. WH: 16C. Var. of dial. *rindle* (from Old English *rinnelle*, from stem of RUN), influ. by RUN.

runt *n.* the smallest or feeblest animal in a litter esp. a piglet. WH: 16C. Orig. unknown.

rupee *n.* the standard monetary unit of various Asian countries including India, Pakistan, Sri Lanka, Nepal, Mauritius and the Seychelles. WH: 17C. Hindi *rupiyā*, *rūpiyā*, from Sanskrit *rūpya* wrought silver.

rupestrian *a.* (of art) done on cave walls. WH: 18C. Modern Latin *rupestris*, from Latin *rupes* rock. See also -AN.

rupiah *n.* the standard monetary unit of Indonesia. WH: mid-20C. Indonesian, from source of RUPEE.

rupture *n.* the act of breaking or the state of being broken or violently parted. *Also v.t., v.i.* WH: 14–15C. Old French, from Latin *ruptura*, from *ruptus*, p.p. of *rumpere* to break. See also -URE.

rural *a.* of or relating to the country, as distinct from *urban*. WH: 14–15C. Old French, from Late Latin *ruralis*, from Latin *rus*, *ruris* the country. See also -AL[1]. Cp. RUSTIC.

Ruritania *n.* an imaginary mysterious or romantic country. WH: 19C. An imaginary kingdom in SE Europe in the novels of Anthony Hope, 1863–1933. Hope introduced the name in *The Prisoner of Zenda* (1894), creating it from Latin *rus*, *ruris* the country + -*tania* as in the names of Roman provinces such as *Lusitania*.

ruru *n.* the New Zealand mopoke. WH: 19C. Maori, of imit. orig. Cp. MOPOKE, BOOBOOK.

rusa *n.* a large Indonesian deer, *Cervus timorensis*. WH: 18C. Modern Latin *Rusa*, former genus name, from Malay.

ruscus *n.* any plant of the genus *Ruscus* of shrubby evergreen plants, containing the butcher's broom. WH: 16C. Latin.

ruse *n.* a stratagem, trick or wile. WH: 14–15C. Old French, from *ruser* to use trickery, (orig.) to drive back, ? ult. from Latin *rursus* back, backwards. The original sense was the doubling back of a hunted animal to avoid being captured. The current sense dates from the 16C.

rush[1] *v.t.* to move or push with haste. *Also v.i., n., a.* WH: 14–15C. Anglo-French *russher*, var. of Old French *russer* (Modern French *ruser*). See RUSE. Many of the current senses may have arisen from the sound of the word. Cp. WHISH, WHOOSH.

rush² *n.* a plant with long thin stems or leaves, of the family Juncaceae, growing mostly on wet ground, used for making baskets, mats, seats for chairs etc., and formerly for strewing floors. *Also a.* WH: pre-1200. Old English *rysc*, from Germanic. The Old English word lies behind such place names as *Ruislip, Rushall* and *Rushmere.*

rusk *n.* a piece of bread or cake crisped and browned in the oven, given to babies. WH: 16C. Spanish and Portuguese *rosca* twist, coil, twisted roll of bread, of unknown orig.

russel *n.* a twilled woollen or cotton fabric or rep. WH: 19C. Orig. unknown.

russet *a.* of a reddish-brown colour. *Also n.* WH: 12–14C. Anglo-French var. of Old French *rosset, rousset,* dim. of *rous* (Modern French *roux*), from Portuguese *ros,* Italian *rosso,* from Latin *russus* red. See also -ET¹.

Russian *a.* of or relating to Russia. *Also n.* WH: 16C. Medieval Latin *Russianus,* from *Russia* Russia, a country in E Europe and N Asia, the central and largest state of the former USSR. See also -AN.

Russophile *n.* a friend or admirer of Russia or the Russians. *Also a.* WH: 19C. *Russ,* old name of Russia and the Russian people + -O- + -PHILE.

Russophobe *n.* a person who fears or is an opponent of Russia or the Russians. *Also a.* WH: 19C. Russo- (RUSSOPHILE) + -PHOBE.

rust *n.* the red incrustation on iron or steel caused by its oxidation when exposed to air and moisture. *Also a., v.i., v.t.* WH: pre-1200. Old English *rūst,* from Germanic base also of RED.

rustic *a.* of or relating to the country, rural. *Also n.* WH: 14–15C. Latin *rusticus,* from *rus* the country. See also -IC. The sense unsophisticated, unrefined evolved in the 16C. The original sense was identical with RURAL.

rustle *v.i.* to make a quick succession of small sounds like the rubbing of dry leaves. *Also v.t., n.* WH: 14–15C. Imit. Cp. Dutch *ridselen, ritselen.*

rustre *n.* a lozenge with a round hole. WH: 18C. French, of unknown orig.

rut¹ *n.* a sunken track made by wheels, a groove. *Also v.t.* WH: 16C. Prob. from Old French *rote, rute* ROUTE.

rut² *n.* the sexual excitement or heat of deer and some other animals. *Also v.i.* WH: 14–15C. Old French, from Latin *rugitus,* from *rugire* to roar.

rutabaga *n.* a swede. WH: 18C. Swedish dial. *rotabagge,* from *rot* root + *bagga* bag.

ruthenium *n.* a white, spongy metallic element of the platinum group, at. no. 44, chem. symbol Ru. WH: 19C. Medieval Latin *Ruthenia* Russia + -IUM. The element is so called because it was first found in ores from the Urals. The name was coined in 1828 for the platinum ore by its discoverer, G.W. Osann, and first applied to the element itself in 1845 by the Russian chemist Karl K. Klaus, who isolated it from the crude ore.

rutherfordium *n.* the artificial radioactive element atom. no. 104, chem. symbol Rf. WH: mid-20C. Ernest *Rutherford,* 1871–1937, New Zealand-born British physicist + -IUM.

ruthless *a.* merciless, cruel. WH: 12–14C. Obs. *ruth* compassion, pity (from RUE¹ + -TH²) + -LESS.

rutile *n.* red titanium dioxide. WH: 19C. Latin *rutilis* reddish.

Rwanda *n.* the official language of Rwanda. WH: early 20C. Bantu *Rwanda,* an E African republic.

-ry *suf.* a business, a place of business, cultivation etc., conduct, things connected with or of the nature etc., as in *foundry, poultry, yeomanry.* WH: Shortening of -ERY.

rye *n.* the seeds or grain of *Secale cereale,* a cereal allied to wheat, used to make (black) bread, whisky etc. *Also a.* WH: pre-1200. Old English *ryge,* from Germanic. Cp. Dutch *rogge,* German *Roggen.*

ryepeck *n.* an ironshod pole used for driving into the bed of a stream to moor a punt etc. WH: 19C. Orig. unknown.

ryokan *n.* a traditional Japanese inn. WH: mid-20C. Japanese, from *ryo* to travel + *kan* building.

ryot *n.* in the Indian subcontinent, a peasant. WH: 17C. Persian, from Persian and Urdu *ra'īyat,* Urdu *raiyat,* from Arabic *ra'iyyat* flock, herd, subjects of a ruler, from *ra'ā* to pasture. Cp. RAYAH.

†'s- *pref.* (esp. in oaths) God's. **WH:** Abbr. of GOD + -'s.

-s¹ *suf.* forming plurals of most nouns. **WH:** Old English *-as*.

-s² *suf.* forming adverbs. **WH:** Old English m. and neut. gen. sing. ending *-es*.

-s³ *suf.* forming nicknames or pet names. **WH:** -s¹.

-s⁴ *suf.* forming the 3rd pers. sing. pres. tense of most verbs. **WH:** Old English dial., prob. from Old English 2nd pers. sing. pres. ending *-es, -as*.

-s' *suf.* forming the genitive (possessive) case of plural nouns and sometimes sing. nouns ending in *s*. **WH:** -s².

-'s *suf.* forming the genitive (possessive) case of sing. nouns and pl. nouns not ending in *s*. **WH:** -s².

sab *n.* a hunt saboteur. *Also v.t.* **WH:** late 20C. Abbr. of *saboteur* (SABOTAGE). The word arose among saboteurs as a name for themselves. Cp. SABAOTH.

sabadilla *n.* a Mexican and Central American liliaceous plant, *Schoenocaulon officinale*, yielding acrid seeds from which veratrine is obtained. **WH:** 19C. Spanish *cebadilla*, dim. of *cebada* barley.

Sabaean *n.* a member of the ancient people of Yemen. *Also a.* **WH:** 16C. Latin *Sabaeus*, Greek *Sabaios*, from *Saba*, from Arabic *Sabā'* Saba, corr. to Hebrew *šĕḇâ* Sheba, an ancient kingdom of the SW Arabian peninsula.

Sabaism *n.* the worship of the stars or the host of heaven. **WH:** 18C. French *sabaïsme*, from Hebrew *ṣābā'* hosts (of heaven). See also -ISM. Cp. SABAOTH.

Sabaoth *n.pl.* hosts, armies (in the title 'Lord God of Sabaoth'). **WH:** 12–14C. Latin, from Greek *Sabaōth*, from Hebrew *ṣĕḇā'ōt*, pl. of *ṣābā'*. See SABAISM. Not rel. to SABBATH.

sabbat *n.* a witches' sabbath. **WH:** pre-1200. Var. of SABBATH.

Sabbatarian *n.* a Jew who strictly observes Saturday as a day of rest and divine worship. *Also a.* **WH:** 17C. Late Latin *sabbatarius*, from Latin *sabbatum*. See SABBATH, also -ARIAN.

sabbath *n.* the seventh day of the week, Saturday, set apart, esp. by the Jews, for rest and divine worship. **WH:** pre-1200. Old French *sabbat* or Latin *sabbatum*, from Greek *sabbaton*, from Hebrew *šabbāt*, from *šāḇaṭ* to rest. The spelling with *-th* is based on the pronunciation of Hebrew *ṭ*. The Hebrew word gave the name of Saturday in many languages, e.g. Italian *sabato*, Spanish *sábado*, Romanian *sâmbătă*, Russian *subbota*, Polish *sobota*.

Sabellian *a.* of or relating to Sabellianism. *Also n.* **WH:** 14–15C. Ecclesiastical Latin *Sabellianus*, from *Sabellius*, *fl. c.*AD 217–220, African heretic leader + -AN.

sabelline *a.* of or relating to the sable. **WH:** 19C. Old French, from Medieval Latin *sabelina* (*pellis*) sable (fur), from *sabel* SABLE. See also -INE.

Sabian *n.* a member of an ancient sect who are classed in the Koran with Muslims, Jews and Christians as worshippers of the true God. *Also a.* **WH:** 17C. Arabic *ṣābī'* + -AN.

sabicu *n.* a W Indian tree, *Lysiloma latisiliqua*. **WH:** 19C. Cuban Spanish *sabicú*.

sabin *n.* a unit of acoustic absorption. **WH:** mid-20C. Wallace Clement Sabin, 1868–1919, US physicist.

Sabine *n.* a member of an ancient Italian people inhabiting the central Apennines. *Also a.* **WH:** pre-1200. Latin *Sabinus*. See also -INE.

Sabin vaccine *n.* a vaccine taken orally to immunize against poliomyelitis. **WH:** mid-20C. Albert Bruce Sabin, 1906–93, Russian-born US microbiologist + *vaccine* (VACCINATE).

sable *n.* a small arctic and subarctic carnivorous quadruped, *Martes zibellina*, allied to the marten, the brown fur of which is very highly valued. *Also a., v.t.* **WH:** 14–15C. Old French *sable* fur, from Medieval Latin *sabelum*, of Slavonic orig. Cp. Russian *sobol'*. The heraldic sense black dates from the 12–14C and is usually identified with the animal's name, even though sable fur is dark brown.

sabot *n.* a simple wooden shoe, usu. made in one piece. **WH:** early 20C. French, from Old French *çabot*, blend of *çavate* (Modern French SAVATE) and *bote* (Modern French *botte*) BOOT¹.

sabotage *n.* malicious damage to a railway, industrial plant, machinery etc., as a protest by discontented workers, or as a non-military act of warfare. *Also v.t.* **WH:** early 20C. French, from *saboter* to make a noise with sabots, to execute badly, to destroy, from SABOT. See also -AGE. The word is popularly said to refer to the action of striking workers who threw their sabots into machinery to damage it, but this origin is not substantiated. A more likely association is with the clumsy, noisy sabots.

sabra *n.* an Israeli born in Israel. **WH:** mid-20C. Modern Hebrew *ṣabbār* or Arabic *ṣabr* prickly pear.

sabre *n.* a cavalry sword having a curved blade. *Also v.t.* **WH:** 17C. French, alt. of obs. *sable*, from German *Sabel*, local var. of *Säbel*, from Hungarian *szablya*. The ultimate source of the word is Slavonic. Cp. Russian *sablya*.

sabretache *n.* a cavalry officer's leather pocket suspended on the left side from the sword-belt. **WH:** 19C. French, from German *Säbeltasche*, from *Säbel* sabre + *Tasche* pocket.

sabulous *a.* sandy, gritty. **WH:** 17C. Latin *sabulosus*, from *sabulum* sand. See also -ULOUS.

sac¹ *n.* a pouch, a cavity or receptacle in an animal or vegetable. **WH:** 18C. French, or Modern Latin use of Latin *saccus*. See SACK¹.

sac² *n.* a right or privilege, such as that of holding a court, granted to a lord of a manor by the Crown. **WH:** pre-1200. Old English *saca*, acc. and gen. pl. of *sacu* SAKE¹.

saccade *n.* a jump of the eye between fixation points. **WH:** 18C. French, from Old French *saquer* to shake, to pull. See SAC¹. See also -ADE. The original sense was a jerking movement in general. The sense jump of the eye dates from the mid-20C.

racchar- *comb. form* sugar. **WH:** Modern Latin *saccharum*, from Medieval Latin, from Greek *sakkharon* sugar. See SUGAR.

saccule *n.* a small sac, esp. the smaller of two cavities in the labyrinth of the inner ear. **WH:** 16C. Latin *sacculus*, dim. of *saccus*. See SACK¹, also -ULE.

sacellum *n.* a small, usu. roofless sanctuary containing an altar in an ancient Roman building. **WH:** 19C. Latin, dim. of *sacrum* shrine, from *sacer* holy.

sacerdotal *a.* of or relating to priests or the priesthood. **WH:** 14–15C. Old French, or from Latin *sacerdotalis*, from *sacerdos, sacerdotis* priest. See also -AL¹.

sachem *n.* a chief of certain tribes of N American Indians. **WH:** 17C. Algonquian (Massachusetts) *sontim*.

sachet *n.* a small ornamental bag or other receptacle containing perfumed powder for scenting clothes etc. **WH:** 15C. French, dim. of *sac*. See SACK¹, also -ET¹.

sack¹ *n.* a large, usu. oblong bag of strong coarse material, for holding coal, vegetables etc. *Also v.t.* **WH:** pre-1200. Old English *sæc*, from Germanic, from Latin *saccus*, corr. to Greek *sakkos*, of Semitic orig. Cp. SAC¹.

sack² *v.t.* to plunder or pillage (a place taken by storm). *Also n.* **WH:** 16C. French *sac*, in *mettre à sac* to put in a bag, from Italian *sacco* sack, bag, from Latin *saccus*. See SACK¹, SAC¹. The original reference was perhaps to filling sacks with plunder. Cp. BAG, POCKET.

sack³ *n.* a white wine, esp. one from Spain and the Canaries.

sackbut WH: 16C. French (*vin*) *sec* dry wine. Cp. SEC², SEKT. The form of the word is partly due to the popular notion that the wine was strained through a sack. The tautologically named brand of sherry, Dry Sack, exploited this association by being sold at one time in bottles encased in a miniature sack.

sackbut *n.* a medieval bass trumpet with a slide like the modern trombone. WH: 15C. French *sacquebute*, from earlier *saqueboute*, *saquebot* hooked lance for pulling a rider off his horse, from *saquer*, var. of Old French *sachier* to pull + *bouter* BUTT⁴. The trumpet is so called from its appearance. The biblical instrument so named (Dan. iii) was actually a SAMBUKE.

sacque *n.* a loose-fitting woman's gown. WH: 16C. Prob. a var. of SACK¹, later assoc. with French SAC¹.

sacrament *n.* a religious rite instituted as an outward and visible sign of an inward and spiritual grace. *Also v.t.* WH: 12–14C. Old French *sacrement*, from Latin *sacramentum* solemn oath, from *sacrare* to hallow, from *sacer* sacred. See also -MENT. The Latin word was used in Ecclesiastical Latin as a translation of Greek *mustērion* MYSTERY¹.

sacrarium *n.* the sanctuary of a church. WH: 18C. Latin, from *sacer* sacred. See also -ARIUM.

sacred *a.* dedicated to religious use. WH: 14–15C. P.p. of *sacre* to consecrate, from Old French *sacrer*, from Latin *sacrare* to dedicate to a divinity, from *sacer* consecrated, holy. See also -ED. Cp. SACRING.

sacrifice *n.* the giving up of anything for the sake of another person, object or interest. *Also v.t.* WH: 12–14C. Old French, from Latin *sacrificium*, rel. to *sacrificus*, from *sacer* sacred, holy + *-ficus* -FIC.

sacrilege *n.* the violation or profanation of sacred things. WH: 12–14C. Old French *sacrilège*, from Latin *sacrilegium*, from *sacrilegus* stealer of sacred things, from *sacer* sacred + *legere* to take possession of.

†sacring *n.* consecration, esp. of the Eucharistic elements in the Mass, and of bishops, kings etc. WH: 12–14C. *sacre* (SACRED) + -ING¹.

sacrist *n.* an officer in charge of the sacristy of a church or religious house with its contents. WH: 16C. Old French *sacriste* or Medieval Latin *sacrista*, from Latin *sacer* sacred + *-ista* -IST.

sacro- *comb. form* sacrum, sacral. WH: Latin (*os*) *sacrum* SACRUM.

sacrosanct *a.* inviolable by reason of sanctity. WH: 15C. Latin *sacrosanctus*, orig. two words, *sacro*, abl. of *sacrum* sacred rite, and *sanctus*, p.p. of *sancire* to make sacred.

sacrum *n.* a composite bone formed by the union of vertebrae at the base of the spinal column, constituting the dorsal part of the pelvis. WH: 18C. Short for Late Latin *os sacrum*, translating Greek *hieron osteon* sacred bone. The bone is so called from the former belief that the soul resided in it.

SAD *abbr.* seasonal affective disorder. WH: Prob. punning on SAD.

sad *a.* sorrowful, mournful. WH: pre-1200. Old English *sæd*, from a Germanic word rel. to Latin *sat*, *satis* enough. The original sense was satisfied, sated, then (to the 17C) steadfast, constant. The current sense dates from the 12–14C.

saddle *n.* a seat placed on an animal's back, to support a rider. *Also v.t.* WH: pre-1200. Old English *sadel*, *sadul*, from a Germanic word ? ult. rel. to the Indo-European base also of SIT, represented in Latin *sella* seat.

Sadducee *n.* a member of a sect among the Jews, arising in the 2C BC, who adhered to the written law to the exclusion of tradition, and denied the resurrection from the dead, existence of spirits etc. WH: pre-1200. Late Latin *Sadducaeus*, from Late Greek *Saddoukaios*, from post-biblical Hebrew *ṣĕdūqī*, from the pers. name *ṣāḏôq* Zadok. The Sadducees were probably associated with Zadok, a high priest under King David, although it is also possible they were connected with a later sage of this name.

sadhu *n.* a Hindu usu. mendicant holy man. WH: 19C. Sanskrit *sādhu* good.

sadism *n.* sexual perversion characterized by a passion for cruelty. WH: 19C. French *sadisme*, from Donatien-Alphonse-François, Comte (known as Marquis) de *Sade*, 1740–1814, French novelist and pornographer. See also -ISM.

safari *n.* a hunting or scientific expedition, esp. in E Africa. WH: 19C. Kiswahili, from Arabic *safar* journey, trip, tour.

safe *a.* free or secure from danger or damage. *Also n.* WH: 12–14C. Old French *sauf*, from Latin *salvus* uninjured, entire, healthy.

safety *n.* freedom from injury, danger or risk. WH: 12–14C. Old French *sauveté*, from Medieval Latin *salvitas*, from Latin *salvus*. See SAFE, also -TY¹.

saffian *n.* leather prepared from goatskin or sheepskin tanned with sumac and dyed yellow or red. WH: 16C. Russian *saf'yan*, alt. of Romanian *saftian*, ult. from Persian *saktiyān* .

safflower *n.* a thistle-like plant, *Carthamus tinctorius*, with orange flowers yielding a red dye, and seeds rich in oil. WH: 14–15C. Dutch *saffloer* or German *Saflor*, from Old French *saffleur*, from obs. Italian *saffiore*, var. of *asfiore*, from Arabic *aṣfar* a yellow plant. The spelling of the English word has been influenced by SAFFRON and FLOWER.

saffron *n.* the dried deep orange stigmas of a crocus, *Crocus sativus*, used for colouring and flavouring food. *Also a., v.t.* WH: 12–14C. Old French *safran*, from Medieval Latin *safranum*, from Arabic *za'farān*.

safrole *n.* a usually colourless liquid obtained from sassafras and used in soaps and perfumes. WH: 19C. SASSAFRAS + -OLE¹.

sag *v.i.* to droop or give way esp. in the middle, under weight or pressure. *Also v.t., n.* WH: 14–15C. Middle Low German *sacken*, rel. to Dutch *zakken* in same sense.

saga *n.* a medieval prose narrative recounting family or public events in Iceland or Scandinavia, usu. by contemporary or nearly contemporary native writers. WH: 18C. Old Norse (Icelandic) SAW².

sagacious *a.* intellectually keen or quick to understand or discern. WH: 17C. Latin *sagax*, *sagacis* of quick perception + -IOUS.

sagamore *n.* a N American Indian chief, a sachem. WH: 17C. Eastern Abnaki *sàkema* SACHEM.

sagan *n.* the deputy of the Jewish high priest. WH: 17C. Late use of Hebrew *sāḡān*, from Akkadian *šaknu* governor.

sagapenum *n.* a gum resin obtained from *Ferula persica*, formerly used to relieve spasms. WH: 16C. Late Latin, from Greek *sagapēnon*.

sage¹ *n.* a grey-leaved aromatic plant of the genus *Salvia*, esp. *S. officinalis*, formerly much used in medicine, now employed in cookery. WH: 12–14C. Old French *sauge*, from Latin *salvia*, from *salvus* safe. Cp. SALVIA. The plant is so called from its supposed healing properties.

sage² *a.* wise, prudent. *Also n.* WH: 12–14C. Old French, from alt. of Popular Latin *sapius*, from Latin *sapere* to be wise.

sagene¹ *n.* a fishing net. WH: 19C. Latin, from Greek *sagēnē*.

sagene² *n.* a Russian measure of length, about 7 ft. (2 m). WH: 18C. Russian *sazhen'*, rel. to obs. *syagat'* to reach. A sagene is the length of the span of both arms. Cp. FATHOM.

saggar *n.* a vessel of fireproof pottery in which delicate porcelain is enclosed while in a kiln. WH: 18C. Prob. contr. of *safeguard* (see SAFE).

sagittal *a.* of, relating to or resembling an arrow. WH: 14–15C. Medieval Latin *sagittalis*, from Latin *sagitta* arrow. See also -AL¹.

sago *n.* a starchy substance obtained from the soft inner portion of the trunk of several palms or cycads and used as food. WH: 16C. Malay *sagu*. The word came into English through Portuguese.

saguaro *n.* a large Central American cactus, *Carnegiea gigantea*, with edible fruit. WH: 19C. Mexican Spanish, prob. from Uto-Aztecan.

sagum *n.* the military cloak worn by ancient Roman soldiers. WH: 18C. Latin, from Late Greek *sagos*.

sahib *n.* (in India) a polite form of address for a man; a gentleman. WH: 17C. Urdu, through Persian, from Arabic *ṣāḥib* friend, lord, master. Cp. MEMSAHIB.

sahlite *n.* a green variety of pyroxene. WH: 19C. *Sahl* (*Sala*), a town west of Uppsala, Sweden + -ITE¹.

sai *n.* a S American capuchin monkey, *Cebus olivaceus*. WH: 18C. French *saï*, from Portuguese, from Tupi *sai*.

saic *n.* a sailing vessel of the eastern Mediterranean. WH: 17C. French *saïque*, from Turkish *şayka*.

saiga *n.* an antelope, *Saiga tartarica*, of the steppes of E Europe and W Asia. WH: 19C. Russian, prob. from a Finnic language. Cp. Finnish *saija*, Estonian *sai*.

sail n. a piece of canvas or other fabric spread on rigging to catch the wind, and cause a ship or boat to move in the water. Also v.i., v.t. WH: pre-1200. Old English segl, segel, from Germanic. Cp. German Segel, Dutch zeil.

sailor n. a member of the crew of a boat or ship, as distinguished from an officer. WH: 17C. Alt. of sailer person who sails, from SAIL + -ER[1]. See also -OR.

sainfoin n. a leguminous herb, Onobrychis viciifolia, resembling clover, grown for fodder. WH: 17C. Obs. French saintfoin (Modern French sainfoin), orig. lucerne, from Modern Latin sanctum foenum, lit. holy hay, alt. of sanum foenum wholesome hay, based on Latin herba medica, erroneous alt. of herba Medica, lit. Median grass, translating Greek Mēdikē poa.

saint n. a person eminent for piety and virtue, a holy person. Also v.t., v.i. WH: pre-1200. Old English sanct, from Latin sanctus, use as n. of p.p. of sancire to confirm, to ratify, to consecrate. The English spelling was influenced by Old French seint (Modern French saint), from Latin sanctus.

Saint-Simonian n. an adherent of the comte de Saint-Simon, who advocated the establishment of State ownership and distribution of earnings according to capacity and labour. Also a. WH: 19C. Comte de Saint-Simon, 1760–1825, French social reformer + -IAN.

sair a. sore. WH: 12–14C. Var. of SORE.

saithe n. the coalfish, Pollachius virens. WH: 16C. Old Norse seithr.

sajou n. a capuchin monkey. WH: 18C. French, abbr. of sajouassu, alt. of cayouassou, from Tupi SAI + guassú large.

sake[1] n. purpose. WH: pre-1200. Old English sacu, from a Germanic word meaning affair, thing, cause, legal action, crime, represented also by Old English sacan to quarrel, to accuse, from base rel. to that of SEEK. Cp. German Sache thing, SAC[2]. The original sense was contention, strife, then (to the 14–15C) guilt, sin, crime.

sake[2] n. a fermented liquor made from rice. WH: 17C. Japanese.

saker n. a large falcon, Falco cherrug, used in hawking, esp. the female. WH: 14–15C. Old French sacre, from Arabic ṣaḳr hawk, falcon.

saki n. any monkey of the S American genera Pithecia or Chiropotes. WH: 16C. French, alt. of obs. Modern Latin cagui, from Tupi saui.

sakieh n. an apparatus used in Egypt for raising water, consisting of a vertical wheel or wheel and chain carrying pots or buckets. WH: 17C. Arabic sāḳiya, use as n. of fem. active part. of saḳā to irrigate.

Sakti n. in Hinduism, the female principle esp. as personified as the wife of a god. WH: 19C. Sanskrit śakti power, divine energy.

sal[1] n. salt (used only with qualifying word). WH: 12–14C. Latin salt.

sal[2] n. a large Indian timber tree, Shorea robusta. WH: 18C. Hindi sāl, from Sanskrit śāla.

salaam n. a ceremonious salutation or obeisance in Eastern countries. Also v.i., v.t. WH: 17C. Arabic salām, rel. to SHALOM.

salacious a. lustful, lecherous. WH: 17C. Latin salax, salacis lustful, from salire to leap. See also -OUS, -IOUS.

salad n. a dish of (mixed) raw vegetables. WH: 14–15C. Old French salade, from Provençal salada, from Latin SAL[1].

salal n. an evergreen shrub, Gaultheria shallon, of California etc., bearing grapelike edible berries. WH: 19C. Chinook Jargon sallal.

salamander n. an amphibian of the family Urodela, esp. the genus Salamandra. WH: 12–14C. Old French salamandre, from Latin salamandra, from Greek, of unknown orig.

salami n. a highly-seasoned Italian sausage. WH: 19C. Italian, pl. of salame, from Popular Latin salamen, from salare to salt, from Latin SAL[1].

salangane n. a Chinese swift of the genus Collocalia, that builds edible nests. WH: 18C. French, from salamga, name of the bird in the Philippines.

salary n. a fixed payment given periodically, usu. monthly, esp. for work not of a manual or mechanical kind. Also v.t. WH: 12–14C. Old French salaire, from Latin salarium (orig.) money allowed to Roman soldiers for the purchase of salt, (later) pay, use as n. of salarius pertaining to salt, from SAL[1]. See also -ARY[1].

salbutamol n. a drug used as a bronchodilator to treat asthma. WH: mid-20C. From salicyl (SALICIN) + BUTYL + AMINE + -OL.

salchow n. an ice-skating jump with turns in the air. WH: early 20C. Ulrich Salchow, 1877–1949, Swedish figure skater.

sale n. the act of selling. WH: pre-1200. Old Norse sala, from base of a Germanic v. meaning to sell. Rel. to SELL.

salep n. a farinaceous meal made from the dried roots of Orchis mascula and other orchidaceous plants. WH: 18C. French, from Turkish sālep, from Arabic ṭa'lab fox, shortening of kuṣa 't-ṭa'lab orchid, lit. testicles of the fox. Cp. SALOOP.

saleratus n. an impure bicarbonate of potash or soda, much used as baking powder. WH: 19C. Modern Latin sal aeratus, lit. aerated salt.

Salesian n. a member of a religious order founded by St Francis of Sales. Also a. WH: 19C. French salésien, from St François de Sales, 1567–1622, French devotional writer and bishop. See also -IAN.

Salian[1] a. of or relating to the Salii or priests of Mars of ancient Rome. WH: 17C. Latin Salii, priests who performed ritual dances, from salire to leap. See SALIENT, also -AN.

Salian[2] a. of or relating to a Frankish tribe on the lower Rhine to which the ancestors of the Merovingians belonged. Also n. WH: 17C. Late Latin Salii Salian Franks. See also -IAN.

salic a. (of minerals) rich in silicon and aluminium. WH: early 20C. From silicon (SILICA) + ALUMINIUM + -IC.

salicet n. organ stops with notes like those of a willow-pipe. WH: 19C. German, from Latin salix, salicis willow. See also -ET[1]. A variant form salicional, from German Salicional, has a suffix of unknown origin.

salicin n. a bitter crystalline compound obtained from the bark of willows and poplars, used medicinally. WH: 19C. French salicine, from Latin salix, salicis willow + -IN[1].

salient a. conspicuous, prominent. Also n. WH: 16C. Latin saliens, salientis, pres.p. of salire to leap. See also -ENT.

salientian n., a. ANURAN. WH: mid-20C. Modern Latin Salientia, from Latin saliens, salientis (SALIENT) + -IA. See also -AN.

saliferous a. (of rock strata) bearing or producing salt. WH: 19C. Latin sal salt + -i- + -FEROUS.

saline a. consisting of or having the characteristics of salt. Also n. WH: 15C. Latin SAL[1] + -INE.

saliva n. an odourless, colourless, somewhat viscid liquid secreted by glands into the mouth where it lubricates ingested food, spittle. WH: 14–15C. Latin spittle.

salix n. a plant of the Salix genus, such as the willow. WH: 18C. Latin willow.

Salk vaccine n. a vaccine against poliomyelitis. WH: mid-20C. Jonas Edward Salk, 1914–95, US virologist + vaccine (VACCINATE).

sallee n. any of several eucalypts and acacias resembling the willow. WH: 16C. Alt. of SALLOW[1].

sallee-man n. a Moorish pirate or pirate ship. WH: 17C. Sallee (French Salé, Arabic Sla), a Moroccan seaport formerly of piratical repute.

sallenders n. a dry scabby inflammation in the hock-joint of a horse's hind leg. WH: 16C. Orig. unknown. Cp. French solandre.

sallet n. a light, hemispherical, crestless helmet with the back curving away, worn by 15th-cent. foot soldiers. WH: 14–15C. French salade, from Provençal salada, Italian celata or Spanish celada, from use as n. of Popular Latin caelata, fem. p.p. of Latin caelare to engrave, from caelum chisel.

sallow[1] n. a willow tree, esp. one of the low shrubby varieties. WH: pre-1200. Old English salh, from Germanic, rel. to Old High German salaha, Old Norse selja, Latin SALIX and Greek helikē.

sallow[2] a. of a sickly yellowish or pale brown colour. Also v.t., v.i. WH: pre-1200. Old English sale, from Germanic. Cp. Middle Dutch salu, saluwe discoloured, dirty, Old High German salo dark-coloured, Old Norse sǫlr yellow.

Sally n. the Salvation Army. WH: early 20C. Abbr. of Salvation Army (see SALVATION), influenced by female forename Sally.

sally[1] n. a sudden rushing out or sortie of troops from a besieged place against besiegers. Also v.i. WH: 14–15C. Old French saillie, fem. p.p. (used as n.) of saillir to leap, alt. of salir, from Latin salire.

sally[2] n. the part of a bell-ringer's rope covered with wool for holding. WH: 17C. ? From SALLY[1].

Sally Lunn n. a sweet teacake eaten hot and buttered. WH: 18C. Prob. from the name of a woman who first sold such cakes in Bath in the late 18C.

salmagundi *n.* a dish of chopped meat, anchovies, eggs, oil, vinegar etc. WH: 17C. French *salmigondis*, obs. *salmigondin*, of unknown orig. 1st element may be French *sel* salt and last rel. to CONDIMENT.

salmanazar *n.* a large wine bottle, holding about twelve times as much as a standard bottle. WH: mid-20C. *Salmanasar*, Late Latin form of *Shalmaneser* king of Assyria (II Kgs. xvii–xviii).

salmi *n.* a ragout, esp. of game birds stewed with wine. WH: 18C. Abbr. of French *salmigondis* SALMAGUNDI.

salmiac *n.* native sal ammoniac. WH: 18C. German *Salmiak*, contr. of Latin *sal ammoniacum*.

salmon *n.* a larger silvery, pink-fleshed fish of the family Salmonidae, esp. of the genus *Salmo*, fished both for food and sport. *Also a.* WH: 12–14C. Old French *saumon*, from Latin *salmo*, *salmonis*.

salmonella *n.* any bacterium of the genus *Salmonella*, many of which cause food poisoning. WH: early 20C. Modern Latin, from Daniel Elmer *Salmon*, 1850–1914, US pathologist + *-ella*, representing Latin dim. suf.

salon *n.* a reception room, esp. in a great house in France. WH: 17C. French. See SALOON.

saloon *n.* a large room or hall, esp. one suitable for social receptions, public entertainments etc., or used for a specified purpose. WH: 18C. French *salon*, from Italian *salone*, augm. of *sala* hall, from Germanic. See also -OON.

saloop *n.* an infusion of sassafras etc., formerly used with milk and sugar as a beverage instead of tea or coffee. WH: 18C. Alt. of French SALEP.

Salop. *abbr.* Shropshire. WH: Shortening of *Salopesberia* and *Salopescire*, Anglo-Norman alt. of Middle English forms of Old English *Scrobbesbyrig* Shrewsbury and *Scrobbesbyrigscīr* Shropshire. *Salop* was the official name of Shropshire from 1974 to 1980.

salopettes *n.pl.* thick usu. quilted trousers with shoulder straps, used for skiing. WH: late 20C. Pl. of French *salopette* dungarees, from *sale* dirty.

Salopian *n.* a native or inhabitant of Shropshire. *Also a.* WH: 17C. *Salop*, a name for Shropshire (see SALOP.) + -IAN.

salpicon *n.* a stuffing or thick sauce made with chopped meat and vegetables. WH: 18C. French, from Spanish, from *salpicar* to sprinkle (with salt).

salpiglossis *n.* any plant of the genus *Salpiglossis*, with trumpet-shaped flowers. WH: 19C. Modern Latin, from Greek *salpigx* trumpet + *glōssa* tongue. The plant is so called from the shape of its corolla.

salping- *comb. form* denoting the Fallopian tubes. WH: Greek *salpigx*, *salpiggos* trumpet. Cp. SALPINX. The tubes are so called from their shape.

salpinx *n.* the Eustachian tube. WH: 19C. Greek. See SALPING-.

salsa *n.* a Puerto Rican dance or the music for this. WH: 19C. Spanish sauce.

salse *n.* a mud volcano. WH: 19C. French, from Italian *salsa*, orig. the name of a mud volcano near Modena.

salsify *n.* a composite plant, *Tragopogon porrifolius*, the long whitish root of which is eaten. WH: 17C. French *salsifis*, from obs. Italian *salsefica* (now *sassefrica*), earlier *erba salsefica*, of unknown orig.

salsilla *n.* the tubers of *Bomarea edulis* and *B. salsilla*, eaten in the W Indies. WH: 19C. Modern Latin, from fem. of *salsillus* salty, from Latin *salsus*, p.p. of *sallere* to salt.

SALT *abbr.* Strategic Arms Limitation Talks. WH: mid-20C. Acronym of *Strategic Arms Limitation Talks*. Cp. START.

salt *n.* chloride of sodium, used for seasoning and preserving food, obtained from sea water or brine. *Also a., v.t., v.i.* WH: pre-1200. Old English *salt*, *sealt*, from Germanic, from Indo-European base represented also by Latin *sal*, Greek *hals*.

saltant *a.* salient (used of figures of small animals). WH: 17C. Latin *saltans*, *saltantis*, pres.p. of *saltare* to dance, freq. of *salire* to leap. See also -ANT.

saltarello *n.* an Italian or Spanish dance characterized by sudden skips. WH: 16C. Italian *salterello*, Spanish *salterelo*, rel. to Italian *saltare*, Spanish *saltar* to leap, to dance, from Latin *saltare* (SALTANT).

saltation *n.* a leaping or bounding. WH: 17C. Latin *saltatio*, *saltationis*, from *saltatus*, p.p. of *saltare* (SALTANT). See also -ATION.

saltigrade *a.* formed for leaping. *Also n.* WH: 19C. Modern Latin *Saltigradae*, from Latin *saltus* leap + *-i-* + *-gradus* walking.

saltire *n.* an ordinary in the form of a St Andrew's cross or the letter X. WH: 14–15C. Old French *sautour*, *sautoir*, *saultoir* stirrup cord, stile with crosspiece, saltire, from Medieval Latin *saltatorium*, use as n. of neut. of Latin *saltatorius*, from *saltator* leaper, dancer, from *saltare* (SALTANT).

saltpetre *n.* potassium nitrate. WH: 14–15C. Old French *salpètre*, Medieval Latin *salpetra*, prob. from *sal petrae* salt of rock, alt. by assim. to SALT.

saltus *n.* a sudden starting aside, breach of continuity or jumping to a conclusion. WH: 17C. Latin leap.

salubrious *a.* (of climate etc.) promoting health, wholesome. WH: 16C. Latin *salubris*, from *salus* health. See also -OUS.

saluki *n.* a Persian greyhound. WH: 19C. Arabic *salūḳī*, from *Salūḳ*, a town in Yemen.

salutary *a.* promoting good effects, beneficial, corrective, profitable. WH: 14–15C. Old French *salutaire* or Latin *salutaris*, from *salus*, *salutis* health, welfare, greeting, rel. to *salvus* safe. See also -ARY².

salute *v.t.* to show respect to (a military superior) by a salute. *Also v.i., n.* WH: 14–15C. Latin *salutare*, from *salus*, *salutis* health. The original sense was to greet in words, to address respectfully on meeting.

salvable *a.* capable of being saved. WH: 14–15C. Late Latin *salvare* SAVE. See also -ABLE.

Salvadorean *a.* of or relating to El Salvador. *Also n.* WH: 19C. *El Salvador*, a republic in Central America + -EAN.

salvage *n.* the act of saving a ship, goods etc. from shipwreck, capture, fire etc. *Also v.t.* WH: 17C. Old French, from Medieval Latin *salvagium*, from *salvare* to save. See also -AGE. The original sense was compensation paid to those who have voluntarily saved a ship or its cargo. The sense saving of waste material dates from the early 20C.

salvation *n.* the act of saving from destruction. WH: 12–14C. Old French *sauvacion* (Modern French *salvation*), from Ecclesiastical Latin *salvatio*, *salvationis* (translating Greek *sōtēria*), from *salvare* SAVE. See also -ION.

salve¹ *n.* a healing ointment. *Also v.t.* WH: pre-1200. Old English *salf*, from Germanic. Cp. German *Salbe*.

salve² *n.* a Roman Catholic antiphon beginning with the words *Salve Regina*, 'Hail, holy Queen', addressed to the Virgin. WH: 14–15C. Latin hail, greetings, imper. of *salvere* to be well.

salve³ *v.t.* to save from destruction. WH: 18C. Back-formation from SALVAGE.

salver *n.* a tray, usu. of silver, brass, electroplate etc., on which refreshments, visiting cards etc. are presented. WH: 17C. French *salve* tray for presenting objects to the king, or Spanish *salva*, orig. sampling of food or drink, tray on which sampled food was placed, from *salvar* to save, to make safe. The ending -er arose by association with PLATTER. Spanish *salva* was used for a tray on which a cup or dish was placed to show that it had been sampled and found to be free of poison.

salvia *n.* any plant of the genus *Salvia*, labiate plants comprising the common sage and many cultivated species with brilliant flowers. WH: 14–15C. Modern Latin, from Latin SAGE¹.

Salvo *n.* a member of the Salvation Army. WH: 19C. Abbr. of *Salvation Army* (see SALVATION). See also -O.

salvo¹ *n.* a discharge of guns etc. as a salute. WH: 16C. French *salve*, Italian *salva* salutation, with substitution of -o for -a.

salvo² *n.* a saving clause, a proviso. WH: 17C. Latin, abl. neut. sing. of *salvus* safe, as in Medieval Latin phr. *salvo iure* without prejudice to the right of (a particular person).

salvor *n.* a person or ship effecting salvage. WH: 17C. SALVAGE + -OR.

sam *v.t.* to dampen (skins) in the process of manufacture, so as to temper them. WH: 19C. Orig. uncertain. ? From some word with *sam-*, from Germanic equivalent of SEMI-.

samadhi *n.* in Buddhism and Hinduism, a state of concentration induced by meditation. WH: 18C. Sanskrit *samādhi* contemplation, lit. a putting together.

samara *n.* a one-seeded indehiscent dry fruit with winglike extensions, produced by the sycamore, ash etc. WH: 16C. Modern Latin use of Latin seed of the elm.

Samaritan *n.* a kind, charitable person, in allusion to the 'good Samaritan' of the parable (Luke x.30–37); also *good Samaritan. Also a.* WH: pre-1200. Late Latin *Samaritanus*, from Greek *Samareitēs*, from *Samareia* Samaria, a region west of the River Jordan. See also -ITE¹, -AN.

samarium *n.* a silvery-grey metallic chemical element, at. no. 62, chem. symbol Sm, one of the rare earth metals. WH: 19C. From *samarskite* a mineral (from V.E. *Samarskii*-Bykhovets, 1803–70, Russian mining engineer + -ITE¹) + -IUM. The element is so called because its spectrum was first observed in samarskite. The name was coined by Paul-Émile Lecoq de Boisbaudran, the French chemist who discovered it in 1880.

Sama-Veda *n.* the third of the four Vedas, mainly made up of extracts from hymns in the Rig-Veda. WH: 18C. Sanskrit *sāman* chant + VEDA.

samba *n.* a Brazilian dance. *Also v.i.* WH: 19C. Portuguese, of African orig.

sambal *n.* a side dish eaten with Malayan and Indonesian curries. WH: 19C. Malay.

Sambo *n.* a black person. WH: 18C. ? Fulah *sambo* uncle. In the sense dark-skinned person of mixed descent the origin is in American Spanish *zambo* a kind of yellow monkey, from Kikongo *nzambu* monkey.

Sam Browne *n.* a military officer's belt with a light strap over the right shoulder. WH: early 20C. Sir *Samuel J. Browne*, 1824–1901, British military commander.

sambuke *n.* an ancient musical stringed instrument of high-pitched tone. WH: 14–15C. Latin *sambuca*, from Greek *sambukē*, rel. to Aramaic *šabbĕḵa*. Cp. SACKBUT.

sambur *n.* a large deer or elk, *Cervus unicolor*, from S Asia. WH: 17C. Hindi *sāar, sābar*, from Sanskrit *śambara*.

same *a.* identical. *Also pron., adv.* WH: 12–14C. Old Norse *same* (m.), *sama* (fem., neut.), from Germanic, from Indo-European base also of Sanskrit *sama*, Greek *homos* (HOMO-). Rel. to SIMILAR. In general use, *same* superseded ILK and SELF.

samfu *n.* an outfit worn esp. by Chinese women, consisting of a blouse or jacket and trousers. WH: mid-20C. Chinese (Cantonese) *shaam foò*, from *shaam* coat + *foò* trousers.

Samhain *n.* 1 November, celebrated as a festival marking the beginning of winter by the ancient Celts. WH: 19C. Irish, from Old Irish *samain* (feast of) All Saints.

Samian *a.* of or relating to Samos. *Also n.* WH: 16C. Latin *Samius*, from Greek *Samos*, an island in the Aegean. See also -AN.

samiel *n.* the simoom. WH: 17C. Turkish *samyeli* hot wind, from Arabic *samm* poison + Turkish *yel* wind.

samisen *n.* a Japanese three-stringed guitar-like instrument played with a plectrum. WH: 17C. Japanese, from Chinese *sānxián*, from *sān* three + *xián* string.

samite *n.* a rich medieval silk fabric with a warp, each thread of which had six strands. WH: 12–14C. Old French *samit*, ult. from Medieval Latin *examitum*, from Medieval Greek *hexamiton*, from Greek HEXA- + *mitos* thread. Cp. DIMITY.

samizdat *n.* the clandestine publishing of banned literature in the former Communist countries of eastern Europe. WH: mid-20C. Russian, from *samo-* self + *izdatel'stvo* publishing house.

samlet *n.* a young salmon. WH: 17C. Contr. of SALMON + -LET.

Samnite *n.* a member of an ancient Italian people eventually subjugated by the Romans. *Also a.* WH: 14–15C. Latin *Samnites* (pl.), rel. to *Sabinus* SABINE. See also -ITE¹.

Samoan *n.* a native or inhabitant of Samoa. *Also a.* WH: 19C. *Samoa*, a group of islands in the Pacific + -AN.

samosa *n.* an Indian savoury of spiced meat or vegetables in a triangular pastry case. WH: mid-20C. Persian and Urdu.

samovar *n.* a Russian tea urn heated by burning charcoal in an inner tube. WH: 19C. Russian, from *samo-* self + *varit'* to boil.

Samoyed *n.* a member of a Mongolian people inhabiting central Siberia. WH: 16C. Russian *samoed*.

samp *n.* maize coarsely ground or made into porridge. WH: 17C. Algonquian (Massachusetts) *nasamp*.

sampan *n.* a Chinese flat-bottomed river boat, frequently used as a houseboat. WH: 17C. Chinese *sānbǎn*, from *sān* three + *bǎn* board.

samphire *n.* a herb, *Crithmum maritimum*, growing on sea cliffs, the aromatic leaves of which are pickled as a condiment. WH: 16C. French (*herbe de*) *Saint Pierre*, lit. (herb of) St Peter. The plant is perhaps associated with St Peter because it grows on rocks. Cp. Late Latin *petra* rock (French *pierre* stone).

sample *n.* a part taken, offered or used as illustrating the whole, an example. *Also v.t., a.* WH: 12–14C. Shortening of Anglo-French *assample*, var. of Old French *essample* EXAMPLE.

samsara *n.* in Hinduism, the cycle of birth, death and rebirth. WH: 19C. Sanskrit *saṃsāra* a wandering through.

samshu *n.* a Chinese alcoholic drink made from fermented rice. WH: 17C. Pidgin English, ult. of unknown orig.

samskara *n.* in Hinduism, a purificatory ceremony or rite. WH: 19C. Sanskrit *saṃskāra* preparation, a making perfect.

samsoe *n.* a firm-textured Danish cheese with a mild flavour. WH: mid-20C. *Samsoe*, a Danish island.

Samson *n.* a man of extraordinary strength. WH: 16C. Latin, Greek *Sampsōn*, from Hebrew *šimšōn*, a blinded Hebrew hero of great strength (Judg. xiii–xvi).

samurai *n.* a Japanese army officer. WH: 18C. Japanese warrior, knight.

san *n.* a sanatorium in a school etc. WH: early 20C. Abbr. of SANATORIUM.

sanative *a.* healing, tending to cure, curative. WH: 14–15C. Old French *sanatif* or Late Latin *sanativus*, from Latin *sanatus*, p.p. of *sanare* to heal. See also -IVE.

sanatorium *n.* an institution for the treatment of chronic diseases. WH: 19C. Modern Latin, from *sanatus*. See SANATIVE, also -ORIUM. The variant N American form *sanitarium* is from Latin *sanitas* health (SANITARY) + -ARIUM.

sanbenito *n.* a penitential garment painted with a red St Andrew's cross worn by heretics who recanted, or painted over with flames and figures of devils, worn at an auto-da-fé by persons condemned by the Inquisition. WH: 16C. Spanish *sambenito*, from *San Benito* St Benedict. The garment is so called from its resemblance to the Benedictine scapular.

sancho *n.* a W African musical instrument like a guitar. WH: 19C. Twi *o-sanku*.

sanctify *v.t.* to make holy, to consecrate. WH: 14–15C. Old French *saintifier* or Late Latin *sanctificare*, from Latin *sanctus* holy. See also -FY.

sanctimonious *a.* making a show of piety or saintliness. WH: 17C. Latin *sanctimonia*, from *sanctus* holy + *-monia* -MONY. See also -OUS.

sanction *n.* the act of ratifying, confirmation by superior authority. *Also v.t.* WH: 14–15C. Old French, from Latin *sanctio, sanctionis*, from *sanctus*, p.p. of *sancire* to make inviolable, from var. of base of *sacer* SACRED. The original sense was law, decree. The sense penalty or reward for disobedience or obedience of a law evolved in the 17C, and that of official permission in the 18C.

sanctity *n.* the state of being holy, holiness. WH: 14–15C. Partly from Old French *sainctité* (Modern French *sainteté*), partly from Latin *sanctitas*, from *sanctus* holy. See also -ITY.

sanctuary *n.* a holy place. WH: 12–14C. Old French *sanctuaire*, from Latin *sanctuarium*, from *sanctus* holy, based on SACRARIUM. See also -ARY¹.

sanctum *n.* a sacred or private place. WH: 16C. Latin, neut. of *sanctus* holy. Latin *sanctum sanctorum* holy of holies translates Hebrew *qōḏeš haq-qŏḏāšīm*.

sanctus *n.* the liturgical phrase 'Holy, holy, holy', in Latin or English. WH: 14–15C. Latin holy, the first word of the hymn. The full version of the hymn that forms the conclusion of the Eucharistic preface in the Latin Ordinary of the Mass is: *Sanctus, sanctus, sanctus, Dominus Deus Sabaoth. Pleni sunt coeli et terra gloria tua. Hosanna in excelsis. Benedictus qui venit in nomine Domini* Holy, holy, holy, Lord God of Hosts. Heaven and earth are full of thy glory. Hosanna in the highest. Blessed is he that cometh in the name of the Lord.

sand *n.* comminuted fragments of rock, esp. of chert, flint and other quartz rocks, reduced almost to powder. *Also v.t.* WH: pre-1200. Old English, from Germanic. Cp. Dutch *zand*, German *Sand*.

sandal[1] *n.* a kind of shoe consisting of a sole secured by straps passing over the foot and often round the ankle. *Also v.t.* WH: 14–15C. Latin *sandalium*, from Greek *sandalion*, dim. of *sandalon* wooden shoe, prob. of Asiatic orig.

sandal[2] *n.* sandalwood. WH: 14–15C. Medieval Latin *sandalum*, *santalum* (SANTAL), ult. from Sanskrit *candana* through Persian *chandal* mangrove, Arabic *ṣandal*, Late Greek *sandanon*, *santalon*.

sandarac *n.* a whitish-yellow gum resin obtained from a NW African tree, *Tetraclinis articulata*. WH: 14–15C. Latin *sandaraca*, from Greek *sandarakē*, of Asiatic orig.

sand-blind *a.* half-blind, dim-sighted. WH: 15C. Prob. alt. of Old English *samblind*, from *sam-* half (rel. to SEMI-) + BLIND, influ. by SAND.

Sandemanian *n.* a follower of Robert Sandeman, principal exponent of the views of John Glass and leader of the movement founded by him, a Glassite. WH: 18C. Robert *Sandeman*, 1718–71, Scottish sectarian + -IAN.

sanderling *n.* a small wading bird, *Calidris alba*. WH: 17C. Orig. uncertain. Poss. from SAND and -LING[1]. The bird's preferred winter habitat is the sandy seashore.

sanders *n.* the red sandalwood, *Pterocarpus santalinus*. WH: 12–14C. Old French *sandre*, var. of *sandle* SANDAL[2].

sandhi *n.* the modification of the sound of a word or affix as a result of its position in an utterance. WH: 19C. Sanskrit *saṃdhi* combination.

sandiver *n.* a saline scum rising to the surface of fused glass in the pot. WH: 14–15C. Appar. from Old French *saïn de verre* (Modern French *sain de verre*), lit. grease of glass.

sandwich *n.* two slices of bread, usu. spread with butter or a similar substance, with meat etc. between them. *Also v.t.* WH: 18C. John Montagu, 4th Earl of *Sandwich*, 1718–92, said to have eaten food in this form in order to avoid leaving the gaming table.

Sandwich tern *n.* a crested tern, *Sterna sandvicensis*. WH: 15C. *Sandwich*, a town in Kent.

Sandy *n.* a Scotsman. WH: 18C. Scottish pet form of male forename *Alexander*, partly influ. by *sandy* (SAND), with ref. to the hair colour of many Scots. Cp. SAWNEY.

sane *a.* sound in mind, not deranged. WH: 17C. Latin *sanus* healthy.

Sanforized® *a.* (of fabric) pre-shrunk by a patented process. WH: mid-20C. *Sanford* L. Cluett, 1874–1968, US inventor of the process + -IZE + -ED.

sanga *n.* a breastwork or wall of loose stones built for defensive purposes in the Himalayas. WH: 19C. Persian and Pashto *sangar*, prob. from Persian *sang* stone.

sangaree *n.* wine and water sweetened, spiced and usu. iced. *Also v.t.* WH: 18C. Spanish *sangría* SANGRIA.

sang-de-boeuf *n.* a dark-red colour such as that of some old Chinese porcelain. *Also a.* WH: 19C. French, lit. ox's blood.

sang-froid *n.* calmness, composure in danger etc. WH: 18C. French, lit. cold blood.

sangria *n.* a Spanish drink of diluted (red) wine and fruit juices. WH: mid-20C. Spanish *sangría*, lit. bleeding.

sanguify *v.i.* to produce blood. WH: 17C. Modern Latin *sanguificare*, from Latin *sanguis* blood. See also -FY.

sanguinary *a.* accompanied by bloodshed or carnage. WH: 12–14C. Latin *sanguinarius*, from *sanguis* blood. See also -ARY[1].

sanguine *a.* cheerful, confident. *Also n., v.t.* WH: 12–14C. Old French, from Latin *sanguineus*, from *sanguis*, *sanguinis* blood. The original sense was blood-red. A ruddy-faced person was believed to have a predominance of blood over the three other bodily humours (phlegm, yellow bile, black bile) and so to be brave and amorous (lustful). Hence the current sense (16C).

Sanhedrin *n.* the supreme court of justice and council of the Jewish nation, down to AD 425, consisting of 71 priests, elders and scribes. WH: 16C. Post-biblical Hebrew *sanhedrīn*, from Greek *sunedrion* council, from *sun-* SYN- + *hedra* seat.

sanicle *n.* any small woodland plant of the umbelliferous genus *Sanicula*, allied to the parsley. WH: 14–15C. Old French, from Medieval Latin *sanicula*, prob. from Latin *sanus* healthy, SANE. See also -ICLE. The plant is so called from its supposed healing properties.

sanies *n.* a thin fetid discharge, usu. stained with blood, from sores or wounds. WH: 14–15C. Latin.

sanify *v.t.* to make healthy or more sanitary. WH: 19C. Latin *sanus* healthy, SANE + -FY.

sanitary *a.* relating to or concerned with the preservation of health, of or relating to hygiene. WH: 19C. French *sanitaire*, from Latin *sanitas* health, from *sanus* healthy. See also -ARY[1].

sanity *n.* saneness, mental soundness. WH: 14–15C. Latin *sanitas*, from *sanus* healthy. See SANE, also -ITY.

sanjak *n.* an administrative subdivision of a Turkish vilayet or province. WH: 16C. Turkish *sancak*, lit. banner.

sannyasi *n.* a Hindu religious man who lives by begging. WH: 17C. Sanskrit *saṃnyāsī*, nom. sing. of *saṃnyāsin* laying aside, abandoning, ascetic, from *saṃ* together + *ni* down + *as* to throw.

sans *prep.* without. WH: 12–14C. Old French *san*, *sanz* (Modern French *sans*), from var. of Latin *sine* without, partly influ. by Latin *absentia* absence. Cp. SENZA.

Sanskrit *n.* the ancient language of the Hindu sacred writings. WH: 17C. Sanskrit *saṃskṛta* prepared, elaborated, perfected, from *saṃ* together + *kṛ* to make, to do. Cp. PRAKRIT.

Santa Claus *n.* a mythical white-bearded old man bringing presents at Christmas and putting them in children's stockings, made popular in Britain in the late 19th cent. WH: 18C. Dutch dial. *Sante Klaas* Saint Nicholas, 4C AD bishop of Asia Minor and patron saint of children. St Nicholas owed his position as Santa Claus to the legend that he gave gifts of gold to three poor girls for their dowries. This led to the exchange of gifts on his feast day, properly 6 December but widely transferred to 25 December, Christmas Day.

santal *n.* sandalwood. WH: 18C. French, from Medieval Latin *santalum*, from Late Greek *santalon*. See SANDAL[2].

santir *n.* an eastern form of dulcimer played with two sticks. WH: 19C. Arabic *sanṭīr*, *sinṭīr*, alt. of Greek *psaltērion* PSALTERY.

santolina *n.* any fragrant shrubby composite plant of the genus *Santolina*. WH: 16C. Modern Latin, perh. alt. of Latin SANTONICA.

santon *n.* a Muslim hermit, a dervish. WH: 16C. French, from Spanish *santo* SAINT. See also -OON.

santonica *n.* a shrubby plant, *Artemisia cina*. WH: 17C. Latin *Santonica* (*herba*) a kind of wormwood, fem. of *Santonicus* pertaining to the Santoni, a Gallic tribe.

sap[1] *n.* the watery juice or circulating fluid of living plants. *Also v.t.* WH: pre-1200. Old English *sæp*, from Germanic. Cp. German *Saft* sap, juice.

sap[2] *v.t.* to undermine. *Also v.i., n.* WH: 16C. French *saper*, obs. *sapper*, from Italian *zappare*, from *zappa* spade, ? from Arabic *sarab* burrow, underground passage, *sabora* to explore.

sap[3] *v.i.* to be studious, to grind. *Also n.* WH: 18C. ? From SAP[2].

sapajou *n.* a small S American prehensile-tailed monkey of the genus *Cebus*; a capuchin. WH: 17C. French, ? from Tupi.

sapanwood *n.* a brownish-red dyewood obtained from trees of the genus *Caesalpinia*, esp. *C. sappan*, from S Asia and Malaysia. WH: 16C. Dutch *sappan*, from Malay *sapang*, of S Indian orig. + WOOD.

sapele *n.* any of several W African trees of the genus *Entandrophragma*. WH: early 20C. *Sapele*, a port on the River Benin, Nigeria.

saphena *n.* either of two prominent veins of the leg. WH: 14–15C. Medieval Latin, from Arabic *ṣāfin*.

sapid *a.* possessing flavour that can be relished, savoury. WH: 17C. Latin *sapidus*, from *sapere* to have a taste. See also -ID. Cp. INSIPID.

sapient *a.* wise, sagacious, discerning, sage (often ironical). WH: 14–15C. Old French, or from Latin *sapiens*, *sapientis*, pres.p. of *sapere* to have a taste, to be sensible. See also -ENT.

sapindaceous *a.* of, relating to or belonging to the *Sapindaceae*, a family of trees, shrubs and lianas which includes the soapberry. WH: 19C. Modern Latin *Sapindaceae*, from *Sapindus* soapberry, prob. from Latin *sapo* soap + *Indus* of India. See also -ACEOUS.

sapi-utan *n.* the wild ox of Celebes. WH: 19C. Malay *sāpi ūtan*, from *sāpi* ox + *ūtan* wild. Cp. ORANG-UTAN.

sapodilla *n.* a large evergreen tree, *Manilkara zapota*, growing in the W Indies and Central America. WH: 17C. Spanish *zapotillo*, dim. of *zapote*, from Nahuatl *zapotl*.

saponaceous *a.* soapy. WH: 18C. Modern Latin *saponaceus*, from Latin *sapo, saponis* soap. See also -ACEOUS.

saponaria *n.* a plant of the genus *Saponaria*, the soapwort. WH: 19C. Modern Latin, use as genus name of fem. of Medieval Latin *saponarius*, a. from Latin *sapo, saponis* soap.

saponify *v.t.* to convert into soap by combination with an alkali. *Also v.i.* WH: 19C. French *saponifier*, from Latin *sapo, saponis* soap. See also -IN[1].

saponule *n.* a soaplike compound formed by the action of an alkali on an essential oil. WH: 18C. Latin *sapo, saponis* soap + -ULE.

sapor *n.* taste. WH: 14–15C. Latin, from *sapere* to have a taste. Cp. SAVOUR.

Sapphic *a.* of or relating to Sappho. WH: 16C. French *saphique*, obs. *sapphique*, from Latin *Sapphicus*, from Greek *Sapphikos*, from *Sapphō* Sappho, *c.*610–*c.*580 BC, Greek lyric poetess of Lesbos, traditionally represented as homosexual. See also -IC.

sapphire *n.* any transparent blue variety of corundum. *Also a.* WH: 12–14C. Old French *safir* (Modern French *saphir*), from Latin *sapphirus*, from Greek *sappheiros* (prob.) lapis lazuli. According to some authorities, the Greek word ultimately derives from Sanskrit *śanipriya*, literally dear to (the planet) Saturn, from *Śani* Saturn + *priya* dear.

sapraemia *n.* septic poisoning. WH: 19C. Greek *sapros* putrid + -AEMIA.

sapro- *comb. form* indicating rotting or dead matter. WH: Greek *sapros* putrid. See also -O-.

saprogenic *a.* producing or produced by putrefaction. WH: 19C. SAPRO- + -GENIC.

saprolegnia *n.* any fungus of the genus *Saprolegnia*. WH: 19C. Modern Latin, from SAPRO- + Greek *legnon* border. See also -IA.

sapropel *n.* slimy sediment that accumulates at the bottom of lakes, oceans etc., largely organic in origin. WH: early 20C. German, from SAPRO- + Greek *pēlos* mud, earth, clay.

saprophagous *a.* feeding on decomposing matter. WH: 19C. SAPRO- + -PHAGOUS.

saprophile *n.* a bacterium feeding on decomposed matter. WH: 19C. SAPRO- + -PHILE.

saprophyte *n.* a plant, bacterium or fungus that grows on decaying organic matter. WH: 19C. SAPRO- + -PHYTE.

saprostomus *n.* halitosis, foulness of breath. WH: 19C. Modern Latin, from SAPRO- + Greek *stoma* mouth.

saprozoic *a.* saprophagous. WH: 19C. SAPRO- + ZOIC.

sapsago *n.* a greenish hard cheese flavoured with melilot, made in Switzerland. WH: 19C. Alt. of *Schabzieger*, from German *Schabzieger*, from *schaben* to grate + *Zieger* a kind of cheese.

sapucaia *n.* a S American tree, *Lecythis zabucajo*, bearing an edible nut. WH: 17C. Portuguese, from Tupi *yasapukaya*.

sar *n.* any fish of the genus *Sargus*, comprising the sea breams. WH: 16C. Latin *sargus*, from Greek *sargos*.

saraband *n.* a slow and stately Spanish dance. WH: 17C. French *sarabande*, from Spanish, Italian *zarabanda*.

Saracen *n.* a nomad Arab of the Syrian-Arabian desert in the times of the later Greeks and Romans. *Also a.* WH: pre-1200. Old French *Sarrazin, Sarracin* (Modern French *Sarrasin*), from Late Latin *Saracenus*, from Late Greek *sarakēnos*, prob. from Arabic *šarķī* eastern, from *šarķ* sunrise, east. Cp. SARSEN, SARCENET. In medieval times the name was often associated with that of *Sarah*, wife of Abraham, as she was believed to be the people's progenitrix.

sarangi *n.* an Indian stringed instrument similar to a violin. WH: 19C. Sanskrit *sāraṅgī*.

Saratoga *n.* a large travelling trunk. WH: 19C. *Saratoga* Springs, a resort in New York State, USA.

sarcasm *n.* an ironical or wounding remark. WH: 16C. French *sarcasme* or Late Latin *sarcasmus*, from Late Greek *sarkasmos*, from *sarkazein* to tear flesh, to gnash the teeth, to speak bitterly, from *sarx, sarkos* flesh.

sarcenchyme *n.* the gelatinous tissue of some higher sponges. WH: 19C. Greek *sarx, sarkos* flesh + -*enchyme*, based on PARENCHYMA.

sarcenet *n.* a thin, fine soft-textured silk used chiefly for linings, ribbons etc. WH: 14–15C. Anglo-French *sarzinett*, prob. dim. of *sarzin* SARACEN, based on Old French *drap sarrasinois*, Medieval Latin *pannus saracenicus* Saracen cloth. See also -ET[1].

sarcine *n.* a nitrogenous compound existing in the juice of flesh. WH: 19C. Greek *sarx, sarkos* flesh + -INE.

sarco- *comb. form* flesh. WH: Greek *sarx, sarkos* flesh. See also -O-.

sarcobasis *n.* a fleshy gynobase. WH: 19C. SARCO- + Latin BASIS.

sarcoblast *n.* a germinating particle of protoplasm. WH: 19C. SARCO- + -BLAST.

sarcocarp *n.* the fleshy part of a drupaceous fruit. WH: 19C. SARCO- + -CARP.

sarcocele *n.* fleshy enlargement of the testicle. WH: 17C. SARCO- + -CELE.

sarcocol *n.* a gum resin from Arabia and Iran. WH: 14–15C. Latin *sarcocolla*, from Greek *sarkokolla*, from *sarko-* SARCO- + *kolla* glue. The resin is so called from its reputed ability to agglutinate wounds.

sarcode *n.* animal protoplasm. WH: 19C. French. See SARCO-, -ODE[1].

sarcoderm *n.* an intermediate fleshy layer in certain seeds. WH: 19C. SARCO- + -DERM.

sarcody *n.* conversion into fleshiness. WH: 19C. SARCODE + -Y[2].

sarcoid *a.* resembling flesh. *Also n.* WH: 19C. SARCO- + -OID.

sarcolemma *n.* the tubular membrane sheathing muscular tissue. WH: 19C. SARCO- + Greek *lemma* husk, shell.

sarcology *n.* the branch of anatomy concerned with the soft parts of the body. WH: 18C. SARCO- + -LOGY.

sarcoma *n.* a tumour of connective tissue. WH: 17C. Modern Latin, from Greek *sarkōma*, from *sarkoun* to become fleshy, from *sarx, sarkos* flesh. See also -OMA.

sarcophagous *a.* feeding on flesh. WH: 18C. SARCO- + -PHAGOUS.

sarcophagus *n.* a stone coffin, esp. one of architectural or decorated design. WH: 14–15C. Latin, from Greek *sarkophagos*, from *sarko-* SARCO- + -*phagos* eating. The coffin is so called from the supposed action of the stone on the body. The Latin word gave French *cercueil* coffin.

sarcoplasm *n.* the substance between the columns of muscle fibre. WH: 19C. SARCO- + -*plasm*, from PROTOPLASM.

sarcoptes *n.* an itch mite of the genus *Sarcoptes*. WH: 19C. Modern Latin, from SARCO- + Greek *koptein* to cut.

sarcosis *n.* a fleshy tumour, a sarcoma. WH: 19C. SARCO- + -OSIS.

sarcotome *n.* an instrument for cutting through the tissues of the body. WH: 19C. SARCO- + -TOME.

sarcous *a.* composed of flesh or muscle tissue. WH: 19C. SARCO- + -OUS.

Sard *a., n.* (a) Sardinian. WH: 19C. Italian *Sardo*, from Latin *Sardus* SARDINIAN.

sard *n.* a precious stone, a variety of cornelian. WH: 14–15C. Old French *sarde* or Latin *sarda* SARDIUS.

sardelle *n.* a small Mediterranean clupeoid fish like, and prepared as, the sardine. WH: 16C. Italian *sardelle*, dim. of *sarda*, from Latin. See SARDINE.

sardine *n.* a fish, *Clupea pilchardus*, caught off Brittany and Sardinia, and cured and preserved in oil. WH: 14–15C. Old French, corr. to Italian *sardina*, from Latin, from *sarda*, from Greek, prob. from *Sardō* Sardinia. The fish was probably caught in large numbers near Sardinia and then exported.

Sardinian *a.* of or relating to the island or the former kingdom of Sardinia, or its language. *Also n.* WH: 16C. *Sardinia*, an island in the Mediterranean, now administratively part of Italy, or the former kingdom of the same name that included territory in mainland Italy besides the island + -AN.

sardius *n.* a precious stone mentioned in Scripture, perhaps the sard or the sardonyx. WH: 14–15C. Late Latin, from Greek *sardios*, prob. from *Sardō* Sardinia. Cp. SARD.

sardonic *a.* forced, insincere. WH: 17C. French *sardonique*, alt. of obs. *sardonien*, from Latin *sardonius*, from Late Greek *sardonios* Sardinian, substituted for *sardanios* of bitter laughter. See also -IC. The reason for the substitution of *sardonios* for *sardanios* was the belief among the Greeks that the former word referred to a 'Sardinian plant' which when eaten produced facial convulsions similar to those accompanying bitter or scornful laughter.

sardonyx *n.* a variety of onyx composed of white chalcedony alternating with layers of sard. **WH:** 12–14C. Latin, from Greek *sardonux*, prob. from *sardios* SARDIUS + *onux* ONYX.

sargasso *n.* any seaweed of the genus *Sargassum*, found floating esp. in the Sargasso Sea in the N Atlantic. **WH:** 16C. Portuguese *sargaço*, of unknown orig.

sarge *n.* a sergeant. **WH:** 19C. Abbr. of SERGEANT, with change of vowel reflecting the pronun.

sari *n.* a Hindu woman's traditional dress, formed from a length of material draped around the body. **WH:** 18C. Hindi *sāṛī*, from Sanskrit *śāṭikā*.

sarin *n.* a compound of phosphorus used as a nerve gas. **WH:** mid-20C. German, of unknown orig.

sark *n.* a shirt or chemise. *Also v.t.* **WH:** pre-1200. Old English *serc*, *syrc*, from Germanic. Cp. BERSERK.

sarkinite *n.* a mineral composed of red arsenate of manganese. **WH:** 19C. Greek *sarkinos* fleshy, from *sarx*, *sarkos* flesh + -ITE¹. The mineral is so called from its flesh-pink colour.

sarky *a.* sarcastic. **WH:** early 20C. Abbr. of *sarcastic* (SARCASM).

Sarmatian *a.* of or relating to ancient Sarmatia, now Poland and part of Russia, or its people. *Also n.* **WH:** 17C. Latin *Sarmatia* land of the Sarmatae. See also -AN.

sarmentose *a.* having or producing runners. **WH:** 18C. Latin *sarmentum*, orig. cut twigs, from *sarpere* to prune. See also -OSE¹.

sarnie *n.* a sandwich. **WH:** mid-20C. Prob. representation of a coll. or dial. pronun. of 1st element of SANDWICH. See also -Y³.

sarod *n.* an Indian instrument like a cello, that may be played with a bow or plucked. **WH:** 19C. Urdu, from Persian *surod* song, melody.

sarong *n.* a loose, skirtlike garment traditionally worn by men and women in the Malay Archipelago. **WH:** 19C. Malay, lit. sheath, quiver.

saros *n.* a cycle of 6585 1/3 days in which solar and lunar eclipses repeat themselves (a misunderstanding from the original cycle of 3600 years). **WH:** 17C. Greek, from Akkadian *šāru*.

sarpanch *n.* an elected head of an Indian village council. **WH:** mid-20C. Urdu *sar-panch*, from *sar* head + *panch* five (from Sanskrit *pañca*).

sarracenia *n.* any plant of the genus *Sarracenia*, insectivorous plants with pitcher-shaped leaves. **WH:** 18C. Modern Latin, from D. *Sarrazin*, 17C Canadian botanist + -IA.

sarrusophone *n.* a brass musical instrument resembling an oboe with a metal tube. **WH:** 19C. V. *Sarrus*, 19C French bandmaster, who invented it in 1856, + -O- + -PHONE. The instrument was actually constructed by René-Louis Gautrot, who generously named it after its original designer.

sarsaparilla *n.* the dried roots of various species of smilax, used as a flavouring and formerly in medicine as an alterative and tonic. **WH:** 16C. Spanish *zarzaparilla*, from *zarza* bramble + dim. of *parra* vine, twining plant.

sarsen *n.* a sandstone boulder such as those scattered over the chalk downs of Wiltshire. **WH:** 17C. Appar. var. of SARACEN. The word presumably originated as a nickname for an incongruous-looking 'alien' object.

sartage *n.* the clearing of woodland for agricultural purposes. **WH:** 19C. French, from *sarter* to clear ground. See also -AGE.

sartorial *a.* of or relating to a tailor or tailored clothing. **WH:** 19C. Latin *sartor* tailor, from *sartus*, p.p. of *sarcire* to patch, to botch. See also -IAL.

sartorius *n.* a muscle of the thigh that helps to flex the knee. **WH:** 18C. Modern Latin *sartorius* (*musculus*), lit. tailor's (muscle). The muscle is so called from the cross-legged seated posture formerly adopted by tailors when sewing.

Sarum use *n.* the rites used at Salisbury cathedral before the Reformation. **WH:** 16C. Medieval Latin *Sarum* Salisbury, prob. from abbr. of Latin *Sarisburia*.

sash¹ *n.* an ornamental band or scarf worn round the waist or over the shoulder, frequently as a badge or part of a uniform. **WH:** 16C. Arabic *šāš* muslin, (length of cloth for a) turban.

sash² *n.* a frame of wood or metal holding the glass of a window. *Also v.t.* **WH:** 17C. Alt. of CHASSIS, taken as pl.

sashay *v.i.* to walk or move in a nonchalant or sauntering manner. **WH:** 19C. Alt. of CHASSÉ.

sashimi *n.* a Japanese dish of thin slices of raw fish. **WH:** 19C. Japanese, from *sashi* to pierce + *mi* flesh.

sasin *n.* the common Indian antelope, *Antilope cervicapra*, also called *blackbuck*. **WH:** 19C. From a local Himalayan word.

sasine *n.* the act of giving legal possession of feudal property. **WH:** 17C. Var. of *seisin* (SEISE), based on law Latin *sasina*.

Sasquatch *n.* a hairy humanoid creature reputedly living in W Canada. **WH:** early 20C. Salish.

sass *n.* impudence, cheek, sauce. *Also v.t.* **WH:** 18C. Var. of SAUCE.

sassafras *n.* a N American tree, *Sassafras albidum*, of the laurel family. **WH:** 16C. Spanish *sasafrás*, ? ult. from Latin *saxifraga* SAXIFRAGE.

Sassanian *a.* of or relating to the Sassanids. *Also n.* **WH:** 18C. *Sasan* (Persian *Sāsān*) *fl.*1C AD?, Persian prince + -IAN. Sasan's grandson, Ardashir, founded the Sassanian dynasty that ruled the Persian empire from 224 to 651.

Sassenach *n.* a Saxon, an English person. *Also a.* **WH:** 18C. Gaelic *Sassunoch*, Irish *Sasanach*, from Latin *Saxones*, Old English *Seaxe*, *Seaxan* Saxons.

sassoline *n.* a mineral composed of a native triclinic form of boric acid. **WH:** 19C. Lago del *Sarso* in Tuscany, W Italy + *-l-* + -INE.

sastrugi *n.pl.* wavelike ridges on snow-covered plains caused by winds. **WH:** 19C. Pl. of *sastruga*, from German, from Russian *zastruga* small ridge, furrow in snow, from *zastrugat'* to plane, to smooth, from *strug* plane.

Satan *n.* the arch-fiend, the Devil. **WH:** pre-1200. Late Latin and Greek, from Hebrew *śāṭān* adversary, from *śāṭan* to oppose, to plot against. 'Be sober, be vigilant; because your adversary the devil ... walketh about' (I Pet. v.8).

Satano- *comb. form* of or relating to Satan. **WH:** SATAN + -O-.

satara *n.* a heavy, horizontally-ribbed woollen or broadcloth. **WH:** 19C. *Satara*, a town and district in W India.

satay *n.* a Malaysian and Indonesian dish of cubed meat served with a spicy peanut sauce. **WH:** mid-20C. Malay *satai*, *sate*, Indonesian *sate*.

satchel *n.* a small rectangular bag, often suspended by a strap passing over one shoulder, esp. for schoolchildren to carry books etc. in. **WH:** 12–14C. Old French *sachel*, from Latin *sacellus*, dim. of *saccus* SACK¹.

sate *v.t.* to satisfy (an appetite or desire). **WH:** 17C. Prob. alt. of obs. *sade* to become sated (from Old English *satian*, from Germanic base of SAD), influ. by SATIATE.

sateen *n.* a glossy woollen or cotton fabric made in imitation of satin. **WH:** 19C. Alt. of SATIN, based on *velveteen* (VELVET). See also -EEN.

satellite *n.* a secondary planet revolving round a primary one. *Also a.* **WH:** 16C. Old French, or from Latin *satelles*, *satellitis* attendant, ? from Etruscan. The earliest sense was a member of an important person's staff. The astronomical sense followed in the 17C.

satiate *v.t.* to satisfy (as a desire or appetite) fully. *Also a.* **WH:** 14–15C. Latin *satiatus*, p.p. of *satiare*, from *satis* enough. See also -ATE³. Cp. SATE.

satin *n.* a silken fabric with an overshot weft and a highly-finished glossy surface on one side only. *Also a., v.t.* **WH:** 14–15C. Old French, from Arabic *zaytūnī* pertaining to (the town of) Zaytun. Zaytun has been identified with Tsinkiang (Chuanchow), a city in S China used as a port in medieval times.

satire *n.* ridicule, sarcasm. **WH:** 16C. Old French, or from Latin *satira*, later form of *satura* poetic medley. The word was formerly associated with SATYR and was spelt thus.

satisfy *v.t.* to supply or gratify to the full. *Also v.i.* **WH:** 14–15C. Old French *satisfier*, from Latin *satisfacere*, from *satis* enough + *facere* to make, to do. See also -FY.

satnav *abbr.* satellite navigation. **WH:** late 20C. Acronym of *satellite navigation*.

satori *n.* in Zen Buddhism, an intuitive enlightenment. **WH:** 18C. Japanese awakening.

satrap *n.* a governor of a province under the ancient Persian empire, a viceroy. **WH:** 14–15C. Old French *satrape* or Latin *satrapa*, *satrapes*, from Greek *satrapēs*, from Old Persian *kšatra-pāvan* protector of the country, from *kšatra-* country + *pā-* to protect.

satsuma *n.* a seedless type of mandarin orange. WH: 19C. *Satsuma,* a province in the island of Kiusiu, Japan.

saturate[1] *v.t.* to soak or imbue thoroughly. WH: 16C. Latin *saturatus,* p.p. of *saturare,* from *satur* full, satiated. See also -ATE[3].

saturate[2] *a.* (of a colour) intense, deep. WH: 14–15C. Latin *saturatus,* p.p. of *saturare.* See SATURATE[1], also -ATE[2].

Saturday *n.* the seventh day of the week, following Friday. *Also adv.* WH: pre-1200. Old English *Sæterndæg, Sæternesdæg,* corr. to Frisian *saterdei,* Middle Low German *saterdach,* Middle Dutch *saterdach* (Dutch *zaterdag*), translating Latin *Saturni dies* day of (the planet) Saturn.

Saturn *n.* the sixth planet from the sun. WH: pre-1200. Latin *Saturnus,* ? of Etruscan orig.

satyagraha *n.* non-violent resistance to authority as practised orig. by Mahatma Gandhi. WH: early 20C. Sanskrit *satyāgraha* force born of truth, from *satya* truth + *āgraha* obstinacy.

satyr *n.* any of a class of ancient sylvan Greek gods represented with the legs of a goat, budding horns, and goatlike ears, identified by the Romans with the fauns. WH: 14–15C. Old French *satyre* or Latin *satyrus,* from Greek *saturos.* Cp. SATIRE.

sauce *n.* a preparation, usu. liquid, taken with foods as an accompaniment or to enhance the taste. *Also v.t.* WH: 12–14C. Old French, from Popular Latin *salsa,* use as n. of fem. of Latin *salsus* salted, salt. Cp. SALAD.

saucer *n.* a shallow dish for placing a cup on and catching drips. WH: 12–14C. Old French *saussier, saussiere* (Modern French *saucière*) sauce-boat, from *sauce* SAUCE, prob. based on Late Latin *salsarium.* The original sense (to the 18C) was a receptacle for holding condiments or sauces. The current sense arose in the 17C.

saucisse *n.* a long tube of gunpowder, etc., for firing a charge. WH: 17C. French SAUSAGE. The variant *saucisson* is an augmentative of *saucisse.*

Saudi *n.* a native or inhabitant of Saudi Arabia. *Also a.* WH: mid-20C. Arabic *sa'ūdī,* from *Sā'ūd* dynasty name + -I[3]. The kingdom of Saudi Arabia, in the Arabian peninsula, was founded by Ibn Sa'ūd, *c.*1880–1953, in 1932.

sauerkraut *n.* finely chopped cabbage compressed with salt until it ferments. WH: 17C. German, from *sauer* sour + *Kraut* cabbage. Cp. KRAUT.

sauger *n.* the smaller N American pikeperch, *Stizostedion canadense.* WH: 19C. Orig. unknown.

sault *n.* a rapid in a river. WH: 12–14C. Old French, earlier spelling of *saut,* from Latin *saltus,* from *salire* to leap.

sauna *n.* a Finnish-style steam bath. WH: 19C. Finnish.

saunter *v.i.* to wander about idly and leisurely. *Also n.* WH: 14–15C. Orig. unknown. Etymologists in the 17C derived the word from French *Sainte-Terre* Holy Land, with reference to pilgrims' journeys. The original sense (to the 16C) was to muse, to wonder, also to chatter. The current sense evolved in the 17C.

saurian *a.* of, relating to or resembling the Sauria, an order of reptiles formerly including the crocodiles and lizards, but now the lizards alone. *Also n.* WH: 19C. Modern Latin *Sauria,* from Greek *sauros* lizard. See also -IAN.

saurischian *a.* of or relating to the Saurischia, an order of dinosaurs. *Also n.* WH: 19C. Modern Latin *Saurischia,* from Greek *sauros* lizard + *iskhion* ISCHIUM. See also -IAN.

sauro- *comb. form* lizard. WH: Greek *sauros* lizard. See also -O-.

saurodont *n.* any of the Saurodontidae, an extinct family of fishes of the Cretaceous age. *Also a.* WH: 19C. SAURO- + -ODONT.

saurognathous *a.* (of birds) having a palate similar to that of the lizards. WH: 19C. SAURO- + Greek *gnathos* jaw. See also -OUS.

sauropod *n.* any of the Sauropoda, an extinct order of gigantic herbivores. WH: 19C. Modern Latin *Sauropoda.* See SAURO-, -POD.

saury *n.* a sea fish, *Scomberesox saurus,* with elongated body ending in a beak. WH: 18C. Appar. from Modern Latin *saurus,* from Greek *sauros* lizard, horse mackerel.

sausage *n.* an article of food consisting of pork or other meat minced, seasoned and stuffed into a length of animal's gut or a similar receptacle. WH: 14–15C. Old Northern French *saussiche,* var. of Old French *salsice* (Modern French *saucisse*), from Medieval Latin *salsicia,* use as n. of neut. pl. of *salsicius,* from Latin *salsus* salted. The spelling with *-age* arose in the 16C, perhaps because the sausage was seen as a food prepared by salting, i.e. resulting from this action (see also -AGE).

saussurite *n.* an impure white, grey or green silicate mineral formed by alteration from feldspar. WH: 19C. Horace Benedict de *Saussure,* 1740–99, Swiss naturalist + -ITE[1].

sauté *a.* lightly fried. *Also v.t., n.* WH: 19C. French, p.p. of *sauter* to leap. The term refers to the tossing action while cooking, done to ensure that the food being cooked does not lie on the surface of the pan continuously.

Sauternes *n.* a sweet white Bordeaux wine. WH: 18C. *Sauternes,* a district near Bordeaux in SW France.

sauve qui peut *n.* a state of panic or chaos. WH: 19C. French, lit. save-who-can.

savage *a.* fierce, cruel. *Also n., v.t.* WH: 12–14C. Old French *sauvage,* from Late Latin *salvaticus,* alt. of Latin *silvaticus* of woodland, wild, from *silva* wood, forest. See also -AGE.

savannah *n.* an extensive treeless plain covered with low vegetation, esp. in tropical America. WH: 16C. Obs. Spanish *zavana, çavana* (now *sabana*), from Taino *zavana.*

savant *n.* a person of learning, esp. an eminent scientist. WH: 18C. French, use as n. of a., orig. pres.p. of *savoir* to know.

savarin *n.* a ring-shaped cake containing nuts and fruit, often flavoured with rum. WH: 19C. Anthelme Brillat-*Savarin,* 1755–1826, French gourmet.

savate *n.* a style of boxing in which the feet are used as well as the hands. WH: 19C. French, orig. a kind of shoe. Cp. SABOT.

save *v.t.* to preserve, rescue or deliver as from danger or harm. *Also v.i., prep., conj., n.* WH: 12–14C. Old French *salver* (Modern French *sauver*), from Late Latin *salvare* to save, from Latin *salvus* SAFE.

saveloy *n.* a highly-seasoned dried sausage of salted pork (orig. of brains). WH: 19C. Alt. of obs. French *cervelat* (Modern French *cervelas*), from Italian *cervellata.* See CERVELAT.

savin *n.* an evergreen bush or low tree, *Juniperus sabina,* with bluish-green fruit, yielding an oil formerly used medicinally. WH: pre-1200. Old French *savine* (Modern French *sabine*), from Latin *sabina,* use as n. of fem. sing. of *Sabinus* SABINE.

saviour *n.* a person who preserves, rescues or redeems. WH: 12–14C. Old French *sauveour* (Modern French *sauveur*), from Late Latin *salvator,* from *salvare* SAVE. Late Latin *salvator* translated Greek *sōtēr* and ultimately Late Hebrew *yēšūã'* Jesus.

savoir faire *n.* quickness to do the right thing, esp. in social situations. WH: 19C. French, lit. to know how to do.

savonette *n.* a toilet preparation of various kinds. WH: 18C. French (now *savonnette*), dim. of *savon* soap. See also -ETTE.

savory *n.* a plant of the aromatic genus *Satureja,* esp. *S. hortensis* and *S. montana,* used in cookery. WH: 12–14C. ? Old English *sætherie* (with alt. of *-th-* to *-v-*), from Latin *satureia,* of unknown orig.

savour *n.* (characteristic) flavour, taste, relish. *Also v.t., v.i.* WH: 12–14C. Old French (Modern French *saveur*), from Latin *sapor* taste, from *sapere* to have a taste. See also -OUR. Cp. SAPOR.

savoy *n.* a hardy variety of cabbage with wrinkled leaves. WH: 16C. French *Savoie,* a region of SE France.

Savoyard *n.* a native or inhabitant of Savoy in SE France. *Also a.* WH: 17C. French, from *Savoie.* See SAVOY, also -ARD.

savvy *v.t., v.i.* to know, to understand. *Also n., a.* WH: 18C. Orig. Black and pidgin English, from Spanish *sabe usted* you know.

saw[1] *n.* a cutting-instrument, usu. of steel, with a toothed edge, worked by hand, or power-driven, as in circular or ribbon form. *Also v.t., v.i.* WH: pre-1200. Old English *saga,* from Germanic. Cp. Dutch *zaag.*

saw[2] *n.* a saying, a proverb. WH: pre-1200. Old English *sagu,* from Germanic, from base of SAY. Cp. SAGA.

sawder *n.* blarney, flattery. WH: 19C. Appar. var. of SOLDER.

Sawney *n.* a Scotsman. WH: 17C. Local var. of SANDY.

sawney *n.* a simpleton. WH: 17C. SAWNEY.

sax[1] *n.* a saxophone. WH: early 20C. Abbr. of SAXOPHONE.

sax[2] *n.* a slate-cutter's chopping and trimming tool with a point for making holes. WH: pre-1200. Old English *seax,* from Germanic, from Indo-European base of Latin *secare* to cut.

saxatile *a.* of, relating to or living among rocks. WH: 17C. French or Latin *saxatilis*, from *saxum* rock, stone. See also -ATILE.

saxboard *n.* the uppermost strake of an open boat. WH: 19C. Prob. from SAX² + BOARD.

saxe *n.* an albumenized photographic paper made in Saxony. WH: 19C. French, from German *Sachsen* Saxony.

saxhorn *n.* a brass musical wind instrument with a long winding tube, a wide opening and several valves. WH: 19C. Charles Joseph *Sax*, 1791–1865, and his son Antoine Joseph 'Adolphe' *Sax*, 1818–94, Belgian instrument-makers + HORN.

saxicavous *a.* hollowing out stone. WH: 19C. Modern Latin *saxicavus*, from *saxum* rock, stone + *cavare* to hollow. See -OUS.

saxicolous *a.* inhabiting or growing among rocks, saxatile. WH: 19C. Modern Latin *saxicola*, from *saxum* rock, stone + *colere* to inhabit. See also -OUS.

saxifrage *n.* any plant of the genus *Saxifraga*, consisting largely of alpine or rock plants with tufted, mossy or encrusted foliage and small flowers. WH: 14–15C. Old French, or from Late Latin *saxifraga*, from *saxum* rock + *frag-*, base of *frangere* to break. The plant is probably so called from its habitat, or because it was used medicinally to dissolve gall stones.

Saxon *n.* a member of a Germanic people from N Germany who conquered England in the 5th and 6th cents. *Also a.* WH: 12–14C. Old French *Saxo*, *Saxons*, from Germanic, ? from base of SAX². Cp. Old English *Seaxe*, *Seaxan* (pl.) Saxons.

saxony *n.* a fine wool or woollen material produced in Saxony. WH: 19C. *Saxony*, a region of Germany (German *Sachsen*) formerly a kingdom, from Late Latin *Saxonia*, from Latin *Saxo*, *Saxonis* SAXON. See also -Y².

saxophone *n.* a brass musical wind instrument with a single reed used as a powerful substitute for the clarinet. WH: 19C. Adolphe *Sax* (see SAXHORN) + -O- + -PHONE.

saxtuba *n.* a bass saxhorn. WH: 19C. Adolphe *Sax* (see SAXHORN) + TUBA.

say *v.t.* to utter in or as words, to speak. *Also v.i., n., adv., int.* WH: pre-1200. Old English *secgan*, from Germanic. Cp. German *sagen*. Rel. to SAGA, SAW².

sayyid *n.* a Muslim title of respect. WH: 17C. Arabic lord, prince.

Sb *chem. symbol* antimony. WH: Abbr. of Latin *stibium*.

sbirro *n.* an Italian police officer. WH: 17C. Italian, now coll.

scab *n.* an incrustation formed over a sore etc., in healing. *Also v.i.* WH: 12–14C. Old Norse *skabb*, from Germanic. Cp. SHABBY. The sense contemptible person arose in the 16C, and from this blackleg in the 18C. A person covered in scabs and sores is to be despised. Cp. LEPER.

scabbard *n.* the sheath of a sword or similar weapon. *Also v.t.* WH: 12–14C. Anglo-French *escauberge*, prob. from Frankish compound of base rel. to SHEAR + base meaning to protect (as in HAUBERK).

scabies *n.* a contagious skin disease, caused by the itch mite. WH: 14–15C. Latin, from *scabere* to scratch. Rel. to SCAB.

scabious *a.* consisting of or covered with scabs. *Also n.* WH: 14–15C. French *scabieux* or Latin *scabiosus*, from SCABIES. See also -OUS. The plant scabious is so called from its supposed effectiveness against certain skin diseases.

scabrous *a.* rough, rugged or uneven. WH: 16C. French *scabreux* or Late Latin *scabrosus*, from Latin *scaber*, rel. to *scabere* to scratch. See also -OUS. The sense indecent, risqué evolved in the 19C.

scad *n.* any fish of the family Carangidae, usu. having large spiky scales, esp. the horse mackerel *Trachurus trachurus*. WH: 17C. Orig. unknown.

scads *n.pl.* large amounts. WH: 19C. Pl. of *scad*, of unknown orig.

scaffold *n.* a temporary structure of poles and ties supporting a platform for the use of workers building or repairing a house or other building. *Also v.t.* WH: 12–14C. Old French *eschaffaut* (Modern French *échafaud*), from expanded form (prob. influ. by *eschace* prop, support) of *chaffaut*, from Popular Latin *catafalicum*. See CATAFALQUE.

scaglia *n.* a red, white or grey Italian limestone corresponding to chalk. WH: 18C. Italian scale, chip of marble, from Germanic. See SCALE¹.

scalar *a.* ladder-shaped. *Also n.* WH: 17C. Latin *scalaris*, from *scala* ladder. See SCALE³, also -AR¹.

scald *v.t.* to burn with or as with a hot liquid or vapour. *Also n.* WH: 12–14C. Old French *eschalder* (Modern French *échauder*), from Late Latin *excaldere* to wash in hot water, from EX- + *calidus* hot, from *calere* to be warm.

scaldino *n.* a small earthenware brazier used for warming the hands etc. WH: 19C. Italian, from *scaldere* to warm.

scale¹ *n.* each of the thin, horny plates forming a protective covering on the skin of fishes, reptiles etc. *Also v.t., v.i.* WH: 12–14C. Shortening of Old French *escale* (Modern French *écale* husk, stone chip), from Germanic base also of SCALE².

scale² *n.* the dish of a balance. *Also v.t.* WH: 12–14C. Old Norse *skál* bowl, from Germanic base also of SHALE, SHELL. Cp. SKOL. The original sense was drinking bowl. The sense pan of a balance evolved in the 14–15C.

scale³ *n.* anything graduated or marked with lines or degrees at regular intervals, such as a scheme for classification. *Also v.t., v.i.* WH: 14–15C. Latin *scala* staircase, ladder, from base of *scandere* to climb. The original sense (to the 19C) was ladder. The musical sense (series of notes) evolved in the 16C.

scalene *a.* (of a triangle) having no two sides equal. *Also n.* WH: 17C. Late Latin *scalenus*, from Greek *skalenos* uneven, unequal.

scallion *n.* a variety of onion or shallot. WH: 14–15C. Old French *escalogne*, from Popular Latin *escalonia*, from Latin *Ascalonia caepa* shallot, lit. Ascalonian onion, from *Ascalo*, *Ascalonis*, a port in SW Palestine (now Askelon, Israel). Cp. SHALLOT.

scallop *n.* any of various bivalve molluscs of the genus *Pecten* or a related genus, with ridges and flutings radiating from the middle of the hinge and an undulating margin. *Also v.t.* WH: 12–14C. Shortening of Old French *escalope* ESCALLOP.

scallywag *n.* a scamp, a rascal. WH: 19C. Orig. uncertain. ? Alt. (influ. by WAG²) of Scottish *scallag* farm servant, rustic, ult. from Latin *schola* SCHOOL¹.

scalp *n.* the top of the head. *Also v.t., v.i.* WH: 12–14C. Prob. of Scandinavian orig. The original sense was skull. The current sense, skin and hair on the top of the head, dates from the 16C, possibly with reference to the biblical passage: 'But God shall wound the head of his enemies, and the hairy scalp of such an one as goeth on still in his trespasses' (Ps. lxviii.21).

scalpel *n.* a small knife used in surgical operations and anatomical dissections. WH: 18C. French, or from Latin *scalpellum*, dim. of *scalprum*, *scalper* cutting tool, chisel, knife, from base of *scalpere* to scratch, to carve. See also -EL. Not rel. to SCALP.

scalpriform *a.* chisel-shaped (as the teeth of rodents). WH: 19C. Latin *scalprum* (SCALPEL) + -i- + -FORM.

scam *n.* a trick or swindle. *Also v.i., v.t.* WH: mid-20C. Orig. unknown.

scammony *n.* an Asian plant, *Convolvulus scammonia*. WH: pre-1200. Old French *escamonie*, *scamonee* or Latin *scammonea*, *scammonia*, from Greek *skammōnia*.

scamp¹ *n.* a worthless person, a knave, a rogue. WH: 18C. Prob. from Middle Dutch *schampen* to slip away, to decamp, from Old French *eschamper*, from Popular Latin *excampare*, from Latin EX- + *campus* field. Cp. SCAMPER.

scamp² *v.t.* to do or execute (work etc.) in a careless manner or with bad material. WH: 19C. ? From SCAMP¹, but similar in sense to SKIMP.

scamper *v.i.* to run rapidly, playfully, hastily, or impulsively. *Also n.* WH: 17C. Prob. from Middle Dutch *schampen*. See SCAMP¹.

scampi *n.* large prawns such as the Norway lobster or Dublin (Bay) prawn, esp. when fried in breadcrumbs or batter. WH: 19C. Italian, pl. of *scampo* a kind of lobster, of Venetian orig.

scan *v.t.* to examine closely or intently. *Also v.i., n.* WH: 14–15C. Late Latin use of Latin *scandere* to climb, to scan verse. A person counting or testing the metrical feet or syllables of a line of verse is like a climber raising and lowering the feet.

scandal *n.* a disgraceful action, person etc. *Also v.t.* WH: 12–14C. Old French *scandale*, from Ecclesiastical Latin *scandalum* cause of offence, from Hellenistic Greek *skandalon* snare for an enemy, cause of moral stumbling (orig. trap). Cp. SLANDER. The original sense was a discredit to religion caused by a religious person. The current sense arose in the 16C, and specifically as an outrage to decency in the 17C.

scandent *a.* climbing, as ivy. WH: 17C. Latin *scandens, scandentis*, pres.p. of *scandere* to climb.

Scandinavian *a.* of or relating to Scandinavia, its language or literature. *Also n.* WH: 18C. Latin *Scandinavia* Scandinavia, a region of NW Europe including Norway, Sweden, Denmark and Iceland + -AN.

scandium *n.* a rare metallic element, at. no. 21, chem. symbol Sc, discovered in certain Swedish yttrium ores. WH: 19C. Latin *Scandia*, contr. of *Scandinavia*. See SCANDINAVIAN, also -IUM. The element is so called because it was found in various minerals in Scandinavia. The name was coined in 1879 by the Swedish physicist Lars F. Nilson.

scansion *n.* the act of scanning verse. WH: 17C. Latin *scansio, scansionis*, from *scandere* to climb. See SCAN.

scansorial *a.* climbing, adapted for climbing. *Also n.* WH: 19C. Latin *scansorius*, from *scansus*, p.p. of *scandere* to climb. See also -IAL.

scant *a.* not full, large or plentiful. *Also v.t., v.i.* WH: 12–14C. Old Norse *skamt*, neut. of *skammr* short, brief, from Germanic.

scantle *v.t.* to divide into small pieces, to partition. *Also n.* WH: 16C. ? Dim. of SCANT. See also -LE[4].

scantling *n.* a beam less than 5 in. (12.7 cm) in breadth and thickness. WH: 16C. Alt., by assoc. with -LING[1], of obs. *scantillon* measuring tool, shortening of Old French *escantillon* (Modern French *échantillon*) sample.

scape *n.* a leafless radical stem bearing the flower. WH: 17C. Latin *scapus*, from Greek *skapos* rod, rel. to *skēptron* SCEPTRE.

-scape *comb. form* scene, view, as in *seascape, townscape*. WH: Extracted from LANDSCAPE.

scapegoat *n.* a person made to bear blame due to another. *Also v.t.* WH: 16C. Obs. *scape*, shortening of ESCAPE + GOAT. The word was coined by William Tyndale in 1530 for his translation of the Bible. It expressed what he believed was the literal meaning of the Hebrew *'azāzēl* (Lev. xvi.8,10,26), which he interpreted as *'ēz 'ōzēl* goat that departs. But the Hebrew word is actually a proper name of unknown origin.

scapegrace *n.* a graceless, good-for-nothing person, esp. a child. WH: 19C. Obs. *scape*, shortening of ESCAPE + GRACE. The literal sense is a person who escapes the grace of God.

scaphite *n.* a cephalopod of the fossil genus *Scaphites*. WH: 19C. Greek *skaphē* boat + -ITE[1]. The fossil is so called from the boat-shaped form of the shell.

scapho- *comb. form* boat-shaped. WH: Greek *skaphē* boat. See also -O-.

scaphocephalic *a.* having a boat-shaped skull, owing to premature union of the parietal bones at the sagittal suture. WH: 19C. SCAPHO- + -CEPHALIC.

scaphoid *a.* boat-shaped, navicular. *Also n.* WH: 18C. Modern Latin *scaphoides*, from Greek *skaphoeidēs*, from *skaphē* boat. See also -OID.

scapolite *n.* any of a group of tetragonal silicate minerals of calcium, aluminium and sodium. WH: 19C. Greek *skapos* (SCAPE) + *lithos* stone. See -LITE.

scapple *v.t.* to reduce (stone) to a level surface without smoothing. WH: 14–15C. Shortening of Old French *escapeler, eschapeler* to dress timber.

scapula *n.* the shoulder blade. WH: 16C. Late Latin, sing. of Latin *scapulae* shoulders, shoulder blades.

scar[1] *n.* a mark left by a wound, burn, ulcer etc. *Also v.t., v.i.* WH: 14–15C. Shortening of Old French *escharre*, from Late Latin *eschara*, from Greek *eskhara* hearth, brazier, scab.

scar[2] *n.* a crag, a cliff, a precipitous escarpment. WH: 12–14C. Old Norse *sker* low reef. Cp. SKERRY.

scar[3] *n.* a parrotfish. WH: 18C. Latin SCARUS.

scarab *n.* an ancient Egyptian sacred beetle, *Scarabaeus sacer*. WH: 16C. Latin *scarabaeus* beetle. The word was originally used for a beetle of any kind.

†scaramouch *n.* a coward and braggart. WH: 17C. Orig. from Italian *Scaramuccia*, a stock character (a cowardly boaster) in the Italian *commedia dell'arte*, from *scaramuccia* SKIRMISH; later from French *Scaramouche*, an equivalent character.

scarbroite *n.* a clayey hydrous silicate mineral of alumina found near Scarborough. WH: 19C. *Scarbro'*, a form of *Scarborough*, a town on the Yorkshire coast + -ITE[1].

scarce *a.* infrequent, uncommon. *Also adv.* WH: 12–14C. Old Northern French *scars*, shortened form of *escars*, Old French *eschars* (Modern French *échars*), from Popular Latin *excarpsus*, lit. plucked out, from p.p. of *excarpere*, alt. of Latin *excerpere* to pluck out, EXCERPT[1]. The original sense (to the 16C) was restricted in quantity, scanty, also (to the 17C), of a person, stingy, parsimonious.

scarcement *n.* a set-off in a wall, or a plain flat ledge resulting from this. WH: 16C. Appar. from SCARCE + -MENT.

scare *v.t.* to frighten, to alarm. *Also v.i., n.* WH: 12–14C. Old Norse *skirra* to frighten, from *skjarr* shy, timid.

scarf[1] *n.* a long strip or square of some material worn round the neck and shoulders or over the head for warmth or decoration. *Also v.t.* WH: 16C. Prob. alt. (by assoc. with SCARF[2]) of SCARP[2].

scarf[2] *v.t.* to join the ends of (timber) by means of a scarf joint. *Also n.* WH: 12–14C. Prob. from Scandinavian. Cp. Swedish *skarv* scarf, seam.

scarf[3] *n.* a cormorant. WH: 17C. Old Norse *skarfr*, prob. of imit. orig.

scarf[4] *v.t.* to eat or drink greedily (usu. with *down*). WH: mid-20C. Var. of SCOFF[2].

scarify[1] *v.t.* to scratch or make slight incisions in. WH: 14–15C. Old French *scarifier*, from Late Latin *scarificare*, alt. of Latin *scarifare*, from Greek *skariphasthai* to scratch an outline, from *skariphos* pencil, stylus. See also -FY.

scarify[2] *v.t.* to scare, frighten. *Also v.i.* WH: 18C. SCARE + -i- + -FY, ? based on *terrify* (TERRIFIC).

scarious *a.* (of bracts etc.) membraneous and dry. WH: 19C. French *scarieux* or Modern Latin *scariosus*.

scarlatina *n.* (a mild form of) scarlet fever. WH: 19C. Modern Latin, from Italian *scarlattina*, fem. of *scarlattino*, dim. of *scarlatto* scarlet.

scarlet *n.* a bright red colour tending towards orange. *Also a.* WH: 12–14C. Shortening of Anglo-French *escarlate* (fem.) (Modern French *écarlate*), from Spanish Arabic *'eškarlāt*, ult. from Latin *sigillatus* decorated with small images.

scarp[1] *n.* a steep or nearly perpendicular slope. *Also v.t.* WH: 16C. Italian *scarpa*. Cp. ESCARP.

scarp[2] *n.* a diminutive of the bend sinister, half its width. WH: 16C. Shortening of Old Northern French *escarpe*, Old French *escherpe* (Modern French *écharpe*), prob. identical with Old French *escarpe, escharpe* pilgrim's scrip suspended from the neck. Cp. SCRIP[2], SCARF[1].

scarper *v.i.* to leave in a hurry. WH: 19C. Prob. from Italian *scappare* to escape, reinforced in and after World War I by rhyming slang *scapa flow* go. Scapa Flow is a landlocked anchorage in the Orkney Islands, N Scotland, where the British Grand Fleet was based in World War I and where the German navy scuttled many of their ships after the war.

scarpines *n.pl.* an instrument of torture similar to the boot. WH: 16C. Pl. of *scarpine*, from Italian *scarpino*, dim. of *scarpa* shoe.

Scart *n.* a 21-pin socket used to connect video equipment. WH: late 20C. Acronym of French Syndicat des constructeurs des appareils radiorécepteurs et téléviseurs Syndicate of radio and television manufacturers, the European committee that designed the connector.

scarus *n.* any fish of the genus *Scarus*, which have brightly coloured scales; also called *parrotfish*. WH: 17C. Latin, from Greek *skaros*.

scat[1] *int.* go away!, be off! *Also v.i.* WH: 19C. ? From a hiss + *cat*, used to drive away cats, or abbr. of SCATTER.

scat[2] *n.* jazz singing in meaningless syllables. *Also v.i.* WH: early 20C. Prob. imit.

scat[3] *n.* excrement. WH: mid-20C. Greek *skōr, skat-*. See SCATOLOGY.

scat[4] *n.* a blow. WH: 18C. Orig. unknown.

scat[5] *n.* tax, tribute. WH: 12–14C. Old Norse *skattr*, rel. to Old English *sceat*, from Germanic. Cp. German *Schatz* treasure.

scathe *v.t.* to hurt, to harm, to injure, esp. by scorching. *Also n.*

WH: 12–14C. Old Norse *skatha*, rel. to Old English *sceathian*, from Germanic. Cp. German *schaden* to hurt, to harm.

scatology *n.* interest in or literature characterized by obscenity. **WH:** 19C. Greek *skōr, skat-* dung (cp. SCORIA). See also -LOGY.

scatter *v.t.* to throw loosely about, to fling in all directions. *Also v.i., n.* **WH:** 12–14C. Prob. var. of SHATTER, with *sc-* substituted for *sh-* under Scandinavian influence.

scatty *a.* incapable of prolonged concentration, empty-headed, giddy. **WH:** early 20C. Prob. from *scatterbrained*. See SCATTER, also -Y[1].

scaturient *a.* gushing out, as from a fountain. **WH:** 17C. Latin *scaturiens, scaturientis*, pres.p. of *scaturire*, from *scatere* to flow out. See also -ENT.

scaup *n.* a diving duck of the genus *Aythya*, esp. *A. marila*, found in the northern regions. **WH:** 17C. Scottish var. of dial. *scalp* shellfish bed, prob. from source of SCALP.

scauper *n.* a wood engraver's gougelike tool. **WH:** 14–15C. Partly from Latin *scalper* (SCALPEL), partly from obs. *scalp* to cut, to engrave, from same source.

scavenger *n.* a person who collects waste or discarded objects. **WH:** 16C. Alt. of *scavager* (15C), officer who collected *scavage*, a toll levied on the goods of foreign merchants, from Old Northern French *escauvage*, from *escauver* to inspect, from Flemish *scauwen*, rel. to Old English *scēawian* SHOW. See also -ER[1]. The *n* entered as with HARBINGER, MESSENGER, PASSENGER, etc.

scavenger's daughter *n.* an instrument of torture for compressing the body. **WH:** 16C. Sir William *Skeffington*, c.1465–1535, Lord Deputy of Ireland, Lieutenant of the Tower (of London) under Henry VIII, its inventor. Skeffington was the inventor or 'father' of the instrument, which was thus his 'daughter'.

scazon *n.* a satiric metre of an irregular or faltering character, esp. an iambic trimeter ending with a spondee or trochee, a choliamb. **WH:** 17C. Latin, from Greek *skazōn*, m. pres.p. (used as n.) of *skazein* to limp, to halt.

Sc.D *abbr.* Doctor of Science. **WH:** Abbr. of Latin *Scientiae Doctor* Doctor of Science.

scena *n.* a long elaborate solo piece or scene in opera. **WH:** 19C. Italian, from Latin SCENE.

scenario *n.* a sketch or outline of the scenes and main points of a play etc. **WH:** 19C. Italian, from Latin *scena* SCENE.

scene *n.* the place where anything occurs or is exhibited as on a stage. **WH:** 16C. Latin *scena, scaena* stage, scene, from Greek *skēnē* tent, booth, stage, scene.

scenography *n.* the painting or design of scenes in a theatre. **WH:** 17C. French *scénographie* or Latin *scenographia*, from Greek *skēnographia* scene-painting, from *skēnē*. See SCENE, -GRAPHY.

scent *v.t.* to perceive by smell. *Also v.i., n.* **WH:** 14–15C. Old French *sentir* to feel, to perceive, to smell, from Latin *sentire* to feel, to perceive.

sceptic *n.* a person of a questioning habit of mind. *Also a.* **WH:** 16C. French *sceptique* or Latin *scepticus*, pl. *sceptici* followers of the Greek philosopher Pyrrho, from Greek *skeptikos*, pl. *skeptikoi*, from *skeptesthai* to look about, to consider, to observe, rel. to *skopein*, *skopos*. See SCOPE[1].

sceptre *n.* a staff or baton borne by a sovereign as a symbol of authority. **WH:** 12–14C. Old French *ceptre* (Modern French *sceptre*), from Latin *sceptrum*, from Greek *skēptron*, from *skēptein*, alt. of *skēptesthai* to prop oneself, to lean on. Cp. SCAPE.

schadenfreude *n.* pleasure in others' misfortunes. **WH:** 19C. German, from *Schaden* harm + *Freude* joy.

schappe *n.* a fabric or yarn made from waste silk. **WH:** 19C. German silk waste.

schedule *n.* a timetable. *Also v.t.* **WH:** 14–15C. Old French *cédule*, from Late Latin *schedula* small slip of paper, dim. of *scheda*, from Greek *skhedē* leaf of papyrus. The original sense (to the 17C) was a slip or scroll of parchment or paper containing writing. The current sense evolved in the 19C.

scheelite *n.* a vitreous variously-coloured mineral, a tungstate of calcium. **WH:** 19C. Karl Wilhelm *Scheele*, 1742–86, German-born Swedish chemist + -ITE[1].

schema *n.* a scheme, summary, outline or conspectus. **WH:** 18C. German, from Greek *skhēma*. See SCHEME.

scheme *n.* a proposed method of doing something. *Also v.t., v.i.* **WH:** 16C. Latin *schema, schematis*, from Greek *skhēma, skhēmatos* form, figure. Cp. SCHEMA.

scherzo *n.* a light playful movement in music, usu. following a slow one, in a symphony or sonata. **WH:** 19C. Italian, lit. sport, jest.

schiavone *n.* a 17th-cent. basket-hilted broadsword. **WH:** 19C. Italian, lit. Slavonian. The sword is so called because it was used by the Slavonian guards of the doge of Venice.

Schick test *n.* a test to determine susceptibility to diphtheria by injecting diluted diphtheria toxin into the skin. **WH:** early 20C. Béla *Schick*, 1877–1967, Hungarian-born US paediatrician.

schiedam *n.* a type of Dutch gin. **WH:** 19C. *Schiedam*, a town in the Netherlands.

schiller *n.* the peculiar bronzelike sheen or iridescence characteristic of certain minerals. **WH:** 19C. German, play of colours.

schilling *n.* the standard monetary unit of Austria. **WH:** 18C. German. See SHILLING.

schindylesis *n.* an articulation in which a thin part of one bone fits into a groove in another. **WH:** 19C. Modern Latin, from Greek *skhindulēsis* splitting into fragments, rel. to *skhizein* to split.

schipperke *n.* a small black variety of lapdog. **WH:** 19C. Dutch dial., lit. little boatman. Cp. SKIPPER. The dog is so called from its use as a watchdog on barges.

schisiophone *n.* an instrument comprising a hammer and induction-balance for detecting flaws in iron rails. **WH:** 19C. Greek *skhisis* cleavage, from *schizein* to split + -O- + -PHONE.

schism *n.* a split or division in a community. **WH:** 14–15C. Old French *scisme* (Modern French *schisme*), from Ecclesiastical Latin *schisma*, from Greek *skhisma* rent, cleft, from base of *skhizein* to cleave, to split.

schist *n.* a rock of a more or less foliated or laminar structure, tending to split easily. **WH:** 18C. French *schiste*, from Latin (*lapis*) *schistos* fissile (stone), from Greek *skhistos*, from base of *skhizein* (SCHISM).

schistosome *n.* a tropical flatworm of the genus *Schistosoma*. **WH:** early 20C. Modern Latin *Schistosoma*, from Greek *skhistos* (SCHIST) + *sōma* body. See -SOME[2].

schizanthus *n.* any plant of the genus *Schizanthus*, with much-divided leaves and showy flowers. **WH:** 19C. Modern Latin, from SCHIZO- + Greek *anthos* flower.

schizo *n.* a schizophrenic. *Also a.* **WH:** mid-20C. Abbr. of *schizophrenic* (SCHIZOPHRENIA).

schizo- *comb. form* marked by a cleft or clefts. **WH:** Greek *skhizein* to split + -O-.

schizocarp *n.* a fruit splitting into several one-seeded portions without dehiscing. **WH:** 19C. SCHIZO- + -CARP.

schizocoele *n.* a perivisceral cavity produced by a splitting of the mesoblast of the embryo. **WH:** 19C. SCHIZO- + Greek *koilon* a hollow.

schizogenesis *n.* reproduction by fission. **WH:** 19C. SCHIZO- + GENESIS.

schizognathous *a.* having the bones of the palate cleft from the vomer and each other, as in the gulls, plovers etc. **WH:** 19C. SCHIZO- + -GNATHOUS.

schizoid *a.* showing qualities of a schizophrenic personality. *Also n.* **WH:** early 20C. SCHIZOPHRENIA + -OID.

schizomycete *n.* any organism of the class Schizomycetes, a class of microscopic organisms comprising bacteria. **WH:** 19C. SCHIZO- + -MYCETE.

schizophrenia *n.* a severe psychological disorder characterized by loss of contact with reality, personality disintegration, hallucinations, delusions etc. **WH:** early 20C. Modern Latin, from SCHIZO- + Greek *phrēn* mind. See also -IA. The term was coined in 1910 by the German psychiatrist Eugen Bleuler.

schizophyte *n.* any of various plants that reproduce by fission, such as bacteria and certain fungi. **WH:** 19C. SCHIZO- + -PHYTE.

schizopod *n.* any of the Schizopoda, a suborder of podophthalmate crustaceans with the feet apparently cleft. **WH:** 19C. SCHIZO- + -POD.

schizothecal *a.* (of birds) having the tarsus divided by scutellation or reticulation. **WH:** 19C. SCHIZO- + Greek *thēkē* case. See also -AL[1].

schizothymia *n.* introversion exhibiting elements of schizophrenia but within normal limits. WH: mid-20C. SCHIZO- + Greek *thumos* mind, temper. See also -IA.

schläger *n.* a German student's duelling sword, pointless, but with sharpened edges towards the end. WH: 19C. German, from *schlagen* to beat.

schlemiel *n.* a bungling clumsy person who is easily victimized. WH: 19C. Yiddish *shlemihl*, prob. from biblical name of *Shelumiel* chief of the tribe of Simeon (Num. vii.36). Shelumiel has been identified in the Talmud with the Simeonite prince Zimri ben Salu, killed while committing adultery with a Midianite woman (Num. xxv.6–15).

schlepp *v.t.* to drag, pull. *Also n.* WH: early 20C. Yiddish *shlepn*, from German *schleppen* to drag.

schlieren *n.* small streaks of different composition in igneous rock. WH: 19C. German, pl. of *Schliere* stria, streak, from earlier *Schlier* marl, from Middle High German *slier* mud.

schlimazel *n.* an unlucky person; a born loser. WH: mid-20C. Yiddish, from Middle High German *slim* crooked + Hebrew *mazzāl* luck.

schlock *n.* shoddy, cheap goods; trash. *Also a.* WH: early 20C. Appar. from Yiddish *shlak* apoplectic stroke, *shlog* wretch, untidy person, from *shlogn* to strike. According to some, the word is from German *Schlacke* dregs, scum, dross.

schloss *n.* a castle (in Germany). WH: 19C. German, rel. to SLOT[3].

schlump *n.* a slovenly person, a slob. WH: mid-20C. Appar. rel. to Yiddish *shlumperdik* dowdy, rel. to German *Schlumpe* slattern.

schmaltz *n.* over-sentimentality, esp. in music. WH: mid-20C. Yiddish, from German *Schmalz* dripping, lard.

schmelze *n.* any one of various kinds of coloured glass, esp. that coloured red and used to flash white glass. WH: 19C. Pl. of German *Schmelz* enamel.

schmo *n.* a stupid or boring person. WH: mid-20C. Alt. of SCHMUCK.

schmooze *v.i.* to gossip, chat. *Also n.* WH: 19C. Yiddish *schmuesn* to talk, to chat, from Hebrew *šĕmū'ōṯ*, pl. of *šĕmū'āh* rumour.

schmuck *n.* a fool. WH: 19C. Yiddish *shmok* fool, penis, ? from Polish *smok* grass snake.

schnapps *n.* any of various spirits resembling genever gin. WH: 19C. German *Schnaps* dram of drink, liquor, from Low German and Dutch *snaps* gulp, mouthful, from *snappen* to seize, to snatch, SNAP. Cp. NIP[2].

schnauzer *n.* a breed of wire-haired German terrier. WH: early 20C. German, from *Schnauze* snout, muzzle + -ER[1]. Cp. SCHNOZZLE. The dog is so called from its 'moustache' and beard, which accentuate its muzzle.

Schneiderian *a.* of or relating to Konrad Victor Schneider. WH: 19C. Konrad Victor *Schneider*, 1610–80, German anatomist. See also -IAN.

schnitzel *n.* an escalope of meat, esp. veal. WH: 19C. German cutlet, slice, from *Schnitz* cut, slice + -el -EL.

schnorrer *n.* a beggar. WH: 19C. Yiddish var. of German *Schnurrer*, from *schnurren* (slang) to go begging.

schnozzle *n.* a nose. WH: mid-20C. Yiddish *shnoytzl*, dim. of *shnoytz*, from German *Schnauze* snout. Cp. SCHNAUZER.

scholar *n.* a learned person. WH: pre-1200. Orig. directly from Late Latin *scholaris*, later shortening of Old French *escoler*, *escolier* (Modern French *écolier*), from Late Latin *scholaris*, from Latin *schola* SCHOOL[1]. See also -AR[1].

scholastic *a.* of or relating to school, schools, universities etc. *Also n.* WH: 16C. Latin *scholasticus*, from Greek *skholastikos* studious, learned, from *skholazein* to be at leisure, to devote one's leisure to learning, from *skholē*. See SCHOOL[1], also -IC.

scholiast *n.* a commentator, esp. an ancient grammarian who annotated the classics. WH: 16C. Late Greek *skholiastēs*, from *skholion*, from *skholē* learned discussion. See SCHOOL[1].

school[1] *n.* an institution for the education of children. *Also v.t.*, *a.* WH: pre-1200. Old English *scōl*, *scolu*, from Germanic, from Latin *schola*, from Greek *skholē* leisure, employment of leisure in discussion, lecture. Later reinforced by shortened form of Old French *escole* (Modern French *école*).

school[2] *n.* a shoal of fish, porpoises etc. *Also v.i.* WH: 14–15C. Middle Low German and Middle Dutch *schōle* troop, multitude, rel. to Old English *scolu* troop, from a Germanic word ? orig. meaning division. Cp. SHOAL[1]. The word is not related to SCHOOL[1] despite the common associated sense of disciplined group.

schooner *n.* a vessel with two or more masts with fore-and-aft rigging. WH: 18C. Orig. uncertain. ? Ult. rel. to obs. *scun* to skim across the water, itself ? from Old Norse *skunda* to speed, to hasten. Cp. *scooter* (SCOOT).

schorl *n.* black tourmaline. WH: 18C. German *Schörl*, of unknown orig.

schottische *n.* a dance resembling a polka. WH: 19C. German (*der*) *Schottische(tanz)* (the) Scottish (dance).

Schottky effect *n.* a reduction in the energy required to remove an electron from a solid surface when an electric field is present. WH: mid-20C. Walter *Schottky*, 1886–1976, German physicist.

schout *n.* a municipal officer in the Netherlands and Dutch colonies. WH: 15C. Dutch, rel. to German *Schulze*.

Schrödinger equation *n.* an equation used in quantum mechanics for the wave function of a particle. WH: early 20C. Erwin *Schrödinger*, 1887–1961, Austrian-born physicist.

schuss *n.* a straight fast ski slope. *Also v.i.* WH: mid-20C. German, lit. shot.

schwa *n.* a neutral unstressed vowel sound. WH: 19C. German. See SHEVA.

sciagraphy *n.* the art of drawing objects with correct shading. WH: 16C. French *sciagraphie*, from Latin *sciagraphia*, from Greek *skiagraphia*, from *skia* shadow. See -GRAPHY.

sciamachy *n.* a fight with a shadow. WH: 17C. Greek *skiamakhia*, from *skia* shadow + *-makhia*, from *makhos* that fights, from base of *makhē* battle.

sciascopy *n.* a method of measuring the refractive power of the eye by projecting light into it from a small mirror, the shadow test. WH: 19C. Greek *skia* shadow + *-scopy* (-SCOPE).

sciatheric *a.* of or relating to a sundial. WH: 17C. Late Greek *skiatherikos*, from *skiatheras* sundial, lit. shadow catcher, from *skia* shadow + *thēran* to catch. See also -IC.

sciatic *a.* of or relating to the hip. WH: 16C. Old French *sciatique*, from Late Latin *sciaticus*, alt. of Medieval Latin *ischiaticus*, from Latin *ischiadicus*, from Greek *iskhiadikos*, from *iskhias*, *iskhiados* pain in the hip, from *iskhion* hipjoint. See also -IC.

science *n.* systematized knowledge about the physical world, developed by observation and experiment. WH: 12–14C. Old French, from Latin *scientia* knowledge, from *sciens*, *scientis*, pres.p. of *scire* to know. See also -ENCE.

scienter *adv.* with knowledge, wittingly, deliberately. WH: 19C. Latin knowingly, from *sciens*, *scientis*, pres.p. of *scire* to know + adv. suf.

sci-fi *n.* science fiction. WH: mid-20C. Abbr. of *science fiction*. See SCIENCE, FICTION.

scilicet *adv.* to wit, videlicet, namely. WH: 14–15C. Latin, from *scire licet* one may understand, it is permitted to know, from *scire* to know + 3rd pers. sing. pres. ind. of *licere* to be permitted. Cp. VIDELICET.

scilla *n.* any plant of the genus *Scilla*, liliaceous plants with bell-shaped flowers. WH: 19C. Latin *scilla*, *squilla* sea onion, from Greek *skilla*. Cp. SQUILL.

Scillonian *n.* a native or inhabitant of the Scilly Isles. *Also a.* WH: 18C. *Scilly* (Isles), off coast of Cornwall + *-onian*, ? based on DEVONIAN.

scimitar *n.* a short Oriental sword, single-edged, curved and broadest towards the point. WH: 16C. French *cimeterre*, *cimiterre* or Italian *scimitarra*, of unknown orig.

scincoid *a.* of, relating to or resembling the Scincidae or skinks. *Also n.* WH: 18C. Modern Latin *Scincoidea*, from use as genus name of Latin *scincus* SKINK. See also -OID.

scintigraphy *n.* a diagnostic technique that uses the radiation emitted following administration of a radioactive isotope to produce a picture of an internal body organ. WH: mid-20C. From *scintillation* (see SCINTILLA) + -GRAPHY.

scintilla *n.* a spark. WH: 17C. Latin spark, glittering speck.

sciography *n.* sciagraphy. WH: 16C. Var. of SCIAGRAPHY.

sciolist *n.* a person who knows many things superficially, a pretender to knowledge. WH: 17C. Late Latin *sciolus*, dim. of Latin *scius* knowing, from *scire* to know. See also -IST.

sciolto *adv.* freely, to one's taste. WH: 19C. Italian, p.p. of *sciogliere* to loosen.

sciomachy *n.* sciamachy. WH: 17C. Var. of SCIAMACHY.

sciomancy *n.* divination through the shades of the dead. WH: 17C. Modern Latin *sciomantia*, from Greek *skia* shadow + *manteia* (-MANCY).

scion *n.* a shoot, esp. for grafting or planting. WH: 12–14C. Old French *ciun, cion, sion* (Modern French *scion*) twig, shoot, from Frankish *kīth* offspring, KID[1] + dim. suf. *-on*.

scire facias *n.* a writ to enforce the execution of or annul judgements etc. WH: 14–15C. Law Latin let (him) know, from *scire* to know + 2nd pers. sing. pres. subj. of *facere* to make, to do.

scirrhus *n.* a hard (cancerous) tumour. WH: 14–15C. Modern Latin, alt. of Latin *scirros*, from Greek *skirros* hard coat, hard covering, rel. to *skiros* hard.

scissel *n.* metal clippings. WH: 17C. Old French *cisaille*, from *cisailler* to clip with shears.

scissile *a.* that may be cut. WH: 17C. Latin *scissilis*, from *scissus*, p.p. of *scindere* to cut, to cleave. See also -IL.

scissors *n.pl.* a cutting instrument consisting of two blades pivoted together that cut objects placed between them; also called *pair of scissors*. WH: 14–15C. Old French *cisoires* (Modern French large shears), from pl. of Late Latin *cisorium* cutting instrument, from Latin *cis-* (CHISEL), later assoc. with *scissus*, p.p. of *scindere* to cut, to cleave.

sciurine *a.* of, relating to or resembling the family Sciuridae, the squirrel family. *Also n.* WH: 19C. Latin *sciurus*, from Greek *skiouros* squirrel (from *skia* shadow + *oura* tail) + -INE. Cp. SQUIRREL.

sclera *n.* the white of the eye; the sclerotic. WH: 19C. Modern Latin, from Greek *sklēros* hard + -A[1].

sclerenchyma *n.* the strong tissue forming the hard or fibrous parts of plants, such as the walls of nuts and fruit-stones, leaf midribs etc. WH: 19C. Modern Latin, from SCLERO- + -enchyma, based on PARENCHYMA.

scleriasis *n.* hardening or induration of tissue. WH: 17C. Modern Latin. See SCLERO-, -IASIS.

sclerite *n.* any one of the definite component parts of the hard integument of various invertebrates. WH: 19C. Greek *sklēros* hard + -ITE[1].

sclero- *comb. form* hard, dry. WH: Greek *sklēros* hard. See also -O-.

scleroderm *n.* a hardened integument or exoskeleton, esp. of corals. WH: 19C. Modern Latin *sclerodermus*. See SCLERO-, -DERM.

sclerogen *n.* the hard matter deposited in the cells of certain plants, as the ivory-nut. WH: 19C. SCLERO- + -GEN.

scleroid *a.* hard in texture. WH: 19C. Greek *sklēros* hard + -OID.

scleroma *n.* hardening of cellular tissue, scleriasis. WH: 19C. SCLERO- + -OMA.

sclerometer *n.* an instrument for determining the hardness of a mineral or a metal. WH: 19C. SCLERO- + -METER.

sclerophyll *n.* any woody plant with leathery leaves. WH: early 20C. German *Sklerophyll*, from SCLERO- + Greek *phullon* leaf.

scleroprotein *n.* an insoluble protein, such as keratin, forming the skeletal tissues of the body. WH: early 20C. SCLERO- + PROTEIN.

sclerosis *n.* hardening of a plant cell wall by the deposit of sclerogen. WH: 14–15C. Modern Latin, from Greek *sklērōsis*, from *sklēroun* to harden. See also -OSIS.

scleroskeleton *n.* the skeletal parts resulting from ossification of tendons, ligaments etc. WH: 19C. SCLERO- + SKELETON.

sclerotic *a.* (of the outer coat or tunic of the eye) hard, indurated. *Also n.* WH: 16C. Medieval Latin *scleroticus*. See SCLEROSIS, also -OTIC.

sclerotium *n.* a compact tuberous mass formed on the mycelium of certain higher fungi, such as ergot. WH: 19C. Modern Latin, from Greek *sklēros* hard. See also -IUM.

sclerous *a.* hard, indurated, ossified. WH: 19C. Greek *sklēros* hard + -OUS.

scoff[1] *v.i.* to mock or jeer (at). *Also v.t., n.* WH: 12–14C. ? Scandinavian. Cp. early Modern Dutch *skof, skuf* jest, mockery, *skuffe* to mock, to jest.

scoff[2] *v.t.* to eat ravenously. *Also n.* WH: 18C. Partly var. of dial. *scaff*, of unknown orig., partly from *scoff* food, from Afrikaans *scof*, from Dutch *schoft* quarter of a day, SHIFT, i.e. each of the four meals of the day.

scold *v.i.* to find fault noisily or angrily. *Also v.t., n.* WH: 12–14C. Prob. from Old Norse *skáld* poet, SKALD. The original meaning was a ribald person, especially a woman, then a persistently nagging woman. The verb evolved from the noun in the 14–15C and originally meant to behave as a scold.

scolex *n.* the larva or embryo in metagenesis. WH: 19C. Modern Latin, from Greek *skōlēx, skōlēkos* worm.

scoliosis *n.* lateral curvature of the spine. WH: 18C. Modern Latin, from Greek *skoliōsis* , from *skolios* bent, curved. See also -OSIS.

scolopendrid *n.* any centipede of the family Scolopendridae. WH: 19C. Modern Latin *Scolopendridae*, from Greek *skolopendra* a mythical marine fish. See also -ID.

scolopendrium *n.* any of a genus of ferns containing the hart's tongue, *Phyllitis scolopendrium*. WH: 14–15C. Modern Latin, from Late Latin *scolopendrium*, from Greek *skolopendrion*. The plant is so called from its supposed resemblance to the *skolopendra* (SCOLOPENDRID).

scombroid *n.* any marine fish of the family Scombridae or the superfamily Scombroidea including the mackerels, tunas and swordfishes. *Also a.* WH: 19C. Latin *scomber, scombris*, from Greek *skombros* tuna or mackerel. See also -OID.

sconce[1] *n.* a flat candlestick with a handle. WH: 14–15C. Shortening of Old French *esconce* hiding place, lantern, or from Medieval Latin *sconsa*, shortening of *absconsa* (*laterna*) dark (lantern), fem. p.p. (used as n.) of *abscondere* to hide. See ABSCOND.

sconce[2] *n.* a blockhouse, a bulwark, a small detached fort. *Also v.t.* WH: 14–15C. Dutch *schans*, obs. *schaatze* brushwood, screen of brushwood for defence, from Middle High German *schanze*, of unknown orig.

†sconce[3] *n.* a fine at Oxford or Cambridge University for a light offence. *Also v.t.* WH: 17C. Orig. uncertain. ? From obs. *sconce* head, itself ? from SCONCE[1].

scone *n.* a soft plain cake, usu. in small round or triangular pieces, cooked on a griddle or in an oven. WH: 16C. ? Shortening of Middle Low German *schonbrot*, Middle Dutch *schoonbroot* fine bread.

scoop *n.* a short-handled shovel-like implement for lifting and moving loose material such as coal or grain. *Also v.t.* WH: 12–14C. Middle Low German and Middle Dutch *schōpe* vessel for bailing, waterwheel bucket, from a Germanic v. meaning to draw water rel. to SHAPE.

scoot *v.i.* to dart off, bolt, to scurry away. *Also n.* WH: 18C. Orig. unknown.

scopa *n.* a brushlike tuft of bristly hairs as on the legs of bees. WH: 19C. Latin, from *scopae* (pl.) twigs, shoots, broom, brush.

scope[1] *n.* range of action or observation. WH: 16C. Italian *scopo* aim, purpose, from Greek *skopos* mark to shoot at, from *skop-, skep-* as in *skopein* to observe, to aim at, to examine, *skeptesthai* to look out.

scope[2] *n.* a periscope, telescope, oscilloscope etc. WH: 17C. Abbr. of many words in -SCOPE, such as MICROSCOPE, TELESCOPE, etc.

-scope *comb. form* denoting an instrument of observation etc., as in microscope, spectroscope. WH: Modern Latin *-scopium*, from Greek *skopein* to look at, to examine.

scopelid *n.* a fish of the deep-water, teleostean group Scopelidae. WH: 19C. Modern Latin *Scopelidae*, from *Scopelus* genus name, from Greek *skopelos* lookout place, promontory, from *skopein* to view. Modern Latin *Scopelus* was introduced in 1817 by the French anatomist Baron Cuvier in the belief that Greek *skopelos* was the name of a fish.

scopolamine *n.* hyoscine hydrobromide, a hypnotic drug used, among other purposes, with morphine for producing twilight sleep. WH: 19C. Modern Latin *Scopolia* genus name + AMINE. The liquid alkaloid on which the drug is based is found in plants of the genus *Scopolia*, itself named after Giovanni A. *Scopoli*, 1723–88, Italian naturalist.

scops owl *n.* an owl of the genus *Otus* (previously *Scops*), having erect tufts of feathers on the side of the head. WH: 18C. Modern Latin *Scops*, former genus name, from Greek *skōps* a kind of owl.

scorbutic *a.* of, relating to, like or affected with scurvy. *Also n.* WH: 17C. Modern Latin *scorbuticus*, from Medieval Latin *scorbutus* scurvy, ? from Middle Low German *schorbūk*, from *schoren* to break, to lacerate + *būk* belly.

scorch *v.t.* to burn the outside of so as to injure or discolour without consuming. *Also v.i., n.* WH: 12–14C. ? Ult. rel. to Old Norse *skorpna* to be shrivelled.

scordato *a.* put out of tune. WH: 19C. Italian, p.p. of *scordare* to be out of tune.

score *n.* the points made by a player or side at any moment in, or in total in certain games and contests. *Also v.t., v.i.* WH: pre-1200. Partly from Old Norse *skor*, tally, twenty, from Germanic base of SHEAR, partly from Old Norse *skora* to make an incision, to count by tallies, from *skor*. The earliest sense was a set of twenty, hence total, hence notch cut in a stick (tally) to record an amount, hence line drawn to mark a boundary. The sense list or total of points in a game dates from the 18C.

scoria *n.* cellular lava or ashes. WH: 14–15C. Latin, from Germanic *skōria* refuse, from *skōr* dung.

scorn *n.* contempt, disdain. *Also v.t.* WH: 12–14C. Old French *escarn*, corr. to Provençal *esquern*, from *eschernir*, from Germanic, from base of Old Saxon *skern* jest, mockery.

scorodite *n.* a mineral consisting of a native arsenate of iron. WH: 19C. German *Skorodit*, from Greek *skorodon* garlic + -ITE[1]. The mineral is so called from its smell when heated.

scorpaenid *n.* any spiny-finned fish of the family Scorpaenidae, including the scorpion fishes. WH: 19C. Modern Latin *Scorpaenidae*, from Latin *scorpaena*, from Greek *skorpaina* a kind of fish, appar. fem. n. formed from *skorpios* SCORPION.

scorper *n.* a gouging-tool for working in concave surfaces in wood, metal or jewellery. WH: 14–15C. Var. of SCAUPER.

Scorpio *n.* a zodiacal constellation. WH: 14–15C. Latin *scorpio*, *scorpionis*. See SCORPION.

scorpion *n.* an arachnid of the order Scorpiones, with claws like a lobster and a sting in the jointed tail. WH: 12–14C. Old French, from Latin *scorpio*, *scorpionis*, extension of *scorpius*, from Greek *skorpios*.

scorzonera *n.* a plant of the family *Scorzonera hispanica* with long tapering roots. WH: 17C. Italian, from *scorzone*, from alt. of Medieval Latin *curtio*, *curtionis* poisonous snake. The plant is presumably so called as it was regarded as an antidote against the snake's venom.

Scot *n.* a native of Scotland. WH: pre-1200. Old English *Scottas* (pl.), from Medieval Latin *Scotus*, from Late Latin *Scottus*, of unknown orig.

scot *n.* a payment, an assessment, a tax. WH: pre-1200. Partly from Old Norse *skot* SHOT[1], partly shortened form of Old French *escot* (Modern French *écot*), of Germanic orig. Cp. SHOT[1].

Scotch *a.* Scottish. *Also n.* WH: 16C. Contr. of SCOTTISH.

scotch[1] *v.t.* to put an end to, frustrate. *Also n.* WH: 14–15C. Orig. unknown. ? From Old French *cocher* to notch, to nick. The original sense was to make an incision in, to cut, to score. The current sense stems from Shakespeare's *Macbeth* (1605): 'we have scotch'd the snake, not kill'd it'. The extended sense to stamp out, to put an end to, dates from the 19C.

scotch[2] *n.* a block for a wheel or other round object. *Also v.t.* WH: 17C. Orig. unknown. ? Rel. to SKATE[1].

scoter *n.* a large sea duck of the genus *Melanitta*. WH: 17C. Orig. unknown.

scotia *n.* a hollow moulding in the base of a column. WH: 16C. Latin, from Greek *skotia*, from *skotos* darkness. The feature is so called from the dark shadow inside the moulding.

Scotice *adv.* in a or the Scottish manner. WH: 19C. Medieval Latin, from Late Latin *Scoticus*, *Scotticus* Scottish.

Scotism *n.* the scholastic philosophy of Duns Scotus. WH: 17C. John Duns *Scotus*, *c.*1266–1308, Scottish scholastic theologian + -ISM. Cp. DUNCE.

Scotland Yard *n.* the headquarters of the London Metropolitan Police. WH: 19C. (Great) *Scotland Yard*, a street off Whitehall in London. The Metropolitan Police were established in Great Scotland Yard in 1829 and took the name with them (as New Scotland Yard) when their headquarters moved to the Thames Embankment in 1890 and again to Broadway, Westminster in 1967.

scoto- *comb. form* dark, dullness. WH: Greek *skotos* darkness. See also -O-.

scotodinia *n.* dizziness, vertigo, with dimness of vision. WH: 19C. SCOTO- + Greek *dinos* whirling, dizziness + -IA.

scotograph *n.* an instrument for writing in the dark or by the blind. WH: 19C. SCOTO- + -GRAPH. In 1891 Lewis Carroll invented a device for writing in the dark which he called a *nyctograph*, from Greek *nux*, *nuktos* night + -GRAPH.

scotoma *n.* a blind spot in the field of vision. WH: 16C. Late Latin, from Greek *skotōma* dizziness, from *skotoun* to darken, from *skotos* darkness.

scotoscope *n.* a telescope enabling one to see objects at night. WH: 17C. SCOTO- + -SCOPE.

Scots *a.* Scottish (applied to the people, language and law). *Also n.* WH: 14–15C. Var. of SCOTTISH. Cp. SCOTCH.

Scottish *a.* of or relating to Scotland or its people. *Also n.* WH: pre-1200. SCOT + -ISH[1], replacing Old English *Scyttisc*. Cp. SCOTCH, SCOTS.

scoundrel *n.* an unprincipled person, a rogue. *Also a.* WH: 16C. Orig. unknown.

scour[1] *v.t.* to clean or polish by friction. *Also v.i., n.* WH: 12–14C. Middle Low German and Middle Dutch *schüren* , from Old French *escurer* (Modern French *écurer*), from Late Latin *excurare*, from Latin EX- + *curare* to take care of, from *cura* CURE.

scour[2] *v.i.* to rove, to range. *Also v.t.* WH: 14–15C. Orig. uncertain. Cp. Old Norse *skúr* a shower of rain. The sense may have been influenced by SCOUR[1].

scourge *n.* a whip with thongs used as an instrument of punishment. *Also v.t.* WH: 12–14C. Shortening of Old French *escurge*, *escorge*, from *escorgier* to whip, from Popular Latin *excorrigiare*, from Latin EX- + *corrigia* thong, whip.

Scouse *n.* the dialect of Liverpool. *Also a.* WH: 19C. Abbr. of LOBSCOUSE.

scout[1] *n.* a person sent out to bring in information, esp. one employed to watch the movements etc. of an enemy. *Also v.t., v.i.* WH: 16C. Shortening of Old French *escoute*, from *escouter* (Modern French *écouter*), alt. of *ascolter*, from Latin *auscultare* to listen.

scout[2] *v.t.* to treat with contempt and disdain, to reject contemptuously. WH: 17C. Prob. of Scandinavian orig., from base of Old Norse *skjóta* SHOOT. Cp. Old Norse *skúta* to taunt.

scow *n.* a large flat-bottomed, square-ended boat. *Also v.t.* WH: 17C. Dutch *schouw*, rel. to Old Saxon *skaldan* to push (a boat) from the shore.

scowl *v.i.* to look sullen or ill-tempered. *Also v.t., n.* WH: 14–15C. Prob. of Scandinavian orig., ? ult. rel. to Old English *scūlēgede* squint-eyed. Cp. Danish *skule* to cast down one's eyes, to give a sidelong look.

scrabble *v.i.* to scratch or grope (about) as if to obtain something. *Also v.t., n.* WH: 16C. Middle Dutch *schrabbelen*, freq. of *schrabben* to scratch, to scrape.

scrag *n.* a lean or bony piece of meat, esp. the lean end of neck of mutton. *Also v.t.* WH: 16C. ? Alt. of dial. *crag* neck, prob. from Low Dutch.

scraggly *a.* sparse and irregular. WH: 19C. SCRAG + -L- + -Y[1], prob. influ. by *straggly* (STRAGGLE).

scram *int.* get out of it! go away! WH: early 20C. Prob. abbr. of SCRAMBLE.

scramble *v.i.* to climb or move along by clambering, esp. with the hands and knees. *Also v.t., n.* WH: 16C. Imit., ? influ. by SCRABBLE.

scran *n.* (leftover) food. *Also v.t.* WH: 18C. Orig. unknown.

scrap[1] *n.* a small detached piece, a bit. *Also v.t.* WH: 14–15C. Old Norse *skrap* scraps, trifles, from base of *skrapa* SCRAPE.

scrap[2] *n.* a fight, a scuffle. *Also v.i.* WH: 17C. ? From SCRAPE.

scrape *v.t.* to rub the surface of with something rough or sharp. *Also v.i., n.* WH: pre-1200. Old English *scrapian*, from Germanic, reinforced later by Old Norse *skrapa* or Middle Dutch *schrapen* to scratch.

scrapie *n.* an encephalopathy affecting sheep, thought to be caused by a prion. WH: early 20C. SCRAPE + -ie (-Y[3]). The disease is so called from the sheep's scraping to relieve the intense itching it causes.

Scratch *n.* the Devil; also *Old Scratch*. WH: 18C. Alt. of obs. *scrat*, from Old Norse *skrati* wizard, goblin, monster, rel. to Old High German *scrato* (German *Schrat*) satyr, sprite.

scratch *v.t.* to tear or mark the surface of lightly with something sharp. *Also v.i., n., a.* WH: 14–15C. Prob. blend of obs. *scrat* to scratch, of unknown orig., and obs. *cratch* to scratch, of uncertain orig., prob. rel. to Middle Low German *kratsen*, Old High German *krazzōn* (German *kratzen*), Old Swedish *kratta*.

scrawl *v.t.* to draw or write clumsily, hurriedly or illegibly. *Also v.i., n.* WH: 17C. ? From obs. *scrawl* to spread the limbs sprawlingly, appar. alt. of CRAWL[1], ? influ. by SPRAWL.

scrawny *a.* excessively lean, bony. WH: 19C. Var. of dial. *scranny*, prob. from *scrannel* thin, meagre (prob. itself ult. from base represented by Norwegian *skran* shrivelled) + -Y[1].

scream *v.i.* to make a piercing, prolonged cry as if in extreme pain or terror. *Also v.t., n.* WH: 12–14C. ? From an Old English word or a rel. Middle Dutch or Old Frisian word. Cp. Middle Dutch *schreem* scream, W Frisian *skrieme* to weep.

scree *n.* loose fragments or debris of rock on a steep slope. WH: 18C. Old Norse *skritha* landslip, rel. to *skritha* to slide, to glide and Old English *scrīthan* to go, to glide.

screech *v.i.* to scream out with a sharp, harsh, shrill voice. *Also v.t., n.* WH: 16C. Alt. of SCRITCH. The lengthening of the vowel represents the sound of a screech.

screed *n.* a long harangue or tirade. WH: 12–14C. Prob. var. of SHRED.

screen *n.* a partition separating a portion of a room from the remainder. *Also v.t.* WH: 12–14C. Shortening of Old Northern French *escren*, var. of *escran* (Modern French *écran*), from Old Frankish, of Germanic orig. Cp. German *Schrank* cupboard.

screeve *v.t.* to write. *Also v.i.* WH: 19C. ? From Italian *scrivere*, from Latin *scribere* to write.

screw *n.* a cylinder with a spiral ridge or groove round its outer surface (called a male screw) or round its inner surface (called a female screw). *Also v.t., v.i.* WH: 14–15C. Old French *escroue* (Modern French *écrou*), either from Germanic (cp. German *Schraube*) or from Latin *scrofa* sow (Medieval Latin female screw).

scribble[1] *v.i.* to write hastily or illegibly. *Also v.t., n.* WH: 14–15C. Medieval Latin *scribillare*, dim. of Latin *scribere* to write. See also -LE[4].

scribble[2] *v.t.* to card roughly. WH: 17C. Prob. from Low German. Cp. German *schrabbeln*, freq. from Middle Low German *schrubben* SCRUB[1].

scribe *n.* a writer. *Also v.t.* WH: 12–14C. Latin *scriba* official writer, from *scribere* to write. In the Vulgate (Latin version of the Bible), Latin *scriba* translates Greek *grammateus* and Hebrew *sōpēr*.

scrim *n.* strong cotton or linen cloth used for lining in upholstery and for cleaning. WH: 18C. Orig. unknown.

scrimmage *n.* a tussle, a confused or rough-and-tumble struggle, a skirmish. *Also v.i., v.t.* WH: 14–15C. Alt. of obs. *scrimish*, var. of SKIRMISH, with assim. of *-ish* to -AGE. Cp. SCRUM.

scrimp *v.t.* to make small, scant or short. *Also v.i., a., n., adv.* WH: 18C. From dial. *scrimp* scant, scanty, ? rel. to SHRIMP.

scrimshander *v.t.* to scrimshaw. *Also n.* WH: 19C. Var. of SCRIMSHAW + -ER[1].

scrimshank *v.i.* to avoid work, to get out of doing one's duty. WH: 19C. Orig. unknown.

scrimshaw *v.t.* to decorate (ivory, shells etc.) with carvings and coloured designs. *Also v.i., n.* WH: 19C. Orig. unknown. ? Influ. by the surname *Scrimshaw* (var. of *Scrimgeour*, from Old French *eskermisseour* fencer; cp. SKIRMISH).

scrip[1] *n.* a provisional certificate given to a subscriber for stock of a bank or company. WH: 16C. ? Alt. of SCRIPT, influ. by SCRAP[1]. The sense provisional certificate of money subscribed to a bank or company arose in the 18C as an abbreviation of *subscription receipt*. See subscription (SUBSCRIBE).

scrip[2] *n.* a small bag, a wallet or satchel. WH: 12–14C. Shortening of Old French *escreppe* purse, bag for alms, var. of *escherpe* (Modern French *écharpe*), or from Old Norse *skreppa* (? also from Old French).

script *n.* a piece of writing. *Also v.t.* WH: 14–15C. Shortening of Old French *escript* (Modern French *écrit*), from Latin *scriptum*, neut.

p.p. (used as *n.*) of *scribere* to write. The original sense was anything written. The sense author's written copy of a work arose in the 19C and was influenced by MANUSCRIPT.

scripture *n.* a sacred writing or book. *Also v.t., v.i.* WH: 12–14C. Latin *scriptura*, from *scriptus*, p.p. of *scribere* to write. See also -URE.

†scritch *n.* a screech. *Also v.t., v.i.* WH: 12–14C. Old English *scriccettan*, of imit. orig. Cp. SCREECH.

scrivener *n.* a person whose business was to draw up contracts or other documents, a notary. WH: 12–14C. Shortening of Old French *escrivein* (Modern French *écrivain*), from Popular Latin *scriba*, *scribanis*, from Latin *scriba* SCRIBE. See also -ER[1].

scrobe *n.* a groove, as that receiving the base of the antenna in a weevil. WH: 17C. Latin *scrobis* trench.

scrod *n.* a young cod or haddock, esp. when prepared for cooking. WH: 19C. Orig. unknown.

scrofula *n.* a form of tuberculosis affecting esp. the lymph glands of the neck. WH: 14–15C. Late Latin *scrofulae* (pl.), Medieval Latin *scrofula* swelling of the glands, dim. of *scrofa* breeding sow. Cp. SCREW. The disease is said to be so called either because the swollen glands caused by the disease resemble the back of a pig, or because sows were subject to it.

scrog *n.* a stunted bush. WH: 12–14C. Var. of dial. *scrag* tree stump, of uncertain orig. (? alt. of CRAG[1]).

scroll *n.* a roll of paper or parchment. *Also v.t., v.i.* WH: 14–15C. Alt. of dial. *scrow* (shortening of ESCROW), based on ROLL.

Scrooge *n.* a miserly person. WH: mid-20C. Ebenezer *Scrooge*, a miserly character in Dickens's *A Christmas Carol* (1843). Dickens probably based the name on English dialect *scrouge*, *scrooge* to squeeze.

scrophularia *n.* any plant of the genus *Scrophularia*, typical of the family Scrophulariaceae, containing the figwort. WH: 14–15C. Medieval Latin, from *scrophula* SCROFULA. The plant is so called from its supposed effectiveness in treating scrofula.

scrotum *n.* the pouch enclosing the testes in the higher mammals. WH: 16C. Latin. Rel. to SHROUD.

scrounge *v.t.* to pilfer. *Also v.i., n.* WH: early 20C. Prob. alt. of dial. *scrunge* to wander about idly, of unknown orig.

scrub[1] *v.t.* to rub hard with something coarse and rough, esp. with soap and water used with a scrubbing-brush for the purpose of cleaning or scouring. *Also v.i., n.* WH: 12–14C. Prob. from Middle Low German and Middle Dutch *schrobben*, *schrubben*, rel. to SCRUB[2], SHRUB[1]. The original sense was to curry-comb a horse. The sense to clean by rubbing with a hard brush dates from the 16C.

scrub[2] *n.* (a tract of) undergrowth or stunted trees. *Also a.* WH: 14–15C. Var. of SHRUB[1].

scruff[1] *n.* the nape or back of the neck, esp. as grasped by a person dragging another. WH: 18C. Alt. of obs. *scuff*, from Old Norse *skoft* hair of the head.

scruff[2] *n.* an unkempt or scruffy person. WH: pre-1200. Alt. of SCURF. The original sense was scurf. The sense untidy or unkempt person dates from the 19C.

scrum *n.* a set struggle in rugby between the forwards of both sides grappling in a compact mass with the ball on the ground in the middle. *Also v.i.* WH: 19C. Abbr. of SCRUMMAGE. Cp. SCRIMMAGE.

scrummage *n.* a rugby scrum. *Also v.i.* WH: 19C. Var. of SCRIMMAGE. Cp. SCRUM.

scrump *v.t., v.i.* to steal (apples) from an orchard. WH: 19C. ? Rel. to dial. *scrimp* scant, scanty. See SCRIMP. The word was originally a dialect name for a small and withered apple.

scrumple *v.t.* to crumple, wrinkle. WH: 16C. Alt. of CRUMPLE.

scrumptious *a.* (of food) delicious. WH: 19C. Orig. unknown. ? Alt. of SUMPTUOUS.

scrunch *v.t.* to crunch. *Also v.i., n.* WH: 18C. Prob. imit. Cp. CRUNCH. The s- intensifies the original word. Cp. SPLASH/ PLASH[2], SQUASH[1]/ QUASH, etc.

scruple *n.* a doubt or hesitation from conscientious or moral motives. *Also v.i., v.t.* WH: 14–15C. French *scrupule* or Latin *scrupulus*, *scripulus* small sharp or pointed stone, smallest division of weight, dim. of *scrupus* rough or sharp pebble, anxiety.

scrutator *n.* a person who scrutinizes, a close inquirer. WH: 16C. Latin, from *scrutatus*, p.p. of *scrutari*. See SCRUTINY, also -ATOR.

scrutiny *n.* close observation or investigation. WH: 14–15C. Latin *scrutinium*, from *scrutari* to search, to examine, (orig.) to sort rags, from *scruta* trash, rubbish. See also -Y².

scruto *n.* a trapdoor with springs, made flush with a theatre stage, for rapid disappearances etc. WH: 19C. Orig. unknown.

scry *v.i.* to practise crystal-gazing. *Also v.t.* WH: 16C. Shortening of DESCRY.

scuba *n.* an aqualung. WH: mid-20C. Acronym of self-contained underwater breathing apparatus.

scud *v.i.* to run or fly swiftly. *Also v.t., n.* WH: 16C. ? Alt. of SCUT, as if to race like a hare.

scudo *n.* an old Italian silver coin and money of account. WH: 17C. Italian, from Latin *scutum* shield. Cp. ESCUDO.

scuff *v.i.* to drag or scrape with the feet in walking. *Also v.t., n.* WH: 16C. ? Imit., or rel. to SCURF, CUFF². Cp. SKIFF². The original sense was to evade, to shirk (duty). The current sense dates from the 18C.

scuffle *v.i.* to fight or struggle in a rough-and-tumble way. *Also n.* WH: 16C. Prob. from Scandinavian base, from Germanic base also of SHUFFLE, SHOVE. See also -LE⁴.

scull *n.* either of a pair of short oars used by one person for propelling a boat. *Also v.t., v.i.* WH: 12–14C. Orig. unknown. Appar. not rel. to SKULL.

scullery *n.* a place where dishes and utensils are washed up, vegetables prepared etc. WH: 14–15C. Anglo-French *squillerie*, from Old French *escuelerie*, from *escuelier* maker of dishes, from *escuele*, from Popular Latin *scutella* (influ. by *scutum* shield), from Latin *scutella* salver, serving platter, dim. of *scutra* wooden dish. See also -ERY. Cp. SCUTTLE¹.

†scullion *n.* a servant who cleans pots, dishes etc., a kitchen drudge. WH: 15C. Orig. unknown, but prob. assim. to SCULLERY. Some authorities derive the word from Old French *escouillon* swab, cloth, from *escouve* broom, twig, from Latin *scopae* (pl.) broom.

sculp *v.t.* to carve, to sculpture. WH: 16C. Latin *sculpere* to carve.

sculpin *n.* any of various N American sea fishes with large spiny heads. WH: 17C. ? Alt. of *scorpene*, anglicized form of Latin *scorpaena*. See SCORPAENID.

sculpture *n.* the art of cutting, carving, modelling or casting wood, stone, clay, metal etc. into representations of natural objects or designs in round or in relief. *Also v.t., v.i.* WH: 14–15C. Latin *sculptura*, from *sculptus*, p.p. of *sculpere*, var. of *scalpere* to carve. See also -URE. Cp. SCALPEL.

scum *n.* impurities that rise to the surface of liquid, esp. in fermentation or boiling. *Also v.t., v.i.* WH: 12–14C. Middle Low German and Middle Dutch *schūm*, from Germanic. Cp. German *Schaum* foam.

scumble *v.t.* to cover (an oil painting) lightly with opaque or semi-opaque colours so as to soften the outlines or colours. *Also n.* WH: 17C. Prob. freq. of SCUM. See also -LE⁴.

scuncheon *n.* a bevelling, splay or elbow in a window opening etc. WH: 12–14C. Shortening of Old French *escoinson* (Modern French *écoinçon*), from *ex-* EX- + *coin* corner.

scunge *n.* dirt, scum. WH: 19C. Orig. uncertain. ? Rel. to SCROUNGE.

scunner *v.t.* to disgust, to nauseate. *Also v.i., n.* WH: 14–15C. Orig. unknown.

scupper¹ *n.* a hole or tube through a ship's side to carry off water from the deck. WH: 14–15C. ? From Anglo-French deriv. of Old French *escopir* (Modern French *écopir*) to spit out, ult. of imit. orig.

scupper² *v.t.* to sink (a ship). WH: 19C. Orig. uncertain. ? From SCUPPER¹. The original sense was to kill (in an ambush). The sense to sink a ship dates only from the late 20C. The possible derivation from SCUPPER¹ lies in the fact that a man killed in action on board ship would roll into the scuppers.

scuppernong *n.* a sweet American wine made from a variety of muscadine grape. WH: 19C. River *Scuppernong* in N Carolina, USA.

scurf *n.* flakes or scales thrown off by the skin, esp. of the head. WH: pre-1200. Old English *sceorf*, from base of *sceorfan* to gnaw, *sceorfian* to cut into shreds, from Germanic. Cp. SCRUFF².

scurrilous *a.* using or expressed in grossly abusive or indecent language. WH: 16C. French *scurrile* or Latin *scurrilis*, from *scurra* buffoon. See also -OUS.

scurry *v.i.* to go with great haste, to hurry. *Also n.* WH: 16C. ? From *hurry-scurry* (see HURRY). Cp. HARUM-SCARUM. The current sense dates from the 19C. The earliest sense, meaning to ride out as a scout, was perhaps from an obsolete noun *scurrier*, itself apparently from Old French *descouvreor* discoverer.

scurvy *n.* a disease caused by lack of vitamin C and characterized by swollen gums, extravasation of blood and general debility, arising orig. esp. among those on shipboard from a deficiency of vegetables. *Also a.* WH: 14–15C. SCURF + -Y¹. The original sense (to the 19C) was worthless, contemptible. The name of the disease evolved from this in the 16C by association with French *scorbut*, Low German *schorbūk*. See SCORBUTIC.

scut *n.* a short tail, esp. of a hare, rabbit or deer. WH: 14–15C. Orig. uncertain. ? Rel. to obs. a. *scut* short and obs. v. *scut* to cut short. The original meaning was a hare. The sense short tail evolved in the 16C.

scutage *n.* money paid by a feudal tenant in lieu of personal attendance on his lord in war. WH: 14–15C. Medieval Latin *scutagium*, from Latin *scutum* shield, based on Old French *escuage* personal service in the field.

scutch *v.t.* to dress (cotton, flax etc.) by beating. *Also n.* WH: 17C. Old French *escoucher*, dial. var. of *escousser* (Modern French *écoucher*), from Latin *excussus*, p.p. of *excutere*, from *ex-* EX- + *quatere* to shake.

scutcheon *n.* an escutcheon. WH: 12–14C. Shortened var. of ESCUTCHEON.

scutellum *n.* a small shield, plate, scale or horny segment in or on a plant or animal. WH: 18C. Modern Latin, appar. from Latin *scutella* platter, as if this were a dim. of *scutum* shield.

scutter *v.i.* to scurry, scuttle. *Also n.* WH: 18C. ? Alt. of SCUTTLE³, with substitution of -ER⁵ for -LE⁴.

scuttle¹ *n.* a metal or other receptacle for carrying or holding coals, esp. for a fireplace, usu. called a coal scuttle. WH: pre-1200. Old English *scutel*, from Old Norse *skutill*, from Germanic, from Latin *scutula* or *scutella*, rel. to *scutra* dish, platter. See also -LE¹. Cp. German *Schüssel*. The original sense (to the 18C) was dish, platter. The sense transferred to that of basket for carrying corn, vegetables, etc. in the 14–15C and to a metal receptacle for coal in the 19C.

scuttle² *n.* a hole with a movable lid or hatch in a wall or roof or the deck or side of a ship. *Also v.t.* WH: 15C. ? From obs. French *escoutille* (Modern French *écoutille*) hatchway, from Spanish *escotilla*, dim. of *escota* cutting out of cloth, from *escotar* to cut out. See also -LE². The sense to sink a ship by letting in water dates from the 17C, and that of to thwart, to spoil, to ruin from the 19C.

scuttle³ *v.i.* to hurry along, to scurry. *Also n.* WH: 15C. Var. of dial. *scuddle*, freq. of SCUD. See also -LE⁴.

scutum *n.* a scute. WH: 18C. Latin oblong shield.

scuzzy *a.* squalid or disgusting. WH: mid-20C. From *scuzz* (prob. abbr. of *disgusting* (DISGUST), ? influ. by SCUM and FUZZ) + -Y¹.

scye *n.* the opening of a coat etc. where the sleeve is inserted. WH: 19C. Scottish and Ulster dial., of unknown orig.

Scylla *n.* either of a pair of alternative risks. WH: 16C. Latin, from Greek *Skulla*, a dangerous sea monster in Greek mythology, personifying a rock on the Italian shore of the Straits of Messina opposite Charybdis. Cp. CHARYBDIS.

scyphozoan *n.* any marine jellyfish of the class Scyphozoa. *Also a.* WH: early 20C. Modern Latin *Scyphozoa*, from Greek *skuphos* cup + *zōa* animals. See also -AN.

scyphus *n.* a bowl-shaped footless Greek cup with two handles. WH: 18C. Modern Latin, use of Latin *scyphus*, from Greek *skuphos* large drinking vessel.

scythe *n.* a long curved blade with a crooked handle used for mowing or reaping. *Also v.t.* WH: pre-1200. Old English *sīthe* , from Germanic, rel. to Latin *secare* to cut. Cp. German *Sense*. The spelling with *sc-* arose in the 15C by association with Latin *scissor* carver, cutter. See SCISSORS.

Scythian *a.* of or relating to ancient Scythia, or the ancient people inhabiting it. *Also n.* WH: 15C. Latin *Scythia*, a region north and north-east of the Black Sea, from Greek *Skuthia*, from *Skuthēs* Scyth. See also -AN.

sd *abbr.* indefinitely. WH: Abbr. of Latin *sine die* without day, from SINE² + *die*, abl. sing. of *dies* day.

se- *pref.* away from, apart, without, as in *secede*, *secure*. WH: Latin, from earlier *se* (also *sed*) without, apart.

sea *n.* the body of salt water covering the greater part of the earth's surface. *Also a.* WH: pre-1200. Old English *sǣ*, from Germanic, of unknown orig. Cp. Dutch *zee*, German *See*.

seaborgium *n.* the artificial radioactive element, at. no. 106, chem. symbol Sg. WH: late 20C. Glenn T. *Seaborg*, 1912–99, US nuclear chemist + -IUM. The name was coined in 1994 for the element formerly known as *unnilhexium* (UNNIL-, HEXA-, -IUM), produced in 1974.

seal[1] *n.* a carnivorous amphibious marine mammal of various species of the family Phocidae, having flipper-like limbs adapted for swimming and thick fur. *Also v.i.* WH: pre-1200. Old English *seol*, base of *seolh*, from Germanic, of unknown orig.

seal[2] *n.* a die or stamp having a device, usu. in intaglio, for making an impression on wax or other plastic substance. *Also v.t.* WH: 12–14C. Old French *seel* (Modern French *sceau*), from Latin *sigillum* small picture, statuette, dim. of *signum* SIGN.

Sealyham *n.* a breed of Welsh terrier. WH: 19C. *Sealyham*, a village in Pembrokeshire, where it was first bred.

seam *n.* a ridge or other visible line of junction between two parts or things, esp. two pieces of cloth etc. sewn together. *Also v.t.* WH: pre-1200. Old English *sēam*, from Germanic base of SEW. Cp. German *Saum*.

Seanad *n.* the upper house, or senate, of the parliament of the Republic of Ireland. WH: early 20C. Irish *Seanad* (*Éireann*) senate (of Ireland).

seance *n.* a meeting for exhibiting, receiving or investigating spiritualistic manifestations. WH: 18C. French *séance*, from Old French *seoir*, from Latin *sedere* to sit. The original sense was a session of a deliberative body. The sense spiritualist meeting arose in the 19C.

sear *v.t.* to burn or scorch the surface of to dryness and hardness. *Also a.* WH: pre-1200. Old English *sēarian*, from Germanic. Rel. to Latin *sudus* dry (of weather). The original sense was to dry up. The sense to cauterize arose in the 14–15C, leading to the current sense in the 16C.

search *v.t.* to go over and examine for what may be found or to find something. *Also v.i., n.* WH: 12–14C. Old French *cerchier* (Modern French *chercher*), from Late Latin *circare* to go round, from Latin *circus* circle.

season *n.* any one of the four divisions of the year, spring, summer, autumn, winter. *Also v.t., v.i.* WH: 12–14C. Old French *seson* (Modern French *saison*), from Latin *satio*, *sationis* sowing, from base of *satus* sown. The origin implies that spring is *the* season. Hence its prime place in the calendar (cp. French *printemps* spring, from Latin *primum tempus* first time, prime season) and in naming the seasons.

seat *n.* something on which a person sits or may sit. *Also v.t., v.i.* WH: 12–14C. Old Norse *sæti*, from Germanic, from base of SIT.

sebaceous *a.* fatty. WH: 18C. Latin *sebaceus*, from *sebum* tallow. See also -ACEOUS.

sec[1] *n.* a second (of time). WH: 19C. Abbr. of SECOND[1].

sec[2] *a.* (of wine) dry. WH: 12–14C. French, from Latin *siccus* dry. Cp. SACK[3], SEKT. The word is only rarely found before the 19C.

sec[3] *abbr.* secant. WH: 18C. Abbr. of SECANT.

secability *n.* capability of being cut or divided into parts. WH: 19C. Late Latin *secabilitas*, from *secabilis*, from Latin *secare* to cut. See also -ITY.

SECAM *n.* a French colour television broadcasting system. WH: mid-20C. Abbr. of French *séquentiel couleur à mémoire* sequential colour with memory. The system is so called because the colour information is transmitted in sequential blocks to a memory in the receiver.

secant *a.* cutting. *Also n.* WH: 16C. French *sécant*, from Modern Latin use of Latin *secans*, *secantis*, pres.p. of *secare* to cut. See also -ANT.

secateurs *n.pl.* pruning scissors. WH: 19C. Pl. of French *sécateur*, from Latin *secare* to cut + -*ateur* -ATOR.

secco *n.* tempera-painting on dry plaster. *Also a.* WH: 19C. Italian, from Latin *siccus* dry. The sense painting on dry plaster derives from Italian *fresco secco*, lit. dry fresco.

secede *v.i.* to withdraw from membership, association or communion, as with a Church. WH: 18C. Latin *secedere*, from SE- + *cedere* CEDE. The original sense was to withdraw from society, to go into seclusion.

secern *v.t.* to separate, to distinguish. WH: 17C. Latin *secernere*, from SE- + *cernere* to separate.

secesh *n.* a secessionist. *Also a.* WH: 19C. Abbr. of *secessionist* (SECESSION).

secession *n.* the act of seceding. WH: 16C. French *sécession* or Latin *secessio*, *secessionis*, from *secessus*, p.p. of *secedere* SECEDE. See also -ION.

sech *abbr.* hyperbolic secant. WH: 19C. SEC[3] + *h* (for *hyperbolic*).

seckel *n.* a small, pulpy variety of pear. WH: 19C. *Seckel*, surname of an early grower.

seclude *v.t.* to shut up or keep (a person, place etc.) apart or away from society. WH: 14–15C. Latin *secludere*, from SE- + *claudere* to shut. The original sense was to shut off, to obstruct access to (something). The current sense evolved in the 16C.

second[1] *a.* immediately following the first in time, place or position. *Also n., v.t.* WH: 12–14C. Old French, from Latin *secundus* following, favourable, second, from base of *sequi* to follow. The Old French word was adopted in English as Old English had no ordinal number corresponding to two. (This sense was expressed by *ōther* OTHER, which was indefinite in its reference.) The sense one sixtieth of a minute dates from the 14–15C and derives from Medieval Latin *secunda pars minuta* second diminished part, since it is the result of the second operation of dividing by 60. Cp. MINUTE[1].

second[2] *v.t.* to retire (a military officer) temporarily without pay in order that they may take a civil or other appointment. WH: 19C. French *en second* in the second rank (of officers).

secondary *a.* coming next in order of place or time to the first. *Also n.* WH: 14–15C. Latin *secundarius* of the second class, of second quality, from *secundus* SECOND[1].

seconde *n.* in fencing, a position in parrying or lungeing. WH: 17C. French. See SECOND[1].

secondo *n.* the second part or the second performer in a duet. WH: 18C. Italian second.

secrecy *n.* the state of being secret. WH: 14–15C. SECRET + -TY[1] or -Y[2], prob. based on pair PRIVATE/ *privacy*.

secret *a.* concealed from notice, kept or meant to be kept private. *Also n.* WH: 14–15C. Old French, from Latin *secretus* separate, set apart, orig. p.p. of *secernere* SECERN.

secretaire *n.* an escritoire, a bureau. WH: 18C. French *sécretaire*. See SECRETARY.

secretary *n.* a person employed to assist in clerical work, correspondence, arranging meetings etc., either by an individual or in an office. WH: 14–15C. Late Latin *secretarius* confidential officer, use as n. of a., from Latin *secretum* SECRET. See also -ARY[1]. The earliest sense (to the 19C) was confidant, person entrusted with secrets.

secrete *v.t.* to conceal, to hide. WH: 18C. Alt., based on Latin *secretus* SECRET, of obs. *secret* to conceal, to keep secret, from SECRET. The sense to produce a substance by means of secretion derives partly from Latin *secretus*. p.p. of *secernere* SECERN, partly as a back-formation from *secretion* (SECRETE).

secretive *a.* given to secrecy, uncommunicative. WH: 19C. Back-formation from *secretiveness*, based on French *secrétivité*, from *secret* SECRET. See also -IVE, -NESS.

sect *n.* a body of persons who have separated from a larger body, esp. an established Church, on account of philosophical or religious differences. WH: 12–14C. Old French *secte* or Latin *secta* party faction, school of philosophy, from *sectus*, var. p.p. of *sequi* to follow. Cp. SEPT. The word is not from Latin *sectus*, p.p. of *secare* to cut, as if a body 'cut' from a larger body.

sectant *n.* a portion of space separated by three intersecting planes but extending to infinity. WH: 19C. Latin *sectum*, neut. p.p. of *secare* to cut + -ANT.

sectile *a.* capable of being cut. WH: 18C. Latin *sectilis*, from *sectus*. See SECTION, also -IL.

section *n.* separation by cutting. *Also v.t.* WH: 14–15C. French, or from Latin *sectio*, *sectionis*, from *sectus*, p.p. of *secare* to cut. See also -ION.

sector n. a distinct part, a section. WH: 16C. Late Latin, from Latin *sector* cutter, from *sectus*. See SECTION, also -OR. The earliest sense was geometrical. The more general sense a distinct part evolved in the 18C, followed by the specific military sense in the early 20C and the economic sense in the mid-20C.

secular a. of or relating to the present world or to things not spiritual or sacred, not ecclesiastical or monastic. *Also n.* WH: 12–14C. Old French *seculer* (Modern French *séculier*), from Latin *saecularis*, from *saeculum* generation, age. See also -AR[1].

secund a. (of flowers etc.) arranged all on one side of the rachis. WH: 18C. Latin *secundus* SECOND[1].

secundine n. the placenta and other parts connected with the foetus, ejected after parturition, the afterbirth. WH: 14–15C. Late Latin *secundinae* (fem. pl.), from Latin *secundus* following. See SECOND[1], also -INE.

secundogeniture n. the right of inheritance belonging to a second son. WH: 19C. Latin *secundo*, adv. form of *secundus* SECOND[1] + -geniture, based on PRIMOGENITURE.

secundum prep. according to. WH: Latin according to.

secure a. free from danger or risk. *Also v.t.* WH: 16C. Latin *securus*, from SE- + *cura* care.

securi- comb. form of or relating to an axe. WH: Latin *securis* axe (from *secare* to cut).

securite n. a high explosive composed of nitrated hydrocarbons, used chiefly for blasting. WH: 19C. SECURE + -ITE[1], based on the orig. German name *Sicherit* (from German *sicher* safe, secure). The explosive is so called because it is flameless when detonated.

security n. the state of being or feeling secure. WH: 14–15C. Old French *sécurité* or Latin *securitas*, from *securus* SECURE. See also -ITY.

sedan n. a covered chair for one person, carried by two people by means of a pole on each side. WH: 17C. ? Alt. of Italian dial. word ult. from Latin *sella*. See SADDLE. A popular etymology linking the word with *Sedan*, a town in NE France, lacks the necessary documentary evidence.

sedate a. calm, staid. *Also v.t.* WH: 14–15C. Latin *sedatus*, p.p. of *sedare* to settle, from *sedere* to sit. See also -ATE[2]. The original sense was not sore, not painful.

sedentary a. sitting. *Also n.* WH: 16C. French *sédentaire* or Latin *sedentarius*, from *sedens, sendentis*, pres.p. of *sedere* to sit. See also -ARY[1].

Seder n. a ceremonial meal eaten on the first night (or the first two nights) of Passover. WH: 19C. Hebrew *sēder* order, procedure.

sederunt n. a sitting of a court etc. *Also v.i.* WH: 17C. Latin (there) were sitting (the following persons), use as n. of 3rd pers. pl. perf. ind. of *sedere* to sit.

sedge n. any coarse grasslike plant of the genus *Carex*, usu. growing in marshes or beside water. WH: pre-1200. Old English *secg*, from Germanic, ult. from Indo-European base represented by Latin *secare* to cut.

sedile n. each of usu. three stone seats, usu. canopied and decorated, on the south side of the chancel in churches, for the priest, deacon and subdeacon. WH: 14–15C. Latin seat, from *sedere* to sit. The original sense was seat in general. The current specialized sense dates from the 18C.

sediment n. the matter which subsides to the bottom of a liquid. WH: 16C. French *sédiment*, or from Latin *sedimentum* settling, from *sedere* to sit. See also -MENT.

sedition n. disorder or commotion in a state, not amounting to insurrection. WH: 14–15C. Old French *sédition* or Latin *seditio, seditionis*, from *sed-* SE- + *itio, itionis* going, from *itus*, p.p. of *ire* to go. See also -ITION.

seduce v.t. to lead astray, esp. to induce (someone) to sexual intercourse. WH: 15C. Latin *seducere*, from SE- + *ducere* to lead. The original sense was to persuade a subject to abandon his allegiance or a soldier his duty. The sense to entice someone into sexual activity dates from the 16C.

sedulous a. assiduous, constant, steady and persevering in business or endeavour; industrious, diligent. WH: 16C. Latin *sedulus* zealous. See also -ULOUS.

sedum n. any fleshy-leaved plant of the genus *Sedum*, including the stonecrop, orpine etc. WH: 16C. Latin.

see[1] v.t. to perceive by the eye. *Also v.i.* WH: pre-1200. Old English *sēon*, from Germanic, from Indo-European, ? from base also of Latin *sequi* to follow. Cp. SIGHT.

see[2] n. the diocese or jurisdiction of a bishop or archbishop. WH: 12–14C. Old French *sied*, from Latin *sedes* seat, from *sedere* SIT. The original sense (to the 16C) was seat in general or specifically throne, place of abode. The sense office or jurisdiction of a bishop dates from the 14–15C.

seed n. the mature fertilized ovule of a flowering plant, consisting of the embryo germ or reproductive body and its covering. *Also v.t., v.i.* WH: pre-1200. Old English *sǣd*, from Germanic word rel. to base of SOW[1]. Cp. German *Saat*.

seek v.t. to go in search of. *Also v.i.* WH: pre-1200. Old English *sēcan*, from Germanic, from Indo-European base represented also by Latin *sagire* to perceive by scent.

†seel v.t. to close the eyes of (a hawk), or close (its eyes) by threads drawn through the lids. WH: 15C. Old French *ciller* or Medieval Latin *ciliare*, from Latin *cilium* eyelid, CILIUM. Not rel. to SEAL[2]. The practice, used chiefly in training, was superseded by hooding.

seem v.i. to give the impression of being, to be apparently though not in reality. *Also v.t.* WH: 12–14C. Old Norse *sœma* to honour, from *sœmr* fitting, seemly. The original sense (to the 17C) was to suit, to befit.

seemly a. becoming, decent. *Also adv.* WH: 12–14C. Old Norse *sœmiligr*, from *sœmr*. See SEEM, also -LY[1].

seep v.i. to percolate, to ooze. *Also v.t.* WH: 18C. ? Dial. development of Old English *sīpian* SIPE[1].

seer n. an Indian weight of about one kilogram or liquid measure of about one litre. WH: 17C. Hindi *ser*, from Prakrit *satera*, from Greek *statēr* hundredweight, STATER.

seersucker n. a thin striped linen or cotton fabric with a puckered appearance. WH: 18C. Indian alt. of Persian *šir o šakar*, lit. milk and sugar. The fabric is so called in allusion to the original alternate smooth and puckered stripes of the material, respectively like the smooth surface of milk and the bumpy surface of sugar.

see-saw n. a game in which two persons sit one on each end of a board balanced on a support in the middle and move alternately up and down. *Also a., adv., v.t., v.i.* WH: 17C. Redupl. of SAW[1] representing alternating movement or imit. of the sound of the action of a two-man saw working on wood or stone. The word was originally a rhythmical refrain in a children's game. It has been in use from the name of the balanced plank for children to play on from the 19C.

seethe v.t. to boil. *Also v.i.* WH: pre-1200. Old English *sēothan*, from Germanic. Cp. German *sieden*.

segment n. a portion cut or marked off as separable, a section, a division, esp. one of a natural series (as of a limb between the joints, the body of an articulate animal, a fruit or plant organ divided by clefts). *Also v.i., v.t.* WH: 16C. Latin *segmentum*, from *secare* to cut. See also -MENT.

segno n. a sign marking the beginning or end of a section to be repeated. WH: 19C. Italian SIGN. Cp. DAL SEGNO.

sego n. a N American liliaceous plant, *Calochortus nuttallii*. WH: 19C. Prob. Ute Indian.

segregate[1] v.t. to separate from others. *Also v.i.* WH: 16C. Latin *segregatus*, p.p. of *segregare* to separate from the flock, from SE- + *grex, gregis* flock. See also -ATE[3].

segregate[2] a. simple, solitary, not compound. WH: 14–15C. Latin *segregatus*. See SEGREGATE[1], also -ATE[2].

segue v.i. to follow on immediately. *Also n.* WH: mid-20C. Italian, 3rd pers. sing. pres. ind. of *seguire* to follow. The word was in earlier use (from the 18C) as a musical direction to proceed to the next movement without a break.

seguidilla n. a lively Spanish dance in triple time. WH: 18C. Spanish, from *seguida* following, sequence, from *seguir* to follow.

Sehnsucht n. yearning. WH: 19C. German, from *sehen* SEE[1].

sei n. a rorqual, *Balaenoptera borealis*. WH: early 20C. Norwegian *sejhval*, from *sei* coalfish + *hval* whale.

seicento n. the 17th cent. in Italian art, architecture or literature. WH: early 20C. Italian six hundred (i.e. 1600s).

seiche *n.* an undulation, somewhat resembling a tidal wave, in the water of Lake Geneva and other Swiss lakes, usu. due to disturbance of atmospheric pressure or to subterranean movements. WH: 19C. Swiss French, ? from German *Seiche* sinking (of water).

Seidlitz powder *n.* a mild aperient, composed of a mixture of Rochelle salt, bicarbonate of soda and finely powdered tartaric acid, mixed separately in water to form an effervescing drink. WH: 18C. *Seidlitz*, a village in SW Bohemia (now *Sedlice*, Czech Republic), where there is a spring impregnated with magnesium sulphate and carbonic acid.

seif *n.* a long sand dune in the form of a ridge. WH: early 20C. Arabic *sayf*, lit. sword.

seigneur *n.* a feudal lord. WH: 16C. Old French, from Latin SENIOR.

seine *n.* a large fishing net with floats at the top and weights at the bottom for encircling. *Also v.t., v.i.* WH: pre-1200. Old English *segne*, from Germanic, from Latin *sagena*.

seise *v.t.* to put in possession of. WH: 12–14C. Var. of SEIZE.

seismic *a.* of, relating to or produced by an earthquake. WH: 19C. Greek *seismos* earthquake (from *seien* to shake) + -IC.

seismo- *comb. form* of or relating to an earthquake. WH: 19C. Greek *seismos* earthquake. See also -O-.

seismogram *n.* a record given by a seismograph. WH: 19C. SEISMO- + -GRAM.

seismology *n.* the study or science of earthquakes. WH: 19C. SEISMO- + -LOGY.

seismometer *n.* a seismograph. WH: 19C. SEISMO- + -METER.

seismoscope *n.* a simple form of seismograph. WH: 19C. SEISMO- + -SCOPE.

seismotic *a.* seismic. WH: 19C. Greek *seismos* (SEISMIC) + -OTIC.

seize *v.t.* to grasp or lay hold of suddenly. *Also v.i.* WH: 12–14C. Old French *seizir* (Modern French *saisir*), from Frankish Latin *sacire* (in *ad proprium sacire* to claim as one's own), from a Germanic base meaning process, procedure, ? rel. to base of SET[1].

sejant *a.* sitting with the forelegs erect. WH: 15C. Alt. of Old French var. of *séant*, pres.p. of *seoir*, from Latin *sedere* to sit. See also -ANT.

Sekt *n.* a German sparkling white wine. WH: early 20C. German. Cp. SACK[3], SEC[2].

selachian *n.* a fish of the subclass Selachii comprising the sharks, dogfish etc. *Also a.* WH: 19C. Modern Latin *Selachii* (from Greek *selakhē*, pl. of *selakhos* shark) + -IAN.

seladang *n.* a Malayan gaur. WH: 19C. Malay.

selaginella *n.* any moss of the genus *Selaginella*, many of which are cultivated for ornamental purposes. WH: 19C. Modern Latin, dim. of Latin *selago* clubmoss.

selah *n.* a word occurring in the Psalms and in Habakkuk, always at the end of a verse, variously interpreted as indicating a pause, a repetition, the end of a strophe etc. WH: 16C. Hebrew *selāh*, ? meaning pause.

seldom *adv.* rarely, not often. *Also a.* WH: pre-1200. Old English *seldan*, from Germanic base represented also by Old English *seldic* strange, wonderful. Cp. German *selten*.

select *a.* chosen, picked out. *Also v.t.* WH: 16C. Latin *selectus*, p.p. of *seligere*, from SE- + *legere* to collect, to choose.

selenium *n.* a non-metallic element, at. no. 34, chem. symbol Se, obtained as a by-product in the manufacture of sulphuric acid, similar in chemical properties to sulphur and tellurium, utilized for its varying electrical resistance in light and darkness. WH: 19C. Modern Latin, from Greek *selēnē* moon + -IUM. The name was coined by the Swedish chemist Jöns Jacob Berzelius, the element's discoverer in 1818, in contradistinction to TELLURIUM, an element with similar properties, named after the earth.

seleno- *comb. form* of or relating to the moon. WH: 19C. Greek *selēnē* moon. See also -O-.

selenocentric *a.* referred to, seen from or measured from the moon as centre. WH: 19C. SELENO- + -CENTRIC.

selenodont *a.* (of molar teeth) having crescent-shaped ridges. *Also n.* WH: 19C. SELENO- + -ODONT.

selenography *n.* a description of the moon and its phenomena. WH: 19C. SELENO- + -GRAPHY.

selenology *n.* the branch of astronomical science treating of the moon. WH: 19C. SELENO- + -LOGY.

selenotropic *a.* (of plant organs) curving towards the moon. WH: 19C. SELENO- + -*tropic* (-TROPE).

self *n.* the individuality of a person or thing, as the object of reflexive consciousness or action. *Also a., pron., v.t.* WH: pre-1200. Old English, from Germanic base of unknown orig. Cp. German *selbe*.

self- *comb. form* expressing direct or indirect reflexive action, as in *self-command.* WH: SELF.

Seljuk *n.* a member of any of various Muslim dynasties in central and W Asia during the 11th and 13th cents., descended from the Turkish chieftain Seljuk. *Also a.* WH: 19C. Turkish *seljūq*, *Selčük*, reputed ancestor of the Seljuk dynasties.

sell *v.t.* to transfer or dispose of (property) to another for an equivalent in money. *Also v.i., n.* WH: pre-1200. Old English *sellan*, from Germanic. Cp. Old Norse *selja* to give up, to sell, Gothic *saljan* to offer sacrifice.

Sellotape® *n.* a cellulose or plastic adhesive tape for mending, binding etc. WH: mid-20C. Alt. of CELLULOSE + -O- + TAPE.

seltzer *n.* an effervescing mineral water. WH: 18C. Alt. of German *Seltserer*, from (*Nieder*)*selters*, a village in W Germany where the water is found.

selva *n.* tropical rain forest in the Amazon basin. WH: 19C. Spanish or Portuguese, from Latin *silva* wood.

selvage *n.* a rope or ring made of spun yarns etc., laid parallel and secured by lashings. WH: 18C. Var. of SELVEDGE.

selvedge *n.* the edge of cloth woven so as not to unravel. WH: 14–15C. SELF + EDGE, based on early Middle Dutch *selfegghe* (now *zelfegge*). The cloth is so called because the edge of the fabric so woven does not unravel and therefore can be its own edging.

semanteme *n.* a unit of meaning conveying an image or idea. WH: early 20C. French *sémantème*, from *sémantique* (SEMANTIC), based on *morphème* MORPHEME, *phonème* PHONEME. See also -EME.

semantic *a.* of or relating to semantics; concerned with the meaning of words and symbols. WH: 17C. French *sémantique*, from Greek *semantikos* significant, from *sēmainein* to show, to signify, from *sēma* sign, work. See also -IC.

semaphore *n.* a system of signalling using the arms or two flags to represent letters of the alphabet. WH: 19C. French *sémaphore*, from Greek *sēma* sign, signal + -*phoros* -PHORE.

semasiology *n.* semantics. WH: 19C. German *Semasiologie*, from Greek *sēmasia* meaning, from *sēmainein* to signify. See SEMANTIC, -LOGY.

sematic *a.* of the nature of a sign, significant, esp. of or relating to markings on animals serving to attract, to warn off enemies etc. WH: 19C. Greek *sēma*, *sēmatos* sign + -IC.

semblance *n.* external appearance, seeming. WH: 12–14C. Old French, from *sembler* to seem. See also -ANCE. The earlier form of the word was *semblant*, a noun formed from the present participle of Old French *sembler*.

semé *a.* (of a field or charge) strewn over with figures, such as stars, crosses etc. WH: 14–15C. French, p.p. of *semer* to sow.

sememe *n.* in linguistics, the meaning of a morpheme. WH: early 20C. Greek *sēma* sign, mark + -EME.

semen *n.* the fertilizing fluid containing spermatozoa, produced by the generative organs of a male animal. WH: 14–15C. Latin, from base of *serere* SOW[1].

semester *n.* a college half-year in German, some American and other universities. WH: 19C. German, from Latin *semestris* of six months, from *sex, se-* SIX + *mensis* month. Cp. TRIMESTER.

semi *n.* a semi-detached house. WH: early 20C. Abbr. of *semi-detached.*

semi- *pref.* half. WH: Latin (partly through French, Italian etc.), corr. to Greek *hēmi-* HEMI-, Sanskrit *sāmi*, from Indo-European base also of Old English *sam-* in SAND-BLIND.

seminal *a.* of or relating to semen or reproduction. WH: 14–15C. Old French *séminal* or Latin *seminalis*, from *semen, seminis* seed. See SEMEN, also -AL[1].

seminar *n.* a group of students undertaking an advanced course of study or research together, usu. under the guidance of a professor. WH: 19C. German, from Latin *seminarium*. See SEMINARY.

seminary *n.* a place of education, a college, esp. a (foreign) Roman Catholic school for training priests. WH: 14–15C. Latin *seminarium* seed-plot, use as n. of neut. of *seminarius*, from *semen*, *seminis*. See SEMEN, also -ARY[1].

semination *n.* the natural dispersal of seeds by plants. WH: 16C. Latin *seminatio*, *seminationis*, from *seminatus*, p.p. of *seminare* to sow, from *semen*, *seminis*. See SEMEN, also -ATION.

semiochemical *n.* a chemical substance such as a pheromone, used for communication between animals. WH: late 20C. Greek *sēmeion* sign (see SEMIOLOGY) + CHEMICAL.

semiology *n.* the study of signs and symbols. WH: 17C. Greek *sēmeion* sign (from *sēma* sign, mark) + -O- + -LOGY.

semiotics *n.* the study of signs and symbols and their relationships in language. WH: 17C. Greek *sēmeiotikos* significance, from *sēmeioun* to interpret as a sign, from *sēmeion* (see SEMIOLOGY). See -OTIC, -IC, -ICS.

Semite *n.* a descendant of Shem, or a member of one of the peoples (including Jews, Phoenicians, Assyrians, Arabs and Ethiopians) reputed to be descended from Shem. *Also a.* WH: 19C. Modern Latin *Semita*, from Late Latin, from Greek *Sēm* Shem, a son of Noah (Gen. x.21–31) + -ITE[1].

semmit *n.* a vest or undershirt. WH: 14–15C. Orig. unknown.

semnopithecus *n.* any monkey of the genus *Semnopithecus*, having long limbs and tail. WH: 19C. Modern Latin, from Greek *semnos* revered, sacred + *pithekos* ape.

semolina *n.* the hard grains of wheat left after bolting, used for puddings etc. WH: 18C. Alt. of Italian *semolino*, dim. of *semola* bran, based on Latin *simila* flour. Cp. SIMNEL.

semper *adv.* always. WH: 17C. Latin always.

sempervirent *a.* evergreen. WH: 17C. Latin *semper* always + *virens*, *virentis*, pres.p. of *virere* to be green.

sempervivum *n.* a fleshy plant of the genus *Sempervivum*, containing the houseleeks. WH: 16C. Latin, use as n. of neut. of *sempervivus* ever-living.

sempiternal *a.* everlasting, eternal, endless. WH: 14–15C. Old French *sempiternel*, from Late Latin *sempiternalis*, from Latin *sempiternus*, from *semper* always + *aeternus* eternal. See also -AL[1].

semplice *adv.* simply, plainly, without embellishment. WH: 18C. Italian simple.

sempre *adv.* in the same manner throughout. WH: 19C. Italian always, from Latin SEMPER.

Semtex® *n.* a malleable plastic explosive. WH: late 20C. Prob. from *Semtín*, a village in the Czech Republic, near its place of manufacture + -ex, ? from *explosive* (EXPLOSION).

semuncia *n.* a Roman coin equal to half an uncia. WH: 19C. Latin half-ounce, from SEMI- + *uncia* OUNCE[1].

sen *n.* a Japanese monetary unit, one-hundredth of a yen. WH: 18C. Japanese.

senarius *n.* in Latin prosody, a verse of six feet, esp. the iambic trimeter. WH: 16C. Latin, use as n. of a., from *seni* six each, from *sex* six.

senate *n.* an assembly or council performing legislative or administrative functions. WH: 12–14C. Old French *sénat*, from Latin *senatus*, from *senex* old (man). See also -ATE[1].

send *v.t.* to arrange for (a letter, message etc.) to go or be taken to some destination. *Also v.i., n.* WH: pre-1200. Old English *sendan*, from Germanic. Cp. German *senden*.

sendal *n.* a light, thin silken fabric used in the Middle Ages for costly attire, banners etc. WH: 12–14C. Old French *cendal*, *sendal*, ult. from Greek *sindōn*, prob. of Oriental orig. See -AL[1].

Senecan *a.* of, relating to or in the style of Seneca. WH: 19C. Lucius Annaeus *Seneca* (the Younger), *c.*4 BC–*c.*AD 65, Roman tragedian and Stoic philosopher + -AN.

senecio *n.* any plant of the genus *Senecio*, including the groundsel and the ragwort. WH: 16C. Latin old man, groundsel. The plant is so called from its white pappus.

senescent *a.* growing old. WH: 17C. Latin *senescens*, *senescentis*, pres.p. of *senescere* to grow old, from *senex* old. See also -ENT.

seneschal *n.* an officer in the houses of princes and high dignitaries in the Middle Ages having the superintendence of feasts and domestic ceremonies, sometimes dispensing justice; a steward or major-domo. WH: 12–14C. Old French (Modern French *sénéchal*), from Medieval Latin *seniscalus*, from Frankish *siniskalk*, lit. old servant. Cp. SENIOR, MARSHAL. See also -AL[1].

senhor *n.* a man, in a Portuguese-speaking country. WH: 18C. Portuguese, from Latin SENIOR. Cp. SEÑOR, SIGNOR.

senile *a.* of, relating to or proceeding from the infirmities etc. of old age. *Also n.* WH: 17C. French *sénile* or Latin *senilis*, from *senex* old (man). See also -IL.

senior *a.* elder (appended to names to denote the elder of two persons with identical names, esp. father and son). *Also n.* WH: 14–15C. Latin, comp. of *senex* old, rel. to Greek *henos* old. See also -IOR. Cp. JUNIOR.

senna *n.* the dried, purgative leaflets or pods of several species of cassia. WH: 16C. Medieval Latin *sena*, from Arabic *sanā* .

sennet *n.* a trumpet-signal for stage entrances and exits in the Elizabethan theatre. WH: 16C. ? Var. of SIGNET.

†sennight *n.* seven nights, a week. WH: pre-1200. Old English *seofon nihta* seven nights. See SEVEN, NIGHT. Cp. FORTNIGHT.

señor *n.* a man, in a Spanish-speaking country. WH: 17C. Spanish, from Latin SENIOR. Cp. SENHOR, SIGNOR.

sensation *n.* the mental state or affection resulting from the excitation of an organ of sense, the primary element in perception or cognition of an external object. WH: 17C. Medieval Latin *sensatio*, *sensationis*, from Latin *sensus* SENSE. See also -ATION.

sense *n.* any one of the five faculties by which sensation is received through special bodily organs (sight, hearing, touch, taste, smell). *Also v.t.* WH: 14–15C. Latin *sensus* faculty or mode of feeling, from *sensus*, p.p. of *sentire* to feel, to perceive by the senses.

sensible *a.* acting with or characterized by good sense or judgement. *Also n.* WH: 14–15C. Old French, or from Latin *sensibilis*, from *sensus*. See SENSE, also -IBLE.

sensillum *n.* a sense organ in insects. WH: early 20C. Modern Latin, neut. n. from dim. of Latin *sensus* SENSE.

sensitive *a.* readily or acutely affected by external influences. *Also n.* WH: 14–15C. Old French *sensitif* or Medieval Latin *sensitivus*, from Latin *sensus*. See SENSE, also -IVE.

sensor *n.* an instrument which responds to, and signals, a change in a physical stimulus, for information or control purposes. WH: mid-20C. From earlier a. *sensor* sensory, from *sensory* (SENSORIUM), based on MOTOR, or from SENSE + -OR.

sensorium *n.* the seat or organ of sensation, the brain. WH: 17C. Late Latin, from Latin *sensus*, p.p. of *sentire* to feel. See also -ORIUM.

sensual *a.* of, relating to or affecting the senses, carnal. WH: 14–15C. Late Latin *sensualis*, from Latin *sensus* SENSE. See also -AL[1]. Cp. SENSUOUS.

sensum *n.* a sense datum. WH: 19C. Modern Latin, that which is sensed, neut. p.p. of Latin *sentire*. See SENSE.

sensuous *a.* of, relating to or derived from the senses. WH: 17C. Latin *sensus* SENSE + -OUS. The word was coined in 1641 by the English poet John Milton to avoid the erotic connotations of SENSUAL.

sensu stricto *adv.* strictly speaking, in the narrow sense. WH: 19C. Latin in the restricted sense.

sentence *n.* a series of words, containing a subject, predicate etc., expressing a complete thought. *Also v.t.* WH: 12–14C. Old French, from Latin *sententia* mental feeling, opinion, philosophical judgement (translating Greek *doxa* and *gnōmē*), from *sentire* to feel. See also -ENCE.

sententious *a.* characterized by many pithy sentences, axioms or maxims. WH: 14–15C. Latin *sententiosus*, from *sententia* SENTENCE. See also -OUS.

sentient *a.* having the power of sense-perception. *Also n.* WH: 17C. Latin *sentiens*, *sentientis*, pres.p. of *sentire* to feel. See also -ENT.

sentiment *n.* an opinion or attitude. WH: 14–15C. Old French *sentement* (Modern French *sentiment*), from Medieval Latin *sentimentum*, from Latin *sentire* to feel. See also -MENT.

sentimental *a.* characterized by sentiment. WH: 18C. SENTIMENT + -AL[1].

sentinel *n.* a person who keeps watch to prevent surprise, esp. a soldier on guard. *Also v.t.* WH: 16C. French *sentinelle*, from Italian *sentinella*, of unknown orig. Cp. SENTRY.

sentry *n.* a sentinel, a soldier on guard. WH: 17C. ? Shortening of obs. *centrinel*, var. of SENTINEL, with assim. to -RY.

senza *prep.* without. WH: 18C. Italian without, prob. from Latin *absentia* absence, influ. by Latin *sine* without. Cp. SANS.

sepal *n.* any one of the segments, divisions or leaves of a calyx. WH: 19C. French *sépale*, Modern Latin *sepalum*, from Greek *skepē* covering, based on French *pétale* petal.

separate[1] *v.t.* to set or keep apart. *Also v.i.* WH: 14–15C. Latin *separatus*, p.p. of *separare*, from SE- + *parare* to make ready. See also -ATE[3].

separate[2] *a.* disconnected, considered apart. *Also n.* WH: 14–15C. Latin *separatus*, p.p. of *separare*. See SEPARATE[1], also -ATE[2].

separatrix *n.* a separating mark, such as a decimal point, or line marking off corrections in the margin of proof, the line of demarcation between light and shade in a picture etc. WH: 17C. Late Latin, fem. of *separator* separator (SEPARATE[1]). See also -TRIX.

separatum *n.* a reprint of one of a series of papers etc. WH: 19C. Latin, use as n. of neut. sing. of *separatus*, p.p. of *separare* SEPARATE[1].

Sephardi *n.* a Jew of Spanish, Portuguese or N African descent. WH: 19C. Modern Hebrew, from *sĕpāraḏ*, a country mentioned in Obad. xx and taken to be Spain.

sepia *n.* a dark reddish-brown colour. *Also a.* WH: 14–15C. Latin, from Greek *sēpia* cuttlefish. The original sense was cuttlefish. The current sense (a brownish pigment prepared from the black secretion of the cuttlefish) dates from the 19C.

sepoy *n.* an Indian soldier under European discipline, esp. one in the former British Indian army. WH: 18C. Persian and Urdu *sipāhī* horseman, soldier, from *sipāh* army. Cp. SPAHI.

seppuku *n.* hara-kiri. WH: 19C. Japanese, from *setsu* to cut + *fuku* abdomen. Cp. HARA-KIRI.

sepsis *n.* septic condition, putrefaction. WH: 19C. Greek *sēpsis*, from *sēpein* to make rotten.

sept *n.* a clan or branch of a clan, esp. in Scotland or Ireland. WH: 16C. Prob. alt. of SECT. Cp. Anglo-Latin *septus* and Medieval Latin *septa*, representing Old French *sette*, Italian *setta* sect.

septarium *n.* a nodule of limestone, ironstone etc., with radiating fissures in the middle filled with some extraneous deposit. WH: 18C. Modern Latin, from SEPTUM. See also -ARIUM.

septate *a.* provided with or divided by a septum or septa, partitioned. WH: 19C. SEPTUM + -ATE[2], based on DENTATE, FOLIATE[2], etc.

septcentenary *n.* a 700th anniversary. *Also a.* WH: early 20C. SEPTI-[1] + *centenary* (CENTENARIAN), based on BICENTENARY, etc.

September *n.* the ninth month of the year. WH: pre-1200. French *septembre*, from Latin *September*, from *septum* seven. The month was originally the seventh of the Roman year. The origin of *-ber* is unknown (cp. OCTOBER, etc.).

septemvir *n.* each of seven people forming a government, committee etc. WH: 18C. Latin, sing. of *septemviri*, from *septem* seven + *viri* men.

septenarius *n.* a verse of seven feet, esp. a trochaic trimeter catalectic. WH: 19C. Latin, from *septeni* seven each, from *septem* seven.

septenary *a.* consisting of or relating to seven. *Also n.* WH: 14–15C. Latin *septeni*. See SEPTENARIUS, also -ARY[1].

septennium *n.* a period of seven years. WH: 19C. Late Latin, from Latin *septem* seven + *annus* year. See also -IUM.

septet *n.* a group of seven, esp. singers, voices, instruments etc. WH: 19C. German *Septett*, from Latin *septem* seven. See also -ET[1].

septfoil *n.* a figure of seven equal segments of a circle, used as a symbol of the seven sacraments etc. WH: 16C. Late Latin *septifolium*, based on CINQUEFOIL, TREFOIL.

septi-[1] *comb. form* seven. WH: Latin *septem* seven + -I-.

septi-[2] *comb. form* septum. WH: Latin SEPTUM + -I-. See also -O-.

septic *a.* causing or tending to promote putrefaction, not aseptic. *Also n.* WH: 17C. Latin *septicus*, from Greek *sēptikos*, from *sēmein* to make rotten. See also -IC.

septicidal *a.* (of the dehiscence of a fruit) taking place through the partitions. WH: 19C. SEPTI-[2] + Latin *caedere*, *-cid-* to cut (-CIDE) + -AL[1].

septifarious *a.* turned seven different ways. WH: SEPTI-[1] + *farious*, from Latin *-farius* as in *multifarius* (MULTIFARIOUS).

septiferous *a.* bearing septa. WH: 19C. SEPTI-[2] + -FEROUS.

septiform[1] *a.* sevenfold. WH: 15C. Old French *septiforme* or Latin *septiformis*. See SEPTI-[1], -FORM.

septiform[2] *a.* shaped like a septum. WH: 19C. Modern Latin *septiformis* or French *septiforme*. See SEPTI-[2], -FORM.

septifragal *a.* breaking away from the partitions (of or relating to a mode of dehiscence in which the septa break away from the valves). WH: 19C. SEPTI-[2] + Latin *frag-*, base of *frangere* to break + -AL[1].

septilateral *a.* seven-sided. WH: 17C. SEPTI-[1] + LATERAL.

septillion *n.* the eighth power of a thousand, 1 followed by 21 ciphers. WH: 17C. French, from SEPTI-[1], based on MILLION, BILLION, etc.

septimal *a.* of, relating to or based on the number seven. WH: 19C. Latin *septimus* seventh + -AL[1], based on DECIMAL.

septivalent *a.* having a valency of seven; heptavalent. WH: 19C. SEPTI-[1] + *-valent*, from Latin *valens*, *valentis*, pres.p. of *valere* to be strong. See also -ENT.

septuagenarian *n.* a person of 70 years of age, or between 70 and 80. *Also a.* WH: 18C. Latin *septuagenarius*, from *septuageni* seventy each, from *septuaginta* seventy. See also -ARIAN.

Septuagesima *n.* the third Sunday before Lent. WH: 14–15C. Latin *septuagesima* (*dies*) seventieth (day), fem. of *septuagesimus*, from *septuaginta* seventy. The day is so called as it falls about 70 days before Easter.

Septuagint *n.* a Greek version of the Old Testament including the Apocrypha (*c.*3rd cent. BC). WH: 16C. Latin *septuaginta* seventy. The version is so called because it is traditionally said to have been made by 72 translators.

septum *n.* a partition, as in a chambered cell, the cell of an ovary, between the nostrils etc. WH: 17C. Latin, from *sepire* to enclose, from *sepes* hedge.

septuple *a.* sevenfold. *Also n., v.t., v.i.* WH: 17C. Late Latin *septuplus*, from Latin *septem* seven, based on *quadruplus* QUADRUPLE.

sepulchre *n.* a tomb, esp. one hewn in the rock or built in a solid and permanent manner. *Also v.t.* WH: 12–14C. Old French *sépulchre*, from Latin *sepulchrum*, from *sepultus*, p.p. of *sepelire* to bury.

sepulture *n.* interment, burial. WH: 12–14C. Old French *sépulture*, from Latin *sepultura*, from *sepultus*. See SEPULCHRE, also -URE.

sequacious *a.* logically consistent and coherent. WH: 17C. Latin *sequax*, *sequacis*, from *sequi* to follow. See also -ACIOUS.

sequel *n.* that which follows. WH: 14–15C. Old French *séquelle*, or from Latin *sequella*, from *sequi* to follow. See also -EL.

sequela *n.* an abnormal condition occurring as the consequence of some disease. WH: 18C. Latin *sequella*, *sequela*. See SEQUEL.

sequence *n.* succession, the process of coming after in space, time etc. *Also v.t.* WH: 14–15C. Late Latin *sequentia*, from Latin *sequens*, *sequentis*, pres.p. of *sequi* to follow. See also -ENCE.

sequester *v.t.* to set apart, to isolate, to seclude. *Also v.i., n.* WH: 14–15C. Old French *séquestrer* or Late Latin *sequestrare* to place in safe keeping, from *sequester* trustee.

sequestrum *n.* a piece of dead and separated bone remaining in place. WH: 19C. Medieval Latin sequestration, thing sequestrated, from *sequester*. See SEQUESTER.

sequin *n.* a small disc of shiny metal, jet etc., used as trimming for dresses etc. WH: 16C. French, from Italian *zecchino*, from *zeccho* mint, from Arabic *sikka* die for coining, coin. Cp. ZECCHINO.

sequoia *n.* either of two gigantic conifers of California, *Sequoia sempervirens* and *Sequoiadendron giganteum*. WH: 19C. Modern Latin, from *Sequoya* (Cherokee *Si:kwa:yi*), *c.*1770–1843, a Cherokee Indian who invented the Cherokee system of writing. The name was coined in 1847 by the Hungarian botanist and ethnologist Stephan L. Endlicher, who knew of Sequoya's achievement.

serac *n.* any of the large angular or tower-shaped masses into which a glacier breaks up at an icefall. WH: 19C. Swiss French *sérac*, orig. the name of a kind of compact white cheese, prob. from Latin *serum* whey.

seraglio *n.* a harem. WH: 16C. Italian *serraglio*, from Turkish *saray* (SERAI) with assim. to Italian *serraglio* cage (from Medieval Latin *serraculum*, dim. of Latin *sera* bolt.

serai *n.* a caravanserai. WH: 17C. Turkish *saray* palace, mansion, from Persian. Cp. SERAGLIO.

serang *n.* a boatman; the leader of a Lascar crew. WH: 18C. Persian and Urdu *sar-hang* commander, from *sar* head + *hang* authority.

serape *n.* a Mexican blanket or shawl. WH: 19C. Mexican Spanish.

seraph *n.* an angel of the highest order. WH: pre-1200. Back-formation from *seraphim* (pl.) (from Late Latin, from Hebrew *šĕrāpīm*), based on pair CHERUB/ *cherubim*.

seraphina *n.* a form of harmonium (invented 1883) with reeds, a keyboard etc. WH: 19C. SERAPH + -INA¹.

seraskier *n.* a Turkish commander, esp. the commander-in-chief or minister of war. WH: 17C. Turkish *serasker, sarasker*, from Persian *sar'askar*, from *sar* head + Arabic *'askar* army, from Latin *exercitus*.

Serb *n.* a native or inhabitant of Serbia in SE Europe. *Also a.* WH: 19C. Serbo-Croat *Srb.*

sere *n.* a series of ecological communities following one another in one area. WH: early 20C. Latin *serere* to join in a series.

serein *n.* a fine rain falling from a clear sky after sunset, esp. in tropical regions. WH: 19C. French, from Latin *serum* evening, use as n. of *serus* late.

serenade *n.* a song or piece of music played or sung in the open air at night, esp. by a lover beneath his lady's window. *Also v.t., v.i.* WH: 17C. French *sérénade*, from Italian *serenata*, from *sereno* SERENE, influ. by *sera* evening.

serendipity *n.* the happy knack of making unexpected and delightful discoveries by accident. WH: 18C. *Serendip*, a former name of Sri Lanka (Ceylon) + -ITY. The word was coined by the writer Horace Walpole in 1754 after the title of a fairy tale, *The Three Princes of Serendip*, whose heroes 'were always making discoveries, by accidents and sagacity, of things they were not in quest of'. *Serendip* and *Ceylon* both ultimately derive from Sanskrit *siṃha* lion, the *-dip* of *Serendip* representing Sanskrit *dvīpa* island.

serene *a.* placid, tranquil. *Also n., v.t.* WH: 14–15C. Latin *serenus* clear, fair, calm (of weather, etc.).

serf *n.* a feudal labourer attached to an estate, a villein. WH: 15C. Old French, from Latin *servus* slave.

serge *n.* a strong and durable twilled cloth, of worsted, cotton, rayon etc. WH: 14–15C. Old French *sarge* (Modern French *serge*), from var. of Latin *serica (lana)* silken (wool), fem. of *sericus*. See SILK.

sergeant *n.* a non-commissioned Army or Air Force officer ranking next above corporal, teaching drill, commanding small detachments etc. WH: 12–14C. Old French *sergent*, from Latin *serviens, servientis*, pres.p. of *servire* to serve. See also -ENT.

serial *a.* of, relating to, consisting of or having the nature of a series. *Also n.* WH: 19C. SERIES + -AL¹.

Seric *a.* Chinese. WH: 19C. Latin *sericus* belonging to the Seres (the inhabitants of the Far Eastern countries from which silk came overland to Europe in ancient times). See SILK.

sericeous *a.* of, relating to or consisting of silk. WH: 18C. Latin *sericus* silken, of the Seres. See SERIC, also -EOUS.

sericin *n.* a gelatinous substance contained in silk. WH: 19C. Latin *sericum* silk + -IN¹.

sericulture *n.* the breeding of silkworms and the production of raw silk. WH: 19C. Contr. of French *sériciculture*, from Late Latin *sericum* SILK + French *culture* CULTURE.

seriema *n.* any long-legged S American bird of the family Cariamidae. WH: 19C. Modern Latin, from Tupi *siriema, sariama*, said to mean crested.

series *n.* a number, set or continued succession of things similar to each other or each bearing a definite relation to that preceding it. WH: 17C. Latin row, chain, series, from *serere* to join, to connect.

serif *n.* any of the fine cross-lines at the top and bottom of printed letters of the alphabet. WH: 19C. Orig. uncertain. ? From Dutch *schreef* dash, line, from Germanic.

serigraph *n.* a silk-screen print. WH: 19C. Latin *sericum* silk + -GRAPH.

serin *n.* a small yellow or green finch, *Serinus serinus*, the wild canary. WH: 16C. French canary, of unknown orig.

serine *n.* a hydrophilic amino acid involved in the synthesis of cysteine. WH: 19C. German *Serin*, from Latin *sericum* silk + *-in* -INE.

seringa *n.* a Brazilian rubber tree, *Hevea brasiliensis*. WH: 18C. French, from Portuguese, from Latin SYRINGA.

serious *a.* grave, thoughtful. WH: 14–15C. Old French *sérieux* or Late Latin *seriosus*, from *serius* weighty, important, grave. See also -OUS.

sermon *n.* a discourse founded on a text of Scripture delivered in church. *Also v.t.* WH: 12–14C. Old French, from Latin *sermo, sermonis* talk, discourse.

sero- *comb. form* serum. WH: SERUM. See also -O-.

serology *n.* the study of blood serum, its composition and properties. WH: early 20C. SERO- + -LOGY.

seronegative *a.* (of a person whose blood has been tested) not showing the presence of a virus etc. WH: mid-20C. SERO- + *negative* (NEGATE).

seropositive *a.* (of a person whose blood has been tested) showing the presence of a virus etc. WH: mid-20C. SERO- + POSITIVE.

seropurulent *a.* composed of serum and pus. WH: 19C. SERO- + PURULENT.

serosa *n.* serous membrane. WH: 19C. Modern Latin *membrana serosa* serous membrane.

serotherapy *n.* serum therapy. WH: 19C. SERO- + *therapy* (THERAPEUTIC).

serotine *n.* a small reddish bat, *Eptesicus serotinus*, flying in the evening. WH: 18C. French *sérotine*, from fem. of Latin *serotinus* belated, from *sero*, adv. of *serus* late. See also -INE. The bat is so called as it flies in the evening.

serotinous *a.* appearing late in the season. WH: 17C. Latin *serotinus* belated, late-flowering. See SEROTINE, also -OUS.

serotonin *n.* a compound found in many body tissues which acts as a vasoconstrictor. WH: mid-20C. SERO- + TONIC + -IN¹.

serous *a.* of, relating to or resembling serum. WH: 14–15C. French *séreux* or Medieval Latin *serosus*, from Latin SERUM. See also -OUS.

serow *n.* a goat-antelope with a thick, dark coat and conical horns, *Capricornis sumatraensis* of S and E Asia, or *C. crispus* of Taiwan and Japan. WH: 19C. Prob. from Lepcha *sā-ro.*

serpent *n.* a reptile with an elongated scaly body and no limbs, a snake. WH: 12–14C. Old French, from Latin *serpens, serpentis*, use as n. of pres.p. of *serpere* to creep, rel. to Greek *herpein*. See also -ENT.

serpigo *n.* a skin disease, esp. a form of herpes or spreading ringworm. WH: 14–15C. Medieval Latin, from Latin *serpere* to creep.

serpula *n.* a serpulid, esp. of the genus *Serpula*. WH: 18C. Modern Latin, from Late Latin small serpent.

serra *n.* a sawlike organ, part or structure. WH: 14–15C. Latin saw, sawfish.

serradilla *n.* a species of clover, *Ornithopus sativus*, grown for fodder. WH: 19C. Portuguese, dim. of *serrado* serrated.

serranid *n.* any marine fish of the family Serranidae, comprising the sea basses, sea perches and groupers. *Also a.* WH: mid-20C. Modern Latin *Serranidae*, from *Serranus* genus name, from Latin SERRA. See also -ID.

serrate¹ *a.* notched on the edge, like a saw, serrated. WH: 17C. Latin *serratus*, from SERRA. See also -ATE².

serrate² *v.t.* to cut into notches and teeth, to give a sawlike edge to. WH: 14–15C. Late Latin *serratus*, p.p. of *serrare*, from Latin SERRA. See also -ATE³.

serried *a.* (esp. of soldiers) close-packed, in compact order. WH: 17C. P.p. of *serry* (16C), prob. from Old French *serré*, p.p. of *serrer* to press close, from Popular Latin *serrare* to bolt, to lock up, var. of Latin *serare*, from *sera* lock, bolt.

serrulate *a.* finely serrated, having minute notches. WH: 18C. Modern Latin *serrulatus*, from Latin *serrulus*, dim. of *serra* saw. See -ULE, -ATE².

serum *n.* the thin transparent part that separates from the blood in coagulation. WH: 17C. Latin whey, watery fluid.

serval *n.* an African wild cat with long legs and a black-spotted tawny coat, *Felis serval*. WH: 18C. Modern Latin or French, from Portuguese (*lobo*) *cerval* lynx, lit. deerlike wolf, from *cervo* deer, from Latin *cervus*.

servant *n.* a person employed by another person to work under direction for wages, esp. in the house of the employer and undertaking domestic tasks or acting as a personal attendant. WH: 12–14C. Old French (Modern French *servante*), use as n. of pres.p. of *servir* SERVE. See also -ANT.

serve *v.t.* to act as servant to, to be in the employment of. *Also v.i., n.* WH: 12–14C. Old French *servir* or Latin *servire*, from *servus* slave.

service[1] *n.* the act of serving. *Also v.t., a.* WH: pre-1200. Old French *servise* (Modern French *service*), or from Latin *servitium* slavery, from *servus* slave. See also -ICE.

service[2] *n.* the service tree. WH: 16C. Orig. pl. of obs. *serve*, from Old English *syrfe*, ult. from Latin *sorbus*. Cp. SORB.

serviette *n.* a table napkin. WH: 15C. Old French towel, napkin, from *servir* SERVE. See also -ETTE.

servile *a.* cringing, fawning. WH: 14–15C. Latin *servilis*, from *servus* slave. See also -IL.

servitor *n.* a male servant or attendant. WH: 12–14C. Old French (Modern French *serviteur*), from Late Latin, from Latin *servitus*, p.p. of *servire* SERVE. See also -OR.

servitude *n.* the condition of a slave, slavery, bondage. WH: 14–15C. Old French, from Latin *servitudo*, from *servus* slave. See also -TUDE.

servo *n.* a servo-mechanism or servo-motor. WH: 19C. French *servo-moteur* servo-motor, from Latin *servus* slave + -o- -O- + French *moteur* MOTOR.

sesame *n.* an African plant, *Sesamum orientale*, with oily seeds used as food. WH: 14–15C. Latin *sesamum*, from Greek *sēsamon*, *sēsamē*, of Oriental orig. Cp. Arabic *simsim*.

sesqui- *comb. form* denoting a proportion of one-and-a-half to one or three to two. WH: Latin, from SEMI- + -que and.

sesquialtera *n.* an interval with the ratio of three to two, a perfect fifth. WH: 14–15C. Latin, fem. of *sesquialter*, from SESQUI- + *alter* second.

sesquicentenary *n.* a 150th anniversary. WH: mid-20C. SESQUI- + *centenary* (CENTENARIAN).

sesquipedal *a.* measuring a foot and a half. *Also n.* WH: 17C. Latin *sesquipedalis*, from SESQUI- + *pes*, *pedis* foot + -*alis* -AL[1].

sessile *a.* attached by the base, destitute of a stalk or peduncle. WH: 18C. Latin *sessilis*, from *sessus*, p.p. of *sedere* SIT. See also -IL.

session *n.* a sitting or meeting of a court, council etc. for the transaction of business. WH: 14–15C. Old French, or from Latin *sessio*, *sessionis*, from *sessus*. See SESSILE, also -ION.

sesterce *n.* an ancient Roman silver (afterwards bronze) coin and money of account worth 2½ asses or ¼ denarius. WH: 16C. Latin *sestertius* that is two and a half, from *semis* half + *tertius* third. See SEMI-, Cp. SESQUI-.

sestet *n.* the last six lines of a sonnet. WH: 19C. Italian *sestetto*, from *sesto*, from Latin *sextus* a sixth + -*etto* -ET[1].

sestina *n.* a form of verse consisting of six six-lined stanzas with a final triplet, each stanza having the same terminal words to the lines but in different order. WH: 19C. Italian, from *sesto*. See SESTET.

set[1] *v.t.* to place, to put. *Also v.i., a.* WH: pre-1200. Old English *settan*, from Germanic base also of SIT. Cp. SEIZE.

set[2] *n.* a number of similar, related or complementary things or persons, a group. WH: 14–15C. Old French *sette*, from Latin *secta* SECT, influ. by and merging with Old English *set* seat, place of the setting sun, from SET[1].

seta *n.* a bristle or bristle-like plant or animal part. WH: 18C. Latin bristle.

seton *n.* a twist of silk, cotton or similar material inserted in a wound to maintain drainage and as a counterirritant, esp. in veterinary surgery. WH: 14–15C. Medieval Latin *seto*, *setonis*, appar. from Latin *seta* bristle.

Setswana *n.* the Bantu language Tswana. *Also a.* WH: 19C. Setswana language pref. *se-* + TSWANA.

sett *n.* a small rectangular block of stone used for road paving. WH: 19C. Var. of SET[2].

settee *n.* a long seat with a back for several persons; a sofa. WH: 18C. ? Fanciful alt. of SETTLE[2]. See also -EE.

setterwort *n.* the bear's foot or stinking hellebore, *Helleborus foetidus*. WH: 16C. Middle Low German *siterwort*, from first element of unknown orig. + *wort* WORT.

settle[1] *v.t.* to place firmly, to put in a permanent or fixed position. *Also v.i.* WH: pre-1200. Old English *setlan*, from *setl* seat. See SETTLE[2].

settle[2] *n.* a long, high-backed seat or bench for several persons. WH: pre-1200. Old English *setl* seat, from Germanic, rel. to Latin *sella* seat. Cp. German *Sessel*.

seven *n.* the number or figure 7 or vii. *Also a.* WH: pre-1200. Old English *seofon*, from Germanic, from Indo-European base also of

Latin *septem*, Greek *hepta*, Old Church Slavonic *sedmĭ* (Russian *sem'*), Sanskrit *sapta*. Cp. German *sieben*.

seventeen *n.* the number or figure 17 or xvii. *Also a.* WH: pre-1200. Old English *seofontīene*, from Germanic base of SEVEN, -TEEN. Cp. German *siebzehn*.

seventh *n.* any one of seven equal parts. *Also a.* WH: pre-1200. Old English *seofotha*, replaced in Middle English by forms from SEVEN + -TH[1].

seventy *n.* the number or figure 70 or lxx. *Also a.* WH: pre-1200. Old English *hundseofontig*, from *hund* of unknown orig. + *seofon* SEVEN + -*tig* -TY[2]. The first element (*hund*) was lost early in Middle English. Cp. EIGHTY.

sever *v.t.* to part, to separate. *Also v.i.* WH: 12–14C. Old French *sevrer* (Modern French to wean), from Popular Latin *seperare*, from Latin *separare* SEPARATE[1].

several *a.* consisting of a number, more than two but not many. *Also n.* WH: 14–15C. Anglo-French, from Anglo-Latin *separalis*, from Latin *separ* SEPARATE[2]. See also -AL[1].

severe *a.* rigorous, strict. WH: 16C. Old French *sévère* or Latin *severus*.

severy *n.* a compartment in a vaulted ceiling. WH: 14–15C. Old French *civoire* ciborium.

Seville orange *n.* a bitter orange used to make marmalade. WH: 14–15C. Anglicized form of Spanish *Sevilla*, a city and province in SW Spain + ORANGE.

Sèvres *n.* porcelain made at Sèvres. WH: 18C. *Sèvres*, a town in N France (now a suburb of Paris), where it was originally made.

sew *v.t.* to fasten together by thread worked through and through with a needle. *Also v.i.* WH: pre-1200. Old English *siwan*, *siowan*, from Germanic, from Indo-European base represented also by Latin *suere*, Greek *kassuein*.

sewer *n.* a channel, underground conduit or tunnel for carrying off the drainage and liquid refuse of a town etc. WH: 12–14C. Old Northern French *seuwiere* channel for carrying off overflow from a fish pond, from Popular Latin *exaquaria*, from Latin EX- + *aquaria*, fem. of *aquarius*, from *aqua* water.

sewin *n.* a variety of sea or salmon trout. WH: 16C. Orig. unknown.

sex *n.* the sum total of the physiological, anatomical and functional characteristics which distinguish male and female. *Also v.t., a.* WH: 14–15C. Old French *sexe* or Latin *sexus*, ? rel. to *secare* to cut, to divide.

sex- *comb. form* containing six. WH: Latin *sex* six.

sexagenarian *a.* 60 years of age or between 60 and 70. *Also n.* WH: 18C. Latin *sexagenarius*, from *sexageni* sixty each, from *sexaginta* sixty. See also -ARIAN, -IAN.

Sexagesima *n.* the second Sunday before Lent. WH: 14–15C. Ecclesiastical Latin, fem. of Latin *sexagesimus* sixtieth, from *sexaginta* sixty, prob. based on QUINQUAGESIMA, QUADRAGESIMA. The day is so called as it falls about 60 days before Easter.

sexcentenary *a.* of, relating to or consisting of 600 years. *Also n.* WH: 18C. SEX- + *centenary* (CENTENARIAN).

sexennial *a.* occurring once every six years. WH: 17C. Latin *sexennis* or *sexennium* + -AL[1].

sexfoil *n.* a six-leaved flower, a six-lobed leaf. WH: 17C. SEX- + -*foil*, based on CINQUEFOIL, TREFOIL, etc. See FOIL[1].

sexivalent *a.* having a valency or combining power of six; hexavalent. WH: 19C. SEX- + -*i*- + -*valent*, from Latin *valens*, *valentis*, pres.p. of *valere* to be strong. See also -ENT.

sexpartite *a.* divided into six. WH: 18C. SEX- + PARTITE, based on BIPARTITE, TRIPARTITE, etc.

sexploitation *n.* the portrayal or manipulation of sex for financial profit in films, magazines etc. WH: mid-20C. Blend of SEX and *exploitation* (EXPLOIT[2]).

sext *n.* in the Roman Catholic Church, the office for the sixth hour or noon. WH: 14–15C. Latin *sexta* (*hora*) sixth (hour), fem. of *sextus* sixth. Cp. PRIME[1].

sextant *n.* the sixth part of a circle. WH: 16C. Latin *sextans*, *sextantis* sixth part, from *sextus* sixth. See -ANT. Cp. OCTANT, QUADRANT.

sextet *n.* a composition for six instruments or voices. WH: 19C. Alt. of SESTET, based on Latin *sex* six. See also -ET[1].

sextillion *n.* the seventh power of a thousand, 1 followed by 21 ciphers. **WH:** 17C. French, from Latin *sex* six, based on MILLION, BILLION, etc.

sexto *n.* a book formed by folding sheets into six leaves each. **WH:** 19C. Italian, abl. of *sextus* sixth. Cp. OCTAVO, QUARTO.

sexton *n.* an officer having the care of a church, its vessels, vestments etc., and frequently acting as parish clerk and a gravedigger. **WH:** 12–14C. Old French *segerstein, secrestein,* from Medieval Latin *sacristanus* SACRIST.

sextuple *a.* six times as many. Also *n., v.t., v.i.* **WH:** 17C. Medieval Latin *sextuplus,* from Latin *sex* six, based on Medieval Latin *quintuplus* quintuple.

sexual *a.* of, relating to or based on sex or the sexes or on the distinction of sexes. **WH:** 17C. Late Latin *sexualis,* from Latin *sexus* SEX. See also -AL¹.

sforzando *adv.* emphatically, with sudden vigour. Also *a., n.* **WH:** 19C. Italian, pres.p. of *sforzare* to use force.

sfumato *a.* (of art) with misty outlines. Also *n.* **WH:** 19C. Italian, p.p. of *sfumare* to shade off, from *s-* EX- + *fumare* to smoke.

sgraffito *n.* decoration by means of scratches through plaster or slip, revealing a differently coloured ground. **WH:** 18C. Italian, from *sgraffiare* to scratch away, with *s-* representing Latin EX-. Cp. GRAFFITI.

sh *int.* used to call for silence. **WH:** 19C. Imit. Cp. HUSH¹, SHUSH, WHISH³.

shabby *a.* ragged, threadbare. **WH:** 17C. Obs. *shab* scab, from Old English *sceabb* + -Y¹. Cp. SCAB.

shabrack *n.* the housing or saddle-cloth of a cavalry saddle. **WH:** 19C. German *Schabracke,* French *schabraque,* of E European orig. Cp. Turkish *çaprak.*

shack *n.* a rude cabin, esp. one built of logs. **WH:** 19C. ? Shortened form of Mexican Spanish *jacal,* Nahuatl *xacatli* wooden hut.

shackle *n.* a fetter or handcuff. Also *v.t.* **WH:** pre-1200. Old English *sceacul,* from Germanic base represented also by Old English *sceac.* See also -LE¹. No related words are known outside Germanic.

shad *n.* any of several anadromous deep-bodied food-fish of the genus *Alosa,* esp. the American or white shad. **WH:** pre-1200. Old English *sceadd,* of unknown orig.

shaddock *n.* the large orange-like fruit of a Malaysian and Polynesian tree, *Citrus grandis.* **WH:** 17C. Captain *Shaddock,* 17C English ship commander, who brought the fruit from the E Indies to Barbados in 1696.

shade *n.* obscurity or partial darkness caused by the interception of the rays of light. Also *v.t., v.i.* **WH:** pre-1200. Old English *sceadu* (fem.), *scead* (neut.). The Old English word's oblique cases are represented by SHADOW.

shadoof *n.* a water-raising contrivance consisting of a long pole with bucket and counterpoise, used on the Nile etc. **WH:** 19C. Egyptian Arabic *šādūf.*

shadow *n.* shade. Also *v.t.* **WH:** pre-1200. Old English *sceaduwe,* oblique forms of *sceadu* SHADE, from Germanic, from Indo-European. Cp. Greek *skotos* darkness.

shaft *n.* the slender stem of a spear, arrow etc. Also *v.t.* **WH:** pre-1200. Old English *scæft, sceaft,* from Germanic, ? rel. to Latin *scapus* shaft, Greek *skapton* staff, *skēptron* SCEPTRE. Cp. German *Schaft.*

shag *n.* a rough coat of hair, a bushy mass. Also *a., v.t., v.i.* **WH:** pre-1200. Old English *sceaga,* rel. to Old Norse *skegg* beard, from Germanic. The word is related to *shaw* thicket, small wood (from Old English *sceaga*) in such place names as *Birkenshaw, Wishaw.*

shagreen *n.* a kind of leather with a granular surface which is prepared without tanning from the skins of horses, asses, camels, sharks and seals, usu. dyed green. **WH:** 17C. Var. of CHAGRIN.

shah *n.* a sovereign of Iran. **WH:** 16C. Persian *šāh,* from Old Persian *kšāyaṭiya* king.

shake *v.t.* to move forcibly or rapidly to and fro or up and down. Also *v.i., n.* **WH:** pre-1200. Old English *sceacan,* from Germanic. No related words are known for certain outside Germanic.

Shakespearean *a.* of, relating to or resembling Shakespeare or his style. Also *n.* **WH:** 18C. William *Shakespeare,* 1564–1616, English playwright and poet + -AN.

shako *n.* a military cylindrical hat, usu. flat-topped, with a peak in front, usu. tilting forward, and decorated with a pompom, plume or tuft. **WH:** 19C. French *schako,* from Hungarian *csákó,* prob. from German *Zacken* peak, point, spike.

shakuhachi *n.* a Japanese bamboo flute. **WH:** 19C. Japanese, from *shaku* a unit of length (approximately 0.33 m) + *hachi* eight (tenths).

shale *n.* a laminated argillaceous rock resembling soft slate, often containing much bitumen. **WH:** 18C. Prob. from German *Schale* (as in *Schalstein* laminated limestone, *Schalgebirge* layer of stone in stratified rock), rel. to SHELL.

shall *v.aux.* (in the 1st pers.) used to express simple futurity or a conditional statement or (stressed) strong intention. **WH:** pre-1200. Old English *sceal* (pres.), *sceolde* (past), from a Germanic v. orig. meaning to owe. Cp. German *(ich) soll* (I) shall, (I) am to; *(ich) sollte* (I) should, (I) was to.

shallot *n.* a plant, *Allium ascalonicum,* allied to garlic with similar but milder-flavoured bulbs. **WH:** 17C. Shortening of ESCHALOT.

shallow *a.* not having much depth. Also *n., v.i., v.t.* **WH:** 14–15C. Rel. to SHOAL².

shalom *n., int.* peace (a greeting used esp. by Jewish people). **WH:** 19C. Hebrew *šālōm* peace.

sham *v.t.* to feign, to make a pretence of. Also *v.i., n., a.* **WH:** 17C. ? Dial. var. of SHAME.

shamanism *n.* a form of religion based on the belief in good and evil spirits which can be influenced by shamans, prevailing among some Siberian and N American peoples. **WH:** 18C. From *shaman* priest with healing and magical powers (from German *Schamane,* Russian *shaman,* from Tungusian *šaman*) + -ISM.

shamateur *n.* a person classed as an amateur in sport, but who accepts payment. **WH:** 19C. SHAM + AMATEUR.

shamble *v.i.* to walk in an awkward, shuffling or unsteady manner. Also *n.* **WH:** 16C. Prob. from *shamble* stool, table, bench. See SHAMBLES.

shambles *n.* utter confusion, a disorganized mess. **WH:** 14–15C. Pl. of *shamble* stool, table, bench, from Old English *sceamul,* from Germanic, from Latin *scamellum,* dim. of *scamnum* bench. The original meaning (as a plural noun) was a row of stalls for the sale of meat or fish, i.e. meat market, fish market. The senses then evolved as follows: slaughterhouse (16C), scene of wholesale bloodshed (16C), scene of devastation and disorder (early 20C).

shambolic *a.* chaotic, utterly confused. **WH:** late 20C. SHAMBLES, in an adjectival form. appar. based on that of *symbolic* (SYMBOL).

shame *n.* a painful feeling due to consciousness of guilt, humiliation etc. Also *v.t., v.i.* **WH:** pre-1200. Old English *sceamu,* from Germanic. Cp. German *Scham.*

shampoo *v.t.* to wash with shampoo. Also *n.* **WH:** 18C. Hindi *cā̃po,* imper. of *cā̃pnā* to press, to knead. The original sense was to massage (as part of the process of a Turkish bath). The sense to wash the hair evolved in the 19C.

shamrock *n.* a species of trefoil, esp. *Trifolium minus, T. repens* or *Medicago lupulina,* forming the national emblem of Ireland. **WH:** 16C. Irish *seamróg,* dim. of *seamar* clover.

shamus *n.* a detective. **WH:** early 20C. Orig. uncertain. ? From Irish male forename *Séamus.*

Shan *n.* a member of a people living on the borders of N Thailand, E Burma (Myanmar) and Yunnan province (China). Also *a.* **WH:** 19C. Burmese.

shandy *n.* a mixture of beer and ginger beer or lemonade. **WH:** 19C. Abbr. of *shandygaff,* of unknown orig.

shanghai *v.t.* to drug and ship as a sailor while stupefied. Also *n.* **WH:** 19C. *Shanghai,* a city and seaport in E China. The reference is to the former practice of kidnapping sailors to serve on ships bound for the Far East.

Shangri-La *n.* a paradise on earth. **WH:** mid-20C. Name of a Tibetan utopia set in a hidden valley in James Hilton's novel *Lost Horizon* (1933). The second part of the name is Tibetan *la* mountain pass.

shank *n.* the leg, esp. the part from the knee to the ankle. Also *v.i.* **WH:** pre-1200. Old English *sceanca,* from Germanic. Cp. German *Schenkel* thigh.

shanny *n.* a blenny, *Blennius pholis.* **WH:** 19C. Orig. unknown.

shantung *n.* a plain fabric woven in coarse silk yarns. **WH:** 19C. *Shantung,* a province in NE China, where orig. manufactured.

shanty[1] *n.* a rude hut or cabin. WH: 19C. ? Canadian French *chantier* lumberjack's log cabin, logging camp.

shanty[2] *n.* a song sung by sailors, esp. one with a strong rhythm sung while working. WH: 19C. Prob. from French *chantez*, imper. of *chanter* to sing.

shape *v.t.* to form, to create. *Also v.i., n.* WH: pre-1200. Old English *sceppan*, from Germanic. Cp. German *schaffen* to create.

shard *n.* a potsherd. *Also v.t.*, *v.i.* WH: pre-1200. Old English *sceard*, from Germanic base also of SHEAR.

share[1] *n.* a part or portion detached from a common amount or stock. *Also v.t., v.i.* WH: pre-1200. Old English *scearu*, from Germanic, from base also of SHEAR. Cp. SHARE[2].

share[2] *n.* a ploughshare. WH: pre-1200. Old English *scær, scear*, from Germanic, from base also of SHEAR. Cp. SHARE[1].

sharia *n.* the body of Islamic religious law. WH: 19C. Arabic *šarī'a*.

shark *n.* a selachoid sea fish of various species with lateral gill openings and an inferior mouth, mostly large and voracious and armed with formidable teeth. *Also v.i., v.t.* WH: 14–15C. Orig. uncertain. The sense worthless rogue evolved in the 16C and is perhaps from German *Schurke*. Cp. SHIRK.

sharon fruit *n.* a kind of persimmon. WH: late 20C. Plain of *Sharon*, Israel, noted for its citrus fruits.

sharp *a.* having a keen edge or fine point. *Also adv., n., v.t., v.i.* WH: pre-1200. Old English *scearp*, from Germanic. Cp. German *scharf*.

shashlik *n.* a lamb kebab. WH: early 20C. Russian *shashlyk*, from Crimean Turkish *şişlik*, from *şiş* skewer. Cp. SHISH KEBAB.

Shasta daisy *n.* a Pyrenean plant, *Leucanthemum maximum*, which has white daisy-like flowers. WH: 19C. Mt *Shasta*, N California, USA. The mountain is itself named from the *Shasta* American Indian people.

Shastra *n.* any of the Vedas and other sacred scriptures of Hinduism. WH: 17C. Sanskrit *śāstra*, lit. instruction, from *śāsti* he punishes, he instructs.

shatter *v.t.* to break up at once into many pieces. *Also v.i.* WH: 12–14C. ? Of imit. orig., with freq. ending. See also -ER[5]. Cp. SCATTER.

shave *v.t.* to remove hair from (the face, a person etc.) with a razor. *Also v.i., n.* WH: pre-1200. Old English *sceafan*, from Germanic. Cp. German *schaben* to scrape.

Shavian *a.* of, relating to or characteristic of the writings of George Bernard Shaw. *Also n.* WH: early 20C. *Shavius*, latinized form of the surname *Shaw*, from George Bernard *Shaw*, 1856–1950, Irish-born dramatist and critic + -IAN.

Shavuoth *n.* the Jewish Pentecost. WH: 19C. Hebrew *šāḇū'ōt*, pl. of *šāḇūā'* week. The name refers to the weeks between Passover and Pentecost. Hence the English name, Feast of Weeks.

shaw *n.* the stalk and leaves of a root-crop plant, e.g. a potato. WH: 19C. Orig. uncertain. ? Var. of SHOW.

shawl *n.* a square or oblong garment worn chiefly by women as a loose wrap for the upper part of the person. *Also v.t.* WH: 17C. Persian and Urdu *šāl*.

shawm *n.* an ancient wind instrument similar to the oboe. WH: 12–14C. Old French *chalemel* (Modern French *chalumeau*), ult. from Latin *calamus* reed, from Greek *kalamos*.

shchi *n.* cabbage soup. WH: 19C. Russian, ? rel. to BORSCH.

she *pron.* the female person, animal or personified thing mentioned or referred to. *Also n., a.* WH: 12–14C. Prob. a phonetic development of Old English *hīo, hēo*, fem. of *hē* HE. The new form would have evolved to avoid confusion between the masculine and feminine pronouns.

s/he *pron.* a written representation of 'he or she'. WH: late 20C. Blend of SHE and HE.

shea *n.* a tropical African tree, *Vitellaria paradoxa*, yielding a kind of butter. WH: 18C. Mande *si, se*.

sheading *n.* any one of the six divisions of the Isle of Man. WH: 16C. Var. of *shedding*, from SHED[1] + -ING[1].

sheaf *n.* a quantity of things bound or held together lengthwise, esp. a bundle of wheat, oats, barley etc. *Also v.t.* WH: pre-1200. Old English *scēaf*, from Germanic, from base also of SHOVE. Cp. German *Schaub*.

shear *v.t.* to cut or clip with shears. *Also v.i., n.* WH: pre-1200. Old English *sceran*, from Germanic base meaning to cut, to divide, to shear, to shave. Cp. German *scheren*.

sheatfish *n.* a large catfish, *Silurus glanis*, the largest European freshwater fish. WH: 16C. Alt. of SHEATH + FISH[1]. The fish is apparently so named from its resemblance in shape to a scabbard.

sheath *n.* a case for a blade, weapon or tool, a scabbard. WH: pre-1200. Old English *scǣth, scēath*, from Germanic, prob. from base also of SHED[1].

sheave[1] *n.* the grooved wheel in a block or pulley over which the rope runs. WH: 12–14C. Corr. to Old Frisian *skīve*, Old High German *scība* (German *Scheibe*), from Germanic base meaning disc, wheel, pulley. The word probably existed in Old English but has not been recorded.

sheave[2] *v.t.* to gather into sheaves, to sheaf. WH: 16C. From *sheaves*, pl. of SHEAF.

shebang *n.* a business, concern, affair. WH: 19C. Orig. unknown. According to some, the word is a variant of CHARABANC. The phrase *the whole shebang* would thus relate to hiring the whole vehicle rather than one or two seats.

Shebat *n.* the eleventh ecclesiastical month, or fifth civil month, of the Jewish year (corresponding to parts of January and February). WH: 16C. Hebrew *šěḇaṭ*.

shebeen *n.* a low public house. WH: 18C. Irish *síbín*, ? var. of *séibín*, dim. of *séibe* bottle, mug, liquid measure.

shechita *n.* the Jewish manner of killing animals for food. WH: 19C. Hebrew *šěḥīṭāh*, from *šāḥaṭ* to slaughter.

shed[1] *v.t.* to let fall, to drop. *Also v.i., n.* WH: pre-1200. Old English *scēadan, scādan*, from Germanic. Cp. SHEATH.

shed[2] *n.* a slight, simple building, usu. a roofed structure with the ends or ends and sides open. *Also v.t.* WH: 15C. Appar. var. of SHADE.

sheen *n.* brightness, splendour. *Also a.* WH: pre-1200. Old English *scēne* beautiful, bright, from Germanic base also of SHOW. Cp. German *schön*. The noun evolved from the adjective in the 12–14C on the assumption it was related to SHINE.

sheep *n.* a gregarious ruminant animal of the genus *Ovis*, esp. the domesticated *O. aries*, or any of its numerous breeds, reared for the sake of their flesh and wool. WH: pre-1200. Old English *scēp, scǣp, scēap*, from Germanic. Cp. German *Schaf*. No related words outside Germanic are known.

sheer[1] *a.* pure, absolute. *Also adv.* WH: 12–14C. Prob. alt. of obs. *shire* bright, shining, from Old English *scīr*, from Germanic base also of SHINE.

sheer[2] *v.i.* to deviate from a course. *Also n.* WH: 17C. ? Middle Low German *scheren*, rel. to SHEAR.

sheerlegs *n.* an apparatus consisting of two masts, or legs, secured at the top, for hoisting heavy weights, esp. in dockyards. WH: 19C. SHEAR + LEG + -S[1].

sheet[1] *n.* a thin, flat, broad piece of anything, esp. a rectangular piece of linen, cotton or nylon used in a bed to keep the blankets etc. from a sleeper's body. *Also v.t., v.i.* WH: pre-1200. Old English *scēte, scīete*, from Germanic base also of SHEET[2], SHOOT, SHOT[1]. One sense of the Germanic base common to all words was to project.

sheet[2] *n.* a rope attached to the clew of a sail for moving, extending it etc. WH: pre-1200. Old English *scēat, scēata*, from Germanic base also of SHEET[1].

sheik *n.* the head of a Bedouin family, clan or tribe. WH: 16C. Ult. from Arabic *šayḵ* old man, elder, from *šāḵa* to be old, to grow old.

sheila *n.* a girl, a young woman. WH: 19C. Orig. uncertain. Later assim. to female forename *Sheila*.

shekel *n.* the main unit of currency of Israel. WH: 16C. Hebrew *šeqel*, from *šāqal* to weigh.

Shekinah *n.* the visible presence of Jehovah above the mercy-seat in the Tabernacle and Solomon's Temple. WH: 17C. Late Hebrew *šěḵīnāh*, from *šākan* to rest, to dwell.

sheldrake *n.* a large wild duck with vivid plumage, of the genus *Tadorna* or *Cascarca*, esp. *T. tadorna*, breeding on sandy coasts. WH: 12–14C. Prob. from *sheld-duck* (from *sheld-* variegated + DUCK[1]) + DRAKE[1]. The reference would be to the vividly contrasting colours of the plumage, common to both sexes.

shelf[1] *n.* a horizontal board or slab set in a wall or forming one of a series in a bookcase, cupboard etc., for standing vessels, books etc. on. WH: 12–14C. Middle Low German *schelf*, rel. to Old English *scylfe* partition, compartment, *scylf* crag, pinnacle.

shelf[2] *n.* an informer. *Also v.t.* WH: early 20C. SHELF[1]. The allusion may be to the phrase *on the shelf* in the sense out of the way.

shell *n.* a hard outside covering etc. *Also v.t., v.i.* WH: pre-1200. Old English *scell, sciell*, from Germanic. Cp. SCALE[1], SHALE.

shellac *n.* a thermoplastic resin obtained by purifying the resinous excreta of certain jungle insects, used in the manufacture of varnishes. *Also v.t.* WH: 17C. SHELL + LAC, translating French *laque en écailles* lac in thin plates.

Shelta *n.* a secret jargon made up largely of Gaelic or Irish words, used by tinkers, beggars etc. WH: 19C. Orig. unknown.

shelter *n.* anything that covers or shields from injury, danger etc. *Also v.t., v.i.* WH: 16C. Orig. uncertain. ? Alt. of obs. *sheltron* close formation of troops, from Old English *scieldtruma*, from *scield* SHIELD + *truma* troop. The original sense is that of a body of men protected by their shields locked to form a roof and a wall.

shelty *n.* a Shetland pony or sheepdog. WH: 16C. Prob. representation of Orkney pronun. of Old Norse *Hjalti* Shetlander.

shelve[1] *v.t.* to place on a shelf or shelves. WH: 16C. From *shelves*, pl. of SHELF[1].

shelve[2] *v.i.* to slope gradually. WH: 14–15C. Orig. uncertain. ? From SHELF[1].

shemozzle *n.* an uproar, a violent row. WH: 19C. Yiddish, prob. var. of SCHLIMAZEL.

shenanigan *n.* trickery, deception. WH: 19C. Orig. unknown. ? From Irish *sionnachuighim* to play tricks, to be foxy, from *sionnach* fox.

Sheol *n.* the Hebrew place of the dead, often translated 'hell' in the Authorized Version. WH: 16C. Hebrew *še'ōl*.

shepherd *n.* a person employed to tend sheep at pasture. *Also v.t.* WH: pre-1200. Old English *scēaphierde*, from *scēap* SHEEP + *hierde* herder.

sherardize *v.t.* to coat (iron or steel) with zinc by heating it in a container with zinc dust. WH: early 20C. *Sherard* O. Cowper-Coles, 1867–1936, English chemist + -IZE.

Sheraton *a.* (of furniture) of a severe style designed and introduced into England by Sheraton towards the end of the 18th cent. *Also n.* WH: 19C. Thomas *Sheraton*, 1751–1806, English furniture-maker and designer.

sherbet *n.* an effervescent powder used in sweets or to make fizzy drinks. WH: 17C. Turkish *şerbet*, Persian *šerbet*, from Arabic *šarbat* draught, drink, from *šariba* to drink. Cp. SHRUB[2], SYRUP.

sherif *n.* a descendant of Muhammad through his daughter Fatima and Hassan Ibn Ali. WH: 16C. Arabic *šarīf* noble, high-born.

sheriff *n.* the chief Crown officer of a county or shire charged with the keeping of the peace, the execution of writs, sentences etc., the conduct of elections etc., a High Sheriff. WH: pre-1200. Old English *scīrgerēfa*, from *scīr* SHIRE + *gerēfa* REEVE[1]. The sheriff was originally the representative of the royal authority in a shire.

Sherpa *n.* a member of a mountaineering people living on the southern slopes of the Himalayas. WH: 19C. Tibetan *sharpa* inhabitant of an eastern country.

sherry *n.* a fortified Spanish white wine. WH: 16C. Alt. of obs. *sherris* (taken as pl.), representing former pronun. of *Xeres* (now Jerez de la Frontera), a town in SE Spain, the original place of production.

Shetland *n.* a Shetland pony. WH: 18C. *Shetland*, a group of islands NE of mainland Scotland.

sheva *n.* the Hebrew sign (:) put under a consonant to denote the absence of a following vowel sound. WH: 16C. Hebrew *šěwā'*, appar. arbitrary alt. of *šāw'* emptiness, variety. The Hebrew word was formerly spelt *Schwa* in German books, giving SCHWA.

Shia *n.* one of the two main branches of Islam (see also SUNNA), which regards Ali (Muhammad's cousin and son-in-law) as the first rightful imam or caliph and rejects the three Sunni caliphs. *Also a.* WH: 17C. Arabic *šī'a* faction, party (i.e. of Ali).

shiatsu *n.* a massage in which pressure is applied to the acupuncture points of the body. WH: mid-20C. Japanese, lit. finger pressure.

shibboleth *n.* a criterion, test or watchword of a party etc. WH: 17C. Hebrew *šibbōleṭ* ear of corn, stream in flood, used as a test of

nationality for foreigners who have difficulty in pronouncing *sh*. The word was said to have been used by the Gileadites to distinguish their own men from the fleeing Ephraimites: 'Then said they unto him, Say now Shibboleth: and he said Sibboleth: for he could not frame to pronounce it right' (Judg. xii.6).

shicer *n.* a crook, a welsher. WH: 19C. German *Scheisser*, lit. shitter, contemptible person. See also -ER[1]. Cp. SHIT, SHYSTER.

shicker *a.* drunk. *Also n.* WH: 19C. Yiddish *shiker*, from Hebrew *šikkōr*, from *šākar* to be drunk.

shield *n.* a broad piece of defensive armour made of wood, leather or metal, usu. carried on the left arm to protect the body, usu. straight across the top and tapering to a point at the bottom. *Also v.t.* WH: pre-1200. Old English *sceld, scield*, from a Germanic word prob. meaning board, from a base meaning to divide, to separate. Rel. to SHELL.

shieling *n.* a hut used by shepherds, sportsmen etc. WH: 16C. Dial. *shiel*, of unknown orig. + -ING[1].

shift *v.t.* to move from one position to another. *Also v.i., n.* WH: pre-1200. Old English *sciftan*, from Germanic base represented also in Old Norse *skipa* to arrange, to assign. Cp. German *schichten* to arrange in layers.

shigella *n.* any bacterium of the genus *Shigella*, some of which cause dysentery in human beings. WH: mid-20C. Modern Latin, from Kiyoshi *Shiga*, 1870–1957, Japanese bacteriologist + -*ella* as in SALMONELLA.

shih-tzu *n.* a small dog with long silky hair, of a Tibetan and Chinese breed. WH: early 20C. Chinese *shīzigǒu*, from *shīzi* lion + *gǒu* dog.

shiitake *n.* a mushroom, *Lentinus edodes*, used in Oriental cookery. WH: 19C. Japanese, from *shii* a kind of oak + *take* mushroom.

shikar *n.* hunting, sport, game. WH: 17C. Persian and Urdu *šikār*.

shiksa *n.* a non-Jewish woman. WH: 19C. Yiddish *shikse*, from Hebrew *šiqṣāh*, from *šeqeṣ* detested thing + fem. suf. -*āh*.

shill *n.* a decoy or person employed to entice others into buying etc. WH: early 20C. ? Abbr. of *shillaber*, of unknown orig.

shillelagh *n.* an oak or blackthorn sapling used as a cudgel. WH: 18C. *Shillelagh*, a town in Co. Wicklow, Ireland. The cudgels would have been cut from the wood there.

shilling *n.* a former British silver (or, later, cupronickel), coin and money of account, equal in value to twelve old pence (five new pence). WH: pre-1200. Old English *scilling*, from Germanic, ? from Indo-European **skel-* to divide, to split. Cp. SCHILLING.

shilly-shally *v.i.* to act in an irresolute manner, to hesitate. *Also n., a.* WH: 18C. Orig. *shill I shall I*, redupl. of *shall I*. Cp. DILLY-DALLY.

shim *n.* a wedge, piece of metal etc., used to tighten up joints, fill in spaces etc. *Also v.t.* WH: 18C. Orig. unknown.

shimmer *v.i.* to emit a faint or tremulous light. *Also n.* WH: pre-1200. Old English *scymrian*, from Germanic base also of SHINE. See also -ER[5]. Cp. German *schimmern*.

shimmy *n.* a chemise. *Also v.i.* WH: 19C. Alt. of CHEMISE.

shin *n.* the forepart of the human leg between the ankle and the knee. *Also v.i., v.t.* WH: pre-1200. Old English *scinu*, prob. ult. from a Germanic word meaning thin piece, narrow piece. Cp. German *Schiene* thin plate.

shindig *n.* a noisy or rowdy ball or dance. WH: 19C. Orig. uncertain. ? From SHIN + DIG, but influ. by SHINDY. The original sense was a blow on the shins, but the sense noisy dance followed soon after.

shindy *n.* a row, a disturbance, a rumpus, a brawl. WH: 19C. ? Alt. of SHINTY.

shine *v.i.* to emit or reflect rays of light. *Also v.t., n.* WH: pre-1200. Old English *scīnan*, from Germanic. Cp. German *scheinen*.

shingle[1] *n.* a thin piece of wood laid in overlapping rows as a roof-covering. *Also v.t.* WH: 12–14C. Appar. from Latin *scindula*, earlier *scandula* a split piece of wood, based on Greek *skhidax*. The sense to cut hair in a style like overlapping shingles evolved in the 19C.

shingle[2] *n.* coarse rounded gravel on the seashore. WH: 14–15C. Orig. unknown. ? Imit. An earlier spelling was *chingle*. Cp. CHINK[2].

shingles *n.pl.* a viral infection, *Herpes zoster*, marked by pain and inflammation of the skin along the path of an affected nerve (usu. on the chest or abdomen). WH: 14–15C. Representation of Medieval Latin *cingulus*, var. of *cingulum* girdle, translating Greek *zōnē*, *zōstēr*. See ZOSTER.

shinny *v.i.* to shin (up, down). WH: 19C. SHIN + -Y³.

Shinto *n.* the indigenous religion of the people of Japan existing along with Buddhism, a species of nature- and ancestor-worship. WH: 18C. Japanese *shin* gods + *tō* way.

shinty *n.* a game somewhat resembling hockey, played by teams of twelve people. WH: 18C. Said to come from the cries of the game, *shin ye, shin you, shin t'ye*, of unknown orig.

ship *n.* a large seagoing vessel. *Also v.t., v.i.* WH: pre-1200. Old English *scip*, from Germanic. Cp. SKIFF¹, SKIPPER.

-ship *suf.* denoting state, condition, the quality of being so-and-so, as in *fellowship, friendship*. WH: Old English *-scipe, -scype*, from German base also of SHAPE. Cp. Germanic *-schaft*, Dutch *-schap* (as in LANDSCAPE).

shiralee *n.* a swag, a tramp's bundle. WH: 19C. Orig. unknown.

shire *n.* an administrative division of England, a county, esp. one whose name ends in '-shire'. WH: pre-1200. Old English *scīr* administrative office. Cp. Old High German *scīra* care, official charge. See also SHERIFF. The word is not related to SHEAR (as if a district 'shorn' off) or SHARE¹ (as if one resulting from a partition).

shirk *v.t.* to avoid or get out of unfairly. *Also v.i., n.* WH: 17C. Rel. to obs. *shirk* swindler, SHARK. The original sense was to practise fraud or trickery. The sense to avoid (work etc.) dates from the 18C.

shirr *n.* an elastic cord or thread inserted in cloth etc. to make it elastic. *Also v.t.* WH: 19C. Orig. unknown.

shirt *n.* a loose garment of linen, cotton, wool, silk or other material, extending from the neck to the thighs, and usu. showing at the collar and wristbands, worn by men and boys under the outer clothes. WH: pre-1200. Old English *scyrte*, from Germanic base also of SHORT. Rel. to SKIRT. Cp. German *Schürze* apron.

shish kebab *n.* a skewer of marinated and cooked meat and vegetables. WH: early 20C. Turkish *şiş kebab*, from *şiş* skewer + KEBAB. Cp. SHASHLIK.

shit *v.i.* to empty the bowels. *Also n., int.* WH: pre-1200. Corr. to Middle Low German *schīten*, Old High German *scīzan* (German *scheissen*), from Germanic. The word was probably already in Old English, but is not recorded as a verb. Cp. the corresponding Old English noun *scitte*. The sense obnoxious person evolved in the 16C. Cp. TURD.

shittim *n.* the wood of the shittah tree used in constructing the Ark of the Covenant and the tabernacle. WH: 14–15C. Hebrew *šiṭṭīm*, pl. of *šiṭṭāh* shittah tree (a kind of acacia).

shiver¹ *v.i.* to tremble or shake, as with fear, cold or excitement. *Also n.* WH: 12–14C. Orig. uncertain. ? Alt. of obs. *chavel* to talk idly, to chatter (from alt. of JOWL), with -ER⁵ substituted for *-el*.

shiver² *n.* a tiny fragment, a sliver. *Also v.t., v.i.* WH: 12–14C. Corr. to Old High German *scivaro* splinter (German *Schiefer* slate), from Germanic. The word was probably already in Old English, but has not been recorded.

shivoo *n.* a (noisy) party. WH: 19C. Var. of dial. *shiveau*, of unknown orig.

shoal¹ *n.* a large number, a multitude, a crowd, esp. of fish moving together. *Also v.i.* WH: 16C. Prob. from Middle Low German, Middle Dutch *schōle*. See SCHOOL².

shoal² *a.* (of water) shallow, of little depth. *Also n., v.i.* WH: pre-1200. Old English *sceald*, from Germanic base also of SHALLOW.

shoat *n.* a young hog. WH: 14–15C. Orig. uncertain. Cp. W Flemish *schoteling* pig under one year old.

shochet *n.* a slaughterer who is qualified to prepare meat and poultry according to Jewish ritual. WH: 19C. Hebrew *šōḥēṭ*, pres.p. of *šāḥaṭ* to slaughter. Cp. SHECHITA.

shock¹ *n.* an impact, a blow. *Also v.t., v.i.* WH: 16C. French *choc*, from *choquer*, corr. to Spanish *chocar*, of unknown orig.

shock² *n.* a collection of sheaves of grain, usu. twelve but varying in number. *Also v.i.* WH: 12–14C. Anglo-Latin *socca, scoka*, either representing an unrecorded Old English word or from Middle Low German, Middle Dutch *schok* shock of corn, group of 60 units (cp. German *Schock* three score), ult. of unknown orig. Cp. SHOCK³.

shock³ *n.* a thick, bushy mass or head of hair. *Also a.* WH: 17C. Orig. uncertain. ? Fig. use of SHOCK² or rel. to SHAG. Some authorities derive the word from obsolete *shough* a breed of lapdog, perhaps itself from this same word in the original sense of hairy dog. The sense bushy head of hair dates from the 19C.

shoddy *a.* inferior. *Also n.* WH: 19C. Orig. unknown.

shoe *n.* an outer covering for the foot, esp. one distinguished from a boot by not coming up to the ankles. *Also v.t.* WH: pre-1200. Old English *scōh*, from Germanic. Cp. German *Schuh*. No related words outside Germanic are known.

shofar *n.* a trumpet made from a ram's horn used in Jewish religious ceremonies and as a battle-signal in ancient times. WH: 19C. Hebrew *šōpār*.

shogun *n.* the hereditary commander-in-chief of the army and virtual ruler of Japan under the feudal regime, abolished in 1868. WH: 17C. Japanese *shōgun*, from Chinese *jiāng jūn* army general.

shoji *n.* a paper screen forming a wall or partition in a Japanese home. WH: 19C. Japanese *shōji*.

shonky *a.* unreliable; unsound. *Also n.* WH: late 20C. ? From *shonk* Jew (alt. of *shonicker*, of uncertain orig.) + -Y¹.

shoo *int.* begone, be off. *Also v.t., v.i.* WH: 14–15C. Natural exclamation.

shook *n.* a set of staves and headings for a cask ready for setting up. *Also v.t.* WH: 18C. Orig. uncertain. ? From *shook*, p.p. of SHAKE.

shoot *v.i.* to go or come (out, along, up etc.) swiftly. *Also v.t., n., int.* WH: pre-1200. Old English *scēotan*, from Germanic base also of Old English *scēat, scīete* (SHEET¹, SHEET²), *scot* SHOT¹, *scotian* to shoot with arrows, *scyttan* SHUT. Cp. SHOUT. The sense young branch springing from a tree arose in the 14–15C, and that of rush of water down a steep place in the 17C. Cp. CHUTE¹.

shop *n.* a building in which goods are sold by retail. *Also v.i., v.t.* WH: 12–14C. Shortening of Old French *eschoppe* (Modern French *échoppe*) lean-to booth, cobbler's stall, from Middle Low German *schoppe*, corr. to Old English *sceoppa* translating Late Latin *gazophylacium* treasury (of the temple), Old High German *scopf* porch, vestibule (German *Schopf* porch, lean-to), rel. to Old English *scypen, shippon*, cattle-shed, cowhouse.

shoran *n.* a system of aircraft navigation using two radar signals. WH: mid-20C. Abbr. of *short-range* navigation. Cp. LORAN.

shore¹ *n.* the land on the borders of a large body of water, the sea, a lake etc. WH: 12–14C. Middle Low German and Middle Dutch *schōre*, ? from base of SHEAR.

shore² *n.* a prop, a stay. *Also v.t.* WH: 12–14C. Middle Low German and Middle Dutch *schōre*, prop, stay.

short *a.* measuring little in linear extension, not long. *Also adv., n., v.t., v.i.* WH: pre-1200. Old English *sceort*, from Germanic. Cp. SHIRT, SKIRT. The word is ultimately related to SHEAR and CURT.

shot¹ *n.* a missile for a firearm, esp. a solid or non-explosive projectile. *Also v.t.* WH: pre-1200. Old English *sceot, scot*, from Germanic base of SHOOT. Cp. SCOT.

shot² *a.* that has been shot. WH: 14–15C. P.p. of SHOOT. The sense as applied to silk dates from the 18C and alludes to the way the warp threads and woof threads of the fabric have been woven ('shot') across each other.

shot³ *n.* a reckoning, a bill. WH: 14–15C. SHOT¹.

shotten *a.* (of a herring etc.) having ejected the spawn. WH: 14–15C. Old p.p. of SHOOT. Cp. SHOT².

shoulder *n.* the part of the body at which the arm, foreleg or wing is attached to the trunk. *Also v.t., v.i.* WH: pre-1200. Old English *sculdor*, from Germanic, of unknown orig. Cp. German *Schulter*.

shout *n.* a loud, vehement and sudden call or expression of a strong emotion such as anger or joy. *Also v.i., v.t.* WH: 14–15C. ? Rel. to SHOOT. Cp. Old Norse *skúta* taunt.

shove *v.t.* to push, to move forcibly along. *Also v.i., n.* WH: pre-1200. Old English *scūfan*, from Germanic. Cp. SCUFFLE, SHUFFLE.

shovel *n.* an implement consisting of a wide blade or scoop with a handle, used for shifting loose material. *Also v.t.* WH: pre-1200. Old English *scofl*, from Germanic base of SHOVE. Cp. German *Schaufel*.

shovelboard *n.* a game played (now usu. on a ship's deck) by shoving wooden discs with the hand or a mace towards marked compartments. WH: 16C. Alt. of earlier obs. *shoveboard*, from SHOVE + BOARD.

show *v.t.* to cause or allow to be seen, to reveal. *Also v.i., n.* WH: pre-1200. Old English *scēawian*, from a Germanic v. meaning to see, to look. Cp. German *schauen* to look. The original sense (to the 12–14C) was to look at, to inspect, to read (in a book).

shower *n.* a fall of rain, hail or snow of short duration. *Also v.t., v.i.* WH: pre-1200. Old English *scūr*, from Germanic. Cp. German *Schauer*.

shrapnel *n.* bullets enclosed in a shell with a small charge for bursting in front of the enemy and spreading in a shower. WH: 19C. General Henry *Shrapnel*, 1761–1842, British soldier, its inventor in *c.*1803.

shred *n.* a piece torn off. *Also v.t.* WH: pre-1200. Old English *scrēad*, from a Germanic word rel. to base of SHROUD. Cp. German *Schrot* meal (of corn, etc.), shot (lead pellets). The original sense was fragment, broken piece. The sense torn scrap of fabric arose in the 12–14C.

shrew *n.* a small mouselike mammal of the family Soricidae. WH: pre-1200. Old English *scrēawa*, rel. to Old High German *scrawazz* dwarf, Old Norse *skrǫggr* fox, Norwegian *skrogg* wolf. The shrew was formerly believed to be injurious to humans. Hence the sense malevolent person from the 12–14C.

shrewd *a.* astute, discerning. WH: 12–14C. Partly from SHREW (in sense malevolent person), partly from obs. *shrew* to curse. The original sense was evil, mischievous. The current sense evolved in the 16C.

shriek *v.i.* to utter a sharp, shrill, inarticulate cry. *Also v.t., n.* WH: 15C. Appar. var. of dial. *screak*, of Scandinavian orig. and prob. imit. Cp. SCREECH.

shrieval *a.* of or relating to a sheriff. WH: 17C. From *shrieve*, obs. var. of SHERIFF + -AL[1].

†shrift *n.* confession to a priest. WH: pre-1200. Old English *scrift*, from *scrīfan* SHRIVE. Cp. German *Schrift* writing.

shrike *n.* a bird of the family Laniidae, especially the butcher-bird, feeding on insects and small birds and having the habit of impaling them on thorns for future use. WH: 16C. Orig. uncertain. ? Rel. to Old English *scrīc* thrush, Middle Low German *schrīk* corncrake, Swedish *skrika* jay. Ult. imit. Cp. SCREECH, SHRIEK.

shrill *a.* high-pitched and piercing in tone. *Also n., v.i., v.t.* WH: 12–14C. Of Germanic orig. Cp. German *schrill*.

shrimp *n.* a slender long-tailed edible crustacean, allied to the prawn. *Also v.i.* WH: 12–14C. Of Germanic orig. and rel. to Middle Low German *schrempen* to contract, to wrinkle (cp. German *schrumpfen* to shrink), Old Norse *skreppa* to slip away. Cp. SCRIMP.

shrine *n.* a chest or casket in which sacred relics were deposited. *Also v.t.* WH: pre-1200. Old English *scrīn*, from Germanic, from Latin *scrinium* case for books or papers. Cp. German *Schrein*. The sense place of worship or devotion dates from the 17C.

shrink *v.i.* to grow smaller. *Also v.t., n.* WH: pre-1200. Old English *scrincan*, rel. to Swedish *skrynka* to wrinkle, Norwegian *skrekka* to shrink.

†shrive *v.t.* to receive the confession of. *Also v.i.* WH: pre-1200. Old English *scrīfan* to impose as a penance, from Germanic, from Latin *scribere* to write. Rel. to SHRIFT. Cp. SHROVETIDE.

shrivel *v.i.* to contract, to wither. *Also v.t.* WH: 16C. ? Old Norse. Cp. Swedish dial. *skryvla* to wrinkle.

shroud *n.* a sheet for wrapping a corpse for burial. *Also v.t.* WH: pre-1200. Old English *scrūd*, from Germanic base meaning to cut, rel. to base of SHRED. The original sense (to the 17C) was garment. The sense winding sheet for a corpse evolved in the 16C.

Shrovetide *n.* the period before Lent, when people formerly went to confession and afterwards made merry. WH: 14–15C. From *shrove*, past tense of SHRIVE + TIDE. The use of the past tense is unusual, but cp. SPOKESMAN.

shrub[1] *n.* a woody plant smaller than a tree, with branches proceeding directly from the ground without any supporting trunk. WH: pre-1200. Old English *scrubb*, *scrybb* shrubbery, underwood, appar. rel. to Norwegian *skrubbe* dwarf cornel, Swedish dial. *skrub* brushwood. Cp. SCRUB[2].

shrub[2] *n.* a drink composed of the sweetened juice of lemons or other fruit with spirit. WH: 18C. Arabic *šurb*, *šarāb*. Cp. SHERBET, SYRUP.

shrug *v.t.* to draw up (the shoulders) to express dislike, doubt etc. *Also v.i., n.* WH: 14–15C. Orig. unknown.

shtick *n.* a comedian's or performer's routine, patter etc. WH: mid-20C. Yiddish, from German *Stück* piece, play.

shtook *n.* trouble, bother. WH: mid-20C. Orig. unknown.

shtoom *a.* quiet, silent. WH: mid-20C. Yiddish, from German *stumm*.

shubunkin *n.* a type of large-finned goldfish. WH: early 20C. Japanese, from *shu* vermilion + *bun* pattern + *kin* gold.

shuck *n.* a shell, husk or pod. *Also v.t.* WH: 17C. Orig. unknown.

shudder *v.i.* to shiver suddenly as with fear; to quake. *Also n.* WH: 12–14C. Middle Low German *schōderen*, Middle Dutch *schūderen*, freq. from a Germanic word meaning to shake represented also in Old Frisian *schedda*, Old High German *scutten* (German *schütten* to tip, to pour). See also -ER[5].

shuffle *v.t.* to shift to and fro or from one to another. *Also v.i., n.* WH: 16C. From (or rel. to) Low German *shuffeln* to walk with dragging feet, ult. from Germanic base also of SHOVE, SCUFFLE. See also -LE[4].

shufti *n.* a (quick) look (at something). WH: mid-20C. Coll. Arabic *šuftī* have you seen?, from *šāfa* to see.

shul *n.* a synagogue. WH: 19C. Yiddish, from German *Schule* school.

shun *v.t.* to avoid, to keep clear of. WH: pre-1200. Old English *scunian*, of unknown orig. Cp. SHUNT. The original sense (to the 12–14C) was to abhor, to loathe. The current sense dates from the 12–14C.

'shun *int.* attention. WH: 19C. Abbr. of ATTENTION, representing a pronun. of its final syl.

shunt *v.t.* to turn (a train etc.) on to a side track. *Also v.i., n.* WH: 12–14C. Orig. uncertain. ? From SHUN. The original sense (to the 18C) was to move aside suddenly, to start. The application to trains dates from the 19C.

shush *int.* used to call for silence. *Also v.i., v.t., n.* WH: early 20C. Imit., representing a repetition of SH. Cp. HUSH[1].

shut *v.t.* to close by means of a door, lid, cover etc. *Also v.i., a.* WH: pre-1200. Old English *scyttan*, from a Germanic v. rel. to base of SHOOT. The original specific sense (to the 17C) was to put a bar or bolt in position so as to fasten a door, then (to the 19C) to fasten any object with a lock or bar. The current general sense evolved from the 12–14C.

shutter *n.* a person who or thing which shuts. *Also v.t.* WH: 16C. SHUT + -ER[1]. The sense movable panel fixed to a window dates from the 17C.

shuttle *n.* a boat-shaped contrivance enclosing a bobbin, used by weavers for passing the thread of the weft between the threads of the warp. *Also v.i., v.t.* WH: pre-1200. Old English *scyttel*, corr. to Old Norse *skutill* harpoon, bolt, from Germanic base also of SHOOT, SHUT. See also -LE[1]. The original sense was dart, arrow, missile. The sense bobbin evolved in the 12–14C.

shuttlecock *n.* a light cone-shaped object with feathered flights, used in the games of battledore and badminton. WH: 16C. SHUTTLE + COCK[1]. The object is so called because it is sent back and forth like a shuttle.

shy[1] *a.* fearful, timid. *Also adv., v.i., n.* WH: pre-1200. Old English *scēoh*, from Germanic base also of Old High German *sciuhen* (German *scheuen* to shun, *scheuchen* to scare). Cp. ESCHEW. The original application (to the 17C) was specifically to a horse. The sense timid, cautious (of humans) dates from the 17C.

shy[2] *v.t., v.i.* to fling, to throw. *Also n.* WH: 18C. Orig. unknown.

Shylock *n.* a miser; a ruthless creditor or moneylender. WH: 18C. *Shylock*, a Jewish moneylender in Shakespeare's *The Merchant of Venice* (1596).

shyster *n.* a tricky or disreputable lawyer. WH: 19C. Orig. uncertain. ? Rel. to German *Scheisser*, from *Scheisse* shit. Cp. SHICER.

si *n.* te. WH: 18C. Initial letters of Latin *Sancte Iohannis* (St John). See UT.

sial *n.* the outer layer of the earth's crust, rock rich in silicon and aluminium. WH: early 20C. From SILICON + ALUMINIUM.

sialic *a.* of or relating to saliva. WH: mid-20C. Greek *sialon* saliva + -IC.

sialo- *comb. form* saliva. WH: Greek *sialon* saliva. See also -O-.

sialogogue *n.* a drug or other substance that stimulates the flow of saliva. WH: 18C. Greek *sialon* saliva + *agōgos* leading, eliciting.

sialoid *a.* resembling saliva. WH: 19C. Greek *sialon* saliva + -OID.

sialorrhoea *n.* excessive flow of saliva. WH: 19C. SIALO- + -RRHOEA.

siamang *n.* a large gibbon with long black hair of the Malay peninsula and Sumatra. WH: 19C. Malay *siāmang*, from *āmang* black.

Siamese *a.* of or relating to Siam, now Thailand, a country of SE Asia, or to its inhabitants or their language. *Also n.* WH: 17C. *Siam* (now Thailand), a country in SE Asia + -ESE.

sib *n.* a brother or sister. *Also a.* WH: pre-1200. Old English, from Germanic, of unknown orig. Cp. German *Sippe* family, kinship group.

sibilant *a.* hissing. *Also n.* WH: 17C. Latin *sibilans*, *sibilantis*, pres.p. of *sibilare* to hiss, to whistle. See also -ANT.

sibyl *n.* one of a number of women who prophesied in ancient times under the supposed inspiration of a deity. WH: 12–14C. Old French *Sibile* (Modern French *Sibylle*), or from Medieval Latin *Sibilla*, from Latin *Sibylla*, from Greek *Sibulla*.

sic¹ *a., adv., pron.* such. WH: 14–15C. Reduced form of SUCH.

sic² *adv.* thus, so (usu. printed after a doubtful word or phrase to indicate that it is quoted exactly as in the original). WH: 19C. Latin so, thus.

Sicanian *n.* a native or inhabitant of Sicily, esp. any of the aboriginal inhabitants of Sicily at the time of Greek colonization. *Also a.* WH: 17C. Latin *Sicanius*, from *Sicani*, pl. of *Sicanus* Sican, from Greek *Sikanoi*.

siccative *a.* drying, causing to dry. *Also n.* WH: 14–15C. Late Latin *siccativus*, from *siccare* to dry. See also -ATIVE.

sice *n.* the number six on dice. WH: 14–15C. Old French *sis* (Modern French *six*), from Latin *sex* six.

Sicilian *a.* of or relating to Sicily, or its inhabitants. *Also n.* WH: 16C. Latin *Sicilia* Sicily, an island off the foot of Italy + -AN.

sick¹ *a.* ill, in bad health. *Also n., v.t.* WH: pre-1200. Old English *sēoc*, from Germanic, ult. of unknown orig. Cp. German *siech* ailing, infirm.

sick² *v.t.* to chase or attack, to set upon. WH: 19C. Dial. var. of SEEK.

sickle *n.* an implement consisting of a long curved blade with a short handle, used for reaping, lopping etc. WH: pre-1200. Old English *sicol*, *sicel*, from Germanic var. of Latin *secula*, from *secare* to cut. Cp. German *Sichel*.

sidalcea *n.* any plant of the genus *Sidalcea*, resembling a mallow. WH: 19C. Modern Latin genus name, from blend of *sida* (from Greek *sidē* pomegranate tree, water lily) and *Alcea*, related genera.

siddur *n.* the Jewish prayer book used for daily worship. WH: 19C. Hebrew *siddūr*, lit. order.

side *n.* any of the bounding surfaces (or lines) of a material object, esp. a more or less vertical inner or outer surface (as of a building, a room, a natural object etc.). *Also v.i., a.* WH: pre-1200. Old English *sīde*, from a Germanic n. prob. from an a. meaning extending lengthways, long, deep, low. Cp. German *Seite*. The original sense of length or breadth is still present in *countryside* (COUNTRY).

sidereal *a.* of or relating to the fixed stars or the constellations. WH: 17C. Latin *sidereus*, from *sidus*, *sideris* star. See also -AL¹.

siderite *n.* native ferrous carbonate. WH: 16C. Orig. from French *sidérite*, or from Latin *siderites*, from Greek *sidēritēs*, from *sidēros* iron; later directly from Greek *sidēros* + -ITE¹.

sidero-¹ *comb. form* iron. WH: Greek *sidēros* iron. See also -O-.

sidero-² *comb. form* the stars. WH: Latin *sidus*, *sideris* star. See also -O-.

siderolite *n.* a meteorite consisting partly of stone and partly of iron. WH: 19C. SIDERO-¹ + -LITE.

siderosis *n.* a lung disease caused by breathing iron or other metal dust. WH: 19C. SIDERO-¹ + -OSIS.

siderostat *n.* an astronomical instrument by which a star under observation is kept within the field of the telescope. WH: 19C. SIDERO-² + -STAT.

sidle *v.i.* to move or edge sideways (e.g. up to someone), esp. in a stealthy or ingratiating manner. WH: 17C. Back-formation from *sidelong* (alt. of *sideling*, from SIDE + -LING²) based on vv. in -LE⁴.

siege *n.* the military operation of surrounding a town or fortified place with troops, cutting its supply lines, and subjecting it to constant bombardment, in order to force its surrender. WH: 12–14C. Old French *sege* (Modern French *siège*) seat, throne, from Popular Latin *sedicum* seat, from Latin *sedere* SIT. The original sense (to the 17C) was chair, seat, especially of a person of rank. But the military sense has also been current from the first. It has the literal idea of 'sitting' before a fortress. Cp. *sit-in* (SIT) as a similar sort of siege.

siemens *n.* the SI unit of electrical conductance, equal to one reciprocal ohm. WH: 19C. Ernst Werner *Siemens*, 1816–92, and his brothers Karl Wilhelm (or Charles William), 1823–83, Friedrich, 1826–1904, and Karl, 1829–1906, German-born electrical engineers.

Sienese *a.* of or relating to Siena, esp. in reference to its 13th- and 14th-cent. school of painting. *Also n.* WH: 18C. *Siena*, a city and province in Tuscany, W Italy + -ESE.

sienna *n.* a pigment composed of a native clay coloured with iron and manganese. WH: 18C. *Siena*. See SIENESE.

sierra *n.* in Spanish-speaking countries and the US, a long mountain chain, jagged in outline. WH: 16C. Spanish, from Latin *serra* saw.

siesta *n.* a short midday sleep, esp. in hot countries. WH: 17C. Spanish, from Latin *sexta* (*hora*) sixth (hour) (of the day), i.e. midday. Cp. SEXT.

sieve *n.* an instrument for separating the finer particles of substances from the coarser, or liquids from solids, having meshes or perforations through which liquid or fine particles pass, while solids or coarse particles are retained. *Also v.t.* WH: pre-1200. Old English *sife*, from Germanic. Cp. German *Sieb*.

sievert *n.* the SI unit of ionizing radiation, equal to 100 rems. WH: mid-20C. Rolf M. *Sievert*, 1896–1966, Swedish physicist.

sifaka *n.* the long-tailed black-and-white lemur of the genus *Propithecus*, native to Madagascar. WH: 19C. Malagasy.

siffleur *n.* a whistling artiste. WH: 18C. French, from *siffler* to whistle + -eur -OR. The word was originally the term for an animal that makes a whistling noise. The current sense dates from the 19C.

sift *v.t.* to separate into finer and coarser particles by means of a sieve. *Also v.i.* WH: pre-1200. Old English *siftan*, from Germanic base also of SIEVE.

sigh *v.i.* to inhale and exhale deeply and audibly, as an involuntary expression of grief, fatigue, relief etc. *Also v.t., n.* WH: 12–14C. Prob. back-formation from past tense of Middle English form of Old English *sīcan* to sigh, of unknown orig.

sight *n.* the faculty of seeing. *Also v.t.* WH: pre-1200. Old English *sihth*, more commonly *gesihth*, from Germanic, ult. rel. to SEE¹. Cp. German *Gesicht* face, look, appearance.

sigil *n.* a seal, a signet. WH: 14–15C. Late Latin *sigillum* sign, trace, impress, dim. of Latin *signum* SIGN.

siglum *n.* a symbol, sign or abbreviation used in a manuscript or document. WH: Late Latin *sigla* (pl.), ? from *singula*, neut. pl. of *singulus* SINGLE.

sigma *n.* the eighteenth letter of the Greek alphabet, Σ, σ, or when final, ς, or, in uncial form, C or c. WH: 14–15C. Latin, from Greek.

sign *n.* a mark expressing a particular meaning. *Also v.t., v.i.* WH: 12–14C. Old French *signe*, from Latin *signum* mark, token. The original sense of the verb was to make the sign of the cross.

signal *n.* a sign in the form of an action, light or sound, agreed upon or understood as conveying information. *Also v.t., v.i., a.* WH: 14–15C. Old French, alt. of earlier *seignal*, from Medieval Latin *signale*, use as n. of neut. of Late Latin *signalis*, from Latin *signum* SIGN. See also -AL¹. The original sense (to the 17C) was distinguishing mark, badge. The current sense evolved in the 16C.

signature *n.* one's name, initials or mark written or impressed with one's own hand in signing a document etc. WH: 16C. Medieval Latin *signatura* sign manual, from Latin *signare* SIGN.

signet *n.* a small seal, esp. for use in lieu of or with a signature as a mark of authentication. WH: 14–15C. Old French, dim. of *signe*, or from Medieval Latin *signetum*, dim. of *signum* seal. See SIGN, also -ET¹.

signify *v.t.* to make known by signs, gestures or words. *Also v.i.* WH: 12–14C. Old French *signifier*, from Latin *significare*, from *signum* SIGN. See also -FY.

signor *n.* an Italian man. WH: 16C. Italian, reduced form of *signore*, from Latin *senior-*. See SENIOR.

sika *n.* a small deer, *Cervus nippon*, native to Japan but introduced into other countries, including Britain. WH: 19C. Japanese deer.

Sikh *n.* a member of a monotheistic religion that takes the Granth as its scripture, founded in the 16th cent. in the Punjab. *Also a.* WH: 18C. Punjabi and Hindi, from Sanskrit *śiṣya* discipline.

silage *n.* any green crop, esp. grass or clover, stored by ensilage, that is, compressed into pits, for use as fodder. *Also v.t.* WH: 19C. Alt. of ENSILAGE, based on SILO.

sild *n.* a young herring, esp. one canned in Norway. WH: early 20C. Danish and Norwegian herring.

sile *n.* a strainer. *Also v.t., v.i.* WH: 14–15C. Of Scandinavian orig. Cp. Swedish *sila*, Norwegian *sile*.

silence *n.* the absence of noise, stillness. *Also v.t.* WH: 12–14C. Old French, from Latin *silentium*, from *silens, silentis*. See SILENT, also -ENCE.

silent *a.* not speaking, not making any sound. *Also n.* WH: 15C. Latin *silens, silentis*, pres.p. of *silere* to be silent. See also -ENT.

silenus *n.* a woodland satyr in the shape of a riotous and drunken old man. WH: 17C. Latin *Silenus*, from Greek *Seilēnos*, in Greek mythology the foster-father of Bacchus and leader of the satyrs.

silesia *n.* a type of twilled cotton or linen cloth used for blinds, dress-linings etc. WH: 17C. *Silesia*, Latinized form of *Schlesien*, German name of a region now mainly in SW Poland.

silex *n.* silica, esp. in the form of quartz or flint. WH: 16C. Latin flint.

silhouette *n.* a portrait in profile or outline, usu. black on a white ground or cut out in paper etc. *Also v.t.* WH: 18C. French, from Étienne de *Silhouette*, 1709–67, French writer and politician. The portrait is said to be so called because it was inexpensive to produce, evoking the petty economies introduced by Silhouette in 1759 to finance the Seven Years' War. Others claim the portraits resembled those made by Silhouette to decorate the walls of his château at Bry-sur-Marne.

silica *n.* a hard, crystalline silicon dioxide, occurring in various mineral forms, esp. as sand, flint, quartz etc. WH: 19C. Latin SILEX, *silicis*, based on ALUMINA, etc.

silici- *comb. form* silicon, silica. WH: From SILICA or SILICON.

silicle *n.* a short siliqua or seed pod. WH: 18C. Modern Latin *silicula*, dim. of SILIQUA. See also -ULE.

silicon *n.* a non-metallic semi-conducting element, at. no. 14, chem. symbol Si, usu. occurring in combination with oxygen as quartz or silica, and next to oxygen the most abundant of the elements. WH: 19C. Latin SILEX, *silicis* + -*on*, from BORON (from CARBON).

siliqua *n.* a dry, elongated pericarp or pod containing seeds, as in plants of the mustard family. WH: 14–15C. Latin pod.

silk *n.* a fine soft glossy fibre spun by the larvae of certain moths, esp. the common silkworm, *Bombyx mori*. *Also a.* WH: pre-1200. Old English *sioloc, seolc*, corr. to Old Norse *silki*, Russian *shëlk*, Old Prussian *silkas* (gen.), or rel. to Late Latin *sericum*, neut. of Latin *sericus*, from Greek *sērikos*, rel. to Latin *Seres*, Greek *Sēres* Seres (SERIC).

sill *n.* a block or timber forming a basis or foundation in a structure, esp. a slab of timber or stone at the foot of a door or window. WH: pre-1200. Old English *syll*, from Germanic. Cp. German *Schwelle* threshold.

siller *n.* silver, money. WH: 12–14C. Var. of SILVER.

sillimanite *n.* the mineral aluminium silicate, found as orthorhombic crystals or fibrous masses. WH: 19C. Benjamin *Silliman*, 1779–1864, US chemist + -ITE[1].

silly *a.* foolish, weak-minded. *Also n.* WH: pre-1200. Alt. of obs. *seely*, from Old English *sælig*, from Germanic base meaning luck, happiness. Cp. German *selig* holy. The original sense was happy, fortunate, then (12–14C) pious, holy, also innocent, harmless, then (14–15C) foolish, simple, as now.

silo *n.* a store-pit or airtight chamber for pressing and preserving green fodder. *Also v.t.* WH: 19C. Spanish, from Latin *sirus*, from Greek *siros*.

silphium *n.* a plant of the Mediterranean region, the juice of which was used by the ancients as a condiment and as a medicine. WH: 18C. Latin, from Greek *silphion*.

silt *n.* fine sediment deposited by water. *Also v.t., v.i.* WH: 14–15C. Prob. from Middle Low German or Middle Dutch *silte, sulte* salt marsh, brine, ult. rel. to SALT. Cp. German *Sülze* brine.

Silurian *a.* of or relating to the period called Silurian or its rock system. *Also n.* WH: 18C. Latin *Silures*, an ancient British tribe of SE Wales + -IAN.

silurid *n.* any fish belonging to a freshwater family that includes the European catfish or sheatfish, *Silurus glanis*. *Also a.* WH: 19C. Modern Latin *Silurus*, genus name, from Greek *silouros* + -ID.

silver *n.* a precious ductile and malleable metallic element of a white colour, at. no. 47, chem. symbol Ag. *Also a., v.t., v.i.* WH: pre-1200. Old English *siolfor, seolfor*, from Germanic, prob. ult. of Oriental orig. Cp. German *Silber*, Russian *serebro*.

silviculture *n.* the cultivation of trees, forestry. WH: 19C. French *sylviculture, silviculture*, from Latin *silva* wood (misspelt *sylva* by assoc. with Greek *hulē* wood) + French *culture* cultivation.

sima *n.* the inner part of the earth's crust, lying deep to the ocean bed as well as to the continental masses. WH: early 20C. SILICA + MAGNESIUM.

simaruba *n.* a tropical American tree of the genus *Simaruba*, esp. *Simaruba amara*. WH: 18C. French *simarouba*, Portuguese *simaruba*, from Galibi *simaruppa*.

Simeonite *n.* a person of low-church sympathies, an evangelical. WH: 19C. Reverend Charles *Simeon*, 1759–1836, a leader of the Evangelical revival in the Church of England + -ITE[1].

simian *a.* of or relating to the anthropoid apes. *Also n.* WH: 17C. Latin *simia* ape, ? from *simus*, from Greek *simos* snub-nosed, flat-nosed + -AN.

similar *a.* having a resemblance (to). WH: 16C. French *similaire*, or from Medieval Latin *similaris*, from Latin *similis* like. See also -AR[1].

simile *n.* a figure of speech that highlights a particular quality that something has by comparing it, esp. using *like* or *as*, to something else proverbial for that quality, as of *eyes like stars; a heart as pure as the driven snow*. WH: 14–15C. Latin, neut. of *similis* like, SIMILAR.

similor *n.* a gold-coloured alloy of copper and zinc used for cheap jewellery. WH: 18C. French, from Latin *similis* like + French *or* gold.

simmer *v.i.* to boil gently. *Also v.t., n.* WH: 17C. Alt. of obs. *simper*, ? imit. See also -ER[5].

simnel *n.* a rich fruit cake decorated with marzipan, traditionally eaten on Mothering Sunday, Easter Day and Christmas Day. WH: 12–14C. Old French *simenel* (Modern French dial. *simnel*), ult. from Latin *simila, similago* or Greek *semidalis* fine flour. Cp. SEMOLINA.

Simon Pure *n.* the genuine article, the real person. WH: 18C. *Simon Pure*, a Quaker character in Susannah Centlivre's play *A Bold Stroke for a Wife* (1717), who is impersonated by another character during part of the comedy.

simony *n.* the buying or selling of ecclesiastical preferments or privileges. WH: 12–14C. Old French *simonie*, from Late Latin *simonia*, from *Simon* Magus, a Samaritan who tried to buy the power of conferring the Holy Spirit (Acts viii.9–14). See also -Y[2].

simoom *n.* a hot dry wind blowing over the desert, esp. of Arabia, raising great quantities of sand and causing intense thirst. WH: 18C. Arabic *samūm*, from *samma* to poison.

simp *n.* a simpleton. *Also a.* WH: early 20C. Abbr. of *simpleton* (SIMPLE).

simpatico *a.* congenial, agreeable, likeable. WH: 19C. Spanish *simpático*, from *simpatía*, or Italian *simpatico*, from *simpatia*, both from Latin *sympathia* SYMPATHY.

simper *v.i.* to smile in an affected manner, to smirk. *Also v.t., n.* WH: 16C. Orig. uncertain. Cp. Danish, Norwegian and Swedish dial. *semper, simper*, German *zimper, zimpfer* elegant, delicate, ? ult. of imit. orig. Cp. SIP.

simple *a.* clear, easy to understand. *Also n.* WH: 12–14C. Old French, from Latin *simplus*. The sense foolish, stupid, mentally handicapped arose in the 14–15C. A simple person is devoid of duplicity.

simulacrum *n.* an image or likeness. WH: 16C. Latin, from *simulare* SIMULATE.

simulate *v.t.* to assume the likeness or mere appearance of. WH: 17C. Latin *simulatus*, p.p. of *simulare*, from *similis* like. See also -ATE[3].

simulcast *n.* (the transmission of) a simultaneous broadcast on radio and television. *Also v.t.* WH: mid-20C. Abbr. of SIMULTANEOUS + *broadcast* (BROAD).

simultaneous *a.* happening, done or acting at the same time. WH: 17C. Medieval Latin *simultaneus*, from Latin *simul* at the same time, prob. based on Late Latin *momentaneus*. See -OUS.

simurg *n.* an enormous fabulous bird of Persian mythology with the ability to think and speak. WH: 18C. Persian *sīmurġ*, from Pahlavi *sēn* eagle + *murġ* bird.

sin *n.* transgression of duty, morality, or the law of God. *Also v.i., v.t.* WH: pre-1200. Old English *synn*, rel. to Indo-European forms with *-d* or *-t*, as Old French *sende*, Old High German *sunta* (German *Sünde*), Old Norse *synd*, prob. rel. to Latin *sons, sontis* guilty.

Sinaitic *a.* of or relating to, or given at, Mount Sinai or the peninsula of Sinai. WH: 18C. Mount *Sinai* or the Sinai peninsula, NE Egypt + -ITIC.

Sinanthropus *n.* any of the primitive apelike hominids represented by Peking man, now regarded as a subspecies of *Homo erectus*. WH: early 20C. Modern Latin, former genus name, from SINO- + Greek *anthropos* man.

sinapism *n.* a mustard plaster. WH: 16C. French *sinapisme* or Late Latin *sinapismus*, from Greek *sinapismos* use of a mustard plaster (*sinapisma*), from *sinapi* mustard, of Egyptian orig. See also -ISM.

since *adv.* after or from a time specified or implied till now. *Also prep., conj.* WH: 14–15C. Contr. of obs. *sithence* from *sithen*, from Old English *siththon*, ult. from Germanic) + -S¹, or from dial. *sin* + -S², with spelling in *-ce* as for HENCE. Cp. SYNE.

sincere *a.* being in reality as in appearance or profession. WH: 16C. Latin *sincerus* clean, pure, sound, ? from *sin-, sim-* one (as in SIMPLE) + base of *crescere* to grow, i.e. of one growth. The word was long popularly derived from Latin *sine cera* without wax, as if to mean genuine.

sinciput *n.* the upper part of the head, especially from the forehead to the crown. WH: 16C. Latin, from *semi* half + *caput* head.

sine¹ *n.* a trigonometric function that is the ratio of the length of the line opposite the angle to the length of the hypotenuse in a right-angled triangle. WH: 16C. Latin *sinus* curve, bay, fold of a toga, used in Medieval Latin to translate Arabic *jayb* bosom, pocket, sine.

sine² *prep.* without, lacking. WH: 17C. Latin without.

sinecure *n.* an ecclesiastical benefice without cure of souls. WH: 17C. Latin (*beneficium*) *sine cura*, from *beneficium* benefice + *sine* without + *cura*, abl. sing. of *cura* care.

sinew *n.* a tendon, a fibrous cord connecting muscle and bone. *Also v.t.* WH: pre-1200. Old English *sinwe, sionwe*, oblique forms of *sinu, seonu*, from Germanic. Cp. German *Sehne*.

sinfonia *n.* a symphony. WH: 18C. Italian. See SYMPHONY.

sing *v.i.* to utter words in a tuneful manner, to render a song vocally, to make vocal melody. *Also v.t.* WH: pre-1200. Old English *singan*, from Germanic. Cp. SONG.

singe *v.t.* to burn slightly, to burn the surface of. *Also n.* WH: pre-1200. Old English *sencgan*, from Germanic. Cp. German *sengen*.

single *a.* consisting of one only, sole. *Also n., v.t.* WH: 12–14C. Old French *single, sengle*, from Latin *singulus*, from *sim-* as in *simplus* SIMPLE.

singspiel *n.* a dramatic entertainment in which the action is expressed alternately in dialogue and song. WH: 19C. German, from *singen* to sing + *Spiel* play.

singular *a.* out of the usual, remarkable. *Also n.* WH: 12–14C. Old French *singuler* (Modern French *singulier*), from Latin *singularis*, from *singulus* SINGLE. The sense remarkable, extraordinary evolved in the 14–15C. Cp. UNIQUE.

singultus *n.* hiccups, hiccuping. WH: 16C. Latin.

sinh *abbr.* a hyperbolic sine. WH: 19C. SINE¹ + *h* (for *hyperbolic*).

Sinhalese *a.* of or relating to Sri Lanka, or to its majority people or their language; Sri Lankan. *Also n.* WH: 18C. Portuguese *Singhalez*, from Sanskrit *Siṅhala*, var. of *Siṁhala* Sri Lanka (Ceylon), from *siṁha* lion. See also -ESE.

Sinic *a.* Chinese. WH: 17C. Medieval Latin *Sinicus*, from Late Latin *Sinae*, from Greek *Sinai*, from Arabic *ṣīn*, name for the Chinese empire. See also -IC.

sinister *a.* ill-looking, malevolent. WH: 14–15C. Old French *sinistre* or Latin *sinister* left, left-hand. Omens observed from one's left were at one time regarded as unlucky.

sink *v.i.* to go downwards, to fall gradually. *Also v.t., n.* WH: pre-1200. Old English *sincan*, from Germanic, of unknown orig. Cp. German *sinken*.

sinkie *n.* a single person with a good income and no children. WH: late 20C. Acronym of *single income no kids* + *-ie* (-Y³). Cp. DINKY², TWINKIE.

sinnet *n.* braided cordage made with three to nine cords. WH: 17C. Orig. unknown.

Sinn Fein *n.* the Irish republican party which was formed in 1905 by the coalescence of all the Irish separatist organizations, and is the political wing of the Irish Republican Army. WH: early 20C. Irish *sinn féin*, lit. we ourselves.

Sino- *comb. form* Chinese, or Chinese and, as in *Sino-Tibetan*. WH: Greek *Sinai*, Latin *Sinae* the Chinese. See also -O-.

sinology *n.* the study of Chinese languages, culture, literature etc. WH: 19C. SINO- + -LOGY.

Sino-Tibetan *n.* a family of languages comprising most Chinese languages, Tibetan, Burmese and usu. Thai. *Also a.* WH: early 20C. SINO- + TIBETAN.

sinsemilla *n.* a specially potent type of marijuana. WH: late 20C. American Spanish, lit. without seed.

sinter *n.* a calcareous or siliceous rock precipitated from (hot) mineral waters. *Also v.t., v.i.* WH: 18C. German CINDER.

sinuate *a.* (esp. of the edges of leaves etc.) bending, curving or winding in and out. WH: 17C. Latin *sinuatus*, p.p. of *sinuare* to bend, to wind, to curve.

sinuous *a.* bending in and out. WH: 16C. French *sinueux*, or from Latin *sinuosus*, from SINUS. See also -OUS. The sense supple, agile evolved in the 19C.

sinupallial *a.* (of a division of bivalve molluscs) having a deeply incurved pallial line for the passage to and fro of the pallial siphons. WH: 19C. From *sinu-*, stem of SINUS + *pallial* (PALLIUM). See also -ATE².

sinus *n.* a cavity or pouchlike hollow, esp. in bone or tissue. WH: 14–15C. Latin curve, bend, bay.

Sioux *n.* a member of a N American Indian people of the upper Mississippi and Missouri rivers. *Also a.* WH: 18C. N American French, from *Nadouessioux*, from Ojibwa (Ottawa dial.) *nātowēssiwak*. The French plural ending *-x* replaced the Ojibwa plural ending *-ak*.

sip *v.t., v.i.* to drink or imbibe in small quantities using the lips. *Also n.* WH: 14–15C. Prob. imit. var. of SUP to express a less vigorous drinking action.

sipe¹ *v.i.* to soak through, to ooze or seep. WH: pre-1200. Old English *sīpian*, corr. to Old Frisian *sīpa*, Middle Low German *sīpen*, of unknown orig. Cp. SEEP.

sipe² *n.* a groove in the tread of a tyre, for improving its grip and helping the dispersal of water. WH: pre-1200. SIPE¹.

siphonophore *n.* any member of an order of marine life (the Siphonophora) variously regarded as a colony of medusoid zooids or as a single individual composed of a cluster of tubular organs. WH: 19C. Greek *siphōn* syphon + -O- + -PHORE.

siphuncle *n.* the tube connecting the chambers of the shell in many cephalopods. WH: 18C. Latin *siphunculus* small tube, dim. of *sipho* SYPHON. See also -UNCLE.

sir *n.* a form of courteous address to a man. WH: 12–14C. Reduced form of SIRE. Cp. SIRRAH.

sirdar *n.* a military leader or commander in the Indian subcontinent or in other Eastern countries. WH: 16C. Persian and Urdu *sar-dār*, from Persian *sar* position of head or chief + *dār* holding.

sire *n.* the male parent of an animal, esp. a stallion. *Also v.t.* WH: 12–14C. Old French, from Popular Latin *seior*, alt. of Latin SENIOR. Cp. SIEUR.

siren *n.* an apparatus for producing a loud warning sound by means of a rotating perforated disc through which steam or compressed air is emitted. WH: 12–14C. Old French *sereine, sirene* (Modern French *sirène*), from Latin *sirena*, fem. form of Latin *Siren*, from Greek *Seirēn*. The original sense (to the 16C) was an imaginary type of snake. The sense half-woman, half-bird who lured sailors to their death in Greek mythology evolved in the 14–15C, and sweet singer, temptress in the 16C. The sense of instrument or apparatus producing a tone or sound evolved in the 19C, originally as an acoustical device for measuring the frequency of sounds, invented by the French physicist Charles Cagniard de la Tour in 1819 and deliberately named after the Greek nymph because it worked through water.

sirloin *n.* the loin or upper part of the loin of beef. WH: 14–15C. Old French *surloigne, var. of *surlonge*, from *sur* SUR-¹ + *longe* LOIN. The spelling with *sir-* arose in the 17C, mainly as a result of the fiction that the cut of beef was so called because it was 'knighted' for its superiority by Henry VIII (or some other king). See SIR.

sirocco n. a hot oppressive wind blowing from N Africa across to Italy etc., often carrying dust or rain. WH: 17C. Italian *scirocco*, ult. from Spanish Arabic *šalūḳ, šulūḳ* south-east wind.

†**sirrah** n. fellow, sir (a term of address used in anger or contempt). WH: 16C. Prob. representation of a form of SIRE with the last syl. eventually assim. to AH. Cp. SIR.

sirree n. sir (used for emphasis often with *yes* or *no*). WH: 19C. Alt. of SIRRAH or SIR + emphat. suf.

sirvente n. a form of ballad or lay, usu. satirical, used by the medieval trouvères and troubadours. WH: 19C. French, from Provençal *sirventes*, of unknown orig. The final -s of the Provençal word was mistaken as a plural ending.

sis n. a sister. WH: 17C. Abbr. of SISTER.

sisal n. the fibre of the Mexican agave used for cordage etc. WH: 19C. *Sisal*, a port in Yucatán, SE Mexico, from which it was exported.

siskin n. a small migratory songbird, *Carduelis spinus*, related to the goldfinch. WH: 16C. Middle Dutch *siseken*, dim. based on Middle Low German *sīsek*, Middle High German *zīsec* (German *Zeisig*), of Slavonic orig. Cp. Russian *chizh*.

sist v.t. to stop, to stay. *Also n.* WH: 17C. Latin *sistere* to cause to stand.

sister n. a female born of the same parents as oneself. *Also a., v.t., v.i.* WH: pre-1200. Old English *sweoster*, from Germanic, from Indo-European base represented in Latin *soror*. The sense nun evolved in the 14–15C, and that of senior nurse in the 19C.

Sistine a. of or relating to any of the Popes named Sixtus, esp. Sixtus IV. WH: 18C. Italian *sistino* of Sixtus. See also -INE. The Sistine Chapel was built for Pope Sixtus IV, 1471–84. Raphael's *Sistine Madonna* was painted for the church of *San Sisto* (St Sixtus) at Piacenza in 1515–19.

sistrum n. a jingling instrument used by the ancient Egyptians in the worship of Isis. WH: 14–15C. Latin, from Greek *seistron*, from *seiein* to shake.

Sisyphean a. (of a task) unceasingly or fruitlessly laborious. WH: 16C. Latin *Sisypheius*, from Greek *Sisupheios*, from *Sisuphos* Sisyphus, a king of Corinth in Greek mythology whose punishment in Hades was to push uphill a stone that rolled down again when he reached the top. See also -EAN.

sit v.i. to set oneself or be in a resting posture with the body nearly vertical supported on the buttocks. *Also v.t., n.* WH: pre-1200. Old English *sittan*, from Germanic, from Indo-European base seen also in Latin *sedere*, Greek *hezesthai*. Cp. German *sitzen*.

sitar n. an Indian stringed musical instrument with a long neck. WH: 19C. Persian and Urdu *sitār*, from *sih* three + *tār* string.

sitatunga n. a grey or brown antelope, *Tragelaphus spekii*, of central and E Africa, the male having spiral horns. WH: 19C. Kiswahili.

sitcom n. a situation comedy. WH: mid-20C. Abbr. of *situation comedy* (SITUATE[1]).

site n. the ground on which anything, esp. a building, stands, has stood, or will stand. *Also v.t.* WH: 14–15C. Anglo-French, or from Latin *situs* local position, ? from *situs*, p.p. of *sinere* to leave, to allow to remain.

sitiology n. dietetics. WH: 19C. Greek *sition, sitos* food made from grain, bread + -O- + -LOGY.

Sitka n. a quick-growing spruce fir, *Picea sitchensis*, cultivated for its timber, native to N America. WH: 19C. *Sitka*, a town in Alaska, USA.

sitrep n. a (military) report on the current situation. WH: mid-20C. Abbr. of *situation* (SITUATE[1]) + REPORT.

sits vac n.pl. situations vacant, jobs offered. WH: mid-20C. Abbr. of *situations vacant* (SITUATE[1]).

situate[1] v.t. to place. WH: 14–15C. Medieval Latin *situatus*, p.p. of *situare*, from Latin *situs* SITE. See also -ATE[3].

situate[2] a. situated. WH: 16C. Medieval Latin *situatus*. See SITUATE[1], also -ATE[2].

sitz-bath n. a bath in which a person sits, a hip bath. WH: 19C. Partial trans. of German *Sitzbad*, from *sitzen* to sit + *Bad* bath.

Siva n. the god who is associated with Brahma and Vishnu in the Hindu triad, known as the destroyer and reproducer of life. WH: 18C. Sanskrit *Śiva*, lit. auspicious one.

Sivan n. the third month of the Jewish ecclesiastical year and ninth of the civil year, comprising parts of May and June. WH: 14–15C. Hebrew *sīwān*.

six n. the number or figure 6 or vi. *Also a.* WH: pre-1200. Old English *siex, six, syx*, from Germanic, from Indo-European base also of Latin *sex*, Greek *hex*. Cp. German *sechs*.

sixte n. a parry in fencing (the sixth of eight parrying positions) in which the hand is opposite the right breast and the point of the sword raised and a little to the right. WH: 19C. French sixth.

sixteen n. the number or figure 16 or xvi. *Also a.* WH: pre-1200. Old English *siextīene*, from Germanic base of SIX, -TEEN.

sixty n. the number or figure 60 or lx. *Also a.* WH: pre-1200. Old English *siextig*, from SIX + -TY[2].

sizar n. any of a number of students at Cambridge University or Trinity College, Dublin, who receive a college allowance towards expenses, and formerly acted as servitors. WH: 16C. SIZE[1] + -AR[3]. The students are so called because they formerly received their sizes (allowances for food and drink) free.

size[1] n. extent, dimensions. *Also v.t.* WH: 12–14C. Old French shortening of *assise* ASSIZE, or shortening of the English word.

size[2] n. a gluey, gelatinous solution used to glaze surfaces (e.g. of paper), stiffen fabrics, prepare walls for papering etc. *Also v.t.* WH: 12–14C. ? Same as SIZE[1].

sizzle v.i. to make a hissing noise as of frying. *Also n.* WH: 17C. Imit. Cp. FIZZLE.

sjambok n. a short heavy whip, usu. of rhinoceros hide. *Also v.t.* WH: 18C. Afrikaans, from Malay *sambuk, chambuk*, from Persian and Urdu *chābuk* horsewhip.

ska n. an early form of reggae music originating in Jamaica. WH: mid-20C. Orig. uncertain. ? Imit.

skag n. a cigarette or the stub of one. WH: early 20C. Orig. unknown.

skald n. in ancient Scandinavia, a bard, a writer and reciter of epic poetry. WH: 18C. Old Norse *skáld*, of unknown orig.

skat n. a three-handed card game resembling piquet. WH: 19C. German, from Italian *scarto* cards laid aside, from *scartare* to discard. Cp. ÉCARTÉ.

skate[1] n. (each of a pair of boots fitted with) a steel blade or runner for gliding on ice, an ice-skate. *Also v.i., v.t.* WH: 17C. Dutch *schaats* (taken as pl.), from Middle Dutch *schaetse*, from Old Northern French *eschasse* (Modern French *échasse*) stilt.

skate[2] n. a fish of the genus *Raja*, distinguished by having a long pointed snout. WH: 12–14C. Old Norse *skata*.

skate[3] n. a mean or dishonest person. WH: 19C. Orig. unknown.

skean n. a long knife or dagger used in Scotland and Ireland. WH: 14–15C. Irish and Gaelic *sgian*.

sked n. a schedule. *Also v.t.* WH: early 20C. Abbr. of SCHEDULE. The spelling represents the usual N American pronunciation of the word.

skedaddle v.i. to run away, as in haste or panic. *Also int., n.* WH: 19C. Orig. unknown. Cp. SKIDOO.

skeet n. a type of clay-pigeon shooting in which targets are hurled in different directions, angles etc. from two traps, to simulate a bird in flight. WH: early 20C. Appar. alt. of SHOOT, as if representing a former pronun.

skeeter n. a mosquito. WH: 19C. Abbr. of a pronun. of MOSQUITO.

skeg n. a stabilizing fin on the underside of a surfboard or sailboard. WH: 12–14C. Old Norse *skegg* beard.

skegger n. a little salmon. WH: 17C. Orig. unknown.

skein n. a quantity of yarn, silk, wool, cotton etc., wound in a coil which is folded over and knotted. WH: 12–14C. Shortened form of Old French *escaigne* (Modern French dial. *écagne*), of unknown orig.

skeleton n. the hard supporting or protective framework of an animal or vegetable body, comprising bones, cartilage, shell and other rigid parts. *Also a.* WH: 16C. Modern Latin, from Greek, use as n. of neut. of *skeletos* dried up, from *skellein* to dry up.

skelf n. a splinter. WH: 14–15C. Prob. from (source of) SHELF[1].

skelly a. squint. *Also n., v.i.* WH: 18C. Old Norse *skjálgr* wry, oblique.

skelp n. a blow, a smack. *Also v.t.* WH: 14–15C. Prob. imit.

skep n. a basket or similar receptacle of wicker, wood etc., or the amount it can carry. WH: pre-1200. Old English *sceppe*, from Old Norse *skeppa* basket, bushel. Cp. German *Scheffel* bushel.

skerrick n. a tiny amount. WH: 19C. Orig. unknown.

skerry n. a rocky islet in the sea. WH: 17C. Orkney dial., from Old Norse *sker*. Cp. SCAR[2].

sketch *n.* a rough, hasty, unfinished or tentative drawing or paint-ing, often one done in preparation for a larger work. *Also v.t., v.i.* WH: 17C. Dutch *schets* or German *Skizze*, from Italian *schizzo*, from *schizzare* to make a sketch, from Latin *schedius*, from Greek *skhedios* done extempore.

skeuomorph *n.* a decorative feature in architecture etc. derived from the material used, or the means of working it. WH: 19C. Greek *skeuos* vessel, implement + -MORPH.

skew *a.* oblique, slanting, crooked, twisted, turned askew. *Also n., v.i., v.t.* WH: 14–15C. Shortening of Old Northern French *eskiuer*, *eskuer*, var. of Old French *eschiver* ESCHEW, or shortening of ASKEW. The adjective evolved from the verb in the 17C.

skewbald *a.* (of an animal, esp. a horse) with spots of white and a colour other than black, as distinct from piebald. *Also n.* WH: 17C. Obs. *skewed* (? from Old French *escu* (Modern French *écu*) shield, from Latin *scutum*) + -*bald*, based on PIEBALD.

skewer *n.* a long pin of wood or metal for holding meat together during cooking. *Also v.t.* WH: 14–15C. Orig. uncertain. ? Of Scan-dinavian orig.

ski *n.* either of a pair of long narrow runners of waxed wood, metal, plastic etc., usu. pointed and curved upwards at the front, fastened one to each foot and used for sliding over snow. *Also a., v.i., v.t.* WH: 18C. Norwegian, from Old Norse *skith* billet of cleft wood, snowshoe. Cp. SKID.

skid *v.i.* (of wheels or vehicles) to slip sideways or diagonally on a slippery surface. *Also v.t., n.* WH: 17C. Orig. uncertain. The form and meaning of the word are close to Norwegian *skith* (SKI).

skidoo *v.i.* to make off, decamp. WH: early 20C. ? From SKEDADDLE.

skiff[1] *n.* a small light boat. *Also v.i.* WH: 15C. French *esquif*, from Italian *schifo*, prob. ult. from Old High German *schif* SHIP.

skiff[2] *v.i., v.t.* to skim (as a stone on water). *Also n.* WH: 18C. ? Alt. of dial. *skift* (from Old Norse *skipta*, rel. to SHIFT) or of SCUFF.

skiffle *n.* a type of music popular in the 1950s played on un-conventional percussion instruments and guitars. WH: early 20C. Orig. unknown.

skill *n.* familiar knowledge of any art or science combined with dexterity. WH: pre-1200. Old Norse *skil*, rel. to *skila* to give reason for, to expound and Middle Low German *schēlen* to differ, to make a difference. Skill implies the ability to differentiate and to be discerning.

skillet *n.* a long-handled cooking pot. WH: 12–14C. Prob. from Old French *escuelete*, dim. of *escuele* (Modern French *écuelle*) platter, from Popular Latin, from Latin *scutella* SCUTTLE[1]. See also -ET[1].

skilling *n.* an outhouse, a lean-to, a shed, esp. with a sloping roof. WH: 14–15C. Orig. unknown.

skilly *n.* thin broth, soup or gruel. WH: 19C. Abbr. of *skilligalee*, appar. a fanciful formation.

skim *v.t.* to clear the scum etc. from the surface of. *Also v.i., n.* WH: 12–14C. Back-formation from *skimmer* (SKIM), or from Old French *escumer* (Modern French *écumer*), from *escume* scum.

skimmia *n.* any evergreen shrub of the Asian genus *Skimmia*, with red berries. WH: 19C. Modern Latin, from Japanese (*miyama*) *shikimi*.

skimp *v.t.* to supply in a niggardly manner, to stint (a person, provisions etc.). *Also v.i.* WH: 18C. Orig. uncertain. Cp. SCRIMP, SCAMP[2].

skin *n.* the natural membraneous outer covering of an animal body. *Also a., v.t., v.i.* WH: pre-1200. Old Norse *skinn*, rel. to Middle Low German *schinden* to flay, to peel, Old High German *scinden* (German *schinden*). The equivalent Old English word was *hȳd* HIDE[2].

skink *n.* a small lizard of the family Scincidae, of Africa and SW Asia. WH: 16C. Obs. French *scinc* (now *scinque*) or Latin *scincus*, from Greek *skigkos*.

skint *a.* hard up for money, penniless. WH: early 20C. Var. of *skinned* (SKIN).

skip[1] *v.i.* to progress by hopping on each foot in turn. *Also v.t., n.* WH: 12–14C. Prob. of Scandinavian orig.

skip[2] *n.* a container for collecting and moving refuse, building materials etc. WH: 14–15C. Var. of SKEP. The sense container for builder's refuse dates from the 19C.

skip[3] *n.* a skipper. *Also v.t.* WH: 19C. Abbr. of SKIPPER.

skipper *n.* a sea captain, the master of a vessel. *Also v.t.* WH: 14–15C. Middle Low German and Middle Dutch *schipper*, from *schip* SHIP. See also -ER[1].

skippet *n.* a flat round box for holding the seal attached to a docu-ment. WH: 14–15C. Orig. unknown.

skirl *n.* the shrill sound of the bagpipes. *Also v.i.* WH: 14–15C. Prob. of Scandinavian orig., ult. imit. Cp. SHRILL.

skirmish *n.* a slight or irregular fight, esp. between small parties or scattered troops. *Also v.i.* WH: 12–14C. Old French *eskermiss-*, *eskirmiss-*, stem of *eskermir*, *eskirmir* (Modern French *escrimer* to fence), from a Frankish v. meaning to defend. See also -ISH[2]. Cp. SCARAMOUCH, SCRIMMAGE.

skirr *v.t.* to pass over rapidly, to range, to scour. *Also v.i.* WH: 16C. Orig. uncertain. ? Rel. to SCOUR[2].

skirret *n.* an umbelliferous plant, *Sium sisarum*, with an edible tuberous root. WH: 14–15C. ? From dial. *skire* pure, clear, bright, from Old Norse *skír* (rel. to SHEER[1]) + WHITE.

skirt *n.* a woman's garment hanging from the waist. *Also v.t., v.i.* WH: 20C. Old Norse *skyrta*, corr. to Old English *scyrte* SHIRT.

skit[1] *n.* a satirical piece, lampoon or humorous theatrical sketch (on a certain situation or topic). WH: 16C. Prob. of Scandinavian orig., ? ult. from Old Norse alt. of stem of *skjóta* SHOOT. Cp. SKITE[1], SKITTISH. The earliest sense was a frivolous woman. The current sense dates from the 18C.

skit[2] *n.* a large number or crowd. WH: early 20C. Orig. unknown.

skite[1] *v.i.* to dart aside, to slip, to slide. *Also v.t., n.* WH: 18C. ? From Old Norse *skýt-*, stem of *skjóta* SHOOT.

skite[2] *v.i.* to boast or brag. *Also n.* WH: 19C. SKITE[1].

skitter *v.i.* to glide, skim or skip rapidly (esp. along a surface). *Also v.t., n.* WH: 19C. Appar. freq. of SKITE[1]. See also -ER[5].

skittish *a.* (of horses) excitable, nervous, easily frightened. WH: 14–15C. Orig. uncertain. ? Ult. from Old Norse alt. of stem of *skjóta* SHOOT + -ISH[1]. Cp. SKIT[1], SKITE[1].

skittle *n.* any one of the pins set up to be bowled at in skittles or ninepins. *Also v.i.* WH: 17C. ? Rel. to SKIT[1]. Cp. Swedish and Danish *skyttel* shuttle, marble.

skive[1] *v.t.* to split (leather) into thin layers. WH: 19C. Old Norse *skifa*, rel. to SHEAVE[1].

skive[2] *v.i.* to avoid performing a duty, task etc. *Also v.t., n.* WH: early 20C. ? French *esquiver* to dodge, to slink away.

skivvy *n.* a maid or general servant. *Also v.i.* WH: early 20C. Orig. unknown.

skol *int.* cheers! good health! (usu. as a toast). WH: 17C. Danish *skaal*, Swedish *skål* toast, from Old Norse *skál* bowl.

skua *n.* a dark-coloured predatory seabird of the family Stercor-ariidae, allied to the gulls. WH: 17C. Modern Latin, from Faeroese *skúvur*, prob. of imit. orig. (but assim. to *skufr* tassel).

skulduggery *n.* underhand behaviour, trickery, cheating or mal-practice. WH: 19C. Alt. of *sculduddery* (18C) sexual impropriety, indecency, of unknown orig.

skulk *v.i.* to lurk, to withdraw and conceal oneself. *Also n.* WH: 12–14C. Of Scandinavian orig. Cp. Norwegian *skulke* to lurk, to lie watching, Swedish *skolka*, Danish *skulke* to shirk, to play truant.

skull *n.* the bony case enclosing the brain, the cranium. WH: 12–14C. Orig. unknown. Cp. Old Norse *skoltr*, Norwegian *skolt, skult*, Swedish *skult*. The native Old English word was *hēafodbolla*, lit. head bowl, or *hēafodpanne*, lit. head pan.

skunk *n.* a N American carnivorous quadruped, *Mephitis mephitica*, with a bushy tail and white stripes down the back, which when on the defence ejects a fetid secretion from the anal glands. *Also v.t.* WH: 17C. Algonquian (prob. Abnaki) *segongw*.

sky *n.* the apparent vault of heaven, the firmament. *Also v.t.* WH: 12–14C. Old Norse *ský* cloud, rel. to Old English *scēo*. The Old Norse word replaced native Old English *heofon* HEAVEN, just as CLOUD replaced native WELKIN.

Skye *n.* a small rough-haired variety of Scotch terrier with a long body and short legs. WH: 19C. *Skye*, the largest island of the Inner Hebrides, NW Scotland.

skyr *n.* a dish of curds. WH: 19C. Icelandic.

slab[1] *n.* a thin, flat, regularly shaped piece of anything, esp. of stone, concrete etc. *Also a., v.t.* WH: 12–14C. Orig. unknown.

slab[2] *a.* thick, slimy, viscous, sticky. *Also n.* WH: 17C. Prob. of Scandinavian orig. Cp. Old Danish *slab* mud, Icelandic, Norwegian, Swedish *slabb* wet filth.

slack[1] *a.* not drawn tight, loose. *Also adv., n., v.i., v.t.* WH: pre-1200. Old English *slæc*, from Germanic, rel. to Latin *laxus* LAX. Rel. to SLAKE. The earliest sense was remiss, negligent. The sense loose, not tight dates from the 12–14C. (One might have expected the other way round.)

slack[2] *n.* a hollow, a dip, a dell. WH: 12–14C. Old Norse *slakki*.

slack[3] *n.* small pieces of coal, or coal dust. WH: 14–15C. Prob. from Low Dutch. Cp. Low German *slakk*, German *Schlacke* dross.

slag *n.* the fused refuse or dross separated in the reduction of ores, clinker. *Also v.i., v.t.* WH: 16C. Middle Low German *slagge*, prob. from *slagen* to strike, with ref. to the fragments made by hammering.

slake *v.t.* to quench, to assuage, to satisfy, to appease (one's thirst, desire etc.). *Also v.i.* WH: pre-1200. Old English *slacian*, from *slæc* SLACK[1]. The original sense (to the 16C) was to slacken. The sense to quench dates from the 12–14C.

slalom *n.* a downhill ski race on a zigzagged course marked with artificial obstacles. WH: early 20C. Norwegian *slalåm*, from *sla* sloping + *låm* track.

slam[1] *v.t.* to shut (a door, lid etc.) suddenly with a loud noise. *Also v.i., n.* WH: 17C. Prob. from Scandinavian. Cp. Old Norse *slamra*, Swedish *slämma*, Norwegian *slemma*.

slam[2] *n.* in whist etc., the winning of every trick (a *grand slam*), or all but one trick (a *little slam* or *small slam*). *Also v.t.* WH: 17C. Orig. unknown.

slander *n.* a false statement maliciously uttered to injure a person. *Also v.t.* WH: 12–14C. Shortening of Old French *esclandre*, alt. of *escandle* SCANDAL.

slang *n.* very informal vocabulary or phraseology that would be out of place in a formal context, and is often confined to a specific context, culture or profession. *Also a., v.i., v.t.* WH: 18C. Orig. unknown. ? Rel. to SLING[1]. Some sources derive the word from French *langue* language.

slant *v.i.* to slope. *Also v.t., a., n.* WH: 14–15C. Var. of dial. *slent*, of Scandinavian orig. Cp. Norwegian *slent* side-slip, Swedish *slänt* slope, slant.

slap *v.t.* to strike with the open hand, to smack. *Also n., adv.* WH: 14–15C. Prob. imit. Cp. SMACK[1].

slash *v.t.* to cut by striking violently at random. *Also v.i., n.* WH: 14–15C. Prob. imit. (cp. FLASH), or shortening of Old French *esclachier* to break, rel. to *esclater* (Modern French *éclater*). See SLAT[1].

slat[1] *n.* a thin narrow strip, usu. of wood or metal, used in Venetian blinds, crates etc. *Also v.i.* WH: 14–15C. Shortening of Old French *esclat* (Modern French *éclat*) splinter, piece broken off, from *esclater*. Cp. SLATE[1].

slat[2] *v.t.* to fling, to dash, to slap, to jerk. *Also v.i., n.* WH: 12–14C. Orig. unknown.

slate[1] *n.* a fine-grained laminated rock easily splitting into thin, smooth, even slabs. *Also v.t., a.* WH: 12–14C. Old French *esclate*, fem. corr. to m. *esclat* SLAT[1]. The rock is so called because it splits easily into thin layers.

slate[2] *v.t.* to criticize savagely, to abuse, to berate. WH: 15C. SLATE[1]. The sense perhaps evolved from the idea of hurling slates. Cp. STONE.

slattern *n.* an untidy or sluttish woman. WH: 17C. Orig. uncertain. The word is probably related to SLAT[2].

slaughter *n.* the killing of animals for market. *Also v.t.* WH: 12–14C. Old Norse *slátr* butcher's meat, rel. to SLAY.

Slav *n.* a member of any of various peoples inhabiting eastern Europe who speak a Slavonic language, including the Russians, Poles, Serbs, Croats, Bulgarians and Slovenes. *Also a.* WH: 14–15C. Orig. from Medieval Latin *Sclavus*, corr. to Medieval Greek *Sklabos*. Later from Medieval Latin *Slavus*. Cp. SLAVE.

slave *n.* a person who is the property of and bound in obedience to another. *Also v.i.* WH: 12–14C. Shortening of Old French *esclave*, use as n. of fem. of *esclaf*, corr. to Medieval Latin *sclavus* captive, identical with *Sclavus* SLAV. A slave is so called because many Slavs were taken captive and sold into slavery by their conquerors in the 9C.

slaver *v.i.* to let saliva flow from the mouth, to slobber, to dribble. *Also v.t., n.* WH: 12–14C. Ult. imit. Cp. SLOBBER.

slaw *n.* sliced cabbage served as a salad, coleslaw. WH: 18C. Dutch *sla*, contr. of *salade* SALAD. Cp. *coleslaw* (COLE).

slay *v.t.* to put to death, to kill. WH: pre-1200. Old English *slēan*, from Germanic. Cp. SLAUGHTER.

sleaze *n.* that which is squalid, distasteful, disreputable, esp. with reference to corrupt behaviour by politicians. *Also v.i.* WH: mid-20C. Back-formation from *sleazy*, of unknown orig.

sled *n.* a sledge. *Also v.i., v.t.* WH: 12–14C. Middle Low German *sledde*, corr. to Middle High German *slitte* (German *Schlitten*) and rel. to Dutch *slede*, *slee* SLEIGH. Cp. SLEDGE[1].

sledge[1] *n.* a vehicle on runners instead of wheels, used for carrying passengers or hauling loads etc., esp. over snow or ice, drawn variously by dogs, horses, reindeer or people; a sleigh. *Also v.i., v.t.* WH: 16C. Middle Dutch *sleedse*, related to *slēde* SLED.

sledge[2] *n.* a sledgehammer. WH: pre-1200. Old English *slecg*, from Germanic base meaning to strike. Cp. SLAY. As *sledge* means hammer, *sledgehammer* is really a tautology.

sleek *a.* (of fur, skin etc.) smooth, glossy. *Also v.t.* WH: 16C. Later var. of SLICK.

sleep *n.* a state of rest in which consciousness is almost entirely suspended, the body is relaxed, the eyes are closed, and the vital functions are inactive. *Also v.i., v.t.* WH: pre-1200. Old English *slēp*, *slǣp*, from a Germanic n. corr. to the v. forming the source of *slǣpan*, rel. to German *schlafen* to sleep. There are no related forms in Scandinavian. Cp. Swedish *sova* to sleep, Norwegian *sove*.

sleet *n.* hail or snow mingled with rain. *Also v.i.* WH: 12–14C. Prob. from an unrecorded Old English form rel. to Middle Low German *slōten* (pl.) hail, Middle High German *slōze* (German *Schlosse*) hailstone, from Germanic.

sleeve *n.* the part of a garment that covers the arm. *Also v.t.* WH: pre-1200. Old English *slēfe*, *slīefe*, ult. related to Middle Dutch *sloove*, *sloof* covering.

sleigh *n.* a vehicle mounted on runners for driving over snow or ice, a sledge, esp. for carrying passengers rather than goods. *Also v.i.* WH: 14–15C. Dutch *slee*. See SLED.

sleight *n.* dexterity, skill in manipulating things. *Also a.* WH: 12–14C. Old Norse *slægth*, from *slœgr* SLY. The phrase *sleight of hand* dates from the 14–15C. Cp. LEGERDEMAIN.

slender *a.* small in circumference or width as compared with length. WH: 14–15C. Orig. unknown.

sleuth *n.* a detective. *Also v.i., v.t.* WH: 12–14C. Old Norse *slóth* track, trail. Cp. SLOT[2].

slew[1] *v.t., v.i.* to turn, twist or swing (round, about etc.) as on a pivot. *Also n.* WH: 17C. Orig. unknown.

slew[2] *n.* a great quantity or large number. WH: 19C. Irish *slua* crowd, multitude.

sley *n.* a weaver's reed for separating threads. WH: pre-1200. Old English *slege*, from base of SLAY.

slice *n.* a broad, thin piece cut off, esp. from bread etc., or a wedge cut from a circular pie, tart, cake etc. *Also v.t., v.i.* WH: 12–14C. Shortening of Old French *esclice* (Modern French *éclisse*) small piece of wood, from *esclicier* to splinter, to shatter, from Frankish *slītjan*, from Germanic. See SLIT. The original sense (to the 16C) was fragment, chip, splinter. The sense thin piece of bread, etc. dates from the 15C.

slick *a.* dexterous, adroit. *Also adv., n., v.t.* WH: 12–14C. From an unrecorded Old English word (seen in *nīgslicod* newly polished) rel. to Old Norse *slíkr* smooth, Icelandic *slíkja*, Norwegian *slikja* to be smooth, to make smooth. Cp. SLEEK. The original sense was slick, slippery. The sense dexterous, adroit evolved in the 19C.

slickenside *n.* a polished and grooved rock surface produced by friction, as in faults, the sides of a vein etc. WH: 18C. From dial. var. of SLICK + SIDE.

slide *v.i.* to move smoothly along a surface with continuous contact, esp. to glide over ice, snow or other slippery surface, without skates. *Also v.t., n.* WH: pre-1200. Old English *slīdan*, rel. to *slidor* slippery and also to SLED, SLEDGE[1].

slight *a.* inconsiderable, insignificant. *Also n., v.t.* WH: 12–14C. Old Norse *sléttr* level, smooth, soft, from Germanic. Cp. German *schlecht* bad, *schlicht* simple. The original sense as a verb (to the 17C) was to make smooth, to level. The sense to treat with contempt dates from the 16C.

slim *a.* tall and narrow in shape. *Also v.i., v.t., n.* WH: 17C. Low German and Dutch, representing Middle Low German *slimm*, Middle Dutch *slimp* slanting, cross, bad, corr. to Middle High German *slimp* slanting, oblique, German *schlimm* grievous, bad, from Germanic.

slime *n.* any soft, glutinous or viscous substance, esp. mucus or soft, moist and sticky earth. *Also v.t.* WH: pre-1200. Old English *slīm*, from a Germanic word rel. to Latin *limus* mud, slime, Greek *limnē* marsh. Cp. German *Schleim* phlegm, slime, mucus.

sling[1] *n.* a band or other arrangement of rope, chains etc., for suspending, hoisting or transferring anything. *Also v.t., v.i.* WH: 12–14C. Prob. from Low Dutch, ult. of imit. orig. Cp. German *Schlinge* noose, snare, arm sling.

sling[2] *n.* a sweetened drink of water mixed with spirits, esp. gin. WH: 18C. Orig. unknown. ? From SLING[1] with idea of drinking rapidly.

slink *v.i.* to steal or sneak (away etc.) in a furtive or cowardly manner. *Also v.t., n.* WH: pre-1200. Old English *slincan*, corr. to Middle Low German *slinken* to subside.

slip[1] *v.i.* to slide unintentionally and miss one's footing. *Also v.t., n.* WH: 12–14C. Prob. from Middle Low German and Dutch *slippen*, from Germanic. Cp. German *schleifen* to slide, to grind, to polish.

slip[2] *n.* a creamy mixture of clay and water used to coat or decorate pottery. WH: pre-1200. Old English *slipa, slyppe*. Cp. SLOP[1].

slip[3] *n.* a small piece of paper for writing messages etc. on. *Also v.t.* WH: 17C. SLIP[1].

slit *n.* a long cut or narrow opening. *Also v.t.* WH: pre-1200. Old English *slītan* to cut, to tear up, from Germanic. Cp. German *schleissen*.

slither *v.i.* to slip, to slide unsteadily (along etc.). *Also n.* WH: 12–14C. Alt. of dial. *slidder*, from Old English *slidrian*, from Germanic. Rel. to SLIDE.

sliver *n.* a thin piece cut from something. *Also v.t., v.i.* WH: 14–15C. From obs. *slive* to cleave, to split, prob. rel. to an Old English v. recorded in past tense *tōslāf*.

slivovitz *n.* a dry plum brandy. WH: 19C. Serbo-Croat *šljivovica*, from *šljiva* plum (cp. SLOE).

Sloane *n.* an upper-class young person, typically female and cultivating the casually elegant look, living in any of the fashionable parts of London. WH: late 20C. From *Sloane* Ranger, punning formation on *Sloane* Square, London and *Lone Ranger*, a fictitious cowboy hero. The term was coined in 1975 by Peter York, an English market researcher.

slob *n.* a messy, slovenly or boorish person. WH: 18C. Irish *slab*, from English dial., from English dial. *slab* muddy place, prob. of Scandinavian orig., ? also partly from SLOBBER. The original sense was mud. The sense boorish fat person arose in the 19C.

slobber *v.i.* to let saliva run from the mouth, to dribble, to slaver. *Also v.t., n.* WH: 14–15C. Prob. from Middle Dutch *slobberen* to walk through mud, to feed noisily. Cp. SLUBBER.

sloe *n.* the fruit of the blackthorn, *Prunus spinosa*, or the shrub bearing it. WH: pre-1200. Old English *slā*, from Germanic base prob. rel. to Latin *livere* to be blue, Slavonic base represented by Russian *sliva* plum (cp. SLIVOVITZ).

slog *v.t.* to hit vigorously and at random, esp. in batting or with the fists. *Also v.i., n.* WH: 18C. Orig. unknown. Cp. SLUG[2].

slogan *n.* a catchy advertising phrase or word. WH: 16C. Gaelic *sluagh-ghairm*, from *sluagh* host + *gairm* cry, shout. The original meaning was war cry, battle cry, specifically a Scottish Highland war cry consisting of a personal name (e.g. 'A Douglas! A Douglas!'). The current sense evolved in the 18C.

sloop *n.* a fore-and-aft rigged vessel with one mast. WH: 17C. Dutch *sloep*, of unknown orig. ? Rel. to SLIP[1].

sloot *n.* an irrigation ditch, a drainage channel. WH: 19C. Afrikaans ditch, from Germanic.

slop[1] *v.t.* to spill or allow to overflow. *Also v.i., n.* WH: 14–15C. Prob. from Old English *sloppe* dung as in *cūsloppe* COWSLIP. Cp. SLIP[2].

slop[2] *n.* a workman's loose overall. WH: 12–14C. From 2nd element of obs. *overslop* loose upper garment, from OVER- + unexplained 2nd element, ult. from Germanic.

slope *n.* an inclined surface, line or direction. *Also v.i., v.t.* WH: 17C. Shortening of ASLOPE.

slosh *v.t.* to strike hard. *Also v.i., n.* WH: 19C. Var. of SLUSH.

slot[1] *n.* the aperture into which coins are put in a slot machine. *Also v.t., v.i.* WH: 14–15C. Old French *esclot*, ult. of unknown orig. The earliest sense was the hollow depression running down the middle of the chest. The current sense (slit in a machine for a coin to be inserted) arose in the 19C.

slot[2] *n.* the track of a deer. WH: 16C. Old French *esclot* horse's hoofprint, prob. from Old Norse *slóth* track. See SLEUTH.

slot[3] *n.* a bar or bolt fastening a door. WH: 12–14C. Middle Low German and Middle Dutch, from Germanic. Cp. German *Schloss* lock, castle, *Schlüssel* key, *schliessen* to close, to lock.

sloth *n.* laziness, indolence, sluggishness, reluctance to exert oneself. WH: pre-1200. SLOW + -TH[2]. The name of the animal evolved in the 17C and refers to its slow movements. It translated Portuguese *preguiça*, the name given it by Portuguese explorers.

slouch *n.* an ungainly or negligent drooping or stooping gait, or movement. *Also v.i., v.t.* WH: 16C. Orig. unknown. ? From Scandinavian and rel. to SLACK[1]. The original sense was a lazy or ungainly person, a lout. The verb evolved from this in the 18C.

slough[1] *n.* a place full of mud, a bog, a quagmire. WH: pre-1200. Old English *slōh*, of unknown orig.

slough[2] *n.* the cast skin of a snake. *Also v.t., v.i.* WH: 12–14C. ? Rel. to Low German *sluwe, slu* husk, peel, shell.

Slovak *n.* any member of a Slavonic people inhabiting Slovakia, formerly the eastern part of Czechoslovakia, but now an independent republic. *Also a.* WH: 19C. Slovak, Czech and Russian, from Slavonic base also of SLOVENE.

sloven *n.* a person who is careless about dress or negligent about cleanliness; an untidy, careless, lazy person. WH: 15C. ? Based on Flemish *sloef* dirty, squalid, Dutch *slof* negligent. The original sense (to the 17C) was a person of low character, a knave, a rascal. The sense untidy person evolved in the 16C.

Slovene *n.* a member of a S Slavonic people inhabiting Slovenia, a republic of S central Europe, formerly part of Yugoslavia. *Also a.* WH: 19C. German *Slowene*, from Slovene *Slovenec* a Slovene, from Slavonic base of SLOVAK, ? ult. from stem of *slovo* word, *sloviti* to speak.

slow *a.* not quick, of low velocity, moving at a low speed. *Also adv., v.i., v.t.* WH: pre-1200. Old English *slāw*, from Germanic, from Indo-European. Cp. German dial. *schleh*, Swedish *slö*, Danish and Norwegian *sløv*.

slow-worm *n.* a small limbless viviparous snakelike lizard, *Anguis fragilis*, the blindworm. WH: pre-1200. Old English *slā-wyrm*, from *slā*, of unknown orig., assim. to SLOW + *wyrm* WORM. The first element was formerly associated with Old English *slēan* SLAY as the creature was believed to be venomous.

slub[1] *n.* a knob or lump in yarn. *Also a.* WH: 19C. Orig. unknown.

slub[2] *n.* wool slightly twisted before spinning. *Also v.t.* WH: 19C. Orig. unknown.

slubber *v.t.* to do lazily, carelessly, or bunglingly. WH: 16C. Prob. var. of SLOBBER.

sludge *n.* thick mud. WH: 17C. Orig. uncertain. Cp. SLUSH.

slug[1] *n.* a shell-less air-breathing gastropod, very destructive to plants. *Also v.t.* WH: 14–15C. Prob. from Scandinavian. Cp. Norwegian dial. *slugg* large heavy body, *sluggje* heavy slow person. The original sense was slothfulness personified, then sluggard. The name of the mollusc dates from the 18C (cp. SLOTH as an animal name). Previous to this a slug was known as a SNAIL.

slug[2] *v.t.* to hit hard. *Also n.* WH: 19C. Orig. unknown. Cp. SLOG.

sluice *n.* a waterway with a sliding gate or hatch by which the level of a body of water is controlled, a sluice-gate or floodgate. *Also v.t., v.i.* WH: 12–14C. Old French *escluce* (Modern French *écluse*), from Late Latin *exclusa*, fem. p.p. (used as n.) of Latin *excludere* EXCLUDE.

slum[1] *n.* a squalid, usu. overcrowded, neighbourhood in a town or city, inhabited by the very poor. *Also v.i.* WH: 19C. Orig. unknown. The original sense was room.

slum² *n.* the non-lubricating part of crude oil. WH: 19C. ? German *Schlamm*, or influ. by *slum*, abbr. of SLUMGULLION.

slumber *v.i.* to sleep, esp. lightly. *Also v.t., n.* WH: 12–14C. Alt. of dial. *sloom*, from Old English *slūma*, from Germanic, or corr. to Middle Low German and Middle Dutch *slūmen*, rel. to German *schlummern*. The *b* has entered as for CHAMBER, EMBER¹, TIMBER, etc.

slumgullion *n.* watery stew, or other sloppy matter. WH: 19C. Prob. a fanciful formation.

slump *v.i.* to fall or sink (down) heavily. *Also n.* WH: 17C. Prob. imit. ? Rel. to Norwegian *slumpe* to fall. Cp. PLUMP².

slur *v.t.* to pronounce indistinctly. *Also v.i., n.* WH: 17C. From obs. *slur* thin mud, of unknown orig. Cp. SLURRY. Some sources relate the word to an earlier verb *slur* to slip a die out of a box so that it does not roll, perhaps related to Low German *slurren* to shuffle, Dutch *sleuren* to drag, to trail.

slurp *n.* a sucking sound produced when eating or drinking noisily. *Also v.i., v.t.* WH: 17C. Dutch *slurpen*, prob. of imit. orig.

slurry *n.* a thin, fluid paste made by mixing certain materials (esp. cement) with water. WH: 14–15C. Rel. to SLUR.

slush *n.* half-melted snow. *Also v.i., v.t.* WH: 17C. Prob. imit. Cp. SLUDGE.

slut *n.* a dirty, slovenly or sexually promiscuous woman. WH: 12–14C. Orig. unknown. ? Ult. rel. to SLATTERN, but not to SLOVEN.

sly *a.* crafty, cunning. WH: 12–14C. Old Norse *slœgr* clever, cunning, orig. able to strike, from *slóg-*, p.p. stem of *slá* to strike. Cp. SLEIGHT.

slype *n.* a covered passage between the transept of a cathedral and the chapter house, deanery etc. WH: 19C. ? Var. of obs. *slipe* narrow strip of ground, prob. alt. of SLIP³.

smack¹ *n.* a blow with the flat of the hand, a slap. *Also v.t., v.i., adv.* WH: 16C. Middle Low German and Middle Dutch *smacken*, of imit. orig. Cp. SLAP. The earliest sense was a loud kiss. The sense blow with the flat of the hand evolved in the 18C.

smack² *n.* a slight taste or flavour (of). *Also v.i.* WH: pre-1200. Old English *smæc*, from Germanic. Cp. German *Geschmack*.

smack³ *n.* a one-masted vessel, like a sloop or cutter, used in fishing etc. WH: 17C. Low German and Dutch *smacke*, of unknown orig.

smack⁴ *n.* heroin or some other illegally sold drug. WH: mid-20C. Prob. alt. of *schmeck*, from Yiddish, lit. sniff, smell.

small *a.* deficient or relatively little in size, stature, amount etc. *Also adv., n.* WH: pre-1200. Old English *smæl*, from Germanic. Cp. German *schmal* narrow.

†smallage *n.* wild celery. WH: 12–14C. SMALL + obs. *ache*, from Old French, from Latin *apium* parsley, from *apis* bee. The plant is so called as it attracts bees.

smalt *n.* a blue glass coloured with cobalt, used in a pulverized state as a pigment. WH: 16C. French, from Italian *smalto*, from Germanic, rel. to SMELT¹.

smarm *v.t.* to plaster, to flatten (hair down) with hair oil etc. *Also v.i., n.* WH: 19C. Orig. unknown.

smart *a.* spruce, formal and stylish. *Also v.i., adv., n.* WH: pre-1200. Old English *smeortan* to be painful, from Germanic base, ? rel. to Latin *mordere* to bite, Greek *smerdnos* terrible. Cp. German *schmerzen* to hurt, to be painful. The original sense was painful, sharp, keen. The current sense dates from the 12–14C.

smash *v.t.* to break to pieces by violence, to shatter. *Also v.i., n., adv.* WH: 17C. Prob. imit., representing a blend of SMACK¹, SMITE, etc. with BASH¹, MASH¹, etc.

smatter *n.* a smattering. WH: 12–14C. Orig. unknown. The noun evolved in the 17C from the verb, which originally meant to make dirty, to pollute, then to talk superficially, to chatter.

smear *v.t.* to rub or daub with anything greasy or sticky. *Also v.i., n.* WH: pre-1200. Old English *smeirwan*, from Germanic, rel. to Greek *muron* ointment, *smuris* EMERY. Cp. German *schmieren*.

smectic *a.* denoting, of or relating to the state, e.g. of liquid crystal, between solid and liquid, with atoms and molecules oriented in parallel planes. *Also n.* WH: 17C. Latin *smecticus*, from Greek *smēktikos*, from *smēkhein* to rub, to cleanse (cp. SMEGMA). See also -IC.

smeddum *n.* fine powder. WH: pre-1200. Old English *smedma*, of unknown orig.

smegma *n.* a sebaceous soapy secretion found in the folds of the skin, esp. under the foreskin. WH: 19C. Latin, from Greek *smēgma* soap, from *smēkhein* to rub, to cleanse.

smell *n.* the sense by which odours are perceived. *Also v.t., v.i.* WH: 12–14C. Orig. unknown. The word was probably already in Old English but is not recorded and no related words are known. It was formerly associated with SMOULDER.

smelt¹ *v.t.* to fuse (an ore) so as to extract the metal. WH: 16C. Middle Low German and Middle Dutch *smelten*, from Germanic base also of MELT. Cp. SMALT.

smelt² *n.* a small food fish, *Osmerus eperlanus*, allied to the salmon. WH: pre-1200. Old English, rel. to various European fish names. Cp. SMOLT.

smew *n.* a small merganser or diving duck, *Mergus albellus*. WH: 17C. Rel. to Dutch *smient*, Low German *smēnt* widgeon, German *Schmeiente* small wild duck (from *Ente* duck).

smidgen *n.* a tiny amount. WH: 19C. Orig. uncertain. ? From *smitch* particle, of unknown orig.

smilax *n.* any climbing shrub of the genus *Smilax*, the roots of many species of which yield sarsaparilla. WH: 16C. Latin, from Greek bindweed, smilax.

smile *v.i.* to express amusement, kindness or pleasure by an instinctive lateral movement of the lips with an upward turn at the corners. *Also v.t., n.* WH: 12–14C. Of Scandinavian orig. Rel. to SMIRK.

smirch *v.t.* to soil, to smear, to stain, to defile, to defame (someone's name or reputation). *Also n.* WH: 15C. Prob. imit. Cp. SMITE, SMUDGE¹, SMUT, etc. The sense to discredit, to defame dates from the 19C.

smirk *v.i.* to smile affectedly or smugly. *Also n.* WH: pre-1200. Old English *smearcian*, from base represented by *smerian* to laugh at. Cp. SMILE. The original sense was to smile in general.

smite *v.t.* to strike, to deal a severe blow to. *Also v.i., n.* WH: pre-1200. Old English *smītan* to smear, to pollute, from Germanic. Prob. of imit. orig. Cp. German *schmeissen* to throw, to fling.

smith *n.* a person who works in metals, esp. someone who forges iron with the hammer, a blacksmith. WH: pre-1200. Old English, from Germanic. Cp. German *Schmied*. Not rel. to SMITE.

smithereens *n.pl.* little bits, tiny fragments. WH: 19C. Prob. from Irish *smidirín*. See also -EEN, -S¹.

smithsonite *n.* carbonate of zinc, calamine. WH: 19C. James L.M. *Smithson*, 1765–1829, British chemist and mineralogist + -ITE¹. The name was coined in 1832 by the French geologist and mineralogist François Beudant.

smock *n.* a loose dress or shirt with a yoke, or smocking forming one, or an artist's overall of similar shape. *Also v.t.* WH: pre-1200. Old English *smoc*, from Germanic. Cp. German *Schmuck* ornament. The word is perhaps related to Old English *smūgan* to creep, to denote a garment into which one 'worms'.

smog *n.* fog thickened by smoke and by fumes from industrial plants or motor vehicles. WH: early 20C. Blend of SMOKE and FOG¹. The word was apparently coined in 1905 by H.A. Des Vœux of the Coal Smoke Abatement Society, London.

smoke *n.* volatile products of combustion, esp. carbonaceous and other matter in the form of visible vapour or fine particles escaping from a burning substance. *Also v.i., v.t.* WH: pre-1200. Old English *smoca*, from Germanic. Cp. German *Schmauch* thick smoke.

smolt *n.* a salmon in its second year when it acquires its silvery scales. WH: 14–15C. Orig. uncertain. Cp. SMELT².

smooth *a.* having a continuously even surface, free from roughness. *Also v.t., v.i., n.* WH: pre-1200. Old English *smōth*, prob. from Germanic but with no known rel. words. The more common Old English word was *smēthe*, the source of London's *Smithfield* (smooth field) and similar place names.

smorgasbord *n.* a buffet or hors d'œuvre of open sandwiches. WH: 19C. Swedish *smörgåsbord*, from *smörgås* (slice of) bread and butter (from *smör* butter + *gås* goose, lump of butter) + *bord* board, table. The word is apt to be confused in English with *smørbrod* or *smørrebrod*, literally bread and butter (actually hors d'oeuvres served on slices of buttered bread), from Norwegian and Danish *smør* butter + *brød* bread.

smorzando *a., adv.* with a gradual fading or dying away. *Also n.* WH: 19C. Italian, pres.p. of *smorzare* to extinguish.

smother *v.t.* to suffocate, to stifle. *Also v.i., n.* WH: 12–14C. From base of Old English *smorian* to suffocate, to choke.

smoulder *v.i.* to burn in a smothered way without flames. *Also n.* WH: 14–15C. Orig. uncertain. Rel. to Low German *smöln*, Middle Dutch *smölen* (Dutch *smeulen*), Frisian *smoel* sultry. The original sense was to smother, to suffocate. The word fell out of use in the 17C and 18C, but was revived by Sir Walter Scott in the 19C: 'Smoulders in Roderick's breast the feud' (*The Lady of the Lake*, 1810).

smriti *n.* a body of Hindu religious teachings from the Vedas. WH: 19C. Sanskrit *smṛiti*, lit. that which is remembered, from *smarati* he remembers.

smudge¹ *n.* a dirty mark, a smear, a blur. *Also v.t., v.i.* WH: 14–15C. Prob. imit. Cp. SMIRCH, SMUT, etc.

smudge² *n.* a smouldering fire for driving away mosquitoes etc. *Also v.t.* WH: 16C. Orig. unknown.

smug *a.* self-satisfied, complacent. WH: 16C. Low German *smuk* pretty. Rel. to SMOCK. The original sense was trim, neat, smart, spruce.

smuggle *v.t.* to import or export illegally without paying customs duties. WH: 17C. Low German *smukkelen*, *smuggelen*, Dutch *smokkelen*, of unknown orig.

smur *n.* fine misty rain, drizzle. *Also v.i.* WH: 19C. Orig. unknown.

smut *n.* a particle of soot or other dirt, a mark or smudge made by this. *Also v.i., v.i.* WH: 14–15C. Imit. Cp. SMIRCH, SMITE, SMUDGE¹, etc. Cp. German *Schmutz*. The sense obscene language, etc. evolved in the 17C.

Sn *chem. symbol* tin. WH: Abbr. of Latin *stannum* tin. Cp. STANNARY.

snack *n.* a quick light meal. *Also v.i.* WH: 14–15C. Middle Dutch, rel. to *snacken*, var. of *snappen* SNAP. Cp. SNATCH. The original sense was snap, bite (as of a dog). The current sense evolved in the 17C.

snaffle *n.* a bridle-bit usu. with a joint in the middle. *Also v.t.* WH: 16C. Prob. from Low Dutch, corr. to Old High German *snabul* (German *Schnabel*) beak, spout, nose. See also -LE¹.

snafu *n.* a state of total confusion or chaos. *Also a., v.t.* WH: mid-20C. Acronym of *situation normal: all fouled (or fucked) up.*

snag¹ *n.* an unexpected or concealed difficulty. *Also v.t., v.i.* WH: 16C. Prob. from Scandinavian. Cp. Norwegian dial. *snage* point of land, Icelandic *snagi* peg. The original sense was a sharp projection. The sense unexpected difficulty arose in the 19C.

snag² *n.* a sausage. WH: mid-20C. Orig. unknown. ? Rel. to SNACK.

snail *n.* a gastropod mollusc of various species with a spirally coiled shell. WH: pre-1200. Old English *snægl*, dim. of *snaca* SNAKE, lit. creeping thing, from Germanic. Cp. German *Schnecke*.

snake *n.* a limbless reptile of the suborder Ophidia, of a venomous or non-venomous type and having a forked tongue and the ability to swallow prey whole. *Also v.t., v.i.* WH: pre-1200. Old English *snaca*, from Germanic. Rel. to SNAIL.

snap *v.i.* to break with a sharp report. *Also v.t., n., a., adv., int.* WH: 15C. Prob. from Middle Low German and Middle Dutch *snappen* to seize, but partly also imit. Cp. SNIP.

snare *n.* a trap, usu. consisting of a noose, for catching birds or other animals. *Also v.t.* WH: pre-1200. Old English *sneare*, from Old Norse *snara*, from Germanic. Cp. Dutch *snaar* string.

snark *n.* an imaginary creature sought in Lewis Carroll's nonsense poem, *The Hunting of the Snark*. WH: 19C. ? A blend of SNAKE and SHARK. The word was invented by Lewis Carroll in *The Hunting of the Snark* (1876).

snarl¹ *v.i.* (of a dog) to growl in a sharp tone with teeth bared. *Also v.t., n.* WH: 16C. Extended form of obs. *snar*, from Germanic (cp. German *schnarren*), prob. ult. of imit. orig. See also -LE⁴.

snarl² *v.t.* to entangle. *Also v.i., n.* WH: 14–15C. Rel. to SNARE. See also -LE¹.

snatch *v.t.* to seize suddenly, eagerly or without permission or ceremony. *Also v.i., n.* WH: 12–14C. Rel. to SNACK and SNECK, suggesting a base represented by Middle Dutch *snakken* to gasp, ? orig. to open jaws suddenly. Cp. SNAP.

snazzy *a.* up to date, showy, smart, attractive (e.g. of clothes). WH: mid-20C. Orig. unknown. The word may be a blend of *snappy* (SNAP) and *jazzy* (JAZZ).

sneak *v.i.* to creep (about, away, off etc.), as if afraid or ashamed to

be seen. *Also v.t., n.* WH: 16C. ? Rel. to obs. *snike*, from Old English *snīcan*, itself prob. related to Old Norse *sníkja* to sneak.

sneck *n.* a latch or catch. *Also v.t., v.i.* WH: 12–14C. Rel. to SNATCH.

sneer *n.* a smile, laugh or verbal expression of contempt. *Also v.i., v.t.* WH: 14–15C. ? Alt. of Old English *fnǣran* to snort. Cp. N Frisian *sneere* to scorn.

sneeze *v.i.* to eject air etc. through the nostrils audibly and convulsively, owing to irritation of the inner membrane of the nose. *Also n.* WH: pre-1200. Old English *fnēosan*, of imit. orig. Cp. NEEZE.

snell *a.* active, keen, smart, severe, stinging, pungent. WH: pre-1200. Old English, from Germanic. Cp. German *schnell* swift, active, quick.

Snell's law *n.* the law of refraction, stating that the sine of the angle of incidence divided by the sine of the angle of refraction is a constant. WH: 19C. Willebrord Van Roijen *Snell*, 1591–1626, Dutch astronomer and mathematician.

snib *n.* a bolt or catch. *Also v.t.* WH: 19C. ? Low German *snilbe* (German *Schnippe*), snib (Swedish *snibb*) beak, beaklike point.

snick *v.t.* to cut, to nick, to notch, to snip. *Also n.* WH: 17C. Prob. from *snick* in obs. phr. *snick or snee* (SNICKERSNEE).

snicker *v.i.* to snigger. *Also v.t., n.* WH: 17C. Imit. Cp. SNIGGER.

snickersnee *n.* a big knife, esp. a bowie. WH: 18C. Alt. of obs. phr. *snick or snee* to cut or thrust in fighting with a knife, from Dutch *steken* (German *stechen*) to thrust, to stick + *snee*, dial. var. of *snijden* (German *schneiden*) to cut, with later assim. of initial *st-* to the *sn-* of *snee*. Cp. SNICK.

snide *a.* malicious, sneering, disparaging, sly, mean. *Also n.* WH: 19C. Orig. unknown. The earliest sense was counterfeit, bogus.

sniff *v.i.* to draw air audibly up the nose in order to smell, clear the nasal passages, inhale a drug, express contempt etc. *Also v.t., n.* WH: 12–14C. Imit. Cp. SNIVEL, SNUFFLE.

snifter *n.* a small drink of spirits. WH: 12–14C. Imit. Cp. obs. *snift* to sniff, to snort.

snig¹ *v.t.* to drag (a heavy log etc.) by means of a rope or chain. WH: 18C. Orig. unknown.

snig² *n.* a small eel. WH: 15C. Orig. unknown.

snigger *v.i.* to laugh in a half-suppressed or discourteous manner. *Also n.* WH: 18C. Later var. of SNICKER.

sniggle *v.i.* to fish for eels by thrusting the bait into their holes. *Also v.t.* WH: 17C. SNIG² + -LE⁴.

snip *v.t.* to cut (cloth etc.) or cut (a hole) in something, quickly and sharply with scissors or shears. *Also v.i., n.* WH: 16C. Low German and Dutch *snippen*, of imit. orig. Cp. SNAP.

snipe *n.* a long-billed marsh- and shorebird of the genus *Gallinago*, esp. the British *G. coelestis*. *Also v.i., v.t.* WH: 12–14C. Prob. of Scandinavian orig. Prob. rel. to Dutch *snip*, German *Schnepfe*.

snit *n.* a rage. WH: mid-20C. Orig. unknown.

snitch *v.i.* to inform, to poach (on). *Also v.t., n.* WH: 17C. Orig. unknown. The original sense was a flick on the nose, also the nose itself. The sense to inform evolved in the 18C.

snivel *v.i.* to weep with nose running, to be tearful. *Also n.* WH: pre-1200. Representation of an unrecorded Old English v. implicit in Old English *snyflung* mucus (of the nose), from *snofl*. Cp. *sniffle* (SNIFF), SNUFFLE.

snob *n.* a person who cultivates or behaves obsequiously towards those of higher social position, or regards the claims of wealth and position with an exaggerated and contemptible respect. WH: 18C. Orig. unknown. The original sense was shoemaker, cobbler, also (in Cambridge University slang) townsman (as opposed to a student). The current sense evolved in the 19C.

SNOBOL *n.* a language used in computer programming for handling strings of symbols. WH: mid-20C. Acronym of *string*-oriented *symbolic language*, based on COBOL and punning on *snowball* (SNOW, BALL¹).

Sno-Cat® *n.* a type of vehicle designed to travel on snow. WH: mid-20C. From *sno*, respelling of SNOW + CATERPILLAR.

snoek *n.* a barracouta. WH: 18C. Dutch pike. See SNOOK².

snog *v.i.* to kiss and cuddle. *Also n.* WH: mid-20C. Orig. unknown. ? Blend of SNUG and COD³.

snood *n.* a fillet or ribbon formerly worn round the hair in Scotland by unmarried girls. WH: pre-1200. Old English *snōd*, of unknown orig. According to some, the word is related to NEEDLE through Celtic links.

snook[1] n. a gesture of derision made with the thumb to the nose and the fingers spread. WH: 18C. Orig. unknown.

snook[2] n. the tropical American fish *Centropomus undecimalis*, and various kinds of sea fish used for food, esp. the S African and Australian pike. WH: 17C. Dutch *snoek* pike, from Middle Low German *snōk*, ? rel. to base of SNACK. Cp. SNOEK.

snooker n. a game played on a billiard table, in which a white cue ball is used to pocket the other 21 balls (15 red and six coloured). *Also v.t.* WH: 19C. Orig. unknown. The word is popularly said to derive from *snooker*, a slang term for a new cadet at the Royal Military Academy, Woolwich, of unknown origin. This was then applied to the game by Colonel Sir Neville Chamberlain, a British army officer stationed in India, with reference to the poor playing skills of a fellow officer.

snoop v.i. to go about in an inquisitive or sneaking manner, to pry. *Also n.* WH: 19C. Dutch *snoepen* to eat furtively. The original sense was to steal and eat. The sense to pry evolved in the early 20C.

snoot n. the nose. WH: 19C. Dial. var. of SNOUT.

snooze v.i. to take a short sleep, esp. in the day. *Also v.t., n.* WH: 18C. Orig. unknown. ? Influ. by SNEEZE or DOZE.

snore v.i. to breathe through the mouth and nostrils with a snorting noise in sleep. *Also v.t., n.* WH: 14–15C. From imit. base represented by Middle Low German and Middle Dutch *snorken*. Cp. SNORT.

Snorkel® n. a fire-fighting platform that is elevated electronically. WH: mid-20C. SNORKEL.

snorkel n. a breathing apparatus used in diving and swimming consisting of a tube which extends from the mouth to above the surface of the water. *Also v.i.* WH: mid-20C. German *Schnorchel* nose, rel. to *schnarchen* SNORE. The word was originally the term for a device on a submarine to draw in air and expel engine exhaust when at periscope depth, so called because it projected like a nose and because when operating it sounded like a snore.

snort v.i. to force air violently and loudly through the nostrils like a frightened or excited horse (e.g. as an expression of contempt). *Also v.t., n.* WH: 14–15C. Ult. imit. Cp. SNORE.

snot n. mucus from the nose. WH: 14–15C. Prob. from Middle Low German and Middle Dutch *snotte*, Dutch *snot*, corr. to Old English *gesnot*, Middle High German *snuz* (German *Schnutz*). Cp. SNOUT. The original sense was the snuff or burnt wick of a candle.

snout n. the projecting nose or muzzle of an animal. WH: 12–14C. Middle Low German and Middle Dutch *snūt* (Dutch *snuit*), ult. from a Germanic word represented also by SNOUT. Cp. SCHNAUZER.

snow n. watery vapour in the atmosphere frozen into crystals and falling to the ground in flakes. *Also v.i., v.t.* WH: pre-1200. Old English *snāw*, from Germanic, rel. to Latin *nix, nivis*. Cp. German *Schnee*, Dutch *sneeuw*.

snub v.t. to rebuke with sarcasm or contempt, to slight in a pointed or offensive manner. *Also n., a.* WH: 12–14C. Old Norse *snubba*, related to Middle Swedish *snybba*, Middle Dutch *snibba*. The original sense was to reprove or rebuke cuttingly.

snuff[1] n. the charred part of the wick in a candle or lamp. *Also v.t.* WH: 14–15C. Orig. unknown. ? Rel. to SNUFF[2].

snuff[2] n. powdered tobacco or other substance inhaled through the nose. *Also v.t., v.i.* WH: 17C. Dutch *snuf*, prob. abbr. of *snuftabak* (cp. German *Schnupftabak*), from Middle Dutch *snuffen* to snuffle. Cp. SNUFFLE.

snuffle v.i. to breathe noisily or make a sniffing noise as when the nose is obstructed. *Also v.t., n.* WH: 16C. Prob. from Low German and Dutch *snuffelen*, from imit. base represented also by SNUFF[2]. See also -LE[4]. Cp. SNIVEL.

snug a. sheltered and comfortable. *Also v.i., n.* WH: 16C. Prob. from Low Dutch. Cp. Low German *snügger, snögger* slender, smooth, dainty, smart, Dutch *snugger* lively, sprightly.

so adv. in such a manner or to such an extent, degree etc. (with *as* expressed or understood). *Also conj., int., a., pron.* WH: pre-1200. Old English *swa, swā* , corr. to Old Frisian *sa, so*, Dutch *zo*, German *so*, from Germanic.

soak v.t. to put (something) in liquid to become permeated, to steep. *Also v.i., n.* WH: pre-1200. Old English *socian*, from *sūcan* SUCK.

soap n. a compound of a fatty acid and a base of sodium or potassium, producing a lather in water, and used for washing and cleansing. *Also v.t.* WH: pre-1200. Old English *sāpe*, from Germanic, rel. to Latin *sapo, saponis* and so to French *savon*. Cp. German *Seife*.

soar v.i. to fly into the air, to rise. *Also n.* WH: 14–15C. Shortening of Old French *essorer* to fly up, to soar, from Popular Latin *exaurare*, from Latin EX- + *aura* air in motion.

sob v.i. to weep violently, catching one's breath in a convulsive manner. *Also v.t., n.* WH: pre-1200. ? Low Dutch. Cp. Dutch dial. *sabben* to suck. Ult. of imit. orig.

sober a. not drunk; temperate in the use of alcoholic liquors etc. *Also v.t., v.i.* WH: 12–14C. Old French *sobre*, from Latin *sobrius*, from *so-*, var. of SE- + *ebrius* drunk (EBRIETY).

soboles n. a creeping or underground stem, a sucker. WH: 18C. Latin, from *sub* under + base of *alescere* to grow up.

sobriquet n. a nickname. WH: 17C. French chuck under the chin, of unknown orig. According to some, the word is from *sous* under + an element of unknown origin.

soc n. the right of holding a local court. WH: pre-1200. Back-formation from *soken*, from Old English *sōcn*, corr. to Old Norse *sókn*, Gothic *sōkns* search, inquiry, from Germanic.

soca n. a type of music popular in the E Caribbean which blends elements of soul and calypso. WH: late 20C. SOUL + CALYPSO.

soccer n. Association Football. WH: 19C. Shortening of *Association* (*Football*) + -ER[6]. Cp. *rugger* (RUGBY).

sociable a. fit or inclined to associate or be friendly, companionable. *Also n.* WH: 16C. French, or from Latin *sociabilis*, from *sociare* to unite, ASSOCIATE[1], from *socius* companion, ally. See also -ABLE.

social a. of or relating to society, its organization or its divisions, or to the intercourse, behaviour or mutual relations of humans. *Also n.* WH: 14–15C. Old French, or from Latin *socialis* allied, confederate, from *socius*. See SOCIABLE, also -AL[1].

society n. a social community. *Also a.* WH: 16C. French *société*, from Latin *societas, societatis*, from *socius*. See SOCIABLE, also -ITY.

socio- comb. form social. WH: Latin *socius* (SOCIABLE) + -O-.

sociobiology n. the study of human or animal behaviour from a genetic or evolutionary basis. WH: mid-20C. SOCIO- + BIOLOGY.

sociocultural a. of, relating to or involving social and cultural factors. WH: early 20C. SOCIO- + *cultural* (CULTURE).

socio-economic a. of, relating to or involving social and economic factors. WH: 19C. SOCIO- + ECONOMIC.

sociolinguistic a. of or relating to the social aspects of language. WH: mid-20C. SOCIO- + *linguistic* (LINGUIST).

sociology n. the science of the organization and dynamics of human society. WH: 19C. French *sociologie*. See SOCIO-, -LOGY. The French word was coined in 1830 by the French philosopher and social reformer Auguste Comte.

sociometry n. the study of social relationships within a group. WH: early 20C. SOCIO- + -METRY.

sociopath n. a person affected by a personality disorder, manifesting itself in antisocial or asocial behaviour, e.g. a psychopath. WH: mid-20C. SOCIO- + -*path*, based on PSYCHOPATH.

sociopolitical a. of, relating to or involving social and political factors. WH: 19C. SOCIO- + POLITICAL.

sock[1] n. a short stocking. WH: pre-1200. Old English *socc*, from Germanic, from Latin *soccus* light low-heeled shoe or slipper, from Greek *sukkhos*. Cp. German *Socke*. The original sense was a light shoe, a slipper. The current sense evolved 12–14C.

sock[2] v.t. to hit or punch (esp. a person) hard with a blow. *Also n.* WH: 17C. Orig. unknown.

socket n. a natural or artificial hollow place or fitting adapted for receiving and holding another part or thing, e.g. an implement or electric plug, or for holding a revolving part such as a limb, eye, head of an instrument etc. *Also v.t.* WH: 12–14C. Anglo-French *soket*, dim. of Old French *soc* ploughshare, prob. of Celtic orig. See also -ET[1]. The earliest sense (to the 16C) was the head of a lance or spear, which resembled a ploughshare. The term then passed (14–15C) to any hollow part or piece designed to receive something fitted into it.

sockeye n. a Pacific blueback salmon, *Oncorhynchus nerka*, with red flesh highly esteemed as a food. WH: 19C. Salish *sukai*, lit. fish of fishes.

socle n. a plain low rectangular block or plinth, forming a base for a statue, column etc. WH: 18C. French, from Italian *zoccolo* wooden shoe, socle, representing Latin *socculus*, dim. of *soccus* SOCK[1].

Socratic a. of, relating to or according to Socrates. Also n. WH: 17C. Latin *Socraticus*, from Greek *Sōkratikos*, from *Sōkratēs* Socrates, 469–399 BC, Athenian philosopher. See also -IC.

sod[1] n. a piece of surface soil cut away, a turf. Also v.t. WH: 14–15C. Middle Low German or Middle Dutch *sode*, of unknown orig. Cp. Dutch *zode*. Some sources relate the word to SEETHE, partly on the grounds that a sod was originally turf used as a fuel. But evidence for this link is lacking.

sod[2] n. a despicable person, esp. male. Also int. WH: 19C. Abbr. of *sodomite* (SODOM).

soda n. any of various compounds of sodium, e.g. sodium carbonate, sodium hydroxide, sodium bicarbonate. WH: 14–15C. Medieval Latin, prob. from Persian *šūrach* saltwort, salt marsh, taken as Arabic *ṣūda'* headache, presumably because the plant was used to make a remedy for headaches.

sodality n. a fellowship, a confraternity, esp. a charitable association in the Roman Catholic Church. WH: 17C. French *sodalité* or Latin *sodalitas*, from *sodalis* companion. See also -ITY.

sodden a. soaked, saturated. Also v.t., v.i. WH: 12–14C. Obs. p.p. of SEETHE.

sodium n. a silver-white metallic element, at. no. 11, chem. symbol Na, the base of soda. WH: 19C. SODA + -IUM. The name was coined in 1807 by the English chemist Sir Humphry Davy, who isolated the element from caustic soda (sodium hydroxide).

Sodom n. a place of utter wickedness or depravity. WH: 16C. Latin, or from Greek *Sodoma*, from Hebrew *sēḏōm*, an ancient city beside the Dead Sea, destroyed together with Gomorrah (GOMORRAH) because of the depravity of its inhabitants (Gen. xviii–xix). The precise application to sodomy arose from the alleged sexual behaviour of the inhabitants of Sodom who wanted to 'know' (in the biblical sense) the two angels staying with Lot (Gen. xix.5).

soever adv. appended, sometimes as a suffix, and sometimes after an interval, to pronouns, adverbs or adjectives to give an indefinite or universal meaning. WH: 12–14C. Orig. two words, SO + EVER.

sofa n. a long stuffed couch or seat with raised back and ends. WH: 17C. French, ult. from Arabic *ṣuffa* long (stone) bench.

soffit n. the undersurface of a cornice, lintel, balcony, arch etc. WH: 17C. French *soffite*, or from Italian *soffito*, ult. from Latin *suffixus*. See SUFFIX[1].

soft a. yielding easily to pressure, easily moulded, cut or worked. Also n., adv. WH: pre-1200. Old English *sōfte*, earlier *sēfte*, from Germanic. Cp. German *sanft*.

softa n. a student of Muslim theology and sacred law. WH: 17C. Turkish, from Persian *sūḵta* burnt, parched, scorched. The student is so called as he is inspired by the teacher, or because he is ardent in study.

soggy a. soaked, sodden, thoroughly wet. WH: 18C. From obs. *sog* marshy ground, swamp, ? from Old Norse + -Y[1].

soh n. the fifth note of a major scale in the tonic sol-fa system. WH: 12–14C. Latin *sol(ve)*. See UT.

soi-disant a. self-styled, pretended, so-called. WH: 16C. French, from *soi* oneself + *disant*, pres.p. of *dire* to say.

soigné a. well-turned-out, well-groomed. WH: 19C. French, p.p. of *soigner* to care for, from *soin* care.

soil[1] n. the ground, esp. the top stratum of the earth's crust, composed of a mixture of crumbled rock and organic matter, whence plants derive their mineral food. WH: 14–15C. Anglo-French *land*, ? representing Latin *solium* seat, by assoc. with *solum* ground. Cp. SOIL[2].

soil[2] v.t. to make dirty. Also v.i., n. WH: 12–14C. Old French *soillier* (Modern French *souiller*), from *soil* tub, wild boar's wallow, from Latin *solium* tub for bathing, seat, prob. rel. to *sedere* SIT. Cp. SOIL[1]. The Old French verb was long said to derive from Popular Latin *suculare*, based on Latin *suculus*, diminutive of *sus* pig (SOW[2]), but recent scholarship has rejected this etymology.

soil[3] v.t. to feed (cattle etc.) with green food, in order to fatten, orig. to purge. WH: 17C. ? From SOIL[2].

soirée n. an evening party or gathering for conversation and social intercourse etc., usu. with music. WH: 18C. French, from *soir* evening. Cp. MATINÉE.

soixante-neuf n. sixty-nine, a sexual position or activity in which a couple engage in oral stimulation of each other's genitals at the same time. WH: 19C. French sixty-nine. The activity is so called because the position of the couple involved resembles the figures 6 and 9.

sojourn v.i. to stay or reside (in, among etc.) temporarily. Also n. WH: 12–14C. Old French *sojourner* (Modern French *séjourner*), ult. from Latin SUB- + Late Latin *diurnum* day. Cp. JOURNAL.

Sol n. the sun personified. WH: 14–15C. Latin sun.

sol n. a colloidal solution. WH: 19C. Abbr. of *solution* (SOLUBLE).

sola n. an E Indian plant with a pithy stem, *Aeschynomene indica*. WH: 19C. Bengali *solā*, Hindi *śolā*.

solace n. comfort in grief, trouble etc. Also v.t. WH: 12–14C. Old French *solas* (Modern French dial. *soulas*), from Latin *solatium*, from *solari* to relieve, to console. An earlier sense (to the 17C) was pleasure, enjoyment, recreation.

solan n. the gannet, *Sula bassana*. WH: 14–15C. Prob. from Old Norse *súla* gannet + *and-*, nom. *ǫnd* duck (cp. German *Ente*). The full name, solan goose, thus comprises three bird names.

solano n. a hot oppressive SE wind in Spain. WH: 18C. Spanish, from Latin *solanus*, from *sol* sun.

solanum n. any plant of the genus *Solanum*, containing the potato, eggplant, nightshades and tobacco. WH: 16C. Latin nightshade, prob. from *sol* sun + *-anum*, neut. of *-anus* -AN.

solar a. of or relating to, proceeding from, measured by or powered by the sun. Also n. WH: 14–15C. Latin *solaris*, from *sol* sun. See also -AR[1].

solatium n. something given as compensation for suffering or loss. WH: 19C. Latin. See SOLACE.

soldanella n. any plant of the dwarf alpine genus *Soldanella*, with bell-shaped flowers that have fringed petals. WH: 16C. Modern Latin, from Italian, of unknown orig.

solder n. a fusible alloy for uniting the edges etc. of less fusible metals. Also v.t., v.i. WH: 12–14C. Old French *soudure*, from *souder*, from Latin *solidare* to fasten together, from *solidus* SOLID.

soldier n. a person engaged in military service, esp. a private or non-commissioned officer. Also v.i. WH: 12–14C. Old French *soudier*, *soldier*, from *soude*, *soulde*, from Latin SOLIDUS. See also -IER. The literal original sense was one serving in the army for pay.

sole[1] n. the flat underside or bottom of the foot. Also v.t. WH: 12–14C. Old French, from Latin *solea* sandal, sill, from *solum* bottom, pavement, sole. The word probably existed in Old English but has not been recorded. There are related Germanic words, as German *Sohle*.

sole[2] n. a flatfish of various species of the family Soleidae, highly esteemed as food. WH: 12–14C. Old French, from Provençal *sola*, from Latin *solea*. See SOLE[1]. The fish is so called from its resemblance to a sandal.

sole[3] a. single, only. WH: 14–15C. Old French *soule* (Modern French *seule*), from Latin *sola*, fem. of *solus*.

solecism n. a deviation from correct idiom or grammar. WH: 16C. French *solécisme* or Latin *soloecismus*, from Greek *soloikismos*, from *soloikos* speaking incorrectly. See also -ISM. The term was said by ancient writers to refer to *Soloi*, an Athenian colony in Cilicia, whose form of the Attic dialect was regarded by the Athenians as barbarous.

solemn a. performed with or accompanied by ceremonies or due formality. WH: 12–14C. Old French *solempne*, from Latin *solemnis*, *solempnis* celebrated regularly, festive customary, from *sollus* whole, entire. The second element is unexplained. It was formerly derived from Latin *annus* year, giving a sense celebrated annually.

solenoid n. a magnet consisting of a cylindrical coil traversed by an electric current. WH: 19C. French *solénoïde*, from Greek *sōlen* channel, pipe, syringe + -OID.

soleus n. a muscle of the calf of the leg beneath the gastrocnemius concerned with plantar flexion, i.e. helping to extend the foot. WH: 17C. Modern Latin, from Latin *solea* SOLE[1].

sol-fa *v.i.* to sing the notes of the musical scale up or down to the syllables *doh* (or *ut*), *re*, *mi*, *fa*, *sol* (or *soh*), *la*, *si* (or *ti*). *Also v.t.*, *n.* WH: 16C. From the syllables *sol* (SOH) and *fa* FAH. See UT.

solfatara *n.* a volcanic vent emitting sulphurous gases. WH: 18C. *Solfatara*, a sulphurous volcano near Naples, from Italian *solfo* sulphur.

solicit *v.t.* to make earnest or importunate requests for. *Also v.i.* WH: 14–15C. Old French *solliciter*, from Latin *sollicitare* to stir, to agitate, from *sollicitus* agitated, from *sollus* whole, entire + *citus*, p.p. of *ciere* (CITE) to set in motion. The original sense (to the 18C) was to disturb, to make anxious.

solid *a.* firm, unyielding. *Also adv.*, *n.* WH: 14–15C. Old French *solide* or Latin *solidus*, rel. to *salvus* safe, *sollus* whole, entire.

solidarity *n.* cohesion, mutual dependence. WH: 19C. French *solidarité*, from *solidaire*, from *solide* SOLID. See also -ARY[1], -ITY.

solidungulate *a.* solid-hoofed, not cloven. WH: 19C. Latin *solidus* SOLID + *ungulatus* ungulate (UNGULA).

solidus *n.* the stroke (/) formerly denoting a shilling (as in 2/6), also used in writing fractions (e.g. 1/4), separating numbers (e.g. in dates) or alternative words (as in *him/ her*) etc. WH: 12–14C. Latin SOLID. Cp. L.S.D..

solifluction *n.* a slow downwards slip of waterlogged soil which usu. occurs in areas of permanent frost (e.g. tundra regions). WH: early 20C. Latin *solum* ground, earth + *-i-* + *fluctus*, p.p. of *fluere* to flow. See also -ION. The term was coined in 1906 by the Swedish archaeologist Johan Andersson.

soliloquy *n.* the activity of talking to oneself. WH: 12–14C. Late Latin *soliloquium*, from Latin *solus*, *soli-* sole, alone + *loqui* to speak. See also -Y[2]. Cp. MONOLOGUE. The Late Latin word was introduced by St Augustine in his *Soliloquia* (6C AD).

soliped *n.*, *a.* (an animal) having solid, as distinct from cloven, hoofs. WH: 18C. Modern Latin *solipes*, *solipedis*, from Latin *solidipes*, from *solidus* SOLID + *pes*, *pedis* foot.

solipsism *n.* the philosophical theory that the only knowledge possible is that of oneself, absolute egoism. WH: 19C. Latin *solus* sole, alone + *ipse* self. See also -ISM.

solitaire *n.* a gem, esp. a diamond, set singly in a ring or other jewel. WH: 18C. French, from Latin *solitarius*. See SOLITARY.

solitary *a.* living or being alone. *Also n.* WH: 12–14C. Latin *solitarius*, from *solus* sole, alone. See also -ARY[1].

solitude *n.* seclusion, loneliness. WH: 12–14C. Old French, or from Latin *solitudo*, *solitudinis*, from *solus*, alone. See also -TUDE.

solmization *n.* the association of the syllables *doh*, *ray*, *me*, *fah*, *soh*, *lah*, *te* with the notes of the musical scale, *doh* being C in the fixed-doh system, or the keynote in tonic sol-fa. WH: 18C. French *solmisation*, from *solmiser*, from *sol* SOH + *mi* ME[2]. See also -IZE, -ATION.

solo *n.* a composition or passage played by a single instrument or sung by a single voice, usu. with an accompaniment. *Also a.*, *adv.*, *v.i.* WH: 17C. Italian, from Latin *solus* sole, alone.

Solomon *n.* a very wise man. WH: 16C. *Solomon*, *c.*970–930 BC, a king of Israel, famed for his wisdom and justice.

Solon *n.* a sage, esp. a wise law-maker. WH: 17C. *Solon*, *c.*638–559 BC, Athenian legislator and sage.

solstice *n.* either of the times (about 21 June and 22 December) and points at which the sun is farthest from the celestial equator (north in summer and south in winter). WH: 12–14C. Old French, from Latin *solstitium*, from *sol* sun + *stitus*, p.p. of *sistere* to stand still. The occasion is so called because the sun appears to stand still when at this point.

soluble *a.* capable of being dissolved in a fluid. WH: 14–15C. Old French, from Late Latin *solubilis*, from Latin *solvere* SOLVE. See also -IBLE.

solus *a.*, *adv.* in stage directions etc., alone. WH: 16C. Latin *solus* sole, alone.

Solutrean *a.* of or relating to the period of Upper Palaeolithic culture between the Aurignacian and Magdalenian periods, including flint and bone instruments and carvings on stone. WH: 19C. French *solutréen*, from *Solutré*, a village in E central France where remains of the period were found. See also -AN.

solve *v.t.* to resolve or find an answer to (a problem etc.). WH: 14–15C. Latin *solvere* to unfasten, to free, to pay. The original sense was to

loosen, to break. The sense to find an answer to a problem etc. arose in the 16C.

soma[1] *n.* the body as distinguished from soul and spirit. WH: 19C. Greek *sōma* body.

soma[2] *n.* an intoxicating liquor used in connection with ancient Vedic worship. WH: 18C. Sanskrit. Cp. HOM.

Somali *n.* a member of a people inhabiting Somalia. *Also a.* WH: 19C. African name, from *Somalia*, a republic in NE Africa.

sombre *a.* dark, gloomy. WH: 18C. Old French, use as a. of n., ult. from Latin SUB- + *umbra* shade, shadow.

sombrero *n.* a wide-brimmed hat worn esp. in Mexico. WH: 16C. Spanish, from *sombra* shade.

some *a.* an indeterminate quantity, number etc. of. *Also adv.*, *pron.* WH: pre-1200. Old English *sum*, from Germanic, from Indo-European, from base represented also by Greek *hamōs* somehow, *hamothen* from some place, Sanskrit *sama* any, every.

-some[1] *suf.* forming adjectives from verbs, nouns or adjectives, denoting qualities, as in *wearisome*, *loathsome*, *toothsome*, *wholesome*. WH: Old English *-sum*, from Germanic. Cp. German *-sam*.

-some[2] *comb. form* a body, as in *chromosome*. WH: Greek *sōma* body.

somersault *n.* a leap, or a forward roll on the ground, in which one turns head over heels and lands on one's feet. *Also v.i.* WH: 16C. Old French *sombresault*, alt. of *sobresault* (Modern French *soubresaut*), from Provençal, from *sobre* above (from Latin *supra*) + *saut* leap (from Latin *saltus*).

somite *n.* a segment of the body of an invertebrate animal such as an earthworm, or of the embryo of a vertebrate animal, a metamere. WH: 19C. Greek *sōma* body + -ITE[1].

sommelier *n.* a wine waiter. WH: 19C. French wine steward, orig. pack animal driver, from Provençal *sauma* pack animal, load of a pack animal. Cp. SUMPTER.

somnambulance *n.* sleepwalking. WH: 18C. Latin *somnus* sleep + *ambulare* to walk (cp. AMBULANCE).

somniferous *a.* causing or inducing sleep. WH: 17C. Latin *somnifer*, from *somnium* dream. See -FEROUS.

somniloquism *n.* the activity or habit of talking in one's sleep. WH: 19C. Latin *somnus* sleep + *-i-* + *loqui* to speak. See also -ISM.

somnolent *a.* sleepy, drowsy. WH: 14–15C. Old French *sompnolent* (Modern French *somnolent*), or from Latin *somnolentus*, from *somnus* sleep. See also -ENT.

son *n.* a male child in relation to a parent or parents. WH: pre-1200. Old English *sunu*, from Germanic, rel. to Greek *huios*. Cp. German *Sohn*, Dutch *zoon*.

sonant *a.* voiced and syllabic. *Also n.* WH: 19C. Latin *sonans*, *sonantis*, pres.p. of *sonare* to sound. See also -ANT.

sonar *n.* a device which detects the presence and position of underwater objects by means of echo-soundings or emitted sound. WH: mid-20C. Acronym of *so*und *na*vigation (and) *r*anging, based on RADAR.

sonata *n.* a musical composition for one instrument, or for one instrument accompanied on the piano, usu. of three or four movements in different rhythms. WH: 17C. Italian, fem. p.p. of *sonare* to sound. Cp. CANTATA.

sondage *n.* in archaeology, a trial excavation or inspection trench. WH: mid-20C. French sounding, borehole.

sonde *n.* a scientific device for gathering information about atmospheric conditions at high altitudes, a radiosonde. WH: early 20C. French sounding line, sounding.

son et lumière *n.* an outdoor entertainment at a historic location which recreates past events associated with it using sound effects, a spoken narration, music, and special lighting. WH: mid-20C. French, lit. sound and light.

song *n.* a short poem intended or suitable for singing, esp. one set to music. WH: pre-1200. Old English *sang*, from Germanic base also of SING. Cp. German *Sang*.

sonic *a.* of, relating to or producing sound waves. WH: early 20C. Latin *sonus* sound + -IC.

sonnet *n.* a poem of 14 iambic pentameter (ten-syllable) lines, usu. consisting of an octave rhyming *a b b a a b b a*, and a sestet with three rhymes variously arranged. *Also v.i.*, *v.t.* WH: 16C. French, or from Italian *sonetto*, dim. of *suono* sound.

sonobuoy *n.* a buoy fitted with instruments for detecting underwater sounds and communicating them by radio to surface vessels etc. WH: mid-20C. Latin *sonus* sound + -O- + BUOY.

sonogram *n.* a visual representation of a sound produced by means of a sonograph. WH: mid-20C. Latin *sonus* sound + -O- + -GRAM.

sonometer *n.* a device for determining the vibration frequency of a string etc. WH: 19C. Latin *sonus* sound + -O- + -METER.

sonorous *a.* giving out sound, resonant. WH: 17C. Latin *sonorus*, from *sonor*, *sonoris* sound. See also -OUS.

sonsy *a.* happy or jolly-looking, buxom, well-favoured, plump. WH: 16C. From dialect *sonse*, from Irish and Gaelic *sonas* good fortune, from *sona* fortunate, happy + -Y[1].

sook[1] *n.* a baby. WH: 19C. Dial. var. of SUCK.

sook[2] *n.* a person who tries to ingratiate themselves, a toady or sycophant. WH: early 20C. Var. of SUCK.

sool *v.t.* to incite (esp. a dog) to attack. WH: 19C. Var. of SOWL.

soon *adv.* in a short time from now. WH: pre-1200. Old English *sōna*, from Germanic, ? rel. to Gothic *suns* immediately. The original sense was also immediately.

soot *n.* a black substance composed of carbonaceous particles rising from fuel in a state of combustion and deposited in a chimney etc. *Also v.t.* WH: pre-1200. Old English *sōt*, from Germanic, from Indo-European base also of SIT. The basic sense is that which settles.

†sooth *n.* truth, reality. *Also a.* WH: pre-1200. Old English *sōth*, from Germanic, from Indo-European. Cp. SOOTHE.

soothe *v.t.* to calm, to tranquillize. WH: pre-1200. Old English *sōthian*, from *sōth* SOOTH. The original sense (to the 16C) was to prove to be true. The current sense emerged in the 17C. To soothe a person is essentially to agree with what they are saying, to accept it as true.

sop *n.* a piece of bread etc. steeped or dipped and softened in milk, broth, gravy etc. *Also v.t., v.i.* WH: pre-1200. Old English *sopp*, corr. to Middle Low German *soppe*, Old High German *sopfa* bread and milk, Old Norse *soppa*, prob. rel. from base of Old English *sūthan* SUP.

sophism *n.* a plausible but specious or fallacious argument. WH: 14–15C. Old French *sophime* (Modern French *sophisme*), from Latin *sophisma*, from Greek clever device, trick, from *sophizesthai* to devise, to become wise, from *sophos* wise, clever. See also -ISM.

Sophoclean *a.* of, relating to or characteristic of Sophocles. WH: 17C. Latin *Sophocleus*, from Greek *Sophokleios*, from *Sophoklēs* Sophocles, 496–406 BC, Athenian tragic poet + -EAN.

sophomore *n.* a second-year student. WH: 17C. From *sophum*, *sophom*, obs. vars. of SOPHISM + -ER[1]. The word is popularly derived from Greek *sophos* wise + *moros* foolish, as if typically descriptive of a student.

Sophy *n.* the title of a Persian sovereign, the shah. WH: 16C. Arabic *Ṣafi-ud-dīn* pure of religion, epithet given to the ancestor of the dynasty of Persia, *c.*1500–1736. The dynasty itself is the *Safavid*, from Arabic *ṣafawī* descended from *Safī-ud-dīn*. Its founder was Ismail I, 1486–1524.

-sophy *comb. form* denoting (a branch of) knowledge. WH: Old French *-sophie*, from Latin *-sophia*, from Greek *sophia* wisdom, from *sophos* skilled, wise + -ia -Y[2].

soporific *a.* causing or tending to cause sleep. *Also n.* WH: 17C. Latin *sopor* deep sleep, rel. to *somnus* sleep + -FIC. Cp. SOMNIFEROUS.

soprano *n.* the highest singing voice, treble. *Also a.* WH: 18C. Italian, from *sopra* above, from Latin *supra*. Cp. SOVEREIGN.

sora *n.* a bird, *Porzana carolina*, inhabiting the Carolina marshes and caught for food. WH: 18C. ? From an American Indian language.

Sorb *n.* a member of a Slavonic people primarily of E Germany, a Wend. WH: 19C. German *Sorbe*, var. of *Serbe* SERB.

sorb *n.* the service tree. WH: 16C. French *sorbe*, or from Latin *sorbus* service-berry. Cp. SERVICE[2].

sorbefacient *a.* promoting absorption. *Also n.* WH: 19C. Latin *sorbere* to absorb + -FACIENT.

sorbet *n.* an ice flavoured with fruit juice, spirit etc., a water ice. WH: 16C. French, from Italian *sorbetto*, from Turkish *şerbet* SHERBET.

Sorbo® *n.* a spongy kind of rubber. WH: early 20C. Appar. from ABSORB + -O-.

sorcerer *n.* a person who uses magic, witchcraft, spells or enchantments, a wizard or magician. WH: 14–15C. Old French *sorcier*, ult. from Latin *sors*, *sortis* lot. See also -ER[2].

sordavalite *n.* a vitreous silicate of alumina and magnesia found in diabase. WH: 19C. *Sordavala*, a town in SE Finland (now *Sortavala*, NW Russia) + -ITE[1].

sordid *a.* foul, dirty. WH: 14–15C. French *sordide* or Latin *sordidus*, from *sordere* to be dirty, to be foul. See also -ID.

sordino *n.* a contrivance for deadening the sound of a bowed instrument or wind instrument, a mute, a damper. WH: 16C. Italian, from *sordo*, from Latin *surdus* deaf, mute.

sore *a.* (of a part of the body) tender and painful to the touch, esp. through disease, injury or irritation. *Also adv., n.* WH: pre-1200. Old English *sār*, from a Germanic word represented also in Finnish *sairas* sick, ill. Cp. German *sehr* very.

sorel *n.* a male fallow deer in its third year. WH: 15C. Var. of SORREL[2].

sorghum *n.* any member of the genus *Sorghum*, which includes the Indian millet, durra etc., much cultivated in the US for fodder etc. WH: 16C. Modern Latin, from Italian *sorgo*, from var. of Medieval Latin *suricum* (*gramen*) Syrian (grass).

sorites *n.* a series of syllogisms so connected that the predicate of one forms the subject of that which follows, the subject of the first being ultimately united with the predicate of the last. WH: 16C. Latin, from Greek *sōreitēs*, from *sōros* heap.

soroptimist *n.* a member of an international organization of women's clubs, Soroptimist International. WH: early 20C. Latin *soror* sister + *optimist* (OPTIMISM). The name may have been based on that of the Optimist Club, founded in 1911.

sororal *a.* of, relating to or characteristic of a sister or sisters. WH: 17C. Latin *soror* sister + -AL[1].

sorosis *n.* a fleshy fruit formed by the cohesion of numerous flowers etc., e.g. the pineapple. WH: 19C. Modern Latin, from Greek *sōros* heap.

sorption *n.* the separate processes, or simultaneous process, of absorption and adsorption. WH: early 20C. From *absorption* (ABSORB) + *adsorption* (ADSORB).

sorrel[1] *n.* a herb with acid leaves, *Rumex acetosa*, allied to the dock. WH: 14–15C. Old French *sorele* (Modern French dial. *surelle*), from *sur*, from Germanic base of SOUR. See also -EL.

sorrel[2] *a.* of a reddish- or yellowish-brown. *Also n.* WH: 12–14C. Old French *sorrel*, from *sor* yellowish, from a Frankish *a.* meaning dry. See also -EL. Ult. rel. to SEAR.

sorrow *n.* mental pain or distress from loss, disappointment etc. *Also v.i.* WH: pre-1200. Old English *sorh*, *sorg*, from Germanic. Cp. German *Sorge*.

sorry *a.* penitent, apologetic. *Also int.* WH: pre-1200. Old English *sārig*, from Germanic base of SORE. See also -Y[1]. Not rel. to SORROW.

sort *n.* a group of instances of a certain thing identifiable, by having the same set of characteristics, a kind. *Also v.t., v.i.* WH: 14–15C. Old French *sorte*, from Latin *sors*, *sortis* wooden voting tablet, lit. share, condition, rank.

sortie *n.* a sally, esp. of troops from a besieged place in order to attack or raid. *Also v.i.* WH: 17C. French, fem. p.p. of *sortir* to go out.

sortilege *n.* divination by drawing lots. WH: 14–15C. Old French *sortilège*, from Medieval Latin *sortilegium* sorcery, divination, from Latin *sortilegus* sorcerer, diviner, from *sors*, *sortis* SORT + *legere* to choose.

sorus *n.* a cluster of spore-producing bodies (sporangia) esp. on the underside of a fern leaf. WH: 19C. Modern Latin, from Greek *sōros* heap.

SOS *n.* an internationally recognized distress call in Morse code. *Also v.i.* WH: early 20C. The letters *s*, *o* and *s*, chosen as easily transmitted (*s* is three dots, *o* three dashes). The letters are popularly regarded as an abbreviation of *save our souls* (or *save our ship*, etc).

sostenuto *a.*, *adv.* (played) in a steadily sustained manner. *Also n.* WH: 18C. Italian, p.p. of *sostenere* to sustain.

sot *n.* a habitual drunkard, a person habitually muddled (as if) with excessive drinking. *Also v.i.* WH: pre-1200. Old English *sott*, from Medieval Latin *sottus*, of unknown orig. The original sense was a foolish person. The sense habitual drunkard dates from the 16C.

soterial *a.* of or relating to salvation. WH: 19C. Greek *sōtēria* salvation. See also -AL[1].

Sothic *a.* of or relating to the star Sirius, esp. with reference to a cycle of 1460 years in Egyptian reckoning, which began with a year whose start coincided with the heliacal rising of Sirius. WH: 19C. Greek *Sōthis*, an Egyptian name for Sirius, the dog-star. See also -IC.

sotto voce *adv.* under one's voice, in an undertone. WH: 18C. Italian *sotto* under + *voce* voice.

sou *n.* a French copper coin worth one-twelfth of a livre. WH: 15C. French, sing. form deduced from *sous*, pl. of Old French *sout*, from Latin *solidus* SOLID. See SOLIDUS.

soubise *n.* a white sauce made from onions, butter, béchamel sauce and consommé. WH: 18C. Charles de Rohan *Soubise*, 1715–87, French general and courtier.

soubrette *n.* a lady's maid. WH: 18C. French, from Provençal *soubreto*, fem. of *soubret* coy, from *soubra* to set aside, from Latin *superare* to be above, to surmount.

souchong *n.* a black China tea made from the youngest leaves. WH: 18C. Chinese *siú chúng* small sort.

souffle *n.* a low whispering or murmur heard in the auscultation of an organ etc. WH: 19C. French breath, from *souffler*. See SOUFFLÉ.

soufflé *n.* any of various savoury or sweet, cooked or uncooked dishes made of beaten whites of eggs etc. *Also a.* WH: 19C. French, p.p. of *souffler* to puff up, from Latin *sufflare*, from *sub* under + *flare* to blow.

sough[1] *v.i.* to make a murmuring, sighing sound, like the wind. *Also n.* WH: pre-1200. Old English *swōgan*, rel. to *swēgan* to sound.

sough[2] *n.* a drain, a sewer, a water channel, esp. in a mine. WH: 12–14C. Orig. unknown.

souk *n.* an outside, often covered market in a Muslim country (esp. in N Africa and the Middle East). WH: 19C. Arabic *sūḳ*.

soul *n.* the spiritual part of a person. *Also a.* WH: pre-1200. Old English *sāwol*, *sāwl*, from Germanic. Cp. German *Seele*.

sound[1] *n.* the sensation produced through the organs of hearing. *Also a., v.i., v.t.* WH: 12–14C. Old French *son*, from Latin *sonus*. The *d* was added in the 15C.

sound[2] *a.* free from injury, defect or decay. *Also adv.* WH: 12–14C. Old English *gesund* sound, safe, healthy, from Germanic. Cp. German *gesund* healthy.

sound[3] *v.t.* to measure the depth of (a sea, channel etc.) or test the quality of (its bed) with a sounding line. *Also v.i., n.* WH: 14–15C. Old French *sonder*, corr. to Spanish and Portuguese *sondar* to use the sounding lead, from Popular Latin *subundare*, from Latin SUB- + *unda* wave.

sound[4] *n.* a narrow passage of water, such as a strait connecting two seas. WH: pre-1200. Old English *sund*, related to Old Norse *sund* swimming, strait, from Germanic base also of SWIM. The original sense (to 14–15C) was the action of swimming. The current sense evolved in the 12–14C. The word is not related to SOUND[3], as if a channel that could be sounded.

soup *n.* a liquid food made from meat, fish or vegetables and stock. WH: 12–14C. Old French *soupe* sop, broth poured on slices of bread, from Late Latin *suppa*, from a v. meaning to soak, ult. from Germanic. Cp. SOP, SUP.

soupçon *n.* a mere trace, taste or flavour (of). WH: 18C. French, from Old French *souspeçon*, from Medieval Latin *suspectio*, *suspectionis*. See SUSPICION.

sour *a.* sharp or acid to the taste, like a lemon, tart. *Also v.t., v.i., n.* WH: pre-1200. Old English *sūr*, from Germanic. Cp. German *sauer*.

source *n.* the spring or fountainhead from which a stream of water proceeds; cause. *Also v.t.* WH: 12–14C. Old French *sours* (m.), *sourse* (fem.) (Modern French *source*), use as n. of p.p. of *sourdre* to rise, to spring, from Latin *surgere* SURGE.

sourdine *n.* a soft stop on an organ etc. WH: 17C. French, from *sourd* deaf, dull.

sous- *pref.* (used before French-derived nouns) under-, subordinate, assistant etc. WH: 12–14C. Old French *sous*, from Latin *subtus* under.

sousaphone *n.* a brass wind instrument like a long curved tuba, carried so as to encircle the player's waist. WH: early 20C. John

Philip *Sousa*, 1854–1932, US bandmaster and composer, based on SAXOPHONE, etc.

souse *v.t.* to pickle. *Also v.i., n.* WH: 14–15C. Old French *sous*, *souz*, from Germanic, from base also of SALT. Cp. German *Sülze* brine.

souslik *n.* any ground squirrel of the genus *Spermophilus*, of Europe and Asia. WH: 18C. French, from Russian *suslik*.

soutache *n.* a narrow, ornamental braid. WH: 19C. French, from Hungarian *sujtás*.

soutane *n.* a cassock. WH: 19C. French, from Italian *sottana*, from *sotto*, from Latin *subtus* under. The garment is so called as it is worn under the vestments in a religious service.

souteneur *n.* a pimp. WH: early 20C. French protector, from *soutenir* to sustain + *-eur* -OR.

souter *n.* a shoemaker, a cobbler. WH: pre-1200. Old English *sūtere*, from Latin *sutor*, from *suere* to sew, to stitch. See also -ER[1].

souterrain *n.* an esp. Iron Age underground chamber. WH: 18C. French, from *sous* under + *terre* earth, based on Latin *subterraneus* SUBTERRANEAN.

south *n.* that one of the four cardinal points of the compass directly opposite to the north, or the direction in which this lies. *Also a., adv.* WH: pre-1200. Old English *sūth*, from Germanic. Cp. German *süd*. The word is perhaps ultimately related to SUN, so that the direction is that towards the region of the sun.

souvenir *n.* a keepsake, a memento. *Also v.t.* WH: 18C. French, use as n. of v. to remember, from Latin *subvenire* to come into the mind, from SUB- + *venire* to come (cp. SUBVENE).

souvlaki *n.* a Greek dish consisting of small pieces of meat grilled on a skewer. WH: mid-20C. Modern Greek *soublaki*, from *soubla* skewer.

sov *abbr.* a sovereign (the gold coin). WH: 19C. Abbr. of SOVEREIGN.

sovereign *a.* supreme. *Also n.* WH: 12–14C. Old French *soverain* (Modern French *souverain*), from Popular Latin *superanus*, from Latin *super* above. The spelling has been influenced by REIGN. Cp. SUZERAIN.

soviet *n.* a local council elected by workers and inhabitants of a district in the former Soviet Union. *Also a.* WH: early 20C. Russian *sovet* council, trans. of Greek *sumboulion* advice, counsel, from *sum-*, SYM- + *boulē* project, plan.

†sovran *n., a.* (a) sovereign. WH: 17C. Alt. of SOVEREIGN, based on Italian *sovrano*.

sow[1] *v.t.* to scatter (seed) for growth. *Also v.i.* WH: pre-1200. Old English *sāwan*, from Germanic, from Indo-European base represented also by Latin *serere* (past tense *sevi*). Cp. SEED, SEMEN.

sow[2] *n.* a female pig. WH: pre-1200. Old English *sugu*, from Germanic, from Indo-European base represented also by Latin *sus* pig, Greek *hus*. Cp. German *Sau*.

sowens *n.* a kind of pudding made from the husks of oats. WH: 16C. Appar. from Gaelic *súghan*, *súbhan* the liquid used in preparing it, from *súgh*, *súbh* sap.

Sowetan *n.* a native or inhabitant of Soweto. *Also a.* WH: late 20C. *Soweto*, a group of Black African townships outside Johannesburg, S Africa + -AN.

sowl *v.t.* to drag about, to tug, to pull by the ears. WH: 17C. Orig. uncertain. Cp. SOOL.

soy *n.* a thin brown salty sauce made from fermented soya beans, used extensively in Japanese and Chinese cookery. WH: 17C. Japanese, var. of *shōyu*, from Chinese *jiàngyóu*, from *jiàng* bean paste + *yóu* oil. Cp. SOYA.

soya *n.* a leguminous herb, *Glycine soja*, native to SE Asia, grown for its seeds. WH: 17C. Dutch *soja*, from Japanese *shōyu*. See SOY.

sozzled *a.* drunk. WH: 19C. P.p. of *sozzle* to wash by splashing, to douse, ? imit. The verb *sozzle* to imbibe intoxicating drink arose in the mid-20C as a back-formation from *sozzled*.

sp *abbr. sine prole*, without issue. WH: Abbr. of Latin *sine prole* without issue, from SINE[2] + abl. of *proles* offspring.

spa *n.* a mineral spring. WH: 17C. *Spa*, a health resort in E Belgium, famous for the curative properties of its mineral springs.

space *n.* continuous extension in three dimensions or any quantity or portion of this. *Also v.t.* WH: 12–14C. Shortening of Old French *espace*, from Latin *spatium*. The application of the word to outer space evolved in the 17C.

spade[1] *n.* an implement for digging, having a broad blade fitted on to a long handle, and worked with both hands and one foot. *Also v.t.* WH: pre-1200. Old English *spadu*, from Germanic, rel. to Greek *spathē* blade, paddle. See SPADE[2].

spade[2] *n.* a playing card with a black figure or figures shaped like a heart with a small triangular handle. WH: 16C. Italian, pl. of *spada*, from Latin *spatha*, from Greek *spathē* blade, paddle, shoulder blade, broadsword. Cp. SPADE[1].

spadille *n.* in the card games ombre and quadrille, the ace of spades. WH: 17C. French, from Spanish *espadilla*, dim. of *espada* sword, from Latin *spatha*, from Greek *spathē*. See SPADE[2].

spadix *n.* a spike of flowers on a fleshy stem, usu. enclosed in a spathe. WH: 18C. Latin, lit. palm branch with its fruit, from Greek.

spae *v.t., v.i.* to prophesy or foretell. WH: 12–14C. Old Norse *spá*, of unknown orig.

spaghetti *n.* a variety of pasta made in long thin cylindrical strings. WH: 19C. Italian, pl. of dim. of *spago* string.

spahi *n.* a Turkish irregular cavalryman. WH: 16C. French, from Turkish *sipahi*, from Persian *sipāhī*. See SEPOY.

spall *n.* a chip, splinter or flake. *Also v.t., v.i.* WH: 14–15C. Orig. unknown.

spalpeen *n.* a scamp, a young rascal. WH: 18C. Irish *spailpín*, ult. of unknown orig. See -EEN.

Spam® *n.* a tinned luncheon meat of chopped and spiced ham. WH: mid-20C. Appar. from *spiced* (from SPICE + -ED) + HAM[1].

span[1] *n.* the space from end to end of a bridge etc. *Also v.t., v.i.* WH: pre-1200. Old English, from Germanic. Cp. German *Spanne*. The original sense was the distance between the tips of the thumb and the little finger when the hand is fully extended, then this distance as a unit of measure (for an adult male on average 9 inches).

span[2] *n.* a rope or chain fastened at both ends to take a purchase. WH: 18C. Low German and Dutch, from *spannen* to stretch, to yoke, from Germanic, rel. to SPAN[1].

span[3] *a.* absolutely new, brand new. WH: 11–12C. Shortening of *span-new*, from Old Norse *spán-nyr*, from *spánn* chip + *nýr* new. Cp. SPICK AND SPAN.

spanaemia *n.* a blood condition in which there is a deficiency of red corpuscles. WH: 19C. Modern Latin, from Greek *spanos, spanios* scarce, scanty + *haima* blood + -IA.

Spandex® *n.* a stretchy fabric made from polymethane fibre. WH: mid-20C. Arbitrary formation, appar. reversing elements of EXPAND.

spandrel *n.* the space between the shoulder of an arch and the rectangular moulding etc. enclosing it, or between the shoulders of adjoining arches and the moulding etc. WH: 14–15C. Orig. uncertain. The word is perhaps from Anglo-French *spaundre* or from *espaundre* to expand. Cp. SPAWN.

spangle *n.* a small disc of glittering metal or metallic material, used for ornamenting dresses etc., a sequin. *Also v.t., v.i.* WH: 14–15C. From obs. *spang* glittering ornament (from Middle Dutch *spange*, from Germanic) + -LE[1].

Spaniard *n.* a native or inhabitant of Spain. WH: 12–14C. Shortening of Old French *Espaignart*, from *Espaigne* (Modern French *Espagne*) Spain. See also -ARD.

spaniel *n.* any of various breeds of dog, distinguished by large drooping ears, long silky or curly coat and a gentle disposition. WH: 12–14C. Old French *espaigneul* (Modern French *épagneul*), from Popular Latin *Hispaniolus* of Spain, dim. of Latin *Hispanus*, from *Hispania* Spain.

Spanish *a.* of or relating to Spain, its people or their language. *Also n.* WH: 12–14C. *Spain*, a country occupying the greater part of the Iberian peninsula in SW Europe + -ISH[1]. The shortened form of the first element dates from the 16C, perhaps influenced by Latin *Hispania* Spain.

spank *v.t.* to strike with the open hand, to slap, esp. on the buttocks. *Also v.i., n.* WH: 18C. Prob. imit.

spanner *n.* an instrument for tightening up or loosening the nuts on screws, a wrench. WH: 17C. German, from *spannen*. See SPAN[2]. The word was originally the name of a device for winding the spring of a wheel-lock gun. The current sense evolved in the 18C.

Spansule® *n.* a capsule for swallowing that releases one or more drugs into the system over a predetermined period. WH: mid-20C. SPAN[1] + CAPSULE.

spar[1] *n.* a round timber, a pole, esp. used as a mast, yard, boom, shears etc. WH: 12–14C. Old Norse *sperra*, or shortened form of Old French *esparre* (Modern French *épar*), from Germanic. Cp. German *Sparren*.

spar[2] *v.i.* to move the arms about in defence or offence as in boxing. *Also n.* WH: pre-1200. Old English *sperran*, corr. to Old Norse *sperrask* to kick out, of unknown orig. The original sense (to the 14–15C) was to dart, to spring. The sense to make the movements of a boxer arose in the 18C.

spar[3] *n.* any of various lustrous minerals occurring in crystalline or vitreous form, e.g. *feldspar*, *fluorspar*. WH: 16C. Middle Low German, rel. to Old English *spær*- in *spærstān*, obs. *spar-stone*, from base recorded also in Old English *spæren* of plaster, of gypsum.

sparable *n.* a headless nail for boot soles. WH: 17C. Contr. of *sparrow-bill*, from SPARROW + BILL[2].

spare *a.* not needed for routine purposes, able to be spared. *Also v.t., v.i., n.* WH: pre-1200. Old English *spær* sparing, frugal, from Germanic. Cp. German *sparen* to spare. The earliest sense was meagre, scanty. The sense additional, extra arose in the 14–15C.

sparge *v.t.* to sprinkle; to moisten by sprinkling, e.g. in brewing. WH: 14–15C. Prob. from Latin *spargere* to sprinkle.

spark *n.* an incandescent particle thrown off from a burning substance, or produced from a match, flint etc. *Also v.i., v.t.* WH: pre-1200. Old English *spærca, spearca*, from Germanic, of unknown orig.

sparkle *n.* a gleam, glitter. *Also v.i., v.t.* WH: 12–14C. SPARK + -LE[4].

sparrow *n.* a small brownish-grey bird of the genus *Passer*, esp. *P. domesticus*, the house sparrow. WH: pre-1200. Old English *spearwa*, from Germanic. Cp. Swedish *sparv*, Danish and Norwegian *spurv*.

sparse *a.* thinly scattered, not dense. WH: 18C. Latin *sparsus*, p.p. of *spargere* to scatter.

Spartan *n.* a native or inhabitant of Sparta. *Also a.* WH: 14–15C. Latin *Spartanus*, from *Sparta*, capital of the ancient Doric state of Laconia.

spartina *n.* any grass of the genus *Spartina*, having rhizomatous roots, growing in marshy ground. WH: 19C. Modern Latin, from Greek *spartinē* rope.

spasm *n.* a convulsive and involuntary muscular contraction. WH: 14–15C. Old French *spasme*, or from Latin *spasmus, spasma*, from Greek *spasmos, spasma*, from *span* to draw, to pull.

spat[1] *n.* a short gaiter fastening over and under the shoe. WH: 19C. Abbr. of *spatterdash*, (from SPATTER + DASH).

spat[2] *n.* a petty quarrel. *Also v.i., v.t.* WH: 19C. Prob. imit.

spat[3] *n.* the spawn of shellfish, esp. oysters. *Also v.i., v.t.* WH: 17C. Anglo-French, of unknown orig.

spatangoid *a., n.* (an urchin) of the Spatangoidea, an order of heart-shaped sea urchins. WH: 19C. Modern Latin *Spatangoides* (now *Spatangoidea*), from *Spatangus* genus name, from Late Latin *spatangius*, Greek *spataggēs* a kind of sea urchin. See also -OID.

spatchcock *n.* a fowl opened out along the backbone and fried or grilled flat. *Also v.t.* WH: 18C. ? Rel. to DISPATCH + COCK[1], but cp. SPITCHCOCK.

spate *n.* a heavy flood, esp. in a mountain stream or river. WH: 14–15C. Orig. unknown.

spathe *n.* a large bract or pair of bracts enveloping the spadix of a plant. WH: 18C. Latin *spatha*, from Greek *spathē*. See SPADE[1].

spathic *a.* resembling spar, esp. in cleavage. WH: 18C. From *spath* spar (from German) + -IC.

spatial *a.* of, relating to, existing or occurring in space. WH: 19C. Latin *spatium* SPACE. See also -AL[1].

Spätlese *n.* a (German etc.) white wine made from late-harvested grapes. WH: mid-20C. German, from *spät* late + *Lese* picking, vintage.

spatter *v.t.* to scatter or splash (water etc.) about. *Also v.i., n.* WH: 16C. Freq. of imit. base represented also by Low German and Dutch *spatten* to burst, to spout. See also -ER[5].

spatula *n.* a broad knife or trowel-shaped tool used for spreading plasters, working pigments, mixing foods etc. WH: 16C. Latin, var. of *spathula*, dim. of *spatha* (SPATHE).

spavin *n.* a disease in horses affecting the hock joint with swelling or a hard excrescence. WH: 14–15C. Shortening of Old French *espavin*, var. of *esparvain* (Modern French *éparvin*), from Germanic, from base represented by E Frisian *spadde*, *sparre*. Old French *esparvain* is probably from Frankish *sparwan* SPARROW. The disease is perhaps so called either because a horse affected with spavin has an awkward gait like a sparrow's, or because the bony swelling resembles a sparrow's round body.

spawn *v.t.* (of fish, amphibians etc.) to deposit or produce (eggs, young etc.). *Also v.i. n.* WH: 14–15C. Shortening of Anglo-French *espaundre* to shed roe, var. of Old French *espandre* (Modern French *épandre*) to shed, to spill, to pour out, from Latin *expandere* EXPAND.

spay *v.t.* to destroy or remove the ovaries of (female animals) so as to make them infertile, to sterilize. WH: 14–15C. Shortening of Old French *espeer*, from *espee* (Modern French *épée*) sword, from Latin *spatha*. See SPATHE.

speak *v.i.* to utter articulate sounds or words in the ordinary tone as distinct from singing. *Also v.t.* WH: pre-1200. Old English *specan*, earlier *sprecan*, from Germanic. Cp. German *sprechen*. The original *r* has been lost as with PANG.

spear *n.* a weapon with a pointed head on a long shaft. *Also v.t.* WH: pre-1200. Old English *spere*, from Germanic. Cp. German *Speer*.

spec¹ *n.* specification. WH: mid-20C. Abbr. of *specification* (SPECIFY).

spec² *n.* speculation. *Also a.* WH: 18C. Abbr. of *speculation* (SPECULATE).

special *a.* exceptionally good or important. *Also n.* WH: 12–14C. Shortening of Old French *especial* (Modern French *spécial*) ESPECIAL, or from Latin *specialis*, from SPECIES. See also -AL¹.

species *n.* a class of things with certain characteristics in common. WH: 14–15C. Latin appearance, form, kind, from *spec-*, base of *specere* to look, to behold. Cp. SPICE.

specify *v.t.* to mention expressly. WH: 12–14C. Old French *spécifier* or Late Latin *specificare*. See also -FY.

specimen *n.* a part or an individual intended to illustrate or typify the nature of a whole or a class. WH: 17C. Latin, from *specere* to look (at).

specious *a.* apparently, but not actually, right or fair, plausible. WH: 14–15C. Latin *speciosus* fair, fair-seeming, from SPECIES. See also -OUS. The original sense (to the 19C) was beautiful, handsome. The sense deceptively attractive evolved in the 17C.

speck *n.* a small spot or blemish. *Also v.t.* WH: pre-1200. Old English *specca*, rel. to Middle Dutch *spekkel* (Dutch *spikkel*) speckle (SPECK).

specs *n.pl.* spectacles, glasses. WH: 19C. Abbr. of *spectacles* (SPECTACLE).

spectacle *n.* something exhibited to the view, a show. WH: 12–14C. Old French, from Latin *spectaculum* public show, from *spectare*. See SPECTATOR.

spectator *n.* a person who looks on, esp. at a show or spectacle. WH: 16C. French *spectateur* or Latin *spectator*, from *spectatus*, p.p. of *spectare* to look, freq. of *specere* to look at. See also -ATE³, -OR.

spectre *n.* an apparition, a ghost. WH: 17C. French, or from Latin *spectrum*, from *specere* to look, to see. Cp. SPECTRUM.

spectro- *comb. form* spectrum. WH: SPECTRUM. See also -O-.

spectrochemistry *n.* a branch of chemistry that studies the spectra of substances. WH: 19C. SPECTRO- + CHEMISTRY.

spectrograph *n.* an apparatus for photographing or otherwise reproducing spectra. WH: 19C. SPECTRO- + -GRAPH.

spectroheliograph *n.* an instrument for photographing the sun using a particular wavelength of light. WH: 19C. SPECTRO- + HELIOGRAPH.

spectrology *n.* the science of spectrum analysis. WH: 19C. SPECTRO- + -LOGY.

spectrometer *n.* an instrument for measuring the refractive index of substances. WH: 19C. SPECTRO- + -METER.

spectrophotometer *n.* an instrument for measuring the intensity of light in different areas of the spectrum, esp. as transmitted by substances or solutions at various wavelengths. WH: 19C. SPECTRO- + PHOTOMETER.

spectroscope *n.* an instrument for forming and analysing the spectra of rays emitted by bodies. WH: 19C. SPECTRO- + -SCOPE.

spectrum *n.* the rainbow-like range of colours into which white light is dispersed, according to the degrees of refrangibility of its components, when passing through a prism, from violet (with the shortest wavelength) to red (with the longest wavelength). WH: 17C. Latin image, appearance, apparition. See SPECTRE.

speculate *v.i.* to pursue an inquiry or form conjectures or views (on or upon). WH: 16C. Latin *speculatus*, p.p. of *speculari* to spy out, to watch, from *specula* lookout, watchtower, from *specere* to see, to look. See also -ATE³. The original sense was to reflect on, to contemplate. The current sense dates from the 17C.

speculum *n.* a surgical instrument for dilating the passages or cavities of the body, to facilitate inspection. WH: 14–15C. Latin, from base of *specere* to look, to see. See also -ULE. Cp. SPIEGELEISEN.

speech *n.* the faculty or act of uttering articulate sounds or words. WH: pre-1200. Old English *spēc*, rel. to *spēcan* SPEAK, replacing earlier *sprǣc*, from Germanic. Cp. German *Sprache* speech, language. The sense formal address, oration dates from the 16C.

speed *n.* rapidity, swiftness. *Also v.i., v.t.* WH: pre-1200. Old English *spēd*, from Germanic base also of Old English *spōwan* to prosper, to succeed. The original sense was abundance, power, success, assistance.

speer *v.i., v.t.* to question, to inquire, to ask. WH: pre-1200. Old English *spyrian*, from Germanic base also of SPOOR.

speiss *n.* a compound of arsenic, nickel, copper etc., produced in the smelting of various ores such as lead. WH: 18C. German *Speise*, orig. food.

spekboom *n.* a large shrub with succulent leaves, *Portulacaria afra*. WH: 19C. Afrikaans, from *spek* fat pork, bacon + *boom* tree. The shrub is so called from its succulent leaves, providing rich fodder for goats and other animals.

spelaean of or relating to a cave or caves. WH: 19C. Latin *spelaeum* (from Greek *spēlaion* cave) + -AN.

spelk *n.* a splinter. WH: pre-1200. Old English *spelc*, corr. to Low German *spalke*, Old Norse *spelkur* (pl.).

spell¹ *v.t.* to say or write the letters forming (a word). *Also v.i.* WH: 12–14C. Shortening of Old French *espeler* (Modern French *épeler*), from Germanic base also of SPELL².

spell² *n.* a series of words used as a charm, an incantation. WH: pre-1200. Old English *spel*, from Germanic base also of SPELL¹. Cp. GOSPEL.

spell³ *n.* a shift or turn of work. *Also v.t., v.i.* WH: 16C. Var. of obs. *spele* to take the place of another, from Old English *spelian*, of unknown orig.

spell⁴ *n.* a splinter of wood etc. WH: 14–15C. ? Var. of obs. *speld* spark, chip, splinter, corr. to Old Norse *speld*, *spjald* (Norwegian *spjeld*, Swedish *spjell*), rel. to German dial. *Spelte* tablet, splinter, chip, from Germanic.

spelt *n.* a variety of wheat, *Triticum spelta*, formerly much cultivated in S Europe etc. WH: pre-1200. Old Saxon *spelta*, Middle Low German and Middle Dutch *spelte*, from Germanic. Cp. German *Spelz*.

spelter *n.* commercial or impure smelted zinc. WH: 17C. Corr. to Old French *espeautre*, Middle Dutch *speauter*, German *Spialter*, ult. rel. to PEWTER.

spelunker *n.* a person who explores or studies caves as a sport or hobby. WH: mid-20C. Latin *spelunca* cave + -ER¹.

†spence *n.* a larder or pantry. WH: 14–15C. Shortening of Old French *despense* (Modern French *dépense*), fem. p.p. (used as n.) of Latin *dispendere* DISPENSE. The Middle English word is the source of the surnames *Spence* and *Spencer*, literally a servant who works in the pantry. Cp. SPENCER¹.

spencer¹ *n.* a short overcoat or jacket, for men or women. WH: 18C. Surname *Spencer*. The overcoat is apparently named after George John Spencer, 2nd Earl Spencer, 1758–1834. Its own name was then probably transferred to the women's undergarment.

spencer² *n.* a fore-and-aft trysail abaft the foremast or mainmast on a barque or ship. WH: 19C. Prob. surname *Spencer*. The name may have been transferred from that of a type of lifebelt, itself apparently designed by a Mr Knight Spencer.

spend *v.t.* to pay out (money etc. on something or someone). *Also v.i., n.* WH: pre-1200. Old English *spendan*, from Germanic, from Latin *expendere* EXPEND. Cp. German *spenden*.

Spenserian *a.* of or relating to or in the style of Spenser or his verse. *Also n.* WH: 19C. Edmund *Spenser, c.*1552–99, English poet + -IAN.

sperm *n.* a spermatozoon, a male gamete. WH: 14–15C. Late Latin *sperma*, from Greek sperm, seed, from base of *speirein* to sow.

-sperm *comb. form* a seed. WH: Greek *sperma* seed.

spermaceti *n.* a white waxy, buoyancy-promoting substance, existing in solution in the oily matter in the head of the sperm whale, used for candles, ointments etc. WH: 15C. Medieval Latin *sperma* sperm + *ceti*, gen. of *cetus*, Greek *kētos* whale. The substance is so called either from its appearance or from the belief that it represents whale spawn. (*Sperm whale* is a shortening of *spermaceti whale.*)

spermary *n.* the male spermatic gland, testicle or other organ. WH: 19C. Modern Latin *spermarium*, from *sperma* SPERM + -ARIUM. See also -ARY[1].

spermatheca *n.* a receptacle in female insects and other invertebrates for spermatozoa. WH: 19C. Greek *sperma* SPERM + *thēkē* case, THECA.

spermatic *a.* consisting of, of or relating to or conveying sperm or semen. WH: 14–15C. Late Latin *spermaticus*, from Greek *spermatikos*, from *sperma* SPERM. See also -ATIC.

spermatid *n.* a male sex cell that may develop directly into a spermatozoon. WH: 19C. SPERMATO- + -ID.

spermato- *comb. form* a seed or sperm. WH: Greek, from *sperma*, *spermatos* SPERM. See also -O-.

spermatoblast *n.* a cell from which a spermatozoon develops. WH: 19C. SPERMATO- + -BLAST.

spermatocyte *n.* a cell produced from a spermatogonium that may divide into spermatids. WH: 19C. SPERMATO- + -CYTE.

spermatogenesis *n.* the development or production of mature spermatozoa. WH: 19C. SPERMATO- + GENESIS.

spermatogonium *n.* a primitive male germ cell which divides to form spermatocytes. WH: 19C. SPERMATO- + Greek *gon*-, stem of *gonē*, *gonos* offspring + -IUM.

spermatophore *n.* a capsule holding spermatozoa, in molluscs and other invertebrates. WH: 19C. SPERMATO- + -PHORE.

spermatophyte *n.* a seed-bearing plant. WH: 19C. SPERMATO- + -PHYTE.

spermatorrhoea *n.* involuntary discharge of seminal fluid. WH: 19C. SPERMATO- + -RRHOEA.

spermatozoon *n.* any of the millions of mature male sex cells contained in the semen. WH: 19C. SPERMATO- + Greek *zōion* animal.

spew *v.t.* to vomit (up). *Also v.i., n.* WH: pre-1200. Old English *spīwan*, from Germanic base rel. to that of Latin *spuere* and Greek *ptuein*, from Indo-European base of imit. orig. Cp. PUKE.

sphagnum *n.* any moss of the genus *Sphagnum*, found in peat or bogs, and used as a fertilizer and as packing material. WH: 18C. Modern Latin, from Greek *sphagnos* a kind of moss.

sphalerite *n.* blende. WH: 19C. Greek *sphaleros* deceptive + -ITE[1]. The blende is so called because its dark-coloured, opaque varieties can be taken for galena, a valuable lead ore. The name was coined in 1847 by the German mineralogist Ernst Friedrich Glocker.

sphene *n.* titanite, occurring as wedge-shaped crystals. WH: 19C. French *sphène*, from Greek *sphēn* wedge.

spheno- *comb. form* the sphenoid bone. WH: Greek *sphēn* wedge. See also -O-.

sphenodon *n.* any member of the genus *Sphenodon* of nocturnal lizard-like reptiles, now confined to New Zealand. WH: 19C. SPHENO- + Greek *odous, odontis* tooth.

sphenogram *n.* a cuneiform or wedge-shaped written character. WH: 19C. SPHENO- + -GRAM.

sphenoid *a.* wedge-shaped. *Also n.* WH: 18C. Modern Latin *sphenoides*, from Greek *sphēnoeidēs*, from *sphēn* wedge. See also -OID.

sphere *n.* a solid bounded by a surface every part of which is equally distant from a point within called the centre. *Also v.t.* WH: 12–14C. Old French *espere*, later (with assim. to Greek or Latin) *sphère*, from Late Latin *sphera*, earlier *sphaera*, from Greek *sphaira* ball, globe.

spherometer *n.* an instrument for measuring the radii and curvature of spherical surfaces. WH: 19C. SPHERE + -O- + -METER.

spherule *n.* a small sphere. WH: 17C. Late Latin *spherula, sphaerula*, dim. of Latin *sphaera* SPHERE. See also -ULE.

sphincter *n.* a ring muscle that contracts or shuts any orifice or tube. WH: 16C. Latin, from Greek *sphigktēr* band, contractile muscle, from *sphiggein* to bind tight.

sphingid *n.* a hawkmoth of the family Sphingidae. WH: early 20C. Modern Latin *Sphingidae*, from SPHINX. See also -ID. The moth is apparently so called because the larva (caterpillar) rests with its head raised, like the figure of a sphinx, or simply because this pose is enigmatic.

sphinx *n.* in Greek mythology, a winged monster, half woman and half lion, said to have devoured the inhabitants of Thebes till a riddle she had proposed should be solved, and on its solution by Oedipus to have flung herself down and perished. WH: 14–15C. Latin, from Greek *Sphigx, Sphiggos*, appar. from *sphiggein* to draw tight. The Sphinx of Greek mythology strangled everyone who could not answer the riddle she posed, and is apparently so called from this action.

sphragistics *n.* the study of engraved seals and signets. WH: 19C. Greek *sphragistikos*, from *sphragis* seal. See also -ICS.

sphygmo- *comb. form* of or relating to a pulse. WH: Greek *sphugmo*-, comb. form of *sphugmos* pulse. See also -O-.

sphygmograph *n.* an instrument for recording the movements of the pulse. WH: 19C. SPHYGMO- + -GRAPH.

sphygmology *n.* the branch of physiology concerned with the pulse. WH: 19C. SPHYGMO- + -LOGY.

sphygmomanometer *n.* an instrument for measuring the tension of blood in an artery. WH: 19C. SPHYGMO- + MANOMETER.

sphygmophone *n.* an instrument for enabling one to hear the action of the pulse. WH: 19C. SPHYGMO- + -PHONE.

sphygmoscope *n.* an instrument for rendering the movements of the pulse visible. WH: 19C. SPHYGMO- + -SCOPE.

sphygmus *n.* a pulse, a pulsation. WH: 19C. Modern Latin, from Greek *sphugmos* pulse.

spic *n.* a Spanish-speaking American, esp. a Mexican. WH: early 20C. Abbr. of *spiggoty*, of uncertain orig. ? Alt. of *speak the* in a phr. such as *no speak the English*.

spica *n.* a spike. WH: 14–15C. Latin ear of grain.

spiccato *n.* a staccato style on a stringed instrument in which the player makes the bow rebound lightly from the strings. *Also a., adv.* WH: 18C. Italian detailed, distinct.

spice *n.* any aromatic and pungent vegetable substance used for seasoning food. *Also v.t.* WH: 12–14C. Shortening of Old French *espice* (Modern French *épice*), from Latin *species* appearance, kind, SPECIES, (pl.) wares, merchandise (based on Late Greek use of pl. of *eidos* form to mean goods, groceries, spices). The original sense (to the 17C) was sort, kind, but the current sense was also in use from the start.

spick and span *a.* new and fresh, clean and smart. WH: 16C. Extended form of *span-new* (SPAN[3]). The first element is prob. from the Dutch equivalent, *spikspelldernieuw* or *spiksplinternieuw*, respectively lit. spike-new, splinter-new. Cp. German *nagelneu*, lit. nailnew.

spicule *n.* a small sharp needle-shaped body, such as the calcareous or siliceous spikes in sponges etc. WH: 18C. Modern Latin *spicula*, dim. of Latin *spica*. See also -ULE.

spider *n.* an eight-legged arachnid of the order Araneae, usu. equipped with a spinning apparatus utilized by most species for making webs to catch their prey. *Also v.i., v.t.* WH: pre-1200. Old English *spithra*, from *spinnan* SPIN. Cp. German *Spinne, spinnen* (SPIN).

spiegeleisen *n.* a white variety of cast iron containing manganese, used in making Bessemer steel. WH: 19C. German, from *Spiegel* mirror (from Latin SPECULUM) + *Eisen* iron.

spiel *n.* the sales patter of a practised dealer, or anyone's well-rehearsed or familiar tale. *Also v.i., v.t.* WH: 19C. German *spielen* to play, to gamble.

spiffing *a.* excellent. WH: 19C. Orig. unknown. The form is that of a present participle, as for *ripping* (RIP[1]), *topping* (TOP[1]), from a verb apparently related to SPIFLICATE.

spiflicate *v.t.* to smash, to crush, to destroy. WH: 18C. Fanciful formation, ? influ. by SUFFOCATE.

spignel *n.* an umbelliferous plant, *Meum athamanticum*, with an aromatic root used in medicine, and finely cut, ornamental leaves, also called *baldmoney*. WH: 16C. Orig. uncertain. ? Anglo-French *spigurnelle*, an unidentified plant.

spigot *n.* a peg or plug for stopping the vent-hole in a cask. WH: 12–14C. ? Provençal *espigou*, rel. to Spanish *espigón*, Italian *spigone* ladder rung, bar of a chair, bung. Cp. Portuguese *espicho* spigot, from Latin *spiculum*, dim. of *spicum*, var. of SPICA.

spike[1] *n.* any pointed object, a sharp point. *Also v.t.* WH: 12–14C. Orig. uncertain. ? Shortened form of Middle Low German and Middle Dutch *spiker* (Dutch *spijker*), or Middle Dutch *spiking*. Rel. to SPOKE.

spike[2] *n.* an inflorescence closely attached to a common stem. WH: 14–15C. Latin *spica*, rel. to *spina* SPINE.

spikenard *n.* a Himalayan herb, *Nardostachys jatamansi*, related to the valerian. WH: 12–14C. Medieval Latin *spica nardi* (SPIKE[2], NARD), translating Greek *nardou stakhus*.

spile *n.* a small wooden plug, a spigot. *Also v.t.* WH: 16C. Middle Low German and Middle Dutch splinter, wooden peg, skewer. Rel. to SPILL[2].

spill[1] *v.t.* to cause (liquid, powder etc.) to fall or run out of a vessel, esp. accidentally. *Also v.i., n.* WH: pre-1200. Old English *spillan* to destroy, to kill, from Germanic, of unknown orig. The original sense was to kill, then (to the 17C) to cause death, to destroy, to devastate. The original reference was thus to spilling blood. The current sense dates from the 12–14C.

spill[2] *n.* a slip of paper or wood used to light a candle, pipe etc. WH: 12–14C. Rel. to SPILE.

spillikin *n.* a small strip or pin of bone, wood etc., used in spillikins. WH: 18C. SPILL[2] + -KIN.

spilosite *n.* a greenish schistose rock spotted with chlorite concretions or scales. WH: 19C. Greek *spilos* spot, speck + -ITE[1].

spin *v.t.* to make (something or someone) rotate or whirl round rapidly. *Also v.i., n.* WH: pre-1200. Old English *spinnan*, from Germanic. Cp. German *spinnen*.

spinach *n.* an annual herb of the genus *Spinacia*, esp. *S. oleracea*, with succulent leaves cooked as food. WH: 12–14C. Prob. from Old French *espinache*, *espinage* (Modern French *épinard*), from Spanish *espinaca*, from Spanish Arabic *isbināḵ*, Arabic *isbānāḵ*, from Persian *aspanāḵ*, *aspanāj*.

spindle *n.* a pin or rod in a spinning wheel for twisting and winding the thread. *Also v.i.* WH: pre-1200. Old English *spinel*, from Germanic base of SPIN. See also -LE[1]. Cp. German *Spindel*.

spindrift *n.* fine spray blown up from the surface of water. WH: 17C. Alt. of *spoondrift*, from *spoon* to run before the wind or sea, of unknown orig. + DRIFT.

spine *n.* the spinal column, the backbone. WH: 14–15C. Shortening of Old French *espine* (Modern French *épine*), or from Latin *spina* thorn, prickle, rel. to *spica* SPIKE[2].

spinel *n.* a vitreous aluminate of magnesium, of various colours, crystallizing isometrically. WH: 16C. French *spinelle*, from Italian *spinella*, dim. of Latin *spina* SPINE. See also -EL.

spinet *n.* an obsolete musical instrument, similar in construction to but smaller than the harpsichord. WH: 17C. Shortening of obs. French *espinette* (now *épinette*), from Italian *spinetta* virginal, spinet, dim. of *spina* SPINE. See also -ET[1]. The instrument is so called because its strings were plucked with quills. Some sources derive the word from the name of the instrument's alleged inventor, Giovanni *Spinetti*.

spini- *comb. form* of or relating to the spine. WH: Latin *spina* SPINE.

spinifex *n.* any coarse, spiny Australian grass of the genus *Spinifex*, growing in sandhills etc. in the arid regions of Australia, and often covering enormous areas of ground. WH: 19C. Modern Latin, from Latin *spina* SPINE + *-fex* maker, from *facere* to make.

spinnaker *n.* a large jib-shaped sail carried opposite the mainsail on the mainmast of a racing yacht. WH: 19C. Said to be a fanciful formation based on *spinx*, a mispronun. of *Sphinx*, the name of the first yacht to use the sail, influ. by *spanker* (SPANK).

spinney *n.* a small wood with undergrowth, a copse. WH: 14–15C. Shortening of Old French *espinei* (Modern French *épinaie*), from alt. of Latin *spinetum* thicket, from *spina* SPINE. See also -Y[3].

spinode *n.* a stationary point on a curve, a cusp. WH: 19C. Latin *spina* SPINE + NODE.

Spinozism *n.* the monistic system of Baruch de Spinoza, who resolved all being into extension and thought, which he considered as attributes of God. WH: 18C. Baruch (Benedict) de *Spinoza*, 1632–77, Dutch philosopher of Jewish descent + -ISM.

spinster *n.* an unmarried woman. WH: 14–15C. SPIN + -STER. The original sense was a woman who spins (cotton, wool etc.) as an occupation. Many such women were unmarried, and the term for the occupation passed to the legal designation of an unmarried woman in the 17C.

spinthariscope *n.* an instrument for showing the rays emitted by radium by the scintillations caused by their impact against a fluorescent screen. WH: early 20C. Greek *spintharis* spark + -SCOPE. The name was coined in 1903 by the English chemist and physicist Sir William Crookes. Cp. THALLIUM.

spinule *n.* a minute spine. WH: 18C. Latin *spinula*, dim. of *spina* SPINE. See also -ULE.

spiracle *n.* an external breathing hole in insects, certain fish, and whales. WH: 14–15C. Latin *spiraculum*, from *spirare* to breathe.

spiraea *n.* any flowering plant belonging to the *Spiraea* genus of Rosaceae, including the meadowsweet. WH: 17C. Modern Latin, from Latin *spiraea* privet, from Greek *speiraia*, appar. from *speira* SPIRE[2]. The plant is so called because it was originally used in garlands.

spiral *a.* forming a spire, spiral or coil. *Also n., v.i., v.t.* WH: 16C. French, or from Medieval Latin *spiralis*, from Latin *spira* SPIRE[2]. See also -AL[1].

spirant *n.* a consonant produced with a continuous expulsion of breath, esp. a fricative. *Also a.* WH: pre-1200. Latin *spirans*, *spirantis*, pres.p. of *spirare* to breathe. See also -ANT.

spire[1] *n.* a tapering, conical or pyramidal structure, esp. the tapering portion of a steeple. *Also v.i., v.t.* WH: pre-1200. Old English *spīr*, from Germanic. Cp. SPEAR.

spire[2] *n.* a spiral, a coil. WH: 16C. French, or from Latin *spira*, from Greek *speira* coil, winding.

spirillum *n.* any bacterium of a genus, *Spirillum*, of bacteria having a spiral structure. WH: 19C. Modern Latin genus name, dim. of Latin *spira* SPIRE[2].

spirit *n.* the vital principle animating a person or animal. *Also v.t.* WH: 12–14C. Anglo-French, shortened form of *espirit*, Old French *esperit* (Modern French *esprit*), from Latin *spiritus* breathing, from *spirare* to breathe.

spiro-[1] *comb. form* of or relating to a coil. WH: Latin *spira*, Greek *speira* SPIRE[2]. See also -O-.

spiro-[2] *comb. form* of or relating to breathing. WH: Latin *spirare* to breathe. See also -O-.

spirochaete *n.* any spiral-shaped bacterium of the genus *Spirochaeta*, which includes the causative agents of syphilis, relapsing fever, and epidemic jaundice. WH: 19C. SPIRO-[1] + Modern Latin CHAETA.

spirograph *n.* an instrument for recording the movement in breathing. WH: 19C. SPIRO-[2] + -GRAPH.

spirogyra *n.* any alga of the genus *Spirogyra*, whose cells contain spiral bands of chlorophyll. WH: 19C. Modern Latin, from *spiro-* SPIRO-[1] + Greek *gura*, *guros* round.

spirometer *n.* an instrument for measuring the capacity of the lungs. WH: 19C. SPIRO-[2] + -METER.

spirophore *n.* an instrument for inducing respiration when animation is suspended. WH: 19C. SPIRO-[2] + -PHORE.

spiroscope *n.* a spirometer. WH: 19C. SPIRO-[2] + -SCOPE.

spirula *n.* a tropical cephalopod mollusc, *Spirula peronii* of the order Decapoda, having a flat spiral shell. WH: 19C. Modern Latin, dim. of Latin *spira* SPIRE[2]. See also -ULE.

†spissitude *n.* density, inspissation. WH: 14–15C. Latin *spissitudo*, from *spissus* thick, dense. See also -TUDE.

spit[1] *v.t.* to eject (saliva etc.), throw (out) from the mouth. *Also v.i., n.* WH: pre-1200. Old English *spittan*, from Germanic imit. base. Cp. German dial. *spützen*.

spit[2] *n.* a long pointed rod on which meat for roasting is skewered and rotated over a fire. *Also v.t.* WH: pre-1200. Old English *spitu*, from Germanic. Cp. German *Spiess*.

spit[3] *n.* a spade's depth of earth. WH: 16C. Middle Low German and Middle Dutch, prob. ult. rel. to SPIT[2].

spitchcock *v.t.* to split and broil (an eel etc.). *Also n.* WH: 15C. Orig. unknown. Cp. SPATCHCOCK. Some sources propose an origin in *spitcook*, from SPIT² + COOK.

spite *n.* ill will, malice. *Also v.t.* WH: 12–14C. Shortening of DESPITE.

spitz *n.* a sharp-muzzled breed of dog, also called *Pomeranian*. WH: 19C. German *Spitz, Spitzhund*, special use of *spitz* pointed, peaked. The dog is so called from its pointed nose and ears.

spiv *n.* a man who dresses flashily and lives by dubious dealing and trading, e.g. in black-market goods. WH: mid-20C. Orig. uncertain. ? From *spiff* to smarten, to make neat, of unknown orig. Cp. SPIFFING.

splake *n.* a hybrid trout found in the lakes of N America. WH: mid-20C. Blend of *speckled* (SPECK) and LAKE¹.

splanchnic *a.* of or relating to the bowels, intestinal. WH: 17C. Modern Latin *splanchnicus*, from Greek *splagkhnikos*, from *splagkhna* entrails. See also -IC.

splanchnology *n.* the branch of medical science dealing with the viscera. WH: 18C. Greek *splagkhna* entrails + -O- + -LOGY.

splanchnotomy *n.* dissection of the viscera. WH: 19C. Greek *splagkhna* entrails + -O- + -TOMY.

splash *v.t.* to bespatter with water, mud etc. *Also v.i., n.* WH: 18C. Alt. of PLASH². The addition of *s* intensifies the original sense. Cp. SQUASH¹/ QUASH.

splat¹ *n.* a flat strip of wood forming the central part of a chair back. WH: 19C. From v. *splat*, to cut up, to split open, rel. to SPLIT.

splat² *n.* the slapping sound made by a soft or wet object striking a surface. *Also adv., v.t., v.i.* WH: 19C. Shortening of SPLATTER.

splatter *v.t.* to bespatter, to splash with dirt, mud, water etc. *Also v.i., n.* WH: 18C. Imit.

splay *v.t.* to form (a window opening, doorway etc.) with diverging sides. *Also v.i., n., a.* WH: 12–14C. Shortening of DISPLAY. The original sense (to the 16C) was to unfurl, to unfold to view.

spleen *n.* a soft vascular organ situated to the left of the stomach in most vertebrates which produces lymphocytes and antibodies, and filters the blood. WH: 12–14C. Shortening of Old French *esplen*, from Latin *splen*, from Greek *splēn*, prob. rel. to *splagkhnon* (SPLANCHNIC), Latin *lien*, Sanskrit *plīhán*.

splen- *comb. form* of or relating to the spleen. WH: Greek *splēn* SPLEEN.

splendid *a.* magnificent, sumptuous. WH: 17C. French *splendide* or Latin *splendidus*, from *splendere* to be bright, to shine. See also -ID.

splenectomy *n.* the surgical removal of the spleen. WH: 19C. SPLEN- + -ECTOMY.

splenetic *a.* affected with spleen; peevish, ill-tempered. *Also n.* WH: 14–15C. Late Latin *spleneticus*, from *splen*. See SPLEEN.

splenic *a.* of or relating to or affecting the spleen. WH: 17C. French *splénique*, or from Latin *splenicus*, from Greek *splēnikos*, from *splēn*. See SPLEEN, also -IC.

splenius *n.* a muscle extending in two parts on either side of the neck and upper back, serving to bend the head backwards. WH: 18C. Modern Latin, from Greek *splēnion* bandage, compress.

splenization *n.* conversion of a portion of the lung into spongy tissue resembling the spleen. WH: 19C. SPLEN- + -*ization* (-IZE).

splenology *n.* scientific study of the spleen. WH: 19C. SPLEN- + -O- + -LOGY.

splenomegaly *n.* morbid enlargement of the spleen. WH: early 20C. SPLEN- + -O- + Greek *megas, megalos* large + -Y².

splenotomy *n.* the dissection of or an incision into the spleen. WH: 19C. SPLEN- + -O- + -TOMY.

spleuchan *n.* a small bag, pouch or purse, esp. a tobacco pouch. WH: 18C. Gaelic *spliùchan*, Irish *spliúchán*.

splice *v.t.* to unite (two ropes etc.) by interweaving the strands of the ends. *Also n.* WH: 16C. Prob. from Middle Dutch *splissen*, from Germanic. Cp. German *splissen, spleissen*. Rel. to SPLIT.

spliff *n.* a cannabis cigarette. WH: mid-20C. Orig. unknown.

spline *n.* a key fitting into a groove in a shaft and wheel to make these revolve together. *Also v.t.* WH: 18C. Orig. E Anglian dial., ? rel. to SPLINTER.

splint *n.* a thin piece of wood or other material used to keep the parts of a broken bone together. *Also v.t.* WH: 12–14C. Middle Low German *splente, splinte*, Middle Dutch *splinte*. Rel. to SPLINTER.

splinter *n.* a thin piece of wood, glass etc. broken, split or shivered off. *Also v.t., v.i.* WH: 12–14C. Middle Dutch and Low German, rel. to SPLINT.

split *v.t.* to break or divide, esp. longitudinally or with the grain. *Also v.i., n., a.* WH: 16C. Middle Dutch *splitten*, rel. to German *spleissen* to split, to cleave, ult. of unknown orig.

splodge *n.* a daub, a blotch, an irregular stain. *Also v.t.* WH: 19C. Imit., or alt. of SPLOTCH.

splore *n.* a noisy frolic, a carousal, a spree. WH: 18C. Orig. unknown.

splosh *v.i., v.t.* to splash; to move with a splashing sound. *Also n.* WH: 19C. Imit.

splotch *n.* a splodge. *Also v.t.* WH: 17C. ? Blend of SPOT and obs. *plotch*, of unknown orig.

splurge *n.* an exuberant or extravagant display. *Also v.i.* WH: 19C. Imit., ? influ. by SPLASH and SURGE.

splutter *v.i.* to speak in an agitated, incoherent manner. *Also v.t., n.* WH: 17C. Imit. Cp. SPUTTER.

Spode® *n.* porcelain made by the factory of Josiah Spode. WH: 19C. Josiah *Spode*, 1754–1827, English maker of china.

†spodium *n.* fine powder obtained from calcined bone and other substances. WH: 14–15C. Latin, from Greek *spodion*, from *spodos* ashes, embers.

spodumene *n.* a monoclinic silicate of aluminium and lithium. WH: 19C. French *spodumène*, German *Spodumen*, from Greek *spodoumenos*, pres.p. of *spodousthai* to be burnt to ashes, from *spodos* ashes, embers.

spoffish *a.* fussy, officious. WH: 19C. Orig. unknown.

spoil *v.t.* to impair the goodness, usefulness etc., of. *Also v.i., n.* WH: 12–14C. Shortening of Old French *espoillier*, from Latin *spoliare*, from *spolium* skin stripped from an animal, booty, or shortening of DESPOIL. The earliest sense was to rob, to plunder. The sense to mar, to damage evolved in the 16C.

spoke *n.* any one of the rods connecting the hub with the rim of a wheel. *Also v.t.* WH: pre-1200. Old English *spāca*, from Germanic base of SPIKE¹. Cp. German *Speiche*.

spokesman *n.* a person who speaks on behalf of another or others. WH: 16C. From *spoke*, p.p. of SPEAK + MAN, based on *craftsman* (CRAFT), etc.

spoliation *n.* robbery, pillage, the act or practice of plundering, esp. of neutral commerce, in time of war. WH: 14–15C. Latin *spoliatio, spoliationis*, from *spoliatus*, p.p. of *spoliare* SPOIL. See also -ATION.

spondee *n.* a metrical foot consisting of two long syllables. WH: 14–15C. Old French *spondée* or Latin *spondeus*, from Greek *spondeios*, use as n. of a. from *spondē* libation. The foot is so called as it was used in chants accompanying libations.

spondulicks *n.pl.* money, cash. WH: 19C. Orig. unknown. According to some authorities, the word is an elaboration of Greek *spondulos* vertebra, kind of mussel, alluding to sea shells used as currency (e.g. the cowrie).

spondyl *n.* a vertebra. WH: 14–15C. Old French *spondyle* or Latin *spondylus*, from Greek *spondulos* vertebra.

spondylitis *n.* inflammation of the vertebrae. WH: 19C. Latin *spondylus* + -ITIS.

sponge *n.* any marine animal of the phylum Porifera, with pores in the body wall. *Also v.t., v.i.* WH: pre-1200. Latin *spongia*, from Greek *spoggia*, from *spoggos, sphoggos*, prob. rel. to FUNGUS.

spongio- *comb. form* of or relating to sponge(s). WH: Latin *spongia* SPONGE. See also -O-.

spongiole *n.* the spongy extremity of a radicle. WH: 19C. French, from Latin *spongiola* matted tuft of asparagus roots, dim. of *spongia* SPONGE.

spongology *n.* the scientific study of sponges. WH: 19C. SPONGIO- + -LOGY.

sponsal *a.* of or relating to marriage. WH: 17C. Latin *sponsalis*, from *sponsus, sponsa* spouse. See also -AL¹.

sponsion *n.* the act of becoming surety for another. WH: 17C. Latin *sponsio, sponsionis*, from *sponsus*. See SPONSOR, also -ION.

sponson *n.* a projection from the sides of a vessel, as supporting the wheel on a paddle steamer, for a gun on a warship, or to support a bearing etc. WH: 19C. Orig. unknown. ? Alt. of EXPANSION.

sponsor n. a person or organization that provides esp. financial support for another person or group or for some activity. Also v.t. WH: 17C. Latin, from *sponsus*, p.p. of *spondere* to promise solemnly. See also -OR. Cp. SPOUSE. The original sense was a godparent (who makes solemn promises on behalf of the godchild).

spontaneous a. arising, occurring, done or acting without external cause. WH: 17C. Late Latin *spontaneus*, from Latin (*sua*) *sponte* of (one's) own accord. See also -OUS.

spontoon n. a kind of short pike or halberd carried by British infantry officers in the 18th cent. WH: 18C. Obs. French *sponton* (now *esponton*), from Italian *spuntone*, from *spuntare* to blunt, from s- EX- + *punto* POINT.

spoof n. a deception, a hoax. Also v.t. WH: 19C. Coined in 1884 by Arthur Roberts, 1852–1933, English comedian, orig. as *Spouf*, the name of a game involving bluff.

spook n. a ghost. Also v.t., v.i. WH: 19C. Dutch, rel. to Middle Low German *spōk*, of unknown orig.

spool n. a small cylinder for winding thread, photographic film etc., on. Also v.t. WH: 12–14C. Shortening of Old French *espole*, from Middle Low German *spōle*, from Germanic, of unknown orig. Cp. German *Spule*.

spoon n. a domestic utensil consisting of a shallow bowl on a stem or handle, used for conveying liquids or liquid food to the mouth etc. Also v.t., v.i. WH: pre-1200. Old English *spōn*, from Germanic. Cp. SPAN³. The original sense (to the 16C) was thin piece of wood, chip, splinter. The current sense dates from the 12–14C.

spoonerism n. an accidental or facetious transposition of the initial letters or syllables of words, e.g. 'I have in my breast a half-warmed fish'. WH: 19C. Reverend W.A. *Spooner*, 1844–1930, English educationist + -ISM. The term derives from Spooner's tendency to make such transpositions when a don at Oxford.

spoor n. the track of a wild animal. Also v.i. WH: 19C. Afrikaans, from Middle Dutch *spoor, spor*, from Germanic. Cp. German *Spur*.

sporadic a. occurring here and there or irregularly. WH: 17C. Medieval Latin *sporadicus*, from Greek *sporadikos*, from *sporas*, *sporados* scattered, dispersed, from base of *spora* sowing, seed.

sporangium n. a sac in which spores are formed. WH: 19C. Modern Latin, from Greek *spora* (SPORE) + *aggeion* vessel. See also -IUM.

spore n. the reproductive body in a cryptogam, usu. composed of a single cell not containing an embryo. WH: 19C. Modern Latin *spora*, from Greek sowing, seed.

sporo- comb. form of or relating to spores. WH: Latin and Greek *spora* SPORE. See also -O-.

sporocarp n. a fructification containing spores or sporangia. WH: 19C. SPORO- + -CARP.

sporocyst n. a cyst containing spores or an encysted organism giving rise to spores. WH: 19C. SPORO- + CYST.

sporogenesis n. spore formation. WH: 19C. SPORO- + GENESIS.

sporogony n. the process of spore formation. WH: 19C. SPORO- + Greek *-gonia* generation, production. See also -Y².

sporophore n. a spore-bearing branch, process etc. WH: 19C. SPORO- + -PHORE.

sporophyte n. the nonsexual phase in certain plants exhibiting alternation of generations. WH: 19C. SPORO- + -PHYTE.

sporozoan n. any of a group of spore-producing parasitic protozoans, that includes the malaria parasite. WH: 19C. Modern Latin *Sporozoa*, from SPORO- + Greek *zōia*, pl. of *zōion* animal. See also -AN.

sporran n. a pouch, usu. covered with fur, hair etc., worn by Scottish Highlanders in front of the kilt. WH: 18C. Gaelic *sporan*, corr. to Irish *sparán* purse, from Latin *bursa* PURSE.

sport n. a competitive pastime, esp. an athletic or outdoor pastime, such as football, running etc. Also v.i., v.t. WH: 14–15C. Shortening of DISPORT. The original sense was diversion, entertainment. The current sense dates from the 16C.

sporule n. a spore, esp. a small or secondary spore. WH: 19C. French, or from Modern Latin *sporula*. See SPORE, also -ULE.

spot n. a small part of a surface of distinctive colour or texture, esp. round or roundish in shape. Also v.t., v.i. WH: 12–14C. ? Middle Dutch *spotte*, Low German *spot*, corr. to Old Norse *spotti* small piece, bit, rel. to Old English *splott* spot, plot of land.

spouse n. a husband or wife. WH: 12–14C. Old French *spus, spous* (m.), *spuse, spouse* (fem.), shortened form of *espous, espouse* (Modern French *époux, épouse*), from Latin *sponsus* bridegroom, *sponsa* bride, m. and fem. p.ps. (used as nn.) of *spondere* to betroth, to promise solemnly. Cp. SPONSOR.

spout n. a short pipe or channelled projection for carrying off water from a gutter, conducting liquid from a vessel etc. Also v.t., v.i. WH: 14–15C. Corr. to Flemish *spuyte*, Dutch *spuit*, from imit. Germanic base represented also by Old Norse *spýta* to spit.

spraddle v.i., v.t. to straddle, spread, sprawl or splay. WH: 17C. ? From *sprad*, dial. p.p. of SPREAD. See also -LE⁴.

sprag n. a chock of wood for locking the wheel of a vehicle. Also v.t. WH: 19C. Orig. unknown.

sprain v.t. to twist or wrench the muscles or ligaments of (a joint) so as to injure without dislocation. Also n. WH: 17C. Orig. unknown.

spraint n. the dung of an otter. WH: 14–15C. Old French *espreintes* (Modern French *épreintes*), use as n. of fem. p.p. of *espraindre* to squeeze out, ult. from Latin *exprimere* EXPRESS².

sprat n. a small food fish, *Clupea sprattus*, related to the herring. Also v.i. WH: 16C. Var. of Old English *sprot*, from Germanic, of unknown orig. Cp. German *Sprotte*. The word is perhaps related to Old English *-sprūtan* SPROUT, as the fish were regarded as the 'small fry' of the herring.

sprauncy a. smart, dapper, swank. WH: mid-20C. Orig. uncertain. ? Rel. to dial. *sprouncey* cheerful.

sprawl v.i. to lie or stretch out the body and limbs in a careless or awkward posture. Also v.t., n. WH: pre-1200. Old English *spreawlian*, rel. to N Frisian *sprawli*, Danish *sprelle* to kick about, to splash about, Norwegian dial. *sprala* to struggle. The original meaning was to move the limbs in a convulsive effort, to toss about.

spray¹ n. water or other liquid flying in small, fine drops. Also v.t., v.i. WH: 17C. Middle Dutch *sprayen*, rel. to Middle High German *spræjen*. Cp. German *sprühen*.

spray² n. a small branch or sprig, esp. with leaves, flowers etc. WH: 12–14C. Old English *esprei* in pers. names and place names, ult. of unknown orig. ? Rel. to SPRIG¹. The original form of the Old English word may have been *spræg. It gave the name of the village of *Spreyton* near Okehampton in Devon, the name meaning farmstead amongst brushwood.

spread v.t. to extend in length and breadth by opening (out), unfolding etc. Also v.i., n. WH: pre-1200. Old English *-sprædan* (in combs.), from a Germanic v. represented by Old High German *sprītan* to be extended. Cp. German *spreiten*.

Sprechgesang n. a style of vocalization between singing and speaking. WH: early 20C. German, lit. speech song.

Sprechstimme n. the type of voice used in Sprechgesang. WH: early 20C. German, lit. speech voice.

spree n. a lively frolic, esp. with drinking. Also v.i. WH: 18C. Orig. unknown. According to some, the word is from French *esprit* spirit. See ESPRIT.

sprig¹ n. a small branch, twig or shoot. Also v.t. WH: 12–14C. Rel. to Low German *sprick*, with final g as for SAG. ? Ult. rel. to SPRING.

sprig² n. a small headless nail or brad. Also v.t. WH: 12–14C. Orig. unknown.

sprightly a. lively, spirited. WH: 16C. Var. of SPRITE (influ. by words in *-ight*) + -LY¹.

spring v.i. to leap, to jump. Also v.t., n. WH: pre-1200. Old English *springan*, from Germanic. Cp. German *springen*. As nouns, the senses first season of the year and metal device to drive clockwork date from the 14–15C. The former is so called because plants spring up then, the latter because it springs back to its original shape when released.

springbok n. a southern African gazelle, *Antidorcas marsupialis*, that runs with a high leaping movement. WH: 18C. Afrikaans, from Dutch *springen* to spring + *bok* goat, antelope.

springe n. a noose, a snare, usu. for small game. Also v.t. WH: 12–14C. Rel. to Old English *sprengen* to sprinkle, from base also of *springan* SPRING.

sprinkle v.i. to scatter in small drops or particles. Also v.t., n. WH: 14–15C. ? Middle Dutch *sprenkelen*, from *sprenkel* speckle, spot. See also -LE⁴.

sprint *v.i., v.t.* to run (a short distance) at top speed. *Also n.* WH: 16C. From Old Norse, ult. of unknown orig. The earlier form was *sprent* (12–14C). The original sense was to dart, to spring. The current sense dates from the 19C.

sprit *n.* a small spar set diagonally from the mast to the top outer corner of a sail. WH: pre-1200. Old English *sprēot*, from Germanic base also of SPROUT. Cp. German *Spriet*.

sprite *n.* a fairy, an elf. WH: 12–14C. Alt. of *sprit*, contr. of SPIRIT. Cp. SPIRIT, SPRIGHTLY.

spritz *v.t.* to squirt or spray. *Also n.* WH: early 20C. German *spritzen* to squirt, to splash.

spritzer *n.* a drink made from white wine and soda water. WH: mid-20C. German splash. Cp. SPRITZ.

sprocket *n.* each of a set of teeth on a wheel etc., engaging with the links of a chain. WH: 16C. Orig. unknown.

sprog *n.* a baby, an infant, a child. WH: mid-20C. Orig. uncertain. ? From dial. *sprag* lively young man, of unknown orig.

sprout *v.i.* to develop shoots, to germinate. *Also v.t., n.* WH: 12–14C. Corr. to Middle Low German *sprūten*, Middle Dutch *spruiten*, from Germanic base represented also by Old English *sprȳtan*, *sprytan*. The word was probably already in Old English but is not recorded.

spruce[1] *a.* neat, smart. *Also v.t.* WH: 16C. Prob. from *spruce leather*, a type of leather from Prussia used esp. for jerkins and considered smart-looking. See SPRUCE[2].

spruce[2] *n.* any conifer of the genus *Picea*, of a distinctive cone shape, with dense foliage and four-angled needles. WH: 14–15C. Alt. of *spruse*, lit. Prussian. See PRUSSIAN. *Spruce* or *Spruce-land* was an early name of Prussia, where the tree was widely grown.

spruce[3] *v.t.* to deceive. *Also v.i.* WH: early 20C. Orig. unknown.

sprue[1] *n.* a hole or channel through which molten metal or plastic is poured into a mould. WH: 19C. Orig. unknown.

sprue[2] *n.* a tropical disease characterized by diarrhoea, anaemia, and wasting, with ulceration of the mucous membrane of the mouth. WH: 19C. Dutch *spruw*, ? rel. to Flemish *spruwen* to sprinkle.

spruik *v.i.* to speak in public, to harangue people. WH: early 20C. Orig. unknown.

spruit *n.* a small tributary stream, esp. one that is dry in summer. WH: 19C. Dutch SPROUT.

sprung *a.* provided with, or as if with, springs. WH: 19C. P.p. of SPRING.

spry *a.* active, lively, nimble, agile. WH: 18C. Orig. unknown. ? Rel. to SPRIGHTLY.

spud *n.* a potato. *Also v.t.* WH: 14–15C. Orig. unknown. The original sense (to the 19C) was short knife, dagger. The sense digging instrument arose in the 17C, and potato in the 19C. The latter is so called from the fork with which it is dug up, perhaps also influenced by POTATO itself.

spumante *n.* a sparkling Italian wine. WH: early 20C. Italian sparkling. Cp. SPUME.

spume *n.* froth, foam. *Also v.i.* WH: 14–15C. Old French *espume*, or from Latin *spuma*.

spun *a.* produced by a spinning process. WH: 12–14C. P.p. of SPIN.

spunk *n.* mettle, spirit, pluck. WH: 16C. ? Blend of SPARK and FUNK[2], but cp. Irish *sponc*, Gaelic *spong* tinder, ult. from Latin *spongia*, Greek *spoggia* SPONGE. Cp. PUNK. The original sense was spark. The sense spirit, mettle evolved in the 18C.

spur *n.* an instrument worn on a horseman's heel having a sharp or blunt point or a rowel. *Also v.t., v.i.* WH: pre-1200. Old English *spora*, *spura*, from Germanic, from Indo-European base also of SPURN. Cp. German *Sporn*.

spurge *n.* a plant of the genus *Euphorbia* with milky, usu. acrid juice. WH: 14–15C. Shortening of Old French *espurge* (Modern French *épurge*), from *espurgier*, from Latin *expurgare* to cleanse, EXPURGATE. The plant is so called from the purgative properties of its juice.

spurious *a.* not genuine, not proceeding from the true or pretended source, false, counterfeit. WH: 16C. Latin *spurius* illegitimate, false + -OUS. The original sense was born out of wedlock, illegitimate. The current sense dates from the 17C.

spurn *v.t.* to reject with disdain; to treat with scorn. *Also v.i., n.* WH: pre-1200. Old English *spurnan*, from a Germanic v. rel. to Latin *spernere* to scorn. Cp. SPUR. The original sense (to the 18C) was to trip, to stumble. The current sense evolved in the 16C.

spurrey *n.* a low annual weed of the genus *Spergula* of the family Silenaceae. WH: 16C. Dutch *spurrie*, prob. rel. to Medieval Latin *spergula*. Cp. German *Spergel*.

spurt *v.i.* to gush out in a jet or sudden stream. *Also v.t., n.* WH: 16C. Orig. unknown. ? Rel. to SPROUT. Some authorities see *spurt* to gush out and *spurt* brief burst of activity as of different origin. In each case the origin is ultimately unknown.

spurtle *n.* a stirring stick for porridge. WH: 16C. Orig. unknown.

sputnik *n.* any of a series of Russian artificial earth satellites, the first of which was launched in 1957. WH: mid-20C. Russian, lit. travelling companion, from *s* with + *put'* way, journey + -*nik* -NIK.

sputter *v.i.* (of frying food etc.) to emit spitting sounds. *Also v.t., n.* WH: 16C. Dutch *sputteren*, of imit. orig. Cp. SPLUTTER.

sputum *n.* spittle, saliva. WH: 17C. Latin, use as n. of neut. p.p. of *spuere* to spit.

spy *n.* a person employed by a government or business to obtain information about, and report on, the movements and operations of an enemy, business rival etc. *Also v.t., v.i.* WH: 12–14C. Shortening of Old French *espie* (Modern French *espion*), from *espier* ESPY, from Germanic, from Indo-European base also of Latin *specere* to look, to behold. Cp. ESPIONAGE.

sq. *abbr.* *sequens*, following. WH: Abbr. of Latin *sequens*, pl. *sequentes* following.

squab *n.* a short fat person. *Also a., adv., v.i.* WH: 17C. Orig. uncertain. Cp. Swedish dial. *skvabb* loose flesh, *skvabba* fat woman, *skvabbig* flabby; ? ult. of imit. orig.

squabble *n.* a petty or noisy quarrel, a wrangle. *Also v.i.* WH: 17C. Prob. imit. Cp. Swedish dial. *skvabbel*.

squacco *n.* a small crested heron, *Ardeola ralloides*, of S Europe, Asia and Africa. WH: 18C. Italian dial. *sguacco*.

squad *n.* a small party of people, e.g. engaged in a task together. WH: 17C. Shortening (based on SQUADRON) of French *escouade*, var. of *escadre*, from Spanish *escuadra*, Italian *squadra*, from Popular Latin *exquadra* SQUARE. Troops were often arranged in a square formation to repel advancing enemy forces.

squadron *n.* an organized group of people. *Also v.t.* WH: 16C. Italian *squadrone*, from *squadra*. See SQUAD.

squail *n.* a game played on a small table or board with discs which are snapped from the edge towards a mark in the centre. *Also v.t., v.i.* WH: 19C. Orig. uncertain. ? Rel. to dial. *squail* (17C) to throw a stick (at something).

squalid *a.* repulsively dirty, filthy. WH: 16C. Latin *squalidus*, from *squalere* to be dry, to be dirty. See also -ID.

squall *n.* a sudden, violent gust or succession of gusts of wind, esp. accompanied by rain, hail, snow etc. *Also v.i., v.t.* WH: 17C. Prob. alt. of SQUEAL by assoc. with BAWL. The sense child's discordant scream is recorded somewhat earlier than that of sudden storm, and the latter may have evolved from the former.

squaloid *a.* resembling a shark. WH: 19C. Latin *squalus* a marine fish of some kind + -OID.

squama *n.* a scale on a plant or animal. WH: 18C. Latin scale.

squander *v.t.* to spend (money, time etc.) wastefully. WH: 16C. Orig. unknown.

square *n.* a rectangle with equal sides. *Also a., adv., v.t., v.i.* WH: 12–14C. Shortening of Old French *esquire*, *esquarre* (Modern French *équerre*), from Popular Latin *exquadra*, from *exquadrare* to square, from Latin EX- + *quadrare* to make square, from *quadrus* square, rel. to *quattuor* four.

squarrose *a.* rough with scalelike projections. WH: 18C. Latin *squarrosus* scurfy, scabby. See also -OSE[1].

squash[1] *v.t.* to crush, to press flat or into a pulp. *Also v.i., n.* WH: 16C. Alt. of QUASH. The added *s* intensifies the original sense. Cp. SPLASH/ PLASH[1], SCRUNCH/ CRUNCH, etc.

squash[2] *n.* the fleshy edible gourdlike fruit of any of several trailing plants of the genus *Cucurbita*, cooked and eaten as a vegetable. WH: 17C. Abbr. of Narragansett *asquutasquash*, from *asq* raw, uncooked + pl. suf. *-ash*. Cp. SUCCOTASH.

squat *v.i.* to sit down or crouch on the haunches. *Also v.t., a., adv.* WH: 12–14C. Old French *esquatir*, from *es-* EX- + *quatir* to press down, to crouch, to hide, from Popular Latin *coactire* to press together, from Latin *coactus*, p.p. of *cogere* (COGENT). The original sense was to dash down violently. The current sense dates from the 14–15C. The sense to settle on unoccupied land arose in the 19C from the earlier noun *squatter* (18C).

squaw *n.* a N American Indian woman or wife. WH: 17C. Narragansett *squaws*, Massachusetts *squa* woman.

squawk *n.* a raucous squeal, esp. as the cry of a fowl. *Also v.i., v.t.* WH: 19C. Imit. Cp. SQUALL, SQUEAK.

squeak *n.* a sharp, shrill cry, like that of a mouse. *Also v.i., v.t.* WH: 14–15C. Imit. Cp. SQUEAL, SHRIEK.

squeal *n.* a more or less prolonged shrill cry, like that made by a pig or a baby. *Also v.i., v.t.* WH: 12–14C. Imit. Cp. SQUALL.

squeamish *a.* easily nauseated or disgusted. WH: 14–15C. Alt. of obs. *squeamous*, from Anglo-French *escoymos*, of unknown orig., with substitution of -ISH¹ for -OUS. Some authorities relate the word to SHAME via its Old English source *sceamu*.

squeegee *n.* a rubber-bladed implement fixed to a handle, for cleaning surfaces such as windows or wiping them dry. *Also v.t.* WH: 19C. From *squeege* to press, alt. of SQUEEZE + -EE.

squeeze *v.t.* to press closely, esp. between two bodies or with the hand, so as to force moisture etc., out. *Also v.i., n.* WH: 16C. Alt. of obs. *queize*, of unknown orig. The added *s* intensifies the original form. Cp. the pair SNEEZE/ NEEZE.

squelch *v.i.* to make a noise as of treading in wet snow. *Also v.t., n.* WH: 17C. Imit. A var. form *quelch* also existed, in a sense relationship as that of QUASH to SQUASH¹.

squib *n.* a firework emitting sparks and hisses, and exploding with a bang. *Also v.i., v.t.* WH: 16C. Prob. imit.

squid *n.* any cephalopod mollusc of the order Teuthoidea, similar to a cuttlefish but with eight arms and two long tentacles, esp. an edible variety of the genus *Loligo*. *Also v.i.* WH: 16C. Orig. unknown.

squidgy *a.* soft and squashy. WH: 19C. Prob. from *squidge*, of imit. orig. + -Y¹.

squiffy *a.* slightly drunk. WH: 19C. Orig. unknown. ? From *skewwhiff* (SKEW) + -Y¹.

squiggle *n.* a wriggly line. *Also v.i., v.t.* WH: 19C. ? Blend of SQUIRM and WIGGLE or WRIGGLE.

squill *n.* any of several liliaceous plants of the genus *Scilla*, e.g. the striped squill, *Puschkinia scilloides*, typically with small blue flowers. WH: 14–15C. Latin *squilla*, var. of SCILLA.

squinch¹ *n.* an arch across the internal angle of a square tower to support a superstructure such as an octagonal spire, dome etc. WH: 15C. Alt. of obs. *scunch*, abbr. of *scuncheon*, shortening of Old French *escoinson* (Modern French *écoinçon*), from *ex-* EX- + *coin* corner.

squinch² *v.t.* to screw (one's face or one's eyes up). *Also v.i.* WH: 19C. ? Blend of SQUINT and PINCH.

squint *v.i.* to look with the eyes differently directed. *Also v.t., a., n.* WH: 16C. Shortening of ASQUINT. The original sense was to have a covert aim. The current sense dates from the 17C.

squire *n.* a country gentleman, esp. the chief landowner in a place. *Also v.t.* WH: 12–14C. Shortening of Old French *esquier* ESQUIRE.

squirm *v.i.* to wriggle, to move (up, through etc.) by wriggling. *Also n.* WH: 17C. Imit. of movement made, prob. assoc. with WORM. (Cp. SQUIGGLE and its assoc. with WRIGGLE).

squirrel *n.* any bushy-tailed rodent of the family Sciuridae, with reddish fur (*red squirrel*) or grey fur (*grey squirrel*) living chiefly in trees. *Also v.t., v.i.* WH: 12–14C. Shortening of Old French *esquireul* (Modern French *écureuil*), from Popular Latin *scuriolus*, dim. of Latin *sciurus*, from Greek *skiouros*, prob. from *skia* shade + *oura* tail. The squirrel is apparently so called because when it sits erect, it raises its tail up against its back and over its head as if to shade itself. But some authorities dismiss this as folk etymology.

squirt *v.t.* to eject (liquid etc.) in a jet or stream from a narrow orifice. *Also v.i., n.* WH: 12–14C. Imit.

squish *n.* a moist squashing or squelching sound. *Also v.t., v.i.* WH: 17C. Imit. Cp. SQUASH¹.

squit *n.* an insignificant person. WH: 19C. Prob. from SQUIRT.

squitch *n.* quitch, couch grass. WH: 18C. Alt. of QUITCH.

squiz *n.* a glance. WH: early 20C. Prob. blend of QUIZ and SQUINT.

Sri Lankan *n.* a native or inhabitant of Sri Lanka. *Also a.* WH: late 20C. *Sri Lanka*, an island in the Indian Ocean (formerly Ceylon) + -AN.

stab *v.t.* to pierce or wound with a pointed, usu. short, weapon. *Also v.i., n.* WH: 14–15C. Orig. unknown.

Stabat Mater *n.* a Latin hymn reciting the seven dolours of the Virgin at the Cross, beginning with these words. WH: 19C. Latin, from the opening words of the hymn, *Stabat mater dolorosa* Stood the mother full of grief. The original hymn is ascribed to Jacopone du Todi, *c.*1230–1306, and others and has the full verse: *Stabat Mater dolorosa, / Iuxta crucem lacrimosa, / Dum pendebat filius* The mother stood in grief, weeping beside the cross while her son was hanging.

stable¹ *a.* firmly fixed, established. WH: 12–14C. Old French *estable* (Modern French *stable*), from Latin *stabilis*, from base of *stare* to stand. See also -BLE.

stable² *n.* a building or part of a building for horses or (sometimes) cattle. *Also v.t., v.i.* WH: 12–14C. Shortening of Old French *estable* stable, pigsty (Modern French *étable* cowshed), from Latin *stabulum*, from base of *stare* to stand.

staccato *a., adv.* (played) with each note sharply distinct and detached, as opposed to *legato*. *Also n.* WH: 18C. Italian, p.p. of *staccare*, shortening of *distaccare* DETACH.

stachys *n.* any labiate plant of the genus *Stachys*, with white or reddish spikes of flowers, also called *woundwort*. WH: 16C. Latin, from Greek *stakhus* ear of wheat.

stack *n.* a pile, a heap, esp. of an orderly kind. *Also v.t.* WH: 12–14C. Old Norse *stakkr* haystack, from Germanic, prob. of Indo-European orig. Cp. Russian *stog* haystack.

stacte *n.* one of the spices used by the ancient Jews in the preparation of incense. WH: 14–15C. Latin, from Greek *staktē*, fem. of *staktos* distilling in drops, from *stazein* to drip.

staddle *n.* a stack-stand. *Also v.t.* WH: pre-1200. Old English *stathol* base, support, tree trunk, fixed position, from Germanic base of STAND. See also -LE¹.

stadia *n.* an instrument, usu. composed of a graduated rod and a telescope, for measuring distances. WH: 19C. Prob. from *stadia*, pl. of STADIUM.

stadium *n.* a sports arena with tiers of benches for spectators. WH: 14–15C. Latin, from Greek *stadion*. The original sense was a unit of length, one-eighth of a Roman mile. The sense course for foot-racing or chariot-racing (originally of this length) evolved in the 17C, and that of sports arena in the 19C.

stadtholder *n.* the chief magistrate of the United Provinces. WH: 16C. Dutch *stadhouder*, translating Latin *locum tenens* (see LOCUM), from *stad* place + *houder* holder, from *houden* HOLD¹. See also -ER¹.

staff¹ *n.* a stick carried for help in walking, climbing etc., or as a weapon. *Also v.t.* WH: pre-1200. Old English *stæf*, from Germanic. Cp. STAVE. The sense body of officers, dating from the first, probably derives from the use of a strong pole to support something. The sense body of employers of an organization, etc. dates from the 19C.

staff² *n.* a composition of plaster of Paris, cement etc., used as building material etc., esp. in temporary structures. WH: 19C. Orig. unknown.

staffage *n.* additional or accessory objects in a painting, such as sheep or cattle in a landscape painting. WH: 19C. German, pseudo-French formation, from *staffieren* to fit out, to decorate, ? from Old French *estoffer*, from *estoffe* STUFF.

Staffordshire bull terrier *n.* a smooth-coated breed of terrier of stocky build. WH: 18C. *Staffordshire*, a county in the N Midlands + *bull terrier* (BULL¹).

stag *n.* the male of the red deer, esp. from its fifth year. *Also v.t., v.i.* WH: 12–14C. Rel. to Old Norse *steggr* (Norwegian *stegg*) male bird, Icelandic *steggi* tomcat, male bird, male fox. The word was probably already in Old English but is not recorded.

stage *n.* a point in a progressive movement, a definite period or phase in development. *Also v.t.* WH: 12–14C. Shortening of Old French *estage* dwelling, stay, situation (Modern French *étage* storey), from Popular Latin *staticum* place for standing, from Latin *stare* to stand. See also -AGE. The sense platform in a theatre on which plays are performed arose in the 16C.

stagflation *n.* a state of the economy in which there is a combination of high inflation and falling industrial output and employment. WH: mid-20C. Blend of *stagnation* (STAGNANT) and *inflation* (INFLATE). The word was coined in 1965 by the English politician Iain Macleod.

staggard *n.* a male red deer in its fourth year. WH: 12–14C. STAG + -ARD.

stagger *v.i.* to move unsteadily in walking, to totter. *Also v.t., n.* WH: 14–15C. Alt. of obs. *stacker*, from Old Norse *stakra*, freq. of *staka* to push, to stagger.

stagnant *a.* (of water) without current, motionless. WH: 17C. Latin *stagnans, stagnantis*, pres.p. of *stagnare*, from *stagnum* pool. See also -ANT.

staid *a.* sober, steady. WH: 16C. Obs. p.p. of STAY[1].

stain *v.t.* to discolour, to soil. *Also v.i., n.* WH: 14–15C. Shortened form of *distain*, from Old French *destaindre, desteign-* (Modern French *déteindre*), from Latin DIS- + *tingere* TINGE.

stair *n.* each one of a series of steps, esp. for ascending from one storey of a house to another. WH: pre-1200. Old English *stæger*, corr. to Middle Low German and Middle Dutch *steiger* scaffolding, quay, ult. from a Germanic v. meaning to climb. Cp. German *steigen* to climb. The original sense was flight of stairs, staircase. The current sense single step arose in the 14–15C.

staithe *n.* a landing stage, a wharf, esp. a staging laid with rails from which coal-wagons etc. may discharge their loads into vessels. WH: pre-1200. Old Norse *stoth*, from Germanic. The original sense was bank, shore. The current sense evolved in the 12–14C.

stake[1] *n.* a stick or post pointed at one end and set in the ground, as a support, part of a railing etc. *Also v.t.* WH: pre-1200. Old English *staca*, corr. to Middle Low German and Middle Dutch *stake*, from Germanic, from base also of STICK[1]. Cp. STAKE[2].

stake[2] *n.* anything, esp. a sum of money, wagered on a competition or contingent event, esp. deposited with a stakeholder. *Also v.t.* WH: 14–15C. ? Special use of STAKE[1]. The sense may have arisen from the placing of an object as a wager on a post or stake.

Stakhanovism *n.* in the former Soviet Union, a system for increasing production by utilizing each worker's initiative. WH: mid-20C. Aleksei Grigor'evich *Stakhanov*, 1906–77, Russian coalminer whose exceptional output was publicized in a Soviet productivity campaign in 1935. See also -ISM.

stalactite *n.* a deposit of carbonate of lime, hanging from the roof of a cave etc., in the form of a thin tube or a large icicle, produced by the evaporation of percolating water. WH: 17C. Modern Latin *stalactites*, from Greek *stalaktos* dropping, dripping, from *stalak-*, base of *stalassein* to drip, to let drip. See also -ITE[1].

Stalag *n.* a German prisoner-of-war camp, esp. for men from the ranks and non-commissioned officers. WH: mid-20C. German, contr. of *Stammlager* main camp. The equivalent camp for officers was the *Oflag*, a contraction of German *Offizierlager* officers' camp.

stalagmite *n.* a deposit of the same material as in a stalactite, in the form of a pointed column or a mound, rising from the floor of a cave. WH: 17C. Modern Latin *stalagmites*, from Greek *stalagma* drop, drip, from *stalak-*. See STALACTITE.

stale[1] *a.* dry, musty. *Also v.t., v.i.* WH: 12–14C. Prob. from an Old French a. (Modern French *étale* stationary), from *estaler* to come to a stand. Cp. STALL[1]. The earliest sense was clear, strong, as applied to alcoholic liquor. The current sense evolved in the 14–15C.

stale[2] *n.* the urine of horses or cattle. *Also v.i.* WH: 14–15C. ? Old French *estaler* to take up a (standing) position. Cp. STALEMATE.

stalemate *n.* in chess, the position when the king, not actually in check, is unable to move without placing itself in check, and there is no other piece that can be moved. *Also v.t.* WH: 18C. From obs. *stale*, from Anglo-French *estale* position, from *estaler* to be placed, from Germanic (cp. STALL[2]) + MATE[2].

Stalinism *n.* the rigid authoritarianism, totalitarianism and centralization associated with the regime of the dictator of the former Soviet Union Joseph Stalin, developed from the communist ideology of Marxism–Leninism. WH: early 20C. J.V. *Stalin* (orig. Dzhugashvili), 1879–1953, Soviet Communist leader and head of state + -ISM.

stalk[1] *n.* the stem or axis of a plant. WH: 12–14C. Prob. dim. (with suf. *k*) of dial. *stale* stile of a ladder, from Old English *stalu*, from Germanic.

stalk[2] *v.t.* to pursue (game or other prey, or an enemy) stealthily by the use of cover. *Also v.i., n.* WH: pre-1200. Old English *-stealcian*, as in *bestealcian* to steal along, ult. from Germanic base also of STEAL. The original sense (to the 16C) was to walk cautiously or stealthily. The current sense arose in the 14–15C.

stall[1] *n.* a booth or shed in a market, street etc., or a bench, table etc. in a building for the sale of goods. *Also v.i., v.t.* WH: pre-1200. Old English *steall*, rel. to Old Norse *stallr* pedestal, stall for a horse, from Germanic, prob. from base also of STAND. In some senses also partly from Old French *estal* (Modern French *étal*) place, stand, stall. The original sense (to the 17C) was place, position.

stall[2] *v.i.* to play for time; to be evasive. *Also v.t., n.* WH: 15C. Anglo-French *estal*, var. of *estale* pigeon used to lure a hawk into a net, from Germanic, prob. from base also of Old English *steall* STALL[1].

stallion *n.* an uncastrated male horse, esp. one kept for breeding purposes. WH: 12–14C. Anglo-French var. of Old French *estalon* (Modern French *étalon*), from Frankish *stal*, from Germanic base also of STALL[1]. The horse is probably so called as it was kept in a stall to service mares there.

stalwart *a.* strong in build, sturdy. *Also n.* WH: 14–15C. Scottish var. of obs. *stalworth*, from Old English *stælwierthe*, from *stæl* place + *weorth, worth* WORTH[1]. The literal sense is having a worthy foundation.

stamen *n.* the pollen-bearing male organ of a flower. WH: 17C. Latin, (thread of) warp, corr. to Greek *stēmōn* warp. Cp. STAMINA. The Latin word was applied by Pliny to the stamens of a lily.

stamina *n.* strength, vigour. WH: 17C. Latin, pl. of STAMEN. The sense derives partly from Latin *stamen* warp, since the warp of a fabric provides its underlying foundation, partly from Latin *stamina* (pl.) threads, with reference to the threads spun by the Fates at a person's birth to determine how long they will live.

stammel *n.* a woollen cloth for making underclothes, usu. dyed red. WH: 16C. Prob. alt. (with var. of suf.) of obs. *stamin* undergarment made of stammel, from Old French *estamine* (Modern French *étamine*), from fem. of Latin *stamineus* consisting of threads, from *stamen, staminis* thread, warp. Cp. STAMEN, STAMINA.

stammer *v.i.* to speak with halting articulation, nervous hesitation, or repetitions of the same sound. *Also n.* WH: pre-1200. Old English *stamerian*, from Germanic base also of STUMBLE, represented by Old English and Old High German *stamm*, Old Norse *stamr*, Gothic *stamms* stammering. Ult. rel. to German *stumm* dumb (cp. SHTOOM).

stamp *v.t.* to bring (one's foot) down heavily. *Also v.i., n.* WH: 12–14C. Prob. from an unrecorded Old English v. corr. to Middle Low German and Middle Dutch *stampen*, Old High German *stampfōn* to pound, from Germanic, prob from a nasalized var. of STEP. The original sense was to beat to a pulp, to mash. The senses to bring one's foot down heavily and to impress or print metal or paper with a pattern, etc. both date from the 14–15C.

stampede *n.* a sudden headlong rush of startled animals, esp. cattle. *Also v.i., v.t.* WH: 19C. Mexican Spanish use of Spanish *estampida* crash, uproar, from *estampar* to stamp, to pound, from Germanic. Cp. STAMP.

stance *n.* the position taken for a stroke in golf, cricket etc. WH: 12–14C. French, from Latin *stans, stantis*, pres.p. of *stare* STAND. Cp. STANZA. The original sense was standing-place, station, position. The sporting sense dates from the 18C.

stanchion *n.* a prop, post, pillar etc., forming a support or part of a structure. *Also v.t.* WH: 12–14C. Anglo-French *stanchon*, from Old French *estanchon, estanson*, from *estance* prop, support, from Germanic base also of STANCE, STANZA.

stand *v.i.* to be in, take or keep an upright position, esp. on the feet, or on a base. *Also v.t., n.* WH: pre-1200. Old English *standan*, from Germanic base also of STADDLE, STOOL, STUD[2], from Indo-European base also of STEAD, Latin *stare* to stand.

standard *n.* a measure of extent, quantity, value etc. established by law or custom as an example or criterion for others. *Also a.* WH: 12–14C. Shortening of Old French *estendart* (Modern French *étendard*), from *estendre* to extend. See also -ARD. The sense upright pillar, etc. has been also influenced by STAND.

stanhope *n.* a light open two- or four-wheeled carriage. WH: 19C. Fitzroy H.R. *Stanhope*, 1787–1864, English clergyman, for whom it was originally built.

staniel *n.* a kestrel. WH: pre-1200. Old English *stāngella*, lit. stone-yeller, from *stān* STONE + suf. rel. to *gellan* YELL. The sense of stone may simply be intensifying, as in *stone-deaf* (STONE).

Stanley knife® *n.* a sharp trimming knife with a replaceable blade. WH: mid-20C. F.T. *Stanley*, US businessman, founder of the Stanley Rule and Level Company in 1843.

stannary *n.* a tin-mining district. *Also a.* WH: 14–15C. Medieval Latin *stannaria* (pl.), from Late Latin *stannum* tin, from Latin *stagnum* alloy of silver and lead, ? of Celtic orig.

stannic *a.* of or containing (tetravalent) tin. WH: 18C. Late Latin *stannum* tin (see STANNARY) + -IC.

stanza *n.* a recurring group of lines of poetry adjusted to each other in a definite scheme, often with rhyme. WH: 16C. Italian standing, stopping-place, room, strophe, from Latin *stans, stantis*, pres.p. of *stare* STAND.

stapelia *n.* any southern African plant of the genus *Stapelia*, whose flowers have an unpleasant smell of carrion. WH: 18C. Modern Latin, from Jan Bode van *Stapel*, d.1636, Dutch botanist + -IA.

stapes *n.* the innermost of the three small bones of the middle ear, shaped like a stirrup and transmitting vibrations to the middle ear from the incus. WH: 17C. Latin stirrup. The bone is so called from its shape.

staphyline *a.* shaped like a bunch of grapes. WH: 19C. Late Greek *staphulinos* pertaining to a bunch of grapes, from *staphulē* bunch of grapes.

staphylitis *n.* inflammation of the uvula. WH: 19C. Greek *staphulē* bunch of grapes, uvula (when swollen) + -ITIS.

staphylo- *comb. form* shaped like a bunch of grapes. WH: Greek *staphulē* bunch of grapes. See also -O-.

staphylococcus *n.* any micro-organism of the genus *Staphylococcus*, forming the bacteria most frequently found in suppurative infections of the skin or mucous membrane. WH: 19C. Modern Latin, from Greek *staphulē* bunch of grapes + *kokkos* berry. The organism is so called because the bacteria form grapelike clusters.

staphyloma *n.* an abnormal protrusion of the sclera or the cornea. WH: 16C. Modern Latin, from Greek *staphulōma*, from *staphulē* bunch of grapes. See also -OMA. The protrusion is so called from its resemblance to a grapestone.

staple¹ *n.* a U-shaped piece of metal driven into a post, wall etc., to receive part of a fastening or to hold wire etc. *Also v.t.* WH: pre-1200. Old English *stapol* post, stake, corr. to Old Frisian *stapul* rung, anvil, Middle Low German and Middle Dutch *stapel* pillar, emporium, Old High German *staffol* foundation, Old Norse *stǫpull* pillar, steeple, from Germanic. See also -LE¹. Ult. rel. to STEP.

staple² *n.* the principal commodity sold or produced in any place, country etc. *Also a., v.t.* WH: 12–14C. Old French *estaple* emporium, mart (Modern French *étape* halting-place), from Middle Low German and Middle Dutch *stapel*. See STAPLE¹.

star *n.* any celestial body appearing as a luminous point, esp. one of the fixed stars or those so distant that their relative position in the heavens appears constant, as distinct from planets or comets. *Also a., v.t., v.i.* WH: pre-1200. Old English *steorra*, from Germanic, from Indo-European base represented also by Latin *stella*, Greek *astēr*. Cp. German *Stern*.

starboard *n.* the right-hand side of a vessel looking forward. *Also v.t.* WH: pre-1200. Old English *stēorbord*, from *stēor* steering paddle, rudder + *bord* (BOARD). The side was formerly the one from which vessels were usually steered.

starch *n.* a white, tasteless, odourless, amorphous compound, found in all plants except fungi, but esp. in cereals, potatoes, beans etc., an important constituent of vegetable foods, and used as a soluble powder to stiffen linen etc. *Also a., v.t.* WH: 14–15C. Rel. to Old Frisian *sterka* to stiffen, Old High German *sterken* to strengthen, from Germanic base of STARK. Cp. German *Stärke*. The word probably existed in Old English but is recorded only in *stercedferhth* resolute of mind.

stare *v.i.* to look with eyes fixed and wide open, as in admiration, surprise etc. *Also v.t., n.* WH: pre-1200. Old English *starian*, from Germanic base meaning to be rigid. Cp. German *starren*.

stark *a.* (of a landscape etc.) bare, desolate. *Also adv.* WH: pre-1200. Old English *stearc*, from Germanic base also of STARE. Cp. German *stark* strong. The original sense was hard, firm. The sense bare, desolate (of a landscape, etc.) dates from the 19C. The phrase *stark naked* was earlier *start naked*, from Old English *steort* tail. Cp. REDSTART.

Stark effect *n.* the splitting of the spectrum into components by applying an electric field. WH: early 20C. Johannes *Stark*, 1874–1957, German physicist.

starling¹ *n.* a small black and brown speckled bird of the genus *Sturnus*, esp. *S. vulgaris*. WH: pre-1200. Old English *stærlinc*, from earlier *stær*, from Germanic, rel. to Latin *sturnus* + -ING¹. Cp. German *Star*.

starling² *n.* an enclosure of piles round or (esp.) upstream of a bridge pier, to protect it from floating rubbish. WH: 17C. ? Alt. of *staddling*, from STADDLE + -ING¹.

START *abbr.* Strategic Arms Reduction Treaty (or Talks). WH: Abbr. of Strategic Arms Reduction Treaty. Cp. SALT.

start *v.i.* to commence, to come into existence. *Also v.t., n.* WH: pre-1200. Old English unrecorded v., from Germanic base represented also by Middle Low German *störten*, Middle Dutch *storten*, Old High German *sturzen* (German *stürzen*) to overthrow, to rush, to fall headlong, to gush out. The original Old English verb may have been *steortian or *stiertan, vars. of *styrtan* to leap up. The original sense (to the 16C) was to jump, to caper. The sense to begin, to commence dates from the 17C.

startle *v.t.* to cause to start in surprise etc. WH: pre-1200. Old English *steartlian*, from base of START. See also -LE⁴.

starve *v.i.* to die of hunger. *Also v.t.* WH: pre-1200. Old English *steorfan*, from Germanic, ult. from base (meaning to be rigid) of STARE. Cp. German *sterben* to die. The original sense was to die (from any cause, but especially slowly). The sense to die or to be in danger of dying from hunger arose in the 14–15C.

stash *v.t.* to store, (money etc.) in a secret place (usu. with *away*). *Also n.* WH: 18C. Orig. unknown.

Stasi *n.* in the German Democratic Republic before 1989, the internal security force. WH: mid-20C. German acronym of *Staatssicherheits* (dienst) state security (service).

stasimon *n.* in ancient Greek drama, an ode sung by the entire chorus, having taken their places after the opening ode, or one sung without interruption by dialogue. WH: 19C. Greek, use as n. of neut. of *stasimos* stationary, from *sta-*, base of *histanai* STAND.

stasis *n.* a state of equilibrium or inaction. WH: 18C. Modern Latin, from Greek, lit. standing, stoppage, party, from *sta-*, base of *histanai* STAND.

stat¹ *n.* a thermostat. WH: late 20C. Abbr. of THERMOSTAT.

stat² *n.* a statistic. WH: mid-20C. Abbr. of *statistic* (STATISTICS). Cp. STATS.

-stat *comb. form* designating a device that causes something to remain stationary or constant, as in *thermostat*. WH: Partly ending of HELIOSTAT, partly back-formation from *-static*, as in *hydrostatic* (HYDROSTATICS).

state *n.* the mode of existence, situation, or relation to circumstances, of a person or thing. *Also a., v.t.* WH: 12–14C. Partly shortening of ESTATE, partly direct from Latin *status* manner of standing, condition, from base of *stare* STAND. Cp. STATUS.

stater *n.* a coin of ancient Greece, esp. the standard gold coin of 20 drachmas. WH: 14–15C. Late Latin, from Greek *statēr*, from *sta-*, base of *histanai* STAND (in the sense to weigh).

static *a.* stationary; not moving, acting or altering; stable, passive. *Also n.* WH: 16C. As a., from Modern Latin *staticus*, from Greek *statikos* causing to stand, pertaining to weighing, from *histanai* to cause to stand, to weigh (see STAND); as n. from Modern Latin *statica*, from Greek *statikē* (*tekhnē*) (science of) weighing, use as n. of fem. of *statikos*.

statice *n.* any plant of a genus *Limonium* that includes the sea lavender. WH: 18C. Latin, from Greek *statikē*, fem. of *statikos* causing to stand still (STATIC). The plant is so called from its use to staunch a flow of blood.

station *n.* a place where railway trains stop to set down or take up passengers or goods, usu. with a platform and administrative buildings and public facilities. *Also v.t.* WH: 12–14C. Old French, from Latin *statio*, *stationis*, from *sta-*, base of *stare* STAND. See also -ION. The earliest sense is a person's position in life. The sense stopping place dates from the 16C.

stationer *n.* a person who sells papers, pens, ink and writing materials. WH: 12–14C. Medieval Latin *stationarius* tradesman having a regular station or shop (i.e. not itinerant), esp. a bookseller. See STATION, also -ER². The original sense (to the 19C) was a bookseller, a person engaged in the book trade. The current sense arose in the 17C.

statistics *n.* the science of collecting, organizing, and analysing numerical data, esp. on a large scale, with the purpose of extrapolating trends in a whole from the representative sample studied. WH: 18C. German *Statistik*, prob. from Modern Latin *statisticum* (*collegium*) (lecture course on) state affairs, from Italian *statista*, from *stato* state. See also -ICS. The German word was coined in 1748 by Gottfried Achenwall, the German scholar reckoned to be the founder of the science of statistics.

stative *a.* (of verbs) expressing a state of mind as distinct from an action, e.g. *know*, *like*, *believe*. WH: 17C. Latin *stativus*, from *status*. See STATUE, also -IVE.

statoblast *n.* an internal bud developed in freshwater sponges and polyzoa. WH: 19C. Greek *statos* standing + -O- + -BLAST.

stator *n.* the fixed part of an electrical generator. WH: 19C. From *stationary* (STATION) + -OR, based on ROTOR.

statoscope *n.* a sensitive aneroid barometer for showing minute fluctuations of pressure. WH: early 20C. Greek *statos* standing + -O- + -SCOPE.

stats *n.pl.* statistics. WH: mid-20C. Abbr. of STATISTICS.

statue *n.* a representation of a person or animal sculptured or cast, e.g. in marble or bronze, esp. about life-size. WH: 12–14C. Old French, from Latin *statura*, from *status*, p.p. of *stare* STAND.

stature *n.* the natural height of a body, esp. of a person. WH: 12–14C. Old French, from Latin *statura*, from *status* (STATUE) + -ura -URE.

status *n.* relative standing or position in society. WH: 17C. Latin, from *status*. See STATUE. The original sense was the crisis of a disease. The current sense dates from the 18C.

status quo *n.* the existing state of affairs. WH: 19C. Latin the state in which, from *status* state + abl. of *qui* which.

statute *n.* a written law enacted by a legislative body. WH: 12–14C. Old French *statut*, from Late Latin *statutum* decree, decision, law, use as n. of neut. p.p. of Latin *statuere* to set up, to establish, from STATUS.

staunch¹ *a.* loyal, trustworthy. WH: 14–15C. Old French *estanche*, fem. of *estanc* (Modern French *étanche*) dried, exhausted, wearied. See STAUNCH². The original sense was impervious to water. The sense loyal, constant evolved in the 17C.

staunch² *v.t.* to stop (blood) flowing, or stop blood flowing from (a wound). *Also v.i.* WH: 12–14C. Old French *estanchier* (Modern French *étancher*), from Popular Latin *stanticare*, prob. from Latin *stans*, *stantis*, pres.p. of *stare* STAND. The original sense (to the 16C) was to restrict or exhaust one's wealth, strength etc. as well as to stop or restrict a flow of blood.

staurolite *n.* an orthorhombic ferrous silicate of aluminium occurring in crosslike twin crystals. WH: 18C. Greek *stauros* cross + -LITE.

stave *n.* each of the curved strips forming the side of a cask etc. *Also v.t.* WH: 14–15C. Back-formation from *staves*, pl. of STAFF¹.

stavesacre *n.* a species of larkspur, *Delphinium staphisagria*, the seeds of which were formerly used as a poison for lice etc. WH: 14–15C. Latin *staphisagria*, from Greek *staphis agria*, lit. wild raisin.

stay¹ *v.i.* to continue in a specified place or state, not to move or change. *Also v.t., n.* WH: 14–15C. Prob. from Anglo-French *estai-*, *estei-*, pres. stem of Old French *ester*, from Latin *stare* STAND. Cp. STAID. The original sense was to come to a halt. The sense to continue to be in the same place dates from the 16C.

stay² *n.* a support, a prop. *Also v.t.* WH: 12–14C. Old French *estaye* (Modern French *étai*) support, prop, from *estayer* (Modern French *étayer*), from Germanic base also of STAY³.

stay³ *n.* a rope supporting a mast. *Also v.t.* WH: pre-1200. Old English *stæg*, corr. to Middle Low German *stach*, Dutch *stag*, from a Germanic v. meaning to be firm. Cp. STEEL. The word is ultimately related to STAY².

stead *n.* place or room which another had or might have had. WH: pre-1200. Old English *stede*, from Germanic, from Indo-European base also of STAND. Cp. German *Statt* place, *Stadt* town. The original sense (to the 14–15C) was a standing still, a stoppage. The current sense, as in *in someone's stead*, dates from the 12–14C.

steadfast *a.* resolute, unwavering. WH: pre-1200. Old English *stedefæst*, from *stede* STEAD + *fæst* FAST¹.

steading *n.* a farmstead. WH: 15C. STEAD + -ING¹.

steady *a.* firmly fixed, not wavering. *Also v.t., v.i., n., adv., int.* WH: 12–14C. STEAD + -Y¹, based on Middle Low German and Middle Dutch *stēdig*, *stādig* stable, constant.

steak *n.* a thick slice of beef, other meat, or fish cut for grilling, frying etc. WH: 12–14C. Old Norse *steik*, rel. to *steikja* to roast on a spit.

steal *v.t.* to take (someone else's property) away without right or permission or intention of returning it. *Also v.i.* WH: pre-1200. Old English *stelan*, from Germanic base also of STALK². Cp. German *stehlen*. The sense to come or go furtively arose in the 12–14C.

stealth *n.* furtiveness, secrecy. WH: 12–14C. Prob. from an unrecorded Old English word rel. to STEAL. See also -TH². The original Old English word would probably have been **stǣlth*. The original sense (to the 18C) was the action of stealing, theft.

steam *n.* water in the form of vapour or the gaseous form to which it is changed by boiling. *Also a., v.i., v.t.* WH: pre-1200. Old English *stēam*, from Germanic.

stearin *n.* a usu. white crystalline glyceryl ester of stearic acid. WH: 19C. Greek *stear* fat, tallow + -IN¹, -INE. The word was coined in 1814 by the French chemist Michel Chevreul.

steatite *n.* soapstone or some other impure form of talc. WH: 18C. Latin, from Greek *steatitēs* (*lithos*) (stone) resembling tallow, from *stear*, *steatos* tallow. See also -ITE¹.

steato- *comb. form* fat. WH: 17C. Greek *stear*, *steatos* stiff fat, tallow, suet. See also -O-.

steatocele *n.* a fatty tumour of the scrotum. WH: 17C. STEATO- + -CELE.

steatoma *n.* a fatty encysted tumour. WH: 16C. Greek *stear*, *steatos* fat + -OMA.

steatopygous *a.* having fat buttocks. WH: 19C. STEATO- + Greek *pugē* rump. See also -OUS.

steatorrhoea *n.* a condition in which there is excessive fat in the faeces. WH: 19C. STEATO- + -RRHOEA.

steed *n.* a horse, esp. a warhorse. WH: pre-1200. Old English *stēda*, from base also of STUD².

steel *n.* iron combined with carbon in various proportions, remaining malleable at high temperatures and capable of being hardened by cooling. *Also a., v.t.* WH: pre-1200. Old English *stēli*, *stǣli*, from a Germanic a. represented by Middle Low German *stāl*, Middle Dutch *stael*, Old High German *stahal* (German *Stahl*), prob. from Germanic base of STAY³.

steelyard *n.* a balance with unequal arms, the article weighed being hung from the shorter arm and a weight moved along the other till they balance. WH: 17C. STEEL + YARD¹.

steenbok *n.* a small southern African antelope, *Raphicerus campestris*. WH: 18C. Dutch, orig. wild goat, from *steen* STONE + *bok* BUCK¹. Cp. STEINBOCK.

steep¹ *a.* sharply inclined, sloping at a high angle. *Also n.* WH: pre-1200. Old English *stēap*, from a Germanic word rel. to STEEPLE, STOOP¹. The original sense was elevated, lofty. The current sense dates from the 12–14C.

steep² *v.t.* to soak (in liquid); to wet thoroughly. *Also n.* WH: 12–14C. Rel. to Swedish *stöpu*, Danish *støbe*, Norwegian *støypa* to steep (seeds, or barley for malting), from a Germanic word rel. to base of STOUP. The word was perhaps already in Old English but is not recorded.

steeple *n.* a lofty structure rising above the roof of a building, esp. a church tower with a spire. WH: pre-1200. Old English *stēpel*, from a Germanic word rel. to STEEP¹. The original sense (to the 19C) was tall tower, but the Old English word was also in use for the tower forming part of a church. The narrower sense spire on the tower or roof of a church evolved in the 15C.

steer¹ *v.t.* to guide (a ship, aeroplane, vehicle etc.) by a rudder, wheel, handle etc. *Also v.i., n.* WH: pre-1200. Old English *stieran*, from Germanic. Cp. German *steuern*.

steer² *n.* a young male of the ox kind, esp. a castrated bullock. WH: pre-1200. Old English *stēor*, from Germanic. Cp. German *Stier*.

steeve¹ *n.* the angle of elevation of a bowsprit. *Also v.i., v.t.* WH: 17C. Orig. unknown. Not rel. to STEEVE².

steeve² *n.* a spar or derrick for stowing cargo. *Also v.t.* WH: 15C. Old Spanish *estibar*. See STEVEDORE. Cp. STIFF.

stegano- *comb. form* covered. WH: Greek *steganos* covered. See also -O-.

steganography *n.* the art of secret writing or writing in cipher. WH: 16C. Modern Latin *steganographia*. See STEGANO-, -GRAPHY.

stegosaur *n.* a quadrupedal herbivorous dinosaur of the Jurassic period, with a double ridge of bony plates along its back. WH: 19C. Modern Latin *stegosaurus*, from Greek *steg-*, base of *stegein* to cover + -O- + Greek *sauros* LIZARD. The dinosaur is so called from its all-covering armour.

stein *n.* a large, usu. earthenware beer mug, often with a hinged lid. WH: 19C. German STONE.

steinbock *n.* a small southern African antelope, a steenbok. WH: 17C. German, from *Stein* STONE + *Bock* BUCK¹. Cp. STEENBOK. The animal is so called from its rocky mountain habitat.

stela *n.* an upright stone slab or column, usu. with sculptured figures and an inscription. WH: 18C. Latin, from Greek *stēlē*. See STELE.

stele *n.* the central cylinder in stems and roots of the higher plants, consisting of vascular bundles with pith and pericycle. WH: 19C. Greek *stēlē* standing block. Cp. STELA.

stellar *a.* of or relating to stars. WH: 17C. Late Latin *stellaris*, from Latin *stella* star. See also -AR¹.

stellion *n.* a lizard belonging to the family Agamidae. WH: 14–15C. Latin *stellio, stellionis*, appar. from *stella* star. The word was originally a heraldic term for a kind of lizard bearing starlike spots.

stem¹ *n.* the stalk, or ascending part of a tree, shrub, or other plant. *Also v.t.* WH: pre-1200. Old English *stemn, stefn*, from Germanic. Cp. German *Stamm*.

stem² *v.t.* to check, to hold back. *Also v.i., n.* WH: 12–14C. Old Norse *stemma*, from Germanic. Rel. to STAMMER. The original sense (to the 16C) was to stop, to delay.

stemma *n.* pedigree, a family tree. WH: Latin, from Greek garland, from *stephein* to crown.

stemple *n.* a crossbar serving as a step or support in the shaft of a mine. WH: 17C. ? Rel. to Middle High German *stempfel* (German *Stempel*).

stemson *n.* a curved timber behind a ship's apron, supporting the scarfs. WH: 18C. STEM¹ + -*son*, based on KEELSON.

stench *n.* a foul or offensive smell. WH: pre-1200. Old English *stenc*, from Germanic base also of STINK. The original sense was a smell in general, whether pleasant or unpleasant.

stencil *n.* a thin plate of metal or other material out of which patterns have been cut for painting through the spaces on to a surface. *Also v.t.* WH: 12–14C. Old French *estanceler, estenceler* to sparkle, to cover with stars, from *estencele* (Modern French *étincelle*) spark, from alt. of Latin SCINTILLA. The noun dates from the 18C.

Sten gun *n.* a light sub-machine gun. WH: mid-20C. Initials of R.V. Shepherd and H.J. Turpin, its designers + Enfield, a town in Middlesex (now a unitary authority), where it was manufactured, based on BREN.

steno *n.* a stenographer. WH: early 20C. Abbr. of *stenographer* (STENOGRAPH).

steno- *comb. form* contracted. WH: Greek *stenos* narrow. See also -O-.

stenochrome *n.* a print taken at one impression from several differently-coloured blocks. WH: 19C. STENO- + Greek *khrōma* colour.

stenograph *n.* a character used in shorthand. WH: 19C. STENO- + -GRAPH.

stenosis *n.* constriction of a bodily passage or orifice. WH: 19C. Modern Latin, from Greek *stenōsis* narrowing, from *stenoun* to narrow, from *stenos* narrow. See also -OSIS.

stenotype *n.* a typewriter-like machine for recording speech as symbols representing phonemes or syllables. WH: 19C. STENO- + TYPE.

Stentor *n.* a person with a loud, strong voice. WH: 17C. *Stentor*, a Greek herald in the Trojan war, famed for his powerful voice.

step *v.i.* to lift and set down a foot or the feet alternately, to walk a short distance in a specified direction. *Also v.t., n.* WH: pre-1200. Old English *steppan, stæppan*, from Germanic. Cp. German *stapfen*. Rel. to STAMP.

step- *comb. form* denoting a family relationship resulting from a remarriage. WH: Old English *stēop-*, from Germanic, rel. to Old English *āstīeped* bereaved, Old High German *stiufen* to bereave. Cp. German *stief-*. The original reference was to children bereaved (orphaned) by the death of a parent, then to the second spouse of the surviving parent when he or she remarried. Thus, *stepchild* originally meant orphan, then stepson or stepdaughter.

stepbrother *n.* a son of a step-parent by a marriage other than with one's mother or father. WH: 14–15C. STEP- + BROTHER.

stepchild *n.* a child of one's husband or wife by a previous marriage. WH: pre-1200. STEP- + CHILD.

stepdad *n.* a stepfather. WH: mid-20C. STEP- + DAD.

stepdaughter *n.* a female stepchild. WH: pre-1200. STEP- + DAUGHTER.

stepfamily *n.* a family that contains a stepchild or stepchildren. WH: early 20C. STEP- + FAMILY.

stepfather *n.* a male step-parent. WH: pre-1200. STEP- + FATHER.

stephanite *n.* a metallic black sulphantimonite of silver. WH: 19C. Archduke *Stephan*, 1816–67, Austrian mining director + -ITE¹. The name was coined in 1845 by the Austrian geologist and mineralogist Wilhelm Haidinger.

stephanotis *n.* any tropical climbing plant of the genus *Stephanotis*, with fragrant waxy flowers. WH: 19C. Modern Latin, from Greek *stephanōtis* fit for a crown, from *stephanos* crown, wreath.

stepmother *n.* a female step-parent. WH: pre-1200. STEP- + MOTHER¹.

stepmum *n.* a stepmother. WH: mid-20C. STEP- + MUM¹.

step-parent *n.* the later husband or wife of a mother or father. WH: late 20C. STEP- + PARENT.

steppe *n.* a vast plain devoid of forest, esp. in Russia and Siberia. WH: 17C. Russian *step'*, ? rel. to STIPE, with ref. to the feather grass that is characteristic of the steppes. Not rel. to STEP.

stepsister *n.* a daughter of a step-parent by a marriage other than with one's mother or father. WH: 15C. STEP- + SISTER.

stepson *n.* a male stepchild. WH: pre-1200. STEP- + SON.

-ster *suf.* denoting a person belonging to a certain category, or involved in a certain activity, as in *youngster, songster, gamester, gangster*. WH: Old English *-istræ, -istre, -estre*, corr. to Middle Low German *-ester*, Middle Dutch *-ster*, from Germanic. The suffix originally denoted a woman engaged in a particular activity. Cp. SPINSTER.

steradian *n.* the SI unit of solid angle, that is the angle subtended at the centre of a sphere by an area on its surface numerically equal to the square of the radius. WH: 19C. Greek *stereos* solid + RADIAN.

stercoraceous *a.* of or relating to, composed of, or like dung. WH: 18C. Latin *stercus, stercoris* dung. See also -ACEOUS.

stere *n.* a cubic metre (35.147589 cu. ft.) used to measure timber. WH: 18C. French *stère*, from Greek *stereos* solid.

stereo *n.* stereophonic reproduction, stereophony. *Also a.* WH: mid-20C. Abbr. of STEREOPHONIC or *stereophony*.

stereo- *comb. form* solid, three-dimensional. WH: Greek *stereos* solid. See also -O-.

stereobate *n.* a solid substructure or base for a building. WH: 19C. French *stéréobate*, from Latin *stereobata*, from Greek *stereobatēs*, from *stereo-* STEREO- + -*batēs* base, from *bainein* to walk. Cp. STYLOBATE.

stereochemistry *n.* chemistry concerned with the three-dimensional disposition of atoms in molecules. WH: 19C. STEREO- + CHEMISTRY.

stereochromy *n.* wall painting with pigments mixed or fixed with water-glass. WH: 19C. German *Stereochromie*, from STEREO- + Greek *khrōma* colour. See also -Y².

stereogram *n.* a three-dimensional picture or image, a stereograph. WH: 19C. STEREO- + -GRAM.

stereoisomer *n.* an isomer of a molecule in which the atoms are linked in the same order but have a different spatial arrangement. WH: 19C. STEREO- + ISOMER.

stereome *n.* a strengthening tissue in vascular plants composed of thick-walled, elongated prosenchymatous cells. WH: 19C. Greek *stereōma* solid body or part, from *stereoun* to make solid, to strengthen, from *stereos* solid.

stereometer *n.* an instrument for measuring the volume of solid bodies. WH: 19C. STEREO- + -METER.

stereophonic *a.* denoting a sound-recording or reproduction system involving the use of two or more separate microphones and loudspeakers to split the sound into separate channels to create a spatial effect. WH: early 20C. STEREO- + PHONIC.

stereopsis *n.* the perception of depth imparted by the combining of images from both eyes, binocular vision. WH: early 20C. STEREO- + Greek *opsis* point of sight.

stereoscope *n.* a binocular instrument for blending into one two pictures taken from slightly different positions, thus giving an effect of three dimensions. WH: 19C. STEREO- + -SCOPE. The term was coined in 1838 by the instrument's inventor, the British physicist Sir Charles Wheatstone.

stereospecific *a.* of or relating to a certain stereoisomer of a substance. WH: mid-20C. STEREO- + *specific* (SPECIFY).

stereotaxis *n.* surgery involving precision-placing of probes in the brain. WH: 19C. STEREO- + TAXIS.

stereotropic *a.* denoting a tendency to turn in response to contact with a solid object. WH: early 20C. STEREO- + *-tropic* (-TROPE).

stereotype *n.* a person or thing that conforms to a standardized image. *Also v.t.* WH: 18C. French *stéréotype*, from *stéréo-* STEREO- + *-type* TYPE. The original sense was a method of replicating a relief printing surface by taking a cast using a mould. This was invented and named in 1797 by the French printer and publisher François Didot. The sense person or thing conforming to a standardized image dates from the early 20C.

steric *a.* of or relating to the spatial arrangement of atoms in a molecule. WH: 19C. Greek *stereos* solid + -IC.

sterigma *n.* a stalk or support. WH: 19C. Modern Latin, from Greek *stērigma* support, from *stērizein* to fix, to support.

sterile *a.* not producing crops, fruit, young etc. WH: 14–15C. Old French *stérile* or Latin *sterilis*, rel. to Sanskrit *starī*, Greek *steira* barren cow, *steriphos* barren.

sterlet *n.* a small sturgeon of the Caspian Sea, *Acipenser ruthenus*. WH: 16C. Russian *sterlyad'*.

sterling *a.* of, relating to, or in, British money. *Also n.* WH: 12–14C. Prob. from an unrecorded Old English n., from *steorra* STAR + -LING[1]. Some early Norman pennies bore a small star.

stern[1] *a.* severe, forbidding. WH: pre-1200. Old English *styrne*, from Germanic, prob. from Germanic base also of STARE.

stern[2] *n.* the hind part of a ship or boat. WH: 12–14C. Prob. from Old Norse *stjórn* steering, from base of *stýra* STEER[1]. There was probably a corresponding form in Old English, but it has not been recorded.

sternum *n.* the breastbone. WH: 17C. Modern Latin, from Latin *sternon* chest, breast.

sternutation *n.* the act of sneezing, a sneeze. WH: 14–15C. Latin *sternutatio, sternutationis*, from *sternutare*, freq. of *sternuere* to sneeze. See also -ATION.

steroid *n.* any of a group of compounds of similar chemical structure, including sterols, bile acids and various hormones. WH: mid-20C. STEROL + -OID.

sterol *n.* any of various solid alcohols, such as cholesterol, ergosterol. WH: early 20C. The ending of CHOLESTEROL, ERGOSTEROL, etc.

stertorous *a.* (of breathing) characterized by deep snoring or snore-like sounds. WH: 19C. Latin *stertere* to snore. See also -OR, -OUS.

stet *v.i.* in proof-reading etc., to let the original stand (cancelling a previous correction), usu. as an instruction 'let it stand'. *Also v.t.* WH: 18C. Latin let it stand, 3rd pers. sing. pres. subj. of *stare* to stand.

stethoscope *n.* an instrument used in listening to the movement of the heart and lungs, consisting of a disc for placing against the chest, attached to a tube dividing into two branches with earpieces. *Also v.t.* WH: 19C. Greek *stēthos* breast, chest + -O- + -SCOPE. The

word was coined in *c.*1819 by the instrument's inventor, the French physicist René-Théophile-Hyacinthe Laënnec.

stetson *n.* a broad-brimmed slouch hat. WH: 19C. John B. *Stetson*, 1830–1906, US hat manufacturer.

stevedore *n.* a person whose occupation is to load and unload ships. WH: 18C. Spanish *estibador*, from Old Saxon *estibar* to stow a cargo, from Latin *stipare* to crowd, to press together. Cp. STIFF.

stevengraph *n.* a brightly coloured woven-silk picture. WH: 19C. Thomas *Stevens*, 1828–88, a ribbon weaver of Coventry + -GRAPH.

stew[1] *v.t.* to cook by boiling slowly or simmering in a closed dish or pan. *Also v.i., n.* WH: 14–15C. Old French *estuver* (Modern French *étuver*), from Popular Latin *extuvare*, prob. ult. from EX- + Greek *tuphos* smoke, steam, ? also influ. by Germanic base of STOVE.

stew[2] *n.* an artificial oyster bed. WH: 12–14C. Old French *estui* place of confinement, fish pond (Modern French *étui* case, sheath), from *estoier* to put into the sheath, to shut up, to conceal, to reserve, from Latin *studium* STUDY. Cp. ETUI, *tweeze* (TWEEZERS).

steward *n.* a passengers' attendant on a ship, aircraft or train, in charge of provisions, accommodation etc. WH: pre-1200. Old English *stigweard, stīweard*, from *stig* (prob.) house, hall + *weard* WARD. The original sense was an official appointed to control the domestic affairs of a household.

sthenic *a.* having a strong athletic physique. WH: 18C. Greek *sthenos* strength, based on *asthenic* (ASTHENIA).

stibium *n.* antimony. WH: 14–15C. Latin, from Greek *stibi, stimmi*, from Egyptian *ṣṭm*.

stich *n.* a metrical line, a verse. WH: 18C. Greek *stikhos* row, rank, line of verse.

stichomancy *n.* divination by passages taken at random in a book. WH: 17C. French *stichomantie*, from Greek *stikhos* STICH + -MANCY.

stichomythia *n.* in ancient Greek drama, dialogue in which the interlocutors speak alternate lines. WH: 19C. Modern Latin, from Greek *stikhomuthia*, from *stikhos* STICH + *muthos* speech, talk.

stick[1] *n.* a shoot or branch of a tree or shrub broken or cut off. *Also v.t.* WH: pre-1200. Old English *sticca* stick, peg, spoon, from Germanic, from base of STICK[2].

stick[2] *v.t.* to thrust the point of (in, into, through etc.). *Also v.i.* WH: pre-1200. Old English *stician* to pierce, to stab, from Germanic, from Indo-European base also of Greek *stigma* STIGMA, Latin *instigare* to spur on, INSTIGATE.

stickle *v.i.* to contend pertinaciously (for some trifle). WH: 16C. Alt. of obs. *stightle*, freq. of obs. *stight* to set in order, from Old English *stihtan*, corr. to Old Norse *stétta* to support, to help.

stickleback *n.* a small spiny-backed, freshwater fish, esp. *Gasterosteus aculeatus*. WH: 14–15C. Old English *sticel* sting, goad, thorn, from Germanic base of STICK[1] + BACK[1]. The fish is so called from its spiny back.

stiff *a.* rigid, not easily bent or moved. *Also n.* WH: pre-1200. Old English *stif*, from Germanic, from base of Latin *stipare*. Cp. CONSTIPATE.

stifle[1] *v.i.* to smother, to suffocate. *Also v.t.* WH: 14–15C. ? From freq. of Old French *estouffer* (Modern French *étouffer*), from Popular Latin *stuffare*, ? ult. of imit. orig. Cp. STOP.

stifle[2] *n.* the stifle-joint. WH: 12–14C. Orig. unknown.

stigma *n.* a mark of discredit or infamy. WH: 16C. Latin, from Greek *stigma, stigmatos*, from base of *stizein* to prick. See STICK[2].

stilb *n.* a unit of luminance equivalent to one candela per square centimetre. WH: mid-20C. French, from Greek *stilbein* to glitter. The term was coined in 1923 by the French physicist André-Eugène Blondel.

stilbite *n.* a vitreous silicate of the zeolite group. WH: 19C. Greek *stilbein* to glitter + -ITE[1]. The name was coined in 1796 by the French crystallographer and mineralogist René-Just Haüy.

stile[1] *n.* a series of steps or other contrivance by which one may get over a wall etc. WH: pre-1200. Old English *stigel*, from Germanic. Cp. German *Stiegel*.

stile[2] *n.* a vertical piece in the frame of a panelled door or wainscot, or in a window frame. WH: 17C. Prob. from Dutch *stijl* pillar, crop, doorpost.

stiletto *n.* a small dagger. *Also v.t.* WH: 17C. Italian, dim. of *stilo* dagger, ult. from Latin *stilus* STYLUS.

still[1] *a.* at rest, motionless. *Also n., adv., v.t., v.i.* WH: pre-1200. Old English *stille*, from Germanic base meaning to be fixed, to stand.

still[2] *n.* a vessel or apparatus employed in distillation, esp. of spirits, consisting of a boiler, a tubular condenser or worm enclosed in a refrigerator, and a receiver. *Also v.t.* WH: 16C. From obs. v. *still* to trickle down, from shortening of DISTIL.

stillage *n.* a frame, stool, bench etc., for placing things on for draining, waiting to be packed up etc. WH: 16C. Appar. from Dutch *stellagie* (now *stellage*) scaffold, stand, from *stellen* to place. See also -AGE. Cp. STILLING.

stilling *n.* a stand for a cask. WH: 17C. ? Dutch *stelling*, from *stellen* to place. Cp. STILLAGE.

Stillson *n.* a powerful wrench whose jaws tighten with increased pressure. WH: early 20C. Daniel C. *Stillson*, 1830–99, US inventor.

stilt *n.* a pole having a rest for the foot, used in pairs, to raise a person above the ground in walking. WH: 12–14C. Corr. to Low German and Flemish *stilte*, from Germanic. Cp. German *Stelze*.

Stilton® *n.* a rich white or blue veined cheese. WH: 18C. *Stilton*, a village in Huntingdonshire (now Cambridgeshire), where (at a coaching inn) the cheese was sold to travellers. It was actually made in Leicestershire, the native county of the inn owner.

stimulus *n.* something that stimulates one to activity, or energizes one; an incitement, a spur. WH: 17C. Latin goad, spur, incentive, prob. from base also of *stilus* STYLUS.

sting *n.* a sharp-pointed defensive or offensive organ, often conveying poison, with which certain insects, scorpions and plants are armed. *Also v.t., v.i.* WH: pre-1200. Old English *stingan*, from Germanic base also of Old Norse *stanga* to pierce.

stingo *n.* strong ale. WH: 17C. STING + -O. The ale is so called from its sharp taste.

stingy *a.* tight-fisted, mean, parsimonious, niggardly. WH: 17C. ? From dial. var. of STING. See also -Y[1].

stink *v.i.* to emit a strong, offensive smell. *Also v.t., n.* WH: pre-1200. Old English *stincan*, from Germanic. Cp. STENCH.

stint *v.t.* to give or allow (someone) money, food etc. scantily or grudgingly. *Also v.i., n.* WH: pre-1200. Old English *styntan*, from Germanic. Cp. STUNT[1]. The original sense was to make blunt or dull. Many senses based on the root meanings to stop, to cease are now obsolete. The current sense evolved in the 18C.

stipe *n.* a stalk, stem or stemlike support. WH: 18C. French, from Latin *stipes* log, post, tree trunk.

stipel *n.* a secondary stipule at the base of a compound leaf. WH: 19C. French *stipelle*, from Modern Latin *stipella*, dim. of Latin *stipula*, straw, stubble.

stipend *n.* a periodical payment for services rendered, a salary, esp. of a member of the clergy. WH: 14–15C. Old French *stipende* or Latin *stipendium*, from *stips, stipis* payment, wages, alms + *pendere* to weigh, to pay. The original specific sense was a soldier's pay.

stipple *v.t.* to engrave, paint or draw by means of dots or light dabs instead of lines etc. *Also v.i., n.* WH: 18C. Dutch *stippelen*, freq. of *stippen* to prick, to speckle, from *stip* point. See also -LE[4].

stipulate *v.t.* to lay down or specify as an essential condition to an agreement, contract or bargain. *Also v.i.* WH: 17C. Latin *stipulatus*, p.p. of *stipulari*, ? from *stipula* straw. See also -ATE[3]. Cp. STUBBLE. The reference would be to the former custom of breaking a straw to confirm a promise.

stipule *n.* a small leaflike appendage, usu. in pairs at the base of a petiole. WH: 18C. French, from Latin *stipula* straw, stubble. See also -ULE.

stir[1] *v.t.* to move a spoon etc. round and round in (a liquid or liquid mixture) to blend the ingredients. *Also v.i., n.* WH: pre-1200. Old English *styrian*, from Germanic. Cp. German *stören* to stir, to poke. The original basic senses were to move, to set in motion and to move, to be in motion. The current senses to move a spoon round and round in a liquid and to poke a fire have been in use from the first.

stir[2] *n.* prison. WH: 19C. Orig. uncertain. ? Romany *sturbin* jail.

stirk *n.* a yearling ox or cow. WH: pre-1200. Old English *stirc*, ? from *stēor* STEER[2] + -*uc* -OCK.

stirps *n.* a classificatory group. WH: 17C. Latin stock, stem.

stirrup *n.* a horse rider's foot support, usu. consisting of an iron loop suspended from the saddle by a strap. WH: pre-1200. Old English *stigrāp*, from Germanic bases of STILE[1], ROPE. The literal sense is a climbing rope.

stitch *n.* a single pass of the needle in sewing. *Also v.t., v.i.* WH: pre-1200. Old English *stice* prick, puncture, from Germanic, from base of STICK[2].

stiver *n.* any very small coin. WH: 14–15C. Middle Dutch *stuiver*, Middle Low German *stūver*, prob. rel. to STUB.

stoa *n.* in ancient Greek architecture, a portico or colonnade. WH: 17C. Greek.

stoat *n.* the ermine, *Mustela erminea*, esp. in its brownish summer coat. WH: 14–15C. Orig. unknown.

stob *n.* in coal mining, a steel wedge used for bringing down coal. WH: 12–14C. Var. of STUB.

stochastic *a.* resulting from a randomly distributed set of probabilities. WH: 17C. Greek *stokhastikos*, from *stokhazesthai* to aim at a mark, to guess, from *stokhos* aim, guess. See also -IC.

stock *n.* the aggregate of goods ready for sale or distribution. *Also a., v.t., v.i.* WH: pre-1200. Old English *stocc* stump, post, from Germanic. Cp. German *Stock* stick. The earliest basic senses are trunk, stem, post. The senses relating to money, assets or a store date from the 14–15C.

stockade *n.* a line or enclosure of posts or stakes. *Also v.t.* WH: 17C. Shortening of obs. French *estocade*, alt. of *estacade*, from Spanish *estacada*, from *estaca*, from Germanic base of STAKE[1]. See also -ADE.

stockfish *n.* cod, ling etc. split open and dried in the sun without salting. WH: 12–14C. Middle Low German and Middle Dutch *stokvisch*, of unknown orig.

stocking *n.* a close-fitting covering for the foot and leg. WH: 16C. STOCK. See also -ING[1]. The reference is to *stock* in the sense of leg covering, sock (15C), probably so called in figurative reference to a log or trunk.

stodge *n.* heavy, starchy, filling food, esp. steamed or baked pudding. *Also v.t.* WH: 17C. Imit., based on STUFF and PODGE. The noun evolved from the verb in the 19C.

stoep *n.* an open, roofed platform in front of a house, a veranda. WH: 18C. Afrikaans, from Dutch, rel. to STEP. Cp. STOOP[2].

stogy *n.* a long cheaply made cigar. WH: 19C. *Conestoga*, a town in Pennsylvania, USA. The cigar is said to be so called because drivers of covered wagons made in Conestoga were associated with cigars of this type.

Stoic *n.* a philosopher or member of the school founded by Zeno, *c.*308 BC, teaching that virtue is the highest good, and that the passions and appetites should be rigidly subdued. *Also a.* WH: 14–15C. Latin *stoicus*, from Greek *stoikos*, from STOA. See also -IC. The reference is to the *Stoa*, the great hall in Athens where the philosopher Zeno lectured.

stoichiology *n.* the study of the elements that compose animal tissue. WH: 19C. Greek *stoikheion* element + -O- + -LOGY.

stoke *v.t.* to tend (a furnace, esp. of a steam engine). *Also v.i.* WH: 17C. Back-formation from *stoker* (STOKE), from Dutch, from *stoken* to feed (a furnace), Middle Low German and Middle Dutch to push, to poke, from base also of STICK[2]. See also -ER[1].

stokes *n.* the centimetre-gram-second unit of kinematic viscosity. WH: 19C. Sir George *Stokes*, 1819–1903, Irish-born physicist and mathematician.

STOL *n.* a system by which aircraft take off and land over a short distance. WH: mid-20C. Acronym of *short take-off and landing*.

stole *n.* a broad band of fabric, fur etc. worn round the neck and shoulders by women. WH: pre-1200. Old English, from Latin *stola*, from Greek *stolē* equipment, array, clothing, garment, from base of *stellein* to place, to array. The original sense was a long robe. The sense woman's long scarf or shawl arose in the 19C.

stolid *a.* dull, impassive, phlegmatic; lacking emotion, or showing none. WH: 16C. Obs. French *stolide*, or from Latin *stolidus*, ? rel. to *stultus* foolish. See also -ID.

Stollen *n.* a spicy German bread containing dried fruit and coated with icing sugar. WH: early 20C. German, from Old High German *stollo* post, support.

stolon *n.* a trailing or prostrate shoot that takes root and develops a new plant. WH: 17C. Latin *stolo, stolonis* shoot, scion.

stoma *n.* a minute orifice, a pore. WH: 17C. Modern Latin, from Greek *stoma, stomatos* mouth.

stomach *n.* the digestive cavity, formed by a dilatation of the alimentary canal, or (in certain animals) one of several such cavities. *Also v.t.* WH: 12–14C. Old French *stomaque* (Modern French *estomac*), from Latin *stomachus*, from Greek *stomakhos* throat, gullet, mouth of an organ, from *stoma* mouth.

stomatitis *n.* inflammation of the mouth. WH: 19C. Modern Latin, from *stoma, stomatos* mouth. See also -ITIS.

stomp *v.i.* to stamp with the feet. *Also n.* WH: 19C. Var. of STAMP.

stone *n.* the non-metallic mineral material of which rock is composed. *Also a., v.t.* WH: pre-1200. Old English *stān*, from Germanic. Cp. German *Stein*.

stonkered *a.* totally exhausted. WH: early 20C. From *stonker* to put out of action (from *stonk* game of marbles, ? of imit. orig.) + -ED.

stooge *n.* a butt, a confederate, a decoy. *Also v.i.* WH: early 20C. Orig. unknown.

stook *n.* a bundle of sheaves set up on end. *Also v.t.* WH: 12–14C. Middle Low German *stūke*.

stool *n.* a seat without a back, for one person, usu. with three or four legs. *Also v.i.* WH: pre-1200. Old English *stōl*, from Germanic base of STAND. See also -LE[1]. Cp. German *Stuhl* chair, throne. The original sense was a chair or seat of authority, a throne. The sense seat without a back arose in the 14–15C.

stoop[1] *v.i.* to bend the body downwards and forward. *Also v.t., n.* WH: pre-1200. Old English *stūpian*, from Germanic base rel. to STEEP[1].

stoop[2] *n.* a flight of steps, a porch, or a small veranda in front of a house. WH: 18C. Dutch STOEP.

stop *v.t.* to cause to cease moving, working etc. *Also v.i., n.* WH: pre-1200. Old English *-stoppian* (in *forstoppian* to stop up, to stifle), from Germanic, from Late Latin *stuppare* to stuff. Cp. German *stopfen* to stuff.

stope *n.* a steplike area of a mine, where ore is being extracted. WH: 18C. Appar. rel. to STEP.

storax *n.* a vanilla-scented resin obtained from *Styrax officinalis*, formerly used in medicine etc. WH: 14–15C. Latin, from Greek, var. of *sturax* STYRAX.

store *n.* a stock laid up for drawing upon. *Also v.t.* WH: 12–14C. Shortening of Old French *estorer*, from Latin *instaurare* to renew, to repair, RESTORE.

storey *n.* a horizontal division of a building, esp. a set of rooms on the same floor. WH: 14–15C. Shortening of Anglo-Latin *historia* picture, floor of a building, from Latin *historia* HISTORY, STORY. A storey is perhaps so called because the fronts of some medieval buildings were decorated with rows of painted windows.

storiated *a.* historiated, decorated with historical or mythical scenes. WH: 19C. From *storiate*, back-formation from *storiation* (from STORY + -ATION) + -ED.

stork *n.* a long-necked, long-legged wading bird of the genus *Ciconia*, allied to the heron, esp. the white or house-stork *C. alba*, nesting on buildings. WH: pre-1200. Old English *storc*, from Germanic, prob. rel. to base of STARK. Cp. German *Storch*. The bird is apparently so called from its rigid stance.

storm *n.* a violent disturbance of the atmosphere accompanied by wind, rain, snow, hail or thunder and lightning. *Also v.i., v.t.* WH: pre-1200. Old English, from Germanic, prob. from base represented also by STIR[1].

stornello *n.* an Italian form of short improvised song. WH: 19C. Italian, prob. from *stornare* to turn aside.

Storting *n.* the Norwegian parliament. WH: 19C. Norwegian, from *stor* great + *ting* assembly. Cp. THING[2].

story *n.* a narrative or recital in prose or verse, of actual or fictitious events, a tale. WH: 12–14C. Shortening of Anglo-French *estorie* (Old French *estoire*, Modern French *histoire*), from Latin *historia* HISTORY. The earliest sense was a true narrative, a historical account. The application of the word to fictitious events began in the 14–15C.

stot *n.* a bullock, a steer. WH: pre-1200. Old English *stott*, ? rel. to Old Norse *stútr* bull. Cp. Anglo-Latin *stottus* steer, *stotta* heifer.

stoup *n.* a basin for holy water. WH: 12–14C. Old Norse *staup*, corr. to Old English *steap*, from Germanic base rel. to Old English *stoppa* pail. Cp. STEEP[2].

stour *n.* a cloud of dust. *Also v.t., v.i.* WH: 12–14C. Old French *estour*, from Germanic base also of STORM.

stoush *v.t.* to fight with or hit. *Also n.* WH: 19C. Orig. unknown.

stout *a.* corpulent, bulky. *Also n.* WH: 12–14C. Old French *estout*, from Germanic, ? rel. to STILT. Cp. German *stolz* proud. The original sense (to the 19C) was proud, haughty, arrogant. The sense corpulent evolved in the 19C.

stove *n.* an apparatus, wholly or partially closed, in which fuel is burned for heating, cooking etc. *Also v.t.* WH: 14–15C. Middle Low German and Middle Dutch *stove*, rel. to Old High German *stuba* (German *Stube* living room), Old English *stofa* bathroom, from Germanic base ? rel. to STEW[1]. The original sense (to the 18C) was a hot-air bath, a sweating-room. The current sense dates from the 16C.

stow *v.t.* to put or pack (often away) in a suitable or convenient place or position. WH: 14–15C. Shortening of BESTOW. The original sense was to lodge or find accommodation for a person. Subsequent senses include to arrest, to imprison (to the 17C) and to spend or invest money (to the 18C).

STP *abbr.* Professor of Sacred Theology. WH: Abbr. of Latin *Sanctae Theologiae Professor* Professor of Sacred Theology.

strabismus *n.* squinting, a squint, produced by a muscular defect of the eye. WH: 17C. Modern Latin, from Greek *strabismos*, from *strabizein* to squint, from *strabos* squinting.

Strad *n.* a Stradivarius. WH: 19C. Abbr. of STRADIVARIUS.

straddle *v.t.* to stand or sit astride of (something) with legs well apart. *Also v.i., n.* WH: 16C. Alt. of obs. *striddle*, back-formation from *striddling*, from base of STRIDE + -LING[2].

Stradivarius *n.* a stringed instrument, esp. a violin, made by Antonio Stradivari. WH: 19C. Latinized form of the name of Antonio Stradivari of Cremona, *c.*1644–1737, Italian violin maker.

strafe *v.t.* to bombard heavily. *Also n.* WH: early 20C. From German *Gott strafe England* may God punish England, a catch phrase in Germany in World War I.

straggle *v.i.* to lose tightness or compactness. *Also n.* WH: 14–15C. ? Alt. of freq. of dial. *strake* to go, to proceed, from Germanic base of STRAKE. See also -LE[4].

straight *a.* not bent or crooked. *Also n., adv.* WH: 12–14C. Obs. p.p. and part. a. of STRETCH.

strain[1] *v.t.* to stretch tight; to make taut. *Also v.i., n.* WH: 12–14C. Old French *estreindre, estreign-* (Modern French *étreindre*), from Latin *stringere* to draw tight, to bind tightly. The original sense (to the 16C) was to bind fast, to confine in bonds. The sense to stretch tight dates from the 14–15C.

strain[2] *n.* family, breed. WH: pre-1200. Old English *strīon*, shortened form of *gestrēon*, rel. to Old English *gestrēonan, gestrīenan* to gain, to get, to beget, from Germanic, rel. to Latin *strues* pile, heap, *struere* to pile up, to build.

strait *n.* a narrow passage of water between two seas. *Also a.* WH: 12–14C. Shortening of Old French *estreit* tight, close, narrow, from Latin *strictus* STRICT. Cp. STRESS.

strake *n.* a continuous line of planking or plates from stem to stern of a vessel. WH: 12–14C. Anglo-Latin *stracus, straca*, prob. from Germanic base of STRETCH. Not rel. to STREAK.

stramash *n.* a disturbance, a fray, a struggle. *Also v.t.* WH: 18C. Appar. imit. Cp. SMASH.

stramineous *a.* straw-coloured. WH: 17C. Latin *stramineus*, from *stramen* straw. See also -OUS.

stramonium *n.* a drug prepared from the thorn apple, *Datura stramonium*, used for asthma and nervous complaints. WH: 17C. Modern Latin, ? rel. to Russian *durman* thorn apple.

strand[1] *v.t.* to run or force aground. *Also v.i., n.* WH: pre-1200. Old English, corr. to Middle Low German *strant*, Old Norse *strǫnd*, from Germanic, of unknown orig. Cp. German *Strand* shore. The verb evolved from the noun in the 17C.

strand[2] *n.* each of the fibres, threads, wires etc. of which a rope etc. is composed. *Also v.t.* WH: 15C. Orig. unknown. ? Of Germanic orig. Cp. German *Strähne* strand.

strange *a.* unusual, surprising. *Also adv.* WH: 12–14C. Shortening of Old French *estrange* (Modern French *étrange*), from Latin *extraneus* EXTRANEOUS. Cp. ESTRANGE. The original sense was belonging to another country, foreign.

stranger *n.* a person from another place; someone who does not know, or is not known in, a certain place. WH: 14–15C. Shortening of Old French *estranger* (Modern French *étranger*), from Latin *extraneus*. See STRANGE, also -ER².

strangle *v.t.* to kill by compressing the windpipe, to choke, to throttle. WH: 12–14C. Shortening of Old French *estrangler* (Modern French *étrangler*), from Latin *strangulare*, from Greek *straggalan*, rel. to *straggalē* halter, *straggos* twisted.

strangulate *v.t.* to strangle. WH: 17C. Latin *strangulatus*, p.p. of *strangulare* STRANGLE. See also -ATE³.

strangury *n.* a disease characterized by pain in passing the urine, which is excreted in drops. WH: 14–15C. Latin *stranguria*, from Greek *straggouria*, from *stragx*, *straggos* drop squeezed out + *ouron* urine. See also -Y².

strap *n.* a long narrow strip of leather or similar material, usu. with a buckle, for fastening round things. *Also v.t.* WH: 16C. Dial. form of STROP. The original sense (to the 17C) was a snare for birds. The current sense dates from the 17C.

strappado *n.* a punishment involving drawing up an offender by a rope and letting them fall to the end of this. *Also v.t.* WH: 16C. French *estrapade*, from Italian *estrapada*, from *strappare* to snatch. See also -ADO.

strass *n.* paste for making false gems. WH: 19C. German, from Josef Strasser, its 18C inventor. According to some sources the word is from G.F. *Stras*, 1700–73, a French jeweller.

stratagem *n.* an artifice, trick or manoeuvre, esp. for deceiving an enemy. WH: 15C. French *stratagème*, from Latin *stratagema*, from Greek *stratēgēma*, from *stratēgein* to be a general, from *stratēgos* general, from *stratos* army + *agein* to lead. Cp. STRATEGY.

strategy *n.* the art of war, generalship, esp. the art of directing military movements so as to secure the most advantageous positions and combinations of forces. WH: 17C. French *stratégie*, from Greek *stratēgia* office of a general, from *stratēgos*. See STRATAGEM.

strath *n.* in the Scottish Highlands, a wide valley through which a river runs. WH: 16C. Gaelic *srath*, rel. to STREET.

strati- *comb. form* layer. WH: STRATUM + -I-.

straticulate *a.* (of rock) composed of narrow layers. WH: 19C. STRATUM + -*iculate*, based on RETICULATE², *vermiculate* (VERMICULAR), etc.

stratiform *a.* composed of layers. WH: 19C. French *stratiforme*. See STRATI-, -FORM.

stratify *v.t.* to form, deposit or arrange in strata. WH: 17C. French *stratifier*. See STRATUM, also -FY.

stratigraphy *n.* the branch of geology dealing with the succession, classification, nomenclature etc. of stratified rocks. WH: 19C. STRATI- + -GRAPHY.

strato- *comb. form* layer, esp. with reference to cloud formations. WH: STRATUS, STRATUM, or back-formation from STRATOSPHERE. See also -O-.

stratocirrus *n.* a cloud formation more compact than cirrostratus. WH: late 20C. STRATO- + CIRRUS.

stratocracy *n.* a military government. WH: 17C. Greek *stratos* army + -CRACY.

stratocumulus *n.* a layer of low cloud in dark round masses. WH: 19C. STRATO- + CUMULUS.

stratopause *n.* the upper boundary of the stratosphere. WH: mid-20C. STRATOSPHERE + -*pause*, based on TROPOPAUSE.

stratosphere *n.* the layer of atmosphere above the troposphere, extending to about 50 km above the earth's surface, in the lower part of which temperature does not vary very much and in the upper part of which temperature increases with height. WH: early 20C. STRATUM + -O- + SPHERE.

stratum *n.* a horizontal layer of any material. WH: 16C. Modern Latin, use of Latin *stratum*, lit. something spread, something laid down, neut. p.p. of *sternere* to lay down, to throw down. Cp. STREET.

stratus *n.* a continuous horizontal sheet of cloud. WH: 19C. Modern Latin, from Latin, p.p. of *sternere*. See STRATUM.

stravaig *v.i.* to roam about idly, to ramble. WH: 18C. Prob. shortening of obs. *extravage* to ramble, from *extravagate* (EXTRAVAGANT) or EXTRAVAGANT.

straw *n.* the dry, ripened stalks of certain species of grain, esp. wheat, rye, oats etc., used as cattle fodder or material for packing, thatching, hat-making etc. *Also a.* WH: pre-1200. Old English *strēaw*, from Germanic base rel. to STREW.

strawberry *n.* a low, stemless perennial plant of the genus *Fragaria*, with trifoliate leaves and white flowers, bearing a fleshy red fruit. *Also a.* WH: pre-1200. STRAW + BERRY. The reason for the name is obscure. Two popular theories are (1) that the seedlike particles on the fruit's surface resemble particles of straw, and (2) that the plant's slender runners track across the ground as if strawn (i.e. strewn) over it.

stray *v.i.* to wander from the direct or proper course. *Also n., a.* WH: 12–14C. Shortening of Old French *estraier*, *estrayer*. See ASTRAY.

streak *n.* an esp. irregular line or long narrow mark of a distinct colour from the background. *Also v.t., v.i.* WH: pre-1200. Old English *strica*, from Germanic base of STRIKE. Cp. STROKE¹, STROKE².

stream *n.* a small river. *Also v.i., v.t.* WH: pre-1200. Old English *strēam*, from Germanic, from Indo-European base also of Greek *rhein* to flow, *rheuma* stream. Cp. German *Strom*.

street *n.* a road in a city or town with houses on one side or on both. *Also a.* WH: pre-1200. Old English *strǣt*, from Germanic, from Late Latin *strata* (*via*) paved (way), use as n. of fem. p.p. of Latin *sternere* to throw down, to lay down. Cp. STRATUM.

strelitzia *n.* any southern African plant of the genus *Strelitzia*, with showy flowers that have a projecting tongue. WH: 18C. Charlotte of Mecklenburg-*Strelitz*, 1744–1818, queen of George III + -IA.

strength *n.* the quality of being strong. WH: pre-1200. Old English *strengthu*, from Germanic base also of STRONG. See also -TH².

strenuous *a.* energetic, vigorous. WH: 17C. Latin *strenuus* brisk, active, valiant + -OUS.

strep *n.* streptococcus. *Also a.* WH: early 20C. Abbr. of STREPTOCOCCUS.

strepitoso *adv.* in a noisy, impetuous manner. WH: 19C. Italian, lit. noisy, loud.

strepto- *comb. form* twisted chain. WH: 19C. Greek, comb. form of *streptos* twisted, from *strephein* to turn, to twist.

streptocarpus *n.* any southern African plant of the genus *Streptocarpus*, with violet or pink funnel-shaped flowers and spirally twisted fruits. WH: 19C. STREPTO- + Greek *karpos* fruit.

streptococcus *n.* any bacterium of the chain-forming genus *Streptococcus*, some of which cause infectious diseases. WH: 19C. Modern Latin, from Greek *streptos* twisted + COCCUS. The bacterium is so called because it usually forms chains.

streptokinase *n.* an enzyme effective in treating blood clots and inflammation, produced by certain streptococci. WH: mid-20C. STREPTOCOCCUS + KINASE.

streptomycin *n.* an antibiotic obtained from a soil bacterium and used in the treatment of tuberculosis and other bacterial infections. WH: mid-20C. *streptomycete* (from Medieval Latin *Streptomyces*, from STREPTO- + Greek *mukēs* fungus) +-IN¹.

stress *n.* tension, pressure or strain exerted on an object; a measure of this, or its amount. *Also v.t., v.i.* WH: 12–14C. Shortening of DISTRESS or partly from Old French *estrece*, *estresse* narrowness, straitness, oppression, ult. from Latin *strictus* STRICT. Cp. STRAIT. The original sense (to the 18C) was hardship, adversity, affliction.

stretch *v.t.* to extend in any direction or to full length. *Also v.i., n., a.* WH: pre-1200. Old English *streccan*, from Germanic. Cp. DISTRAUGHT, STRAKE.

stretto *adv.* at a quicker tempo. WH: 18C. Italian, lit. narrow.

strew *v.t.* to scatter, to spread. WH: pre-1200. Old English *strēowian*, from Germanic, from Indo-European base represented by Latin *sternere* to lay down, to throw down. Cp. STRAW.

strewth *int.* used to express surprise or alarm etc. WH: 19C. Abbr. of *God's truth*.

stria *n.* a superficial furrow, a thin line or groove, mark or ridge. WH: 16C. Latin furrow, grooving.

stricken *a.* affected, esp. severely, by e.g. disease, disaster or sorrow. WH: 15C. P.p. of STRIKE.

strickle *n.* a straight-edge for levelling grain in a measure. WH: pre-1200. Old English *stricel*, rel. to STRIKE.

strict *a.* defined or applied exactly, accurate. WH: 12–14C. Latin *strictus*, p.p. of *stringere* to draw tight. Cp. STRAIT, STRINGENT. The original sense was restricted. The sense severe arose in the 16C.

stricture *n.* a censure, a sharp criticism. WH: 14–15C. Latin *strictura*, from *strictus*, p.p. of *stringere* to draw tight, to touch lightly. See also -URE.

stride *v.i.* to walk with long steps. Also *v.t.*, *n.* WH: pre-1200. Old English *strīdan*, prob. ult. from Germanic. ? Rel. to STRIFE, STRIVE. The original sense was to stand or walk with the legs wide apart. The current sense dates from the 12–14C.

stridence *n.* loudness or harshness of tone. WH: 19C. From *strident* (from Latin *stridens*, *stridentis*, pres.p. of *stridere* to creak) + -ENCE.

strife *n.* conflict, hostile struggle. WH: 12–14C. Shortening of Old French *estrif*, rel. to *estriver* STRIVE.

striga *n.* a short stiff hair, bristle or hairlike scale. WH: 18C. Latin row, strip.

strigil *n.* a skin-scraper used in baths by the ancient Romans and Greeks. WH: 16C. Latin *strigilis*, from base of *stringere* to graze, to touch lightly. See also -IL.

strike *v.t.* to hit, to inflict (a blow etc.). Also *v.i.*, *n.* WH: pre-1200. Old English *strīcan*, from Germanic base of STREAK. Cp. STRICKLE, STROKE[1].

Strimmer® *n.* an electrically operated grass trimmer with a rapidly rotating nylon cutting cord. WH: late 20C. Prob. blend of STRING and *trimmer* (TRIM), or shortening of *grass trimmer*, from GRASS + *trimmer*.

Strine *n.* Australian English, comically transliterated, e.g. *afferbeck lauder*, for *alphabetical order*. WH: mid-20C. Representation of an alleged Australian pronun. of AUSTRALIAN.

string *n.* twine, usu. thicker than thread and thinner than cord. Also *v.t.*, *v.i.* WH: pre-1200. Old English *streng*, from Germanic base of STRONG. Cp. German *Strang* cord, rope.

stringendo *adv.* in accelerated time. WH: 19C. Italian, pres.p. of *stringere* to press, to squeeze, to bind together, from Latin *stringere* to bind.

stringent *a.* strict, precise, binding, rigid. WH: 17C. Latin *stringens*, *stringentis*, pres.p. of *stringere* to bind. See also -ENT. Cp. STRICT.

stringhalt *n.* a convulsive movement of a horse's hind legs in walking. WH: 16C. STRING + HALT[2]. A variant form *springhalt* (17C) is an unexplained alteration of *stringhalt*.

strip[1] *v.t.* to pull the clothes or covering from, to skin. Also *v.i.*, *n.* WH: 12–14C. Corr. to Middle Dutch *stroopen*, Old High German *stroufen* (German *streifen* to strip off), from Germanic. The word probably existed in Old English but is unrecorded.

strip[2] *n.* a long narrow piece. WH: 14–15C. Rel. to Middle Low German *strippe* strap, thong, and prob. to STRIPE.

stripe *n.* a long, narrow band of a distinctive colour or texture. Also *v.t.* WH: 14–15C. ? Back-formation from *striped* (? orig. from Low Dutch, later from v. *stripe* + -ED), ult. rel. to Middle Low German and Middle Dutch *strīpe*, from Germanic. Cp. STRIP[1]. The sense stroke with a whip, etc. is probably of different origin, but ultimately related.

stripling *n.* a youth, a lad. WH: 12–14C. Prob. from STRIP[2] + -LING[1].

strive *v.i.* to try hard, to make a great effort (for something, to do something etc.). WH: 12–14C. Shortening of Old French *estriver*, rel. to *estrif* STRIFE. The original sense was to quarrel, to wrangle.

strobe *n.* a stroboscope. Also *v.t.*, *v.i.* WH: mid-20C. Abbr. of *stroboscope* (19C), from Greek *strobos* a twisting, a whirling round + -SCOPE.

strobila *n.* a chain of segments forming the body of a tapeworm. WH: 19C. Modern Latin, from Greek *strobilē* plug of lint twisted into the shape of a fir cone. Cp. STROBILE.

strobile *n.* a pine cone or a multiple fruit such as this. WH: 18C. French, from Late Latin *strobilus*, from Greek *strobilos* twisted thing, fir cone.

Stroganoff *n.* a dish of meat, usu. beef in strips, cooked with onions and mushrooms in a sour-cream sauce. Also *a.* WH: mid-20C. French, from Count Pavel Aleksandrovich *Stroganov*, 1772–1817, Russian diplomat.

stroke[1] *n.* an act of striking, the impact, noise etc., of this. Also *v.t.* WH: 12–14C. Var. of STRIKE. Cp. STREAK. The word was probably already in Old English but is not recorded. The original form would have been *strāc. Cp. STROKE[2].

stroke[2] *v.t.* to pass the hand over the surface of (fur, hair, an animal etc.) caressingly. Also *n.* WH: pre-1200. Old English *strācian*, from Germanic var. of base of STRIKE. Cp. STREAK.

stroll *v.i.* to walk in a leisurely way, to saunter. Also *v.t.*, *n.* WH: 17C. Prob. from German *strollen*, *strolchen* to loaf, to wander as a vagrant, from *Strolch* vagabond, of unknown orig.

stroma *n.* the framework of tissue of an organ or cell. WH: 19C. Modern Latin use of Late Latin bed covering, from Greek *strōma* thing spread out for lying or sitting on, from base of *strōnnunai* to spread.

stromb *n.* any gastropod of the genus *Strombus* or the family Strombidae, chiefly found in tropical seas. WH: 19C. Latin *strombus* spiral shell, from Greek *strombos* spirally twisted thing.

strong *a.* able to withstand force; not easily damaged. Also *adv.* WH: pre-1200. Old English *strong*, *strang*, from Germanic base also of STRING. Cp. German *streng* strict, stern.

strontium *n.* a soft silvery-white metallic element, at. no. 38, chem. symbol Sr, resembling calcium. WH: 19C. *Strontian*, a parish west of Loch Linnhe in western Scotland, where the mineral was discovered in lead mines + -IUM. The name was coined in 1808 by the English chemist Sir Humphry Davy.

strop *n.* a strip of leather etc., for sharpening razors etc. on. Also *v.t.* WH: 14–15C. Middle Low German and Middle Dutch, from Germanic, from Latin *struppus*, *stroppus*, prob. from Greek *strophos*. Cp. STROPHE. The equivalent Old English form *strop* did not survive.

strophanthus *n.* any plant of the genus *Strophanthus* of Asia and Africa, belonging to the periwinkle family. WH: 19C. Modern Latin, from Greek *strophos* twisted cord + *anthos* flower. The plant is so called from the long segments of the corolla.

strophe *n.* the turning of the chorus from right to left in an ancient Greek drama. WH: 17C. Greek *strophē*, lit. turning, from *stroph-*, of base of *strephein* to turn.

strophiole *n.* an appendage like an aril attached to the hilum of some seeds. WH: 19C. Modern Latin *strophiolum*, from Latin dim. of *strophium* chaplet, from Greek *strophion*, from *stroph-*. See STROPHE.

stroppy *a.* rowdy, angry. WH: mid-20C. ? Abbr. of OBSTREPEROUS, with alt. of *-strep-* to *strop-*. Cp. Swedish *stroppig* stuck-up, pompous.

structure *n.* a combination of parts, as a building, machine etc., esp. the supporting framework. Also *v.t.* WH: 14–15C. Old French, or from Latin *structura*, from *structus*, p.p. of *struere* to build. See also -URE.

strudel *n.* a thin pastry rolled up with a filling (e.g. apple) and baked. WH: 19C. German, lit. eddy, whirlpool.

struggle *v.i.* to make violent movements in trying to break free from restraint etc. Also *n.* WH: 14–15C. From a freq. base of unknown orig., ? imit. See also -LE[4]. Some sources relate the word to Old Norse *strúgr* ill will, contention, or to German *straucheln* to stumble.

strum *v.t.*, *v.i.* to play noisily or carelessly, to thrum on a stringed instrument. Also *n.* WH: 18C. Imit. Cp. THRUM[1].

struma *n.* scrofula. WH: 16C. Modern Latin, from Latin scrofulous swelling.

†**strumpet** *n.* a prostitute, a harlot. Also *v.t.* WH: 12–14C. Orig. unknown. Some authorities derive the word from Latin *stuprata*, fem. p.p. of *stuprare* to have illicit sexual relations with, to violate the chastity of, but such a connection remains putative.

strut[1] *v.i.* to walk with a pompous, conceited gait. Also *n.* WH: pre-1200. Prob. from source of obs. *strut* strife, contention, from Germanic base ? orig. meaning to stand out, to project. The original sense (to the 19C) was to protrude stiffly, to stick out, to stick up. The current sense dates from the 16C.

strut[2] *n.* a timber or iron beam inserted in a framework so as to keep other members apart, a brace. Also *v.t.* WH: 16C. Orig. uncertain. ? Rel. to STRUT[1].

struthious *a.* of or relating to the ostrich; ostrich-like. WH: 18C. Latin *struthio* OSTRICH + -OUS.

strychnine *n.* a highly poisonous alkaloid obtained from certain plant species of the genus *Strychnos*, esp. *S. nux-vomica*, used in medicine as a stimulant etc. WH: 19C. French, from Modern Latin *strychnos*, use as a genus name of Latin a kind of nightshade, from Greek *strukhnos* + -INE.

stub n. a stump, end or remnant of anything, e.g. of a cigarette or a pencil. Also v.t. WH: pre-1200. Old English stybb, from Germanic.

stubble n. the stumps of wheat, barley etc. covering the ground after harvest. WH: 12–14C. Old French estuble (Modern French éteule), from Latin stupula, stipula straw. Cp. STIPULE.

stubborn a. unreasonably obstinate, refractory. WH: 12–14C. Orig. unknown. The sense, but not the form, suggests a source in STUB. The original sense was untameable, ruthless, fierce.

stucco n. fine plaster for coating walls or moulding into decorations in relief. Also v.t. WH: 16C. Italian, ult. from Germanic. Cp. STOCK.

stud[1] n. a large-headed nail, knob, head of a bolt etc., esp. fixed as an ornament. Also v.t. WH: pre-1200. Old English studu, from Germanic, rel. to German stützen to prop, to support. The original sense was wooden post, upright prop. The sense large-headed nail etc. arose in the 14–15C.

stud[2] n. a number of horses kept for riding, racing, breeding etc. Also a. WH: pre-1200. Old English stōd, from Germanic base also of STAND. Cp. German Stute mare.

studding-sail n. an additional sail set beyond the sides of a square sail in light winds. WH: 16C. Orig. of first element is uncertain, ? from Middle Low German and Middle Dutch stōtinge, from stoten to thrust, from Germanic; second element is SAIL.

student n. a person engaged in study, esp. someone receiving instruction at a university, college or other institution for higher education or technical training. WH: 14–15C. Latin studens, studentis, pres.p. of studere. See STUDY, also -ENT.

studio n. the working room of a sculptor, painter, photographer etc. WH: 19C. Italian, from Latin studium. See STUDY.

studious a. devoted to study. WH: 12–14C. Latin studiosus, from studium STUDY. See also -IOUS.

study n. mental application to books, art, science etc., the pursuit of knowledge. Also v.t., v.i. WH: 12–14C. Shortening of Old French estudie (Modern French étude), from Latin studium eagerness, affection, painstaking application. Cp. ÉTUDE.

stuff n. the material of which anything is made or may be made. Also v.t., v.i. WH: 12–14C. Shortening of Old French estoffe (Modern French étoffe) material, furniture, prob. from estoffer (Modern French étoffer) to equip, to furnish, from Greek stuphein to draw together, to contract, rel. to stupeion oakum, Latin stuppa tow. Cp. STOP, STUPE[1].

stultify v.t. to dull the mind of. WH: 18C. Late Latin stultificare, from Latin stultus foolish, fool. See also -FY.

stum n. unfermented grape juice, must. Also v.t. WH: 17C. Dutch stom, use as n. of a., dumb.

stumble v.i. to trip in walking or to strike the foot against something without falling. Also v.t., n. WH: 12–14C. From an Old Norse word represented by Norwegian and Danish dial. stumle, Swedish dial. stumla, from Germanic base also of STAMMER.

stumer n. a cheque that has no money to back it; a returned cheque. WH: 19C. Orig. unknown.

stump n. the part left in the earth after a tree has fallen or been cut down. Also v.i., v.t. WH: 12–14C. Middle Low German stump, stumpe, Middle Dutch stomp, from Germanic. Cp. German Stumpf.

stun v.t. to render senseless with a blow. WH: 12–14C. Shortening of Old French estoner (Modern French étonner). See ASTONISH.

stunt[1] v.t. to check in growth or development, to dwarf, to cramp. Also n. WH: 16C. From obs. stunt foolish, stupid, from Germanic, ? from base of STUMP. Cp. STINT. The original sense (to the 17C) was to irritate, to provoke to anger. The current sense arose in the 17C.

stunt[2] n. a thing done to attract attention. WH: 19C. Orig. unknown. The word originated as American college athletics slang.

stupa n. a domed Buddhist shrine, a tope. WH: 19C. Sanskrit stūpa. Cp. TOPE[3].

stupe[1] n. a compress of flannel or other soft material used in fomentations etc. Also v.t. WH: 14–15C. Latin stuppa tow, from Greek stuppē.

stupe[2] n. a stupid person. WH: 18C. Abbr. of STUPID. Cp. SIMP.

stupefy v.t. to make stupid or senseless. WH: 14–15C. French stupéfier, from Latin stupefacere, from stupere. See STUPID, also -FY.

stupendous a. astounding in magnitude, force, degree etc., marvellous, amazing, astonishing. WH: 16C. Latin stupendus, ger. of stupere. See STUPID, also -OUS.

stupid a. slow in understanding, unintelligent. Also n. WH: 16C. French stupide or Latin stupidus, from stupere to be annoyed (at), to be stunned. See also -ID.

stupor n. a dazed condition, torpor, deadened sensibility. WH: 14–15C. Latin, from stupere. See STUPID, also -OR.

sturdy[1] a. robust, lusty, vigorous, hardy. WH: 12–14C. Shortening of Old French estourdi stunned, dozed, reckless (Modern French étourdi thoughtless), ult. from Latin EX- + turdus thrush. The thrush is frequently characterized in Romance languages as drunk or dizzy. Cp. French soûl comme une grive drunk as a thrush. The current sense of the word evolved in the 14–15C.

sturdy[2] n. a disease in sheep characterized by giddiness caused by a tapeworm in the brain. WH: 16C. STURDY[1].

sturgeon n. a large anadromous fish of the genus Acipenser, characterized by bony scales, esp. A. sturio, which yields caviare and isinglass. WH: 12–14C. Anglo-French, from Old French esturgeon, from Germanic base of Old English styrga, Middle Dutch störe (Dutch steur), Old High German sturjo (German Stör), Old Norse styrja. The original sense appears to be stirrer, disturber.

Sturm und Drang n. a late 18th-cent. German literary and artistic genre typified by stirring action, and the expression of strong passion or emotional unrest. WH: 19C. German, lit. storm and stress, title of a 1776 play by Friedrich Maximilian Klinger.

sturnoid a. like a starling. WH: 19C. Latin sturnus starling + -OID.

stutter v.i. to keep hesitating or repeating sounds spasmodically in the articulation of words. Also v.t., n. WH: 16C. Freq. of obs. stut, rel. to Germanic base of Middle Low German stöten, Old High German stozan (German stossen) to strike against. See also -ER[5].

sty[1] n. a pen or enclosure for pigs. Also v.t., v.i. WH: pre-1200. Old English stī- in comb. such as stī-fearh sty-pig, ? identical with stig hall (see STEWARD), from Germanic. Cp. Middle Low German stege, Old Norse stía pen, fold.

sty[2] n. a small inflamed swelling on the edge of the eyelid. WH: 17C. Back-formation from obs. styany from obs. styan (from Old English stīgend, lit. riser, use as n. of pres.p. of stīgan to rise) + EYE[1].

Stygian a. of or relating to the river Styx, in Greek mythology. WH: 16C. Latin Stygius, from Greek Stugios, from Stux Styx, in Greek mythology a dark and gloomy river in Hades, over which Charon ferried the souls of the dead. See also -IAN.

style n. a sort, pattern, esp. with reference to appearance. Also v.t. WH: 12–14C. Old French, from Latin stilus, influ. in spelling by assoc. with Greek stulos column. Cp. STYLUS.

stylet n. a long pointed instrument, a stiletto. WH: 17C. French, from Italian STILETTO.

stylite n. a religious recluse in ancient and medieval times who lived on the top of a pillar. WH: 17C. Ecclesiastical Greek stulitēs, from Greek stulos column. See also -ITE[1].

stylo n. a stylograph. WH: 19C. Abbr. of STYLOGRAPH.

stylobate n. a continuous base for a range of columns. WH: 17C. Latin stylobata, from Greek stulobatēs, from stulos column + -batēs base, from bainein to walk. Cp. STEREOBATE.

stylograph n. a pen with a tubular point fed with ink from a reservoir in the shaft. WH: 19C. STYLUS + -GRAPH.

styloid a. penlike, stylus-like. Also n. WH: 17C. Modern Latin styloides, from Greek stuloeidēs like a style, from stulos column. See also -OID.

stylus n. a pointed instrument for writing by means of carbon paper. WH: 18C. Alt. of Latin stilus. See STYLE.

stymie n. in golf, the position when an opponent's ball lies between the player's ball and the hole. Also v.t. WH: 19C. Orig. uncertain. ? Scottish dial. styme in not to see a styme to be unable to see at all, of unknown orig.

styptic a. (of a drug or application) that stops bleeding. Also n. WH: 14–15C. Latin stypticus, from Greek stuptikos, from stuphein to contract. See also -IC.

styrax n. any tree or shrub of the genus Styrax, certain species of which yield benzoin and storax. WH: 16C. Latin, from Greek sturax. Cp. STORAX.

styrofoam *n.* a type of expanded polystyrene. WH: mid-20C. POLY-STYRENE + -O- + FOAM.

suable *a.* capable of being sued. WH: 17C. SUE + -ABLE.

suasion *n.* persuasion as opposed to compulsion. WH: 14–15C. Old French, or from Latin *suasio, suasionis*, from *suasus*, p.p. of *suadere*. See PERSUADE.

suave *a.* agreeable, polite. WH: 14–15C. Old French, or from Latin *suavis* sweet, agreeable. See SWEET. The original sense (to the 16C) was gracious, kindly. The current sense dates from the 19C.

sub- *pref.* to, at or from a lower position, as in *submerge, substratum, subvert*. WH: Latin pref., from prep. *sub* under, close to, up to, towards. For reasons of pronunciation *b* is often assimilated to a subsequent consonant. See SUC-, SUF-, SUG-, SUP-, SUR-², SUS-.

subabdominal *a.* situated below the abdomen. WH: 19C. SUB- + *abdominal* (ABDOMEN).

subacid *a.* slightly acid or sour. *Also n.* WH: 17C. Latin *subacidus*. See SUB-, ACID.

subacute *a.* (of illness) intermediate between acute and chronic. WH: 18C. SUB- + ACUTE.

subadult *a.* (of an animal) not quite adult. *Also n.* WH: early 20C. SUB- + ADULT.

subaerial *a.* being, acting or produced in the open air, as opposed to *submarine, subterranean*, etc. WH: 19C. SUB- + AERIAL.

subagent *n.* a person employed by an agent. WH: 19C. SUB- + AGENT.

subalpine *a.* of or relating to elevated regions not above the timberline. WH: 17C. Latin *subalpinus*. See SUB-, *alpine* (ALP).

subaltern *n.* a junior army officer, one below the rank of captain. *Also a.* WH: 16C. Late Latin *subalternus*, from Latin SUB- + *alternus* every other (see ALTERNATE¹). The literal sense is that of a person subordinate to another.

subantarctic *a.* of or relating to the region bordering on the Antarctic. WH: 19C. SUB- + ANTARCTIC.

subapostolic *a.* of or relating to the period succeeding that of the apostles. WH: 19C. SUB- + *apostolic* (APOSTLE).

sub-aqua *a.* of or relating to underwater sports. WH: mid-20C. SUB- + Latin *aqua* water.

subarctic *a.* of or relating to the region bordering on the Arctic. WH: early 20C. SUB- + ARCTIC.

subassembly *n.* an assembled unit forming part of a larger product. WH: early 20C. SUB- + *assembly* (ASSEMBLE).

subastral *a.* terrestrial. WH: 18C. SUB- + ASTRAL.

subatomic *a.* of or occurring inside an atom. WH: early 20C. SUB- + *atomic* (ATOM).

subaudition *n.* the act of understanding something not expressed or of mentally supplying a missing word etc. WH: 17C. Late Latin *subauditio, subauditionis*, from *subauditus*, p.p. of *subaudire* to supply mentally, from *sub-* SUB- + *audire* to hear, based on Greek *upakouein*.

subaxillary *a.* situated beneath the armpit or the wing cavity, or under the axil formed by a petiole and stem etc. WH: 18C. SUB- + *axillary* (AXIL).

sub-base *n.* the lowest part of a base horizontally divided. WH: 19C. SUB- + BASE¹.

sub-basement *n.* a storey underneath a basement. WH: 19C. SUB- + *basement* (BASE¹).

sub-branch *n.* a subordinate branch. WH: 17C. SUB- + BRANCH.

sub-breed *n.* a secondary or less distinguished breed. WH: 19C. SUB- + BREED.

subcategory *n.* a secondary or subordinate category. WH: early 20C. SUB- + CATEGORY.

subcaudal *a.* situated under the tail, or relating to this part. WH: 18C. SUB- + CAUDAL.

subcelestial *a.* terrestrial. WH: 16C. Late Latin *subcelestis*, from Latin SUB- + *caelestis* CELESTIAL. See also -IAL.

subclass *n.* a secondary or subordinate class. WH: 19C. SUB- + CLASS.

sub-clause *n.* a subsidiary part of a clause. WH: 19C. SUB- + CLAUSE.

subclavian *a.* situated or extending under the clavicle. WH: 17C. Modern Latin *subclavius*, from Latin SUB- + *clavis* key (see CLAVICLE). See also -IAN.

subclinical *a.* having symptoms sufficiently slight as to be undetectable clinically. WH: mid-20C. SUB- + *clinical* (CLINIC).

subcommittee *n.* a small committee appointed from among its members by a larger committee to consider and report on a particular matter. WH: 17C. SUB- + COMMITTEE¹.

subconical *a.* roughly conical. WH: 18C. SUB- + *conical* (CONIC).

subconscious *a.* existing in the mind but without one's full awareness. *Also n.* WH: 19C. SUB- + CONSCIOUS.

subcontinent *n.* a large land mass, not of sufficient size to be a continent. WH: 19C. SUB- + CONTINENT¹.

subcontract¹ *v.t.* to employ a company etc. to carry out (work) as part of a larger project. *Also v.i.* WH: 17C. SUB- + CONTRACT¹.

subcontract² *n.* a secondary or subsidiary contract, e.g. to supply labour, materials or equipment. WH: 19C. SUB- + CONTRACT².

subcontrary *a.* (of a proposition in relation to another differing from it only in quality) contrary in an inferior degree, such that at least one must be true. *Also n.* WH: 16C. Late Latin *subcontrarius*, translating Late Greek *upenantios*. See SUB-, CONTRARY¹.

subcordate *a.* roughly heart-shaped. WH: 18C. SUB- + CORDATE.

subcortical *a.* below the cortex. WH: 19C. SUB- + *cortical* (CORTEX).

subcostal *a.* below the ribs. WH: 19C. SUB- + *costal* (COSTA).

subcranial *a.* below the cranium. WH: 19C. SUB- + *cranial* (CRANIUM).

subcritical *a.* (of or relating to nuclear fuel) of insufficient mass to sustain a chain reaction. WH: mid-20C. SUB- + *critical* (CRITIC).

subculture *n.* a social or ethnic group with a characteristic culture differing from that of the national or predominant culture. WH: 19C. SUB- + CULTURE.

subcutaneous *a.* beneath the skin. WH: 17C. SUB- + CUTANEOUS.

subdeacon *n.* a minister of the church ranking below a deacon. WH: 12–14C. Old French *subdekne*, or from Ecclesiastical Latin *subdiaconus*. See SUB-, DEACON.

subdelirium *n.* a mild or intermittent form of delirium. WH: 19C. SUB- + DELIRIUM.

subdivide *v.t., v.i.* to divide again or into smaller parts. WH: 14–15C. Late Latin *subdividere*. See SUB-, DIVIDE.

subdominant *a., n.* (of or relating to) the tone next below the dominant, the fourth of the scale. WH: 18C. SUB- + DOMINANT.

subduction *n.* the sideways and downward thrust of the edge of a tectonic plate into the mantle beneath another plate. WH: 14–15C. Latin *subductio, subductionis*, from *subductus*, p.p. of *subducere*, from SUB- + *ducere* to lead, to bring.

subdue *v.t.* to conquer, to overcome. WH: 14–15C. Old French *souduire* to deceive, to seduce, from Latin *subducere* to withdraw, to evacuate (see SUBDUCTION). The sense derives from Latin *subditus*, p.p. of *subdere* to conquer, to subdue, from SUB- + *dere* to put.

subdural *a.* sited or occurring between the dura mater and the arachnoid membrane of the brain and spinal chord. WH: 19C. SUB- + *dural*, from DURA MATER + -AL¹.

sub-edit *v.t.* to prepare (a manuscript) for printing. WH: 19C. Back-formation from *sub-editor*. See SUB-, EDIT.

subentry *n.* a subsidiary entry. WH: 19C. SUB- + ENTRY.

suberect *a.* (of an animal or plant) more or less erect. WH: 19C. SUB- + ERECT.

subereous *a.* of the nature or texture of cork; of, relating to or derived from cork. WH: 19C. Late Latin *subereus*, from Latin *suber* cork. See also -EOUS.

subfamily *n.* a taxonomic subdivision of a family. WH: 19C. SUB- + FAMILY.

subfloor *n.* a foundation for a floor. WH: 19C. SUB- + FLOOR.

subform *n.* a secondary form. WH: mid-20C. SUB- + FORM.

sub-frame *n.* a supporting frame, e.g. for a door frame or window frame. WH: early 20C. SUB- + FRAME.

subfusc *a.* dusky, sombre. *Also n.* WH: 18C. Latin *subfuscus*, from SUB- + *fuscus* dark, dusky.

subgenus *n.* a taxonomic subdivision of a genus. WH: 19C. SUB- + GENUS.

subglacial *a.* at the bottom of, or next to, a glacier. WH: early 20C. SUB- + GLACIAL.

sub-group *n.* a subdivision of a group. WH: 19C. SUB- + GROUP.

sub-head *n.* a heading, often explanatory, underneath the main heading of a book, article etc. WH: 19C. SUB- + HEAD¹.

subhuman *a.* less than human or that which is normal to humans. WH: 18C. SUB- + HUMAN.

subimago *n.* a stage in the metamorphosis of certain insects preceding the imago. WH: 19C. SUB- + IMAGO.

subintrant *a.* (of a fever) characterized by paroxysms that succeed each other so rapidly as to be almost continuous. WH: 17C. Latin *subintrans*, *subintrantis*, pres.p. of *subintrare* to steal in, from SUB- + *intrare* ENTER. See also -ANT.

sub-irrigation *n.* irrigation by underground pipes. WH: 19C. SUB- + *irrigation* (IRRIGATE).

subito *adv.* suddenly, immediately. WH: 18C. Italian suddenly, from Latin *subitus* sudden, unexpected.

subjacent *a.* underlying; lower in position. WH: 16C. Latin *subiacens*, *subiacentis*, pres.p. of *subiacere* to lie below, from SUB- + *iacere* to lie.

subject¹ *n.* the topic under consideration. *Also a.* WH: 12–14C. Old French *suget* (Modern French *sujet*), from Latin *subiectus*, p.p. of *subicere*, from SUB- + *iacere* to throw, to cast.

subject² *v.t.* to expose, to make liable (to). WH: 14–15C. Old French *subjecter* or Latin *subiectare*, freq. of *subicere*. See SUBJECT¹.

subjoin *v.t.* to add at the end, to append, to affix. WH: 16C. Obs. French *subjoindre*, from Latin *subiungere*, from SUB- + *iungere*. See JOIN.

sub judice *a.* under consideration, esp. by a court or judge. WH: 17C. Latin, lit. under a judge, from *sub* under + abl. sing. of *iudex* judge.

subjugate *v.t.* to subdue, to conquer, to bring into subjection, to enslave. WH: 14–15C. Latin *subiugatus*, p.p. of *subiugare*, from SUB- + *iugum* yoke. See also -ATE³.

subjunctive *a.* denoting the mood of a verb expressing condition, wishes, hypothesis or contingency. *Also n.* WH: 16C. French *subjonctif* or Late Latin *subjunctivus*, from Latin *subiunctus*, p.p. of *subiungere* SUBJOIN. See also -IVE. Late Latin *subjunctivus* probably translates Greek *hupotaktikos* subordinated, so called because in Greek the subjunctive mood is used almost exclusively in subordinate clauses.

subkingdom *n.* a primary division of the animal or plant kingdom. WH: 19C. SUB- + *kingdom* (KING).

sublapsarian *n.* any member of a group of moderate Calvinists believing that God permitted the Fall of Adam without preordaining it; an infralapsarian. *Also a.* WH: 17C. Modern Latin *sublapsarius*. See SUB-, LAPSE, also -ARIAN.

sublate *v.t.* to treat as untrue, to deny. WH: 16C. Latin *sublat-*, from SUB- + *latus*, p.p. of *tollere* to take away.

sub-lease¹ *n.* a lease of property by a tenant or lessee. WH: 19C. SUB- + LEASE.

sub-lease² *v.t.* to grant or obtain a sublease of (property). WH: 19C. SUB- + LEASE.

sub-let¹ *n.* a sub-letting, a sub-lease. WH: 18C. SUB- + LET¹.

sub-let² *v.t.* to sub-lease, to let (property already rented or held on lease). WH: 18C. SUB- + LET¹.

sublibrarian *n.* a subordinate librarian. WH: 18C. SUB- + *librarian* (LIBRARY).

sub-lieutenant *n.* a British naval officer next in rank below a lieutenant. WH: 18C. SUB- + LIEUTENANT.

sublimate¹ *v.t.* to divert by sublimation. WH: 14–15C. Latin *sublimatus*, p.p. of *sublimare* SUBLIME. See also -ATE³. The original sense was to sublime. The current sense arose only in the early 20C, first recorded in A.A. Brill's 1910 translation of Freud's *Drei Abhandlungen zur Sexualtheorie* (*Three Essays on the Theory of Sexuality*) (1905).

sublimate² *n.* the product of sublimation. WH: 16C. Latin *sublimatum*, neut. p.p. (used as n.) of *sublimare*. See SUBLIME, also -ATE¹.

sublime *a.* of the most lofty or exalted nature. *Also v.t., v.i.* WH: 16C. Latin *sublimis*, from SUB- + an element prob. either from *limen* threshold or *limen* oblique. The verb *sublime* dates from the 14–15C and derives from Old French *sublimer* or Latin *sublimare* to lift up, to elevate, from *sublimis*.

subliminal *a.* not reaching the threshold of consciousness, hardly perceived. WH: 19C. SUB- + Latin *limen*, *liminis* threshold + -AL¹, orig. translating German *unter der Schwelle* (*das Bewusstseins*) below the threshold (of consciousness). The German phrase was used by the German philosopher, psychologist and educator Johann Friedrich Herbart, 1776–1841.

sublingual *a.* under the tongue. WH: 17C. SUB- + LINGUAL.

sublittoral *a.* (of plants, creatures etc.) found close to the low-water mark on the seashore. WH: 19C. SUB- + LITTORAL.

sublunary *a.* situated beneath the moon. WH: 17C. Late Latin *sublunaris*. See SUB-, LUNAR, also -ARY¹.

subluxation *n.* partial dislocation. WH: 17C. SUB- + *luxation* (LUXATE).

sub-machine gun *n.* a light automatic or semiautomatic rapid-firing gun fired from the hip or shoulder. WH: early 20C. SUB- + *machine-gun*. See MACHINE, GUN.

subman *n.* a brutal, subhuman or stupid person. WH: early 20C. SUB- + MAN.

submarginal *a.* not meeting minimum requirements, esp. in economic terms. WH: 19C. SUB- + MARGINAL.

submarine *n.* a vessel, esp. a warship, that may be submerged, equipped with a periscope. *Also a.* WH: 17C. SUB- + MARINE.

submaster *n.* an assistant master in, or the assistant headmaster of, a school. WH: 14–15C. SUB- + MASTER.

submaxillary *a.* of or relating to the lower jaw, esp. to a pair of salivary glands situated beneath it. WH: 18C. SUB- + *maxillary* (MAXILLA).

submediant *a., n.* (of) the sixth note of the diatonic scale. WH: 19C. SUB- + MEDIANT.

submental *a.* situated below the chin. WH: 19C. SUB- + MENTAL².

submerge *v.t.* to put under water etc., to flood. *Also v.i.* WH: 17C. Latin *submergere*. See SUB-, MERGE.

submicroscopic *a.* too small to be viewed under a normal microscope. WH: early 20C. SUB- + *microscopic* (MICROSCOPE).

subminiature *a.* of very reduced size. WH: mid-20C. SUB- + MINIATURE.

submission *n.* the act of submitting, or the process of being submitted. WH: 14–15C. Old French, or from Latin *submissio*, *submissionis*, from *submissus*, p.p. of *submittere* SUBMIT.

submit *v.t.* to yield or surrender (oneself) to the domination of someone else. *Also v.i.* WH: 14–15C. Latin *submittere*, from SUB- + *mittere* to send, to put. The original sense was to place (oneself) under a particular control or authority.

submontane *a.* situated at the foot of a mountain or range of mountains. WH: 19C. SUB- + MONTANE.

submultiple *n.* a number capable of dividing another without remainder, a factor or aliquot part. WH: 17C. Late Latin *submultiplus*, from SUB- + *multiplus* MULTIPLE.

subnivean *a.* situated beneath the snow. WH: 19C. SUB- + Latin *niveus* of snow, from *nix*, *nivis* snow. See also -AN.

subnormal *a.* less than normal, below the normal standard. WH: early 20C. SUB- + NORMAL.

sub-nuclear *a.* occurring in, or smaller than, an atomic nucleus. WH: mid-20C. SUB- + NUCLEAR.

subocular *a.* situated below the eyes. WH: 19C. SUB- + OCULAR.

suboptimal *a.* less than optimal; not of the best kind or quality. WH: early 20C. SUB- + *optimal* (OPTIMUM).

sub-orbital *a.* beneath the orbit of the eye. WH: 19C. SUB- + *orbital* (ORBIT).

suborder *n.* a subdivision of a taxonomic order. WH: 19C. SUB- + ORDER.

subordinary *n.* a device or bearing that is common, but not as common as an ordinary. WH: 18C. SUB- + ORDINARY.

subordinate¹ *a.* inferior (to) in rank, importance etc. *Also n.* WH: 14–15C. Medieval Latin *subordinatus*, p.p. of *subordinare*. See SUBORDINATE², also -ATE¹.

subordinate² *v.t.* to make subordinate. WH: 16C. Medieval Latin *subordinatus*, p.p. of *subordinare*, from SUB- + *ordinare* ORDAIN. See also -ATE³.

suborn *v.t.* to induce (e.g. a witness) by underhand means, esp. bribery, to commit perjury or some other criminal act. WH: 16C. Latin *subornare*, from SUB- + *ornare* to equip.

suboxide *n.* an oxide of an element that contains less oxygen than its common oxide. WH: 19C. SUB- + OXIDE.

subpanation *n.* the doctrine that the body and blood of Christ are locally and materially present in the Eucharist in the form of the bread and wine. WH: 17C. Medieval Latin *subpanatio*, *subpanationis*, from *subpanatus*, p.p. of *subpanare*, from SUB- + *panis* bread. See also -ATION.

subphylum n. a taxonomic subdivision of a phylum. WH: 19C. SUB- + PHYLUM.

sub-plot n. a secondary or subordinate plot in a novel, play etc. WH: early 20C. SUB- + PLOT.

subpoena n. a writ commanding a person's attendance in a court of justice under a penalty. Also v.t. WH: 14–15C. Latin *sub poena* under penalty, the first words on the writ.

sub-postmaster n. a person in charge of a sub-post office. WH: 17C. SUB- + *postmaster*. See POST³, MASTER.

sub-post office n. a small local post office offering a restricted range of services. WH: early 20C. SUB- + *post office*. See POST³, OFFICE.

subprogram n. a subroutine. WH: mid-20C. SUB- + *program* (PROGRAMME).

subregion n. a division of a region, esp. in relation to natural life. WH: 19C. SUB- + REGION.

subreption n. the act of obtaining something by surprise or fraudulent representation. WH: 17C. Latin *subreptio, subreptionis*, from *subreptus*, p.p. of *subripere*, from SUB- + *rapere* to snatch. See also -ION. Cp. SURREPTITIOUS.

subrogation n. the substitution of one person in the place of another with succession to their rights to a debt etc. WH: 14–15C. Late Latin *subrogatio, subrogationis*, from Latin *subrogatus*, p.p. of *subrogare*, from SUB- + *rogare* to ask, to offer for election. See also -ATION.

sub rosa adv. secretly. WH: 17C. Latin, lit. under the rose. The rose was formerly an emblem of secrecy.

subroutine n. a sequence of computer instructions for a particular, usu. recurring, task that can be used at any point in a program. WH: mid-20C. SUB- + ROUTINE.

sub-Saharan a. of, relating to or forming part of the regions of Africa south of the Sahara Desert. WH: mid-20C. SUB- + *Saharan*, from *Sahara*, the great desert in N Africa + -AN.

subscribe v.t. to contribute or pledge to contribute (an annual or other specified sum) to or for a fund etc. Also v.i. WH: 14–15C. Latin *subscribere*, from SUB- + *scribere* to write.

subsection n. a subdivision of a section. WH: 17C. SUB- + SECTION.

subsellium n. a misericord. WH: 18C. Latin, from SUB- + *sella* seat.

subsequence n. WH: early 20C. SUB- + SEQUENCE.

subsequent a. coming immediately after in time or order; following. WH: 14–15C. Old French *subséquent*, or from Latin *subsequens, subsequentis*, pres.p. of *subsequi*, from SUB- + *sequi* to follow. See also -ENT.

subserve v.t. to serve as a means or instrument in promoting (an end etc.). WH: 14–15C. Latin *subservire*. See SUB-, SERVE.

subset n. a set contained within a larger set. WH: early 20C. SUB- + SET².

subshrub n. a low-growing woody plant with nonwoody tips. WH: 19C. SUB- + SHRUB¹.

subside v.i. to settle down, to become tranquil. WH: Latin *subsidere*, from SUB- + *sidere* to sit down.

subsidiary a. auxiliary, supplemental. Also n. WH: 16C. Latin *subsidiarius*, from *subsidium*. See SUBSIDY, also -ARY¹.

subsidy n. money granted by the state or a public body to keep down the price of essential commodities. WH: 14–15C. Old French *subside*, from Latin *subsidium* reserve of troops, support, assistance, rel. to *subsidere*, from SUB- + *sedere* SIT.

subsist v.i. to exist, to remain in existence. Also v.t. WH: 16C. Latin *subsistere* to stand still, to stand firm, to cease, from SUB- + *sistere* to stand.

subsoil n. the stratum of earth immediately below the surface soil. WH: 18C. SUB- + SOIL¹.

subsonic a. of, relating to, using or travelling at speeds less than that of sound. WH: mid-20C. SUB- + SONIC.

subspecies n. a taxonomic subdivision of a species. WH: 17C. SUB- + SPECIES.

substage n. an apparatus underneath the stage of a microscope carrying the condenser etc. WH: 19C. SUB- + STAGE.

substance n. that of which a thing consists. WH: 12–14C. Old French, from Latin *substantia* being, essence, material property, from *substans, substantis*, pres.p. of *substare*, from SUB- + *stare* to stand. See also -ANCE.

sub-standard a. below an accepted or acceptable standard. WH: early 20C. SUB- + STANDARD.

substantial a. of considerable importance, amount etc. Also n. WH: 12–14C. Old French *substantiel*, or Latin *substantialis*, from *substantia*. See SUBSTANCE, also -AL¹.

substantiate v.t. to establish, to prove. WH: 17C. Medieval Latin *substantiatus*, p.p. of *substantiare* to give substance to, from Latin *substantia* SUBSTANCE. See also -ATE³.

substantive a. independently existent, not merely implied, inferential or subsidiary. Also n. WH: 14–15C. Old French *substantif* or Late Latin *substantivus*, from *substantia* SUBSTANCE. See also -IVE.

sub-station n. a subsidiary station, esp. one in which electric current from a generating station is modified before distribution. WH: 19C. SUB- + STATION.

substituent a. (of a group of atoms) replacing another atom or group in a compound. Also n. WH: 19C. Latin *substituens, substituentis*, pres.p. of *substituere* SUBSTITUTE.

substitute n. a person or thing put in the place of or serving for another. Also v.t., v.i. WH: 14–15C. Latin *substitutus*, p.p. of *substituere*, from SUB- + *statuere* to set up.

substratum n. that which underlies anything. WH: 17C. Modern Latin, use as n. of neut. p.p. of Latin *substernere*, from SUB- + *sternere*. See STRATUM.

substructure n. an understructure or foundation. WH: 18C. SUB- + STRUCTURE.

substyle n. the line on which the style or gnomon of a dial stands. WH: 16C. SUB- + STYLE.

subsume v.t. to include under a more general class or category. WH: 16C. Medieval Latin *subsumere*, from SUB- + *sumere* to take.

subsurface n. the stratum or strata below the surface of the earth. Also a. WH: 18C. SUB- + SURFACE.

subsystem n. a system within a larger system. WH: 19C. SUB- + SYSTEM.

subtangent n. the portion of the axis of a curve intercepted between an ordinate and a tangent both drawn from the same point. WH: 18C. SUB- + TANGENT.

subtemperate a. of or relating to slightly colder than temperate regions. WH: 19C. SUB- + TEMPERATE.

subtenant n. a tenant holding property from someone who is also a tenant. WH: 14–15C. SUB- + TENANT.

subtend v.t. (of a chord relatively to án arc, or the side of a triangle to an angle) to extend under or be opposite to. WH: 16C. Latin *subtendere*, from SUB- + *tendere* to stretch.

subterfuge n. a deception, prevarication etc. used to avoid an inference, censure etc., or to evade or conceal something. WH: 16C. French, or from Late Latin *subterfugium*, from Latin *subterfugere* to escape secretly, from *subter* below, underneath + *fugere* to flee.

subterminal a. almost at the end. WH: 19C. SUB- + TERMINAL.

subterranean a. underground. WH: 17C. Latin *subterraneus*, from SUB- + *terra* earth. See also -AN, -EAN.

subtext n. an unstated message or theme in a speech or piece of writing, conveyed in the tone of voice, choice of words etc. WH: 18C. SUB- + TEXT.

subtilize v.t. to make subtle. Also v.i. WH: 16C. French *subtiliser* or Medieval Latin *subtilizare*, from Latin *subtilis* SUBTLE. See also -IZE.

subtitle n. an additional or subsidiary title of a book etc. Also v.t. WH: 19C. SUB- + TITLE.

subtle a. delicate, elusive. WH: 12–14C. Old French *sutil*, from Latin *subtilis*.

subtonic n. the note next below the tonic. Also a. WH: 19C. SUB- + TONIC.

subtopia n. unsightly suburbs, badly planned rural or urban areas. WH: mid-20C. Blend of SUBURB and UTOPIA. The term was coined in 1955 by the British architect Ian Nairn.

subtopic n. a secondary topic. WH: 19C. SUB- + TOPIC.

subtotal n. the total resulting from adding a group of figures which form part of the overall total. WH: early 20C. SUB- + TOTAL.

subtract v.t. to take away (a part, quantity etc.) from the rest. WH: 16C. Latin *subtractus*, p.p. of *subtrahere*, from SUB- + *trahere* to draw.

subtriangular *a.* approximately triangular. WH: 18C. SUB- + *triangular* (TRIANGLE).

subtribe *n.* a subdivision of a tribe. WH: 19C. SUB- + TRIBE.

subtriplicate *a.* expressed by the cube root. WH: 17C. SUB- + *triplicate* (TRIPLE).

subtropical *a.* characterized by features common to both the temperate and tropical zones. WH: 19C. SUB- + *tropical* (TROPIC).

subulate *a.* awl-shaped. WH: 18C. Latin *subula* awl + -ATE[2].

subungulate *a.* hoofed, but having several digits. WH: 19C. SUB- + *ungulate* (UNGULA).

subunit *n.* a distinct part, esp. one of the polypeptide chains in a large protein. WH: mid-20C. SUB- + UNIT.

suburb *n.* an outlying part of a city or town. WH: 12–14C. Old French *suburbe* or Latin *suburbium*, from SUB- + *urbs* city.

subvariety *n.* a subdivision of a variety. WH: 19C. SUB- + VARIETY.

subvene *v.i.* to happen so as to aid or effect a result. WH: 18C. Latin *subvenire*, from SUB- + *venire* to come.

subvert *v.t.* to overthrow, to destroy, to overturn. WH: 14–15C. Old French *subvertir* or Latin *subvertere*, from SUB- + *vertere* to turn.

subvocal *a.* subtonic. WH: mid-20C. SUB- + VOCAL.

subway *n.* an underground passage, tunnel, conduit etc. WH: 19C. SUB- + WAY.

subwoofer *n.* a component in a loudspeaker which reproduces very low bass frequencies. WH: late 20C. SUB- + *woofer* (WOOF[1]).

sub-zero *a.* below zero (degrees). WH: mid-20C. SUB- + ZERO.

suc- *pref.* to, at or from a lower position, as in *succeed, succinct.* WH: Latin *pref.*, from SUB- with *b* assim. to *c*.

succade *n.* a fruit candied and preserved in syrup. WH: 14–15C. Old Northern French, of unknown orig. See also -ADE.

succedaneum *n.* something used instead of something else, a substitute. WH: 17C. Modern Latin, neut. sing. of Latin *succedaneus*, from *succedere* to come close after. See SUCCEED.

succeed *v.i.* to be successful, to end well or prosperously. *Also v.t.* WH: 14–15C. Old French *succéder* or Latin *succedere* to go under, to go up, to come close after, to go near, from SUC- + *cedere* to go. The senses to come after and to be successful have both been current from the first.

succentor *n.* a deputy precentor in a cathedral. WH: 17C. Late Latin, from Latin *succinere* to sing to, to accompany, to agree, from SUC- + *canere* to sing. See also -OR.

succès de scandale *n.* success owing to notoriety. WH: 19C. French, lit. scandalous success.

success *n.* the act of succeeding, favourable result. WH: 16C. Latin *successus*, from p.p. of *succedere* SUCCEED.

succession *n.* a following in order. WH: 12–14C. Old French, or from Latin *successio, successionis*, from *successus*. See SUCCESS, also -ION.

successive *a.* following in order or uninterrupted succession, consecutive. WH: 14–15C. Medieval Latin *successivus*, from Latin *successus*. See SUCCESS, also -IVE.

succinct *a.* compressed into few words, concise. WH: 14–15C. Latin *succinctus*, p.p. of *succingere*, from SUC- + *cingere* to gird.

succinite *n.* amber; a yellow variety of garnet. WH: 19C. Latin *succinum* + -ITE[1].

succory *n.* chicory. WH: 16C. Alt. of obs. French *cicorée* (CHICORY), based on Middle Low German *suckerie*, Middle Dutch *sūkerie*.

succose *a.* juicy. WH: 19C. Latin *succosus*, from *succus* juice. See also -OSE[1].

succotash *n.* a dish made of green maize and beans cooked together. WH: 18C. Narragansett *msiquatash* (pl.). Cp. SQUASH[2].

Succoth *n.* the Jewish harvest festival commemorating the Israelites' sheltering in the wilderness. WH: 19C. Hebrew *sukkōt*, pl. of *sukkāh*, lit. hut. The festival's alternative English name is *Feast of Tabernacles* (TABERNACLE).

succour *n.* aid in time of difficulty or distress. *Also v.t.* WH: 12–14C. Old French *sucurs* (Modern French *secours*), from Medieval Latin *succursus*, from Latin, p.p. of *succurrere*, from SUC- + *currere* to run.

succuba *n.* a demon believed to assume the shape of a woman and have sexual intercourse with men in their sleep. WH: 16C. Late Latin prostitute, from *succubare*, from SUC- + *cubare* to lie. A variant

form *succubus* dates from the 14–15C as a Medieval Latin masculine form (with feminine meaning) corresponding to *succuba*, based on INCUBUS.

succulent *a.* juicy and delicious. *Also n.* WH: 17C. Latin *succulentus*, from *succus* juice. See also -LENT, -ULENT.

succumb *v.i.* to yield, to submit (to). WH: 15C. Old French *succomber* or Latin *succumbere*, from SUC- + *-cumbere* to lie. The original sense was to bring down, to bring low, to overwhelm. The current sense dates from the 17C.

succursal *a.* (of an ecclesiastical building, such as a chapel of ease) auxiliary. WH: 19C. French *succursale*, from Medieval Latin *succursus*. See SUCCOUR, also -AL[1].

succus *n.* a body juice or fluid secretion. WH: 18C. Latin juice.

succuss *v.t.* to shake suddenly, esp. in medical diagnosis. WH: 19C. Latin *succursus*, p.p. of *succutere*, from SUC- + *quatere* to shake.

such *a.* of that, or the same, or the like kind or degree (as). *Also adv., pron.* WH: pre-1200. Old English *swilc, swelc, swylc*, ult. from Germanic base of SO, ALIKE. Cp. ILK, WHICH.

suck *v.t.* to draw (milk etc.) into the mouth by the action of the lips. *Also v.i., n.* WH: pre-1200. Old English *sūcan*, rel. to Latin *sugere*, from Indo-European base of imit. orig. Rel. to SOAK.

suckle *v.t.* to give milk from the breast or udder to. *Also v.i.* WH: 14–15C. Prob. back-formation from *suckling*, from SUCK + -LING[1], prob. based on Middle Dutch *sūgeling* (Dutch *zuigeling*).

sucre *n.* the standard unit of currency of Ecuador. WH: 19C. Antonio José de *Sucre*, 1795–1830, S American popular leader, who fought under Simón Bolívar (BOLIVAR) against Spanish rule.

sucrose *n.* sugar as obtained from sugar cane or sugar beet. WH: 19C. French *sucre* SUGAR + -OSE[2].

suction *n.* the act or process of sucking. WH: 17C. Late Latin *suctio, suctionis*, from Latin *suctus*, p.p. of *sugere*. See SUCK, also -TION.

sudamina *n.pl.* minute transparent vesicles arising from a disorder of the sweat glands. WH: 16C. Modern Latin, pl. of *sudamen*, from Latin *sudare* to sweat.

Sudanese *a.* of or relating to Sudan. *Also n.* WH: 19C. *Sudan*, a region and republic in NE Africa + -ESE.

sudatory *a.* promoting perspiration. *Also n.* WH: 14–15C. Latin *sudatio, sudationis*, from *sudatus*, p.p. of *sudare* to sweat. See also -ORY[2].

sudd *n.* a floating mass of vegetation, trees etc. obstructing navigation in the White Nile. WH: 19C. Arabic obstruction, dam, from *sadda* to obstruct, to block, to congest.

sudden *a.* happening unexpectedly, without warning. WH: 12–14C. Old French *soudain*, from Late Latin *subitanus*, alt. of Latin *subitaneus*, from *subitus* sudden.

sudoriferous *a.* producing or secreting perspiration. WH: 16C. Late Latin *sudorifer*, from Latin *sudor* sweat + -OUS. See also -FEROUS.

Sudra *n.* a member of the lowest of the four great Hindu castes. WH: 17C. Sanskrit *śūdra*.

suds *n.pl.* soapy water forming a frothy mass. *Also v.i., v.t.* WH: 19C. Pl. of *sud* (16C), prob. from Middle Low German and Middle Dutch *sudde*, Middle Dutch *sudse* marsh, bog, from Germanic base also of SEETHE. See also -S[1].

sue *v.t.* to prosecute or to pursue a claim (for) by legal process. *Also v.i.* WH: 12–14C. Anglo-French *suer*, from *siu-, seu-*, pres. stem of Old French *sivre* (Modern French *suivre*), from Popular Latin *sequere*, from Latin *sequi* to follow. The original sense was generally to follow, but the sense to take legal action also dates from the first.

suede *n.* undressed kid or similar leather given a nap surface by rubbing. *Also a.* WH: 17C. French (*gants de*) *Suède* (gloves of) Sweden.

suet *n.* the hard fat about the kidneys and loins of oxen, sheep etc. WH: 12–14C. Ult. from Old French *seu, siu, sif* (Modern French *suif*), from Latin *sebum* fallow, suet, grease.

suf- *pref.* to, at or from a lower position, as in *suffix, suffuse.* WH: Latin *pref.*, from SUB- with *b* assim. to *f*.

suffer *v.i.* to undergo or endure pain, grief, injury, loss etc. *Also v.t.* WH: 12–14C. Old French *soffrir* (Modern French *souffrir*), from Popular Latin *sufferire*, from Latin *sufferre*, from SUF- + *ferre* to bear. The sense to tolerate dates from the first, but the sense to allow (a thing to be done) became obsolete in the 17C.

suffice *v.i.* to be enough, to be adequate or sufficient (for or to do etc.). *Also v.t.* WH: 12–14C. Old French *suffire*, *suffis-*, from Latin *sufficere*, from SUF- + *facere* to make, to do. An early sense (to the 19C) was to have the capacity for doing something, to be competent.

suffix[1] *n.* a letter or syllable appended to the end of a word to form an inflection or derivative. WH: 18C. Modern Latin *suffixum*, use as n. of neut. of *suffixus*, p.p. of Latin *suffigere*, from SUF- + *figere* FIX.

suffix[2] *v.t.* to add as a suffix, to append. WH: 17C. Partly from Latin *suffixus* (SUFFIX[1]), partly from SUFFIX[1].

suffocate *v.t.* to choke, to kill by stopping respiration. *Also v.i.*, *a.* WH: 15C. Latin *suffocatus*, p.p. of *suffocare*, from SUF- + *fauces* throat. See also -ATE[3].

Suffolk *n.* a breed of black-faced sheep. WH: 16C. *Suffolk*, a county in SE England, forming part of E Anglia.

suffragan *a.* assisting: denoting a bishop consecrated to assist another bishop or any bishop in relation to the metropolitan. *Also n.* WH: 14–15C. Old French, from Medieval Latin *suffraganeus*, from Latin *suffragium*. See SUFFRAGE, -AN. The bishop is so called because he may be summoned by his archbishop to attend synods and give his 'suffrage', i.e. support.

suffrage *n.* the right to vote, esp. in parliamentary elections. WH: 14–15C. Latin *suffragium*, from *suffragari* to express support, to vote for, from SUF- + *fragor* noise of breaking, din, outbreak of shouts (of approval from a crowd).

suffruticose *a.* having a woody perennial base with nonwoody branches. WH: 18C. Modern Latin *suffruticosus*, from *suffrutex*. See SUF-, FRUTEX, also -OSE[1].

suffuse *v.t.* (of a blush, fluid etc.) to overspread from within. WH: 16C. Latin *suffusus*, p.p. of *suffundere*, from SUF- + *fundere* to pour.

Sufi *n.* a Muslim pantheistic philosopher and mystic. WH: 17C. Arabic *ṣūfī*, lit. woollen, prob. from *ṣūf* wool. The mystic is so called from the rough woollen garment associated with ascetics. The word is not related to SOPHY.

sug *v.t.* to pretend to be conducting market research while actually trying to sell a product to. WH: late 20C. Acronym of *sell under guise*.

sug- *pref.* to, at or from a lower position, as in *suggest*. WH: Latin pref., from SUB- with *b* assim. to *g*.

sugar *n.* a sweet, crystalline substance obtained from the expressed juice of various plants, esp. the sugar cane and the sugar beet. *Also v.t.* WH: 12–14C. Old French *çukre*, *sukere* (Modern French *sucre*), from Italian *zucchero*, prob. from Medieval Latin *succarum*, from Arabic *sukkar*, from Persian *shakar*, from Prakrit *śakara*, from Sanskrit *śarkarā*. Cp. SACCHAR-. The word is common to all European languages: French *sucre*, Italian *zucchero*, Spanish *azúcar*, German *Zucker*, Dutch *suiker*, Russian *sakhar*, Polish *cukier*, Hungarian *czukor*, Finnish *sokeri*, Modern Greek *zakharē*, Turkish *şeker*, Irish *siúcra*, Welsh *siwgr*, etc.

suggest *v.t.* to propose (a plan, idea etc.) for consideration. WH: 16C. Latin *suggestus*, p.p. of *suggerere*, from SUG- + *gerere* to bear, to carry.

suicide *n.* the act of intentionally taking one's own life. *Also a.*, *v.i.* WH: 17C. Modern Latin *suicidium*, *suicida*, from Latin *sui* of oneself. See -CIDE.

sui generis *a.* unique, of its own kind. WH: 18C. Latin of its own kind, gen. of *suus genus* own kind. Cp. GENUS.

sui juris *a.* of age; legally competent. WH: 17C. Latin, lit. of one's own right, gen. of *suus ius* own law.

suilline *a.* piglike. *Also n.* WH: 19C. Medieval Latin *suillinus*, from Latin *suillus*, from *sus*, *su-* pig.

suint *n.* the natural grease of wool. WH: 18C. French, from *suer* to sweat.

suit *n.* a set of outer clothes (now usu. a jacket and trousers or a skirt), esp. when made of the same cloth. *Also v.t.*, *v.i.* WH: 12–14C. Old French *siute* (Modern French *suite*), from Popular Latin *sequita*, fem. of *sequitus*, alt. of Latin *secutus*, p.p. of *sequi* to follow. Cp. SUE.

suite *n.* a set (of connecting rooms, matching furniture etc.). WH: 17C. French. See SUIT.

suitor *n.* a man who wants to marry a particular woman. WH: 12–14C. Anglo-French *seutor*, *suitour*, from Latin *secutor* follower, from *secutus*, p.p. of *sequi* to follow. See SUE, also -OR.

suivez *v.i.* a direction to an accompanist to follow the tempo of the soloist. WH: 19C. French follow, 2nd pers. pl. imper. of *suivre* to follow.

sukiyaki *n.* a Japanese dish of thin slices of meat and vegetables cooked together with soy sauce, saki etc. WH: early 20C. Japanese, from *suki* spade + *yaki* roasting.

sulcate *a.* having longitudinal furrows, grooves or channels. WH: 18C. Latin *sulcatus*, from *sulcus* furrow, trench, ditch. See also -ATE[2].

sulk *v.i.* to be silent and bad-tempered. *Also n.* WH: 18C. ? Back-formation from *sulky*, ? from obs. *sulke* hard to sell, ? from base of Old English *āseolcan* to become sluggish. The horse-drawn vehicle *sulky* (18C) is apparently so called because it has room for only one person. Cp. SULLEN.

sullage *n.* filth, refuse; sewage; silt. WH: 16C. ? Anglo-French *suillage*. See SOIL[2], also -AGE.

sullen *a.* persistently morose, cross. *Also n.pl.* WH: 12–14C. Anglo-French *sulein*, *solein*, from *sol*, corr. to Old French *soule* SOLE[3]. The original sense (to the 15C) was single, sole, also strange, unusual.

sully *v.t.* to defile, to disgrace. *Also v.i.*, *n.* WH: 16C. ? French *souiller* SOIL[2].

sulph- *comb. form* containing sulphur. WH: SULPHUR. See also -O-.

sulpha *n.* any drug derived from sulphonamide. WH: mid-20C. Abbr. of SULPHANILAMIDE.

sulphadiazine *n.* a sulpha drug used to treat pneumonia and meningitis. WH: mid-20C. SULPHA + *diazine*, from DI-[2] + AZINE.

sulphadimidine *n.* a sulpha drug used to treat urinary infections in humans and respiratory disease in pigs. WH: mid-20C. SULPHA + DI-[2] + PYRIMIDINE.

sulphamic acid *n.* an amide of sulphuric acid, used in weedkiller. WH: 19C. SULPH- + AMIDE + -IC + ACID.

sulphanilamide *n.* a sulphonamide drug administered orally and by injection for combating streptococcal and other bacterial diseases. WH: mid-20C. SULPH- + *anilic* (from ANIL + -IC) + AMIDE.

sulphate *n.* a salt of sulphuric acid. WH: 18C. French *sulfate*, from Latin SULPHUR. See also -ATE[1].

sulphide *n.* a compound of sulphur, with an element or radical. WH: 19C. SULPHUR + -IDE.

sulphite *n.* a salt of sulphurous acid. WH: 18C. French *sulfite*, arbitrary alt. of *sulfate* sulphate. See also -ITE[1].

sulphonamide *n.* an amide of a sulphonic acid. WH: 19C. SULPHONE + AMIDE.

sulphonate *n.* a salt or ester of sulphonic acid. *Also v.t.* WH: 19C. From *sulphonic* (SULPHONE) + -ATE[1].

sulphone *n.* an organic compound containing the divalent group SO_2 linked to two carbon atoms. WH: 19C. German *Sulfon*, from *Sulfur* sulphur. See also -ONE.

sulphur *n.* a pale yellow non-metallic element, at. no. 16, chem. symbol S, insoluble in water, occurring in crystalline or amorphous forms, used in the manufacture of chemicals, gunpowder, matches etc. *Also a.* WH: 12–14C. Old French *soufre*, from Latin *sulfur*, *sulphur*, ? from a Mediterranean language. The native Old English word was BRIMSTONE.

sultan *n.* a Muslim sovereign, esp. a former ruler of Turkey. WH: 16C. French, or from Medieval Latin *sultanus*, from Arabic *sulṭān* power, ruler.

sultry *a.* very hot, close and heavy. WH: 16C. From obs. *sulter* to swelter, of unknown orig. (? Rel. to SWELTER). See also -Y[1].

sum *n.* the aggregate of two or more numbers, the total. *Also v.t.* WH: 12–14C. Old French *summe* (Modern French *somme*), from Latin *summa* main thing, substance, sum total, use as n. of fem. of *summus* highest. Cp. SUMMIT.

sumac *n.* a tree or shrub of the genus *Rhus or Cotinus*, the dried and powdered leaves of which are used in tanning, dyeing etc. WH: 12–14C. Old French, or from Medieval Latin *sumach*, from Arabic *summāḳ*.

Sumatran *a.* of or relating to Sumatra. *Also n.* WH: 17C. *Sumatra*, an island of the Malay Archipelago, now part of Indonesia + -AN.

Sumerian *a.* of or relating to Sumer. *Also n.* WH: 19C. French *sumérien*, from *Sumer*, a district in SE Mesopotamia (now S Iraq) + -IAN.

summa *n.* a comprehensive survey of a subject. WH: 14–15C. Latin. See SUM.

summa cum laude *adv., a.* with the highest distinction. WH: 19C. Latin, lit. with the highest praise, from *cum* with + abl. of *summa laus* highest praise.

summary *n.* an abridged or condensed statement. *Also a.* WH: 16C. Latin *summarium*, from *summa*. See SUM, also -ARY¹. The adjective *summary* dates from the 14–15C and derives from Medieval Latin *summarius*, from Latin *summarium*.

summation *n.* the act or process of making a sum, addition. WH: 18C. SUM + -ATION.

summer¹ *n.* the season of the year when the sun shines most directly upon a region, the warmest season of the year. *Also a., v.i., v.t.* WH: pre-1200. Old English *sumor*, from Germanic, rel. to Sanskrit *samā* year, Avestan *ham-* summer. Cp. German *Sommer*.

summer² *n.* a heavy horizontal beam or glider. WH: 12–14C. Old French *somier* (Modern French *sommier*), from Late Latin *sagmarius*, from *sagma*, from Greek *sagma* packsaddle.

summit *n.* the highest point, the top. WH: 14–15C. Old French *somet* (Modern French *sommet*), from *som, sum*, from Latin *summum*, neut. sing. of *summus* (SUM).

summon *v.t.* to call or command to meet or attend. WH: 12–14C. Old French *sumun-, sumon-*, pres. stem of *somondre* (Modern French *semondre*), from Popular Latin *summonere*, from Latin, from SUB- + *monere* to warn.

summons *n.* the act of summoning. *Also v.t.* WH: 12–14C. Old French *somonce* (Modern French *semonce*), from alt. of Latin *summonita*, fem. p.p. (used as n.) of *summonere* SUMMON.

summum bonum *n.* the highest or supreme good. WH: 16C. Latin highest good.

summum genus *n.* a genus which cannot be considered as a species of another genus. WH: 16C. Latin highest kind.

sumo *n.* traditional Japanese wrestling in which a contestant attempts to force his opponent out of the designated area or to touch the ground with a part of the body other than the feet. *Also a.* WH: 19C. Japanese *sūmo* wrestling.

sump *n.* a well in the floor of a mine, to collect water for pumping. WH: 12–14C. Middle Dutch *somp* or Middle Low German *sump*, from Germanic, from Indo-European base also of SWAMP.

sumph *n.* a stupid person, a simpleton. WH: 18C. Orig. unknown.

sumpitan *n.* a Malay blowpipe. WH: 17C. Malay, from *sumpit* shooting with a blowpipe.

†**sumpter** *n.* an animal employed to carry packs, a packhorse etc. WH: 12–14C. Old French *sommetier*, from Popular Latin *sagmatarius*, from Late Latin *sagma, sagmatis*. See SUMMER², also -ER¹. Cp. SOMMELIER.

sumptuary *a.* of, relating to or regulating expenditure. WH: 17C. Latin *sumptuarius*, from *sumptus* expenditure, expense, from p.p. of *sumere* to take. See also -ARY².

sumptuous *a.* costly, expensive. WH: 14–15C. Old French *sumptueux*, from Latin *sumptuosus*, from *sumptus*. See SUMPTUARY, also -OUS.

sun *n.* the heavenly body round which the earth revolves and which gives light and heat to the earth and other planets of the solar system. *Also v.t., v.i.* WH: pre-1200. Old English *sunne*, from Germanic, from an Indo-European word rel. to Greek *hēlios*, Latin *sol*, Old English *sōl*, Old Norse *sól*. ? Ult. rel. to SOUTH.

sundae *n.* an ice cream served with fragments of nuts and various fruits. WH: 19C. Appar. alt. of SUNDAY. The dish is perhaps so called either as it was made from leftover ice cream that could not be sold on a Sunday, or because it was served only on Sundays. According to some accounts, the spelling was altered in order not to offend religious people's respect for the word *Sunday*.

Sunday *n.* the first day of the week, the Christian Sabbath. *Also adv.* WH: pre-1200. Old English *sunnandæg*, from Germanic, translating Latin *dies solis*, itself translating Late Greek *hēmera hēliou* day of the sun.

†**sunder** *v.t.* to part, to separate. *Also v.i.* WH: pre-1200. Old English *sundrian*, earlier *āsundrian, gesundrian*, from intens. pref. *ā-*, perfective pref. *ge-* + *sundor* separately, apart, from Germanic. Cp. German *sondern*.

sundry *a.* various, miscellaneous. *Also n.* WH: pre-1200. Old English *syndrig*, from Germanic. See SUNDER, also -Y¹. The original sense (to the 18C) was different for each respectively, individually assigned. Hence the phrase *all and sundry* everyone and each one.

sunn *n.* a hemplike fibre obtained from a southern Asian plant. WH: 18C. Hindi *san*, from Sanskrit *śáṇá* hempen.

Sunna *n.* the traditional part of the Muslim law, based on the sayings or acts of Muhammad, accepted as of equal authority to the Koran by one branch of Islam, the Sunni, but rejected by the Shiites. WH: 18C. Arabic custom, normative rule.

sup *v.t.* to take (soup etc.) in successive sips or spoonfuls. *Also v.i., n.* WH: pre-1200. Old English *sūpan*, from Germanic. Cp. Dutch *zuipen*, German *saufen* to drink, to booze.

sup- *pref.* to, at or from a lower position, as in *supplant, suppose*. WH: Latin pref., from SUB- with *b* assim. to *p*.

Supadriv® *n.* a type of screwdriver which holds a screw on its tip until the hole is located. WH: mid-20C. Prob. from SUPER¹ + *screwdriver* (DRIVE).

super¹ *a.* excellent, very good, enjoyable. WH: 19C. Abbr. of various aa. beginning with SUPER-.

super² *n.* a supernumerary actor. WH: 19C. Abbr. of SUPERNUMERARY.

super- *comb. form* above, beyond or over. WH: Latin pref., from prep. *super* above, on the top (of), beyond, besides, in addition. Cp. HYPER-, OVER-. See also SUR-¹.

superable *a.* able to be overcome, conquerable. WH: 17C. Latin *superabilis*, from *superare* to overcome. See also -ABLE. Cp. INSUPERABLE.

superabound *v.i.* to be more than enough. WH: 14–15C. Ecclesiastical Latin *superabundare*, from SUPER- + *abundare* ABOUND.

superaccommodating *a.* extremely accommodating. WH: 19C. SUPER- + *accommodating* (ACCOMMODATE).

superaccomplished *a.* extremely accomplished. WH: 19C. SUPER- + *accomplished* (ACCOMPLISH).

superactive *a.* extremely active. WH: 17C. SUPER- + ACTIVE.

superadd *v.t.* to add over and above (something else). WH: 14–15C. Latin *superaddere*. See SUPER-, ADD.

superaltar *n.* a consecrated slab for placing on an unconsecrated altar. WH: 12–14C. Medieval Latin *superaltare*, from SUPER- + Late Latin *altar* ALTAR.

superambitious *a.* extremely ambitious. WH: 19C. SUPER- + *ambitious* (AMBITION).

superannuate *v.t.* to pension off on account of age. WH: 17C. Back-formation from *superannuated*, from Medieval Latin *superannuatus*, from SUPER- + *annus* year, assim. to Latin *annuus* ANNUAL. See also -ATE³, -ATE², -ED.

superaqueous *a.* above water. WH: 19C. SUPER- + AQUEOUS.

superb *a.* grand, magnificent. WH: 16C. Old French *superbe*, from Latin *superbus* proud, superior, distinguished.

superbold *a.* extremely bold. WH: 19C. SUPER- + BOLD.

supercalendered *a.* (of paper) highly finished. WH: 19C. SUPER- + CALENDER¹ + -ED.

supercargo *n.* an officer in a merchant ship who superintends sales etc. and has charge of the cargo. WH: 17C. Alt. of obs. *supracargo*, from Spanish *sobrecargo*, from *sobre* over + *cargo* CARGO, based on SUPER-.

supercelestial *a.* above the heavens. WH: 14–15C. Late Latin *supercaelestis*, from SUPER- + *caelestis*. See CELESTIAL.

supercharge *v.t.* to charge or fill greatly or to excess with emotion, vigour etc. *Also n.* WH: early 20C. SUPER- + CHARGE.

superciliary *a.* of, relating to or situated above the eyebrows. WH: 18C. Latin *supercilium* eyebrow (SUPER-, CILIUM) + -ARY¹.

supercilious *a.* contemptuous, overbearing, haughtily indifferent, arrogant, disdainful. WH: 16C. Latin *superciliosus*, from *supercilium*. See SUPERCILIARY, also -OUS. The eyebrow is used to express sternness or haughtiness.

superclass *n.* a taxonomic category between a phylum or division and a class. WH: early 20C. SUPER- + CLASS.

supercolossal *a.* extremely huge. WH: mid-20C. SUPER- + *colossal* (COLOSSUS).

supercolumnar *a.* having one order of columns placed over another. WH: 19C. SUPER- + *columnar* (COLUMN).

supercomplex *a.* extremely complex. WH: early 20C. SUPER- + COMPLEX.

supercomputer *n.* a very powerful computer capable of over 100 million arithmetic operations per second. WH: mid-20C. SUPER- + COMPUTER.

superconductivity *n.* the total loss of electrical resistance exhibited by some metals and alloys at very low temperatures. WH: early 20C. SUPER- + *conductivity* (CONDUCT²).

superconfident *a.* extremely confident. WH: 19C. SUPER- + *confident* (CONFIDE).

superconformity *n.* extreme conformity. WH: 17C. SUPER- + *conformity* (CONFORM).

supercongested *a.* extremely congested. WH: early 20C. SUPER- + *congested* (CONGEST).

superconscious *a.* beyond human consciousness. WH: 19C. SUPER- + CONSCIOUS.

superconservative *a.* extremely conservative. WH: early 20C. SUPER- + CONSERVATIVE.

supercontinent *n.* any of several large land masses believed to have split to form the present continents. WH: mid-20C. SUPER- + CONTINENT¹.

supercool *v.t.* to cool (a liquid) below its freezing point without solidification. *Also v.i., a.* WH: 19C. SUPER- + COOL.

supercriminal *n.* an arch-criminal. WH: early 20C. SUPER- + CRIMINAL.

supercritical *a.* of more than critical mass. WH: 17C. SUPER- + *critical* (CRITIC).

supercurious *a.* extremely curious. WH: 19C. SUPER- + CURIOUS.

supercynical *a.* extremely cynical. WH: 19C. SUPER- + *cynical* (CYNIC).

superdeficit *n.* a very large deficit. WH: early 20C. SUPER- + DEFICIT.

superdevotion *n.* extreme devotion. WH: 19C. SUPER- + *devotion* (DEVOTE).

superdifficult *a.* extremely difficult. WH: 19C. SUPER- + DIFFICULT.

superdiplomacy *n.* extreme diplomacy. WH: early 20C. SUPER- + DIPLOMACY.

superdominant *n.* the submediant. WH: 19C. SUPER- + DOMINANT.

superdose *n.* a larger-than-usual dose. WH: early 20C. SUPER- + DOSE.

supereffective *a.* extremely effective. WH: early 20C. SUPER- + *effective* (EFFECT).

superefficient *a.* extremely efficient. WH: early 20C. SUPER- + EFFICIENT.

superego *n.* the unconscious inhibitory morality in the mind which criticizes the ego and condemns the unworthy impulses of the id. WH: early 20C. SUPER- + EGO, translating German *Über-Ich*, coined by Sigmund Freud.

superelevation *n.* the difference in height between the opposite sides of a curved section of road, railway track etc. WH: 17C. SUPER- + *elevation* (ELEVATE).

supereminent *a.* extremely remarkable. WH: 16C. Latin *supereminens, supereminentis*, pres.p. of *supereminere* to rise above, from SUPER- + *eminere*. See EMINENT.

supererogation *n.* performance of more than duty requires. WH: 16C. Late Latin *supererogatio, supererogationis*, from *supererogatus*, p.p. of *supererogare*, from SUPER- + *erogare* to pay out, from E- + *rogare* to ask. See also -ATION.

superexcited *a.* extremely excited. WH: 19C. SUPER- + *excited*, from EXCITE + -ED.

superexpressive *a.* extremely expressive. WH: 19C. SUPER¹ + *expressive* (EXPRESS²).

superfamily *n.* a taxonomic category between a suborder and a family. WH: 19C. SUPER- + FAMILY.

superfatted *a.* (of soap) containing excess of fatty matter relatively to alkali. WH: 19C. SUPER- + *fatted* (FAT).

superfecundation *n.* the conception of two embryos from ova produced at one time, by separate acts of sexual intercourse. WH: 19C. SUPER- + *fecundation* (FECUND).

superfetation *n.* the conception of a second embryo or litter during the gestation of the first. WH: 17C. French *superfétation* or Modern

Latin *superfetatio, superfetationis*, from *superfetare* to conceive by superfetation. See SUPER-, FOETUS, also -ATION.

superficial *a.* of or relating to or lying on the surface. WH: 14–15C. Late Latin *superficialis*, from Latin SUPERFICIES. See also -AL¹.

superficies *n.* a surface. WH: 16C. Latin, from *super-* + *facies* (FACE).

superfine *a.* exceedingly fine, of extra quality. WH: 14–15C. SUPER- + FINE¹.

superfinite *a.* absolutely finite. WH: 19C. SUPER- + FINITE.

superfluidity *n.* the property of flowing without friction or viscosity. WH: mid-20C. SUPER- + *fluidity* (FLUID).

superfluous *a.* more than is necessary or sufficient, excessive. WH: 14–15C. Latin *superfluus*, from *superfluere*, from SUPER- + *fluere* to flow. See also -OUS.

superfrontal *n.* the part of an altar cloth covering the top. *Also a.* WH: 19C. Medieval Latin *superfrontale*, from SUPER- + *frontale* frontal (FRONT).

supergenerous *a.* extremely generous. WH: 19C. SUPER- + GENEROUS.

supergiant *n.* a very large, very bright star of low density. WH: early 20C. SUPER- + GIANT.

superglue *n.* an adhesive that gives an extremely strong bond on contact. *Also v.t.* WH: late 20C. SUPER- + GLUE.

supergrass *n.* a police informer whose information implicates many people or concerns major criminals or criminal activities. WH: late 20C. SUPER- + GRASS.

superheat *v.t.* to heat (a liquid) above boiling point without vaporization. WH: 19C. SUPER- + HEAT.

superhero *n.* a comic-strip character with superhuman powers who fights against evil. WH: early 20C. SUPER- + HERO.

superhet *n.* superheterodyne. WH: early 20C. Abbr. of SUPERHETERODYNE.

superheterodyne *n.* a radio receiver with a high degree of selectivity. *Also a.* WH: early 20C. SUPERSONIC + HETERODYNE.

superhighway *n.* a motorway. WH: early 20C. SUPER- + HIGHWAY.

superhive *n.* a removable upper storey of a beehive. WH: 19C. SUPER- + HIVE.

superhuman *a.* beyond normal human ability. WH: 17C. Late Latin *superhumanus*, from SUPER- + *humanus* HUMAN.

superhumeral *n.* something worn upon the shoulders, such as an archbishop's pallium, or a Jewish sacerdotal ephod. WH: 17C. Late Latin *superhumerale*, from SUPER- + *humeralis* humeral (HUMERUS).

superignorant *a.* extremely ignorant. WH: 19C. SUPER- + *ignorant* (IGNORANCE).

superimportant *a.* extremely important. WH: 19C. SUPER- + *important* (IMPORTANCE).

superimpose *v.t.* to lay on top of something else. WH: 18C. SUPER- + IMPOSE.

superincumbent *a.* lying or resting on something. WH: 17C. SUPER- + INCUMBENT.

superindifference *n.* extreme indifference. WH: 19C. SUPER- + *indifference* (INDIFFERENT).

superinduce *v.t.* to bring in as an addition. WH: 16C. Latin *superinducere* to cover over, (Late Latin) to bring in, to add. See SUPER-, INDUCE.

superinsist *v.i., v.t.* to insist strongly. WH: 19C. SUPER- + INSIST.

superintellectual *a.* extremely intellectual. WH: 17C. SUPER- + *intellectual* (INTELLECT).

superintelligent *a.* extremely intelligent. WH: mid-20C. SUPER- + INTELLIGENT.

superintend *v.t.* to have or exercise the management or oversight of, to direct, to control. *Also v.i.* WH: 17C. Ecclesiastical Latin *superintendere*, translating Greek *episkopein*. See SUPER-, INTEND.

superior *a.* of higher position, class, rank etc. *Also n.* WH: 14–15C. Old French *superiour* (Modern French *supérieur*), from Latin *superior*, comp. of *superus* situated above, from SUPER-. See also -IOR.

superjacent *a.* lying on or above something. WH: 16C. Latin *superiacens, superiacentis*, pres.p. of *superiacere*, from SUPER- + *iacere* to lie down. See also -ENT.

superlative *a.* of the highest degree, consummate, supreme. *Also n.* WH: 14–15C. Old French *superlatif*, from Late Latin *superlativus*, from Latin *superlatus* (use as p.p. of *superferre*), from *super-* SUPER- + *latus*, p.p. of *tollere* to take away. See also -IVE.

superlogical *a.* extremely logical. WH: 19C. SUPER- + *logical* (LOGIC).

superlucky *a.* extremely lucky. WH: early 20C. SUPER- + *lucky* (LUCK).

superluminal *a.* of or relating to a speed greater than the speed of light. WH: mid-20C. SUPER- + Latin *lumen, luminis* light. See also -AL[1].

superlunar *a.* above the moon, celestial, not mundane. WH: 18C. Medieval Latin *superlunaris*, from SUPER- + *luna* moon. See also -AR[1].

superluxurious *a.* extremely luxurious. WH: early 20C. SUPER- + *luxurious* (LUXURY).

superman *n.* a hypothetical superior being, esp. one who is advanced in intellect and morals. WH: early 20C. SUPER- + MAN. A translation by G.B. Shaw of German ÜBERMENSCH, popularized by the German philosopher Friedrich Nietzsche. Shaw introduced the word in his play *Man and Superman* (1903).

supermarket *n.* a large, self-service shop where food and domestic goods are sold. WH: mid-20C. SUPER- + MARKET.

supermodel *n.* a well-known, highly-paid fashion model. WH: late 20C. SUPER- + MODEL.

supermundane *a.* above or superior to worldly things. WH: 17C. Medieval Latin *supermundanus*, from SUPER- + *mundus*. See MUNDANE. Cp. SUPRAMUNDANE.

supernal *a.* divine, lofty. WH: 14–15C. Old French, or from Medieval Latin *supernalis*, from Latin *supernus*, from *super* above. See also -AL[1].

supernatant *a.* floating on the surface of a solid residue after precipitation etc. *Also n.* WH: 17C. Latin *supernatans, supernatantis*, pres.p. of *supernatare*, from SUPER- + *natare* (NATANT).

supernatural *a.* due to or exercising powers above the usual forces of nature. *Also n.* WH: 14–15C. Medieval Latin *supernaturalis*. See SUPER-, NATURAL.

supernegligent *a.* extremely negligent. WH: 19C. SUPER- + *negligent* (NEGLIGENCE).

supernormal *a.* beyond what is normal. WH: 19C. SUPER- + NORMAL.

supernova *n.* a nova up to 100 million times brighter than the sun, produced by the eruption of a star following its implosion. WH: mid-20C. SUPER- + NOVA.

supernumerary *a.* being in excess of a prescribed or customary number. *Also n.* WH: 17C. Late Latin *supernumerarius* excessive in number (of soldiers added to a legion after it is complete), from Latin *super numerum* beyond the number. See SUPER-, also -ARY[1].

superobligation *n.* a pressing obligation. WH: 19C. SUPER- + OBLIGATION.

superoctave *n.* a coupler in an organ causing a note to sound an octave higher than the key struck. WH: 19C. SUPER- + OCTAVE.

superofficious *a.* extremely officious. WH: early 20C. SUPER- + OFFICIOUS.

superoptimist *n.* a supreme optimist. WH: early 20C. SUPER- + *optimist* (OPTIMISM).

superorder *n.* a taxonomic category between an order and a subclass or a class. WH: 19C. SUPER- + ORDER.

superordinate *a.* superior in rank or status. *Also n.* WH: 17C. SUPER- + ORDINATE, based on SUBORDINATE[1].

superorganic *a.* superior or external to the organism, psychical. WH: 19C. SUPER- + ORGANIC.

superovulation *n.* the production of large numbers of ova at a single time. WH: early 20C. SUPER- + *ovulation* (OVULE).

superphosphate *n.* a mixture of phosphates used as a fertilizer. WH: 18C. SUPER- + PHOSPHATE.

superphysical *a.* unable to be explained by physical causes. WH: 17C. SUPER- + PHYSICAL.

superpose *v.t.* to lay over or on something. WH: 19C. French *superposer*, from *super-* SUPER- + *poser* POSE[1], based on Latin *superponere*.

superpower *n.* a very powerful nation, esp. the US or the former USSR. WH: early 20C. SUPER- + POWER. The original sense was superior power. The sense a very powerful nation dates from the mid-20C.

superrefine *v.t.* to refine to a high degree. WH: 18C. SUPER- + REFINE.

super-royal *a.* larger than royal (denoting a size of printing paper). WH: 17C. SUPER- + ROYAL.

supersaturated *a.* containing more material than a saturated solution or vapour. WH: 18C. SUPER- + *saturated* (SATURATE[1]).

superscribe *v.t.* to write on the top or outside of something or above. WH: 15C. Latin *superscribere*, from SUPER- + *scribere* to write.

supersede *v.t.* to put a person or thing in the place of. WH: 15C. Old French *supercéder*, later *superséder*, from Latin *supersedere* to set above, to be superior to, to refrain from, from SUPER- + *sedere* to sit. The original sense was to postpone, to defer. The sense to take the place of dates from the 17C.

supersensitive *a.* extremely sensitive. WH: 19C. SUPER- + SENSITIVE.

supersimplicity *n.* extreme simplicity. WH: 19C. SUPER- + *simplicity* (SIMPLE).

supersonic *a.* of or relating to sound waves with such a high frequency that they are inaudible. WH: early 20C. SUPER- + SONIC.

supersophisticate *n.* an extremely sophisticated person. WH: mid-20C. SUPER- + *sophisticate* (SOPHISM).

superspecialize *v.i., v.t.* to specialize to a high degree. WH: early 20C. SUPER- + *specialize* (SPECIAL).

superstar *n.* a very popular film, music, sports etc. star. WH: early 20C. SUPER- + STAR.

superstate *n.* a powerful political state formed from a union of several nations. WH: early 20C. SUPER- + STATE.

superstition *n.* credulity regarding the supernatural, the occult or the mysterious. WH: 12–14C. Old French, or from Latin *superstitio, superstitionis*, from *superstare* to stand on, to stand over, from SUPER- + *stare* to stand. See also -ION. The original sense of the Latin word perhaps evolved from the notion of someone or something standing over one to give a feeling of awe or dread.

superstore *n.* a very large supermarket; a very large store selling goods other than food. WH: mid-20C. SUPER- + STORE.

superstratum *n.* a stratum resting on another. WH: 19C. Modern Latin, neut. sing. (used as n.) of p.p. of Latin *supersternere* to spread over. See SUPER-, STRATUM.

superstring *n.* a particle in a theory of cosmic strings that incorporates supersymmetry. WH: late 20C. SUPER- + STRING.

superstructure *n.* the part of a building above the ground. WH: 17C. SUPER- + STRUCTURE.

supersymmetry *n.* a postulated type of symmetry relating fermions and bosons. WH: late 20C. SUPER- + SYMMETRY.

supertanker *n.* a very large tanker ship. WH: early 20C. SUPER- + *tanker* (TANK).

supertax *n.* a tax in addition to the basic income tax, levied on incomes above a certain level. WH: early 20C. SUPER- + TAX. Cp. SURTAX.

superterrestrial *a.* of or relating to a region above the earth. WH: 18C. SUPER- + TERRESTRIAL.

supertonic *n.* the note next above the tonic in the diatonic scale. WH: 19C. SUPER- + TONIC.

supervene *v.i.* to come or happen as something extraneous or additional. WH: 17C. Latin *supervenire*, from SUPER- + *venire* to come.

supervise *v.t.* to have oversight of, to oversee. WH: 15C. Medieval Latin *supervisus*, p.p. of *supervidere*, from Latin SUPER- + *videre* to see. The original sense (to the 18C) was to look over, to survey, to inspect. The current sense dates from the 16C.

superwaif *n.* a young, very thin, childlike fashion model. WH: late 20C. SUPER- + WAIF.

superwoman *n.* an exceptionally strong or capable woman. WH: early 20C. SUPER- + WOMAN.

supinate *v.t.* to turn the palm of (the hand) upwards or forwards, as distinct from *pronate*. WH: 19C. Back-formation from *supination*, from Latin *supinatio, supinationis*, from *supinatus*, p.p. of *supinare*, from *supinus*. See SUPINE, also -ATION.

supine *a.* lying on the back with the face upwards, as distinct from *prone*. *Also n.* WH: 14–15C. Latin *supinus*, from base of *super* above, *superus* higher. See also -INE.

suppedaneum *n.* a footrest on a cross or crucifix. WH: 19C. Late Latin footstool, use as n. of neut. of *suppedaneus* under the feet, from Latin SUP- + *pes, pedis* foot.

supper *n.* the last meal of the day, esp. a light one. WH: 12–14C. Old French *soper, super* (Modern French *souper*), use as n. of *soper* SUP. See also -ER[4].

supplant *v.t.* to take the place of or oust, esp. by craft or treachery. WH: 12–14C. Old French *supplanter* or Latin *supplantare* to trip up, to overthrow, from SUP- + *planta* sole of the foot. The original sense (to the 17C) was to trip up, to cause to fall by tripping, hence (to the 18C) to cause the downfall of, to overthrow.

supple *a.* pliant, easily bent. *Also v.t., v.i.* WH: 12–14C. Old French *souple*, from Latin *supplex, supplicis* submissive, suppliant, from SUP- + *plicare* to fold, to bend.

supplement[1] *n.* an addition, esp. one that supplies a deficiency. WH: 14–15C. Latin *supplementum*, from *supplere* SUPPLY. See also -MENT.

supplement[2] *v.t.* to make additions to. WH: 19C. SUPPLEMENT[1].

suppliant *a.* entreating, supplicating. *Also n.* WH: 14–15C. Old French, pres.p. of *supplier*, from Latin *supplicare* SUPPLICATE. See also -ANT.

supplicate *v.t.* to beg or ask for earnestly and humbly. *Also v.i.* WH: 14–15C. Latin *supplicatus*, p.p. of *supplicare*, from SUP- + *placere* to propitiate. See also -ATE[3].

supply *v.t.* to furnish with what is wanted, to provide (with). *Also n., a.* WH: 14–15C. Old French *soupleer, supplier* (Modern French *suppléer*), from Latin *supplere* to fill up, to make good, to complete, from SUP- + *plere* to fill.

support *v.t.* to bear the weight of, to sustain. *Also n.* WH: 12–14C. Old French *supporter*, from Latin *supportare*, from SUP- + *portare* to carry.

suppose *v.t.* to take to be the case, to accept as probable. WH: 12–14C. Old French *suposer*, based on Latin *supponere* to place under, to substitute, from SUP- + *ponere* to place, but re-formed on *suppositus*, p.p. of *supponere*, and Old French *poser* (POSE[1]). An early sense (to the 18C) was to expect.

supposititious *a.* substituted for something else, not genuine, spurious. WH: 17C. Latin *supposititius*, from *suppositus*, p.p. of *supponere*. See SUPPOSE, also -ITIOUS[2].

suppositive *a.* including or implying supposition. *Also n.* WH: 14–15C. Late Latin *suppositivus*, from *suppositus*. See SUPPOSE, -IVE.

suppository *n.* a solid block of medicine introduced into the vagina or rectum, and left to dissolve. WH: 14–15C. Medieval Latin *suppositorium*, use as n. of neut. sing. of Late Latin *suppositorius* placed underneath, from *suppositus*. See SUPPOSE, also -ORY[1].

suppress *v.t.* to overpower, to quell. WH: 14–15C. Latin *suppressus*, p.p. of *supprimere*, from SUP- + *premere* PRESS[1].

suppurate *v.i.* to generate pus, to fester. WH: 14–15C. Latin *suppuratus*, p.p. of *suppurare*, from SUP- + *pus, puris* PUS. See also -ATE[3].

supra *adv.* above; earlier on. WH: 16C. Latin. See SUPRA-.

supra- *pref.* above. WH: Latin, from *supra* above, beyond, in addition to, before (in time). Rel. to SUPER-.

supralapsarian *n.* a Calvinist holding that God decreed the salvation of the elect before the Fall (as opposed to INFRALAPSARIAN). *Also a.* WH: 17C. Modern Latin *supralapsarius*, from Latin SUPRA- + *lapsus* fall, LAPSE. See also -ARIAN.

supramaxillary *a.* of or relating to the upper jaw. *Also n.* WH: 19C. SUPRA- + *maxillary* (MAXILLA).

supramundane *a.* above the world. WH: 17C. Var. of SUPER-MUNDANE. See SUPRA-.

supranational *a.* overriding national sovereignty. WH: early 20C. SUPRA- + NATIONAL.

supraorbital *a.* being above the eye socket. WH: 19C. SUPRA- + *orbital* (ORBIT).

suprarenal *a.* situated above the kidneys. WH: 19C. SUPRA- + RENAL.

supreme *a.* highest in authority or power. *Also n.* WH: 15C. Latin *supremus*, superl. of *supernus* situated above, from *super* above. See SUPER-.

suprême *n.* a rich, creamy sauce or a dish served in this. WH: 19C. French SUPREME. The name may also have been intended literally for a sauce that was poured over the dish.

supremo *n.* a supreme leader or head. WH: mid-20C. Spanish (*generalísimo*) *supremo* supreme general.

sur-[1] *pref.* above, beyond or over, as in *surfeit, survive*. WH: French (earlier *sour*-), from Latin SUPER-.

sur-[2] *pref.* to, at or from a lower position, as in *surreptitious, surrogate*. WH: Latin pref., from SUB- with *b* assim. to *r*.

sura *n.* a chapter of the Koran. WH: 17C. Arabic *sūra*, prob. from Syriac *ṣūrtā* scripture.

surah *n.* a soft, twilled, usu. self-coloured silk material. WH: 19C. Representation of French pronun. of SURAT.

sural *a.* of or relating to the calf of the leg. WH: 17C. Modern Latin *suralis*, from *sura* calf of the leg. See also -AL[1].

surat *n.* coarse, short cotton grown near Surat. WH: 17C. *Surat*, a port and district in NW India.

surbase *n.* the cornice or moulding at the top of a pedestal or base. WH: 17C. SUR-[1] + BASE[1].

†surcease *n.* cessation. *Also v.i., v.t.* WH: 14–15C. Old French *sursis*, p.p. of *surseoir* to refrain, to delay, to suspend, from Latin *supersedere* SUPERSEDE, assim. early to CEASE.

surcharge[1] *n.* an extra charge or cost. WH: 15C. SURCHARGE[2].

surcharge[2] *v.t.* to put an extra charge on. WH: 14–15C. Old French *surcharger*. See SUR-[1], CHARGE.

surcingle *n.* a belt or girth put round the body of a horse etc., for holding a saddle or blanket on its back. *Also v.t.* WH: 12–14C. Old French *surcengle*, from SUR-[1] + *cengle*, from Latin CINGULUM.

surcoat *n.* an outer coat, esp. a loose robe worn over armour. WH: 12–14C. Old French *surcote*. See SUR-[1], COAT.

surculus *n.* a shoot rising from a rootstock, a sucker. WH: 18C. Latin young branch, shoot.

surd *a.* not capable of being expressed in rational numbers. *Also n.* WH: 16C. Latin *surdus* deaf, silent, mute. The mathematical sense derives ultimately from a translation of Greek *alogos* not expressible, irrational, through Arabic *jiḍr aṣamm*, literally deaf root.

sure *a.* certain, undoubting. *Also adv., int.* WH: 12–14C. Old French *sur*, earlier *seür* (Modern French *sûr*), from Latin *securus* SECURE. The original sense (to the 17C) was safe, secure, but the current sense has also been in use from the first.

surety *n.* a person undertaking responsibility for payment of a sum, discharge of an engagement or attendance in court by another, a guarantor. WH: 12–14C. Old French *seürté* (Modern French *sûreté*), from Latin *securitas* SECURITY. See also -TY[1].

surf *n.* the swell of the sea breaking on the shore, rocks etc. *Also v.i., v.t.* WH: 17C. ? Alt. of obs. *suff* the inrush of the sea towards the shore, of unknown orig., with assim. to SURGE.

surface *n.* the exterior part of anything, the outside. *Also a., v.t., v.i.* WH: 17C. French, from SUR-[1] + *face* FACE, based on Latin SUPERFICIES.

surfactant *n.* a surface-active substance, such as a detergent. WH: mid-20C. SURFACE + ACTIVE + -ANT.

surfeit *n.* excess, esp. in eating or drinking. *Also v.t., v.i.* WH: 12–14C. Old French *surfet, surfait*, use as n. of p.p. of *surfaire* to overdo, from SUR-[1] + *faire* to make, to do.

surge *n.* a sudden onset. *Also v.i.* WH: 15C. Old French *sourgen* (Modern French *surgeon*), from *sourge-*, stem of *sourdre* or *sorgir* (Modern French *surgir*), from Catalan *sorgir* to anchor, *surgir* to land, from Latin *surgere* to rise. The original sense was fountain, stream. The sense sudden onset evolved in the 16C.

surgeon *n.* a medical practitioner treating injuries, deformities and diseases by manual procedure, often involving operations. WH: 12–14C. Anglo-French *surgien*, contr. of *serurgien, cirurgien* (Modern French *chirurgien*), ult. from Latin *chirurgia* surgery, from Greek *kheirourgia*, from *kheir* hand + *ergon* work.

surgery *n.* (the branch of medicine dealing with) the treatment of injuries, deformities or diseases by manual procedure, often operations. WH: 12–14C. Old French *surgerie*, contr. of *serurgerie, cirurgerie*, from *serurgien, cirurgien*. See SURGEON, also -ERY.

suricate *n.* a small southern African meerkat, *Suricata suricata*, allied to the weasel. WH: 18C. French, of African orig.

Surinamese *a.* of or relating to Suriname. *Also n.* WH: mid-20C. *Suriname*, a country in NE S America + -ESE.

surly *a.* rude and bad-tempered. WH: 16C. Alt. of obs. *sirly*, from SIR + -LY[1]. The original sense was lordly, majestic, then (to the 18C) masterful, imperious, haughty.

surmise *n.* a supposition on slight evidence, a guess, a conjecture. *Also v.t., v.i.* WH: 14–15C. Old French *surmis*, p.p. of *surmettre* to accuse, from Late Latin *supermittere*, from Latin SUPER- + *mittere* to put. The original sense (to the 18C) was an allegation, a charge, esp. a false one. The current sense dates from the 16C.

surmount *v.t.* to overcome, to vanquish, to rise above. WH: 14–15C. Old French *surmonter*. See SUR-[1], MOUNT[1].

surmullet *n.* the red mullet. WH: 17C. French *surmulet*, from Old French *sor* (Modern French *saur*) red, of unknown orig. + MULLET[1].

surname *n.* a name added to the first or Christian name; a family name (orig. an appellation signifying occupation etc., or a nickname ultimately becoming hereditary). *Also v.t.* WH: 12–14C. Old French *surnom*, from SUR-[1] + *nom* NAME, based on Medieval Latin *supernomen, supranomen.*

surpass *v.t.* to excel, to go beyond in amount, degree etc. WH: 16C. French *surpasser*, from *sur-* SUR-[1] + *passer* PASS.

surplice *n.* a loose, flowing vestment of white linen, with full sleeves, worn by clergy and choristers at divine service. WH: 12–14C. Old French *sourpelis* (Modern French *surplis*), from Medieval Latin *superpellicium*, use as n. of neut. of *superpellicius*, from SUPER- + *pellicia* fur garment (PELISSE). The garment is so called because it was worn over furs in unheated medieval churches.

surplus *n.* an amount which remains over, excess beyond what is used or required. *Also a.* WH: 14–15C. Old French, from Medieval Latin *superplus*, from SUPER- + *plus* more.

surprise *n.* an unexpected event. *Also a., v.t.* WH: 14–15C. Old French *surpris*, use as n. of p.p. of *surprendre*, from Medieval Latin *superprehendere*, from SUPER- + *prehendere* to grasp, to seize, to catch, earlier *praehendere*, from *prae* PRE- + Latinized form of Greek *khandanein* to take in, to hold.

surra *n.* a serious disease of horses, cattle etc. in Asia and NE Africa, transmitted by horseflies. WH: 19C. Marathi *sūra* air breathed through the nostrils.

surreal *a.* having the qualities of surrealism. WH: mid-20C. Backformation from SURREALISM.

surrealism *n.* an artistic and literary movement of the 20th cent. which aimed at expressing the subconscious activities of the mind by presenting images with the chaotic incoherency of a dream. WH: early 20C. French *surréalisme*. See SUR-[1], REALISM. The word was coined in *c.*1917 by the French poet Guillaume Apollinaire and adopted in *c.*1924 by the French poet André Breton in his *Manifeste du Surréalisme* (1924).

surrebut *v.i.* to reply to a defendant's rebutter. WH: 18C. Backformation from *surrebutter* (16C), from SUR-[1] + *rebutter* (REBUT), based on *surrejoinder* (SURREJOIN).

surrejoin *v.i.* to reply to a defendant's rejoinder. WH: 16C. Backformation from *surrejoinder*, from SUR-[1] + *rejoinder* (REJOIN).

surrender *v.t.* to give up possession of, esp. upon compulsion or demand. *Also v.i., n.* WH: 14–15C. Old French *surrendre*, from SUR-[1] + *rendre* RENDER.

surreptitious *a.* done by stealth or fraud. WH: 14–15C. Latin *surrepticius*, from *surreptus*, p.p. of *surripere* to seize secretly, from SUR-[2] + *rapere* to seize. See also -ITIOUS[2]. Cp. SUBREPTION.

surrey *n.* a light, four-wheeled horse-drawn carriage. WH: 19C. *Surrey cart*, from *Surrey*, a county in S England, where it was originally made and from which the later carriage was adapted.

surrogate *n.* a deputy; a substitute. WH: 17C. Latin *surrogatus*, p.p. of *surrogare*, var. of *subrogare* to put in another's place, from SUB- + *rogare* to ask, to offer for election. See also -ATE[1].

surround *v.t.* to lie or be situated all round, to encompass. *Also n.* WH: 14–15C. Old French *suronder*, from Late Latin *superundare*, from *super-* SUPER- + *undare* to rise in waves, from *unda* wave. The original sense was to overflow, to inundate. The current sense dates from the 17C, by association with ROUND.

surtax *n.* an additional tax. *Also v.t.* WH: 19C. French *surtaxe*, from SUR-[1] + *taxe* TAX. Cp. SUPERTAX.

surtitle *n.* a printed translation of part of the text of an opera etc. projected on a screen above the stage. *Also v.t.* WH: late 20C. SUR-[1] + TITLE, based on SUBTITLE.

surtout *n.* a man's overcoat, esp. one like a frock coat. WH: 17C. French, from *sur* above + *tout* everything. Cp. *overall*.

surveillance *n.* observation, close watch, supervision. WH: 19C. French, from *surveiller* to watch over, from SUR-[1] + *veiller* to keep watch, from Latin *vigilare*. See also -ANCE.

survey[1] *v.t.* to look over, to take a general view of. *Also v.i.* WH: 14–15C. Anglo-French *surveier*, from *sorvey*, pres. stem of Old French

sorveeir, from Medieval Latin *supervidere*, from Latin SUPER- + *videre* to see. Cp. SUPERVISE, *oversee*.

survey[2] *n.* the act or process of surveying. WH: 15C. SURVEY[1]. The original sense (to the 17C) was supervision, superintendence. The current sense dates from the 16C.

survive *v.i.* to be still alive or in existence. *Also v.t.* WH: 14–15C. Old French *sourvivre* (Modern French *survivre*), from Latin *supervivere*, from SUPER- + *vivere* to live.

sus *n.* suspicion of loitering with criminal intent. WH: mid-20C. Var. of SUSS.

sus- *pref.* to, at or from a lower position, as in *suspect, sustain*. WH: Latin pref., from SUB- with *b* assim. to *p, t*. In some Latin derivatives this assimilated form is also used before *c*, as in *susceptible*.

susceptible *a.* impressionable, sensitive. WH: 17C. Late Latin *susceptibilis*, from Latin *susceptus*, p.p. of *suscipere* to take up, from SUS- + *capere* to take. See also -IBLE.

†**suscitate** *v.t.* to rouse, to excite. WH: 16C. Late Latin *suscitatus*, p.p. of *suscitare* from SUS- + *citare* to set in rapid motion. See CITE, also -ATE[3].

sushi *n.* a Japanese dish of cold rice cakes with a vinegar dressing and garnishes of raw fish etc. WH: 19C. Japanese.

suspect[1] *v.t.* to have an impression of the existence of without proof, to surmise. *Also v.i.* WH: 14–15C. Latin *suspectus*, p.p. of *suspicere* to look up, to admire, to suspect, from SUS- + *specere* to look.

suspect[2] *n.* a person suspected of crime etc. *Also a.* WH: 12–14C. Old French, or from Latin *suspectus*, p.p. of *suspicere* SUSPECT[1]. The noun evolved in the 16C and was obsolete after the 17C until revived in the 19C following the French use of the word for a person suspected of hostility (or indifference) to the Revolution.

suspend *v.t.* to hang up, to hang from something above. WH: 12–14C. Old French *suspendre* or Latin *suspendere*, from SUS- + *pendere* to hang.

suspense *n.* a state of uncertainty or apprehensive waiting. WH: 14–15C. Old French *suspens* abeyance, delay, from Medieval Latin *suspensum*, use as n. of neut. of Latin *suspensus*, p.p. of *suspendere* SUSPEND.

suspicion *n.* the act or feeling of a person who suspects. WH: 12–14C. Anglo-French *suspeciun*, var. of Old French *sospeçon* (Modern French *soupçon*), from Medieval Latin *suspectio, suspectionis*, later assim. to Old French *suspicion* from Latin *suspicio, suspicionis*, from *suspicere* SUSPECT[1]. See also -ION.

suss *v.t.* to suspect of a crime. *Also n., a.* WH: mid-20C. Abbr. of SUSPECT[1], SUSPICION.

Sussex *n.* an English breed of fowl. WH: 18C. *Sussex*, a county in SE England.

sustain *v.t.* to bear the weight of, to keep from falling. WH: 12–14C. Old French *sostein-, soustein-*, stem of *sostenir, soustenir* (Modern French *soutenir*), from Latin *sustinere*, from SUS- + *tenere* to hold, to keep.

sustenance *n.* something which sustains, the means of support or maintenance. WH: 12–14C. Old French *sostenance, soustenance* (Modern French *soutenance*), from *sostenir, soustenir*. See SUSTAIN, also -ANCE.

sustentaculum *n.* a supporting body part, tissue etc. WH: 19C. Modern Latin, from Latin *sustentatus*, p.p. of *sustentare*, freq. of *sustinere*. See SUSTAIN, also -ATE[3], -CULE.

sustentation *n.* support, maintenance. WH: 14–15C. Old French, or from Latin *sustentatio, sustentationis*, from *sustentatus*. See SUSTENTACULUM, also -ATION.

susurrant *a.* whispering, rustling, murmuring. WH: 18C. Old French, pres.p. of *susurrer*, from Latin *susurrare*, from *susurrus* whisper, of imit. orig. See also -ANT.

sutler *n.* a person following an army and selling provisions, liquor etc. WH: 16C. Obs. Dutch *soeteler*, from *soetelen* to befoul, to perform menial duties, to follow a low trade, from Germanic base also of SUDS.

Sutra *n.* in Hindu literature, a rule, a precept, an aphorism. WH: 19C. Sanskrit *sūtra* thread, string, rule.

suttee *n.* a Hindu custom by which the widow was burnt on the funeral pyre with her dead husband. WH: 18C. Sanskrit *satī* faithful wife, fem. of *sat* good.

suture *n.* the junction of two parts by their margins as if by sewing, esp. of the bones of the skull. *Also v.t.* WH: 14–15C. French, or from Latin *sutura*, from *sutus*, p.p. of *suere* SEW. See also -URE.

suzerain *n.* a feudal lord. WH: 19C. French, from Old French *suserain*, prob. from *sus* above, up (from Latin *sursum* upward), based on *souverain* SOVEREIGN.

svelte *a.* (esp. of a woman's figure) slender, lissom. WH: 19C. French, from Italian *svelto*, lit. pulled out, lengthened, p.p. of *svellere* to pluck out, to root out, from Popular Latin *exvellere*, var. of Latin *evellere*, from E- + *vellere* to pluck, to pull, to stretch.

Svengali *n.* a person who control's another's mind, esp. for a sinister purpose. WH: early 20C. *Svengali*, a sinister musician in George du Maurier's novel *Trilby* (1894).

swab *n.* a mop for cleaning floors, decks, the bore of a gun etc. *Also v.t.* WH: 17C. Back-formation from *swabber*, from early Middle Dutch *zwabber*, ult. from Germanic base meaning to sway, to splash in water, represented also in Middle Low German *swabben* to splash, to sway, to slap, Norwegian *svabba* to splash, to wade, Low German *swabber* (German *Schwabber*) mop, swab.

Swabian *a.* of or relating to Swabia, a duchy of medieval Germany. *Also n.* WH: 17C. *Swabia*, earlier *Suabia*, Latinized form of German *Schwaben*, a region and former duchy in SW Germany + -AN.

swaddle *v.t.* to wind or swathe in or as in a bandage, wrap or wraps. WH: 12–14C. SWATHE + -LE[4].

Swadeshi *n.* a movement in India for self-government, and agitation until this was obtained. WH: early 20C. Hindi *svadeśī*, from Sanskrit *svadeśīya* of one's own country, from *sva* own + *deśa* country. Cp. SWARAJ.

swag *n.* booty obtained by robbery, esp. burglary. *Also v.t., v.i.* WH: 12–14C. Prob. of Scandinavian orig. Cp. Norwegian dial. *svagga* to sway. The original sense was a bulging bag. The senses bundle of personal belongings carried by a traveller, burglar's booty arose in the 18C.

swage *n.* a tool for shaping wrought iron etc. by hammering or pressure. *Also v.t.* WH: 14–15C. Old French *souage* (Modern French *suage*), of unknown orig.

swagger *v.i.* to strut or go (about etc.) with an air of defiance, self-confidence or superiority. *Also v.t., n., a.* WH: 16C. Appar. from SWAG + -ER[5].

Swahili *n.* a member of a Bantu-speaking people of Tanzania. WH: 19C. Kiswahili, lit. pertaining to the coasts, from Arabic *sawāḥil*, pl. of *sāḥil* coast. The Swahili inhabit Zanzibar and the adjacent coasts of Tanzania.

swain *n.* a young rustic; a country gallant. WH: pre-1200. Old Norse *sveinn* boy, servant, attendant, corr. to Old English *swān* swineherd, from Germanic. Cp. BOATSWAIN, COXSWAIN. The original sense (to the 16C) was young man attending a knight, then (to the 17C) male servant, young man, boy. The sense country gallant evolved in the 16C.

swale *n.* a moist depression between ridges. WH: 16C. Orig. unknown.

swallow[1] *v.t.* to take through the mouth and throat into the stomach. *Also v.i., n.* WH: pre-1200. Old English *swelgan*, from Germanic. Cp. German *schwelgen* to revel, to feast.

swallow[2] *n.* any small, swift, migratory bird of the family Hirundinidae, with long, pointed wings and a forked tail. WH: pre-1200. Old English *swealwe*, from Germanic. Cp. German *Schwalbe*.

swami *n.* a Hindu religious teacher. WH: 18C. Sanskrit *svāmin*, nom. *svāmī* master, prince.

swamp *n.* a tract of wet, spongy land. *Also v.t., v.i.* WH: 17C. Prob. ult. from Germanic base meaning sponge or fungus. Cp. German *Schwamm* sponge. The word was perhaps already in Old English (as *swamp*) but is not recorded.

swan *n.* a large, web-footed aquatic bird of the genus *Cygnus*, with a long neck and usu. white plumage, noted for its grace in the water. *Also v.i.* WH: pre-1200. Old English, from Germanic, poss. from same source as Old English *swinsian* to sing, to make music. See SOUND[1]. If this origin is correct, the reference would probably be to the 'singing' throb of the swan's flight, not to its voice, which in most species is silent.

swank *n.* swagger, bluster. *Also v.i., a.* WH: 19C. Orig. unknown.

swap *v.t., v.i.* to exchange, to barter. *Also n.* WH: 12–14C. Prob. imit. of a sharp resounding blow. Cp. SLAP. The original sense was to move something quickly so as to hit something else, then (14–15C) to strike hands in token of a bargain or agreement. The sense to exchange evolved from the latter (16C).

Swaraj *n.* home rule for India. WH: early 20C. Hindi *svarāj*, from Sanskrit *svarājya*, from *sva* own + *rājya* rule. Cp. SWADESHI, RAJ.

sward *n.* a surface of land covered with thick short grass. WH: pre-1200. Old English *sweard*, from Germanic. Cp. German *Schwarte* bacon rind, crust. The original sense was skin of the body. The current sense evolved in the 14–15C.

swarf *n.* grit, metal filings, chips, grindings. WH: 16C. Ult. from Old English *geswearf*, *gesweorf* filings (cp. SWERVE), or from Old Norse *svarf* file dust.

swarm[1] *n.* a cluster of bees issuing from a hive with a queen bee and seeking a new home. *Also v.i.* WH: pre-1200. Old English *swearm*, from Germanic, prob. rel. to Sanskrit *svarati* it sounds, Latin *susurrus* whisper (SUSURRANT). Cp. German *Schwarm*. Some sources relate the word to SWERVE, with reference to the motion of the bees rather than to their sound.

swarm[2] *v.i.* to climb up (a tree, rope, pole etc.) by embracing it with the arms and legs. *Also v.t.* WH: 16C. Orig. unknown. ? Ult. rel. to SWARM[1].

†swart *a.* of a dark colour; swarthy. WH: pre-1200. Old English *sweart*, from Germanic. Cp. German *schwarz* black.

swarthy *a.* dark or dusky in complexion. WH: 16C. Alt. of obs. *swarty*, from SWART + -Y[1].

swash[1] *v.i.* to make a noise as of splashing water. *Also v.t., n.* WH: 16C. Imit. Cp. SWISH.

swash[2] *a.* sloping. WH: 17C. Orig. unknown.

swastika *n.* a cross with arms bent at a right angle, used as a symbol of anti-Semitism or Nazism. WH: 19C. Sanskrit *svastika*, from *svasti* well-being, luck, from *su* good + *asti* being. The cross is so called because it was originally believed to bring good luck.

swat *v.t.* to hit sharply. *Also n.* WH: 17C. Dial. alt. of SQUAT. The original sense was to SQUAT. The sense to hit sharply evolved in the 18C.

swatch *n.* a sample of cloth. WH: 16C. Orig. unknown. The original sense was counterfoil, then tally fixed to a piece of cloth before it is dyed. The current sense arose in the 17C.

swath *n.* a row or ridge of grass, corn etc. cut and left lying on the ground. WH: pre-1200. Old English *swæth*, *swathu*, from Germanic. Cp. German *Schwade*. The original sense was track, trace. The current sense dates from the 12–14C.

swathe *v.t.* to bind or wrap in or as in a bandage, cloth etc. *Also n.* WH: pre-1200. Old English *swathian*, from Germanic. ? Rel. to SWAY.

sway *v.i.* to move backwards and forward, to oscillate irregularly. *Also v.t., n.* WH: 12–14C. Orig. uncertain. Corr. in form to Old Norse *sveiga* to bend, to give way, but in meaning to Dutch *zwaaien* to swing, to wave, Low German *swäjen* to move to and fro (in the wind). The original sense (to the 16C) was to go down, to fall. The current sense evolved in the 14–15C.

Swazi *a.* of or relating to Swaziland, southern Africa. *Also n.* WH: 19C. Nguni *Mswati*, *c.*1820–68, king of the Swazi, son of Sobhuza I, the founder of Swaziland (*c.*1820).

swear *v.i.* to affirm solemnly invoking God or some other sacred person or object as witness or pledge. *Also v.t., n.* WH: pre-1200. Old English *swerian*, from Germanic base represented also by Old Norse *svara* to answer (ANSWER). Cp. German *schwören*. The sense to use profane or indecent words dates from the 12–14C.

sweat *n.* the moisture exuded from the skin of a person or animal. *Also v.i., v.t.* WH: pre-1200. Old English *swāt*, from Germanic, from Indo-European base represented also by Latin *sudor*. Cp. German *Schweiss*.

Swede *n.* a native or inhabitant of Sweden, or a descendant of one. WH: 17C. Middle Low German and Middle Dutch *Swēde*, prob. from Old Norse *Svíthjóth* people of the Swedes, Sweden, a country occupying the eastern part of the Scandinavian peninsula, from *Svíar* Swedes + *thjóth* people. The name of the large turnip dates from the 19C.

Swedenborgian *a.* of or relating to Swedenborg or Swedenborgianism. *Also n.* WH: 18C. Emmanuel *Swedenborg*, 1688–1772, Swedish philosopher + -IAN.

Swedish *a.* of or relating to Sweden. *Also n.* WH: 17C. From *Sweden* or SWEDE. See also -ISH¹.

Sweeney *n.* the members of a flying squad. WH: mid-20C. *Sweeney Todd*, rhyming slang for *flying squad*, from the name of a fictitious barber who murdered his customers in George Dibdin Pitt's play *A String of Pearls, or the Fiend of Fleet Street* (1847), later known as *Sweeney Todd, the Demon Barber of Fleet Street*.

sweeny *n.* atrophy of a muscle, esp. of the shoulder in horses. WH: 19C. Prob. from German dial. *Schweine* emaciation, atrophy.

sweep *v.t.* to clear dirt etc. from or clean with or as with a broom. *Also v.i., n.* WH: pre-1200. Old English *swāpan*, from Germanic. Cp. SWIPE.

sweepstake *n.* a lottery in which a number of people stake sums on an event, esp. on a horse race, the total amount staked being divided among the winning betters. WH: 15C. SWEEP + STAKE². The word originally denoted a person who takes ('sweeps') the whole of the stakes in a gambling game. The term passed in the 18C to the race or contest serving as a basis for the game.

sweet *a.* having a taste like the taste of honey or sugar. *Also n., adv.* WH: pre-1200. Old English *swēte*, from Germanic, from an Indo-European word represented by Sanskrit *svādu*, Greek *hēdus*, Latin *suavis*. Cp. German *süss*.

swell *v.i.* to increase in bulk or extent, to expand. *Also v.t., n., a.* WH: pre-1200. Old English *swellan*, from Germanic. Cp. German *schwellen*.

swelter *v.i.* (of the weather etc.) to be hot, moist and oppressive, to cause faintness, languor or oppression. *Also n.* WH: 12–14C. From base of Old English *sweltan* to die, to perish, from Germanic + -ER⁵.

swerve *v.i.* to turn to one side, to diverge from the direct or regular course. *Also v.t., n.* WH: pre-1200. Old English *sweorfan*, from Germanic. Cp. Middle Dutch *swerven* to stray, to wander, Old High German *swerban* to wipe, Old Norse *sverfa* to file. Rel. to SWARF. The original sense was to file, to scour.

swift *a.* moving or able to move with great rapidity, quick. *Also adv., n.* WH: pre-1200. Old English, from Germanic base of SWIVEL.

swig *v.t., v.i.* to drink in large draughts. *Also n.* WH: 16C. Orig. unknown.

swill *v.t., v.i.* to wash, to rinse. *Also n.* WH: pre-1200. Old English *swillan*, with no certain rel. words. ? Rel. to SWALLOW¹.

swim *v.i.* to move progressively in the water by the motion of the hands and feet, or fins, tail etc. *Also v.t., n.* WH: pre-1200. Old English *swimman*, from Germanic. Cp. German *schwimmen*.

swindle *v.t., v.i.* to cheat. *Also n.* WH: 18C. Back-formation from *swindler*, from German *Schwindler* giddy person, extravagant speculator, from *schwindeln* to be giddy, to act extravagantly, to swindle.

swine *n.* a pig, a hog. WH: pre-1200. Old English *swīn*, from Germanic, from Indo-European base represented also by Latin *sus*, *su-* pig, Greek *hus*. Cp. German *Schwein*. The Old English word was originally an adjective from SOW¹. Cp. SUILLINE.

swing *v.i.* to move to and fro, like an object suspended by a point or one side, hang freely. *Also v.t., n.* WH: pre-1200. Old English *swingan*, from Germanic base also of SWINK. Cp. German *schwingen* to brandish. The original sense was to whip, to strike (a blow), also to move or go rapidly, to rush. These senses were obsolete by the 16C, when the current sense emerged.

swingeing *a.* severe, great, huge. WH: 16C. From dial. *swinge* to cut down with a scythe, from Old English *swengan*, rel. to *swingan* SWING + -ING².

swingle *n.* a wooden instrument for beating flax to separate the woody parts from the fibre. *Also v.t.* WH: 12–14C. Middle Dutch *swinghel*, from base of SWING + -LE¹.

†swink *v.i.* to labour, to toil. *Also v.t., n.* WH: pre-1200. Old English *swincan*, from base also of *swingan* SWING.

swipe *v.t.* to hit with great force. *Also v.i., n.* WH: 18C. Prob. var. of SWEEP. The original sense was to swallow in one gulp. The current sense dates from the 19C.

swipple *n.* the swingle of a flail. WH: 14–15C. Prob. orig. from SWEEP + -LE¹.

swirl *v.i.* to form eddies, to whirl about. *Also v.t., n.* WH: 14–15C. ? Of Low Dutch orig. (cp. Dutch *zwirrelen* to whirl), prob. freq. formation of imit. base represented also by Middle Low German *swirren*, German *schwirren* to whirl.

swish *v.i.* to make a whistling sound in cutting through the air. *Also v.t., n., a.* WH: 18C. Imit. Cp. WHISH.

Swiss *a.* of or relating to Switzerland. *Also n.* WH: 16C. French *Suisse*, from Middle High German *Swīz* Switzerland, a country in central Europe. Cp. SWITZER. Switzerland derives its name from what is now the canton of *Schwyz*.

switch *n.* a mechanism for diverting railway trains or vehicles from one line to another, or for completing or interrupting an electric circuit, transferring current from one wire to another etc. *Also v.t., v.i.* WH: 16C. Prob. from Low German. Cp. Hanoverian dial. *swutsche*, var. of Low German *swukse* long thin stick. The original sense was a thin riding whip. The application to an electric switch arose in the 19C.

swither *v.i.* to hesitate, to vacillate. *Also n.* WH: 16C. Orig. unknown.

Switzer *n.* a Swiss, esp. a member of the Swiss Guard. WH: 16C. Middle High German *Switzer*, *Schwytzer*, from *Swīz*. See SWISS.

swivel *n.* a link or connection comprising a ring and pivot or other mechanism allowing the two parts to revolve independently. *Also v.i., v.t.* WH: 12–14C. From base of Old English *swīfan* to move in a course, to sweep, from Germanic, from Indo-European base also of SWIFT. See also -EL.

swivet *n.* a panic, a fluster. WH: 19C. Orig. unknown.

swizz *n.* something unfair; a disappointment. WH: early 20C. Abbr. of SWIZZLE.

swizzle *n.* a mixed alcoholic drink of various kinds. *Also v.t., v.i.* WH: 19C. Orig. unknown. The sense cheat, fraud, dates from the early 20C and is probably an alteration of SWINDLE.

swoon *v.i.* to fall into a fainting fit, esp. from excitement. *Also n.* WH: 12–14C. Back-formation from *swooning*, from obs. *swown* in a swoon (shortening of Old English *geswōgen*, p.p. of stem of *āswōgan*, *oferswōgan* to suffocate, to choke) + -ING¹.

swoop *v.i.* (of a bird of prey) to descend upon prey etc. suddenly. *Also v.t., n.* WH: 16C. ? Dial. development of Old English *swāpan* SWEEP. The original sense (to the 17C) was to move in a stately manner, to sweep along. The sense to descend upon prey dates from the 18C.

swoosh *v.i.* to move with or make a rushing sound. *Also n.* WH: 19C. Imit. Cp. WHOOSH.

sword *n.* a weapon, usu. consisting of a long blade fixed in a hilt with a guard for the hand, used for cutting or thrusting. WH: pre-1200. Old English *sweord*, *sword*, from Germanic, of uncertain orig. Cp. German *Schwert*.

swot *v.i., v.t.* to study hard. *Also n.* WH: 19C. Var. of SWEAT. The original figurative sense of *sweat* was to work hard, to labour.

swy *n.* the game of two-up. WH: early 20C. German *zwei* two.

-sy *suf.* forming diminutive adjectives and nouns, as in *folksy*, *mumsy* etc. WH: Var. of -Y³.

sybarite *n.* a sensual and luxurious person. *Also a.* WH: 16C. Latin *Sybarita*, from Greek *Subaritēs*, from *Subaris* Sybaris, an ancient Greek city of S Italy traditionally noted for the luxury and indulgence of its way of life. See also -ITE¹.

sycamine *n.* the black mulberry tree, *Morus nigra*. WH: 16C. Greek *sukaminon* mulberry, from Hebrew *šiḳmāh*, assim. to Greek *sukon* fig. The word is found chiefly in biblical translations (Luke xvii.6).

sycamore *n.* a large Eurasian maple, *Acer pseudoplatanus*, having winged seeds. WH: 12–14C. Old French *sicamor* (Modern French *sycomore*), from Latin *sycomorus*, from Greek *sukomoros*, from *sukon* fig + *moron* mulberry. The tree is so called because its leaves are somewhat similar to those of the mulberry.

syce *n.* esp. in the Indian subcontinent, a groom. WH: 17C. Persian and Urdu *sā'is*, from Arabic.

sycee *n.* pure uncoined silver cast into ingots, usu. bearing the seal of a banker or assayer, and formerly used in China by weight as a medium of exchange. WH: 18C. Cantonese pronun. of Chinese *xī sī*, lit. fine silk. The silver is so called because, if pure, it can be drawn out into fine threads.

sycomore *n.* the sycamore fig. WH: 12–14C. Var. of SYCAMORE.

syconium *n.* an enlarged receptacle which develops into a multiple fruit, such as the fig. WH: 19C. Modern Latin, from Greek *sukon* fig.

sycophant *n.* a servile flatterer, a parasite. *Also v.i., v.t.* WH: 16C. French *sycophante* or Latin *sycophanta*, from Greek *sukophantēs*, from *sukon* fig + base of *phainein* to show. The literal sense is fig-shower, i.e. one who makes the insulting gesture of the 'fig' by sticking the thumb (representing the penis) between two fingers (representing the vulva). The derogatory name was used in ancient Greece for an informer, perhaps originally one who informed against the illegal exportation of figs from Athens.

sycosis *n.* a pustular eruption or inflammation of the scalp or bearded part of the face. WH: 16C. Modern Latin, from Greek *sukōsis*, from *sukon* fig. See also -OSIS. The original sense was an ulcer on the skin resembling a fig.

Sydenham's chorea *n.* a form of chorea in children, associated with rheumatic fever. WH: 19C. Thomas *Sydenham*, 1624–89, English physician.

Sydneysider *n.* a resident of Sydney. WH: 19C. *Sydney*, the capital of New South Wales, Australia + *sider*, from SIDE + -ER[1].

syenite *n.* a granular igneous rock consisting of orthoclase and hornblende, with or without quartz. WH: 18C. Latin *syenites* (*lapis*) (stone of) *Syene*, from Greek *Suēnē* Aswan, a city and region of SE Egypt. See also -ITE[1].

syllable *n.* a sound forming a word or part of a word, containing one vowel sound, with or without a consonant or consonants, and uttered at a single effort or vocal impulse. *Also v.i.* WH: 14–15C. Anglo-French *sillable*, alt. of Old French *sillabe* (Modern French *syllabe*), from Latin *syllaba*, from Greek *sullabē*, from *sullambanein* to collect together, to bring together, from *sun-* SYN- + *lambanein* to take.

syllabub *n.* a dessert made by mixing cream with wine etc., adding flavouring and frothing it up. WH: 16C. Orig. unknown.

syllabus *n.* a list, outline, summary, abstract etc., giving the principal points or subjects of a course of lectures, teaching or study, examination requirements, hours of attendance etc. WH: 17C. Modern Latin, orig. a misreading of *sittybas*, acc. pl. of *sittyba*, from Greek *sittuba* title-slip, label.

syllepsis *n.* the application of a word in both the literal and metaphorical senses at the same time. WH: 14–15C. Late Latin, from Greek *sullēpsis* taking together, from *sun-* SYN- + *lēpsis* taking.

syllogism *n.* a form of argument consisting of three propositions, a major premiss or general statement, a minor premiss or instance, and a third deduced from these, called the conclusion. WH: 14–15C. Old French *sillogisme*, earlier *sillogime* (Modern French *syllogisme*), or from Latin *syllogismus*, from Greek *sullagismos*, from *sullogizesthai*, intens. of *logizesthai* to reckon, to conclude, from *logos* reasoning, discourse. See SYN-, LOGOS, also -ISM.

sylph *n.* a supposed elemental being inhabiting the air, intermediate between material and immaterial beings. WH: 17C. Modern Latin pl. *sylphes*, *sylphi*, German pl. *Sylphen*, ? based on Latin *sylvestris* of the woods + *nympha* nymph.

sylva *n.* the trees of a particular time or place. WH: 17C. Latin *silva* wood, woodland, misspelt *sylva* by assoc. with Greek *hulē* wood.

sylvanite *n.* a gold or silver telluride mineral. WH: 18C. *Transylvania*, a region of Romania + -ITE[1].

sym- *pref.* with, as in *symbiosis*, *symphony*. WH: Greek *sum-*, from *sun-* SYN- with *n* assim. to *b, m, p*.

symbiont *n.* an organism living in a state of symbiosis. WH: 19C. SYM- + Greek *biount-*, pres.p. stem of *bioun* to live, from *bios* life.

symbol *n.* an object typifying or representing something by resemblance, association etc., a type, an emblem. *Also v.t.* WH: 14–15C. Latin *symbolum*, from Greek *sumbolon* mark, token, watchword, outward sign, from *sum-* SYM- + base of *bolē, bolos* throw.

symmetry *n.* due proportion of the several parts of a body or any whole to each other, congruity, parity, regularity, harmony. WH: 16C. Obs. French *symmétrie* (now *symétrie*) or Latin *symmetria*, from Greek *summetria*, from *summetros*, from *sum-* SYM- + *metron* measure. See -METRY.

sympathy *n.* the quality of being affected with the same feelings as another person, or of sharing emotions, affections, inclinations etc. with another person. *Also a.* WH: 16C. Latin *sympathia*, from Greek *sumpatheia*, from *sumpathēs* having a fellow feeling, from *sum-* SYM- + base of PATHOS. See also -Y[2].

sympatric *a.* occurring in the same geographical area, as distinct from *allopatric*. WH: early 20C. SYM- + Greek *patra* fatherland. See also -IC.

sympetalous *a.* having the petals joined. WH: 19C. SYM- + *petalous* (PETAL).

symphony *n.* a complex and elaborate composition for an orchestra, usu. consisting of four varied movements. WH: 12–14C. Old French *simphonie* (Modern French *symphonie*), from Latin *symphonia* instrumental harmony, voices in concert, from Greek *sumphonia*, from *sumphōnos* harmonious, from *sum-* SYM- + *phōnē* sound, voice. See also -Y[2].

symphyllous *a.* having the leaves joined. WH: 19C. SYM- + Greek *phullon* leaf. See also -OUS.

symphysis *n.* (the joint formed by) the union of two parts of the skeleton by growing together or the intervention of cartilage. WH: 16C. Modern Latin, from Greek *sumphusis* growing together, from *sum-* SYM- + *phusis* growth.

sympiesometer *n.* an instrument for measuring the pressure or velocity of a current of water. WH: 19C. Greek *sumpiesis* compression, from *sumpiezein* to compress, from *sum-* SYM- + *piezein* to press + -O- + -METER.

symploce *n.* the repetition of a word or phrase at the beginning and of another at the end of successive clauses. WH: 16C. Late Latin, from Greek *sumplokē* an interweaving, from *sum-* SYM- + *plekein* to twine, to plait, to weave.

sympodium *n.* a false plant axis or stem composed of superimposed branches. WH: 19C. Modern Latin, from Greek *sum-* SYM- + *pous, podos* foot. See also -IUM.

symposiarch *n.* the president or director of a feast. WH: 17C. Greek *sumposiarkhos*, from *sumposion* SYMPOSIUM + *arkhos* chief.

symposium *n.* a conference or formal meeting at which several speakers give addresses on a particular topic. WH: 16C. Latin, from Greek *sumposion*, from *sumpotēs* fellow drinker, from *sum-* SYM- + *potēs* drinker. The word was originally the term for a convivial meeting held by the ancient Greeks for drinking, conversation, philosophical discussion, etc. The current sense evolved in the 18C.

symptom *n.* a perceptible change in the appearance or functions of the body indicating disease. WH: 14–15C. Medieval Latin *synthoma*, from Late Latin *symptoma*, from Greek *sumptōma* chance, accident, mischance, from *sumpiptein* to fall upon, to happen to, from *sum-* SYM- + *piptein* to fall.

syn- *pref.* with. WH: Latin, from Greek *sun-*, from *sun* with. For reasons of pronunciation, *n* is often assimilated to a subsequent consonant. See SYM-.

synaeresis *n.* the contraction of two vowels or syllables into one. WH: 16C. Late Latin, from Greek *sunairesis*, from *sun-* SYN- + *hairesis*, from *hairein* to take.

synaesthesia *n.* the subjective sensation of a sense other than the sense being stimulated. WH: 19C. SYN- + -*aesthesia*, based on ANAESTHESIA.

synagogue *n.* a Jewish congregation for religious instruction and observances. WH: 12–14C. Old French *sinagoge* (Modern French *synagogue*), from Late Latin *synagoga*, from Greek *sunagōgē* meeting, assembly, from *sunagein* to bring together, to assemble, from *sun-* SYN- + *agein* to lead, to bring.

synalepha *n.* a blending of two syllables into one, esp. by the suppression of a final vowel before an initial vowel. WH: 16C. Late Latin *synaloepha*, from Greek *sunaloiphē*, from *sunaleiphein* to melt together, from *sun-* SYN- + *aleiphein* to melt.

synallagmatic *a.* (of a contract or treaty) imposing reciprocal obligations. WH: 18C. Greek *sunallagmatikos*, from *sunallagma* covenant, contract, from *sunallassein*, from *sun-* SYN- + *allassein* to exchange. See also -IC.

synantherous *a.* having the anthers growing together. WH: 19C. SYN- + Modern Latin *anthera* ANTHER + -OUS.

synanthous *a.* having flowers and leaves appearing at the same time. WH: 19C. SYN- + Greek *anthos* flower + -OUS.

synaphea *n.* continuity between lines or portions of lines in verse, esp. when the last syllable of a line is made long or elided by synalepha with the initial syllable of the next. WH: 19C. Greek *sunapheia* connection, from *sunaphēs* connected, united, from *sun-* SYN- + *haptein* to fasten, to fix.

synapse *n.* the point at which a nerve impulse is transmitted from one neuron to another. WH: 19C. Modern Latin *synapsis*, from Greek *sunapsis* connection, junction, from *sun-* SYN- + *hapsis* joining, from *haptein* to join.

synarthrosis *n.* a fixed bone joint. WH: 16C. Greek *sunarthrōsis*, from *sun-* SYN- + *arthrōsis* (ARTHRO-, -OSIS).

sync *n.* synchronization. *Also v.t., v.i.* WH: early 20C. Abbr. of *synchronization* (SYNCHRONOUS).

syncarp *n.* an aggregate fruit, such as the blackberry. WH: 19C. Modern Latin *syncarpium*, from Greek *sun-* SYN- + *karpos* fruit.

syncategorematic *a.* denoting words that can express only parts of terms, such as adverbs, prepositions etc. WH: 19C. Medieval Latin *syncategorematicus*, from Greek *sugkatēgorēmatikos*, from *sugkatēgorēma*, from *sugkatēgorein* to predicate jointly. See also -IC.

synchondrosis *n.* the almost immovable articulation of bones by means of cartilage, as in the vertebrae. WH: 16C. Modern Latin, from Late Greek *sugkhondrōsis*, from *sun-* SYN- + *khondros* cartilage. See also -OSIS.

synchoresis *n.* in rhetoric, a concession made for the purpose of retorting more effectively. WH: 18C. Greek *sugkhōrēsis*, from *sugkhōreein* to agree, to yield ground, from *sun-* SYN- + *khōros* space.

synchro- *comb. form* synchronized. WH: Abbr. of SYNCHRONOUS, *synchronized*. See also -O-.

synchrocyclotron *n.* a cyclotron which can achieve higher frequencies by decreasing the frequency of the accelerating field as the energy and mass of the particles increase. WH: mid-20C. SYNCHRO- + CYCLOTRON.

synchromesh *a.* of or relating to a system of gearing in which the drive and driving members are automatically synchronized before engagement, thus avoiding shock and noise in changing gear. *Also n.* WH: early 20C. SYNCHRO- + MESH.

synchronology *n.* comparative chronology. WH: 18C. SYN- + CHRONOLOGY.

synchronous *a.* occurring simultaneously. WH: 17C. Late Latin *synchronus*, from Greek *sugkhronos*, from *sun-* SYN- + *khronos* time. See also -OUS.

synchrotron *n.* a very high-energy particle accelerator. WH: mid-20C. SYNCHRO- + -TRON.

synchysis *n.* a confused arrangement of words in a sentence. WH: 16C. Late Latin, from Greek *sugkhusis*, from *sugkhein* to mingle, to confuse, from *sun-* SYN- + *khein* to pour.

synclastic *a.* having uniform curvature, convex or concave in every direction. WH: 19C. SYN- + Greek *klastos* broken (here, bent) + -IC.

synclinal *a.* sloping downwards towards a common point or line, as distinct from *anticlinal*. WH: 19C. SYN- + Greek *klinein* to lean, to slope + -AL[1].

syncopate *v.t.* to modify (a musical note, rhythm etc.) by beginning on an unaccented and continuing with an accented beat. WH: 17C. Late Latin *syncopatus*, p.p. of *syncopare* to shorten. See SYNCOPE, also -ATE[3].

syncope *n.* the elision of a letter or syllable from the middle of a word. WH: 14–15C. Late Latin, from Greek *sugkopē*, from *sun-* SYN- + *kop-*, stem of *koptein* to strike, to cut off.

syncretism *n.* the attempted reconciliation of various philosophic or religious schools or systems of thought, for example against a common opponent. WH: 17C. Modern Latin *syncretismus*, from Greek *sugkrētismos*, from *sugkrētizein* to combine against a common enemy. See also -ISM. Some sources see an origin in Greek *sun-* SYN- + *Krēs*, *Krētos* Cretan, as if referring to an alliance in the manner of the Cretans. But this is usually regarded as a folk etymology.

syncytium *n.* a mass of cytoplasm containing several nuclei. WH: 19C. SYN- + Greek *kutos* receptacle, vessel. See -CYTE, also -IUM.

syndactyl *a.* having the digits united, as in webbed feet. WH: 19C. SYN- + Greek *daktulos* finger.

syndesis *n.* synapsis. WH: early 20C. SYN- + Greek *desis* binding together, from *desmos* bond, connection.

syndesmosis *n.* an articulation of bones by ligaments. WH: 16C. Greek *sundesmos* binding, ligament, from *sun-* SYN- + *desmos* bond, connection. See also -OSIS.

syndetic *a.* serving to connect, copulative. WH: 17C. Greek *sundetikos*, from *sundein* to bind together, from *sun-* SYN- + *dein* to bind. See also -IC.

syndic *n.* an officer or magistrate invested with varying powers in different places and times. WH: 17C. French delegate, chief representative, from Late Latin *syndicus* delegate of a corporation, from Greek *sundikos* defendant's advocate, from *sun-* SYN- + base of *dikē* judgement, *deiknusthai* to show. See also -IC.

syndicalism *n.* the economic doctrine that all the workers in any trade or industry should participate in the management and control and in the division of the profits. WH: early 20C. French *syndicalisme*, from *syndical*, from *syndic*. See SYNDIC, also -AL[1], -ISM.

syndicate[1] *n.* an association of people or firms formed to promote some special interest or undertake a joint project. WH: 17C. French *syndicat*, from Medieval Latin *syndicatus*, from Late Latin *syndicus*. See SYNDIC, also -ATE[1].

syndicate[2] *v.t.* to combine in a syndicate. WH: 17C. SYNDICATE[1].

syndrome *n.* the aggregate of symptoms characteristic of any disease or disorder. WH: 16C. Modern Latin, from Greek *sundromē*, from *sun-* SYN- + *dromos* running, from *dramein* to run.

syne *adv., conj., prep.* since. WH: 12–14C. Contr. of obs. *sithen*, from Old English *siththon*, *siththan*, ult. from Germanic. Rel. to SINCE.

synecdoche *n.* a figure of speech by which a part is put for the whole or the whole for a part. WH: 14–15C. Latin, from Greek *sunekdokhē*, from *sunekdekhesthai*, lit. to take with something else, from *sun-* SYN- + *ekdekhesthai* to take, to take up.

synechia *n.* an abnormal adhesion of the iris to the cornea or to the capsule of the crystalline lens. WH: 19C. Greek *sunekheia* continuity, from *sunekhēs* continuous, from *sun-* SYN- + *ekhein* to have, to hold. See also -IA.

synecology *n.* the ecology of plant and animal communities. WH: early 20C. SYN- + ECOLOGY.

synecphonesis *n.* synaeresis. WH: 17C. Late Latin, from Greek *sunekphōnēsis*, from *sunekphōnein* to utter together, from *sun-* SYN- + *ekphōnein* to utter, to pronounce, from *ek-* EX- + *phōnein* to speak, to utter, from *phōnē* sound, voice.

synergy *n.* the working together of two drugs, muscles etc. so that their combined action exceeds the sum of their individual actions. WH: 17C. Modern Latin *synergia*, from Greek *sunergia*, from *sunergein* to work together. See also -Y[2].

synesis *n.* a grammatical construction according to the sense rather than syntax. WH: 18C. Modern Latin, from Greek *sunēsis* union, intelligence, from *sunienai* to bring together, to perceive, to understand.

syngamy *n.* sexual reproduction by union of gametes. WH: early 20C. SYN- + -GAMY.

syngenesious *a.* having the anthers cohering. WH: 18C. Modern Latin *syngenesia*, from *syn-* SYN- + Greek GENESIS + -ia -IA. See also -OUS.

syngenesis *n.* reproduction by the union of the ovum and the spermatozoon. WH: 19C. SYN- + GENESIS.

synizesis *n.* synaeresis involving the combination into one syllable of two vowels that cannot make a diphthong. WH: 19C. Late Latin, from Greek *sunizēsis*, from *sunizanein* to sink down, to collapse, from *sun-* SYN- + *hizanein* to seat, to sit, to settle down, from *hizein* to seat, to sit.

synod *n.* an ecclesiastical council. WH: 14–15C. Late Latin *synodus*, from Greek *sunodos* assembly, meeting, from *sun-* SYN- + *hodos* way.

synoecious *a.* having male and female organs in the same inflorescence or receptacle. WH: 19C. SYN- + -oecious, based on DIOECIOUS, MONOECIOUS.

synonym *n.* a word having much the same meaning as another of the same language. WH: 14–15C. Latin *synonymum*, from Greek *sunōnumon*, use as n. of neut. sing. of *sunōnumos*, from *sun-* SYN- + *onuma* name.

synopsis *n.* a general view, a conspectus, a summary. WH: 17C. Late Latin, from Greek *sunopsis*, from *sun-* SYN- + *opsis* view. Cp. CONSPECTUS.

synostosis *n.* union of different parts of the skeleton by means of bone. WH: 19C. SYN- + Greek *osteon* bone + -OSIS.

synovia *n.* an albuminous lubricating fluid secreted by the synovial membranes lining joints and tendon sheaths. WH: 17C. Modern Latin *sinovia, synovia, sinophia*, of uncertain orig. The term was probably invented arbitrarily by Paracelsus for a nutritive body fluid and for gout. It is traditionally derived from Greek *sun-* SYN- + *ōon*, Latin *ovum* egg, from the resemblance of synovia to the white of an egg. But this is simply an attempt to explain a word of unknown origin.

syntagma *n.* a word or phrase forming a syntactic unit. WH: 17C. Late Latin, from Greek *suntagma*, from *suntassein*. See SYNTAX.

syntax *n.* (the part of grammar that deals with) the due arrangement of words forming units or the construction of sentences etc. WH: 16C. French *syntaxe*, or from Late Latin *syntaxis*, from Greek *suntaxis*, from *suntassein*, from *sun-* SYN- + *tassein* to arrange.

synteresis *n.* the habit of mind which enables one to make primary moral judgements, conscience; remorse. WH: 14–15C. Medieval Latin, from Greek *suntērēsis* careful guarding, careful watching, from *suntērein* to guard, to watch over, from *sun-* SYN- + *tērein* to guard, to keep.

synth *n.* a synthesizer. WH: late 20C. Abbr. of *synthesizer* (SYNTHESIS).

synthesis *n.* the building up of a complex whole by the union of elements, esp. the process of forming concepts, general ideas, theories etc. WH: 14–15C. Latin, from Greek *sunthesis*, from *suntithenai*, from *sun-* SYN- + *tithenai* to put, to place.

sypher *v.t.* to join (planks etc.) with bevelled and overlapping edges so as to leave a flush surface. WH: 19C. Var. of CIPHER.

syphilis *n.* an infectious venereal disease caused by the spirochaete *Treponema*, introduced into the system by direct contact or due to heredity, affecting first the genitals, then the skin and mucous membranes and finally the muscles, bones and brain. WH: 18C. Modern Latin, orig. in *Syphilis, sive Morbus Gallicus* Syphilis, or the French Disease, title of a Latin poem (1530) by Girolamo Fracastoro, 1483–1553, Veronese physician, from *Syphilus*, a shepherd in it, the supposed first sufferer of the disease.

syphon *n.* a tube shaped like an inverted U or V, having one branch longer than the other, used for conveying liquid over the edge of a cask, tank etc., to a lower level, through the force of atmospheric pressure. *Also v.t., v.i.* WH: 14–15C. French *siphon* or Latin *sipho, siphonis*, from Greek *siphōn* pipe, tube.

Syrian *a.* of or relating to Syria. *Also n.* WH: 12–14C. Old French *sirien* (Modern French *syrien*), from Latin *Syrius*, from Greek *Surios*, from *Suria* Syria, a country in the Middle East. See also -AN.

syringa *n.* the mock orange. WH: 17C. Modern Latin, from Greek *surigx, suriggos* pipe, SYRINX. The plant is so called from the former use of the stems to make pipe-stems.

syringe *n.* a cylindrical instrument with a piston used to draw in a quantity of liquid by suction and eject or inject it in a stream, spray or jet. *Also v.t.* WH: 14–15C. Medieval Latin *syringa*. See SYRINX.

syringo- *comb. form* a syrinx. WH: Latin *syrinx, syringis*, or from Greek *surigx*. See SYRINX, also -O-.

syrinx *n.* a set of pan pipes. WH: 17C. Latin, from Greek *surigx, suriggos* pipe, tube, channel, fistula.

Syro- *comb. form* Syrian, Syriac. WH: Greek *Suro-*, comb. form of *Suros* a Syrian. Cp. SYRIAN.

Syroarabian *a.* of, relating to or comprising Syriac and Arabic. WH: 19C. SYRO- + *Arabian* (ARAB).

Syrophoenician *a.* of or relating to Syrophoenicia, a Roman province in W Asia. WH: 16C. Latin *Syrophoenix, Syrophoenicis*, from Greek *Surophoinix, Surophoinikos*. See SYRO-, PHOENICIAN.

syrphid *a.* of or relating to the dipteran family Syrphidae, including the hoverflies. *Also n.* WH: 19C. Medieval Latin *Syrphidae*, from *Syrphus* genus name, from Greek *surphos* gnat. See also -ID.

syrup *n.* a saturated solution of sugar in water, usu. combined with fruit juice etc. for use in cookery, as a beverage etc., or with a medicinal substance. WH: 14–15C. Old French *sirop* or Medieval Latin *siropus, sirupus*, ult. from Arabic *šarāb* wine, beverage, drink, fruit syrup. Cp. SHERBET, SHRUB².

SYSOP *n.* a system operator. WH: late 20C. Abbr. of *system operator*.

syssarcosis *n.* a connection of parts of the skeleton by intervening muscle. WH: 17C. Modern Latin, from Greek *sussarkōsis*, from *sussarkoun* to unite by flesh, to cover over by flesh, from *sun-* SYN- + *sarx* flesh.

systaltic *a.* (of the heart) alternately contracting and dilating, pulsatory. WH: 17C. Late Latin *systalticus*, from Greek *sustaltikos*, from *sun-* SYN- + *staltos*, verbal a. from *stal-*, stem of *stellein* to put, to place. See also -IC.

system *n.* coordinated arrangement, organization. WH: 17C. French *système* or Late Latin *systema*, from Greek *sustēma, sustēmatos*, from *sunistanai*, from *sun-* SYN- + *sta-*, base of *histanai* to set up.

systole *n.* the contraction of the heart forcing the blood outwards, as distinct from *diastole*. WH: 16C. Late Latin, from Greek *sustolē*, from *sustellein* to contract.

systyle *a.* having columns set only two diameters apart. WH: 18C. Latin *systylos*, from Greek *sustulos*, from *sun-* SYN- + *stulos* column.

syzygy *n.* the conjunction or opposition of any two of the heavenly bodies, esp. of a planet with the sun. WH: 17C. Late Latin *syzygia*, from Greek *suzugia* yoke, pair, copulation, conjunction, from *suzugos* yoked, paired, from *sun-* SYN- + stem of *zeugnunai* to yoke.

ta *int.* thank you. WH: 18C. Childish form of *thank you* (THANK).

taal *n.* the Afrikaans language. WH: 19C. Dutch language, speech, from Middle Dutch *tāle*, corr. to Old English *talu* TALE.

tab[1] *n.* a small flap, tag, tongue etc., as the flap of a shoe, the tag or tip of lace etc. *Also v.t.* WH: 14–15C. Orig. uncertain. Cp. TAG.

tab[2] *n.* a tabulator on a computer or typewriter keyboard. *Also v.t.* WH: early 20C. Abbr. of *tabulator* (TABULAR).

tab[3] *n.* a tablet or small piece of paper impregnated with a drug, esp. an illegal one. WH: mid-20C. TAB[1], influ. by TABLET.

tabard *n.* a sleeveless jacket, tunic or overall. WH: 12–14C. Old French *tabart*, of unknown orig.

tabaret *n.* a fabric of alternate satin and watered-silk stripes used for upholstery. WH: 18C. Prob. from TABBY.

Tabasco® *n.* a hot, capsicum sauce, used for flavouring Mexican dishes, tomato juice etc. WH: 19C. *Tabasco*, a river and state of Mexico.

tabbouleh *n.* a type of Mediterranean salad made from cracked wheat, tomatoes and cucumber and flavoured with mint, lemon juice and olive oil. WH: mid-20C. Arabic *tabbūla*.

tabby *n.* a tabby cat. *Also v.t., a.* WH: 16C. Old French *tabis*, watered silk, from Arabic a. *'attābī*, from *al-'Attābiyya*, a quarter of Baghdad where the fabric was manufactured. The name of the striped cat dates from the 18C, originally as *tabby cat* (17C).

tabernacle *n.* a tent, booth or other building of light construction, and usu. movable, used as a habitation, temple etc. *Also v.i., v.t.* WH: 12–14C. Old French, or from Latin *tabernaculum* tent, booth, shed, dim. of *taberna* TAVERN. See also -CLE.

tabes *n.* wasting away, emaciation. WH: 16C. Latin wasting away.

tabla *n.* a pair of small Indian drums with variable pitch, played with the hands. WH: 19C. Persian and Urdu *tabla*, Hindi *tablā*, from Arabic *ṭabl* drum.

tablature *n.* a system of notation for instruments such as the lute, violin or guitar, showing string and fret position, and indicating rhythm and fingering. WH: 16C. French, from Latin *tavolatura* prick song, from *tavolare* to set to music.

table *n.* an article of furniture consisting of a flat surface resting on one or more supports, used for serving meals, working, writing, playing games etc. *Also v.t.* WH: pre-1200. Latin *tabula* plank, tablet, list. The form in Middle English was adopted from French *table*, from Latin.

tableau *n.* a presentation resembling a picture. WH: 17C. French, from Old French *tablel*, dim. of *table* TABLE. See also -EL.

tablet *n.* a small apron or apron-like part of a woman's dress. WH: 12–14C. Old French *tablete* (Modern French *tablette*), from dim. of Latin *tabula* TABLE. See also -ET[1]. The original sense was a small flat slab of stone, metal etc. The medicinal tablet dates from the 14–15C.

tablier *n.* a small apron or apron-like part of a woman's dress. WH: 12–14C. Old French, ult. from Latin *tabula*. See TABLE, also -ER[2]. The original sense (to the 15C) was backgammon board. The sense apron dates from the 19C.

tabloid *n.* a cheap daily newspaper that usually offers a more sensationalist view of the news than the broadsheet papers give. WH: 19C. Orig. the proprietary name of a medicinal or pharmaceutical preparation sold in tablet form, from TABLET + -OID. The name was registered as a trademark in 1884 by Burroughs, Wellcome & Co., London, but subsequently applied generically to a compressed form of anything. It was applied to a popular newspaper in the early 20C.

taboo *n.* something which is very strongly disapproved of in a particular society etc. *Also a., v.t.* WH: 18C. Tongan *tabu*.

tabor *n.* a small drum used to accompany the pipe. WH: 12–14C. Old French *tabur*, *tabour*, also *tanbor*, *tambour*, appar. of Oriental orig. Cp. Persian *tabīra*, *tabūrāk* drum, ? influ. by Arabic *ṭunbūr* a kind of lute or lyre.

tabouret *n.* a small seat, usu. without arms or back. WH: 17C. French, dim. of *tabour*. See TABOR, also -ET[1].

tabular *a.* set out, arranged in, or computed from tables. WH: 17C. Latin *tabularis*, from *tabula* TABLE. See also -AR[1].

tabun *n.* an organic phosphorus compound, formula $C_2H_5OP(O)(CN)N(CH_3)_2$, used as a lethal nerve gas in chemical warfare. WH: mid-20C. German, of unknown orig.

tacamahac *n.* a resin obtained from various S American trees, esp. of the genus *Calophyllum*. WH: 16C. Obs. Spanish *tacamahaca* (now *tacamaca*), from Aztec *tecomahiyac*.

tac-au-tac *n.* in fencing, the parry combined immediately with the riposte. WH: early 20C. French, lit. clash for clash, from imit. *tac*.

tacet *v.i.* to be silent (used in the imperative as an instruction to a particular voice or instrument). WH: 18C. Latin is silent, 3rd pers. sing. pres. ind. of *tacere* to be silent.

tach *n.* a tachometer. WH: mid-20C. Abbr. of TACHOMETER.

tachism *n.* a form of action painting with haphazard blobs of colour. WH: mid-20C. French *tachisme*, from *tache* spot, blot. See also -ISM.

tachistoscope *n.* an instrument which flashes images on to a screen for very brief spaces of time, usually a fraction of a second, used in the study of learning and perception. WH: 19C. Greek *takhistos* swiftest + -SCOPE.

tacho *n.* a tachometer. WH: mid-20C. Abbr. of TACHOMETER.

tacho- *comb. form* speed. WH: Greek *takhos* speed. See also -O-.

tachogram *n.* a visual record produced by a tachograph. WH: early 20C. TACHO- + -GRAM.

tachograph *n.* a tachometer in a motor vehicle, esp. a lorry or bus, which records its speed and the distance travelled between stops. WH: early 20C. TACHO- + -GRAPH.

tachometer *n.* an instrument for measuring the rate of rotation of a revolving shaft in a vehicle's engine and which can therefore also indicate the vehicle's speed. WH: 19C. TACHO- + -METER. The word was coined in 1810 by the English engineer and inventor Bryan Donkin.

tachy- *comb. form* swift. WH: Greek *takhus* swift.

tachycardia *n.* abnormally rapid beating of the heart. WH: 19C. TACHY- + Greek *kardia* heart.

tachygraphy *n.* shorthand, stenography, esp. any of the ancient Greek or Roman systems. WH: 17C. TACHY- + -GRAPHY.

tachylyte *n.* a black, vitreous basalt. WH: 19C. TACHY- + -*lyte* (LYSIS). The basalt is so called as it is easily fusible.

tachymeter *n.* a surveying instrument for measuring distances rapidly. WH: 19C. TACHY- + -METER.

tachyon *n.* a hypothetical elementary particle which travels faster than the speed of light. WH: mid-20C. TACHY- + -ON. The term was coined in 1967 by the US physicist Gerald Feinberg.

tachyphylaxis *n.* the rapid development of tolerance or immunity to the effects of a specific drug. WH: early 20C. TACHY- + Greek *phulaxis* protection.

tacit *a.* implied but not actually expressed. WH: 17C. Latin *tacitus*, p.p. of *tacere* to be silent.

taciturn *a.* habitually silent, reserved or uncommunicative. WH: 18C. French *taciturne* or Latin *taciturnus*, from *tacitus* TACIT.

tack[1] *n.* a small, sharp, flat-headed nail. *Also v.t., v.i.* WH: 12–14C. Prob. from an unrecorded var. of Old French *tache* fibula, clasp, large nail. Any relation with ATTACH, DETACH etc. is uncertain.

tack[2] *n.* a horse's saddle, bridle, harness etc. **WH:** 18C. Abbr. of TACKLE.

tack[3] *n.* something shoddy, cheap or vulgarly ostentatious. **WH:** late 20C. Back-formation from *tacky* (TACK[1]).

tack[4] *n.* food, fare. **WH:** 16C. Orig. unknown.

tack[5] *n.* a letting contract, a lease. **WH:** 12–14C. Prob. from Old Norse *tak* seizure, hold, bail, security, from *taka* TAKE[1].

tackle *n.* apparatus, esp. of ropes, pulleys etc., for lifting, hoisting etc., or for working spars, sails etc. *Also v.t.* **WH:** 12–14C. Prob. from Middle Low German *takel*, from *taken*, corr. to Middle Dutch *tacken* to lay hold of. See also -LE[1]. ? Rel. to TAKE[1].

taco *n.* a type of thin pancake or tortilla from Mexico, usually with a spicy meat or vegetable filling. **WH:** mid-20C. Mexican Spanish.

tact *n.* an intuitive sense of what is fitting or right. **WH:** 17C. Old French, or from Latin *tactus* touch, from p.p. of *tangere* to touch. The original meaning was sense of touch. The current sense, deriving direct from French *tact*, evolved in the 19C.

tactics *n.* the art of manoeuvring military or naval forces, esp. in actual contact with the enemy. **WH:** 17C. Modern Latin *tactica*, from Greek *ta taktika*, neut. pl. of *taktikos*, from *taktos* ordered, arranged, from base of *tassein* to set in order. See also -ICS.

tactile *a.* of, relating to or perceived by the sense of touch. **WH:** 17C. Latin *tactilis*, from *tactus*, p.p. of *tangere* to touch. See also -IL.

tad *n.* a small amount. **WH:** 19C. Orig. uncertain. ? Shortening of TADPOLE.

tadpole *n.* the larva of an amphibian, esp. of a frog or toad, before the gills and tail disappear. **WH:** 15C. TOAD + POLL[1].

taedium vitae *n.* weariness of life. **WH:** 18C. Latin, from *taedium* TEDIUM + gen. sing. of *vita* life.

tae kwon do *n.* a type of Korean martial art, similar to karate, involving kicks and punches. **WH:** mid-20C. Korean, lit. art of hand and foot fighting, from *tae* kick + *kwon* fist + *do* art, method.

tael *n.* a Chinese and Far Eastern weight of 1 1/3 oz. (38 g) or a weight close to this. **WH:** 16C. Portuguese, from Malay *tahil* weight.

taenia *n.* a band or fillet separating a Doric frieze from an architrave. **WH:** 16C. Latin, from Greek *tainia* band, fillet, ribbon.

taffeta *n.* a light, thin, glossy silk fabric. **WH:** 14–15C. Old French *taffetas* or Medieval Latin *taffata*, ult. from Persian *tāfta*, use as n. of p.p. of *tāftan* to shine.

taffrail *n.* the rail round a ship's stern. **WH:** 19C. Alt. of *tafferel*, from Dutch *taffereel* panel, picture, dim. of Latin *tafel* TABLE, with assim. of -*rel* to RAIL[1]. The *tafferel* (17C) was the upper part of the flat portion of a ship's stern, usually decorated with carvings, etc.

Taffy *n.* a Welshman. **WH:** 17C. Representation of a pronun. of the Welsh male forename *Dafydd*, English *David*. The name is common in Wales and is that of the principality's patron saint.

taffy *n.* toffee. **WH:** 19C. Earlier form of TOFFEE.

tafia *n.* a variety of rum distilled from molasses. **WH:** 18C. French, from W Indian creole, alt. of RATAFIA.

tag *n.* any small appendage, such as a metal point at the end of a lace. *Also v.t.* **WH:** 14–15C. Orig. unknown. Cp. DAG. The original sense was a pointed hanging section of a slashed garment. The children's game of the name arose in the 18C, perhaps as a variant of TIG.

tagetes *n.* any plant of the genus *Tagetes* of the aster family. **WH:** 18C. Modern Latin, from *Tages*, the name of an Etruscan god who sprang from the ploughed earth.

tagliatelle *n.* pasta in the form of thin strips. **WH:** 19C. Italian, from *tagliare* to cut.

tahini *n.* a thick paste made from ground sesame seeds. **WH:** mid-20C. Modern Greek *takhini*, from Arabic *ṭaḥīnā*, from *ṭaḥana* to grind, to crush, to pulverize.

Tahitian *n.* a native or inhabitant of Tahiti. *Also a.* **WH:** 19C. *Tahiti*, an island in the S Pacific + -AN.

tahr *n.* a beardless Himalayan goatlike mammal, *Hemitragus jemlahicus*. **WH:** 19C. Local (Himalayan) name.

tahsil *n.* a division for revenue and other administrative purposes in some Indian states. **WH:** 19C. Persian and Urdu *taḥṣīl*, from Arabic collection, levying of taxes.

taiaha *n.* a Maori carved long-handled club, now ceremonial. **WH:** 19C. Maori.

t'ai chi ch'uan *n.* a Chinese form of exercise and self-defence based on slow controlled movements. **WH:** mid-20C. Chinese *tàijí quán*, from *tài* great + *jí* limit + *quán* fist.

Taig *n.* in N Ireland, a Roman Catholic. **WH:** late 20C. Var. of *Teague* (17C), a nickname for an Irishman, from Anglicized spelling of Irish name *Tadhg*.

taiga *n.* the spruce-dominated coniferous forests found in subarctic N America and Eurasia. **WH:** 19C. Russian *taïga*, from Mongolian.

tail[1] *n.* the part of an animal, bird, fish or insect that extends from the end or the back of the body, esp. when it forms a movable or flexible appendage. *Also v.t., v.i.* **WH:** pre-1200. Old English *tægl*, *tægel*, rel. to Middle Low German *tagel* twisted whip, rope's end, Old High German *zagal* animal's tail (German dial. *Zagel*), Old Norse *tagl* horse's tail, from Germanic.

tail[2] *n.* limitation of ownership, limited ownership. *Also a.* **WH:** 12–14C. Old French *taille*, from *taillier* (Modern French *tailler*) to cut, from Latin *talea* rod, twig, cutting. The original sense (to the 17C) was a subsidy levied by a king, a tax. The current sense dates from the 14–15C.

tailor *n.* a person whose occupation is to cut out and make clothes, esp. outer clothes for men. *Also v.i., v.t.* **WH:** 12–14C. Old French *tailleur* cutter, from Late Latin *taliare* to split, from Latin *talea*. See TAIL[2], also -OR.

Taino *n.* a member of an extinct American Indian people of the W Indies. **WH:** 19C. Taino noble, lord.

taint *n.* a stain, a blemish, a disgrace. *Also v.t., v.i.* **WH:** 14–15C. Partly shortening of ATTAINT, partly from Old French *teint*, *taint*, from Latin *tinctus*, p.p. of *tingere* TINGE.

taipan[1] *n.* a large and extremely venomous Australian snake, *Oxyuranus microlepidotus*. **WH:** mid-20C. Australian Aboriginal (Wik-Mungkan) *dhayban*.

taipan[2] *n.* the head of a foreign business in China. **WH:** 19C. Chinese *tài* great + *bān* team.

Taiwanese *n.* a native or inhabitant of Taiwan. **WH:** mid-20C. *Taiwan*, an island in SE Asia + -ESE.

taj *n.* a crown, a head-dress of distinction, esp. a tall cap worn by Muslim dervishes. **WH:** 19C. Persian *tāj* crown.

Tajik *n.* a native or inhabitant of Tajikistan, a republic in central Asia. **WH:** 19C. Persian *tājik* a person who is neither an Arab nor a Turk, a Persian.

take[1] *v.t.* to lay hold of, grasp, seize, capture etc. *Also v.i.* **WH:** pre-1200. Old Norse *taka*, rel. to Middle Dutch *tāken* to grasp, to seize, to catch, ult. of unknown orig. The earliest sense was to get possession by force, to capture.

take[2] *n.* the act of taking. **WH:** 16C. TAKE[1].

takin *n.* a hollow-horned ruminant, *Budorcas taxicolor*, of SE Tibet. **WH:** 19C. Local Tibetan-Burman name.

talapoin *n.* a Buddhist priest or monk in Burma (Myanmar), Sri Lanka etc. **WH:** 16C. French, from Portuguese *talapão*, from Mongolian *tula pói*, lit. lord of merit, a respectful title for a Buddhist monk.

talaria *n.pl.* in Roman mythology, the winged boots or sandals of Hermes, Iris etc. **WH:** 16C. Latin, neut. pl. of *talaris*, from *talus* ankle. See also -AR[1].

talbot *n.* a large variety of hound, usu. white with large pendulous ears and massive jaws, now extinct but formerly used for tracking and hunting. **WH:** 14–15C. Prob. from English family name *Talbot*.

talbotype *n.* a process invented in 1840 of producing a latent image upon sensitized paper, the basis of the photographic process. **WH:** 19C. William Henry Fox *Talbot*, 1800–77, English photographer + -*type* (TYPE). Cp. CALOTYPE.

talc *n.* talcum powder. *Also v.t.* **WH:** 16C. Medieval Latin *talcum*, from Arabic *ṭalk*, from Persian.

tale *n.* a narrative, an account, a story, true or fictitious, esp. an imaginative or legendary story. **WH:** pre-1200. Old English *talu*, from Germanic base also of TELL[1]. Cp. German *Zahl* number, *Erzählung* story. The original sense (to the 16C) was the action of telling or relating. The sense story told for entertainment arose in the 12–14C.

talent *n.* a particular aptitude, gift or faculty. **WH:** pre-1200. Old English *talente*, from Old High German *talenta*, from Latin *talenta*, pl. of *talentum* weight, sum of money, from Greek *talanton*. The word was originally an ancient unit of weight or money. The current sense evolved in the 15C from the biblical parable of the talents (Matt. xxv.14–30).

tales *n.* a writ for summoning jurors to make up a deficiency. WH: 15C. Latin, pl. of *talis* such in *talis circumstantibus* such of the bystanders, the opening words of the writ.

Taliban *n.pl.* members of a fundamentalist Islamic militia in Afghanistan. WH: late 20C. Persian, lit. students.

taligrade *a.* walking on the outer side of the foot. WH: 19C. Latin TALUS¹ + -GRADE.

taliped *a.* club-footed. WH: 19C. Modern Latin *talipes, talipedis*, from Latin TALUS¹ + *pes, pedis* foot.

talipot *n.* a S Indian palm, *Corypha umbraculifera*, with very large fan-shaped leaves used in thatching and as sunshades. WH: 17C. Malayalam *tālipat*, from Sanskrit *tālīpatra*, from *tālī* fan palm + *patra* leaf.

talisman *n.* a charm or an amulet that is believed to have magical powers, esp. one thought to protect the wearer from evil and to bring them good luck. WH: 17C. French or Spanish, appar. from Medieval Greek *telesmon*, alt. of Late Greek *telesma* completion, performance, religious rite, consecrated object, from *telein* to complete, to perform (a rite), to consecrate, from *telos* result, end.

talk *v.i.* to communicate ideas or thoughts in spoken words. Also *v.t.*, *n.* WH: 12–14C. From Germanic base of TALE or TELL¹ + freq. suf. -*k*. Cp. LURK.

tall *a.* high in stature, above the average height. Also *adv.* WH: 14–15C. Old English *getæl* swift, prompt, from Germanic. Rel. to TALE. The original sense (to the 17C) was prompt, ready, also handsome, fine. The current sense dates from the 16C.

tallage *n.* a tax on towns levied by the king (abolished 1340). WH: 12–14C. Old French *taillage*, from *taillier*. See TAIL¹, also -AGE.

tallith *n.* a fringed scarf worn over the head and shoulders by Jewish men during prayer. WH: 17C. Rabbinical Hebrew *ṭallīt*, from biblical Hebrew *ṭillel* to cover.

tallow *n.* a substance composed of the harder or less fusible fats, chiefly of animals, esp. beef or mutton fat, used for making candles, soap etc. Also *v.t.* WH: 12–14C. Middle Low German *talg, talch*, of unknown orig.

tally *n.* a reckoning, an account. Also *v.t., v.i.* WH: 14–15C. Anglo-Latin *tallia*, from Latin *talea* cutting, rod, stick. Cp. TAIL². The sense thing that corresponds with another arose in the 17C from the practice of splitting a tally-stick lengthwise, the debtor and creditor each retaining one of the halves.

tally-ho *int.* used to encourage hounds when the quarry is sighted. Also *n., int., v.t.* WH: 18C. Appar. alt. of French *taïaut*, of unknown orig. Cp. YOICKS.

Talmud *n.* the body of Jewish civil and religious law not included in the Pentateuch, including the Mishna and the Gemara. WH: 16C. Post-biblical Hebrew *talmūḏ* instruction, from Hebrew *lāmaḏ* to learn.

talon *n.* a claw, esp. of a bird of prey. WH: 12–14C. Old French, from Latin TALUS¹.

†talpa *n.* an encysted tumour, a wen. WH: 14–15C. Latin mole.

talus¹ *n.* the ankle-bone. WH: 16C. Latin ankle, ankle-bone.

talus² *n.* a mass or sloping heap of fragments accumulated at the base of a cliff or scree. WH: 17C. French, of unknown orig.

tam *n.* a tam-o'-shanter. WH: 19C. Abbr. of TAM-O'-SHANTER. Cp. TAMMY.

tamale *n.* a Mexican dish of highly seasoned maize and meat. WH: 17C. Mexican Spanish *tamal*, pl. *tamales*, from Nahuatl *tamalli*.

tamandua *n.* any small tropical American anteater of the genus *Tamandua*. WH: 17C. Portuguese, from Tupi *tamanduá*, from *ta* (contr. of *taly*) ant + *monduar* hunter.

tamarack *n.* an American larch, *Larix laricina*. WH: 19C. Canadian French *tamarac*, prob. from Algonquian.

tamari *n.* a concentrated wheat-free sauce made from soya beans. WH: late 20C. Japanese.

tamarillo *n.* the fruit of the tree tomato. WH: mid-20C. Invented word. Cp. TOMATILLO.

tamarin *n.* any small monkey of the genera *Saguinus* or *Leontopithecus* of the forests of Central and S America. WH: 18C. French, from Galibi.

tamarind *n.* a tropical tree, *Tamarindus indica*. WH: 14–15C. Medieval Latin *tamarindus*, from Arabic *tamr hindī* Indian date.

tamarisk *n.* an evergreen shrub of the genus *Tamarix*, with slender feathery branches and white and pink flowers. WH: 14–15C. Late Latin *tamariscus*, var. of Latin *tamarix*, of unknown orig.

tamasha *n.* in the Indian subcontinent, a show, a public function. WH: 17C. Persian and Urdu *tamāšā* walking about for amusement, from Arabic *tamāšā* to walk about together, from *mašā* to walk.

tambour *n.* a drum, esp. a bass drum. Also *v.t., v.i.* WH: 15C. French. See TABOR.

tambourine *n.* a small percussion instrument composed of a hoop with parchment stretched across one head and loose jingling discs in the sides, played by striking with the hand etc. WH: 16C. French *tambourin*, dim. of TAMBOUR. See also -INE.

tame *a.* (of an animal) having lost its native wildness, domesticated, not wild. Also *v.t.* WH: pre-1200. Old English *tam*, from Germanic, from Indo-European base represented also by Latin *domare*, Greek *daman* to tame, to subdue. Cp. German *zahm*.

Tamil *n.* a member of the Dravidian people who inhabit S India and Sri Lanka. Also *a.* WH: 18C. Tamil, corr. to Prakrit *Damiḷa, Daviḷa*, Sanskrit *Dramiḍa, Draviḍa*. Cp. DRAVIDIAN.

Tammany *n.* a corrupt political organization. WH: 19C. *Tammany* Hall, the building housing the central organization of the Democratic Party in New York. The hall was itself named after *Tammanend*, a wise and benevolent Delaware Indian chief.

Tammuz *n.* the fourth month in the Jewish calendar according to biblical reckoning, the tenth in the civil year, usually falling in June and July. WH: 16C. Hebrew *tammūz*.

tammy *n.* a tam-o'-shanter. WH: 19C. TAM + -Y³.

tam-o'-shanter *n.* a cap fitted closely round the brows but wide and full above. WH: 19C. *Tam o' Shanter*, the hero of a poem by Robert Burns (1790). In the poem named after him, Tam o' Shanter is described as having a 'gude blue bonnet'. His name means Tom of Shanter, the latter being a farm near Kirkoswald, S Ayrshire.

tamoxifen *n.* a drug that suppresses the effects of the hormone oestrogen and which is used in the treatment of women's breast cancer and infertility. WH: late 20C. Alt. of TRANS- + AMINE + OXY-² + PHENOL, elements of the full chemical name.

tamp *v.t.* to fill up (a blast-hole) with rammed clay above the charge. Also *n.* WH: 19C. Prob. back-formation from var. of *tampion*, as if *tamping*. A related word is *tampon* plug of soft material, a nasalized variant of French *tapon*, from a Frankish word related to TAP².

tamper *v.i.* to meddle (with). WH: 16C. Alt. of TEMPER.

tam-tam *n.* a large metal gong. WH: 19C. ? Hindi *ṭam-ṭam* TOM-TOM.

tan¹ *n.* a deepening of the skin's colour, esp. from pinkish-white to bronze, caused by exposure to the sun's rays or to artificial ultra-violet rays. Also *a., v.t., v.i.* WH: pre-1200. Prob. from Medieval Latin *tannare*, ? from Celtic. The noun evolved from the verb in the 14–15C. The sense brown skin colour evolved in the 18C.

tan² *abbr.* tangent. WH: 17C. Abbr. of TANGENT.

tanager *n.* an American bird of the subfamily Thraupinae, related to the finches, usu. with brilliantly coloured plumage. WH: 17C. Tupi *tangará*.

tandem *n.* a bicycle or tricycle for two riders one behind the other. Also *adv., a.* WH: 18C. Latin at length, as a punning use of the Latin word, originally applied to a carriage drawn by two horses harnessed one behind the other.

tandoor *n.* a clay oven as used in N India and Pakistan. WH: 19C. Urdu *tandūr*, Persian *tanūr*, ult. from Arabic *tannūr* oven, furnace.

Tang *n.* a dynasty that ruled in China, AD 618–906. Also *a.* WH: 17C. Chinese *táng*.

tang¹ *n.* a strong taste or flavour. Also *v.t.* WH: 12–14C. Old Norse *tange* point, spit of land, tang of a knife. Cp. TWANG.

tang² *n.* a ringing or clanging sound. Also *v.t., v.i.* WH: 17C. Imit.

tanga *n.* pants, briefs or bikini bottoms that consist of two small joined triangular pieces, held in place by a string or thong waistband. WH: early 20C. Portuguese, ult. of Bantu orig.

tangelo *n.* a tangerine and pomelo hybrid. WH: early 20C. TANGERINE + POMELO.

tangent *n.* a straight line meeting a circle or curve without intersecting it. Also *a.* WH: 16C. Latin *tangens, tangentis*, pres.p. of *tangere* to touch. See -ENT.

tangerine *n.* a small, loose-skinned orange. Also *a.* WH: 19C. *Tanger, Tangier*, a seaport in Morocco on the Strait of Gibraltar + -INE.

tangible *a.* perceptible by touch. *Also n.* WH: 16C. French, or from Late Latin *tangibilis*, from Latin *tangere* to touch. See also -IBLE.

tangle[1] *v.t.* to knot together or intertwine in a confused mass. *Also v.i., n.* WH: 12–14C. Prob. from Scandinavian. Cp. Swedish dial. *taggla* to disorder. The original sense was to entangle. The current sense dates from the 16C.

tangle[2] *n.* any of various seaweeds, esp. the edible ones of the genus *Laminaria*. WH: 16C. Prob. from Norwegian *tångel, tongul*, from Old Norse *thongull*.

tango[1] *n.* a Latin American dance that is characterized by highly stylized, often erotic, body movements punctuated by glides and pauses. *Also v.i.* WH: 19C. American Spanish, ? of African orig.

tango[2] *n.* a bright orange colour. *Also a.* WH: early 20C. Abbr. of TANGERINE, prob. influ. by TANGO[1]. See also -O.

tangram *n.* a Chinese puzzle consisting of a square cut into seven differently shaped pieces which have to be fitted together. WH: 19C. Orig. unknown. The Chinese name is *qīqiǎotú*, from *qī* seven + *qiǎo* skilful, clever + *tú* picture, plan. The English name is probably based on words in -GRAM denoting puzzles, such as ANA-GRAM, CRYPTOGRAM.

tanh *n.* hyperbolic tangent. WH: 19C. TAN[2] + *h* (for *hyperbolic*).

tank *n.* a cistern or vessel of large size for holding liquid, gas etc. *Also v.t., v.i.* WH: 17C. Gujarati *tākū*, Marathi *tākē* underground cistern, ? also influ. by Portuguese *tangue*, rel. to Spanish *estanque*, French *étang*, from Latin *stagnum* pond. The military combat vehicle was so named in 1915 to conceal its true nature. It was supposedly a portable watertank designed to be used in desert warfare.

tanka *n.* a Japanese verse form with five lines and 31 syllables, the first and third lines having five syllables and the others having seven. WH: 19C. Japanese, from *tan* short + *ka* song.

tankard *n.* a large drinking-vessel, usu. of metal and often with a cover. WH: 12–14C. Orig. uncertain. Cp. Middle Dutch *tanckaert*, Anglo-Latin *tancardus*.

tanner *n.* a sixpence. WH: 19C. Orig. unknown. According to some, the word is from *simon* (18C), a slang term for a sixpence, by punning allusion to the biblical character 'one Simon a tanner' (Acts ix.43).

Tannoy® *n.* a public announcement and loudspeaker system. WH: mid-20C. Abbr. of *tantalum alloy*, originally used in the manufacture of accumulators to power radio receivers.

tansy *n.* a yellow-flowered perennial herb, *Tanacetum vulgare*, with much-divided, bitter, aromatic leaves, formerly used in cookery and medicine. WH: 12–14C. Old French *tanesie* (Modern French *tanaisie*), prob. as shortening of Medieval Latin *athanasia*, from Greek immortality. The plant is so called either from its use as a medicinal herb or from the durability of its flowerheads and stems. It is also difficult to remove once established in a garden.

tantalize *v.t.* to torment or tease by seeming to offer something badly wanted but continually withholding it. WH: 16C. Latin TANTALUS + -IZE.

tantalum *n.* a rare hard greyish-white metallic element, at. no. 73, chem. symbol Ta, which is highly resistant to heat and acid corrosion. WH: 19C. Latin TANTALUS + -*um*, var. of -IUM. The element is so called because it cannot absorb acid even when immersed in it. The name was coined in 1802 by the Swedish chemist Anders Ekeberg.

tantalus *n.* a spirit-stand in which the decanters remain in sight but are secured by a lock. WH: 18C. Latin *Tantalus*, from Greek *Tantalos*, a mythical king of Phrygia punished for killing his son by being placed near water which receded whenever he tried to drink, and near branches of fruit which drew back whenever he tried to eat.

tantamount *a.* equivalent (to) in value or effect. WH: 17C. Italian *tanto montare* to amount to as much.

tantivy *n.* a hunting cry. *Also a., adv., v.i.* WH: 17C. Prob. imit. of the sound of galloping horses, or of a huntsman's horn.

tant mieux *int.* so much the better. WH: 18C. French so much the better. Cp. TANT PIS.

tanto *adv.* too much. WH: 19C. Italian, from Latin *tantum* so much.

tant pis *int.* so much the worse. WH: 18C. French so much the worse. Cp. TANT MIEUX.

tantra *n.* any of a class of later Sanskrit Hindu and Buddhist textbooks dealing chiefly with magical powers. WH: 18C. Sanskrit loom, warp, groundwork, system, doctrine.

tantrum *n.* a burst of ill temper, a fit of passion. WH: 18C. Orig. unknown.

Taoiseach *n.* the Prime Minister of the Republic of Ireland. WH: mid-20C. Irish, lit. chief, leader.

Taoism *n.* the Chinese religious system based on the teachings of Laoze (b.604 BC), primarily concerned with achieving harmony with the universe. WH: 19C. *Tao*, from Chinese *dào* way, path, right way + -ISM.

tap[1] *v.t.* to strike lightly or gently. *Also v.i., n.* WH: 12–14C. Old French *taper* or imit. Cp. CLAP[1], FLAP, RAP[1].

tap[2] *n.* a device that allows water or other fluid to be drawn out at a controlled rate; a faucet, a spigot. *Also v.t.* WH: pre-1200. Old English *tæppa*, from Germanic. Cp. German *Zapfen*. The original sense was a peg or stopper for closing and opening the hole in a cask or barrel.

tapa *n.* a kind of tough clothlike paper made from the bark of a tree, used by Polynesians for clothes, nets etc. WH: 19C. Polynesian.

tapadero *n.* a leather guard worn in front of the stirrup in California and other parts of the western US. WH: 19C. Spanish cover, lid, stopper, from *tapar* to stop up, to cover.

tapas *n.pl.* various light savoury snacks or appetizers, as served in Spain. WH: mid-20C. Pl. of Spanish *tapa*, lit. cover, lid.

tape *n.* a continuous strip of paper or magnetized flexible material on which sound, pictures or other data can be recorded using various types of recording machines. *Also v.t.* WH: pre-1200. Old English *tæppa, tæppe*, ? rel. to Old Frisian *tapia*, Middle Low German *teppen* to pluck, to tear.

taper *n.* a small wax candle. *Also v.i., v.t., a.* WH: pre-1200. Old English *tapor, taper*, from Latin *papyrus* PAPYRUS, with *p*- becoming *t*-. The candle is so called with reference to the use of the pith of the papyrus for a wick.

tapestry *n.* a textile fabric in which the wool is supplied by a spindle instead of a shuttle, with designs or pictures applied by stitches across the warp. *Also a., v.t.* WH: 14–15C. Old French *tapisserie*, from *tapissier* tapestry worker or *tapisser* to cover with carpet, from *tapis* carpet, TAPIS.

tapetum *n.* a layer of cells lining the cavity of anthers in flowering plants or of the sporangia in ferns. WH: 18C. Late Latin, from Latin *tapete* carpet.

taphonomy *n.* the study of fossilization processes. WH: mid-20C. Greek *taphos* grave + -O- + -NOMY.

tapioca *n.* a starchy, granular substance produced by beating cassava, forming a light farinaceous food. WH: 18C. Tupi-Guarani *tipioca*, from *tipi* residue, dregs + *ok, og* to squeeze out.

tapir *n.* an ungulate mammal of the genus *Tapirus* of Central and S America and parts of Asia, related to the rhinoceros and the horse, with a short, flexible snout which it uses for feeding on vegetation. WH: 18C. Spanish or Portuguese, from Tupi *tapyra*.

tapis *n.* a tapestry, a thick table-covering. WH: 15C. Old French *tapiz* (Modern French *tapis*), from Late Latin *tapetium*, from Greek *tapētion*, dim. of *tapēs, tapētos* tapestry.

tapotement *n.* the use of light rapid tapping as a form of massage. WH: 19C. French, from *tapoter* to tap. See also -MENT.

tappet *n.* a projecting arm or lever that gives intermittent motion to some part in machinery. WH: 18C. Appar. from TAP[1] + -ET[1].

tappit *a.* topped, crested. WH: 18C. Var. of *topped* (TOP[1]).

tapu *a.* sacred, taboo. WH: 18C. Var. of TABOO.

tar[1] *n.* a thick, dark, viscid oily liquid produced by the dry distillation of organic bodies and bituminous minerals, used in surfacing roads, preserving wood and the manufacture of antiseptics. *Also v.t.* WH: pre-1200. Old English *teru, teoru*, from Germanic, prob. ult. rel. to TREE. Cp. German *Teer*.

tar[2] *n.* a sailor. WH: 17C. ? Abbr. of TARPAULIN.

ta-ra *int.* goodbye. WH: mid-20C. Alt. of TA-TA.

taradiddle *n.* a lie, a fib. WH: 18C. Orig. unknown. Second element ? rel. to DIDDLE.

taraire *n.* a New Zealand forest tree, *Beilschmiedia tarairi*, with white wood. WH: 19C. Maori.

tarakihi *n.* an edible fish, *Cheilodactylus macropterus*, found in the waters of New Zealand. WH: 19C. Maori.

taramasalata *n.* a pale pink creamy Greek pâté, made from smoked cod roe or, less commonly, the roe of other fish, blended with olive oil and garlic. WH: early 20C. Modern Greek *taramosalata*, from *taramas* preserved roe + *salata* salad.

tarantass *n.* a large four-wheeled Russian carriage without springs. WH: 19C. Russian *tarantas*.

tarantella *n.* a rapid S Italian dance in triplets for one couple. WH: 18C. Italian, dim. of *Taranto* (Latin *Tarentum*), a seaport in S Italy. Pop. assoc. with *tarantola* TARANTULA. Cp. TARANTISM. The dance was attributed to the bite of the tarantula, which was believed to cause tarantism.

tarantism *n.* a form of nervous disorder characterized by uncontrollable dancing movements, prevalent in S Italy during the 15th, 16th and 17th cents. and at that time believed to be caused by venom from the bite of a tarantula. WH: 17C. Italian *tarantismo*, from *Taranto*. See TARANTELLA.

tarantula *n.* any large hairy spider of the family Theraphosidae, found in tropical regions. WH: 16C. Medieval Latin, from Old Italian *tarantola*, from *Taranto*. See TARANTELLA. The spider is so called as it has been found near Taranto. Cp. TARANTISM.

taraxacum *n.* any plant of the genus *Taraxacum*, which includes the dandelion. WH: 18C. Medieval Latin *altaraxacon*, from Arabic and Persian *ṭarakšakūn, ṭarakšakūk* dandelion, wild endive, ult. from Persian *talk* bitter + *čakūk* purslane.

tarboosh *n.* a brimless cap or fez, usu. red. WH: 18C. Egyptian Arabic *ṭarbūš*, from Ottoman Turkish *terpōš, tarbuš*, from Persian *sarpūš*, from *sar* head + *pūš* cover.

Tardenoisian *a.* belonging or relating to a mesolithic culture known to exist in S and W Europe and characterized by the use of small flint tools. *Also n.* WH: early 20C. French *Tardenoisien*, from Fère-en-*Tardenois*, a town in NE France, where first discovered + -IAN.

tardigrade *n.* any of various slow-moving invertebrates of the phylum Tardigrada, which have eight legs and live in wet soil, ditches etc. *Also a.* WH: 17C. French, or from Latin *tardigradus*, from *tardus* slow + -*i*- + -*gradus* walking.

tardy *a.* moving slowly, slow, sluggish. WH: 16C. Old French *tardif*, from Latin *tardus* slow. *Tardy* superseded *tardive* in the 15C.

tare[1] *n.* a vetch, esp. *Vicia sativa*, the common vetch. WH: 12–14C. Orig. unknown.

tare[2] *n.* an allowance for the weight of boxes, wrapping etc. in which goods are packed. *Also v.t.* WH: 14–15C. French, waste in goods, deficiency, tare, from Medieval Latin *tara*, from Arabic *ṭarḥ* that which is thrown away, from *ṭaraḥa* to reject, to deduct.

targa *n.* a sports car that has a removable hard roof which fits over a roll bar or goes into the boot when not in use. *Also a.* WH: late 20C. Italian plate, shield. The word was originally the name of a model of Porsche car (introduced in 1965) with a detachable hood, perhaps itself named after the *Targa Florio* (Florio Shield), an annual motor time trial held in Sicily.

†**targe** *n.* a light shield. WH: pre-1200. Old English *targa, targe*, Old Norse *targa* shield, Middle High German *zarge* edging, border, reinforced in Middle English from Old French. Cp. TARGET.

target *n.* an object set up as a mark to be fired at in archery etc., painted with concentric bands surrounding a bull's eye. *Also v.t.* WH: 14–15C. Dim. of TARGE. See also -ET[1]. The original sense was a light round shield or buckler. Hence anything resembling a shield. The current sense evolved in the 18C.

Targum *n.* any of various ancient Aramaic versions or paraphrases of the Old Testament Scriptures. WH: 16C. Hebrew, from Aramaic *targūm* interpretation, from *targēm* to interpret. See DRAGOMAN.

tariff *n.* a table of charges. *Also v.t.* WH: 16C. French *tarif*, from Italian *tariffa*, from Turkish *tarife*, from Arabic *ta'rifa*, from *'arrafa* to notify, to apprise. The original sense was an official list of customs duties. The sense of table charges arose in the 18C.

tarlatan *n.* a fine, transparent muslin. WH: 18C. French *tarlatane*, alt. of *tarnatane*, prob. of Indonesian orig.

Tarmac *n.* a mixture of stones or slag held together by tar and used in surfacing roads, runways etc. WH: early 20C. Abbr. of *tarmacadam* (19C), from TAR[1] + MACADAM.

tarn *n.* a small mountain lake. WH: 12–14C. Old Norse *tjǫrn*, Swedish dial. *tjärn*, Norwegian *tjörn*, Danish *tjern*. Like GILL[2] and FELL[3], the word became widely known through the works of Wordsworth and other Lake Poets in the 19C.

tarnish *v.t.* to diminish or destroy the lustre of. *Also v.i., n.* WH: 14–15C. French *ternir, terniss-*, from *terne* dark, dull. See also -ISH[2].

taro *n.* a tropical plant of the arum family, esp. *Colocasia esculenta* and *C. macrorhiza*, the roots of which are used as food by Pacific islanders. WH: 18C. Polynesian name.

tarot *n.* a figured playing card, one of a pack of 78, used in an old (orig. Italian) card game. *Also a.* WH: 16C. French, from Italian *tarocchi*, pl. of *tarocco*, of unknown orig.

tarp *n.* (a) tarpaulin. WH: early 20C. Abbr. of TARPAULIN.

tarpan *n.* an extinct small wild horse that formerly lived on the steppes of Russia and central Asia. WH: 19C. Turkic (Kirghiz).

tarpaulin *n.* a canvas cloth coated with tar or other waterproof compound. WH: 17C. Prob. from TAR[1] + PALL[1] + -ING[1].

tarpon *n.* a large and powerful game fish, *Tarpon atlanticus*, of the herring family, found in tropical Atlantic waters. WH: 17C. Prob. from Dutch *tarpoen*, ? ult. from a Central American language.

tarragon *n.* a perennial herb, *Artemisia dracunculus*, related to wormwood, used as a flavouring in cookery etc. WH: 16C. Medieval Latin *tragonia* and *tarchon*, ? an Arabic deformation of Greek *drakōn*, assoc. with *drakontion* dragonwort.

†**tarry** *v.i.* to stay, to remain behind, to wait. *Also v.t.* WH: 12–14C. Orig. uncertain. Hardly from Old French *tarier* to provoke, despite the similarity of form. The original sense (to the 16C) was to delay, to retard, to defer. The sense to stay, to remain, evolved soon after.

tarsia *n.* an Italian mosaic or inlaid woodwork. WH: 17C. Italian, INTARSIA.

tarsier *n.* a small nocturnal arboreal primate of the genus *Tarsius* found in the Philippines and Malaysia, with very large eyes and ears, and long tarsal bones. WH: 18C. French, from *tarse* TARSUS. The animal is so called from its long tarsal bones.

tarsus *n.* the set of bones (seven in humans) between the lower leg and the metatarsus, the ankle. WH: 14–15C. Modern Latin, from Greek *tarsos* the flat part of the foot, the eyelid.

tart[1] *n.* a pie containing fruit or some other sweet filling. WH: 14–15C. Old French *tarte*, from Medieval Latin *tarta*, of unknown orig.

tart[2] *n.* a prostitute, a promiscuous woman. WH: 19C. Prob. abbr. of *sweetheart* (SWEET).

tart[3] *a.* sharp to the taste, acid. WH: pre-1200. Orig. unknown. Later assoc. with TART[1], from the fruit often used in tarts.

tartan[1] *n.* a chequered pattern of crossing stripes of various colours, esp. one of those distinguishing the various Scottish Highland clans. *Also a.* WH: 15C. Prob. from Old French *tertaine*, var. of *tiretaine* a type of strong cloth, ? from Old French *tiret, tire* silk stuff, from Latin *tyrius*, from place name *Tyre*.

tartan[2] *n.* a small Mediterranean one-masted vessel with bowsprit and lateen sail. WH: 17C. French *tartane*, from Italian *tartana*, ? ult. from Arabic *ṭarīda*.

Tartar *n.* a member of a group of peoples, such as the Mongols and Turks, who live in central Asia. WH: 14–15C. Old French *Tartare* or Medieval Latin *Tartarus* (influ. by Latin TARTARUS), from *Tatar*, Turkish name of a Tartar tribe.

tartar *n.* a yellowish incrustation of calcium phosphate deposited on the teeth. WH: 14–15C. Medieval Latin *tartarum*, from Medieval Greek *tartaron*, of unknown orig.

tartare *a.* in cookery, in a Tartar style. WH: 19C. French, TARTAR. The term is apparently a punning allusion to the fieriness of the Tartars.

Tartarus *n.* in Greek mythology, a deep abyss below Hades where the Titans were confined. WH: 16C. Latin, from Greek *Tartaros*.

Tartuffe *n.* a hypocritical pretender. WH: 17C. *Tartuffe*, the religious hypocrite who is the principal character of the comedy of the same name by Molière (1664). The character's own name apparently derives from Italian *Tartufo*, from *tartufo* truffle. A hypocrite conceals his true feelings as a truffle is concealed in the ground.

tarwhine *n.* any of several edible Australian sea fish, esp. a bream, *Rhabdosargus sarba*. WH: 19C. Australian Aboriginal (Dharuk) *darrawayin*.

Tarzan n. a man of great physical strength and agility. WH: early 20C. *Tarzan*, the hero of a series of novels by Edgar Rice Burroughs, 1875–1950. Tarzan is orphaned in Africa as a baby and reared by apes in the jungle, where he communes with animals, rescues damsels in distress, and discovers a number of lost civilizations.

tash n. a moustache. WH: 19C. Abbr. of MOUSTACHE.

Tashi Lama n. PANCHEN LAMA. WH: 18C. *Tashi* Lhunpo, a Tibetan Buddhist monastery + LAMA.

tasimeter n. an instrument for measuring changes in atmospheric pressure. WH: 19C. Greek *tasis* tension + -METER.

task n. a piece of work. *Also v.t.* WH: 12–14C. Old Northern French *tasque*, var. of Old French *tasche* (Modern French *tâche*), from Medieval Latin *tasca*, alt. of *taxa*, from *taxare*. See TAX.

Tasmanian a. of or relating to Tasmania. *Also n.* WH: 19C. *Tasmania*, an island state of Australia + -IAN.

Tass n. the official news agency of the former Soviet Union. WH: early 20C. Acronym of Russian *Telegrafnoe agentstvo Sovetskogo Soyuza* Telegraphic Agency of the Soviet Union. Cp. ITAR-TASS.

tass n. a cup, a goblet. WH: 15C. Old French *tasse*, from Arabic *ṭās* cup, from Persian *tašt* bowl.

tasse n. any of a series of overlapping plates of armour hanging from a corslet as a sort of kirtle to protect the thighs. WH: 14–15C. ? Old French, purse, from Middle High German *tasche* pouch, pocket, from Old High German *tasca*, rel. to Old Saxon *dasga* pouch, Middle Dutch *tassche*, prob. ult. from Latin *tasca*. See TASK.

tassel[1] n. a pendent ornament, usu. composed of a tuft of threads, cords, silk etc. attached to the corners of cushions, curtains etc. *Also v.t., v.i.* WH: 12–14C. Old French clasp, of unknown orig. Cp. Anglo-Latin *tassellus* tassel, fringe. Prob. not. rel. to TASSEL[2].

tassel[2] n. a small piece of wood or stone fixed into a wall for a beam or joist to rest on. WH: 17C. Old French (Modern French *tasseau*), from Popular Latin blend of Latin *taxillus* small die and *tessella* small square piece of stone.

taste n. the sensation excited by the contact of various soluble substances with certain organs in the mouth, flavour. *Also v.t., v.i.* WH: 12–14C. Old French *tast*, from *taster* (Modern French *tâter*) to touch, to feel, to try, appar. from Popular Latin blend of Latin *tangere* to touch and *gustare* to taste. The original meaning was a sense of touch. The current sense evolved in the 14–15C.

-tastic suf. added to words to indicate approval, enthusiasm etc. WH: late 20C. Extracted from FANTASTIC.

tat[1] n. rubbish, rags. WH: 19C. Prob. back-formation from TATTY[1].

tat[2] v.t. to make by knotting. *Also v.i., n.* WH: 19C. Back-formation from *tatting* a kind of knotted lace, of unknown orig.

ta-ta int. goodbye. WH: 19C. Orig. unknown. Prob. orig. a child's word.

tatami n. a traditional woven straw or rush mat of standard size, used as a floor covering in Japanese houses. WH: 17C. Japanese.

tater n. a potato. WH: 18C. Alt. of POTATO. Cp. TATTIE.

tatter n. a rag. *Also v.i.* WH: 14–15C. Old Norse *tǫtrar* rags, rel. to Old English *tættec* rag.

tattersall n. material with stripes in a checked pattern. WH: 19C. Richard *Tattersall*, 1724–95, English horseman, founder of a firm of horse auctioneers in 1776. The material is so called from the traditional design of horse blankets.

tattie n. a potato. WH: 18C. Alt. of POTATO. Cp. TATER.

tattle v.i. to chatter, to gossip. *Also n.* WH: 15C. Middle Flemish *tatelen*, of imit. orig. Cp. PRATTLE, TITTLE-TATTLE, TWATTLE.

tattoo[1] n. the beat of drum recalling soldiers to their quarters. *Also v.i.* WH: 17C. Dutch *taptoe*, lit. to close the tap (of the cask), from *tap* TAP[2] + *toe*, from *doe toe* to close. The drum beat is so called because the police visited taverns in the evening to close the taps of the casks. The soldiers then returned to their quarters.

tattoo[2] v.t. to mark (the skin) by pricking and inserting pigments. *Also n.* WH: 18C. Polynesian, e.g. Tahitian *ba-tau*, Marquesan *ta-tu*.

tatty[1] a. untidy, unkempt. WH: 16C. Appar. ult. rel. to Old English *tættec* rag (cp. TATTER). Cp. TAT[1]. The original sense was having tangled or matted hair. The more general sense of untidy, scruffy evolved in the middle 20C.

tatty[2] n. in the Indian subcontinent, a matting of khus-khus for hanging in doorways and other openings, usu. kept wet to cool the air. WH: 18C. Hindi *ṭaṭṭī* wicker frame.

tau n. the 19th letter of the Greek alphabet (Τ, τ). WH: 12–14C. Greek. Cp. *taw* final letter of the Hebrew alphabet, from Hebrew *tāw*.

taunt[1] v.t. to reproach or upbraid sarcastically or contemptuously. *Also n.* WH: 16C. French *tant* (in *tant pour tant* so much for so much, tit for tat), from Latin *tantum*, neut. of *tantus* so great.

taunt[2] a. (of masts) exceptionally tall. WH: 17C. Prob. shortening of obs. *ataunt* (16C) fully shipshape, from Old French *autant* as much.

taupe n. a brownish-grey colour. *Also a.* WH: early 20C. French, from Latin *talpa* mole.

Taurus n. a constellation close to Orion, said to represent a bull; the Bull. WH: pre-1200. Latin *taurus* bull, Taurus.

taut a. tight, not slack. WH: 12–14C. ? Alt. of var. of TOUGH. The original sense was distended. The current sense (of a rope, etc.) dates from the 17C.

tauto- comb. form same, identical. WH: Greek *tauto*, contr. of *to auto* the same.

tautog n. a food fish, *Tautoga onitis*, common on the Atlantic coast of the US. WH: 17C. Narragansett *tautauog*, pl. of *taut*.

tautology n. repetition of the same thing in different words. WH: 16C. Late Latin *tautologia*, from Greek, from *tautologos* repeating what has been said. See TAUTO-, -LOGY.

tautomerism n. the ability of two isomers to change into one another so that they may co-exist in equilibrium. WH: 19C. TAUTO- + ISOMER + -ISM.

tautonym n. a two-part taxonomic name in which the specific name repeats or reflects the generic name, e.g. *Rattus rattus* (black rat). WH: early 20C. TAUTO- + -ONYM.

tautophony n. the repetition of sounds. WH: 19C. TAUTO- + Greek *phōnē* sound, voice.

tavern n. a public house, an inn. WH: 12–14C. Old French *taverne*, from Latin *taberna* hut, tavern.

taw[1] v.t. to dress or make (skins) into leather with mineral agents, as alum, instead of tannin. WH: pre-1200. Old English *tawian*, from Germanic base meaning to do, to make, to prepare. Cp. TOOL.

taw[2] n. a game of marbles. WH: 18C. Orig. unknown.

tawdry a. showy without taste or elegance. *Also n.* WH: 17C. Shortening of obs. *tawdry lace* a silk cord or ribbon worn as a necklace, contr. of *St Audrey's lace*, from *St Audrey*, Etheldrida, d.679, patron saint of Ely, in whose honour a fair was held, at which such necklaces were sold + LACE. St Audrey believed that her fatal throat cancer was divine retribution for wearing magnificent necklaces in her youth.

tawny a. brownish-yellow, tan-coloured. *Also n.* WH: 12–14C. Old French *tané*, from *tan* TAN[1]. Cp. TENNÉ.

taws n. a leather strap, usually with the end cut into thin strips, formerly used as an instrument of punishment, esp. in schools. WH: 16C. Appar. pl. of obs. *taw* tawed leather, from TAW[1], but recorded earlier.

tax n. a compulsory contribution levied on a person, property or business to meet the expenses of government or other public services. *Also v.t.* WH: 12–14C. Old French *taxer*, from Latin *taxare* to censure, to charge, to compute, ? from Greek *tassein* to order, to fix. The sense task was current from the 14–15C to the 17C. Cp. TASK.

taxi n. a motor car usu. fitted with a taximeter and licensed to carry fare-paying passengers. *Also v.i.* WH: early 20C. Coll. abbr. of TAXIMETER.

taxidermy n. the art of preparing and mounting the skins of animals so that they resemble the living forms. WH: 19C. Greek *taxis* arrangement + *derma* skin.

taximeter n. an automatic instrument fitted in a cab for registering the distance travelled on a particular journey and the fare to be paid. WH: 19C. French *taximètre*, from *taxe* tariff, tax + -*mètre* -METER.

taxis n. the methodical application of manual pressure to restore displaced body parts to their normal positions. WH: 16C. Greek arrangement, from *tassein* to arrange.

taxonomy n. the branch of natural history that deals with the principles, theories and techniques of classification. WH: 19C. Greek TAXIS + -O- + -NOMY. The word was coined by the Swiss botanist Augustin Pyrame de Candolle in his *Théorie élémentaire de la botanique* (1813).

tayberry *n.* a type of hybrid plant produced by crossing blackberry and raspberry plants. WH: late 20C. *Tay,* a river in Scotland + BERRY. The plant was introduced by the Tay in 1977.

Tay–Sachs disease *n.* a rare hereditary genetic disorder affecting the brain and spinal cord, causing death in early childhood. WH: early 20C. Warren *Tay,* 1843–1927, English ophthalmologist + Bernard *Sachs,* 1858–1944, US neurologist.

tazza *n.* a flattish or saucer-shaped cup, esp. one on a high foot. WH: 19C. Italian, from Arabic *ṭasa.* See TASS.

te *n.* the seventh note of a major scale in the sol-fa system of notation. WH: 19C. Later form of SI.

tea *n.* a small evergreen shrub or tree, *Camellia sinensis,* grown in India, China, Japan and other parts of SE Asia for its leaves. *Also v.i., v.t.* WH: 17C. Prob. from Dutch *tee* (now *thee*), from Chinese *te,* (Mandarin) *chá* CHA.

teach *v.t.* to cause (a person etc.) to learn (to do) or acquire knowledge or skill in, to instruct or train in. *Also v.i.* WH: pre-1200. Old English *tǣcan,* rel. to base also of TOKEN, from Germanic base meaning to show, from Indo-European base represented by Greek *deiknunai* to show, *deigma* sample. The original sense was to show, to present to view.

teak *n.* a large tree, *Tectona grandis,* grown in India and SE Asia for its heavy timber which does not crack, warp, shrink or corrode iron, used largely for shipbuilding, furniture etc. WH: 17C. Portuguese *teca,* from Tamil and Malayalam *tēkku* .

teal *n.* a small Eurasian freshwater duck of the genus *Anas,* esp. *A. crecca,* the common teal, related to the mallard. *Also a.* WH: 12–14C. Orig. unknown. Rel. to Middle Low German *tēlink,* Middle Dutch *tēling* (Dutch *teling*).

team *n.* a group of people who form a side in a game or sport. *Also v.t.* WH: pre-1200. Old English *tēam,* from Germanic base meaning to draw, to pull, rel. to Latin *ducere* to lead. Cp. TEEM[1]. The early basic sense (to 12–14C) was the bearing of children, also (to 14–15C) offspring, family, race, stock. The first current sense was a set of draught animals working together. This was extended to humans in the 16C.

teapoy *n.* a small three- or four-legged table for holding a tea service etc. WH: 19C. Hindi *ti-* three + Urdu and Persian *pāī* foot. Cp. CHARPOY, TRIPOD. The sense and spelling have been influenced by TEA.

tear[1] *v.t.* to pull forcibly apart. *Also v.i., n.* WH: pre-1200. Old English *teran,* from Germanic, from Indo-European base represented also by Greek *derein* to flay. Cp. German *zehren* to wear out, to sap.

tear[2] *n.* a drop of the saline liquid secreted by the lachrymal glands, moistening the eyes or flowing down in strong emotion etc. WH: pre-1200. Old English *tēar,* from Germanic, from Indo-European base represented also by Old Latin *dacruma* (Latin *lacrima*), Greek *dakru.*

tease *v.t.* to annoy, torment, irritate or vex with petty requests, importunity, jesting or raillery. *Also n.* WH: pre-1200. Old English *tǣsan,* from Germanic. Cp. German dial. *zeisen* to pluck wool. The original sense was to pull or pick wool etc. into separate fibres, to comb or card wool, flax etc. for spinning. The sense to worry, to irritate evolved in the 17C.

teasel *n.* a plant of the genus *Dipsacus,* with large burs or heads covered with stiff, hooked awns, used for raising a nap on cloth. *Also v.t.* WH: pre-1200. Old English *tǣsl, tǣsel,* from Germanic base also of TEASE. See also -EL. The plant is so called because it was used for teasing woven cloth so as to raise a nap.

teat *n.* the nipple of the mammary gland, esp. of an animal, through which milk is drawn. WH: 12–14C. Old French *tete* (Modern French *tette*), prob. of Germanic orig., replacing earlier TIT[2].

Tebeth *n.* the fourth month of the civil and tenth month of the Jewish ecclesiastical year, comprising parts of December and January. WH: 14–15C. Hebrew *ṭēbēt.*

Tebilize® *v.t.* to treat (cotton and linen fabrics) by a proprietary method to prevent creasing and shrinking. WH: mid-20C. Abbr. of *Tootal Broadhurst Lee* Company Ltd, the Manchester company that invented and patented the process in 1937 + -IZE.

tec *n.* a detective, esp. a private detective. WH: 19C. Abbr. of *detective* (DETECT).

tech *n.* a technical college. WH: early 20C. Abbr. of *technical college* (TECHNICAL).

techie *n.* a person with a great enthusiasm for or a good understanding of the latest technology (esp. computing). WH: mid-20C. TECH + *-ie* (-Y[3]).

technetium *n.* a chemical element, at. no. 43, chem. symbol Tc, whose radioisotope is used in radiotherapy. WH: mid-20C. Modern Latin, from Greek *tekhnētos* artificial, from *tekhnasthai* to make by art, from *tekhnē.* See TECHNIC. The element is so called as it was produced artificially. The name was coined in 1947 by the Italian mineralogist Carlo Perrier and the Italian-born US physicist Emilio Segrè.

technic *n.* technology. *Also a.* WH: 17C. Latin *technicus,* from Greek *tekhnikos* pertaining to art, from *tekhnē* art, craft. See also -IC.

technical *a.* of or relating to the mechanical arts and applied sciences. *Also n.* WH: 17C. Partly from TECHNIC, partly from Latin *technicus* (or direct from Greek *tekhnikos*) + -AL[1].

technician *n.* a person skilled in the technical side of a subject, a technical expert. WH: 19C. TECHNIC + -IAN.

Technicolor® *n.* a colour cinematography process. WH: early 20C. TECHNICAL + COLOUR.

technique *n.* a mode of artistic performance or execution. WH: 19C. French, use as n. of a., from Latin *technicus* TECHNIC.

techno *n.* a type of dance music with insistent repetitive beats performed on electronic instruments. WH: late 20C. Abbr. of *technological* (TECHNOLOGY).

techno- *comb. form* technology, technological. WH: Greek *tekhno-,* comb. form of *tekhnē* art, craft. See also -O-.

technobabble *n.* meaningless technical jargon. WH: late 20C. TECHNO- + BABBLE.

technocracy *n.* government or industrial control by technical experts. WH: early 20C. TECHNO- + -CRACY. The word was coined in 1919 by the US engineer and inventor William H. Smyth.

technology *n.* the study of the mechanical arts and applied sciences; the practical application of science to industry and other fields. WH: 17C. Greek *tekhnologia* systematic treatment, from *tekhnē* art, craft. See also -O-, -LOGY.

technophile *n.* a person with an enthusiasm for new technology. *Also a.* WH: late 20C. TECHNO- + -PHILE.

technophobe *n.* a person who distrusts, avoids or cannot master new technology. WH: mid-20C. TECHNO- + -PHOBE.

technothriller *n.* a sensational or exciting novel, film etc. in which an amazing technological innovation is crucial to the plot. WH: late 20C. TECHNO- + *thriller* (THRILL).

tectonic *a.* of or relating to building or construction. WH: 17C. Late Latin *tectonicus,* from Greek *tektonikos,* from *tektōn, tektonos* carpenter, builder. See also -IC.

tectorial *a.* forming a covering. *Also n.* WH: 19C. Latin *tectorium* covering, cover + -AL[1].

tectrix *n.* the covert of a bird's flight feather. WH: 19C. Modern Latin, from Latin *tectus,* p.p. of *tegere* to cover. See also -TRIX.

Ted *n.* a Teddy boy. WH: mid-20C. Abbr. of TEDDY BOY.

ted *v.t.* to turn over and spread (hay, grass or straw) so as to expose to the sun and air. WH: 12–14C. Old Norse *tethja,* past tense *tadda,* rel. to *tad* dung, *toddi* small piece (see TOD[2]).

teddy *n.* a stuffed toy bear. WH: early 20C. *Teddy,* pet name of *Theodore* Roosevelt, 1858–1919, US president (1901–9), famous as a bear hunter. Roosevelt was shown sparing the life of a bear cub in a cartoon reputedly drawn by C.K. Berryman in 1902 as a spoof on the president in the role of an ardent conservationist.

Teddy boy *n.* a young man, esp. of the 1950s, characteristically wearing a long jacket, drainpipe trousers and other styles of dress associated with the Edwardian period. WH: mid-20C. *Teddy,* pet form of *Edward,* with ref. to the style of dress in the reign of Edward VII (1901–10) (see EDWARDIAN) + BOY.

Te Deum *n.* a hymn of praise sung at morning service or as a special thanksgiving. WH: pre-1200. Latin *Te Deum laudamus* We praise thee, O God, opening words of the hymn.

tedious *a.* boring, tiring and continuing for a long time. WH: 14–15C. Old French *tedieus* or Late Latin *taediosus,* from Latin *taedium* TEDIUM. See also -OUS, -IOUS.

tedium *n.* monotony, boredom. WH: 17C. Latin *taedium* weariness, tediousness, from *taedere* to be disgusted, to be weary.

tee[1] *n.* in golf, the area at the start of each hole where players strike the first ball of the hole. *Also v.t.* WH: 17C. Orig. unknown. Orig. recorded as *teaz* and back-formed from this, as if a pl.

tee[2] *n.* the 20th letter of the alphabet, T, t. WH: 15C. Representation of the pronun. of *T*, *t* as letter's name.

tee-hee *int.* used to express restrained amusement. *Also n., v.i.* WH: 12–14C. Imit. Cp. TITTER.

teem[1] *v.i.* to be prolific or abundant. *Also v.t.* WH: pre-1200. Old English *tēman*, *tīeman*, from Germanic base of TEAM. The original sense was to bring forth, to give birth to. The current sense dates from the 16C.

teem[2] *v.i.* to pour (down), as rain etc. *Also v.t.* WH: 12–14C. Old Norse *tœma* to empty, from *tómr* empty. The original sense was to empty (a vessel), to drain the liquid from. The sense to pour (of rain) dates from the 19C. Not rel. to TEEM[1].

teen *a.* teenage. *Also n.* WH: 16C. -TEEN.

-teen *suf.* denoting the addition of ten (in numbers 13–19). WH: Old English *-tēne*, *-tȳne* (TEN), from Germanic.

teens *n.pl.* the time in a person's life from age 13 to 19 years. WH: 16C. TEEN + -S[1].

teensy *a.* tiny. WH: 19C. Prob. from TEENY + -SY.

teeny *a.* tiny. WH: 19C. Var. of TINY.

teeter *v.i.* to move to and fro unsteadily, to sway or wobble. *Also v.t., n.* WH: 19C. Var. of dial. *titter* (14–15C) to move unsteadily, from Old Norse *titra* to shake, to shiver, rel. to Old High German *zittarōn* (German *zittern* to tremble).

teethe *v.i.* to cut or develop teeth, esp. first or milk teeth. WH: 14–15C. From *teeth*, pl. of TOOTH.

teetotal *a.* characterized by, relating to, pledged to or advocating total abstinence from intoxicants, esp. alcoholic drink. WH: 19C. Redupl. or extension of TOTAL. The word was apparently first used by Richard Turner of Preston, Lancashire in 1833 in a speech advocating total abstinence from all alcoholic liquor, as opposed to abstinence from spirits only.

teetotum *n.* a toy, orig. four-sided, turning like a top, used in a game of chance. WH: 18C. Orig. *T totum*, from *T* (standing for *totum*, and inserted on one side of the toy) + Latin *totum* all, the whole (of the stakes). The *T* was later interpreted as standing for English *take-all*.

teff *n.* an African cereal, *Eragrostis tef*, used as a fodder-plant and sometimes as a source of flour. WH: 18C. Amharic *ṭēf*.

TEFL *abbr.* teaching English as a foreign language. WH: Abbr. of teaching of English as a *foreign language*.

Teflon® *n.* polytetrafluoroethylene, used as a non-stick coating for saucepans etc. WH: mid-20C. TETRA- + FLUOR + -*on* (cp. NYLON, RAYON).

teg *n.* a sheep in its second year. WH: 16C. Orig. uncertain. Cp. Old Swedish *takka*, Swedish *tacka* ewe. The word was originally used only of a female sheep.

tegmen *n.* a covering of an organ or part in an animal or plant. WH: 19C. Latin covering, from *tegere* to cover.

tektite *n.* a small, dark, glassy stone, thought to be of meteoric origin. WH: early 20C. Greek *tēktos* molten (from *tekein* to make molten). See also -ITE[1].

tela *n.* a web, a weblike membrane, structure etc. WH: 19C. Modern Latin, from Latin web. See TOILS.

telaesthesia *n.* the supposed perception of objects or events beyond the normal range of sense perceptions. WH: 19C. TELE- + Greek *aisthēsis* perception. See also -IA. The word was coined in 1882 by the English writer and psychic researcher Frederic W.H. Myers.

telamon *n.* a male figure functioning as a column or pilaster supporting an entablature. WH: 17C. Latin *telamones* (pl.), from Greek *telamōnes*, pl. of *Telamōn* Telamon, a mythical hero. The female equivalent is a CARYATID.

telco *n.* a company in the telecommunications industry. WH: late 20C. Abbr. of *tele*communications *co*mpany.

tele- *comb. form* far, distant, as in *teleport*. WH: Greek *tēle-*, comb. form of *tēle* far off.

tele-ad *n.* a classified advertisement sent to a newspaper etc. by telephone. WH: late 20C. TELE- + AD.

telebanking *n.* a computerized system of banking that allows transactions to be carried out by telephone. WH: late 20C. TELE- + *banking* (BANK[2]).

telecamera *n.* a camera designed for filming in television studios. WH: early 20C. TELE- + CAMERA.

telecast *n.* a programme or item broadcast by television. *Also v.t.* WH: mid-20C. TELE- + *broadcast* (BROAD).

telecine *n.* the broadcasting of film, esp. cinema film, on television. WH: mid-20C. TELE- + CINEMA.

telecommunication *n.* communication at a distance, by cable, telephone, radio etc. WH: mid-20C. French *télécommunication*. See TELE-, *communication* (COMMUNICATE).

telecommute *v.i.* to work at home, keeping in contact with the office etc. by telephone, e-mail, fax, the Internet etc. WH: late 20C. TELE- + COMMUTE.

telecoms *n.* telecommunications. WH: mid-20C. Abbr. of TELECOMMUNICATION + -S[1].

teleconference *n.* a meeting, discussion or conference where the participants are linked by video, audio or computer connections. WH: mid-20C. TELE- + *conference* (CONFER).

telecottage *n.* a place with personal computers, fax, e-mail, Internet etc. facilities where people can work away from a central office while still being in close contact with it. WH: late 20C. TELE- + COTTAGE, translating Swedish *telestuga*, from *stuga* cottage.

teledu *n.* a badger, *Mydaus javanensis*, of Java and Sumatra, which emits an offensive odour if disturbed or attacked. WH: 19C. Javanese.

telefacsimile *n.* an act or the process of sending a fax. WH: mid-20C. TELE- + FACSIMILE.

telega *n.* a four-wheeled springless Russian cart. WH: 16C. Russian.

telegenic *a.* (of a person) having the looks or personal qualities desirable for working in or appearing on television. WH: mid-20C. TELE- + -GENIC, based on PHOTOGENIC.

telegnosis *n.* knowledge of distant events not obtained through normal sense perceptions. WH: early 20C. TELE- + GNOSIS.

telegony *n.* the supposed influence that a female's first mate has on her offspring by subsequent mates. WH: 19C. TELE- + Greek *-gonia* generation, production.

telegram *n.* a communication sent by telegraph, now used only for international messages and superseded in 1981 by the telemessage for internal messages. WH: 19C. TELE- + -GRAM, based on TELEGRAPH.

telegraph *n.* an apparatus or device for transmitting messages or signals to a distance, esp. by making and breaking electrical connections. *Also v.t., v.i.* WH: 18C. French *télégraphe*. See TELE-, -GRAPH. The word was coined in 1792 by the French diplomat André-François Miot de Mélito. It originally denoted a kind of semaphore. Hence the various locations named *Telegraph Hill* (one is in Hampstead, NW London).

telekinesis *n.* the movement of objects at a distance supposedly without their being physically touched or interfered with. WH: 19C. TELE- + KINESIS.

telemark *n.* a swinging turn in skiing, performed to change direction or to stop. *Also v.i.* WH: early 20C. *Telemark*, an administrative district in S Norway.

telemarketing *n.* a way of trying to boost the sales of a product by making unsolicited telephone calls to potential customers. WH: late 20C. TELE- + *marketing* (MARKET).

telemessage *n.* a message sent by telex or telephone (superseding the telegraph). WH: late 20C. TELE- + MESSAGE.

telemeter *n.* a device that records readings, esp. meteorological data, and transmits it by way of electric or radio signals to a distant point. *Also v.t., v.i.* WH: 19C. TELE- + -METER.

telencephalon *n.* the front part of the brain, made up of the cerebrum, parts of the hypothalamus and the third ventricle. WH: 19C. TELE- + ENCEPHALON.

teleology *n.* the doctrine that asserts that everything in the universe has been designed for a purpose. WH: 18C. Modern Latin *teleologia*, from Greek *telos* end + *-logia* -LOGY. The term was coined in 1728 by the German philosopher Christian von Wolff.

teleosaur *n.* a Mesozoic fossil saurian of the genus *Teleosaurus*. WH: 19C. Greek *teleos* complete, perfect, from *telos* end + *sauros* lizard.

teleost *n.* any fish of the subclass Teleostei, which includes all fish with bony skeletons, but excludes those such as sharks, rays, skates etc., which have cartilaginous skeletons. *Also a.* WH: 19C. Greek *teleos* complete, perfect, from *telos* end + *osteon* bone. The fish are so called because their skeleton is (usually) completely ossified.

telepathy *n.* the supposed communication between minds at a distance without using any of the five recognized senses, thought-transference, mind-reading. WH: 19C. TELE- + -PATHY. The term was coined in 1882 by the English writer and psychic researcher Frederic W.H. Myers. Cp. TELAESTHESIA.

telephone *n.* a means of transmitting sounds to distances by a wire or cord, esp. by converting sound vibrations into electrical signals. *Also v.t., v.i.* WH: 19C. TELE- + -PHONE.

telephotograph *n.* a picture reproduced at a distance. *Also v.t.* WH: 19C. Back-formation from *telephotographic* or *telephotography*. See TELE-, PHOTOGRAPH.

telepoint *n.* a type of socket where a cordless telephone can be connected to a telephone system. WH: late 20C. TELE- + POINT.

teleport *v.t.* to move (an object, oneself or another person) by tele-kinesis. WH: mid-20C. Back-formation from *teleportation*, from TELE- + *transportation* (TRANSPORT¹).

telepresence *n.* the use of virtual reality technology esp. for remotely controlling machinery or for allowing someone to seem to take part in events that are happening at some distance. WH: late 20C. TELE- + PRESENCE.

teleprinter *n.* a telegraphic apparatus with a keyboard transmitter and a receiver which prints incoming messages. WH: early 20C. TELE- + *printer* (PRINT).

teleprompter *n.* an apparatus which enables a speaker on tele-vision to see the text without this being visible to the viewers. WH: mid-20C. TELE- + *prompter* (PROMPT).

telerecording *n.* a recording for broadcasting on television. WH: mid-20C. TELE- + *recording* (RECORD¹).

telesales *n.pl.* the selling of items by telephone. WH: late 20C. TELE- + SALE + -S¹.

telescope *n.* an optical instrument that uses lenses, mirrors or both for increasing the apparent size of distant objects. *Also v.t., v.i.* WH: 17C. Italian *telescopio*, Modern Latin *telescopium*. See TELE-, -SCOPE.

teleshopping *n.* the buying of goods (usu. displayed or listed on a television or computer screen) through a telephone or computer link. WH: late 20C. TELE- + *shopping* (SHOP).

telesoftware *n.* software that is sent to and downloaded from remote terminals. WH: late 20C. TELE- + *software* (SOFT, WARE¹).

telespectroscope *n.* an instrument for spectroscopic examination of the heavenly bodies. WH: 19C. TELE- + SPECTROSCOPE.

telestereoscope *n.* an optical instrument presenting distant objects in relief. WH: 19C. TELE- + STEREOSCOPE.

telestich *n.* a poem in which the final letters of each line make up a word or words. WH: 17C. Greek *telos*, *tele-* end + *stikhos* row, line of verse, based on ACROSTIC.

teletext *n.* data, such as news, local information etc., transmitted by television companies and viewable as text and graphics on a television that has a special adaptor or decoder. WH: late 20C. TELE- + TEXT.

telethon *n.* a very long television programme, usu. to raise funds for charities. WH: mid-20C. TELE- + -THON.

Teletype® *n.* a brand of teleprinter. WH: early 20C. TELE- + *typewriter* (TYPE).

teleutospore *n.* a spore produced at the end of the season of fructification in the rust-fungi. WH: 19C. Greek *teleutē* completion, end (from *telos* end) + -O- + SPORE.

televangelist *n.* a person who regularly appears on television to hold religious services, preach (often a fundamentalist doctrine) and appeal for funds. WH: late 20C. Blend of TELEVISION and *evangelist* (EVANGELISM).

televiewer *n.* a person who watches television. WH: mid-20C. TELE- + *viewer* (VIEW).

televirtuality *n.* virtual reality in which more than one user can interact over a computer link. WH: late 20C. TELE- + abbr. of *virtual reality*. See VIRTUAL, REALITY.

television *n.* the transmission by radio or other means of visual images, usu. with accompanying sound, so that they are displayed on a cathode-ray tube screen. WH: early 20C. TELE- + VISION. The word is first recorded in 1907.

telework *v.i.* TELECOMMUTE. WH: late 20C. TELE- + WORK.

telex *n.* an international telegraphy service that uses public telecom-munications systems to send and receive printed messages by way of teleprinters. *Also v.t.* WH: mid-20C. TELEPRINTER + EXCHANGE.

telic *a.* (of a clause or phrase) expressing end or purpose. WH: 19C. Greek *telikos* final, from *telos* end. See also -IC.

tell¹ *v.t.* to relate, to recount. *Also v.i.* WH: pre-1200. Old English *tellan*, from Germanic base also of TALE. Cp. German *zählen* to reckon, to count, *erzählen* to recount, to relate.

tell² *n.* in Middle Eastern archaeology, a mound that is composed of the remains of successive settlements. WH: 19C. Arabic *tall* hill, hillock.

tellurian *a.* of, relating to or living on the earth. *Also n.* WH: 19C. Latin *tellus*, *telluris* earth + -IAN.

telluric *a.* of or relating to the earth's status as a planet. WH: 19C. Latin *tellus*, *telluris* earth + -IC.

tellurium *n.* a rare silvery-white non-metallic element, at. no. 52, chem. symbol Te, found in association with gold, silver and bismuth. WH: 19C. Latin *tellus*, *telluris* earth + -IUM. The name was coined in 1798 by the German chemist Martin Klaproth, who based it on that of URANIUM (from Greek *ouranos* heaven), which he had discovered earlier.

telly *n.* television. WH: mid-20C. Shortening of TELEVISION. See also -Y³.

telophase *n.* the final stage in cell division which results in the formation of the nuclei of the daughter cells. WH: 19C. Greek *telos* end + PHASE.

telpher *n.* a form of suspended monorail on which a truck runs, carrying its load hanging below the level of the truck and rail. WH: 19C. Contr. and alt. of TELE- + -PHORE. The word was coined (as *telpherage*) in 1883 by the Welsh electrical engineer H.C. Fleeming Jenkin, perhaps partly by association with the name of Thomas Telford, 1757–1834, the Scottish civil engineer who did much work in Wales.

telson *n.* the last segment in the abdomen of crustaceans and arach-nids. WH: 19C. Greek limit.

Telugu *n.* a Dravidian language spoken in parts of SE and central India and parts of Sri Lanka. WH: 18C. Kannada and Taino. Cp. Telugu *teluṅgu*.

temazepam *n.* a sedative drug used as a premedication or as a treat-ment for insomnia, and sometimes taken in quantity for a euphoric effect. WH: late 20C. From *tem-*, of unknown orig. + *azepam*, based on *oxazepam* (mid-20C), a type of tranquillizer, from OXY-¹ + AZO- + -epine (from EPI- + -INE) + AMIDE.

temblor *n.* an earthquake or tremor. WH: 19C. American Spanish.

temerity *n.* excessive rashness, recklessness. WH: 14–15C. Latin *temeritas*, from *temere* blindly, rashly. See also -ITY.

temp *n.* a temporary, usu. secretarial or clerical, worker. *Also v.i.* WH: early 20C. Abbr. of TEMPORARY.

temp. *abbr.* temperature. WH: 19C. Abbr. of TEMPERATURE.

temper *n.* a disposition of mind, esp. with regard to emotional stability. *Also v.t., v.i.* WH: pre-1200. Old English *temprian*, from Latin *temperare* to mingle, to restrain oneself, with sense prob. influ. by Old French *temprer* (Modern French *tempérer*) to temper, to moderate. The noun evolved from the verb in the 14–15C. The sense mental balance arose in the 16C.

tempera *n.* a method of artistic painting that uses an emulsion of powdered pigment mixed with egg yolk and water. WH: 19C. Italian, in phr. *pingere a tempera* to paint in distemper.

temperament *n.* a person's individual character, natural disposition. WH: 14–15C. Latin *temperamentum* due mixture, from *temperare* TEMPER. See also -MENT.

temperance *n.* moderation, self-restraint, esp. where indulgence in food, alcohol etc. is concerned. *Also a.* WH: 12–14C. Anglo-French *temperaunce*, from Latin *temperantia* moderation, from *temperans*, *temperantis*, pres.p. of *temperare* TEMPER. See also -ANCE.

temperate *a.* self-restrained. WH: 14–15C. Latin *temperatus*, p.p. of *temperare* TEMPER. See also -ATE².

temperature *n.* degree of heat or cold in a body or the atmosphere, esp. as registered by a thermometer. WH: 14–15C. French *tem-pérature* or Latin *temperatura*, from *temperatus*, p.p. of *temperare* TEMPER. See also -URE.

tempest *n.* a violent storm of wind, esp. with heavy rain, hail or snow. WH: 12–14C. Old French *tempeste* (now *tempête*), from Latin *tempestas* season, weather, storm, from *tempus* time, season.

Templar *n.* a lawyer or a law student having chambers in the Temple, in London. WH: 12–14C. Old French *templier*, from Medieval Latin *templarius*, from Latin *templum* TEMPLE[1]. See also -AR[2].

template *n.* a pattern, gauge or mould, usu. of thin wood or metal, used as a guide in shaping, turning or drilling. WH: 17C. Prob. from TEMPLE[3] + -ET[1], influ. by PLATE.

temple[1] *n.* an edifice dedicated to the service of some deity or deities, esp. of the ancient Egyptians, Greeks or Romans. WH: pre-1200. Latin *templum* open space, consecrated area.

temple[2] *n.* the flat part at either side of the head between the forehead and ear. WH: 12–14C. Old French (Modern French *tempe*), from alt. of Latin *tempora*, pl. of *tempus*. Latin *tempus* meaning temple in this sense was probably associated with *tempus* meaning span, as of time. Cp. TEMPORAL[1], TEMPORAL[2].

temple[3] *n.* an attachment in a loom for keeping the fabric stretched. WH: 14–15C. French, ? ult. identical with TEMPLE[2].

tempo *n.* the specified speed at which a piece of music is or should be played. WH: 17C. Italian, from Latin *tempus* time.

temporal[1] *a.* of or relating to this life. WH: 12–14C. Old French *temporel* or Latin *temporalis*, from *tempus, temporis* time. See also -AL[1].

temporal[2] *a.* positioned at the temples. WH: 14–15C. Late Latin *temporalis*, from *tempora* the temples. See TEMPLE[2], also -AL[1].

temporary *a.* lasting, designed or intended only for a limited length of time. *Also n.* WH: 16C. Latin *temporarius*, from *tempus, temporis* time. See also -ARY[1].

temporize *v.i.* to pursue an indecisive, procrastinating or time-serving policy. WH: 16C. French *temporiser* to bide one's time, from Medieval Latin *temporizare* to delay, from Latin *tempus, temporis* time. See also -IZE.

tempt *v.t.* to incite or entice (to or to do something wrong or forbidden). WH: 12–14C. Old French *tempter*, var. of *tenter*, from Latin *temptare* to handle, to test. The sense to incite, to entice (a person) to do something is also partly a shortening of ATTEMPT.

tempura *n.* a Japanese dish of vegetables, seafood and fish coated in batter and deep-fried. WH: early 20C. Japanese, prob. from Portuguese *tempêro* seasoning.

ten *n.* the number or figure 10 or x. *Also a.* WH: pre-1200. Old English *tēne, tiene*, from Germanic, from Indo-European base also of Latin *decem*, Greek *deka*, Sanskrit *daśa*. Cp. German *zehn*.

tenable *a.* capable of being held, retained or maintained against attack. WH: 16C. Old French, from *tenir* to hold. See also -ABLE.

tenace *n.* in whist, etc., the best and third best cards of a suit held in the same hand. WH: 17C. French, from Spanish *tenaza*, lit. pincers, tongs. The cards are so called because they act like pincers (one above and one below) on the card held by one's opponent (the second best).

tenacious *a.* holding fast. WH: 17C. Latin *tenax, tenacis* holding fast (from *tenere* to hold) + -OUS. See also -ACIOUS.

tenaculum *n.* a sharp hook used in surgery for picking up blood vessels. WH: 17C. Latin holder, holding instrument, from *tenere* to hold.

tenaille *n.* in fortification works, a low outwork in the enceinte ditch in front of the curtain between two bastions. WH: 16C. Old French, from Latin *tenacula*, pl. of TENACULUM.

tenant *n.* a person who rents land or property from a landlord. *Also v.t.* WH: 12–14C. Old French, use as n. of pres.p. of *tenir* to hold, from Latin *tenere* to hold. See -ANT. The original sense was a person who holds land or property. The sense person who rents land or property evolved in the 14–15C.

tench *n.* a freshwater fish, *Tinca tinca*, of the carp family. WH: 12–14C. Old French *tenche* (Modern French *tanche*), from Late Latin *tinca*.

tend[1] *v.i.* to have a bent, inclination or attitude, to be inclined (to). WH: 12–14C. Old French *tendre*, from Latin *tendere* to stretch. The original sense was to direct a course. The sense to be inclined (to) dates from the 16C.

tend[2] *v.t.* to attend, to watch, to look after, to take charge of. *Also v.i.* WH: 12–14C. Shortening of ATTEND. The original sense (to the 19C) was to listen to. The current sense arose in the 14–15C.

tender[1] *a.* (of food) easily chewed. WH: 12–14C. Old French *tendre*, from Latin *tener* tender, delicate.

tender[2] *v.t.* to offer, to present for acceptance. *Also v.i., n.* WH: 16C. Old French *tendre*, from Latin *tendere* to stretch, to hold forth (cp. TEND[1]). Unusually, the French infinitive ending has been retained. Cp. RENDER.

tendon *n.* any of the strong bands or cords of connective tissue forming the termination or connection of the fleshy part of a muscle. WH: 14–15C. French, or from Medieval Latin *tendo, tendonis* (from Latin *tendere*; see TEND[1]), translating Greek *tenōn* sinew, use as n. of aorist p.p. of *teinein* to stretch.

tendril *n.* a leafless organ by which a plant clings to another body for support. WH: 16C. Prob. alt. (based on obs. French dim. *tendrillon*) of Old French *tendron* tender part, cartilage, from Latin *tener* TENDER[1].

Tenebrae *n.pl.* in the Roman Catholic Church, the offices of matins and lauds for the last three days in Holy Week. WH: 17C. Latin darkness. The offices are so called as candles were formerly extinguished one by one in memory of the darkness during the crucifixion (Matt. xxvii.45, etc.).

tenement *n.* an apartment or set of apartments used by one family or set of residents. WH: 12–14C. Old French (Modern French *tènement*), from Medieval Latin *tenementum*, from Latin *tenere* to hold. See also -MENT. The original sense (to the 17C) was tenure. The sense apartment dates from the 16C.

tenesmus *n.* a continual need, accompanied by effort and straining, to evacuate the bowels or bladder. WH: 16C. Medieval Latin, from Latin *tenesmus*, from Greek *tēnesmos, teinesmos* straining, from *teinein* to stretch, to strain.

tenet *n.* an opinion, principle, doctrine or dogma held by a person, school or organization. WH: 16C. Latin, lit. he holds, 3rd pers. sing. pres. of *tenere* to hold.

tenné *n.* an orangish-brown colour. *Also a.* WH: 16C. Obs. French, var. of Old French *tané* TAWNY.

tennis *n.* a racket game for two (singles) or four (doubles) players where the object is to hit the ball over a net so that it lands within the confines of a grass or hard court. WH: 14–15C. ? Old French *tenez*, imper. of *tenir* to hold, to take, as the server's call to an opponent. No mention of such a call has been found in French. The Old French name of the game was *la paulme*, lit. the palm, because in the early form of the game the ball was struck with the palm of the hand.

tenno *n.* the Emperor of Japan, esp. in his capacity as divine ruler. WH: 19C. Japanese *tennō*, from *ten* heavenly + *nō* power.

Tennysonian *a.* of, relating to or in the style of Tennyson. WH: 19C. Alfred (Lord) *Tennyson*, 1809–92, English poet + -IAN.

tenon *n.* the projecting end of a piece of timber fitted for insertion into a mortise etc. *Also v.t.* WH: 14–15C. French, from *tenir* to hold + -on. See also -OON.

tenor *n.* the highest of male voices between baritone and alto. *Also a.* WH: 12–14C. Old French *tenour* (Modern French *teneur* course, import), from Latin *tenor* continuous course, substance, from *tenere* to hold. See also -OR. The sense high male voice evolved in the 14–15C and is so called because it carried or held the melody.

tenore *n.* a tenor voice or singer. WH: 18C. Italian TENOR.

tenosynovitis *n.* swelling and inflammation in the tendons, usu. in joints, caused by repetitive use of the joint concerned. WH: 19C. Greek *tenōn* tendon + *synovitis* (SYNOVIA).

tenotomy *n.* the cutting of a tendon. WH: 19C. Greek *tenōn* tendon + -O- + -TOMY.

tenrec *n.* any of several small insectivorous mammals similar to the hedgehog, esp. the tailless variety, *Tenrec ecaudatus*, found in Madagascar. WH: 18C. French *tanrec*, from Malagasy *tàndraka, tràndraka*.

tense[1] *a.* stretched tight, strained to stiffness. *Also v.t., v.i.* WH: 17C. Latin *tensus*, p.p. of *tendere* to stretch.

tense[2] *n.* a form taken by a verb to indicate the time, and also the continuance or completedness, of an action. WH: 12–14C. Old French *tens* (Modern French *temps*), from Latin *tempus* time. The original meaning was time. The grammatical sense of the word dates from the 14–15C.

tension n. the act of stretching. WH: 16C. Old French, or from Latin *tensio*, *tensionis*, from *tensus*, p.p. of *tendere* to stretch. See also -ION.

tent[1] n. a portable shelter consisting of canvas or other flexible material stretched over and supported on poles. *Also v.t.*, *v.i.* WH: 12–14C. Old French *tente*, ult. from Latin *tentus*, p.p. of *tendere* to stretch.

tent[2] n. a Spanish wine of a deep red colour, used for sacramental purposes. WH: 14–15C. Spanish *tinto* dark-coloured, from Latin *tinctus*, p.p. of *tingere* to dye, to colour.

tent[3] n. a small roll of lint, sponge etc., inserted in a wound, ulcer etc., to keep it open. *Also v.t.* WH: 14–15C. Old French *tente*, from *tenter*, from Latin *temptare* to touch, to feel, to try. Cp. TEMPT.

tentacle n. a long slender organ, esp. in invertebrates, such as an arm of an octopus, used for touching, grasping, moving etc. and, if suckers are present, for attaching the animal to a surface. WH: 18C. Modern Latin *tentaculum*, from *tentare*, var. of *temptare* to feel, to try. See TEMPT, also -CLE.

tentative a. consisting or done as a trial, experimental. *Also n.* WH: 16C. Medieval Latin *tentativus*, from Latin *tentatus*, p.p. of *tentare*, var. of *temptare* to try. See TEMPT, also -IVE.

tenter[1] n. a frame or machine for stretching cloth to dry to make it set even and square. WH: 12–14C. Medieval Latin *tentorium*, from Latin *tentus*, p.p. of *tendere* to stretch.

tenter[2] n. a person who is in charge, esp. of factory machinery. WH: 19C. From obs. *tent* to pay attention to, shortening of obs. *attent*, from Old French *atente* (Modern French *attente*), fem. p.p. (used as n.) of *atendre* ATTEND + -ER[1].

tenuity n. thinness, slenderness. WH: 14–15C. Latin *tenuitas*, from *tenuis* thin. See also -ITY.

tenuous a. insignificant, not able to stand up to much scrutiny. WH: 16C. Latin *tenuis* + -OUS.

tenure n. the act, manner or right of holding property, esp. real estate or office. WH: 14–15C. Old French, from *tenir* to hold, from Latin *tenere*. See also -URE.

tenuto a., adv. sustained, held on for the full time. *Also n.* WH: 18C. Italian, p.p. of *tenere* to hold.

teocalli n. a pyramidal mound or structure, usu. surmounted by a temple, used for worship by the ancient peoples of Mexico, Central America etc. WH: 17C. American Spanish, from Nahuatl *teo:kalli*, from *teo:tl* god + *kalli* house.

teosinte n. a type of Mexican fodder grass, *Zea mexicana*. WH: 19C. French *téosinté*, from Nahuatl *teocintli*, appar. from *teo:tl* god + *cintli*, *centli* dried ear of maize.

tepal n. any of the subdivisions of a perianth which is not clearly differentiated into the calyx and corolla. WH: 19C. French *tépale*, blend of *sépale* SEPAL and *pétale* PETAL. The word was coined in 1827 by the Swiss botanist Augustin Pyrame de Candolle. Cp. TAXONOMY.

tepee n. a N American Indian tent, usu. cone-shaped and made by stretching animal skins over a framework of poles. WH: 18C. Sioux *típi* dwelling.

tepefy v.t. to make tepid. *Also v.i.* WH: 17C. Latin *tepefacere* to make tepid, from *tepere* to be lukewarm. See also -FY.

tephra n. the solid debris thrown up in a volcanic eruption. WH: mid-20C. Greek ashes.

tepid a. moderately warm, lukewarm. WH: 14–15C. Latin *tepidus*, from *tepere* to be warm.

tequila n. a Mexican spirit distilled from agave which forms the basis of many drinks. WH: 19C. Mexican Spanish, from *Tequila*, a district of central Mexico.

ter- comb. form three, thrice, three times, as in *tercentenary*. WH: Latin *ter* thrice.

tera- comb. form 10 to the power of 12. WH: Greek *teras* monster.

teraflop n. a unit of computing speed equal to one million million floating-point operations per second. WH: late 20C. TERA- + acronym of *f*loating-point *op*erations *p*er *s*econd (with *-s* taken as -S[1]). Cp. MEGAFLOP.

terai n. a wide-brimmed felt hat, often with ventilation holes and a double crown, worn in subtropical regions. WH: 19C. *Terai*, a belt of marshy jungle between the southern foothills of the Himalayas.

teraph n. a small household god or image which ancient Semitic peoples consulted as an oracle. WH: 19C. Back-formation from *teraphim* (pl.) (14–15C), from Late Latin *theraphim*, from Greek *theraphin*, from Hebrew *tĕrāpīm*. Cp. SERAPH.

teratism n. a monster, a malformed person or animal, esp. at the foetal stage. WH: early 20C. Greek *teras*, *teratos* monster + -ISM.

terato- comb. form of or relating to a monster. WH: Greek *teras*, *teratos* monster. See also -O-.

teratogen n. something which results in the malformation of an embryo. WH: mid-20C. TERATO- + -GEN.

teratology n. the study of congenital malformations. WH: 17C. TERATO- + -LOGY.

teratoma n. a tumour or group of tumours composed of tissue that is foreign to the site of growth, most usually occurring in the testes or ovaries. WH: 19C. TERATO- + -OMA.

terawatt n. a unit of power equivalent to 10^{12} watts or a million megawatts. WH: late 20C. TERA- + WATT.

terbium n. a rare metallic element, at. no. 65, chem. symbol Tb, found in association with erbium and yttrium. WH: 19C. *Ytterby*, a town in Sweden + -IUM. The term was coined by the Swedish chemist Carl Gustaf Mosander, who discovered the element in 1843. Cp. YTTERBIUM.

terce n. in the Roman Catholic Church, the third canonical hour of divine office when prayers are said around 9 a.m. WH: 14–15C. Old French, var. of *tierce*, from Latin *tertia*, use as n. of fem. of *tertius* THIRD. Cp. TIERCE.

tercentenary n. a 300th anniversary. *Also a.* WH: 19C. TER- + *centenary* (CENTENARIAN).

tercet n. in prosody, a set of three consecutive lines of verse that either all rhyme or which rhyme with another set of three lines coming before it or after it. WH: 16C. French, from Italian *terzetto*, from *terzo* (from Latin *tertius* third) + *-etto* -ET[1].

terebene n. a liquid hydrocarbon obtained by treating oil of turpentine with sulphuric acid, used as an antiseptic, disinfectant, expectorant etc. WH: 19C. TEREBINTH + -ENE.

terebinth n. a small tree, *Pistacia terebinthus*, found around the Mediterranean and once used as a source of a form of turpentine. WH: 14–15C. Old French *terebinte* (Modern French *térébinthe*), corr. to Spanish and Italian *terebinto*, Latin *terebinthus*, from Greek *terebinthos*, earlier *terbinthos*, *terminthos*. Cp. TURPENTINE.

teredo n. any of several molluscs, esp. *Teredo navalis*, that bore into submerged timber, the shipworm. WH: 14–15C. Latin, from Greek *terēdōn*, from base of *teirein* to rub hard, to wear away, to bore.

Terentian a. of, relating to or in the style of Terence. WH: 20C. Latin *Terentianus*, from *Terentius* Terence, 190–159 BC, Roman comic dramatist. See also -AN.

terephthalic acid n. a white crystalline carboxylic acid which is insoluble in water and is widely used in the manufacture of synthetic fibres, esp. plastics and polyesters. WH: 19C. From *terebic* (TEREBENE) + PHTHALIC (+ ACID).

terete a. rounded, cylindrical and smooth. WH: 17C. Latin *teres*, *teretis* rounded (off).

tergiversate v.i. to change sides. WH: 17C. Latin *tergiversatus*, p.p. of *tergiversari* to turn one's back, to be evasive, from *tergum* back + *versus*, p.p. of *vertere* to turn. See also -ATE[3].

tergum n. the upper or dorsal plate of a somite or segment of an articulate animal. WH: 19C. Latin back.

-teria suf. indicating that an establishment is self-service, as in *washeteria*. WH: Extracted from CAFETERIA.

term n. a word or expression that has a precise meaning and is used in a particular, often specialized, field. *Also v.t.* WH: 12–14C. Old French *terme*, from Latin TERMINUS. The original sense was limit (in space or time). The sense word or expression arose in the 14–15C.

termagant n. a shrewish, abusive, violent woman. *Also a.* WH: 12–14C. Old French *Tervagant*, from Italian *Trivigante*, *Trivagante*, said to come from Latin TRI- + *vagans*, *vagantis*, pres.p. of *vagari* to wander, ref. to the moon 'wandering' between heaven and hell. See also -ANT. The current sense dates from the 16C.

terminal a. (of a disease) ending in death. *Also n.* WH: 15C. Latin *terminalis*, from *terminus* end, boundary. See also -AL[1].

terminate *v.t.* to put an end to. *Also v.i.* WH: 16C. Latin *terminatus*, p.p. of *terminare* to limit, to end, from *terminus* end, boundary. See also -ATE³.

terminism *n.* the doctrine that there is a limited period in each person's life for repentance and grace. WH: 19C. Latin *terminus* end, limit + -ISM.

terminology *n.* the set of terms used in any art, science, discipline etc. WH: 19C. German *Terminologie*, from Latin *terminus* (in its Medieval Latin sense) term. See -LOGY.

terminus *n.* the point where a railway or bus route ends. WH: 16C. Latin end, limit, boundary. The original sense was the point at which motion or action ends. The application to a transport route dates from the 19C.

termite *n.* any of several kinds of small social insects of the order Isoptera, found chiefly in tropical regions and often causing damage to trees and wood in buildings, also called *white ant*. WH: 18C. Latin *termes, termitis* woodworm, alt. of earlier *tarmes*, ? by assim. to *terere* to rub.

tern¹ *n.* any small gull-like seabird of the family Sternidae, having slenderly-built bodies, forked tails and narrow, sharp-pointed wings. WH: 17C. Of Scandinavian orig. Cp. Norwegian *terna*, Danish *terne*, Swedish *tärna*, from Old Norse *therna*.

tern² *a.* ternate. *Also n.* WH: 18C. Latin *terni* three each.

terne *n.* an alloy of lead and 10–20% tin, often also with a small percentage of antimony. WH: 19C. Prob. from French *terne* dull, tarnished.

terotechnology *n.* the application of managerial, financial and engineering skills to the installation and efficient operation of equipment and machinery. WH: late 20C. Greek *tērein* to watch over, to take care of + -O- + TECHNOLOGY.

terpene *n.* any one of various isomeric oily hydrocarbons derived chiefly from coniferous plants. WH: 19C. German *Terpentin* TURPENTINE + -ENE.

Terpsichorean *a.* characteristic of or relating to dancing or Terpsichore, the Muse of dancing. WH: 19C. *Terpsichore*, from Greek *Terpsikhorē* the Muse of dancing (from *terpein* to delight + *khoros* dance, CHORUS) + -AN.

terra *n.* in legal contexts, earth or land. WH: 17C. Latin earth.

terrace *n.* a raised level space or platform, artificially constructed or natural and used for growing grapes etc. *Also v.t.* WH: 16C. Old French (Modern French *terrasse*) rabble, platform, from Latin *terra* earth. The word originally denoted an open gallery, then a raised, level, paved area adjoining a house or in a garden.

terracotta *n.* a hard, unglazed earthenware used as a decorative building material and for making pottery, models etc. *Also a.* WH: 18C. Italian *terra cotta* baked earth, from Latin *terra cocta*.

terrain *n.* a region, a tract, an extent of land of a definite geological character or as thought of in terms of military operations. WH: 18C. French, from Popular Latin var. of Latin *terrenum*, use as n. of neut. of *terrenus* TERRENE.

terramare *n.* a dark earthy deposit found at the sites of some prehistoric lakeside settlements, esp. in Italy. WH: 19C. French, from Italian dial. *terramara*, from *terra marna*, from *terra* earth + *marna* marl.

Terramycin® *n.* an antibiotic used to treat a wide range of bacterial infections. WH: mid-20C. Latin *terra* earth + -MYCIN.

terrapin *n.* any of several small turtles of the family Emydidae, esp. *Emys orbicularis*, which lives on land and in freshwater ponds and rivers in Europe. WH: 17C. Alt. of an Eastern Algonquian word (cp. Eastern Abnaki *turepé* turtle), with *-in* of unknown orig. Not rel. to Latin *terra* land.

terrarium *n.* an enclosed container where small land animals are kept. WH: 19C. Modern Latin, from Latin *terra* earth, based on AQUARIUM.

terrazzo *n.* a mosaic floor-covering made by setting marble or other chips into cement, which is then polished. WH: early 20C. Italian terrace, balcony.

terrene *a.* of or relating to the earth, earthly. *Also n.* WH: 12–14C. Anglo-French, from Latin *terrenus*, from *terra* earth.

terreplein *n.* the upper surface of a rampart where guns are mounted. WH: 16C. French *terre-plein*, from Italian *terrapieno*, from

terrapienare to fill with earth, from *terra* earth + *pieno* (from Latin *plenus*) full.

terrestrial *a.* of or relating to or existing on the earth, not celestial. *Also n.* WH: 14–15C. Latin *terrestris*, from *terra* earth. See also -IAL.

terret *n.* each of the rings or loops on harness through which the driving reins pass. WH: 15C. Old French *toret, touret*, dim. of *tour* TOUR. See also -ET¹.

terre-verte *n.* a soft green mineral used by artists as a pigment. WH: 17C. French green earth.

terrible *a.* dreadful, appalling. WH: 14–15C. Old French, from Latin *terribilis*, from *terrere* to frighten. See -IBLE.

terricolous *a.* living on or in the earth. WH: 19C. Latin *terricola* earth dweller, from *terra* earth. See -COLOUS.

terrier¹ *n.* a small active dog of various breeds orig. bred to pursue its quarry underground. WH: 14–15C. Old French (*chien*) *terrier*, from Medieval Latin *terrarius*, from Latin *terra* earth. The dog is so called as it was originally trained to turn out foxes, etc. from their earths.

terrier² *n.* a book or roll in which the lands of private persons or corporations are described by site, boundaries, acreage etc. WH: 15C. Old French, use as n. of a., from Medieval Latin *terrarius*, from Latin *terra* land.

terrific *a.* excellent, wonderful. WH: 17C. Latin *terrificus*, from *terrere* to frighten. See also -FIC.

terrigenous *a.* formed in the sea from debris from land erosion. WH: 17C. Latin *terrigenus* earth-born + -OUS.

terrine *n.* a type of coarse pâté, usu. made by incorporating vegetables into a meat or fish base. WH: 18C. French large earthenware pot, fem. of Old French *terrin* earthen, from Latin *terra* earth. Cp. TUREEN.

territory *n.* the extent of land within the jurisdiction of a particular sovereign, state or other power. WH: 14–15C. Latin *territorium*, from *terra* land, based on *dormitorium* dormitory, *praetorium* (PRAETOR), etc.

terror *n.* extreme fear. WH: 14–15C. Old French *terrour* (Modern French *terreur*), from Latin *terror*, from *terrere* to frighten. See also -OR.

terry *n.* a pile fabric in which the loops are not cut, used esp. for towels, bathrobes etc. *Also a.* WH: 18C. Orig. unknown. According to some, the word is from French *tiré*, p.p. of *tirer* to draw out.

terse *a.* (of style, language etc.) neat and compact. WH: 17C. Latin *tersus*, p.p. of *tergere* to wipe, to polish. The original sense (to the 19C) was wiped, brushed, polished. The current sense dates from the 18C.

tertial *a.* of or relating to a bird's tertiary feathers. *Also n.* WH: 19C. Latin *tertius* third + -AL¹.

tertian *a.* (of a fever) occurring or recurring every third day, taking the first and last days into account. *Also n.* WH: 14–15C. Latin (*febris*) *tertiana*, from *tertius* third. See also -AN.

tertiary *a.* of the third order, rank or formation. *Also n.* WH: 16C. Latin *tertiarius* of the third rank, from *tertius* third. See also -ARY¹.

tertium quid *n.* a third (or intermediate) something. WH: 18C. Late Latin, translating Greek *triton ti* some third thing. The entity is so termed as it is related in some way to two definite or known things, but distinct from both.

Terylene® *n.* a synthetic polyester used as a textile fibre. WH: mid-20C. From inversion and shortening of the two words of *polyethylene terephthalate*. See POLYTHENE, TEREPHTHALIC ACID.

terza rima *n.* in prosody, an arrangement of tercets with a linking rhyme scheme of aba, bcb, cdc etc. WH: 19C. Italian third rhyme.

terzetto *n.* a group of three performers or singers. WH: 18C. Italian TERCET.

TESL *abbr.* teaching of English as a second language. WH: Cp. TEFL.

tesla *n.* the SI unit of magnetic flux density equal to a flux of one weber per square metre. WH: 19C. Nikola *Tesla*, 1856–1943, Croatian-born US physicist.

TESSA *n.* a tax exempt special savings account. WH: late 20C. Abbr. of *tax-exempt special savings account*, punning on female forename *Tessa* and poss. also on an inversion of *asset* (ASSETS).

tessellate *v.t.* to make (a mosaic, pattern etc.) using tesserae or checks. WH: 18C. Late Latin *tessellatus*, p.p. of *tessellare*, from *tessella*, dim. of TESSERA.

tessera *n.* a small cubical piece of marble, earthenware etc., used in mosaics. WH: 17C. Latin, from Greek, neut. of *tesseres*, var. of *tessares* four.

tessitura *n.* the range that encompasses most of the tones of a voice part. WH: 19C. Italian, lit. texture.

test¹ *n.* a critical trial or examination. *Also v.t.* WH: 14–15C. Old French (Modern French *têt*), from Latin *testum*, var. of *testa* tile, earthen vessel, pot. The word originally denoted a type of shallow vessel used to assay or refine precious metals. Hence the assaying process itself. The current sense dates from the 16C.

test² *n.* a shell, a hard covering or exoskeleton. WH: 14–15C. Latin *testa*. See TEST¹. The word was originally the term for a piece of earthenware, a potsherd. The current biological sense arose in the 19C.

testa *n.* a hard seed covering. WH: 18C. Latin. See TEST¹.

testaceous *a.* characterized by a hard outer covering. WH: 17C. Latin *testaceus*, from *testa*. See TEST², also -ACEOUS.

testament *n.* a solemn instrument in writing by which a person disposes of their personal estate after death, a will. WH: 12–14C. Latin *testamentum* will, from *testari* to bear witness, to make a will, from *testis* witness. See also -MENT. The special sense division of the Christian Bible derives from Late Latin *testamentum* covenant, translating Greek *diathēkē*.

testate *a.* having made and left a valid will. *Also n.* WH: 14–15C. Latin *testatus*, p.p. of *testari* to bear witness, to make a will. See also -ATE².

tester¹ *n.* a canopy, esp. over a four-poster bedstead. WH: 14–15C. Medieval Latin *testerium*, *testrum*, from *testera* headstall, from Late Latin *testa* (*capita*) skull, from Latin *testa* tile.

†tester² *n.* a shilling bearing the head of Henry VIII. WH: 16C. Appar. alt. of obs. *teston* a silver coin bearing a head, from Italian *testa* head, from Latin tile. See also -OON.

testicle *n.* either of the two reproductive glands which secrete the seminal fluid in males. WH: 14–15C. Latin *testiculus*, dim. of TESTIS. See also -CLE.

testify *v.i.* to bear witness (to, against, concerning etc.). *Also v.t.* WH: 14–15C. Latin *testificare* to bear witness, to proclaim, from *testis* witness. See also -FY.

testimony *n.* a statement under oath or affirmation. *Also v.t.* WH: 12–14C. Latin *testimonium*, from *testis* witness. See also -MONY.

testis *n.* a testicle. WH: 18C. Latin witness. The organ is so called as it is a witness to virility. Cp. Greek *parastatei* testicles, lit. bystanders.

testosterone *n.* a steroid hormone secreted by the testes, controlling the growth and functioning of male sex organs and stimulating the development of male secondary sexual characteristics. WH: mid-20C. TESTIS + -O- + *sterone* (from STEROL + KETONE).

testudo *n.* a type of protective barrier formed by attacking Roman soldiers who raised their shields above their heads so that they overlapped and made a screen. WH: 14–15C. Latin, from *testa* pot, shell, *testu* pot lid.

testy *a.* irritable, peevish, pettish, petulant. WH: 14–15C. Anglo-French *testif*, from Old French *teste* (Modern French *tête*) head, from Latin *testa*. See TEST¹. The original sense was headstrong, impetuous, then aggressive, contentious. The current sense evolved in the 16C.

tetanus *n.* a disease caused by the bacterium *Clostridium tetani* and marked by long-continued spasms of voluntary muscles, esp. those of the jaws. WH: 14–15C. Latin, from Greek *tetanos* muscular spasm, from *teinein* to stretch.

tetchy *a.* fretful, irritable, touchy. WH: 16C. Prob. var. of *tache* spot, blot (TACHISM) + -Y¹.

tête-à-tête *n.* a private interview, a close or confidential conversation. *Also a., adv.* WH: 17C. French, lit. head to head.

tête-bêche *a.* (of a postage stamp) printed so that it is upside down or facing the other way in comparison to the other stamps on a sheet. WH: 19C. French, from *tête* head + *bêche* (reduced form of *béchevet*), lit. double bedhead.

tether *n.* a rope or halter by which an animal is prevented from moving too far. *Also v.t.* WH: 14–15C. Old Norse *tjóthr*, corr. to Middle Dutch *tüder*, Old High German *zeotar* forepole, from Germanic base meaning to fasten.

tetra *n.* any of various small tropical fish of the characin family that are often kept in home aquaria for their attractive brightly-coloured appearance. WH: mid-20C. Abbr. of Modern Latin *Tetragonopterus*, lit. tetragonal finned, former genus name.

tetra- *comb. form* four, as in *tetragon*. WH: Greek, comb. form of *tettares* four.

tetrabasic *a.* (of an acid) having four replaceable hydrogen atoms. WH: 19C. TETRA- + *basic* (BASE¹).

tetrabranchiate *a.* having four branchiae or gills. WH: 19C. Modern Latin *tetrabranchiata*, from Greek TETRA- + *bragkhia* gills. See also -ATE².

tetrachord *n.* a scale series of four notes where the interval between the first and last notes encompasses a perfect fourth, esp. as used in ancient music. WH: 17C. TETRA- + CHORD¹.

tetracyclic *a.* having four circles or whorls. WH: 19C. TETRA- + *cyclic* (CYCLE).

tetrad *n.* a collection, group or set of four things. WH: 17C. Greek *tetras*, *tetrados* a group of four. See also -AD¹.

tetradactyl *n.* an animal having four digits on each limb. *Also a.* WH: 19C. TETRA- + Greek *daktulos* finger, toe.

tetraethyl *a.* having four ethyl groups. WH: early 20C. TETRA- + ETHYL.

tetragon *n.* a plane figure having four angles and four sides. WH: 17C. Late Latin *tetragonum*, from Greek *tetragōnon* quadrangle, use as n. of *tetragōnos* quadrangular, from TETRA- + *-gōnos* -GON.

tetragram *n.* a word of four letters. WH: 17C. TETRA- + -GRAM.

tetragynous *a.* (of a flower) having four pistils. WH: 19C. TETRA- + -GYNOUS.

tetrahedron *n.* a solid figure bounded by four planes, esp. equilateral, triangular faces. WH: 16C. Late Greek *tetraedron*, use as n. of neut. of *tetraedros* four-sided. See TETRA-, -HEDRON.

tetralogy *n.* a collection of four dramatic works, esp. in ancient Greek a trilogy or three tragedies, followed by a satyric piece. WH: 17C. Greek *tetralogia*. See TETRA-, -LOGY.

tetramerous *a.* consisting of four parts. WH: 19C. TETRA- + Greek *meros* part + -OUS.

tetrameter *n.* in prosody, a verse consisting of four measures. WH: 17C. Late Latin *tetrametrus*, from Greek *tetrametros*, from TETRA- + *metron* measure.

tetrandrous *a.* (of a flower) having four stamens. WH: 19C. TETRA- + -ANDROUS.

tetraplegia *n.* quadriplegia, paralysis of both arms and both legs. WH: early 20C. TETRA- + PARAPLEGIA.

tetraploid *a.* having four times the haploid number of chromosomes. *Also n.* WH: early 20C. TETRA- + -PLOID.

tetrapod *n.* a four-footed animal. *Also a.* WH: 19C. Modern Latin *tetrapodus*, from Greek *tetrapous*, *tetrapodos* four-footed. See TETRA-, -POD.

tetrapterous *a.* having four wings. WH: 19C. TETRA- + Greek *pteron* wing + -OUS.

tetrarch *n.* a governor of the fourth part of a province under the Roman empire. WH: pre-1200. Late Latin *tetrarcha*, from Latin *tetrarches*, from Greek *tetrarkhēs*, from TETRA-, ARCH-.

tetraspore *n.* a group of four spores asexually produced, as in some algae. WH: 19C. TETRA- + SPORE.

tetrastich *n.* a stanza, poem or epigram consisting of four lines of verse. WH: 16C. Latin *tetrastichon*, from Greek *tetrastikhon*, use as n. of neut. of *tetrastikhos* containing four rows, from TETRA- + *stikhos* row, line of verse.

tetrastyle *n.* a building, portico etc. having four pillars. *Also a.* WH: 18C. TETRA- + Greek *stulos* pillar.

tetrasyllable *n.* a word of four syllables. WH: 16C. TETRA- + SYLLABLE.

tetratheism *n.* the doctrine that the Godhead comprises four elements, the three persons of the Trinity and a divine essence from which each of these proceeds. WH: 19C. TETRA- + THEISM.

tetrathlon *n.* a competition that comprises four distinct events, esp. a sporting one featuring running, swimming, shooting and riding events. WH: mid-20C. TETRA- + Greek *athlon* contest, based on PENTATHLON, etc.

tetratomic *a.* having four atoms to a molecule. WH: 19C. TETRA- + *atomic* (ATOM).

tetravalent *a.* having a valency of four, quadrivalent. WH: 19C. TETRA- + *-valent*, from Latin *valens, valentis*, pres.p. of *valere* to be strong. See VALENCE.

tetrode *n.* a thermionic valve containing four electrodes. WH: early 20C. TETRA- + -ODE[2].

tetroxide *n.* any oxide having four oxygen atoms per molecule. WH: 19C. TETRA- + OXIDE.

tetryl *n.* a yellow crystalline explosive solid, used as a detonator. WH: 19C. TETRA- + -YL.

tetter †*n.* any of several skin conditions such as eczema. *Also v.t.* WH: pre-1200. Old English *teter*, rel. to Sanskrit *dadru* skin disease.

Teucrian *a.* of or relating to ancient Troy. *Also n.* WH: 18C. Latin *Teucri*, from Greek *Teukros* Teucer, mythological ancestor of the kings of Troy + -IAN.

Teuton *n.* a member of any Teutonic people, esp. a German. WH: 18C. Latin *Teutoni, Teutones* (pl.), from Indo-European base meaning people, country, land, as also in German *Deutschland* Germany.

Texan *n.* a native or inhabitant of Texas. *Also a.* WH: 19C. *Texas*, a large state in the SW USA + -AN.

Tex-Mex *a., n.* (of, relating to or denoting) the Texan version of something Mexican, such as food, music, language etc. WH: mid-20C. TEXAN + MEXICAN.

text *n.* the words of something as printed, written or displayed on a video display unit. WH: 14–15C. Old Northern French *tixte* (Modern French *texte*), from Latin *textus* tissue, style of literary writing, from *textus*, p.p. of *texere* to weave. Cp. TEXTURE. The words of a written work are its 'texture', as if woven into it.

textile *n.* a woven, bonded or felted fabric. *Also a.* WH: 17C. Latin *textilis*, from *textus*. See TEXT, also -IL.

texture *n.* the quality of something as perceived by touch. *Also v.t.* WH: 14–15C. Latin *textura* weaving, from *textus*. See TEXT, also -URE.

-th[1] *suf.* forming ordinal and fractional numbers from the cardinal number four and upwards, as in *sixth, sixteenth, sixtieth*. WH: Old English *-tha, -the, -otha, -othe*, ult. from Indo-European.

-th[2] *suf.* forming nouns from verbs of action of process, as in *growth*. WH: Old English *-thu, -tho, -th*, from Germanic, from Indo-European.

Thai *n.* a native or inhabitant of Thailand (formerly Siam). *Also a.* WH: 19C. Thai free.

thalamus *n.* either of two oval masses of grey matter at the base of the brain whose function is to relay sensory information to the cerebral cortex. WH: 17C. Latin, from Greek *thalamos* inner chamber.

thalassaemia *n.* a hereditary disorder of the blood due to defects in the synthesis of haemoglobin, sometimes fatal in children. WH: mid-20C. Greek *thalassa* sea + *haima* blood + -IA. The disorder is so called because it was originally discovered in Mediterranean countries. The name was coined in 1932 by the US pathologist George H. Whipple.

thalassic *a.* of or relating to the sea or seas, marine. WH: 19C. French *thalassique*, from Greek *thalassa* sea. See also -IC.

thaler *n.* an old German silver coin. WH: 18C. German (now *Taler*) DOLLAR.

thalidomide *n.* a drug formerly used as a sedative, withdrawn from use in 1961, as it was shown to be associated with malformation of the foetus when taken by pregnant women. WH: mid-20C. PHTHALIC + IMIDE + -O- + IMIDE, elements of the full chemical name, *phthalimidoglutarimide*.

thallium *n.* a rare soft, white, crystalline metallic element, at. no. 81, chem. symbol Tl, the spectrum of which contains a bright-green line from which it was named, used in alloys and glass-making. WH: 19C. Greek *thallos* green shoot (from *thallein* to bloom) + -IUM. The element is so called from the vivid green band in its spectrum. The name was coined in 1861 by the English chemist Sir William Crookes.

thallophyte *n.* any plant, such as algae, fungi and lichens, that has a thallus. WH: 19C. Modern Latin *Thallophyta* (pl.), from Greek *thallos* green shoot (from *thallein* to bloom). See -PHYTE.

thallus *n.* a plant-body without vascular tissue and lacking differentiation into root, stem or leaves. WH: 19C. Greek *thallos* green shoot, from *thallein* to bloom.

thalweg *n.* the longitudinal line where the opposite slopes of a river, valley or lake meet. WH: 19C. German, from *Thal* (now *Tal*) valley + *Weg* way. Cp. DALE, WAY.

than *conj., prep.* used to introduce the second element in a comparison. WH: pre-1200. Old English *thanne, thonne, thænne*, orig. the same word as THEN, from which it was not finally differentiated until the 18C.

thanatology *n.* the scientific study of death. WH: 19C. Greek *thanatos* death + -O- + -LOGY.

thane *n.* in feudal times in England, a freeman holding land by military service and ranking between ordinary freemen and the nobles. WH: pre-1200. Old English *thegn, thegen*, corr. to Old Saxon *thegan* man, Old High German *degan* boy, servant, warrior, hero (German *Degen* warrior), Old Norse *thegn* freeman, liegeman, from Germanic, from Indo-European base also of Greek *teknon* child, *tokeus* parent. Cp. THEGN. The original sense (to the 16C) was a servant, especially of Christ.

thank *v.t.* to express gratitude (to or for). *Also n.* WH: pre-1200. Old English *thancian*, from Germanic base also of THINK. Cp. German *danken*. To thank someone is to express a favourable thought towards them.

that *pron.* used to refer to someone or something already known, indicated, mentioned etc. *Also a., adv., conj.* WH: pre-1200. Old English *thæt*, nom. and acc. sing. neut. of the demonstrative pron. and a. *se* (m.), *sēo* (fem.). See THE. Cp. THIS, THOSE.

thatch *n.* a roof covering of straw, rushes, reeds etc. *Also v.t., v.i.* WH: 14–15C. Alt. of dial. *thack* (from Old English *thæc*), based on *thatch* (v.) from Old English *theccan* to cover, from Germanic. Cp. German *decken* to cover. Rel. to DECK.

Thatcherism *n.* the political, economic etc. philosophy and policies of Margaret Thatcher. WH: late 20C. Margaret *Thatcher* 1925–, British Conservative politician and Prime Minister (1979–90), + -ISM.

thaumato- *comb. form* of or relating to wonder or miracles. WH: Greek *thauma, thaumatos* wonder, marvel. See also -O-.

thaumatrope *n.* an optical toy consisting of a disc with figures on opposite sides which appear to combine and perform movements when the disc is rotated. WH: 19C. THAUMATO- + Greek *-tropos* turning.

thaumaturge *n.* a worker of miracles; a wonder-worker, a magician or conjuror. WH: 18C. Medieval Latin *thaumaturgus*, from Greek *thaumatourgos*, from *thaumat-* THAUMATO- + *-ergos* working. The original Latin form *thaumaturgus* was later assimilated in English to the French form.

thaw *v.i.* (of ice, snow etc.) to melt, dissolve or become liquid. *Also v.t., n.* WH: pre-1200. Old English *thawian*, from Germanic. Cp. German *tauen*.

the *a.* used to refer to a particular person or thing, or to particular people or things, already mentioned, known to be familiar etc. *Also adv.* WH: pre-1200. Old English *se* (m.), *sēo, sīo* (fem.), *thæt* (neut.) (cp. THAT), ult. superseded by forms in *th-*, from Germanic. Cp. German *der* (m.), *die* (fem.), *das* (neut.). Ult. rel. to Greek *ho* (m.) *hē* (fem.), *to* (neut.).

theandric *a.* relating to or existing by the union of divine and human nature in Christ. WH: 17C. Ecclesiastical Greek *thandrikos*, from *theandros* god-man, from *theos* god + *anēr, andros* man. See also -IC.

theanthropic *a.* being both human and divine. WH: 17C. Ecclesiastical Greek *theanthrōpos* god-man, from *theos* god + *anthrōpos* man. See -IC.

thearchy *n.* government by God or gods. WH: 17C. Ecclesiastical Greek *thearkhia*, from *theos* god + *arkheia* government, rule.

theatre *n.* a building or outdoor area designed for the performance of plays, ballets, operas etc. *Also a.* WH: 14–15C. Old French *theatre* (Modern French *théâtre*) or Latin *theatrum*, from Greek *theatron*, from *theasthai* to behold.

theatrical *a.* of or relating to the theatre. *Also n.* WH: 16C. Late Latin *theatricus*, from Greek *theatrikos*, from *theatron* THEATRE. See also -IC, -AL[1].

thebaine *n.* a poisonous crystalline alkaloid obtained from opium. WH: 19C. Greek *Thēbai* Thebes, an ancient Egyptian city + -INE. The substance is so called because Egypt was a leading source of opium.

Theban *a.* of or relating to ancient Thebes (in Greece or in Egypt). *Also n.* WH: 14–15C. Latin *Thebanus*, from *Thebae*, Greek *Thēbai* Thebes, capital of ancient Boeotia in Greece, also ancient capital of Upper Egypt (cp. THEBAINE). See also -AN.

theca *n.* a part in a non-flowering plant such as moss that functions in a similar way to a receptacle. WH: 17C. Latin, from Greek *thēkē* case.

thé dansant *n.* a dance held during afternoon tea, popular in the 1920s and 1930s. WH: 19C. French, lit. dancing tea.

†thee *pron.* objective (accusative and dative) of THOU¹. WH: pre-1200. Old English *thec*, *theh*, later *thē* (acc.), *thē* (dat.), both from Germanic, from Indo-European (base of acc. also represented by Latin *te*, Greek *se*). Cp. THOU¹.

theft *n.* the act or an instance of stealing. WH: pre-1200. Old English *thiefth*, *thēofth*, from Germanic base of THIEF.

thegn *n.* an English thane. WH: 19C. Modern representation of Old English *thegn* THANE. The form was adopted in the 19C as a spelling to distinguish the Old English use of *thane* from the Scottish use (meaning lord) made familiar by Shakespeare in *Macbeth* (1605), in which Macbeth is hailed as 'Thane of Cawdor'.

theine *n.* caffeine (found in tea leaves). WH: 19C. Modern Latin *Thea*, former genus name of the tea plant, from Dutch *thee*. See TEA, also -INE.

their *a.* possessive of THEY. WH: 12–14C. Old Norse *theira*, *theirra*, gen. pl. of *sá* (m.), *sú* (fem.), *that* (neut.) THE, THAT. Cp. THEIRS, THEM, THEY.

theirs *pron.* something belonging to or associated with them. WH: 12–14C. THEIR + -'S.

theism *n.* belief in the existence of gods or a God, as opposed to atheism. WH: 17C. Greek *theos* god + -ISM.

them *pron.* objective (accusative and dative) of THEY. *Also a.* WH: 12–14C. Old Norse *theim* to those, to them, dat. pl. of *sá* (m.), *sú* (fem.), *that* (neut.) THE, THAT, pl. *their* THEY.

theme *n.* a subject on which a person thinks, writes or speaks. *Also v.t.* WH: 12–14C. Old French *tesme*, from Latin *thema*, from Greek *thema* proposition, from *the-*, base of *tithenai* to place. The Old French form was soon conformed in spelling to the Latin.

themselves *pron.* the emphatic and reflexive form of THEM. WH: 12–14C. THEM + SELF. See also -S¹.

then *adv.* at that time. *Also conj.*, *a.*, *n.* WH: pre-1200. Old English *thænne*, *thanne*, *thonne*, from base also of THAT, THE. Cp. THAN.

thenar *n.* the part of the palm at the base of the thumb. *Also a.* WH: 17C. Greek palm of the hand, sole of the foot.

thence *adv.* from that place. WH: 12–14C. From obs. *thenne* (from Old English *thanone*, *thanon*, from Germanic) + -S². The spelling with *-ce* phonetically represents the unvoiced sound denoted by *-s* in the original spelling. Cp. HENCE, WHENCE.

theo- *comb. form* of or relating to God or a god. WH: Greek, from *theos* god. See also -O-.

theobromine *n.* a bitter alkaloid resembling caffeine contained in cacao seeds. WH: 19C. Modern Latin *Theobroma*, genus name, lit. food of the gods, from Greek *theos* god + *brōma* food + -INE. The seeds of the tree *Theobroma cacao* are the source of cocoa and chocolate.

theocentric *a.* having God as its centre. WH: 19C. THEO- + -CENTRIC.

theocracy *n.* government by the immediate direction of God or through a class of priests. WH: 17C. Greek *theokratia*. See THEO-, -CRACY.

theocrasy *n.* mixed worship of different gods, polytheism. WH: 19C. Greek *theokrasia* a mingling with God, from *theos* god + *krasis* mingling.

theodicy *n.* a vindication of divine justice in respect to the existence of evil. WH: 18C. French *théodicée*, title of a work by the German philosopher G.W. Leibniz (1710), from Greek *theos* god + *dikē* justice.

theodolite *n.* a portable surveying instrument for measuring horizontal and vertical angles. WH: 16C. Modern Latin *theodelitus*, ult. of unknown orig. See also -ITE¹. The word is said to have been coined in 1571 by the English applied mathematician Leonard Digges or his son Thomas.

theogony *n.* the genealogy of the gods. WH: 17C. Greek *theogonia* birth of the gods, from *theos* god + *-gonia* generation, production.

theology *n.* the study of theistic religion, esp. Christianity. WH: 14–15C. Old French *théologie*, from Latin *theologia*, from Greek, from *theologos* a person who discourses on the gods, a theologian. See THEO-, also -LOGY.

theomachy *n.* a combat against or among the gods. WH: 16C. Greek *theomakhia*, from *theos* god + *-makhia*, from base of *makhē* battle.

theomancy *n.* divination by oracle or by people inspired by a god. WH: 17C. Greek *theomanteia* spirit of prophecy. See THEO-, -MANCY.

theomania *n.* religious insanity. WH: 19C. THEO- + -MANIA.

theomorphic *a.* having the form or semblance of God. WH: 19C. Greek *theomorphos*, from *theos* (THEO-) + *morphē* form. See also -IC.

theopathy *n.* emotion excited by the contemplation of God. WH: 18C. Ecclesiastical Greek *theopatheia* suffering of God. See THEO-, -PATHY.

theophany *n.* a manifestation or appearance of God to humans. WH: pre-1200. Ecclesiastical Latin *theophania*, from Greek *theophaneia*, neut. pl. *theophania*, from *theos* god + *phainein* to show.

theophoric *a.* derived from or bearing the name of a god. WH: 19C. THEO- + Greek *pherein* to bear. See also -IC.

theophylline *n.* a white alkaloid similar to theobromine found in plants such as tea, used to treat heart disease and headaches. WH: 19C. Modern Latin *Thea* (THEINE) + PHYLLO- + -INE.

theopneusty *n.* divine inspiration. WH: 19C. Greek *theopneustia*, from *theos* god + *-pneustos* inspired, from *pneu-*, stem of *pnein* to breathe, to blow.

theorbo *n.* a stringed instrument resembling a two-necked lute used in the 16th–17th cents. WH: 17C. Italian *tiorba*, with alt. of ending as in some words in -ADO. Some sources derive the Italian word from Venetian dialect *tiorba* travelling bag, from Slovenian *torba*, from Turkish bag. The instrument may have been so called because it was carried by wandering mendicants.

theorem *n.* a rule or law, esp. one expressed by symbols etc. WH: 16C. French *théorème* or Latin *theorema*, from Greek *theōrēma* speculation, theory, proposition to be proved, from *theōrein* to be a spectator, to look at, from *theōros* spectator.

theoretical *a.* of, relating to or founded on theory not facts or knowledge, not practical, speculative. WH: 17C. Late Latin *theoreticus*, from Greek *theōrētikos*, from *theōrētos* that may be seen, from *theōrein*. See THEOREM, also -IC, -AL¹.

theory *n.* a supposition explaining something, esp. a generalization explaining phenomena as the results of assumed natural causes. WH: 16C. Late Latin *theoria*, from Greek *theōria* contemplation, speculation, sight, from *theōros* spectator, from base of *theasthai* to look on, to contemplate.

theosophy *n.* a form of speculation, mysticism or philosophy aiming at the knowledge of God by means of intuition and contemplative illumination or by direct communion. WH: 17C. Medieval Latin *theosophia*, from Late Greek wisdom concerning God, from *theosophos*, from *theos* god + *sophos* wise.

theotechny *n.* the employment of supernatural intervention in a literary composition. WH: 19C. Greek *theos* god + *tekhnē* art.

therapeutic *a.* of or relating to healing or curing disease. WH: 16C. French *thérapeutique*, or from Late Latin *therapeutica* (pl.), from Greek *therapeutika*, use as n. of neut. pl. of *therapeutikos*, from *therapeutēs* minister, from *therapeuein* to minister to, to treat medically. See also -IC.

therapsid *n.* any fossil reptile of the order Therapsida, considered to be the ancestors of mammals. *Also a.* WH: early 20C. Modern Latin *Therapsida*, from Greek *thēr* animal + *hapsis*, *hapsidos* arch. See also -ID. The order name was coined by the S African palaeontologist Robert Broom in 1905 with reference to the skull, which is bounded below by a bony arch.

Theravada *n.* a form of Buddhism practised esp. in SE Asia. WH: 19C. Pali *theravāda*, lit. doctrine of the elders.

there *adv.* in or at that place, point or stage. *Also n.*, *int.* WH: pre-1200. Old English *thær*, *thēr*, from Germanic base also of THAT, THE. Cp. German *da*.

†theriac *n.* an antidote against the bite of poisonous animals. WH: 14–15C. Latin *theriaca*. See TREACLE.

therianthropic *a.* of or relating to deities represented as half man and half beast or to their worship. WH: 19C. Greek *thērion* wild animal + *anthrōpos* man. See also -IC.

therm *n.* a British unit of heat, equal to 100,000 British thermal units. WH: 19C. Greek *thermos* hot, *thermē* heat.

thermae *n.pl.* public baths in ancient Greece and Rome. WH: 16C. Latin (pl.), from Greek *thermai* hot baths, from *thermē* heat.

thermal *a.* of or relating to heat. *Also n.* WH: 18C. French, from Greek *thermē* heat + -AL[1].

thermion *n.* an ion or electron emitted by an incandescent body. WH: early 20C. THERMO- + ION. The term was coined in 1904 by the English physicist Owen W. Richardson, based on his earlier coinage *thermionics*.

thermistor *n.* a semiconducting device whose resistance decreases with rising temperature. WH: mid-20C. Contr. of *thermal resistor*. See THERMAL, RESIST.

thermite *n.* a mixture of finely divided aluminium and a metallic oxide, esp. of iron, producing intense heat on combustion, used in welding, incendiary bombs etc. WH: early 20C. THERMO- + -ITE[1]. The name was coined in 1895 by the German chemist Hans Goldschmidt.

thermo- *comb. form* heat. WH: Greek, from *thermos* hot, *thermē* heat. See also -O-.

thermochemistry *n.* the branch of chemistry dealing with the relations between chemical reactions and the heat liberated or absorbed. WH: 19C. THERMO- + CHEMISTRY.

thermocline *n.* a layer of water in a lake etc., in which the water temperature decreases rapidly between the epilimnion and hypolimnion. WH: 19C. THERMO- + Greek *klinein* to incline.

thermocouple *n.* a device for measuring temperature consisting of two wires of differing metals joined at both ends, one wire of a fixed temperature, the other at the temperature to be measured, the voltage developed being proportional to the difference in temperature. WH: 19C. THERMO- + COUPLE.

thermodynamics *n.* the branch of physics dealing with the relations between heat and other forms of energy. WH: 19C. THERMO- + *dynamics* (DYNAMIC). See also -ICS.

thermoelectricity *n.* electricity generated by differences of temperature. WH: 19C. THERMO- + *electricity* (ELECTRIC).

thermogenesis *n.* the production of heat, esp. by physiological processes. WH: 19C. THERMO- + GENESIS.

thermography *n.* the use of thermographic imaging to detect abnormalities in the body. WH: 19C. THERMO- + -GRAPHY.

thermolabile *a.* (of a substance) unstable when subjected to heat. WH: early 20C. THERMO- + LABILE.

thermoluminescence *n.* phosphorescence produced by heating an irradiated substance. WH: 19C. THERMO- + *luminescence* (LUMINESCE).

thermolysis *n.* loss of body heat. WH: 19C. THERMO- + -*lysis* (LYSIS).

thermometer *n.* an instrument for measuring temperature, usu. by the expansion or contraction of a column of mercury or alcohol in a graduated tube of small bore with a bulb at one end. WH: 17C. French *thermomètre* or Modern Latin *thermometrum*. See THERMO-, -METER.

thermomotor *n.* an engine producing force from the expansion of hot air or fluid. WH: early 20C. THERMO- + MOTOR.

thermonuclear *a.* relating to the fusion of nuclei at very high temperatures. WH: mid-20C. THERMO- + NUCLEAR.

thermophile *n.* a bacterium thriving in a high temperature. *Also a.* WH: 19C. THERMO- + -PHILE.

thermopile *n.* a series of thermocouples, esp. one employed to measure small quantities of radiant heat. WH: 19C. THERMO- + PILE[1].

thermoplastic *n., a.* (a substance) which softens under heat without undergoing any chemical change, and can therefore be heated repeatedly. WH: 19C. THERMO- + PLASTIC.

Thermos® *n.* a vacuum flask. WH: early 20C. Greek *thermos* warm, hot. The name was registered as a trademark in 1907.

thermoscope *n.* an instrument for indicating changes of temperature without measuring them. WH: 17C. THERMO- + -SCOPE.

thermosetting *a.* (of plastics) softening initially under heat but subsequently hardening and becoming infusible and insoluble. WH: mid-20C. THERMO- + *setting* (from SET[1] + -ING[2]).

thermosphere *n.* the part of the earth's atmosphere above the mesosphere, from about 50 miles (80 km), in which the temperature rises steadily with height. WH: early 20C. THERMO- + SPHERE.

thermostable *a.* (of a substance) stable when subjected to heat. WH: early 20C. THERMO- + STABLE[1].

thermostat *n.* an automatic device for regulating temperatures. WH: 19C. THERMO- + -STAT.

thermotaxis *n.* the movement of an organism in reaction to heat stimulus. WH: 19C. THERMO- + TAXIS.

thermotropism *n.* the orientation of a plant in response to temperature difference. WH: 19C. THERMO- + TROPISM.

theroid *a.* relating to or resembling a beast. WH: 19C. Greek *thēr* wild animal + -OID.

theropod *n.* any carnivorous saurischian dinosaur of the genus *Theropoda*, including the tyrannosaurs and megalosaurs. *Also a.* WH: early 20C. Greek *thēr* wild animal + -O- + -POD.

thesaurus *n.* a collection of words, phrases etc. arranged as groups of synonyms or by concept. WH: 16C. Latin, from Greek *thesauros* store, treasure, storehouse. Cp. TREASURE. The word was originally the term for a dictionary in general. The sense dictionary of synonyms dates from the 19C.

these *pron.* the plural of THIS. *Also a.* WH: pre-1200. Old English *thǣs*, pl. of *this*. Cp. THOSE.

thesis *n.* a proposition advanced or maintained. WH: 14–15C. Late Latin, from Greek putting, placing, proposition, affirmation, from *the-*, base of *tithenai* to put, to place.

thespian *a.* of or relating to tragedy or drama. *Also n.* WH: 17C. Greek *Thespis*, 6C BC Greek poet, the traditional founder of Greek tragedy + -AN.

theta *n.* the eighth letter of the Greek alphabet (Θ, θ), corresponding to *th*. WH: 14–15C. Greek *thēta*.

theurgy *n.* divine or supernatural agency, esp. in human affairs. WH: 16C. Late Latin *theurgia*, from Greek *theourgia* sorcery, from *theos* god + *-ergos* working.

thew *n.* muscles, sinews. WH: pre-1200. Old English *thēaw* usage, conduct, from Germanic, ult. of unknown orig. The original sense (to the 19C) was custom, habit, a person's manner of behaving. The current sense evolved in the 12–14C and was popularized by Sir Walter Scott, who associated it with *sinew*: 'My fellow traveller, to judge by his thewes and sinews, was a man who might have set danger at defiance' (*Rob Roy*, 1818).

they *pron.* the plural of HE, SHE or IT[1] (subjective). WH: 12–14C. Old Norse *their*, nom. pl. of *sá* (m.), *sú* (fem.), *that* (neut.) THE, THAT, superseding Old English *hī*, *hīe*, pl. of *hē* (m.), *hēo* (fem.) *hit* (neut.). Cp. THEIR, THEM.

thiamine *n.* a vitamin found in unrefined cereals, beans and liver, important for metabolism and nerve function, the lack of which can cause beriberi; vitamin B_1. WH: mid-20C. THIO- + AMINE.

thick *a.* having great or specified extent or depth from one surface to the opposite. *Also adv., n.* WH: pre-1200. Old English *thicce*, from Germanic, of unknown orig. Cp. German *dick*.

thief *n.* a person who steals, esp. furtively and without violence. WH: pre-1200. Old English *thīof*, *thēof*, from Germanic. Cp. German *Dieb*.

thigh *n.* the thick, fleshy portion of the leg between the hip and knee in humans. WH: pre-1200. Old English *thēh*, *thēoh*, from Germanic.

thigmotropism *n.* movement when touched. WH: early 20C. Greek *thigma* touch + -O- + TROPISM.

thill *n.* the shaft of a cart, carriage or other vehicle. WH: 12–14C. Orig. unknown.

thimble *n.* a cap of metal, plastic etc., worn to protect the end of the finger in sewing. WH: pre-1200. Old English *thȳmel*, from *thūma* THUMB. See also -LE[1]. The original sense was a protective sheath for the thumb. The current sense evolved in the 14–15C.

thin *a.* having the opposite surfaces close together, of little thickness, slender. *Also adv., v.t., v.i.* WH: pre-1200. Old English *thynne*, from Germanic, from Indo-European base represented also by Latin *tenuis*. Cp. German *dünn*.

†**thine** *a.* THY (before a vowel). *Also pron.* WH: pre-1200. Old English *thin*, used as gen. case of *thu* THOU[1] and as poss. a.

thing[1] *n.* any object or thought. WH: pre-1200. Old English, corr. to Old High German *ding* assembly for deliberation (German *Ding* affair, matter, thing), Old Norse *thing*, from Germanic. Cp. THING[2]. The original sense was meeting, assembly, court, council, then (to the 16C) cause, reason, sake.

thing² n. a Scandinavian public assembly, esp. a legislative body. WH: 18C. Old Norse *thing*, Danish, Norwegian and Swedish *ting*. See THING¹. Cp. STORTING, TYNWALD.

think v.t. to regard or examine in the mind, to reflect, to ponder (over etc.). *Also v.i., n.* WH: pre-1200. Old English *thencan*, from Germanic, from Indo-European. Cp. THANK, THOUGHT.

thio- *comb. form* sulphur. WH: Greek *theion* sulphur. See also -O-.

thiol n. any organic compound analogous to alcohol containing sulphur in place of oxygen. WH: 19C. THIO- + -OL.

thiopentone n. a barbiturate drug used, as a sodium salt, in medicine as a general anaesthetic and hypnotic. WH: mid-20C. THIO- + PENTOBARBITONE.

thiosulphuric a. applied to an acid corresponding to sulphuric acid in which one atom of oxygen is replaced by one of sulphur. WH: 19C. THIO- + *sulphuric* (SULPHUR).

thiourea n. a white crystalline compound used in photographic fixing, rubber vulcanization and the manufacture of synthetic resins. WH: 19C. THIO- + UREA.

third n. any one of three equal parts. *Also n., a.* WH: pre-1200. Old English *thirdda, thridda*, from Germanic, from Indo-European. Cp. Latin *tertius*, Greek *tritos*.

†thirl v.t. to pierce through, to perforate. *Also n.* WH: pre-1200. Old English *thyrlian*, from *thȳrel*, from THROUGH + -EL. Cp. THRILL.

thirst n. the uneasiness or suffering caused by the need to drink liquid. *Also v.i.* WH: pre-1200. Old English *thurst*, from Germanic, from Indo-European base represented also by Latin *torrere* to dry, to parch (cp. TORRID). Cp. German *Durst*.

thirteen n. the number or figure 13 or xiii. *Also a.* WH: pre-1200. Old English *thrēotīene*. See THREE, -TEEN.

thirty n. the number or figure 30 or xxx. *Also a.* WH: pre-1200. Old English *thrītig*. See THREE, also -TY².

this a., pron. used to denote the person or thing that is present or near in place or time, or already mentioned, implied or familiar. *Also adv.* WH: pre-1200. Old English *this* (neut.), *thes* (m.), *thēos* (fem.), from Germanic bases of THAT, THE. Cp. THESE, THOSE.

thistle n. any plant of the genera *Circium, Carlina, Carduus* etc. having prickly stems, leaves and involucres. WH: pre-1200. Old English *thistel*, from Germanic, of unknown orig. Cp. German *Distel*.

thither adv. to that place. WH: pre-1200. Old English *thider*, alt. (by assim. to HITHER) of *thæder*, corr. to Old Norse *thathra*, from Germanic base of THE, THAT + suf. meaning towards. Cp. WHITHER.

thixotropic a. (of certain gels, e.g. non-drip paints) becoming fluid when shaken or stirred. WH: early 20C. Greek *thixis* touching + -O- + -*tropic* (-TROPE).

thole¹ n. a pin in the gunwale of a boat serving as fulcrum for the oar. WH: pre-1200. Old English *thol, tholl*, corr. to Middle Dutch *dolle* (Dutch *dol*), Old Norse *thollr* fir tree, tree, peg.

thole² v.t. to suffer, to endure, to bear, to undergo. WH: pre-1200. Old English *tholian*, from Germanic, from Indo-European base meaning to raise, to remove.

tholus n. a dome, cupola, or lantern. WH: 17C. Latin, from Greek *tholos*.

Thomism n. the scholastic philosophy and theology of Aquinas. WH: 18C. St *Thomas* Aquinas, 1225–74, Italian scholastic philosopher and theologian + -ISM.

-thon *comb. form* a large-scale event or related series of events lasting a long time or demanding endurance of the participants, as in *telethon*. WH: Extracted from MARATHON. Cp. -ATHON.

thong n. a strip of leather used as a whiplash, for reins, or for fastening anything. *Also v.t.* WH: pre-1200. Old English *thwang, thwong*, from Germanic. Cp. German *Zwang* compulsion.

thorax n. the part of the trunk between the neck and the abdomen. WH: 14–15C. Latin, from Greek *thōrax, thōrakos* breastplate, chest.

thorium n. a radioactive metallic element, at. no. 90, chem. symbol Th, found chiefly in thorite and monazite. WH: 19C. *Thor*, the Norse god of thunder + -IUM. The element is so called as it was found in *thorite* (from *Thor* + -ITE¹). It was named in 1832 by the Swedish chemist Jöns Jakob Berzelius, who discovered it in 1828–9.

thorn n. a spine, a sharp-pointed projection on a plant, a prickle. WH: pre-1200. Old English, from Germanic, from Indo-European. Cp. German *Dorn*.

thorough a. complete, total, unqualified, not superficial. *Also n.* WH: 15C. Old English *thuruh*, alt. of *thurh* THROUGH. The word, originally a preposition and adverb, was adopted subsequently for use as an adjective.

†thorp n. a village, a hamlet (esp. in place names). WH: pre-1200. Old English *throp, thorp*, corr. to Old Saxon *thorp* (Dutch *dorp*), Old High German *dorf* (German *Dorf*), Old Norse *thorp*, from Germanic. Place names containing *thorp* are most common in NE and E England, especially in Yorkshire, Lincolnshire, Northamptonshire, Leicestershire and Norfolk. Examples are *Bishopthorpe, Caythorpe, Grimsthorpe, Saxthorpe, Scunthorpe*. Cp. TROOP.

those pron. the plural of THAT. *Also a.* WH: pre-1200. Old English *thās, thōs*, pl. of THIS (cp. THESE), but later used as pl. of *that*, replacing obs. *tho*.

†thou¹ pron. the second personal pronoun singular (subjective), denoting the person spoken to. *Also v.i.* WH: pre-1200. Old English *thu*, from Germanic, from Indo-European base represented also by Latin *tu*, Greek (Doric) *tu*, (Attic) *su*. Cp. THEE, THINE, THY.

thou² n. a thousand. WH: 19C. Abbr. of THOUSAND.

though *conj.* notwithstanding that, despite the fact that. *Also adv.* WH: pre-1200. Old English *thēah*, superseded in Middle English by forms from Old Norse *thó*, from Germanic, from Indo-European base of THE, THAT. Cp. German *doch*.

thought n. the act or process of thinking. WH: pre-1200. Old English *thōht, gethōht*, from Germanic base of THINK. Cp. German *Bedacht* thoughtfulness, consideration.

thousand n. ten hundred, 1000. *Also a.* WH: pre-1200. Old English *thūsend*, from Germanic. Cp. Dutch *duizend*, German *Tausend*. Related words outside Germanic are Lithuanian *túkstantis*, Russian *tysyacha*, Polish *tysiac*.

thrall n. a state of slavery or enthralment. *Also a., v.t.* WH: pre-1200. Old English *thrēl*, from Old Norse *thrɛ̋ll*, ? from Germanic base meaning to run (cp. Old High German *dregil, drigil* servant, runner).

thrang a. thronged, busy. WH: 12–14C. Alt. of THRONG.

thrash v.t. to beat severely, esp. with a stick etc. *Also v.i., n.* WH: pre-1200. Var. of THRESH. The original sense was to strike, to knock.

thrasher n. a N American songbird of the family Mimidae, resembling the thrush. WH: 19C. Said to be a survival of an English dial. name for the song thrush.

†thrasonical a. bragging, boastful. WH: 16C. Latin *Thraso, Thrasonis*, from Greek *Thrasōn* Thraso, a boastful soldier in Terence's comedy *Eunuchus* (161 BC), from *thrasus* bold, spirited. See also -IC, -AL¹.

thrave n. 24 sheaves or two stooks of corn. WH: pre-1200. Of Scandinavian orig. Cp. Old Norse *threfi*, Swedish *trave*, Danish *trave*.

thrawn a. twisted, misshapen. WH: 14–15C. Scottish p.p. of THROW.

thread n. a slender cord consisting of two or more yarns doubled or twisted, for sewing or weaving. *Also v.t.* WH: pre-1200. Old English *thrɛ̄d*, from Germanic base also of THROW. Cp. German *Draht*.

threap v.t. to scold. *Also v.i., n.* WH: pre-1200. Old English *thrēapian*, of unknown orig.

threat n. a declaration of an intention to inflict punishment, loss, injury etc. WH: pre-1200. Old English *thrēat*, rel. to Old Norse *thraut* struggle, labour, from Germanic. Prob. also rel. to Latin *trudere* to thrust (cp. INTRUDE). Cp. German *verdriessen* to annoy.

three n. the number or figure 3 or iii. *Also a.* WH: pre-1200. Old English *thrī, thrīe* (m.), *thrīo, thrēo* (fem., neut.), from Germanic, from Indo-European base also of Latin *tres, tria*, Greek *treis, tria*, Sanskrit *trayaḥ, trī*. Cp. Dutch *drie*, German *drei*.

thremmatology n. the branch of biology dealing with the breeding of animals and plants. WH: 19C. Greek *thremma, thremmatos* nursling + -O- + -LOGY. The term was coined in 1888 by the English zoologist Sir Edwin R. Lankester.

threnody n. a song of lamentation. WH: 17C. Greek *thrēnōidia*, from *thrēnos* funeral lament + *ōidē* song, ODE.

threonine n. an amino acid essential for growth and health found in certain proteins. WH: mid-20C. From *threose* a hygroscopic solid tetrose sugar (from letters of *erythrose* a liquid tetrose sugar, itself from ERYTHRITE + -OSE²) + -*n*- + -INE. The acid is so named as having a similar molecular configuration to threose.

thresh v.t. to beat out or separate the grain (from corn etc.). *Also v.i.* WH: pre-1200. Old English *therscan*, later *threscan*, from Germanic, from Indo-European. Cp. German *dreschen*. Related words outside Germanic include Lithuanian *traszketi* to rattle, to make a noise, Russian *treskat'* to crash, to crackle.

threshold n. the stone or plank at the bottom of a doorway. WH: pre-1200. Old English *therscold*, *threscold*, from Germanic, from a 1st element rel. to THRESH and a 2nd element of unknown orig. Cp. German dial. *Drischaufel*.

thrice adv. three times. WH: pre-1200. Old English *thrīga*, *thrīwa*. See THREE, also -s². Cp. ONCE, TWICE.

thrift n. frugality. WH: 12–14C. Old Norse, from *thrífask* THRIVE.

thrill v.t. to affect with emotion so as to give a sense as of vibrating or tingling. *Also v.i., n.* WH: 12–14C. Alt. of THIRL. Cp. NOSTRIL. The original sense (to the 18C) was to pierce, to bore, to penetrate (of a material object or a sound, emotion, etc.). The current sense dates from the 16C.

thrips n. a minute insect of the order Thysanoptera, often injurious to plants, esp. grain, the thunderfly. WH: 18C. Latin, from Greek *thrips*, pl. *thripes* woodworm.

thrive v.i. to prosper, to be fortunate, to be successful. WH: 12–14C. Old Norse *thrífask*, reflex. of *thrífa* to grasp, to lay hold of suddenly. The original sense was to grow, to increase.

throat n. the front part of the neck, containing the gullet and windpipe. *Also v.t.* WH: pre-1200. Old English *throte*, *throtu*, from Germanic, represented also by Old Norse *throti* swelling, Old English *thrūtian*, Old Norse *thrutna* to swell. Cp. German *Drossel*.

throb v.i. to vibrate, to quiver. *Also n.* WH: 14–15C. Prob. imit., the -r- representing the beat of the heart, pulse, etc.

throe n. the pains of childbirth or death. *Also v.i.* WH: 12–14C. Orig. uncertain. ? Rel. to Old English *thrēa*, *thrawu* threat, calamity, influ. by *thrōwian* to suffer.

thrombosis n. local coagulation of the blood in the heart or a blood vessel. WH: 18C. Modern Latin, from Greek *thrombōsis* curdling, from *thrombousthai*, from *thrombos* lump, piece, clot of blood, curd of milk.

throne n. a royal seat, a chair or seat of state for a sovereign, bishop etc. *Also v.t., v.i.* WH: 12–14C. Old French *trone* (Modern French *trône*), from Latin *thronus*, from Greek *thronos* elevated seat.

throng n. a multitude of people or living things pressed close together, a crowd. *Also v.i., v.t.* WH: pre-1200. Old English *gethrang* throng, crowd, tumult, rel. to *thringan* to push, to press, from Germanic. Cp. German *Drang* stress.

throstle n. the song thrush. WH: pre-1200. Old English, from Germanic, from Indo-European base represented also by Latin *turdus* thrush. Cp. THRUSH¹.

throttle n. a throttle-lever. *Also v.t.* WH: 16C. ? Dim. of early form of THROAT. The original sense was throat. The current sense evolved in the 19C.

through prep. from end to end of, from side to side of, between the sides or walls of. *Also adv., a.* WH: pre-1200. Old English *thurh*, from Germanic. Cp. German *durch*. An alternative Old English form *thuruh* developed into THOROUGH and came to be used as an adjective, while *through* is used as the preposition and adverb.

throw v.t. to fling, to hurl, to cast, esp. to a distance with some force. *Also v.i., n.* WH: pre-1200. Old English *thrāwan*, from Germanic, from Indo-European base represented also by Latin *terere* to rub, Greek *teirein* to wear out, *trēma* hole. Cp. THREAD. The original basic sense was to twist, to turn. The sense to project through the air evolved in the 12–14C.

thrum¹ v.i. to play carelessly or unskilfully (on a stringed instrument). *Also v.t., n.* WH: 16C. Imit. Cp. STRUM.

thrum² n. the fringe of warp threads left when the web has been cut off, or one of such threads. *Also v.t.* WH: pre-1200. Old English, from Germanic, from Indo-European base represented also by Latin *terminus*, Greek *terma* end, term. Cp. German *Trumm* end-piece, *Trümmer* remnants.

thrush¹ n. a bird of the family Turdidae, esp. the song thrush, *Turdus philomelos* or mistle thrush, *T. viscivorus*. WH: pre-1200. Old English *thrysce*, rel. to *thræsce* in same sense. Cp. THROSTLE.

thrush² n. a disease of the mouth and throat, usu. affecting children, caused by the fungus *Candida albicans* and resulting in white patches. WH: 17C. Orig. unknown. Cp. Swedish *torsk*, Danish *troske* in sense disease of mouth and throat.

thrust v.t. to push suddenly or forcibly. *Also v.i., n.* WH: pre-1200. Old Norse *thrýsta*, prob. from Indo-European base also of Latin *trudere* to thrust (cp. INTRUDE).

thud n. a dull sound as of a blow on something soft. *Also v.i.* WH: 14–15C. Prob. from Old English *thyddan* to thrust, to push, rel. to Old English *thoddettan* to push, to beat, *thoden* violent wind.

thug n. a violent or brutal ruffian. WH: 19C. Hindi *thag* cheat, swindler. The word was originally the name of a member of an organization of professional robbers in India, who strangled their victims.

thuja n. any coniferous tree or shrub of the genus *Thuja*, also called *arbor vitae*. WH: 18C. Modern Latin, from Greek *thuia*.

thulium n. a rare silver-grey malleable metallic element, at. no. 69, chem. symbol Tm. WH: 19C. *Thule*, a land believed by ancient Greek and Roman geographers to be the most northerly in the world + -IUM. The element was named in 1879 by its discoverer, the Swedish chemist Per Theodor Cleve, who identified Thule with Scandinavia.

thumb n. the short thick digit of the human hand. *Also v.t., v.i.* WH: pre-1200. Old English *thūma*, from Germanic, from Indo-European base also of Latin *tumere* to swell (cp. TUMID). Cp. German *Daumen*. For the added -b, cp. DUMB.

thump v.t. to strike with something giving a dull sound, esp. with the fist. *Also v.i., n.* WH: 16C. Imit. Cp. BUMP¹, JUMP.

thunder n. the sound following a flash of lightning, due to the disturbance of the air by the electric discharge. *Also v.i., v.t.* WH: pre-1200. Old English *thunor*, from Germanic, from Indo-European base also of Latin *tonare* to thunder. Cp. German *Donner*.

thunk n. a thud. *Also v.i.* WH: mid-20C. Imit.

thurible n. a censer. WH: 14–15C. Old French, or from Latin *thuribulum*, from *thus*, *thuris* incense.

Thursday n. the fifth day of the week, following Wednesday. *Also adv.* WH: pre-1200. Old English *thuresdæg*, var. of *thunresdæg* day of thunder, from gen. of *thunor* THUNDER, partly assoc. with Old Norse *thorsdagr*, lit. Thor's day, after Thor, the Norse god of thunder, corr. to Middle Dutch *donderdag*, Old High German *donarestac* (German *Donnerstag*), translating Late Latin *Jovi dies* Jupiter's day (cp. French *jeudi* Thursday).

thus adv. in this manner. WH: pre-1200. Old English, rel. to Old Saxon *thus*, Middle Dutch *dus*, of unknown orig.

thwack v.t. to hit with a loud heavy blow, esp. with something flat. *Also n.* WH: 14–15C. Imit. Cp. WHACK.

thwaite n. a piece of ground reclaimed and converted to cultivation. WH: 12–14C. Old Norse *thveit* piece of land, paddock, lit. cut-piece, rel. to Old English *thwītan* to cut (off).

thwart v.t. to cross, to frustrate. *Also n., prep., adv., a.* WH: 12–14C. Old Norse *thvert*, orig. neut. of *thverr* transverse, cross, corr. to Old English *thwerh* crooked, cross, perverse, from Germanic, from Indo-European base also of Latin *torquere* to twist.

†thy a. of or relating to you. WH: 12–14C. Reduced form of THINE (orig. used before consonants except *h*).

thylacine n. a carnivorous marsupial of Tasmania, *Thylacinus cynocephalus*, perhaps extinct. WH: 19C. Modern Latin *Thylacinus*, from Greek *thulakos* pouch. See also -INE.

thyme n. any plant of the genus *Thymus*, esp. the garden thyme, *T. vulgaris*, a pungent aromatic herb used in cookery. WH: 12–14C. Old French *thym*, from Latin *thymum*, from Greek *thumon*, from *thuein* to burn, to sacrifice. The plant is so called as it was originally used as incense.

thymine n. one of the bases in DNA and RNA, containing nitrogen. WH: 19C. From *thymic* (from THYMUS + -IC) + -INE.

thymol n. a phenol obtained from oil of thyme, used as an antiseptic. WH: 19C. Greek *thumon* THYME + -OL.

thymus n. a gland situated in the lower region of the neck, usu. degenerating after puberty. WH: 16C. Greek *thumos* warty excrescence like a thyme bud.

thyristor n. a semiconductor rectifier in which the flow of current between the anode and the cathode is initiated by a signal applied to a third electrode, the gate. WH: mid-20C. Blend of *thyratron* a type of thermionic valve (from Greek *thura* door + -TRON) and TRANSISTOR.

thyroid n. the thyroid gland. *Also a.* WH: 18C. Obs. French *thyroïde* (now *thyroïde*) or Modern Latin *thyroides*, from Greek (*khondros*) *thureoïdēs* shield-shaped (cartilage), from *thureos* oblong shield. See also -OID.

thyrsus n. in ancient Greece and Rome, a spear or shaft wrapped with ivy or vine branches and tipped with a fir cone, an attribute of Bacchus. WH: 16C. Latin, from Greek *thursos* stalk of a plant, Bacchic staff.

thysanuran a. belonging to the Thysanura, a division of wingless insects comprising the springtails. *Also n.* WH: 19C. Modern Latin *Thysanura*, from Greek *thusanos* tassel, fringe + *oura* tail. See also -AN.

ti n. a cabbage tree. WH: 19C. Polynesian.

tiara n. a jewelled coronet or headband worn as an ornament by women. WH: 16C. Latin, from Greek, partly through Italian.

Tibetan a. of or relating to the country of Tibet or its language. *Also n.* WH: 19C. *Tibet*, a country in central Asia, now an autonomous region of China + -AN.

tibia n. the shin bone, the anterior and inner of the two bones of the leg. WH: 14–15C. Latin shank, pipe, shin bone.

tic n. a habitual convulsive twitching of muscles, esp. of the face. WH: 19C. French, from Italian *ticchio*.

tick[1] v.i. to make a small regularly recurring sound like that of a watch or clock. *Also v.t., n.* WH: 12–14C. Prob. rel. to Dutch *tikken* to pat, to tick, Old High German *zekōn* to pluck, Middle High German *zicken* to push. Cp. TICKLE, TIG.

tick[2] n. any of various parasitic arachnids of the order Acarina, infesting some animals and occasionally humans. WH: pre-1200. Old English *ticia*, from Germanic, from Indo-European. Cp. German *Zecke*.

tick[3] n. credit, trust. *Also v.i.* WH: 17C. Appar. abbr. of TICKET in phr. *on the ticket*.

tick[4] n. a cover or case for the filling of mattresses and beds. WH: 14–15C. Prob. from Middle Low German and Middle Dutch *tēke*, also Middle Dutch *tīke*, rel. to Old High German *ziahha*, *ziehha* (German *Zieche* bedtick, pillowcase), from Germanic, from Latin *theca*, from Greek *thēkē* case.

ticket n. a card or paper with written or printed contents entitling the holder to admission to a concert etc., conveyance by train etc., or other privilege. *Also v.t.* WH: 16C. Shortening of obs. French *étiquet*, from Old French *estiquette*, from *estiquier*, *estiquier*, *estichier* to fix, to stick, from Middle Dutch *steken*. See also -ET[1]. Cp. ETIQUETTE. The original sense was a short written document, a memorandum, also a notice posted in a public place. The current sense as a paper or card giving entitlement dates from the 17C.

tickety-boo a. satisfactory, all right, fine. WH: mid-20C. Orig. uncertain. ? Hindi *ṭhīk hai* all right, influ. by TICKET.

tickle v.t. to touch lightly so as to cause a thrilling sensation usually producing laughter. *Also v.i., n., a.* WH: 12–14C. Orig. uncertain. ? Freq. of TICK[1] or alt. of KITTLE. The original sense (to the 17C) was to be excited. The current sense arose in the 14–15C.

tiddler n. a stickleback or other very small fish. WH: 19C. Prob. rel. to *tittlebat*, child's var. of STICKLEBACK. See also -ER[1].

tiddly a. slightly drunk, drunk. *Also n.* WH: 19C. Orig. uncertain. Cp. TIDDLYWINK.

tiddlywink n. a small counter or disc flicked into a cup or tray with another. WH: 19C. Orig. uncertain. ? Rel. to TIDDLY.

tide n. the alternative rise and fall of the sea, due to the gravitational attraction of the sun and moon. *Also v.i.* WH: pre-1200. Old English *tīd*, from a Germanic word rel. to TIME. Cp. German *Zeit* time. The original sense was time. The sense rise and fall of the sea evolved in the 14–15C.

tidings n.pl. news, intelligence, a report. WH: pre-1200. Pl. of *tiding*, from Old English *tīdung*, as if from Old English *tīdan* to happen + -ING[1], but prob. from Old Norse *títhendi*, *títhindi* (news of) events or occurrences, from *títhr* occurring.

tidy a. in good order, neat, trim. *Also n., v.t.* WH: 12–14C. TIDE + -Y[1]. The original sense (to the 18C) was timely, seasonable, opportune. The current sense evolved in the 18C.

tie v.t. to fasten with a cord etc., to secure, to attach, to bind. *Also v.i., n.* WH: pre-1200. Old English *tīgan*, earlier *tīegan*, *tēgan*, from Germanic.

tier n. a row, a rank, esp. one of several rows placed one above another. *Also v.t.* WH: 15C. Old French *tire* sequence, rank, order, from *tirer* to draw (out). Cp. TIRADE.

tierce n. in fencing, the third position for guard, parry or thrust. WH: 14–15C. Var. of TERCE.

tiercel n. a male falcon. WH: 12–14C. Old French *tercel* (Modern French *tiercel*), from dim. of Latin *tertius* THIRD. The bird is said to be so named either from the belief that the third egg of a clutch hatched a male or because the male is a third smaller than the female.

tiff n. a slight quarrel. *Also v.t., v.i.* WH: 18C. Prob. a dial. word of imit. orig. Cp. HUFF.

tiffany n. a kind of thin silklike gauze. WH: 17C. Old French *tifanie*, from Ecclesiastical Latin *theophania*, from Greek *theophaneia*. See THEOPHANY. The reason for the name is obscure. It may actually derive from Greek *diaphaneia* transparency, with reference to its thinness. Cp. DIAPHANOUS.

tiffin n. a lunch or light repast between breakfast and dinner, formerly taken by the British in India. *Also v.i.* WH: 19C. Appar. from *tiffing*, from dial. *tiff* to drink, of unknown orig.

tig v.t. to touch in the game of tag. *Also v.i., n.* WH: 14–15C. Var. of TICK[1]. Cp. TAG.

tiger n. a large Asian carnivorous feline mammal, *Panthera tigris*, tawny with black stripes. WH: 12–14C. Old French *tigre*, from Latin *tigris*, from Greek.

tight a. drawn, fastened, held, or fitting closely. *Also adv.* WH: 12–14C. Prob. alt. of dial. *thight*, from Old English *thīht*, from Germanic. Cp. German *dicht* dense, close.

tigon n. the offspring of a tiger and a lioness. WH: early 20C. Blend of TIGER and LION. Cp. LIGER.

Tigrayan a. of or relating to Tigray. *Also n.* WH: 19C. *Tigray*, *Tigre*, a province of N Ethiopia + -AN.

tiki n. a Maori neck ornament or figurine, a stylized representation of an ancestor etc. WH: 18C. Maori image. Cp. HEI-TIKI.

tikka n. an Indian dish of kebabs (esp. chicken or lamb) marinated in spices and dry-roasted in a clay oven. WH: mid-20C. Punjabi *ṭikkā*.

tilapia n. any freshwater mouthbrooding fish of the African genus *Tilapia* or related genera. WH: 19C. Modern Latin, of uncertain orig. ? From Greek *tilōn* a kind of fish (mentioned by Aristotle) + *apios* distant.

tilbury n. a light, two-wheeled open horse-drawn carriage. WH: 19C. Said to be so named from one *Tilbury*, its orig. manufacturer.

tilde n. a diacritical sign (~) in Spanish put over *n* to indicate the sound *ny* as in *señor*, in Portuguese and phonetics put over vowels to indicate nasalization. WH: 19C. Spanish, from Latin *titulus* TITLE. Cp. TITTLE.

tile n. a thin slab of baked clay, used for covering roofs, paving floors, constructing drains etc. *Also v.t.* WH: pre-1200. Old English *tigele*, from Latin *tegula*, from Indo-European base meaning to cover. Cp. German *Ziegel*.

tiliaceous a. of or relating to the family Tiliaceae of flowering plants and trees, related to or resembling the linden or lime tree. WH: 19C. Latin *tiliaceus*, from *tilia* lime tree + -OUS. See also -ACEOUS.

till[1] prep. up to, up to the time of, until. *Also conj.* WH: pre-1200. Old English *til*, prob. from use as adv. of Germanic n. meaning aim, goal, represented by Old English *till* fixed point. Cp. TILL[3].

till[2] n. a money drawer in or on a counter. WH: 14–15C. Orig. unknown.

till[3] v.t. to cultivate for crops. WH: pre-1200. Old English *tilian* to strive after, to cultivate, from Germanic base also of TILL[1]. Cp. German *zielen* to aim, to strive.

till[4] n. an unstratified clay containing boulder, pebbles, sand etc., deposited by glaciers. WH: 17C. Orig. unknown.

tiller[1] n. the lever on the head of a rudder by which this is turned. WH: 14–15C. Anglo-French *telier* weaver's beam, from Medieval Latin *telarium*, from Latin *tela* web. See also -ER[1].

tiller[2] n. the shoot of a plant springing from the base of the original stalk, a sucker. *Also v.i.* WH: 17C. Appar. from Old English *telgor*, *tealgor*, extended form of *telga* branch, bough, twig.

Tilley lamp® n. a portable oil or paraffin lamp where the burner is supplied with fuel by air pressure. WH: mid-20C. *Tilley*, name of orig. manufacturer + LAMP.

tilt *v.i.* to heel over, to tip, to be in a slanting position. *Also v.t., n.* WH: 14–15C. Prob. from an Old English form rel. to *tealt* unsteady, or of Scandinavian orig. (cp. Norwegian *tylten* unsteady, Swedish *tulta* to totter). The original sense was to cause to fall, to push over, to overthrow. The current sense dates from the 16C, as does the historical sense to engage in a joust.

tilth *n.* tillage, cultivation. WH: pre-1200. Old English, from *tilian* TILL³ + -TH².

†**timbal** *n.* a kettledrum. WH: 17C. French *timbale*, alt. (based on *cymbale* cymbal) of obs. *tamballe*, from Spani.sh *atabal* (with assim. to *tambour* drum), from Arabic *aṭ-ṭabl*, from *aṭ* the + *ṭabl* drum.

timbale *n.* a dish of meat or fish pounded and mixed with white of egg, cream etc., and cooked in a drum-shaped mould. WH: 19C. French *timbale* TIMBAL.

timber *n.* wood suitable for building, carpentry etc. *Also v.t., int.* WH: pre-1200. Old English building, structure, from Germanic, from Indo-European base meaning to build. Cp. German *Zimmer* room.

timbre *n.* the quality of tone distinguishing particular voices, instruments etc., due to the individual character of the sound waves. WH: 19C. French, from Medieval Greek *timbanon* timbrel, kettledrum, from Greek *tumpanon* TYMPANUM. Cp. TIMBREL.

timbrel *n.* an ancient instrument like the tambourine. WH: 16C. Prob. dim. of obs. *timbre* in same sense. See TIMBRE, also -EL.

Timbuctoo *n.* any distant place. WH: 19C. *Timbuktu*, a town on the edge of the Sahara in Mali, W Africa, legendary for its remoteness and difficulty of access.

time *n.* the general relation of sequence or continuous or successive existence. *Also v.t., v.i.* WH: pre-1200. Old English *tīma*, corr. to Old Norse *tími* time, good time, prosperity, from Germanic, from base of TIDE (which was superseded by *time* in the temporal senses).

timid *a.* easily frightened, shy. WH: 16C. French *timide*, or from Latin *timidus*, from *timere* to fear. See also -ID.

timocracy *n.* a form of government in which a certain amount of property is a necessary qualification for office. WH: 15C. Old French *timocratie*, from Medieval Latin *timocratia*, from Greek, from *timē* honour, value. See -CRACY.

Timorese *n.* a native or inhabitant of Timor. *Also a.* WH: 19C. *Timor*, an Indonesian island off the NW coast of Australia + -ESE.

timoroso *adv.* with hesitation. WH: 19C. Italian, from Medieval Latin *timorosus* TIMOROUS.

timorous *a.* fearful, timid. WH: 14–15C. Old French *temoros, temoreus*, from Medieval Latin *timorosus*, from Latin *timor* fear, from *timere*. See TIMID, also -OUS.

timothy *n.* a valuable fodder grass, *Phleum pratense*. WH: 18C. *Timothy* Hanson, 18C US farmer, said to have introduced it from New England to the Southern States in *c.*1720.

timpani *n.pl.* orchestral kettledrums. WH: 19C. Italian, pl. of *timpano* kettledrum, from Latin *tympanum* drum.

tin *n.* a lustrous white metallic element, at. no. 50, chem. symbol Sn, easily beaten into thin plates, much used for cooking utensils etc., esp. in the form of thin plates of iron coated with tin. *Also v.t.* WH: pre-1200. Old English, from Germanic. Cp. German *Zinn*. No related words outside Germanic are known.

tinamou *n.* any S American quail-like game bird of the family Tinamidae. WH: 18C. French, from Carib *tinamu*.

tincal *n.* borax in the crude state. WH: 17C. Prob. from Portuguese *tincal, tincar*, from Persian and Urdu *tinkār, tankār*, ult. from Sanskrit *ṭaṅkaṇa*.

tincture *n.* a slight taste or flavour, a spice (of). *Also v.t.* WH: 14–15C. Latin *tinctura* dyeing, from *tinctus*, p.p. of *tingere*. See TINGE, also -URE.

tinder *n.* any dry, very combustible substance used to kindle fire from a spark. WH: pre-1200. Old English *tynder*, corr. to Middle Low German *tunder* (Dutch *tonder*), Old High German *zuntara* (German *Zunder*), Old Norse *tundr*, from Germanic.

tine *n.* the prong, point or spike of an antler, fork, harrow etc. WH: pre-1200. Old English *tind*, rel. to Middle Low German *tinne*, Old High German *zinna* (German *Zinne* pinnacle).

tinea *n.* a fungal disease of the skin, athlete's foot, ringworm. WH: 14–15C. Latin gnawing worm, moth, bookworm.

ting *n.* a tinkling sound, as of a small bell. *Also v.i., v.t.* WH: 14–15C. Imit. Cp. TWINKLE.

tinge *v.t.* to colour slightly, to stain (with). *Also n.* WH: 15C. Latin *tingere* to dye, to colour.

tingle *v.i.* to feel a stinging, prickly sensation. *Also v.t., n.* WH: 14–15C. ? Var. of TINKLE, by assoc. with RING².

tinker *n.* an itinerant mender of pots, kettles, pans etc. *Also v.t., v.i.* WH: 12–14C. Orig. unknown. First recorded as surname *Tynker*.

tinkle *v.i.* to make a succession of sharp, metallic sounds as of a bell. *Also v.t., n.* WH: 14–15C. Freq. of *tink* in same sense, of imit. orig. See also -LE⁴.

tinnitus *n.* ringing in the ears. WH: 19C. Latin *tinnire* to ring, to tinkle, of imit. orig. Cp. TINTINNABULATION.

tinsel *n.* brass, tin or other lustrous metallic substances in extremely thin sheets and used in strips, discs or spangles to give a sparkling effect in decoration. *Also a., v.t.* WH: 14–15C. Old French *estincele* (Modern French *étincelle*) spark, from Popular Latin form of Latin SCINTILLA. The original sense (to the 18C) was a fabric interwoven with metallic thread or decorated with spangles. The current sense dates from the 16C.

tint *n.* a variety of colour, esp. one produced by admixture with another colour, esp. white. *Also v.t.* WH: 18C. Alt. of *tinct* colour, from Latin *tinctus*. See TINCTURE.

tintinnabulation *n.* a ringing, tinkling or jingling of bells, plates etc. WH: 19C. Latin *tintinnabulum* bell, from *tintinnare* to ring + -*bulum* suf. of instrument + -ATION. Cp. TINNITUS.

tiny *a.* very small. WH: 16C. Extension with -Y¹ of obs. *tine* in same sense, of unknown orig.

-tion *suf.* denoting action or condition, as in *mention, expectation, vacation.* WH: French, from Old French -*cion*, from Latin -*tio, -tionis*, combining with v. stems in -*t*. See also -ATION, -ION.

tip¹ *n.* the point, end or extremity, esp. of a small or tapering thing. *Also v.t.* WH: 14–15C. Old Norse *typpi*, from Germanic base also of TOP¹.

tip² *v.t.* to cause to lean, to tilt (up, over etc.). *Also v.i., n.* WH: 14–15C. Prob. from Scandinavian, ? later influ. by TIP¹. The sense to strike lightly could have evolved from the notion of touching with a point.

tippet *n.* a fur covering for the neck and shoulders, worn by women. WH: 12–14C. Prob. from Anglo-French deriv. of TIP¹. See also -ET¹.

Tipp-Ex® *n.* a usu. white correction fluid. *Also v.t.* WH: mid-20C. German *tippen* to type + Latin *ex* out. The product was originally in the form of white paper strips over which one typed to erase the lettering underneath.

tipple *v.i.* to drink alcoholic liquors habitually. *Also v.t., n.* WH: 15C. Back-formation from *tippeler* (TIPPLE) tapster, of unknown orig. Cp. Norwegian dial. *tipla* to drip slowly, *tippa* to drink in small quantities.

tipsy *a.* fuddled, partially intoxicated. WH: 16C. TIP² + -SY. To be tipsy is to be intoxicated to such an extent that one is unsteady on one's feet.

tipula *n.* any fly of the family Tipulidae, a group of dipterous insects containing the crane-flies. WH: 18C. Latin *tippula* water spider, water bug, adopted by Linnaeus as a genus name.

TIR *abbr.* international road transport. WH: Abbr. of French *transit international par route* international transit by road.

tirade *n.* a long, vehement speech, declamation, or harangue, esp. of censure or reproof. WH: 19C. French, from Italian *tirata* volley, from Late Latin *tirare* to draw.

tirailleur *n.* a skirmisher. WH: 18C. French, from *tirailler* to fire in skirmishing order, from *tirer* to draw, to shoot + -*eur* -OR.

tire¹ *v.t.* to exhaust the strength of by toil or labour, to fatigue, to weary. *Also v.i.* WH: pre-1200. Old English *tēorian*, of unknown orig. The original sense (to the 17C) was to fail, to cease to supply. The sense to become weak or weary evolved soon after.

tire² *n.* a band of iron, steel etc., placed round the rim of a wheel. WH: 15C. Prob. from *tire* equipment, shortening of ATTIRE. Cp. TYRE.

tisane *n.* a herbal tea. WH: 14–15C. Old French *tisane, ptisane*, from Latin *ptisana*, from Greek *ptisanē* peeled barley, barley water, rel. to *ptissein* to peel.

Tishri *n.* the first month of the Hebrew civil year and the seventh of the ecclesiastical year, corresponding to parts of September and October. WH: 17C. Late Hebrew *tišrī*, from Aramaic *šěrā* to begin.

tissue *n.* a fabric of cells and their products, forming the elementary substance of plant and animal organs. *Also v.t.* WH: 14–15C. Old French *tissu*, use as n. of p.p. of *tistre*, from Latin *texere* to weave.

tit[1] *n.* any small songbird, esp. of the family Paridae and esp. of the genus *Parus*, e.g. the blue tit, great tit, a titmouse. WH: 16C. Of Scandinavian orig. Cp. Old Norse *titlingr*, Icelandic *titlingur* sparrow, Norwegian dial. *titling* small size of stockfish. The word was originally the term for a small horse. The sense small songbird arose in the 18C. Cp. TITMOUSE.

tit[2] *n.* a woman's breast. WH: pre-1200. Old English, TEAT. The current sense arose in the early 20C, although originally *tit* was the regular word until replaced in the 12–14C by TEAT.

tit[3] *n.* an unpleasant or contemptible person. WH: mid-20C. Orig. uncertain. ? From TIT[2]. Cp. TIT[1], TWIT[2].

tit[4] *n.* a tap, a slight blow. WH: 16C. Alt. of TIP[2]. The phrase *tit for tat* was originally *tip for tap*.

titan *n.* a person of superhuman strength or genius. *Also a.* WH: 14–15C. Latin, from Greek *Titan*, name of the elder brother of Kronos in Greek mythology, a member of a race of giants.

titanium *n.* a dark-grey metallic element, at. no. 22, chem. symbol Ti, found in small quantities in various minerals. WH: 18C. TITAN + -IUM, based on URANIUM. The name was coined in 1795 by the German chemist Martin Klaproth. In Greek mythology, the Titans were the firstborn sons of Uranus and Gaea.

titbit *n.* a delicate or dainty morsel of food. WH: 17C. In 16C *tyd bit*, ? from dial. *tid* tender, soft + BIT[1].

titch *n.* a very small person. WH: mid-20C. Little *Tich*, stage name of the tiny music hall comedian Harry Relph, 1868–1928. The comedian took his stage name from the so called 'Tichborne claimant', the nickname of Arthur Orton, who in 1866 claimed to be Roger Charles Tichborne, the heir to an English baronetcy.

titfer *n.* a hat. WH: early 20C. Shortening of *tit for tat* (TIT[4]), rhyming slang for *hat*.

tithe *n.* a tax of one-tenth, esp. of the yearly proceeds from land and personal industry, payable for the support of the clergy and Church. *Also v.t.* WH: pre-1200. Old English *tēotha*, contr. of *teogotha* tenth (see TEN).

titi[1] *n.* any small brightly-coloured S American monkey of the genus *Callicebus*. WH: 18C. Aymara.

titi[2] *n.* any evergreen shrub or small tree of the family Cyrillaceae, found in SE US. WH: 19C. ? Of American Indian orig.

Titian *a.* (of hair) reddish-brown in colour. WH: 19C. Anglicized form of name of *Tiziano* Vecelli, *c.*1488–1576, Venetian painter.

titillate *v.t.* to excite or stimulate pleasurably. WH: Latin *titillatus*, p.p. of *titillare* to tickle. See also -ATE[3].

titivate *v.t., v.i.* to dress up, to adorn, to make smart. WH: 19C. ? From TIDY, based on CULTIVATE.

title *n.* an inscription serving as a name or designation, esp. of a book, chapter, poem etc. *Also v.t.* WH: pre-1200. Old French (Modern French *titre*), from Latin *titulus* placard, inscription, title. The original sense (to the 17C) was an inscription placed over an object to name it or describe it. The current sense evolved in the 12–14C.

titmouse *n.* the small insectivorous songbird, the tit. WH: 12–14C. TIT[1] + Old English *māse*, corr. to Middle Low German and Middle Dutch *mēse* (Dutch *mees*), Old High German *meisa* (German *Meise*), from Germanic. Assim. to MOUSE[1] (16C).

Titoism *n.* the kind of Communism introduced by Marshal Tito in Yugoslavia as opposed to that of the USSR. WH: mid-20C. *Tito*, name adopted by Josip Broz, 1892–1980, premier of Yugoslavia (1945–80) + -ISM.

titrate *v.t.* to determine the amount of a particular constituent in (a solution) by adding a known quantity of another chemical capable of reacting with it. WH: 19C. French *titrer*, from *titre* title, qualification, fineness of alloyed gold or silver. See TITLE, also -ATE[3].

ti-tree *n.* a ti, a cabbage tree. WH: 19C. TI + TREE.

titter *v.i.* to laugh in a restrained manner, to snigger, to giggle. *Also n.* WH: 17C. Imit. Cp. TEE-HEE.

tittle *n.* any small diacritic or punctuation mark. WH: 14–15C. Latin *titulus* TITLE, in medieval sense of little stroke, accent.

tittle-tattle *n.* gossip. *Also v.i.* WH: 16C. Redupl. of TATTLE. Cp. PRITTLE-PRATTLE.

tittup *v.i.* to go, act or behave in a lively manner, to prance, to frisk. *Also n.* WH: 17C. Appar. imit., representing the sound of the horse's feet.

titubation *n.* fidgeting or stumbling caused by nervous disorder. WH: 17C. Latin *titubatio*, *titubationis*, from *titubatus*, p.p. of *titubare* to stagger. See also -ATION.

titular *a.* existing in name or in title only, or holding a title without the office or duties attached, nominal. *Also n.* WH: 16C. French *titulaire*, or from Modern Latin *titularis*, from *titulus* TITLE. See also -ULAR.

tizzy *n.* a state of extreme agitation. WH: mid-20C. Orig. unknown.

tmesis *n.* the separation of the parts of a compound word by inserting one or more words between (e.g. *Get it your-blooming-self!*). WH: 16C. Greek *tmēsis* cutting, from *temnein* to cut.

to *prep.* in a direction towards (a place, person, thing, state or quality). *Also adv.* WH: pre-1200. Old English *tō*, from Germanic. Cp. German *zu*.

toad *n.* a tailless amphibian of the family Bufonidae, esp. of the genus *Bufo*, being like a frog, usu. with a warty body, terrestrial except during breeding. WH: pre-1200. Old English *tāda*, *tādde*, shortening of *tādige*, *tādie*, of unknown orig.

toadstone *n.* a stone coloured and shaped somewhat like a toad, or supposed to have been found in the body of a toad, formerly worn as a talisman. WH: 16C. TOAD + STONE, translating Latin *batrachites*, Greek *batrakhitēs*, or Medieval Latin *bufonitis*, *crapadinus*, French *crapaudine*.

toadstool *n.* an umbrella-shaped fungus, esp. a poisonous mushroom. WH: 14–15C. TOAD + STOOL, a fanciful name.

toady *n.* an obsequious person, a sycophant. *Also v.i.* WH: 19C. Prob. back-formation from *toad-eater* (TOAD). A *toad-eater* was originally a charlatan's assistant who pretended to eat toads (regarded as poisonous) so that his master could display his skill in expelling the poison.

toast *n.* a slice of bread browned by radiant heat. *Also v.t., v.i.* WH: 14–15C. Old French *toster* to roast, to grill, from Latin *tostus*, p.p. of *torrere* to parch. The sense person in whose honour a company is requested to drink arose in the 18C from the notion that a woman's name flavours the drink as spiced toast would.

tobacco *n.* a plant of American origin of the genus *Nicotiana*, with narcotic leaves which are used, after drying and preparing, for smoking, chewing, snuff etc. WH: 16C. Spanish *tabaco*, said to come from a Carib word meaning a pipe through which smoke was inhaled, or from a Taino word for a primitive cigar, but poss. actually from Arabic.

toboggan *n.* a long low sled used for sliding down snow or ice-covered slopes. *Also v.i.* WH: 19C. Canadian French *tabaganne*, from Micmac *topaģan* sled.

toby jug *n.* a mug or jug shaped like an old man wearing a three-cornered hat. WH: 19C. *Toby*, pet form of male forename *Tobias* + JUG[1].

toccata *n.* a keyboard composition orig. designed to exercise or display the player's touch. WH: 18C. Italian, fem. p.p. (used as n.) of *toccare* to touch.

Toc H *n.* a society formed after the First World War to encourage Christian fellowship and perform social work, esp. among ex-servicemen. WH: early 20C. *toc*, arbitrary syllable for letter *t* in telecommunication messages + *H*, initials of Talbot House, a military resthouse and club for soldiers. The first Talbot House was founded in 1915 at Poperinghe, Belgium, and named after Gilbert Talbot, son of the Bishop of Winchester, who had been killed in battle the previous year.

Tocharian *n.* an extinct Indo-European language of central Asia from the first millennium AD. *Also a.* WH: early 20C. French *tocharien*, from Latin *Tochari*, from Greek *Tokharoi*, a Scythian tribe in central Asia.

tocher *n.* a woman's dowry. *Also v.t.* WH: 15C. Irish *tochra*, Gaelic *tochradh*.

tocology *n.* obstetrics. WH: 19C. Greek *tokos* offspring + -LOGY.

tocopherol *n.* any of a group of antioxidants thought to be required for healthy animal and human reproduction and found in wheatgerm, egg yolk etc.; vitamin E. WH: mid-20C. Greek *tokos* offspring + *pherein* to bear + -OL.

tocsin *n.* an alarm bell, signal etc. WH: 16C. Old French *touquesain* (Modern French *tocsin*), from Provençal *tocasenh*, from *tocar* to strike, TOUCH + *senh* bell, SIGNAL.

tod¹ *n.* own, only in the phrase *on one's tod*. WH: mid-20C. Short for *Tod Sloan* (US jockey, 1874–1933), rhyming slang for *own* or *alone*.

tod² *n.* a bush, esp. of thick ivy. WH: 14–15C. Prob. of Low Dutch orig. Cp. Low German *todde* bundle, pack. The word originally denoted a unit of weight of wool. The sense ivy bush arose in the 16C.

today *adv.* on or during this or the present day. *Also n.* WH: pre-1200. Old English *tō dæge* on (the) day, from *tō* TO + *dæge*, dat. of *dæg* DAY. Cp. TONIGHT, TOMORROW.

toddle *v.i.* to walk with short unsteady steps, as a child does. *Also v.t., n.* WH: 16C. Orig. unknown.

toddy *n.* a beverage of spirit and hot water sweetened. WH: 17C. Marathi *tāḍī*, Hindi *tāṛī*, from Sanskrit *tāḍī* palmyra.

tody *n.* any small W Indian insectivorous bird of the genus *Todus*, related to the American kingfishers. WH: 18C. French *todier*, from Latin *todus* a small bird.

toe *n.* any one of the five digits of the foot. *Also v.t.* WH: pre-1200. Old English *tā*, from Germanic. Cp. German *Zehe*.

toff *n.* a swell, a dandy, a person of consequence. *Also v.t.* WH: 19C. ? Alt. of TUFT. A toff is presumably so called from *tuft* as a nickname for a titled undergraduate at Oxford or Cambridge who wore a gold tassel on his cap.

toffee *n.* boiled sugar or molasses and butter made for sucking or chewing. WH: 19C. Alt. of TAFFY, of unknown orig. The expression *toffee-nosed* puns on *toffy*, i.e. like a TOFF.

toft *n.* a homestead. WH: pre-1200. Old English, from Old Norse *topt* beside.

tofu *n.* unfermented soya bean curd. WH: 18C. Japanese *tōfu*, from Chinese *dòufu*, from *dòu* beans + *fu* to rot, to turn sour.

tog¹ *v.t.* to dress (up or out), esp. in one's best. WH: 18C. Prob. from TOG².

tog² *n.* a unit of measurement of the heat insulation of clothing, fabrics etc. WH: 18C. Appar. abbr. of obs. *togemans* cloak, coat, from obs. *toge* TOGA or direct from TOGA itself + *-mans* as in obs. *darkmans* night or *lightmans* day. The original sense was a coat, an outer garment. The current sense as a unit of thermal resistance arose in the mid-20C.

toga *n.* a loose flowing robe, the principal outer garment of an ancient Roman citizen. WH: 17C. Latin, rel. to *tegere* to cover.

together *adv.* in a company or union, conjointly, unitedly. *Also a.* WH: pre-1200. Old English *tōgædere*, from *tō* TO + *gædere* together, rel. to Old English *gadrian* GATHER, from Germanic. Cp. Old English *gæd* fellowship, *gegada* companion.

toggle *n.* a crosspiece for fastening a garment, securing a watch-chain etc. WH: 18C. Orig. unknown.

Togolese *a.* of or relating to Togo. *Also n.* WH: mid-20C. *Togo*, a state in W Africa + *-ESE*, based on French *togolais*.

toheroa *n.* an edible mollusc, *Mesodesma ventricosum*, of New Zealand shores. WH: 19C. Maori.

toil *v.i.* to labour with pain and fatigue of body or mind. *Also v.t., n.* WH: 12–14C. Old French *tooillier* (Modern French *touiller* to mix, to stir up), from Latin *tudiculare* to stir about, from *tudicula* machine for crushing olives, from base of *tundere* to beat, to crush. The original sense was to contend verbally, to dispute, also to contend in battle, to fight. The current sense evolved in the 14–15C.

toile *n.* cloth, esp. for clothes. WH: 14–15C. Old French, from Latin *tela* web, from base also of *texere* to weave. Cp. TOILS.

toilet *n.* a lavatory. *Also v.t.* WH: 16C. French *toilette* cloth, wrapper, dim. of TOILE. See also *-ET¹*. The original sense was a piece of fabric used as a wrapper for clothes. Hence articles required for dressing, etc. (17C), dressing table (17C), action of dressing (17C), dressing room (17C), dressing room with washing facilities (19C), lavatory (early 20C).

toils *n.pl.* a net or snare. WH: 16C. Pl. of TOIL, from Old French *toile* cloth, linen, web. See TOILE.

tokamak *n.* a toroidal reactor used in thermonuclear experiments involving magnetic effects on hot plasma. WH: mid-20C. Russian, from *toroidal'naya kamera s magnitnym polem* toroidal chamber with magnetic field.

Tokay *n.* a rich aromatic wine made around Tokaj in Hungary and elsewhere. WH: 18C. *Tokaj*, a town in NE Hungary.

tokay *n.* a grey gecko with orange and blue spots, *Gekko gecko*, of SE Asia. WH: 18C. Malay dial. *toke'*, from Javanese *tekèk*, of imit. orig. Cp. GECKO.

token *n.* something representing or recalling another thing, event etc. *Also a., v.t.* WH: pre-1200. Old English *tācn*, *tācen*, from a Germanic word rel. to TEACH. Cp. German *Zeichen*. The original sense was a sign or symbol, esp. (to 16C) a sign of the zodiac. The current sense evolved in the 14–15C.

tola *n.* a unit of weight for gold and silver, usu. about 180 grains troy. WH: 17C. Hindi *tolā*, from Sanskrit *tolaka*.

Toledo *n.* a sword or sword blade made at Toledo in Spain. WH: 16C. *Toledo*, a city in central Spain, long famous for the manufacture of sword blades.

tolerate *v.t.* to suffer, to endure, to permit by not preventing or forbidding. WH: 16C. Latin *toleratus*, p.p. of *tolerare* to bear, to endure. See *-ATE³*.

toll¹ *n.* a tax or duty charged for some privilege, service etc., esp. for the use of a road, bridge, market etc. *Also v.i., v.t.* WH: pre-1200. Old English, from Germanic, from Medieval Latin *toloneum*, alt. of Late Latin *teloneum*, from Greek *telōnion* tollhouse, from *telōnēs* tax collector, from *telos* tax. Cp. German *Zoll*.

toll² *v.t.* to cause (a bell) to sound with strokes slowly and uniformly repeated. *Also v.i., n.* WH: 14–15C. Prob. orig. a special use of dial. *toll* to attract, to entice, rel. to Old English *fortyllan* to seduce.

Toltec *n.* a member of a people who ruled in Mexico during the 7th–11th cents., before the Aztecs. *Also a.* WH: 18C. Spanish *tolteca*, from Nahuatl *toltecatl*, lit. person from Tula (an ancient Toltec city).

tolu *n.* a balsam derived from the S American trees *Myroxylon balsamum* and *M. toluifera*. WH: 17C. Santiago de *Tolú*, a town in NW Colombia.

tom *n.* a male animal, esp. a tom-cat. *Also v.i.* WH: 14–15C. *Tom*, abbr. of male forename *Thomas*.

tomahawk *n.* a N American Indian battleaxe or hatchet with a stone, horn or steel head. *Also v.t.* WH: 17C. Virginia Algonquian.

tomalley *n.* the soft, fatty, greenish so-called liver of the lobster. WH: 17C. French *taumalin*, from Carib *taumali*.

toman *n.* a former Persian gold coin worth about 10,000 dinars. WH: 16C. Persian *tūmān*, from Old Turkish *tümen*, from Tocharian A *tmān*, prob. ult. from base of Chinese *wàn* ten thousand.

tomatillo *n.* a Mexican ground cherry, *Physalis philadelphica*. WH: early 20C. Spanish, dim. of *tomate* TOMATO.

tomato *n.* the red or yellow pulpy edible fruit (used as a vegetable) of a trailing plant, *Lycopersicon esculentum*, of the nightshade family or Solanaceae, orig. S American. WH: 17C. French, Spanish or Portuguese *tomate*, from Nahuatl *tomatl*.

tomb *n.* a grave. *Also v.t.* WH: 12–14C. Anglo-French *tumbe* or Old French *tombe*, from Late Latin *tumba*, from Greek *tumbos* mound, tomb.

tombac *n.* any one of various copper and zinc alloys, used for making cheap jewellery. WH: 17C. French, from Portuguese *tambaca*, from Malay *tembaga* copper, brass, ? from Sanskrit *tāmraka* copper.

tombola *n.* an instant lottery at a fête etc. WH: 19C. French or Italian, from Italian *tombolare* to turn a somersault, to tumble. The lottery is so called from the revolving container from which the tickets are drawn.

tombolo *n.* a narrow spit joining an island to the mainland or to another island. WH: 19C. Italian sand dune.

tome *n.* a volume, esp. a ponderous one. WH: 16C. French, from Latin *tomus*, from Greek *tomos* slice, piece, roll of papyrus, volume, rel. to *temnein* to cut. The word was originally used (to the 18C) for each of the (numbered) volumes of a literary work.

-tome *comb. form* forming nouns denoting instruments for cutting. WH: Greek *-tomon*, neut. of *-tomos* that cuts. See *-TOMY*.

tomentum *n.* a down on stems and leaves consisting of matted woolly hairs. WH: 17C. Latin stuffing for cushions.

tommy *n.* a British private soldier. WH: 18C. Dim. or pet form of TOM. See also *-Y³*. The original sense was brown bread supplied to soldiers. The sense British private soldier arose in the 19C from

Thomas Atkins, a name used in specimens of completed official forms. The *tommy-gun* (early 20C) was originally officially the *Thompson sub-machine gun*, from John T. *Thompson*, 1860–1904, the US general who introduced it.

tomography *n.* diagnostic radiography of plane sections of the human body. WH: mid-20C. Greek *tomos* slice, section + -GRAPHY.

tomorrow *n.* the next day after today. *Also adv.* WH: 12–14C. Old English *tō morgenne* on (the) morrow, from *tō* TO + *morgenne*, dat. of *morgen* morning, MORN.

tom-tom *n.* a long, narrow, hand-beaten drum used in India, Africa etc. *Also v.i.* WH: 17C. Telugu *ṭamaṭama*, Hindi *ṭam ṭam*, of imit. orig. Cp. TAM-TAM.

-tomy *comb. form* forming nouns denoting cutting, esp. of the surgical type, as in *lobotomy*, *phlebotomy*. WH: Greek *-tomia*, from *-tomos* cutting, from *temnein* to cut. Cp. -ECTOMY.

ton[1] *n.* any of various measures of weight or volume, usu. large, as the long ton, short ton etc. WH: 12–14C. Var. of TUN.

ton[2] *n.* the prevailing fashion or mode. WH: 18C. French, from Latin *tonus* TONE.

tonal *a.* of or relating to tone or tonality. WH: 18C. Medieval Latin *tonalis*, from Latin *tonus* TONE. See also -AL[1].

to-name *n.* a distinguishing name added to a surname. WH: pre-1200. TO + NAME.

tondo *n.* a circular easel painting, relief carving etc. WH: 19C. Italian a round, circle, compass, shortened from *rotondo* round.

tone *n.* sound, with reference to pitch, quality and volume. *Also v.t., v.i.* WH: 12–14C. Old French *ton*, from Latin *tonus*, from Greek *tonos* tension, tone, from *teinein* to stretch.

tong *n.* a Chinese secret society. WH: 19C. Chinese *táng* hall, meeting place.

tonga *n.* a light two-wheeled horse-drawn cart for four persons used in India. WH: 19C. Hindi *tãgā*.

Tongan *a.* of or relating to Tonga, its people or language. *Also n.* WH: 19C. *Tonga*, an island kingdom in the SW Pacific + -AN.

tongs *n.pl.* an implement consisting of two limbs, usu. connected near one end by a pivot, used for grasping coals etc.; also called *pair of tongs*. WH: pre-1200. Old English *tange*, from Germanic, from Indo-European base represented also by Greek *daknein* to bite. Cp. German *Zange*.

tongue *n.* a fleshy muscular organ in the mouth, used in tasting, swallowing and (in humans) speech. *Also v.t., v.i.* WH: pre-1200. Old English *tunge*, from Germanic, rel. to Latin *lingua*. Cp. German *Zunge*.

tonic *n.* a tonic medicine. *Also a.* WH: 17C. French *tonique*, from Greek *tonikos* for stretching, from *tonos* TONE. See also -IC.

tonight *n.* the present night. *Also adv.* WH: pre-1200. Old English *tō niht* on (the) night, from *tō* TO + *niht*, dat. of *niht* NIGHT. The word was written as two words to the 18C.

tonka bean *n.* the fragrant seed of a S American tree, *Dipteryx odorata*, used in perfumery. WH: 18C. From *tonka*, name in Guyana + BEAN.

tonnage *n.* the carrying capacity or internal cubic capacity of a vessel expressed in tons. WH: 14–15C. TON[1] + -AGE.

tonne *n.* the metric ton. WH: 19C. French. Cp. TON[1].

tonneau *n.* the rear part of a car containing the back seats, esp. of an open car. WH: 18C. French barrel, cask. Cp. TUN. The original sense was a unit of capacity for French wine. The term for the rear part of a car evolved in the early 20C.

tonsil *n.* either of two organs situated to the rear of the mouth on each side of the fauces. WH: 16C. French *tonsilles* (pl.) or Latin *tonsillae*, of unknown orig.

tonsorial *a.* of or relating to a hairdresser or hairdressing. WH: 19C. Latin *tonsorius*, from *tonsor* barber, from *tonsus*. See TONSURE, also -IAL.

tonsure *n.* the shaving of the crown (as in the Roman Catholic Church before 1972) or of the whole head (as in the Greek Church) on admission to the priesthood or a monastic order. *Also v.t.* WH: 14–15C. Old French, or from Latin *tonsura*, from *tonsus*, p.p. of *tondere* to shear, to clip.

tontine *n.* a form of annuity in which the shares of subscribers who die are added to the profits shared by the survivors, the last of whom receives the whole amount. WH: 18C. French, from Lorenzo

Tonti, 1630–95, Neapolitan banker, who started such a scheme to raise government loans in France in *c.*1653.

tonus *n.* the normal elasticity of a muscle at rest, tonicity. WH: 19C. Latin, from Greek *tonos* TONE.

Tony *n.* an annual American award for work in the theatre. WH: mid-20C. Antoinette (*Tony*) Perry, 1886–1946, US actress and producer. The first Tony was awarded in 1947.

too *adv.* in excessive quantity, degree etc. WH: pre-1200. Stressed form of TO, spelt *too* from 16C. The notion is that of addition. Add icing *to* a cake and the cake will have icing *too*.

toodle-oo *int.* goodbye. WH: early 20C. Orig. unknown. According to some, the phrase is an alteration of French *à tout à l'heure* see you soon.

tool *n.* a simple implement, esp. one used in manual work. *Also v.t., v.i.* WH: pre-1200. Old English *tōl*, from Germanic base meaning to prepare. Cp. TAW[1].

toon *n.* a large Indian, SE Asian and Australian tree, *Cedrela toona*, with close-grained red wood. WH: 19C. Hindi *tun*, *tūn*, from Sanskrit *tunna*.

toot *v.i.* to make a short sharp noise like that of a horn, whistle etc. *Also v.t., n.* WH: 16C. Prob. from Middle Low German *tūten*, or some similar imit. formation.

tooth *n.* any one of the hard dense structures, originating in the epidermis, growing in the mouth or pharynx of vertebrates, and used for mastication. *Also v.t., v.i.* WH: pre-1200. Old English *tōth*, pl. *tēth*, from Germanic, from Indo-European base represented also by Latin *dens*, *dentis*, Greek *odous*, *odontis*, Sanskrit *dan*, *dant-*. Cp. German *Zahn*.

tootle *v.i.* to toot gently or continuously, as on a flute. WH: 19C. TOOT + -LE[4].

tootsy *n.* a foot or toe (used by or to children). WH: 19C. Alt. of FOOT + -SY. See also -Y[3].

top[1] *n.* the highest part or point of anything, the summit. *Also v.t., a.* WH: pre-1200. Old English *topp*, rel. to Middle Dutch *top* crest, summit, tip, Old High German *zopf* plait, tress, Old Norse *toppr* top, tuft, from Germanic. Cp. TIP[1], TOUPEE.

top[2] *n.* a wooden or metal toy, usu. conical or pear-shaped, made to rotate with great velocity on a metal point underneath, by the rapid unwinding of a string or spring or with the hand. WH: pre-1200. Old English, of unknown orig. ? Special use of TOP[1]. The word was not widely current until the 14–15C.

toparch *n.* the ruler of a small place or country, a petty king. WH: 17C. Greek *toparkhēs*, from *topos* place + *arkhos* ruler.

topaz *n.* a transparent or translucent aluminium silicate, usu. white or yellow, but sometimes green, blue, red or colourless, valued as a gem. WH: 12–14C. Old French *topace* (Modern French *topaze*), from Latin *topazus*, from Greek *topazos*, *topazion*, prob. of Asian orig.

tope[1] *v.i.* to drink alcoholic liquors excessively or habitually, to tipple. WH: 17C. ? Alt. of TOP[1] (in sense to slant a yard by tilting up one arm).

tope[2] *n.* a grove, esp. of mango trees. WH: 17C. Telugu *tōpu*, Tamil *tōppu*.

tope[3] *n.* a Buddhist monument in the form of a dome, tower or mound, usu. containing relics, a stupa. WH: 19C. Punjabi *thūp*, *thop* barrow, mound, appar. rel. to Sanskrit *stūpa* STUPA.

tope[4] *n.* a small European shark, *Galeorhinus galeus*. WH: 17C. Orig. uncertain. ? Cornish.

Tophet *n.* hell. WH: 14–15C. Hebrew *tōpeṭ*, a place in the valley of Hinnom near Jerusalem, used for idolatrous worship including the sacrifice of children (Jer. xix.6).

tophus *n.* calcareous matter deposited round the teeth and at the surface of the joints in gout. WH: 16C. Latin *tophus*, *tofus* loose porous stones. Cp. TUFA, TUFF.

topi[1] *n.* a sunhat, a pith helmet. WH: 19C. Hindi *ṭopī* hat.

topi[2] *n.* a large African antelope, *Damaliscus lunatus*, with a sloping back and reddish-brown colouring. WH: 19C. Mende.

topiary *n.* the art of cutting and clipping trees or shrubs etc. into fanciful shapes. *Also a.* WH: 16C. French *topiaire*, from Latin *topiarius* pertaining to ornamental gardening, from *topia* ornamental gardening, from Greek *topia*, pl. of *topion*, dim. of *topos* place. See also -ARY[1].

topic *n.* the subject of a discourse, argument, literary composition or conversation. WH: 15C. Latin *topica*, from Greek *topika* in *ta topika*, lit. matters concerning commonplaces (title of a treatise by Aristotle, 4C BC), from *topos* place, commonplace.

topography *n.* the detailed description of particular places. WH: 14–15C. Late Latin *topographia*, from Greek, from *topos* place. See -GRAPHY.

topology *n.* the study of geometrical properties and relationships which are not affected by distortion of a figure. WH: 17C. Greek *topos* place + -LOGY.

toponym *n.* a place name. WH: 19C. Greek *topos* place + -ONYM.

topos *n.* a basic theme or concept in literature, rhetoric etc. WH: mid-20C. Greek. See TOPIC.

topple *v.i.* to totter and fall. *Also v.t.* WH: 16C. TOP¹ + -LE⁴.

topsy-turvy *a.* upside down. *Also adv., n., v.t.* WH: 16C. 1st element prob. from TOP¹, 2nd element prob. from obs. *terve* to turn (over), from Germanic, with -Y¹ added to both elements to make a jingle. Cp. ARSY-VERSY.

toque *n.* a small, brimless, close-fitting hat. WH: 16C. French, from Spanish *toca*, of unknown orig. Some sources relate the word to German *Tuch* cloth, fabric.

toquilla *n.* a S American palmlike tree, *Carludovica palmata*. WH: 19C. American Spanish use of Spanish small gauze headdress, dim. of *toca* TOQUE.

tor *n.* a prominent hill or rocky peak, esp. on Dartmoor and in the Peak District. WH: pre-1200. Old English *torr*, ? of Celtic orig. Cp. Old Welsh *torr* bulge, belly, Gaelic *tòrr* bulging hill.

Torah *n.* the Pentateuch. WH: 16C. Hebrew *tōrāh* direction, instruction, doctrine, law, from *yārāh* to throw, to show, to direct, to instruct.

torc *n.* a twisted necklace of gold or other metal, worn by the ancient Gauls etc. WH: 19C. French, var. of TORQUE.

torch *n.* an electric torch. *Also v.t.* WH: 12–14C. Old French *torche*, from Latin *torqua*, var. of *torques* necklace, wreath, from *torquere* to twist. A torch was originally a length of twisted tow dipped in wax and lit for illumination.

torchon *n.* a kind of coarse bobbin lace. WH: 19C. French duster, dishcloth, from *torcher* to wipe, from *torche* TORCH. A handful of twisted straw will serve to wipe with.

tore *n.* a torus. WH: 17C. French, from Latin TORUS.

toreador *n.* a bullfighter, esp. one who fights on horseback. WH: 17C. Spanish, from *torear* to fight bulls, from *toro* bull, from Latin TAURUS.

torero *n.* a bullfighter, esp. one who fights on foot. WH: 18C. Spanish, from *toro* bull, from Latin TAURUS. Cp. TOREADOR.

toreutic *a.* of or relating to carved, chased or embossed work, esp. in metal. WH: 19C. Greek *toreutikos*, from *toreuein* to work in relief. See also -IC.

torgoch *n.* a red-bellied Welsh variety of char. WH: 17C. Welsh, from *tor* belly + *goch*, alt. of *coch* red.

torii *n.* a gateless gateway composed of two uprights with (usu.) three superimposed crosspieces, at the approach to a Shinto temple. WH: 18C. Japanese, from *tori* bird + *i* to sit, to perch.

torment¹ *n.* extreme pain or anguish of body or mind. WH: 12–14C. Old French (Modern French *tourment*), from Latin *tormentum* engine for firing missiles, instrument of torture, from *torquere* to twist. The original sense was the infliction or suffering of torture.

torment² *v.t.* to subject to torment. WH: 12–14C. Old French *tormenter* (Modern French *tourmenter*), from *torment* TORMENT¹.

tormentil *n.* a low-growing herb, *Potentilla erecta*, with four-petalled yellow flowers, the astringent rootstock of which is used for medicine. WH: 14–15C. Old French *tormentille*, from Medieval Latin *tormentilla*, of unknown orig. According to some, the word is ultimately from Latin *tormentum* TORMENT¹, with reference to the herb's medicinal properties, especially to ease gripes. Cp. TORMINA.

tormina *n.pl.* severe griping pains in the bowels. WH: 17C. Latin, ult. from *torquere* to twist.

torn *a.* having been cut or ripped. WH: 14–15C. P.p. of TEAR¹.

tornado *n.* a storm of extreme violence covering a very small area at once, but progressing rapidly, usu. having a rotary motion with electric discharges. WH: 16C. Prob. alt. of Spanish *tronada* thunderstorm, from *tronar* to thunder, later assim. to *tornar* to turn. See also -ADO.

toroid *n.* a figure shaped like a torus. WH: 19C. TORUS + -OID.

torose *a.* muscular, knobby. WH: 18C. Latin *torosus*, from *torus* bulge, brawn. See also -OSE¹.

torpedo *n.* a long, cigar-shaped, self-propelled apparatus charged with explosive, used for attacking a hostile ship below the waterline. *Also v.t.* WH: 16C. Latin stiffness, numbness, also the electric ray, from *torpere*. See TORPID. The electric ray was so called from the numbing effect of its discharges. The explosive device was so called because it was towed or propelled through water and somewhat resembled an electric ray. The latter sense dates from the 18C.

torpid *a.* dull, sluggish, inactive. *Also n.* WH: 14–15C. Latin *torpidus*, from *torpere* to be sluggish. See also -ID.

torque *n.* the movement of a system of forces causing rotation. *Also v.t.* WH: 19C. French, from Latin *torquere* to twist.

torr *n.* a unit of pressure, equal to 133.32 pascals, 1/760 of a standard atmosphere. WH: mid-20C. From *Torricelli*. See TORRICELLIAN.

torrefy *v.t.* to dry or parch. WH: 17C. French *torréfier*, from Latin *torrefacere* to dry by heat, from *torrere* to scorch. See also -FY.

torrent *n.* a violent rushing stream (of water, lava etc.). *Also a.* WH: 16C. French, from Italian *torrente*, from Latin *torrens, torrentis*, use as n. of pres.p. of *torrere* to scorch. See also -ENT.

Torricellian *a.* of or relating to Torricelli. WH: 17C. Evangelista *Torricelli*, 1608–47, Italian scientist + -IAN.

torrid *a.* dried up with heat, parched, scorching, very hot. WH: 16C. French *torride* or Latin *torridus*, from *torrere* to scorch. See also -ID. Ult. rel. to THIRST.

torse¹ *n.* a wreath. WH: 16C. Obs. French *torse, torce*, from Latin *torta*, fem. p.p. of *torquere* to twist.

torse² *n.* a surface generated by a straight line continuously moving about some point or other in its length. WH: 19C. Medieval Latin *torsus*, from Latin *tortus*, p.p. of *torquere* to twist.

torsel *n.* a twisted ornament, such as a scroll. WH: 17C. Var. of TASSEL².

torsion *n.* the act of twisting or the state of being twisted. WH: 14–15C. Old French, from Late Latin *torsio, torsionis*, alt. of *tortio, tortionis*, from *tortus*, p.p. of *torquere* to twist. See also -ION.

torsk *n.* an edible fish, *Brosme brosme*, allied to the cod. WH: 18C. Norwegian *torsk, tosk*, from Old Norse *thorskr, thoskr*, prob. from base of *thurr* dry.

torso *n.* the trunk of a statue or body without the head and limbs. WH: 18C. Italian stalk, stump, trunk of a statue, from Latin THYRSUS.

tort *n.* a private or civil wrong leading to liability for damages. WH: 12–14C. Old French, from Medieval Latin *tortum*, use as n. of neut. of Latin *tortus*, p.p. of *torquere* to twist.

torte *n.* a rich gateau or tart, with fruit, cream etc. WH: 18C. German *Torte* tart, pastry, cake, from Italian *torta*, from Late Latin. Prob. rel. to TART¹.

tortelli *n.* a dish of small pasta parcels filled with a meat, cheese or vegetables mixture. WH: mid-20C. Italian, pl. of *tortello* small cake, fritter, dim. of *torta*, from Late Latin.

torticollis *n.* a rheumatic disease of the neck muscles, causing abnormal bending and stiffness. WH: 19C. Modern Latin, from Latin *tortus* crooked, twisted + *collum* neck. Cp. wryneck. See WRY, NECK.

tortile *a.* twisted, wreathed, coiled, curved. WH: 17C. Latin *tortilis*, from *tortus*, p.p. of *torquere* to twist. See also -IL.

tortilla *n.* in Mexican cooking, a thin flat maize cake baked on an iron plate. WH: 17C. Spanish, dim. of *torta* cake, from Late Latin. See TORTE.

tortoise *n.* a slow-moving herbivorous land reptile of the family Testudinidae, having a dome-shaped leathery shell. WH: 14–15C. Old French *tortue*, Spanish *tortuga*, from Medieval Latin *tortuca*, prob. alt. of Late Latin *tartaruchus* of the underworld. See TURTLE. The Medieval Latin word may have been influenced by Latin *tortus* twisted, with reference to the shape of the tortoise's feet.

tortrix *n.* any moth of the family Tortricidae, esp. *Tortrix viridana*, whose larvae live in rolled-up leaves. WH: 18C. Modern Latin, fem. of *tortor*, lit. twister, from Latin *tortus*, p.p. of *torquere* to twist. The moth is so called from the leaf-rolling habits of its larvae.

tortuous *a.* twisting, winding, crooked. WH: 14–15C. Old French (Modern French *tortueux*), from Latin *tortuosus*, from *tortus* twisting, from p.p. of *torquere* to twist. See also -OUS.

torture *n.* the infliction of extreme physical pain as a punishment or to extort confession etc. *Also v.t.* WH: 14–15C. Old French, from Late Latin *tortura* twisting, writhing, torment, from *tortus*. See TORTUOUS, also -URE. Cp. TORMENT[1].

torula *n.* a microscopic yeastlike fungus of the genus *Torula*. WH: 19C. Modern Latin, dim. of TORUS. See also -ULE.

torus *n.* a ring-shaped surface generated by a circle rotated about a line which does not intersect the circle. WH: 16C. Latin swelling, bolster, round moulding.

Tory *n.* a member of the Conservative Party. *Also a.* WH: 17C. Prob. from Irish *toraidhe* pursuing person, highwayman, from *tóir* to pursue. The word was originally a derogatory term for a dispossessed Irishman, some of whom turned to outlawry and attacked the new English landholders and soldiers. The name was then extended to other marauders, especially in the Scottish Highlands. The political use of the name dates from 1689. It was formally superseded by *Conservative* in *c.*1830.

tosa *n.* a smooth-haired large heavy dog bred from the mastiff, orig. kept for dogfighting. WH: mid-20C. *Tosa*, a former province on the island of Shikoku, Japan.

tosh[1] *n.* rubbish, nonsense. WH: 19C. Orig. unknown.

tosh[2] *n.* used as a casual form of address, esp. to an unknown person, pal, chum. WH: mid-20C. Orig. unknown.

toss *v.t.* to throw up with the hand, esp. palm upward. *Also v.i., n.* WH: 16C. Orig. unknown. ? From Scandinavian.

tot[1] *n.* a small child. WH: 18C. Orig. dial. Cp. TIT[1].

tot[2] *v.t.* to add (up). *Also v.i., n.* WH: 18C. Abbr. of TOTAL or Latin *totum* the whole.

tot[3] *v.i.* to collect items for resale from waste disposal sites etc., esp. as a licensed operator. *Also n.* WH: 19C. Orig. unknown.

total *a.* complete, comprising everything or constituting the whole. *Also n., v.t., v.i.* WH: 14–15C. Old French, from Medieval Latin *totalis*, from *totum* the whole, use as n. of neut. of Latin *totus* entire, whole.

totara *n.* a New Zealand conifer, *Podocarpus totara*, yielding dark red wood. WH: 19C. Maori *tótara*.

tote *v.t.* to carry, to bear. WH: 17C. Prob. of dial. orig.

totem *n.* a natural object, usu. an animal, taken as a badge or emblem of an individual or clan on account of a supposed relationship. WH: 18C. Ojibwa *nindoodem* my totem.

tother *a., pron.* the other. WH: 12–14C. Misdivision of neut. of THE (Old English *thæt*) + OTHER.

totipalmate *a.* having all four toes webbed. WH: 19C. From *toti-*, comb. form of Latin *totus* whole + *palmate* (PALM[2]).

totter *v.i.* to walk or stand unsteadily, to stagger. WH: 12–14C. Middle Dutch *touteren* to swing, from Old Saxon, corr. to Old English *tealtrian* to totter, to stagger.

toucan *n.* a brilliantly-coloured tropical American bird of the family Ramphastidae, with an enormous beak. WH: 16C. French, from Portuguese, from Tupi *tucan*, imit. of the bird's call.

touch *v.t.* to meet the surface of, to have no intervening space between at one or more points, to be in contact with, to come into contact with. *Also v.i., n.* WH: 12–14C. Old French *tochier, tuchier* (Modern French *toucher*), from a Romance word of imit. orig. Cp. Romanian *tocà* to knock.

touché *int.* used to acknowledge a hit in fencing, or a point scored in argument. WH: early 20C. French, p.p. of *toucher* to touch.

touchy *a.* apt to take offence, irascible, irritable. WH: 17C. TOUCH + -Y[1], influ. by TETCHY.

tough *a.* firm, strong, not easily broken, resilient, not brittle. *Also n.* WH: pre-1200. Old English *tóh*, from Germanic. Cp. German *zäh*.

toupee *n.* a small wig to cover a bald spot, a hairpiece. WH: 18C. Alt. of French *toupet* tuft of hair, from Old French *toup* tuft, from base also of TOP[1]. See also -ET[1].

tour *n.* a journeying round from place to place in a district, country etc. *Also v.i., v.t.* WH: 12–14C. Old French *tour*, earlier *tor, torn*. See TURN. The original sense (to the 18C) was circular motion, revolution. The sense journey or period of travel dates from the 17C.

tourbillion *n.* a whirlwind. WH: 15C. French *tourbillon*, from Old French *torbeillon*, from Latin *turbellae* bustle, stir, blended with *turbo* whirlwind.

tour de force *n.* an outstanding feat of performance, skill, strength etc. WH: 19C. French, lit. turn of strength. See TOUR, FORCE[1].

Tourette's syndrome *n.* a neurological disorder characterized by involuntary outbursts of shouting, swearing etc. and sudden involuntary movements. WH: 19C. Gilles de la *Tourette*, 1857–1904, French neurologist.

tourmaline *n.* a black or coloured transparent or translucent silicate with electrical properties, some varieties of which are used as gems. WH: 18C. French, ult. from Sinhalese *tôramalli* cornelian.

tournament *n.* any contest of skill in which a number of people take part. WH: 12–14C. Anglo-French var. of Old French *torneiement*, from *torneier*. See TOURNEY, also -MENT.

tournedos *n.* a thick round fillet steak. WH: 19C. French, from *tourner* to turn + *dos* back. The dish is said to be so called because it was not placed directly on the table but passed behind the back of the guests. But this may well be folk etymology.

tourney *n.* a tournament. *Also v.i.* WH: 12–14C. Old French *tornei* (Modern French *tournoi*), from *torneier*, ult. from Latin *tornus* TURN.

tourniquet *n.* a bandage for compressing an artery and checking haemorrhage. WH: 17C. French, ? alt. of Old French *tournicle*, var. of *tounicle, tunicle* coat of mail, tunicle (TUNIC), by assoc. with *tourner* TURN.

tousle *v.t.* to disarrange, to rumple, to dishevel, to put into disorder. *Also v.i., n.* WH: 14–15C. Freq. of *touse* to pull about, from Germanic (cp. German *zausen*). See also -LE[4]. Cp. TUSSLE. It was *touse* that gave the dog's name *Towzer*, as if meaning tearer, worrier.

tous-les-mois *n.* a food starch from the roots of species of a canna, esp. *Canna indica*, a perennial Peruvian herb. WH: 19C. French all the months, every month, but prob. alt. of *toloman*, the name in the French Antilles.

tout[1] *n.* a person employed to solicit custom in an obtrusive way. *Also v.i., v.t.* WH: pre-1200. Old English *týtan*, from Germanic base represented also in Middle Low German *tûte* horn, funnel, Middle Dutch *tûte* (Dutch *tuit* spout, nozzle), Old Norse *tûta* nipple, teat. The word was originally a verb in the sense to peer, to look out. Hence (17C) to keep watch, to be on the lookout. The noun evolved from the verb in the 18C, initially in the sense thieves' scout.

tout[2] *a.* all, whole. *Also adv.* WH: 18C. French, from Latin *totus* all, whole. Cp. TOTAL.

tovarish *n.* in Russia, the former Soviet Union etc., comrade. WH: early 20C. Russian *tovarishch*, from Turkic, ? Tatar.

tow[1] *v.t.* to pull (a vehicle) behind another. *Also n.* WH: pre-1200. Old English *togian*, from Germanic. Cp. German *ziehen*. The original sense (to the 16C) was to draw by force, to drag. The sense to draw or pull a vehicle or vessel dates from the 14–15C.

tow[2] *n.* the coarse broken part of hemp or flax after combing out. WH: pre-1200. Old English *tow-* in *towcræft* spinning, *towhûs* spinning house, from Germanic.

†toward *a.* docile, obedient. WH: pre-1200. Old English *tôweard* directed towards. See TO, -WARD.

towards *prep.* in the direction of. *Also adv.* WH: pre-1200. TOWARD + -S[2].

towel *n.* an absorbent cloth for wiping and drying after washing, washing up etc. *Also v.t., v.i.* WH: 12–14C. Old French *toaille* (Modern French *touaille*), from Germanic base also of Old English *thwêan*, Old High German *dwahan*, Old Norse *thvá* to wash.

tower *n.* a structure lofty in proportion to the area of its base, and circular, square or polygonal in plan, frequently of several storeys, often forming part of a church, castle or other large building. *Also v.i.* WH: pre-1200. Old English *torr*, reinforced in Middle English by Old French *tur, tor* (Modern French *tour*), from Latin *turris*, from Greek *turris, tursis*.

towhee *n.* any of several buntings of the genus *Pipilo*, found in N America. WH: 18C. Imit. of the bird's call.

town *n.* an urban area larger than a village, esp. one not constituting a city. WH: pre-1200. Old English *tûn*, from Germanic, rel. to Old Irish *dún*, Welsh *din* fort, camp, castle, fortified place. Cp. German

Zaun fence. Rel. to DOWN³, DUNE. The original sense was enclosure, and specifically the enclosed land belonging to a single dwelling, a farm with its farmhouse. This is usually the sense of *-ton* in place names such as *Newton, Easton, Weston* etc., and by extension *-don* (hill) as in *Maldon, Swindon*.

toxaemia *n.* blood poisoning. WH: 19C. Greek *toxikon* poison + *haima* blood. See also -IA.

toxic *a.* poisonous. WH: 17C. Medieval Latin *toxicus* poisoned, from Latin *toxicum* poison, from Greek *toxikon pharmakon* poison for use on arrows. Greek *toxikos* originally meant pertaining to the bow, from *toxon* bow.

toxico- *comb. form* poisonous; poison. WH: Greek *toxikon* poison or TOXIC. See also -O-.

toxicology *n.* the branch of medicine treating of poisons and their antibodies. WH: 19C. TOXICO- + -LOGY.

toxicosis *n.* any disease or condition due to the action of toxic matter. WH: 19C. TOXICO- + -OSIS.

toxin *n.* a poisonous compound causing a particular disease. WH: 19C. TOXIC + -IN¹.

toxocara *n.* any parasitic worm of the genus *Toxocara*, esp. the common roundworm causing toxocariasis. WH: mid-20C. Modern Latin, from Greek *toxon* bow + *kara* head.

toxophilite *n.* a person skilled in or devoted to archery. *Also a.* WH: 18C. From *Toxophilus*, title of a book by Roger Ascham (1545) intended to mean 'lover of the bow' (from Greek *toxon* bow + *philos* loving). See also -ITE¹. Ascham apparently based his title on the personal name *Theophilus*, meaning lover of God or loved by God.

toxoplasmosis *n.* an infectious disease caused by the sporozoan *Toxoplasma gondii*, characterized by jaundice, enlarged liver and spleen and convulsions, transmitted esp. through badly-prepared food and cat faeces. WH: mid-20C. Modern Latin *Toxoplasma* (from Greek *toxon* bow + *plasma* PLASMA) + -OSIS. The sporozoan is so called as it is crescentic (bow-shaped).

toy *n.* a plaything, esp. for a child. *Also v.i., a.* WH: 14–15C. Orig. unknown. Appar. rel. to Middle Dutch *toi* (Dutch *tooi*) attire, finery, but this does not correspond with the sense. The original sense was frivolous speech, idle tale, jest, joke. The sense plaything evolved in the 16C.

tra- *pref.* across, through, as in *tradition, travesty*. WH: Latin assim. form of TRANS-.

trabeate *a.* built of horizontal beams, as distinct from arches and vaults. WH: 19C. Latin *trabs, trabis* beam, timber + -ATE². See also -CULE.

trabecula *n.* a band or bar of connective tissue, esp. one forming the framework of an organ. WH: 19C. Latin, dim. of *trabs, trabis* beam, timber. See also -CULE.

tracasserie *n.* a turmoil, an annoyance. WH: 17C. French, from *tracasser* to bustle, to worry oneself. See also -ERY.

trace¹ *n.* a token, vestige, or sign of something that has existed or taken place. *Also v.t., v.i.* WH: 12–14C. Old French, from *tracier* (Modern French *tracer*), from Latin *tractus*. See TRACT¹.

trace² *n.* either of the two straps, chains or ropes by which a vehicle is drawn by horses etc. WH: 12–14C. Old French *trais*, pl. of *trait* draught, harness strap, from Latin *tractus*. See TRACT¹.

trachea *n.* the windpipe, the air passage from the larynx to the bronchi and lungs. WH: 14–15C. Medieval Latin, from Late Latin *trachia*, from Greek *trakheia*, short for *artēria trakheia* rough artery. The windpipe is so called from the rings of cartilage that form it.

tracheo- *comb. form* of or relating to the trachea. WH: TRACHEA. See also -O-.

tracheotomy *n.* the operation of making an opening into the windpipe. WH: 18C. TRACHEO- + -TOMY.

trachoma *n.* a disease of the eye characterized by papillary or granular growths on the inner surface of the lids. WH: 17C. Greek *trakhōma* roughness, from *trakhus* rough. See also -OMA.

trachyte *n.* a gritty-surfaced volcanic rock containing glassy feldspar crystals. WH: 19C. Greek *trakhus* rough or *trakhutēs* roughness. See also -ITE¹.

track *n.* a series of marks left by the passage of a person, animal or thing, a trail. *Also v.t., v.i.* WH: 15C. Old French *trac*, ? from Low Dutch *treck* drawing, draught, pull. Cp. TREK.

tracklement *n.* a condiment, an accompaniment to food, esp. a jam, jelly etc. WH: mid-20C. Orig. unknown.

tract¹ *n.* a region or area of land or water of a considerable but undefined extent. WH: 14–15C. Latin *tractus* drawing, draught, from p.p. of *trahere* to draw, to drag. The original sense was a period of time. The sense stretch of land, water etc. dates from the 16C.

tract² *n.* a short treatise or pamphlet, esp. on religion or morals. WH: pre-1200. Appar. abbr. of Latin *tractatus* TRACTATE. The original sense was a treatise in general. The sense pamphlet on a religious or political topic dates from the 19C and was made widely current by J.H. Newman's *Tracts for the Times* (1833–41). Cp. TRACTARIAN.

tract³ *n.* in the Roman Catholic Church, an anthem sung in place of the Alleluia. WH: 14–15C. Medieval Latin *tractus* (*cantus*), lit. drawn-out (song), from Latin *tractus*. See TRACT¹.

tractable *a.* easily led, managed, or controlled, docile, manageable. WH: 14–15C. Latin *tractabilis*, from *tractare* to handle, freq. of *trahere* to draw, to drag. See also -ABLE. Cp. TREAT.

Tractarian *n.* any one of the authors of *Tracts for the Times*, 1833–41, a series enunciating the principles of the Oxford Movement. *Also a.* WH: 19C. TRACT² + -ARIAN.

tractate *n.* a treatise. WH: 15C. Latin *tractatus*, from p.p. of *tractare*. See TRACTABLE, also -ATE¹. Cp. TRACT².

tractile *a.* capable of being drawn out, ductile. WH: 17C. Latin *tractus* (TRACT¹) + -IL. Cp. DUCTILE.

traction *n.* the act of drawing something along a surface, esp. by motive power. WH: 14–15C. French, or from Medieval Latin *tractio, tractionis*, from *tractus*. See TRACT¹, also -ION.

tractor *n.* a motor vehicle capable of drawing other vehicles, farm implements etc. WH: 18C. Latin *tractus* (TRACT¹) + -OR. The original sense was a person or thing that draws or pulls something. The sense agricultural motor vehicle arose in the early 20C.

trad *n.* traditional jazz. *Also a.* WH: mid-20C. Abbr. of *traditional* (TRADITION).

trade *n.* the exchange of commodities, buying and selling, commerce. *Also v.i., v.t.* WH: 14–15C. Middle Low German track, corr. to Old Saxon *trada*, Old High German *trata*, from Germanic. Rel. to TREAD. The original sense was way, course, manner of life. The current sense evolved in the 16C.

tradescantia *n.* any usu. trailing plant of the genus *Tradescantia*, with large colourful flowers and striped variegated leaves. WH: 18C. Modern Latin, from John *Tradescant*, 1570–1638, English naturalist. See also -IA.

tradition *n.* the handing down of opinions, practices, customs etc., from ancestors to posterity, esp. by oral communication. WH: 14–15C. Old French *tradicion, tradition* or Latin *traditio, traditionis*, from *tradere* to hand over, to deliver, from TRA- + *dare* to give. See also -ITION. Cp. TRAITOR. The original sense was orally delivered instruction. The current sense dates from the 16C.

traditor *n.* any one of the early Christians who, to save their lives, gave up copies of the Scriptures or the goods of the Church to their persecutors. WH: 14–15C. Latin. See TRAITOR. The original sense was betrayer, traitor. The specific sense dates from the 16C.

traduce *v.t.* to defame, to misrepresent, to speak ill of. WH: 16C. Latin *traducere*, from TRA- + *ducere* to lead.

traducianist *n.* a person believing in the transmission of souls by parents to children. WH: 19C. Ecclesiastical Latin *Traduciani*, use as n.pl. of *traducianus* transmitting, transmitter, deriv. of Latin *tradux*, vine shoot for propagation. See also -IAN, -IST.

traffic *n.* the vehicles etc. passing on a road etc. *Also v.i., v.t.* WH: 16C. French *trafique* (now *trafic*), Spanish *tráfico*, Italian *traffico*, from *trafficare* to carry on trade, of unknown orig. According to some, the word is from Popular Latin *transfricare* to rub across, from Latin TRANS- + *fricare* to rub. The original sense of Italian *trafficare* might thus have been to make contact frequently, to handle.

tragacanth *n.* a whitish or reddish demulcent gum obtained from the Asian plant of *Astragalus gummifer*, used in pharmacy, calico-printing etc. WH: 16C. French *tragacante*, from Latin *tragacantha*, from Greek *tragakantha* goat's thorn, from *tragos* goat + *akantha* thorn.

tragedy *n.* a fatal or calamitous event, esp. a murder or fatal accident. WH: 14–15C. Old French *tragédie*, from Latin *tragedia*, from Greek *tragōidia*, appar. lit. from *tragos* goat + *ōidē* song, ODE. The word may have arisen because the actors or singers in Greek tragedies were dressed in goatskins to represent satyrs, or because a goat was the prize for the best performance.

tragic *a.* lamentable, sad, calamitous. WH: 16C. French *tragique*, from Latin *tragicus*, from Greek *tragikos*, from *tragos* goat (but assoc. with *tragōidia* TRAGEDY). See also -IC. The Greek reference would probably have been to a satyr personified by a singer or actor.

tragopan *n.* any Asian pheasant of the genus *Tragopan*, having brilliant plumage and erect fleshy processes on its head. WH: 19C. Modern Latin, from Greek name of a horned bird, from *tragos* goat + *Pan* (the god) Pan.

tragus *n.* a small process on the front of the orifice in the external ear. WH: 17C. Late Latin, from Latin, from Greek *tragos* goat. The process is so called because it often bears a tuft of hair, like a goat's beard.

trahison des clercs *n.* the betrayal of standards by intellectuals influenced by politics. WH: early 20C. French *La Trahison des Clercs* The Treachery of the Intellectuals, a work by Julien Benda (1927), in which he denounces as moral traitors those who betray truth and justice for racial and political considerations.

trail *v.t.* to drag along behind, esp. along the ground. *Also v.i., n.* WH: 12–14C. Old French *traillier* to tow, or from Middle Low German and Middle Flemish *treilen* to haul (a boat), ult. from Latin *tragula* dragnet. Cp. DRAIL, TRAWL.

train *n.* a series of railway carriages or trucks, either self-powered or drawn by an engine. *Also v.t., v.i.* WH: 12–14C. Old French, from *trahiner, traîner* (Modern French *traîner*), from Popular Latin *traginere*, extension of *tragere*, from Latin *trahere* to draw. The original sense was a body of attendants or followers. The current sense as applied to railway transport was originally in the form *train of carriages* (19C).

train-oil *n.* oil obtained from the blubber or fat of whales. WH: 16C. From obs. *train* (from Middle Low German *trān*, Middle Dutch *traen*, rel. to German *Träne* tear, drop) + OIL.

traipse *v.i.* to trudge, to drag along wearily. *Also n.* WH: 16C. Orig. unknown. ? Rel. to TRESPASS.

trait *n.* a distinguishing or peculiar feature, esp. of a person's character or behaviour. WH: 15C. French, from Latin *tractus* drawing, draught. See TRACT[1]. Cp. TRET.

traitor *n.* a person guilty of disloyalty, treason or treachery, esp. to their country. *Also a.* WH: 12–14C. Old French *traïtour*, from Latin *traditor*, from *tradere* to deliver, to betray, from TRA- + *dare* to give. See also -OR. Cp. TRADITION.

trajectory *n.* the path taken by a body, comet, projectile etc., under the action of given forces. WH: 17C. Medieval Latin *trajectorius* pertaining to trajection, from Latin *traiectus*, p.p. of *traicere* to throw across, from TRA- + *iacere* to throw. See also -ORY[2].

tra-la *int.* used to express joy, pleasure etc. WH: 19C. Imit. of a refrain or a fanfare.

tram[1] *n.* a public passenger vehicle, usu. powered electrically from an overhead cable, running on lines set in or near ordinary roads. *Also v.t., v.i.* WH: 16C. Middle Low German and Middle Dutch *trame* baulk, beam, ult. of unknown orig. The original sense was one of the two shafts of a cart, wagon etc., then a frame or barrow for transporting baskets in a coal mine. The sense tracks in or from a coal mine arose in the 19C, and passed soon after to the vehicle running on the rails that evolved from such tracks. The word is still popularly associated with the name of the English civil engineer Benjamin *Outram*, 1764–1805, who introduced iron railways for colliery traffic.

tram[2] *n.* silk thread made up of two or more strands twisted together, used for the weft of the finer kinds of silk goods. WH: 17C. Old French *trame* woof, from Latin *trama*.

trammel *n.* anything restraining freedom or activity. *Also v.t* WH: 14–15C. Old French *tramail* (Modern French *trémail*), from Medieval Latin *tramaculum*, var. of *tremaculum, trimaculum*, ? from TRI- + *macula* spot, mesh.

tramontane *a.* lying, situated or coming from beyond the mountains, esp. the Alps (as seen from Italy), transmontane. *Also n.* WH: 12–14C. Italian *tramontana* north wind, polestar, *tramontani* dwellers beyond the mountains, from Latin *transmontanus*, from TRANS- + *mons, montis* MOUNT[2]. See also -ANE.

tramp *v.i.* to walk, to go on foot, esp. for a considerable distance. *Also v.t., n.* WH: 14–15C. Prob. of Low Dutch orig., from Germanic. Cp. Middle Low German *trampen*. ? Ult. rel. to TRAP[1].

trample *v.t.* to tread underfoot, esp. carelessly or in scorn, triumph etc. *Also n.* WH: 14–15C. TRAMP + -LE[1]. Cp. Middle High German and Low German *trampeln*.

trampoline *n.* a sheet of canvas suspended by springs from a frame, used for bouncing on or for assisting jumps in gymnastics. *Also v.i.* WH: 18C. Italian *trampolino*, from *trampoli* stilts.

trance *n.* a state of mental abstraction, with no response to external surroundings or stimuli. *Also v.t.* WH: 14–15C. Old French *transe* (Modern French *trance*), from *transir* to depart, to die, to fall into a trance, from Latin *transire*. See TRANSIENT.

tranche *n.* a portion, esp. of a larger sum of money, block of shares etc. WH: 15C. Old French, from *trancher*. See TRENCH.

tranny *n.* a transistor radio. WH: mid-20C. Abbr. of TRANSISTOR. See also -Y[3].

tranquil *a.* (of a person) calm and not showing any worry, excitement or strong feeling. WH: 14–15C. French *tranquille* or Latin *tranquillus*.

trans- *pref.* across, over. WH: Latin pref., from prep. *trans* across, over.

transact *v.t.* to do, to perform, to manage, to carry out. *Also v.i.* WH: 16C. Latin *transactus*, p.p. of *transigere* to drive through, to accomplish, from TRANS- + *agere* to drive, to do.

transalpine *a.* lying or situated beyond the Alps (usu. as seen from Italy). *Also n.* WH: 16C. Latin *transalpinus*. See TRANS-, *Alpine* (ALP).

transatlantic *a.* lying or being beyond the Atlantic; American as seen from Europe, European as seen from N America. WH: 18C. TRANS- + ATLANTIC.

transceiver *n.* a device for transmitting and receiving radio signals. WH: mid-20C. From *transmitter* (TRANSMIT) + *receiver* (RECEIVE).

transcend *v.t., v.i.* to rise above, to surpass, to excel, to exceed. WH: 12–14C. Old French *transcendre* or Latin *transcendere* to climb over, to surmount, from TRANS- + *scandere* to climb.

transcode *v.t., v.i.* to convert (information represented in one code) into another code. WH: mid-20C. TRANS- + CODE.

transcontinental *a.* extending or travelling across a continent. *Also n.* WH: 19C. TRANS- + *continental* (CONTINENT[1]).

transcribe *v.t.* to copy in writing, to write out in full (shorthand notes etc.). WH: 16C. Latin *transcribere*, from TRANS- + *scribere* to write.

transcurrent *a.* running or passing across or transversely. WH: 17C. TRANS- + CURRENT.

transducer *n.* a power-transforming device for which the input and output are of different kinds, electrical, acoustic, optical etc., e.g. loudspeaker, microphone, photoelectric cell etc. WH: early 20C. Latin *transducere* to lead across, to transfer, from TRANS- + *ducere* to lead. See also -ER[1].

transect[1] *v.t.* to cut across. WH: 17C. Latin TRANS- + *sectus*, p.p. of *secare* to cut.

transect[2] *n.* a sample strip of land used to study the geography, natural history etc. of a wider area. WH: early 20C. TRANSECT[1].

transept *n.* either of the transverse arms extending north and south in a cruciform church. WH: 16C. Modern Latin *transeptum*. See TRANS-, SEPTUM.

transfer[1] *v.t.* to convey, remove or shift from one place or person to another. *Also v.i.* WH: 14–15C. French *transférer* or Latin *transferre*, from TRANS- + *ferre* to bear, to carry.

transfer[2] *n.* the removal or conveyance of a thing from one person or place to another. WH: 17C. TRANSFER[1].

transferase *n.* an enzyme that acts as a catalyst in the transfer of a chemical group from one molecule to another. WH: mid-20C. TRANSFER[1] + -ASE.

transferrin *n.* a blood protein that transports iron. WH: mid-20C. TRANS- or TRANSFER[1] + FERRO- + -IN[1].

transfiguration *n.* a change of form or appearance. WH: 14–15C. Old French, or from Latin *transfiguratio, transfigurationis*, from *transfiguratus*, p.p. of *transfigurare*, from TRANS- + *figura* FIGURE. See also -ATION. The earliest sense is the change in the appearance of Jesus when on a mountain with three of his disciples (Matt. xvii.1–9, Mark ix.2–8, Luke ix.28–36).

transfinite *a.* beyond or surpassing what is finite. WH: early 20C. TRANS- + FINITE.

transfix *v.t.* to pierce through, to impale. WH: 16C. Latin *transfixus*, p.p. of *transfigere*, from TRANS- + *figere* to fix, to fasten.

transform[1] *v.t.* to change the form, shape or appearance of, to metamorphose. Also *v.i.* WH: 12–14C. Old French *transformer*, or from Latin *transformare*, from TRANS-, FORM.

transform[2] *n.* the result of a mathematical or linguistic transformation. WH: 19C. TRANSFORM[1].

transfuse *v.t.* to permeate, to cause to pass from one vessel etc. into another. WH: 14–15C. Latin *transfusus*, p.p. of *transfundere*, from TRANS- + *fundere* to pour.

transgenic *a.* (of an animal or plant) containing genetic material artificially transferred from another species. WH: late 20C. TRANS- + GENE + -IC.

transgress *v.t.* to break (a rule or rules), to violate, to infringe. Also *v.i.* WH: 15C. Old French *transgresser* or Latin *transgressus*, p.p. of *transgredi*, from TRANS- + *gradi* to proceed, to walk.

transhumance *n.* the seasonal migration of livestock from one grazing ground to another. WH: early 20C. French, from *transhumer*, ult. from Latin *trans* across + *humus* ground. See also -ANCE.

transient *a.* not lasting or durable, temporary. Also *n.* WH: 16C. Latin *transiens, transeuntis*, pres.p. of *transire* to go across, to pass over, from TRANS- + *ire* to go.

transilluminate *v.t.* to send a powerful light through (an organ or part) in diagnosis. WH: early 20C. TRANS- + ILLUMINATE[1].

transire *n.* a customs warrant authorizing the passage of dutiable goods. WH: 16C. Latin. See TRANSIENT.

transistor *n.* a device made primarily of a semiconductor (germanium or silicon) capable of giving current and power amplification. WH: mid-20C. Blend of TRANSFER[1] and *resistor* (RESIST).

transit *n.* the act of passing, conveying or being conveyed, across, over or through. Also *v.t., v.i.* WH: 14–15C. Latin *transitus*, from *transire*. See TRANSIENT.

transition *n.* passage or change from one place, state or action to another. WH: 16C. Old French, or from Latin *transitio, transitionis*, from *transitus*. See TRANSIT, also -ION.

transitive *a.* (of verbs) expressing an action passing over from a subject to an object, having a direct object. WH: 16C. Late Latin *transitivus*, from *transitus*. See TRANSIT, also -IVE.

transitory *a.* lasting only a short time, transient, not durable, short-lived. WH: 14–15C. Old French *transitoire*, from Late Latin *transitorius*, from Latin *transitus*. See TRANSIT, also -ORY[2].

Transjordanian *n.* a native or inhabitant of the former Transjordan. Also *a.* WH: early 20C. TRANS- + *Jordan*, a river of SW Asia flowing south from Syria across Israel into Jordan + -IAN. *Transjordan* was the name of the present Jordan from 1921 to 1949.

translate *v.t.* to render or express the sense of (a word, passage or work) into or in another language. Also *v.i.* WH: 12–14C. Latin *translatus*, p.p. of *transferre* TRANSFER[1]. See also -ATE[3].

transliterate *v.t.* to represent (words, sounds etc.) in the corresponding or approximately corresponding characters of another language or alphabet. WH: 19C. TRANS- + Latin *litera* letter + -ATE[3].

translocation *n.* movement from one place to another. WH: 17C. TRANS- + *location* (LOCATE).

translucent *a.* allowing light to pass through but not transparent. WH: 16C. Latin *translucens, translucentis*, pres.p. of *translucere* to shine through, from TRANS- + *lucere* to shine. See also -ENT.

translunar *a.* situated beyond the moon, opposed to *sublunary*. WH: early 20C. TRANS- + LUNAR.

transmarine *a.* situated beyond the sea. WH: 16C. Latin *transmarinus*, from TRANS- + *marinus*. See MARINE.

transmigrate *v.i.* to pass through one place, country or jurisdiction en route to another, to migrate. WH: 14–15C. Latin *transmigratus*, p.p. of *transmigrare*, from TRANS- + *migrare* MIGRATE.

transmit *v.t.* to send, transfer or convey from one person or place to another. WH: 14–15C. Latin *transmittere*, from TRANS- + *mittere* to send.

transmogrify *v.t.* to transform, esp. as if by magical means. WH: 17C. Orig. uncertain. ? Alt. of TRANSMIGRATE, based on vv. in -FY. The word was originally applied to people.

transmontane *a.* situated beyond the mountains, tramontane. WH: 14–15C. Latin *transmontanus*. See TRAMONTANE.

transmute *v.t.* to change from one form, nature or substance into another; to transform (into). WH: 14–15C. Latin *transmutare*, from TRANS- + *mutare* to change.

transoceanic *a.* situated or coming from beyond the ocean. WH: 19C. TRANS- + *oceanic* (OCEAN).

transom *n.* a horizontal bar of wood or stone across a window or other opening. WH: 14–15C. Old French *traversin*, from *travers*. See TRAVERSE[2].

transonic *a.* relating to or being a speed near the speed of sound. WH: mid-20C. TRANS- + SONIC, based on SUPERSONIC, *ultrasonic*.

transpacific *a.* lying or being beyond the Pacific. WH: 19C. TRANS- + PACIFIC.

transparent *a.* having the property of transmitting rays of light without diffusion, so that objects are distinctly visible. WH: 14–15C. Old French, from Medieval Latin *transparens, transparentis*, pres.p. of *transparere* to shine through, from TRANS- + *parare* to come into view. See also -ENT.

transpersonal *a.* going beyond the personal. WH: early 20C. TRANS- + *personal* (PERSON).

transpierce *v.t.* to pierce through. WH: 16C. TRANS- + PIERCE, based on French *transpercer*.

transpire *v.t.* to emit through the excretory organs (of the skin or lungs), to emit as vapour, to exhale. Also *v.i.* WH: 14–15C. French *transpirer* or Medieval Latin *transpirare*, from TRANS- + *spirare* to breathe. The sense to become known indirectly dates from the 18C.

transplant[1] *v.t.* to remove and plant in another place. WH: 14–15C. Late Latin *transplantare*, from TRANS- + *plantare* PLANT. The sense originally applied to plants. The medical sense evolved in the 18C.

transplant[2] *n.* the surgical procedure for transplanting an organ. WH: 18C. TRANSPLANT[1].

transponder *n.* a radio or radar device which automatically transmits a signal in response to a signal received. WH: mid-20C. TRANSMIT + RESPOND + -ER[1].

transpontine *a.* on the other side of a bridge. WH: 19C. Latin TRANS- + *pons, pontis* bridge. See also -INE. A second sense on the other side of the ocean derives from TRANS- + Latin *pontus* sea.

transport[1] *v.t.* to carry or convey from one place to another. WH: 14–15C. Old French *transporter* or Latin *transportare*, from TRANS- + *portare* to carry.

transport[2] *n.* transportation, conveyance from one place to another. WH: 14–15C. TRANSPORT[1], or from Old French. The original sense (to the 17C) was the transfer or conveyance of property. The current sense evolved in the 17C.

transpose *v.t.* to cause to change places. WH: 14–15C. Old French *transposer*. See TRANS-, POSE[1].

transputer *n.* a powerful microchip which has its own RAM facility and is designed to process in parallel rather than sequentially. WH: late 20C. TRANSISTOR + COMPUTER.

transsexual *n.* a person who dresses and lives for all or most of the time as a member of the opposite sex. Also *a.* WH: mid-20C. TRANS- + SEXUAL.

trans-ship *v.t.* to transfer from one ship, vehicle etc., to another. WH: 18C. TRANS- + SHIP.

transubstantiate *v.t.* to change the substance of. WH: 14–15C. Medieval Latin *transubstantiatus*, p.p. of *transubstantiare*, from Latin TRANS- + *substantia* SUBSTANCE.

transude *v.i.* to pass or ooze through the pores or interstices of a membrane etc. WH: 17C. French *transsuder*, from Old French *tressuer*, ult. from Latin TRANS- + *sudare* to sweat.

transuranic *a.* (of an atomic element) having an atomic number higher than uranium. WH: mid-20C. TRANS- + URANIUM + -IC.

Transvaal daisy *n.* a S African gerbera, *Gerbera jamesonii*, which has large daisy-like flowers. WH: early 20C. *Transvaal*, a former province of S Africa + DAISY.

transvalue v.t. to evaluate by a different or new principle. WH: 19C. TRANS- + VALUE.

transverse a. lying, being or acting across or in a cross direction. Also n., v.t. WH: 14–15C. Latin transversus, p.p. of transvertere to turn across, from TRANS- + vertere to turn.

transvestism n. the wearing of clothing belonging to the opposite sex, esp. for sexual stimulation. WH: early 20C. Latin TRANS- + vestire to clothe. See also -ISM.

Transylvanian a. of or belonging to Transylvania. WH: 17C. Transylvania, a former region of Austria-Hungary, now in W Romania + -IAN.

trap[1] n. a contrivance for catching an animal, consisting of an enclosure or mechanical arrangement, esp. with a spring, often baited. Also v.t., v.i. WH: pre-1200. Old English træppe, corr. to Middle Dutch trappe, Medieval Latin trappa, Old French trape (Modern French trappe), Portuguese trapa, Spanish trampa.

trap[2] n. a dark igneous rock, esp. a variety of dolerite or basalt, presenting a columnar or stairlike aspect. WH: 18C. Swedish trapp, from trappa stair. The rock is so called from its frequent stairlike appearance.

trap[3] v.t. to adorn, to caparison. Also n. WH: 12–14C. Alt. of Old French drap. See DRAPE.

trapeze n. an apparatus consisting of a suspended bar or set of bars on which acrobats perform swinging, balancing and other feats. WH: 19C. French trapèze, from Late Latin trapezium, from Greek trapezion, from trapeza table. The apparatus is probably so called because the ropes originally formed a trapezium with the crossbar and the roof.

Trappist n. a member of a Cistercian order, following the strict rule of La Trappe, a monastery founded at Soligny-la-Trappe, in 1664. Also a. WH: 19C. French trappiste, from La Trappe, near Soligny, N France. See also -IST.

trash n. any waste or worthless matter, refuse, rubbish. Also v.t. WH: 14–15C. Orig. unknown.

trass n. a light-coloured type of tuff rock, often used to make hydraulic cement. WH: 18C. Obs. Dutch tarasse, terras, tiras, ult. from Latin terra earth. Cp. TERRACE.

trattoria n. an Italian restaurant. WH: 19C. Italian, from trattore innkeeper.

trauma n. a psychological shock having a lasting effect on the subconscious. WH: 17C. Greek wound.

travail n. painful toil, painful exertion or effort. Also v.i., v.t. WH: 12–14C. Old French travailler, from Popular Latin tripaliare to torture, from Medieval Latin trepalium instrument of torture, prob. from Latin tres three + palus stake. Cp. TRAVEL. The Medieval Latin word for the instrument of torture presumably alludes to its structure. The original sense was a painful or laborious task (to the 18C) as well as specifically the pains of childbirth.

travel v.i. to make a journey, esp. to distant or foreign lands. Also v.t., n. WH: 12–14C. Var. of TRAVAIL. The reference is presumably to the hardships and difficulties of early travel.

traverse[1] v.t. to travel across. Also v.i. WH: 12–14C. Old French traverser, from Late Latin transversare, from Latin transversus TRANSVERSE.

traverse[2] a. lying or being across, transverse. Also adv., n. WH: 15C. Old French travers, partly from traverser (TRAVERSE[1]), partly from Medieval Latin transversum, neut. p.p. (used as n.) of transversare TRANSVERSE, partly representing Late Latin traversa, fem. p.p. (used as n.) of Latin transvertere to turn across.

travertine n. a light yellow porous rock formed by calcareous deposit from streams, hardening on exposure, used for building. WH: 18C. Italian travertino, earlier tivertino, from Latin tiburtinus, from Tiburs, Tiburtis Tibur (now Tivoli), a region of ancient Latium, Italy.

travesty n. a parody, burlesque imitation or ridiculous misrepresentation. Also v.t. WH: 17C. French travesti, p.p. of travestir, from Italian travestire, from tra- TRA- + vestire to clothe. Cp. TRANSVESTISM.

travois n. a N American Indian vehicle consisting of two poles joined by a frame and pulled by a horse etc. WH: 19C. Alt. of French travail, ? ult. from Latin trabs, trabis beam. According to some, the word is from the source of TRAVAIL.

travolator n. a moving pavement. WH: mid-20C. TRAVEL + -ator, based on ESCALATOR.

trawl n. a net, shaped like a flattened bag, for dragging along the sea bottom. Also v.i. WH: 16C. Prob. from Middle Dutch traghelen to drag, rel. to traghel dragnet, ? from Latin tragula dragnet, from trahere to draw. Cp. TRAIL.

tray n. a flat shallow vessel, used for holding or carrying small articles on. WH: pre-1200. Old English trīg, from Germanic base also of TREE.

treacherous a. violating allegiance, disloyal, perfidious. WH: 12–14C. Old French trecherous, tricherous, from trecheor, tricheor (Modern French tricheur), from trechier (Modern French tricher) to cheat, to trick. See TRICK, also -ER[2], -OUS.

treacle n. a syrup drained from sugar in refining. WH: 12–14C. Old French triacle, from Latin theriaca, from Greek thēriakē, use as n. of fem. of a. from thērion wild animal, poisonous animal. The original sense was a medicinal salve used as an antidote against poisons, venomous bites, etc. The current sense evolved in the 17C, either because syrup or molasses resembled the ancient compound, or because it was itself considered a medicine in its use as a laxative.

tread v.i. to set the foot on the ground. Also v.t., n. WH: pre-1200. Old English tredan, from Germanic. Cp. TRADE.

treadle n. a lever worked by the foot giving motion to a lathe, sewing machine, bicycle etc. Also v.i. WH: pre-1200. Old English tredel, from tredan. See TREAD, also -LE[1]. The original sense (to the 19C) was step, stair. The current sense arose in the 14–15C.

treason n. a violation of allegiance by a subject against the sovereign or government, esp. an overt attempt to subvert the government, high treason. WH: 12–14C. Old French traïson (Modern French trahison), from Latin traditio, traditionis. See TRADITION.

treasure n. precious metals in any form, or gems. Also v.t. WH: 12–14C. Old French tresor, from Latin THESAURUS.

treasurer n. a person who has charge of a treasure or treasury. WH: 12–14C. Old French tresorier, from tresor TREASURE, based on Late Latin thesaurarius. See also -ER[2].

treasury n. a place or building in which treasure is stored. WH: 12–14C. Old French tresorie, from tresor TREASURE, based on Medieval Latin thesauraria, thesaurarium. See also -Y[2].

treat v.t. to act or behave to or towards. Also v.i., n. WH: 12–14C. Old French tretier, traitier (Modern French traiter), from Latin tractare to drag, to manage, to handle, from tractus, p.p. of trahere to draw.

treatise n. a literary composition expounding, discussing and illustrating some particular subject in a thorough way. WH: 14–15C. Anglo-French tretis, from Old French traitier TREAT. See also -ISE[1].

treatment n. any medical procedure intended to bring about a cure. WH: 16C. TREAT + -MENT.

treaty n. an agreement formally concluded and ratified between different states. WH: 14–15C. Old French traité, from Latin tractatus TRACTATE. See also -Y[2].

treble a. triple, threefold. Also n., v.t., v.i. WH: 12–14C. Old French, from Latin triplus TRIPLE. The musical sense probably arose from the fact that in early contrapuntal music the chief melody was given to the tenor (the 'first voice') and the voice parts added above were the alto ('second') and treble ('third').

trebuchet n. a medieval military engine for hurling stones. WH: 12–14C. Old French trébuchet, from trébucher to overturn, to overthrow, ult. from trabuc, from tra- (from Latin trans, expressing displacement) + buc trunk (of the body), bulk, from Frankish būk belly.

trecento n. the 14th cent. as characterized by a distinctive style of Italian literature and art. WH: 19C. Italian three hundred (i.e. the 1300s).

tree n. a perennial woody plant rising from the ground with a single supporting trunk or stem. Also v.t. WH: pre-1200. Old English trēo, trēow, from Germanic var. of Indo-European base represented by Sanskrit dāru, dru- tree, Greek doru wood, spear, drus tree, oak.

treenail n. a pin or peg of hard wood used in fastening timbers, esp. in shipbuilding. WH: 12–14C. TREE + NAIL.

tref *a.* in Judaism, not kosher. **WH:** early 20C. Hebrew *ţĕrēpāh* flesh of an animal torn or mauled, from *ţārap* to tear, to rend. The dietary law follows the biblical ordinance: 'Neither shall ye eat any flesh that is torn of beasts in the field; ye shall cast it to the dogs' (Exod. xxii.31).

trefoil *n.* a plant with three leaflets or three-lobed leaves, esp. of the genus *Trifolium*, such as the clover, the black medick etc. **WH:** 12–14C. Anglo-French *trifoil*, from Latin *trifolium*, from TRI- + *folium* leaf, FOIL[1].

trehala *n.* a kind of manna formed by the substance of the cocoons of a coleopterous insect in Asia Minor. **WH:** 19C. Turkish *tigale*, from Persian *tīgāl*.

treillage *n.* a light frame of posts and rails to support espaliers. **WH:** 17C. French, from *treille*, from Latin *trichila* bower, arbour. See also -AGE.

trek *v.i.* to journey, esp. with difficulty on foot. *Also n.* **WH:** 19C. Afrikaans and Middle Dutch *trekken* to draw, to pull, to travel. Cp. TRACK.

trellis *n.* openwork of strips of wood crossing each other and nailed together, used for verandas, summer houses etc. *Also v.t.* **WH:** 14–15C. Old French *trelis*, *trelice*, from Latin *trilix*, *trilicis*, from TRI- + *licium* thread of a warp.

trematode *n.* any parasitic flatworm of the class Trematoda, esp. a fluke. **WH:** 19C. Modern Latin *Trematoda*, from Greek *trēmatōdēs* perforated, from *trēma* hole, orifice. See also -LE[4]. The worms are so called from their perforated skin.

tremble *v.i.* to shake involuntarily, as with fear, cold, weakness etc. *Also n.* **WH:** 12–14C. Old French *trembler*, from Medieval Latin *tremulare*, rel. to Latin *tremulus* TREMULOUS. See also -LE[4].

tremellose *a.* (of some fungi) tremulous, jelly-like, gelatinous. **WH:** 19C. Modern Latin *Tremella* genus name, dim. of Latin *tremulus* TREMULOUS. See also -OSE[1].

tremendous *a.* terrible, dreadful. **WH:** 17C. Latin *tremendus*, ger. of *tremere* to tremble (at), rel. to TREMOR. See also -OUS. Cp. HORRENDOUS, STUPENDOUS. The original sense was inspiring dread or awe, fearsome. The current general sense evolved in the 19C.

tremolite *n.* a calcium magnesium metasilicate crystallizing in the monoclinic system. **WH:** 18C. *Tremola*, a valley in Switzerland + -ITE[1].

tremolo *n.* a tremulous or quavering effect in singing, playing etc. **WH:** 18C. Italian, from Latin *tremulus* TREMULOUS.

tremor *n.* a trembling, shaking or quivering. *Also v.i.* **WH:** 14–15C. Old French *tremour*, Latin *tremor*, rel. to *tremere* tremble. See also -OR.

tremulous *a.* trembling, shaking, quivering. **WH:** 17C. Latin *tremulus*, from *tremere* to tremble. See also -ULOUS.

trench *n.* a long narrow cut or deep furrow in the earth, a ditch, esp. a long narrow ditch, usu. with a parapet formed by the excavated earth, to cover besieging troops etc. *Also v.t., v.i.* **WH:** 14–15C. Old French *trenche* cutting, cut, ditch, slice, from *trenchier* (Modern French *trancher*) to cut, ult. from Latin *truncare*. See TRUNCATE[2].

trenchant *a.* cutting, biting, incisive. **WH:** 12–14C. Old French (Modern French *tranchant*), pres.p. of *trenchier*. See TRENCH, also -ANT.

trencher *n.* a wooden plate of a type formerly used for serving food, now for cutting bread on. **WH:** 12–14C. Old French *trencheoir*, from *trenchier*. See TRENCH, also -ER[2].

trend *n.* a general tendency, bent or inclination. *Also v.i.* **WH:** pre-1200. Old English *trendan*, from Germanic base represented also by Old English *trinda* round lump, ball, *ātrendlian* to roll away. Cp. TRUNDLE. The noun evolved from the verb in the 17C, originally in the sense rounded bend of a stream. The current sense dates from the 18C.

trente-et-quarante *n.* a gambling card game played by a 'banker' and a number of people on a table marked with red and black diamonds. **WH:** 17C. French, lit. thirty-and-forty. The reference is to winning and losing scores in this game.

trepan[1] *n.* a surgeon's cylindrical saw for removing portions of the skull. *Also v.t.* **WH:** 14–15C. Medieval Latin *trepanum*, from Greek *trupanon* borer, from *trupan* to pierce, to bore, *trupē* hole.

†trepan[2] *v.t.* to entrap, to ensnare. *Also n.* **WH:** 17C. Prob. from TRAP[1].

trepang *n.* the sea slug or bêche-de-mer. **WH:** 18C. Malay *teripang*.

trephine *n.* an improved trepan with a centre-pin. *Also v.t.* **WH:** 17C. Latin *tres fines* three ends, appar. partly based on TREPAN[1].

trepidation *n.* a state of alarm or agitation. **WH:** 15C. Latin *trepidatio*, *trepidationis*, from *trepidatus*, p.p. of *trepidare*, from *trepidus* scared, alarmed. Cp. INTREPID.

treponema *n.* a member of a genus of spirochaetes *Treponema*, that cause syphilis and other diseases. **WH:** early 20C. Modern Latin, from Greek *trepein* to turn + *nēma* thread.

trespass *n.* a wrongful act involving injury to the person or property of another, esp. unauthorized entry into another's land. *Also v.i.* **WH:** 12–14C. Old French *trespas*, from *trespasser* to pass beyond (Modern French *trépasser* to die), from Medieval Latin *transpassare*. See TRANS-, PASS.

tress *n.* a lock or plait of hair, esp. from the head of a girl or woman. *Also v.t.* **WH:** 12–14C. Old French *tresse*, ? from Popular Latin *trichia* braid, rope, and ult. from Greek *trikha* threefold.

tressure *n.* a diminutive of the orle, usually borne double and emblazoned with fleurs-de-lis. **WH:** 12–14C. Old French *tressour*, from *tresse*. See TRESS, also -OUR, -URE.

trestle *n.* a movable frame for supporting a table, platform etc., usu. consisting of a pair of divergent legs, fixed or hinged. **WH:** 12–14C. Old French *trestel* (Modern French *tréteau*), from Popular Latin *trastellum*, dim. of Latin *transtrum* beam. See also -EL, -LE[2].

tret *n.* an allowance to purchasers of goods of certain kinds for damage or deterioration during transit, usu. 4 lb. (1.8 kg) in every 104 lb. (47.2 kg). **WH:** 15C. Old French, var. of *trait* draught. See TRAIT.

trevally *n.* any Australian fish of the genus *Caranx*. **WH:** 19C. Appar. alt. of *cavally* (CAVALLA).

trews *n.pl.* trousers, esp. made of tartan. **WH:** 16C. Irish *triús*, Gaelic *triubhas* (sing.). Cp. TROUSERS.

trey *n.* the three at cards or dice. **WH:** 14–15C. Old French *treis* (Modern French *trois*), from Latin *tres* THREE.

tri- *comb. form* three, three times, triple. **WH:** Latin and Greek comb. form of Latin *tres* three, Greek *treis* three, *tris* thrice.

triable *a.* subject to judicial trial. **WH:** 14–15C. Anglo-French, from Old French *trier*. See TRY, also -ABLE.

triacetate *n.* a cellulose derivative containing three acetate groups. **WH:** 19C. TRI- + ACETATE.

triacid *a.* (of a base) capable of reacting with three molecules of a monobasic acid. **WH:** 19C. TRI- + ACID.

triad *n.* a collection of three. **WH:** 16C. French *triade*, or from Late Latin *trias*, *triadis*, from Greek *trias*, *triados*, from TRI-. See also -AD[1].

triadelphous *a.* (of a plant) having the stamens in three bundles. **WH:** 19C. TRI- + Greek *adelphos* brother (here, stamen) + -OUS.

triage *n.* the sorting of hospital patients, casualties in war etc. according to urgency of treatment and likelihood of survival. **WH:** 18C. Old French, from *trier*. See TRY, also -AGE.

trial *n.* the judicial examination and determination of the issues in a cause between parties before a judge, judge and jury or a referee. *Also v.t., v.i., a.* **WH:** 14–15C. Anglo-French, or from Medieval Latin *triallum*, from *trier*. See TRY, also -AL[1].

triandrous *a.* having three stamens. **WH:** 19C. TRI- + -ANDROUS from Greek *anēr*, *andros* man (here, stamen). Cp. TRIGYNOUS.

triangle *n.* a figure, esp. a plane figure, bounded by three lines, esp. straight lines. **WH:** 14–15C. Old French, or from Latin *triangulum*, use as n. of neut. of *triangulus* three-cornered, from TRI- + *angulus* ANGLE[1].

triarch *n.* the ruler of one of three divisions of a country. **WH:** 19C. TRI- + -*arch*, based on TETRARCH.

Trias *n.* the division of rock strata between the Carboniferous and the Jurassic (divided in Germany into three groups, whence the name). **WH:** 19C. German, from Latin. See TRIAD.

triathlon *n.* an athletic contest consisting of three events. **WH:** late 20C. TRI- + Greek *athlon* contest, based on DECATHLON, etc.

triatomic *a.* having three atoms in the molecule. **WH:** 19C. TRI- + *atomic* (ATOM).

triaxal *a.* having three axes. **WH:** 19C. TRI- + Latin *axis* AXIS[1] + -AL[1].

tribade *n.* a lesbian. **WH:** 17C. French, or from Latin *tribas*, *tribadis*, from Greek *tribas*, from *tribein* to rub.

tribal *a.* belonging to, of or relating to a tribe. *Also n.* WH: 17C. TRIBE + -AL[1].

tribasic *a.* having three atoms of hydrogen replaceable by a base or basic radical. WH: 19C. TRI- + *basic* (BASE[1]).

tribe *n.* a group of people ethnologically related and forming a community or a political division. WH: 12–14C. Old French *tribu*, or from Latin *tribus*, ? rel. to *tri-* three. The group is said to be so called from the supposed division of the Roman people in early times into three tribes (Ramnes, Tities, Luceres).

triblet *n.* a mandrel used in forging tubes, nuts and rings etc. WH: 17C. French *triboulet*, of unknown orig.

tribo- *comb. form* friction, rubbing. WH: Greek *tribos* rubbing. See also -O-.

triboelectricity *n.* electricity generated by friction. WH: late 20C. TRIBO- + *electricity* (ELECTRIC).

tribology *n.* the study of friction, lubrication and wear between interacting surfaces. WH: mid-20C. TRIBO- + -LOGY. The term was coined in 1965 by the Scottish classicist Colin G. Hardie.

triboluminescence *n.* luminescence produced by friction. WH: 19C. TRIBO- + *luminescence* (LUMINESCE).

tribometer *n.* a sledlike apparatus for measuring sliding friction. WH: 18C. French *tribomètre*. See TRIBO-, -METER.

tribrach *n.* a metrical foot of three short or unstressed syllables. WH: 16C. Latin *tribrachys*, from Greek *tribrakhus*, from TRI- + *brakhus* short.

tribulation *n.* severe affliction, suffering, distress. WH: 12–14C. Old French, from Ecclesiastical Latin *tribulatio*, *tribulationis*, from Latin *tribulare* to press, to oppress, to afflict, from *tribulum* a board with sharp points on the underside used in threshing, prob. from var. of stem of *terere* to rub.

tribunal *n.* a court of justice. WH: 14–15C. Old French, or from Latin *tribunal* raised platform for the seats of magistrates, elevation, from *tribunus* TRIBUNE[1]. See also -AL[1].

tribune[1] *n.* a champion of popular rights and liberties. WH: 14–15C. Latin *tribunus*, prob. orig. use as n. of a., magistrate of a tribe, from *tribus* TRIBE.

tribune[2] *n.* a bishop's throne in an apse; an apse containing this. WH: 17C. French, from Italian *tribuna*, from Medieval Latin *tribuna*, alt. of Latin TRIBUNAL.

tributary *n.* a stream or river flowing into a larger one or a lake. *Also a.* WH: 14–15C. Latin *tributarius*, from *tributum*. See TRIBUTE, also -ARY[1]. The original sense was a person paying tribute. The sense stream or river flowing into a larger one evolved in the 19C from an earlier (17C) adjective meaning subsidiary.

tribute *n.* a contribution, gift or offering (of praise etc.). WH: 14–15C. Latin *tributum*, use as n. of neut. of *tributus*, p.p. of *tribuere* to assign, to allot, to grant, lit. to divide among the tribes, from *tribus* TRIBE. The word was originally the term for a payment made periodically by one state to another as a sign of dependence. The current general sense evolved in the 16C.

tricar *n.* a motor car with three wheels. WH: early 20C. TRI- + CAR.

trice[1] *n.* an instant. WH: 14–15C. TRICE[2]. The original sense was a sharp pull, a tug. Hence the time taken for this, an instant.

trice[2] *v.t.* to haul. WH: 14–15C. Middle Dutch *trīsen*, from *trīse* windlass, pulley, of unknown orig. The original sense (to the 17C) was to pull sharply, to tug.

triceps *a.* (of muscles) three-headed, having three points of attachment. *Also n.* WH: 16C. Latin, from TRI- + *-ceps*, *caput* head. Cp. BICEPS.

triceratops *n.* a large herbivorous dinosaur of the Cretaceous period, of the genus *Triceratops*, with three horns and a bony crest on the hood. WH: 19C. Modern Latin, from Greek *trikeratos* three-horned + *ōps* eye, face.

trichiasis *n.* entropion or inversion of the eyelashes. WH: 17C. Late Latin, from Greek *trikhiasis*, from *trikhian* to be hairy. See also -IASIS.

trichina *n.* any hairlike nematode parasitic worm of the genus *Trichinella*, esp. *T. spiralis*, infesting the intestine or muscles of pigs, humans etc. WH: 19C. Modern Latin, from Greek *trikhinos* of hair, from *thrix*, *thrikhos* hair.

trichite *n.* a minute hairlike form occurring in certain vitreous volcanic rocks. WH: 19C. Greek *trikho-* TRICHO- + -ITE[1].

trichloroethane *n.* a volatile nonflammable colourless liquid used as a solvent; also called *methyl chloroform*. WH: mid-20C. TRI- + CHLORO- + ETHANE.

tricho- *comb. form* hair. WH: Greek *trikho-*, comb. stem of *thrix* hair. See also -O-.

trichogenous *a.* promoting growth of the hair. WH: 19C. TRICHO- + -GENOUS.

trichology *n.* the study of the human hair. WH: 19C. TRICHO- + -LOGY.

trichome *n.* a hair, filament, scale, prickle or an outgrowth. WH: 19C. Greek *trikhōma* growth of hair, from *trikhoun* to cover with hair. See also -OME.

trichomonad *n.* any parasitic protozoan of the order Trichomonadida, occurring in the digestive system of humans and animals such as cattle. WH: 19C. TRICHO- + MONAD-.

trichomoniasis *n.* an infection caused by trichomonads, esp. a vaginal infection, *Trichomonas vaginalis*. WH: early 20C. TRICHOMONAD + -IASIS.

trichopathy *n.* the treatment of hair diseases. WH: 19C. TRICHO- + *-pathy* (-PATH).

trichopteran *n.* any insect of the order Trichoptera, containing the caddis-flies. WH: 19C. Modern Latin *Trichoptera*, from *tricho-* TRICHO- + Greek *pteron* wing. See also -AN. The insects are so called from their hairy wings.

trichosis *n.* any disease or unhealthy condition of the hair. WH: 17C. Greek *trikhōsis* growth of hair, from *trikhoun*. See TRICHOME.

trichotomy *n.* division into three, esp. of the human being into body, soul and spirit. WH: early 20C. Greek *trikha*, *trikhē* triply + -O- + -TOMY.

trichroism *n.* the property of exhibiting different colours in three different directions when viewed by transmitted light. WH: 19C. Greek *trikhroos*, *trikhrous* three-coloured + -ISM.

trichromatic *a.* three-coloured, having the normal three fundamental colour-sensations (of red, green and purple). WH: 19C. TRI- + CHROMATIC.

trick *n.* an artifice, an artful device or stratagem. *Also a., v.t., v.i.* WH: 14–15C. Old French *trique*, dial. var. of *triche*, from *trichier* (Modern French *tricher*) to deceive, to cheat, of unknown orig. Cp. TREACHEROUS.

trickle *v.i.* to flow in drops or in a small stream. *Also v.t., n.* WH: 12–14C. Imit.

triclinic *a.* (of a mineral) having the three axes unequal and inclined at oblique angles. WH: 19C. TRI- + *-clinic*, based on *monoclinic* (MONOCLINAL).

triclinium *n.* a set of couches arranged round three sides of a dining table. WH: 17C. Latin, from Greek *triklinion*, dim. of *triklinos* dining room with three couches, from TRI- + *klinē* couch, bed.

tricolour *n.* a flag or banner having three colours, esp. arranged in equal stripes, such as the national standard of France of blue, white and red, divided vertically. *Also a.* WH: 18C. French *tricolore*, from Late Latin *tricolor*, from TRI- + *color* COLOUR.

tricorn *a.* having three horns. *Also n.* WH: 18C. French *tricorne* or Latin *tricornis* three-horned, from TRI- + *cornu* horn.

tricot *n.* a hand-knitted woollen fabric or a machine-made imitation. WH: 18C. French, from *tricoter* to knit.

tricrotic *a.* (of the pulse etc.) having three distinct undulations for each beat. WH: 19C. TRI- + *-crotic*, based on DICROTIC.

tric-trac *n.* a complicated form of backgammon. WH: 17C. French, imit. of the clicking sound made by the pieces when being played.

tricuspid *a.* (of molar teeth, a valve of the heart etc.) having three cusps or points. *Also n.* WH: 17C. TRI- + Latin *cuspis*, *cuspidis* CUSP. See also -ID.

tricycle *n.* a three-wheeled cycle. *Also v.i.* WH: 19C. TRI- + CYCLE.

tricyclic *a.* (of a compound) having three rings in its molecule. *Also n.* WH: 19C. TRI- + Greek *kuklos* circle + -IC.

tridactyl *a.* having three fingers or toes. WH: 19C. TRI- + Greek *daktulos* finger, toe. See also -OUS.

trident *n.* a three-pronged implement or weapon, esp. a fish-spear. WH: 14–15C. Latin *tridens*, *tridentis*, from TRI- + *dens*, *dentis* tooth.

Tridentine *a.* of or relating to Trent, or the Council held there 1545–63. *Also n.* WH: 16C. Medieval Latin *Tridentinus*, from *Tridentum* Trent (Italian *Trento*), a city in N Italy. See also -INE.

tridimensional *a.* having three dimensions. WH: 19C. TRI- + *dimensional* (DIMENSION).

triduum *n.* in the Roman Catholic Church, a three days' service of prayer etc. WH: 18C. Latin, use as n. of a., from TRI- + *dies* day.

tridymite *n.* a vitreous form of silica usu. occurring in small hexagonal tables composed of groups of three individual crystals. WH: 19C. Greek *tridumos*, from TRI- + -*dumos*, as in *didumos* twin (cp. DIDYMOUS). See also -ITE[1]. The silica is so called because its compound forms consist of three individual crystals.

triennial *a.* lasting for three years. *Also n.* WH: 16C. Late Latin *triennis* of three years, *triennium* period of three years, from TRI- + *annus* year. See also -AL[1].

trierarch *n.* in ancient Greece, the commander of a trireme. WH: 17C. Latin *trierarchus*, or from Greek *triērarchos*, *triērarchēs*, from *triērēs* trireme + *arkhos* chief.

trifacial *a.* threefold and of or relating to the face (as the trigeminus). *Also n.* WH: 19C. TRI- + FACIAL.

trifecta *n.* a form of betting in which a punter must predict the first three places in a race. WH: late 20C. TRI- + *perfecta* (PERFECT[2]).

trifid *a.* divided wholly or partially into three. WH: 18C. Latin *trifidus*, from TRI- + *fid*-, stem of *findere* to split.

trifle *n.* a thing, matter, fact etc. of no value or importance. *Also v.i., v.t.* WH: 12–14C. Old French *truffle*, var. of *truffe* deceit, gibe, corr. to Italian *truffa*, Spanish and Portuguese *trufa*, of unknown orig. The original sense (to the 17C) was false story, joke, jest. The sense matter of little importance arose at the same time and gave the name of the dessert dish in the 16C. This was originally cream boiled up with flavourings and as such was relatively insubstantial. Cp. FOOL[2].

trifloral *a.* bearing three flowers. WH: 19C. TRI- + Latin *flos, floris* FLOWER + -AL[1].

trifocal *a.* having three focuses or focal lengths. WH: 19C. TRI- + *focal* (FOCUS).

trifoliate *a.* three-leaved, consisting of three leaflets. WH: 18C. TRI- + FOLIATE[2].

triforium *n.* a gallery or arcade in the wall over the arches of the nave or choir, or sometimes the transepts, in a large church. WH: 18C. Anglo-Latin, of unknown orig. On the face of it, the origin appears to be in Latin TRI- + Latin *foris* door + -IUM, as if referring to a gallery or arcade with three openings. But the term specifically applies to Canterbury cathedral, where there is no such gallery.

triform *a.* having three shapes, parts or divisions. WH: 14–15C. Salish *triformis*, from *tri-* TRI- + *forma* FORM.

trifurcate *a.* having three branches or forks. *Also v.t., v.i.* WH: 19C. Latin *trifurcus* three-forked, from TRI- + *furca* FORK. See also -ATE[2].

trig[1] *n.* trigonometry. WH: 19C. Abbr. of TRIGONOMETRY.

trig[2] *a.* neat, trim, spruce. *Also n., v.t.* WH: 12–14C. Old Norse *tryggr*, corr. to Gothic *triggws* true, faithful. See TRUE. The original sense was true, faithful. The current sense dates from the 16C.

trig[3] *v.t.* to stop, check or skid (a wheel). *Also n.* WH: 16C. Orig. uncertain, ? from Old Norse *tryggja*, Old Danish *trygge* to make firm, from *trygg*. See TRIG[2].

trigamous *a.* married three times. WH: 19C. Greek *trigamos*, from TRI- + *gamos* marriage. See also -OUS.

trigeminal *a.* threefold. *Also n.* WH: 19C. TRI- + Latin *geminus* born at the same birth + -AL[1].

trigger *n.* a catch or lever for releasing the hammer of a gunlock. *Also v.t.* WH: 17C. Dutch *trekker*, from *trekken* to pull. See TREK, also -ER[1].

triglyceride *n.* any ester of glycerol and three acid radicals. WH: 19C. TRI- + *glyceride* (GLYCEROL).

triglyph *n.* an ornament on a Doric frieze consisting of a tablet with three vertical grooves. WH: 16C. Latin *triglyphus*, from Greek *trigluphos*, from TRI- + *gluphē* carving, GLYPH.

trigon *n.* a triangle. WH: 16C. Latin *trigonum*, from Greek *trigōnon*, neut. of *trigōnos* three-cornered, from TRI- + *gōnos* -GON.

trigonometry *n.* the branch of mathematics treating of the relations of the sides and angles of triangles, and applying these to astronomy, navigation, surveying etc. WH: 17C. Modern Latin *trigonometria*, from Greek *trigōnon* (TRIGON) + -METRY.

trigram *n.* a group of three letters representing a single sound, a trigraph. WH: 17C. TRI- + -GRAM.

trigraph *n.* a group of three letters representing a single sound. WH: 19C. TRI- + -GRAPH.

trigynous *a.* having three pistils. WH: 18C. TRI- + -GYNOUS, from Greek *gunē* woman (here, pistil). Cp. TRIANDROUS.

trihedron *n.* a figure having three sides. WH: 19C. TRI- + -HEDRON.

trihydric *a.* containing three hydroxyl groups. WH: 19C. TRI- + HYDRIC.

trike *n., v.i.* a tricycle. WH: 19C. Abbr. of TRICYCLE. Cp. BIKE[1].

trilabiate *a.* three-lipped. WH: 19C. TRI- + *labiate* (LABIAL).

trilateral *a.* of or having three sides. *Also n.* WH: 17C. TRI- + LATERAL.

trilby *n.* a man's soft felt hat with a dent in the middle. WH: 19C. *Trilby*, the heroine of George du Maurier's novel of the same name (1894). The hat is so called from that worn by one of the characters, Little Billee, in du Maurier's illustrations for the book.

trilemma *n.* a syllogism involving three alternatives. WH: 17C. TRI- + DILEMMA.

trilinear *a.* consisting of three lines. WH: 18C. TRI- + LINEAR.

trilingual *a.* able to speak three languages. WH: 19C. TRI- + Latin *lingua* tongue, language + -AL[1].

triliteral *a.* (esp. of Semitic roots) consisting of or using three letters. *Also n.* WH: 18C. TRI- + Latin *litera* letter + -AL[1].

trilith *n.* a megalithic monument usu. consisting of two uprights supporting an impost. WH: 18C. Greek *trilithon*, use as n. of neut. of *trilithos*, from TRI- + *lithos* stone.

trill *v.i.* to sing or emit a sound with a tremulous vibration. *Also v.t., n.* WH: 17C. Italian *trillare*, prob. of imit. orig.

trillion *n.* a million million. WH: 17C. French, or from Italian *trilione*, from TRI- + MILLION. The word originally denoted a million million million (10^{18}).

trillium *n.* any herbaceous plant of the genus *Trillium*, with a single central flower above three leaves. WH: 19C. Modern Latin, appar. alt. of Swedish *trilling* triplet. The plant is so called from its three leaves.

trilobate *a.* having three lobes. WH: 18C. TRI- + *lobate* (LOBE).

trilobite *n.* any of the Palaeozoic group of articulates with a three-lobed body. WH: 19C. Modern Latin *Trilobites*, from Greek TRI- + *lobos* LOBE + -ITE[1].

trilocular *a.* having three cells or chambers. WH: 18C. TRI- + *locular* (LOCULUS).

trilogy *n.* a group of three plays, operas, novels etc., each complete in itself, but connected. WH: 17C. Greek *trilogia*, from TRI- + *logos*. See -LOGY.

trim *v.t.* to put in good order, to make neat and tidy. *Also v.i., a., n.* WH: pre-1200. Old English *trymman*, *trymian* to strengthen, to make ready, from *trum* strong, stable. The original sense was to make firm, to arm (a force), to arrange. The current sense dates from the 16C.

trimaran *n.* a sailing vessel with three hulls. WH: mid-20C. TRI- + CATAMARAN.

trimensual *a.* happening or issued every three months. WH: 19C. TRI- + Late Latin *mensualis*, from Latin *mensis* month. See also -AL[1].

trimer *n.* a polymer whose molecule is formed from three molecules of a monomer. WH: mid-20C. TRI- + -MER.

trimester *n.* a period of three months. WH: 19C. French *trimestre*, from Latin *trimestris*, from TRI- + *mensis* mouth. Cp. SEMESTER.

trimeter *n.* a verse consisting of three measures of two feet each. *Also a.* WH: 16C. Latin *trimetrus*, from Greek *trimetros*, from TRI- + *metros* METRE[2].

trimonthly *a.* occurring every three months. WH: 19C. TRI- + *monthly* (MONTH).

trimorphism *n.* the existence in certain species of plants and animals of three distinct forms, colours etc., esp. having flowers with pistils or stamens of three different relative lengths. WH: 19C. Greek *trimorphos*, from TRI- + *morphē* form. See also -ISM.

trine *a.* threefold, triple. *Also n.* WH: 14–15C. Old French, fem. of *trin*, from Latin *trinus* threefold, from *tres*, *tria* THREE.

Trinidadian *n.* a native or inhabitant of Trinidad. *Also a.* WH: early 20C. *Trinidad*, an island in the W Indies + -IAN.

trinitrotoluene *n.* a chemical compound, usually known as TNT, largely used as a high explosive. WH: early 20C. TRI- + NITRO- + *toluene* (TOLU).

trinity n. a group or union of three individuals, a triad. WH: 12–14C. Old French *trinité*, corr. to Portuguese and Spanish *trinidad*, Italian *trinità*, from Latin *trinitas*, from *trinus* trio, triad, TRINE. See also -ITY. The original sense was theological, with reference to the existence of God in three persons.

trinket n. a small personal ornament of no great value as a jewel, esp. a ring. WH: 16C. Orig. unknown. According to some, the word comes from Old Northern French *trenquet*, from *trenquer* to cut, a variant of Old French *trenchier*. See TRENCH. But this origin does not accord with the meaning. The original sense (to the 18C) was a small article, a small tool.

trinomial a. consisting of three terms, esp. connected by the signs + or –. Also n. WH: 17C. TRI- + -*nomial*, based on BINOMIAL.

trio n. a set of three. WH: 18C. Italian, from Latin *tres*, *tria* THREE, based on DUO.

triode n. a thermionic valve with three electrodes. WH: 19C. TRI- + -ODE².

trioecious a. having male, female and hermaphrodite flowers, each on different plants of the same species. WH: 19C. TRI- + Greek *oikos* house + -OUS.

triolet n. a poem of eight lines with two rhymes arranged *ab aa ab ab*. WH: 17C. French, from Italian *trio*. See TRIO, also -LET.

trioxide n. an oxide having three oxygen atoms. WH: 19C. TRI- + OXIDE.

trip v.i. to move, step, walk or run lightly or nimbly. Also v.t., n. WH: 14–15C. Old French *triper*, *treper*, from Provençal *trepar*, from Middle Dutch *trippen* to skip, to hop, rel. to Old English *treppan* to tread, to trample. Ult. rel. to TRAP¹.

tripartite a. consisting of three parts. WH: 14–15C. Latin *tripartitus*, p.p. of *tripartire*. See TRI-, PARTITE.

tripe n. a part of the stomach of ruminating animals prepared for food. WH: Old French, rel. to Provençal *tripa*, Italian *trippa*, of unknown orig.

tripersonal a. consisting of three persons (esp. of the Godhead). WH: 17C. TRI- + PERSON + -AL¹.

triphibious a. on land, on sea and in the air. WH: mid-20C. TRI- + *amphibious* (AMPHIBIAN).

triphthong n. a combination of three vowels forming one sound. WH: 16C. French *triphthongue*, from *tri-* TRI- + -*phthongue*, based on DIPHTHONG.

tripinnate a. triply pinnate. WH: 18C. TRI- + PINNATE.

triplane n. an aeroplane with three supporting wings. WH: early 20C. TRI- + PLANE⁴.

triple a. consisting of three parts or three things united, threefold. Also n., v.t., v.i. WH: 12–14C. Old French, or from Latin *triplus*, from Greek *triplous*. Cp. TREBLE.

tripod n. a three-legged stand, stool, utensil, seat, table etc. WH: 17C. Latin *tripus*, *tripodis*, from Greek *tripous*, *tripodos*, from TRI- + *pous*, *podos* foot.

tripoli n. rotten-stone, a friable siliceous limestone. WH: 17C. *Tripoli*, either of two towns on the Mediterranean, one in Lebanon, the other the capital of Libya. The stone was originally found in the region of the named towns.

tripos n. either part of the examination for an honours BA at Cambridge University. WH: 16C. Alt. of Latin *tripus* TRIPOD. The original sense was tripod, but in the 17C the term was adopted for a Cambridge graduate appointed to make a satirical speech while sitting on a three-legged stool (tripod), and the current sense evolved from this in the 19C.

trippet n. a projecting part of a machine which regularly strikes another part of the mechanism. WH: 19C. TRIP + -ET¹.

triptane n. a very powerful aviation fuel, trimethyl butane. WH: mid-20C. TRI- + -*p*- + BUTANE.

tripterous a. having three winglike parts. WH: 19C. TRI- + Greek *pteron* wing, based on DIPTEROUS.

triptych n. a picture, carving or other representation, on three panels side by side, frequently used for altarpieces. WH: 18C. TRI- + -*ptych*, based on DIPTYCH.

triptyque n. a customs pass, made out in triplicate, for importing or exporting a motor vehicle. WH: early 20C. French TRIPTYCH.

triquetra n. an ornament composed of three interlacing arcs. WH: 16C. Latin, fem. of *triquetrus* three-cornered, triangular.

triradial a. having three rays or radiating branches. WH: 19C. TRI- + RADIAL.

trireme n. a war-galley with three benches of oars. WH: 16C. Old French *trirème*, or from Latin *triremis*, from TRI- + *remus* oar.

trisaccharide n. a sugar that consists of three monosaccharide molecules. WH: early 20C. TRI- + *saccharide* (SACCHAR-).

Trisagion n. a hymn with a threefold invocation of God as holy, in the liturgies of the Greek and Eastern Churches. WH: 14–15C. Greek, neut. of *trisagios* thrice holy, from *tris* thrice + *hagios* holy.

trisect v.t. to divide into three (esp. equal) parts. WH: 17C. TRI- + Latin *sectus*, p.p. of *secare* to cut, based on BISECT.

trishaw n. a three-wheeled rickshaw. WH: mid-20C. TRI- + RICK-SHAW.

triskaidekaphobia n. fear of the number 13. WH: early 20C. Greek *treiskaideka* thirteen + -*phobia* (-PHOBE). The Greek numeral represents *treis* three + *kai* and + *deka* ten.

triskelion n. a form of fylfot, usu. consisting of three human legs, bent, and joined at the thigh, as in the arms of the Isle of Man. WH: 19C. Greek TRI- + *skelos* leg.

trismus n. lockjaw. WH: 17C. Modern Latin, from Greek *trismos* squeak, grinding.

trisoctahedron n. a solid having 24 equal faces. WH: 19C. Greek *tris* thrice + OCTAHEDRON.

trisomy n. a condition in which one chromosome type is represented three times instead of twice. WH: mid-20C. TRI- + -SOME² + -Y².

triste a. sad, gloomy. WH: 14–15C. Old French, from Latin *tristis*.

tristesse n. sadness. WH: 14–15C. Old French *tristesce* (Modern French *tristesse*), from Latin *tristitia*, from *tristis*. See TRISTE, also -ESS².

tristich n. a strophe or set of three lines. WH: 19C. TRI- + -*stich*, based on DISTICH.

trisyllable n. a word of three syllables. WH: 16C. TRI- + SYLLABLE.

tritagonist n. the third actor in a classical Greek play. WH: 19C. Greek *tritagōnistēs*, from *tritos* third + *agōnistēs* AGONIST.

tritanopia n. a reduced ability to distinguish the colour blue. WH: early 20C. TRITO- + *an*- (A-⁶) + -OPIA. The condition is so called because blue, the third primary colour, cannot be distinguished. Cp. PROTANOPIA, in which red, the first primary colour, cannot be distinguished, and *deuteranopia* (DEUTERO-), in which green, the second primary colour, cannot.

trite a. commonplace, hackneyed, stale. WH: 16C. Latin *tritus*, p.p. of *terere* to rub.

tritheism n. the doctrine that the three persons of the Trinity are each distinct Gods. WH: 17C. TRI- + THEISM.

tritium n. an isotope of hydrogen with a mass three times that of ordinary hydrogen. WH: mid-20C. TRITO- + -IUM. The isotope is so called because its nucleus, consisting of one proton and two neutrons, has triple the mass of ordinary hydrogen.

trito- comb. form third. WH: Greek *tritos* third. See also -O-.

Triton n. a newt. WH: 16C. Latin, from Greek *Tritōn* Triton, in Greek mythology a minor sea-god, the son of Poseidon and Amphitrite, often represented carrying a trident and a shell trumpet.

tritone n. an augmented fourth, containing three whole tones. WH: 17C. Medieval Latin *tritonus*, from Greek *tritonos*, from TRI- + *tonos* TONE.

triturate v.t. to rub or grind down to a fine powder. WH: 18C. Latin *trituratus*, p.p. of *triturare* to thresh corn, from *tritura* rubbing, threshing, from *tritus*, p.p. of *terere* to rub. See TRITE, also -URE, -ATE³.

triumph n. the state of being victorious. Also v.i. WH: 14–15C. Old French *triumphe* (Modern French *triomphe*), from Latin *triumphus*, earlier *triumpus*, prob. from Greek *thriambos* hymn to Bacchus. Cp. TRUMP¹.

triumvir n. any one of three men united in office, esp. a member of the first or second triumvirate in ancient Rome. WH: 14–15C. Latin, from *triumviri* (pl.), back-formation from *trium virorum*, gen. of *tres viri* three men.

triune a. three in one. WH: 17C. TRI- + Latin *unus* one.

trivalent a. having a valency or combining power of three. WH: 19C. TRI- + -*valent*, from Latin *valens*, *valentis*, pres.p. of *valere* to be strong. See VALENCE.

trivet *n.* a three-legged stand, esp. a metal tripod or movable bracket for supporting a cooking vessel or kettle. WH: 14–15C. Old English *trefet*, from Latin *tripes, tripedis*, from TRI- + *pes* foot, based on Greek *tripous* TRIPOD. The precise meaning of the Old English word is uncertain.

trivia *n.pl.* trifles, inessentials. WH: early 20C. Modern Latin, pl. of Latin *trivium*. See TRIVIAL.

trivial *a.* of little value or importance, trifling, inconsiderable. WH: 14–15C. Latin *trivialis*, from *trivium*, place where three ways meet, from TRI- + *via* way. Latin *trivialis* meant commonplace, vulgar, i.e. pertaining to the crossroads.

tri-weekly *a.* happening, issued or done three times a week or once every three weeks. WH: 19C. TRI- + *weekly* (WEEK).

-trix *suf.* forming feminine agent nouns. WH: Latin fem. suf. corr. to m. *-tor*.

troat *n.* the cry of a buck in rutting time. Also *v.i.* WH: 17C. Orig. uncertain. Cp. Old French *trout, trut* a cry to urge on hunting dogs.

trocar *n.* an instrument for draining an internal part of fluid, used in dropsy, hydrocele etc. WH: 18C. French *trocart*, also *trois-quarts*, from *trois* three + *carre* (Latin *quadra*) face (of an instrument). The instrument is so called from its triangular shape.

trochanter *n.* any one of several bony processes on the upper part of the thigh bone. WH: 17C. French, from Greek *trokhantēr*, from *trekhein* to run.

troche *n.* a lozenge, usu. circular, of medicinal substance. WH: 16C. Alt. of obs. *trochisk*, from French *trochisque*, from Late Latin *trochiscus*, from Greek *trokhiskos* small wheel, lozenge, pill, dim. of *trokhos* wheel.

trochee *n.* a metrical foot of two syllables, long and short. WH: 16C. Latin *trochaeus*, from Greek *trokhaios* (*pous*) running (foot), from *trokhos*, from *trekhein* to run.

trochil *n.* an Egyptian plover said by the ancients to enter the mouth of crocodiles and feed on parasites. WH: 16C. Latin *trochilus*, from Greek *trokhilos*, from *trekhein* to run.

trochlea *n.* a pulley-like anatomical part or surface, esp. that of the humerus articulating with the ulna. WH: 17C. Latin. Cp. Greek *trokhilia* sheave of a pulley.

trochoid *a.* rotating on its own axis, pivotal. Also *n.* WH: 18C. Greek *trokhoeidēs* wheel-like, from *trokhos* wheel. See also -OID.

trochophore *n.* a free-swimming ciliate larva of many invertebrates. WH: 19C. Greek *trokhos* wheel + -O- + -PHORE.

trog[1] *v.i.* to walk, esp. wearily. WH: late 20C. Orig. uncertain. ? Blend of TRUDGE, SLOG, JOG etc.

trog[2] *n.* a lout or hooligan. WH: mid-20C. Abbr. of TROGLODYTE.

troglodyte *n.* a cave dweller. WH: 15C. Latin *troglodyta*, from Greek *trōglodutēs*, from *trōglē* hole + *duein* to go in, to dive in.

trogon *n.* any of a family of tropical American insectivorous birds, the Trogonidae, with brilliant plumage. WH: 18C. Modern Latin, from Greek *trōgōn*, pres.p. of *trōgein* to gnaw.

troika *n.* a team of three horses harnessed abreast. WH: 19C. Russian *troĭka*, from *troe* set of three.

troilism *n.* sexual activity involving three people of both sexes. WH: mid-20C. ? French *trois* three. See also -ISM.

Trojan *a.* of or relating to ancient Troy. Also *n.* WH: 12–14C. Latin *Troianus*, from *Troia* Troy, an ancient city in Asia Minor. See also -AN.

troll[1] *v.t.* to roll or reel out (a song) in a careless manner. Also *v.i., n.* WH: 14–15C. Orig. uncertain. Cp. Old French *troller* (Modern French *trôler*) to quest, to wander casually, Middle High German *trollen* to stroll, to toddle.

troll[2] *n.* a giant or giantess in Scandinavian mythology, endowed with supernatural powers. WH: 14–15C. Swedish, from Old Norse, of unknown orig. Cp. Danish *trylla*, Swedish *trolla* to bewitch, to charm, Old Norse *trolldómr* witchcraft.

trolley *n.* a set of shelves with wheels, used for moving things, e.g. trays of food, around. WH: 19C. Of dial. orig., prob. from TROLL[1].

trollop *n.* a careless, slovenly woman, a slattern. WH: 17C. Orig. unknown. Cp. TRULL.

trombone *n.* a large and powerful wind instrument of the trumpet kind usu. played by means of a sliding tube. WH: 18C. French or Italian, from *tromba* TRUMP[2].

trommel *n.* a rotating cylindrical sieve for cleaning and sizing ore. WH: 19C. German drum.

tromometer *n.* an instrument for measuring earth tremors. WH: 19C. Greek *tromos* trembling + -METER.

trompe *n.* an apparatus worked by a descending column of water for producing a blast in a furnace. WH: 19C. French trumpet.

trompe l'œil *n.* (a painting etc. giving) a very deceptive appearance of reality. WH: 19C. French, lit. deceives the eye, 3rd pers. sing. pres. of *tromper* to deceive + *l'* the + *œil* eye.

-tron *suf.* elementary particle, as in *electron*. WH: Extracted from ELECTRON or from Greek instr. suf. *-tron*.

trona *n.* a native hydrous carbonate of soda. WH: 18C. Swedish, from Arabic *naṭrūn* NATRON.

tronc *n.* a system whereby waiters and other employees in a restaurant share in the tips. WH: early 20C. French collecting box, TRUNK.

troop *n.* an assemblage of persons or animals, a crowd, a company. Also *v.i., v.t.* WH: 16C. French *troupe*, back-formation from *troupeau* flock, herd, dim. of Medieval Latin *troppus* herd, prob. of Germanic orig. Cp. German *Dorf* village.

troopial *n.* any of various American orioles of the genus *Icterus*, in some respects resembling the starling. WH: 19C. French *troupiale*, alt. (based on *troupe* flock) of American Spanish *turpial*, of Carib orig.

tropaeolum *n.* a S American climbing plant of the genus *Tropaeolum*, with trumpet-shaped flowers. WH: 18C. Modern Latin, dim. of Latin *tropaeum* TROPHY. The plant is so called from the resemblance of its leaf to a shield and its flower to a helmet. The name was coined by Linnaeus in 1737.

trope *n.* a figurative use of a word. WH: 16C. Latin *tropus* figure of speech, from Greek *tropos* turn, rel. to *trepein* to turn.

-trope *comb. form* forming nouns indicating a turning towards or affinity for. WH: Greek *tropē* turn.

trophic *a.* of or relating to nutrition. WH: 19C. Greek *trophikos*, from *trophē* nourishment. See also -IC.

-trophic *comb. form* relating to nutrition. WH: TROPHIC.

tropho- *comb. form* nourishment. WH: Greek *trophē* nourishment, from *trephein* to nourish. See also -O-.

trophoblast *n.* a membrane enclosing the mammalian embryo which absorbs nourishment from the uterine fluids. WH: 19C. TROPHO- + -BLAST.

trophotropism *n.* the movement of the organs of a growing plant towards or away from nutrient substances, induced by the chemical nature of its surroundings. WH: 19C. TROPHO- + TROPISM.

trophy *n.* anything, esp. a cup, preserved as a memorial of victory or success. WH: 15C. French *trophée*, from Latin *trophaeum*, earlier *tropaeum*, from Greek *tropaion*, use as n. of neut. of *tropaios*, from *tropē* turning, putting to flight, defeat. The literal sense is a monument to mark the defeat of an enemy. The current sense evolved in the 16C.

-trophy *comb. form* a specified form of nourishment or growth. WH: Greek *trophē* nourishment.

tropic *n.* the parallel of latitude 23° 26′ north of the equator. Also *a.* WH: 14–15C. Latin *tropicus*, from Greek *tropikos* pertaining to a turn, from *tropē* turn. See also -IC. The tropic is so called with reference to the apparent turning of the sun at the solstice.

tropism *n.* the direction of growth in a plant or other organism that is due to an external stimulus. WH: 19C. Extracted from *heliotropism* (HELIOTROPE).

tropo- *comb. form* turn(ing). WH: Greek *tropos* turning. See TROPE, also -O-.

tropology *n.* the use of tropical or figurative language. WH: 14–15C. Late Latin *tropologia*, from Greek, from *tropos* TROPE + -O- + -LOGY.

tropopause *n.* the boundary between the troposphere and the stratosphere. WH: early 20C. TROPOSPHERE + PAUSE.

troposphere *n.* the hollow sphere of atmosphere surrounding the earth, bounded by the stratosphere, in which temperature varies and the weather functions. WH: early 20C. TROPO- + SPHERE.

troppo[1] *adv.* too much, excessively. WH: Italian too much.

troppo[2] *a.* affected mentally by a tropical climate; crazy. WH: mid-20C. TROPIC + -O.

Trot *n.* a Trotskyite or other left-winger. **WH:** mid-20C. Abbr. of *Trotskyite* (TROTSKYISM).

trot *v.i.* (of a horse or other quadruped) to move at a steady rapid pace by simultaneously lifting one forefoot and the hind foot of the opposite side alternately with the other pair, the body being unsupported at intervals. *Also v.t., n.* **WH:** 14–15C. Old French *troter* (Modern French *trotter*), from Latin *trottare*, of Germanic orig. Rel. to TREAD.

†troth *n.* faith, fidelity, truth. **WH:** 12–14C. Var. of TRUTH.

Trotskyism *n.* the political theories of Trotsky, esp. that of worldwide proletarian revolution. **WH:** early 20C. Leon *Trotsky*, 1879–1940, Russian revolutionary + -ISM.

troubadour *n.* any one of a class of lyric poets who flourished in Provence in the 11th cent., writing chiefly of love and chivalry. **WH:** 18C. French, from Provençal *trobador*, from *trobar* to compose in verse, to invent, to find. Cp. TROUVÈRE.

trouble *v.t.* to agitate, to disturb. *Also v.i., n.* **WH:** 12–14C. Old French *trubler* (Modern French *troubler*), from Popular Latin *turbulare*, alt. of Late Latin *turbidare*, from Latin *turbidus* TURBID.

trou-de-loup *n.* a conical pit with a stake in the centre, used against enemy cavalry. **WH:** 18C. French, lit. wolf-pit.

trough *n.* a long, narrow, open receptacle of wood, iron etc., e.g. for holding water, fodder etc., for domestic animals. **WH:** pre-1200. Old English *trog*, from Germanic, from Indo-European base also of TREE. Cp. TRUG.

trounce *v.t.* to beat severely. **WH:** 16C. Orig. unknown.

troupe *n.* a company of actors, performers etc. **WH:** 19C. French TROOP.

trousers *n.pl.* a two-legged outer garment reaching from the waist to the ankles; also called *pair of trousers*. **WH:** 17C. Extension (with added *r*) of *trouse* (14–15C) garment from the waist to the knees, from Irish *triús* or Gaelic *truibhas* (sing.), ult. of unknown orig. Cp. TREWS.

trousseau *n.* the clothes and general outfit of a bride. **WH:** 12–14C. French, dim. of *trousse* TRUSS.

trout *n.* any of various freshwater fishes of the genus *Salmo* or *Salvelinus*, esp. *Salmo trutta*. *Also v.i.* **WH:** pre-1200. Old English *truht*, from Late Latin *tructa*, from Greek *trōktēs* gnawer, a marine fish, from *trōgein* to gnaw.

trouvaille *n.* a lucky find. **WH:** 19C. French, from *trouver* to find.

trouvère *n.* a medieval poet of N France, composing chiefly narrative poems. **WH:** 18C. Old French *trovere* (Modern French *trouvère*, *trouveur*), from *troveor*, from *trover* (Modern French *trouver* to find) to compose in verse, to invent, to find, ult. of unknown orig. Cp. TROUBADOUR.

trover *n.* the acquisition or appropriation of any goods. **WH:** 16C. Anglo-French use as n. of Old French *trover* (Modern French *trouver*). See TROUVÈRE, also -ER[4].

†trow *v.t., v.i.* to think, to suppose, to believe. **WH:** pre-1200. From Old English *trēowian*, *trēowan*, from *trēow* (TRUCE), partly from Old English *trūwian*, from Germanic. Cp. TRUE.

trowel *n.* a flat-bladed, usu. pointed, tool used by masons etc., for spreading mortar etc. *Also v.t.* **WH:** 12–14C. Old French *truele* (Modern French *truelle*), from Medieval Latin *truella*, alt. of Latin *trulla* ladle, scoop, from *trua* skimmer, spoon.

troy *n.* a system of weights (based on the grain, in which one pound troy equals 12 oz. av. (340 g) or 5760 grains) used chiefly in weighing gold, silver and gems. **WH:** 14–15C. Prob. from a weight used at the fair of *Troyes*, a city in N France.

truant *n.* a child who stays away from school without leave. *Also a., v.i.* **WH:** 12–14C. Old French (Modern French *truand*) beggar, vagabond, rogue, prob. of Celtic orig. Cp. Welsh *truan* wretched, miserable. The current sense evolved in the 14–15C.

truce *n.* a temporary cessation of hostilities. **WH:** pre-1200. Old English *trēowa*, pl. (used as sing.) of *trēow*, corr. to Old Frisian *trouwe*, Old High German *triuwa* (German *Treue*), from Germanic base also of TRUE. Cp. TROW. The *-ce* of the modern word represents -S[1].

truck[1] *n.* a strong, usu. four-wheeled vehicle for conveying heavy goods; a lorry. *Also v.t., v.i.* **WH:** 12–14C. ? Shortening of TRUCKLE.

truck[2] *n.* exchange of commodities. *Also v.t., v.i.* **WH:** 12–14C. From unrecorded Anglo-French and Old French vv. reflected in Medieval Latin *trocare* to barter, of unknown orig. The noun evolved from the verb in the 16C.

truckle *v.i.* to give way obsequiously (to the will of another), to cringe, to be servile (to). *Also n.* **WH:** 14–15C. Anglo-French *trocle*, from Latin *trochlea*, from Greek *trokhilia* sheave of a pulley. The original sense was a small wheel in a pulley block, then a small roller or wheel placed under a heavy object to move it, then a low bed (*truckle-bed*) on such rollers. The verb arose in the 17C, originally in the sense to sleep in a truckle-bed, hence to take a subordinate position, to submit.

truculent *a.* defiant or sullen. **WH:** 16C. Latin *truculentus*, from *trux, trucis* fierce, savage. See also -ULENT.

trudge *v.i.* to travel on foot, esp. with labour and fatigue. *Also v.t., n.* **WH:** 16C. Orig. unknown.

trudgen *n.* a swimming stroke with the arms brought over the head alternately, and a scissors leg action. **WH:** 19C. John *Trudgen*, 1852–1902, English swimmer, who first demonstrated the stroke in 1873.

true *a.* conformable to fact or reality, not false or erroneous. *Also v.t., adv.* **WH:** pre-1200. Old English *trīewe*, *trēowe*, from Germanic base also of TRUCE. Cp. TROW.

truffle *n.* any fleshy fungus of the order Tuberales, used for seasoning etc. **WH:** 16C. Prob. from Dutch *truffel*, from obs. French *truffle* (now *truffe*), ? ult. from Popular Latin var. of Latin *tubera*, pl. of TUBER.

trug *n.* a wooden basket used by gardeners, greengrocers etc. **WH:** 14–15C. ? Dial. var. of TROUGH.

truism *n.* a self-evident or unquestionable truth. **WH:** 18C. TRUE + -ISM.

†trull *n.* a prostitute. **WH:** 16C. German *Trulle*. Cp. TROLLOP.

truly *adv.* sincerely. **WH:** pre-1200. TRUE + -LY[2].

trumeau *n.* a piece of wall, a pier or pillar, between two openings or dividing a doorway. **WH:** 19C. French, lit. calf of the leg. Cp. JAMB (from French *jambe* leg).

trump[1] *n.* any card of a suit ranking for the time being above the others. *Also v.t., v.i.* **WH:** 16C. Alt. of TRIUMPH.

†trump[2] *n.* a trumpet blast. **WH:** 12–14C. Old French *trompe*, from Frankish *trumpa*, of imit. orig.

trumpery *n.* worthless finery. *Also a.* **WH:** 14–15C. Old French *tromperie*, from *tromper* to deceive, of unknown orig. See also -ERY.

trumpet *n.* a musical wind instrument, usu. consisting of a long, straight, curved or coiled tube with a wide termination, usu. of brass, with a cup-shaped mouthpiece. *Also v.t., v.i.* **WH:** 12–14C. Old French *trompette*, dim. of *trompe* TRUMP[2]. See also -ET[1].

truncate[1] *v.t.* to cut the top or end from. **WH:** 15C. Latin *truncatus*, p.p. of *truncare* to maim. See also -ATE[3].

truncate[2] *a.* cut short, truncated. **WH:** 16C. Latin *truncatus*, p.p. of *truncare*. See TRUNCATE[1], also -ATE[2].

truncheon *n.* a short staff, club or cudgel, esp. one carried by a police officer in Britain. *Also v.t.* **WH:** 12–14C. Old French *tronchon* (Modern French *tronçon*), from Popular Latin *truncio, truncionis*, from Latin *truncus* TRUNK. The original sense was a fragment of a spear or lance but the sense policeman's club has also been current from the first.

trundle *v.t., v.i.* to move heavily (as if) on wheels. *Also n.* **WH:** 16C. Var. of Old English *trendel* ring, disc, from Germanic. See also -LE[1]. Cp. TREND.

trunk *n.* the main stem of a tree, as opposed to the branches or roots. **WH:** 14–15C. Old French *tronc*, from Latin *truncus*. The sense elephant's proboscis arose in the 16C, apparently by association with TRUMP[2]. The plural sense short breeches arose in the 19C from earlier *trunk-hose*.

trunnion *n.* a cylindrical projection on the side of a cannon or mortar. **WH:** 17C. Old French *trognon* core of fruit, trunk of a tree, of unknown orig.

truss *v.t.* to support or brace with a truss. *Also n.* **WH:** 12–14C. Old French *trusser* (Modern French *trousser*), Medieval Latin *trossare*, prob. from Late Latin *torsus*, p.p. of *torquere* to twist.

trust *n.* confident reliance on or belief in the integrity, veracity, justice, friendship, power, protection etc. of a person or thing. *Also v.t., v.i.* **WH:** 12–14C. Old Norse *traust*, rel. to *tryggr* TRUE.

truth *n.* the state or quality of being true. **WH:** pre-1200. Old English *trīewth, trēowth.* See TRUE, also -TH².

try *v.t.* to test, to examine by experiment. *Also v.i., n.* **WH:** 12–14C. Old French *trier* to sift, to pick out, of unknown orig. The original sense was to distinguish, to separate out, to select. The sense to test also dates from the first, and in the 16C this gave the sense to attempt to find out by experiment.

tryma *n.* a drupelike fruit, the outer wall of the pericarp of which is dehiscent, as in the walnut. **WH:** 19C. Greek *truma* hole, from *truein* to rub down.

trypanosome *n.* any protozoan parasite of the genus *Trypanosoma,* causing sleeping sickness and other diseases. **WH:** early 20C. Modern Latin *Trypanosoma,* genus name, from Greek *trupanon* borer + *sōma* body.

trypsin *n.* a ferment contained in the pancreatic juice etc. **WH:** 19C. Appar. from Greek *tripsis,* from *tribein* to rub. The ferment is so called because it was first obtained by rubbing down the pancreas with glycerine.

†tryst *n.* an appointed meeting, an appointment. *Also v.i., v.t.* **WH:** 14–15C. Var. of obs. *trist,* from Old French *triste* or Medieval Latin *trista,* ? rel. to TRUST.

tsar *n.* the emperor of Russia. **WH:** 16C. Russian *tsar',* Old Church Slavonic *cěsarĭ,* ult. representing Latin CAESAR, prob. through Germanic.

tsessebi *n.* a large southern African antelope, *Damaliscus lunatus.* **WH:** 19C. Setswana *tsessébe, tsessábi.*

tsetse *n.* any fly of the genus *Glossina,* the bite of which is often fatal to cattle, horses, dogs etc., and transmits to humans the trypanosomes of sleeping sickness. **WH:** 19C. Setswana.

tsk *int., n., v.i.* TUT-TUT. **WH:** mid-20C. Imit.

tsotsi *n.* a violent criminal operating esp. in black townships. **WH:** mid-20C. ? Nguni *-tsotsa* to dress in exaggerated clothing.

tsunami *n.* a very large wave at sea caused by a submarine earthquake, volcanic eruption etc. **WH:** 19C. Japanese, from *tsu* harbour + *nami* wave.

tsutsugamushi disease *n.* an acute infectious rickettsial disease common in Asia, esp. scrub typhus. **WH:** early 20C. Japanese dangerous insect, from *tsutsuga* harm, evil, hurt + *mushi* insect (+ DISEASE).

Tswana *n.* a member of a southern African people living chiefly in Botswana. *Also a.* **WH:** mid-20C. Bantu. Cp. SETSWANA.

tuan¹ *n.* a flying phalanger, *Phascogale tapoatafa,* of Australia. **WH:** 19C. Australian Aboriginal (Wathawurung) *duwan.*

tuan² *n.* (in Malay-speaking countries) sir, lord (used as a title of respect). **WH:** 18C. Malay.

Tuareg *n.* a member of a nomadic Berber people of the Sahara. **WH:** 19C. Berber.

tuart *n.* a W Australian tree, *Eucalyptus gomphocephala,* yielding an intensely hard and durable wood valuable for boat-building. **WH:** 19C. Australian Aboriginal (Nyungar) *duward.*

tuatara *n.* the largest New Zealand reptile, the lizard-like *Sphenodon punctatum,* now the last survivor of the class Rhyncocephalia. **WH:** 19C. Maori, from *tua* on the back + *tara* spine. The reptile is so named from the row of yellow spines down its back.

tub *n.* an open wooden (usu. round) vessel constructed of staves held together by hoops, used for washing, holding butter etc. *Also v.t., v.i.* **WH:** 12–14C. Prob. from Low Dutch. Cp. Middle Low German and Middle Dutch *tubbe,* Dutch *tobbe.*

tuba *n.* a brass wind instrument of the saxhorn kind, with a low pitch. **WH:** 14–15C. Italian, from Latin.

tube *n.* a long hollow cylinder for the conveyance of fluids and various other purposes, a pipe. *Also v.t.* **WH:** 17C. French, or from Latin *tubus,* rel. to TUBA.

tuber *n.* a short, thick portion of an underground stem, set with eyes or modified buds, as in the potato. **WH:** 17C. Latin hump, swelling. Cp. TRUFFLE.

tubercle *n.* a small prominence, esp. in bone. **WH:** 16C. Latin *tuberculum,* dim. of TUBER. See also -CLE, -CULE.

tuberose¹ *a.* tuberous. **WH:** 14–15C. Latin *tuberosus,* from TUBER. See also -OSE¹.

tuberose² *n.* a bulbous plant, *Polianthes tuberosa,* with fragrant white flowers. **WH:** 17C. Latin *tuberosa,* fem. of *tuberosus* TUBEROSE¹.

The plant is so named from its tuberous root. The word is not related to ROSE.

tubi- *comb. form* tube. **WH:** Latin *tubus* TUBE.

tubicolous *a.* inhabiting a tubular case. **WH:** 19C. TUBI- + -COLOUS.

tubifex *n.* any reddish annelid worm of the genus *Tubifex,* used as food for aquarium fish. **WH:** mid-20C. TUBI- + Latin *-fex,* from *facere* to make, to do.

tubiform *a.* having the shape of a tube. **WH:** 18C. TUBI- + -FORM.

tubular *a.* tube-shaped. **WH:** 17C. Latin *tubulus* small tube. See also -AR¹.

tuchun *n.* a Chinese military governor or warlord. **WH:** early 20C. Chinese *dūjūn,* from *dū* to govern + *jūn* military.

tuck¹ *v.t.* to press close together or press, fold, or roll the loose ends or parts of compactly (up, in etc.). *Also v.i., n.* **WH:** pre-1200. Old English *tūcian,* from Germanic base rel. also to TUG. Cp. German *zucken* to twitch, to snatch. The original sense (to the 12–14C) was to punish, to chastise, to torment. The current sense dates from the 14–15C.

tuck² *n.* the beat or roll of a drum. **WH:** 14–15C. Old Northern French *toquer* to touch, to strike, var. of Old French *tochier* TOUCH.

†tuck³ *n.* a long, narrow sword, a rapier. **WH:** 16C. Prob. from French dial. *étoc,* Old French and Provençal *estoc,* from Germanic. Cp. German *Stock* stick.

tucker¹ *n.* an ornamental frilling of lace or muslin round the top of a woman's dress, covering the neck and shoulders, worn in the 17–18C. **WH:** 14–15C. TUCK¹ + -ER¹.

tucker² *v.t.* to exhaust (often with *out*). **WH:** 19C. TUCK¹ + -ER⁵.

†tucket *n.* a flourish on a trumpet, a fanfare. **WH:** 16C. TUCK² + -ET¹.

tucotuco *n.* any of various burrowing S American rodents of the genus *Ctenomys.* **WH:** 19C. Imit. of the cry of some species.

-tude *suf.* forming abstract nouns, as in *altitude, beatitude, fortitude.* **WH:** French, from Latin *-tudo, -tudinis.*

Tudor *a.* of or relating to the English royal line (from Henry VII to Elizabeth I) founded by Owen Tudor. *Also n.* **WH:** 18C. Owen *Tudor, c.*1400–61, Welsh squire who married Catherine of Valois, widow of Henry V.

Tuesday *n.* the third day of the week, following Monday. *Also adv.* **WH:** pre-1200. Old English *Tīwesdæg,* from gen. of *Tīw,* a Teutonic god identified with Mars (from Germanic word rel. to Latin *deus* god) + *dæg* DAY, translating Latin *dies Marti* day of Mars. Cp. French *mardi* Tuesday.

tufa *n.* a soft calcareous rock deposited by springs and streams. **WH:** 18C. Italian, obs. local var. of *tufo,* from Late Latin *tofus* TOPHUS. Cp. TUFF.

tuff *n.* an earthy, sometimes fragmentary, deposit of volcanic materials of the most heterogeneous kind. **WH:** 16C. French *tuffe, tufe,* from Italian *tufo.* See TUFA.

tuffet *n.* a tuft of grass etc. **WH:** 16C. Alt. of TUFT.

tuft *n.* a cluster, a bunch, a collection of hairs, threads, feathers, grass etc. held or fastened together at one end. *Also v.t., v.i.* **WH:** 12–14C. Prob. from Old French *toffe, tofe* (Modern French *touffe*), of unknown orig. Cp. TOFF, TUFFET. For alt. of *-ff* to *-ft,* cp. GRAFT¹.

tug *v.t.* to pull or draw with great effort or with violence. *Also v.i., n.* **WH:** 12–14C. From base also of TOW¹.

tugrik *n.* the standard unit of currency in Mongolia. **WH:** mid-20C. Mongolian *dughurik,* lit. round thing, wheel.

tui *n.* a New Zealand honeyeater, *Prosthemadura novaeseelandiae.* **WH:** 19C. Maori.

tuition *n.* teaching, instruction, esp. in a particular subject or group of subjects and separately paid for. **WH:** 14–15C. Old French, from Latin *tuitio, tuitionis* protection, from *tuitus,* p.p. of *tueri* to watch, to guard. See also -ITION. The original sense (to the 18C) was the action of looking after, protection. The sense teaching evolved in the 16C. Cp. TUTOR.

tularaemia *n.* an acute infectious bacterial disease of rodents, sometimes communicated to humans by flea or tick bites, causing fever etc. **WH:** early 20C. Modern Latin *tularensis,* specific epithet, from *Tulare* a county in California. See -AEMIA.

tulip *n.* any plant of the genus *Tulipa,* bulbous plants of the lily family, with bell-shaped flowers of various colours. **WH:** 16C. Obs. French *tulipan* (now *tulipe*), from Turkish *tülbend,* from Persian *dulband* TURBAN. The plant is so called from the shape of the flower when in full bloom.

tulle *n.* a fine silk net, used for veils etc. WH: 19C. *Tulle*, a town in SW France, where originally made.

tum[1] *n.* the stomach. WH: 19C. Abbr. of STOMACH. Cp. TUMMY.

tum[2] *n.* the sound of a stringed musical instrument like the banjo. WH: 19C. Imit.

tumble *v.i.* to fall (down etc.) suddenly or violently. *Also v.t., n.* WH: 12–14C. Middle Low German *tummelen*, rel. to Old High German *tumalōn* (German *tummeln*), freq. from base of Old High German *tūmōn*, *tūmalōn* (German *taumeln*). See also -LE[4]. Cp. Old English *tumbian* to dance, Old Norse *tumba* to tumble.

tumbler *n.* a person who or thing which tumbles. WH: 12–14C. TUMBLE + -ER[1]. The earliest sense is an acrobat. The sense drinking vessel arose in the 17C. It is so called as it originally had a rounded base so could not stand upright.

tumbril *n.* a two-wheeled cart for carrying ammunition and tools for mining and sapping. WH: 12–14C. Old French *tumberel*, *tomberel* (Modern French *tombereau*), from *tomber* to fall. See also -EL. Cp. TUMBLE. The word was originally the term for an instrument of punishment, from the 16C identified with a cucking-stool. The sense open cart dates from the 14–15C.

tumid *a.* swollen, enlarged, distended. WH: 16C. Latin *tumidus*, from *tumere* to swell. See also -ID.

tummy *n.* the stomach. WH: 19C. Alt. of STOMACH. Cp. TUM[1].

tumour *n.* a swelling on some part of the body, esp. if due to an abnormal growth of tissue. WH: 14–15C. Latin *tumor*, from *tumere* to swell. See also -OR.

tump *n.* a hillock, a mound. *Also v.t.* WH: 16C. Orig. unknown.

tum-tum *n.* a W Indian dish of boiled plantain beaten soft. WH: 19C. Orig. unknown.

tumult *n.* the commotion, disturbance or agitation of a multitude, esp. with a confusion of sounds. WH: 14–15C. Old French *tumulte*, or from Latin *tumultus*. Cp. Sanskrit *tumula* noisy. Not rel. to MULTITUDE.

tumulus *n.* a mound of earth, sometimes combined with masonry, usu. sepulchral, a barrow. WH: 14–15C. Latin, rel. to *tumere* to swell.

tun *n.* a large cask, esp. for alcoholic liquors. *Also v.t.* WH: pre-1200. Old English *tunne*, corr. to Middle Low German and Middle Dutch *tunne*, *tonne* (Dutch *ton*), Old High German *tunna* (German *Tonne*), from Medieval Latin *tunna*, prob. of Gaulish orig. Cp. TON[1].

tuna[1] *n.* any marine fish of the family Scombridae found in warmer waters; also called *tunny*. WH: 19C. American Spanish, ? rel. to Latin *thunnus*, *tunnus* tunny.

tuna[2] *n.* a prickly pear, esp. *Opuntia tuna*, or its fruit. WH: 16C. Spanish, from Taino.

tundra *n.* a marshy treeless plain in the Arctic and subarctic regions, with permanently frozen subsoil and covered largely with mosses and lichens. WH: 16C. Russian, from Lappish *tundar* elevated wasteland.

tune *n.* a melodious succession of musical tones forming a coherent whole, an air, a melody, esp. as a setting for a song, hymn etc. *Also v.t., v.i.* WH: 14–15C. Alt. of TONE. The reason for the variant form is unknown. The original sense (to the 19C) was sound, tone, especially the sound of the voice. The current sense of melody gradually evolved from this.

tung *n.* a tree of the genus *Aleurites*. WH: 19C. Chinese *tóng*.

tungsten *n.* a heavy, greyish-white metallic element, at. no. 74, chem. symbol W, of unusually high melting point; also called *wolfram*. WH: 18C. Swedish, from *tung* heavy + *sten* stone. The name was coined by K.W. Scheele, the discoverer of SCHEELITE.

Tungus *n.* a member of a people occupying parts of Siberia and China. WH: 17C. Yakut.

tunic *n.* a military or police officer's jacket. WH: pre-1200. Old French *tunique* or Latin *tunica*, prob. from Semitic. Cp. CHITIN.

tunnel *n.* an artificial underground passage or gallery, esp. one under a hill, river etc., for a railway, road or canal. *Also v.t., v.i.* WH: 14–15C. Old French *tonel* (Modern French *tonneau* tun, cask), from *tonne* TUN. See also -EL. The original sense (to the 19C) was the shaft or flue of a chimney. The current sense dates from the 18C.

tunny *n.* TUNA[1]. WH: 16C. Old French *thon*, from Provençal *ton*, corr. to Italian *tonno*, from Latin *thunnus*, from Greek *thunnos*. The -*y* ending is unexplained.

tup *n.* a ram or male sheep. *Also v.t., v.i.* WH: 12–14C. Orig. unknown.

Tupamaro *n.* a member of a Marxist urban guerrilla group in Uruguay. WH: mid-20C. *Tupac Amaru* I, d.1571, and II, *c.*1740–81, Inca leaders. Tupac Amaru II, born José Gabriel Condorcanqui, was a descendant of Tupac Amaru I and was identified with him.

tupelo *n.* a N American or Asian tree of the genus *Nyssa*, living in swampy conditions. WH: 18C. Creek *ito* tree + *opilwa* swamp.

Tupi *n.* a member of a S American people of the Amazon region. *Also a.* WH: 19C. American Indian name.

tupik *n.* an Eskimo (Inuit) animal-skin tent. WH: 19C. Eskimo (Inuit) *tupiq*.

Tupperware® *n.* a range of plastic kitchen equipment, esp. food containers. WH: mid-20C. *Tupper* Corporation, its US manufacturers + WARE[1]. The business was founded in 1938 by Earl S. *Tupper*, an American chemical engineer, as the Tupperware Plastics Company.

tuque *n.* a Canadian cap made by tucking in one end of a knitted cylindrical bag both ends of which are closed. WH: 19C. Canadian French, from French TOQUE.

turaco *n.* any African bird of the family Musophagidae, which have crimson and green plumage. WH: 18C. French *touraco*, from a W African name.

Turanian *n.* the group of Asian languages that are neither Indo-European nor Semitic, esp. the Ural-Altaic group. *Also a.* WH: 18C. Persian *Tūrān*, the region north of the Oxus + -IAN.

turban *n.* a (Muslim or Sikh) man's headdress consisting of a sash or scarf wound round a cap or the head. WH: 16C. Obs. French *tolliban*, *tulban*, *turbant*, obs. Italian *tolipano* (now *turbante*), from Turkish *tülbend*, from Persian *dulband*. Cp. TULIP.

turbary *n.* the right of digging turf on another's land. WH: 14–15C. Old French *tourberie*, from *tourbe* TURF. See also -ARY[1].

turbellarian *n.* any flatworm of the class Turbellaria, with ciliated skin. *Also a.* WH: 19C. Modern Latin *Turbellaria*, from Latin *turbella* bustle, stir, dim. of *turba* crowd. See also -ARY[1], -AN.

turbid *a.* muddy, discoloured, thick, unclear. WH: 14–15C. Latin *turbidus* full of confusion, muddy, from *turba* crowd, disturbance. See also -ID. Ult. rel. to STIR[1].

turbinate *a.* top-shaped, like an inverted cone. WH: 17C. Latin *turbinatus*, from *turbo*, *turbinis* TURBO[2]. See also -ATE[2].

turbine *n.* a waterwheel or motor enclosed in a case or tube in which a flowing stream acts by direct impact or reaction upon a series of vanes or buckets. WH: 19C. French, or from Latin *turbo*, *turbinis* TURBO[2].

turbit *n.* a variety of domestic pigeon with a flattened head and short beak. WH: 17C. Appar. from Latin *turbo* (TURBO[2]), so called from its shape.

turbo[1] *n.* a model of car etc. incorporating a turbocharger. WH: early 20C. Abbr. of *turbocharger*. See TURBO-, CHARGE.

turbo[2] *n.* any gastropod of the genus *Turbo*. WH: 17C. Modern Latin, from Latin *turbo*, *turbinis* spinning top, whirlwind, whirl, twirl. The gastropods are so called from their shape.

turbo- *comb. form* having or driven by a turbine. WH: TURBINE. See also -O-.

turbot *n.* a large European flatfish, *Scophthalmus maximus*, with bony tubercles, highly valued as food. WH: 12–14C. Old French, from Old Swedish *tornbut*, from *törn* THORN + *but* BUTT[5]. Cp. HALIBUT. The fish is so called from its 'thorns' (spines).

turbulent *a.* disturbed, tumultuous. WH: 14–15C. Latin *turbulentus*, from *turba* crowd, *turbare* to disturb, to agitate. See also -ULENT.

Turco *n.* an Algerian sharpshooter in the French army. WH: 20C. Spanish, Portuguese and Italian TURK.

Turco- *comb. form* Turkish; Turkish and. WH: Medieval Latin *Turcus* TURK + -O-.

turd *n.* a lump of excrement or dung. WH: pre-1200. Old English *tord*, from Germanic. Cp. Old English *tordwifel*, Old Norse *tordýfill* dung-beetle.

turdine *a.* of, resembling or characteristic of thrushes. WH: 19C. Latin *turdus* thrush + -INE.

tureen *n.* a deep covered dish or vessel for holding soup etc. WH: 18C. Alt. of TERRINE, ? influ. by *Turin*, a city in N Italy.

turf *n.* surface earth filled with the matted roots of grass and other small plants. *Also v.t.* WH: pre-1200. Old English, from Germanic, from Indo-European base represented also by Sanskrit *darbha* tuft of grass. Cp. German *Torf.*

turgid *a.* swollen, bloated, morbidly distended, tumid. WH: 17C. Latin *turgidus*, from *turgere* to swell. See also -ID.

Turing machine *n.* a hypothetical computer that can write its own program. WH: mid-20C. A.M. *Turing*, 1912–54, English mathematician.

turion *n.* a young scaly shoot rising from the ground, as in asparagus. WH: 18C. French, from Latin *turio.*

Turk *n.* a native or inhabitant of Turkey. WH: 14–15C. French *Turc*, Italian, Spanish and Portuguese *Turco*, Medieval Latin *turcus*, Byzantine Greek *Tourkos*, from Turkish *türk* Turk, prob. ult. a Turkish name. The Turks gave the name of *Turkey*, a country in SW Asia and SE Europe between the Mediterranean and the Black Sea. Cp. TURKEY.

turkey *n.* a large gallinaceous bird, *Meleagris gallopavo*, allied to the pheasant, orig. introduced from America. WH: 16C. Short for *turkeycock* (TURKEY), appar. orig. the guinea fowl, a bird native to Africa imported through Turkey (TURK). Subsequent confusion between the two birds led to the name's passing to the American bird.

Turki *a.* of or relating to the Turkic languages or their speakers. *Also n.* WH: 18C. Persian *turkī*, from *turk* TURK.

Turkish *a.* of or relating to Turkey or the Turks or their language. *Also n.* WH: 16C. TURK + -ISH[1].

Turkmen *n.* a member of any of various Turkic peoples of Turkmenistan and parts of Iran and Afghanistan. *Also a.* WH: early 20C. Persian *turkmān*, from Turkish *türkmen*, from *türk* TURK + *-man*, prob. augm. suf. Cp. TURKOMAN.

Turkoman *n.* a Turkmen. *Also a.* WH: 17C. Medieval Latin *Turcomannus*, French *turcoman*, from Persian *turkmān*. See TURKMEN. Not rel. to MAN.

turmeric *n.* an Asian plant, *Curcuma longa*, of the ginger family. WH: 14–15C. Appar. from French *terre mérite*, Modern Latin *terra merita*, lit. deserving earth, ? alt. of an Oriental word, with ending assim. to -IC. The French or Modern Latin derivation is appropriate for a plant that grows underground and that thus has its essence imparted from the earth.

turmoil *n.* a commotion, disturbance, tumult. *Also v.t.* WH: 16C. Orig. unknown. According to some, the word is an alteration (influenced by TURN and MOIL) of Old French *tremouille* mill hopper, with reference to the constant motion to and fro.

turn *v.t.* to cause to move round on or as on an axis, to give a rotary motion to. *Also v.i.*, *n.* WH: pre-1200. Old English *tyrnan, turnian*, from Latin *tornare* to turn in a lathe, to round off, from *tornus* lathe, from Greek *tornos* lathe, circular movement.

turnip *n.* a plant, *Brassica rapa*, with a fleshy globular root used as a vegetable and for feeding sheep. WH: 16C. From 1st element of unknown orig. + NEEP. Cp. PARSNIP.

turpentine *n.* an oleoresin exuding naturally or from incisions in several coniferous trees, esp. the terebinth. *Also v.t.* WH: 12–14C. Old French *terebentine*, from Latin *terebenthina*, from *terebinthus* TEREBINTH. See also -INE.

turpeth *n.* the root of an Asian plant, *Ipomoea turpethum*, used as a drastic purgative. WH: 14–15C. Medieval Latin *turbithum, turpetum*, from Persian *turbid*, from Sanskrit *triputā.*

turpitude *n.* baseness, depravity. WH: 15C. French, or from Latin *turpitudo, turpitudinis*, from *turpis* base, disgraceful. See also -TUDE.

turquoise *n.* a sky-blue or bluish-green translucent or opaque precious stone. *Also a.* WH: 14–15C. Old French *turqueise*, later *turquoise*, from *pierre turqueise*, lit. Turkish stone. The stone is so called because it was originally found in Turkestan or the Turkish dominions.

turret *n.* a small tower attached to a building, and rising above it. WH: 12–14C. Old French *torete, tourete*, dim. of *tur, tor, tour* TOWER. See also -ET[1].

turriculate *a.* (of shells) having a long spire. WH: 19C. Latin *turriculatus*, dim. of *turris* tower + -ATE[2] (+ -ED).

turtle *n.* a marine reptile of the order Chelonia, encased in a carapace, like a tortoise, with flippers used in swimming. *Also v.i.* WH: 16C. ? Alt. of French *tortue* TORTOISE or from a Bermudian name.

turtle-dove *n.* any wild dove of the genus *Streptopelia*, esp. *S. turtur*, noted for its soft cooing and its devotion to its mate and young. WH: 12–14C. From obs. *turtle* turtle-dove, from Old English *turtla, turtle*, from Latin *turtur*, of imit. orig. + DOVE.

Tuscan *n.* a native or inhabitant of Tuscany. *Also a.* WH: 14–15C. Old French (Modern French *toscan*), Italian *toscano*, from Latin *Tuscanus*, from *Tusci*, pl. of *Tuscus*, corr. to *Etruscus* ETRUSCAN. The *Tusci* gave the name of Tuscany, a region of W Italy.

tusche *n.* a substance used in lithography for drawing in the design which resists the printing medium. WH: 19C. German, backformation from *tuschen*, from French *toucher* to touch.

†tush[1] *int.* used to express contempt or impatience. WH: 14–15C. Natural exclamation. Cp. PISH, TUT-TUT.

tush[2] *n.* a long pointed tooth, esp. a horse's canine tooth. WH: pre-1200. Old English *tusc*. See TUSK.

tush[3] *n.* the buttocks. WH: mid-20C. Abbr. or dim. of *tokus*, from Yiddish *tokhes*, from Hebrew *taḥaṭ* beneath.

tusk *n.* a long pointed tooth, esp. one permanently protruding from the mouth as in the elephant, narwhal etc. *Also v.t.* WH: pre-1200. Old English *tux* (var. of *tusc* TUSH[1]), rel. to Old Frisian *tusk, tosk* and prob. ult. to TOOTH.

tussis *n.* a cough. WH: 19C. Latin cough.

tussle *v.i.* to struggle, to scuffle (with or for). *Also n.* WH: 14–15C. Appar. orig. Scottish and dial., ? from *touse* (TOUSLE). See also -LE[4]. The original sense was to pull or push about roughly. The current sense evolved in the 17C.

tussock *n.* a clump, tuft or hillock of growing grass. WH: 16C. Prob. alt. of obs. *tusk* tuft of grass, of unknown orig., assim. to words in -OCK.

tussore *n.* an Indian silkworm moth, *Antheraea mylitta*, feeding on the jujube tree etc. WH: 16C. Hindi *tasar, ṭasar*, appar. from Sanskrit *tasara* shuttle. The spelling with -ore was probably influenced by Indian place names such as *Mysore.*

tutelage *n.* guardianship. WH: 17C. Latin *tutela* keeping, from *tutus.* See TUTOR, also -AGE.

tutenag *n.* zinc or spelter from China or SE Asia. WH: 17C. Portuguese *tutunaga, tutenaga*, from Tamil *tuttunākam.* Cp. Kannada *tuttu, tutte* copper sulphate, Sanskrit *nāga* tin, lead, ult. from Akkadian *anāku* tin.

tutiorism *n.* in the Roman Catholic Church, the doctrine that in cases of moral doubt the course should be followed that seems the safer or more in accord with the letter of the law. WH: 19C. Latin *tutior*, comp. of *tutus* safe, from *tutus.* See TUTOR, also -ISM.

tutor *n.* a private teacher, esp. one having the general care and instruction of a pupil in preparation for a university etc. *Also v.t.*, *v.i.* WH: 14–15C. Old French *tutour* (Modern French *tuteur*) or Latin *tutor*, from *tutus*, p.p. of *tueri* to watch, to look after, to protect. See also -OR. The original sense (to the 17C) was custodian, keeper, protector, but the current sense private teacher was also in use from the first. (The sense university teacher evolved in the 17C.)

tutsan *n.* a species of St John's wort, *Hypericum androsaemum*, formerly held to be a panacea for wounds etc. WH: 14–15C. French *toute-saine*, from *toute*, fem. of *tout* all + *saine*, fem. of *sain* healthy.

Tutsi *n.* a member of a Bantu-speaking people in Rwanda. *Also a.* WH: mid-20C. Bantu.

tutti *adv.* all together. *Also n.* WH: 18C. Italian, pl. of *tutto* all, from Latin *totus.*

tutti-frutti *n.* a confection, such as ice cream, made of or flavoured with different fruits. WH: 19C. Italian all fruits. Cp. TUTTI.

tut-tut *int.* used to express disapproval, impatience or contempt. *Also n.*, *v.i.* WH: 16C. Natural exclamation. Cp. TSK.

tutty *n.* an impure oxide of zinc collected from the flues of smelting furnaces, used as polishing powder. WH: 12–14C. Old French *tutie*, from Medieval Latin *tutia*, from Arabic *tūtiyā.*

tutu[1] *n.* a New Zealand shrub, *Coriaria arborea*, with poisonous berries. WH: 19C. Maori.

tutu[2] *n.* a ballet dancer's short, stiff skirt that spreads outwards. WH: early 20C. French, childish alt. of *cucu*, dim. of *cul* buttocks, bottom.

tu-whit tu-whoo *int.*, *n.* used to imitate the cry of an owl. WH: 16C. Imit. The phrase is first recorded in Shakespeare's *Love's Labour's Lost* (1594).

tuxedo *n.* a dinner jacket. WH: 19C. *Tuxedo* Park in New York, USA, location of a country club where it was first worn.

tuyère *n.* the blast-pipe or nozzle in a furnace, forge etc. WH: 18C. French, from *tuyau* pipe.

twaddle *v.i.* to talk unmeaningly. Also *n.* WH: 18C. Alt. of TWATTLE.

†**twain** *a.* two. Also *n.* WH: pre-1200. Old English *twegen* TWO.

twang *v.i.* to make a ringing metallic sound as by plucking the string of a musical instrument. Also *v.t., n.* WH: 16C. Imit., with -*w*- representing the reverberation of the string. Cp. TANG². The sense nasal pronunciation or intonation arose in the 17C.

twat *n.* the female genitals. WH: 17C. Orig. unknown. ? Rel. to dial. *twitchel* narrow lane.

twattle *n.* meaningless talk, twaddle. WH: 16C. ? Alt. of TATTLE. Cp. TWADDLE.

twayblade *n.* any orchid of the genus *Listera* etc., with two broad, ovate, radical leaves, and green or purplish flowers. WH: 16C. From obs. *tway*, from Old English *twe* shortened from *twegen* TWAIN + BLADE, translating Medieval Latin *bifolium*. The plant is so named from its two broad stem-leaves.

tweak *v.t.* to pinch and twist or pull with a sudden jerk, to twitch. Also *n.* WH: 17C. Prob. alt. of obs. *twick*, from Old English *twiccian*, from Germanic base of TWITCH¹.

twee *a.* excessively dainty and prettified. WH: early 20C. Representation of a childish pronun. of SWEET, ? influ. by TWEET.

tweed *n.* a twilled woollen or wool-and-cotton fabric with an unfinished surface, used chiefly for outer garments. WH: 19C. Orig. a misreading of *tweel*, Scottish var. of TWILL, influ. by assoc. with River *Tweed*.

Tweedledum and Tweedledee *n.* an indistinguishable pair; distinction without difference. WH: 18C. From *tweedle* (17C) to play on a light-pitched instrument, of imit. orig. + -*dum*, representing a note from a low-pitched instrument, -*dee* a note from a high-pitched instrument. The two words, originally nicknames of the rival 18C composers Handel and Bononcini, were popularized by twin characters so named in Lewis Carroll's *Through the Looking-Glass* (1871).

†**'tween** *adv., prep.* between. WH: 12–14C. Shortening of BETWEEN.

tweet *n.* the chirp of a small bird. Also *int., v.i.* WH: 19C. Imit.

tweezers *n.pl.* a small pair of pincers for picking up minute things, plucking out hairs etc. WH: 17C. Pl. of *tweezer*, from obs. *tweeze* etui, case of surgical instruments (from obs. *twee*, shortening of *etwee*, var. of ETUI + -S¹) + -ER¹.

twelfth *n.* any one of twelve equal parts. Also *n., a.* WH: pre-1200. Old English *twelfta*, from Germanic, from base of TWELVE, -TH¹. Cp. German *zwölfte*.

twelve *n.* the number or figure 12 or xii. Also *a.* WH: pre-1200. Old English *twelf*, from Germanic, prob. from base of TWO + base represented also by ELEVEN. Cp. German *zwölf*.

twenty *n.* the number or figure 20 or xx. Also *a.* WH: pre-1200. Old English *twentig*, from Germanic, ? from base of TWO. See also -TY². Cp. German *zwanzig*.

twerp *n.* a contemptible or silly person. WH: 19C. Orig. unknown.

twi- *comb. form* two. WH: Old English *twi-, twy-*, from Germanic, rel. to Latin BI-, Greek DI-², Sanskrit *dvi-*, from base rel. to that of TWO.

twibill *n.* a double-bladed battleaxe. WH: pre-1200. Old English, from TWI- + BILL², BILL³.

twice *adv.* two times. WH: pre-1200. Old English *twiges*, from *twige*, from base also of TWO. See also -S². Cp. THRICE.

twiddle *v.t.* to rotate. Also *v.i., n.* WH: 16C. Appar. imit., based on TWIRL, TWIST and FIDDLE, PIDDLE.

twig¹ *n.* a small shoot or branch of a tree, bush, etc., a branchlet. WH: pre-1200. Old English *twigge*, rel. to *twig, twī*, corr. to Old Danish *tvige* fork, Middle Low German *twīch* (Dutch *twigg*), Old High German *zwīg* (German *Zweig*), ult. from Germanic, from Indo-European base also of TWAIN, TWIN, TWINE, TWO. A twig is so called as it forms a twofold fork or division with a larger branch.

twig² *v.t.* to understand, to comprehend, to catch the drift of. Also *v.i.* WH: 18C. Orig. unknown.

twilight *n.* the diffused light from the sky appearing a little before sunrise and after sunset. Also *a., v.t.* WH: 14–15C. TWI- + LIGHT¹. The light is probably so called as a half light rather than from its occurrence twice daily.

twill *n.* a fabric in which the weft threads pass alternately over one warp thread and then under two or more, producing diagonal ribs or lines. Also *v.t.* WH: 12–14C. Scottish and dial. var. of obs. *twilly*, from Old English *twili*, from TWI- + base of Latin *licium* thrum, thread, based on Latin *bilix, bilicis* two-threaded. The fabric is so called as the weft threads pass over one and under two (or more) threads of the warp, instead of over and under in regular succession.

twin *a.* being one of two born at a birth. Also *n., v.t., v.i.* WH: pre-1200. Old English *twinn*, earlier *getwinn*, corr. to Old Norse *tvinnr, tvennr* twofold, double, from Germanic base also of TWI-.

twine *v.t.* to twist. Also *v.i., n.* WH: pre-1200. Old English *twīn, twigin* linen, from Germanic base of TWI-. Twine is so called because its thread or string is made of two (or more) twisted strands.

twinge *v.t.* to affect with a sharp, sudden pain. Also *v.i., n.* WH: pre-1200. Old English *twengan*, from Germanic base also of Middle High German *zwange* tongs, *zwangen* to pinch.

twinkie *n.* a person from a two-income household without children. WH: late 20C. From *two* incomes, *no* kids.

twinkle *v.i.* to shine with a broken quivering light, to gleam fitfully, to sparkle. Also *v.t., n.* WH: pre-1200. Old English *twinclian*, from Germanic. See also -LE⁴. Cp. German *zwinkern* to blink, to wink, to twinkle.

twirl *v.t.* to cause to rotate rapidly, esp. with the fingers, to spin. Also *v.i., n.* WH: 16C. Prob. alt. (by assoc. with WHIRL) of obs. *tirl, tirl* of obs. *trill* (14–15C) to turn round, to cause to revolve, ? rel. to Swedish *trilla*, Danish and Norwegian *trille* to roll, to trundle.

twist *v.t.* to wind (a thread, filament, strand etc.) round another. Also *v.i., n.* WH: pre-1200. Old English -*twist* (in combs.), from Germanic, prob. ult. from base also of TWIN, TWINE. To twist is to wind two (or more) strands together.

twit¹ *v.t.* to reproach, taunt or upbraid (with some fault etc.). WH: pre-1200. Old English *ætwītan* to blame, to reproach, from *æt* AT + *wītan* to know, WIT². The shortened form of the Old English verb is not recorded until the 16C.

twit² *n.* a fool. WH: 16C. TWIT¹. The original sense was a act of twitting. The sense fool arose only in the mid-20C.

twitch¹ *v.t.* to pull with a sudden or sharp jerk. Also *v.i., n.* WH: 12–14C. Corr. to Low German *twikken*, Old High German *gizwickan*, Middle High German *zwicken*, from Germanic, represented also by Old English *twiccian* to pluck. See TWEAK.

twitch² *n.* couch grass. WH: 16C. Alt. of QUITCH.

twite *n.* a N European finch, *Acanthis flavirostris*, which resembles the linnet. WH: 16C. Imit. of the bird's call.

twitter *v.i.* to utter a succession of short, tremulous, intermittent notes. Also *v.t., n.* WH: 14–15C. Imit. See also -ER³. Cp. TWEET.

†**'twixt** *prep.* between. WH: 12–14C. Shortening of BETWIXT.

twizzle *v.i., v.t.* to twist round and round, to spin. Also *n.* WH: 18C. Appar. imit. based on TWIST.

two *n.* the number or figure 2 or ii. Also *a.* WH: pre-1200. Old English *twā*, from Germanic, rel. to Greek and Latin *duo*, Sanskrit *dvau* (m.), *dve* (fem. and neut.). Cp. German *zwei*.

twocking *n.* taking a car without the owner's permission. WH: late 20C. Acronym of *t*aking *w*ithout (the) *o*wner's *c*onsent + -ING¹.

-ty¹ *suf.* forming abstract nouns, as in *bounty, cruelty, fealty*. WH: Old French -*te* (Modern French *té*), from Latin -*itas, -itatis*. Cp. -ITY.

-ty² *suf.* denoting tens, as in *fifty, twenty*. WH: Old English -*tig*, corr. to Old Frisian -*tich*, Old Saxon -*tig* (Dutch -*tig*), Old High German -*zug* (German -*zig*) and Old Norse *tigr*, Gothic *tigus* ten.

tychism *n.* the theory that chance is at work in the universe, esp. in evolutionary adaptations. WH: 19C. Greek *tukhē* chance + -ISM.

tycoon *n.* a financial or political magnate. WH: 19C. Japanese *taikun* great lord, great prince, from Chinese *dà* great + *jūn* prince.

tyke *n.* a dog. WH: 14–15C. Old Norse *tík* bitch. Cp. Middle Low German *tike* bitch.

tylopod *a.* having the digits enclosed in a cutaneous pad, as the camels. Also *n.* WH: 19C. Greek *tulos* knob or *tulē* callus, cushion + -O- + -POD.

tylosis *n.* a growth in the cavity of a duct intruding from the wall of a contiguous cell. WH: 19C. Modern Latin, from Greek *tulōsis* formation of a callus, from *tulē* callus + -OSIS.

tylote *n.* a cylindrical spicule, in a sponge, knotted at each end. WH: 19C. Greek *tulōtos* knobbed, from *tuloun* to make knobby, from *tulos* knob.

tympan *n.* a frame stretched with paper cloth or parchment, used for equalizing the pressure in some printing presses. WH: pre-1200. Old English *timpana*, from Latin TYMPANUM.

tympanum *n.* the middle ear. WH: 16C. Latin, from Greek *tumpanon* drum, from nasalized var. of base of *tuptein* to strike.

Tynesider *n.* a native or inhabitant of Tyneside. WH: 19C. *Tyneside*, an area adjacent to the River Tyne, NE England + -ER[1].

Tynwald *n.* the legislature of the Isle of Man. WH: 14–15C. Old Norse *thingvollr* place of assembly, from *thing* assembly, THING[2] + *vollr* field, level ground, WOLD. The name of *Dingwall*, a town in NE Scotland, is of identical origin.

type *n.* a kind, a class, a category. *Also v.t., v.i.* WH: 15C. Latin *typus*, from Greek *tupos* blow, impression, image, figure, from base of *tuptein* to strike, to beat. The original sense was a symbol. The sense kind, class dates from the 19C. The technical sense character for printing arose in the 18C.

typhlitis *n.* inflammation of the caecum. WH: 19C. Greek *tuphlon* caecum, blind gut (use as n. of neut. of *tuphlos* blind) + -ITIS.

typhoid *a.* of, relating to or resembling typhus. *Also n.* WH: 19C. TYPHUS + -OID.

typhoon *n.* a violent cyclonic hurricane occurring in the China Seas and the W Pacific. WH: 16C. Partly from Portuguese *tufão*, from Urdu *ṭūfān* hurricane, tornado, from Arabic, ? from Greek *Tuphōn* Typhon, in Greek mythology a hundred-headed fire-breathing monster believed to raise hurricanes and whirlwinds, partly from Chinese dial. *tai fung* big wind, from Chinese *dà* big + *fēng* wind.

typhus *n.* a contagious rickettsial fever marked by an eruption of dark purple spots, great prostration, stupor and delirium. WH: 17C. Greek *tuphos* smoke, vapour, stupor, from *tuphein* to smoke.

typical *a.* of the nature of or serving as a type. WH: 17C. Medieval Latin *typicalis*, from Late Latin *typicus*, from Greek *tupikos*, from *tupos* TYPE. See also -IC, -AL[1].

typo *n.* a typographical error. WH: 19C. Abbr. of *typographical* (error) (TYPOGRAPHY).

typography *n.* the art of printing. WH: 17C. French *typographie* or Modern Latin *typographia*, from Greek *tupos* TYPE + -O- + -*graphia* writing. See -GRAPHY.

typology *n.* the study and interpretation of types, esp. those of the Bible. WH: 19C. Greek *tupos* TYPE + -O- + -LOGY.

tyramine *n.* a colourless crystalline amine found in cheese, ergot, decayed animal tissue and mistletoe, which is similar in action to adrenaline. WH: early 20C. TYROSINE + AMINE.

tyrannosaurus *n.* a large flesh-eating dinosaur, *Tyrannosaurus rex*, which had small front legs and powerful hind legs. WH: early 20C. Modern Latin, from Greek *turannos* TYRANT + *sauros* lizard. The name was coined in 1905 by the US palaeontologist and zoologist Henry F. Osborn.

tyrant *n.* an arbitrary or despotic ruler. WH: 12–14C. Old French *tyrant, tiran* (Modern French *tyran*), from Latin *tyrannus*, from Greek *turannos*. See also -ANT. For the added -*t*, cp. PEASANT, PHEASANT.

tyre *n.* an air-filled rubber casing round the outside of a wheel. WH: 15C. Var. of TIRE[2]. The current sense dates from the 18C.

Tyrian *a.* of or relating to ancient Tyre. *Also n.* WH: 12–14C. Latin *Tyrius*, from *Tyrus* Tyre, an ancient Phoenician city and commercial port, now in S Lebanon + -AN.

tyro *n.* a beginner, a novice. WH: 14–15C. Latin *tiro, tironis* young soldier, recruit, beginner.

Tyrolean *a.* of or relating to the Tyrol. *Also n.* WH: 19C. *Tyrol*, an Alpine region of Austria and N Italy + -EAN.

tyrosine *n.* an amino acid formed by the decomposition of proteins. WH: 19C. Greek *turos* cheese + -INE.

†Tyrrhene *a.* Etruscan. *Also n.* WH: 14–15C. Latin *Tyrrhenus* of the Etruscans or Etruria.

tzatziki *n.* a Greek dip of yogurt flavoured with cucumber, garlic etc. WH: mid-20C. Modern Greek, from Turkish *cacık*.

tzigane *n.* a Hungarian gypsy. *Also a.* WH: 18C. French, from obs. Hungarian *czigany* (now *cigány*). Cp. ZINGARO.

tzimmes *n.* a sweetened stew of vegetables and/or fruit. WH: 19C. Yiddish *tsimes*, of unknown orig.

U[1] *a.* (of words, phrases, behaviour etc.) associated with the so-called upper classes. WH: mid-20C. Abbr. of *upper-class* (UPPER).

U[2] *n.* a Burmese (Myanmar) title of respect used before a man's name. WH: mid-20C. Burmese (Myanmar).

UB40 *n.* a card issued to a person registered as unemployed. WH: late 20C. Abbr. of *unemployment benefit* (UN-[1], EMPLOY, BENEFIT) + serial number 40.

Übermensch *n.* a superman. WH: 19C. German, back-formation from *übermenschlich* superhuman, from *über* over + *menschlich* human, from *Mensch* person, man. Cp. SUPERMAN, UNTERMENSCH.

uberty *n.* fruitfulness, fertility. WH: 14–15C. Old French *uberté*, or Latin *ubertas*, from *uber* rich, fruitful, from *uber* udder. See also -TY[1].

ubiety *n.* the state of being in a particular place. WH: 17C. Medieval Latin *ubietas*, from Latin *ubi* where. See also -ITY. Cp. *ubiquity* (UBIQUITOUS).

-ubility *suf.* forming nouns that correspond to adjectives in -*uble*, as in *dissolubility*. WH: Latin -*ubilis* (-UBLE) + -ITY.

ubiquitous *a.* present everywhere or in an indefinite number of places at the same time. WH: 19C. Modern Latin *ubiquitas*, from *ubique* everywhere + -OUS.

-uble *suf.* that can or must be, as in *dissoluble*, *voluble*. WH: French, from Latin -*ubilis*, form taken by suf. -*bilis* (-BLE) when added to vv. in -*vere*, as *solubilis* SOLUBLE, from *solvere*, *volubilis* VOLUBLE, from *volvere*.

U-boat *n.* a German submarine used in World Wars I and II. WH: early 20C. German *U-Boot*, abbr. of *Unterseeboot*, lit. undersea boat.

udal *n.* freehold tenure based on uninterrupted possession, as in N Europe before feudalism and in Orkney and Shetland. WH: 15C. Norwegian and Swedish *odal*, Danish *odel*, from Old Norse *othal* property held by inheritance, from Germanic source also of ATHELING.

udder *n.* the milk-secreting organ of a cow, ewe etc., having several teats. WH: pre-1200. Old English *ūder*, from Germanic. Cp. German *Euter*.

udometer *n.* a rain gauge. WH: 19C. French *udomètre*, from Latin *udus* wet. See -METER.

UFO *n.* an unidentified flying object. WH: mid-20C. Acronym of unidentified flying object.

ugh *int.* used to express disgust or horror. WH: 18C. Imit.

Ugli® *n.* a cross between a grapefruit and a tangerine. WH: mid-20C. Alt. of UGLY.

ugly *a.* unpleasing to the sight or ear. WH: 12–14C. Old Norse *uggligr* to be feared, from *ugga* to fear, to dread, to apprehend. The original sense was having an appearance that causes dread or horror. The current sense evolved in the 14–15C.

Ugrian *n.* a member of the eastern branch of the Finno-Ugric peoples, esp. the Magyars. *Also a.* WH: 19C. Russian *Ugry* (UGRIC). See also -AN, -IAN.

Ugric *a.* of or relating to the Magyars and other eastern Finnic peoples. *Also n.* WH: 19C. Russian *Ugry*, a people living east of the Urals. See also -IC.

uh-huh *int.* used to express assent or show understanding. WH: early 20C. Imit.

uhlan *n.* a cavalryman armed with a lance, in the old German and some other European armies. WH: 18C. French *uhlan*, German *Ulan*, *Uhlan*, from Polish *ułan*, *hułan*, from Turkish *oğlan* youth, servant.

Uitlander *n.* a foreigner. WH: 19C. Afrikaans, from Dutch *uit* OUT + *land* LAND. Cp. OUTLANDISH.

ujamaa *n.* a system of village cooperatives set up by President Nyerere in Tanzania in the 1960s and designed to encourage self-reliance. WH: mid-20C. Kiswahili consanguinity, brotherhood, from *jamaa* family, from Arabic *jamā'a* group (of people), community.

ukase *n.* an edict or decree of the Imperial Russian Government. WH: 18C. Russian *ukaz* ordinance, edict, from *ukazat'* to show, to order, to decree.

Ukrainian *n.* a native or inhabitant of Ukraine. *Also a.* WH: 19C. *Ukraine*, a country of SW Asia bordering the Black Sea, formerly a republic of the USSR. See also -IAN.

ukulele *n.* a small four-stringed instrument resembling a guitar. WH: 19C. Hawaiian, lit. jumping flea, from *uku* louse, flea + *lele* to fly, to leap. The instrument is said to be so called from the Hawaiian nickname of Edward Purvis, a British army officer noted for his small size and agility, who popularized it when it was brought to Hawaii by the Portuguese in *c.*1879.

-ular *suf.* forming adjectives, as in *corpuscular*, *avuncular*. WH: Latin -*ularis*, from dim. suf. -*ul-* + -*aris* -AR[1].

ulcer *n.* an open sore on the outer or inner surface of the body, often accompanied by a secretion of pus or other discharge. WH: 14–15C. Latin *ulcus*, *ulceris*, rel. to Greek *helkos* wound, sore.

-ule *suf.* forming diminutive nouns, as in *globule*, *pustule*. WH: Latin dim. ending -*ulus*, -*ula*, -*ulum*.

ulema *n.* a body of Muslim doctors of law and interpreters of the Koran. WH: 17C. Arabic *'ulamā'*, pl. of *'ālim*, *'alīm* learned, from *'alima* to have (religious) knowledge. Cp. ALMA.

-ulent *suf.* forming adjectives meaning full of, abounding in, as in *succulent*, *virulent*. WH: Latin -*ulentus*.

uliginose *a.* growing in swampy or muddy places. WH: 14–15C. Latin *uliginosus*, from *uligo*, *uliginis* moisture. See also -OSE[1].

ullage *n.* the quantity by which a cask falls short of being full. WH: 14–15C. Old French *eulliage* (Modern French *ouillage*), from *euiller* (Modern French *ouiller*) to fill (a barrel), ult. from Latin *oculus* eye (in sense bung-hole). See also -AGE.

ulmaceous *a.* of, relating to or characteristic of the elm. WH: 14–15C. Modern Latin *Ulmaceae* order name, from Latin *ulmus* ELM.

ulna *n.* the longer and thinner of the two bones in the forearm. WH: 14–15C. Latin, rel. to Greek *ōlenē* and Old English *eln* ELL. Cp. ELBOW.

ulotrichan *a.* having tightly curled hair. *Also n.* WH: 19C. Greek *oulos* crisp + *thrix*, *thrikhos* hair + -AN.

-ulous *suf.* forming adjectives, as in *querulous*, *nebulous*. WH: Latin -*ulosus*, -*ulus*.

ulster *n.* a long, loose overcoat, usu. with a belt, made of rough cloth. WH: 16C. *Ulster*, a former province of Ireland comprising the present N Ireland and the counties of Cavan, Donegal and Monaghan.

Ulsterman *n.* a native or inhabitant of Ulster. WH: 19C. ULSTER + MAN.

ult *adv.* ultimo. WH: 18C. Abbr. of ULTIMO.

ulterior *a.* lying behind or beyond what is admitted or disclosed; hidden. WH: 18C. Latin further, more distant. See also -IOR.

ultima *n.* the last syllable of a word. WH: early 20C. Latin, fem. of *ultimus* last.

ultimate *a.* last, final. *Also n.* WH: 17C. Late Latin *ultimatus*, p.p. of *ultimare* to come to an end, from *ultimus* last, final. See also -ATE[2].

ultimatum *n.* a final proposal or statement of conditions by one party, the rejection of which may involve rupture of diplomatic relations of a declaration or war etc. WH: 18C. Use as n. of neut. of Late Latin *ultimatus* in the Medieval Latin senses final, completed. See ULTIMATE.

ultimo *a.* in or during last month. WH: 16C. Latin *ultimo*, abl. sing. m. of *ultimus* last, final, in phrs. *ultimo die* on the last day, *ultimo mense* in the last month. Cp. PROXIMO.

ultimogeniture *n.* inheritance by the youngest son. WH: 19C. Latin *ultimus* last + -O- + -*geniture*, based on PRIMOGENITURE.

ultra *a.* extreme; advocating extreme views or measures. *Also n.* WH: 19C. Independent use of ULTRA-, esp. orig. as abbr. of French *ultra-royaliste*.

ultra- *pref.* beyond, on the other side of, as in *ultramundane*. WH: Latin *ultra* beyond, used as a pref. in Late Latin and Medieval Latin.

ultramarine *a.* deep blue. *Also n.* WH: 16C. Obs. Italian *oltramarino* (Modern Italian *oltremarino*), in *azzuro oltramarino*, lit. azure from overseas, later assim. to Medieval Latin *ultramarinus*, from Latin *ultra* beyond + *mare* sea. See also -INE. The colour is so called as it was originally created from imported lapis lazuli.

ultra vires *a., adv.* beyond one's legal power or authority. WH: 18C. Latin beyond the powers. See ULTRA-, VIS.

ultromotivity *n.* the power of spontaneous movement or action. WH: 19C. Latin *ultroneus*, from *ultro* of one's own accord + *motivity* (MOTIVE).

ululate *v.i.* (of a dog, wolf etc.) to howl. WH: 17C. Latin *ululatus*, p.p. of *ululare* to howl, of imit. orig. See also -ATE³. Cp. HOWL.

um *int.* used to express hesitation or a pause in speaking. WH: 17C. Natural exclamation. Cp. HUM².

umbel *n.* an inflorescence in which the flower stalks spring from one point and spread like the ribs of an umbrella forming a flattish surface, as in parsley. WH: 16C. Obs. French *umbelle* (Modern French *ombelle*) or Latin *umbella* parasol, dim. of *umbra* shade, shadow. See also -EL.

umber *n.* a dark yellowish-brown pigment derived from a mineral ferric oxide containing manganese. *Also a., v.t.* WH: 16C. French (*terre d'*) *ombre* or Italian (*terra di*) *ombra*, from Latin *umbra* shade, shadow or *Umbra*, fem. of *Umber* UMBRIAN.

umbilical *a.* of, relating to or situated near the navel. *Also n.* WH: 16C. Obs. French (Modern French *ombilical*), from *umbilic*, from Latin *umbilicus*, from base of UMBO, rel. to Greek *omphalos* (OMPHALO-) and Indo-European base of NAVEL.

†umbles *n.pl.* the entrails of a deer. WH: 14–15C. Alt. of NUMBLES. Cp. *humble-pie* (HUMBLE, PIE¹).

umbo *n.* the boss or projecting point in the centre of a shield. WH: 18C. Latin shield-boss, knob. Cp. UMBILICAL.

umbra *n.* the darker part of a shadow cast by an opaque object, esp. that cast by the moon on to the earth during a solar eclipse. WH: 16C. Latin shadow, shade.

umbrage *n.* a sense of injury; offence. WH: 14–15C. Old French (Modern French *ombrage*), from Latin *umbra* shadow. See also -AGE. The original sense (to the 18C) was shade, shadow, then (17C) ground for suspicion, also shelter, protection. The current sense dates from the 17C. To take umbrage is to take offence at being under the shadow of suspicion.

umbrella *n.* a light screen of fabric, stretched on a folding frame of radiating ribs on a stick, for holding above the head as a protection against rain or sun. WH: 17C. Italian *ombrella*, *ombrello*, dims. of *ombra*, from Latin *umbra* shade, shadow, based on *umbella* UMBEL. The umbrella was originally used as a protection against the heat and glare of the sun (see PARASOL) rather than as a protection against rain.

Umbrian *a.* of or relating to Umbria. *Also n.* WH: 17C. Latin *Umber*, *Umbria*, a province of central Italy + -IAN, -AN.

umiak *n.* an Eskimo (Inuit) boat made of skins stretched on a framework, used by women. WH: 18C. Eskimo (Inuit) *umiaq*.

umlaut *n.* a change of the vowel in a syllable through the influence of an *i*, *r* etc. (now usu. lost or modified) in the following syllable. *Also v.t.* WH: 19C. German, from *um*- about + *Laut* sound.

ump *n.* an umpire. WH: early 20C. Abbr. of UMPIRE.

umpire *n.* a person chosen to enforce the rules and settle disputes in a game, esp. cricket or football. *Also v.t., v.i.* WH: 14–15C. Old French *nonper*, from *non-* NON- + *per, pair* PEER², with loss of initial *n-* through Middle English misdivision of *a noumpere* as an *oumpere* (cp. ADDER, APRON). An umpire is so called as an impartial third person who is not on the same level as the two contending persons or parties.

umpteen *a.* very many. *Also pron.* WH: early 20C. From *umpty* (19C), arbitrary formation based on TWENTY, THIRTY, etc. + -TEEN. The formation may have been influenced by *umpty*, military slang representing the dash in Morse code. (The dot was *iddy*, so that *iddy-umpty* was a slang term for an army signaller.)

un-¹ *pref.* giving a negative sense to adjectives, adverbs and nouns, as in *unappealing*, *unerringly*, *unpretentiousness*. WH: Old English, rel. to Old Saxon, Old High German and Gothic *un-*, Old Norse *ú-*, *ó-*, and corr. to Old Irish *in-*, *an-*, Latin IN-², Greek *an-* (A-³), Sanskrit *an-*, *a-*, all from Indo-European base of NE NOT.

un-² *pref.* denoting 'one' and used in combination with other numerical roots (as in UNNIL-) to form names of elements based on their atomic number. WH: Latin *unus* one. Cp. UNI-.

'un *pron.* one. WH: 19C. Alt. of ONE.

una corda *a., adv.* using the soft pedal. WH: 19C. Italian one string. The depression of a piano's soft pedal causes the hammer to strike only one of the three strings. The direction to release the pedal is thus *tre corde*, Italian three strings.

unanimous *a.* being all of one mind. WH: 17C. Latin *unanimus*, from *unus* one + *animus* spirit, mind. See also -OUS.

uncate *a.* hooked. WH: 19C. Latin *uncatus*, from *unca* hook. Cp. UNCINATE, UNCUS.

uncial *a.* denoting a kind of majuscule writing somewhat resembling modern capitals, used in manuscripts of the 4th–8th cents. *Also n.* WH: 17C. Latin *uncialis*, from *uncia* OUNCE¹, inch. The kind of writing derives from Late Latin *unciales litterae*, literally inch-high letters.

uncinate *a.* hooked at the end. WH: 18C. Latin *uncinatus*, from *uncinus*, from UNCUS + -*inus* -INE. See also -ATE².

uncle *n.* the brother of one's father or mother. WH: 12–14C. Old French *oncle* from Late Latin *aunculus*, alt. of *avunculus* maternal uncle. Cp. AVUNCULAR.

-uncle *suf.* forming nouns, esp. diminutives, as *furuncle*. WH: Old French *-uncle*, *-oncle*, from Latin *-unculus*, *-uncula*.

unco *a.* strange, extraordinary. *Also n., adv.* WH: 14–15C. Alt. of UN-COUTH.

uncouth *a.* lacking in refinement or manners. WH: pre-1200. Old English *uncūth* unknown, uncertain, unfamiliar, from *un-* UN-¹ + *cūth* well-known, p.p. of *cunnan* to know. See CAN¹. Cp. COUTH. The original sense (to the 17C) was unknown, uncertain. The current sense emerged in the 16C. A person or thing that is unfamiliar or strange may seem odd or awkward.

unction *n.* the act of anointing with oil or an unguent, as a symbol of consecration or for medical purposes. WH: 14–15C. Latin *unctio*, *unctionis*, from *unctus*, p.p. of *unguere* to smear. See also -ION.

uncus *n.* a hook, claw, or hooklike part or appendage. WH: 19C. Latin hook.

undate *a.* having a wavy surface, undulate. WH: 15C. Medieval Latin *undatus*, from Latin *unda* wave. See also -ATE².

undecagon *n.* a plane figure having eleven angles and eleven sides. WH: 18C. Latin *undecim* eleven + -GON.

under *prep.* in or to a place or position lower than. *Also adv., a.* WH: pre-1200. Old English, from Germanic base from Indo-European comp. formation meaning lower, below, rel. to Latin INFRA-. Cp. German *unter*.

under- *pref.* under, below, as in *underpass*. WH: UNDER, in early use as trans. of Latin SUB-.

understand *v.t.* to know or perceive the meaning of. *Also v.i.* WH: pre-1200. Old English *understandan* to comprehend, lit. to stand in the midst of, from *under-* UNDER- + *standan* STAND. Cp. German *verstehen* to understand, lit. to stand before.

undertake *v.t.* to take upon oneself (a task, enterprise, responsibility etc.). *Also v.i.* WH: 12–14C. UNDER- + TAKE¹, superseding Old English *underfōn*, from *fōn* to seize, to take (cp. FANG), and *underniman*, from *niman* to take (cp. NIM). An *undertaker* was originally a person who undertook some task or kind of work. The specific current sense evolved in the 17C.

undies *n.pl.* women's underwear. WH: early 20C. Abbr. of *underclothes* or *undergarments* (UNDER, CLOTHE, GARMENT), prob. based on *frillies* (FRILL).

undine *n.* a female water spirit without a soul, but capable of obtaining one by marrying a mortal and bearing a child. WH: 19C. Modern Latin *undina*, *undena*, from Latin *unda* wave. See also -INE. The word was popularized by the fairy romance *Undine* (1811) by the German writer Baron Friedrich de la Motte Fouqué.

und so weiter *adv.* and so on. WH: 19C. German and so forth.

undulate[1] *v.i.* to have a wavy motion. *Also v.t.* WH: 17C. Prob. from Late Latin *undulatus* waved, from *undula*, from Latin *unda* wave. See also -ULE, -ATE[3].

undulate[2] *a.* wavy, moving in and out or up and down. WH: 17C. Prob. from Late Latin *undulatus*. See UNDULATE[1], also -ATE[2].

ungainly *a.* clumsy, awkward. WH: 17C. UN-[1] + GAINLY.

unguent *n.* any soft composition used as an ointment or for lubrication. WH: 14–15C. Latin *unguentum*, from *unguere* to anoint.

unguis *n.* a nail or claw. WH: 17C. Latin nail, claw. Cp. UNGULA.

ungula *n.* a hoof, claw or talon. WH: 14–15C. Latin claw, hoof, from UNGUIS. See also -ULE.

uni *n.* a university. WH: 19C. Abbr. of UNIVERSITY.

uni- *comb. form* one, single, as in *unisex*, *unipolar*. WH: Latin, comb. form of *unus* one, single. Cp. UN-[2].

Uniate *n.* a member of any of the Eastern Churches acknowledging the supremacy of the Pope but retaining their own liturgy, rites and ceremonies. *Also a.* WH: 19C. Russian *uniat*, from *uniya* union, from Latin *unio* UNION. The members are so called from their union with the Roman Catholic Church.

unicorn *n.* a fabulous animal like a horse, but with a long, straight, tapering horn. WH: 12–14C. Old French *unicorne*, from Latin *unicornis* one-horned, *unicorn*, from *unus* one + *cornu* horn, translating Greek *monokerōs*. In early biblical translations, *unicorn* represents Latin *unicornis*, *rhinoceros*, translating Hebrew *rĕ'em* wild ox, e.g. 'His glory is like the firstling of his bullock, and his horns are like the horns of unicorns' (Deut. xxxiii.17).

uniform *a.* having an unchanging form, appearance, quality, character etc.; the same, not varying, not changing. *Also n.*, *v.t.* WH: 16C. Old French *uniforme* or Latin *uniformis*, from *unus* UNI- + *forma* FORM.

unify *v.t.* to make one. WH: 16C. Old French *unifier*, or from Late Latin *unificare*. See UNI-, also -FY.

union *n.* the act of uniting; the state of being united. WH: 14–15C. Old French, or from Ecclesiastical Latin *unio*, *unionis* the number one, unity, from Latin *unus* one. See also -ION.

unique *a.* having no like or equal. *Also n.* WH: 17C. French, earlier *unic*, from Latin *unicus* one and only, alone of its kind, from *unus* one. See also -IC.

UNISON *n.* a trade union for employees in the public services, formed in 1993 from an amalgamation of COHSE, NALGO and NUPE. WH: late 20C. (Pun on) blend of UNION and UNISON.

unison *n.* coincidence of sounds proceeding from equality in rate of vibrations; unity of pitch. *Also a.* WH: 14–15C. Old French (Modern French *unisson*), or from Late Latin *unisonus* of the same sound, from Latin *unus* one + *sonus* SOUND[1].

unit *n.* a single person, thing, or group, regarded as complete. WH: 16C. Latin *unus*, prob. based on DIGIT. Cp. UNITY.

unite *v.t.* to join together so as to make one. *Also v.i.* WH: 14–15C. Latin *unitus*, p.p. of *unire* to join together, from *unus* one.

unity *n.* the state or condition of being one or individual, oneness as opposed to plurality or division. WH: 12–14C. Old French *unité*, from Latin *unitas*, from *unus* one. See also -ITY.

universal *a.* of or relating to the whole world or all persons or things in the world or in the class under consideration. *Also n.* WH: 14–15C. Old French *universel*, or from Latin *universalis*, from *universus*. See UNIVERSE, also -AL[1].

universe *n.* all existing things; all created things viewed as constituting one system or whole, the cosmos. WH: 14–15C. Old French *univers* or Latin *universum* the whole world, use as n. of neut. of *universus* all taken together, lit. turned into one, from UNI- + *versus*, p.p. of *vertere* to turn.

university *n.* an educational institution for both instruction and examination in the higher branches of knowledge with the power to confer degrees, often comprising subordinate colleges, schools etc. WH: 12–14C. Old French *université*, from Latin *universitas* the whole, the whole number (of), the universe, (later) society, guild, from *universus*. See UNIVERSE, also -ITY. A university is so called as a 'whole' of teachers and students.

Unix® *n.* a multi-user computer operating system. WH: late 20C. UNI- + -ix, representing -ICS, punning on *Multix* (mid-20C), a similar system designed for use with mainframe computers, acronym of *mul*tiplexed *in*formation and computing service. Unix has *uni-* one, instead of *multi-* many, with reference to its relative compactness by comparison with the earlier system. (It is designed for use with minicomputers.)

unkempt *a.* (of hair) uncombed. WH: 14–15C. UN-[1] + KEMPT.

unless *conj.* if it be not the case that; except when. WH: 14–15C. ON + LESS, orig. two words. The two words coalesced as *onless*, in which *on-* was assim. to UN-[1]. The original sense (as a preposition) was on a less condition (than). It was the negative connotation of the word that led to the alteration of *on-* to UN-[1].

unnil- *pref.* formerly forming names of chemical elements of atomic numbers 104–109. WH: UN-[2] + NIL, i.e. 1 + 0. The six elements were respectively named *unnilquadium*, *unnilpentium*, *unnilhexium*, *unnilseptium*, *unniloctium* and *unnilennium*. See QUADRI-, PENTA-, HEXA-, SEPTI-[1], OCTA-, ENNEA-. The current names of the elements are respectively RUTHERFORDIUM, DUBNIUM, SEABORGIUM, BOHRIUM, HASSIUM and MEITNERIUM.

unready *a.* badly or insufficiently advised (used as a nickname of Ethelred II, 968–1016, king of England). WH: 16C. Alt. of obs. *unredy*, from UN-[1] + REDE + -Y[1]. The word is not related to *unready* (UN-[1], READY), but became popularly associated with it.

Untermensch *n.* a person who is regarded as socially or racially inferior. WH: mid-20C. German, from *unter* UNDER + *Mensch* person, man. Cp. ÜBERMENSCH.

until *prep.* up to the time of. *Also conj.* WH: 12–14C. Old Norse *und*, corr. to Old English *und* up to, as far as + TILL[1]. The word is an etymological tautology, duplicating the meaning.

†unto *prep.* to. WH: 12–14C. UNTIL, with TO replacing *-til* TILL[1].

unwitting *a.* unconscious. WH: pre-1200. UN-[1] + *witting*, pres.p. of WIT[2].

up *adv.* to or at a higher place or position. *Also prep.*, *a.*, *n.*, *v.t.*, *v.i.* WH: pre-1200. Old English, from Germanic. Cp. Dutch *op*, German *auf*. Rel. to OVER.

up- *pref.* up; upwards; upper. WH: UP.

Upanishad *n.* any one of the philosophical treatises forming the third division of the Vedas. WH: 19C. Sanskrit *upaniṣad*, from *upa* near + *ni-ṣad* to sit down. The treatise is so called from the notion of sitting at the foot of a teacher.

upas *n.* the upas tree. WH: 18C. Malay (*pohun*) *upas* poison. The upas is noted for its poisonous milky sap.

upbraid *v.t.* to reproach; to reprove with severity. *Also v.i.* WH: pre-1200. Old English *upbrēdan*, prob. based on an unrecorded Old Norse v., from *upp-* UP- + *bregtha* BRAID[1]. The original sense (to the 18C) was to bring forward (a matter) as a ground for censure. The current sense dates from the 12–14C.

upholster *v.t.* to provide (chairs etc.) with stuffing, cushions, coverings etc. WH: 19C. Back-formation from *upholsterer* or *upholstery* (UPHOLSTER), from *upholder*. See also -ER[1], -ERY. The noun *upholsterer* (17C) is an expanded form of the synonymous obsolete noun *upholster* (14–15C), from *uphold* (UP-, HOLD[1]) + -STER. An upholsterer upholds (i.e. maintains) upholstery. The word is not related to HOLSTER.

uphroe *n.* a long wooden block pierced with holes for reeving a cord, esp. for adjusting an awning. WH: 17C. Dutch *juffrouw*, lit. maiden, from *jong* young + *vrouw* woman. Cp. GASKET. The term is of obscure, possibly sexual origin.

upon *adv.* on. WH: 12–14C. UP + ON, based on Old Norse *upp á*. Cp. Swedish *på*, Norwegian and Danish *paa*.

upper *a.* higher in place. *Also n.* WH: 12–14C. UP + -ER[1]. Cp. *downer* (DOWN[1]).

uppish *a.* self-assertive, pretentious or snobbish. WH: 17C. UP + -ISH[1]. The original sense was plentifully supplied with money. The current sense dates from the 18C.

uppity *a.* uppish. WH: 19C. UP + *-ty* as in HAUGHTY, prob. based on UPPISH.

upright *a.* erect, perpendicular. *Also adv.*, *n.* WH: pre-1200. Old English *upriht*, from Germanic. See UP, RIGHT. Cp. German *aufrecht*.

uproar *n.* a noisy or violent disturbance. *Also v.i.* WH: 16C. Middle Dutch *uproer* (Modern Dutch *oproer*), from *op-* UP + *roer* confusion. The word is not related to ROAR but became associated with it.

upset[1] *v.t.* to overturn. *Also v.i.* WH: 14–15C. UP- + SET[1]. The original sense (to the 17C) was to set up, to raise, to erect. The current sense dates from the 18C and may have been influenced by obsolete *overset* (OVER-, SET[1]).

upset[2] *n.* the act of upsetting. *Also a.* WH: 14–15C. UPSET[1], or UP- + SET[2].

upside down *a., adv.* with the upper part under. WH: 12–14C. Orig. *up so down*, with *so* prob. meaning as if. The word was subsequently associated with SIDE, as if meaning with the up side down.

upsilon *n.* the 20th letter in the Greek alphabet (Υ, υ). WH: 17C. Greek *u psilon* simple u, slender u, from *psilos* slender. The letter is so called from the need to distinguish upsilon from the diphthong *oi* formed by omicron and iota, which was pronounced the same way.

upsydaisy *int.* used as a reassuring expression to accompany the lifting up of someone, esp. a child, who has stumbled or fallen. WH: 19C. Alt. of obs. *up-a-daisy* (18C), from UP + extended form of *a-day*. Cp. LACKADAISICAL.

uptight *a.* tense, nervy. WH: mid-20C. UP- + TIGHT.

upward *a.* directed, turned or moving towards a higher place. *Also adv.* WH: pre-1200. Old English *upweard*, from UP- + -WARD.

ur- *comb. form* original, primitive, as in *Urtext*. WH: 19C. German.

uracil *n.* a pyrimidine making up one of the four bases of RNA and found in all living cells. WH: 19C. ? From UREA + ACETIC + -IL.

uraemia *n.* a condition caused by the retention of urea and other noxious substances in the kidneys and bladder. WH: 19C. Modern Latin, from Greek *ouron* URINE + *haima* blood.

uraeus *n.* the serpent emblem worn on the headdress of ancient Egyptian divinities and kings. WH: 19C. Modern Latin, from Greek *ouraios* (? from *oura* tail), representing the Egyptian word for cobra.

Ural-Altaic *a.* of or relating to the Ural and Altaic mountain ranges or the people inhabiting them. *Also n.* WH: 19C. *Ural* Mountains, forming the NE boundary between Europe and Asia + ALTAIC.

Uralic *n.* a language group comprising the Finno-Ugric and Samoyed languages. *Also a.* WH: 19C. *Ural* Mountains (URAL-ALTAIC) + -ITE[1].

uranium *n.* a radioactive, fissionable, silvery-white metallic element, at. no. 92, chem. symbol U, found in pitchblende, and used as a source of nuclear energy. WH: 18C. URANUS + -IUM. The name was coined in *c.*1790 by the German chemist Martin Klaproth in honour of the discovery of the planet Uranus (1781). Cp. TELLURIUM.

urano- *comb. form* sky, the heavens. WH: Greek *ouranos* sky, heavens, roof of the mouth. See also -O-.

†**uranography** *n.* descriptive astronomy. WH: 17C. Greek *ouranographia*. See URANO-, -GRAPHY.

Uranus *n.* the seventh planet from the sun. WH: 19C. Latin, from Greek *Ouranos*, in Greek mythology the husband of Gaea (Earth) and father of Kronos (Saturn), himself the father of Zeus (Jupiter). The names of the fifth, sixth and seventh planets from the sun, Jupiter, Saturn and Uranus, reflect the family relationship of the mythological characters whose names they bear.

urate *n.* a salt of uric acid. WH: 19C. URIC + -ATE[1].

urban *a.* of or relating to a city or town. WH: 17C. Latin *urbanus*, from *urbs, urbis* city. See also -AN.

urbane *a.* polite; suave. WH: 16C. Old French *urbain*, or from Latin *urbanus*. See URBAN, also -ANE. For the difference in meaning and pronunciation of URBAN and URBANE, cp. HUMAN and HUMANE.

urbanity *n.* the quality of being urbane. WH: 16C. Old French *urbanité* or Latin *urbanitas*, from *urbanus* URBAN. See also -ITY.

urchin *n.* a roguish, mischievous child, esp. one dressed in rags. *Also a.* WH: 12–14C. Old Northern French *herichon*, var. of Old French *heriçon* (Modern French *hérisson*), from Latin *hericius*, late form of *ericius* hedgehog. The sense mischievous child dates from the 14–15C, and that of ragged child from the 16C. The former alludes to sharpness of wit, like the hedgehog's prickles, the latter to the child's unattractive appearance.

Urdu *n.* a language closely related to Hindi but with many Persian and Arabic words, an official language of Pakistan, also widely used

in India esp. by Muslims. WH: 18C. Persian and Urdu (*zabān i*) *urdū* (language of the) camp, from Persian *urdū*, from Turkish *ordu* camp. Cp. HORDE.

-ure *suf.* forming nouns indicating process or action, as in *censure, portraiture, seizure.* WH: Old French, from Latin *-ura.*

urea *n.* a soluble crystalline compound contained in urine, esp. of mammals. WH: 19C. French *urée*, from Greek *ouron* URINE or *ourein* to urinate.

ureter *n.* the duct conveying the urine from the kidneys into the bladder. WH: 16C. French *uretère* or Modern Latin *ureter*, from Greek *ourētēr*, from *ourein* to urinate, from *ouron* urine.

urethane *n.* a crystalline amide, $NH_2COOC_2H_5$, used esp. in plastics and as an anaesthetic. WH: 19C. UREA + ETHANE.

urethra *n.* the duct by which the urine is discharged from the bladder. WH: 17C. Late Latin, from Greek *ourēthra*, from *ourein* to urinate.

urethroscope *n.* an instrument for examining the interior of the urethra. WH: 19C. URETHRA + -O- + -SCOPE.

uretic *a.* of or relating to urine. WH: 19C. Late Latin *ureticus*, from Greek *ourētikos*, from *ourein* to urinate.

urge *v.t.* to drive or force onwards. *Also n.* WH: 16C. Latin *urgere* to press, to drive, to compel.

-uria *comb. form* indicating a diseased condition of the urine, as in *dysuria.* WH: Late Latin, from Greek *-ouria*, from *ouron* urine.

uric *a.* of or relating to urine. WH: 18C. French *urique*, from *urine* URINE. See also -IC.

urinal *n.* a receptacle fixed to a wall for men to urinate into. WH: 12–14C. Old French, from Late Latin, use as n. of neut. of *urinalis* urinary, from Latin *urina* URINE. See also -AL[1]. The original sense (to the 19C) was a glass vessel for the medical inspection of urine. The current sense dates from the 19C.

urine *n.* a pale-yellow fluid with an acid reaction, secreted from the blood by the kidneys, stored in the bladder, and discharged through the urethra, the chief means for the removal of nitrogenous and saline matters resulting from the decay of tissue. WH: 12–14C. Old French, from Latin *urina*, rel. to Greek *ouron.*

urn *n.* a vase with a foot and a usu. rounded body used for preserving the ashes of the dead, for holding water, as a measure, and other purposes. *Also v.t.* WH: 14–15C. Latin *urna*, rel. to *urceus* pitcher.

uro-[1] *comb. form* tail, hind part. WH: Greek *oura* tail. See also -O-.

uro-[2] *comb. form* urine. WH: Greek *ouron* urine. See also -O-.

urochord *n.* the notochord of larval ascidians and some tunicates. WH: 19C. URO-[1] + CHORD[2].

urodele *n.* any amphibian of the order Urodela, having a tail and four short limbs and including newts and salamanders. WH: 19C. French *urodèle* or Modern Latin *Urodela*, from Greek *oura* URO-[1] + *dēlos* evident.

urogenital *a.* of or relating to the genital and urinary organs. WH: 19C. URO-[2] + GENITAL.

urology *n.* the branch of medicine concerned with the study of the urinary system. WH: 18C. URO-[2] + -LOGY.

uropod *n.* an abdominal appendage of lobsters and related crustaceans. WH: 19C. URO-[1] + -POD.

uropygium *n.* the terminal part of the body of a bird. WH: 18C. Medieval Latin, from Greek *ouropugion*, from *ouro-* URO-[1] + *pugē* rump.

urostyle *n.* a bone forming the last part of the vertebral column in tailless amphibians. WH: 19C. URO-[1] + STYLE.

Ursa *n.* Ursa Major. WH: pre-1200. Latin (female) bear, the Great Bear.

ursine *a.* of or relating to or resembling a bear. WH: 16C. Latin *ursinus*, from *ursus* bear. See also -INE.

Ursuline *n.* a member of an order of nuns devoted chiefly to nursing and the education of girls. *Also a.* WH: 17C. St *Ursula*, 4C patron saint of the founder + -INE. The order was founded in 1535 by St Angela Merici, 1474–1540.

urticaceous *a.* of or having the character of nettles. WH: 19C. Latin *urtica* nettle, from *urere* to burn. See also -ACEOUS.

us *pron.* objective (acc. and dat.) of WE. WH: pre-1200. Old English *ūs*, from Germanic, from Indo-European. Cp. German *uns*, Sanskrit *nas.*

usage *n.* the manner of using or treating, treatment. WH: 12–14C. Old French *us* USE[1] + -AGE.

usance *n.* a period of time allowed for payment of a foreign bill of exchange. WH: 14–15C. Old French, from Medieval Latin *usantia*, *usancia*, from base of USE². See also -ANCE.

use¹ *n.* the act of using. WH: 12–14C. Old French *us*, from Latin *usus* use, usage, from *usus*. See USE².

use² *v.t.* to employ, to apply to a purpose. *Also v.i.* WH: 12–14C. Old French *user* (Modern French *user de*) to employ, to consume, to wear out, from Popular Latin *usare*, from Latin *usus*, p.p. of *uti*.

usher *n.* a seat-attendant at a cinema, theatre etc. *Also v.t.* WH: 14–15C. Old French *ussier*, *uissier* (Modern French *huissier*), from Medieval Latin *ustiarius*, from Latin *ostiarius* doorkeeper, from *ostium* door + *-arius* -ER².

usquebaugh *n.* whisky. WH: 16C. Gaelic *uisge beathe* water of life, from *uisge* water + *beatha* life. Cp. WHISKY.

†ustion *n.* the act of burning. WH: 16C. Old French, from Latin *ustio*, *ustionis*, from *ustus*, p.p. of *urere* to burn. See also -ION.

usual *a.* such as ordinarily occurs. *Also n.* WH: 14–15C. Old French *usual* (Modern French *usuel*), from Late Latin *usualis*, from Latin *usus* USE¹. See also -AL¹.

usucaption *n.* the acquisition of the title or right to property by uninterrupted possession for a certain number of years. WH: 17C. Latin *usucaptio*, *usucaptionis*, from *usucaptus*, p.p. of *usucapere* to acquire ownership by prescription, from *usu*, abl. of *usus* USE¹ + *capere* to take, to seize. See also -ION.

usufruct *n.* the right to the use and enjoyment of property belonging to another without waste or destruction of its substance. *Also v.t.* WH: 17C. Latin *usufructus*, from *usus (et) fructus* use (and) enjoyment, from *usus* USE¹ + *fructus* FRUIT.

usurer *n.* a person who lends money at (esp. exorbitant) interest. WH: 12–14C. Old French *usureor* (Modern French *usurier*), from *usure*, from Latin *usura* usury (USURER), from *usus* USE¹. See also -ER².

usurp *v.t.* to seize or take possession of without right. *Also v.i.* WH: 12–14C. Old French *usurper*, from Latin *usurpare* to seize for use, from *usus* USE¹ + *rapere* to seize.

ut *n.* the first note or keynote in Guido's musical scale. WH: 12–14C. Latin, the lowest of the series *ut, re, mi, fa, sol, la*, the initial syllables of each half-line, and *si* the initial letters of the closing words *Sancte Iohannes* (St John), of a stanza of the Latin office hymn for the Nativity of St John the Baptist. Cp. GAMUT. The first note, *ut*, has now been superseded by DOH. The Latin hymn itself runs: *Ut* queant laxis / *resonare fibris* / *Mi*ra gestorum / *fa*muli tuorum / *sol*ve polluti / *la*bii reatum / *Sancte Iohannes*, That with full voices thy servants may be able to sing the wonders of thy deeds, purge the sin from their unclean lips, O Holy John.

ute *n.* a utility truck. WH: mid-20C. Abbr. of UTILITY.

utensil *n.* an implement, esp. one used in cookery or domestic work. WH: 14–15C. Old French *utensile* (Modern French *ustensile*), from Medieval Latin *utensile*, use as n. of Latin *utensilis* fit for use, useful, from *uti* to use.

uterus *n.* the womb. WH: 14–15C. Latin, rel. to Greek *hustera* womb. See HYSTERIA.

utilitarian *a.* concerned with or made for practical use rather than beauty. *Also n.* WH: 18C. UTILITY + -ARIAN.

utility *n.* usefulness, serviceableness. *Also a.* WH: 14–15C. Old French *utilité*, from Latin *utilitas*, from *utilis* useful, from *uti* to use. See also -ITY.

utilize *v.t.* to make use of. WH: 19C. French *utiliser*, from Italian *utilizzare*, from *utile*, from Latin *utilis*, from *uti* to use. See also -IZE.

-ution *suf.* forming nouns, as in *execution*. WH: French, from Latin *-utio*, *-utionis*.

utmost *a.* being or situated at the farthest point or extremity; extreme; greatest. *Also n.* WH: pre-1200. Old English *ūtmest*, from *ūt* OUT + *-mest* -MOST.

Utopia *n.* a place or state of ideal perfection. WH: 16C. Modern Latin, lit. no-place (from Greek *ou* not + *topos* place; see -IA), title of a book (1516) by Sir Thomas More. The term is sometimes popularly interpreted as meaning good place, from Greek *eu-* good (EU-) + *topos* place.

utricle *n.* a cell of an animal or plant. WH: 18C. French *utricle*, or from Latin *utriculus*, dim. of *uter* leather bottle. See also -CULE.

ut sup. *abbr.* ut supra, as mentioned above. WH: 14–15C. Abbr. of Latin *ut supra*, from *ut* as + SUPRA.

utter¹ *a.* total, absolute. WH: pre-1200. Old English *ūtera*, *ūterra* comp. formed on *ūt* OUT (see -ER³), from Germanic. Cp. German *äusser*. The original sense was outer. The sense total, entire dates from the 14–15C.

utter² *v.t.* to emit audibly. WH: 14–15C. Middle Dutch *ūteren* to drive away, to speak, to show, to make known, rel. to Middle Low German *ūtern* to turn out, from *ūter* outer, assim. to UTTER¹.

UVA *abbr.* ultraviolet radiation with a range of 320–380 nanometres. WH: Abbr. of *ultraviolet A*.

UVB *abbr.* ultraviolet radiation with a range of 280–320 nanometres. WH: Abbr. of *ultraviolet B*.

UVC *abbr.* ultraviolet radiation of very short wavelengths. WH: Abbr. of *ultraviolet C*.

uvea *n.* the inner coloured layer of the iris. WH: 14–15C. Medieval Latin, from Latin *uva* grape.

uvula *n.* the fleshy tissue hanging from the posterior margin of the soft palate at the back of the throat. WH: 14–15C. Late Latin, dim. of Latin *uva* grape. See also -ULE.

uxorious *a.* excessively fond of one's wife. WH: 16C. Latin *uxoriosus*, from *uxor* wife. See also -OUS.

Uzbek *n.* a member of a Turkic people of Uzbekistan. WH: 17C. Turkish and Uzbek *özbek*.

Uzi *n.* a type of sub-machine gun designed in Israel. WH: mid-20C. *Uziel* Gal, the Israeli army officer who developed it after the Arab–Israeli war of 1948.

V

vac¹ *n.* a vacation, esp. a university holiday. **WH:** 18C. Abbr. of VACA-TION.

vac² *n.* a vacuum cleaner. *Also v.i., v.t.* **WH:** late 20C. Abbr. of *vacuum cleaner* (VACUUM).

vacant *a.* unfilled, empty, unoccupied. **WH:** 12–14C. Old French, from Latin *vacans, vacantis*, pres.p. of *vacare*. See VACATE, also -ANT.

vacate *v.t.* to make vacant, to give up occupation or possession of (a room, property). **WH:** 17C. Latin *vacatus*, p.p. of *vacare* to be empty, to be unoccupied. See also -ATE³.

vacation *n.* a period of cessation of legal or other business, or of studies at university etc. *Also v.i.* **WH:** 14–15C. Old French, or from Latin *vacatio, vacationis*, from *vacatus*. See VACATE, also -ATION.

vaccinate *v.t.* to inoculate with the modified virus of any disease so as to produce a mild form of the disease and prevent a serious attack. **WH:** 19C. From *vaccine* (VACCINATE), from Latin *vaccinus* (as in Modern Latin *variolae vaccinus* cowpox, *virus vaccinus* cowpox vaccine), from *vacca* cow. See also -INE. The Modern Latin term was coined by the English physician Edward Jenner in 1798.

vacherin *n.* a dessert consisting of whipped cream, ice cream, fruit etc. in a meringue shell. **WH:** mid-20C. French, from *vache* cow.

vacillate *v.i.* to oscillate from one opinion or resolution to another, to be irresolute. **WH:** 16C. Latin *vacillatus*, p.p. of *vacillare* to sway, to totter. See -ATE³. The original sense was to swing unsteadily, to stagger. The sense to alternate between different opinions arose in the 17C.

vacuole *n.* a minute cavity in a cell, containing air, fluid etc. **WH:** 19C. French, from Latin *vacuolus*, dim. of *vacuus* empty. See also -OLE².

vacuous *a.* showing no signs of feeling or intelligence. **WH:** 17C. Latin *vacuus* empty, void. See also -OUS. The original sense was empty, containing nothing. The sense unintelligent, expressionless dates from the 19C.

vacuum *n.* a space completely devoid of matter. *Also v.t., v.i.* **WH:** 16C. Latin, mod. use as n. of neut. sing. of *vacuus* empty.

vade-mecum *n.* a pocket companion or manual for ready reference. **WH:** 17C. French, from Modern Latin use as n. of Latin *vade mecum* go with me. The phrase is recorded in the Modern Latin writings of the German humanist Petrus Lotichius Secundus, 1528–60.

vadose *a.* of or relating to water found above the water-table. **WH:** 19C. Latin *vadosus*, from *vadum* shallow stretch of water. See also -OSE¹. Cp. WADE.

vagabond *n.* a person who wanders about without any settled home, a wanderer, esp. an idle or disreputable one, a vagrant. *Also a., v.i.* **WH:** 12–14C. Old French, or from Latin *vagabondus*, from *vagari* to wander. Cp. VAGRANT.

vagary *n.* a whimsical idea, an extravagant notion, a freak. **WH:** 16C. Latin *vagari* to wander, to roam. The original sense (to the 18C) was wandering journey, excursion, ramble. The current sense evolved in the 17C.

vagina *n.* the genital passage of a female from the vulva to the uterus. **WH:** 17C. Latin sheath, scabbard.

vagrant *n.* a person wandering about without a settled home or visible means of subsistence, a tramp. *Also a.* **WH:** 14–15C. Anglo-French *vagrant, vagaraunt*, ? alt. of *wakerant, walcrant*, by assoc. with Old French *vaguer*, from Latin *vagari* to wander. See also -ANT.

vague *a.* of doubtful meaning or application; not expressed or understood clearly. **WH:** 16C. French, or from Latin *vagus* wandering, uncertain.

vagus *n.* the tenth cranial nerve, which regulates the heartbeat, rhythm of breathing etc. **WH:** 19C. Latin wandering, straying. The nerve is so called from its length and wide distribution in the brain.

†vail¹ *v.t.* to lower (a topsail etc.) or doff (one's cap etc.), esp. in token of respect or submission. *Also v.i.* **WH:** 12–14C. Shortening of obsolete *avale* to sink, to drop, from Old French *avaler*, from *à val* at the bottom, down, from Latin *ad vallem* to the valley. Cp. AVALANCHE.

†vail² *v.i., v.t.* to avail. *Also n.* **WH:** 12–14C. Old French *valoir, vail-* to be of value, from Latin *valere* to be strong, to be powerful. Cp. AVAIL.

vain *a.* excessively proud of one's appearance or attainments, conceited, self-admiring. **WH:** 12–14C. Old French, from Latin *vanus* empty, without substance.

vair *n.* a squirrel fur used extensively in the Middle Ages for linings and trimmings. **WH:** 12–14C. Old French, from Latin *varius*. See VARIOUS.

Vaishnava *n.* a member of a sect that worships Vishnu as supreme among the Hindu gods. **WH:** 18C. Sanskrit *vaiṣṇava* relating to Vishnu, worshipper of Vishnu.

Vaisya *n.* the third of the four chief Hindu castes, the traders. **WH:** 17C. Sanskrit *vaiśya* peasant, tradesman.

valance *n.* a short curtain or hanging round the frame or tester of a bedstead, along a shelf, above a window etc. to conceal structural details. **WH:** 14–15C. ? Anglo-French, from *valer*, shortened form of Old French *avaler*. See VAIL¹, -ANCE. According to some, the word is from *valents*, a noun adopted from the plural of the present participle of *valer*.

vale¹ *n.* a valley. **WH:** 12–14C. Old French *val*, from Latin *valles, vallis*. Cp. VALLEY.

vale² *int.* farewell. *Also n.* **WH:** 16C. Latin, imper. of *valere* to be strong, to be well.

valediction *n.* the act or an instance of bidding farewell. **WH:** 17C. Latin *vale* (VALE²) or *valedictus*, p.p. of *valdicere* to say 'vale', based on BENEDICTION. See also -ION.

valence *n.* the combining or replacing power of an element or radical reckoned as the number of monovalent elements it can replace or combine with. **WH:** 14–15C. Var. of *valency*, from Latin *valentia* power, competence, from *valere* to be powerful. See also -ENCE.

Valenciennes *n.* a fine variety of lace, the design of which is made with and of the same thread as the ground. **WH:** 18C. *Valenciennes*, a town in NE France.

valentine *n.* a letter or card of an amatory or satirical kind sent to a person, often anonymously, on St Valentine's day. **WH:** 14–15C. Old French *Valentin*, from Latin *Valentinus*, name of either of two Italian saints whose feast day falls on 14 February, a day traditionally associated with the choosing of sweethearts and the mating of birds.

valerian *n.* a herbaceous plant of the genus *Valeriana*, esp. *V. officinalis*, with clusters of pink or white flowers. **WH:** 14–15C. Old French *valériane*, from Medieval Latin *valeriana*, appar. fem. sing. of Latin a. *Valerianus*, from pers. name *Valerius*. See also -IAN. According to some, the word is from Latin *valere* to be healthy, alluding to the medicinal properties of some species.

valet *n.* a manservant who acts as a personal attendant to his employer, looking after his clothes, serving his meals etc. *Also v.t., v.i.* **WH:** 15C. Old French, var. of *vaslet, varlet* VARLET, ult. rel. to VASSAL.

valetudinarian *a.* morbidly anxious about one's state of health. *Also n.* **WH:** 18C. Latin *valetudinarius* in ill health, from *valetudo, valetudinis* state of health, from *valere* to be strong, to be well. See also -ARIAN.

valgus *a.* twisted away from the midline of the body. *Also n.* **WH:** 19C. Latin knock-kneed.

Valhalla *n.* in Norse mythology, the palace of immortality where the souls of heroes slain in battle were carried by the Valkyries. WH: 17C. Modern Latin, from Old Norse *Valhǫll*, from *valr* those slain in battle, rel. to Old English *wæl* slaughter + *hǫll* HALL. Cp. VALKYRIE.

valiant *a.* brave, daring. WH: 12–14C. Old French *vailant* (Modern French *vaillant*), from Latin *valens, valentis*, pres.p. of *valere* to be strong. See VAIL², also -ANT.

valid *a.* based on sound reasoning. WH: 16C. French *valide* or Latin *validus* strong, from *valere* to be strong. See also -ID.

valine *n.* an amino acid that is essential to health and growth in humans and other vertebrates. WH: early 20C. From *valerianic* (from VALERIAN + -IC) + -INE.

valise *n.* a bag or case, usu. of leather, for holding a traveller's clothes etc., esp. one for carrying in the hand, a travelling bag. WH: 17C. French, from Italian *valigia*, corr. to Medieval Latin *valesia*, of unknown orig.

Valium® *n.* the tranquillizer diazepam. WH: mid-20C. Orig. unknown. ? From Latin *valere* to be well + -IUM.

Valkyrie *n.* in Norse mythology, each of twelve maidens of Valhalla who were sent by Odin to select those destined to be slain in battle and to conduct their souls to Valhalla. WH: 18C. Old Norse *Valkyrja*, lit. chooser of the slain, from *valr* those slain in battle (see VALHALLA) + *-kyrja* chooser, ult. from *kjósa* CHOOSE.

vallecula *n.* a groove or furrow. WH: 19C. Late Latin, var. of Latin *vallicula*, dim. of *valles, vallis* VALLEY. See also -CULE.

valley *n.* a depression in the earth's surface bounded by hills or mountains, and usu. with a river or stream flowing through it. WH: 12–14C. Old French *valée* (Modern French *vallée*), from Latin *valles, vallis*. See VALE¹, also -Y².

vallum *n.* an ancient Roman rampart, an agger. WH: 17C. Latin collect. n., from *vallus* stake, pallisade.

valonia *n.* the large acorn-cups of the valonia oak, used for dyeing, tanning, ink-making etc. WH: 18C. Italian *vallonia*, from obs. Modern Greek *balania*, pl. of *balani*, from Greek *balanos* acorn.

valorize *v.t.* to increase or stabilize the price of (an article) by an officially organized scheme. WH: early 20C. French *valoriser*, from *valeur* value. See also -IZE.

valour *n.* personal bravery, courage esp. as displayed in fighting. WH: 12–14C. Old French *valour* (Modern French *valeur* value), from Late Latin *valor*, from *valere* to be strong. See also -OUR.

valse *n.* a waltz. WH: 18C. French, from German *Walzer* WALTZ.

value *n.* worth, the desirability of a thing, esp. as compared with other things. *Also v.t.* WH: 12–14C. Old French, fem. p.p. formation from *valoir* to be worth, from Latin *valere* to be strong, to be worth.

valuta *n.* the value of one currency in terms of another. WH: 19C. Italian value.

valve *n.* an automatic or other contrivance for opening or closing a passage or aperture so as to permit or prevent passage of a fluid, such as water, gas or steam. WH: 14–15C. Latin *valva* leaf of a door (usu. pl. *valvae* folding door).

vambrace *n.* armour for the arm from the elbow to the wrist. WH: 12–14C. Anglo-French *vauntbras*, shortening of Old French *avantbras*, from *avant* before + *bras* arm. Cp. VAMPLATE.

vamoose *v.i.* to decamp, to be gone, to be off. WH: 19C. Spanish *vamos* let us go.

vamp¹ *n.* the part of a boot or shoe upper in front of the ankle seams. *Also a., v.i.* WH: 12–14C. Shortening of Old French *avantpié* (Modern French *avantpied*), from *avant* before + *pié* foot. The verb evolved from the noun in the 16C, originally in the sense to fit with a new vamp, hence to make by patching together, to compile (17C), to improvise a tune or accompaniment (18C), to extemporize generally (19C).

vamp² *n.* an adventuress, a woman who exploits her sexual attractiveness to take advantage of men. *Also v.t., v.i.* WH: early 20C. Abbr. of VAMPIRE, ? influ. by TRAMP in similar sense.

vampire *n.* a ghost of a heretic, criminal or other outcast, supposed to leave the grave at night and suck the blood of sleeping persons. WH: 18C. French *vampire* or German *Vampir*, from Hungarian *vampir*, ? from Turkish *uber* witch.

vamplate *n.* an iron plate fixed on a lance as a guard for the hand. WH: 12–14C. Anglo-French *vauntplate*, var. of *vant-*, shortening of *avant* before + *plate* PLATE. Cp. VAMBRACE.

van¹ *n.* a motor vehicle, usu. covered, for conveying goods, furniture etc. *Also v.t.* WH: 19C. Abbr. of CARAVAN.

van² *n.* the foremost division of an army or fleet, the advance guard. WH: 17C. Abbr. of VANGUARD.

van³ *n.* a test of the quality of ore by washing on a shovel etc. *Also v.t.* WH: 14–15C. Dial. var. of FAN¹, reinforced by Old French *van* or Latin *vannus*. Cp. VANE.

van⁴ *n., int.* in tennis, advantage. WH: early 20C. Abbr. of ADVANTAGE.

vanadium *n.* a rare, silver-white metallic element, at. no. 23, chem. symbol V, used to give tensile strength to steel and, in the form of its salts, to produce an intense permanent black colour. WH: 19C. Modern Latin, from Old Norse *Vanadis*, a name of the Scandinavian goddess Freyja + -IUM. The name was coined in 1830 by the Swedish chemist Nils Sefström.

Van Allen belt *n.* a belt of intense particle radiation in the earth's outer atmosphere. WH: mid-20C. James A. *Van Allen*, 1914–, US physicist.

vandal *n.* a person who wilfully or ignorantly destroys or damages anything. *Also a.* WH: pre-1200. Old English *Wendlas* (pl.), from Germanic. Reintroduced 16C from Latin *Vandalus*, from Germanic. The current sense evolved in the 17C from the name of the Germanic people who sacked Rome on a marauding expedition in AD 455.

van de Graaff generator *n.* a device for generating a very high electrostatic charge on a hollow metal sphere by means of a continuous belt. WH: mid-20C. R.J. *van de Graaff*, 1901–67, US physicist.

van der Waals forces *n.pl.* weak attractive forces between atoms or molecules caused by transient dissymmetries in electron distribution. WH: 19C. Johannes *van der Waals*, 1837–1923, Dutch physicist.

vandyke *n.* any one of the series of points forming an ornamental border to lace, linen etc. *Also a., v.t.* WH: 18C. Sir Anthony *Vandyke* (Anglicized spelling of Van Dyck), 1599–1641, Flemish painter.

vane *n.* a weathercock, flag or arrow pointing in the direction of the wind. WH: 14–15C. Dial. var. of obs. *fane* flag, banner, from Old English *fana*, from Germanic. Rel. to Latin *pannus* (piece of) cloth, and so to PANE. Cp. VAN³.

vanessid *n.* a butterfly with notched wings, belonging to any of several brightly coloured species, such as Camberwell Beauty, red or white admiral, tortoiseshell etc. WH: early 20C. Modern Latin *Vanessa*, genus name, from female forename coined by Jonathan Swift for *Esther Vanhomrigh* + -ID.

vang *n.* either of a pair of guy ropes running from the peak of a gaff to the deck to steady it. WH: 18C. Var. of FANG.

vanguard *n.* the troops who march in the front or van of an army, an advance guard, the van. WH: 14–15C. Shortening of Old French *avant-garde*, from *avant* before + *garde* GUARD. Cp. AVANT-GARDE, VAN².

vanilla *n.* any member of a genus, *Vanilla*, of tall, epiphytal orchids, natives of tropical Asia and America, bearing fragrant flowers. *Also a.* WH: 17C. Spanish *vainilla*, dim. of *vaina* sheath, from Latin VAGINA. Assim. to French *vanille*. The plant is so called from its pods. The sense extract obtained from dried vanilla pods dates from the 18C.

vanish *v.i.* to disappear suddenly. *Also v.t.* WH: 12–14C. Shortening of Old French *esvanir, esvaniss-*, from Latin *evanescere* EVANESCE. See also -ISH².

Vanitory® *n.* a vanity unit. WH: mid-20C. VANITY + -ORY¹, based on LAVATORY.

vanity *n.* the quality or state of being vain. WH: 12–14C. Old French *vanité*, from Latin *vanitas*, from *vanus* VAIN. See also -ITY.

vanquish *v.t.* to conquer, to overcome, to subdue. WH: 12–14C. Old French *vencus*, p.p., *venquis*, past tense of *veintre, vaintre* (Modern French *vaincre*), from Latin *vincere* to conquer. The first syllable was altered by association with later Old French *vain-*, and the ending assimilated to -ISH².

vantage *n.* superiority or elevation, esp. such as to give a commanding view. *Also v.t.* WH: 12–14C. Anglo-French, shortening of Old French *avantage* ADVANTAGE. See also -AGE.

vapid *a.* lacking interest or excitement. WH: 17C. Latin *vapidus* savourless, insipid. See also -ID.

vaporetto n. a small motor vessel (orig. a steamship) used for public transport on the canals of Venice. WH: early 20C. Italian small steamboat, dim. of *vapore*, from Latin *vapor* steam. See VAPOUR.

vapour n. moisture in the air, light mist. *Also v.i.* WH: 14–15C. Old French *vapeur* or Latin *vapor* steam, heat. See also -OUR.

vaquero n. in Mexico and Spanish-speaking parts of America, a herdsman, a cowherd. WH: 19C. Spanish, from *vaca* cow.

vara n. a Spanish-American measure of length, varying from 33 to 43 in. (84–110 cm). WH: 17C. Spanish and Portuguese rod, yardstick, from Latin forked pole, trestle, from *varus* bent.

varactor n. a two-electrode semiconductor device in which capacitance varies with voltage. WH: mid-20C. Shortening of *vari*able re*actor*.

Varangian n. any of the Norse sea rovers in the 8th–12th cents. who ravaged the coasts of the Baltic and conquered part of Russia. WH: 18C. Medieval Latin *Varangus*, from Medieval Greek *baraggos*, through Slavonic languages, from Old Norse *Væringi* (pl. *Væringjar*), prob. from *vár* (pl. *várar*) pledge. See also -IAN.

varec n. kelp or the ash obtained from kelp. WH: 17C. French, from Middle Low German and Dutch *wrak* WRACK.

variable a. capable of varying, liable to change. *Also n.* WH: 14–15C. Old French, or from Latin *variabilis*, from *variare*. See VARY, also -ABLE.

variance n. the fact of varying, the state of being variant, disagreement, difference of opinion, dissension, discord. WH: 12–14C. Old French, from Latin *variantia*, from *variare* VARY. See also -ANCE.

variation n. the act, process or state of varying. WH: 14–15C. Old French, or from Latin *variatio*, *variationis*, from *variatus*, p.p. of *variare* VARY. See also -ATION.

varicella n. chickenpox. WH: 18C. Modern Latin, from VARIOLA + dim. suf. *-ella*.

varicoloured a. variously coloured, variegated, particoloured. WH: 17C. Latin *varius* VARIOUS + *coloured* (COLOUR).

varicose a. (of veins) permanently dilated, affected with varix. WH: 14–15C. Latin *varicosus*, from VARIX, *varicis*. See also -OSE[1].

variegate v.t. to diversify in colour, to mark with patches of different hues, to dapple, to chequer. WH: 17C. Latin *variegatus*, p.p. of *variegare* to make varied, from *varius* VARIOUS. See also -ATE[3].

variety n. the quality or state of being various; diversity, absence of sameness or monotony, many-sidedness, versatility. *Also a.* WH: 15C. Old French *variété* or Latin *varietas*, from *varius* VARIOUS + *-itas* -ITY.

varifocal a. having a variable focal length, allowing the focusing range to alter gradually to accommodate near, intermediate and far vision. *Also n.* WH: mid-20C. VARIABLE + *focal* (FOCUS).

variform a. varying in form, of different shapes. WH: 17C. Latin *varius* VARIOUS + -FORM.

variola n. smallpox. WH: 18C. Late Latin pustule, pox, from Latin *varius* VARIOUS.

variometer n. a device for varying the inductance in an electric circuit. WH: 19C. VARIABLE + -METER.

variorum a. (of an edition of a work) with notes of various commentators inserted. *Also n.* WH: 18C. Latin, lit. of various (people), gen. pl. of *varius* VARIOUS. The usual full phrase was *editio cum notis variorum* edition with the notes of various (commentators).

various a. differing from each other, diverse. WH: 14–15C. Latin *varius* changing, diverse, variegated. See also -OUS.

varistor n. a semiconductor with two electrodes which has a resistance dependent on the strength of the voltage applied. WH: mid-20C. VARIABLE + *resistor* (RESIST).

varix n. a permanent dilatation of a vein or other vessel. WH: 14–15C. Latin dilated vein. Cp. VARICOSE.

varlet n. a page, an attendant preparing to be a squire. WH: 14–15C. Old French, var. of *vaslet*, *varlet*, VALET. The sense rogue evolved in the 16C.

varmint n. a troublesome or mischievous person or animal. WH: 16C. Alt. of VERMIN, with added *-t*. The word is not related to VARLET, despite the similarity of sense.

varna n. any of the four great Hindu castes. WH: 19C. Sanskrit *varṇa*, lit. appearance, aspect, colour.

varnish n. a thin resinous solution for applying to the surface of wood, metal etc., to give it a hard, transparent, shiny coating. *Also v.t.* WH: 12–14C. Old French *vernis*, from Medieval Latin *veronix*, *veronicis* fragrant resin, sandarac, or Medieval Greek *berenikē*, prob. from *Berenice*, a town in Cyrenaica.

varsity n. university. WH: 17C. Abbr. of UNIVERSITY. The spelling represents the former pronunciation. Cp. CLERK, SERGEANT, where the pronunciation has changed similarly but is not reflected in the spelling.

varus n. a variety of club foot in which the foot is bent inwards. WH: 19C. Latin bow-legged.

varve n. a seasonal layer of clay deposited in still water, used to fix ice age chronology. WH: early 20C. Swedish layer, turn.

vary v.t. to change, to alter in appearance, form or substance. *Also v.i.* WH: 12–14C. Old French *varier* or Latin *variare*, from *varius* VARIOUS.

vas n. a vessel or duct. WH: 16C. Latin vessel.

vascular a. of, consisting of, or containing vessels or ducts for the conveyance of blood, chyle, sap etc. WH: 17C. Modern Latin *vascularis*, from Latin *vasculum*, dim. of VAS. See also -AR[1].

vasculum n. a botanist's collecting case, usu. of tin. WH: 18C. Latin, dim. of VAS. See also -CULE.

vase n. a vessel of pottery etc., of various forms but usu. circular with a swelling body and a foot or pedestal, used for various ornamental and other purposes, esp. holding flowers. WH: 14–15C. French, from Latin *vas* vessel.

vasectomy n. excision of the vas deferens or part of it to produce sterility. WH: 19C. VAS + -ECTOMY.

Vaseline® n. a soft, medicated paraffin jelly employed as a lubricant etc. WH: 19C. German *Wasser* water + Greek *elaion* oil + -INE. The name was coined in 1872 by the US manufacturer Robert A. Chesebrough.

vasiform a. having the form of a vas. WH: 19C. Latin VAS, *vasi*- + -FORM.

vaso- comb. form relating to a vas, vessel or duct. WH: 19C. Latin VAS + -O-.

vasoactive a. vasomotor. WH: mid-20C. VASO- + ACTIVE.

vasoconstrictor a. causing constriction of a blood vessel. *Also n.* WH: 19C. VASO- + *constrictor* (CONSTRICT).

vasodilator a. causing dilatation of a vessel. *Also n.* WH: 19C. VASO- + *dilator* (DILATE).

vasoinhibitor n. a drug that inhibits the action of the vasomotor nerves. WH: 19C. VASO- + *inhibitor* (INHIBIT).

vasomotor a. causing constriction or dilatation in a vessel. *Also n.* WH: 19C. VASO- + MOTOR.

vasopressin n. a polypeptide hormone secreted by the pituitary gland that reduces diuresis and increases blood pressure. WH: early 20C. VASO- + PRESSOR + -IN[1].

vassal n. a person holding land under a superior lord by feudal tenure, a feudatory. *Also a.* WH: 14–15C. Old French, from Medieval Latin *vassallus* manservant, retainer, of Celtic orig. Cp. VAVASOUR.

vast a. of great extent, immense, huge, boundless. *Also n.* WH: 14–15C. Latin *vastus* void, immense.

vat n. a large tub, tank or other vessel used for holding mash or hop liquor in brewing and in many manufacturing operations in which substances are boiled or steeped. *Also v.t.* WH: 12–14C. Var. of FAT. For a similar change of *f* to *v*, see southern and western English speech, cp. VIXEN. 'A certain man planted a vineyard, and set an hedge about it, and digged a place for the winefat' (Mark xii.1).

vatic a. of or relating to a prophet. WH: 17C. Latin *vates* seer, poet + -IC.

Vatican n. the palace of the Pope on the Vatican Hill in Rome. WH: 16C. French, or from Latin *Vaticanus* (*collis* hill, or *mons* mountain), a hill in Rome on which stands the Vatican, the palace and official residence of the Pope.

vaticide n. the murder or murderer of a prophet. WH: 19C. Latin *vates*, *vati*- seer, prophet + -CIDE.

vaticinate v.t., v.i. to prophesy. WH: 17C. Latin *vaticinatus*, p.p. of *vaticinari* to prophesy, from *vates*, *vati*- seer, prophet. See also -ATE[3].

vatu n. the standard monetary unit of Vanuatu. WH: late 20C. Shortening of *Vanuatu*.

vaudeville *n.* a miscellaneous series of sketches, songs etc., a variety entertainment. WH: 18C. French, earlier *vau de ville*, *vau de vire*, from *chanson du Vau de Vire* song of the valley of the Vire (in NW France), influ. by *ville* town. The title is said to have been originally applied to the songs composed by Olivier Basselin, a 15C fuller who lived in the Vire valley. French etymologists, however, generally prefer an origin in dialect *vauder* to go round and *virer* to turn, referring to the 'circulating' nature of the songs and sketches.

Vaudois[1] *n.* a native or inhabitant of Vaud. Also *a.* WH: 19C. French, from *Vaud*, a canton of Switzerland.

Vaudois[2] *n.* any of the Waldenses. Also *a.* WH: 16C. French, from Medieval Latin *Valdensis*. See WALDENSES.

vault[1] *n.* an arched roof; a continuous arch or semi-cylindrical roof; a series of arches connected by radiating joints. Also *v.t.* WH: 12–14C. Old French *voute*, *vaute* (Modern French *voûte*), from alt. of Latin *voluta*, fem. p.p. (used as n.) of *volvere* to roll, to turn.

vault[2] *v.i.* to leap, to spring, esp. with the hands resting on something or with the help of a pole. Also *v.t.*, *n.* WH: 16C. Old French *volter*, *voulter* to turn (a horse), to gambol, to leap, from an assumed var. of Latin *volvere* to roll. Assim. to VAULT[1].

vaunt *v.i.* to boast, to brag. Also *v.t.*, *n.* WH: 14–15C. Old French *vanter*, from Late Latin *vanitare*, freq. of *vanare* to speak empty words, from *vanus* vain, empty.

†vaunt-courier *n.* a forerunner, a harbinger. WH: 16C. Shortening of French *avant-coureur* avant-courier (AVANT, COURIER).

vavasour *n.* a vassal holding land from a great lord and having other vassals under him. WH: 12–14C. Old French *vavassour* (Modern French *vavasseur*), from Medieval Latin *vavassor*, prob. from *vassus vassorum* vassal of vassals. Cp. VASSAL.

Veadar *n.* a supplementary or intercalary month inserted into the Jewish calendar every third year after the month Adar. WH: 14–15C. Hebrew *wĕ-'ăḏār*, lit. and Adar (i.e. the second Adar). See ADAR.

veal *n.* the flesh of a calf as food. WH: 12–14C. Anglo-French *vel*, from Old French *veel* (Modern French *veau*), from Latin *vitellus*, dim. of *vitulus* calf.

vector *n.* a quantity having both magnitude and direction but not temperature. Also *v.t.* WH: 18C. Latin carrier, traveller, rider, from *vectus*, p.p. of *vehere* to carry, to convey. See also -OR.

Veda *n.* the ancient Hindu scriptures, divided into four portions or books (the *Rig-*, *Yajur-*, *Sāma-*, and *Artharva-Veda*). WH: 18C. Sanskrit (sacred) knowledge, sacred book, ult. from Indo-European base meaning to know, represented also in WIT[2].

Vedda *n.* a member of an aboriginal people of Sri Lanka. WH: 17C. Sinhalese *vaddā* archer, hunter.

vedette *n.* a sentinel (usu. mounted) stationed in advance of an outpost. WH: 17C. French, from Latin *vedetta*, alt. (based on *vedere* to see) of southern Italian *veletta*, ? from Spanish *vela* watch, from *velar* to keep watch, from Latin *vigilare*.

vee *n.* the letter V, v. WH: 19C. Representation of pronun. of *V*, *v* as letter's name.

veep *n.* a vice-president. WH: mid-20C. From initials *V.P.*

veer[1] *v.i.* to change direction; esp. (of the wind) in the direction of the sun (i.e. clockwise in the northern hemisphere and anticlockwise in the southern hemisphere). Also *v.t.* WH: 16C. Old French *virer*, corr. to Spanish *virar*, Italian *virare*, ? from alt. of Latin *gyrare* GYRATE.

veer[2] *v.t.* to let out or slacken (a rope etc.). WH: 14–15C. Middle Dutch *vieren* to let out, to slacken, rel. to Old High German *fiaren*, *fieren* to give direction to.

veery *n.* a tawny N American thrush, *Catharus fuscescens*. WH: 19C. ? Imit.

veg *n.* a vegetable. WH: 19C. Abbr. of VEGETABLE.

vegan *n.* a person who uses no animal products whatsoever for food, clothing etc. Also *a.* WH: mid-20C. VEGETABLE + -AN.

Vegeburger® *n.* a vegetarian burger. WH: late 20C. VEGETABLE + BURGER.

vegetable *n.* a plant, esp. a herbaceous one, used for culinary purposes or for feeding cattle etc. Also *a.* WH: 14–15C. Old French (Modern French *végétable*), or from Late Latin *vegetabilis* animating, vivifying, from Latin *vegetare*, from *vegetus* active, from *vegere* to be active. See also -ABLE.

vehement *a.* proceeding from or exhibiting intense fervour or passion, ardent, passionate, impetuous. WH: 14–15C. Old French *véhément* or Latin *vehemens*, *vehementis*, impetuous, violent, ? from an unrecorded a. meaning deprived of mind, alt. by assoc. with *vehere* to carry.

vehicle *n.* any kind of carriage or conveyance for use on land, having wheels or runners. WH: 17C. French *véhicule* or Latin *vehiculum*, from *vehere* to carry. The original sense was means, medium, but the current specific sense means of conveyance followed soon after.

veil *n.* a more or less transparent piece of cloth, muslin etc., usu. attached to a hat or headdress, worn to conceal, shade or protect the face. Also *v.t.* WH: 12–14C. Old French *voil* (Modern French *voile*), from Latin *vela* (pl.) sails, *velum* (sing.) sail, curtain, veil. Cp. VELUM. The Latin words respectively gave French *voile* (fem.) sail and *voile* (m.) veil. The former sense did not pass to English. Cp. VOILE.

veilleuse *n.* a night-lamp, shaded and usu. artistically decorated. WH: 19C. French, fem. of *veilleur*, from *veiller* to stay awake, to keep watch.

vein *n.* any of the tubular vessels in animal bodies conveying blood to the heart. Also *v.t.* WH: 12–14C. Old French *veine*, from Latin *vena*.

velamen *n.* a membraneous covering or envelope, esp. of the aerial roots of some orchids. WH: 19C. Latin covering, from *velare* to cover, to veil.

velar *a.* of or relating to a velum. Also *n.* WH: 18C. Latin *velaris*, from VELUM. See also -AR[1].

velarium *n.* the great awning stretched over the seats in an ancient Roman theatre or amphitheatre as a protection against rain or sun. WH: 19C. Latin awning, sail, from VELUM. See also -ARIUM.

Velcro® *n.* a fastening for clothes etc. which consists of two nylon strips, one consisting of hooks and the other of loops, which stick together when pressed. Also *v.t.* WH: mid-20C. Abbr. of French *velours croché* hooked velvet. Cp. VELOUR, CROCHET.

veld *n.* open country suitable for pasturage, esp. the high treeless plains in N Transvaal and NW Natal. WH: 18C. Afrikaans, from Dutch field. Cp. FIELD.

veldskoen *n.* an ankle-length boot, orig. made of raw hide, now usu. of soft suede or leather. WH: 19C. Afrikaans field shoe, alt. (by assim. to VELD) of earlier *velschoen*, from *fel* skin, FELL[2] + *schoen* shoe.

veleta *n.* a dance or dance tune in slow waltz time. WH: early 20C. Spanish weathervane. The dance is so named from its revolving movements.

veliger *n.* a free-swimming larva of a mollusc, which has a ciliated velum for feeding and movement. WH: 19C. VELUM + -*i*- + Latin *-ger* bearing.

†velitation *n.* a slight skirmish. WH: 17C. Latin *velitatio*, *velitationis*, from *velitari* to skirmish, from *veles* skirmisher. See also -ATION.

velleity *n.* a low degree of desire or volition unaccompanied by effort. WH: 17C. Medieval Latin *velleitas*, from Latin *velle* to wish, to will. See also -ITY.

vellicate *v.t.*, *v.i.* to twitch spasmodically. WH: 17C. Latin *vellicatus*, p.p. of *vellicare*, freq. of *vellere* to pluck. See also -ATE[3].

vellum *n.* a fine parchment orig. made of calfskin. Also *a.* WH: 14–15C. Old French *vélin*, from *veel* VEAL + -*in* -INE. The final *n* has changed to *m* as with PILGRIM, VENOM.

veloce *adv.* with great quickness. WH: 19C. Italian rapid, from Latin *velox*, *velocis* swift.

velocimeter *n.* an apparatus for measuring velocity. WH: 19C. Latin *velox*, *velocis* swift + -*i*- + -METER.

velocipede *n.* an early kind of bicycle propelled by the feet. WH: 19C. French *vélocipède*, from Latin *velox*, *velocis* swift + *pes*, *pedis* foot.

velociraptor *n.* a small carnivorous dinosaur of the Cretaceous period which stood upright and had a large curved claw on each hind foot. WH: late 20C. Modern Latin genus name, from Latin *velox*, *velocis* swift, rapid + RAPTOR.

velocity *n.* swiftness, rapidity, rapid motion. WH: 14–15C. Old French *vélocité* or Latin *velocitas*, from *velox*, *velocis* swift, rapid. See also -ITY.

velodrome *n.* a building containing a cycle-racing track. WH: 19C. French *vélodrome*, from *vélo* bicycle (abbr. of *vélocipède* VELOCIPEDE) + -*drome* -DROME.

velour *n.* velvet, velveteen or other fabric resembling velvet. *Also v.t.* WH: 18C. French *velours* velvet, from Old French *velour, velous,* from Latin *villosus* hairy, from *villus* hair. Cp. VELVET.

velum *n.* a membrane, a membraneous covering, envelope etc., esp. the soft palate. WH: 18C. Latin sail, curtain, veil. Cp. VEIL. Not rel. to VELLUM.

velvet *n.* a closely-woven fabric, usu. of silk, with a short, soft nap or cut pile on one side. *Also a.* WH: 12–14C. Old French *veluotte,* from *velu* velvety, from Medieval Latin *villutus,* from Latin *villus* hair.

vena *n.* a vein. WH: 14–15C. Latin.

venal *a.* ready to be bribed or to sacrifice honour or principle for sordid considerations. WH: 17C. Latin *venalis,* from *venum* something sold, something for sale. See also -AL[1]. The original sense was available for purchase. The current sense evolved from this in the 18C.

venatic *a.* of, relating to or used in hunting. WH: 17C. Latin *venaticus,* from *venatus,* p.p. of *venari* to hunt. See also -ATIC.

vend *v.t.* to sell. WH: 17C. Old French *vendre* or Latin *vendere* to sell, from *venum* (VENAL) + *-dere,* var. of *dare* to give.

vendace *n.* a small and delicate whitefish, *Coregonus albula,* found in some lakes. WH: 18C. Old French *vendese, vendoise* (Modern French *vandoise*), from a Gaulish word rel. to Old Irish *find,* Welsh *gwyn* white.

Vendéan *a.* of or relating to La Vendée. *Also n.* WH: 18C. French *vendéen,* from *La Vendée,* a maritime department in W France + -AN.

Vendémiaire *n.* the first month of the French revolutionary calendar (22 September–21 October). WH: 18C. French, from Latin *vindemia* (VINTAGE) + *-aire* -ARY[1].

vendetta *n.* a blood feud, often carried on for generations, in which the family of a murdered or injured man seeks vengeance on the offender or any member of his family, prevalent esp. in Corsica, Sardinia and Sicily. WH: 19C. Italian, from Latin *vindicta* vengeance. Cp. VINDICTIVE.

vendeuse *n.* a saleswoman, esp. in a fashionable dress shop. WH: early 20C. French, fem. of *vendeur,* from *vendre* to sell.

veneer *v.t.* to cover with a thin layer of fine or superior wood. *Also n.* WH: 18C. German *furnieren,* from French *fournir* FURNISH.

venenose *a.* poisonous. WH: 17C. Late Latin *venenosus,* from *venenum* poison. See also -OSE[1].

venerable *a.* worthy of reverence, esp. on account of old age and good character. WH: 14–15C. Old French *vénérable* or Latin *venerabilis,* from *venerari* VENERATE. See also -ABLE.

venerate *v.t.* to regard or treat with profound deference and respect, to revere. WH: 17C. Latin *veneratus,* p.p. of *venerari* to adore, to revere. See also -ATE[3].

venereal *a.* of or relating to, or produced by sexual intercourse. WH: 14–15C. Latin *venereus,* from *venus, veneris* love + -AL[1]. Cp. VENUS.

†**venery** *n.* hunting, the chase. WH: 12–14C. Old French *vénerie,* from *vener* to hunt, from Latin *venari.* See also -ERY. Cp. VENISON.

Venetian *a.* of or relating to Venice. *Also n.* WH: 14–15C. Old French *Venicien* (Modern French *Vénitien*), later assim. to Medieval Latin *Venetianus,* from Latin *Venetia* Venice, a city and former republic in NE Italy (Italian *Venezia*). See also -IAN.

vengeance *n.* punishment inflicted in return for an injury or wrong, retribution. WH: 12–14C. Old French, from *venger,* from Latin *vindicare* VINDICATE.

venial *a.* that may be pardoned or excused. WH: 12–14C. Old French (Modern French *véniel*), from Late Latin *venialis,* from *venia* forgiveness. See also -AL[1].

venin *n.* any of the poisonous substances found in animal venom. WH: 12–14C. Old French, from Latin *venenum* poison.

venison *n.* the flesh of deer as food. WH: 12–14C. Old French *veneson, venison* (Modern French *venaison*), from Latin *venatio, venationis,* from *venatus,* p.p. of *venari* to hunt. See also -ISON.

Venite *n.* Psalm xcv, 'O come let us sing', used as a canticle. WH: 12–14C. Latin, 2nd pers. pl. imper. of *venire* to come, first word of Vulgate (Latin) version of Ps. xcv. The first full phrase of the psalm is *Venite, exultemus Domino* O come, let us sing unto the Lord.

Venn diagram *n.* a diagram in which sets and their relationships are represented by intersecting circles or other figures. WH: early 20C. John *Venn,* 1834–1923, English logician.

venom *n.* a poisonous fluid secreted by snakes, scorpions etc., and injected by biting or stinging. *Also a., v.t.* WH: 12–14C. Old French *venim, venin,* from alt. (based on Latin words in *-imen*) of Latin *venenum* potion, drug, poison. The final *n* has changed to *m* as with PILGRIM.

venose *a.* veiny, having many or very marked veins. WH: 17C. Latin *venosus,* from *vena* vein. See also -OSE[1].

vent[1] *n.* a hole or aperture, esp. for the passage of air, water etc. into or out of a confined place. *Also v.t., v.i.* WH: 14–15C. Partly from French *wind,* partly based on French *évent,* from *éventer* (AVENTAIL).

vent[2] *n.* a slit in a garment, esp. in the back of a coat or jacket. *Also v.t.* WH: 14–15C. Alt. of FENT. Not rel. to VENT[1].

ventail *n.* in a suit of armour, the part of the helmet that covers the lower part of the face and is often movable to admit fresh air. WH: 12–14C. Old French *ventaille,* from *vent* wind, from Latin *ventus.* See also -AL[1].

venter *n.* the belly, the abdomen, any large cavity containing viscera. WH: 16C. Latin belly.

ventiduct *n.* a passage or conduit, esp. subterranean, for ventilation. WH: 17C. Latin *ventus* wind + *-i-* + Latin *ductus* DUCT.

ventifact *n.* a pebble shaped or polished by wind-blown sand. WH: early 20C. Latin *ventus* wind + *-i-* + Latin *factus,* p.p. of *facere* to make, based on ARTEFACT.

ventil *n.* a valve in a wind instrument. WH: 19C. German, from Italian *ventile,* from Medieval Latin sluice, rel. to Latin *ventus* wind.

ventilate *v.t.* to supply with fresh air, to cause a circulation of air in (a room etc.). WH: 14–15C. Latin *ventilatus,* p.p. of *ventilare* to brandish, to fan, to winnow, from *ventus* wind. See also -ATE[3].

Ventolin® *n.* a preparation of salbutamol. WH: mid-20C. Orig. unknown. ? From VENTILATE + -OL + -IN[1].

Ventôse *n.* the sixth month of the French revolutionary year (19 February–20 March). WH: 19C. French, from Latin *ventosus,* from *ventus* wind. See also -OSE[1].

ventouse *n.* in obstetrics, a vacuum suction cup that may be placed on the baby's head to assist the delivery. WH: mid-20C. French, orig. cupping glass, from Late Latin *ventosa,* use as n. of fem. of Latin *ventosus,* from *ventus* wind.

ventre à terre *adv.* flat out, at full speed. WH: 19C. French, lit. belly to the ground. The reference is to a painting of a horse running at full speed with its legs stretched out in line with its belly.

ventricle *n.* a cavity or hollow part in an animal body, esp. in the heart and brain. WH: 14–15C. Latin *ventriculus,* dim. of *venter, ventris* belly. See also -CLE.

ventriculite *n.* any of a family of fossil sponges common in flint nodules. WH: 19C. Modern Latin *Ventriculites* genus name, from Latin *ventriculus.* See VENTRICLE, also -ITE[1].

ventriloquism *n.* the act or art of speaking or producing sounds so that the sound appears to come not from the person speaking but from a different source. WH: 16C. Modern Latin *ventriloquium,* from *ventriloquus,* from *venter, ventris* belly + *loqui* to speak. See also -ISM.

venture *n.* the undertaking of a risk, a hazard. *Also v.t., v.i.* WH: 14–15C. Shortening of ADVENTURE, partly taken as *a venture.*

venturi *n.* a tube or duct, wasp-waisted and expanding at the ends, used in measuring the flow rates of fluids, or as a means of accelerating air flow, or to provide a suction source for vacuum-operated instruments. WH: 19C. Giovanni Battista *Venturi,* 1746–1822, Italian physicist.

venue *n.* a place chosen as the site of an organized event or meeting. WH: 12–14C. Old French, use as n. of fem. p.p. of *venir* to come, from Latin *venire.* The original sense was sally, attack, then (16C) location where a cause must be tried and a jury gathered. The current sense dates from the 19C.

Venus *n.* the second planet from the sun, the brightest heavenly body after the sun and moon. WH: pre-1200. Latin, in Roman mythology the goddess of beauty and (sexual) love. Cp. VENEREAL.

veracious *a.* habitually speaking or disposed to speak the truth. WH: 17C. Latin *verax, veracis,* from *verus* true. See also -ACIOUS.

veranda *n.* a light external gallery or portico with a roof on pillars, along the front or side of a house. WH: 18C. Hindi *varaṇḍā*, from Portuguese *varanda* railing, balustrade, balcony, of unknown orig.

veratrine *n.* a highly poisonous amorphous compound obtained from hellebore and other plants, used as a local irritant in neuralgia, rheumatism etc. WH: 19C. Latin VERATRUM + -INE.

veratrum *n.* the hellebore. WH: 16C. Latin hellebore.

verb *n.* that part of speech which predicates, a word or group of words that denotes an action performed or state undergone by something else (the subject). WH: 14–15C. Old French *verbe* or Latin *verbum* word, verb.

verbal *a.* of or relating to words. *Also n., v.t.* WH: 15C. Old French, or from Late Latin *verbalis*, from Latin *verbum*. See VERB, also -AL¹.

verbascum *n.* a plant of the genus *Verbascum*, a mullein. WH: 16C. Latin mullein.

verbatim *adv., a.* word for word. WH: 15C. Medieval Latin, from Latin *verbum* word. Cp. LITERATIM.

verbena *n.* any of a large genus of plants, *Verbena*, of which *V. officinalis*, the common vervain, is the type. WH: 16C. Latin genus name, sing. of *verbenae* sacred boughs (of laurel, olive or myrtle). Cp. VERVAIN.

verbiage *n.* an excess of words, unnecessary words. WH: 18C. French, from obs. *verbeier* to chatter, from *verbe* word. See also -OSE¹.

verboten *a.* forbidden by authority. WH: early 20C. German forbidden, p.p. of *verbieten* FORBID.

verb. sap. *int.* used to indicate that there is no need for a more explicit statement, warning etc. WH: 19C. Abbr. of Latin *verbum sapienti sat est* a word is sufficient for a wise person. The proverb echoes a line from Plautus: *Dictum sapienti sat est*, A sentence is enough for a sensible man (*Persa*, 2C BC).

verdant *a.* green. WH: 16C. Prob. from Old French *verdeant*, pres.p. of *verdoier* (Modern French *verdoyer*), from Popular Latin *viridiare* to grow green, from Latin *viridis* green. See also -ANT.

verd-antique *n.* an ornamental stone composed chiefly of serpentine, usu. green and mottled or veined. WH: 18C. Obs. French *verd* (now *vert*) *antique*. See VERT, ANTIQUE.

verderer *n.* a judicial officer who had charge of the royal forests. WH: 16C. Anglo-French, extended form (see -ER¹) of *verder*, from Old French *verdier*, ult. from Latin *viridis* green. See VERT, also -ER².

verdict *n.* the decision of a jury on an issue of fact submitted to them in the trial of any cause, civil or criminal. WH: 12–14C. Old French *verdit*, *voirdit*, from *veir*, *voir* (from Latin *verum* true) + *dit* (from Latin *dictum* saying, speech, use as n. of neut. p.p. of *dicere* to say). See VERY.

verdigris *n.* a green crystalline substance formed on copper by the action of dilute acetic acid, used as a pigment and in medicine. WH: 12–14C. Old French *verte-gres*, earlier *vert de Grece* (Modern French *vert-de-gris*), lit. green of Greece. See VERT. The English and French forms have been influenced by French *gris* grey. The reason for the name is unknown.

verdure *n.* greenness of vegetation. WH: 14–15C. Old French, from *verd* (Modern French *vert*) green. See VERT, also -URE.

verecund *a.* bashful, modest. WH: 16C. Latin *verecundus*, from *verere* to revere, to fear.

verge¹ *n.* an edge, border or boundary. *Also v.t.* WH: 14–15C. Old French, from Latin *virga* rod. The sense edge, border relates to the expression *within the verge*, meaning within the authority of the Lord High Steward (originally a 12-mile radius round the King's court), whose staff of office was the *verge* or rod. Cp. VERGER.

verge² *v.i.* to move or incline in a particular direction, esp. downwards. WH: 17C. Latin *vergere* to bend, to incline.

verger *n.* an official in a church acting as caretaker, attendant, usher etc. WH: 12–14C. Anglo-Latin *virgarius*, from Latin *virga* rod. See also -ER². A verger is so called from his rod of office.

verglas *n.* a film of ice on rock. WH: 19C. French, from *verre* glass + obs. *glas* (now *glace*) ice.

veridical *a.* truthful, veracious. WH: 17C. Latin *veridicus*, from *verum* truth + *dic-*, stem of *dicere* to speak. See also -AL¹.

verify *v.t.* to confirm the truth of. WH: 12–14C. Old French *vérifier*, from Medieval Latin *verificare*, from Latin *verus* true. See also -FY.

†verily *adv.* in very truth, assuredly. WH: 12–14C. VERY + -LY¹, based on Old French *verraiment* (Modern French *vraiment*).

verisimilitude *n.* the appearance of or resemblance to truth. WH: 17C. Latin *verisimilitudo*, *veri similitudo*, from *verisimilis*, *veri similis* like the truth, from *veri*, gen. sing. of *verus* true + *similis* like. See also -AR¹.

verism *n.* extreme naturalism in art or literature. WH: 19C. Latin *verum* or Italian *vero* true + -ISM.

verity *n.* truth, correspondence (of a statement) with fact. WH: 14–15C. Old French *vérité*, var. of *verté*, from Latin *veritas*, from *verus* true. See also -ITY.

verjuice *n.* an acid liquid expressed from crab apples, unripe grapes etc. and used in cooking and for other purposes. WH: 12–14C. Old French *vertjus* (Modern French *verjus*), from *vert* green + *jus* juice. See VERT, JUICE.

verkrampte *a.* opposed to liberalization, esp. in matters of racial segregation. *Also n.* WH: mid-20C. Afrikaans narrow, cramped.

verligte *n., a.* (a person) of more liberal outlook, esp. in matters of racial segregation. WH: mid-20C. Afrikaans enlightened.

vermeil *n.* silver gilt. *Also a.* WH: 14–15C. Old French. See VERMILION.

vermi- *comb. form* of or relating to worms. WH: Latin *vermis* worm + -i-.

vermian *a.* of or relating to worms, wormlike. WH: 19C. VERMIS + -IAN.

vermicelli *n.* pasta in the form of long slender tubes or threads like macaroni. WH: 17C. Italian, pl. of *vermicello*, dim. of *verme* worm, from Latin *vermis*.

vermicide *n.* a medicine or drug that kills worms, an anthelmintic. WH: 19C. VERMI- + -CIDE.

vermicular *a.* of or relating to worms; caused by intestinal worms. WH: 17C. Medieval Latin *vermicularis*, from Latin *vermiculus*, dim. of *vermis* worm. See also -CULE.

vermiform *a.* worm-shaped. WH: 18C. VERMI- + -FORM.

vermifuge *n.* a medicine or drug that destroys or expels intestinal worms, an anthelmintic. WH: 17C. VERMI- + -FUGE.

vermilion *n.* a brilliant red pigment consisting of mercuric sulphide, obtained by grinding cinnabar or by the chemical treatment of mercury and sulphur. *Also a., v.t.* WH: 12–14C. Old French *vermeillon*, from *vermeil*, from Latin *vermiculus*, dim. of *vermis* worm. The pigment is so called with reference to the kermes, the scale insect from which the red dye was obtained.

vermin *n.* certain harmful or troublesome animals, such as the smaller mammals or birds injurious to crops or game, noxious or offensive insects, grubs or worms, esp. lice, fleas etc. WH: 12–14C. Old French, ult. from Latin *vermis* worm. Cp. VARMINT. The original sense was reptiles, snakes, or other animals regarded as harmful.

vermis *n.* the middle lobe connecting the two halves of the cerebellum. WH: 19C. Latin worm.

vermivorous *a.* feeding on worms. WH: 18C. VERMI- + -VOROUS (-VORE).

vermouth *n.* a drink consisting of wine flavoured with wormwood and other aromatic herbs. WH: 19C. French *vermout*, from German *Wermut* wormwood. See WORMWOOD.

vernacular *n.* the native language or dialect of a particular place or country. *Also a.* WH: 17C. Latin *vernaculus* native, indigenous, domestic, from *verna* homeborn slave. See also -AR¹.

vernal *a.* of or relating to, prevailing, done or appearing in spring. WH: 16C. Latin *vernalis*, from *vernus* of the spring, from *ver* spring. See also -AL¹.

vernicle *n.* a veronica, a cloth bearing the image of Christ's face. WH: 12–14C. Old French, alt. (with added *l*) of *vernique*, from Medieval Latin VERONICA. See also -CLE.

vernier *n.* a movable scale for measuring fractional portions of the divisions of the scale on a measuring instrument, a barometer, theodolite etc. WH: 18C. Pierre *Vernier*, 1580–1637, French mathematician.

Veronal® *n.* a hypnotic drug, diethylbarbituric acid, also called barbitone. WH: early 20C. *Verona*, a city in N Italy + -AL². The drug is so called because its inventor, the German chemist Emil Fischer, was working at the time in Verona.

Veronese *a.* of or relating to Verona. *Also n.* WH: 17C. Italian, from *Verona*, a city in N Italy. See -ESE.

veronica n. a herb or shrub of the genus *Veronica*, with blue, purple or white flowers; the speedwell. WH: 16C. Medieval Latin, ? alt. of Greek *benedikion*. The sense cloth bearing a portrait of Christ dates from the 17C and is so called after St *Veronica*, who is said to have wiped Christ's face with a cloth as he went to his crucifixion. The female forename itself is popularly derived from Latin *vera* true (cp. VERACIOUS) + Greek *eikōn* image, ICON.

veronique a. (*used after the noun*) served with white grapes, e.g. *sole veronique*. WH: early 20C. French *Véronique* Veronica. The dish *sole véronique* was invented in 1903 by the French chef Auguste Escoffier, who named it after André Messager's light opera *Véronique* (1898), then still popular.

verricule n. a dense tuft of upright hairs. WH: 19C. Latin *verriculum* dragnet, from *verrere* to sweep.

verruca n. a wart, esp. a contagious wart on the sole of the foot. WH: 14–15C. Latin wart.

vers n. verse. WH: 18C. French VERSE.

versant n. an area of land sloping in one direction. *Also a.* WH: 19C. French, use as n. of pres.p. of *verser* to turn.

versatile a. readily adapting or applying oneself to new tasks, occupations, subjects etc., many-sided. WH: 17C. French or Latin *versatilis*, from *versatus*, p.p. of *versare*, freq. of *vertere* to turn. See also -ATILE.

verse n. metrical composition as distinct from prose. *Also v.t., v.i.* WH: pre-1200. Old English *fers*, from Germanic, from Latin *versus* turn of the plough, furrow, line, row, line of writing, from *versus*, p.p. of *vertere* to turn.

versed a. skilled, familiar, experienced, proficient (in). WH: 17C. French *versé* or Latin *versatus*, p.p. of *versari* to stay, to be situated, to be occupied, pass. of *versare*. See VERSATILE, also -ED.

versicoloured a. changeable from one colour to another, with differences of light. WH: 18C. Latin *versicolor*, from *versus*, p.p. of *vertere* to turn + *color*. See COLOUR, also -ED.

†**versiform** a. varying in form. WH: 18C. Latin *versiformis*, from *versus*, p.p. of *vertere* to turn + -FORM.

versin n. a versed sine. WH: 19C. Abbr. of *versed sine* (VERSED).

version n. a statement, account or description of something from a person's particular point of view. WH: 14–15C. Old French, from Latin *versio, versionis*, from *versus*, p.p. of *vertere* to turn.

verso n. a left-hand page of a book lying open. WH: 19C. Latin (*folio*) *verso* (the leaf) being turned, abl. neut. sing. of *versus*, p.p. of *vertere* to turn.

verst n. a Russian measure of length, 3500.64 ft., nearly two-thirds of a mile (about 1 km). WH: 16C. Russian *versta*, rel. to *vertet'* to turn, itself rel. to Latin *vertere* to turn. The original literal sense was a turn of the plough.

versus prep. against. WH: 14–15C. Medieval Latin use of Latin *versus* towards, in sense of *adversus* against (cp. ADVERSE).

vert n. in English law, everything in a forest that grows and bears green leaves; the right to cut green or growing wood. *Also a.* WH: 14–15C. Old French, from Latin *viridis* green, rel. to *virere* to be green. Cp. VERDANT.

vertebra n. any one of the bony segments of which the spine or backbone consists. WH: 17C. Latin, from *vertere* to turn.

vertex n. the highest point, the top, summit, or apex. WH: 14–15C. Latin whirl, vortex, crown of the head, highest point, from *vertere* to turn.

verticil n. a whorl, an arrangement of parts in a circle round a stem etc. WH: 18C. Latin *verticillus* whorl of a spindle, dim. of VERTEX.

vertigo n. giddiness, dizziness, a feeling as if one were whirling round. WH: 14–15C. Latin whirling about, giddiness, from *vertere* to turn.

vervain n. a wild plant or weed, with small purplish flowers, of the genus *Verbena*, esp. *V. officinalis*, formerly credited with medical and other properties. WH: 14–15C. Old French *verveine*, from Latin VERBENA.

verve n. spirit, enthusiasm, energy, esp. in literary or artistic creation. WH: 17C. Old French vigour (earlier, form of expression, empty chatter), from Latin *verba*, pl. of *verbum* word. The original sense was a special talent in writing. The current sense emerged in the 19C.

vervet n. a small southern African monkey, *Cercopithecus aethiops*, usu. black-speckled greyish-green, with reddish-white face and abdomen. WH: 19C. French, of unknown orig.

very adv. (used as an intensifier) in a high degree, greatly, extremely. *Also a.* WH: 12–14C. Old French *verrai* (Modern French *vrai*), from Popular Latin *veracus*, from Latin *verus* true, with ending assim. to -Y[1]. The earliest sense was real, genuine, then (to the 16C) truthful, (to the 17C) exact, precise, also faithful, sincere. The current sense began to emerge in the 14–15C.

Very light n. a flare for lighting up the surroundings or for signalling. WH: early 20C. Edward W. *Very*, 1847–1910, US naval officer.

vesica n. a bladder, cyst etc., the gall bladder, the urinary bladder. WH: 17C. Latin bladder, blister.

vesper n. the evening star, Venus, appearing just after sunset. *Also a.* WH: 14–15C. Partly from Latin evening star, evening, corr. to Greek *hesperos* HESPERUS, partly from Old French *vespres* (Modern French *vêpres*), from Ecclesiastical Latin *vesperas*, acc. pl. of Latin *vespera* evening, based on *matutinas* MATINS.

vespiary n. a nest of wasps, hornets etc. WH: 19C. Latin *vespa* wasp, based on *apiary* (APIARIAN).

vessel n. a hollow receptacle, esp. for holding liquids, as a jug, cup, dish, bottle, barrel etc. WH: 12–14C. Old French *vaissel* (Modern French *vaisseau*), from Late Latin *vascellum* small vase, dim. of *vas* vase. See VASE, also -EL.

vest n. an undergarment for the upper part of the body, a singlet. *Also v.t., v.i.* WH: 17C. French *veste* garment, from Italian, from Latin *vestis* clothing, garment. The word was originally the term for a loose outer garment. The current sense evolved in the 19C.

vesta n. a wax match igniting by friction. WH: 17C. Latin *Vesta*, the Roman goddess of the hearth and household.

vestal a. of or relating to the goddess Vesta or the vestal virgins. *Also n.* WH: 14–15C. Latin *vestalis*, from *Vesta*. See VESTA, also -AL[1].

vestiary a. of or relating to dress. *Also n.* WH: 12–14C. Latin *vestiarius*, from *vestis* clothes, clothing. See also -ARY[1]. The noun derives from Old French *vestiarie* (Modern French *vestiaire*), from Latin *vestiarium* clothes chest, wardrobe, a noun use of Latin *vestiarius*. Cp. VESTRY.

vestibule n. a small hall, lobby or antechamber next to the outer door of a house, from which doors open into the various inner rooms. WH: 17C. French (? from Italian *vestibulo*), or from Latin *vestibulum* forecourt, of unknown orig.

vestige n. a sign, a mark or trace of something no longer present or in existence. WH: 14–15C. French, from Latin *vestigium* sole of the foot, footprint, trace.

vestiture n. anything covering a surface, such as hair, scales etc. WH: 14–15C. Medieval Latin *vestitura*, from Latin *vestire* to clothe. See VEST, also -URE.

vestment n. any of the ritual garments of the clergy, choristers etc., esp. a chasuble. WH: 12–14C. Old French *vestiment, vestement* (Modern French *vêtement*), from Latin *vestimentum* clothing, from *vestire* to clothe. See VEST, also -MENT.

vestry n. a room or place attached to a church in which the vestments are kept and in which the clergy, choristers etc. robe. WH: 14–15C. Anglo-French alt. of Old French *vestiaire* (VESTIARY), by assoc. with -*erie* -ERY. See also -RY.

vesture n. dress, clothes, apparel. *Also v.t.* WH: 12–14C. Old French (Modern French *vêture*), from Medieval Latin *vestura*, from Late Latin *vestitura*, from Latin *vestire* to clothe. See also -URE.

vesuvian n. a variety of fusee for lighting cigars etc. in the open air. *Also a.* WH: 17C. *Vesuvius*, an active volcano on the Bay of Naples in Italy + -AN.

vet[1] n. a veterinary surgeon. *Also v.t.* WH: 19C. Abbr. of *veterinary surgeon* (VETERINARY).

vet[2] n. a veteran. WH: 19C. Abbr. of VETERAN.

vetch n. a plant of the genus *Vicia* of the bean family, including several wild and cultivated species used for forage, esp. the common vetch or tare. WH: 12–14C. Anglo-French *veche*, from Old French *vece* (Modern French *vesce*), from Latin *vicia*.

veteran a. grown old or experienced, esp. in the military service. *Also n.* WH: 16C. Old French *vétéran* or Latin *veteranus*, from *vetus, veteris* old. See also -AN.

veterinary *a.* of or relating to treatment of the diseases of animals, esp. domestic or farm animals such as cows, horses, dogs etc. *Also n.* WH: 18C. Latin *veterinarius*, from *veterinus* pertaining to cattle, from *veterinae* (fem. pl.), *veterina* (neut. pl.) cattle, ? from *vetus*, *veteris* old. See also -INE, -ARY[1].

vetiver *n.* khus-khus grass and root. WH: 19C. French *vétiver*, from Tamil *veṭṭivēr*, from *vēr* root.

veto *n.* the power or right of a sovereign, president or branch of a legislature to negative the enactments of another branch. *Also v.t.* WH: 17C. Latin I forbid, 1st pers. sing. pres. ind. of *vetare* to forbid. The word was used by Roman tribunes of the people to oppose measures of the Senate or actions of the magistrates.

vex *v.t.* to cause trouble or annoyance to, to irritate. WH: 14–15C. Old French *vexer*, from Latin *vexare* to shake, to agitate, to disturb.

vexillum *n.* in ancient Rome, a square flag carried by a vexillary, forming the standard of a maniple. WH: 18C. Latin flag, banner, from *vehere*, *vex-*, *vect-* to carry, to convey.

via *adv.* by way of, through. WH: 18C. Latin, abl. sing. of *via* way, road.

viable *a.* likely to become actual or to succeed, practicable, feasible. WH: 19C. French, from *vie*, from Latin *vita* life. See also -ABLE.

viaduct *n.* a bridgelike structure, esp. one composed of masonry and a considerable number of arches carrying a road or railway over a valley etc. WH: 19C. Latin *via* way, road + -*duct*, based on AQUEDUCT.

vial *n.* a small vessel, usu. cylindrical and of glass, for holding liquid medicines etc. *Also v.t.* WH: 12–14C. Alt. of PHIAL.

viameter *n.* a hodometer. WH: 19C. Latin *via* way, road + -METER. Cp. ODOMETER.

viand *n.* an article of food. WH: 14–15C. Old French *viande* food, (now) meat, from alt. of Latin *vivenda*, neut. pl. ger. of *vivere* to live.

viaticum *n.* the Eucharist as given to a person at the point of death. WH: 16C. Latin, use as n. of neut. of *viaticus* pertaining to a journey, from *via* way, road.

vibes *n.pl.* feelings, intuitions or sensations experienced or communicated. WH: mid-20C. Abbr. of *vibration* (VIBRATE) + -S[1].

vibraculum *n.* any one of the filamentous whiplike appendages of many polyzoa, bringing particles of food within reach by their lashing movements. WH: 19C. Modern Latin, from Latin *vibrare*. See VIBRATE, also -CULE.

vibrant *a.* vibrating, tremulous. WH: 16C. Latin *vibrans*, *vibrantis*, pres.p. of *vibrare* VIBRATE. See also -ANT.

vibraphone *n.* a percussion instrument similar to a xylophone but with metal bars placed over electronic resonators. WH: early 20C. VIBRATO + -PHONE.

vibrate *v.i.* to move to and fro rapidly, to swing, to oscillate. *Also v.t.* WH: 14–15C. Latin *vibratus*, p.p. of *vibrare* to move rapidly to and fro, to brandish, to shake. See also -ATE[3].

vibrato *n.* a pulsating effect, esp. in singing or string-playing, produced by the rapid variation of emphasis on the same tone. WH: 19C. Italian, p.p. of *vibrare* to vibrate.

vibrio *n.* a bacterium of the genus *Vibrio*, more or less screw-shaped with a filament at each end, such as that causing cholera. WH: 19C. Modern Latin genus name, from Latin *vibrare* VIBRATE, based on French *vibrion*.

vibrissa *n.* a stiff coarse hair or bristle in the nostrils of humans and about the mouths of most mammals. WH: 17C. Latin, from *vibrare* VIBRATE.

vibronic *a.* of, relating to or caused by electronic vibration. WH: mid-20C. From *vibrational* (VIBRATE) + ELECTRONIC.

viburnum *n.* a shrub or small tree of a genus *Viburnum*, containing the guelder rose and the laurustinus etc., of the honeysuckle family. WH: 18C. Modern Latin use as genus name of Latin wayfaring tree. The shrub's French name, *viorne*, from the same source, is popularly derived from Latin *vias ornans*, literally decorating the ways.

vicar *n.* in the Church of England, the priest in charge of a parish. WH: 12–14C. Anglo-French *vicare*, from Old French *vicaire* (now) assistant curate, deputy, from Latin *vicarius* substitute, deputy, from *vic-* change, alteration, from **vix* (found only in oblique cases). See also -AR[3]. A vicar was originally a priest appointed by a monastery to perform parochial duties as its deputy when it had appropriated the tithes and other revenues that had formerly gone to the incumbent. Cp. CURATE, RECTOR.

vicarious *a.* experienced at second hand by imaginative or sympathetic participation in the pleasure, satisfaction etc. of someone else. WH: 17C. Latin *vicarius*. See VICAR, also -ARIOUS.

vice[1] *n.* an evil or immoral practice or habit. WH: 12–14C. Old French, from Latin *vitium*.

vice[2] *n.* an instrument with two jaws, brought together by a screw or lever, between which an object may be clamped securely. *Also v.t.* WH: 12–14C. Old French *vis*, from Latin *vitis* vine (stem), tendril, plant with tendrils.

vice[3] *prep.* in place of.' WH: 18C. Latin, abl. of *vic-* (VICAR).

vice[4] *n.* a vice-president, vice-chairman etc. WH: 16C. Independent use of VICE-.

vice- *pref.* forming nouns denoting a person acting or qualified to act in place of another or next in rank below another. WH: Latin, from *vice* in place of. See VICE[3].

vicegerent *a.* having or exercising delegated power. *Also n.* WH: 16C. Medieval Latin *vicegerens*, *vicegerentis* deputy, from Latin VICE- + *gerens*, *gerentis*, pres.p. of *gerere* to carry on, to manage. See also -ENT.

vicenary *a.* consisting of or relating to 20. WH: 17C. Latin *vicenarius*, from *viceni* twenty each, from *viginti* twenty. See also -ARY[1].

viceroy *n.* a ruler exercising authority in a colony, province etc. in the name of a sovereign or government. WH: 16C. Old French (Modern French *viceroi*), from *vice-* VICE- + *roy* (Modern French *roi*) king.

vice versa *adv.* the order or relation being inverted, the other way round. WH: 17C. Latin, lit. the position being reversed, from *vice* (VICE[3]) + *versa*, abl. fem. sing. of *versus*, p.p. of *vertere* to turn.

vichyssoise *n.* a cream soup usu. served chilled, with ingredients such as leeks and potatoes. WH: mid-20C. Short form of French *crème vichyssoise glacée*, lit. iced cream soup of Vichy (a town in central France).

vicinage *n.* neighbourhood, vicinity, surrounding places, environs. WH: 12–14C. Old French *visenage*, *visné* (Modern French *voisinage*), from alt. of Latin *vicinus* neighbour.

vicinity *n.* the neighbourhood, the adjoining or surrounding district. WH: 16C. Latin *vicinitas*, from *vicinus* neighbouring. See also -ITY.

vicious *a.* likely, disposed or intended to attack, hurt or wound. WH: 12–14C. Old French (Modern French *vicieux*), from Latin *vitiosus*, from *vitium* VICE[1]. See also -IOUS. The original sense was pertaining to vice. The current sense evolved in the 18C.

vicissitude *n.* a change of condition, circumstances or fortune, a mutation, a revolution. WH: 16C. Old French, or from Latin *vicissitudo*, from *vicissim* by turns, from *vic-*. See VICAR, also -TUDE.

victim *n.* a person killed or injured as a result of an event such as an accident or epidemic. WH: 15C. Latin *victima* sacrifice, of unknown orig.

victor *n.* a person, organization, nation etc. that conquers in battle or wins in a contest. WH: 12–14C. Anglo-French *victour* or Latin *victor*, from *victus*, p.p. of *vincere* to conquer. See also -OR.

victoria *n.* a four-wheeled carriage with a raised seat for the driver, seats for two persons over the back axle and a low seat for two persons over the front axle, and a collapsible top. WH: 19C. Queen *Victoria* of Great Britain and Ireland, reigned 1837–1901.

victual *n.* food, provisions. *Also v.t., v.i.* WH: 12–14C. Old French *vitaille* (Modern French *victuaille*), from Late Latin *victualia*, neut. pl. of *victualis*, from Latin *victus* livelihood, food, from base of *vivere* to live. See also -AL[1].

vicuña *n.* a S American animal, *Vicugna vicugna*, allied to the camel, a native of the Andean regions of Bolivia and N Chile. WH: 17C. Spanish, from Quechua *wikúña*.

vide *int.* (as an instruction in a book) see, consult. WH: 16C. Latin, imper. sing. of *videre* to see.

videlicet *adv.* namely, that is to say, to wit (usu. abbreviated to *viz.*). WH: 14–15C. Latin, from *vide*, stem of *videre* to see + *licet* it is permissible. Cp. SCILICET.

video *n.* a video recorder. *Also a., v.t., v.i.* WH: mid-20C. Latin *videre* to see + -O, based on AUDIO.

vidicon *n.* a small television camera tube, used in closed-circuit systems and for outside broadcasts, that operates by photoconductivity. WH: mid-20C. VIDEO + ICONOSCOPE.

vidimus *n.* an examination or inspection of accounts etc. WH: 14–15C. Latin we have seen, 1st pers. pl. perf. of *videre* to see.

vie *v.i.* to strive for superiority, to contend, to compete (with). WH: 16C. Prob. shortening of obs. *envy*, from Old French *envier*, from Latin *invitare* to challenge, INVITE[1].

vielle *n.* a hurdy-gurdy. WH: 18C. French. See VIOL.

Viennese *a.* of or relating to Vienna or its inhabitants. *Also n.* WH: 19C. *Vienna*, the capital of Austria + -ESE.

Vietnamese *a.* of or relating to Vietnam, its people or their language. *Also n.* WH: mid-20C. *Vietnam*, a country in SE Asia + -ESE.

vieux jeu *a.* old-fashioned, hackneyed. WH: 19C. French, lit. old game.

view *n.* sight, range of vision. *Also v.t., v.i.* WH: 12–14C. Old French *vëue* (Modern French *vue*), use as n. of fem. p.p. of *vëoir* (Modern French *voir*) to see, from Latin *videre* to see.

vigesimal *a.* relating to or based on the number twenty. WH: 17C. Latin *vigesimus*, var. of *vicesimus*, from *viceni* twenty each, from *viginti* twenty + -AL[1].

vigia *n.* a warning of a suspected rock, shoal etc., whose existence is unconfirmed, on a hydrographical chart. WH: 19C. Portuguese lookout, from *vigiar*, from Latin *vigilia*. See VIGIL.

vigil *n.* keeping awake during the customary hours of rest, watchfulness. WH: 12–14C. Old French *vigile*, from Latin *vigilia* watch, wakefulness, from *vigil* awake, alert, rel. to *vigere* to be vigorous, to be lively.

vigneron *n.* a wine-grower. WH: 14–15C. French, from *vigne* VINE.

vignette *n.* a short descriptive essay or sketch. *Also v.t.* WH: 14–15C. Old French, dim. of *vigne* VINE. See also -ETTE. A vignette was originally a running ornament of vine leaves, tendrils and grapes on the title page of a book or at the beginning or end of a chapter.

vigoro *n.* a team ball game (esp. for women) combining elements of cricket and baseball and played with a paddle-shaped bat. WH: early 20C. From *vigorous* (VIGOUR) + -O.

vigoroso *adv.* with energy. WH: 19C. Italian *vigorous* (VIGOUR).

vigour *n.* active physical or mental strength or energy. WH: 12–14C. Old French (Modern French *vigueur*), from Latin *vigor* liveliness, activity, from *vigere* to be lively, to flourish. See also -OUR.

vihara *n.* a Buddhist or Jain temple or monastery. WH: 17C. Sanskrit *vihāra*.

Viking *n.* any of the Scandinavian seafaring warriors of the 8th–11th cents., who raided and colonized large parts of N and W Europe. WH: 19C. Old Norse *víkingr*, Icelandic *víkingur*, either from *vík* creek, inlet, or from Old English *wīc* WICK[2]. See also -ING[3]. The word is not related to KING, despite the synonymous *sea king*. Old Norse *vík* would mean a person coming from the inlets of the sea, i.e. the fjords, while Old English *wīc* would refer to a person who made a temporary camp while invading foreign territory.

vilayet *n.* an administrative division of Turkey. WH: 19C. Turkish *vilâyet*, from Arabic *wilāyat* government, rule, administrative district. Cp. BLIGHTY.

vile *a.* foul, disgusting. WH: 12–14C. Old French *vil*, from Latin *vilis* of low value, cheap, mean, base.

vilify *v.t.* to say unpleasant things about. WH: 14–15C. Late Latin *vilificare*, from Latin *vilis*. See VILE, also -FY.

†vilipend *v.t.* to treat or regard with contempt. WH: 14–15C. Old French *villipender* or Latin *vilipendere*, from *vilis* VILE + *pendere* to consider.

vill *n.* a feudal township. WH: 17C. Old French *ville* farm, country house (Modern French town), from Latin *villa*. See VILLA.

villa *n.* in ancient Rome, a country house or farmhouse with subsidiary buildings on an estate. WH: 17C. Partly from Latin *villa* country house, farm, partly from Italian *villa*, from Latin.

village *n.* a small assemblage of houses, smaller than a town or city and larger than a hamlet. *Also a.* WH: 14–15C. Old French, from Latin *villa*. See VILLA, also -AGE.

villain *n.* a person guilty or capable of crime or great wickedness. *Also a.* WH: 12–14C. Old French *vilein* (Modern French *vilain*), from Medieval Latin *villanus* villager, farmhand, from Latin VILLA. The original sense was simple person, rustic, boor, hence by implication scoundrel, knave, evil person. The word is not related to EVIL.

villanelle *n.* a poem in five tercets and a final quatrain on two rhymes. WH: 16C. French, from Latin *villanella*, fem. of *villanello* rural, rustic, from *villano* peasant, rustic, from Medieval Latin *villanus* villager, from Latin VILLA.

-ville *comb. form* a place, condition or quality with a character as specified, as in *dullsville*, *dragsville*, *squaresville*. WH: 16C. French *ville* town, as in many US town names, e.g. *Charlottesville*, *Nashville*.

villeggiatura *n.* retirement to or a stay in the country. WH: 18C. Italian, from *villeggiare* to live at a villa, from *villa* VILLA.

villein *n.* a feudal serf, a bondsman attached to a feudal lord or to an estate. WH: 12–14C. Var. of VILLAIN.

villus *n.* any of the short hairlike or finger-like processes on certain membranes, such as those on the inner surface of the small intestine. WH: 18C. Latin tuft of hair, shaggy hair.

vim *n.* energy, vigour. WH: 19C. Prob. from Latin *vim*, acc. sing. of *vis* strength, energy. Cp. VIS.

vimineous *a.* of or relating to, producing, or consisting of twigs or shoots. WH: 17C. Latin *vimineus*, from *vimen*, *viminis* osier. See also -EOUS.

vin *n.* (a) wine. WH: 17C. French. Cp. VINHO VERDE, VINO.

vina *n.* an Indian stringed instrument with a fretted fingerboard over two gourds. WH: 18C. Sanskrit and Hindi *vīṇā*.

vinaceous *a.* of or relating to wine or grapes. WH: 17C. Latin *vinaceus*, from *vinum* wine. See also -ACEOUS.

vinaigrette *n.* a salad dressing consisting of oil, vinegar and seasoning. WH: 14–15C. French, from *vinaigre* VINEGAR. See also -ETTE.

vinasse *n.* a residual product containing potassium salts left after distilling spirits, esp. brandy, or obtained from beets from which sugar has been extracted. WH: 19C. French, from Latin *vinacea*, fem. of *vinaceus* VINACEOUS.

vinca *n.* any plant of the periwinkle genus, *Vinca*. WH: 19C. Modern Latin, from Late Latin *pervinca*. See PERIWINKLE[1].

vincible *a.* capable of being conquered, not invincible. WH: 16C. Latin *vincibilis*, from *vincere* to overcome. See also -IBLE. The word is of later origin than its converse, INVINCIBLE.

vincristine *n.* an alkaloid substance derived from the tropical periwinkle, used in the treatment of some types of leukaemia. WH: mid-20C. Modern Latin *Vinca* genus name (VINCA) + ? CRISTA + -INE.

vinculum *n.* a straight line drawn over several terms in an equation to show that they are to be treated as if they were in brackets. WH: 17C. Latin, from *vincere* to bind. See also -ULE.

vindaloo *n.* a type of hot Indian curry. WH: 19C. Prob. from Portuguese *vin d'alho* wine and garlic sauce, from *vinho* wine + *alho* garlic.

vindicate *v.t.* to clear from blame, suspicion, criticism etc. WH: 16C. Latin *vindicatus*, p.p. of *vindicare* to claim, to set free, to punish, to avenge, from *vindex*, *vindicis* claimant, avenger. See also -ATE[3].

vindictive *a.* characterized or prompted by a desire for revenge. WH: 17C. Latin *vindicta* vengeance, revenge + -IVE.

vine *n.* a slender climbing plant of the genus *Vitis*, esp. *V. vinifera*, the grapevine. WH: 12–14C. Old French *vine* (Modern French *vigne*), from Latin *vinea* vineyard, vine, use as n. of fem. of *vineus* pertaining to wine, from *vinum* WINE.

vinegar *n.* an acid liquid obtained by oxidation or acetous fermentation from wine, cider etc., used as a condiment and as a preservative in pickling. *Also v.t.* WH: 12–14C. Old French *vyn egre* (Modern French *vinaigre*), ult. from Latin *vinum* wine + *acer*, *acre* sour.

vingt-et-un *n.* a card game in which the object is to make the aggregate number of the pips on the cards as near as possible to 21 without exceeding this; pontoon. WH: 18C. French twenty-one. Cp. PONTOON[1].

vinho verde *n.* any of a number of light, immature, sharp-tasting Portuguese wines. WH: 19C. Portuguese, lit. green wine.

vini- *comb. form* of or relating to wine or vines. WH: Latin *vinum* wine + -*i*-.

vinic *a.* of, relating to, contained in or derived from wine. WH: 19C. Latin *vinum* wine + -IC.

viniculture *n.* the cultivation of grapevines. WH: 19C. VINI- + CULTURE. Cp. VITICULTURE.

viniferous *a.* wine-producing. WH: 19C. VINI- + -FEROUS.

vinify *v.t.* to convert (grape juice) into wine. WH: 19C. VINI- + -FY.

vino *n.* wine, esp. cheap wine. WH: 17C. Spanish and Italian wine. Cp. VIN, VINHO VERDE.

vinous *a.* of, relating to or resembling wine. WH: 14–15C. Latin *vinum* wine + -OUS.

vint *n.* a Russian card game similar to auction bridge. WH: 19C. Russian, of uncertain orig. ? From German *Gewinde* thread.

vintage *n.* the yield of grapes or wine from a vineyard or vine district for a particular season, esp. the wine obtained in a particularly good year. *Also a., v.t.* WH: 14–15C. Old French *vendange*, from Latin *vindemia*, from *vinum* WINE + *demere* to take away, alt. by assoc. with VINTNER and assim. to -AGE.

vintner *n.* a wine merchant. WH: 14–15C. Anglo-Latin *vintenarius*, var. of *vinetarius*, from Anglo-French *viniter*, *vineter*, Old French *vinetier*, from Medieval Latin *vinetarius*, *vinatarius*, from Latin *vinetum* vineyard, from *vinum* wine. See also -ER².

vinyl *n.* an organic radical CH₂CH-, derived from ethylene. *Also a.* WH: 19C. Latin *vinum* wine + -YL. The connection with wine is through ethylene, since ethyl alcohol forms the base of common alcohol and so is present in wine.

viol *n.* any of a family of medieval stringed musical instruments, the predecessor of the violin family, that had six strings and were held on or between the knees and played with a curved bow. WH: 15C. Old French *vielle*, alt. of *viole*, from Provençal *viola*, *viula*, prob. rel. to FIDDLE.

viola¹ *n.* an instrument like a large violin, the alto instrument in the violin family tuned an octave above the cello. WH: 18C. Spanish and Italian, prob. from Provençal. See VIOL.

viola² *n.* a plant or flower of the genus *Viola*, containing the violet and pansy. WH: 14–15C. Latin violet, later used as a genus name.

violate *v.t.* to infringe or transgress, to break, to disobey (a law, obligation, duty etc.). WH: 14–15C. Latin *violatus*, p.p. of *violare* to treat with violence. See also -ATE³.

violence *n.* the state or quality of being violent. WH: 12–14C. Old French, from Latin *violentia*, from *violens*, *violentis* or *violentus*, of unknown orig. See also -ENCE.

violet *n.* a plant or flower of the genus *Viola*, esp. the sweet violet, *V. odorata*, the dog-violet, *V. riviniana*, and some other species with small blue, purple or white flowers. *Also a.* WH: 12–14C. Old French *violet*, *violette*, dims. of *viole*, from Latin VIOLA². See also -ET¹. The word for the colour comes from the name of the flower. Cp. PINK¹.

violin *n.* a musical instrument with four strings, held under the chin and played with a bow, the most important of modern string instruments and the one with the highest pitch. WH: 16C. Italian *violino*, from *viola* VIOLA².

violoncello *n.* a cello. WH: 18C. Italian, dim. of VIOLONE.

violone *n.* a medieval double-bass viol. WH: 18C. Italian, from *viola* VIOLA².

viper *n.* a venomous snake of the family Viperidae, esp. the European viper or adder, the only poisonous British snake. WH: 16C. Latin *vipera* snake, from *vivus* alive + *parere* to bring forth. Cp. WYVERN. The viper is so called from the former belief that it does not lay eggs but gives birth to live young. Cp. VIVIPAROUS.

virago *n.* a bad-tempered, violent or scolding woman, a termagant, a shrew. WH: pre-1200. Latin, from *vir* man. The original sense (to the 16C) was woman, with specific reference to the name given by Adam to Eve in Gen. ii.23, 'This schal be clepid virago, for she is takun of man' (Wyclif's translation, 1388), 'she shall be called Woman, because she was taken out of Man' (AV, 1611).

viral *a.* of, relating to or caused by a virus. WH: mid-20C. VIRUS + -AL¹.

virelay *n.* an old form of French verse with two rhymes to a stanza and usu. a refrain. WH: 14–15C. Old French *virelai*, alt. of *vireli* (? orig. a meaningless refrain), based on *lai* LAY³.

virement *n.* a transfer of funds from one account to another. WH: early 20C. French, from Old French *virer* VEER¹. See also -MENT.

vireo *n.* any American passerine insectivorous songbird of the genus *Vireo*. WH: 19C. Latin name of some bird, ? the greenfinch. Cp. *virere* to be green.

virescent *a.* green, tending to become green, viridescent. WH: 19C. Latin *viriscens*, *viriscentis*, pres.p. of *viriscere* to turn green. See also -escent (-ESCENCE).

virga *n.* streaks of precipitation appearing under a cloud but evaporating before they reach the ground. WH: mid-20C. Latin rod.

virgate¹ *a.* long, straight and erect, rodlike. WH: 19C. Latin *virgatus*, from *virga* rod.

virgate² *n.* an ancient measure of land, usu. taken as equivalent to 30 acres (12.15 ha). WH: 17C. Medieval Latin *virgata*, from VIRGA. See also -ATE¹. The Medieval Latin word translates Old English *gerdland* yardland, i.e. yard of land. See YARD¹, LAND.

Virgilian *a.* of, relating to or in the style of Virgil. WH: 16C. Latin *Virgilianus*, from Publius *Virgilius* Maro, 70–19 BC, Roman poet. See also -IAN. The contemporary spelling of Virgil's name was with an *e*, i.e. as *Vergilius*.

virgin *n.* a person, esp. a woman, who has never had sexual intercourse. *Also a., v.i.* WH: 12–14C. Old French *virgine* (Modern French *vierge*), from Latin *virgo*, *virginis*, prob. rel. to *virga* twig, young shoot.

Virginia *n.* tobacco from Virginia. WH: 17C. *Virginia*, a state in the SE USA, so named for Queen Elizabeth I of England, 1558–1603, the Virgin Queen.

Virgo *n.* one of the 12 ancient zodiacal constellations, the Virgin. WH: pre-1200. Latin *virgo* VIRGIN, Virgo.

virgule *n.* a slanting line used as a division within or between words, a solidus. WH: 19C. French comma, from Latin *virgula*, dim. of *virga* rod. See also -ULE.

viridescent *a.* greenish. WH: 19C. Late Latin *viridescens*, *viridescentis*, pres.p. of *viridescere* to become green, from Latin *viridis*, from *virere* to be green. See *-escent* (-ESCENCE).

virile *a.* characteristic of a man, masculine, manly; strong, forceful, vigorous. WH: 15C. Old French *viril* or Latin *virilis*, from *vir* man. See also -IL.

virino *n.* an agent postulated as the cause of BSE and related diseases, thought by some to be a fragment of nucleic acid surrounded by a protein coat derived from the host cell. WH: late 20C. VIRUS + dim. suf. -*ino*.

virion *n.* a virus in an infective form consisting of an RNA particle within a protein covering. WH: mid-20C. VIRUS + -*i*- + -ON.

virtu *n.* a taste for or knowledge of the fine arts. WH: 18C. Italian *virtù* VIRTUE.

virtual *a.* being such in effect or for practical purposes, though not in name or by strict definition; near, practical. WH: 14–15C. Medieval Latin *virtualis*, from Latin *virtus* VIRTUE, based on Late Latin *virtuosus*, from Latin *virtus*. See also -AL¹.

virtue *n.* moral excellence, goodness, uprightness, rectitude. WH: 12–14C. Old French *vertu*, from Latin *virtus* valour, merit, moral perfection, from *vir* man.

virtuoso *n.* a skilled performer in some fine art, esp. music. *Also a.* WH: 17C. Italian learned, skilful, from Late Latin *virtuosus*. See VIRTUAL.

virulent *a.* extremely poisonous. WH: 14–15C. Latin *virulentus* poisonous, from VIRUS. See also -ULENT.

virus *n.* a very small infective agent capable of self-propagation only in living matter, the causative agent of many diseases, consisting of a single nucleic acid molecule in a protein coat. WH: 14–15C. Latin slimy liquid, poison, offensive odour.

vis *n.* force, energy, potency. WH: 17C. Latin. Cp. VIM.

visa *n.* an official endorsement on a passport showing that it has been examined and found correct, esp. one enabling the holder to travel to or through a particular country. *Also v.t.* WH: 19C. French, from Latin things seen, neut. pl. of p.p. of *videre* to see.

visage *n.* the face, the countenance. *Also v.t.* WH: 12–14C. Old French, from *vis* (cp. VIS-À-VIS), from Latin *visus* sight, appearance, from p.p. of *videre* to see. See also -AGE.

vis-à-vis *prep.* in relation to. *Also adv., n.* WH: 18C. French, lit. face to face, from Old French *vis* VISAGE + *à* to + *vis*.

viscacha *n.* a S American burrowing rodent of the genus *Lagostomus* or *Lagidium*, related to the chinchilla. WH: 17C. Spanish *vizcacha* (obs. *bizcacha*), from Quechua *huiscacha*.

viscera *n.pl.* the internal organs of the great cavities of the body, such as the skull, thorax, and abdomen, esp. those of the abdomen, the intestines. WH: 17C. Latin internal organs, pl. of VISCUS.

viscid *a.* sticky, adhesive. WH: 17C. Late Latin *viscidus*, from Latin *viscum* birdlime. See also -ID.

viscoelastic *a.* having both viscous and elastic properties. WH: mid-20C. VISCOUS + ELASTIC.

viscometer *n.* an apparatus for determining the viscosity of liquids. WH: 19C. Late Latin *viscosus* VISCOUS + -METER.

viscose *n.* the highly viscous cellulose sodium salt used in the manufacture of artificial silk. *Also a.* WH: 19C. Late Latin *viscosus* VISCOUS + -OSE².

viscount *n.* a British peer ranking next below an earl, and above a baron. WH: 14–15C. Old French *visconte* (Modern French *vicomte*), from Medieval Latin *vicecomes*, *vicecomitis*. See VICE-, COUNT².

viscous *a.* (of liquids) thick and sticky. WH: 14–15C. Anglo-French, or from Late Latin *viscosus*, from *viscum* birdlime. See also -OUS.

viscus *n.* any of the viscera. WH: 18C. Latin, pl. VISCERA.

Vishnu *n.* the preserver god of the Hindu sacred triad, appearing in many incarnations and worshipped by some as the saviour. WH: 17C. Sanskrit *Viṣṇu*.

visible *a.* capable of being seen, perceptible by the eye. WH: 12–14C. Old French, or from Latin *visibilis*, from *visus*, p.p. of *videre* to see. See also -IBLE.

Visigoth *n.* a member of the western Goths who settled in S Gaul and Spain in the 4th and 5th cents. WH: 16C. Late Latin *Visigothus*, usu. in pl. *Visigothi*. The first element may mean west, as opposed to OSTROGOTH.

vision *n.* the act or faculty of seeing, sight. *Also v.t.* WH: 12–14C. Old French, from Latin *visio*, *visionis* sight, thing seen, from *visus*. See VISIBLE, also -ION.

visit *v.t.* to go or come to see, as an act of friendship, civility, business, curiosity etc. *Also v.i., n.* WH: 12–14C. Old French *visiter*, or from Latin *visitare* to go to see, freq. of *visare* to view, to see to, to visit, from *visus*, p.p. of *videre* to see.

visor *n.* the movable perforated part of a helmet defending the face. WH: 12–14C. Old French *visière*, from *vis* face. See VISAGE, also -OR.

vista *n.* a long view shut in at the sides, as between rows of trees. WH: 17C. Italian view.

visual *a.* of, relating to or used in sight or seeing. *Also n.* WH: 14–15C. Late Latin *visualis*, from *visus* sight. See also -AL¹.

vital *a.* very important and necessary. *Also n.pl.* WH: 14–15C. Old French, from Latin *vitalis*, from *vita* life + -AL¹.

vitamin *n.* any of a number of naturally occurring substances which are necessary, though in minute quantities, for normal metabolism. WH: early 20C. Latin *vita* life + AMINE. The term was coined in 1912 (as *vitamine*) by the US biochemist Casimir Funk in the belief that vitamins contain amino acids. The spelling was altered to *vitamin* in 1920.

vitellus *n.* yolk of egg; the protoplasmic contents of the ovum. WH: 18C. Latin yolk of an egg.

vitiate *v.t.* to impair the quality of; to render faulty or imperfect. WH: 16C. Latin *vitiatus*, p.p. of *vitiare*, from *vitium* VICE¹. See also -ATE³.

viticulture *n.* the cultivation of the grapevine. WH: 19C. Latin *vitis* vine + CULTURE. Cp. VINICULTURE.

vitiligo *n.* an abnormal skin condition in which pigment is lost from areas of the skin, causing whitish patches. WH: 16C. Latin tetter.

vitreous *a.* consisting of or resembling glass. WH: 14–15C. Latin *vitreus*, from *vitrum* glass. See also -EOUS.

vitrine *n.* a glass showcase. WH: 19C. French, from *vitre* glass. See also -INE.

vitriol *n.* sulphuric acid as made from copperas. WH: 14–15C. Old French, or from Medieval Latin *vitriolum*, from Latin *vitrum* glass. The acid is so called from its glassy appearance in certain states.

Vitruvian *a.* of or in the style of Marcus Vitruvius Pollio. WH: 18C. Marcus *Vitruvius* Pollio, 1C BC Roman architect and writer + -IAN.

vitta *n.* an oil-tube in the fruit of the parsley family etc. WH: 17C. Latin band, fillet, chaplet.

†vittles *n.pl.* victuals. WH: 16C. Var. of *victuals*. See VICTUAL, also -S¹.

vituline *a.* of or relating to a calf or veal. WH: 14–15C. Latin *vitulinus*, from *vitulus* calf. See also -INE. Cp. VEAL.

vituperate *v.i.* to use violently abusive language. *Also v.t.* WH: 16C. Latin *vituperatus*, p.p. of *vituperare*, from *vitu-*, alt. of *viti-*, stem of *vitium* VICE¹ + *parare* to prepare. See also -ATE³. The original sense was to blame, to vilify, to revile. The current sense dates from the 19C.

viva¹ *n.* an exclamation of joy or applause. *Also int.* WH: 17C. Italian live!, 3rd pers. sing. pres. subj. of *vivere* to live, from Latin. Cp. VIVAT, VIVE.

viva² *n.* a viva voce examination. *Also v.t.* WH: 19C. Abbr. of VIVA VOCE.

vivace *adv.* in a brisk, lively manner. WH: 17C. Italian brisk, lively, from Latin *vivax*, *vivacis*. See VIVACIOUS.

vivacious *a.* lively, animated, sprightly, high-spirited. WH: 17C. Latin *vivax*, *vivacis* conscious of life, long-lived, lively, vigorous, from *vivus* alive, from *vivere* to live. See also -ACIOUS.

vivandière *n.* a female sutler attached to a Continental, esp. French, regiment. WH: 16C. French, fem. of *vivandier*, from *viande* food, (now) meat. See VIAND, also -IER.

vivarium *n.* a park, enclosure or other place artificially prepared in which animals etc. are kept alive as nearly as possible in their natural state. WH: 17C. Latin warren, fish pond, use as n. of *vivarius*, from *vivus* alive, from *vivere* to live. See also -ARIUM.

vivat *n., int.* (a shout of) long live. WH: 16C. Latin may he live, 3rd. pers. sing. pres. subj. of *vivere*. Cp. VIVE.

viva voce *adv.* by word of mouth, orally. *Also a., n.* WH: 16C. Medieval Latin, lit. by the living voice, abl. of *viva vox* living voice.

vive *int.* long live, up with. WH: 16C. French may he live, 3rd pers. sing. pres. subj. of *vivre* to live, from Latin *vivere*. Cp. QUI VIVE.

viverrid *n.* any of the Viverridae, a family of carnivorous mammals containing the civets, genets, mongooses etc. *Also a.* WH: early 20C. Modern Latin *Viverridae*, from *Viverra* genus name, from Latin ferret.

vivers *n.pl.* food, provisions. WH: 16C. Old French *vivres*, use as n. of *vivre* to live.

vivid *a.* (of colour, light) very bright, intense, brilliant. WH: 17C. Latin *vividus*, from *vivere* to live, *vivus* alive, lively. See also -ID.

vivify *v.t.* to give life to, to quicken, to animate, to enliven. WH: 14–15C. Old French *vivifier*, from Late Latin *vivificare*, from Latin *vivus* alive, from *vivere* to live. See -FY.

viviparous *a.* giving birth to young alive, as distinct from *oviparous* and *ovoviviparous*. WH: 17C. Latin *viviparus*, from *vivus* alive. See -PAROUS. Cp. VIPER.

vivisection *n.* the dissection of, or performance of inoculative or other experiments on, living animals. WH: 18C. Latin *vivus* alive + SECTION, based on *dissection* (DISSECT).

vivo *adv.* with life and animation, vivace. WH: 18C. Italian alive, lively, from Latin *vivus*. Cp. VIVACE.

vixen *n.* a female fox. WH: pre-1200. Old English *fyxe*, fem. of FOX, from Germanic. Cp. German *Füchsin*. The initial *f* has become *v* (from English southern speech) as with VAT, VANE.

Viyella® *n.* a soft woven fabric made from cotton and wool, used esp. for blouses and shirts. WH: 19C. From *Via Gellia*, a road and valley in Derbyshire, where it was first made. The road name, based on the surname *Gell*, imitates a typical Roman road name such as *Via Devana*. See VIA.

viz. *adv.* namely, that is to say, to whit. WH: 16C. Abbr. of VIDELICET. The *z* represents the standard Medieval Latin symbol of contraction for -*et*.

†vizard *n.* a means of disguise, a mask, a visor. WH: 16C. Alt. of VISOR, with confusion of ending. See also -ARD. For a similar substitution, cp. MAZARD.

vizier *n.* a high officer or minister of state in some Muslim countries, esp. in the former Ottoman empire. WH: 16C. French *visir*, *vizir* or Spanish *visir*, from Turkish *vezir*, from Arabic *wazīr* helper, assistant, (later) minister. See also -IER.

vizsla *n.* a Hungarian breed of hunting dog with a smooth red or rust-coloured coat. WH: mid-20C. *Vizsla*, a town in Hungary.

Vlach *n.* a member of a people inhabiting Romania and parts of the former Soviet Union, a Wallachian. *Also a.* WH: 19C. Bulgarian and Serbo-Croat, corr. to Old Church Slavonic *Vlachŭ*, ult. from a Germanic word for foreigner rel. to WALLACH.

vlei *n.* a swampy tract, a place where water lies in rainy seasons. WH: 18C. Afrikaans, from Dutch *vallei* valley.

vocable *n.* a word, esp. as considered phonologically. WH: 14–15C. French or Latin *vocabulum*, from *vocare* to call. See also -ABLE.

vocabulary *n.* a list or collection of words used in a language, science, book etc., usu. arranged in alphabetical order, and explained. WH: 16C. Medieval Latin *vocabularius, vocabularium*, from Latin *vocabulum* VOCABLE. See also -ARY[1].

vocal *a.* of or relating to the voice or oral utterance. *Also n.* WH: 14–15C. Latin *vocalis*, from *vox, vocis* voice. See also -AL[1].

vocation *n.* a call or sense of fitness for and obligation to follow a particular career. WH: 14–15C. Old French, or from Latin *vocatio, vocationis*, from *vocatus*, p.p. of *vocare* to call. See also -ATION. The earliest sense was that of a religious calling (by God). The current sense dates from the 16C.

vocative *a.* used in addressing a person or thing. *Also n.* WH: 14–15C. Old French *vocatif*, or from Latin *vocativus*, from *vocatus*. See VOCATION, also -IVE.

vociferate *v.i.* to cry loudly, to bawl, to shout. *Also v.t.* WH: 16C. Latin *vociferatus*, p.p. of *vociferari*, from *vox, vocis* voice + *fer-*, stem of *ferre* to carry. See also -ATE[3].

vocoder *n.* an electronic device, similar to a synthesizer, that produces synthetic speech. WH: mid-20C. VOICE + CODE + -ER[1].

Vodafone® *n.* a British cellular telephone system; a handset used for this. WH: late 20C. VOICE + DATA + *fone*, alt. of PHONE[1]. The name was coined in 1984 by Racal Electronics, the manufacturers of the system.

vodka *n.* a strong alcoholic liquor distilled from rye, orig. from Russia. WH: 19C. Russian, dim. of *voda* water. Cp. WHISKY.

voe *n.* in Orkney or Shetland, a small inlet, bay or creek. WH: 17C. Norwegian *våg*, Icelandic *vogur* bay, inlet, from Old Norse *vágr* creek, bay.

voetsek *int.* go away. WH: 19C. Afrikaans, from Dutch *voort zeg ik* be off I say.

vogue *n.* a fashion prevalent at any particular time. WH: 16C. French, from Italian *voga* rowing, fashion, from *vogare* to row, to be going well.

voice *n.* the sound uttered by the mouth, esp. by a human being, in speaking, singing etc. *Also v.t.* WH: 12–14C. Old French *vois, voiz* (Modern French *voix*), from Latin *vox, vocis* voice, sound.

void *a.* empty, unfilled, vacant. *Also n., v.t.* WH: 12–14C. Old French *voide*, dial. var. of *vuide* (Modern French *vide*) (fem.), superseding *vuit* (m.), from Popular Latin *vocitus*, appar. replacing Latin *vocivus, vacivus*, rel. to *vacare* (VACANT).

voile *n.* a thin, semi-transparent dress material. WH: 19C. French VEIL.

voir dire *n.* the preliminary examination of a witness by a judge; an oath administered to such a witness. WH: 17C. Law French, from Old French *voir* true, truth + *dire* to say.

voix céleste *n.* a soft organ stop with a distinctive tremulous sound. WH: 19C. French, lit. heavenly voice. The stop is so called as its undulating tone was held to be reminiscent of celestial voices.

vola *n.* the palm of the hand. WH: 17C. Latin.

volant *a.* flying, able to fly. WH: 16C. French, pres.p. of *voler* to fly, from Latin *volare*. See also -ANT.

volante *n.* a two-wheeled covered horse-drawn vehicle with very long shafts and a body slung in front of the axle. WH: 18C. Spanish, from pres.p. of *volar* to fly, from Latin *volare*. Cp. VOLANT.

Volapük *n.* a universal language invented (1879) by Johann Maria Schleyer. WH: 19C. From *vol*, representing English *world* + -*a*- + *pük*, representing English *speak, speech*.

volar *a.* relating to flight or flying. WH: 19C. Latin *volare* to fly.

volatile *a.* readily evaporating. *Also n.* WH: 12–14C. Old French *volatil* (Modern French *volatile*) or Latin *volatilis*, from *volatus*, p.p. of *volare* to fly. See also -ATILE.

vol-au-vent *n.* a small, round puff pastry case filled with a filling, often savoury. WH: 19C. French, lit. flight in the wind. The pie is so called because it is light and delicate. Cp. PUFF.

volcano *n.* an opening in the earth's surface through which lava, cinders, gases etc. are ejected from the interior, esp. at the top of a hill or mountain formed by the successive accumulations of ejected matter. WH: 17C. Italian, from Latin *Volcanus, Vulcanus* Vulcan, the Roman god of fire and metal working, believed by the Romans to have his seat in Mount Etna.

vole[1] *n.* a mouselike or ratlike rodent of the family Cricetidae, with a stocky body, blunt nose, short tail and inconspicuous ears. WH: 19C. Norwegian *voll* field (+ *mus* mouse). Cp. *field mouse* (FIELD). The animal was originally known as a *vole-mouse*.

vole[2] *n.* the act of winning all the tricks in a deal. *Also v.i.* WH: 17C. French, appar. from *voler*, from Latin *volare* to fly.

volet *n.* a wing or panel of a triptych. WH: 19C. French, lit. shutter, from *voler*, from Latin *volare* to fly. See also -ET[1].

volitant *a.* flying, flitting. WH: 19C. Latin *volitans, volitantis*, pres.p. of *volitare*, freq. of *volare* to fly. See also -ANT.

volition *n.* exercise of the will. WH: 17C. French or Latin *volitio, volitionis*, from *volo, velle* to wish, to will. See also -ITION.

volk *n.* the people or nation, esp. that of the Afrikaners. WH: 19C. Afrikaans (from Dutch) and German nation, people. See FOLK.

Völkerwanderung *n.* a migration of peoples, esp. that of the Germanic and Slav peoples into S and W Europe in the 2nd–11th cents. WH: mid-20C. German, from *Völker* nations (VOLK) + *Wanderung* migration (WANDER).

volley *n.* a simultaneous discharge of missiles. *Also v.t., v.i.* WH: 16C. Old French *volée*, ult. from Latin *volare* to fly. See also -Y[2].

volplane *v.i.* to glide down to earth in an aircraft with the engine shut off. *Also n.* WH: early 20C. French *vol plané*, from *vol* flight + *plané*, p.p. of *planer* PLANE[1].

volt[1] *n.* the SI unit of electric potential or potential difference, the difference of potential between two points in a conductor carrying a current of 1 ampere when the power dissipated between them is 1 watt. WH: 19C. Alessandro *Volta*, 1745–1827, Italian physicist who perfected a chemical action used in the electric battery.

volt[2] *n.* a circular tread, the gait of a horse going sideways round a centre. *Also v.i.* WH: 16C. French *volte*, from Italian *volta* turn, use as n. of fem. p.p. of *volgere* to turn, from Latin *volvere* to roll.

volta *n.* a lively Italian dance of the 16th and 17th cents.; a piece of music to accompany this. WH: 16C. Italian turn. Cp. LAVOLTA.

volte-face *n.* a complete change of opinion, attitude etc. WH: 19C. French, from Italian *voltafaccia*, from *voltare* to turn (ult. from freq. of Latin *volvere* to roll) + *faccia* (ult. from Latin *facies*) face. Cp. *about-face*.

voluble *a.* producing or characterized by a flow of words, fluent, glib, garrulous. WH: 14–15C. French, or from Latin *volubilis*, from *volu-*. See VOLUME, also -IBLE. The original sense was readily rotating, moving easily. The current sense dates from the 16C.

volucrine *a.* of or relating to birds. WH: 19C. Latin *volucris* bird + -INE.

volume *n.* a collection of (usu. printed) sheets of paper, parchment etc., bound together forming a book or work or part of one. WH: 14–15C. Old French *volum* (Modern French *volume*), from Latin *volumen* roll (of writing), book, from *volu-*, base of *volvere* to roll.

voluminous *a.* of great volume, bulk or size. WH: 17C. Partly from Late Latin *voluminosus* with many coils, sinuous, partly from Latin *volumen, voluminis* VOLUME. See also -OUS.

voluntary *a.* acting, performed, given etc. of one's own free will or choice, not under external constraint. *Also n.* WH: 14–15C. Partly from Latin *voluntarius*, from *voluntas* will, partly from Old French *volontaire* VOLUNTEER. See also -ARY[1].

volunteer *n.* a person who undertakes a job etc. voluntarily. *Also a., v.t., v.i.* WH: 16C. Old French *volontaire*, from Latin *voluntarius* VOLUNTARY, with ending assim. to -EER.

voluptuary *n.* a person given to luxury or sensual pleasures. *Also a.* WH: 17C. Latin *voluptuarius*, var. of *voluptarius*, from *voluptas* pleasure. See also -ARY[1].

volute *n.* a spiral, a whorl. *Also a.* WH: 16C. French, or from Latin *voluta*, use as n. of fem. of *volutus*, p.p. of *volvere* to roll, to wrap.

volvox *n.* a spherical colony of simple, freshwater, greenish organisms, composed of minute flagellate cells which set up a revolving motion. WH: 18C. Modern Latin genus name, from misreading (in Pliny) of *volvocem* for *volucrem* (acc.) a pest of vines, as if from Latin *volvere* to roll.

volvulus *n.* a twisting of an intestine causing obstruction of the intestinal canal. WH: 17C. Medieval Latin, from Latin *volvere* to roll, to twist.

vomer *n.* a small thin bone forming the chief portion of the partition between the nostrils in human beings. WH: 18C. Latin ploughshare.

vomit *v.t.* to eject from the stomach by the mouth. *Also v.i., n.* WH: 14–15C. Latin *vomitus*, p.p. of *vomere*, from Latin freq. *vomitare*. Rel. to EMETIC.

voodoo *n.* a cult involving animistic deities, witchcraft and communication in trances practised by Creoles and blacks in Haiti and other parts of the W Indies and in the southern US. *Also v.t.* WH: 19C. Louisiana French *voudou*, from Fon *vodū* tutelary deity, fetish. Cp. HOODOO.

voortrekker *n.* any of the Dutch farmers from Cape Colony who took part in the Great Trek into the Transvaal in 1836 and following years. WH: 19C. Afrikaans, from *voor-* before + *trekken* TREK.

voracious *a.* greedy in eating. WH: 17C. Latin *vorax, voracis*, from *vorare* to devour. See also -IOUS.

-vore *comb. form* forming nouns denoting creatures that live on a certain type of food, as in *carnivore, herbivore*. WH: French, from Latin *-vorus*, from *vorare* to devour.

vortex *n.* a whirling or rotating mass of fluid, esp. a whirlpool. WH: 17C. Latin (var. of VERTEX) eddy of water, whirlwind, from *vortere, vertere* to turn.

vorticella *n.* a protozoan of the genus *Vorticella* of ciliated infusoria with the cilia restricted to a fringe around the mouth. WH: 18C. Modern Latin, dim. of Latin VORTEX,*vorticis*.

votary *n.* a person who is devoted or consecrated by a vow or promise. WH: 16C. Latin *votus*, p.p. of *vovere* to vow. See also -ARY[1].

vote *n.* a formal expression of opinion, will or choice, in regard to the election of a candidate, the passing or rejection of a resolution, law etc., usu. signified by voice, gesture or ballot. *Also v.i., v.t.* WH: 14–15C. Latin *votum* vow, wish, use as n. of neut. of p.p. of *vovere* to vow, to desire.

votive *a.* given, paid or dedicated in fulfilment of a vow. WH: 16C. Latin *votivus*, from *votum* vow, VOTE. See also -IVE.

vouch *v.t.* to uphold or guarantee by assertion, proof etc., to confirm, to substantiate. *Also v.i., n.* WH: 12–14C. Old French *vocher, voucher* to summon, ult. from Latin *vocare* to call. The original sense was to summon a person to court to give proof of a title to property. The current sense evolved in the 16C.

vouchsafe *v.t.* to condescend to grant. *Also v.i.* WH: 12–14C. VOUCH + SAFE. Orig. two words.

voussoir *n.* any of the wedge-shaped stones forming an arch. WH: 12–14C. Old French *vausoir, vaussoir* (Modern French *voussoir*), from Popular Latin *volsorium*, ult. from Latin *volsus*, p.p. of *volvere* to roll, to turn.

vow *n.* a solemn promise or pledge, esp. made to God or to a saint etc., undertaking an act, sacrifice, obligation etc. *Also v.t., v.i.* WH: 12–14C. Old French *vo, vou* (Modern French *vœu*), from Latin *votum* vow, VOTE.

vowel *n.* a sound able to make a syllable or to be sounded alone; an open and unimpeded sound as distinct from a closed, stopped or mute sound or consonant. WH: 12–14C. Old French *vouel*, var. of *voiel* (Modern French *voyelle*), from Latin *vocalis*, from VOX, *vocis* + *-alis* -AL[1].

vox *n.* a voice. WH: 16C. Latin voice, sound.

voyage *n.* a journey by water or air or through space, esp. to a distant place. *Also v.i., v.t.* WH: 12–14C. Old French *veiage, voiage* (Modern French *voyage*), from Latin VIATICUM. See also -AGE.

voyeur *n.* a person who derives sexual gratification from watching sexual acts, people undressing etc. WH: early 20C. French, from *voir* to see + *-eur* -OR.

vraisemblance *n.* an appearance of truth, verisimilitude. WH: 19C. French, from *vrai* true + SEMBLANCE.

vroom *v.i.* (of an engine) to make a loud revving noise. *Also v.t., n., int.* WH: mid-20C. Imit.

vug *n.* a small cavity in a rock or vein lined with crystals. WH: 19C. Cornish *vooga*, ? ult. rel. to Breton *mouger* cave.

vulcanian *a.* of or relating to a volcanic eruption that discharges gas and ash but little or no lava. WH: 16C. Latin *Vulcanius*, from *Vulcanus* Vulcan (see VOLCANO), in later senses ? partly also from *vulcano*, obs. var. of VOLCANO. See also -IAN.

vulcanism *n.* volcanic activity and phenomena collectively. WH: 19C. Latin *vulcanisme*, var. of *volcanisme* volcanism (VOLCANO).

vulcanite *n.* vulcanized rubber, ebonite. WH: 19C. From *Vulcan* (VOLCANO) + -ITE[1].

vulgar *a.* of, relating to or characteristic of the common people. *Also n.* WH: 14–15C. Latin *vulgaris*, from *vulgus* the common people. See also -AR[1]. The original sense was common or ordinary (time, distance, use, etc.). The sense offensively coarse evolved in the 19C.

Vulgate *n.* the Latin translation of the Bible made by St Jerome, 383–405. WH: 17C. Late Latin *vulgata* (fem.), *vulgatus* (m.), p.ps of Latin *vulgare* to make public, from *vulgus*. See VULGAR, also -ATE[2]. The Late Latin adjective was represented in phrases such as *editio vulgata* common edition, *lectio vulgata* common reading, *textus vulgatus* common text.

vulnerable *a.* capable of being wounded physically or emotionally. WH: 17C. Late Latin *vulnerabilis* wounding, from *vulnerare*, from *vulnus, vulneris* wound. See also -ABLE.

vulpine *a.* of or relating to or characteristic of a fox. WH: 17C. Latin *vulpinus*, from *vulpes* fox. See -INE. Latin *vulpes* is related to Greek *alōpēx* (ALOPECIA).

vulture *n.* a large bird of the family Accipitridae (Old World) or Cathartidae (New World) with head and neck almost naked, feeding chiefly on carrion. WH: 14–15C. Old French *voltour* (Modern French *vautour*), from Latin *vulturius*, from *vultur, voltur*, ? rel. to *vellere* to pull, to tear, or to *vulnus* wound.

vulva *n.* the external female genitals, esp. the opening of the vagina. WH: 14–15C. Latin *vulva, volva* womb, matrix, from *volvere* to turn, to roll.

W *chem. symbol* tungsten. **WH:** Abbr. of Modern Latin *wolframium* WOLFRAM.

†wabster *n.* a weaver. **WH:** 12–14C. Var. of *webster* (WEB).

wack *n.* friend (used as a term of address). **WH:** mid-20C. Prob. from WACKER.

wacke *n.* an earthy or clayey rock produced by the decomposition of igneous rocks. **WH:** 19C. German, from Middle High German large stone, from Old High German *wacko* pebble.

wacker *n.* a Liverpudlian. **WH:** 18C. Orig. unknown.

wacko *a.* crazy, eccentric. *Also n.* **WH:** late 20C. WACKY + -O.

wacky *a.* crazy, eccentric, absurd. *Also n.* **WH:** 19C. WHACK + -Y[1].

wad[1] *n.* a small, compact mass of some soft material, used for stopping an opening, stuffing between things etc. *Also v.t.* **WH:** 16C. Rel. to Dutch *watten*, French *ouate*, Italian *ovatta* padding, cotton wool, Spanish *bata* dressing gown.

wad[2] *n.* an earthy ore of manganese. **WH:** 17C. Orig. unknown.

waddle *v.i.* to walk with an ungainly rocking or swaying motion and with short, quick steps, as a duck or goose does. *Also n.* **WH:** 14–15C. ? Freq. of WADE. See also -LE[4]. The original sense was to fall heavily. The current sense dates from the 16C.

waddy *n.* an Australian war club, usu. bent like a boomerang or with a thick head. *Also v.t.* **WH:** 18C. Australian Aboriginal (Dharuk) *wadi* tree, stick of wood, wooden weapon.

wade *v.i.* to walk through water or a semi-fluid medium, such as snow, mud etc. *Also v.t.* **WH:** pre-1200. Old English *wadan*, from a Germanic v. meaning to go, to go through, from Indo-European base represented by Latin *vadere* to go, *vadere* to wade through, *vadum* ford. The original sense (to the 17C) was to go, to move forward. The current specialized sense evolved in the 12–14C.

wadi *n.* the valley or channel of a stream that is dry except in the rainy season. **WH:** 17C. Arabic *wādī* valley, river bed. The Arabic word forms the 1st element of the Spanish river name *Guadalquivir*, literally great river.

wafer *n.* a small, thin, sweet biscuit, esp. one eaten with ice cream. *Also v.t.* **WH:** 14–15C. Anglo-French *wafre*, var. of Old Northern French *waufre*, Old French *gaufre* (GOFFER), from Middle Low German *wāfel* WAFFLE[1].

waffle[1] *n.* a thin batter cake baked in a waffle-iron. **WH:** 18C. Dutch *wafel*, *waefel*, from Middle Low German *wāfel* (WAFER). Cp. GOFFER.

waffle[2] *v.i.* to talk or write aimlessly and at length. *Also n.* **WH:** 17C. Freq. of dial. *waff* to bark (of a puppy), to yap, to yelp, of imit. orig. Cp. WOOF[1]. The original sense was to yap, to yelp (of a dog). The current sense dates from the early 20C.

waft *v.t.* to carry or convey through the air. *Also v.i., n.* **WH:** 16C. Back-formation from obs. *wafter* armed vessel used as a convoy, from Low German and Dutch *wachter*, from *wechten* to guard. Rel. to WAKE[1], WATCH. The original sense (to the 17C) was to escort a fleet of ships, also (to the 19C) to sail about, to sail along. Hence the current sense, from the 17C.

wag[1] *v.t.* to shake up and down or backwards and forwards lightly and quickly, esp. in playfulness, reproof etc. *Also v.i., n.* **WH:** 12–14C. Old English *wagian* to wave, to shake, to totter, from Germanic. Rel. to WEIGH. The original sense (to the 15C) was to totter, to stagger. The current sense dates from the 14–15C.

wag[2] *n.* a facetious person, a wit, a joker. **WH:** 16C. ? Shortening of obs. *waghalter* gallows bird, lit. person likely to swing in a halter, from WAG[1] + HALTER.

wage *n.* payment for work done or services rendered, esp. fixed periodical pay for labour of a manual kind. *Also v.t., v.i.* **WH:** 12–14C. Old Northern French, from Old French *guage* (Modern French *gage*), from Germanic, rel. to GAGE[1].

wager *n.* something staked or hazarded on the outcome of a contest etc., a bet. *Also v.t., v.i.* **WH:** 12–14C. Anglo-French *wageure*, from *wager* WAGE.

waggle *v.t., v.i.* to wag or swing to and fro, esp. quickly and frequently. *Also n.* **WH:** 16C. Freq. of WAG[1]. See also -LE[4]. Cp. WIGGLE.

Wagnerian *a.* of, relating to or in the style of Wagner's music or operas. *Also n.* **WH:** 19C. Richard *Wagner*, 1813–83, German operatic composer + -IAN.

wagon *n.* a strong four-wheeled vehicle for the transport of heavy loads, usu. with a rectangular body, often with a removable cover, usu. drawn by two or more horses. **WH:** 15C. Dutch *wagen*, rel. to Old English *wægn* WAIN. Cp. German *Wagen*.

wagon-lit *n.* a sleeping car on a Continental train. **WH:** 19C. French, from *wagon* railway coach (from WAGON) + *lit* bed.

wagtail *n.* any of various small, long-tailed birds, chiefly of the genus *Motacilla*. **WH:** 16C. WAG[1] + TAIL[1]. The bird is so named from its long tail which continually wags up and down.

Wahabi *n.* a member of a sect founded about the middle of the 18th cent. cultivating a strict form of Islam. **WH:** 19C. Arabic *wahhābī*, from Muḥammad ibn 'Abd-al-*Wahhāb*, 1703–92, founder of the sect.

wahine *n.* a Maori or Polynesian woman. **WH:** 18C. Maori woman, wife. The variant form *vahine* is familiar from the titles of paintings by the French artist Paul Gauguin, 1848–1903, e.g. *Vahine no te tiare* Woman with a Flower (1891).

wahoo[1] *n.* a N American elm, *Ulmus alata*, also called *winged elm*. **WH:** 18C. Orig. unknown.

wahoo[2] *n.* a N American shrub or small tree, *Euonymus atropurpureus*. **WH:** 19C. Dakota *wanhu*, lit. arrowwood.

wahoo[3] *n.* a fast-swimming food fish, *Acanthocybium solanderi*, of tropical seas. **WH:** early 20C. Orig. unknown.

wahoo[4] *int.* used to express exultation, excitement etc. **WH:** mid-20C. Prob. natural exclamation. Cp. WHEE, WOW[1].

wah-wah *n.* the sound made by alternately covering and uncovering the bell of a brass instrument. **WH:** early 20C. Imit.

waif *n.* a homeless wanderer, esp. a forsaken child. **WH:** 14–15C. Anglo-French *waif*, *weif*, var. of Old Northern French *gaif*, prob. of Scandinavian orig. Cp. Old Norse *veif* something wavering, flapping thing, rel. to *veifa* to wave. The word was originally a legal term for a piece of property that was found ownerless and that went to the lord of the manor if unclaimed. The current sense dates from the 17C.

wail *v.i.* to lament. *Also v.t., n.* **WH:** 12–14C. Of Scandinavian orig. Cp. Old Norse int. *vei*, rel. to Old English *wā* WOE.

wain *n.* a four-wheeled vehicle for the transportation of goods, a wagon. *Also v.t.* **WH:** pre-1200. Old English *wægn*, *wǣn* wagon, from Germanic, from Indo-European root represented also by WAY, WEIGH. Cp. WAGON.

wainscot *n.* a wooden, usu. panelled, lining or casing of the walls of a room. *Also v.t.* **WH:** 12–14C. Middle Low German *wagenschot*, appar. from *wagen* wagon + *schot*, ? boarding, planking. The word was originally a term for high-quality imported oak, hence (to the 17C) a piece or board of such oak. The current sense dates from the 16C.

waist *n.* the part of the human body below the ribs or thorax and above the hips. **WH:** 14–15C. Appar. from unrecorded Old English **wæst*, **weahst* growth, size, from Germanic base of WAX[2]. The original reference was to a man's waist, rather than a woman's, regarded as being the part of the body with the greatest circumference. The waist of a ship is still its widest part.

wait *v.i.* to remain inactive or in the same place until some event or time for action, to stay. *Also v.t., n.* **WH:** 12–14C. Old Northern

French *waitier*, var. of Old French *guaitier* (Modern French *guetter* to watch for), from Germanic base represented also by WAKE[1]. The original sense (to the 16C) was to watch for, to lie in wait (for). The current sense dates from the 14–15C.

waive *v.t.* to decide officially that something can be ignored. WH: 12–14C. Anglo-French *weyver*, var. of Old French *gaiver*, *guesver* to allow to become a waif, to abandon, from *gaif* WAIF. The original sense (to the 17C) was to abandon, to give up. The current sense evolved in the 14–15C.

wake[1] *v.i.* to be aroused from sleep, to cease to sleep. *Also v.t.*, *n.* WH: pre-1200. Old English *wacan* to become awake, *wacian* to be awake, rel. to *wæccan* to be awake (see WATCH), from Germanic, from Indo-European. Cp. German *wachen*. The original sense was to be awake, to stay awake. The sense to wake up arose in the 12–14C.

wake[2] *n.* the track left by a vessel passing through water. WH: 15C. Prob. from Middle Low German *wake*, from Old Norse *vaka*, *vok* hole in ice (? orig. one made by a vessel).

waken *v.t.* to rouse from sleep. *Also v.i.* WH: pre-1200. Old English *wæcnan*, from Germanic base also of WAKE[1]. See also -EN[5].

Waldenses *n.pl.* a religious sect founded in S France about 1170 by Peter Waldo, in a reform movement leading to persecution by the Church. WH: 16C. Medieval Latin, appar. from *Waldensis*, var. of (Peter) *Valdes*, d.1205, Lyonnese merchant, founder of the sect. Cp. VAUDOIS[2].

waldgrave *n.* a German title of nobility, orig. a head forester. WH: 19C. German *Waldgraf*, from *Wald* forest (WEALD, WOLD) + *Graf* count. Cp. BURGRAVE, LANDGRAVE, MARGRAVE, PALSGRAVE.

wale *n.* a ridge on the skin, a weal. *Also v.t.* WH: pre-1200. Old English *walu*, from Germanic. Cp. WEAL[1].

waler *n.* a riding horse (orig. as supplied by military authorities in New South Wales). WH: 19C. New South *Wales*, state of SE Australia + -ER[1].

walk *v.i.* to go along by raising, advancing and setting down each foot alternately, never having both feet off the ground at once. *Also v.t.*, *n.* WH: pre-1200. Old English *wealcan* to toss, to roll, from Germanic base of unknown orig. Cp. Old Norse *valka* to drag about, to torment. The original sense was to toss (to the 14–15C), to journey, to wander (to the 16C). The current sense dates from the 12–14C. The surname *Walker* is unrelated and comes from obsolete *walk* in the sense to full (FULL[2]).

wall *n.* a continuous structure of stone, brick etc. forming an enclosure, a side or internal partition of a building etc. *Also v.t.* WH: pre-1200. Old English, corr. to Middle Low German and Middle Dutch *wal*, from Latin *vallum* rampart, from *vallus* stake. A wall was originally a purely defensive structure.

wallaby *n.* a marsupial of the family Macropodidae, similar to but smaller than the kangaroo. WH: 19C. Australian Aboriginal (Dharuk) *walabi*.

Wallach *n.* a Wallachian or Vlach, a Romance-speaking inhabitant of Romania. WH: 18C. Var. of VLACH.

wallah *n.* an agent, worker or any person concerned with a usu. specified thing. WH: 18C. Hindi *-vālā*, suf. expressing relation, from Sanskrit *pālaka* keeper. The Hindi suffix is conventionally understood by Europeans as a noun meaning man, fellow.

wallaroo *n.* a large species of kangaroo, *Macropus robustus*. WH: 19C. Australian Aboriginal (Dharuk) *walaru*.

wallet *n.* a small case for carrying paper money, credit cards etc. WH: 12–14C. Prob. from Anglo-French, from Germanic base of WELL[2]. A wallet was originally a bag or pouch slung over the shoulder to carry food, clothing etc. on a journey. The current sense evolved in the 19C.

wall-eye *n.* a condition of the eye characterized by opacity of the cornea. WH: 16C. Back-formation from *wall-eyed* (14–15C), from Old Norse *vagleygr*, from a 1st element of unknown orig. rel. to Icelandic *vagl* film over the eye, Swedish *vagel* sty on the eye + -*eygr* -eyed (from *auga* EYE[1]). See also -ED.

Walloon *n.* a member of a French-speaking people in SE Belgium and the adjoining parts of France. *Also a.* WH: 16C. French *Wallon*, from Medieval Latin *Wallo*, *Wallonis*, from Germanic. See also -OON. Cp. WELSH.

wallop *v.t.* to thrash, to flog. *Also v.i.*, *n.* WH: 14–15C. Old Northern

French *waloper*, var. of Old French *galoper*, ? a blend of Frankish *wala* WELL[1], *hlaupen* to run, ult. from Germanic. Cp. GALLOP, LEAP. The original sense was to gallop, then (16C) to boil with noisy bubbling, then (18C) to move clumsily. The sense to beat, to thrash arose in the 19C.

wallow *v.i.* to roll or tumble about in mud, water etc. *Also v.t.*, *n.* WH: pre-1200. Old English *walwian*, *wealwian*, ult. from Germanic, from Indo-European base represented by Latin *volvere* to roll. The original sense was to roll about, to toss about while lying down.

wally *n.* an incompetent or stupid person. WH: mid-20C. Orig. uncertain. ? Shortening of male forename *Walter*. Cp. CHARLIE.

walnut *n.* a tree of the genus *Juglans*, esp. *J. regia*, bearing a nut enclosed in a green fleshy covering. WH: pre-1200. Old English *walhhnutu*, from *walh* foreign, WELSH + *hnutu* NUT, from Germanic. Cp. German *Wallnuss*. Not rel. to WALL. The nut is so called as it was originally introduced into the Germanic region from Gaul and Italy.

Walpurgis night *n.* the eve of 1 May, when witches are supposed to hold revels and dance with the Devil, esp. on the Brocken mountain in Germany. WH: 19C. German *Walpurgisnacht*, from *Walpurgis*, gen. of *Walpurga* Walburga, d.779, Anglo-Saxon saint, abbess of Heidenheim, Germany + *Nacht* NIGHT. Walpurga's feast day, 1 May, coincided with a pagan feast for the beginning of summer and the revel of witches. Hence the adoption of her name for Walpurgis night.

walrus *n.* a large, amphibious, long-tusked, seal-like mammal of the Arctic seas, *Odobenus rosmarus*. WH: 18C. Prob. from Dutch *walrus*, *walros*, alt. (based on *walvisch* whale), with inversion of the elements, of such forms as Old English *horschwæl*, Old Norse *hrosshvalr*, lit. horse-whale.

waltz *n.* a dance in triple time in which the partners pass round each other smoothly as they progress. *Also v.i.*, *v.t.* WH: 18C. German *Walzer*, from *walzen* to roll, to revolve, to waltz. Cp. VALSE. Rel. to WELTER[1].

wampum *n.* small beads made of shells, used by N American Indians formerly as money, or for decorating belts, bracelets etc. WH: 17C. Abbr. of obs. *wampumpeag* (mistakenly analysed as *wampum* + *peag*), from Algonquian *wap* white + *umpe* string + pl. suf. *-ag*. The Algonquian word refers to a string of shells used as money.

wan *a.* pale or sickly in hue, pallid. WH: pre-1200. Old English *wann* dark, gloomy, black, of unknown orig. The original sense was gloomy, dark, as of the sea or other water. The current sense dates from the 12–14C.

wand *n.* a long, slender rod, esp. one used by conjurors or as a staff of office. WH: 12–14C. Old Norse *vǫndr*, rel. to Gothic *wandus*, prob. from Germanic base meaning to turn, to wind. Cp. WEND.

wander *v.i.* to travel or go here and there without any definite route or object, to rove, ramble or roam. *Also v.t.*, *n.* WH: pre-1200. Old English *wandrian*, from a Germanic v. rel. to WEND, WIND[2]. See also -ER[5]. Cp. German *wandern*.

wanderoo *n.* a macaque, *Macaca silenus*, with a large greyish beard, of India and Sri Lanka. WH: 17C. Sinhalese *vandaru* monkey, from Sanskrit *vānara*.

wandoo *n.* a white eucalyptus tree, *Eucalyptus redunca*, of W Australia. WH: 19C. Australian Aboriginal (Nyungar) *wandu*.

wane *v.i.* (of the illuminated portion of the moon) to diminish in size and brilliance. *Also n.* WH: pre-1200. Old English *wanian* to lessen, from Germanic base represented also by Latin *vanus* vain. The original sense was to decrease in size, to dwindle, but the application to the moon dates from the first also.

wangle *v.t.* to achieve or gain by devious means. *Also n.* WH: 19C. Orig. uncertain. ? Based on WAGGLE and obs. *wankle* unsteady, insecure, from Old English *wancol*, from Germanic (cp. German *wanken* to waver, to totter).

wank *v.i.*, *v.t.* to masturbate. *Also n.* WH: mid-20C. Orig. uncertain. ? Alt. of WHANG[2]. Cp. *whang* penis.

Wankel engine *n.* a type of internal-combustion engine in which a curved, triangular piston rotates in an elliptical combustion chamber. WH: mid-20C. Felix *Wankel*, 1902–88, German engineer and inventor.

wanna *contr.* want to. WH: 19C. Representation of a pronun. of *want to*.

wannabe *n.* a person anxious to be like somebody, esp. a famous person, or to become something. WH: late 20C. Representation of a pronun. of *want to be.* Cp. WANNA.

want *n.* the state or condition of not having, lack, deficiency, absence (of). *Also v.t., v.i.* WH: 12–14C. Old Norse *vant,* n. of *vanr* lacking, missing, rel. to Old English *wana.* Rel. to WANE.

wanton *a.* behaving in a licentious manner, with uncontained immorality. *Also n., v.i.* WH: 12–14C. Old English *wan* wanting (WANE) + *togen,* p.p. of *tēon* to discipline, to train, from Germanic base rel. to that of TEAM. The original sense was undisciplined, rebellious. The current sense evolved in the 14–15C.

wapentake *n.* in certain English counties, a division corresponding to a hundred. WH: pre-1200. Old English *wǣpentæc,* from Old Norse *vápnatak,* from *vápna,* gen. pl. of *vápn* WEAPON + *tak* act of taking, from *taka* TAKE[1]. The reference is to a brandishing of weapons. The subdivision is found chiefly in northern and midland counties, i.e. in the Danelaw.

wapiti *n.* a N American stag, *Cervus canadensis,* related to the red deer. WH: 19C. Shawnee *wa:piti,* lit. white rump.

war *n.* a contest carried on by force of arms between nations, or between parties in the same state. *Also v.i.* WH: pre-1200. Old Northern French *werre,* var. of Old French *guerre,* from Frankish *werra,* rel. to Old High German *werra* confusion, discord, strife, Old High German *werran* to bring into confusion, from Germanic base represented by WORSE. Cp. German *wirren* to confuse, to perplex.

waratah *n.* an Australian shrub, *Telopea speciosissima,* with a large, brilliant crimson flower. WH: 18C. Australian Aboriginal (Dharuk) *warrada.*

warble[1] *v.i.* (esp. of birds) to sing in a continuous quavering or trilling manner. *Also v.t., n.* WH: 14–15C. Old Northern French *werbler* to trill, to sing, from Frankish *hwirbilōn* to whirl, to trill. Cp. German *Wirbel* whirlwind. The original sense was to proclaim by a flourish of trumpets. The current sense to sing (of birds) arose in the 15C.

warble[2] *n.* a small hard tumour on a horse's back caused by the galling of the saddle. WH: 14–15C. Orig. unknown.

ward *n.* an administrative or electoral division of a town or city. *Also v.t.* WH: pre-1200. Old English *weard,* rel. to Old High German *warta* watch (German *Warte* watchtower), from stem of a Germanic v. meaning to be on guard (cp. WARE[2]) reinforced in Middle English by Old Northern French *warde,* from Old French *garde* GUARD. The original sense was protection, defence, hence place for guarding, person to be guarded.

-ward *suf.* used to form adjectives and adverbs expressing direction, as in *backward, forward, homeward, inwards, outwards* etc. WH: Old English *-weard, -weardes,* from Germanic base meaning to turn (cp. Latin *vertere* to turn). Old English *-weardes* is the genitive singular form.

warden *n.* a keeper, a guardian. WH: 12–14C. Old Northern French *wardein,* var. of Old French *guarden* GUARDIAN.

warder *n.* a keeper. WH: 14–15C. Anglo-French *wardere,* from Old Northern French *warder.* See WARD, also -ER[1].

wardrobe *n.* a tall cupboard with rails, shelves etc. where clothes are hung up. WH: 12–14C. Old Northern French *warderobe,* var. of Old French *garderobe,* from *garder* GUARD + *robe* ROBE. The original sense (to the 17C) was bedroom, hence (to 19C) room adjoining a bedroom, dressing room. The sense of cupboard for clothes dates from the 16C.

ware[1] *n.* manufactured articles of a specified kind, as *tableware, glassware, silverware, hardware* etc. WH: pre-1200. Old English *waru,* from Germanic, ? from same base as WARE[2] with a meaning object of care.

†ware[2] *a.* conscious, aware. *Also v.t., int.* WH: pre-1200. Old English *wær,* from Germanic base meaning to observe, to take care. Cp. WARE[1], WARN.

warehouse[1] *n.* a building in which goods are stored, kept for sale or in bond. WH: 12–14C. WARE[1] + HOUSE[1].

warehouse[2] *v.t.* to deposit, secure or store (furniture, bonded goods etc.) in a warehouse. WH: 18C. WAREHOUSE[1].

warfarin *n.* a compound used as a rodent poison and to prevent blood clotting. WH: mid-20C. Abbr. of *Wisconsin Alumni Research Foundation* + *-arin,* based on COUMARIN. See also -IN[1].

†warlock *n.* a wizard, a sorcerer. WH: pre-1200. Old English *wǣrloga,* corr. to Old Saxon *wārlogo,* from Old English *wǣr* covenant + base of *lēogan* LIE[1]. The spelling with *-ck* is from Scottish. The original sense was oath-breaker, traitor. The current sense dates from the 12–14C.

warm *a.* at a rather high temperature. *Also v.t., v.i., n.* WH: pre-1200. Old English *wearm,* from Germanic, prob. from Indo-European base represented by Latin *formus* warm, Greek *thermos* hot, Sanskrit *gharma* heat. Cp. German *warm.*

warn *v.t.* to give notice to, to inform beforehand. *Also v.i.* WH: pre-1200. Old English *warnian, wearnian,* from Germanic base meaning to be cautious. Cp. WARE[2].

warp *n.* the state of being twisted or distorted, a twist or distortion in timber etc. *Also v.t., v.i.* WH: pre-1200. Old English *wearp,* from *weorpan* to throw, from Germanic. Cp. German *werfen* to throw. The original sense of the verb was to throw, to fling. The sense to weave, then to arrange yarn to form a warp, dates from the 12–14C.

warrant *v.t.* to answer or give an assurance for, to guarantee. *Also n.* WH: 12–14C. Old French *warantir,* var. of *guarantir,* from *guarant* (Modern French *garant*), from Frankish *werēnd,* from *giwerēn,* corr. to Old Frisian *wera* to be surety for, to guarantee. Cp. GUARANTEE. The original sense (to the 16C) was to keep safe from danger, to protect.

warren *n.* a piece of ground with a network of underground tunnels where rabbits live and breed. WH: 14–15C. Old Northern French *warenne,* var. of Old French *garenne* game park (Modern French rabbit warren), from a Gaulish base meaning post (cp. Irish *farr* pillar, post).

warrigal *n.* a dingo. *Also a.* WH: 18C. Australian Aboriginal (Dharuk).

warrior *n.* a person experienced or distinguished in war, a distinguished soldier. WH: 12–14C. Old Northern French *werreior,* var. of Old French *guerreieor* (Modern French *guerroyeur*), from Old French *guerreier* (Modern French *guerroyer*), from *guerre* WAR. See also -ER[2], -OR.

wart *n.* a small hard excrescence on the skin of the hands etc. due to irregular growth of the papillae, caused by a virus. WH: pre-1200. Old English *wearte,* from Germanic. Cp. German *Warze.* Rel. to VERRUCA.

wary *a.* cautious, watchful against deception, danger etc. WH: 15C. WARE[2] + -Y[1].

wash *v.t.* to cleanse with water or other liquid. *Also v.i., n.* WH: pre-1200. Old English *wæscan, wascan,* from Germanic, from base also of WATER. Cp. German *waschen.*

Wasp *n.* an American of N European descent, considered in N America as belonging to a privileged class. WH: mid-20C. Acronym of *White Anglo-Saxon Protestant,* punning on WASP, ? with ref. to their self-importance or aggressiveness.

wasp *n.* a predatory hymenopterous insect of solitary or social habits, esp. the common wasp, *Vespula vulgaris,* a European insect with a slender waist, black and yellow stripes and a powerful sting. WH: pre-1200. Old English *wæsp, wæps,* from Germanic, from Indo-European base meaning WEAVE[1]. Cp. German *Wespe.* The insects are so called with reference to the construction of their paper nest.

†wassail *n.* a festive occasion, a drinking-bout. *Also v.i.* WH: 12–14C. Old Norse *ves heill* be healthy, from *ves,* imper. of *vera* to be (see *was* under BE) + *heill* healthy, HALE[1]. The word was originally a drinking toast.

Wassermann test *n.* a diagnostic test for the presence of syphilis. WH: early 20C. August Paul *Wassermann,* 1866–1925, German bacteriologist.

waste *v.t.* to consume, to spend, to use up unnecessarily, carelessly or lavishly, to squander. *Also v.i., a., n.* WH: 12–14C. Old Northern French *waster,* var. of *guaster,* ult. from Latin *vastare,* from *vastus* waste, desert. The original sense was to lay waste, to devastate.

wastrel *n.* a wasteful person. WH: 16C. WASTE + derog. suf. *-rel,* as in MONGREL, SCOUNDREL.

wat *n.* a Thai Buddhist temple or monastery. WH: 19C. Thai, from Sanskrit *vāta* enclosure.

watch *n.* the act or state of watching. *Also v.i., v.t.* WH: pre-1200. Old English *wæcce,* from same source as *wacian.* See WAKE[1]. The original meaning (to the 17C) was the state of being awake, wakefulness. The sense timepiece dates from 14–15C and originally applied to an alarm clock. A watch has to be 'watched' (looked at) to find out the time, whereas a clock strikes and can be listened to.

water *n.* a colourless, transparent liquid, without taste or smell, possessing a neutral reaction, a compound of two parts by weight of hydrogen with one of oxygen. *Also a., v.t., v.i.* WH: pre-1200. Old English *wæter*, from Germanic, from Indo-European base represented also by Old Church Slavonic and Russian *voda* (cp. VODKA). Cp. Dutch *water*, German *Wasser*. Rel. to WET.

Waterford glass *n.* a type of clear colourless glass. WH: 18C. *Waterford*, a city in SE Ireland.

Watergate *n.* a scandal involving a political cover-up. WH: late 20C. *Watergate*, a building in Washington, DC, USA, containing the headquarters of the Democratic Party. The bugging and burglary of the headquarters by people connected with the Republican administration led to a national scandal and the resignation of President Richard M. Nixon in 1972.

Waterloo *n.* a downfall, a decisive defeat. WH: 19C. *Waterloo*, a village (now a town) near Brussels, Belgium, where Napoleon was finally defeated in 1815.

watt *n.* a unit of power or rate of doing work, equal to a rate of working of one joule per second or the power available when the electromotive force is one volt and the current is one ampere. WH: 19C. James *Watt*, 1736–1819, Scottish engineer, inventor of the steam engine.

wattle *n.* a construction of interwoven twigs or wickerwork used to make fences, walls etc. *Also v.t.* WH: pre-1200. Old English *watul*, of uncertain orig. ? Rel. to Old English *wætla* bandage. The sense coloured fleshy lobe hanging from the head or neck of certain birds dates from the 16C and is probably of different origin.

waul *v.i.* to cry like a cat, to wail or squall. WH: 16C. Imit. Cp. WAIL.

wave *v.i.* to move to and fro with a sinuous or sweeping motion like a flag in the wind, to flutter or undulate. *Also v.t., n.* WH: 12–14C. Old English *wafian*, from Germanic, partly from Germanic base also of WAVER. The sense undulation of water on the sea dates from the 15C, replacing earlier *waw*, related to Old English *wagian* WAG[1].

waver *v.i.* to be in a state of indecision, to hesitate, to vacillate. WH: 12–14C. Old Norse *vafra* to move unsteadily, to flicker, from Germanic. See also -ER[5]. Cp. WAVE.

WAVES *n.* the women's reserve of the US navy. WH: mid-20C. Acronym of *Women Appointed* (later, *Accepted*) for *Volunteer Emergency Service*, punning on pl. of WAVE.

wax[1] *n.* a yellow, mouldable, fatty substance excreted by bees and used for the cells of honeycombs; beeswax. *Also a., v.t.* WH: pre-1200. Old English *wæx, weax*, from Germanic. Cp. German *Wachs*.

wax[2] *v.i.* to increase gradually in size and brilliance, as the illuminated portion of the moon between new and full. WH: pre-1200. Old English *weaxan*, from Germanic, from Indo-European base represented also by Greek *auxanein* to increase, Latin *augere*, Sanskrit *ukṣ* to grow. Cp. German *wachsen*.

wax[3] *n.* a rage. WH: 19C. ? From a phr. such as *to wax angry* (WAX[2]).

way *n.* a road, path, track or other place of passage. *Also adv.* WH: pre-1200. Old English *weg*, from Germanic base meaning to move, to journey, to carry (cp. WAIN, WEIGH), represented also by Latin *vehere* to carry. Cp. German *Weg*.

-ways *suf.* forming adverbs of position, direction, manner etc., as in *always, lengthways*. WH: WAY + -'s. Cp. -WISE.

wayward *a.* selfish, stubborn and difficult to control. WH: 14–15C. Shortening of obs. *awayward* in a different direction, away, from AWAY + -WARD.

wayzgoose *n.* an annual dinner, picnic or other entertainment given to or held by the persons employed in a printing house. WH: 18C. Alt. of earlier obs. *way goose*, of unknown orig. The meal was perhaps originally a dish of GOOSE.

we *pron.* the plural of I, denoting the person speaking and others associated with or represented by that person. WH: pre-1200. Old English *wē, we*, from Germanic. Cp. Dutch *wij*, German *wir*.

weak *a.* deficient in physical strength, not robust, vigorous or powerful. WH: pre-1200. Old English *wāc*, from Germanic base meaning to yield, to give way. Cp. German *weich* soft. The original sense (to the 16C) was pliant, flexible. The sense lacking in strength dates from the 12–14C.

weal[1] *n.* a ridge or raised streak made by a rod or whip on the flesh. *Also v.t.* WH: 19C. Var. of WALE, based on obs. *wheal* pimple, pustule. Cp. WHELK[2].

weal[2] *n.* a sound, healthy or prosperous state of persons or things. WH: pre-1200. Old English *wela*, from Germanic base also of WELL[1].

weald *n.* a tract of open forest land, esp. the Weald. WH: pre-1200. Old English var. of *wald* WOLD.

wealth *n.* riches, large possessions of money, goods or lands. WH: 12–14C. WELL[1] or WEAL[2] + -TH[2], based on HEALTH.

wean[1] *v.t.* to accustom (a child or animal) to nourishment other than its mother's milk, to teach to feed other than from the breast or bottle. WH: pre-1200. Old English *wenian*, from Germanic. Cp. German *entwöhnen*.

wean[2] *n.* a child. WH: 17C. Contr. of *wee ane*. See WEE, ONE. Not rel. to WEAN[1].

weapon *n.* an instrument of attack or defence, a thing used to inflict bodily harm. WH: pre-1200. Old English *wǣpen, wǣpn*, from a Germanic v. of unknown orig. Cp. German *Waffe*.

wear[1] *v.t.* to have on the person as clothing, ornament etc. *Also v.i., n.* WH: pre-1200. Old English *werian*, from Germanic, from Indo-European base represented also by Old Norse *vest* cloak, Latin *vestis* clothing (VEST). The original sense was to bear, to carry. The sense to waste away, to diminish dates from the 12–14C, to move, to pass (as of time) from the 14–15C.

wear[2] *v.t.* to bring (a ship) about by turning the bow away from the wind. *Also v.i.* WH: 17C. Orig. unknown. According to some, a variant of VEER[1].

weary *a.* tired, fatigued, exhausted. *Also v.t., v.i.* WH: pre-1200. Old English *wērig, wǣrig*, corr. to Old Saxon *sithwōrig* weary from a journey, Old High German *wuarag* drunk, from Germanic.

weasel *n.* a small reddish-brown, white-bellied mammal, *Mustela nivalis*, related to the stoat, ferret etc., with a long lithe body and short legs, preying on small birds, mice etc. *Also v.i.* WH: pre-1200. Old English *wesule, wesle*, from a Germanic noun of unknown orig. Cp. German *Wiesel*.

weather *n.* the state of the atmosphere, esp. at a given time or place, with reference to cold or heat, humidity, rain, pressure, wind, electrical conditions etc. *Also v.t., v.i., a.* WH: pre-1200. Old English *weder*, from Germanic, prob. from base of WIND[1]. Cp. German *Wetter*.

weave[1] *v.t.* to form (threads, yarns etc.) into fabric by interlacing. *Also v.i.* WH: pre-1200. Old English *wefan*, from Germanic, from Indo-European base represented also by Greek *huphē, huphos* web, *huphainein* to weave, Sanskrit *ūrṇavābhi* spider, lit. wool-weaver. Cp. WASP, WEB, WEEVIL, WEFT.

weave[2] *v.i.* to take a zigzag course, esp. to avoid obstructions. WH: 16C. Prob. from Old Norse *veifa* to move from place to place, to wave, to brandish, from Germanic, ult. rel. to Latin *vibrare* VIBRATE. Not rel. to WEAVE[1].

web *n.* a network of threads constructed by spiders to catch their prey, a cobweb. *Also v.t., v.i.* WH: pre-1200. Old English *webb, web*, from Germanic base also of WEAVE[1].

weber *n.* the SI unit of magnetic flux. WH: 19C. Wilhelm Eduard *Weber*, 1804–91, German physicist.

wed *v.t.* to marry. *Also v.i., n.* WH: pre-1200. Old English *weddian*, from Germanic base rel. to Latin *vas, vadis* surety. See GAGE[1], WAGE. Cp. German *wetten* to pledge, to wager. The original basic sense was to make a covenant.

wedge *n.* a piece of wood or metal thick at one end and tapering to a thin edge at the other, used for splitting wood, rocks etc., for exerting great pressure, for fixing or fastening etc. *Also v.t.* WH: pre-1200. Old English *wecg*, from Germanic. Cp. German *Wecke* wedge-shaped piece of cake. Cp. WODGE.

Wedgwood® *n.* a type of fine pottery, made by Josiah Wedgwood and his successors, often bearing a white cameo-like design in relief. WH: 18C. Josiah *Wedgwood*, 1730–95, English potter.

wedlock *n.* matrimony, the married state. WH: pre-1200. Old English *wedd* pledge + -*lāc*, n. suf. Not rel. to LOCK[1].

Wednesday *n.* the fourth day of the week, following Tuesday. *Also adv.* WH: pre-1200. Old English *wōdnesdæg*, corr. to Middle Low German *wōdensdach*, Old Norse *óthinsdagr* Odin's day, translating Late Latin *Mercurii dies* day of Mercury (cp. French *mercredi* Wednesday). The Roman historian Tacitus equated Odin (Woden) with Mercury in his *Germania* (AD 98).

wee *a.* little. WH: 12–14C. Ult. from Old English *wǣge* weight. See WEIGH. Cp. WEY.

weed *n.* a useless or troublesome plant in cultivated land, a wild plant springing up where not wanted in a garden etc. *Also v.t., v.i.* WH: pre-1200. Old English *wēod*, rel. to Old High German *wiota* fern, of unknown orig.

†weeds *n.pl.* mourning worn by a widow. WH: pre-1200. Pl. of *weed*, from Old English *wǣd* garment, from Germanic, of disputed orig.

week *n.* a period of seven days, esp. from Sunday to Saturday inclusively. WH: pre-1200. Old English *wice, wicu*, from a Germanic n. prob. meaning series, succession and rel. to Latin *vic-*. See VICE[3], VICE-. Cp. German *Woche*.

†ween *v.i.* to be of the opinion. WH: pre-1200. Old English *wēnan*, from Germanic base also of WISH, WONT. Cp. German *wähnen* to suppose wrongly.

weeny *a.* very small, tiny. WH: 18C. WEE, based on TINY. Cp. TEENY.

weep *v.i.* to shed tears. *Also v.t., n.* WH: pre-1200. Old English *wēpan*, from Germanic, prob. of imit. orig.

weever *n.* any marine fish of the genus *Trachinus*, such as *T. vipera*, inflicting painful wounds with their dorsal and opercular spines. WH: 17C. Prob. from Old French *wivre* serpent, dragon, var. of *guivre*, from Latin *vipera* VIPER. Cp. WYVERN. The fish is so called from its stinging spines.

weevil *n.* a small beetle, esp. of the family Curculionidae, with the head prolonged into a rostrum or proboscis, feeding on grain, nuts, roots, leaves etc. WH: pre-1200. Old English *wifel* beetle, from Germanic base meaning to move briskly, represented also by WAVE, WEAVE[1]. Cp. German *Wiebel*.

wee-wee *v.i.* to urinate (used esp. by or to children). *Also n.* WH: mid-20C. Imit., ? influ. by WEE. Cp. *biggies* (mid-20C), child's slang for excrement (see BIG).

weft *n.* the threads passing through the warp from selvedge to selvedge, the woof. WH: pre-1200. Old English, from Germanic base also of WEAVE[1].

Wehrmacht *n.* the armed forces of Germany from 1921–45. WH: mid-20C. German, lit. defence force.

weigela *n.* any shrub of the genus *Weigela*, esp. *W. florida*, grown for its showy pink, red, purple or white flowers. WH: 19C. Modern Latin, from Christian E. *Weigel*, 1748–1831, German physician + -A[1].

weigh *v.t.* to find the weight of by means of scales etc. *Also v.i., n.* WH: pre-1200. Old English *wegan*, from Germanic, from Indo-European base represented also by Latin *vehere* to convey. Cp. WAIN.

weight *n.* the force with which bodies tend towards a centre of attraction, esp. the centre of the earth; the downward tendency caused by gravity less the centrifugal tendency due to the earth's rotation. *Also v.t.* WH: pre-1200. Old English *gewiht*, from Germanic. Cp. German *Gewicht*. The current form has been influenced by WEIGH.

Weil's disease *n.* a severe form of leptospirosis transmitted via contaminated water. WH: 19C. H. Adolf *Weil*, 1848–1916, German physician.

Weimaraner *n.* a type of gun dog with a very short, usu. grey coat. WH: mid-20C. *Weimar*, a city in E Germany + -*aner* of (the place named). The dog is so called as it is a breed developed by German nobles of the court of Weimar.

weir *n.* a dam across a river or stream for raising the level of the water above it. WH: pre-1200. Old English *wer*, from *werian* to dam up, from Germanic. Cp. German *Wehr*.

weird *a.* supernatural, unearthly, uncanny. *Also n.* WH: pre-1200. Old English *wyrd* fate, destiny, from Germanic. The adjective dates from the 14–15C and was originally given currency in *weird sisters*, the three Fates or goddesses who control human destiny. The phrase was popularized by the *weird sisters*, the three witches in Shakespeare's *Macbeth* (1605).

Weismannism *n.* the doctrine maintaining the continuity of germ plasm and the impossibility of transmitting acquired characteristics. WH: 19C. August F.L. *Weismann*, 1834–1914, German biologist + -ISM.

weka *n.* a flightless New Zealand rail, *Gallirallus australis*. WH: 19C. Maori, imit. of the bird's cry.

Welch *a.* Welsh (now only in *Royal Welch Fusiliers, Welch regiment*). WH: pre-1200. Var. of WELSH.

welcome *a.* admitted or received with pleasure and cordiality. *Also n., int., v.t.* WH: pre-1200. Old English *wilcuma*, from *wil-* desire, pleasure + *cuma* comer. The 1st element *wil-* was later altered to *wel-* WELL[1], influenced by French *bien venu* or Old Norse *velkominn*.

weld[1] *v.t.* to unite or join (pieces of metal) together by heat or by compressing, esp. after they have been softened by heat. *Also v.i., n.* WH: 16C. Alt. of WELL[2], influ. by *welled*, its past tense and p.p.

weld[2] *n.* a plant, *Reseda luteola*, from which a yellow dye was formerly prepared. WH: 14–15C. Middle Low German *waude*, Middle Dutch *woude*, ? rel. to WEALD, WOLD. The word was perhaps already in Old English, but it has not been recorded.

welfare *n.* prosperity, success. WH: 12–14C. Contr. of *well fare*, from WELL[1] + FARE.

welkin *n.* the sky, the vault of heaven. WH: pre-1200. Old English *weolcan, wolcen* cloud, from Germanic. Cp. German *Wolke*. The original sense was cloud, hence heaven, sky.

well[1] *adv.* in a good or right manner, properly, satisfactorily. *Also a., n., int.* WH: pre-1200. Old English *wel*, from Germanic, prob. from Indo-European base also of WILL[1]. Cp. WEAL[2].

well[2] *n.* a shaft bored in the ground to obtain water, oil, gas etc. *Also v.i.* WH: pre-1200. Old English *wella*, from Germanic. Cp. German *Welle* wave, Old Norse *vella* boiling heat.

wellington *n.* a waterproof boot. usu. rubber, coming up to the mid-calf or knee. WH: 19C. Arthur *Wellesley*, 1st Duke of *Wellington*, 1769–1852, British statesman and general. The boot is named from the original type of high boot worn by the Duke of Wellington.

wellingtonia *n.* a sequoia, *Sequoiadendron giganteum*. WH: 19C. Modern Latin, from Arthur *Wellesley*, 1st Duke of Wellington (WELLINGTON) + -IA. The tree is so named as it stands taller than other trees, just as Wellington was regarded as greater in stature than his contemporaries.

welly *n.* a wellington boot. WH: mid-20C. Abbr. of WELLINGTON. See also -Y[3].

wels *n.* a large European freshwater catfish, *Siluris glanis*, the sheat fish. WH: 19C. German.

Welsh *a.* of or relating to Wales, its inhabitants or their language. *Also n.* WH: pre-1200. Old English *Wēlisc, Wǣlisc, Wīlisc, Wȳlisc*, from *Wealh, Walh* Celt, Briton, Welshman, non-Germanic foreigner, from Germanic, from Latin *Volcae*, a Celtic people, of unknown orig. Cp. VLACH. Old English *-sc* in the adjective gave the *-sh* of Welsh as a form of -ISH[1].

welsh *v.i.* (of a bookmaker) to make off from a racecourse without paying up bets. WH: 19C. Orig. unknown. Prob. not rel. to WELSH.

welt *n.* a strip of leather sewn round a boot or shoe between the upper and the sole to attach them together. *Also v.t.* WH: 14–15C. Orig. uncertain. ? From Old English.

Weltanschauung *n.* a view of the world as an entity, a personal philosophy of life etc. WH: 19C. German, from *Welt* world + *Anschauung* perception.

welter[1] *v.i.* to roll, to tumble about, to wallow. *Also n.* WH: 12–14C. Middle Low German and Middle Dutch *welteren*, from Germanic. Cp. German *wälzen*. Rel. to WALTZ.

welter[2] *n.* a heavy boxer or rider. WH: 19C. Orig. uncertain. ? From WELT + -ER[1] in sense one who causes welts by beating.

Weltpolitik *n.* a policy aiming at the participation or predominance of a country, specifically Germany, in the affairs of the whole world. WH: early 20C. German, from *Welt* world + *Politik* politics.

Weltschmerz *n.* a melancholic or pessimistic outlook on life. WH: 19C. German, from *Welt* world + *Schmerz* pain.

welwitschia *n.* a plant of SW tropical Africa, *Welwitschia mirabilis*, with a very short, wide trunk and a single pair of leaves, which attain a development of 6ft (1.8 m) or more. WH: 19C. Modern Latin, from Friedrich *Welwitsch*, 1806–72, Austrian botanist + -IA.

wen¹ *n.* a sebaceous cyst, frequently occurring on the scalp or neck. WH: pre-1200. Old English, prob. rel. to Middle Low German *wene*, Low German *wehne* tumour, wart, of unknown orig.

wen² *n.* a runic letter replaced by *w*. WH: pre-1200. Old English *wyn*, *wynn*, lit. joy, from Germanic base also of WISH. Cp. WINSOME.

wench *n.* a girl or young woman. *Also v.i.* WH: 12–14C. Abbr. of obs. *wenchel* child, servant, slave, prostitute, ? rel. to obs. *wankle* unsteady, insecure (WANGLE).

Wend *n.* a member of a Slavic people inhabiting Saxony and Prussia (now N and E Germany). WH: pre-1200. Old English *Winedas*, corr. to Old High German *Winida*, Old Norse *Vindr*, of unknown orig. The name was readopted in the 18C from German *Wende*, plural *Wenden*.

wend *v.t.* to go or direct (one's way). *Also v.i.* WH: pre-1200. Old English *wendan* to turn, to go, from Germanic base rel. to WIND². Cp. WANDER. It was this verb that gave *went* as the past tense of GO¹.

Wendy house *n.* a small toy house for children to play in. WH: mid-20C. *Wendy* Darling, the little girl who had a small house built around her in J.M. Barrie's play *Peter Pan* (1904).

Wensleydale *n.* a type of crumbly white cheese. WH: 19C. *Wensleydale*, a district of N Yorkshire.

wentletrap *n.* any snail of the genus *Clathrus*, with a many-whorled shell. WH: 18C. Dutch *wenteltrap* winding staircase, spiral shell, from earlier *wendeltrap*, from *wenden* to wind, to turn + *trap* stair.

werewolf *n.* a person turned into or supposed to have the power of turning into a wolf. WH: pre-1200. Old English *werewulf*, prob. from *wer* man (cp. VIRILE) + *wulf* WOLF. Cp. *lycanthrope* (LYCANTHROPY).

†wergild *n.* in Old English and Germanic law, a fine or monetary compensation for manslaughter and other offences against the person, paid by the kindred of the offender to the kindred of the injured person. WH: pre-1200. Old English *wergeld*, from *wer* man + *gield* YIELD.

Wesleyan *a.* of or belonging to the Church founded by John Wesley. *Also n.* WH: 18C. John *Wesley*, 1703–91, English evangelist + -AN.

west *adv.* at, in or towards the quarter opposite the east, or where the sun sets at the equinox. *Also n., a.* WH: pre-1200. Old English, from Germanic, from Indo-European base represented also by Greek *hesperos*, Latin *vesper* evening.

western *a.* in, facing or directed towards the west. *Also n.* WH: pre-1200. Old English *westerne*, from WEST + -*erne*, suf. denoting direction.

Westinghouse brake *n.* a brake worked by compressed air for use on railway trains and motor cars. WH: 19C. George *Westinghouse*, 1846–1914, US inventor and manufacturer.

Westminster *n.* the British Parliament. WH: 16C. *Westminster*, a borough of inner London where the Houses of Parliament are located.

wet *a.* moistened, soaked, saturated or covered with water or other liquid. *Also n., v.t.* WH: pre-1200. Old English *wæt*, *wēt*, ult. rel. to WATER.

weta *n.* a wingless insect of the family Stenopelmatidae, with long spiny legs, found in New Zealand. WH: 19C. Maori.

wether *n.* a castrated ram. WH: pre-1200. Old English, from Germanic, of disputed orig. Cp. German *Widder*. According to some, the word is related to Latin *vitulus* and so to VEAL.

wey *n.* a former weight or measure varying with different articles (of wool, 182 lb/ 82.5 kg, of cheese, 224 lb/ 101.6 kg etc.). WH: pre-1200. Old English *wæg*, *wæge*, from Germanic, rel. to WEIGH.

whack *v.t.* to strike heavily. *Also n.* WH: 18C. Imit., or ? alt. of THWACK.

whacko *int.* used to express delight. WH: mid-20C. WHACK + -O.

whale¹ *n.* any large marine fishlike mammal of the order Cetacea, several of which are hunted chiefly for their oil and whalebone. *Also v.i.* WH: pre-1200. Old English *hwæl*, from Germanic. Cp. German *Wal*, *Walfisch*.

whale² *v.t.* to beat, to flog. WH: 18C. Prob. var. of WALE.

wham *n.* a forceful blow. *Also v.i., v.t.* WH: early 20C. Imit.

whammy *n.* an evil influence, a curse. WH: mid-20C. WHAM + -Y³.

whang¹ *v.t.* to beat noisily, to bang. *Also v.i., n.* WH: 19C. Imit., influ. by WHANG².

whang² *n.* a tough leather strap or thong. *Also v.t.* WH: 17C. Var. of THONG.

whangee *n.* a flexible bamboo cane. WH: 18C. Chinese *huáng* old bamboo shoots, hard white-skinned bamboo.

whare *n.* a Maori hut or other simple dwelling place. WH: 19C. Maori.

wharf *n.* a landing place for cargo beside a river, harbour, canal etc., usu. consisting of a platform, pier or quay of timber, masonry etc. *Also v.t.* WH: pre-1200. Old English *hwearf*, *wearf*, from Germanic. Cp. German *Werft* wharf, shipyard.

what *pron.* which thing or things. *Also a., adv.* WH: pre-1200. Old English *hwæt*, from Germanic, from Indo-European neut. form of base of WHO. Cp. WHEN, WHERE, WHY.

whaup *n.* the curlew. WH: 16C. Imit.

wheal *n.* in Cornwall, a mine (usu. a tin mine). WH: 19C. Cornish *huel*, from obs. *wheyl* work.

wheat *n.* any annual cereal grass of the genus *Triticum*, cultivated for its grain which is ground into flour for bread. WH: pre-1200. Old English *hwæte*, from Germanic base also of WHITE. Cp. German *Weizen*.

wheatear *n.* a small white-rumped bird of the genus *Oenanthe*, esp. *O. oenanthe*. WH: 16C. Appar. from WHITE + ARSE, with assim. to WHEAT, EAR². Cp. REDSTART. The bird is so called from its white rump.

Wheatstone bridge *n.* a device for measuring an unknown electrical resistance by means of a known resistance. WH: 19C. Sir Charles *Wheatstone*, 1802–75, English physicist.

whee *int.* used to express delight or excitement. WH: early 20C. Natural exclamation. Cp. WAHOO⁴, WOW¹.

wheedle *v.t.* to entice, to win over, to persuade by coaxing or flattery. WH: 17C. ? German *wedeln* to fawn (on), to cringe (to), from *Wedel* tail, fan.

wheel *n.* a circular frame or solid disc turning on its axis, used in vehicles, machinery etc. to reduce friction and facilitate motion. *Also v.t., v.i.* WH: pre-1200. Old English *hwēol*, from Germanic, from Indo-European base represented by Sanskrit *cakra-* wheel, circle, Greek *kuklos* CYCLE, redupl. of a v. meaning to move around, represented by Greek *polos* axis, Latin *colus* distaff.

wheeze *v.i.* to breathe hard and with an audible sound, as in asthma. *Also v.t., n.* WH: 14–15C. Prob. from Old Norse *hvæsa* to hiss.

whelk¹ *n.* a marine spiral-shelled gastropod of the family Buccinidae, esp. the common whelk, used for food. WH: pre-1200. Old English *weoloc*, *wioloc*, rel. to Modern Dutch *willoc*, *wilc* (Modern Dutch *wulk*). The spelling with *wh*- may have come about by association with WHELK² or with other words beginning with *wh*- such as WHALE¹, WHELP.

whelk² *n.* a small pustule or pimple. WH: pre-1200. Old English *hwylca*, rel. to obs. *wheal* pimple, pustule, of unknown orig.

whelm *v.t.* to engulf, to submerge. WH: 12–14C. Representation of an unrecorded Old English v. rel. to *hwielfan* to arch, to bend over.

whelp *n.* the young of a dog, a pup. *Also v.i., v.t.* WH: pre-1200. Old English *hwelp*, from Germanic. Cp. German *Welf*. No related words outside Germanic are known.

when *adv.* at what or which time? *Also conj., pron., n.* WH: pre-1200. Old English *hwenne*, *hwænne*, *hwanne*, from Germanic, from Indo-European base also of WHO, WHAT. Cp. German *wenn* if, *wann* when.

whence *adv.* from what place? where from? *Also conj., pron.* WH: 12–14C. From obs. *whenne* (from Old English *hwanon*, *hwonan*, from Germanic, from Indo-European base also of WHEN) + -S². The spelling with -*ce* represents the unvoiced sound denoted in an earlier spelling by -*s*. Cp. HENCE, THENCE.

where *adv.* at or in what place, situation, case, circumstances? *Also conj., pron., n.* WH: pre-1200. Old English *hwær*, *hwar*, from Germanic, from Indo-European base also of WHO, WHAT. Cp. Dutch *waar*, German *wo*.

wherry *n.* a light shallow rowing boat for plying on rivers. WH: 14–15C. Orig. unknown. Prob. assoc. with FERRY.

whet *v.t.* to sharpen by rubbing on a stone or similar substance. *Also n.* WH: pre-1200. Old English *hwettan*, from Germanic v. from an *a.* meaning sharp, represented by Old English *hwæt* quick, active, brave.

whether *conj.* introducing (an indirect question in the form of) an alternative clause followed by an alternative *or*, *or not*, or *or whether*, or with the alternative unexpressed. *Also a., pron.* **WH:** pre-1200. Old English *hwether, hwæther* which of two, from a Germanic word from base of WHO + comp. suf. represented also in OTHER. Cp. German *weder* neither.

whew *int.* used to express relief, astonishment or consternation. **WH:** 14–15C. Imit. Cp. PHEW.

whey *n.* the watery part of milk that remains after the curds have formed and been separated. **WH:** pre-1200. Old English *hwæg, hweg,* from Germanic. Cp. Dutch *wei.*

which *pron.* what person, thing or persons or things of a definite number. *Also a.* **WH:** Old English *hwilc,* ult. from Germanic bases of WHO, ALIKE. Cp. EACH, SUCH.

whicker *v.i.* to neigh softly. **WH:** 17C. Imit. Cp. NICKER[2], SNICKER.

whiff *n.* a sudden expulsion of smoke etc., a puff, a light gust, esp. one carrying an odour. *Also v.i., v.t.* **WH:** 16C. Imit. Cp. PUFF.

whiffle *v.i.* (of the wind etc.) to veer about. *Also v.t.* **WH:** 16C. WHIFF + -LE[4].

whiffletree *n.* a swingletree. **WH:** 18C. Var. of WHIPPLETREE.

Whig *n.* a member of the British political party that contended for the rights and privileges of Parliament in opposition to the Tories, supported the Revolution of 1688 and the principles it represented, and was succeeded by the Liberals. **WH:** 17C. Prob. abbr. of obs. *whiggamore* member of a party of rebels from W Scotland who marched on Edinburgh in opposition to Charles I in 1648, prob. from Scottish *whig* to urge forward, to drive briskly, of unknown orig. + MARE[1]. Not rel. to WIG[1].

while *n.* a space of time, esp. the time during which something happens or is done. *Also conj., adv.* **WH:** pre-1200. Old English *hwīl,* from Germanic, from Indo-European base represented also by Latin *quies* QUIET, *tranquillus* TRANQUIL. Cp. German *Weile.*

†whilom *adv.* formerly, once, of old. *Also a.* **WH:** pre-1200. Old English *hwīlom,* dat. pl. of *hwīl* WHILE.

whim *n.* a sudden fancy, a caprice. **WH:** 17C. Orig. unknown. The original sense was a pun, a play on words.

whimbrel *n.* a small curlew, *Numenius phaeopus.* **WH:** 16C. From dial. *whimp* or WHIMPER + dim. suf. *-rel* as in COCKEREL. The name is imitative, with reference to the bird's cry.

whimper *v.i.* to cry with a soft, broken, whining voice. *Also v.t., n.* **WH:** 16C. From dial. *whimp* to whimper, of imit. orig. + -ER[5]. Cp. WIMP.

whin[1] *n.* furze, gorse. **WH:** 14–15C. Prob. from Scandinavian. Cp. Swedish *hven,* Old Danish *hvine,* Norwegian *hvine,* the names of certain grasses.

whin[2] *n.* a very hard, resistant rock, esp. basalt, chert or quartzite. **WH:** 12–14C. Orig. unknown.

whine *v.i.* to make a plaintive, long-drawn cry. *Also v.t., n.* **WH:** pre-1200. Old English *hwīnan* to whiz, to whistle in the air. Cp. WHINGE. The original sense was to whistle through the air (of an arrow). The current sense arose in the 12–14C.

whinge *v.i.* to cry fretfully. *Also n.* **WH:** pre-1200. Old English *hwinsian,* from Germanic. Cp. WHINE. The word is not recorded between the time of its original Old English use and the 16C.

whinny *v.i.* to neigh, esp. in a gentle or delighted way. *Also n.* **WH:** 14–15C. Imit. Cp. HINNY[2].

whip *v.t.* to lash, to flog. *Also v.i., n.* **WH:** 12–14C. Prob. from Middle Low German and Middle Dutch *wippen* to swing, to vacillate, to leap, from Germanic base meaning to move quickly, represented also in Dutch *wipplank* see-saw, *wipstaart* wagtail. Cp. WIPE. The original sense was to move swiftly or abruptly. The sense to lash, to flog dates from the 14–15C.

whippet *n.* a racing-dog similar to but smaller than a greyhound. **WH:** 15C. Partly from WHIP + -ET[1], partly from obs. *whippet* to move briskly, appar. from *whip it.* See WHIP.

whippletree *n.* a swingletree. **WH:** 18C. 1st element appar. from WHIP + TREE.

whippoorwill *n.* a small N American nocturnal bird, *Caprimulgus vociferus,* allied to the nightjars. **WH:** 18C. Imit. of the bird's call.

whir *v.i.* to revolve, move or fly quickly with a buzzing sound. *Also n.* **WH:** 14–15C. Prob. of Scandinavian orig. from an unrecorded Old Norse v. rel. to *hvirfla* (WHIRL), but later prob. also imit.

whirl *v.t.* to swing round and round rapidly. *Also v.i., n.* **WH:** 12–14C. Old Norse *hvirfla* to turn about, to whirl, rel. to *hvirfill* circle, ult. from Germanic base meaning to turn. Cp. WHORL.

whish *v.i.* to move through the air or water with a whistling sound. *Also n.* **WH:** 16C. Imit.

whisht *int.* hush! silence! *Also v.t.* **WH:** 16C. Natural exclamation. Cp. HIST, HUSH[1], SHUSH.

whisk *v.t.* to sweep, brush or flap (away or off). *Also v.i., n.* **WH:** 14–15C. Prob. from Scandinavian. Cp. Swedish *viska* to whisk (off), Danish *viske.* The original sense was to become entangled. The current sense dates from the 15C.

whisker *n.* any one of the bristly hairs growing round the mouth of a cat or other animal. **WH:** 14–15C. WHISK + -ER[1]. The word was originally used of hair growing on a man's chin, etc. The application to a cat's bristly hairs evolved in the 17C.

whisky *n.* a spirit distilled usu. from malted barley, sometimes from wheat, rye etc. **WH:** 18C. Var. of obs. *usque,* abbr. of USQUEBAUGH.

whisper *v.i.* to speak with articulation but without vocal vibration. *Also v.t., n.* **WH:** pre-1200. Old English *hwisprian,* from Germanic imit. base also of WHISTLE. Cp. German *wispeln.*

whist *n.* a card game, usu. for four persons, played with the entire pack of 52 cards. **WH:** 17C. Alt. of obs. *whisk,* ? from WHISK. The game is perhaps so called from the act of whisking up the cards after each trick is won. The alteration to *whisk* may have come from the notion that it was a game played in silence. Cp. WHISHT.

whistle *v.i.* to make a shrill musical sound by forcing the breath through a small opening of the lips or with an instrument, an appliance on a steam engine etc. *Also v.t., n.* **WH:** pre-1200. Old English *hwistlian,* corr. to Old Norse *hvísla* to whisper, Swedish *vissla* to whistle, Danish *hvistle* to hiss, from Germanic imit. base also of WHISPER. The original meaning was to play on a pipe.

whit *n.* a jot, the least amount, an iota. **WH:** 14–15C. Appar. alt. of WIGHT.

white *a.* being of the colour produced by reflection of all the visible rays in sunlight, as of pure snow, common salt etc. *Also v.t., n.* **WH:** pre-1200. Old English *hwīt,* from Germanic, from Indo-European. Cp. German *weiss.*

Whitehall *n.* the British Government. **WH:** 19C. *Whitehall,* a street in London in which Government offices are located.

whither *adv.* to what or which place, where. *Also conj.* **WH:** pre-1200. Old English *hwider,* from Germanic base also of WHICH. Cp. HITHER, THITHER.

whiting[1] *n.* a sea fish, *Merlangus merlangus,* used for food. **WH:** 12–14C. Middle Dutch *wijting,* from *wijt* white. See also -ING[3]. The fish is so called from its white colour.

whiting[2] *n.* fine chalk pulverized, washed and prepared for use in whitewashing, polishing etc. **WH:** 14–15C. WHITE + -ING[1].

whitleather *n.* leather dressed with alum, white leather. **WH:** 14–15C. WHITE + LEATHER.

whitlow *n.* a pus-filled inflammation, esp. round the nail of a finger or toe. **WH:** 14–15C. Prob. from WHITE + FLAW[1], but ? rel. to Dutch *fijt,* Low German *fit* whitlow, abscess.

Whitsun *a.* of or relating to Whit Sunday or Whitsuntide. *Also n.* **WH:** 12–14C. From *Whit Sunday,* analysed as *Whitsun Day,* from Old English *Hwīta Sunnandæg,* lit. White Sunday. The festival is probably so called from the white robes worn by those baptized at Pentecost.

whittle *v.t.* to trim, shave or cut pieces or slices from with a knife. *Also v.i., n.* **WH:** 14–15C. Var. of obs. *thwittle* knife, from Old English *thwītan* to cut off, rel. to Old Norse *thveita* small axe. See THWAITE.

whity *a.* whitish, inclining to white (usu. *in comb.,* as *whity-brown*). **WH:** 16C. WHITE + -Y[1].

whiz *v.i.* to make or move with a hissing sound, like an arrow or ball flying through the air. *Also n.* **WH:** 16C. Imit. Cp. WHISTLE.

who *pron.* what or which person or persons? **WH:** pre-1200. Old English *hwā,* from Germanic, from Indo-European base also of Latin *quis* who, what. Cp. German *wer.*

whoa *int.* stop! (used chiefly to horses). **WH:** 14–15C. Var. of HO.

whole *a.* complete or entire. *Also n.* **WH:** pre-1200. Old English *hāl, gehāl.* Rel. to HALE[1]. The spelling with *wh-* reflects a dialect pronunciation with the sound of *w.* Cp. WHORE.

whoop *v.i.* to utter a 'whoop'. *Also v.t., n.* **WH:** 14–15C. Prob. imit.

whoosh *n.* a rushing or hissing sound as of something moving swiftly through the air. *Also int., v.i.* WH: 19C. Imit.

whop *v.t.* to beat, to thrash. *Also v.i., n.* WH: 14–15C. Var. of dial. *wap*, of unknown orig. Cp. SWAP.

whore *n.* a prostitute. *Also v.i., v.t.* WH: pre-1200. Old English *hōre*, from Germanic base represented also by Old Norse *hórr* adulterer, from Indo-European base also of Latin *carus* dear. The change of spelling from *h-* to *wh-* was as for WHOLE.

whorl *n.* a circular set or ring of leaves, sepals or other organs on a plant. WH: 14–15C. Appar. var. of WHIRL.

whortleberry *n.* the bilberry. WH: 16C. Dial. var. of HURTLEBERRY.

whump *n.* a dull thud or thump. *Also v.i., v.t.* WH: 19C. Imit.

why *adv.* for what reason or purpose? *Also n., int.* WH: pre-1200. Old English *hwī, hwȳ*, instr. of *hwæt* WHAT corr. to Old Saxon *hwī*, Old Norse *hví*, from Germanic, from Indo-European loc. form of base of WHO, WHAT.

whydah *n.* any small black African weaver-bird of the genus *Vidua*, the male of which has mainly black plumage and four long tail feathers. WH: 18C. Orig. *widow-bird*, with spelling alt. by assoc. with *Whidah* (now Ouidah), a town in Benin, W Africa.

Wicca *n.* the cult or practice of modern witchcraft. WH: mid-20C. Revival of Old English *wicca*. See WITCH.

wick¹ *n.* a piece or bundle of fibrous or spongy material used in a candle or lamp to convey the melted grease or oil by capillary action to the flame. *Also v.t.* WH: pre-1200. Old English *wēoc* (in *candel-wēoc*), from Germanic, of unknown orig. Cp. German *Wieche*.

wick² *n.* a town, village or municipal district (chiefly in place names). WH: pre-1200. Old English *wīc*, prob. from Germanic, from Latin *vicus* row of houses, street, village, rel. to Greek *oikos* house. The word is common in place names as *-wick* or *-wich*.

wicked *a.* sinful, addicted to evil or vice, immoral, depraved. WH: 12–14C. Prob. from Old English *wicca* (WITCH) + -ED.

wicker *n.* twigs or osiers plaited into a material for baskets, chairs etc. *Also a.* WH: 12–14C. Scandinavian, from base of Swedish *vika* to bend. Rel. to WEAK.

wicket *n.* a set of three stumps surmounted by two bails at which the bowler directs the ball in cricket. WH: 12–14C. Old Northern French *wiket*, from Old French *guichet*, prob. from Germanic base seen also in Old Norse *víkja* to move, to turn. The original sense was a small door or large one. The application to cricket dates from the 17C, when the stumps took the form of a little gate.

wickiup *n.* a hut or shelter used by nomadic American Indians, comprising an oval frame covered with grass etc. WH: 19C. Algonquian (Menominee) *wikiop*, ? a var. of *wikiwam* WIGWAM.

widdle *v.i.* to urinate. WH: mid-20C. Alt. of PIDDLE, ? influ. by *wee* (WEE-WEE).

wide *a.* having a great relative extent from side to side, broad, as opposed to *narrow*. *Also adv., n.* WH: pre-1200. Old English *wīd*, from Germanic, of unknown orig. Cp. German *weit*.

widget *n.* a gadget. WH: mid-20C. ? Alt. of GADGET.

widow *n.* a woman who has lost her husband by death and has not remarried. *Also v.t.* WH: pre-1200. Old English *widewe, wuduwe*, from Germanic, from Indo-European base represented by Sanskrit *vidhavā* widow, Greek *ēitheos* unmarried man, Latin *viduus* bereft, void, widowed. Cp. German *Witwe*.

width *n.* the extent of a thing from side to side, breadth, wideness. WH: 17C. WIDE + -TH². The word was formed on the analogy of BREADTH to replace *wideness* (WIDE).

wield *v.t.* to handle, hold, use or employ. WH: pre-1200. Old English *wealdan, wieldan*, from Germanic. Cp. German *walten*.

wiener *n.* a type of frankfurter. WH: 19C. German of Vienna, from *Wien* Vienna + -ER¹.

Wiener schnitzel *n.* a cutlet of veal or pork, coated with a breadcrumb mixture and fried. WH: 19C. German. See WIENER, SCHNITZEL.

wife *n.* a married woman, esp. in relation to her husband. WH: pre-1200. Old English *wīf*, from Germanic, of unknown orig. Cp. German *Weib* woman. The original meaning was woman, but the current sense soon evolved in Old English. The sense woman is still current in *fishwife* (FISH¹), MIDWIFE and *old wives' tale*.

wig¹ *n.* a covering for the head composed of false hair, worn to conceal baldness, as a disguise, for ornament or as part of an official costume, esp. by judges, lawyers etc. WH: 17C. Shortening of PERIWIG.

wig² *v.t.* to reprimand, to scold. WH: 19C. WIG¹. The original sense was to put a wig on. The current sense probably refers to a reprimand given by a *bigwig* (BIG).

wigeon *n.* a wild duck of the genus *Anas*, esp. *A. penelope* or *A. americana*. WH: 16C. ? From imit. base, with spelling influ. by PIGEON¹.

wiggle *v.i.* to move (oneself) jerkily, esp. from side to side. *Also v.t., n.* WH: 12–14C. Middle Low German and Middle Dutch *wiggelen*, freq. of Low German *wiggen*. See also -LE⁴. Cp. WAG¹, WAGGLE, WRIGGLE.

†wight *n.* a person. WH: pre-1200. Old English *wiht*, from Germanic. Cp. German *Wicht* creature, being, infant. The original sense (to the 16C) was creature, living being. The sense human being, person dates from the 12–14C.

wigwag *v.t.* to wag to and fro. *Also v.i.* WH: 16C. Redupl. of WAG¹.

wigwam *n.* a N American Indian hut or cabin, usu. consisting of a framework covered with bark, matting, hides etc. WH: 17C. Ojibwa *wigwaum, wigiwam*, var. of Algonquian *weekuwom, wikiwam*, lit. their house.

wilco *int.* used in radio communications etc. to indicate that a message received will be complied with. WH: mid-20C. Abbr. of *will comply*.

wild *a.* living in a state of nature, esp. inhabiting or growing in the forest or open country. *Also n., adv.* WH: pre-1200. Old English *wilde*, from Germanic. Cp. German *wild*.

wildebeest *n.* a gnu. WH: 19C. Afrikaans, from *wild* wild + *beest* beast. Cp. HARTEBEEST.

†wilder *v.t.* to lead astray. WH: 17C. Orig. unknown. ? From WILDERNESS. Cp. BEWILDER.

wilderness *n.* an uninhabited or uncultivated land, a desert. WH: pre-1200. Old English *wildēornes*, from *wildēor, wilddēor* (WILD, DEER) + -*nes* -NESS. The literal sense is a place of wild animals.

wile *n.* a trick, an artifice, a stratagem or deception. *Also v.t.* WH: 12–14C. ? From an unrecorded Old Norse n. rel. to *vél* craft, artifice.

wilful *a.* intentional, voluntary, deliberate. WH: 12–14C. WILL² + -FUL.

wilga *n.* a tree of the genus *Geijera*, esp. *G. parviflora*. WH: 19C. Australian Aboriginal (Wiradhuri) *wilgarr*.

will¹ *v.t.* to desire, to wish, to choose, to want (a thing, that etc.). *Also v.aux.* WH: pre-1200. Old English *wyllan*, from Germanic, from Indo-European base also of Latin *velle* to wish, to will, *volo* I wish, I will. Cp. German *wollen*.

will² *n.* the mental power or faculty by which one initiates or controls one's activities, as opposed to *impulse* or *instinct*. WH: pre-1200. Old English *willa*, from Germanic, from base also of WILL¹. Rel. to WILL¹.

will³ *v.t.* to intend or bring about by the exercise of one's will, to resolve, to determine. *Also v.i.* WH: pre-1200. Old English *willian*, from Germanic base of WILL².

willet *n.* a N American sandpiper, *Catoptophorus semipalmatus*, allied to the snipe. WH: 19C. Imit. of the bird's call.

willies *n.pl.* nervousness, apprehensiveness. WH: 19C. Orig. unknown.

willing *a.* inclined, ready, not averse or reluctant (to). WH: pre-1200. WILL¹ + -ING².

will-o'-the-wisp *n.* an ignis fatuus. WH: 17C. *Will*, abbr. of male forename *William* + O' + THE + WISP. The literal sense is Will of the wisp, i.e. a person called Will holding a burning handful of hay, used as a torch. Cp. *jack-o'-lantern* (JACK¹).

willow *n.* any tree or shrub of the genus *Salix*, usu. growing near water, characterized by long, slender, pliant branches, largely yielding osiers and timber used for cricket bats etc. WH: pre-1200. Old English *welig*, from Germanic. Cp. Dutch *wilg*.

willy *n.* the penis. WH: early 20C. *Willy*, pet form of male forename *William*. Cp. DICK¹.

willy-nilly *adv.* willingly or unwillingly. *Also a.* WH: 17C. Representation of *will I, nill I* or *will he, nill he*, from WILL¹ + obs. *nill* to be unwilling, from Old English *ne* not + WILL¹. Cp. NOLENS VOLENS.

willy wagtail *n.* a black-and-white Australian flycatcher, *Rhipidura leucophrys*. WH: 19C. WILLY + WAGTAIL.

willy-willy *n.* a tropical cyclone, esp. one that sweeps over NW Australia in the late summer. WH: 19C. Australian Aboriginal (Yinjibarndi) *wili wili*.

wilt *v.i.* to wither, to droop. *Also v.t.*, *n.* WH: 17C. ? Alt. of obs. *welk* to wilt, to droop, prob. of Low Dutch orig. Cp. Middle Low German and Middle Dutch *welken*.

Wilton *n.* a carpet with the loops cut open into an elastic velvet pile. WH: 18C. *Wilton*, a town in Wiltshire noted for the manufacture of carpets.

wily *a.* using or full of wiles, cunning, crafty. WH: 12–14C. WILE + -Y[1].

Wimbledonization *n.* the giving of preferential treatment to foreign companies etc. in the UK. WH: late 20C. *Wimbledon*, a district of SW London where an annual international tennis championship is played + -*ization* (-IZE).

WIMP *n.* denoting a computer operating system with features designed to help the non-expert user. WH: late 20C. Acronym of *windows*, *icons*, *mouse*, *program* (or *pointer*, *product*, *pull-down menu*, etc.) prob. punning on WIMP (whom they are intended to assist).

wimp *n.* a feeble, ineffectual person. WH: early 20C. Orig. uncertain. ? From WHIMPER.

wimple *n.* a covering of silk, linen etc., worn over the head, neck and sides of the face by some nuns and formerly by other women. *Also v.i.*, *v.i.* WH: pre-1200. Old English *wimpel*, from Germanic. See also -LE[1]. Cp. German *Wimpel* streamer, pennon.

Wimshurst machine *n.* a friction machine by which static electricity can be generated and stored. WH: 19C. James *Wimshurst*, 1832–1903, English engineer.

win *v.t.* to gain, obtain, achieve or attain by fighting or superiority in a contest, competition, wager etc. *Also v.i.*, *n.* WH: pre-1200. Old English *winnan*, from Germanic, of unknown orig. Cp. German *gewinnen* to earn, to gain, to produce. The original sense (to the 12–14C) was to work, to strive, to fight.

wince[1] *v.i.* to shrink, recoil or flinch, as from pain, trouble or a blow. *Also n.* WH: 12–14C. From an unrecorded Anglo-French variant of Old French *guencir*, *guenchier* to turn aside, to avoid. See WINCH. The original sense was to kick restlessly from impatience. The sense to flinch dates from the 18C.

wince[2] *n.* a roller for moving fabric through dyeing vats. WH: 18C. Var. of WINCH.

wincey *n.* a cotton cloth with wool filling. WH: 19C. Appar. alt. of *woolsey* in LINSEY-WOOLSEY.

winch *n.* a windlass, a hoisting machine. *Also v.t.* WH: pre-1200. Old English *wince*, from Germanic base also of WINK. The original basic sense was reel, roller, pulley. The sense windlass evolved in the 16C.

Winchester *n.* a breech-loading repeating rifle. WH: 19C. Oliver F. *Winchester*, 1810–80, US manufacturer.

winchester *n.* a large cylindrical bottle for transporting chemicals. WH: 16C. *Winchester*, a city in Hampshire.

wind[1] *n.* air in motion, a natural air current, a breeze, a gale. *Also v.t.* WH: pre-1200. Old English, from Germanic, from Indo-European base represented also by Latin *ventus*. Cp. German *Wind*.

wind[2] *v.i.* to turn, move or be twisted or coiled in a spiral, curved or tortuous course or shape. *Also v.t.*, *n.* WH: pre-1200. Old English *windan*, from Germanic base rel. to WANDER, WEND. Cp. German *winden*.

wind[3] *v.t.* to sound (a horn, bugle etc.) by blowing. WH: 14–15C. WIND[1].

windlass *n.* a machine consisting of a cylinder on an axle turned by a crank, used for hoisting or hauling. *Also v.t.* WH: 14–15C. Appar. alt. of obs. *windas*, from Old French *guindas*, from Old Norse *vindáss*, from *vinda* WIND[2] + *áss* pole.

window *n.* an opening in the wall or roof of a building, vehicle or other structure, usu. with the wooden or metal glazed framework filling it, for the admission of light or air. WH: 12–14C. Old Norse *vindauga*, from *vindr* WIND[1] + *auga* EYE[1]. The Old Norse word replaced native Old English *ēagthyrl*, lit. eyehole or *ēagduru*, lit. eye-door.

Windsor *a.* of or relating to the British royal family from 1917. WH: 15C. *Windsor*, a town west of London, the site of the royal residence Windsor Castle.

wine *n.* the fermented juice of grapes. *Also v.i.*, *v.t.* WH: pre-1200. Old English *wīn*, from Germanic, from Latin *vinum*, prob. (together with Greek *oinos* and words for wine in other non-Germanic languages) from a Mediterranean source.

wing *n.* each of the limbs or organs of flight in birds, insects etc. *Also v.t.*, *v.i.* WH: 12–14C. Old Norse *vængir* (acc.), *vengi* (pl.) of *vængr* wing (of a bird), aisle. The Old Norse word replaced native Old English *fethra* wings, pl. of *fether* FEATHER.

wingding *n.* a riotous party or celebration. WH: early 20C. Orig. unknown.

wink *v.i.* to close and open one eye quickly. *Also v.t.*, *n.* WH: pre-1200. Old English *wincian*, from Germanic, from Indo-European base also of WINCE[1]. Cp. German *winken* to wave, to wink. The original sense (to the 19C) was to close the eyes. The sense to blink arose in the 12–14C, and the sense to close and open one eye to convey a message in the 19C.

winkle *n.* an edible marine mollusc of the genus *Littorina*, a periwinkle. WH: 16C. Abbr. of PERIWINKLE[2].

winnow *v.t.* to separate and drive the chaff from (grain). WH: pre-1200. Old English *windwian*, from *wind* WIND[1]. The literal sense is to expose grain to the wind so that the chaff is blown away.

wino *n.* an alcoholic, esp. one who drinks mainly wine. WH: early 20C. WINE + -O.

winsome *a.* engaging, winning, charming, attractive. WH: pre-1200. Old English *wynsum*, from *wynn* pleasure, delight + -*sum* -SOME[1]. Rel. to WISH, WONT. The word is not related to WIN, despite an association of sense with *winning* (WIN).

winter *n.* the coldest season of the year, astronomically from the winter solstice to the vernal equinox, usu. regarded in northern latitudes as including December, January, February. *Also a.*, *v.i.*, *v.t.* WH: pre-1200. Old English, from Germanic, prob. from nasalized var. of Indo-European base of WATER, WET. Cp. German *Winter*.

winze *n.* a shaft sunk from one level to another for communication or ventilation. WH: 18C. ? From WIND[2].

wipe *v.t.* to rub with something soft in order to clean or dry. *Also v.i.*, *n.* WH: pre-1200. Old English *wīpian*, rel. to Germanic base of WHIP.

Wiradhuri *n.* an extinct Aboriginal language of SE Australia. WH: 19C. Australian Aboriginal, appar. from Wiradhuri word for no, *wirai*, contrasted with the equivalent word in rel. languages.

wire *n.* metal drawn out into a slender and flexible rod or thread of uniform diameter. *Also a.*, *v.t.*, *v.i.* WH: pre-1200. Old English *wīr*, from Germanic, prob. from base of Latin *viere* to plait, to weave. Cp. Old Norse *víravirki* filigree work, Old High German *wiara* finest gold.

wireless *n.* any process or method whereby messages, music or other sounds can be transmitted by electromagnetic waves without the intervention of wires; radio. *Also a.*, *v.t.*, *v.i.* WH: 19C. WIRE + -LESS. The process is so called as it operates by the transmission of radio waves, without the use of connecting wires.

†wis *v.i.* to know. WH: pre-1200. Old English *wissan*, alt. of *wīsian* to show the way, to guide, to lead, to instruct. See WISE[1]. Cp. IWIS.

wisdom *n.* the quality or state of being wise. WH: pre-1200. Old English *wīsdōm*, from Germanic. See WISE[1], -DOM. Cp. German *Weistum* legal sentence, precedent.

wise[1] *a.* having or showing the power or faculty of discerning or judging rightly; sagacious, sensible, discreet, prudent, judicious. WH: pre-1200. Old English *wīs*, from Germanic, from Indo-European base also of WIT[2].

†wise[2] *n.* a manner, way or mode of acting, behaving etc. WH: pre-1200. Old English *wīse*, from Germanic base also of WIT[2]. Cp. GUISE.

-wise *suf.* forming adverbs of manner, as in *lengthwise*, *likewise*. WH: WISE[2]. Cp. -WAYS.

wiseacre *n.* a person pretending to learning or wisdom. WH: 16C. Middle Dutch *wijsseggher* soothsayer, prob. (with assim. to *segghen* to say) from Old High German *wīssago*, alt. (by assoc. with *wīs* WISE[1] + *sagēn* to say) of *wīzago*, corr. to Old English *witega* prophet, from Germanic base also of WIT[2]. The assimilation to ACRE is unexplained.

wisent *n.* the European bison, *Bison bonasus*. WH: 19C. German. See BISON.

wish *v.t.* to have a desire, aspiration or craving (for). *Also v.i.*, *n.* WH: pre-1200. Old English *wȳscan*, from Germanic base also of WEEN, WONT. Cp. German *wünschen*.

wish-wash *n.* thin weak liquor or drink. WH: 18C. Redupl. of WASH.

wisp *n.* a small bunch or handful of straw, hay etc. WH: 12–14C. Orig. uncertain. Cp. W Frisian *wisp* wisp, twig, handful of straw, from Germanic base also of WHISK.

wisteria *n.* any leguminous climbing shrub of the genus *Wisteria*, with racemes of lilac-coloured flowers. WH: 19C. Modern Latin, from Caspar *Wistar* (or *Wister*), 1761–1818, US anatomist + -IA. The name was coined by Thomas Nuttall, an English botanist who went to the USA in 1808.

wistful *a.* full of vague yearnings, esp. for unattainable things, sadly longing. WH: 17C. Appar. from obs. *wistly* intently, ? var. of obs. *whistly* silently (from *whist*, var. of WHISHT + -LY²), influ. by *wishful* (WISH). See also -FUL.

wit¹ *n.* intelligence, understanding, sense, sagacity. WH: pre-1200. Old English *wit, gewit*, from Germanic base of WIT². Cp. German *Witz*.

†wit² *v.t., v.i.* to know. WH: pre-1200. Old English *witan*, from Germanic base also of WISE¹, ult. from Indo-European base also of Sanskrit *veda* (VEDA), Latin *videre* to see. Cp. GUIDE.

witch *n.* a woman having dealings with evil spirits or practising sorcery. *Also v.t.* WH: pre-1200. Old English *wicce*, fem. of *wicca* sorcerer, from Germanic, of unknown orig. Cp. WICKED.

witchetty *n.* the edible larva of a beetle or moth. WH: 19C. Australian Aboriginal (Adayamadhanha) *wityu* hooked stick + *varti* grub. The word was originally the term for a hooked stick used to obtain witchetty grubs, then the word for the grub itself.

witenagemot *n.* the Anglo-Saxon national assembly or parliament. WH: pre-1200. Old English *witena gēmot* assembly of wise men. See WIT², MOOT.

with *prep.* in or into the company of, in or into the relation of accompaniment, association, simultaneousness, cooperation, harmoniousness etc. WH: pre-1200. Old English, prob. shortening of a Germanic prep. meaning against. Cp. German *wider* again. The original sense was in a position opposite, over against. The current sense dates from the 12–14C and took over the sense formerly expressed by Old English *mid*, from Germanic (cp. German *mit* with). The original sense is still present in WITHSTAND.

†withal *adv.* with the rest, in addition, at the same time, further, moreover. *Also prep.* WH: 12–14C. Orig. two words, from WITH + ALL.

withdraw *v.t.* to draw back, aside or apart. *Also v.i.* WH: 12–14C. Old English *with-* WITH in sense away, back + DRAW.

withe *n.* a tough, flexible branch, esp. of willow or osier, used in binding things together. WH: pre-1200. Old English *withthe*, from Germanic, ult. from base represented by WIRE. Cp. WITHY.

wither *v.t.* to cause to fade, shrivel or dry, to shrivel and dry (up). *Also v.i.* WH: 14–15C. Appar. var. of WEATHER. A plant will wither if exposed to intemperate weather.

withers *n.pl.* the ridge between the shoulder blades of a horse. WH: 16C. Pl. of *wither*, appar. a reduced form of *widersome*, ? from obs. *wither* hostile, adverse (from Old English, from Germanic, from an Indo-European root denoting separation or division) + SINEW. Cp. German *Widerrist* withers. Rel. to WITH. The ridge is presumably so called because the withers are the parts that the horse opposes to its load.

withershins *adv.* anticlockwise, in the contrary direction, esp. to the left or opposite to the direction of the sun. WH: 16C. Middle Low German *weddersinnes*, from Middle High German *widersinnes*, from *wider-* counter- + gen. of *sin* direction, way. The second element subsequently came to be associated with Scottish *sin* SUN.

withhold *v.t.* to keep back, to refuse to grant or give; to deduct. WH: 12–14C. Old English *with-* WITH in sense away, back + HOLD¹.

within *adv.* inside, in or to the inside, in the inner part or parts, internally. *Also n., prep.* WH: pre-1200. Old English *withinnan*, from WITH + *innan* within, assim. to IN.

without *adv.* in, at or to the outside. *Also n., prep., conj.* WH: pre-1200. Old English *withūtan*, from WITH + *ūtan* from the outside, from *ūt* OUT.

withstand *v.t.* to stand up against, to resist, to oppose. *Also v.i.* WH: pre-1200. Old English *with-* WITH in sense against + STAND.

withy *n.* a withe. WH: pre-1200. Old English *wīthig*, rel. to Old High German *wīda* (German *Weide*), Old Norse *vīthir* willow. Cp. WITHE.

witness *n.* a person who has seen an incident etc., a spectator, a person present at an event. *Also v.t., v.i.* WH: pre-1200. Old English *witnes*, from WIT¹ + *-nes* -NESS. The original sense (to the 15C) was knowledge, wisdom, but the current sense soon followed.

witter *v.i.* to talk without purpose or at length, to chatter or babble. WH: 19C. Prob. imit. Cp. NATTER, YATTER.

witting *a.* conscious, knowing, intentional. WH: 14–15C. WIT² + -ING².

†wive *v.t.* to take for a wife, to marry. *Also v.i.* WH: pre-1200. Old English *gewīfan*, from *wīf* WIFE.

wiz *n.* a person with remarkable skill. WH: early 20C. WHIZ, influ. by WIZARD.

wizard *n.* a sorcerer, a magician, a conjuror. *Also a.* WH: 14–15C. WISE¹ + -ARD. The original sense was philosopher, sage. The current sense evolved in the 16C.

wizen *v.t., v.i.* to wither, to dry up, to shrivel. *Also a.* WH: pre-1200. Old English *wisnian*, from Germanic base rel. to Latin *viescere* to wither.

woad *n.* a plant, *Isatis tinctoria*, yielding a blue dye. WH: pre-1200. Old English *wād*, from Germanic. Cp. German *Waid*.

wobbegong *n.* an Australian shark, *Orectolobus maculatus*, with mottled skin, one of the carpet sharks. WH: 19C. Australian Aboriginal.

wobble *v.i.* to incline to one side and then the other alternately, as when not properly balanced. *Also v.t., n.* WH: 17C. Corr. to Low German *wabbeln*, Old Norse *vafla* (var. of *vafra* WAVER), from Germanic base also of WAVE, WAVER. See also -LE⁴.

wodge *n.* a thick slice or chunk. WH: 19C. Alt. of WEDGE.

woe *n.* sorrow, affliction, distress, overwhelming grief. WH: pre-1200. Old English *wā*, from Germanic, from Indo-European, ult. a natural exclamation. Cp. German *Weh*, Latin *vae*, Welsh *gwae*.

wog¹ *n.* any dark-skinned person. WH: early 20C. Orig. uncertain. ? Abbr. of GOLLIWOG. The word is popularly explained as an acronym of westernized (or worthy) oriental gentleman.

wog² *n.* an illness. WH: mid-20C. Orig. uncertain. ? Alt. of BUG¹. The original sense is small insect.

woggle *n.* a leather ring used to fasten a Scout's neckerchief at the front. WH: mid-20C. Orig. unknown. ? Blend of WIGGLE and TOGGLE.

wok *n.* a large metal bowl with curved sides and handles used in Chinese cooking. WH: mid-20C. Chinese.

wold *n.* a tract of open country, esp. downland or moorland. WH: pre-1200. Old English *wald, weald* (WEALD), from Germanic, rel. to WILD. Cp. German *Wald* wood, forest. The original sense was forest land. The current sense dates from the 12–14C. The change of sense matches the gradual deforestation of England.

wolf *n.* a grey, tawny-grey, reddish or white carnivorous quadruped, esp. *Canis lupus*, closely allied to the dog, preying on sheep, calves etc. and hunting larger animals in packs. *Also v.t.* WH: pre-1200. Old English *wulf*, from Germanic, from an Indo-European word represented also by Latin *lupus*, Greek *lukos*, Sanskrit *vṛka*. Cp. German *Wolf*.

wolfram *n.* tungsten. WH: 18C. German, from *Wolf* WOLF + Middle High German *rām* soot. The word presumably originated as a pejorative term for an ore regarded as inferior to the tin with which it was found.

Wolof *n.* a member of a W African people living mainly in Senegal. WH: 19C. Wolof.

wolverine *n.* a small carnivorous animal, *Gulo gulo*, also called the glutton or carcajou. WH: 16C. Appar. from *wolv-*, stem of WOLF + -ING¹. The animal would be so called from its 'wolfish' appetite.

woman *n.* an adult human female. *Also a., v.t.* WH: pre-1200. Old English *wīfman*, from *wīf* woman, WIFE + *man* human being, MAN.

womb *n.* the organ in a woman or other female mammal in which the young is developed before birth, the uterus. WH: pre-1200. Old English *wamb*, from Germanic, of unknown orig. Cp. German *Wamme* animal's womb. A basic sense belly, stomach was current to the 19C.

wombat *n.* any burrowing Australian marsupial of the family Vombatidae, resembling a small bear. WH: 18C. Australian Aboriginal (Dharuk) *wambad*.

won *n.* the standard monetary unit in N and S Korea. WH: mid-20C. Korean *wǎn*.

wonder *n.* a strange, remarkable or marvellous thing, person, event, action etc., a miracle, a prodigy. *Also a., v.i., v.t.* WH: pre-1200. Old English *wundor*, from Germanic, of unknown orig. Cp. German *Wunder*.

wonga-wonga *n.* a large Australian pigeon, *Leucosarcia melano-leuca*. WH: 19C. Australian Aboriginal (Dharuk) *wanga wanga*.

wonky *a.* askew, crooked. WH: early 20C. Appar. fanciful formation.

wont *a.* used, accustomed (to). *Also n., v.i., v.t.* WH: pre-1200. P.p. of Old English *gewunian* to stay, to reside, to be accustomed, from Germanic. Cp. German *gewohnt* accustomed.

wonton *n.* a small Chinese dumpling with a savoury filling, usu. served in soup. WH: mid-20C. Chinese (Cantonese dial.) *wǎn t'ǎn*.

woo *v.t.* to court, esp. with a view to marriage. *Also v.i.* WH: pre-1200. Old English *wōgian, āwōgian*, of unknown orig.

wood *n.* the fibrous substance of a tree between the bark and the pith. WH: pre-1200. Old English *wudu*, earlier *widu, wiodu*, from a Germanic word rel. to Old Irish *fid* tree, wood, Irish *fiodh*, Welsh *gwŷdd* trees.

woodchuck *n.* a N American marmot, *Marmota monax*. WH: 17C. Alt. of N American Indian name (prob. Algonquian), by assoc. with WOOD.

woof[1] *n.* the sound of a dog barking or growling. *Also v.i.* WH: 19C. Imit.

woof[2] *n.* the threads that cross the warp, the weft. WH: pre-1200. Alt. of *abb* coarse wool (from A-[1] + WEB), based on WEAVE[1]. Later also influ. by WARP.

woofter *n.* a male homosexual. WH: late 20C. Alt. of *poofter* (POOF[1]).

wool *n.* the fine, soft, curly hair forming the fleece of sheep, goats and some other animals, used as the raw material of cloth etc. *Also a.* WH: pre-1200. Old English *wull*, from Germanic, from Indo-European base also of Latin *lana* wool, *vellus* fleece. Cp. German *Wolle*.

woomera *n.* a stick used in throwing a spear or dart. WH: 18C. Australian Aboriginal (Dharuk) *wamara*.

woop woop *n.* any remote place, real or imaginary. WH: early 20C. Mock Australian Aboriginal, prob. influ. by the redupl. used in Australian Aboriginal languages to indicate plurality or intensity.

woozy *a.* suffering from giddiness, nausea etc. WH: 19C. Orig. unknown. ? Alt. of *boozy* (BOOZE).

wop *n.* any person of S European origin, esp. an Italian. WH: early 20C. ? Italian *guappo* bold, showy, from Spanish *guapo* dandy.

Worcester sauce *n.* a dark sauce made by mixing soy sauce, vinegar, spices etc. WH: 16C. *Worcester*, a city in W England.

word *n.* an articulate sound or combination of sounds uttered by the human voice or written, printed etc., expressing an idea or ideas and usu. forming a constituent part of a sentence. *Also v.t.* WH: pre-1200. Old English, from Germanic base rel. also to Latin *verbum* word (cp. VERB). Cp. German *Wort*.

Wordsworthian *a.* of, relating to or after the manner or spirit of Wordsworth or his poetry. *Also n.* WH: 19C. William *Wordsworth*, 1770–1850, English poet + -IAN.

work *n.* the exertion of physical or mental energy, effort or activity directed to some purpose. *Also v.i., v.t.* WH: pre-1200. Old English *weorc, werc, worc*, from Germanic, from Indo-European base also of Greek *ergon*. Cp. German *Werk*.

working *a.* engaged in work, esp. manual labour. *Also n.* WH: 14–15C. WORK + -ING[2], -ING[1].

world *n.* the earth with its lands and seas. *Also a.* WH: pre-1200. Old English, from Germanic base rel. to Latin *vir* man + Germanic base of obs. *old*, from Old Norse *ǫld* age, an age. Cp. German *Welt*. The literal sense is age of man.

worldly *a.* of or relating to the present, temporal or material world. WH: pre-1200. WORLD + -LY[1].

worm *n.* any of various invertebrate creeping animals with a long limbless segmented body. *Also v.i., v.t.* WH: pre-1200. Old English *wyrm*, later *wurm*, from Germanic base rel. to Latin *vermis* worm, Greek *rhomos, rhomox* woodworm. Cp. German *Wurm*. The original sense was serpent, snake, dragon.

wormwood *n.* a shrub of the genus *Artemisia*, esp. *A. absinthium*, having bitter and tonic properties, used in the manufacture of vermouth and absinthe and in medicine. WH: pre-1200. Old English *wermōd*, from Germanic alt. (14–15C) as if from WORM + WOOD. Cp. VERMOUTH. The altered form arose partly through the use of wormwood as a worm medicine.

worn *a.* tired, exhausted. WH: 14–15C. P.p. of WEAR[1].

worrit *v.t., v.i.* to worry, to cause mental distress to. *Also n.* WH: 18C. Appar. alt. of WORRY.

worry *v.t.* to cause mental distress to. *Also v.i., n.* WH: pre-1200. Old English *wyrgan* to strangle, from Germanic. Cp. German *würgen*. The original sense was to strangle. Hence (12–14C) to seize by the throat with the teeth and pull about (of a dog or wolf). The current sense did not fully evolve until the 19C.

worse *a.* more bad, bad in a higher degree. *Also adv., n.* WH: pre-1200. Old English *wiersa, wyrsa*, from Germanic base represented also by WAR.

worship *n.* the act of paying divine honour to God or some other deity, esp. in religious services. *Also v.t., v.i.* WH: pre-1200. Old English *weorthscipe*, from *weorth* WORTH[1] + *-scipe* -SHIP. The original basic sense was worth, dignity. To worship a person or thing is to acknowledge their worth.

worst *a.* most bad, bad in the highest degree. *Also adv., n., v.t.* WH: pre-1200. Old English *wierresta, wyrresta*, from Germanic. See WORSE, also -EST[1].

worsted *n.* a fine woollen yarn used for making fabric, knitting stockings etc. *Also a.* WH: 12–14C. *Worsted, Worstead*, a village in Norfolk.

wort *n.* a plant, a herb (*usu. in comb.*, as *moneywort, soapwort*). WH: pre-1200. Old English *wyrt*, from Germanic base rel. to that of ROOT[1].

worth[1] *a.* equal in value or price to. *Also n.* WH: pre-1200. Old English *weorth, worth, wurth*, from Germanic. Cp. German *wert*.

†worth[2] *v.t.* to betide, to befall. WH: pre-1200. Old English *weorthan, wurthan*, from Germanic, from Indo-European base also of Latin *vertere* (earlier *vortere*) to turn. Cp. German *werden*.

worthy *a.* having worth, estimable. *Also n.* WH: 12–14C. WORTH[1] + -Y[1].

-worthy *comb. form* safe or suitable for, as in *seaworthy*. WH: WORTHY.

wotcher *int.* a form of greeting. WH: 19C. Representation of a pronun. of *what cheer?* See CHEER.

Woulfe bottle *n.* a bottle with three or more necks used in the handling and washing of gases. WH: 19C. Peter *Woulfe*, c.1727–1803, English chemist.

wound *n.* an injury caused by a cut or blow to the skin and flesh of an animal or the bark or substance of plants, esp. one involving disruption of the tissues. *Also v.t., v.i.* WH: pre-1200. Old English *wund*, from Germanic, of unknown orig. Cp. German *Wunde*.

wove *a.* (of paper) having a uniformly smooth surface. WH: 18C. Var. of *woven*, p.p. of WEAVE[1].

wow[1] *int.* used to express astonishment, wonder etc. *Also n., v.t.* WH: 16C. Natural exclamation, ? influ. by WHY as expression of surprise.

wow[2] *n.* a variation in pitch occurring at low frequencies in sound-reproducing systems. WH: 18C. Imit. Cp. *woofer* (WOOF[1]). The original sense was a bark or similar sound. The current sense dates from the mid-20C.

wowser *n.* a spoilsport. WH: 19C. ? From WOW[1]. See also -ER[1].

wrack *n.* seaweed thrown upon the shore. WH: 14–15C. Middle Dutch *wrak*, rel. to Old English *wræc* vengeance, revenge, from var. of base of *wreccan* WREAK. The sense moving or driving clouds is a variant of RACK[5]. The sense seaweed cast ashore is related to VAREC. The sense destruction, ruin is from Old English *wræc*. Cp. WRECK.

wraith *n.* the double or phantom of a living person. WH: 16C. Orig. unknown.

wrangle *v.i.* to dispute, argue or quarrel angrily, peevishly or noisily, to brawl. *Also v.t., n.* WH: 14–15C. Prob. from Low Dutch. Cp. German dial. *wrangeln* to wrestle, freq. of Middle Low German *wrangen*, rel. to *wringen* (WRING).

wrap *v.t.* to fold or arrange so as to cover or enclose something. *Also v.i., n.* WH: 12–14C. Orig. unknown. Cp. N Frisian *wrappe* to stop up, Danish dial. *vrappe* to stuff.

wrasse *n.* a sea fish of the family Labridae, having thick lips and strong teeth. WH: 17C. Cornish *wrah*, from Middle Cornish *gwrah*, corr. to Welsh *gwrach*, lit. old woman, hag. The fish is so called from its appearance.

wrath *n.* deep or violent anger, indignation, rage. WH: pre-1200. Old English *wrǣththu*, from *wrǎth* WROTH.

wreak *v.t.* to carry out, to inflict, to execute. WH: pre-1200. Old English *wrecan*, from Germanic, from Indo-European base prob. represented also in Latin *urgere* URGE, Greek *eirgein* to shut up. Cp. WRACK, WRECK, WRETCH.

wreath *n.* a band or ring of flowers or leaves tied, woven or twisted together for wearing on the head, decorating statues, walls, graves etc. WH: pre-1200. Old English *writha*, from *writhan* WRITHE. The original sense was a circular band of metal worn as an ornament. The current sense evolved from this in the 14–15C.

wreathe *v.t.* to form (flowers, leaves etc.) into a wreath. *Also v.i.* WH: 16C. Prob. partly back-formation from obs. *wrethen*, later *wreathen* formed in coils, twisted, appar. var. of *writhen*, p.p. of WRITHE, partly from WREATH. Cp. WRITHE.

wreck *n.* destruction, ruin, esp. of a ship. *Also v.t., v.i.* WH: 12–14C. Anglo-French *wrec*, from Old Norse, from v. meaning to drive represented also in WREAK.

Wren *n.* a member of the former Women's Royal Naval Service. WH: early 20C. From abbr. WRNS, influ. by WREN.

wren *n.* a small songbird of the family Troglodytidae, esp. *Troglodytes troglodytes*, with a short erect tail and short wings. WH: pre-1200. Old English *wrenna*, rel. to Old High German *wrendo*, *wrendilo*, Old Norse *rindill*.

wrench *n.* a violent twist or sideways pull. *Also v.t.* WH: pre-1200. Old English *wrencan*, corr. to Old High German *renchen* (German *renken*) to twist, of unknown orig.

wrest *v.t.* to pull or wrench (away) forcibly. *Also n.* WH: pre-1200. Old English *wræstan*, rel. to Icelandic *reista*, Middle Danish *vreste* (Danish *vriste*).

wrestle *v.i.* to fight by grappling with and trying to throw one's opponent, esp. in a sporting contest under recognized rules. *Also v.t., n.* WH: pre-1200. Old English *wræstlian*, freq. of *wræstan* WREST. See also -LE[4].

wretch *n.* a miserable or unfortunate person. WH: pre-1200. Old English *wrecca*, from Germanic base represented also by WREAK. Cp. German *Recke* warrior, hero.

wrick *v.t.* to sprain or strain. *Also n.* WH: 19C. Var. of RICK[2].

wriggle *v.i.* to turn, twist or move the body to and fro with short motions. *Also v.t., n.* WH: 15C. Middle Low German *wriggelen*, freq. of *wriggen* to twist, to turn. See also -LE[4]. Cp. WIGGLE, WRY.

wright *n.* a person who is occupied in making, building, repairing or creating something (*usu. in comb.*, as in *shipwright, wheelwright*). WH: pre-1200. Old English *wryhta*, var. of *wyrhta*, from Germanic base represented by WORK.

wring *v.t.* to twist and squeeze or compress. *Also n.* WH: pre-1200. Old English *wringen*, from Germanic base rel. to WRONG.

wrinkle[1] *n.* a small ridge, crease or furrow caused by the folding or contraction of a flexible surface. *Also v.t., v.i.* WH: 14–15C. Orig. uncertain. Prob. from stem of rare Old English p.p. form *gewrinclod* winding, of which no inf. is recorded.

wrinkle[2] *n.* a useful bit of information or advice, a bright idea, a tip, a dodge. WH: 19C. WRINKLE[1]. The original sense was a clever device, a cunning expedient, so called as it was 'devious' or tortuous, like the crease of a wrinkle.

wrist *n.* the joint uniting the hand with the forearm. WH: pre-1200. Old English, from Germanic, prob. ult. from base also of WRITHE. Cp. German *Rist* instep, wrist.

writ *n.* a written command or precept issued by a court to a person commanding them to do or refrain from doing some particular specified act. WH: pre-1200. Old English, from Germanic base also of WRITE. The original sense was written matter, writing. The legal sense dates from the 12–14C.

write *v.t.* to form or trace (words, a sentence etc.) in letters or symbols, with a pen, pencil or the like on paper or other material. *Also v.i.* WH: pre-1200. Old English *wrītan*, from Germanic base of unknown orig. Cp. German *reissen* to sketch, to tear, to drag. The original basic sense was to score, to outline, to draw the shape of something. An early form of writing was scratching runes on bark.

writhe *v.i.* to twist, turn or roll the body about, as in pain. *Also v.t., n.* WH: pre-1200. Old English *wrīthan*, from Germanic. Rel. to WREATHE, WROTH.

wrong *a.* false, inaccurate, incorrect, mistaken, erroneous. *Also adv., n., v.t.* WH: 12–14C. Corr. to Old Norse *rangr* awry, unjust, from Germanic. Rel. to WRING. The word has not been recorded as an adjective in Old English but it probably existed as such. The corresponding Old English noun was *wrange*.

wrot *n.* wrought timber. WH: mid-20C. Alt. of WROUGHT.

wroth *a.* angry, wrathful. WH: pre-1200. Old English *wrāth*, from Germanic base also of WRITHE. Cp. WRATH.

wrought *a.* worked, formed or fashioned (*often in comb.*, as *well-wrought*). WH: 12–14C. Early p.p. of WORK.

wry *a.* twisted, distorted, crooked. *Also v.i., v.t.* WH: pre-1200. Old English *wrīgian* to strive, to go forward, to tend. Cp. AWRY, WRIGGLE. The noun evolved from the verb in the 16C.

Wu *n.* a dialect of Chinese spoken around the Yangtze delta. WH: early 20C. Chinese *wú*.

wunderkind *n.* a child prodigy. WH: 19C. German, from *Wunder* wonder + *Kind* child.

wurst *n.* a type of large German or Austrian sausage. WH: 19C. German.

wuss *n.* a weak or cowardly person. WH: mid-20C. Orig. uncertain. ? From *pussy-wussy*, redupl. of *pussy* (PUSS[2]).

Wyandot *n.* a member of a N American Indian people from Ontario. *Also a.* WH: 18C. French *Ouendat*, from Huron *Wendat*.

wych *a.* drooping. WH: 17C. Var. of *witch*, from Old English *wice*, *wic*, appar. from Germanic base of WEAK.

Wycliffite *a.* of or relating to Wycliffe, his tenets or his followers. *Also a.* WH: 16C. John *Wycliffe*, c.1320–84, English theologian and reformer + -ITE[1].

Wykehamist *n.* a member (past or present) of Winchester College. *Also a.* WH: 18C. Modern Latin *Wykehamista*, from William of *Wykeham*, 1324–1404, Bishop of Winchester and founder of Winchester College. See also -IST. Wykeham is *Wickham*, a village near Fareham, Hampshire.

wynd *n.* an alley. WH: 12–14C. Appar. from stem of WIND[2].

WYSIWYG *a.* denoting or relating to a computer or word processor which can print out exactly what is shown on the screen. WH: late 20C. Acronym of *what you see is what you get*.

wyvern *n.* a two-legged dragon with erect wings and barbed tail. WH: 14–15C. Old French *wivre* (Modern French *guivre*), from Latin *vipera* snake. See VIPER. The original sense was viper. The heraldic sense dates from the 16C.

xanthate *n.* a salt or ester of xanthic acid. WH: 19C. XANTHIC + -ATE[1].

xanthein *n.* the part of the yellow colouring matter of flowers that is soluble in water. WH: 19C. XANTHO- + IN, with inserted -*e*- to differentiate from *xanthin* (19C) insoluble yellow colouring matter in flowers.

xanthic *a.* of a yellowish colour. WH: 19C. XANTHO- + -IC.

Xanthippe *n.* a shrewish, quarrelsome or nagging woman. WH: 16C. *Xanthippe*, 5C BC, wife of Socrates, traditionally said to be quarrelsome and shrewish.

xanthium *n.* any hardy composite plant of the genus *Xanthium*. WH: 18C. Modern Latin, from Greek *xanthion*, from *xanthos* yellow. The plant is so called as it was used to dye the hair yellow.

xantho- *comb. form* yellow. WH: Greek *xanthos* yellow. See also -O-.

xanthochroism *n.* a condition where all skin pigments apart from yellow disappear, as in some goldfish. WH: 19C. XANTHO- + Greek *ōkhros* pale. See also -ISM.

xanthoma *n.* a skin disease characterized by a growth of yellowish tubercles, usu. in flat patches, on the eyelids. WH: 19C. XANTHO- + -OMA.

xanthophyll *n.* the yellow carotenoid pigment of withered leaves. WH: 19C. XANTHO- + -PHYLL.

xanthous *a.* belonging to one of the peoples having yellowish hair and a light complexion, xanthochroic. WH: 19C. Greek *xanthos* yellow + -OUS.

xebec *n.* a small three-masted vessel with lateen and square sails, used in the Mediterranean. WH: 18C. French *chebec*, obs. Spanish *xabeque* (Modern Spanish *jabeque*) or Catalan *xabec*, ult. from Arabic *šabbāk* small warship, fishing vessel.

xeno- *comb. form* strange, foreign; foreigner. WH: Greek *xenos* stranger, guest, foreigner. See also -O-.

xenogamy *n.* cross-fertilization. WH: 19C. XENO- + -GAMY.

xenogenesis *n.* the (imagined) production of offspring completely unlike either parent, heterogenesis. WH: 19C. XENO- + GENESIS.

xenoglossia *n.* in psychical research, the knowledge of a language one has not learned, claimed by some mediums. WH: late 20C. XENO- + Greek *glōssa* tongue, language. See also -IA.

xenograft *n.* a tissue graft from a member of a different species, a heterograft. WH: mid-20C. XENO- + GRAFT[1].

xenolith *n.* a fragment of rock enclosed in a different type of rock. WH: 19C. XENO- + -LITH.

xenomorphic *a.* not having its characteristic crystal form but an irregular shape due to surrounding minerals. WH: 19C. XENO- + -morphic (-MORPH).

xenon *n.* an inert gaseous element, at. no. 54, chem. symbol Xe, found in the atmosphere and solidifying at the temperature of liquid air. WH: 19C. Greek, neut. of *xenos* foreign, strange. The gas was so named in 1898 by its discoverers, the British chemists Sir William Ramsay and Morris W. Travers. They called it thus because it was obtained from liquid air along with KRYPTON, which they had discovered shortly before.

xenophile *n.* a person who likes foreign people and things. WH: mid-20C. XENO- + -PHILE.

xenophobia *n.* fear or hatred of strangers or foreigners. WH: early 20C. XENO- + -*phobia* (-PHOBE).

xeransis *n.* the state of drying up or being dried up, desiccation. WH: 19C. Greek *xēransis* a drying up, from *xēros* dry.

xeranthemum *n.* an annual plant of the genus *Xeranthemum*, with everlasting flowers. WH: 18C. Greek *xēros* dry + *anthemon* flower.

xeric *a.* (of a habitat) very dry. WH: early 20C. XERO- + -IC.

xero- *comb. form* dry. WH: Greek *xēros* dry. See also -O-.

xeroderma *n.* an abnormal dryness of the skin. WH: 19C. XERO- + Greek *derma* skin. See also -IA.

xerography *n.* a photographic process in which the plate is sensitized electrically, and the latent image developed by a resinous powder. WH: mid-20C. XERO- + -GRAPHY, based on *photography* (PHOTOGRAPH).

xerophilous *a.* (of a plant) adapted to living in a hot, dry climate. WH: 19C. XERO- + -*philous* (-PHILIA).

xerophthalmia *n.* a dry inflammation of the lining membrane of the eye, caused by a deficiency of vitamin A. WH: 17C. XERO- + OPHTHALMIA.

xerophyte *n.* a plant adapted to living in a region of little moisture, such as a cactus, a xerophile. WH: 19C. XERO- + -PHYTE.

xerosis *n.* abnormal dryness of certain parts of the body. WH: 19C. XERO- + -OSIS.

xerostomia *n.* abnormal dryness of the mouth. WH: 19C. XERO- + Greek *stoma* mouth. See also -IA.

Xerox® *n.* a xerographic copying process. WH: mid-20C. Greek *xēros* dry, with substitution of -*x* for -*s*. Cp. XEROGRAPHY.

Xhosa *n.* a member of one of the Bantu-speaking peoples in the Cape Province, S Africa. *Also a.* WH: 19C. Nguni.

xi *n.* the 14th letter of the Greek alphabet (Ξ, ξ). WH: 14–15C. Greek.

Xian *n.* a Christian. WH: 19C. Abbr. of CHRISTIAN, with *X* for the Greek letter CHI, transliterated *kh*, as the first letter of Greek *Khristos* Christ. Cp. XMAS.

-xion *suf.* used to form nouns from Latin participial stems in -*x*-, usu. involving action, as in *crucifixion*, *connexion*. WH: French -*xion*, from Latin -*xio*, -*xionis*. Cp. -TION.

xiphoid *a.* sword-shaped. *Also a.* WH: 18C. Greek *xiphoeidēs*, from *xiphos* sword. See also -OID.

Xmas *n.* Christmas. WH: 16C. Abbr. of CHRISTMAS, from *X* (see XIAN) + -*mas*.

xoanon *n.* a primitive carved image of a god, supposed by ancient Greeks to have fallen from heaven. WH: 18C. Greek, rel. to *xein* to carve.

xu *n.* a unit of currency in Vietnam, equal to one-hundredth of a dong. WH: mid-20C. Vietnamese, from French *sou*. See SOU.

xylem *n.* woody tissue, wood parenchyma, as opposed to *phloem*. WH: 19C. Greek *xulon* wood + pass. suf. -*ēma*.

xylene *n.* any one of three isomeric colourless, volatile, liquid hydrocarbons distilled from coal or wood tar. WH: 19C. XYLO- + -ENE.

xylo- *comb. form* relating to wood. WH: Greek *xulon* wood. See also -O-.

xylocarp *n.* a hard, woody fruit such as the coconut, or a tree bearing this. WH: 19C. XYLO- + -CARP.

xylograph *n.* a woodcut or engraving, esp. in a primitive style, or an impression from one. WH: 19C. XYLO- + -GRAPH.

xyloid *a.* of or resembling wood, ligneous. WH: 19C. Greek *xuloeidēs*, from *xulon* wood. See also -OID.

xyloidine *n.* a high explosive prepared by the action of nitric acid on starch or wood fibre. WH: 19C. French *xyloïdine*, from Greek *xuloeidēs*. See XYLOID, also -INE.

Xylonite® *n.* a type of celluloid. WH: 19C. XYLO- + -*n*- + -ITE[1].

xylophagous *a.* (of insects) boring into wood. WH: 19C. XYLO- + -PHAGOUS.

xylophone *n.* an instrument consisting of a graduated series of wooden or metal bars vibrating when struck or rubbed. WH: 19C. XYLO- + -PHONE.

xylose *n.* a white crystalline pentose found in wood and straw, wood sugar. WH: 19C. XYLO- + -OSE².

xylotomous *a.* (of an insect) eating wood. WH: 19C. XYLO- + Greek *-tomos* cutting. See also -OUS.

xyster *n.* a surgeon's instrument for scraping bones. WH: 17C. Latin, from Greek *xustēr*, from *xuein* to scrape.

xystus *n.* a long covered portico or colonnade used for athletic exercises in ancient Greece. WH: 17C. Latin, from Greek *xustos* smooth, from *xuein* to scrape.

†y- *pref.* forming past participles, collective nouns etc., as in *yclept, ywis.* WH: Old English *ge-*, from Germanic (German *ge-*), ? identical with Latin *co-* (CO-).

-y¹ *suf.* forming adjectives from nouns and adjectives, as in *lucky, pricey.* WH: Old English *-ig*, from Germanic.

-y² *suf.* forming abstract nouns etc., as in *memory, remedy.* WH: Latin *-ia*, Greek *-eia*, *-ia.*

-y³ *suf.* forming diminutives, pet names etc., as in *laddy, Jimmy, sonny, Mickey, nightie.* WH: Orig. unknown.

yabber *v.i.* to talk, to chatter. *Also n.* WH: 19C. Australian Aboriginal.

yabby *n.* a freshwater crayfish of the genus *Charax.* WH: 19C. Australian Aboriginal (Wemba-wemba) *yabij.*

yacht *n.* a light sailing vessel, esp. one designed for racing. *Also v.i.* WH: 16C. Early Modern Dutch *jaghte* (now *jacht*), from *jaghtschip* fast pirate ship, from *jaght* hunting + *schip* ship.

yaffle *n.* the green woodpecker. WH: 18C. Imit. of the bird's call.

Yagi antenna *n.* a highly directional aerial used for television, radio, radio astronomy etc., consisting of parallel elements fixed at right angles to a central bar that points in the direction of strongest reception. WH: mid-20C. Hidetsugu *Yagi*, 1886–1976, Japanese electrical engineer.

yah¹ *int.* used to express dismissal, scepticism or derision. WH: 17C. Natural exclamation.

yah² *int.* yes. WH: 19C. Representation of an affected pronun. of YES.

yahoo *n.* a coarse, brutish person, a lout. WH: 18C. *Yahoo*, imaginary race of brutish creatures resembling human beings in Jonathan Swift's *Gulliver's Travels* (1726), prob. based on YAH¹.

Yahweh *n.* the Hebrew name for God in the Old Testament, Jehovah. WH: 19C. Hebrew YHWH, with added vowels. Cp. JEHOVAH, YHVH.

yak¹ *n.* a long-haired ox, *Bos grunniens*, from the mountainous regions of central Asia. WH: 18C. Tibetan *gyag.*

yak² *n.* noisy, unceasing, trivial chatter. *Also v.i.* WH: 19C. Imit.

yakitori *n.* a Japanese dish of boneless chicken pieces, grilled on skewers and served with a thick sweet sauce. WH: mid-20C. Japanese, from *yaki* toasting, grilling + *tori* bird. Cp. TORII.

yakka *n.* work. WH: 19C. Australian Aboriginal (Yagara) *yaga.*

Yakut *n.* a member of a mixed Turkic people living in the basin of the Lena, in E Siberia. WH: 18C. Russian, from Yakut.

Yale® *n.* a type of lock with a revolving barrel, turned by a flat key with a serrated edge. WH: 19C. Linus *Yale* Jr., 1821–68, US locksmith.

yam *n.* the fleshy edible tuber of various species of the genus *Dioscorea*, tropical climbers orig. from India. WH: 16C. Portuguese *inhame*, or from obs. Spanish *iñhame* (Modern Spanish *ñame*), prob. of W African orig. Cp. Fulani *nyami* to eat.

yamen *n.* the office or official residence of a Chinese mandarin. WH: 18C. Chinese *yámen.*

yammer *v.i.* to cry out, to whine, to complain peevishly. *Also n.* WH: 14–15C. Alt. of obs. *yomer* to murmur, to complain (from Old English *geōmrian*, from *geōmor* sorrowful), based on Middle Dutch and Middle Low German *jammeren.*

yandy *v.t.* to separate (seed) from other material by a particular form of shaking. *Also n.* WH: mid-20C. Australian Aboriginal (Yinjibarndi) *yandi.*

yang *n.* the masculine, positive, bright principle in nature, according to Chinese philosophy, which interacts with its complement, *yin.* WH: 17C. Chinese *yáng* sun, positive, male genitals.

Yank *n.* an American, a native or inhabitant of the US. WH: 18C. Abbr. of YANKEE.

yank *v.t.* to pull sharply. *Also v.i., n.* WH: 19C. Orig. unknown.

Yankee *n.* an American, a native or inhabitant of the US. *Also a.* WH: 18C. ? Dutch *Janke*, dim. of *Jan* John. The word is recorded in the 17C as a nickname. According to some, it is from Dutch *Jan Kees*, literally John Cheese, a nickname for a Dutchman, with reference to early Dutch settlers.

yap *v.i.* to yelp or bark snappishly. *Also n.* WH: 17C. Imit. Cp. YAWP.

yapok *n.* a small opossum, *Chironectes minimus*, with webbed hind feet and aquatic habits. WH: 19C. River *Oyapock*, flowing from Brazil into French Guiana.

yapp *n.* a style of bookbinding, usu. in leather, with flaps at the edges. WH: 19C. William *Yapp*, 1854–75, owner of a London bible warehouse, for whom it was first produced.

yarborough *n.* in whist, bridge etc., a hand containing no card higher than a nine. WH: early 20C. Appar. from an Earl of *Yarborough*, said to have bet 1000 to 1 against the occurrence of such a hand.

yard¹ *n.* a unit of length, 3 ft. or 36 in. (0.9144 m). WH: pre-1200. Old English *gerd* rod, stick, from Germanic. Cp. German *Gerte* switch, rod. A yard was originally a rod used for measuring, then the measurement itself. The sense spar on a ship's mast dates from the first.

yard² *n.* a small piece of enclosed ground, esp. adjoining or enclosed by a house or other building. *Also v.t.* WH: pre-1200. Old English *geard*, from Germanic base rel. to Old Church Slavonic *gradŭ* city, garden (Russian *gorod* town). Cp. GARDEN, GARTH, ORCHARD. The original sense was building, house, home, then a piece of land around a house.

†yare *a.* ready, prepared. *Also adv.* WH: pre-1200. Old English *gearu*, from Germanic. Cp. German *gar* ready, prepared.

yarmulke *n.* a skullcap worn all the time by Orthodox Jewish men, and during prayer by others. WH: early 20C. Yiddish *yarmolke*, from Polish *jarmułka* cap, prob. from Turkish *yağmurluk* raincoat, cape, from *yağmur* rain.

yarn *n.* any spun fibre prepared for weaving, knitting, rope-making etc. *Also v.i.* WH: pre-1200. Old English *gearn*, prob. from Germanic base represented also by Old Norse *gǫrn*, pl. of *garnar* guts. The sense long tale evolved in the 19C, probably originally in sailors' slang.

yarran *n.* any of several Australian acacias, esp. *Acacia omalophylla*, a small hardy tree used esp. for fencing, fuel and fodder. WH: 19C. Australian Aboriginal (Kamilaroi) *yarraan.*

yarrow *n.* a perennial herb of the genus *Achillea*, esp. *A. millefolium*, the milfoil, with white flowers, a pungent odour and astringent properties. WH: pre-1200. Old English *gearwe*, from Germanic, ult. of unknown orig. Cp. German *Garbe.*

yashmak *n.* the veil worn by many Muslim women in public. WH: 19C. Turkish *yaşmak*, use as n. of *yaşmak* to hide oneself.

yataghan *n.* a Turkish sword or scimitar with a double-curved blade and without a guard or crosspiece. WH: 19C. Turkish *yatağan.*

yatter *v.i.* to talk at length, gossip, chatter, esp. irritatingly. WH: 19C. Imit., ? based on YAMMER and CHATTER.

yaupon *n.* an evergreen shrub, *Ilex vomitoria*, growing in the southern US, the leaves of which are used to make a tea and by the Indians as an emetic and purgative medicine. WH: 18C. N American Indian.

yaw *v.i.* (of a ship, aircraft etc.) to steer out of the direct course, to move unsteadily, esp. from side to side. *Also v.t., n.* WH: 16C. Orig. unknown.

yawl¹ *n.* a small two-masted sailing boat with a small jigger-mast towards the stern. WH: 16C. Middle Low German *jolle* or Dutch *jol*, ult. of unknown orig. Cp. JOLLY².

yawl[2] *v.i.* to howl, to yell, to yowl. *Also n.* WH: 12–14C. Var. of YOWL. Cp. Low German *jaulen* to howl (of a cat).

yawn *v.i.* to open the mouth wide or to have the mouth open involuntarily through drowsiness, boredom, bewilderment etc., to stand agape. *Also v.t., n.* WH: pre-1200. Old English *geonian, ginian,* from Germanic. Cp. German *gähnen.* The original sense (to the 17C) was to open the mouth wide to swallow something. The current sense, as a reflex action when sleepy, dates from the 14–15C.

yawp *n.* a hoarse or raucous cry. *Also v.i.* WH: 12–14C. Imit. Cp. YAP, YELP.

yaws *n.* an infectious tropical disease whose symptoms include sores, caused by spirochaetes; also called *framboesia.* WH: 17C. Prob. Carib *yaya,* ult. from S American Indian. The *-s* is probably the plural suffix -s[1].

†yclept *a.* called, named. WH: pre-1200. Y- + *clept,* obs. p.p. of *clepe* to call, from Old English *cleopian,* from Germanic.

†ye[1] *pron.* the plural of THOU[1], you people (orig. nom. or subjective). WH: pre-1200. Old English *gē,* modified form (based on WE) of Germanic root represented by Gothic *jūs,* from *ju-* (with pl. ending). See YOU, YOUR. Cp. German *ihr.*

ye[2] *a.* the. WH: 16C. Old way of printing THE, with substitution of *y* for the runic consonant letter known as thorn (representing voiced or voiceless *th*).

†yea *adv.* yes. *Also n.* WH: pre-1200. Old English *gē, gēa,* from Germanic. Cp. YES.

yeah *adv.* yes. WH: early 20C. Representation of an informal pronun. of YES. Cp. YAH[1].

†yean *v.t., v.i.* (of sheep and goats) to give birth to (young). WH: 14–15C. Representation of an Old English v. rel. to *geēan* pregnant, from *ge-* Y- + *ēanian,* from Germanic.

year *n.* the period of time occupied by the revolution of the earth round the sun, the time taken by the sun in returning to the same equinox, in mean length, 365 days, 5 hrs., 48 min. and 46 sec. WH: pre-1200. Old English *gēr, gēar,* from Germanic, from Indo-European base represented also by Greek *hōra* season. Cp. German *Jahr.*

yearn *v.i.* to feel a longing desire (for). WH: pre-1200. Old English *giernan,* from Germanic. Cp. German *gern* gladly, willingly.

yeast *n.* a yellowish, viscous substance consisting of a growth of fungous cells developed in contact with saccharine liquids and producing alcoholic fermentation by means of enzymes, used in brewing, distilling etc. and for raising dough for bread etc. WH: pre-1200. Old English *gist,* from Germanic, rel. to Greek *zein* to boil, *zestos* boiled. Cp. German *Gischt* sea foam.

yegg *n.* a safe-breaker. WH: early 20C. Orig. unknown.

yell *v.i.* to cry out with a loud or inarticulate cry as in rage, agony, terror or uncontrollable laughter. *Also v.t., n.* WH: pre-1200. Old English *gellan, giellan,* from Germanic base represented also by Old English *galan* to sing. Cp. German *gellen.*

yellow *a.* of a colour between green and orange in the spectrum or like that of gold, brass, sulphur, lemon or, the duller form, like that of discoloured old paper etc. *Also n., v.t., v.i.* WH: pre-1200. Old English *geolu, geolo,* from Germanic, rel. to Latin *helvus,* Greek *khloos.* Cp. GOLD.

yelp *v.i.* to utter a sharp, quick cry, as a dog in pain, or in fear or anticipation. *Also n.* WH: pre-1200. Old English *gielpan, gelpan,* from Germanic imit. base. The original sense (to the 14–15C) was to boast. The current sense arose in the 16C.

Yemeni *n.* a native or inhabitant of the Republic of Yemen. *Also a.* WH: early 20C. Arabic *yamanī.* See also -I[3].

yen[1] *n.* the standard unit of currency of Japan. WH: 19C. Japanese *en* round. Cp. YUAN.

yen[2] *n.* ambition, yearning, desire, longing. *Also v.i.* WH: 19C. Chinese *yăn* craving.

yeoman *n.* a freeholder not ranking as one of the gentry. WH: 12–14C. Prob. reduced form of *young man.*

yep *adv.* yes. WH: 19C. Alt. of YES. Cp. NOPE.

-yer *suf.* forming nouns, esp. from words in *-w,* denoting an agent, as in *lawyer, sawyer.* WH: Var. of -IER.

yerba *n.* Paraguay tea, maté. WH: 19C. Spanish herb. Cp. MATÉ.

yes *adv.* as you say, it is true, agreed (indicating affirmation or consent). *Also n.* WH: pre-1200. Old English *gēse, gīse, gȳse,* prob. from an unrecorded form equivalent to YEA + *sīe* may it be (so). The word was originally used in response to a negative question, as distinct from YEA.

yeshiva *n.* a Jewish school devoted to the study of the Talmud. WH: 19C. Hebrew *yĕšīḇāh,* from *yāšhaḇ* to sit.

yester- *comb. form* of or relating to yesterday. WH: pre-1200. Old English *geostra, giestra,* from Germanic base + comp. suf. *-ter,* from Indo-European base represented also in Greek *khthes,* Sanskrit *hyas,* Latin *heri* yesterday. Cp. German *gestern.*

yet *adv.* up to this or that time. *Also conj.* WH: pre-1200. Old English *gēet, gīeta,* of unknown orig. The only known related form is Old Frisian *ieta, ēta, īta.*

yeti *n.* a hypothetical manlike, apelike or bearlike creature, whose tracks are alleged to have been found in the snows of the Himalayas, also called *Abominable Snowman.* WH: mid-20C. Tibetan *yeh-teh* little manlike animal.

yett *n.* a gate, a door. WH: 12–14C. Var. of GATE[1].

yew *n.* a dark-leaved evergreen shrub or tree of the genus *Taxus,* esp. *T. baccata,* a large tree with spreading branches, the wood of which has long been valued for making bows and used in cabinet-making. WH: pre-1200. Old English *īw, ēow,* from Germanic. Cp. German *Eibe.*

Yggdrasill *n.* in Scandinavian mythology, an ash tree binding together heaven, earth and hell with its roots and branches. WH: 18C. Old Norse, appar. from *Yggr,* a name of Odin + *drasill* horse.

YHVH *n.* Yahweh, the Tetragrammaton. WH: 19C. Hebrew. See YAHWEH.

Yiddish *n.* a language spoken by Jews of E Europe and N America, based on a Hebraized Middle German, with an admixture of Polish, French and English, and usually written in Hebrew characters. *Also a.* WH: 19C. Yiddish *yidish,* short for *yidish daytsh,* from Middle High German *jüdisch diutsch* Jewish German. Cp. German *jiddisch* Yiddish.

yield *v.t.* to bring forth as fruit or result. *Also v.i., n.* WH: pre-1200. Old English *geldan, gieldan,* from Germanic base meaning to pay, to requite. Cp. GUILD. The original sense (to the 17C) was to pay, to render as due. The current sense dates from the 12–14C.

yikes *int.* used to express surprise, astonishment, alarm etc. WH: late 20C. Orig. unknown. Cp. YOICKS.

yin *n.* the feminine, passive, dark principle in nature, according to Chinese philosophy, which interacts with its complement and opposite, yang. WH: 17C. Chinese *yīn* shade, feminine, the moon.

yip *n.* a short sudden cry, a yelp. *Also v.i.* WH: 14–15C. Imit. The original sense was to cheep, as a young bird. The current sense dates from the early 20C.

yippee *int.* used to express delight, pleasure, exuberant anticipation etc. WH: early 20C. Natural exclamation.

yips *n.pl.* an attack of nerves, particularly in sport and esp. when putting in golf. WH: mid-20C. Orig. unknown.

-yl *suf.* denoting a radical, as in *ethyl, methyl.* WH: Greek *hulē* wood, material.

ylang-ylang *n.* a Malayan tree, *Cananga odorata,* of the custard-apple family. WH: 19C. Tagalog *ilang-ilang.*

-yne *comb. form* denoting a triple bond, as in *alkyne.* WH: Alt. of -INE.

yo *int.* used as a greeting, to gain someone's attention, etc. WH: 14–15C. Natural exclamation.

yob *n.* an aggressive, loutish youth, a hooligan. WH: 19C. Back slang for BOY.

yocto- *comb. form* denoting a factor of 10^{-24}. WH: late 20C. Var. of OCTO-. Cp. YOTTA-.

yod *n.* the tenth letter of the Hebrew alphabet. WH: 18C. Hebrew *yōḏ.* Cp. IOTA. The letter is the smallest of the Hebrew alphabet.

yodel *v.t., v.i.* to sing or shout in a musical fashion with alternation from the natural voice to the falsetto. *Also n.* WH: 19C. German *jodeln,* from *jo,* exclamation of joy, of imit. orig.

yoga *n.* a Hindu system of abstract meditation and rigid asceticism by which the soul is supposed to become united with the eternal spirit of the universe. WH: 18C. Sanskrit, lit. union. See YOKE.

yogh *n.* a Middle English letter (ȝ) used to represent *g* and *y* sounds. WH: 12–14C. Orig. unknown.

yogurt *n.* a custard-like food made from milk fermented in a special way. WH: 17C. Turkish *yoğurt.*

yo-ho *int.* used to attract attention. WH: 18C. YO + HO.

yoicks *n., int.* a fox-hunter's cry. WH: 18C. Orig. unknown.

yojan *n.* a measure of distance in the Indian subcontinent, usu. about 5 miles (8 km). WH: 18C. Sanskrit *yojana* yoking, distance travelled without unyoking. Cp. YOGA, YOKE.

yoke *n.* a frame or crossbar fitting over the necks of two oxen or other draught animals and attaching them to a plough or vehicle. *Also v.t., v.i.* WH: pre-1200. Old English *geoc*, from Germanic, from Indo-European stem corr. to Latin *iugum*, Greek *zugon*, Sanskrit *yuga*, from base represented also by Latin *iungere* to join, Greek *zeugnunai*, Sanskrit YOGA.

yokel *n.* a rustic, a country bumpkin. WH: 19C. Orig. unknown. ? From German dial. *Jokel*, dim. of male forename *Jakob* Jacob, as a derogatory nickname for a rustic. Cp. HICK, RUBE.

yolk[1] *n.* the yellow part of an egg, the contents of the ovum, esp. that nourishing the embryo, the vitellus. WH: pre-1200. Old English *geoloca, geolca*, from YELLOW.

yolk[2] *n.* the natural grease in sheep's wool, suint. WH: 17C. Backformation from *yolky* full of yolk, from Old English *eowocig*, ult. from *ēowu* EWE. See also -Y[1]. The spelling has been influenced by association with YOLK[1].

Yom Kippur *n.* the Day of Atonement, a Jewish day of fasting. WH: 19C. Hebrew *Yōm Kippūr*, from *yōm* day + *kippūr* atonement.

yomp *v.i.* to trek, often with heavy equipment, over heavy terrain. WH: late 20C. Orig. unknown. Cp. HUMP.

yon *a., adv.* yonder. *Also pron.* WH: pre-1200. Old English *geon*, rel. to Greek *enē* day after tomorrow, *enioi* some, Sanskrit *ana-* this one. Cp. German *jener* that one.

yonder *a.* that over there. *Also adv., n.* WH: 12–14C. Corr. to Old Saxon *gendra*, W Frisian *gindra* on this side, Middle Dutch *ghinder* (Dutch *ginder*). Cp. YON.

yoni *n.* the Hindu symbol of the fertility of nature under which the consort of a male deity is worshipped, represented by an oval figure (the female genitalia). WH: 18C. Sanskrit source, womb, female genitals.

yonks *n.pl.* a long time, ages. WH: mid-20C. ? Rel. to *donkey's years* a very long time.

yoo-hoo *int.* used to attract someone's attention. WH: early 20C. Natural exclamation, ? influ. by YOU. Cp. COOEE.

yore *n.* long ago, old time. WH: pre-1200. Old English *geāra, geāre*, of unknown orig.

yorker *n.* in cricket, a ball bowled so as to pitch immediately under the bat. WH: 19C. Prob. from *York*, a city in NE England + -ER[1]. The bowling style is said to have been introduced by Yorkshire players. Cp. YORKSHIRE.

yorkie *n.* a Yorkshire terrier. WH: mid-20C. YORKSHIRE + -ie (-Y[3]).

Yorkist *a.* of or relating to the house of York, or the White Rose party supporting this in the Wars of the Roses. *Also n.* WH: 17C. *York* (see YORKER), a royal house + -IST. The house of York descended from Edmund Langley, 1341–1402, 5th son of Edward III, 1st Duke of York. It ruled England from 1461 to 1485.

Yorkshire *a.* of or derived from Yorkshire. WH: 17C. *Yorkshire*, a former county of NE England, divided into E, N and W Riding (RIDING) (now into N Yorkshire and the E Riding of Yorkshire). Its county town was York (see YORKER).

Yoruba *n.* a member of a people living in the coastal regions of W Africa, esp. SW Nigeria. WH: 19C. Yoruba.

yotta- *comb. form* denoting a factor of 10^{24}. WH: late 20C. Var. of YOCTO-, appar. based on Italian *otto* eight. Cp. OCTA-.

you *pron.* the person, animal, thing or persons etc. addressed. WH: pre-1200. Old English *īow, ēow*, from Germanic. Cp. THEE, THOU[1], YE[1].

young *a.* being in the early stage of life, growth or development. *Also n.* WH: pre-1200. Old English *geong, gung*, later *iung*, from Germanic, ult. from Indo-European base represented also in YOUTH

and in Sanskrit *yuvaśa* youthful, Latin *iuvencus* young bull. Cp. Dutch *jong*, German *jung*.

Young's modulus *n.* a measure of elasticity for wire etc., equal to the ratio of the stress acting on the material to the increase in length produced. WH: 19C. Thomas *Young*, 1773–1829, English physician and physicist.

†younker *n.* a youngster. WH: 16C. Middle Dutch *jonckher*, from *jonc* young + *hēre* lord. Cp. JUNKER.

your *a.* possessive of YOU. WH: pre-1200. Old English *ēower*, gen. of YE[1], from Germanic. Cp. YOU.

youth *n.* the state of being young. WH: pre-1200. Old English *geoguth*, later *iuguth*, from Germanic, from base represented by YOUNG. See also -TH[2]. Cp. German *Jugend*. The sense young male person dates from the 12–14C.

yowl *n.* a howl or yell of distress. *Also v.i.* WH: 12–14C. Imit. Cp. YAWL[2].

yo-yo *n.* a toy which consists of a spool winding up and down on a string. *Also v.i.* WH: early 20C. Prob. ult. from a Philippine language.

ytterbium *n.* a rare metallic element, at. no. 70, chem. symbol Yb, used to improve the mechanical properties of steel. WH: 19C. *Ytterby*, a quarry in S Sweden + -IUM. The name was coined in 1878 by the Swiss chemist Jean-Charles-Golinard de Marignac. Cp. TERBIUM, YTTRIUM. It was originally applied to a mixture that was later separated into ytterbium proper and lutetium.

yttrium *n.* a rare metallic element, at. no. 39, chem. symbol Y, belonging to the cerium group, used in alloys, lasers and in making superconductors. WH: 19C. *Ytterby* (YTTERBIUM) + -IUM. The name was coined in 1822 by the Swedish chemist Carl Gustaf Mosander, from earlier *yttria* (1800), a heavy white powder, the oxide of yttrium, which had been isolated by the Finnish chemist Johan Gadolin in 1794 (cp. GADOLINITE).

yuan *n.* the standard monetary unit of China. WH: early 20C. Chinese *yuán*, lit. round. Cp. YEN[1].

yucca *n.* any liliaceous subtropical American flowering plant of the genus *Yucca*, with rigid lanceolate leaves and an erect cluster of white flowers, many species of which are grown for ornament. WH: 16C. Carib.

yuck *int.* used to express disgust or distaste. *Also n., v.i.* WH: mid-20C. Imit. of the sound of vomiting. Cp. UGH.

yuga *n.* any of the Hindu ages or cycles of the world. WH: 18C. Sanskrit YOKE, an age of the world.

Yugoslav *a.* of or relating to the southern Slav peoples or countries, esp. the former Yugoslavia. *Also n.* WH: 19C. Austrian German *Jugoslav*, from Serbo-Croat *jugo-*, comb. form of *jug* south + SLAV. Yugoslavia itself was formed in 1918 as the Kingdom of the Serbs, Croats and Slovenes and did not formally adopt the one-word name until 1929.

yulan *n.* a Chinese tree, *Magnolia denudata*, with large, brilliant, snow-white or rosy flowers. WH: 19C. Chinese *yùlán*, from *yù* gem + *lán* plant.

Yule *n.* Christmas time or the festival of Christmas. WH: pre-1200. Old English *gēol* Christmas Day, corr. to Old Norse *jól* (pl.) heathen feast lasting twelve days, (later) Christmas. Ult. of unknown orig. Cp. Swedish, Norwegian and Danish *jul* Christmas. ? Rel. to JOLLY[1].

yum-yum *int.* used to express pleasure, esp. anticipation of delicious food. WH: 19C. Redupl. of *yum*, imit. of the smacking of lips.

yuppie *n.* a young financially successful professional person who spends much money on their lifestyle. *Also a.* WH: late 20C. Acronym of *young urban* (or *upwardly mobile*) *professional* (person).

yurt *n.* a circular, collapsible tent made of skins and used by nomads in central Asia. WH: 18C. Russian *yurta*, from Turkish *jurt*.

Z

zabaglione *n.* a warm whipped dessert of egg yolks, sugar and marsala. WH: 19C. Italian, ? ult. from Late Latin *sabaia*, an Illyrian drink.

zaffre *n.* impure cobalt oxide used for enamelling and as a blue pigment for painting on glass, porcelain etc. WH: 17C. Italian *zaffera*, or from Old French *safre*, ? rel. to to SAPPHIRE.

zag *n.* a sharp change of direction in a zigzag course. *Also v.i.* WH: 18C. Extracted from ZIGZAG.

Zairean *n.* a native or inhabitant of Zaire. *Also a.* WH: late 20C. *Zaire*, a country in central Africa (now Congo) + -EAN.

zakuska *n.* a snack, an hors d'oeuvre. WH: 19C. Russian (usu. as pl. *zakuski*), from *kusat'* to bite. Cp. MORSEL.

Zambian *n.* a native or inhabitant of Zambia. *Also a.* WH: mid-20C. *Zambia*, a country in S central Africa + -AN.

zamia *n.* any palmlike tree or low shrub of the genus *Zamia*, from the W Indies and America. WH: 19C. Modern Latin, from *zamiae*, misreading of *azaniae* pine cones (in a passage of Pliny).

zamindar *n.* a member of a class of Bengali landowners formerly paying a certain land tax to the British government. WH: 17C. Urdu, from Persian *zamīndar*, from *zamīn* land + *dār* holder.

zander *n.* a large European freshwater pikeperch, *Stizostedion lucioperca*. WH: 19C. German.

zany *a.* comical, absurd. *Also n.* WH: 16C. French *zani*, or from Italian *zanni*, orig. Venetian and Lombardic form of *Gianni*, shortening of *Giovanni* John, stock name of servants acting as clowns in the *commedia dell'arte*. It was originally the word for a comic performer accompanying a clown, acrobat, etc. and imitating him.

zap *v.t.* to hit, smack, strike suddenly. *Also v.i., n., int.* WH: early 20C. Imit.

zapateado *n.* a flamenco dance characterized by much clicking of the heels, and stamping and tapping of the feet. WH: 19C. Spanish, from *zapato* shoe.

zaratite *n.* a hydrous nickel carbonate, usu. occurring as an incrustation. WH: 19C. G. *Zárate*, 19C Spanish mineralogist + -ITE[1].

zarf *n.* an ornamental cup-shaped holder for a hot coffee cup. WH: 19C. Arabic *zarf* vessel.

zariba *n.* a stockade, hedge or other enclosure for a camp or village in Sudan. WH: 19C. Arabic *zarība* pen for cattle.

zarzuela *n.* a traditional Spanish form of musical comedy or comic opera. WH: 19C. Spanish, prob. from *La Zarzuela*, royal residence near Madrid where it was first performed 17C. The name of the palace comes from Spanish *zarza* bramble.

zeal *n.* ardour, enthusiasm. WH: 14–15C. Latin *zelus*, from Greek *zēlos* jealousy, fervour.

zebra *n.* a black and white striped, asslike mammal of the genus *Equus*, esp. *E. burchelli*, from the mountainous regions of southern Africa. WH: 17C. Italian, Spanish and Portuguese wild ass, ? ult. from Latin *equiferus*, from *equus* horse + *ferus* wild.

zebu *n.* the humped Indian ox, *Bos indicus*. WH: 18C. French *zébu*, of unknown orig.

zecchino *n.* a Venetian gold coin, the sequin. WH: 16C. Italian SEQUIN.

zed *n.* the letter Z. WH: 14–15C. Old French *zède*, from Late Latin *zeta*, from Greek *zēta*. Cp. ZEE, ZETA.

zedoary *n.* a tropical Asian plant, *Curcuma zedoaria*, similar to turmeric. WH: 14–15C. Medieval Latin *zedoarium*, from Persian *zadwār*.

zee *n.* the letter Z, zed. WH: 17C. Var. of ZED.

Zeeman effect *n.* the splitting of the spectrum line of a substance into several parts when the substance is placed in a magnetic field. WH: 19C. Pieter *Zeeman*, 1865–1943, Dutch physicist.

zein *n.* a protein found in maize, used in the manufacture of inks, coatings, adhesives etc. WH: 19C. From *zea*, a species of cereal grass (from Late Latin, from Greek *zeia*) + -IN[1].

Zeitgeist *n.* the spirit, or moral and intellectual tendency, of the times. WH: 19C. German, from *Zeit* time + *Geist* spirit.

zeloso *adv.* with energy. WH: 19C. Italian, from *zelo* ZEAL.

zemstvo *n.* a Russian elective local assembly dealing with economic affairs in the decades preceding the Russian Revolution. WH: 19C. Russian, from obs. *zem'* (now *zemlya*) land.

Zen *n.* a form of Mahayana Buddhism teaching that truth is in one's heart and can be learned only by meditation and self-mastery. WH: 18C. Japanese, from Chinese *chán* quietude, from Sanskrit *dhyāna* meditation.

zenana *n.* in the East (esp. India or Iran), the portion of the house in a Hindu or Muslim household which is reserved for the women. WH: 18C. Persian and Urdu *zanānah*, from *zan* woman, rel. to Greek *gunē* (cp. QUEAN).

Zend *n.* a section of commentary on the Avesta. WH: 18C. French, abstracted from Persian *Awastā wa Zand*, lit. Avesta and interpretation. See AVESTA.

Zener cards *n.pl.* a set of 25 cards, each having one of five different symbols, used in research into ESP. WH: mid-20C. Karl Edward *Zener*, 1903–61, US psychologist.

Zener diode *n.* in electronics, a semiconductor diode in which a certain reverse voltage produces a sudden increase in reverse current, making it useful as a voltage regulator. WH: mid-20C. Clarence M. *Zener*, 1905–93, US physicist.

zenith *n.* the point in the heavens directly overhead to an observer, as opposed to *nadir*. WH: 14–15C. Old French *cenit* (Modern French *zénith*) or Medieval Latin *cenit*, ult. from Arabic *samt* in *samt-ar-ra's* path over the head. Cp. AZIMUTH. The *n* of *zenith* may have developed from a misreading of *m* in the transliteration of Arabic *samt*.

zeolite *n.* any one of a group of hydrous silicates found in cavities of eruptive rocks, which gelatinize in acid owing to the liberation of silica. WH: 18C. Greek *zein* to boil + -O- + -LITE. The name was coined in 1756 by the Swedish mineralogist Axel Fredrik Cronstedt.

zephyr *n.* any soft, gentle breeze. WH: pre-1200. Old English *zefferus*, from Latin *zephyrus*, from Greek *zephuros* the west wind, prob. rel. to *zophos* the west, darkness. The sense soft breeze evolved in the 17C.

Zeppelin *n.* a large dirigible airship. WH: early 20C. Count Ferdinand von *Zeppelin*, 1838–1917, German general, its first constructor.

zepto- *comb. form* denoting a factor of 10[-21]. WH: late 20C. Alt. of SEPTI-[1]. Cp. ZETTA-.

zero *n.* the figure 0, nought. *Also a., v.t.* WH: 17C. French *zéro* or Italian *zero*, from Old Spanish *zero* (Modern Spanish *cero*), from Arabic *ṣifr*. Cp. CIPHER.

zest *n.* keen enjoyment. WH: 15C. French *zeste* thick skin dividing a walnut kernel, orange peel, lemon peel, of unknown orig. The original sense was orange or lemon peel used as a flavouring. Hence the sense piquant quality (18C), keen relish, gusto (18C), appetizer (19C). Cp. SPICE.

zeta *n.* the sixth letter of the Greek alphabet (Z, ζ). WH: 14–15C. Greek *zēta*. Cp. ZED.

zetetic *a.* proceeding by enquiry. *Also n.* WH: 17C. Greek *zētētikos*, from *zētein* to seek, to inquire. See also -IC.

zetta- *comb. form* denoting a factor of 10[21]. WH: late 20C. Alt. of ZEPTO-, appar. based on Italian *sette* seven.

zeugma *n.* a figure in which a verb or adjective governs or modifies two nouns to only one of which it is logically applicable. WH: 14–15C. Latin, from Greek, lit. yoking, from *zeugnunai* to yoke, rel. to *zugon* yoke.

zibeline *a.* of, relating to or resembling the sable. *Also n.* WH: 16C. French, from Slavonic. See SABLE, also -INE.

zibet *n.* an Indian and Asian civet, *Viverra zibetha.* WH: 16C. Medieval Latin *zibethum.* See CIVET.

zidovudine *n.* a drug derivative of thymine used to alleviate the symptoms of Aids sufferers, AZT. WH: late 20C. Appar. arbitrary alt. of *azidothymidine,* from AZIDE + -O- + *thymidine* (from THYMINE + -IDE + -INE).

ziff *n.* a beard. WH: early 20C. Orig. unknown.

zig *n.* a sharp change of direction in a zigzag course. *Also v.i.* WH: mid-20C. Shortening of ZIGZAG. Cp. ZAG.

ziggurat *n.* an ancient Mesopotamian temple tower of a rectangular or tiered design. WH: 19C. Akkadian *ziqquratu* height, pinnacle.

zigzag *a.* having or taking sharp alternate turns or angles to left and right. *Also n., adv., v.t., v.i.* WH: 18C. French, from German *Zickzack,* of imit. orig., suggesting abrupt alternation of direction. The word was originally used of fortifications.

zilch *n.* nothing, zero. WH: mid-20C. Orig. unknown. ? Based on NIL, with *z* from ZERO.

zillah *n.* an administrative district in India or Bangladesh. WH: Persian and Urdu *zila,* from Arabic *ḍila'* division.

zillion *n.* a huge unspecified amount, quantity or number. WH: mid-20C. Arbitrary alt. of MILLION, ? based on *z* as algebraic unknown quantity.

Zimbabwean *n.* a native or inhabitant of Zimbabwe. *Also a.* WH: mid-20C. *Zimbabwe,* a country in southern Africa + -AN.

Zimmer® *n.* a metal walking frame used as a means of support by those with walking difficulties. WH: late 20C. *Zimmer* Orthopaedic Ltd., manufacturing company. The firm's name is said to derive from Mongolian *zhima,* a sledge drawn by a *zho* (DZO) and guided by a man walking at the rear holding an upright frame.

zinc *n.* a bluish-white metallic element, at. no. 30, chem. symbol Zn, used in the manufacture of brass and other alloys, for coating sheet iron, as roofing material, in electric batteries etc. *Also v.t., a.* WH: 17C. German *Zink,* rel. to *Zinke* prong, point. The element is perhaps so called from the shape that it assumes after cooling.

zinfandel *n.* a variety of grape grown esp. in California for making red wine. WH: 19C. Orig. unknown. ? A European place name.

zing *n.* energy, go, zest. *Also v.i.* WH: early 20C. Imit. Cp. ZIP.

Zingaro *n.* a gypsy. WH: 17C. Italian gypsy, from Greek *Athigganoi,* an Oriental people.

zingiber *n.* any monocotyledonous tropical herb of the genus *Zingiber* with creeping, jointed, woody rootstocks, esp. the common ginger, *Z. officinale.* WH: early 20C. Modern Latin. See GINGER.

zinjanthropus *n.* the fossil hominid found in Tanzania in 1959, *Australopithecus boisei.* WH: mid-20C. Former Modern Latin genus name, from *Zinj,* early medieval (Arabic) name for E Africa (preserved in the name of *Zanzibar*) + Greek *anthrōpos* man.

zinnia *n.* a plant of the genus *Zinnia* (daisy family) with showy rayed flowers in single terminal heads. WH: 18C. Modern Latin, from Johann Gottfried *Zinn,* 1727–59, German physician + -IA.

Zion *n.* a hill in ancient Jerusalem, the royal residence of David and his successors. WH: pre-1200. Ecclesiastical Latin *Sion,* Greek *Seōn,* from Hebrew *ṣiyôn* hill. Biblical references to 'Mount Zion', typically in Psalms and Isaiah, are thus really a tautology.

zip *n.* a zip fastener, a zipper. *Also v.i.* WH: 19C. Imit.

Zip code *n.* a postal code. WH: mid-20C. Acronym of Zone Improvement *Plan,* punning on ZIP.

zircon *n.* a translucent, variously-coloured zirconium silicate, some varieties of which are cut into gems. WH: 18C. German *Zirkon.* See JARGON².

zit *n.* a spot, a pimple. WH: mid-20C. Orig. unknown.

zither *n.* a simple stringed instrument consisting of a flat sounding-board and strings plucked by the fingers. WH: 19C. German, from Latin CITHARA.

zizania *n.* any tall aquatic grass of the genus *Zizania,* including the different species of wild rice. WH: 12–14C. Late Latin, from Greek *darnel,* pl. of *zizanion.* The Late Latin plural noun was adopted as a (feminine singular) genus name.

zizz *n.* a nap, a short sleep. *Also v.i.* WH: 19C. Imit.

zloty *n.* a coin and monetary unit of Poland. WH: early 20C. Polish *złoty,* from *złoto* gold.

-zoa *comb. form* denoting groups of animals, as in *Metazoa, Protozoa.* WH: Pl. of -ZOON.

zoarium *n.* a polyzoan colony, a polyzoary. WH: 19C. Modern Latin, from Greek *zōiarion,* dim. of *zōion* animal, but taken as if from *zōion* + -ARIUM.

zodiac *n.* the zone or broad belt of the heavens, extending about 8° to each side of the ecliptic, which the sun traverses during the year. WH: 14–15C. Old French *zodiaque,* from Latin *zodiacus,* from Greek *zōidiakos* (*kuklos*) circle of figures, from *zōidion* sculptured figure (of an animal), dim. of *zōion* animal. See also -AC.

zoetic *a.* of or relating to life, vital. WH: 19C. Greek *zōētikos,* from *zōē* life. See also -ETIC.

zoetrope *n.* an optical instrument in which a series of pictures on the inner face of a rotating cylinder gives an impression of continuous motion when viewed through slits in the cylinder. WH: 19C. Greek *zōē* life + -TROPE.

zoic *a.* of or relating to animals or animal life. WH: 19C. Greek *zōikos,* from *zōion* animal. See also -IC.

-zoic *comb. form* indicating a geological era, as in *Mesozoic, Palaeozoic.* WH: Greek *zōē* life + -IC.

zoilean *a.* savagely critical, esp. malignantly so. WH: 17C. *Zoilus,* 4C BC, a Greek critic and grammarian famous for his criticism of Homer + -EAN.

zoisite *n.* a translucent calcium and aluminium silicate, first found in Carinthia in Austria. WH: 19C. Baron S. von Edelstein *Zois,* 1747–1819, Austrian scholar + -ITE¹.

Zöllner's lines *n.pl.* rows of parallel lines made to appear not parallel by short oblique intersecting lines in something similar to a herringbone pattern. WH: 19C. Johann Karl Friedrich *Zöllner,* 1834–82, German astronomer and physicist.

zollverein *n.* a customs union among states maintaining a tariff against imports and usu. having free trade with each other. WH: 19C. German, from *Zoll* TOLL¹ + *Verein* union.

zombie *n.* a stupid, apathetic or slow-moving person. WH: 19C. Bantu. Cp. Kikongo *nzambi* god, *zumbi* fetish.

zonda *n.* a hot dry west wind blowing from the Andes, usu. during July and August, in Argentina. WH: 19C. American Spanish.

zone *n.* an area sectioned off for a particular function. *Also v.t.* WH: 14–15C. Old French, or from Latin *zona* girdle, from Greek *zōnē.*

zonk *v.t.* to hit sharply or suddenly. *Also n.* WH: early 20C. Imit.

zoo *n.* a place with a collection of living wild animals on public display or kept in captivity as a conservation measure. WH: 19C. Abbr. of *zoological gardens* (ZOOLOGY). The word was originally used with reference to the zoological gardens of the London Zoological Society, established in Regent's Park, London in 1828.

zoo- *comb. form* of or relating to animals or to animal life. WH: Greek *zōion* animal. See also -O-.

zooblast *n.* an animal cell. WH: 19C. ZOO- + -BLAST.

zoochemistry *n.* the chemistry of the substances occurring in the animal body. WH: 19C. ZOO- + CHEMISTRY.

zoogamy *n.* sexual reproduction of animals. WH: 19C. ZOO- + -GAMY.

zoogeny *n.* the origination of life. WH: 19C. ZOO- + -GENY.

zoogeography *n.* the study of the distribution of animals. WH: 16C. ZOO- + GEOGRAPHY.

zoogony *n.* the formation of animal organs. WH: 17C. ZOO- + Greek *-gonia* begetting.

zoography *n.* the branch of zoology concerned with describing animals. WH: 16C. ZOO- + -GRAPHY.

zooid *n.* a more or less independent invertebrate organism developed by fission or budding. *Also a.* WH: 19C. ZOO- + -OID.

zoolatry *n.* the worship of animals as deities. WH: 19C. ZOO- + -LATRY.

zoolite *n.* a fossil animal or animal substance. WH: 19C. ZOO- + -LITE.

zoology *n.* the natural history of animals, the branch of biology dealing with the structure, physiology, classification, habits and distribution of animals. WH: 17C. Modern Latin *zoologia,* Modern Greek *zōologia,* from Greek *zōion* animal. See ZOO-, -LOGY.

zoom *v.i.* to move quickly (as) with a deep loud buzzing noise. *Also n.* WH: 19C. Imit.

zoomancy *n.* divination by means of observation of the movements and behaviour of animals. WH: 19C. ZOO- + -MANCY.

zoometry *n.* comparative measurement of the parts of animals. WH: 19C. ZOO- + -METRY.

zoomorphic *a.* of, relating to or exhibiting animal forms. WH: 19C. ZOO- + -*morphic* (-MORPH).

zoon *n.* the total product of a fertilized ovum. WH: 19C. Modern Latin, from Greek *zōion* animal.

-zoon *comb. form* animal, as in *spermatozoon*. WH: Greek *zōion* animal.

zoonosis *n.* a disease which can be transmitted to humans by animals, e.g. rabies. WH: 19C. ZOO- + Greek *nosos* disease.

zoopathology *n.* animal pathology. WH: 19C. ZOO- + PATHOLOGY.

zoophagous *a.* feeding on animals, carnivorous. WH: 19C. ZOO- + -PHAGOUS.

zoophile *n.* an animal lover. WH: 19C. ZOO- + -PHILE.

zoophobia *n.* abnormal fear or hatred of animals. WH: early 20C. ZOO- + -*phobia* (-PHOBE).

zoophorus *n.* a continuous frieze carved with figures of people and animals in relief. WH: 16C. Latin, from Greek *zōiophorus*, from *zōion* animal + -*phoros* bearing.

zoophyte *n.* an invertebrate animal presenting many external resemblances to a plant, such as a coral, sea anemone, sponge etc. WH: 17C. Modern Latin *zoophyton*, from Greek *zōiophuton*, from *zōion* animal. See ZOO-, -PHYTE.

zooplankton *n.* the minute floating animal life of a body of water. WH: early 20C. ZOO- + PLANKTON.

zooscopy *n.* a form of hallucination involving visions of animals, esp. snakes. WH: 19C. ZOO- + -*scopy* (-SCOPE).

zoospore *n.* a spore of fungi, algae etc. having the power of independent motion, usu. by means of cilia. WH: 19C. ZOO- + SPORE.

zootaxy *n.* the classification of animals. WH: 19C. ZOO- + Greek -*taxia*.

zootechnics *n.* the science of breeding and of the domestication of animals. WH: 19C. ZOO- + TECHNIC + -S[1]. See also -ICS.

zootheism *n.* the attribution of divine qualities to animals. WH: 19C. ZOO- + THEISM.

zootomy *n.* the dissection or anatomy of animals. WH: 17C. Modern Latin *zootomia*, prob. from Late Latin *anatomia* ANATOMY. See ZOO-, -TOMY.

zootoxin *n.* a toxin produced by an animal, e.g. snake venom. WH: early 20C. ZOO- + TOXIN.

zootrophic *a.* of or relating to the nourishment of animals. WH: 19C. ZOO- + -TROPHIC.

zoot suit *n.* a man's baggy suit popular in the late 1940s, consisting of a long jacket with fitted waist and padded shoulders, and wide trousers tapering into narrow turn-ups. WH: mid-20C. Rhyming formation on SUIT.

zopilote *n.* any small American vulture of the family Cathartidae, esp. the turkey buzzard. WH: 18C. Spanish, from Nahuatl *azopilotl*.

zori *n.* a Japanese flat sandal of straw or rubber, similar to a flip-flop. WH: 19C. Japanese *zōri*, from *sō* grass, straw + *ri* footwear, sole.

zorilla *n.* a small carnivorous quadruped, *Ictonyx striatus*, allied to the skunks and polecats, found in Africa and Turkey. WH: 18C. Modern Latin former genus name, or from French *zorille*, Spanish *zorilla*, *zorillo*, dim. of *zorra*, *zorro* fox.

Zoroastrian *a.* of or relating to Zoroaster (or Zarathustra) or the religious system expounded by him and his followers in the Zend-Avesta, based on the dual principle of Ormazd, the god of light and good, and Ahriman, the god of darkness and evil. *Also a.* WH: 18C. Latin *Zoroastres*, from Greek *Zōroastrēs*, from Avestan *Zaratuštra* Zoroaster, Persian founder of Zoroastrianism (10 BC or earlier). See also -IAN.

zoster *n.* the condition shingles, herpes zoster. WH: 17C. Latin, from Greek *zōstēr* girdle.

Zouave *n.* a soldier belonging to a French light infantry corps, orig. composed of Algerian recruits and still wearing an Oriental uniform. WH: 19C. French, from Kabyle *Zouaoua*, name of a tribe.

zouk *n.* a kind of lively music combining Latin American, African and Western influences, originating in the French Caribbean. WH: late 20C. French, appar. from Guadeloupian Creole, lit. to party. Cp. JUKEBOX.

†zounds *int.* used to express anger, surprise etc. WH: 16C. Abbr. of (*God*)'s *wounds*.

zucchetto *n.* the skullcap of a Roman Catholic ecclesiastic, black for a priest, purple for a bishop, red for a cardinal, white for a pope. WH: 19C. Italian *zucchetta*, dim. of *zucca* gourd, head.

zucchini *n.* a courgette. WH: early 20C. Italian, pl. of *zucchino* small marrow, courgette, dim. of *zucca* gourd.

zugzwang *n.* a blocking position in chess making any move by an opponent disadvantageous. *Also v.t.* WH: early 20C. German, from *Zug* move + *Zwang* compulsion, obligation.

Zulu *n.* a member of a branch of the Bantu-speaking people of SE Africa. *Also a.* WH: 19C. Zulu *umzulu*, pl. *amazulu*.

Zuñi *n.* a member of an American Indian people of New Mexico. WH: 19C. *Zuñi*, a river in New Mexico, USA.

zwieback *n.* a type of biscuit or rusk. WH: 19C. German, lit. twice-bake. Cp. BISCUIT.

Zwinglian *a.* of or relating to Zwingli or his doctrines (esp. the denial of 'real presence' in the Eucharist). *Also n.* WH: 16C. Ulrich *Zwingli*, 1485–1531, Swiss religious reformer + -IAN.

zwitterion *n.* an ion that carries both a positive and a negative electric charge. WH: early 20C. German, from *Zwitter* hybrid + *Ion* ION.

zydeco *n.* a kind of Afro-American dance music, orig. from S Louisiana. WH: mid-20C. Louisiana Creole, ? from a pronun. of French *les haricots* the beans, in a dance tune title.

zygapophysis *n.* any one of the processes by which a vertebra articulates with another. WH: 19C. ZYGO- + *apophysis* protuberance from a bone, from Modern Latin, from Greek *apophusis*, from APO- + *phusis* growth.

zygo- *comb. form* union, pairing. WH: Greek *zugon* yoke. See also -O-.

zygobranchiate *a.* (of certain gastropods) having the right and the left gills alike. WH: 19C. ZYGO- + *branchiate* (BRANCHIA).

zygodactyl *a.* (of birds) having the toes disposed in pairs, two in front and two behind. *Also n.* WH: 19C. ZYGO- + Greek *daktulos* finger, toe.

zygoma *n.* the arch joining the cheekbone and temporal bone. WH: 17C. Greek *zugōma*, from *zugon* yoke. See also -OMA.

zygomorphic *a.* (of flowers) divisible into similar halves only in one plane. WH: 19C. ZYGO- + -*morphic* (-MORPH).

zygon *n.* a connecting bar, such as the crossbar of an H-shaped fissure of the brain. WH: 19C. Modern Latin, from Greek *zugon* yoke.

zygophyllaceous *a.* of, relating to or belonging to the Zygophyllaceae, a family of desert and steppe plants including the genus *Zygophyllum*. WH: 19C. ZYGO- + Greek *phullon* leaf. See also -ACEOUS.

zygophyte *n.* a plant reproduced by means of zygospores. WH: 19C. ZYGO- + -PHYTE.

zygopleural *a.* bilaterally symmetrical. WH: 19C. ZYGO- + Greek *pleura* side. See also -AL[1].

zygosis *n.* conjugation. WH: 19C. Greek *zugōsis*, from *zugoun* to yoke, from *zugon* yoke. See also -OSIS.

zygospore *n.* a spore formed by conjugation of two similar gametes within certain fungi or algae. WH: 19C. ZYGO- + SPORE.

zygote *n.* the product of the fusion between the oocyte and the spermatozoon, the fertilized ovum. WH: 19C. Greek *zugōtes* yoked, from *zugoun* to yoke, from *zugon* yoke.

zymase *n.* a mixture of enzymes obtained from yeast. WH: 19C. Greek *zumē* leaven + -ASE.

zymo- *comb. form* relating to fermentation. WH: Greek *zumē* leaven. See also -O-.

zymogen *n.* a substance developing by internal change into an enzyme. WH: 19C. ZYMO- + -GEN.

zymology *n.* the science of fermentation. WH: 18C. ZYMO- + -LOGY.

zymolysis *n.* the action of enzymes. WH: 19C. ZYMO- + -*lysis* (LYSIS).

zymometer *n.* an instrument for measuring the degree of fermentation. WH: 19C. ZYMO- + -METER.

†zymosis *n.* the process of fermentation, esp. that by which disease was supposed to be introduced into the system. WH: 18C. Greek *zumōsis* fermentation. See also -OSIS.

zymurgy *n.* the branch of applied chemistry concerned with fermentation as it is used in brewing etc. WH: 19C. ZYMO- + -*urgy*, based on METALLURGY, *thaumaturgy* (THAUMATURGE).